The American Directory of

Writer's Guidelines

More than 1,700 Magazine Editors and Book Publishers Explain What They Are Looking for from Freelancers

2007-2008

6th Edition

Compiled by
Stephen Blake Mettee,
Michelle Doland,
and Doris Hall

Quill Driver Books

Sanger, California

Published by
Quill Driver Books/Word Dancer Press, Inc.
1254 Commerce Way
Sanger, CA 93657
(559) 876-2170
FAX (559) 876-2180
QuillDriverBooks.com

Printed in The United States of America

Quill Driver Books/Word Dancer Press books may be purchased at special prices for educational, fund-raising, business or promotional use. Please contact:

Special Markets
Quill Driver Books\Word Dancer Press, Inc.
1254 Commerce Way
Sanger, CA 93657
Info@QuillDriverBooks.com
1-800-497-4909

To order an additional copy of this book please call 1-800-497-4909 or visit QuillDriverBooks.com

ISBN 1-884956-58-0

QUILL DRIVER BOOKS and colophon are trademarks of Quill Driver Books/Word Dancer Press, Inc.

Library of Congress Cataloging-in-Publication Data

The American directory of writer's guidelines : more than 1,600 magazine editors and book publishers explain what they are looking for from freelancers 6th edition / edited and compiled by Stephen Blake Mettee, Michelle Doland, Doris Hall
    p. cm.
  ISBN 1-884956-58-0
  1. Authorship—Handbooks, manuals, etc. 2. Journalism—Authorship—Handbooks, manuals, etc. I. Mettee, Stephen Blake, 1947- II. Doland, Michelle III Hall, Doris, 1932-

PN147.A479 2004
808'.02—dc22

2004011497

What Are Writer's Guidelines?

For years, editors at magazines have prepared writer's guidelines to advise and direct freelance writers who wish to write for their magazines. Today, editors at many book publishers also prepare writer's guidelines for writers with book-length projects in mind.

Yet, while supporting writers is important to editors (who are most often writers themselves), they don't provide writer's guidelines for purely altruistic reasons. They do it with the hope that the pool of material submitted to them will increase both in quality and in adherence to the needs of the press.

In theory, the editor's ability to pick and choose from this enriched reservoir will enhance the publisher's success—and the editor's job security.

Whether this works as anticipated is a still a topic of discussion among editors—most material that arrives on an editor's desk still does not fit the editor's needs. What is certain is that savvy writers save time and limit the number of rejection slips they receive by perusing a publisher's guidelines before querying or submitting material.

The best writer's guidelines convey a plethora of information. The basics, such as whether material should be fiction or nonfiction, which subject matters or topics are to be dealt with, and the approximate word count required, are almost universally spelled out. Yet, many guidelines go well beyond the basics, instructing the writer in such matters as tone, voice, use of first person or third person point of view, use of humor, and the appropriateness of political, sexual, or violent content.

Guidelines often provide information about photographs and other illustrations to be used, deadlines for seasonal material, which rights are acquired, which columns or features are open to freelancers and which are staff written, and which style guide (*The Associated Press Stylebook and Libel Manual* and *The Chicago Manual of Style* are two common examples) the publisher wishes the author to follow. Some guidelines even list the rates the publisher will pay.

How this Book Is Organized

This book is broken into two main sections, "Periodicals' Guidelines," which lists guidelines for magazines and other periodicals in alphabetical order, and "Book Publishers' Guidelines," which does the same for book publishing houses. Contact information—with names of the editors to whom submissions should be addressed—follows each of the guidelines. Since editors change jobs and publishers change addresses, it is wise to invest in a phone call to verify this information before submitting.

The "Topic Index" beginning on page 873 lists publishers by areas of interest. This is the place to start when you know what subject you want to write about.

Contents

Periodicals' Guidelines

Book Publishers' Guidelines

Author's Tool Kit

Query Letters

The job of a query letter is to convince an editor to ask to see a full book proposal or to assign an article to you.

The first rule of a query letter is to address it to the proper editor—by name. Never use "Dear Editor" or "To Whom It May Concern." Triple-check the correct spelling of the editor's name.

The second rule is to be brief. What's brief? Conventional wisdom dictates never exceeding one page in length, but Donna Elizabeth Boetig, author of *Feminine Wiles: Creative Techniques for Writing Women's Feature Stories that Sell,* says this advice is "a scam propagated by published writers who want to keep new ones from nipping at their assignments." She advises, "...don't shortchange yourself. If you've got something to say—and you better if you're writing to [an editor]—then relax and allow yourself space to make your point." Boetig says for her, "...one and a half to two pages seems comfortable."

A query letter should begin with an opening that will "hook" the editor. This might be a colorful anecdote, an intriguing question, or some other arresting device. Whatever you use, the first paragraph or two must pique the editor's interest, or he may not read on.

After you have caught his attention, explain why you have chosen to contact this particular editor. How do the interests of his magazine or book publishing house coincide with what you are proposing?

Your query must present a specific idea. Don't ask if the editor would like an article on snowboarding; ask if he would like one on septuagenarians who snowboard in their underwear.

Describe the main points your article or book will cover and how the reader will benefit from having read it. Suggest a catchy title for the work. Explain how your article or book will be fresh and different than other articles or books on the same subject.

Explain why you are the one to write the article or book. How will you get your material? Will you research the subject, conduct polls, interview experts?

Estimate the approximate word count for the project, fitting this number to what you have learned from this publisher's writer's guidelines.

Throughout the query, show your passion for the subject.

When not to query

Most publishers of short stories don't wish to receive a query letter. They prefer that the complete short story be submitted. In fact, many suggest foregoing a cover letter as well, the point being that the short story must stand on its own—without any tangential information that is included in the cover letter—when published.

If you have already written a nonfiction article—and tailored it to a specific periodical—you might wish to send the whole article with a short cover letter explaining what the article is about and why you chose to send it to this particular periodical.

When you are suggesting a nonfiction book project to a publisher, Stephen Blake Mettee, author of *The Fast-Track Course on Writing a Nonfiction Book Proposal*, advises skipping the query letter stage and instead submitting a full proposal. He contends a query letter asking if an editor wishes to see a full book proposal is simply giving the editor an additional chance to say no. Where the full proposal might secure a contract with the editor, a query letter never will. If you choose to skip the query stage, a brief cover letter explaining why you chose to contact this particular editor would be appropriate.

Query letter format

Query letters are business letters and as such take the form of business letters. Single space queries. Use a businesslike font such as Times New Roman. Use your letterhead or center your name and contact information at the top of the sheet.

Writing "On Spec"

If you are a new writer, an editor interested in the article you are suggesting may ask to see it "on spec." On spec is short for "on speculation," meaning the author writes the article speculating that the editor will purchase it. While, at this point, the editor *has* shown an interest in the article, all he has agreed to do is to consider it when it comes in. This is a common practice and may be necessary for the new author trying to break in.

Getting a Response: Self-Addressed, Stamped Envelopes (SASEs)

It is customary for an author to enclose a self-addressed, stamped envelope with unsolicited queries, book proposals, or other submissions. This isn't absolutely necessary; if the editor is interested in what you are suggesting, he will undoubtedly contact you, but, if he isn't, most will simply trash or recycle your material without responding.

This may sound harsh and unbusiness like, but an editor who receives hundreds or even thousands of submissions each year, as most do, simply doesn't have the time to address and affix the correct postage to that many envelopes.

While a business-sized (#10) envelope will suffice, it is a good idea to enclose a self-addressed, stamped envelope large enough to return everything you sent—many editors jot notes on the material and these notes may provide information you can use to tweak your submission when sending it out to another editor.

Selling Your Book to a Publisher

Nonfiction books

Most nonfiction books, even those by first-time authors, are sold to a publisher before the book has been completely written. This is done via a ten- to fifty-page book proposal.

Most successful book proposals have the following five components:

- A synopsis of the book, including a suggested title, the subject matter and how it will be approached, the main points the book will cover, the book's potential readership, other similar books and how yours will be different or better, the anticipated word count, and why you are the person to write this book.
- A table of contents
- A chapter-by-chapter outline
- Two or three sample chapters
- Additional supporting material. This may be copies of charts or photographs to be included in the book, current newspaper clippings that deal with the subject matter, photocopies or a list of your previously published works, and any other material that will help the editor get an overall view of the project.

For more on writing nonfiction book proposals, including a successful proposal and sample book contracts, see *The Fast-Track Course on How to Write a Nonfiction Book Proposal* by Stephen Blake Mettee.

Novels

First-time novelists usually acquire the attention of an agent or an editor by submitting a complete synopsis of the book and the first two or three chapters. The synopsis should provide an overview of the main characters and the intricacies of the plot and subplots. Unlike with nonfiction book publishers, most publishers of novels will want to see the complete novel before offering a contract to a first-time author.

> ## Writing a book proposal sounds like a lot of work. Won't the editor just see the brilliance of my idea and jump at it?
>
> Nonfiction books are sold to editors in many different ways, and a formal book proposal isn't always necessary—Dean Koontz could get a contract for a book on how to write scary stories with a phone call as could O.J. Simpson for his memoirs—if he decided to confess.
>
> Sometimes an author meets an editor socially, and a deal for a book ensues. Experts or other high-profile people are occasionally contacted by an editor in need of a book on a specific subject and a contract is signed without a formal book proposal being produced.
>
> But, for the rest of us with average fame and average luck, the chances of selling an editor on a book project are increased immensely with a professional, well-thought-out and well-organized book proposal.

The Author's Bundle of Rights

According to United States copyright law, the writer's work is considered copyrighted from the moment it is written. This automatically gives the author ownership of a bundle of rights to his or her work.

This bundle of rights may be divided and sold in any number of pieces and with any limitations the author can conceive of and get a publisher to agree to. The writer assigns the right to use the work to a publisher according to the contract between the writer and the publisher.

While it isn't necessary, many people in the industry suggest that writers list on the manuscript just what rights are being offered. For example, type "First North American Serial Rights" on the upper right hand corner of a short story or article, just above the word count. Always check your contract (or letter of acceptance from the editor) to see what rights the publisher expects to receive.

Below is a brief summary of some of the components of the bundle of rights. For specific questions, it is always best to consult an attorney who specializes in communications, copyright, or publication law.

All rights—This is just what it suggests. When a writer sells "all rights" to a work to a publisher, the writer no longer has any say in future publication of the piece. If he wants to use it again, say to include it in an anthology, he would need to get permission from the publisher to whom he sold the rights. It's always a good idea to avoid selling "all rights," unless the amount offered is excellent or the writer decides that the sale—for prestige or another reason—is worth abdicating all rights to the piece.

Electronic rights—This is a term used to define a bundle of rights related to computer technology. It may include the right to reproduce the material on CD-ROMs, in online databases, in multimedia or interactive media, on web sites, or with publishing-on-demand systems. Just like all other rights, an author may wish to assign certain electronic rights and retain others.

First North American rights—A specific form of first serial rights. This is an agreement to let a periodical publish the material before any other periodical within North America publishes it. This is probably the most common type of rights purchased when short stories and articles are acquired by a periodical published in the United States.

First serial rights—The right to be the first periodical to publish the material. May be limited geographically.

Foreign language rights—The right to reproduce the material in one or more foreign languages. This also may involve geographic limitations, such as Spanish language rights for Mexico, but not Spain.

Foreign rights—These include the right to publish the material outside of the originating country. These may be broken down by country or by some other geographical division, such as European rights, and may involve foreign language rights.

One-time rights—This is generally used when a writer sells an article to more than one noncompeting newspaper or magazine. This means the periodical buys nonexclusive rights to use the piece once.

Second serial rights—Also called reprint rights. This gives a periodical the right to print a piece that has already appeared somewhere else. Like one-time rights, these are usually nonexclusive.

Simultaneous rights—The right to publish the material at the same time as another publisher. An example would be when a writer sells the same article to more than one of the many regional periodicals published.

Subsidiary rights—This is a term that refers to any secondary rights including, but not limited to:

- Audio rights
- Book club rights
- Condensation rights
- TV rights
- Film rights
- Mass-market paperback rights
- Merchandising rights
- Trade paperback rights
- Translation rights

Subsidiary rights usually come into play with books. Often an author will assign these rights to a book publisher with the agreement that the author will share in the profits when the publisher exploits these rights or licenses others to exploit them.

Dealing with Rejection

There are many reasons a publishing company turns down a project that have nothing to do with the quality of the work or its publishability. When you get a form rejection letter, don't get discouraged. It may be that the editor used a form letter because he didn't want to tell you how awful your work was, but chances are, something else came into play.

There are at least four other reasons editors are reluctant to give you a concrete reason for declining your work:

- It takes time out of an already too-busy day.
- Giving a reason suggests that the door is still open and appears to the author as an opportunity to begin a dialogue with the editor, when, if he wanted to discuss your fixing or changing something and resubmitting the work, he would have said so.
- Explaining how elements particular to his company's publishing program came into play to nix your project might be sharing confidential corporate information with an outsider.
- Editors know they aren't the final authority on what will please the reading public and they don't want to discourage you.

Persistence is frequently the key to getting published. Mark Victor Hansen and Jack Canfield had their fabulously successful *Chicken Soup for the Soul* rejected by publishers 140 times before Health Communications picked it up.

Rejection is part of most writers' lives. Remember, you aren't defeated until you quit submitting.

Questions to Ask Literary Agents

The following is a list—prepared by the Association of Author's Representatives, Inc.—of suggested topics for authors to discuss with literary agents after an agent has offered to represent them. There is reason for concern if an agent balks at answering these questions or says he or she doesn't have the time.

1. Is your agency a sole proprietorship? A partnership? A corporation?

2. Are you a member of the Association of Authors' Representatives?

3. How long have you been in business as an agent?

4. How many people does your agency employ?

5. Of the total number of employees, how many are agents, as opposed to clerical workers?

6. Do you have specialists at your agency who handle movie and television rights? Foreign rights? Do you have subagents or corresponding agents overseas and in Hollywood?

7. Do you represent other authors in my area of interest?

8. Who in your agency will actually be handling my work? Will the other staff members be familiar with my work and the status of my business at your agency? Will you oversee or at least keep me apprized of the work that your agency is doing on my behalf?

9. Do you issue an agent-author contract? May I review a specimen copy? And my I review the language of the agency clause that appears in contracts you negotiate for your clients?

10. What is your approach to providing editorial input and career guidance for your clients or for me specifically?

11. How do you keep your clients informed of your activities on their behalf? Do you regularly send them copies of publishers' rejection letters? Do you provide them with submission lists and rejection letters on request? Do you regularly, or upon request, send out updated activity reports?

12. Do you consult with your clients on any and all offers?

13. Some agencies sign subsidiary contracts on behalf of their clients to expedite processing. Do you?

14. What are your commissions for: 1) basic sales to U.S. publishers; 2) sales of movie and television rights; 3) audio and multimedia rights; 4) British and foreign translation rights?

15. What are your procedures and time-frames for processing and disbursing client funds? Do you keep different bank accounts separating author funds from agency revenue?

16. What are your policies about charging clients for expenses incurred by your agency? Will you list such expenses for me? Do you advance money for such expenses? Do you consult with your clients before advancing certain expenditures? Is there a ceiling on such expenses above which you feel you must consult with your clients?

17. How do you handle legal, accounting, public relations or similar professional services that fall outside the normal range of a literary agency's function?

18. Do you issue 1099 tax forms at the end of each year? Do you also furnish clients upon request with a detailed account of their financial activity, such as gross income, commissions and other deductions, and net income, for the past year?

19. In the event of your death or disability, or the death or disability of the principal person running the agency, what provisions exist for continuing operation of my account, for the processing of money due to me, and for the handling of my books and editorial needs?

20. If we should part company, what is your policy about handling any unsold subsidiary rights to my work that were reserved to me under the original publishing contracts?

21. What are your expectations of me as your client?

22. Do you have a list of Do's and Don'ts for your clients that will enable me to help you do your job better?

Reprinted by permission of Association of Authors' Representatives, Inc. (www.aar-online.org)

Standard Manuscript Format

There is no single correct page format for a manuscript, but following common format conventions, as shown here, is a good way to say to an editor: "I am a professional." Always use letter-sized, white paper. Always be sure the print is dark and legible. Paper clip sheets together or use a manuscript box; never staple. Be sure to check individual guidelines for special requirements.

List the rights you're offering to sell.

Some say a copyright notice is the mark of a novice. Most editors won't care either way.

With articles and short stories, list the aproximate word count, rounding off to the nearest 50 or 100.

Social security number is necessary for government reporting of payments.

Come down about one-third and type the title in all caps. Double space and type "by" and the author's name.

Leave four blank lines, then start the text.

Indent paragraphs.

Double space text. Do not right-justify it or hyphenate words at the end of a line.

Left, right and bottom margins should be 1"-1½" wide.

Place a slug line: last name/a key word from the title/page number, approximately one-quarter of an inch down, right justified, on all but first page.

Leave 1½" blank at top of sheet.

With articles and short stories, drop 4 lines below end of text and type MORE," except on the last page type "-30-" or "END".

Author's Tool Kit

Submission Tracking Sheet

Photocopy this page and use for each item submitted

Title: _____

Notes:

① Publisher: _____ Editor: _____ Phone: _____

Address: _____ Date submitted: _____ Multiple Submission? No Yes

Date to follow up: _____ Date followed up: _____ Follow-up note: _____

Date accepted: _____ Pub date: _____ Payment due date: _____ Payment amount: _____ Clips received: _____ Rejection date: _____

② Publisher: _____ Editor: _____ Phone: _____

Address: _____ Date submitted: _____ Multiple Submission? No Yes

Date to follow up: _____ Date followed up: _____ Follow-up note: _____

Date accepted: _____ Pub date: _____ Payment due date: _____ Payment amount: _____ Clips received: _____ Rejection date: _____

③ Publisher: _____ Editor: _____ Phone: _____

Address: _____ Date submitted: _____ Multiple Submission? No Yes

Date to follow up: _____ Date followed up: _____ Follow-up note: _____

Date accepted: _____ Pub date: _____ Payment due date: _____ Payment amount: _____ Clips received: _____ Rejection date: _____

④ Publisher: _____ Editor: _____ Phone: _____

Address: _____ Date submitted: _____ Multiple Submission? No Yes

Date to follow up: _____ Date followed up: _____ Follow-up note: _____

Date accepted: _____ Pub date: _____ Payment due date: _____ Payment amount: _____ Clips received: _____ Rejection date: _____

⑤ Publisher: _____ Editor: _____ Phone: _____

Address: _____ Date submitted: _____ Multiple Submission? No Yes

Date to follow up: _____ Date followed up: _____ Follow-up note: _____

Date accepted: _____ Pub date: _____ Payment due date: _____ Payment amount: _____ Clips received: _____ Rejection date: _____

Banish Writer's Block Forever

Definition: **writer's block** – *When the only thing more blank than the screen in front of you is your mind.*

Perhaps nothing is more dreaded among writers than writer's block. Oh sure, we've all read the Sunday *Times*' interviews of famous authors who express surprise that anyone suffers from writer's block when, for these gods of literature, the words simply come tumbling out, elbowing each other in their haste to get to the screen. And, who knows, maybe these writers never have to deal with writer's block, but the rest of us, mere mortals that we are, must occasionally battle this particular demon.

To know one's enemy is to have a leg up on one's enemy, so let's take a look at three common causes of writer's block—and a few strategies you can use to beat it into submission.

Cause number one: You've got nothing to say

This malady in itself exists for at least three reasons. One is lack of passion for what you are writing about. How can you wax elegant about something if you have no real interest in it?

Clear this hurdle by changing subjects when possible or, when not, by looking for an angle on the subject in which you can get interested. Find you need 500 words on golf, but hate the sport? Write about why you hate it. Maybe it's distasteful to you because every time you and your husband take a weekend vacation, he deserts you to play a five-hour round. In this case, you might write about how you and other golf widows fill these lonely hours, offering positive strategies such as visiting a day-spa or museum hopping.

Another reason you might have nothing to say is because you don't have enough information on the topic. This becomes apparent when you find yourself trying to pad whatever it is you're writing just to get the word count up. The cure here is to go back to the library or the Internet and do more research. When you have plenty of information, there will be plenty to write.

This works with fiction too. Need to provide background on a 90-year-old character's tendency to hoard? Pull out Marc McCutcheon's authoritative *Writer's Guide to Everyday Life from Prohibition Through World War II* (Writer's Digest Books) and research the Great Depression for ideas on what this fellow may have lived through while he was raising his family.

A third reason writers find themselves with nothing to say is that they have no plan for what they are going to write. Even if only in your head, you have to have some idea of the structure of what it is you intend to write. Make a simple outline by jotting down the key concepts you want to get across and then rearrange them until they form a logical order. Pick one concept and write what it is you want to say about it, then go on to the next. Pretty soon, the piece will have written itself.

Cause number two: Perfectionism

If you allow your internal editor—probably in the voice of your high school English teacher—to interfere with comments like, "Does a comma really belong there?" or "That's not how you spell 'liaison,'" you'll never get anything written. Allow yourself to write a flawed first draft—then go back and edit what you wrote.

Cause number three: Self-doubt

Entertaining negative thoughts such as "I'm never going to get this published" or "My writing stinks," drains your creativity and sets you up for failure. If you can't banish such thoughts outright, build up your confidence in stages. Obtain objective opinions on your writing by joining a critique group or taking a writing class. Write and publish short pieces in lesser-known periodicals—nothing increases confidence like seeing your own byline, no matter what the venue.

Next time this demon visits you, put these strategies to work and send it scurrying back into it's barren lair.

Writers on Writer's Block

Wherever writers gather, the conversation is, sooner or later, bound to turn to writer's block. Here are some thoughts on it by some of the best in the business.

"Generally, when I hit writer's block, I stop. I can break away and work on other books. Or, I will pace around in circles downstairs in my house and talk to my dog about it."
—Amelia Atwater-Rhodes, author of *In the Forests of the Night*

"I think writer's block is simply the dread that you are going to write something horrible. But as a writer, I believe that if you sit down at the keys long enough, sooner or later something will come out."
—Roy Blount, Jr. author of *Crackers* and *One Fell Soup*

"You don't know what it is to stay a whole day with your head in your hands trying to squeeze your unfortunate brain so as to find a word."
—Gustave Flaubert, author of *Madame Bovary*

"Writer's block is only a failing of the ego."
—Norman Mailer, author of *The Naked and the Dead*

"This may seem oversimple, but if you think you have writer's block or are taking too long to write, the problem is probably that you are spending too much time writing (or trying to) and not enough time thinking."
—Steven D. Stark, author of *Writing to Win*

"I was trained as a newspaper reporter, so there's no such thing as writer's block. You get fired for having writer's block."
—Nora Ephron, author of *When Harry Met Sally*

"If I don't know my character well enough, then I'll have writer's block. That's a clear sign I haven't delved deep enough into the personalities of my characters."
—Lee Wardlaw, author of *Punia and the King of Sharks*

"If I'm stuck, I write something else, do laundry, or take a nap."
—Karen Cushman, author of *Catherine Called Birdy*

"I've never had the luxury of having writer's block. When I do, I think about my mortgage."
—Larry Dane Brimner author of *The Littlest Wolf*

"Trust the process. Acknowledge your doubts and then write anyway."
—Mary Pearson author of *Scribbler of Dreams*

Editors and Agents Can Smell Your Fear

By: Stephen Blake Mettee

When I was a little boy, some well-meaning adult told me that dogs could smell your fear. Thereafter, when I encountered a barking dog, I would extrapolate what that adult told me into "...and, if it smells your fear, it is more likely to a eat you all up." This thought, of course, only made me more fearful, which in turn, I imagined, made me smell more like a tasty bunny rabbit, which in turn made me more scared, which...well you get the picture.

I think this paranoid cycle often comes into play when writers approach literary agents and book editors. The first problem is that, for some reason, as authors (yes, I'm an editor, but I'm also an author), we have in our minds that editors and agents are inexorably important to us. They, and only they, can grant our grandest desires. They are gods. Omnipotent beings who hold the key to our success and happiness. It is an awesome power. And they wield this power whimsically.

Or so it seems.

First let me disavow you of this "gods" stuff. I know for a fact that cab drivers and maitre 'ds are just as surly to these immortals as they are to the rest of us. And it is only at writer's conferences that editors and agents can be seen walking across hotel swimming pools.

Omnipotent? Please. There isn't an agent or editor who bats 1,000. Most would be thrilled if ten percent of their projects went into a second printing. Bat that kind of percentage and they kick you out of Little League.

Whimsical? Not on your life. Most editors and agents know exactly what kind of material they can use—or at least they know it when they see it. Give them apples when they need oranges and you won't get a sale. However, deliver big juicy oranges, ripe for publishing, and you'll end up seeing your name on book spines time and again.

Here are four things you can do to get over your fear of editors and agents.

1.) Concentrate on the fact that you have something of value to offer and that the editor or agent is in the market for what you have. Be polite and friendly but don't be obsequious. What you are proposing is a business deal like any other business deal. You aren't asking for a favor or some kind of charity.

2.) If you are likely to encounter the editor or agent in person, have an "elevator speech" prepared. An elevator speech (so named because it is short enough to deliver between floors) is a one- to three-sentence description of your book idea. Here's an example for a book titled *Long Distance Grandparenting*: "My book is about the positive effect good grandparenting can have on children even though the grandparents live in a distant city, and it details strategies on how to achieve this. *Long Distance Grandparenting* will fill the need for grandparents who wish to be a stable part of their grandchildren's lives even in today's mobile society." Practice your elevator speech until you can say it without stumbling.

3.) When corresponding with the editor or agent, do the little things that say "I am a professional": Spell the editor or agent's name correctly; explain in your query letter why you chose to approach this particular person; use correct manuscript format; double check for spelling or other errors, include a SASE (self-addressed, stamped envelope) with queries and proposals. If you are certain you are coming across as a professional, your fear will decrease.

4.) If none of the above does the job, picture the editor or agent in his or her underwear. This works every time.

Listen!

How to use dialogue to light up your characters until they attract readers like moths to a flame

By Parke Godwin

Narrative is no problem, but I have an awful time with dialogue." Of all the writers I know, only one ever said dialogue was easy for her. She then added that she couldn't plot worth a damn. For far more writers, by admission or demonstration, the opposite seems to be true.

Good dialogue convinces the reader, depicts the characters clearly and moves the plot. After I decided to throw some light on this subject, I found myself worrying at the root of the problem like a pup at a slipper. Why is dialogue a common stumbling block? Why should something writers hear and speak every day suddenly freeze them up when they try to capture it on the page?

Hearing is one key. We all hear English differently as the words sift through our experience of and meanings for them. In the positive sense this makes for diversity of style; in the negative the writers aren't hearing conversation at all, they're writing for the eye and mind, not the ear.

Why? I'll give it a shot: Their education gets in the way.

Trying to nail down this insight, I thought back through the whole uninspired educational process America foists on children. We're taught to write in complete sentences with punctuation in the right places, and we're graded on the relative success of our results. We are necessarily writing for a judicial eye. "This has got to be the best I can do, gotta be right or I won't get a good mark, get the job, impress the person I'm writing to." Small wonder that when we try to put words into fictional mouths, we restimulate these memories and freeze up, even to an avoidance of letter writing. The words come stiff and awkward because habit is working dead against talent and instinct, so you don't get the ring of truth—and remember, ring is a sound, not a word on paper. Unconsciously the writer strives by habit to be correct, putting down not how they would sound but how they should.

Granted, professional fiction requires a certain literacy. More than this it takes a supple facility with language, but don't let grammar lessons or the layered habits of school get in the way; they can be ruinous inhibitors. There are legions of highly educated people (and, God knows, educators) unable to write or even converse without putting you to sleep. Their graduate and doctoral theses molder undisturbed in university libraries.

The first rule in writing "natural" dialogue—hey, like someone's saying it for real—is to forget your grammar and education and *hear* it.

People don't usually think or speak in complete sentences. A person with a grammatical tic may annoy purists, but such verbal habits can illuminate the character and bring him to life. You've heard the guy who buttonholes his listener by adding "know what I mean?" to so many sentences. Or the speaker who makes a redundant sentence out of what should be a subordinate clause: "...a love affair between two men, which she didn't approve of that at all."

You hear this often in conversation, if you listen like a writer, and I wonder if the person isn't compulsively honoring the moss-grown rule about not dangling a preposition at the end of a sentence. But people *do* when they speak naturally. I've used both of the above tics to good advantage in fiction.

Given that good dialogue lights up the character with his own spontaneous words, you should have a clear idea of that person's "sound"—which is compounded of his background, education and experience, and his emotional makeup, all within the work's chosen style. People don't talk in any consistent style all the time, but in fiction dialogue must be appropriate to the story setting, tone and characters. Let's consider four basic types.

Informal dialogue

Naturalistic or "kitchen sink" dialogue is people expressing themselves informally and the hell with grammar, if the characters knew it to begin with. A classic example is the famous taxi scene from *On the Waterfront*:

> "You don't understand, Charley. I coulda been a contender. I coulda been somebody. Instead of a bum which is what I am, let's face it."

The Brando character, Terry Molloy, probably never went beyond the tenth grade or his own neighborhood and sounds like it. The ear again. The advantage of good naturalistic dialogue is that it moves like a shot, carries the reader along with it. Also the short conversational lines leave a good deal of white space on the page, much more attractive and restful to the reader's eye than long, thick paragraphs.

Here's a good technique that's worked well for me. When I have to talk about a character in narrative, whenever suitable, I like to have him or her break in to the narrative, often in the middle of a sentence, with their own typical comments, like this passage from my *Lord of Sunset*:

> Mother was everywhere, badgering the cooks, fretting over supplies not arrived, upstairs and down...counting linens twice over, seeing to the hanging of holly ropes—
> "Don't put it there; it goes *there*. And use smaller nails. It's holly you're putting up, not a gallows."
> —and finding time that afternoon before the wedding to bathe and dress me herself.

The above example is a very long single sentence, giving the sense of a mother's perpetual motion preparing for Christmas and her daughter's wedding all at once. I made it more palatable and vivid by breaking in with the mother's harried line of dialogue.

One of my major gripes in naturalistic dialogue, one which dulls much modern fiction and too many films, is excessive profanity or obscenity. This seems to be a pitfall for very young writers or those who never have or never will grow up. "Look at me being gritty and street smart." Come on, we're all big people, we know all the nasty words. Beyond a certain point—very quickly reached—this verbal grime doesn't move the story or illuminate character. It's a lazy copout that no longer frightens horses in the street, merely annoys and ultimately bores an intelligent reader. Sure, people use pungent language and always have, but art cannot imitate life completely and remain art. In this case, "wherein a little more than a little is by much too much"— trust me, less is more.

Then again, if it's right for the character to be salty, make sure you and the reader know why. Justify the choice. In *Limbo Search*, my science fiction novel, the burnout fighter pilot Janice Tyne is a woman at the end of her career and psychological rope at 27. She can't be what she's been anymore, but she's terrified of the future. Her X-rated dialogue is a symptom of fear and tension; otherwise she'd be an unattractive character with no more than a habitually dirty mouth, and that's never very interesting.

Realistic dialogue

Realistic dialogue, while appearing deceptively natural, is more organized. The vast bulk of modern plays and fiction employ this style combined with naturalistic. Classic examples are Miller's *Death of a Salesman*, Chayefsky's screenplay for *Network*, or William Goldman's piquant tongue-in-cheek dialogue for *Butch Cassidy and the Sundance Kid* or *The Princess Bride*. From the last:

> "You seem a good fellow. I hate to kill you."
> "You seem a good fellow. I hate to die."

Pitfalls in realistic lines are the lack of accurate ear and the old bugaboo of educational freeze-up. One can be so organized, correct and formal that the lines go flat and lose the sound of people talking to each other. Read it aloud and *listen*, please. Your reader will thank you. If that reader is I, I'll thank you profusely and maybe buy your next book as well.

Another dangerous copout in realistic is putting quote marks around what is obviously pure plot exposition and passing it off as dialogue. This needs little explanation; we've all seen examples. The following horror is not from any published source, but one I made up during a lecture to demonstrate:

> "Meanwhile, alarmed by the growth of the Protestant Reformation in the north, Rome's answer was to found the Jesuit order."

Writers who call this dialogue should be restricted to occasional postcards. They haven't taken the trouble to put exposition where it belongs, and they don't fool anyone.

Heightened realism

Here we come to a style I've loved since discovering the riches of Anouilh, Shaw, Dylan Thomas and others of that silver-tongued ilk. Heightened realism is realism with music and the lights turned up high. The language shimmers with wit and a cutting edge. Your ear *and* your syntax are vital here because of the economy and crispness the style demands. Nothing dulls a lucid passage more than too many words. Nothing kills a good line deader than one word too many or in the wrong place. More than once I've winced at my own finished work on the printed page and moaned, "Why didn't I cut that word? Why didn't I invert the whole line?" Never mind how well it reads; how does it *play*?

In *Robin and the King*, a son of William the Conqueror is speaking of his royal father. I could have given him the line thus:

> "My father is very devout. He wants to understand the will of God and the English people but cannot comprehend either."

Historically and hopelessly correct with none of the tart flavor of bluff, rowdy Rossel who became William II. The line carried the same meaning with far more bite and economy this way:

> "Father is fascinated by things he can't understand. Like God and England."

And in *Camelot*, Arthur wonders of Guinevere:

> "Why is Jenny in that castle? How did we come to this agonizing absurdity? Where did I stumble?...Should I not have loved her? Then I should not have been born."

Read that line again. Taste the flavor and the lean muscularity of "agonizing absurdity." Not a phrase you'd hear in realistic dialogue, but so beautifully expressive and precise, a bonus HR affords to those who work for it. Another favorite example is Eleanor of Acquitaine to her sons in *The Lion in Winter*:

> "Good, good Louis. If I'd managed sons for him instead of all those little girls, I'd still be stuck with being queen of France and we should not have known each other. Such, my angels, is the role of sex in history."

The last two examples are from stage works, true, but there's no reason why such supple language won't work as HR in prose. Because in HR you're going a little beyond realism, slightly larger than life. The style is more suited to fantasy and historical fiction than a contemporary setting. The main danger here is going too far, falling in love with verbal agility and cleverness for its own sake (said one of the guilty), but there's a sturdy cure. In rewrite be a hanging judge with an honest ear and a long blue pencil.

For a moment let's consider that honest ear, so necessary to any style from "kitchen sink" to the transcendent lines of Shakespeare. Good dialogue convinces, bad does not. The magic difference is human truth, which we achieve by living and listening for what makes humans tick. "The players cannot keep counsel; they'll tell all." So they will, but you have to listen in depth. Bearing this in mind, let's come to the last category.

Larger than life

Call it lyrical or poetic if you will. In LTL you're presenting truth in a big way. The nature of this style pretty much limits its use in prose to works of high fantasy or magic realism, although Ray Bradbury's early and middle period work made brilliant use of LTL and HR combined. Since the dumbing-down of media-addicted America, many people might find this hard to read, if they read at all, so economy, concision and truth are all-important. You have to be secure in your ear, cadence and command of language. Nothing falls flatter than lyrical language that doesn't sing or soar. So put this down in large letters over your word processor: *High language does not mean highflown.*

Highflown is what you get when words for their own effect inflate beyond the emotional truth they're charged to convey. Put another way, you can take the language as high as the emotional truth is real. When you no longer bear the reader along with language—that labored point where he is simply slogging through *words*: "Look at me writing pretty"—you've lost him.

In LTL you present the pure thought or emotion, all meat and muscle. There's little or no room for the vagaries or digressions of naturalism/realism in which the character may honestly grope for a meaning or even try to conceal it for personal reasons. Try a good modern translation of *Oedipus Rex, Antigone* or *Medea*; better, see them staged and hear them. The action develops like a taut thriller.

The anonymous eighth-century tale of Beowulf plays on a poetic stage as vast and dark as any envisioned by Richard Wagner in his *Ring* cycle. In my novel adaptation, *The Tower of Beowulf*, Grendel and his mother, Sigyn, are hideous creatures, halfling children of gods and giants, but a merciful spell gives them the illusion of beauty. While Sigyn has long known the truth, young Grendel can't bear the horrible revelation of his true appearance. When Sigyn comforts him, to give her a realistic tone would be ludicrously flat and wrong, as perhaps something like this:

> "I don't know, I can't say why we're this way. It seemed kinder to let you believe a lie. I would make it different if I could, believe me. Because I love you. I am so sorry."

Sure, honest enough, but not *big* enough for LTL. The speech doesn't fill the scene at all or do justice to creatures trapped between two worlds and larger than life themselves. Their joy or sorrow needs far richer orchestration:

> "We are (men's) nightmares. If there were more of us than them, I suppose they would be ours. Surely they have been mine. Loki was not unkind. He gave me a little beauty for a little time…oh, Grendel, I would be beautiful for you if I could. I would have all women and all worlds fair for you—and for myself while the wishing. But I am a god's get in the body of a beast. Pity, but can Hrothgar and his kind say more? Deal with what you are, my son."

Never easy, the balancing of high language with emotional truth, so find the truth first and always trust instinct before intellect. Emotional truth is different and more elusive than the cerebral kind, which may intrigue and entertain as it does so effervescently in the works of G.B. Shaw, but rarely invokes deep emotional response. Remember that intellect proceeds from the simple to the complex, wisdom from the complex to the profoundly simple, which is where you'll find the truth of any dialogue, whatever the style.

Parke Godwin has been a published novelist since 1973. His work has been published in England, France, Germany, Holland and Poland.. He is best known for his Arthurian novels Firelord *and* Beloved Exile *and for his novels of Robin Hood,* Sherwood *and* Robin and the King.

He is the author of the satires Waiting for the Galactic Bus *and* The Snake Oil Wars *and the historical novel* Lord of Sunset, *a novel of the Norman Conquest and prequel to* Sherwood. *This was followed by* The Lovers, *his first Arthurian novel in twelve years, and* Watch By Moonlight, *a novel based on the popular poem "The Highwayman" by Alfred Noyes.*

In recent years Godwin has turned his attention to short stories, his second collection The Night You Could Hear Forever *due out from Wildside Press late summer 2006. Currently he has sold film rights to* Sherwood *and the black-humor short story "A Matter of Taste," plus posting all his work for film possibilities.*

Periodicals' Guidelines

Periodicals

12th Planet Literary Journal

You have entered the realm of *12th Planet*, one of the premiere internet literary magazines. In existence since, February of 1999 (a dinosaur in on-line time!) we are proud to have showcased some of the best authors on the web.

Submission Guidelines

We welcome your work! Please submit your poetry and/or essays according to the following guidelines!

WHAT WE ACCEPT

You may submit up to 3 poems at one time. We tend to shy away from rhyming poetry and gravitate towards poems that are rich in imagery.

You may also submit one essay at one time. We are looking for essays with a satirical bent. Think "A Modest Proposal".

Please do not submit additional work until we have responded to your initial submission. Any additional work submitted before we have a chance to respond to your initial submission will not be reviewed and will be deleted or destroyed.

We do NOT publish chapbooks or collections of poetry. Please do not query us asking how we can publish your manuscript!

HOW TO SUBMIT YOUR WORK

All e-mail submissions must be submitted in the body of an the e-mail. NO ATTACHMENTS ARE ACCEPTED!!!! To forewarn you, we delete any submission that is in attachment form. E-mail your submissions to twelfthplanet@worldnet.att.net. Please list "submission" in the subject line, and enclose all work in ONE e-mail.

All snail mail submissions must be accompanied by a self-addressed stamped envelope (SASE) or an e-mail address to which we can respond. We are usually slower at responding to snail mail submissions, since we function mainly electronically. However, we understand not everyone feels comfortable using email, and may not have easy access to the Internet. That being said, please address submissions to:

NOTE! U.S. Postal prices are increasing, effective June 30. If you send a submission via the mail from this point on, please be certain the SASE has enough postage.

PAYMENT & COPYRIGHT

We pay $10 per accepted piece, payable upon publication.

We claim one-time electronic publishing rights. After publication all rights revert back to the author. If your piece is published in another forum at a later date, you must list *12th Planet* at the original publisher. We also retain the right to re-publish your work in print, should we decide to do a "Best of" collection in the future. At that time we would notify you of our intent to publish your work in this forum, which will include further monetary compensation.

We will do our best to reply to your submission within 2 months. However, the volume of submissions we receive does not always allow for this. If you haven't heard from us by then, please drop us a line to make certain we received your original submission!

Finally, please make certain that the email address you use to make your submission will be valid for the next 2-3 months. We get email returned to us on a regular basis because the address is not longer in use, or the mailbox is full. If you do not hear from us, make certain it isn't for this reason!

Categories: Poetry—Short Stories

CONTACT: Rachel Baron, Editor
Material: All
4111 Circle Court, Ste. 1
Williamsville NY 14221
E-mail: twelfthplanet@worldnet.att.net
Website: www.12thplanetmagazine.com

360 Magazine

360 Magazine is presently accepting articles on all topics related to the wheelchair community. Our overall tone is informative and entertaining. A general familiarity with our editorial content is the best guideline for submissions, but don't hesitate to surprise us.

Submit story ideas and edit questions to: editor@360mag.com

Here are some points to keep in mind:

Audience: Our core readers are men and women between the ages of 18 to 45. They are living with a spinal cord injury, cerebral palsy, multiple sclerosis, post-polio syndrome, spina bifida, amputation or other physical disability that frequently requires use of a wheelchair.

Regular Departments

360 Profile: We don't focus exclusively on celebrities. We're just interested in people doing inspiring, unusual stuff.

From Our Readers: All 360 members are welcome to contribute. In terms of content, surprise us. Focus on specific experiences and observations, rather than drawn out life stories. No payment, but writer retains all rights. We also accept excerpts from newly published or upcoming works of nonfiction.

Sports: From surfing to sled hockey, we write about it. But we rarely use play-by-play narratives.

Travel: We cover the exotic as well as the well-known spots. Our readers need tangible information not general travel stuff. Don't give us moment-by-moment travelogues. That is more appropriate for our forums.

Nutrition & Health: Article sources should be medical professionals. That said, we intend to have fun with this section so we're open to suggestions.

Sex & Relationships: One month we'll provide insight from a well-respected researcher, the next we'll focus on strip clubs. Anything goes, but nothing beyond an R rating.

Why Me: Readers inspire our illustrated story section. There is no financial arrangement. If a reader's tale is chosen, he or she receives a 360 cap and story credit. All submissions become the property of 360 Magazine, L.L.C.

Bookmark: From criminals to long-lost loves to alien planets, we love a good story. All fiction genres are welcome. No payment, but author retains all rights. We also accept excerpts from newly published or upcoming works of nonfiction.

Length
- Articles: 700 - 1,300 words
- From Our Readers: 650 words
- Fiction: 1,200 - 2,000 words

Payment
- Ranges from 10 cents to 25 cents per word, depending on research required.
- Payment on acceptance. No payment for works of fiction and personal essays, but author retains all rights.
- Byline given.

Rights
We purchase first electronic rights and nonexclusive archival rights. On occasion, we use reprints

Queries
Response time is usually about two weeks. Maybe three if the weather is nice. We do not accept simultaneous submissions

Place all information in the body of the email, including writing clips. No attachments please; we won't even open the file. Attachments can wreak havoc with our system and make our wonderful Web guys cranky. Never a good thing.

Categories: Fiction—Nonfiction—Health—Nutrition—Sports—Travel—Wheelchair Community

CONTACT: Nora Wood, Editor
PO box 922
Clifton NJ 07014
Phone: 917-568-4077
E-mail: editor@360mag.com
Web site: 360usainc.com

4-Wheel Drive & Sport Utility

Circulation: 50,440
Frequency: monthly
Published by the PRIMEDIA Enthusiast Group.

Features in-depth articles about Jeeps, Broncos, Explorers, Blazers and domestic and imported four-wheel drive trucks and sport utility vehicles. Editorial also includes technical how-to information and reviews of aftermarket products and accessories.

For more information, visit the magazine's Web site at: www.4wdandsportutility.com.

Editorial submissions are welcomed, but the editor recommends that contributors query first. All contributions must be accompanied by a self-addressed, stamped envelope. Solicitations for editorial coverage, including car feature articles, should be submitted via US mail. Please include a photograph of the vehicle/project, a quick reference sheet and a few paragraphs detailing the editorial significance of your work. Due to busy travel and work schedules, the editor is not able to field calls related to potential editorial coverage. We assume no responsibility for loss or damage of any unsolicited materials.

Due to the volume of letters received we cannot directly answer any tech inquiry letter. Published letters may be edited for style, length or content. Be sure to include your full name and mailing address in all correspondence.

Categories: Nonfiction—Automobiles—Sports/Recreation—Technical

CONTACT: Editor
Material: All
PRIMEDIA Anaheim (McMullen Argus)
2400 E. Katella Ave, Ste 1100
Anaheim CA 92806
Phone: 714-939-2400
Fax: 714-939-6390
E-mail: 4wd@mc mcmullenargus.com
Website: www.mcmullenargus.com

5.0 Mustang & Super Fords

Formal guidelines not available. Please read a number of issues to ascertain the publication's style and needs.

Send queries to address below.

Categories: Nonfiction—Automobiles—Hobbies—Technical

CONTACT: Steve Turner, Editor-in-Chief
Material: All
3816 Industry Blvd.
Lakeland FL 33811
Phone: 863-644-0449
Website: www.50mustangandsuperfords.com

5280 Magazine

5280 is Denver's premier guide to the arts, entertainment, dining, and lifestyle issues in the Mile-High City. First published in 1993, the magazine has a circulation of 80,000, which translates to a total readership of approximately 184,000. The vast majority of these readers live in the Denver metro area. Most are in their late 30s or early 40s, and have an average household income in excess of $100,000 per year. Ninety-one percent are college educated, and an almost equal number own their own homes. All of which means that our articles must be targeted specifically to the needs and interests of an affluent, educated audience.

With only nine issues per year, we must be highly selective in the articles we choose to publish. Because Denver is such a competitive media market—few American cities of its size still have two daily newspapers, not to mention a strong alternative weekly and numerous TV and radio news organizations—this task becomes all the more difficult.

WHAT WE'RE LOOKING FOR
In a nutshell, we're looking for writers who understand the difference between newspaper and magazine writing. This is a subjective matter, of course, but it boils down to a difference both in how we approach a story and how we tell it.

Newspapers (and television) typically cover the Who, What, When, and Where. That leaves us with the Why and How. Put another way, a good magazine article should answer the question "What does it mean?"

Because our readers are well-informed, they may already be aware of the topic you're covering. This means that your article must offer insight that goes beyond a simple recitation of facts. For example, the dailies may be reporting that monthly home sales figures continue to soar. It's up to you to step back, put the numbers in perspective, and offer guidance to the reader who wonders whether now is the time to put his or her home on the market.

Newspapers tend to rely on official sources. It's our job to also include the voices of the people whose lives are actually affected by the issues being covered. If the newspapers report that burglaries are up in a particular Denver neighborhood, it's up to us to find the victims of those crimes and to convey their experiences in a compelling way.

Finally, a magazine story is told with style. Tom Wolfe once likened newspaper writers to golf announcers, whispering in the background so as to not interrupt the play. The magazine writer's aim is to craft a story that is every bit as entertaining to read as it is informative.

WHAT WE EXPECT
Too often, writers who are new to magazines think that they have been freed from the drudgery of old-fashioned reporting, and can now exercise their long repressed literary aspirations. Not so. Because we have longer to prepare an issue, our articles deserve to be held to an even higher standard of accuracy and professionalism than those published in the dailies.

But unlike a newspaper story, which typically presents both sides of an issue and leaves the reader to draw his or her own conclusion, our writers must be able to formulate a reasoned and well-grounded reaction to the subject matter. Again, your article should answer the question "What does it mean?"

Articles should be strongly organized and clearly presented. Unlike the newspaper's inverted pyramid, magazine articles have a beginning, a middle, and an end. The magazine writer has many of the novelist's tools—dialog, description, narrative, and point of view, to name a few—at his or her disposal. Your writing should have personality.

It's worth pointing out, however, that this is not a license for self indulgence. Remember that Picasso was an accomplished traditional painter before embracing more abstract techniques. In particular, the first person should be used only when it truly advances the story. No one cares that you arrived late for your interview, or that you ordered the fish and she had the veal.

Above all else, of course, your finished product must have a strong local feel. Our mission is to help our readers get the most out of living in this very unique city. If your story could run in any other city magazine with only minor changes, you haven't done your job.

HOW TO BREAK IN
It should go without saying that your first step should be to read

the magazine. Become familiar with our style and understand the kinds of articles we publish. Then submit a written query that succinctly summarizes your idea and explains why you're the writer to bring the story to our readers. If possible, also include published clips that give us an idea of your abilities. A self-addressed, stamped envelope should accompany all queries. Do not telephone us with story proposals.

A query should propose a story with a specific angle, not just a broad topic. Rather than suggesting a story on skiing, tell us that you want to write a guide to the best powder trails in Colorado. Almost any topic is fair game, provided that it has a strong connection to life in Denver.

The best places for new writers to break into the magazine are our Profiles (800-1,000 words), Getaways (1,000 words), or Atmosphere (300-400 words) sections. You can also propose feature stories (2,000-4,000 words), though these assignments are less likely to go to newcomers. Our restaurant reviews are written by our regular restaurant critic and are not assigned to other writers. We do not publish fiction or poetry.

Don't simply offer your services for whatever stories we may be looking to assign. Queries give us a chance to see how a prospective writer's mind works. (Stories proposed by our editors always are assigned to writers we have already worked with.)

When proposing a story, keep in mind that we generally assign stories at least 10 weeks prior to an issue's cover date. For this reason, when writing about events, we usually look forward to upcoming events rather than reviewing what has already occurred.

Copy should be prepared according to the conventions of the Associated Press Style Book. Submit articles in electronic format, accompanied by a printed manuscript. Microsoft Word for Macintosh is our preferred file format. If your word processor doesn't support this format, please contact us to arrange an alternate format.

Along with the article itself, you should submit a list of your sources (including phone numbers) and notes from your interviews (including transcriptions of taped interviews). These will be used for fact-checking purposes.

TERMS

Once assigned a story, you will be required to sign a contract which grants 5280 Publishing, Inc. first-time North American rights to publish the article in both print and electronic formats. **Fees for articles vary, depending on writer and piece.** In order to be paid, you must submit an invoice with your article. Invoices should include your Social Security Number or Federal Tax ID Number.

Categories: Nonfiction—Culture—Entertainment—Food—Lifestyle—Recreation—Denver

CONTACT: Editor
Material: All
5280 Publishing, Inc.
1514 Curtis St., Ste. 300
Denver, CO 80202
Phone: 303-832-5280
Fax: 303-832-0470

5678 Country
5678 Swing

Champion Media Group publishes two magazines *5678 Swing* and *5678 Swing*. Each is published six times per year focused on dance in its perspective genre. 5678 is a niche publication that has approximately 10,000 readers per month. *5678 Country* features articles pertaining to Country Western couples, line, and team dancing in its many forms.

5678 Swing features articles pertaining to West coast Swing, Lindy Hop, Salsa, Shag, Hustle and other forms of Swing Type social dance.

Areas of Interest:

We are interested in articles of many different natures.

• *Celebrity Interviews:* Today's stars of the dance world

• *Dance Technique:* How to do the steps, connection, lead and follow and more

• *Event Reviews:* How did it go?

• *Social Dancing:* Where to go, what to do, who does what where.

• *Personal Profiles*: Teachers, Studios, Dance Clubs.... what's up?

• *Dance Humor:* Something true or fictitious.... just funny.

• *Just Dance:* Doesn't fit into a category above, so what, if it's dance we might just want it.

Submission Format:

All articles accepted by email or attached file only. We accept Microsoft Word or a text file.

We pay upon printing of the article and purchase all rights. We pay anywhere from $35 to $100 for features. Material is subject to editing for length, style and format. We encourage photos and prefer to receive them by email as well in 300 dpi jpeg format at regular size. If that is not possible they can be sent hard copy. Photos are paid depending on quantity of use and size.

Categories: Fiction—Nonfiction—Arts—Dance—Entertainment—Music

CONTACT: Barry Durand, Publisher
Material: All
PO Box 8886
Gaithersburg MD 20898
E-mail: durand5678@aol.com
Website: www.5678magazine.com

9-1-1 Magazine

Established 1988, Circulation 18,000. Editor: Randall D. Larson.

9-1-1 Magazine is the magazine for the public safety communications industry. Serving law enforcement, fire, emergency medical services, and disaster management, 9-1-1 Magazine provides valuable information to readers in all aspects of the public safety communications and response community. Each issue contains a blending of product-related, technical, operational, and people-oriented stories, covering the skills, training, and equipment which these professions all share in common. We run stories on provocative issues and cover major incidents from both a responder and a communications standpoint.

SUBMISSIONS

Eighty-five percent free-lance. Our primary need is for 1,000-2,500 word articles, accompanied if possible by appropriate high-quality photography (see below for Photography Guidelines, or click here). Each manuscript should include a 25-word biography of the author. All submissions must include social security number, address, and phone number.

We prefer queries, but will look at manuscripts on speculation. Most positive responses to queries are to be considered on spec, but occasionally we will make assignments. In such cases, we offer a 20-percent kill fee.

9-1-1 Magazine adheres to standard rules of manuscript formatting. All printed submissions must be double spaced, clear and readable. Handwritten manuscripts are not acceptable. Emailed files in MS Word format preferred. Hard copies must be accompanied by SASE if to be returned. We will return material first class unless appropriate additional postage is included. We assume no responsibility for unsolicited manuscripts, photos, or other material, nor for loss due to postal negligence or damage beyond our control.

We do not use poetry or fiction. We do not consider simultaneous submissions.

PREVIOUS USE

We rarely accept a manuscript or photograph that has been published elsewhere. Upon acceptance by 9-1-1 Magazine, authors and photographers will be asked to certify the material's exclusivity to 9-1-1 Magazine.

MANUSCRIPT PAYMENT

We pay 10-20 cents per word for feature articles. Stories submitted on behalf of vendors or agencies are usually not compensated. Columns pay a flat rate of $50 each.

9-1-1 Magazine buys first North American serial rights to manuscripts accepted, with a two-year option to purchase second (reprint) editorial rights at the original payment rate. All subsequent rights revert to the author. Payment is on publication.

PHOTOGRAPHY

9-1-1 Magazine has maintained a reputation for outstanding photography for many years.

Primary needs include dramatic photographs of incidents and unusual situations for covers, From the Field, and to illustrate articles. We especially need communications-related photos and law enforcement images. Query for specific topics in need of photography.

We do not use stock photos, and insist that all photography submitted to 9-1-1 Magazine be for our exclusive use.

Photo submissions should be transparencies or high resolution digital images (300 dpi jpg, minimum). Low resolution samples can be sent for consideration. All photos must be accompanied by date and description of the incident or situation pictured. Photos must be labeled with the name of the person to be credited.

9-1-1 Magazine pays $50 for color interior photos (if used at half page=$75; if full page=$100), $300 for cover photo. One-time editorial rights are purchased, with a two year option to purchase second (reprint) editorial rights at the original payment rate.

THE IMPORTANT STUFF

Our editorial schedule is planned several issues in advance, and broad themes are planned a year ahead. Freelancers are encouraged to submit queries or material of a seasonal nature well in advance. Email is the preferred method of contact.

9-1-1 Magazine is published for a knowledgeable, professional audience. Our target readership consists of 9-1-1 center administrators and dispatch managers and supervisors, and emergency services chiefs. Our primary considerations in selecting material are: quality; appropriateness of material; brevity, knowledge of our readership; accuracy; accompanying photography; originality, wit and humor; a clear direction and vision; and proper use of the language.

Categories: Nonfiction—Public Safety

CONTACT: Randall Larson, Editor
18201 Weston Pl
Tustin CA 92780
Phone: 714-544-7776
Fax: 714-838-9233

96 Inc.

About *96 Inc*: *96 Inc* Artists' Collaborative has received national attention over the past twelve years for its innovative ways of supporting new and established artists. Its goal is that of integrating the arts into the community and to bring together the professional and the beginner, the artist and the artisan. Using writing and literature as a base, *96 Inc* has created and presented new works in usual and unusual spaces. Since February 1995, 96 has been the resident company at the Lansdowne Street Playhouse, where it presented the New Works on Tuesdays series and afternoon workshops for high school students. Founded on inclusiveness, *96 Inc* places a strong belief in the potential of young people and in the potential and accomplishments of young artists of all ages.

96 Inc magazine has a national distribution in bookstores and is currently being used in several high schools and colleges in other parts of the country—Colorado, Kentucky, Minnesota, Ohio, South Carolina, Vermont, and West Virginia. In addition, the Lithuanian Translators Society translates the magazine and uses it in literature and language classes at the University of Vilnius.

Submissions: *96 Inc* considers submissions in short fiction and poetry.

When to Submit: *96 Inc* accepts submissions on an ongoing basis. The magazine is published annually.

Payment: Writers whose submissions are accepted for publication receive four free copies of the magazine.

Categories: Fiction—Arts—Poetry—Short Stories

CONTACT: Vera Gold or Nancy Mehegan, Editors
Material: All
PO Box 15559
Boston MA 02215
Phone: 617-267-0543
Fax: 617-262-3568
E-mail: mail@96inc.com
Website: www.96inc.com

A&U

A&U is a national, nonprofit HIV/AIDS magazine. We are interested in publishing original literature, art, opinion, and reportage relating in any way to the AIDS pandemic. With any submission, please include a brief personal biography (no longer than 25 words).

Submissions may be mailed to: A&U Magazine, Att: Submissions, 25 Monroe St. Suite 205, Albany, NY 12210. Electronic submissions, as Word attachments, may be mailed to Chael Needle, Managing Editor, at chaelneedle@mac.com or editor@aumag.org. Pay rate schedule available upon request.

Be sure to include your address, phone number, and e-mail address!

Fiction/Drama:
no longer than 1,000 words. Excerpts of longer works may be accepted; please include full work as well as excerpt
unpublished work only
if plays have been performed, please include any important performance information
include biography
Poetry:
any length/style accepted, shorter works preferred
include biography
Viewpoint/Essays:
around 700 words
include biography
Feature Articles:
submit proposals, please do not send completed stories or interviews; feature articles: about 1,200 words, cover stories: about 2,000 words
include personal resume
Reviews:
reviews of film, theater, books, art exhibits, video, music, and other media accepted
no longer than 300-600 words
include visuals such as film stills or dust jackets
include biography
preface every review in the following manner:
title of work or exhibit
subtitle (if applicable)
author(s) (or editor, director, artist)
publisher (or film/video distributor, art gallery)
year of publication, length (pages or minutes)
Manuscripts cannot be returned
Guidelines for Submitting Visual Material:
include SASE for return of visual materials
please do not send original works of art*
please attach a photo credit and description to each piece submitted
please include a standard photographer's release, allowing *A&U* to publish the work sent.
Only the following formats are accepted (listed in order of preference):
Transparencies
35 mm, medium format, large format (up to 4x5 inches)

color or black and white
no negatives
Prints
color or black and white
no smaller than 5x7 inches
no larger than 8x10 inches
glossy finish only please
please have custom prints made at a professional photo lab. Do not send consumer-grade machine prints
Electronic
High resolution JPEG (300 dpi, no less than 4x6 inches)
Also acceptable: high resolution tiffs and pdfs
Contact us for other exceptions
* to submit works of art:
please have paintings, sculptures and installations photographed in a manner suitable for printing press reproduction
if professional photography is not available please follow these guidelines:
subject should be brightly lit
use more than one light source
avoid shadows (use diffused or indirect light)
use color slide film
use film with the proper color balance for your light source
properly align the subject and the camera
check slides after processing for color accuracy and sharpness
use professional,not consumer-grade, film
please include a full resume
please label all slides in the following manner:
title of work
media
year of creation
artist name
photographers credit
if slides are courtesy of a gallery or artist rep., please credit
if the work is part of a private or public collection please state
Categories: Fiction—Nonfiction—Art—Drama—Essays—Health—Poetry—Reviews

CONTACT: Submissions, A&U Magazine
Material: All
25 Monroe St Ste 205
Albany NY 12210
CONTACT: Chael Needle, Managing Editor
Material: Electronic submissions
E-mail: chaelneedle@mac.com or editor@aumag.org

AAA Going Places

Please refer to *Going Places*

AAA Midwest Traveler

Please refer to *Midwest Traveler*

AAA Southern Traveler

Please refer to *Southern Traveler.*

AARP, The Magazine

Query letters for specific features and departments should be one page in length and accompanied by recent writing samples. The letter should explain the idea for the piece, tell how you would approach it as a writer, give some sense of your writing style, and mention the section of the magazine for which the piece is intended. **Your samples should not include the actual story that you are proposing.**

Features and departments cover the following categories:
Finance: investments, legal matters, and work issues
Health: tips, trends, studies
Food: recipes, emphasis on healthy eating
Travel: domestic and international
Consumerism: practical information and advice
General interest: new thinking, research, information on timely topics, trends
Profiles or first-person accounts of people who have made a dramatic change in their lives
AARP The Magazine discourages the submission of unsolicited manuscripts and assumes no responsibility for their return. Also, we do not print articles that have been previously published.
Rate of Payment
AARP The Magazine pays on acceptance at the minimum rate of $1.00 per contracted word. A kill fee of 25% will be paid for assigned articles that are not accepted for publication.
AARP The Magazine does not accept queries by fax. You may submit your query by email to member@aarp.org, but please do not send actual manuscripts via email.
Categories: Nonfiction—Consumer—Food—General Interest—Health—Travel

CONTACT: Editorial Submissions
AARP The Magazine
AARP
601 E St NW
Washington DC 20049

ABA Journal

Thank you for your inquiry about submitting an article. The *ABA Journal*, the official magazine of the American Bar Association, is published 12 times a year and distributed to more than 376,000 readers. We also publish the *ABA Journal* eReport, a weekly e-mail publication that is sent to more than 200,000 members who have submitted their e-mail addresses.

The *ABA Journal* does not publish unsolicited manuscripts. Our articles are written by in-house legal writers or by freelance journalists we hire for specific assignments.

The Journal will consider queries. We prefer to hire freelancers who have a law degree and experience as a reporter for a legal or consumer publication. If you are interested in freelancing for the Journal, we urge you to include your resumé and published clips when you contact us with story ideas.

We are interested in queries about legal news or practice-oriented topics.

Please send queries to Sarah Randag by e-mail at releases@abanet.org or by fax to (312) 988-6025.
WRITERS' GUIDELINES
The *ABA Journal*'s content is designed to appeal to the association's diverse membership, with some emphasis on general practitioners in smaller law firms.

In writing an article for possible publication in the Journal, please be familiar with the following guidelines:

1. Type of article. The focus of the Journal is on current events in the law and on ideas that will help lawyers to practice better and more efficiently. Articles should emphasize practical, rather than theoretical or esoteric material.

2. Readership. As you write, keep your audience in mind. The typical reader of the Journal is a lawyer whose age is 43, and who is in private practice in a small law firm. Most are general practitioners.

3. Writing Style. The Journal is a magazine that covers topical issues involving lawyers. STORIES WRITTEN IN THE STYLE OF LAW REVIEWS, ACADEMIC JOURNALS OR LEGAL BRIEFS WILL NOT BE ACCEPTED. Articles should be written in an infor-

mal, journalistic style. Short quotations from people and specific examples will improve an article.

4. Length. Feature articles should be NO MORE THAN 3,500 WORDS. News stories or departments are 650 words.

5. Title. Developing a working title for an article may help you keep it in focus. The working title may be accepted as is or altered by the Journal staff as it deems appropriate.

6. Editing. All articles are subject to editing by the Journal. All articles are edited to conform to the Journal editorial style, which generally follows the AP Stylebook. The Journal inserts subheads, captions and readouts as needed.

7. Copyright. By having an article published in the Journal, authors thereby grant all property rights in the article to the American Bar Association and consent to an unqualified right by the ABA to copyright the work. This grant includes the right of the ABA to republish the article in other media, including electronic databases. This applies unless other arrangements are made in writing.

8. Citations. Citations to cases and other materials should be incorporated into the text; FOOTNOTES ARE NOT PERMITTED.

9. Structure. It is suggested that articles open with an interesting catchy lead, followed by a "nut paragraph" that tersely states the gist of the article.

10. Biographical data. At the end of an article, give your name, whether you are a lawyer, your place of employment, and whether you serve on an ABA committee or other entity. This data may be shortened.

11. Manuscripts. Manuscripts should be typewritten in a standard font (not all italics or all capitals) and double spaced. A cover letter should accompany the manuscript, indicating your name, address and telephone number. You also can submit your article via e-mail to releases@abanet.org.

12. Graphics. The Journal obtains appropriate artwork or photographs, if any, to illustrate articles.

Categories: Nonfiction—Law

CONTACT: Debra Cassens, Managing Editor
Material: All
American Bar Association
750 N. Lake Shore Drive
Chicago IL 60611
Phone: 312-988-6009
Fax: 312-988-6025
Website: abanet.org/journal

Abilities
Canada's Lifestyle Magazine for People with Disabilities

ABILITIES is Canada's foremost cross-disability lifestyle magazine. It is widely read by people with disabilities, their families and professionals engaged in disability issues.

The mission of the magazine is to provide:

INFORMATION: to the readership about stories, events and services.

INSPIRATION: to the readership to participate in organizations and events that are or could/should be made accessible to them.

OPPORTUNITY: to the readership through exposure, four times a year, to a wealth of Canadian resources that facilitate self-empowerment of people with disabilities.

ABILITIES is distributed nationally and internationally. The publication is available in print, and on computer disk. Back issues are also available on the Internet. In addition to its subscriber base, ABILITIES is circulated to thousands of organizations across Canada committed to the advancement and well-being of people with disabilities, as well as thousands of professionals, corporations and government agencies.

The editorial scope of the magazine includes travel, health, sport, recreation, employment, education, transportation, housing, social policy, sexuality, movie/book reviews and personality profiles. Other topics such as specific events or conferences are also considered.

The style of the magazine is "conversational" in that it is important for each article to be appreciated by as many of the readers as possible.

Articles are considered on the following basis:

Organizations and businesses are welcome to purchase space in the ABILITIES Forum section, as long as the editorial provided is of relevance to our readership and falls within the guidelines of the publication's philosophy. A one-page space in the magazine accommodates approximately 800 words - or fewer if a photograph or illustration is to be incorporated. "Advertorial" that is strictly product or company specific will be tagged as advertising. Information considered of generic interest may be treated simply as editorial.

Voluntary contributors wishing to shed light on a particular area of interest or provide personal perspective on any given matter are encouraged to submit a brief abstract of their idea for consideration, accompanied by a writing sample. The magazine cannot be responsible for unsolicited material. A self-addressed stamped envelope should be included. Finished articles, in general terms, should be between 500 and 2000 words.

Professional writers are welcome to submit abstracts or proposals for consideration, accompanied by writing samples, or unsolicited completed manuscripts. ABILITIES, as a not-for-profit organization, is generally able to award only honoraria as remuneration for professional work. Honoraria range from $50 to $350, depending on the length of the article and whether it was assigned by ABILITIES as needed information or brought to the publication as a matter of interest. Again, a self-addressed, stamped envelope should be included with any submission. Finished articles, unless otherwise specified, should range from 500 to 2000 words. We prefer not to receive simultaneous submissions.

Written contributions may also target specific regular departments in ABILITIES, such as coping methods in "FYI," and humour in "The Lighter Side."

Please note that all queries and manuscripts submitted by e-mail for consideration must include the writer's full regular mailing address and phone number.

ABILITIES purchases first-time rights only for all material used. This includes the right to publish all material printed in ABILITIES in our alternate formats as well as in electronic format on the Internet. A "kill fee" of 50% is available to writers where a financial agreement has been established.

If possible, all material should be provided both electronically (computer disk or e-mail), and as hard copy. The hard copy can be mailed, but faxing or e-mail is essential if it is close to a deadline. The disk should be in an IBM-compatible format. Any available photographs that illustrate an article should also be collected and included.

All material is subject to the editorial prerogative of the publication as to word count, logical flow, grammatical accuracy and choice of terms as they relate to people with disabilities.

Categories: Nonfiction—Disabilities—Lifestyle

CONTACT: Jaclyn Law, Managing Editor
Material: All
Canadian Abilities Foundation
340 College St., Ste. 401
Toronto, Ontario M5T 3A9
Phone: 416-923-1885

Fax: 416-923-9829
E-mail: jaclyn@abilities.ca
Website: www.abilities.ca

About Teens on-line magazine

Humor and short fiction for young adults. Updated monthly.
GUIDELINES: We will consider publishing your article, essay, short story, book review, or joke unless it is obscene, racist, offensive or fails to meet *all* the following criteria:

1. Send it to us by Email, and include
a. Your Name
b. The city and country where you live
c. The Category of your submission (joke, short story, etc.) in the "Subject" space of the Email
2. FICTION / ESSAY / ARTICLE / BOOK REVIEW:
a. It must be less than 2,000 words
b. It must be unpublished previously
c. You must review and spell check it before submitting. If posted, it will be as submitted—mistakes and all.
d. Include it in the body of your email message, or send it as an attachment in one of the following formats: Microsoft Word (.doc, .txt, .rtf, or .html.)
e. Copyright remains yours, and we are not responsible for plagiarism from this site.
f. We do not pay for submitted material that is used
g. Anytime you want your work removed from AboutTeens, Email us with the word "remove" along with the title of your piece in the Email "Subject" space.
3. FUNNY FOTO
a. Must be sent as a .jpg file attached to email
Email submissions to aboutteens@worldnet.att.net
Categories: Young Adult

CONTACT: Paul Wagner, Editor
Address: 5721 Garden Hwy
Sacramento, CA 95837
Email: aboutteens@worldnet.att.net
Website: http://www.aboutteens.org

Absolute Magnitude

Absolute Magnitude is a full-sized, quarterly science fiction magazine. We do not use fantasy, horror, satire, or funny science fiction; while we will not reject the following out of hand, they are almost impossible to sell to us: present tense, police procedural, time travel, clones, alternate history, or stories with religious overtones. We're looking for character-driven action/adventure based technical Science Fiction stories from 1,000-25,000 words; 3,000 to 8,000 words are best. We want tightly plotted stories with memorable characters. Characters should be the driving force behind the action of the story, and should not be thrown in as an afterthought. We need to see both plot development and character growth. Stories that are resolved without action on the protagonist's part do not work for us; characters should not be spectators in situations completely beyond their control or immune to their influence. The ideal *Absolute Magnitude* story will have the plot resolution and character growth tied together. That is, the plot resolution will happen as a result of character growth, or vise versa. Payment: 2 to 6 cents per word on publication for First English Language Serial Rights. All rights revert to the author upon publication.
Categories: Fiction—Science Fiction

CONTACT: Warren Lapine, Editor
Absolute Magnitude
PO Box 2988
Radford VA 24143-2988

Absolute Write

Absolute Write is seeking original and reprint articles. We publish articles and interviews related to the craft and/or marketing of writing only— please do not submit fiction! We recommend that writers read articles published on this site to get an idea of our style and the types of articles that we publish. We are not geared to beginners; our target audience is intermediate and advanced-level writers. Very occasionally, we publish articles about the "basics," but in general, we're looking for articles that will be helpful to writers who have already had work published, taken writing courses, etc.
Article Submissions
Absolute Write is seeking "how-to" type articles about any branch of writing— screenwriting, freelance writing, technical writing, greeting cards, novels, nonfiction, playwriting, comic writing, and so on.

If you have never been published, please don't submit an article about how to get published. If you've never sold a screenplay, please don't submit an article about how to sell a screenplay. (You'd think this would be obvious, right?)

We are ALSO looking for the following things:
Interviews with working writers or those connected to the publishing or film industries— we particularly need interviews with agents, editors, and producers.
News stories or trends related to writing.
Perspectives from working writers. Can cover any aspect of a writer's life— business, craft, or "life" (balancing work and family, overcoming writer's block, increasing creativity, etc.).
Departments
• Debate Desk: be controversial. Tackle a subject like writing on spec, writing for free, plagiarism, etc. Don't be afraid to be opinionated!
• First Person: first-person essays about writing.
• Just for Fun: humor columns and funny poetry about writing.
Articles should be approximately 800-2000 words in length. Feel free to query first if you're considering writing an original article for us. For reprints, just send the complete manuscript with original publication name and date in the BODY of the e-mail message (please, no attachments, except for photos. We delete them unread, as we've gotten far too many viruses— even from writers who didn't know they had them).

We particularly like informational and humorous articles... the best are the ones that manage to combine those two qualities. You are welcome to write from a first-person perspective and editorialize, as long as your subject matter is relevant to other writers.

Articles must be the work of the original author. We accept simultaneous submissions. *Absolute Write* retains non-exclusive electronic publishing rights with the right to archive the material indefinitely on the website— thought the writer can ask me to pull it down at any time, and I'm happy to comply. All other rights remain with the author.
Bios
It'll save time if you include the bio that you'd like us to include along with the article. Of course, you can always send it after we accept an article, but if you have it ready, please send it along when you submit. (Just paste it below the article.)

All submissions should be sent to managing editor Amy Brozio-Andrews at amy@absolutewrite.com.
Payment
Did you skip right to this section? (Yeah, can't blame you.) I don't want to let you down, but we probably won't make you rich. There are two payment options:
• We pay $5 per article, interview, essay, or column— originals or reprints. We do not pay for book reviews (but, of course, you keep any book we send you). We also do not pay for syndicated columns (those that are published widely on the 'net). That said, it's very unlikely for us to accept a column that's been widely published on the 'net. Payments can be made by PayPal or check.
• Or you can have a free 1-year subscription to the Absolute Markets Premium Edition (a $15 value— see www.absolutemarkets.com).

We are happy to run your bio (with any links you like), your photo, ordering info if you've got books published. We have more than 75,000 subscribers and hope it brings you great publicity!

Product and Book Submissions

If you would like to submit your product or book for review by *Absolute Write* staff, or for use as a prize in our writing contests, please e-mail amy@absolutewrite.com to let us know. I'm sorry, but we do NOT review self-published/vanity-published/subsidy-published books anymore.

Categories: Nonfiction—Book Reviews—Interview—Writing

CONTACT: Amy Brozio-Andrews, Managing Editor
Material: All
E-mail: amy@absolutewrite.com
Website: www.absolutewrite.com

Accounting Today

Accounting Today is mostly staff-written, though we do occasionally run articles, commentaries and opinion pieces from outside, generally ranging from 600-1,200 words. They must be of specific interest to our readership of practicing accountants. There's no need to query first, though you may if you like; all submissions should be made via e-mail or snail mail — no phone calls or faxes.

Categories: Money & Finances—Accounting/CPAs

CONTACT: Bill Carlino, Editor-in-Chief
Material: All other
CONTACT: John Covaleski, Senior Editor
Material: Technology
395 Hudson St., 5th Floor
New York NY 10014
Phone: 212-337-8433

ACM
Another Chicago Magazine

We happily read submissions between February 1 and August 31; submissions received any other time are returned unread.

• Please send a SASE for reply.

• Double-space all fiction and keep stories under 25 pages (though once or twice we've published stories a little longer).

• Send one story only, unless you write shorts, and then you may send up to three (if indeed they are very short).

• It's very unlikely we would accept a "strictly genre" piece (e.g., Fantasy, Mystery, Scifi, etc.)

• No inspirational or religious stuff.

• Keep poetry to 4 pages unless you're convinced your long poem is irresistible.

• We welcome creative non-fictions personal essay, memoir, pastiche-that are factual and urgent, that had to be written. We publish short-short essays as well as longer pieces.

• Simultaneous submissions are okay, but we expect to be notified immediately when work has been accepted elsewhere and is therefore withdrawn from ACM consideration.

Replies/Acceptance/Payments: Like most literary magazines, we're a nonprofit, struggling operation which can't afford to pay much-a barely token honorarium when funding permits; but you do get a contributor's copy and a year's subscription. We try to send notice within 10 weeks, though it too often takes longer. We get about 75 manuscripts a week, which is a lot for your volunteer editors to handle.

If we accept the work, we understand you grant us first serial rights; all subsequent rights are yours, though we expect any future publication to carry acknowledgment that the work first appeared in ACM.

Photo guidelines—We're especially interested in presenting strong documentary photography and possibly some fine art photography. For more information, contact photo editor Karen Kring kkring@anotherchicagomag.com. You may include a URL for reviewing images on the web. No attachments please. Submitting scans or prints for production purposes-this work will be returned promptly.

Support literary publishing—To ensure the survival of literary journals—and a place to publish your writing—consider subscribing to at least one literary journal (if you don't already). If not ours, another.

Thanks—Tom Moss

Categories: Fiction—Poetry—Short Stories

CONTACT: Editors
Material: All
3709 N Kenmore
Chicago IL 60613
E-mail: editors@anotherchicagomag.com
Website: www.anotherchicagomag.com

Acorn

Acorn is a small biannual journal dedicated to publishing the best of contemporary English-language haiku. In particular, it showcases the individual poem and the ability of haiku to reveal the extraordinary moments found in everyday life. A. C. Missias, editor.

Original, unpublished haiku, not under consideration elsewhere, are welcomed from all writers, and should be accompanied by a self-addressed stamped envelope (SASE). (Appearance in an edited online journal or 'zine constitutes prior publication.) Payment will be made upon acceptance; all copyrights revert to author upon publication. Submissions via email also acceptable (with subject line "acorn" and complete mailing address included) at: missias@@earthlink.net (remove second @ before sending)—be sure that haiku are in the body of the message, formatted as plain text, to ensure that poems are readable.

Acorn publishes in October and April; submissions are due by the end of August and February, respectively.

Ordering information: (US funds only)

Individual issues: #1-7 = $5 ea. #8 on = $6 ea. Overseas orders add $1 per single issue (or inquire about postage for larger orders)

Annual subscriptions: 1-year (2 issues) US = $11.50 Can = $13 elsewhere = $15; 2-year (4 issues + Supplement) US = $27 Can = $30 elsewhere = $35

Supplement volumes: North America = $6 elsewhere = $8

Categories: Haiku

CONTACT: Redfox Press
Material: All
PO Box 186
Philadelphia PA 19105
E-mail: missias@earthlink.net

Acoustic Guitar

QUERIES

If you are working on an assignment for Acoustic Guitar, you can skip this section. If you want an assignment, send a written query to the editors describing your proposed submission and your interest in the subject. If you have a manuscript, send it with a self-addressed stamped envelope. If you have previously published work that will give us a sense of your writing, send a copy with the understanding that it will not be returned. We will respond to your query within 60 days.

ASSIGNMENTS

If we assign you an article, we will send you two copies of a letter confirming the details of the assignment (deadline, length, content, etc.) and your acceptance of the terms of these Guidelines; please sign one copy and return it to us in the envelope provided. Even if we do not receive your signed copy, your submission of an assigned article constitutes agreement to the terms of the letter and the Guidelines.

CONTENT

The readers of Acoustic Guitar are musicians and/or instrument makers, so you may safely suppose that all have some basic knowledge of musicianship, music reading, etc. Remember, however, that many guitarists are self-taught or play only by ear, and that their musical interests and ability levels vary widely. Try to keep your article accessible and interesting to a reader who might be unfamiliar with the genre or style you are discussing, without getting bogged down in explaining every musical detail. Similarly, articles about guitars and gear should be catered to players, but they need to speak to readers with greatly varying degrees of knowledge and expertise.

INTERVIEWS/PROFILES

We publish stories on individual players because their musical contributions are enduring and important. Your job is to bring those contributions to light in an entertaining and illuminating way, not to hype them as personalities or stars. Treat artists with respect, but don't suspend your critical faculties or shy away from difficult questions. The musician-to-musician communication in the magazine should be as open and honest as possible.

• A sidebar list of recommended, currently available recordings is often useful for readers. Supply listings with full title, record company (with mail, phone, and Web address if it's a small label), catalog number, and year. If videos, publications, or Web sites relating to the artist's work are available, include details on those as well.

• Artist profiles written for the magazine's feature section, Song Craft, Jump Street, or Off the Record should include a "What They Play" sidebar on the artist's choice of guitar(s) and related equipment: strings, picks, and other accessories, plus stage amplification and recording setups. Include addresses for any small, hard-to-find companies. The best "What They Play" sidebars are more than straight listings, including quotes from the artists on why they use a particular piece of gear.

REVIEWS

We expect all writers who are evaluating products or the work of an artist to be free from conflicts of interest. If you have any questions about what might constitute a conflict of interest, speak to your editor.

FORMAT

Please submit your article electronically as well as on hard copy. If you're working on a PC, send us files in Microsoft Word for Windows (versions up to 97), RTF, or text-only format. If you use a Macintosh, send Word, WordPerfect, RTF, or text-only files. Stories should be emailed (preferably as attached Word files) to the editor who assigned the piece or editors.ag@stringletter.com.

FACTS

Make sure all name spellings, album titles, song titles, dates, company and product names, and other facts are correct when you're writing, and double-check them before you submit an article. We do as much fact-checking of material as we can, but our resources are limited, so don't count on us to catch errors. It can be useful to check facts with your original sources, but do not submit your full manuscript to an artist or company you're writing about. Doing so frequently leads to disagreements over the content and will compromise the integrity of your article.

MUSIC

If your contribution includes previously published music, we need either the original or a clear photocopy of the published example (original preferred), including full identification of the publisher and name of work. If the music has not been published, please provide a fair copy

and any relevant information about the composer, copyright, etc. In the case of a transcription from a recording, we will need the same type of information. Whenever possible, please provide computer-notated scores on a disk in Encore or Finale (up to version 2002) format or as a standard MIDI file. Include a printout of the piece with the disk. Music files can be emailed to music editor Andrew DuBrock: andrew@stringletter.com. Details about our notation style can be found in the Music Style Guide, which is available from our music editor.

PHOTOS

If you are providing black-and-white prints, please be sure they are on glossy paper; sized as large as possible, up to 8" x 10"; clearly identified; properly credited to the photographer and/or owner of copyright; safely packed (not paperclipped!); and unmarred by writing on front or back. We can also use color transparencies or good-quality color prints. You may e-mail JPEG or TIFF photo files (300 dpi or better and as large as possible) to agart@stringletter.com.

DEADLINES

For magazine articles, we need your draft manuscript approximately 120 days before the cover date (the magazine actually comes out a month before the cover date). Your exact deadline will be included in your assignment letter.

PROOFS

After initial editing, we will send proofs for your approval.

PAYMENT

For all articles except Hit List reviews and Great Acoustics articles, you will be paid 25 cents per word, upon publication. We pay a flat rate of $75 for Great Acoustics and $25 per published Hit List review. For instructional articles, you will be paid $75 per published page of music that you contribute. Consult the editors about rates for photographs. On the rare occasion when we find an assigned article to be unpublishable, we will pay you 50 percent of the fee for that article at its assigned length, up to $200. (For example, the normal fee for a 1,000-word article would be $250, so the "kill fee" for that article would be $125.) We do not pay kill fees for unpublished Hit List reviews. See below for information on payments for article reprints. You will receive two complimentary copies of the issue in which your contribution appears. As a contributor, you may purchase any of our products (magazine subscriptions or back issues) at a 50 percent discount.

EXPENSES

We do not reimburse you for routine expenses such as phone calls, postage, or local travel. If you anticipate unusual expenses, please discuss these in advance with your editor.

COPYRIGHT

By submitting a manuscript, you are representing to us that you are its original author and that it has not been published previously. You must notify us in advance if your article contains any copyrighted material (whether text, artwork, or music), or if any of it has appeared, or is slated to appear, in another publication. The entire content of each issue of Acoustic Guitar is copyrighted as "work for hire," meaning that we, not you, hold the copyright. This copyright covers all uses of the material, including electronic or digital reproduction and our Web site. If you are providing us with a work that is already under copyright, such as an excerpt from a book, please furnish complete copyright information. If you are authorized to give permission to reprint it, please do so in writing. If someone else must grant us permission, furnish us with their name, address, and phone number. If you wish us to reassign the copyright to you, please consult your editor.

REPRINT RIGHTS

String Letter Publishing has an active book publishing program in which we frequently reprint material written for the magazine; we also reprint material written for our books in the magazine. If we reprint your article, you will be notified in advance and paid 12.5 cents per word for the reprinted text. (The rate for reprinted music will depend on whether you provide a recording for a lesson book/CD). The same principle applies when other publishers request permission to reprint articles. In the case of a publisher with limited resources and circulation-a local guitar club newsletter or a fan Web site, for example-we generally assign permission without a fee. But in the case of a publication that can pay for rights, we will negotiate the fee and share the reprint proceeds with you on a 50/50 basis.

—Scott Nygaard, Editor

Categories: Nonfiction—Biography—Music

CONTACT: Derk Richardson, Associate Editor
Material: All
255 West End
San Rafael, CA 94901
Phone: 415-485-6946 ext. 611
Fax: 415-485 0831
Website: www.acousticguitar.com

Across the Board

The editors present business perspectives on timely issues, including management practices, foreign policy, social issues, and science and technology. We are neither an academic business journal nor a "popular" manual. That means we aren't interested in highly technical articles about business strategy. It also means we don't publish over-simple "how-to" articles. We are an idea magazine, but the ideas should have practical overtones.

We let Forbes, Fortune, and Business Week do most of the straight reporting, while we do some of the critical thinking; that is, we let writers explore the implications of the news in depth. Across the Board tries to provide different angles on important topics, and to bring to its readers' attention issues that they might otherwise not devote much thought to. A few examples from past issues: ethics overseas; how and why a company should set up shop on the Internet; and business lessons learned from the art world. We emphasize the human side of organizational life at all levels. We're as concerned with helping managers who are "lonely at the top" as with motivating workers and enhancing job satisfaction.

All this we try to do without any particular political or ideological bias. Though *Across the Board* represents the interests of The Conference Board's corporate members, we feel obligated to present a range of viewpoints over time.

Manuscript requirements.

Our style fits our content—thoughtful, authoritative, more akin to Harper's than to People magazine. We like the usual things—bright writing, solid research, illuminating quotes, sharp opinions. Our articles range from 1,000 to 3,500 words. Payment varies. The editors prefer detailed story proposals that show your writing style as well as the bare bones of your article. Double-spaced manuscripts submitted on speculation will be considered. Please enclose the usual self-addressed stamped envelope

Categories: Nonfiction—Foreign Policy—Management—Social Issues—Science—Technology

CONTACT: Al Vogl
Across the Board
845 Third Ave
New York NY 10022

Action Pursuit

Make it clear and clean, with plenty of photographs! We are most likely to accept articles under 400 words with photos. (Gear reviews may be longer.)

All submitted articles and photos are considered to have been submitted exclusively to Action Pursuit Games unless clearly marked otherwise. Editors may be contacted at: editor@actionpursuitgames.com or paintballmag@mindspring.com

STORY RIGHTS, PHOTOGRAPHER, MODEL RELEASES: When submitting an article, fill out and send the Electronic Releases

(below) for writer, photographer, models. Then download and print out the Story Rights, Photographer, and Model Releases, and submit the hard copy signed with the article and/or photos. Send the story/photos and releases to the editor. Be sure to use the same "working title" as you put on the electronic release. Articles without releases will go on "hold" until releases are received.

Press releases, news items, new product and promotional type releases must be marked as such. Include contact information. These types of items are not paid items.

Exclusives: Mark them "exclusive." DO NOT submit to APG any feature or photos (same or substantially the same) that you have submitted to any other magazine. Questions: email the editor.

Payment: Payment is made in the month on the cover of the issue in which the item appears.

Assignments: Request specific assignments ahead of time by email to editor@actionpursuitgames.com (APG) or paintballmag@mindspring.com (Paintball)

Style: Send without formatting (no underlines, fonts, italics, etc.). Use plain text. Word Perfect or MSWord preferred. Use News Pro style: put only one space after end punctuation. Start each paragraph flush left. Double space down between paragraphs.

Editing: "During his stint as a reporter, he volunteered for what was considered the magazine's dullest beat, profiling mutual-fund managers, and didn't grouse when tough-minded editors chewed up his copy. By his mid-20s though, it had become clear to all that his father had anointed him as his successor." (from an article about Steve Forbes appearing in the Wall Street Journal)

PHOTOS: All photos need photo credit and a caption. Identify photo with a small number on the back in a corner. Number the captions to match the photos, and include the captions with the electronic text.

DIGITAL IMAGES: High Resolution TIF, and use a photo i.d. that's easy to understand.

The photo releases must be matched to the photos submitted.

DO NOT write on the photos with black or dark markers, or with ink. Use a thin tip felt marker only. Take care the marker has dried before stacking photos to send.

Captions: write the caption, and include the location where photo was taken, date photo was taken, and the name of the photographer. (Flag pull! SC Village, Corona, California, May 19, 2000. Photo by John Doe). When identifying people in the photo: identify by row (front/back), kneeling, standing, holding blue marker, etc. A group photo may be identified by group name plus the location, date, and photographer.

Color prints, slides, or transparencies are highly preferred. We reject low resolution digital images. We will consider original digital images that are high resolution (please submit on CD or disk). Instead of a scan, send the original photo. Non-photographic prints (such as prints made on an ink jet printer) are not acceptable.

Photos are not returned without prior arrangement.

Persons in shooting areas must be following all current industry safety rules. They must wear full unmodified factory head protection systems (no cut down masks, ears must be covered by the headgear, must have full factory facemask; bottom of facemask is not allowed to be rolled up, etc.).

Persons in non-shooting areas must be following all current industry safety rules. They must have a barrel plug in the paintball marker, must not have a finger on the trigger, muzzle must be pointed in a safe direction and not pointing at a person or animal.

The paintball marker must NEVER be pointed at the reader.

TO GET PAID YOU MUST DO THESE THINGS

1. Have a current W-9 form on file. These are IRS forms readily available. A W-9 can be downloaded from the Internal Revenue web site or from other web sources.

Fill out/sign the W-9, attach a note saying "APG/Paintball Writer" and mail it directly to:

Accounting, Action Pursuit Group Media LLC, 265 S. Anita, Ste. 120, Orange, CA 92868-3310.

2. Provide Original Signed Annual Releases (writer, photographer, model as appropriate) for all your articles/photographs.

The forms are available at actionpursuitgames.com.

Send these forms in the Complete Package that you submit (see Writer Guidelines for details).

The Complete Packages go directly to the Editor: Dan Reeves, Editor, PO Box 417, Licking, MO 65542.

3. Apprise Enthusiast Media LLC, will not issue checks until all these forms are on file.

Questions: editor@actionpursuitgames.com

Releases

Annual Releases cover all articles or photographs submitted or modeling done during the calendar year you indicate on the Release.

Releases may be filled out online to get the process started. You will receive a copy at the email address you enter so be sure the email address is correct. After you submit the online version you MUST print out the text version and complete it so that it matches the information submitted online. SIGN the Release(s) (and have your parent/guardian complete and sign it if you are under 18) and send it to the Editor listed above. It is IMPORTANT you fill out BOTH the electronic and the printed version. Receipt of the Release(s) is mandatory before an article can be published.

Categories: Nonfiction—Games

CONTACT: Dan Reeves, Editor
Material: All
PO Box 417
Licking MO 65542

Adirondack Life

Editorial Guidelines

Adirondack Life is the only publication that addresses the unique natural and social aspects of New York State's Adirondack Park, and that gives those concerns local and national exposure. The magazine offers an important window into understanding this region.

In addition to the regular bimonthly issues of *Adirondack Life* — describing the history, culture, recreation, wildlife and personalities of the area—are two special issues: the Annual Guide to the Adirondacks and the Collectors Issue. The Guide's emphasis is on outdoorsy how-to and where-to articles that meet the needs of new visitors and offer in-depth information about an array of recreational offerings. The theme of the Collectors Issue changes each year—the premiere Collectors Issue was "At Home in the Adirondacks" and in 1999 that issue celebrated the magazine's thirtieth anniversary.

Writers should become familiar with the magazine and can do so by requesting a sample copy. Please send an address label and a check for $3.00 to cover postage. Along with a writer's query we like to see a few published stories. For new writers, the best way to break into the magazine is through departments, which, save for Adirondack Made (see below), run from 1,200 to 2,400 words. Features run from approximately 2,500 to 5,000 words.

Payment is $0.25 per published word approximately sixty days after acceptance. Currently we are not interested in poetry, editorial cartoons or short essays of less than 1,000 words.

All work submitted must be the original property of the writer and should not have appeared in another publication. *Adirondack Life* buys first North American serial print rights.

Facts in all articles must be verified or substantiated in the text. Please double space manuscripts. Include an SASE with all correspondence.

Departments

Special Places: Focused articles about unique locations that underline the special character of the Adirondacks. Recent examples include a visit to Up Yonda Farm, in Bolton Landing, and a history of the Crater Club, on Lake Champlain. Watercraft: Pieces on boats, boatbuilders and boat-related events. A recent example profiled sailboat builder Jack Manley, of Northville.

Barkeater: Short essays, from personal to political. Recent examples: an essay on winter camping on Azure Mountain's summit and a proposal for a trail around the Hudson River Gorge.

Wilderness: Descriptions of specific wild places and observations about legal or environmental issues affecting wilderness areas. In 1998 we described the search, semantical and actual, for "pristine" ponds.

Working: Stories of uncommon occupations in the Adirondack Park as well as characteristic employment. Recent Working departments include a story on a theatrical-lighting company in North Creek and a reflection on summer jobs in Lake George.

Home: Stories of Adirondack crafts or skills and techniques of interest to homeowners. A recent example describes family tree farms.

Yesteryears: Vignettes from regional history. Recent examples include an account of the former keeper of the Arab Mountain fire tower and a profile of "The Bishop of North Lake."

Adirondack Made: Short (500-600 words) describing a unique Adirondack business, past or present, and the people behind it. Recent examples profiled the Sunfeather Natural Soap Company, in Parishville, and the Crown Point Bread Company.

Other departments include Kitchen (distinctly Adirondack recipes), Profile (local individuals and families), Historic Preservation (important structures), North Country (catch-all), Sporting Scene (outdoor recreation and competitions), Environment and Wildlife.

The *Annual Guide* generally includes departments on hiking, biking, paddling, climbing, fishing, family activities, touring, access, learning and so forth.

*We accept queries, BUT NOT UNSOLICITED MANU-SCRIPTS, via e-mail.

Categories: Nonfiction—Architecture—Conservation—Culture—Ecology—Environment—Fishing—Gardening—History—Lifestyle—Outdoors—Photography—Recreation—Regional—Sports/Recreation—Travel

CONTACT: Galen Crane or Mary Thill, Editors
Material: All
PO Box 410
Jay NY 12941-0410
Phone: 518-946-2191
Website: www.adirondacklife.com

Adoptive Families

Adoptive Families is the leading information resource for families before, during, and after adoption. The award-winning national bimonthly magazine provides independent, authoritative adoption information in an accessible and reader-friendly format.

Each issue of *Adoptive Families* is built around stories of adoption written by people who read the magazine closely and regularly. This active community of readers also offers thoughtful, deeply felt responses to the pieces we publish.

We want to hear your stories. We encourage you to share your insights and experiences with other adoptive families. And we're always looking for great writing.

The Magazine

Core topics covered in every issue:

Preparing for adoption; health issues; school and education; family, friends, and community; birthfamilies; talking about adoption; parenting tips and guidelines

Departments:

The Waiting Game: A special section for pre-adopters

Parenting the Child Who Waited: Raising children who have lived without a permanent family

About Birthparents: Stories about, and sometimes by, birth families

Been There: Adults speak honestly about their experiences of growing up adopted

Adoption & School: Advice from teachers, parents, and experts on education-related issues

In My Opinion: An editorial on a controversial subject

At Home: A personal essay

Single Parent: Single parents share their experiences

Living with Diversity: For and by families who've adopted transracially or from other cultures

Parent Exchange: Readers share information with the Adoptive Families community

Letters: Responses from readers to past articles and other readers' letters

Lois Melina's Adopted Child: A regular column by the nation's leading expert on parenting adopted children

Growing Up Adopted: Age-specific developmental information from experts, including adoption pediatricians, members of the American Academy of Pediatrics

Legal Q&A: Leading adoption attorneys answer readers' questions

Calendar of Events: Parents support group events around the country

Book Reviews: Reviews by knowledgeable reviewers

Adoption New and Notes: Legislative and policy updates, with occasional "News Focus" articles elaborating on a particular item or issue in the news

Bulletin Board: Resources for Adoptive Families

(Departments listed above from "The Waiting Game" down through "Letters" are ones for which we typically accept submissions.)

How to Submit an Article or Essay

Personal essays:

Before sending us your personal essay, we recommend that you take a look at the suggestions below, under "What We're Looking For."

Reported articles on adoption-related topics:

In the case of reported articles on adoption-related topics, we prefer that you send a query letter (via e-mail or regular mail) before sending in your article. Again, take a look at recent issues of the magazine; we're less likely to publish a piece on a topic we've recently covered.

Query letters should include:

• A brief description or outline of your idea

• Why you think it belongs in our magazine

• Why you should be the one to write it

• If possible, a sense of where in the magazine you believe your story might fit, whether as a feature or in a particular department; see list of departments above

• Any recent clips you may have

How to send them:

• We prefer to receive submissions via e-mail, as attachments. But we accept submissions via US mail, as well.

• You may also wish to send family photographs with your story, particularly in the case of personal essays. We prefer scanned photos e-mailed as attachments. We can also use prints sent by mail, but we cannot guarantee that unsolicited photographs will be returned.

When you'll hear from us, payment, etc.:

• It generally takes us 6-8 weeks to respond to a submission.

• Writers of personal essays we publish will receive a one-year subscription to the magazine. Payment for reported articles varies. We're a small magazine; our pay rates are scaled accordingly.

• We consider all submissions on a speculative basis. We cannot guarantee that a proposed article, even one that we've expressed interest in, will be published.

• We cannot assume responsibility for unsolicited material or guarantee its return.

• You should submit a brief, two- or three-sentence biographical note at the end of each submission.

What we're looking for

Whether you consider yourself a writer or simply someone with a story to share, the following strategies will go a long way toward making your piece an Adoptive Families story:

• Know the magazine. Look through past issues. Get a sense of our general tone. Familiarize yourself with the topics we generally cover. Consider which of our departments your story might best fit.

• Have a clear sense of your central theme. (E.g., "How I included extended family in our adoption process," "Traditions and rituals bind families together," "Networking can help to make the waiting period less agonizing.") Think about what makes your story unique—or what useful information families in similar situations might gain from it.

• Keep it active. Describe not only what happened to you, but how you chose to deal with it.

• Focus on choices made and strategies used to deal with a particular situation. (E.g., "We realized our parents weren't ready to be supportive, and we didn't have the energy to deal with their criticism on every single point, so we offered them only general information as we progressed through the adoption process;" "When my daughter started being questioned by her classmates about her adoption, I offered her teacher tips on how to inform the class about adoption in general without invading any individual student's privacy.") Keep it active. Describe not only what happened to you, but how you chose to deal with it.

• Be specific. The more specific the details you provide, the more useful—and engaging—your story will be for other adoptive families. And bear in mind, even the most "ordinary" of experiences—the ones many people share—can be extraordinarily inspiring to read about. Other readers can learn from your experiences—even from your mistakes. We do receive many, many "How I Adopted" stories. But each of these can offer something unique if it maintains a strong focus on a central theme.

Typical subjects and themes:

For a quick glimpse of themes and subjects other *Adoptive Families* writers have explored, read the "decks" (the lines that appear between the title and the beginning of the story) in articles from past issues.

Areas we are currently looking to cover

• Middle-school and teen years

• Relatives and community

• Adoptive parent support groups

• School

• Foster adoption

• Transracial adoption

• Domestic adoption

• Adoptive parents of color

Categories: Nonfiction—Children—Education—Family—Parenting

CONTACT: Susan Caughman
Adoptive Families
39 W 37th St 15th Floor
New York NY 10018
E-mail: letters@adoptivefamilies.com

The Advocate

The best guide to whether your idea is right for the magazine is a good knowledge of what the magazine has published in recent issues. For example, flipping through recent issues would tell you that *The Advocate* does not publish fiction or poetry, has only one first-person guest columnist or essayist per issue, and runs almost exclusively reported stories that are typically 200 to 1,000 words long.

We are a biweekly newsmagazine with a focus on the breaking news, news analysis, and developing arts & entertainment stories that involve out gay and lesbian people or are of direct interest to a national readership of out gay and lesbian readers. Because we are a newsmagazine rather than a "lifestyle" magazine, we do not publish travel destination stories, fashion or grooming tips, fitness articles, advice columns, or other "service" or "how-to" pieces. Because *The*

Advocate is sold only in the United States and Canada, with some U.K. distribution, it focuses principally on news and entertainment from those countries.

Payment rates are negotiated upon assignment.

If the above summary confirms for you that your pitch is right for *The Advocate*, you should also know that new writers should provide samples of their relevant published work to the appropriate editor at the same time they are submitting their pitches. Published clips are best sent via snail mail, as photocopies; articles that have been posted on the Web may be submitted as e-mailed URLs. Printouts of unpublished or unedited articles or personal Web postings should not be submitted.

A detailed query letter of 500 or fewer words is always preferred to a completed article submitted on spec. Be specific, have a timely news hook, and refer to particular departments or past features of the print or online magazine in making your pitch.

Submissions of articles already printed or posted elsewhere, blog entries, "open letters" or other correspondence, and "simultaneous submissions"—queries or articles sent to more than one publication at the same time—will not be considered or answered.

Queries may be submitted by snail mail, fax, or e-mail but must in all cases include an e-mail address for response. Self-addressed, stamped envelopes are not necessary and will not be used. While clips should be sent via snail mail, sending pitches via e-mail is preferred and is the method most likely to result in a personal response. Free sample copies of the magazine are not available.

If you have any further questions, please feel free to e-mail the appropriate editor, or newsroom@advocate.com.

Photographer Guidelines

We are happy to consider unsolicited photography submissions for possible publication. Before making any submissions to us, please familiarize yourself with our magazine. It is available at most newsstands throughout the country. Keep in mind that *The Advocate* is a newsmagazine. As such, we publish photos of interest to the gay and lesbian community based on their newsworthiness and timeliness. We do not publish art photography or portfolios of individual photographers. The majority of photos appearing in *The Advocate* were assigned by us to our photographers in the field, or were taken by other newsgathering organizations.

We are always looking for talented news and feature photographers around the country. If you would like to submit your work for our consideration:

• Send prints or crisp photocopies, promo cards, or duplicate 35mm slides of your work. Do not send originals.

• Include your name, address, and telephone number.

• Due to the volume of material we receive, we regret we are unable to return any unsolicited submissions.

• If we are interested we will contact you.

PORTFOLIO REVIEW: If you would like us to see your book, you may drop it off at our offices. However, be prepared to leave it for up to 48 hours before picking it back up.

Illustrator Guidelines

We are happy to consider unsolicited illustration submissions to use as a reference for making possible assignments to you in the future. Before making any submissions to us, please familiarize yourself with our magazine. It is available at most newsstands throughout the country.

Keep in mind that *The Advocate* is a newsmagazine. As such, we publish items of interest to the gay and lesbian community based on their newsworthiness and timeliness. We do not publish unsolicited illustrations or portfolios of individual artists. We do not publish cartoons or humorous illustrations. Any illustration appearing in The Advocate was assigned by us to an artist to illustrate a specific article.

We are always looking for talented illustrators from around the country. If you would like to submit your work for our consideration:

• Send samples of your work in the mail. Include either crisp photocopies, or duplicate 35mm slides of your work. Do not send originals.

Be sure to include some material we can keep on file for future reference. If you wish to have your work returned, include a self-addressed, stamped envelope with sufficient postage. We cannot be responsible for any material sent to us.

• Submissions by e-mail that include URLs to artists' pages may be sent to gstoll@advocate.com

• Include your name, address, e-mail address, and telephone number.

• If we are interested we will contact you.

PORTFOLIO REVIEW: We do not accept unsolicited portfolio drop-offs at the editorial offices.

Categories: Nonfiction—Arts—Entertainment—Gay/Lesbian

CONTACT: Editors, The Advocate
Material: All
PO Box 4371
Los Angeles CA 90078
Phone: 323-871-1225
Fax: 323-467-6805
E-mail: letters@advocate.com
CONTACT: Photo Editor
Material: Photos
6922 Hollywood Blvd Ste 1000
Los Angeles CA 90028
CONTACT: Art Director
Material: Art
6922 Hollywood Blvd Ste 1000
Los Angeles CA 90028

Adventure Time

AdventureTime is an extreme sports e-zine that covers mountain biking, skateboarding, inline skating, climbing, skatedogging, snowskating, whitewater rafting, kayaking, sport humor & product reviews.

AdventureTime Magazine is looking for Writers!

Who we are: AdventureTime was founded in 1990 by publisher Gary Grant Fassbach as a print newsletter published bi-monthly and distributed in the Western Pennsylvania Region of the United States. In 1993, with the addition of Gary Winterhalter as sales agent and co-publisher, AdventureTime became a large-format print magazine distributed through free distribution and paid subscription throughout the United States. In 1995, AdventureTime was placed on the World Wide Web and the print version was discontinued.

We have been online for over 2 years and have built a respectable following in the extreme sports genre. We offer extreme sports products via our Extreme Mall and website design and maintenance services for extreme sport companies. We have good working relationships with extreme sport companies and organizations worldwide.

Our mission statement: To encourage active participation in extreme sports by providing readers with information and training resources delivered in an entertaining format.

What we can offer: At present, we cannot offer an unproven writer financial compensation but we will be offering small fees in the near future to those writers whose work we would like to use on a regular basis.

Who we are looking for: We are looking for spirited submissions preferably from writers who have an interest in extreme sports. We are looking specifically for writing of original extreme sport articles--both fiction and non-fiction, extreme product reviews (free gear a possibility!), and composition of an online one page monthly newsletter that would be condensed from the main AdventureTime website and "pushed" to registered subscribers.

Familiarity with electronic publishing and electronic mail is helpful for those writers who would like to become future staff writers. Interested candidates should send along samples of their writing in the form of text documents or url addresses.

What about copyrights? Copyright stays with the author. Work is published herewith the author's express consent and permission and on a one-time basis unless otherwise contracted by AdventureTime.

How to Respond: If this sounds like something that you would be seriously interested in doing, please reply with samples of work/urls attached. All entries will remain confidential and receive a reply. Thank-you for your consideration. Editors: Gary Grant Fassbach, Amy Krut.

CONTACT: lisa@adventuretime.com
E-mail: mudhog@adventuretime.com
Website: www.adventuretime.com

Affaire de Coeur

1. AFFAIRE DE COEUR no longer accept short stories, except through our contest. For the contest we will accept short stories of two thousand words maximum. *Short stories must be stories of romance with the following guidelines:*

a. There are no limitations with regard to setting. Time of setting may be historical, contemporary or futuristic.

b. Plots may be general romance or may include suspense, mystery or intrigue.

c. There are no age restrictions on the couple. Romances can range from young adult romances to twilight romances. There are no restrictions on previous relationship.

d. There are no racial or ethnic restrictions on the couple. We welcome diversity as long as the portrayal of the race or ethnic groups are realistic and non-stereotypical.

e. Because of the short length of the story, we discourage a love scene unless it is vital to the story.

f. The story should end on a positive note. That does not necessarily mean that the couple ends up together and lives happily ever after. It may mean that the heroine realizes she is better off without the hero or vice versa.

g. In order to avoid the feel of a true confession we encourage the author to write the story in the third person. However, if he/she does write it in the first person and it works, it may be accepted.

2. AFFAIRE will not accept previously printed short stories. We require a contract to the effect that the work submitted is original.

3. AFFAIRE pays up to $35.00 per published short story depending on the length. Payment is made at the end of the quarter in which the story appears.

4. AFFAIRE reserves the right to edit all short stories. While it is not our intent to change the context or complexion of a story, we will alter it for the purposes of length and correct spelling or grammar.

5. Short stories printed in AFFAIRE become the property of AFFAIRE DE COEUR magazine and may not be reprinted without the expressed written permission of AFFAIRE DE COEUR.

Categories: Fiction—African-American—Reference—Romance—Women's Fiction

CONTACT: Submissions Editor
Material: All
3976 Oak Hill Rd.
Oakland CA 94605
Phone: 510-569-5675
Fax: 510-632-8868
E-mail: Sseven@aol.com
Website: www.affairedecoeur.com

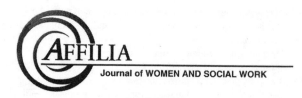

Affilia
Journal of Women and Social Work

The Editorial Board of *Affilia: Journal of Women and Social Work* invites the submission of manuscripts, poetry, articles, reports, and essays that relate to its mission: to the discussion and development of feminist values, theories, and knowledge as they relate to social work and social welfare research, education, and practice. All forms of writing and analysis will be considered and a range of feminist perspectives will be encouraged. The intent of *Affilia* is to bring insight and knowledge to the task of eliminating discrimination and oppression, especially with respect to gender, race, ethnicity, class, age, disability, and sexual and affectional preference. The editors seek manuscripts from people both in and outside the field of social work that offer a critical analysis of the condition of women in this and other societies, apply these ideas to social welfare purposes, and work toward the empowerment of women in an equitable society.

Manuscripts should be submitted in quadruplicate, typewritten and double spaced in 12-point font. Maximum length of a manuscript for an article is 20 pages (25 pages for manuscripts reporting on history or qualitative research), including text, tables, references, and all else. Authors must submit manuscripts in the reference style specified in the *Publication Manual of the American Psychological Association* (5th ed.). Authors should supply a separate cover sheet with name of the author(s) and other identifying information. An abstract of fewer than 100 words should accompany the manuscript. It is assumed that manuscripts are submitted for exclusive consideration of *Affilia* and have not been simultaneously submitted elsewhere.

Authors are required to submit written permission to reprint, from the original publisher, any quoted material of 300 words or more from a single source (journal article or book); any quoted material from a newspaper (especially the *New York Times*), a poem, or a song (even a phrase); and any table or figure reproduced from another work.

After editing, a corrected copy of the manuscript saved on a disk as an ASCII text file must be returned with the final hard copy (see letter of acceptance). Text references use the author's surname and the year of publication; superior figures are not used. The References section at the end of each article contains the full citation, alphabetized by author, with initials for the author's first name, followed by the year of publication in parentheses. Titles of articles, chapters, and books are to be typed lowercase except for the initial letter, and no quotation marks are used with titles of articles or chapters. Titles of journals and publishing companies, however, follow the usual style of capitalizing the appropriate letters. This style affords no place for notes or comments in the References section or footnotes in the text. Such notes should be incorporated into the text if they are pertinent. Simple asides will not be included.

Submission of a manuscript implies commitment to publish in this journal. Authors submitting manuscripts to the journal should not simultaneously submit them to another journal, nor should manuscripts have been published elsewhere in substantially similar content. Authors in doubt about what constitutes prior publication should consult the editor.

Categories: Nonfiction—Family—Feminism—Health—Multicultural—Sexuality—Social Work —Society—Women's Issues

CONTACT: Fariyal Ross-Sheriff, Editor-in-Chief, *Affilia*
Material: All
School of Social Work

Howard University
601 Howard Pl. NW
Washington, D.C. 20059
Phone: 202-806-7305
E-mail: fross-sheriff@howard.edu
Website: www.affiliajournal.org

African American Family

Please refer to *Metro Parent Magazine*.

The African American Pulpit!

Unsolicited materials are gladly received. Please follow these specifications for publication: Only sermons and articles by African American preachers will be published. Any sermon submitted for consideration should be prefaced with a brief synopsis of its context and point of origin.

Submission of material to Judson Press or to the editors assumes the right of Judson Press to publish the material in an issue of *The African American Pulpit*. Prior to actual publication, the writers will sign a formal publishing agreement granting permission to Judson Press to publish the piece. All manuscripts submitted for publication to *The African American Pulpit* are subject to editorial revision (grammar, punctuation, conformity with house style, and length). Only original work will be considered. Any previously published material chosen for use will be obtained by the editorial team.

The following are some specifics to remember:

• Written manuscripts should be submitted printed on 8 1/2" x 11" paper, typed double-spaced, and on computer diskette (a non-MAC format). Sermons should not exceed 2,500 words. Articles should not exceed 1,500 words. •

• When a Scripture verse is quoted or paraphrased, make sure to specify chapter, verses, and version used. •

• Sources of direct quotations must be cited with full publishing author, title, place of publication, publisher, year of publication, and page number(s) of quoted material. For periodicals, include author, title of article, name of periodical, date, volume and number if applicable, and page number(s). •

• For quotations longer than one sentence, contributors must supply a photocopy of the original. If this is not available, the editors will, in most instances, paraphrase or delete the quotation rather than risk reprinting it incorrectly. •

• Permission from the copyright holder is needed for any quote of significant length and for any music or poetry that is not in public domain. •

• Please be sure to include a photograph (black and white preferred) of yourself with your submission. If your submission is published, we will include your photograph alongside your piece.

Categories: Nonfiction—African-American—Book Reviews—Christian Interests—Inspirational—Men's Issues—Multicultural—Music—Poetry—Public Speaking—Religion—Spiritual—Sermans—Women's Issues—Homiletics

CONTACT: Editorial Department—Judson Press
Material: All
Judson Press, 588 North Gulph Road
King of Prussia PA 19406
Phone: 610-768-2128

African American Review

African American Review publishes essays on African American literature, theater, film, art, and culture generally; interviews; poetry; fiction; bibliographies; and book reviews.

Those submitting article manuscripts should prepare them in accordance with the most recent edition of *The MLA Style Manual*, which encourages the use of intratextual documentation wherever possible and mandates the inclusion of a list of works cited (with full pagination) at the manuscript's end. Essays between 4,000 and 9,000 words are preferred—the word count does not include notes and works cited. We strongly encourage you to submit your work online at http://mc.manuscriptcentral.com/aar. If you prefer to submit via US mail, please send *three* blind copies of submissions, along with a cover letter, self-addressed envelope and sufficient postage to permit your manuscript's return, to Dr. Joycelyn Moody, *African American Review*, Saint Louis University, Humanities 317, 3800 Lindell Blvd., St. Louis, MO 63108.

Poets should submit *two* copies of no more than six poems at a time, along with a self-addressed, stamped envelope (with sufficient postage to return work), to the Editor at the above address.

Fiction writers should also submit *two* copies of a story, along with a self-addressed, stamped envelope (sufficient postage to return work), to the Editor at the above address. (Stories between 2,500-5,000 words are preferred.)

Artists should submit artwork on slides, along with a self-addressed, stamped envelope (with sufficient postage to return work), to the Editor at the above address.

Inquiries regarding book review assignments should be addressed to: Dr. Yoshinobu Hakutani, Book Review Editor—AAR, Kent State University, Dept. of English, Kent, OH 44242. You may also contact him by e-mail: yhakutan@kent.edu.

Individuals whose works are accepted for publication must provide *African American Review* with a brief biographical sketch. Moreover, because the magazine is set from computer disk, accepted work should, whenever possible, be provided on floppy diskette.

The editors do not assume responsibility for loss of or damage to submitted materials. Materials published in AfricanAmerican Review do not necessarily represent the views of the journal's editors, staff, or financial supporters, and these parties therefore disavow any legal responsibility for the materials.

Categories: African-American—Book Reviews—Literature

CONTACT: Dr. Joycelyn Moody, Editor
Material: All
Saint Louis University, Humanities 317
3800 Lindell Boulevard
St. Louis MO 63108-3414

African-American Career World

Please refer to Equal Opportunity Publications, Inc.

Agni

Submission Guidelines
The Big Picture

AGNI publishes poetry, short fiction, and essays. Writers whose work has appeared in the magazine include Derek Walcott, Louise Glüück, David Foster Wallace, Seamus Heaney, Jhumpa Lahiri, Ha Jin, Olga Broumas, Tom Sleigh, Jill McCorkle, Thomas Sayers Ellis, Gail Mazur, Noam Chomsky, Ilan Stavans, and Rosanna Warren. *AGNI* regularly features emerging writers and "among readers around the world . . . is known for publishing important new writers early in their careers, many of them translated into English for the first time" (PEN American Center). Most of what we publish is unsolicited.

The *print* magazine appears twice yearly, in spring and fall. The website grows weekly with postings of new *online-only* fiction, poetry, essays, reviews, and interviews.

AGNI welcomes unsolicited manuscripts between September 1st and May 31st. We adhere strictly to postmark dates, and submissions mailed outside that period will be returned unread, provided that sufficient return postage is included. *AGNI*'s reporting time is approximately 2-4 months.

Each submission may be accepted for publication in *AGNI* or (with a writer's permission) *AGNI Online*. We pay $10 per printed (or printed-out) page for all accepted work ($20 minimum for the print magazine; $150 maximum for both), along with a year's subscription, and, for the print magazine, two contributor's copies and four gift copies of the issue.

The Nitty-Gritty
A list of DOs

Please submit poetry, fiction, and nonfiction SEPARATELY and addressed to the genre editor (Fiction, Poetry, or Nonfiction). Translations and essays are welcomed.

Please send no more than one story, one essay, or five poems at a time. Note that for prose we have **no word limits**, but generally the longer a piece is, the better it needs to be to justify taking up so much space in the magazine. We will consider novel excerpts provided that they are cohesive enough to stand alone.

Please enclose a self-addressed, stamped envelope (SASE) if you would like *AGNI* to return your submission. Envelopes that are too small or have insufficient postage for a manuscript's return will get our response, but the manuscript will be recycled. If you do not require the return of your manuscript and would like to be notified by email, please indicate clearly an email address where we may contact you (and skip the SASE).

Before submitting, please familiarize yourself with *AGNI* by ordering a copy of a recent print issue or by perusing the work that appears online. This site includes selected pieces from the latest print *AGNI*s (e.g., 60 and 61), current web-only work, and archived fiction, poetry, and nonfiction from both *AGNI* and *AGNI Online*.

A list of DON'Ts

WE DO NOT READ EMAILED SUBMISSIONS; please send your manuscript to our mailing address (see below).

Simultaneous submissions are acceptable and encouraged, but please notify us immediately if the work we are considering has been accepted elsewhere.

Please do not send submissions to *AGNI* between June 1st and August 31st; manuscripts received during this time will be returned UNREAD provided sufficient return postage is included. These dates do not apply to subscribers, whose work the editors will read year-round.

While we endeavor to deal with each submission quickly and fairly, we cannot, due to the overwhelming number of submissions we receive, accept responsibility for your manuscript. **Do not send us your only copy.**

CONTACT: Genre editor (Fiction, Poetry, Nonfiction)
AGNI Magazine
Boston University
236 Bay State Rd
Boston MA 02215
Website: www.bu.edu/AGNI

Air & Space

AIR & SPACE/Smithsonian is a general interest magazine about flight. Its purpose is to enlighten and to entertain. Its goal is to show readers, both the knowledgeable and the novice, facets of the enterprise of flight that they are unlikely to encounter elsewhere. The emphasis is on the human rather than the technological, on the ideas behind events, rather than a simple recounting of details.

Style points:

• Writing should be clear, accurate, and engaging. It should be free of technical and insider jargon, and generous with explanation and background.

• The first step every aspiring contributor should take is to study recent issues of the magazine. If back issues are unavailable at your public library, you may obtain a sample copy by sending a check or money order for $5.00 (includes postage) payable to Air & Space/Smithsonian. Our address is below; please be sure to include yours. Back issues may be searched for headline contents at our back issue page.

• The next step is to submit a one-page proposal introducing the article you envision. Describe the approach, the sources, and the possibilities for illustration, as well as your credentials. Editors read proposals especially to evaluate writing skill and imaginativeness of approach. Clips should accompany the proposal.

• For first time contributors, writing a department—a short piece that often has a personal point of view—offers the best chance for acceptance. Payment for departments is usually between $500 and $1,000, except for Soundings and Reviews, which generally pay $150 to $300.

Departments include:

Soundings: a compilation of newsy, somewhat offbeat short reports on the less illuminated corners of aerospace activities, from aeromodeling to music and the arts, from proceedings and events at group meetings to new technologies that have gone unreported in the mass media. The raw material of a good Soundings would probably appear as a story in a local paper and should provide a close-up of people involved in a unique aerospace enterprise.

Above & Beyond: a first person narrative of an adventure in air or space. Many have been written by pilots and astronauts. An "I was there" flavor is essential. (1,500 words)

Flights & Fancy: a whimsical, brief reflection that should leave the reader chuckling quietly. This department offers the opportunity for a range of tones, from nostalgic to mischievous to satiric. (800-1,000 words)

Soundings: short news items reporting oddball or amusing events, efforts, or situations; also, the stories behind the news. Soundings need to be fairly current. (300 to 1,000 words)

Reviews & Previews: a description and critique of a recent or soon-to-be-released book, video, movie, aerospace-related recreational product, or software. Reviewers should have specific experience or knowledge that enables them to give informed evaluations. Quotations from the text must be accompanied by page numbers. (200-1,000 words)

Oldies and Oddities: a bit of funky, little-known history; generally records the rise and fall of a design or idea that was ingenious but doomed. Descriptions of the personalities behind the brainstorms are especially encouraged. (1,500 words)

Feature articles: These require substantial research and reporting and average 2,500 words. Fees vary widely, depending on the type of treatment proposed but are generally between $1,000 and $2,500. In the event that an article is not accepted for publication, a kill fee is negotiated. Payment for first North American Serial Rights is made upon acceptance.

Categories: Nonfiction—Aviation—History

CONTACT: AIR&SPACE Magazine
Smithsonian Institution
PO Box 37012
Victor Bldg 7100 MRC 951
Washington, DC 20013-7012

Air Line Pilot

Air Line Pilot is published 10 times a year by the Air Line Pilots Association (ALPA), an AFL-CIO union of airline pilots. The magazine recognizes the airline pilot as the primary reader audience, and editorial content is developed to fill airline pilot needs. A list of airlines whose pilots are members of ALPA is attached.

Please Note: All unsolicited manuscripts, photographs, and cartoons must include sufficient return postage (stamps only) and packaging materials to ensure their safe return. Although all reasonable care will be taken with materials received, no responsibility can be assumed for any unsolicited materials.

WRITERS

We seek editorial material of aviation industry information, (e.g., economics, avionics equipment, aircraft systems, aviation safety, regulations) that affects the life of a professional airline pilot from a profession and a career standpoint.

Further, we seek editorial material pertinent to a pilot's life from a job security and work environment standpoint.

We prefer writers to query first in writing. Include content summary, length estimate, description of available illustrations (photos or art), and date when article could be ready. Be specific about why you think the article is right for our audience. SASE is appreciated to ensure reply.

Any airline pilot featured in an article must be an ALPA member in good standing. Please note in query that standing has been verified or provide complete name and address of the pilot.

Article length should be determined by subject matter, within a general range of 6 to 12 pages on 8½ x 11 inch white paper. Manuscripts must be typed and double-spaced; page one should include author's name, mailing address, and daytime telephone number.

Articles prepared on 3½-inch hard disks may be submitted. Such manuscripts must be prepared on an IBM-compatible computer using word processing with at least ASCII language—but preferably Microsoft Word 97. Disks should be mailed in suitable protective envelopes to ensure that data is not erased enroute. If requested, the disks will be returned. The manuscript file name, author's name, address, and day telephone number must be included on the disk label. Articles may also be sent by e-mail to magazine@alpa.org

Accompanying black-and-white photographs should be in the form of 8 x 10 inch glossy prints; color should be in 35mm transparencies, prints, or high-resolution (300 dpi) digital images. When a large selection of original photos is available, send proof sheets and negatives, a CD-ROM disk, or Zip disk. When a large number of transparencies is submitted, plastic slide pages are recommended. Maps, drawings, and charts may be submitted in black and white or color and should be

suitable for reproduction without additional work.

Payment is made on acceptance, which follows a four- to six-week review process. Range for features is $100 to $500, depending on length and extent of research required. Higher fees may be negotiated with writers on assignment or with a writer who becomes a regular contributor. *Air Line Pilot* buys all rights except book rights. By accepting an article, we make no commitment to a publication date.

An additional fee will be paid for each author-supplied photo used with a story, depending on the quality of the print and the problems involved in securing it. No payment is made for public-domain photos furnished to the author free of charge. All prints and negatives supplied by the author, including those used, will be returned upon request.

PHOTOGRAPHERS
Cover

Our greatest need is for strikingly original color cover photographs featuring ALPA flight deck crew members and their airlines in their operating environment. Only ALPA member airlines will be featured (see list). Visual emphasis is on a sharp image, good color, and strong composition. Only vertical compositions will be considered. We prefer to work exclusively from original transparencies, 35mm or larger. Exceptionally sharp 8 x 10 color prints may be acceptable. We pay $350 for all rights.

Inside Color and Stock Photography

Primarily, subject matter should be ALPA crews and ALPA member aircraft but can include almost any scene that relates directly to the airline pilot's world. Of particular interest are photographs showing aircraft flying in bad weather, nighttime operations, noise pollution problems/solutions, and aircraft operating in areas with obvious regional characteristics (i.e., Rocky Mountains in the background). Again, original 35mm or larger slides, using Fuji Velvia 50 film, are preferred. If possible, stay away from Ektachrome. We generally buy onetime rights for inside color; fees are negotiated on the basis of use. Rights and fees for stock photos are negotiated on an individual basis.

Any material accepted must be for the exclusive use of *Air Line Pilot*. It is understood that the material is not being offered simultaneously to other magazines. *Air Line Pilot* reserves the right to edit freelance material as necessary to meet the requirements of the publication. The act of mailing material to *Air Line Pilot* shall constitute a warranty by the contributor that the material is original and in no way an infringement upon the rights of others.

Categories: Nonfiction—Aviation

CONTACT: Air Line Pilots Association, Intl.
1625 Massachusetts Ave NW
Washington DC 20036
Phone: 703-689-2270

Alaska Airlines

Alaska Airlines Magazine is the monthly in-flight magazine for Alaska Airlines, reaching more than a million travelers in Alaska, California, Washington, Oregon, Arizona, Nevada, Western Canada and Mexico each month. Our mission is to inform and entertain our target audience—business travelers, the majority of whom are between the ages of 35 and 54. We produce a superior magazine with high-quality writing and striking photography. We look for writing with vivid visual images, anecdotes and a strong narrative flow. We are always looking for writers of national-magazine caliber. We are interested in writers who can cover business with insight and style; in local writers who can lend inside perspectives to our destination and travel columns; in journalists who write with a sense of humor, though we do not publish a humor column. Our magazine is 80 percent freelance written.

The best way for writers to get started with us is to send clips of previously published work and a well-written query that includes a sample lead that represents the direction, tone and style proposed for the story. The query should demonstrate advance research and original thought on the part of the writer.

Columns are the best way to break into *Alaska Airlines* Magazine. Our columns include Journal (arts and culture), Business, On Location, Profiles, Sports, Technology and Travel. We are not interested in fiction, poetry or book reviews. Our Business column examines innovative companies and business people in the route system, current trends in business and contemporary corporate issues. Topics in the Technology and Science columns range from computers to new resource development processes or scientific phenomena, clearly explained. Journal and Itinerary pieces are short, succinct and timely articles about events and places in our route system. All travel-oriented ideas must focus on destinations within the Alaska Airlines route system.

Features are generally on assignment only. If you take your own photographs, please ask for our photography guidelines. Assignments are acknowledged by written contract. Alaska Airlines Magazine pays within 30 days of publication, buying first North American rights with reprint rights. We pay a kill-fee of one-third the contracted price. Rates begin at $50 to $ 100 for Journal and Itinerary shorts (100 to 400 words); $100 to $200 for short articles or meals and lodging reviews (400 to 800 words); $300 for columns (1,600 words); and $500 for features (2,000 to 2,500 words). Expenses, if agreed to in advance, are paid on invoice. Expenses and rates vary in special circumstances. All queries should be written; they will not be accepted over the telephone. Features should be queried about six months in advance. Include a self-addressed, stamped envelope. You will receive a written response within six weeks. Please do not send original manuscripts, artwork or slides as we cannot be responsible for their receipt, or their return.

Categories: Nonfiction—Adventure—Arts—Entertainment—Food—Leisure—Outdoors—Regional—Science—Technology—Travel

CONTACT: Paul Frichtl, Editor-in-Chief
Material: All
2701 1st Ave Ste 250
Seattle WA 98121
Phone 206-441-5871
Fax 206-448-6939

Alaska Business Monthly

Alaska Business Monthly is written, edited and published by Alaskans for Alaskans and other U.S. and international audiences interested in the business affairs of the 49th state. Its goal is to provide thorough and objective analysis of the issues and trends affecting Alaska's businesses, and to feature stories on the individuals, organizations and companies that shape the Alaska economy. *Alaska Business Monthly* emphasizes the importance of all enterprise, and stresses a statewide approach to business coverage.

We seek informative articles on everything from entrepreneurs to heavy industry. We cover all Alaska industry to include mining, tourism, timber, transportation, oil & gas, fisheries, finance, insurance, real estate, communications, medical services, technology and construction. We also cover Native and environmental issues, and occasionally feature Seattle and other communities in the Pacific Northwest.

As our magazine is on most in-state airlines and in many major hotels, our reach extends beyond the businessperson to include tourists and the general public. Though circulation is at minimum 11,500 issues per month, we have a total statewide readership of approximately 100,000 individuals per month.

SUBMISSION CRITERIA

Approximately 80 percent of the features appearing in *Alaska Busi-* *ness Monthly* are written by free-lancers. All queries should be directed to the editor via mail, e-mail (editor@akbizmag.com), mail, fax or phone. We also welcome queries from individuals who would like to write columns in their fields of expertise. Anyone interested in writing for *Alaska Business Monthly* should submit three clips or sample articles.

Articles are assigned at least three months in advance. Each year we publish an editorial calendar that lists about half of each issue's topics. A copy of the editorial calendar will be provided upon request.

We purchase all rights of articles and reserve the right to make reprints of articles or to republish them in special ABM editions (such as an anniversary edition) or use them on our Web Site. We generally do not provide additional payment for such uses. Even though we purchase rights, we typically do not deny request for authors to have the piece published elsewhere, provided it appears in ABM first.

We prefer submissions via e-mail. When submitting by e-mail, send the article as an attachment(Microsoft Word doc or rtf format only), and also place a copy of the text in the e-mail itself.

PAYMENT

In the last reviewed survey, we discovered that *Alaska Business Monthly* pays the second-highest free-lance rates of any statewide business magazine in the western states. *Payment for articles is set at the time of assignment and will generally conform to the following standards:*

Business Spotlight	1-2 sources	500 words	$125
Short Feature	1-2 sources	500-750 words	$150
Short Feature	3+ sources	500-850 words	$175
Regular Feature	1-2 sources	750-1,000 words	$175
Regular Feature	Multi-source	1,000-1,500 words	$225
Full-length Feature	Multi-source	1,500-1,800 words	$250
Full-length Feature	Multi-source	1,800-2,000 words	$275
Full-length Feature	Multi-source	2,000+ words	$300
Sidebar to Feature			$15-$50

We will reimburse writers for long-distance charges, provided total charges for any article do not exceed $20. Charges in excess of $20 must be approved in advance. We generally do not reimburse for other expenses (gas, travel, meals). Writers must invoice for payment.

PHOTOGRAPHY GUIDELINES

We prefer electronic images, dropped onto our ftp site. Call or e-mail for instructions). ideally, digital photos should be high-resolution (i.e. 8-inch by 6 - inch at 300 dpi or 22.222 - inch by 16.667 - inch at the 72 dpi). Please do not send in digital photos that are low-resolution, such are 72 dpi, 2 - inch or 3 - inch height/width. There is not enough digital information in these photos to try to enhance them and prepare them for printing purposes. CMYK format is necessary. We only accept JPEG and TIFF images.

In addition, we accept black-and-white prints or negatives, color slides, color prints or color negatives. The name and address of the photographer must be on the back of every print or on the margin of every slide, or included in a text document in case of electronic submission. Photographers must always provide caption/credit information and guarantee permission to publish. We will not accept original images.

Photo payment is determined by the published size of the photograph, unless otherwise agreed upon at the time of assignment. Generally, the following rates for payment will apply for one-time use of an assigned photograph. (When we are asked for reprints of articles or sections of our magazine, we generally do not provide additional payment to the photographer). Payment for stock photography is less.

Cover:	up to $400
Stock:	up to $100
Full-page:	up to $200 color
	up to $175 B/W
Stock:	up to $50
Three-quarters-page:	up to $150 color
	up to $125 B/W
Stock:	up to $40
Half-page:	up to $125 color
	up to $100 B/W
Stock:	up to $35

Quarter-page: up to $75 color
                         up to $50 B/W
Stock: up to $25

ABM will only pay full-price for photography that is professionally done. Payment for slides and photographs of lesser quality will be substantially less. There is no payment for photos provided by businesses or nonprofits. In special cases ABM will reimburse the photographer for film and processing. Arrangements should be made with the editor at the time of assignment. Photographers must invoice for payment. (Call or e-mail editor for amount to invoice.)

Categories: Nonfiction—Business—Regional: Alaska

CONTACT: Debbie Cutler, Editor
Material: All
PO Box 241288
Anchorage AK 99524-1288
Phone: 907-276-4373

Alaska Quarterly Review

Alaska Quarterly Review is a literary journal devoted to contemporary literary art, publishing fiction, short plays, poetry and literary non-fiction in traditional and experimental styles. The editors encourage new and emerging writers, while continuing to publish award winning and established writers.

The editors invite submissions of fiction, short plays, poetry, and literary nonfiction in traditional and experimental styles:

FICTION: Short stories and novel excerpts in traditional and experimental styles (generally not exceeding 50 pages).

POETRY: Poems in traditional and experimental styles but no light verse (up to 20 pages).

PROSE: Literary nonfiction in traditional and experimental styles (generally not exceeding 50 pages).

DRAMA: Short plays in traditional and experimental styles (generally not exceeding 50 pages).

Please include your contact information in your cover letter and/ or on your manuscript: mailing address, phone number, and email address if available. All manuscripts must be typed and accompanied by a self-addressed, stamped envelope (SASE). Unless a SASE is enclosed with your submission, you will not hear from us unless we are interested in publishing your manuscript. We try to reply within 4 to 12 weeks.

Important notes:

(1) Unsolicited manuscripts are read between August 15 and May 15.

(2) Although we respond to e-mail queries, we *cannot* review electronic submissions.

(3) We review simultaneous submissions and request that they be identified as such in the cover letter.

Categories: Fiction—Nonfiction—Drama—Literature—Poetry—Short Stories

CONTACT: Editors
Alaska Quarterly Review
University of Alaska Anchorage
3211 Providence Dr
Anchorage AK 99508

Albemarle Kids Magazine

Parenting Magazine on topics for parents about kids and family life: health, education, trends, etc.

Rights: varies

Needs: We write for local parents so stories will likely get a local sidebar attached. Please email for current needs.

Length: regular columns are 550, features 100, 1400, 1800.

Payment: Varies from 15-65/piece dependent on length, originality etc.

How to Submit: microsoft word attaached as well as full story in body of email.

Response Time: 1-2 weeks

Tips for Writers: We want something fun and useful. Personal essays are particularly encouraged.

Sample Copies/Subscription Information: visit www.albemarlekids.com

Categories: Family

CONTACT: Jen
935 Owensville Rd
Charlottesville VA 22901
Phone: 434-984-4713
Fax: 434-984-4813
E-mail: editor@albemarlekids.com
Website: www.albemarlekids.com

Alberta Views

Writers/Illustrators/Photographers

AlbertaViews is a bimonthly magazine dedicated to providing well-written and well-researched commentary on the culture, politics and economy of Alberta. Each issue contains three feature articles of between 3000–5000 words on matters of social concern to Albertans. *AlbertaViews* is a regional magazine; therefore we are only interested in articles with a strong Albertan focus.

Please do not send unsolicited manuscripts.

AlbertaViews will consider synopses for feature ideas, reviews and garden articles, as well as reprints from various Alberta media of up to 1000 words for our readings section entitled Eye on Alberta. We also accept queries from photographers for submissions to View, our regular photographic feature on the inside front cover, or from artists who wish to showcase their work in Eye on Alberta. We do not accept unsolicited fiction or poetry. No materials will be returned without a self-addressed, stamped envelope (S.A.S.E.).

WE DO NOT ACCEPT PHONE QUERIES. But email is an excellent way to query us.

Queries:

Please read *AlbertaViews* before querying in order to fully understand the mandate of the magazine. With at least two months lead time for every issue, *AlbertaViews* covers issues as opposed to news, so please be aware of time-sensitive material or ideas. Back issues of the magazine are available for $5, which includes first class postage.

In any query, please include:

1) A written proposal of 300–500 words outlining your intended contribution to *AlbertaViews*, why you feel qualified to write about your chosen subject and what sources you intend to use.

2) A resume outlining your experience and education, complete with references and their phone numbers.

3) Recent examples of your published work (tear sheets).

4) A self-addressed stamped envelope (S.A.S.E.) if you require your submission material returned.

To submit a piece that has been previously published–such as an editorial or news item relevant to a current issue–please e-mail us the text and send a clear photocopy of the published piece. Provide the name of the publication and the date the piece appeared. We do not pay for reprints, art or anything else published in the Eye on Alberta section of the magazine, but we are interested in receiving speeches, memos, e-mails, web site excerpts and letters that might be of interest to the public.

For queries, expect a reply in six to eight weeks.

Format

For matters of style such as spelling, please refer to the Canadian Oxford Dictionary and the Globe and Mail style guide. Send all material in a double-spaced, paragraphed format with one space after periods.

Provide us with both a hard copy of the text (preferably mailed) and a computer version on disk or via e-mail. When e-mailing text, please attach the file if it is a Microsoft Word document, and include plain text in the body of the e-mail if you are not using Word. We require disks to be IBM or PC formatted (Microsoft Word if possible. If not, please send plain text).

Accompanying artwork or photos are welcome, but please provide them as 5x7 or 4x5 transparencies, 35 mm slides, or on disk, saved as Adobe Photoshop scans of a minimum 300 dpi using the CMYK color system and saved as a .tiff file.

For clarity of communication, we expect all writers to sign an agreement. We buy First North American Serial Rights, and the right to use an excerpt of the article on our web site. *AlbertaViews* pays about $.30 to $.50 per word depending on the writer's experience and qualifications. We pay about $50.00 for reviews. Photos vary. We pay upon publication. The writer must also provide a brief autobiographical sketch to be included with the article, a title for the article and suggested pull quotes. For emailing, please send only 3 to 5 files (no larger than 100kb each). Thank you.

Thank you for your interest in *AlbertaViews*. If you have any further questions, please feel free to e-mail us.

If you would like *AlbertaViews* to see your work, please send samples to: Scott Dutton, Art Director (see address below).

Categories: Nonfiction—Arts—Culture—Economics—Politics—Regional

CONTACT: Jackie Flanagan, Publisher and Executive Editor
Material: Queries
(QUERIES) 320 23rd Ave SW Ste 208
Calgary AB P2SOJ2
Phone: 403-243-5334
Fax: 403-243-8599
E-mail: (QUERIES) contactus@albertaviews.ab.ca
CONTACT: Scott Dutton, Art Director
Material: Photos and Illustrations
602 - 815 1st Street SW
Calgary AB T2P 1N3
E-mail: (PHOTOS, ILLUSTRATION)
creative@albertaviews.ab.ca
Website: www.albertaviews.ab.ca

Alfred Hitchcock's Mystery Magazine

Finding new authors is a great pleasure for all of us here, and we look forward to reading the fiction you send us. Since we do read all submissions, there is no need to query first; please send the entire story. You don't need an agent.

Because this is a mystery magazine, the stories we buy must fall into that genre in some sense or another. We are interested in nearly every kind of mystery, however: stories of detection of the classic kind, police procedurals, private eye tales, suspense, courtroom dramas, stories of espionage, and so on. We ask only that the story be about a crime (or the threat or fear of one). We sometimes accept ghost stories or supernatural tales, but those also should involve a crime.

You might find it useful to read one or more issues of *AHMM*; that should give you an idea of the kind of fiction we buy. For a sample copy, send a check made out to *AHMM* for $5.00 to 475 Park Ave. South, 11th floor, New York, NY 10016.

Style. We prefer that stories not be longer than 12,000 words; most of the stories in the magazine are considerably shorter than that. They

should, of course, be well-written. We are looking for stories that have not been previously published elsewhere, and among them for those that are fresh, well-told, and absorbing. They should be entirely fiction: please do not send us stories based on actual crimes, for instance, or other real-life events.

Manuscript preparation. Manuscripts should be typed on plain white paper (not erasable paper) and double-spaced (not space-and-a-half), with your name and address at the top of the first page. The title of the story as well as the byline you want to use should be on the first page of the story also. (We prefer that there not be a separate title page.) If you use a word processor, please do not justify the right-hand margin. Every page of the story should be numbered, preferably in the upper right-hand corner. If you number the pages by hand, be sure before you start that no page has been omitted. Do not use the italic, large-size, or boldface characters some computers are capable of generating. Underline words to indicate italics.

Indent for each paragraph. Do not leave 1-line spaces between paragraphs. The number of lines per page should be uniform, or mostly so.

Stories should be mailed to us flat, with the pages bound together by a paper clip only—not stapled or enclosed in a binder. A cover letter isn't necessary. If you want the manuscript returned in the event we cannot use it, you must include a self-addressed stamped envelope; contributors outside the U.S.A. should send International Reply Coupons in lieu of stamps. If you have sent us a photocopy and do not want it back, please advise us of that and enclose a smaller SASE for our response. Please keep a copy of any material submitted, since we cannot be responsible for lost or misdelivered mail.

Revisions. Revised versions of a story should be submitted only on our request, as a rule. At the very least, tell us in a cover letter that the story has been submitted before but has been revised, and explain how.

NOTE: Stories submitted to *AHMM* are not also considered by or for *Ellery Queen's Mystery Magazine*, though we share the same address. Submissions to *EQMM* must be made separately. We do not accept simultaneous submissions.

Categories: Fiction—Crime—Mystery—Short Stories

CONTACT: Submissions Editor
Material: All
AHMM
475 Park Ave. South, 11th Floor
New York NY 10016
Phone: 212-686-7188
Website: www.themysteryplace.com

Alien Q

AlienQ Science Cyber Fiction Ezine, alien contact on the web. Interactive Ask the Alien, stories, articles, glossary of alien terms, and more.

Guidelines

Write a quick paced interesting story.

Subjects should include alien encounters—real or imagined, universal history, possible futures, out-of-body experiences, spiritual abilities and powers, interstellar technologies and anything that broadens the scope of man's thought processes.

We like stories around 2000 to 5000 words.

Submit as an attachment or within the email text. We prefer Microsoft word documents. We pay $50.00 within a month after publication.

Categories: Science Fiction

CONTACT: Editor@alienq.com
Editors: Art Bacon, Verna Mitchell
11231 San Fernando Rd
San Fernando CA 91340
E-mail: aq@alienq.com
Website: www.alienq.com

Alienskin

Free online science fiction, fantasy and horror magazine

Guidelines

AlienSkin magazine **ONLY** accepts Email submissions. Submissions can be made 3 ways:

1. As a Plain Text Format (.txt) attachment;
2. As a Rich Text Format (.rtf) attachment; or by,
3. Copying and Pasting the story into the body of an email to us.

Submissions are to be made via email to: **Submit@Alien SkinMag.com**.

We **DO NOT** accept Simultaneous Submission, Reprints, Novel Excerpts, Serialized Stories, Snail Mail Submissions. Nor do we accept stories containing excessive blood, gore, vulgarity, erotica or child abuse. No inflammatory, hate pieces. No stories under 500 words or over 3,500 words.

Each author is limited to a total to 2 submissions per author per month. This does not include submissions to our contests.

All submissions **MUST** include the following information:

Response time on ALL submissions is about 1-2 months.

AlienSkin seeks First Electronic/Web Rights on all accepted stories for the 2 month period in which the story appears online, and a 60 day online archive of the First Paragraph only of the story in our **Shed Skins** section.

Payments for accepted stories are made in US$ via mailed Check or to a valid Paypal account. Payment is made upon publication, generally 2-3 weeks after the issue in which the story appears online. **AlienSkin** pays 100% kill fee to writers for stories that have been promised publication but do not get published do to magazine restructuring, etc.

PLEASE NOTE: AlienSkin offers a paragraph or two of critique on rejected stories, if you are a writer who can not accept honest criticism of your work (as to what we felt didn't work for us in regards to your story), then please note so in your cover letter that you prefer a form rejection. **AlienSkin** is not a market that attempts to thwart anyone's desire to write, we are working writers who attempt to offer honest comments on the stories your send us. But to some writers, even well-meaning criticism is an insult.

So if you are over protective of your work or you get red-faced reading the phrases, such as, "we pass on this story " or "this just didn't work for us", then we prefer you tell us so upfront. By doing so you will save us the time of writing a critique and spare us from receiving a nasty email from you if you don't like or agree with what we say.

Again, our critique comments are just the opinions of seven of our staff members. There is a whole world of people beyond us who may have a different perspective of your work. Other markets may agree to publish your story even if we did not.

To Avoid Receiving An Auto-Rejection Follow Our Submission Guidelines. Please Use A Normal 12pt font, such as, Times New Roman or Courier.

We Accept Submissions For The Following Categories:

Featured Fiction - Submissions Are Open:

We pay 1/2 centUS/word for stories of 1,001-3,500 words

Works of Short Fiction of 1,001-3,500 words are being accepted for our upcoming issues. Stories must fit within the genres of Science Fiction, Fantasy, or Horror. All stories MUST contain story basics of character, conflict, action and resolution. No excessive blood or gore. No erotica or blatant abuse of vulgarity. Please avoid sending us stories written in the present tense.

AlienSkin accepts 9 - 12 **Featured Fiction** pieces per issue.

Flash Fiction - Submissions Are Open:

We pay $5.00US/story of 500 - 1,000 words

We seek Flash Fiction, also known as Short-Shorts, of 500 to 1,000 words in length. Word length does not include story title or author byline. Stories must fit within the genre of Science Fiction, Fantasy, or Horror. All stories MUST contain story basics of character, conflict,

action, and resolution. We do not accept stories containing excessive blood, gore or vulgarity, nor does it accept stories containing erotica or child abuse. Please avoid sending us stories written in the present tense.

AlienSkin accepts 12 - 15 Flash Fiction pieces per issue.

Poetry - Submissions Are Open:

We pay a flat $2.50US/poem of 100 - 500 words

We seek poetry of 100 - 500 words. Poetry **MUST** fit within the genres of Science Fiction, Fantasy, or Horror. Our taste in poetry varies and is basically 'if we like it, we'll publish it.' Poems are published in our Flash Fiction section.

Round Robin Paragraphs - FREE to ALL

AlienSkin accepts paragraph submissions for the **Round Robin Work-In-Progress** section. Only one paragraph per Round Robin will be selected as the winner per issue.

Submissions should be made in Plain Text Format or Rich Text Format by COPYING and PASTING the story into the body of an email. Submissions are made via email to: **Submit@AlienSkinMag. com**.

Submissions **MUST** be emailed to **AlienSkin** Magazine by Midnight EST (Eastern Standard Time) of the **Paragraph Submission Deadline Date** as listed within the Round Robin section in order for the submission to qualify for consideration and inclusion in the following issue's Round Robin.

The submission should be roughly one paragraph in length, or may be one scene long. The paragraph/submission content must fits in with the material of the preceding paragraphs of the Round Robin for which it is intended, following character, plot, etc.; and the paragraph/submission content must fit within the genre of that particular Round Robin.

Any submissions containing excessive use of blood, gore, erotica, or vulgarity will automatically be disqualified for inclusion in the Round Robins.

Paragraphs chosen as the winner for each of the Round Robins will be selected by a panel of judges from our staff from the submissions we receive that follow the above guidelines.

The winning paragraph is published as a continuation of the Round Robin Stories in the issue of **AlienSkin** following the Paragraph Submission Deadline. Honorable Mentions, listing of the 1st and 2nd paragraph runners up, will be posted in each of the Round Robin section.

AlienSkin does not pay for the accepted paragraph nor is there a fee to participate. **AlienSkin** retains the copyright of the partial and/or finished Round Robin story as a conglomerated piece of fiction published within our Round Robins. Completed stories will not be published elsewhere.

Categories: Science Fiction—Fantasy—Horror

CONTACT: Katherine Patterson and Phil Adams, Editors
PO Box 495
Beaver PA 15009
E-mail: alienskin@alienskinmag.com
Website: www.alienskinmag.com

Alive Now

Our Mission

Alive Now is a devotional magazine that supports the spiritual lives of small groups as well as individuals. The magazine invites readers to enter an ever-deepening relationship with God, helps them reflect on contemporary issues from a faith perspective, and supports them in acting on these issues.

General Guidelines

Each issue of this bimonthly, 64-page magazine focuses on a contemporary topic that impacts the faith life. Divided into sections that move readers through exploration and reflection on the theme, the magazine may be used weekly by individuals or members of small groups. The sections contain scripture, prayers, meditations, stories, poetry, reflection aids, photographs, and art. Seasonal material, both theological and liturgical, is appropriate.

Readership

Alive Now is ecumenical, including both lay persons and church professionals. Our readers are primarily adults — from young adults to older adults — and include persons of many cultures and ethnic backgrounds.

Style and Format

Your submissions should invite readers to seek God in the midst of daily life by exploring how contemporary issues impact their faith lives. We do not pretend to have the final answer to life's dilemmas. But we hope that the magazine will provide a glimpse of the life of faith to which we all are called.

Submit for a theme. We make selections based on a list of upcoming themes. Manuscripts which do not fit a theme will be returned. To receive a current themes list by mail, please send your request to us with a self-addressed, stamped envelope. (See *Alive Now* address below.) *Alive Now* also posts upcoming themes online. We place manuscripts on long-term hold for specific issues. Authors are free to request that their manuscripts be returned to them at any time during the long-term hold.

Meditations and stories should be 250 to 500 words. Send your best work. Use language that is inclusive. Material that contains sexist language and imagery is difficult to use.

Manuscript Preparation

Contributions should be typed, double-spaced, on 8 1/2" x 11" paper and should be accompanied by a self-addressed, stamped envelope for return. If you are submitting material for more than one theme, send an SASE for each theme represented. On each page you submit, include your name, address, and the theme for which the piece is being sent.

Notification and Payment

Payment will be made at the time of acceptance for publication. We will notify contributors of manuscript status when we make final decisions for a theme, three months before the issue date. Unusable material will be returned if an SASE was sent with the manuscript. We purchase newspaper, periodical, and electronic rights so that we can respond to requests for reprints from local church publications and other periodicals as well as promote the magazine on the World Wide Web. We may purchase one-time use. The usual fee is $35 and up.

Categories: Arts—Inspirational—Photography—Poetry—Religion—Spiritual

CONTACT: Melissa Tidwell
Material: All
1908 Grand Ave.
PO Box 340004
Nashville TN 37203-0004
Phone: 615-340-7216
E-mail: AliveNow@upperroom.org
Website: www.alivenow.org

Alive!
A Magazine for Christian Senior Adults

No longer accepting submissions.

All About Kids

About Us

All About Kids, now in its 17th year of production, is a local, national award-winning magazine that serves as the premier parenting resource in the Greater Cincinnati and Northern Kentucky area.

All About Kids is a valuable guide for parents, educators and child care providers. Each monthly issue features timely articles on a variety of parenting topics, as well as a comprehensive calendar of family events.

Pick up a free copy at any Greater Cincinnati or Northern Kentucky Kroger Store or one of our more than 600 distribution points throughout the area including The Museum Center, The Art Museum, Cincinnati Public Libraries and a multitude of local public, private and parochial schools.

If you have any questions, comments or suggestions please contact us at:

All About Kids is nearly 100% freelance written and depends on talented freelance writers to fill the magazine with timely and informative editorial content each month.

Although we utilize an annual editorial calendar, there are some topics you simply can't plan for; thus, assignments become critical and maintaining a wide variety of talented writers is crucial.

We accept queries via e-mail, phone, fax and mail. Please note that we do adhere to AP style and require documentation of all sources.

Each issue also includes regular columns such as Expert Advice, Middle Years, Rave Reviews, Women's and Family Health, News You Can Use and our award-winning Calendar of Family Events.

For more information, or to submit an article, please e-mail our the Editor.

Categories: Nonfiction—Children—Parenting—Relationships—Teen—Women's Issues

CONTACT: Shelly Bucksot, Editor
Material: All
Midwest Parenting Publications
1077 Celestial St. Ste. #101
Cincinnati OH 45202-1629
Phone: 513-684-0501
Fax: 513-684-0507
E-mail: editor@aak.com
Website: www.aak.com

All For You

***ALL for YOU*'s Philosophy**

ALL for YOU is in business to help people discover feeling good everyday, so we print only positive stories about life experiences. ALL for YOU does not dwell on negative aspects of any related subject matter. Please do not be critical of competing products or services. If you do mention a product or service, please give us a contact name for possible advertising.

***ALL for YOU*'s Editorial Requirements**

ALL for YOU is interested in where to go and how to do it stories on fitness, nutrition, self-health/alternative health options in the Chicagoland suburbs, primarily western and northwest. Material should provide information readers can use in this immediate vicinity and in areas they can travel to on weekends or a short vacation.

The accent in *ALL for YOU* is on:
• Fitness
• Nutrition
• Health
• Spirituality
• Healing Arts

Related subjects are healthy eating/cooking, well-being, massage, meditation, acupuncture, hypnosis, intuitive healing, bicycling, yoga, pilates, golf, education related to any of these areas, intuitive/awareness information, chiropractic.

Remember, you are writing for publication one or two months in advance, and your subject matter should reflect that time lapse if necessary. We never want to lose sight of our primary goal which is to provide useful information for the reader.

Any material accepted is subject to such revision as is necessary to meet the requirements of this publication. Manuscripts and photos not used will be returned if a stamped, self-addressed envelope is provided, but we assume no responsibility for lost materials.

Please include a title of the article on each page. Also include an overline or subtitle (example: Pilates: The Miracle I Found). Include a byline and page number on each page and please include your social security number. If you submit a timely item, please indicate the month for suggested use.

ALL for YOU's Acceptance Policy

Please read before calling.

If you make an editorial submission to ALL for YOU and it is not returned in 30 days, you can assume we do plan to use it. However, we do keep some material for as long as 12 to 18 months before using it.

ALL for YOU Web Site Permission Form

The ALL for YOU web site may feature a sampling of articles found in the magazine. These articles are chosen at random from the current issue. If your article appears in ALL for YOU and you do not wish to see it on the web page, please let us know. The use of an article on the web site involves no additional compensation from ALL for YOU.

ALL for YOU Deadline Schedule:

35 Days Preceding Publication. Example: April 25th for the June issue.

Stories

• Should be accompanied by jpg, tif or gif files, black and white or color photos

• Should be between 600 and 1,200 words with shorter stories preferred. The story's focus should be on where to and how to. Stories should impart information in an entertaining fashion, and not in a text book or preachy tone.

• Can be submitted in the following forms:

—via e-mail. We have had best results with email.

—on a 3½" diskette if you use a Macintosh or IBM computer. We use Microsoft Word for word processing.

Photos

• ALL for YOU can accept color or black and white or color slides. A good photo is usually one that catches the action of the story.

• Please send no more than 3 to 4 photos per story.

• You must place your return address on the back of the photo if you want it returned. Caption sheet, with the title of the story it accompanies should be taped to the back of the photo. There is no better way to insure that your photo will not be used with another writer's story.

Important Checklist before Sending in Material

• Your name is on all pages and photos.

• You have included your social security number.

• You have indicated what month the material is for.

• You have written a headline and subheadline.

• You have written a caption for each photo.

Please Remember: If we do not plan on using your material, it will be returned to you within 10 days of receipt.

Categories: Food/Drink—Health—Spiritual

CONTACT: Submissions Editor
Material: All
161 Hawkins Circle
Wheaton IL 60187
E-mail: ALL4YOUWRITERS@aol.com

All Info-About Freelance Writing

An ezine for freelance professionals and keen hobbyists to stay up to date with current news, views and trends, seek practical assistance and browse market resources.

Rights: We acquire non-exclusive one-time rights, plus permission to archive your work on our web site.

Needs: We are pleased to accept well-crafted essays, how-tos, interviews, book reviews and articles concerning writers and writing for use in our ezine and on the main website. We will also considerand any other appropriate contribution.

Length: Open.

Payment: We offer a full by-line: brief bio, two links to the websites of your choice and a contact email address (optional). You will automatically receive a copy of the ezine.

How to Submit: All Info-About Freelance Writing currently accepts e-mail submissions only. Please submit your work to the e-mail address: freelancewriting@allinfoabout.com with

Response Time: We will attempt to respond within 28 days of receiving your submission/s. However, please don't lose hope if we take slightly longer!

Sample Copies/Subscription Information: Please send an e-mail to freelancewriting@allinfoabout.com with the words 'sample free' in the subject line.

Submission Guidelines For Writers

See your articles, essays and reviews published on this site

Would you like to submit your work for publication in our newsletter or write a leading feature for All Info-About Freelance Writing? Here's how:

What is All Info-About Freelance Writing?

A place for freelance professionals and keen hobbyists to stay up to date with current news, views and trends, seek practical assistance and browse market resources.

What to submit?

We are pleased to accept well-crafted essays, how-tos and articles concerning writers and writing - we will also considerand any other appropriate contribution. Pieces containing excessive use of bad language or other types of unacceptable subject matter (based on the sole discretion of the Editor at All Info-About Freelance Writing), may be rejected.

How to submit?

All Info-About Freelance Writing currently accepts only e-mail submissions. Submit your work to the e-mail address: freelancewriting@allinfoabout.com with "submission free" in the subject heading. Please **do not send attachments**. Submissions with attachments will automatically be deleted. Please include your name; address (including zip/post code and country); e-mail address; title of work; details concerning when and where your work was previously published (if applicable) and up to 100 words about yourself in the form of a brief biography.

Rights:

All Info-About Freelance Writers acquires non-exclusive one-time rights and permission to archive your work on our web site. In other words, once the author has submitted his or her work for consideration, they are giving All Info-About Freelance Writers permission to publish their work in our weekly newsletter and on the main All Info-About Freelance Writers web site.

By submitting your work, you agree that we reserve the right to edit all submissions for spelling (this will include anglicising your spelling) and grammar, and to make minor revisions if necessary. Upon submission, you confirm that it is your work and that you are the legal copyright holder of the submitted work. We will not be held responsible for any and all copyright disputes or actions which may result because of copyright infringement issues.

Compensation: Currently, All Info-About Freelance Writers is unable to pay contributors. However, we can offer you a full byline, two links to the websites of your choice and a contact email address (optional).

Reply time: All Info-About Freelance Writers will attempt to respond within 28 days of receiving your submission/s.

Categories: Nonfiction—Writing

CONTACT: Paula Bardell, Editor
Email: freelancewriting@allinfoabout.com
http://freelancewriting.allinfoabout.com

Alternatives

Alternatives is a journal dedicated to in-depth analysis of environmental issues, including ecological, social and economic dimensions. It combines the learned rigour of an academic journal with the accessible style and format of a general-audience magazine. This unique hybrid has proved itself by its staying power: the journal has been publishing continuously in Canada since 1971, making it the oldest environmental policy journal in the country. *Alternatives* is published by Alternatives Inc., a non-profit charitable corporation.

Alternatives aims to publish the best environmental writing in the country—writing that is engaging to read and that provides a deeper level of analysis and insight than can be gained from the mainstream press. We invite feature articles, shorter reports, notes, interviews, resource guides, visual images related to article themes, cultural commentary and humour.

Features (2000-3000 words, including endnotes) cover a topic in-depth. Features may be written in an essay style where the author ruminates on a topic, a journalistic style, where the author tells a story based on interviews with stakeholders and published documents, or an academic style that sets out a logical framework and systematically explores an issue.

Feature articles must meet the highest standards in terms of the analytical rigour and reliability of the information presented. However, they must also be lively, well-written and accessible to a non-expert readership. Authors are encouraged to use illustrative cases for theoretical or general points and to avoid using specialized language (i.e., jargon). Manuscripts are subject to blind review by experts in the field.

Reports (500 -1200 words) are less analytical than features and are usually written to convey a story or inform the reader of new initiatives or recent developments in policy, thought, technology or action. They are usually written in a balanced, news style approach with some analytical content, but other styles will be considered: e.g., case study, research report, recounting a personal experience, etc.. Shorter reports normally do not have endnotes.

Notes (up to 500 words) are intended to inform busy readers about interesting topics that can be summarized quickly. They are written in a to-the-point news style.

Style Guidelines

Alternatives requires all submissions to be written in a non-sexist manner. Quotes that include sexist terms should be avoided. If a sexist term is unavoidable, it should be followed by "[sic]". For reference see Bobbye D. Sorres, The Nonsexist Communicator (New Jersey: Prentice-Hall, 1983).

Alternatives follows the Oxford Canadian Dictionary for spelling and the Globe and Mail and Canadian Press Style Guides for style.

At the end of articles, under the subheading "Notes", authors should provide explanatory notes and references, where appropriate. A literary style of documentation should be used, presented as follows:

For a journal:
A.B. Author, "Article Title," Journal Name, 2:3 (1982), pp. 123-25.

For a book:
A.B. Author, Book Title (Place of publication: Publisher, 1982), p. 101.

For a web site:
Name of Organization, "Title of Document or Page" (accessed Date) <URL>.

Figures and tables should appear on separate pages, be numbered and have appropriate titles.

Accepted submissions will be illustrated with photographs, drawings or other graphics. If possible, please submit illustrative graphic material, or suggest sources of appropriate photos. All original art work supplied will be returned.

For all articles, authors should supply web gaddresses where readers can find further information about the topic.

Themes

Each issue of *Alternatives* contains both theme and non-theme material. Recent themes have included Industrial Redesign, Green Energy, Community Redesign, Biodiversity, Urban Transportation, Food, Sex and Nature, and Development and the Environment. Upcoming themes are listed on our Call for Submissions page.

Procedure for Submission

Although we do consider completed manuscripts, we prefer to work with authors from the proposal stage to a finished manuscript. Proposals should explain what you plan to cover and how you will proceed with the writing. The proposal should convey your approach, tone, and style; and should indicate the approximate length of the proposed article.

Keep in mind that our lead time is several months and submissions should not be so time-bound that they will appear dated once published.

Both proposals and finished manuscripts should be submitted electronically (as an e-mail attachment) to:
Tara Flynn, Executive Editor, Alternatives Journal
Email:
While we work with Microsoft Word on Macintosh computers, we can accept files created with most other word processing software on other platforms.

In cases where an author is unable to send attachments by email, please call (519) 888-4442 to make alternative arrangements.

While we do not normally accept material that has already appeared in other major publications, we will consider articles that have already received a very limited or regional audience.

Revisions

Initial acceptance of a proposal or a manuscript, or the assignment of a commission, does not guarantee publication. After initial acceptance, authors are expected to work with an Alternatives editor to revise the manuscript. Authors are asked to respond to requests for revisions within a delay of two weeks. Final copy is sent to authors for approval prior to publication. Although the author's views are taken into account, the title to be used on the article is chosen by Alternatives' editors.

Honoraria

Full time academics, students writing for course credit, and other authors who submit articles written in a context related to their employment are not offered payment. In other cases, honoraria are negotiated with the author on a case-by-case basis. Authors who wish to be considered for an honoraria should indicate their wish to the editor with whom they are working when the article is assigned or accepted for publication. Payment is made upon publication. If an article has been commissioned or accepted for publication but is not (for whatever reason) eventually published, the author will be paid half the negotiated fee.

Copyright

Alternatives purchases first North American serial rights. We distribute some articles for not-for-profit research and educational purposes. These include some ongoing arrangements with library and research databases that make our articles available as reference materials. We also promote the copying of articles for use as university course texts.

Style Guidelines

Alternatives follows the Oxford Canadian Dictionary and The Globe and Mail Style Book.

At the end of articles, under the subheading "Notes," authors should provide explanatory notes and references, where appropriate. A literary style
of documentation should be used, presented as follows:

For a journal: A.B. Author, "Article Title," Journal Name, 2:3 (1982), pp. 123-25.

For a book: A.B. Author, Book Title (Place of publication: Publisher, 1982), p. 101.

For a web site: Name of Organization, "Title of Document or Page" (accessed Date) <URL>.

Figures and tables should appear on separate pages, be numbered and have appropriate titles.

Accepted submissions will be illustrated with photographs, drawings or other graphics. If possible, please submit illustrative graphic material, or suggest sources of appropriate photos. All original artwork supplied will be returned.

For all articles, authors should supply web addresses where readers can find further information about the topic.

Categories: Nonfiction—Ecology—Environment

CONTACT: Nicola Ross, Editor, Alternatives Journal
Faculty of Environmental Studies, University of Waterloo
Waterloo Ontario Canada N2L 3G1
Phone: 519-888-4442
Toll free: 866-437-2587
Fax: 519-746-0292
E-mail: editor@alternativesjournal.ca
Website: alternativesjournal.ca

Amazing Journeys Magazine

Amazing Journeys is a new magazine of Science Fiction and Fantasy. *Amazing Journeys* is a quarterly print magazine. Currently the magazine is a digest sized, black and white only issue.

Rights: We purchase first serial rights for Amazing Journeys Magazine. Books and anthology rights will be discussed after acceptance.

Needs: Journey Books is seeking great authors who are willing to work at building a name for themselves while building a reputation for Journey Books. We'll work hard for you, but as a new and relatively small press we need authors who are willing to help sell their work. Currently, we a seeking short works for Amazing Journeys Magazine. The first issue is due for release this fall. Those authors whose work generates the most interest from readers may be given an opportunity to participate in one of our upcoming anthologies. It is our hope to develop a "stable" of authors for our publishing house by using the magazine, and later the anthologies, as a test vehicle for writers. Those who pass may find themselves with a book deal a few years down the road. Our initial payments will be very small, but hopefully as our presence grows and our authors names become know so will the money.

Length: For books, send a brief synopsis and the first three chapters.

For Amazing Journeys Magazine and our anthologies we are looking for works with lengths from 3000-20,000 words but prefer the 5k-8k range.

Payment: For Amazing Journeys Magazine: As stated above, we're just getting started. Our payment is terrible, but we hope it will get better. We pay $10.00 per story upon acceptance for First North American Serial Rights for Amazing Journeys Magazine. Additional rights may be purchased later. An additional $10.00 will be paid to each author for each $1000.00 in subscription revenue the magazine brings in for the edition in which the work appears.

Works accepted for book and anthology publication will receive a contract stating rights, advances and /or royalty payments on an individual basis.

How to Submit: Snail Mail all submissions to address below.

Response Time: 3-6 weeks

Tips for Writers: We accept works in most science fiction and fantasy genres, but we shy away from the really dark stuff and will never publish gay or lesbian work, so don't bother.

Sample Copies/Subscription Information: Single issues are a reasonable $2.99. Save with a yearly subscription. That's four issues for $9.99. Order now to receive the first issue this Fall. Mail payment to: Journey Books, 3205 Hwy. 431, Spring Hill, TN 37174. Please indicate that you are purchasing *Amazing Journeys Magazine.*

Journey Books Writers Guidelines

We're seeking fresh voices with a Golden Age flare.

Journey Books is seeking great authors who are willing to work at building a name for themselves while building a reputation for Journey Books. We'll work hard for you, but as a new and relatively small press we need authors who are willing to help sell their work.

Currently, we are seeking short work s for Amazing Journeys Magazine. Those authors whose work generates the most interest from readers may be given an opportunity to participate in one of our upcoming anthologies. It is our hope to develop a "stable" of authors for our publishing house by using the magazine, and later the anthologies, as a test vehicle for writers.

(Authors must be published in the magazine before anthology and book length works will be considered.)

Here's what we want:

We are looking for G and PG rated material. We prefer Golden Aged styled Science Fiction but will use work in all speculative genres. ABSOLUTELY NO SEXUAL CONTENT WILL BE ACCEPTED. Profanity is greatly restricted (fewer than two mildly profane words per story please).

For *Amazing Journeys Magazine*, we are looking for works with lengths from 3,000 to 10,000 words but prefer the 3k-6k range. We also are looking for two poetry pieces for each issue. Poems must be between 20 and 40 lines.

We accept works in most science fiction and fantasy genres We do not accept work that promotes gay lifestyles.

We do not accept reprints. (This includes stories that have ever appeared on the net in any format.)

We will accept multiple submissions of no more than two short stories or four poems. We do not accept simultaneous submissions.

We are not seeking artwork at this time. All art work is handled in house.

Work must be formatted using traditional manuscript conformities.

We now accept email submissions. Email subs must be mailed to: subs@journeybookspublishing.com. We accept MS Word (.doc) or .rtf attachments. Shorter pieces my be included in the body of an email.

Send snail mail submissions to address below.

All snail mail submissions must include a SASE.

All submissions must contain the author's email address as part of the contact information. Submissions without email contact information will be returned unread.

We will answer email queries and answer questions about the guidelines.

We usually respond within six to twelve weeks but if we don't, do not call us. We'll contact you if we like it. The longer we hold your story, the more likely we are to be thinking about acceptance.

Don't be discouraged if you get a rejection letter. We're like all the rest and are biased by our own taste. Send us something else.

Payment:

For *Amazing Journeys Magazine*. Short story payments will be made at the rate of 1/4 cent per word. One lead story each issue will receive our Editor's Choice award and payment of 1/2 cent per word. We will pay $5.00 for each poem. We purchase First North American Serial Rights.

Categories: Fantasy

CONTACT: Edward Knight, Donnie Clemons, Editors
Journey Books
3205 Hwy 431
Spring Hill TN 37174
E-mail: subs@journeybookspublishing.com
Website: www.journeybookspublishing.com

America@Work

About Us

America@work (monthly magazine). Union leaders and front-line activists creating change for working families find their ideas, info and ammo in America@work, the monthly magazine of the AFL-CIO. The AFL-CIO was formed in 1955 by the merger of the American Federation of Labor and the Congress of Industrial Organizations.

What is the AFL-CIO?

The American Federation of Labor-Congress of Industrial Organizations (AFL-CIO) is the voluntary federation of America's unions, representing more than 13 million working women and men nationwide.

Guidelines

Formal guidelines not available. Please read a number of issues to ascertain the publication's style and needs.

Send queries to address below.

Categories: Nonfiction, Careers

CONTACT: Submissions Editor
Material: All
AFL-CIO, 815 16th Street, N.W.
Washington DC 20006
Phone: 202-637-5000
Fax: 202-637-5058
Website: www.aflcio.org

America West

Published by Skyword Marketing Inc., *America West* magazine is the monthly publication aboard *America West* Airlines. Each month, more than 1.6 million passengers fly on *America West* to destinations across the continental United States, several Canadian cities, Mexico and Costa Rica. The airline's operational hubs are Phoenix and Las Vegas.

Feature

• One Good Read: The magazine's centerpiece story might be a thoughtful news feature, an essay, a piece of fiction (short story or excerpt from a longer work) or a photo essay. Subjects that evoke a strong sense of place within the airline's route system are particularly welcome. The length ranges from 1,500- 3,000 words; sidebars often are staff-generated.

Departments

• Flights of Fancy: A regular compendium of fribble and froth to amuse and inform. Discrete components of short narratives and lists in a graphically sharp design. Demands excellent research, reporting and snappy writing with an attitude. Staff written. Each issue includes several of the following, plus other material as warranted:

• Dept. of Commerce: A look at new and notable business trends in *America West* destination cities. Approximately 450 words; assigned to a regular contributor.

• Dateline: Las Vegas—a monthly slice of commercial, cultural or recreational life in and around • Las Vegas. 300-400 words; assigned to a regular contributor.

• Language Arts—words, phrases, vocabulary. Etymology rendered entertainment.

• Briefs—goofy news stories, trivia and cool stuff we can't fit anywhere else.

• Creature Feature—descriptions of bizarre animals, traits, animal behavior and research.

• Extreme Science—reports of wacky research studies we wonder ever got funded.

• Who, What, When, Where, Why?—brief descriptions of quirks in history keyed to destination cities.

The length of this section ranges from 1,200-2,000; currently staff written and not open to freelancers.

• Opposites Attract: Two writers assume opposing positions on a topic of wide interest. Balanced, civil expressions by people with no agenda other than to communicate well a passionate belief; politicians, stuffy academics need not apply. The length is 500-800 words each; open to freelancers and contributors among our readers.

• City Lights: a digest of interesting, entertaining and serviceable information about our cover destination. The length is 500 words; assigned to a regular contributor.

• Transitions: how people solved problems, confronted demons and prejudices, or overcame odds in business, personal relationships, adventure/survival, competition, etc. The length is 1,000- 1,500 words; open to freelancers.

• Location, Location, Location: Real estate writ engagingly conceptual and pegged to destination cities. The length is 1,000- 1,500 words; open to freelancers.

• Hometown: Writers wax eloquent/amusing/ passionate/quirky about an aspect of their city of origin or residence. No sweeping "everything you always wanted to know about" destination stories. Must be personal and opinionated. No wimps allowed. The length is 1,000-1,500 words; open to freelancers.

• Who's On First?: A humorous, sports-information Q&A with questions submitted by our readers. The length is 1,000- 1,500 words; assigned to a regular contributor.

Terms and Rights

The magazine buys first North American print rights and pays on acceptance. Rates range from 60 cents to $1 per word, depending on the degree of difficulty and research. If, after one rewrite as directed by the editor, the work is not suitable for publication, the kill fee is 25%. Reasonable expenses are reimbursed if cleared with the editor in advance and invoiced with receipts and a Social Security number.

Terms and Assignments

Please query the editors by snail mail at the address below. Expect four to eight weeks for a reply. A business-sized SASE guarantees a faster response. Sample copies are available for $3: Please include an self-addressed, 9-inch by 12-inch envelope with sample-copy requests. Stories are assigned four to six months in advance of publication. Assignments must be submitted via e-mail or on disk in Microsoft Word. Meeting deadlines is critical. Writers should also be prepared to submit a list of source material for fact-checking.

Categories: Fiction—Nonfiction—Adventure—Animals—Careers—Comedy—Conservation—Cooking—Culture—Entertainment—Family—Food/Drink—General Interest— Inspirational—Language—Literature—Money and Finances—Multicultural—Native Americans—Photography—Recreation—Rural America—Science—Short Stories—Society—Travel—Western—Writing

CONTACT: Ellen Alperstein, Editor in Chief
Material: All
CONTACT: David Proffit, Associate Editor
Skyword Publishing
4636 E. Elwood St., Ste. 5
Phoenix, AZ 85040-1963
Phone: 602-997-7200
Website: www.skyword.com

American Artist Watercolor

What we are looking for:

The readers of *American Artist* and *Watercolor* magazines are professional or advanced amateur artists who want to learn from other artists. Our articles therefore profile an accomplished artist in any fine-art medium (no photography) and his or her techniques, featuring large full-color reproductions of the artwork and a step-by-step demonstration whenever possible. The artists are primarily realists, interested in traditional techniques and subjects.

American Artist always features a "Watercolor Page" and a "Pastel Page." These articles are often written by the artist (or ghost-written in the artist's voice) and focus on one technical aspect, rather than providing an overview of the artist's work. In addition, the "Business & Professional Practices" articles cover the business side of being an artist, such as gallery representation, pricing artwork, framing, and obtaining grants and fellowships.

The stories in *Watercolor* are similar in content to those in *American Artist*, except that they must be on watermedia (acrylic on paper, casein, gouache, and watercolor). *Watercolor* often features a "Lives in Art" story that focuses on one artist's career path.

In both magazines we also publish stories with an art historical bent. These stories are always oriented toward what a practicing artist today can learn from a master of a certain medium or technique.

Finally, some of our stories focus on recent exhibitions. In these pieces, we aim to provide insight into an assembled group of pictures in terms of their subject matter. In this way, we hope to provide readers with a greater understanding of how contemporary artists are incorporating more meaningful content into their work.

What to submit:

For editorial consideration, please send a letter outlining your proposal, along with your résumé. (A Web site address is not acceptable.) Be as specific, and concise, as possible in your proposal.

Please send a stamped return envelope with your submission.

What we pay:

Upon the article's publication, we generally pay $500 for articles of about 1,500 to 2,000 words.

Final notes:

We acquire the copyright for the article, but not the artwork.

We receive a large volume of material every day. It can take six to eight weeks for us to respond to your query. Please be patient. We seriously consider every proposal we receive.

We work about four and a half months in advance of the publication date.

Categories: Arts—Biography—Trade: Art Exhibition

CONTACT: M. Stephen Doherty, Editor-in-Chief
American Artist and Watercolor
770 Broadway
New York, NY 10003
Phone: 646-654-5506
Website: www.myamericanartist.com

American Baby

ABOUT THE MAGAZINE AND OUR READERS

AMERICAN BABY is a monthly, national publication dedicated to being a knowledgeable guide for pregnant couples and new parents, particularly those having their first child or those whose child is birth to age 2. Mothers are the primary readers, but fathers are involved also.

Parenthood is a new and engrossing experience for our readers. They want to keep up with the latest issues affecting their new family, particularly health and medical news, but they don't have a lot of spare time to read. They are not interested in abstract or theoretical issues, or in subjects they can read about in general-interest magazines.

We forgo the theoretical approach to offer quick-to-read, hands-on information that can be put to use immediately. And we present a balanced view of some controversial issues, such as childhood immunizations, so the readers can make their own decision. Our readers want to feel connected to other parents, both to share experiences and to learn from one another. They want reassurance that the problems they are facing are solvable and not uncommon.

TOPICS ACCEPTED

Full-Length Articles: Submitted articles or query letters for them should offer helpful information on some aspect of pregnancy or child care; should cover a common problem of child-raising, along with solutions; or should give advice to the parents on a psychological or practical subject. Articles about products, such as toys and nursery furniture are not accepted, as these are covered by staff members.

Medical subjects are acceptable as long as at least two medical doctors or medical authorities are mentioned. A list of sources and contacts will be expected with submission of the article.

Most feature articles run between 1,000 and 2,000 words. If practical, query first.

SHORT ITEMS: We accept items of 50-350 words for Crib Notes (news and feature topics) and Medical Update (health and medicine). Items must appeal to a nationwide audience. Dated or seasonal material must be received at least three months in advance. If practical, query first.

We do not accept fiction, fantasy pieces, dreamy musings, or poetry.

WRITING STYLE

A simple, straightforward, clear approach is mandatory. We are an understanding shoulder to lean on, an experienced friend to lend a helping hand. Articles can focus on the reality, the humor, and the delight of child-rearing, but not on its mystical or magical qualities. A preachy or know-it-all tone is unacceptable. Researched topics should include real-life anecdotes.

Articles should contain approximately four to five subheads and a suggested headline. Articles submitted with sidebars and other short, additional elements are preferred.

QUERY LETTERS: Include published clips, if available, and a brief outline/synopsis of the article idea. One article idea per query letter, please. Do not send queries by fax.

SAMPLE COPY: For a sample copy of AMERICAN BABY, send a 9" X 12" self-addressed envelope and $2 or equivalent postage to:AMERICAN BABY Magazine, 125 Park Avenue, 16th floor, New York, NY 10017.

PAYMENT: Between $800 and $1,000 for feature articles, depending on article length and whether the author has written for AMERICAN BABY before, is paid upon acceptance. First-person experiences pay $500 upon acceptance. Our kill fee for rejecting assigned articles is 25 percent of the stated payment.

Thank you for your interest in writing for AMERICAN BABY. We work successfully with a large number of new writers each year.

Categories: Nonfiction—Children—Health—Parenting

CONTACT: Editor, AMERICAN BABY Magazine
Material: All
125 Park Ave 16th floor
New York NY 10017

American Business Review

The American Business Review welcomes both empirical and theoretical articles that can be applied or be pertinent to current business issues and practices or contribute to academic research in finance and business.

Authors' articles should not exceed 25 double-spaced typewritten pages, and footnotes should appear on a separate page and follow A.P.A. style. The author should send three copies of his manuscript plus a short biography. Include also an abstract of not more than 75 words summarizing the paper.

All articles are anonymously reviewed by the editorial board entirely in terms of scholarly content.

Previously published articles cannot be accepted.

Categories: Nonfiction—Business—Money & Finances

CONTACT: Editor
Material: All
University of New Haven, 300 Orange Ave.

West Haven CT 06516
Phone: 203-932-7118
Fax: 203-931-6084
E-mail: mharvey@newhaven.org

American Bungalow

Inquiry Letter: Please send a brief pitch letter with a summary of the article you propose and several photographs of the subject matter if possible. We will return any materials with a SASE. Expect a response within six weeks and include an e-mail address if at all possible.

Clips: If you are a published writer, please include one to three samples of your previous work. If you write for competitive magazines, or if the material you are pitching has been published previously, please let us know the names of those publications.

Topics: American Bungalow covers a wide range of topics: the Arts and Crafts movement, collecting, bungalow neighborhoods, new construction, gardens, art, period lodges and home renovation, among others. Surprise us; we love to publish little-known gems.

Tone: We're looking for writers whose personalities come through in their work, and first-person storytelling is fine. Factual information should be leavened with quotes when possible, and please avoid footnotes and other academic approaches.

Length: Typically, American Bungalow articles run between 800 and 1,200 words. Sidebars containing resource information, brief historical overviews, etc. are also fine to include. Short (100–400 word) pieces may be published in our b&w newsletter within the magazine without compensation.

Format: If your idea is accepted for further development, you may submit final text in a hard copy, an MS Word-based floppy or an electronic document.

Artwork: Strong graphic elements are very important to the look of American Bungalow. Your proposal has a much better chance of being accepted if you are able to provide quality photographs, drawings or period illustrations to accompany your piece.

Some specifics: We can work with transparencies, slides or prints of photographs. Scanned images need to be saved at 300 dpi; please do not e-mail photos to us without prior arrangement. Please include the name of the photographer so we can give them proper credit. Period photos are welcome as well. Elevations, floor plans and the like should be a reasonable size—they need to fit on our scanners. We are happy to return all of your materials, but will need to work with them for approximately three months.

Show Us What You've Done: American Bungalow publishes architect and homeowner renovations, and new construction articles that have slightly different guidelines than our features. We're looking for firsthand experiences—the challenges or special characteristics of your project and how you solved them—that will resonate for other readers. Humor, how the experience impacted your family, what made you decide to build a bungalow—all are welcome. These articles are also the one category where we can accept amateur snapshots—but we still need sharp, well-exposed photos to illustrate the piece. Flash-on-camera interiors are often unusable, so if you're shooting indoors, please use a tripod and available light. Professional-quality photography is most welcome as well, and elevations, floor plans and resource lists are strongly encouraged.

Compensation: American Bungalow will send you several copies of the issue in which your article appears, along with your returned art materials. Articles are often written in exchange for a nationally published clip, a comp book from the Bungalow Bookstore, or a subscription to the magazine. If you have a business that deals with Arts and Crafts products or services, we may be able to trade out ad space for the feature; each case is unique, so please let us know on what basis your proposal is predicated. We do offer modest compensation for some features, in the $175–$250 range.

Back Issues: If you are not a regular reader, the best way to get a sense of our style is to review several back issues of American Bunga-

low. The current issue is posted on our website, www.ambungalow.com, and past issues are available through the site or by calling 800 350-3363.

We look forward to receiving your proposals; thanks for your inquiry.

Categories: Nonfiction—Architecture—Collectibles—History—Sheltor

CONTACT: Michelle Gringeri-Brown, Editor
Material: All
PO Box 756
Sierra Madre, CA 91025-0756
Phone: 800-350-3363
E-mail: editor@ambungalow.com
Website: www.ambungalow.com

American Careers

American Careers is published once a year for high school students and once a year for middle/junior high school students. Each issue contains up-to-date career information, how-to articles, self-assessments and other stories designed to promote career development and career education.

Assignment Procedures

1. Individuals in business, government and education provide some stories at no charge. Career Communications, Inc., makes work-for-hire assignments or buys all rights for other stories in *American Careers*.

2. Often stories are assigned based on ideas proposed by writers. Before making assignments, we need a résumé and writing samples on file.

3. We assign stories by phone, letter or e-mail detailing the story idea and focus, possible contacts, deadline, etc. We may ask you to include photographs or request photographs or other art from interviewees to illustrate your article.

4. A signed contract must be on file before any payment is made.

5. We accept late copy only if you consult with us first. Writers who do not meet deadlines may not receive future assignments.

Payment

1. Payment rate varies with assignment.

2. Payment is made within 30 days of receipt of assigned work.

3. Reasonable expenses, approved in advance and documented, will be reimbursed within 30 days.

Copy/Photo Requirements

1. You may e-mail your manuscript using Macintosh-compatible Microsoft Word or QuarkXPress programs. We also request a hard copy of your manuscript, which you may submit by fax or mail. Use 1" margins, double-space your copy and place a page number on each page.

2. Include a one-sentence author biography at the end of your story.

3. Submit a list of all resources and the names, addresses, phone numbers and e-mail addresses of interviewees with each article.

4. When possible, we would appreciate photographs complementing your article, particularly photos of specific people addressed in your story. Submit permission slips or release forms from all people photographed and all photographers.

Style

1. Reading Level/Story Length. Articles should be written at a seventh-grade reading level, or they will be returned for rewrite. Ar-

ticles in *American Careers* usually run from 300-750 words. Some topics may require additional space for impact and clarity. These topics are discussed on an individual basis. Sometimes we run half-page or single-page items on topics such as recent career news or people who have been successful climbing the career ladder.

2. Focus. Stories should exhibit a balanced national focus, unless the assignment covers only one region or school.

3. Style. Use the Associated Press Stylebook as a guide for style. Style matters particular to *American Careers* will be handled in editing. Career Communications, Inc., reserves the right to edit and revise all materials for publication.

Categories: Nonfiction—Careers—Education—Interview—Science—Math & Science Factoids

CONTACT: Submissions Editor
Material: All
6701 W. 64th St.
Overland Park KS 66202
Phone: 800-669-7795
Fax: 913-362-4864
E-mail: ccinfo@carcom.com

American City & County

Everything you need to know to get your article published
General Information

American City & County is received by more than 82,000 elected and appointed local and state government officials and public and private engineers. Included in the circulation list are administrators, supervisors and department heads of municipal, county, township, state and special district governments.

The interests of these readers span all areas of state and local government concern, including, but not limited to: street and highway construction and maintenance, water supply, wastewater collection and treatment, solid waste collection and disposal, resource recovery, street lighting, public transit, parks and recreation, traffic engineering, public housing, urban renewal, financing, community development, office automation and computer application, management techniques, and security and public safety.

Our goal is to provide a voice for local government by addressing the issues and concerns of public officials, offering ideas and solutions to problems and publishing information of interest to managers at all levels of local government. This goal is accomplished through the publication of in-depth discussions of major topics and supporting features, shorter news and feature items and various departments devoted to federal legislation, news of people in the industry, new products, product literature and manufacturers' news.

Before submitting any editorial material, you should take a few moments to read a copy of the magazine. This should give you information about what we cover and at whom our editorial material is aimed. Be aware of several things, including:

• We use only third-person articles. We do not tell the reader what to do; we offer the facts and assume the reader will make his or her own informed decision;

• We cover state, city and county government. We do not cover the federal government, except as it affects local government;

• If you are submitting a case history or application story, be aware that a company or product may be mentioned once in the article unless a byline is included, in which case the author's bio will list the company. We do not run articles about products no matter how clever or useful. To be considered, the article must be about the product's usefulness to a particular city or county. In other words, tell us how the product or service helped the local government solve a unique problem. Only in rare instances will we use quotes from company spokespeople; quotes must generally be from city or county officials.

What We Use

FEATURES AND SPECIAL REPORTS—Each month, three to five major topics are given in-depth coverage of 1,500 to 2,200 words. These stories are written in news magazine format and are generally authored by magazine staff members or paid freelancers. Occasionally, however, experts on particular subjects are retained to write features. Sources and ideas for these articles must be approved by the editor in order to assure placement and proper writing style. Features should generally discuss all pertinent aspects of a subject and use quotes from local government officials and industry leaders. Dissertations or thesis-like articles are not used for features, nor is promotional copy.

ISSUES AND TRENDS—This section includes four articles per month on rotating topics that include public safety (including EMS services and 911 systems,) water supply, wastewater, grounds maintenance (including landscaping and pest control,) information technology (including GIS, imaging, surveying and computer services,) fleet maintenance (including trucks and automated fleet systems,) streets and highways and solid waste collection and disposal. These 500- to 700-word articles should reflect information on timely developments and trends within the specific topics. Graphics are encouraged.

DOTTED LINE—Briefs on services offered or contracts awarded are used in this department. A state or local government or government agency must be involved. We do not use material about contracts between private companies.

ROLL CALL—This department reports on promotions, job changes, new appointments and honors received by local government officials or those companies that serve the state, municipal and county market. Releases should include the name of the individual community or company name, location and the person's responsibilities. Black and white photographs will be considered.

WAYS & MEANS—Case histories between 500 and 800 words appear in this section. When available, color or black-and-white photographs or artwork should accompany the case history. They should be written from the local government perspective and should not be promotional in nature. Case histories should discuss how a particular local government solved a unique problem and should be non-technical in nature.

ACROSS AMERICA—Short news articles of general interest to local governments are included in this section. Technical or dated material will not be used. Articles should not be promotional but may mention company names germane to the subject matter. Articles about community projects should be written in a third person, news feature format with quotes from local officials. Items that include black-and-white prints or color slides are preferred. Articles should not exceed 600 words.

FINANCIAL MANAGEMENT—This column is bylined by experts in local government financing, both from the public and private sectors. These 500- to 600-word articles discuss local government financial options and techniques in generic terms. Published articles will include a byline and brief biography; no other reference to a company or specific service is allowed. Ideas for submission should be cleared with the editor first. Deadline is six weeks prior to publication.

GOVERNMENT TECHNOLOGY—This column is bylined by public officials or companies serving local governments. It deals with information technology trends in local government operations. This 500- to 600-word column is not limited to administrative operations; discussions of the automation of public works functions are equally important. The contributor receives a byline and short biography for this generic article. Ideas should be cleared with the editor. Deadline is six weeks prior to publication.

BUYER'S INDEX—Items should include a brief, clearly written summary of important features of the product, video or literature and the significance to the local government field. We file the hundreds of product releases we receive each week, so we would prefer that you not call to request information on the status of a particular one. We clean out these files every six months, so, if your product release has not appeared within that time, it most likely will not appear. You are welcome to re-submit releases. Black and white photos are encouraged. Length: 50-100 words.

Submitting Articles

American City & County accepts articles on CDs and via e-mail. We will also accept a clean, double-spaced manuscript for scanning. The magazine's word processing software is Microsoft Word, and its desktop publishing software is Adobe InDesign. Other software can be translated. Editorial is prepared two months in advance of the publication date. Signed copyright forms are required and will be sent out before publication. Advance phone calls and query letters are welcome but not necessary, except regarding feature stories.

You should be aware of certain considerations, including:

• We do accept unsolicited articles, which we keep on file for a year. We use these articles when the topic appears on the editorial calendar. It is generally a good idea to call to make sure your article has been received, although it is unlikely that you will receive the promise of a certain publication date;

• Rather than calling with an article query, it is generally better to write a short paragraph describing a potential story idea and to follow up a week or so later with a phone call;

• We will never guarantee either publication or placement of a story. We deal with too many variables—space considerations, length of other articles, etc. If we specifically ask you to write an article for us, we will do everything possible to see that it is published;

• Our copyright forms are not open to negotiation. They basically serve to protect us against the possibility of your article appearing in our magazine and those of our competitors. We don't want that, and neither do they. If your article has been accepted for publication elsewhere, please inform us of that fact, so we do not count on it;

• Your article has a better chance of being published if it is accompanied by artwork (photographs, charts or graphics.) Color slides are preferred, but we will accept black and white and color photographs, as well as digital images. Please call if you have questions about digital formats;

• We stick closely to our editorial calendar, so if the topic of your article is not listed on the calendar, it is highly unlikely we will make an exception and publish it;

• We edit all submitted material for style. We will try to work with you on edits if we get the material early enough; however, we cannot guarantee that you will see the finished article before it is published.

Categories: Nonfiction—Government

CONTACT: Bill Wolpin, Editorial Director
Material: Feature Articles
Phone: 770-618-0112
E-mail: bwolpin@prismb2b.com
Lindsay Isaacs, Managing Editor
Material: Government Technology, Project Profiles
Phone: 770-618-0199
E-mail: lisaacs@prismb2b.com
Ed Brock, Associate Editor
Material: Issues and Trends, Dotted Line, Roll Call
Phone: 770-618-0401
E-mail: ebrock@prismb2b.com
Deanna Hart, Assistant Editor
Material: All Product Releases and Submissions for
Across America, Buyer's Index, Financial Management
Phone: 770-618-0120
E-mail: dhart@prismb2b.com
Fax: 770-618-0349
Web site: www.americancityandcounty.com

The American Dissident

Read the FOCUS section of *The American Dissident* to better understand what this literary journal is about and what it seeks to publish. Send no more than three or four well-written, unpublished poems and/or one unpublished essay (250-950 words max), preferably relating or stemming from a PERSONAL EXPERIENCE with corruption, any kind, and, even better yet, that RISKED something on the part of the poet/writer, be it ostracism from fellow poets or even one's job because it was published or read in public. Include an SASE. Send books for review consideration. Pays one copy. Acquires first North American serial rights. Submit a short biography not including credits or letters of recommendation, but rather deprogramming and personal dissident information. What pushed you to shed the various skins of indoctrination? When did you stand apart from your friends or colleagues to "speak the rude truth" a la Emerson? Why are you submitting poems to a journal called The American Dissident? Subscriptions are $18 per year (two issues). Purchase one copy of the most recent issue for $8. *The American Dissident* is professionally printed, flatbound and 48-56 tight pages virtually crammed, though neatly, with poems, essays, book reviews, literary letters, tough rude truth quotations, and sociopolitical cartoons and drawings. All correspondence should be sent to and checks made out to G. Tod Slone, Ed., The American Dissident, 1837 Main St., Concord, MA 01742 -3811. E-mail submissions accepted only from subscribers.

Categories: Nonfiction—Literature—Poetry

CONTACT: G. Tod Slone, Editor
Material: All
ContraOstrich Press
1837 Main St.
Concord MA 01742-3811
E-mail: todslone@yahoo.com
Website: www.theamericandissident.org

American Educator

American Educator is the quarterly professional magazine of the American Federation of Teachers. We are interested in articles on a wide range of topics, including new trends in education, politics, well-researched news features on current problems in education, education law, professional ethics, and thoughtful or thought-provoking pieces and essays that explore current social issues relevant to American society. We also welcome articles on international affairs and labor issues of interest to teachers as AFT members.

Articles should be written in a journalistic style that avoids education and research jargon. We do not publish research papers, doctoral theses, etc., as articles. If you have been involved in a study or research project that you think would be of interest to our readers, write a story about that research and summarize the pertinent findings. Cite sources within the copy rather than by footnotes.

Personal narratives of classroom experience are read with interest, but few are published. Those selected for publication are short, to the point, and timely.

Articles may vary in length from 500 to 2,500 words, depending on the topic. Avoid overwriting. A well-written article of 700 words, for example, has a much better chance of being accepted than a lengthy, rambling story. Pay careful attention to grammar, spelling, and sentence structure. As teachers, our readers are very quick to point out grammatical errors. We use the University of Chicago Press, A Manual of Style as our stylebook.

We prefer queries to manuscripts. If sending a manuscript (typed, double-spaced), please enclose a stamped, self-addressed envelope large enough to accommodate the manuscript. Although we attempt to answer every manuscript query within four to six weeks, we cannot be responsible for unsolicited manuscripts and strongly suggest that you keep at least one copy of your article on file.

Authors are paid upon publication. Payment varies according to length and topic. The minimum payment for an article is $300.

If your article is accepted for publication, you will receive a release form for your signature. Unless otherwise indicated, we assume that your article has not been published elsewhere in North America. We purchase all rights to articles (although rights may be returned to author upon request), and the editor reserves the right to edit manuscripts for style, format, and length requirements.

Categories: Nonfiction—Education—Ethics—Law—Politics

CONTACT: Ruth Wattenberg, Editor
555 New Jersey Ave NW
Washington DC 20001
E-mail: amered@aft.org

American Falconry

American Falconry is a magazine that is devoted entirely to the sport of falconry and is produced by practicing falconers.

We have tried to keep our requirements for submissions loose so as not to discourage potential writers. Manuscripts don't even have to be typed. We understand that some falconers live in remote areas and don't have access to a computer or typewriter. If you do have access to a computer you may submit your article on disk, or as an email attachment.

Anytime we do any editing, other than spelling or simple punctuation corrections, a proof copy will be sent to the author for approval.

We are happy to accept multiple part articles, but we will not normally print part one until we receive the complete series. We encourage authors submitting articles over 5000 words to write them as a series.

Good photographs accompanying an article increase the likelihood it will be used. We prefer slides or prints with negatives, but will accept quality prints without negatives. Please include captions and authors of all photos submitted.

Tables, graphs, and other illustrations need to be professional in appearance if they are to be used. Frequently we can help in this area so don't hesitate to call.

Remuneration for articles will start at $50.00. Exact amount will depend on length (longer isn't always better), photos included, amount of editing needed, and notoriety of the author.

If you have any questions at all, feel free to call any time. During the hawking season, you will have better luck reaching me after dark.

Categories: Falconry

CONTACT: Steve Jones, editor
Material: All
PO Box 187
Dayton, WY 82836-0187
(307) 655-2467
E-mail: sjones@americanfalconry.com

American Fitness

American Fitness welcomes unsolicited and queried manuscripts for publication on the subjects of health, fitness, aerobic exercise, sports nutrition, sports medicine, innovations and trends in aerobic sports, fitness marketing, tips on teaching exercise and humorous accounts of fitness motivation, physiology and women's health and fitness issues (pregnancy, family, pre- and post-natal, menopause and eating disorders). Profiles and biographical accounts of fitness leaders are also used. Query with published clips or send complete manuscript. Length: 1,000-1,200 words. Pays $200. *No first person accounts.*

American Fitness also accepts material for its columns and departments: "Health," "Adventure" (treks, trails and global challenges), "Strength" (the latest breakthroughs in weight training), "Clubscene" (profiles and highlights of the fitness club industry), "Food" (low-fat/non-fat, high-flavor dishes), "Homescene" (home workout alternatives) and "Clip 'n' Post" (concise exercise research to post in health clubs, offices or refrigerators). Query with published clips or send complete

manuscript. Length: 800-1,000 words. Pays $100-140.

Review: All manuscripts are reviewed, refereed and edited according to the editors' discretion. Solicited manuscripts receive referee notification within three to four months. Only accurate, scientifically valid and well-documented material is accepted for educational articles. Manuscripts that deal with lighter, non academic material are not processed through the editorial review board.

Preparation: Manuscripts should be emailed or, typed, double-spaced, with 1.25-inch margins. Due to our scanning capabilities, dot matrix submissions are now unacceptable. Manuscripts must be submitted on pure white paper with no last-minute, penciled notations. All italic type must be indicated with an underline. Electronic submissions on Macintosh compatible disks in Microsoft Word are welcome. SASE must be enclosed. Every attempt will be made to return artwork, line drawings, photographs and slides. However, neither the editors nor AFAA are responsible for lost or damaged submissions.

Exclusivity: It is understood that accepted manuscripts are not being considered for publication in any other magazine or journal.

Categories: Nonfiction—Adventure—Alternate Life-style—Children—Consumer—Exercise—Food/Drink—Health—History—Inspirational—Interview—Physical Fitness—Senior Citizen—Sports/Recreation—Travel—Nutrition—Nostalgia—Personal Experience—Pregnancy—Medicine—Home—Eating Disorders—Humor

CONTACT: Meg Jordan, Editor-at-large
Material: All
15250 Ventura Blvd.
Sherman Oaks CA 91403
Phone: 818-905-0040
Fax: 818-990-5468

American Forests

American Forests—the magazine of trees and forests for those interested in all facets of forestry—is the nation's oldest conservation magazine, having begun regular publication in 1894. It emphasizes the trends, issues, policies, management, and enjoyment of America's forest resources, including trees in and around communities. The best way to get an idea of the kind of articles and photographs we commission and buy is to study the magazine. A sample copy will be sent to those who send a self-addressed, magazine-size envelope with $1.70 in postage.

ARTICLES FORMAT: We're looking for factual articles that are well written, well illustrated, and will inform, entertain, and perhaps inspire. Most of our articles are now assigned, but we welcome informative news stories on controversial or current topics, as long as they are well documented and present the issue fairly. We do not, at this time, accept fiction or poetry. Articles should be neither too elementary nor too technical. About 80 percent of our readers have had college training, and about 30 percent have either a Master's or a Ph.D. degree.

Written queries are required, and we work four to 12 months in advance of an issue.

Most of our published manuscripts come to us on disc. Because the magazine is produced on Macintosh computers, we prefer Microsoft Word, but we can accept WordPerfect saved as ASCII text (DOS). Your disc must be accompanied by a paper manuscript. We can also accept articles via e-mail [or mailed] to the address below.

Although we are always willing to consider a submission, the acceptance of an article for review in no way constitutes a contract for publication. All submissions and queries are reviewed by the editors, and the author is informed of our decision within 12-16 weeks.

PAY RATES: Payment for full-length articles—with photo or other illustrative support—ranges from $250 to $2000, and is authorized upon acceptance.

PHOTOGRAPHS
FORMAT: Many of the photos used in American Forests are sent by the authors to illustrate their articles. These photographs should be

related to the article and must be clear and sharp. A caption sheet, keyed to numbers on the photos, should describe each shot and name any people shown.

We accept good quality digital images that are at least 300 dpi. We also accept original—not duplicate—color transparencies; 35mm is the most common, although 4"x5" or 5"x7" transparencies are good choices for cover shots.

PAY RATE: Payment for cover photos is $400. For photos submitted with articles, payment is included in a check to the author. Inside shots not submitted with an article are paid for at a rate that depends on size, quality and placement in the magazine.

SUBMITTING ARTICLES AND/OR PHOTOGRAPHS

All material will be returned, provided a self-addressed, stamped envelope of suitable size accompanies your submission. Send submissions to the address below.

ADDITIONAL INFORMATION FOR PHOTOGRAPHERS

American Forests has long been noted for its coffee table quality covers and inside photographs, and we intend to improve upon that reputation. We strive for the photos in our magazine to be more than simply a record of a place or event, but rather a creative interpretation that's pleasing to the eye and evokes an understanding of what is happening in the scene and/or a longing to be in that particular place, usually outdoors. Some detailed guidelines on outdoor photography follow for the semi-pros and nonprofessionals among our contributors.

BEST TIME OF DAY: The ideal time to photograph is when the sun is low on the horizon—from sunrise until about 10:30 and from 3:30 until sunset. A low sun lights a person's face or any vertical object, so that you can distinguish detail. When the sun is directly overhead, all the features are in dark shadows. Also, the light of a low sun is warmer, because it is passing through more atmosphere on its slanted approach.

Obviously, there are situations when the time of day cannot be prearranged and photographs must be taken when the opportunity arises.

POSING YOUR SUBJECTS: When working with people in your photos, it's best to have them doing their "thing," whatever that may be, rather than looking at the camera. If they are scientists, for example, they should appear to be studying some object that relates to the article. Posed shots usually are undesirable; when taking a portrait, strive for a more relaxed shot.

CAMERA EQUIPMENT: Because we are trying to portray a three-dimensional subject in two-dimensional form without the help of other senses, you should portray nature not exactly the way it appears, but a bit larger than life. To accomplish this, most photographers use lenses other than the "normal" 50mm lens that comes on most cameras. The lenses used most by professional photographers are wide-angle—either 35mm or 28mm—or short telephotos of 75mm or 135mm. These lenses produce a slightly exaggerated view of nature and appear fresh to the reader, who with the unaided eye has never seen nature quite that way.

Packages to be handled by Federal Express, UPS, or other fast-delivery services should be sent to our street address below.

Categories: Nonfiction—Conservation—Ecology—Environment—General Interest—Outdoors—Politics—Recreation—Reference

CONTACT: Michelle Robbins, Editor
Material: All
734 15th St NW, 8th Floor
Washington DC 20005
Phone: 202-737-1944, x203
Fax: 202-737-2457
E-mail: mrobbins@amfor.org
Website: www.americanforests.org

The American Gardener

The American Gardener is the official publication of the American Horticultural Society (AHS), a national, nonprofit, membership organization for gardeners founded in 1922. By advancing the art and science of horticulture through its publications and programs, AHS is dedicated to educating and inspiring people of all ages to become successful and environmentally responsible gardeners.

The bimonthly *American Gardener* goes out to the more than 30,000 members of the American Horticultural Society.

EDITORIAL CONTENT

The magazine is primarily free-lance written, and its content differs considerably from that of other gardening publications. Our readers are mainly experienced amateur gardeners; about 20 percent are horticultural professionals. Articles are intended to bring this knowledgeable group new information, ranging from the latest scientific findings that affect plants, to the history of gardening and gardens in America. We introduce readers to unusual plants, personalities, and issues that will enrich what we assume is already a passionate commitment to gardening.

Among the topics of particular interest to us are profiles of individual plant groups; innovative approaches to garden design; profiles of prominent horticulturists whose work has a national impact; plant research and plant hunting; plant conservation, biodiversity, and heirloom gardening; events or personalities in horticultural history; people-plant relationships (horticultural therapy, ethnobotany, and community gardening); environmentally appropriate gardening (choosing plants suited to one's region, using native plants, conserving water, etc.); and plant lore and literature. We are also seeking articles that describe and show how to construct simple garden features such as ponds or paths, or illustrate gardening techniques such as grafting, pollarding, or propagation.

We stress environmentally-responsible gardening: minimal use of synthetic pesticides and water, not collecting plants from the wild, and avoiding plants with the potential to escape and damage natural ecosystems. Proposals for articles on specific plants or plant families, public or private gardens, or garden design should stress a unique approach to the topic.

QUERIES

We prefer that authors query us before developing a manuscript. Queries must be accompanied by a self-addressed stamped envelope. Please note: We do not accept phone, fax, or e-mail queries, or simultaneous submissions.

Queries should include a description of the proposed topic and an explanation of why it is of interest to a national audience of knowledgeable gardeners, as well as an outline of the major points to be covered in the manuscript.

When querying for the first time, authors should submit relevant writing samples, and explain why they believe they are qualified to write on the subject they are proposing. We look for writers with a knowledge of plants, but also an ability to write in a strong journalistic style, complete with lively quotes from interviews or written sources. While ideas for articles are evaluated separately from photographs or artwork, it is helpful to the evaluation process for submissions to include information on possible sources for photographs or illustrations.

Acceptance of an idea outlined in a query does not constitute acceptance of an article. All contributors to *The American Gardener* are sent a formal contract outlining the rights being purchased, payment terms, and deadlines.

Feature articles run 1,500 to 2,500 words, depending on subject and assignment.

DEPARTMENTS

The American Gardener has a number of departments for which we accept free-lance submissions.

• Natural Connections. Explains a natural phenomenon or symbiotic relationship-plant and pollinator relationships, plant and fungus relationships, plant and soil relationships, parasites, etc.-that may be observed in nature or in the garden. Runs 750- 1,000 words.

POLICIES

We make every effort to report back to the author within 90 days of receiving a query. Accepted articles are scheduled and published at the discretion of the editorial staff.

We do not knowingly consider manuscripts simultaneously submitted to other publishers, and we retain the right to return at any time manuscripts that appear or have been published as a whole or in part in another publication, regardless of whether the manuscripts have already been accepted or scheduled.

The staff of *The American Gardener* retains the right to edit manuscripts as it deems necessary, for clarity, style, length, and accuracy. We do not as a matter of policy provide authors with revised manuscripts prior to publication. However, this can sometimes be negotiated at the time that an article is accepted.

Although all work submitted to *The American Gardener* is handled with great care, the Society cannot accept responsibility for any materials that are lost or damaged.

PAYMENT

Payment for feature articles ranges from $300 to $600 upon publication, depending on the article's length and complexity, and the author's horticultural background and publishing experience. Reimbursement for travel and other expenses can sometimes be negotiated.

Payment for departments is $150 to $200. Payment for photographs used with department articles is $50 each.

We pay a 25-percent kill fee in those instances where an author has completed revisions of the text requested by our editorial staff, and the article is still for any reason considered unacceptable.

All contributors receive three complimentary copies of the issue in which their work is published. Additional copies are available to contributors at a reduced rate of $1 each; shipping fees will be charged for contributor orders of 10 copies or more. Extra copies must be ordered prior to publication in order to ensure availability and avoid additional handling fees.

RIGHTS

Information on specific rights purchased is included in a contract sent to all contributors. All articles in *The American Gardener* are also published in the members-only section of the American Horticultural Society's website (www.ahs.org).

Mechanical Requirements On ACCEPTANCE

• Submit material typewritten and double spaced. Include a self-addressed, stamped return envelope.

• Accompany the article with a brief biography plus your name, address, social security number, and telephone number.

• After a manuscript has been accepted, e-mail it to us in Rich Text Format (.rtf) or in Microsoft Word. In preparing a computer document, please do not include formatting such as automatic indents, centering, italics, etc.

• Feature articles should be limited, whenever possible, to eight to 10 double-spaced, typewritten pages, excluding bibliography or sidebars.

• Avoid using footnotes. Incorporate citations or attributions in the body of the text. To assist us in editing, authors should include a bibliography of reference books or previously published articles used for background, and addresses, telephone numbers, and e-mail addresses of individuals interviewed.

• For articles relating to particular plants or types of plants, we appreciate a list of retail mail-order sources-including the names, addresses, phone numbers, and web site-and whether the nurseries charge for their plant lists or catalogs.

• Authors who are submitting photographs or illustrations to accompany an article should request a copy of our Photographer's Guidelines before doing so. Authors writing in detail about plants should request a copy of our "Rules for Botanical Nomenclature."

SAMPLE COPIES

Sample copies of the magazine are available for $5; specific back issues are available for $8. Send checks payable to AHS with your request for sample issues or back issues to the address below; back issues can also be ordered by credit card from the AHS website (www.ahs.org). Photographer's guidelines are available by e-mail to editor@ahs.org or by sending an SASE with the request to the address below.

Categories: Conservation—Ecology—Environment—Gardening

CONTACT: David J. Ellis, Editor
Material: All
7931 E. Boulevard Dr.
Alexandria VA 22308
Phone: 703-768-5700

American Girl

Thanks for your interest in writing for *American Girl*.

American Girl is a bimonthly, four-color magazine for girls ages 8 and up. *American Girl* readers are girls in the formative years, girls who dream big dreams. We hope to encourage that dreaming and to reinforce each reader's self-confidence, curiosity, and self-esteem as she prepares to navigate adolescence in the years ahead. Our lead time is approximately six months.

Fiction

We're looking for contemporary fiction up to 2,300 words. The protagonist should be a girl between 8 and 12 who captures the hopes, thoughts, and emotions unique to that precarious age between childhood and teenager. We look for top quality writing and thoughtfully developed characters and plots. Stories should engage readers quickly and have a satisfying conclusion. We are always looking for humor and seasonal stories. We don't publish science fiction, romance, or horror stories.

Nonfiction

We're looking for individual girls, or groups of girls who are doing something other girls would love to read and learn about. Find a topic about which girls are passionate. Past pieces have featured synchronized swimmers, rhythmic gymnasts, ballerinas, and girl bands. Some of our most successful pieces are sports-related, but that doesn't mean we won't consider other contemporary topics or profiles. Look for new twists on familiar topics. Please send queries rather than finished manuscripts.

Girls Express

This section offers the most opportunities for freelance writers. We're looking for short profiles of girls who are into sports, the arts, interesting hobbies, cultural activities, and other areas. We are also looking for true stories about girls who have had unusual experiences. The girl must be the "star" and the story must be from her point of view. Be sure the include the age of the girls you're pitching to us. Let us know if you have any photo leads. We also welcome how-to stories—how to send away for free things, hot ideas for a cold day, or how to write the President and get a response. Stories should be no more than 150 words. In addition, we're looking for easy crafts and recipes that can be explained in a few simple steps, ideas for contests, and current products and trends for girls to review.

Craft and Cooking

We welcome original craft and cooking ideas that are new and exciting to our readers. Projects should require limited parental involvement and supplies should be inexpensive and readily available. Keep in mind the skill level of our readers. Safety is a priority. Query with a short explanation of the project and an example, photograph, or sketch.

Brain Waves

We're looking for visual puzzles, mazes, math puzzles, word games, simple crosswords, cartoons, and other ideas. Seasonal ideas are especially welcome.

Sample issues

American Girl costs $3.95 per issue and is available in many children's bookstores. To get a sample copy, send a check for $3.95 made out to *American Girl*, plus a self-addressed stamped 9x12 envelope with $1.98 in postage on it.

Address

All queries and request for sample magazines should be addressed to : Magazine Department Assistant, American Girl, 8400 Fairway Place, Middletown, WI 53562-2554

Please Note

American Girl cannot reply or return a manuscript unless you enclose a self-addressed stamped envelope. Please allow at least 12 weeks for a reply.

Categories: Fiction—Nonfiction—Cooking—Crafts/Hobbies—Entertainment—Games—Juvenile—Young Adult

CONTACT: Magazine Editorial Assistant
Material: All queries and requests for sample magazines
PO Box 620986
8400 Fairway Place
Middleton WI 53562
Phone: 608-836-4848
Website: americangirl.com

American History

Please refer to WEIDER History Group.

American Hunter

American Hunter, an official journal of the National Rifle Association, is one of the most popular hunting magazines in the nation. Approximately 1.3 million NRA members receive it each month. For most issues, *American Hunter* buys out 50 percent or more of its editorial material and photos. The following information is intended to reduce confusion during the query, submission, and publication process and to inform contributors of our editorial needs and policies.

Feature Articles-*American Hunter feature* stories typically run 1,800 to 2,000 words. However, the editors are more concerned with content than length. If an article is short (1,000 to 1,500 words) but good, we'll buy it. Subject matter for feature articles falls into five general categories that run in each issue: deer, big game, upland birds, waterfowl, and varmints/small game. Features may be written in a number of styles, including expository how-to, where-to, and general-interest pieces; humor; personal narratives; and technical articles on firearms, ammunition, optics, wildlife management, or hunting. *American Hunter* does not buy poetry or articles on firearms legislation. Story angles should be narrow, but coverage must have depth. How-to articles are popular with readers and might range from methods for hunting to techniques on making gear used on successful hunts. Where-to articles should contain contacts and information needed to arrange a similar hunt. All submissions are judged on three criteria: story angle (it should be fresh, interesting, and informative); quality of writing (clear and lively-capable of holding the readers' attention throughout); and quality and quantity of accompanying photos (sharpness, reproduction quality, and connection to the text are most important).

Departments-We solicit material for three monthly departments: "Public Hunting Ground," "Hunting Skills," and "Hardware." "PHG" covers how to and where to hunt different game on public lands throughout the nation. "Skills" covers techniques and "tricks of the trade" used in the field; marksmanship, first aid, field-dressing, and calling techniques are just some worthy topics. "Hardware" is our technical department covering new firearms, ammunition, and optics used for hunt-

ing. Contributors should study back issues for appropriate subject matter and style for this column. Copy length should be 800 to 1,200 words.

Photographs-Photo requirements are demanding. We use color transparencies and prints throughout the magazine to illustrate features and departments. The editors prefer article packages containing a good selection of 35mm color transparencies. We will accept color prints, however, overall criteria for selection includes content and technique. Captions should be detailed and should explain how the photo relates to the text. Photos should be given an identifying code to correspond to the caption sheet, and the name of the photographer should appear on every print or slide. Color slides should be protected in plastic sleeves (either individually or within sheets that hold 20 or more). If a submitted photograph has been published previously, photographers are required to advise the editor of the title and date of publication. *American Hunter rates for photographs submitted and purchased separately and not as part of a photo package supporting a manuscript are:*

- Cover: $450-$600
- Centerspread, full bleed: $300-$400
- Two-page spread, partial coverage: $250-$300
- Full page: $200-$250
- Fractional page: $75-$150

Query Letters-Although unsolicited manuscripts are welcomed, detailed query letters outlining a proposed topic and approach are appreciated and will save both writers and editor and given direction on how we'd like the topic covered. American Hunter accepts all manuscript and photographs for consideration on a speculative basis only. On those rare occasions when an advance assignment is made, it will be done in writing only if signed by the Editor or the Executive Editor of American Hunter.

Payment-We pay for articles on acceptance and for freelance photos on publication. We purchase first North American serial rights plus the subsequent reprint rights for NRA Publications. *American Hunter* currently pays up to $800 for full-length feature articles with complete photo packages. Payment may be reduced if we have to supplement your photo package or if your manuscript requires extensive clean-up or rewrite. Payment for departments and other short articles ranges from $300 to $450. Upon publication, all photographs and other material is returned to the contributor. *American Hunter* does not pay kill fees.

Specifications-All manuscripts must be typed double-spaced. No photocopied or hand-written submissions will be accepted and simultaneous submissions will not receive consideration. Please avoid script typefaces. Manuscripts should be submitted in both hard-copy form and on 3 s considerable time. If we like your story idea you will be contacted by mail, phone, or e-mail ½-inch, IBM-compatible diskettes in Microsoft Word or WordPerfect word-processing programs. We work specifically with Word, and would rather see the article come in on this program, but others are accepted so long as we can open a file and read it. Disks will be returned after publication or upon decline or purchase.

Replies-*American Hunter* receives more than a thousand queries and manuscripts a year, and although the editors try to respond within a month it may take longer for an author to receive a reply. The editors are not responsible for unsolicited manuscripts or photos.

Categories: Nonfiction—Animals—Computers—Fishing—General Interest—Internet—Law—Outdoors—Politics—Recreation—Sports/Recreation—Hunting——Humor—Firearms—Personal Experience—How-to: Camping

CONTACT: Scott Olmstead, Editor in Chief
Material: All
11250 Waples Mill Rd.
Fairfax VA 22030-9400
Phone: 703-267-1335
Fax: 703-267-3971

Remember: Editors change jobs and publishers change addresses. It is wise to invest in a phone call for the current information before submitting.

American Indian Art Magazine

American Indian Art Magazine is a quarterly art journal that presents the art of the American Indian through articles and illustrations appealing to both lay people and professionals. We prefer articles that utilize the magazine's illustrated format—in other words, articles that tie the illustrations to the text. Our readers are collectors, dealers, scholars, students and other interested individuals. Some of our readers are knowledgeable about the field and some know very little; American Indian Art Magazine seeks articles which offer something to both groups.

Manuscript Review

Any article, whether solicited or volunteered, is subject to review by members of the magazine's Editorial Advisory Board and/or other authorities in the field. These readers may suggest revisions to be made by authors or may recommend additional material and illustrations. Manuscripts will be returned to the author for any substantive changes. An article must be approved by members of the Editorial Advisory Board before it is published in the magazine. Articles reflecting original research and expressing new hypotheses are preferred over summaries and reviews of previously discussed material. Acceptance of an article for publication does not guarantee its appearance in the next issue of the magazine.

In addition to research articles, the magazine publishes museum collection and exhibition features that are designed to give readers a sense of the overall strengths and weaknesses of the collection, in addition to answering questions about collection history, quality or problems of documentation and the like.

Style

Manuscripts published in the magazine generally run between twelve and eighteen pages in typescript form, exclusive of bibliography, captions and footnotes. We prefer to receive manuscripts on computer disc (Macintosh Microsoft Word) with a hard copy.

We would like an article to be as detailed and specific as possible; try to limit the article to a particular subject, small geographical area, particular object(s) or selected design style. For example, if the subject is Plains Indian shields, try to limit the article to one group or one type of shield or design. In an article discussing changes in style with time, try to explain how to date the changes, and what other contemporaneous styles were. Authors should discuss aesthetics as well as the anthropological context of a subject, if possible.

An article usually requires between eight and fifteen photographs, with a choice from both black and white and color. It is often a good idea to shoot all the subjects in both ways so that the article can be adapted to the technical limitations of the printing process. Please send photographs in individual sleeves with figure numbers clearly marked.

In obtaining photographs, make certain the photographer and processor know that the photographs will be used for reproduction in a magazine. Black-and-white photographs should be glossy 8"x10" prints. Color photographs should be transparencies and 35mm slides are acceptable. Use plain backdrops.

As a matter of policy, we prefer to illustrate material from public collections, avoiding items in private collections unless comparable material is not available elsewhere.

Other Illustrations

Occasionally an article will require a diagrammatic drawing to illustrate a particular manufacturing method. If the author provides a clear sketch or a standard reference source, the magazine will prepare a reproducible line drawing.

Permission

American Indian Art Magazine needs permission in writing to use illustrations which belong to other publications, historical societies, institutions, and private individuals. Sometimes it is necessary to obtain permission separately from the owner of the object in the picture, as well as from the owner of the photograph and/or photographer. With contemporary objects it is also necessary to obtain permission from the artist. Obtaining such permission is the responsibility of the author.

The magazine can supply copies of the printed article to the person or institution allowing use of the photograph; this is frequently a condition for receiving permission. Make certain any special phrases—e.g., "used by permission of"—stipulated by the permission-giver are included in the photograph caption.

Photograph Usage and Fees

American Indian Art Magazine buys onetime publication rights to photographs and returns the originals after the magazine has been printed. Fee schedules and reimbursable expenses are arranged for single photographs and for multiple photograph assignments; the magazine and the author jointly decide on these arrangements.

Conclusion

The Editor and staff of American Indian Art Magazine make every effort to help authors in preparing manuscripts, obtaining illustrations and permission, and generally assisting in article preparation. Authors are encouraged to make preliminary contact with the magazine before committing many long hours to work on the article: proposals and draft outlines will be reviewed if an author requests.

Style

Note: In preparing accepted manuscripts for publication, the editorial staff of the magazine attempts to conform to standard spelling and usage procedures. Reference works consulted include Webster's Ninth Collegiate Dictionary (Merriam-Webster Inc., Springfield, Massachusetts, 1985); A Manual of Style (University of Chicago Press, 1969, twelfth edition, revised); and Ethnographic Bibliography of North America by George Peter Murdock and Timothy J. O'Leary (Human Relations Area Files Press, New Haven, 1975, fourth edition).

Categories: Nonfiction—Arts—Native American

CONTACT: Roanne Goldfein, Editor
Material: All
7314 E. Osborn Dr.
Scottsdale AZ
Phone: 480-994-5445
Fax: 480-945-9533

American Indian Quarterly

The complexity and excitement of the burgeoning field of Native American studies are captured in *American Indian Quarterly* (AIQ), a peer reviewed interdisciplinary journal of the histories, anthropologies, literatures, religions, and arts of Native America. Wide-ranging in its coverage of issues and topics, AIQ is devoted to charting and inciting debate about the latest developments in method and theory. It publishes original articles, shorter contributions, review articles, and book reviews.

Subscription Information

Quarterly/ISSN 0095-182X
Individuals $25.00
Institutions $50.00
Single issue $14.00

For foreign subscriptions please add $20.00. Payment must accompany order. Make checks payable to University of Nebraska Press and mail to:

University of Nebraska Press
233 N 8th St
Lincoln, NE 68588-0255
or call: 1-800-755-1105 U.S. Orders and customer service.
1-800-526-2617 U.S. Fax orders and customer service.
1-402-472-3584 Foreign orders and customer service.
1-402-472-6214 Main fax line.
Telephone and fax orders must be prepaid.

Submission Information

AIQ accepts submissions that make original contributions to scholarship within the broad interdisciplinary framework of American Indian Studies and that meet the following requirements:

- 35 pages or less
- submit 4 copies
- prepare according to Chicago Manual of Style, 14th edition
- include a one-sentence personal bio
- typed double-spaced (including quotations and endnotes)
- 8 1/2 x 11" paper
- 1" margins
- 12 pt. type
- paragraphs not blocked
- footnotes and author date systems are not acceptable

Authors whose manuscripts are accepted for publication will be required to submit their article on a 3.5-inch Macintosh-formatted disk. Submissions to AIQ will not be returned to authors and all submissions, except for book reviews, will be subjected to peer review. All reviewers will remain anonymous unless specifically requesting otherwise. The decisions of the editor with respect to the acceptance of manuscripts are final.

All material published in AIQ is copyrighted by the University of Nebraska Press. Photocopies for course or research use that are supplied to the end user at no cost may be made without explicit permission or fee. Photocopies that are provided to end users for a photocopying fee may not be made without payment of permissions fees to the University of Nebraska Press.

Categories: Nonfiction—Culture—Health—History—Native American

CONTACT: Devon A. Mihesuah, Editor
Material: All
Department of Applied Indigenous Studies
Northern Arizona University
PO Box 15020
Flagstaff AZ 86011-5020
Phone: 928-523-5159
Website: jan.ucc.nau.edu/~mihesuah/aiq/

The American Legion Magazine

The America Legion magazine is 50% freelance writer. Monthly magazine. Feature articles in The American Legion magazine must address compelling issues in American society. Issues relating to veterans affairs, the U.S. military, national security, foregin affairs, American values, and patriotism often are preferred. We also publish selected general-interest articles and question-and-answer interviews with prominent national and world figures. Articles are not required to have a military angle. We make all assignments based on a 300-word query letter.

Prefers to work with published/established writers. Estab. 1919. Circ. 2,550,000. Buys first North American serial rights. Reports in 8 weeks on submission. **Pays upon acceptance.** Byline given. Sample copy for $3.50 and 9x12 SASE. Writer's guidelines for #10 SASE.

Nonfiction: Query letter should convince us that we should cover the subject, outline its basic structure and content, and demonstrate the writer's bonafides and firm understanding of the proposed topic. Writers should list relevant experience or background. We rarely accept essays, news columns, articles or letters previously published in other books, newspapers, newsletters, magazines, pamphlets, or items from the Internet. No regional topics or promotions. **Buys 30-40 mss/year.** Length: 500-2,000 words. Pay individually negotiated.

Photos: On assignment.

Tips: Submit suitable material showing you have read several issues. Your query letter should provide us an opportunity to judge your writing ability. Unsolicited opinion pieces, jokes, or poetry will not be considered or returned. No phone queries.

Categories: Nonfiction—Associations—General Interest

CONTACT: John B. Raughter, Editor
Material: All
PO Box 1055
Indianapolis IN 46206-1055
Phone: 317-630-1200
Fax: 317-630-1280
E-mail: magazine@legion.org
Website: www.legion.org

American Letters & Commentary

American Letters & Commentary is a literary annual particularly interested in innovative and challenging writing. Past contributors include Charles Bernstein, Gillian Conoley, Lydia Davis, Stephen Dixon, Stephen Dixon, Elaine Equi, Barbara Guest, Ann Lauterbach, Donald Revell, Stephanie Strickland, Cole Swensen, Susan Wheeler, and John Yau. Writers unfamiliar with these names are encouraged to read a copy of the magazine before submitting material. For a sample send $6.00 to the address below, requesting a sample back issue.

All submissions must include a self-addressed stamped envelope (SASE) for response. We cannot be responsible for returning items without an SASE. A brief cover letter is always welcome, but please do not send resumes, reviews of your work, or lengthy lists of previous publications. Submit to the address below.

Only previously unpublished work is considered. Simultaneous submissions are accepted providing we are notified at once should the work be accepted elsewhere.

Poetry
Send 3 to 5 poems, 10 pages maximum. We prefer that poetry submissions be sent in a standard #10 envelope.

Fiction
Stories of 12 pages or less have the best chance. Most of our stories are shorter than that. Please query before sending more than 20 pages of fiction.

Non-fiction (essays, reviews)
We are interested in personal literary essay and in critical essays on writers that are slanted for the general reader (i.e., not academic prose). Please see past issues for examples. Reviews are usually assigned. If you are interested in reviewing books, please query first. We regret the size of our staff makes these restrictions necessary. We also regret that the publication of just one issue each year means that we must turn down many worthy pieces that come our way.

Payment is in copies. All rights are returned to the author upon publication.

Thank you for your interest in our magazine.

Categories: Fiction—Nonfiction—Poetry—Short Stories

CONTACT: Submissions Editor
Material: All
850 Park Avenue, Suite 5B
New York NY 10021
Website: www.amletters.org

American Libraries

American Libraries is ALA's [American Library Association] four-color monthly magazine and the primary perquisite of membership in the Association. Each issue features articles on professional concerns and developments, along with news of the Association, library-related legislation, and libraries around the country and the world. Expression of diverse viewpoints and critical interpretation of professional issues make the magazine the premier forum for the exchange of ideas crucial to the fulfillment of ALA Goal 2000. Annual subscriptions are available to institutions at $60, $70 foreign.

STYLE: Informal, but informative. Factual article must be inviting and readable, with all statements backed by responsible research and interviews. The Chicago Manual of Style may be used in styling articles for publication, but extensive footnoting is discouraged.

FORMAT: Letter- or near-letter quality. One copy suffices.

SUBMISSIONS BY E-MAIL: In addition to considering manuscripts submitted by surface mail, American Libraries considers manuscripts sent by e-mail. When e-mailing a submission, please include your surface-mail address to expedite our sending a contributor's contract if your submission is accepted for publication.

WORD PROCESSING REQUIREMENTS: Manuscripts should be submitted via email or on a 3½" diskette (high density, 1.44 megabytes in size) and accompanied by a paper printout of the text. While American Libraries is capable of handling a wide range of word processing programs in both the PC and Mac formats, we prefer that manuscripts be in Word 6.x for Windows. When submitting a manuscript, indicate the word processing program used.

LENGTH: 600-2,000 words.

PAYMENT: Honoraria of $100 to $250 are offered for most articles, paid upon receipt of an acceptable manuscript.

EXCLUSIVE SUBMISSION: It is assumed that no other publisher is or will be simultaneously considering a manuscript submitted to American Libraries until that manuscript is returned or written permission is provided by the *American Libraries* editors.

RIGHTS: According to the contract provided to authors, exclusive North American rights are retained until three months after publication, unless another arrangement is made in writing. American Libraries retains rights to have the published material reproduced, distributed, and sold in microform or electronic text.

REPRINT POLICY: No reprints can be provided, but permission is usually granted for authors to reproduce their contributions as published in American Libraries. Others wishing to republish the text of an article are referred to the author for permission and fee information. A reasonable number of copies are sent to each author. Special arrangements may be necessary to reproduce illustrations.

ACKNOWLEDGEMENT: Unsolicited manuscripts are acknowledged when received.

REPORTS: The editors try to report on manuscripts within 4-8 weeks. Written reminders from the author after this period are welcome, and usually result in a prompt reply.

PUBLICATION DATE: On acceptance, an estimated date of publication may be provided to the author. Usually manuscripts can be published no sooner than two months after receipt.

EDITING: On accepted manuscripts, the editors reserve the right to make editorial revisions, deletions, or additions which, in their opinion, support the author's intent. When changes are substantial, every effort is made to work with the author.

GALLEYS: Galleys are not provided to the author.

PHOTOGRAPHS: Color prints, taken in natural light, are preferred for use with manuscripts or as picture stories. Transparencies and black-and-white prints are also considered for possible use. High-resolution digital photos (300 dpi, approximate size of 3 x 5 inches) can be sent to americanlibrariesproduction@ala.org. Payment is negotiated.

CARTOONS: Cartoons of the highest professional quality that relate to library interests and avoid librarian stereotypes will be considered. Average payment $50.

ILLUSTRATIONS: Illustrations are commissioned for certain articles and features.

Categories: Education—Trade—Libraries

CONTACT: Submissions Editor
Material: All
50 E. Huron
Chicago IL 60611
Phone: 312-280-4216
Fax: 312-440-0901
E-mail: americanlibraries@ala.org
Website: www.ala.org

American Medical News

American Medical News is the nation's most widely circulated newspaper focusing on socioeconomic issues in medicine. Published weekly by the American Medical Association, AMN covers the full spectrum of non-clinical news affecting physicians' practices. Our primary readers are about 320,000 physicians, most of whom receive the publication free as part of their AMA membership. Readers also include administrators of health-care organizations, government health-care policymakers and others with a professional interest in physicians and the U.S. health-care system.

AMN contracts with a relatively small group of freelance writers for news and feature articles that focus on policy development, legislation, regulation, economic trends, and physician-impact coverage in the categories that follow. We also seek articles about innovative efforts by individuals or groups to improve health-system functioning or physician practice in these areas.

Population health & related trends
- Health promotion and disease prevention: tobacco, alcohol and drug use; family and community violence; maternal and child health, including immunization; clinical preventive services
- Infectious diseases: AIDS; tuberculosis
- Treatment issues: health of targeted groups, including minorities, women, children, adolescents elderly and disabled; access to care for homeless, medically indigent and rural residents; organ transplantation
- Health protection: environmental and occupational health; accident prevention; food and drug safety• Impact of health care market trends and policy developments on patients and population health
- How doctors are helping to implement public health goals
- Physician health, well-being and job satisfaction
- Physician-patient relationships
- Consumerism and patients' rights
Topic Editor: Wayne Hearn

Professional issues
- Medical education and training, including undergraduate, graduate and continuing medical education, specialty training, certification, credentialing and physician supply issues
- Medical-legal matters, including professional liability, antitrust, fraud, abuse and related questions
- Quality assurance, including licensure, discipline, professional regulation, peer review, outcomes measurement and practice standards
- Professional and clinical ethics
- Technology, medical informatics, the pharmaceutical industry and related biomedical research
- The institution of organized medicine

Health system structure and finance
- Developments in public policy and the private marketplace that affect the structure of the health care industry and determine the conditions, quality and financial rewards of the practice of medicine
- Physician services financing issues, including Medicare, Medicaid, other government payers, Blue Cross and Blue Shield, commercial insurers and managed care; physician pay
- Physician relations with health care delivery systems, including HMOs, PPOs, group practices, hospitals and integrated hospital/physician networks
- Workforce issues: supply of physicians, the mix between specialists and generalists, relations between physicians and other health professions
- Federal and state health system reform efforts

Business
- Practice management, including general small-business issues (i.e. taxes, employment policies, salary and benefits), small-business issues unique to medical practices (i.e. CPT coding, relations with other physicians and third-party payers), contracting with insurers, strategic planning, raising capital, integrating new technology in practice settings, forming partnerships and managing groups

Please submit written queries of about one typewritten page, containing a detailed account of what you intend to cover and beginning with a lead you consider suitable for a finished article. Alternatively, you may submit the story to us on speculation.

Categories: Health—Medicine

CONTACT: Kathryn Trombatore, Editor
Material: All
515 N. State St.
Chicago IL 60610
Phone: 312-464-4429
Fax: 312-464-4445

The American Poetry Review

The American Poetry Review is unique in American publishing. With its eclectic editing, its newsprint- tabloid format, and its circulation of 17,000, APR reaches a worldwide audience six times a year with the poetry and prose of living modern masters, of new poets and critics just arriving on the scene, and of a diverse range of cultures and ethnic groups. Over the past 30 years, the magazine has helped to make poetry a more public art form without compromising the art of poetry.

Writers' Guidelines

The American Poetry Review publishes original poetry, literary criticism, interviews, essays and social commentary. Please use the following guidelines when submitting manuscripts for consideration.

Manuscripts should snail mailed. Do not send manuscripts by fax or E-mail.

Each manuscript must be accompanied by a self-addressed envelope, stamped with sufficient postage for its return. (International submissions should be accompanied by Universal Postal Union International Response Coupons.) No reply will be made to unaccepted manuscripts that are not accompanied by sufficient return postage.

Keep a copy of your manuscript and an accurate record of the date you mailed it.

Do not send previously published material or material that is currently under consideration by another magazine or periodical. Please do not send work that is under consideration by APR to another magazine or periodical.

Our reporting time is approximately ten weeks. We will inform you of acceptance or return your manuscript. Please do not inquire about the status of your manuscript during the ten-week reporting period.

All work submitted to APR is considered for publication in *The American Poetry Review* only.

Copyright: APR holds first serial rights for material that we publish. The copyright automatically reverts to the author upon publication. We do not require that material be copyrighted prior to submission.

Contests: APR does not conduct a poetry contest. All work submitted to APR is considered for publication in *The American Poetry Review* only.

Prizes: The Jerome J. Shestack Poetry Prizes of $1000 are awarded annually to each of two poets whose work has appeared in APR during the preceding calendar year.

Thank you and best wishes. The Editors

Categories: Literature—Poetry—Writing

CONTACT: The Editors
Material: All
117 South 17th Street Ste 910
Philadelphia PA 19103
Phone: 215-496-0439
Website: www.aprweb.org

American Profile

American Profile's audience lives in communities with an average population of 7,000. Our articles are useful, informative, human, and concise; full of detail and color, writing and reporting at its best. Our readers are intelligent and discriminating, our standards are high. This is not a market for beginners; send only your most professional work. No fiction, nostalgia, or poetry. Coverage of people and places must be enlightening and instructional, and have a broad regional or national relevance. We also cover health, food, gardening, home projects, nature, and finances. Articles should be topical, but have a long shelf life. Length varies from 450 to 1,200 words. Payment within 30 days of acceptance. Fees are competitive but vary widely. Byline and one-sentence bio given. Mostly freelance written. No reprints. Buys exclusive first-time print rights and all electronic rights to unpublished pieces for six months, non-exclusive rights thereafter.

Queries: Send a one-paragraph query with clips and SASE. No phone, fax, or e-mail submissions. Read our magazine before sending a query.

Categories: Nonfiction—Book Reviews—Education—Entertainment—Family—Gardening—General Interest—Health—History—Inspirational—Music—Rual America—Travel—Hometown Heroes—Hometown Spotlight

CONTACT: Peter V. Fossel, Executive Editor
Material: All
Publishing Group of America
341 Cool Springs Blvd., Suite 400
Franklin TN 37067
Phone: 615-468-6000
Fax: 800-720-6323
Website: www.americanprofile.com

American Rifleman

WRITER'S AND PHOTOGRAPHER'S GUIDELINES

The publisher of *American Rifleman* regularly purchases material submitted by freelancers. While we buy only a small portion of the material submitted, we do pay upon acceptance. Articles are received on speculation only, and we do not pay kill fees. Assignments are made only on written approval of the editor or the executive editor of *American Rifleman*. The editorial staff is not responsible for unsolicited manuscripts and/or photographs.

WHAT WE ARE LOOKING FOR: We want fresh material on all aspects of firearms and shooting. These can include gunsmithing, handloading, gun collecting, law enforcement training, competitive shooting, blackpowder, handguns, rifles or shotguns. Personality and firearms industry-related feature articles are also considered.

WHAT WE DON'T NEED: While we can use equipment-related articles that involve hunting, we do not run straight hunting pieces. Consider sending those to American Hunter at the same address. Nor can we use verse, fiction, essays or articles on gun legislation. We occasionally purchase pieces on the gun control issue, but the circumstances must be compelling or the material a new scholarly contribution to the literature.

NRA DOES NOT BUY GUN TESTS: Tests of new firearms and related equipment are conducted exclusively by the NRA Technical Staff and Contributing Editors.

ILLUSTRATIONS: Pictures sell articles. We need good quality color images. We want technically excellent photographs that are well-focused and properly exposed. We can supplement photo packages but give first consideration to articles that have good photo support. A completed NRA Publications Division Model Release Form is required for each identifiable individual appearing in a photograph. (They will be supplied upon request.) While we can handle other formats, we strongly prefer 35 mm slides or medium-or large-format transparencies. We may be able to get more out of them than your local processor. You may submit images electronically as high-resolution (300 d.p.i.) RGB, TIF, or .JPG files. The file size needs to be large enough for magazine format publication (example, 4"x 6" photo'8mgs; full page '25mgs.) We return illustrative material approximately three months after publication.

ARTICLE PREPARATION: Articles should be typed double-spaced, with only one space between sentences, with 22" margins and may range in length from 1,600 to 2,200 words. Manuscripts may be submitted on 32" disks or via e-mail (addressed to Publications@NRAHQ.org) on an IBM compatible operating system. Articles may be submitted in WordPerfect versions 4.2, 5.0, 5.1 or 6.0 or in other convertible word processing format (Microsoft Word) or in ASCII format along with a legible printout. Disks will be returned after publication or upon decline of purchase. Submissions must be accompanied by a postage-paid, self-addressed return envelope.

REPLIES: We generally purchase or reject manuscripts within 3 months of receipt. Occasionally, this process may take a little longer.

WRITING FOR US: Aspiring writers should study carefully the content of past issues of the magazine to get an understanding of the type of material we publish. Inexperienced writers might consider first submitting a AFavorite Firearms@ article for publication. While American Rifleman does not currently pay for these pieces, they generally represent good, concise writing and provide an opportunity for new writers to Atest the water.@

COPYRIGHT: The Copyright Law Revision of January, 1978 provides that, unless otherwise stipulated, a publisher purchases first publication rights only. The purpose of this notice is to include in addition to first publication rights the NRA's right to reprint any manuscript or illustrative material purchased by the NRA in future publications of the NRA. The right to offer this material to publishers other than the NRA remains with the author.

Categories: Nonfiction—Firearms—Shooting
CONTACT: Mark A. Keefe IV, Executive Editor
Material: All
11250 Waples Mill Rd.
Fairfax VA 22030-9400
Phone: 703-267-1300
Fax: 703-267-3971
Website: www.nra.org

American Salesman

The *American Salesman* is a monthly magazine for sales professionals. Its primary objective is to provide informative articles which develop the attitudes, skills, personal and professional qualities of the sales representative, enabling them to use more of their potential to increase their productivity and achieve goals.

CONTENT: *The American Salesman* contains seven feature articles each month. Most of the articles are contributed by people with practical experience in sales. No advertising is used in this publication. Articles involving successful and innovative sales trends or case histories are considered.

NEEDS: We are interested in articles addressing the following: improving sales productivity, reviewing sales fundamentals, motivating sales staff, determining customer needs, customer service, knowing and analyzing competition, making sales presentations, handling objections, closing sales, following up, telephone selling, managing sales territory, planning, goal setting, time management and new innovative sales concepts.

SUBMISSION OF ARTICLES: We work in advance. Therefore, articles may be retained up to six months before tentative scheduling. Finished articles should contain from 900 to 1,200 words. A sample is mailed to the copy originator.

Manuscripts should be high-quality typed (suitable for scanning—do not submit articles on a low quality dot matrix printer). The Associated Press Stylebook is followed for editing. The author should indicate address, current byline containing background employment, company affiliation and educational degrees listing alma mater. Submissions must include a stamped, self-addressed return envelope.

Your experience and your ideas are valuable. We are always happy to receive inquiries from potential writers.

Categories: Business—Careers—Economics—Money & Finances—Sales

CONTACT: Teresa Levinson, Editor
Material: All
National Research Bureau, 320 Valley St.
Burlington IA 52601-5513
Phone: 319-752-5415

The American Scholar
Phi Beta Kappa

Articles
The Scholar is a quarterly journal published by Phi Beta Kappa for general circulation. Our intent is to have articles by scholars and experts but written in non-technical language for an intelligent audience. The material that appears in the magazine covers a wide range of subject matter in the arts, sciences, current affairs, history, and literature. We prefer articles between 3,500 and 4,000 words, and we pay up to $500. To be accepted for publication, a manuscript must receive the affirmative votes of the editor and at least two members of the editorial board.

Poetry
Poems for submission to *The Scholar* should be typewritten, on one side of the paper, and each sheet of paper should bear the name and address of the author and the name of the poem. We have no special requirements of length, form, or content for original poetry. A look at several recent issues of the Scholar should give a good idea of the kind of poetry we publish and the way poems look on our pages. We suggest, too, that, from the author's point of view, it is probably most effective if not more than three or four poems are submitted at any one time. We pay $50.00 for each accepted poem.

We do not have arrangements for sending sample copies of the Scholar to prospective contributors. It would be possible, of course, for you to purchase the latest issue for $8.00. If you do not care to purchase a copy, your library would probably have copies you could see.

Categories: Nonfiction—Arts—General Interest—History—Literature—Poetry

CONTACT: Submissions Editor
Material: All
Phi Beta Kappa Society
1606 New Hampshire Ave., N.W.
Washington DC 20009
Phone: 202-265-3808
Website: www.pbk.org

American Snowmobiler

American Snowmobiler welcomes stories and photos from its readers and freelance writers.
WHAT WE LIKE
We are particularly fond of
Travel stories that give our readers a look at, and solid information about, new areas where they can snowmobile. We require that the author also provide us pictures and trail maps.

Sled modification stories, where an individual has customized his or her sled. Be sure to tell us what parts were used and how much was spent overall! We also will want some pictures of the project sled, before and after.

How-to stories describing how to modify or improve your sled, complete with pictures of the steps.

Personality stories about interesting people of note in the snowmobile world. Again we would want several pictures of the story subject.

Photos of trail adventures with family and friends, accompanied by an explanation of why the picture is particularly meaningful and identifying everyone in the photo, plus when and where it was taken. (These might be used in the magazine or in our Photo of the Week feature on the internet!)

Photos and stories about vintage sleds.

Anything interesting or newsworthy. If you're not sure if we would want your story, email us at address below.

The editor will then respond, telling you to go ahead with your story, or no thanks, we already have had that story, or one like it, in the recent past. Generally we ask that your stories be no longer than 1,200 words, but exceptions are possible.

We prefer that submitted stories be written in and sent to us in an attached Microsoft Word document. In most cases we buy exclusive industry rights, although again, some exceptions are made.

TO SUBMIT A PHOTO

E-mail your photos for the Web or magazine to: amsnow@amsnow.com

The higher resolution and clearer your photos the more likely they will be used.

View our digital image photo submission guidelines.

If prints are submitted, they should include the photographer's name on the back, along with caption information about the picture.

For other questions about digital image submissions, email us at address below.

PAYMENT

Pay for stories varies depending on length, time required to gather the information, quality and type of story. Likewise, pay will vary for photos.

The editor will explain payment before accepting a story (or photo), or assigning one. After acceptance you'll be sent a contract with an explanation of copyrights and payment. To be paid, we will need your Social Security or Federal Taxpayer I.D. numbers. Your payment will follow the return of a signed contract.

We do NOT pay for photos sent to us for the Photo of the Week feature on the Web, or for those used in our Mail Bonding (Letters) page in the magazine.

If you have further questions, please e-mail them to: amsnow@amsnow.com.

Categories: Nonfiction—Adventure—Recreation—Sports—Travel

CONTACT: Editor
Material: All
E-mail: editor@amsnow.com
CONTACT: Photo Editor
Material: photos
E-Mail: photoeditor@kalmbach.com

AmericanStyle

AmericanStyle is a magazine for people who love art. Our mandate is to nurture collectors with information that will increase their knowledge of and passion for contemporary craft and the artists who create it.

AUDIENCE:

AmericanStyle's primary audience is contemporary craft collectors and enthusiasts. Readers are primarily college educated, age 35-plus, high-income earners with the financial means to collect art and craft, and to travel to national art and craft events in pursuit of their passions.

CONTENTS:

Every issue of *AmericanStyle* contains a wealth of information about American crafts in all mediums, including a collector profile, a city/regional arts tour, interviews with artists, museum curators and gallery directors, visits to regional arts enclaves, and state-by-state listings of museum and gallery craft exhibitions, retail craft fairs and annual craft events. About 75 percent of the articles in *AmericanStyle* are written by freelancers; the balance is staff-produced.

AmericanStyle is interested in purchasing well-researched articles on themes in contemporary craft art; profiles of American craft collectors; arts tours of American cities or regions of the country; major craft fairs and events; established craft artists and their work; trends in studio art; and regional art enclaves, craft workshops and educational institutions.

It is essential that stories be written for readers who already have considerable expertise and background knowledge of studio art and contemporary crafts; straight general interest articles will be discouraged.

STORY CONSIDERATIONS:

Regular features in *AmericanStyle* include collector profiles, arts tours, Collector's Corner articles, themes in craft art and artist profiles. Keep in mind the following as you work to complete manuscripts in these specific areas:

COLLECTOR PROFILE:

Article should be written in a clear, lively, conversational style, and answer the following questions of the subject being interviewed: how did you first become interested in collecting? how has your collection grown and/or changed over the years? how do you feel about these works from an investment standpoint? what advice would you give to a new collector? did you have a mentor when you first started collecting? how do you make your selections? where do you find new talent? is your family involved in your collecting endeavors?

Profiles generally run 1000-1200 words, with possible accompanying sidebars on topics such as a brief history of a particular craft medium; information on technique or a brief profile of a specific artist in the collection.

ARTS TOUR:

City and regional arts tours in *AmericanStyle* focus specifically on art, artists, galleries, museums and arts-oriented open studios, tours and events in a given city or region. They are NOT generic travel stories and should not be written as such.

Stories generally run about 900 words for the main feature, and are accompanied by possible sidebars of varying lengths that highlight gallery group events, gallery crawls, interesting arts centers, sculpture gardens or art coops, plus a mandatory "If You Go" box with details about contacting travel bureaus and arts organizations for more information.

The main story must include quotes from a variety of gallery owners, artists or museum directors about the city or region's growing arts scene.

For this assignment, the writer is also expected to ask galleries contacted to supply 35mm slides, transparencies, or high-resolution electronic images of their establishments and/or artists' works for the feature. All slides will be returned by *AmericanStyle* to the galleries after publication.

The arts tour also includes a list of galleries and art museums in the city or region being featured. A primary list of galleries in the region will be supplied to the writer at the time the assignment is made; the writer, in turn, is expected to compile the galleries and museums sidebar for the arts tour, with specifics on address, phone number and a brief description of what a reader can expect of the establishment and its artists.

ARTS WALK:

Arts Walk is a regular department of the magazine that virtually walks readers through an arts enclave, small arts town or gallery district. Stories generally run 600-800 words, with addresses and phone numbers for each gallery highlighted included in parentheses in the running text. General guidelines for writing Arts Walk columns follow the same considerations as for Arts Tours (see above).

ARTIST PORTFOLIO:

A regular department of the magazine, the Portfolio column focuses on emerging artists and their work, and provides readers with details about their background and education, ongoing editions of their work, gallery affiliations and, where applicable, museum representation.

Portfolio columns run approximately 600 words and should be written in a lively conversational style. Hints: focus on the human side of craft artists, uncovering for the reader interesting tidbits about where artists get their inspiration, what their work space is like, how they came to work in their chosen medium, who their mentors were/are, and what path their work is now taking.

For Portfolio submissions, the writer is also expected to ask the artist to supply 4 to 8 35mm slides, transparencies, or high-resolution electronic images of their recent work PLUS a color slide, transparency, or electronic image of themselves, preferably a candid (rather than formal) portrait at work in their studio.

SUBMISSION REQUIREMENTS:

Most manuscripts are transmitted electronically by e-mail to hoped@rosengrp.com, followed by hard-copy manuscripts (to verify materials and proof against) sent by regular mail.

QUERIES:

Freelancers interested in contributing to *AmericanStyle* should submit a clear, specific, concise outline of the topic they wish to write about. They should explain why they think it would be of interest to *AmericanStyle* readers and also provide reasons why they have the background or experience to sucessfully carry out the assignment. Subject, sources, projected length of the article, types of interviews and angle should all be clearly explained in written form. Submissions by e-mail are acceptable and generally assure a quicker response.

First-time writers submit articles on speculation; after an article has been accepted, the editor will negotiate a fee with the writer for the material to be used. Payment is made for published stories at the time of publication.

When an article is assigned to a writer, article length is set by the editor at the time the assignment is made. The average length of feature articles in *AmericanStyle* is about 1000-1200 words; lengths of secondary features, columns and departments at the front and back of the magazine range from 500 to 800 words.

AmericanStyle buys First North American serial rights to all its articles. Contributors are free to resell their articles after publication, but not before.

AmericanStyle's lead time is 6 to 12 months.

Categories: Arts—Collectibles—Crafts/Hobbies—Interview

CONTACT: Hope Daniels, Editor
Material: All
3000 Chestnut Ave., #304
Baltimore, MD 21211
Phone: No phone queries
E-mail: hoped@rosengrp.com
Website: www.americanstyle.com

American Theatre

When submitting material, please allow for *American Theatre's* two month lead time for each issue.

Writers Guidelines

American Theatre typically publishes two or three features and four to six back-of-the-book articles covering trends and events in all types of theatre, as well as economic and legislative developments affecting the arts. The main focus, however, is on professional, nonprofit theatre. We usually are not interested in academic or community theatre, nor in "how-to" articles. While significant productions are high-lighted in our "Critic's Notebook" section, *American Theatre* does not publish reviews.

Writers wishing to submit articles to *American Theatre* should send a query letter to editor Jim O'Quinn outlining a particular proposal; unsolicited material is rarely accepted. Please include a brief resume and sample clips, along with a self-addressed, stamped envelope—average response time is two months. Lead time for finished pieces is at least two months. While fees are negotiated per manuscript, *American Theatre* pays on average $350 for full-length (2500-3500 words) features, less for shorter pieces, upon publication. All manuscripts are subject to editing.

Categories: Arts—Drama

CONTACT: Jim O'Quinn, Editor
Material: All
American Theatre
520 8th Ave., 24th Floor
New York, NY 10018
Website: www.tcg.org

American Turf Monthly

Specific approaches or insights relating to Thoroughbred handicapping, researched angles, methods or trends, non-fiction stories of general racing interest, interviews with racing personalities.

Double-spaced manuscripts, three to five typewritten pages. For handicapping angles and systems, accompanying past performance lines, results charts and workout of results preferred

Unsolicited manuscripts and photographs O.K. Queries welcome.

Fee: Approx. $75 per published page.

Categories: Nonfiction—Book Reviews—Games—Sports/Recreation—Gambling—Equine—Sports Betting

CONTACT: James Corbett, Editor-in-Chief
Material: All
All Star Sports, Inc.
299 East Shore Rd., Ste. 204
Great Neck, NY 11023
Phone: 516-773-4075

American Western Ezine

Monthly publication celebrating the traditions of ranch & rural life thru short fiction, nonfiction, Cowboy poetry, articles, author interviews, & weekly columns. Western authors visit on forum board.

Writers Guidelines for submissions to American Western Magazine.

Now accepting Western short stories, Essays, Equine Columns, and articles on Old West History, Western Personalities, Re-enactors, Travel, Home Decor, Lifestyle, Art, Fashion, and Food/Cooking...By ..."Submit an article & see your name here!"

American Western Magazine is the Internet's premier monthly online magazine of the American West and has quickly become the leading Western magazine online. Our quality online publication celebrates Western life and ranching traditions through short fiction/nonfiction, columns, history, essays, humor, food & cooking articles, travel, equine articles, rodeo articles, author interviews/profiles, reviews, exclusive book excerpts, plus features on celebrities, music, film and art. Our readership spans the globe.

Although we prefer original work, we will *occasionally* accept submissions of previously published nonfiction articles, interviews, profiles, columns, and book reviews—as long as the work does not or has not appeared elsewhere on the Internet. We also actively seek nonexclusive book excerpts, cuts, and novel serializations from published novels *only*.

TERMS OF ACCEPTANCE

Byline given. Also, if the writer has published books, the title, cover image, and brief synopsis of each will be listed in the sidebar of each article written by the writer.

Payment is not issued at this time for any material, including short stories, history articles, features, interiviews, article reprints, book excerpts or reviews. Since we've managed to keep the magazine free of advertising, there is no advertising income that we can draw upon to pay for submissions.

American Western Magazine acquires First Electronic Rights, and only accepts works that have not been accepted or published in other online publications. This includes the right to publish and archive the material for an unlimited period of time on the World Wide Web, but excludes the right to redistribute or sell material on CD ROM; All rights revert to author thirty days after publication.Our goal is to present only the very best in Western. With that in mind, on very rare occasion we may also ask to be granted Exclusive Internet Rights for a period of 3-12 months; however, this point will be discussed individually with each author prior to acceptance.

Categories

Presently, we are actively seeking **quality submissions** for the following categories only. The word counts below are supplied as a general guideline, however, we prefer not to accept material that falls below the suggested word count. No poetry is being accepted at this time.

Short Story (fiction) 2000-3500 - literary quality only. No hunting or Sci-Fi stories. No excerpts or stand-alone chapters from books. (*QUERY FIRST,* supply 3-paragraph sample with bio).

General articles 1000-2500 (supply prior publication experience). Areas we are most interested in at this time are Equine, Rodeo, Travel, Fashion, Home, Crafts, Food/Cooking, Guest Ranches, Cowboy Re-enactors, Personality Profiles & History of the American West.

Book, Music Reviews 300-700.

Book Excerpts From published novels only. Please, no e-book excerpts or material from self-published novels.

Interviews, Profiles Film & Art 800-1500 (*QUERY FIRST, include bio*).

Columns, Commentary 600-1000 (supply proposed column idea & prior publication experience).

Humor Article (Rural/ranch) BOOKED: Currently not accepting.

Cartoon Art Must be appropriate to magazine theme. Color art only. Supply online source where work may be previewed for consideration.

GUIDELINES

Do not submit unpublished novel manuscripts, chapters from unpublished novels, self-published novels or works-in-progress. Do not ask if we can help you place your work with an agent or publishing house. Do not request that we critique your work; we will not.

General article submissions must be geared to topics that relate to the West or affect the West in some way, preferably with a rural, ranching, historical, rodeo, or cowboy/cowgirl theme. Because this publication reaches a crossover audience, articles or essays about Western writing or Western films/film stars are also welcome. We also seek articles on Bit and Spur Makers, Braiders, Cattle Dogs, Cowboy Shooting/Re-enactor Groups, Guest Ranches, Hat Makers, Leather Crafters, Saddle Makers, Western Collectibles and Western Fashion.

Short stories may be set in the contemporary, modern or historical West or have a Civil War theme. No hunting or Sci-Fi type stories. Traditional westerns of exceptional quality are also welcome. We look for stories that are fully developed and realistic. The characters should be multi-dimensional and placed within a well-plotted story-line that has a true sense of place. Story must have detail, offering at least one nugget of information from which most readers can learn something new. The story should be fresh and original; please do not send rehashed versions of old TV westerns, or stories whose characters are drawn from country/western songs. No shoot 'em ups. Stories that are comprised of mostly dialogue, or otherwise suffer from the "talking

heads" syndrome are the most likely to be rejected. Please QUERY FIRST for short story considerations: include brief synopsis along with first 3 paragraphs, word count of your story, plus your bio including prior publication experience.

Submit your material in a professional manner, and please keep in mind that our first and foremost obligation is to our readership. Above all be prepared to accept rejection with grace; too many new writers attempting to enter the market have made the fatal flaw of taking rejection personally and use the ease of email as a way to vent their frustrations—for those writers it is suggested they simply toughen up. Good writing is a craft, not a hobby, and your submitted work should be polished, without errors, and be wholly representative of a professional who actively engages in the craft of writing.

We will not accept anything with excessive profanity, or any material that is pornographic, obscene, or racially demoralizing or inflammable.

All submissions and queries must be made through our online Content Submissions Form. Please do not submit material via postal mail, email or FAX, unless you have made prior arrangements with us. PLEASE NOTE: We DO NOT accept simultaneous submissions, i.e. material that is currently under consideration by other publishers, be they online or off. Our goal is to use our ranking wisely by providing our readers with FRESH content that cannot be found elsewhere on the Internet.

Lastly, please be patient. We read all submissions, however due to the sheer volume that we receive, we are not able to answer each submission directly. If you have not heard back from us within eight weeks, please assume we will not be able to use your idea or submission.

Categories: Western

CONTACT: T. S. Fogarty, Editor
Material: All
PO Box 73
Cowdrey CO 80434
Email: ezine@readthewest.com
www.readthewest.com

America's Civil War

Please refer to *Primedia History Group*

Analog Science Fiction & Fact

Analog Science Fiction features science fiction short stories by current authors, science fact articles, and book reviews.

Analog will consider material submitted by any writer, and consider it solely on the basis of merit. We are definitely eager to find and develop new, capable writers.

We have no hard-and-fast editorial guidelines, because science fiction is such a broad field that I don't want to inhibit a new writer's thinking by imposing Thou Shalt Nots. Besides, a really good story can make an editor swallow his preconceived taboos.

Basically, we publish science fiction stories. That is, stories in which some aspect of future science or technology is so integral to the plot that, if that aspect were removed, the story would collapse. Try to picture Mary Shelley's *Frankenstein* without the science and you'll see what I mean. No story!

The science can be physical, sociological, psychological. The technology can be anything from electronic engineering to biogenetic engineering. But the stories must be strong and realistic, with believable people (who needn't be human) doing believable things—no matter how fantastic the background might be.

Fact Articles Fact articles for Analog should be about 4,000 words in length and should deal with subjects of not only current but future interest, i.e., with topics at the present frontiers of research whose likely future developments have implications of wide interest. Illustrations should be provided by the author in camera-ready form.

In writing for Analog readers, it is essential to keep in mind that they are, in general, very intelligent and technically knowledgeable, but represent a very wide diversity of backgrounds. Thus, specialized jargon and mathematical detail should be kept to a necessary minimum. Also, our readers are reading this magazine largely for entertainment, and a suitable style for our articles is considerably more informal than that in many professional journals. Manuscript Format Manuscripts must be computer-printed or typed, double-spaced, on white paper, one side of the sheet only. Please avoid unusual or very small typefaces. Indent paragraphs but do not leave extra space between them. Please do not put manuscripts in binders or folders. We *do not* accept e-mail or fax submissions.

Author's name and address should be on the first page of the manuscript. No material submitted can be returned or acknowledged unless accompanied by sufficient postage, stamped and addressed envelope (not a postcard), or stamped International Reply Coupons. No simultaneous submissions please.

Payment Analog pays 6-8 cents per word for short stories up to 7,500 words, $450-600 for stories between 7,500 and 10,000 words, and 5-6 cents per word for longer material. We prefer lengths between 2,000 and 7,000 words for shorts, 10,000-20,000 words for novelettes, and 40,000-80,000 for serials. Fact articles are paid for at the rate of 6 cents per word.

Other Information Please query first on serials only. A complete manuscript is strongly preferred for all shorter lengths.

Payment is on acceptance.

Categories: Science Fiction

CONTACT: Stanley Schmidt, Editor
475 Park Ave. South, 11th Floor
New York, NY 10016
E-mail: analog@dellmagazines.com
Website:www.analogsf.com

And Baby

About Us

When publisher Michelle Darné and her partner Kathleen Weiss made the commitment to become parents, they shared the excitement, fear and questioning that all parents-to-be experience. Yet as a lesbian couple, they had questions and concerns that others did not share.

They began to look for information appropriate to their needs. In the initial research, they were frustrated to find limited resources appropriate to the unique situations faced by gay parents. They networked profusely for feedback and advice on what options they had as gay parents, where to go and how to get started. They spent hours surfing the web for gay-friendly insemination doctors and donor facilities, went to every local bookstore in search of pregnancy and parenting guides and consulted several financial and legal advisors.

Most of the fragmented information they collected came from mainstream materials that did not address the unique obstacles faced by Gay/Lesbian/Bisexual/Transgender (GLBT) parents-to-be. The GLBT materials, on the other hand, did not include the broad scope or light-hearted content they liked seeing in mainstream publications. As a 20-year veteran of the advertising and publishing industries, Michelle realized the potential for a magazine that combined both sensibilities in a way that would appeal to a broad audience and be a valuable resource for others in the community looking for answers and inspiration. Twelve months later she launched *And Baby* Magazine.

Since our inception in July 2001, we have been embraced by experts, professionals, contributors, vendors and advertisers. And as our visibility increases, the positive response from the community, both here and abroad, has been overwhelming.

Submission guidelines:

All of *And Baby's* stories are written by assignment, work-for-hire projects.

Our editorial manifest is brainstormed at a staff meeting prior to each issue. Prior to each manifest meeting, an email is sent out to writers calling for ideas for stories, which they then write if the idea is selected.

If you would like to be included in the email call for story ideas, please email a few of your clips (or sample stories), copied into the email (not as an attachment) and a list of publications you have written for before to info@andbabymag.com.

If you're a good fit for *And Baby*, your name will be added to our list.

Categories: Gay Lesbian—Parenting

CONTACT: Editor
Material: All
E-mail: info@andbabymag.com
Website: www.andbabymag.com

Ancestry Magazine

Ancestry Magazine is a bimonthly publication of Myfamily.com, Inc. The magazine is primarily aimed at genealogists and hobbyists who are interested in getting the most out of their research. The focus on Column and Department articles is to instruct, inform, provide historical information, and help genealogists advance their work. Feature articles are given a more liberal approach. While still expected to be appealing and beneficial to genealogists, these articles should also generate interest and appeal among lay people. Topics should focus on human interest, historical, biographical, or personal aspects of genealogy, generally following a theme determined by *Ancestry's* editorial staff.

Each issue of *Ancestry* also features a case study. The case study focuses on getting past a brick wall and the many unique discoveries a researcher makes that will benefit other family historians. The editors are interested in the unique story of your family as well as the steps you took to solve the problem, the research methods you used, and the sources you consulted. Illustrations and photographs are a plus. Entries should be between 1,800 and 2,000 words.

The final page of each issue of *Ancestry* is dedicated to a Bare Bones essay, limited to between 600 and 800 words. The essay is nostalgic, humorous, or sentimental in nature, and contributes largely to the human nature of family history.

Ancestry seeks articles that rise above the standard levels of writing, are informative, and appeal to its genealogy-focused audience. As a consequence of these expectations, the editor reserves the right to make alterations to an article to maintain consistency of tone, style, and clarity. Editors will make every effort to respect the author's voice and artistic freedom, within reasonable bounds. Writers should keep careful notes and provide sources and documentation for all facts. Articles should conform to The Chicago Manual of Style. Interested individuals are encouraged to submit articles appropriate to the focus and format of the publication. Family histories, genealogies, pedigree charts, and queries are not solicited.

Electronic text files must be submitted along with a double-spaced hard copy. Please label disks with the name of the article and program used. WordPerfect and Microsoft Word files are preferred; e-mail and faxed submissions are also acceptable. Authors should include a very brief biography with their submission. Quality illustrations or photographs that enhance the article are appreciated, but authors are not expected to generate headlines and titles or gather art.

The editor considers all submissions and usually responds within six weeks. Upon acceptance of an article, *Ancestry* sends the author a standard contract of agreement. An honorarium will be paid to the author upon publication.

Ancestry Magazine purchases the copyright as work for hire.

Categories: Nonfiction—Family—Geneology

CONTACT: Jennifer Utley, Managing Editor
Material: All
360 E. 4800 North
Provo UT 84602
Phone: 801-705-7301
Fax: 801-705-7120
E-mail: editoram@ancestry.com
Website: www.ancestry.com

Angels on Earth

Angels on Earth publishes true stories about God's messengers at work in today's world. We are interested in stories of heavenly angels and stories involving humans who have played angelic roles in daily life. The best stories are those where the narrator has been positively affected in some distinct way. Look for unusual situations; we have a surplus of stories about illness and car accidents. We are also especially on the lookout for recent stories. A typical *Angels on Earth* story is first-person narrative written in dramatic style, with a spiritual point that the reader can "take away" and apply to his or her own life. It may be your own or someone else's story. Please observe the following in writing your Angels on Earth story: ·The emphasis should be on one person, and is usually told from the vantage point of the individual most deeply affected by the angelic experience. But don't try to tell an entire life story; focus on one specific life event. Bring only as many people as needed to tell the story so the reader's interest stays with the dominant character. ·Decide what your spiritual point will be. We like to see a positive and specific change in the narrator as a result of the angelic experience. Don't forget: We want our readers to take away a message or insight they can use in their own lives. Everything in the story should be tied in with this specific and inspiring theme. ·Don't leave unanswered questions. Give all the relevant facts so the reader can clearly understand what took place. Let the reader feel as if he were there, seeing the characters, hearing them talk, feeling what they felt. Use dialogue, set scenes, build tension—dramatize the story. Show how the narrator becomes a new, or different person. ·The best rule of all: STUDY THE MAGAZINE! Payments: ·For full-length manuscripts (1500 words): $100 - $400, and is made when the story is approved and scheduled for publication. ·For quotes, anecdotes to use as fillers, and material for our short features (50 - 250 words): ·"Messages": brief, mysterious happenings, or letters describing how a specific Angels on Earth article helped you. Payment is usually $25. ·"Earning Their Wings": unusual stories of good deeds worth imitating. Payment is usually $50. ·"Only Human?": short narratives in which the angelic character may or may not have been a human being. The narrator is pleasantly unsure and so is the reader. Payment is usually $100. Please do not send essays, sermons or fiction. We rarely use poetry and do not evaluate book-length material. We receive thousands of unsolicited manuscripts each month, so allow three months for a reply. At this time we cannot accept electronic submissions.

Categories: Nonfiction—Inspirational—Psychology—Religion—Self Help—Society—Personal Experience

CONTACT: The Editor
Material: All
16 East 34th St.
New York NY 10016
Phone: 212-251-8100
Fax: 212-684-0679
E-mail: submissions@angelsmag.com
Website: www.angelsonearth.com

Animal People

ANIMAL PEOPLE welcomes freelance submissions of articles, informed guest opinion columns, original art, and photography, subject to the following terms and conditions:

• Material submitted for our consideration must not be simultaneously submitted to any other animal-related publication of national distribution. We must be informed if an item is simultaneously submitted to or has previously been published by some other type of publication, e.g. a local humane society newsletter or a general circulation magazine or newspaper.
• All submissions of writing will be either accepted or rejected within two weeks of receipt. Our usual turn-around time is less than one day.
• We buy either first North American serial rights or one-time reprint rights, depending on whether or not the material has been previously published, including the right of publication in both our newsprint and electronic editions. All other rights remain with the author.
• Because we are a nonprofit publication, we prefer to receive freelance materials as donations. However, recognizing that many contributors need to earn their livings by their work, we do pay the following honorariums: $25 per assigned book review, $15 per photograph or drawing, 10¢ a word for profiles and features. Payment is upon acceptance. We do not pay for guest opinion columns.
• Assignments will be made (or confirmed) in writing only, and only to contributors whose work we have previously published. Please do not query by telephone.
• We do not assign spot news coverage to freelancers.
• Profile submissions are particularly welcome, especially if accompanied by photographs. Although we may occasionally be receptive to a profile of a well-known subject, or a subject who has engineered a uniquely effective protest, our preference is to salute seldom recognized individuals of unique and outstanding positive accomplishment, in any capacity that benefits animals or illustrates the intrinsic value of other species. We are also particularly interested in those individuals who combine active concern for animals with active concern for fellow human beings.
• Profiles of organizations should be accompanied by a copy of the organization's most recent IRS Form 990 (unless we already have it on file.)
• We require independent verification of the animal care conditions at facilities whose reputations and administrations are unknown to us.
• We prefer to consider photography and art submissions on a portfolio basis. Query first, with examples of your work. If we think we might be able to use your material with reasonable frequency, we will invite you to send us prints of photos that might be appropriate, as you take them, identified with your name on the back of each. We will file them according to subject (aardvark to zebra mussel), and use them and pay you for them as our need to illustrate news items requires.
• We do not publish fiction or poetry.
• We are not interested in atrocity stories, essays on why animals have rights, or material that promotes or defends animal abuse, including hunting, fishing, trapping, and slaughter. ANIMAL PEOPLE is the leading independent newspaper providing original investigative coverage of animal protection worldwide, founded in 1992. Our readership of 30,000-plus includes the decision-makers at more than 8,300 animal protection organizations. We have no alignment or affiliation with any other entity.
• We prefer to receive manuscript submissions by e-mail and/or in hard copy format.

Categories: Animals—Animal Protection

CONTACT: Submissions Editor
Material: All
PO Box 960
Clinton WA 98236-0960
Phone: 360-579-2505
Fax: 360-579-2575
E-mail: anmlpepl@whidbey.com
Website: www.animalpeoplenews.org

The Animals' Agenda
Helping People Help Animals

The *Animals' Agenda* is a bimonthly magazine that seeks to inspire action for animals by informing people about animal rights and cruelty-free living. Agenda is committed to serving —and fostering cooperation among—all animal advocates from the grassroots to the national levels. The magazine is published by The Animal Rights Network Inc., an IRS 501(c)(3) federal tax-exempt, not-for-profit organization founded in 1979.

Submissions

The *Animals' Agenda* does not accept unsolicited manuscripts.

Article proposals or outlines, as well as letters to the editor, should be sent to The *Animals' Agenda* mailing address (see below). Once an article has been commissioned, we prefer it to be submitted via e-mail or on a 3.5" computer disk saved in standard ASCII format (with hard copy attached). Typed copy may also be faxed (letters to the editor may be neatly handwritten). Articles are due two months preceding the month of publication, and may be edited for space or clarity. Agenda reprints articles infrequently. Please indicate if an article is being submitted to other publications in addition to Agenda. We generally welcome other periodicals' reprinting articles from Agenda if those articles are credited properly. Agenda generally does not offer payment for articles.

Contents

• Letters to the editor allow readers to comment on articles or letters that have appeared in previous issues of Agenda, to voice opinions about matters of concern to animal advocates, and to offer advice on solving animal-abuse problems. Maximum length: 300 words.

• "Bulletin Board" is a collection of concise and late-breaking news briefs relating to animals and their well-being. These items may be obtained from magazines, newspapers, newsletters, or computer forums. Contributors should identify the sources of the "Bulletin Board" items they submit. Maximum length: 100 words.

• "Making a Difference" highlights victories and successes on behalf of animals, and is similar in style and format to "Bulletin Board."

• "Happy Endings" briefly recounts the true story of an animal(s) who was rescued from abusive, exploitative, or dangerous conditions, and who now lives a comfortable and secure life. Must include a photo of the animal(s). Maximum length: 400 words.

• "News" is a compilation of brief reports that describe animal abuse or exploitation practices, organizational campaigns for animals, recent pertinent developments, etc. A report should include information on how readers can help and a contact organization (if applicable), and may be accompanied by a photo. Maximum length: text, 400 words; photo with caption, 100 words.

• "Unsung Heroes" profiles individuals who work diligently, without major recognition, to protect the well-being and/or rights of animals—whether through direct hands-on assistance or other ongoing advocacy efforts. The individual should reflect a "regular" activist, not movement leaders or other professional advocates. Must include a photo of the activist. Maximum length: 500 words.

• "Investigations" are based on investigative reporting. They present considerable detail about a major source of animal exploitation or about a campaign to reduce or eliminate that exploitation. Must include photographs and material for "Your Agenda," outlining action readers can take to help. Maximum length: 1,200 words.

• "Analysis" serves a variety of functions: discussing strategies to reduce or to end animal exploitation, reviewing in detail a book or movie about animals or animal liberation, presenting a historical analysis of some facet of animal abuse, discussing the status of animals in society, etc. Must include photographs and material for "Your Agenda." Maximum length: 1,200 words.

• The cover feature presents in-depth and extensively detailed coverage of a major news story or development concerning the treatment or status of animals. Must include photographs, at least one sidebar, and material for "Your Agenda." Maximum length: 2,500 words.

• "Resources" presents brief reviews describing recently produced materials including books, computer software, CDs, campaign matter, videos, etc. that are intended to serve as educational or activist tools. Maximum length: 100 words.

• Reviews, while generally devoted to books about animal liberation or abuse, also may discuss the latest movies or CDs that treat these subjects. Must include the dust jacket or cover of the work reviewed. Maximum length: 800 words.

• "Commentary," provides a forum for guest columnists to offer a perspective on important issues and developments affecting the animal rights movement. Must include a photo of the author. Maximum length: 700 words.

• "Toward Kinship," an essay in which an author is free to consider any aspect of animal rights, should approach its subject in a personal, expansive, even offbeat manner. Whenever appropriate, submit a photograph or other image to illustrate the text. Maximum length: 1,200 words.

• "Activities" lists forthcoming conferences, demonstrations, protests, seminars, and other events of interest to animal advocates. Must include the name of a person and/or organization to contact about the listed event, as well as the address and phone number of that individual or organization. Maximum length: 50 words.

Categories: Animals—Animal Rights

CONTACT: Kirsten Rosenberg, Managing Editor
Material: All
PO Box 25881
Baltimore MD 21224
Phone: 410-675-4566
Fax: 410-675-0066
E-mail: office@animalsagenda.org
Website: www.animalsagenda.org

Animals Magazine

Overview:

Animals is a full-color, quarterly magazine written and edited to deliver timely, reliable, and provocative coverage of wildlife issues, pet-care topics, and animal-protection concerns. It also publishes natural-history pieces that educate readers about animals' needs and behaviors.

The magazine circulates to a national audience (around 50,000), consisting mostly of members of the Massachusetts Society for the Prevention of Cruelty to Animals and the American Humane Education Society, its publishers.

What We Publish From Freelance Sources:

About 90 percent of our editorial coverage is from freelance sources.

Feature Stories: Well-researched articles (1,200 to 2,000 words) on national and international wildlife, domestic animals, wildlife/conservation issues, controversies involving animals and/or their use, animal-protection issues, pet health, and pet care. Articles must engage readers who are interested in knowing more about a variety of creatures as well as those who consider themselves animal protectionists.

Reviews: Newly released books and videos on animals, animal-related issues, and the environment. These reviews run from 300 to 500 words and are for our Books column.

Profiles: Short pieces on individuals at work to save both domestic and wild animals, to make conditions better for animals, or on others whose interactions with animals makes them of interest to a wide-ranging audience. These reviews run about 800 words and are published in our ProFiles column.

What We Pay:

Because payment depends on the length of the article and the amount of research necessary to complete it, payment varies.

How to Query:

Please query by letter and allow four to six weeks for a response. Query letters should include:

• a pointed summary describing the article's focus, purpose, approximate length, and finish date;

• a list of sources that you plan to contact or have already contacted. When dealing with controversies, sources should be from both sides of the issue;

• writing samples, preferably of comparable pieces;

• information on when and where you may have published, or plan to publish, a similar story, if applicable.

Additional Information:

For a sample copy of *Animals Magazine*, please send a check in the amount of $3.95, payable to Animals Magazine, to the address below.

For a copy of *Animals Magazine's* photography guidelines, please send a stamped, self-addressed envelope to the address below.

Thank you for your interest in *Animals Magazine*.

Categories: Animals

CONTACT: Paula Abend, Editor
Material: Wildlife and Pet/Domestic queries
350 S. Huntington Ave.
Boston MA 02130
Phone: 617-522-7400
Fax: 617-522-4885

Annals of Improbable Research (AIR)

The Journal of Record for Inflated Research and Personalities

The Annals of Improbable Research (AIR) publishes original articles, data, effluvia and news of improbable research. The material is intended to be humorous and/or educational, and sometimes is. We look forward to receiving your manuscripts, photographs, x-rays, drawings, etc. Please do not send biological samples. Photos should be black & white if possible. Reports of research results, modest or otherwise, are preferred to speculative proposals.

Keep it short, please. Articles are typically 500-2,000 words in length. (Items intended for mini-AIR* should be much, much, much shorter.) Please send two neatly printed copies. Alternatively, you may submit via e-mail, in ASCII format.

Please don't spend a lot of efforting in elaborate text formatting. If the article is accepted for publication we will take care of that.

Sincerely and improbably,

Marc Abrahams, Editor

Categories: Humor— Internet—Interview—Science

CONTACT: Submissions Editor
Material: All
PO Box 380853
Cambridge MA 02238
Phone: 617-491-4437
E-mail: AIR@improbable.com
Website: www.improbable.com

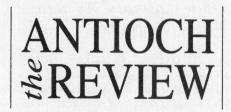

Antioch Review

GUIDELINES FOR PROSPECTIVE CONTRIBUTORS

The best answer we can give on inquiries relating to what kind of material the ANTIOCH REVIEW uses is, "read the magazine." Look through a few representative issues for an idea of subjects, treatment, lengths of articles, and stories we have used; it will be far more rewarding than any theories we might try to formulate.Unfortunately, we cannot honor requests for free sample copies. The REVIEW is expensive to produce and operates on a precarious financial margin. If copies are not available at your local newsstand or library, we will be happy to send you a back issue for $7.00, which includes postage and handling. Please note that we do not read simultaneous submissions, nor do we consider submissions sent via email. Review the section below on style, lengths, and payment for more information about submissions.

ARTICLES

Our audience is made up of educated citizens, often professional people, who are interested in matters beyond their fields of special activity. With few exceptions, our subjects cover most of the range of social science and humanities. Our approach tries to steer a middle course between scholars speaking exclusively to other scholars in their field, and workaday journalists appealing to a broad popular audience; both these approaches have their own journals and audiences. We try for the interpretive essay on a topic of current importance, drawing on scholarly materials for its substance and appealing to the intellectual and social concerns of our readers. We are also interested in reviving the moribund art of literary journalism. We DO NOT accept essay submissions from June 1 to September 1. Submissions received during this period will be returned unread (is SASE enclosed) or discarded.

FICTION

We seldom publish more than three short stories in each issue. Although the new writer as well as the previously published author is welcome, it is the story that counts, a story worthy of the serious attention of the intelligent reader, a story that is compelling, written with distinction. Only rarely do we publish translations of well known or new foreign writers; a chapter of a novel is welcome only if it can be read complete in itself as a short story. We DO NOT accept fiction from June 1 to September 1. Submissions received during this period will be returned unread (if SASE enclosed) or discarded.

POETRY

Like fiction, we get far more poetry than we can possibly accept, and the competition is keen. Here, where form and content are so inseparable and reaction is so personal, it is difficult to state requirements or limitations. Studying recent issues of the REVIEW should be helpful. No "light" or inspirational verse. Any poetry received without a self addressed stamped envelope will be discarded if rejected and no notice will be sent. No need to enclose a post card for the purpose of acknowledging receipt of a submission. Do not mix poetry and prose in the same envelope. Please submit three to six poems at one time. We DO NOT read poetry from May 1 to September 1. Submissions received during this period will be returned unread (if SASE enclosed) or discarded.

REVIEWS

We do not publish unsolicited book reviews and very seldom do we publish essays on literary problems or the canons of significant contemporary writers. The editors and their associates regularly prepare a section of short book evaluations, selectively treating recent publications.

STYLE, LENGTHS, PAYMENT, ETC.

Our literary standards are as high as we can enforce them; we do not have the staff to engage in major editorial rewriting, except on rare occasions when the content justifies the effort.

Actually, we have no rigid expectations of length, preferring the content and treatment to determine size. Rarely, however, do we use articles or stories over 5,000 words—and 8,000 at the outside limit.

In order to be returned to you, *all manuscripts must be accompanied by a self-addressed stamped envelope.* Others will be discarded, as we cannot be responsible for the return of manuscripts for which the postage has not been provided. If you want the manuscript discarded, say so and enclose a postcard or stamped envelope which we can use if we do not accept your submission.

Manuscripts should be typed, double-spaced on one side of white, 8.5 x 11 paper. Please spare the editors the task of reading carbons or dirty Xerox copies or pages with excessive inter-linear corrections and revisions. We also prefer manuscripts to be mailed flat, fastened by paper clip only, and one at a time except for poetry. Please note the type of submission—FICTION, NONFICTION, or POETRY—on the envelope, and do not mix prose and poetry in the same envelope.

We try to report on manuscripts as quickly as possible, but because material that interests us is occasionally read by several members of our staff, the process can sometimes take up to four to six months. We acknowledge receipt of a manuscript only if it is accompanied by a return postcard for that purpose.

Payment is upon printed publication at the rate of $15.00 per printed page (about 425 words) plus 2 copies of the issue. Authors may buy additional copies at an authors' discount of 40% off the cover price.

All material sent to the ANTIOCH REVIEW is read and considered, although we cannot comment on each rejection. As noted above, we do not read simultaneous submissions. They will be returned unread (if SASE enclosed) or discarded.

Categories: Fiction—Nonfiction—Literature—Poetry

CONTACT: Robert Fogarty, Editor
Material: Fiction, Nonfiction
CONTACT: Judith Hall, Poetry Editor
Material: Poetry
PO Box 148
Yellow Springs OH 45387
Phone: 937-769-1365
Website: www.review.antioch.edu

Antiques & Collecting Magazine

Editorial Submissions

We accept unsolicited manuscripts featuring a particular antique, collectible, artist, or company of interest to collectors, dealers, auction houses and others involved in the antiques & collecting industry. We buy first publication rights only, with pay ranging from $50-$300 (story and illustrative materials) depending on length and quality. A publication contract will be mailed out after the article has been accepted. Payment and four copies of the magazine are provided after publication.

We consider articles about collectibles made after 1980, but prefer to focus on those made prior to 1980. Query letters via e-mail are appreciated. Please include previously published writing samples, if

available. Writers are also encouraged to send in complete articles and images for consideration. Please include a self-addressed, stamped envelope with sufficient postage if you would like us to return the submitted materials.

What are we looking for?

• **Length:** 1,000-1,600 words. Longer and shorter submissions are considered.

• **Values:** Please include current pricing information if possible.

• **Photos:** Please include 6-10 (or more), high quality photographs to illustrate your article. High resolution digital images are preferred (300 DPI+), but we do accept photographs and slides. Leave the cropping to us! Full-color images are preferred. Photographs and slides will be returned after publication.

• **Format:** We cannot accept hand-written or typed manuscripts. Please submit your articles via email, on a floppy disc, Zip, or CD-ROM. Microsoft Word is preferred.

• **Event coverage:** Normally, we do not buy articles that focus on auction coverage (pre-or post), or antique shows (pre-or post) except for our annual August "Show Spectacular."

• **Style:** We follow the basic journalistic style of the *Associated Press Stylebook*. Please proofread articles carefully before submitting them. All stories are subject to editing and rewriting for accuracy, clarity, conciseness and space considerations.

You may request a sample copy via U.S. Post at adddress below.

Categories: Nonfiction—Antiques—Arts—Crafts/Hobbies

CONTACT: Editor
Material: All
1006 S Michigan Ave
Chicago IL 60605
Phone: 312-939-4767
E-mail: editor@acmagazine.com
Website: www.acmagazine.com

Antique Trader Weekly

Editorial Submissions

Unsolicited manuscripts are welcome, but must include a self-addressed, stamped envelope (SASE) with sufficient return postage. Query letters are appreciated with samples of the author's previously published writing. Writers are encouraged to send in completed articles for consideration.

Queries are accepted via e-mail at korbecks@krause.com.

Content

Antique Trader is published weekly and includes feature stories, news items and regular columns. Articles are of general interest to collectors, dealers and others actively involved in the antiques and collectibles hobby.

What are we looking for?

• *Profiles.* These 500 to 800-word profiles could feature interesting stories about "super" collectors, enterprising dealers, fledgling businesses or other personalities in the hobby. They should be creatively written in story form, rather than question and answer format.

• *Feature stories.* Subject matter should focus on the collectibility of specific antiques or manufacturers' lines. Features should not be too narrow, but rather hit the highlights of a particular type of antique. Smaller features may focus on more specific topics (tin wind-up toys, Wallace Nutting furniture, Red Wing pottery, milk glass, etc.)

• *Event coverage. Antique Trader* regularly covers news of events such as antique shows and auctions. These features should include highlights of the events (special guests, prices realized, major announcements), quotes from promoters, dealers and attendees and high-quality photos with identification.

Most stories bear an author's byline, and all stories are subject to editing and rewriting for accuracy, clarity, conciseness and space considerations.

Current values of antique and other pricing information should be incorporated into features or placed in an accompanying sidebar. Our readers want to know not only the historical information about toys, but also what is available and how much it's worth. Please note the source of the pricing (online auction, auction prices realized, dealer list, etc.).

• *Word count.* To accommodate our new, more user-friendly design, word count should be limited to 500 to 800 words. Sidebar and pricing text is not included in that count.

• *Illustrations.* Appropriate photos (line art, illustrations, etc.) must accompany each column. This can include color or black/white slides, prints or transparencies or digital images. Digital images (TIFF or JPG) must be at least 200 dpi (72 dpi JPGs are NOT acceptable for print) and sent via e-mail, disk or CD. Images downloaded from Web sites are discouraged since screen resolution does not frequently translate well to print.

Photos should be identified on a separate sheet or on a Post-It note on the back of the photo. Do NOT use ink on the backs of photos.

It is the columnist's responsibility to secure photos for his/her column; photos from outside sources are acceptable with proper permissions. Photos should not be indiscriminately downloaded from Web sites without the owners' and/or author's permission. Photos must not be taken from other books or publications without permission from the respective publishers.

• *Quotes.* In an effort to make our editorial content more interactive and community driven, quotes from at least two outside sources must be incorporated into each column or feature. Depending on content, these quotes could be from dealers, collectors, show promoters, clubs or other related sources. Sources should be tapped to comment on what's hot, what's not, a particular controversy, a new product, an old standard or anything applicable to your column that month.

• *Sidebars.* At least one sidebar must be included with each column or feature. Sample sidebars could include (but are not limited to):

• Resources (clubs, books, web sites, etc.)

• *Hot News.* (a late-breaking addition, an especially interesting trend or controversy, a show report, historical timeline, etc.)

• *Pricing.* All features must include secondary market pricing or retail pricing (depending on what is appropriate). Pricing sidebars can include values from various sources including Krause Publications price guides, secondary market dealers, retail price lists, other outside "expert" resources or prices realized (from auctions or completed online auctions). In any case, proper citation must be given.

Prices should be worked into a sidebar, but you are also free to incorporate pricing into the body of the column or feature. Top 10 lists are encouraged as well (top-selling Rookwood, best bets of the month, etc.).

Rights and Payment

Krause Publications purchases exclusive rights to manuscripts for *Antique Trader* Publications. Krause Publications retains the right to republish the material (online or in other Krause publications).

Previously published articles can be submitted for consideration; please specify previous publisher/date with query.

Editorial contracts are mailed out after the article has been accepted, but the editor retains the right to withhold publication due to space, time or other considerations. At such time, a lesser kill fee may be offered.

Payment for articles accepted is based on a per-story basis (story plus illustrative material) at the editor's discretion. Payment is upon publication, unless other arrangements have been agreed upon. Contact Editor Sharon Korbeck for specific, current rates.

Manuscript Format

Hard copy submitted must be typewritten and double-spaced on white paper with the author's name, address and phone number at the top. Please leave at least one-inch margins on all sides of the page. Do not submit copy typed in ALL CAPS.

Computer submissions should be on a DS/HD disk in ASCII (text) or Microsoft Word format with accompanying hard copy.

Electronic submissions are accepted only for solicited or assigned stories. No unsolicited manuscripts via e-mail, please. Send e-mail submissions to korbecks@krause.com.

Style

We follow the basic journalistic style guidelines in *The Associated Press Stylebook.* Consult Strunk & White's *The Elements of Style* for additional considerations. Please proofread stories carefully before submitting them.

Publication

Authors will not be notified prior to publication and will be sent two copies of the issue containing their story.

Please note: Publication time may be anywhere from two months to 24 months following acceptance.

Contact

Interested free-lance writers should query via mail or via e-mail.

For a sample copy of *Antique Trader* or other Krause publications, call (800) 258-0929.

For more information about our company's books and magazines, visit our Web sites www.krause.com or www.collect.com.

Categories: Nonfiction—Antiques—Collectibles—Hobbies

CONTACT: Sharon Korbeck, Editor
Material: Queries
700 E. State St.
Iola WI 54990-0001
Phone: 715-445-4612, ext. 468v
Fax: 715-445-4087
E-mail: korbecks@krause.com
Website: www.krause.com

ANVIL
M A G A Z I N E

Anvil Magazine

For the past 21 years, ANVIL Magazine has been The Voice of the Farrier and Blacksmith. This international monthly is distributed throughout the United States and in over 20 foreign countries and enjoys a readership of over 10,000 per issue.

Our staff is always interested in your submission. We read and consider every contribution forwarded, as we sincerely believe that the responsibility of a good editor is to listen to many voices and to encourage writers to grow. We appreciate the efforts of our contributors, and when editing is necessary, we attempt to offer comment that promotes clarity. We reserve the right to edit in the interests of available space and clarity.

Contribution Categories

• Feature/Pictorial Events, personal profiles, question-and-answer interviews, local color, points of interest (e.g., museums, schools)

• Blacksmithing

• How-To-Do-It articles—illustrated step-by-step smithing processes. Metallurgy, history, craft hints, tools and techniques

• Farriery

• How-To-Do-It articles—illustrated step-by-step shoeing processes. Craft hints and techniques, shoeing experience with horses.

• Veterinary/Technical: Research, studies, documented reports by professional individuals.

• Equine Training Information

• Reports, studies and personal experiences related to handling, training and locomotion of the horse.

• Humor: As it pertains to the farrier and blacksmith.

• Safety/Health/Psychology: Personal aspects of the industry: individual experiences, shop safety tips, exercise and nutrition information, psychology of working with horses.

- Book Reviews on books of interest to the industry.
- Business articles for the farrier and equine industry.
- Guest Editorial: Personal opinion or consideration of an existing condition within the industry. Individual's name must be included with submission.
- Horse Owner Information: Equine hoof, nutrition and handling, pertaining to farriery, written to inform the horse owner.

Submission Format and Requirements

Text: Formats listed in order of preference.

1. Commitment of material to a 5¼" or 3½" floppy disk with one (1) hard copy representation (printout, typewritten text, photocopy) of each submission. Computer files must be IBM compatible and utilize either WordPerfect, Word or ASCII text files. Hard copies are required, should there be complications involved in disk submission retrieval.

2. Computer printout or photocopy of typewritten material.

3. Handwritten articles.

All submissions must be legible and must include the name, address and phone number of author. If previously published material, full credit information of prior publication and written release to reprint are required. In the case of technical, historical or controversial submissions, the reference sources, bibliography or verification may be requested. Illustrations in the form of original art work and photographs enhance the literature. Contributors are encouraged to illustrate articles whenever possible.

Photography: Formats listed in order of preference.

1. High-contrast, high-clarity black-and-white 5"x7" photographs, labeled on backs for article reference.

2. Black-and-white proof sheets with negatives.

3. High-contrast color photographs.

4. Color slides.

All photo submissions must be clearly identified and must include photographer's name, address and phone number. Each individual photo should be clearly marked, preferably with paper label on the back with reference to the article. Names of subjects, dates and places or reference numbers to written sheet of captions are required. If previously published material, include full credit information of prior publication and written release to reprint.

Cartoons, Graphics, Illustrations: Must be original and the work of the artist of submission. Submissions must be clearly marked with name, address and phone number of the artist. In the case of illustration to text referrals, illustrations must be clearly marked in sequence. Black-and-white material is preferred. Computer files (TIFF or other formats) of art work are welcomed.

Submission Dates

Material targeted for a particular issue must be in our editorial offices two months prior to the first day of the month of issue. In case of important events, special arrangements can be made to accommodate time-sensitive material.

Publishing Policy

ANVIL Magazine publishes first-run material and reprints of previously published articles. We reserve the right to reject material and to professionally edit any first-run works submitted.

ANVIL Magazine reserves the right to offer articles for reprints, which are available at cost.

In addition, ANVIL Magazine reserves the right to place articles on the ANVIL Magazine World Wide Web Page. These articles will carry the copyright of the author, e.g., "© John Smith." The ANVIL Magazine Web Page is an information resource.

Material Appearance Policy

First-run material under contract to ANVIL Magazine may not appear in another publication prior to its appearance in ANVIL Magazine.

No material will be accepted for publication prior to review. No material will be considered in part, but must be forwarded in its entirety for editorial review.

Tear sheets of article/graphic appearance and a complimentary copy of the issue in which it appears are forwarded directly to author within 30 days of publication.

Disclaimer

ANVIL Magazine and its staff do not manufacture, test, warrant, guarantee or endorse any of the tools, materials, instructions or products contained in any articles published. ANVIL Magazine disclaims any responsibility or liability for damages or injuries as a result of the use or application of any information published in ANVIL Magazine.

Payment for Contributions

Payment for submissions is made directly to the author within 30 days of material acceptance. Rate of payment is determined on each individual submission and is based upon, but not limited to, article length, quality, complexity, timeliness and number of photos or graphics. ANVIL Magazine payments range from $25.00 to $250.00.

Categories: Book Reviews—Blacksmithing—Ferriery—Veterinary

CONTACT: Bob Edwards, Publisher/Editor
Material: All
PO Box 1810
Georgetown CA 95634
Phone: 530-333-2142
Fax: 530-333-2906
E-mail: anvil@anvilmag.com
Website: www.anvilmag.com

Appaloosa Journal

Appaloosa Journal is the official publication of the Appaloosa Horse Club, the international breed registry for the Appaloosa horse. We strive to cover all aspects of the breed, from breeding and training to showing and racing.

We do not publish poetry, fiction or purely sentimental stories. We seek interesting, informative, fresh and well-written pieces that have an impact on the Appaloosa industry.

We seek feature-length (1,800 words) and article-length (600 to 800 words) submissions about breeders, trainers, specific training methods, influential horses, youth and non-pro competitors, breed history, trail riding and artists using Appaloosa subjects. Article-length reports of timely and newsworthy events, such as shows, races and overseas competition, are welcome but must be pre-approved by the editor.

All submissions must specifically involve the Appaloosa breed or Appaloosa events. Coverage of Appaloosas competing outside the Appaloosa circuit may also be of interest.

Manuscripts must be sent on a CD or 3.5-inch disk for Apple Macintosh or via e-mail in Microsoft Word or text-only format. An accompanying hard copy should be printed, double spaced, following the guidelines set in *Writers Market.*

Authors are responsible for accuracy of material, and a byline is required for any published material. Thoroughbreds, Quarter Horses and Arabians, as well as any other breed, must be identified as such. Spellings of horses' names must exactly match the names listed on registration papers.

Payment for accepted material is made upon publication but arranged prior to acceptance. Return of writer's contract is required. Typically, accepted material may not be submitted to another publication for six months after publication in *Appaloosa Journal.*

Submitted photos should be clear, relevant and of the highest quality. Prints (slides are rarely accepted) can be no smaller than 5x7 inches, although 8x10-inch prints are preferred. Captions, including identification of all horses and people pictured, are required. Model releases, photographer's name and other pertinent information must accompany the image. To avoid marring a photo, never write on either side of the print. Horses pictured should be Appaloosa and should display the breed's color characteristics.

An SASE must be enclosed for material returns. *Appaloosa Jour-*

nal is not responsible for unsolicited materials. All freelance correspondence for *Appaloosa Journal* should be directed to Diane Rice, editor, at address below, subject line "freelance." All queries must be in writing, via mail* or e-mail.

Categories: Nonfiction—Animals

CONTACT: Diane Rice, Editor
Appaloosa Journal
2720 W Pullman Rd
Moscow ID 83843
E-mail: drice@appaloosa.com

Appleseeds

General Information

APPLESEEDS is a 36-page, multidisciplinary, nonfiction social studies magazine for children ages 8 and up (primarily in grades 3 & 4). Writers are encouraged to study recent back issues for content and style. (Sample issues are available at $4.95 plus $2.00 shipping and handling. Send 7 1/2 " x 10 1/2 " self-addressed envelope.) We are looking for articles that are lively, age-appropriate, and exhibit an original approach to the theme. Scientific and historical accuracy is extremely important. Authors are urged to use primary sources and up-to-date resources for their research. And remember, your article must stimulate the curiosity of a child. APPLESEEDS purchases all rights to material.

Procedure

Writers may propose an article for any issue. The article idea must be closely related to the theme of the issue. Please include a completed query.

• Each query must be written separately.

• Feel free to include copies of published writing samples with your query if you have not yet written for APPLESEEDS.

• After the deadline for query proposals has passed, the editors will review the suggestions and assign articles. This may take several months - don't despair! We may suggest modifications to your original proposal or assign an entirely new idea.

Please do not begin work until you've received a detailed assignment sheet from us!

Guidelines

Feature articles:

1-4 pages, (Most issues contain about 6-8 feature articles.)

Includes: nonfiction, interviews, and how-to

Departments:

• Fun Stuff (games or activities relating to the theme, 2 pages)

• Reading Corner (literature piece, 2-4 pages)

• By the Numbers (math activities relating to the theme, 1 page)

• Where in the World (map activities, 2 pages)

• Your Turn (theme-related opportunities for children to take action, 1 page)

• Experts in Action (short profile of professional in field related to theme, 1 page)

• The Artist's Eye (fine or folk art relating to theme, 1 page)

• From the Source (age-appropriate primary source material, 1-2 pages)

Assume 150 words per page; payment approximately $50 per page

Photo Guidelines

To be considered for publication, photographs must relate to a specific theme. Writers are encouraged to submit available photos with their query or article. We buy one-time use.

Our suggested fee range for professional quality photographs follows:

1/4 page to full page

b/w $15 to $100
color $25 to $150

• Please note that fees for non-professional quality photographs are negotiated.

• Cover fees are set on an individual basis for one-time use, plus promotional use. All cover images are color.

• Prices set by museums, societies, stock photography houses, etc., are paid or negotiated. Photographs that are promotional in nature (e.g., from tourist agencies, organizations, special events, etc.) are usually submitted at no charge.

• If you have photographs pertaining to any upcoming theme, please contact the editor by mail or fax, or send them with your query. You may also send images on speculation.

Write a brief description of your idea, including a list of sources you plan to use, your intended word length, and any unique angle or hook you think will make your piece irresistible to its intended audience (8 - 10-year-olds and their teachers and parents).

• E-mail queries only. To avoid problems in downloading attachments, always include your query in the body of the email. You may also include attachments if you wish.

• Queries may be submitted at any time before the deadline. Due to the volume of queries received, only accepted queries will receive notification.

• Assignments are made approximately one month before manuscripts are due.

E-mail queries to: swbuc@aol.com
Mail sample requests to:
Editorial Department
Cobblestone Publishing
Attn: Sample Requests
30 Grove Street, Suite C
Peterborough, NH 03458
Categories: Nonfiction—Children—History—Juvenile—Science—Society

CONTACT: Susan Buckley, Editor
Material: All
AppleSeeds
140 E 83rd St.
New York NY 10028
E-mail: swbuc@aol.com
Website: www.cobblestonepub.com

The Appraisers Standard

• Articles should be approximately 700 words in length. Longer articles may be broken in two or more parts if necessary in order to cover the topic as required.

• Black and white photos should accompany the article and assist the reader with appraising the articles being covered.

• Current auction/market prices should be included whenever applicable.

• Topics for articles should be appropriate for appraisers of personal as well as real estate property.

• Articles should be geared to provide information which will help the appraisers with ascertaining value, detecting forgeries or reproductions, or simply providing advice on appraising the articles.

• A short biography of the author should be sent to be added to story to supply reader with credentials of author.

• Payment of $60 is made when story is published.

Categories: Nonfiction—Antiques—Arts—Collectibles—Appraising

CONTACT: Linda Tucker, Editor
Material: All
5 Gill Terrace
Ludlow VT 05149-1003
Phone: 802-228-7444

Remember: Editors change jobs and publishers change addresses. It is wise to invest in a phone call for the current information before submitting.

Apex Science Fiction & Horror Digest

Quarterly magazine for science fiction & horror.

Want to send your fiction to Apex Digest?

We submit every issue of *Apex Science Fiction and Horror Digest* to reviewers at Locus, Whispers of Wickedness, Tangent, SciFiDimensions and more. We also make sure the editors of the yearly 'Best Of' short story anthologies receive every issue of Apex. So you'll know that your stories will be seen by the best in the business.

We pay upon publication.

Ok, the particulars...

We want dark sci-fi. All stories require a sci-fi element. Most stories we print will be a mix of sci-fi and horror, but occasionally we'll buy an exceptional work of straight sci-fi (see "Allergies" in issue one).

Must be sent electronically in Word Doc format as an attachment to your email. Save your stamps, we don't accept mailed submissions. Submit to submission@apexdigest.com.

Must be no more than 10,000 words.

Double spaced. Please use Courier 12 point as your font. Put your last name on each page. In fact, our feelings wouldn't be hurt if you used http://www.shunn.net/format/story.html as a format reference.

Only one submission at a time.

We don't accept poetry. Flash fiction is ok.

Artists need to query.

Query about reprints for Apex Digest. Reprints will be considered for Apex Online.

We ask for First North America Serial Rights. We also ask for the exclusive electronic rights to your manuscript for up to 90 days after the publication date of the issue in which you appear.

If we like your story, we will email and ask if you are willing to let us publish your work. If you agree, then we will either fax or email our standard publication contract. This has to be signed and returned to Apex before we can print your work.

Payment for fiction is 1.5 cents per word. Additionally, you will receive two free contributor copies of the issue in which you appear. And...you will be given props on the Apex website, along with a bio and byline in the magazine.

We will try to answer all submissions within four weeks. Right now, estimated response time is 20-30 days.

Categories: Science Fiction

CONTACT: Jason Sizemore, Editor
Material: All
PO Box 2223
Lexington KY 40588
Phone: 859-312-3974submission@apexdigest.com
E-mail: jason@apexdigest.com
Website: www.apexdigest.com

AQR
Alaska Quarterly Review

Alaska Quarterly Review, a journal devoted to contemporary literary art, and published by the University of Alaska Anchorage, invites submissions in the following areas:

FICTION: Short stories and novel excerpts in traditional and experimental styles (generally not exceeding 50 pages).

POETRY: Poems in traditional and experimental styles but no light verse (up to 20 pages).

PROSE: Literary nonfiction in traditional and experimental styles (generally not exceeding 50 pages).

DRAMA: Short plays in traditional and experimental styles (generally not exceeding 50 pages).

No cover letter is necessary. Your submission will be judged on its own merits. If you do send a letter, please include your publication credits. You may submit a legible photocopy. Unless a SASE is enclosed with your submission, you will not hear from us unless we are interested in publishing your manuscript. We try to reply within 4 to 12 weeks. Unsolicited manuscripts are welcome between August 15 and May 15.

Rates for individuals: $10.00 (1 yr.); $20.00 (2 yrs.); $30.00 (3 yrs.)

Rates for institutions: $10.00 (1 yr.); $20.00 (2 yrs.); $30.00 (3 yrs.)

Note: Add $4.00 per year for subscriptions outside of the USA.

Sample copies: $6.00 (Outside the USA add $2.00)

Prices for back issues and special issues available upon request. Please make checks payable to: *Alaska Quarterly Review.*

Categories: Fiction—Nonfiction—Poetry

CONTACT: Editor
Material: All
University of Alaska Anchorage, 3211 Providence Dr.
Anchorage AK 99508
Phone: 907-786-6916
Fax: 907-786-6916
Website: aqr.uaa.alaska.edu

Archaeology

Archaeology magazine is one of two publications of the Archaeological Institute of America. While our sister publication, the *American Journal of Archaeology*, is widely read in the academic world, Archaeology shares this world of discovery with a general audience. Our circulation is 225,000.

Our readers are well-read, well-traveled professionals interested in global history, discovery, culture and adventure. They are acutely aware of the fact that archaeology often corrects and rewrites history, and provides a voice to peoples whom often have had no presence in the historical record.

Authors include not only professional journalists but professional archaeologists as well. If you are a scientist interested in writing about your research for *Archaeology*, see below for tips and suggestions on writing for a general audience.

What we publish:

Our feature—length articles cover all corners of the globe, from frozen settlements in Alaska to ancient temples on South Asian islands. Archaeology isn't just about digging, and we're always looking for a new angle on a subject. Recent articles (which generally range from 1,000 to 3,500 words) have covered such diverse topics as how to make a mummy, the terror of Moche ritual sacrifice, cultural heritage in Afghanistan under the Taliban, objects featured in the odd paintings of Hieronymous Bosch that have been found in excavations of his hometown, how increased tourism has boosted archaeological investigation in Old Havana, and royal nomad burials in Kazakhstan; as well as photo essays on Angkor Wat, the artifacts of the steel industry, and Australian rock art; and profiles of people who have made great contributions to archaeology, from volcanologists to tree-ring specialists to Mayanists to novelists. Archaeology encompasses the full breadth of human history—there's a lot out there; don't be afraid to think outside the box.

Along with new archaeological discoveries, our news department publishes short (250 to 500 word) articles on criminal, environmental, and political developments that impact global heritage. Significant or exclusive archaeological news is featured in our 1,000-1,500-word *Special Report section*. Recent Special Reports have included an unlikely Israeli-Palestinian archaeological program that sprung up during the current Intifada, as well as prospects for archaeology and the preservation of cultural heritage in Pakistan during military actions in neighboring Afghanistan.

Our reviews department looks for short (250 to 500 word) articles on museums, books, television shows, movies, and websites of interest to our readers. While the material reviewed may not be purely archaeological in nature, it should have a strong archaeological element to it. Reviews should not simply summarize the material, but provide an critical evaluation.

Letter From… is often a personal rumination on a particular topic or site. Recent "Letters" have included a look at how metal detectorists and archaeologists in Britain have learned to cooperate, the ongoing dispute over construction work at Jerusalem's ancient Temple Mount, and a humble stone monument that keeps causing a lot of political friction between Japan and Korea. "Letters" are usually about 2,500-3,000 words in length.

Conversations is a one-page interview in Q&A format with someone who has made a considerable impact on the field of archaeology. The interview may explain the researcher's general approach to his or her subject, or concentrate on a specific, and often controversial, discovery or theory.

Field Note: features a compelling and intriguing photograph of someone (layperson or professional) involved in an archaeological activity, together with a 300-word first-person narrative of what the subject in the photograph is doing and thinking.

We do not accept fiction, poetry, or previously published articles.

Queries: Preliminary queries should be no more than one or two pages (500 words max.) in length and may be sent to the Editor-in-Chief, *Archaeology*, 36-36 33rd Street, Long Island City, NY 11106 or via email to editorial@archaeology.org. If you would like a reply to your query mailed to you, please enclose a self-addressed stamped envelope. We do not accept telephone queries. Check our online index (link) to make sure that we have not already published a similar article.

Your query should tell us the following: who you are, why you are qualified to cover the subject, how you will cover the subject, and why our readers would be interested in the subject. Clips and credentials are helpful.

While illustrations are not the responsibility of the author, it helps to give us a sense of how the article could be illustrated; if possible, email an example of 2 or 3 images that might accompany the article. Please do not email unusually large images or too many images at a time; we will request additional images if needed. Please do not mail us unsolicited diskettes, photographs, or transparencies as they will not be returned. If you do not have access to images, referrals to professional photographers with relevant material are appreciated.

Unsolicited queries should receive a reply within six to eight weeks. Commissioned articles found unsuitable for publication will receive a kill fee of one-quarter of the agreed payment price.

Please be familiar with our magazine and what we publish before you write up a query. For a sample copy of *Archaeology*, send a self-addressed stamped 9"x12" envelope to Guidelines, *Archaeology*, 36-36 33rd Street, Long Island City, NY 11106. Back issues can be ordered on our website.

Manuscripts: Accepted manuscripts should be sent electronically in a universal format, with no embedded images. The author's name, social security number and contact information must be included. Authors should be prepared to provide a list of publications and people consulted, along with contact information for each source. In addition, we request a list of five to seven general-interest books and/or websites, with a brief description of each, that may be of interest to readers who would like to learn more about the subject you've written about.

Style: Dates use A.D. and B.C., measures must be in miles and feet. When in doubt, refer to *The Chicago Manual of Style*.

Rights and payment: Payments range from $100 for a short news article to $1500 for a feature. We purchase non-exclusive worldwide publication rights for texts and photographs. News and review articles are included in full on the magazine's website; feature articles are abstracted. Material published in *Archaeology* may be reproduced on our web site as purchasable html or pdf format files, and via third-party

data bases such as EBSCO, in books of collected articles from Archaeology, and in translated form.

Things to keep in mind when writing for a general audience: This is not an academic publication. It's critically important to remember that less than one-half of one percent of our readers are professional archaeologists. Your proposed article must clearly spell out why the other 99.5% of our readers—bank tellers, doctors, librarians, corporate raiders—would be interested in your story. Some research—say, the variance in arsenic levels of metal objects produced in the Near East from the beginning to end of the Assyrian period—is a hard sell for a popular publication. On the other hand, such unlikely topics as Sumerian beer and a fish bone conference have made for entertaining and accessible articles that give our readers what they're looking for—a fresh and interesting perspective on human history.

Put yourself in the piece: Many scientists are consistently surprised by the fact that the general public is not just interested in what they do, but who they are. This is especially true for archaeologists: chances are you've traveled to a lot more interesting places, met a lot more interesting people, and had many more interesting adventures than most people. Nobody becomes an archaeologist to get rich, they do it for the experience; let the guy who grew up wanting to be an archaeologist but ended up a lawyer live vicariously through you!

Enable your readers to see through your eyes, but don't lose them in technical details. If you're writing about a fabulous discovery you made in the depths of the rain forest, bring the complete experience to your readers: what does the jungle look like, smell like? What sort of animals are about? What's camp like? If you only have a limited number of sentences to evoke a site for a lay reader, you're better off describing the looming mountains or sun-baked bricks rather than the fact that the 4.5x10-foot structure is 3.3 feet south of the 15-foot-square platform, which is 10 feet from the two cooking pits, each averaging 24 inches in diameter. Explain or avoid technical or local terms.

Engage the locals: If you're ready to tell us about the remarkable discoveries you've made in your ten years of work at site X, solicit thoughts and opinions from the people who live around site X. Does it give them a new perspective on where they live? Has it taught them something about themselves? How has having an archaeological expedition around for a decade affected their lives? What role will they have in managing the site you've excavated? Are they glad to see your noisy Land Rovers go?

Talk to us: *Archaeology* understands the importance of sharing your research with the public, and we've been helping archaeologists do just that for over fifty years. If you'd like to explore the possibility of publishing your work in the world's largest-circulation archaeology magazine, please contact us at editorial@archaeology.org and we'll put you in touch with the editor who can best assist you.

Categories: Nonfiction—Environment—Politics—Science—Archaeology

CONTACT: Editor-in-Chief
Material: All
36-36 33rd St.
Long Island City NY 11106
Phone: 718-472-3050
Fax: 718-472-3051
E-mail: edit@archaeology.org
Website: www.archaeology.org

Architectural Digest

Thank you for contacting *Architectural Digest* regarding how to submit to the magazine. Due to the volume of submissions we adhere to a strict policy.

Below is the best way to submit a project or person for publication consideration:

Our submission procedure requires that the designer, architect, resident (or representative) send 35mm transparencies, slides or prints to the attention of Ms. Paige Rense, Editor-in-Chief, 6300 Wilshire Boulevard, Los Angeles, CA 90048. *We do not accept anything via e-mail, disk, fax or cd-rom.*

For a private home, these images should cover the main rooms of the residence, (living room, dining room and master bedroom in particular) as well as a few exterior shots. We are not necessarily interested in bathrooms or kitchens unless they are extremely interesting or spectacular as they are rarely featured. Children's rooms and nurseries are not normally featured either.

Please include information on antiques, art works, and special design elements as well. Please also make sure information is typed and legible. Please also include a short bio on the owners of the property as well as the architect and or interior designer. With any and all submissions, we would like to know if the residence has been published previously.

To submit for an artist, photographs of different works as well as a bio will be sufficient. Please also send a list of your clients, designer and architects, who shop with you or have used your work. Send this information to Nina Farrell at the above address. I am sorry to say that we do not feature commercial spaces, except for hotels, gardens and museums.

After the editors have carefully reviewed the images, the submitter will be notified of our decision. If selected for publication, we will assign a photographer and a writer to do the story. If not, all materials will be returned. We do not visit or 'scout' homes in person. Normally it takes at least seven months from the submission date for the article to be published.

This letter is not a solicitation for materials and *Architectural Digest* is not responsible for unsolicited photos and other submitted materials.

Thank you for your interest in *Architectural Digest* and please let me know if I may be of further assistance.

Categories: Nonfiction—Architecture

CONTACT: Ms. Paige Rense, Editor-in-Chief
Material: Architectural Reviews
CONTACT: Nina Farrell
Material: Artist Reviews
6300 Wilshire Blvd.
Los Angeles CA 90048
Website: www.condenet.com/mags/archdigest

Area Development

Area Development is an economic development publication. It has consistently maintained a quality of editorial unmatched by any other magazine in this field. Writers for *Area Development* should have an understanding of its advertising market and readership to avoid submission of unsuitable material.

Area Development's advertising market consists of countries, states, provinces, counties, cities, utilities, railroads, industrial and business parks, industrial real estate firms, port authorities, foreign-trade zones, enterprise zones, and location specialists/ consultants. These advertisers are in *Area Development* because they want to attract industry to their areas. However, editorial in *Area Development* is not directed towards its advertisers.

Editorial in *Area Development* is directed to corporate decision-makers responsible for selecting sites and planning facilities for their companies. The magazine's more than 40,000 readers are primarily chief executives of industrial corporations. Feature articles must be useful to them in making decisions involving expansion or relocation. A basic guideline for editorial is stated in the magazine's masthead: "sites and facility planning." *This broad statement covers various factors including the following:*

- Labor availability and costs
- Availability of raw materials
- Infrastructure (highways, rail service, airports, ocean ports, inland ports and waterways)
- Proximity to (and association with) colleges and universities
- Utilities (electricity and gas availability and costs)
- Financing and incentives
- Training of employees
- Taxes
- Quality-of-life factors (schools, housing, cultural opportunities, recreational facilities)
- Availability of land and facilities for future expansion
- Community acceptance and relations
- Government requirements and controls
- Telecommunications requirements and services
- Access to markets
- Security (crime prevention, fire protection)
- Support services for constructing and maintaining plants and equipment
- Pollution controls and environmental regulations
- Legislation affecting economic development
- Working with architects, construction companies, and construction management firms
- Technical equipment (such as robotics and CAD/CAM) when it is a factor in site selection and facility planning.
- Start-up and operating costs

When writing feature articles for *Area Development*, it is necessary to avoid blatant promotional or "puff" material. It is also necessary to avoid negative comments about any areas or comparisons of areas. With a few exceptions, *Area Development* does not publish case studies or information specifically about any area.

If there are any questions about the suitability of feature material for *Area Development*, please call the editor.

Categories: Business—Site and Facility Planning

CONTACT: Geraldine Gambale, Editor
Material: All
400 Post Ave.
Westbury NY 11590
Phone: 516-338-0900
Fax: 516-338-0100
E-mail: gerri@areadevelopment.com
Website: www.areadevelopment.com

Arizona Foothills Magazine

Formal guidelines not available. Please read a number of issues to ascertain the publication's style and needs.

Send queries to address below.

Categories: General Interest—Lifestyle—Regional

CONTACT: Melissa Castleman, Features Editor
Material: Features
CONTACT: Elizabeth Exline, Departments Editor
Material: Departments
8132 N. 87th Place
Scottsdale AZ 85258
Phone: 480-460-5203
Fax: 480-443-1517
E-mail: publishersassistant@azfoothillsmag.com
Website: www.azfoothillsmag.com

Arizona Highways

Arizona Highways is a monthly magazine that encourages travel to and within Arizona. It does this by featuring stories on places to go and things to do, on the state's unique scenic environment, on its flora and fauna, on its people and on the history and culture of the Old West. We use experience-based travel stories, rather than guidebook or list stories, and we particularly like adventure-travel stories and stories on Indian arts, crafts and customs.

CIRCULATION: The magazine sells about 350,000 copies monthly, mostly to subscribers outside Arizona (about 25 percent are in Arizona). The magazine circulates in every state and in about two-thirds of the countries of the world.

AUDIENCE: Our typical reader is a 50-something person with the time, the inclination and the means to travel. Our subscribers are equally divided between men and women, are outdoor-oriented and have a strong interest in the Old West and in the arts, crafts and culture of Native Americans.

QUERIES: Nearly all the features and departments are free-lance written and photographed. And nearly all assignments result from written queries. We prefer query letters that are brief and to the point, by e-mail. The letter should detail the story, the angle or angles you will pursue; what makes this story important and useful for *Arizona Highways*; and why you are the person to write it. We do not accept queries for fiction, humor stories or Along the Way columns. For these, we must see the manuscript before making a decision to purchase. If you include a SASE, we normally respond to queries within a month. Replies to manuscript submissions may take longer. No phone queries, please.

BREAKING IN: The easiest way to break into the magazine for writers new to us is to (1) propose short items for the Off-ramp section, (2) contribute short humor anecdotes for the Humor page, or (3) submit 650-word pieces for the Along the Way column.

DEPARTMENTS: The maximum word length and fees paid for departments are: Along the Way (650 words, $450), Back Road Adventure (1,000 words, $900), Hike of the Month (500 words, $275), Humor (200 words, $50), Off-ramp (200 words, $50), Destination (1,000 words, $750). Check the magazine for content of these departments.

FEATURES: Feature stories should be between 1,200 and 1,800 words (two-page stories should be 650 to 800 words), depending on the subject. Travel stories, cover stories and lead stories pay $1 a word. Other features pay 55 cents a word.

TRAVEL STORIES: Our travel stories are of three types: travel-destination (involves experience at a specific location/tourist attraction), travel adventure (involves hiking, climbing, boating or some other physical activity) and travel history (involves a backdrop or running theme of a historical event/person). We have a style for travel stories that is distinctly Arizona Highways. As this style starts with outstanding photographs that not only depict an area but interpret it as well, our travel stories need not dwell on descriptions of what can be seen.

Concentrate instead on the experience of being there, whether the destination is a hiking trail, a ghost town, a trout stream, a forest or an urban area. What thoughts and feelings did the experience evoke? What was happening? What were the mood and comportment of the people? What were the sounds and smells? What was the feel of the area? Did bugs get into the sleeping bag? Were the crows curious about intruders? Could you see to the bottom of the lake, and if so, what was there? We want to know why you went there, what you experienced and what impressions you came away with.

These experiences and impressions should be focused into a story with a beginning, middle and end, and it should be as evocative and interesting as you can make it. We do not want a rambling series of thoughts or vignettes, diary entries or a travelogue (a piece that begins in the morning, goes hour-by-hour through the day and ends in the evening). We want a story that opens by introducing us to a story line or theme, then develops the tale and finally concludes. We want an ending, a logical conclusion to the story we are telling. Just stopping the story won't do.

Because the piece will not be a general guide to an area, we need a short sidebar detailing the service information. (Some departments also require this sidebar.)

The sidebar, called "When You Go," should explain how to get to the destination, where to stay, restrictions, special requirements and what to see and do in the area. It also should include places to call for further information. (You will receive a separate format sheet with contractual paperwork.)

APPROACH: Our style is informal yet polished, with a readable, literary quality. The story should use the techniques of the fiction writer to create a narrative the reader will be unable to put down. We do not want choppy, shallow/Sunday-supplement treatments. First-person or third-person narrative is okay; present tense, fine. Use strong verbs in the active voice and avoid overuse of the verb "to be" in all its forms, especially "it was" and "there are."

CONTRACT AND PAYMENT: We buy first print rights, and we expect original work. Payment is 35 cents to $1 a word, on acceptance. For travel stories as well as cover stories and lead stories (determined by the editor), we pay $1 a word.

SUBMISSIONS: We require written queries, preferably on page; no unsolicited manuscripts (except for consideration for Fiction or Along the Way). Send all queries to Arizona Highways, Query Editor, 2039 W. Lewis Ave., Phoenix, AZ 85009. Send short humorous anecdotes to Humor Department, editor@arizonahighways.com. Queries may be sent via e-mail to: queryeditor@arizonahighways.com. Effective March 2002.

Categories: Adventure—Culture—Environment—History—Regional—Travel—Western

CONTACT: Query Editor
<queryeditor@arizonahighways.com >
Material: Queries
CONTACT: Humor Dept. <editor@arizonahighways.com>
Material: Short humorous anecdotes
CONTACT: Photography Editor
Material: Photographs
2039 W. Lewis Ave.
Phoenix AZ 85009-9988
Website: www.arizhwys.com

Arkansas Review
A Journal of Delta Studies

Arkansas Review: A Journal of Delta Studies focuses on the seven-state Mississippi River Delta. Interdisciplinary in scope, we welcome contributions from all the humanities and social sciences, including anthropology, art history, folklore studies, history, literature, musicology, political science, and sociology. Articles should be aimed at a general academic audience and follow the format specified in the Chicago Manual of Style, 14th edition. Submit articles in hard copy and on disk to the General Editor.

Photographs and other visual materials to accompany articles are encouraged. Do not submit originals until after the article has been accepted. When submitted, photographs should be black-and-white prints no larger that 8"x10" in either glossy or matte finish.

Arkansas Review also publishes creative material, especially fiction, poetry, essays, and visual art that evoke or respond to the Delta cultural and natural experience.

All material sent to the *Arkansas Review* will be refereed by the relevant editor and at least one other reviewer—in the case of articles, a specialist in the field of the article. We will attempt to respond to submissions within four months.

Contributors may also want to submit proposals for special issues of the *Review*, ones dealing with specific Delta topics. Such proposals should be sent to the General Editor.

Contributors will receive three (3) copies of the issue of the *Arkansas Review* in which their work appears and a years subcription.

Categories: Fiction—Nonfiction—African-American—Arts—Culture—History—Literature—Multicultural—Music—Poetry—Regional—Short Stories

CONTACT: Tom Williams, General Editor and Creative Materials Editor
Material: All written submissions
CONTACT: Kim Vickrey, Art Editor

Material: Visual Art
PO Box 1890
State University AR 72467-1890
Phone: 870-972-3043
Fax: 870-972-2795
E-mail: delta@astate.edu
Website: www.clt.astate.edu/arkreview

Army Magazine

Length

Features are typically 1,000 to 1,500 words long. Shorter articles such as sidebars to features or photo essays are 250 to 500 words.

Include a brief explanation of why your submission (if it is a feature article) is timely, innovative or important.

Book reviews, guest columns (such as "Sounding Off" and articles for "Front & Center") are preferably 500 to 1,000 words long. We do not accept unsolicited book reviews. If you are interested in book reviewing, write us regarding your areas of interest and expertise. Send writing samples also.

Format

Please send your article on a CD or other media (disk), via email as a word attachment, or typed in the body of an email (last resort), and also send a double-spaced hard copy (in the case of sending media). Indicate the type of software used if not standard Microsoft Office™. For the article itself, use only standard, double spaced word processing (like a term paper, but with no footnotes). Do not insert pictures or graphics in the article; however, you may certainly suggest insertion points for images if they are of importance. Ensure that images (see below) are clearly marked so that any references to them are clear.

Photographs and Other Artwork (see next page for electronic image details)

"Front and Center" essays usually don't run with images. For features, however, we are interested in seeing photographs or artwork that may enhance your article. We can use hardcopy black and white or color prints as well as color slides. **Please include caption and credit information for each photograph.** Digital photo and caption information is explained below.

Headlines

We take your suggestions for headlines seriously. Please send headline suggestions with your article.

Author Biographies

Biographical information should be submitted with the text of the article. Include as much information as possible, preferably a vita.

Submissions

Please do not send us articles that have been submitted or published elsewhere. We do not accept simultaneous submissions.

Send all letters of query and submissions to:
The Editor in Chief
Army Magazine
2425 Wilson Blvd.
Arlington, VA 22201
E-mail: armymag@ausa.org

Electronic Images

—NO POWERPOINT SUBMISSIONS—We would prefer that electronic images be supplied on either a CD or zip disk, but can accept photos via e-mail. Each image must be sent as a stand-alone graphic file. In other words, if you have image files (pictures) contained in a POWERPOINT presentation, don't send us the presentation, but send us the original image files that were inserted into the presentation. Similarly, PLEASE DO NOT IMBED IMAGES IN A WORD DOCUMENT or send retouched images (like collages or pictures that have had text or other graphics added to them). Accompanying caption information is also critical; see below for particulars.

For the technically inclined, the resolution for photographic images that appear in ARMY magazine is 300ppi. This means that we require high resolution digital images to ensure quality reproduction in print. We can accept Photoshop EPS, TIFF and JPEG files. The following chart is a guide for submitting electronic images for publication in the magazine, and is based on **CMYK EPS** files. It shows the file size necessary to print at common dimensions in the magazine.

File Size	Size in Magazine	Approx. Size in Pixels
6.5 MB	quarter page	1530 x 1115
13 MB	half page	2160 x 1570
32 MB	full page bleed	2475 x 3400

For the layman, a simple rule of thumb is that high resolution image files are at least .5 MB in size, and usually closer to 1 MB; if your image file is smaller than this, then it probably won't reproduce for print. Or put another way, once compressed to meet resolution requirements, a standard 72dpi image shrinks to 1/3 its size (so a low resolution image has to be very large to work, but a high resolution image will hold its size or can actually be expanded to fit a space).

Captions

To ensure best use, each image should have its own caption. Include all captions in a **separate** word file, clearly indicating which captions go with which images. Do not imbed photos and captions in a word document together. Do not use photo software to overwrite captions or to place labels on images themselves. Descriptive file names are helpful, but they are not substitutes for good captions. Avoid acronyms if possible, and spell them out if used. Please make your captions complete sentences and as specific to the image and what is depicted in it as possible (people, equipment, activity, place, etc).

EXAMPLE SUBMISSION WITH IMAGES: A typical submission, with 3 images, would have the following five files:

Item	Form	Example
Article*	Word document	(your file name).doc
Captions	Word document captions	(your file name).doc
Picture	jpeg, tiff	image1.jpeg
Picture	jpeg, tiff	image2.jpeg
Picture	jpeg, tiff	image3.jpeg

*author bio information included at the end of the article

Art&Antiques

Art & Antiques

Proposal Tips

Art & Antiques is the authoritative source for elegant, sophisticated coverage of the treasures collectors love, the places to discover them and the unique ways collectors use them to enrich their environments. From fine art to folk art, from Louis XIV to Louis Tiffany, *Art & Antiques'* award-winning articles and lush photography meld the past to the present to reflect the passion of collecting.

Submission Guidelines: Unless noted above, query first with visuals of the subject. No article will be considered without scouting shots (pre-printed material is accepted, but slides or transparencies are better. All material will be returned.) Editorial lead-time: 6 months. Payment upon acceptance.

Unless otherwise noted, send proposals to Patti Verbanas, Managing Editor, *Art & Antiques* Magazine, 2100 Powers Ferry Rd., Ste. 300, Atlanta, GA 30339.

No phone calls, please.

Ideas pitched for any of these departments are also considered for feature treatment.

***Art & Antiques* Update**

Definition: A mix of trend coverage and timely news of the issues and personalities that move the world of art and antiques. Word length: 100-350.

Visuals not necessary for pitch, but must be attainable if assigned.

We are seeking these pitches on an on-going basis.

Send proposals for this section directly to Rebecca Grilliot at rgrilliot@billian.com or to Rebecca via regular mail.

Buying Buzz

Definition: A monthly, 300-word column that focuses on emerging collecting trends. Writers interview top dealers and auctioneers. While this column does report post-sale results from a few key events, its goal is to provide collectors with practical information rather than to merely report the latest market news. If a writer attends a fair and learns from several sources that a certain type of furniture is likely to skyrocket in value, those interviews and related sales figures could form the basis for an excellent Buying Buzz column. A general post-mortem on the fair itself would be of less interest. Writers are responsible for providing a few high-quality images of artworks/antiques, along with the appropriate caption and credit information. Send proposals for this section directly to Rebecca Grilliot at rgrilliot@billian.com or to Joel via regular mail. Fee: $300.

Review

Definition: A criticisms on a variety of worldwide art exhibitions throughout the year. If it is a European show, it must have a destination in the United States. Visuals preferred, but not necessary. Word length: 600-800.

Value Judgments

Definition: Experts in various fields highlight popular to undiscovered areas of collecting and discuss crucial aspects of connoisseurship. Provides readers with an in-depth look at specific categories of high-end art and antiques collecting. Pitches should include recent auction results and why now is an important time to report on this collectible. This is a popular department; competition is stiff. Visuals required. Word length: 600-900.

Emerging Artists

Definition: This department highlights an artist on the cusp of discovery. What "unknowns" should readers be watching? Send the artist's c.v. and 7-15 slides or cards to show work. Entrants are juried by an international team of art scholars, and response time can reach 10-12 months. Word length: 600-800.

Features

Definition: Features are expanded, more in-depth articles that fit into any of the other categories noted here. We publish one "interior design with art and antiques" focus feature a month. Visuals required for all feature pitches. Word length: 1,000-2,000.

A&A Insider

Definition: A "How-To" column for beginning an expert collectors on how to collect and collecting issues. Examples include: "How To Collect Contemporary Art," "Best Lighting Techniques," "How to Find an Art Advisor," etc. Word length: 800–900. Fee: $750.

Discoveries

Definition: Art & Antiques takes to the road to seek out collections in lesser-known museums and homes that are open to the public. It is similar to the Traveling Collector, but without shopping as the focus. In your proposal note why now (issue month) is the time to visit? Visuals required. Word length: 800-900.

Studio Session

Definition: A peek into the studio of an artist who currently is hot or is a revered veteran that allows the reader to watch the artist in action. In your proposal, note a timely angle to the story and if we should look at the pitch for a particular month). This is a very competitive department. Visuals required. Word length: 800-900.

Then & Now

Definition: Highlights the best reproductions being created today and the craftspeople behind the work. In your proposal, tell us the artists who would be discussed as the "Thens" and the contemporary artists/manufacturers who are the "Nows." Visuals required. Word length: 800-900.

World View

Definition: A report on major art and antiques news worldwide. Visuals preferred, but not necessary. Do let us know where we would be able to obtain images and how easy that will be. Word length: 600-800.

Traveling Collector

Definition: Guides readers to the hottest art and antiques destinations.

Featured are the best in local art and antiques, and unique places and events of interest to readers in their many travels. Destinations are selected one time a year (during Editorial Calendar meeting in May); suggestions are welcomed. Visuals necessary. In the past, the winning destinations have been those where the writer sends us a contact list of the galleries and antiques shops that can be profiled. Word length: 800-1,800.

Essay

Definition: A forum for the writer's opinion, expressed within the magazine's guidelines. It is a first-person piece that tackles a topic in a non-academic way. Can send completed manuscript. Visuals preferred, but not necessary. Word length: 600-800.

Categories: Nonfiction—Antiques—Arts

**CONTACT: Patti Verbanas, Managing Editor
Material: All
TransWorld Publishing, Inc.
2100 Powers Ferry Rd. Ste. 300
Altanta GA 30339
Website: www.artantiquesmag.com**

ART PAPERS

Art Papers

GENERAL GUIDELINES

We prefer proposals to completed articles. For features, the proposal should be 125—250 words; for columns and reviews, 50 words is plenty. Tell us what and who you want to discuss, and what you plan to say. If you haven't written for ART PAPERS before, please include two brief writing samples (1,000—2,000 words), together with a short bio (40 words) describing your background and interests. We evaluate proposals based on quality, appropriateness and available space, and strive to notify writers of a decision within two months. Proposals must be submitted by email to editor@artpapers.org. We will not consider queries not accompanied by writing samples.

If we accept your proposal, we will negotiate a mutually acceptable length, deadline and fee. We reserve the right to terminate our acceptance of your proposal without compensation if we discover you have misrepresented yourself, or if the final form of the article diverges markedly from the agreed-upon topic, format or deadline.

TYPES OF ARTICLES

Features range from 2,400 to 2,700 words, and express fully developed viewpoints about a particular work, artist or trend.

The staff of ART PAPERS, Inc. appreciates the value of historical investigation and academic work. However, ART PAPERS does not print densely theoretical arguments or detailed archival research. Nonetheless, we expect our writers to develop and support their theses rigorously, and to have a sophisticated understanding of any philosophies, histories or theoretical concepts they invoke.

Columns in ART PAPERS cover a wide range of topics. These columns differ from those of most other magazines in that none of them appear regularly and they do not "belong" to any one writer. Rather, our columns offer opportunities for writers to address topics of current interest in brief, exploratory essays. These pieces generally are around 1,000 words, with four pictures.

Reviews cover solo and group shows of regional, national or international significance. We are especially interested in regionally significant artists who have not yet reached a national or international audience. Reviews are 600 words when covering the work of a single artist and 800 words when discussing the work of more than one artist (in both cases, plus or minus ten words). Faculty and student exhibitions do not constitute acceptable group shows.

CONFLICT OF INTEREST

a) The editors will not consider submissions in which a writer: writes about his/her work, the work of someone with whom the writer has a personal relationship, the work of someone with whom the writer has a financial relationship, any gallery that represents his/her work, any relative, any gallery institutionally related to the organization employing the writer or a colleague in the institution employing the writer.

b) The editors will not consider submissions by a writer who has been hired to write a catalogue essay for the same artist or gallery within the past year. The exception, to be determined by the editors, shall be a curator who has shown an artist's work and whose expertise on the artist would be considered an advantage in writing the article.

c) The editors will not consider submissions by a writer whom the gallery or artist has paid or commissioned to write the article in question. Suggestions from galleries are permitted but the editors make the final decision.

d) The editors will not consider a submission by a writer who collects the work of the artist in question.

e) Writers may not write reviews or articles for ART PAPERS on exhibitions that they already have covered for other publications.

f) The editors shall decide whether to cover exhibitions curated by, featuring or including the work of any writer for ART PAPERS.

Categories: Arts

CONTACT: Sylvie Fortin, Editor-in-Chief
Material: All
PO Box 5748
Atlanta GA 31107
Phone: 404-588-1837 ext 20
Fax: 404-588-1836
E-mail: editor@artpapers.org
Website: www.artpapers.org

Art Times

WRITER'S GUIDELINES FOR FIRST SERIAL RIGHTS

FICTION: Short Stories up to 1,500 words. All subjects but no excessive sex, violence or racist themes. Our prime requisite is high literary quality and professional presentation. Pay $25 upon publication, six extra copies of issue in which work appears and one year's complimentary subscription beginning with that issue. We do not publish reprints.

POETRY: Up to 20 lines. All topics; all forms. Same requisite high quality as above. Pay is six extra copies of issue in which work appears and one year's complimentary subscription beginning with that issue. We do not publish reprints. We do not encourage simultaneous submissions of poetry.

(Note: We are usually on about a 36-month lead for fiction; 24-month lead for poetry.)

Readers of ART TIMES are generally over 40, literate and arts conscious. Our distribution is heaviest in New York State (along the "Hudson River Corridor" from Albany into Manhattan). We are sold by subscription; copies may be obtained free at selected art galleries. Subscription copies are mailed across the US and abroad. In addition to short fiction and poetry, feature essays on the arts make up the bulk of our editorial. (Note: Articles and Essays are not solicited).

Sample copy: $1.75 plus 9"x12" SASE with 3 first class stamps.

Categories: Arts Crafts/Hobbies Culture Dance Drama Entertainment—Film/Video—Literature—Multicultural—Music—Poetry—Short Stories—Theatre

CONTACT: Submissions Editor
Material: All
PO Box 730
Mt. Marion NY 12456-0730
Phone: 845-246-6944
Fax: 845-246-6944
E-mail: info@arttimesjournal.com

Artemis Magazine
Science and Fiction for a Space-Faring Age

About the Magazine: *Artemis Magazine* publishes science for an educated audience interested in space development, flight, and travel and the best in near-term, near-Earth, hard science fiction. Formed as an adjunct to the Artemis Project (a commercial venture to build a lunar colony), *Artemis Magazine* and its parent company, LRC Publications, are independent entities.

Science: Articles should generally be limited to 5,000 words. We're looking for articles related to the devvelopment of lunar and near-Earth industries, including the role of the Moon in further development of space travel. Remember that the readers, in general, want to know how to get to, build, and live in a lunar colony. Target your work toward a general audience of educated, but not necessarily technically sophisticated, people. Include charts, tables, or photos if necessary, and explain them in the text.

Illustrations should be separate from the text, with captions on a separate page.

Fiction: We're looking for near-term, near-Earth, hard science fiction. As a supporter of the Artemis Project, we're looking especially for stories that aim at lunar and space development, but a good story is a good story. We want well-plotted, character-oriented stories. Technical accuracy is an absolute requirement, but don't bog down the story with unnecessary technical detail; remember that in good "science fiction", both terms ought to receive equal emphasis.

We'll consider any length up to 15,000 words. Shorter is better.

Mechanics: This is standard: on the first page, put your name, address(es), and phone number in the upper left corner; put the word count in the upper right corner.

Print your manuscript double-spaced on 8.5" x 11" paper (or the local equivalent) in a legible font with 1-inch margins all around. Do not put it in a binder or staple the pages together. You don't need a separate title page. On every page after the first, in the upper right-hand corner, put your name, the page number, and enough of the title that we can reassemble your manuscript after we drop it on the floor and get it mixed up with a bunch of other papers.

Don't use your word processor's ability to do fancy fonts, italics, or typesetting. Simply underline text to be italicized.

Include an "about the author" paragraph with your manuscript.

Include a self-addressed envelope with your manuscript with sufficient postage to get it back to you. If you don't want your manuscript back, mark it DISPOSABLE and include a business-size self-addressed, stamped envelope for our reply (it's very difficult to fold a check into a postcard). From outside the US, include International Reply Coupons. We will not respond to any submissions without return postage. And no, we do NOT accept electronic submissions.

Art: We need artists to illustrate articles and stories. Send disposable photocopies of examples of your work along with notes about prior publication and the type of art you prefer to do.

Cartoons and stock submissions are welcome.

Payment: We pay be on acceptance, 3 to 5 cents a word, for science and fiction.

About the Artemis Project: The Artemis Project is a commercial venture to establish a permanent lunar colony and to exploit the Moon's resources for profit. Our strategy for this project is to use its entertainment value as much as possible to pay for its initial development. The Project is sponsored by The Lunar Resources Company. For more information on the Project, check out the web site at http://www.asi.org.

A final note: These guidelines describe what we want. If you can write something that fits this bill, we want you. However, we're also open-minded enough to be interested in a story that contradicts everything written here, and yet won't let us reject it. You want us to read your manuscript: save us both some time, and read the magazine first.

Categories: Fiction—Nonfiction—Adventure—Agriculture—Architecture—Arts—Aviation—Business—Careers—Cartoons—Children—Comedy—Computers—Conservation—Consumer—Cooking—Crafts/Hobbies—Ecology—Economics—Education—Electronics—Engineering—Entertainment—Environment—Fashion—Food/Drink—Games—General Interest—Government—Health—History—Hobbies—Interview—Law—Lifestyle—Literature—Military—Money & Finances—Outdoors—Photography—Physical Fitness—Politics—Psychology—Recreation—Recreation Vehicles—Reference—Regional—Satire—Science—Science Fiction—Short Stories—Society—Software—Sports/Recreation—Technical—Trade—Travel—Aerospace

CONTACT: The Editor
Material: All
Ian Randal Strock, Editor
Material:1380 E. 17th St., Suite 201
Brooklyn NY 11230-6011
Phone: 718-375-3862

ARTFUL DODGE

Artful Dodge
The College of Wooster

Even from the beginning, *Artful Dodge* has strived to expand the wide but not infinite boundaries of American literature. We have developed an ongoing interest in translation, especially from Eastern Europe and Third World, and have published well-received special sections on poetry from the Polish underground and the Middle East. One of our more recent issues, *Artful Dodge* 31/32, featured a section of poetry written and translated from the Native American Ahtna by John Smelcer accompanied by an eye-opening essay entitled "Poems from a Vanishing Language."

Rather than looking at these other literatures as rare exotica, we recognize that American literature right now is particularly open to writing form other languages, to fresh air from mythologies beyond our huge but not infinite cultural and metaphorical borders. We are always on the look out for excellent translations of contemporary literature.

However, *Artful Dodge*'s doors are open to much more than just translations or works rooted in foreign culture. What it boils down to is this: *Artful Dodge* has always been attracted to writing with a sense of place and looks for work that combines the aesthetic and the human in fresh, unexpected ways. However, don't ask us what that statement means—all we can say is that the work we print shows awareness of the cultural landscape out of which it comes, the words and deeds of people, the language of the bus stop and bar. It involves an illumination of the particular and the concrete, and the transforming of this here-at-hand to the level of the permanent, the mythic. This can be accomplished in ways as diverse as William Carlos Williams' wheelbarrows, Elizabeth Bishop's maps, Langston Hughes' rivers, or William S.

Burroughs' disrobed lunches. But some sort of interplay between focus and transcendence must be at work.

So, read *Artful Dodge* to get an idea of what we print. If you can't afford a copy, then ask your local library to order a subscription—it might as well be *Artful Dodge* (or some other literary journal) sitting on those shelves instead of Fortune and Cosmo and Gourmet. And, after you've taken a look at the world around you, at the words surrounding you, take a deep breath and send us your work.

Some basic guidelines for submitting work to *Artful Dodge* are as follows: SASE, typed manuscripts; simultaneous submissions are okay but no previously published material; allow one week to six months for response. Please send no more than 30 pages of prose or six poems, though long poems are encouraged. We pay in copies, plus $5 a page, thanks to support from the Ohio Arts Council. Translations should be submitted with original texts. We also prefer that you indicate you have copyright clearance and/or author permission.

Categories: Fiction—Poetry

CONTACT: Daniel Bourne, Editor
Material: All
Dept. of English, The College of Wooster
Wooster OH 44691
Phone: 330-263-2577
Website: www.wooster.edu/artfuldodge

Arthritis Today

About *Arthritis Today*

Arthritis Today is an award-winning, national consumer health magazine published by the Arthritis Foundation. It is written for the 43 million Americans who have arthritis or an arthritis-related condition as well as for the millions of other people whose lives are touched by these conditions. The magazine is a comprehensive and authoritative source of information about arthritis research, treatment, self-care and emotional coping.

Our magazine has a diverse audience because there are more than 100 arthritis-related conditions, including osteoarthritis, rheumatoid arthritis, fibromyalgia and lupus. These conditions can affect anyone of any age, from children and young adults to middle-aged and older people. Our magazine speaks to all of these groups.

The editorial content of *Arthritis Today* is designed to empower people with arthritis to live healthier lives overall, emphasizing upbeat, informative articles that provide practical advice and inspiration. Feature articles of approximately 1,000 to 4,000 words focus on treatment options, research advances, ways of coping with physical and emotional challenges, empowerment, and exercise. Our "Research Spotlight" section reports on research advances in the understanding and treatment of arthritis, based on studies from respected medical journals and scientific meetings. The magazine also includes shorter items that address the whole person, such as brief items of 150 to 300 words on general health and medical topics, travel, nutrition, hobbies, leisure and relationships. We also include personal, inspirational essays of 500 to 1,200 words written by people who have arthritis-related conditions. Each issue is extensively reviewed by our medical editor, by the Arthritis Foundation's medical director and by individual experts on our medical advisory board.

What we're looking for in a freelance writer

We prefer to work with professional writers who have experience writing for other consumer magazines, but will consider pieces – specifically first-person accounts of life with arthritis or a related condition – from people who have not been previously published.

What we need from you

A resume and nonreturnable clips of articles you've written that have been published in other consumer magazines plus a query for article(s) you are interested in writing.

Queries should include the following information:

• a general synopsis of the idea and the specific angle to be addressed in the article;

• research or other material you plan to cite to support the article;

• experts, such as researchers, health professionals or real people, whom you plan to interview and quote in the article.

When you can expect to hear from us

After reviewing your query, the editors will respond within six to eight weeks. At that time, we may ask for more details or request the manuscript on speculation.

A caveat

We prefer not to receive unsolicited manuscripts or telephone queries.

Tell Us Your Personal Story

Hardly a day goes by that we at Arthritis Today don't hear from readers who want a chance to share a personal story about how they've encountered – and bested – arthritis.

Categories: Nonfiction—Consumer—Health

CONTACT: Assistant Editor
Material: All
1330 West Peachtree St.
Atlanta GA 30309
Phone: 404-872-7100
Fax: 404-872-9559
E-mail: writers@arthritis.org. (queries)
E-mail: my.story@arthritis.org. (poem or personal essay)
Website: www.arthritis.org/resources/arthritistoday

The Artist's Magazine

Article Submission Guidelines

The Artist's Magazine is a monthly publication for working artists. Unlike coffee-table magazines for art collectors, *The Artist's Magazine* is a nuts-and bolts, instructional resource for the working artist in search of artistic and professional success. We show readers how other artists have dealt with various issues-painting techniques, media and materials, design and composition, specific subjects, special effects, marketing and other business topics.

Opportunities for professional artists and writers to work with *The Artist's Magazine* lie basically with feature articles. Freelance writers must have the ability to write from the artist's viewpoint using the language of art.

Where to Start

Artists and writers should query in advance rather than send unsolicited manuscripts. Queries should include:

• A cover letter giving us a clear picture of the slant and purpose of the proposed article (including a possible title and subtitle).

• The artist's résumé, credits and approximately 8-12 slides or larger transparencies of his or her work. (Note: All slides should be in protective plastic slide sleeves.)

• The writer's résumé, credits and photocopies of no more than two clips (if different than the artist).

• A self-addressed stamped envelope (SASE) large enough and with sufficient postage for returning the slides.

Note: We cannot accept digital images on disk or sent by e-mail, or a referral to an artist's Web site, in lieu of slides or transparencies. Our publication decisions are based heavily on the quality of the artwork submitted, and we've found that slides and transparencies capture the color, depth and texture of a painting in a way that digital images cannot. The only exception to this requirement would be in the case of digitally-created art, but we very rarely feature computer-generated art in *The Artist's Magazine.*

Let your query demonstrate that you know where you want to go and how to get there. If we like your idea, we'll do one of two things: 1) ask for a comprehensive, detailed outline or 2) assign the piece to you.

We will attempt to respond to your query within three months.

All About Features

Our most consistent need is for instructional articles written in the artist's voice, rather than in newspaper-style reporting or Q&A interview styles. All features should emphasize the how-to: how an artist works with a medium, solves problems and conducts business. You're talking to artists, not the general public, so techniques and methods must be specifically explained and demonstrated. Writers should try to avoid clichés and concentrate on basic, practical, step-by-step instruction with a friendly, conversational tone. The goal is for the reader to be able to pick up a brush (or whatever) and duplicate the described process or technique after reading the article.

Feature themes will generally fall into the following categories:

• Genres of art, including basic, new or unusual techniques of still life, landscape, portraiture or wildlife painting. Example: 10 ways to arrange a still life.

• Specific objects, such as flowers, animals, trees—objects commonly found in paintings and drawings. Example: the visual structure in painting a sky.

• Basic application techniques and how they're used with different media. Examples: color mixing in watercolors, drybrushing with acrylics.

• Special effects, covering new or time-tested techniques in any one medium. Example: using stencils with water-based media.

• Introduction to unusual media, including the necessary tools, materials and basic techniques of mastering a medium. Examples: alkyds, encaustics, casein.

• Techniques of the masters—how a great artist created his or her works. Example: paint like the Impressionists.

• New markets for art sales, including the scope and potential of market categories, and how an artist can break in. Examples: religious market, romance book cover market.

• Business articles on any subject that the beginning artist needs to master to become a professional. Examples: recordkeeping, pricing, selling, portfolio building, etc.

One tip: The Artist's Magazine typically deals with realistic and semi-realistic painting; we rarely feature abstract art. Therefore, we suggest that you peruse recent copies of the magazine and compare them to the work of the artist you have in mind before you send in your submission.

Feature articles typically range from 1,200 to 2,200 words. Pay is $300 for most features. Articles are usually used within one year of acceptance.

Manuscripts should be submitted as typed, double-spaced hard copy and on a 3-1/2" disk if possible, and should include captions, author bio and artist bio. The artwork package should contain at least 8-12 slides or larger transparencies of the artist's work for use in illustrating the article. It should also include at least one set of progressives—a series of slides that show how a painting is developed from concept to finish; include at least four distinct steps per set. The slides/transparencies should be professionally shot, either by yourself or by a photographer; poorly shot artwork will not be reproducible. All slides should be correctly labeled with artist's name, address, medium, dimensions, title and indication of top and front. (For more information on correctly shooting slides of artwork, please see our Photography Guidelines.) A complete set of writer's guidelines will be provided upon acceptance of query. Slides and transparencies will be returned after publication of the article.

Inside Our Columns

Artists interested in submitting for a particular column should clearly indicate which one, both in the query letter and on the envelope. We recommend that potential contributors familiarize themselves with the structure and style of several recent columns before submitting. Queries should include a brief outline of the topic and how it would be approached, illustrations and/or slides as appropriate, and an artist's résumé including any expertise or credentials especially relevant to the topic. Payment varies by column and length.

• Drawing Board covers basic drawing skills. Recent examples include improving your sketching techniques, using grids to improve composition, drawing realistic trees and grass, and rendering textural hair and fur.

• Color Corner focuses on how to use color effectively in your paintings. Some recent examples include tips for using white, possibilities for fleshtones, and how to make use of sedimentary colors.

• Landscape Basics deals with issues fundamental to landscape painting. Recent examples include autumn scenes, painting wind and rain, and painting mountains.

• Brushing Up is concerned with defining and illustrating art terms. Recent examples include pointillism, contour drawings and underpainting.

• The Business column deals with the business-related issues of artmaking. Recent examples include hanging art for shows, writing news releases, entering the greeting card market, and writing the artist's résumé.

For More Information

Query letters with art should be sent to: Editor, *The Artist's Magazine*, 4700 E. Galbraith Rd., Cincinnati OH 45236. Sample copies can be ordered by sending $6.50 per copy to: Back Issue Manager, *The Artist's Magazine*, PO Box 2031, Harlan IA 51593.

Categories: Nonfiction—Arts—Business—Painting

CONTACT: The Editor
Material: Queries
4700 E. Galbraith Rd.
Cincinnati OH 45236
Phone: 513-531-2690 ext. 1467
Fax: 513-531-2902
E-mail: TAMedit@fwpubs.com

The Asian Pacific American Journal

The Asian Pacific American Journal is now accepting submission. THERE IS NO SPECIFIC THEME — so send those essays, short stories, poems, plays and art pieces that have been ripening in the deepest caverns of your heart and mind.

Send four typed copies with your name, address, email and phone number on each piece (all pages must be numbered and double-spaced, only one story/essay per submission). Include cover letter with a list of submitted pieces, brief author bio and SASE for reply. Please send print-outs of manuscripts, no disks please. We do not take general submissions by email. Please send art in transparency or slide form. Due to the volume of submissions, manuscripts cannot be returned.

Categories: Nonfiction—Arts—Asian-American—Drama—Poetry—Short Stories

CONTACT: Editors
Material: All
16 West 32nd Street, Ste 10A
New York NY 10001
Phone: 212-228-7718
Fax: 212-228-7718
E-mail: apaj@aaww.org

Asimov's Science Fiction

PAYMENT & RIGHTS *Asimov's Science Fiction* magazine is an established market for science fiction stories. We pay on acceptance, and beginners get 6.0 cents a word to 7,500 words, 5.0 cents a word for stories longer than 12,500 words, and $450 for stories between those lengths. We seldom buy stories longer than 15,000 words, and we don't serialize novels. We pay $1 a line for poetry, which should not exceed 40 lines. We buy First English Language serial rights plus certain nonexclusive rights explained in our contract. We do not publish reprints, and we do not accept "simultaneous submissions," (stories sent at the same time to a publication other than Asimov's). Asimov's will consider material submitted by any writer, previously published or not. We've bought some of our best stories from people who have never sold a story before.

STORY CONTENT In general, we're looking for "character oriented" stories, those in which the characters, rather than the science, provide the main focus for the reader's interest. Serious, thoughtful, yet accessible fiction will constitute the majority of our purchases, but there's always room for the humorous as well. Borderline fantasy is fine, but no Sword & Sorcery, please. Neither are we interested in explicit sex or violence. A good overview would be to consider that all fiction is written to examine or illuminate some aspect of human existence, but that in science fiction the backdrop you work against is the size of the Universe.

MANUSCRIPT FORMAT Manuscripts submitted to Asimov's must be neatly typed, double-spaced on one side of the sheet only, on bond paper (no erasable paper, please). Any ms. longer than 5 pages should be mailed to us flat. Dot matrix printouts are acceptable only if they are easily readable. Please do NOT send us submissions on disk. When using a word processor, please do not justify the right margin. If sending a printout, separate the sheets first. The ms. should include the title, your name and address, and the number of words in your story. Enclose a cover letter if you like. All manuscripts must be accompanied by a self-addressed stamped envelope (if ms. is over 5 pages, use a 9" x 12" envelope) carrying enough postage to return the ms. If you wish to save on postage, you may submit a clear copy of your story along with a standard (#10) envelope, also self-addressed and stamped. Mark your ms. "DISPOSABLE," and you will receive our reply only. We do not suggest that you have us dispose of your original typescript. If you live overseas or in Canada, use International Reply Coupons for postage, along with a self-addressed envelope.

OUR REPLY Finally, we regret that it's become necessary for us to use form letters for rejecting manuscripts, but time limitations are such that we have no choice. Unfortunately, we are unable to provide specific criticism of each story. Our response time runs about five weeks. If you have not heard from us within three months from the day you mailed your ms., you can assume it was lost in the mail, and are welcome to resubmit it to us. We do NOT keep a record of submissions, but if you would like to know if we received your story or poem, include a self-addressed stamped postcard, which we will return to you on the day it arrives in the office. Thanks for your interest in Asimov's and good luck!

Categories: Fiction—Experimental Fiction—Fantasy—Literature—Science Fiction—Short Stories

CONTACT: Sheila Williams, Editor
Material: All
475 Park Ave. South, 11th Floor

New York NY 10016
Phone: 212-686-7188
E-mail: asimovs@asimovs.com
Website: www.asimovs.com

Aspen Magazine

Aspen Magazine is published six times a year with a mission of providing a voice for the life of the town. We strive to capture the flavor of all that is Aspen—the latest news, local personalities, businesses, controversies, the best dining, skiing, gallery openings, live music, outdoor adventure, festivals, and events. Stories are geared towards a well-traveled, well-educated, savvy audience with a special interest in the area, either as resident or as tourist.

Guidelines

• Issues appear in January (Midwinter), March (Spring), May (Summer), July (Midsummer), August (Fall), and November (Holiday). Lineups are created no later than two-and-a-half months before the publication date and writing deadlines fall no later than a month-and-a-half before

publication. For example, a story for the Midsummer issue (on sale by mid-July) would be assigned no later than early May and due in early June.

• Queries are accepted ONLY in writing. We look for an "only in Aspen" angle: whether it be a local triumph or tragedy or a special event, it must be timely and newsworthy.

• We do not accept unsolicited articles.

• Aspen Magazine buys first North American serial rights to any work assigned and must be notified if articles of similar content will appear in any other publications.

Departments

• Aspen Insider. Short takes on the latest news, personalities, or businesses. Departments include Around Town, Sports, Arts & Performance, Shopping, Home & Lifestyle, Design, and Health. About 50 to 150 words.

• Middle-of-the-Book. Voice-oriented, mid-length stories for departments including Art, Trends, Business, Film, Health. About 500 to 1,000 words.

• Features. In depth coverage of any number of cutting-edge Aspen-related topics. About 1000 to 3500 words.

• Scene. Short, newsy, and up-to-date information on the latest in events, art, dining, and nightlife in Aspen and the Roaring Fork valley. Written in a sophisticated tone, usually about 150 to 300 words per piece.

Categories: Nonfiction—Adventure—Arts—Automobiles—Business—Computers—Conservation—Culture—Entertainment—Health—Lifestyle—Outdoors—Recreation—Regional—Rural America—Sports/Recreation—Travel

CONTACT: Dana Butler, Managing Editor
Material: All
720 E. Durant Ave Ste E8
Aspen CO 81611
Phone: 970-920-4040
Fax: 970-920-4044
E-mail: edit@aspenmagazine.com

ASU Travel Guide
The Guide for Airline Employee Discounts

The *ASU Travel Guide* is published quarterly: January (winter issue); April (spring issue); July (summer issue); and October (fall issue). The publication comprises two sections. The first section contains four travel articles and other pertinent editorial matter. The second section, which is the bulk of the publication, is a directory of dis-

counts available only to airline employees, their families, parents of airline employees and retired airline employees. Articles must be aimed at this well-traveled audience.

Style: Clean and simple; use active verbs. You may use whatever narrative you deem best. Focus on what is unique about a destination: do not write descriptions that could apply to any tourist destination.

Photographs: We do not buy photos. They are mostly obtained from tourist and convention bureaus.

Payment: $200 upon acceptance-including one rewrite if needed—for 1,800-word articles.

Tips:

• Reader surveys indicate that most of our subscribers are interested in how to visit a destination inexpensively, so please include some cost-cutting hints.

• If you have information indirectly related to the article, such as a side trip, it is best presented as a sidebar.

• Send us a sample of your published travel writing and a list of destinations about which you can write. A list of recent articles is shown below. Be aware that we publish travel destination articles only (i.e., do not submit pieces on luggage or currency tips).

• Be patient. The next year's editorial calendar is made each April, so an idea may not be acted upon immediately. We answer all mail as long as a self-addressed, stamped envelope is enclosed. To receive a sample copy of the publication, please submit a 6"x9" envelope (minimum) with $1.41 postage affixed.

Categories: Travel—Airline

CONTACT: Christopher Gil, Managing Editor
Material: All
1525 Francisco Blvd. E
San Rafael CA 94901
Phone: 415-459-0300
Fax: 415-459-0494
E-mail: christopher_gil@asutravelguide.com
Website: www.asutravelguide.com

Atlanta Baby

Please refer to *Atlanta Parent.*

Atlanta Homes and Lifestyles

GENERAL GUIDELINES

Atlanta Homes & Lifestyles is published twelve times a year. Much of the content is written by freelance writers working on assignment for the magazine. Writers are paid between $100 and $500 per article, depending on the assignment.

We always welcome inquiries from qualified freelance writers. Interested parties should submit a resume and photocopies of three published articles to Lisa Frederick, Managing Editor, *Atlanta Homes & Lifestyles*, 1100 Johnson Ferry Road, Suite 595, Atlanta, GA 30342. We regret we cannot return writing samples or unsolicited photos.

We will review story proposals, but such queries should be limited to lifestyle topics, personality profiles or home and garden feature candidates in the Atlanta area. Food, wine and garden stories are written by regular columnists and are not generally assigned to outside freelancers.

Thank you for your interest in *Atlanta Homes & Lifestyles*. We look forward to hearing from you.

ADDITIONAL GUIDELINES
Features—home or garden

Length is 500-800 words (approximately 2-4 pages, double-spaced). All articles should include three suggested heads and two to three decks (subheads). Please include cutlines (captions) and resources (study our format for both; Resources is located in the back of the magazine).

When writing the article, keep the following guidelines in mind:

• Homeowners are first introduced in the story as, for example, John and Jane Doe (not Mr. and Mrs. Doe, except where appropriate, such as former President and Mrs. Carter). In subsequent mentions, they are referred to as John and Jane. Professionals associated with the home, such as builders, interior designers and landscape architects, are mentioned by last name on second reference. (In departments, such as Short Takes or Snapshots, all second references are with last names.)

• Limit discussion of rooms or gardens to areas seen in photography (if photos are available at the time), unless it's particularly relevant or self-explanatory even without a photo.

• Avoid stating the obvious, such as the colors of things (unless particularly relevant) or furniture arrangement. Captions, also, should state some new information: what type of furnishings, from where, why bought, etc.

• Avoid including overused phrases, such as "I wanted to create an environment that reflects me" or "I created this garden because flowers bring such joy." Focus instead on unusual angles or approaches in design. Some features might be slanted towards the homeowner and his or her interests and talents; a remodeling story, on the other hand, may deal primarily with the chronological progress of the project.

• Avoid lapses into first-person reporting.•

• No gushing over the homeowner or home.

• Remember that houses are not homes until someone is living in them. A "new home" is realtor- speak. Condominiums and apartments can also be homes, of course.

• Don't include specific streets where gardens or homes are located; we don't print that. Add geographical interest, though, by being more specific than "north Atlanta," such as "a quiet cul- de-sac near Roswell's historic square."

Features—Food & Entertaining

In general, F & E articles should have no more than 500 words intro before recipes. Sidebars elaborating on something mentioned in the article are encouraged. As always, include three suggested heads and decks, plus cutlines with the article. Recipe guidelines:

• Must include name of dish and source of recipe, if known.

• List yield at end of recipe.

• Teaspoon, tablespoon, pounds, etc. are always spelled out.

• Ingredients listed in the order they're used.

• List generic rather than brand names, when possible (mayonnaise vs. Hellman's).

• Try to keep directions as succinct as possible without confusing the reader.

Department — A la Carte (restaurants)

Themed to a specific topic (best chicken salad, al fresco dining, for example), this 300-500 word article usually includes one intro paragraph and paragraphs on four or five restaurants.

Include phone number and general location (Virginia-Highland area, historic Marietta, for example) for each restaurant. Mention several special dishes, but no more than six for each restaurant. No overly negative comments. Text should be personal without being written in first person.

Department—Short Takes

Short Takes articles can range in size from one paragraph to 500 words; brevity is always appreciated! Topics may include Finds (new, unique stores; new products or services); People (focus on an entrepreneur or personality in one of our subject matters); or Causes (charities with some tie-in to our subjects). Stories should focus on a benefit to the reader, and what's unusual about the subject. Include a phone number and Web site (if applicable).

Department—Big Fix or Quick Fix

Most articles should have a before-after component and be written with a Problem-Solution-Cost intro (see past issues for examples). Articles should also include a Spec Sheet, a listing of professionals and products involved in the project. Any projects under $5,000 are considered a Quick Fix. Average length is 300-500 words.

Department—Great Escapes (travel)

All hotels, inns, etc. mentioned must include prices/packages, and phone numbers. Average length is 500 words. Travel features should go beyond brochures and press kit copy, focusing on unique finds and interesting anecdotes about the area. We like off-the-beaten-path suggestions.

Department—House Hunting (real estate)

Subjects can be broad, such as "Who's Buying What Where," unusual subdivision amenities or female builders; can be a real estate-related web-site; can be a blurb, sidebar or one-page article, depending on subject. Includes a one-page "Homing in On" article about a specific area, i.e., Vinings, Marietta, Decatur. Write articles to be of the most benefit to readers. All must have a metro Atlanta-area slant. Whenever possible, include house prices, square footage, etc.

Remember: a house on the market isn't a "home" yet, no matter what the real estate agents call it.

Whenever possible, obtain supplied photography.

Department—Second Home

An article about an Atlantan's vacation home, approximately 400-500 words. Articles should have an emphasis on the area, the home itself and the activities the Atlantans enjoy there. (Avoid overused phrases such as "We designed this second home for relaxing.")

Department-Cheap Chic

This short (200-300 words) article focuses on a clever idea that doesn't cost a lot. It can be written from a how-to standpoint or one person's story of how he or she executed the idea. Often we have two examples of a related idea, such as two inexpensive headboards or two uses of outdoor furniture in an indoors setting. Writing tone is light.

ADDITIONAL GUIDELINES

Please obtain very specific resources from designers, architects and homeowners when applicable (any home piece). This is a service to our readers. Resources can include builders, designers, architects, cabinetry, wallpaper (pattern name and manufacturer), paint (manufacturer, color name or number), furniture, accessories, window treatments, flooring, landscaping, artwork, etc. Please provide phone numbers as well.

Include photography (preferably slides or transparencies) with your article if you are able to. If more photography is needed or you are unable to obtain photography, please include suggestions for photography. Also provide a contact name and phone number for the subject to be photographed. Please suggest specific shots, as you wrote the article and are most familiar with the subject matter.

Include the names, addresses and phone numbers of anyone contacted, quoted or mentioned in the article so that we can send them a complimentary copy of the magazine.

List several suggestions for a story head (headline should be catchy) and deck (should be an explanatory sentence).

Please include an invoice for your services with your article. Delays can occur if your paperwork is not submitted.

If you have photos for the article, please write cutlines (captions). This helps us tremendously.

Provide both a hard copy of your article and a disk (on Microsoft Word 6.0 or a compatible software). If you are using a PC save as rich text or Microsoft Word. You may also e-mail to lfrederick@ atlantahomesmag,com.

Strange things happen to text in our computers, so please follow these formatting guidelines. Don't use tabs or indent paragraphs in your text. And, though it goes against everything you were taught, please try to leave only one space after a period. Also, no fancy organizing, styling (like bold or italics) or centering of text is necessary (we try to let the art director have some fun). Simply double space, justify left and return to start a new paragraph.

We refer to homeowners in a feature by their first names (after first mention of first and last names) and designers, architect, etc., by their last names (unless homeowner is anonymous and designer or architect is the primary interviewee). In department articles refer to people by their last names after first mention (unless it is a couple with the same last name).

Spell out all numbers from one to nine. Over nine use the numeral, unless it is the first word of a sentence. In feature articles always spell out state names. (ex. The beach house in Mobile, Alabama, is tacky. In departments use state abbreviations (AP style).

When in doubt, refer to the *AP Style Book* and *Webster's Unabridged Dictionary.*

Categories: Nonfiction—Antiques—Architecture—Arts—Book Reviews—Cooking—Food/Drink—Gardening—Lifestyle—Real Estate—Regional—Society—Travel

CONTACT: Lisa G. Frederick, Managing Editor
Material: All
Weisner Publishing LLC, 1100 Johnson Ferry Rd., Suite 595
Atlanta GA 30342
Phone: 404-965-4471
Fax: 404-252-6673
E-mail: lfrederick@atlantahomesmag.com
Website: www.atlantahomesmag.com

Atlanta Parent
Atlanta Baby

Atlanta Parent Magazine is a monthly magazine aimed at parents with children from birth to 18 years old.

Atlanta Baby is aimed at parents from the time of pregnancy through when baby is 2 years old. *Atlanta Baby* is published 4 times a year.

For both publications:

• Send submissions to: LWhite@atlantaparent.com (in word attachments); 2346 Perimeter Park Drive, Suite 101, Atlanta, Georgia 30341; 770-454-7699 (fax). E-mailed submissions are preferred.

• Authors should include name, address, phone number and e-mail address at the top of the first page, along with the word count. On the following pages, please include your name - top pages frequently get detached from the rest of the manuscript.

• For publication in our magazines, please use only one space after a period at the end of a sentence - not two. All articles should be typed and double-spaced. Lengths typically run from 800 to 1,200 words. Indent paragraphs with a tab.

• Articles should address the parent, not the child.

• All of our articles are very down-to-earth - we do not print philosophical or theoretical articles. Most are third person - we do VERY little first person, except for humor pieces. We do not publish short stories, poetry or fiction.

• *Atlanta Parent* Magazine and *Atlanta Baby* are both service journalism publications. When writing about a problem, give parents the symptoms or signs of the problem and then the solution or where they can turn to for help. We encourage you to include the addresses, phone numbers and web addresses for local and national resources and support groups so our readers can obtain reliable information.

• We will not accept articles with quotes from experts located in only one region of the country. For *Atlanta Parent* Magazine and *Atlanta Baby*, the article should include either quotes from local experts or experts from around the country.

• Our readers also want to read articles that are activity-based. Keep the instructions short and to the point. Using the directions, do the activity yourself or ask another person to follow the instructions to make sure they are accurate.

• Articles will not be returned.

• All articles are submitted on speculation unless specifically assigned in advance.

• If we like your article but have no immediate plans to use it, our normal procedure is to keep your article on file for possible future publication.

• Photos and illustrations may be submitted with the story. Nominal payment may be offered, if used.

• Payment is upon publication.

Categories: Children—Disabilities—Education—Family—Juvenile—Parenting

CONTACT: Liz White, Publisher
Material: All
2346 Perimeter Park Dr, Ste 101
Atlanta GA 30341
Phone: 770-454-7599
Fax: 770-454-7699
E-mail: LWhite@atlantaparent.com (in word attachments)
Website: www.atlantaparent.com

Atlanta Tribune

The award-winning *Atlanta Tribune* is a monthly newsmagazine targeted at metropolitan Atlanta's African-American executives, professionals and entrepreneurs.

Thanks for your interest in writing for *Atlanta Tribune: The Magazine*; Black Atlanta's No. 1 resource for information on business, careers, technology and wealth-building.

Please read these guidelines carefully, as they are important to creating a successful relationship between us, you and, ultimately, our reader.

Editorial Mission Statement - *Atlanta Tribune: The Magazine* is Black Atlanta's leading source for relevant, thought-provoking news and information on business, careers, technology, wealth-building, politics and education.

Our audience is metropolitan Atlanta's progressive, politically concerned, culturally aware, family-oriented Black executives, professionals and entrepreneurs.

We educate our readers and present ideas, viewpoints and possible solutions that economically, politically and socially empower them.

We are timely, accurate, credible, in-depth, progressive and always strive to make our readers think.

Our Editorial Focus - The primary editorial focus of *Atlanta Tribune: The Magazine* is business, careers, technology, wealth-building, politics and education.

Atlanta Tribune: The Magazine does not publish poetry or fiction and does not publish feature articles about entertainment or celebrity figures.

Freelance Opportunities - *Atlanta Tribune: The Magazine* is approximately 30 percent freelance written and we welcome queries from experienced freelancers. We accept freelance articles as cover stories, features and in our regular sections.

Given the sophistication of our readers, any current news development that has significant impact on Atlanta's African-American executives, professionals and entrepreneurs might qualify for feature treatment in *Atlanta Tribune: The Magazine.*

Submitting Queries - Article queries on subjects appropriate to *Atlanta Tribune: The Magazine* are always welcome. Unsolicited manuscripts are not accepted.

Please note that *Atlanta Tribune: The Magazine* does not publish syndicated columns or stories that have run in other publications. All features, cover stories and profiles published in *Atlanta Tribune: The Magazine* are original materials written exclusively for *Atlanta Tribune: The Magazine*. Please do not submit queries for syndicated columns or manuscripts of previously published materials.

All feature articles and cover stories are assigned. Stories are usually assigned three to six months in advance of publication date, and it generally takes four to six weeks for the editors to respond to queries. If yours is a time-sensitive topic, please submit your proposals accordingly. A separate query letter should be sent for each topic. Please keep all queries to one page in length.

We accept queries by **e-mail only.**

If you have not written for us before, be sure to include a current resume and no less than three, but no more than five samples of your previously published, business-oriented works. These items will be accepted via fax, mail or e-mail.

Writers with specific story ideas should submit a query via e-mail that clearly, succinctly and persuasively answers the following questions:

What is your story idea and why is it newsworthy?

How and why is the story significant to *Atlanta Tribune: The Magazine*'s readers?

What specific insights about the topic will your story deliver?

What primary and secondary sources will you use for reporting the story?

What experience have you had as a freelance writer, and why are you qualified to handle this assignment?

A good query will convince us that your article is a must-read feature for *Atlanta Tribune: The Magazine*'s audience. A great one will tell us why the article should be a cover story.

Story Elements - Upon receiving your submission, our editors will evaluate it based on the following criteria. Your chances of acceptance will be greatly increased if you take them into consideration during the research and writing phases. The editors will read it carefully, sometimes more than once, to see what's in it and what's not. After reading it, the editors will ask themselves the following seven questions about the piece. Does the piece have: *

A clear angle? The piece must be about something—not all about something, but something about something. If it's a profile, for example, it should not be a biography; it should be about some part or aspect of the subject's life. Other material may be included, but the piece should focus on something specific. The piece should convey a main message, a central idea or major theme. It should not be merely a fact sheet or encyclopedia entry. It ought to make one big, overriding point—but not more than one. More than one angle is no angle. Furthermore, if it's an assigned piece, the angle should be the same one described to the author when the piece was assigned.

An effective lead? A lead is supposed to (a) stop the perusing reader, (b) introduce the subject and (c) draw the reader into the piece. What's more, the lead should not merely introduce the subject, but should introduce it within the context of the angle. For example, if the piece is about the governor's wife being her husband's most enthusiastic campaigner, the lead should show her in connection with a campaign, not in her kitchen or selecting new draperies. The editor must decide if the author's lead does what a lead is supposed to do.

A clear justifier? The justifier—or peg—is a sentence or paragraph, maybe more than one paragraph, that (a) tells the reader what's going on in the lead if it isn't obvious, (b) tries to establish newsworthiness, or relevance, in order to give the reader a reason to read the piece and (c) hints at what is to come and what the reader will find out by reading the piece. The justifier is the link between the lead and the body of the piece.

Anecdotes and other narrative? The piece, whatever its subject or angle, must be readable—interesting and easy to read—and the most effective way to make it readable is to use anecdotes and/or other narrative. The piece should have anecdotes that illustrate, that support generalizations, that show the subject to the reader. Narrative is the kind of writing that shows action, unlike exposition, which merely explains or tells. The piece ought to show, not just tell.

Lively quotes, descriptive detail and other specifics? A piece needs voices. It should let the reader hear someone other than the author. The piece should also let the reader see—and hear and smell and feel—

for himself. Insofar as possible, the piece ought always be showing the reader something, making pictures form in the reader's mind, because pictures, particularly action pictures, are much more interesting and much more likely to hold the reader's interest than abstractions. The piece should avoid vagueness and generalities by giving the reader specifics—names, dates, places, times, identifications, numbers, all the appropriate and needed details.

A logical organization? The material shouldn't be simply dumped onto the pages of the manuscript and left for the reader to sort out. It should be arranged and presented to the reader in a logical, make-sense, what-does-the-reader-need-to-know-next sequence.

An appropriate conclusion? The piece should not simply peter out or end abruptly. It should have a conclusion that lets the reader feel satisfied by the piece in the same way a diner, having eaten the dessert, feels satisfied by a meal.

Supplying Resource Information - Resource information is usually supplied to our readers through the liberal use of sidebars. Each story in *Atlanta Tribune: The Magazine* usually contains one to three such resource information sidebars and we consider these as part of the story. Writers are responsible for researching and supplying information for accurate and informative sidebars for each submission.

Fact-Checking Requirements - Writers are required to conduct their own fact checking and are responsible for accuracy. Please provide a complete list of all sources mentioned in your article, including names, current addresses and phone numbers so the editors can verify names, titles, professional associations, etc.

If a book is referred to in the article, you must include the author's name, the book's publisher, year of publication and the book's price if it is still in print. If statistics are quoted, complete information on the source of the data must be included so editors can verify their accuracy.

Submission Format - All submissions (initial submissions, articles submitted on speculation, articles accepted for publication and work turned in on assignment) will be accepted by e-mail only (no disk submissions). The article text should be attached to the e-mail message as a Microsoft Word document (PC format). If you are not using Microsoft Word or are working in a Macintosh format, the file can be attached as an ASCII text document. DO NOT paste the text of the article directly into the body of the e-mail message.

Material not submitted in this format will not be reviewed or accepted and no writer's fees will be paid.

Publication Rights - *Atlanta Tribune: The Magazine* purchases all print and electronic rights to all assigned articles. We purchase first North American serial rights, electronic rights and non-exclusive reprint rights to articles submitted on speculation.

Deadlines and Late Penalties - Writers are usually given between two and eight weeks to complete an assignment based on the article length and the complexity of the research involved. If a writer fails to meet the submission deadline agreed to in the "Assignment Letter," there is an initial twenty-five percent (25%) penalty and a five percent (5%) penalty each day thereafter on the remaining balance. Writers should note that deadline policies and associated late penalties are strictly adhered to.

How to Contact Us - All queries and any questions concerning these Writers' Guidelines or other editorial policies should be directed to Fredrick Robinson, editor. All submissions should be sent directly to the attention of the editor.

Categories: Culture—African American

CONTACT: Cicely Bland, Editor
Atlanta Tribune: The Magazine
875 Old Roswell Rd, Ste C-100
Roswell GA 30076
Phone: 770-587-0501
Fax: 770-642-6501
E-mail: cbland@atlantatribune.com

The Atlantic Monthly

The *Atlantic Monthly* is always interested in poetry, fiction, and articles of the highest quality. A general familiarity with what we have published in the past is your best guide to what we're looking for. Simply send your manuscript—typewritten, double-spaced, and accompanied by a stamped self-addressed envelope.

Categories: Fiction—General Interest—Poetry

CONTACT: Submissions Editor
Material: All
77 North Washington St.
Boston MA 02114
Website: www.atlantic.com

Attaché
The Inflight Magazine of US Airways

No longer accepting submissions.

Audio Video Interiors

Rarely accepts unsolicited submissions.
Categories: Nonfiction—Technical—Technology—Audio-Video

CONTACT: Mary Ann Giorgio, Editor
Material: All
774 S. Placentia Ave
Placentia CA
92870
Phone: 714-939-2628
E-mail: magiorgio@mcmullenargus.com
Website: www.audiovideointeriors.com

Audubon

Audubon articles deal with the natural and human environment. They cover the remote as well as the familiar. What they all have in common, however, is that they have a story to tell, one that will not only interest *Audubon* readers, but that will interest everyone with a concern for the affairs of humans and nature.

We want good solid journalism. We want stories of people and places, good news and bad; humans and nature in conflict, humans and nature working together, humans attempting to comprehend, restore and renew the natural world.

We are looking for new voices and fresh ideas. Read the magazine, both features and departments before sending queries. Every story suggestion should be submitted in a brief query letter, accompanied by a stamped, self-addressed envelope; no telephone or FAX queries please. Be sure the query not only outlines the subject matter, but also indicates the approach you would take and how you would handle the material. Please estimate how many words you would need to cover the subject. Also, include some samples of your writing.

Among the types of stories we seek: profiles of individuals whose life and work illuminate some issues relating to natural history, the environment, conservation, etc.; balanced reporting on environmental issues and events here in North America; analyses of events, policies, and issues from fresh points of view. We do not publish fiction or poetry. We're not seeking first person meditations on "nature," or accounts of wild animal rescue or taming.

Queries should be accompanied by a stamped, self-addressed envelope of sufficient size. If you are submitting photographs with a queries, be sure your submission includes the stiffeners, sufficient postage, and instructions we need to return the photos the way you want them returned.

Author identification should be included; name, address, telephone number, fax number. Computer printouts and photocopies are acceptable though we will not consider simultaneous submissions. *Audubon* is vigorously fact-checked. Once an article is accepted, the author must be prepared to submit source materials that back up the text and enable us to verify all facts.

We pay for articles on acceptance, and our rates vary according to length, the amount of work and thought required.

Categories: Nonfiction—Book Reviews—Conservation—Ecology—Environment—History—Interview—Outdoors—Nature—Essay—Humor —Opinion

CONTACT: The Editor
Material: All
700 Broadway
New York NY 10003-9501
Website: magazine.audubon.org

Austin Home & Living

Austin Home & Living is published six times a year. Much of the content is written by freelance writers working on assignment for the magazine. Writers are paid between $100 to $300 per article, depending on the assignment.

We always welcome inquiries from qualified freelance writers. Interested parties should submit a resume and photocopies of published articles to address below.

We regret we cannot return writing samples or unsolicited photos.

We will review story proposals, but such queries should be limited to lifestyle topics, personality profiles, gardening features, and Austin area home profiles.

Thank you for your interest in AH&L. We look forward to hearing from you.

Categories: Nonfiction—Home—Gardening—Lifestyle—Regional

CONTACT: AH&L
11675 Jollyville Rd Ste 201
Austin TX 78759

Austin Monthly
"Austin's City Magazine"

Heading:
At the top of each story please include, in this complete format:
• Full Name
• Contact Info (E-mail &/or Phone No.)
• Section article goes in (e.g. Talk, Character, Features)
• Month & Year article will be in: Nov. 2003
• Word Count
• Suggested Title(s) of the Article:
• Suggested Deck (An auxiliary headline that adds info. to the title):
• Image Status: (Here, TK, on CD, etc.)
(Note: You can usually check your word count in Microsoft Word under Tools on the Menu bar.)

Please do not include notes to the staff, invoices, etc. within the same document as your story. Please put this information in the e-mail itself or a separate attachment.

Submission:
Please submit your stories in a Microsoft Word or Quark document, if possible, and note if you use a computer other than a Macintosh (We receive stories on Macs.). Please submit your stories via e-mail to srichardson@austin.rr.com and editor@austinmonthly.com. Please do

not send images to these addresses! (See Photography and Artwork section.)

Photography and Artwork:

If you need our office to supply imagery for your piece, please let us know as soon as possible.

To aid in caption writing, please submit the following, complete information along with each image:

Full names (correct spellings) of everyone in the picture

As many details as you can: who it is, what it's of, where it was taken, when it was taken and why the event was held or why it was important.

Any images used in the magazine need to be a minimum of 300 dpi, preferably in TIF format (JPEG as a second option). Images must be able to be enlarged to a minimum of 5x7 and maintain a 300 dpi. Slides are also acceptable, but transparencies should be used as a last resort.

Please send all images to designer@austin.rr.com. Images are due by the 10th of the month (same time as the stories); however, if the image cannot be submitted by the deadline, please let Shannon Richardson (editor) or Lyn Brady (publisher) know. (Images for features are due on the 10th three months in advance, unless the photos cannot be taken until a later date.) We understand that photographers usually have to read the story before they can shoot pictures and extensions will be given when necessary.

Text:

Articles should be single-spaced with an extra space in between paragraphs. Please do not make indentions.

Please fact check all of your work: This means verifying all facts with a credible source, especially the spellings of all proper names. Please contact a credible source directly (in person, by phone or e-mail) and avoid using the phone book or Internet as references—they might not always be accurate.

Carefully edit the entire story for errors in spelling, grammar and punctuation before submission.

Please write like you know your topic intimately. If you're writing about someone, meet him or her in person. If you're writing about a place, visit it.

Style:

We follow AP Style (*The Associated Press Stylebook and Briefing on Media Law*, Norm Goldstein, ed., 2002) and refer to *The Elements of Style* (William Strunk Jr. and E.B. White, 2000) and a standard English dictionary, in addition to the following *Austin Monthly* modifications/additions:

• Attribution: Please use present tense ("says", not "said") and keep it in subject-verb order ("Bob says", not "says Bob"). We do not use courtesy titles (Miss, Ms., Mrs., Mr.), and we generally use last names for reference unless the piece is especially personal or informal ("Smith ran," not "Bob ran").

• Composition Titles: Italicize the names of movies, books, newspapers, magazines, plays, songs, TV shows, etc. Don't use quotes.

• Fonts: To bold a word, please insert double brackets around the bolded word: [[bold]]. To italicize a word, please insert single fancy brackets around the italicized word: {*italicize*}. This way, when your document is transferred to our designers who work in Quark (our layout program), we won't lose any of your bolded or italicized words.

• Foreign Words: Italicize non-English words, and provide a translation if the word is not commonly known.

• Percentages: Use the numeral and the word "percent" spelled out (14 percent; 6.5 percent)

• Phone Numbers: Use hyphens only (263-9133; 214-561-0341). The local area code 512 is not needed.

• The University of Texas at Austin: Use this as the official name on first reference. On second reference, The University is acceptable when referring to the University of Texas at Austin. Use the university on second reference for another institution of higher learning. UT is used only as a modifier, not a noun.

• Street names: Every street mentioned should have a St., Blvd., Ave., Road, Circle, etc. with it. Follow AP Style to determine what's abbreviated and what's not.

• Time of Day: We use Central Daylight (CDT) time or Central Standard Time (CST). We use a.m. and p.m. (not am, AM, pm, or PM) with numerals. Use midnight or noon, not 12 a.m. or 12 p.m.

• Web addresses: Please use this format for a Web site: www.austinmonthly.com

Grammar and Punctuation Reminders:

• Commas: In a series of three or more terms with a single conjunction, use a comma after each term except the last (apples, oranges and bananas; not apples, oranges, and bananas). Place a comma before a conjunction introducing an independent clause. Do not join independent clauses with a comma.

• Dashes (———), rather than hyphens (-), should be used within a sentence to designate abrupt change or a series within a phrase. Hyphens are often used in order to avoid ambiguity or with compound modifiers. There should be no spaces on either side of a dash or hyphen.

Be aware of:

• Dangling modifiers—The writer knows what is intended but doesn't say it, forcing the reader to rearrange a sentence to grasp its meaning (Short and readable, I finished it in about 45 minutes.) Avoid these!

• Misuse of relative pronouns—Who is nominative, like the personal pronouns he, she and they. Whom is objective, like him, her and them.

• Possessives—Singular common nouns ending in s take 's unless the next word begins with s: the hostess' invitation; the hostess' seat.

• Singular proper nouns ending in s take only an apostrophe: Socrates' life.

• Cliches—Try to avoid and instead come up with fresh, original language

• Clutter—Avoid unnecessary words; be concise.

• Passive Voice—Active voice (the subject performs the action) is preferred over passive voice (the subject is acted upon).

QUERY PROCEDURE

Editorial mission

Austin Monthly is not content to sit back and watch the city; we are active participants, chronicling and contributing to the vitality of the community. We strive to create a magazine that is lively and relevant—a utilitarian "owner's manual," written with an insider's edge, geared to help life-long residents and newcomers alike get the most out of living in this city. We will challenge the status quo, criticize when warranted, heap praise when deserved and season everything with a passion for this place we call home.

Austin Monthly stories are by, for and about this city. The magazine examines our city's people, politics, services, development, economy, culture, shopping, faults, quirks—everything that makes the city unique—through useful service pieces, personality profiles and investigative stories.

The editorial style of *Austin Monthly* is bright, lively and utilitarian wherever possible. We like to feature at least one sidebar per story (features and departments)—they don't have to be long, just relevant to the piece. We must lead readers into each story, making it relevant to their lives, answering the "so what/what's in it for me" and trying to anticipate readers' questions. Pieces should provide insight into the subject that goes beyond the obvious, beyond what the dailies and weeklies are saying, and provide insider information the reader cannot find elsewhere. Stories should be well researched and facts triple-checked (including phone numbers, addresses, titles, etc.).

Target reader

Austin Monthly is targeted to an urban, affluent Austin metro resident. Primary age range: 30s-60s. 60% female, 40% male. They live in Austin, the surrounding city neighborhoods and suburbs. They are into cooking, dining out, the restaurant scene, their homes, fitness/outdoor activities, their children, style, shopping, culture, art, music and events—but they also want to read in greater depth about politics, personalities and other important issues that shape the city and come with rapid growth (crime, traffic, city government, public transportation, etc.).

Editorial format and departments

On average we run three to four feature stories per issue, each one usually opening with a two-page spread. We have several regular departments in the magazines as well as several rotating departments. Please study the magazine before you query us to know what types of stories we like to run. You'll be way ahead of the game if you query us with a story idea for a specific department or genre in the magazine.

Query Procedure

WE DO NOT ACCEPT QUERIES OVER THE PHONE.

Queries should be submitted in writing via e-mail, fax or mail and consist of three parts:

1. What is the story? A brief synopsis written in the style of your proposed piece.

2. How will you tell it? Detail what sources you will use and how you will research the story.

3. Why? Answer the "so what?" Why is this story important now? Why should you be the one to tell it? Why is this story right for *Austin Monthly*?

PLEASE ALSO SEND THREE OF YOUR BEST MAGAZINE-STYLE WRITING CLIPS.

How will I know if you've accepted my query?

Sometimes it takes us months to get around to reading queries. We will do our best to respond to your query in the timeliest manner possible. We prefer that you follow up with us via email. NO PHONE CALLS PLEASE.

Sometimes your pitch isn't exactly what we're looking for, but we like your tone, your approach and the way you think. If that happens, we'll usually keep your pitch and clips on file and contact you if a story comes up that we think you might be interested in.

If you want the opportunity to sell your story to another publication after we've had a chance to review it, please indicate a time frame (e.g. "If I don't hear from you within 30 days, I'll assume you're not interested and will begin to pitch the story to other publications.") We won't take it personally.

If you are to get an assignment from us, style and content, as well as deadline and payment, are negotiated when the assignment is made.

Questions?

For questions concerning editorial matters, contact Jeff Brady, managing editor, at editor@austinmonthly.com.

We cannot be responsible for unsolicited manuscripts, slides, photographs or other **material.**

Categories: Non-Fiction—Art—Business—Cooking—Children—Culture—Economy—Family—Food/Drink—General Interest—Government—Lifestyle—Music—Politics—Regional

CONTACT: Submissions Editor
Material: All
11612 Bee Caves Rd., Bldg. II, Ste. 125
Austin, TX 78738
Phone: 512-263-9133
Fax: 512-263-1370
E-mail: editor@austinmonthly.com
Website: www.austinmonthly.com

Authorship

Purpose: Authorship magazine is the "in-house" publication for the National Writers Assn. It is read by the thousands of members on a quarterly basis. Currently the magazine is online.

Scope: Articles submitted for consideration to *Authorship* should have a writing slant. Material should deal with writing "how-to's" or current market trends. We are overstocked on inspirational "How I became a successful writer…" type material and will not be interested in any of these articles. Articles slanted toward aspects of fiction–creating characters, setting scenes, etc. are of interest and will be our primary interest. Humor is a plus–writing is serious enough without a totally serious article.

We do not accept fiction. Poetry is published in our Winter issue, if it has a writing theme.

Submissions: All submissions should be in standard manuscript format, approximately 750 words, accompanied by an SASE if the material is to be returned. *Authorship* used AP style with the exception of state abbreviations. If the author is not aware of proper manuscript format, they should request NWA RR#35 prior to submitting. Manuscripts accepted for publication will be requested on disk 3½ IBM compatible in Microsoft Word format in text files with line breaks. NO tabs, fancy fonts, bullets, charts, or tables. If charts or tables are necessary submit them like art work. Disks will be given preferred treatment as this prevents typos in final copy. Sharp clear photos of article authors will be requested if material is accepted.

Payment: We are currently paying $10 honorarium per article or a $10 reduction on membership dues.

Reporting Time: Currently we are reporting in approximately 8 weeks, however this varies at different times of the year and with the amount of material received.

Themes: The issues will have the following themes: Winter-Poetry; Spring-Conference, Creative Nonfiction; Summer-Children's Writing; Fall-The Business of Writing, Fiction, Screenplays.

Categories: Nonfiction—Biography—Writing How-To's

CONTACT: Sandy Whelchel, Managing Editor
Material: All
National Writers Association
10940 S. Parker Road #508
Parker CO 80134
Phone: 303-841-0246
Fax: 303-841-2607

Auto Sound & Security

Circulation: 44,754
Frequency: monthly
Published by the PRIMEDIA Enthusiast Group.

Showcases the excitement, quality and technology of sound systems designed for specific use in vehicles, whether simply for the listener's enjoyment or as the hottest equipment competing in sound-off events. Features include coverage of industry events, vehicle protection, and sound-system protection tips.

For more information, visit the magazine's Website.

Editorial submissions are welcomed, but the editor recommends that contributors query first. All contributions must be accompanied by a self-addressed, stamped envelope. Solicitations for editorial coverage, including car feature articles, should be submitted via US mail. Please include a photograph of the vehicle/project, a quick reference sheet and a few paragraphs detailing the editorial significance of your work. Due to busy travel and work schedules, the editor is not able to field calls related to potential editorial coverage. We assume no responsibility for loss or damage of any unsolicited materials.

Categories: Nonfiction—Automobiles

CONTACT: Editorial Feedback, Submissions
Material: All
McMullen Argus Publishing Inc.
2400 E. Katella Ave., 11th Floor
Anaheim CA 92806
Phone: 714-939-2400
Fax: 714-978-6390
Website: www.autosoundsecurityweb.com

Automated Builder

Automated Builder publishes articles on all seven segments of the automated building industry: Production (Big Volume Site) Builders; Panelized/Precut (including Log and Dome) Home Manufacturers; Residential Modular Manufacturers; Commercial (Special Unit) Modular; HUD-Code Home Manufacturers; Component Manufacturers and Dealers and Builders for the above companies.

Deadlines

Editorial deadlines are the 21st day of the second preceding month. Advertising deadlines are on the first day of the preceding month. Call for extensions.

Profile Features

Articles range in length from 500 to 1,000 words with a preferred length of 750 words. Color photographs (slides, prints or electronic format) are required. A query about subject matter is suggested before submitting work.

General News

Automated Builder publishes departmental items in these categories: newslines (general industry news); company news, coming events, letters to the editor, new software, new literature and new products.

Electronic Specifications

Material sent for publication should be submitted on floppy (3.5) diskette, CD, ZIP disk or JAZ disk, formatted for IBM PC. Fonts and images used in the material submitted should accompany the material on the disk.

Text should be formatted in text (.txt) or MSWord. If files are compressed, please include the unzipping utility on the disk.

Image files should be saved in .tif or .eps format at 300 dpi. Line art should be scanned at 800 dpi or above and saved in .tif format.

Automated Builder used Pagemaker 6.5 and Photoshop 5.0 for IBM and processes 1200 dpi negative film. Copy should also be submitted in hard copy form.

Categories: Nonfiction—Business—Trade: Building & Construction

CONTACT: Don O. Carlsen, Editor, Publisher
Material: All
CMN Associates, Inc.
1445 Donlon St., Ste 16
Ventura Ca 93303
Phone: 805-642-9735
Fax: 805-642-8820
E-mail: info@automatedbuilder.com
Website: www.automatedbuilder.com

Automobile Quarterly
The Connoisseur's Magazine of Motoring Today, Yesterday, and Tomorrow

Automobile Quarterly is a quality hardbound, advertising-free, 112-page journal of automotive history with excellent photography. Established in 1962, circ. approx. 10,000. It is 85% freelance written.

Submission and Style

Contact for queries and submissions: Tracy Powell, managing editor. No phone calls please. Query by e-mail, fax or snail mail.

AQ accepts queries regarding historical stories about automakers, individual automobile models, and historical figures, past competition, automotive art and collectibles, as well as automotive technology. Queries need to address available sources of information and illustrative materials. Queries will be responded to within 2 weeks, manuscripts within 2 months. Although AQ reviews unsolicited manuscripts, queries are preferred. Unsolicited manuscripts will be returned only if accompanied by a self-addressed, stamped envelope. Submissions should arrive on disc (3 1/2-in. floppy, zip or CD) and hard copy (8 1/2 x 11, double-spaced). Although we prefer Word for Mac, we can convert most PC-based word-processing programs. AQ expects its stories to be based on original and primary research sources and to be accurate and well written. Previously published sources must be used sparingly and be carefully documented. The magazine does not accept repackaged stories that have already been published in English.

Sections frequently freelanced include:
- Brass Era (1904-1917)
- Grand Classic (1918-1929)
- Racing History
- Great Cars of the 30s
- Great Cars of the 40s
- Great Cars of the 50s
- Of Inventors & Innovations
- Of Collectors and Collections
- Art Gallery
- Short-Lived Marque
- Cars of the World
- Biography

AQ's audience consists of enthusiasts from all eras, a group of knowledgeable car aficionados that pay a premium subscription for lively, insightful stories accompanied by top-notch photography. For a sample of what AQ is looking for, visit www.autoquarterly.com and read Featured Articles, or request an issue for $20 (normal price: $25.99). Style bibles include the latest *AP Stylebook* and *Webster's Ninth Collegiate Dictionary*. Bylines are given; authors receive one comp issue.

Photos

AQ reviews 4x5, 35mm and 120 transparencies, historical prints, and high-resolution digital photography (300 dpi minimum).

Compensation

AQ pays on acceptance within 30 days of assigned deadline, unless otherwise contracted. Feature stories range from 1,500 to 4,500 words. Payment is negotiated (depending primarily on word length, the writer's expertise, writing ability and professionalism) but generally ranges between $500 and $2,000 per story. AQ often relies on authors to assist in locating and supplying historical photos. Writer/photographers are sometimes used to provide a complete package of words and color or black-and-white images. Fees will be negotiated. AQ offers a 33% kill fee. Manuscripts are published an average 1 year after acceptance with byline. Editorial lead time: 9 months. Currently, AQ purchases first international rights for articles (including excerpting for book compilation and Web site use) and all rights for photographs.

Contributors receive two (2) complimentary copies; additional copies are available at $15 per copy.

Categories: Nonfiction—Automobiles—Consumer—History

CONTACT: Tracy Powell, Managing Editor
Material: Queries and submissions
137 E. Market St.
New Albany IN 47150
Phone: 866-838-2886
Fax: 812-948-2816
E-mail: editor@autoquarterly.com
Website: www.autoquarterly.com

Aviation History

Please refer to WEIDER History Group.

Aviation Maintenance

About Us

Monthly—12 issues.

Aviation Maintenance is the number-one source for information on the worldwide aviation aftermarket. Maintenance managers in all segments of the industry—corporate flight departments, regional and major airlines, general aviation, repair stations and the military turn to *Aviation Maintenance* for the latest new business trends, regulatory developments, technical advancements, and new products and services. Subscriptions to *Aviation Maintenance* are complimentary to aviation maintenance industry professionals.

Guidelines

No formal guidelines, but writers must be intimately familiar with the Aviation Industry, especially the maintenance side of the industry.

Categories: Nonfiction—Aviation—Trade: Aircraft Maintenance Issues

CONTACT: Matt Thurber, Editor
Material: All
Access Intelligence, LLC
4 Choke Cherry Road, 2nd Floor
Rockville MD 20850
Phone: 301-354-2000
Website: www.aviationmx.com

Aviation Safety World

Foundation Charter Built on Communication

Flight Safety Foundation (FSF) is dedicated to improving worldwide aviation safety. Nonprofit and independent, the Foundation was launched in 1947 to respond to the aviation industry's need for a neutral clearinghouse to disseminate objective safety information. FSF is a credible and knowledgeable body that identifies threats to safety, studies the problems and recommends practical solutions for them.

Articles Emphasize Safety

Safety is a necessary ingredient in manuscripts selected for publication. The Foundation's scheduled periodical, *Aviation Safety World*, addresses several broad subject areas, and few aviation topics are outside its scope.

Clarity

Aviation Safety World is written in English, but is distributed to many persons whose primary language is not English. Thus, clear writing is especially important.

Follow Guidelines to Prepare Manuscripts

Documents should be sent in both digital and hard copy format. The author may be asked to incorporate or review editorial changes that will lead to acceptance for publication.

Art should accompany the manuscript.

Attribution. Identify information that is copied from another source by quotation marks. Cite the quoted information accurately and attribute its source. Quote only information that can be attributed to specific individuals or publications, not to unidentified or "company representative" sources.

Confirm your facts. Verify the accuracy of numerical data, especially information taken from graphs, charts and tables.

List and number sources at the end of the manuscript, in the same order in which they are cited in the text, in a section called "Notes." Number endnotes sequentially, beginning with "1" (see Notes).

Author's Biography. Outline your current position, background, education and special accomplishments that reflect the experience and knowledge that qualifies you to write credibly about the manuscript's subject.

Hard Copy Specifications. One copy of the manuscript on white paper is required. Use a plain 12-point typeface. Leave the back side of each page blank. Double-space text.

Cover Letter. Provide daytime and evening telephone numbers, fax number (if applicable) and your e-mail address. If you are a U.S. citizen or resident, provide your Social Security number or your business' tax identification number.

Editing. The editorial staff, which must protect the credibility and reputation of the Foundation, reserves the right to edit all manuscripts. Authors are consulted if substantive changes are necessary.

Manuscripts are edited to comply with the Foundation's standards and styles, which are based on The Associated Press Stylebook and Libel Manual, The Chicago Manual of Style and the FSF style book.

First Printing Rights. The Foundation reserves first printing rights. The author must agree that the manuscript shall appear in the Foundation publication before being republished elsewhere. The director of publications can waive this requirement under certain circumstances.

Graphs, Tables, Charts and Illustrations. Visual display of quantitative information reduces the need for lengthy explanations, summarizes data, clarifies relationships and emphasizes/reinforces article content.

Authors are welcome to provide photographs, graphs, tables, charts and illustrations as digital documents or as paper documents (hard copy art). Digital documents are preferred whenever possible, but either rough sketches or refined visual presentations (with adequate data) can be adapted for publication.

Do not fold or crease hard copies of graphs, tables, charts or illustrations for shipment.

Photographs. Digital photos in TIFF or JPEG format must be of sufficient resolution to produce a 300 dpi image at a useable size. Photo prints and transparencies are also accepted.

Write brief captions in the present tense; they should add information that is not obvious from looking at the image. Identify each person from left to right (clockwise). Use complete names, titles and affiliations. If appropriate, provide other information such as date, location and photo credit.

The Foundation prefers to retain all published photographs; if requested by the author, prints, transparencies and negatives will be returned after publication.

Payment. Flight Safety Foundation buys all rights to the author's manuscript, and payment is made at the rate of US$300 per full page as published, to a maximum of $1,500. An additional payment of $50 is made for each published piece of original art—photographs, charts, figures, illustrations and tables—that is prepared by the author. A check for payment is mailed within 10 days after publication. If there are multiple authors, the check is usually issued to the first author listed on the manuscript.

Each author will receive a complimentary one-year subscription to *Aviation Safety World*.

Extra Copies. At no charge, you will be mailed six copies of the periodical in which your article is published. The editorial staff can arrange to print additional copies at minimum cost to you, but you must make this request well before the periodical goes to press.

Publication and Copyright. Generally, the manuscript must be unpublished and must not be under consideration for publication elsewhere. In some circumstances, the Foundation may consider a previously published manuscript if it has been rewritten and adapted for Foundation readers. If your manuscript has been copyrighted, a copyright transfer may be required before your manuscript will be published by the Foundation. Contact the director of publications for more information.

To disseminate credible and objective safety information as widely as possible, the Foundation buys all rights to each manuscript, and the author must sign a transfer of copyright. Nevertheless, the public is encouraged to reproduce information, in whole or in part, from reports, proceedings of seminars and scheduled periodicals that are published by the Foundation.

Notes. Cite the sources that support your manuscript's text by following the examples listed below:

Book: Author's last name, first name [omit degrees and affiliations, but middle initial can be included in all examples]; second author's last name, second author's first name [if applicable]. Title of Book. City, state, country [publisher's location]: publisher, year.

Collier, Basil. A History of Air Power. New York, New York, United

States: Macmillan Publishing Co., 1974.

Meeting Paper [published]: Author's last name, first name. "Title of Paper." In [Name of Publication or Proceedings], edited by [omit if no editor's name is given]. City, state, country [publisher's location]: Publisher, year.

Koplin, Klaus. "The JAA Safety Strategy Initiative." In Keeping Safety a Worldwide Priority: Proceedings of the 55th annual International Air Safety Seminar, IFA 32nd International Conference and IATA. Alexandria, Virginia, United States: Flight Safety Foundation, 2002.

Meeting Paper [unpublished]: Author's last name, first name. "Title of Paper." Paper presented at [name of meeting, location of meeting, month and year of meeting].

Mason, Jeanette. "Safety Adds Up." Paper presented at the 54th Annual Meeting of Aerospace Chief Financial Officers, Mesa, Arizona, United States, May 2001.

Periodical: Author's last name, first name. "Title of Article." Name of Periodical Volume number (issue number or date of issue): page range.

Veillette, Patrick R. "Most Fatal U.S. Commercial Helicopter Accidents Occur in Instrument Meteorological Conditions." Flight Safety Digest Volume 22 (January 2003): 1–56.

Reports: Author's last name, first name [or organization if no author is listed]. Title of Report, contract number or serial number [if provided]. A special report prepared at the request of [name of agency]. Month and year.

Flight Safety Foundation. Air Carrier Voluntary Flight Operational Quality Assurance Program, Contract No. DTFA01-92-C-00010. A special report prepared at the request of the U.S. Federal Aviation Administration. March 1993.

Style. Spell out all names on first usage, followed by the abbreviation or acronym in parentheses. For example, write "Civil Aviation Authority (CAA)." Many abbreviations and acronyms may not be familiar to all readers.

Categories: Nonfiction—Aviation

CONTACT: J.A. Donoghue, director of publications
Flight Safety Foundation
601 Madison St Ste 300
Alexandria VA 22314-1956
Phone: 703-739-6700, ext 116

Babybug

For a sample issue of BABYBUG, please send $5.00 to: BABYBUG Sample Copy • P.O. Box 300 • Peru, IL 61354. **NOTE:** Sample copy requests from foreign countries must be accompanied by International Postal Reply Coupons (IRCs) valued at US $5.00. Please do NOT send a check or money order.

BABYBUG, a listening and looking magazine for infants and toddlers ages six months to two years, is published by Cricket Magazine Group. BABYBUG features simple stories and poems, words and concepts, illustrated in full color by the best children's artists from around the world. BABYBUG measures 6-1/4" x 7", contains 24 pages, and is printed in large (26-point) type on high-quality cardboard stock with rounded corners and no staples. We hope that the following information will be useful to prospective contributors.

Published: Monthly, except for combined May/June and July/August issues.

Price: $35.97 for 1-year subscription (ten issues)

Manuscripts: Stories very simple and concrete; 4 to 6 short sentences maximum.

Poems: rhythmic, rhyming; 8 lines maximum.

Nonfiction: very basic words and concepts; 10 words maximum.

Activities: parent/child interaction; 8 line maximum.

Rates vary $25 minimum.

Payment upon publication.

Art by assignment only: Artists should submit review samples of artwork to be kept in our illustrator files. We prefer to see tear sheets or photoprints/photocopies of art.

• If you wish to send an original art portfolio for review, package it carefully, insure the package, and be sure to include return packing materials and postage.

• Author-illustrators may submit a complete manuscript with art samples. The manuscript will be evaluated for quality of concept and text before the art is considered.

• Rate: $500/spread ($250/page).

• Payment within 60 days of acceptance. We purchase all rights; physical art remains the property of the illustrator and may be used for artist's self promotion.

Comments:

• BABYBUG would like to reach as many children's authors and artists as possible for original contributions, but our standards are very high, and we will accept only top-quality material. Before attempting to write for BABYBUG, be sure to familiarize yourself with this age child.

• PLEASE DO NOT QUERY FIRST. We will consider any manuscripts or art samples sent on speculation and accompanied by a self-addressed, stamped envelope. Submissions without a SASE will be discarded.

• Please allow 8 to 10 weeks response time for manuscripts, 12 weeks for art samples.

• We do not distribute theme lists for upcoming issues.

BABYBUG normally purchases the following rights. For stories and poems previously unpublished, BABYBUG purchases all rights. Payment is made upon publication. For stories and poems previously published, BABYBUG purchases second North American publication rights. Fees vary, but are generally less than fees for first publication rights. Payment is made upon publication. Same applies to accompanying art.

For recurring features, BABYBUG purchases the material outright. The work becomes the property of BABYBUG and is copyrighted in the name of Carus Publishing Company. A flat fee per feature is usually negotiated. Payment is made upon publication.

For commissioned artwork, BABYBUG purchases all rights plus promotional rights (promotions, advertising, or in any other form not offered for sale to the general public without payment of an additional fee) subject to the terms outlined below:

(a) Physical art remains the property of the illustrator.

(b) Illustrator may use artwork for self promotion.

Categories: Fiction—Nonfiction—Children—Literature—Poetry—Short Stories

CONTACT: Submissions Editor
Material: Manuscripts
CONTACT: Suzanne Beck, Art Director
Material: Art Samples
Cricket Magazine Group
PO Box 300
Peru IL 61354 (after Mar. 1, 2007: 70 E Lake St, Ste 300
Chicago IL 60601)
Website: www.cricketmag.com or www.cobblestonepub.com

BabyLife

Please refer to *ParentLife*.

BabyTalk

BabyTalk reaches 1.8 million readers, primarily women, who are expecting a child or are the parents of a child under the age of 18 months. Every area we cover–pregnancy, the basics of baby care, infant health, growth and development, juvenile equipment and toys, work and day care, marriage and relationships–is approached from a how-to service perspective. The message "here's what you need to know and why" is delivered with smart, crisp style. The tone is confident and reassuring (and, when appropriate, humorous and playful)–advice you can trust, backed up by experts, from someone who's been there.

BabyTalk is largely freelance written, although we use regular contributors for many of the departments. Fees average a dollar a word, depending on the degree of difficulty and the writer's previous experience. Features generally run between 1,000 and 2,000 words. Departments range from 100 to 1,000 words.

Queries should be addressed to the editor of the department in question (Your Body Editor, Table for 2 Editor, Healthy Baby Editor) or, for essays or features, to the Articles Editor. Relevant clips and samples of your work are appreciated, although they can not be returned.

Put all queries in writing (no phone calls, please) and enclose a stamped, self-addressed business-size envelope for a reply. We cannot return any unsolicited manuscripts or material. Please allow at least six to eight weeks for a response. *BabyTalk* will not consider simultaneous submissions. We do not publish poetry.

The best guide for writers is *BabyTalk* itself. Please familiarize yourself with the magazine before submitting a query and take the time to focus your story idea; scattershot queries are a waste of time and postage. Thank you for your interest in *BabyTalk*.

Categories: Fiction—Nonfiction—Arts—Book Reviews—Cartoons—Conservation—Ecology—Environment—Recreation—Short Stories—Writing

CONTACT: Caitlin Stine, Editorial Assistant
Material: All
The Parenting Group, Inc.
530 5th Ave, 4th Floor
New York NY 10036
Phone: 212-522-8989
E-mail: letters@babytalk.com
Website: www.babytalk.com

Back Home In Kentucky

Writer/Photographer Guidelines - Effective: May 2005
NOTES:
Images accompanying articles may be slides, good quality prints, or digital. Digital images MUST be high resolution (at least 300 dpi) suitable for printing on glossy stock.

Images may be emailed in pdf format. If image is larger than 4 mgs, it should be sent on a CD.

Photographer's name and phone number must accompany all images.

Articles may be emailed as text in Microsoft Word.

Rather than word count, length of articles is listed by page count. (A page is 8½ x 11 inches, typed, double-spaced in 10-11-point type.)

BACK HOME IN KENTUCKY is a standard size (8.5 x 11) format magazine printed on glossy stock, generally 48 pages per issue, published bi-monthly, 6 issues per year.

It is a "coffee-table" magazine reflecting a dynamic and contemporary Kentucky, rich in history, hospitality, and natural beauty. Back Home fosters interest and pride in Kentucky, entertaining and educating the reader. The magazine draws attention to the state's little-known sites and events as well as its most popular and interesting places and events.

Queries: We welcome queries and manuscripts on speculation that have a Kentucky connection and fall within these general areas: Kentucky history (Chronicles), Kentucky locations (Field Trip), interesting people and people with interesting jobs or hobbies (Profile), nostalgia (Memories), arts and crafts/crafts (Made In Kentucky), cookbooks by Kentucky author or group (In the Kitchen).

Focus: Each issue focuses on a Kentucky "Destination," which is the main feature of the issue and will be accompanied by a front cover photograph from the area of destination and from 2-6 pages of editorial copy (text and photos). The Destination piece is generally staff written or assigned.

Field Trip: This is a mini-destination piece, featuring a place that perhaps is not as widely known but interesting for its historic significance, natural beauty, architecture, etc.

These can be any size, from a one-page feature with photo, to a 2-4-page spread. Good photos are important to this piece.

Kentucky Treasure: Generally a one- to two-page feature of an historic site, building, park, old-stand forest area, etc.

Profile/Pursuit: "Profile" and "Pursuit" are so closely related in content that they are listed together here. These are features about people who have a Kentucky connection - an individual with an interesting hobby, vocation, or career. These can be 2-3 page features. An example is a recent feature on a champion ice skater. (May-June 2005)

Made in Kentucky: This features a product made in Kentucky, generally something unusual or interesting such as a hobby that evolved into a marketable product. A good example is the "Spirits of Design" (July/Aug 2005) featuring the melting and flattening of liquor bottles to create cheese trays, etc. that retain the shape and label of the original bottle. This feature can be 2-3 pages with photos.

Memories: A first person anecdotal feature of 2-3 pages in length. This feature could be accompanied by old family photos.

Commonwealth Chronicle: A feature relating to Kentucky history. This could be about one individual, an historic place, event, or category (medicine, exploration, aviation). Length can be up to 4 pages. Photos and/or illustrations desirable.

In the Kitchen: This is our recipe source and our opportunity to help a Kentucky group or author sell their cookbook. Send us a free sample along with brief information about the group or author, price of the cookbook, and how to order. We select about a dozen recipes for our "In the Kitchen" feature, and give How to Order information at the end. All orders for the cookbook go directly to the group/author.

Payment: Payment for all materials is upon publication. Payment is for first-time North American rights, unless otherwise negotiated. Writers receive a by-line and three copies of the magazine containing their article. Material is subject to editing and is placed in the magazine as content merits and space allows. Materials will be returned if requested and ONLY if a self-addressed, stamped envelope is enclosed with submitted materials. The editor determines suitability of material for inclusion, as well as in which issue the material appears. Payment is negotiated with the author but ranges from $50-$100 depending on department or category, and other criteria. Photos accompanying articles are paid for as part of the manuscript purchase.

Photographs: Photo essay submissions are welcome. Back Home welcomes submissions of color transparencies for cover consideration, but please query as to editorial calendar as covers are determined by our "Destination" feature. We use about 25 photos per issue, less than 10% on assignment.

Photos submitted MUST BE IDENTIFIED as to location—BE SPECIFIC. Don't identify as "a Kentucky barn" or "Snow-covered log." Kentucky is a very county-oriented state. We want to know the county name where it was taken, and anything else you can tell us about your photo. We accept 35mm slides and larger format transparencies, prints and digital (300dpi or higher resolution). Payment for photo submissions is negotiated. No payment is made for photos submitted for the Fairs & Festivals section, as it is assumed their publication benefits the event.

DEADLINES: Back Home In Kentucky editorial content is

planned several months in advance. If an author wishes his/her work to appear in a particular month, it is advisable to work closely with the editor. Material should be in the editor's hands no later than ten (10) weeks prior to the month of the issue (i.e.: May/June material is due Feb. 15).

DON'T FORGET: All submissions should include author/ photographer's name, mailing/shipping address, and a TELEPHONE NUMBER, for the editor's convenience should questions arise. Include an e-mail address if you have one. Manuscripts should be typed, one-sided, double-spaced with word-count included. We accept emailed manuscripts in Microsoft Word and a variety of formats, but please query before sending it in a format that may not be compatible.

Copies: Single-issue copies are available for $3 plus $1.87 postage for first class mailing.

NOTE: Back Home In Kentucky, Inc. also publishes 2-4 bonus issues each year, as well as other publications. Examples:

(1.) Kentucky's Civil War 1861-1865: Published Annually: Volume I-2002; Volume II-2003; Volume III- 2004.

(2.) Lewis and Clark – Corps of Discovery: Published in 2003 commemorating the 200th anniversary of the exploration. (Copies available at $5.00 each plus $2.50 s/h.)

(3.) Family Guide to Kentucky Museums and Historic Sites (Copies of the 2004 edition are available through the Kentucky History Center, Frankfort.) *Will be updated in 2006.*

(4.) Kentucky Arts & Artisans: Publication date – 2006.

(5.) *Kentucky's Civil War 1861-1865*: A hard-cover book scheduled for release in August 2005, contains some of the articles which were in Vols. I, II, and III, and additional information including a fold-out map of Civil War battles and skirmishes in Kentucky.

(6.) Kentucky Festivals & Events: Launched in 2003, this is a tabloid newsprint publication about festivals and events throughout the state, published 6 times each year. Subscription to Kentucky Festivals & Events is $12/year or $10 to Back Home subscribers. For information about advertising in or submitting information to Kentucky Festivals & Events, contact Festivals Editor Lisa Matthews, P.O. Box 278, Shelbyville KY 40065, PH: 502-633-7766; FAX: 502-633-7850, Email: Smilla88@aol.com.

Categories: Nonfiction—Animals—Antiques—Architecture—Arts—Biography—Civil War—Collectibles—Cooking—Crafts/Hobbies—History—Rural America—Travel—Regional (Kentucky-related only)

CONTACT: Jerlene Rose, Editor/Publisher
Material: All
PO Box 710
Clay City KY 40312-0710
Phone: 606-663-1011
Fax: 606-663-1808
E-mail: info@backhomeinky.com
Website: www.backhomeinky.net

Back to College

Rights: Exclusive, first-use one-time electronic rights only. We also retain the non-exclusive right to archive all published articles on an indefinite basis. For certain articles we will also accept reprints.

Needs: Articles of interest to the returning student, including real-life experiences of adults returning to school, advice on maximizing financial aid, academic success tips, and accelerating a degree plan. Open to ideas.

Length: open
Art/Photo Needs: Prefer a photo with article.
Payment: $75-$100 for original feature articles.
How to Submit: http://www.back2college.com/submit.htm
Response Time: 30 days maximum, usually within two weeks.
Tips for Writers: Please send the full article for best consideration. If submitting a query, please attach clips of former work.

Writer's Guidelines

Back to College® is a news and information resource for adult re-entry students pursuing professional development or an advanced degree.

Content

Feature articles must address issues that are of importance to the older student: obtaining financial aid, distance education, finding the right program (comparing costs and quality of curriculum), graduate school, or attaining academic excellence (study skills and success strategies). Career management and articles on successful transition are appreciated. We are especially looking for stories on the re-entry student experience. Articles may be anecdotal, or include examples, direct quotes, and resources where readers can obtain more information. Web resources cited are desirable for an online publication. Please do not submit articles or queries proposing content already covered in previous features or elsewhere on the Website.

(**Please note**: Articles will not be accepted for payment if they may be considered promotional in nature or provide testimonials for a Web site, book, product, or service.)

Feature articles must be submitted in electronic form via e-mail or through our online submissions form below (no attachments, please.)

Terms and Conditions

Feature Articles: Payment is $50.00 - $75.00 for feature articles ($25.00 - $35.50 for reprints), approximately 1,250 - 1,500 words in length (payment is rendered according to depth), and is rendered by check 30 days from publication.

Columns: $50.00 - $65.00 for 850-1,000 words.

Editorial Cartoons: $125.00 for each set of four cartoons looking at the lighter side of returning to school.

By submitting articles for publication on Back to College, you grant WD Communications LLC exclusive first-serial rights to the articles for the first six months, non-exclusive serial rights thereafter (including the right to archive the article online on an indefinite basis), and the world-wide, royalty free and non-exclusive license to use, distribute, reproduce, publish, and incorporate the article (in whole or in part) in any ancillary or subsidiary product or reprint. If you republish the article after the six month period, we ask that you mention that the article first appeared on Back to College®.

Compensation

By submitting an article, you represent that you are its sole author or creator, or that you are submitting it with the permission of its author or creator who has agreed to these terms and conditions. You also grant WD Communications LLC permission to publish your photo in any publication or Web site in relation to your article. WD Communications LLC reserves the right to edit articles for grammar and style.

Author receives a byline and photo with a short summary of biographical information. Back to College was listed as one of The 50 Best Places to Get Published Online by Writer's Digest in 2001.

Queries

For best consideration, send the article itself. Writers may submit proposed articles to the editor by using the online submission form. All queries must include full article details or outline, a writing sample, biographical information, any publishing credits or references, and estimated length of article.

Before submission, **check article** for factual correctness, style and content: (strong article lead, body, and ending). Completed articles need to be tight, concise and professional and include a short biography and color digital photo of the author (author photos should be a headshot and be in .jpeg or .gif format.) Please include proposed article title and word count. If a query or submission is accepted, you will be notified within 30 days of submission. No phone queries, please.

Publication Deadlines

Back to College is updated weekly. Submissions are preferred by Wednesday afternoon before 5:00 p.m. Pacific Standard Time for the upcoming week.

Catergories: College

CONTACT: D. Rickerd, Editor
WD Communications
PO Box 2001
Fullerton, CA 92837
Phone: 714-447-0734
E-mail: webmaster@back2college.com
Website: www.back2college.com

BackHome Magazine

Suggestions for BackHome Contributors

BackHome is a down-to-earth, how-to magazine whose primary purpose is to help people gain more control over their own lives by doing more for themselves. We are looking for interesting, lively, preferably first-person articles based upon actual experience in the fields of gardening, home construction and repair, workshop projects, cooking, crafts, outdoor recreation, family activities and vacations, livestock, home business, home-based and other education, and community/neighborhood action.

In general, we'll consider any article that will help our readers improve the quality of life—for themselves, their families, their community, and their environment. We seldom publish essays or basically philosophical contemplations.

You can query or make submissions by e-mail (backhome@ioa.com). We try to answer queries within a reasonable time. You are welcome to send complete articles, but in most cases sending a query in advance may save you the trouble of writing an article only to discover that we have a similar one in our files.

At present our base rate of pay is $35 a printed page, payable upon publication. We pay extra for good clear photographs: color prints are preferable but transparencies are OK. We return all photos sent to us. Photos sent electronically should be at least 300 dpi. We prefer to buy first North American serial rights, in which case you're free to sell the article elsewhere after we run it, but we may hold your accepted submission for a considerable time before finding a spot for it. (We sometimes use second-rights material if its previous appearance was not in a major publication.) If after accepting an article we find we can't use it, we pay a kill fee of $25.

When submitting an article, please include your full name, address, and phone number. If you submit hard copy it is helpful if you can provide your manuscript on computer disk or transmit it by modem. A stamped self-addressed envelope, or your e-mail address, will speed up our answers to your queries, and an envelope with correct postage is essential if you want your manuscript and photos returned. If you haven't seen BackHome, we strongly suggest you read at least an issue or two to get a better feel for the magazine before you try to write for us. If you can't find BackHome locally, you can order a sample from us for $5.00 or a one-year subscription for $21.97 (six issues).

Thank you very much for your interest in BackHome.

Categories: Environment—Family—Gardening—Sustainable Living—Alternative Energy—"Green" Building

CONTACT: Lorna K. Loveless, Editor
PO Box 70
Hendersonville NC 28793
E-mail: backhome@ioa.com
Website: www.backhomemagazine.com

Backpacker

BACKPACKER is a proud sponsor of Leave No Trace (check out our book, Leave No Trace, available from The Mountaineers Press). All articles and photos that appear in the magazine must adhere to Leave No Trace's ecologically friendly practices. Likewise, we do not promote motorized use in the wilderness or backcountry.

Our readers are knowledgeable and experienced backpackers, therefore we accept only authentic, well-researched, well-crafted stories (see the section on "Accuracy," below). We're not interested in slavish imitations of stories we've already done. As always, you should carefully study several issues of the magazine before submitting a query. The best articles have style, depth, emotional impact, and take-away value for the reader.

Good *BACKPACKER* articles contain the following attributes:

• Foot-based travel: BACKPACKER primarily covers hiking. When warranted, we cover canoeing, kayaking, snowshoeing, cross-country skiing, and other human-powered modes of travel.

• Wilderness or backcountry: The true backpacking experience means getting away from the trailhead and into the wilds. Whether a dayhike or a weeklong trip, out-of-the-way, unusual destinations are what we're looking for.

• North American destinations: We only occasionally cover foreign locales. Our defined market is North American destinations.

• Advice for improving the backcountry experience: Our readers want to know how to, when to, where to, and with what. Every *BACKPACKER* article incorporates one or more of these things. We write not merely to inspire our readers to do something, but to help them identify and research new places to go, techniques and skills to use, or the gear to take.

While a large portion of *BACKPACKER* is written by staff and regular contributors, we encourage freelance authors to submit query letters for features and departments. Approximately 50 percent of our features and more than half of our departments are written by freelancers. Please note that it's rare for a writer new to *BACKPACKER* to break into the magazine with a feature assignment. Direct your efforts toward establishing a working relationship with us via department assignments first.

FEATURES

BACKPACKER features usually fall into one of several distinct categories: destinations, personality, technique, or gear. Gear features are generally staff written. In order to make the grade, a potential feature needs an unusual hook, a compelling story, a passionate sense of place, or unique individuals finding unique ways to improve or enjoy the wilderness.

• Destinations: *BACKPACKER* uses pieces that go beyond a mere description of a trail or place. Our destination stories are almost always first person and based upon the author's recent trip experience. Readers should come away with a strong sense of that particular outdoor experience, a firm grasp of the location's character, and the inspiration to duplicate the trip. Journal-style articles are generally unacceptable. Typical word count is 1,250 to 1,750 words, plus a full Expedition sidebar (contact, permit, season, hazards, map, guidebook, and other useful information; look at past *BACKPACKER* issues for examples and style).

• Personality: Backpacking doesn't have star athletes like you find in bicycling or some other outdoor sports, but plenty of unique personalities exist to write about. Colorful, controversial, historically significant, amusing, unusual, or unique people are what we're looking for, especially those who have a direct impact on how or where others hike.

• Technique: Skill-based articles in *BACKPACKER* feature high levels of take-away value. A good technique piece also has information relevant to all skill levels (e.g., beginner, intermediate, and advanced hikers). Often our technique pieces take non-narrative forms.

• Gear: Our Field Tests and comparative gear reviews are always written by writers we've worked with before. If you're interested in writing such articles, start by querying our equipment editor about the Outfitting department (see "Departments," below).

DEPARTMENTS

Freelancers most often break into *BACKPACKER*'s pages in the departments. These shorter assignments (100 to 1,200 words) have specific topics and focus.

• Signpost: the news, issues, views, trends, and people that influence the backpacking world.

• Skills: the how-to, techniques, and tips department that covers all essential hiking and camping skills plus the following categories:

Food—centers on all aspects of trail nutrition, cooking, and food preparation. Tested recipes are a must.

Fitness/First Aid—covers the physical and psychological aspects of fitness, health, first aid, and occasionally nutrition as it relates to backpacking.

Wild Things—covers animals, plants, geology, any nature-oriented topic, provided it is presented in a way that provides substantive information a reader can actively apply on a backcountry trip.

• Outfitting: This department is filled with short reviews of gear that has been field-tested. Note: Outfitting, unlike the other departments, is done by assignment only. Instead of submitting a query regarding a specific piece of equipment, query the equipment editor with your qualifications for testing and reviewing gear. All gear reviewed in Outfitting is acquired by *BACKPACKER* editors only and shipped by us to assigned reviewers. All reviewed gear must be returned to us at the end of the test so that we may photograph it and return it to the manufacturer. This is not a way to fill your gear closet.

• Getaways: This is where we print short, fact-filled destination pieces on trails that can be hiked in a weekend or week. Destinations must be backcountry and offer overnight camping.

Most *BACKPACKER* departments take a single topic within the scope of that section and cover it thoroughly. Again, the more take-away value for the reader, the more appropriate it is for *BACK-PACKER*.

ACCURACY

BACKPACKER prides itself on providing outdoor enthusiasts with reliable information. It's important that our contributors check all facts and figures. A full set of guidelines for fact checking will be provided to you with your first contracted assignment for us. In general, however, we require:

Confirmation of all facts and figures used within an article from a primary source.

For medical, nutrition, and technical advice, direct quotes from accepted professionals or experts.

Full contact information for every source used in creating an article.

An extra copy for our files of any map, catalog, brochure, or other primary source you may have acquired from a land agency or manufacturer.

QUERIES

We prefer queries to completed manuscripts. Send samples of your published work with your first query. Include a SASE envelope if your samples must be returned. We are not responsible for unsolicited artwork, photographs, and manuscripts, so please don't send originals or anything that you can't afford to lose. Allow 6 to 8 weeks for replies.

ASSIGNMENTS AND PAYMENT

All *BACKPACKER* assignments are made in writing, and require a signed contract with you, the freelance author, in order to be valid. The contract will specify payment amount, payment terms, and rights purchased. In general, we pay on acceptance and buy all rights. We pay $.60 to $1.00 per word, depending upon the complexity and demands of the article, as well as the proven experience of the writer.

PHOTOGRAPHY

BACKPACKER uses stock photography and assigns photographers for magazine-sponsored trips. We use high-quality color transparencies in any format. We prefer photographs that meet the following requirements:

The activity shown does not violate local agency guidelines or Leave No Trace principles (e.g., unless specifically allowed in that location, no tents within 200 feet of water).

No visible roads and no frontcountry shots, unless specifically required by the article. *BACKPACKER* is about the backcountry experience and hiking in wildlands; photos taken at scenic outlooks on a road are not what the backpacking experience is about.

Packs and equipment shown in photos should reflect backpacking, not dayhiking or car camping. We're not likely to run a photo of someone wearing a fanny pack on a trail, nor are we likely to use a photo showing someone cooking on a two-burner stove set up on a campground table.

Because we use unbleached, recycled paper stock for the magazine, transparencies shot on film that saturates colors work best for us (e.g., Fuji Velvia, Fuji Provia, Kodak Ektachrome 100VS, etc.). This is especially true for gear photos.

Other things that we look for in photos, especially in gear shots for use in technique stories or • • • Outfitting: Hikers should not be shown wearing sneakers or jeans. At least one person should be in every shot to give a sense of scale to the equipment.

No dogs in the photo (unless we've requested it).

Packs should fit the hiker properly, and features like bottle holders should be utilized.

Tents should be fully staked out and the fly should be tight.

Smaller products, such as purifiers, stoves, and headlamps, should be shot in use.

A variety of images to choose from (two or three dozen), both vertical and horizontal, as well as varying viewpoints and framing.

• Stock Requirements: While we use a large amount of stock photography to illustrate articles, we usually have very specific requirements (e.g., "overnight hiker on McConnell Lake Trail, Desolation Wilderness, preferably with Horseshoe Lake in background"). For each issue, our photo editor sends out via e-mail a list of photos we need for upcoming articles. If you believe you have stock photos that may meet our needs, contact Liz Reap (lreap@*BACKPACKER*.com) indicating your interest in receiving our monthly call list. We require a stock list and a leave-behind example of your work. Portfolios are welcome, however please contact us first to let us know it's coming. If your work meets our photographic standards, you will be added to our database.

• Assignments: *BACKPACKER* is one of the few magazines that still hires photographers on a contract basis and sends them out on assignment. These assignments are grueling, as they often involve lots of mileage over rough terrain. Not only that, but you have to get your pictures while moving through the terrain, carrying your own photo and backpacking gear. Because we're a small publication, our budgets and time restraints are quite restrictive in this area, thus we tend to work only with photographers that we know to be capable of always bringing back results, no matter what the conditions. Interested photographers should contact photo editor Liz Reap and be prepared to present a portfolio of photographs taken in the backcountry.

Our pay rates for photography varies depending on how the photograph is used, and at what size:

• Cover photos: $550 to 800

Photo use inside magazine: $100 to 400 (depends upon size and placement)

Assignment day rate: $450 to 500

STATISTICS

Publishing frequency: 9 issues annually, one of which is the Gear Guide (March)

Circulation: 300,000 (2004)

Lead time: 6 months

Categories: Outdoor—Sports/Recreation—Travel

CONTACT: Peter Flax, Features Editor
Material: Features
E-mail: pflax@BACKPACKER.com
CONTACT: Dave Howard, Senior Associate Editor
E-mail: dhoward@BACKPACKER.com
Material: Getaways, Signpost
CONTACT: Michelle Hamilton, Assistant Editor
Material: Getaways, Skills
E-mail: mhamilton@BACKPACKER.com
CONTACT: Dennis Lewon, Equipment Editor,
Material: Outfitting
E-mail: dlewon@BACKPACKER.com
33 E. Minor St.
Emmaus, PA 18098.
Website: www.BACKPACKER.com

Backroads
Motorcycle Tour Magazine

Introduction

The concept of *Backroads* is simple. It is a publication created with the idea of giving our readers places of interest to ride to and getting the most enjoyment out of their motorcycles. Although *Backroads* is geared towards the motorcycling population, it is not by any means limited to just motorcycle riders. Non-motorcyclists enjoy great destinations too. As time has gone by, *Backroads* has developed more and more into a cutting edge touring publication. We like to see submissions that give the reader the distinct impression of being part of the ride they're reading. Words describing the feelings and emotions brought on by partaking in this great and exciting lifestyle are encouraged.

Aim and Query Before Shooting and Writing

Backroads does not send out rejection letters, just emails and notes to let you know we are interested. Being a touring publication, we are always interested in your travels, especially when they lead our readers to exciting new destinations, but sometimes we have a backlog of articles that cover the same area, idea or situation. To save you and us a lot of time, it is best to email us a note on your intentions regarding your article before submission.

We love pictures. The more the merrier. Particularly shots of motorcycles on the move, great scenery and creative photography. *Backroads* is about riding, and although we will use party pictures when appropriate, we discourage photography showing only indoor "end of the ride" shots.

Backroads Dos and Don't

What *Backroads* does not want is any "us vs. them" submissions.

We are decidedly non-political and secular. *Backroads* is about getting out and riding, not getting down on any one particular group, nor do we feel this paper should be a pulpit for a writer's beliefs…be they religious, political or personal.

Please do not take any returns or criticism to heart. If we rejected an article perhaps another regional or national publication could use it. Don't give up or stop sending in submissions, you're already doing more than most folks…keep writing!

Backroads does not want submissions that push any one particular dealership or shop. Of course, if a shop is part of an event or charitable cause, mentioning the shop is the right thing to do. But a mention is not a 100 word description of everything the shop or dealer does. Articles are not ads, nor do we feature any one dealer or shop as an article by itself.

When writing a piece for *Backroads* try not to go overboard mentioning everybody's name. This paper is not here to make points for people personally. Stick to the story.

How to Submit

All submissions must be accompanied by images (negatives or slides), with an SASE of adequate size to return all material sent as well as a copy of the issue in which they were published, and a hard copy printout of the article, including your name, address and phone number. If none is enclosed, the materials will not be returned.

Text submissions are accepted via US mail on CD. Color images must be no smaller than 250 dpi, with B&W acceptable at 170 dpi. *Backroads* accepts both negatives, with accompanying prints for verification, and slides.

Please do not submit faded photocopies or badly developed film, as we will not use them. Photos should be properly exposed, neither light and washed out looking nor so dark that detail is hard to make out. Be aware of the five Ws of journalism, pertaining both to photography and writing: who, what, when, where and why. *Backroads* does not use photos that do not accompany an article, and vice versa.

What *Backroads* Is Looking For

Backroads has several monthly columns which are open to freelance writers. They include:

The Great All American Diner Run. An eatery destination story accompanied by directions, affectionately called a "Rip & Ride Route Sheet." These should be about 500 to 750 words, with a few good photos, at least one showing the eatery (with motorcycle in shot). Focus on ride area, eatery and what makes it a great motorcyclist's destination are suggestions for inclusioin. Payment on publication: $50

Big City Getaway. A day trip, either including a specific destination or just an enjoyable day's ride, about 500 to 750 words, with a few good photos along the route and of the destination, and route sheet. Payment on publication: $50

Mysterious America. Dr. Seymour O'Life founded this column. Since he is frequently gallivanting around the world, he needs help filling the spot. These stories should feature some mysterious, amazing, bizarre or just head-scratching destination. Story should be about 500 to 750 words, with photos, of course, of destination, although route sheet is not mandatory. Payment on publication: $50

We're Outta Here. *Backroads'* multi-day destination column, aimed towards couples looking for a quick weekend getaway, or perhaps a club ride, if the destination warrants larger groups. This should feature overnight accommodations, such as a hotel, B&B or such, route sheet, and photos of area and destination. Length from 500 to 750 words. Payment on publication: $50

Thoughts from the Road. This column gives the writer an opportunity to reflect on motorcycling, whether it be a specific instance that meant something in their life, a person that influenced them, or just something that ticked them off. As mentioned before, no pontificating, please, but rather thoughtful reflection. Length should be 400 to 600 words. Payment on publication: $50

Full Length Travel Features. This type of story offers a good opportunity for prospective contributors. They MUST feature spectacular photography, color preferable, and may be used as a cover story, if of acceptable quality. (Please query before submitting.) Payment on publication varies from .05¢ to .10¢ a word.

Travel Feature Dos and Don't

Don't write a blow-by-blow diary filled with minute, personal details. Structure your story with an opening that makes the reader want to read more. Include hotels or campgrounds in the area, key attractions and how to get to them, interesting places to eat, and special regional events, if applicable. Make sure that all information is current. A route sheet, with a loop of the area, would be a good feature. Photo suggestions include scenic shots with and without rider(s) and action shots. A mini tripod is always a good accessory to include in your tankbag on such trips.

Other avenues open to freelance are product review and Club Spotlights. Payment on publication varies–please query before submission.

Payment and Rights

Payment for all articles is upon publication, and varies from $50 and upward. *Backroads* buys one-time publication rights. We will accept articles that have been previously printed with a gap of at least six months from submission to *Backroads*. Please do not send us an article that has been simultaneously submitted to another publication! We reserve the right to edit any material we accept.

We hope these guidelines will be of help to you and we look forward to reading your submissions. If you have any questions regarding these guidelines, please drop us a line.

Categories: Adventure—Trade—Motorcycles Travel

CONTACT: Brian Rathjen, Publisher
Material: All
PO Box 317
Branchville NJ 07826
Phone: 973-948-4176
Fax: 973-948-0823
E-mail: editor@backroadsusa.com

Backwoodsman Magazine

Subjects: Muzzleloading guns, muzzleloading hunting, 19th century woodslore, early cartridge guns, primitive survival, craft items from yesteryear, American history, grass roots gardening, leather crafting projects, homesteading, log cabin construction, mountain men, Indians, Indian bow & arrow construction, building primitive weapons, etc.

We are not particularly interested in fictional stories, or material that has the tone of a novel. Any material of this type submitted to *Backwoodsman Magazine* will be sent back. It is important that any material submitted also have illustration or photo, many times this is the determining factor whether an article is published. Pen and ink drawings, or b/w and color pictures will reproduce. No pencil drawings. Length of material is left up to the author, but lengthy material that covers a subject in depth is always favored over a short piece. We do not count words at Backwoodsman, only the depth by which a subject is covered.

Pay: *Backwoodsman Magazine* is not a paying magazine. In the near future it's possible that we can become a paying magazine, but at this time we can't afford to pay. We are willing to trade a 1/24 page display ad (value $55) for each article submitted and accepted. Several of our regular writers who have something to sell have chosen this route. In the event you don't have anything to sell in the buckskinning field we are willing to trade a subscription for an article accepted. We want writers who care about a special publication, not writers who care more for the money they might earn. If you can gain satisfaction from submitting subject material of importance to our BWM family of readers, then you are our type of people.

Misc.: We do not deal in world affairs, personal vendettas, or bad mouthing products. Our whole basis is yesteryear. This is not to say that you can't speak your mind. We also do not publish racially motivated material of any type. We don't need a law suit.

If you desire correspondence with us, please send a SASE.

Categories: Crafts/Hobbies—History—Hobbies—Native American—Western—Buckskinning: Fur Trade—Historical (how-to)—Primitive Archery

CONTACT: Submissions Editor
Material: All
PO Box 627
Westcliffe CO 81252
Phone: 719-783-9028
Fax: 719-783-9028
E-mail: bwmmag@rif.net
Website: www.backwoodsmanmag.com

Baja Life

Baja Life is a magazine devoted to promoting tourism, culture, environmental concerns and economic development in the Baja peninsula. Contributors should have a strong basic understanding of their subject matter.

Subjects of interest include Recreational Activities, Tourist Interests, The People of Baja, Environmental Issues, Historical Figures, Retirement Living, Historical Events, Cultural Events, The Arts and Business Development.

Both a double-spaced hard copy and a computer file of an article should be submitted. If forwarding by E-mail, take out double spacing and put the file in some kind of 10 point type (ASCII format). Double space only between paragraphs and use a tab. Do not use ### at all. Use -30- at the end of text. Send as a text file, not a binary file.

E-mail: erik@bajalife.com. Payment for articles may be reduced if *Baja Life* or Baja Communications Group manually enters an article. Also be sure to include your full name, address, phone number and social security number.

Acceptable Computer Formats: PC or Mac formatted. Acceptable formats include MS Word, WordPerfect Mac, MacWrite II or any ASCII

format on 3½" disks.

Terms:
Payment is made upon publication. Since all payment requests are submitted monthly to our Accounts Payable Department, delivery of payment may take up to 30 days from publication.

Feature Articles:
Payment for feature articles of 2,000 words plus are paid at a rate of $.10 per word. The author is expected to provide accurate, researched facts and correct spellings of all proper names. Spanish words must include appropriate punctuation.

Columns and Travel Reports:
Columns and travel reports of 600 to 1,000 words are paid at a rate of $.10 per word. Writers are expected to deliver an unbiased, accurate description of the resort or location. Instructional columns and technical subjects should be written for the average reader. Please educate our readers by defining.

Baja Communications Group, publishers of Baja Life magazine, assumes no responsibility for the return of material and considers for publication only those manuscripts that are previously unpublished and checked for factual accuracy, unless otherwise agreed upon by the interested parties.

Categories: Nonfiction—Arts—Business—Culture—Environment—History—Recreation

CONTACT: Baja Life Magazine
Material: All
PO Box 4917
Laguna Beach CA 92652
Phone: 949-376-2252
Fax: 949-376-7575
E-mail: admin@bajalife.com

Bakersfield Magazine

Bakersfield Magazine is written by both staff and freelance writers. We seek writers with the ability to pull the reader into the story through character development and dramatic illustration. We demand accuracy, strict adherence to deadlines and the ability to self-edit.

Story concepts are generally developed in-house, then assigned, but we are always open to new ideas. To propose an article, submit a query letter—no longer than one page—via e-mail or post. E-mail elicits the quickest response.

As a city magazine, serving the Greater Bakersfield Metropolitan area, our focus is on local people, places, things and events. We do not cover statewide or national issues unless there is a direct local connection. We do not buy articles or pursue topics previously published in other local media. And due to our two-month lead time, we cannot cover breaking news or time-sensitive topics. Article length typically ranges between 1,500 and 2,500 words.

If you would like to join our stable of freelance writers, submit a query letter and clips demonstrating your ability to handle facts, narrative and character development. We favor writers who offer fresh perspectives and/or present a sharp, sophisticated style. If you do not have clips, the best way to break into *Bakersfield Magazine* is through Kern Facts, a section of short articles (100 to 300 words) found in the front of the publication. Query the editor with your idea(s).

Please abide by assignment word lengths and deadlines. Apprise you editor if it appears your story will greatly exceed or fall short of its assigned length. It is preferable to submit shorter, tightly edited articles than to insert useless information to reach a specified word count.

Submit manuscripts in a single-spaced format, with an extra space between paragraphs. Do not indent and use only one space after a period. Do not use any special formatting within the body of the text. E-mail completed articles to your editor on or before your deadline. Should circumstances prevent you from meeting your deadline (ie: problems making contact with sources or you find you are unable to complete your assignment), immediately notify your editor. We do not give additional assignments to writers who cannot meet their deadlines.

Bakersfield Magazine pays on publication, seven (7) cents per word, based on final edit. Writers with photography skills are welcome to submit photos to accompany their stories. *Bakersfield Magazine* pays $8 for the first photo and $5 for each additional photo used in a single issue. A brief caption and the photographer or owner's name must accompany each photo. Photos remain with *Bakersfield Magazine* until publication. If you use a digital camera or plan to submit photography electronically, please contact the production department for format specifications.

Writers and photographers must complete and sign Contributer's Contract and Photography Release Form(s) before *Bakersfield Magazine* can accept submissions of any materials. These forms can be downloaded from the magazine's website.

Categories: Nonfiction—General Interest—Regional: Bakersfield, CA

CONTACT: Bakersfield Magazine
Material: All
1601 New Stine Rd Ste 200
Bakersfield CA 93309
Phone: 651-834-4126
Fax: 561-834-5495
E-mail: editorial@bakersfieldmagazine.net
Website: bakersfieldmagazine.net

Balanced Living Magazine

We always encourage article submissions and welcome those who believe in our endeavor to make our world a healthier, happier place.

The following are editorial guidelines for preparing article submissions for *Balanced Living Magazine.*

1. Articles—length should be 700–1,000 words.

2. Mainstream Demographic—Assume a mainstream demographic of our readership. Assume that readers have little to no background knowledge of given subjects. Make sure articles begin with point A and follow through to point Z.

3. Clear Writing—Articles should be easy reads. While an article's subject matter may be complex, the writing style and presentation of information and/or ideas should be clear and deliberate. Utilize paragraphs that convey clear points and move successively from one point to the next. If an article is a difficult read due to writing style, a re-write will be requested of the author or the article will not be considered.

4. Mainstream Content—Content should not be too far from mainstream ideologies. Picture an "open-minded, mainstream reader" and present information they would be interested in and/or accept. We understand that this criterion is highly subjective because everyone has their own idea of what is mainstream; but aim to keep articles and ideas within an open-minded view of normalcy.

5. Formal Writing—Articles should embrace a standard of excellence. While certain magazine departments may accept a slightly casual style of writing, the overall aim should be to present information utilizing very professional literary and grammatical standards. A reader's willingness to accept a new idea hinges on the idea's presentation.

6. Keep it Balanced—Articles should not be overtly one-sided when arguing a sensitive point such as religion or politics. There may be an exception to this standard if we are preparing a Point/Counterpoint feature.

7. Accredited Writing—As much as possible, the author should have a demonstrated knowledge of subject matter.

8. Unbiased and Objective—Articles should be unbiased and objective, unless the article is specifically an opinion piece.

9. Supported Writing—Articles and points should be supported by facts and/or evidence wherever possible. Unsubstantiated statements or statements loaded with senseless propaganda and generalizations should be examined carefully or not submitted.

Categories: Nonfiction—Book Reviews—Environment—Health—Lifestyle—New Age—Physical Fitness—Psychology—Spiritual

CONTACT: Editor-in-Chief
Material: All
Balanced Living Magazine, LLC
13314 Detroit Ave.
Lakewood, OH 44017
Phone: 216-226-6094
Fax: 216-226-6095
E-mail: articles@balancedlivingmag.com
Website: www.balancedlivingmag.com

Balloon Life

Articles should be 1,000 to 1,500 words. Shorter articles in the 300 to 500 word range will be considered. Longer articles may be submitted, but are generally reserved for more technical or historical subjects. In addition, the writer may wish to present additional information as a separate item for use as a sidebar to the article.

Types of articles considered for publication:

• *Balloon events/rallies:* May be written on events that have recently taken place. Post-event articles should be submitted as soon as possible after the completion of the event. Types of information to include would be: the event's name, its history, its organizers, participating balloonists, other attractions in the area (famous restaurants, river raft trips, shopping, etc.), value of the event to the community, etc. Short articles (±300 words) will be accepted for our Logbook section, which deals with an event that has recently taken place.

• *Safety seminars:* Because this is an educational event, the article should be written as an educational piece that can be used by the readers to further their knowledge. If not written by the presenter whose information is being used, you must secure his/her permission.

• *Balloon clubs/organizations:* Tell us the history of the organization, what they do, meetings, events, projects, activities, etc. How the club helps to promote the sport of ballooning and handles public relations.

• *General interest stories:* Can be interviews or biographies of people that have made a contribution to the sport of hot air ballooning, or other general interest items.

• *Crew Quarters:* A regular column devoted to some aspect of crewing. May be educational, tell as story of a crew experience, or share some other aspect of the sport. 900 words preferred.

The above contributions should include pictures (color and black & white) with captions (pictures should be able to tell the story), charts, maps, or additional information that would be helpful in conveying the story to the readers.

All material submitted will be on a speculation basis only. The writer will be notified in writing within two weeks of receipt of the material whether it is being considered for publication. BALLOON LIFE will only consider articles for publication which have not previously been published. BALLOON LIFE will pay $50 for the first time North American rights of articles selected for publication and $20 for short article (our Logbook Section) balloon events that have recently taken place. Payment schedule for pictures is $15 inside and $50 for the cover.

Freelance pictures that are submitted will be considered for publication but generally only if they are of an unusual nature or used for the cover photo. See photo guidelines below for more information.

Those individuals who are interested in writing on a specific, technical topic may contact the editor to discuss subject areas, deadlines, and needs of the magazine. For these topics BALLOON LIFE will pay $100-200 for article(s) used on a specific subject, and provide assistance in researching the subject.

Photo Guidelines

BALLOON LIFE is a 4-color monthly magazine dedicated to the sport of hot air ballooning. Only photographs of the highest quality are considered. Photos should be of sharp exposure, good contrast and with excellent color saturation. The use of photos in the magazine is editorially driven; all photos, including the cover, must relate directly to inside editorial.

Submissions should be 35mm color transparencies. Color or black & white prints may also be acceptable. All photographs should be originals. (Duplicate transparencies will be considered but should be so identified.) Copyright must rest with photographer or written permission must be secured from third-party owners. Captions and model releases are preferred. Unless specific written assignment is made, all photos are accepted on a speculation basis only. Photographs will not be returned unless accompanied by a self-addressed, stamped envelope. The photographer generally will be notified within two weeks to confirm receipt of submissions. Simultaneous submissions and previously published work is okay.

• *Stock Needs:* BALLOON LIFE rarely buys stock photography. As mentioned above, the magazine is editorially driven. Occasionally we are interested in "stock subjects" such as winter flying, mountain flying, commercial balloons, special shape balloons, etc. Photographers should query first for information on these anticipated needs. Please include an indication of the contents of your files.

• *Event Coverage:* BALLOON LIFE targets a variety of balloon events for coverage each year and freelance photographs are often used with these articles. Photo coverage should include not only balloons, but other shots which help the reader to capture the true spirit of the event. For example, celebrities, scenics (with and without balloons) faces in the crowd, related events (arts & crafts fairs, chili cookoffs, polo games), etc. Photographers are welcome to query the magazine for interest if they will be attending an upcoming balloon event.

• *Assignments:* Occasionally assignments are made to shoot either specific events, flights, or subjects. In these cases, BALLOON LIFE will provide the photographer with specific direction, contacts and other assistance. Assignment rates are negotiable.

• *Rates:* BALLOON LIFE buys first North American serial rights. Payment schedule is $50 for the cover and $15 for inside color or B&W. Photos are returned and payment is made upon publication.

Categories: Nonfiction—Aviation—Outdoors—Sports/Recreation

CONTACT: Submissions Editor
Material: All
2336 47th Ave. SW
Seattle WA 98116-2331
Phone: 206-935-3649
Fax: 206-935-3326
E-mail: TOM@balloonlife.come
Website: www.balloonlife.com

Baltimore Magazine

As a regional magazine serving the Baltimore metropolitan area, we're almost obsessive in our focus on local people, events, trends, and ideas.

We sometimes write about national issues, but only those of immediate interest to our readers in Baltimore and surrounding coun-

ties. About 50 percent of our magazine is written by staff members.

We seek feature stories that are rich with character and drama or that provide new insight into local events. These stories range from 1,600 to 2,500 words. To propose one, send a query letter and clips.

Unless you already have a great set of feature clips and a powerful idea, though, the best way to break into Baltimore is through the shorter articles that run before and after the features, in the front of the book sections like B-Side and Baltimore Inc., which run from 300-700 words. Another good place to start is our departments beat, such as "Hot Shots" and "Health." These stories range from 1,400 to 2,000 words. To propose one, send a query letter and clips.

We generally develop story ideas ourselves and sometimes assign them to freelancers. To be considered for such assignments, send clips and a letter about your specialties.

Throughout the magazine we need originality, so don't propose anything that you've seen in *The Sun*, the *Baltimore Business Journal*, or other local media, unless you offer a fresh perspective or important new information. Because of our two-month lead time, we can't do much with breaking news.

You're most likely to impress us with writing that demonstrates how well you handle character, dramatic narrative, and factual analysis. We also admire inspired reporting and a clear, surprising style.

We prefer receiving queries via e-mail.

If you use standard U.S Mail, your query should fit on one page. If you want a response, you must include a stamped, self-addressed envelope with your submission.

Thank you for your interest.

Categories: Nonfiction—General Interest—Regional: Baltimore, Maryland

CONTACT: Submissions Editor
Material: All
Inner Harbor East
1000 Lancaster Street, Ste 400
Baltimore MD 21202
Phone: 410-752-4200
Fax: 410-625-0280
E-mail: iken@baltimoremag.com
Website: www.baltimoremagazine.com

The Baltimore Review

Submit 1-5 poems or 1 work of either fiction or creative non-fiction. Traditional and experimental forms welcome. No themes. Length for essays and short stories: short-short to 6,000 words max. No previously published work. Simultaneous submissions are accepted, but notify us immediately if your work is accepted elsewhere.

Response time is 2-6 months and submissions are read year-round. Payment is in copies; readings are held for our local writers.

The Baltimore Review is distributed through:

Ingram Periodicals, Inc., P.O. Box 7000, 1240 Heil Quaker Blvd., Vergne, TN 37086-7000—(615) 793-5522

Categories: Nonfiction—Poetry—Short Stories

CONTACT: Fiction, Poetry, or Nonfiction Editor
Material: All
PO Box 36418
Towson MD 21286
Website: www.baltimorereview.org

The Bark

The Bark is a quarterly publication for the modern dog enthusiast. We bring to our readers a literate and entertaining approach to dog-life through essays, reviews, interviews and artwork.

The Bark is a quarterly magazine about life with dogs; we pay homage to the age-old relationship between our two species. We seek to bring our readers a literate and entertaining approach to dog-centric articles and stories. We also wish to provide a new forum for writers who have a special appreciation for dogs. *The Bark* is read by 75,000 loyal dog lovers. It is very important for you to become familiar with the "voice" of our magazine before submitting your work. *The Bark* has been publishing for seven years and we have covered many subjects and themes that you might be interested in, we do not repeat ourselves.

Commentaries, essays, stories, fiction and well-researched non-fiction will be considered but all work must include dogs in a prominent manner. Articles and stories should not exceed 2,000 words. Ideally an article should be no longer than 1,200 words, and will stand a better chance of publication if it is below this limit. We also accept short pieces (less than 600 words) on general tips, how-to articles and on other topics as well. All work is subject to editing. We urge you to strive for universal themes and not to discuss any one particular breed of dog. A journalistic approach is one that would be most attractive to us—memoirs are strongly discouraged. If submitting a non-fiction article, primary sources must be provided for fact checking.

We do accept poetry, but we do not have space for all the poems that we would like to publish. We have already selected the poetry that will take us into 2006. But the shorter the poem, the more likely we might be to find space for it.

If you are interested in doing an original book review, please send us a writing sample and let us know what subject matter interests you, or you can simply send us a completed review or the title of the book. Book reviews of current or past work is accepted.

Essay tributes to dogs that have died are discouraged; we have received an abundance of this type of heartfelt writing and simply do not have room for it.

Manuscripts must be typed with author's name, address, phone number and e-mail address on each page; it is very important to include the word count. A short bio would also be appreciated.

It is important to include a SASE. If your submission or query does not include one, your submission will not be considered and you will not receive any notification. Do not send original photos/artwork/slides. Notification time is approximately eight to ten months. E-mail submissions and queries are not accepted. Inquiries about the status of your work cannot be answered, so please do not call, write or e-mail us regarding this.

Payment: *The Bark* pays upon publication, prices vary according to quality and length of the article.

Categories: Animals

CONTACT: Claudia Kawczynska, editor
2810 Eighth Street
Berkeley, CA 94710
Email: editor@thebark.com
Website: www.thebark.com

The Baseball Research Journal

Please refer to the Society of American Baseball Research.

Bass West
A Magazine for Western Bass Anglers

Our goal is to make BASS WEST the most authoritative reference guide in the West. As western water problems continue to grow and fisheries budgets suffer more cutbacks, bass will become even more important to the western fishing scene. With your expertise, we can make BASS WEST a major resource for bass anglers in the West. BASS WEST magazine focuses on western techniques for the deep, clear water and tough fishing conditions found in the West. Each issue has three main sections:

1. Columns by western bass pros such as Mike Folkestad, Don Iovino, Jay Yelas, and Dub LaShot.

2. In-depth features of 2,000 to 3,000 words on western techniques, strategies, issues, etc. Additional standard-length articles of 750 to 1,800 words about projects, tips or other items of interest to western bass anglers.

3. Serious reports on the West's best bass destinations. Up to 4,500 words.

EDITORIAL REQUIREMENTS
• Content geared to both the serious western bass angler and occasional western tournament angler
• Lots of quotes from other authorities on the subject-guides, manufacturers, and biologists
• Specific lures and equipment and identification of manufacturers
• Articles based on current scientific research—western-based biological data
• New facts, not rehashed or outdated opinions

SPECIFICATIONS
• FEATURE ARTICLES: In-depth. hands-on western bass information including seasonal and regional variations-Southwest, Northwest and Intermountain may vary. Educational content is important, as are practical solutions to tough fishing problems. Subjects: techniques, biology, technology, seasonal conditions, etc. Include any slides, photos, charts, maps or illustrations you may have. We also like to clarify subjects with sidebar explanations, illustrations and charts or graphs.
• STANDARD ARTICLES: Unique projects, tidbits, short technical pieces, innovative projects, etc. If helpful, use quotes from experts. Include slides, diagrams, etc.
• DESTINATIONS ARTICLES: We want to know the nuts and bolts-why, where, how. Include information on seasonal variations, good detailed maps and interviews with experts-guides, biologists, and major tournament anglers. List lodges, guides and camping areas with phone numbers.
• PHOTOS AND ILLUSTRATIONS: We require 35mm color slides. We strongly encourage fishing action shots and photos showing tackle, techniques, rigging, lures, locations (especially western scenic locations) and some big fish photos. Please send photo captions with names, places and pertinent information.
• HUMOR/REAL LIFE ADVENTURES: Creative entertainment.
• PHOTOS: Cover shot must include angler; bass, western scenery, and action in one shot.

RATES
Rates are based upon how well the article is written and how closely the author follows the writers' guidelines. Payment for articles and photographs payable 30 to 45 days after publication.
• Feature articles: 2,000 to 3,000 words—$200 to $500.
• Standard articles: 750 to 1,800 words—$75 to $300.
• Destinations articles: 2,000 to 4,500 words—$200 to $500.
• Humor/real life adventure: 750 to 1,000 words—$75 to $250.
• Photos: Independent inside use—$25 to $75. Cover shot-angler, bass, western scenery, and action—Up to $400.

Categories: Fishing

CONTACT: Mark Mendez, Publisher
Material: All
1145 2nd St A-286
Brentwood CA 94513
Phone: 800-591-7111
Fax: 925-240-9450
E-mail: info@basswest.com
Phone: 800-240-9450
Website: www.basswest.com

Bay Area Parent

Please refer to United Parenting Publications.

Bay Area Parent's B.A.B.Y.

Formerly *Bay Area Baby*. Please refer to United Parenting Publications.

Bead & Button

Bead&Button is a bimonthly magazine devoted to techniques, projects and designs, and materials relating to beads, buttons, and accessories. Our readership includes both professional and amateur bead and button makers, hobbyists, and enthusiasts who find satisfaction in making beautiful things. Our authors are skilled artisans (not necessarily skilled writers) who are willing to share what they know, as well as professional writers with technical knowledge in the field.

Our format it 8.5 x 11, four-color throughout, and more than 50% graphic. Most articles are uninterrupted by advertising. Regular departments include: Letters, News & Reviews, Your Work, Origins, Tips & Techniques, Pattern Gallery, Anything Goes, and several projects.

We are looking for beadworking and button hobby articles about techniques, projects and patterns, materials, and people and design concentrated in the areas of jewelry, accessories, and clothing embellishment. We also examine fashion and style and present home furnishings.

Point of View

Our emphasis is on learning to design jewelry and accessories and developing the skills necessary for producing professional looking results. Most articles are or include projects and patterns, both for their own sake and also as a way to encourage experimentation in design. Thus we prefer projects that offer alternatives: in fashion—youthful, mature, and sophisticated styles; in design—suggestions for variation in size, materials, style or technique.

We report on what's available and new in tools, supplies, and materials. We review books, videos, schools or workshops, galleries, and organizations. We report on artists working with beads and buttons from the viewpoint of the enthusiast who is as curious about the artist's life as about her/his methods of work. And we explore trends in accessory fashion and contemporary beads and buttons.

Simultaneous Submissions

We don't accept simultaneous submissions. Please do not send your piece, proposal, or manuscript to us if you are sending it another magazine. If we seem slow in responding to your submission, please call or write to give us the opportunity to accept or release your submission within two weeks.

Article Proposals

If you want to write an article for *Bead&Button*, begin by sending us a proposal. Summarize your project, your knowledge of it, and the focus of your article in two or three paragraphs. Include an outline or a descriptive list of the topics and points you plan to cover. Please include photos and any supporting swatches, samples. And drawings you have or ideas about what you think should be illustrated. At this stage none of the art you submit needs to be publishable. We'll review your proposal and do our best to respond within eight weeks. Whenever sending us your goods, be sure to insure them

Manuscripts

When we ask you to proceed to a finished manuscript, we'll negotiate a deadline for the first draft of the text and supporting materials. For reference, please include all photos and drawings that you think the article requires (or sample of the work at the appropriate step for each photo), captioned and keyed to the text. The more good-quality visual information you can provide, especially photos of work in process that gives step-be-step information about how to make the item or shows what the tricky parts of the process are, the better the magazine article we can produce together.

We are most comfortable working with original color slides or transparencies—preferably 35mm—but sharply focused prints and negatives are fine. We usually arrange to reshoot step-by-step photos and finished work, but be sure to include photo and model credits and the photographer's and model's permission for us to use the photos. We will almost always redraw drawings; those you submit should be labeled so that all the information is clear.

If appropriate, include sources of supply with current addresses and phone numbers and an annotated Further reading list. We need your social security number for payment purposes, so please include it with your manuscript submission.

We'll evaluate your article and get back to you as soon as possible—our goal is within six weeks. We may accept the article immediately and tentatively schedule it for a particular issue (usually six months to a year hence); we may accept it but not yet schedule it (in this case the wait for publication might be up to two years); we may ask you to revise or rewrite before deciding, or we may reject the article. Because each issue of the magazine is a careful blend of techniques, projects, and information, our editorial scheduling must remain flexible. Acceptance of your article is not a promise to publish it but a good-faith acknowledgment of our intention to do so.

When your article has been scheduled for publication, an editor will be assigned to work with you throughout its production. This editor is likely to ask for revisions or clarification. She/he may ask for additional photography or for the loan of your item(s) so that we can rephotograph them. An illustrator will also be assigned to develop the final art for your article. In most cases, you will see an edited version of the manuscript before publication so that you can review it for accuracy and answer an outstanding questions.

Payment

Once we accept your article and have all the necessary materials, we'll send you copyright-agreement forms to sign. We pay for the article upon receipt of the signed contract. We'll also send you complimentary copies of the issue in which your article appears, and you'll have the right to buy up to 50 additional copies at half price while the issue is current. You must notify us before we go to press, however, if you want to buy more than 20 copies of the issue.

We'll reimburse you for out-of-pocket photo expenses that we request (film and processing only). All requests for reimbursement must be cleared with us in advance. We can only reimburse for expenses that are verified with dated receipts.

Contributing to Departments

To contribute to Tips & Techniques (hints, advice, sources for hard-to-find materials, techniques), you don't need to send a proposal. Just send the complete tip together with any necessary rough sketches or photos. For Patterns send a color diagram of your design. We'll pay $20 for each tip and $40 for each pattern upon receipt of your signed contract.

News & Reviews may be opinion or reportage (usually less than 400 words and one or two photos) on current or upcoming books, videos, or new products. A sample of the product must accompany the request for review samples will not be returned. Not all items submitted for review will appear in the magazine.

Anything Goes relates hilarious or amusing experiences with beads, buttons, or accessories or is a short article out of our normal format. Origins explains little-known facts, history, or superstitions about beads, buttons, or body or garment adornments. Your Work (unpaid) presents photos of readers' best work along with a short paragraph about it. Please address your proposals to the appropriate department.

We'd be delighted to discuss your article ideas with you or answer your questions.

Categories: Crafts/Hobbies

CONTACT: Editorial Submissions
Material: All
PO Box 1612
Waukesha, WI 53187-1612
Phone: 262-796-8776
E-mail: web@beadandbutton.com
Website: www.beadandbutton.com

Beadwork

Beadwork is a bi-monthly magazine devoted to every kind of bead stitching and bead making. Always providing clear-cut instruction for beaders of all skill levels, we also inspire readers to find their own creative voice. Articles focus on the latest innovations in the craft, including seed bead stitching, wireworking, lampwork, polymer clay, bead knitting, bead crochet, and beaded embroidery.

Beadwork welcomes fresh ideas to share with our readers, and we appreciate new approaches to standard topics. Our articles fall into two catagories:

Project instructions provide the basics for beginners, but challenge the advanced beadworker with new beadworking ideas. All are beautifully illustrated and provide clear step-by-step instructions.

Feature articles broaden our readers' perspective of their craft. This includes interviews of beadworking pros, exhibit and book reviews, historical surveys, and helpful tips.

Written proposals to *Beadwork* should display in-depth knowledge of the subject matter based on experience and research. Though the material is often technical, the tone of articles should be informal and accessible. If you are not already familiar with the content, style, and tone of the magazine, we suggest you read our previous issues.

Submissions

Send a detailed proposal or a completed manuscript along with supporting slides, sketches, and a brief biography. We do not accept articles that have been published, and discourage simultaneous submissions. If any portion of your submission has been published previously, please let us know when and by whom.

Manuscripts range from two to ten typed pages (from 500 to 2,500 words). Please submit your article on a 3 1/2" X 5" disk and include a hard copy of the article. Please save your files in Word for Windows 98, if possible. If not, our preference is Word 2.0, MS DOS-based Word, DOS-based WordPerfect, text only (*.txt), or a flat ASCII file. Although we can have MacIntosh disks read by our production department and emailed to us as flat ASCII files, we prefer DOS formats. Double-space your manuscript on 8 1/2 x 11 white bond paper with at least 1-inch margins. Place your name, address, and telephone number in the upper right-hand corner of each page. Photocopies and computer printouts should be legible. If you submit your article via fax or email, please follow your electronic submission with a hard copy and disk in the mail.

We will need to have your finished pieces at Interweave Press for at least eight to ten weeks for photography, illustration, and technical editing. If you need them returned by a specific date, please let us know.

Drawings and diagrams should be done in black ink on white paper ready for redrawing by a staff artist. All slides, artwork, and other materials will be returned.

Keep a copy of everything. Enclose a self-addressed envelope with sufficient return postage for return of your materials. Receipt of your submission will be promptly acknowledged, but please be patient while we decide whether to use it.

Deadlines and Payment

Submissions are accepted at any time and are scheduled as space permits. Projects are due about 4 1/2 months before publication date (ie. 8/16/00 project due date for Jan/Feb 2001 issue). About 1 month before the publication date, we will send a contract for you to sign which states that we are purchasing first North American serial rights for publication in *Beadwork* and subsequent nonexclusive rights for use in other Interweave Press publications and promotions. As author, you retain the publication rights for the original materials.

We reserve the right to edit your material as necessary to fit the style, format, or other requirements of *Beadwork*. A copy of the edited manuscript will be submitted to you for approval before publication.

Payment for *project instructions* is $50 per page. Payment for *feature articles* is 12.5 cents per published word. Payment is made upon publication unless other arrangements are made.

Categories: Nonfiction—Arts—Crafts/Hobbies—Hobbies

CONTACT: Submissions Editor
Material: Written and visual submissions
Interweave Press, Inc.
201 East Fourth St.
Loveland CO 80537
Phone: 970-669-7672 x 625
Fax: 970-669-6117
E-mail: beadwork@interweave.com
Website: www.interweave.com/bead

The Bear Deluxe Magazine

Thank you for your interest in *The Bear Deluxe* Magazine. Published quarterly, the magazine celebrates the big tent theory of literary arts, including investigative reporting, fiction, essay, poetry, news, creative opinion, reviews and interviews in each issue. Unsolicited submissions and query letters are encouraged. *The Bear Deluxe* has included nationally published authors as well as emerging and unpublished writers. As with any publication, writers are encouraged to review a sample copy for a clearer understanding of the magazine's editorial approach.

Established in 1993, *The Bear Deluxe* was recognized by *Utne Reader* as one of the country's best new titles and has received acclaim from media sources around the country. *The Bear Deluxe* is published by Orlo, a nonprofit organization exploring environmental issues through the creative arts. In 1998, *The Bear Deluxe* changed its name from *The Bear Essential*.

Twenty thousand copies of each issue are distributed free of charge across the Western United States and beyond. Stories, however, are not limited to a regional focus.

While informative, the magazine has the additional goal of engaging new audiences. Cross-town appeal is achieved by including the full spectrum of literary forms and divergent styles, including satire and parody, while complementing the writing with original artwork and graphic design. Finally, the magazine draws connections to other related social concerns such as the media, social justice and human rights.

Nonfiction in General

Unsolicited nonfiction manuscripts are considered, but it is less common that they find a home in *The Bear Deluxe*. More often, nonfiction writers approach editors with a story idea or are asked to write on ideas generated by the magazine. Specific ideas should be presented in a query letter format and accompanied by writing samples and suggestions for artwork. Given its limited travel budget, the magazine is working to develop relationships with free-lance workers who can take assignments and offer story ideas from their home areas.

Features

Two to five independent features are included in each issue. Features are typically more timely, have an overarching perspective or appeal and require strong elements of reporting. Word range: 750-4000 words.

Departments

Portrait of an Artist: Profile of artist or arts group with unique environmental focus. 750-1500 words. Reviews: New titles, lost classics, films, videos, products, theater, fast food and pop corn. Almost anything goes. 100-1000 words. New Dept.: Front of the Book: Unique mix of news shorts, lists, found writing, cartoons, opinion, others. 100-750 words.

Fiction/Essay/Poetry/Other

The Bear Deluxe maintains an open submission policy for fiction, essay, poetry and other forms. The Creative Review Group considers submissions on an ongoing basis. The magazine is moving away from using the term "environmental writing." Quality writing which furthers the magazine's goal of engaging new and divergent readers will garner the most attention. News essays, on occasion, are assigned out if they have a strong element of reporting.

The magazine welcomes submissions and appreciates writers who see it as appropriate for their work. Generally, authors are informed on their submissions 3-6 months after they are received. Manuscripts are returned only if accompanied by appropriate SASE. Fiction: 1-3 fiction pieces published per issue. 750-4000 words. Essays: Zero to two essays per issue. 750-3000 words. Poetry: 5-10 poems published per issue. Please submit only 3-5 poems.

Theme Section

One issue each year will focus on a specific theme. Theme stories tend to be developed in close consultation with the editorial staff. Contact the magazine for upcoming themes.

Copyright & Compensation

The Bear Deluxe pays for first time publishing rights only. After publication, all rights revert to the authors. *The Bear Deluxe* compensates its writers with five cents per published word ($10 per poem), contributor copies and a one-year subscription. The magazine may cover incidental costs (including phone and postage) upon prior agreement.

Deadlines

The magazine has moved away from strict deadlines and is considering submissions and story ideas on an ongoing basis. Writers are encouraged to join our e-mail list-serve for occasional updates on our publishing schedule.

E-mail Submissions

E-mail submissions are accepted but not roundly encouraged. Please send stories as e-mail text, not as attached documents. The magazine can only respond to those e-mail submissions chosen for publication.

Submission Formats

Submit double-spaced text on clean hard copy. Do not send discs. Writers are encouraged to suggest headlines, subheads and pull-quotes, though final decisions in these areas are made by the editorial staff. Include a 20-word biographical statement. Send submissions to appropriate editor: i.e. "poetry editor," "fiction editor," or "nonfiction editor." Do not send material to the street address.

Contact the editorial staff with further questions.

Categories: Conservation—Ecology—Environment—Government—Literature—Poetry—Politics—Short Stories

CONTACT: Tom Webb, Editor
Material: Nonfiction
CONTACT: Poetry Editor
Material: Poetry
CONTACT: Fiction Editor
Material: Fiction
c/o Orlo
PO Box 10342
Portland OR 97296
Phone: 503-242-1047
Fax: 503-243-264
E-mail: bear@orlo.org
Website: www.orlo.org

The Beauty Spot
News You Can Use

Description: Quarterly publication of topics of interest to employees of Fortune 500 companies. Employees receive this publication at work.

(From permission form: "Very infrequently do we use freelance material. We do use material from press releases.")

No formal guidelines available

Categories: Nonfiction—Arts—Automobiles—Book Reviews—Business—Careers—Cartoons—Computers—Consumer—Cooking—Culture—Diet/Nutrition—Drama—Directories—Entertainment—Fashion—Feminism—Food/Drink—General Interest—Health—Internet—Interview—Lifestyle—Literature—Men's Issues—Money and Finances—Poetry—Public Speaking—Real Estate—Relationships—Society—Theater—Travel—Women's Issues

CONTACT: C.G. Bradford, Editor in Chief
Material: All
24 Fifth Ave., 6th Floor
New York, NY 10011
Phone: 212-614-9683

Beginnings

Beginnings is a magazine dedicated to the unpublished, but talented writer.

Guidelines: This is a website and publication for the aspiring writer. Sharing your work with other writers is very important when first starting out. Please post your ideas, thoughts and insights and keep the board hopping! Let's be supportive and helpful with each other. Get on the *Beginnings* road to publication!

You do have the option of submitting your work through the Bulletin Board. You will be notified via e-mail if your work has been accepted for the print publication. In the meantime, enjoy the friendly camaraderie and comments from the other writers.

We welcome the submissions of short stories (3,000 words or fewer) human-interest stories, and articles pertaining to the craft of writing. Fiction genres include humor, mystery, science fiction, fantasy, western, romance and drama. No graphic sex, violence or offensive language. Please, no essays. *DO NOT* send fiction via email.

Poetry of reasonable length is also considered. Please send all poetry submissions via email to scbeginnings@juno.com Write "Poetry submissions" in the subject line. Cut and paste work in the body of the email. Attachments will ***not be read.*** Do not send more than five poems per submission.

Simultaneous submissions accepted but **not** multiple submissions. Cover letters are appreciated. *It is strongly suggested that you familiarize yourself with the magazine before submitting.* We are also looking for cartoons related to the writing life only; pay is five dollars per cartoon. *Beginnings* is distributed through all Borders book stores on Long Island, with subscribers in many other parts of the world. We must sell magazines to stay in business. Send in your manuscripts, but also send in your subscription order. Together, let us create a special kind of writing-publishing success. New writers must stick together!

YOUNG ADULT & CHILDREN'S SECTION: Short stories, poetry, or artwork accepted ***by children***. Not written work by adults for children. For artwork submitted, any age is acceptable. Written work: ages 5-12. ***Young Adult*** section: 13-19 years. Poetry, artwork, short stories. Artwork must be on plain, un-ruled white paper. The inside of the magazine is black and white.

Beginnings magazine takes only one-time publication rights and all rights revert to authors and artists upon publication. Publishers reserve the right to edit for spelling, grammar, and punctuation. Please send copies, never originals, and send sufficient postage if you want your work returned. Published authors receive free copy. Additional and current copies $5.00 Back issues: $3.00 Subscriptions are $9.00 for two issues, winter and summer. Send $10.50 and receive a free back issue with your subscription order.

Categories: Writing

CONTACT: Jenine Boisits, Editor
Material: All
CONTACT: Freada Dillon, Poetry Editor
PO Box 92
Shirley NY 11967
E-mail: scbeginnings@juno.com
Website: www.scbeginnings.com

Bellevue Literary Review

Bellevue Hospital, the oldest public hospital in the United States, has been witness to nearly 270 years of human drama. In this tradition we have created the *Bellevue Literary Review*, a forum for illuminating humanity and human experience. *BLR* is published by the Department of Medicine at New York University. We invite submissions of previously unpublished works of fiction, nonfiction, and poetry that touch upon relationships to the human body, illness, health and healing. We encourage creative interpretation of these themes.

Submission Guidelines:

1. Prose should be limited to 5000 words. Please submit only one manuscript at a time. Manuscripts should be double-spaced with full author information (including address, phone number, email address) on the first page. Please specify word count, and indicate fiction or nonfiction.

2. Submit up to 3 poems at one time. Please do not submit poetry along with prose.

3. We read submissions year-round, but all of our reviewers and editors are volunteers. We strive to provide several readers for each manuscript in order to give it maximum exposure, but this takes time. We respectfully ask for your patience and forbearance. If you have not heard from us within six months, feel free to inquire about your manuscript.

4. *BLR* acquires first-time North American rights. After publication, all rights revert to the author and may be reprinted as long as appropriate acknowledgement to *BLR* is made.

5. Someday soon we hope to pay lavish stipends, but for now we will thank you with two copies of the issue in which your work appears, an additional 1-year subscription to the *BLR*, as well as a gift subscription for a lucky friend. You will also be eligible for an author discount when you purchase extra copies.

6. We now accept online submissions. To submit your manuscript electronically, please visit our website: www.BLReview.org

7. We continue to accept paper manuscripts. Please include SASE with sufficient postage for reply.

Categories: Fiction—Nonfiction—Poetry

CONTACT: Editor
Material: All
NYU School of Medicine
Dept. of Medicine, 550 First Ave., OBV-A612
New York, NY 10016
E-mail: info@BLReview.org
Website: www.BLReview.org

Bellingham Review

Simultaneous submissions are considered, as long as the *Bellingham Review* is notified immediately if the work is accepted elsewhere. All submissions must be previously unpublished in North America.

General Submission Guidelines

The *Bellingham Review* is a nonprofit literary arts magazine affiliated with Western Washington University. The magazine is biannual, published spring and fall. Sample copies are available for $7.00 each.

Our general submission period is from September 15th through March 15th, although contest submission dates may vary. Manuscripts arriving between February 2nd and September 14th will be returned unread. The editors welcome submissions of poems, stories, and essays. There are no limitations on form or subject matter. Prose must be under 9,000 words. The editors prefer poetry submissions of 3-5 poems. Please indicate the approximate word count on prose pieces. We do not currently accept electronic mail submissions.

All submissions should be accompanied by a self-addressed stamped envelope (SASE). Submissions from other countries should be accompanied by a sufficient number of international postal reply coupons.

Reporting time normally varies from one to six months. We pay upon publication as funds permit.

Categories: Fiction—Nonfiction—Literature—Poetry

CONTACT: Fiction Editor
Material: Fiction
CONTACT: Nonfiction Editor
Material: Nonfiction
CONTACT: Poetry Editor
Material: Poetry
MS—9053
Western Washington University
Bellingham WA 98225
Phone: 360-650-4863
Website: www.wwu.edu/~bhreview

Bellowing Ark

We began publishing *Bellowing Ark* in 1984 because no market existed for the kind of literature that we wanted to read and wanted to see published; we set out to create such a market, and, by example, encourage others to do the same. We believe that there is more to art than the desire to shock and the glib and facile expression of nihilism and despair. We are also convinced that artists, particularly literary, have a responsibility to their audience and are required to present the world as meaningful, for, if the world has no meaning, how can life? The material we publish is the best expression of that responsibility that we can command.

We feel *Bellowing Ark* stands solidly in the Romantic tradition which passes from Blake and Wordsworth through the American Transcendentalists to Whitman, Frost, Roethke and Nelson Bentley then on to current writers Natalie Reciputi, Marshall Pipkin, L.L. Ollivier, Muriel Karr, Teresa Noelle Roberts and others. While we are in the Romantic tradition, we also take pride in being one of the most eclectic magazines ever published. There are essentially no restrictions on genre, length, or style.

We have published plays, serialized novels, short stories, poems, long-poems, epic poems (Nelson Bentley's Tracking the Transcendental Moose ran to 20,000 lines, published in 14 books, serialized sequentially), essays, memoirs, drawings, photographs, all forms of self expression, in fact, that we consider to meet our single, and sufficient criterion: everything that we publish demonstrates, to our satisfaction, that life is both meaningful and worth living. We are biased toward the narrative, both in poetry and fiction; that is, stories should have a plot, characterization, a beginning, a middle, and an end.

We have not, in our years of publication, ever published a fiction, nor anything pointlessly minimalist or surrealist—it seems to us that practitioners of those elegantly academic artforms have deliberately cut themselves off from an audience. We are interested in audience, since we believe art must be shared to be art.

We do ask that material submitted to *Bellowing Ark* be carefully presented. Please double-space prose, single space poetry, one poem per page. If you use a dot-matrix printer please make sure the print is dark enough to be legible: we read hundreds of submissions every month and eyestrain is always a danger. And, always submit a stamped, self-addressed envelope with every submission. Note: we do not consider simultaneous submissions.

Payment is in copies of the issue containing the artist's work, that is, on publication. Sample copies, and it never hurts to read a magazine to see if your work fits, are $3.00, postpaid from the address below.

Thank you for your interest in *Bellowing Ark*; we do hope to hear from you again.

Robert R. Ward, Editor

Categories: Fiction—Literature—Poetry

CONTACT: Submissions Editor
Material: All
PO Box 55564
Seattle WA 98155
Phone: 206-440-0791

BELOIT POETRY JOURNAL
WWW.BPJ.ORG

Beloit Poetry Journal

Beloit Poetry Journal is a quarterly in continuous publication since 1950. BJP peoms are regularly featured by the Poetry Daily and Verse Daily websites. Our own website, www.bpj.org, contains a full-text archive of the journal from its inception. We have been the first or early publisher of such poets as Galway Kinnell, Anne Sexton, Sharon Olds, Maxine Kumin, W. S. Merwin, James Dickey, Philip Larkin, Charles Bukowski, Adrienne Rich, Philip Levine, and more recently Sherman Alexie, Victor Lodato, and Mary Leader.

We seek only unpublished poems or translations of poems (which we publish en face) not already available in English. The reviews are by our editors. The magazine is copyrighted, with rights reverting to the poet on publication. Payment is in copies.

We receive as many as twenty envelopes of poetry a day and return most within days of their arrival. The rest we circulate among the editors and continue to winnow. At quarterly meetings of the editorial board we read the surviving poems aloud and put together an issue of what we consider the best work. The Chad Walsh Poetry Award ($3,000 in 2006) goes to the author of the poem or group of poems that the editors judge to be the strongest we have published during the previous year.

We are always watching for new poets, quickened language, fresh insights into a troubled world. Our occasional chapbooks are special collections of categories of poems we want to bring to our readers' at-

tention, for example, *Poets Under Twenty-Five*.

How to Submit Poems—to the BPJ or Most Literary Magazines

1. Be familiar with any publication before you submit. Half of the poems we get are from poets who have obviously never seen an issue. A year's subscription to the BPJ is $18. A sample copy is only $5. Hundreds of libraries subscribe.

2. Type no more than one poem on a page, single-spaced. Put your name and address on every sheet.

3. Limit your submission to what will go for one first-class stamp-about four pages—unless it's a long poem or a poem sequence.

4. Always enclose an SASE (self-addressed stamped envelope). From overseas send an International Reply Coupon for each half-ounce (from Canada, U.S. or Canadian coins are acceptable), or include your email address and we'll respond by email. Tell us if you don't want your manuscript returned.

5. Keep copies of your work in case the originals disappear.

6. No cover note is necessary, unless you have something to say to us—but many other editors do like them. We use no contributors' notes. Our emphasis is on the poem.

7. Keep a record of when and where you mail every poem. Never send a poem to two places at once, unless they explicitly invite simultaneous submissions. We do not. If you have no reply after four months, send a query, including a new SASE. If after a month you still hear nothing, send a card announcing that you are withdrawing the poems.

8. Don't expect any comment on your work. Editors read as a labor of love, in spare moments, and if they fall behind they may have to read several hundred poems in a day.

9. Don't be discouraged by rejections. Just keep writing and mailing-and reading what is being published.

10. We do not accept electronic submissions from within the U.S. For further information, consult our website: www.bpj.org.

Categories: Poetry

CONTACT: John Rosenwald and Lee Sharkey, Editors
Material: All
PO Box 151
Farmington, ME 04938
Phone: (207)778-0020
E-mail (for information only): bpi@bpi.org
Website: www.bpj.org

Bend of the River® Magazine

We are always looking for interesting articles about past events that have happened in Northwestern Ohio. Query or send 1500 word typewritten double-spaced hard copy with SASE.

It is our pleasure to include pictures of a nostalgic nature along with articles. We lean heavily on local history, but feature a nostalgic slant. We want positive, up-beat articles on "famous people" and or events that have their birth in the State of Ohio.

We buy one-time rights, pay accordingly one month after publication. And encourage first time writers and/or never published enthusiasts.

Thanks for your interest. We enjoy "delighting" our audience with wonderful, homespun stories of the early Black Swamp, life in Pioneer America, World War II and Great Depression subjects, along with the Prohibition Era.

Categories: Nonfiction—History—Regional

CONTACT: Ms. Lee Raizk
Material: All
PO Box 859
Maumee OH 43537
Phone: 419-893-0022

International Foundation
OF EMPLOYEE BENEFIT PLANS

Benefits & Compensation Digest
(Formerly Employee Benefit, Digest and Employees Benefit Journal)

The International Foundation Publications Department is looking for authors to write articles on the newest and most relevant employee benefits and compensation topics. We are looking for U.S. and Canadian articles in the areas of health care, pensions, retirement, and general benefits and compensation topics. If you would like to write an article for our publications, please see the following guidelines and suggested topics.

GENERAL INFORMATION
The guidelines are intended to make the writing process easier and more enjoyable for you. Please do not hesitate to call the Foundation editorial staff at any time. We are looking forward to working with you.

Our publications include articles on subjects directly or indirectly related to the employee benefits, compensation and related fields. Articles covering new or developing topics are particularly appropriate. We welcome suggestions or outlines of proposed articles. The editors will respond promptly.

We assume all material submitted is the original work of the listed authors and has not been accepted for publication elsewhere. In the event of any potential conflict, it is the author's responsibility to notify the editor prior to publication. We will ask you to sign a copyright transfer agreement.

ARTICLE LENGTH AND CONTENT
The recommended length for a printed article is 2,000-3,200 words.

In addition, we are accepting longer, in-depth articles of more than 3,200 words. We will post these longer articles on our Web site in a special online showcase called Web Exclusives. The full text of new articles, plus a permanent online archive of past articles, is available to all on the Foundation Web site at www.ifebp.org. Follow the article submission guidelines included in this article.

You will be notified whether your article has been accepted within approximately two weeks.

Articles should be educational in nature. Pieces promoting a specific product or company will not be accepted.

WRITING THE ARTICLE
Organize your article carefully. Avoid overly specialized jargon.
HOW TO SUBMIT
Send your article via e-mail to cindyb@ifebp.org. or judys@ifebp.org.
CONTENT
Send us your complete manuscript in its final version, including any tables, graphs/charts, etc. at the same time.
REFERENCES
It is the author's responsibility to obtain any necessary permission for the use of lengthy quotations or other material (charts, surveys, etc.) originally prepared by others.
HEADINGS
Provide headings and subheadings that are succinct and that include words useful for information retrieval.
GRAPHS AND TABLES
If you use tables or graphs/charts, construct them so they are completely understandable on their own.

Tables and figures should be referenced correctly in the text.

If you are using:

Simple text tables: Tabular material can simply be part of your text document.

Pie charts/bar charts: Please DO NOT EMBED them into your Word documents. You may reference the placement, i.e., **Place table 3 here** but please do not embed any kind of image in Word. Please send charts and graphs as a separate file.

Best option: Separate high-resolution tif, eps or jpg files (600 dpi for line art or 300 ppi for grayscale or color), e.g., created in Illustrator or Photoshop.

Next best: Original Excel or PowerPoint documents. Do not make any conversions or embed them in Word; please send the original .xl or .ppt files.

Almost never usable: Charts taken from the Web, anything at 72 dpi or 96 dpi, Word charts.

LEGAL CASE CITATIONS
Check legal citations for accuracy. They will be included in the text as they are submitted.
COPYRIGHTED MATERIAL AND ACKNOWLEDGMENTS
If you use copyrighted materials from another publication, secure permission for reprint. Submit this with your manuscript, and inform the editor if a cost is associated with reprint approval.
AUTHOR NOTE
Write a brief biographical note, including present position title, responsibilities and address. Include a photo of the author at a resolution of 300 dpi or 600 dpi, whether scanned from hard copy or shot with a digital camera.
AUTHOR COPIES AND REPRINTS
Authors will receive ten copies of the issue containing their material. Reprints are available for a nominal charge.

Categories: Nonfiction—Employee Benefits

CONTACT: Cindy Berg, Editor, Publications Department (cindyb@ifebp.org)
Material: All
CONTACT: Judy Sankey, CEBS, Editor, Publications Department (judys@ifebp.org)
Material: All
International Foundation of Employee Benefit Plans
18700 W. Bluemound Rd.
PO Box 69
Brookfield, WI 53008-0069
Phone: 262-786-6710 (ext. 7632 for Cindy; ext. 7633 for Judy)
Website: www.ifebp.org

Best of Times
Grandparents Magazine

Please refer to Metro Parent/Metro Baby.

Better Homes and Gardens

Only about ten percent of our editorial material comes from freelance writers, artists, and photographers; the rest is produced by staff.

We read all freelance articles submitted, but much prefer to see a letter of query than a finished manuscript. The query should be directed to the department where the story line is the strongest. See appropriate editor and department below.

A freelancer's best chance lies in the areas of travel, health, parenting and education. We do not deal with political subjects or with areas not connected with the home, community, and family. We use no poetry, beauty, or fiction. The best way to find out what we do use, and to get some idea of our style, is to study several of our most recent issues.

We buy all rights and pay on acceptance. Rates are based on our estimate of the length, quality, and importance of the published article.

Categories: Nonfiction—Automobiles—Computers—Cooking—Environment—Family—Gardening—Health—Home—Money & Finances—Parenting—Physical Fitness—Software—Travel—Decorating—Remodeling

CONTACT: Sarah Egge
Material: Home Design
CONTACT: Nancy Hopkins
Material: Food and Nutrition
CONTACT: Becky Mollenkamp
Material: Travel
CONTACT: Mark Kane
Material: Garden
CONTACT: Lamont Olson
Material: Money Management, Automotive
CONTACT: Lora O'neil
Material: Environment
CONTACT: Steve Mumford
Material: Environment
CONTACT: Martha Miller
Material: Health/Fitness, Cartoons
CONTACT: Richard Sowienski
Material: Education and Parenting, BH&G Kids
CONTACT: Stephen George
Material: Health/Fitness and Cartoons
CONTACT: Stephen George
Material: Education and Parenting, BH&G
1716 Locust St.
Des Moines IA 50309-3023
Phone: 515-284-3000
Website: www.bhg.com

Bible Advocate/Now What?

Identity

The Bible Advocate is one of the oldest religious magazines in America, founded in 1863. *Now What?* has been on the Internet since late 1996. Both are published by the Bible Advocate Press, the publication agency of the General Conference of the Church of God (Seventh Day). *Now What?* is monthly; the print version is published eight times a year.

Readership

Readers of the print magazine have a wide range of denominational and religious backgrounds. About half of them are not members of the Church of God (Seventh Day).

Editorial focus

The Bible Advocate is geared to help Christians understand and obey God's Word, with articles on Bible doctrine, current social and religious issues, Christian living, Bible topics, textual or biblical book studies, prophecy, and personal experience. We also print fillers (sidebars), and poetry (traditional, free, and blank verse).

Now What? addresses more of the "felt needs" of people (grief, depression, sickness, etc.). Each issue centers around a personal experience, with articles related to the topic. Material for this e-zine is more inclusive of non-Christians. Personal experience stories show a person's struggle that either led him to faith in Christ or deepened his walk with God. No opinion pieces or poetry.

Payment

We pay an honorarium, on publication, of $25 per printed magazine page, up to $55, for print and electronic rights. Online articles run $25-$55, depending on published length. For poetry and fillers, we pay $20.

Rights

We buy first, electronic, and one-time rights. We also accept reprints and simultaneous submissions.

Format

We prefer e-mail submissions, to bibleadvocate@cog7.org, copied into the e-mail message box. No attachments, please.

Writers should include their name, address, and telephone number in the upper left-hand corner of the first page. The word count and indication of rights offered should appear in the upper right-hand corner of the first page.

Submissions

Please include an SASE or SASC with all hard copy submissions. Unsolicited manuscripts will not be returned unless accompanied by an SASE or SASC. Computer submissions on disk are welcomed if the material is compatible with our program. *The Bible Advocate* is produced in Word 2001 on Macintosh computers. Word programs that are 1998 and newer are compatible with ours.

No fax or handwritten submissions, please.

Documentation

When stating important facts likely to be questioned, please list your sources so we can verify. When preparing a manuscript, writers should reference all Scripture quotations and enclose them in parentheses. Specify the main translation used, and note specifically where any other translation is used.

Length

• Feature articles 1000-1500 words
• Fillers 100-400 words
• Poetry 5-20 lines

Online:

• Feature articles, 1,000-1500 words-personal experience

Contact

Address manuscripts to the person listed below. Or send via e-mail to bibleadvocate@cog7.org. Allow 4-8 weeks for a response.

Tips

Articles must be in keeping with the doctrinal understanding of the Church of God (Seventh Day). Therefore, the writer should become familiar with what the Church generally accepts as truth as set forth in its doctrinal beliefs.

We reserve the right to edit manuscripts to fit our space requirements, doctrinal stands, and Church terminology. Significant changes are referred to writers for approval.

Categories: Christian Interests—Culture—Lifestyle—Religion

CONTACT: Sherri Langton, Associate Editor, Bible Advocate/Now What?
Material: All
PO Box 33677
Denver CO 80233
E-mail: bibleadvocate@cog7.org
Website: http//.nowwhat.cog7.org

Bibliophilos
A Journal of History, Literature, and the Liberal Arts

Audience: Literate persons, academically and scholastically-oriented. Topics range throughout the liberal arts, including fiction and non-fiction, literature and criticism, history, art, music, theology, philosophy, natural history, educational theory, contemporary issues and politics, sociology, economics. A refereed journal, with articles published in English, French, German, Romanian. Circulates throughout the United States, Canada, Mexico, United Kingdom, France, elsewhere. *Bibliophilos* was nominated for the Writer's Digest listing as one of the best 100 small press magazines in the country for the year 2000.

Bi-monthly magazine format: averages 72 pages per issue. Price $5.25 per issue, $18.00 per year, $35.00 for two years. Library rate available. Query first, unsolicited manuscripts not considered. MSS must be accompanied by large (#10) SASE (sufficient postage please–if it costs $1.03 to send the material to us, then it can't be returned with an SASE bearing only $.39.) Along with query or manuscript send check or money order for $5.25 handling fee, which also pays for sample issue along with our answer, and specifications. Initial answer in two weeks, final decision normally within thirty days. Payment varies, often including complimentary subscription, and money in some instances. Photocopied or simultaneous submissions ok, but we expect notification immediately if your material is accepted elsewhere. Acquires First North American Serial rights.

Non-fiction: Should be scholarly, with clarity of writing and well-defined and documented thesis. Footnotes are to be Turabian/Chicago Manual of Style only, and may be typed ordinally on the final page of the MS for convenience, but not in the text. Remember that paraphrased material must also be footnoted. The word "quote," moreover, is a verb, and not a noun. Lively and variegated prose is preferable to turgid thesis language. Literate and informative essays in literature, comparative studies, and critical review essays rather than the superficial standard "book review," are welcome. Length: 1500-3000 words for feature articles, 750-1250 words for reviews.

Fiction: Short stories, fantasy, satire, "genre pieces," mainstream, horror, humorous, historical, ethnic, regional and local color, suspense. Length 1500-3000 words, typed, double-spaced. We use 25-30 per year. Avoid obscenities and scatological language; curse words and vulgarisms should be minimized and serve a specific function. We do not use gay or lesbian themes, nor will we use historically anachronistic terminology for the sake of political correctness.

Poetry: we publish an annual poetry issue, containing the winners of an annual poetry contest. Send for a sample issue.

Photographs: we use a limited number, B & W submitted with MSS, glossies only; supply captions. Original art work and cartoons also welcome.

Reviews of books, art or photographic exhibitions, films: We assign almost all book reviews specifically, so do not submit unsolicited book reviews, please. We publish an annual book review number, but reviews are in every issue as well, averaging about 30+ per year. 750-1250 words. Consult the guidelines for book reviewers published in *Bibliophilos* Book Reviews '99, Vol. II, No. 3, pp. 188-191.

Notes & Notices section: for appropriate notices, plaudits, upcoming features announcements, and extravagant praise from readers. See sample issue. The majority of this is devoted to information about the contributors in that number, so if your material is accepted, we need 25-30 words about yourself. Best to send a brief biographical sketch with your original material.

Submissions are to be typed, double-spaced, on 8½" by 11" paper, with approximately 250 words per page, paper-clipped, not stapled, with pages numbered. Please do not clutter your query letters or MSS with e-mail addresses, fax numbers, and other electronic detritus, and please do not suggest that we use them to get in touch with you, because we will not. Please do not suggest that we telephone you, or that you will call us; we operate through the postal service only, such as it is.

MSS should be free as possible of jargon, cant, or short-cut language. The word is not "rehab," but rehabilitation, it is political science and not "poli sci," it is not "ad" but advertisement, not TV but television. Kindly remember that "quote" is a VERB, not a noun, and "access" is a NOUN, not a verb. If your material contains the word "hopefully" used as an expletive or adverbially, don't bother sending it at all. Grammar and punctuation and typographical errors should be fixed before sending your material. We want to invest our time considering its merit and literary value, not correcting apostrophes and possessives.

Kindly consult our listings in *The Writer's Market, the Poet's Market, the Novel & Short Story Writer's Market, The Writer* magazine, the *Small Press Review*, and the like to inform yourself of our tone and philosophy, and for further elaboration of some of the above items.

Recap for those publishing for the first time, or publishing with *Bibliophilos* for the first time:

1. *Query first*, before you send anything.

2. Along with your query (and again with any submitted material) send a large, self-addressed stamped envelope, with sufficient postage, and $5.00 for a sample issue, specifications, and answer.

3. *Nota Bene*. Once you have had your material accepted for publication, and an agreement has been concluded between you and the editor/staff, then embrace the words of Anthony Trollope that "some time must elapse before your story actually appears in print." Do not send us continual inquiries about "when will my stuff be published?" and thus force us to engage in needless extra correspondence, the normal volume of which is practically overwhelming as it is. The more you pester an editor, the farther down in the pile your story goes. We have a large backlog, we receive 20 submissions per week, at least, and answer each one personally, and with six issues annually it takes time to use up so much material. If you think your piece will appear two weeks after acceptance, you had better send it elsewhere.

4. *Equally important*: once your story has been accepted and/or published, this does not mean that you immediately send us another, or empty out your file cabinet and assume that you now have an automatic forum for everything you write. Query for each individual submission and expect each one to be judged on its own merits. But above all wait until submission #1 has been published before you start flooding us with Nos. 2, 3, and 4.

Categories: Fiction—Nonfiction—Adventure—Animals—Antiques—Arts—Biography—Book Reviews—Cartoons—Civil War—College—Culture—Drama—Economics—Education—Entertainment—Film/Video—Folklore—General Interest—Government—History—Interview—Language—Law—Literature—Military—Music—Poetry—Politics—Religion—Rural America—Satire—Short Stories—Textbooks—Travel—Western—Writing

CONTACT: Gerald J. Bobango, Editor
Material: All
The Bibliophile Publishing Co
200 Security Building
Fairmont WV 26554
Phone: 304-366-8107

Bike

Thank you for your interest in writing for *Bike* magazine. *Bike* delivers the excitement and passion of the sport better than the other mountain bike magazines do. We are vivid, unbiased, irreverent, probing, fun, humorous, funky, quirky, smart, good. And we're always on the lookout for new talent.

Bike has a section devoted to news and odds and ends. It has product reviews. It has travel stories that are *true* stories. It has unparalleled photography. It has regional columns. It has personality profiles, long and short ones. It has debates.

What *Bike* needs from you, then, are lots of story ideas. They can be about anything so long as there's a connection, however remote, to mountain biking. For instance, a Peace Corps worker describes what it was like peddling from village to village in Senegal. A whole essay devoted solely to the feeling of mud. Why bike messengers give us all a bad name. Odd things you've overheard. Whatever. Have fun, bust out, be a spin doctor, cut your teeth, tell us about things you'd tell a friend, write stories you've always wanted to write. Do anything. The only rule is that there are no rules.

We're vigorous editors, but we aren't saboteurs. You'll get great layouts with spectacular photography; in other words, your stuff will look good in *Bike*. As for buyouts, our basic rate is 50 cents per word. It's not a lot, but if you wanted riches you'd be an investment banker instead of some overgrown child splashing through creeks and whooping to an empty forest.

We'd love to hear what you've got to say, but we prefer that you say it in a certain way—as in a double-spaced, 12-point-font, typed hard copy. Feel free to include additional writing samples, photography (prints or slides) or anything else you think we should know about—within reason, of course. If we like what we see, we'll let you know. If we don't like what we see, we'll let you know too. So either way, we'll get back to you as soon as we're able. Oh, and kick us a SASE so we can return your materials. Thanks.

Categories: Nonfiction—Adventure—Recreation—Sports—Recreation

CONTACT: Sarah Smith
Material: All
33046 Calle Aviador
San Juan Capistrano, CA 92675
Phone: 949-661-5127
Fax: 949-496-7849
E-mail: sarah.smith@primedia.com
Website: www.bikemag.com

Birds & Blooms

There are plenty of opportunities to contribute to every issue of *Birds & Blooms*. Just jot down your personal backyard experiences and send us your photographs to help fill this magazine, which is basically "written by our readers." **If you'd like to share a story or photos, here are some guidelines:**

1. Be sure to print your name, address and daytime telephone number (and E-mail address, if you have one) on the first page of each item or manuscript. We receive a lot of mail, so please keep your stories under 800 words.

2. Print your name, city and state or province on the back of each photo lightly with pencil or indelible marker. Address labels work extremely well on the backs of photographs.

3. We do not publish fiction. Instead, we want you to tell us your real-life stories and share some of the tried-and-true tips and ideas that make your backyard a birds or blooms haven.

We can only print a limited amount of the mail we receive. Published stories are edited, and in many cases, only an excerpt of the original letter or manuscript is used.

4. Please enclose a self-addressed stamped envelope (SASE) if you want your materials returned or are requesting a response. Because of our small staff size and large mail volume, we simply cannot respond to most inquiries and letters.

Don't worry, submissions without SASEs are equally considered. We'll let you know if your story is published.

5. If you choose to enclose a SASE with your submission, please be patient. Submissions that do not fit in the magazine may be considered for our *Birds & Blooms* Web site (www.birdsandblooms.com) or for other projects.

6. Mail your submissions to *Birds & Blooms*, 5925 Country Lane, Greendale WI 53129.

7. Send E-mail submissions to editors@birdsandblooms.com. Be sure to include your full mailing address, daytime telephone number and E-mail address.

8. Feel free to E-mail electronic photographs. However, it's important that these photos are saved as "jpeg" files and measure at least 3 x 5 inches at 300 dpi (that's dots per inch).

Categories: Fiction—Animals—Family—Gardening—Hobbies—Lifestyle—Nature—Outdoors

CONTACT: Jeff Nowak, Managing Editor
Material: Manuscripts and manuscript/photo combination
CONTACT: Trudi Bellin, Photo Coordinator
Material: Photos Only
5400 S. 60th St
Greendale WI 53129
Phone: 414-423-0100
E-mail: editor@birdsandblooms.com
Website: www.birdsandblooms.com

BPR

Birmingham Poetry Review

Subscription Information
Birmingham Poetry Review is published semiannually in the fall and spring. Subscriptions are $5.00 per year. Sample copies are $2.50. Tax-deductible contributions of $12.00 or more are welcomed and entitle patrons to a two-year subscription.

Submission Information
Unsolicited manuscripts of no more than five poems are welcomed but must be accompanied by a stamped, self-addressed envelope for consideration. Deadlines are December 1 and June 1. At the present time, we do not accept electronic submissions. Reprints are permitted with appropriate acknowledgement. All rights revert upon publication.

From Poet's Market:
Birmingham Poetry Review uses poetry that is, according to editor Robert Collins and associate editor Randy Blythe, of "any style, form, length, or subject. Style is secondary to the energy, the fire, the poem possesses. We don't want poetry with cliché-bound, worn-out language."

The magazine is composed of 64 pages, 5.5" x 8.5" offset print, with a color cover, usually a photograph. The press run is 600 for fall and 600 for spring. Currently, we have over 300 subscriptions.

Guidelines for submission are available for a SASE. Pay is two copies and a one-year subscription. Authors should submit 3-5 poems, without cover letters: "We are impressed by good poetry, not by publication credits." Be absolutely certain that you enclose sufficient postage on your SASE if you expect us to return your work. Simultaneous submissions are not accepted. Reprints are accepted in a very few cases — translations being the most common. We report on submissions within 1-3 months, and we occasionally comment on rejections. Our editors suggest that beginning writers "Read as much good contemporary poetry, national and international, as you can get your hands on. Then be persistent in finding your own voice."

Categories: Poetry
CONTACT: Robert Collins, Editor
Material: Any
CONTACT: Tina Harris, Editor
Material: Any
English Department
University of Alabama - Birmingham
HB 205
1530 3RD AVE S
Birmingham AL 35294-1260
Phone: 202-934-4250
Fax: 205-975-8125
Website: www.uab.edu/english/bpr

The Birthkit

Please refer to *Midwifery Today*.

BIZLife Magazine

About the submission process:
Articles should be original work that does not infringe on the copyrights of other authors or publications.

After receiving the article, it may be edited for conciseness, correctness and clarity. Content should support the title. If substantial revision is required, writers will have the option to resubmit article at a later date.

Articles that pass editorial review will be published on a space-available basis.

BIZlife Magazine is under no obligation to print submissions, and there is no compensation for guest column articles.

BIZlife Magazine follows Associated Press style.

What should I submit?

Authors are advised to review recent BIZlife articles prior to submission to ensure that their article provides a perspective that is relevant to BIZlife business readers. Columns and articles offering fresh insights, ideas and trends will be given first consideration.

Columns should run between 800-900 words. Drafts should not be submitted.

All columns must be in paragraph form: no lists, charts, graphs, and article should not contain promotional information about your company or product.

Columnist should include byline to include name, company, area of expertise, contact phone and contact email address (if applicable).

Send your article as a Microsoft Word attachment or by pasting into an email to the editor.

Where will my article appear?

Articles submitted to BIZlife will be considered for publication in our monthly magazine and on the BIZlife website. For more information, please contact our editor.

Categories: Nonfiction—Business

CONTACT: Altina Layman, Editor
4101 A Piedmont Parkway
Greensboro NC 27410
Phone: 336-812-8801, ext. 3014
Fax: 336-812-8832
E-mail: alayman@bizlife.com
Website: bizlife.com

BLACK BELT.
COMMUNICATIONS INC.

Black Belt

Thank you for your interest in writing for *Black Belt*, the oldest martial arts publications in the United States. The magazine's subjects include martial arts styles and techniques, training methods, historical pieces, health and fitness articles, and interviews with prominent martial artists.

Before mailing a completed manuscript to *Black Belt*, we advise you to send a query letter. It will save your time and ours. Describe your proposed article, including a sample lead or story outline. If the subject attracts our interest and has not been covered too recently, we may request to see the article on a speculation basis. Please enclose a self-addressed stamped envelope if you want your materials returned.

Articles must address an area of specific interest or concern for the serious martial artist. The vast majority of our stories are educational; they either teach technical and strategic skills, or enlighten the reader about historical and philosophical matters. The writing should capture the reader's interest with a strong lead, then hold it with information that is exact, concrete and focused around a strong central theme. All quotes and anecdotes should pertain to that theme.

Black Belt seldom uses first-person accounts, because most are of interest only to the author and his or her friends. In addition, while many instructors are dedicated and high-ranking, the magazine rarely requests personality profiles. (If you do choose to write about an individual, your article should prove that your subject is unique or particularly significant in the martial arts community.) Remember: if you have a chance to meet or train with a great martial artist and want to write an article afterward, discuss what that person knows rather than how his or her life has unfolded.

All statements and quotes must be accurate and verifiable. Use authoritative sources and cross-check your information. Be certain of all spellings—especially names and foreign words—and define foreign terms in parentheses after first usage only.

Manuscripts should be 1,000 to 3,000 words long, typed and double-spaced. If you use a computer, feel free to send a floppy disk with a Microsoft Word or plain text (ASCII) file. Please include full-color lead and step-by-step photos—with the negatives, if possible—taken in front of a plain, contrasting background. Be careful not to chop off the subjects' feet or hands when you frame the image, and verify that your camera is focused on the subjects and not on the background. Feature articles receive $150 to $300, which is paid upon publication. Simultaneous or previously published submissions must be identified as such.

Categories: Martial Arts

CONTACT: Robert Young, Executive Editor
Material: All
Black Belt Communications, Inc.
24900 Anza Dr., Unit E
Valencia CA 91355
Phone: 661-257-4066
Fax: 661-257-3028

The Black Table

The Black Table welcomes a staggering array of submissions, from the serious to the satirical to the servicey and back again. Few topics are off limits, provided they are well written with a sharp point of view and cover something that hasn't completely saturated the media yet.

Before submitting, readers are encouraged to take some time to peruse the archive to get a feel for the tone, topics and treatment we give our stories. We're big fans of sidebars and artwork, so feel free to suggest stories that are driven by visuals, especially in service pieces. Q&A style interviews are always welcome and an easy way to break in, especially if the source or the line of questioning is especially sharp.

When it comes to length, *The Black Table* feels it's what you do with the words that counts most, so we refuse to adhere to a strict word count. Some of our stories have clocked in at 400 words and others have pushed 30,000. It all depends on the topic and what you have to say. Interviews can run long, whereas criticism should be kept short. Only professors like reading term papers. Typically, the best submissions are around 1,000 words.

The Black Table has few rules about what we will not run, but they're rather hard and fast. Excuse the boldness here, but *The Black Table* does not run personal reflections, or the kinds of first-person memoirs that show up on diary sites. We no longer run Life as a Loser, and we're not looking to publish personal essays, late-night musings or disposable tales of drunken mayhem. There are plenty of places for your personal essays to live outside of *The Black Table*. Generally speaking, we're aiming for original journalism here, hard-hitting stories that involve real people out there in the world, and a measure of reporting—not just one person's view on their own life.

It may be helpful to think of *The Black Table* as a home for the random magazine ideas you never have time to pitch or felt qualified enough to write. We're the excuse for you to write those. We're the place those can go.

Most come from like-minded strangers with good ideas, people with a passion for writing and a need to have that writing seen. We don't play favorites here, we just want good content on a daily basis. Don't be shy about dropping us a line.

All submissions are voted on by the editor-in-chief and the three managing editors and you're gonna need three votes in order for something to run. Our tastes kinda run the gamut, but we'll be very nice about it if we have to reject something. If you're accepted, you will be added to the masthead promptly.

Oh, yes. And *The Black Table* doesn't pay for stories, mostly because *The Black Table* has no money. Fire off your ideas to: theblacktable@hotmail.com. See you on the playground.

Categories: Culture—Current Affairs—Humor—Interviews—Satire

CONTACT: Eric Gillin, Editor-in-Chief
Material: All
E-mail: theblacktable@hotmail.com
Website: www.blacktable.com

Black Warrior Review

The *Black Warrior Review* publishes contemporary fiction, poetry, nonfiction, comics, art, and photography. General guidelines are below (along with specific guidelines for each genre).

FICTION Up to 1500 words. We'd like to see more short-short fiction, but are open to longer work. Please send only one story or novel excerpt per envelope (short-shorts excluded). We generally consider excerpts only from novels already completed and contracted for publication.

POETRY Limit poetry submissions to seven poems.

ESSAYS We consider creative personal essays, lyric essays, and such. We do not typically publish academic articles.

ART Each issue of *Black Warrior Review* features cover art and a 6-12 page internal feature on an artist.

SIMULTANEOUS SUBMISSIONS are fine, if noted (understanding that you must notify us immediately if the work is accepted somewhere else).

GENERAL GUIDELINES *Black Warrior Review* does NOT accept unsolicited email submissions. E-mail queries, however, are welcomed.

We read submissions year-round, though our response time is slower in the summer.

The average response time for submissions is between 2 and 4 months. If you have not received a response after 4 months (excepting the summer), send a query and SASE through the mail, or email us at <bwr@ua.edu>, and we'll check on the status of your submission.

Unsolicited manuscripts will not be returned unless accompanied by a self-addressed, stamped envelope (SASE) and proper postage.

We can't respond to submissions that come without an SASE.

Please do not mix genres in the same envelope.

We encourage you to read *Black Warrior Review* before submitting. Sample issues are available for $10; one-year subscriptions for $16.

Address all submissions and other correspondence to the attention of the appropriate editor.

RIGHTS Manuscripts accepted for publication become the property of the *Black Warrior Review* unless otherwise indicated. All rights reserved. All rights revert to the author upon publication.

PAYMENT *Black Warrior Review* pays a one-year subscription, and up to $150 for stories or $75 for poems.

AWARDS The annual Black Warrior Review Fiction and Poetry Contests award $1000 each to the best poetry and fiction entry. Postmark deadline for this year's contest is October 1, 2006. Reading fee is $15 and includes one year subscription.

CIRCULATION *Black Warrior Review* is published bianually with a circulation of 2,000.

Categories: Fiction—Nonfiction—Arts—Book Reviews—Cartoons—Experimental Fiction—Interview—Literature—Poetry—Short Stories—Writing

CONTACT: Editor (Indicate Department)
Material: Queries and submissions
PO Box 862936
Tuscaloosa AL 35486-0027
Phone: 205-348-4518
E-mail: bwr@ua.edu (for queries only)
Website: www.webdelsol.com/bwr

Blackfire

Overview

Blackfire features the erotic images, experiences and fantasies of black men in the life. Without compromising the sensual spell, it also includes provocative articles, useful information, delicious interviews and fresh poetry. *Blackfire* is designed for the sophisticated reader as well as those who want to take matters into their own hands.

Submissions

Blackfire seeks stories, articles, photography, models, illustration and a very limited amount of poetry all related to black men unclothed or in erotic situations.

STORIES AND ARTICLES

The best way to determine our needs is to read and study several recent issues. Here is a partial list of our needs:

• Full-length erotic fiction of 2,000-4,000 words detailing the exploits of black men in the life.

• Nostalgia and humor pieces are welcome if they are black, ITL and erotic. We also publish historical articles and first-person accounts that meet these criteria.

• Where-to articles that include details on where black men in the life congregate. These can range from the latest local bar to out-of-the-way resorts. Thoroughness and accuracy are the keys to acceptance of these articles.

• Shorts. We use articles of 400 to 700 words with one to two photos for one-pagers. Subjects include fresh, sharply focused erotic ideas.

• We do not solicit product reviews, games or puzzles. Subjects considered inappropriate include stories that refer to minors, illegal drugs, bestiality, water sports and scat.

WRITING STYLE

Blackfire seeks erotic material of the highest quality, but it need not be written by professional writers. The most important thing is that the work be erotic and that it feature black men in the life or ITL themes. We are not interested in stories that demean black men or place them in stereotypical situations.

Erotic fiction can range from descriptions of idealized men having idealized sex ("his 13-inch dick spurted a cupful of love juice"), to depictions of typical men in plausible encounters ("homeboy didn't have no meat, but I didn't care; I wanted that booty"), to unconsummated hints at sex ("ballet is the politically correct way for men to stare at other men's dicks in public"). We are partial to the latter two categories.

We want to publish concise, well-organized articles, so material must be tightly written. We reserve the right to edit submissions and to change titles as necessary.

Study the magazine to see what we do and how we do it. Some fiction is very romantic; other is highly sexual. Most articles in *Blackfire* cater to black men between these two extremes.

SPECIFICS

Include your name and address on the title page as well as your pseudonym, if you intend to use one. If the work you submit to us is being submitting to others as well, please let us know.

RIGHTS

Blackfire secures first North American rights and the right to anthologize accepted work. You retain all other rights to your work. If the material you're submitting has appeared elsewhere, tell us when you submit it. Payment for articles averages about 10 cents per word. This payment is based on quality of the material, research required to complete the piece, length of the copy and how badly we want the story. Writers whose work is included in an anthology receive an additional payment.

ACCEPTANCE

Individuals whose works are accepted for publication must provide *Blackfire* with a brief biographical sketch. Accepted works should, whenever possible, be provided on diskette in either PC or Macintosh format. You should provide the original or a reproduction-quality duplicate of accepted artwork.

PEP TALK

Because you're reading these guidelines, you're one step closer to having us accept your work than are many others. We want to hear from you by way of a tantalizing query, a top-notch completed manuscript, or an article we can't resist featuring on the cover. Every year we work with a few unpublished writers, and in our pages you can also find the bylines and credits of established professionals. It doesn't matter if you're a pro or a novice. If the material meets our needs and standards, we use it.

PHOTOGRAPHY AND ILLUSTRATION

If you are a photographer or an artist, submit your work.

MODELS

If you have a nice face, a great body or are heavy in the meat department and want to appear in *Blackfire*, let us know. In fact, if you don't have a nice face, you've got an average body and God sent your dick elsewhere, and you want to appear in *Blackfire*, contact us anyway.

DEADLINES

We accept submissions year-round. Submit seasonal material six months in advance. For instance, a piece about Kwanzaa in December must be received in June, and an April piece about Easter must be in our hands in October.

DELIVERY

Submissions may be mailed to Editor, *Blackfire*, PO Box 83912, Los Angeles, CA 90083-0912. Please include a self-addressed, stamped envelope with adequate postage if you want your work returned. Submissions may be faxed to the Editor at 310-410-9250. Submissions may be emailed to: newsroom@blk.com. We usually respond within a month.

LEGALESE

The Editors do not assume responsibility for loss of or damage to submitted materials. Publication of the name, photograph or likeness of any person or organization in articles or advertising in *Blackfire* is not to be construed as any indication of the sexual orientation of such persons or organizations. The opinions of *Blackfire* are expressed only in editorials. Other opinions are those of the writers and do not necessarily represent the opinions of *Blackfire*.

Categories: Fiction—African-American—Erotica—Fantasy—Gay/Lesbian—Men's Fiction—Men's Issues—Poetry—Sexuality

CONTACT: Alan Bell, Editor
Material: All
PO Box 83912
Los Angeles CA 90083-0912
Phone: 310-410-0808
Fax: 310-410-9250
E-mail: newsroom@blk.com
Website: www.blackfire.org

Blacque's Literary Machine

Blacque's Literary Machine publishes short fiction, reviews, articles and market listings.

Rights: First electronic rights (60 days). All rights revert to author after that time.

Needs: We seek science fiction; fantasy; horror; mainstream; gay/lesbian/alternative tales; ethnic; stories about woman; paranormal.

Will consider any well-written story that resonates.

Length: 1500-3000 words

Payment: Author bio and link to your website/e-mail. Also will receive free subscription and copies of print version when available.

How to Submit: Submit all work to e-mail address below.

Submissions should be in the body of an e-mail. Will also accept attachments in MS Word, WordPerfect and RTF formats.

Response Time: Please allow 7-10 days for response.

Tips for Writers: Unlike most publications these days, we still like old-fashioned monster tales and vampire stories-but be original! Use humor or add a new twist to an old story. Don't be afraid to shake things up-shock us, shock the reader.

Follow standard manuscript format, give an accurate word count. Above all else, we want honesty in writing.

Writer's Guidelines

Blacque's Literary Machine is intended as a site for fans of the experimental, the different and the new.

Most genres are considered, as long as proper manuscript format is followed. The editor"s job is not to teach anyone how to spell or correct grammar usage. If you are a new writer, please consider purchasing texts on proper manuscript format (Writers Digest Books are a great resource) or search the web's professional writer's sites.

Be professional-that means submitting your best product in a neat, concise fashion. Submissions that are not up to standards **will not** be accepted for publication. In short, treat this resource as you would any professional writer"s publication-we"ll show you the same respect.

We read July-December.

The copyright remains with the author-we just ask for first electronic rights. This means that for at least sixty (60) days, your material should not appear in any other print or e-zine. After that time, all rights revert to author.

Here's what we"re looking for:

FICTION. I like sci/fi, fantasy, horror, lesbian/gay/alternative stories; ethnic experience and tales about women are strongly welcomed; mainstream lit with verve is also considered. Metaphysical tales (witchcraft, astrology, paranormal, New Age lore, Mythology, etc.) are a big plus-we notice these subjects are usually handled in the "Swords & Sorcerer" like way. Got a new spin on an old formula? Send it!

Give me your vampire stories (but for godsakes be original!). Like aliens? Me too. Make me believe they enter my bedroom at night. Girl/girl and boy/boy scenes can be a real turn-on. Make them spicy or sweet without too much smut or sentiment.

Sex is nice, but has its limits; I reserve my porn intake for the video/DVD player. No romance epics or Movie-Of-The-Week style, "And then she dies." stories. No trademarked characters from films or television shows.

NON-FICTION. Articles between 500-1000 words on the writing craft, essays (sometimes); reviews of other webzines (what they offer, format, readability, etc.) and articles which discuss specific methodology for breaking into markets, i.e. "How To Make The Sale."

And at least for now—NO POETRY.

The Internet is a medium made for people with short attention spans—if you can't say what you need to in 3,000 words or less, submit elsewhere.

We **DO** edit submissions for clarity (when necessary) and will notify the author of any and all changes.

I prefer to receive e-mail submissions at this time via text copied directly into the e-mail's body (some people think viruses are funny). I may make concessions in special cases (MS Word ,WordPerfect or RTF). A short bio should accompany your submission. If you use a pseudonym, please include this (after your real name) and use this symbol (*) for clarification. In the Subject Box, add **BLM Submission, "Genre"** (genre is important!!!).

We **DO** accept works that were previously published on the Internet or in print publications, though original works are preferred. Should you submit a previously published work, please let us know the original publication (this will also look good in your contributor profile.) Let us know if you wish for your e-mail address (or any additional contact info) to be available to our readers. Contributors are also free to send pictures.

Blacque's Literary Machine is not offering monetary payment at this time, but hopes to join the paying markets soon. We know it's hard to write part/full time and pay the bills, too.

Categories: Science Fiction

CONTACT: Lilith Blacque, Editor
E-mail: lblacque@yahoo.com
Website: blacques.faithweb.com/index.htm

The Blessed Bee

Please refer to *SageWoman Magazine*.

Bloomsbury Review

The Bloomsbury Review is a magazine about books that has been publishing since 1980 and is distributed throughout the U.S. and Canada. TBR accepts submissions of book reviews, essays, poetry, interviews, and other book-related articles.

Editorial Policy: *The Bloomsbury Review* does not announce reviews prior to publication. We do send copies of the issue to the publisher if and when a review appears. With that in mind, we ask that writers not contact the publisher or the author of a book when they have submitted a review to TBR.

TIPS ON WRITING A BOOK REVIEW

As in any good writing, there should be a strong introduction and conclusion, and smooth transitions between paragraphs. The writing should be intelligent without being too pedantic, critical without being condescending, and lively and colorful without being frivolous.

A good book review should tell the reader what the book is about, why the reader may or may not be interested in it, whether or not the author is successful in his/her intent, and whether or not the book should be read.

Never review a book on a subject you are not familiar with. It is not necessary to be an expert on the subject, but good working knowledge of the author or subject matter is imperative.

Be objective. Never review the work of a personal or ideological friend or enemy.

Never review a book you haven't read at least once and understood.

Review the author's ideas, not your own. Do not compete with the subject, but instead respond or react to it.

A review should be more than just a summary of the book's contents. It should be an involved and informed response to the style, theme, and content.

If you have any questions regarding the writing of a book review or any other feature, please do not hesitate to contact one of our editors. It is our obligation to provide our readers with informative, entertaining statements about books and the ideas presented in them.

For Style: Follow *The Chicago Manual of Style*. It is our policy to use nonsexist language. TBR's editors will make minor editorial alterations, if necessary, to conform to the house style. If substantial editing of your review is required, you will be notified and a copy of your edited review can be sent to you for your approval or final changes prior to publication.

Length: Upon assignment of a review or feature, an editor will assign an approximate length (usually from 100 to 1,000 words, as some subjects or books may warrant more or less space). If you find that a book you have been assigned does not warrant the time and effort it would take to review it, please contact your editor. This does not mean, however, that we will not publish negative criticism provided it is properly substantiated.

Quoted Material: It is extremely important to include a photocopy of all materials quoted in a review.

If the quotes are directly from the text of the book you are reviewing, please either photocopy those pages and indicate the passage quoted with brackets or, if you are returning the book to TBR along with the review, indicate on your manuscript (in the left margin) the page from which the quote is taken.

If you are quoting from a book other than the one you are reviewing, indicate the title of the book, the author, and the year of publication as well as a photocopy of the page with the quoted passage in brackets.

If you are quoting from a journal or magazine, please indicate the title of the periodical, the title of the article, the author of that piece, and the volume and issue date, as well as a photocopy of the quote.

Reviewer Information: Please include a bio/byline of up to 30 words at the end of each submission.

Headline: Writers are welcome to suggest a headline for their reviews, interviews, or essays, although such will be subject to editorial discretion and space limitations.

FORMAT FOR SUBMISSIONS

We use a PC. Our preferred format for submissions is in DOS text file stored on a 3¼" diskette (with one hard copy) formatted in Word Perfect version 5 or 5.1 or ASCII. We will also accept your review at our e-mail address (BloomsB@aol.com — only in ASCII or Word Perfect 6.0) or as hard or faxed copy. Please also send to our office one photocopy (keep your original), byped and double-spaced.

Please include your name, mailing address, and phone number on page 1, and your name only at the top of each following page; allow eight weeks for reply.

FORMAT FOR BOOK REVIEWS

At the top of the first page, include the following information:
1. Title of book
2. Subtitle (if any)
3. Author/Editor/Translator/Illustrator/Photographer
4. Publisher/price/binding/ISBN (please include price and ISBN for both cloth and paper editions, when available, as well as the address for small presses)
5. The year the book was published

Payment: Reviewers may opt for gift subscriptions in lieu of cash payment. The scale is as follows: book reviews (of 600 or more words) = $10 to $15 (1-year subscription); poetry = $5 to $10 per poem (1-year subscription); essays, features, and interviews = $20 to $50 (2- to 4-year subscription). Payment is made upon publication. Submissions of less than 600 words in length are welcome but not paid.

The book business is an exciting field, and we welcome your thoughts, comments, and submissions.

Categories: Fiction—Nonfiction—Book Reviews—Interview—Literature—Writing

CONTACT: Tom Auer, Publisher
Material: All
Marily Auer, Associate Publisher
1553 Platte St., Ste 206
Denver CO 80202-1667
Phone: 303-455-3123
Fax: 303-455-7039

Blue Ridge Country Magazine

Blue Ridge Country is a bi-monthly, full-color magazine embracing the feel and spirit of the Blue Ridge region—the traditions and recipes, the husbandry and farming, the country stores and bed-and-breakfast inns, the things to visit and learn about. In short, it is everything that will allow and encourage the reader to "take a trip home for the weekend" even if he or she has never lived in the region.

Our territory extends from Western Maryland south through Virginia's Shenandoah Valley of Virginia down into northern Georgia and Alabama and including all territory within about a half day's drive of the Blue Ridge Parkway. It includes the mountain regions of Kentucky, Maryland, West Virginia, Virginia, North Carolina, South Carolina, Tennessee, Alabama and Georgia.

We encourage writers to submit story ideas with sample clips; we rarely publish unsolicited manuscripts.

Main Pieces: 750-2,000 words

PLACES

Everything there is to find out and tell about a great Blue Ridge town, city or locale. The history, the current economic status, the quaint spots and characters, the best places to eat. A profile so complete our readers can make hard decisions on going to spend a weekend or even moving there.

HISTORY AND LEGENDS

From people and events to unexplained occurrences or phenomena, full magazine prints, fascinating tales of past and present. In particular, we are seeking stories from "baby boomer" history—the 1940s to present.

THE BLUE RIDGE PARKWAY AND THE APPALACHIAN TRAIL

There's a wealth of wildlife, beauty, history and future plans involving the parkway and the trail and the areas immediately surrounding each. We'll bring our readers a new piece of America's favorite scenic highway and favorite footpath in each issue.

ENVIRONMENT

Well-researched, objective stories on environmental issues of relevance to the Appalachian mountains.

GENERAL ARTICLES

Anything that is well-researched, well-written and brings us some of the flavor of the region will get strong consideration. We'll be looking for at-home kinds of things—environmental issues, arts and crafts, natural history and wildlife, and especially pieces that embrace the whole of the region. Plus humor, first-person adventure or discovery and the "bests" of the region.

Departments (100-400 words)

Very much like the main pieces, but in shorter versions; places to see, things to do, recipes to try, great people doing great things, new books, etc. – anything and everything that contributes to the sense of the place. Regular departments include Country Roads (travel/environmental news, book reviews, etc.), Mountain Delicacies, Mountain Inns, Almanac (festivals and events), On the Mountainside (outdoor recreation) and The Hike.

RIGHTS

We buy exclusive first North America serial rights until the off-sale date of the issue in which material is published, as well as exclusive rights to the work for promotional reprint and use. We prefer attribution any time an article is reprinted elsewhere that has appeared in our magazine; *Blue Ridge Country* rarely publishes reprints (the usual exception is book preview excerpts). Please inform us if you are simultaneously submitting the same story to another publication.

STYLE

We adopt AP style for all magazine content. Stories must include interview material from primary sources only (person-to-person interview or, if necessary, e-interview). We expect accuracy and thorough research in all submissions. We encourage first person writing for outdoor recreation and travel writing.

PAY

We pay from $25 (for department shorts) up to about $250 for major pieces. Original photos (shot by writer) are paid $50 per photo accepted. Payment is upon publication. Sample copies of the magazine are available. Send $3 and a magazine-size SASE.

PHOTOGRAPHY

We use primarily color photographs that can be submitted as slides, high-resolution digital files (.jpgs or .tiffs, 300 dpi at a minimum print size of 5"x7") or high-quality prints. We pay $25 (interior minimum) to $150 (cover maximum) for exclusive first North American serial rights until the off-sale date of the issue in which the material is published, as well as rights to the work for promotional and reprint use. See photographic guidelines for more details.

Send queries, ideas, and stories with SASE.

Categories: Nonfiction—Animals—Book Reviews—Civil War—Conservation—Cooking—Culture—Ecology—Entertainment—Environment—Family—Fishing—Folklore—Food/Drink—Gardening—General Interest—History—Interview—Lifestyle—Music—Native Americans—Outdoors—Photography—Real Estate—Recreation—Regional—Rural America—Travel—Appalachian Events & Festivals

Material: All
CONTACT: Cara Ellen Modisett, Editor
3424 Brambleton Ave
Roanoke VA 24018
Phone: 540-989-6138
Fax: 540-989-7603
Website: www.blueridgecountry.com

Boating Life
The Authority on Recreational Boating

Boating Life is published 9 issues per year. BL does not have any formal writers' guidelines, but we publish articles on the following:
• Boating in crafts up to 40 feet
• Electronics
• Engines
• Fishing
• Product Reviews
• Tips, Techniques, & Travel
• Water sports

Categories: Nonfiction—Adventure—Fishing—Lifestyle—Outdoors—Sports/Recreation—Travel

CONTACT: Robert Stephens, Editor
Material: All
World Publications, LLC
460 N. Orlando Ave., Ste 200
Winter Park, Florida 32789
Phone: 407-628-4802
Website: www.boatinglifemag.com

Boca Raton

Story Queries

We at Boca Raton magazine value the concerns, ideas, and interests of our readers. All story queries should be submitted by mail, with an SASE, to Managing Editor Gaspar Gonzalez (see address below). It is our goal to respond to all queries; however, due to the large volume that we receive, this may not be possible.

Letters

Your thoughts and comments are important to us. All letters to the editor are proofread for style and grammar. We reserve the right to withhold any letters deemed inappropriate for publication. To submit a letter, see address listed below or e-mail us.

Diversions

Where to go, and what to see and do in South Florida. Please submit information regarding fund-raisers, art openings, plays, readings, concerts, dance, or other performances, etc., two and a half months prior to the event. (e.g., to list an event in the March/April Datebook, submit information by December 15; for the May/June issue, the deadline is February 15). Address submissions to Assistant Editor Chelsea Greenwood or e-mail her: chelsea@bocamag.com

Dining

Our comprehensive listing of restaurants in South Florida. A reliable resource for fine and casual dining for residents and tourists. For more information about the Dining Guide, call Lulu Chesterfield at ext. 234.

People

A photo collage of recent social gatherings and events in South Florida. All photographs submitted to "People" should be accompanied by a brief description of the event (who, what, where and when). Photos will be returned only upon request. Submissions should be addressed "People," attention Brenna Fisher.

Categories: Nonfiction—Entertainment—Foor—General Interest—Regional: Boca Raton, FL

CONTACT: Boca Raton Magazine
Material: All
6413 Congress Ave Ste 100
Boca Raton FL 33487
Phone: 561-997-8683
Fax: 561-997-8909
e-mail: magazine@bocamag.com

body & brain

body & brain

Integrating mind, body and spirit for an authentic, balanced life
WRITERS GUIDELINES

body & brain represents a beacon of hope for its readers, offering innovative ways to enhance their well-being with a wide range of subjects: natural health solutions, nutritional alternatives, thought-provoking features, compelling brain research updates and spiritual enlightenment.

A quarterly holistic health/yoga magazine published by Healing Society, Inc., in Sedona, Ariz., it is inspired by Dahn Yoga* philosophy, whose main teachings are self-healing and listening to the inner voice. Designed for holistic health enthusiasts and Dahn Yoga practitioners alike, its stimulating articles help readers make the connection between mental and physical balance.

As part of the magazine's overall readership of 100,000 in the U.S., Canada and Great Britain, it provides more than 50,000 Dahn Yoga practitioners with simple tools to enhance their practice. At the same time, it serves those who wish to experience greater health, happiness and peace by presenting the latest information about health and nutritional trends, advancements in neuroscience and inspiration for inner growth and spiritual development.

Our editorial objective is to provide a wealth of information that helps people make informed, holistic choices. Those who have made mind-body practices an important part of their daily lifestyle will find guidance in practical tips and moving stories for heartfelt personal changes.

ABOUT US
• Established: Spring 2004
• Publisher: Healing Society, Inc.
• Circulation/readership: 100,000, mostly throughout North America.
• Distribution: Barnes & Noble and major bookstore chains, health food markets, paid subscriptions and more than 170 Dahn Yoga Centers in the U.S., Canada and Great Britain.
• Editorial Focus: We serve our readers by presenting them with a forum of ideas, including the latest scientific research and holistic trends, to help them make their own decisions for achieving balance in their everyday lives. Articles focus on mind-body practices, Dahn Yoga workouts, holistic health, brain research, green living, optimal nutrition, natural beauty solutions, balanced living and spiritual growth.
• Content: 90% freelance written.
• Publication dates: Spring issue: March.1; Summer issue: June 1; Fall issue: Sept. 1; Winter issue: Dec. 1.
• Related Web sites: www.bodynbrain.com, www.Dahnyoga.com.
OUR AUDIENCE: Who reads *body & brain*?
We serve a general audience and Dahn Yoga practitioners of primarily affluent, physically active, intelligent women age 47+ who are interested in health, fitness, nutrition, mind-body practices, brain enhancement, wellness trends and alternatives, personal growth and spiritual development.

• While we aim to serve Dahn members, our focus is based on a general audience. Therefore, our content appeals to a mass market as well as Dahn practitioners.
• Our current reader survey shows 90% of our readers are women with college or higher degrees, 90% of them consider spiritual enlightenment important, and 70% prefer to use alternative medicine to treat any illness.
• Our readers are sharp, observant, aware and in touch with their minds, bodies and souls.
WHAT WE'RE LOOKING FOR
Fascinating, timely, exciting and lively magazine-style articles about mind-body practices and holistic health that serve both Dahn Yoga practitioners as well as the general public. Each issue offers new Dahn Yoga postures designed to promote people's well-being plus practical tools to enhance their brain power.

We seek well-researched, informative, intelligent stories that encourage readers to think. We look for clinical studies and compelling research information transformed into exciting, thought-provoking, vital stories that offer simple guidelines for readers to achieve balance in their lives.

Our readers want healthy tips for managing stress, losing weight, eating right and increasing their energy. They enjoy higher wisdom, positive thinking and self-empowerment articles with a spiritual perspective. While we like to see stories make a connection with Dahn philosophy and principles, it is not a prerequisite for every article. Above all, we like material that reaches out and touches all readers on a personal level, inspiring them to live happier, healthier lives.
WHAT WE'RE *NOT* LOOKING FOR
Fiction; poetry; first-person narratives; spa, travel or retreat articles; academic or textbook articles; opinion pieces; standard consumer beauty pieces or others oriented toward female cosmetic appearance and traditional gender roles. First-person accounts are reserved for the Insight column, where writers can share their inner wisdom, lessons learned and other personal insights on life (see specific guidelines for this column below).
QUERY LETTERS AND STORY PROPOSALS
GOT A GREAT STORY IDEA? WE WANT TO KNOW!
We are always willing to consider your ideas whether you are a new or unpublished writer.

1. Read our magazine before submitting your proposal! Check our current and past issues at www.bodynbrain.com to see if we have featured your subject in a prior edition.

2. We look for stories specifically tailored for our audience and magazine style. Is your idea suitable for our mission? Is it consistent with our editorial focus? Will it inspire readers to be happier, healthier and more aware? You can obtain copies of the current issue at any Barnes & Noble or Borders bookstore, as well as your local Dahn Yoga Center. Call 1-877-HSP-YOGA to find a center near you.

3. Since *body & brain* is a quarterly publication, please submit seasonal queries at least four months in advance. Final assignments are made at the end of every August, November, February and May for each seasonal issue.

4. Your proposal should consist of a brief but specific story outline of one or two pages highlighting the major points you intend to make in bullet or paragraph form. Note how your story would benefit our readers and why it would enhance our editorial appeal in a timely manner. What approach would you take to present your subject on a personal level for readers?

5. Articles should appeal to the general public as well as Dahn practitioners. Is there some way your story can weave in a theme from basic Dahn principles?

6. If you are proposing a new angle on a previously covered topic, specify how your outline differs from that story. What new studies, findings or information makes it newsworthy for our readers four months from now? Mention why it would be of particular interest to our audience. What current research trends support your premise?

7. Incorporate the tone your story will take into your proposal

where possible. A query that starts with a compelling angle and links it to a national trend or concern will get our attention.

8. Who are you? What qualifies you to write the story? We prefer to hire published writers but will consider first-time authors who can demonstrate their skill based on writing samples. Whether experienced or novice, all writers must include samples of their work.

9. Include a short bio or summary (approximately 60 words) about yourself, your profession and your practice or philosophy, as well as your full name, address, phone and e-mail.

10. See Submission Formats for Queries and Proposals below before sending your document. This will provide you with tips for preparing your material.

11. **Do not call**. E-mail all queries to editor@bodynbrain.com with attachments or links to samples of your work. We will respond within four weeks.

12. Clips may also be faxed to 928-282-8467 or sent to our mailing address below. Include a SASE with any material if you want it returned.

POLICIES, RATES AND ETHICS: OUR WRITER-FRIENDLY APPROACH

1. All queries and stories must be submitted via e-mail either as a Word attachment or as part of the text.

2. We do not accept multiple submissions.

3. Assignments are made via e-mail letter of agreement, with story guidelines, deadline and word count, and confirmed upon writer's acceptance. We do not offer writing contracts. Assignments do not guarantee acceptance or publication.

4. We reserve the right to edit stories for clarity and length in accordance with our publications standards. Our editors take every measure to preserve the writer's voice.

5. Please allow us two weeks for reading and editing your material. We may request revisions up to 3 or 4 weeks after your submission. Revisions are standard and stories sometimes require more than one draft from the writer.

6. Callbacks and questions are de rigueur and writers should not feel put down about an editor's request for clarification. We consider great articles a team effort orchestrated by the editor and writer in concert.

7. Bylines are given on all stories.

8. We pay upon acceptance after our approval of the final draft. We reserve the right to reject a story at any stage of the editorial/production process. A kill fee of 20% is paid to writers whose stories we do not run after completion and submission on deadline. Please note that killing stories is the exception, not the norm. All materials will be returned to the contributor with the opportunity to resubmit at a later date.

9. We provide writers with a 1099 form and they remain responsible for filing their own income taxes.

10. Rates vary by column, department and length of story and include the purchase of electronic rights. Features range from $200-$500 and department articles pay anywhere from $50-$75 for short pieces (Balanced Living, Media Review) to $150-350 for full stories.

11. We buy first North American serial rights with the nonexclusive right to post the article or an excerpt on our affiliated Web sites, with full credit given to the author.

12. Any illustrations must meet our art director's approval. Photographs must be in a jpeg format with a resolution of 300 dpi or better.

13. Proposals remain the writer's intellectual property. If we decide not to use your idea, we would never use your material.

14. We do not use freelance material for books or other publications without the writer's permission.

15. We cannot be held responsible for loss or damage to unsolicited manuscripts or artwork.

FREELANCE DEPARTMENTS

Every issue of *body & brain* presents some of the most important developments in mental, physical and spiritual well-being. We currently use freelance writers for the following departments:

Feature Stories—General Word Count: 1500 - 2800

We usually publish three or four per issue, all freelance written and on a wide range of topics. Each issue includes one Dahn Yoga training feature and one inner growth/spiritual development story. Other topics include healing and brain research.

Balanced Living

Balanced Living consists of the following components: seasonal wisdom, body wise, green living, brain update, alt adventure, healing products and medical perspectives. The latter addresses a health issue and provides alternative approaches for healing, including allopathic and Western medical traditions, without taking sides so readers can decide what modality will work best for them.

Brain Up—General Word Count: 1300

Designed to educate readers with practical tips to boost their brain power, this column features the latest in Brain Respiration techniques, brain research and technology. Previous topics have included the power of a smile and toys that build brain power, as well as tools that build confidence, strengthen family ties and manage stress.

In a Nutshell—General Word Count: 1400

The purpose of In a Nutshell is to educate the public about an important brain-related scientific subject. Stories provide an in-depth look at how innovations in neuroscience can affect people's brains and therefore their lives. Previous stories have addressed hypnosis, meditation, memory, guided imagery and the effect of hope in healing. The topic can be about the latest research, a controversial topic in the news or a basic function of the brain with a new/interesting/educational angle. Basically, the article should do its job of summarizing what would otherwise be a difficult topic "in a nutshell," making that topic accessible and interesting to the general public.

Media Review—Sections include film, books, CDs, DVDs and other media and may include unique games or novelty items that educate and enlighten the reader.

Books/Author Excerpts: We welcome queries from authors to feature their works that are in alignment with our philosophy. Authors can write their own stories or we will assign a writer to complete a feature on the book, with permission to quote excerpts from the author. We also feature book reviews in our Media Review column.

Dahn Articles

We prefer to have these written by practitioners, healers and instructors fluent in Dahn Yoga techniques and principles. We welcome free-lance writers who can demonstrate an ability to weave Dahn principles in their writings to submit proposals for this section.

1. Training Article—Serves as our main feature story and cover theme. Word count varies and usually ranges between 800-900 words for the intro text and around 900 words for the postures for a 7 to 10-page article. The article consists of two pages of text (approximately 800 words) introducing approximately six or seven Dahn Yoga postures that promote better mental and physical well-being. Recent articles include Jung-Choong Breathing and postures to open the Heart Chakra.

2. For Beginners—Offers exercises that new Dahn Yoga practitioners can use to enhance their practice. Word count is 850 for both text and exercise guidelines that cover two pages. Example articles include modifications for Jung-Choong Breathing postures, harnessing more energy, correct form and muscle aches.

3. Health Solution—Provides Dahn Yoga techniques that anyone can use to help alleviate a physical challenge. Past topics have addressed healing tense shoulders, back pain, insomnia solutions, allergy relief, headache antidotes, flu remedies and detoxification methods. Word count: 800 (200 intro; 600 exercises).

4. Feature Story—Focuses on inner growth, positive thinking and spiritual development with tools and tips for applying them to everyday life. Word count varies from 1500-2000 words.

5. Dahn Community News—Are you a Dahn Yoga practitioner who has something exciting to share with us? These pages offer short community news briefs and blurbs that highlight the following categories: People, New Programs, News & Events and Dahn Voices. Dahn Voices

features short healing stories and testimonials of approximately 50 words from members about the way the practice has changed their lives.

Insight—General Word Count: 450

We welcome short, dramatic yet simply moving essays in anecdotal style for our

Insight column, which always displays on the last page of *body & brain* magazine. You can write about anything you want — something about your practice, growth, a lesson learned, epiphany, revelation, awareness or point of view. Writers should share some profound pearl of wisdom – as long as it is inspirational and not just a dry opinion – versus nuts-and-bolts type of tips. It does not have to be Dahn-related and should appeal to a wide audience. Submissions that offer a profound yet simple "twist" and strike an emotional chord with the reader have the best chance of publication.

A riveting, emotional or anecdotal first-person narrative is more suited to this column than a strictly third-person opinion that sounds like "preaching the choir." Since it is the last story that readers see before closing the magazine, we like it to reflect something that really moves them or leaves them with a sense of wonder, inspiration or awe – that kind of "aha!" awareness or wondrous lesson of sheer simplicity. The story should leave readers of *body & brain* magazine with a sense of completion and give them a message or insight they can apply to their own lives. Writers are strongly urged to read previous Insight columns at www.bodynbrain.com.

BEFORE YOU CLICK THE "SEND" BUTTON:
SUBMISSION FORMATS FOR QUERIES AND STORIES
ALL DOCUMENTS:

1. Format in Microsoft WORD—Please do not send files written in other applications.

2. Please use black type only since we reserve colors for editing purposes.

3. Must be e-mailed. Attachments must be in WORD format.

4. Font: Times New Roman, 12-pt.

5. SINGLE SPACE paragraphs; double space in between paragraphs; one space between sentences.

6. Keep margins flush left; do not justify.

7. Do not indent paragraphs.

8. Please spell check.

9. While we prefer AP style, writers are not required to submit their work as such.

QUERIES AND PROPOSALS

1. Include your name, address, phone and e-mail on the first page.

2. Submit an outline specifying how you plan to structure your story, noting sources or experts you may interview.

3. Attach any clips or links to your published work (or fax hard copies).

4. If you are not a published writer, please include a writing sample.

5. Include a resume or short bio.

ASSIGNED STORIES

body & brain magazine is committed to excellence and accuracy in the printed word. This guarantees that our readers who believe something simply because they read it in *body & brain* have not misplaced their trust.

1. Sentence format: one space between sentences.

2. Use present tense.

3. Stick as close to the word count as possible.

4. Please spell-check your story.

5. body & brain is vigorously fact-checked. Please help us ensure accuracy by verifying the spelling of all proper names and nouns. Indicate that you checked them by bold-facing all proper nouns or underlining them. For example: Which is correct: Association for Research & Enlightenment—or—Association for Research and Enlightenment? We must publish the name exactly as it appears for the organization and don't assume titles provided by a source are correct. Always check the Web site or materials for verification.

6. Font: Times New Roman, 12 point

7. Paragraph format: Single space, no paragraph indents, double

space between paragraphs

8. At the top left of the first page of your story, please list the following:

a. Draft: Note whether this is the first, second or final version

b. List magazine dept. (e.g., "Feature")

c. Title:

d. Subhead:

e. By: your name

f. Word count: does not include title or subhead but does include sidebars and author's tagline at the end

9. Please use paragraph subheads wherever possible. Do not put a space between the subhead and its accompanying paragraph.

10. Create a couple of short sidebars with reference info as part of your story wherever possible. Look at our magazine for effective examples.

11. At the end of your story, please include your bio tagline: E.g., Jane Doe is a freelance writer from New York City, New York, USA, who… (add whatever you want, personally or professionally, that pertains to the story).

12. Submit your story by the assigned deadline date. If you cannot meet the deadline, please contact the editor as soon as possible.

13. Always keep a copy of your work.

WRITING TIPS

1. Crown your story with a title and subtitle.

2. Seduce readers with an exciting lead and keep them entertained with informal yet polished prose they find impossible to put down. Hold their attention through the last sentence by constantly introducing a fresh stream of material throughout the story.

3. Use colorful, vivid, lucid, flowing, feature-style magazine writing. Please avoid dry, scientific textbook tones.

4. We favor simplicity, clarity and real-life language versus academic approaches.

5. Avoid technical jargon and cryptic acronyms that readers may not understand.

6. Explore your topic by going the extra mile in your research. Dig a little deeper to go "just beyond" the ordinary. Give us the extraordinary. Offer strong supporting evidence for the article's premise.

7. Stick with the story outline and focus.

8. Offer solutions wherever possible.

9. Keep your article in third or second person and avoid first-person narrative unless you are writing a personal account for our Insight column.

10. Reach out and touch the reader with warmth yet authority; establish a personal connection with them with the use of anecdotes where appropriate. Get inside their minds and address their needs, hopes, fears and desires.

11. Keep sentences short.

12. Break up long paragraphs wherever possible. Use subheads.

13. Avoid passive voice (has been, etc.) and exhaustive use of "to be" verbs (is, was, are, etc.). Use colorful action verbs whenever possible instead of dry, boring, repetitive ones.

14. Avoid any editorial opinion.

15. Use quotes from veritable experts, examples, anecdotes and interesting statistics. Offer credible reports that provide meaningful options or practical advice for our readers.

16. When referring to any scientific studies, take clinical research and translate it into fascinating, lively copy for the readers.

17. Provide solid, reliable sources, including both mainstream and alternative experts.

18. Distinguish fact from fiction. Have you made any statements based on cultural assumptions or are they based upon unbiased fact? We don't assume mainstream or government authorities are necessarily aligned with updated facts in the best public interest. Include them, but get the opinion of alternative sources as well to let our readers decide for themselves what is best.

19. End with a solid conclusion or unique twist that provokes thought.

20. Include a short, one-sentence bio that we can use as a tagline at the end of your story. This should include any Dahn-related or professional info, including the location of your Dahn center, as well as the city and state where you reside.

21. READ YOUR STORY before sending it in! Spell-check often misses words that are in the dictionary yet used incorrectly in your story. Example: "One you turn your story in" should read "Once you turn your story in" but spell check reads "one" as a correct word and not for its context.

22. Check how many action verbs versus passive verbs you have. Highlight each word you can see, feel, taste, hear or smell. For example, "chocolate chip" conjures up more taste, sight and smell than mere "ice cream." Review your story to ensure the reader enjoys a total sensational experience.

23. Styles differ; be true to your natural voice. We are not looking for uniform voice and tone in *body & brain* stories, but for lively style.

Categories: Nonfiction—Exercise—Health—Yoga

CONTACT: Catherine J. Rourke. Editor in Chief
body & brain magazine
6560 Hwy 19, Ste 114
Sedona AZ 86351
Fax: 928-282-8467
E-mail: editor@bodynbrain.com
Web site: www.bodynbrain.com

Body & Soul

Thank you for your interest in contributing to BODY & SOUL magazine.

BODY & SOUL is a national bimonthly magazine. Our editorial objective is to serve as an inspirational guide for all those who want to live healthier, more balanced lives. We cover a wide range of subjects: integrative medicine, nutrition, self-help psychology, spirituality, the mind/body connection, work and money issues, and organic living. We provide the information readers need to take an active role in improving their lives and preserving the planet. We are looking for quality writing and thorough reporting to inform and entertain our audience. We are also interested in new, cutting-edge thinking.

We publish up to six features per issue (1,500 to 3,500 words); up to eight columns that run under headings such as Holistic Health, Food/Nutrition, Spirit, Home, Community, Travel and Life Lessons (600 to 1,300 words); book and music/media sections that include a variety of reviews (200 to 750 words); and an Insight section that includes short news items (50-250 words). Please note that we do not publish fiction, poetry, or previously published articles.

Our payment rates for published material are comparable to those of other small national magazines and range from $50 for a short news piece to $1,500 or more for a feature story. Fees are determined on an individual basis by assignment and vary depending on the nature of the story and the experience of the writer. Fees include the purchase of electronic rights.

Although we consider unsolicited manuscripts, it is best to send a query letter before preparing a lengthy article. When sending queries, please include clips of recent work and a résumé. Due to the volume of mail we receive, only manuscripts accompanied by an SASE with sufficient postage will be returned. We cannot consider submissions sent via e-mail. Please do not send originals, as the magazine cannot be held responsible for loss or damage of unsolicited material. We will attempt to respond to all submissions within 12 weeks of receipt. No phone calls please.

Categories: Nonfiction—Alternate Life-style—Arts—Book Reviews—Diet/Nutrition—Environment—Health—Inspirational—Lifestyle—Music—New Age—Physical Fitness—Self-Help—Spiritual

CONTACT: Liz Phillips, Executive Editor
Material: Spirituality, Work, Environment
CONTACT: Tania Hannan, Managing Editor
Material: Fitness, Health

CONTACT: Frances Lefkowitz, Senior Editor
Material: Food, Nutrition, Creativity
New Age Publishing, Editorial Department
42 Pleasant St.
Watertown MA 02472
Phone: 617-926-0200
Fax: 617-926-5021
E-mail: editor@bodyandsoulmag.com
Website: www.bodyandsoulmag.com

Book/Mark Quarterly Review

Book/Mark Small Press Quarterly Review (1994-present) is dedicated to publishing reviews of books and magazines by small presses and non-corporate publishing entities. We are distributed by the Suffolk Cooperative Library System and can be found in the New York Public Library, in colleges, bookstores and arts councils on Long Island. We have subscribers and contributors across the country and abroad. *Book/Mark* is a member of CLMP, and is listed in, among other references, the *International Directory of Small Presses & Magazines* and *The American Humanities Index*.

We welcome inquiries regarding reviews, books (especially by local writers, artists, and faculty), and internship possibilities for students seeking experience in publishing/public relations. Our content is eclectic, including reviews of books on a variety of topics/genres (literary, political, popular culture, the arts, children's books, history, science, critical essay). *Book/Mark* seeks to promote and publicize the efforts of small press book publishers (including independents, university presses, cooperative, alternative and arts presses). We have sponsored literary forums such as a Women's History Month panel and discussion at Borders Books, and created/hosted the Long Island Small Press Book Fair.

Reviews generally run from 600 - 900 words (sometimes a bit longer, especially when using excerpts/author quotes).

Book/Mark is available by subscription: $12.00 yr/$15.00 Institutions; $3.50 a copy pp. Back issues available for $2.00 pp. Advertising rates available. We print gratis notices for arts/non-profits (readings/conferences/credible contests) and exchange ads where appropriate. We thank you for your interest and support!

Categories: Nonfiction—Book Reviews—Literature

CONTACT: Mindy Kronenberg, Editor-In-Chief
Material: All
PO Box 516
Miller Place NY 11764
Phone: 631-331-4118
E-mail: cyberpoet@msn.com

Books & Culture

Books and Culture magazine is a Christianity Today Publication.

Books and Culture magazine does not have any writers guidelines, however, we do accept unsolicited submissions.

See our website for an overview of our publication.

Categories: Christian Interests—Culture—Literature—Religion—Spiritual

CONTACT: John Wilson, Editor
Material: All
465 Gundersen Drive
Carol Stream IL 60188
Phone: 630-260-8428
E-mail: bceditor@booksandculture.com
Website: www.booksandculture.com

Boston Magazine

No formal guidelines available.

Categories: Book Reviews—Business—Culture—Economics—Education—Entertainment—Fashion—Food/Drink—General Interest—Health—Lifestyle—Politics—Real Estate

CONTACT: Jon Marcus, Editor
Material: All
CONTACT: Kim Atkinson, Executive Editor
Material: Lifestyle
CONTACT: Don Armstrong, Features Editor
Material: Features
Metro Corp
300 Massachusetts Ave.
Boston, MA 02115
Phone: 615-262-9700
Fax: 617-267-1774
E-mail: editor@bostonmagazine.com
Website: www.bostonmagazine.com

Boston Review

Boston Review is a bimonthly magazine of cultural and political analysis, reviews, fiction, and poetry. The editors are committed to a society and culture that foster human diversity and a democracy in which we seek common grounds of principle amidst our many differences. In the hope of advancing these ideals, the *Review* acts as a forum that seeks to enrich the language of public debate.

The best way to get a sense of the kind of material the *Review* is looking for is to read the magazine (sample copies are available for $5.00). Recent issues have featured articles by Stephen Lerner on rebuilding American unions, Sven Birkerts on the decline of reading, and Atilio Boron on prospects for Latin American democracy. Also poetry by Robert Pinsky, Charles Simic, and Jorie Graham, fiction by Tom Paine, Patricia Traxler, and Elizabeth Graver, and criticism by Richard Howard, Raphael Campo, and Marjorie Perloff.

FICTION: From Jodi Daynard, fiction editor: "I'm looking for stories that are emotionally and intellectually substantive and also interesting on the level of language. Things that are shocking, dark, lewd, comic, or even insane are fine so long as the fiction is controlled and purposeful in a masterly way. Subtlety, delicacy and lyricism are attractive too." Work should be polished—clearly revised, grammatical, proofread. Length should be no less than 1,200 and no more than 5,000 words.

NONFICTION: Please query with clips before devoting time to an article or essay. Also realize that the editors plan issues well in advance, and the *Review*'s bimonthly publication schedule often cannot accommodate topical or especially timebound material.

REVIEWS: We do not accept unsolicited book reviews: if you would like to be considered for *Review* assignments, please send your resume along with several published clips.

GENERAL: *Boston Review* acquires first serial rights on accepted pieces; copyright reverts to the author after publication. We do not consider previously published material. Simultaneous submissions are fine as long as we are notified of the fact; however, we do not accept electronic submissions. Payment varies. Response time is generally 6-8 weeks. A self-addressed stamped envelope must accompany all submissions.

Thank you for your interest in *Boston Review*.

Categories: Fiction—Nonfiction—Culture—Economics—Education—Literature—Multicultural—Poetry—Politics—Short Stories—Society—Writing

CONTACT: Jodi Daynard, Fiction Editor
Material: Short Stories
CONTACT: Mary Jo Bang, Timothy Donnelly, Poetry Editors
Material: Poetry
CONTACT: Ian Lague, Managing Editor
Material: Nonfiction Submissions
E53-407; MIT
30 Wadsworth St.
Cambridge MA 02139
Phone: 617-253-3642
Fax: 617-252-1549
E-mail: bostonreview@mit.edu

Boulevard

Boulevard strives to publish only the finest in fiction, poetry, and non-fiction (essays, interviews, etc.). Therefore we ask that you send only your best work. While we frequently publish writers with previous credits, we are *very* interested in publishing less experienced or unpublished writers with exceptional promise. If you have practiced your craft and your work is the best it can be, send it to *Boulevard*.

As with any magazine, before submitting, read several recent issues to get a feel for style, content, quality, and form of the work we publish. Sample issues can be purchased as a cost of $8.00 each (please include five first-class stamps for postage). Our subscription rates are as follows: $15/3 issues (double issues count as one issue); $22/6 issues; $25/9. (For subscriptions outside of the US add $6.) Please make checks payable to Opojaz, Inc. and mail to address below.

All submissions, and all correspondence, *must* include SASE (with sufficient postage) for response. Keep abreast of changes in postal rates, remembering that our responses tend to take about two months.

No submissions will be accepted from May 1 to October 1.

All submissions must include author's name and address on each submission (including multiple submissions) and must include the author's first and last name on every page of the submission.

Authors retain rights to their work from the time of publication in *Boulevard*.

Boulevard does allow, and even encourages, simultaneous submissions, but we want to be notified of this fact. Photocopies and computer printed submissions are acceptable; handwritten ones are not.

Cover letters with previous credits are appreciated but not required.

Send only fully complete, fully proofread work. Send only your best work.

Submit no more than five poems at a time.

POETRY

We accept poems of up to 200 lines. We do not accept light verse. We pay $25-$300 (sometimes higher) for accepted work.

FICTION

We accept fiction works up to 8,000 words. We do not accept science fiction, erotica, westerns, horror, romance, or children's stories. We pay $50-$300 (sometimes higher) for accepted work.

Because of the high volume of submissions received, *Boulevard* makes no assurances, and is in no way responsible for unsolicited manuscripts that are lost, damaged or misplaced for any reason whatsoever.

Categories: Fiction—Poetry—Short Stories

CONTACT: Boulevard Magazine
Material: All
6614 Clayton Rd
Box 325
Richmond Heights MO 63117

Remember: Editors change jobs and publishers change addresses. It is wise to invest in a phone call for the current information before submitting.

BOYS' LIFE®

Boys' Life

Boys' Life is a general interest, four-color monthly, circulation 1.3 million, published by the Boy Scouts of America [BSA] since 1911. We buy first-time rights for original, unpublished material.

NONFICTION. Major articles run 500 to 1,500 words; payment is $400 to $1,500. Subject matter is broad. We cover everything from professional sports to American history to how to pack a canoe. A look at a current list of the BSA's more than 100 merit badge pamphlets gives an idea of the wide range of subjects possible. Even better, look at a year's worth of recent issues. We are found in libraries and BSA council offices.

Columns run 300 to 750 words; payment is $150 to $400. Column headings are science, nature, earth, health, sports, space and aviation, cars, computers, entertainment pets, history, music and others. Each issue uses seven columns, on average. We also have back-of-the-book how-to features that bring $250 to $300.

FICTION. Fiction runs 1,000 to 1,500 words. Payment is $750 and up. All stories feature a boy or boys. We use humor, mystery, science fiction and adventure. We use one short story per issue.

Articles for *Boys' Life* must interest and entertain boys ages 8 to 18. Write for a boy you know who is 12. Our readers demand crisp, punchy writing in relatively short, straightforward sentences. The editors demand well-reported articles that demonstrate high standards of journalism. We follow T*he New York Times Manual of Style and Usage.*

We receive approximately 100 queries and unsolicited manuscripts and 75 fiction manuscripts per week. Unsolicited nonfiction manuscripts are returned unread.

Please query by mail, not by phone.

Thank you for your interest in *Boys' Life*.

Categories: Fiction—Nonfiction—Adventure—Animals—Automobiles—Aviation—Careers—Cartoons—Children—Computers—Conservation—Crafts/Hobbies—Ecology—Education—Electronics—Entertainment—Environment—Fishing—Games—General Interest—Health—History—Hobbies—Juvenile—Outdoors—Science—Science Fiction—Short Stories—Sports/Recreation—Humor—Technology

CONTACT: Fiction Department
Material: Fiction Manuscripts
CONTACT: Mike Goldman, Senior Editor
Material: Nonfiction Queries (NO mss.)
1325 W. Walnut Hill Ln., PO Box 152079
Irving TX 75015-2079
Phone: 972-580-2366
Website: www.boyslife.org

Boys' Quest

A Word At The Outset:

Every BOYS' QUEST contributor must remember we publish only six issues a year, which means our editorial needs are extremely limited. It is obvious that we must reject far more contributions that we accept, no matter how outstanding they may seem to you or to us.

With that said, we would point out that BOYS' QUEST is a magazine created for boys from 6 to 13 years, with youngsters 8, 9, and 10 the specific target age. Our point of view is that every young boy deserves the right to be a young boy for a number of years before he becomes a young adult. As a result, BOYS' QUEST looks for articles, fiction, nonfiction, and poetry that deal with timeless topics, such as pets, nature, hobbies, science, games, sports, careers, simple cooking, and anything else likely to interest a young boy.Each issue revolves around a theme. A list of future themes can be view at our website.

Writers, we are looking for lively writing, most of it from a young boy's point of view - with the boy or boys directly involved in an activity that is both wholesome and unusual. We need nonfiction with photos and fiction stories—around 500 words—puzzles, poems, cooking, carpentry projects, jokes, and riddles. Nonfiction pieces that are accompanied by black and white photos are far more likely to be accepted than those that need illustrations.

The ideal length of a BOYS' QUEST piece - nonfiction or fiction - is 500 words. We will entertain simultaneous submissions as long as that fact is noted on the manuscript. Computer printouts are welcome if they are (as all submissions should be) double-spaced. BOYS' QUEST prefers to receive complete manuscripts with cover letters, although we do not rule out query letters. We do not answer submissions sent in by fax or e-mail. All submissions must be accompanied by a self-addressed, stamped envelope, with sufficient postage.

We will pay a minimum of five cents a word for both fiction and nonfiction, with additional payment given if the piece is accompanied by appropriate photos or art. We will pay a minimum of $10 per poem or puzzle, with variable rates offered for games, carpentry projects, etc.

BOYS' QUEST buys first American serial rights and pays upon publication. It welcomes the contributions of both published and unpublished writers. Sample copies are available for $6.00 within the US and $7.00 outside the US. All payment must be in US funds. A complimentary copy will be sent to each writer who has contributed to a given issue.

Photographers, we use a number of black and white photos inside the magazine, most in support of articles used. Payment is $5-10 per photo and $5 for color slides.

Artists, most art will be by assignment, in support of features used. The magazine is anxious to find artists capable of illustrating stories and features and welcomes copies of sample work, which will remain on file. Our work inside is pen and ink. We pay $35 for a full page and $25 for a partial page.

BOYS' QUEST is the companion to HOPSCOTCH magazine, and like HOPSCOTCH, the issues each revolve around a theme. We often choose new themes as the result of a submission on a topic we haven't covered. We work far into the future. If you don't receive a quick response on your submission, it means we are holding it and giving it serious consideration. We strive to treat all of our contributors and their work with respect and fairness.

Categories: Fiction—Nonfiction—Adventure—Animals—Cartoons—Children—Games—Hobbies—Nature—Outdoors—Sports/Recreation

CONTACT: Marilyn Edwards, Editor
Material: All
PO Box 227
Bluffton OH 45817-0227
Phone: 419-358-4610
Website: www.boysquest.com

A-E

Brain, Child

Brain, Child is for and by mothers who like to think about what raising children does for and to the mind and soul. Includes essays, features, contrasting opinions, humor, reviews, fiction, art, cartoons, and readers' own stories.

WRITER'S GUIDELINES

For all submissions (except features, news items, and debate essays), please either send your double-spaced manuscript with a cover letter and an SASE if you'd like our reply and/or your manuscript back, or e-mail the manuscript in the body of the e-mail to editor@brainchildmag.com with "Submission" as the subject heading. For features, new items, and debate essays, please query with clips first. Simultaneous submissions are okay—just let us know immediately if the manuscript is accepted elsewhere. We respond in about two months. We believe writers are the lifeblood of this publication; we pay as much as we can, although our fees are still modest for now.

PERSONAL ESSAYS (800 to 4,500 words): These are the signature pieces of the magazine, the heart and soul of our endeavor. We're looking for essays that share certain qualities—specificity and insight primary among them. These pieces should employ illustrative anecdotes, a personal voice, and a down-to-earth tone. We will avoid essays that fall back on big concept words—"magic," "joy," "wonder"—to get across the transformative nature of motherhood. Poignancy is fine; sentimentality isn't. Humor is a big plus.

Topics: We've broken down our areas of interest into six rough categories, although we understand that many essays will occur at the intersection of two or more of them:

1. The Domestic Life. These essays deal primarily with the nuts and bolts of mother in a reflective (as opposed to didactic) way. Example subjects: naming the baby; the isolation of parenting a wild child; and what building your child's self-esteem did to his work ethic.

2. Identity. These pieces touch on the integration of motherhood into the rest of a woman's identity. Example subjects: how much of your checkered past you choose to divulge; feelings about "the empty nest"; and housewifery.

3. Memory/Family. These essays dip into the memory well. Example subjects: a portrait of your mother as a young woman; the class reunion; an ode on travel and what makes a home.

4. The World at Large. These pieces offer perspectives on politics, spirituality, career, and other matters of the mind and soul. Example subjects: belonging to the Christian left; home business; the similarities between new moms and cloistered nuns.

5. Crisis. Essays of this sort revisit the moments (or weeks or years) of trial or terror in mothering. Example subjects: your child and her mental institution; inexplicable childhood rage; third grade, the second time around.

FEATURE (3000 words): Each issue, we devote space to at least one traditional feature, a piece that relies more heavily on reporting than introspection. Examples of this sort include an in-depth look at the home-schooling movement and an investigation into the frontiers of genetic testing. We're open to both New Journalism and old, but high-quality research and reporting are a must. Please query with clips and a one-page story outline.

NUTSHELL (200 to 800 words): Nutshell is our news section, offering both stories you won't find in the mainstream media and unique perspectives on hot topics. Example stories include: a profile of pediatrician whose own children watched three hours of TV a day; a report on a new study of lesbian adoptive mothers; and an interview with a mother whose child left home for college at fourteen. Please query with clips and a pitch.

DEBATE (700 words): Our section of friendly fire, where two writers square off on a topic of controversy. We're looking for concise, thoughtful words on issues such as sex education, the Barbie question, and whether sleeping with your kids is okay. Brief anecdotes helpful; very strong opinion required. Please query with clips and the issue.

FICTION (1500 to 4500 words): We look for strongly developed characters and, more ephemerally, a sense that we trust the writer. We get a lot of stories that address the daily grind of the characters' lives; if your story does this, you might ask yourself if this is the moment in the character's life you want to capture in story. Since much of *Brain, Child* is made of personal essays, we have to walk a strict line between the essay and short story forms.

BOOK REVIEWS (200 words for mini-reviews; 800-1200 for longer reviews): We review new and not-so-new books of fiction, memoir, autobiography, and nonfiction. Reviews should be critical. We are interested in multi-book reviews for longer reviews.

PARODY (800 words): The parodies we like most are ones that target people, institutions, or media who don't take mothers seriously. We're open to a variety of forms (e.g., narrative, letter, quiz, etc.)—as long as it make us laugh.

Categories: Young Adult

CONTACT: Jennifer Niesslein, Stephanie Wilkinson, Editors
PO Box 1161
Harrisonburg VA
E-mail: editor@brainchildmag.com
Website: www.brainchildmag.com

BrandPackaging

We're always looking for good freelance articles, but they have to reflect business savvy and support our magazine's niche in the packaging industry. Freelancers should thoroughly understand our editorial platform before proposing articles. We focus on the marketing impact of packaging for marketing professionals at consumer packaged goods companies. We identify consumer and packaging industry trends at their earliest stages and publish articles that help marketers capitalize on these trends by more effectively using packaging as a marketing tool. Our readers include brand managers/marketers, product managers, category managers, senior vice president-marketing, package designers, and anyone else who is involved in package creation. They're very pressed for time, highly educated, cynical and dislike being sold to in print. They want ideas on how to innovate. Our job is to digest things down to the top-line information they want, written in the language of marketers. We do not publish "news," or "cover" industry events. Rather, we address topics such as color, shape, labels, special-effects materials, the psychology of packaging and the consumer's mind-set when looking at packaging. We work from the premise that 70 percent of consumer buying decisions are made at the store shelf, and more than half of all brands carry no advertising support, so packaging must act as the "silent salesman."

Submission format: We prefer that articles be submitted electronically or provided on a CD. All "hard-packaging" articles that include information from packaging suppliers must include the name, phone number and e-mail address of the initial contact person at the supplier for our readers. Articles must be accompanied by well-lit, clear color photos or digital images of packaging referenced in the article. Photos should be either 4x6 or 5x7 in size, glossy finish. Digital images should be 300 dpi, jpeg or pdf format, 4 inches wide. We pay up to $1,200 for features, depending on length and complexity. We pay on acceptance and purchase all rights. Material is subject to editing for length, style and format. Tip: Our readers love bulleted and numbered lists, as well as sidebars. All articles should answer these three questions: What does it do? How does it do it? How can marketers use it in packaging to achieve their business objectives? Freelancers should look through the magazine archives at www.packaginginfo.com, and click on "Visit *BrandPackaging*" to familiarize themselves with our writing approach.

Categories: We are a "horizontal" magazine. We could use examples from a number of product categories in dissecting a trend in a single article. We also take an occasional look at product categories vertically. Our categories include food, beverage, housewares, hardware, automotive aftermarket, toys, health and beauty aids, and OTC drugs.

Categories: Packaging—Marketing

CONTACT: Bob Swientek, Editor-in-Chief
Material: All
CONTACT: Jim George, Senior Editor
Material: All
Independent Publishing Co.
210 S. Fifth St., Ste. 204
St. Charles IL 60174
Phone: 630-377-0100

Bravehearts

BRAVE HEARTS is a quarterly magazine from Ogden Publications. The magazine is written by and for ordinary people who have an inspirational message to share.

BRAVE HEARTS seeks short manuscripts (up to 900 words), photographs, prayers, and related material on special inspirational subjects for each issue. A nominal payment of $5 to $12 is made upon publication. An additional payment of $2 is made for each item used on our Web site.

BRAVE HEARTS purchases all publishing rights to the items used. No simultaneous submissions are accepted. No e-mail submissions accepted.

Material should be submitted at least six months in advance of publication. Notification of acceptance or rejection will be made within approximately six months of receipt.

No queries: Send complete mss. to the address below.

Categories: Nonfiction—General Interest—Inspirational—Lifestyle—Religion—Romance—Spiritual

CONTACT: Ann Crahan, Editor-in-Chief
Material: All
1503 SW 42nd St
Topeka KS 66609
Phone: 785-274-4300
Fax: 785-274-4305
Website: www.braveheartsmagazine.com

Bridal Guide

Bridal Guide is interested in articles about relationships, marriage, sexuality, fitness, psychology, finance, and travel. Please do not send queries concerning fashion, beauty, or home design stories, since we produce these pages in house. We do accept wedding-planning ideas, but these should cover broad subjects, such as planning a long-distance or theme wedding, or emotional subjects, such as dealing with divorced parents. Shorter, how-to pieces (such as finding a band or choosing a cake) are written in-house. We also do not accept fiction or poetry.

We are looking for service-oriented, well researched pieces that are journalistically written and have a length of 1,000 to 2,000 words. Payment, made on acceptance, is 50 cents per word. Writers we work with consult at least 3 expert sources, such as physicians, book authors, and business people in the appropriate field. Our tone is conversational yet authoritative. Features are also generally filled with real-life anecdotes. We also do features that are completely real-person

based–such as finding roundtables of bridesmaids discussing their experiences, or grooms-to-be talking about their feelings about getting married.

In queries, we are looking for a well thought-out idea, the specific angle or focus the writer intends to take, and the sources he or she intends to use. Queries should be brief and snappy–and titles should be supplied to give the editor an even better idea of the direction the writer is going in.

Feature ideas and ideas for the Confident Bride column should be sent to Cybele Eidenschenk, executive editor. Travel feature ideas should be directed to Laurie Bain Wilson, travel editor. Submit queries only, along with clips of work published in a national consumer magazine, and a self-addressed, stamped envelope. You will get a reply within one to three months, but we cannot return any materials such as manuscripts, clips, or photos, so do not send any originals.

Categories: Fiction—Nonfiction—Health—Marriage—Money & Finances—Poetry—Psychology—Relationships—Sexuality—Travel

CONTACT: Cybele Eidenschenk, Executive Editor
Material: Relationships, planning & financial issues
CONTACT: Laurie Bain Wilson, Travel Editor
Material: Honeymoon Travel
R.F.P., LLC.
3 East 54th St., 15th Floor
New York NY 10022
Phone: 212-838-7733

BrideAgain Magazine

Magazine Objective

BrideAgain is an on-line publication designed for the encore bride. It is targeted to women over 30 who have been married at least once before, have children from a previous marriage or are marrying someone with children and are currently planning to be remarried. They have a career, a median household income of $61,500 per year, and are more mature and sophisticated than the 24-year-old first time bride. They are looking for information about not just the wedding day itself, but about remarriage, blending families and beating the odds the second time around.

All articles are to be double spaced, compatible with Microsoft WORD 6.0 and can be emailed to staff@brideagain.com. We do not accept queries. Although there is no financial compensation for on-line articles, all articles will feature the author's byline and bio if supplied.

Articles must be specific to encore brides and remarriage.

Word count for all topics is 300 words.

Please e-mail submissions to: staff@brideagain.com

Categories: Women

CONTACT: Beth Reed Ramirez, Publisher
1240 N Jefferson, Ste G
Anaheim CA 92807
E-mail: publisher@brideagain.com
Website: www.brideagain.com

Bridge

About

Bridge is a triannual publication, a hybrid of a journal and a magazine, as well as an event space at 119 North Peoria in Chicago.

The simple belief that provided the motivation to launch *Bridge* as a publication in November 2000 was that separate fields of inquiry can and should be thought of as having shared horizons. Every existing world view, whether scientific, philosophic, aesthetic, religious, political, or literary must acknowledge its limits or risk being defined as obsolete, unachievable, and incoherent. The goal of *Bridge* has been to make the relationships between these isolated fields of inquiry clear, exposing the basic humanity from which every idea originates.

This *idée-force* led to the development of a publication where innovative and discerning artistic expression in the fields of literature, poetry, visual art, music, and more could be stated without inhibition, alongside intellectual work exploring a similarly unrestricted scope of thoughts, images and conceptions.

Our event space, launched in June 2002, is an extension of this purpose, a place where, through art events, symposia, author events, artists' talks, colloquia and more, an independent physical space can exist in which to put aside the incommensurability of these disparate fields of inquiry and participate in an examination of the particulars as well as the contexts of intelligibility that surround them.

General Editorial Guidelines

Submissions sent to *Bridge* should be addressed to the relevant department (Culture and Critique, Fiction, Literary Criticism, Poetry, Visual Arts, or Music), for which specific guidelines are available below. We consider unsolicited submissions.

For email submissions to all departments, please paste the first 300 words of your submission in the body of your email, and attach a Word document to that email, unless otherwise noted. Submissions shorter than 300 words need not be accompanied by a Word file. E-mail submissions are acceptable as an attachment in Microsoft Word format only. All email submissions must include the author's name, address, telephone number and date submitted. This will help us to prioritize. All email submissions should be sent to submissions@bridgemagazine.org. Please allow up to six months for a response, unless otherwise noted. After six months, please inquire as to the status of your submission with the appropriate editor or by email with Michael Workman, *Bridge* Publisher and Editor-in-Chief. If after completing these steps you receive no response, please feel free to submit elsewhere.

Editing of articles will consist primarily of lengthening or shortening, at the editor's discretion, to suit available space restrictions. Additionally, changes may be made to suit proper grammar. Editorial standards for nonfiction submissions are usually consistent with the most recent version of MLA style or *The Chicago Manual of Style: The Essential Guide for Writers, Editors, and Publishers* (14th Edition).

There is no payment for publication, unless otherwise noted. If we accept work for the print version, we will not necessarily accept that work for website publication.

Submission Guidelines for Bridge Readings Dept.

General Guidelines: Bridge is currently seeking submissions of ephemera, office memos, found notes, zine excerpts, website excerpts and the offbeat for its Readings department. Average length of submissions is 400 words unless otherwise stipulated by the editor. Material that otherwise fits into the Culture and Critique, Fiction, Literary Criticism, Poetry, Music, and Visual Arts Departments submitted for the Readings department should be sent directly to the editor of that department.

Submissions may be emailed directly to Michael Workman, Publisher and Editor-In-Chief, or mailed to us at *Bridge*, ATTN: Readings Department, 119 North Peoria, #3D, Chicago, IL 60607. E-mail submissions must include "Readings Section" in the subject line.

Submission Guidelines for Culture & Critique Dept.

General Guidelines: Essays should be submitted electronically as a Word attachment. Generally, they should be 500-2500 words long (although we will consider longer pieces) and double-spaced in a 12-point font. Endnotes are acceptable. The preferred citation method is the most recent version of MLA style; please triple-check quotations before submission. Essays may be emailed directly to Mark Tschaepe, Culture and Critique Editor-At-Large, or mailed to us at *Bridge*, ATTN: Culture & Critique Dept., 119 North Peoria, #3D, Chicago, IL 60607. Culture and Critique department queries (preferred) and submissions should also include the following:

1) Two (2) writing samples
2) Curriculum Vitae
3) Letter of Intent

Culture and Critique Portfolio:

The Culture and Critique department at *Bridge* does not normally accept unsolicited essays for its portfolios—which are typically devoted to a single subject—but if you would like to submit an essay for possible inclusion in a future portfolio, contact Culture and Critique Editor-At-Large Mark Tschaepe to find out what the focus of our upcoming issue is.

Other: Bridge is also willing to publish high-quality cultural and critical writing outside its portfolio format. We seek analysis and exploration of contemporary theory and writing that actively participates in a critical exchange relevant to an identifiable public forum, from the institutional to the obscure. *Bridge* is not interested in peer review, writing that merely evidences a position or issue while offering unconditional support, political-scientific exegesis, or in mere discursive conceptual exercise, regardless how well-researched. Any discussion of ideas, concepts, methods and accessory citation of texts should only be used to support your own unique, cohesive argument.

Primarily, we are interested in philosophical writing that articulates qualitative distinctions and offers informed commentary on the practices of and tensions current in the social and cultural forces of the modern West. Strong writing for the Culture and Critique department will present thoroughly-examined investigations of particular subjects while providing contexts of intelligibility that successfully strive after verisimilitude. A readable prose that avoids utilizing literary devices is preferred, with styles that fall in the margin between academic journal writing and more popular intellectual writing (eg., *The New Yorker, Harper's, Atlantic Monthly*); unsolicited travel narratives or personal essays are not acceptable. No dissertation excerpts or class papers, please.

Feel free to submit unsolicited essays to the email address above, following the general guidelines. Allow up to six months for a response. Simultaneous submissions are fine so long as you contact *Bridge* immediately should your essay be accepted elsewhere.

Submission Guidelines for Fiction Dept.

General Guidelines: We are seeking provocative, well crafted short fiction by newer and established writers.

In broad terms, we eschew stories bound by expectations and allegiance to pre-defined 'schools', in favor of dynamic, risky material that forces the writer to take a stand on his or her intentions, rather than flooding the work with their authorial presence. Some developing veins of fictive expression which we admire include: the cunning consumerist dreams of George Saunders and Alex Shakar, the astringent moral landscapes of Denis Johnson and Thom Jones, the lapidary compressions of Stephen Milhauser and William Gaddis, the reactionary genre implosions of Robert Coover and James Ellroy, the psychopathic melodramas of Charles Willeford and Stephen Wright, the formalized rage of Mary Caponegro and Thomas Bernhard, the gonzo Gothic of Barry Hannah and Harry Crews, the broader disordered histories pursued by Don DeLillo. We welcome those writers cruising beneath radar who will cause us to re-calibrate these already stiffening priorities.

Younger writers, and those of culturally diverse or under-represented backgrounds, are particularly encouraged to submit. However, all interested writers are urged to read a recent issue of *Bridge* to consider the work we've already included, and likewise urged to read those writers who cut the paths we walk upon: John Barth, Flann O'Brien, Cynthia Ozick, Grace Paley, Donald Barthelme, Flannery O'Connor, Thomas Pynchon, Joan Didion, Chester Himes, and many others.

The fine print: please send only previously unpublished, legible (non-dot matrix) manuscripts of approximately 2 - 20 pages, along with a business SASE for response (or an appropriately sized and stamped envelope for manuscript return). Simultaneous submissions are fine so long as you contact *Bridge* immediately should your work be accepted elsewhere. Fiction may be emailed directly to Mike Newirth, Fiction Editor

NOTE: Do Not send email attachments to this email address, please paste your submission in the body of the email or submit attachments to the main submission email address, submissions-@*Bridge*magazine.org), or mailed to us at *Bridge*, ATTN: Fiction Dept., 119 North Peoria, #3D, Chicago, IL 60607.

Submission Guidelines for Poetry Dept.

General Guidelines: We read with interest every poem submitted to *Bridge* and are, quite frankly, looking to be as much informed and inspired by our poets as the other way around. Our emphasis is on the new—or the newly discovered—and we entertain, if sometimes briefly, all arguments in sympathy with this idea.

Poetry submissions sent via email should be addressed to Greg Purcell, Poetry Editor, or send a typewritten group of two to six unpublished poems to *Bridge*, ATTN: Greg Purcell, Poetry Dept., 119 North Peoria, #3D, Chicago, IL 60607. Please include a self-addressed stamped envelope with your submission. Contributors living outside the United States should include international reply coupons. We will not consider simultaneous submissions or poems that have been previously published.

Several pieces of original poetry will appear per issue. We generally hold a standard of printing no more than ten (10) one-page poems per issue, but everything depends on the merit of the work we receive.

Submission Guidelines for Literary Criticism Dept.

General Guidelines: Essays should be submitted electronically as a Word attachment. Generally, they should be 5-10 pages long (although we will consider longer pieces) and double-spaced in a 12-point font. Footnotes are okay. The preferred citation method is the most recent version of MLA style; please triple-check quotations before submission. Essays may be emailed directly to David Andrews, Lit Crit Associate Editor, at or mailed to us at *Bridge*, ATTN: Literary Criticism Dept., 119 North Peoria, #3D, Chicago, IL 60607.

Critical Portfolios: The literary criticism department at *Bridge* does not normally accept unsolicited essays for its critical portfolios—which are typically devoted to a single literary figure—but if you would like to submit an essay for possible inclusion in a future portfolio, contact Lit Crit Associate Editor David Andrews to find out who the focus of our upcoming issue is.

Other: Bridge is also willing to publish high-quality critical essays outside its portfolio format. Feel free to submit unsolicited essays to the email address above, following the general guidelines. Typically, we are looking for analytical, text-based criticism rather than biography, anecdotal essays, or "art appreciation." And feel free, as well, to mix your media—*Bridge* always encourages this approach to the arts. Allow six to eight weeks for a response. Simultaneous submissions are fine so long as you contact *Bridge* immediately should your essay be accepted elsewhere.

Submission Guidelines for Music Dept.

General Guidelines: Bridge welcomes unsolicited articles on music-related topics for consideration and possible publication. We are looking for lucid and engaging writing on contemporary music as it relates to culture, art and society. Sample areas of interest include, but are not limited to: popular music, jazz, folk, blues, contemporary classical, oral histories, electronic music, experimental sound, independent or underground rock, politics and music, conceptual art, and music technology, as well as music-related fiction or artwork. Record reviews and band profiles are discouraged. Historical and musicological writing are welcome, but must be of interest to a general audience (not overly-technical or academic). Humor and wit are especially encouraged.

The above guidelines are flexible, and all works will be judged on their individual merits. Please proofread and fact-check before submitting. Submissions will not be returned without SASE. Essays may be emailed directly to Justin McKinley Niimi, Music Editor, at or mailed to us at *Bridge*, ATTN: Music Dept., 119 North Peoria, #3D, Chicago, IL 60607.

Submission Guidelines for Visual Art Dept.

General Guidelines, Writing: Bridge is interested in writing on contemporary art, though we're particularly interested in writing not limited to contemporary art. That is, we prefer writing that looks at work relevant to something old with a fresh eye. Strong writing will focus less on critique and more on theory, attempt to form ideologies based on trends in contemporary art and sum what's happening now as well as what's around the bend.

Essays should be submitted electronically as a Word attachment. Generally, they should be 500-2500 words long (although we will consider longer pieces) and double-spaced in a 12-point font. Endnotes are acceptable. The preferred citation method is the most recent version of MLA style; please triple-check quotations before submission. Essays may be emailed directly to Marie Walz, Art Editor, or Howard Fonda, Associate Art Editor, or mailed to us at *Bridge*, ATTN: Visual Art Dept., 119 North Peoria, #3D, Chicago, IL 60607. *Visual Art department queries (preferred) and submissions should also include the following:*

1) Two (2) writing samples
2) Curriculum Vitae
3) Letter of Intent

Images: If images are required, writers are responsible for making sure that *Bridge* receives an image to be published with the essay by the deadline. You may send the image yourself, or ask the artist, museum or gallery to send it. If mailed, an SASE must be included for return of materials. Images should be color where possible. Digital images should be Macintosh-formatted tif files, minimum 300 DPI. *Images must be labeled with the following information:*

- Artist's name
- Title of work, date, dimensions, media
- Credit line (photographer's name, gallery's name, etc.)

General Guidelines, Visual Art:

Slides or jpegs (via email) are acceptable. Include resume and artists statement. ALL materials must include a self-addressed, stamped envelope for return of materials. Inquiries may be emailed directly to Marie Walz, Art Editor, or Howard Fonda, Associate Art Editor, or mailed to us at *Bridge*, ATTN: Visual Art Dept., 119 North Peoria, #3D, Chicago, IL 60607.

Project Pages: Bridge does not normally accept unsolicited work for its project pages but if you would like to submit images for possible inclusion in a future project, contact Marie Walz, Art Editor, or Howard Fonda, Associate Art Editor or mailed to us at *Bridge*, ATTN: Visual Art Dept., 119 North Peoria, #3D, Chicago, IL 60607.

Sketchbook Pages: Bridge does not normally accept unsolicited work for its Sketchbook Pages, which appear only periodically in *Bridge*. Inquiries should be made to Marie Walz or Howard Fonda at the email addresses above or mailed to us at *Bridge*, ATTN: Visual Art Dept., Sketchbook Pages, 119 North Peoria, #3D, Chicago, IL 60607.

Comix Panels: Bridge does not normally accept unsolicited comix panels, which appear only periodically in *Bridge*. Inquiries should be made to Marie Walz or Howard Fonda at the email addresses above, to Michael Workman, or mailed to us at *Bridge*, ATTN: Visual Art Dept., Comix, 119 North Peoria, #3D, Chicago, IL 60607.

Illustrations: We are looking for spot illustrations and story-specific illustrations. Slides or jpegs (via email) are acceptable. Include resume and artists statement. ALL materials must include a self-addressed, stamped envelope for return of materials. Inquiries should be emailed to Howard Fonda or Marie Walz, or mailed to us at *Bridge*, ATTN: Visual Art Dept., Illustrations, 119 North Peoria, #3D, Chicago, IL 60607.

Online Book & Art Reviews: Bridge is currently accepting book reviews and reviews of art exhibitions to appear online ONLY. Art and book reviews will NOT be considered for publication in the print version of *Bridge*.

Online Book Reviews

Bridge does not publish unsolicited reviews. Writers wishing to be considered for book review assignments should send samples of previous reviews, a cover letter listing any areas of special interest (i.e., in covering contemporary experimental fiction, literature in translation, philosophy, etc.), and a brief resume.

Reviews are assigned by the editors. Ideas for reviews may also be pitched by writers. Reviews should be of contemporary authors publishing in the field of fiction, poetry, or an academic specialty (e.g. philosophy, psychology, literary or art criticism, etc.). For established authors or authors reviewed by *Bridge* in the past, reviews should be of new work. We generally do not review chapbooks, "pulp" fiction, online publishing, journal writing and reprints, etc.

Length:
- Short reviews: 500 words
- Long reviews: 750 words
- Unless otherwise stipulated by the editor.

Writing the review: Title information should appear in the upper left-hand corner of the first page of the review.

Information must include:
- Author's name/title of book
- Publisher name
- Publisher city/Year of publication
- ISBN #
- Hardcover or softcover/Page count/price

A review should include:
- Explanation of content - What is the subject matter?
- Contextualization - It is helpful to establish a context for the author's work in relation to his or her peers, in relation to the history in which they are participating (past and present), and in relation to his or her previous work.
- Interpretation - What does it mean?
- Judgment - Is it good or bad. Why? The writer's opinion of the work is the backbone of a review.

Fact-checking: Please take extra care with factual data (dates, spelling of names, and other information). We are not able to check every fact, and rely on the accuracy and integrity of our writers. If you mention a name or place, identify it, e.g. author Mary Caponegro.

Quotations: In general, reviews should not contain quotations. Avoid quoting the author or press release in reviews and do not extensively quote writers who have written reviews of the same title.

Byline: Include a writer's byline for yourself at the end of the review, such as "Sally Smith is a writer based in New York."

Editing: Reviews by writers who have not written for *Bridge* before are accepted "on spec."

All major editorial changes will be shown to the writer prior to publication. Unsatisfactory reviews will be returned for emendation.

Ethics and integrity: If you suspect an assignment may pose a potential conflict of interest, please check the situation with your editor. *Conflicts include, but are not limited to the following:*
- If you work for a commercial publisher, you may not review titles released by other publishers in your area.
- Do not review titles by people with whom you have personal relationships; i.e. relatives, close friends, significant others.
- Do not review titles with which you have any involvement (i.e. as an editor).
- Review content must be kept confidential until publication.

Bridge does not publish reviews of titles that are or will be reviewed by the writer in other publications.

Submitting: All review assignments must be cleared with your editor prior to submission. *Bridge* does not accept unsolicited reviews.

If possible, submit a press release from the publisher with your review. Sending the review via email is preferred. Send as an attached document in Microsoft Word format, or in the text of an e-mail message to: submissions@*Bridge*magazine.org and write "Book Review" in the subject line. Reviews may also be submitted on a 3.5" Macintosh floppy disk accompanied by a double-spaced hard copy.

Cover Images: Writers are responsible for making sure that *Bridge* receives a cover image of the title being reviewed. You may send the image yourself, or ask the publisher to send it. If mailed, an SASE must be included for return of materials. Images should be color where possible. Digital images should be Macintosh-formatted jpg files. Images should be formatted for 3 x 5 inches for reviews.

Online Art Reviews

Bridge does not publish unsolicited reviews. Writers wishing to be considered for art review assignments should send samples of previous reviews, a cover letter listing any areas of special interest (i.e., in covering photography, performance art, film, etc.), and a brief resume.

Reviews are assigned by the editors. Ideas for reviews may also be pitched by writers. Reviews should be of contemporary artists showing at museums, galleries, or alternative spaces. The work should participate in current national and international dialogues on contemporary art in some way. For established artists or artists reviewed by *Bridge* in the past, reviews should be of new work. We generally do not review faculty shows, student shows, annual competitions and invitationals, etc.

Length:
- Short reviews:500 words
- Long reviews: 750 words
- Unless otherwise stipulated by the editor.

Writing the review: Exhibition information should appear in the upper left-hand corner of the first page of the review.

Information must include:
- Artist's name/title of show
- Gallery, museum, or other venue
- Gallery's street address, including city, state, and zip code
- Area code and phone number
- Dates of exhibition

A review should include:
- Physical description - Describe in detail what the work looks like: scale, materials, color, shape. The reader should be able to visualize the art from your brief descriptions of it. It is not necessary to mention every piece, likewise in a group show it is not necessary to mention every artist. Only write about those that substantiate the points you are making.
- Explanation of content - What is the subject matter?
- Contextualization - It is helpful to establish a context for the artist's work in relation to his or her peers, in relation to art history (past and present), and in relation to his or her previous work.
- Interpretation - What does it mean?
- Judgment - Is it good or bad. Why? The writer's opinion of the work is the backbone of a review.

Style: Write as clearly as possible. Reviews can become confusing when the writer relies too heavily on poetic license (ie, stretching the meaning of words), academic or theory-based language, or personal narrative and other prose or poetic structures.

As a rule, always use past tense. Exceptions are made if the show will still be on view when the review is published, or if you are discussing a piece that will still be in existence after the show closes (the work is not site-specific).

Fact-checking: Please take extra care with factual data (dates, spelling of names, and other information). We are not able to check every fact, and rely on the accuracy and integrity of our writers. If you mention a name or place, identify it, e.g. performance artist Meg Duguid.

Quotations: In general, reviews should not contain quotations. Avoid quoting the artist, press release, or catalogue in reviews and do not extensively quote writers in book reviews.

Byline: Include a writer's byline for yourself at the end of the review, such as "Sally Smith is a writer based in New York."

Editing: Reviews by writers who have not written for *Bridge* before are accepted "on spec."

All major editorial changes will be shown to the writer prior to publication. Unsatisfactory reviews will be returned for emendation.

Ethics and integrity: If you suspect an assignment may pose a potential conflict of interest, please check the situation with your editor. *Conflicts include, but are not limited to the following:*
- If you work for a commercial gallery, you may not review other commercial galleries in your area; likewise for alternative spaces, museums, schools, etc.
- Do not review exhibitions of work by people with whom you have personal relationships; i.e. relatives, close friends, significant others.

• Do not review exhibitions with which you have any involvement (i.e. as a catalogue essayist, guest lecturer, curator, or consultant).

• Review content must be kept confidential until publication.

• *Bridge* does not publish reviews of exhibitions that are or will be reviewed by the writer in other publications.

Submitting: All review assignments must be cleared with your editor prior to submission. *Bridge* does not accept unsolicited reviews.

If possible, submit a press release or announcement card from the exhibition with your review.

Sending the review via email is preferred. Send as an attached document in Microsoft Word format, or in the text of an e-mail message to: submissions@*Bridge*magazine.org and write "Art Review" in the subject line. Reviews may also be submitted on a 3.5" Macintosh floppy disk accompanied by a double-spaced hard copy.

Images: Writers are responsible for making sure that *Bridge* receives an image to be published with the review by the deadline. You may send the image yourself, or ask the museum or gallery to send it. If mailed, an SASE must be included for return of materials. Images should be color where possible. Digital images should be Macintosh-formatted jpg files. Images should be formatted for 3 x 5 inches for reviews.

Images must be labeled with the following information:
• Artist's name
• Title of show if it is a group show
• Title of work, date, dimensions, media
• Credit line (photographer's name, gallery's name, etc.)

Categories: Fiction—Arts—Culture—Literature—Music—Poetry

CONTACT: Michael Workman, Publisher and Editor-In-Chief
Material: Submission for Bridge Readings Dept
E-mail: mworkman@bridgemagazine.org
CONTACT: Mike Newirth, Fiction Editor
Material: Fiction
E-mail: submissions@bridgemagazine.org
CONTACT: Mark Tschaepe, Culture & Critique Editor
Material: Culture & Critique
CONTACT: Greg Purcell, Poetry Dept
Material: Poetry
CONTACT: David Andrews, Lit Crit Associate Editor
Material: Literary Criticism
CONTACT: Marie Walz, Art Editor
Material: Visual Art <mwalt@bridgemagazine.org> or
119 North Peoria, #3D
Chicago IL 60607
Phone: 312-421-2227
Fax: 312-421-2228
E-mail: submissions@bridgemagazines.com
Website: www.bridgemagazine.org

British Heritage

Please refer to WEIDER History Group.

Budget Living

While, as a new magazine, we have yet to prepare formal guidelines, we are open to freelancers. Please take a look at a recent issue or our website to get an idea of how to target submissions.

Categories: Nonfiction—Antique—Consumer—Crafts/Hobbies—Fashion—Food/Drink—Money & Finances—Recreation—Travel

CONTACT: Caroline Whitbeck, Editorial Assist.
Material: All
317 Madison Ave Ste 2003
New York NY 10017
Phone: 212-657-6060
Website: www.budgetliving.com

Budget Travel

Budget Travel accepts submissions from freelance writers. To be considered, send a copy of published work as a sample, your pitch (not a completed article) and a cover letter to address below. We cannot return submitted materials.

Categories: Nonfiction—Travel

CONTACT: Submissions, Budget Travel
530 Seventh Ave 2nd Fl
New York NY 10018
E-mail: Letters@BudgetTravelOnline.com

Buffalo Spree

As Buffalo's only city magazine, *Buffalo Spree* tries to provide a wide range of engaging and compelling feature articles uniquely relevant to Buffalo and Western New York. We also offer regular coverage of home and garden design, arts and entertainment, food and dining, health and fitness, and travel and leisure. We prefer submissions in query format, rather than as unsolicited manuscripts. We encourage potential writers to keep Spree's mission as a city/regional publication in mind.

Spree accepts queries for possible feature or department articles. Send a letter with your story idea, along with samples of other published writing, and a resume to:

Categories: Fiction—Nonfiction—Arts—Entertainment—Health—Poetry—Regional—Short Stories

CONTACT: Elizabeth Licata, Editor
Material: Fiction and Nonfiction
CONTACT: Janet Goldenberg, Poetry Editor
Material: Poetry
5678 Main St.
Williamsville NY 14221
Phone: 716-839-3405
Fax: 716-839-4384
E-mail: elicata@buffalospree.com
E-mail: info@buffalospree.com
Website: www.buffalospree.com

Bugle
Elk Country and the Hunt

The *Bugle* editorial staff is seeking manuscripts depicting the world of elk and the hunt. We accept fiction, non-fiction and scientific articles geared to the layman. Query letters are encouraged, but we also accept unsolicited manuscripts.

By reading *Bugle* prior to submitting (it's available on newsstands), you will gain a better sense of the kinds of stories we might publish. Thoughtful hunting stories and elk-related human interest stories are always high on our need list, as are essays on issues affecting hunting and conservation. Stories we use generally range from 1,500-4,500 words (1,000 to 3,000 words for departments like Women in the Outdoors or Situation Ethics), but we have no set length requirements.

We prefer hunting stories in which the hunter's satisfaction lies at least as much in appreciation for elk and other wildlife and for wild country and the total outdoors experience as in shooting a large bull. Sometimes it is the sheer difficulty or novelty of a hunt which attracts our interest. We do not publish how-to articles, or stories which indicate serious concern over who has taken the better trophy.

We will evaluate your story based on content, writing quality and our needs for the coming year. This process may take several months. If we decide not to publish it, the story will be returned in your self-addressed, stamped envelope with a letter to that effect.

The Rocky Mountain Elk Foundation is a nonprofit conservation organization committed to putting membership dollars into wildlife habitat, management and research. Donated manuscripts enable the Elk Foundation to devote more funds to habitat, and are tax deductible. We encourage and appreciate donated manuscripts, but gladly purchase them if that is the writer's preference. Our basic rate is 20 cents per word, paid on acceptance. Should your story appear in *Bugle*, you will receive three complimentary copies.

Please feel free to inquire into the status of your manuscript at any time.

Categories: Nonfiction—Sports/Recreation

CONTACT: Don Burgess, Hunting Editor
Material: Elk/Hunting
CONTACT: Paul Queneau, Conservation Editor
Material: Elk/Conservation/Natural History
CONTACT: Jan Brocci, Managing Editor
Material: Elk/Women Hunting
CONTACT: PJ DelHomme
Material: Elk/Poetry
5705 Grant Creek Rd
Missoula MT 59808
Phone: 406-523-4570
Fax: 406-543-7710
E-mail: bugle@rmef.org
Website: www.rmef.org/bugle/bugle.html?main=/bugle/features.html

Business 2.0

Business 2.0 is the essential tool for navigating today's relentlessly changing marketplace, particularly as it's driven by the Internet and other technologies. It discovers and reports on the smartest, most innovative business practices and the people behind them. It delivers surprising, useful insights, and explains how to put them to work.

In the magazine we deliver great journalism that provides business people with useful, actionable insights to help them navigate and benefit from change.

On the website we offer daily editorial features and columns, in addition to resources that give readers an opportunity to research issues and network with people who have similar interests.

SUBMIT A PITCH

Our Website, www.business2.com/whatworks is a place for readers to share stories about successes and failures in the world of business and technology. We decided to create this feature online because we realized that our readers are eager to learn not just from the pages of *Business 2.0*, but also from each other. Our hope is that many of our hundreds of thousands of readers will provide their own personal "case studies" and that What Works will become the Web's greatest repository of grassroots information about what works (and what doesn't!) in business and technology. Please visit the website, if you'd like to share a story.

Note: If you are a software or hardware vendor, or a services provider, you'll do better if you get your customers to contact us directly with their stories, rather than you telling us what you've done for them.

Independent freelance writers and artists may send pitches, clips, and resumes to freelancers@business2.com with the words "freelance writer" or "freelance artist" in the subject line. (DO NOT, UNDER ANY CIRCUMSTANCES, SEND PR-RELATED MATERIALS TO THIS ADDRESS!) We use a few freelance writers, and the most suc-

cessful freelance proposals come from established writers who have familiarized themselves with the magazine and our recent articles, and who can provide us with clear, smart, fresh-angled pitches on department topics. We're particularly interested in hearing about businesses that are using the Web or new technologies to achieve some measurable success.

We apologize that we can't respond directly to every e-mail, but we will contact you if we're interested in your work.

Categories: Business—Money & Finances—Technology

CONTACT: Submissions Editor
Material: Pitches, clips and resumes
One California St., 29th Floor
San Francisco CA 94111
Phone: 415-293-4800
Fax: 415-293-5900
E-mail: freelancers@business2.com (preferred submissions method)
Website: www.business2.com

Business Fleet

Business Fleet goes to 100,000 companies operating small fleets of from 10 to 50 vehicles. We run articles on such subjects as driver management, maximizing trade-in values, maintenance, telematics, fuel management, safety and accident prevention, dealer relationships, purchasing, and lifecycle costing.

We know that our target audience is very busy — they are often the owners of the company — so we make the magazine graphics-intensive and attractive to the eye. With the writing, we strive for readability and an informal tone, even while presenting material that is information-rich and sometimes slightly technical.

We pay $100 per page (500 words); in special circumstances (such as difficult assignments or short deadlines), we pay up to $150 per page. Our deadlines typically fall about three weeks after you receive an assignment. These assignments typically involve, in the case of *Business Fleet*, calling three or four vendors, such as fleet management or telematics companies, and three or four fleet managers and/or small company owners who use the products.

A good example of a recent *Business Fleet* article for which we used a freelancer is "Evaluating Diesel vs. Gasoline for Medium-Duty Trucks." This article (with background sources/leads provided by us) looked at the pros and cons of both fuels, including price, fuel efficiency, vehicle longevity, and other factors. It contained quotes from small-fleet managers in the field (we can help with these contacts) on why they chose one over the other.

We tend to go back again and again to authors who do a good job for us and demonstrate a willingness to get a "feel" for the magazines and for our target audiences, so there is an excellent possibility of an ongoing, mutually beneficial relationship.

The best way to get a feel for the "voice" of *Business Fleet* is to read a few back issues. These are available, free of charge, to serious and interested freelancers.

Categories: Nonfiction—Automobiles—Trade—Business Vehicles

CONTACT: Submissions Editor
Material: All
Bobit Publishing
21061 S. Western Ave.
Torrance CA 90501-1711
Phone: 310-533-2592
Fax: 310-533-2503
E-mail: Steve.Elliott@bobit.com
Website: www.businessfleet.com

The Business of Writing

An ezine dedicated to helping writers understand the business of writing. The Business of Writing is a free subscription based ezine.

Rights: non-exclusive

Needs: Nonfiction only:

Articles on how to get published, find an agent/publisher, or any other aspect of the process of getting published

Horribly worded, funny, ridiculous rejection letters from publishers.

Success Stories.

Articles on writing in general, ie. Discussion on Genre differences. Reviews of publishing companies, agents, books for writers, software for writers, ect.

Any other relevant articles

Length: open

How to Submit: Email the editor at jeff@domynoes.net

Include your article in the body of the email, do not send as an attachment. If the article has pictures then you may include the pictures as attachments. In the subject please put: Article submission - TITLE: AUTHOR.

Include a picture of yourself (in gif format) if you would like to include that in your byline.

Response Time: 2-3 weeks

Payment:

Currently The Business of Writing is a non-paying market.

Categories: Writing

CONTACT: Jeff Johnston, Publisher
E-mail: jeff@domynoes.net
Website: http://bizwriter.4t.com

ByLine

Always include a self-addressed, stamped envelope with submissions. Manuscripts without SASE will not be read or returned. No e-mail submissions, please, but e-mail queries are okay.

We purchase first North American rights only; no reprints. Submissions must follow standard manuscript format. List your full name, address and telephone number in the upper left corner of the first page and an accurate word count (line count for poetry) in the upper right corner. Send a #10-sized SASE or larger.

Please do not confuse manuscript submissions with contest entries; these are two different processes. Send contest entries separately, following the rules on the contest page (see our website).

Manuscript Submission

Please do not e-mail complete manuscripts. Queries by e-mail are welcome, to robbi@bylinemag.com.

Fiction - *General short fiction, mainstream, literary or genre*; 2,000 to 4,000 words. Good writing is the main criterion. No explicit sex or violence. Payment is $75 on publication.

Features - *Instructive or motivational articles* that could be of genuine help to writers, especially how-to-write or how-to-sell to specific market areas. Length should be 1,500 to 1,800 words; query or submit full manuscript. We also solicit interviews with editors of freelancer-friendly publications for our Inside Information feature. Query with editor's name and sample of his publication; we'll provide specific guidelines. Payment is $100 on publication for all features.

End Piece - *A strong, thoughtful, first-person essay* of 700 words, related to writing. May be humorous, motivational or philosophical. Read several back issues as examples. Payment is $35 on publication.

Departments - *Read the magazine for examples*. First $ale carries 250-300 word accounts of a writer's first sale. Payment is $20 on publication. Writing-related humor of 50-600 words needed for Only When I Laugh. Pays $15 to $25 on publication. Great American Bookstores! features outstanding independent bookstores in 500-600 words. Stores should be unique in some way and also promote writers. No chains, children's only, or used bookstores. Pay is $30, or $40 with one good photo.

Poetry - *Our poetry also deals with the subject of writing*. We lean toward free verse but will accept skillful rhyme if it is not predictable. We seek good quality, serious or humorous poetry. Poems about writer's block, "the muse," and inspiration that comes in the middle of the night have been overdone. Payment for poems is $10 upon publication.

How to subscribe

Mention our Web page when you subscribe and get a $5 coupon for contest entries by return mail. Send your check for $24 for one year (11 issues) or $42 for two years, along with your complete name and address (zip + four, please) to the address below.

For Canada: $28 per year in U.S. funds.

Overseas: $40 per year in U.S. funds.

To order ByLine with your credit card, see our website.

Sample copies are available from the same address for $5, postpaid.

Categories: Fiction—Nonfiction—Literature—Poetry—Short Stories—Writing

CONTACT: **Donna Marbach, Poetry Editor**
Material: Poetry
E-mail:dmarbach@rochester.rr.com
CONTACT: **Robbi Hess, Editor**
Material: Short stories
CONTACT: **Robbi Hess, Editor**
Material: All other manuscripts or queries
PO Box 111
Albion NY 14411
Phone: 585-355-3290
E-mail: robbi@bylinemag.com (Queries only)
Website: www.bylinemag.com

Cadet Quest

Formerly Crusader: A Magazine for Cadets and Their Friends
About the Magazine

Cadet Quest is a Christian-oriented magazine for boys ages 9-14. It is published by the Calvinist Cadet Corps—a ministry of over 600 boys' clubs throughout churches in the United Sates and Canada. The goal of the Cadet Corps is "helping boys to grow more Christlike in all areas of life." *Cadet Quest* is one way we reach boys.

Cadet Quest is looking for fiction stories about sports, camping, athletes, or nature; craft and hobby projects; cartoon; puzzles; and illustrations.

Fiction (1000-1300 words)

Fast-moving, entertaining stories that appeal to a boy's sense of adventure or to his sense of humor are welcomed. Stories must present Christian life realistically and help boys relate Christian values to their own lives. Stories must have action without long dialogues. Favorite topics for boys include sports and athletes, humor, adventure, mystery, friends, etc. They must also fit the theme of that issue of *Cadet*

Quest. Stories with preachiness and/or cliches are not of interest to us.

Nonfiction Articles (up to 1500 words)

Articles about Christian athletes, coaching tips, and developing Christian character through sports are appreciated. Photos of these sports or athletes are also welcomed. Be original in presenting these topics to boys.

Articles about camping, nature, and survival should be practical—the "how-to" approach is best. God in nature articles, if done without being preachy, are appreciated.

Nonfiction articles do not have to fit the issue's theme (though it helps, of course), but do need to fit within the *Cadet Quest* goals.

Project/Hobby Articles

Articles with clear and accurate instructions for projects boys can do with easily accessible materials are especially appreciated. Our artists can illustrate these articles, but photos are also appreciated.

Cartoons and Puzzles

Wholesome and boy-oriented, of course. Unique and/or theme puzzles or games appreciated—simple logic, crosswords, and hidden pictures are favorites.

Illustrations

Illustrations are done on a contracted basis to fit stories and articles. Send sample work for consideration. Photos should be at least 5x7, but snapshots are acceptable if sharp and clear. Action shots are preferred.

About *Cadet Quest* Readers

Generally speaking, *Cadet Quest* boys are active, inquisitive, and imaginative. They imitate their heroes and they love adventure. They are sociable and form groups easily. Many of them make decisions for Jesus Christ that will affect them the rest of their lives. Because our goal is to help boys see how God is working in and around them, every article and story for every issue is chosen for a specific purpose or reason. It must be wholesome, Christian, and age-appropriate.

Although *Cadet Quest* is the "official" publication of the Cadet Corps, it is designed to appeal to every pre-adolescent boy.

Method of Selection

Manuscripts submitted to *Cadet Quest* are read as they are received—we try to read them within four to eight weeks. If your manuscript doesn't fit our needs, it is returned in your SASE within one week of our decision, or recycled at your request or if you haven't included an SASE.

Themes for the new editorial season are chosen in January. By the end of April, all fiction selections are made for that editorial season. Fiction manuscripts are normally not purchased between May and December. After selecting material, we notify authors whose material will be published and return anything not selected. The new season's theme list is made available following their selection in January. (Include an SASE for your copy, or visit our website.)

Editing

The *Cadet Quest* staff reserves the right to edit any accepted manuscript or cartoon. Editing is done with a conscious effort to retain the author's style and intent.

Basis for Rejection of Material

1. Inappropriate. Does not show boys how God is working in their lives or world.

2. Not age/gender appropriate for 9-14 year old boys.

3. Simplistic, unrealistic, too predictable or preachy, or theological perspective too different from our own.

4. Does not fit themes.

5. Too similar to material already published/submitted.

6. Editorial needs already filled.

7. Very limited need for poetry.

8. Poor writing. Poor opening, transitions, grammar. Lacks excitement or adventure that appeals to readers.

Rights

We purchase all rights, first rights, and second rights. We have no qualms about purchasing rights to articles/stories that have been printed elsewhere, providing the audiences do not overlap.

Payment

Payment is made upon final acceptance of the material, varying according to the rights purchased and amount of editing needed. Current rates:

Manuscripts: 5¢ per word and up (first rights with no major editing)
Cartoons: $5 and up for single gags; $15 and up for full-page panels
Puzzles: Rates vary
Photos: $5 for each photo used with an article

Submissions

Please do not send queries before submitting a manuscript.

Mail: Send complete manuscript, typed, double-spaced, one-sided copy on white opaque paper. Include your name, desired byline, and address on the first page. Also indicate what publishing rights are offered and approximate number of words. On succeeding pages, include page number and your name.

Submit cartoons as camera-ready art.

Puzzle submissions must include answers.

Please include an SASE with correct postage if you would like your materials returned. Any material without an SASE will be recycled.

Online: Submit stories or articles (text) online at submissions@calvinistcadets.org. Submissions must be included in the body of the e-mail, not as an attachment. We will not open any material sent as attachments.

Tips for Acceptance

Write to our audience and to the issue's theme. Keep stories or articles exciting and entertaining. Include humor. The best time to send your submissions to Cadet Quest is between January and April. Remember our purpose of showing God's work in boys' lives!

Themes/Guidelines/Sample

For editorial theme list and/or author guidelines, send a #10 envelope with sufficient postage. For a free sample copy, simply write and ask, including a 9x12 SASE ($1.01 US postage, $1.14 Cdn postage). Requests sent without the required SASE will be recycled. Send your request to: Managing Editor, *Cadet Quest*, PO Box 7259, Grand Rapids, MI 49510-7259.

CONTACT: G. Richard Broeme, Editor
Material: All
PO Box 7259
Grand Rapids, MI 49510-7259
Phone: 616-241-5616
Fax: 616-241-5558
E-mail: submissions@calvinistcadets.org
Website: www.calvinistcadets.org

California Lawyer

California Lawyer is a monthly magazine about legal affairs, with related looks at social issues and politics. It is distributed to more than 140,000 members of the California bar, who practice both in California and nationally. We are interested in concise, well-researched articles on news and trends in the legal profession, legal aspects of current events, and general interest articles of benefit or interest to attorneys.

In an average month, we assign two feature articles. In addition, we publish columns on technology, the courts, language, and strategies of sole practitioners.

In our California, Esq. section, we publish about six news stories on current case law, state and national politics, and shifts in the legal marketplace. In our Technicalities section, our columnist writes reviews and personal reflections on how software, hardware, and the Internet affect the practice of law.

Our editors will review unsolicited manuscripts, though contributors can send query letters describing proposed articles. Letters should include a brief outline of the story and the intended approach. Please enclose copies of previously published work.

Payment for feature articles of 2,000-4,000 words ranges from $750 to $2,000, depending on the nature of the assignment and the writer's experience. Payment for columns of 1,000-1,500 words is $500. Payment for news articles ranges from $50 to $350.

Articles should be double-spaced, with wide margins and numbered pages. Unsolicited manuscripts should be accompanied by a stamped, self-addressed envelope if you would like us to return your article. Please address correspondence to Tema Goodwin, Managing Editor.

Categories: Nonfiction—General Interest—Government—Politics—Society—Law

CONTACT: Tema Goodwin, Managing Editor
Material: All
California Lawyer
44 Montgomery St., Ste. 250
San Francisco CA 94104
Fax: 415-296-2482

California Wild
California Academy of Sciences

California Wild is the quarterly natural history magazine of the California Academy of Sciences. Launched as *Pacific Discovery* in 1948, it has a circulation of approximately 30,000. The Academy, located in San Francisco, encompasses research facilities, a natural history museum, Steinhart Aquarium, and Morrison Planetarium.

Proposing A Story

We're always eager to hear your story ideas, but would prefer to receive them in query form rather than as completed manuscripts. Before you query, please take the time to search our online article index (www.calacademy.org/calwild/search) to see if we have already covered a topic. Queries should begin with the story's opening paragraphs, followed by a description of the remaining points to be covered. Mention the people you might interview, explain why you are the best person to write the story, and attach several writing samples or published clips. We accept queries by regular mail and email to calwild@calacademy.org

Source documentation must be available for every manuscript, including contact information for each source or publication.

We encourage all writers, artists, and photographers interested in contributing to *California Wild* to review a printed copy of the magazine. To obtain a sample issue, send a self-addressed 9" x 12" envelope with $1.75 in postage and a check for $4.00 to *California Wild*, California Academy of Sciences, 875 Howard Street, San Francisco, CA 94103.

Our readers are well educated, and most are residents of California. They are fascinated by the natural world and concerned about wildlife and the fate of our environment.

Our article topics range from ecology to cosmology, animal intelligence to global warming, ecological restoration to indigenous cultures. We primarily seek stories about California and the West, but almost every issue includes topics that roam farther afield.

Our story needs are most acute for the following departments:
Skywatcher: An account of recent research in a field of astronomy: (2,000-3,000 words). **Wild Lives**: Reveals the surprising talents and peculiar habits of a particular plant or animal species. (1,000 words). *A Closer Look:* Describes how geology, climate, ecological interactions, and/or other forces link residents of a micro-ecosystem such as a vernal pool or treetop (1,000 words). *In Pursuit of Science:* Spotlights innovative programs bringing science to the general public, and people who have parlayed their science training into unusual but rewarding careers (1,500 words).

Rates and rights We purchase first North American serial rights. We may also request electronic rights, as a version of *California Wild* is available online. Payment is 30 cents per word, two weeks before publication. We ask most authors to submit on speculation.

Our contributors are typically professional writers or scientists with experience writing for popular audiences. We encourage first-time authors to pitch stories for our departments.

Writing should be lively and geared toward a popular audience. We prefer to emphasize possible solutions to conservation and environmental issues rather than list problems. Paint a vivid picture of your subject whenever possible—flesh out the personality of a scientist; bring a historical event to life; depict the beauty of a landscape with your words. It is fine to take a stance on controversial issues, but remember to air opposing arguments. Please keep jargon to a minimum and clearly define all scientific terms

Style tips Include scientific names in parentheses after common names of species. Spell out numbers from one to twelve and use numerals for measurements. Use either the metric or English system to express measurements, but not both. When in doubt, refer to *The Chicago Manual of Style.*

Photography

California Wild seeks quality photographs from emerging and established nature photographers. We publish photo essays as well as unusual images that tell a story of interest to our readers.

We purchase one-time publication rights to all images published. Payment ranges from $75 to $175 inside, to $250 for a cover. In the unlikely event that an original transparency is lost or damaged, the California Academy of Sciences" liability is limited to fair market value. We are not bound by any arbitrary valuations.

Caption material must accompany all submissions. Please identify all plants and animals using scientific names in addition to common names. If a photograph includes people, the names of all subjects must be correctly spelled. It is the photographer's responsibility to have model clearances on file for all human subjects.

Submissions We prefer original color transparencies or reproduction quality duplicates. Any 35mm color slides must be protected with individual slide protectors and mounted in transparent slide pages. Transparencies must be clearly marked on the slide mount with subject, location, and photographer's name and mailing address. Please enclose a stamped, self-addressed envelope, return mailing instructions, and sufficeint postage to cover safe return. We strongly recommend insuring your photographic submissions against loss and using Return Receipt Mail or a next-day courier.

Digital images may be submitted as jpegs via email, CD, or light box for approval. "Photo submission" should be included in the subject line. Do not send high resolution images via email unless prior permission has been given. All digital images must be available at 300 dpi at 3" x 5" or larger to be considered for publication.

Our current photography needs are listed on The Guilfoyle Report, www.agpix.com; call 212-929-0959 to subscribe. All unsolicited mailed submissions must be accompanied by a self-addressed envelope with sufficient postage to ensure safe return.

Categories: Animals—Conservation—Ecology—Environment—Outdoors—Science—Western

CONTACT: Keith Howell, Editor
Material: California Natural History/Traditional Cultures
Golden Gate Park
San Francisco CA 94118-4599
Phone: 415-750-7116
Fax: 415-221-4853

The Caller

The Caller is the official newsletter of the NWTF, which is comprised of 2,200 local chapters. It is published as an insert to *Turkey Call* magazine six times per year. The primary purpose of *The Caller* is twofold: to communicate to the membership news related to hunting, wildlife habitat management and the programs available to them through the national office of the NWTF; and to give the membership an outlet to publicize the work of local chapters.

NWTF members are encouraged to submit information, with photos, about their chapter to The Caller. Deadlines for each issue are available on the NWTF/s Web site. No payment is ussed for publication unless noted by editor.

CONTACT: Jake Fagan, Editor
jfagan@nwtf.net

About the NWTF: The National Wild Turkey Federation is a non-profit conservation/education organization dedicated to the conservation of the North American wild turkey and the preservation of the hunting heritage. Established in March 1973, the NWTF has members throughout the United States, Canada, Mexico and 10 other countries.

Calliope Magazine

General Information

CALLIOPE covers world history (East / West) and we are looking for lively, original approaches to the subject. Keep in mind that our magazine is aimed at youths from ages 8 to 14. Writers are encouraged to study recent back issues for content and style. (Sample issues are available at $5.95. Send 7 ½ " x 10 ½ " self-addressed $2.00 stamped envelope.) All material must relate to the theme of a specific upcoming issue in order to be considered. CALLIOPE purchases all rights to material.

Procedure

In order for your idea to be considered, a query must accompany each individual idea (however, you can mail them all together) and must include the following:

• A brief cover letter stating the subject and word length of the proposed article,

• A detailed one-page outline explaining the information to be presented in the article,

• An extensive bibliography of materials the author intends to use in preparing the article,

• A self-addressed stamped envelope.

Authors are urged to use primary resources and up-to-date scholarly resources in their bibliography. Writers new to CALLIOPE should send a writing sample with the query. In all correspondence, please include your complete address as well as a telephone number where you can be reached.

A writer may send as many queries for one issue as he or she wishes. All queries must be typed.

GUIDELINES

Feature Articles:
700-800 words
Includes: in-depth nonfiction, plays, and biographies

Supplemental Nonfiction:
300-600 words
Includes: subjects directly and indirectly related to the theme. Editors like little-known information but encourage writers not to overlook the obvious.

Fiction:
Up to 800 words
Includes: authentic historical and biographical fiction, adventure, retold legends, relating to the theme. The above three pay 20 to 25 cents per printed word.

Activities:
Up to 700 words.
Includes: crafts, recipes, woodworking, or any other interesting projects that can be done either by children alone or with adult supervision. Sketches and description of how activity relates to theme should accompany queries.

Puzzles and Games:

(please, no word finds). Crossword and other word puzzles using the vocabulary of the issue's theme. Mazes and picture puzzles that relate to the theme.

The above two pay on an individual basis.

Photo Guidelines

To be considered for publication, photographs must relate to a specific theme. Writers are encouraged to submit available photos with their query or article. We buy one-time use.

See our website for suggested fee range for professional quality photographs.

• Please note that fees for non-professional quality photographs are negotiated.

Cover fees are set on an individual basis for one-time use, plus promotional use. All cover images are color.

Prices set by museums, societies, stock photography houses, etc., are paid or negotiated.

Photographs that are promotional in nature (e.g., from tourist agencies, organizations,

special events, etc.) are usually submitted at no charge.

If you have photographs pertaining to any upcoming theme, please contact the editor by mail or fax, or send them with your query. You may also send images on speculation.

NOTE

Queries may be submitted at any time, but queries sent well in advance of deadline MAY NOT BE ANSWERED FOR SEVERAL MONTHS. Go-aheads requesting material proposed in queries are usually sent five months prior to publication date. Unused queries will be returned approximately three to four months prior to publication date. Hard copy queries ONLY, no email.

Categories: Nonfiction—Children—Education—History—Young Adult

CONTACT: Rosalie Baker, Editor
Material: All Queries
Cobblestone Publishing
30 Grove Street, Suite C
Peterborough NH 03458
Phone: 603-924-7209
Fax: 603-924-7380
Website: www.cobblestonepub.com

CALYX Journal
A Journal of Art and Literature by Women

Thank you for your interest in CALYX. *CALYX Journal* accepts submissions of poetry, short fiction, visual art, essays, reviews, and interviews. The writer's/artist's guidelines are as follows:

Prose (includes essays) should be double-spaced and not exceed 5,000 words.

Poetry submissions are limited to 6 poems.

Interviews should be double-spaced and are limited to 2,500 words.

Book reviews should be double-spaced and are from 500 to a maximum of 1,000 words. If you are interested in reviewing books, please send a resume, published samples of review writing, and an SASE. After reviewing these, we will contact you about the book review list. Always open for reviews.

Visual Art should be submitted on 35mm slides or 5"x7" or 8"x10" black and white glossy photographs (limit 6 slides and/or photos). All art media are considered. Please label all slides and photos with your name, titles, media, dimensions, and date. Also mark the top of the work. Do not write on photos! Attach all necessary information on a label. Include a brief biographical statement and a separate 50-word statement about your artwork. **CALYX is always open for art submissions.**

All submissions should include author's name on each page and be accompanied by a brief (50-word or less) biographical statement, a self-addressed, stamped envelope (SASE), a phone number, and e-mail address. Even if you indicate that it is unnecessary to return your submission(s), enclose an SASE for your notification. Prose and poetry should be submitted separately with separate SASEs for each submission category.

CALYX assumes no responsibility for submissions received without adequate return postage, packaging, or proper identification labels. CALYX can only respond to submission queries accompanied by a self-addressed, stamped envelope. We do not accept electronic submissions—either e-mail or fax. Every effort is made to respond to submissions in a timely manner, but CALYX receives a large number of submissions when open, and it may take up to six to nine months to read and review everything received. Simultaneous submissions are accepted.

PLEASE NOTE: *CALYX Journal* is only open for submissions for prose and poetry once annually, October 1-December 31.

Sample copies of CALYX are available for $9.50 plus $3.00 postage (U.S.) and handling. Send to CALYX, PO Box B, Corvallis, OR 97339.

Categories: Fiction—Nonfiction—African-American—Asian-American—Feminism—Gay/Lesbian—General Interest—Hispanic—Literature—Multicultural—Native American—Poetry—Short Stories—Women's Fiction—Women's Issues

CONTACT: Beverly McFarland, Senior Editor
Material: Any
PO Box B
Corvallis OR 97339
Phone: 541-753-9384
Fax: 541-753-0515
E-mail: calyx@proaxis.com
Web site: www.calyxpress.org

Camping Today

We appreciate your interest. *Camping Today* is a 32 page, ten times per year magazine which serves the 15,000 member families of the Family Campers & RVers (founded as NCHA, National Campers & Hikers Association). The July/August and January/February issues are combined. Because organization news is a priority we can only buy one or two articles a month. We print on a two month lead time.

Seventy-five (75) percent of our readers are over age 55 and most are owners of recreational vehicles such as travel trailers, fifth wheels, and motorhomes. They enjoy reading nonfiction articles around 1,500 words on interesting places to visit by rv, how-to-do-it features related to camping, and topics of general interest to campers.

Payment is in the range of $35 to $150 depending on the type of article and photographs. We prefer b&w prints, but sharp, clear color prints or slides will work. We can use slides (vertical preferred) for covers. Please send the photos with the article.

We prefer prints, but digital photos may be submitted in tiff, eps, or jpeg file formats, 300 d.p.i. resolution. Photo files sent in 72 d.p.i. need to be 20" x 30" in size. Please do not e-mail photos.

We buy one-time rights and will consider previously published articles (at minimum rates). We can't use poems or essays on "our first or worst campout."

When submitting articles please include a stamped, self-addressed envelope so that materials may be returned if unused. Allow 60 days for a response. Send to Camping Today at address below.

Categories: Recreation Vehicles—RV/Camping

CONTACT: DeWayne Johnston, Editor
Material: RV Travel
126 Hermitage Rd.
Butler PA 16001

Phone: 724-283-7401
E-mail: D_Johnston01@msn.com

Campus Life

Meet *Campus Life*

Campus Life's contemporary and relevant editorial deals with the real life issues of high school and college students, including sex, spiritual concerns, friendships, school and music.

Campus Life is published bimonthly by Christianity Today International, 465 Gundersen Drive, Carol Stream, Illinois 60188. Please send all e-mail to clmag@campuslife.net

WRITER's GUIDELINES

Who Writes for *Campus Life*?

Writers who understand and empathize with a Christian world view is a good start, but that's not enough. Freelancers must be pros who understand our unique style and editorial philosophy. Don't query until you've studied at least one issue of *Campus Life* (Sample copy available for $3.00).

What Type of Article Works Best?

First-person stories that capture experiences from the lives of teenagers are our readers' favorite. These can be dramatic narratives or stories that highlight a "life lesson" learned through common everyday adolescent experiences. A first-person story must be highly descriptive and incorporate fictional technique. While avoiding simplistic religious answers, the story should demonstrate that Christian values or beliefs brought about a change in the young person's life. Since this is our editorial bread and butter, experienced freelancers should consider writing "as told to" first-person stories based on an experience from an interviewee's life Guidelines for writing first-person stories are available upon request.

What Else Does *Campus Life* Print?

Humor, fiction, and information for teens considering a Christian college. All such writings must be tied to the teenager's life experience. We also offer several regular departments that are largely staff written. Specific writer's guidelines for fiction, first person and humor pieces are available upon request.

What Doesn't Work?

Essays and how-to articles are not wanted. There are a few exceptions, yet even exceptions must be highly anecdotal and demonstrate a clear understanding of our style and editorial philosophy. Manuscripts are rejected if they: become moralistic or preachy; offer simplistic solutions; take an adult tone; use religious clichés and overuse/misuse religious language; lack respect and empathy for teenagers.

Guide for Writing First-Person Stories

The first-person or "as told to" first-person story is the best way for a new writer to break into our freelance pool. It is also the best way for a seasoned writer to remain there. It's no overstatement to say that the personal narrative is our editorial "mainstay." Follow these guidelines and your manuscript will receive serious consideration.

Study first-person stories. Guideposts© and Reader's Digest© are excellent resources. Most of all, study the first-person stories that appear in *Campus Life* before submitting anything. (Sample copy available for $3.00.).

Interview thoroughly. For "as told to" stories, be sure to tape a thorough interview with your subject. During the interview, probe for details that will add life and color to your story.

Show, don't tell. Appeal to the five senses through strong descriptive writing. Use fictional technique: Pay attention to plot (problem focus), character and scene development, setting, dialogue, and credible resolution.

Focus on the best scenes. Don't try to "tell it all." Pick scenes that are germane and develop those to the fullest. If possible, try to keep your story within a short interval of time.

Don't force your message. Weave your "life lessons" into the fabric of the story.

Think readers. Your story needs to have "universal appeal" to all of our teenage readers, both male and female.

Don't force religious values. A Christian world view should be represented, yet creatively and in a manner that won't alienate or puzzle the non-churched teenager. If the story becomes preachy, brings characters "out of character" to deliver a message or uses religious clichés, it won't work for us.

Mechanics. Campus Life does not accept unsolicited manuscripts. Query first. Requested manuscripts should be typed/keyboarded and double-spaced. Simultaneous submissions must be indicated on the first page. Length should be between 1,200 and 2,500 words. Based on difficulty and length, we pay 15 cents to 20 cents per word. Expect a response in three to six weeks.

Guide for Writing Fiction

It's not uncommon for a writer to query us with: "I know a teenager who had a problem and I have written a fictional piece based on that problem. ..." Our usual response: "So why not tell the story in a true, first-person narrative?" That is the most helpful advice we can offer. At tops we print three short stories a year, and those are usually written by experienced, seasoned professionals. With that caution, consider these guidelines.

Know Campus Life. Do not query without a thorough understanding of this magazine. (Sample copy available for $3; when requesting a copy be sure to ask for fiction samples.).

Style and technique. Pay attention to strong descriptive scenes, credible dialogue, and realistic action, conflict and resolution.

Setting/perspective/tone. Story must take place in the world of today's high-school or college student and must be told from a teenager's perspective. Tone must not be condescending and/or adult. The overall "feel" must show a respect and empathy for the teenager's life and experiences.

Language. Strive for simplicity. Keep adjectives and adverbs to a minimum. Go instead with active, appropriate verbs. Remember: Lions roar, parents yell; rain trickles, people cry; cars travel, eyes look; etc. Exchange clichés for fresh expressions. Use metaphorical language sparingly and without mixing. Faddish, teen colloquialisms are not acceptable.

Predictability. We quickly reject stories that are simplistic, dependent on coincidences or end too neatly. A good fictional piece reflects life's shades of gray and complexities.

Point and message. In keeping with our editorial philosophy, each story we publish must contain a "lesson life" that represents a Christian world view. Yet this life lesson must be natural—not forced. "Religious message writing" is out. Give the reader credit for a good measure of intelligent, analytical thinking. Offer a credible resolution, yet strive for subtlety.

Mechanics. Campus Life does not accept unsolicited manuscripts. Query first. Requested manuscripts should be typed/keyboarded and double-spaced. Simultaneous submissions must be indicated on the first page. Length should be no longer than 2,000 words. Based on difficulty and length, we pay 15 cents to 20 cents per word. Expect a response in three to six weeks.

Categories: Campus Life—Education—Juvenile—Lifestyle—Music—Relationships—Sexuality—Spiritual—Young Adult

CONTACT: Marilyn Roe, Editorial Administrator
Material: All
Campus Life
465 Gundersen Drive
Carol Stream IL 60188
Phone: 630-260-6200
Fax: 630-260-0114
E-mail: clmag@campuslife.net
Website: www.christianitytoday.com

Canoe & Kayak Magazine

Editorial Submissions

Thank you for your interest in *Canoe & Kayak*! If you haven't already done so, we suggest that you review a recent issue of our magazine so that you can see what kinds of stories and photos we are using. You'll find *Canoe & Kayak* Magazine at many bookstores, large newsstands, and paddlesports retail shops. If you have trouble finding a copy, we'll send you a sample if you send us a self-addressed, 9-by-12-inch envelope with seven first-class stamps. Subscriptions are $17.95 per year.

Our readers include flatwater and whitewater canoeists and kayakers of all skill levels. We provide comprehensive information on destinations, technique, and equipment. Beyond that, we cover a variety of subjects of interest to our readers, including canoe and kayak camping, safety, the environment, and the history of boats and sport. We publish a limited number of personality pieces on people of national importance.

Most issues contain at least three feature articles of 2,000 to 2,500 words each. These features cover the range of subjects appropriate for our audience and are distinguished from departments by more in-depth coverage in the story and more liberal use of accompanying photographs. Regular departments, of 500 to 1,200 words, cover specific subjects such as techniques, new equipment, and boat reviews. Traditions and Take Out are devoted to reflective, personal essays on paddling.

The Put-In section uses short (700 words or less), newsy pieces that cover conservation, interesting people, and events. Keep in mind that you are writing for a national audience.

Our Destinations articles emphasize canoeing and kayaking trips that take no more than a few days to complete. Submissions should be a maximum of 1,500 words in length and include a map of the area showing the put-in, take-out, towns, tributaries, and features mentioned in the article; copies of materials we may need to check facts (name spelling, phone numbers, prices, etc.); a selection of quality color slides with captions; a sidebar giving driving directions to the put-in from the nearest town; trip length; seasonal information; permit requirements for paddling and camping; whitewater classification and hazards; recommended guidebooks (author, title, publishing information); and phone numbers of local sources.

Submissions

You can either query or submit material on speculation. If querying, give a brief outline of the proposed article. You can submit queries either by post or e-mail (editor@canoekayak.com). Allow at least six weeks for a response. To ensure return of your material, provide a self-addressed, stamped envelope of proper size. Please note: we will treat submissions with care, but we are not responsible for unsolicited manuscripts or photographs.

We prefer submissions in both hard copy and on disk. Please note whether your files are in Mac or IBM format on your disk, and please DO NOT double-space electronic copy or set tabs. We can accept most popular word-processing formats, but to be safe, please save a copy of the file in text format as well. Hard copies should be double-spaced.

We follow the *AP Stylebook* and *The Chicago Manual of Style*.

Preference will be given to writers who can supply color photographs with articles (see photo guidelines below).

Payment and Rights

Our base rate is 15¢ per published word. Rate for assigned articles may vary. Payment is made on publication. We purchase first international rights, which includes first anthology rights and electronic rights.

Photo Submissions

Canoe & Kayak is always looking for strong images appropriate for the magazine in 35mm, 2 1/4 x 2 1/4, or 4x5 slide formats. We prefer duplicates for selection purposes, provided that they are of good quality. We require a model release when the subject of the photo is easily identifiable.

We prefer unpublished images and do not use images that show a lack of common sense, lack of knowledge about paddlesports, or disregard for safety or the environment. People are usually wearing life preservers in photos we select. We do not use images of people in sailboats, rowing craft, or powerboats.

Payment

Canoe & Kayak Magazine pays on publication and purchases one-time or international serial rights. Rates are based on the published size and use (color or b/w) of the image:

Color
- $500 for a cover
- $350 for a full spread
- $300 for a three-quarter spread
- $250 for a full page
- $150 for a half page
- $75 for a quarter page or smaller
- $25 for second use of image in same publication

Black and White
- $200 for a full page
- $125 for a half page
- $75 for a quarter page or smaller
- $25 for second use of image in same publication

Place your name, address, and phone number on each image. *Canoe & Kayak* Magazine will handle each submission with due care, but we assume no liability for unsolicited original or duplicate slides, prints, or transparencies. Include a self-addressed envelope with proper postage for the return of your material. We normally reply to unsolicited material within six weeks.

Categories: Nonfiction—Adventure—Boating—Consumer—Family—Outdoors—Recreation—Sports/Recreation—Travel

CONTACT: Editor
Material: Editorial submissions
CONTACT: Art Director
Material: Photo submissions
PO Box 3146
10526 NE 68th St.
Kirkland WA 98033
Phone: 206-827-6363
Website: canoekayak.about.com

Canter Magazine

Canter Magazine is a quarterly consumer magazine aimed at equestrians and horse enthusiasts. *Canter* is a brand new publication, but it has a distinct voice and focus that a writer should understand before submitting a query. Please read a sample copy before querying.

Articles Published: *Canter* is particularly interested in articles that appeal to a horse person's literary interests. This includes: horse-related art and literature (past or present day artists and writers who have represented the horse in some unique way), historical (either individual horses and riders, or the horse's role in a particular era), cultural (how horses are valued in other parts of the world), travel (horse-related destinations such as Kentucky or the Spanish Riding School—not necessarily just "riding" destinations), collectibles (antique cavalry bits, Breyer horses, etc.), profiles (people or horses in the horse world who are doing something besides just winning ribbons and trophies), breed profiles (which should include information about the breed's historical development or cultural significance), reviews of horse-related books and movies, and some fiction and poetry. Canter is not interested in articles about riding, training, or veterinary care.

Audience: The bulk of *Canter*'s audience are horse owners, but we also appeal to people who are interested in horses, but may not have the time or practical knowledge necessary for horse ownership. Most of our readers are female, ages 30 to 50. They are life-long horse enthusiasts. They travel often, they like to read, and they are interested in history. They have very "horsey" lifestyles, even if they are not necessarily owners. They collect horse related art and literature, and, especially, information about horses.

Submissions: Send a one-page query by email only to canter@equinepost.com. Include a detailed outline of what you will be writing about, and what specific or unique angle you have on the subject. The letter should demonstrate your ability to write and your knowledge of the subject. Please don't send one-sentence subject proposals or questions. If possible, attach links to writing samples. Let us know if and where you have been published in the past.

Assignments: Once your idea has been accepted, an assignment letter and transfer-of-rights agreement will be sent to you by mail. The letter will outline length, payment, deadline, and any guidelines we'd like you to follow for the story. All submissions are reviewed for quality and suitability, and are edited to conform to *Canter Magazine* style.

Length: Most stories are between 1,000 and 2,000 words.

Photographs: State availability of photographs with query. All articles should include photographs or drawings of some kind. Travel or cultural articles will not be accepted without photos. When submitting queries on historical subjects, include information about where you will be obtaining archived photographs, where applicable. Professional quality 35mm transparencies are preferred. Include a variety of different subjects. For example, if your article is historical, include one or two archived photographs, several different modern or "scene-setting" photographs from the historical site, close ups of associated artifacts, maps or diagrams of an event location, etc. Photographs should be well-exposed and in sharp focus.

Departments: We have several regular departments and are always looking for good writers to fill them:

Bits are very short (300 words or less), timely discussions of cultural events associated with horses. These can be unusual events in and around the horse world (such as Internet adoption of wild mustangs), or newsworthy causes (such as the Inner Vision competition for blind dressage riders). They should not be announcements of winners in traditional horse shows or other equestrian competitions.

Tales Retold is a 500 word department in which horse-related mythology and legend is recounted for readers. This department can include an analysis of what horses meant to the culture where a particular legend originated, or it can be a simple retelling of the legend.

Art. We occasionally print profiles of equestrian artists, but we very much prefer to feature artists who can use their work to illustrate a theme. For example, an artist's work might illustrate the history of horses on the Arabian peninsula. The artist can choose to write the article, or we may assign it to someone on our staff. Payment for pieces such as these is usually a half or full page color ad and a sidebar providing readers with the artist's contact information and purchasing information for the works featured in the article. Artists should query with a short outline of the proposed piece and a few thumbnails of relevant works.

Fiction. We publish very short fiction (between 300 and 500 words), and occasionally longer pieces depending on the availability of accompanying graphics, or the availability of space in the magazine.

Happenings are generally announcements and reviews of upcoming or ongoing events. These should be events that are open to the public—particularly "artsy" events such as theatre productions, films, museums, expos, and exhibitions, though any event with an equine theme will be considered. Again, we do tend to avoid reviews of traditional equestrian events such as horse shows and equestrian competitions, unless they have a very unusual perspective.

The Book Barn contains short, 300-word reviews of new horse-related books. We prefer to review books with a historic or cultural theme, memoirs, and essays. We don't generally cover how-to or discipline-specific books. We will also publish in-depth reviews of up to 1,500 words, especially those with a theme closely associated with our own.

Hoofnotes is a 500 word personal experience department. This is the only place in the magazine where we publish stories told in the first person, especially stories that are associated with the ownership of horses. This department is generally a personalized account of what horses have meant to the author.

Payment: Payment for feature-length articles is $25. Departments and columns pay $10, except for *Bits* and *The Book Barn*, which pay $5. These are preliminary rates, which will be in effect for the first two years of publication. Writers who work with us in the early stages of the magazine will be given preference for future assignments, and the rate of pay will scale accordingly. The magazine buys first-time rights. Payment is on publication. We offer a 25% kill fee for accepted, completed articles not deemed suitable for publication in our magazine.

What not to do: If your idea is practical, we are probably not interested in it. This includes anything that can be considered a "how-to" article, such as "how to build your dream barn," "ten ways to improve your balance," etc. If your idea is general, we are probably not interested in it. A general piece is any overview of a subject without a distinctive or unique angle, such as "Dressage in England," or "Arabian Horse Racing." Don't send personal experience stories, such as "My Weekend Horse Camping Trip," or "My Horse's Bout with Colic." We are not interested in articles about So-and-So, who won the Burghley Horse Trials in 1999.

What to do: Find some unique new way of looking at your subject. Instead of proposing an article on Arabian horse racing, tell us how Arabian horse racing is shaping the economy of an isolated village in Spain. Tell us how three generations of townspeople have thrived by taking bets on the outcome of the annual race. Tell us about the festival that proceeds and follows the event. Tell us how the races were founded by a man who challenged his fellow villagers to try and beat his unbeatable stallion. We want to hear something we've never heard before. In particular, we want to know the intricacies of how the horse's history and presence in the world is indivisibly intertwined with our own. We want to know why horses are important to us, and how we can make them a part of our lives.

Categories: Fiction—Nonfiction—Animals—Art—Book Reviews—Collectibles—History—Poetry—Short Stories—Travel

CONTACT: Canter Magazine
PO Box 720322
San Jose, CA 95172
E-mail: canter@EquinePost.com
Website: www.EquinePost.com

Capper's

ABOUT US

CAPPER'S has been taken to heart by families for more than 120 years, striving to enlighten and entertain while concentrating on traditional American values. CAPPER'S emphasizes life's positive perspectives and offers the opportunity to earnestly share joys and tears within the caring community of readers. CAPPER'S is a rural American tradition, growing from its Kansas roots to spread across the country. CAPPER'S takes a positive approach to the art of living, and subscribers in all 50 states love it and believe in it, often passing their copies

among family and friends. Reader interest is the key to CAPPER'S continued popularity. The Heart of the Home is CAPPER'S most popular section. It is composed of reader-submitted letters, sharing humorous, heartwarming, poignant and nostalgic experiences of life. It also includes patterns and down-home recipes, including a special Kate Marchbanks feature recipe in every issue.

CAPPER'S columns include the well-loved Reader to Reader, in which subscribers help each other find old friends, family, and songs, and plan for reunions. Garden Clippings presents gardeners, old and new, with timely advice and suggestions for new plantings. Medical advice from Dr. Paul G. Donohue and a financial column by Bruce Williams are reader favorites. Reader questions are answered in Social Security Connections.

News stories, feature articles, photos, editorials and news briefs keep CAPPER'S readers in touch with the world.

CAPPER'S offers a wide selection of poetry in each issue, and serialized fiction remains a reader favorite.

SUBMISSION GUIDELINES

CAPPER's is a nationally distributed biweekly tabloid publication with a national paid circulation of approximately 240,000. It emphasizes home and family to readers who live mainly in the rural Midwest.

CAPPER's publishes manuscripts an average of two to 12 months after acceptance. It purchases first North American serial rights, with the exception of Heart of the Home letters, in which all rights are retained. Seasonal or holiday material should be submitted at least four months in advance. Notification of acceptance or rejection is made within two to three months, six months for serialized novels. No simultaneous submissions. Query for novel-length manuscripts only; submit all others complete.

If you wish to be notified of the status of your manuscript, please send a self-addressed, stamped envelope. If you wish to have your manuscript returned, send SASE with adequate postage. No manuscripts will be returned without adequate postage.

Features

CAPPER's uses historical, inspirational, nostalgic, family-oriented, travel and human-interest stories; unusual accomplishments, collections, occupations, hobbies, etc. Approximately 75 manuscripts are purchased annually (not including Heart of the Home). Use journalistic style. Payment is made upon publication at the rate of approximately $2.50 per printed inch. Length: 900 words maximum. Good quality accompanying photos considered.

CAPPER's uses 1-2 cartoons per issue Payment of $10-15 is made upon acceptance. Submit in batches of no more than 15.

Poetry

Free verse and light verse, traditional, nature and inspirational poems are purchased. Those selected are easy to read, with down-to-earth themes. Five or six poems are used in each issue. Limit submissions to batches of 5-6, length 4-16 lines. Payment of $10-$15 is made upon acceptance; tear sheet sent upon publication.

Jokes

CAPPER's buys 5-10 jokes per issue. Jokes published earn a $2 gift certificate. Limit submissions to batches of 5-6. Sorry, no jokes returned.

SERIALIZED NOVELS

Fiction: Query first, with brief description of plot and characters. Manuscripts accepted omit profanity, violence, sex and alcohol use. Four to six manuscripts are purchased annually. Payment of $100-$400 is made upon acceptance. Manuscripts of 12,000 to 25,000 words preferred; 7,500 words minimum, 50,000 maximum.

Manuscripts should be double-spaced with numbered pages and accurate word count. Use readable fonts; no italics or scripts.

PHOTOS

Color: Submit 35 mm color slides, transparencies or sharp color prints in batches of no more than 40. Include caption material. Payment of $40 for front page, $20-40 inside, made upon publication.

Black and white: Good quality photos accompanying manuscripts are considered. Payment is $5-15, depending on size and quality.

Heart of the Home

"Kate Marchbanks" uses letters sharing humorous, heartwarming, poignant and nostalgic experiences of life. These are mostly reader-written. Submissions may be held up to one year, especially if they are seasonal. Payment of $2 per printed inch is made upon publication. Length: 300 words maximum. Payment for recipes is $5 each. Hints used earn a $2 gift certificate.

"Space Place" is for original drawings, poems, jokes, stories, etc., by children 12 and under. Contributors receive T-shirts. (Include birth date, home address and shirt size with submission.)

CAPPER's retains all rights for Heart of the Home material.

We do not accept electronic submissions.

Items used on our Web site receive an additional $5.

Categories: Agriculture—Culture—Family—Gardening—General Interest—Inspirational—Lifestyle—Mystery—Outdoors—Poetry—Recreation—Regional—Romance—Rural America—Senior Citizen—Travel—Western

CONTACT: Dennis McLaughlin, Managing Editor
Material: All
c/o Ogden Publications, Inc.
1503 SW 42nd St
Topeka KS 66609
Phone: 785-274-4300
Fax: 785-274-4305
Website: www.cappers.com

Car and Driver

We do not accept unsolicited manuscripts, but story ideas in writing are accepted.

Categories: Nonfiction—Automobiles—History—Recreation—Sports/Recreation—Satire—Humor—Nostalgia

CONTACT: Csaba Csere, Editor-in-Chief
Material: All
2002 Hogback Rd.
Ann Arbor MI 48105-9736
Phone: 734-971-3600
Fax: 734-971-9188
E-mail: editors@caranddriver.com
Website: www.caranddriver.com

CardMaker

General Information

CardMaker is published bimonthly by Annie's Attic (DRG Publishing)—Jan., Mar., May, July, Sept. and Nov.

Editor: Tanya Fox, Associate Editor: Sue Reeves

All correspondence should be sent to *CardMaker* at the address below. The magazine's editorial offices are open each weekday from 8 a.m. to 5 p.m. EST. Feel free to contact the editor or associate editor by phone (260-589-4000) or via e-mail at Tanya_Fox@DRGnetwork.com or Sue_Reeves@DRGnetwork.com.

CardMaker mission statement:

CardMaker magazine appeals to card crafters of all experience levels, and contains a wide variety of technique articles and projects featuring greeting cards, invitations, announcements and postcards. Created primarily from paper, many of these innovative card projects also include easy-to-make coordinating envelopes and instructions for finishing the *inside* of the card.

CARDMAKER IS ALWAYS LOOKING FOR:

• Original, attractive designs and patterns for card projects that readers of all skill levels can easily follow. Techniques featured in the magazine include, but are not limited to: rubber stamping, air-dry clay, quilling, paper weaving, paper piercing, handmade paper, embossing, paper folding, etc.

• Your ideas for issue themes, project types to feature, etc.

• New products and printed materials to review.

SUBMITTING PROPOSALS TO *CARDMAKER*

If we have not worked together before, we *strongly recommend* you first send an overview of your design concept, including a color sketch, project notes and a SASE. Include in the project notes the pertinent information about your craft, such as materials used, as well as any details that you feel will help "sell" your project.

While we will consider submission of completed projects, we reserve the right to request revisions to allow for photography in a coordinated setting with other projects.

SUBMIT PROPOSALS TO:
Tanya Fox, Editor
CardMaker
306 East Parr Rd
Berne IN 46711

E-mail submissions may be sent to: submissions@CardMaker magazine.com.

Please make sure *everything* you submit is labeled with your name, complete address and daytime phone, and the *issue for which the submission should be considered.*

CONTRACTS & PAYMENT

• When your project and instructions are approved, we will send you an agreement with our payment offer and a business reply envelope. You should complete it with your signature and phone number. Return the original to us in the postage-paid envelope—the photocopy we send is for your records. (You always have the right to reject or negotiate a contractual offer.) If this is the first time we've worked with you or if it has been a while since we've accepted a project, you will also receive a W-9 (or a W-8 if you live outside the United States) which must be completed and returned before payments can be issued.

• You will be issued a check for payment within 45 days of the date we receive your signed contract.

• We will keep your project until the magazine issue is published. Your project will be returned to you after publication unless other arrangements are made. All manuscripts, diagrams, etc., remain our property. Since we purchase all rights to design, you should not sell that design—or one very similar to it—to another publication. If you have questions as to what constitutes an original design, please give us a call.

GUIDELINES FOR MANUSCRIPTS

Once a concept is approved, you will need to provide complete written instructions for the project. Please observe the following guidelines.

• Please type your instructions double-spaced on white paper, leaving generous margins all around. Label the first page with your name, complete address, daytime phone number and the title of your project; label *all* pages with your name and the title of the project. Number the pages if there is more than one.

• Include a complete materials list for your project, listing each item on a separate line. The materials list should precede the instructions.

• Give complete instructions on how the item is to be used. Label the top and bottom. It may be apparent to you, but it can be very confusing for us.

• Give sources (including addresses and product numbers) for any products used in your project which are not readily available at any general craft or fabric store. Refer to specific brand names whenever possible; if the same kind of project is offered by different manufacturers under different names, include two or three options to give our readers a choice. When referring to specific brand names of materials, please be accurate. Please do not use discontinued products in your design.

• List instruction steps numerically.

• Label all diagrams, photos, etc.

• If your project uses pattern pieces, please submit full-size pieces.

• *Proofread all aspects of your submission for accuracy.* Are instructions clear? Is the materials list complete? Are all pattern pieces and diagrams labeled properly? *Remember:* Your instructions should be clearly understood by a *beginner.* We will return projects with instructions that are not written clearly enough for our needs, and will pay less if your instructions need considerable editorial help.

• If at all possible, e-mail instructions directly to both the editor and associate editor and include a hard copy in the box with the completed sample.

FINALLY...

We appreciate your interest in our magazine! These guidelines are meant to be just that—guidelines. If you have questions, special circumstances, etc., feel free to contact us. We will make every effort to work with you!

Categories: Arts—Crafts/Hobbies

CONTACT:
Tanya Fox, Editor
Tanya_Fox@DRGnetwork.com
Sue Reeves, Associate Editor
Sue_Reeves@DRGnetwork.com
Phone: 260-589-4000

The Magazine For Those Who PLAY TO WIN!

Card Player

OUR MISSION STATEMENT

Our mission is to bring you a well-written, interesting, accurate, and informative magazine that will tweak your poker interest, knowledge, and comportment to make poker more enjoyable for you.

STANDARD TERMS AND CONDITIONS

These Standards Terms and Conditions (the "Standard Terms"), made and entered into as of the date of the Magazine Articles Submission Letter (the "Submission Letter"), are expressly incorporated into and made a part of the Submission Letter. The Standard Terms together with the Submission Letter govern the relationship between SM and Writer with respect to Writer submitting the Articles to SM for the purpose of being published in the Publication. (Capitalized terms not otherwise defined shall have the meanings set forth in Section 1 below.) By countersigning the Submission Letter, Writer is expressly agreeing to comply with and be bound by all the terms and conditions set forth in these Standard Terms and in the Submission Letter.

1. Definitions. As used herein, the following defined terms shall have the following meanings:

a. "Agreement" means, collectively, the Standard Terms and the Submission Letter.

b. "Articles" means, collectively, those magazine articles that Writer is submitting to SM for the purpose of being published in the Publication.

c. "SM" means Shulman Media, LLC, a Nevada limited liability company.

d. "Publication" means SM's biweekly publication entitled *"Card Player."*

e. "Writer" means the party who wrote the Articles and who is submitting the Articles to SM for the purpose of being published in the Publication.

2. Grant of Rights. For the consideration set forth in the Submission Letter, and subject to Section 3 below, Writer hereby irrevocably grants, conveys, and assigns exclusively to SM, forever and throughout the universe: (i) all right, title, and interest in and to the Articles, and any and all parts thereof, free and clear of any and all claims, liens, and encumbrances, including interactive media rights, Internet rights and book rights, and the right to utilize, reproduce, and exploit any of the foregoing rights; (ii) the right to utilize, reproduce, exploit, advertise, and promote Writer's name, likeness, photograph, and biography in connection with the Publication, SM's Web site located at www.cardplayer.com, and any advertising and publicity relating thereto; and (iii) the right to edit the Articles in any manner SM deems appropriate.

3. Rights Reserved to Writer. Notwithstanding the foregoing, Writer reserves the nonexclusive right to use and reuse the Articles in any form, manner, and media that Writer determines, so long as Writer does not use or reuse the Articles in connection with or for the benefit of any magazine that competes with the Publication. SM will have the sole discretion to determine whether a magazine competes with the Publication, and SM will periodically provide Writer with a list of those magazines that are determined to be in competition with the Publication. Presently, only Poker Pages and Poker Digest are prohibited publications. Except as set forth in the foregoing sentences, Writer reserves no other rights of any kind or nature whatsoever in or to the Articles, all such rights being granted to SM pursuant hereto.

4. Writer's Representations and Warranties. Writer hereby represents and warrants to SM that: (i) Writer has full and complete right, title, and interest in and to the Articles, has not sold, granted, conveyed, or assigned any of Writer's right, title, or interest in or to the Articles to any person or entity and has the full power, capacity, and authority to grant to SM the rights granted herein; (ii) no liens, encumbrances, claims, proceedings, and/or litigation presently exist or are pending with respect to the Articles; and (iii) the Articles are wholly original with Writer and shall not infringe upon or violate any statutory copyright, common law rights, proprietary rights or any other rights whatsoever of any person or entity.

5. Writer's Indemnification. Writer indemnifies, defends, protects, and holds harmless SM, and each of its members, managers, employees, licensees, agents, representatives, successors, and assigns, as well as any third parties claiming rights through SM, from and against any and all claims, liabilities, damages, losses, and costs of any kind resulting in connection with or otherwise resulting from the breach by Writer of any of the foregoing warranties.

6. Writer's Release. Writer releases, discharges, and acquits SM and each of its members, managers, employees, licensees, agents, representatives, successors, and assigns, from any and all claims, liabilities, damages, losses, and costs of any kind that Writer may now or hereafter have against SM, whether for defamation, invasion of right of privacy or publicity, or otherwise, arising out of or in connection with the exercise of any rights granted hereunder.

7. Entire Agreement. This Agreement constitutes the entire agreement among the parties and supersedes and cancels any prior agreements, representations, warranties, or communications, whether oral or written, among the parties to this Agreement relating to the transactions contemplated by this Agreement or the subject matter herein.

8. Miscellaneous. This Agreement will be governed by and construed in accordance with the laws of the state of Nevada (without regard to conflicts of law principles), and the parties hereby consent to the jurisdiction of Nevada State and Federal courts located within Clark County, over all matters relating hereto. In the event of any litigation between or among the parties arising out of this Agreement, the successful or prevailing party will be entitled to recover its reasonable attorneys' fees and other costs in connection therewith. This Agreement may not be amended, modified or supplemented except pursuant to an instrument in writing signed by each of the parties. This Agreement may not be assigned by any party without the other Party's prior written consent, and any attempted unauthorized assignment will be null and void.

Categories: Nonfiction—Games—Poker Gaming

CONTACT: Submissions Editor
Material: All
3140 S. Polaris, Ste. 8
Las Vegas NV 89102
Phone: 702-871-1720
Fax: 702-871-2674
E-mail: cardplay@wizard.com
Website: www.cardplayer.com

Careers & the Disabled

Please refer to Equal Opportunity Publications, Inc.

Caribbean Travel & Life

Caribbean Travel & Life is now in its 22nd year of providing stories and photos about the fascinating region of the world that is the Caribbean. Potential writers for the magazine should understand, first and foremost, that our audience is made up of upscale, sophisticated and experienced Caribbean travelers: our research indicates that they visit the islands repeatedly. Therefore, our readers look to CT&L to guide them to the new and interesting places to visit, to explore the many facets of Caribbean culture and to highlight the fascinating people of the islands.

The editors of CT&L are always open to ideas from writers. Our only requirements are that the writing be superb, the subject be something unique and interesting, and the writer must know his/her subject. To understand what kind of stories we buy, read the magazine. We do NOT run generalized travelogues, guidebook-like island profiles, or stories about well-known, over-publicized or commonly visited places. Our readers demand behind-the-scenes stories, off-the-beaten-path destinations, ahead-of-the-curve knowledge about the Caribbean.

Most of the major features in CT&L are assigned to staff or to writers with whose work we are familiar. New writers will have better success starting off in one of our departments. Always keep in mind that the availability of good photographs to illustrate a story is essential.

TO SUBMIT
To submit a query, send a brief letter to Bob Friel, Editor, Caribbean Travel & Life, 460 N. Orlando Ave., Suite 200, Winter Park, FL 32790; FAX to 407-628-7061; or e-mail to editor@worldpub.net. Please do not call and do not send a complete manuscript unless requested by an editor.

Categories: Nonfiction—Culture—Entertainment—Regional—Travel

CONTACT: Bob Friel, Editor
Material: All
World Publications
460 N. Orlando Ave. Ste 200
Winter Park FL 32790
Phone: 407-628-4802
Fax: 407-628-7061
E-mail: editor@worldpub.net
Website: www.carribeantravelmag.com

Carolina Quarterly
The University of North Carolina

History
Since 1948 *The Carolina Quarterly* has served as a forum for the best work by writers with established reputations and by writers at the very beginnings of their careers. Among the many fine writers whose work has appeared in *The Carolina Quarterly* are Conrad Aiken, Wendell Berry, Anthony Burgess, Raymond Carver, Don DeLillo, Annie Dillard, Louise Erdrich, Lawrence Ferlinghetti, Paul Green, Michael

S. Harper, Archibald MacLeish, Joyce Carol Oates, Reynolds Price, Kenneth Rexroth, and Thomas Wolfe. Among contributors to recent issues are Doris Batts, Mark Doty, Stephen Dunn, Clyde Edgerton, George Garrett, Barry Hannah, William Harmon, X. J. Kennedy, James Laughlin, Denise Levertov, Robert Morgan, and Gregory Orr.

Guidelines for Writers
The editorial board of *The Carolina Quarterly* welcomes submissions of fiction, poetry, reviews, nonfiction, and graphic art. Prose and poetry in all styles and on all subjects are of interest. The board also considers translations of work originally written in languages other than English. Black-and-white graphic art is used to illustrate prose in each issue and to decorate each cover.

Despite its name, *The Carolina Quarterly* goes to press three times a year, so manuscripts and artwork may be kept under serious consideration for four months or more. The editorial board considers unpublished work only and does not consider simultaneous submissions. All correspondence may be sent to the editorial board at the address below. Writers and artists should send only clear copies of their work.

Contributors of writing and art receive two copies of the issue in which their work appears and a 50% discount on additional copies. *The Carolina Quarterly* acquires first-publication rights to each work accepted for publication; subsequent to publication, rights revert to the author. Writers without major publication credits are eligible for the yearly Charles B. Wood Award for Distinguished Writing, a $500 prize for the best poem or story by an unestablished writer published in each volume.

Sample Copies and Subscriptions
Writers and artists may find it helpful to look at a sample copy of *The Carolina Quarterly*. A sample copy of a recent issue costs $5 (including shipping and handling). Yearly subscriptions to *The Carolina Quarterly* are just $12 to individuals. International subscriptions to individuals are $15.

Categories: Fiction—Nonfiction—African-American—Book Reviews—Gay/Lesbian—Interview—Literature—Men's Fiction—Men's Issues—Poetry—Short Stories—Women's Fiction—Women's Issues—Writing—Reviews

CONTACT: Fiction Editor
Material: Fiction
CONTACT: Poetry Editor
Material: Poetry
Editorial Board
CB 3520 Greenlaw Hall
University of North Carolina
Chapel Hill NC 27599-3520
Phone: 919-962-0244
Fax: 919-962-3520
Website: www.unc.edu/depts/cqonline

Cascades East Magazine
Central Oregon's Quarterly

Two types of articles offer limited opportunities for freelancers:
• First-Person Accounts of Outdoor Activities
• First-person accounts, with black & white or color photos, of outdoor activities in Central Oregon (Deschutes, Jefferson & Crook counties) are of particular need. Activities can include fishing, hunting, camping, hiking, backpacking, spelunking, etc. These would be strong narratives although treatment can be dramatic, factual or humorous. No "travel folder" tours. Queries are considered, however finished articles of 1,000 to 2,000 words are preferred.

Historical Features
Each issue includes a "Little Known Tales from Oregon History" feature. Query letters are preferred along with a statement of the availability of black & white photos. Length from 1,000 to 2,000 words.

Payment for the Above

5 to 15 cents a word with additional payment for photos. Payment is made upon publication.

Color Photos

Vertical, color transparencies of superior quality are needed, on a limited basis, for the magazine cover.

Editing

Any material accepted is subject to such revision necessary in our sole discretion to meet the requirements of *Cascades East*.

Categories: Adventure—Fishing—History—Outdoors—Physical Fitness—Recreation—Sports/Recreation

CONTACT: Geoff Hill, Editor
Material: All
PO Box 5784
Bend OR 97708
Phone: 541-382-0127
Fax: 541-382-7057
E-mail: Sunpub@sun-pub.com

Cat Fancy

Writer's Guidelines: Thank you for your interest in *Cat Fancy*, a consumer magazine directed to the love of cats. Before submitting any materials, read several issues to become acquainted with the type of material we use. Our magazine is available at many pet stores, bookstores and other places magazines are sold. **Do not send unsolicited feature manuscripts.** We will return them unread (if accompanied by a self-addressed stamped envelope) or discard them unread. If you have an idea for an article, please send a written query with a self-addressed stamped envelope. See Departments and Columns for acceptable unsolicited manuscript submissions.

Feature Articles

We are open to working with new contributors and fresh voices in addition to drawing from a talented crop of established contributors. Each month, we provide our readers with a mix of informative articles, including breed profiles, feline health, nutrition, grooming, behavior, training, as well as special interest articles on cat culture, the human-animal bond and personalities. Length: 300-1,200 words.

Departments and Columns

Regular contributors write most of our monthly departments and columns. Exceptions include:

1. Flights of Fancy. Short fiction, nonfiction, poetry, artwork or other creative expressions of feeling for cats (include artwork or photo if applicable). Length: up to 500 words. Payment: a complimentary copy of the issue in which your story appears. Submissions are accepted between January and March.

2. Cats for Kids. Puzzles, games and how-to pieces for our younger readers. Payment: a complimentary copy of the issue in which your story appears.

3. Purrsonalities. Personality profiles of people (including celebrities and public figures) who love cats, work with cats, or make a difference in the lives of cats. Length: 500 words. Payment varies with subject and experience. Please include photos. Query first (see below).

4. Homeless to Housecat. Profiles of a cat's journey from homeless (rescued or shelter) to housecat. Length: 500 words. Payment varies with subject and experience. Please include photos. Query first (see below).

Queries

Please note: We accept queries between January 1 and May 1. Queries sent after then will be returned (if SASE is included) or discarded unread. Your typewritten, single-page query should include the following:

The topic of your proposed article, expressed in one or two sentences.

Why this topic will interest our readers.

Key points you will cover in your article.

Sources you will interview.

How you will present this topic in a fresh, appealing way.

Please include one or two previously published samples of your best writing, plus information regarding your experience and qualifications. Mail your query to: Cat Fancy, Attn: Query Editor, PO Box 6050, Mission Viejo, CA 92690, or e-mail it to *query@catfancy.com*. Include your telephone number and e-mail address. **We do not accept phone of fax queries.** We may take up to 8 weeks to respond.

Terms

Cat Fancy pays following publication and buys exclusive first-time rights for one North American edition and one of each foreign language edition of the magazine for a period of six months from the date of first publication, after which the licensed rights are non-exclusive. (The contracted license grants rights for reproduction, distribution, syndication, online rights and the right to engage third parties.) We cannot assume responsibility for materials you submit, but we assure you that we will take all reasonable care in handling your work.

Categories: Fiction—Nonfiction—Animals—Children—Crafts/Hobbies—Games—Health—History—Hobbies—Poetry—Short Stories—Pets—How To—Humor—Personal Experience—News

CONTACT: Query Editor
Material: All
PO Box 6050
Mission Viejo CA 92690
Phone: 949-855-8822
Fax: 949-855-3045
Website: www.catfancy.com

The Catholic Answer

The mission of *The Catholic Answer* magazine is to help readers answer important questions about Catholic faith, practice and tradition, and to apply these insights to their everyday lives. Our goal is to publish articles and columns that are faithful to the teachings of the Church. They must also be engaging, clear, concise, convincing, compelling, charitable, accessible, informed by the best available scholarship and sensitive to pastoral concerns.

Our Focus

The word *answer* in the name of the magazine is an important key to maintaining its focus. We always ask about any piece we consider for publication: "If this is the Catholic answer, then what's the question?" Our readers, too, after finishing the piece, should be able to identify not only the subject matter addressed, but also the particular question (or cluster of related questions) answered.

Our goal, then, is not simply to inform, persuade, and inspire. We aim to do these things by *answering specific questions of importance to Catholics.* These questions will usually fall into one of three categories:

Important questions Catholics often ask

Important questions Catholics are often asked by non-Catholics

Important questions Catholics should be asking

The cover letter (email) accompanying your manuscript should identify the question(s) answered. In addition, the question should appear somewhere in the manuscript itself, either within the text or as a title, subtitle or subheading.

Topics of Interest

the Scripture

the Sacraments

Catholic doctrine

Catholic moral teaching

Catholic liturgy

Other Catholic practices (sacramentals, devotions, the Church calendar, etc.)

Catholic history (especially the lives and writings of the saints)

Application of Catholic faith to common situations in everyday life

Understanding and responding to other religious traditions in light of the Catholic faith

Issues in secular culture and society of interest to Catholics

Style, Format, Specifications

Write for a popular readership.

For specific matters of style, consult the *Associated Press Stylebook* or, if you have access to it, the *Catholic News Service Stylebook on Religion.*

Contrary to these style guides, however, we ask you to capitalize all pronouns referring to Deity (except *who, whose,* and *whom*).

Manuscripts should be no longer than 1200 words without prior consultation with the editor. Shorter than 1200 words is fine, with a minimum of 500. We especially need shorter pieces of about 1000 words.

Boxes and sidebars related to your article are welcome, but they should be included in the 1200-word limit.

When you quote Scripture, please note the Bible translation you are using.

Keep in mind that brief subheadings within the text help move the reader along.

Quotes of up to fifty words should be attributed to a particular source within the text. Quotes of more than fifty words must include a footnote with full bibliographic data for the source. (You may also include such a footnote for shorter quotes if you think the typical reader would appreciate having that information.) Keep quotations brief.

Include a one- or two-sentence author biographical statement.

We prefer to receive manuscripts by email. To avoid the transfer of viruses, please cut and paste your manuscript into the body of the email message rather than sending it as an attachment. Send to the editor, Dr. Paul Thigpen, at pthigpen@osv.com.

If you prefer to send your manuscript by mail, please make sure the hard copy is typed and double-spaced on standard 8½ x 11 paper.

The publisher provides all artwork and photos.

Normal payment is $200 upon acceptance. To receive payment, you must include your full name, Social Security number, and current mailing address. Please include as well your daytime phone number in case we have questions for you.

Thanks for your interest in writing for *The Catholic Answer.* We look forward to hearing from you!

Categories: Nonfiction—Religion—Catholicism

CONTACT: Dr. Paul Thigpen
PO Box 30157
Savannah GA 31410-0157
E-mail: pthigpen@osv.com

Catholic Digest

What material *Catholic Digest* uses:

Non-fiction articles: 700-2,000 words on almost any topic. Our readers have a wide range of interests—religion, family, science, health, human relationships, nostalgia, good works and more. • *Catholic Digest* article rates: $100 for reprints, $200-400 for originals. For re-use in electronic form, we pay half of all traceable revenue derived from use to owner/author. Online-only articles receive $100, plus half of any traceable revenue from electronic use. A copy of the issue is included with payment if published in *Catholic Digest.* Finders' fees are $15 per article published. • Send submissions to: Articles Editor, *Catholic Digest,* 1 Montauk Ave, Ste 200, New London, CT 06320,or by email to cdsubmissions@bayard-inc.com. If submitting by mail, enclose a self-addressed, stamped envelope (SASE). Be Well submissions may be sent to cdfillers@bayard-inc.com, attn: Be Well. Fillers: *Catholic Digest* features regular fillers each month plus a variety of other fillers.

Open Door: Statements of true incidents through which people are brought into the Catholic faith, or recover the Catholic faith they had lost. (200-500 words)

Other fillers: Jokes, short anecdotes, quizzes, and informational paragraphs (one-liners to 500 words)

***Catholic Digest* filler rates:**

To authors, we pay $2 per published line (full-page width) upon publication. For this payment, your filler may be published in any *Catholic Digest* publication, including but not limited to *Catholic Digest, Catholic Digest Reader en Español,* and our Web site (www. CatholicDigest.com). A copy of the issue is included with payment if published in *Catholic Digest.* Finders' fees are $5 or $ 10, depending on length.

Tips on selling a manuscript to *Catholic Digest*:

Before you submit a manuscript, study a copy of *Catholic Digest* for article tone and style, or visit our Web site, (www.Catholic Digest.com).We favor the anecdotal approach. Stories submitted must be strongly focused on a definitive topic. This topic is to be illustrated for the reader by way of a well-developed series of true-life, interconnected vignettes. Most articles we use are reprinted—i.e., they have appeared in another periodical or newspaper. But we also consider original submissions. Don't query. Send the article itself. We don't consider fiction, poetry, or submissions simultaneously sent to other publications. Include your name, address, and telephone number on each submitted page. If you are submitting an article for reprint consideration, you must include the name, address, and editor of the original publication source, the copyright line from the original source, and the page number and date of the original publication. If you are submitting an original manuscript by mail, please send a double-spaced, typewritten photocopy and, if possible, a text file saved on a CD-R disc; e-mail submissions should be included in the text of your message rather than as an attached file.

Categories: Nonfiction—Family—Health—Humor—Relationships—Religion—Science—Spiritual—Catholic Church—Cartoons—Christian Interests—Hispanic—Inspirational—Lifestyle—Senior Citizens

CONTACT: Articles Editor
Material: Non-Fiction
CONTACT: Filler Editor
Material: Filler: Jokes, cartoons, short anecdotes and quizzes
CONTACT: Katie Collings, Managing Editor
Material: Submissions to Catholic Digest en Espanol
Catholic Digest
1 Montauk Ave, Ste 200
New London, CT 06320
Phone: 800-321-0411
E-mail: cdsubmissions@bayard-inc.com

Catholic Near East

Please refer to *CNEW World.*

Catholic Parent

Catholic Parent emphasizes practical, useful information for today's busy parents. We are most interested in features dealing with the real-life issues of real-life Catholic parents. In our editorial mix, we look for practical, useful articles on topics of interest to moms and dads who are building families with solid, Catholic values in today's changing world.

We are presently limiting the freelance material we accept, as we are primarily an assignment-only publication. We are not interested in new columnists at this time. However, queries on features, especially how-to's and parenting topics of broad, widespread interest to Catholic parents are always welcome. We will consider features if they are well-written and directly tied to the concerns and needs of other parents. A few sample clips of representative work should be included with any query.

We are not interested in long, philosophical, theological or argumentative essays. We do not use poetry, short stories or fiction. Presently we are not using reprints or Bible studies. We do not want didactic or overly scholarly material.

What's the best way to have your work accepted in *Catholic Parent*? Query first. Then write a tight story or feature (not more than 1,000 words) on an issue of concern to Catholic parents. Keep it anecdotal and practical, with an emphasis on how-to. Whatever you do, don't preach! Share your experiences as a parent, but don't try to hand down wisdom from the mountaintop. Keep it short and concise. For shorter submissions, This Works!, our column of parenting tips, accepts material without query. Any Scripture quotations should preferably be from the Catholic New American Bible.

Computer and FAX submissions are accepted with prior approval of the editor. With rare exceptions, articles do not exceed 1,000 words. Most features run about 800 words.

For a sample copy, send a check for $3, payable to Catholic Parent, with a 10-by-13-inch SASE with $1.29 in postage affixed.

Categories: Nonfiction—Children—Family—Religion

CONTACT: Our Sunday Visitor
200 Noll Plaza
Huntington IN 46750
E-mail: cparent@osv.com

Cats & Kittens Magazine

Cats & Kittens Magazine is your source for the very best about cats and the people who love them.

Payment: The compensation structure is 10 cents a word on the final edited published word count, payable upon publication of the article. Short articles are defined as 500 to 1,000 words, and features are defined as 1,200 to 2,000 words.

Photography and Editorial Guidelines

Dog & Kennel, *Cats & Kittens* and *Bird Times* are published bimonthly. These magazines contain beautiful full-color photographs, informative, authoritative and educational articles about the species and their care. The articles are written to educate and entertain the readers. In addition to articles on popular species, we include human-interest stories. The magazines contain columns dealing with training, questions and answers, grief, horoscopes, snips of information from the Internet, art and collectibles and special reports.

Photo Needs

Color photography of publication quality is required. Slides or transparencies are preferred.

We are always looking for photographs of common pet birds such as cockatiels, parakeets, lovebirds, canaries, finches, doves and pigeons, and softbills—plus other exotics such as Amazons, cockatoos and macaws. Natural or colored portraiture type backgrounds are acceptable. Interactive people-bird shots are needed. In addition to portrait-type shots, we have an ongoing need for attractive photos of birds in household situations—in their cage, on a playpen, eating, bathing, etc. as well as clutches and baby birds in all stages of growth.

Photographs of all breeds of purebred dogs, random bred dogs and rare breeds in all life stages of growth from puppy through veteran years. Photographs are needed of dogs performing tasks for which they were bred, engaging in sports with their owners or sports developed specifically for dogs such flyball, interactive people-dog shots, portrait-type shots, attractive shots in all types of situations. Photos may be of dogs alone, with kids, adults and other dogs and animals.

Photographs of all breeds of cats, pedigreed as well as non-pedigreed in all life stages of growth from kitten through veteran years. Photographs are needed of cats in all types of situations. Photos may be of cats alone, with kids, adults and other cats and animals.

All material should be labeled with the breed of dog, cat or bird, the telephone number, name and address of the photographer. Note: photographer is responsible for correctly identifying the breeds/species of dogs, cats or birds in the photos. Photographs identified incorrectly in print due to photographers error cannot be paid.

We prefer to hold submissions on file for at least three months. Slides and transparencies intended for future consideration will be scanned to a CD-ROM and photographers' material will be returned.

Payment

Payment is upon publication. Fee for inside usage/partial page is $25; for inside usage/full page, $50; for cover usage, $150.

Freelance Editorial Submissions

Submissions for consideration may cover all aspects of dogs, cats and birds including breed/species profiles, breeder-kennel profiles, medical-technical articles, training, humorist, stories of pet dogs, cats and birds that go to work with their owners, heroic tales, etc.

The compensation structure is 10 cents a word on the final edited published word count, payable upon publication of the article. Short articles are defined as 500 to 1,000 words, and features are defined as 1,200 to 2,000 words.

Upon acceptance of your article, you will be sent a contract for permission to publish.

Categories: Animals

CONTACT: Rita Davis, Executive Editor
7-L Dundas Circle
Greensboro NC 27407
Website: www.catsandkittens.com

The Cattleman

Editorially, *The Cattleman* covers all aspects of the beef industry in Texas, Oklahoma and the Southwest. In the most recent readership survey, subscribers said they were most interested in the following topics in this order: range/pasture, property rights, animal health, water, new innovations and marketing.

Our feature stories are generally more in-depth than other livestock publications. Word counts average between 1,500 to 2,000. We ask all writers to fax their drafts to all sources to verify the accuracy of any quotes before sending the final copy into the office. *The Cattleman* uses AP style for punctuation and grammar, with a few exceptions.

Manuscripts should be e-mailed to ehumphries The Cattleman

Editorially, *The Cattleman* covers all aspects of the beef industry in Texas, Oklahoma and the Southwest. In the most recent readership survey, subscribers said they were most interested in the following topics in this order: range/pasture, property rights, animal health, water, new innovations and marketing.

Our feature stories are generally more in-depth than other livestock publications. Word counts average between 1,500 to 2,000. We ask all writers to fax their drafts to all sources to verify the accuracy of any quotes before sending the final copy into the office. *The Cattleman* uses AP style for punctuation and grammar, with a few exceptions.

Manuscripts should be e-mailed to ehumphries@texas cattleraisers.org and sent as an attachment. Microsoft Word is the preferred format. The deadline is the first of the month, 60 days prior to the issue. Photographs or illustrations are desired; color, black and white, print and slides are all welcome. All people in the photos should be clearly identified.

Most features run in four color. Fees are negotiated and depend upon the amount of research, travel and photography required and terms of payment are on acceptance. *The Cattleman* prefers to work on an assignment basis. However, prospective contributors are urged to write the editor of the magazine to inquire of interest on a proposed subject. Occasionally, the editor will return a manuscript to a potential contributor for cutting, polishing, checking, rewriting or condensing.

Categories: Nonfiction—Animals—Beef Industry—Regional: Texas, Oklahoma, Southwest

CONTACT: Ellen Humphries
The Cattleman

1301 W Seventh St
Fort Worth TX 76102
E-mail: ehumphries@texascattleraisers.org

CC Motorcycle News Magazine

CC Motorcycle News Magazine is always happy to review freelance articles, stories, and poetry, but will only accept unsolicited material that meets the following guidelines:

1. Articles and stories must have a word count of no less than 750 words and no more than 2500 words. Poetry can be of varying lengths (within reason).

2. Articles, stories, and poetry can be about any subject, fiction or non-fiction, as long as the subject pertains to motorcycles or the world of motorcycling. Examples would include fiction or non-fiction stories about traveling cross-country on a motorcycle, biker lifestyle or perspective, motorcycling/biker humor, etc. Poetry can have a serious focus but light or humorous verse is generally preferred. Submissions need not be concerned about the date of the subject — motorcycling is rich in history, and stories about older bikes or past experiences are always welcome. Still, reading the publication thoroughly is the best way to understand what we seek from our writers.

3. Submissions MUST be sent in electronic form, on computer disk, text-only format or .rtf (Interchange Format) for IBM or Mac (Word 5.1 files may be sent as "Normal") or via e-mail with files attached. A printed copy is also welcome but is not necessary. If photos accompany an article or story, a written explanation for each photo MUST also be given. DO NOT write on the back of the photo (use Post-It™ notes or peel and stick labels). Identify the event, the motorcycles (if they are the subjects), and all people whose faces can be seen.

4. We will gladly return all submissions for which a SASE is provided.

We purchase all rights then license them back to you for $1.00 — this is because we need to own all rights for our copyright but also want to allow you to sell your work to other markets. Payment is $150 maximum for stories with photos from regular contributors; $10 minimum to $100 for all others depending on quality and need for editing. Tearsheets or contributor copies will be provided with payment. Payment is made at or within 30 days of publication.

Copies of current or past issues are available for $3.00 or you can read past articles on our website: www.motorcyclenews.cc.

Categories: Fiction—Nonfiction—Automobiles—Humor—Lifestyle—Short Stories—Travel

CONTACT: Mark Kalan
Material: All
Motomag Corp.
PO Box 808
Nyack NY 10960
Phone: 845-353-MOTO (6686)
Fax: 845-353-5240
E-mail: CCMNeditor@yahoo.com
E-mail: mark@motorcylenews.cc
Website: www.motorcylenews.cc

Cemetery Dance

Fiction: Horror, dark mystery, and suspense short stories up to 5,000 words. Query for longer material. We want tales that are powerful and emotional—creepy, chilling, disturbing, and moody. Suspense/mystery/crime tales with a horror element are always welcome. Both supernatural and psychological stories are fine. Most common reasons for rejection are: lack of power, lack of originality, slow pacing, poor writing, boring themes. Read the magazine, see what type of fiction we are publishing—don't submit with a blind eye!

Submission Format: Send us manuscript and SASE. No electronic submissions. Simultaneous submissions are okay, if noted in cover letter. Authors outside the United States should send disposable manuscripts with a business sized SAE and proper US postage. US postage can be purchased online at usps.com from anywhere in the world. No IRCs, please.

Response Time: Averages 2-4 months.

Artwork: We solicit all our cover and interior artwork directly. Query first with samples.

Payment: Professional rates, minimum of five cents per word, plus two contributor copies. Payable within 30 days of publication. Up to 5,000 words; maximum payment of $250. All rights revert to the author upon publication.

Reading Period: We are open to submissions year round.

Please do not send any email submissions, proposals, or pitches.

If you have a book, disk, or other product that you'd like to have considered for review in *Cemetery Dance*, please send copies to each of the addresses below.

Categories: Fiction—Crime—Horror—Mystery—Short Stories

CONTACT: Robert Morrish
ATTN: CD Reviews
22393 Old Logging Rd
Los Gatos CA 95033
CONTACT: Richard Chizmar
ATTN: CD Reviews
PO Box 623
Forest Hill MD 21050

Central PA Magazine

EDITORIAL FOCUS

The central heartland of Pennsylvania ranges from rural expanses and small-town charm to vibrant cities with surprisingly diverse populations and cultural offerings. It's home to the state capital and Amish country, firehouse barbecues and world-class arts centers, ubiquitous outdoor recreation and a bustling economy. To sample the life of the region each month, *Central PA* magazine expresses a downhome knowledge of its territory with a sophisticated eye and literate writing. Our writers tell the stories of the region's people, history, places and events in intelligent prose and experiential narratives. Our storytelling component is tempered by analytical pieces on issues and initiatives that affect the region or informational articles about lifestyle trends that enable our readers to make better use of all the region has to offer.

MONTHLY FEATURES

Central Shorts and Central Stories comprise our opener section, with glances (175-750 words) into useful, suprising or quirky aspects of life in the region — the joys and trials of working as a costumed Hershey candy character, a look into the state treasury's mysterious underground vault, a visit to a ferret-rescue shelter or a local computer security firm with international scope. It's spiced with occasional quotes from the region's newspapers, mini-reviews of local books or CDs, or interesting local websites we've noticed.

In our departments, Opinion addresses an overlooked or unique angle on some aspect of state, local or national politics or public affairs. Our Essay department showcases the musings of some of the best writers in the region, on virtually any topic — humorous, serious, reflective or analytical, but always a good read. Our interview feature, Cameo, presents a monthly encounter with an interesting *Central PA* resident, from an opera singer to a rock vocalist, from the matron of a soft-pretzel empire to a female boxer.

Thirty Days is our events calender, highlighting noteworthy goings-on in 18 counties, plus a sprinkling of happenings in nearby urban areas.

Food is essential to identity in the region that invented shoofly pie, where (mostly locally produced) potato chips and pretzels take up a whole aisle in the grocery store, and where new dining establishments seem to be opening almost daily. Anchoring our Food section is The Phantom Diner, in which our anonymous restaurant critic sits down at one the region's tables each month and reports on the experience in detail. We also elicit a recipe and some thoughts on cooking from a *Central PA* chef each month, review cookbooks, provide entertaining tips and give a nod to local markets and drinking establishments.

A local duo of world-class puzzle creators whose credits include Atlantic Monthly and the Boston Globe supplies our crossword on *Central PA* themes.

ANNUAL FEATURES

In January, *Central PA* releases its much-awaited annual Dining Guide, with more than 1,000 restaurants throughout the region, picked by our readers as places where they like to eat. Winners are chosen in dozens of categories, including best overall restaurant in the region.

Our July issue is our annual Insider's Guide, giving natives and visitors alike a portrait of our 18-county region's offerings in the arts, educational and historic sites, tourist attractions and festivals, nightlife, day-trips, sports and outdoor recreation.

We finish off the year with a bow to the Best of *Central PA*, a lighthearted look by a panel of writers and editors at things throughout the region that stand out in their admittedly arbitrary categories.

WRITERS' GUIDELINES

Central PA magazine, a publication of WITF, Inc., is a general-interest regional magazine serving more than 43,000 families in 18 counties of Central Pennsylvania.

SUBJECT MATTER & POLICIES:

Central PA magazine publishes feature articles about interesting people, places, cultural and social issues, and activities that relate to life in Central Pennsylvania. The editorial content also includes essays, Q&As and short articles reviewing or discussing books, theater, music, news, food, dining, sports and outdoors. Features should be of broad interest, have a strong regional connection and be based on more than one source. The editors seek writing that is lively and literate. Writers must submit source information for fact-checking and be willing to work closely with editors before, during and after the submission process. Article lengths in the magazine range from 175-word vignettes to 3,000-word feature articles, although queries for the shorter pieces are much more likely to meet our editorial needs.

SUBMISSIONS:

Written queries are required for all articles and should be sent via mail, fax or e-mail to the attention of—Steve Kennedy, Senior Editor.

Telephone queries will not be accepted. Submissions will be considered on speculation only from writers with whom *Central PA* magazine has not previously worked. Articles are assigned by contract to established writers.

Revised 9/5/01

Categories: Nonfiction—Arts—Cooking—Culture—Education—Entertainment—Environment—Family—Food/Drink—Gardening—Health—History—Interview—Lifestyle—Multicultural—Outdoors—Regional

CONTACT: Steve Kennedy, Senior Editor
Material: All
CONTACT: Tracy Erb, Managing Editor
Material: All
WITF, Inc.
1982 Locust Lane
Harrisburg PA 17109
Phone: 717-221-2800 or 800-366-9483
Fax: 717-221-2630
E-mail: centralpa@centralpa.org
Website: www.centralpa.org

Remember: Editors change jobs and publishers change addresses. It is wise to invest in a phone call for the current information before submitting.

Ceramics Monthly

The following information is intended to serve as a guide for the submission of materials for publication in *Ceramics Monthly* magazine. If you have additional questions, please contact the editorial department: telephone (614) 895-4213; e-mail editorial@ceramicsmonthly.org.

About *Ceramics Monthly*

Recognized as "the world's most widely read ceramic arts magazine," *Ceramics Monthly* engages a wide variety of readers. Artists/potters, educators, students, gallery and museum personnel, and collectors alike enjoy full-color articles on studio artists/potters and exhibition coverage, as well as news, commentary and process-oriented articles.

Who Writes for *Ceramics Monthly*?

Our authors come from many walks of life. Although most are directly associated with ceramics, we also receive manuscripts from engineers, chemists, art critics, historians, collectors, publicists and others who have a topic of interest to CM subscribers.

What Kinds of Articles Are Needed?

Because of our readers' diverse interests, many kinds of articles are accepted, but the following categories are typical of what CM publishes most:

Profiles

This is perhaps the most popular article format in *Ceramics Monthly*. We prefer first-person accounts covering the full range of the potter's or sculptor's experience, including aesthetic concerns, business practices, technical data, etc. See "A Lot to Think About" by Craig Martell (May 2002) or "Intentional Serendipity" by Scott Ruescher (November 2001) as examples.

• Informational Articles: CM publishes a range of articles relating to the making and selling of ceramic art and craft. These include such topics as recipes for glazes and clay bodies, forming methods, innovative processes, studio layout and production flow, business practices, ceramics history, and ceramics in higher education. Technical articles on the leading edge of the field are also welcome.

• News and Exhibition Articles: Submissions concerning exhibitions, workshops, symposia and other ceramics-related events should include the location, date, names of the presenters/exhibitors (with their complete mailing addresses) and a description of the work(s) shown. Additional information (such as artists' statements, clay and glaze recipes, or details about forming or decorating techniques) may be of interest to a larger audience, thus increasing chances for publication.

For exhibition reviews, we prefer texts that include critical analysis of the work (what makes it good, bad, innovative, controversial, etc.), as well as pertinent background information of value to potters, ceramics sculptors, students and educators, and collectors. Publishable images of each work discussed must accompany the text.

• Commentary: Well-reasoned, substantiated thoughts on any ceramic craft- and art-related issues are particularly sought for the Comment column. (Responses to previous Comments are not eligible, but may be submitted to the Letters column.)

Manuscript Preparation

The average manuscript ranges from 750 to 1500 words. Thus, it should be approximately 2 to 6 pages, typed double-spaced with ample margins. Please place your name, mailing address, telephone/fax number and e-mail address (if available) on the title page. Consecutively number each page, including the first. Unillustrated texts or submissions with digital graphics may be e-mailed to editorial@ceramicsmonthly.org, but please mail a printed copy as well. Texts submitted on disk (as a text-only file) should also be accompanied by a printed copy. We will need only one copy of your manuscript, but you may wish to keep a copy for your own reference.

Copyright

We ask for exclusive worldwide rights for the text (both print and electronic versions, including but not limited to publishing on demand, database online services, reprints or books), and nonexclusive rights for use of the photographic materials in print or electronic media.

Payment

We do not pay for news items or exhibition announcements. All other articles receive our standard fee following publication. Current rates are 10¢ per printed word and $25 per image. An article published in the Comment column receives the flat rate of $75.

Images

The quality of images is extremely important in determining manuscript acceptance. Slides and transparencies submitted for publication should be in focus, properly exposed and with a full range of contrast. No part of the work should be completely hidden by shadow. In most cases, the photographer should use a neutral background (typically gray, black, white or earthtones; avoid primary colors). Images of a work-in-progress should all have the same axis (either vertical or horizontal). It is best to submit as many images as possible (including bracketed exposure variations, if available).

• Slides/transparencies: We prefer professional-quality, large-format (2 1/4-inch-square or 4x5-inch) transparencies shot with any low ASA (ISO) film, but we can also work with original (not duplicate) 35mm color slides on a high-resolution film, such as Kodachrome 25 or Ektachrome 64T. Of course, slides or transparencies taken using other film types will also be considered, provided film grain or contrast does not detract from image quality.

• Photographs: Glossy prints in color or black-and-white are also used on occasion, primarily for candid action shots; however, color photocopies and laser prints are not suitable for publication.

• Digital images: We prefer professional digital images for publication. Digital images should be delivered as uncompressed four-color (CMYK), 300 dpi image files (preferably tiff or eps format). Do not e-mail images! Image files should be burned to a CD and mailed to our editorial offices with your complete submission (see address above), or uploaded to our ftp site. Uploaded files must be stuffed or zipped. For instructions and settings, call (614) 895-4213 or e-mail editorial@ceramicsmonthly.org.

Graphics

We also accept drawings for visual explanation of hard-to-photograph tools, equipment and processes, and charts for technical data.

Captions

Caption information should include the title of the work (when applicable), dimensions, specific ceramic medium (e.g., earthenware, stoneware, porcelain, etc.), brief description of forming and glazing techniques, firing temperature or cone, year made, and price (specify retail or wholesale). Number the slide mount or transparency sleeve and list captions with corresponding numbers on a separate sheet of paper.

Credits

Please provide the photographer's name so that credit may be duly noted. Whenever images by more than one photographer are used to illustrate an article, each photo should be identified with the appropriate photographer's name. It is the author's responsibility to secure permission to use photographic materials. CM does not credit collectors or collections.

Sending a Complete Submission

Enclose a cover letter, text, images and any other support materials in one package. Include a self-addressed, padded envelope with sufficient postage if you would like your materials to be returned. Protect the photographic materials with cardboard on both sides, and mark the package "Contains Photographs-Do Not Bend." Mail the package first class to: The Editor, *Ceramics Monthly*, 735 Ceramic Place, Ste 100, Westerville, OH 43081. Timely, unillustrated manuscripts may also be faxed to (614) 891-8960.

Evaluation and Acceptance

When your submission arrives, it will receive immediate attention. A member of the editorial staff will acknowledge receipt and perhaps ask for additional information or images. Once the submission is complete, the editors will consider it for publication.

Acceptance decisions are made at monthly review meetings, after which publication contracts are mailed to the authors. We ask that you give *Ceramics Monthly* exclusive worldwide rights to the text, and nonexclusive rights for any other use of the photographic materials in any other form, such as electronic media, reprints or books. This nonexclusive agreement allows for the continued use of the photographic material in any way the artist chooses after the article has The average time from acceptance to publication is between two months and one year, depending on article length and subject. The author and artist(s) are notified approximately one month prior to publication.

Editing and Proofs

Texts are edited first for style, grammar and punctuation, as well as technical accuracy, then to meet layout requirements. Because changes may take place up to the time the presses roll, we are unable to provide final proofs; however, galley proofs are available on request.

Layout

Article design takes place after initial editing. CM does not accept layouts from authors or subjects.

Copies

Following publication, two complimentary copies of the magazine containing your feature article will be mailed to you; additional copies are available for purchase on a first-come, first-served basis. Authors/subjects of Upfront items receive one complimentary copy.

Categories: Arts—Ceramics—Crafts/Hobbies

CONTACT: Editor
Material: All
735 Ceramic Place, Ste 100
Westerville, OH 43081
Phone: 614-895-4213
Fax: 614-891-8960
E-mail: editorial@ceramicsmonthly.org
Website: www.ceramicsmonthly.org

Cerca

Cerca magazine promotes enjoyment and respect for the region surrounding Las Vegas, primarily within 300 miles, including parts of Nevada, Utah, Arizona, and Southern California. It does not accept material about casinos, resorts, or gambling but is interested in the region's natural beauty and opportunities for outdoor recreation, its wildlife, its small towns, and its history. It seeks free-lance contributions from the best photographers in these fields and from professional writers. Most content is free-lance.

Created by the state's largest newspaper, the Las Vegas Review-Journal, *Cerca* is distributed separately to its own subscriber list, and is sold at bookstores and newsstands. Many subscribers live in Las Vegas, but others live outside the state, so contributors should strive for treatments that seem fresh to both audiences.

Cerca first appeared in October 2001 as a quarterly; in 2003 it will publish six bi-monthly issues.

SUBJECT MATTER

Cerca needs both photos and stories on scenic areas, outdoor adventures, interesting small towns, back road trips, hikes, scientific and educational subjects uniquely linked to this region, Native American people of this region, and a few personalities who have made unique contributions to the region.

Some of the categories for which we will purchase submissions are:

PORTFOLIO - Photo packages about a specific beautiful location easily reached from Las Vegas, or about a subject especially associated with the region. A short text of 200 words may accompany photos, or we can arrange to have it written.

TRAVEL - Photo-heavy packages with longer texts (up to 1500-word narratives, but length will be dictated by subject) concentrating on the experience of visiting an area. Not necessarily first-person but should give details of a specific trip (or trips) by an identified visitor or visitors. Provide the how-tos (minimum includes directions and mileage from Las Vegas, accommodation information, a telephone number for further information, but most writers include restaurants, campgrounds, whatever writer considers useful to visitors)separately, in list form, for display as a sidebar. Include web addresses wherever possible. Sidebar does not count against word limit.

ADVENTURES - Off-beat or high-energy travel stories involving mountain climbing, pack-train travel, whitewater, hang-gliding, etc. at specific locations in this region. Should also meet "Travel" requirements above, but how-to-go box will lean toward campgrounds and climbing information, etc. for a more active reader. Up to 1200 words, plus sidebar.

SETTLEMENTS - Concentrates on some interesting community. Up to 1500 words, plus getting-there sidebar, for town with major attractions, perhaps 800 for a colorful backwater village.

EDUCATIONAL-SCIENTIFIC - Involves archaeology, biology, and other scientific subjects specific to our area. Word length 400-1,200.

HISTORY - Historical events in this region, which should lend themselves to thorough photo documentation. Length 600-1,200 words.

DIRT ROADS, BACK ROADS, AND COWPATHS - Routes off the beaten track to and through interesting places. Must be lawfully negotiable by motor vehicle but not necessarily a 2-wheel-drive sedan; you must specify the kind of vehicle needed and other necessary details, and include with your submission a good map or photocopy thereof, with the route marked on it. (We'll use it to draw our own map for publication.) Up to 1,000 words.

HIKES - Choice hikes, usually of one-day duration, in the region. Narratives of 500-800 words; photos will show the country's appearance. Put how-to details (directions, length of hike in hours and miles, difficulty, time of year to do it, etc.) in separate box for display as sidebar.

WILDLIFE - Short feature on some animal (or bird or fish or insect) of the region. Try to make it multi-dimensional; the most interesting aspect may not be its natural history but its importance in Indian lore, pioneer diet, or effect on its environment. About 800 words.

PERSONALITIES - Profiles of people uniquely associated with region. Have used an Arizona Strip rancher, operator of diner on Rt. 66, and ballerina who performs in Death Valley. About 800 words.

MAN VS. NATURE - A single, outstanding photo juxtaposing the presence of man with a spectacular and/or beautiful natural setting in our region. These photos will always be given full-page display. A caption is the only text required, but if there's an anecdote about how you got this picture, send it along and we'll try to use that also.

AROUND THE BEND -Tidbits (100-400 words) about regional history, plants, artifacts, and outdoor lore.

PHOTO REQUIREMENTS

Photos must be of high professional quality and we prefer large-format transparencies. Black-and-white may be acceptable for historical pieces. We cannot work from color negatives or prints, or digital images, at this time. Stories and photos are often bought as a package. However, all categories of photos and stories are accepted separately with *Cerca* management assuming responsibility for arranging the other half of the package. But to appear in *Cerca*, every story should lend itself to outstanding photography.

Please do not send photos or manuscripts until we have answered your query. Telephone queries okay in case of looming deadlines.

QUERY EARLY FOR SEASONAL STORIES

Ideally, photos and stories are suitable to the season in which they appear, so contributors seeking assignments should submit queries and be prepared to cover the subject a year ahead of publication. This is why we tend to pay on acceptance for assigned work.

Cerca also buys many stock photos, as well as stories based upon the writer's earlier experiences. *Cerca* normally buys first North American Rights, and expects original work, but occasionally considers previously published material.

TERMS OF SALE

Terms of each sale are arranged individually.

In most cases contributors cover an assignment for a pre-arranged fee and work at their own pace. Rarely, *Cerca* agrees to pay day rate, $500 for photographers and $300 for writers. By prearrangement, *Cerca* pays reasonable expenses but requires documentation.

Cerca pays a fee agreed upon in advance taking into account the importance of the story and the perceived difficulty of doing it. We do not pay by the word; however, for purposes of comparison to other markets, that payment has usually worked out to 35-80 cents per published word.

Front Cover $480; Man vs. Nature $350; 2-page spread $350
Full page plus $280; Full page $200; Half page plus $120
Minimum $100
Internet use:
Reused from magazine $25
Assigned photos by negotiation

TIMELY PAYMENT

On package deals where the amount owed is clear upon acceptance, we pay at that point. In cases where the amount owed depends on flexible factors such as number of photos we select or display we are able to give them, we will pay promptly on publication.

Categories: Nonfiction—Adventure—Education—Nature—Travel—Wildlife

CONTACT: A.D. Hopkins, editor
Cerca magazine
PO Box 1600
Las Vegas NV 89125-1600
Phone: 702-383-0270.
E-mail: ad@cercamagazine.com

Change
The Magazine of Higher Learning

SCOPE

Change is a magazine dealing with contemporary issues in higher learning. It is intended to stimulate and inform reflective practitioners in colleges, universities, corporations, government, and elsewhere. Using a magazine format, rather than that of an academic journal, *Change* spotlights trends, provides new insights and ideas, and analyzes the implications of educational programs, policies, and practices.

Over the past few years it has included articles on trend-setting institutions and individuals, innovative teaching methods, technology, liberal learning, the curriculum, the financing and management of higher education, for-profit and entrepreneurial higher education, faculty, the changing needs and nature of students, the undergraduate experience, administrative practice and governance, public policy, accountability, and the social role of higher education. The topics of the coming year's issues can be found on the Heldref Website, at http://www.heldref.org/. We encourage you to submit articles—whether brief expressions of a point of view (750 to 1,500 words) or more extended articles of from 2,500 to 5,000 words—on one of those topics or on others of current importance to higher education.

AUDIENCE

Change, which is published six times a year, is intended for individuals responsible for higher learning in college, university, and other settings, including faculty, administrators, trustees, state and federal officials, and students, as well as corporation, union, and foundation officers.

MANUSCRIPTS

Owned by Heldref Publications, a division of the nonprofit Helen Dwight Reid Education Foundation in Washington, *Change* is one of the 43 journals and magazines published by Heldref. The magazine staff at Heldref includes a full-time managing editor, Nanette Wiese, and an associate editor, Lea Pasternak. It is to Heldref that you direct all manuscripts, letters to the editor, and queries about guidelines for writers, as well as questions about advertising and subscriptions. (See below for relevant contact information.)

All manuscripts must be submitted in hard copy, on 8 1/2" x 11" paper, 12 point font, double spaced, with one inch margins, and page numbers, in triplicate. If the article is accepted, we will request an electronic copy of the article.

Because *Change* is a magazine rather than a journal, footnotes should not be included. References can be worked into the text or given parenthetically when necessary. A short list of "Related Readings" or "Resources" can be provided with the article where appropriate, and URLs can be provided for Web sites containing more extensive documentation.

A separate title page should provide short biographical information (up to four or five lines) and contact information, including the complete address, telephone, and fax number, and e-mail of the author(s). The first-named author of a multi-authored article will receive the notification of acceptance, rejection, or need for revision.

REVIEW PROCESS

When we receive your manuscript, we will send you a postcard verifying that your article has entered the review process. All manuscripts are read first by Barbara Cambridge to determine their suitability for *Change*. If the fit is not good, you will hear within six weeks. Those that are promising she sends to two consulting editors, who evaluate them for accuracy, argument, style, and interest to the readership. Barbara reads returned reviews to assign those that are positive to another executive editor. This process takes from three to four months to complete. (Should the manuscript be held for longer than usual, you will be notified at the end of four months and offered the option of withdrawing the manuscript from consideration.)

If the article is accepted, you will be contacted to discuss editing procedures and the production schedule for the issue of the magazine in which your article will appear. Each author receives six complimentary copies of the issue in which the article is included. Authors may also order additional copies or reprints (minimum order of 100) at their expense.

Manuscripts should be submitted exclusively to this publication.

CONTRIBUTING TO *Change*

By agreement with Heldref, AAHE is responsible for all editorial judgments about the magazine: its themes, articles, and editorial voice. AAHE exercises that judgment through a team of four executive editors—Barbara Cambridge, Cheryl Fields, Peter Ewell, and Margaret Miller.

Even the best manuscripts compete for limited space: We publish just six times a year and given that many of the articles are solicited, we can use but 20 or so of the hundreds of manuscripts submitted. What accounts for acceptance or rejection? Topics that have been exhausted (the culture wars) or that are too broad (the history of universities in 2,000 words or less) or too specific for our broad audience (preventing dormitory theft) will not be published, nor will those written in the style of a journal—heavy on jargon and footnotes, light on analysis and point of view.

This last criterion is important. *Change* is a magazine, and the magazine article is a genre unto itself. A good article compels attention to an important matter. It shows a mind at work, one that reaches judgment and takes a stance. It is credible: it knows its subject and the context. And it is concrete: It names people, places, dates, and events. For a good idea of the kind of writing that works for *Change*, we encourage you to read a few past issues.

Change doesn't start with an ideological predisposition; we court good ideas from all sides. But tracts, broadsides, and grand plans seldom impress reviewers (or readers), who prefer real, usable ideas that someone has actually tried out and evaluated.

Beyond writing for *Change*, we encourage you to write to the magazine. Feedback is not plentiful in the magazine business, and any reader comment gets full attention. Your reactions to what we publish help your editors make *Change* better and more valuable for all of us.

—Barbara Cambridge, Cheryl Fields, Peter Ewell, and Margaret Miller

Categories: Nonfiction—College—Education

CONTACT: Managing Editor
Material: All

Heldref Publications
1319 Eighteenth Street, NW
Washington DC 20036-1802
Phone: 202-296-6267, Ext 222
Fax: 202-296-5149
E-mail: ch@heldref.org
Website: www.aahe.org/change

Charleston Magazine

Charleston Magazine has been a Low-country institution for more than 30 years, distilling the essence of Charleston and her outlying districts into a lively, informative, entertaining, and sophisticated resource. We welcome submissions and story proposals. These guidelines are intended to help writers match their story ideas to our editorial mission.

All articles must have a direct and obvious connection to Charleston. Ideally, each focuses on someone or something special to Charleston and contributes to a better understanding of this community's unique identity.

Typical issues of *Charleston* include articles on outstanding houses and gardens; notable residents; significant Charleston businesses and institutions; social and political issues facing Low country residents; local history, artists, and architecture; wildlife, natural history, and environmental research; antiques, wine, and food; and natural and cultural points of interest within the county. Stories with a visual nature are preferred. Articles range in length from 500-word profiles to 2,000-word features. We also publish illuminating personal narratives and reminiscences, think-pieces on Charleston subjects and occasional short fiction.

The pages of each bimonthly issue of *Charleston Magazine* deliver editorial and artistic excellence in a glossy, four-color format.

Editorial Content:

Profiles of the region's most provocative and influential personalities. Thorough reporting on issues and concerns facing Low country residents today. Beautifully photographed, in-depth features revealing the subtle charms of our Low country lifestyle: uniquely beautiful homes and gardens, the natural beauty of the Low country and its environmental issues, our rich histories and traditions, and the lively arts community and cultural institutions.

Departments:

Channel Markers: Charleston's newsy snippets including The Insider and Mystery History.

Style File: Local style and fashion layouts for him, her, and home.

Local Seen: Outstanding, colorful Low country characters.

Southern View: Humorous first-person essays on life in the Low country.

In Good Taste/Chef at Home: Revolving departments featuring regional chefs, culinary trends, and recipes.

Fête Set: The Charleston social scene benefits good causes.

CityScape: A comprehensive guide to arts and events in Charleston: performing arts, visual arts and architecture, literary and cultural events, weddings, dining guides, sports and nature, family and youth activities, and special charitable events.

More! photo essays, history, and local weddings.

Categories: Nonfiction—Architecture—Arts—General Interest—Lifestyle—Regional

CONTACT: Darcy Shankland, Editor
Material: All
782 Johnnie Dodds Blvd., Suite C
Mt. Pleasant SC 29464
Phone: 843-971-9811
Fax: 843-971-0121
E-mail: dshankland@charlestonmag.com
Website: charlestonmag.com

The Chattahoochee Review
Georgia Perimeter College

The Chattahoochee Review pays $25.00 per Chattahoochee page for fiction, $20.00 per Chattahoochee page for essays, $100 per omnibook review, $50.00 per review of a single book, $100.00 per interview, and $50.00 per poem.

The aim of The *Chattahoochee Review* is to encourage unacknowledged writers and to provide printing space for published authors, striking a balance between the two. We are open to poetry and prose, both fiction and nonfiction. The *Chattahoochee Review* is copyrighted in its entirety. However, we are happy to grant reprint rights upon written request; we require only that the Review receive printed acknowledgement as first publisher.

All manuscripts should be typed. Prose should be double-spaced, and poetry should be single-spaced within stanzas, and double-spaced between stanzas. One poem to a page, please. Send originals or clear photocopies. The author's name, address, telephone numbers (including fax number, and e-mail address if available) should appear on the first page of each poem or prose piece. Send no more than one short story or nonfiction piece and no more than five (5) poems per submission. Your cover letter should provide sufficient information for us to compile a two- to three-sentence biography for our "Notes on Contributors" page, should the work be accepted. Do not send any work that is being simultaneously submitted to other publishers. Submit only work that has not been previously published.

Reviews: We usually review the categories that we publish: collections of poems or short stories. If you are submitting an omnibook review, please submit more of an essay than just a review-a piece that reflects the writer's other books and other relevant information. Please give the review a title inclusive of the book's title and provide the following bibliographic information: title of piece, author, title of book, publisher, date, number of pages, price.

Interviews: We are interested in a wide range of subjects, but favor interviews with notable Southern authors. If you wish to interview a writer for The *Chattahoochee Review*, please contact the editor.

Essays: We prefer literary essays that focus on aesthetics, essays that are intelligent, insightful, and artful. We also welcome essays that address literary trends and activities. Submissions of personal essays should reveal human truths in evocative styles: essays in the traditions of Thoreau, Monette, and Rodriguez-masters of the personal essay. The human experience is powerful, especially if shared with beautiful language, honest reflection, and clear prose.

Subscriptions: $20.00 per year, $30.00 for two years, $6.00 per copy.

Categories: Fiction—Nonfiction—Arts—Book Reviews—Literature—Poetry—Short Stories

CONTACT: Marc Fitten, Editor
Material: Any
CONTACT: Jo Ann Yeager Adkins, Managing Editor
Material: Any
2101 Womack Rd.
Dunwoody GA 30338
Phone: 770-274-5145

Chef
The Food Magazine for Professionals

Chef magazine, "The Food Magazine for Professionals," focuses almost exclusively on food preparation and presentation for the modern chef and cook.

That's why we scheduled more than 100 food-related focuses in 2000. To that end, a writer for *Chef* should have a thorough knowledge of the food service industry and, more specifically, the needs of chefs and cooks in both commercial and noncommercial kitchens. Occasionally, we are happy to work with established writers with strong food backgrounds who may be less familiar with the food service industry, but are eager to learn.

Manuscripts for *Chef* magazine:
• speak to the professional, not the cooking enthusiast.
• tend to be short, usually no longer than 1,500 words; 1,200 words (including sidebar) is an average length. Our audience has little time to read, so we have to package features economically.
• usually feature a number of chefs in both commercial and noncommercial operations executing a particular application(s) or preparing a certain type or style of dish in a variety of markets nationwide.
• are light on basic information or instruction (such as history of an ingredient or how to prepare something simple or commonplace) and heavy on application, particularly novel or unique preparations and presentations. Our audience is almost solely professional, and mostly comprised of individuals who work in establishments grossing $1 million or more in F&B sales. We reach a negligible number of students.

Chef magazine does NOT accept:
• first-person editorials.
• travel features, except in very few cases, and then only when they have a strong cooking-application focus. (No "I dined on this here and on that there…")
• everything-you-wanted-to-know manuscripts on raw ingredients (garlic, pecans, watermelon, et al.).
• profiles of people or institutions, except when the angle is unusual and entertaining, and then only when that angle includes a strong cooking-application focus.
• manuscripts from representatives of entities selling a product or service.
• manuscripts on industry issues, except when real or potential impact on working chefs is considerable, and then only when they haven't been covered greatly in like publications or when the angle is unique.
• manuscripts on non-food-preparation topics such as management issues, computer software or the Internet, personal financial management, lifestyle issues and the like.

A few tips:
• Request our editorial calendar. We are committed to most of the focuses we plan for the year. We are interested, however, in topics not on the calendar, but you'll want to determine whether they've already been covered this year or soon will be.
• Read a sample issue or two to review our focus and style.
• Query with an idea in writing first, with published clips. Please include a daytime telephone number where you can be reached. Include in your letter why the topic you propose is of interest to our readers. Also, please make us aware of availability of color photography and the costs, if any, of such.

Payment starts at $300 for first-time North American serial rights, on acceptance, based on the writer's experience, expertise and relationship to our magazine. *Chef* will reimburse telephone and postage expenses. Other expenses must be approved prior to beginning assignment.

"Profiles" Articles Guidelines

Chef magazine "Profiles" are intended to be informational and educational articles that illustrate the breadth and variety of expertise in the culinary community. These articles identify the chefs who are influencing the industry, the new trends, and new upbeat ideas. These articles should inspire the reader through a clear description of the fresh and useful ideas of the chef being profiled. Profile articles "let the chef do the talking." Finished articles are approximately 750 words.

The "Profile" focuses attention on the chef's career by describing:
• Background;
• How the chef came to the industry;

- Mentors;
- Why the chef remains in the industry;
- Exciting accolades of the chef;
- What the chef is doing now;
- Areas of special interest;
- How he/she approaches challenges; and
- What he/she sees for the future.

The "Profile" article describes the chef's dishes by discussing:
- Some of the chef's techniques;
- Important steps in his/her procedures;
- The ingredients; and
- Advice and tips.

Artwork:

Artwork should reflect the personality of the chef. Authors are expected to provide suitable artwork.

A few Don'ts:

Do not include quotes or opinions that are negative or those that can have a deleterious effect on the industry, a supplier, or a market segment. Do not include quotes that reflect a political perspective or personal opinions of products or equipment. That's advertising.

Categories: Food—Design/Decor

CONTACT: Robert Benes, Senior Editor
Material: All
Melanie Wolkoff, Managing Editor
Material: All
20 W. Kinizig, Ste. 1200
Chicago, IL 60610
Phone: 312-849-2220
Fax: 312-849-2174
E-mail: ChefMag@aol.com
Website: www.chefmagazine.com

Chesapeake Family

Writers' Guidelines 2006
Who We Are

Chesapeake Family is a free, monthly parenting publication serving Anne Arundel, Calvert, Bowie and Upper Marlboro areas of Prince George's and Kent Island area in Queen Anne's counties of Maryland.

Who Our Readers Are

We have a circulation of about 40,000 with an estimated 90,000 readers. They get the magazine at schools, libraries, doctors' offices, grocery stores and toy stores. Our readers are parents (mostly moms) of children from the cradle to college age. They're well educated and strive to do the best for their children even as they juggle busy lives and try to watch their budgets. They tend to pick up *Chesapeake Family* initially for the calendar of monthly activities and the sections on health and education.

What We're About

Our goal is to make our readers' everyday lives easier by anticipating the sort of information they will need, identifying and sifting through available resources and gathering it for them so they can just read it and go. We strive to present unique stories that readers won't find in any other local publication.

Our Writing Approach

Our readers may have only 5 minutes over a slice of toast to glance at the magazine so we want to use an easy-to-read, accessible tone but also pack plenty of punch into the few words we get. Through our pages, we want our readers to feel understood, supported and empowered to make healthy parenting and life choices.

What We're Looking For
- We are looking for professional writers who are conscientious and fact check their work.
- Our articles are short (about 1,000 words for a feature and 750 for a column) so pick your main theme and develop it well. Know the main point you want the reader to take away and present it clearly.
- Talk to three local sources considered authorities on the topic at hand.
- Perform all the legwork for the reader and list local resources, answering the obvious questions: Where? When? How much? Whom can I call? What's the number?
- Our magazine serves readers outside of Annapolis (see Who We Are above) so be sure to talk to authorities and include resources in other areas as well.
- Where appropriate, use local, real-life situations and people to illustrate your topic.
- We generally do not run first person or personal essays unless they are unusually compelling.

What We Pay

For assigned articles, we start at $75 and go up to $150. Articles that require more research can generate more. We pay around $35 for reprints but note that we try not to overlap coverage with the other parenting publications in the region: Maryland Family, Baltimore's Child, Washington Families, Washington Parent and ParentLine. We're buying one-time print rights and web rights. Articles are subject to editing for space and clarity. We pay upon publication and sometimes must hold articles over when space is shy. If we assign an article and do not run it for any reason, we will pay a kill fee of $25.

Deadlines and Submissions

Articles are due on the 15th of the month, two months before the publication issue (so articles for the July issue are due on May 15, for example). Please submit your article with a creative title/headline suggestion and brief bio to run at the end. Articles may be submitted as a Word attachment and/or embedded in an e-mail. Attach a separate invoice that includes your name, address, phone number, e-mail address, social security number, the date, title of article and agreed-upon rate.

Unsolicited Articles

We will consider unsolicited articles, but we have very limited space. We encourage writers, especially local ones, who feel strongly that they have a story for *Chesapeake Family* to send a query/outline.

Contacting Us

Preferred method of contact is via e-mail. You may also send faxes.

Categories: Nonfiction—Children—Education—Family—Health—Regional: areas of Maryland

CONTACT: Editor
929 West St Ste 307
Annapolis MD 21401
Fax: 410-280-0255
E-mail: editor@chesapeakefamily.com

Chess Life
School Mates

WRITERS' & PHOTOGRAPHERS' GUIDELINES

Chess Life is the official publication of the United States Chess Federation. Each monthly issue covers news of many major chess events, both here and abroad, with special emphasis on the triumphs and exploits of American players. It also includes regular columns of instruction, general features on chess in other fields (computer science, psychology, art, war, etc.), historical articles, personality profiles, interviews, cartoons, quizzes, and humor.

Of special interest to free-lance writers is the feature section, which can include articles on relatively unknown chess personalities and "chess in everyday life," along with the usual chess news and tournament reports.

There is only one all-encompassing injunction: The game of chess must be central to every item. *Chess Life* readers include everyone from the professional grandmaster to the discerning amateur and hobbyist. Therefore, articles like "My first Chess Tournament" or quizzes containing the names of world champions have all been tried too many times before. We give little or no attention to other games or variants of chess. We no longer publish fiction.

School Mates is the national chess magazine for children. It includes instructional articles, chess news, tournament reports, quizzes, puzzles, humor, tips, cartoons, and pictures. Material is aimed at 8-12 year old beginning to intermediate chess players.

MANUSCRIPTS

Rates: Payment for *Chess Life* is generally $100 per page; a page is generally defined at 800 to 1,000 words. For the computer-minded, the general guide is approximately 5,000 bytes per page.) Writers with IM or GM titles should inquire about special rates. Payment is upon publication. This policy can be changed only under special circumstances.

Payment for *School Mates* is generally $50 per page (80-1000 words). Unsolicited promotional material is not paid.

TABLE FOR MANUSCRIPTS SUBMITTED TO *Chess Life*

The following shows a word count table for rates and dollar amounts based on such:

Size	Word Count	CL Rate
Full Page	900 to 1,100 words	$100 a pg.
2/3 Page	600 to 899 words	$6
1/2 Page	400 to 599 words	$50
1/3 Page	300 to 399 words	$35
1/4 page	200 to 299 words	$25
1/8 page or below	Below 200 words	$15

Writers with IM or GM titles should inquire about special rates. Payment is upon publication. This policy can be changed only under special circumstances.

TABLE FOR MANUSCRIPTS SUBMITTED TO *School Mates*

The following shows a word count table for rates and dollar amounts based on such:

Size	Word Count	SM Rate
Full Page	600 to 899 words	$50 a pg.
2/3 Page	450 to 599 words	$30
1/2 Page	300 to 449 words	$25
1/3 Page or below	Below 300 words	$10 or negotiable with editor

Writers with IM or GM titles should inquire about special rates. Payment is upon publication. This policy can be changed only under special circumstances.

Rights: All rights are reserved unless otherwise negotiated at the time the article is accepted.

Form: Submissions should be made on diskette (3½" or Zip and IBM compatible) or e-mailed. Word Perfect and Microsoft Word are acceptable word processing programs. If you don't have access to either, .txt or ASCII format is fine. Hard copy (printout) should be sent with the diskette.

The writer should include full name, address, telephone number, and e-mail address on the first page. Subsequent pages should include a short title and page number. Chess notation should be in simple algebraic (1. e4 e5 2.f4 exf4, etc.). Descriptive is, however, acceptable.

Getting in Touch: Unsolicited manuscripts, on speculation, are welcomed, but queries with clippings of the writer's previous work are preferred. No queries are necessary for fiction. Unsolicited manuscripts and query contents are not returned.

PHOTOGRAPHS

Inside: Chess Life: Black-and-white, one-time use: $25; color, one-time use: $35. *School Mates*: $25 for first time rights; $15 for each subsequent use. Additional photograph rights will be negotiated by the photographer and the editor.

Covers: Chess Life - up to $300. *School Mates* - up to $150 in special cases. All rights may be negotiated.

Format: Black-and-white: 5x7 or 8x10 glossies. Color: Slides are preferred, but 5x7 or 8x10 glossies are acceptable. FULL NAME MUST BE INCLUDED ON THE BACK OF EACH PHOTO. If this remains undone, we take no responsibility for either payment or for giving photo credit. Address and telephone number of the photographer must also accompany submissions. Captions and, when necessary,

model releases must accompany each picture.

Getting in Touch: Unsolicited work, on speculation, is welcomed, but queries with contract sheets, samples, or clippings are preferred. Unsolicited photographs and query contents are not returned.

OTHER MATERIALS

Unsolicited cartoons, poems, puzzles and fillers submitted on speculation are welcomed. Payment is generally $25 upon acceptance for initial work. Subsequent work paid on publication. Rights purchased are the same as those for manuscripts. Cartoonists may submit sketches with captions and samples of published work. Unsolicited materials are not returned.

Contact Editor Peter Kurzdorfer for further information on *Chess Life* and *School Mates* (845) 562-8350 ext. 152 magazines@uschess.org

Categories: Children—Games—Sports/Recreation—Young Adult

CONTACT: Peter Kurzdorfer, Editor
Material: Chess
CONTACT: Jean Bernice, Editorial Asst.
Material: Chess
CONTACT: Jami Anson, Sr. Art Director
Material: Art, Photos
United States Chess Federation, 3054 US Route 9W
New Windsor NY 12553-7698
Phone: 845-562-8350, ext 152
E-mail: 845-236-4852
Website: magazines@uschess.org

Chicago Magazine

A major magazine that covers a wide metropolitan area with a limited number of articles each month has to be highly selective about what it prints. Naturally, articles written with our readers in mind will interest us most. Our typical readers live along the lakefront or in other affluent communities, mainly in the suburbs. They have had more than four years of college and hold unusually high-paying jobs, often professional or managerial. Many are parents. They are well read and are interested in the arts and social issues. They go out several times a week to the city's theatres, music halls, and restaurants. They travel widely.

Procedures. Usually we assign or buy articles only after they have been discussed in editorial conferences, so put your queries in writing and send us samples of your best published work. In your query, tell us why you think your idea would interest our particular readers and why you are especially well qualified to write it.

Should we assign the story, you will be contacted by an articles editor, who will negotiate deadline and payment and outline the main features of the article we expect to receive. We will then send you a contract to sign and return.

Payment is on acceptance. What we pay depends on the length of your manuscript, the extent and nature of your research, and the importance we attach to the subject. You will be reimbursed for all reasonable expenses. *Although we have paid both more and less, the following ranges will give you an idea of our rates:*

- Feature articles (including sidebars) $350-$1,500
- Supplemental sidebars $150- $250
- Short articles (columns) $275- $600
- Standards. These are not hard-and-fast rules, and they don't apply to every article. If you have questions, discuss them with your articles editor.

1. A well-organized story usually answers a single question-often a very simple one. You may not know what it is at first, but after a little research you and your articles editor should be able to formulate one, and the answer ought to be the core of your story.

2. Your research should help you support a point of view. Your story is less likely to be successful if you merely present all sides of an issue and hope that the reader will discern the truth, or if you force a

point of view that is not substantiated by your research, or if you tailor your research to validate a preconception.

3. A good magazine story is a good story. It doesn't just describe a state of affairs. It tells how and why the situation came about, who was instrumental in making it happen, what it means to the reader, and what the future holds. Often, novelistic devices can be effective: description, narrative, anecdote, dialogue, sensory detail. But if the situation in the story is not intrinsically interesting or does not have consequences that affect our readers, it might not be appropriate for us.

4. A good story usually focuses on individuals. Although institutions take action, it is ultimately individuals who make them act and whose lives are affected. A writer can make almost any story more vivid, and even more truthful, by concentrating on the people involved-their personalities, backgrounds, and motives-on what they stood to gain and lose, and on how they fared.

5. Good stories are rewritten stories. Our readers' time is limited; your manuscript should be a distilled version of your original draft. Remember: We don't pay by the word.

6. Above all, a good magazine story is believable and fair. Any person or institution whose character or actions have been impugned by the author or by anyone quoted in the article has a right to rebut those charges within the article. If that person or institution declines comment, say so in your story. Chicago magazine's libel insurance does not cover free-lance writers.

Chicago Magazine does not publish fiction, poetry or cartoons.

Categories: Fiction—Nonfiction—Literature—Poetry—Regional—Short Stories—Writing

CONTACT: Senior Editor
Material: All
CONTACT: Andrew Rathmann, Editor
Material: Nonfiction
5801 S. Kenwood Ave.
Chicago IL 60637
Phone: 773-702-0887
Fax: 773-702-0887
Website: www.chicagomagazine.com

Chicago Parent

Chicago Parent seeks to include new voices and is happy to respond to queries, although we strongly prefer local writers. Articles submitted by writers who have not previously written for *Chicago Parent* are on speculation. We offer a lively editorial mix with a distinctly local focus and a "we're all in this together" spirit. This includes:

Short stuff is the port of entry for new writers. If you haven't written for *Chicago Parent*, chances are we'll ask you to start here. It is a section in the front of the magazine that looks at local people, places and things of interest to families. Several readers who started with Short stuff, graduated to writing book reviews and went on to other feature stories. We ask first-time writers to pitch us an idea so we can tell if you are familiar with the magazine. Some writers prefer to submit the full article on speculation, but there is no guarantee of publication.

Feature articles tackle a wide range of timely topics for local families, including issues relating to childcare and education, balancing work and family and handling the everyday joys and challenges of parenting. We ask writers to use the best experts on a subject—national and local, but almost every story should use local parent voices. We also publish profiles of remarkable local people and institutions, interviews of local parenting experts, reviews of parenting books and whimsical looks at the lives of typical Chicago parents. Typically, these are assigned but we will look at submissions. The Museums column also offers opportunities to writers.

Reader essays are 800-word pieces about all aspects of parenting. We welcome submissions from local writers only, on speculation.

Our regular columns are written by freelancers who have a long standing relationship and a contract with *Chicago Parent*. They are Everyday amazements, our parenting essay; Smart love, our parenting Q&A column; Healthy child, covering health issues; Tweens and teens, advice on the later years; Going places, our comprehensive calendar of family events and guide to local parenting resources, and Kid culture, where we review books, videos, music, software and Web sites and the arts.

Basics
Queries and Pitches
Send to Susy Schultz, editor, at address below. Please include clips, a resume, your phone number and e-mail.

Payment
Short stuff articles are 200 to 400 words in length, payment is $25. Museums are about 500 words; payment is $50. Reader essays pay $100 for 800 words. The average feature story is 800 to 2,500 words in length. Payment varies depending on the writer's experience and the relationship with *Chicago Parent*, but begins at $100 for a one-page story of 800 words. We pay on publication. Checks are disbursed on the first day of the month of the publication. Invoices are necessary only for the writer's record keeping.

Illustrations
Chicago Parent also purchases illustrations to accompany articles. Payment depends upon the quantity.

Rights
We buy one-time print publication rights for *Chicago Parent* and an exclusive for Illinois parenting publications. We also purchase the electronic rights and may place material on our Web site. If we choose to reprint an article in one of our other publications, such as the semi-annual *Chicago Baby*, we pay an additional 20 percent of the original manuscript payment. If we successfully place the material in another parenting publication, we pass along half of our earnings to the writer. (Writers are free to sell their work after we publish it. If there ever is a question about who is responsible for getting it published elsewhere, all payment goes to the writer.)

Submissions
Articles should be submitted electronically. Text files may be sent to us at sschultz@chicagoparent.com. Please include your name, address, phone number, fax number, e-mail and social security number.

Kill Fee
For commissioned material, typically we pay 10 percent of the manuscript fee. There is no kill fee for first-time submissions, even when commissioned.

Categories: Nonfiction—Book Reviews—Children—Education—Family—Health—Regional: Chicago

CONTACT: Susy Schultz, Editor
Chicago Parent
141 S Oak Park Ave
Oak Park IL 60302
E-mail: sschultz@chicagoparent.com

Chicago Reader

More than half the articles published in the *Reader* each week come from freelancers, and once or twice a month we publish one that's come in "over the transom"—from a writer we've never heard of and may never hear from again. We think that keeping the *Reader* open to the greatest possible number of contributors makes for a fresher, less predictable, more interesting paper. So we not only publish unsolicited freelance writing, we depend on it.

Below are our answers to the questions freelancers most commonly ask:

What kind of articles are you looking for? Generally speaking, our greatest need is for magazine-style feature stories of varying lengths on Chicago topics. Beyond saying this, we usually answer this question with a list of the things we're not looking for: hard news (What the Mayor Said About the Schools Yesterday), commentary and opinion (What I Think About What the Mayor Said About the Schools Yesterday), poetry. We are not particularly interested in national stories unless there's a local angle, or in celebrity for celebrity's sake (a la *Rolling Stone*, *Details*, etc).

We value good writing more than we value any particular topic—and, it should be added, more than we value the above list of rules. We are always willing to violate our own guidelines—to publish news, commentary, a celebrity interview—if we like a particular article enough. Virtually any topic can make a good *Reader* story if it's written well enough. Similarly, any terrific-sounding article can miss the mark, no matter how fascinating the idea, if it's butchered badly enough.

We publish quite a bit of arts and entertainment criticism—reviews of movies, music, theater, dance, art, etc. Don't be put off if these essays seem to be written by the same people every week—we're always open to new reviewers who can do as well as or better than our regulars. Be aware, however, that many reviews are reserved by our regulars in advance. You can ask if the art exhibit or movie you want to review has been reserved by someone else. Or, better, you can just go ahead and review it anyway. If we like your piece but can't print it, we'll get back to you and suggest something we can print. If you'd like to become one of our regulars, submitting freelance material on spec is the only way to audition.

We also run short articles (typically 250-1,000 words) on places to go, things to do, restaurants, shops, etc. We welcome short profiles and humor pieces. A good rule of thumb: if you don't see it in the *Reader* (whatever it is), don't assume we don't want it.

We have occasional special issues focusing, among other things, on fashion, books, fiction, and stories from around the region. Fiction submissions are welcome year-round, but see below for our caveat about slow response time.

Should I send a query? Sure. Occasionally we know in advance that we don't want a particular story—because we've just published it, or someone else has, or the idea is patently revolting (What Julia Roberts Thinks About What the Mayor Said About the Schools Yesterday). But the rest of the time we're likely to respond: "We'll publish it if we like it—why don't you give it a try?" Feel free to e-mail us with a query anytime.

What about contracts? We usually encourage newcomers to submit completed manuscripts on spec. If we've worked with you before, we might make an assignment and discuss a deadline and payment. An e-mail exchange is usually sufficient as a contract. We do our best to make sure assigned stories make it into the paper, but if an assigned story or rewrite doesn't work out we'll pay at least 25 percent of the agreed-upon minimum.

What lengths do you prefer? We run short features of 250-1,200 words. Our larger feature stories start at about 2,500 and are often much longer. Reviews are generally 600-1,200 words but can be more. If we make an assignment, we'll likely recommend a length.

Once my story's accepted, will your editors destroy my deathless prose? We have a healthy appreciation for writerly idiosyncrasies but little patience for lazy reporting or bad logic. If we have to edit your story heavily, we'll explain our changes, and we show edited work to writers before publication. Naturally, a writer can refuse at any time to submit a rewrite or withdraw a story from consideration. Stories that need a lot of editing tend to migrate to editors' back burners. If we want your story but it's taking a long time to get it edited, we'll be happy to give you an advance.

How much do you pay? As of this writing (December 2005), from a minimum of $75 (the shortest items) to a maximum of $3,000 (the best and longest of our cover features). Short features usually run $200-$500, and reviews pay set rates of $150 or $250, depending on length. A more complete schedule of fees is available upon request. Freelance payments are made monthly, by the 15th of the month following the month of publication.

Do you pay expenses? Since most of our stories are local, writers don't incur many expenses, but when necessary we pay for things like long-distance phone bills. We pay for mileage when you need to travel more than 20 miles to get the story. Check with us ahead of time if you plan to spend our money. Expense requests, including receipts, should be submitted within a month of publication.

What rights are you buying? Unless a different arrangement is made prior to publication, our freelance fee includes first-time serial rights, archival rights (microfilm, microfiche, etc), the nonexclusive right to publish on our Web sites, and the right to use your material (1) in our online archive, for additional payment per download; (2) in the suburban *Reader's Guide to Arts & Entertainment*, for an additional payment of 20 percent; (3) in anthologies, for an additional amount to be negotiated. We also assume permission to make articles available via third-party online databases such as Proquest Alt-Press Watch and AltWeeklies.com. Freelancers are free to exclude their articles from our online archive and/or third-party databases. Please contact us for details.

How soon do you report on acceptance/rejection? Usually pretty quickly, but if we don't love your article or hate it, we could hold it for weeks or even months, waiting for the right time to publish it. If you know that you'll need a response in a hurry, inform us in a cover note.

How about artwork and photos? We prefer to take care of art ourselves. You're welcome to submit drawings, diagrams, photos, etc, but we may decide we can do better with our own artists and photographers. Of course, if it's going to be impossible for our people to do the artwork—the subject of your story is leaving town for six months, or the art requires technical expertise that you happen to have—it may be to your advantage to supply us with something.

Artists and photographers who want to contribute to the *Reader* should send samples to the editor and art director or arrange a portfolio review with the art director. Assignments may follow. Occasionally we accept unsolicited photographs, photo essays, and comics. Our basic rate for photos is $100 per print. Comics pay a minimum of $10. Illustrations (on assignment only) pay $50-$400.

Do you accept rewrites or simultaneous submissions? We have on rare occasion accepted rewritten versions of articles that have already appeared elsewhere, and we have no objection in principle to simultaneous submissions (manuscripts submitted to several publishers at the same time). But in both cases we need to know up front what we're dealing with: please inform us in your cover note.

What manuscript form do you prefer? We prefer e-mail with your text pasted into the message rather than sent as a file attachment. If you're sending paper, please triple space. Don't forget to include your name, address, phone number(s), and SSN.

If you'd like to drop your manuscript by in person, our office is at 11 E. Illinois in Chicago, just a block south of the Red Line subway stop at Grand Avenue and State Street. Please leave it at the front desk with our receptionists—we can't take the time to discuss your story when you drop it off.

Feel free to e-mail or call us if you have any further questions. And thanks for your interest in the *Reader*.

Categories: Nonfiction—Art—Dance—Entertainment—Music—Theater—Regional: Chicago

CONTACT: Editors, Chicago Reader
11 E Illinois St
Chicago IL 60611
Phone (all departments): 312-828-0350
E-mail (general): mail@chicagoreader.com

Chicago Review

Thank you for your interest in *Chicago Review*. Since 1946, *Chicago Review* has published innovative fiction, poetry, and essays, including work by John Ashbery, Leslie Silko, Joyce Carol Oates, William Burroughs, Susan Sontag, Thom Gunn, Robert Pinsky, Nikki Giovanni, Charles Simic, and many others.

The editors welcome submissions of unpublished poetry, fiction, and nonfiction (i.e., reviews, interviews, essays, and the like). We strongly recommend that unsolicited authors familiarize themselves with recent issues of *Chicago Review* before submitting. Submissions that demonstrate familiarity with the journal tend to make it towards the top of the pile more quickly than those that appear to be part of a carpet-bombing campaign.

We have established the following guidelines for submission:

• All submissions should include a self-addressed, stamped envelope with sufficient postage or International Reply Coupons for return of manuscript.

• Simultaneous submissions are strongly discouraged. If work is accepted elsewhere, please notify our office at once.

• There are no strict length requirements. The poetry editors prefer 3-7 pages of poetry. Fiction and nonfiction submissions average about 20 pages.

• Citations follow the most recent edition of *The Chicago Manual of Style.*

• Contributors receive three copies of the issue in which their work appears, plus a one-year subscription.

• Due to the increasing volume of unsolicited submissions, the average response time is three to six months; it is especially slow during the summer.

• Unsolicited electronic submissions are gleefully deleted unread.

• Address submissions to the appropriate genre staff: Poetry, Fiction, or Nonfiction.

We do not accept submissions by e-mail or fax.

Potential contributors are encouraged to read a copy of *Chicago Review*. Many bookstores and libraries carry the magazine. Sample issues are available for $10; see our subscription page for more information.

Categories: Fiction—Nonfiction—Poetry

CONTACT: Sam Eccleston, Fiction Editor
Material: Fiction
CONTACT: Lee Glidewell, Non-Fiction Editor
Material: Non-Fiction
CONTACT: Joshua Kotin, Poetry Editor
Material: Poetry
5801 South Kenwood Ave.
Chicago IL 60637

Chicken Soup for the Soup

Dear Friend of *Chicken Soup for the Soul®*,

We owe most of our success to writers like you for the wonderful contributions of inspiration, hope, overcoming life's challenges and realized dreams.

We hope that this letter finds you well and sitting atop a plethora of stories that you just don't know what to do with. We welcome stories from contributors of any age.

Recipe for A Winning *Chicken Soup for the Soul®* Story

A *Chicken Soup for the Soul®* story is an inspirational, true story about ordinary people doing extraordinary things. It is a story that opens the heart and rekindles the spirit. It is a simple, interdenominational, living art piece that touches the soul of the readers and helps them discover basic principles they can use in their own lives. They are personal and often filled with emotion and drama.

They are filled with vivid images created by using the five senses. In some stories, the readers feel that they are actually in the scene with the people.

Chicken Soup stories have a beginning, middle and an ending that often closes with a punch, *creating emotion* rather than simply talking about it. *Chicken Soup for the Soul®* stories have heart, but also something extra...an element that makes us all feel more hopeful, more connected, more thankful, more passionate and better about life in general. A story that causes tears, laughter, goosebumps or any combination of these. A good story covers the range of human emotions. The most powerful stories are about people extending themselves, or performing an act of love, service or courage for another person.

Guidelines for a *Chicken Soup for the Soul®* Story

1. Tell an exciting, sad or funny story about something that has happened to you or someone you know. Make sure that you introduce the character(s).

2. Tell your story in a way that will make the reader cry, laugh or get goose bumps (the good kind!) Don't leave anything out — how did you feel?

3. The story should start with action; it should include a problem, issue or situation. It should include dialogue and the character should express their feelings though the conflict or situation. It should end in a result, such as a lesson learned, a positive change or pay-off.

4. Above all, let it come from your HEART! Your story is important!

What a *Chicken Soup for the Soul®* story IS NOT:

1. A sermon, an essay or eulogy.

2. A term paper, thesis, letter or journal entry.

3. About politics or controversial issues.

4. A "My Grandma Just Died, and Let Me Tell You What A Wonderful Person She Was" or "Let Me Tell You About My Disease or Operation" or "I Gave a Bum Some Money, Aren't I Incredible?" or "Why My Mother Is the Best Mother" or a personal testimony that may mean nothing to the reader.

Story Specifications

1. It is preferred that all submissions are sent via our website at www.chickensoup.com. If you don't have access to the Internet, please submit your stories preferably typed on plain white 8½" x 11" paper, in 12-point Times New Roman font.

2. Please be sure to type the author's name and contact information on the first page of each and every story.

3. Stories should be non-fiction, ranging in length between 300-1200 words.

4. Mail your submissions in a flat, 9x12 envelope if possible.

5. No anonymous or author unknown submissions please.

6. Send only one copy of each submission.

7. We do not return submissions, so please don't send the original.

Chapters

Every book is divided into topic chapters with the following as a guideline for typical chapters:

1) On Love This chapter contains stories that describe acts of love and kindness; the healing power of love; acts of tenderness and compassion; acts of generosity; and events that transcend racism, sexism, ageism and nationalism.

2) On Parenting: This chapter contains stories that demonstrate love and caring in the act of parenting and grand parenting.

3) On Teaching and Learning: This chapter contains stories that demonstrate caring, compassion and creativity in the art of teaching—both in the classroom and outside the classroom.

4) Overcoming Obstacles: This chapter contains stories that demonstrate how we have triumphed over our own personal obstacles or supported one over theirs, and how individually each should be celebrated.

5) A Matter of Perspective: This chapter contains stories that demonstrate how our experience of all events is effected by our point of view, that there is more than one way to see and interpret the same event, and that as we change our point of view, we actually change our experience. These stories may be humorous.

6) A Matter of Attitude: This chapter, like the previous one, will contain stories that demonstrate how our attitudes and beliefs control our perception of reality and our behavior.

7) On Death and Dying: This chapter will contain stories about the power of the human spirit to confront the loss of loved ones through spiritual understanding, healing acts of love and kindness, and through humor.

8) On Aging: This chapter will contain stories about people over 60 years old who are making remarkable contributions to society, who are challenging the stereotypes of aging, and who are living without limitations.

9) On Living Your Dream: This chapter will contain stories that demonstrate the power of believing in your dream, the power of goal setting, the wisdom of trusting and following your heart, the power of giving encouragement and the importance of asking for and being open to receiving assistance from both other people and God.

10) Eclectic Wisdom: This chapter contains stories that don't fit into any other chapters. The stories are what about any aspect of life that is emotionally moving, touching, inspiring and insightful.

Also include a bio—a short paragraph (of about 50 words or less) about you, promoting your latest book, project, etc. It has been reported to us that those paragraphs have been great advertisements for sales of books and other endeavors. Dr. Cherie Carter Scott, author of *If Life is a Game, These are the Rules*, has sold hundreds of thousands of books as a result of people writing her after reading her bio in *A 2nd Helping of Chicken Soup for the Soul*. She also appeared on the Oprah Winfrey show as a result of this!

If the story you wrote is published, you will be paid upon publication of the story. Payment amount will be determined at that time.

Please note that our policy has changed. We will no longer be mailing acknowledgment cards after receiving your story if it arrives via postal mail or fax. The only way to receive an acknowledgment of your submission at this time is by submitting through our website, http://www.chickensoup.com. By submitting through the website, you will be taken to an acknowledgment screen on our website directly after hitting "send." This screen will inform you that the story has been accepted into our submission process. We strongly encourage you to submit stories online as it is both the fastest and easiest way to process and review your submission. If you do not have Internet access at home, you can always visit a local library.

It can take up to three or four years for Chicken Soup for the Soul® books to develop. Please be patient, as this is an important, yet time-consuming process. If your story is chosen for a future edition of Chicken Soup for the Soul or any other projects, you will be notified by mail and your permission to print it will be requested. However, if your story is not chosen, you will not receive a letter due to the fact that there are future books for which it may be considered for.

Feel free to submit more than one story if you'd like. If you do not have a personal story of your own, but have a pre-published favorite or a story written by someone else, these stories are welcomed as well. Don't forget to include who the author is, source, etc.

You can submit your story three different ways, on the Internet, by mail, or by fax. See addresses below.

Respectfully, Chicken Soup for the Soul® Enterprises, Inc.

Here Are Some of Our Up-Coming Titles:

-Adopted Soul: 101 uplifting stories that share the experiences of adoption.

-Alzheimer's Soul: Stories for all those suffering at the hands of this terrible disease.

-Athlete's Soul: Stories to inspire everyone to reach for their physical best.

-Blended Family Soul: Uplifting and enriching stories celebrating all forms of family life!

-Boy's Soul: Stories about the adventures, challenges, and humorous moments that boys encounter.

-Breast Cancer Survivor's Soul: A collection of stories about overcoming breast cancer.

-Celtic Soul: Stories of Celtic decent, including Irish, Scottish, Welsh, Cornish, Breton, and Manx.

-Christian Kid's Soul: Sharing the experiences of Christian Kids and how faith works in their lives.

-Christian Music Lover's: Embrace the measures of faith and melodies in these uplifting stories.

-Dieter's Soul: Inspirational stories to aid those on their quest toward weight loss.

-Divorced Soul: Stories for divorced people offering hope and encouragement.

-Doctor's Soul: Humorous and touching stories celebrating the professionals who heal others.

-Entrepreneur's Soul: Encouraging stories by business owners as they run their own companies.

-Father and Daughter Soul: Inspiring and healing stories of the father/daughter bond.

-Grandmother's Soul: Stories and lessons that connect grandmothers to their grandchildren.

-Hero's Soul: Words of thanks and love for the professionals who have risked it all to save a life.

-Hip Hop Soul: Stories about the meaning and inspirations found in this urban phenomenon.

-Young Horse Lover's Soul: Stories from and for today's young horse lovers.

-Latino Soul: Stories that open the door to Latino culture and family.

-Laughing Soul: A collection of the funniest stories in the Chicken Soup series!

-Life Lessons for Teens: Stories and lessons encompassing the inspiration, strength and dreams of teens.

-Life Lessons for Teachers: Stories and lessons encompassing the inspiration, strength and dreams of teachers.

-Living Your Dreams for Women: Inspirational stories, powerful principles and practical techniques to help women realize their goals and dreams.

-Military Wives Soul: Stories to acknowledge, entertain and inspire the un-sung heroines who also defend and protect family and homeland.

-Mother and Son Soul: Stories to celebrate the unique bond between Mothers and their sons.

-Music Lover's Soul: Find notes of hope in stories of melodies that are able to touch all of us.

-Peace Lover's Soul: Stories about using the creative power of non-violence to resolve conflicts and nurture relationships.

-Pre-Teen's Soul: Not yet an adult, but not a kid anymore, pre-teens have a special place in the world.

-Quilter's Soul: A collection of stories celebrating the art of quilting.

-Scrapbooker's Soul: A collection of stories that celebrate all those that enjoy the art of scrapbooking.

-Single Parent's Soul: Stories of encouragement, support and hope, letting single dads and moms know they are not alone.

-Teen's Soul: Stories to help teens get through the difficult changes they face while growing up.

Categories: Nonfiction—Inspiration

CONTACT: Chicken Soup for the Soul, Attn: Story Submissions
PO Box 30880
Santa Barbara CA 93130
Phone: 805-563-2935
Fax: 805-563-2945
Website: www.chickensoup.com

The Chief of Police Magazine

Please refer to *Police Times Magazine*.

Child

Have a story idea for *Child*? Tell us about it:

Freelance writers are invited to submit QUERY LETTERS ONLY, on the following topics.

* Children's health
* Parenting and marital relationship issues
* Child behavior and development
* Personal essays pertaining to family life

Child purchases first-time rights for articles and pays upon acceptance. Fees vary depending on the length and positioning of articles.

Writers must include clips of previously published work and a stamped, self-addressed envelope with their queries. Please allow 8 weeks for a reply. No electronic submissions will be accepted.

Categories: Nonfiction—Children—Marriage—Parenting—Relationships

CONTACT: Submissions
Child Editorial Department
375 Lexington Ave 9th floor
New York NY 10017

Child Life

Please refer to Children's Better Health Institute.

Child Magazine

Child Magazine is published 10 times a year, with combined issues in June/July and December/January.

Child provides parents of children from birth to age 12 with the newest thinking, information, and advice they need to raise their families in a constantly changing, time-pressed world.

Freelance writers are invited to submit query letters only, on the following topics:

• Children's health
• Parenting and marital relationship issues
• Child behavior and development
• Personal essays pertaining to family life

Child purchases first-time rights for articles and pays upon acceptance. Fees vary depending on length and positioning of articles.

Writers must include clips of previously published work and a SASE with their queries. Please allow 8 weeks for a reply. No electronic submissions will be accepted.

Categories: Nonfiction—Children—Consumer—Parenting

CONTACT: Submissons Editor
Material: All
Child Editorial Dept.
375 Lexington Ave., 9th Floor
New York NY 10017
Phone: 212-499-2000
Fax: 212-499-2038

Children's Better Health Institute

We at the Children's Better Health Institute have a constant need for high quality stories, articles, and activities with health related stories, articles, and activities with health-related themes. "Health" is a broad topic that includes exercise, sports, safety, nutrition, hygiene, and drug education.

Health information can be presented in a variety of formats, including fiction, nonfiction, poems, recipes, and puzzles. Fiction stories with a health message need not have health as the primary subject, but they should include it in some way in the course of events. Characters in fiction should adhere to good health practices, unless failure to do so is necessary to a story's plot.

Remember that characters in realistic stories should be up-to-date. Many of our readers have working mothers and/or come from single-parent homes. We need more stories that reflect these changing times but at the same time communicate good, wholesome values.

We are especially interested in material concerning sports and fitness, including profiles of famous amateur and professional athletes; "average" athletes (especially children) who have overcome obstacles to excel in their areas; and new or unusual sports, particularly those in which children can participate.

Nonfiction articles dealing with health subjects should be fresh and creative. Avoid an encyclopedic or "preachy" approach. We try to present our health material in a positive manner, incorporation humor and a light approach wherever possibly without minimizing the seriousness of the message.

We also welcome recipes that children can make on their own with minimal adult supervision. Ingredients should be healthful, so avoid using fats, sugars, salt, chocolate, and red meat. In all material submitted, please avoid reference to eating sugary foods, such as candy, cakes, cookies, and soft drinks.

Although our emphasis is on health, we certainly use material with more general themes. We would especially like to see more holiday stories, articles, and activities. Please send seasonal material at least eight months in advance.

Reading our writers guidelines is not enough. Careful study of current issues will acquaint writers with each title's "personality," various departments, and regular features, nearly all of which are open to freelancers. Sample copies are $2.95 each (U.S. currency) from the Children's Better Health Institute, P.O. Box 567, Indianapolis, IN 46206.

Manuscript format

Manuscripts must be typewritten and double or triple-spaced. The author's name, address, telephone number, Social Security number, date of submission, and the approximate word count of the material should appear on the first page of the manuscript. Title pages are not necessary. Keep a copy of your work. We will handle your manuscript with care, but we cannot assume responsibility for its return. Please submit to a specific magazine, not just to CBHI or the Children's Better Health Institute. This aids us in tracking your manuscript.

Please send the entire manuscript. All work is on speculation only; queries are not accepted, nor are stories assigned. The editors cannot criticize, offer suggestions, or enter into correspondence with an author concerning manuscripts that are not accepted, nor can they suggest other markets for material that is not published. Material cannot be returned unless it is accompanied by a self-addressed stamped envelope and sufficient return postage.

Photos and Illustrations

We do not purchase single photographs. We do purchase short photo features (up to 6 or 8 Picture) or photos that accompany articles to help illustrate editorial material. (Please include captions and model releases.) Suggestions for illustrations are not necessary but are permissible. Please do not send drawings or artwork. We prefer to work with professional illustrators of our own choosing.

Review Time

About three months are required to review manuscripts properly. Please wait three months before sending status inquiries. If a manuscript is returned, it should not be resubmitted to a different you publication at this address. Each manuscript is carefully considered for possible use in all magazines, not only the one to which it was originally addressed.

Rates and Payment Policies

Turtle: up to 22¢ a word, Fiction/nonfiction — up to 350 words

Humpty Dumpty: up to 22¢ a word, Fiction/nonfiction — up to 350 words

Children's Playmate: up to 17¢ a word, Fiction/nonfiction — 300 to 700 words

Jack and Jill: up to 17¢ a word, Fiction/nonfiction — 500 to 800 words

Child Life: not accepting manuscripts at this time

Children's Digest: up to 12¢ a word, Fiction — 500 to 1500 words/ nonfiction 500 to 1000 words

Poetry: $25.00 minimum
Photos: $15.00 minimum
Puzzles and games: no fixed rate
Rights

We purchase all rights to manuscripts. We buy one-time rights to photos. Simultaneous submissions are discouraged. One-time book rights may be returned when the author had found an interested publisher and can provide us with an approximate date of publication.

Children's Contributions

Except for items that are used in children's columns, the editors do not encourage submissions from children. Even highly talented young people are not usually experienced enough to compete on a professional level with adult authors. There is no payment for children's contributions.

ARTISTS GUIDELINES
Art Requirements

Artists interested in being considered for assignments may mail samples of their artwork accompanied by a stamped, self-addressed return envelope.

When an artist accepts an assignment, type proofs of the material are sent to him, together with layout sheets showing the page size of the magazine. Deadline dates for receipt of sketches and finished are included.

The artist should read the proofs carefully, then cut them close to the edge of the type matter and place the trimmed strips on the layout sheets. This will show how much space is available for illustration so artists can plan accordingly. Large illustrations for dramatic impact, and/or a scattering of small spots are preferred. Illustrations may bleed off the page, but any important art, such as lettering or parts of a person's body, must be kept within 1/4" from bleed lines, to avoid being cut when the magazine is trimmed. Avoid having a full page of copy without an illustration.

After the layout is planned and the type has been pasted down on the layout sheet, the artist should make actual-size sketches, the material is returned to the artist along with any comments and changes.

Sketches and finished artwork should be actual size. Sketches must be returned to us with the finished art for layout purposes. Color separations of the art are made on a color scanner; art must be prepared on a flexible surface to wrap around the scanner drum. The artist supplies color overlays for two-color work.

We welcome cover ideas with health, exercise, nutrition, and safety themes. Rough sketches should be submitted in color, the actual size of the magazine, with space allowed for the logo. The artist's name and return address should be noted on the back. These sketches are returned when the editors have reviewed them.

Payment for completed artwork is customarily mailed within a three-week period prior to the publication date. Each contributor is sent two copies of the printed issue containing his/her work. The art director should be contacted if additional copies are needed. All artwork is considered work for hire. We buy all rights and retain work after publication.

All artwork is considered work for hire.

Kill fees rarely occur. If they should, they will be handled on a case-by-case basis.

The artist is responsible for any costs incurred in mailing sketches and finished artwork—please do not bill federal express or other mailing costs to us. Children's Better Health Institute is a non-profit organization; we do not pay state taxes on artwork.

An invoice should be submitted with your finished artwork. It should contain the following information: Your name, address, social security or federal tax reporting number, the date, the magazine for which the assignment has been made, the issue date, the title of the story and the total payment. The total is to be determined according to the above schedule and confirmed wit the art director at the time your sketches are submitted. We will hold your check until we have received your invoice.

Categories: Nonfiction—Health—Physical Fitness

CONTACT: Editor (Magazine Name)
Material: All
100 Waterway Blvd., Box 567
Indianapolis IN 46202
Phone: 317-634-1100
Fax: 317-684-8094
Website: www.cbhi.org

Children's Digest
Children's Playmate

Please refer to Children's Better Health Institute.

Chiron Review

Chiron Review presents the widest possible range of contemporary creative writing — fiction and non-fiction, traditional and off-beat — in an attractive, professional tabloid format, including artwork and photographs of featured writers.

All submissions are invited. No taboos. Send up to five poems, and/or one short story (up to 3000 words), typed or printed legibly. Photocopies are okay. We do NOT consider simultaneous submissions, previously published material or e-mail submissions. Must include SASE for reply. We recommend writers see a sample copy ($5) before submitting. Report in 2-6 weeks. Pays 1 copy. CR is copyrighted; writers retain all rights to their work.

About a quarter of each issue is devoted to news, views and reviews of interest to writers and the literary community. We are always on the lookout for intelligent non-fiction, as well as talented reviewers who wish to write in-depth, analytical reviews of literary books and magazines.

Past contributors include Charles Bukowski, William Stafford, Marge Piercy, Gavin Dillard, Edward Field, Antler, Robert Peters, Joan Jobe Smith, Fred Voss, Janice Eidus, Felice Picano, Lyn Lifshin, Will Inman, Richard Kostelanetz, Lorri Jackson, Ruth Moon Kempher, Charles Webb and a host of others, well-known and new.

A one-year subscription is $15 (four issues). A sample copy is $5.
Categories: Arts—Gay/Lesbian—Literature—Poetry

CONTACT: Michael Hathaway, Editor
Material: All
522 E. South Ave.
St. John KS 67576-2212
Phone: 620-786-4955
Website: geocities.com/SoHo/Nook/1748

The Christian Century

The editors assume that our readers are deeply engaged in thinking about the Christian faith and in trying to live it out. Many are church leaders, either in congregations or church-related agencies.

The Christian Century aims to be a magazine for Christians who are thoughtful about theology, church life, and contemporary culture, but who are not likely to be scholars of any academic discipline. We are not likely, therefore, to publish a treatise on, say, Augustine's doctrine of the Trinity. We might well be interested, however, in a fresh investigation of how that doctrine has been ignored—or perhaps made freshly relevant to contemporary life. Similarly, we probably won't publish an article on apocalyptic sects of the 19ᵗʰ century—but we might well be interested in an article on apocalyptic movements of our time and their relation to earlier groups.

When we read a submission, we tend to ask: Why this? Why now? What does this contribute to the ongoing discussion of the topic and people's everyday encounters? We also ask: What will cause someone to pick up this article? Is it lively? Is it provocative? Does it grab the reader with the importance of the subject? Does it generate some drama? Does it cover a neglected aspect of a familiar topic, or approach a classic topic in a new and engaging way?

If you are writing about a local event or program or about a conference, we encourage you to shape your account around the most crucial and broadly significant issues. No need to provide a step-by-step, or speaker-by-speaker, account.

Feature articles run about 3,000 words. Articles for the "comments and reports" section run about 1,500 words. We don't use footnotes or endnotes. We usually pay an honorarium of about $150 for feature articles.

We urge you to examine a copy of the magazine before submitting a manuscript. If you want your manuscript returned, please enclose a self-addressed stamped envelope.

Categories: Religion

CONTACT: Manuscripts, The Christian Century
Material: All
104 S. Michigan, Ste. 700
Chicago, IL 60603
Phone: 312-263-7510
E-mail: main@christiancentury.org
Website: www.christiancentury.org

HOME & SCHOOL
CHRISTIAN

Christian Home & School

Christian Home & School is published by Christian Schools International for parents who send their children to Christian schools. The magazine aims to promote Christian education and to address a wide range of parenting topics. The magazine is published six times during the school year and has a circulation of 66,000 (75% U.S.; 25% Canada).

Some suggested topics can be found here, but don't limit yourself to these ideas. We are interested in articles that deal with timely issues that affect Christian parents. We are also interested in articles about Christian schooling and the relationship of parents to Christian schools. Each year we also include seasonal articles dealing with such topics as the beginning of the school year, Christmas, graduation, summer activities, and vacations. Send seasonal articles 4-5 months before the event. (We don't publish poetry or fillers.)

Articles should reflect a mature, biblical perspective. Use an informal, easy-to-read style rather than a philosophical, academic tone. Try to incorporate vivid imagery and concrete, practical examples from real life. You may wish to suggest a sidebar that contains further information or resources related to your subject.

A query is not necessary. Manuscripts can range from 1,000 to 2,000 words and should be typed (double spaced). Submissions as Word attachments to e-mails are welcomed. Include your name and address at the top of the first page; also include a sentence or two about yourself for us to use as a contributor's note.

We pay $175-$250 upon publication, depending on the length of the edited article. We prefer to buy first rights only. We also look for brief parenting tips of 100 to 250 words for our Parentstuff pages and pay $25 to $40 for these.

If you would like a sample copy of the magazine, please send a 9" x12" self-addressed envelope with four first-class stamps affixed.

Categories: Nonfiction—Education—Family—Parenting

CONTACT: Roger W. Schmurr, Senior Editor
Material: All
3350 E. Paris Ave. SE
Grand Rapids MI 49512
Phone: 616-957-1070 ext. 239
Fax: 616-957-5022
E-mail: RogerS@CSIonline.org

Christian Living

Does not accept unsolicited submissions.

*Christian*New Age Quarterly*

Thank you for your interest in writing for *Christian*New Age Quarterly*. We welcome your creativity and insights, focused upon some facet of the *Christian-New Age* relationship.

C*NAQ is a forum for clear, respectful dialog between Christians and New Agers. Here we entertain, but do not assume, an underlying compatibility of the two. While we allow for the possibility of irreconcilable ideological differences, we have yet to see a single reason which precludes honest, mutually supportive communication. Moreover, we have discovered many reasons why such genuine communication is warranted, even crucial.

Our readership is comprised of Christians and New Agers, as well as those exploring other avenues of spiritual expression. While extraordinarily diverse, our readers also tend to be keenly observant, intelligent and in touch with spirituality. Consequently, we do not accept material marked by either a patronizing style, which assumes the reader needs to be taught some self-evident spiritual insight, or self-circular reasoning, which confuses subjective truth with observable fact.

As you select words for your insight or observation, aim for vital, flowing, yet precise language. C*NAQ especially looks for a certain caliber of vantage that surprises us with a slant we've yet to consider. Take a look at a topic, then wrestle with it, contemplatively and vigorously. Capture and submit it in simple style and fine polish.

If yours is a controversial theme, we would be pleased to consider it—as long as you have thought it through with research and sensitivity. Here, you needn't be wary of words considered taboo in other journals; "church," "Savior," "feminism" and "Goddess" are all functional terms in C*NAQ. But pieces that put forth an exclusivistic stance would best be submitted to one of the more singularly Christian or New Age periodicals which abound.

Besides staff-composed columns and "The Letters Library," we publish 2-3 articles per issue. Recommended word length is 400-1,500 words. The more peripheral the content is to our main focus, the shorter it needs to be. Articles with content especially pertinent may aim for the upper end of the range. Still, if you have composed an outstanding piece that exceeds length recommendations, we might consider it. We do try to be flexible when it comes to truly noteworthy pieces.

We do not accept poetry, photos, trendy pieces, channeled wisdom or fiction. We do, however, welcome original line drawings and cartoons. If you are in doubt regarding the propriety of an intended subject, feel free to query prior to investing your energies in its composition.

As to blind submissions, we at C*NAQ find it presumptuous when authors submit work with no knowledge of our periodical's focus. If one is drawn to Christian-New Age dialog to the extent that one would write on the subject, it would seem reasonable to expect interest in at least examining C*NAQ. Doing so provides the opportunity not only to explore our stylistic preferences, but also to learn from the views of other writers who are published here. Though our acceptances are not prejudiced by whether or not a writer reads C*NAQ, those who have familiarized themselves with our work are far more likely to create the kind of piece we seek to publish. If you are not currently a subscriber, you may obtain a sample by sending your check or money order, payable to *Christian*New Age Quarterly*, in the amount of $3.50.

C*NAQ rarely accepts material offered on a basis other than "first rights." Please indicate "first rights" on your manuscript or detail, in your cover letter, why first rights are not available. Never do we consider simultaneous submissions; don't send them here. We require a note of assurance, accompanying your submission, that we are the sole periodical considering the piece. After your work has been published in C*NAQ, you are free to submit it elsewhere.

We reserve the right to edit. Although C*NAQ honors the personal style of our authors, editing may be necessary for clarity or length. If you are opposed to revising your manuscript yourself or allowing us to do so, clearly state this in your cover letter. Our preliminary evaluation of submissions often is based on their "editability." Rest assured that we would not print a piece requiring substantial editing without first obtaining the author's approval on necessary changes.

The request of a revision does not ensure eventual acceptance. It does mean we are seriously interested. But acceptance depends upon our approval of your final copy.

For accepted articles, you'll receive, as payment, a one-year complimentary subscription or an extension to your current subscription. For each drawing or cartoon, you'll receive one copy of the issue in which your work appears.

Our decisions are commitments. If we accept a piece for publication, you may rest assured that it will be published. Although we try to publish accepted material as soon as possible, we work carefully to achieve a balance of content in each issue. Therefore, we may wait upon an appropriate issue to include accepted articles.

Please enclose an SASE with sufficient postage in all correspondence. We are not responsible for returning manuscripts, advising you of our decision, or answering inquiries which arrive without SASEs. Please help us to be responsive to you!

C*NAQ's Editor, Catherine Groves—as well as our readers—will look forward to the opportunity to explore your thoughts.

Categories: Book Reviews—Christian Interests—Inspirational—New Age—Occult—Religion—Spiritual

CONTACT: Catherine Groves, Editor
Material: All
PO Box 276
Clifton NJ 07015-0276
E-mail: info@christiannewage.com
Website: www.christiannewage.com

Christian Reader
Stories of Faith, Hope and God's Love

Please refer to Today's Christian.

Christian Science Monitor

International, general-interest daily newspaper published as a public service of the Christian Science Church. Pulitzer-Prize winning; est. 1908.

Needs: The Home Forum section is looking for upbeat, personal essays of from 400 to 1,000 words. We also publish poetry (25 lines is a long poem, for us). Every Tuesday we publish Kidspace, feature stories (main story and at least one sidebar) aimed at children ages 6 to 13.

Payment: Personal essays: $75 to $150, depending on the way it's used, length, and the editor's subjective assessment.
Poetry: $20 (haiku) to $40.
Kidspace articles: $150 for main story of 750 to 900 words, $50 to $75 per sidebar. We like to have at least one sidebar per Kidspace, ideally two.

Contributors guidelines for other sections
Note: Please inquire about up-to-date Copyright terms

The Christian Science Monitor is an international daily newspaper produced by The Christian Science Publishing Society, which is owned and operated by The First Church of Christ, Scientist, in Boston. Mary Baker Eddy, who founded the Monitor in 1908, set the paper's high goal: "To injure no man, but to bless all mankind." That mandate endures. What does it mean?

It means we look for the greater public significance of a story, and we seek to convey it with as much fairness and accuracy as possible. It means we care about social problems and people in trouble, and we're especially interested in finding progress against those problems. We want our stories to be reported and told with an honest and open-minded balance that is not partisan or polemic. We want to appeal to the curious and compassionate in our readers, the part of them that seeks to understand the world better. We don't want to lead them to conclusions or to disrespect their worldviews. Monitor stories should shed light, not heat, on their subjects.

We love historical and international context whenever either is appropriate. We're always interested in the social and cultural trends that underly events. We like good, tight writing that speaks to heart as well as mind. We strive for a mix of subject, tone, and treatment as varied as the world we cover. We are open to creative approaches to stories.

Monitor readers are well-educated, curious, and engaged. But assume they bring no special knowledge or interest in the subject you're covering. This means stories need to establish quickly—in the first few lines—why they are interesting and worth the read. Always ask why readers would care about the story, and answer as you write.

Story lengths may range from 500 words for fairly simple stories to 1,400 words for more in-depth pieces. After this general introduction, you will find a section-by-section guide to the paper, including rates for photographic work.

Copyright information and terms of acceptance
When you file a story with us, it is assumed that the piece is original and exclusive to us for 90 days from the date of publication. We have the right to distribute the story via The Christian Science Monitor News Service, which provides Monitor stories to about 122 client newspapers in the US, and to post it on the Monitor's Web site. Please ask to see the standard contract, which asks you to grant us worldwide rights to your story for the 90-day period. Once you have been given the go-ahead to write, please sign the contract and return it to your assigning editor by fax or mail. We cannot publish your work without it.

Except in unusual circumstances, we accept a new writer's work "on spec" only. That means you give us the opportunity to read your piece before we decide whether to accept it; and our agreeing to look at something on spec implies no financial obligation on our part. We try to render verdicts on pieces quickly, but we are often inundated, and you should feel free to pester us for an answer on a perishable story. Please check the policy set by the editor of the section to which you are pitching a story.

If we ask you for stories, there is a financial obligation on our part. If you file a commissioned piece that fulfills what you pitched to us, we will pay you our basic rate for the piece whether we run it or not. If the commissioned piece you deliver is unsatisfactory, we will ask you to rework it or we will pay a kill fee, usually half the basic rate. We may not pay a fee, however, if the story arrives too late for avoidable reasons.

It's important that freelancer and editor clarify whether we are commissioning a piece or asking to see a story on spec.

Payment and expenses

Our basic rate for a story is $200 to $225. But please be in touch with individual news and section editors (see entries below) about any variation from this rate. Longer stories can pay appreciably more. Short stories or sidebars often pay half the basic rate.

Targeting your written work

International news

Editor: David Scott

Deputy editor: Amelia Newcomb

Preferred e-mail(s) for inquiries: Appropriate regional editor (see below), with copy to Amelia Newcomb

Overview

The Monitor has long been valued for its thoughtful and balanced coverage of world affairs. Stringers make an essential contribution toward that end with the incisive analysis and vivid description that comes with on-the-ground reporting. Writing for us has its challenges: Our deadlines are early; we require lively, concise writing that sets events in context; and we expect you to back up your analysis with the voices of intelligent observers and to enliven your stories with a sense of place.

Best opportunities for freelancers

We are almost always disappointed with a spot-news, day-one account of a news event. Our readers like us because we step back, sum up, and look ahead. Monitor coverage—though you may have to write it before journalists from other US dailies file their day-one stories—almost always has to read like a day-two analysis.

How to pitch and follow up

For stories that aren't tied to breaking events, we prefer a written pitch. Please e-mail us a brief description of the story, specifying the number of words you think you need and when you could deliver it. E-mail addresses and fax numbers are listed below. Transmitting approved stories: E-mail the story or phone us if you need to make other arrangements.

Copy deadline for news is 7 a.m. EST the day before publication. This is an inflexible deadline; we make final decisions on the content of the next day's paper at 8:00 a.m. EST. If you foresee a problem delivering a perishable story on time, you must call us at 7 a.m., and we will discuss how to proceed. The rule to remember: You must file or call at 7 a.m. Boston time.

If news happens after 7 a.m., we nonetheless appreciate a call. In certain circumstances we can make arrangements to take stories as late as 10 a.m. or make changes to stories in hand as late as noon.

Regional contacts (all numbers in area code 1-617)

International News Editor: Dave Scott 450-2410

Asst. Int'l News Editor: Amelia Newcomb 450-2440

Regional editors:

Europe/Former USSR: Christa Case 450-2415

Latin America/Africa: Matt Clark 450-2433

Asia: Matt Bradley 450-2915

Middle East: Mike Farrell 450-2447

Foreign desk fax: 450-7506

Payment and expenses

In commissioning a piece from you, it is understood that we will pay the costs you incur in discussing the piece with us, before and after filing, and the costs you incur in transmitting the story to us. We do not pay filing and communication costs associated with on-spec pieces unless we accept the story.

All other expenses—travel, long-distance phone costs for your reporting, or anything else—must be approved in advance of expenditure. In other words, you must estimate what these costs will be and receive our approval before you proceed to spend the money. Otherwise we will not reimburse it to you.

We do not accept material produced by journalists receiving benefits (such as free travel) from any entity or person who could be perceived as an interested party to the story in question. So if you are proposing to travel from your place of residence and write stories for us on your trip, we will want to know who is funding your travel.

Please note

Until we commission a story from you, you may not represent yourself to officials, sources, or credentialing authorities (or anyone else, for that matter) as a representative of The Christian Science Monitor. Until we designate you as our stringer in a particular locality, you may not identify yourself as a Monitor writer in researching a prospective piece prior to pitching it to us. And you may not identify yourself as a Monitor writer for the purpose of obtaining a visa or a credential as a resident correspondent from a foreign government without the express written consent of the International News Editor.

Obviously, once we have established a relationship, you have more leeway in identifying yourself as the Monitor's representative. Nonetheless, we ask that you do so judiciously.

National news

Editor: Cheryl Sullivan

Preferred e-mail(s) for queries: US News

Overview

The asset we value most in freelancers is quality of thought. In every case, the stories that we want are not simply a recounting of events, but rather an insightful look into why something happened and what it means—not only to the people directly involved, but also to people across the country. As a national newspaper, each story must have currency and relevance to readers nationwide.

Best opportunities for freelancers

We're interested in stories of national import from all over the country.

We want to stay on top of what is in the news—and in public thought—as much as possible, but there's also an opportunity for news features with a sense of place. Regardless of the setting or situation, though, we look for history and an eye for detail that show what makes peoples and places the way they are, influencing events.

How to pitch and follow up

Pitch your stories to the e-mail address above. Keep them brief (no more than a paragraph or two) and focus on telling us why your story is important to readers from Maine to Georgia to California.

Payment

We always take the first two articles on spec. Starting pay is $200 per article plus up to $50 phone expenses. Any travel or other expenses would have to be cleared by the department beforehand.

All pieces must be original for the Monitor. We cannot accept stories that have been or will be published elsewhere.

Opinion page

Editor: Josh Burck

Preferred e-mail(s) for queries: oped@csps.com

Overview

The Op-Ed page invites a written version of what you might imagine the conversation would be like at a cozy dinner party with interesting people: serious, funny, broad-ranging discussion on any topic imaginable. The Op-Ed page provides a forum for opinions and commentary on politics, life, family, society, and culture. We aim to provide fodder for the public conversation that's both engaging and enlightening. If it's a subject people care about, and it's well-written, we'd probably be interested in seeing it.

Best opportunities for freelancers

You don't have to be a policy wonk to write for the Op-Ed page, but you should be qualified to speak about your subject. Our contributors include ambassadors writing on foreign affairs, parents and teachers on standardized testing, foreign journalists on the human side of wars. While we like to receive articles of 750 words or less, we are always looking for shorter pieces.

How to pitch and follow up

We prefer to see completed submissions rather than queries. Contributors should e-mail oped@csps.com or fax (617/450-2317) their submissions. The Op-Ed editor is Josh Burck.

We publish only submissions that are exclusive to The Christian Science Monitor. Due to the volume of submissions we receive, we can neither acknowledge nor return unpublished manuscripts. Due to volume, only the occasional query can be answered. If we choose your submission, we will always contact you to verify that it is still available exclusively to us, and you will be included in the editing process. If you haven't heard from us within 48 hours for articles pegged to news events, or within 2 weeks for articles without a news peg, please feel free to submit your piece elsewhere. Please do not call to check on the status of your piece. Any item submitted by e-mail will receive an automated reply as confirmation of receipt.

If we have commissioned you to write a piece, or have accepted a concept on speculation, you may not represent yourself to officials, sources, or credentialing authorities (or anyone else, for that matter) as a representative of The Christian Science Monitor. And you may not identify yourself as a Monitor writer for the purpose of obtaining a conference or event credential, nor may you use a Monitor assignment to obtain visas from a foreign government without the express written consent of the Op-Ed editor.

Payment
Pay starts at $150 and is determined on a case-by-case basis.

Please note
The average size of an Op-Ed is 700 words. While all manuscripts are given attention, the editor will not review dissertation-length papers. Any manuscript of more than 1,200 words risks being disqualified purely out of lack of staff time to edit it to a publishable length.

The Home Forum
Editor: Judy Lowe

Preferred e-mail for queries and submissions: homeforum @csps.com.

Overview
The Home Forum is looking for upbeat, personal essays of from 400 to 1,000 words. (We cannot consider any essay longer than 1,200 words.) We also publish short poems. Every Tuesday we publish Kidspace, feature stories (main story and at least one sidebar) aimed at children ages 9 to 14. The best way to understand what we're all about is to read our five-days-a-week section online for several weeks. Go to The Home Forum section on our website, www.csmonitor.com, and click on Essays, Kidspace, or Poetry.

More on essays:
These are first-person, nonfiction explorations of how one responded to a place, a person, a situation, an event, or happenings in everyday life. Tell a story; share a funny true tale. The humor should be gentle.

At the moment, we are looking for more submissions on parenting (your experiences in solving a family situation), gardening, home, family, and food (even including, if it's pertinent, a recipe. All recipes must have been tried, however, since the Monitor tests all recipes before printing them.)

An essay is more than a description: A theme should be present. The essay should have a beginning, a middle, and an end. The best essays contain fresh observations and take the reader along with you on a journey of self-discovery. They are surprising and unselfish; they have a point; they share. They are personal, but not self-serving. They are honest and anecdotal. They are rooted in experience. Nostalgia may work, but it should not be mere nostalgia. We're still looking for a theme, insight.

The two mistakes we see most frequently: "essays" that are mere descriptions, that lack forward motion or a theme; essays in which the story has obvious meaning for the author, but he or she has failed to communicate the significance to the reader, to show why anyone else would care.

Essays on time-sensitive subjects (Christmas, Father's Day, first day of spring, etc.) should reach us a minimum of four weeks in advance.; earlier is better.

Payment ranges from a minimum of $75 for short pieces (300 words) up to $160, and is paid upon publication. See below for submission details. All submissions should be by e-mail. We prefer a Microsoft Word attachment, if possible. We cannot consider queries for essays; only completed manuscripts.

More on poetry:
Poetry that appears in The Home Forum explores and celebrates life. It provides a respite from daily news and from the bleakness that appears in so much contemporary verse. We do not publish work that presents people in helpless or hopeless states. Nor do we print poetry about death, aging, or illness. Poems that are dark, violent, or sensual won't work for us. Nor do we want poems that are overtly religious or falsely sweet.

One of the biggest mistakes we see is "poetry" that does not go beyond a brief, saccharin description. Good poems take the reader—and writer—somewhere new. A sense of discovery is present, as is solid narrative, music, and engaging language. "Uplifting" poems can be very challenging to write successfully.

We publish poems in free verse and fixed forms. We are always in need of seasonal material. However, we are flooded with "first" poems—first snowfall, first berries, first fall leaves. These topics are fine, but they have a limited shelf life. We also need poems that span the entire season. Snow, for instance, can be part of the scenery and not the poem's focus.

Due to time constraints, submissions are now accepted only by e-mail, one poem per e-mail; no more than 5 poems submitted at one time. In order to preserve line breaks and indents, you may want to consider using a Microsoft Word attachment. Payment ($20 for a haiku, $40 per poem) is made upon publication.

More on Kidspace:
We're looking for stories on high-interest topics that will engage, empower, entertain, and educate kids ages 6 to 13. You should stand as close to your subject as possible: Interview an engineer in the locomotive cab, for instance; go on an expedition to collect fossils; try out the high-tech sled. The best stories have this "live action" component. Consult primary sources: experts in magnetism, for instance, not encyclopedia entries on magnets (though you should read those, too, for background). Any expert worth his salt should be able to respond satisfactorily to the question: "And how would you explain that to an intelligent 9-year-old?" You have to know enough about the subject to explain it simply and accurately. No hiding behind a quote that you don't understand.

The writing should be simple, but not condescending. One idea per sentence, as a rule. The writing must be lively and pull the reader along. This is a tough audience: They have to WANT to read what you've written, because this story is optional. As often as possible, include a "hands on" sidebar - an activity of some kind. An annotated list of books, websites, or other resources for further information is also welcome. Once kids get interested in something, how can they find out more, experience it more?

Topics have included: tagging along with a skywriter; where does a candy bar come from? (short histories, anecdotes about sugar, peanuts, chocolate, etc.); how animated cartoons are made (visit to a Hollywood studio); riding on a US Navy sub. We've interviewed people who are celebrities to kids (Tomie de Paola, a visit to Eric Carle's studio). Even "strange but true" stories/origins about office supplies (in Nazi-occupied Norway, you could be arrested for wearing a paper clip on your lapel, a symbol of resistance).

Some of the most-successful stories are ones that help children see the wonder in everyday things, things they can relate to, things they see and interact with every day—pencils, traffic lights, pizza, crows, bees, snow. We've also done stories on "kids who do interesting things," such as a teen radio host, a "ball boy" for the Utah Jazz, a 12-year-old composer whose composition has been performed by major city orchestras.

Query first by e-mail. Let us know if you have online clips we can access, or if you can fax us clips. Word lengths: 700 to 1,000 for the main story, plus at least one 250-to-400-word sidebar and another even shorter one (a resource list, bulleted items, etc.) We pay from $150 up for the package. We need visuals, too. We pay extra for writer-provided photos.

How to pitch and follow up
1. Personal essays and poetry: Submit finished work only, via e-mail. homeforum@csps.com.

2. Query on Kidspace articles. In an e-mail (The Home Forum), tell us what you know about the topic, how you would like to cover it, your experience, and what you see as visual possibilities.

You will receive an acknowledgment of receipt by return e-mail. If you do NOT receive an acceptance letter within three weeks of the acknowledgment, you can assume that we are not able to use the submission.

Please do not e-mail the section's editors directly; that will only slow down consideration of your work.

Please note

Be sure to include all of your contact information (e-mail address, daytime telephone, mailing address) with your submission or query. Please include a word count with essays.

ONE submission per e-mail, please. ONE essay submission per author per week. Five poems at a time is sufficient.

We are unable to accept:
Faxed submissions
Telephone queries
Simultaneous submissions
Previously published material

Daily Article on Christian Science
Editor: Clare Turner
Preferred e-mail for queries: jshwrite@csps.com.

Overview

This is the column in the newspaper where spiritual topics are freely discussed, including those that respond to events in the news as well as those that are perennial features. The goal is not just to promote Christian Science but to offer readers from various backgrounds a thoughtful perspective on how God relates to the issues and problems of the day. The article has traditionally carried no byline, although authors frequently share how prayer and Bible study have brought healing to their lives. We look for lively writing that isn't preachy.

Best opportunities for freelancers

Articles need to be consonant with the basic tenets of Christian Science (see "Science and Health with Key to the Scriptures," by Mary Baker Eddy, page 497). We strongly suggest that you become familiar with the column before sending a submission.

Word count: 625-675

Articles for children are also welcome.

How to pitch and follow up

If you want to write an article that will respond to the news or a particular event or holiday, please e-mail Clare Turner (turner@csps.com) to see if something is already being planned on that issue or to discuss the approach you'd like to take.

You are welcome to send manuscripts on more timeless topics for consideration with or without prior contact.

Contributors should e-mail CS Submissions (jshwrite@csps.com) or fax (617-450-2707) their submissions and note that they are for the Monitor article on Christian Science.

Payment

Standard rate is $100 per published article.

Books

Editor: Marjorie Kehe

How to pitch and follow up

Pitch should be a paragraph or two at most, and always come as e-mail. Book review queries should go directly to the book editor, Marjorie Kehe. Section editor will always answer an e-mail upon receipt with a yes, no, or "tell me more."

Payment

Pay is from $150 to $250, depending on length, degree of difficulty, and quality.

Weekend

Editor: Stephen Humphries
Deputy Editor: David S. Hauck
Preferred e-mail(s) for queries: Weekend

Overview

In a word, the Monitor's Weekend section is about everything—everything people do when they're not at work. We cover movies, TV, music, fine arts, reading, recreation, leisure, lifestyle, and all points in between. We're interested in trends, what's new, and what's next. We want to give our readers practical information—how they can participate and reviews they can trust. And we want them to enjoy their stay in Weekend—we put a premium on snappy, engaging writing.

Best opportunities for freelancers

We will take pitches from all parts of the US, but we are always looking for things from a noncoastal perspective. And leisure stories are of particular interest, especially those for and about women, seniors, and the family.

How to pitch and follow up

Pitch your stories to the e-mail addresses above. Keep them brief (no more than a paragraph or two) and focus on telling us why your story is important to readers from Maine to Georgia to California.

Payment

We always take the first two articles on spec. Starting pay is $225 per article plus up to $50 filing expenses. Any travel or other expenses would have to be cleared by the department beforehand.

All pieces must be original for the Monitor. We cannot accept stories that have been or will be published elsewhere.

Targeting your images
Photography
Editor (news): Alfredo Sosa
Preferred e-mail(s) for queries: Alfredo Sosa

Overview

Most photographs published in the Monitor illustrate a story idea and have strong visual appeal. We favor images that both respect the dignity of the subjects and the family sensibilities of our readers. We are not interested in the graphic portrayal of violence, even for the most serious stories. All photographs are printed in color.

Best opportunities for freelancers

We are interested in developing long-term freelance relationships with skilled professional photojournalists. Since we have staff photographers based in Boston, Los Angeles, and Washington, D.C., we are most interested in hiring photographers who live and work in other areas. We hire freelance photographers every week, both in the United States and in other countries. The assignments are almost always at our "half day rate" of $175 plus pre-approved expenses.

We are also interested in discussing appropriate photo stories that a photographer has already begun or has completed.

How to pitch a photo idea (or yourself)

Send a brief letter of introduction and resume to Alfredo Sosa, the news photo editor, at Alfredo Sosa. A follow-up phone call to Alfredo Sosa at 617-450-2340 two days later is recommended. We would like to see a portfolio that demonstrates your strengths and experience as a photojournalist. A digital portfolio is preferred, but slides are acceptable. Do not send originals.

Illustrations and cartoons
Contact: John Kehe (Design director)
Preferred e-mail for queries: John Kehe

Overview

Freelance artists should be familiar with the many art styles used in current newspapers, books, and magazines. Artists should be proficient in Adobe Illustrator and/or conversant in Adobe Photoshop.

How to pitch and follow up

Artists should send samples of their work either electronically and/or by regular mail to John Kehe (John Kehe), Graphics Designer, The Christian Science Monitor.

In case we need to contact you, please send current address: street number, state, country, e-mail, fax number, pager number, and phone number.

Categories: Family

CONTACT: Appropriate Editor as listed
One Norway St

Boston MA 02115
E-mail: addresses as listed
Website: www.csmonitor.com

Christian Science Quarterly

The spirituality.com community is all about individuals sharing experiences that show how an understanding of Christian Science can lead to healing and to other practical, positive solutions. These insights and results help anyone see how their lives—and their community—can be made better through prayer. We'd love to have you share the experiences and healings that come about through your study and practice of Christian Science. Here are some simple guidelines for article submissions:

Write for a global audience—spiritual seekers from all backgrounds, countries, professions, ages.

Include the spiritual idea(s) from the Bible or Mary Baker Eddy's writings that helped you or those you're writing about.

Don't try to cover too many points. Focus on just one spiritual concept.

Use clear, simple reasoning to explain this concept, but develop the idea thoroughly in a way that any reader can understand.

Show how these spiritual concepts changed your thought in a way that led to healing or that gave you spiritual inspiration.

Be sure to describe how the situation or condition changed as your thought about it was spiritualized.

Give enough detail about the subject of the story so that site visitors can directly relate to what happened.

Since this is a site meant to help visitors find healing and comfort, remember to let your writing touch the hearts of your fellow spiritual seekers.

When your article is ready for submission, send it to JSHWrite@csps.com. To ensure it reaches us, please write **"For the Web"** in the subject line. And thank you for sharing with this community of seekers.

After you've submitted:

You can expect an acknowledgement of your submission within one business day. If you don't receive such an acknowledgement, it could be because it didn't make it through net-space to the site, so please try to send it again.

After receipt, you will be contacted via email or phone as to your submission's publication status.

If your article published on the site, be sure to let everyone know by emailing a link to it to your friends!

Note: Accounts that include examples of physical cure through spiritual means require independent verification.

Categories: Nonfiction—Spirituality—Christian Science

CONTACT: Christian Science Quarterly
E-mail: JSHWrite@csps.com
Website: csps.com

Christian Single

Thanks for your interest in writing for *Christian Single*. We are always looking for qualified Christian writers who deliver professional Christian journalism. These guidelines will give you a glimpse into who we are, what we look for in writers, our editorial voice, and how we work with writers.

WHO WE ARE

Our Vision

All articles submitted should be consistent with the vision for our publisher, LifeWay Christian Resources, as well as our magazine.

Christian Single vision: *Christian Single* is the magazine for successful single living, providing practical answers to the real-life needs of today's single adults, challenging them to intensify their faith and impact their community.

LifeWay vision: As God works through us...we will help people and churches know Jesus Christ and seek His kingdom by providing biblical solutions that spiritually transform individuals and cultures.

Our Audience

Our primary readership is comprised of men and women (approximately 40% male; 60% female) between the ages of 25 and 35. We also have secondary readership in the 20-25 and 35-45 age ranges. Approximately 70% have never been married, with 26% divorced or separated, and 4% widowed. Approximately 30% have completed at least some college, with 30% completing bachelor's degrees and 20% graduate degrees. The majority attend church more than once a week (65%) and half are involved in a singles group.

First Contact

Christian Single doesn't accept unsolicited queries or manuscripts. In your initial contact with our editors, we ask that you please provide the following:

1. Resume

Outline your qualifications as a writer, including but not limited to researching, interviewing, and writing skills or particular areas of expertise. What we tend to look for is (1) formal writing training (such as degrees in journalism, communications, English, etc.); (2) experience in feature writing (such as with newspapers, magazines, or books); and (3) recent publishing credits.

2. Clips

Send recently published pieces, including your original drafts as available. This is your opportunity to give us a look at your best work, and with the original drafts, it's our chance to see what it took to get it there.

3. Areas of interest

Share topics or areas of interest/expertise you'd be interested in covering for the magazine. We find that it's better for both the writers and editors if writers cover areas in which they already have an interest or investment.

4. A brief description of your testimony/journey with Christ.

It's important to us that our writers share the same worldview as our readers.

Journalists will be evaluated on the above and their ability to convey the tone and general worldview of the CS audience (see audience demographics above). What we hope to develop at CS are "surrogate staff writers"–a stable of strong writers who are able to deliver consistently in terms of reaching our audience and matching our editorial voice.

Categories: Nonfiction—Christian Interests—Lifestyle—Religion—Singles—Spiritual

CONTACT: Christian Single Writer
Material: All
127 Ninth Ave.
North TN 37234-0140
Phone: 615-251-2000

CHRISTIANITY TODAY

Christianity Today

WHAT WE LOOK FOR IN CHRISTIANITY TODAY ARTICLES:

A. Good Thinking

1. Creative ideas; new angles on old themes.

2. Theses that fit the purpose and stance of CHRISTIANITY TODAY.

3. Fresh insights, wisdom, judgment, analysis, interpretation.

4. Of interest to and useful for CHRISTIANITY TODAY readers.

B. Evidence of Hard Work

1. No superficial generalities.

2. Strong supporting evidence for the article's thesis.

3. Careful diagnosis and solutions.

4. Related to the real world.

    a. Not limited to academic research.

    b. Addressing problems and needs Christians face.

5. Interaction with Christian values and principles.

C. A Strong Logical Case

1. Point-by-point, with transitions.

2. Show the reader where you are going and why.

3. Makes clear what you are trying to prove.

D. Compelling Opening and Conclusion

1. Introductory paragraphs that hold attention.

2. Thesis/transition sentence that clearly states the thesis.

3. An ending that summarizes and provokes thought.

E. Careful Craftsmanship.

1. High regard for language and style, words, punctuation, grammar, etc.

2. Colorful, vivid, moving language.

3. Simplicity, clarity, readability.

4. Generous, and appropriate, use of quotes, anecdotes, stories.

5. No technical jargon or professional academic language.

6. Adherence to our word limits, usually 1,500 to 3,000 words. The Speaking Out columns use 800-word articles. Book reviews are usually commissioned. Letters of inquiry are requested before these are sent out.

7. An electronic copy, as a text file or a Microsoft Word file, preferred. For hard copy we prefer a clean legible manuscript, double-spaced, typed. We prefer exclusive original submissions. If you have sent your manuscript to another magazine, please advise. We prefer these to be on 8-1/2 x 11 inch sheets.

8. Please include a self-addressed, stamped envelope with your submission.

CHRISTIANITY TODAY expects query letters before manuscripts are sent.

1. Material should not be submitted without first becoming thoroughly familiar with the magazine's content over a period of time.

2. Outline your article proposal. State your subject, theme, unique angle, proposition and your main points.

3. Outline your research, experience, qualifications.

4. Tell us something about yourself. Why are you qualified to write this particular article?

5. CT if NOT in the market for fiction or poetry.

PAYMENT SCHEDULE:

Articles are purchased at 20 cents per published word and higher. Reimbursement is usually sent upon publication.

Categories: Nonfiction—Christian Interests—Religion—Spiritual

CONTACT: Mark Galli, Managing Editor
Material: All (No poetry or fiction)
Christianity Today International
465 Gundersen Dr.
Carol Stream IL 60188
Phone: 630-260-6200
Fax: 630-260-8428
E-mail: cteditor@christianitytoday.com
Website: www.christianitytoday.com

> *Remember: Editors change jobs and publishers change addresses. It is wise to invest in a phone call for the current information before submitting.*

Christian Women Today

Article Categories

• We publish non-fiction only; we do not publish poetry.

• Spiritual Content: Our prayer, life stories, spiritual growth and training tools channels are the heartbeat of the site. Suggested maximum word count: 800.

• Life Stories: We publish first-person life stories of Christian women that reflect how they have discovered the Holy Spirit's power for living. We value international representation in life stories. Word count: 500-800 words.

• Training Tools: This channel features practical, how-to articles that equip women for the ministries of prayer, evangelism and discipleship. We also have a special section for leaders in ministry. Word count: 500-800 words.

• Lifestyle Content: We seek authoritative, relevant articles on beauty, health, the workplace, personal finances, and parenting and relationships. Generally, lifestyle pieces are 200-500 words.

Writing for the Internet

To offer ease of online reading for our audience, we like to use sub-headings or bulleted lists that break up longer articles. For more information on writing for the Internet, see How Users Read on the Web.

Submissions

We ask that you complete a preliminary application form before submitting your article. (You will not have to fill out this form in the future if you decide to submit more articles.) Once your preliminary application is received, we will e-mail you information on how to submit articles.

The preliminary application form is available at
http://www.christianwomentoday.com/volunteer/writingappl.html

Categories: Nonfiction—Beauty—Career—Christian Interest—Evangelism—Family—Health—Marriage—Ministry—Money and Finances—Parenting—Relationships—Spiritual

CONTACT: Editor
Material: All
Campus Crusade for Christ
Christian Women Today
Box 300 Stn A
Vancouver, BC V6C 2X3
Phone: 604-514-2000
Fax: 604-514-2124
E-mail: editor@christianwomantoday.com (preferred)
Website: www.christianwomentoday.com

The Chronicle of the Horse

The Chronicle of the Horse, founded in 1937, is a national weekly magazine with approximately 20,000 subscribers. The magazine focuses primarily on dressage, hunters and jumpers, eventing, foxhunting, and steeplechase racing.

In addition to reporting news about these disciplines, we feature articles on horse care and profiles of prominent horse people. We also occasionally accept humor, human interest and historical articles. No poetry, please, and no clinic reports.

Eighty percent of our editorial material comes from freelance writers. We review submissions for acceptance or rejection within four to eight weeks of receipt. We pay for feature articles the month following acceptance; for news articles the month following publication.

Articles appear in the magazine and on the website (www.chronofhorse.com).

The following special issues are published:

Winter Circuit Preview Issue (January); Steeplechasing (January);

American Horses In Sport (February); Show Jumping (February); Horse Show (March); Intercollegiate (March);

Rolex Kentucky Preview (April);
Junior and Pony (May);
Dressage (June);
Horse Care (July);
Eventing (August);
Hunt Roster (September);
Amateur (November); Pony Breeding (November);
Stallion (December).

The Chronicle of the Horse is the official publication of the following national organizations:

Masters of Foxhounds Association, U.S. Equestrian Team Foundation, U.S. Pony Clubs, National Riding Commission, American Foxhound Club, U.S. Dressage Federation, American Vaulting Association, North American Riding for the Handicapped Association, Inc., and The Roster of Packs of the National Beagle Club of America, Inc.

News stories may be submitted to: results@chronofhorse.com.

Feature stories may be sent to: bethr@chronofhorse.com.

Types of Material

Publisher assumes no responsibility for lost or damaged manuscripts and photographs. Precise publication dates of accepted articles cannot be predetermined.

NEWS STORIES - Before covering any competition, clear the assignment with us.

Approx. 1,500 words. $165-$220.

FEATURE ARTICLES - We advise sending a query letter.

Approx. 1,500-2,500. $150 - $250.

PHOTOS - Black and white or color, print, or digital. 3 1/2" x 5" minimum print size. 300 dpi minimum resolution for digital images.

ALL SUBJECTS MUST BE IDENTIFIED. $30 - $50 for each photo published. Photographer's guidelines available on request.

Categories: Nonfiction—Animals

CONTACT: results@chronofhorse.com
Material: News stories
CONTACT: bethr@chronofhorse.com
Material: Feature stories
PO Box 46
MiddleburgVA 20118
108 The Plains Rd.
Middleburg, VA 20117
Phone: 540-687-6341
Fax: 540-687-3937
Website: www.chronofhorse.com

Chronicle of the Old West

Chronicle of the Old West is a monthly 1800's newspaper for Old West enthusiasts. These are people for whom the Old West is a time and place of the heart.

WRITING STYLE: We are looking for articles that educate, entertain and excite people about the Old West. The articles should be historically accurate. – We do not do fiction. We are looking for the real flavor and atmosphere of the Old West, not technical or dry scholarly accounts. *Articles should be written as if the author is a reporter for* Chronicle of the Old West *writing about a current event. We want to give the reader the feeling the event just took place, and the reader is at the time and location of the subject of the article.* The author should not make reference to himself within the article. (A sample article is at the end of the writer's guidelines.)

Subjects can be about the adventure or daily life of outlaws and lawmen, ranchers and farmers, trappers and settlers, Native Americans and cavalry.

If the article is about a well-known person or event, it should include new or not commonly known information.

The format is newsprint tabloid size in sepia tone ink, giving the flavor of a vintage Old West newspaper.

We accept original or reprint articles. Please indicate if the material has previously been published and where. We purchase the rights not only to print the material in *Chronicle of the Old West*, but also the rights to reprint in our web site and an anthology.

Original sources are best (newspaper accounts, memoirs, documents), rather than compilations from previous publications. Do not include your sources within the article itself, but do include them as an addendum for our review.

So that our readers will get a better feeling of the timing of the article, it will appear in the issue of the month in which the article's final outcome took place.

TIMELINE & GEOGRAPHIC COVERAGE: The age of the Old West was from 1800 to 1900. We give a special emphasis to what is known as the "Wild West" from 1860 to 1900. The Old West covers the Mississippi River to the Pacific Ocean, and the Canadian border to the Rio Grande River.

QUERY LETTER: Provide a one-page summary of the story with sources and short bio explaining your expertise and credits. If you would like your submission returned, please include a self-addressed stamped envelope.

SUBMISSIONS: Manuscripts should be typed, single space, on one side of standard white 8 ½ x 11 paper in Times or Arial fonts. Use bond paper and one inch margins on all sides. Name, address, telephone number and approximate word count should be at the top of the first page. Sources and additional reading should be included at the end of the manuscript. You can also submit manuscripts on an IBM compatible computer disk or via e-mail atOldPress@RavenHeart.com

In addition to byline and payment, we will provide authors with two copies of *Chronicle of the Old West* in which the article appears. When we buy a manuscript, we reserve the right to edit, rewrite and shorten it. Please allow up to two month's response time for queries and manuscripts.

PHOTOS/ART: Photos, maps and art are encouraged and may sway a decision. Material can be black and white, color slides or archival material. Private photos are especially valued. Submit photocopies with query.

ARTICLE LENGTH: Feature articles can vary in length from short 500 word clips to 1,500 word essays. Articles can be one-time, a series of related articles or a continuing saga. We also have special departments. *They include:*

• "The Chuck Wagon." Recipes of the Old West. It is necessary to include information on the history of the recipe.

• "The Old West on Celluloid." How current and past western movies portray the Old West.

• "The Old West Today." Descriptions of places and events where people can experience the Old West through participation and observation. This needs to be submitted four months prior to the event.

PAYMENT: Payment is made within 30 days following publication. *Chronicle of the Old West* pays five to eight cents per word with the exception of the column "The Chuck Wagon." The payment for "The Chuck Wagon" is $10.00 per recipe.

Categories: Nonfiction—History—Western

CONTACT: Dakota Livesay, Publisher
Material: All
PO Box 2859
Show Low AZ 85901
E-mail: info@chronicleoftheoldwest.com
Website: www.chronicleoftheoldwest.com

Chronicles

A MAGAZINE OF AMERICAN CULTURE

Chronicles
A Magazine of American Culture

CHRONICLES is a monthly magazine of ideas devoted to discussions of first principles in all branches of humane learning. It is not an academic journal. Our special concern is with the intersection of arts and letters with social and political issues. While our editorial policy can be described as traditionalist or conservative, our pages are open to a broad spectrum of opinions.

The ideal contributor to CHRONICLES is a writer or scholar who can express his ideas clearly enough to reach the general reader. We try to avoid both ideological polemics and academic jargon in favor of liveliness and clarity.

"VIEWS": Two or three essays are commissioned for each CHRONICLES issue and are usually devoted to some aspect of the issue's theme. These pieces run anywhere from 1,500-3,000 words long.

"OPINIONS": These are our longer review essays of about 1,500 words on a theme derived from a current book or number of books. The subject of the essay is not just the books themselves but a topic suggested by the books. The main part of the essay should be devoted to developing the writer's own ideas.

"REVIEWS": These are our shorter reviews in 500-1,200 words, reviewers are asked to identify the primary themes of a book and put them into perspective. In the case of fiction, please resist the temptation to summarize the plot.

"VITAL SIGNS": This is our cultural section, in which we run movie, theater, and art reviews. This is also the place for reportage on subjects such as legal cases, academic issues, and the like.

"CORRESPONDENCE": Our "Letters From..." fall into this section, which has the loosest criteria. In the past we have run reportage, personal essays, and more philosophical pieces.

When reviewing books, please be sure to include all book review information: title, author (or editor), publisher, city, state, price, and page number.

To assist us in fact-checking, please include at the end of the article sources of any quotations used within the text.

We will need you to provide us with a short bio, one or two sentences long.

CHRONICLES does not accept unsolicited fiction.

Categories: Nonfiction—Christian Interests—Culture—Education—Environment—Government—Literature—Poetry—Politics—Regional

CONTACT: Scott P. Richert, Exec. Editor
Material: All
928 N. Main St.
Rockford IL 61103
Phone: 815-964-5054
Fax: 815-964-9403
E-mail: submissions@chroniclesmagazine.org
Website: www.chroniclesmagazine.org

Chronogram

Chronogram is a regional magazine of arts, lifestyle, politics, environmental issues, holistic health and culture published monthly. *Chronogram* is an outlet for reportage and point of view that are not often found in the mainstream media. We like to think of ourselves as "progressive" in the broadest sense: We believe that an enlightened, democratic society is attainable as long as citizens-our readers a small group among them-are informed with reliable information. Our writers write the critiques, praises, philosophizings and personal anecdotes that provide the detail to the larger picture, the colors to the outline (often coloring outside the lines).

The editor's ears are always open for new voices and all story ideas are invited for pitching. *Chronogram* welcomes all voices and viewpoints as long as they are expressed well. We discriminate solely based on the quality of the writing, nothing else. The length of articles we usually run are from 1000-3500 words.

While for the most part *Chronogram* covers local events and profiles local people, our political and environmental coverage is nationally and internationally focused. *Chronogram* is also committed to publishing insightful first person essays, short stories and poetry.

Chronogram pays on a sliding scale based on a contract between the editor and the writer. We do not offer kill fees or any other compensation for stories we choose not to publish; we cannot afford that luxury. *Chronogram* reserves the right not to publish any story submitted to us if it does not meet our editorial standards, even if the editor has initially given a writer the 'go-ahead' for a story idea. If a story is purchased, *Chronogram* reserves first-time North American print and Web rights, which revert to the writer after a period of three months.

Now that you know what we want, get to it. For longer article ideas, please contact the editor, via e-mail bmahoney@chronogram.com, or regular post, before submitting the piece. Submissions should be double-spaced, with only one carriage return between paragraphs (no spaces between the paragraphs) and no paragraph indents. All accepted editorial submissions (not poetry) must be submitted electronically or on disk. Send it all, and if you want it returned, include an SASE.

Brian K. Mahoney, Editorial Director

Chronogram Artists' Guidelines

Since *Chronogram* is a magazine of the arts, we strive to feature the best available art for our monthly Cover and Parting Shot features. Both are full page venues for local/semi-local artists to display their work. Along with both are (approximate) 100-word bios about the artist and gallery where and when to find the original work. Please send samples via e-mail or snail mail to the address above.

As well as the Cover and Parting Shot opportunities, there are many other ways artists can be seen in *Chronogram*. We are always looking for new talent to grace our pages. Assignment photographers, illustrators and cartoonists are needed every month! *Chronogram* pays $40-$80 per assignement. Please send samples via e-mail or snail mail to the address above.

COVER SUBMISSIONS:

Paintings/mixed media/photographs: original work*, large-format transparencies (sorry, no 35mm slides accepted for the cover)

PARTING SHOT SUBMISSIONS:

• Photographs/mixed media: original work* (no larger than 8.5x14), 35mm slide, large-format transparency, 300 dpi 8x10 BW scan (tiff/jpg/psd)

• Original work can be submitted, though is not recommended. We can direct large-format painters on how to get a 4x5 transparency shot for easier submission. Photographers, please submit original prints no larger than 8.5x14 inches.

Please note: Chronogram does not pay for Cover or Parting Shot art. All mailed artwork must come with a SASE in order to be returned. All measurement requirements listed above are in inches.

Categories: Nonfiction—Arts—Cartoons—Culture—Ecology—Interview—Music—Poetry—Regional

CONTACT: Brian K. Mahoney, Editorial Director
Material: All, except poetry
CONTACT: Franci Levine Grater, Poetry Director
Material: Poetry
Luminary Publishing, PO Box 459
New Paltz NY 12561
Phone: 845-255-4711
Website: www.chronogram.com

THE CHRYSALIS READER

Chrysalis Reader
Journal of the Swedenborg Foundation

What Is the Chrysalis Reader? *Chrysalis*, originally a journal issued three times a year, has evolved into a book series titled The Chrysalis Reader, published once a year in the Autumn by the Swedenborg Foundation. Each Reader focuses on a theme, from which a book title evolves based on the essays, stories, and poetry collected for that issue. Themes include modern yet timeless topics related to human nature that resonate the approach and insightfulness of Emanuel Swedenborg (1688–1772)—scientist, inventor, and mystic—who used his rational and scientific orientation to explore the world of spirit. The Reader explores contemporary questions on spirituality and seeks to give fresh and diverse perspectives from many traditions.

The Chrysalis Reader Audience The Chrysalis Reader audience includes people from numerous faiths and backgrounds. Many of them work in psychology, education, religion, the arts, or one of the helping professions. The style of writing may be humorous, serious, or some combination of these approaches. Essays, poetry, and fiction that are not evangelical but rather that are unique in addressing the Chrysalis Reader theme are more likely to be accepted. Our readers are interested in expanding, enriching, or challenging their intellects, hearts, and philosophies, and many also just want to enjoy a good read. For these reasons the editors attempt to publish a mix of writings. Articles and poetry must be related to the theme, however, you may have your own approach to the theme not written in our description. Upcoming themes and copy deadlines are available at www.swedenborg.com.

Writer's Guidelines The *Chrysalis Reader* does not accept material that has been published previously. We do accept simultaneous submissions.

In editing, our primary goal is to maintain the integrity of the author's style and point of view. Editing is designed to clarify and to keep the writing in the Reader lively and interesting.

The *Chrysalis Reader* style follows *The Chicago Manual of Style.* Manuscripts should be typed, double-spaced, and no longer than 3,000 words. The final copy of an accepted manuscript should be submitted in hard copy (snail mail) and electronically either on disc or as an attached file via e-mail (chrysalis@hovac.com). Manuscripts will not be returned to authors. Please keep a copy of your manuscript for your records and include a self-addressed, stamped envelope for our response and other correspondence.

The interval between submission of the accepted manuscript and the final draft may involve communication between author, reviewers, and editors. Our schedule is designed to allow flexibility and a liberal amount of time for such communication. If you have missed the date for a rough draft but feel you have a solid idea for a piece, send us your article or poem. We look forward to your contribution. For potential authors, previously issued titles are $7 each; current titles are $10 each. At the bookstore, Readers sell for $14.95. You can visit www.swedenborg.com to view back issues of The Chrysalis Reader.

Categories: Fiction—Nonfiction—Arts—Literature—Poetry—Spiritual—Philosophy

CONTACT: Richard Butterworth, Editorial Associate
Material: All
Route 1, Box 4510
Dillwyn VA 23936
Phone: 434-983-3021
Fax: 434-983-1074
E-mail: chrysalis@hovac.com
Website: www.swedenborg.com

Cicada

Submissions Guidelines

For a sample issue of CICADA, please send $8.50 to CICADA Sample Copy • P.O. Box 300 • Peru, IL 61354 *NOTE: Sample copy requests from foreign countries must be accompanied by International Postal Reply Coupons (IRCs) valued at US $8.50. Please do NOT send a check or money order.* CICADA is a literary magazine for teenagers and young adults and is published by Cricket Magazine Group. CICADA, for ages 14 and up, publishes original short stories, poems, and first-person essays written for teens and young adults. In some cases, CICADA purchases rights for excerpts from books yet to be published. Each issue also includes several reprints of high-quality selections. CICADA measures 5-1/2" x 8-1/2", contains 128 pages, has a full-color cover, and is perfect bound. Black-and-white illustrations of the highest quality appear throughout the magazine. We hope the following information will be useful to prospective contributors.—Editor-in-Chief, Marianne Carus; Executive Editor, Deborah Vetter.

Published: Bimonthly, 6 times a year.

Price: $35.97 for 1-year subscription (6 issues).

Comments:

CICADA would like to reach as many authors and illustrators as possible for original contributions, but our standards are very high, and we will accept only top-quality material. PLEASE DO NOT QUERY FIRST. CICADA will consider any manuscripts or art samples sent on speculation and accompanied by a self-addressed, stamped envelope. For art, send tear sheets or photoprints/photocopies. PLEASE DO NOT send original artwork. Be sure that each sample is marked with your name, address, and phone number. Allow 12 weeks for a reply.

CICADA normally purchases the following rights for works appearing in the magazine. For stories and poems previously unpublished, rights vary. Payment is made upon publication.

For stories and poems previously published, CICADA purchases second North American publication rights. Fees vary, but are generally less than fees for first publication rights. Payment is made upon publication. Same applies to accompanying art.

For recurring features, CICADA purchases the material outright. The work becomes the property of CICADA, and it is copyrighted in the name of Carus Publishing Company. A flat fee per feature is usually negotiated. Payment is made upon publication.

For commissioned artwork, rights vary, but in all cases the terms outlined below apply:

a. Physical art remains the property of the illustrator.

b. Payment is made within 45 days of acceptance.

c. Illustrators may use artwork for self promotion.

Manuscripts:

Fiction, realistic, contemporary, historical fiction, adventure, humor, fantasy, science fiction (Main protagonist should be at least 14, preferably older; stories should have a genuine teen sensibility and be aimed at readers in high school or college). Nonfiction first-person experiences that are relevant and interesting to teenagers Poetry serious or humorous; rhymed or free verse. Other book reviews providing in-depth, thoughtful commentary. Length Fiction/articles up to 5,000 words .

Novellas up to 15,000 words (We run one novella per issue) .

Poems up to 25 lines.

Book review 300 to 500 words. An exact word count should be noted on each manuscript submitted. For poetry, indicate number of lines instead. Word count includes every word, but does not include the title of the manuscript or the author's name.

Rates:

Fiction and articles up to 25¢ per word.

Poems up to $3.00 per line.

Payment upon publication.

Categories Fiction—Nonfiction—Book Reviews—Juvenile—Poetry—Teen—Young Adult

CONTACT: Submissions Editor
Material: Manuscripts
CONTACT: John Sandford, Art Director
Material: Art
CONTACT: Diane Sikora, Rights and Permissions Coordinator
Material: Inquiries regarding permissions
PO Box 300
Peru IL 61354 *(please check our website in 2007 for new mailing address for submissions)*
Phone: 312-701-1720
Fax: 312-701-1728
Website: www.cricketmag.com

Cimarron Review

Please read carefully these guidelines before submitting.

We accept submissions year-round in poetry, fiction, non-fiction, and art. All work must be accompanied by a SASE. Cover letter encouraged.

Please send 3–6 poems, one piece of fiction or non-fiction (2–3 o.k. if work is under 1500 words), and prints for cover art and portfolios. Address all work to the appropriate editor (fiction, poetry, non-fiction, art) and mail to:

Cimarron Review
205 Morrill Hall, English Dept.
Oklahoma State University
Stillwater, OK 74078

We do not accept the following:
• Previously published work (includes work published online).
• E-mail submissions from authors living in the United States.

We will accept E-mail submissions from writers living outside the US, but please query first, and follow our guidelines listed here.

Simultaneous submissions are welcomed, but please notify us immediately through postal or E-mail should your work be accepted elsewhere.

We do not publish theme issues. We are interested in any strong writing of a literary variety, but are especially partial to poetry with an awareness of narrative and fiction in the modern realist tradition. We have no set page lengths for any genre, but we seldom publish short-shorts or pieces over 25 pages. There are, however, exceptions to every rule. Our guiding aesthetic is the quality of the work itself.

We strongly encourage those interested in submitting to first read a copy of the magazine in order to better understand our likes and/or dislikes.

Categories: Fiction—Nonfiction—Culture—Literature—Native American—Poetry—Short Stories—Writing

CONTACT: Fiction Editor
Material: Fiction
CONTACT: Poetry Editor
Material: Poetry
CONTACT: Non-Fiction Editor
Material: Non-Fiction
CONTACT: Art Editor
Material: Art
205 Morrill Hall, English Dept.
Oklahoma State University
Stillwater OK 74078-4069
Phone:405-744-9476
Fax: 405-744-6326
E-mail: cimarronreview@yahoo.com (no submissions)
Website: www.cimarronreview.okstate.edu

Remember: Editors change jobs and publishers change addresses. It is wise to invest in a phone call for the current information before submitting.

Cincinnati Woman Magazine

Cincinnati Woman is a magazine relating to woman's issues in the Cincinnati area.

Please send a sample of your writing along with your story idea. E-mail submissions are okay.

Payment
$80 for feature stories of about 1,000 words.
$50 for other department articles.

Categories: Nonfiction—Animals—Antiques—Architecture—Arts—Biography—Boating—Book Reviews—Careers—Children—Christian Interests—Collectibles—College—Computers—Cooking—Crafts/Hobbies—Dance—Diet/Nutrition—Drama—Education—Electronics—Entertainment—Family—Fashion—Film/Video—Fishing—Food/Drink—Games—Gardening—Health—Hobbies—Human Rights—Internet—Interview—Jewish Interest—Juvenile—Law—Lifestyle—Literature—Marriage—Men's Issues—Money & Finances—Multicultural—Music—New Age—Outdoors—Parenting—Photography—Physical Fitness—Politics—Public Speaking—Real Estate—Recreation—Regional—Relationships—Religion—Rural America—Science—Self-Help—Sexuality—Singles—Society—Spiritual—Sports/Recreation—Teen—Textbooks—Theatre—Travel—Women's Issues—Writing

CONTACT: Alicia Wiebe, Publisher
Material: All
Niche Publishing & Media, LLC
PO Box 30
Milford OH 45150-0030
Phone: 513-697-6433
Fax: 513-697-6473
E-mail: cincinnatiwoman@cinci.rr.com

CINEASTE
AMERICA'S LEADING MAGAZINE ON
THE ART AND POLITICS OF THE CINEMA

Cineaste

Published quarterly, and appearing regularly since 1967, *Cineaste* is today internationally recognized as one of America's foremost film magazines. An independent publication, with no financial ties to the film industry or academic institutions, *Cineaste* features contributions from many of America's most articulate and outspoken writers, critics, and scholars. Focusing on both the art and politics of the cinema, and always stressing a popular, readable style displayed in an attractive, lavishly illustrated format, *Cineaste* offers colorful and thought-provoking coverage of the entire world of cinema, *including*:

• Probing and informative interviews with directors, screenwriters, performers and other creative and technical film production personnel.
• Feature articles on topical issues and contemporary film trends
• In-depth reviews of the latest Hollywood movies, independent productions and foreign films
• Regular coverage of films from developing nations in the Third world
• Critical symposiums and debates on such controversial films as *JFK, Do the Right Thing, Thelma & Louise, Boyz N the Hood,* and *Malcolm X*
• Special supplements on such subjects as Central and Eastern European Cinema, The Arab Image in American Cinema, The Restoration of Spartacus, and Sound and Music in the Movies
• A continuing series on "Race in Contemporary American Cinema"

- Regular columns such as "Book Reviews," "Homevideo," "A Second Look," "Festivals," and "Short Takes"

Guidelines for Writers

Cineaste offers a social, political and esthetic perspective on the cinema. We are not affiliated with any organization or institution. We are interested in all areas of the cinema, including Hollywood films (old and new), American independents, quality European films, and the cinema of the Third World. Familiarity with our editorial policies is a must for authors. The most frequent reason we reject material is that the potential contributor has sent material which, because of length or style or orientation, is clearly out of place in our pages.

STYLE: Our target audience is the intelligent general public, a public that is fairly sophisticated about both art and politics. No matter how complex the ideas or arguments advanced, we demand readability. We think it is the job of the writer to clarify his or her thoughts and not for the reader to decipher clumsy formulations. We dislike academic jargon, obtuse Marxist terminology, film buff trivia, trendy 'buzz' phrases, and show biz references. We do not want our writers to speak of how they have 'read' or 'decoded' a film, but to view, analyze and interpret same. The author's processes and quirks should be secondary to the interests of the reader. Warning the reader of problems with specific films is more important to us than artificially 'puffing' a film because its producers or politics are agreeable.

FEATURE ARTICLES: Articles should discuss the subject (a film, film genre, a career, a theory, a movement, etc.) in depth. The author should detail the particular sociopolitical and artistic content. When appropriate, provide documentation or quotes on the producer's intentions rather than your speculations. Be aware of the political implications of the work and its social perspectives, whatever the actual plot or genre. Whenever possible, sources should be incorporated into the text rather than footnoted. Preferred length for feature articles is 3,000-4,000 words. Send a letter of inquiry on a feature idea or provide an outline. Do not call the office to speak to an editor about article ideas. We want to see your proposal in writing.

One article format we encourage is an omnibus review of several current films, preferably those not reviewed in a previous issue. Such an article would focus on films that perhaps share a certain political perspective, subject matter, or generic concerns (e.g., films on suburban life, or urban violence, or revisionist Westerns). Like individual Film Reviews, these articles should incorporate a very brief synopsis of plots for those who haven't seen the films. The main focus, however, should be on the social issues manifested in each film and how it may reflect something about the current political/social/esthetic climate.

INTERVIEWS: Interviews may be with directors, performers, writers, composers, producers, distributors, technicians, or anyone else involved in the creative or business side of filmmaking. We expect the interview to be hard hitting in that challenging (not necessarily hostile) questions are posed and difficult or controversial points pursued. Our experience is that most interviewees respect a well-prepared interviewer who takes their work seriously enough to ask demanding questions. 'Puff' pieces are boring. We are interested in 1) In-depth career interviews with major personalities; 2) Medium-length interviews usually on a current production or issue; and 3) Very short interviews of a few questions which can be used as a sidebar interview with a review.

An interview is more than a transcript of questions and answers. Transcripts must be edited, condensed, and, if necessary, rearranged to bring major themes into focus. The interviewee should see this material for approval before submission to us. It is helpful, but not necessary, to provide a brief, straightforward introduction and a suggested title. Photos are also appreciated. We wish to emphasize that the focus of the interview is the interviewee, not the interviewer. A typical sign of a poor interview is the inordinate length of the questions which are as long, or even longer, than the answers.

FILM REVIEWS: We prefer reviews that focus on one current film. The review should tell what is of merit and what is not in the film under discussion. It should incorporate a very brief synopsis or description of the plot for those who haven't seen the film. Your review should not be a long plot outline with appended evaluations. We are concerned with esthetics as well as content, with how cinematic techniques affect a film's impact. Preferred length is about 1,500 words for feature reviews

BOOK REVIEWS: Book reviews should deal with newly published books, although recent books as much as two years old may be covered depending on the work's importance. Reviewers may focus on one title or cover several related ones. We encourage review-essays in which the discussion serves as a vehicle for a broader treatment of ideas or issues; but, to be fair to authors, their works deserve to be treated seriously rather than merely as launching pads for general essays. Preferred length for feature reviews is 1,000-2,000 words; capsule reviews are 300-400 words. Provide complete publication information (e.g., publisher, year of publication, number of pages, illus., etc.), following the format used in the "Book Reviews" section. In general, writers should query the Book Review Editor before submitting book reviews.

COLUMNS: "Homevideo" articles (1,000-1,500 words) should deal with topics of general interest or a related group of films; individual title reviews should be 300-500 words. "A Second Look" articles (1,000-1,500 words) should offer a new interpretation of a film classic or a reevaluation of an unjustly neglected release of more recent vintage. "Lost and Found" articles (1,000-1,500 words) should discuss a film that may or may not be released or otherwise seen in the U.S. but which is important enough to be brought to the attention of our readers. "Festivals" columns (1,000-1,500 words) should focus on film festivals of particular political importance, providing as much broader social and artistic context as possible for the specific films discussed since many of the latter may not be released or otherwise screened in the U.S.

SUBMISSIONS: We assume that all manuscripts are not reworked versions of previously published or simultaneously submitted material. Manuscripts will be responded to in from 2-4 weeks. Unsolicited material will be given serious consideration, but it is best to query first in case the film, book, or topic has already been assigned. No term papers, please! Do not call the office about submissions unless more than a month has elapsed since making your submission. Long distance phone calls will be returned collect.

REVISIONS: If we feel the material needs further work, we will either 1) Return the material to you with suggestions for changes, or 2) Make changes and submit the revised manuscript for your approval before publication. A Writer's Agreement Form will be sent for all manuscripts accepted for publication.

PAYMENT: We currently pay a minimum of $50 for film reviews and other short pieces, $40 for book or video reviews (the author also gets to retain the book or video reviewed), and a minimum of $100 for feature material, on publication. Contributors also receive three copies of the issue for short pieces and six copies for feature material. We hope to raise these rates, knowing that good writing merits adequate compensation. Kill fees (50% of the above rates) may be paid for material originally solicited by the editors. Royalties from subsequent publication in foreign journals or anthologies will be split 50/50 with the author. Our percentage will be waived when the book is a collection of the author's work or is edited by the author.

All material submitted will be carefully read. Although we have published some of the best known writers on film, we have also been the first place of publication for many writers. All the editors are themselves writers and are aware of the curt treatment writers so often receive from indifferent editors. The least you can expect from us is a thoughtful reading of your work, even though we may not be able to write you with detailed comments.

Categories: Film/Video

CONTACT: Submissions Editor
Material: All
304 Hudson St., 6th Floor

New York NY 10013-1015
Phone: 212-366-5720
Fax: 212-366-5724
E-mail: CINEASTE@cineaste.com
Website: www.cineaste.com

Circle K

Thank you for your interest in CIRCLE K magazine. CIRCLE K is a sixteen-page collegiate publication distributed five times during each academic year (October, November/December, January/February, March, and April) to the 11,000 members of Circle K International, as well as additional subscribers.

Circle K International is the world's largest collegiate service organization, and its members are above-average college students, primarily residing in the United States and Canada, who are committed to community service and leadership development.

Articles published in CIRCLE K are of two types: serious and light nonfiction. Most articles purchased for publication in CIRCLE K address broad areas of interest to all college students but specifically to service-minded individuals, such as current trends (social, collegiate, etc.), leadership and career development, self-help, and community involvement. No fiction, short humor, or travel pieces are accepted. Also, we do not publish historical or philosophical pieces, nor do we accept profiles.

CIRCLE K articles average between 1,500 and 2,000 words (six to eight pages, typed double-spaced); payment is "on acceptance" and ranges from $150 to $400, depending on depth of treatment, appeal to our special audience, and other factors. Query letters are preferred to finished manuscripts.

Proposed articles are tested against two major criteria: They should (1) cover a broad subject rather than an individual person, place, or event; and (2) be applicable to the lives and concerns of today's college students.

Some of our recently published articles include "Student Legal Woes," "Mum's the Word" (political correctness), "The Black and White of How to Get a Job," "Cultural Diversity 101," "Television's College Cult," "Crossing the Student/Mentor Line," "When Children and Collegians Click," "The Graduate School Climb," "Last Call for Alcohol," and "Students of Divorce."

In all articles, treatment must be objective and in-depth, and each major point should be substantiated by illustrative examples and quotes from expert sources. Authors are required to base their stories on interviews and research rather than on personal insights and experiences, and serious articles should avoid intrusions of writers' views. Single-source articles and essays are quickly rejected.

Writing style should be smooth, personable, and to the point, with strong narration, anecdotes, and use of descriptive detail where appropriate. An article's lead must be strong, capturing the readers' attention and setting the tone of the piece. It should be followed by a clear thesis statement of the article's central point. The reader should know quickly what he or she is going to read about and why.

Treatment of light subjects must be as authoritative as serious subjects, but humorous examples and comparisons, as well as a lighter writing style, also are valued when appropriate.

Writers should be aware that CIRCLE K is not exclusively a US publication but has readers in Canada and the Caribbean as well. Avoid terms such as "our nation" and "our president," and strive for some quotes and examples from non-US sources, if practical.

Photographs (color and/or black-and-white) are not essential but are when they are of high quality and add substantially to the impact of article. Photos and artwork are purchased as part of the manuscript with consideration given to the extra time and expense of the author.

Mail or fax query letters.

Categories: Campus Life—College—Education—Young Adult

CONTACT: Amy Wiser, Executive Editor
Material: All
3636 Woodview Trace
Indianapolis IN 46268-3196
Phone: 317-875-8755
Fax: 317-879-0204
E-mail: ck.magazine@kiwanis.org

Circle Track

Circulation: 130,212
Frequency: monthly
Readers turn to *Circle Track* as the voice of authority and technical guide to oval track racing. The title focuses on the latest in racing technology and competition strategies. It also provides readers with in-depth articles on performance modifications.

Guidelines: *Circle Track* has no formal guidelines.

Visit *Circle Track* on-line at www.circletrack.com

Categories: Nonfiction—Automobiles—Sports/Recreation—Technology

CONTACT: Ron Lemaster Jr., Editor-in-Chief
Material: All
3816 Industry Blvd.
Lakeland FL 33811
Website: www.circletrack.com

The Circle

We love reading submissions. By submitting, you agree that if we chose to publish your work, we have permission to publish it in our print issue and put it on our website.

We pay in copies of the print edition (even if your work only appears on the website) so include your address with any submission.

Poetry
3-5 poems
No file attachments - put in body of email
any length/style
Note, however, that we have published only one rhyming poem since 1997.

Include your name, address, phone number & email address with submission. Submissions can be emailed to circlemag@aol.com or snail mailed.

Artwork/photographs
Please do not send originals until artwork is accepted! Attach as .jpg file or mail color photocopies. we are currently seeking art/photographs for cover and inside the print edition, as well as on the website. if the piece is for sale, please let us know that as well!

Submissions can be emailed to circlemag@aol.com or snail mailed.

Short stories
Word count is flexible but longer pieces have little chance of making the print issue most any style/topic - we shy away from anything religious or predictable can be attached as a TEXT FILE (not .doc) or in the body of email submissions can be emailed to circlemag@aol.com or snail mailed.

Features
Check with us first!

Columns
We are currently seeking new columnists on a weekly/monthly/quarterly basis. most of these columns will appear on the website with infrequent appearance in print edition. we are open to ideas and will work with writers to get their voice heard! email us for more information or with ideas. Note: pays in copies of print edition

Reviews
CD, website, movie, book, zine, etc. - email editor and ask!
helpful suggestions

1. The word "you" is not spelled "u," nor is "your" or "you're" spelled "ur."

2. If English is not your native language, make sure we don't know it from your writing.

Categories: Fiction—Nonfiction—Arts—Comedy—Culture—Interview—Literature—Music—Paranormal—Photography—Poetry—Science—Science Fiction—Short Stories—Writing—Humor—Philosophy

CONTACT: Penny Talbert, Editor
Material: Short stories, Artwork, Photos, Poetry
173 Grandview Road
Wernersville PA 19565
Phone: 610-678-6550
Fax: 610-678-6550
E-mail: circlemag@aol.com
Website: www.circlemagazine.com

Civil War Times

Please refer to WEIDER History Group.

Clamor
New Perspectives on Politics, Culture, Media and Life

Clamor magazine is built from everyday folks like you. Please take some time to contact us if you have any ideas that you would like to see in clamor. *Below are the guidelines for contributing to clamor:*

REQUIREMENTS

When approaching us with a proposal, we simply need to know the topic, expected length, whether or not you will provide graphics to accompany your piece, and what deadline you can commit to.

Final drafts should be submitted via email or disk, and should include title, how you want to be credited (how you want your name listed), and a few lines of biographical inormation or the contributors page. You also need to tell us if want your address or e-mail to accompany your bio. This needs to be submitted with each article.

You always have the option of using your payment towards advertisement, a subscription, or a donation. Please let us know how you would like your payment (and what name to make payments to), when you submit your final draft.

PLEASE REMEMBER:

Do not feel obliged to send a big, feature length piece each time you contribute. We will happily take short columns, reviews, single panel/stand alone artwork and photography, etc.

WRITING REVIEWS FOR CLAMOR:

If you think you might be interested in writing reviews of books, zines, movies or CDs for *Clamor*, see our website for a list of available items.

Categories: Book Reviews—Film/Video—Mass Communications—Music

CONTACT: Submissions Editor
Materials: All
PO Box 1225
Bowling Green OH 43402
E-mail: info@clamormagazine.org
Website: www.clamormagazine.org

Class Act

Practical ideas for language arts teachers in grades 5-12.

Rights: We purchase all rights.

Needs: We need practical, tested ideas for English classrooms, grades 5-12. We look for articles that have ideas that teachers can use the day they read them. It helps to know what teenager don't know in

order to write for them. Writing with a sense of humor helps, too.

Length: 500-200 words.

Payment: Payment ranges from $10-$40, plus an author's copy. We do not have a kill fee; we pay the full amount upon receiving a signed contract.

How to Submit: Please send to Dotty Denton in a cut-and-paste form (no attachments).

Response Time: Generally we respond in less than 1 month.

Tips for Writers: We are seeing far too many submissions that are not geared toward our format or our audience. Please be familiar with both.

Sample Copies/Subscription Information: Samples=$3. Subscription (for nine issues)=$25.

Categories: Education

CONTACT: Dolly Denton
PO Box 802
Henderson KY 42419
E-mail: classact@henderson.net
Website: www.henderson.net/~classact/

Classic Toy Trains

Formal guidelines not available. Please read a number of issues to ascertain the publication's style and needs.

Send queries to address below.

Categories: Antiques—Collectibles—Crafts/Hobbies—Hobbies—Juvenile

CONTACT: Kelly Shaw, Editorial Assistant
Material: All
Kalmbach Publishing Co.
21027 Crossroads Circle
Waukesha WI 53186
Phone: 262-796-8776
E-mail: manuscripts@ClassicToyTrains.com
Website: ClassicToyTrains.com

Click Magazine

Mission: The goal of CLICK is to allow young children access to the world of ideas and knowledge in an age-appropriate yet challenging way. It is often assumed that many areas of human endeavor and knowledge are uninteresting and beyond the understanding of young children. However, CLICK assumes otherwise and attempts to provide children with a clear and inviting introduction to many of the same phenomena and questions about the world that intrigue their adult counterparts. CLICK also attempts to introduce children to the processes of investigation and observation and encourages children to be active participants in the search for knowledge and understanding of their world.

Criteria for an Acceptable Article or Story: Each issue of CLICK is built around a central theme; CLICK themes introduce children to ideas and concepts within the natural, physical, or social sciences; the arts; technology; math; and history. CLICK presents nonfiction concepts to young children through a variety of formats, stories, articles, poems, photo essays, and activities. CLICK seeks **articles** that explain the how and why of something in a friendly, engaging, perhaps humorous way. CLICK prefers a more informal, conversational style to a formal, textbook style. The best articles tackle one idea or concept in depth rather than several ideas superficially. CLICK also seeks **stories** that contain and explain nonfiction concepts within them. Since it is part of CLICK's mission to encourage children to question, observe, and explore, successful stories often show children engaged in finding out about their universe—with the help of supportive, but not all-knowing, adults.

Queries: CLICK editors do not accept unsolicited manuscripts or queries. All articles published in CLICK are commissioned from professional authors. Authors interested in being considered for commissioned work should send a resume, writing samples, and detailed story ideas. Please allow 12 weeks for a reply.

Categories: Nonfiction—Arts—Children—Education—History—Juvenile—Nature—Science—Technology

CONTACT: Submissions Editor
Material: Queries
CONTACT: Art Director
Material: Art Samples
Carus Publishing Company
332 S. Michigan Ave., Ste 1100
Chicago IL 60604
Website: www.cricketmag.com

Climbing

Writers, Photographers, Illustrators and Artists
(digital media included)

Climbing magazine, which celebrates its 30th anniversary in 2000, covers the sport in all its forms. The magazine's editorial spectrum includes rock *Climbing* — from sport climbing to big walls — and mountaineering, with its steep ice routes, alpine classics, and expeditions to the world's great ranges. International in scope, but with a strong North American emphasis in its coverage, *Climbing* is published every six weeks.

If you are considering writing for *Climbing*, carefully read several recent issues to get an idea of our style and focus. Please query us prior to submitting any article, preferably enclosing a detailed outline of your proposal. E-mail queries are preferred. Also, mention the availability of photographs or illustrations to accompany the proposed article. *Send your query to:* climbing@climbing.com (formatted for Macintosh).

All written materials submitted should be typewritten and on disk if possible. Include a self-addressed, stamped envelope for their return.

Payment

Payment for photographs used is made on publication according to the following scale:
• Cover: $700
• Table of Contents: paid at rates listed below for size actually used, or $50/photo for second use in same issue.
  • Two-page spread: $400
  • Full page: $300
  • 2/3 page: $200
  • ½ page: $150
  • 1/4 page & smaller: $75

Mailing Instructions

All editorial materials should be packaged carefully and shipped via certified or insured mail. All materials must include return postage.

Features

We publish both creative and documentary-type features. We strive to include personal accounts of climbing adventures, profiles of interesting climbers, and surveys of different areas in each issue. We look for lively, authoritative writing that captures the spirit of our varied sport. Think about the articles you've read that stimulated you to action, made your palms sweat, or gave you something new to dream about. That's the feeling we're looking for.

Features are from 2000 to 5000 words in length; payment, made on publication, is $.35 per word for final copy.

High-quality photography is another cornerstone of *Climbing*'s editorial product. A regular feature is the Climbing Gallery, a photo section that showcases our sport's finest images, from action shots to mountain scenery. Gallery pays $300 per photo.

Departments

• Off the Wall, Hot Flashes, and Inside Game: Off The Wall is a mostly lighthearted section that highlights the unusual and the humorous. Hot Flashes concentrates on state-of-the-art ascents, from rock to alpine.

Off the Wall and Hot Flashes are written by *Climbing* editors, although we do occasionally accept short news stories and pay $.25 per word. Otherwise, we welcome tips and information, and pay regular rates for photos used in both columns.

• Inside Game: We are on the lookout for correspondents; anyone interested should be involved in the local scene and willing to do the research required to provide accurate information. Competitions covers the rapidly growing field of local, national, and international climbing competitions; please call or write beforehand if you want to cover an event. Photos are used liberally and are paid for at our regular rates.

• Roadworthy: These destination mini-features range from 500 to 1500 words, and are information-oriented. The story should both give a feel for the area and enough information for the reader to plan a trip. Stories pay $400, with regular rates for photos.

• High and Wild: These information-oriented stories are primers to both well-known and obscure mountain destinations. Include all pertinent information necessary for travel. Stories are 1000 to 2000 words. Pay is $500.

• Training: Subjects for this column can vary from nutrition to weight lifting. Concentrate on practical information for climbers of all levels, including theory and step-by-step workouts. Stories should be 1000 to 1500 words. Pay is $500.

• Medicine: Articles range from the prevention and treatment of tendinitis to what to take in an expedition medical kit. Length ranges from 1000 to 1500 words. Pay is $500.

• Equipment: This department reviews technical climbing gear, from rock shoes to bivy tents, and explains its use. Evaluations should be hard-hitting and research driven. Length varies from 1000 to 2000 words. Pay is $.35/word for final text.

• Just Out: Similar to our regular equipment reviews, but covers one piece of equipment only. Equipment reviewed should be new and innovative. Text reveals how a specific product worked in the field, based on the author's experiences. Length is 500 to 600 words. Pay is $150.

• Tech Tip: Concise how-to description of useful techniques for all types of climbing. Text is 250 to 500 words. Pay is $150.

• Players: Short (750-word) profiles of climbers. Players features those who are interesting as much or more for their personalities or lifestyle as their pure climbing accomplishments. Pay is $400.

• Reviews: This department covers new books, both fiction and non-fiction, as well as guidebooks, films, CD-ROMs, and videos. Length should be 200 to 300 words. Pay is $150.

• Perspective: The most varied department in the magazine, this is a personal opinion or experience column. Virtually any subject related to climbing is appropriate. Length should be 1000 to 1500 words. Pay is $300.

Photography

Climbing is renowned for its photography. While many of the images we use are solicited from regular contributors, we are always on the lookout for high-quality work.

Images must be sharp and properly exposed. If you are shooting for an article, variety is also important; a selection of both horizontal and vertical compositions, shot from different angles and with different lenses, will help us in layout. Please don't send multiple images that are virtually the same — edit your selection to "the best of the best." We accept negatives or prints, but typically use original 35mm transparencies. We also accept medium- and large-format transparencies. Please do not send duplicates. Submit your slides in plastic file sheets and make sure that your name and address are clearly printed on each slide mount. Include complete captions, including climbs' and climbers' names, for every photo submitted. Unsolicited submissions must be accompanied by return postage.

Contributor Guidelines for Illustrators and Artists

What happens to your art when we receive it?

Your illustrations will be scanned or downloaded to one of our Macintosh computers here in *Climbing*'s production department. Traditional art is scanned on an Agfa Studioscan IIsi 30bit color scanner. This is a high-quality flatbed scanner that is capable of scanning images at up to 2400dpi (with interpolation). In other words, if there are any marks on the art other than the art work it will digitize this information. We will only alter digitized information if it needs to be cleaned or if a file is not in the right format. Files that are already digitized will appear as you deliver them. The digitized files are imported into QuarkXPress and scaled to the layout.

Guidelines for traditional media illustrators.

All art should be as clean as possible. Your art will be digitized and everything you can see will be seen by the scanner. Keep art clean, please. Using high-quality art paper will minimize the chance that your original art will be altered by tonal adjustments after scanning.

Pen and ink drawings should have solid blacks and pure whites unless you desire a grayscale image. Again, working on high-quality paper will produce the best results.

Any text in your work should not be hand drawn unless you are asked to do so by an editor. We suggest using an overlay of tracing paper and making notes on the overlay to indicate where you would like text to be placed.

Color work should be cleared by the editor you are working with and a proof will ensure that your work looks the way you intend it to.

If you are sending original art you want returned, please include return address information. Protective covers are recommended for original art.

Guidelines for digital artwork.

We can translate most digital files, but if you are using an obscure or old program please contact us before sending files. If you are sending an illustration done in any vector-based drawing program, such as Adobe Illustrator or Macromedia Freehand, save in an EPS file format or as an Illustrator file.

Our primary graphic and photographic applications are:
- Adobe Illustrator (currently version 8.x-10.x)
- Adobe Photoshop (currently version 5.x-7.x)
- Fractal Design Painter (currently version 6.x-7.x)
- Macromedia Freehand (version 8.x-9.x)

If you are going to be adding your own text to a file please design using Helvetica unless we specify another font. If you are unsure of text use in the illustration you are submitting, print a copy/proof and attach a tracing-paper overlay to indicate text placement. Whenever possible convert text to outlines in programs such as Adobe Illustrator or Macromedia Freehand.

Important: Always include fonts for your work!

NOTE: The mandatary use of Helvetica font does not apply to advertisers or illustrations used in advertisements.

All digital files are imported into QuarkXPress. Please send all files as EPS. Send files at 100% size, or slightly oversized if you are unsure of our final layout size. If you want size information contact John McMullen <webmaster@climbing.com> or Mike Freeman <freeman@climbing.com> . Please notify us if you have any questions about the final size of your work.

The following are recommended settings for Adobe Photoshop 3.x-4.0 digital files:

Black and White EPS files can be bit mapped at 600dpi, 50% threshold (or your preference). *Save as EPS settings:*
- Macintosh (1 bit/pixel)
- Binary
- Halftone screens OFF
- Transfer function OFF

Grayscale EPS settings:
- Macintosh (8 bits/pixel)
- Binary
- Halftone screens OFF
- Transfer function OFF

Full- and spot-color files should be at least 288dpi (300dpi if you have enough room on your disk), converted to CMYK and saved as EPS files. *Settings should be:*
- Macintosh (8 bits/pixel)
- DCS, OFF
- Binary
- Halftone screens OFF
- Transfer function OFF

Disk drives we have available to read your data are:
- SyQuest 200c drive, reads 44MB, 88MB and 200MB SyQuest disks.
- SyQuest 540 drive, reads 540, 270 and 105 SyQuest disks.
- SyQuest 270 drive, reads 105 and 270 SyQuest disks.
- 600MB Sony Optical drive, reads double sided optical disks.
- 100MB Zip Drive.
- 1gig Jaz Drive.
- 2gig Jaz Drive, reads 1gig and 2gig disks.
- 1.4MB Super Floppy and 800k Floppy drives.
- CDROM and DVD readers.

If you are sending disks you will want returned, please include return address information.

Climbing is printed using a 155-line screen. You can set the resolution of your digital files using this information if disk space is tight. Scale them up just a bit to give us some working room.

If you need assistance with this please call, (970) 963-9449, or send e-mail to John McMullen <webmaster@climbing.com>

Thank you, and we look forward to seeing your work.

Categories: Nonfiction—Outdoors—Recreation—Sports,—Travel

CONTACT: Submissions Editor
Material: All
0326 Hwy 133, Ste 190
Carbondale CO 81623
Phone: 970-963-9449
Fax: 970-963-9442
E-mail: climbing@climbing.com
Website: www.climbing.com

Cloth Paper Scissors™

So, you want to write for us?

If you have a technique, project, or body of work to share, *Cloth Paper Scissors*™ Magazine would like to know about it. We want to show other artists—from beginners to the advanced—the latest, edgiest, most unusual collage and mixed media techniques and applications.

Who?

We are looking for writers who are artists themselves, with intimate knowledge of the subjects they wish to write about. We want sparkling, grammatically correct — even humorous — prose, of course, but what's most important is that you are an expert in your subject. Please note that regular features, including Artist Profiles, Product Reviews, Book Reviews, and Reader Challenges are all written by our in-house staff.

What?

Cloth Paper Scissors™ is most interested in publishing previously unpublished articles that cover unique collage and mixed media techniques geared to beginner, intermediate, or advanced artists. Feature articles may explore motifs and methods that will inspire and inform collage and mixed-media artists. Shorter "Spotlight" pieces focus on photos of projects with a brief explanation of how the work was done. *We are actively seeking queries on the following topics for publication:*

• Collage and mixed media artists to feature in our Artist Profiles (Please note: All profiles are written by CPS staff members.)
  • Collage techniques
  • Altered books
  • Art dolls
  • Assemblage
  • Image and text transfer techniques
  • Beaded embellishments
  • Working with found objects
  • Paper folding techniques
  • Transformative art
  • Embossing on fabric or paper
  • Unique painting and dyeing methods
  • Unusual stamping techniques
  • Book arts
  • Working with vintage materials
  • Punching and cutting techniques
  • Burning and distressing techniques
  • Inspiration and the creative process

Bottom Line

So, what do we pay? The pay for feature articles in *Cloth Paper Scissors*™ (other than staff-written pieces) varies depending on the length of the piece and the depth of the subject matter, but generally we pay $150 and up for shorter pieces and $300 and up for longer ones. We pay within 45 days after publication.

Guidelines for Submissions

Query first, please. We prefer that you send us a query by mail only (no e-mails, please), that succinctly describes your story idea or your artwork and process, explaining how you would handle the story and summarizing your writing experience. Please include slides or prints of artwork or samples (these are just to give us an idea and do not need to be professionally shot.

Note: Our editors will consider complete articles submitted on spec, but queries will get first priority.

Consider our tone. We know, we know, we're just getting started, so you don't have much to go by. But here are some hints: *Cloth Paper Scissors*™ is fun, creative, quirky, spiritual, surprising, inspiring and sassy. We're upbeat. How-to articles should combine the excitement of discovery with accuracy and easy-to-follow instructions. Personal stories should show how you worked through a problem with your art and go on to show others how to use similar techniques or solve similar creative issues.

Give length some thought. Ultimately, we will decide how long the piece is, but please tell us what you have in mind. Though our story length varies greatly, main feature articles range from 800 to 2,500 words while shorter pieces run 400 to 1,000 words.

Include all your information. Please include your address, phone number, e-mail address, and a brief biographical paragraph that includes your title, affiliation, any other relevant experience, if applicable, as well as how you'd like your byline to appear. If you want us to return your query materials, please include a SASE (self-addressed, stamped envelope). Please do not send original artwork at this point in the process.

Copyright Issues

No submissions which may violate copyright laws will be accepted. If your artwork could be perceived by Quilting Arts, LLC as a potential copyright violation, please provide written consent by the party which may have standing with regard to the copyright issue. Thank you for cooperation.

Categories: Nonfiction—Crafts/Hobbies

CONTACT: Patricia Bolton, Editor
Material: All
PO Box 685
Stow, MA 01775
Phone: 978-897-7750
E-mail: CPSEditor@quiltingartsllc.com
Website: www.quiltingarts.com

Club Connection

Club Connection, Girls Edition

Club Connection is an fun, full-color quarterly magazine for Missionettes ages 6 to 12. *Club Connection* includes articles dealing with girls' common interests such as school, friends, God, family, music, and fun activities like crafts, games, puzzles, snack recipes, etc. Also included are devotionals; fun facts and news; book, video, and music reviews; missions facts and trivia; a write-in question-and-answer column; and other great features. The salvation message is presented in each issue.

Club Connection, Leader Edition

Club Connection, Leader Edition, is targeted to leaders of Missionettes clubs. Leader's Connection provides leadership ideas and resources, discipleship materials, write-in questions and answers, fundraising and graduation ideas, information on important current issues, and missions lesson plans that correspond with the missions features in the Girls Edition.

Topics for *Club Connection*, Girls Edition
• Fictional short stories
• Girls' personal experiences
• Adventures—Nature, camping, fine arts, professional, industrial
• Sports
• Unique craft and snack ideas
• Pets/animals
• Unique puzzles and games (Please do not send Word Search or Crossword puzzles)

Topics for *Club Connection*, Leader Edition
• Club meeting ideas
• Sponsors' personal experiences
• Social, Awards Presentation, Adventure (field trip) and project ideas
• Assisting girls with special needs
• Missionettes Celebrations
• Missionettes and outreach ministries
• Discipline in the clubroom
• Leadership development
• Spiritual growth
• Discipleship
• Program questions

SUBMITTING MANUSCRIPTS FOR *Club Connection*
Formatting

Copy should be typed double-spaced. Check grammar, spelling, and punctuation before submitting your manuscript. Make theologically correct statements, and confirm all illustrations, Scripture references, and facts (history, nature, etc.). Give the version of the Bible you are using when quoting Scripture.

Manuscripts 350 words or less will be considered a one-page article. Manuscripts 700 words or less will be two-page spreads.

Indicate if the manuscript is gratis, if the article has been submitted to another publisher, and if the article has previously been printed.

Please avoid any use of names of actual businesses and people. Also, indicate if your article is fact or fiction.

Print your name, address, and social security number on your manuscript, as well as the approximate number of words and a short bio. Include photos relevant to the manuscript (see "Photo Guidelines" below). Enclose a self-addressed stamped envelope if you would like your manuscript returned.

Photo Guidelines

Do not staple or paper clip photos to anything. Do not write directly on the back of photos. Instead attach a label or tape a piece of paper to the back of the photo with your name, address, and phone number and a fun caption describing the action or event. List the names and ages of girls who appear in the picture.

Photos which do not include name and address information cannot be returned.

Photos must be production quality-not blurry or over- or underexposed.

Manuscript Evaluations

Each manuscript is read and evaluated, then either returned or held in a planning file for further evaluation and possible use. Because *Club Connection* is a quarterly publication, this process may take several months. If your material is published, you will be notified. Writers will receive payment upon publication, as well as two complimentary copies of the issue in which their article appears when the issue is printed. The editors of *Club Connection* reserve the right to edit your manuscript for clarity and space.

Enjoy writing!

Categories: Nonfiction—Children—Christian Interests—Inspirational—Girls

CONTACT: Kelly Kirksey, Associate Editor
Material: All
Assembly of God Publications
1445 N. Boonville Ave.
Springfield MO 65802-1894
Phone: 417-862-2781
E-mail: clubconnection@ag.org
Website: www.clubconnection@ag.org

Clubhouse

Clubhouse readers are 8- to 12-year-old boys and girls who desire to know more about God and the Bible. Their parents (who typically pay for the membership) want wholesome, educational material with Scriptural or moral insight. The kids want excitement, adventure, action, humor or mystery. Your job as a writer is to please both the parent and child with each article.

Fiction needs:

• humor with a point (500-1500 words)
• historical fiction featuring great Christians or Christians who lived during great times (1200-1500 words)
• contemporary, exotic settings (1200-1500 words)
• holiday material (Christmas, Thanksgiving, Easter, President's Day)
• parables (500-1000 words)
• fantasy, avoiding graphic descriptions of evil creatures and sorcery (1200-15– words)
• mystery stories (1200-1500 words)
• choose-your-own adventure stories (1500-1800 words)
• westerns (1200-1500 words)
• biblical: enhancing Bible stories without changing content or message (900 words)

Fiction flops:

• contemporary, middle-class family settings (existing authors meet this need)

• poems (rarely printed)
• stories dealing with boy-girl relationships
Nonfiction needs:
• fun-filled fact essays (12 to 18 off-the-wall facts on a certain subject or theme)
• interviews with noteworthy Christians or Christians who experienced noteworthy events
• scripts for Bible comics (10-12 panels)
• activity theme pages with 4 to 7 fun things for kids to do (800 words)
• top-10 how-to lists: 10 ways to get good grades, save money, etc.
• top-10 humor lists: 10 reasons to avoid family photograph sessions, 10 things not to do in a car while vacationing, 10 foods that do not mix well, etc.
• short, humorous essays with a point
• short news articles adapted to bring out a biblical lesson in a humorous way
Nonfiction flops:
• bible stories without a unique format or overt visual appeal
• information-only science or educational articles
• biographies told encyclopedia or textbook-style
Payment:
• 15 to 25 cents a word for nonfiction
• $200 on up for feature-length fiction stories
• $150 on up for Bible stories
Mail your article with a SASE.

You will receive a response within eight weeks. We accept printed manuscripts only; no query letters. Seasonal material should be sent at least 6 months in advance.

Categories: Fiction—Nonfiction—African-American—Asian-American—Children—Christian Interests—Cooking—Crafts/Hobbies—Family—Games—Hispanic—Home—Juvenile—Multicultural—Religion—Spiritual

CONTACT: Suzanne Hadley, Associate Editor
Material: All
Focus on the Family
8605 Explorer Dr.
Colorado Springs CO 80920
Phone: 719-531-3400

Clubmex

We look for positive, upbeat stories that pertain to a specific travel destination, a small village or big city in Mexico, that tells our readers where to go, what to see, where to stay and shop, and possible interesting things to do. The essential purpose of the Newsletter is to encourage our readers to drive into Mexico. Thus articles involving travel by air, train or ship will be less favored than those involving travel by auto, RV, or any road use vehicle.

For our feature articles, our large international readership base is interested in retirement area, fishing, camping, swimming, lodging (i.e., hotels, resorts, motels, RV parks, etc.), exploring, wind surfing, and/or snorkeling, boating, restaurants, shopping, whale watching, local colorful events—fiestas, and interesting people.

We pay $65.00 for the cover story and $50.00 for other articles, if and when used. Length can vary from 300 to 1000+ words. Photos or slides are strongly encouraged but not mandatory. We pay $5.00 for each photo or slide published.

We reserve the right to edit, delay printing and/or not print any and all stories due to editorial constraints and as space requirement dictate.

I sincerely hope that you send us some articles, photos and slides! I know that we would certainly appreciate your contribution. We will be looking forward to hearing from you soon.

Categories: Nonfiction—Hispanic—Travel

CONTACT: Chuck Stein, Vice President
Material: All
3450 Bonita Rd., Suite 103
Chula Vista CA 91910-5200
Phone: 619-422-3022
Fax: 619-422-2671
E-mail: igib@igib.com
Website: www.igib.com

CNEWA World

CNEWA World was formerly known as *Catholic Near East.*

CNEWA World magazine strives to educate its readers about the culture, faith, history, issues and people who form the Eastern Christian churches.

Established in 1974 by Catholic Near East Welfare Association, this bimonthly publication also attempts to inform its readers of the presence and work of the Association and its sister agency, the Pontifical Mission, in those nations that many Eastern Christians call home.

The goal of CNEWA World is to inform, but its contents should not be academic. People, details of contemporary life, history and "local color" should be woven together. Eastern Christians—Catholic and Orthodox—are frequently depicted as relics of the past. Our goal is to portray these communities as living bodies of men, women and children living and coping in a confused and often troubled world.

CNEWA World is also a tool of ecumenical and interreligious dialogue. Eastern forms of Christianity, Catholic and Orthodox, should be highlighted. However, the Jewish, Hindu and Muslim communities should not be ignored.

The most successful articles are written by those in the field. Stringers in each PM city and in other CNEWA countries offer the most objective, accurate and sensitive portraits of their subjects. Articles should not exceed 1,500 words. This stipulation allows for the lavish use of color photographs.

Photographers, if they are not writers as well, should work with the respective author (the editor should coordinate these efforts). Photographs must illustrate what is described in the article—people, places, festival, etc. General or thematic illustrations are exceptions.

Categories: Nonfiction—Christian Interests—Culture—History—Religion—Spiritual

CONTACT: Michael La Civita, Executive Editor
Material: All
1011 First Ave.,15th Floor
New York NY 10022-4195
Phone: 212-826-1480
Fax: 212-826-8979
E-mail: cnewa@snewa.org
Website: www.CNEWA.org

Coal People Magazine

THEME:
Coal industry business profiles; focus on people in different facets of the coal mining industry; and industry news and related features.

Please note: story ideas related to coal mining will be reviewed, however special assignments must be approved by the editors of COAL PEOPLE MAGAZINE.*

OTHER:
Payment upon publication only
All submissions must be typed or sent via email.
Computer CD acceptance (PC or Mac) in Word format
Please allow 3 months after date of submission.
Short Stories: $35.00 (1,500 words or under)
Regular Features: $60.00 (under 5,000 words)
Features: $75.00 (5,000 words or more)

Puzzles/Fillers: $15.00
Pictures: Cost, plus 15%
*Special assignment payments will be determined.
Categories: Fiction—Coal Mining

CONTACT: Submissions Editor
Material: All
PO Box 6247
Charleston WV 25362
Phone: 304-342-4129
Fax: 304-343-3124
E-mail: cpm@newwave.net or alskinner@ntelos.net
Website: www.coalpeople.com

Coast to Coast

Coast to Coast

As the membership publication for *Coast to Coast* Resorts, *Coast to Coast* is mailed to 200,000 readers eight times a year. *Coast to Coast* Resorts unites nearly 1,000 private camping and resort clubs across North America. A portion of the magazine is devoted to news about the *Coast to Coast* network: its programs, products and services, and, of course, its members. The remainder of the magazine focuses on travel, recreation and good times. *Coast to Coast* strives to be a fun, unpretentious but well-written and informative publication that offers a balanced mix of articles on things to do, places to visit, people to meet and ways to ensure a safe and happy trip.

Destination features in *Coast to Coast* should focus on a city or region of North America and should strive to convey the spirit of the place. The most readable place pieces go beyond typical tourist stops to interview locals and synthesize anecdotes and first-person observations in a way that is useful, entertaining and enlightening. Keep in mind that *Coast to Coast*'s readers already have more than 1,000 camping resorts at which to stay, so reporting on accommodations is almost always beside the point.

Activity or recreation features should introduce readers to or rekindle their interest in a sport, hobby or other diversion. As with the general public, most of our audience can be assumed to possess a basic knowledge of, say, golf or bicycling, but few have experienced rock climbing or skydiving. Nor would they care to, for the most part.

Many of our readers own recreational vehicles, so we feature the RV lifestyle in at least one article per issue. This is where lively, concise writing is especially in demand. If the writing is dry, the article will be, at best, unappealing; at worst, deadly. What's essential in these features is that readers identify with the situations they're reading about, that they pick up new information and at the same time are engaged and entertained.

The editors of *Coast to Coast* encourage queries and manuscripts. If you possess the requisite professional ability and have a lively writing style, please summarize your story idea, supplement it with a few opening paragraphs and forward it to our editorial offices with a selection of your best published clips or other writing samples. The editors are also pleased to review completed manuscripts.

Coast to Coast publishes first North American serial rights; articles must not appear in other publications for 90 days after they are first published in *Coast to Coast*. In accepting an assignment from *Coast to Coast*, writers agree to submit stories on or before the stated deadline and agree to rewrite them, if required, in a timely fashion. Assigned stories should be submitted electronically, either on disk or via e-mail, with an accompanying hard copy. Payment is made upon acceptance.

Categories: Recreation Vehicles—Travel

CONTACT: Valerie Law, Editorial Director
Material: All
2575 Vista Del Mar Dr.
Ventura CA 93001
Phone: 805-667-4100

Coastal Living

Welcome to the award-winning world of *Coastal Living* magazine. Many kudos have come our way since the first issue date, May-June 1997, but Folio: may have said it best. When this watchtower of the magazine industry presented its Editorial Excellence Award for Best Regional Magazine, *Coastal Living* was cited as "Beautifully designed, well written and nicely conceived and balanced. The breezy style, pace and rhythm of this issue make you want to shake the beach sand from its pages."

WHO WE ARE

Coastal Living is a lifestyle magazine that occupies a unique and well-defined niche. As stated on every cover, we are "The Magazine for People Who Love the Coast." Our editorial lineup takes readers to homes, destinations, activities, and people along the Atlantic, Pacific, and Gulf shores of North America. We include Hawaii and Alaska as well as coastal Canada and Mexico. We also visit the multinational Caribbean islands from time to time, and we recently expanded coverage to the waterside ways of life along the U.S. Great Lakes. Our rule of thumb: With the exception of features on the Great Lakes, or "North Coast," *Coastal Living* stories spotlight topics within sight, sound, taste, touch, or smell of salt water.

OUR VOICE

A tone of casual sophistication unfolds between the covers of *Coastal Living*. Regardless of the subject—decorating, entertaining, gardening, travel, nature, or zany beach characters—insider knowledge and ease prevail in the language of our stories. Our syntax welcomes humor but avoids cuteness.

Well-balanced and poised, *Coastal Living* is an accessory on the coffee table, a workhorse in the kitchen, and a friend in the hammock.

VITAL STATS

- *Frequency:* 6 times per year
- *Circulation:* 500,000 paid subscribers nationwide
- *Readership:* 1.5 million (average of 3 readers per issue)
- *Distribution:* 81% subscription; 19% newsstand
- *Editorial-to-Advertising Ratio:* +/-60 to +/-40
- *Publisher:* Southern Progress Corporation (SPC), a division of AOL Time Warner
- *SPC Editorial Offices:* 2100 Lakeshore Dr., Birmingham, AL 35209
- *Web site:* coastalliving.com
- *Word Counts:* 500-1,000

PLANNING SCHEDULE

Coastal Living stories are planned one year in advance during an annual series of editorial meetings from about November 1 through February 1. For example, the slate for 2003 was finalized as of February 2002. Flexibility allows some adjustment as the year progresses, but editors generally stick to the plan. That allows time for research, photography, writing, and production. This lead time is particularly crucial if a story has a seasonal angle, such as fall color or holiday decorating.

PRODUCTION SCHEDULE

Depending on the type of article, the deadline for text to be researched, written, and submitted to the assigning editor is four to six months prior to publication date.

OUR READERS

Subscription renewals and growing newsstand sales tell us that *Coastal Living* succeeds in transporting people to their dreams. Letters, E-mails, and focus groups reveal countless ways readers use our information to make those dreams come true. Surveys show the average time spent perusing a typical issue is 90 minutes an impressive statistic in this fast-paced age. Reader characteristics include:

- *Gender:* 65% women; 35% men
- *Median age:* 44.7
- *Median household income:* $84,824
- *Own a vacation home:* 28%
- *College educated:* 72%
- *Geographic location (percentages rounded):* South and Southeast 47%; Northeast 21%; West 17%; Midwest 15%.
- *Travel frequency:* 4.5 vacation trips per year; $4,000 + average annual vacation expenditure; 54% maintain a valid passport.

EDITORIAL DEPARTMENTS

Four overall subject areas (homes, travel, lifestyle, and food and entertaining) define the content of each issue. Divided into features and regular columns, stories depicting each of these areas are included in all three sections of the magazine: front of book, well (the middle section, with no advertising), and back of book.

The magazine also has special sections—such as ones focusing on summer entertaining and building a coastal home—typically written and produced by staff editors.

Behind every story, in all departments, is the desire to serve our readers—to give them ideas, techniques, or inspiration applicable to their own lives. Woven into our stories is an awareness of nature, the environment, and the importance of coastal conservation. Often those topics form the backbone of a story.

Homes

With a mission to promote comfort, livability, and style, the Homes section makes up more than 50% of editorial. Story focus may be on decorating, building and renovating, architecture, products, community development, or gardens and landscaping. Our tone of casual sophistication is unmistakable here: Informal scenes sport just-right touches of grace and taste; otherwise luxurious locations project a "come in and make yourself at home" personality. Homes stories are staff- and freelance-written.

Travel

Coastal Living issues a passport to fun in our destination, outdoor activity, nature experience, and lodging and dining stories. We strive for angles that reveal the essential character of a place in fresh and lively ways no other magazine would capture. The sight, sound, taste, touch, and smell of surf and sand are ever-present in text and photography. A travel/community hybrid is "So You Want to Live In . . . " This popular column, appearing in every issue, includes many of the earmarks of a travel story because it evokes a sense of place. But it takes the reader beyond what might otherwise be a great weekend getaway spot to the practicalities of year-round life with the resident cast and culture of a specific seaside town or village. Travel stories are staff- and freelance-written.

Lifestyle

Stories in this category may feature a family or other cluster of people with a common tie, or they may profile an individual person. They also may be hybrids—partly home/partly lifestyle. The latter depicts homeowners, architects, designers, or landscapers pertinent to the homes, gardens, or communities within the story. Lifestyle columns include:

"The Good Life," which showcases a person or family with a will to live on the coast and a way to do it.

"Coastal Character," which portrays one person who may be a quirky local or a semicelebrity but, either way, is intrinsically connected to the coastal environment.

"Collectibles" highlights rare, valuable, or otherwise treasured items and accessories with a marine connection or motif and is often presented in situ and/or with the owner's path in assembling the collection.

Lifestyle stories are staff- and freelance-written.

Food & Entertaining

In a word, "convivial" describes our approach to putting food and wine on the table or on the picnic cloth. We profile a lively gathering in each issue's well section feature. Other columns include:

"Seafood Primer," a popular what's it and how-to in each issue. The column features a type of (or method of cooking) fish or shellfish.

"Host Notes," which a modern-day Emily Post would find handy at the beach.

NOTE: Recipes in all food features and columns are professionally tested in the *Coastal Living* kitchens to ensure accuracy and quality. Food & entertaining stories are primarily staff-written. Currents— Encompassing the above subject areas, this section opens every issue of *Coastal Living* and is home to a variety of short items (25-200 words). Travel news, cool home products, beach fashion, and seaside events are among the topics that populate its pages. "Currents" is primarily staff-written.

FROM QUERY TO CONTRACT

No manuscripts, please! *Coastal Living* does not accept prepared text, but we are happy to consider a well-developed idea expressed in a query letter.

Winning Queries:

Indicate that the writer has read our magazine well enough to grasp our style and subject matter.

Do not propose a topic recently addressed in a published *Coastal Living* story.

Present a fresh and surprising angle on a widely acknowledged topic; or present a new story idea that is uniquely suited to *Coastal Living*.

Convince our editors that the writer is highly qualified to write on the topic according to his/her experience and familiarity with the subject.

Express the idea in language that captures and holds our attention.

Express the idea concisely.

Include scouting shots or photocopies of photographs whenever possible. This is mandatory for any query related to home and garden stories.

Maintain 100% perfect spelling and grammar.

Are accompanied by clips of published work by the writer unless samples are already on file with *Coastal Living*. (In the latter case, the cover letter should remind us that we have clips and offer to send more if necessary.)

NOTE: Query letters may be sent via e-mail, with clips sent by regular mail in a separate package, with a copy of the query enclosed.

Assignments

Assigning editors will contact the writer if *Coastal Living* decides to pursue an idea. The specific angle, fees, expenses, and deadlines are discussed. That editor prepares and sends a story-focus sheet to the writer to confirm the story approach.

NOTE: Per the planning process followed by *Coastal Living* editors (see Planning Schedule), queried ideas typically will be considered on an annual basis for a future editorial lineup. (For example, all 2003 stories are planned by early 2002.)

The *Coastal Living* office manager issues a story contract, which should be signed and promptly returned by the writer. Accompanying the contract are expense guidelines and a list of items for the writer's submitted story package to include. (The story Focus Sheet also may be included or may be sent separately—see above.)

FEES

Coastal Living typically pays $1 per word, plus reasonable expenses (such as transportation, lodging, and dining for travel stories) agreed upon in advance. Compliance of our expense guidelines is mandatory.

Payment is issued within 24 weeks of story acceptance. NOTE: Following story acceptance, the assigning editor may still request text revisions by the writer.

Kill fees are 25% of the assigned fee, as noted in the contract.

Finder's fees are paid when and where pertinent. The range varies according to the story.

PAYMENT

To ensure prompt payment, writers must:

Meet the deadline specified in the contract.

Send a complete story package to the assigning editor as specified in the directions that accompany the contract. That includes 1) story text; 2) all fact-checking material; 3) names and complete and legible addresses of all story sources or participants who should receive complimentary copies of the issue featuring the story.

Put themselves in the shoes of our fact checkers and think about what they need to do their job. Writers must not fail to include complete fact-checking material in the story package. This is mandatory for payment. Such material includes but is not limited to: 1) names and contact points for all story sources and anyone quoted; 2) brochures and/or business cards showing up-to-date data pertinent to lodging and other referenced facilities; 3) restaurant menus if applicable; 4) photocopies of pages from historical documents, Web sites, or other information sources used.

Submit an invoice along with the complete story package. The contract does not serve as an invoice.

Categories: Nonfiction—Entertainment—Gardening—Home— Humor—Lifestyle—Regional

CONTACT: Cathy Still-Johnson, Senior Editor
Material: Homes & gardens
Phone: 205-445-6722
E-mail: cathy_still@timeinc.com
CONTACT: Susan Haynes, Senior Editor
Material: West Coast travel
Phone: 205-445-8580
E-mail: susan_haynes@timeinc.com
CONTACT: Steve Millburg, Travel Editor
Material: All non-West Coast travel
Phone: 205-445-6294
E-mail: steve_millburg@timeinc.com
CONTACT: Jennifer Chappell, Lifestyle Editor
Material: Lifestyle
E-mail: jennifer_chappell@timeinc.com
Phone: 205-445-6264
CONTACT: Julia Rutland, Foods & Entertaining Editor
Material: Food & Entertaining
Phone: 205-445-6053
E-mail: julia_rutland@timeinc.com
2100 Lakeshore Dr.
Birmingham AL 35209
Phone: 205-445-6007
Fax: 205-445-8655
Website: www.coastalliving.com

Cobblestone Magazine
Discover American History

General Information

COBBLESTONE is interested in articles of historical accuracy and lively, original approaches to the subject at hand. Do not forget that our magazine is aimed at youths from ages 8 to 14. Writers are encouraged to study recent back issues for content and style. (Sample issues are available at $4.95. Send 7 ½" x 10½" self-addressed envelope with $2.00 worth of postage.) All material must relate to the theme of a specific upcoming issue in order to be considered. COBBLESTONE purchases all rights to material.

Procedure

In order for your idea to be considered, a query must accompany each individual idea (however, you can mail them all together) and must include the following:

• A brief cover letter stating the subject and word length of the proposed article,

• A detailed one-page outline explaining the information to be presented in the article,

• An extensive bibliography of materials the author intends to use in preparing the article,

• A self-addressed stamped envelope.

Authors are urged to use primary resources and up-to-date scholarly resources in their bibliography. Writers new to COBBLESTONE should send a writing sample with the query. If you would like to know if your query has been received, please also include a stamped postcard that requests acknowledgment of receipt. In all correspondence, please include your complete address as well as a telephone number where you can be reached.

A writer may send as many queries for one issue as he or she wishes, but each query must have a separate cover letter, outline, bibliography, and self-addressed stamped envelope. All queries must be typed.

Articles must be submitted on disk using a word processing program (preferably Microsoft Word - MAC). Text should be saved as ASCII text (in MS Word as "text only"). Disks should be either MAC - (preferred) or DOS - compatible 3½".

GUIDELINES

Feature Articles:

700-800 words

Includes: in-depth nonfiction, plays, first-person accounts, and biographies

Supplemental Nonfiction:

300-600 words

Includes: subjects directly and indirectly related to the theme. Editors like little-known information but encourage writers not to overlook the obvious.

Fiction:

up to 800 words

Includes: authentic historical and biographical fiction, adventure, retold legends, relating to the theme.

The above three pay 20 to 25 cents per printed word.

Activities:

Up to 700 words.

Includes: crafts, recipes, woodworking, or any other interesting projects that can be done either by children alone or with adult supervision. Sketches and description of how activity relates to theme should accompany queries.

Poetry:

up to 100 lines. Clear, objective imagery. Serious and light verse considered. Must relate to theme.

Puzzles and Games:

(please, no word finds). Crossword and other word puzzles using the vocabulary of the issue's theme. Mazes and picture puzzles that relate to the theme.

The above three pay on an individual basis.

Photo Guidelines

To be considered for publication, photographs must relate to a specific theme. Writers are encouraged to submit available photos with their query or article. We buy one-time use.

See our website for suggested fee range for professional quality photographs.

Please note that fees for non-professional quality photographs are negotiated.

Cover fees are set on an individual basis for one-time use, plus promotional use. All cover images are color.

Prices set by museums, societies, stock photography houses, etc., are paid or negotiated.

Photographs that are promotional in nature (e.g., from tourist agencies, organizations, special events, etc.) are usually submitted at no charge.

If you have photographs pertaining to any upcoming theme, please contact the editor by mail or fax, or send them with your query. You may also send images on speculation.

Note

Queries may be submitted at any time, but queries sent well in advance of deadline MAY NOT BE ANSWERED FOR SEVERAL MONTHS. Go-aheads requesting material proposed in queries are usually sent five months prior to publication date. Unused queries will be returned approximately three to four months prior to publication date.

Categories: Fiction—Adventure—Biography—Games—History—Poetry

CONTACT: Meg Chorlian, Editor
Material: All
Cobblestone Publishing
30 Grove Street, Ste C
Peterborough NH 03458
Phone: 603-924-7209
Fax: 603-924-7380
Website: www.cobblestonepub.com

Collector Editions

PAYMENT: To be negotiated on an individual basis, meeting the agreement of both the writer and publisher. Payment will follow 60 days after publication. A complimentary copy of this issue will be mailed to the writer.

ARTICLE TOPICS: Free-lance articles introducing new artists in the collectibles and giftware industry; comprehensive documentaries of core companies, lifestyle articles with décor focus, seasonal. Contact the editor for assignments.

COPY: Electronic files are preferred. Submissions may be by e-mail, cd, floppy or zip discs.

ILLUSTRATIONS: 8–10 full color images for layout options. Electronic/digital images are preferred, hi res 300 dpi and approx. 4" x 5" or larger in size. MacIntosh platform; tifs, eps, jpeg, or hi res pdf files. Materials are retained on file, unless return is requested by the author.

Categories: Collectibles—Gifts—Home Décor—Lifestyle

CONTACT: Joan Pursley, Editor
Material: All
Pioneer Communications, Inc.
PO Box 306
Grundy Center IA 50638
Phone: 800-352-8039
Fax: 319-824-3414
E-mail: lkruger@thepioneergroup.com
Website: www.collectors-news.com

Collectors News

SUBJECT MATTER: Free-lance article topics sought: 1. Articles about individuals and their collections, emphasizing personal insights. 2. Informational articles on antiques and collectibles. Themes: Show, Furniture, Beauty, Food, Art and Music, Sports/Military, Housewares, Textiles, Toys/Video Games, Holiday, Jewelry, Movie/TV/Electronics.

CONTENT: • Tips on how to collect, where to locate items, and brief histories with information that will enhance the collecting process are encouraged in copy whenever appropriate. • It is preferred that current values of your subject matter are included, either within copy or as a sidebar. Be sure to credit sources for the prices. • Sidebars containing Reproduction Alerts and/or topical Resources (books, clubs, etc.) also are recommended.

PHOTOS: Illustrations are required. Color electronic images at 300 resolution are best. Sharply focused pictures of individual items with an uncluttered background work best. When appropriate, images including collectors and/or a grouping of collectibles add interest to an article. A selection of 4 to 8 images is suggested.

FRONT PAGE PHOTOS: Articles are eligible for full-color front page consideration when accompanied by color electronic images.

LENGTH: Shorter articles of 900 words or less are preferred; longer articles sometimes must await space availability or may be published in a serial.

COPY: Manuscripts are preferred in electronic files, but are accepted as typed double-spaced copy by mail. Specifics are available upon request.

PAYMENT: Basic payment is $1.10 per column inch, including space for published photos. Articles providing a color image selected for front page use receives an additional $25. Payment is routinely sent upon publication.

Basis of Purchase of Editorial Material by Collectors News:

All news articles and related editorial materials purchased by Collectors News are purchased on the basis of exclusive, First Serial Rights, for use in the magazine Collectors News and possible use on the Internet, unless otherwise stipulated by the author and agreed to by Collectors News at the time of submission and/or acceptance.

Categories: Nonfiction—Antiques—Collectibles—Hobbies—Lifestyle

CONTACT: Linda Kruger, Managing Editor
Material: All
Pioneer Communications, Inc.
PO Box 306
Grundy Center IA 50638
Phone: 800-352-8039
Fax: 319-824-3414
E-mail: lkruger@thepioneergroup.com
Website: www.collectors-news.com

CollegeBound Teen

Misson:

CollegeBound Teen is designed to provide high school students with an inside look at all aspects of college life. College students (and those young at heart!) from around the country are welcome to serve as Correspondents to provide our teen readership with real-life accounts and cutting-edge, expert advice on the college admissions process and beyond.

Frequency:

CollegeBound Teen is published six times a year in New York, New Jersey, and Connecticut; in the fall, winter, and spring in California, Illinois, Florida, Texas, and New England; and nationally each September and February.

Style/Tone:

The tone of most articles in *CollegeBound Teen* is light-hearted and informative. Imagine you're relaying advice to a younger sibling or friend. You want to give them "the inside scoop" and offer helpful pointers for making a successful transition from high school to college. Teenage lingo and pop-culture references are totally acceptable (and encouraged!); however, a responsible journalistic blend of down-to-earth authority is important as well.

The Make-up:

CollegeBound Teen is comprised of departments, columns, and full feature articles. Our payment rates depend upon length of story, topic, and research involved.

Features:

Feature articles are usually 800-1,500 words. We look for well-researched articles packed with real-life student experiences and expert voices. Share with readers stories and survival tips on everything from dealing with dorm life, choosing the right college, and joining a fraternity or sorority, to college dating, cool campus happenings, scholarship scoring strategies, and other scholastic issues. Be original, real, and creative! Pays $70-$100.

Columns/Departments:

Straight Up Strategies (Think fun service pieces: Campus survival skills, admissions advice, professor tips, etc.—150-400 words); Cash Crunch (Money-related tips, scholarship advice, news—150-400 words); Savvy Scope (Lifestyle issues, student profiles, etc.—150-300 words); Athletics (standout student-athlete profiles—150-400 words); Celeb 101 (entertainment tidbits with a scholastic scope—200-600 words). Department payments range from $40-$75.

Rights/Payments:

We usually buy first rights to a piece; we also purchase electronic rights if we are interested in featuring the article at the online version of *CollegeBound Teen Magazine* (CollegeBoundTeen.com) or one of The CollegeBound Network affiliate sites (CollegeBound.net). We will not accept second rights to an article that has appeared in a similar publication. Payments are generated 60 days upon publication, with two complimentary issues.

All accepted articles must be accompanied by a source sheet (interview transcripts and research documentation may be requested).

How to Query Us:

Familiarize yourself first. Get to know our style and the kinds of articles we love. (You may receive a sample issue by sending a 9"x12" SASE [$3.85]).

We recommend you query us (via mail or e-mail) with a well-structured article proposal. *Hint:* Follow this format:

• Begin with the lead you expect to put in the article. Make it catchy—grab our attention!

• Write a summary of your intended areas of coverage, including sidebar ideas.

• Give specifics about experts you plan to interview, the types of student anecdotes you'll iclude, which resources you plan to utilize, and what conclusion the story might reach.

Writing Clips/Sample:

Send two or three clips or samples of your writing from your college newspaper, journalism class, etc. Photocopies are a good idea, as we do not return clips. All queries should be accompanied by a SASE. Our response time to all correspondence is approximately eight weeks.

Categories: Nonfiction—Campus Life—College—Education—Lifestyle—Self-Help—Teen—Young Adult

CONTACT: Gina LaGuardia, Editor-in-Chief
Material: All
CONTACT: Dawn Kessler, Senior Editor
Material: All
1200 South Ave., Ste. 202
Staten Island NY 10314
Phone: 718-761-4800
Fax: 718-761-3300
E-mail: editorial@collegebound.net
Website: www.collegebound.net

Colorado Homes & Lifestyles Magazine

1. Format: If possible, submit material by e-mail to mdakotah@coloradohomesmag.com. Please call to let us know it is on the way. Either send in the body of the letter, or attach as text only.

We use Microsoft Word 6.0 on an IBM computer system, so you can send a double-sided, double- or high density IBM disk formatted in Microsoft Word. Please save the information as a text-only file—even if you are using a Mac disk.

If you re mailing a disk, please include a hard copy of your article.

Laser-printed, double-spaced copy in basic fonts (such as Courier, Times, or Helvetica) to allow us to scan the article into our system if your electronic transmission fails.

2. Style: *Colorado Homes & Lifestyles Magazine* uses the *Associated Press Stylebook* for style and punctuation. Other style guidelines:

• Do not use courtesy titles (such as Dr., Mr., Mrs.) unless the person is an actual medical doctor or if there is no other way to avoid confusion.

• Book titles, exhibition names and series are in italics. Place quotation marks around artwork titles.

• Italicize foreign words that are not shown in the dictionary in plain type.

• Write in present tense.

3. Headlines: Give your article three headline choices and three deck (article introduction or subtitle) choices. Headlines are usually 3-8 words. Decks can range from a phrase to two full sentences. Please look at past issues of the magazine for examples.

4. Source List: A list of sources used in the article should accompany your submission to be published on our Resources page. These should include the homeowner, the architect, the designer, artists, manufacturers, retailers, distributors, etc. Give the contact name, title and name of company, phone/fax number, mailing address, and e-mail address (if applicable).

5. References: If applicable to your article, include a publishable list of sources to which readers can refer to find out more about your topic. Sources include, books, people, organizations, and websites. Often this is used as sidebar material. This information should not be included in your total word count.

6. Sidebars: A story that falls under the heading of department may require a sidebar that includes such information as a reference-book listing, ingredients, facts, figures, etc.

7. Departments:

• **Travel:** Provide 35 mm slides or transparencies (that you ve taken yourself or from other sources).

• **Artist s Workshop:** Ask artist to provide 35mm slides or transparencies of their work, and one of the artist as well—preferably showing him/her working.

• **Gardening:** Provide 35mm slides or transparencies of plants, flowers, etc. relevant to the story.

8. Photographers: Provide information on each photo (for editors to use in captioning), and full name/name of studio of photographer for proper photo credit.

9. Invoices: Submit an invoice for the contracted amount, plus expenses (previously agreed upon by editor and/or art director), along with your article or photography. Please include your name, address, phone/fax, and social security number on all invoices. Checks may be delayed if invoices are not included.

10. Length and Payment: Department articles usually run 1,000-1,200 words; payment is generally $150-$175. Features run 1,200-1,300 words; payment is generally $200-$250. Expenses must be approved before story is submitted.

11. Writer biography: Include a short (no more than two sentences) biography.

Categories: Nonfiction—Architecture—Cooking—Culture—Gardening—General Interest —Home—Lifestyle

CONTACT: Editor
Material: All
7009 S. Potomac St., Ste. 200
Centennial, CO 80112
Phone: 303-397-7600
Fax: 303-397-7619
E-mail: mdakotah@coloradohomesmag.com
Website: www.coloradohomesmag.com

ColoradoBiz Magazine

ColoradoBiz was formerly known as *Colorado Business Magazine.* With its January 1999 re-launch, *ColoradoBiz* took on a new tone, name, direction and look. We strive for fresh, vivid coverage of the people and issues affecting the entire state's business scene. Our readers are Colorado's business owners and top management, earning high-end and six-figure salaries. We seek and use writers who present accurate, professional work that's strong, humorous, touching, insightful, analytical, active, sound, witty, acerbic, droll, detailed, business-oriented—or any combination of those.

Queries

ColoradoBiz welcomes written, e-mail and phone queries with solid, original ideas and angles. In fact, it's required before we'll assign you a story.

We want analysis, forecasts, profiles, and pieces on trends, businesses, people and activities. As a full-color monthly, our editorial deadlines are about 10 to 12 weeks out from the first of the issue's month.

We seek features ranging between 650 and 1,200 words, and we always look for corresponding sidebar and chart material. Pay is a flat fee based on the story's complexity, length and time frame. Pay can range from $50 for a department item to $400 for a feature, including any sidebars. Our departments use stories in the 50- to 250-word range and cover people, companies, trends, unusual products, facts and more. *ColoradoBiz* also pays such expenses as phone and 25 cents a mile in certain cases.

We do not accept general business articles (they specifically must target Colorado's business scene), general how-to columns, book reviews, commentaries, collect calls, syndicated work, articles written by PR people about their clients, humor columns and poetry. Read back issues to gauge what we do want.

Photos

We usually shoot our own, although it can't hurt to ask sources to send us what they've got. If you shoot well, or know someone who does, we continuously seek contributions to our Last Look page in the back. This page tries to capture, in one shot, the unusual, offbeat, reminiscent, humorous or ironic in Colorado's business sectors.

What to Include

Although *ColoradoBiz* is a consumer magazine, our content is business-oriented. We want strong business angles, as well as clarity and accuracy.

Our features must start with a good lead and a clear (two- or three-line) nut graf summing up the story.

We like numbers. The more strong, solid, attributed numbers you include to support your story and facts, the better.

Active writing fits more into your word count and lessens your chances of heavy editing.

Do not use jargon

Do use several sources. Because this is a statewide magazine, include sources away from the Front Range.

Clearly attribute each quote. Include names, complete titles, company names, cities and for companies outside of Colorado, states.

Is it a public company? Include its stock exchange information: Wallace Computer Services (NYSE:WCS).

Where pertinent, include affiliates: Moore & Co. and Coldwell Banker Van Schaack, part of Parsippany, N.J.-based NRT Inc., a residential real estate brokerage and consolidator.

Verify data with the original source, especially with surveys and numbers. Do not use information published in other media, without verifying it for yourself. Get survey names, etc.

Check and double-check names and titles. Fact-check your work. We might, too.

Separately, give us your sources and phone numbers for photos and fact-checking.

We need your full name, address, phone, fax, e-mail, and Social Security number on the story to pay you. Include a brief biography of your experience.

Policies

New Wiesner Publishing policy requires a signed, dated, complete writer's contract for each article, before invoices will be paid. Do not alter the contracts. Please call Mike Taylor at 303-662-5223 with questions or comments.

Absolutely do not fax or send stories or portions of stories to anyone, including sources. We will read back direct quotes to sources after editing, if they want to know. If there are any questions about sources or anyone seeing a story, refer them to us.

Deadlines

Meet them. Call in advance if you can't. Have a good reason ready.

Format

Send the stories either on disk or via e-mail, in text or Word for Windows. Put MAC files on a PC disk in text. Include a hard copy.

Send attached e-mail files in text or paste the copy into your e-mail message.

Do not embellish the copy with indents of any kind, formatting of any kind, bold or italic type, or other aesthetic touches that we just have to take the time to remove.

Expenses

We pay long-distance phone bills for interviews (see writer contract). We also pay mileage (25 cents/mile) in some cases, which must be approved by the editor. *ColoradoBiz* is not responsible for expenses incurred without prior approval of the editor.

Photography and Illustration Guidelines

With its January 1999 relaunch, *ColoradoBiz* took on a new tone, name, direction and look. We are a full-color monthly business magazine that strives for fresh, vivid coverage of the people and issues affecting the entire state's business scene. Our readers are Colorado's business owners and top management, earning high-end and six-figure salaries.

We seek and use photographers and illustrators who want to have fun with their art, and who turn that into accurate, professional work with excellent composition, proper lighting, creative content and technical expertise. It should tell a story in itself and further the content of the article it illustrates. Our preference is for art with strong visual and emotional impact that captures the essence of the article.

Queries

ColoradoBiz welcomes written, e-mail and phone queries from artists and photographers. We use photos and renderings to illustrate articles on Colorado-specific business people, places, events, issues and concepts.

Last Look

Our Last Look page is dedicated to good photos and illustrations that make a fast and direct point. This page tries to capture, in one shot, the unusual, offbeat, reminiscent, humorous, ironic or other tones and looks of Colorado's business sectors.

Other photos and illustrations are by assignment for features or our departments. They may include studio shots, on-location shots and photojournalism. Read several issues of *ColoradoBiz* to gauge our style, tone and direction.

As a full-color monthly, our art deadlines are about three to four weeks out from the press date (typically the 3rd week of the month). Deadlines are assigned by the art director.

Format, Pay and Other Details

We use original color transparencies and slides, which we scan in-house. We also accept digital art and photos. Digital work should be scanned to 8 x 10, 300 dpi, CMYK in TIF format in MAC. We pay full- and half-day rates based on the assignment's complexity, length and size (no higher than $400 per day and no lower than $100 per half day). Pay is set by *ColoradoBiz* prior to the assignment, based on the assignment's logistics. The art director will state the pay at the time of the assignment. This rate is non-negotiable.

We also pay 25 cents a mile and reasonable film and processing expenses. Roughly, full-day rates apply to assignments of four ordered shots or more; half-day rates to three or fewer shots. Reasonable film and processing expenses are based on shooting 10 photos for every one ordered (five ordered, 50 shots).

All expenses must be approved by the art director prior to the shoot. *ColoradoBiz* is not responsible for expenses incurred without the art director's prior approval.

Illustrations should be distinctive, professional renderings in any media — preferably 8 x 10 or smaller, depending on its intended use. Digital renderings should follow the specifications for digital photos. Rates for illustrations range from $45 to $350, depending on complexity and size, and include reasonable revisions or alterations at the art director's discretion.

Do not e-mail digital art.

ColoradoBiz pays on publication. Space may dictate how many photos ultimately will be used and when they will be used.

What to Include

Although *ColoradoBiz* is a consumer magazine, our content is business-oriented. We want art that renders a story in itself with a strong business focus.

ColoradoBiz is striving to move away from cliches and stereotypes in portraying business, whether in photos or illustrations. We do not want traditional posed shots, power shots, staid businessman shots, Venetian blinds, computers in the backgrounds and other dull office props - unless creatively used. We do want fresh, vivid work using activity, conceptualization, humor where appropriate, dignity where appropriate - in short, the photo (or art) should tell an interesting story.

Without fail, on photo shoots, get subjects' correct name spellings, complete titles, complete company names and locations, and their positions in the photos. Accuracy is critical for the cutlines.

Aside from good composition, proper lighting and creative content, art should be clear technically and in content. Focus photos. Some shots may be blown up several hundred percent.

Color should be well-saturated, not washed out, with good value contrast. As a general rule, use a variety of color. The paper we use may affect the colors. Check with the art director when in any doubt.

Art should have contrast in color, shape and sizes, and show attention to detail.

Read the stories (we will send the one you're illustrating for) to help determine art content. If you do not clearly understand or have difficulty with the assignment, contact the art director immediately. Reshoots are options only in special circumstances.

Do not show stories to sources. They are for your use only.

Photographers are responsible for arranging photo shoots with the subjects, which may include coordinating with art director and story author.

Wiesner Publishing requires a photographers' or illustrators' contract for each article illustrated (four articles or assignments, four contracts). These must be complete, signed, dated and returned in order to be paid. Do not alter the contract. Please call the managing editor with questions.

Provide exact wording for photo credits.

New artists also must fill out and return a W-9 before being paid.

Finally, we must have your full name, company name, address, phone, fax, e-mail and Social Security number with the photo in order to pay you. Expenses must have receipts. Please send contracts and invoices to Anne Kerven, managing editor, at the above address.

Upon submission, we must also have the photo credit wording and a brief two- or three-line bio of yourself for our contributors' list.

We will return art work to you after the issue is printed.

Deadlines

Meet them. Our production department generates a minimum of nine titles and extensive special projects. Our scanning schedule is tight. We schedule according to when your art is expected.

Categories: Nonfiction—Business

CONTACT: Robert Schwab, Editor, (303) 662-5283
Material: Manuscripts
CONTACT: Jurgen Mantzke, Art Director, (303) 662-5251

Material: Illustrations/Photography
7090 E. Potomac St.
Englewood CO 80112
Phone: 303-397-7600
Fax: 303-397-7619
E-mail: rschwab@cobizmag.com (Robert Schwab)
E-mail: jmantzke@wiesnerpublishing.com (Jurgen Mantzke)
Website: www.cobizmag.com

Colored Stone

Queries and Submissions: Because of the specialized nature of the colored stone trade, *Colored Stone* prefers to receive queries on story ideas before the manuscript itself is submitted.

Correspondents: The bulk of the articles published in each issue are generated from leads gathered by *Colored Stone* staff and assigned to one of a standard list of writers. If you do not have a specific story proposal, but would like to be considered for a story assignment, send your resume, and writing samples to the Editor at the below address. We also have "foreign correspondent" positions available for freelance writers in gem-producing or gem-trading centers outside the United States.

Readership: People in the wholesale end of the jewelry business, principally manufacturing jewelers and jewelry designers, gemstone dealers, and retail jewelers.

Subjects: New sources for colored gemstones, mining and processing, manufacturing, retail sales, consumer buying trends, marketing and promotion, gem cutting and jewelry design, and technological developments pertaining to the colored gemstone trade.

Style: Mostly feature style with an edge; some hard news.

NOTE: Because we are a trade magazine, our articles assume familiarity with the gem business, as well as a certain pre-knowledge about different types of colored gemstones, their sources, and how they are marketed and sold. If you are not familiar with the trade, we will provide background information for any articles we assign, and can also recommend some general reference books.

Length: Features: 1400-2000 words; Short Stories: 900-1200 words.

Artwork: Transparencies, slides, and prints. All photographs should be labeled and include captions. We prefer slides to prints and color to black and white. We cannot scan photos from pre-printed material such as postcards, brochures, or magazine pages.

Digital files submitted via e-mail are also acceptable. All pictures must be a minimum of 266 dpi at the size the picture will run in the magazine. We cannot take pictures directly from Web sites.

Manuscripts: E-mail submissions preferred, especially from writers outside the United States. Story text should be pasted into the body of the e-mail message rather than sent as an attached file.

Conditions: Writers must be able to substantiate any and all material as accurate. All articles are subject to editing. All material shall be submitted solely and exclusively for publication in *Colored Stone*, unless approved by the Editor in advance. Writers must sign a copyright agreement form before publication.

Fees: Payment is generally on a per-article rather than a per-word basis; fees are negotiated through the Editor. Fees generally run at 25-30 cents per word, depending on the complexity of the article, the experience of the writer, and the cost of living in the writer's home base. We pay a $15 finder's fee per photo submitted by the author and published. Phone/fax expenses are reimbursed upon submission of the phone bill; other expenses may be reimbursed with the pre-approval of the Editor.

Categories: Nonfiction—Trade—Gemstones

CONTACT: Morgan Beard, Editor-in-Chief
Material: All
300 Chesterfield Pkwy, Ste 100
Malvern PA 19355
Phone: 610-232-5700
Fax: 610-232-5756
E-mail: Morgan.Beard@primedia.com
Website: www.colored-stone.com

COMBAT Magazine

Original essays, stories, and poetry on the ramifications of war
Rights: first English language serialization
Needs: original essays (800wds), stories (800wds), and poetry (800wds) on the ramifications of war
Length: essay @800 words; story @800 words; poetry @800 words
Art/Photo Needs: original illustrations, with or without accompanying literature, but with caption, on the ramifications of war
Payment: presently, only byline and lit bio (w/link)
How to Submit: electronic format by e-mail or surface mail
Response Time: three weeks
Tips for Writers: see editorial policies and guidelines in S-1 Admin section of website
Writer's Guidelines

This literary magazine was conceived as a successor to its wartime namesake, formerly published by Albert Camus, the existentialist philosopher and resistance fighter. This *little magazine* is in the tradition of the "National Tribune" and "The Land We Love," the "Century" and "The Southern Magazine"; but authors should aspire to the intellectual rigor of the "New Individualist Review," and to emulate the verbal breadth in "**Antaeus.**"

This periodical is not a celebration of war; but is an acknowledgement of what war has begotten. Although war stories *per se* are not excluded, this publication is focused on **interpreting the meaning** of such encounters. Compositions should be both transparently evocative and poignantly authentic; but valid speculations and legitimate retrospectives are not precluded, as long as they somehow refer to one of the *touchstones* common to veterans and survivors. Cognizance of contextual elements integral to human conflict constitutes an essential criterion for publication. Relevant submissions for this publication that reveal and explore the ramifications of war upon combatants, noncombatants, and their families will be welcomed.

Categories: History—Literature—Military

CONTACT: Ed Staff, Editor
PO Box 3
Circleville WV 26804
E-mail: majordomo@combat.ws
Website: www.combat.ws

Commercial Investment Real Estate Magazine

Commercial Investment Real Estate magazine is the member publication of the CCIM Institute. *CIRE* provides practical, how-to information, market analyses and trends, and business strategies for commercial real estate professionals.

Selecting a Topic

CIRE readers are interested in how-to, trend, and forecast articles on a variety of topics, including development, brokerage, leasing, financing, property management, technology, and investment. Submit a detailed outline on a topic at least one month in advance of the manuscript. To discuss the topic with the editor, call (312) 321-4460.

Preparing the Manuscript

Submit articles as a Microsoft Word attachment to an e-mail. Article length should range between 1,800 and 3,000 words.

Supply a brief professional biography, including present title, designations, place of employment, published articles, and expertise in the subject about which you are writing.

Graphics

Include charts, graphs, original color or high-resolution digital photos, and illustrations when possible to emphasize and clarify points in your article.

Style

Aim for clear, concise, and lively writing, even if your topic is technical. *CIRE* follows AP style. When appropriate, include case studies.

Editors will remove any promotional material from articles before publication.

The Review Process

All articles are reviewed by the editorial review board, composed of commercial investment real estate professionals. The board determines whether an article is appropriate for publication in *CIRE*. If your manuscript is approved "with revisions," it may be returned with recommendations for more information or clarification. After receiving the revised article, the editor will discuss possible publication with you.

Copyright

CIRE is seeking original, unpublished material, and it owns the copyright for all of its contents. If your manuscript has been published elsewhere, please provide us with full information about the publication in which it appeared. Please inform us if your manuscript is currently under consideration or scheduled for publication elsewhere.

The Benefits of Writing

Share your knowledge and receive national recognition in your field by joining the ranks of well-respected CIRE authors. You will receive 5 complimentary copies of the issue in which your article appears. Online, your article will be linked to your e-mail address (if provided).

In addition, article reprints are available at a reasonable cost and make excellent handouts to current and potential clients.

Categories: Nonfiction—Associations—Business—Money & Finances—Real Estate

CONTACT: Jennifer Norbut, Editor and Associate Publisher (312-321-4531)
Material: Feature article ideas and outlines, regional info., CCIM Deal Makers submissions, and marketing information
CONTACT: Sara Drummond, Staff Editor (312-321-4469)
Material: Industry news
CONTACT: Stephanie Bell, Publishing Coordinator (312-321-4477)
Material: Product Information, Advertising, Reprints
430 N. Michigan Ave., Ste. 800
Chicago IL 60611-4092
Phone: 312-321-4460
Fax: 312-321-4530
E-mail: jnorbut@cciminstitute.com (Jennifer Norbut)
E-mail: sdrummond@cciminstitute.com (Sara Drummond)
Website: www.ciremagazine.com

Founded in 1924
Commonweal

Commonweal

COMMONWEAL is a biweekly journal of opinion edited by Catholic lay people. Founded in 1924, the magazine welcomes original manuscripts dealing with topical issues of the day on culture, religion, politics, and the arts. We look for articles that are timely, accurate, and well-written. *Articles fall into three categories:*

1. "Upfronts," running between 750-1,000 words, are brief, "newsy" reportorials, giving facts, information, and some interpretation behind the "headlines of the day."

2. Longer articles, running between 2,000-3,000 words, are more reflective and detailed, bringing new information or a different point of view to a subject, raising questions, and/or proposing solutions to the dilemmas facing the world, nation, church, or individual.

3. "Last Word" column, a 750-word reflection, usually of a personal nature, on some aspect of the human condition: spiritual, individual, political, or social.

Please send a query with outline and resume. We do not consider simultaneous submissions.

Articles should be written for a general but well-educated audience. While religious articles are always topical, we are less interested in devotional and churchy pieces than in articles which examine the links between "worldly" concerns and religious beliefs.

Notes and footnotes are discouraged. Please allow 3-4 weeks for an editorial decision.

Manuscripts should be emailed (see below). Please send as a MS Word attachment. Payment for articles is generally made on publication.

Poetry: We publish about 20 high quality poems a year.

Categories: Nonfiction—Culture—Literature—Politics—Regional—Public Policy

CONTACT: Patrick Jordan, Managing Editor
Material: All
475 Riverside Dr., Ste. 405
New York NY 10115
Phone: 212-662-4200
E-mail: editors@commonwealmagazine.org
Website: www.commonwealmagazine.org

Communications News

Communications News is written for enterprise telecommunications, data communications and network managers who are looking for solutions for their corporate or organization networks that are practical, proven and cost-effective.

What we are looking for

Features: The majority of our features are vendor-contributed, solutions-based, real-world application stories in a case-study format. We also publish tutorials that discuss technology developments important to enterprises (i.e., corporate, educational and government organizations). Articles should be focused on enterprise end-user solutions, or solutions provided by service providers to enterprise end-users. Our focus is NOT on internal operations solutions for carriers/telcos or service providers (e.g., billing, OSS, CRM).

Guest Columns: Every month, we feature a one-page guest columnist, writing in an opinion or trends style. Any subjects pertaining to the enterprise end-user voice and data network areas are eligible. Guest columns are selected based on timeliness and appropriateness to our audience and do not have to match scheduled editorial calendar topics for a given month.

Product Sections: Product-review information should be sent to the Products Editor (products@comnews.com). This will ensure that it gets handled correctly. If you send it to the wrong editor, it may be misplaced. We publish New Product Announcements relevant to our enterprise end-user audience. We do not do product testing or reviews. Please send your new product announcements as soon as the product is shipping, and do not try to target it to a specific issue.

Calling to follow up on product press releases does not help or speed up the process. Please do not follow up by phone to "check on the status" of the product submission. Please submit files of less than 3 megabytes. **NOTE:** Do not send screenshots or company logos as artwork. Artwork guidelines at: Product Submission Guidelines: comnews.com/about/prod_submission.htm

Getting Started

First, send us an abstract proposal. After defining the topic, write two or three paragraphs describing what you want to say in your article. Make sure that you identify, with the abstract, the month and editorial focus subject you feel the article fits in, as well as the vendor supplying the article. To do this, visit the editorial calendar on our Web site at www.comnews.com/mediakit/CALENDARCN04.pdf.

DO NOT submit an abstract unless the companies involved (vendor and customer, if appropriate) have agreed to have the article published.

In addition, identify with the abstract what audience the article is meant for: enterprises, service providers, carriers, etc.

Send the proposal to the editor (e-mail is the best way) at least 14 weeks prior to publication date (e.g., Dec. 15 for the April issue). Our policy is to review proposals shortly after the abstract deadline date and to inform all potential contributors whether or not their abstract has been accepted for development into a feature. Please do not follow up by phone to "check on the status" of the abstract.

Important: Please submit with your abstract the vendor name, address, phone, fax, contact person for reader inquiries, e-mail and Web addresses.

Writing the Article

Case histories should be solution-based, providing practical and useful information to enterprise end-users (i.e., corporations, educational, government). A simple and effective formula is this: "Here is a problem we had; here is the way we solved it; these are the products and techniques we used; this is how we're working now."

A case history should include all the elements of the solution, not just the vendor's products (if there are more elements than one). We prefer third-person accounts, so it is generally better to include quotes from the end-user, rather than use that person as the author. Case studies should not carry the vendor's byline, since the vendor and products are mentioned in the story. A case study should focus on just ONE enterprise situation. Here is some of the information we would like included in the article:

Describe the problem solved and the improvement made. How was the problem increasing expenses, hindering operations, causing staff to be unproductive? When did corrective action first start and how was it accomplished? How was a final solution selected? Site visits? Vendor demos? How many products were reviewed before deciding? How long did the process take. Describe the most important components of the solution, or the network where the solution was installed: hardware, software, networks, consultants, training, etc.

Also, what was the approximate cost of all components of the solution? What was the cost justification? Who had to approve the purchase or installation? How many staff and/or customers are served by the system? What are the benefits, in terms of: savings, productivity, customer care or service, etc.? Are enhancements planned? Any anecdotes that speak to the value and benefits of the solution? Please include quotes of principals of the subject company throughout the article to describe the process. Do not include quotes from the vendor or vendor partners.

The importance of "Warts." Warts are journalistic imperfections in an article-not errors but rather negatives about the subject. Articles that paint too rosy a picture often are dismissed by readers as self-promotional. Articles that include "warts" become more believable by readers because the warts provide a dose of realism and truth that says to the reader, "We are presenting the problems associated with this solution, as well as the benefits." The article immediately becomes more believable, as a result. A journalist would seek out these imperfections in order to write a more balanced article. We encourage you to include warts in your article whenever possible.

Quotes in case histories: Often, with case histories that we receive, it is apparent that someone has concocted quotes for the case history subject, instead of actually interviewing the customer for real quotes. Invariably, these quotes say something like: "XYZ company did a fantastic job with the implementation and their products are saving us lots of time and money." These types of quotes do not lend any useful information to our readers, and generally will be deleted from the article. Also, quotes from the vendor generally are inappropriate for case histories.

Contact information. In addition to contact information for the vendor submitting the article, we will need the name, phone number and e-mail address of a person at the company that is the subject of the case history. This person preferably should be the one interviewed for and quoted within the article. Editors routinely call these contacts to verify information or to ask additional questions. Failure to provide this contact information can result in your article being turned down.

The Tutorial

A second type of story is a tutorial, which examines a basic or advanced technology in a new or updated context. We cover a broad range of enterprise end-user networking and communications topics, and it is not reasonable to expect every reader to have detailed knowledge of all aspects of every topic or to have access to the very latest developments. A tutorial style article should still be readable and, where possible, cite specific examples and cases. A tutorial can carry a byline from a vendor representative, but the vendor's products will not be mentioned in the article.

Please do not submit an opinion piece as a tutorial, and remember, we want discussion of solutions, not problems. Your article should explain how the technology is used by and benefits the enterprise end-user. Avoid too much historical background. Do not criticize competing technologies; instead focus on the features, implementation, benefits, etc., of the technology of your focus.

Articles that are self-serving or recite the technical specifications of a particular product are unacceptable. The article should not serve as a thinly disguised promotion for a product or company.

Any submission of articles must be exclusive to Communications News. We do not accept articles that have been published in another trade journal, newspaper, periodical, on the Web, company literature or conference proceedings.

Acceptance Frequency Policy

In order to be fair to all potential contributors, we limit the frequency of articles accepted for publication from any one company to no more than one article every four months.

Length

Our feature stories generally run from 700 words to 1,200 words. Most stories are on the shorter side.

Submission

If your article is accepted for publication, it will be assigned a file name to use in future references (e.g., c04XYZcompany.doc). Please be aware that your manuscript will be edited for style, space requirements and ease of reading. We can accommodate your article and graphics on 3-1/2" IBM-compatible PC disks, Syquest (44 or 88) or Zip disks, or as an attached file to an e-mail message (preferred). Our preferred word processing program is Microsoft Word (pre-97).

Important: Make sure the manuscript you send us has the name and address of a contact person within the vendor company submitting the article to whom we can send reader inquiries.

Illustrations

Photos and artwork help to set a tone for articles, and provide important visual interest. We encourage you to provide photos and/or artwork for the article. For case histories, we prefer photos at the customer site, preferably including the main person who is quoted (no head shots, please). Artwork, graphics or photographs should be high-quality photographs, transparencies, 35-mm slides or electronic files. Line drawings such as tables, charts or schematics also are acceptable. Graphics may be submitted in digital format or via hard copy. The graphics should be in Adobe Photo Shop or Adobe Illustrator-compatible TIF, JPG and PPT files. EPS is not recommended. The best quality comes in 300 dpi high-resolution or higher.

Important: Do not embed graphics, artwork or photos in the Word document containing the article. Also, include captions with all photos and artwork.

Contact Us

Editorial Assistant, ljudd@comnews.com, phone 941-966-9521 x182. Check this number first with questions about deadlines, topics, media kits, contributed articles, editorial calendar, etc.

Editor

To propose cover stories or feature articles, send a short abstract first. Indicate the month, focus and story in the subject line of your e-mail.

Product reviews editor

Send product information. Indicate "Product Review" in the subject line of your e-mail. Product Submission Guidelines: comnews.com/about/prod_submission.htm

Categories: Nonfiction—Communications—Technology

CONTACT: Communications News
2500 Tamiami Trail N
Nokomis FL 34275
Phone: 941-966-9521
FAX: 941-966-2590
E-mail: Ken Anderberg, Editor

COMPLETE WOMAN

Complete Woman

Thank you for your interest in submitting material to *Complete Woman*. We welcome all manuscripts and cartoons or illustrations that address the concerns of today's woman. Topics may vary over a range, including positive approaches to home, family, career, health, relationships, and self-improvement. Subject matter is limited only by your imagination and understanding of what it means to be a complete woman in today's society.

Manuscripts should be between 1,000 and 2,200 words in length, including any sidebar or supplementary material. Because all materials are received on speculation only, we suggest you query us with clips before sending your articles.

Complete Woman is published bimonthly. We pay upon publication (during the month of the cover, and after publication).

We look forward to seeing your work.

Sincerely,

Bonnie L. Krueger, Editor-in-Chief

Categories: Confession—Diet/Nutrition—Entertainment—Fantasy—Fashion—General Interest—Interview—Lifestyle—Marriage—Physical Fitness—Relationships—Self Help—Sexuality—Singles—Teen—Women's Issues

CONTACT: Bonnie L. Krueger, Editor-in-Chief
Material: All
CONTACT: Lora M. Wintz, Executive Editor
Material: All
875 N. Michigan Ave., Ste. 3434
Chicago IL 60611-1901
Phone: 312-266-8680

The Compulsive Reader

The Compulsive Reader reviews literary fiction, cookbooks, and books for writers. If your book fits this category, please send a brief (1-2 paragraph) synopsis to maggieball@compulsivereader.com, and if we feel that the book fits the site, we will contact you directly to let you know where to send a review copy. Our reviews are quite detailed, honest, and specific, and will cover such things as stylistics, theme, characterisation, narrative voice, and plot development.

WHAT ARE WE LOOKING FOR IN REVIEW SUBMISSIONS?

We are looking for detailed, and informative reviews of literary fiction, cookbooks, or books for writers, as well as articles on any literary topic, including literary criticism. Reviewers retain all copyrights to their work and are free to publish their review or article in other venues as long as it doesn't conflict with our rights while your review remains on our site. Although we are unable to offer monetary compensation for reviews and articles at this time, we provide all contributors with a byline located directly under the title, up to six lines of Author Bio information at the end of the article, and links. Regular contributors are also featured in the "Who are We" section of our site and are offered books for review. Submit reviews in the body of the text (rather than as an attachment) to: maggieball@compulsivereader.com

Categories: Nonfiction—Book Reviews—Writing

CONTACT: Maggie Ball, Editor
Material: All
E-mail: maggieball@compulsivereader.com
Website: www.compulsivereader.com/html

ComputorEdge
San Diego's Computer Magazine

ComputorEdge is the nation's largest regional computer weekly magazine.

A Profile of CE Writers

Freelance writers contribute to most sections of the magazine. CE writers use a style that is easily understood by novice and intermediate computer users, as well as well-educated readers and experts. Our writers are clear and conversational. They share their technical expertise in a relaxed, personable manner without unnecessary techno-jargon. This is a rare combination of talents.

Rights and Compensation

We buy First North American Serial Rights, as well as subsequent electronic publishing rights in order to maintain an archive on our Web site. Feature articles should be 1,000 to 1,200 words in length. The columns Mac Madness and The Linux Link are open to freelance writers. They should consist of approximately 900 words.

Payment is rendered 30 days after publication. Feature articles pay $100; columns pay $75.

How to Submit Your Ideas

Become familiar with the magazine-each issue has a specific theme. You'll find the current issue and archived copies of at www.computoredge.com. Access the Editorial Calendar at www.computoredge.com/sandiego/edcal.pdf or request one from editor@computoredge.com.

If you have a feature story or column idea for an upcoming issue, submit an e-mail query to submissions@computoredge.com. Do not include any attachments. We do not open attachments from unknown senders; your entire query will be deleted immediately. This is important: Put the Issue Number for which you wish to write in the Subject line of your e-mail message. Keep in mind that we assign stories up to three months ahead of the publication date. You should also provide:

• A brief but detailed description of the article you would like to write.

• A summary of your writing credits, credentials, or brief bio if you have never written for *ComputorEdge* before.

If your article is accepted, an editor will contact you. Be sure to provide your current e-mail address. If you do not hear from us within a reasonable amount of time, your submission has probably been rejected. If you wish, you may send a "reminder" e-mail to check on the status of your submission. Please do not send unsolicited manuscripts.

After Acceptance

When finalized, e-mail your accepted article or column to assigned@computoredge.com. It needs to be received by the Writer's Deadline, which is indicated on the Editorial Calendar. This is important:

In the Subject line of your e-mail, put "Issue Number" and the number of the issue for which your article is slated.

We prefer to receive the article in Microsoft Word format or as part of the body of the e-mail.

It is important that assigned articles be directed to assigned@computoredge.com. It is important that submissions be directed to submissions@computoredge.com. It is important that no other e-mail be directed to these mailboxes. Questions and comments should be addressed to editor@computoredge.com.

Acceptance of a piece does not guarantee its immediate publication. On occasion, a scheduled article may be moved to another issue.

Revised 10/12/05

Categories: Nonfiction—Computers—Technical—Technology

CONTACT: Submissions Editor
Material: All
4740 Murphy Canyon Rd, Ste 250
San Diego CA 92123
Phone: 858-573-0315
E-mail: editor@computoredge.com
Website: www.computoredge.com

---

conceive magazine

conceive magazine is for any woman contemplating or actively trying to start or expand a family: by natural conception, fertility treatments and assisted reproductive technologies, or adoption. We are not a pregnancy or parenting magazine, but are focused on all aspects of fertility, conception, and adoption.

If you have a personal story to tell, please post it on the "Success Stories" section of this website. Because of the volume of submissions we receive, we cannot respond to every story. But if your story is chosen to be featured in the magazine, you will be contacted. Although we try to respond quickly, because of the volume of stories we receive it may take several months.

If you want to let us know about something newsworthy—a new program, medical study, book or product—you can email the Editor in the contactus.asp

All other queries should be posted by regular mail. conceive magazine is published quarterly. We receive many queries from writers but can only use a small percentage of what we receive. Most of our writers are longtime professionals specializing in women's health coverage.

If you are a professional freelance writer interested in writing assignments for conceive, please send samples of your published work, a resume or description of your publishing career, and a few story ideas—no completed articles, please—to the address below.

Enclose a self-addressed, stamped envelope if you want your work returned. And please allow several months for a response, due to the large number of unsolicited queries we receive. Thank you for your interest in conceive magazine.

Categories: Nonfiction—Family—Women's Health

CONTACT: Editors, conceive magazine
622 E Washington St Ste 440
Orlando FL 32801
Website: www.conceiveonline.com

Confrontation
A Literary Journal

Formal guidelines not available. Please read a number of issues to ascertain the publication's style and needs.

Send queries to address below.

Categories: Drama—Experimental Fiction—Literature—Men's Fiction—Poetry—Theatre—Women's Fiction—Writing

CONTACT: Jonna Semeiks, Associate Editor
Material: Fiction
CONTACT: Isaac Cates, Assistant Editor
Material: Poetry
English Dept, C.W. Post of Long Island University
Brookville NY 11548
Phone: 516-299-2720

Connecticut Magazine

Connecticut Magazine is a general interest, service and issue-oriented magazine that covers all aspects of life in the state—arts, politics, travel, people, business, health, environment and newsworthy issues. Connecticut Magazine readers are generally affluent and well-educated. They enjoy intellectual pursuits, entertainment, dining out and recreation. They are inquisitive, active. They are concerned about the state in which they live and are looking for information and entertainment in our pages.

Unsolicited Articles: Many of the articles we publish, including restaurant reviews, interiors, politics, and gardening, are written by our regular contributing writers. Connecticut Magazine does, however, purchase unsolicited articles from free-lancers. We look for service articles, investigative pieces, personality profiles and other pieces of interest to Connecticut readers. We do not publish fiction or poetry. Writers are encouraged to read recent issues of Connecticut Magazine to get a sense of the types of articles and styles appropriate for the magazine.

Query Letters: The editors request that free-lancers query their ideas by letter and not by telephone. A query letter should contain a detailed outline of the proposed piece and a list of sources. Copies of articles previously published should be attached, if possible. Query letters are reviewed by the editors, and if the idea is accepted, the piece may be assigned.

Deadlines: Our deadline is two months prior to publication date. For example, the final manuscript for a piece slated or intended for the December issue is due on or before October 1. Because most issues are planned well in advance, queries should be submitted as early as possible, in the case of seasonal pieces four to six months ahead of the proposed publication date.

Manuscript Requirements: Manuscripts must be typed, double- or triple-spaced, on 8½" by 11" paper with 1½" margins. All pages must be numbered. Onion skin and corrasable paper are unacceptable. Writers should retain a copy. Writer's name, address, phone number and social security number should appear on the first and last page of each article. Phone numbers and addresses of article subjects and resource persons as well as a SASE should be included with all manuscripts submitted. Length requirements vary from piece to piece, but generally range from 1,800 words for columns and departments to 3,000 words or more for features. If possible, a choice of titles should be included.

Expenses: In certain circumstances, and if agreed to by the editor at the time of assignment, Connecticut Magazine will reimburse writers for expenses incurred with their articles. In these situations, copies of itemized phone bills and other receipts for expenses incurred must be submitted before reimbursement can be made.

Payment: The amount of payment is determined at the time of assignment and is made within one month of publication. A kill fee not to exceed 20 percent may be paid in the event a commissioned article is still unpublishable after reasonable attempts at revision either by the assigned writer or the magazine staff. Payment is determined on an individual basis. Articles assigned on speculation and unsolicited articles carry no kill fee and no expenses unless otherwise stated in writing.

Artwork: Photos and/or illustrations to accompany articles are independently assigned by the art department. However, if a writer has appropriate photos or a lead on available ones, this information should be made known. Photographers and illustrators should contact the art department for a portfolio review.

Categories: Nonfiction—Entertainment—Food—Gardening—General Interest—Politics—Regional: Connecticut

CONTACT: Dale Salm, Managing Editor
Material: All
Connecticut Magazine
35 Nutmeg Drive
Trumbull CT 06611
E-mail: dsalm@connecticutmag.com

Conscience
The Newsjournal of Catholic Opinion

Conscience is a quarterly newsjournal of Catholic opinion, with a circulation of approximately 12,500, including members of Congress, librarians, members of the clergy, and members of the press.

Focusing on ideas and values, *Conscience* presents an ethical discussion of reproductive rights and choices, the role of women in society and the church, conscience and dissent in the church, church-state issues, and social conditions and policies affecting women's choices in childbearing and child-rearing.

The editor seeks manuscripts that will be of interest to concerned individuals of all denominations, as well as to leaders in the fields of theology, ethics, and women's studies. Articles should be written for an educated audience that is diverse professionally, culturally, and geographically.

Simultaneous submissions are acceptable, but writers should notify the editor at once when a manuscript is accepted elsewhere. Likewise, we ask writers to notify other publications considering the manuscript of any agreement to publish the article in *Conscience*. Some previously published articles are accepted; all such submissions must include the original publisher's name and address.

Manuscripts accepted for publication are subject to editing for clarity and conformity with *Conscience* style. Authors will generally receive an edited draft of the manuscript for evaluation before it is typeset and will be asked to answer any editorial queries and return the manuscript by a specified date. In the case of multiple authorship, one author should be designated as correspondent.

Submission
Manuscripts should be submitted in Microsoft Word version 6.0/95 or higher, and may be submitted on disk or via e-mail.

Length
Articles should be approximately 1,200 to 2,000 words; *Conscience* may run longer articles by agreement with the editor. Book reviews should be 800 to 1,500 words, and letters to the editor should be 100 to 350 words.

Title Page
In addition to the title of the manuscript, the title page should include the author's name, academic or professional title and degree, current affiliation, complete address, phone number, fax number, and e-mail address. For articles with multiple authorship, please provide complete information for each author.

Formatting
Submitted manuscripts should be double-spaced and use common system fonts such as Times New Roman, Courier, or Arial. Formatting, such as bolding, italics, underlining, tabs, indents, etc., should be kept to the minimum amount necessary to organize the text.

References
References should be numbered sequentially in the text, with full information for each citation. CFFC follows *The Chicago Manual of Style*, 15th Edition and the *Associated Press Stylebook*.

Illustrative Material
If permission to reproduce any illustration, photograph, or excerpt is needed, it is the responsibility of the author to secure such permission. Written notice of the permission should be included with the submission, or if the manuscript has been submitted via e-mail, sent via U.S. mail with the title page of the article to be published in *Conscience*.

When graphs, illustrations, line drawings, or other figures accompany the manuscript, they should be supplied as camera-ready art whenever possible. High-quality photographs that are relevant to the manuscript may be submitted. Accompanying tables should be put at the end of the manuscript, with a note in the text to show where they should appear in the published version.

Copyright
Conscience reserves first international and website rights to all original material accepted for publication unless otherwise specified. Thereafter, authors retain copyright of their work. Simultaneous submissions are accepted, but upon notice of intent to publish in *Conscience*, authors are expected to withdraw all simultaneous submissions.

Compensation
CFFC offers *Conscience* contributors five to ten copies of the issue in which their article appears; additional copies are available upon request. Some articles are paid on publication; payment for these is arranged on a case-by-case basis.

Categories: Nonfiction—Book Reviews—Culture—Feminism—Health—Human Rights—Politics—Religion—Sexuality—Women's Issues

CONTACT: Editor, Conscience
1436 U Street, NW, Ste 301
Washington DC 20009-3997
Phone: 202-986-6093
Fax: 202-332-7995
E-mail: conscience@catholicsforchoice.org

Contract Management

The Magazine and Its Audience
Contract Management (CM) magazine is the NCMA flagship publication for people and businesses working in the buying and selling communities of both the public and private sectors.

CM is a full-color, monthly magazine written and edited specifically for contract management professionals. Each issue provides comprehensive reporting on issues and trends relevant to contract management of all shapes and sizes ¾ covering the public and private sectors.

Readers are usually members of National Contract Management Association (NCMA), typically with more than 15 years of contract management experience.

Before You Write
CM seeks original and useful articles dealing with contract management problems, insights, applications, and opinions. As a contract management professional, your personal experiences in the field can become valuable to readers. Apply your practical insights, solutions, and encountered problems to their situations. Focus on the lessons learned, rather than chronology of events. *Before you begin to write an article for CM, you should ask yourself these questions:*
- Is this topic practical to the reader?
- Do I have specific examples of lessons learned?
- How can other professionals adapt what I have done?
- What kinds of pitfalls might they run into?
- What are the costs involved?

Avoiding the Pitfalls
Articles often are not accepted in Contract Management magazine because the article topic:
- Is not related to contract management,
- Is poorly organized,

• Lacks valuable insight,

• Offers too few examples, or is overly promotional and self-serving.

In order to avoid these pitfalls, we recommend that you send an inquiry including a brief summary (150 words) of the proposed article to the editor-in-chief before you write the article.

If you cannot capture your idea in 150 words, you may be trying to tackle too broad of a topic. Your topic should be focused sufficiently in 12 to 30 pages, double-spaced, plus a double-spaced sidebar.

Your topic may not be best suited for a feature article, but rather a special interest corner article. Corner articles (four to 11 pages, double-spaced) can be written about the following topics: alternative disputes resolution, commercial contracting, construction contract management, environmental contracting, information technology, e-commerce, e-business, education, grants management, health care contracting, international acquisition, program management, small business, state and local government contracting, and professional development.

Writing Your Article

Here are our suggestions for an easy-to-read, successful CM article.

• Create a clever working title using active verbs. Try to keep it brief, between three and six words.

• Provide a byline. Include the author(s') full name(s), suffixes, degrees, etc.

• Provide a two- to three-line biography. Include the author's name, title, affiliation/employer, employer's city and state, and NCMA chapter membership information.

• Use subheadings in the article to help the reader focus on the direction of the story at least every two pages.

• Pay attention to tone. Avoid lecturing. Convey your ideas by showing the reader what to do, rather than telling them what to do. Explain your ideas clearly by avoiding excessive jargon, and define jargon you must use.

• Be comprehensive. Use details¾such as dates, statistics, references, and quantities¾to clarify and support your points. Sometimes pertinent information that is self-contained can be used as a sidebar. Steps of a process or a list of resources can be boxed off as a nice design element and easy-to-read sidebar.

• Explain the relevance to others. Make your points using examples from your experience, and then tell readers how they can apply your experience to their situations.

• Avoid the passive voice. Active language is straightforward and simple.

• Edit your article at least twice. Delete unnecessary words and phrases. Turn passive sentences into active ones. Move paragraphs to achieve continuity and use transition sentences to help paragraph-to-paragraph flow. Make sure paragraphs flow logically.

• Check the accuracy of your article. Using your original source material, verify every date, name, fact, and figure. Accuracy is your responsibility, not that of CM magazine editors.

• Test market your article. Ask a few colleagues to review your article. They may help point out ways to clarify your message.

Submitting Your Article

Members write most of the articles published in *Contract Management* (CM), although one does not have to be an NCMA member to be published in the magazine. Articles should concern some aspect of the contract management profession, whether at the level of a beginner or that of an advanced practitioner.

When submitting an article, accompany it with a cover letter that includes your daytime telephone number and preferred mailing address. If making a query, contact the Communications Team-see information below.

The Communications Team publishes an editorial calendar each year as a guide for potential writers on particular topics. Writers should not feel limited by the "topic of the month." CM is interested in receiving articles on all topics of interest to those engaged in the contract management profession. Particularly of interest are articles of a "how-to" nature with practical, problem-solving instruction that can be used on the job.

Note: The magazine has a three-month lead-time for any given issue.

Disk/Article submission guidelines

• Send the manuscript on a 3.5" disk formatted in Word or a compatible program; or e-mail your manuscript to miedema@ncmahq.org.

• Accompany the disk with hard copy, double-spaced on 8.5 x 11" sheets, on one side of each page only.

• Include a two to three sentence "abstract" describing what the article is about and how it will benefit the reader.

• Keep manuscripts in the range of 12 to 30 pages in length (double-spaced) for features, four to 12 pages in length for corners.

• Do not use all upper-case type for headings or text.

• Indent the beginning of each paragraph.

• Use illustrative charts, graphs, figures, and tables when appropriate.

• Use endnotes rather than footnotes.

• Include a brief biography of the author(s) at the end. This should include job title, employer name and location, and NCMA affiliation-chapter name, CPCM/CACM, Fellow, whether a member of a Special Topic Committee, etc.

Evaluation and Acceptance

The editor-in-chief will send an acknowledgment letter, but cannot guarantee when or if an article will be published. Articles are evaluated based on readability, soundness of content, timeliness, and interest to our readers. We also consider whether you support you ideas with concrete examples.

Articles that essentially only promote a particular company, product, and service are not considered publishable.

We may accept your article outright or accept it contingent on your revision. If an article is accepted, an editor will contact the author to advise him/her of the issue of publication. All accepted articles are subject to editing for style, clarity, language, and length.

Rejection of articles is confirmed through written correspondence.

Copyright Transfer

Once the article has been accepted and edited, you will be asked to sign a copyright release form that gives National Contract Management Association (NCMA) copyright to the article. The copyright only gives NCMA right to the copyedited version of your article in print and electronic format. You retain the rights to your original. If you have questions or concerns about copyright transfer, please call Amy Miedema, editor-in-chief, at 703-734-5412.

Categories: Nonfiction—Business—Government

CONTACT: Amy Miedema, Editor-in-Chief
Material: All
CONTACT: Kathryn Mullan, Assistant Editor
Material: All
National Contract Management Association
1912 Woodford Road
Vienna VA 22182
Phone: 703-448-9231 or 800-344-8096
Fax: 703-448-0939
E-mail: cm@ncmahq.org
E-mail: Miedema@ncmahq.org
Website: www.ncmahq.org

Remember: Editors change jobs and publishers change addresses. It is wise to invest in a phone call for the current information before submitting.

Conversely

No longer accepting submissions.

A-E

Cooking Light

Cooking Light, The Magazine of Food and Fitness, is the recipe for healthy living. Nearly 85% of our 11.6 million readers are women, most between the ages of 30 and 60. Our readers are affluent, sophisticated, well-educated, professional, and interested in living holistically healthy life styles. They come first to the magazine for our recipes, but the lively writing as well as health and fitness coverage help keep them coming back issue after is sue. *Here's what the editors of Cooking Light look for when assigning articles:*

• *Knowledge of the Magazines:* You can now find *Cooking Light* — the nation's largest epicurean magazine — at just about any supermarket or newsstand.

Lead Time: For food articles, it's anywhere from a year to 18 months, due largely to seasonality and the extensive work our Test Kitchens must do on every recipe. For healthy life styles articles, it's anywhere from three to eight months.

• *Story Ideas:* Those lead times acquire that our stories be seasonal, long-range, or forward-looking. A trend of today can be old news in a six months, so please keep that in mind when developing queries. We're looking for fresh, innovative stories that yield worthwhile information for our readers — a cooking tip, a trend, a suggestion of how they can use a particular recipe, nutritional information that may not be common knowledge, reassurance about their lifestyle or health concerns, etc.

• *Food Queries: Cooking Light* strives to offer new ideas and information than help readers make informed meal-planning, food-purchasing, and food-preparation decisions for a healthier way of eating — with more starch, dietary fiber, and water, but less fat, sodium, sugar, and alcohol. Our principles involve replacing the old, adapting the traditional, and creating the new. We expect our writers to adhere to the ethical standards set by the national Association of Food Journalists to keep our stories free of any commercial bias.

• *Submitting Queries:* All story ideas must be submitted in writing. Please enclose a paragraph or two about each idea, your resume, and some sample clips. Because of the volume of mail we receive, we guarantee a response only if you include a self-addressed, stamped envelope with your query. We'll get back to you, even if by form letter, within about a month.

Our street address (for overnight services) is 2100 Lakeshore Drive, Birmingham, AL 35209.

Categories: Nonfiction—Cooking—Diet/Nutrition—Food/Drink—Health—Physical Fitness—Travel

CONTACT: Alison Ashton, Senior Food Editor
Material: Food
CONTACT: Senior Editor, Healthy Living
Material: Fitness/Healthy Living
PO Box 1748
Birmingham AL 35201
Phone: 205-445-6000
Website: cookinglight.com

Cooks Illustrated

Does not accept unsolicited submissions.

The Cooperator
The Co-op and Condo Monthly

Requirements

Structure: Whereas newspaper articles are structured in a top-down format, *The Cooperator* articles are structures like those in magazines–composed as an entire piece. Every article must flow from beginning to end. Both a lead and a conclusion are necessary.

Title: Every title has a "header" and a "kicker"…Don't Get Soaked! *Waterproofing Your Masonry Facade,* Saving For a Rainy Day. *The Five-Year Budget Planning-Process*

Byline: Use capital B; no colon: By John Smith

Subheads: Sections of the article should be preceded with a subhead, organizing the information and breaking it up a bit. Arrange the article so that the story evolves from one section to the next.

Include @ 3 or 4 per article. Begin the body of the article with the first subhead following the introduction (around the second or third paragraph).

Subhead titles should generalize the information to follow, but be specific: "A Past of Many Disciplines" instead of just "the Past."

Author Blurb: (at end of article) indent blurb, and begin with Mr. Or Ms.: "Mr. Smith is a freelance writer based in Manhattan"; "Ms. Smith is executive director of the Bla Bla Foundation, a non-profit organization in Brooklyn that promotes safe bla bla practices."

Acronymns: First spell out the title and then put the acronym in parentheses. The acronym can then be used freely throughout the article: the Real Estate Board of New York (REBNY)…

Commas: Don't use a comma in a string of simple words: a dog, a cat and a bird.

Use comma in a string of phrases: The project succeeded because of a well-planned marketing program, long-term financing by several institutions, and much dedication from the developer's New York employees.

Colon: Capitalize the word following a colon only if it is a proper noun or the beginning of a new sentence.

Remember this: It is better to be…

There are two kinds: normal and strange.

Dash: Never use a dash to replace the words to or between and and: "10 a.m. to 11 a.m." instead of "10 a.m.-11 a.m." "Between eight and ten things" instead of "8-10"

Dates: Days of the week are not abbreviated: Monday instead of Mon.

Geography: Write out the names of cities, states and countries unless they are in a long list of cities and states or states and countries: New York, New York; or Philadelphia, PA, Knoxville, TN, and Quebec, Can.

Hyphens: Use hyphens when two or more words are used together as an adjective: five-year plan; 70-unit building.

Measurements: Use symbols when describing dimensions of furniture or space: The painting is 48" by 18".

Money:; Use decimal only if cents are indicated: $10 and $10.50.

Numbers: Spell out one through ten; use numerals above ten (11, 12…)–maintain this style within quotes.

BUT, spell out numerals when they begin a sentence.

Below one, use fractions: 3/4, 1/8…

For larger numbers, spell out: 16 million instead of 16,000,000.

Percent: Write out the word: two percent; 16 percent.

Quotes: All periods, commas, etc. fall inside quotes (even simple quotes): She says, "I love The Cooperator."

The meter dials had "turned over."

Quotes within quotes are single: According to Knight, "The coalition was created as a 'grassroots organization.'"

Quoting Sources: While it's not necessary to put every other sentence in quotes, back up much of what you say with "words" from a professional.

If a quote is not directly attributed to a person, make sure it's obvious who you're paraphrasing.

All quotes are present tense: So and so of blank says, "…"

Titles are lower case: Robert Grant, director of property management at Diversified Property Management in Brooklyn…

Give a brief description of the firm (what it is and where) unless it is obvious (like Diversified above): Jane Jones, president of Kaye Waterproofing, an exterior restoration firm in Manhattan.

Don't include words like "Inc." or "Co." unless it's a necessary part of a firm's title: "Insignia Financial Group" instead of "Insignia Financial Group, Inc."; "Samuel Klein & Co." is OK.

Text: Indent paragraphs ½"; double-space lines.

Use only one space between sentences.

Time: A.M. and P.M. are upper-case, "small caps" with periods and put a space between the number and the a or p.

Use colons only if minutes are indicated: "10 a.m. and 10:15 p.m."

Miscellaneous

"co-op" is hyphenated; "cooperative" isn't.

Generally use "co-op" for "cooperative" and "condo" for "condominium."

Use lower case for:
• the "b" in "board members"
• the "b" in "bylaws" (bylaws is not hyphenated)
• the "m" and "a" in "managing agent" (or the "a" in attorney, etc.)

Only use an ampersand (&) when it is part of a company's formal name.

Use the terms "managing agent" and "management company."

Simplify! It is better to break a sentence into two or three (or seven…) than to continue with a number of semi-colons, commas and dashes. If a sentence seems a bit confusing, that's because it is. The Cooperator's tone is one of straight-forward simplicity. Present things in "layman's" terms as clearly as possible.

Categories: Fiction—Business—Real Estate

CONTACT: Delora A. Estock, Editor
Material: All
Yale Robbins, LLC
31 E. 28th Street, 12th Floor
New York NY 10016
Phone: 212-683-5700
Website: www.cooperator.com

COPIOUS

Following your bliss can be painful but there is no other option for the artist. We are interested in redemption. We like to take risks.

We are seeking high quality art, photography, poetry, and articles about music and film. We focus on the multidimensionality of the artistic nature, and like to show the real person behind the art. Let us know if you work in more than one medium……tell us your secrets.

The first step to publication in COPIOUS is by email. Please send your PROFESSIONAL bio and credits to: submissions@ copiousamounts.com. Include written samples in the body of the email. If your work is visual, send a link to your artist"s web site. No attachments will be accepted.

If your work is selected for publication, COPIOUS will ask you to talk about 3 things (under 250 words please):

1. Your artistic aesthetic—not how your agent wants to market you, but your true philosophy. Talk about the burning rapture of the muse. Make it personal. Maybe something dramatic happened to set you on this path. We won't be shocked. Try to sum it up in 3 sentences.

2. Tell us how others describe your work versus how you see it? Do they get it?

3. We would like one story/example of obstacles you have overcome or are currently struggling with. You can be critical, you can vent. Show your humanity. Tell us what we want to know. Tell us the truth. THANK YOU.

Categories: Comics

CONTACT: E-mail: Submissions@copiousmagazine.com

Cornerstone

These are the writers' guidelines for *Cornerstone* magazine. We appreciate your interest and hope you will find these guidelines helpful.

As of August 22, 2001, *Cornerstone* magazine will no longer be accepting unsolicited article manuscripts of any kind. Our publication dates (twice a year) preclude the likelihood that we would use any unsolicited materials, including general articles, book reviews, or fiction manuscripts.

Poetry:

One specific exception to this is poetry; we will still accept poetry submissions. We are interested in a variety of poetic styles (e.g., avant-garde, free and light verse, haiku), but if it has a "churchy," singsong rhythm or form, it is not for *Cornerstone*. We print 2 or 3 poems per issue at $10.00 per 1 to 15 line poem, $25.00 per 16+ line poem. We are looking for good use of imagery, words that elicit a sensory response, a poem that has memorable quality. The most important thing you can do: read the magazine. More poetry is rejected for not being familiar with *Cornerstone* than for any other reason. By reading back issues, you can familiarize yourself with our outlook on poetry.

Submissions:

Please send only email submissions (if email is unavailable to you, we accept hard copies—no SASEs please).

Send the submission in the body of the email message as ASCII or HTML text, or send as an attachment created in MS-Word, RTF (rich text format), or Word Perfect. If you send a file attachment, please tell us in the message body which word processor, version number, and operating system were used to produce it.

We do not mind simultaneous or previously published submissions.

Please DO NOT expect rejection slips. Due to the large volume of material we receive, we will only be able to respond to works we wish to publish. However, please rest assured that all material sent to *Cornerstone* is read and considered.

We look forward to hearing from you.

Sincerely,

Jon Trott, Editor in Chief

Categories: Christian Interests—Poetry

CONTACT: Book Review Editor
Material: Short Fiction, Articles
CONTACT: Tammy Perlmutter, Poetry Editor
Material: Poetry
Cornerstone Communications
939 W. Wilson
Chicago IL 60640
Phone: 773-561-2450
Fax: 773-989-2076
E-mail: poetry@cornerstonemag.com
Website: www.cornerstonemag.com

Corrections Compendium

Submission Guidelines

Corrections Compendium is a peer-reviewed research-oriented publication of the American Correctional Association (ACA). Its international readership includes individuals involved in every sector of the corrections and criminal justice fields.

Our readers are committed to the advancement of the corrections field. They cut across the spectrum of corrections, from individuals employed in correctional institutions, community corrections, and probation and parole, to those in juvenile services and academia.

AUTHOR GUIDELINES

What kind of articles do we want? We're very open-minded—as long as the article idea is interesting and relates to corrections. We are interested primarily in articles that are research-based and scholarly.

We don't like puff pieces or promotional articles. We want information that can help our readers better understand their profession and the critical issues they face day to day. For this reason, *our policy is that any article written by a consultant or an employee of a private firm must be co-authored by a corrections professional*. In other words, at least one author must be a practitioner employed by a public agency or nonprofit organization, or currently working in an adult/juvenile institutional or academic setting.

If you have not written for us before, send a written query telling us who you are and what kind of article you wish to submit. We'll let you know if your idea has possibilities. If you have an article that already is written and conforms to these guidelines, send the completed manuscript. All submitted manuscripts are reviewed by at least two members of the *Corrections Compendium* Editorial Advisory Board. Final publication decisions are based on the recommendations of these reviewers. We'll respond as soon as possible, usually within eight to 10 weeks.

What Makes a Good *CC* Article?

Most articles are organized in a simple format. First is the introduction. This captures the readers' attention and lets them know what the article will be about. It orients them to time and place and tells them why the subject is important enough for them to take the time to read about it.

The middle section of the article develops the topic. This is the meat of the article and should explain, simply and clearly, the important points you'd like to make about your research-oriented topic. When writing this section, try to put yourself in your readers' shoes. Make sure you're being detailed enough and giving enough examples to illustrate your point so they clearly understand the situation you are describing.

The final section is the conclusion. This should restate the main point of the article and should include any evaluations or recommendations you may have.

Finally, every good article has three main qualities: an interesting subject, thorough research and reporting, and an organized writing style. Your article doesn't have to be perfect—our editors will help you enhance it if it is accepted—but it's up to you to give the article focus.

Suggestions on Style

You can do a number of things to make your article come alive for readers. First, you should be familiar with the journal and the type of material we publish. Reading *Corrections Compendium* is the best way to figure out how to make your article fit our readers' needs.

Second, write clearly. In *The Elements of Style*, William Strunk makes these suggestions:

• use the active rather than passive voice;
• be specific, concrete and definite;
• don't overstate; and
• avoid fancy words and jargon.

Submission Specifics

Corrections Compendium is a peer-review publication. This means that unsolicited manuscripts are sent to editorial advisory board members with expertise in the article's subject area for evaluation. For this reason, you should provide us with two copies of the manuscript. Other submission guidelines include:

• Manuscripts must be typed and double-spaced. If possible, send us the article in WordPerfect or Microsoft Word. Manuscripts will not be returned.
• Ideally, articles should be 3,000 to 6,000 words.
• Include your name, title, agency name, address, office or home telephone number, and fax number.
• We must be notified in writing at the time of submission if you are submitting the article to any other publications. *Corrections Compendium* is a copyrighted journal.
• Do not use footnotes. Endnotes are fine.
• Any references discussed or referenced in the text must be cited in a reference list at the end of the article.
• Include a resume or biographical information with your article.
• Submit charts, graphs or diagrams at the end of the manuscript to illustrate the topic.

If Your Article Is Accepted

Articles published in *Corrections Compendium* will be edited to conform to Associated Press (AP) style. You will be given a chance to review the edited version of your article before publication. The Association reserves the right to write article headlines.

A Note on References

Please follow the guidelines below when submitting references:

• **Reference for a magazine article with one author:**

Doe, John. 1997. Rhetoric in contemporary culture. *Professional Writing Quarterly*, 40(3):151-155. [40(3):151-155 refers to Volume 40, issue number 3, pages 151 through 155]

• **Starting a reference for an article/book with two or more authors:**

Doe, J. and S. Smith.

Doe, J., S. Smith and R. Jackson.

• **Reference for a book:**

Doe, John. 1997. *Analyzing modern poetry*. Attica, N.Y.: Exciting Press.

• **Reference for a pamphlet/gov. document:**

Federal Bureau of Prisons. 1988. *A report to the attorney general on disturbances at the federal detention center*. Washington, D.C.: U.S. Government Printing Office. (February).

• **Reference for an article in a book with an editor(s):**

Doe, J. 1997. Perspectives on best practices in corrections. In *Exciting ideas in corrections*, ed. S. Smith, 545-549. Washington, D.C.: Georgetown University Press.

Doe, J. 1997. Perspectives on best practices in corrections. In *Exciting ideas in corrections*, eds. S. Smith and R. Jackson, 545-549. Washington, D.C.: Georgetown University Press.

• **Reference for a speech/paper:**

Doe, J. 1997. How to travel across country. Paper presented at the National Travel Symposium, 3-5 April in Pittsburgh, Pa.

*Note: If you are unable to attribute material within your text (i.e., According to researcher Michael Rutter of the University of Maryland, ...), use the following method of citation—

Positive interaction is critical to the development of healthy social relationships (Rutter, 1995).

CONTACT: Susan L. Clayton, Managing Editor
Corrections Compendium
American Correctional Association
206 N. Washington St., Suite 200
Alexandria VA 22314
Phone: 1-800-224-0000, ext. 0190; 703-224-0190
Fax: 703-224-0179
E-mail: susanc@aca.org

Corrections Today

Submission Guidelines

Corrections Today is the professional membership publication of the American Correctional Association (ACA). Its international readership includes individuals involved in every sector of the corrections and criminal justice fields. The magazine, begun in 1939, currently has a circulation of 21,000, with a pass-along readership estimated as high as 65,000.

Our readers are committed to the advancement of the corrections field, and most play active roles in operating and administrating correctional facilities and systems. They cut across the spectrum of corrections, from individuals employed in correctional institutions, community corrections, and probation and parole to those in juvenile services and academia.

The magazine serves as a forum for presenting and discussing important issues related to corrections, including the presentation of minority or conflicting points of view. Its primary purpose is to offer practical information to promote the development of the field and those working in the field.

AUTHOR GUIDELINES

What kind of articles do we want? We're very open-minded—as long as the article idea is interesting and relates to corrections. We're interested in a variety of articles, including service ("how to") pieces, articles outlining new programs and case studies, and articles on how agencies or systems handle controversial issues. We also accept opinion pieces for our "Speak Out" column and personal accounts of on-the-job experiences for "A View From the Line."

We don't like puff pieces or promotional articles. There should be news, information or an opinion behind the story. Articles should be written in journalistic style using third person rather than first person (avoid using "I, we, me, us," etc.). We want information that can help our readers better understand their profession and the critical issues they face day to day. For this reason, our policy is that any article written by a consultant or an employee of a private firm must be co-authored by a corrections professional or academician. In other words, at least one author must be a practitioner employed by a public agency or non-profit organization, or currently working in an adult/juvenile institutional or academic setting.

If you have not written for us before, send a written query telling us who you are and what kind of article you wish to submit. We'll let you know if your idea has possibilities. If you have an article that already is written and conforms to these guidelines, send the completed manuscript. We'll respond as soon as possible, usually within eight to 10 weeks.

What Makes a Good CT Article?

Most magazine articles are organized in a simple format. First is the introduction. This captures the readers' attention and lets them know what the article will be about. It orients them to time and place and tells them why the subject is important enough for them to take the time to read about it. An anecdote or sample situation often is useful in the introduction—it can be a great way to pique readers' interest.

The middle section of the article develops the topic. This is the meat of the article and should explain, simply and clearly, the important points you'd like to make about your topic. When writing this section, try to put yourself in your readers' shoes. Make sure you're being detailed enough and giving enough examples to illustrate your point so they clearly understand the program, strategy or situation you are describing.

The final section is the conclusion. This should restate the main point of the article and should include any evaluations or recommendations you may have.

Finally, every good magazine article has three main qualities: an interesting subject, thorough research and reporting, and an organized writing style. Your article doesn't have to be perfect — our editors will help you enhance it if it is accepted — but it's up to you to give the article focus.

Suggestions on Style

You can do a number of things to make your article come alive for readers. First, you should be familiar with the magazine and the type of material we publish. Reading *Corrections Today* is the best way to figure out how to make your article fit our readers' needs.

Second, write clearly. In *The Elements of Style*, William Strunk makes these suggestions:
- use the active rather than passive voice;
- be specific, concrete and definite;
- don't overstate; and
- avoid fancy words and jargon.

Submission Specifics

Corrections Today is a peer-review publication. This means that unsolicited manuscripts are sent to ACA members with expertise in the article's subject area for evaluation. For this reason, you should provide us with two copies of the manuscript. Other submission guidelines include:
- Manuscripts must be typed and double-spaced. If possible, send us the article in WordPerfect or Microsoft Word. Manuscripts will not be returned.
- Ideally, articles should be 8 to 10 double-spaced, typed pages (2,000 to 2,500 words).

- Include your name, title, agency name, mailing address, e-mail address, office or home telephone number, and fax number.
- We must be notified in writing at the time of submission if you are submitting the article to any other publications. *Corrections Today* is a copyrighted magazine.
- Any references discussed in the text must be cited at the end of the article.
- Please do not format the article, as it will need to be reformatted to fit the style of the magazine.
- Include a resume or biographical information with your article.
- Submit photos or slides, as well as charts, graphs or diagrams with the manuscript to illustrate the topic. These should be placed at the end of the document.

If Your Article Is Accepted

Articles published in *Corrections Today* will be edited to conform to AP style, as well as *Corrections Today* style. You will be given a chance to review the edited version of your article before publication. The Association reserves the right to write article headlines and photo captions and to illustrate articles with art or file photos when more suitable photos are not provided by you.

PHOTOGRAPHY GUIDELINES

Photos are the first thing readers see when they look at a page. Photos draw attention to the page, leading the eye to the text. Often, important copy goes unread because a photograph is not striking enough to stop the browsing reader.

Techniques

Two qualities of good photographs are technical excellence and composition of interesting subject matter. Detail is achieved through proper picture-taking, sharp focus, correct exposure and a steady hand. Photographs also must have satisfactory contrast: An ideal print for reproduction should have a full range of tones—from very white, through many intermediate grays, to deep black.

Make sure to carefully frame your pictures. Define what you want in both the foreground and background; this is called "composing" the picture. You should be certain that the subject appears level and then center on the subject. Move in as close as possible to eliminate nonessential details in the foreground, background and sides. If your camera takes pictures that are larger in one dimension than the other, don't forget to turn the camera to see if you can frame the subject better.

Types of Photos

The best photo is the one that appears unposed. Action photos make excellent shots. Action does not necessarily refer to physical movement, but rather to the subjects' keeping busy—their being occupied with something that holds their attention. This prevents a picture from appearing static.

Take photos showing people, focusing on one or two. Crowd scenes (unless you're showing prison crowding) make it difficult to see what you're trying to illustrate. A dramatic closeup photo may do a better job of making a statement.

If your article mentions a particular service, program or case study, photograph those involved—the employees, participants, family, etc. Familiar scenes can be photographed from an unusual perspective. For example, a typical counseling setting might dramatize the situation between a client and a correctional officer, capturing their facial expressions and body language.

Captions and Credits

Identify the subjects in the photos through a caption. Tell us what's going on and who's in the photo. Supply the name of the photographer or the person/agency who supplied the photo to you. But please do not write directly on the backs of photos because ink tends to bleed through and ruin the photo. It's best if you mount the photo on a piece of paper and write the necessary caption/credit information on it.

Photo Releases

When photographing inmates, whether juveniles or adults, a release must be signed by the individual or individuals giving permission for the photo to be taken for publication. We require a release for any person photographed—even if the photo shows a back or side view. A

A-E

copy of an existing release already on file for a photo you are submitting also is permissible. Securing a release takes a little extra work, but in the long run, it protects you and *Corrections Today* from any liability.

A Note on References

Corrections Today encourages authors to include references with their articles to allow our readers to do follow-up reading on the subjects. Because *Corrections Today* is a magazine and not a scholarly journal per se, we favor the use of references in lieu of citations directly within the text. Please follow the guidelines below when submitting references:

• **Reference for a magazine article with one author:**

Doe, John. 1997. Rhetoric in contemporary culture. *Professional Writing Quarterly*, 40(3):151-155. [40(3):151-155 refers to volume 40, issue number 3, pages 151 through 155] Lanham, Md.: ACA Press. (November).

• **Starting a reference for an article/book with two or more authors:**

Doe, John and Jane Doe.

Doe, John, Jane Doe and James Doe.

• **Reference for a book:**

Doe, John. 1997. *Analyzing modern poetry*. Attica, N.Y.: Exciting Press.

• **Reference for a pamphlet/government document:**

Federal Bureau of Prisons. 1988. *A report to the attorney general on disturbances at the federal detention center*. Washington, D.C.: U.S. Government Printing Office. (February).

• **Reference for an article in a book with an editor(s):**

Doe, Jane. 1997. Perspectives on best practices in corrections. In *Exciting ideas in corrections*, ed. James Doe, 545-549. Washington, D.C.: Georgetown University Press.

Doe, Jane. 1997. Perspectives on best practices in corrections. In *Exciting ideas in corrections*, eds. James Doe and Jeffrey Doe, 545-549. Washington, D.C.: Georgetown University Press.

• **Reference for a speech/paper:**

Doe, Jeffrey. 1997. How to travel across the country. Paper presented at the National Travel Symposium, 3-5 April in Pittsburgh, Pa.

If you are unable to attribute material within your text (i.e., According to researcher Michael Rutter of the University of Maryland, ...), and you need to use endnotes:

DO NOT use the following method of citation: Positive interaction is critical to the development of healthy social relationships (Rutter, 1995).

DO use the following method of citation:

Positive interaction is critical to the development of healthy social relationships.[1]

On a separate page at the end of the article:

[1]Rutter, M. 1995. *Maternal deprivation reassessed*, second edition. New York: Penguin Books.

Categories: Nonfiction—Law Enforcement

CONTACT:
Susan Clayton, Managing Editor
Material: All
American Correctional Association
206 N. Washington St., Suite 200
Alexandria VA 22314
1-800-222-5646, ext. 0190
703-224-0190
Fax: 703-224-0179
E-mail:susanc@aca.org

Remember: Editors change jobs and publishers change addresses. It is wise to invest in a phone call for the current information before submitting.

Corvette Fever

Writers and Photographers Guidelines

Thank you for your inquiry. *Corvette Fever* is devoted to Corvettes of all eras, although our readers have little interest in highly or unusually modified cars. All featured vehicles must have Corvette engines or they will be rejected outright. The major focus of the magazine is technical maintenance, restoration and hop-up articles, features about exceptional Corvettes and racing coverage.

Features

Photography for feature cars should be submitted in color using 35mm slides or medium format photography. Our graphic arts department likes 100 ASA slide film. For tech articles and certain historical features, 400 ASA black and white film would be preferable. When submitting B&W, please submit the negatives with contact sheets. Color prints are not acceptable for feature car photography. For small, secondary photos inside a story, color prints are acceptable, but not preferable. Features in *Corvette Fever* normally focus on restored older Corvettes and '84-and-up in exceptional condition with an interesting hook. Race cars are also featured on an occasional basis, but we focus more on actual racing events. If you are not sure if a car is suitable for publication, please check it with us.

Stories from readers on their own Corvettes are welcome for consideration in our "Editor's Spotlight" section each month, and for our annual "Corvettes USA" July issue. These use reader-generated photography and information, and are never assigned to professional journalist/photographers.

When photographing feature cars, be aware of background clutter and reflections; we need clean, simple backgrounds. We think *Corvette Fever* is a dynamic, stimulating magazine, so don't be afraid to experiment with dramatic or unusual camera angles. However, keep in mind the four basic shots we request for every feature car: an engine shot, interior shot, front three-quarter view and rear three-quarter view. Beyond that, feel free to let those creative juices flow!

Study recent issues for examples. Shoot interiors with the doors open; convertibles can be shot top up or down, although down is usually the better choice.

One commonly overlooked approach to feature car photography is action. If possible, have your subject drive by so you can pan to blur the background, wheels, and tires. We really enjoy action photography, so the extra effort often pays off. However, keep in mind the photos will be enlarged considerably and must be very sharp. Thus, get close to the subject and keep the car large in the frame. Use the fastest shutter speed possible that will not freeze the background or tires. The idea is to have a razor-sharp shot of the car with the background blurred. If you have the people, cars, and time, shooting car-to-car is the best way of getting these shots.

For text, the average two-page color feature story runs about 500 words, more for detailed historical features or interviews. When writing about feature cars, focus on the history and unusual characteristics of that particular car, with perhaps some general history of that model thrown in. Information like this can frequently best be presented in chart or graph form. When writing features, always remember our readers have heard the old historical stories too many times already. Strive to put the humanity behind the subject car into the story. Above all, make your feature text more-than a simple listing of what original parts remain on the car and what options were originally installed, or which aftermarket parts have been installed. With late model Corvettes, if feasible, document performance by quarter-mile time, lap times, top speed, lateral acceleration or whatever. We want to know how hard it runs besides how good it looks, when that is appropriate.

Technical

Our readers expect the very best, up-to-date, detailed, accurate tech advice on restoring, maintaining or improving performance on their Corvettes. Make sure B&W photography is sharp, not too dark or light, and crop as necessary ON THE CONTACT SHEET. Photos are sent to scan and cannot include crop marks for the process.

Categories: Nonfiction—Automobiles—Technical

CONTACT: Ronnie Hartman, Editor-in-Chief
Material: All
3816 Industrial Blvd.
Lakeland FL 33811
Phone: 863-644-0449
Website: www.corvettefever.com

Cosmopolitan

Cosmopolitan magazine is aimed at young, sophisticated women between 18 and 34. All non-fiction should tell readers how they can 1) navigate their relationships, 2) attain their goals, and 3) better enjoy their lives. *Cosmo* covers relationships, self-development, health, work, and news of interest to young women. Writing must be crisp, clear, and in *Cosmo's* unique voice. Articles range from 1,000 words to 1,800 words. *Cosmopolitan* assigns stories to seasoned writers only and rarely accepts pitches.

Payment is open to negotiation.

Categories: Nonfiction—Careers—Diet/Nutrition—Entertainment—Fashion—Health—Lifestyle—Money & Finances—Physical Fitness—Relationships—Romance—Sexuality—Travel—Women's Issues—Self-Help—Beauty—Personal Development—Home —Essay—Interior Decorating—Celebrities—How-to—Humor—Personal Experience

CONTACT: Michele Promaulayko, Executive Editor
Material: All non-fiction
CONTACT: John Searles, Senior Books Editor
Material: Fiction
224 W. 57th St.
New York NY 10019
Phone: 212-649-2000
Fax: 212-956-3268
Website: www.hearstcorp.com

Cottage Magazine

Cottage Magazine is a bi-monthly publication about Country Living in Western Canada. Topics include do-it-yourself projects, profiles of people and their innovative solutions to building and maintaining their country homes, issues that affect rural individuals and communities and the R&R aspect of country living.

Our readers want solid, practical information about living in the country—including alternative energy, and sustainable living. They also like to have fun in a wide range of recreational pursuits, from canoeing, fishing and sailing to water skiing, snowmobiling and entertaining.

COLUMNS: Not all columns run every issue. Length 800 words

Utilities or Maintenance - Septic, water, electrical, woodburning, solar and wind power, energy efficiency etc. Past topics: woodstove maintenance, collecting and conserving water, do-it-yourself hydro systems, propane appliances.

Weekend Project - A how-to that most homeowners can do themselves. Requires strong illustrations/photos and clear instructions. Past topics: willow chairs, sheds, benches, cribbage boards, etc. Do-it-yourself projects are also in cluded in "Inroads".

Government - New regulations, processes, problems. Recent topics: road maintenance.

Diversions- Advisories, ideas, and how-to's about the fun things that people do.

InRoads - A catch-all of product reviews, short news items, book reviews, follow-ups to previous articles or events, essays, flora and fauna, quick tips etc. Length 50-600 words.

This Land - Personal essays or news-based story with a broader context. Recent topics: Cottage leases on First Nations land; cottage associations at work. Length 800 words.

Last Word or Cabin Life - Personal essays and experiences. Length 800 words. Illustrations welcome.

Elements - A short article focusing on a single feature of a cottage, like a hot tub or an outhouse. 600 words.

Alternatives - Applied alternative energy—how real people use it to solve cottage problems. Past topics: ram pumps, solar shower modifications, microhydro energy. 600 words.

FEATURE ARTICLES: Three or four per issue. Includes a main article of up to 1,500 words plus one or two sidebars (150 words) and box "tip" info (25 words). Recent features: Cob Building, Sharing a Cottage. Every issue also has at least one Feature Cottage, chosen for its unusual design, building techniques/process, energy conservation elements etc.

VISUALS: Writers usually also provide photos [slides or negatives] as well as other accompanying visuals such as house plans, diagrams [for how-to's] and maps, logos or line art as appropriate to the article. Photos should be slides or prints with negatives; digital images can be discussed.

SUBMISSIONS: We use Canadian spellings and CP style. Unsolicited articles/essays welcome. If submitted by email include in body of message since attachments will be deleted. Queries by email or fax. If by snail mail incl.an SASE with Canadian postage. Response within a month. Assignments made an average 6 months in advance of publication.

RATES: 1st Nth. Am. Rights. Payment is within 30 days of publication. Will negotiate 50% on Acceptance for assigned articles. Columns: 20 cents/published word. Features: $200-$450 [including visuals]. Photos: $15-$25. Cover submissions are also accepted.

TIPS FROM THE EDITOR: (1) We serve all of Western Canada so while it's ok to have a main focus on one region, reference should be made to similarities/differences in other provinces. (2) Even technical articles should have some anecdotal content. Some of our best articles come from readers themselves or from writers who can relay that "personal" feeling. (3) Cottaging is about whimsy and fun as well as maintenance and chores. (4) Images, images images: we require sharp, quality photos, and the more the better.

Categories: Nonfiction—Entertainment—Recreation—Rural—Sports—Regional: Western Canada

CONTACT: Editors, Cottage Magazine
1080 Howe St Ste 900
Vancouver BC V6Z 2T1
Phone: 604-606-4644
Fax: 604-687-1925
Website: cottagemagazine.com

Country Living

While we do not commission work based on query letters, we are happy to review completed manuscripts.

Manuscripts should be triple-spaced, allowing wide margins on both sides, as well as at the top and bottom of the page. Please use white bond paper only.

Our fees vary depending on the nature of the work and on the inclusion of supplemental photos and/or art work.

All manuscripts should be sent to our Features Editor, Lynne Constantin, at the address below.

Categories: Nonfiction—Antiques—Collectibles—Conservation—Cooking—Crafts/Hobbies—Entertainment—Family—Food/Drink—Gardening—Hobbies—Marriage—Real Estate—Travel—Home—Interior Decorating—Nature

CONTACT: Lynne Constantin, Features Editor
Material: All
224 W. 57th St., 7th Floor

New York NY 10019
Phone: 212-649-3509

Country Magazine
Country Extra Magazine

Country is for people who "live in or long for the Country"—and our editorial matter reflects the rural life-style with relaxed, conversational writing and top-quality rural and scenic photography. We showcase the pleasures and benefits of Country life, the beauty of rural America and folks with interesting tales to tell. In fact, much of each issue is based on what we receive from our readers, who send us thousands of pieces of mail every month.

Country is full-color throughout, printed on high-quality glossy paper, with an extra-heavy varnished cover. Published six times per year, it contains no paid advertising and is available primarily by subscription. The magazine was launched in 1987 and has a very loyal following.

Country EXTRA includes the same type of photo and editorial material as *Country*. CX is published "in between" the bimonthly issues of *Country*, thereby offering these enthusiastic subscribers monthly frequency through six extra issues.

Each editorial and photo submission is reviewed thoroughly. The ideal time for free-lance submissions is 4 months before the issue date. Unless a specific assignment is made, all freelance material will be considered on a speculative basis.

Photography: We welcome submissions. See separate Reiman Publications Photo Guidelines for payment schedule.

Feature Articles: We are always looking for a variety of rural-oriented features. Past stories have covered such diverse topics as the reason most barns are red, an essay on windmills and a first-person account of riding on a cattle drive. At the end of many features, we ask readers to respond with their own stories and photos.

Payment, upon publication, varies according to length, quality of photos, and amount of editing required to make it fit the format and style of *Country* and CX.

In most cases, payment is $100-$200 per story.

"God's Country", the regular 10-page photo feature in *Country*, is paid at a flat rate of $1,000 for photos and text.

Aside from the above guidelines, editors will negotiate a package rate for other multi-page features that use extensive amounts of photography.

"Country People Section": "Country People" features brief articles about rural "characters" with unusual hobbies, interests and enterprises. Photo-illustrated pieces should be 500-1,000 words, with a conversational tone; at least half should be direct quotes. Payment, upon publication, ranges from $75-$150, depending on length and quality.

We prefer transparencies for all color work (including photos submitted along with feature articles). Color prints are acceptable if they are of high quality. Be sure every image is identified for proper return.

Potential contributors are encouraged to obtains samples of *Country* and CX to learn about our needs. With high production costs and our no-advertising policy—we're supported solely by subscriptions—we regret that we can't give away samples.

Issues are $2 plus a 9- x 12-inch envelope with $1.93 in postage. Freelancers may subscribe at a special rate of $10.98 per year (regularly $17.98). Contributors receive a complimentary copy of the issue in which their work appears. Always include return postage with submissions.

Please direct manuscripts and manuscript/photo combinations to Jerry Wiebel, editor. Photo submissions should be sent to Trudi Bellin, photo coordinator. The address for both is:

Categories: Nonfiction—Adventure—Agriculture—Animals—Cooking—Food/Drink—Lifestyle—Multicultural—Nature—Outdoors—Recreation—Rural America—Travel

CONTACT: Submissions Editor
Material: Manuscripts
CONTACT: Trudi Bellin, photo coordinator
Material: Photo submissions
5400 S. 60th St.
Greendale WI 53129
Phone: 414-423-0100
E-mail: editors@country-magazine.com
Website: www.country-magazine.com

Country Woman

Country Woman is a 68-page, full-color, bimonthly magazine for women who live in or long for the country. It is a positive, upbeat, entertaining and informative publication that reflects the many interests and roles of its readers through short, photo-illustrated profiles of rural women…recipes, decorating, antiques and gardening articles… nostalgic photos and reader remembrances.

The publication also includes informative articles on health, finance and lifestyle issues related to rural living. While *Country Woman* readers are women of all ages, we target baby boomers, or women born between 1946 and 1965.

Free-lance material should have a rural link and be of specific interest to women who live on a farm or ranch, or women who live in a small town or country home and/or simply have an interest in country-oriented topics.

Many of the stories, columns, anecdotes and photos in *CW* come directly from its readers. But we count on freelancers such as you for the balance of each issue. Here are some of our regular features that freelancers help us with:

Features/Profile Stories …In each issue, we feature about half a dozen profile pieces, stories about country women doing unique and/or interesting things. Stories must be told in a light, entertaining, conversational style with plenty of direct quotes from the featured country woman. This is her story; so you can write it in first person as though she were telling it. Stories should have a strong, readily identifiable angle. Stories must be country related, and the "why" behind what the woman is doing must be clearly explained.

Many of our profile pieces focus on cottage industries or small businesses women have started themselves. Recent issues have included profile pieces on: a farm woman who has become a wool spinner and whose husband has begun to make spinning wheels as a result of her craft…a country artist who paints and sells floor rugs…a grade school teacher who takes the chicks she raises on her farm into her grade school classroom and uses them as "teaching aids."

These profile pieces are not limited to farm women; features on women who live on a country place or in a small town are also acceptable. We are also interested in stories about recent "transplants" to the country, including retirees.

Bright and beautiful color photos must accompany all profile pieces. We prefer to work with 35 mm or 2-1/4 Kodachrome transparencies, but we have had remarkable luck with bright, clear color prints. *CW* is looking for top-quality color, focus and lighting in all photos. While not our first choice, digital photographs are acceptable if they are at least 300dpi. Profile pieces are most often rejected because of poor quality photos! Please take good action, not posed, shots of your featured country woman in her natural environment—at work on the ranch, cutting out Christmas cookies, stitching a quilt or doing whatever it is that you are focusing on in your story. Your subject should be colorfully dressed and she should be wearing carefully-applied makeup. Manuscript length should be about 1,000 words, accompanied by a variety of photos—give us lots to choose from, please! Payment for a photo-feature package, on acceptance: $300-$600.

Cover shots …We are always in the market for strong cover photos! Cover shots must be strong verticals, with bright and vibrant colors...focus must be razor-sharp-no soft-focus shots will be accepted. No hot spots either! Use fill-in lighting where necessary to avoid hulking shadows. We have found that Kodachrome film generally provides the best color saturation, although other brands in the hands of skilled photographers have also met our standards. We can work from either 35 mm or 2-1/4 transparencies, but we prefer the larger-format photos. Photos usually focus on a close-up shot of a country woman in her natural surroundings. The subject should be attractive, but in a natural way. We ask that you help us locate a skilled professional make-up artist.

The subject must be a true country woman. We prefer subjects in their 30's to mid-40's, although attractive older women are acceptable as well. It is our cover woman's "job" to invite the reader into the magazine. The woman should look as if she's just stopped whatever she was doing for a moment to glance up and smile warmly out at the reader. Try for as spontaneous a look as possible. While the magazine's logo does not overprint the cover photo, several small lines of type do—so try to plan a small solid area somewhere in the background to accommodate them. When possible, covers should portray a strong seasonal look as well. We always need at least one additional pose for the inside cover story.

Cover prices are somewhat negotiable, but generally range around $300-$800, depending on the situation. Inside shot: $50-$200, depending on quality and size at which it's used.

Service Features ...these must relate specifically to the lives of country women. Some "how-to" articles we've bought recently include: how to start your own at-home business...how to market your crafts...how to sell your work to publishers...how to preserve old family photos...a listing of mail-order sources for holiday baking. Maximum length: 500-600 words. Color photos are generally needed. Rate: $150-$300.

Country Crafts, Sewing, Needlework ...emphasizing quick, easy and inexpensive country crafts. Include a list of all materials needed, detailed patterns, instructions and illustrations. Actual item must be enclosed so we can check it against instructions and photograph it. Rate: $50-$200, depending on quality and degree of difficulty.

Also, we welcome features on contemporary sewing methods, ideas for recycling, quilting tips, practical wardrobe planning, etc. Good color photos where appropriate. Rate: $300-$600 for a 2-page article, depending on length and quality.

Decorating ...We're always looking for features on home improvements along with before and after photos, short tips on decorating and exciting features on how to accomplish that "country look". Again, good quality color transparencies or high resolution digital photos are a must. If appropriate, photos can be from a corporation or trade organization. Rate: $300-$600 for a 2-page spread.

Nostalgia ...We're looking for well-written nostalgic pieces for our "I Remember When..." department. This is a country woman's recollection of a past event that the vast majority of readers can identify with. Length: 300-500 words. Rate: $100-$300, depending on length and quality.

Inspirational ...We are looking for inspirational (not overtly religious) material for the back cover. This can be in the form of a paragraph, poem or a short (300 words or less) article. Rate: $50-$100.

Fiction ...Well-written short fiction is a continuing need. The subjects should center on life in the country, its problems and joys, as experienced by women. The main character must be a country woman. Length: 1,000-2,000 words. Rate: $300-$600.

Health, Beauty and Fitness ...We are interested in these subjects, providing they have a "country woman" angle. We ask that you supply good quality color photos. Photos can be original or from a corporation or trade organization. Rate: $300-$600 for a 2-page spread.

Travel and Other Experiences ...Today's country women are interested in a variety of life experiences, including travel. However, articles must be of interest to women living in all states and Canada. We ask that you supply good quality color photos. Photos can be original or from a corporation or trade organization. Rate: $300-$600 for a 2-page spread.

Other Information

Unless a specific assignment is made, all freelance material will be considered on a speculative basis. That is, we must be able to review the article and photos before we make a decision to purchase it. *CW* is published 6 times per year. The ideal deadline for free-lance material is 6 months before the date of the issue. Manuscripts should be typed and double-spaced.

Please enclose a self-addressed stamped return envelope with all manuscript and photo submissions if you want your material returned. For craft submissions, send return postage in the form of a check or money order. Submissions without adequate return postage will not be returned. *CW* is not responsible for lost material.

Country Woman reserves the right to rewrite any and all material it buys to comply with our in-house style.

A decision on free-lance material is generally made within 2-3 months after receipt of the article. Payment is upon acceptance. If querying first (and do query on all feature/profile pieces), please enclose a self-addressed stamped envelope.

If you are notified that your manuscript is being held for future publication and later on you have an inquiry about its status, please enclose a self-addressed return envelope. Be sure to remind us of the subject matter of the article in your letter—don't just give the title. This will help us locate it in our files. Of course, articles we hold are not available for resale until we've notified you of publication. We sometimes hold articles several years before publishing.

Contributors are strongly urged to study the magazine carefully before querying or submitting. Free-lancers may subscribe at a special rate of $10.98 per year (regularly $17.98). To obtain a sample copy, send $2.00.

Categories: Consumer—Cooking—Crafts/Hobbies—Family—Lifestyle—Rural America

CONTACT: Marilyn Kruse, Managing Editor
Material: All
5400 S. 60th St.
Greendale WI 53129
E-mail: editors@countrywomanmagazine.com
Website: www.countrywomanmagazine.com

Country Extra

Please refer to *Country Magazine*.

Crab Creek Review

Submission Guidelines

Literary alchemy is what we're after: Ferociously original prose, and poems that flash off the page on bright wings to tickle our noses! We admire prosodic innovators and obsessive paragraph-crafters. Wit? Yes! Punch? Yes. Dry toast? No thanks.

Rivet us with your masterful concoctions:
· Send up to five poems
· Short stories or novel excerpts up to 6,000 words, double-spaced
· Art submissions for our covers. See website for full guidelines.

We review manuscripts between September 1 and May 31 (postmark dates). ***All submissions sent from June through August will be returned unread.***

All submissions should be previously unpublished. Should you submit something that is under simultaneous consideration elsewhere, you must indicate this in your cover letter, and notify us immediately if it has been accepted elsewhere. We aim for a response time between three and five months.

All manuscripts should be accompanied by a self-addressed, stamped envelope (SASE) for a response. Please note that we do not accept email submissions.

Our current payment is in the form of two copies of the issue for which your work has been accepted. We buy first rights as well as the rights to use your name and the accepted work (whole or part) on our website. Beyond this use, and following publication, rights revert to the author. We ask that **Crab Creek Review** be acknowledged in any subsequent publication of the work.

Categories: Fiction—Poetry

CONTACT: Editors
Material: All
PO Box 85088
Seattle WA 98145-1088
Website: http://www.crabcreekreview.org

The Cream City Review
University of Wisconsin, Milwaukee

The Cream City Review, founded in 1975, is a non-profit literary magazine operated entirely by students and published semi-annually in association with the creative writing concentration of the English Department of the University of Wisconsin—Milwaukee.

Our review takes its name from the "City of Cream-colored Bricks" or "Cream City," as Milwaukee was once known. The first "cream" brick was made in 1835. Pale yellow, the bricks proved more durable and aesthetically pleasing than the traditional red bricks produced by East Coast kilns. Popular throughout the 1800s, cream city bricks were used for ornamental architecture in the United States and Europe.

Our magazine is perfect bound in the standard magazine format of 5½"x8½" inches, with a four-color cover, averaging 250 pages. It is distributed to major university and public libraries and independent bookstores throughout the United States. We are indexed by *The American Humanities Index, the Index of American Periodical Verse*, and the *Annual Index to Poetry in Periodicals*, and are members of CLMP and COSMEP.

Submissions
Of course the best way to figure out what we really want is to read the magazine. Check out the samples and the preview of issue 19.2 or just go ahead and subscribe.

Submission Guidelines
First of all, we are sorry to say that we cannot accept electronic submissions at this time. We just don't yet have a reliable way of distributing an electronic manuscript among our various editors. So until further notice, you must rely on the US Postal Service.

Author's name and address should appear on the first page of the manuscript or on each individual piece of art work. Address submissions to the editors of the appropriate genre followed by our full address. Simultaneous submissions are acceptable as long as TCCR is notified at the time of submissions and in the event that work is accepted elsewhere. Submissions which do not include an SASE will not be read or returned.

We seek to publish all forms of writing, from traditional to experimental. We strive to produce issues which are challenging, diverse, and of lasting quality. We are not interested in sexist, homophobic, racist, or formulaic writings.

Please include a few lines about your publication history and other information you think of interest. TCCR seeks to publish not only a broad range of writing but a broad range of writers with diverse backgrounds as well. Both beginning and well established writers are welcome.

Reporting time is at least eight weeks. We do not read from April 1-Sept. 1. Contributors are given a one-year subscription to TCCR beginning with the issue in which their work appears. Copyright automatically reverts to the author upon publication, although TCCR retains the right to republish in future issues of the magazine.

GENRES
Fiction: Preferably under thirty pages, although we occasionally consider longer material. Please submit no more than one story at a time.

Poetry: No length restrictions. Please submit no more than five poems at a time.

Nonfiction: We are interested in reviews (one to ten pages), interviews, and personal essays.

Art: We are interested in camera-ready black-and-white artwork and photography. Please submit prints or slides. We use approximately twelve pieces of art per issue. As with text, we can accept submissions only through the mail.

Categories: Fiction—Nonfiction—Arts—Literature—Poetry—Short Stories—Writing

CONTACT: Erica Wiest
Material: Any
CONTACT: Beth Bretl or Jennifer Sworshack-Kinter, Poetry Editor
Material: Poetry
CONTACT: Steve Nelson or Zeke Jarvis, Fiction Editor
Material: Fiction
CONTACT: Oody Petty
Material: Nonfiction Editors
UW-Milwaukee English Dept., PO Box 413
Milwaukee WI 53201
Website: www.uwm.edu/Dept/English/ccr

Creative Knitting

Creative Knitting is a full-color, 100-page bimonthly magazine.
Submissions
1. Project submissions or manuscripts:
• Send (1) proposal sketch with swatches; (2) your completed project; or (3) photo. Be sure to label everything with your name and address. Keep a copy of all materials.
• Project review: Knitting reviews are held six times a year for the magazine. Check the editorial calendar for dates. These projects are seasonal. Design topics and suggestions are sent to knitters in our database. They can also be requested.
• If we accept your design (s), we will contact you within two weeks after the swatch review date. Other designs will be returned within four weeks after the swatch review date.
2. Accepted projects or manuscripts:
• Be sure to label every page and tag every project with your name (as you would like it published) and e-mail and mailing address. Also list the publication in which the project will appear.
• Send the completed model and paper copy of instructions and drawings to Bobbie Matela (see address below).
• At the same time that you send the project and instructions, send us an electronic copy on disk (either MAC or PC files are acceptable) as well if you do not have email. If you have email, send a copy of magazine instructions to Joy Slayton at joyknits@joyknits.com.
   • Put the pattern name in the subject line.
   • In the message state Creative Knitting and the issue it will be in.
   • If the instructions are sent as an attachment, state in the message what format it's in (MacWord, Wordperfect, Microsoft Word, etc.)
3. Writing guidelines:
• Type and double-space all instructions in step-by-step form, following a current magazine.
• Pay special attention to pattern stitch instructions, i.e. use k2, p2, not the upper case equivalent of K2, P2. Notice there is no space between the k or p and the stitch number.
• Do not use all caps for any part of the instructions.
• Do not use lowercase L's in place of numeral 1's.
• Complete and label graphs, diagrams and color keys. Do not use blue graph paper or a pencil because they do not photocopy well. Be sure lines are dark enough to photocopy, using ink if possible. Include

charts of stitch patterns whenever possible.

• Use the abbreviations given in Creative Knitting magazine. Explain any non-standard abbreviations in your instructions.

• Write a descriptive sentence describing your project.

• State skill level, using the guidelines given in Creative Knitting magazine.

Give sizes (a minimum of three sizes, preferably four or five) and finished measurements.

• Give the model size in the instructions and on the tag on the project.

Include in the materials list the types of materials, quantities used (for all sizes) and ordering information if unavailable at most craft stores. Include any extras such as cable needles, stitch holders, markers, buttons.

• State needle size(s), including length of circular needles.

Give yardage and weight per skein/ball, fiber content, manufacturer and/or distributor (for imported yarns), color number and name (if given) and specify weight (baby/fingering, sport, DK, worsted, bulky).

• Send a yarn band for each color and kind of yarn if at all possible.

Give gauge (including approximate gauge before felting for a felted project). Measure stitches and rows/rnds over 4 inches/10cm and specify pattern (St st, stitch pattern, color pattern, etc.) and needle size used.

• Include source references for pattern stitches when available (such as Barbara Walker's books).

• Provide stitch counts at the end of all increase and decrease rows.

When increasing, specify type of increase: Knit in front & back of stitch, Make 1 (M1), etc. When decreasing, specify ssk, k2tog, etc.

• Write out any reverse shaping for all experience levels.

• Explain any technique a knitter of that experience level may not know.

4. Mailing address: Send submissions and completed projects to Bobbie Matela, Creative Knitting, 2420 Grand Avenue, Suite H, Vista, CA 92081.

5. Return of published projects: Projects accepted for publication will be returned to the designer (unless otherwise arranged) after the publication is printed. All manuscripts, diagrams, etc., remain the property of the publisher.

6. For all other questions, contact Bobbie Matela. If you have a question about the status of a design, contact Mary Ann Frits. If you have a question about pattern writing, contact Kathy Wesley.

Contracts and payment

When we receive the completed project, instructions and all related materials, we will send you a contract and a business-reply envelope. Sign the contract and return it in the postage-paid envelope. Keep the photocopy of the contract for your records and return the original to us.

Payment will be made within 45 days of the time we receive your signed contract. Amount will be determined by accuracy, creativity, workmanship, skill level, overall quality and instruction format. Average fees range from $50 to $550. Because all rights to designs are purchased, unless otherwise arranged, designers should not sell the purchased design or one very similar to it to another publisher.

We look forward to working with you in the coming months!

Categories: Nonfiction—Crafts—Hobbies

CONTACT: Bobbie Matela,, Editor
Material: All
2420 Grand Ave., Ste. H
Vista, CA 92081
Phone: 760-597-4801 ext. 129
E-mail: Bobbie_Matela@ASNpub.com
Website: www.knittingdigest.com

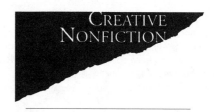

Creative Nonfiction

"Now that you have established this journal called *Creative Nonfiction*," people ask, "what does it mean?"

It's surprising how many writers (and readers) don't understand, exactly, the elements of the form in which they are writing. Some are attracted by the word "creative" and think that because their prose is unusual or distinctive and because the stories they are telling are true, they are writing "*Creative Nonfiction.*"

Others, usually people with a journalistic background, are put off by the word "creative," maintaining that if it is creative, it certainly can't be accurate, believable, or ethical, which are the essence and anchor of nonfiction prose.

But there is no conflict between being a good "reporter" and a good writer, creative in technique and approach. The essays published in each issue of *Creative Nonfiction* are models of the truest forms of *Creative Nonfiction*, in that they simultaneously "showcase" or "frame" fact in creative context.

"Truth"—which should not be confused with the factual or informational aspects of the genre—is another important element of the "classic" *Creative Nonfiction* form-and often a more personal one. A writer's concept of the truth may not be universally accepted and may even conflict with the facts as others understand or remember them. Good *Creative Nonfiction* does not deny personal opinion: to the contrary, it welcomes the subjective voice.

Take, for example, Hilary Masters' essay, "Son of Spoon River," in our summer, 1996 "Five Fathers" issue. Masters discusses the ways in which the media and the publishing industry tend to brand or categorize people for their own comfort and pleasure, despite the personal and professional damage such "public" judgments may cause. Masters is the son of Edgar Lee Masters, of Spoon River Anthology fame; he and his father were the victims about whom he writes. The writer's message is often called the "theme" or "main point of focus."

As it was in Masters' piece, it is often the writer's personal depiction of the message that makes the work unique. Presenting the theme with a personal take makes the writer's work creative. But there are other ways in which writers can go about making their nonfiction creative.

Fiction techniques often capture a subject and add a distinctive feel that conventional journalism may not. Action-oriented scenes contain dialogue and evocative description with great specificity and detail. Fiction techniques include the use of dialogue, characterization, description, and point of view. But using the devices of fiction does not give the *Creative Nonfiction* writer a license to fabricate. John McPhee once noted that *Creative Nonfiction* is "an attempt to recognize that a piece of writing can be creative while using factual materials,that creative work can respect fact."

Writers must always respect fact-as distinguished from universal truth-in their work. Writers for *Creative Nonfiction* must present their personal interpretation of the truth without becoming overly experimental or egocentric. Though we encourage the subjective voice and encourage a unique approach, writers are still bound to the fundamental duty of journalism: to inform or teach the reader.

An essay from our third issue, "Emerging Women Writers," serves as a good example of a highly subjective voice that adheres to the principle of accuracy. The author, Lauren Slater, a practicing psychologist, used her skills as a fiction writer to give her readers insight into her struggles as a professional counselor and her own recovery from a debilitating mental illness. The reader feels close to Slater as she describes how she was assigned to counsel a patient in a hospital in which she herself had once been a patient. Every aspect of her essay was true, though she used scene and dialogue to embellish the facts into a larger and more universal truth.

There are no length requirements, although we are always searching for writers who can communicate a strong idea with drama and humor in a few pages. Payment is $10 per published page. We report in five months. Query for author profiles only.

Points to Remember When Submitting to *Creative Nonfiction*:
• Strong reportage.
• Well-written prose, attentive to language, rich with detail and distinctive voice.
• An informational quality or "teaching element" offering the reader something to learn-for example, an idea, concept, collection of facts-strengthened with insight, reflection, interpretation.
• A compelling, focused, sustained narrative that's well-structured, makes sense, and conveys a meaning.
• Manuscripts will not be accepted via fax or e-mail.
Categories: Nonfiction—General Interest—Literature—Writing

CONTACT: Submissions Editor
Material: all
5501 Walnut St., Ste. 202
Pittsburgh PA 15232
Phone: 412-688-0304
Fax: 412-688-0262
E-mail: information@creativenonfiction.org
Website: www.creativenonfiction.org

Creative With Words!

CWW will accept well-written manuscripts that focus on.
Folklore
• Writing/Painting (why do I write/paint; why did I start, where do I plan to go with it)
• Photography (What can I photograph, how can I embellish my photographs, what will I do with my photographs?)
• Slogans/Idioms (take any slogan/idiom, research what it means, indicate for what purposes you would use it, whom have you convinced to use it as well)
• Quality of light, of water, of air, of fire
• Flashback (start your writing with "I remember..." or "I will never forget..."
• Wishes ("If I had, I would")
• I feel positive about.../I feel negative about...(write about it, how it influences your life; the life of others)
• Color (select a color, observe your environment for an entire day, jot down every time you see the color; then write a story about that particular color) When writing on the above topics, make sure you follow CWW's guideline before submitting your manuscripts. Manuscripts can be fiction or nonfiction.
• For further information, send CWW a FAX (831-655-8627) or an E-mail (geltrich@mbay.net),addressed to Brigitta Geltrich, Editor & Publisher; or visit CWW at its website: members.tripod.com/Creative withwords
Standard Subscription Rates remain the same, please check CWW's guidelines.
CWW Guidelines
1. Focus: a) folkloristic matter; b) poetry, prose, language/ computer art by children (state age of child and verify authentic- city of writing); and by all ages; special interest groups, senior citizens (state age), disabled (state why), shut-ins (state why).
2. Language: English; translations by a native English speaker from another language. All manuscripts will be edited by CWW.
3. Manuscripts: Typed or legibly written: prose double-spaced, 1 poem per page, 1" margin (all sides); give name, home address, age (if child, up to 19) top left on every page; number pages.
Use standard font, size 12. Do not fax manuscripts. You may E-mail manuscripts. Send no more than 3 poems/prose by one author to any CWW theme.

4. Length: Poetry: up to 20 lines, up to 46 characters across any line. Prose: 800 words maximum. Shorter poems/prose have a better chance, if of quality. Our staff readers do count the words. Longer poems, if of quality, are converted to prose, or they are returned. Longer prose are returned with request to rewrite.
5. Format: Title poems (except haikus); do not indent each line differently, nor put a single word on a separate line. Title prose. If not titled, CWW will provide title.
6. Style: Poetry: any; folkloristic tales: any; folkloristic research: use MLA Handbook for Writers of Research Papers, Theses, and Dissertations. Prose: Quality writing. Use no brand names, names of companies, movies, television shows, etc. CWW is not their endorser.
7. Content: CWW publishes according to set themes. Violence of any nature, over-preoccupation with death, racial slurs or preferences, pornographic material, or current sensationalism will not be accepted.
8. Cover Letter: Include cover letter or CWW submittal form, stating name of project submitted to.
9. Multiple Submissions: Are not accepted.
10. Previously-Published Manuscripts: Are not accepted. If of folkloristic nature, permission of reprint must be enclosed.
11. SASE (self-addressed-stamped envelope with sufficient postage + 2 oz. for CWW material): Must accompany all manuscripts & correspondence. Rule: Manuscripts and correspondence submitted without SASE are destroyed at end of month submitted. A self- addressed envelope without postage is not a SASE. You may use E-mail, make sure to give return E-mail, for CWW to respond.
12. Query: Is preferred. CWW does not publish self- contained books. CWW publishes anthologies according to set themes. See theme list for the each year.
13. Copyright: CWW Publications. After publication, rights revert back to author for submission elsewhere. CWW requests a credit line be given to CWW for having published the item first. Content and graphics submitted must be copyright-free or a copyright-clearance statement must be included.
14. Evaluation: By CWW staff or guest readers; folkloristic items are read by guest scholars of folklore. CWW editors take the readers' and scholars' suggestions into consideration when further evaluating manuscripts. All manuscripts must reflect the standards of CWW. CWW offers suggestions how to improve rejected stories/ poems.
15. Reading Time: One month after deadline of theme. First notice might come one year after submitting to a specific theme. It is the writer's responsibility to notify CWW of any changes in the status of the manuscript or in change of writer's address.
16. Payment: Writers/poets published by CWW receive 20% discount on copies purchased of issue containing the writing; orders of 10 to 19 copies, writers receive a 30% discount; on orders of 20 or more copies, writers/schools/libraries receive 40% off. Note: A poet/writer does not have to order a copy to get published; however, a poet/writer should not use the services of CWW to claim "acceptance" only. There are neither tear sheets nor free copies. Accepted material is not returned. Byline: name of writer/ poet, age (if child/senior), city and state. Online issue contest winner receives a 3-month subscription to CWW, runner-ups receive a prize.
17. Contract: No contract. A statement of publishing intent is forwarded with acceptance notification and guidelines, at which time a writer/poet may withdraw manuscript within a given time.
18. Publications per Annum: 4-6 anthologies, written by all ages; 4 anthologies written by children (must be written by children, up to 19 years of age, not by well-meaning adults); 4 the Eclectics by adults (20 and over) only.
19. Market/Readership: Family, schools, libraries, universities- ties, editors,physicians, political and religious leaders, shut- ins. CWW publications are evaluated at trade fairs and trade conferences and are presented at book fairs; some are used in reading classes.

20. Editors/Advisors: Editor-in-Chief/Publisher: Brigitta Geltrich; Visiting Editor: Bert Hower; Advisor: D.G. Spencer Ludgate; Web-site advisors: D. G. Spencer Ludgate and K. Peter Geldreich; Wood Sculpture/Artist: Henning Kristensen.

21. Editorial Office: P.O. Box 223226, Carmel, CA, USA 93922; FAX 831-655-8627 (this is not a telephone).

22. Cost of Issues: Single: US$12. *Special:* US$15-$20; Back Issues: US$6. Subscription: 12 issues for US$60; 6 issues for US$36; 3 issues for US$21 (state whether to include the four children only issues or the four adults only issues). Credit-card orders are not accepted at this time. Libraries and schools receive a 10% discount. Back-order status is set by CWW. Most issues do not make it to back- order status.

23. Reading Fees: Are reasonable and available. Write to CWW for information and fee, include SASE.

24. Check: Make check payable to: Brigitta Ludgate. Thank you! (Sorry, we must charge a $20 fine on returned checks.)

See our website to download the CWW Manuscript Submittal Form Thank you for submitting your manuscript to *Creative With Words* Publications (CWW). Manuscripts will be placed in appropriate theme file and processed after deadline of theme. You will be notified one way or the other within two to four weeks after deadline.

Categories: Fiction—Adventure—Animals—Children—Comedy—Culture—Education—Family—Gardening—History—Juvenile—Outdoors—Poetry—Relationships—Senior Citizen—Short Stories—Teen—Travel—Writing—Young Adult—Folklore—Humor—Nature

CONTACT: Brigitta Geltrich, Editor/Publisher
Material: All
PO Box 223226
Carmel CA 93922
Phone: 831-655-8627
Fax: 831-655-8627
E-mail: geltrich@mbay.net
Website: member.tripod.com/Creativewithwords

Cricket

For a sample issue of CRICKET, please send $5.00 to: CRICKET Sample Copy • P.O. Box 300 • Peru, IL 61354. NOTE: Sample copy requests from foreign countries must be accompanied by International Postal Reply Coupons (IRCs) valued at US $5.00. Please do NOT send a check or money order. In September 1973, Open Court Publishing Company started publication of CRICKET, a literary magazine for young people. CRICKET is now published by Carus Publishing Company. CRICKET, for readers ages 9 to 14, publishes original stories, poems, and articles written by the world's best authors for children and young adults. In some cases, CRICKET purchases rights for excerpts from books yet to be published. Each issue also includes several reprints of high-quality selections. CRICKET measures 8" x 10", contains 64 pages, has a full-color cover, and is staple bound. Full-color and black-and-white illustrations of the highest quality appear throughout the magazine. We hope the following information will be useful to prospective contributors. —Editor-in-Chief, Marianne Carus

Published: 12 months a year

Price: $35.97 for 1-year subscription (12 issues)

Comments: CRICKET would like to reach as many illustrators and authors as possible for original contributions, but our standards are very high, and we will accept only top-quality material. PLEASE DO NOT QUERY FIRST. CRICKET will consider any manuscripts or art samples sent on speculation and accompanied by a self-addressed, stamped envelope. For art, send tear sheets or photo prints/photocopies. PLEASE DO NOT send original artwork. Be sure that each sample is marked with your name, address, and phone number. Allow 12 weeks for a reply. Themes CRICKET does not publish an advance list of themes. Submissions on all appropriate topics will be considered at any time during the year. CRICKET normally purchases the following rights for works appearing in the magazine. For stories and poems previously unpublished, rights vary.

Payment is made upon publication.

For stories and poems previously published, CRICKET purchases second North American publication rights. Fees vary, but are generally less than fees for first publication rights. Payment is made upon publication. Same applies to accompanying art.

For recurring features, CRICKET purchases the material outright. The work becomes the property of CRICKET, and it is copyrighted in the name of Carus Publishing Company. A flat fee per feature is usually negotiated. Payment is made upon publication.

For commissioned artwork, rights vary. However, in all cases, the terms outlined below apply:

a. Physical art remains the property of the illustrator.

b. Payment is made within 45 days of acceptance.

c. Illustrator may use artwork for self promotion.

Art Submissions: CRICKET commissions all art separately from the text. Any review samples of artwork will be considered. Samples of both color and black-and-white work (where applicable) are appreciated. It is especially helpful to see pieces showing young people, animals, action scenes, and several scenes from a narrative (i.e., story) showing a character in different situations and emotional states. CRICKET accepts work in a number of different styles and media, including pencil, pen and ink, watercolor, acrylic, oil, pastels, scratch board, and woodcut. While we need humorous illustration, we cannot use work that is overly caricatured or "cartoony." We are always looking for strong realism. Many assignments will require artist's research into a particular scientific field, world culture, or historical period.

TYPES OF WORK IN CRICKET.

Fiction: realistic, contemporary, historical, humor, mysteries, fantasy, science fiction, folk tales, fairy tales, legends, myths.

Nonfiction: biography, history, science, technology, natural history, social science, archeology, architecture, geography, foreign culture, travel, adventure, sports (A bibliography is required for all nonfiction articles. Be prepared to send other backup materials and photo references—where applicable—upon request).

Poetry: serious, humorous, nonsense rhymes.

Other: crossword puzzles, logic puzzles, math puzzles, crafts, recipes, science experiments, games and activities from other countries, plays, music, art.

LENGTH

Stories: 200 to 2,000 words (2 to 8 pages).

Articles: 200 to 1,500 words (2 to 6 pages).

Poems: not longer than 50 lines (1 page, 2 pages maximum) An exact word count should be noted on each manuscript submitted. For poetry, indicate number of lines instead. Word count includes every word, but does not include the title of the manuscript or the author's name.

RATES

Stories and articles up to 25¢ per word

Poems up to $3.00 per line.

Payment upon publication.

Categories: Fiction—Nonfiction—Children—Literature—Poetry—Short Stories

CONTACT: Submissions Editor
Material: Manuscript Submissions
CONTACT: Ron McCutchan, Senior Art Director
Material: Art Samples
CONTACT: Mary Ann Hocking, Rights and Permissions Manager
Material: Rights and Permissions
PO Box 300
Peru IL 61354
Phone: 815-224-5803, ext. 656
Fax: 815-224-6615
Website: www.cricketmag.com

Critical Ceramics

SUBMISSION INFORMATION

Critical Ceramics is commited to publishing the widest range of articles relevant to the contemporary ceramic artist, including those on creativity, aesthetics, contemporary art, culture, artistic movements, art criticism, and individual artists. To this end, Critical Ceramics is always looking for new writers and critics.

Critical Ceramics does not represent any set viewpoint. In fact, authors arguing opposing view points are sought by Critical Ceramics. Articles which take a strong position and defend it well are encouraged. Of course, all submissions are subject to the editorial process.

Each submission must include the writer's name, address, daytime phone number, and email address. Emailed contributions are preferred. Alternatively, disks may be mailed if this will not hamper the timeliness of the article. Each submission should include a brief description of the writer's background, relevant url's, and 2 images, if desired, to be included in Critical Ceramics' contributors' gallery.

Words

In general, Critical Ceramics publishes two types of articles. The first type is a feature article of 1000 to 1500 words in length. An article of this kind should explore in some depth the major points of the topic. Feature articles may be on artists, new genres of work, or particular aesthetic view points for example. The author should supply 5 to 10 images in support of the article.

The second type of article is a review. These are shorter articles, approximately 500 words, critiquing an exhibition, book, or video. Any exhibition held in a legitimate, publicly accessible context may be reviewed. Critical Ceramics would like to post reviews within days of the show opening. Reviews are featured for the duration of the exhibition. After the show closes, reviews will be indexed and maintained as a reference archive. Accompanying each review should be 3 to 5 supporting images.

Images

In almost all instances, images are necessary to properly represent the ideas in the article or review. If at all possible, each image shouid be a 24-bit (16 million color) uncompressed JPEG file no larger than 500 pixels in either dimension. If electronic files are not possible, slides or transparencies may be submitted for scanning.

Compensation

Critical Ceramics compensates writers and reviewers for each work published. Authors and artists retain their copyrights to their work, but allow Critical Ceramics to publish it in perpetuity.

Interested? Please email the editor with your idea.

Categories: Hobbies

CONTACT: Editor
Material: All
E-mail: editor@criticalceramics.com
Website: www.criticalceramics.com

Crochet World

General Information

House of White Birches publishes Crochet World magazine, a full-color, 48-page bimonthly.

Submissions/Designer Guidelines

Project submissions or manuscripts:

Send (1) proposal sketch with swatches; (2) your completed project; or (3) photo. Be sure to label everything with your name and address. Keep a copy of all materials. Correct return postage is required.

Project review: Reviews are held approximately every eight weeks. Check the editorial calendar for dates. Many of these projects are seasonal. Editorial calendars can be requested.

If we accept your design(s), we will contact you within two weeks after the review date. Other designs will be returned within four weeks after the review date.

E-mail projects or manuscripts:

If we have accepted your project after seeing the swatch or photo, e-mail the pattern instructions to Susan Tullis at editor@crochet-world.com. Send the completed model and paper copy of the instructions and drawings to Susan Tullis.

Put the pattern name in the subject line.

In the message, state the project will appear in Crochet World.

If the instructions are sent as an attachment, state in the message what format they're in (MacWord, Microsoft Word, etc.)

Be sure to label every page and tag every project with your name (as you would like it published) and address.

Mailing address: Send submissions and completed projects to address below. Correct return postage is required.

Writing Guidelines:

Type and double-space all instructions in step-by-step form in 12 point font size, following a current publication.

Pay special attention to pattern stitch instructions

Do not use all caps for any part of the instructions.

Do not use lowercase Ls in place of numeral 1's.

Complete and label graphs, diagrams and color keys. Do not use blue graph paper or a pencil because they do not photocopy well. Be sure lines are dark enough to photocopy, using ink if possible.

Use the abbreviations given in Crochet World magazine. Explain any non-standard abbreviations in your instructions.

Write a descriptive sentence describing your project.

State skill level: Beginner, intermediate or advanced.

Give sizes (a minimum of three sizes, preferably four or five) and finished measurements.

Give the model size in the instructions and on the tag of the project.

Include in the materials list the types of materials, quantities used and ordering information if unavailable at most craft stores. Include any extras such as stitch holders, markers, buttons, sequins, ribbon, fiberfill, etc.

State hook size(s).

Give yardage and weight per skein or ball, fiber content, manufacturer and/or distributor (for imported yarns), color number and name (if given) and specify weight (baby/fingering yarn, sport, DK, worsted, bulky, etc.)

Send a yarn or thread band (label) for each color and kind of yarn if at all possible.

Give gauge. Measure stitches and rows/rnds over 1 or 2 inches (example: 4 sc = 1 inch; 5 sc rows = 1 inch).

Provide stitch counts at the end of all increase and decrease rows.

Explain any technique a crocheter of that experience level may not know.

Small poems (less than 3 typeset column inches) pay $20; on rare occasions we publish non-pattern manuscripts that must relate to crochet in some way. They must be less than one typeset page.

Payment is $50-$125.

Proofread your instructions several times to eliminate possible errors. Suggestions: Have a crocheting friend read over your patterns to help spot errors or hard-to-follow sections.

House of White Birches will be responsible for all photography.

Contracts and payment

After our review and decision of acceptance, we will send you a contract and a business-reply envelope. Sign the contract and return it in the postage-paid envelope. Keep the photocopy of the contract for your records and return the original to us.

Payment will be made within 45 days of the time we receive your contract. Amount will be determined by accuracy, creativity, workmanship, skill level, overall quality and instruction format. Average fees range from $50 to $400. Because HWB purchases all rights to designs unless otherwise arranged, designers should not sell the purchased design or one very similar to it to another publisher.

Categories: Nonfiction—Crafts/Hobbies—Hobbies—Needlework

CONTACT: Susan Tullis, Editor

Material: All
6 Pearl Street
PO Box 776
Henniker NH 03242-0776
Phone: 206-589-4000
Fax: 206-589-8093
E-mail: editor@crochet-world.com
Website: www.crochet-world.com

Crone Chronicles
A Journal of Conscious Aging

No longer accepting submissions.

Cross & Quill

The Christian Writers Newsletter

Cross & Quill
The Christian Writers Newsletter

Cross & Quill serves an audience of writers, speakers, editors, conference directors, group leaders, researchers, and agents involved in the Christian publishing industry. Please keep that in mind when submitting. Need more nuts and bolts (this is how to write it) articles. Rarely use personal experiences except for Writing Rainbows!

Our purpose is to inform, instruct, encourage, and equip Christians in publishing to produce writing of the highest biblical and professional standards.

OUR NEEDS ARE AS FOLLOWS:

Meet the Pro: Assigned. Front page features one of our professional members.

This Side of the Desk: Written in-house.

Writing Rainbows!: 500 to 600 word devotional thought including Scripture and prayer that comes from your writing experience. Give Bible translation.

Writers Helping Writers: 200 to 800 words. More instructional and how-to articles, fewer personal experiences. Need more articles directed to the veteran, rather than the beginning writer. (Feature Article)

Tots, Teens, & In Betweens: 200 to 800 word how-to and informational articles on writing for the juvenile marketplace. (Feature Article)

Editors Soapbox: Assigned. Dave Fessenden, Contributing Editor.

Editors Round Table: 200 to 800 word interviews with editors on current needs of the publication or publishing house. Ask questions that help writers understand the joys, frustrations, and challenges of editorial work. Find out what the editor has often wanted to tell writers to make the editor's and the writer's jobs easier, more productive, and more profitable. Professional quality photo of editor improves chances of acceptance. (Feature Article)

Computer Wise: Assigned. Kay Hall, Contributing Editor.

Business Wise: 200 to 800 how-to and informa tional articles on the business side of writing such as tax information, recordkeeping, and other related topics.

Legal Ease: 200 to 800 words on various legalities in the writing profession: contracts, copyright, etc. (Feature Article)

Connecting Points: 200 to 800 word how-to's on leading and attending writers groups. Especially want articles on how to critique various kinds of writing such as nonfiction, fiction, poetry, and others. Also group program ideas.

The Conference Circuit: Organizing and operating writers workshops and conferences â " successes and learning experiences. Also profiles of Christian writers conferences. State availability of photos.

Poetry: 1 to 8 line poems on helpful and inspirational topics, limit 3 per envelope.

Fillers: 25 to 100 word helpful hints, newsbreaks, tips, cartoons. Book and other writing product reviews, 100 to 300 words.

Submissions: Submit by regular mail or e-mail. No simultaneous submissions.

Rights: Buys first or reprint rights. If manuscript is a reprint, state when and where the piece has been used.

Payment: Honorarium on publication and 3 contributors copies.

Sample copy of *Cross & Quill* available for $2 and 9x12 SASE w/ 2 first class stamps.

E-mail Submissions to: CQArticles@cwfi-online.org or CQArticles@aol.com.

Postal submissions not accompanied by SASE will not be returned.

Categories: Nonfiction—Arts—Associations—Careers—Christian Interests—Education—Internet—Language—Literature—Poetry—Religion—Writing

CONTACT: Sandy Brooks, Editor/Publisher
Material: All
c/o Christian Writers Fellowship International
1624 Jefferson Davis Rd.
Clinton SC 29325-6401
Phone: 864-697-6035
E-mail: CQArticles@cwfi-online.org (submissions)
E-mail: sandybrooks@cwfi-online.org
Website: www.cwfi-online.org

Cruising World

Although *Cruising World's* editorial inventory is already planned and almost filled for 2002, we continue to welcome author inquiries and unsolicited manuscripts. All manuscripts should be typed double-spaced and accompanied by an electronic version, as well as by appropriate artwork such as transparencies or color prints. Color prints do not generally reproduce well, but if submitted should be accompanied by negatives. Good sketches are also acceptable. Manuscripts submitted for Feature consideration (center of the magazine) should be written in the first person and not exceed approximately 2,500 words. Manuscripts submitted for consideration as Non-features (technical articles and general interest, front and back of the magazine) should not exceed 2,000 words. "Log style" articles are generally unacceptable.

Due to the volume of manuscripts we receive, we regret we cannot offer critiques of unacceptable material. Payment varies depending on the type of article, ranging from $50 to $200 for short, newsworthy items and $300 to $800 for technical and feature articles. We buy all World Periodical Rights and pay within 90 days of acceptance.

Write your name and address on every page of your manuscript and on each photograph, slide or sketch. We cannot be responsible for anything that does not bear the sender's name. Also number and identify each slide and print on a brief caption sheet. If your manuscript involves a cruise, please include a photocopy of a map or chart with the places you visited clearly marked on it. Please enclose an author bio note with sailing history and identify the people and type of boat in the story.

Manuscripts submitted to *Cruising World* must not be sent to other magazines for consideration during the same time period. Such simultaneous submissions could cause an infringement of copyright laws. If, however, your manuscript has previously been published in part or in whole, let us know. Our rates vary with each individual submission.

Within about six weeks after we receive your manuscript, after the editors have had a chance to review your contribution, we will either accept it for publication or return it to you. Dates of publication remain tentative. Generally, it takes one year for a piece to reach publication.

Please be sure that you use a consistent permanent (not transient) address in all correspondence with *Cruising World*. Also, please note your telephone number and e-mail address on your cover letter, and enclose a self-addressed, stamped envelope large enough to contain your submission and any accompanying artwork.

Categories: Nonfiction—Boating—Lifestyle—Outdoors—Recreation—Sports/Recreation

CONTACT: Manuscripts Editor
Material: All
5 John Clarke Rd.
PO Box 3400
Newport RI 02840-0992
Phone: 401-845-5141
Website: www.cruisingworld.com

Crusader
A Magazine for Cadets and Their Friends

Please refer to *Cadet Quest* in the periodical section.

The Culture Star Reader

The Culture Star Reader is seeking submissions from short fiction writers and poets of all genres. We are interested in work that is brash, ribald, hilarious, evocative, and unconventional; let your work snap at us. We suggest that you take a look at an issue or two before submitting. Writers may submit two pieces of short fiction or three pieces of poetry. Short fiction submissions should be 3000 words or less. Work should be submitted as an attachment via email. Type the word count on top of the first page. Name, address, e-address, phone number, and a short bio must appear on the first page. We accept simultaneous submissions and ask that, should you decide to publish your work elsewhere, you let us know immediately. We publish monthly.

If we publish your work: We pay $10 for Short Fiction. We pay $5 for Poetry.

All entries must be original and in English. Manuscripts above the stated word count will not be considered. The Culture Star Reader reserves one-time publication rights to your entry. All submissions must be in their final form upon submission. The Culture Star Reader will not accept any story or poetry revisions after acceptance of the submission except when specifically requested by the editor.

Categories: Fiction—Poetry—Short Stories

CONTACT:
Culture Star Reader Magazine
45 Hudson Ave Ste 743
Albany New York 12207
E-mail: submissions@culturestarreader.com

Custom Rodder

Circulation: 45,000
Frequency: Bi-monthly
Published by the PRIMEDIA Enthusiast Group.

Devoted to the modification and upgrading of American-made automobiles from the late forties to the present. Editors who appreciate and work on these cars themselves share their enthusiasm via on-the-spot participation and color coverage of events, immersing the leader in the beauty and nostalgia of these one-of-a-kind vehicles. Editorial includes how-to tech articles, tips, advice, and expertise. For more information, visit the magazine's Web site at: www.customrodderweb.com.

Editorial Submissions

Contributions Welcomed, but editors recommend that contributors query first. Contribution must be accompanied by return postage

and we assume no responsibility for loss or damage thereto.

Manuscripts must be typewritten and submitted on white paper, with a disc copy enclosed enclosed (Microsoft Word format preferred). All photographs must be accompanied by captions.

Electronic images, Polaroid photographs and color copies are not acceptable for print publication. Photo model releases are required for all persons in photos.

Categories: Nonfiction—Automobiles—Hobbies

CONTACT: Editor
Material: All
Corporate Headquarters
McMullen Argus Publishing Inc.
2400 E. Katella Avenue, 11th Floor
Anaheim CA 92806
Phone: 714-939-2400
Fax: 714-978-6390
E-mail: robt@mcmullenargus.com
Website: www.customrodderweb.com

CutBank
University of Montana

Guidelines for Artists and Writers

CutBank is interested in art, poetry and fiction of high quality and serious intent. We regularly print work by both well-known and previously unpublished artists. All manuscripts are considered for the Richard Hugo Memorial Poetry Award and the A.B. Guthrie, Jr. Short Fiction Award.

We accept submissions from August 15 until March 15. The deadline for the spring issue is November 15, and for the fall issue it's March 15.

Include an SASE for response or return of submitted material.

Manuscripts must be typed or letter quality printout, double-spaced, and paginated. Your name should appear on each page. We encourage the use of paper clips over staples.

Fiction writers should submit only one story at a time, no longer than 40 pages. Poets may submit up to 5 poems.

Artists and photographers may submit up to 5 works at one time. Send slides or reproductions only; do not send original art.

If a piece has been submitted simultaneously to another publication, please let us know.

Please address all submissions to the appropriate editor—poetry, fiction, or art.

Categories: Fiction—Nonfiction—Poetry—Short Stories

CONTACT: Poetry Editor
Material: Poetry
CONTAC: Sarah Aswell, Fiction Editor
Material: Fiction/Nonfiction
Department of English
The University of Montana-Missoula
Missoula MT 59812
Phone: 406-243-6156
Fax: 406-243-4076
E-mail: cutbank@selway.umt.edu
Website: www.umtedu/cutbank

Cutting Tool Engineering

Editorial Mission Statement:

CUTTING TOOL ENGINEERING is published for managers and engineers in the machining industry. The magazine provides timely and practical information on the procurement, use, and maintenance of cutting and grinding equipment, tools, and related accessories. CTE readers work in a wide variety of market segments, but the heaviest concentration is in the automotive and aerospace industries. The magazine has been published since 1955 and has a BPA-audited circulation of 35,000.

Submissions: We urge you to submit article documents electronically. In order of preference, documents may be sent in Word or Rich Text Format (RTF). E-mail communication is strongly encouraged, but disk or CD submission is acceptable. Artwork that illustrates the article is primarily your responsibility unless prior permission is granted in advance. The availability of artwork is a serious consideration for timely publication. Please review our artwork guidelines.

Style: We ask, if possible, that you follow the Associated Press writing style and use Webster's Ninth edition dictionary to resolve spelling and non-technical conflicts concerning word definition. Please write in the present tense. We encourage the use of common industry trade terms, but please spell out all acronyms on the first reference.

Any company mentioned in an article must include a city and state reference. Any person mentioned in the article must also include their job title, employer, city and state.

All articles must contain your byline. Please include a brief biography, including your current title and your employer's name and location.

Content: We will work with all authors to establish a working title. The author and editor work together to develop deadlines for an outline, first rough draft, final rough draft and the submission of artwork.

A narrow focus is essential. Providing relevant technical detail and a complete explanation of a subject are hallmarks of CTE articles. We ask that you maintain this tradition. If you can picture yourself telling a competent machine apprentice about why it works-and the cookbook recipe needed to correctly apply it on the shop floor-then you should find yourself at the right level of detail.

CTE readers are technically astute and very careful readers that want direct, unbiased information. Therefore, we do not accept so-called "advertorials," including case history/application stories. Submissions must be generic in nature and not specific to a single vendor's product or process unless that product or process is truly revolutionary and receives prior approval from CTE before an outline is submitted.

Length: Articles can range from 1,000 to 2,500 words, depending on the subject. However, our experience has shown that feature articles submitted below 2,000 words do not explain the subject in sufficient detail. On the other hand, articles that approach 3,000 words indicate a subject that is too broad for a magazine article.

Artwork: Photos, charts, graphs, and other visuals are necessary for any article that is being considered for publication. There is a distinct acceptance advantage for authors that can provide-or identify sources-of artwork for their articles. The most desirable photo shows a process in action, and an action photo is essential for a cover story. Unfortunately, great application photos are not commonplace in the industry. And most digital cameras that take great photos for Web pages and other types of screen viewing are useless for publication work. Technical requirements for submitting electronic files for publication in CUTTING TOOL ENGINEERING:

Photographic images: We accept black-and-white and 4-color photographic images, saved in either .TIFF or .EPS format.

To achieve the best print quality, images should have a resolution of approximately 266 dpi. Color images should be saved in CMYK (not RGB) format. Black-and-white images should be saved in grayscale mode. Mac files are preferable, but we can read correctly formatted images created on an IBM platform.

Art files (ads, illustrations, etc.): We accept black-and-white and color art files, MACINTOSH FORMAT ONLY, in the following applications: Quark Xpress, Adobe Illustrator, Adobe PageMaker, Adobe Photoshop, and Macromedia Freehand. All fonts and supporting graphics files used in creating the art must be included. Contact the production department for guidelines when preparing your files.

• *Quark/PageMaker:*
  Save files as native Quark or PageMaker files — do not save as EPS or postscript files.
  Include all linked images.

Include all fonts used in document, (both screen and printer fonts).
If your file is to print black-and-white, all graphic elements must be black-and-white.
If your file is to print 4-color, graphic elements must be black-and-white or 4-color process (CMYK).
If your file is to print with pms colors and includes color graphics, please contact production department to verify ad color.
Provide a laser proof and/or a color proof.

• *Adobe Illustrator*
  Save files as Illustrator 6.0 or Illustrator EPS for Macintosh.
  Set preview to "Color Macintosh"
  Convert all text to outlines—or—include all fonts on disk (both screen and printer fonts).
  Provide a laser proof and/or a color proof.

• *Macromedia Freehand*
  Save files as Freehand Document or export as Macintosh EPS.
  Convert all text to paths - or — include all fonts on disk (both screen and printer fonts).
  Provide a laser proof and/or a color proof.

• *We accept electronic files on the following media only:*
  3.5" floppy (Mac or PC)
  Zip 100 disk (Mac or PC)
  Syquest 44MB, 88MB, 135 MB EZ-drive cartridges (Mac only)
  CD-Rom (Mac or PC)

We currently do not accept files over the Internet.

Questions?

Contact Claudia Gray, Art Director @ 847-714-0178.

Authors must plan for artwork very early. The author should submit possible sources of artwork with the outline. You may initially get very positive responses for artwork. But responses can and do get rescinded because of trade secret concerns or customer objectives. Progressive companies understand that continuous improvement is the key to protecting market position. Those companies will likely have an enlightened view regarding artwork-but don't count on it.

For more information contact Don Nelson, editorial director and publisher @ 847-714-0173 or dnelson@jwr.com.

Categories: Nonfiction—Engineering—Technical—Trade: Metal Working

CONTACT: Don Nelson, Editorial Director and Publisher
Material: All
John Wm.. Roberts & Associates, Inc.
400 Skokie Blvd., #395
Northbrook IL 60062-7903
Phone: 847-714-0175
E-mail: dnelson@jwr.com

Dakota Outdoors
Premier Outdoor Magazine of the Dakotas

Dakota Outdoors is a regional, monthly (12 issues per year) outdoor publication for and about the Dakotas. *Dakota Outdoors* contains feature articles about fishing, hunting and other outdoor pursuits. *Dakota Outdoors* focuses on how- and where-to articles, written by local sportsmen, that provide a local perspective on outdoor life in the Dakotas that you cannot get elsewhere. We also cover legislative, governmental and regulatory concerns, as well as product information, hints and tips, personalities, and humor relative to our *Dakota Outdoors*. Articles from writers outside our region are welcome, so long as they cover topics of concern to Dakotans.

Articles submitted should be applicable to the outdoor life in the Dakotas.

Topics: Topics should center on fishing and hunting experiences and advice. Other topics, such as boating, camping, hiking, environmental concerns and general nature, will be considered as well.

Rights: Exclusive rights to an article are not mandatory, but we would like to have exclusive rights in our area. Please inform us if the article has been, or will be, published elsewhere.

Deadlines: Timely articles are important. Typically, copy deadline is the 10th of the month prior to the month of publication.

Photos: Photos will also be considered for publication. We prefer digital files of 300 dpi or greater. If submitted with an article, the photo should be pertinent to the article. All photos should be identified with the photographer's name and address as well as the name and address of the subject(s). The location where the photo was taken should be included as well.

Format: Articles should be submitted via e-mail. A headline and byline should be included on the submission. Please inquire for other formats. If submitting on disk, please let us know what format the file is in.

Rates: Rates are negotiable and depend upon the quality of the article and the amount of work necessary to put it into final form. Rates typically run from $5 to $50 per article. If a specific rate is requested, the price should be negotiated prior to publication.

Kids Korner: *Dakota Outdoors* publishes a kids outdoors column each month. We look for articles addressing kids from 12 to 16 years of age, from 50 to 500 words in length. Payment will generally range for $5 to $15.

Shorts & Fillers: *Dakota Outdoors* accepts shorts and fillers and uses them on an as needed basis. There is generally no payment for these items. If you submit a short of filler item and require payment, please notify us in advance.

Payment: Payment will be made for articles and photos after the issue is published, unless other arrangements are made.

Categories: Nonfiction—Outdoors—Recreation

CONTACT: Lee Harstad, Managing Editor
Material: All
PO Box 669
Pierre SD 57501-0669
Phone: 605-224-7301
Fax: 605-224-9210
E-mail: editor@dakotaoutdoors.net

Dance Spirit

SUBJECT MATTER

DS is about all idioms of dance as well as choreography, fitness, nutrition, education and competitions. All articles are assigned; send pitches rather than unsolicited finished copy. Our approach is educational/instructional. Use quotes from the company or individual artist as a way of teaching the lesson to be learned.

The most successful queries demonstrate a familiarity with our regular columns and departments. When pitching, please send your resume, indicating all dance experience, as each issue focuses on a theme you may or may not be qualified to write about.

Readership: Most of our readers are in their mid-teens to mid-20s. They are pre-professional dancers with aspirations of careers on Broadway, in professional companies and in music videos. They want to know how to get there.

Language: upbeat and peppy, but intelligent

SUBMISSIONS

All submissions must be in electronic format. E-mail is preferred. Please include a title and a deck with all submissions. All manuscripts should follow Associated Press style.

Artwork: Art must be submitted with each story unless otherwise arranged. Do not pitch a story without first knowing that there is quality artwork to accompany it. Send as much art as you can so we have options. Performance photos are preferred. Label the back of each piece of artwork with a return address if you need it returned. Do not use a pen that will bleed ink onto another picture.

Caption and credit all artwork: Captions should include names of performers, name of choreographer, title of piece, name of company and photographer or photo credit. EX: Sally Smith and Jane Brown of Ballet Company in Susan Camp's [ital: Energetic Flight]. Credit: John Jump

We accept high-contrast photos, slides and e-mail submissions. Please make sure that the images submitted via e-mail are high-resolution, CMYK or greyscale and that they are 300 dpi (minimum). Images saved for Web pages are generally not acceptable as they are low-resolution.

When sending images taken by a digital camera, please capture them at the highest resolution setting the camera is capable of taking.

Manuscript: Do not use serial commas before "and". EX: ballet, jazz and modern.

DO NOT FORMAT YOUR DOCUMENTS. All italics and bold-faced words should be in brackets, indicating the correct formatting. EX: [BF: Don't Forget:] George Delancey's piece [Ital: On The Fence] will be performed April 3.

Do not leave more than one space after periods.

Columns are 600 words; features are between 800 and 1200 words.

CONTRACT

Pay is received after your work is published. We own all rights to your work, including the right to post it on our website. Missed deadlines will not get you another assignment. We pay a 25 percent kill fee.

Categories: Nonfiction—Arts—Dance—Entertainment

CONTACT: Editor: Sara Jarrett
Material: Broadway/Celebrities/Special Events & Awards/
Hip Hop Dance/Dancewear/Dance Competitions & Conventions
CONTACT: Managing Editor: Kristin Lewis
Material: Features/Nutrition/Modern or Lyrical Dance/
Dance Team/Fitness
CONTACT: Assistant Editor: Kathryn Holmes
Material: Dance News/Jazz/Tap/Ballet/Dance Books,
Products and Shoes
McFadden Performing Arts Media, LLC
110 William St., 23rd Floor
New York NY 10038
Phone: 646-459-4800
Fax: 646-459-4890
E-mail: editor@dancemedia.com
Website: www.dancespirit.com

Dance Teacher
The Practical Magazine of Dance

Founded in 1979, *Dance Teacher* is the only magazine exclusively about dance education. Its mission is to provide practical information written in a clear, simple, conversational style, that readers can put to immediate use, and to provide a forum for communication among dance educators.

Readership

Dance Teacher has a national circulation with additional subscribers in more than 35 countries. The readers are teachers, dancers, choreographers, and serious students in independent studios, dance departments and in the schools associated with major dance companies. They participate in all forms of dance—ballet, jazz, modern, tap, hip hop, character, folk and ethnic, ballroom/DanceSport, aerobic and fitness dance, dance drill, sacred dance and creative movement. Artistic directors, administrators of schools, dance historians, critics and writers also read *Dance Teacher*.

Topics

Articles focus on subjects specific to the teaching of dance: the business of running a studio; nutrition, injuries and health; publicity; performance production; people in dance education; and other subjects of interest to dance educators. *Dance Teacher* accepts queries for the following sections of the magazine: Business, Health, Higher Ed, K-12 and Teaching. Stories should have a practical, how-to approach and provide easy-to-follow advice that readers can take into their studio or classroom. "Problem Solved!" pieces, which focus on one problem and its solution, may also be submitted.

In addition, some issues include a "Spotlight" on a successful teacher. This is a teacher or dancer involved in dance education who has made a unique impact, and should include how-to information (even sample lesson plans) so readers can emulate, rather than merely admire, the success enjoyed by the subject.

Special Sections

Dance Teacher has a theme for each issue of the year. Queries on articles appropriate to any of these sections are welcome, and should be submitted at least four months prior to the issue date.

January: Summer Study & Continuing Education includes information on summer workshops for students, as well as teacher training programs.

February: The Boys Issue is dedicated to educating male dancers and addressing their needs in all sectors of dance.

March: The Health & Wellness Issue includes articles on a variety of health topics, such as injury prevention, healthy habits and fitness products.

April: Summer Travel & Competition offers advice for making the most of time off during the summer, as well as maximizing the competitive experience.

May: The Age-Appropriate Teaching Issue is full of suggestions for how to tailor instruction to work most effectively with a variety of age groups.

June: The Business Issue is all about the nuts and bolts of running a studio, from flooring to plumbing, accounting to marketing.

July: Annual Dance Directory is Dance Teacher magazine's resource guide for everything dance, from costumes to flooring.

August: The Multimedia & Back-to-School Issue provides a variety of strategies for starting off the new school year right.

September: The K-12 & Convention Issue details the unique experience of teaching dance in public schools along with solutions for improvement. Tips on taking students to conventions are also included.

October: The Competition Issue helps teachers prepare students to participate in competitive dance events.

November: The Costume Preview Issue gives advice on choosing costumes for students, as well as other ideas for running great recitals and shows.

December: Higher Ed & Career Issue focuses on the college and university dance scene, including articles for and about professors in the field.

Length: Feature articles run 1,500 to 2,000 words and columns run 600-1,200 words. All articles must have artwork accompanying them. (No additional fee is paid for artwork, although appropriate credit is given.)

Style: Articles are written in a conversational style, using the second-person pronoun. Take into consideration the body of knowledge readers of *Dance Teacher* already have about dance. Include dollar amounts, titles, dates, names—as many specifics as possible. Use present tense, direct quotes. Include anecdotes, illustrations and examples.

Editing: All articles submitted are subject to editing for style and length. Stories will also be checked for accuracy. *Dance Teacher* generally follows the style rules of the Chicago Manual of Style, 15th edition.

Submissions: A query letter or e-mail is preferred, but a completed article may be submitted for consideration. E-mail submissions are preferred with the piece contained in the body of the message. Please do not send submissions as e-mail attachments. Stories may also be submitted through the mail, typed, double-spaced, with the author's name, address, telephone and e-mail address.

Simultaneous submissions must be clearly indicated. Submissions will not be returned unless accompanied by a self-addressed, stamped envelope. Prepublication drafts will be sent to the author as well as primary sources for verification (by request only), so please provide names, phone numbers and addresses of persons quoted at length. An author's bio runs with each article. Please include 75 words about yourself and your dance and writing credentials.

DT purchases all rights. Authors are given full credit unless otherwise requested.

Photos/Illustrations: *Dance Teacher* uses photographs and artwork in conjunction with articles and pays one fee for text and artwork. All art must be royalty-free or cleared for publication by the artist or holder of copyright. First generation slides, transparencies, or prints are acceptable. Color is preferred but we do accept black & white. In general, the closer-up and fewer people in a photograph, the better. Action photos are preferred. All photos or illustrations should be submitted with photographer's name and suggested caption clearly printed on an attached label.

2006 *Dance Teacher* Editorial Calendar

January - *Summer Study & Continuing Ed Issue* -2005 Summer Study & Continuing Ed Guides; comprehensive listings of summer and continuing education programs for teachers -Shoe Preview: the latest dance shoes -Sub-focus: Ballet

February - *Boys Issue* -How to develop male role models -Style: fashion: costumes and dancewear for boys and men -Sub-focus: Hip hop

March - *Health & Wellness Issue* -Supplementary and alternative training methods 101 -Exploring diet fads and supplements

April - *Summer Travel & Competition Issue* -Teaching Resources: new book & DVD releases -Shoe Preview: the latest dance shoes

May - *Age-Appropriate Teaching Issue* -Spotlight: National Tap Day -Ideas for teaching the preschool crowd

June - *Business Issue* -Teaching: my view: renovation diary -Shoe Preview: the latest dance shoes

July - *2007 Dance Directory* -The dance teacher's ultimate guide: completely updated resource listings for everything from costumes and competitions to music and health organizations

August - *Multimedia & Back-to-School Issue* -2006 Music Guide: comprehensive listings of music resources for teachers -Teaching: resources: new books, videos & DVDs -Spotlight on new teaching techniques and methods

September - *K-12 & Convention Issue* -2006-2007 Convention Guide: comprehensive listings of the year's dance conventions -Shoe Preview: the latest dance shoes

October - *Competition Issue* -2006-2007 Competition Guide: comprehensive listings of the year's dance competitions -Sub-focus: jazz

November - *Costume Preview Issue* -2007 Costume Preview: a survey of the newest costume styles -Shoe Preview: all the latest dance shoes

December - *Higher Ed and Career Issue* -2006 Higher Ed Guide: comprehensive listings of college and university dance programs -Holiday gift guide: new books, videos & DVDs -Helping students stay healthy in college -Sub-focus: modern

Writers' Fees: Dance Teacher pays $250-300 for feature articles and up to $200 for columns. We pay within 30 days of publication and after having received the appropriate invoice.

Thank you for your interest in *Dance Teacher*.

Categories: Arts—Dance—Drama

CONTACT: Jeni Tu, Managing Editor
Material: Queries and manuscripts
Dance Spirit
110 William St, 23rd Floor
New York NY 10038
Fax: 646-459-4900
E-mail: editor@dance-teacher.com

Dark Energy Speculative Fiction

Needs: Anything that makes us go, "Wow! That was good!" Speculative fiction is a wide and open genre, which includes a bit of horror, and a bit of supernatural. We're even willing to look at mainstream fiction as long as it has a strange feel to it. This is a good place to try that odd story that doesn't seem to fit in any particular "box."

As to story length, keep in mind that your readers will be reading your stories online. The fact is, not many people enjoy reading a long manuscript on a computer screen. Anything 10,000 words and above will be stretching it, but if you feel you have something we must see, despite the length, go ahead and submit it.

We are not looking for reprints, but if you have a story that's only appeared somewhere for a short period of time, or was published in small press with limited circulation, we'll still consider it equally.

Length: Open, but prefer under 10,000 words

Art/Photo Needs: None

Payment: Dark Energy Speculative Fiction is a market whose sole purpose is to award exposure to new and little-known talent. We pay a flat $10 fee for each story accepted, which we know isn't a whole lot, but it's better than a poke in the eye.

Also, each story will be presented with a PayPal donations button, so that readers may tip the writer directly. So, in a way, there is the possibility of more remuneration, but nothing is guaranteed. Dark Energy SF will not keep any of the donated money for expenses, etc. This publication is not out to make money. It's not even a goal. We only want to reward talent and entertain readers. Period.

How to Submit: Use standard manuscript formatting, and save the file in RTF format. Attach this file to an email and send it, with a brief note or cover letter, to: submissions@darkenergysf.com

This is important: Put the words "FICTION SUBMISSION" in the subject field. If you don't, we won't see it. The SPAM filter will have sent it directly to the trash. Also, make sure to include a current, working email address on your manuscript, because as soon as we download your story, your email will be deleted so as to save space on the mail server.

Thus: If you don't include your email address on the manuscript you will not hear back from us. This would be a shame especially if we decided we wanted to publish you.

When writing your cover letter, you don't have to address it to anyone in particular, as we have guest editors coming in from time to time to choose stories. "Dear Editor," will work perfectly.

Response Time: If you don't hear back in 33 days assume it's been lost and resubmit.

Tips for Writers: The stranger your story, the better.

Sample Copies/Subscription Information: See website: www.darkenergysf.com

What We're Looking For

We are particularly fond of End Of The World type stories, and never see enough of them. Stories dealing with hard science, and also stories dealing with religion, are both of particular interest to us.

Lately, we've been seeing far too much horror. We're not really a horror market. It will have to be very different than the standard horror fare to catch our fancy.

The same thing goes with fantasy stories. While we like *Lord Of The Rings*, etc., the main problem we have is that it's all alike. It's the same as the stories that have already been published time and time again. This is rather odd, if you think about it, because there are no boundaries at all to the fantasy genre. Your imagination can run as wild as you want. So, why write the same old thing?

Akin to horror and fantasy are ghost stories. Now, we love a really good ghost story, but writing one is very difficult, because if you think about it, all the good ones are actually mystery stories ... but yet we never see these, we always see quick little ghost stories that try to end with a shocker, and are never really satisfying.

We'd also like to see more experimental stories, and mainstream stories that have a strange angle to them ... like something's a bit off.

Think *Twilight Zone*. Think *Donnie Darko*.

Above all, what we're looking for are stories that are 100% character driven. Stories that draw us in to the character so much we really don't care what the genre is. A story that really goes behind the curtain, deep into the well, and taps into that dark energy that's inside all of us.

As to story length, keep in mind that your readers will be reading your stories online. The fact is, not many people enjoy reading a long manuscript on a computer screen. Anything 10,000 words and above will be stretching it, but if you feel you have something we must see, despite the length, go ahead and submit it.

We are not looking for reprints, but if you have a story that's only appeared somewhere for a short period of time, or was published in small press with limited circulation, we'll still consider it equally.

What We Don't Want

Anything written using characters or settings that are not entirely your own creation. We don't want stories featuring Star Trek, Star Wars, Babylon-5, The Wizard of Oz, or anything like that. There are specific underground markets for this type of thing and that's where you need to send it.

Note: This doesn't include historical figures, or characters that have been in the public domain for a long time. They're fair game.

We are not looking for pornographic stories. Not that we don't like it, it just doesn't belong in *Dark Energy SF*. You can try us with something that has an erotic edge to it, but, nothing really overboard. Kids have access to this website.

Also, please, nothing overtly grotesque and disgusting unless it absolutely *has to be that way* for the story to work.

Money

Dark Energy Speculative Fiction is a market whose sole purpose is to award exposure to new and little-known talent. **We pay a flat $20 fee for each story accepted**, which we know isn't a whole lot, but it's better than a poke in the eye.

Also, each story will be presented with a PayPal donations button, so that readers may tip the writer directly. So, in a way, there is the possibility of more remuneration, but nothing is guaranteed. *Dark Energy SF* will not keep any of the donated money for expenses, etc. This publication is not out to make money. It's not even a goal. We only want to reward talent and entertain readers. Period.

Note: PayPal, however, *may* get a percentage of each donation before it reaches the author. It's the price of doing business with PayPal.

Rights

We are seeking web-publishing rights only, and after the story is cycled into the Archive section, we'll reassign these rights back to the author upon request. You are free to continue marketing your story in other venues as you see fit.

All stories will appear with a copyright notice attributed to the author. The author retains the right to request removal of his/her story after it is moved into the Archive section.

How To Submit

Please, NO SIMULTANEOUS SUBMISSIONS, and only one story at a time.

Use standard manuscript formatting, and save the file in RTF format. Simply attach this file to an email and send it, with a brief note or cover letter, to: darkenergy.editor@gmail.com

This is important: Put the words "FICTION SUBMISSION" in the subject field. If you don't, we won't see it. The SPAM filter will have sent it directly to the trash. Also, make sure to include a current, **working email address** on your manuscript, because as soon as we download your story, your email will be deleted so as to save space on the mail server.

Thus: If you don't include your email address on the manuscript you may not hear back from us. This would be a shame especially if we decided we want to publish you.

When writing your cover letter, you don't have to address it to anyone in particular, as we have guest editors coming in from time to time to choose stories. "Dear Editor," will work perfectly.

Because of the non-existent budget and dependence upon free mail services, some submissions may be lost. **If you haven't heard back from us within 33 days, assume it didn't reach us**, and send it again. Also, if your email bounces back with an error, it's probably because our inbox is full and the current editor hasn't yet had a chance to download all the manuscripts. Try again in a few days, and if that doesn't work, contact us directly via the Contacts Page.

How Often Do You Publish?

The problem with emulating a magazine on the Internet is that you start trying to force the publication into issues and volumes which, if you think about it, doesn't translate well. This is a new medium. It's not paper. It doesn't "go to press."

So how often do we publish? *Continuously*. It can change from day to day. This is not a magazine, and it's not an eZine. It's a website.

So when you get your story accepted, it will be put up in the current stories list. After a story is up for a month or so, it will be put into the archive. Or, if you wish, deleted.

Hey, I Was Rejected!

Why? This is a fact of life: fiction writers get rejection slips. If nothing else, we hope to help you get used to the fact. There's no way around it. Even Stephen King collected a huge pile of rejection slips while he was learning the craft.

Just because we don't like a particular story doesn't mean someone else won't like it. It also doesn't mean we won't like your next story. So please don't take it personally.

Do You Give Feedback?

Time permitting, we'll try to give you some help, but if you want feedback on your stories, we strongly suggest you join a writer's group. If you can find a good one it can do more than anything else to improve your writing.

Stories are the children of a writer. It's hard to see flaws in your own children. You love them too much. It hurts when others reject them.

Put the story away and don't look at it for a long time. Write several more stories. Then take that one out and look at it again. Whoa! The parts you loved are now terrible, and the parts you didn't like are the good parts. Weird how that works, huh?

Fix it and then send it out again. And again. And again.

And remember to give us a try every once in a while.

Categories: Science Fiction

CONTACT: The Editor
E-mail: editor@darkenergysf.com
Website: www.darkenergysf.com

DCM

About *DCM*: This slick, four-color, fifty-plus page bimonthly magazine is the members-only publication of AFCOM with a 50/50 split between editorial and advertising. Our readers are data center managers, MIS directors, CIOs, and other IS professionals.

Each issue of *DCM* has five feature articles of about 2,000 words each. Typically, four deal with some aspect of data center technology and one addresses a management issue. All articles must be written in a journalistic style with a strong, practical slant toward the data center management community without any trace of preferential treatment toward a product, service, or vendor. Articles from freelancers (average three per issue) may report feedback from data center managers on products and services. However, articles from vendors (average two per issue) may discuss technologies and techniques, but not specific products or services.

DCM includes regular bimonthly columns. In addition to our time-honored Best Practices, Data Center Profile, Data Center Insights, and Data Center Institute Report columns, the following column is new for 2006: "Ask the Experts" – This column features topics based on recent AFCOM hotline inquiries; experts in the field provide practical, thoughtful responses to these pertinent end-user questions.

"Data Center Manager Profile" – This is a twist on the popular "Data Center Profile" column. Instead of featuring an entire data center, we present a Q and A with a member of an innovative staff.

What Else is New in 2006? Our editorial focus for 2006 continues with themed issues of *DCM* magazine. The themes are as follows:

January-February 2006 – Emerging Technologies
March-April 2006 – Vendor Relations/Vendor Management
May-June 2006 – Successful IT Management
July-August 2006 – Everything You Need to Know about Storage
September-October 2006 – Disaster Recovery
November-December 2006 – Year-End Wrap-Up (Topics vary)

Feature articles are required to have practical depth. This means we want specific examples of how challenges in data center management can be met, particularly by leveraging existing resources or the judicious selection of new ones. What especially appeals to us are the detailed descriptions of how "in-the-trenches" data center managers solve problems, face crises, and pioneer best practices. Accompanying sidebars of "how to" checklists, pros and cons, recommended resources, interviews with experts, and so on are key to providing practical depth. Feature articles must be insightful, hands-on resources that our readers will use as problem-solving guides and recommend to their peers. Bottom line: The content they read must make their jobs easier.

Case Studies: Very few case studies submitted to *DCM* by vendors are selected for publication. Most are rejected because they focus on the vendor rather than the solution. We are looking for the vendor to remain "invisible" until his or her bio at the end of the study.

How to Submit Articles: Send the managing editor a separate e-mail for each article you are submitting or proposing with the topic clearly noted in the subject line. Query letters, 75-word abstracts, press releases, or completed articles are welcome. Please include your full contact information with each submission.

What to Expect: The editor does not consider previously published material (including online content), self-promoting material, product-specific material, or simultaneous submissions for publication in *DCM* magazine. Your original submission will be acknowledged upon receipt. If a personal editorial reply does not arrive within 30 days of the acknowledgement, you may conclude that the submission was not accepted. If your original article is accepted, your signature on AFCOM's publication policy will be required. If your abstract is approved, you will receive information confirming the assignment on speculation.

Payment and Rights: *DCM* acquires all rights to original articles. Freelancers are paid according to their expertise, but must cover their own assignment-related expenses. Kill fees are offered at the discretion of *DCM*. Assigned articles are paid for—upon receipt of an author's invoice—on the fifth and twentieth of each month. Unsolicited articles are paid for upon publication.

Reprinting Your Article Later: Requests to reprint articles elsewhere after they have appeared in *DCM* are routinely granted at no charge, but prior permission is required. Details are available in the reprint policy. Please e-mail the managing editor to request a copy of the policy. (cstichter@afcom.com).

Sample Copies, Media Kits, Advertising Rates: Freelancers may request sample copies from the managing editor. Vendors may request a full media kit and advertising details from sales manager Tom Bauchard at 714-997-7966, ext. 217 or tbauchard@afcom.com.

Editorial Deadlines – 2006

January-February 2006 – Deadline: November 4, 2005
March-April 2006 – Deadline: January 6, 2006
May-June 2006 – Deadline: March 3, 2006
July-August 2006 – Deadline: May 5, 2006
September-October 2006 – Deadline: July 7, 2006
November-December 2006 – Deadline: September 8, 2006

About AFCOM

AFCOM is one of the most respected names in the data center industry, offering its members exceptional services and resources. The association counts among its prestigious members data center managers, MIS directors, CIOs, and other IS professionals from the largest corporations and government agencies throughout the world.

Founded in 1980 by Len Eckhaus, AFCOM is dedicated to supporting and helping data center managers achieve excellence. This is accomplished through facilitating networking among members, creating industry alliances, providing an interactive Web site and a troubleshooting hotline, publishing a bimonthly magazine (DCM) and a monthly electronic newsletter (The Communiqué), and hosting two major educational conferences annually. The fall Data Center World conference is held in varying locations throughout the United States (Orlando in 2006). The spring Data Center World conference is traditionally held in Las Vegas, but will be in Atlanta in 2006. The conference includes keynote addresses, educational sessions, virtual data center tours, Vision2Vision open forum sessions and a luncheon, comprehensive trade show, optional tutorials, and much more.

Significant among AFCOM's features is the Data Center Institute. Formed by AFCOM in 2001, the DCI board is a select group of senior data center managers and information technology vendors joined to examine and appraise issues and trends relevant to data center operations. Its charter is to provide thought leadership and direction for the industry and the press on data center-related matters. Through this group, experienced industry professionals and their organizations will have the opportunity to ensure that informed opinions about data center issues are properly disseminated to the public.

AFCOM's expanded online Resource Center has an ongoing need for editorial content, templates, white papers, and so on. DCM editorial requirements apply to online content.

Categories: Nonfiction—Associations

CONTACT: Chelsey Stichter, managing editor
Phone: 714-997-7966 ext 219
E-mail: cstichter@afcom.com

DECA Dimensions

DECA is...the international association of marketing education students—ambitious, talented students eager to explore their career interests in marketing, merchandising, and entrepreneurship.

A nonprofit educational association, DECA has 180,000 members in all 50 states, Guam, Puerto Rico, Germany and Canada. The majority of members are of high school age, 15-19, while those in the postsecondary division, Delta Epsilon Chi, are 18 and older.

For more than 50 years, DECA has provided a program of leadership and professional development designed to merge with the marketing education curriculum. DECA is not extracurricular, but is a part of classroom instruction.

Working hand-in-hand with the education and business communities, DECA utilizes on-the-job experience, chapter projects and an outstanding program of competency based competitive events in specific occupational areas including sales, advertising, finance, retailing, wholesaling, fashion merchandising, restaurant management, tourism and hospitality among others.

Formerly known as the Distributive Education Clubs of America, DECA is governed by a board of directors and guided by councils of educators, as well as two advisory boards—the National Advisory Board (NAB) consists of representatives from more than 60 of America's major businesses and corporations; the Congressional Advisory Board (CAB) is made up of select members of the United States Congress.

DECA helps its members develop a "career success kit" to carry with them from school to work.

Dimensions is... the journal magazine for DECA's membership. Published four times a year during the school year, i.e., September/October, November/December, January/February and March/April, Dimensions reaches 160,000 young people and the adults who support their goals. It is a glossy publication, 8¼"x10¾", printed in four-color. Its audience is primarily high school students ages 15-19.

Because it is an education journal with a unique audience, Dimensions is a publication of substance but with the appeal of a commercial magazine for young adults. Its approach is direct and conversational—not academic.

Advertising and freelance articles are accepted. Topics covered include general business—corporate and small business; management and marketing—domestic and international; leadership development; entrepreneurship; fashion merchandising and trends; sales; business technology; personal and business finance; advertising and visual display; security; tourism and hospitality industries; food service—quick and full-serve; the retail food industry; career opportunities; employment and academic tips and helps; job skills; school-to-work incentives; current issues of interest to the association or audience, including school and peer issues.

Dimensions feature articles are approximately 1,000 words; columns approximately 500 words. A short bio statement should accompany bylined articles. Submissions on Mac disk along with hard copy are preferred. Small honorariums may be paid upon use.

Preparing to Write

Writing a column, a feature piece or a book is an experience that can be satisfying for you and rewarding for your reader. Producing a well-written, accurate work clearly conveys your knowledge and expertise to the audience. Each author has his own style and editors try diligently to maintain that flavor in the finished piece. However, once your writing has been submitted to the publisher, it is assumed that editorial changes can and will be made as needed without consultation. Most often this will be done to accommodate available publication space.

To minimize editorial changes to your work, you will want to observe the following points:

• Keep in mind the audience you are trying to reach. The readers may be young, but they are knowledgeable in their areas and accustomed to a professional presentation. They will expect valuable, timely information that they can learn from or practice.

• Don't talk down to your reader, but at the same time don't use wordy or jargon-filled language. Whatever style you adopt, casual or formal, stay consistent throughout.

• Avoid language or content that could be interpreted as humiliating or slighting to any minority group or specific segment.

• The use of specific examples or stories to explain concepts is always a good idea.

• Laws governing what may or may not be used from another source are very complex and often difficult to interpret. You, as the author, are legally responsible for obtaining permissions, whether for text or illustration. Permission must be obtained not only for the directly quoted material but also for significant material that has been paraphrased or condensed. It is best to get permissions in writing and submit copies of them for our files along with your article. Sources must be acknowledged in the text or in a credit line.

Categories: Business—Careers—Education—Teen—Young Adult

CONTACT: Traci Molnar, Editor
Material: All
1908 Association Dr.
Reston VA 20191
Phone: 703-860-5000
Fax: 703-860-4013
E-mail: deca_dimensions@deca.org
Website: www.deca.org

Decision

Before sending *Decision* your manuscript, consider ...

Decision magazine's purpose is to set forth the Good News of salvation in Jesus Christ with such clarity that readers will be drawn to make a commitment to Christ; to encourage, teach and strengthen Christians to walk daily with Christ and to reach out to others for Christ; and to inform readers about the ministry of the Billy Graham Evangelistic Association.

We look for articles that communicate the hope that is found in the Gospel of the Lord Jesus Christ. Readers should see how Christ makes a difference in your life and how you are applying biblical truth.

Our Editorial Needs:

We are considering only articles that have some connection with a ministry of BGEA either through the author's participation in the ministry or through the author being touched by the ministry.

Finding Jesus—Did you make a decision for Christ as a result of a Billy Graham Crusade, a Franklin Graham Festival, or a ministry of BGEA such as a telecast, film or radio, Web site, or *Decision* magazine? Tell us about it—and what you are doing now. Length: 500-900 words.

Personal Experience—How have you applied biblical principles to everyday living or to a crisis experience? Or, how did you grow closer to Christ through a specific experience? The story should have some connection with a ministry of BGEA or of Billy Graham or Franklin Graham. Length: 500-900 words.

Decision magazine is published 11 times a year by the Billy Graham Evangelistic Association.

Your Submissions:

Note: We are no longer able to give a personalized response to all submissions. We will let you know by form letter if we cannot use your article, and we will respond personally only if we are interested in using your article. Please enclose a self-addressed envelope for our response.

1. Type your manuscript in standard manuscript form: double-spaced; name, address and telephone number in the top left-hand corner (include fax number if available); word-count and rights offered in the top right-hand corner. Keep at least one copy of your manuscript for your files.

2. When using Scripture quotations, specify the version. Include sources for quotations and for comments attributed to other persons. When a quotation is directly from a book or a magazine, photocopy the page from which the quotation is taken, the title page and the copyright page, and include them with your manuscript.

3. Send your manuscript to Bob Paulson, editor, at address below.

Categories: Nonfiction—Christian Interests—Religion—Spirituality

CONTACT: Bob Paulson, Editor
DECISION
1 Billy Graham Parkway
Charlotte NC 28201-0001
E-mail: submissions@bgea.org

Decorative Artist's Workbook

About Us

Decorative Artist's Workbook's mission is to inspire, instruct, inform and entertain decorative painters across the country and around the world. Our aim is to teach beginning, intermediate and advanced decorative painters the processes and techniques of painting firsthand from other artists via step-by-step instructions and illustrations. To encourage a reader's success, we: 1) provide patterns for every feature project, 2) teach the fundamentals of decorative painting, 3) present techniques in a variety of media, and 4) have experienced master painters answer their questions.

Writer's & Artist's Guidelines

Decorative Artist's Workbook (DAW) is a bimonthly publication for decorative painters of all skill levels. The magazine covers a wide range of decorative painting subjects, including folk art (such as rosemaling), stroke work, stenciling, fabric painting and faux finishing methods, just to name a few. Paintings are done in acrylics, oils, alkyds and watercolors on such surfaces as tin, wood, canvas, fabric and glass. Whatever the medium or surface, we're seeking the new, the unique and the traditional presented in a fresh way.

FEATURES

Our most consistent need is for instructional articles. We use between six and 10 features per issue, and all features should emphasize the how-to: the step-by-step process used to complete a project or master a technique. These features range from 1,000 to 2,000 words in length, but we certainly welcome short features on quick projects that can be explained in one or two pages.

Articles that introduce a traditional folk art style, for instance, or new technique, are usually combined with a finished project. This type of article explains how a style or technique originated, the history of the technique (if applicable), the materials used, and how it can be completed.

Pay for all features ranges from $200 to $300. and is, of course, dependent upon the complexity of the artwork, the writing, the article's length and the total package submitted by the writer. To submit a feature idea, see "How to Query" below.

COLUMNS

Opportunities with DAW lie primarily with feature articles. Most of the columns are written by our staff, contributing editors or editorial board members. We will, however, accept queries for "Stenciling," "By Design" (which covers the principles of design), "Home Decor" (decorative painting for the home), "Creative Painting" (new ideas, techniques and trends in decorative painting), and "Artist of the Issue" (profiles of up-and-coming artists).

Submissions for columns should follow the same format as for features. Pay varies depending on the length and content. To submit a column idea, see "How to Query" below.

OTHER NEEDS

"Ask the Masters" is a column that offers expert answers to your painting questions from the country's top decorative painters. To participate, send your questions to "Ask the Masters," *Decorative Artist's Workbook*. (See address below.)

In "Brush Talk," we share our reader mail – projects, creative ideas, painting solutions and opinions – that were inspired by the pages of *Decorative Artist's Workbook*. To participate, send your letters to "Brush Talk" at the address below.

ORIGINALITY AND RIGHTS

All material submitted must be original and unpublished. If accepted, DAW purchases First North American Serial Rights for one-time use in the magazine and all rights for use of the article (text and illustration/art) in any F&W promotional material/product or reprint.

You always retain copyright of your work and are free to use it in any way you wish after it appears in the magazine. We ask, however, that you do not publish this same material for at least six months from the time it appears in our publication.

HOW TO QUERY

Please query in advance rather than send unsolicited manuscripts and artwork. You may query with more than one idea at a time. Your query should include:

• A self-addressed, stamped envelope for the return of your material.

• A brief outline of the proposed article, telling us the skill level, medium and surface used, and anything else about the project that makes it special or unique.

• A color photo or slide of the project/s.

• A short biographical sketch. Include your accomplishments, address and a daytime phone number.

MANUSCRIPT SUBMISSION

Once your article query has been given the go-ahead, here's what you'll need to send next:

1. The Manuscript: This should be typed and double-spaced on white 8-1/2 x 11-inch paper. (If you have a computer, you may submit the article on a 3-1/2 inch disk along with the printed copy. Check with an editor for details.) Place your full name, address and phone number on the first page. *Your manuscript should include the following:*

• Title

• Introduction

• Describe an important point about your project or subject. What made you develop the idea or design for it? You might note an unusual technique, surface or medium, how it can be used, or why it's one of your favorites.

• Preparation: Explain any necessary pre-painting steps such as sanding, sealing, etc.

• Painting Instructions: Writing in a conversational style, go step-by-step through the painting process, explaining each point clearly and concisely, as if a beginning painter were looking over your shoulder. Make sure you include every detail (such as the brush size and pigment being used). Spell out the full names of paint colors, and please don't shorten terms (e.g., P.G. for Paynes Gray).

• Finishing: Give complete instructions on how to finish the painted project (varnishing, sanding, heat setting, etc.).

• Closing: Close your article with a brief statement that ties everything together. Also, if you can, add an estimate of the approximate time needed to complete the project.

• Materials: Please provide a complete list of the materials used to complete the project. We ask that you include the following with the assumption that any product mentioned carries your endorsement for quality:

• Palette: paint brand, medium and colors (be sure these are spelled correctly).

• Brushes: brand name, type and size.

• Surface: size (if applicable), supplier's name, address, phone number and the price of the surface (including shipping charges).

• Miscellaneous: Note every other item used, from pencils to glue and sprays.

• About the Artist: This sidebar runs with every feature. Tell us about yourself, including the following information:

> How long have you been painting and how did you get "hooked?"
> Have you won any awards?
> Have you published any painting books or pattern packets?
> If you teach, give the what, when and how.
> Any anecdotes about painting.
> Your philosophy regarding decorative art.
> Your advice for beginners.
> Include a photo of yourself.

2. Visual Aides: Visual aids are an important part of instruction and are essential for project articles, so remember to submit quality painted work-sheets of key painting steps for each element of the design (such as petal leaves, and flower center). These work-sheets should show the painting progression, corresponding as much as possible with the written instructions.

For example, if the first step is base coating, the first illustration would show only that. If the second step is adding the shading, the second illustration would show that, and so on. (Please note: If adding written instructions on the illustrations, do not do so directly on the art. Instead, place them on a tracing paper overlay, and we'll compile the information into captions.)

Also include on the worksheets paint swatches for the paint mixtures used for the project.

Step-by-step worksheets should be painted on canvas, canvasette or sturdy paper, and should be neat and easy to see with plenty of contrast between the painted step and the background color. Also, keep plenty of blank space around each step as we may need to cut out illustrations for art purposes.

3. Sidebars: If a certain technique is important in the project, such as dry brushing or cross blending, make a suggestion for a special "sidebar" explaining that technique. Tips and hints to ensure success also make good sidebars.

4. Alternate Instructions: Whenever possible, we like to provide instructions for painting a project in an alternate medium. So, if you've painted your project in oils, for instance, and are able to translate those instructions or suggest tips for acrylic painters, please include them in your package.

5. The Pattern: Include a "drawn-to-scale" line drying of the pattern (neatly drawn with a technical pen) for inclusion in the pull-out pattern section of the magazine.

6. The Project: Please send the completed project, ready to be photographed. (If the project is on canvas or watercolor paper, please frame it.)

All artwork, photos and drawings will be returned after publication. **Categories:** Arts—Crafts—Painting

CONTACT: Anne Hevener
Material:4700 E. Galbraith Rd.
Cincinnati OH 45236
Phone: 513-531-2690 ext. 1461
Fax: 513-531-2902
E-mail: dawedit@fwpubs.com
Website: www.decorativeartist.com

Deep Outside SFFH

Who We Are: Outside is a paying professional magazine of SF and dark imaginative fiction, aimed at people who love to read well-plotted, character-driven genre fiction. We are interested in fiction that transcends the limitations and ventures outside the stereotypes of genre fiction.

What We Publish: short (1500-4000 words) Science Fiction, Horror, and darkly imaginative fiction. We seek well-written, professionally executed fiction, with attention to basics - grammar, punctuation, usage. We do not accept Sword & Sorcery, pornography, or excessive violence and gore beyond the legitimate needs of a story. Also no derivative works (e.g., emulating TV shows and movies - no Star Trek stories, for example).

Our goals: We strive to be both writer-friendly and reader-friendly. We eagerly look forward to receiving top quality, professional material from you.

Requirements: We no longer accept snail mail submissions. All stories must be submitted via e-mail to storysub@clocktowerfiction.com.

The subject line of the e-mail must begin with **[storysub]** followed by the name of the author, followed by the title of the story. For example:

Correct: [storysub] Edgar Poe - The Fall of the House of Usher
Incorrect:
[Story Sub] Edgar Poe - The Fall of the House of Usher
storysub - Edgar Poe - The Fall of the House ofUsher
[submission] Edgar Poe - The Fall of the House of Usher

Because we have automated mechanisms for routing submissions, it is extremely important that you follow the "correct" format above, including the brackets in the subject line. Ensure that it follows the format exactly. The body of the e-mail should contain the author's full name, social security number (if you have one), and address, followed by an approximate word count. No simultaneous submissions, please. Submissions that do not follow the format above will not be considered. The story you are submitting may be submitted as either plain text pasted into the body of the e-mail or as an attached RTF file. We DO NOT ACCEPT Microsoft Word DOC files—please save your file as RTF (Rich Text Format)—most word processors, including Microsoft Word have a "Save As..." feature that will allow you to save your story in RTF format. For plain text submissions, place an underscore ("_") on either side of text that should be italicized (since formatting is not retained in plain text) and paste your story directly into the body of your e-mail.

Grammar, punctuation, spelling, and usage weigh heavily as we consider the story. You must master these essentials to be a professional writer. We expect that a professional writer owns, and regularly uses, a dictionary and at least one or two usage books (e.g. Strunk & White, Fowler). To be a successful writer, you should be a voracious but discriminating reader. Many books are available about the craft of writing—read them all for free through your public library. Join a writers' group. Write constantly to improve your craft—it's a tough discipline, as difficult and time consuming as learning to play symphony-quality violin or piano. Visit SharpWriter.Com for a comprehensive writer's resource. Finally, despite all these somewhat dire words, we wish you a passionate and successful love affair with writing.

We pay three cents per word upon acceptance of your manuscript for First Serial Rights for one year. Acceptance constitutes final editorial approval of content. We strive to pay as promptly as possible, but please allot a reasonable amount of time (6-8 weeks after acceptance) for your check to arrive.

Manuscripts must be sent by e-mail to **storysub@clocktower fiction.com** only. Postal mail submissions will be disposed of without being read (as will submissions not mailed to the above e-mail address).

We usually respond within twelve weeks after receiving a submission. Depending on many variables, however, it can sometimes take longer. Please give us ample time before you begin writing to inquire about a submission's status. No simultaneous or previously published work.

Categories: Science Fiction

CONTACT: **Brian Callahan and John Cullen, Editors**
6549 Mission Gorge Pl, Box 260
San Diego CA 92120
E-mail: **outside@clocktowerfiction.com**
Website: **www.clocktowerfiction.com**

Defenders

General Information

DEFENDERS magazine is published quarterly for the membership of Defenders of Wildlife, a national nonprofit organization devoted to wildlife conservation. DEFENDERS has a circulation of about 260,000. Content reflects the organization's focus on endangered species, public lands, habitat and bio-diversity conservation, the international wildlife trade and similar subjects. Most issues contain four full-length features as well as departments and an organizational "newsletter." Most content deals with North American wildlife, although we print international articles from time to time. Please study an issue of the magazine and send a query before submitting any material.

Manuscripts

Query first. Include a self-addressed stamped reply envelope (SASE). Include a brief description of your background and qualifications along with some published writing samples. Most articles are assigned after a query.

We do not accept fiction or poetry. Essays are accepted rarely.

Length and Format

Usual length: 1,500 to 3,500 words.

Proposals and manuscripts submitted simultaneously to other publications are not acceptable, nor is previously published work.

The content is directed to a general audience, but scientific accuracy is essential. We do not want encyclopedia extracts or other second-hand natural history descriptions. We emphasize current threats to wild species and habitat, worthwhile action to save wildlife and informed discussions of government programs and policies. We seek to maintain a high literary, reportorial and graphic standard.

Categories: Nonfiction—Animals—Conservation—Ecology—Environment—Nature—Politics

CONTACT: **Submissions Editor**
Material: **All**
1101 Fourteenth Street, NW, Ste 1400
Washington DC 20005
Phone: 202-682-9400
Fax: 202-682-1331
E-mail: **JDEANE@defenders.org**
Website: **www.defenders.org**

Delicious Living

Thank you for your interest in writing for *Delicious Living*, a monthly consumer magazine that is distributed primarily through natural products stores nationwide. Our goal is to inspire health-conscious men and women to take responsibility for their health and well being. To do this, we educate readers on topics such as nutrition, disease prevention, integrative medicine, healthy cooking, and personal care. Our approach to health is proactive, emphasizing disease prevention rather than symptom fighting.

Delicious Living articles are lively, informative, and conversational in tone. Our audience comprises savvy, educated women and men who demand facts to back up health claims. Therefore, we provide up-to-date health information in a clear, easy-to-understand manner. We ask writers to consult varied sources for their stories, including health professionals, research journals, and books written by health professionals. We require that writers cite research in stories and make every attempt to reference first-hand research.

The first step in getting an article published in *Delicious Living* magazine is to send a query letter, resume, and published clips to the editors. Queries should reflect familiarity with the magazine's content and tone. Stories that present new information about or a fresh angle on integrative medicine, women's health, nutrition, disease prevention, natural cuisine, profiles, or personal care are among the most desirable topics. While we accept freelance queries for most of our features and departments, we do not read unsolicited material.

FEATURES

Delicious Living considers both issue- and service-oriented stories that focus on trends and information relating to nutrition, health, alternative medicine, and natural living and natural products. We generally publish two non-food focused features per issue, ranging from 1,200 to 2,000 words. We usually ask the writer to generate one or two sidebars.

Science/Issue feature. This feature offers an in-depth, research-based look at current health topics, including herbs and supplements relevant to the topic. Recent subjects include children's food allergies, water conservation, the science of aging, GMO facts, and foods that help fight cancer. Science articles run about 1,500 words each.

Lifestyle, trend, and profile features. This feature story focuses on topics that are related to natural living. Recent stories include natural living books to change your life, profiles of those making a difference in the environment, eco-clothing, refrigerator/diet makeovers for the new year, and a look at five of the most inspiring and healthy U.S. cities to live in. Lifestyle, trend, and profile stories usually run about 1,500 words each.

Cuisine. There are usually one to two natural cuisine features in each issue, featuring a 300-word intro, six original recipes, and one sidebar. We publish a wide variety of cuisine articles, from internationally focused pieces, such as Caribbean cuisine, to articles on soy foods, mushrooms, quick weeknight dinners, grilling, and much more. We generally ask for two recipes that are easier than the others, with a shorter ingredient list and easier preparation. Ingredients used in the recipes should be easily found in natural food stores, and all recipes should be focused on mindful, healthy cooking. The sidebar should relate to the topic of the story (for example, how to brew a perfect pot of tea to accompany six afternoon-tea recipes).

DEPARTMENTS

Update is the natural news section of *Delicious Living*, featuring brief reports on what's new and notable in natural living. Regular sections include What's in Season, Good Read, Ask the Expert, Make a Difference, and Why I Do What I Do. Stories run 100 to 300 words.

Shop Talk provides shopping insights from an experienced grocer. Stories run about 300 words.

Herbs/Supplements feature specific herbs and supplements and their roles in disease prevention or as remedies for health problems. Herbs/Supplements columns generally run 600 words.

Women's Health provides readers with up-to-date information about how various complementary healing therapies—homeopathy, traditional Chinese medicine, massage therapy, herbs and supplements, ayurveda and mind-body work, for example—can help address women's health needs. Recent topics include how to get pregnant after 35, seasonal affective disorder (SAD), and women's sleep disorders. Our **Men's Health** department is published approximately every third month. Articles are 1,000 words.

Nutrition offers the reader current ideas and health information about a variety of nutrition-related topics, with two related original recipes. Past Nutrition topics include foods to lower cholesterol, pet nutrition, trans fats, nondairy milks, and cooking with beans. Articles run 750 words plus two recipes and one short sidebar.

Spirit, Fitness, and Beauty. This is a rotating column in the magazine, each month offering a look at something new and interesting in one of these three areas. Recent stories include the power of forgiveness (Spirit), tips to keep you motivated and exercising all year long (Fitness), and a guide to natural makeup (Beauty). Articles run 1,000 words.

If you'd like us to consider a story idea, please send your query and clips to *Delicious Living* at address below. Queries may be e-mailed; however, we do not review clips sent electronically.

Categories: Nonfiction—Cooking—Food—Nutrition—Men's Health—Women's Health

CONTACT: The *Delicious Living* Staff
1401 Pearl St
Boulder Co 80302
Phone: 303-939-8440
Fax 303-440-8884
E-mail: deliciousliving@newhope.com
Website: www.deliciouslivingmag.com

Dermascope

As a trade publisher to the aesthetics, body therapy and spa industries, our subscribers have come to depend on DERMASCOPE as their source of clear educational information.

All articles submitted for consideration must meet the following criteria:

Style: Written from an aesthetic educators point-of-view, articles must be educational, comprehensive and positive.Whenever practical, alternative options and techniques should be mentioned. Overall, articles must remain generic in nature. Therefore, manuscripts cannot promote particular products, procedures or people. Instead, press releases, new products, industry profiles, news items, etc., will be considered for inclusion within courtesy sections: Essentials, or Pulse depending on space availability and other editorial criteria.

Furthermore, articles must not be slanted against a particular segment of the trade. Support your hypothesis based on documented facts about your subject; theory must be able to stand on its own merits, without referring negatively to other industry services, procedures or products. Please include research and other reference materials that support your claim.

Topics/Length: How-to, body therapy, diet, nutrition, spa, equipment, medical procedures, make-up and business articles should be approximately 1,500-2,000 words. Feature stories are usually between 1,800-2,500 words. Stories that are more than 2,500 may be printed in part and run in concurrent issues of the magazine.

Acceptance Policy: No simultaneous submissions, please. Reprints are rarely accepted.

All articles should be submitted in electronic form, whenever possible (MS Word), as well as a hard copy. (The hard copy will only serve as a backup, in case we are unable to read the electronic version.) The hard copy should be typed with 1" margins, double-spaced on single side of paper.

Artwork: Articles should include quality photographs or recommendations for photos, graphics, charts or other illustrations that would enhance the article. Electronic images (jpg or tiff) are preferred, but transparencies, slides, or glossy prints (no smaller than 3.5x5) may be acceptable.

Photo credits, model releases, and identification of subjects or techniques shown in photos are required. Side bars are a plus. Photos will not be returned, therefore we ask that you do NOT send Original artwork.

Authors are requested to supply their biographies, limited to a maximum of 80 words. A professional color headshot is also needed to accompany the bio. Photos will not be returned, therefore we ask that you do NOT send Original artwork.

DERMASCOPE acquires all rights and a signed release form is required. We publish manuscripts on an average of four to six months after acceptance and reserve the right to final edit all materials, kill an article or reschedule its publication date.

Categories: Nonfiction—Health—Aesthetics

CONTACT: Editorial Department
Material: All
2611 N. Belt Line Rd., Ste. 101
Sunnyvale TX 75182
Phone: 972-226-2309
Fax: 972-226-2339
E-mail: saundra@dermascope.com
Website: www.dermascope.com

Desktop Engineering

Desktop Engineering is for design and mechanical engineers who use and specify the purchase of computer hardware and software for the design for manufacture/process industries. DE covers all computer platforms, operating systems, applications software, and peripherals. DE clarifies technologies, explains operational theories and practices, and offers hands-on reports of how hardware and software affects engineers.

DE's readers are well educated and technically knowledgeable. They are interested in comprehensive technical and scientific information on new and existing technologies and products so that they can make informed business and technological decisions. They are not computer geeks, but they are computer savvy. They are engineers.

Write an Outline

Before you write an article for DE, please submit a complete outline. E-mail inquiries are acceptable. Please supply your daytime phone number. An outline includes a working title, a paragraph or two summarizing the article's major points, a paragraph outlining the major graphical elements that will accompany your article, and a short biography detailing your qualifications to write on the subject matter.

If your idea is accepted, an editor will work with you on all other details, such as deadline and length.

Unacceptable and unsolicited manuscripts will be returned if accompanied by a self-addressed envelope with sufficient first-class postage.

What to Write

DE offers various types of articles, including focus topics, resource guides, features, application stories, and product reviews.

Focus topics, feature articles, and cover stories are in-depth discussions of leading-edge computer technologies. These articles range in size from 1,200 to 1,600 words.

Application stories and product reviews range in size from 900 to 1,200 words. Here, you test drive products and provide readers with a hands-on report.

Things to Remember

No matter what type of article you write, support and enhance your article visually. Visual information can include screen shots, photos, schematics, tables, charts, checklists, time lines, reading lists, and program code. The exact mix will depend on your particular article. Your article also must be original, noncommercial, unpublished elsewhere, and not under consideration by another publication. All articles are subject to editing and significant rewrites. DE is not responsible for lost manuscripts, disks, or artwork.

Ethics Matter

DE will arrange to have products shipped to you. Never request a product from a company or accept one if offered. Please disclose any and all professional ties, grudges, or investments relating to companies or products you cover.

Submission Guidelines

Articles should be submitted via e-mail as Word attachments preferably saved in RTF or Text only format. Attach illustrations as well. Captions can be a separate attachment or be written at the end of the text of the article.

Print out all text and illustrations at the highest quality possible. Number illustrations sequentially and reference them in the text. Provide captions for all illustrations. Captions should not repeat the main text. Identify all printouts with your name and article title.

Reference sidebars, book lists, program code, and other textual elements in text by item title. Such elements should appear sequentially after the main text.

Submit graphics on disk, as color glossies or as slides (in that order of preference). Electronic files should be TIFF, JPG, or EPS (resolution must be 300+ dpi). Only use a common utility such as StuffIt or PKZip to compress graphics files. Please call about any images that must be sent on a CD-ROM, ZIP disk, or on another medium.

Acceptance & Payment

DE pays for articles upon publication. In most cases, all article rights revert to DE.

Categories: Nonfiction—Computers—Engineering—Trade—Design Engineering

CONTACT: Dennis Barker, Editor-in-Chief
Material: All
CONTACT: Jennifer Runyon, Managing Editor
Material: All
Helmers Publishing
174 Concord St, PO Box 874
Peterborough NH 03458
Phone: 603-924-9631
Fax: 603-924-4004
E-mail: DE-Editors@helmers.com

Development Director's Letter
Practical Advise for the Nonprofit Manager

We seek practical tips for nonprofit managers, particularly tips designed for fundraisers and executive directors. Typical areas of interest include: campaigns, direct mail, technology, proposal writing, public relations, Washington Watch and book reviews.

Articles are generally 500-800 words in length. We prefer articles based on interviews and which include a significant number of quotes.

Categories: Fundraising—Nonprofit Organizations

CONTACT: Lynn O'Connell, Editor
Material: All
4848 Virginia St.
Alexandria, VA 22312
Phone: 703-867-4942
Website: www.cdpublications.com/pubs/
developmentdirector.php

Devo'Zine

The daily meditations in Devo'Zine are written by real people — like you! These meditations are 250 words in length or less and are grouped according to weekly themes. Be sure to mention which theme you are writing for, and send your meditation to us by e-mail, Fax, US Mail, or submit it online.

WHAT IS THE PURPOSE?

Our purpose is to help youth develop a lifelong practice of prayer and spiritual reflection. Devo'Zine is designed to help readers grow in their faith and explore the relevancy of the Christian faith for the issues they face. Undergirded by scripture, Devo'Zine will aid youth in their prayer life, introduce them to spiritual disciplines, help them shape their concept of God, and encourage them in the life of discipleship.

WHAT IS Devo'Zine?

A bimonthly, 64-page magazine for youth
Written by youth and adults who care about them
Each issue focuses on nine themes.

Each theme includes weekday readings and weekend features, enough for two months.

Meditations may be read in chronological or random order.

Themes may be expressed through scripture, prose, poetry, prayers, stories, songs, art, or photographs.

Readers and writers include persons of many different denominations and cultures.

WHO WILL ENJOY IT?

Youth ages 12-18 who seek personal devotional readings
Youth groups who seek devotional reflections
Adults who seek to understand youth spirituality

HOW DO I WRITE FOR THE PUBLICATION?

Daily meditations should be 150-250 words long.

Poetry and prayers should be short to moderate in length — 10 to 20 lines.

Think about the purpose of the meditation — what do you want it to evoke in the reader?

Style notes: Simply written (preferably in youth language), realistic and relevant to life experiences of youth, does not need to be overtly religious but should help to open youth to the life of faith that we all seek, inclusive of multicultural experiences

Language guidelines: Try to use language that is non-sexist and inclusive of everyone (examples are words such as *humankind, persons,* or *everyone* instead of *mankind* or *men* in the familiar generic sense). We encourage the use of a wide range of biblical images for God.

May include scripture verse or suggested text (state version of Bible used)

May include a reflective element: brief prayers, quotes, reflection or journaling questions, action ideas, or other items. Prayers should use honest, straightforward, conversational language.

WHAT ARE SOME TIPS FOR DEVOTIONAL WRITING?

Devotional writing should invite people to come closer to God.

Devotional writing should tell about real experiences of real people who are struggling to apply their faith to daily life.

Devotional writing should express only one main idea. It should leave one memorable image with the reader.

Devotional writing should lead persons into further conversation with God after they finish reading the meditation.

Your journal can be a great source of devotional writing because your journal records your real thoughts about your experiences.

HOW DO I PREPARE MY MEDITATION?

Typed or handwritten, doubled-spaced on 8 1/2" x 11" paper/or on email

If the meditation is mailed in, it needs to be accompanied by a self-addressed, stamped envelope for return. We cannot acknowledge or return meditations submitted without an SASE, so please keep a copy of what you submit.

HOW WILL I KNOW IF MY MEDITATION IS ACCEPTED?

If we choose to use your meditation, we will notify you before publication. Otherwise, you will not hear from us unless you send an SASE.

We pay $25 for weekday meditations. Payment will be made at the time of acceptance.

HOW CAN I FIND OUT ABOUT UPCOMING THEMES?

Check out our upcoming themes — or send us an SASE to receive themes for upcoming issues.

WHAT OTHER INFORMATION DO I NEED TO INCLUDE?

Name, Age/Birthdate (if you are younger than 25), Mailing Address, Phone, Email, FAX

You may have noticed that *Devo'Zine's* format includes brief devotional meditations to be read on the weekdays and a longer, more in-depth article for Saturday/Sunday reading. We invite you to consider writing one of these longer articles. The *Devo'Zine* staff assigns these articles; so if you'd like to write one, please contact us about what you'd like to write. We may have already assigned this particular article, so we don't want you to write an article for us that we can't publish. Contact us with your idea by mail or email. (See the last section of this document for addresses.) Give us as much notice as you can.

WHAT IS THE PURPOSE?

Our purpose is to help youth develop a lifetime pattern of prayer and spiritual reflection. *Devo'Zine* is designed to help readers grow in their faith and explore the relevancy of the Christian faith for the issues they face. Undergirded by scripture, it will aid youth in their prayer life, introduce them to spiritual disciplines, help them shape their concept of God, and encourage them in the life of discipleship.

WHAT IS *Devo'Zine*?

A bimonthly, 64-page magazine for youth

Written by youth and adults who care about them

Each issue focuses on nine themes

Each theme includes weekday readings and weekend features

Meditations may be read in chronological or random order

Themes may be expressed through scripture, prose, poetry, prayers, stories, songs, art, or photographs

Readers and writers include persons of many different denominations and cultures

WHO WILL ENJOY IT?

Youth ages 12-18 who seek personal devotional readings

Youth groups who seek devotional reflections

HOW SHOULD I WRITE?

Weekend feature articles should be 350-500 words long and should be related to the theme for the week — with a "twist."

Think about ideas for graphics and suggest them to the editor.

As you write, think about what you can do to give the feature a reflective element — the Next Day Stretch for the Sunday reading. You may want to use a question or questions, a suggestion for action, tips for ongoing practice of spiritual disciplines, a directed or open-ended prayer, or a suggestion for journaling or starting a journal.

Format. Try not to have long blocks of copy. Make your article invitational and reader-friendly. Use subtitles to break up copy; use sidebars; or use bulleted lists.

Language guidelines. We seek to use language that is non-sexist and inclusive of everyone (examples: *humankind, persons, everyone,* instead of *mankind, men* in the familiar generic sense). We encourage the use of a wide range of biblical images of God.

Payment is $100. Please include your legal name, name as you wish it to appear on article, address and email address, and a short bio (youth-friendly, please!).

MAIL, FAX, OR E-MAIL MANUSCRIPTS TO THE ADDRESS BELOW:

Categories: Arts—Christian Interests—Inspirational—Photography—Poetry—Religion—Spiritual

CONTACT: Sandy Miller, Managing Editor
Material: All
1908 Grand Avenue   PO Box 340004
Nashville TN 37203-0004
FAX: 615-340-1783
E-mail: devozine@upperroom.org
Website: www.upperroom.org/devozine

Diabetes Health

Diabetes Health Writer's Guidelines

Diabetes Health provides patients, educators and healthcare professionals with practical advice and the latest information on new methods, technologies and research related to diabetes.

Diabetes Health accepts solicited submissions from contributing writers for feature-length stories. Our feature stories run at a maximum of 1,500 words. Features should have at least three to five outside sources.

We also accept shorter opinion pieces, columns (500 words each) and letters to the editor.

We are not responsible for returning unsolicited content or photos.

All content should be balanced, informative, lively, timely, concise and easy to read for a lay audience.

Diabetes Health does not accept manuscripts that promote a product, philosophy or personal view. When discussing products or treatment techniques, you should include experiences of a person with diabetes. Never make sweeping generalizations that cannot be supported by published research or highly credible sources.

All manuscripts should be sent as a Word file. Do not fax or mail manuscripts. Do not copy and paste manuscript into the body of an email.

All manuscripts will be edited for style, length and substance.

Upon receiving a manuscript, we will either query you for additional information or, if the material is unacceptable, return the manuscript with rewrite instructions.

Payment varies with experience and is based on the final length as it appears in the magazine.

All submissions are **"on spec" only**.

We encourage writers to submit photographs or other art that will help illustrate the story.

Categories: Nonfiction—Health—Diabetes

CONTACT: Daniel Trecroci
Phone: 415-258-2828 x 108

Diabetes Self-Management

Diabetes Self-Management is written for the growing number of people with diabetes who want to know more about controlling and managing their diabetes. Our readers need up-to-date and authoritative information on nutrition, pharmacology, exercise, medical advances, self-help, and a host of other how-to subjects. We address the day-to-day and long-term concerns of our readers in a positive and upbeat manner and enable them to make informed choices about managing their diabetes.

The rule of thumb for any article we publish is that it must be clear, concise, interesting, useful, and instructive, and must have immediate application to the day-to-day life of our readers. For that reason, we do not publish personal experiences, personality profiles, exposés, or research breakthroughs.

Our audience ranges from the newly diagnosed diabetic—who has little knowledge of diabetes—to people who have been intimately involved in their own treatment for many years and often know more about diabetes than well-informed health writers. We do not assume knowledge of our audience, but we do assume intelligence and are careful not to write down to our readers.

Most articles range between 1,500 and 2,500 words. We do not accept previously published material. While we buy all rights, we are extremely generous regarding permission to republish. Articles are published with bylines and payment is made on publication. Payment rates vary depending on the quality of the material and the skill and effort required of the writer. Kill fees are 20%.

Tips

Use plain English; avoid medical jargon, but where appropriate for understanding, explain technical terms in simple, easily understood language. Writing style should be simple, upbeat, and leavened with tasteful humor where possible. Information should be accurate, up-to-date, and from reliable sources. References from lay publications are not acceptable.

Tables, charts, drawings, and sidebars are particularly useful when they are concise, illustrative, and help explain the text. Photographs are generally not accepted. Authors are required to include with their article a list of suggested reading to be published as a sidebar to the article.

Query with a one-page rationale and outline, and include writing samples. Reports will be made within six weeks. If your query is accepted, expect heavy editorial supervision.

Categories: Diet/Nutrition—Health

CONTACT: James Hazlett, Editor
Material: Any
CONTACT: Ingrid Strauch, Managing Editor
Material: Any
150 W. 22nd St.
New York NY 10011
Phone: 212-989-0200
Fax: 212-989-4786

Dialogue

Blindskills, Inc. welcomes the submission of freelance material for possible publication. The best way to get an idea of the kind of material we publish is to request a sample copy of *Dialogue* and review it. Sample copies are available at no charge in large print, four-track cassette, braille, or via e-mail. If the sample is requested by a fully sighted author, we will charge $5 to cover the cost of shipping and handling. Samples sent to blind and visually impaired individuals are shipped via the Free Matter for the Blind designation.

Current Needs: Personality profiles of interest to newly blind and other visually impaired people, examples of career, education and leisure experiences, and descriptions of technological solutions, coping strategies and helpful resources.

Material that is religious, controversial, political, or that contains explicit descriptions of sex is not accepted.

Payments: Since *Dialogue* is entirely dependent upon public contributions for its support, payment is modest. We think we offer an unusual opportunity for beginning writers. We send an explanatory letter along with each returned manuscript. Writers whose articles are published in *Dialogue* receive a complimentary large print copy. Payment for articles will be made at the rate of $15 to $35. All payments for articles used in an issue are made after all formats of *Dialogue* have been shipped to our readers.

Policies: 1) No simultaneous submissions to other publications are permitted while being considered by Blindskills, Inc.

2) We reserve the right to do minor editing.

3) Manuscripts must be the original and unpublished work of the writer.

4) Authors who are legally blind are given priority. Exceptions are sometimes made when topics are judged to be of reader interest.

Rights: We purchase all First North American Serial Rights (FNASR) including first electronic rights and nonexclusive archival rights.

Reprints: For reprint permission, contact Blindskills, Inc. in writing and state the following:

Name of Publication:
Publisher:
Address:
Telephone:
E-mail:
Date of Publication:
Formats of Publication:

If possible, send a print copy of the publication in which the article is reprinted to Blindskills, Inc. The following statement is required to appear at the end of a reprinted article from *Dialogue*. Include the issue date in which the article appeared. "The above article was first published in *Dialogue*, Summer 2004. *Dialogue* is published by Blindskills, Inc., P.O. Box 5181, Salem, OR 97304-0181; Phone: 800-860-4224; E-mail: info@blindskills.com; Web site: www.blindskills.com. For a free sample copy of *Dialogue* or information about other publications offered by Blindskills, Inc. contact the office directly."

Deadlines: For publication in the January-February issue, material must be received by November 1; for the March-April issue by January 1; for the May-June issue by March 1; for the July-August issue by May 1; for the September-October issue by July 1; and for the November-December issue by September 1.

Specific Guidelines: Nonfiction: Although the freelance portion of any issue is generally representative of the kind of material we are buying, freelance articles on subjects now being staff-written are always welcome. Currently, we are especially interested in first-person accounts of career or education experiences, travel experiences, stories about participation in sports, information on new high-tech and low-tech products useful to people who are visually impaired, features on seniors and veterans who have experienced vision loss, articles about the concerns of parents raising children with vision impairments or blind parents raising children, and descriptions of feelings and coping methods of people who are currently losing vision or who are blind.

Manuscripts: While we accept unsolicited manuscripts, we prefer e-mail queries. Both queries and manuscripts may be e-mailed. Include your last name and the query topic or the first three or four words of the article title in the subject line. In the body of the message, please also indicate for which column you think your proposed article is best suited. All text must be placed in the body of the message—absolutely no attachments, please. You may e-mail queries and manuscripts to magazine@blindskills.com .

Please accompany manuscripts with a cover letter that includes your mailing address, e-mail address, and telephone number. Manuscripts in printed form are acceptable. Blindskills, Inc. cannot be responsible for manuscripts lost in the mail. Writers are therefore advised to retain a copy of each submission.

Length: Articles of 200, 500, and from 800 to 1,000 words are preferred. Articles of more than 1,000 words are rarely used. We do occasionally run longer articles if the importance of the topic or nature of the material warrants.

Notification of Receipt: We acknowledge receipt of material by e-mail or postcard. Only submissions accompanied by a self-addressed stamped envelope bearing sufficient postage will be returned upon rejection.

Time Needed For Reply: At least one month.

Where To Send Freelance Material: Send all queries and manuscripts to magazine@blindskills.com.

Categories: Nonfiction—Careers—Computers—Consumer—Disabilities—Family—Hobbies—Recreation—Self-Help—Senior Citizen—Sports/Recreation

CONTACT: Carol M. McCarl, Executive Director
Material: All
Blindskills, Inc.
PO Box 5181
Salem OR 97304-0181
Phone: 800-860-4224
Fax: 503-581-0178
E-mail: info@blindskills.com
Website: www.blindskills.com

The Diamond Registry Bulletin

Formal guidelines not available. Please read a number of issues to ascertain the publication's style and needs.

Send queries to address below.

Categories: Nonfiction—Fashion—Marriage—Trade—Diamonds and Jewelry

CONTACT: Submissions Editor
Materials: All
580 Fifth Ave.
New York NY 10036
Phone: 212-575-0445
Fax: 212-575-0722
E-mail: diamond@58@aol.com
Website: www.diamondregistry.com

DIG™

DIG™ focuses on archaeology—recent discoveries, techniques used in the field and in the laboratory, archaeologists past and present, innovative "dig" programs for our age audience (8- to 14-year olds), rethinking of popular theories, and creative activities that entertain as well as inform. Accuracy is essential. Writers are encouraged to study recent back issues for content and style. (Sample issues are available at $5.95 plus $2.00 shipping and handling. Send 10" x 13" self-addressed envelope.)

Illustrators, please click on Illustrators Guidelines on our website.

Procedure

In order for your idea to be considered, a query must accompany each individual idea (however, you can mail them all together) and must include the following:

• a brief cover letter stating the subject and word length of the proposed article,

• a detailed one-page outline explaining the information to be presented in the article,

• an extensive bibliography of materials the author intends to use in preparing the article,

• a self-addressed stamped envelope.

Authors are urged to use primary resources and up-to-date scholarly resources in their bibliography. Writers new to DIG™ should send a writing sample with the query. If you would like to know if your query has been received, please also include a stamped postcard that requests acknowledgment of receipt. In all correspondence, please include your complete address as well as a telephone number where you can be reached.

A writer may send as many queries for one issue as he or she wishes, but each query must have a separate cover letter, outline, bibliography, and self-addressed stamped envelope. All queries must be typed.

Articles must be submitted on disk using a word processing program (preferably Microsoft Word MAC). Text should be saved as ASCII text (in MS Word as "text only.") Disks should be either MAC (preferred) or DOS compatible 3½".

Guidelines

Feature Articles: 700-800 words. Includes: in-depth nonfiction, plays, and biographies

Supplemental Nonfiction: 300-600 words. Includes: subjects directly and indirectly related to the theme. Editors like little-known information but encourage writers not to overlook the obvious.

Fiction: up to 800 words. Includes: authentic historical and biographical fiction, adventure, retold legends, relating to the theme.

The above three pay 20 to 25 cents per printed word.

Activities: up to 700 words. Includes: crafts, recipes, woodworking, or any other interesting projects that can be done either by children alone or with adult supervision. Sketches and description of how activity relates to theme should accompany queries.

Poetry: up to 100 lines. Clear, objective imagery. Serious and light verse considered. Must relate to theme.

Puzzles and Games: (please, no word finds). Crossword and other word puzzles using the vocabulary of the issue's theme. Mazes and picture puzzles that relate to the theme.

The above three pay on an individual basis.

Photo Guidelines

To be considered for publication, photographs must relate to a specific theme. Writers are encouraged to submit available photos with their query or article. We buy one-time use.

Our suggested fee range for professional quality photographs* follows:

b/w - ¼ page to full page - $15 to $100

color - ¼ page to full page - $25 to $100

* Please note that fees for non-professional quality photographs are negotiated.

Cover fees are set on an individual basis for one-time use, plus promotional use. All cover images are color.

Prices set by museums, societies, stock photography houses, etc., are paid or negotiated. Photographs that are promotional in nature (e.g., from tourist agencies, organizations, special events, etc.) are usually submitted at no charge.

If you have photographs pertaining to any upcoming theme, please contact the editor by mail or fax, or send them with your query. You may also send images on speculation.

Note

• Queries may be submitted at any time, but queries sent well in advance of deadline MAY NOT BE ANSWERED FOR SEVERAL MONTHS. Go-aheads requesting material proposed in queries are usually sent five months prior to publication date. Unused queries will be returned approximately three to four months prior to publication date. **Hard copy queries ONLY, no email.**

Categories: Nonfiction—Archaeology

CONTACT: Editorial Department
Cobblestone Publishing
Attn: Rosalie Baker
30 Grove St Ste C
Peterborough NH 03458

Digger Magazine
Farwest Magazine

Publications

Digger Magazine—published monthly, including the triple-size *Digger: Farwest Edition* produced in August for our annual Farwest Show trade show—is a trade publication produced by the Oregon Association of Nurseries. that serves the Northwest's nursery and greenhouse industry. Our circulation averages 6,700 monthly, 13,500 in August. Two-thirds of our readers are in the Northwest, and we have a growing national readership as well.

Mission Statement:

Digger is an Oregon Association of Nurseries-produced monthly publication designed to improve the quality and viability of Oregon's nursery industry. Editorial content and supporting advertisements supply OAN-member nursery and greenhouse growers and retail operations with timely and critical information on market trends, production methods and business management practices, as well as providing coverage of state and federal industry-related activities and other news affecting Oregon's nursery indsutry.

Magazine Sections. The magazines are divided into these sections:

• Feature articles. Usually two features of varying lengths are used each month. Articles are staff- or freelance-written. Most of our freelance needs are for feature-length articles.

• Continuing departments: Northwest News, Events, Calendar, Around the State, New Members and National News.

• Continuing columns by our executive director and president, a retail-related column called What I'm Hearing by Mike Darcy, 10-Minute Marketing by Miles McCoy and legal and business advice pieces.

• *Farwest Magazine* only: Farwest Show information, including exhibitors listings, seminars information, Portland and Northwest attractions, in addition to several more meaty feature articles to fill the triple-size issue.

Editorial Focus

Because we are an association title, our editorial—features and news items—mostly centers on our members (primarily those in the Northwest), their companies, products or information that can benefit them in keeping with our purpose. Topics may include:

• New plants and cultivars.

• Industry trends. What do business and consumer markets demand now and in the future.

• Regulatory and legislative aspects. What regulations are upcoming, how regulations or legislation affect Oregon or Northwest nursery operators.

• Resource management. What demands are placed on resources (water, media, by-products, etc.) and how they are changing.

• Pests, disease and their management (specific pests, pesticide use, safety and IPM).

• Research. How we can apply horticultural research to practical use.

• Business skills. How the industry can improve its marketing, management, etc.

Editorial Calendar. Contact the editor for a list of topics for general or thematic issues. Our planned calendar is subject to change, however, as topics and space warrant.

Freelance Submissions.

Contact the editor in advance of all submissions, for story ideas or for an assignment before you proceed. As a general rule, we do not buy unsolicited articles (manuscripts and related visuals). We are not responsible for unsolicited articles and related visuals. By visuals we generally mean photos, illustrations, graphs, charts, etc.

Acceptance. Articles accepted for publication are determined by the editor. We are under no obligation to publish an article and related visuals, either unsolicited or purchased.

Usually, an agreement form will be provided by the editor to sig-nal a commitment with an author for an article, news item or visual. We expect the author to fully honor the agreement. Conditions as stipulated are subject to change upon mutual agreement.

Upon acceptance of the topic and/or agreement form, the author shall provide Social Security number, address and telephone and fax numbers for our recordkeeping.

Credit. Author will be credited with by-line credit for feature articles, source credit for shorter pieces. Supplied visuals will be credited as to their source.

Deadlines. All articles and related visuals must be submitted at least by the first of the month in advance of the targeted issue. For features, we prefer submissions six weeks in advance of the scheduled run.

Length. Features generally run 1,000-2,000 words.

Articles format. We require articles to be submitted in the following formats (listed in order of preference):

• Microsoft Word or text file attached to e-mail sent to editor. Also include story in e-mail body text as a backup. Fax hard copy of article to editor, also as a backup.

• On CD a word-processing application (Microsoft Word desired) or ASCII text, and Macintosh (desired), Windows or DOS operating systems.

• An original hard copyi s required in all cases as a back-up. Mail or fax to the editor.

Visuals format. Visual elements include charts, tables and graphs, illustrations and photography. They should be submitted by e-mail as PDFs. Faxed visuals are meant to be an example only; an original must be delivered.

Faxed visuals are meant to be an example only; an original must be delivered.

• Computerized. Contact editor or graphic design coordinator for software compatibility of computer applications well in advance of submission deadline.

• Photography. Digital format is preferred. Photos should be raw digital images or a minimum of 300 resolution sized at least to 4-inch by 5-inch. TIFs or JPGs are preferred. No Web images (resolution is too small for print.) Prints or slides can be submitted when necessary. Prints should be 3x5 at a minimum.

• Permission. It is the responsibility of the author to secure any releases or other permission to use photographic images, logos, illustrations or other visual elements. Items will be returned to the author after publication upon request.

Visuals must include identification or description of subjects and products for cutlines.

Visuals should be mailed to the editor's attention in protective packaging.

Payment. Rate of pay ranges from $125 for shorter articles to $400 for special feature-length articles and related visuals to qualified freelancers. Compensation depends on the quality of the article (length, number of sources, complexity of subject, etc.) and is solely the judgment of the editor.

Payment generally will be made upon receipt and acceptance of the article and all related visuals. Allow two to three weeks for payment to arrive.

Certain expenses, such as film, film processing, and toll telephone calls, will be paid if agreed upon by editor and freelancer beforehand.

Rights: Upon acceptance, the Oregon Association of Nurseries will assume first North American rights to the article and related visuals. The article shall not be published in other relevant industry publications (local, regional or international) before or concurrent with publication in *Digger* or *Digger: Farwest Edition*, or the author forfeits compensation, unless prior agreement is reached. The author retains all copyrights. Most Digger features also appear on the OAN Web site and are archived.

Editing. We reserve the right to edit all manuscripts and visuals for space, style, grammar or content at the discretion of the editor. Manuscripts will be returned to author for major revisions.

Categories: Nonfiction—Agriculture—Trade—Nursery—Greenhouse—Horticulture

CONTACT: Cam Sivesind, Editor
Material: All
Oregon Association of Nurseries
29750 S.W. Town Center Loop W.
Wilsonville OR 97070
Phone: 503-682-5089
Fax: 503-682-5727
E-mail: csivesind@oan.org

DISCIPLESHIP JOURNAL

Discipleship Journal

Guidelines for Writers
Our Purpose
Discipleship Journal strives to help believers develop a deeper relationship with Jesus Christ, and to provide practical help in understanding the Scriptures and applying them to daily life and ministry.

Content
Most of the articles we publish fall into one of three categories:
• **Teaching on a Scripture passage**, such as a study of an Old Testament character or a short section of an epistle, explaining the meaning and showing, through illustrations and examples, how to apply it to daily life
• **Teaching on a topic**, such as what Scripture says about forgiveness or materialism
• **How-to**, such as tips on deepening your devotional life or witnessing in the workplace
We **do not** publish testimonies, devotionals, personal profiles, purely theological material, book reviews, poetry, fiction, news articles, or articles about Christian organizations.

Word Count
Articles generally run from 1,200 to 2,800 words. (The word count varies according to the complexity of the article's thesis.)

Topics
Though part of each issue is devoted to a theme topic, there is no need to coordinate your article with our theme topics. We are always looking for nontheme articles, which can touch on any aspect of living as a disciple of Christ. Recent issues have dealt with subjects such as rekindling passion for God, our focus in prayer, developing a gentle spirit, key dynamics for personal discipling, dealing with stress, and principles for reaching unbelieving friends.

We'd like to see more articles that (1) apply biblical principles to everyday issues or relationships, (2) help readers with personal ministry such as evangelism, follow-up, and discipling, (3) show how to develop a deeper relationship with Jesus, (4) focus on an aspect of God's character, or (5) show how to grow in an area of Christian character.

Our Readers
Be sure to consider our audience as you choose a topic and approach:
• Two thirds are women.* Median age is 47.
• Close to half lead a small-group Bible study or meet individually with younger Christians to help them grow.
• Most are professionals with at least some college education. However, they are not pastors or in full-time ministry.
• They describe themselves as maturing Christians rather than as new believers.
• Many consider busyness the greatest obstacle to their spiritual growth.
• Nearly all have regular personal devotions.

However, we are not a women's magazine. Make sure your approach and topic are appropriate for both men and women.

Keys for Successful Articles
• **Derive your main principles from a thorough study of Scripture.** You should include some personal experience, but this should not form the basis of your article.
• **Illustrate each principle.** Use analogies, examples, and illustrations to aid the reader.
• **Show how to put each principle into practice.** Show the reader what applying this principle would look like in everyday life.
• **Be vulnerable.** Show the reader that you have wrestled with the subject matter in your own life. Write from the perspective of a fellow pilgrim, not someone who has "arrived."

How to Submit a Query
Due to an increasing volume of submissions, we can no longer accept unsolicited manuscripts. Instead, send a query letter. Query letters should include
(1) the working title,
(2) a short statement of purpose or the article's thesis (be sure this includes a clear benefit to the reader),
(3) a tentative outline of your main points (include the scripture you will use and how you will incorporate your personal experience with the topic),
(4) some indication of the style and approach you plan to use,
(5) the prospective word count, and
(6) a short description of your qualifications to write the article.
• Before you submit a query, study several recent issues of Discipleship Journal. Look at the types of articles we publish, common writing styles, and the way our writers approach their topics. For samples, visit our archives at www.discipleshipjournal.com or mail a request (see below).
• Please include a self-addressed, stamped envelope (SASE) with all query letters. If possible, include one or two samples of your published work. Queries may also be submitted by email. We do not accept phone queries or simultaneous queries.
• Queries may be mailed or emailed to Sue Kline, Editor, at the address below.
• Response time is usually within four to six weeks. Feel free to drop us a note if you haven't heard from us after two months; some manuscripts do get lost in the mail. If you receive a positive response to your query, you will be invited to send your article on speculation.

If Your Query Is Accepted (do not send your manuscript unless invited to do so)
• All articles should be typed, double-spaced, on one side of the paper only. On the first page, type your name, address, phone number, and email address in the upper left corner. At top right, indicate an approximate word count and rights offered (first or reprint). Please use page numbers.
• We prefer Bible quotes from the New International Version. If quoting from a version other than the NIV, indicate which version is being quoted with each reference.
• Again, response time is four to six weeks. Articles will not be returned unless requested (include a SASE with appropriate postage).

Payment
Payment is made upon acceptance. The current rate is 25 cents per word for first rights plus an additional 10 percent for limited electronic rights.

Reprints
Reprints from noncompeting publications are acceptable but must be queried in the same form as other articles. In your query letter, indicate the publication in which the article originally appeared and the date of publication. Reprints are paid at five cents per word.

Samples
To obtain a sample copy of *Discipleship Journal*, send a manila envelope with $2.64 in postage to the address below.

Department Guidelines
Separate guidelines are available for the DJ Plus department. To request these guidelines, send a SASE to the address below, or download them from www.discipleshipjournal.com.

Categories: Nonfiction—Christian Interests—Inspirational—Religion—Spiritual

CONTACT: Sue Kline, Editor
Material: All
PO Box 35004
Colorado Springs CO 80935
E-mail: dj.writers@naupress.com
Web site: www.discipleshipjournal.com

Discover

If you are interested in writing for *Discover*, we encourage you to submit a focused article proposal. While we do not issue formal guidelines to prospective writers, we suggest that you look carefully at the style and content of articles in *Discover* and shape your story proposal accordingly. Include samples of your previously published work and a brief biography. We do not accept proposals for our R&D (news) section. Feature proposals should be sent to the attention of Submissions Editor, *Discover*, 114 Fifth Ave., 15th floor, New York, NY 10011. Due to the large volume of mail we receive, please allow six to eight weeks for a response.

Please note that we do not accept e-mail proposals.
Categories: Nonfiction—Health—Science—Medicine

CONTACT: Submissions Editor
Material: Feature Proposals
114 Fifth Ave., 15th floor
New York NY 10011
Website: www.discover.com

Diver

DIVER Magazine (ISSN 0706-5132) is published nine times a year by Seagraphic Publications Ltd. It is Canada's Premier *Diving Magazine. Subject matter includes the following:*

- Travel Adventures
- Canadian Diving
- U/W Photography
- Equipment Reviews
- Dive Boat Reviews
- Wreck Diving
- Marine Life
- Technical Diving

EDITORIAL GUIDELINES

In order to have a manuscript considered for publication it must be submitted as follows:

Subject Preferences: Well written and illustrated Canadian and North American regional dive destination articles. Travel features should be brief and accompanied by a sleeve or more of outstanding original slides and/or prints and a map. Most travel articles are committed up to a year in advance and there is limited scope for new material.

Submission: Copy should be on disc-PC or Mac in MS Word, with a hard copy. Copy should be concise and clear; other materials enclosed should be marked for easy identification and reference. Only complete articles as described with illustrations will be considered. Package only one completed article per submission.

Length: Between 500 and 1000 words. Shorter pieces are welcome.

Illustrations: Original slides, 5"x7" colour prints, glossy 5"x7" black and white prints, maps, drawings, digital images at 300 dpi or greater. Each item should be labelled with name, address and description. Cap-

tions and credits on separate sheet must be numbered to match. Photos by other than writer of article must be clearly indicated on each picture. (Payment made only to author or submitter.)

Return Envelope: Please enclose a self-addressed stamped envelope if you wish your manuscript returned. International Reply Coupons accepted. DIVER Magazine assumes no responsibility for loss or damage of unsolicited manuscripts or photographs.

Scheduling: Unsolicited travel articles will be viewed only from July through August for possible use in the following year (eight issues). Material sent prior to that period is subject to being unopened until then or returned. Photos only may be submitted after ascertaining what features are planned for the upcoming year. Photos will be considered only if approved manuscripts are not adequately supported by illustrations.

Acknowledgment: We will acknowledge receipt of articles or return immediately if not suitable. Acknowledgement does not mean acceptance. We may hold material for up to 90 days before deciding (except travel articles see "Scheduling" above).

Payment: Payment to author for text and photos will be made by cheque six to eight weeks after the date of publication. Rights purchased are First North American. Any story may be archived on our website unless its exemption is requested in writing. Rates are $2.50 per column inch text, $25 for images. Cover shots $300.

Categories: Nonfiction—Outdoors—Recreation—Regional—Sports/Recreation

CONTACT: Peter Golding
Material: All
Seagraphic Publications Ltd
241 E 1st St
North Vancouver BC V7L 1B4 Canada
Phone: 604-988-0711
Fax: 604-988-0747
E-mail: editor@divermag.com
Website: www.divermag.com

Dog & Kennel Magazine

Dog & Kennel is your source for entertaining, informative and authoritative information about dogs.

Photography and Editorial Guidelines

Dog & Kennel, Cats & Kittens and *Bird Times* are published bimonthly. These magazines contain beautiful full-color photographs, informative, authoritative and educational articles about the species and their care. The articles are written to educate and entertain the readers. In addition to articles on popular species, we include human-interest stories. The magazines contain columns dealing with training, questions and answers, grief, horoscopes, snips of information from the Internet, art and collectibles and special reports.

Photo Needs

Color photography of publication quality is required. Slides or transparencies are preferable.

We are always looking for photographs of common pet birds such as cockatiels, parakeets, lovebirds, canaries, finches, doves and pigeons, and softbills—plus other exotics such as Amazons, cockatoos and macaws. Natural or colored portraiture type backgrounds are acceptable. Interactive people-bird shots are needed. In addition to portrait-type shots, we have an ongoing need for attractive photos of birds in household situations—in their cage, on a playpen, eating, bathing, etc. as well as clutches and baby birds in all stages of growth.

Photographs of all breeds of purebred dogs, random bred dogs and rare breeds in all life stages of growth from puppy through veteran years. Photographs are needed of dogs performing tasks for which they were bred, engaging in sports with their owners or sports developed specifically for dogs such flyball, interactive people-dog shots, portrait-type shots, attractive shots in all types of situations. Photos may be of dogs alone, with kids, adults and other dogs and animals.

Photographs of all breeds of cats, pedigreed as well as non-pedigreed in all life stages of growth from kitten through veteran years. Photographs are needed of cats in all types of situations. Photos may be of cats alone, with kids, adults and other cats and animals.

All material should be labeled with the breed of dog, cat or bird, the telephone number, name and address of the photographer. Note: photographer is responsible for correctly identifying the breeds/species of dogs, cats or birds in the photos. Photographs identified incorrectly in print due to photographers error cannot be paid.

We prefer to hold submissions on file for at least three months. Slides and transparencies intended for future consideration will be scanned to a CD-ROM and photographers' material will be returned.

Payment

Payment is upon publication. Fee for inside usage/partial page is $25; for inside usage/full page, $50; for cover usage, $150.

Freelance Editorial Submissions

Submissions for consideration may cover all aspects of dogs, cats and birds including breed/species profiles, breeder-kennel profiles, medical-technical articles, training, humorist, stories of pet dogs, cats and birds that go to work with their owners, heroic tales, etc.

The compensation structure is 10 cents a word on the final edited published word count, payable upon publication of the article. Short articles are defined as 500 to 1,000 words, and features are defined as 1,200 to 2,000 words.

Upon acceptance of your article, you will be sent a contract for permission to publish.

Categories: Animals

CONTACT: Rita Davis, Executive Editor
7-L Dundas Circle
Greensboro NC 27407
Website: www.dogandkennel.com

Dog Gone Newsletter

EDITORIAL GUIDELINES

Dog Gone Newsletter is a 16-page printed, bimonthly publication about fun places to go and cool stuff to do with your dog. The editorial focus is split between travel pieces and activity articles, as well as regular columns. Dog-friendly vacation spots, resorts, hotels, campgrounds, beaches, hiking trails, dining and shopping establishments, weekend getaways, and festivals or events are profiled. Also highlighted are fun activities, such as: flyball, jogging, walking or skiing with your dog, lure coursing and obedience trials. In short, it's a travel and activity newsletter for dog owners - Travel & Leisure for our four-legged pals.

Dog Gone Newsletter readers range in age from young singles to families to retired folks. All are dog owners and their pooches range from the most highly prized pedigree to those of questionable ancestry. *Dog Gone Newsletter* readers are typically active folks who like to travel and never leave home without the dog. Many are outdoor types who enjoy hiking, camping, roller-blading, skiing, and other activities. Some subscribers are physically impaired and thus enjoy those activities that are conducive to their limitations. Some readers prefer luxury accommodations, while others are looking for moderate or budget lodgings. Some simply like to camp or stay in their RV.

What We're Looking For: *Dog Gone Newsletter* is looking for lively, entertaining, intelligently, and creatively written articles on travel and dog-friendly activities. A sampling of travel features includes resort destinations, B&Bs, camping, and air-travel tips - all written from a dog angle.

Activities features can be dog sports or people activities to enjoy with your best pal.

For travel pieces, resorts and inns which are especially dog-friendly (perhaps even offering a "Pampered Pooch Package") warrant a profile. Other accommodations that welcome dogs can be incorporated into a theme article (i.e. fall foliage destinations, ski resorts, or suite hotels).

For destination articles (such as "Boston With Terrier" or "Viszlas in Vegas"), it is important to find fun activities in the area for owners to take their dogs, such as nearby parks, hiking trails, pet-friendly tourist attractions, yearly festivals that allow dogs, gardens or zoos that permit pets, and transportation services that accommodate dogs. Our readers aren't bringing their dogs on vacation just to leave them in a hotel room! Destination features should include lodging recommendations that allow any size of dog. Contact phone numbers and addresses should be included, along with rates, number of dogs permitted in rooms, pet fees or deposits, and any pet restrictions.

Combination travel/activity articles include themes such as "dogs-allowed" beaches, hiking trails, skiing trails, etc.

Transportation articles could include international travel documentation requirements, railroads that permit pets, rating the airlines on their treatment of pet passengers, sailboat or houseboat travel with your dog, and the like.

Activity features will introduce readers to new hobbies to enjoy with their pooches. Dog-related sports, such as agility, field trials, skijoring, obedience trials, and pet therapy are possibilities, as are including your dog in your spare-time activities, such as backpacking, rock-hounding, cross-country skiing or bird-watching.

Short submissions are accepted for
***Dog Gone Newsletter's* regular departments:**
• "Beyond Fetch (offering creative suggestions for games to play with your pooch)
• "Roving Rv'er (profiling pet-friendly campground resorts)
• "Road Trip" (featuring dog-allowed national, state, regional, or local parks, forests and recreations areas)
• "Dining With Dogs" (restaurants for dogs or that allow dogs.
Photos are required for most submissions.

Style: Upbeat, humorous and/or easy-to-read articles are the main criteria for *Dog Gone Newsletter*'s style. AP style is loosely adhered to; however, we prefer articles to sound colloquial. Therefore, a sentence does not necessarily have to be "complete" in a conversational style article. Because there are so many freelance writers who are not familiar with the publication, and thus the style, (and submit articles that are outside of the focus or style), freelancers are encouraged to subscribe to the newsletter ($25/6 issues), or to send $5 for a current issue, to become better acquainted with the nature and focus of *Dog Gone Newsletter*.

Addresses and phone numbers of destinations and accommodations can be included in the text or can appear as a sidebar or blurb at the end of an article. All information should be fact-checked personally; chamber of commerce and other published info is often outdated. For activity articles, it is important to include contacts for further information, as we will only be able to introduce readers to the activity.

Articles can be anywhere from 300 to 750 words. An approximate word count will be agreed upon at acceptance so we can plan the rest of the newsletter accordingly. Articles may be submitted via e-mail or by snail mail (see addresses below). Articles with photos should be sent via USPS or other ground transportation. A SASE (9x12) is required for photos to be returned and a current newsletter sent to you.

Artwork: Articles MUST include photos. Location photos of guests with dogs are preferred.

Line art may be interspersed with photography, but it cannot be the sole graphic for a destination feature.

Color or B&W prints are accepted (no slides). Activity articles may be accompanied by a photograph of a dog and its owner participating in the featured activity.

Pay rate: This depends on the article. Generally speaking, however, an article of at least 300 words pays $35; 600 words pays $70; and 700-750 words pays $80-85. No article will pay more than $85 and there is no extra fee for photos or other graphics. A one-year subscription to *Dog Gone Newsletter* can be payment or partial payment for the article.

Queries: If you have an article you feel would fit into *Dog Gone Newsletter*'s focus and format, submit a query or the actual article (including word count) in writing to: Robyn Peters, Owner and Publisher, *Dog Gone Newsletter*, PO Box 1846, Estes Park, CO 80517; or via e-mail to: roblipete@earthlink.net. Response time is generally 2-4 weeks. You may be requested to submit your entire article for consideration. All submissions are subject to editing if necessary.

(Articles may not have been published prior to acceptance and cannot be published elsewhere for a year after they appear in *Dog Gone Newsletter*.)

Categories: Nonfiction—Animals—Outdoors—Recreation—Senior Citizen—Sports/Recreation—Travel

CONTACT: Robyn Peters, Owner and Publisher
Material: Queries or articles
PO Box 1846
Estes Park, CO 80517
Phone: 303-449-2527
E-mail: roblipete@earthlink.net
Website: www.doggonefun.com

Doll World
The Magazine for Doll Lovers

General Information

Doll World is an 84-page, full-color, bimonthly magazine with readers from all age sectors. They are interested in informative, well-written articles about collectible dolls of all kinds, doll history, preservation, restoration, dollmakers, plus discerning articles about the world of dolls. Nostalgia and humor are welcome touches. We occasionally include full-size paper dolls.

SUBMISSIONS

1. Manuscript Submissions

• To submit your ideas: At the review date you may send an outline and summary of what you wish to cover in your story, as well as a list and color photocopies of the graphic images you will include. If accepted; send the complete manuscript at the manuscript deadline date listed.

• Complete manuscripts should include subtitles throughout, as well as a small paragraph at the beginning of the story as an introduction. Keep your photo captions short but lively, as some readers believe captions "tell the whole story!"

• You must include a SASE to receive a reply and have images or photos returned. Please allow one month for a response. Only written submissions will be considered. No phone or fax queries.

• Type your manuscript double-spaced on 8 1/2 x 11-inch white paper. Use one-inch margins. Be sure to number all pages. Our corporate style follows the Associate Press Style.

• Label everything! Be sure your name and contact information is on your written materials and photos or items to be photographed.

• Manuscripts should be written independently from the photos. Do not include any portion in the main text of the manuscript that would have to be cut if the photos were not printed. Captions should be at least two sentences in length and written on a separate page.

• Occasionally we use full-size paper dolls. This feature is a one-to two page spread. Color copies may be sent for query purposes. Origi-

nals are requested when accepted, and will be returned after published.

• Proofread all aspects of your manuscript for accuracy. Then read it again!

2. Illustrations, Photos, Slides and Your Dolls

• We are happy to do the photography of your dolls in our studio. Dolls will be returned (at our expense) as our production process nears completion, usually a three-month period.

• If sending your dolls is not possible we require high-quality transparencies, slides, disk images (TIFF, high resolution, 300 dpi, CMYK color, Mac format) or clear, crisp photos to accompany your manuscript. They should be of excellent quality, particularly in regards to focusing, lighting and complete view of subject with a contrasting background.

• Please number each image and type the captions at the end of your manuscript numbered to correspond. Label the individual images with a stick-on address label.

• If you are sending digital images, title them to match your caption title.

• If there are not usable images to go with your manuscript, it may render your submission unacceptable.

Mailing address: Send submissions to Vicki Steensma, *Doll World*, 306 E. Parr Rd., Berne, IN 46711.

Contracts and payment

If your submission is accepted, you will be notified and will be sent a contract at the "manuscript deadline" listed on the editorial calendar. Payments vary depending on length (1000-1200 words are preferred), graphic images, form of submission (e-mailed submissions as a Word document are preferred), adherence to the guidelines and experience of the writer. We purchase all rights, however first rights contracts are available for a lower fee. Payment is made within 45 days after receipt of your signed contract.

If you have any questions, contact Vicki Steensma.
jkn02/02

Categories: Nonfiction—Arts—Biography—Collectibles—Crafts/Hobbies—Entertainment—Family—Fashion—Hobbies—Interview—Photography—Technology—Trade: Dolls

CONTACT: Vicki Steensma, Editor
Material: All
House of White Birches
306 East Parr Rd.
Berne IN 46711
Phone: 206-589-4000
Fax: 206-589-8093
E-mail: Vicki_Steensma@whitebirches.com
Website: www.whitebirches.com

The Dollar Stretcher

Who we are: The Dollar Stretcher is a group of publications dedicated to "Living Better...for Less." The goal is to provide readers with ways to help them save time and money. Occasionally we will also include material on ways to make money at home.

The monthly print version of the newsletter made it's debut in January 1998. We offer it with different covers and lengths for use by private organizations. So, in effect we're creating more than one newsletter with the same content. Our online newsletters go out weekly with a circulation of 200,000. We also have a web site <www.stretcher.com>.

Compensation: Monthly Print Version. Payment is at the rate of $0.10 per published word. We are buying the rights to use the article in the different formats of our newsletter.

Payment is made at the time of acceptance and will be sent to the address provided. Payment will be by check in US$. At present we are only able to pay for material that appears in the monthly hardcopy version of the newsletter.

Online Version & Website. At this time we are unable to pay for material that's used in the online newsletter and website. However, it can provide an excellent opportunity to showcase your talents. We do have a large audience and send out press releases to newspapers, radio, TV and online media regularly. Recently the site has been mentioned in The Chicago Tribune, Washington Post, MSNBC.com, and other publications. Our authors have been contacted by various media outlets including the Rosie O'Donnell Show.

Rights:

Monthly Print Version. We are purchasing first time rights including reprint rights. Reprints will be provided free of charge to non-profit organizations and may also be used for promotional purposes. Non-profits may be asked to cover the cost of production and shipping. Any other potential sale will be negotiated seperately with the author or referred to the author.

Online Version & Website: We are obtaining the one time rights to include a story in the online newsletter and website. No further rights are implied. Any inquiries on usage are referred back to the author.

Writer's Qualifications:

You need not be a professional in the area being discussed. But you must be knowledgeable. Knowledge is more important than literary skill. Personal, hands-on, experience is valued. Unpublished authors are welcome.

Article Length: We are interested in articles up to 800 words in length. The majority of articles that will be used will be in the 550 to 750 word range.

Type of Material Used:

• how to articles based on personal or professional experience

• profiles of people who are successfully living the frugal lifestyle

• time and space saving techniques

• creative ways to save on food, housing, auto and clothing

• stage-of-life material for babies, children, teens, college students, singles, couples, the divorced, single parents, empty nesters and retirees.

• Material targeting different levels of experience with frugal living is welcome. We are looking for articles for the newcomer as well as the experienced tightwad.

• Material on dealing with non-frugal partner, children or significant others

Interviews: We are also interested in interviews with people who have successfully found ways to save time and money. An emphasis is put on those who have found new and creative ways to accomplish the frugal lifestyle and who can share ideas that can be imitated by our readers.

Book Reviews:

When reviewing a book, include:

• book title in Capitals

• author, publishing company, year of publication, soft or hard cover, number of pages and price.

• suggestions for discussion

• general description

• who would it appeal to

• author's goal in writing the book

• author's qualifications

• merits of the book

• any weaknesses of the book

• quality of indexes, recipes or financial aids

Your Article:

The article should be submitted in the body of an email. If you're mailing your submission please include a diskette with the article. Our typist is too busy already! Please make sure that your email and postal addresses, as well as your daytime phone number, are included in the email or on the disk label.

Please include a brief one or two sentence bio statement with your text, and any title suggestions that you may have.

If your article includes resources, please make sure that you provide the necessary addresses and phone numbers. And that they are correct!

Please make sure that your lead 'hooks' the reader. In a newsletter dedicated to saving time and money our readers are very quick to skip to the next article.

How to Submit:

• email to: gary@stretcher.com with the article included in the body of the email. Please do not send attachments. Please indicate hardcopy submission in the subject of the email. We also publish material in the online newsletter without paying the writers. Neither one of us would be happy if your work was used without payment!

• by mail to: The Dollar Stretcher, 6695 Cortez Rd W, Bradenton, FL 34210.

A Final Note: As you would expect, the monthly print version has limited space. We can be much more generous in the online and web versions. Since the online version is a weekly, we'll use about 7 times more material online than in the print version. But, remember that we're not able to pay for that material except to get your work displayed before a sizeable audience. Please mark your submission "Print Version" or "Online Version." If a submission is not marked we need to go back to you before we can begin to review it.

Categories: Nonfiction—Consumer—Economics—General Interest—Money & Finances—Parenting

CONTACT: Submissions Editor
Material: All
6695 Cortez Rd W
Bradenton FL 34210
E-mail: gary@stretcher.com
Website: www.stretcher.com

Dollars & Sense

Dollars & Sense is a national popular economics magazine. It presents progressive analysis of current economic issues and trends. Our goal is to offer a range of left perspectives, and to address economic issues of concern to different constituencies—such as labor, women, environmentalists, people of color, the poor—that mainstream publications often ignore. We also view *Dollars & Sense* as a link between the academic economics community and the general community by helping academic economists communicate with a popular audience.

Our subscribers are progressives, many are activists, social scientists (particularly economists, sociologists, and urban planners), union members, and journalists. We also have a large college and high school student audience. Our articles are reprinted frequently in economics readers for high school and college students, including our own readers, *Real World Macro*, *Real World Micro*, and *Real World Banking*.

Though we have many readers who are economists, we aim our articles at those who are mystified and intimidated by economics. Our readers look to the magazine for concise, lively, and understandable writing.

Toward this end, use a conversational tone and avoid writing as if for a technical journal. It is best to define all terms, eliminate jargon, and use active, simple sentences. Colorful leads, examples and analogies, and anecdotes will help you get your ideas across. The more clearly you as a writer express your ideas, the more likely you are to gain and hold readers' attention and influence their thinking.

We look for articles that provide new and useful information to our readers, and interpret the larger political and economic issues from a left perspective. Articles may explain technical terms or mechanisms, present a new policy proposal, report on a grassroots struggle or political or economic trend, or review an interesting new book or film.

The editorial process

Dollars & Sense is a collective of journalists, economists and other social scientists, activists, and students. Staff members are part of the collective. We meet every Thursday night (except major holidays). At these meetings, we read and discuss the outline and first (and sometimes second) draft of articles in groups of four to six. Your article will be read by editors and non-editors; you might think of this group as a representative sample of our subscribers. Since the collective meets only on Thursday nights, a draft must arrive by Thursday morning to be discussed on schedule. The best time for editors to reach authors with comments is between Friday and Monday, so it is helpful for us to have both your work and home numbers.

After an article is read in the collective, our "edcom committee" reads the next version of the article. The edcom committee is made up of our two staff editors and a collective member. After that read, the article goes through a final copy edit and three proofreading stages.

Start by submitting a one- or two-page synopsis of the article you are planning to write. This may be written in outline or letter form. This step saves you and us time and trouble because it allows us to agree on what you are going to cover, and how, before you start writing. The synopsis should describe the main ideas you want to write about, show how you plan to organize them, give your point of view, and tell who or what your sources are. A Thursday collective group will read this synopsis, and your editor will contact you with suggestions and guidelines.

We then set up an editorial schedule, leaving room for a first draft, second draft, and edcom draft, before production. When the first draft arrives, an editor will read it and will either return it to you for furthers work or submit it to a Thursday collective read. After the read, your editor will then ask you to fill in any missing information, answer questions, and in general revise the article as needed.

When the revised article is completed, it will then be read in a Thursday group or submitted to an "edcom" read. Once again, the editor will get back to you with comments. At this stage, you or the editor may make changes, depending on the degree and type of work needed. The editor sharpens points in the piece that seem unclear and may make organizational changes to help readers focus on the main ideas. This process inevitably introduces mistakes, so please bear with us. The editor will also make copy-editing changes, smoothing out language, correcting grammar, and checking the logic.

Although this editorial process can seem long and tedious, most authors find that the final product is worth the effort.

You may be asked to review editing changes quickly because of production pressures. We apologize for any inconvenience and ask for understanding and help in keeping to a tight schedule. We will receive the final edited version before design and production. If any changes beyond grammatical changes are made at the final production stage, you will be called for approval. If you would like to see the complete final produced version, please request that of your editor. You will be asked to approve the version the day you receive it.

Articles usually appear about six to eight weeks after editing is completed, although they may have to be held for later publication because of considerations of space and timeliness.

If at any time in this process, you ever have questions about your article, please call one of the editors. And, if at any time, you cannot make an arranged deadline, please let your editor know as soon as possible.

Illustrations

Graphs, charts, diagrams, illustrations, and photos help make your ideas concrete and accessible to readers. When possible, please submit any of these with the original manuscript, or discuss any ideas for these with the editor.

The specs

Feature articles range from 2000 to 3500 words

Dollars & Sense does not use footnotes, but we may include a short list of sources or suggested readings with articles. Please attach a one to three-sentence biographical sketch as well.

Categories: Nonfiction—Economics—Money and Finances

CONTACT: Chris Sturr
E-mail: sturr@dollarsandsense.org
CONTACT: Amy Gluckman
E-mail: gluckman@dollarsandsense.org

Dovetail
A Journal by and for Jewish/Christian Families

Writers' Guidelines

Thank you for your interest in Dovetail: A Journal by and for Jewish/Christian Families. We have no denominational affiliation or agenda. Articles may reflect any of a variety of approaches and strategies (e.g., conversion of one partner or maintaining both religions), but should not have a proselytizing or negative tone. Personal experiences are welcome, as are articles based on research, but remember that Dovetail readers tend to be knowledgeable on this topic: avoid trite observations or broad generalizations. Each issue is geared to a particular theme. Upcoming topics planned (subject to change), with article deadlines:

Publication Date and Deadline

Sep/Oct/Nov: Back to School/Fall Holiday Issue - August 15
Dec/Jan/Feb: Winter Holiday Issue - November 15
Mar/Apr/May: Wedding/Spring Holiday Issue - February 1
June/July/Aug: Summer Issue (Various Topics) - May 15

Please let me know if you are interested in writing on any of these topics. We pay $25 plus 2 copies for an 800-1,000 word article; $15 plus 2 copies for a 500-word book review.

Note: we have suspended publication of our print edition; all issues of Dovetail are now published for subscribers in pdf form on our website. Since we receive no income from these postings, there will be no further compensation to authors above the original sum. Submission of an article to Dovetail constitutes your agreement to these terms. We prefer electronic submission as unformatted text file. It should be sent to me at DI-IFR@Bardstown.com. I look forward to hearing from you.

Sincerely, Mary Helene Rosenbaum, General Editor. Dovetail Journal

Categories: Family—General Interest—Parenting—Relationships—Religion

CONTACT: Editor
Material: All
775 Simon Greenwell Lane
Boston KY 40107
Phone: 800-530-1596
Fax: 502-549-3543
Website: www.dovetailinstitute.org

Downstate Story

We publish each November, and decide what to use in the fall. The deadline is always on June 30 for the issue coming out in the fall.

We aim to present a variety of work so every reader who looks at *Downstate Story* will find something fascinating.

Copies cost $8, postpaid in the USA. We encourage writers to buy a copy so they will be familiar with our publication.

Story guidelines, in general: short fiction or narrative written to the standards of fiction, under 2,000 words, never published before. Shorter is better. We prefer some connection with Illinois or the Midwest. We also need illustrators. All contributors are paid $50 on acceptance for their work. We buy first rights only. Anyone can submit work. Simultaneous submissions are OK with us. Just let us know if the story is accepted elsewhere.

Always enclose a SASE both for a response, and for the mss. itself, if you want it returned.

We prefer disposable mss. for the postage savings, as well as Internet correspondence. But no Internet submissions, please.

Categories: Fiction—Short Stories

CONTACT: Submissions Editor
Material: All
1825 Maple Ridge
Peoria IL 61614
E-mail: ehopkins@prairienet.org
Website: www.wiu.edu/users/mfgeh/dss

Dr. Dobb's Journal

Most of the articles that appear in *Dr. Dobb's Journal* are written by readers just like you—programmers who have something they're interested in and would like to share it with fellow programmers. In other words, articles can be described as real solutions for real programmers, usually going well beyond the familiar "hello world" type of article. The best *Dr. Dobb's* articles are those that are grounded in your real-world experiences with programming tools and techniques.

It is important to remember that *Dr. Dobb's* readers begin receiving the magazine about 5 weeks prior to the cover date. This means that articles need to be complete and in our hands at least 3½ months before the cover date.

Is *Dr. Dobb's* interested in my article?

If you're a programmer who has done something you think is interesting, odds are that other programmers will also think it's interesting. Writing for *Dr. Dobb's* will give you the chance to share your innovations and insights with other programmers who can appreciate what you've done. *Dr. Dobb's* articles tend to be fairly narrow in focus, looking at a single technique or problem. A magazine article is too short to discuss an entire large development effort, but it's just the right size for discussing how you solved a single, specific problem.

Dr. Dobb's readers are serious programmers who look to *Dr. Dobb's Journal* for useful information. They read *Dr. Dobb's* for descriptions of algorithms, specific language implementations, and edifying examples of solutions to more general programming concerns. Many articles in *Dr. Dobb's* are "task specific" — they solve a specific problem or provide a unique technique. (Keeping this point in mind helps you focus your writing.)

Most articles in *Dr. Dobb's* have source code with them, ranging from a few dozen lines to illustrate a particular technique or language feature to tens of thousands of lines implementing a complete application. Good source code is not very useful by itself, however. A good article describes why the source code is interesting. Is this technique faster than other techniques? How does your tool compare to other similar tools? If your program is an implementation of a protocol, algorithm, or data structure, tell us about the protocol, algorithm, or data structure.

Not all articles are about software, however. We publish articles on hardware issues (especially if there is a software component), as well as articles covering legal, social, and business issues of direct interest to software developers.

Dr. Dobb's is both platform- and language-independent. We cover operating environments including DOS, Windows 3/95/NT, MacOS, OS/2, UNIX, Linux, and real-time operating systems. In addition to C and C++, we routinely cover Java, Tcl, Perl, Visual Basic, Python, Cobol, Delphi, Fortran, Modula-3, Basic, Smalltalk, assembler, Bob, and other

familiar (and unfamiliar) programming languages.

What kinds of articles does *Dr. Dobb's* print?

Feature Articles

Dr. Dobb's Journal has "themes" that tell readers what they can expect in that issue. Feature Articles are responsible for delivering on that theme. Most articles submitted by our readers are considered as possible feature articles. If you are proposing a possible feature article, you should consider what theme issue it might fit. However, our themes are quite flexible, and we'll print a good article whenever we have space, even if it doesn't precisely match that month's theme.

Embedded Systems

Every month, *Dr. Dobb's Journal* publishes an article on some aspect of embedded systems. These are computer systems which are developed for a specific task, from controlling a car engine to putting a rocket in orbit. These types of systems have some unique requirements: special hardware, new communications protocols, custom operating systems, different languages, development tools, and development methodologies. We're not afraid of block diagrams or schematics, but you should make a clear tie to the software side of embedded systems development. Articles about emulators or real-time operating systems are also appropriate here.

Internet Programming

Especially with the rapid growth of the Internet, software developers are very interested in all aspects of network programming, from client-server database development and distributed operating systems to Web applets and networked coffee machines. This section is your chance to talk about network protocols, systems, and development strategies.

Programmer's Toolchest

The Programmer's Toolchest is where *Dr. Dobb's Journal* looks at specific products. Unlike typical product reviews, which give a feature checklist and a "thumbs up" or "thumbs down" conclusion, we want to know what it's like to use the product. This is your chance to tell us about the tools you've used, and how they helped or hindered you in solving specific problems.

Programmer's Toolchest articles vary in their approach. Some focus on a particular problem, and show how to solve that problem with different tools. Others focus on a particular, little-known aspect of a common tool and show how it can be useful. Some of our most popular Programmer's Toolchest articles show how to combine two or more tools to solve a particular problem. Often, this involves circumventing certain mis-matched features, taking advantage of different strengths of otherwise competitive products, or taking an unusual approach to a problem, one that might not have occurred to someone else.

Like all of our articles, Programmer's Toolchest articles usually provide a healthy dose of code. Those who already own the products can put that code to work immediately, and those who are assessing it can use the code to take a firsthand look. Your fellow programmers are looking for your expert knowledge and experience in using a tool under real-world conditions; this is more valuable than just knowing that a tool exists.

Ultimately, the reader should walk away with a sense that he or she has actually used those tools. Although you're certainly free to throw in your own recommendations, this hands-on approach should allow readers to make their own conclusions about whether that tool will work for them.

Columns

For the most part, individual columns are written by our contributing editors. However, three of our columns regularly feature contributed articles—"Java Q&A," "Algorithm Alley," and the "Programmer's Bookshelf."

If you have the answer to a challenging Java question and are interested in writing an article describing your solution, then we'd like to hear from you. Contact us at editors@ddj.com.

If you've come up with a new algorithm or refined an old one, we have someone to help you develop your idea. Contact editors@ddj.com if you have an algorithm you'd like to present in our "Algorithm Alley."

If you have read a valuable programmer's book or two, contact Jonathan Erickson (jerickson@ddj.com), who will help you turn your opinions into an article. *Dr. Dobb's* views books as important programmer tools and treats them as such in the column. We usually like to spend no more than 750 or so words on an individual book, and prefer to cover two or three in the same issue.

How do I propose an article?

If you have an article idea, you should first send us an article proposal. This is a short statement (about a page) that says what your article will be about. You can mail it to our office or e-mail it to editors@ddj.com. Be sure to give us several ways to contact you (such as phone number, e-mail address, fax number, and mailing address). We'll look at your idea and get back to you, usually within a month.

Although many people simply write their entire article and send it to us, there are several advantages to sending us a proposal. We can look at your idea and possibly suggest a particular slant you hadn't considered. We can also help you to organize the article.

How do I write an article?

Writing Style

Write as if you are giving a brief, informal talk to a group of co-workers. You want to be concise and well organized because you don't want to waste their time, but you don't want to be too stuffy or formal because you know them. If there's an issue or example that's important, but slightly off topic or more difficult, consider separating that into a 300-400 word sidebar.

We encourage you to describe in depth all of the algorithms your program uses. Go into as much detail as possible. Your article should provide something useful to the readers, even if they never look at the code. Ideally, your article should begin with a concrete, general perspective on how the algorithms can or have been used practically.

Teach something in your article. Though *Dr. Dobb's* readers are, by and large, a knowledgeable lot, many of them are reading your article to learn something new. Consequently, your article should contain more than a technical description of the code. It should explain how a program works and why you made each important programming decision. Describe a few basics before jumping into a very technical discussion. Of course, you can't explain everything about your topic in a short magazine article. Nevertheless, a reader should be able to understand the basics of how your program works by reading your article.

Address the issue of portability. Even if your program is very machine specific, your underlying algorithms and tricks will transfer. Say how.

If applicable, provide a bibliography at the end of the article that includes a description of each of the referenced sources. It is essential that you include the full bibliographic information of all sources! This means title, publisher, date of publication, author, issue (if a periodical), place of publication, and any other information that is pertinent.

Do not hype your product. An article that amounts to little more than a product description or lengthy press release will have to be rewritten.

Parts of a Typical Article

A typical article contains several parts:

Article text

Articles usually range from 2000-3500 words of text. However, you should make your article the right length for your topic. The most common problem with submitted articles is that they are too long, with a lot of details that don't really belong.

Text within the main article should stand alone, rather than relying on the illustrations. For example, you should first explain a topic then refer to the illustration: "Although the Trend function is useful in some applications, a more flexible approach is to use the equation <I> as a matrix operator, as shown in Figure A."

Tables

Tables are a concise way to give particular types of information. Give each table a clear, detailed caption, and refer to it in the text by number. ("As Table 1 shows, ...")

Figures

Illustrations and screen captures offer an opportunity to lure anyone looking through an issue into reading your article. They can also provide succinct summaries of complex ideas. Since we redraw most figures anyway, to conform to our size and style requirements, you should not worry about making your images very high quality. Many authors prefer to sketch them by hand and fax or mail them.

Please provide any screen captures you think are relevant. We don't necessarily have the time or equipment to run your program and make our own screen captures. Screen captures should be in a common graphics format (such as GIF, PCX, TIFF, or BMP)

Please don't embed your images in a word-processing document.

Examples

Short pieces of code (less than 20 lines) can be placed near the text as Examples. Like Tables or Figures, they should have clear captions and be referred to by number. ("A better approach is to use Knuth's algorithm, outlined in Example 1.")

Tables, Figures, and Examples are placed at the top or bottom of the page in the magazine. Although we do try to place them near where they are needed in the text, space constraints sometimes force them onto a later page. Keep this in mind as you write.

Listings

Longer pieces of source code are printed at the back of the magazine or on the pages following the article. For space reasons, these should be less than about 400 lines. Often, these will be a few important excerpts from a longer piece of source code.

Complete Source Code

Although we can't publish the complete source code to large projects (or binaries), we do make this code available to our readers in many ways, including our FTP sites, the Web, and so on. You can (and should) refer to this code in your article, but be careful since the reader will not have the source code immediately available.

Other Information

Please include suggested headline (title), decks (subtitle), subheads (section titles), and a two-sentence author biography. Also, please provide short captions for all examples, figures, and tables. All should be in active voice.

General Writing Guidelines

Keep your writing informal and concise. Here are some concrete suggestions:

· Use the active voice when possible. (Avoid excessive use of forms of "to be." For example, don't say "The problem is that XXX", just say "XXX is a problem.")

· Don't use "we" or "our" unless there are multiple authors; use "I" instead. Similarly, refer to the reader as "you." (For example, "Although I chose a simpler approach, you might find the full algorithm necessary in some situations.")

· Avoid needless duplication. Read your article carefully and ask yourself whether each sentence and paragraph adds to the article or simply duplicates a point you've already made.

· Many writers find it useful to put their article aside for a few days after they write it, and then come back and read it again.

· Get a friend to read and comment on your article before you send it to us.

· Make sure that every Figure, Table, Example, or Listing is referred to somewhere in the article.

· Don't put lengthy code excerpts, tables, or figures into the text. Any piece of code longer than a few words should go into an "Example" or a "Listing" (see above.)

· Refer to parts of a listing by using function names or other apparent locations ("...the definition of variable cpLine..."). Do not use line numbers.

· If you refer to source code that isn't going to be printed in the magazine, use the name of the source file and the function or other apparent location.

Take the same care in preparing your Listings that you do in polishing your article. People will be reading your source code; make sure it is clearly formatted, no more than 70 columns wide, and reasonably commented.

How do I send a completed article?

Once you have something you like, it's time to package it all up. Although we accept articles in a variety of formats, here are some of our preferences:

· Save each figure, table, example, or listing as a separate file.

· If you want to e-mail, build a ZIP/PKZIP archive containing the separate files, then UUENCODE or use MIME to e-mail it to us.

· If you want to mail it, include all of the files on a 3.5" diskette.

· Don't forget the complete source code for inclusion on our FTP site.

· Provide all listings and examples as plain text files.

· Provide graphics in a common graphics format (GIF, TIFF, PCX, BMP). Don't worry about making it perfect; we recreate most graphics so they look as good as possible. However, if you have screen shots or the output of a program you're demonstrating, be certain to tell us, so we won't unintentionally alter them.

· The article text should be provided in a plain text format, which is what we often work from. Especially if there are formulas or other special symbols, please provide a hard-copy printout as a reference. Word processor files are often useful, but don't waste much effort formatting them, and please don't embed figures in the word processor file.

· Remember to include your name, work and home address, work and home phone numbers, e-mail address, and any other information that might help us contact you. (We can't publish your article unless we can contact you and mail you a contract.)

To include an article in a particular issue, we request that you give us the final article at least four months ahead of the cover date. It typically requires at least a month to review and edit an article, another month to typeset and prepare the magazine, and our magazine actually ships to subscribers one full month prior to the cover date.

Whom do I send my article to?

If you've first sent a proposal, then you should already have the name and address of an editor you're working with. You should send it directly to them.

Otherwise, you can mail them to "Editors" at our office or e-mail them to editors@ddj.com.

What happens next?

Once we receive an article, we go through a number of steps to evaluate it and prepare it for publication:

· If you send us a proposal, we'll assign an editor to work with you. That editor will discuss your proposal with you and help you refine your idea.

· After we receive the finished article, we'll decide if we want to publish your article. If we do, we'll send you a publishing agreement. This agreement tells you that we want to publish your article; it's not a guarantee that we will publish your article. However, if we don't publish it within 12 months, the contract will expire, and you can offer it to another magazine if you wish. The publishing agreement will specify the fee you will receive for publishing the article (yes, we do pay for all articles in *Dr. Dobb's*), along with the rights we need to acquire. Essentially, we request the rights to publish your article and accompanying code in *Dr. Dobb's* magazine, include it on our annual CD-ROM, publish it on the *Dr. Dobb's* web site, and so on.

· One of our technical editors will carefully go through the entire article. They'll check that your article makes sense, and may rewrite sections of your article to make it clearer. Our technical editors are experienced software developers and writers, and our authors usually find their work is improved in this process. If an article requires more extensive changes, the editor will frequently ask the author to make the changes. Please be patient at this stage. Our technical editors are very careful; it sometimes takes a full week to edit a single article. As a result, an editor that has three or four articles to work on may not be able to give you useful feedback for a while.

· Our Editor-In-Chief will take the edited article and decide which

issue it goes into. Notice that although the contract specified a particular issue, that was only a guess.

· About three months before the cover date, the article goes to our production staff. They produce a galley proof of the article and send it to the author for any final changes. They also create a mock-up of the magazine containing all of the articles. This mock-up is thoroughly edited by our entire editorial staff, which checks every article for grammar, style, punctuation, and other minor problems. Any corrections the author makes to the galley proof are incorporated at this stage.

· About two months before the cover date, the final magazine goes to the printers, and it is mailed to subscribers and newstands about a month before the cover date.

There are times when our office is extremely busy, so we will sometimes not be able to respond to a proposal or article for several weeks. If you've not heard anything for more than a month, however, please call us.

Categories: Computers

CONTACT: Dr. Dobb's Journal
Material: All
2800 Campus Drive
San Mateo, CA 94403
Phone: 650-513-4300
Fax: 650-513-4618
Email: editors@ddj.com
Website: www.ddj.com

DRAGON

DRAGON WRITERS' GUIDELINES
THE GROUND RULES

With few exceptions, submitting an article to *DRAGON* requires these important steps:

1. Review these guidelines.
2. Send a query. Send an outline if it's requested.
3. Submit the manuscript if approved.
4. Wait patiently.

The Guidelines

The Writers' Guidelines outline what we expect as far as format and style, but they also give specific advice about how to write certain kinds of articles. Before sending any query, review these guidelines for information about what we're looking to see and on how to write the kind of articles you'll propose in your query. Forearmed with such knowledge, your queries and articles have a much greater chance of being accepted.

These guidelines do not address one of the most important subjects any writer should know: the proper way to prepare and submit a manuscript for possible publication. You can check out any number of resources for manuscript preparation, but we don't care much about specific format except for two things: Your manuscript must be easy to read, and it must follow D&D style. Note that all rules articles should be written for the current edition of the DUNGEONS & DRAGONS game. See Writing for *DRAGON* for more details.

The Query Query us with an email to **dragon@paizo.com** before you submit an article manuscript; that way, we can tell you which articles we're most likely to accept. Please send queries in the body of your email and not as an attachment. We do not accept unsolicited articles.

We recommend you list a few possible article ideas with each query. Write a brief description of each article and the game content you'll include in the article. If we're interested, we'll ask you to send in the article or to email an outline.

An outline should give more detail, providing a description of every part of the article. For instance, if you want to write an article containing new magic items, your outline should tell us about the items and what special powers each will have.

You don't need to have the whole article written before you send a query or outline, but you should be able to give us a good idea of what the final article will look like. Give a rough estimate of each article's length, which should be less than 5,000 words in most cases. Certain types of articles have specific word counts they must meet, and longer articles of those types have little chance of being accepted. See the Familiars section of the Writers' Guidelines for more details.

Also, it's frustrating for the editors to see proposals for articles similar to articles that have already been printed. If you subscribe to the magazine and are familiar with its content, you'll save yourself and the editorial staff time by not submitting ideas for articles that have already been published, and you're more likely to write the article in a style appropriate to the magazine.

Send queries to: **dragon@paizo.com**. It may take about a month for us to review and reply to your proposal.

The Submission

After you have received a request to write an article, email the completed submission to **dragon@paizo.com** as a Word document (preferably) or in rich text format. There are two important rules for your submission:

1. Always include your name, current email address, home address, and word count on the first page of your article. Articles without this information will automatically be rejected. If either address changes before you receive a response, send an email to **dragon@paizo.com** noting the address change and the article or articles to which the change is relevant so we can send a response to the appropriate place.

2. Always include a standard disclosure form. You'll find the standard disclosure from attached to these guidelines. You can scan the form with your signature, mail a signed copy, or include it in the file at the end of the article.

The Waiting

An editor should reply to your emailed submission within two weeks to let you know the article was received. We might need as long as twelve weeks to make our evaluation of your submission. If you have not heard from us after this much time, feel free to inquire by email about the status of your material. While you wait, feel free to send more queries. Do not contact us by phone to ask about the status of your manuscript.

Revisions

If your article is acceptable, expect to do some revision. We often ask for changes to articles to adjust style, game balance, length, or focus. Send your revision in Word (preferably) or rich text format attached to an email to the editor who requested it or to **dragon@ paizo.com** if no email address is provided. Put "revision" in the title of your email and give a brief description of the article in the body of your email. When we ask for a revision, it is not a guarantee of acceptance of the article. If you are unwilling or unable to revise your work as we require, we will not print your article. Again, we might need as long as twelve weeks to make our evaluation of your submission. Please do not contact us about the status of you submission until that time has passed.

Rejections

Your article might be deemed unacceptable, even after revisions, and we will not often have time to provide you with an explanation. Although we would like to help writers improve their skills and better inform our freelancers of how to get articles accepted, the quantity of articles we receive already exceeds our ability to respond to them in a timely manner. If you receive a form rejection letter, please save your article for future inspiration and query us about new article ideas.

Articles are most often rejected because of poor writing quality, imprecise game mechanics, failure to present information in D&D styles, poor formatting and organization, clichéd approaches to topics, or differences between the query and the final article. These are problems that all freelancers should be aware of and looking for in their writing. We strongly recommend that you have another person or several others review your work before you send it in. Another person's point of view can often reveal problems or missed opportunities invisible to you.

Acceptance

Once your article is accepted an editor will contact you and explain our plans for it. Although we tentatively place accepted articles into future issues, the challenges and changes inherent in producing a monthly magazine prevent us from saying with assuredness exactly when most articles will see publication. Contracts for articles will be sent to authors in the month we begin working on the issue your article is slotted for, which is roughly two months before the issue's publication date. Even at this point articles have the potential to be bumped to future issues. Authors should also expect changes to be made to their articles for the purposes of game balance and to better suit the needs of the magazine.

WRITING FOR DRAGON

Writing for *DRAGON* can be an easy, exciting experience, but you must do your homework before writing and familiarize yourself with *DRAGON*'s guidelines and the D&D system.

What Do We Want?

We usually don't assign specific article ideas to freelance writers. It's easier and almost always better to write about subjects that interest you. Still, there are some generalities about the articles we prefer that you should keep in mind.

D&D Focus: *DRAGON* magazine serves D&D players, *DUNGEON MASTERS*, and fans of the game in general. Our favorite articles include some things for players on both sides of the DM screen, with compelling writing and inspiration to satisfy even general readers who may not be D&D experts.

New Rules: Articles that provide new feats, races, spells, magic items, equipment, or prestige classes are welcome additions to *DRAGON*, although all articles should have compelling backgrounds that inspire the new rules. Stories, backgrounds, and inspiration for new rules should be interesting enough to stand alone without their rules element. Articles that present rules almost exclusively might make better "Familiars," as we call our regular articles, than features. See the Familiars section of the Writers' Guidelines.

We also like new rules systems that deal with new concepts in the game or rules that cover certain aspects of game play that the current D&D rules might gloss over. Ensure that your rules article adds to the existing D&D game rather than replacing parts of it.

Unearthed Arcana: *DRAGON* has a history of presenting new rules systems and alternative play methods for the D&D game, much like in the book *Unearthed Arcana*. Thus, articles that seek to present such new rules systems make welcomed feature articles. These features should follow the standards applied to all features and strive to have equally strong stories and inspirational elements in addition to the new mechanics.

In addition, being the official DUNGEONS & DRAGONS magazine, *DRAGON* has the ability to present articles other publications cannot. In few other places do writers have the opportunity to discuss and detail creatures like beholders and mind flayers, familiar names like Bigby and Vecna, or exciting campaign worlds like the FORGOTTEN REALMS or EBERRON.

Published Worlds: We don't mind reviewing articles that stem from a published world, but we're not interested in presenting articles that are deeply rooted in any particular setting. An article describing a race from SPELLJAMMER that is useful in all D&D games without requiring the SPELLJAMMER setting or ships-in-space motif is fine, but an article that delves deeply into the politics of a region in GREYHAWK or the rites of a religion in the FORGOTTEN REALMS is not useful enough to most readers.

Iconic Topics: When submitting your article ideas to *DRAGON*, remember that the closer your ideas are to the core experience of playing D&D, the more they'll appeal to the majority of readers and the more likely they will be accepted.

No New Columns: We are not looking for any new columns.

Format and Style

A-E

Article manuscripts should use the current style of D&D game products. For instance, the names of magic items and spells should be italicized, and feat names should be capitalized. See the Rules Content section for more information about how to present game elements.

Note that we will not publish an article written in the first person. This means that you should not use the words "I" or "my" in your article unless some character other than yourself is saying them. If you must refer to some example from personal experience, do not use the first person to do so.

If your article begins with a narrative vignette or piece of example dialog, it should be no more than 200 words long. Being more concise pieces, Class Acts should not include such length introductions.

A full page of text in *DRAGON* contains about 750 words. Submissions should not exceed 5,000 words or the specified word count for the Familiars article unless the editor specifically responds to a query that a longer article is desired.

Use proper bibliographic style when listing book and magazine references in your article. If your article quotes material verbatim from other sources, identify the sources (including page numbers) and be sure that each quote is written exactly as it appears in the original source.

Consistently poor spelling, grammar, and sentence structure will almost certainly cause an article to be rejected. We don't insist that manuscripts be perfect, but we prefer those that require little editing. Especially avoid passive writing, particularly "to be" verbs, and always spell check your work.

Do not submit any manuscript simultaneously to *DRAGON* and to any other magazine, website, or d20 publisher. Do not copy material from another source and pass it off as your own (i.e., commit plagiarism). Authors will bear full legal responsibility for such actions.

Drawings and sketches may accompany your article if they are necessary to illustrate important points. Such pictures need not be for publication as drawn but should still be clearly and neatly rendered. We can sometimes use photographs, but they must be clear, crisply focused, and high in contrast.

Rules Content

D&D is precise and consistent. This precision makes the game-stalling and argument-provoking questions of other games and previous editions a thing of the past. The designers of the game put a lot of thought into how the various rules and game elements interact and are balanced. *DRAGON* articles must be held to this high standard. If there is one thing you must remember when creating new game elements for D&D, it is this: **Be precise.**

The more work you do to adhere to the rules and the formats presented in the rulebooks, the greater the chances that we'll be able to accept the article you write and the less revision you will be required to do. When you've gotten the go-ahead to write an article that contains rules, make sure that you have a good grasp of any other similar rules that exist and that you use all the resources you have available.

If you plan on creating new rules elements, you should be aware of other such rules elements that have been published in *DRAGON* and other D&D products. It's a good idea to keep a library of these materials so that you do not duplicate content. Unique new game elements garner our attention; highly derivative or duplicated rules will not be published. The other benefit is for comparison. When creating new rules elements be sure to check your work against similar existing rules. For example, spells should be checked for power against other spells of the same level, while magic item costs should be compared to existing ones to fine-tune values.

Book References: If your article uses rules elements from D&D products other than the *Player's Handbook*, *DUNGEON MASTER's Guide*, or *Monster Manual*, reproduce the integral elements in your article for readers' reference. You will not be paid for those words, and too much reprinting of such information will make an article unacceptable. It's to your advantage and the readers' to provide content that can be used with just the three Core Rulebooks.

Show Your Work: When you calculate the skill points for a monster, figure out the cost of a magic item, or set the level of a spell, provide the calculations or the thought process behind the decisions you made. Notes to the editor should be noted in red colored text within the body of your work at the relevant point. Documents that don't allow for colored text should include notes at the end of the article.

Standard Text: When you give an established ability (such as scent or sneak attack) to a monster or prestige class, use the full text from the most recent product available. If your article would repeat that text many times, use the full text just the first time, and note in later instances that the earlier text should be used. Copying rules language from published Wizards of the Coast products for our needs is not plagiarism, but rather adheres to the game's precision. It should also be understood that specific words and formats have specific meanings in D&D and writers should be watchful for and use the styles presented in *DRAGON* and Wizards of the Coast products. For example, the word "enchanted" refers only to creatures under the effects of a spell of the enchantment school, while the names of size categories are always capitalized (a spider eater is a Large monstrous beast).

d20 Resources and References: Do not use or reference material produced in d20 products by companies other than Wizards of the Coast, even if it is labeled as open game content. In certain rare circumstances, the editors might grant permission to reprint or reference certain d20 content, but for the most part *DRAGON* is devoted to giving readers new official D&D elements for their games.

Sidebars

Your article might include a number of sidebars (text set apart from the main body of the article). When you include a sidebar, it's helpful if you indicate its presence with text in brackets, such as: [[begin sidebar]] and [[end sidebar]]. If you present a table, use the same indicators.

There are a couple sidebars that appear regularly in *DRAGON*, and you should always check if your article would benefit from the inclusion of one or more of them. Unless otherwise noted, sidebars should consist of no more than 300 words long.

New Feats, Equipment, Rules, Spells, Etc: These sidebars present new useful rules elements to players related to the topic of the article (nonmagic weapons, armor, alchemical items, spells, feats, tools, magic items, etc).

How-To: This sidebar explains how readers might construct something from your article. For instance, if you devise a new kind of quality for a magic item, you might explain how to arrive at that quality's cost and thereby how to create other similar properties.

Table Talk

DRAGON has several standard articles that appear in the front section of the magazine. These articles have specific guidelines that you must follow in addition to those noted above. Adhering to these guidelines greatly increases your chances of having an article accepted.

Scale Mail (Up to 300 Words)

"Scale Mail" is *DRAGON*'s letters column. It's a place for readers to give their opinions and let other gamers know their thoughts. We do not pay for letters sent to "Scale Mail," but we'd love to hear from you. Send emails to **scalemail@paizo.com**.

First Watch (Up to 300 Words)

"First Watch" features upcoming products or events of interest to D&D players. We do not pay for submissions to first watch, but if you have a product you'd like to see featured in the magazine, we'd be happy to review it for inclusion. Send product samples to: Dragon at Paizo Publishing; 2700 Richards Road, Suite 201; Bellevue, WA 98005-4200.

Under Command (2,600 Words)

The "Under Command" column is currently being retooled to a new format. If you are interested in the D&D Miniatures game and would like to write for this column, please show your interest by dropping a line to **dragon@paizo.com**. Full guidelines for this column will be available shortly.

Divine Inspiration (2,800 Words)

This new article combines and broadens the vision of the former

"Novel Approach" and "Silicon Sorcery" articles. The purpose of these articles is to show how inspiration for D&D games can be taken from books, video games, comics, movies, television shows, manga, or any other form of media. These articles are divided into at least three sections.

The first section is about 1,200 words on the work itself. This should summarize the plot, characters, and unique elements of the story without spoiling the story. If the work has an author, artist, or designer of note, a brief sidebar should mention why the creator is of interest, along with his other works. A 200-300 word sidebar in this section should also note what about the work appeals to D&D players and DMs.

The second section presents 800 words of thematic ideas for use in D&D. These might be new plot hooks, reasons to go adventuring, character concepts, ways to get groups of PCs together, etc. This section should not present new rules elements.

The last section should consist of approximately 800 words of new rules, magic items, spells, monsters, or similar modular rules elements. These rules elements should be inspired by the work being covered and cannot be wholesale interpretations into D&D rules. For example, we cannot publish official D&D rules for the One Ring, but an intelligent evil ring that grants *invisibility* at the risk of summoning 1d4 wraiths might be more acceptable. These new rules should be useful in nearly any D&D campaign.

Features

DRAGON's Features section presents longer articles on a diverse array of topics of interest to D&D players, DMs, and game enthusiasts alike. If you have an idea for an article that doesn't fit one of the other types noted in the guidelines, or you have an article like them that does not fit the specified word count, your article idea is a Features article. Typically, the Features section contains an advice article for players, a general interest article, an article that delves into detail about some aspect of the D&D (not a specific setting), and a couple rules articles. Sometimes the Features section contains fiction.

Advice Articles (up to 5,000 Words)

Longer advice articles make great articles for the Features section. Advice articles should be focused on players or DMs, while still offering useful information to the other side of the DM screen. Advice articles about elements central to adventuring or D&D play have the greatest chance of acceptance. Example topics include: surviving and fighting in a specific environment, developing a new campaign theme, picking or building a base of operations, creating better challenges, and deciding what class to play.

General Interest Articles (up to 5,000 Words)

General interest articles discuss something of interest to D&D players without necessarily discussing an aspect of D&D. Example topics include: the history of the crossbow, an encyclopedia of fantasy movies, elements of a typical castle, and a guide to plagues.

D&D Detail Articles (up to 5,000 Words)

This type of Features article takes an element central to the D&D game and describes it in greater detail. The "Ecologies" article are an example of doing this kind of thing for monsters. Example topics include: elven names and language, fostered dragons, the design of gnomish communities, and holidays of the core D&D races.

Rules Articles (up to 5,000 Words)

Longer rules articles make great articles for the Features section. Many rules articles will fit in other parts of the magazine. Rules elements that don't have a place in a recurring column make the best Features articles. These articles should include a rich and sustaining background, compelling enough to stand alone without the rules content. Example topics include: a knightly order, complete with hierarchy, prestige class, feats, and magic items, a group of new monsters, tied together by a similar theme, and a planar article detailing a few monsters, environmental effects, and magic items.

Fiction

DRAGON does not accept unsolicited fiction. We publish just twelve issues a year, and not all of those issues contain a short story. In the past this meant an unfair competition between thousands of unsolicited fiction submissions and fiction solicited from established fantasy authors.

DRAGON will continue to feature great fiction, but *DRAGON* can't be the place for potential fiction authors and novelists to break into the industry. There are other outlets for short fantasy fiction better equipped to showcase a new author's work.

Familiars

DRAGON has several standard articles that appear regularly in issues. These articles have specific guidelines that you must follow in addition to those noted above. Adhering to these guidelines greatly increases your chances of having an article accepted.

Spellcraft (2,000 Words) "Spellcraft" features original spells. **These articles present a unique named spellbook** and the new spells found within. The spellbook should provide a compelling backdrop for the spells and might even include its own unique rules (such as inflicting a curse upon its user or needing some extra check to decipher). It does not need to be a book per se, but it should be some collection of spells (either arcane or divine). When creating new spells, reread the Magic and Spells chapters in the *Player's Handbook*. Make sure you understand the divisions between the various schools of magic and that you use the proper formats for school, subschool, descriptors, level, components, casting time, range, area, effect, target, duration, and other spell description elements. Pay particular attention to the guidelines for how much damage a spell of a particular level should do. If you have them available, check out the spells sections of other D&D books like *Complete Arcane, Tome and Blood, Magic of Faerûn,* and *Defenders of the Faith.* The "Abuse Your Illusions" article in issue #292 is an excellent resource to learn how to design illusion spells. Present the spells with the proper formatting and include a "New Spells" sidebar including brief descriptions of each new spell (as at the beginning of chapter 11 of the *Player's Handbook*).

Do not design spells that are simply variations on standard themes, such as a *fireball* that deals acid damage or an *entangle* spell that constricts to damage foes. These are easy spells to design and can be represented by rules already in place.

On average, submissions that follow these guidelines will only present 5–8 new spells, which is perfectly acceptable.

Ecologies (3,000 Words)

An "Ecologies" article delves into greater detail about a particular monster from the *Monster Manual* or another Wizards of the Coast published bestiary. In general, an "Ecology" article should have a hunter's guidebook approach, although it should not be written "in voice." The purpose of these articles is both to make DMs excited about using these monsters and educate players on how to survive encounters with them. A number of sections must be included in each "Ecologies" article. **Remember:** Don't describe new features of the creature or add to it in such a way that it would change game mechanics.

Introduction: Draw a reader in with a strong introduction of only a paragraph or two. It should include something tantalizing, such as a cool or oft-overlooked feature of the monster that makes the reader want to continue with the article.

History or Origin Myths: Relate a brief version of the creature's history or origin myth as described in other D&D books. This is perhaps most important for intelligent creatures with complex societies, but unnatural creatures and constructs might also have interesting histories. It's important in this section that you rely on what has been written. We do not want a new origin story for a monster.

Knowledge Check Sidebar: This sidebar should offer sample bits of knowledge depending on the DC result of an appropriate Knowledge check. See the *Player's Handbook*, page 78, for the different Knowledge skills and what type of Knowledge a monster falls into. This knowledge should scale from DC 0 to DC 30 (assuming there's enough interesting things to know about the creature) with DC 10 representing the limit of common knowledge and what PCs would know with an unskilled Knowledge check.

Physiology: Describe the creature in more detail than the *Monster Manual*. Include physical descriptions of adults and young. This is also the section to include a dissection-table analysis of the creature or a part of the creature. See the first chapter of the *Draconomicon* for some examples of what you might do.

Psychology and Society: Describe the creature's eating and sleeping cycles, procreation, hunting methods, lifespan, and other such information related to how the creature lives. Especially important for creatures with near-human or greater intelligence, this section details how the creature thinks and why it acts the way it does. Try to strike a balance between simplification and psychoanalysis. Many creatures have drastically different mentalities that are completely alien to humans. This is the place to explore those differences. Obviously, creatures without an Intelligence score don't have psychologies, and therefore don't need this section.

Additional Information/Abilities Sidebars: These sidebars highlight some element of the creature or its society in greater detail. This might be a description of a race's god, an examination of a lair, a new item or magic item uniquely relevant to a creature, examples of how to creatively use a specific ability, etc. This sidebar should be shorter than 300 words.

Vs.: This section explains tactics and tips for defeating the creature in combat. It should describe the creature's tactics and offer counter tactics that PCs should use. Each piece of advice or tactic should appear with a bold title at the beginning of the paragraph (much like this one for Vs.). Think about the mundane and magical equipment PCs should have to defeat the monster and which spells might prove especially useful. Avoid obvious basics such as "use magic," "use ranged weapons," or "wear armor."

Bazaar of the Bizarre (2,000 Words)

Bazaar of the Bizarre articles present new magic items for the D&D game. We prefer that each Bazaar of the Bizarre article follow a specific theme. If possible, a magic item for each "item slot" (see Magic Items on the Body on page 214 of the *DUNGEON MASTER's Guide*) or a magic item for each item creation feat (see the *Player's Handbook*) should appear. Items should be useful to player characters, and unless an editor has given you specific exception player characters should have the ability to buy or create the items (i.e. no artifacts). As with new spells, the best items have an interesting background and description. Each item should have at least one paragraph describing what it looks like and a sentence or two of its history.

Reread the Magic Items chapter in the *DUNGEON MASTER's Guide.* Pay special attention to the rules for creating magic items for the game and how the costs for magic items are devised. **Magic items must have their aura, caster level, prerequisites, price, and weight listed.** Understand what these terms are and how their values are derived. Note that saving throws for magic item effects are usually calculated by the minimum ability bonus needed to cast the spell. Please show your work, in red text or in an accompanying file, of how you established the price for each item.

The easiest magic items to design are those that duplicate spell effects or that stack current magic item qualities. While an item that does this in a creative way might be acceptable, we prefer that you attempt something more difficult and ingenious. We will reject articles that feature magic items that are too derivative or that simply reproduce existing effects.

Class Acts (700 Words)

A Class Acts article presents 700 words for a single core class from the *Player's Handbook.* Each issue features one such article for each of the eleven classes. Class Acts articles should follow a "toolkit" approach, providing players (and DMs) of all experience levels something useful that they can immediately implement in their games. New class-specific feats, equipment, or magic items make good Class Acts articles. Alternative versions of a class (such as those presented in *Unearthed Arcana*) or class-substitution levels (as presented in the *Planar Handbook*) also make solid Class Acts. **We are not currently looking for advice articles.**

Other topics to explore might include gear packages; alternative class starting packages (see the *Player's Handbook*); new or alterna-tive animal companions, familiars, or mounts; new martial arts styles; societies and schools (with organization stat blocks); new combat styles; expansion of overlooked class abilities (see "Optional Special Abilities for Rogues" in DRAGON #326); and so on.

Power Plays: "Power Plays" sidebars present a combination of feats, spells and feats, spells, magic items, or other game rules that results in a particularly puissant effect. They briefly show how a game element or a few game elements can be used by players to the greatest effect. "Power Plays" are accepted in groups of 700 words (usually 5 or 6 "Power Plays") and each should be no longer than 150 words long. These sidebars should be relevant to a variety of classes. "Power Plays" are not published as a single article but are divided through several Class Acts as they are required.

Prestige Classes (4,000 Words)

Generally speaking, we now solicit all of our prestige classes. However, if your longer submission includes a prestige class, **please make sure to use the new prestige class format (see *Races of Destiny* and Dragon #330).** Prestige classes using the older format will be sent back for revision and expansion. Note that the new format provides more background information and flavor to allow you to integrate the prestige class more fully into your campaign.

Prestige classes are fun to design, but they can be difficult to design well. Be especially careful when assigning a prestige class sneak attack damage, all good saves, a high Hit Die type, the fighter attack progression, or +1 level of existing class at each level for the purposes of determining spells per day; these are elements that can quickly make a prestige class too powerful. A prestige class should be better than a base class in some way, but not better at everything or so much better at one thing that everyone would take the prestige class.

The prestige class should have a consistent and unique feel; we don't want to see a better version of the barbarian or a prestige class with abilities that have nothing to do with its theme. Each level of the prestige class should tempt the player, but not necessarily because of the powerful ability that it grants. Ideally, a character who starts on the path of your prestige class will want to follow through on the whole thing, not switch to another class after gaining one particular ability at a low level of the prestige class. Look at all the D&D references you have for prestige classes and use them as examples of how your prestige class and its abilities should be presented.

A prestige class useful to multiple character types is better than one with highly specialized requirements or that is only good for one kind of character. The assassin is a great prestige class (because there are many ways to qualify for it), but a prestige class designed for dwarven druid/bards is not.

In general, we are largely no longer interested in submissions exclusively detailing prestige classes. That doesn't mean we won't look at them, but such articles face an uphill battle to acceptance.

RIGHTS

If we like your manuscript, we'll ask to purchase the rights to print it. Once we have accepted your article, be patient when waiting for contracts. Contracts are sent when we begin work on the issue in which the article appears, which might not be for several months. We will send three copies of a contract to you if we want to purchase the rights to your manuscript. Sign all three and return two. If you are under 18, a parent or guardian must sign or co-sign your contracts. Contracts are sent when work on an issue intended to contain an article begins, which may still be several months before an issue's release date.

PAYMENTS

Payments for most articles are made 30 days after publication of the issue in which the article appears, usually at a rate of about 5 cents per word. We pay a flat fee for the use of an article, and we do not offer royalties. If two or more persons collaborate on an article, send us a signed statement from all authors concerning the division of payments.

All authors must keep us up to date on any address changes. American writers (only) must also provide us with their Social Security numbers, for tax purposes. If you have not received a check 60 days after your article's publication, contact the editors by mail or email.

Good luck!

FAQ

Q: I've sent in twelve proposals and they've all been rejected. What am I doing wrong?

A: Putting out a magazine every month often means that our editorial staff can't spend muchtime detailing the specifics of all our editorial decisions. Between dozens of contributors, knowledge of past successes and failures, future plans, and simple personal preferences, it's likely that numerous proposals will be rejected before we ask to see one in more detail. Keep sending proposals and one is bound to take hold eventually.

Q: I've sent queries and haven't been responded to in over a week, what's up?

A: We *try* to respond to all queries soon after we receive them, but things can be pretty hectic at times (especially from December to February and the summer convention season). Please be patient and if you haven't heard back after a few weeks feel free to gently inquire.

Q: I haven't received my contract yet, should I be worried?

A: You will receive a contract when we begin working on the issue in which your article willappear. That might be up to a year from when we accepted the article.

Q: The article printed in *DRAGON* is different from the one I submitted. What happened?

A: *DRAGON*'s editorial staff is more than just a team of copy editors, also being knowledgable game designers and developers. Any article that undergoes editing for inclusion in the magazine undergoes scrutiny not only by the *DRAGON* staff but Wizards of the Coast's R&D department. Every facet of each new rule is considered for balance and fairness as it relates to the entire D&D game. Thus, if an article is accepted it is possible that some rules element might need extensive revision. We may like the ideas and background, but sometimes the rules just need the professional treatment.

Q: How can I break into the industry?

A: You've got to be cool, suave, and sophisticated. Actually, you need to be persistent,deadline-oriented, knowledgeable about the game, and able to write well. Becoming a frequent submitter to *DRAGON* doesn't hurt.

Q: Does Wizards of the Coast look at what I write for *DRAGON*?

A: Yes. Wizards of the Coast approves everything we put in the magazine.

Q: Can I use stuff that isn't in the SRD?

A: Yes. Wizards of the Coast owns *DRAGON* so we can use anything in their IP.

Q: What is passive voice and why should I avoid it?

A: There is an excellent answer to this question here:http://owl.english.purdue.edu/handouts/grammar/g_actpass.html

Q: I want to submit my artwork to *DRAGON*, who should I send it to?

A: Feel free to send a link to your website to **dragon@paizo.com**.

Q: Is it true that if I fly out to Bellevue and wash Mike's truck my article will be accepted?

A: It depends on whom you ask and what your article is.

PAIZO PUBLISHING STANDARD DISCLOSURE FORM

I wish to submit the following materials for consideration for publication by Paizo Publishing, subject to all of the conditions below.

Working Title of submission and brief description (please type or print legibly)

I submit my materials voluntarily and on a nonconfidential basis. I understand that this submission by me and its review by Paizo Publishing does not, in whole or in part, establish or create by implication or otherwise any relationship between Paizo Publishing and me that is not expressed herein. I further understand and agree that Paizo Publishing in its own judgment, may accept or reject the materials that are submitted with this Disclosure Form and shall not be obligated to me in any way with respect to my submission until Paizo Publishing shall, at its own election, enter into a properly executed written agreement with me, and only then according to the terms of such an agreement.

I agree that Paizo Publishing may have a reasonable period in which to review this submission. Paizo Publishing will return my submission to me provided that it is received by Paizo Publishing with a self-addressed, stamped envelope. Paizo Publishing shall not be held responsible, however, for items or materials that are accidentally damaged or lost. I hereby agree to retain a copy of the submitted materials.

I understand and agree that the review by Paizo Publishing of the materials that accompany this Disclosure Form does not imply or create (1) any financial or other obligation of any kind on the part of Paizo Publishing, (2) any confidential relationship or guarantee of secrecy, or (3) any recognition or acknowledgment of either novelty or originality.

I also understand and agree that if the submission utilizes or is based on characters, settings, or other materials that are owned by Paizo Publishing or Wizards of the Coast, Inc. or if the submission contains trademarks and/or other proprietary materials that are owned by Paizo Publishing or Wizards of the Coast, Inc., then I shall not be free to submit the submission for publication to any person or firm other than Paizo Publishing.

I warrant that the submission (check one, and provide information if necessary):

[ ] has never been published.

[ ] has been published by_____ in _____

I further warrant that the submission is original, and that its publication will not violate the rights of any third party, and that the person identified herein as the submitter is the sole owner of the submission. Furthermore, I am of legal age and am free to make agreements relative to this submission, or I am the authorized representative of the submitter (check one: [ ] Parent; [ ] Legal Guardian; [ ] Agent; [ ] Other: _____). Signature and Date.

Submitter's Name (please type or print), Phone, Email, and Mailing Address

Categories: Hobbies

CONTACT: www.dragon@paizo.com
Material: All

Dramatics
The Magazine for Students and Teachers of Theatre

The magazine and its readers

Dramatics is an educational theatre magazine published since 1929 by the International Thespian Society, a nonprofit honorary organization dedicated to the advancement of secondary school theatre. (In 1989 the Educational Theatre Association was formed to operate the Society as well as a separate professional association for teachers.) *Dramatics* is published nine times a year, September through May. It has a circulation of about 42,000. Approximately 80 percent of its readers are high school theatre students; about 10 percent are high school theatre teachers. Other subscribers include libraries, college theatre students and teachers, and others interested in educational theatre.

The primary editorial objectives of the magazine are: to provide serious, committed young theatre students and their teachers with the skills and knowledge they need to make better theatre; to be a resource that will help high school juniors and seniors make an informed decision about whether to pursue a career in theatre, and about how to do so; and to prepare high school students to be knowledgeable, appreciative audience members for the rest of their lives.

Opportunities for contributors We buy four to eight articles for each issue, ranging in length from 800 to 4,000 words.

Articles are accepted on any area of the performing arts, including film, video, and dance. A typical issue might include an interview with someone who has made a significant contribution to the theatre; an article describing some innovative approach to blocking, costume design, or set construction; a survey of leading theatre schools describing what they look for in students; and a photo spread, with copy, on some ground-breaking performer or theatre group.

Short news items, book reviews, and humor pieces (provided they're actually funny) are also part of the mix.

The test we apply, in deciding whether to accept an article, is whether it would engage an above-average high school theatre student and deepen his or her understanding and appreciation of the performing arts. We also look for pieces a theatre teacher might use in the classroom, studio, or rehearsal hall, although articles of this kind are more likely to be published in our quarterly journal Teaching Theatre (see separate guidelines).

Plays We print seven one-act and full-length plays a year. We occasionally reprint plays, but prefer that they be unpublished. Plays should be performable in high schools, which places some restrictions on language and subject matter; however, we tend not to publish children's theatre pieces, teen angst dramas, and overtly didactic "message" plays.

We buy one-time, non-exclusive publication rights to plays. The playwright retains all other rights.

Graphics Photos and illustrations to accompany articles are welcomed, and when available, should be submitted at the same time as the manuscript. Acceptable forms: color transparencies, 35mm or larger; color or black and white prints, 5 x 7 or larger; line art (generally used to illustrate technical articles); JPEG and TIFF files of high-quality scans. Unless other arrangements are made, payment for articles includes payment for photos and illustrations.

We occasionally buy photo essays.

Rights and returns

We buy first publication rights (unless we make other arrangements with an author), pay on acceptance, report in 4-6 months (or notify authors if a longer period is needed for review), and return all material that is accompanied by a self-addressed stamped envelope.

Queries and sample copies We prefer to see a finished manuscript but will respond to queries by letter or e-mail.

Phone queries are discouraged. Sample copies of the magazine cost $2.50. Subscriptions cost $24 a year.

Payment

Honorariums of $25 to $400 are paid for accepted work. Payment is based on quality of work, amount of editing or rewriting needed, length of work, and inclusion of photos or graphics. Contributors also receive five free copies of the issue in which their piece appears and may obtain additional copies at a minimal charge.

MS specifications

We edit manuscripts to conform to the Chicago Manual of Style. Manuscripts should be typed double-spaced on a sixty-character line. Photocopies are acceptable as long as they are clearly legible. Contributors should keep an exact copy of any manuscript submitted. Once articles are accepted, authors can score big points with the editorial staff by supplying their work electronically via e-mail (our address: dcorathers@edta.org; jpalmarini@edta.org) or on diskettes, sent to Dramatics magazine, 2343 Auburn Avenue, Cincinnati, OH 45219. We work on Windows-based computers; MS Word is the text program of choice.

All submissions are subject to editing, and we try to involve authors in that process as much as possible.

Whenever time allows, we send galley proofs to authors for review—usually by fax.

A CONTRIBUTORS CHEAT SHEET:

What makes us cranky

• Writers who are too lazy or careless to do basic reporting and research. Very few articles are complete with only one quoted source.

• Writers who represent themselves as experts when they're not.

• Writers who are not up front about if and where a piece has been previously published.

• Submissions that ignore or misunderstand our audience; articles that either talk down to our readers or are way over their heads. (If a piece has footnotes, it's probably too academic for us.)

• Contributors who create an impression of conflict of interest by writing about an organization in which they themselves are involved (although we do sometimes publish first-person accounts).

• Would-be playwrights who do not understand the basic conventions of the stage.

• Writers who are impossible to get ahold of, or who do not return messages.

What makes us happy

• Writers who really understand our audience.

• Writers who bring lots of strong, specific article ideas to the table, and keep abreast of topics recently covered by the magazine.

• Contributors who submit written queries or complete articles, rather than interrupting our work to make a sales pitch by phone.

• Writers who understand the need for editorial input, and can make and/or accept necessary changes gracefully.

• Writers who can provide good quality photography to go along with their pieces (snapshots are not publishable). Illustration ideas are also appreciated.

• Writers who include student voices in their pieces when appropriate, as well as a variety of other sources.

• Writers whose work is well organized, factual, and clean.

• Writers who are willing to work cheerfully for what we can afford to pay.

Categories: Fiction—Nonfiction—Arts—Book Reviews—Children—Culture—Diet/Nutrition—Dance—Drama—Directories—Education—Entertainment—Film/Video—General Interest—Interview—Literature—Teen—Theatre—Writing

CONTACT: Don Corathers, Editor
Material: All
2343 Auburn Ave.
Cincinnati OH 45219
Phone: 513-421-3900
Fax: 513-421-7077
E-mail: dcorathers@edta.org
E-mail: jpalmarini@edta.org

Dream Network
A Quarterly Journal
Exploring Dreams & Myth

The *Dream Network* invites articles, interviews, news items, photographs and artwork which will, in some way, inspire, inform or otherwise encourage our readers to value their dreams. Recommended are dream and myth related experiential articles, accounts of a personal/transformative nature and/or educational information that will empower readers in learning to understand the symbolic and metaphoric language of dreams and mythology. Our writers and readers consist of lay persons, students & professional dreamworkers. It is our goal to unite individuals who respect their dreams, to demystify dream work and to integrate dreamsharing into our culture. We also publish a few short poems in each issue.

Strictly promotional material is discouraged, since this is best addressed through advertising, also available in the Journal. (Send for publicity packet.)

Articles which attack, demean, or otherwise negate other people, organizations, philosophies, or systems are not accepted. Intelligently written articles which analyze or disagree with issues are welcomed as such material helps us understand one another better.

One section in each issue revolves around questions that were asked in the previous issue, i.e., our theme. Please contact us directly, by phone or mail, if you wish to be made aware of upcoming questions/ themes. Other special sections are The Art of Dreamsharing and The Mythic Connection.

If you are not familiar with *Dream Network*, we ask that you avail yourself of several back issues so as to experience the texture and purpose of our mission.

LENGTH OF ARTICLES & FORMAT

If you enter your submission on a personal computer, please send copy of the article via email to Publisher@DreamNetwork.net or on computer disk, ideally with complementary illustrations and/or photographs. Include a one-sentence biographical statement and address at the end of each article submitted.

A page consists of approximately 900 words with room for title and a 2-5/8"x2-5/8" illustration and/or photograph of yourself. Preferred length, 2 to 3 pages, including photos &/or illustrations. Maximum length of articles, 1,800 words or approximately 3/4 pages, including illustrations/photos.

Please indicate copyright preference and date on submissions. DNJ reserves the right to edit all materials submitted for publication.

ART MATERIAL & PHOTOGRAPHS

Reproducible black and white original artwork and photographs are preferred. We use one color (black and white) graphics of many types—line drawings with washes, and photographs. Graphics need to be of high quality and camera ready. Art/graphic submissions can also be transmitted via email as .jpg file/300dpi or as .pdf files to Publisher@DreamNetwork.net

TIMING

Once an article is accepted for publication, we do our best to publish it in the next available issue. However we are routinely blessed with more material than we can publish. If you do not see your article in print immediately, please be patient. If you want us to consider your material for a specific issue, please indicate and/or advise us. We should be in receipt of the article no later than six weeks prior to the publication "Lifeline" and preferably much sooner. We do not promise any particular publication date for articles.

PAYMENT

In appreciation, we offer a free one year subscription and several complimentary copies of the issue in which your submission appears.

We do not pay money for articles nor do we give free advertising in exchange. If you are in business, we will also print a brief (no more than 40 words) statement of who you are and how people can reach you.

The reason we do not pay for articles is based on philosophical as well as financial considerations. The *Dream Network* exists to provide a community forum in which we learn from one another as well as a place for us to dialogue with one another. Once acceptance of articles is based upon financial remuneration, a certain segment of the population is denied access. Those denied such access would be those whose ability to express themselves well enough in writing is not such that they can earn a fee, i.e., only professional writers would be heard. Obviously, we encourage well-written articles and professional writers do write for us out of a desire to share with the dream community.

Approximate 'Lifelines' (formerly 'deadlines'):

All Saints Day/Halloween (Winter); Valentine Day (Spring); Memorial Day (Summer) Labor Day (Autumn)

Approximate Distribution Dates: January (Winter); April (Spring); July (Summer); October (Autumn)

Thank you for your interest in dreams & the *Dream Network*.

Categories: Fiction—Nonfiction—Arts—Children—Culture—General Interest—Health—Inspirational—Interview—New Age—Paranormal—Parenting—Psychology—Self Help—Senior Citizen—Spiritual—Mystery in the true sense

CONTACT: Submissions Editor
Material: All
PO Box 1026
Moab UT 84532
Phone: 435-259-5936
Website: DreamNetwork.net

Dreams of Decadence

Vampire poetry up to 2 pages and vampire fiction 1k–15k words. Pays 1-5¢/word on publication for FNASR for original fiction. In general, reprints will be considered on a for-copy basis and only if last published at least two years ago. Looking for atmospheric, well-written stories. The emphasis is on dark fantasy rather than horror. Vampires may be either protagonists or villains, but in either case characters should be well-developed. We want to see original ideas and story concepts, not rehashes. I like stories that take the traditional concept of the vampire into new territory, or offer a new perspective. I like elegantly-crafted, poetic prose with a Gothic feel, but remember: stories do need well-developed characters and plot no matter how lovely the writing style may be. I do NOT want to see any more stories about posers or wanna-be's; Dracula (historical or Stoker's); vampire monks/priests; or Jesus Christ, Santa Claus, or the Easter Bunny as vampires. The following are NOT STORIES; please do not send them to me: Someone becomes a vampire; Vampire feeds; Vampire gets laid; Vampire gets staked. If that is all that happens in your story, this is NOT the market for it. It is okay for any of those things to happen in a story, but none of those is a sufficient plot. "Vampire feeds" is equivalent to "Someone eats a hamburger": It happens all the time, but it doesn't make much of a story. Looking for all forms of poetry, up to 2 pages in length; however, the less horrific and the more explicitly vampiric a poem is, the more likely it is to be accepted. I do not buy horror poetry. Poetry payment: $3.00 per short poem, $5.00 per longer poem, $20.00 for featured poet. Simultaneous subs ok if so noted. No e-mail submissions. Sample $5.

Categories: Fiction—Fantasy—Poetry

CONTACT: Angela Kessler, Editor
Material: All
PO Box 2988
Radford VA 24143-2988
Please mark clearly as being for Dreams of Decadence

Drum Business

Drum Business is designed exclusively for individuals involved in the sale of acoustic and electronic percussion and related equipment. The primary objective is to help the dealer run his or her operation more effectively by delivering relevant information on other successful operations. Other editorial will consist of manufacturer profiles, industry news, and in-depth coverage on new product information. While it is not crucial that all of our writers have worked in a drum shop or drum department, it is necessary that they know enough about drums, drum retailing, and retailing in general to be able to write about managing, merchandising, advertising, sales tips, and other topics associated with running a retail establishment.

Additionally, DB is looking for journalists who can present information in an objective manner so as to avoid making value judgements. Therefore, keep all articles as objective as possible. We are interested in how and why a particular store owner or manager operates a certain way; the reader can make their own decisions about whether or not they can adapt it for use in their own store.

Before you attempt to write an article for *Drum Business*, you should ask yourself the following questions: Will this article help a substantial numbers of retailers improve their operations? Will it enlighten them on a particular phase of retailing? Will it save them time, money, or effort? Is the topic interesting enough to attract a large number of readers? Will the article help them arrive at a decision or draw a conclusion? Will the article help retailers do their jobs better or run their stores more efficiently? Not every article will do all of those things, but if the article does not do any of them, the DB will probably not be interested in it.

Please query us on lengthy material before you begin writing. This helps us avoid receiving articles we cannot use, and it will help you avoid having your articles returned. Send us a brief outline of the subject matter and your angle on the story. The editors will then be able to guide you in tailoring the material to the exact needs of the magazine. Also, if your idea has already been assigned or covered, we can notify you before you begin working. If you are writing for DB for the first time, or if your idea is somewhat out of the ordinary, you will be asked to submit your piece on speculation.

The above information should guide you in submitting material to *Drum Business*. If you need any further information, please write to us. We are always interested in acquiring good editorial material and in finding talented, competent writers.

PAYMENT

Drum Business pays upon publication. Rates vary depending upon the length of the story after editing, whether the article will be used as a feature article or column, and, to some extend, the length of the writer's association with *Drum Business*.

GENERAL RATES

Feature article: $250 - $350. Buys all rights.

Column: $100 - $200. Buys all rights. (Receipt of payment generally occurs three to six weeks after publication.)

OPEN COLUMNS

*Retailing Column*s – Column material can be technical, conceptual, or philosophical in nature.

Topics should be very specific, and we encourage the use of drawings, photos, or illustrations where applicable. (750 – 1000 words)

Progressive Management: Insightful management techniques for everything from computer usage to hiring and firing.

Effective Merchandising: Tips and practical ideas on merchandising drum and related equipment store layout, displays, etc.

Sales Seminar: Tips on retail sales techniques.

Advertising Basics: How to run cost-effective ad campaigns.

Studio Insights: Setting and running a teaching program.

Retailer Profile: A look at the management of successful drum/music shops.

A Closer Look: A look at one vertical aspect of a particular company and how it relates to over-all operation of the company.

Site Seeing: Everything about drums, drummers, and retail on the Web.

Manuscripts are edited to conform to style policies, as well as for consistency and readability.

This may involve condensing, rearranging, retitling, and, to some extent, rewording the article.

Please refer to the DB Style sheet for specific style preferences. Final decisions regarding style, grammar, and presentation are the right of the editorial staff of *Drum Business* magazine.

STYLE SHEET - Manuscript Layout

Margins: First page—three-inch margin at top, one-inch margin at bottom and sides. Subsequent pages—one-inch top, bottom, and sides.

Type specs: Copy must be typed and double spaced. Pica preferred, elite acceptable, no script.

For those using computers, manuscripts should look at much like typewritten manuscripts as possible, i.e., double spaced, margins as specified above, common typeface.

E-mail submissions are acceptable. Please attach Word or text file to email document and send to kevk@moderndrummer.com.

COPY LENGTHS

Feature material should range from 2,500 to 3,000 words.

Column material should range from 750 to 1,000 words.

PUNCTUATION

Album, film, and book titles, as well as periodicals, should be underlined. Trademarks and model names should also be underlined, e.g. Tama Titan hardware, Paiste Rude crash cymbal, Remo Pinstripe head, Pro-Mark 5A drumsticks, Ludwig Black Beauty snare drum. Do not hyphenate words at the end of lines.

Dashes should be typed as a double hyphen with a space before and after (-). The initial letter of each word in album, film, and book titles, and in the names of periodicals, should be capitalized.

GEOGRAPHIC TERMS

Specific locations should be capitalized, e.g., Midwest, East Coast, West Coast. General directions should be in lowercase, e.g., east, west, north, south.

MUSICAL GENRES

Capitalize Gospel, Latin, and Dixieland. All other musical genres should be lower case, e.g., rock, jazz, etc. R&B or rhythm & blues; C&W or country & western; rock 'n' roll.

STYLE NOTES

Use words for number most of the time, except in a list of measurements or specific scientific measurements. '70s, '80s, 90s when dealing with decades. Forties, fifties, and sixties when dealing with age. LP (LPs), 45 (45s) CD (CDs)

PARAGRAPHING

The first paragraph of an article should be aligned entirely with the left margin. The first line of subsequent paragraphs should be indented one tab when using a computer, with subsequent lines aligning with the left margin. Do not insert line spaces between paragraphs.

INTERVIEWS

A. For question and answer format, introduction should follow paragraph format described in VII above. Uppercase initials of interviewer (followed by a colon) should precede questions, and initials of interviewee (also followed by a colon) should precede responses.

B. Interviews that follow narrative format should follow paragraph rules outlined in VII above.

PREFERRED SPELLINGS

A. Okay

B. Alright, Tom-tom, Hi-hat, Drumset, Drumkit, Drumheads, Drumsticks, Mic' (microphone), (noun) plural—mic's, e.g., I use three mic's. Miking, miked, mike (verb), e.g., I mike my sound room. Setup (noun), e.g., The article describes my store setup. Set up (verb), e.g., I will set up the new display. " (inch), e.g., 2" x (by), e.g., 5x4

LANGUAGE

A. Do not use gonna for going to, gotta for got to, or 'cause for because. In general, stay away from contracting verbs by omitting the ending "g," e.g., sayin' or playin'.

B. Language should be reasonably "clean." Obscenities should be kept to a minimum, or avoided, if possible.

Categories: Nonfiction—Arts—Business—Money & Finances—Music

CONTACT: Kevin W. Kearns, Associate Publisher/Editor
Material: All
12 Old Bridge Road
Cedar Grove NJ 07009-1288
Phone: 973-239-4140
E-mail: kevk@moderndrummer.com

E Magazine
The Environmental Magazine

As the largest independent environmental magazine on the newsstand today, with a circulation of 50,000, *E* serves an important role as the voice for the environmental movement and as a vital information source on national and international coverage of environmental issues. Founded in 1990, E is sponsored by Earth Action network, a nonprofit organization located in Norwalk, CT. In an attempt to stay consistent with our values and goals, we print our magazine on recycled paper and screen our advertisers carefully.

1. We request that writers send an e-mail (preferred) or written query when first contacting *E* with a story idea. FAXed queries are acceptable. Please indicate approximate article length and which section of the magazine you are targeting, allowing a three-month lead time. We will contact you on acceptance of an article and assume no responsibility for unsolicited manuscripts. Please include writing samples and a self-addressed, stamped envelope (SASE) with your submission. We do not send free issues to potential freelancers.

2. Payment: *E* pays 30 cents per word upon publication. We do not usually pay for product or book reviews. Please submit an invoice upon acceptance.

3. Articles should be submitted on deadline in typed form with an approximate word count indicated. E-mail transmissions are preferred, although IBM-compatible disks are also acceptable. Please include a few sentences about yourself for the brief "author bio" we include at the end of many articles.

4. Articles for *E* should be written in a journalistic style in order to be easily understood by those not immersed in the environmental movement. Unfamiliar terms, scientific language and jargon should be avoided or explained for the benefit of the lay reader. We are not interested in strident, opinionated writing. We want a balanced tone that will not alienate the casual reader; *E* is an "advocacy" magazine that aims to broaden the base of the environmental movement, not to preach to the converted.

5. We are interested in articles dealing with environmental issues, currents of environmental thought and action and the dynamics of the movement (see "Section Guidelines" below). We are also interested in articles that explore the connections between environmental and other social change/humanitarian issues. We like articles which suggest ways to become involved and include places to write letters of support or protest, contact names and addresses, resources to tap, etc.

6. If photos and/or artwork are available, please indicate so in your query. PLEASE DO NOT SEND ANY ART MATERIALS UNTIL THEY ARE REQUESTED. We are not responsible for unsolicited artwork. Rates for images are negotiable.

7. We reserve the right to edit for grammar, brevity, clarity and tone. We prefer gender-neutral phrasing—i.e., "humankind" instead of "mankind."

8. We do not publish poetry, fiction or nature writing.

9. *E*'s "Green Living" section features regular departments: Your Health, Eating Right, House and Home, Going Green, Money Matters, Consumer News and Tools for Green Living. These articles individualize the environmental movement and discuss ways readers can implement environmental practices into their homes and family lifestyles.

Section Guidelines

E seeks submissions for the following sections, with word lengths as indicated. Please examine back issues of *E* to get an idea of the style, tone and content of articles we publish.

Features: In-depth articles on key national and international environmental issues. i.e., population, transportation, children's environmental health, biotechnology, environmental education and energy. Length: 3,200 to 4,200 words.

Currents: News articles. i.e., environmental racism, cloning controversies, Maine forests for sale, cactus poachers, profiles of key organizations/campaigns. 1,000 words; five per issue.

In Brief: Short news articles. i.e., garbage art, AmeriCorps, sea cucumber conservation. 400 words; four to five per issue.

Money Matters: Information, resources and tips on greening personal finance and investments. i.e., eco-friendly stocks, saving money with community supported agriculture, shareholder activism. 750 words.

Going Green: This section follows the fast-growing eco-tourism industry and highlights notable trends and destinations. i.e., Costa Rica Rainforest Eco-Lodges, Alaska ANWR Experience and vegetarian vacations. 750 words.

Consumer News: Examines green consumer products and trends. i.e., recycled or "tree-free" paper, natural cosmetics, and "smart" wood. 1,200 words.

House & Home: Looks at services and products beneficial in the creation of a green home. i.e., eco-paints, home energy-saving tips, organic cotton bedding. 750 words.

Your Health: Explores environmental aspects of personal health. i.e., autism and the environment, antibiotic-pumped livestock, endocrine disruptors, mercury poisonings. 1,200 words.

Eating Right: Discusses the environmental implications of food choices. i.e., organic cereals, sustainable seafood. 1,2 00 words.

Tools for Green Living: Brief introductions/reviews of new green products and services. i.e., Nature's Way Feline Pine cat litter and eco-friendly shoes. 100 words; unpaid. The Books section profiles new publications. i.e., Earth Odyssey. 100 words; unpaid.

Categories: Conservation—Ecology—Environment—Politics

CONTACT: Jim Motavalli, Editor
Material: All
PO Box 5098
Westport CT 06881
Phone: 203-854-5559 ext. 109
Fax: 203-866-0602
E-mail: jimm@emagazine.com
Website: www.emagazine.com

Eagle Magazine

FOE.com is the official website of the Fraternal Order of Eagles, its design and maintenance is provided mainly by Volunteer Eagle Webmasters at the International, State, Provincial and Local levels. For this reason you will find many different styles as you browse through the sections of our website.

The website is overseen by the Grand Aerie Website Committee which is comprised of the following Eagle members:

Heather Callahan - Assistant Webmaster, Coeur D'Alene Idaho #486

Gregory Colburn - Committee Chairman, Webmaster, San Jose California #8

Chuck Cunningham - Assistant Webmaster, Assistant to the Grand Secretary, Akron Ohio #2736

Dwight Dennings - Assistant Webmaster, Gladwin Michigan #4121

Linda Heffner - PGMP, Assistant to the GMP, Brunswick Maryland #1136

Tom McGrath - Past Grand Officer, Vergennes Vermont #3801

Don Westfall - Webmaster of one of the very first Eagle websites, Orlando Florida #3496

If you have any questions, comments, suggestions or submissions for the website you can email us at websupport@foe.com.

Categories: Nonfiction—Fraternal Order of Eagles

CONTACT: Gregory Colburn
San Jose #8
1036 Lincoln Ave
San Jose CA 95125

Early American Life

Early American Life (formerly *Early American Homes*) is a bi-monthly magazine about the details of the American domestic past. Our time period ranges from the Pilgrim Century to 1850 and extends later if the subject warrants.

Our readers are interested in material and social history. They value what this information adds to their own lives and surroundings. They want to know more, in-depth, about the history inherent in objects—houses, gardens, textiles, painted decoration, furniture, pottery, food—indeed every element that was commonplace to early America. They like to see, and read about, the details.

This magazine is about reproductions as well as antiques. Fine craftsmanship—the work of someone who lived and worked at a certain time in a particular place—is integral to the value of objects past and present. We feature new houses, textiles, furniture, ceramics and other decorative objects and techniques made with attention to their historic precedents. Projects our readers can try themselves are also appealing, provided they, too, have an early American background.

We're receptive to articles that explore travel to historic places, discuss preservation issues, the antiques and reproductions market, journals, diaries, and inventories. We are always interested in articles that examine the human dimensions of American history; in the regular department called Life in Early America we explore what went on day to day in a particular place in a certain period. Academic writing and images of past grandeur do not appeal.

Photographs accompanying article queries are helpful to us; their quality need not be professional, just informational. We do return them. We pay for articles on acceptance.

Categories: Antiques—Architecture—Arts—Biography—Collectibles—History—Travel

CONTACT: Jeanmarie Andrews, Editor
Material: American life, social history, and arts before 1850
PO Box 221228
Shaker Heights OH 44122
E-mail: queries@firelandsmedia.com
Web site: www.ealonline.com

The East Bay Monthly

The East Bay Monthly, as you might have guessed, is a magazine published monthly and distributed throughout the East Bay (Oakland, Berkeley and environs). The Monthly's circulation—81,000—is the largest in the East Bay.

The Monthly's editors welcome queries from freelance writers. You should know that our first commitment is to fine writing. We appreciate the passionate essay, the deft parody, the tale well-told, first-person narratives, historical pieces, personality profiles, as well as carefully reported features and in-depth investigative articles. Just about the only genres we are not interested in are poetry and fiction.

We aim to be a forum for distinctive, intelligent, individual voices on every conceivable topic of interest to our audience. We like stories about local people and issues. We are generally only interested in topics outside the East Bay's borders if, a) the writer is a recognized East Bay writer, or b) the article idea can still be tied to East Bay history or culture.

We suggest you spend some time looking over recent issues of The Monthly to get a sense of what we publish and what might appeal to us.

To propose an article, send us some recent writing samples, a self-addressed stamped envelope and a cover letter with the following information: your story idea, how you will approach it, your point of view, whom you will interview, a proposed length, and why you think your idea will make our readers sit up and take notice.

Expect to receive a reply from us in four to six weeks. Please note that if you do not send us an SASE, we are not responsible for the fate of your submission.

The Editors
Categories: Nonfiction—Culture—Lifestyle—Regional

CONTACT: Kira Halpern, Co-editor
Material: Any
CONTACT: Kate Rix, Co-editor
Material: Any
1301 - 59th St.
Emeryville CA 94608
Phone: 510-658-9811
E-mail: editorial@themonthly.com
Website: www.themonthly.com

East End Lights
The Quarterly Magazine for Elton John Fans

WHAT ARE WE LOOKING FOR?

Anything, so long as it is related to Elton John. We want the voice of the fans to be heard, whether it be in a story, photos, original artwork, fan letters, ramblings, ravings... you get the idea.

You could write a deep piece about a personal experience related to a song, or a funny story about how your co-workers make fun of you for listening to Elton's music. Close encounters with EJ, the first song which turned you on to his music, lyric analysis, album critique, an outstanding concert experience, and so on.

Be creative. Write what you like. Use your own voice. As editors we try to keep our influence to a minimum. But if you should have questions, or even writer's block, we're just an email away.

East End Lights is not an Elton John love-fest. We do not subscribe to the "artist can do no wrong" policy. Be objective. *East End Lights* provides readers with historical accounts and interviews with Elton band members and associates and does not lend itself to "gossip" type stories and articles. Just the facts.

East End Lights has an open-door policy regarding submissions. You don't have to be a seasoned journalist — just a fan!

WHAT FORMAT DO I SUBMIT MY WRITTEN WORK IN?

Very simply. Electronic. You can email it to us at eel@accessthemusic.com. It can be any just about any word processing program out there (Word, Quark Epress, Simple Text, etc). Please send the file as an attachment and not embedded into your message window.

PHOTOS & ARTWORK

We accept photos and original artwork. Copyright laws are applicable; if you are not the original photographer or author of the work, we cannot accept your submission.

We accept 35mm prints only — color laser copies and inkjet prints are generally not acceptable. Photos mailed to use are not returned, so don't send anything you cannot part with.

You may also send photos via email. Scanned images should be 300dpi at 100% scale, and saved as a JPEG with a high quality setting.

Be sure to include the pertinent details about the photo, such as the date it was taken and a brief description of the subject. When submitting original artwork, include the medium used, and perhaps your inspiration for the work.

If you have any questions about submitting your photos or artwork, please contact eel@accessthemusic.com.

HOW DO I SUBMIT?

There are two kinds of submissions: unsolicited, and comissioned. The short story is, if you don't care about getting paid for your work, you can simply send it in as an unsolicited submission. However, if you would like to be paid for your efforts, you must begin with a query letter to let us know about your ideas.

UNSOLICITED SUBMISSIONS

An unsolicited submissions is a piece which, regardless of size or content, is sent to us without first being assigned to you. To get a story assignment, you must first send us a query letter. *East End Lights* is not obligated to use, nor do we pay for, unsolicited submissions.

WHAT IS A QUERY LETTER?

A query letter is simply the starting point... if you have an idea for an article, let us know what you have in mind before you before you put pen to paper.

We do not have a "standard format" for query letters. Just tell us who you are, what you want to write about, and how we can contact you. Samples of your previous works are helpful. Just drop us a line at eel@accessthemusic.com.

COMMISSIONED WORK

If your idea is accepted, we will contact you with further details on what we need for your story. If you accept the assignment, it becomes a commissioned piece.

If you write your piece before we have commissioned it, you do so at your own risk. *East End Lights* is not obligated to use, nor do we pay for, unsolicited submissions.

WHAT'S IN IT FOR ME?

Apart from international exposure and the joy of seeing your name in print, *East End Lights* will actually pay you for your commissioned work!

$50 for features and columns
$20 for fillers*
$20 kill fee**
pays on publication
byline given
does not pay expenses*** of writer on assignment
author usually handles major revisions
accompanying photos are appreciated, but not required

All authors who receive payment for their work will receive a Tax Form 1099 for the IRS if applicable.

For material which isn't time-sensitive, we may hold an article for use in a future issue due to space constraints.

GET IT RIGHT

We're pretty relaxed as far as content, but we do ask that you follow some basic tenets of writing. Proper grammar and accurate spelling are as important as the story itself.

Fact checking is equally important. If you quote a lyric, get out the liner notes and make sure you get it right. Check dates, verify quotes, and in general try not to leave holes in your work.

Edit thyself. If the story is about the EJ concert you attended, make sure that is the story. Skip the details of the sumptuous meal you ate before the show, the lovely hotel you stayed in the night before, the screaming child behind you on the plane, or the three hour delay at the airport. Focus. Tell the story you set out to tell.

And above all, have fun!

NOTES

Generally speaking, fillers are much shorter than features and columns. *East End Lights* will determine whether a piece constitutes a filler, feature, or column, and will inform you of this at the time of the assigment.

The kill fee is the amount paid for commissioned work which, for reasons beyond our control, is never published.

We will never ask you to spend any money for the sake of a story, so there will never be any expenses as a result of an assignment. If you choose to jet off to see Elton John in concert, you do so at your own expense.

Categories: Fiction—Nonfiction—Arts—Biography—Entertainment—Gay/Lesbian—Music

CONTACT: Mark Norris, Editor
Material: All
Access Entertainment, LLC
PO Box 621
Joplin MO 64802-0621
Phone: 417-782-9911
E-mail: eel@accessthemusic.com

East Texas Historical Journal
Stephen F. Austin State University

The *East Texas Historical Journal* is published in the Spring and Fall of each year. It includes articles and reviews of recently published books, mainly on Texas history, especially East Texas history. Submission must be on disk (3.5") or via email as an MS-Word attachment as well as hard copy. Notes should be placed at the end. Articles that do not exceed twenty-five to thirty pages, notes included, are preferred. We also welcome new book reviewers. Potential book reviewers should email a brief statement of their fields of expertise.

Categories: Nonfiction—History

CONTACT: Archie P. McDonald, Director and Editor
Material: All
Box 6223, Stephen F. Austin State University
Nacogdoches TX 75962
Phone: 936-468-2407
Fax: 936-468-2190
E-mail: amcDonald@sfasu.edu
Website: www.easttexashistorical.org

Eastern Fly Fishing

Thanks for your interest in *Eastern Fly Fishing* magazine. To receive consideration for publication you should read and follow these guidelines closely.

ABOUT THE MAGAZINE

Eastern Fly Fishing magazine is a destination specific publication to be viewed as an inspiring, collectible reference of Eastern angling destinations. The staff at *Eastern Fly Fishing* takes pride in our editorial content. Our writing is refreshing, our photography, captivating. *Eastern Fly Fishing* is issued bimonthly.

FEATURE ARTICLES

Our goal is to give an inspiring and complete report on specific Eastern angling destinations. Angling destinations include both the famous and the lesser know waters, and include all species found in our diverse geographical region. If more than one species is found in any given water, writers should cover each species, as well as every season that water is fishable. In short, feature articles should be concise, and leave no holes. Our goal is to cover specific angling destinations as no other publication has done in the past. **The best way to get a feel for what we want is to study one of our magazines.**

Photography is very important. *Eastern Fly Fishing* has set high standards for all images used in our magazine. Writers have a much better chance of being published if articles are accompanied by stunning photography. We will not publish dead fish, poorly exposed or composed shots, and we prefer not to use "hero shots."

The area of coverage for our features includes the Eastern United States, Eastern Canada, and the Caribbean.

Feature Article Requirements
- Provide practical traveling and angling information to specific destinations, including personal anecdotes
- Included should be pertinent angling history and thorough description of the fishery
- Detailed description of angling techniques, tackle and flies, and local perspectives
- Articles should be thorough and specific so as to sufficiently inform and give the angler confidence to effectively fish the presented water
- Included with each article should be any applicable hatch chart and detailed map of the coverage area
- Conservation issues and future considerations should be addressed
- Selection of 35mm (or larger) slides **(captioned and placed at the end of the manuscript)**
- Three popular flies of the fishery should be included for us to photograph, as well as a material list for each pattern.
- Feature article length should be 2,500 to 3,500 words

DEPARTMENTS

Most department material is staff-written. Exceptions are as follows:

Eastern Fly Tying: This department covers one Eastern fly pattern each issue. New, unusual and exciting patterns are encouraged, but we will also represent the time-proven standards. Flies for any Eastern species can be considered. Articles should include a little history and use of the fly, as well as step-by-step photos of the tying sequence, shot against a neutral-colored background. Two finished flies should accompany the article for photographic purposes.

Notes, News & Reviews: This department covers news events, and mini destinations (200 to 500 words). As with all material submitted, query first.

Conservation: Any conservation issue concerning our coverage area. Maximum length 850 words.

Exposure: Photo essay of 8 to 10 images depicting angling in our coverage area.

Digital Image Submission Guidelines
Feature Articles/Exposure
1) We only except files from digital SLR cameras with a minimum of 6-megapixels, 8-megapixel or higher are preferred! **Note:** A 35-megabyte file is needed for full page offset printing.
2) When making a submission please include 2 images per image file, the unedited RAW file and a processed JPEG.
3) Include a color contact sheet with file names of your images.
4) If the RAW file or contact sheet is not included, the submission will automatically be rejected.
5) Please do not submit images that are out of focus or overexposed.

Departments
1) Image files must be a minimum of 5-megabytes (11-megabyte files are preferred).
2) Files submitted for use in our departments may be sent in RAW, TIFF or JPEG format. If submitting files in JPEG, please use the maximum quality when saving images from your camera.
3) Please do not submit images that are out of focus or overexposed.

MANUSCRIPT SUBMISSIONS AND PAYMENTS

Initial contact with the editor by e-mail is preferred. A formal query letter, outlining the proposed article, should be sent to the editor before making a submission. A selection of slides **must** accompany the formal query. Unsolicited manuscripts must include a self-addressed, stamped envelope (**S.A.S.E.**) for their return. *Eastern Fly Fishing* is not responsible for submissions in transit to and from our editorial office.

Text and photos are purchased as a package. Manuscripts accepted without the appropriate photographic support will warrant less money for their use. *Eastern Fly Fishing* buys first North American serial publication rights. We reserve the option to edit all articles, however, we will make every effort to minimize editing to avoid changing the style or content of manuscripts.

All manuscripts should be submitted in typewritten form, double spaced. The author's name, address, phone number and manuscript word count should appear on the first page of the manuscript. A 3½" computer disk needs to be included with your submission. Manuscripts should also be e-mailed to the managing editor using a .doc or .rtf extension.

Payment is made approximately one month prior to publication, and the pay rate varies with the length and completeness of the submission. Inclusion of high-quality slides has a major impact in determining the pay rate for any given article. Our pay rate is as follows:

Feature Articles $400 to $600; Northwest Fly Tying $250 ; Notes, News & Reviews $100 to $125; Conservation $150

PHOTO SUBMISSIONS, ARTWORK AND PAYMENTS

Eastern Fly Fishing usually buys text and photos as a package. There are exceptions, however, and additional photography may be purchased on occasion. Contributors must query first.

We accept 35mm (or larger) transparencies only. Slides should be shipped in a clear sleeve, with concise captions. The photographer's name and address should appear on each slide mount. Payment varies for size used and impact. Our pay rate is as follows:

Cover $500; Exposure $600; Inside use $25 to $300; Illustrations and artwork $25 to $300

Categories: Nonfiction—Fishing—Sports/Recreation

CONTACT: Steve Probasco, Editor-in-Chief
Eastern Fly Fishing
PO Box 708
Raymond WA 98577
E-mail: probasco@matchthehatch.com
CONTACT: John Shewey, Managing Editor
Material: Manuscripts/slides
Eastern Fly Fishing
PO Box 12275
Salem OR 97309
E-mail: shewey@matchthehatch.com
Website: www.matchthehatch.com

EatingWell

An Introductory Note

EatingWell is edited for intelligent, discriminating readers who know that what they eat directly affects their well-being. They believe that, with the right approach, one can enjoy both good food and good health. They are suspicious of additives and junk foods and personally concerned about saturated fat, "empty" carbohydrates, sodium, calories, and the nutritional value of the foods they eat.

The magazine's distinguishing characteristics are:

A strong journalistic voice

Authoritative, timely coverage of nutrition issues

An avoidance of the "for women only" tone of many food magazines

Healthy recipes that emphasize good ingredients, simplicity of preparation and full flavor

A scrupulous balance of good writing and beautiful photography presented through the highest-quality printing and binding

A sense of humor

The best way to understand us, and the type of material we publish, is to read a recent issue. This will give you an accurate picture of EatingWell's scope, approach and style.

Feature Articles

Each issue of EatingWell contains a mix of solid journalistic profiles, science reports, investigative articles and travel pieces in combination with several cooking/recipe-oriented service features. We expect thorough, accurate research (vetted by our staff nutritionist and scientific advisory panel) and thought-provoking writing. At the same time, articles must be readable—filled with detail and the creative use of anecdotes.

Features range from 1,500 to 3,000 words, for which we pay $1.00 to $1.50 per word. Recipes rates range from $100 to $175 per recipe.

On assigned articles, we will negotiate expenses. While we will consider unsolicited manuscripts, contributors are urged to query first with a one- or two-page letter. We accept queries accompanied by clips via standard mail or electronic mail. Virtually all the features we use are specific assignments made after extensive discussion with an experienced writer whose work we know. Some samples:

Heart of the Matter: Cholesterol & the heart-smart consumer: foods to eat, foods to avoid, *By Peter Jaret*

Faux Food: Where have all our nutrtients gone? *By Rachael Moeller Gorman*

Cranberries: The tart, versitile American fruit of the holiday season. *By Nancy Baggett*

Departments

The best way for a first-time contributor to introduce us to his or her work is through one of our four regular departments. Several of these are staff-written or done by "regulars," but our two short-feature departments, "NutritionWatch: The Science of Eating Well" and "Observer: News From the World of Food," rely heavily on freelancers. Newcomers are welcomed. Stories in these departments run from 200 to 500 words and payment is generally $150 to $200. As with longer features, query first in writing. A paragraph or two is sufficient.

Photography

EatingWell's photographic standards equal or surpass those of any other publication in our category. Guidelines for submission of digital photography are being developed.

We use color throughout the magazine. Transparencies, 35 mm or larger, are preferred. Prints, while acceptable, are a distant second choice to transparencies. Some photographs used in the departments are purchased from stock, but whenever possible, we prefer to assign.

Photographers who would like to be considered for assignments or who wish to contribute from existing files should send samples of their work and sufficient return postage to the art director. We prefer two or three sheets of transparencies accompanied by tearsheets. While every care will be taken, we regret that we cannot be responsible for unsolicited material sent to us.

Assignment rates and expenses are negotiated individually. Unless stated otherwise, rates for stock photography are as follows:

Cover: $500 One-half page: $150

Spread (2-page): $325 Less than one-half page: $100

Full page: $225

Illustrations

Illustration plays an important part in the graphic personality of EatingWell. Typically, it is used to open at least one major feature and appears throughout the departments. Artists wishing to be considered for assignments are encouraged to send reproductions of their work to the art director.

Technical Details

Contributors are responsible for assuring that their material is delivered safely to our offices. Original artwork should be sent via Federal Express or trackable UPS.

Electronic text files should be compatible with Microsoft Word. Submissions may be made on disk or via e-mail, with the manuscript sent as an attachment. Writers should always retain a copy of their work.

Payment for assigned material reaches contributors within 45 days of acceptance. We pay on publication for stock material.

Unless otherwise stated, we purchase first North American serial rights and we retain the nonexclusive right to reuse material in our own publications and digital media. If we do reuse it, additional payment is made, typically 20% of the original fee for each distinct use.

EatingWell cannot be responsible for unsolicited material. Such submissions will not be returned unless accompanied by return postage or courier fees.

Categories: Nonfiction—Food—Nutrition—Science—Travel

CONTACT: Eating Well, Inc.
Material: All
PO Box 1010
823A Ferry Rd
Charlotte VT 05445
Phone: 802-425-5700
Fax: 802-452-3700
E-mail: editors@eatingwell.com - foodeditors@eating well.com - artdirector@eatingwell.com

Education in Focus

Education in Focus is a 6-page newsletter that enlightens readers to urgent concerns in education in a fundamental way. All material must maintain a humane premise, rationally defended, and be suitably documented. Length is limited to about 3,000 words (more in exceptional cases). Please don't submit articles that support the failures of the education system or that lack sensible solutions to urgent problems. Payment is modest. Comp copy available (provide SASE—#10, one stamp).

Categories: Education

CONTACT: Joe David, Editor
Material: All
PO Box 202
Warenton,VA 20188
Phone: 540-428-3175
E-mail: staff@bfat.com
Website: www.bfat.com

Education Week

Guidelines for *Education Week* Commentary Writers:

Education Week considers unsolicited manuscripts for inclusion in the Commentary section, provided they follow the guidelines below.

Essays should run approximately 1,200 to 1,500 words (five to six double-spaced pages) in length.

Submissions should treat issues in precollegiate education or child development. In organization and tone, the piece should take the form of an opinion essay rather than a scholarly paper or research report.

Our audience includes elementary and secondary teachers, principals, superintendents, school-board members, education-school faculty members, chief state school officers, education researchers, and others. Most of our readers are already aware of basic issues in education; for this reason, we usually accept only essays that treat specific topics in a detailed and analytical way.

If your submission is accepted for publication in the Commentary section, you will be contacted about possible publication dates and the amount of your honorarium; payments are made within two weeks of publication.

Because *Education Week* has specific style rules, it is likely that we will make at least a few changes to your essay. Please provide us with daytime and evening/weekend phone numbers where you can be reached to approve any changes or answer any questions we might have.

We often receive requests from other publications to reprint Commentaries. Our procedure is to grant permission. Our credit line and the date of publication must also be printed with the essay. The person making the request is asked to contact the author of the essay. If you are contacted, it is up to you to give final permission and to discuss the subject of your payment. If you receive the initial call from someone who wants to reprint your piece, please tell the caller he or she must contact *Education Week*.

Please submit a hard copy of your manuscript as well as a copy on a computer diskette, or if you prefer, e-mail the submission to Amy E. Conrad at aconrad@epe.org. Please include a mailing address where the contract, honorarium, and other materials can be sent.

Manuscripts and diskettes cannot be returned.
Categories: Nonfiction—Child Development—Education

CONTACT: Amy E. Conrad
Material: All
6935 Arlington Rd.
Suite 100
Bethesda, MD 20814-5233
Phone: 301-280-3100
E-mail: aconrad@epe.org
Website: www.edweek.org

Educational Leadership

Educational Leadership is the official journal of the Association for Supervision and Curriculum Development (ASCD). Its contents are intended for all persons interested in curriculum, instruction, supervision, and leadership in education. Each issue contains articles by leading educators, reports of effective programs and practices, interpretations of research, book reviews, and columns.

Issues are organized around themes. In general, the more appropriate your article is for a theme issue, the more likely we will be able to publish it. We also accept articles on "Special Topics" if the subject is of great interest but not related to a theme. In addition, we invite international contributions all year long, but especially for those three to four issues designated as having an International Section.

Other important information: ASCD offers no remuneration for articles by professional educators.

Decisions regarding publication are made by the Editor and the editorial staff. ASCD reserves the right to reject material, whether solicited or otherwise, if it is considered lacking in quality or timeliness.

WHAT WE LOOK FOR...

The editors look for brief (1,500-2,500 words) manuscripts that are helpful to practicing K-12 educators. We are not looking for term papers or reviews of literature, and we rarely publish conventional research reports. We prefer articles in which the writer speaks directly to the reader in an informal, conversational style. The treatment of the topic should be interesting, insightful, and based on the writer's experiences. Practical examples should be used to illustrate key points. When reporting their own research, writers should emphasize explanation and interpretation of the results, rather than the methodology. We usually don't find query letters helpful; we prefer to read the manuscript.

HOW TO PREPARE YOUR MANUSCRIPT...

To prepare your manuscript, number all pages and show your name, address, phone number, fax number, and e-mail address on the cover sheet only. We prefer manuscripts that look like manuscripts, not like typeset articles from desktop publishing. On page one, just above the title, please indicate the number of words in the manuscript, including references, figures, and the like.

Cite references in the text like this (Jones 1988), and list them in bibliographic form at the end of the article; or use citations in the form of numbered endnotes. See a recent issue of *Educational Leadership* for examples of citations. Authors bear full responsibility for the accuracy of citations, quotations, figures, and the like.

For other matters of style, refer to *The Chicago Manual of Style and Webster's Collegiate Dictionary.*

HOW TO SUBMIT YOUR MANUSCRIPT...

Send two copies. It is not necessary to send unsolicited manuscripts by overnight mail-our deadlines are target dates, not factors in selection. You can expect to receive a postcard telling you that the manuscript has arrived; a response from an editor should arrive within eight weeks.

If you discover a small error after mailing your manuscript, please do not send a correction; small errors can be corrected in the editing process.

WHAT HAPPENS NEXT...

If your manuscript is accepted, even provisionally, we will ask you to send a computer disk or a letter-quality original of your article. Then your manuscript enters the pool of manuscripts on hand for a particular theme issue (or for use in "Special Topics"). When the editors assemble a particular issue, they review all manuscripts to make selections for the table of contents. All manuscript selections are tentative until we go to press.

When we select articles for each issue, we consider many factors, such as the balance of perspectives, locations, grade levels, and topics. If your manuscript becomes a contender for the final table of contents, you will be notified, and we'll ask you to send a computer disk or a letter-quality original. During the editing and layout process, however, we may have to make last minute adjustments, with resultant disappointments to authors.

WHAT TO DO ABOUT COMPUTER DISKS...

We edit on computer, so we'd like you to submit your manuscript on disk as well as on paper. We can use IBM-compatible or Mac disks but not Apple. Write on the disk both the kind of computer and the name of the word processing program you used-and be specific: include version numbers where applicable. If your disk has been formatted high-density, indicate this, too. And please indicate on the disk your last name and the file name of your manuscript.

If you cannot send a disk, we will use an electronic scanner to transfer your manuscript to a disk. We can only scan it, however, if it's a high-quality (clear and sharp) typewritten text or print-out.

We will also accept articles scheduled for publication sent to us via the Internet. Our e-mail address is shown below.

HOW TO SURVIVE THE EDITING PROCESS...

If your manuscript becomes a contender for the issue's table of contents, it is assigned to a staff editor, who shepherds it through all the editing and layout processes. Once your manuscript is edited, you will receive an edited version for your review, correction, and approval. At this time you will have a chance to correct errors, answer our queries, and update any outdated information. The style requirements of *Educational Leadership*—as well as space limitations—dictate heavy editing, and we appreciate collaboration with the authors in the process.

One more word about correcting your edited manuscript:

Please do not retype it! Just mark your corrections directly on the manuscript, and mail or fax it back to us. If you have insertions, please type or write them on separate pieces of paper; and indicate on the manuscript where they are to be inserted.

When you receive the edited version of your manuscript, you should also receive a transfer of copyright form, which includes permission to record your article (in case the editors select it for EL on Tape), and permission to use your article online. Please indicate your preferences on these forms, and return them by first-class mail or fax as soon as possible.

ABOUT ARTWORK AND PHOTOGRAPHS...

The editors like to have photographs and artwork related to the manuscripts, but these do not influence editorial selection. We appreciate having the opportunity to see your artwork-photos (black and white or color) or slides, and student papers and artwork. Send artwork when you are notified that your manuscript has been accepted or when the editors request it. Send photos to us by overnight mail.

Authors are responsible for ensuring that all persons in each photograph have given their permission for the photograph to be published; they are also responsible for ensuring that they have permission to use all other artwork, such as student work. Please include the name of the photographer or the source so that we may give proper credit; and, on the back of each item, tape a small piece of paper with your name and address. (Do not write directly on the back of the photo.) And please add a note to explain what's happening in each photo, including the name and location of the school, or a note to explain the artwork. This information helps us when it's time to write captions.

WHEN YOUR ARTICLE COMES OUT...

As soon as the issue is off press-about the first of each month of issue-we'll send your complimentary copies. Article authors receive five copies; column authors, two copies; book reviewers, one copy. We'll also send an "Author's Feedback Form" to gather your comments about our work. Fill that out quickly, and it's time to arrange your autograph party.

Categories: Nonfiction—Education

CONTACT: Marge Scherer, Editor
Material: All
ASCD, 1250 N. Pitt St.
Alexandria VA 22314-1453
E-mail: el@ascd.org
Website: www.el@ascd.org

Educators Edition
Teachers Magazine

Please refer to Metro Parent/Metro Baby.

Elbow Creek Magazine

Fiction, poetry and articles about the American West during the golden age of the cowboy.

Rights: We retain 90 day exclusive rights, with an added nine month electronic rights. That is, the item will remain on our site for at least one year, longer with writer's permission.

Needs: Cowboy fiction, poetry and articles. Stories should be set in the 1800s, though an occaisional exception will slip through. No pornography.

Length: Open

Art/Photo Needs: None at this time.

Payment: Payment is currently $20 per item.

How to Submit: Accept submissions via e-mail only. Please include the item within the text of your e-mail rather than as an attachment.

Response Time: 1-3 weeks

Submission Guidelines For Elbow Creek Magazine

Elbow Creek will focus on the American West, primarily the 1800s. While we may occasionally break from tradition and purchase a story that is based on modern times, that will be an exception.

No sexual content. We are an open readership, from ages ten to ninety. Innuendo is fine, courtship encouraged, but let the reader savor your words rather than your character's hooters.

Gunplay is fine, I mean c'mon, this is the west, but let's not focus on horrific, graphic death scenes. If your story is built around a gruesome death, you're not trying hard enough.

Stories should be more than straight out shoot 'em ups. I want the reader to pause after finishing your story and reflect a moment on the ending or on the slant of the story.

Characters should learn from their actions or seek to improve themselves, even if they "die trying." Throw a moral in there, if you can be subtle about it.

Story length can be anywhere from 1,500 words to 10,000, but keep in mind, we pay by the story, not the word.

Current payment is $20 per item, whether it is an article, a story or a poem. Additionally, one story per issue will be designated as the "featured" story, with payment of $50.

For independent stories, articles and poetry, we purchase exclusive, 120 day rights, with archive rights up to one full year. After that point, the story will remain archived on our web-site until you request that it be removed. The contract that you acknowledge after acceptance will reflect specific days, so there will be no confusion. This means that you may resell the story/poem/article after it has been posted at our site for 120 days, with the understanding that it will remain posted at our site for a total of 365 days. All that we ask is that you acknowledge, in the next printing, that your item was first published electronically at "Elbow Creek Magazine."

PLEASE NOTE: For rights and payment of our shared world

environment, please refer to the document entitled ""Elbow Creek Shared World Guidelines."

We welcome all independent submissions of articles, fiction and poetry. However, submissions to the shared world environment are by inquiry only. Because we will need to be careful about character and story development, it will be much more difficult to get published in this section of the magazine.

Include all submissions within the text of your e-mail. No attachments, please! Use Times New Roman, if possible, 12 pt. Submissions should be sent to editor@elbowcreek.com. Good luck to you, and thank you for your interest in Elbow Creek Magazine.

Categories: Western

CONTACT: Tom Rice, Editor
Material: All
PO Box 216
Gosport IN 47433
E-mail: editor@elbowcreek.com
Website: www.elbowcreek.com

The Electron
Cleveland Institute of Electronics and World College

How to write for *The Electron*

Articles in *The Electron* have "news value." We cover recent developments and trends in electronics and high technology. Because *The Electron* is published every other month, the editors and writers can't report breakthrough immediately when they occur. However, any items covered must be timely to justify its publication in our newspaper.

Cover Stories

The Electron's front page features must be written in the journalistic style, have news value, and contain quotes based on interviews with one or more sources.

Other elements the editors look for are strong lead paragraphs, a good angle, descriptive language and general readability.

You may use news releases as source material, but a manuscript that reads like a sales pitch will be rejected. Avoid an obvious slant toward a particular product or company. (An exception to this would be a "corporate profile," in which activities of a company in the forefront of electronics technology are examined. AT&T Bell Laboratories is a good example of one organization we have covered.)

You should have the ability to write about electronics/high technology in a manner the layperson can understand. Define terminology with a brief line of explanation set off with dashes or parentheses, or with a concise one or two line paragraph. Practical examples are helpful:

"Requirement at startup will be 75 kilowatts—enough to power a small radio station..."

Acronyms or terms common in everyday usage—IC, LCD, semiconductor, solid-state—do not require an explanation.

Suggested length for a cover story is 800 words.

The above guidelines also apply to articles written for *The Electron*'s various departments. However, we do not necessarily require that you interview sources or include quotes. If you are well-versed in an area (computers, broadcasting, avionics, etc.), you may rely upon your knowledge of, or expertise in that field to write your article.

Main Features

The Electron's main (photo) feature covers in depth a broad area in electronics/high technology. Examples of topic areas we have already covered include: Artificial Intelligence; Medical Electronics; Robotics;

and Telecommunications.

The main feature, run on a semi-regular basis, reflects that issue's editorial theme. Other articles in the issue will relate to the main feature, particularly the cover stories.

You should follow the cover story guidelines for style, content and readability. Remember, this is a photo feature. Ask about the availability of photographs when interviewing sources for facts and quotes.

Due to the length of the main feature (2,000 words), we recommend that you take the following approach. Break down the topic area by writing a main/overview article and one sidebar. In the main article, review trends and developments relating to the general topic. For the sidebar, you may write a retrospective of the technology, or interview a prominent person in the field.

We will consider your suggestions for alternative approaches to the main feature.

Technical Features

The Electron's technical articles focus on a timely topic in technology. The preferred writing style here is "tutorial" (essay form is best). Thus, technical articles in *The Electron* have news and educational value.

Most of your readers will be the students of The Cleveland Institute of Electronics and World College. Knowledge of electronics in relation to *The Electron*'s readers range from an electronics technician (associate degree level) to an electronics engineer (bachelor's degree level.) As a technical writer for *The Electron*, you are a teacher. Help the readers understand difficult points and concepts by providing illustrations. Supplement text discussion with tables and figures. These may be submitted as clean freehand drawings or sketches.

Your choice of topic should relate to the issue's editorial theme, if possible. Suggested length for a technical feature is 1,000 words.

Categories: Education—Electronics

CONTACT: Ted Sheroke, Advertising Manager
Material: All
1776 E 17th St
Cleveland OH 44136
Phone: 216-781-9400
Fax: 216-781-0331

Electronic Servicing & Technology

These writers' guidelines describe the kinds of articles published in *Electronic Servicing & Technology*, give some idea of the recommended length, and suggest a format for manuscripts.

Also included is a list of possible article subjects as well as a list of vocabulary words that we would like to define in depth in the magazine. These are meant as idea starters, and are not intended to exclude from consideration subjects that are not on the lists.

Also included are specific guidelines for preparing materials for publication in the SYMCURE and Troubleshooting Tips departments.

Sincerely, Conrad Persson, Editor

Electronic Servicing & Technology is written primarily for servicing technicians who sell, install, and service home electronics equipment.

Articles for *Electronic Servicing & Technology* should be technical in nature and be about an electronics or electronics-related subject. *Articles published in ES&T ordinarily fall into the following general categories:*

• Specific servicing procedures for specific electronic products.
• General troubleshooting/servicing procedures.
• Theory/operation of specific items of test equipment.
• Reports of new electronics technology of interest to electronic servicing technicians.
• Tutorial articles on electronics theory.
• Symptom/cure type brief articles.
• Troubleshooting tips.
• Articles on business, as related to consumer electronics servicing.

ES&T article coverage is not limited to these subject areas, however, and we welcome inquiries from prospective authors.

We use drawings, schematics, and photos, both B&W and color. For color photos, we prefer transparencies, although we can work from prints. We have access to artists who can create finished art, so don't be hesitant to include rough hand drawings. We can put them in final form.

We especially welcome articles that are on computer disk. We use IBM format, and can accept either 3½" or 5¼" disks. Preferred format is ASCII, but we can usually accept output from any word processor. Please be sure to include information that tells us what word processor you used to create the document.

Article length for a feature article should ordinarily be between three and fifteen typewritten pages. That's just a rough guide, though, not a hard and fast rule. Articles should be as long as they have to be to cover the subject thoroughly. Other manuscripts like Symcure, Troubleshooting Tips and others may be very brief.

It might be to the writer's advantage to submit a query beforehand, outlining a proposed article. That would allow the editors to comment specifically on whether an article is appropriate and/or needed, as well as to suggest to the writer information that should be included.

In any case, do not hesitate to write or call the editors to request comments and guidance on writing for ES&T.

Symcure

The term Symcure is a contraction of the two words: Symptom/cure. Problems that are published in ES&T in the Symcure department are those that have occurred more than once.

This is the kind of problem that you can solve without even a second thought because you've already seen so many of that particular brand and model of set with those symptoms and in almost every case it was the same component that had failed, or the same solder joint that had opened.

Because of the manner in which we publish Symcure, submissions, if they are to be considered, must follow these rules:

1. Each submission must consist of seven individual symptom/cure units on a single brand and model of television set. Seven are requested so we may choose the most appropriate for publication.

2. We must have the following information about the set:
• Manufacturer's name
• Model and chassis number or ID
• Sams Photofact number if you know it
• A rough sketch of the schematic where the fault was found. Each sketch should contain a major component such as a transformer, a tube, a transistor or an IC to provide a landmark for the ES&T staff.

3. Because the very nature of Symcure is based on schematics, if for any reason there is no Sams Photofact on the unit, we cannot accept the submission.

Troubleshooting Tips

A troubleshooting tip is a description of the procedure used by a servicing technician to diagnose, isolate and correct an actual instance of a specific problem in a specific piece of electronic equipment. Its value to readers, however, lies in the general methods described rather than its applicability to the repair of the specific piece of electronic equipment.

A good, useful troubleshooting tip has the following elements:
• A brief but complete, accurate and concrete description of the problem symptoms.
• A complete identification of the set, including manufacturer's name, model and chassis number and the Sams Photofact number, if known.
• A rough, simplified, schematic sketch of the area where the trouble occurred. Include some major component such as a transformer, tube or transistor, to serve as a landmark to the ES&T staff.
• A detailed step-by-step description of the procedure used to track down the cause of the problem. This should include the thinking process used—for example, "the absence of B+ voltage led me to believe...etc." • A mention of any symptoms that misled you and per-

haps caused you to follow false trails.

• A narrative telling why the defect was suspected and how it was determined to be the cause of the problem (e.g., tested open, shorted, etc.).

• A description of how the repair was performed, including any precautions about possibility of damage to the set or injury to the servicing technician, if applicable.

The characteristics of a good candidate for troubleshooting tips are as follows:

1. The cause of the problem should be relatively uncommon.

2. The diagnosis and repair should not be obvious, and preferably should present something of a challenge to a competent servicing technician.

Article Ideas

This is a list of ideas for articles for *Electronic Servicing & Technology* that readers have suggested, and that the editorial staff has added to. It is not meant to limit articles in *Electronic Servicing & Technology* to these subjects, merely to serve as a list of possible articles and idea starters.

• One type of article that many readers have requested is the article, or more usually a series of articles, that examines a relatively new model of TV set from end to end, describing all of the circuitry, and especially dwelling on any new type of circuitry.

Other article subjects:
• Power conditioning
• Troubleshooting HV and LV circuits and how they work
• Understanding and servicing TV shutdown circuits
• Understanding TV startup circuits
• Understanding TV voltage regulator circuits
• Troubleshooting horizontal circuits
• Troubleshooting vertical circuits
• Troubleshooting TV power supply circuits
• Servicing cellular telephones
• Specific troubleshooting procedures for specific brands and models of TV
• Dealing with newer, more exotic TV
• Understanding the NTSC waveform
• Preventive maintenance for printers
• Understanding electronic tuners and tuning
• DC motor control
• Servicing two-way radio
• IBM PC computer servicing
• The personal computer as a servicing tool
• Servicing CB radio
• Personal computer servicing: general and product specific
• Servicing compact disc players
• Servicing VCRs
• Understanding and servicing VCR control systems
• Servicing TVRO: downconverters, LNAs, actuators
• Understanding new circuitry: SAW filters, phase-lock loops, comb filters
• Using a spectrum analyzer in troubleshooting
• Fundamentals of electronics
• Fundamentals of electronic servicing
• Servicing projection TV
• Servicing video cameras/camcorders
• Test equipment use and operation
• Do-it-yourself circuit construction
• Diagnosing antenna problems
• Servicing consumer electronic instruments: keyboards, organs, etc.
• Troubleshooting older TVs
• Servicing microwave ovens
• Servicing, repair and calibration of test equipment
• Inexpensive test equipment/accessories
• Testing methodology
• Suggested general troubleshooting techniques/tips/hints
• Servicing audio equipment
• Detailed descriptions of how circuits work
• New methods of soldering/desoldering for new soldering technology

• Suggestions on finding/tailoring general replacements when exact replacements are no longer offered by manufacturer
• Lightning and surge protection
• TV tuner repair
• Understanding digital circuit design and operation
• Troubleshooting/repairing digital circuits
• Signal injection/signal tracing
• CIB calculations for MATV
• Identifying sources of TV interference and correcting problems
• Electronics in home appliances: what they are, how to fix
• Test equipment for personal computers
• Servicing mechanical components
• Understanding wire and cable
• Sources of replacement parts
• Description of the evolution of consumer electronic servicing
• The new multistandard TVs
• A step-by-step approach to troubleshooting: using the senses, what's the next step, etc.
• Equipping a test bench
• Troubleshooting logic circuits with logic probes, pulsers, etc.
• Training/studying
• Multichannel TV sound
• Understanding digital circuit test equipment
• Component testing: resistors, capacitors, inductors, diodes, transistors, ICs
• How switching power supplies work, and are there a lot of TVs or other consumer electronics with switchers in them
• Something like SYMCURE and Troubleshooting Tips for computers/VCR
• Information on electronics societies, organizations
• ESD protection
• Servicing the new Sanyo power supplies
• What is "HQ" circuitry in VCRs
• One reader would like to see a shop hints department showing better ways to make repairs faster in the shop.
• How about a mini course in relay and control logic for such purposes as microwave oven controls?
• Here's an idea I've toyed with from time to time: Would it be possible to start with a bare bones TV receiver and add colored overlays showing how TV has evolved from its inception to today?
• Troubleshooting using an oscilloscope
• Understanding electronics math
• Logs, R/C time constants, Kirchhoff's laws, Trigonometric functions, math primer
• Finding schematics is a problem, but is it possible in some instances to recreate the schematic by tracing the wiring and doing your own drawing?
• How does detection actually work?
• Math Cad review
• Remote control cable converters
• How does AGC work?
• How does AFC work?
• How does a VCO work?
• Discuss filters: high pass, low pass, band pass, active. And how about the word "filter"? Is it really a good word? In one sense, a filter is used to pass a band of frequencies while rejecting others. In another it is used to "smooth" a pulsating dc after rectifying an ac waveform. How should a tech think about filters?
• Why do we use Q to identify a transistor, CR or Y to identify a diode, etc.?
• What does sampling rate mean when we're talking about, for example, a digitizing oscilloscope?
• Why not a primer on transistors, explaining, among other things, why the base, emitter and collector are so called, why use a and ß for amplification, getting into PNP and NPN to a certain degree. That, then, gets into another interesting question: should bipolar transistors and FETs in fact be both called transistors? What are the similarities that get them both the name "transistor" (transfer/resistor), and what

A-E

are the differences?

• Modulation: among other things, we call the modulating waveform the "carrier", when in fact it can be suppressed before transmitting the signal. It seems like it's a poor choice of terminology.

• An article on antique radio, phono, etc. What the rewards are. What the equipment is. What people, organizations, companies are involved, etc.

• The organizations that ES&T readers belong to, or that might be able to help readers: NESDA, ETA, FIA, etc. What is a CET from the point of view of NESDA and ETA, etc.

• What is a "waveform analyzer"? Is it simply an oscilloscope with some other features like a built in DMM, etc.?

• How about an article on reading manufacturers model numbers: do the numbers mean anything?

• Correcting VCR loading problems

• Correcting VCR speed selection circuit problems

• One thing I'd like to do if possible is to track and publish information on companies that seem to disappear: like Symphonette, Bohsei, etc. I'd welcome any thoughts on how to do that.

• An article that looks at herringbone on screen, and describes what problem causes it and examines the circuits involved and the mechanics of the problem.

• We frequently talk about a two-port or three-port device. How about an explanation of what we mean by that?

• Ways to deal with intermittent problems

• Sorting out all of the transistor and IC part numbers

• How about an article on closed-captioning circuitry for TVs for the hearing impaired?

• What is an "eye" pattern on an oscilloscope? What is it used to measure and how is it used?

• What is a parametric amplifier and where is it used?

• What do ferrite beads do, what are they made of, when were they introduced, etc.?

• What books, catalogs, etc. are essential to a servicing technician's library?

• Warranties, manufacturer's and extended

• Satellite TV scrambling and descrambling

• Such things as active high, active low, Vdd, Vss, etc.

• Charge pump?

• Swallow counter

• Prescaler

• How to go about estimating a job

• Reading a schematic diagram

• Technical support from manufacturers. Tech help phone lines and price and availability of service literature.

• Frequency synthesis and frequency division—what do we mean by these?

• What are servos used for and how do they work?

• On a digital multimeter, why is there a 1/2-digit, and what does "an accuracy of "2% + 2 digits (or whatever) mean?

• Bar-code scanners. Bar codes are now being used to program VCRs

• This one was suggested by a reader who sent in a Reader Service card. An article on a complete sales/service center management software package.

• I'd like to see us do an article on transformers. Describe line isolation transformers, variable transformers, autotransformers, variable isolation transformers, discuss trademarks like Variac, step up, step down, coupling.

• How about a rundown of the safety related components in a consumer electronics product? What are their special characteristics, and why can't they be replaced with universal replacements.

Vocabulary

Here are some words that we would like to define in the magazine at some convenient time. One possible way would be for a writer to write an article on a subject to which several of the words relate, and define the terms in the article. Most vocabularies or glossaries provide just a brief definition of the word. I would like to include in-depth definitions.

Something to keep in mind, is that where the term is not particularly apt, this should be pointed out. For example, I'm not sure that the

terms "active" and "passive" are really descriptive of the characteristic they describe, although they come fairly close. Another example is the term "carrier" in regard to electromagnetic transmission. If you can transmit without the "carrier", then it really isn't a carrier, is it?

• Here's another term I have a hard time with - Injection, as of a signal or a voltage? What does "injection" mean, and is it apt?

• Slew rate

• Synchronous/asynchronous

• Prescaler

• Preemphasis

• PWM

• How about an article on abbreviations concerning computers, like MS-DOS, etc.

• Ramp up

• Bio of Lord Kelvin

• Why do we use U followed by a number to designate an IC?

• Scan-derived

• It would be interesting to delve into why the elements of a transistor: base, emitter and collector are so called.

• Why do we call certain portions of a TV circuit a driver?

• A to D and D to A conversion

• What is heat sink grease made of?

• In cable TV, what is meant by head end?

• What is a balun?

• What is meant by the term "leaky" in conjunction with electronic components? For example, transistors can be leaky, or capacitors. Anything else?

• Piecrusting

• Motorboating

• Barkhausen lines

• Turbo (in connection with computers)

• Servo

• WWV

• Alignment: TV, FM, VCR, Disc drive, other?

• Bias (There's forward and reverse bias on semiconductor junctions, and a bias used on magnetic tape). Any others?

• What do we mean by sampling rate when it comes to A to D conversion?

• Where does the term "capacitor" come from.

• What does "peak reading" mean when it comes to capacitors?

• Why not do a simple article to reveal the difference between "linear" and "nonlinear"? You could use actual resistors and diodes to do the research and suggest the readers do the same experimentation to find out what's going on.

• What is meant by "dynamic range"?

• There seems to be more than one meaning of "saturation": one, for example when talking about a circuit current condition, and one when talking about tape recording. What do they mean? Are there other meanings?

• Describe modulation: AM and FM. Come to think of it, why not include PCM, and any other Ms that come to mind?

• Define "harmonics".

• Dropout

• Retrace: Is this a good term, or is it misleading?

• Damper

• Keystoning

• Explain abbreviations like BNC, DIN, etc.

• Active filters

• Data communications "protocol"

• algorithm

• excursion

• Why is the supply voltage (in some cases the "scan derived" voltage) called a B+ voltage

• The term "flyback" would be one worth exploring at some time.

• Coupling, decoupling

• Neutralization as regards transistor amplifiers

• Countdown, as in TV output circuits

• Parasitic, as in parasitic oscillations.

It saves us a great deal of time, not to mention typographical errors, if writers who submit articles to ES&T are able to submit a floppy disk containing the text along with the manuscript. All of the computers used by the ES&T editorial staff are IBM compatible, and we can handle either to 5¼" or 3½" floppy disks formatted at any density.

Our preferred formats for articles that are submitted on disk are ASCII, or Word Star format, but we can work with files created on most word processors. If you submit an article on disk in any format other than pure ASCII, please include information that tells us what word processor you used to create the file.

There really are few stringent requirements for preparation of manuscripts for ES&T, but *here are a few suggestions for writers who submit manuscripts on computer disc, that will make it easier for the editors.*

1. If you feel that a term, or some kind of description requires emphasis, make a note of it on the manuscript, with your suggestion of the type of emphasis: italic, boldface, etc. Please don't include such things as underline or all caps, because we don't do that kind of emphasis in the magazine. And don't include that kind of emphasis in your document if you're submitting it on disc, because we would have to eliminate those imbedded commands and change to our typesetting codes for that emphasis.

2. Don't leave large open spaces in the text to show where figures go. Simply refer to the art in the text, for example "see Figure 1." The art department will try to put the art in the right place.

3. Don't put the caption at the point in the article text where the art goes. At the end of the article type in the word Captions, leave a couple of line spaces, and type in the captions, like this:

Figure 1. Connect the probe of the oscilloscope to

4. If you're submitting hand drawn art to be prepared in final form by the ES&T artist, it would be very helpful to the editors if you could type the callouts for all of the art on a separate sheet of paper, as well as writing them in on the hand drawn diagram, in all capitals. This has to be done by someone before the callouts can be sent to the typesetter.

Categories: Electronics—Technology

CONTACT: Conrad Persson, Editor
Material: All
PO Box 12487
Overland Park KS 66282-2487
Phone: 913-492-4857
Fax: 913-492-4857
E-mail: cpersedit@aol.com
Website: www.electronic-servicing.com

The Elks Magazine

The Elks Magazine is published 10 times a year for the 1.1 million members of the Benevolent and Protective Order of Elks. In addition to our mission of being "the voice of the Elks," we carry features of general interest. Articles should be fresh, provocative, thought provoking, well researched, and well documented. A thumbnail profile of the average reader would be a person over 40, with some college, an above-average income, and living in a town of 500,000 or less.

What We Can Use: Each year we buy 20 to 30 articles. We're looking for informative, upbeat, entertaining writing on a variety of subjects, including technology, science, sports, history, and seasonal items. Articles should be authoritative (please include sources) and geared toward the lay person. Articles should run between 1,500 and 2,500 words.

Not Needed: Fiction, travel, business, health, political or religious articles, humor, filler, or poetry. We usually do not publish first-person pieces.

Editorial Requirements

Rates: We prefer to see complete manuscripts. We review articles on speculation and pay 20 cents a word on acceptance.

Format: Articles should be typewritten and double-spaced in a 12-point type size. Do not send computer disks nor e-mails with attachments, as we are sensitive to viruses. Please include your telephone number or the best method to contact you. If we wish to buy your manuscript, we'll contact your for your Social Security number so that we can begin the payment process.

Photos: If we use any of your photos in the article, we pay $25 per photo. We take responsibility for securing illustrations/photographs for the article, but appreciate any assistance you might give.

Rights: First North American serial rights in print only. The author retains all other rights. Upon publication, all print rights revert to the author, and we forward all reprint queries to the author.

Response time: We read you manuscript within a day or so of receipt and either hold it for further consideration or reject the article. Basically, the longer (up to 6 weeks) it is until you hear from us, the greater the probability is that your work will be purchased.

SASE: YES. *The Elks Magazine* cannot accept responsibility for manuscripts sent without a self-addressed, stamped envelope.

Categories: Nonfiction—Associations—Aviation—Biography—General Interest—History—Rural America—Science—Sports/Recreation

CONTACT: Anna L. Idol, Managing Editor
Material: All
425 W. Diversey Pkwy.
Chicago IL 60614-6196
Phone: 773-528-0433
Fax: 773-755-4792
E-mail: annai@elks.org
Website: www.elks.org/elksmag

Elle

Formal guidelines not available. Please read a number of issues to ascertain the publication's style and needs.

Send queries to address below.

Categories: Fiction—Beauty—Diet/Nutrition—Entertainment—Fashion—Health—Lifestyle—Women's Issues

CONTACT: Submissions Editor
Material: All
1663 Broadway, 4th Floor
New York NY 10019
Phone: 212-767-5800
Website: www.elle.com

ELLERY QUEEN
THE WORLD'S LEADING MYSTERY MAGAZINE

Ellery Queen's Mystery Magazine

Ellery Queen's Mystery Magazine welcomes submissions from both new and established writers. We publish every kind of mystery short story: the psychological suspense tale, the deductive puzzle, the private eye case—the gamut of crime and detection from the realistic (including the policeman's lot and stories of police procedure) to the more imaginative (including "locked rooms" and "impossible crimes"). We need hard-boiled stories as well as "cozies," but we are not interested in explicit sex or violence. We do not want true detective or crime stories. With the exception of a regular book review column and a mystery crossword, *EQMM* publishes only fiction. We are especially happy to review first stories by authors who have never before published fiction professionally. First-story submissions should be addressed to *EQMM*'s Department of First Stories.

EQMM has been in continuous publication since 1941. From the beginning three general criteria have been employed in evaluating submissions: We look for strong writing, an original and exciting plot, and professional craftsmanship. We encourage writers whose work meets these general criteria to read an issue of *EQMM* before making a submission. *EQMM*'s range in the mystery genre is extensive: Almost any story that involves crime or the threat of crime comes within our purview. However, like all magazines, *EQMM* has a distinctive tone and style and you can only get a sense of whether your work will suit us by reading an issue. To receive a sample copy send a check or money order for $5.00 to the address below.

EQMM uses stories of almost every length. 2,500-8,000 words is the preferred range, but we occasionally use stories of up to 12,000 words and we feature one or two short novels (up to 20,000 words) each year, although these spaces are usually reserved for established writers. Shorter stories are also considered, including minute mysteries of as little as 250 words. Our rates for original stories are from 5 to 8 ¢ a word, sometimes higher for established authors. *EQMM* does not accept stories previously published in the United States.

It is not necessary to query *EQMM* as to subject matter or to ask permission to submit a story. All manuscripts should be printed on one side of the paper and double-spaced. If you would like the manuscript returned in the event that we cannot use it, please enclose a SASE of suitable size. If you do not want the manuscript returned, please indicate this and enclose a SASE for a reply; if you live outside the U.S., please use International Postal Reply coupons for return postage.

We regret that we cannot provide criticism with returned stories. Response time is up to three months.

Categories: Fiction—Crime—Literature—Mystery—Short Stories

CONTACT: Janet Hutchings, Editor
Material: Mystery Fiction
475 Park Ave. South
New York NY 10016
Phone: 212-686-7188
Website: www.themysteryplace.com

Embedded

Here's How to Start:

First, send us an abstract of your article. An abstract is just a one-page e-mail overview of what your article will cover, like an outline or a summary. There's no need to send the entire article unless you've already finished it. Send your abstract to Editor in Chief Jim Turley at jturley@cmp.com.

Next, wait for us to contact you. This might take several weeks. Embedded Systems Design comes out monthly, and if your abstract happens to arrive right at the beginning of our frenzied production cycle we may not read it for three or four weeks. Don't panic; we'll certainly get to it before long. Alas, not all abstracts are accepted. We receive dozens of article ideas every month (that's the good news), but we only have space for a few (that's the bad news). If your first idea isn't accepted, try sending a new abstract on a different idea.

If we decide your abstract looks promising, we'll ask to see the full article. If the full article still looks good, we'll let you know that we'd like to publish it and ask you to sign a contract. Your article might appear anywhere from three months even a year after that. It might appear in the magazine, online, or both.

What To Write About:

Your article could be about almost anything, but like you, our readers prefer hands-on, real-life examples of embedded problem-solving. Tutorials, educational, and explanatory articles are good. You can write about hardware or software, programming or engineering, design or debugging. You can describe an algorithm, a programming technique, or a device; present an inside look at a processor, a program, or a product. Think about what your colleagues discuss over lunch, or what you'd ask an interview candidate. If you're still stumped for ideas, here are a few:

- Real-time, low-latency, or deterministic programming
- Handling hardware interrupts or software exceptions
- Managing a large project or a team of off-site engineers
- Using low-cost processors for high-end tasks
- Implementing algorithms or standards in real code
- Programming tricks or features of specific processors
- Making hardware and software work better together

The Time Scale:

It takes a long time to produce an article for Embedded Systems Design (kind of like developing software for an embedded system). So the first rule is, send your abstract in early. It takes at least four months from the time we receive your abstract to the time your article hits the streets. Plan ahead.

After your article has been accepted, we'll notify you three months before the issue it will be published in. For instance, if your article is going in the June issue, we'll notify you around April 1st and tell you when to expect your proof draft of the article. You'll see one proof draft of the article just as it will appear in the magazine (or online).

This final proofing is important. You'll need to be available by telephone and e-mail for two days so we can ask you any final questions about your article before it goes to the printer. We might also need your approval if we've made any spelling or grammar changes that could affect the meaning of your text. You must be available on these dates. If we can't reach you to approve changes, we'll postpone publishing your article for one month, at least.

That's it! We're looking forward to seeing your abstract.

Tips for Writing Better Articles:

Here are some tips and tricks that we've collected over the years. Read these through and keep a copy under your pillow.

Three-Star Super-Important Rules and Time-Savers

- Don't try to sell or otherwise promote your own product or service. This should be obvious. Your fellow readers are eager for your technical insight and acumen, not your employer's propaganda. We already have advertisements in the magazine, thank you very much.

- Write like you talk. For some reason, lots of people adopt a stiff, formal tone when they start writing articles. They use big words and long sentences with lots of "inasmuch" and "wherefores." Resist the urge to sound like a lawyer or an English Lit professor. We want to hear what you have to say, in your own words. Think about how you talk to your colleagues over lunch or at a conference (like the Embedded Systems Conference), and write your thoughts the same way.

- Tell a story. Think about how you've discussed problems and interesting solutions with your coworkers. You probably started with, "we had this weird bug we couldn't figure out . . ." and talked about how you tracked it down, and then finished with a happy or surprising ending.

- Send us a Word document. Paste your code listings, tables, and figures directly in the document and give them each a title and number (i.e., Listing 1: A Goertzel implementation). Don't worry about making your illustrations pretty; we'll have a professional illustrator redraw them for you. You just need to provide a sketch, line drawing, PowerPoint picture, Excel spreadsheet, or other starting point—and then be available to review and correct the final figures we create. If you have really long code listings that you'd like posted on our Web site, provide those in a different file.

Two-Star Rules and Tips to Improve Your Article

- Avoid the following words. We hate these words; they sound like marketing-speak, and we'll ruthlessly edit them out of your article if we see them.

- Methodology. This isn't a real word. The word you're looking for is method.

- Functionality. This isn't a real word, either. Function is a perfectly good word; use it.

· Solution. Unless you're describing a powder dissolved in a liquid or a mathematical proof, we don't want to hear about solutions. Try product, service, chip, or program instead.

· Engine. An engine is a device for converting fossil fuel into mechanical motion, not a catch-all term for all products and services.

· Platform. This is a horizontal surface bearing weight, not a chip, computer, or operating system. Carpenters make platforms; embedded systems developers make products.

· Impact. This is a noun, not a verb. In other words, a comet can have an impact on your home town; your device driver can't impact performance. Don't even think about impactful.

· Target. This is a noun; the verb you want is aim. You aim at a target, you don't target an aim.

· Seamless. Reserve this for particularly good sewing, not for particularly elegant software engineering.

· Price point. The first word, price, works much better.

· Utilization or utilize. You're probably thinking of use or usage, which are much better words.

· Try to use active voice instead of passive voice. This is English-grammar-speak for sentences that sound like someone talking, not someone writing a legal brief. Here are some examples of active versus passive voice. See how much clearer the active-voice sentences are to read?

· It's surprisingly difficult to break the habit of using passive voice once you're accustomed to it. Don't obsess over this; we have professionals who can fix this during the editing process.

One-Star Bonus Points

· It's nice to start your article with a one-paragraph introduction or "hook" that grabs the reader and makes everyone want to know more. These are sometimes called executive summaries or thesis statements.

· Likewise, you get bonus points for concluding your article with a paragraph or two that reviews what you just said and maybe finish up with your own opinion, forecast, or pronouncement.

· Be a little careful about using abbreviations, acronyms, and other technical terms that other engineers might not understand. Yes, Embedded Systems Design is a professional's journal but that doesn't mean everyone reading it shares your expertise. For example, telecommunications standards and abbreviations are gibberish to most engineers who don't also work in that field.

· Leave out trademark symbols like (R) (TM) or other legal stuff in your article. Yes, we know your marketing or legal staff might ask for this. Ignore them. Magazines like Embedded Systems Design are exempt from trademark-protection rules. Trust us on this, we're professionals.

· Speaking of trademarks and copyrights, you are writing the article and collecting all the supporting data yourself, right? It's easy to copy a chart or reuse a paragraph you've seen somewhere else. That's not okay. You must ask for — and receive — written permission from the original author or publisher. Newspaper and magazine articles are not open source; you can't borrow from them without permission.

Final Notes: When finished, your entire article should be somewhere between 2,000 and 5,000 words long but don't worry about hitting exact numbers. We don't pay by the word, so don't bother padding it out any longer than it needs to be. Illustrations — we like articles that have interesting charts, code listings, block diagrams, schematics, or other eye candy. Try to add two or three of these to your article.

That's it! Have fun and good luck! We're looking forward to publishing your first article.

Categories: Computers

CONTACT: Submission
Email: jturley@cmp.com

Employee Benefit Journal
Employee Benefit Digest

Please refer to *Benefits & Compensation Digest.*

ENCOUNTER

Who We Are: ENCOUNTER™ is an 8-page, full-color, weekly magazine for teenagers to encourage their relationships with Jesus. It is published quarterly by Standard Publishing and designed to correlate with the company's Young Teen and High School curriculum. It is distributed mainly through churches and Christian bookstores.

What We Need: Nonfiction (1100 words maximum): We use articles on current issues from a Christian point of view. Topics should be of interest to teens, including school, family life, recreation, friends, part-time jobs, dating, and music. Articles should speak directly to teens without being preachy. We are also interested in quizzes, interviews, and teen profiles. (Please send snapshots to accompany teen profiles along with a release form signed by a guardian for each teen under 18 who is photographed. We can provide release forms upon request.)

Fiction (1100 words maximum): Stories must appeal to younger and older teenagers and have well-constructed, interesting plots. The main characters should be contemporary teens who cope with modern-day problems using Christian principles. Stories should be authentic and realistic.

"my story" (400 words maximum): This is a feature for teens only. Here teens can share personal testimonies of ways God has worked in their lives.

Poetry & art are accepted from teens only. We include these features in our special section by teens called Expressions.

Note to teens: Please include your date of birth with each submission so we can include your age if your poem, testimony, article, or work of art is printed.

* Send all submissions and correspondence to: encounter@standardpub.com

What We Offer

* Payment is on acceptance. ENCOUNTER pays 8¢ per word for first rights on unsolicited manuscripts, 6¢ per word for one-time or reprint rights, and $20 for poetry and art (from teens only).

* We require all authors to sign a contract if their work is accepted.

What We Require

* We prefer manuscripts sent via e-mail (encounter@standardpub.com). However, if you do send manuscripts via postal mail, please include an e-mail address where we can contact you or a self-addressed, stamped envelope.

* We prefer full manuscripts. (Queries are optional, not required.)

* At the top of the first sheet of the manuscript include your name, address, phone number or e-mail address, and approximate word count.

* Please indicate what rights you are offering to us on the top of your manuscript as well.

* Allow 10-15 weeks for reply.

* All manuscripts are submitted on speculation.

What We Suggest

* Get to know teens before you begin to write for them. Evaluate their ideas, language, thoughts, and trends in order to effectively reach the teen market. Many manuscripts are rejected simply because the plot or vocabulary is outdated for modern teens.

* We produce ENCOUNTER™ long before its publication date. Send seasonal material 9-12 months in advance.

* We look for material that correlates with our Sunday school curriculum, so each quarter we are considering specific topics. You may request our latest theme list by contacting us at: encounter@standardpub.com

* If you would like a sample copy, please send a request along with a 9 by 12 SASE.

Categories: Religion—Young Adults

CONTACT: ENCOUNTER
Standard Publishing
8121 Hamilton Ave
Cincinnati OH 45231
E-mail: encounter@standardpub.com
Website: www.standardpub.com

Endless Vacation RCI

Now in its 31st year, *Endless Vacation (EV)* magazine is published six times a year. Our circulation is 1.9 million subscribing members, the nation's largest ABC-measured consumer travel magazine.

Ev provides engaging, award-winning travel journalism and photography; the experience and insight of well-traveled, professional freelance travel writers; information on domestic and international RCI resort destinations, as well as other popular travel destinations and activities; and travel resources (phone numbers, Web sites, and contact information) to assist in vacation planning.

When writing for *EV*, the following six attributes should be reflected in the story's voice:

• **Highly enthusiastic regarding travel**—*EV* is ready to share the best of what we've discovered in travel with our readers

• **Relaxed, with a lack of pretension**—*EV* readers enjoy relaxed, resort-style vacations. They have little need for pretense or formal address

• **A planner**—*EV* knows how to plan a trip, where to go for the latest info, who to contact, and shares that expertise in every story

• **Value-oriented**—*EV* knows our readers want the best value for the dollar. Value comes in all price ranges and should fit any budget

• **Understands vacation ownership**—*EV* can address the special needs of timeshare vacationers—activities to fill a week (or more), accommodations that include cooking facilities, resorts built around activities such as the beach, golf, or skiing

• **Confident**—Readers look to *EV* as the "expert" in providing complete information devoted to vacation ownership travel

In addition to destination travel, we're also looking for activity-based editorial—golf, ski, family travel, etc. Destination travel is carefully planned to reflect areas of resort growth and development and to present familiar destinations in a new and dynamic way. International coverage is limited to allow greater focus on domestic, Mexico, Canada, and Caribbean travel.

Department topics for which *Endless Vacation* accepts some freelance contributions include regionalized weekend travel destinations, family travel, cruising trends, getting the most value out of travel, health and safety on the road, food and dining, short travel service and news-oriented pieces, and hot news tips and trends in travel.

Before You Write Your Manuscript or Query

1. The editors strongly suggest that you read the magazine thoroughly to get an understanding of our style and approach. Reading the magazine may also prevent you from querying us on a topic that has recently been covered. You can also visit www.evmediakit.com to view our current editorial calendar and learn interesting facts about our readers.

2. Features should have a good balance between "you are there" narrative and service information. We are not looking for guidebook material, but finely written, well-constructed travel stories. Personal observations and experiences, interviews with other vacationers or local guides, and solid facts are elements we look for. Many publications are competing for our readers' time. Brevity, clarity, and conciseness should be hallmarks of your article.

3. Audience (Source: 2004 MRI Database)
• Circulation: 1.6 million
• Sex: 61 percent female; 38 percent male
• Median age: 47
• College graduates: 73 percent
• Married: 77 percent
• Income: $78,961 median

In addition, *Endless Vacation* readers are passionate about travel, averaging 4 weeks away from home per year. Other research shows that 99 percent own a timeshare condominium and rank their most important activities while on vacation as: sight-seeing, shopping, attending a specific event, visiting a national park, golfing, biking, and skiing.

For more information, visit www.evmediakit.com. Single copies of the magazine are $5 each, and subscriptions are available to freelance writers for $42 (standard subscription rate is $84). Please mail requests to the attention of Stephanie Dawson.

How to Submit Manuscripts and Queries

Our editorial calendar is booked many months in advance, and currently we have extremely limited space for freelance submissions. We will review manuscripts on speculation; for a writer who is unfamiliar to us, this may be the best entry to our publication.

Query letters should include three to four concise paragraphs indicating the focus and tone of the proposed article. Please include samples of your travel writing so that we may give your query full consideration. Materials will be returned only if you include a self-addressed, stamped envelope. We generally respond to queries by letter in 30 days.

Although we attempt to return unsolicited manuscripts and slides accompanied by a SASE, we assume no responsibility for doing so. Additionally, we do not encourage writers to submit photos. **Queries must be received in written form, not by phone.**

Manuscript Payment

Payment is negotiated upon assignment and tendered upon acceptance. The following ranges will give you an idea of our rates:
• **Feature articles (1,500 words):** $1,200 to $1,800
• **Departments (up to 1,200 words):** $800 to $1.200
• **News briefs (50-200 words):** $100 to $300

Expenses are not guaranteed and are negotiated individually.
Categories: Nonfiction—Travel

CONTACT: Julie Woodard, Senior Editor, *Endless Vacation Magazine*
Material: All
9998 N. Michigan Rd
Carmel IN 46032
E-mail: julie.woodard@rci.com

The Engineering Economist

The Engineering Economist is a quarterly, refereed publication published jointly by the Engineering Economy Divisions of the American Society for Engineering Education (ASEE) and the Institute of Industrial Engineers (IIE). *The Engineering Economist* publishes articles, case studies, readers' comments, and reviews that represent current research and practice involving problems of capital investment. Opinions expressed in *The Engineering Economist* are those of the authors and do not necessarily represent those of ASEE or IEE.

Submissions

Manuscripts are to be sent in quadruplicate.

Style Requirements

Electronic submission of manuscripts accepted for publication is required and must meet the following criteria.

Submit the manuscript in an IBM PC-compatible format on a diskette in Microsoft Word format.

Word process the entire manuscript double-spaced in 10-point Times Roman type.

Submit a hard copy of the manuscript, including Figures.

Number figures, tables, equations, references, and end notes, and make sure these numbers match those cited in the text.

All Tables and Figrues must be submitted in a form ready to reproduce without further modification, enlargement, or reduction, and fit within a space no larger than 4.5 x 7.5 inches, including the title of the Table or Figure. List Table and Figure captions on a separate page.

Tables must be typed using the Microsoft Word Tables feature.

Minimize table rules. Use horizontal rules above and below the column headings, inside the table body to show totals and at the table bottom. Use vertical rules only when necessary for clarity. Do not use side rules.

Photocopies of illustrations will not be accepted.

Figures submitted in electronic form must be compatible with Microsoft Word; otherwise, they must be submitted in hard copy form.

In eithe rform, Figure captions must be separate - not within the Figures.

Equations, both in-line and displayed, must be typed using Microsoft Word Equation Editor.

Abstract

Manuscripts must include a nonmathematical abstract of 50 - 100 words.

Mathematical Notation

Make mathematical expressions as simple as possible. Lengthy mathematical derivations should be placed in an Appendix. Number equations; put the equation number in parentheses, flush with the right margin of the page. Authors should restrict themselves to the English alphabet and standard Greek symbols. For interest factors, follow the functional format of ANSI Standard Z94.5-1990, "Symbology Manual of Standard Notation for Engineering Economy Parameters and Interest Factors".

Tables and Figures

Tables are lists of numbers. All other illustrations are Figures. Tables should be numbered with Arabic numerals and provided with titles at the top. Figures should be numbered with Arabic numerals and numbered and titled at the bottom.

Footnotes

Footnotes should be avoided because they disrupt the readers' train of thought and create confusion with the references. If the material is important enough for the reader to seek it out, it is important enough to be included in the text.

Acknowledgments

If any, these should be made in a separate section following the Conlusion or Summary and prior to References.

References

Use the alpabetical numbering method. References should be numbered, enclosed in square brackets (e.g., [1]) and listed in alphabetical order in the list of references. Only references cited in the text should be listed. (If material is removed or added, be sure to revise numbering.)

Biographical Sketch

A biographical sketch of 200 or fewer words for each author should be submitted on a separate page with the manuscript.

Categories: Nonfiction—Engineering

CONTACT: Latha S. Bhavnani, Managing Editor
Material: All
Dept. of Industrial and Systems Engineering
Auburn University AL 36849-5346
Phone: 334-844-1419
Fax: 334-844-1381
E-mail: bhavna1s@eng.auburn.edu
Website: www.eng.auburn.edu/~park/journal

Enrichment
A Journal for Pentecostal Ministry

Enrichment is a quarterly journal for Assemblies of God ministers and other Pentecostal, charismatic leaders. It carries articles and feature material on a wide range of ministry-related topics. It exists for the purpose of enriching and encouraging Pentecostal ministers to equip and empower Spirit-filled believers for effective ministry.

Its Free-Lance Market

Free-lance material is accepted on a limited basis in the following areas:

• Slanted to ministers on preaching, pastoral practice, and any ministry-related subject (1,200-2,100 words).

• How-to Features

• Program and ministry ideas for ministers/church leaders (200-500 words)

Sermon Illustrations

Original and previously published material with the original source indicated if the material has been previously published.

Rate of payment

Up to 10 cents per word for first rights; payment on publication.

Categories: Nonfiction—Religion—Spiritual

CONTACT: Rick Knoth
Material: All
The General Council of the Assemblies of God
1445 N. Boonville Ave.
Springfield MO 65802
Phone: 417-862-2781, ext. 4095
E-mail: fhamilton@ag.org
Website: www.enrichmentjournal.ag.org

Entrepreneur Magazine

Our Mission

Business ownership is not what it used to be. *Entrepreneur* helps entrepreneurs thrive in today's fast-paced environment, offering actionable information and practical inspiration that successful business owners can use to achieve their vision of growth.

Our Readers

Our readers are energetic entrepreneurs who are not content with the status quo. They're risk-takers who thrive on growth and innovation, constantly seeking cutting-edge ideas to improve their businesses. They're the thinkers shaping the new face of entrepreneurship.

Our Content

Entrepreneur reports on innovative methods and strategies to help readers improve their business operations. We also cover current issues and trends that affect entrepreneurial companies, as well as new business ideas and opportunities. We provide detailed how-to information in an entertaining, intriguing and evocative fashion, with a writing style that is punchy, sophisticated and chatty.

What We're Looking For

Don't give us the obvious, or merely touch on the surface of a subject. Our readers are not beginners, and they don't have time to waste reading what they already know.

We're looking for in-depth reporting, with information culled from many sources to give readers a broad perspective on a topic. Can you offer a fresh angle on a familiar subject? Can you convey atmosphere and personality when interviewing entrepreneurs and experts? Can you elicit interesting quotes from people, and find sources who don't say the same old thing in the same old way? Can you write about business with authority and passion? Then you're the kind of writer we're looking for.

Features

Features are 1,700 words, plus sidebars, charts and/or boxes. Types of features we are seeking include:

• In-depth articles examining how a current business issue, such as the tight labor market or the health-insurance crisis, affects small businesses.

• Psychological topics, such as "Can you have a business and still have a life?" or "What is the line between taking advantage of opportunities and being an opportunist?"

• How-to articles, such as how to get your product into Wal-Mart, how to bounce back from a business failure, how to market to a certain demographic group (such as teens) or how to sell your product to the U.S. government.

Columns

Entrepreneur's upfront section, "Forward," features brief, punchy articles on news and trends affecting small-business owners. We purchase short (300 words) articles for $1 per word in the following topic areas:

• *Money*—business financing, finanacial management and personal finance issues. Recent examples: Is the housing boom hurting investment in small business?; A group of small businesses is suing the major credit-card issuers over excessive fees; Unusual ways entrepreneurs are financing their businesses.

• *Marketing*—sales and marketing issues. Recent examples: Getting your product on a reality TV show; "Techfluential" consumers—who they are and why you should care; What are the current marketing clichés?

• *Management*—management and operations issues. Recent examples: Some retail stores and restaurants are starting to ban children—should you?; After years of only targeting big chains, more malls are seeking small boutiques again; More states are encouraging "managed-competition" health care.

• *Technology*—tech issues. Recent examples: "Green" web hosting is a new trend; Should you send your IT person to hacker bootcamp?; What it's really like to switch to VoIP in your office.

• *Viewpoint*—thought-provoking, controversial first-person essay on some aspect of entrepreneurship. Could cover politics, ethics, personal life and more.

• *Miscellaneous*—We also purchase short (300- to 500-word) articles for the Forward section that do not fall into the above categories, but simply report on interesting trends or ideas. For example: Why pork rinds are suddenly a hot snack item; what your sleeping position says about you as an entrepreneur; how the Internet is revolutionizing the crafts industry.

Within the Sell, Money, Lead and Tech sections, we buy Snapshot articles—Brief (150-word) profiles of entrepreneurs who use innovative marketing, business financing or management strategies, or who run an innovative technology company.

Other columns are not open to freelancers. However, if you have an idea for a new column—or you think you could write better than one of our existing columnists—query us and prove it.

StartUp. Targeted at start-up entrepreneurs, "StartUp" is a mini-magazine within a magazine. The monthly feature within "StartUp" is open to freelancers. It is 2,000 words long and covers how-to topics of interest to start-up entrepreneurs—for example, what it's really like to launch a business from an incubator; the best places to find start-up capital; how to overcome the mental roadblocks that keep you from starting a business.

Where to Start

• Please read several issues of the magazine before querying us. Pay particular attention to the columns. We have dozens of columns on topics including management, sales and marketing, business ideas, technology and finance. Many of the queries we receive are rejected because they duplicate topics covered in our columns. Only a topic that is too extensive to be covered in one of our columns warrants feature coverage.

• Submit queries only. Full-length manuscripts are discouraged.

• If submitting queries via regular mail, send them to the attention of Karen Axelton, Executive Editor, at 2445 McCabe Way, Suite 400, Irvine, CA 92614. Enclose a self-addressed stamped envelope and a few clips of past articles you've written. Queries may also be e-mailed to kaxelton@entrepreneur.com.

• Queries should describe the topic clearly and succinctly. Avoid vagueness and generalities. Be as specific as possible about what aspects of the subject you will cover, people you will interview, how the story will help our readers and why you're qualified to write it.

• Allow a minimum of six weeks for a response. No phone calls, please.

• Include a return address and both day and evening phone numbers on all correspondence.

• Entrepreneur Media buys first worldwide rights and pays upon acceptance.

• Entrepreneur Media assumes no responsibility for unsolicited manuscripts, photos or tapes.

Sample copies

You can find *Entrepreneur* at most newsstands and bookstores, or you can order the magazine by sending $7.20 ($4.00/issue + $3.20 shipping) to: Entrepreneur Media, PO Box 432, Newburgh, NY 12551.

Categories: Nonfiction—Business

CONTACT: Karen Axelton, Executive Editor
Material: Queries
Entrepreneur Media, Inc., 2445 McCabe Way
Irvine CA 92614
Phone: 949-261-2325
Fax: 949-261-0234
E-mail: kaxelton@entrepreneur.com
Website: Entrepreneur.com

Entrepreneur.com

People who visit or are members of *Entrepreneur.com* are seeking a variety of accessible, easy-to-digest information. *Our readers consist of four primary groups:*

• They may be small-business owners (those with fewer than 20 employees) who have been in business for several years and are seeking innovative methods and strategies to improve their business operations but are also interested in new business ideas and opportunities as well as current issues that affect their companies.

• They may be people who are either dreaming of starting their own business or have a business that's less than 2 years old. These individuals don't necessarily have a lot of money, so they're looking for businesses that don't require mountains of start-up cash. In addition to start-up ideas, they're looking for how-to advice to help them run and grow their businesses, articles that keep them on top of business trends, and motivational articles to get (and stay) psyched up.

• They may be individuals who already run or want to start a homebased business. Like the entrepreneurs described above, they're seeking information that will help them run their businesses better.

• Finally, they may be people interested in purchasing a franchise or business opportunity. They want accurate, reliable, unbiased information from a company they can trust. They want to know what they need to know before plunking down any cash—as well as where to find the cash to plunk down. Before pitching a story to us, be sure to read a variety of the articles on our site so you can tailor your pitches to meet our content needs. Many of the queries we receive are rejected because the subject matter in no way matches what we're looking for.

Submission Guidelines

• Submit queries or queries with clips only. Full-length manuscripts are discouraged.

• If you're querying an article about a successful entrepreneur, you must include his/her age and some indication of the company's sales.

• Include your day and evening phone number, return address and e-mail address on all correspondence.

• Please send queries in writing via e-mail to Karen Spaeder, Editor, or via snail mail (include a self-addressed, stamped envelope) to 2445 McCabe Way, Irvine, CA 92614. Allow a minimum of eight weeks for a response—no phone calls, please.

• Entrepreneur Media Inc. assumes no responsibility for unsolicited manuscripts or photos.

• Entrepreneur Media Inc. pays upon acceptance.

Editorial Voice: We want our articles to sound as if they were written by people who are on the same level as—or maybe just a step above—our readers, people who are part of the community, not above the community. We want you to sound experienced, so you can point our readers in the right direction. We don't want our editorial copy to sound as if we're talking down to our readers or patronizing them. We're here to help; we want to be their mentors.

No matter what the topic or audience is, the articles you provide us should be informative yet entertaining. The style should be lively and relaxed—never dry or boring. In addition, the voice of our articles needs to be inviting. We want to involve the community. We need to inform them, but we also want to promote thought and discussion.

If you've received a writing assignment from us, we have a few helpful hints about mechanics:

• Articles should be concise and specific. They need to communicate information quickly: We can't be long-winded, or we'll lose our Web readers. Columns should be approximately 600 words long. Features, approximately 1,000.

• Headlines should concisely convey the basic information in the article. They should not be obtuse or clever for the sake of being clever.

Examples: Advertising on the Cheap; Beat Those Wintertime Blahs; E-Promotions Done Right; Decks should also be concise. They may or may not be full sentences that briefly convey the essence of the article.

Examples: Think advertising is beyond your means? Not with these low-cost and no-cost options; Follow these 10 steps to stave off the cold-weather blues; How to promote your online business on a shoestring budget.

• Where appropriate, articles should include real-life examples of entrepreneurs—more than one example is better—as well as information from an expert. Before including a specific entrepreneur, clear it with Karen Spaeder.

• Bulleted or numbered lists are always a plus. Web readers like information they can digest easily, and bulleted/numbered lists seem to go over well.

• Additional resources should be included with each article. This information could be from the *Entrepreneur.com* site, such as related articles or tools, an appropriate message board or link to an expert, or links to related areas of the site, such as the Franchise Zone or a specific area of Your Business. You could also include non-*Entrepreneur.com* resources, such as related books or Web sites. This information should be set off at the end of the main article with a note to include it in a box.

• Specific information must be included in every article, where appropriate. This information includes: full names and titles of all individuals mentioned or quoted in article; names of all partners or co-founders of companies; complete names and brief descriptions of all companies, organizations or associations (including Inc., Corp., and Co.); city and state where companies are located; the year a company was founded; current annual sales of companies; Web site addresses of all companies, organizations and associations; and street prices of any products mentioned.

• Contact information for all individuals mentioned in the article must be included at the end of the article so we can easily complete our fact checking.

This should include each person's name, phone number, e-mail address and Web address.

If you are not a regular contributor, please provide a brief writer's bio.

• We like to include a bio at the end of every article. And if you wouldn't mind, please provide a way for readers to contact you if they'd like to. An e-mail address would be just fine.

Categories: Nonfiction—Business

CONTACT: Karen Spaeder, Editor
Material: Queries
Entrepreneur Media, Inc., 2445 McCabe Way
Irvine CA 92614
Phone: 949-261-2325
Fax: 949-261-0234
E-mail: kspaeder@entrepreneur.com
Website: Entrepreneur.com

Environment: Science and Policy for Sustainable Development

Environment welcomes manuscripts and proposals that make an original contribution to the public's understanding of global and regional environmental issues. The award-winning magazine, now in its 48th year of publication, has a broad audience that includes world-renowned scientists, researchers, and policymakers; university professors and high school teachers (who read the magazine for themselves as well as assign it to their students); and concerned citizens. The peer-reviewed magazine offers readers extended articles on key environmental issues, shorter articles that explore parts of these issues, reviews of major governmental and institutional reports, commentaries that provide different points of view than those in the articles, book recommendations, pointers to the best environmental web sites and other digital media, and staff-written news briefs. Readers enjoy thought-provoking articles that provide balanced, authoritative analyses written in an accessible way. The goal, similar to that of a policy "white paper," is for those interested in but not necessarily familiar with the topic (including undergraduate and graduate students, faculty members in other disciplines, and the educated public) to be able to easily grasp the key science and policy issues without wading through jargon or overly technical material.

Environment's executive editors review all submissions and may request other experts, including contributing editors, to review manuscripts and proposals. The executive editors may accept the piece as submitted, accept it pending revision, or reject the manuscript. *Final publication decisions rest with them on the five types of manuscripts:*

• Main article submissions (between 2,500 to 4,000 words) should expose readers to the major scientific and policy issues surrounding a significant topic. Articles must be concise, objective, technically accurate but free of jargon, and factually supported. They should also give appropriate weight to alternative points of view. We encourage authors to include endnotes that offer readers suggestions for further reading and document more technical information or controversial points (an average number of references is 30). We also encourage the use of maps, tables, graphs, and sidebar boxes to illustrate key points, describe relevant case studies, or provide background information for readers unfamiliar with the topic discussed. The introduction and conclusion are especially important. The introduction should entice the reader to read further as well as provide a solid foundation for understanding the article. Conclusions must follow logically from the facts and analyses presented, must give the reader an idea of what is likely to happen in the future, and must indicate the implications for both research and policy. This section is more detailed than that of the typical magazine or journal article.

• "Departments" (1,000 to 1,700 words) focus on special topics such as education, energy, economics, and public opinion. These manuscripts should elucidate a small portion of a larger issue. Though not as comprehensive in coverage as the main articles, these manuscripts should also be objective, free of jargon, factually supported, technically accurate, and well referenced. As examples of the appropriate scope, one piece presented a geographic breakdown of U.S. membership in Environmental organizations while another explored the Environmental implications of local currencies.

• The "Report on Reports" section provides lengthy reviews (1,500 to 2,000 words) of institutional and governmental reports. The reviews subject new research reports produced by government agencies and private institutions to the same scholarly scrutiny usually given to an individually authored book or monograph. Topics of recently reviewed reports include the constitutionality of the Clean Air Act, the role of pesticides in U.S. agriculture, acidic deposition, and dams and development.

• "Commentary" (maximum of 750 words) seeks to broaden the debate on various topics by providing thoughtful alternative points of view to those expressed elsewhere in the magazine.

• The "Books of Note" section provides short (100 to 150 words) notices of recent print publications to call readers' attention to a wide range of important books rather than provide detailed critical evaluations. Reviewers and books to be reviewed are selected by the magazine's contributing editors, executive editors, and managing editor. A book's relevance to *Environment*'s general themes and its accessibility to a nonspecialist audience are crucial.

More detailed guidelines for these sections are available from the editorial offices.

Editing and Style References

Once a manuscript is accepted for publication, it is edited thoroughly by the editorial staff for style, substance, and clarity. Because the magazine brings complex and technical analyses to a broad audience, we edit more extensively than do most journals or magazines. Articles that exceed the specified length may be shortened. We compose titles and subheads without consultation but query authors concerning any substantive editorial changes. We offer rapid publication of timely material, so we require a rapid turnaround when we send authors typescripts of the edited manuscript. The staff works closely with authors to ensure a mutually satisfying product.

Environment follows the 14th edition of *The Chicago Manual of Style*, published by the University of Chicago Press, and the *American Heritage Dictionary* for spelling.

Manuscript Submission and Technical Requirements

1. Send three clean copies of your manuscript to Barbara T. Richman, Managing Editor, *Environment*, Heldref Publications, 1319 Eighteenth Street, N.W., Washington, DC 20036-1802. Manuscripts can also be sent via e-mail, with a cover letter, to env@heldref.org. The preferred format is Microsoft Word 6.1 for Macintosh; DOS-based formats are also acceptable.

2. Double space everything, including endnotes and tables. Use 1-inch or greater margins and confine the page length to 10 inches or less. Sidebar boxes, tables, and figures must be on separate pages at the end of the manuscript.

3. Authors' names, positions, titles, places of employment, mailing addresses, and telephone numbers must appear on the cover page. Include fax numbers and e-mail addresses.

4. It is extremely helpful to submit figures electronically. The preferred program is Illustrator 8.0 or lower (Mac versions) with Postscript fonts (no Truetype). Colors must be in CMYK format, not RGB. Tiff and EPS files are also acceptable. Each figure should be sent as a separate e-mail. Authors must also send print-outs of the figures.

5. Authors are encouraged to submit photographs and original artwork of professional quality to accompany the text. Authors are responsible for obtaining permission to use such materials. Captions and a credit line identifying the photographer must accompany each photograph. The editorial and graphics staffs determine use of all photographs based on relevance, aesthetic value, and space availability. Maps and figures are also useful and may be redrafted to match *Environment*'s style.

6. Authors are responsible for the accuracy of endnotes, and all references and quotations must be checked against the original sources by the author. Authors are also responsible for securing permission to use material quoted from copyrighted publications as well as for use of tables and figures from other sources.

7. Do not use the endnote function in your word-processing program. All endnotes must be double-spaced and placed at the end of the article. Do not use endnotes in headlines or author affiliations or use more than one per sentence. Provide enough information to allow the reader to retrieve the referenced material from the most available source. Provide specific page numbers for general reference to articles (e.g., "For more on this topic, see…"), quotations, or references to specific facts or arguments. Where possible, include a printed source along with Internet references. *Environment* uses the following styles:

Book:
1. D. Scheberle, *Federalism and Environmental Policy: Trust and the Politics of Implementation* (Washington, D.C.: Georgetown University Press, 1997), 95-98.

Book with more than five authors:
1. G. Atkinson et al, *Measuring Sustainable Development: Macroeconomics and the Environment* (Cheltenham, U.K.: Edward Elgar Publishing, 1997), 95-98.

Chapter in a book:
1. L. White Jr., "The Historical Roots of Our Ecologic Crisis," in L. Gruen and D. Jamieson, eds., *Reflecting on Nature: Readings in Environmental Philosophy* (New York: Oxford University Press, 1994), 5-14 at 12.

Scholarly journal:
Monthly or less frequently:

1. S. T. Phillips, *"Lessons from the Dust Bowl: Dryland Agriculture and Soil Erosion in the United States and South Africa*, 1900-1950." *Environmental History* 4, No. 2 (1999): 245-66.
Weekly:
2. G. Hardin, "Extensions of 'The Tragedy of the Commons'," *Science.* 1 May 1998, 683-83.
Magazine:
Popular magazine:
1. C. Gordon, "The Warm Lessons of the Ice Storm '98," *Macleans.* 16 February 1998, 14.
Newspaper or regular newsletter:
1. K. Schneider, "New Breed of Ecologist to Lead EPA," *New York Times.* 17 December 1992, B20.
Interview or personal communication:
1. Robin L. Rivett, attorney, Pacific Legal Foundation, letter to Robert Burford, director, Bureau of Land Management, 2 February 1993.
2. Simon Smith, manager of regulator innovations, New South Wales *Environment*al Protection Authority, personal communication with the authors. Beijing, 23 November 1997.
Additional references to a previous note:
5. Lundgren, note 1 above, page 7.
Reference to an immediately preceding note:
6. Ibid., page 17.
Government report:
1. U.S. General Accounting Office, EPA and the States: *Environmental Challenges Require a Better Working Relationship.* GAO/RCED-95-64 (Washington, D.C., 1995).
International treaty:
1. "Protocol on Substances That Deplete the Ozone Layer," Montreal, 1987, in *International Legal Materials* 26 (1987): 1550.
U.S. federal law:
1. Endangered Species Act of 1973, U.S. Code, vol.16, sec. 1531(1973).
Congressional bill where title of bill appears in the text of the manuscript:
1. H.R. 3055, 94th Cong., 2nd sess., Congressional Record, 122, no.5, daily ed. (15 July 1976): H16,870.
Congressional bill where title of bill does not appear in the text:
1. Food Security Act of 1985, 99th Cong., 1st sess., H.R. 2100, Congressional Record, 131, no.132, daily ed. (8 October 1985): H8461-66.
Press release:
1. U.S. Bureau of Land Management, "BLM Announces Major Policy Change," press release (Washington, D.C., 1 November 1997).
Unpublished discussion papers:
1. F. Butera and U. Farinelli, "Lessons of Technology Transfer from Developing World Experience (paper presented at the Royal Institute of International Affairs Workshop on International Technology Transfer. London, March 1991).

For other types of notes, refer to the 14th edition of the Chicago Manual of Style or to a recent issue of *Environment*.

Updated January 2002
Categories: Nonfiction—Agriculture—Animals—Ecology—Environment—Science—Environmental Science & Policy—Energy

CONTACT: Barbara T. Richman, Managing Editor
Material: All
1319 - 18th St. NW
Washington DC 20036-1802
Phone: 202-296-6267
Fax: 202-296-5149
E-mail: env@heldref.org
Website: www.heldref.org

Equal Opportunity Publications, Inc.

WRITER'S GUIDELINES

Thank you for your interest in writing for our *career-guidance magazines*, which provide college-level and professional women, members of minority groups, and people with disabilities with information on how to find employment and develop their careers.

Since 1968, Equal Opportunity Publications, Inc. (EOP) has led the way from affirmative action to diversity recruitment by publishing career-guidance and recruitment magazines for women, members of minority groups, and people with disabilities. "First in diversity, best in results" is the slogan that summarizes EOP's successful record of helping job-seekers from under represented groups find employment and in aiding companies and government agencies eager to recruit from this diversified workforce.

Our Publications

Lana Russo is the Editor for the following magazines:

• *Woman Engineer*: Aimed at advancing the careers of women engineering students and professional engineers.

• *Workforce Diversity For Engineering And IT Professionals*: Addresses workplace issues affecting technical professional women, members of minority groups, and people with disabilities.

• *Hispanic Career World*: Focused on the careers of Hispanic students and entry-level professionals in a variety of industries, including health care, banking, retail, hospitality and travel, and information technology.

James Schneider is the Editor for the following magazines:

• *Careers & the disABLED*: Developed to promoting the personal and professional growth of individuals with disabilities.

• *Equal Opportunity*: Dedicated to advancing the professional interests of blacks, Hispanics, Asians, and Native Americans.

• *Minority Engineer*: Focused on advancing the careers of minority engineering students and professional engineers.

• *African-American Career World*: Focused on the careers of African-American students and entry-level professionals in a variety of industries, including insurance, government and military, computer science, and transportation.

GUIDELINES

• First North American serial rights are owned by EOP, Inc. Previously published articles are also acceptable. Please note that we may choose an excerpt of a published article for our Website.

• The rate for articles is ten cents per word paid within 6 weeks after publication. The rate for each photograph used is $15.00; cartoons, $25. All manuscripts are submitted on speculation.

• Articles may be submitted via E-mail. Please include social security, address, and telephone number.

Forward your query electronically to: Lana Russo (*Woman Engineer*, *Workforce Diversity For Engineering And IT Professionals*, and *Hispanic Career World*), E-mail: Ldamico@eop.com.

Mail your query to James Schneider (*Equal Opportunity*, *Minority Engineer*, *Careers & the disABLED*, *African-American Career World*) at 445 Broad Hollow Road, Suite 425, Melville, NY 11747.

Categories: Nonfiction—African-American—Asian-American—Book Reviews—Campus Life—Careers—College—Disabilities—Education—Engineering—Feminism—Hispanic—Multicultural—Native Americans—Women's Issues

CONTACT: James Schneider, Director, Editorial & Production (ext.12)
Material: Submissions for Equal Opportunity, Minority Engineer, Careers & the disABLED, and African-American Career World
CONTACT: Lana Russo, Editor (ext.17)
Material: Submissions for Woman Engineer, Workforce Diversity For Engineering And IT Professionals, Hispanic

Career World
Editorial Department
445 Broad Hollow Rd, Ste 425
Melville NY 11747
Phone: 631-421-942
Fax: 631-421-0359
E-mail: JSchneider@eop.com (James Schneider)
E-mail: *Lrusso*@eop.com (Lana Russo)
Website: www.eop.com

Equine Journal

Freelance

The *Equine Journal* welcomes freelance submissions. Following are the basic guidelines we suggest.

1. Submissions should be neatly typed double-spaced. We do accept e-mailed submissions, however they must not be in the form of attachments (simply paste all text into the body of the e-mail message).

2. Most of our features run approximately 2,000-3,000 words in length. Occasionally, a topic is such that it cannot be adequately covered within this range; two-part features are arranged in this instance.

3. Photographs, if available, are welcome. It is better to note their availability rather than enclose them.

4. An Editorial Calendar listing each month's primary topics is available.

Depending on length and complexity of the topic, features pay between $75-$100. Photographs used receive an additional $10/photo.

We do our best to respond to each submission. However, if after four to six weeks you have not heard back on an article you sent, please follow up with a phone call to our editor, Kathleen Labonville, at 800-742-9171.

Solicited

The *Equine Journal* requests the following guidelines be followed when submitting event coverage.

1. Coverage must have been pre-approved and assigned by the editor or assistant publisher of the *Equine Journal*.

2. Submissions should be neatly typed and double spaced. Mail, fax and e-mail (editorial@equinejournal.com, no attachments please) are all accepted.

3. Articles must run approximately 600 words in length; photographs, a minimum of two, should also be mailed to our office.

4. The writer is asked to request from the show secretary the show results. They should be forwarded to the Journal at the Keene, New Hampshire, address or faxed to 603-357-7851. Show results are not accepted via e-mail.

5. The writer is also requested to distribute Journals at the show, which will be shipped to them via UPS. Or, you may provide us with the show's address and we will send issues directly there.

6. To ensure proper payment, an invoice (needn't be formal) should accompany the submission addressed to the editor's attention.

7. Payment will be a flat fee of $50, unless otherwise agreed to. Checks will be mailed within 30 days of the cover date of the issue bearing the write-up.

8. Write ups must be submitted within 10 days of the show unless otherwise pre-approved by the editor.

Should you have any questions, please call the editor, Kathleen Labonville, at 800-742-9171.

Spotlight

1. Spotlight articles are intended to highlight a business, farm, individual or program within the equine industry. Its primary intent is to inform our readers of what the business has to offer, by. The article should be centered around the writer's telephone or personal interview with the subject being spotlighted. Topics covered may include but are not limited to a history of the business, what they have to offer, where they plan to go in the future, etc.

2. Submissions should be neatly typed and double-spaced, then mailed or faxed to our office. We welcome e-mailed submissions, however they must not be in the form of attachments (simply paste all text

into the body of the e-mail message).

3. Spotlights should be roughly 1,000 words in length and pay $50 each. If a telephone interview is conducted, please submit your phone bill for reimbursement.

4. Please request that the spotlight subject send two photographs to the *Equine Journal* office.

If you have any questions, do not hesitate to call Kathleen Labonville, editor, at 800-742-9171.

Categories: Nonfiction—Animals—Trade—Horses

CONTACT: **Kathleen Labonville, Managing Editor**
Material: All
103 Roxbury St.
Keene NH 03431-8801
Phone: 603-357-4271
E-mail: editor@equinejournal.com
Website: www.equinejournal.com

Equities Magazine

Formal guidelines not available. Please read a number of issues to ascertain the publication's style and needs.

Send queries to address below. No submissions by email.

Subscription Terms
1 Year $19.95 (Four Issues)
3 Years $39.95 (Twelve Issues)
We Accept Visa, MasterCard, American Express, Discover.
Categories: Nonfiction—Business—Economics

CONTACT: **Greg Bergman, Assistant Editor**
Material: All
Equities Magazine
2118 Wilshire Blvd. #722
Santa Monica CA 90403
Phone: 800-709-7005
Website: www.equitiesmagazine.com

Erased, Sigh, Sigh

Erased, Sigh, Sigh is VDP's literary journal. It was formed in late 1994 to print the more serious poetry and fiction submissions we received for our early magazine *In Ravens' Eyes*. Since that time, *ESS* has become the premier journal for what we refer to as "death poets and suicide writers." Quite a few of the writers who submit their poems and stories to *ESS* go on to become authors published through Via Dolorosa Press.

If you are interested in submitting to this journal, you should use the same guidelines that are listed in the VDP section. However, we do not accept non-fiction pieces. We mostly print poetry, though we will consider very short stories. We do not charge reading fees, and we accept both simultaneous submissions and previously-published work (as long as you currently hold the rights to it). There is no limit to the number of items you may submit to us at one time. But, if you want rejected work returned, you must enclose enough return postage.

Payment for accepted work is a contributor's copy for each issue in which the writer's work appears.

Send all ESS submission to the attention of Ms. Hyacinthe L. Raven at: *Erased, Sigh, Sigh*, at the address below.

Queries are not necessary, but we do appreciate cover letters. We print bylines for accepted work, so please feel free to include one.

Enclose a SASE (or SAE with IRC) with your submission for our response. We do not respond by email and will not acknowledge submissions without a SASE enclosed.

Categories: Fiction—Experimental—Language—Poetry—Short Stories

CONTACT: **Ms. Hyacinthe L. Raven, Editor**
Material: All
701 E. Schaaf Rd.
Cleveland, OH 44131-1227

Erosion Control

Please refer to Forester Communications.

Esquire

In all correspondence with us:

1. Please consult a recent issue of the magazine for content and style and consider carefully before making your submission.

2. Materials sometimes get lost in the mail or in the great wave of submissions we receive daily. We cannot track down wayward or unanswered manuscripts.

For fiction:

1. It is best to send the finished manuscript. We will consider short stories only; please do not send full-length novels.

2. We do not accept query letters for fiction.

3. Please send one story at a time; we will not read entire collections.

4. We do not publish pornography, science fiction, poetry or "true romance" stories.

5. We receive so many manuscripts that it is impossible for us to comment individually on them.

For nonfiction:

1. While we rarely publish unsolicited manuscripts, all submissions are read and answered within four to six weeks

2. We prefer receiving a query letter together with some published feature samples, rather than receiving a finished manuscript.

3. Suggested length for nonfiction manuscripts is 1,500 to 4,000 words.

4. Fees vary. We pay upon acceptance of an article.

Categories: Men's Issues

CONTACT: **Adrienne Miller**
Material: Fiction
CONTACT: **Mark Warren**
Material: Nonfiction
1790 Broadway
New York NY 10019

Essence

Thank you for your interest in writing for ESSENCE, the magazine for African-American and Caribbean women. We feature personal-growth articles, celebrity profiles, and well-reported pieces on political and social issues. We are also looking for how-to pieces on careers, money, health and fitness, and relationships. And we run short items on people in the arts and community activists. Word length is given upon assignment.

Please send a query letter rather than submitting a completed manuscript. The only exceptions are for the Interiors, Our World, Brothers and Back Talk columns. Essays submitted for these pages should run no longer than 600 words and should be clearly addressed to the editor of the column.

We cannot discuss story ideas over the telephone, nor can we respond to queries that come by fax or e-mail.

Give us a clear outline of your story; one page is sufficient. It would also help to include a brief biography that describes your writing experience, and some clips. If you would like to submit more than one idea, write a separate query for each topic. Check our masthead in the current issue for the names of the appropriate editors.

If we think your subject is of interest to our readers but you are a writer new to ESSENCE, you may be asked to submit the completed manuscript on speculation. Payment will be made if the article is accepted for publication.

All manuscripts must be typed and double-spaced. (We suggest that you keep a copy of your original manuscript.) We cannot be responsible for unsolicited material. Be sure to include your name, address and daytime phone number, and include a self-addressed stamped envelope. Allow six to eight weeks for review.

We look forward to hearing from you!

WRITER'S GUIDELINES FOR "Interiors"

We are looking for short personal essays that delve into the emotional lives of African-American women and/or explore issues that are of general concern to women from the writer's viewpoint. The essay should be well-written, clearly focused and help the reader understand herself and the world better. We welcome essays relating to women's lives on a broad range of subjects.

Manuscripts should be approximately 700 words, typed, double-spaced and submitted with a S.A.S.E. (self-addressed-stamped-envelope). Be sure to include a phone number where you can be reached during business hours. Mail manuscripts to Interiors, ESSENCE, 1500 Broadway, New York, NY 10036. Please allow six to eight weeks for review.

WRITER'S GUIDELINES FOR "Brothers"

We are looking for personal essays that explore and reveal aspects of men's feelings and concerns from the writer's subjective viewpoint. We'd like to be able to look inside the writer's heart and hear about his feelings and experiences, rather than just hear his opinions. Our readers want Brothers to help them understand what Black men are experiencing, how they are perceiving their world and how this might impact on their relationships with women, other men, children, their families and friends.

If you have an essay that meets our specifications, we'd love to see it.

SUGGESTED BROTHERS TOPICS:

• Being single • married • divorced • a father • incarcerated
• unemployed/underemployed • homosexual • celibate
• politically active • Growing older • Sports—meaning/importance
• Interacting with family • Friendship with men/women
• Cross-cultural experiences
And please suggest topics of your own!

Manuscripts should be approx. 800 words, typed, double-spaced and submitted with a S.A.S.E. (self-addressed-stamped-envelope). Be sure to include a phone number where you can be reached during business hours.

WRITERS GUIDELINES for "Our World"

"Our World" is a column in ESSENCE magazine written by people of varied ethnic and cultural backgrounds. These essays should transport our eight million readers across cultural and/or racial boundaries and provide insight into the lives of other people.

Using a first-person approach, writers should feel free to use anecdotes, phrases in her native language and descriptions of rituals and customs. But we hope you will go beyond mere descriptions to express how they feel about cultural references. "Our World" pieces should be written from the heart.

We prefer to read query letters rather than completed manuscripts. (A manuscript can be sent on speculation with the understanding that it will not be returned.) If an assignment is made, manuscripts should be no more than 800 words, typed and double-spaced. Be sure to include your name, address and daytime telephone number, and a self-addressed stamped envelope. Please allow eight weeks for review. Thank you for your interest in writing for ESSENCE.

WRITERS GUIDELINES for "Back Talk"

Think of this column as a forum page; it's your chance to make a point, deliver an opinion, build a case — or even pick a bone. Whether it revolves around an incident that happened to you, a trend or attitude you think is worth shedding light on or some timely issue of the day, it's important that you give us a concrete, distinctive perspective or new insight. Most Back Talk essays are persuasive; they exhort readers to think a certain way or do something. Others, however, simply highlight, celebrate or analyze some part of the human condition. As you write your Back Talk, or select a topic, the overriding concern should be whether or not your statements are important, relevant or of interest to Black women, Black people, or any social thinker.

Keep the language and tone of your essay as conversational or personable as possible. The most popular and effective Back Talks have been those that did not set up a large distance between the author and reader. So think of yourself as having a chat with someone, rather than giving a speech to masses. Avoid academic jargon or aimless rhetoric at all cost. As you're pulling your essay together, ask yourself questions such as: Does each point I make move toward or relate to the main theme? Have I included any examples or illustrations to make my point? Does the whole piece hold together or revolve around one major statement or theme?

Remember, what we're looking for in a Back Talk essay is clarity, unity, and substance. Whether your essay's tone is humorous or alarmist, realist or visionary, the readers should come away with her mind made up or changed: she should come away feeling resolved, enlightened, amused, provoked or encouraged.

Manuscripts should be 7-800 words, typed, double-spaced and submitted with a S.A.S.E. (self-addressed-stamped-envelope) and a color photograph that reflects the tone of your essay. Be sure to include your name and a phone number where you can be reached during business hours atop each page. Please allow four to six weeks for a written response.

Categories: Fiction—Nonfiction—African-American—General Interest—Health—Relationships—Self-Help

CONTACT: Submissions Editor
Material: All
1500 Broadway
New York NY 10036
Website: www.essence.com

Et cetera
A Review of General Semantics

The International Society for General Semantics, founded in 1943, publishes articles, essays, fiction, and correspondence related to general semantics. Our publications include a quarterly journal, *ETC: A Review of General Semantics*, and numerous books and anthologies.

General semantics, a science-oriented, educational discipline first formulated by Alfred Korzybski, applies to a wide range of human activities: communication, evaluating, perception, problem-solving, inference-making, critical thinking, to name a few.

As a writer, you communicate. You communicate your view of the world, based on your assumptions, observations, inferences, and conclusions. General semantics offers a wealth of material for the writer because it helps you understand some of the processes underlying thinking, evaluating, and communicating.

Our publishing covers many areas, including: • Humor • Multi-Media • Effective Writing • Comment • How to Apply General Semantics • Book Reviews • Self-Esteem • Fiction • Language & Behavior • Education • Research Results • Self-improvement Through General Semantics • Metaphor • The Media • Problem-Solving with General Semantics • Popular Culture • Critical Thinking • Communication • Science & Language • The Press • Psychology • Folklore • History of Thought • Computers & Networks

We produce books on using and teaching general semantics, including a number of anthologies of original material and reprints from *ETC: A Review of General Semantics*. We use material from published and unpublished writers.

Preparing to Write

Read about general semantics. Before making submissions, study *ETC: A Review of General Semantics* in order to familiarize yourself with content and style.

Read some of the recent general semantics books, such as Thinking and Living Skills: General Semantics for Critical Thinking, To Be or Not: An E-Prime Anthology, and More E-Prime: To Be or Not II. The latter two books have examples of general semantics fiction.

Our anthologies now in print also include: Classroom Exercises in General Semantics, Bridging Worlds Through General Semantics, Teaching General Semantics, Enriching Professional Skills Through General Semantics.

Manuscripts Needed

We need material for a forthcoming anthology of general semantics-related fiction. We also need submissions for *ETC: A Review of General Semantics*. As we have done in the past, we may select material from *ETC: A Review of General Semantics* for reprinting in future anthologies.

The Society, a nonprofit educational organization which exists to disseminate information related to general semantics, pays for publication with contributor's copies.

You may have noticed that we wrote these guidelines without to be verbs: is, was, am, were, be, being, been, etc. We call this variant of English E-Prime. Perhaps you heard about E-Prime on National Public Radio's All Things Considered or read about it in *The Atlantic Monthly* (February 1992). You may wish to find out how E-Prime can help improve your writing.

Preparing Submissions

Please use standard ms. preparation: Submit two copies. We cannot accept handwritten submissions. Put your name, address, and phone number on the first page at top left. Keep length of ms. below 4,000 words. Include a biography of up to thirty words. For reference style, see copies of *ETC: A Review of General Semantics*. Please advise us if you have a word processing disk available.

If you would like a sample copy of *ETC: A Review of General Semantics*, please let us know.

Meanwhile, do the important thing—keep on writing!

Categories: Education—General Interest—Language—Literature—Psychology—Writing

CONTACT: Jeremy Klein, Editor-in-Chief
Material: All
CONTACT: Paul D. Johnston, Managing Editor
Material: All
PO Box 728
Concord CA 94522
Phone: 925-798-0311
Fax: 510-798-0312
E-mail: isgs@generalsemantics.org
Website: www.generalsemantics.org

Evangel

Evangel a publication of Light and Life Communications, is printed quarterly and is geared toward adults. All submissions should reflect the needs, interests, and struggles of adults striving to maintain a vital relationship with Christ in the midst of everyday experiences—or seeking to know Christ in these same experiences. (In general, stories should be aimed at young to middle-aged adults.)

We accept both fiction and nonfiction work. Material can range from first person stories to Christian growth and living articles to devotional articles. Material should not be preachy or overly predictable. First-time rights are preferred, although second rights and reprints will be considered.

Materials should be limited to 1,200 words or less. We can use a larger quantity of short articles compared to long ones.

Short anecdotes and humor articles are welcome, although use is less frequent. Poetry is used on a very limited basis.

SUBMISSIONS: In the upper left-hand corner of the first page, include your name, address, phone number and e-mail contact if you have one. In the upper right-hand corner, specify the number of words in the manuscript, what rights you are offering and if the piece is fiction or nonfiction. One-third of the way down the page, give the manuscript title and your name. All subsequent material must be double-spaced, with one-inch margins. Number your pages.

Always include a word count, and a cover letter which introduces yourself and your work.

If we accept your article, we may ask you to provide the manuscript in a computer format by email. When preparing computer manuscripts:

- Do not justify margins.
- Use single spaces after periods and colons.
- Use tabs to begin paragraphs (not 5 spaces).

Allow six to eight weeks for response. Send seasonal material at least 9-12 months in advance.

PAYMENT: Rate of pay is four cents per word as published. Minimum payment is $10.00. Your check and complimentary copy are sent on publication.

PHOTOGRAPHY: Good-quality black-and-white or color photographs relating to your article are welcome. Rate of pay is $10.00 per selected photo. Include photo credit.

COMPLIMENTARY: If you would like to examine the style and content of *Evangel*, sample issues are available when [requests are] accompanied by a self-addressed, stamped envelope (business size).

MISSION STATEMENT: The *Evangel*, a weekly adult publication, seeks to increase the reader's understanding of the nature and character of God and the nature of a life lived under the lordship of Christ. Devotional in character, it directly and unashamedly lifts up Christ as the Source of salvation and hope.

Hints: • *Evangel* is limited in space. • Don't ramble, stick to your thesis or theme. • Don't be unnecessarily redundant. • Brevity and simplicity of content makes for a more readable piece. • Material not accompanied by a self-addressed stamped envelope is not returned and may not receive a reply. • Rhyming poetry is seldom seriously considered.

Categories: Fiction—Nonfiction—Christian Interests—Family—General Interest—Inspirational—Poetry

CONTACT: Julie Innes, Editor
Material: All
PO Box 535002
Indianapolis IN 46253-5002
Phone: 317-244-3660

Extra!!
Serving Southern Wisconsin

Columns are 200-500 words.
Submit by email.
Payment varies by piece.
Categories: General Interest

CONTACT: Mark T. Onosko, Editor/Publisher
Material: All
Union-Cooperative Publishing
3030-39th Ave., Ste 110
Kenosha WI 53144
Phone: 262-657-6116
Fax: 262-657-6153

Fabricator

Ornamental & Miscellaneous Metal

Fabricator

National Ornamental & Miscellaneous Metal Association

Articles can be from 800 to 2,000 words on topics related to the Ornamental and Miscellaneous Metal Industry.

These guidelines provide general tips on producing high-quality, easy-to-read articles for *Fabricator* magazine.

Tip #1: Articles should be written in a clear, concise, easy-to-read format. When writing, put yourself in the shoes of the reader and ask yourself such questions as, "Does this make sense?," "Is this interesting?," "Would I read this article if I were a *Fabricator* subscriber?"

Tip #2: Make sure the "Five W's" are included in the story: Who, What, When, Why, Where. Do not assume the reader knows what you're talking about. Explain highly technical terms in plain English.

Tip #3: As a writer, remember your goal is to benefit the reader. Whether your article is to educate, entertain, or inspire, always keep your reader in mind.

Tip #4: Place emphasis on things of special interest about your topic: Trivia, facts about the project's history, anecdotes, etc. Feel free to throw in humor and consider approaching your topic in a creative manner.

Tip #5: Once you have received an assignment, give yourself a couple of days to think about how to approach the story and what to include. If you are excited about the article, and it flows out easily, then chances are you have a great story. If a story must be forced out, line for line, then you may want to take a step back and consider another angle.

Tip #6: Always try to come up with artwork for a story—either drawings or photos. An illustrated article will catch the reader's eye, while a gray article will usually turn a reader off. If you can't find suitable artwork, then consider including a mug shot or photo of your business (all photos and artwork will be returned unharmed in about four weeks).

Tip #7: If you are a supplier, never make your articles sound like an "advertorial" or free advertisement. The purpose of the article is to provide helpful and interesting information as a valuable industry service—not to be self-serving. No "puff" pieces, please.

All articles published must be original material (i.e. you must control the copyright). If you use published information, it must be done in accordance with U.S. copyright laws. The article should not infringe on any existing copyrights.

When writing the article, you must honor any agreements on publicity that may have been signed with owners, architects, primary contractors, or other fabricators. As a matter of fairness, please credit subcontractors, partners, or employees when credit is due.

Transmission Methods

1) **U.S. Mail**—All stories will be scanned into our computer. Thus, they should be printed in dark ink on plain white paper.

2) **CD is OK.**

3) **E-mail**—Either as e-mail or as an "attached file."

4) **Fax**—You can fax directly into our computer. When faxing, please set your machine on the highest-quality setting.

Editing: All articles in *Fabricator* are subject to editing. Stories are typically edited for grammar, style, clarity, transition, voice, and length. If a story is edited, the editor will make every effort to preserve the author's original idea and intent. If a story requires complete rewriting, the editor will contact the writer. If a story is highly technical in nature, with lots of figures, the editor will likely send a proof after editing.

Statement of Purpose: *Fabricator*'s mission is to inform, educate, and inspire the industry. The magazine's long-term goal is to strengthen both the industry and NOMMA by fostering the free flow of information and knowledge.

For Freelance Writers: *Fabricator* welcomes unsolicited articles and photos.

Categories: Nonfiction—Trade—Metalworking

CONTACT: Fabricator Magazine Editor
Material: All
1535 Pennsylvania Ave
McDonough GA 30253
Phone: 423-413-6436
Fax: 888-516-8585
E-mail: fabricator@nomma.org

Faces
The Magazine About People

General Information

Lively, original approaches to the subject are the primary concerns of the editors in choosing material. Writers are encouraged to study recent back issues for content and style. (Sample issues available at $4.95. Send 7 ½" x 10 ½" (or larger) self-addressed stamped envelope.) All material must relate to the theme of a specific upcoming issue in order to be considered (themes and deadlines given below). FACES purchases all rights to material.

Procedure

A query must consist of all of the following information to be considered:

• please use non-erasable paper
• a brief cover letter stating the subject and word length of the proposed article,
• a detailed one-page outline explaining the information to be presented in the article,
• an extensive bibliography of materials the author intends to use in preparing the article

Writers new to FACES should send a writing sample with the query.

If you would like to know if your query has been received, please also include a stamped postcard requesting acknowledgment of receipt.

In all correspondence, please include your complete address as well as a telephone number where you can be reached.

Manuscripts should be typed double-spaced and include final word count. Authors are requested to supply a 2- to 3-line biographical sketch.

Articles must be submitted on disk using a word processing program (preferably Microsoft Word - MAC). Text should be saved as ASCII text (in MS Word as "text only"). Disks should be either MAC - (preferred) or DOS - compatible 3 ½ ".

GUIDELINES

Feature Articles

(about 800 words)

Includes: in-depth nonfiction highlighting an aspect of the featured culture, interviews, and personal accounts.

Supplemental Nonfiction

(300-600 words)

Includes: subjects directly and indirectly related to the theme. Editors like little-known information but encourage writers not to overlook the obvious.

Fiction

(up to 800 words)

Includes: Retold legends, folktales, stories, and original plays from around the world, etc., relating to the theme.

The above three pay 20 to 25 cents per printed word.

Activities

(up to 700 words)

Includes: crafts, games, recipes, projects, etc., which children can do either alone or with adult supervision. Should be accompanied by sketches and description of how activity relates to theme.

Poetry

(up to 100 lines)

Clear, objective imagery. Serious and light verse considered. Must relate to theme.

Puzzles and Games

Crossword and other word puzzles using the vocabulary of the issue's theme. Mazes and picture puzzles that relate to the theme.

The above three pay on an individual basis.

Photo Guidelines

To be considered for publication, photographs must relate to a specific theme. Writers are encouraged to submit available photos with their query or article. We buy one-time use.

See our website for suggested fee range for professional quality photographs.

• Please note that fees for non-professional quality photographs are negotiated.

• Cover fees are set on an individual basis for one-time use, plus promotional use. All cover images are color.

• Prices set by museums, societies, stock photography houses, etc., are paid or negotiated. Photographs that are promotional in nature (e.g., from tourist agencies, organizations, special events, etc.) are usually submitted at no charge.

• If you have photographs pertaining to any upcoming theme, please contact the editor by mail or fax, or send them with your query. You may also send images on speculation.

Note

Queries may be submitted at any time before the deadline, but queries sent well in advance of deadline MAY NOT BE ANSWERED FOR SEVERAL MONTHS. Go-aheads requesting material proposed in queries are usually sent at least seven months prior to publication date. Unused queries will be returned if a SASE is supplied.

Categories: Children—Culture—Juvenile—Multicultural—Young Adult

CONTACT: Elizabeth Crooker Carpentiere, Editor
Material: All
Cobblestone Publishing
30 Grove Street, Ste C
Peterborough NH 03458
Phone: 603-924-7209
Fax: 603-924-7380
E-mail: www.cobblestonepub.com
E-mail: facesmag@yahoo.com

Faith Today

Faith Today uses freelance writers for most articles and news reports. The following information outlines Faith Today's goals and the type of material we publish.

I. Non-writers can find answers to their frequently asked questions (FAQ) about Faith Today by jumping to http://www.evangelical fellowship.ca/about/faq.asp#Set_46.

II. Purpose

Founded in 1983 by the Evangelical Fellowship of Canada (EFC), Faith Today is a bi-monthly national magazine that seeks to inform, equip and inspire Christians across Canada. Faith Today is one facet of the EFC's communication ministry, which seeks to build community and understanding among Christians in Canada.

The EFC's purpose is to "bring Christians together for greater impact in mission, ministry and witness." It is an association of denominations, ministry organizations and congregations in Canada that collaborate in shared ministry and who speak into public forums to influence Canadians on the values and vision of the Christian perspective.

III. What's New

Faith Today has shifted its focus. Once a newsmagazine intended to inform Canadian evangelicals on thoughts, trends, issues and events, Faith Today has become a general interest publication for Christians in Canada. While still providing national news and comment, Faith Today now includes more feature articles that seek to inspire and equip lay leaders and ministry staff. As well, it provides profiles of individuals and ministries that have overcome challenges through God's intervention.

For writers this means that Faith Today is mainly interested in features ranging from 800-1,750 words that provide analysis and interpretation, rather than straight newsmagazine-style reports. (See below for more details.)

As well, two sections of short articles are open to writers: Kingdom Matters and Arts & Culture. (See below.)

IV. Readership Profile

Our readers include a wide spectrum of Christian men and women, many of them in their 40s and 50s, most often from the evangelical sector of the Church in Canada. More than half of the evangelical Church is formally affiliated with the EFC (see here) but there are also many evangelical individuals and institutions not formally affiliated with the EFC, including a large number in "mainline" denominations.

Our readers want to: understand current trends and issues in Canadian society and in Christian communities; learn how God is working among other Canadians, especially among believers and ministries they don't regularly communicate with; understand the diversity of thought and practice among Christians in Canada; connect with others to gain spiritual insights and other perspectives; gain analysis and resources to equip them in their personal and professional ministries.

Some informal reader surveys suggest that:

About half the readers of Faith Today are male, half female. Average age: 45. Average household income: $61,000 (Canadian dollars adjusted for inflation to 2004 levels). Average education: Bachelors or college degree. Most give more than 10 percent of their income to charities and churches.

About one third live in cities or suburbs of 500,000 or more residents. Another third live in medium-sized urban or suburban municipalities. The final third live in rural areas or municipalities of less than 25,000 residents.

About half live in the province of Ontario. A third live in British Columbia and Alberta (combined). About one eighth live in Saskatchewan and Manitoba (combined). The rest are distributed pretty evenly throughout Canada's other provinces and territories.

Most attend church services more than once per week. Faith Today has readers among virtually all of Canada's Christian groups, the largest numbers in Baptist, Pentecostal, Christian and Missionary Alliance, non-denominational, Christian Reformed, Mennonite Brethren and Anglican congregations.

V. Articles: What Faith Today Uses

A. Cover and feature articles

Each issue of Faith Today publishes a mix of 4-6 feature stories, one of which is selected as the cover story. They are assigned at least five weeks—more often five months—in advance. Each feature must address one or more of the desired outcomes stated in our "tag line": Faith Today seeks to inform, equip and inspire Christians across Canada.

Cover stories focus on Canadian trends, issues and ministry initiatives of interest to Christians.

Some features could also be described this way. But features can also include: service articles ("how to" pieces, treating topics from prayer to web sites); faith profiles of people or ministries; slices of life that help readers understand their own experiences; background articles such as an overview of the new Bible translations; and transformation stories that show how a situation was turned around.

One final kind of feature is the essay, which Faith Today publishes only occasionally. An essay is usually an extended report or opinion piece by a writer who draws on a particular area of expertise to provide an intriguing, Christian-based exploration of a group of ideas (e.g. spiritual or social issues). Some essays we published recently include examinations of reconciliation, technology, why we weep at the deaths of public figures, and how the church should respond to terrorism.

We don't normally publish a "theme" list like many other periodicals. We rely instead on a dynamic flow of topics suggested by editorial staff and freelance writers.

Features vary from 800 to 1,750 words and always require submitting an outline two weeks before due date. Cover stories are 2,000 words. Longer articles have sidebars, which may include statistics, a profile or a related story. They are calculated in the total word count. Essays are 650–1,200 words.

A typical feature article for Faith Today is written in the third person and has a point of view that is supported by clear arguments based on sound research and interviews with Canadian sources.

Successful features will: begin with a captivating and colourful lead that draws readers into the topic by enabling them to experience the issue. This should be human focused, anecdotal and interesting; include a clear theme statement (or indicator paragraph) that identifies the issue which the feature will address and why Christian readers should care about it. This tells the readers where the article is headed and convinces them to continue; reflect Canadian and Christian diversity (depending on the type of article, this can be in the perspective, denominational background, geography, sex, age, ethnicity or other characteristics); include contrary views as appropriate, thus anticipating the reader's questions. However the feature should have a sense of closure and a point of view. A good feature persuades and "shows" the reader rather than "tells" them the important issues being addressed. Readers should be left with a balanced understanding of the issue at hand; contain analysis and opinions from a variety of sources; create a lively style using anecdotes, metaphor, vivid descriptions of settings and people to keep the reader in the piece and caring for the issue; provide a simple explanation of the research in the writer's words, illustrated by occasional succinct quotes. Features should not be merely source quotes strung together; close with an ending that ties into the lead and theme statement. It should not only sum up the article but possibly point to the future (without suddenly introducing a new idea in the last paragraph).

B. Kingdom Matters section

This section of Faith Today includes a lively collection of short items that reflects how God is at work in the Church in Canada, both in formal ministry and in daily life. The articles are tightly focused on one aspect of a topic. Writing must be concise and concrete.

Topics include achievements, effective initiatives, short profiles and coverage of time-sensitive events that don't fit into Faith Today's news section.

Length: 50-300 words. Faith Today looks for strong photos to illustrate and accompany the items.

C. News section

In each issue Faith Today includes several articles about current Canadian events of interest to Christians. These articles are 300 to 700 words each. Common topics include: education, media, social issues, courts, native concerns, missions, churches, politics/government and youth.

News stories are written in inverted pyramid style, third person, using Canadian research.

For controversial news stories, interviews with representatives of all sides of a story are essential. Unlike the features, the news stories should be neutral and balanced, with no cheerleading. Original research is expected—no rewriting of media releases. Local news is acceptable as long as there is an element with national appeal. Photos welcomed.

D. Arts & Culture section:

Reviews of Christian books, music (and rarely theatre and art) are limited to 300 words. Preference is given to items with a Canadian connection. Short reports on special events and contests are also used.

Keep in mind the 50-50 split in our readership between leaders and laity: write so that both audience segments can read the review. Reviews should summarize content, describe the intended audience for the product, and include opinion as to quality, usefulness and entertainment value as appropriate. Some mention of where the product "fits" in relation to existing products is also welcome (e.g. is the influence of other artists/thinkers/producers evident in the work? does it fit squarely in an accepted genre or not?)

Please make explicit the Canadian connection, e.g. "The author is a professor at XYZ school in Ponoka, Alta." Please also cite the following details (which we print under an image of the book cover alongside the review): Publisher name, year, number of pages, price for Canadian customers in Canadian dollars, noting if the price is for paperback or hardcover.

E. Letters and Milestones section:

Comments on previously published issues are subject to editing for clarity and length; maximum length is 300 words. To be published, a writer must include his/her name and location as well as a phone number (this will not published).

In each issue Faith Today includes milestones such as announcements of appointments, resignations, organizational name changes, awards and other items of interest to the wider Christian community.

VI. Writing Style

Faith Today follows the Canadian Press Stylebook for spelling, grammar, capitalization, etc. as well as the Faith Today Style Guide, available for free at http://www.faithtoday.ca/article_viewer.asp?Article_ID=54. The CP stylebook is available at www.cp.org and elsewhere for $32.

VII. What Faith Today Doesn't Use

Bible studies, poetry, serialized articles and most seasonal material. (To clarify: we welcome short Easter-themed submissions but only print one per year.)

VIII. Queries: Getting an Assignment

To propose a cover or feature article, query Faith Today in writing by e-mail at FTeditor@efc-canada.com. Describe the topic and the angle you wish to address; why it would be of interest to a Christian audience in Canada; the research you intend to conduct; the people you intend to interview; your writing background and any qualifications that you have to write about the topic.

Show in the query letter that you have already done a few minutes of research. This may involve using an Internet search engine that excludes non-Canadian sites (www.crosscanadasearch.com, www.praize.ca, www.google.ca); consulting a print reference such as the annual Christian Ministry Sourcebook; or materials produced by Christian Info Society.

For cover stories, Faith Today works with experienced writers who can do diverse research and provide analysis as well as write a lively article.

For Kingdom Matters, News, or Arts & Culture: Send a query by e-mail, fax or letter. Outline the story and whom you plan to interview. If you are new to us please include your writing background.

Contacting Faith Today: We prefer carefully composed query letters sent by e-mail or fax. If you are mailing hardcopy, include a SASE with Canadian postage (or international reply coupon) for prompt reply. If your idea is time-sensitive, call 905-479-5885 and ask for the senior editor.

Unsolicited manuscripts are not accepted. They will not be returned.

A special way to get to know Faith Today editors is to attend one of the many training events organized by www.thewordguild.com. Faith Today editors attend and sometimes teach at Word Guild seminars across Canada. Canada is currently blessed with at least three national associations for writers and editors who are Christian. Besides the Word Guild, consider joining www.inscribe.org and www.canadianchurchpress.com. All these groups serve professionals as well as beginners and are less expensive than mainstream counterparts such as the Periodical Writers Association of Canada (www.pwac.ca). Faith Today editors recommend that writers who aspire to be more than hobbyists join mainstream associations; the cost may seem high at first but pays off in the long run. All of the organizations mentioned in this paragraph can help writers, from beginners to pros, to improve their craft and their career.

IX. Rate Schedule

Rates include both first North American serial print rights as well as perpetual web rights.

Cover story: $Cdn 0.30/word; Regular features: $Cdn 0.25/word; Kingdom Matters and News: $Cdn 0.20/word; Essays: $Cdn 0.15/word; Reprints: $Cdn 0.15/word.

Writers who request it can have their cheques made out in American funds (i.e., we convert the amount owing in Cdn funds to the equivalent in U.S. funds, and prepare a cheque in U.S. funds).

Expenses: Telephone expenses are covered though they must be submitted with an itemized copy of the phone bill. These may also be limited to a certain amount. Other expenses must be negotiated in advance.

Web Rights: All features and material published in Faith Today may be selected for posting on several web sites owned by the Evangelical Fellowship of Canada or on web sites that promote Faith Today, unless permission is refused by the writer at acceptance of the assignment. (The EFC web sites currently include www.evangelical fellowship.ca and www.christianity.ca and www.faithtoday.ca. We are not currently posting articles on any promotional web sites.)

Kill Fee: Faith Today reserves the right not to publish an assigned article if it is not of publishable quality or does not meet the terms of the assignment. The payment is 30-50 percent of the assigned fee, plus agreed upon expenses.

X. Publishing Practices

Payment is made within six weeks of the acceptance of a publishable story and the submission of contact information for all research sources. Two copies of the issue in which the author's article appears will be provided for the author. Goods and Services Tax (GST), where charged, are paid in addition to rates. Writers who charge GST must invoice us.

We often require writers to submit more than one draft of an article, and payment will only be requisitioned after production of a final draft by the writer and approval by an FT editor.

Copyright: Faith Today purchases first North American periodical rights only, with these exceptions: we grant reproduction permission without consultation with the author for: an anthology of collected works of Faith Today material; audio services for the handicapped; photocopies for use in a local church or classroom.

Reprinting: Freelance writers and columnists own their work. We will direct any requests for reprint permission to them. (Articles by Faith Today staff are owned by the magazine, which generally forbids reprints for commercial uses, e.g. for advertising, advertorial or fundraising copy.) Reprints must include a credit line indicating Faith Today as the source and date of first publication. Please also add a line saying, "For a free sample copy of Faith Today, please call 905-479-6071 ext. 255." Please send a copy of the reprinted article to us for our files.

Publication of an opinion, event or advertisement does not indicate endorsement by Faith Today staff or its publisher, the Evangelical Fellowship of Canada.

Simultaneous publication: Writers may re-sell an assigned article after Faith Today has published it. For breaking stories, Faith Today may accept an article from a person who writes for several publications using the same research or interviews and whose work will appear elsewhere before Faith Today has published its story. However in that case the situation must first be discussed with an FT editor and the FT story must be significantly different from the other articles. In the event that there is a conflict, Faith Today may choose not to publish the story.

Photos: Writers are asked to arrange for sending photos to Faith Today of their main interviewee, due five days after the article. A stock photo (e.g. mug shot) is acceptable, but we prefer a casual photo or an action shot (perhaps taken by the writer). Photos should be in colour. Photos can be prints or sent in high-resolution electronic form. Our minimum for an image sized 4" by 4" is 266 dots per inch (a smaller image must have more dpi). The format can be jpg or pretty much anything. If your photo file is less than 150 kilobytes, it's probably not good enough. If an expert did not scan your photos, we prefer that you send prints to us by mail so that we can scan them. We will return prints to the source at no charge upon request.

Pseudonyms: Faith Today generally does not publish material under pseudonyms.

Filing method: Articles should be submitted by e-mail. We currently use Microsoft Word 2000, but can handle text in all major formats. All articles must be accompanied by a list of research sources, with MAILING ADDRESSES and phone numbers. We may need to contact them to finalize photo arrangements, to check facts with them, or to send them tear sheets of the article once the magazine is printed.

Categories: Nonfiction—Religion

CONTACT: Faith Today M.I.P.
Box 3745
Markham ON L3R 0Y4Canada
Phone: 905-479-5885
Fax: 905-479-4742
E-mail: ft@efc-canada.com Web page: www.faithtoday.ca

Family Business

• Your audience consists primarily of owners and managers of family-owned businesses. Their various needs are covered by many publications; only *Family Business* focuses on the family aspect of businesses, and the business aspect of families. For example: Succession, estate planning, sibling rivalries, cousin jealousies, attracting and holding non-family talent, compensating family members vs. non-family employees, raising capital without giving up control. Make these "family business" concerns paramount.

• In a family business, many problems that appear to be financial or technical actually stem from emotional roots. Try to delve beneath the surface and get your subjects to talk candidly and introspectively about the human side of the business.

• Your readers are busy people. You must entice them to read your story with a compelling lead. Thereafter, you must hold their attention. Any one of the following devices will probably suffice:

1. Dramatize your subject. Ask yourself: What's the problem here? How was it solved—or, conversely, how was it fumbled?

2. Humanize. Wherever possible, illustrate your general points with specific examples, either from your own research or from business news or history. Pseudonymous examples are better than none, but real people are preferable. That's what readers can relate to.

3. Paint word pictures. Visual words and images stick to people's minds. Ask yourself: Would you rather attend a lecture or a movie?

• Your article must have a compelling point. Before you plunge too far into the details of your story, ask yourself, "So what?"—and answer that question in your text.

• E-mail is the preferred method for submitting queries. Freelance writers are encouraged to propose article ideas. Identify the family business owners you plan to interview.

Information for company/public relations representatives

• General business success stories are covered in numerous business publications. *Family Business* is a niche publication that focuses specifically on the family aspect of businesses, and the business aspect of families. The story we're interested in is how the business leaders at your company have resolved issues of succession, sibling or cousin compensation, family conflict, governance (e.g., inactive vs. active shareholders), raising capital without relinquishing control, employment of family and non-family members and other concerns involving the connection between family and business.

• Members of your organization must be willing to speak candidly and introspectively to our reporters about areas of family disagreement and the ways in which these issues were resolved.

• *Family Business* accepts contributed articles from attorneys, accountants, M&A specialists, organizational psychologists and other family business advisers. To be considered for publication, articles must explicitly address the concerns of *family* business owners. Wherever possible, please try to cite real-life family business examples, using real names. (One suggestion: Use famous names drawn from your own research or from the news—or cite historical examples.)

• E-mail is the preferred method for submitting author inquiries.
Categories: Nonfiction—Business—Family

CONTACT: Barbara Spector, Editor-in-Chief
1845 Walnut St
Philadelphia PA 19103
Phone: 215-405-6084
Fax: 215-405-6078
e-mail: bspector@familybusinessmagazine.com

Family Circle

Writers are sometimes surprised to find out that most of the articles *Family Circle* publishes are written by freelancers. We are always looking for new contributors.

If you want to submit an article proposal to *Family Circle*, please pay careful attention to the following points:

• Take a close look at *Family Circle* for some knowledge of format and an understanding of the subjects we have tackled in the past, remembering that we are a general interest women's magazine which focuses on the family. We are looking for true stories with strong plot lines and characters, or newsworthy reports on social issues and trends that affect American families. We are especially interested in women who make a difference in their community, news and information on health, child care, relationships, finances and other matters of concern to today's family; as well as dramatic personal experiences.

• Submit a detailed outline first, and include a brief cover letter describing your publishing history and two representative clips.

• Manuscripts should be typed, double-spaced, on letter-size paper. Handwritten submissions will be returned.

• Maximum length for articles is usually 2,500 words.

• *Family Circle* does not consider multiple submissions.

• Submissions must be accompanied by self-addressed stamped envelopes of sufficient size or, if mailed from abroad, by International Reply Coupons, which are available at post offices throughout the world.

• *Family Circle* takes good care of submissions; however, owing to the fact that mail is sometimes mislaid by the U.S. Post Office, we cannot assume responsibility. Be sure to have a copy of every submission you send to us.

Categories: Nonfiction—Children—Family—General Interest—Health—Money & Finances—Relationships—Personal Experiences

CONTACT: Appropriate Editor from Masthead
Material: As appropriate
375 Lexington Ave.
New York NY 10017-5514
Phone: 212-499-2000

The Family Digest

"The joy and fulfillment of Catholic family life"

Family Digest

Submission Guidelines for *Family Digest* magazine & Web site.
Publisher's note: In a world that has ignored, demeaned, devalued and berated the Black family, we stand forth to celebrate and empower Black mothers, fathers, husbands and wives. Come join us in this movement!

What's In It For Our Readers? "Smarter, Healthier, Happier Black Families."

Family Digest magazine is a magazine for Black Moms/Female heads-of-household; helping them get more out of their roles as wife, mother, home-manager - with special emphasis on areas of interest to Black Americans.

Editorial coverage includes parenting, health, love & marriage, family finances, recipes, and beauty & style,... all designed to appeal to Black Moms/Female heads-of-household. Most of our readers are married with kids.

Please note: Articles published in *Family Digest* are positive in nature and focus on providing information and solutions, not just analysis. The articles are conversational, factual and authoritative. When the reader reads *Family Digest* it is as if she is having a discussion with a friend who is an expert in a particular field.

Important: We love it when you can deliver photos appropriate for the article.

Family Digest's Interest Areas include:

1. Family: Articles in this section help parents help their children in a variety of areas, such as: how to effectively discipline their child, how to talk to kids about drugs, how to build their kids self-esteem, etc.

2. Family Travel: This is a section that we're really excited about. The key to this section is affordable, interesting vacation destinations for the family. This could be: cruises in the Caribbean, auto travel to destinations in the U.S., Club Med, Skiing, Hawaii, trips out West, air/land packages, etc. We want the trips to be accessible.

3. Auto Review: We're interested in this piece (to run in every issue) that reviews various family vehicles... This piece should always be written from the standpoint of, and the benefit of, what a Mom with kids would like in a family vehicle.

4. Enjoy Life!: This section focuses on articles that strengthen moms so that they can be better people. Articles in this section are uplifting and leave the reader feeling they can do anything. Example topics include: how to get negative people out of your life, job strategies, networking tips.

5. Love & Marriage: The articles that appear in this section allow readers to strengthen their relationship with their spouse. Features in this section focus on: improving communication between partners, tips on how to have a strong relationship and pleasing your partner (these articles can include information on healthy sexual relations).

6. Health: The focus here is on health and medical issues of particular interest to Black women. Topics include breast cancer, fibroids, diabetes, sickle-cell, cystitis, etc... These articles should offer factual information regarding available treatments and resources.

7. Family Finances: These are tips regarding saving money and investing. Articles should provide immediately usable information and how-tos. Examples include how to save on groceries, how to choose life insurance, how to develop an investment strategy, saving for the kids' college, ...

8. Beauty & Style: This section provides information on the latest in hair and skin care, as well as relevant fashion trends. Examples might be: best skin care products for busy moms, how to effectively moisturize African-American skin, taking care of particular hair styles, the age at which it is safe to do certain things to children's hair (for in-

stance, at what age is it safe to perm a child's hair), ...

9. Meal Time!: This section features recipes and information on food. Articles should feature foods that are easily found in a typical grocery store. Also, meals should be relatively easy to prepare.

10. Horoscope: This section should be written about adult females, in a tone that is relevant to the female head-of-household.

Submission Guidelines:

1. Please submit story ideas, and your thoughts on the angle you'd like to take to editor@familydigest.com . Ideas will be judged according to their fit with the information outlined above.

2. If you have not written for us before, please submit 3 writing samples that are representative of your work. These should also be sent to editor@familydigestbaby.com via EMail.

3. Length: Generally, articles should be 1,000 to 2,000 words.

4. Article Approach: We encourage a mix of approaches including narratives, profiles, how- tos and Q&As. Please indicate the direction you would like to take along with each story idea (see #1 above).

5. Deadlines: Inquire

6. Completed story submission: All work must be submitted by EMail to editor@familydigest.com (unless other arrangements agreed to).

7. Rewrites: If retooling is necessary, we will contact you within 3 weeks of article submission to discuss.

8. Send photos to: Angel Morning at the address below. Include your name and story title with all photos.

9. We pay upon publication. Writing fees vary based on budget and need. We will contact you with rate at time of initial contact.

Please feel free to contact editor@familydigest.com with any questions or comments.

Categories: Nonfiction—Children—Culture—Family—Parenting—Relationships

CONTACT: Submissions Edito
Material: All
Family Digest Media Group
696 San Ramon Valley Blvd., Ste. 349
Danville CA 94526
Phone: 925-838-4800
Fax: 925-838-4948
E-mail: editor@familydigest.com
Website: www.familydigest.com

Family Fun

Thank you for inquiring about freelance opportunities at *FamilyFun*, the country's number one magazine for families with children ages three to twelve. Founded in 1991 and with a circulation now exceeding 1.9 million, our publication celebrates all the fun things families can do together, from throwing parties and making crafts to taking trips and cooking great food. Our goal is to inspire families to spend time together by providing the sure-fire ideas and activities that will make that time a success. In other words, we take fun seriously. Please note that our heavy emphasis on activities and ideas distinguishes us from other parenting and family magazines (as one of our descriptive slogans points out, we provide "100% activities for 100% fun"). This format means that we are always looking for freelancers who are experts in the art of being a fun-loving, creative parent.

We accept submissions by standard mail from published writers. Queries should describe the content, structure, and tone of the proposed article. Since we receive many queries on the same topics, please be as specific as possible about what makes your idea unique and your qualifications to write it. If appropriate, include photographs or sketches of the finished project, food, or craft. Also, with each query, please enclose two or three relevant clips for our review. Unfortunately, we no longer accept unsolicited manuscripts for feature stories. We will continue to accept manuscripts for the following departments: Everyday Fun, Family Getaways, Creative Solutions, My Great Idea, Healthy Fun, and Family Home (please note department on envelope). Unless otherwise indicated below, articles are scheduled and assigned at least five months in advance of their publication date. We generally take at least four to eight weeks to respond and regret that we cannot, under any circumstance, consider queries over the telephone, via email, or fax. Please enclose a self-addressed stamped envelope with correct postage for our response to your query.

FEATURES

Our features present activities that are entertaining for the whole family, relatively inexpensive, and easy to do. The specific topics include food, crafts, parties, holiday celebrations, sports, games, creative solutions to common household problems, and educational projects. Our travel features highlight moderately priced destinations, generally within the United States, that offer an exceptional value and specifically cater to the needs of families. Similarly, our food features present recipes that have a proven track record with families, dishes that are fun both to make and to eat. In all our articles, our style is upbeat, personal, and straightforward. Features generally run 850 to 3,000 words and pay $1.25 per word upon acceptance. We consider ideas in query form only.

DEPARTMENTS

Everyday Fun provides readers with simple, fun, practical, and inexpensive ideas and projects (outings, crafts, games, nature activities, learning activities, kid-friendly recipes, and so on). Its tone is direct and cheerful. We read both freelance manuscripts and queries for Everyday Fun. Pieces are assigned from 100 to 300 words; we pay $1.25 per word upon acceptance. We also pay $100 for ideas in the event that we decide to use a staff writer. We consider ideas in query or manuscript form.

Family Getaways consists of short, newsy items about family travel—what's new, what's great, and what's a good deal. We cover festivals, civic and cultural events, museum exhibits, family hotel packages, state and national park programs, and more. We also present longer articles on such topics as road trips, city weekends, and roundups of themed attractions or destinations. Because we are budget-conscious, we rarely cover international travel or expensive American resorts or programs. We pay $100 upon acceptance for 100- to 125-word pieces. We pay $1.25 per word upon acceptance for other Family Getaways articles. We also pay $100 for ideas in the event that we decide to use a staff writer. We consider ideas in query or manuscript form.

Creative Solutions showcases a practical, innovative idea that the writer used to solve a common household problem: a chart that got the kids excited about doing chores, say, or a trick that persuaded some reluctant letter writers to keep up their correspondence with Grandpa. Each essay also presents the story of how this Creative Solution changed or inspired the family. The column runs 800 to 1,200 words, and pays $1250 upon acceptance. We consider ideas in query or manuscript form, though manuscripts are preferred.

My Great Idea consists of ideas and solutions from writers and readers. These, like Creative Solutions above, showcase simple, clever ideas that solve common household problems, but they are presented in an abbreviated format with less narrative detail. My Great Idea runs 100 to 200 words and pays $100 upon publication.

Healthy Fun features refreshingly practical strategies and creative ideas for staying active, eating well, and feeling great. It offers a humorous, knowing, down-to-earth, parent-to-parent look at ways of working healthy habits and exercise into your life. The light approach and conversational tone underscore the fundamental challenge: sure, you know your kids should eat more veggies and get moving, but how do you really entice them? How do you make it fun for you and them? We're looking for real-world solutions to the health challenges today's families face. Healthy Fun runs 1,300 words in length and pays $1500 upon acceptance. We consider detailed queries only.

Family Fun features creative and useful ideas for the home, yard, and garden. We look for practical solutions for staying organized, new products, and easy, unique ways to decorate. The ideas must be affordable and realistic, such as those in the "success stories" (sent in by families around the country) that we regularly run. The column is usually written by a select group of contributing editors, but we do buy individual ideas. The column runs 1,000 words in length and pays @1250 upon acceptance. We also pay $100 to $200 for ideas in the event that we decide to use a staff writer. We consider specific ideas in query form. Photos are appreciated but cannot be returned.

Please address all submissions to:
ATTN: (name of appropriate editor)
FamilyFun
47 Pleasant St
Northampton MA 01060

If you would like to receive a sample copy of our magazine, send a check for $3 made out to *FamilyFun* to:
FamilyFun, PO Box 37032, Boone IA 50037-0032

Subscriptions ($14.95 for one year) can also be ordered through the above address, online at https://commerce.cdsfulfillment.com/FAF/subscriptions.cgi or by calling 800-289-4849.

Categories: Nonfiction—Crafts/Hobbies—Family—Parenting

CONTACT: Features Editor
Material: Feature Queries
CONTACT: Adrienne Stolarz, Associate Editor
Material: Everyday Fun Submissions
CONTACT: Nicole Blasenak, Senior Associate Editor
Material: Family Getaway Submissions
CONTACT: Debra Immergut, Senior Editor
Material: Creative Solutions Submissions
CONTACT: Nicole Blasenak, Senior Associate Editor
Material: My Great Idea Submissions
CONTACT: Jodi Butler, Senior Editor
Material: Healthy Fun Submissions
CONTACT: Cindy Littlefield, Senior Editor
Material: Family Home Submissions
47 Pleasant St
Northampton MA 01060
Phone: 413-585-0444
Fax: 413-586-5724
Website: www.familyfun.com

Family Safety and Health

No longer acceoting submissions.

Family Therapy
The Journal of the California Graduate School of Family Psychology

The editor welcomes succinct, well-written papers within the broad field of family and marital therapy. Clinical articles devoted to techniques, and richly endowed with illustrative dialogue, are most highly regarded.

MANUSCRIPTS, REFERENCES AND REPRINTS: Manuscripts must be type-written in duplicate. All manuscripts must include an abstract of 100-150 words and typed on a separate sheet of paper. Footnotes, charts, tables, graphs, etc. should be kept to a minimum and submitted in the original, camera-ready copy. (We prefer that, when practical, the information contained in this material be incorporated into the text instead.) References to books and articles should appear

at the end of the manuscript under the heading "References," with items listed alphabetically by name of author.

Authors will be furnished galley proofs which must be returned to the editor within two days. Corrections should be kept to a minimum. A schedule of reprint costs and an order blank for reprints will be sent with galley proofs.

SUBSCRIPTIONS: All business communications, including subscriptions, renewals, and remittances should be addressed to:
Libra Publishers, Inc.
3089C Clairemont Dr., Suite 383
San Diego, CA 92117
SUBSCRIPTION RATES
Individuals-U.S.A.: One year $62; Two years $122; Three years $182 Other countries: One year $69; Two years $136; Three years $203
Institutions-U.S.A.: One year $70; Two years $138; Three years $206 Other countries: One year $75; Two years $148; Three years $221

Copies of current or back issues are available at $22.00 each from Libra Publishers.

Categories: Nonfiction—Counseling—Family—Marriage—Psychology—Relationships—Family and Marital Therapy

CONTACT: Martin G. Blinder, M.D., Editor
Material: All
50 Idalia Rd.
San Anselmo CA 94960
Phone: 858-571-1414
Fax: 858-571-1414

Family Tree Magazine

Family Tree Magazine is a general-interest consumer magazine that helps readers discover, preserve and celebrate their family's history. We cover genealogy, ethnic heritage, personal history, genealogy Web sites and software, scrapbooking, photography and photo preservation, and other ways that families connect with their past.

Articles are geared to beginners—our readers don't necessarily think of themselves as "genealogists"—but never talk down to the audience. Readers may be experts in one area of our coverage, yet novices in another. We emphasize sidebars, tips and other reader-friendly "packaging," and each article aims to provide the resources necessary to take the next step in the quest for one's personal past.

Writing for *Family Tree Magazine*

· Always query with an SASE. If we've never worked with you before, a paper query with samples of your writing is preferred over an e-mail query. (Though please do include your e-mail address for faster response.) Please don't call with queries or to check on the status of your query.

· The ideal *Family Tree Magazine* writer is both a writer—able to explain complex topics in clear, friendly, easy-to-read articles and sidebars—and an expert (or interested amateur) in one of our coverage areas. Your query should indicate both why you're right for this topic and why you're able to write it.

· Please query with a specific story idea. In general, we're looking for stories that are right for our magazine, not writers to assign articles to. Please do not submit finished articles (except for our Everything's Relative section; see #9) or articles previously published in other genealogical magazines.

· Issues are planned well in advance. Though our lead time is technically about six months, we'll have a plan for the December issue by January of that year. Better to look too far ahead than to miss the boat.

And we do like to be timely—scheduling a story on wedding records in June, for example.

· Our style is bright, breezy, helpful and encouraging. We're NOT an academic journal or a genealogy-research journal.

· Articles need to be broad in scope to appeal to a general audience, yet narrow enough to support specific, useful information. "Getting Started with the National Archives" might be a good article for us; "1840 North Carolina Census Records" is not.

· We do NOT publish personal experience stories (except in Everything's Relative) or the histories of specific families. Nor do we publish generic family or parenting articles—keep in mind that our focus is family history.

· Query with specific suggestions on accompanying sidebars, tip boxes, resource lists and other elements, as well as ideas for content that might be appropriate for posting on our Web site, www.familytreemagazine.com.

· For writers new to *Family Tree Magazine*, we are most open to short submissions for Branching Out (lively, newsy upfront section) and brief writeups of new resources for genealogists, scrapbookers and family history buffs for our Toolkit section. We also invite short, amusing stories of "the lighter side of family history" for our Everything's Relative page; accepted submissions here pay $25.

· Please read a copy of the magazine before querying.

· For more advice on writing and marketing your work, see writersdigest.com at www.writersdigest.com.

· **Payment and rights:** Pay on acceptance. Buy first rights and online rights. Rates vary widely depending on difficulty of assignment. Offer 25% kill fee.

· **Sample copy:** Order from our Web site, www.familytreemagazine.com.

Categories: Family

CONTACT: Editor
Material: All
4700 E Galbraith Rd
Cincinnati OH 45236
Website: www.familytreemagazine.com

Fantastic Stories

Fantastic Stories is a full size, quarterly fantasy and science fiction magazine. Each issue has a full color glossy cover and is filled with imaginative stories, poetry, interviews and art, by professional and small press writers. *Fantastic Stories* features fantasy and science fiction in all their forms. While elements in the story must be SF/F oriented, mixing genres is permissible (e.g., an SF Mystery.) All stories must be well written, factually correct and, of course, entertaining. Stories should be entirely fictional; do not send stories based on actual events. 2,000 to 15,000 words; average is 4,000 to 5,000 words. Payment is 1 to 5 cents per word for First North American Serial Rights.

POETRY: All forms and styles, 3-20 lines, within the stated genres; payment up to $1 per line for First North American Serial Rights.

ART: Fantastic Stories is always in need of good art. Send B&W samples for interior and color photocopied samples for cover work. Payment for interior and cover art is negotiated with each artist.

Follow standard manuscript format; manuscripts with type smaller than 12 point will be returned unread; submissions without a self-addressed stamped envelope (with IRCs for international submissions) will be destroyed unread. No e-mail submissions. Do not send rewrites unless they are specifically requested. Response time is 1-2 months. Include cover letter w/credits. Sample $5.

Categories: Fiction—Art—Interviews—Poetry—Short Stories

CONTACT: Ed McFadden, Editor
PO Box 329
Brightwaters NY 11718-0329

Fantasy&ScienceFiction

Fantasy & Science Fiction

The Magazine of Fantasy & Science Fiction, founded in 1949, is the award-winning SF magazine which is the original publisher of SF classics like Stephen King's *Dark Tower*, Daniel Keyes's *Flowers for Algernon*, and Walter M. Miller's *A Canticle for Leibowitz*.

Each 160 page issue offers: Compelling short stories and novellas by writers such as Ray Bradbury, Ben Bova, Ursula K. Le Guin, Esther M. Friesner, Terry Bisson and many others. The science fiction field's most respected and outspoken opinions on Books, Films and Science (samples are available via our Departments link)

Writer's Guidelines

We have no formula for fiction. We are looking for stories that will appeal to science fiction and fantasy readers. The SF element may be slight, but it should be present. We prefer character-oriented stories. We receive a lot of fantasy fiction, but never enough science fiction or humor. Do not query for fiction; send the entire manuscript. We publish fiction up to 25,000 words in length. Please read the magazine before submitting. A sample copy is available for $6 (to NJ address).

We do not accept simultaneous or electronic submissions. Please type your manuscript on clean white bond, double spaced, with one inch margins. Put your name on each page, and enclose a self-addressed, stamped envelope. Writers from abroad are encouraged to send recyclable manuscripts with a letter-sized SASE and an International Reply Coupon or 84 cents in US postage (63 cents to Canada and Mexico).

Allow 8 weeks for a response. Please write and enclose a self-addressed stamped envelope if you have any questions.

Payment is 6-9 cents per word on acceptance. We buy first North American and foreign serial rights and an option on anthology rights. All other rights are retained by the author.

Our columns and non-fiction articles are assigned in house. We do not accept freelance submissions in those areas.

Since we use so little art—just eleven covers a year, no interiors—we have no separate artist's guidelines. Please send art samples to Gordon Van Gelder at the address below.

Categories: Fiction—Fantasy—Literature—Science Fiction—Short Stories—Young Adult

CONTACT: Gordon Van Gelder, Editor
Material: Story submissions, cartoon queries and art samples
PO Box 3447
Hoboken NY 07030
Phone: 201-876-2551
E-mail: fsfmag@fsfmag.com
Website: www.sfsite.com/fsf

Farm & Ranch Living

Unlike other farm magazines, *Farm & Ranch Living* does not tell readers how to grow crops or raise animals. Instead, F&RL is a lifestyle magazine for and about farmers and ranchers. We aren't interested in yields, costs, trends or topical issues. We are interested in stories about people and how they live. Ours is the magazine folks read not for profit, but for pure pleasure.

Our kind of story might be about a farmer who has collected dozens of antique tractor and implement seats and hung them in neat rows on his barn wall…or about a farm wife who, between chores, picks and dries wildflowers, then sells them in beautiful wreaths and arrangements. We recently ran a story about a 73-year-old dairy farmer who, in more than 50 years of farming, has spent only $15 to buy cattle!

Back in 1937, when he was a teenager, that $15 purchased a heifer for a 4-H project. Later, he started his herd by breeding the heifer...and today, all his cows are descended from her!

We've also had stories about a Louisiana dirt farmer who put nine kids through college...an Indiana farmer who is an expert on American Indian history...and a Utah turkey raiser who is that state's "Cookout King." Feature stories should focus on folks who farm or ranch under interesting or unusual circumstances or have out-of-the-ordinary crops or sidelines. Stories should be a celebration of living and working on the land and can be upbeat...poignant...lighthearted—even inspirational.

Like the other magazines we publish, F&RL carries no advertising, has full-color throughout and appears six times a year. The ideal time for freelance submissions is 4 or 5 months before the issue date. We are happy to consider either queries or actual submissions. Often, even with a query, we will ask the contributor to submit on speculation. We prefer photos to be included with submissions and usually buy a package of text and photos.

Typically, payment is upon publication, but exceptions can be made. Payment varies according to quality of text and photos and to space used in the magazine. Rates range from a minimum of $25 for a filler to a maximum of $300 for a package of text and photos. We use color photos only...unless, of course, the story is nostalgic or recollective and calls for old black and white photos. We accept color prints, slides and large-format transparencies.

Potential contributors are encouraged to obtain a sample copy of the magazine to better understand our needs. Because we carry no advertising and rely solely on subscription revenue, we must charge freelancers $2.00 for a sample copy (to cover the cost of postage). Contributors receive a complimentary copy of the issue in which their work appears.

Each issue of F&RL contains a special feature called "Prettiest Place in the Country." Writers/photographers interested in contributing to this feature should first obtain a copy of the magazine, then query the editors. "Prettiest Place" is a photos-and-text "tour" of a particularly attractive farm or ranch, including the home. Payment for this feature is negotiated with the editors.

Send query or submission, along with SASE, to Nick Pabst, Editor. Queries and manuscripts may be sent via E-mail to editors@farmandranchliving.com. Please remember, however, that we seldom, if ever, accept something for publication unless we can also see photos. There are instances when photos are not available (such as in the case of a personal essay), and we will illustrate the story if need be.

We also buy scenic farm photos without text. For Photo Guidelines send a stamped, self-addressed, business-size envelope to: Trudi Bellin, Photo Coordinator, Reiman Publications, 5400 S. 60th St., Greendale, WI 53129. Electronic photos must be sent at 300 dpi.

Thanks for your interest!

Categories: Nonfiction—Agriculture—Lifestyle—Rural America

CONTACT: Nick Pabst, Editor
Material: All
CONTACT: Trudi Bellin, Photo Coordinator
Material: Photos
5400 S 60th St
Greendale WI 53129
Phone: 414-423-0100
E-mail: editors@ farmandranchliving.com
Website: www.farmandranchliving.com

Farwest Magazine

Please refer to *Digger Magazine*.

Fast & Fun Crochet

General Information

Fast & Fun Crochet is a full-color digest-size 48-page quarterly magazine published by House of White Birches, a Dynamic Resource Group (DRG) publishing company.

The magazine features creative crochet patterns that use popular stitches and readily available yarns (either in yarn shops, craft stores or mail order). Yarn and thread designs include, but are not limited to, apparel, home decor, winter accessories, bazaar items, doilies and afghans.

SUBMISSIONS

Project submissions or manuscripts: Send us your completed project, a photo or proposal sketches and swatches. IMPORTANT: Label your project! Write your name, address and project name on a tag and attach it to your project.

Instructions: Send typed, double-spaced, step-by-step instructions following the *Fast & Fun Crochet* format and stitch abbreviations. Keep a copy of all instructions, diagrams and graphs.

Garment instructions must include a minimum of three sizes.

Materials list must include types of materials, quantities used and ordering information if available. If design materials were supplied free of charge, indicate which materials should be credited and to whom.

Send complete and labeled graphs, diagrams and color keys all correctly labeled. If you send preliminary sketches, it is not necessary to include the finished graphs, material amounts, etc., at this time.

Include your name (as you prefer to have it in print) address, telephone number and e-mail address.

Project review: We will review submissions according to our editorial calendar. We return items that we do not accept within two weeks of the review. See the Editorial Calendar for specific issue deadlines. Please do not call to check on the status of your design until at least two weeks after the review date.

Return of published projects: Published projects will be returned to the designer (unless otherwise arranged) after the issue is published. All manuscripts, diagrams, etc. remain the property of HWB.

Contracts and payment

If the editor accepts your project for publication, we will send you an agreement with HWB's payment offer and a business-reply envelope. If the agreement is acceptable, sign it and return it in the postage-paid envelope. Keep a photocopy of the agreement for your records and return the original to us.

Payment will be made within 45 days of acceptance. Amount will be determined by accuracy, creativity, workmanship, skill level, overall quality and instruction format. Average fees range from $50 to $400. Because HWB purchases all rights to designs unless otherwise arranged, designers should not sell the purchased design or one very similar to it to another publisher.

If you have any questions, contact Vicki Blizzard by phone or e-mail, or write to the address at the left. If you have a question about the status of a design or payment, contact Cathy Reef at HWB.

We look forward to working with you in the coming months!

Categories: Nonfiction—Crafts/Hobbies—Hobbies

CONTACT: Vicki Blizzard, Editor
Material: Completed project, photo or proposal sketches and/or swatches
House of White Birches, Publications
306 East Parr Rd
Berne IN 46711
Phone: 260-589-4000
E-mail: Vicki_Blizzard@whitebirches.com
Website: www.whitebirches.com

FATE

Fate
True Reports of the Strange and Unknown

Thank you for your interest in writing for FATE. We've prepared these guidelines to show you what we look for in a manuscript. Please know that we cannot accept every good article we receive; we simply don't have room.

If possible, please submit your article both on computer disk and in hard-copy form.

Because of the volume of submissions we receive, you can expect to wait one to several months for a response. If you want to be sure your submission has arrived here, include a self-addressed, stamped postcard.

FATE does not publish book-length manuscripts.

TOPICS

FATE magazine reports a wide variety of strange and unknown phenomena. We are open to receiving any well-written, well-documented article. (FATE does not publish poetry or fiction.) Our readers especially like reports of current investigations, experiments, theories, and experiences. *Here is a partial list of typical FATE topics:*

• Psychic Phenomena Dreams, prophecies, telekinesis.

• Recent Fortean Phenomena Strange creatures, mysterious events, unexplained coincidences.

• *Life After Death* Near-death experiences, mediumship, spirit contact, reincarnation, astral travel, and other proof of life after death.

• *Healing Alternative* healing systems and experiences, including acupuncture, herbalism, and psychic techniques.

• *Ghosts and Hauntings Experiences* and investigations of ghosts, hauntings, and poltergeists.

• *Scientific Breakthroughs* Including free energy, new discoveries about matter, lost continents, ley lines, and mind machines.

• *Recent UFO Occurrences* UFO sightings, encounters, abductions, activity, investigations, and disclosures.

• *How-To Healing*, divination, mediumship, dowsing, ghost hunting, astrology, dream analysis, graphology, visualization, and the like.

• *Sacred, Mystic, and Historic Sites* Modern archaeological discoveries and reinterpretations of old ones, the true stories behind myths and folklore, and ancient religions and cultures.

• *Alternative Spirituality*

DEPARTMENTS

True Mystic Experiences and My Proof of Survival

Articles for "True Mystic Experiences" and "My Proof of Survival" departments should be fewer than 1,000 words. They should recount personal mystic or psychic experiences of the writer. All details must be true. If your account is accepted for publication, you will be required to send a notarized affidavit attesting that the incident described is true.

Contributors should include a photo of themselves, at least 3" x 5", either color or black and white. We will return photos unharmed after publication.

Many photos we receive are poor quality. Make sure your picture has good contrast and detail. A plain background is best. Make sure your face shows and is not shadowed by hats or trees, and that glasses don't create a glare. Photocopies, color printouts, pictures cut from larger photos, large group shots in which you are one tiny face among many, and I.D. cards are not acceptable. Our graphics designer will "cut you out" electronically.

Payment is $25, including photo use.

PHOTOS AND ARTWORK

We want FATE to be as visually appealing as possible. Articles with accompanying photographs and illustrations are more likely to be accepted and published faster.

Articles, illustrations, and photos must be legally reproducible. If you are using illustrations, photos, or text from other published sources, they may fall under copyright law. You are responsible for obtaining permissions for use from either the publisher or copyright holder before the manuscript is accepted for publication. We cannot assume items are in the public domain unless you tell us so and give the source and year of publication.

Attach a slip of paper to the back of photos and illustrations, with your name, the story title, and captions.

Keep copies in case of loss.

STYLE
Write to Entertain and Inform

Articles should be lively, personal, and informative. They should play up the wonder of the subject matter and/or develop practical benefits. Avoid academic-style writing, and please be aware that we rarely publish theoretical articles.

Although FATE publishes relatively brief articles, we look for depth of content. We rarely want round-ups that merely list a variety of sightings or events. In general, it is best to focus on one event or type of event, or one time period, and provide convincing detail. Let the reader feel what it was like to be at the event.

LENGTH

• Features run 1,500 to 3,000 words.

• Briefs are 500 to 1,000 words.

• Fillers are less than 500 words.

TRUTHFULNESS

FATE is non-fiction. All articles should be documented in these ways:

• Personal experience articles should include full details of names, dates, times, and places. Although some of this material may be withheld from publication if you specifically request it, we must have it all correctly documented for our files.

• You may be asked to provide contact information for all participants. You may be asked for a sworn and notarized statement from yourself and other participants or witnesses verifying facts described. You will be reimbursed for this cost after publication if you provide a copy of the receipt.

• Sources for quotes and unusual information must be included.

• Articles that are not based on personal experience should include references.

FORMAT

• We encourage email submissions (fate@fatemag.com) and submissions on CDs. Label disks with your name, article title, whether the disk is Macintosh or PC, and the software used. If you are using an unusual word processing program, save it as a plain text or ASCII file. Include a printed copy of the article.

• Use 8" x 11" white paper, a standard typeface, and do not use all caps. Please double space.

• On the first page, include your full name, address, and phone number.

• Place identification at the top of each page. Include your name, the article's title, and page numbers.

• Include a cover letter with your submission.

• Whether you use a typewriter, word processor, or computer, output should be letter quality. Faxed articles are not acceptable.

• Keep a copy of your manuscript in case of loss. We do not accept responsibility for materials sent to us.

• Include a self-addressed, stamped envelope with enough postage to return your article if it is not accepted. (From outside the United States, send several International Reply Coupons, available at any post office.) If return postage is not included and your submission is not accepted, you will receive notification but your article will be discarded.

PAYMENT

Standard payment for feature articles is 10 cents per word, payable after publication. FATE does not pay kill fees if an article is not used, except for contracted, assigned articles where an arrangement has been specified, in writing, in advance.

Contributors who live outside of the U.S. may choose to avoid currency conversion costs by opting to be paid in kind with a FATE subscription or with other FATE merchandise.

Payment for "True Mystic Experiences" and "My Proof of Survival" is $25, including the use of the photograph, which will be returned.

Photos and illustrations that accompany news and feature articles will be paid for after publication, at a rate of $10 per item. (We do not pay for the use of author photos or contributor's photos in "True Mystic Experiences" and "My Proof of Survival.") Photo use will be determined by the graphics designer.

We will send you three copies of the issue in which your article appears, with a coupon enabling you to buy additional copies at a discount price.

POLICIES

FATE normally purchases the right to assign copyright and all rights, literary, electronic, and otherwise, to all articles and photos we accept. FATE generally retains all rights to the articles, illustrations, and photographs that we publish. This entitles FATE to use the article again, in print or in any other media, including but not limited to radio, film, and electronic media. It does not prevent you from sending a substantially different article on the same subject to another publication.

We like to see our writers published! If you are having a book published that includes material from an article you have published in FATE, write to us, giving details, and we will send you written authorization to use the article at no charge as long as FATE is credited as the original source (month and year of issue).

If you have questions about this policy or about re-selling your work elsewhere, please write to us with your specific question and we will send a detailed reply.

Original manuscripts, photographs, illustrations, documentation, etc., that are published will remain FATE's property.

FATE looks for new writers and encourages them. We hope that your inquiry is the beginning of a long and mutually beneficial relationship!

Phyllis Galde, Editor-in-Chief

Categories: Nonfiction—Folklore—History—New Age—Occult—Religion—Science—Spiritual

CONTACT: Fate Magazine, Inc.
Material: All
PO Box 460
Lakeville MN 55044-0460
Phone: 952-431-2050
Fax: 952-891-6091
E-mail: fate@fatemag.com
Website: www.fatemage.com

FBI Law Enforcement Bulletin

GENERAL INFORMATION

The FBI Law Enforcement Bulletin is an official publication of the Federal Bureau of Investigation and the U.S. Department of Justice.

Frequency of Publication: Monthly

Purpose: To provide a forum for the exchange of information on law enforcement-related topics.

Audience: Criminal justice professionals, primarily law enforcement managers.

MANUSCRIPT SPECIFICATIONS

Length: Feature article submissions should be 2,000 to 3,500 words (8 to 14 pages, double-spaced). Submissions for specialized departments, such as Police Practice, Case Study, and Sound Off, should be 1,200 to 2,000 words (5 to 8 pages, double-spaced).

Format: All pages should be numbered, and three copies should be submitted for review purposes. When possible, an electronic version of the article saved on computer disk should accompany the typed manuscript.

References should be used when quoting a source exactly, when citing or paraphrasing another person's work or ideas, or when referring to information that generally is not well known. Authors should refer to *A Manual for Writers of Term Papers, Theses, and Dissertations*, 6th ed., by Kate L. Turabian, for proper footnote citation format.

Research papers, reports, and studies should be revised to reflect the editorial needs of *The Bulletinn*. Subheadings and lists should be used to break up the text and provide direction to readers.

Writing Style and Grammar: Articles generally should be written in the third person. (Point of View and Sound Off submissions are exceptions.) *The Bulletinn* follows *The New York Public Library Writer's Guide to Style and Usage*. Potential authors should study several issues of the magazine to ensure that their writing style meets *The Bulletinn*'s requirements.

PHOTOGRAPHS AND GRAPHICS

A photograph of the author(s) should accompany the manuscript. Other suitable photos and illustrations that support the text and enhance reader comprehension also should be furnished. Black-and-white glossy prints of a moderate size (3"x5" to 5"x7") reproduce best. Prints are preferred over negatives or slides.

PUBLICATION

Basis for Judging Manuscripts: Material that has been published previously or that is under consideration by other magazines will be returned to the author. Submissions will be judged on the following points: Relevance to audience, factual accuracy, analysis of information, structure and logical flow, style and ease of reading, and length. Generally, articles on similar topics are not published within a 12-month period. Because *The Bulletinn* is a government publication, favorable consideration cannot be given to articles that advertise a product or service.

Query Letters: Authors may submit a query letter along with a detailed 1- to 2-page outline before writing an article. Editorial staff members will review the query to determine suitability of topic. This is intended to help authors but does not guarantee acceptance of any article.

Author Notification: Receipt of manuscript will be confirmed. Notification of acceptance or rejection will follow review. Articles accepted for publication cannot be guaranteed a publication date.

Editing: The Bulletinn reserves the right to edit all manuscripts for length, clarity, format, and style.

Categories: Crime—Law Enforcement

CONTACT: Editor
Material: All
Madison Bldg. Rm. 206, FBI Academy
Quantico VA 22135
Phone: 703-632-1952
Fax: 703-632-1968
E-mail: leb@fbiacademy.edu
Website: www.fbi.gov

Feed-Lot

Feed-Lot is published 6 times per year. Circulation is approximately 11,000. A subscription costs $29.95 (foreign $50).

Feed-Lot is a trade publication for large feedlots and their related cow and calf operations and 500-plus head and stocker operations. The magazine covers all phases of production from breeding, genetics, animal health, nutrition, equipment design, research through finishing fat cattle-serious articles with information readers can use. Writers need to have knowledge of the industry and good sources of information for research.

Editorial content is reviewed by the Editor.

Categories: Agriculture—Cattle Feeding

CONTACT: Robert Strong, Editor
Material: All
PO Box 850
Dighton KS 67839
Phone: 316-397-2838
Fax: 316-397-2839

Feline Magazine

Feline Magazine is a new magazine dedicated to women artists and writers. We are looking for submissions for our first publication.

Rights: We reserve first publications rights.

Needs: Feline Magazine is looking for the strange and bizarre, funny, dark, thrilling, exotic tales. We want to be shocked by the ending; we want to be grabbed by the first line. For our first issue we are looking for stories about beauty, unconventional, out of the box, contradicting.

Length: nothing more than 2,000

Art/Photo Needs: For our first issue we are looking for artwork reflecting beauty and women, but not typical beauty but beauty that is against society's standard of beauty.

Payment: We pay contributor copies, author/artists bios, we pay $50.00 for cover artwork/photography.

Response Time: 1 to 2 weeks

Tips for Writers: Please feel free to ask questions, and please read our guidelines.

Feline Magazine Submission Guidelines

We are now taking submissions for our second issue - *The Exhibitionist.*

Fiction:

What we want:

Feline Magazine is looking for the strange, bizarre, funny, dark, thrilling, and exotic tales. We want to be shocked by the ending; we want to be taken by the first line.

What we DON'T want:

We do not, and I say DO NOT want sappy love stories (unless there is a strong presence of something dark or funny lingering). We don't want blood and gore, unless it is crucial to the story. Nor do we want so much profanity that we forget what the story is about. Please don't send us love making near the fierce ocean waves or moonlight.

Categories: Fiction—Women

CONTACT: Kim Rivera, Editor
Material: All
74-31 88th Ave
Woodhaven NY 11421
Phone: 718 296 3177
Email: editor@felinemagazine.com
Website: www.felinemagazine.com

Fellowship
a magazine of peacemaking

Thank you for your interest in submitting work to *Fellowship* magazine.

In lieu of payment, *Fellowship* offers a 2-year subscription (or gift transfer) to the magazine and 3 free copies of the issue containing the author's article.

For specific themes/issues please query several months in advance of the deadline for assurance that your article will be considered. *Fellowship* is published six times a year: January/February, March/April, May/June, July/August, September/October, November/December.

Manuscripts can vary in length from 800 to 3,200 words.

Always keep a copy of your work, and include an SASE with your submission if you want it returned. We cannot be held responsible for unsolicited manuscripts, photographs, or artwork.

Please ensure that photographs and artwork are marked with a brief description (caption) and the name of the photographer/artist if credit line is desired.

We reserve the right to edit those articles accepted for publication for length and clarity.

Deadline:

For articles and reviews, deadline is two months prior to the first day of the first month of the issue. Accompanying photographs and graphics six weeks prior to that date.

Maximum length:

For articles: 3,200 words

For book reviews: 500 words.

Format:

Hard copies must be typed, double-spaced, and clean (i.e. free of italics, corrections, white-out, or pen or pencil markings). Late changes may be indicated on another copy–we will incorporate them.

Computer diskettes (3.5") are acceptable in either PC or Mac format, with the documents saved as text files or made otherwise readable by Microsoft Word 6.0 for Macintosh. We cannot be responsible for returning your diskettes. If possible, include multiple formats of the article to ensure our computer will be able to read it, particularly if you send something in PC format (we use a Macintosh). Please also send a hard copy, if possible.

E-mail submissions, with the article attached in the format specifications listed above or included in the body of the e-mail, are preferable.

Note: Do not send faxes for submission! Faxes do not scan well. They are useful for reference, but cannot be used for publication.

Book Reviews–Additional Guidelines:

At the top of your review, include the full title and subtitle of the book, full author listing, full publisher's address, year of publication, and number of pages. Please note whether the book is paperback or hardcover, or both, and the prices in either case. We must have this information in order to publish the review.

Example:

The Challenge of Shalom: The Jewish Tradition of Peace and Justice

Murray Polner and Naomi Goodman, editors.

New Society Publishers, 4722 Baltimore Avenue, Philadelphia, PA 19143.

1994, 278 pages, (paper) $18.95.

For all submissions, please include your mailing address and two lines of biographical information to serve as an author's note.

Categories: Nonfiction—Book Reviews—Politics—Religion—Spiritual—Peace—Justice —Nonviolence

CONTACT: Submissions Editor
Material: All
Fellowship of Reconciliation
PO Box 271
Nyack NY 10960
Phone: 845-358-4601
Fax: 845-358-4924
E-mail: editor@forusa.org
Website: www.forusa.org

Feminist Studies
University of Maryland

Guidelines for Contributors

Feminist Studies is committed to publishing an interdisciplinary body of feminist knowledge that sees intersections of gender with racial identity, sexual orientation, economic means, geographical location, and physical ability as the touchstone for our politics and our intellectual analysis. Whether work is drawn from the complex past or the shifting present, the pieces that appear in *Feminist Studies* address social and political issues that intimately and significantly affect women and men in the United States and around the world.

We invite submissions that are not presently under consideration elsewhere and that fall under or integrate the following categories.

Research and Criticism

FS publishes research and criticism that address theoretical issues and offer analyses of interest to feminist scholars across disciplines. Although many, if not most, of the articles we publish draw on the methodology of a single discipline, we especially encourage scholars to pursue truly interdisciplinary research and research methods that not only showcase but integrate contributions from multiple disciplines. Submissions should not exceed 12,500 words, approximately 35 pages, including endnotes.

How to submit: Authors should mail two (2) double-spaced copies and a 200-word (or less) abstract of their manuscripts to our office address, and E-mail an electronic copy to submit@feministstudies.org. Author's name should only appear on a separate title page. Please include a cover note and contact information (mailing and E-mail address).

Creative Writing

Feminist Studies is deeply committed to publishing creative work. Beginning with our very first issue published in 1972, we have included creative work in every issue. We have published such distinguished authors as Meena Alexander, Nicole Brossard, Jayne Cortez, Toi Derricote, Diane Glancy, Marilyn Hacker, Lyn Hejinian, June Jordan, Audre Lorde, Cherrie Moraga, Sharon Olds, Grace Paley, Ruth Stone, and Mitsuye Yamada.

We continue to welcome all forms of written creative expression, including but not limited to poetry and short fiction in all forms. We are interested in work that addresses questions of interest to the Feminist Studies audience, particularly work that pushed past the boundaries of what has been done before. We look for creative work that is intellectually challenging and aesthetically adventurous, that is in complicated dialog with feminist ideas and concepts, and that shifts our readers into new perspectives on women/gender.

Deadlines for submission are May 1 and December 1. Authors should mail one (1) hard copy of their work to our office and E-mail an electronic bopy to creative@feministstudies.org. Author's name should only appear on a separate title page.

Art and Art Essays

We are always interested in displaying contemporary women artists and have done much in recent years to promote their work in the journal. The collective accepts art work three times a year at our board meetings. Artists are therefore encouraged to submit images that reflect the range and scope of their portfolio. We also publish an artist's statement or an essay written either by the artist or another author along with art work. Feel free to submit a statement with your work; if you have suggestions of someone who could write an accompanying art essay, please include their curriculum vitae and writing sample (or essay).

How to submit: Please submit art in digital format (as TIFF files at 300dpi, preferably, or high quality JPEG files). We also accept prints, slides, or negatives. Do not send original works of art or anything that must be returned. For electronic submissions, send E-mail attachments to art@feministstudies.org.

Book Review Essays

The *Feminist Studies* collective selects a few books each year for review on the basis of their scholarly merit and their implications for feminist scholars and activists. Due to space limitations we do not publish reviews of individual books, but rather review essays of clusters of important books on the same general theme. Although the collective commissions most essays, we also accept unsolicited review essay proposals. Such proposals should identify the books to be reviewed, state why these books are important and deserve consideration as a cluster, and briefly present the concepts or questions that will be developed in the article.

How to submit: E-mail proposal, curriculum vitae, and a writing sample to submit@feministstudies.org.

Other Forms of Written and Visual Work

We are actively seeking political and social commentaries, activist reports from the field, political manifestos, interviews, and other forms of writing that are not easily categorized. To this end, we encourage authors and artists to submit individual or collaborative projects that cross established boundaries of scholarship, activism, visual culture, memoir and creative writing. Through such work we hope to ensure that *FS* continues to engage, challenge, and reevaluate standard domains of inquiry to create new forms and objects of knowledge.

How to submit: Authors should submit two (2) double-spaced hard copies to our office address and E-mail an electronic copy to submit@feminist studies.org. Author's names should appear only on a separate title page. Please include mailing and E-mail addresses with a cover note.

Graduate Students

Feminist Studies offers an annual *Feminist Studies Award*, a prize of $500, to honor the best article submitted by a graduate student and accepted for publication. With this prize we aim both to encourage and to learn from a new generation of feminist scholars. There is no deadline for submission; articles will be eligible for consideration in the year they are accepted. Although graduate students who finish their doctoral work before their article is accepted are still eligible for the prize, they must be a graduate student when they originally submit their work.

Citations and References

Scholarly articles should follow *Chicago Manual of Style* (15th ed.). *Feminist Studies* articles use endnotes, limited to only essential material and specific textual citation. We do not publish discursive notes. We may ask for full revision of manuscripts that do not follow *CMS* requirements for documentation.

Examples of Work Cited

Notes

1. Sarah Franklin and Helena Ragone, *Reproducing Reproduction: Kinship, Power, and Technological Innovation* (Philadelphia: University of Pennsylvania Press, 1998), 9.

2. Rosalind Petchesky, "The Body as Property: A Feminist Revision," in *Conceiving the New World Order: The Global Politics of Reproduction*, ed., Faye Ginsburg and Rayna Rapp (Berkeley: University of California Press, 1995), 394.

3. Mary Poovey, "The Abortion Question and the Death of Man," and Vicki Schultz, "Women 'before' the Law: Judicial Stories about Women, Work, and Sex Segregation on the Job," in Feminists Theorize the Political, ed. Judith Butler and Joan Scott (London: Routledge, 1992), 239-56.

4. Natalie Zemon Davis, "Women on Top," in her *Society and Culture in Early Modern France* (Stanford: Stanford University Press, 1975), 124.

5. Luce Irigaray, *This Sex Which Is Not One*, trans. Catherine Porter (Ithaca: Cornell University Press, 1985), 209.

6. William Farmwinkile, *Humor of the American Midwest*, vol. 2 of Survey of American Humor (Boston: Plenum Press, 1983), 132.

7. Phyllis Turnball, "The Politics of Toys: Politicization of Child Development" (Ph.D. diss., University of Hawaii, 1978), 134.

8. Memorandum to Bill, 6 June 1942, Lillan Wald Papers, reel 94, Columbia University.

9. Pepe Karmel, "Behind Folk Forms, Classical Modes," *New York Times*, 27 Oct. 1995, sec. C, 25.

10. James B. Jacobs, introduction to *Drunk Driving: An American Dilemma* (Chicago: University of Chicago Press, 1989).

11. Carla Williams, "Naked, Neutered, or Noble: Extremes of the Black Female Body and the Problem of Photographic History," www.carlagirl.net.

Further Inquiries:

Questions on submissions policy can be directed to Managing Editor Karla Mantilla at kmantilla@feministstudies.org or submission@feministstudies.org.

Categories: African-American—Arts—Book Reviews—Culture—Experimental Fiction—Feminism—Gay/Lesbian—History—Human Rights—Literature—Poetry—Short Stories—Women's Fiction—Women's Issues

CONTACT: Feminist Studies
Material: All
0103 Taliaferro, University of Maryland
College Park MD 20742
Phone: 301-405-7415
Fax: 301-405-8395
E-mail: submit@feministstudies.org
Website: www.feministstudies.org

Fencers Quarterly Magazine

About Us

Founded in 1996 by Bruce Darling as *Veteran Fencers Quarterly*, *FQM* underwent its formal name change to *Fencers Quarterly Magazine* with the June, 2000, issue.

Our purpose is to keep the fencing enthusiast informed about some of the issues that affect you, to illuminate the history and art of fencing, and to provide a forum for your thoughts and ideas.

We are eager to read reports about your tournaments, schools, individuals, special programs, or other unique features of your group. We are also especially interested in your opinions and personal experience of fencing—today or in the past.

Feel free to send us any articles of interest to the fencing community, including local newspaper clippings, your photos, or even your own stories and comments.

We reserve the right to edit for length and clarity.

FQM is published quarterly in March, June, September, and December for a measly $19.95 annual subscription cost. We think this is awfully cheap for the quality articles, superior writers, and wide-open forum that *FQM* represents!

Want to write for *FQM*?

Great! We want to read your writing! We are interested in articles, stories, poetry, and fiction related to all aspects of fencing.

What are the basics?

First, even though you've heard it a thousand times, read a couple recent issues of the magazine — that'll give you the best examples of what we buy, the style of writing, and how we approach fencing issues.

Next, decide what you want to say to the thousands of dedicated fencers who read our magazine. Remember, you will be speaking to young beginners, mature fencers, current and former Olympians, classically trained or sport-oriented, members of re-creation groups, and people interested in the history of swordplay. We don't expect your work to appeal to ALL of them — but it must be of interest to SOME of them!

Finally, what we look for is logical progression in your writing (i.e., make a point in an orderly manner!), good command of language, spell-checked writing, and a length that fits the magazine.

What are the specifics?

Length: typically, 250-2000 words. Average article is about 1,000 words. When published, this works out to 1-2 magazine pages. We have gone as high as 4,000 words and serialized the work — but this was material from one of the top people in the discipline.

Publication: usually within 3 months of acceptance, though it can run longer.

Payment: "modest". We pay a flat rate, varying from $15 to $60, depending on how much we like the piece — pretty subjective, but that's how we do it. Occasionally, we've gone as high as $200, but this is RARE! You'll also receive 5 copies of the issue in which your piece is published. Sometimes, we trade a published article for advertising space, so if you have a product to sell and an issue you'd like to write about, please contact us to discuss the matter.

Tips: We use fiction and poetry very rarely, so it better be concise, well written, and strongly fencing-related. Most past rejections were because material was WAY too long or lacked an understanding of fencing. We like controversial material as long as it is logically presented — use the language of fencing and explain your point so that a beginner would understand.

We like new writers, and fully understand how anxiety-producing it can be! We will make every effort to help you create material that will work for *FQM*. And, if we don't use your stuff, we'll explain why!

E-mails: We prefer email submissions, in .RTF format.

Photographs: We love them! Must be clear and show proper form. $5 to $10.

Categories: Nonfiction—History—Recreation—Sports

CONTACT: Anita Evangelista, Managing Editor
Material: All
848 S. Kimbrough
Springfield MO 65806
Phone: 417-866-4370 (No phone queries)
E-mail: editor@fencersquarterly.com
Website: www.fencersquarterly.com

FIBERARTS

Fiberarts Magazine

Fiberarts magazine, started in 1975, strives to inspire and inform our readers about exciting, innovative contemporary textile art and craft. Our readers are professional artists, textile students, fashion designers, collectors, educators, museum curators, gallery owners, and other fiber aficionados. They are interested in a broad range of textile art–related subjects, particularly contemporary artwork in the following media: fiber sculpture, surface design, weaving, quilting, needlework, papermaking, basketry, artwear, and mixed-media art. Historical and ethnographic textiles, while not our primary focus, are also of interest. We publish five times a year.

We are interested in the conceptual background of artists' work as well as their creative process. While our readers like to know how artworks are made, we don't publish how-to, step-by-step articles.

Fiberarts welcomes submissions from writers and artists. Our magazine is visually driven, so great images are key to successful proposals.

Feature Articles

Feature articles cover a broad range of topics. For example, they may profile a textile artist or visionary collector; compare the work of two or three artists; discuss the work and workings of a textile group, school, or exhibition venue; evaluate a current trend; focus on creative process or work spaces; or present artwork created using an important technique. Excellent visuals are particularly important to this section. 1000–1500 words. Payment: $300–$425.

Departments

News & Notes: Short news items and blurbs on textile art–related topics, accompanied by visuals if appropriate. 150–250 words. Payment: $25–$50.

Previews: Short articles about upcoming exhibitions, conferences, or textile-related events, accompanied by appropriate visuals. 150–250 words. Payment: $25–$50.

Roots: Articles about the origins or historical aspects of the contemporary textile-art field, accompanied by appropriate visuals. 250–400 words. Payment: $75–$125.

Books: Short reviews of new books on contemporary textile art and related topics. We need to see the book first in order to assign a review. 100–200 words. Payment: $25.

Creative Process: First-person descriptions by artists of how they approach an aspect of creativity or a technique, accompanied by images of work in progress. 300–350 words. Payment: $100.

Collecting: Profiles of textile-art collectors, with details such as why they collect, how they got started, how they acquire objects, and how they display their collections. Visuals ideally should show the collection in its home setting; a picture of the collector and images of individual objects are also appropriate. 400 words. $125.

Profiles: Profiles of textile artists, with details such as their backgrounds, their creative lifestyles, the inspiration for and themes of their work, and their signature techniques. Accompanied by images of recent work and a picture of the artist. 450 words. $150.

Reviews: Articles about recent textile-art exhibitions, to include a description of the focus and content of the exhibition, as well as commentary on the quality and significance of the show. We are interested in honest and thought-provoking criticism. Reviewers should not have participated in the exhibition as an artist, organizer, curator, or juror; have submitted their work for consideration for the show; or have close ties to an artist, organizer, curator, or juror. Please query with visuals well in advance of the show. Solo show: 400 words ($125). Group show: 450–500 words ($150).

Travel & Traditions: Articles about ethnographic-textile traditions and fiber art–oriented travel destinations such as cities, museums, or galleries, accompanied by appropriate visuals. 250–400 words. Payment: $60–$125.

How to Submit

Submissions from writers should be in the form of a prose synopsis of the proposed article, publication-quality visuals, and a couple of writing samples. If the topic is an artist, please include the artist's resume and artist statement and a list of his or her upcoming shows.

We prefer to receive submissions by mail rather than e-mail. Please note that we can only consider submissions that are accompanied by visuals.

Visuals

Unless other arrangements are made with the editor, authors are responsible for collecting all visual material to illustrate their articles and for providing caption information. Feature articles may include 4–8 images; departments, 1–4 images. We like to receive more images than will be used so that we have some flexibility in layout. We'd suggest 15–20 images for feature articles and 5–10 for departments. Visuals will be returned after publication.

We can use high-resolution digital images, which should be accompanied by a printout of the images. Digital images should be 300 dpi and at least 8x10" for a feature article and 4x6" for departments. TIFF format is preferable, JPEGs are also acceptable. If your images are high resolution, please do not convert their format; we will let you know if they won't work. We can also use slides or transparencies. We cannot use prints.

For each visual, please include complete caption information: artist name, title of work, year of execution, materials, techniques, dimensions (HxWxD, in inches), and photographer credit. Please include the contact information of the artist or entity to whom we should send our visual-use permission form.

We prefer that if specific objects are discussed in an article, excellent visuals of the selected objects be available because readers like to see visuals of the pieces discussed.

Editorial Guidelines

Tone: Our readers range from those who have a fairly sophisticated knowledge of the field to newcomers who are just learning about fiber art. Please explain terms and techniques that aren't familiar to the general reader. We prefer an accessible rather than scholarly tone. Notes and references should be incorporated into the text rather than footnoted.

Accuracy: Writers are responsible for accuracy of facts and correct spelling of names, places, titles, etc. Please fact-check your article before submitting it.

Endnotes: We use short endnotes to provide information on related exhibitions or events that will take place after the magazine is printed, to provide information on exhibition catalogs, and to provide resources for further information, such as the artist's website.

Format: The text of assigned articles can be accepted by e-mail as Microsoft Word attachments or incorporated into the body of the e-mail.

Contributor bio: Authors of assigned articles will be asked to send a short one- to two-sentence author bio and a picture of themselves for our Contributors page.

Editing: Articles will be edited for clarity, organization, grammar, and magazine style. In our editing, we strive to preserve the author's voice. Authors will have a chance to review the edited text. The editor may request revisions of the article, and final editing of the material is at the editor's discretion.

Acceptance: The editor reserves the right to refuse, without a kill fee, any articles that are not submitted by the agreed-upon deadline, that vastly exceed the assigned word count, or that differ substantially from the requested content.

Payment and tearsheets: Authors will receive a complimentary copy of the issue in which their work appears, tearsheets of the article, and payment after publication. The signed author's agreement is confirmation of total amount due. Additional expenses, such as travel and phone bills, are usually not covered.

Categories: Nonfiction—Arts—Crafts/Hobbies—Multicultural

CONTACT: Sunita Patterson, Editor
Material: All
CONTACT: Liz Good, Assistant Editor
Material: All
201 E. Fourth St.
Loveland CO 80537-5655
Phone: (970) 669-7672
Fax: (970) 669-6117
E-mail: lizg@fiberarts.com
Website: www.fiberarts.com

FIELD
A Journal of Contemporary Poetry and Poetics

Guidelines for Poetry Submissions to *FIELD: A Journal of Contemporary Poetry and Poetics. FIELD* accepts poetry only. Translations are welcome if publication permission has been acquired from the author of the original work. All manuscripts must be accompanied by a self-addressed stamped envelope for a response. Be sure to include sufficient postage for return of manuscript or indicate that you expect a reply only. We do not accept simultaneous submissions or electronic submissions. Poems (2-6 at a time) may be sent to the address below.

FIELD is published twice yearly, in spring and fall. We read submissions year-round and usually reply within six weeks, though occasionally we may take longer. Please keep in mind that *FIELD* is one of the most selective small poetry journals in the country. We suggest you familiarize yourself with our journal before submitting.

Sample issues are available for $7.00 (check or money order payable to Oberlin College Press). An annual subscription (2 issues) is $14.00 and a two year subscription (4 issues) is $24.00.

Categories: Poetry

CONTACT: Submissions Editor
Material: All
Oberlin College Press
50 N Professor St
Oberlin OH 44074
Phone: 440-775-8408
Fax: 440-775-8124
E-mail: oc.press@oberlin.edu
Website: www.oberlin.edu/ocpress

Field & Stream

FIELD & STREAM is a tightly focused magazine. All material is related to hunting and fishing, with the articles ranging from basic how-it's-done pieces to carefully crafted features with a philosophical edge. There are many opportunities for freelancers, including:
• Short pieces (500 to 750 words) on hunting and fishing tactics and techniques, and DIY [Do-It-Yourself] projects with a hunting/fishing slant.
• Longer how-to features (1,500 words maximum) on hunting and fishing.

Writers are encouraged to submit queries. These should be no more than a page, and should include a summary of the idea, including the angle you will hang the story on, and a sense of what makes this piece different from all others on the same or a similar subject.

Pieces that depend on writing style, such as humor, mood, and nostalgia or essays often can't be queried and may be submitted in manuscript form. The same is true of short tips. All submissions to FIELD & STREAM are on an on-spec basis.

Before submitting anything, however, we encourage you to study, not simply read, the magazine. Many pieces are rejected because they do not fit the tone or style of the magazine, or fail to match the subject of the article with the overall subject matter of FIELD & STREAM.

FIELD & STREAM does not pay by the word. Payment ranges from $100 to as much as several thousand dollars, depending on the quality of the work, the experience of the author, and the difficulty of obtaining the story.

All queries and completed manuscripts submitted to FIELD & STREAM must be typed and double spaced. The magazine also accepts electronic submissions.

FIELD & STREAM needs an accurate word count for every submission. Include them at the top of the first page of every submission.

Categories: Nonfiction—Conservation—Environment—Fishing—Outdoors—Sports/Recreation—Hunting—Animals (big game)

CONTACT: Editor
Material: All Submissions
2 Park Ave.
New York NY 10016-5295
Phone: 212-779-5000
Fax: 212-779-5114
E-mail: FSLetters@time4.com

Field Trial Magazine

Feature Articles are 2,000 to 3,000 words in length and cover a variety of subjects, including but not limited to the following:

Important Places - field trial sites, kennels, training areas, etc.

Important People - current and historic competitors, judges, trainers, breeders and owners.

Important Dogs - to be considered, a dog should have an impressive record either as a producer of great dogs or as winner, preferably both—top quality photos of the dog a must.

Important Birds - articles on managing for wild and released birds that are pursued in field trials, special consideration to articles written by professional wildlife managers.

Training Articles will be a regular part of the magazine and must pertain specifically to training field trial dogs. (If you don't know the difference between training a field trial dog and training a hunting dog don't attempt it.) Special attention will be paid to articles that rely on the top professional trainers for their expertise.

Breeding and Health Related Articles will be a regular part of the magazine and must provide our readers with the latest advances in veterinary science. Special attention will be given to articles written by vets. We would rather get the science right and work on the writing, than have great writing with inaccurate science.

Controversial Articles will be considered. We want the magazine to function as a clearinghouse for the problems that affect our sport. We will not shy away from a controversy if it is well researched and presented in an objective fashion.

Illustrations we are always looking for top quality photos, line art and paintings that show pointing dogs and field trials. Will buy illustrations without articles and on occasion will commission work, especially for covers.

Statement of Purpose: We publish a quarterly magazine dedicated to the breeding, training, and field trialing of pointing dogs. It is our intent to provide interesting and informative articles that will appeal to a knowledgeable audience which has been, is currently, or would like to be involved in some aspect of field trials for pointing dogs. We are interested in any article that is well written and well illustrated, and is related to field trials.

It is important that all writers submitting to *Field Trial Magazine* be experienced field trialers or use the expertise of someone who is. Quality illustrations are extremely important at FTM. It is our intent to provide our readers with interesting visuals to go along with every article. Payment will be on publication. Query first with SASE or by e-mail.

Categories: Nonfiction—Animals: Dogs

CONTACT: Craig A. Doherty, Editor
PO Box 98
Milan NH 03588
Phone: 603-449-6767
Fax: 603-449-2462
E-mail birddog@ncia.net

Filipinas

Mission Statement
Filipinas magazine—The magazine for all Filipinos aims to provide Filipino Americans with a sense of identity, community and pride through accurate, fair and sensitive coverage of the second largest immigrant population in the United States. It is the chronicler of the Filipino American experience. It showcases pioneers, role models and future leaders. It presents the struggles that bring about the change and successes in the community. It presents issues that affect Filipinos in North America. It is the source of knowledge about Filipino culture and the Philippine social, economic, and political state. *Filipinas* magazine aims to be the close friend who will inform, entertain, include and

invigorate the Filipino in North America.

Audience

Filipinas magazine targets Filipinos in North America—immigrants and native-born; the old and the young; the ones still searching for cultural identity and the ones who take pride in their culture and heritage.

Fees

• Upon publication, writers will be paid $50-$100 depending on length and complexity. $10 for published "Buhay Pinoy Abroad" contributions.

• We pay $15 for each black and white published (non-stock) photos, and $25 for each colored published photo taken by the author. Publicity shots and personal album photos are not subject to payment.

• Payment is mailed on the 15th of the month the article or photo is published.

• Unsolicited materials are not subject to payment. The writer assigns titles, rights and all interests to the story to Filipinas Publishing, Inc.

Departments

Entree (recipe and restaurant reviews), Cultural Currents (Filipino traditions, beliefs), Travel (destinations in the Philippines or other places with a Philippine slant, e.g. Spain), "Here and There" (150 words or less profile with photo of a noteworthy Filipino personality).

Non-Fiction Articles

Expose; general interest; interview/profiles of prominent Filipinos and non-Filipinos who are important to the Filipino community or the Philippines; Filipino recipes and reviews of Filipino restaurants; travel articles; "how-to" articles, e.g. making a parol (Philippine Christmas lantern) or tips on starting an export/import business or other small business; personal experience.

Word count on articles: Cover story 1,000-1,500; profiles 750-1,000; reviews and other features 600-1,200; "Here & There" 50-150.

Photos

Color photos should be 35mm slides or 120mm transparencies or 4 x 5 transparencies or 4 x 6 prints. Black and White prints: 5" x 7" or 8" x 10", captions, photo credits and model releases required. Electronic photos should be sent as 300 dpi, 4x5 or final size, scanned as tiff or jpeg file. Captions and photo credits are required.

Terms

We require that a writer send a query letter along with a resume and three writing samples of preferably previously published work. *Filipinas* Publishing has exclusive rights to any solicited articles. (Unsolicited manuscripts are not subject to payment even if published. They will not be returned.) Once published, the article may be reprinted with permission and credit to *Filipinas* magazine. Writer agrees to a one-time rewrite, if necessary.

Submission

Articles and queries may be electronically sent. We also accept hard copy submissions with 3.5 computer diskette, preferably using Microsoft Word. Diskettes will not be returned.

Categories: Nonfiction—Asian-American—Multicultural

CONTACT: Greg Macabenta, Publisher
Material: All
Filipinas Publishing, Inc.
1580 Bryant St
Daly City CA 94015
Phone: 650-985-2530
Fax: 650-985-2532
E-mail: mail@filipinasmag.com
Website: www.filipanasmag.com

Film Quarterly

In preparing material for submission to *Film Quarterly*, keep in mind that while many of our contributors are academics, not all of our readers are. By the standards of the commercial magazine world, *Film Quarterly* is quite specialized and its circulation is small-about 7,000, which means perhaps 8,000 to 10,000 readers (since library copies have multiple readers). But by the standards of the narrower academic journals, this is very large. Since its inception in 1958, *Film Quarterly's* mission has been to bring intelligent, original, and rigorous thinking about film to as large a readership as possible (including filmmakers, incidentally). The journal is sold about two-thirds by subscription and one-third by retail sales in bookstores. We also have numerous subscribers scattered throughout the world.

The English-language film journal universe includes several publications whose contents are aimed at scholars, such as *Cinema Journal*, *Screen*, and *The Quarterly Review of Film and Video*, among others. Popular magazines, such as *Film Comment* and *Sight & Sound*, seek a wide audience of moviegoers. *Film Quarterly*, somewhat like *Cineaste* and *Framework*, occupies a middle ground, making specialized ideas accessible to literate and "cinemate" readers. It is, however, peer-reviewed by academics, like other scholarly journals, and has over the years published the work of some of the most distinguished film studies scholars-and continues to do so to this day. We aim at the whole community of educated readers seriously concerned with film (and, to an increasing degree, video and television) and are particularly interested in the work of emerging writers both within and outside the academy.

Careful study of back issues is imperative for new writers hoping to have their work accepted by *Film Quarterly*. (If your library does not subscribe, you might wish to call the journal to the attention of the periodicals librarian.) We like to surprise our readers with unusual material, but we have certain emphases and do not publish certain kinds of writing: we never use personality or reportage pieces, for instance, nor do we cover festivals. We are interested in important theoretical developments, but when we run theoretical articles they include treatments of films and thus demonstrate a connection between theory and practice. We publish pieces on older films that are readily available on video or DVD, and more wide-ranging historical articles. Documentaries, experimental and avant-garde works, national cinemas, reassessments of classic works, Hollywood, the business world, foreign filmmakers, new works and new filmmakers-all these are included in our pages. We also encourage submissions on television and video. We often run interviews, mostly with film- and video-makers, but occasionally with writers, directors of photography, etc. (Interviews are best done by someone who knows the interviewee's work thoroughly, can obtain the time and attention for an extended conversation, and can prepare a solid introduction.)

We welcome communications and submissions from writers. There is no closed group of contributors to the magazine, and many now well-known writers and scholars published their first articles or reviews with us. We are eager to find innovative approaches deployed with energy, and we relish making unknown or esoteric films accessible to American audiences. We also welcome commentary and critiques on the journal and any particulars of its contents.

II. MANUSCRIPT SUBMISSION

Send in one hard copy copy of your manuscript only. You should always submit the completed manuscript, since the Editor and the Editorial Board read and assess all submissions and cannot accept anything on the basis of a query or an outline. You may, of course, check with the Editor to make sure your article idea or film review is not already in the *FQ* pipeline. Book reviews are assigned separately; if you are interested in writing a review of a particular book, check with the Book Review Editor (see below).

Our working rule of thumb for article length is that it should not exceed 25 double-spaced manuscript pages, or about 6,500 words, although we occasionally run longer pieces and can certainly consider shorter ones. If you contemplate a really long manuscript, it may be helpful to query the Editor before setting to work. Film reviews ideally amount to around ten pages, but we do run longer pieces if the issues involved seem sufficiently substantial. We seek reviews with analytic treatments that (1) give readers (who may not have seen the film) a clear idea of what it is like, in stylistic as well as plot/narrative terms; (2) provide some implicit or explicit "theory" to account for what the film seems to be trying to do-structurally, emotionally, politically, etc.; and (3) offer an estimate of its success and general quality. We are more impressed with analytic power than by vehemence or charm of opinions, and we are always searching for that elusive ideal, the "definitive" review-essay that treats a film so intelligently and substantially that the review will remain readable in ten or even twenty years.

When submitting a manuscript, please include your name, home and work addresses, phone numbers, and email address at the top, and a brief biographical description at the end. Should you want to have your manuscript returned if it is not accepted, include a self-addressed stamped envelope. If you happen to possess stills or photos relevant to your topic, please mention this, but do not send them; they will be required only if your piece is accepted. Everything in the manuscript should be double-spaced, including quotations and notes (which should be formatted as endnotes); film titles should be italicized, TV titles in quotes. If you need guidance on detailed points of manuscript preparation, you should follow the *Chicago Manual of Style*. Printouts should *not* be right-hand justified. We do not use disks or attachments at first submission, but if your manuscript is accepted, we will then need a digital version.

Manuscripts are discussed by our editorial board at quarterly meetings (in early February, May, August, and November-deadlines for submission are one month before the meeting dates). Decisions about acceptance take about a month to reach the writer. We always have some backlog of manuscripts, and you should count on it taking about a year from acceptance to publication. Payment for a published manuscript is slightly above the magnificent sum of two cents per word, plus two gratis copies.

III. BOOK REVIEWS

Book reviews are assigned to individual writers by the Book Review Editor. If you are interested in contributing, or have a specific book you want to review, please contact Matthew Bernstein, Film Studies Department, 109 Rich Building, 1602 Fishburne Drive, Emory University, Atlanta, GA 30322 (email: mbernst@emory.edu). Send him a brief outline of your credentials, your areas of interest, and any sample book reviews you may already have written.

Categories: Film/Video—Television/Radio

CONTACT: Ann Martin, Editor, Film Quarterly
Material: All
University of California Press
2000 Center St., Ste. 303
Berkeley, CA 94704-1223
E-mail: ann.martin@ucpress.edu

FilmFax Magazine

Filmfax Magazine is a bi-monthly, nationally distributed publication. The entertainment media we cover includes radio, television, and film, both live action and animated, produced from the late 1920s up to and including the mid 1970s.

Although the members of the editorial staff are all media fans, *Filmfax* is *not* a fanzine. The entertainment media we cover includes radio, television, and film, both live action and animated, produced from the late 1920s up to and including the mid 1970s. We do not cover new productions.

Filmfax encourages writers to research their articles. Our basic goal is to historically document the entertainment field and the people involved in it. We give preference to articles including an interview, having a new slant on an old subject, or ones bringing to light new information of interest to our readers. Before submitting an article proposal, we would request that a writer carefully examine several current issues of the magazine. A sample copy will be provided on request at our discretion.

GENERAL INFORMATION:

At the present time, *Filmfax* pays 3 cents per word for an accepted article.

All articles submitted to *Filmfax* are done so on speculation. Please note that this also includes article ideas accepted on query and assignments.

Filmfax does not guarantee specific publication dates.

Filmfax reserves the right to edit all articles. If extensive re-writing is required, the manuscript will be returned to you, with suggestions if possible and time permits.

Filmfax buys only first rights for an article. After your article is published you are free to do with it as you wish.

Payment for an article is on publication. Immediately upon publication, you will receive your check, two copies of the issue in which your article appears, and any graphics that were submitted (see "Graphics" below).

Filmfax is a 100% freelance publication. Therefore, we are unable to pay the expenses of writers. Exceptions include articles mailed by Federal Express, Overnight Mail, etc. at our request.

Filmfax does not pay for the use of graphics.

The length of an article is not as important as its content. Your article should be as long as it is required to cover your topic properly. We look for articles in all three length ranges: short (approximately 2500 words); medium (approximately 5000 words); long (5000 words on up). Long, extensively researched articles may be broken into two parts, if necessary.

Cover Page: Include Name, address, home and work phone.

Manuscript: All articles are to be submitted in either typewritten form or on a hard disc compatible with the Macintosh computer systems. (Microsoft Word is prefer- able). If you plan to submit your article on computer disc, please contact us for details and verification of compatibility.

Double or triple space the article.

Paragraphs should be indented three spaces; Single space after periods.

Number all pages.

If using printed materials as your sources (books, magazine articles etc), include a bibliography. Be sure all direct quotes are credited.

Proofread your article, paying particular attention to the spelling of proper names.

Film titles in the context of the article should include the year of their release. Example: *War of the Worlds* (1953).

If your article includes an interview, include the address and/or phone number of the person so that we may contact them directly and send them copies of the magazine.

After reading several issues of *Filmfax*, you should have a good idea of the proper structure we expect in a submitted article. Following are a few specific suggestions:

Make sure the article has a distinct beginning, middle and end. Your opening paragraph is the most important and should be written to capture the attention and interest of your reader.

Interviews submitted in the "Q & A" format must have an introduction identifying the subject and their background. The final sentence of that introduction should lead directly into your first question. When interviewing an actor or director, please keep in mind that the films they have done may *not* be the most important story. The story may be the *person*.

Questions should be (re)written with the answer in mind. They should also include information not covered in your introduction, but required for clarification in the body of the interview. The verbatim questions you asked during the verbal interview may not suffice for the transcribed interview in its final form. *Rewrite them as is necessary for the education and entertainment of the reader.*

Narrative articles should also have an introductory paragraph which focuses specifically on the subject of the piece. If the article is about an individual film, the name of the film should appear in your opening. Do not wait until page two or three to let your reader know what you are writing about. Also, please try not to have your second paragraph begin—"Big Movie Star was born." Be creative.

For examples of articles which may be used as guides, see the following:

1. *Johnny Jupiter* (Issue #34): A good example of a well researched article on an obscure topic. Note the companion interview with Wright King.

2. *Cohn Clive* (Issue #35): While this article focuses specifically on the actorts career, it keeps the personality of the man in the fore front.

3. *Russ Tamblyn* (Issue #27): An interview article in the Q & A style. Note the short introduction leading into the first question. Also note that the interview quickly shifts its focus from the actor's well-known film role, to the man himself and his personal history.

Please keep in mind that (metaphorically speaking) an article is a circle. The beginning leads to the end, and vice versa. Make sure paragraphs have segues; each paragraph should lead to the next.

If you have any questions on how to conduct an interview or on writing the article itself, please feel free to ask. It's a sign of intelligence.

Please do not use first person references such as "When I met with so-and-so," or "I have always thought that so-and-so." Our readers are interested in your subject, not your personal opinions.

Graphics: We always appreciate it if graphics are submitted with an article. These will be returned to you immediately upon publication by certified mail. Please note the following requirements for submitting graphics (still photos, lobby cards, newspaper ad mattes etc.):

Be sure your name is written clearly on the back of each graphic submitted.

Number each graphic on the back.

Include a numbered list of your graphics describing each one. The list should include the following information: Number of item; identification of film and/or person or persons involved;. a brief caption if possible. Please be as specific as you can.

If anyone other than yourself is to be credited for the photo, still, etc., please indicate this clearly.

Conduct of Writers: No writer, including those on the *Filmfax* masthead, may use the name of the magazine for personal gain. This includes:

Contacting publishers for review copies of books.

CinemaSourcebook reviews are assigned by *Filmfax*. If review copies are provided to you in this manner, (without receiving prior approval from the *Filmfax* editorial staff), and we print your review, the book becomes the property of *Filmfax* and should be submitted with your review.

Contacting video or laser disc companies—both corporate and individually owned—for review Copies.

Videoscan reviews are assigned by *Filmfax*. If video tapes or laser discs are provided to you in this manner, (without receiving prior approval from the *Filmfax* editorial staff), and we print your review, the video tape/disc becomes the property of *Filmfax* and should be submitted with your review.

Contacting any celebrity in the anticipation that *Filmfax* will publish your interview/ article.

We may not be interested in the individual in question, or another writer may already be covering the same material. Also, *Filmfax* prefers to deal directly with the individual, when possible.

Gaining access to any production set, television or movie, by using the *Filmfax* name. Arrangements must be made through *Filmfax*.

Gaining access or special consideration at any convention, media event, film screening, etc. Writers must contact *Filmfax* prior to the event for approval.

Obtaining any items offered by our advertisers free of charge. This includes video tapes, books, T-shirts, magazines, collectibles, model kits, etc.

Finally, no writer, including those listed on the masthead as contributing editors or special consultants, may indicate in any way that he or she represents *Filmfax* Magazine without receiving specific individual approval from a member of the *Filmfax* editorial staff.

Categories: Entertainment

CONTACT: Website: www.filmfax.com
Materials: All

Film Quarterly

In preparing material for submission to *Film Quarterly*, keep in mind that while many of our contributors are academics, not all of our readers are. By the standards of the commercial magazine world, *Film Quarterly* is quite specialized and its circulation is small-about 7,000, which means perhaps 8,000 to 10,000 readers (since library copies have multiple readers). But by the standards of the narrower academic journals, this is very large. Since its inception in 1958, *Film Quarterly*'s mission has been to bring intelligent, original, and rigorous thinking about film to as large a readership as possible (including filmmakers, incidentally). The journal is sold about two-thirds by subscription and one-third by retail sales in bookstores. We also have numerous subscribers scattered throughout the world.

The English-language film journal universe includes several publications whose contents are aimed at scholars, such as *Cinema Journal*, *Screen*, and *The Quarterly Review of Film and Video*, among others. Popular magazines, such as *Film Comment* and *Sight & Sound*, seek a wide audience of moviegoers. *Film Quarterly*, somewhat like *Cineaste* and *Framework*, occupies a middle ground, making specialized ideas accessible to literate and "cinemate" readers. It is, however, peer-reviewed by academics, like other scholarly journals, and has over the years published the work of some of the most distinguished film studies scholars-and continues to do so to this day. We aim at the whole community of educated readers seriously concerned with film (and, to an increasing degree, video and television) and are particularly interested in the work of emerging writers both within and outside the academy.

Careful study of back issues is imperative for new writers hoping to have their work accepted by *Film Quarterly*. (If your library does not subscribe, you might wish to call the journal to the attention of the periodicals librarian.) We like to surprise our readers with unusual material, but we have certain emphases and do not publish certain kinds of writing: we never use personality or reportage pieces, for instance, nor do we cover festivals. We are interested in important theoretical developments, but when we run theoretical articles they include treatments of films and thus demonstrate a connection between theory and practice. We publish pieces on older films that are readily available on video or DVD, and more wide-ranging historical articles. Documentaries, experimental and avant-garde works, national cinemas, reassessments of classic works, Hollywood, the business world, foreign filmmakers, new works and new filmmakers-all these are included in our pages. We also encourage submissions on television and video. We often run interviews, mostly with film- and video-makers, but occasionally with writers, directors of photography, etc. (Interviews are best done by someone who knows the interviewee's work thoroughly, can obtain the time and attention for an extended conversation, and can prepare a solid introduction.)

We welcome communications and submissions from writers. There is no closed group of contributors to the magazine, and many now well-known writers and scholars published their first articles or reviews with us. We are eager to find innovative approaches deployed with energy, and we relish making unknown or esoteric films accessible to American audiences. We also welcome commentary and critiques on the journal and any particulars of its contents.

II. MANUSCRIPT SUBMISSION

Send in one hard copy copy of your manuscript only. You should always submit the completed manuscript, since the Editor and the Editorial Board read and assess all submissions and cannot accept anything on the basis of a query or an outline. You may, of course, check with the Editor to make sure your article idea or film review is not already in the *FQ* pipeline. Book reviews are assigned separately; if you are interested in writing a review of a particular book, check with the Book Review Editor (see below).

Our working rule of thumb for article length is that it should not exceed 25 double-spaced manuscript pages, or about 6,500 words, although we occasionally run longer pieces and can certainly consider shorter ones. If you contemplate a really long manuscript, it may be helpful to query the Editor before setting to work. Film reviews ideally amount to around ten pages, but we do run longer pieces if the issues involved seem sufficiently substantial. We seek reviews with analytic treatments that (1) give readers (who may not have seen the film) a clear idea of what it is like, in stylistic as well as plot/narrative terms; (2) provide some implicit or explicit "theory" to account for what the film seems to be trying to do-structurally, emotionally, politically, etc.; and (3) offer an estimate of its success and general quality. We are more impressed with analytic power than by vehemence or charm of opinions, and we are always searching for that elusive ideal, the "definitive" review-essay that treats a film so intelligently and substantially that the review will remain readable in ten or even twenty years.

When submitting a manuscript, please include your name, home and work addresses, phone numbers, and email address at the top, and a brief biographical description at the end. Should you want to have your manuscript returned if it is not accepted, include a self-addressed stamped envelope. If you happen to possess stills or photos relevant to your topic, please mention this, but do not send them; they will be required only if your piece is accepted. Everything in the manuscript should be double-spaced, including quotations and notes (which should be formatted as endnotes); film titles should be italicized, TV titles in quotes. If you need guidance on detailed points of manuscript preparation, you should follow the *Chicago Manual of Style*. Printouts should *not* be right-hand justified. We do not use disks or attachments at first submission, but if your manuscript is accepted, we will then need a digital version.

Manuscripts are discussed by our editorial board at quarterly meetings (in early February, May, August, and November-deadlines for submission are one month before the meeting dates). Decisions about acceptance take about a month to reach the writer. We always have some backlog of manuscripts, and you should count on it taking about a year from acceptance to publication. Payment for a published manuscript is slightly above the magnificent sum of two cents per word, plus two gratis copies.

III. BOOK REVIEWS

Book reviews are assigned to individual writers by the Book Review Editor. If you are interested in contributing, or have a specific book you want to review, please contact Matthew Bernstein, Film Studies Department, 109 Rich Building, 1602 Fishburne Drive, Emory University, Atlanta, GA 30322 (email: mbernst@emory.edu). Send him a brief outline of your credentials, your areas of interest, and any sample book reviews you may already have written.

Categories: Film/Video—Television/Radio

CONTACT: Ann Martin, Editor, Film Quarterly
Material: All
University of California Press
2000 Center St., Ste. 303
Berkeley, CA 94704-1223
E-mail: ann.martin@ucpress.edu

Financial Planning

No longer accepting submissions.

Fine Gardening

Fine Gardening is a bimonthly magazine for enthusiastic landscape and ornamental gardeners. Filled with practical information and innovative ideas, *Fine Gardening* seeks to inform, assist, and inspire gardeners of all skill levels. What makes *Fine Gardening* unique is that all articles are written by home gardeners, horticulturists, or landscape professionals based on their own experience and knowledge-whether it be about a plant, gardening technique, design approach, or project.

Style

All of our stories are written in first person, based on first-hand experience. The tone should be friendly, yet informative. The style should be casual, that of one gardener sharing information with another as they walk through the garden together.

Features

Fine Gardening features ornamental plants and home landscaping ideas. Most of our feature stories fall into the following categories: design, techniques, plants, or garden structures. Most stories are how-to or instructional in nature; many are projects. We often include other related stories, such as those on tools or garden pests and diseases. While we do not publish general garden profiles, we illustrate most stories with photographs taken in our authors' gardens. Content should appeal to both beginning and experienced gardeners. Accurate botanical names, USDA Hardiness Zones, and cultural information must be provided for all plant profiles.

Departments

Tips, Q&A, Regional Reports (6), Lawn Talk and Tool Hound are all reader-written departments. Of these, we pay for published tips.

Plants to Know and Grow, Reviews, and Container Gardening are most often assigned to horticulture professionals, but we welcome queries. Last Word features gardening essays; humorous, insightful, or sentimental; that are selected from among unsolicited manuscripts.

Most of the photography in *Fine Gardening* is taken by our editors. We occasionally use professional photographers or accept photography supplied by the author. Additional fees are paid for any published photographs not taken by staff members.

Copyright and Payment

At *Fine Gardening*, we generally purchase the following rights:
• The right to be the first magazine to publish the article.
• The right to reprint the article in one or more of our anthology books.
• The right to use portions of the article in materials promoting *Fine Gardening* or The Taunton Press.
• The right to publish the article on our *Fine Gardening* web page.

We pay for all stories on a project basis. Payment runs from $200 - $1,000 per story, depending upon its length and complexity. A portion of this fee is paid upon acceptance of a publishable manuscript and signed copyright agreement. The balance is paid upon publication. Please note that by signing a copyright agreement with you, we do not guarantee publication of your article. We reserve the right to decide later not to publish it. This doesn't happen often, but if it does, you are entitled to keep your advance as a kill fee.

We pay $35 - $50 per published tip. For individual photographs, we pay $75– per published photograph, depending upon size and use. For assignment photography, we pay day rates, plus reasonable expenses.

Submitting a Query

If you would like to propose a story, please send a brief query explaining why the subject would be of interest to our readers. Be sure to highlight key points that would be covered in the story, and enclose any snapshots, sketches, or other materials that will help us evaluate story potential.

With the exception of Last Word, we prefer that a proposal precede the development of any manuscript.

All queries, tips, and reader contributions should be sent to the address below. Please submit only one story idea per query and allow

4-6 weeks for a response. If your proposal is accepted, an editor will be assigned to work with you. If at any time you have a question regarding the status of your proposal or story, please contact our editorial secretary at 800-926-8776, ext. 509.

Categories: Nonfiction—Gardening

CONTACT: Todd Meier, Editor
Material: All Features
CONTACT: Virginia Small, Associate Editor
Material: Last word
PO Box 5506
Newtown CT 06470
Phone: 203-426-8171
Fax: 203-426-3434
E-mail: fg@taunton.com
Website: www.taunton.com

Fine Homebuilding

Submitting an article proposal to *Fine Homebuilding* is simple. You don't need to write a manuscript or take professional photographs. We ask that you mail us a cover letter and photos introducing your project. Tell us what makes the project interesting and briefly explain the problems, challenges, solutions and results. The photos should be comprehensive. We recommend that you shoot interior and exterior, before, during and completed photos. If drawings or blueprints best illustrate the project, please include them in your presentation. If we decide to pursue the article an editor will be assigned, and will contact you. If not, we will return all of your material. Please include a self addressed stamped envelope. Good luck.

Categories: Nonfiction—Carpentry—Home

CONTACT: Submissions Editor
Material: All
The Taunton Press
63 South Main St.
PO Box 5506
Newtown, CT 06470-5506
Phone: 800-309-8919
E-mail: fh@taunton.com
Website: www.taunton.com/fh

Fine Woodworking

Fine Woodworking is a bimonthly magazine for all those who strive for and appreciate excellence in woodworking, veteran professional and weekend hobbyist alike. We have always been a reader-written magazine, relying on skilled woodworkers to share their practical experience and knowledge about the best methods of work, tools, construction and design.

We're looking for good articles on almost all aspects of woodworking from the basics of tool use, stock preparation and joinery to specialized techniques and finishing. We're especially keen on articles about shop-built tools, jigs and fixtures or any stage of design, construction, finishing and installation of cabinetry and furniture. Whether the subject involves fundamental methods or advanced techniques, we look for high-quality workmanship, thoughtful designs, safe and proper procedures.

We do not require our readers/writers to be professional authors. Our staff of editors are woodworkers themselves and are experienced with standard woodworking practices, as well as in working with first-time authors. We'll do everything we can step by step to make the writing process a smooth and pleasurable experience.

• **Start with a proposal**—If you'd like to write an article for *Fine Woodworking*, start by sending us a proposal. Summarize your topic and point of view in a paragraph or so and include an informal outline of the material you plan to cover in the article. Include a paragraph about yourself and your woodworking background. The better the quality of the visual information you can supply—especially photographs of actual work in progress—the better we will be able to appreciate your ideas. But don't worry if the images are not publishable quality, we'll reshoot photos if we decide to develop your article. Finally, please include a self-addressed stamped envelope large enough to hold all the materials you send. We'll take good care of everything, and we'll return it all at the appropriate time.

Once we receive your proposal, we'll send you a letter to let you know everything arrived. You'll hear from us again within a month, with a decision about whether we want you to go ahead with the article. If we do, you'll be assigned a staff editor to work with you. This editor will be your primary contact with the magazine. You and the editor will discuss and agree on an outline for the article, as well as a deadline for a first draft. Remember though, that final acceptance of your article depends on whether we can use your manuscript.

• **Preparing the manuscript**—What makes *Fine Woodworking* special is that most of our articles are written by people who actually do the work they write about. Therefore, we're more interested in your experiences, point of view and technical expertise than in your writing style or ability to provide grammar-perfect English. But even so, there are a few things to keep in mind when writing for us. First, stick to the outline that you and your editor agreed upon. If you want to reorganize it or add new information, let your editor know what you're up to.

As far as the writing goes, it's best to adopt an easy, conversational style, as if you were describing something to a friend in a letter. Be sure to define any terms you think might be obscure or specialized; not everyone will have a specialized knowledge of your subject. Note any particular tools, hardware or materials that played a part in your operation or project. And be sure to provide us with the product name, along with the manufacturer's name, current address and telephone number.

Strive to explain technical procedures in clear, simple sentences, and organize your flow of ideas logically. If you're trying to describe parts, operations or assemblies that are hard to verbalize, don't hesitate to use a drawing. Sketches should be clear, but don't have to be works of art; an artist will redraw anything that we decide to use. Drawings should be supplied with dimensions and labeled so that the visual information is correct and complete. If appropriate, include sources of supplies (complete with up-to-date addresses) or a list of books for further reading. We'll also need your Social Security number for payment purposes, so please send it along with your manuscript.

We'd prefer to receive your manuscript in typed, double spaced pages. If you work on a computer, tell your editor; it's likely that we'll be able to translate from your word processing program to ours, in which case we'll ask you to send a floppy disc as well as the printed pages.

• **Photography**—To assure that an article will be accompanied by high quality images, our editors usually visit authors and take most of the photographs. Since our editors are trained photographers, this assures us of getting photos that accurately support the processes and projects described in the text. A visit also gives authors a chance to meet their editor and work out any details involved in preparing the article. For project articles that involve building a piece of furniture, we rarely will ask you to build the piece from start to finish. We will work with you to select and stage certain process shots, to visually convey the most important operations described in the article. By the way, don't worry about writing photo captions—your editor will prepare those when the article is edited.

While we may occasionally photograph finished pieces during a visit, we more commonly hire a professional, as it's much more complex to shoot finished work than just process photos. We may ask to borrow small finished pieces (such as a jewelry box, a turning, jigs and fixtures) or tools to photograph at Taunton's photo studio. If you already have high quality (or professionally shot) photos of your work, we'll naturally want to consider using them. original color transparencies (slides) are best for magazine reproduction, but we can work from black and white or color negatives, if need be. Unless you tell us otherwise in writing, we assume that any photographs and drawings you supply with your article belong to you, and can be covered in a copyright agreement for our use. If a professional photographer owns the copyright to photos of your work, we'll need to sign a copyright agreement with the photographer separately, in which case you'll need to supply the address and phone number.

• **Payments and copyrights**—Our basic rate is $150 per published magazine page. We'll also reimburse you for out-of-pocket expenses, such as for film purchases and photo processing (only if we approve the project before you begin shooting). We'll also reimburse you for shipping or courier charges and for materials purchased for making samples or building projects specifically for the article. All requests for reimbursement must be accompanied by a photocopy of your dated receipts (the IRS says you should keep the originals). Any other reimbursements must be cleared with us in advance.

Once your editor has a manuscript that's ready for editing, we'll send you a copyright agreement to sign. The agreement constitutes our acceptance of the article for publication. It's not a difficult document to understand, and simply states that we are buying three things:

1. The right to be the first North American magazine to publish your article.

2. The right to reprint your article in one or more of our anthology books, such as the *Fine Woodworking on...* series.

3. The right to use portions of the article, including photographs and drawings, in materials promoting the magazine or The Taunton Press.

As author, you retain all other rights, including the right to publish the article elsewhere after it has appeared in *Fine Woodworking*. If photographs were taken by a professional photographer, we'll ask the photographer to sign a similar copyright agreement. Once you sign the copyright agreement and return the original to us, we'll send you an advance of $150. We'll pay the balance at time of publication. We'll also send you two complimentary copies of the issue in which your article appears.

• **Publication and scheduling**—We don't usually schedule an article for publication until we have an acceptable manuscript in hand. And because we have to schedule our issues almost a year in advance of publication, it may seem as though we're asking you to hurry up and deliver you material only to have you wait to see it in print. Putting together the best possible magazine from available material often means juggling the mix of articles for a given issue, often right up to our publication deadline. We think the results are worth waiting for and we appreciate your understanding and patience in the meantime. You're always welcome to call your editor to find out how things are going.

Please note that by signing a copyright agreement with you, we do not guarantee publication of your article. Even if we schedule the article for a specific issue, our editorial needs and direction sometimes change. Therefore, we reserve the right to decide later not to publish your article, but that rarely happens. If it does happen, the advance will serve as a "kill fee." The material would be returned to you and released from the copyright agreement, freeing you to sell it to another magazine.

• **Editing and author corrections**—Once your manuscript is accepted and scheduled for publication, we'll assign a sponsoring editor to work closely with you throughout its production, which can take anywhere from a week to a month. The editor may ask you to supply additional information, or to rewrite or revise sections of your manuscript. The editor will try to be sensitive to your individual writing style and retain as much of the character of the original writing as possible. If any major changes are warranted or if we have any doubts about changes we're considering during the editing process, your editor will call you to discuss the matter. Remember that changes to your writing made by the sponsoring editor are done in the interest of making your writing more effective and accurate, to make for the best possible presentation of your ideas.

After your manuscript has been edited, we'll mail you a galley—a computer printout of the edited version of the text—so that you'll have a chance to review it before it goes to press. Read it carefully and check the text for technical accuracy, typos and errors in facts. Make sure your editor hasn't inadvertently misinterpreted your original material. Also, answer any questions the editor has included on the printout. Please try to limit your changes to repair of facts; this isn't the time for rewriting the entire article. If your article includes complex drawings, you may also receive the artist's pencil drawings for corrections; please check these for accurate dimensions and labels as well.

Mark any corrections directly on the printouts and drawings and call your sponsoring editor at 1-800-926-8776 to discuss changes as soon as possible. Also, please mail us back the marked-up galley and drawing, so we can later refer to them if necessary. Small additional changes are typically made by the editors after author's corrections. These changes are typically minor, and are necessary to fit the manuscript into the page layout.

• **Contributing to departments**—In addition to our articles, *Fine Woodworking* features a number of regular departments, including "Methods of Work," "Q & A," "Books," "Tool Forum," and "Notes and Comments." We invite you to contribute to these sections of the magazine as well. Be sure to address all submissions to the appropriate department, in care of *Fine Woodworking*. "Methods of Work" submissions, which include "Quick Tips," don't require a proposal first; just send us your idea about an innovative jig, shop device, tool design or mode of operation, including rough sketches and photos. We'll pay $35 for each method we accept, $10 for quick tips.

The "Books" department includes reviews of new books and videos on woodworking and related topics (e.g. upholstery). Reviews should be concise and informative as to the content and quality of information in the item reviewed. We discourage unsolicited reviews; if you have a book in ming, contact us first. If we're interested, we'll arrange to have a copy sent to you. Payment is $35 per review, plus you get to keep the book. "Tool Forum" features short reviews of new woodworking tools and gadgets. We prefer that you first contact us with ideas for tools to review and then let us make the arrangements. Payment for "Tool Forum" reviews is prorated from our standard page rate of $150/page. Articles for "Notes and Comments" are generally less than 500 words and may include one or more photos. Subjects may include reports on woodworking-related current events, trade shows, gallery shows, woodworking seminars or school programs, personal profiles or humorous essays. Payment is prorated from our standard page rate.

• **Extra copies and reprints**—If you need more copies of the issue your article is in, authors are entitled to purchase additional copies at a discount of 50% off the cover price of the issue (plus shipping). Reprints of an individual article are available only by request, are run on heavier paper than the issue and can be produced any time after the issue has been printed. Reprints are fairly expensive to produce (you must order a minimum of 500 copies), and they take about a month to complete. If you'd like more information about reprints, contact *Fine Woodworking's* editorial secretary.

• **Questions?**—Thank you for your interest in *Fine Woodworking* magazine. If you have any further questions, feel free to call us toll free at 1-800-926-8776 and ask for the *Fine Woodworking* editorial department.

Categories: Nonfiction—Crafts—Hobbies

CONTACT: Editorial Department
Material: All
• **The Taunton Press**
63 South Main St., PO Box 5506
Newtown, CT 06470
Phone: 203-426-8171
Fax: 203-270-6753
E-mail: jdeeds@taunton.com
Website: www.taunton.com

FineScale Modeler

FineScale Modeler

How you can contribute to *FineScaleModeler*

Most *FineScaleModeler* (FSM) articles are contributed by modelers, not professional writers. This means that if you have a modeling story to tell, you can be an FSM author! In evaluating manuscripts we look first at the quality of your photos and illustrations, second at how you present your how-to information, and only third at your writing style.

If you have a modeling technique that FSM readers would like to learn about, our editors can rework your writing to the magazine's format and style. Most FSM feature articles concern how-to-do-it technique: How to build a kit into a more accurate or more representative model; how to make parts you can't buy or parts that are better than what you can buy; how to paint a model or how to paint a particular color scheme; how to build a display or diorama; and so on.. Virtually every how-to aspect of modeling, including hints, tips, and workshop techniques, is a worthwhile subject for an FSM article.

By far, the best way to learn what FSM needs is to study how stories are presented in current issues. However, we don't consider articles that are submitted simultaneously to other modeling publications, or articles previously published in other magazines.

Preparing a manuscript

We prefer typed manuscripts, and if you can also send your manuscript on a computer disk, that's even better. Almost any format will work. Be sure to enclose a paper copy even if you send a disk. In the upper right corner of the first page of your text, type your name, address, home and work telephone numbers, e-mail address if you have one, and the date you submit the article. In addition to the main text, provide captions for all photos you submit. Provide these on a separate sheet, and please make sure you describe everything shown in each photo.

Writing style

Keep your writing simple and direct, but give lots of detail. Our readers need a clear description of what you did to the model, how you did it, and what tools and materials you used. Be specific. Did you use sheet or tube styrene? Tell us the sizes. What brands and colors of paint — exactly — did you use? What sort of putty — epoxy, acrylic — did you use? Don't simply say "I scratchbuilt the transmission from sheet, tube, and rod styrene." Tell us how you did it, step by step. The best way to do this is to write as if you were telling a friend how to duplicate your modeling project. The best method for organizing your text is in chronological order, from the start of the project to its completion. Be sure to provide a complete list of materials you used and a list of references, if applicable.

Articles should be brief; most range from 750 to 3,000 words. While big features such as "How I Scratchbuilt the Hughes Spruce Goose in 1/24 Scale" are used occasionally, FSM has a greater need for short articles. Such reports usually cover only a single aspect of a project — like just the painting, or just the conversion, or just the detailing. Your best chance for breaking into print is to contribute a short article that focuses on a single modeling technique.

For first-time FSM contributors, we often run a "meet the author" box with a three- or four-paragraph biography (please concentrate on your modeling interests) and a photo showing you engaged in some modeling or research activity. Please include these with your first article.

Before you mail...

We strongly recommend that you send a written inquiry to the Editor describing your proposed article, and ask for comments or interest before preparing a complete article package. We prefer letters or e-mail, but sometimes clear up our requirements in a brief phone call.

Payment and copyright

FSM pays for feature articles upon acceptance — when we accept a complete feature for publication, you get a check. We normally purchase all rights to the material. We pay based on the estimated length of the published story, and if we underestimate the space your article requires, we issue a second payment upon publication.

Our payment rates vary; they're highest when an author does a particularly good job, or when the material is especially timely or interesting. Articles that include camera-ready scale drawings or how-to artwork also qualify for special rates.

Publishing your photographs in FSM

Photography makes or breaks most FSM articles, and by far our most common reason for rejecting a story is poor photos.

We need color slides or glossy prints from 35mm or larger film. Black-and-white photos usually are acceptable if color is not available, such as with historical photos. How-to shots should be taken against a plain background.

In-progress, how-to-do-it photos are especially important for selling your article to FSM. We often have to reject excellent material simply because it does not include photos taken while the model was being built. Showing the model before painting tells a lot about what you did to it.

In addition to the main text, provide captions for all photos you submit. Provide these on a separate sheet, and please make sure you describe everything shown in each photo.

Taking better model pictures

If you haven't taken pictures of models before, it can be a little tricky. Here are some tips from a September 1999 FSM article, "Great model photos are a snap," in case you're not pleased with your initial results. A free copy of the complete article is available from FSM on request.

Depth of field. The amount of depth of field (how much of the model is in focus) in a photo is controlled primarily by the lens aperture, or opening. The smaller the aperture, the more of your model from front to back will be sharp and in focus. Shoot your photos using the smallest aperture possible; it's usually f22 or f23 on most lenses.

Use a tripod. Small apertures mean long exposure times. Placing the camera on a tripod and using a cable release will keep camera motion from blurring your photos.

Show the whole model. Although close-up lenses make detail shots easier to take, don't forget to take a few shots showing the whole model!

Background check. A cluttered background draws attention away from your masterpiece. A poster-sized piece of colored art paper, curved up behind the model, makes a simple backdrop and helps concentrate the viewer's attention on the subject model.

Choose the right film. Use daylight-balanced film outdoors or with electronic flash; use tungsten-balanced film indoors with incandescent light. Films with "slow" speeds (ASA 50 or 100) produce sharper images than "fast" films (ASA 200, 400, or higher).

Digital photography

At this time, we need conventional transparencies, slides, or color prints. Consumer-quality digital cameras don't have the resolution that film provides, so except in special circumstances, we cannot use digital images in FSM.

If you send snapshot-quality 4 x 6 prints and negatives we can make reproduction-quality prints in our photo lab. Please include the negatives regardless of the quality of your prints. Negatives and 4 x 6 prints can be sent in a standard business size envelope, inside the larger envelope of your manuscript, to help keep them from being bent or scratched in transit.

Scale drawings and how-to illustrations

Please include sketches, patterns, templates, or plans with your article. Our artists can work from rough sketches. Draw the roughs as carefully and neatly as you can. If you can furnish reproduction-quality artwork your article will qualify for higher rates of payment. We often include arrows, circles, and words in photos to point out what's going on. You can suggest such pointers by attaching a tracing-paper flap to your photo and writing on the flap.

Payment and copyright

FSM pays for feature articles (but not Gallery images) upon acceptance. See payment and copyright information above.

Gallery, Portfolio, and Showcase stories

FSM pays on publication for photos published in the Reader Gallery, and buys all right. Published Gallery photos will not be returned. Portfolio and Showcase articles feature photos of a modeler's completed work, and usually are two magazine pages long. FSM pays on acceptance for these staff-written articles, and will follow up via questionnaire to get information needed for the text.

Categories: Nonfiction—Hobbies

CONTACT: Mark Thompson, Editor
Material: Any
CONTACT: Dick McNally, Managing Editor
Material: Any
21027 Crossroads Circle
Waukesha WI 53187
Phone: 414-796-8776
Fax: 414-796-1383
E-mail: RMCNALLY@finescale.com
Website: www.finescale.com

Firehouse Magazine
Firehouse.com

Firehouse® is the world's largest publication devoted exclusively to the fire service. Our primary editorial objectives are to educate, inform and entertain our audience of 1.5 million career and volunteer firefighters and thousands of fire buffs.

Generally, we are interested in all incidents, innovations, controversies and trends that affect the fire service world. Specifically, we concentrate on the following areas:

• MAJOR FIRES AND DISASTERS: detailed accounts and technical analyses of firefighting operations at major incidents (see "On the Job" specifications).

• APPARATUS AND EQUIPMENT: innovations in fire apparatus and other equipment (including protective gear), advice on purchasing, new and best uses of equipment, converting and repairing equipment, analysis/critique of equipment.

• COMMUNICATIONS: equipment, dispatch systems and dispatchers, command centers, fireground communications systems.

• TRAINING: methods and tools, new, successful courses, training simulations.

• HAZARDOUS MATERIALS: incidents, training, equipment, command, protective equipment.

• ARSON: investigation, prevention, analysis, trends.

• LAW: fire-related legislation at local and national levels.

• FIRE SAFETY: new and successful ways of educating the public.

• MEDICINE: health concerns, fitness of firefighters.

• LEADERSHIP: improving command skills and systems on the fireground, interviews with high-ranking fire service personnel (commissioners and chiefs of major fire departments).

• RESCUE: unusual incidents, successful methods and tools.

• EMS: major events involving EMTs, concerns of medical technology in the fire service.

• FIREFIGHTING HISTORY: great fires of the past, collectibles and memorabilia, fire museums, old-time equipment.

• HEALTH AND SAFETY: issues pertaining to firefighter health and safety.

• PUBLIC RELATIONS: improving relations with the community, fundraising.

• HUMAN INTEREST: lifestyles, profiles of firefighters with unusual hobbies and interests.

Query us first so we can give you more specific guidance, required length of the manuscript and deadlines. *Firehouse®* does not accept multiple submissions; that is, the material submitted must be an exclusive to *Firehouse®*. The writer must verify, in writing, that the material submitted is his original work, it has not been published previously and that it is not under consideration at another publication.

We would appreciate receiving manuscripts that are submitted on computer disk accompanied by a printed copy. Please use Microsoft Word for text documents, saved on a CD or floppy disk. For those writers who do not yet have word processing capability, clean, original typewritten pages are required. Please use a Courier 10-point typeface (the standard issue of typewriters) or comparable with one-inch margins throughout the document. If you make corrections, apply White-Out and retype. Do not handwrite corrections on typewritten copy. Handwritten, dot matrix-printed (without floppy disk) or Xeroxed or faxed manuscripts will be returned.

Please keep in mind that you are writing a magazine article. Most magazine readers, including those of *Firehouse®*, want to be able to learn the important aspects of a given topic without having to read through numerous paragraphs of background information. The average length of each article in *Firehouse®* is between two and three pages including visuals. In the past, we have received manuscripts that would be suitable for the first chapter of a book. Making these stories fit in the allocated space requires a great deal of editing on our part. More importantly, we may be cutting material that you would rather have included. A good rule of thumb is that one typeset page in *Firehouse®* is equal to about four double-spaced, typewritten pages.

Firehouse® is a visually-oriented publication. Please include photographs (color preferred) with captions (or a description of what is taking place in the photo), illustrations, charts or diagrams that support your manuscript. The highest priority is given to those submissions that are received as a complete package. Please keep a copy of all of your material, including visuals. *Firehouse®* makes every effort to ensure that all material is returned to the writer, whether it is published or not; however, we cannot guarantee the return of unpublished material. Enclose a stamped, self-addressed envelope (SASE) with all submissions. Submissions lacking the necessary SASE will not be returned. Please make sure that the return envelope is large enough to house your material. Also, please make sure the envelope has sufficient postage; do not include payment (checks or cash) for postage.

Please include your current mailing address as well as a daytime telephone, cell phone and fax number (if available). If we have any questions regarding copy or additional information is needed, we will contact you directly. If you have any stories ready to send prior to deadline dates, please send them along. We appreciate early arrivals.

Firehouse® makes payment only upon publication of written and photographic material. Once accepted, articles are published depending on timeliness and space availability. We cannot guarantee a publication date. Please include your social security number so that payment is not delayed.

If you have any story ideas, questions, hints, tips, etc., please do not hesitate to call. We appreciate and thank you for your assistance, enthusiasm and promptness.

Categories: Nonfiction—Health—Hobbies—Law—Lifestyle—Technical—Trade—Emergency Response—Fire-related

CONTACT: Firehouse Magazine, Editorial
Material: All Firehouse Magazine Submissions
3 Huntington Quadrangle, Ste 301N
Melville NY 11747
Phone: 631-845-2700
Fax: 631-845-7218

Chris Hebert, Firehouse.com Editor
Material: All Firehouse.com Submissions
11720 Beltsville Dr. Ste 300
Beltsville MD 20705
Phone: 301-486-7500
Fax: 301-486-4556
Website: www.Firehouse.com

First for Women

First for Women provides today's busy, on-the-go woman with a wealth of information packed into quick-reading articles. We are looking for service pieces on health and fitness, relationships and sex, happiness and parenting. We also feature real women's stories, stories of inspiration or life-changing events. Before submitting a query, please read the magazine to familiarize yourself with our style and editorial needs.

Please send a query letter rather than a completed manuscript. Clips are welcome. We regret that we do not accept email submissions, and we do not accept unsolicited fiction or poetry. Payment for articles is made upon acceptance for publication.

Please include your name, address, and daytime phone number with your query. Material not accompanied by a self-addressed stamped envelope will not be returned. *First for Women* accepts no obligation to return any material.

Categories: Nonfiction—Beauty—Cooking—Fashion—Food/Drink

CONTACT: Barbara Moff
Material: Fashion, Beauty
CONTACT: Kate Keating
Material: Food
CONTACT: Linda Moore, Features Editor
Material: All Other
Bauer Publishing Co., L.P.
270 Sylvan Ave.
Englewood Cliffs NJ 07632
Phone: 201-569-6699
Fax: 201-569-6264
Website: www.ffwmarket.com

The First Line

Fiction: All stories must be written with the first line provided. The line cannot be altered in any way, unless otherwise noted by the editors. The story should be between 300 and 3,000 words. The sentences can be found on the home page of The First Line's Web site, as well as in the prior issue.

Non-fiction: 300-600 word critical essays about your favorite first line from a literary work.

All Stories: Writers should include a two- to three-sentence biography of themselves that will appear in the magazine should their story run.

Multiple Submissions: We don't mind if you want to submit multiple stories for the same issue. However, it is unlikely we will use more than one of your stories in the same issue. We ask that you do not submit a story using our first line to another publication until after our issue with that first line is published. Also, please do not post your story to your personal Web site (or blog) until after we have made a decision.

Continuing Series: We will consider only four-part stories using all the sentences for a single year. All the stories must be submitted at once (a single e-mail or snail mail) before the February 1st deadline.

Submissions: We prefer you send manuscripts via e-mail to submission@thefirstline.com. We accept stories in MS Word or Word Perfect format (we prefer attachments). Make sure your name and contact information, as well as your bio, are part of the attachment.

Stories also can be sent to The First Line's post office box. No manuscripts will be returned without an accompanying SASE with sufficient return postage. Here is the submission schedule for this year's sentences: Spring Issue Deadline: February 1st; Summer Issue Deadline: May 1st; Fall Issue Deadline: August 1st; Winter Issue Deadline: November 1st.

Notification: We don't make any decisions about stories until after each issue closes. We typically send notices out within three to four weeks after the issue's deadline to everyone who submitted a story. You can also check the home page of the website as we will indicate each issue's production status there.

Payment: Payment is $20.00 (U.S.) for fiction and $10.00 (U.S.) for nonfiction. We also send you a copy of the magazine in which your story or nonfiction appears. We pay on publication. You'll receive your money and magazine at the same time.

Categories: Fiction—Nonfiction

CONTACT: Editors
E-mail: submissions@thefirstline.com
Website: www.thefirstline.com

First Things
A Monthly Journal of Religion and Public Life

FIRST THINGS does accept unsolicited manuscripts. Guidelines are as follows:

Opinions: 1,00-2,000 words. Honorarium of $400.
Articles: 4,000-6,000 words. Honorarium of $1000.
Book Reviews: 1,500-1,800 words. Honorarium of $400.
Review Essays: 4,000-6,000 words. Honorarium of $1000.

Manuscripts should be typed, double-spaced and on one side of the page. We prefer to receive submissions via e-mail. Manuscripts submitted by surface mail should include a SASE and return postage.

Categories: Nonfiction— Book Reviews—Christian Interests—Culture—Education—General Interest—Government—Jewish Interest—Law—Politics—Religion—Spiritual—Philosophy—Public Policy

CONTACT: Joseph Bottum, Editor
Material: All
156 Fifth Ave., Ste. 400
New York NY 10010
Phone: 212-627-1985
Fax: 212-627-2184
E-mail: ft@firstthings.com
Website: www.firstthings.com

Fishing Facts

Fishing Facts Magazine has been teaching people how to fish for the past 40 years. Every issue features stories on how-to and where-to fish at some of the hottest spots in the United States.

1) Every article submitted should be between 750 and 1,500 words.
2) They should contain color photos and/or charts, graphs and maps.
3) Clearly outline the techniques used to fish successfully.
4) Clearly outline where the author was fishing, either the specific body of water or the area.
5) Articles must be submitted in the following forms:
  • via e-mail, e-mail address: info@midwestoutdoors.com
  • on a CD (We use Microsoft Word for word processing.)

Please remember, the tone of Fishing Facts Magazine is positive and upbeat.

Important checklist before sending in material:
- You have included your name, address and social security number.
- Your name is on all pages and photos.
- You have indicated what issue the material is for.
- You have written a headline and sub-headline.
- You have written a caption for each photo.

Please read: If we do not plan on using your material, it will be returned to you within 10 days of receipt. The best check you have for knowing if we have used your material, is if you receive payment from Fishing Facts. Payment for each article published is $30 paid upon publication.

Categories: Nonfiction—Fishing—Recreation—Sports/Recreation

CONTACT: **Dena Kollman, Assistant Editor**
Materials: All
111 Shore Drive
Burr Ridge IL 60527
Phone: 630-887-7722
Fax: 630-887-1958
E-mail: info@midwestoutdoors.com.
Website: www.fishingfacts.com

Fitness Management

Categories: Health—Fitness

CONTACT: **Ronale Rhodes, Editor**
Material: Feature Articles
CONTACT: **Anne B. McDonnell, Senior Editor**
Material: New Products
PO Box 409
Danville PA 17821
Phone: 800-722-8764
Fax: 570-271-1201
E-mail: edit@fitnessmanagement.com
Website: www.fitnessmanagement.com

Five Points

Fiction: Stories or self-contained novel excerpts in the 7500-word range preferred, but we will consider longer pieces. One story per submission. Each publication year the editors select one author whose work has appeared in *Five Points* to receive The Paul Bowles Prize for Fiction, an award of $1000.

Poetry: High-quality poems. Send up to three poems per submission. Poems should not exceed fifty lines each.

Essays: Literary or personal essays, no criticism. We prefer the 7500-word range. Send one essay per submission.

Photographs and Artwork: Send slides, cd, or duplicates. Black and white photography is preferable, but we will consider color.

Payment: $15 per printed page (prose), $50 per poem, $250 for photographs and artwork plus complimentary copies and subscription.

Manuscripts must be typed, double-spaced, on one side only of 8½" x 11" paper. Be sure your name, address, and phone number appear on all pages. Enclose a sufficiently stamped SASE if you want your work returned to you and indicate so on your cover letter.

We do not accept simultaneous submissions. We do not accept unsolicited submissions during the months of May, June, July, and August. Please send no more than two submissions per reading period. We do not accept submissions via email. We also do not respond to inquiries concerning the status of manuscripts via email or the telephone. Please send your written inquiries to the address below and include a SASE.

Categories: Fiction—Essays—Poetry—Short Stories

CONTACT:
Five Points
PO Box 3999
Atlanta GA 30302-3999

Flight Journal

The first part of these guidelines describes the kinds of articles that fit our editorial formula and how to propose articles to us. The second part describes the kind of photography we are seeking.

Writers' Guidelines - Subject Matter

Flight Journal presents aviation-oriented material, for the most part with a historical overtone, but also with some modern "history in the making" reporting. Many articles have an "I was there" or "from the cockpit" human-interest emphasis, typically in a manner that is not being done in other magazines. We are trying to "... sing the note no one else is singing ...."

It is important that prospective writers understand that we are NOT a general aviation magazine—so we are not interested in articles such as "My Flight to Baja in my 172," or "My friend's Homebuilt." Nor do we wish to publish articles that are simply detailed recitations of the technical capabilities of an aircraft.

A typical issue of *Flight Journal* will include, among other features:

2-3 articles on WW II.

1 modern jet story; it could be hardware and operations with pilot interviews, or a personal story.

1 historical piece, e.g., early airlines, barnstormers.

1 semi-technical piece with historical overtones, e.g. low aspect ratio airplanes, Burnelli lifting-body aircraft.

When considering a story idea, *Flight Journal* places a premium on the following:

1. Does the basic idea fit our mission?

2. Is there an unusual slant to the idea that makes it unique?

3. Does it lend itself to an exciting presentation because of unusual pictures? Is it a fantastic but true personal account?, etc.

4. Is there a lot of human interest? We want as much human interest in every story as possible. The designers, builders, pilots and mechanics are what aviation is all about.

An Example

Basic idea: WW II Gunner Aces (idea appears unique and is certainly not overdone). The article, by Barrett Tillman, was published in our February 1997 issue.

Slant: difficulties faced by gunners.

They were often just kids.

How accurate were the gunners, how many of them, how many kills?

Quotes from German fighter pilots would be desirable, e.g., how it was to attack a bomber box?

Excitement potential: is good WW I and WW II photography available? Are personal accounts?

Human interest: what was it like to be a kid in that position? Paint a picture of the fear, the cold, the blood, etc., using quotes and anecdotal stuff wherever possible.

How to Submit your Idea

Send a single page outline of your idea to the address listed below. Feel free to use the intro to the story as the lead paragraph.

Indicate the story's angle, uniqueness, technical or historical interest value, human interest.

If practical, provide one or more samples of prior articles so we can get a feel for your style.

We'll respond and let you know what we think of the idea and whether you should send it in.

Submitting Articles

The article should come to us by email or on a disk along with a double-spaced hard copy.

Average article length is 2,500–3,000 words, or approximately 8 pages, when double-spaced, on typing paper or printed from a word processor. Lengthier pieces should be discussed in advance with the editors.

Categories: Nonfiction—Aviation

CONTACT: Roger Post
Air Age Publishing
100 E Ridge
Ridgefield CT 06877-4606
Fax: 203-431-3000
E-mail: rogerp@airage.com

Florida Hotel & Motel Journal

Market: Our magazine is a reference tool for managers and owners of Florida's hotels, motels and resorts—circulation 8,000+. It is mailed on the first of each month, except Dec. & Aug.

Editorial content: Nonfiction only. Preference is given to articles that include references to mem- ber properties and general managers affiliated with the Florida Hotel and Motel Association. Since the association acquires new members weekly, queries may be made prior to the scheduling of interviews. This does not preclude the use of materials or ideas based on non-member properties, but member property sources are preferable.

Approach: Queries are encouraged. Unsolicited manuscripts must be accompanied by SASE with sufficient postage for first class return. Articles submitted for an issue with a specific theme must be received two months in advance of the publication date.

Format: Length is determined by nature and import of subject matter, not to exceed 2000 words unless specified by the editor. Shorter articles with accompanying sidebars are preferred. Manuscripts should be typed, double-spaced.

Attributions: All opinions, quotations and statements used should be attributable to a creditable source, i.e., a person in the lodging industry, a footnoted quotation from texts or clearly identified as the personal viewpoint of the author.

Writing and editing: Clarity and organization of content are essential. The editor reserves the right to edit for grammar, punctuation and simplification of subject matter, as necessary, without changing the author's intent.

Photos and Artwork: Submissions accompanying an article should be of professional quality and authorized in advance by the editor. Color slides and/or b&w glossy prints are acceptable.

Rates and Rights: Payment is $.10 per word upon publication for first U. S. A. rights. Travel and/ or telephone expenses must have the editor's advance approval. Three complimentary copies of the issue in which a commissioned article appears will be mailed to the author. Additional copies may be purchased.

Categories: Nonfiction—Business—Trade—Hotel & Motel Management

CONTACT: Lytha Belrose, Editor
Material: All
200 W. College Ave.
Tallahassee FL 32301
Phone: 850-224-2888
Fax: 850-222-3462
Website: www.flahotel.com

Remember: Editors change jobs and publishers change addresses. It is wise to invest in a phone call for the current information before submitting.

Florida Leader
For College Students

Please refer to Oxendine Publishing, Inc.

Florida Leader
For High School Students

Please refer to Oxendine Publishing, Inc.

Florida Wildlife

Florida Wildlife is a not-for-profit, bimonthly magazine published by the Florida Fish and Wildlife Conservation Commission (FWC) focused on hunting, fishing, outdoor activities and FWC initiatives. Limited paid advertising is accepted.

Florida Wildlife began in 1947 and continued to publish for 56 years until its "final" issue published in November of 2003 due to lack of state funding. In 2004, the Florida Legislature renewed its funding of *Florida Wildlife*, stipulating that the magazine be dedicated to promoting the heritage of hunting and fishing in Florida and providing both Floridians and visitors with information regarding additional outdoor recreational opportunities.

Submissions

We prefer to purchase first-time, one-time rights to manuscripts and photographs. If submissions are being considered by other publishers, please notify us of this fact. Articles, artwork and photographs may appear on the *Florida Wildlife* Web site.

Submissions are on speculation. *Florida Wildlife* reserves the right to use either all or part of your submission and to edit for content and/ or size. Proper credit is given to authors, writers and photographers. Submissions are acknowledged upon arrival. Queries will be answered as time permits. Self-addressed return envelopes with sufficient postage should accompany all submissions you wish returned.

Writers Guidelines

Florida Wildlife is looking for well-written and exciting Florida fishing, hunting and nature-based recreation stories. These stories should emphasize the appreciation of the overall outdoor experience and not focus solely on the taking of game. Stories should also reflect the concern hunters, anglers and other outdoor enthusiasts have about conserving wildlife and the habitat.

Typed manuscripts of 500 to 1,200 words may be submitted via e-mail, computer disc or in hard copy format. We prefer that electronic copy be composed in MS Word, but will accept other formats. The first page should include the writer's name, address, Social Security number, telephone number and e-mail address. Poetry and handwritten manuscripts will not be considered for publication.

Manuscripts that include photographs or artwork are more likely to be considered for publication. Include the photographer's pertinent information (if not the same as the writer's) and a brief description of the action, person or place being pictured.

We are looking for:

· Freshwater and saltwater fishing articles.

· Hunting and hunting-related stories.

· Articles about outdoor activities such as tracking, diving, boating, hiking, wildlife watching, etc.

· How-to articles with tips and techniques for both beginners and experienced enthusiasts.

· Game recipes — for camp sites, backyard grilling and kitchen cooking.

Photographers' Guidelines

Florida Wildlife has a long history of showcasing outstanding and award-winning photography and artwork. In order to continue this tradition, only extremely sharp, in-focus and well lit photographs are considered for publication. We prefer high-resolution scans rather than film to avoid damage to or loss of original work. Low-resolution images enlarged via a computer program or other obviously retouched images will not be considered. We cannot accept soft focus or blurred images.

Each image submitted, whether digital, transparency or glossy print, should be labeled with the photographer's name and a number. The number should correspond with a separate caption sheet. The caption sheet should describe the action, place and/or person pictured. Include the name, address, Social Security number, telephone number and e-mail address of the photographer.

Images may be cropped, rotated, flipped or otherwise edited by a graphic artist to suit the magazine's style or to fit in available space.

We accept:

· High-resolution digital images, at least 300dpi and 2M-15M. If e-mailed, larger files should be sent singly and as JPEGs. If submitted via CD, images may be JPEG, TIFF or EPS)

· 35mm or larger first-generation slides or negatives.

· High quality color prints, preferably 8x10.

All images should:

· Be shot in Florida or illustrate species living in Florida.

· Portray hunting, fishing and all other activities conforming to Florida's legal regulations, safety practices and to high ethical standards.

Other Policies

All submissions are on speculation, and payment is made upon publication. Payment varies, depending on length, complexity and quality.

Materials will be handled carefully, but due to the risk of mailing and shipping, *Florida Wildlife* and its agents will not be responsible for damage or loss of submitted material.

Stories and photographs will not be accepted for publication if they:

· Refer to alcohol or tobacco products.

· Use profanity or picture profane printed products such as explicit t-shirts.

· Advertise or promote a business or product.

· Fail to show respect for the game being taken and/or contain overly graphic details of the harvest.

· Are strictly "trophy" in content—pictures of a sportsperson with harvest or "how I got my biggest…" stories.

Categories: Animals—Boating—Conservation—Ecology—Environment—History—Native American—Nature—Outdoors—Recreation—Travel—Bass Fishing—Habitat—Wildlife

CONTACT: Editor
Material: All
Florida Wildlife
620 S Meridian St
Tallahassee FL 32399-1600
Phone: 850-410-4944 or 1-866-967-5600
Fax: 850-488-8974
E-mail: floridawildlife@MyFWC.com

Fly Fisherman

NOTES TO CONTRIBUTORS

Fly Fisherman is the nation's first and largest consumer magazine devoted solely to the sport of fly fishing. We don't assume that all of our readers are expert fly fishes, nor do we assume that they are all novices. We select material for publication that, educates accomplished fly fishers, beginners and even non-fly fishers. Similarly, we provide geographic coverage that meets our responsibility as an international publication.

Our contributors are avid readers of the magazine, and their submissions reflect a familiarity with the style and content of material used in the magazine. Potential contributors should likewise familiarize themselves with the kind of material *Fly Fisherman* uses by looking over recent issues.

Over Eighty percent of *Fly Fisherman*'s readers are college educated, and ninety percent are male. However, the magazine is regularly read by other members of the household—including non-fly fishers. Our readers fish in fresh or salt water for almost any species of fish that will take a fly.

Editorial Format

The types of articles that we publish include:

1. Main features of 2,000-3,000 words, illustrated with black-and-white prints or

color transparencies (slides) and illustrations. These articles embrace a wide variety of subjects, including major destinations (where to fish), instruction about fishing techniques, and how to tie flies. Fiction, humor and personality profiles are seldom used.

2. Short features of about 750-1,500 words, usually illustrated in black-and-white or color. These articles highlight a specific aspect of the sport; most are short destination or how-to-do-it articles. The short feature is an important component of our magazine. It allows us to present a wide variety of information and topics to our readers.

3. Destination features of about 2,000-3,000 are feature articles that highlight a particular stream or the waters of a specific region. These features include good photos of fish from the waters discussed and anglers fishing in scenic surroundings. They also may include a hatch chart, a map with each water clearly indicated, local fly shop information, lodging information, and any other details that can make it easy to plan a trip to the area. The text should inform the reader about the area and techniques and flies needed to catch fish there. It should not be an account of your trip to a particular destination.

4. Technical feature articles of about 2,000 words, illustrated in black-and-white or color, deal with subjects that lend themselves to presentation in the Improving Your Skills, Fly Tier's Bench or Tips From The Experts departments. Sometimes these are used in the main feature section of the magazine. The text usually includes step-by-step instructions (such as fly-tying instructions), and if such instructions are included, appropriate photos, illustrations, or diagrams should accompany the text.

All submissions to *Fly Fisherman* containing factual information must be thoroughly and carefully documented. Double-check stream or lake locations and names (especially spelling); if you're unsure of any factual detail and can't document it, leave it out. When referring to insects or fish by their Latin names, consult a standard college text for correct spelling and nomenclature.

Photographs and Artwork

We can't overemphasize the importance of quality illustrations to accompany submissions. See the attached Artist/Photographers

If you don't have photos, send the article anyway—we may have the appropriate photos and illustrations on file. However, good photos often sell an article that is less than complete. Quality color or black-and-white art is always welcome. All photographic submissions should be accompanied by a caption sheet.

Maps and diagrams should be submitted with articles when called for by the text. When submitting fly-tying articles, drawings or photographs showing tying steps should be included when appropriate.

Submissions of cartoons are welcome.

Preparation of Material and Submission Procedures

Manuscripts must be typed and double-spaced. We do not accept handwritten manuscripts. Computer printouts are acceptable. If possible, send the manuscript on computer disk (3-1/2" disk in Microsoft Word text or ASCII format). The name, address and phone number of the author should be on the first page of the manuscript. The name of the article, the name of the author and the page number should be on each ensuing page of the manuscript. The author's name (or appropriate credit line) should be marked on each piece of photographic material or artwork submitted. Care should be taken to package all material properly before mailing. Please enclose a self-addressed envelope and attach or enclose sufficient postage for return of material.

An excellent, concise and handy guide to style is *The Elements of Style* by William Strunk, Jr. and E.B. White (2nd ed., Macmillan Publishing Co., New York, 1972, $1.95) and we recommend it highly.

Queries

We strongly recommend that you query us in advance on a specific article or article idea. A query allows us to suggest a slant on the article, or at least to inform you in advance of our interest in your proposed story idea.

Acknowledgment of Submissions

Upon receipt of a submission we'll send an acknowledgment; within six to eight weeks after receipt, material will either be returned or purchased. Sometimes we may ask for a rewrite. Article queries will be answered within four weeks, and queries concerning the status of submissions (after our reply deadline of six to eight weeks) will be answered immediately.

Payment

Payment is made within 30 days of publication or acceptance of material. *Fly Fisherman* buys First Time World Publishing Rights and all nonexclusive World Publishing Rights (for use on our internet site, www.flyshop.com). *Fly Fisherman* does not accept simultaneous submissions or previously published material. Shortly after publication, all photos, illustrations, diagrams, maps, etc. will be returned. Original manuscripts will be kept here on file. (Writers who regularly make submissions to any publication should familiarize themselves with the current copyright laws.)

Fees to contributors vary according to the manuscript's professional level, frequency of accepted contributions, and length of article. The same applies to photographs and artwork. Fees range from $400 to $700 for main features, from $100 to $300 for short features, from $200 to $300 for technical features. We pay $100 for book reviews. Contact us before writing the review.

Fees are paid for complete packages, which include manuscript, artwork, and photographs. Payment for photographs and artwork purchased without manuscripts is determined by the size and use inside the magazine and ranges from $50 to $300. We pay $600 for a photograph used on the cover of the magazine.

Publication Schedule

Fly Fisherman magazine is published six times per year. The editor usually purchases manuscripts one year in advance.

Please advise us of any change in your address or telephone number so that we may keep our files up-to-date and ensure that your submissions are returned safely. Include both home and office phone numbers as well as any seasonal addresses and e-mail.

Style Guide for Potential Contributors

1. Indent the first line of each paragraph.

2. Show the end of a story by writing End, The End, 30, #, or similar mark.

3. Use standard scientific nomenclature when referring to insects: Consult standard references, such as "Mayflies of North and Central America," Edmunds et al, for correct spellings.

4. The common names of insects are lower case, the proper names of fly patterns are capitalized: The black gnats were a nuisance that night, but I caught four trout on a Black Gnat dry fly.

5. The common names of fish are lower case unless the name includes a proper noun: I like to fish for coho salmon, Chinook salmon,

Atlantic salmon and brown trout.

6. Some preferred spellings: caddisfly, drys (dry flies), fish-for-fun, fly-fishing, fly-fishing-only, fly rod, fly-rodder, fly tier, fly-tying, Matuka, marabou, mayfly, mylar, no-kill, Opening Day, snowmelt, snowpack, stonefly, whip-finish.

Guidelines

Color photographs should be in the form of 35mm slides or 2¼" x 2¼" transparencies, as color prints do not reproduce satisfactorily. The preferred format for black-and-white photographs is 8" x 10" glossy prints. Articles are best accompanied by both black-and-white and color, giving us the option of using one or the other or both to illustrate your work.

Categories: Nonfiction—Fishing

CONTACT: The Editor
Material: All
6405 Flank Dr.
Harrisburg PA 17112-2753
Website: www.flyfisherman.com

Fly Fishing in Salt Waters

Formal guidelines not available. Please read a number of issues to ascertain the publication's style and needs.

Send queries to address below

Categories: Fishing—Sports/Recreation—Travel

CONTACT: David Ritchie, Editor
Material: All
2001 Western Ave., Ste. 210
Seattle WA 98121
Phone: 206-443-3273
Fax: 206-443-3293
Website: www.flyfishinsalt.com

Flyfisher

We're looking for writing and photography that help us reinforce our mission to conserve, restore and educate through fly fishing.

Founded in 1965, the Federation of Fly Fishers (FFF) is the nation's largest, oldest and most influential fly-fishing organization. The *Flyfisher*, first published in 1968, is the Federation's flagship publication and this country's oldest fly-fishing magazine.

Circulation of each issue is a minimum of 12,500 copies. More than 10,000 copies are delivered by mail to FFF members. The balance is distributed by the FFF to its nearly 200 affiliated local fly-fishing clubs around the country, to retail fly shops, at fly-fishing shows and expositions and in FFF promotions.

Mirroring the FFF's mission to "conserve, restore and educate through fly fishing," each issue of the *Flyfisher* takes a hard look at resource issues affecting cold-water, warm-water and saltwater game fish and their habitats.

The magazine also serves as an educational tool for the FFF and its International Fly Fishing Center, providing practical information focusing on fly fishing techniques—including emphasis on fly tying, which many FFF members enjoy. *Flyfisher* editorial also aims to attract and support new constituencies for the sport, particularly women and youths.

Feature stories

We carry features that have been the hallmark of the *Flyfisher* for nearly 30 years. We're particularly interested in how-to and technique features, fly-fishing history and tradition, personality profiles and interviews, personal narratives, fly-fishing trends, conservation profiles, fly tying and, on rare occasions, fiction. We'll run occasional where-to-fish stories that feature a fishing destination, but feel these types of stories predominate in the for-profit magazines and are less reflective of the FFF mission. Length should be from 750 to 1,500 words. Payment: $50 to $150.

Conservation stories

We run conservation-oriented stories as short news stories of not more than 400 words, or as longer stand-alone features not exceeding 1,500 words. At various times the *Flyfisher* will also feature a longer story or package of stories focusing on a conservation issue of national concern that impacts the quality of freshwater or saltwater fishery habitats or resources. We're looking for top-notch environmental journalism that 1) gets *Flyfisher* readers interested in the topic and concretely demonstrates how it affects the sport of fly fishing; and 2) provides easily assimilated information that will further reader knowledge. Length should be from 750 to 1,500 words for an individual story, or up to 2,500 words for a package of stories. If querying a conservation package idea, please suggest possible sidebar subjects and visual support. Payment: $20 to $40 for short conservation stories; $50 to $150 for stand-alone feature stories; or $150 to $250 for a package of stories.

Photography

We're always interested in photography to accompany writing, and good photos make a story more attractive to us. Although we assign very little photography, we use several stock images per issue. We encourage interested photographers to submit a list of subjects in stock and a resume of credits. If you wish to submit photos for consideration, the *Flyfisher* staff responds within one month of receiving materials with an Acknowledgment of Receipt and will hold materials with potential for use for up to 90 days.

Solicited material will be returned via Postal Service certified mail.

We use black-and-white photos which should be submitted as 5"x7" or 8"x10" prints, or as negatives with proof sheets. For color, we use 35mm or larger format transparencies. We may wish to reproduce a color photograph in black-and-white; if you object to this, please specify when submitting. Payment: $10 to $25 for black-and-white usage, $15 to $50 for color, $100 for cover. Credit line is given on all photographs. Model release is required when subject is easily identifiable and potential for litigation exists.

General guidelines

Although we'll look at unsolicited manuscripts, we encourage writers to submit query letters. If you are simultaneously submitting your story or photos elsewhere, please specify this. We also like to see one or two clips or writing samples from authors with whom we are unfamiliar.

Accuracy is of paramount importance. Writers are responsible for the accuracy of their stories, and for ensuring names and proper nouns are correctly spelled. For some subjects we may require writers to send us background material and a source list to help us perform fact checking.

Keep the length of your story within the guidelines set forth above. We strongly favor concisely written stories. Also, remember the *Flyfisher* is published in February, April, July and November; bear in mind our seasonal needs and query at least 120 days prior to the season for which your story is appropriate.

The first page [of your manuscript] should include your name, address, phone number and social security number. We use a Macintosh computer system and welcome submissions on disk in any word processing program. If you write on an IBM compatible, simply save in ASCII (text only) format on a 3.5" floppy. If you do send a disk, be sure to send along a hard copy, too.

We may also receive your story via e-mail. At this time, however, we prefer that queries be sent by regular U.S. mail, rather than as e-mail.

The *Flyfisher* buys first North American serial rights, and payment is made on publication. Writing is done on speculation unless a kill fee is agreed to in advance.

Categories: Nonfiction—Conservation—Ecology—Education—Environment—Fishing—Nature—Sports/Recreation

CONTACT: Nick Amato, Editor
Material: All
Frank Amato Publications

PO Box 82112
Portland OR 97282
Phone: 503 653-8108
Fax: 503 653-2766
E-mail: nick@amatobooks.com
Website: www.fedFlyfishers.org

Flyfishing & Tying Journal
A Compendium for the Complete Fly Fisherman

Publisher: Frank Amato
Editor: Dave Hughes
Managing Editor: Kim Koch
Writer's and Photographer's Guidelines

Flyfishing & Tying Journal (FTJ) is a quarterly *fly-fishing* magazine with issues designated Winter, Spring, Summer, and Fall. As its name implies, the magazine has two major focal points of interest, *fly fishing* and *fly tying*, that reflect the interests of its readers.

The majority of FTJ readers, 98%, fly-fish for trout, most of them many days each year. 60% also fly-fish for steelhead and salmon. 50% fly-fish for bass and panfish. 30% go after bonefish, tarpon, permit, and other saltwater species at least once a year. A high percentage of our readers tie their own flies. Three-quarters are over 40 years old, 90% have education beyond high school, and most have been fly-fishing five years or more, though we can never forget that many readers of every issue have more eagerness than they have experience.

More than half of our readers, 60%, live in the West: the Pacific coast states and Rockies. 15% live in New England and on the East Coast. 15% live in the Midwest and Great Lakes region. Many in all regions travel to other areas to fish.

Articles accepted for publication in the magazine will be balanced to reflect the above preferences for species and areas in which readers live and fish. Article selection will also reflect a balance between the two focal points of the magazine: fly fishing and fly tying. Each issue is divided into two cores, the major one the fly-fishing core toward the front and the fly-tying core toward the back. Articles for each core are very different from those for the other, and must be tailored to one or the other to fit our requirements.

Fly-fishing core feature articles. The fly-fishing core of each issue will consist of 4 to 6 feature articles, each from 1,200 to 2,000 words long, on a specific fishing technique, an insect hatch or natural food form and the flies and methods that work to take fish, a range of methods to solve a specific situation or type of fishery, or any other subject deemed by the editors to be of sufficient interest to our readers. Each feature should include one or two short sidebars, 100 to 250 words each, that illuminate or enlarge the subject. One sidebar should almost always deal with the flies used in the fishing featured. The dressing for each fly should be given in the sidebar, and a finished sample of each fly should be furnished for our photographer. If a fly pattern is written about in an article, its dressing should be given in a sidebar, and a copy of the fly, tied, should be provided for our photographer. Please use barbless hooks, or de-barb them.

Our desire is to publish informative articles that our readers can have fun reading, learn from, and put to use in their own fishing. We rarely buy articles in which a destination itself is the subject; we commonly buy articles about solutions to fishing problems with the supporting anecdotes set in a specific destination. If a destination is dealt with in any article, the article should be about the fishing, not the destination, and all high praise not directly related to the fishing should go into a sidebar along with contact information: address, phone number, e-mail address, and website.

Each fly-fishing feature will require enough high-quality color slides to illustrate it attractively. Twenty to forty slides should be submitted with any full feature. Slide selection should include lead shots to set the scene for the article, action shots, fish shots, scenery, flies, and peripheral flora and fauna.

The formula is often denigrated in outdoor writing, but it dates back to the 1500s and Montaigne's highly regarded essays, and is to this day a very fine format to follow for any feature. If you don't have a better outline, and you should rarely write an article without an outline in mind, use it:

Introduction: the fishing problem to be solved.

Part 1. the first part of the solution (e.g. recognizing an insect).

Part 2. the second part of the solution (e.g. choosing the right fly to match it).

Part 3. (optional) the third part of the solution (e.g. using the right presentation).

Conclusion: summation of the solving of the problem.

Sidebar 1. The flies used (dressings listed and flies provided for photographer).

Sidebar 2. Some peripheral part of the solution, or contact info for a destination.

This has been summed up as: tell them what you're going to tell them, tell them, tell them, then tell them what you told them. That's not far from wrong. Brief anecdotes, set on the water in the midst of the action, should be used to enliven at least one or two parts of each article. These give an immediacy to the problem and its solution, and in general makes an article more fun to read. Your editors strongly prefer first person past tense, and are known to frown on second or third person present tense.

Fly-tying core feature articles. The fly-tying core of each issue will consist of 4 to 6 features ranging from 400 to 800 words long, about a fly or fly style, and specifically instructive for tying the fly or style. These articles can focus on individual patterns, pattern styles, new tying techniques, new and innovative tools, new materials, new uses of old materials, specific imitations, or any other fly-tying subject deemed of sufficient interest to our readers. Emphasis should be on usefulness of the flies; all patterns should be related to an actual fishing situation.

Each tying feature should include a short introduction to the fly and the problem it solves, then should list one or at most two dressings with the materials listed in the order they'll be tied to the hook, followed by numbered tying steps. Steps should usually be limited to from 4 to no more than 8; captions for each step should be 25 to 75 words long. Look at previous issues of the magazine to see how these articles are laid out. Please use barbless hooks, or de-barb them.

Chances of acceptance of a fly-tying feature will be enhanced by the inclusion of handsome slides of the fishing situation the flies solve. If the flies imitate an insect, include a shot of the natural if possible, though we can often find an appropriate picture in our files.

Unless you're an expert at step photography, tie a hook to the level of each numbered step, leave the thread attached, and include these-one hook for each step, plus two finished flies-for our staff photographer to shoot. If you're an expert, include the hooks tied to each step, along with your photos of each step and the finished flies, so our photographer can shoot them if we deem this necessary.

Query letters. Each issue is planned from six months to a year in advance. Queried and approved articles, delivered on time and of the quality expected, find secure seats in the slot to which they've been assigned. Articles submitted without a query cannot be planned, though they might be accepted and then either assigned to a slot or to the waiting list for the next open slot. Your editors prefer to work from query letters, though if your work is not known to us, you can send it in, and we'll give it full consideration.

Each query should cover the following: subject of the proposed article, whether it's for the fly-fishing or fly-tying core, tentative title, brief outline, projected word count, sidebar ideas, and the extent of your expertise-tell us why you're the one to write this article. Keep queries to one page, at most two. If you have photos, send them and they'll help us make our decision. Always include a self-addressed stamped envelope (SASE).

E-mail queries will be considered, but they often print out awk-

wardly and therefore become strikes against you. Always send e-mail queries as a Word attachment. However, give yourself the best chance by submitting queries in an envelope, with an SASE. E-mail is becoming very undependable; with all the spam receieved by your editors, it's becoming a 50/50 chance, or even less, that we'll be able to sort out your message as important and open it. If you send us an e-mail and don't hear back, don't assume we've ignored you. Send us the same message by mail, and we'll be sure to get it and read it.

Round-Up. This news section of FTJ includes short conservation notes, legislative problems, regional issues, happy or unhappy news events, or any other news item related to fly-fishing and fly-tying. Word count is 200 to 800 words, depending on the demands of the subject. Round-Up pieces can be queried or submitted with an SASE. Photographic support makes a stronger presentation; please provide color slides, or call to discuss electronic files.

Photography. With each fly-fishing feature submitted, we'll be looking for one or two strong lead photos, plus several supporting shots. It's wise to submit photos from different views: wide angle, normal, telephoto, and close-up, in both vertical and horizontal formats. The better the lead photos and the mix of photos, the better your chance of acceptance. Use of a tripod is usually beneficial.

Use color slide film, 35mm or 2-1/4", the slower the film speed the better. We cannot use prints. Most pros use 100 ASA Fuji slide film as their standard. A selection of 20 slides with an article is minimal; 40 to 60 is better. Slides should be submitted in 20-slide plastic sheets, numbered consecutively, and captioned at the end of the article. Each caption can reinforce material covered in the article, or better yet mention new information. If people, fly patterns, fish, or insects are in the photo, please identify them by name, and if appropriate, Latin name.

We rarely use photographs submitted separate from articles, unless they are vertical shots sent for cover consideration. Always send an SASE with any photos.

Illustrations. We occasionally use artwork with articles. We'd like to know who is out there and willing to work on somewhat short notice. If you're interested, send a brief portfolio with SASE. We will return the portfolio, but will keep a file of artists to call when the need arises.

Manuscript preparation. Articles should be submitted in both hard copy-printed on paper-and on a 3-1/2" disk or a CD in Microsoft Word. The hard copy should have your name, address, phone, FAX, and e-mail address on the front page. The title of the article should start ten spaces down. **The hard copy must be double-spaced.** Your name, article title, and page number should be on the top of each subsequent page. At the end of each piece, add a short 2- 4-line bio about yourself.

The computer disk label should have your name, title of the piece, the program you've worked in, and whether you use a PC or Mac. **Place all information-text, bio, sidebars, captions, notes-in one file.**

Do not vary your text, headings, or anything: use one type size and style for everything from one end to the other, preferably Times New Roman 12 or Courrier New 12. No bold, no underlining, nothing to make it pretty. Simplicity, please!

The package. Every submission, queried or not, should arrive as a neat and orderly package containing the following: cover letter, hard copy of text and captions, disk, SASE, and stiffener to protect the photos and disk.

Payment. FTJ buys one-time rights and pays as soon as possible after publication of the issue that includes your work. Payment rates vary with length and quality of the piece, and the amount of work we have to do on it, or the photos we must buy to support it.

Fun. Please remember in your queries and submissions that fly-fishing is fun or should be, and that we'd like the magazine to reflect that important fact. Direct queries and submissions to the address below.

Categories: Fishing—Outdoors—Recreation

CONTACT: Dave Hughes, Editor
Material: All
CONTACT: Kim Koch, Associate Editor

Material: Any
Frank Amato Publications, PO Box 82112
Portland OR 97282
Phone: 503-653-8108
Fax: 503-653-8108
E-mail: dave@amatobooks.com or kim@amatobooks.com
Website: www.amatobooks.com

Food & Wine

Formal guidelines not available. Please read a number of issues to ascertain the publication's style and needs.

Send queries to address below.

Categories: Nonfiction—Cooking—Entertainment—Food/Drink

CONTACT: Submissions Editor
Material: All
1120 Ave of the Americas
New York NY 10036
Phone: 212-382-5618

Forester Communications

OUR PUBLICATIONS
- *MSW Management*
- *Erosion Control*
- *STORMWATER, The Journal for Surface Water Quality Professionals*
- *Grading & Excavation Contractor*

MSW Management—OUR AUDIENCE
MSW Management - selected in 1999 by the Solid Waste Association of North America as its official journal - has grown to become the preeminent journal focusing on public-sector municipal solid waste issues. It is well known throughout the industry and at all levels of government, looked upon by all as a fair and viable forum for ideas. Its departments and feature articles are informative, to the point, and readable, even when dealing with highly technical subjects.

ABOUT OUR AUDIENCE
MSW Management's audience is composed of solid waste professionals employed by local municipal governments (city/county/township), regional solid waste management authorities, and their engineers (both outside, independent, consulting engineers and those employed by the municipality). Our readers are responsible for all aspects of integrated solid waste management (source reduction, composting, recycling, incineration, landfilling, etc.). Over 20% of our readers are engineers and since the audience is made up entirely of working professionals in the field, you must assume that they have a high level of expertise and familiarity with your subject matter.

The prevailing perspective and the bulk of interviews, ascriptions, and quotes should belong to MSW managers and staff, or to private sector affiliates performing solid waste tasks. If you find yourself writing about non-municipal activities or people, take another look at the assignment and see if you're headed in the right direction

GENERAL GUIDELINES
Think like your audience. Put yourself in an MSW manager's boots. What makes this subject important enough that you would take time out from your busy schedule to stop and read the article? Where's the hook? How best to bait it, cast it, troll it, and sink it? When you've satisfied yourself on those scores, you're ready to write.

Engage your reader. Leave no doubt in anyone's mind who you are writing to and why it is important. Rivet your full attention on your readers and drag them into the middle of your subject, address them directly and personally.

Don't shy away from technical aspects of your subject. Make your readers "reach," but never "write down" to them. Aim high in your expectations of the reader's knowledge and expertise.

Also assume that your readers appreciate sound use of language or grammar. If the article is too simple or basic, we can't use it.

Identify yourself as a writer on assignment for MSW Management and conduct yourself and the interview in an open, friendly manner. Think about the article's appearance as you conduct your interviews. How might graphics underscore an important point? What may entice a browser to take the plunge? Gather as much graphic material as possible (photos, charts, illustrations, etc.). The more options our art director has, the better.

As far as rules are concerned, follow the latest version of The Chicago Manual of Style. We have a set of conventions of our own (see the Forester Style Guide), however, we'll apply them as appropriate leaving you to concentrate on more important matters.

If it is your intention to write for Forester Communications, please sign and date where indicated, acknowledging that you have read and understand the contents of this guide.

Name:_____

Date:_____

The above general guidelines have applicability to *Erosion Control*, *Grading and Excavation Contractor* and *Stormwater* magazines

Erosion Control—OUR AUDIENCE
Erosion Control is the premier journal for erosion and sediment control professionals. The official journal of the International Erosion Control Association since 1994, it is the most widely read and highly respected magazine in its sector.

Our audience is composed of planning, engineering, construction, development, operations, and regulatory professionals employed in activities involving erosion and/or sediment control. As the audience is made up entirely of working professionals in the field, you should assume a high level of expertise and familiarity with your subject matter.

The prevailing perspective and the bulk of interviews, ascriptions, and quotes should belong to direct participants in erosion or sediment control activities. If you find yourself writing about nonparticipants, take another look at the assignment and see if you're headed in the right direction

GENERAL GUIDELINES
Think like your audience. Put yourself in an erosion control professional's boots.

Identify yourself as a writer on assignment for Erosion Control and conduct yourself and the interview in an open, friendly manner.

For further information, please refer to the General Guidelines for *MSW Management*.

STORMWATER
Around the world, awareness of the importance of surface water quality is rapidly increasing. The impacts on surface water quality made by society have been made abundantly clear, and you are the person with primary responsibility for complying with the increasing rules and regulations addressing these issues. In the United States, you are probably the person responsible for NPDES Phase 2 compliance and the other significant regulatory and business changes that impact us all.

Before *STORMWATER, The Journal for Surface Water Quality Professionals*, there has been no single publication written specifically for you - the professional involved with surface water quality issues, protection, projects, and programs. Regardless of whether you work for the government, a watershed protection agency, or a private business, a single professional publication written to assist you in your day to day work has not existed before. The need or such a magazine has never been stronger.

STORMWATER, the Journal for Surface Water Quality Professionals. If you're in stormwater, this is your magazine. Each issue, each article, each dot of ink on each page (and each pixel on your monitor) is put there specifically to meet your professional needs. We don't write for all engineers, or every municipal official, or all contractors, or the entire environmental industry. Just those with specific surface water quality responsibilities.

Every interview, every article, every news item, every facet of editorial is focused on various aspects of stormwater programs and surface water quality improvement or protection operations and is edited for that specific reader. This is a practical business journal, edited for professionals with an increasingly complex job to do. We endeavor to assist you in meeting your day-to-day professional responsibilities. With technology advancing rapidly and legislation changing almost daily, the need for STORMWATER is stronger than at any time in the past.

STORMWATER, the Journal for Surface Water Quality Professionals, is available on a complimentary basis for qualified readers.

Grading & Excavation Contractor—OUR AUDIENCE

Grading & Excavation Contractor focuses on the management of grading, excavating, site preparation and earthmoving projects, as well as the equipment and tools involved. Topics include Business Management Methods & Practices, Equipment Acquisition & Maintenance, Regulatory Updates, Insurance & Financial Matters, and other relevant issues. As our audience consists of working professionals in the field, you should assume a high level of expertise and familiarity with your subject matter.

The prevailing perspective and the bulk of interviews, ascriptions, and quotes should belong to participants in grading and excavation activities. If you find yourself writing about nonparticipants, take another look at the assignment and see if you're headed in the right direction.

GENERAL GUIDELINES

Think like your audience. Put yourself in an grading or excavation contractor's boots.

Identify yourself as a writer on assignment for Grading & Excavation Contractor and conduct yourself and the interview in an open, friendly manner.

For further information, please refer to the General Guidelines for *MSW Management.*

Categories: Nonfiction—Business—Environment—Trade: Construction

CONTACT: MSW Management Editor
Material: Submissions for *MSW Management*
CONTACT: Erosion Control Editor (eceditor@forester.net)
Material: Submissions for *Erosion Control*
CONTACT: STORMWATER Editor (sweditor@forester.net)
Material: Submissions for STORMWATER
CONTACT: Grading & Excavation Contractor Editor
(geceditor@forester.net)
Material: Submissions for *Grading & Excavation Contractor*
5638 Hollister Ave., Ste 301
Santa Barbara CA 93117
Phone: 805-681-1300
Fax: 805-681-1311
E-mail: msweditor@forester.net
Website: www.forester.net

Fourteen Hills
The SFSU Review

About Us

Since its inception in 1996, *Fourteen Hills* has held an impressive reputation within international literary magazines for publishing the highest-quality innovative poetry, fiction, short plays, and literary nonfiction. Representing a culmination of one of the best-known Creative Writing departments in the United States, the bi-annual journal is committed to presenting a great diversity of experimental and progressive work by emerging and cross-genre writers, as well as by award-winning and established authors.

Proud of (and part of) the vibrant literary heritage of the west coast and the San Francisco Bay area, *Fourteen Hills* is honored to be an active participant in the contemporary creative community. As a nonprofit press, its staff, editors, and contributors bring readers of the

journal some of the most exciting offerings of independent literature-from the postmodern to the traditional, *Fourteen Hills* is a testimony to the fact that independent, innovative, experimental literature is not only alive and thriving, but also overflowing with ebullience, energy, and an irresistible embrace of what comes next.

Submissions

We accept submissions of fiction, short-shorts, poetry, short drama, and creative non-fiction in traditional and experimental styles, as well as camera-ready artwork to be considered for upcoming issues. The editors especially encourage new and emerging writers, while continuing to publish award winning poets and established writers. Writers may submit up to five selections of poetry, and up to three selections of prose or drama; word count may not exceed 4,000 words per piece. Artwork should be camera-ready, and fit the dimensions of our cover design. Manuscripts and artwork MUST be accompanied by a self-addressed, stamped envelope. We accept simultaneous submissions; however, please note that we do not accept unsolicited electronic submissions at this time. The deadline for the Fall issue is around September 1, and February 1 for the Spring issue; please contact us for precise dates. We do not read unsolicited manuscripts from March through July. Response time can be anywhere from two weeks to four months. The Editors strongly suggest that writers interested in submitting familiarize themselves with our editorial style and vision.

Categories: Fiction—Nonfiction—Drama—Gay/Lesbian—Literature—Poetry—Short Stories—Women's Fiction

CONTACT: Editor-in-Chief
Material: All Other
CONTACT: Poetry Editor
Material: Poetry
CONTACT: Fiction Editor
Material: Fiction
CONTACT: Drama Editor
Material: Drama
Dept. of Creative Writing
San Francisco State University
1600 Holloway Ave.
San Francisco CA 94132-1722
Phone: 415-338-3083
Fax: 415-338-7030
E-mail: hills@sfsu.edu
Website: mercury.sfsu.edu/~hills

France Today

INFORMATION FOR FREELANCE JOURNALISTS/PHOTOGRAPHERS

FORMAT: 32-40 page magazine of French travel and culture written entirely in English. Sold nationally and largely by subscription. Published 10 times a year. Circulation: 6,000.

READERSHIP: Highly educated (over 90% college educated, more than 50% with graduate degrees), upscale (over 50% of households have income exceeding $80,000 per annum) and well-traveled. Most *FRANCE TODAY* readers have already visited France several times and are familiar with popular tourist attractions in Paris and throughout the country. Many have traveled extensively and return on a regular basis. Close to 50% say they visit France once a year. Almost two-thirds stay a minimum of one month.

CONTENTS: Feature articles are open to freelancers. Articles on travel, sociocultural issues and trends are given top priority. Three features are published per issue, one a travel story (with an insider's perspective), one a sociocultural piece, and one a historical article. Best buys and value per dollar/euro should be stressed in travel articles, which should give readers an informed sense of place and history. Our readers are highly knowledgeable about France and we try to explore in depth the little-known parts of the familiar or make familiar the little-known (the Forest of Brocéliande, the Ile de Ré). Participatory travel stories (canoeing, paragliding, sailing, cooking, birdwatching, etc.) are encouraged. Besides our features, we also look for first-person essays—on general topics (e.g., "Why do the French think they are logical?") and more personal appreciations, such as "Mon Quartier/My City."

STYLE: *FRANCE TODAY* is "The insider's guide to France—in English." Our regular contributors are highly accomplished professionals with longtime experience in France. Our tone is opinionated and personal, informed up to the minute. Specific "how to" or "where to" information for North American travelers is featured, such as "How to buy real estate in France," "How to plan a winter skiing vacation in the Alps," "How to arrange a wine-tasting visit to a château in Bordeaux," etc.

LENGTH: Travel and sociocultural features are approximately 1400 words.

RATES: According to length, originality and style. Travel & sociocultural articles are $100-$300. Payment 30 days after publication.

PHOTOGRAPHS: Query first. We are looking for quality photographs, not snapshots of what I did on my vacation. Payment $25 per published photo.

USE OF ARTICLES: FrancePress reserves the right to use articles printed in France Today on any FrancePress Web site.

SUBMISSIONS: Query first, via e-mail preferably. Articles to be submitted by e-mail. We are not responsible for unsolicited manuscripts.

RETURNS: Unsolicited articles and photos will only be returned when accompanied by a self-addressed, stamped envelope (with adequate postage for weight and destination).

KILL FEES: Only commissioned will be paid a kill fee of 33%.

Categories: Nonfiction—Culture—Travel

CONTACT:
Editor
Material: All
944 Market St #210
San Francisco CA 94115
Phone: 415-981-9088
Fax: 415-981-9177
E-mail: editorial@francetoday.com

Freelance Writer's Report

Since its first issue (March 1982), FWR's main purpose has been to help serious, professional freelance writers—whether full-time or part-time—improve their earnings and profits from their editorial businesses.

The bulk of our content is market news and marketing information—how to build a writing/editing business, how to maximize income. But we don't need the basics, like how to write a query letter. It's critical to remember our target audience.

Our target readers — members of Cassell Network of Writers — are established writers. Many of them have published hundreds of magazine articles, several books, and/or worked for dozens of business clients. We are interested only in information these writers can learn from and put to immediate use.

Because FWR is a newsletter and not a magazine, we do not use lengthy, magazine-style articles. We also do not use jumps, so our length is restricted to one page—and shorter than that is even better. Our readers are busy professionals; they hardly have time to read a newsletter at all. So we try to provide only the meat of the information, none of the fat. For example, we like bulleted copy and lists. Because our format is so specific, most of our freelance material is written by our readers—they know what we've already covered recently and how we want information presented.

We pay 10 cents per edited word; a check is sent along with a copy of the issue in which the item appears. We lease only one-time rights. Because we use outside material for "filling in" the empty columns after our regular market columns and in-house material is laid out, it can be several months before a spot the right size becomes available for an outside piece.

Queries—e-mail or regular mail with SASE—are OK, but because we have more use for shorter material, it usually makes more sense to send in the completed piece. E-mail here is preferred because we don't have to rekey it or scan it. We usually respond within a few days.

For a sample back issue, e-mail your name and address; for a current issue, send $4 to CNW Publishing, PO Box A, North Stratford NH 03590 (the $4 can be applied toward a subscription if you decide to join CNW within 30 days of receiving the isssue).

E-mail queries or manuscripts to submission@writers-editors.com.

Contributor Guidelines for writers-editors.com

We have not yet purchased outside material, but plan to begin doing so sometime over next several months. See our website for guidelines, payment policies, and other pertinent details.

In the meantime, if you have an article or tips of interest to freelance writers or book authors, and would like us to consider posting some or all of them in exchange for mention of your book or website or other item of interest to our visitors, plus links to where people can learn more about your products and services, email Dana Cassell at contributor@writers-editors.com

Categories: Writing

CONTACT: Dana K. Cassell, Editor
Material: All
CNW Publishing
PO Box A
North Stratford NH 03590-0167
E-mail: contributor@writers-editors.com (writers-editors.com submissions)
E-mail: submission@writers-editors.com (Queries or manuscripts)
Website: www.writers-editors.com

The Freeman
Ideas on Liberty

We welcome the opportunity to consider thoughtful articles exploring the principles underlying a free society: private property, the rule of law, voluntary exchange,

individual rights, morality, and responsibility, and limitations on power. We publish both scholarly and popularly written nonfiction articles.

Although a necessary part of the literature of freedom is the analysis of collectivist and interventionist errors, we emphasize the positive case for freedom. We advocate self-improvement rather than compulsory reform of others. We avoid name- calling and partisan, electoral politics. We do not advocate political action as a cure for problems caused by government intervention.

Preparation
• Query before submitting articles and book reviews.
• Articles should be submitted via e-mail, in Word (or WordPerfect) format. Include the author's name, address, telephone number, e-mail address, Social Security number, and a sentence or two that we may use to identify the author to our readers. (If electronic submission is impossible other arrangement may be made.)
• Suggested manuscript length: 1,200-2,000 words.
• Facts and quotations must be fully documented.
• We prefer to purchase full rights to an article, but we will withhold reprint rights at the author's request. By submitting an article, the author warrants that he has unencumbered rights to it and that it has not been submitted, accepted, or published elsewhere. Authors are paid on publication.

Send manuscripts and queries by snailmail or email to the address below. —December 1, 2003

Categories: Nonfiction, Biography (of entrepreneurs)—Economic (Free-market)— Theory—Economy—History—Libertarian—Politics (public-issue analysis)

CONTACT: Sheldon Richman, Editor
Material: All
Foundation for Economic Education
Irvington-on-Hudson, NY 10533
E-mail: freeman@fee.org

Freeskier

FREESKIER is a magazine for, about, and by skiers who love the sport of skiing and the skiing lifestyle. Our editorial focus is everything new school: freeskiing, moguls, terrain park, halfpipe skiing and anything else that is young, hip and fun in skiing. From features on the best ski-town brewpubs to the hottest mountain outerwear, we emphasize the skiing lifestyle as well as the sport itself fin our editorial mix. Readers are skiiers ages 18-29, about three-quarters male and dedicated skiiers.

FREESKIER provides user-friendly, service-oriented editorial that speaks directly to our readers — informing them about the sport, inspiring them to get out on the mountains, enticing them to get involved in the new school of skiing.

Most features run about 2,000 — 3,000 words. Departments include Cliff Notes, the front-of-the-book section covering news, issues, humorous anecdotes and anything else related to the skiing lifestyle. Try anything new, funky and short for this section.

Most stories are 250 words or less. We are always looking for humorous, newsy pieces here. Savoir Faire, a regular 1,500 word feature, explores how to do ski towns like a local. Writers must know the towns inside and out. Untameable Terrain highlights some of the most difficult lift-serviced terrain in the nation.

Queries should present a clear, original and well-conceived focus, and stories must be tailored specifically for our audience and the tone of our magazine. While we are always willing to review people's ideas, new/unpublished writers have the best chance by writing for one of our departments. Queries will be accepted by mail or email. Phone queries will be hung up on. If you want a reply, include a SASE — period.

Please include at least two relevant clips with queries. Unsolicited manuscripts are welcome. Payment is negotiable. For a copy of the magazine, send us a check for $3.50 made out to Storm Mountain Publishing.

Categories: Nonfiction—Lifestyle—Recreation—Sports/Recreation—Travel

CONTACT: Patrick Crawford, Senior Editor
Material: All
1630 30th St.
Boulder CO 80302
Phone: 877-LIVE2SKI or 877-548-3275
Fax: 303-449-2427
E-mail: patrick@freeskier.com
Website: www.freeskier.com

French Forum

French Forum is a journal of interest to all scholars and students of French and Francophone literatures. It accepts articles of all critical persuasions on all periods and genres of French and Francophone literary production. Founded by Virginia and Raymond La Charité, *French Forum* is produced by the French Section of the Department of Romance Languages at the University of Pennsylvania. All articles are peer reviewed by an editorial committee of external readers. The journal has a book review section which highlights a selection of important new publications in the field.

French Forum is available electronically through Project MUSE.

Subscription Information
Triannual
ISSN 0098-9355
Individuals $35.00
Institutions $80.00
Single issue $25.00

For foreign subscriptions please add $15.00. Payment must accompany order. Make checks payable to University of Nebraska Press and mail to:
University of Nebraska Press
233 N 8th St
Lincoln, NE 68588-4555
or call: 1-800-755-1105 U.S. Orders and customer service.

Submission Information
French Forum is a journal of French and Francophone literature. It publishes articles in English and French on all periods and genres in the field and welcomes a multiplicity of approaches. Submissions must meet the following requirements:
4,000 to 6,000 words submit
3 copies (a word count should be included)
Prepare according to Chicago Manual of Style, 14th edition.
Please do not send diskettes

French Forum observes a "blind reading" policy. The author's name should not appear on the manuscripts. Receipt of articles will only be acknowledged if a post-card or an e-mail address is included.

Send a self-addressed envelope and sufficient postage to permit the return of your article.

Categories: Fiction—Nonfiction—Book Reviews—History—Language—Literature

CONTACT: Editors
Material: Articles and books
Dept. of Romance Languages
University of Pennsylvania
Philadelphia PA 19104-6305
Website: www.nebraskapress.unl.edu/journals.html

Fresh Cut
The Magazine for Value-Added Produce

Editorial Focus: *Fresh Cut* magazine is written for people in the food business who manufacture, sell, use or distribute packaged salads or cut and packaged fresh fruits and vegetables. Articles can be written for actual produce processors as well as retail grocers, restaurant or food service operators, and others who handle or distribute these products.

Article Length: No more than 1,200 to 1,500 words, 1,000 words for guest opinion.

Suitable Articles

Feature stories: Again, fresh-cut processors can be the focus of such articles, but retailers who have had success with specific items or with their fresh-cut section in general and food service operators who use fresh-cut products successfully can also be feature material.

New Technology: Articles can include new equipment, packaging, supplies, processes or other advances which make the world a better place for processors or users of fresh-cut products.

Eating Trends: Time is the commodity of the 90s and articles illustrating how consumers are turning to convenient, healthful fresh-cut produce items are meat for *Fresh Cut* magazine. Any new and exciting fresh-cut product is fair game. Reports on health and nutrition as they relate to fresh fruits and vegetables and the 5 A Day Program are also of interest. Even information from other magazines can be reported or quoted in *Fresh Cut*.

Meeting Reports: Speakers who address topics related to fresh-cut produce often relate important news for our readers. Reporting their messages makes excellent copy.

Food Safety: Articles could include sanitation techniques, sanitary plant and equipment design and even keeping the "cold chain" intact to assure optimum product shelf life.

Categories: Nonfiction—Business—Food/Drink—Technology—Produce & Processing

CONTACT: Submissions Editor
Material: All
417 N. 20th Ave.
Yakima WA 98902
Phone: 509-248-2452
Fax: 509-248-4056
E-mail: brent@freshcut.com
Website: www.freshcut.com

Friction Zone

Friction Zone is a monthly motorcycle publication with a circulation of 33,000 copies. It is distributed throughout Arizona, California, Idaho, Nevada, Oregon, Utah, and Washington. Our editorial focus is on local travel, motorcycle information, and rider safety.

In each issue we publish at least 15 feature articles ranging from 800 to 1500 words in length. We assign stories based on writers' proposals. We do not accept unsolicited submissions, and we do not accept any first-person (using the words "I" or "me") writing. We are most interested in creative writers whose work requires minimal editing.

Before you submit article ideas, please read several issues of Friction Zone to familiarize yourself with our requirements. Back issues are available for $4.50 an issue. We rarely accept proposals that are not accompanied by a writing sample.

We pay $.20/published word (except for travel articles) and $15/photo/illustration upon publication for first North American rights. We do not pay for news items, product or press releases, or product reviews. Payment is always made upon publication, and no payment is made if we decide not to publish the article. The only reason we would not publish an assigned article is because a writer does not follow the guidelines or cannot write.

Articles are only accepted via e-mail and should be sent to the editor. Submitted articles must include writer's name, address, social security number, telephone number, fax, and e-mail address.

Photos or slides must be taken with 100 speed film (slide or print). Negatives must accompany photos. Digital photos are preferred provided they are submitted at a minimum of 3 megapixels. All photos must be accompanied by captions. A model release must be submitted for any picture that shows a recognizable person unless you are covering a newsworthy event.

We reserve the right to edit and restructure your material to ensure that it fits with the writing style of Friction Zone. When time permits, we will work with you throughout the editing process.

Submitting your story to Friction Zone constitutes an express warranty that the material is original and there is no infringement on the rights of others. Simultaneous submissions are not accepted. Please do not query us using a shotgun approach. If we accept your query only to find out you have given it to someone else, no further queries will be accepted.

Features

Friction Zone contains several monthly features that are provided by freelance writers. We are only interested in publishing articles that fit into those features. Features that are open to freelance writers outside of California include Cover Story, Health Zone, Motorcycles 101, Pulp Friction, Special Feature, and Spotlight. All features are open to freelance writers/riders who live in California. You must ride your own street bike to be a contributor to Friction Zone. Regular features that are provided by freelance writers include:

Cover Story

Typically 1200-1500 words. This feature offers the greatest amount of freedom for writers because the only requirement is that it be related to motorcycling. Some examples of past Cover Stories include: How Helmets are Tested, The True Story of Easy Rider, Harley-Davidson's 100th Anniversary Party, Mentoring Done Right, California's Motorcycle Awareness Program, How to Increase Event Participation, and Making Better Travel Photos. Unless you are a professional photographer, we will provide the cover artwork to go along with your article. If you supply an acceptable cover photo (must be 6 Megapixel if it's digital, otherwise the original negative or slide must be submitted), you will be paid $100 for its use.

Discover Arizona, California, Idaho, Nevada, Oregon, Utah, or Washington

Typically 1200 words. A review of a motorcycle-friendly hangout and surrounding roads. Please contact the editor for specific guidelines and a list of roads and eateries already reviewed.

Health Zone

Typically 1000 words. A health issue is discussed along with how it relates to a motorcyclist. Examples of topics previously published in this section include Hyperthermia, Treating Road Rash, Managing an Accident Scene, Tattoo Removal, Accidents and Memory Loss, and Hypothermia. Health Zone typically contains tables, graphs, and photos that enhance the reader's ability to understand the topic while making the layout more appealing. Credentials may be required depending on your topic. Please contact the editor for specific guidelines and a complete list of health-related topics already covered.

Pulp Friction

Typically 700 words. A review of a motorcycle-related book. Please contact the editor for specific guidelines and a list of books already reviewed.

Road Trip

Typically 1500 words. A review of a place of lodging, fine dining establishment, and roads in Arizona, California, Idaho, Nevada, Oregon, Utah, or Washington. Please contact the editor for specific guidelines and a list of roads and places already reviewed.

Special Feature

Typically 1000 words. A Special Feature usually concerns a current event in the sport of motorcycling and must be of interest to riders in the western United States. Past stories include Update on Assembly Bill 1200, Helmet Testing Results, and San Francisco Motorcyclists Take a Stand on Parking. Guidelines are given after acceptance of your idea.

Spotlight

Typically 1000 words. A Spotlight highlights a special figure, event, or item that is of interest to motorcyclists in the western United States. Past Spotlights have included The Gourmet Biker, Motorcycling HAMS, Italian Motorcycle Exhibit in Santa Paula, and the National Motorcycle Patrol. We do not spotlight dealerships, and we do not routinely cover events. When we do "cover" an event, it is to publish information about the event before it happens in order to bring interest to the event just prior to its occurrence. Guidelines are given after acceptance of your idea.

Categories: Nonfiction—Automobiles—Motorcycles

CONTACT: Editor, Friction Zone
60166 Hop Patch Spring Rd
Mountain Center CA 92561
Phone: 877-713-9500

Frontiers
A Journal of Women Studies

About Us

Frontiers: A Journal of Women Studies began publication in 1975. The original Editorial Collective chose the title to symbolize the new territories of feminist scholarship and accomplishment the journal planned to explore. Since 1975, however, understandings of "frontiers" have changed. The current editorial staff of Frontiers completely rejects any one-sided, expansionist, and racist use of the term. What we mean by "frontiers" are zones of interaction between two or more different cultures. Following Gloria Anzaldúa, we revision "frontiers" from boundary to borderlands, a concept especially suitable to our interdisciplinary and multicultural feminist purpose. With this definition in mind, Frontiers encourages submissions in all areas of women's studies that cross and/or reexamine boundaries, and that explore the diversity of women's lives as shaped by factors such as race, ethnicity, class, sexual orientation, and region.

Frontiers: A Journal of Women Studies invites you to submit articles, personal essays, photo essays, art, short stories, and poetry Submissions should be sent blind, in triplicate, with a cover letter.

Submission Guidelines

Frontiers is published three times a year at the University of Nebraska Press under the editorship of Sue Armitage and the Frontiers Editorial Collective of Washington State University, Pullman, Washington. The Frontiers Editorial Collective includes Delia D. Aguilar, Mary Bloodsworth, Jo Hockenhull, Linda Kittell, Yolanda Flores Niemann, Marian Sciachitano, Shawn Michelle Smith, Noël Sturgeon, Karen Weathermon, and Amy Wharton. The Collective is joined by a distinguished roster of contributing editors. Frontiers has published feminist scholarship and literary works since 1975.

Frontiers: A Journal of Women Studies is a juried publication committed to the discussion of the full variety of women's lives as they are shaped, for example, by such factors as gender, race, class, and sexual orientation. We seek papers that explore this variety through interdisciplinary scholarly work as well as literary and artistic contributions. We encourage unsolicited submissions. We are especially interested in work that places its topic within a broader literary, historical, political, social, or cultural framework and that argues a thesis encompassing more than a single text or event.

All textual submissions must be word-processed, double-spaced, unstapled, and accompanied by a title page with the author's name. No other page in the manuscript should identify the author. Two copies of the text should accompany the original. One set of visual materials is sufficient and slides are preferred. Art should be identified only by title, medium, and number. A list of all work sent, which includes the artist's name and address, should accompany the submission. Artists are responsible for insuring work, and only copies of originals (35mm slides or black and white photos) should be submitted for editorial review. Most published work will be in black and white.

If you want your submission returned, please provide a self-addressed, stamped envelope with correct postage. Scholarly articles must follow *The Chicago Manual of Style*, 14th edition, for text and endnotes. Permissions are the responsibility of the author.

Rights and Payment

Manuscripts are judged by the members of the Editorial Collective and by readers who have competence in the applicable field(s). This initial process usually requires three months. If the article is accepted for publication, we reserve the right to edit and/or revise it, in consultation with the author, in accordance with our space limitations and editorial guidelines. Contributors receive two copies of the issue in which their work appears.

Copyright for published material belongs to the Frontiers Editorial Collective, Inc. We do not consider previously published material or work under consideration by other journals.

Correspondence regarding editorial matters should be sent to the address below.

Categories: Nonfiction—Alternate Life-style—Feminism—Gay/Lesbian—Hispanic—History—Multicultural—Women's Fiction—Women's Issues—Scholarly

CONTACT: Managing Editor
Material: All
Women's Studies Program
PO Box 644007
Pullman WA 99164-4007
Phone: 509-335-7268
Fax: 509-335-4377
E-mail: frontier@wsu.edu

Fun for Kidz

Every *Fun For Kidz* contributor must remember we publish only six issues a year, which means our editorial needs are extremely limited.

It is obvious that we must reject far more contributions than we accept, no matter how outstanding they may seem to you or to us.

With that said, we would point out that *Fun For Kidz* is a magazine created for boys and girls from 6 to 13 years, with youngsters 8, 9, and 10 the specific target age. The magazine is designed as an activity publication to be enjoyed by both boys and girls on the alternate months of *Hopscotch* and *Boys' Quest* magazines.

Our point of view is that every child deserves the right to be a child for a number of years before he or she becomes a young adult.

As a result, *Fun For Kidz* looks for activities that deal with timeless topics, such as pets, nature, hobbies, science, games, sports, careers, simple cooking, and anything else likely to interest a child Each issue revolves around a theme. You may request a theme list by sending in a self-addressed, stamped envelope.

Writers

We are looking for lively writing that involves an activity that is both wholesome and unusual. We are looking for articles around 500 words as well as puzzles, poems, cooking, carpentry projects, jokes, riddles, crafts, and other activities that complement the theme. Articles that are accompanied by good photos are far more likely to be accepted than those that need illustrations.

We will entertain simultaneous submissions as long as that fact is noted on the manuscript. Computer printouts are welcome if they are (as all submissions should be) double-spaced.

Fun For Kidz prefers to receive complete manuscripts with cover letters, although we do not rule out query letters. We do not answer submissions sent in by fax or e-mail. All submissions must be accompanied by a self-addressed, stamped envelope, with sufficient postage.

We will pay a minimum of five cents a word for both fiction and nonfiction, with additional payment given if the piece is accompanied by appropriate photos or art. We will pay a minimum of $10 per poem or puzzle, with variable rates offered for games, carpentry projects, etc.

Fun For Kidz buys first American serial rights and pays upon publication. It welcomes the contributions of both published and unpublished writers.

Sample copies are available for $6.00 within the US & $7.00 outside the US. All payment must he in US. funds. A complimentary copy will be sent each writer who has contributed to a given issue.

Photographers

We use a number of black and white photos inside the magazine, most in support of articles used. Payment is $5-10 per photo.

Artists

Most art will be by assignment, in support of features used. We are anxious to find artists capable of illustrating stories and features and welcome copies of sample work, which will remain on file. Our inside art is pen and ink. We pay $35 for a full page and $25 for a partial page.

There's one more thing.

Fun For Kidz is a new publication. It is the companion to Boys' Quest, and Hopscotch. Like Hopscotch and Boys' Quest, the issues each revolve around a them. We often choose new themes as the result of a submission on a topic we haven't covered. We work far into the future. If you don't receive a quick response on your submissions, we are holding it and giving it serious consideration. We strive to treat all of our contributors and their work with respect and fairness. We are always in need of cute and clever recipes, well-written and illustrated crafts, riddles, and jokes.

Categories: Fiction—Nonfiction—Animals—Children

CONTACT: Marilyn Edwards, Editor
Material: Any
CONTACT: Virginia Edwards, Associate Editor
Material: Any
PO Box 227
Bluffton OH 45817-0227
Phone: 419-358-4610
Fax: 419-358-5027
Website: www.funforkidz.com

Funny Times

Dear Writer/Cartoonist Person,

Thanks for your interest in the *Funny Times*. We are currently looking for material and welcome your submissions. We are especially interested in written humor columns, interviews, book reviews, stories, and 1-2 page comics.

Here are some guidelines:

• Your submissions should be funny. If it isn't funny, don't bother sending it to us.

• Most of our material is reprinted from other sources or syndicated. We welcome submission of previously published material.

• Our pay rates vary, but in all cases are pitifully small. We pay upon publication. Figure about $25 for a single panel cartoon and $60 for a humor essay.

• We buy one-time rights; all other rights stay with the copyright holder.

• Send copies only, no originals. We cannot promise you will ever receive back anything you send us.

• Include a SASE; if not, you can simply assume you've been rejected unless we call or write you.

• There are only two of us reading these, and sometimes it takes a long time to get through it all. Don't expect a lightning-fast response and don't bug us.

• Send only complete work. No query letters.

Now get to work! Make us laugh!

Sincerely,

Raymond Lesser and Susan Wolpert, Co-editors

Categories: Cartoons—Humor—Satire—Humor

CONTACT: Submissions Editor
Material: All
2176 Lee Rd.
Cleveland Hts. OH 44118
Phone: 800-811-5267
Fax: 216-371-8696
E-mail: FT@funnytimes.com
Website: www.funnytimes.com

Fur-Fish-Game

For more than 75 years, *FUR-FISH-GAME* has been a monthly magazine dedicated to serious outdoorsmen of all ages. We purchase 150 manuscripts a year. Topics include hunting, trapping, freshwater fishing, predator calling, camping, boating, woodcrafting, conservation and related outdoor topics.

We mostly buy feature articles of a "how-to" or informative nature. We also purchase real-life tales of wilderness adventure and survival. Stories of historic or nostalgic value are also considered, as are unique personal experiences and an occasional personality profile. We buy few "where to" stories and no book, video or product reviews.

We prefer articles with a specific slant or theme that explain how to hunt, trap or fish for species that are popular with the everyday outdoorsman. Articles about trapping, especially those of an instructional nature, are used throughout the year and are very popular with our readers. Other recommended topics include hunting dogs, living off the land, and do-it-yourself outdoor projects. **No fiction**, but will consider humor pieces based on real experiences. It is strongly recommended that writers familiarize themselves with the magazine before querying article ideas.

NO phone queries, please. Written queries need to explain the specific slant or angle that sets the story apart; unsolicited manuscripts may be reviewed at the editor's discretion. All manuscripts submitted on a speculation-only basis, unless otherwise agreed.

Solid photo or art support greatly enhances the value of a manuscript. Photos or slides should be submitted with manuscript and are purchased as a package (although we do buy some photos separately). We prefer color slides, black-and-white or color prints sized 5x7 or 8x10. A variety of photos is preferred, especially closeup shots that illustrate a particular aspect of the manuscript, and overall shots that set the "scene." Hand drawings may help to illustrate aspects that cannot be adequately shown photographically. These illustrations may be redone by our staff artist. All photos and artwork should be accompanied by caption information and the name of the photographer or artist. We do hold free-lance photos for separate use, paying $25 for each use.

Feature manuscripts should be 2,000-3,000 words. Shorter how-to, humor, and human interest articles also needed. All submissions should be typed and double-spaced, with page numbers and author's name on every page. If you prepare your manuscript on a computer and can enclose a CD, please do. If you want your manuscript or photos returned, they MUST be accompanied by a self-addressed stamped envelope.

Payment for feature length articles usually falls between $150 and $250, depending upon length, quality of photo support, quality of writing, originality, and importance to the magazine. We may pay more for manuscript packages of particular interest to our readers. Shorter articles generally pay less. *FUR-FISH-GAME* buys one-time rights to photos and first North American Serial Rights to all manuscripts–no manuscripts reprints or secondary rights considered. Payment is made upon acceptance, and bylines are given. All correspondence should be directed to Mitch Cox, editor.

Categories: Nonfiction—Animals—Ecology—Environment—Fishing—Outdoors—Recreation—Sports/Recreation

CONTACT: Mitch Cox, Editor
Material: All
2878 E. Main St.
Columbus OH 43209-9947

Futures Mysterious Anthology Magazine

FMAM considers itself a stepping stone for many younger writers as well as a magazine with tremendous variety and creative power for seasoned writers and artists. Please consider that many proudly show their family the content and use appropriate language. When in doubt, feel free to inquire. We nominate for the Pushcart Prize Award each year and are honored to do so; profanity will exclude a Pushcart nomination by their own rules.

We accept submissions via email only. Save your story in plain text and then insert it into the body of your email message. Do not use attachments—often they cannot be opened at this end. Please get into the habit of checking back here for any new guidelines or just to refresh yourself. Keep in mind that even if you have been featured in FMAM we expect all the information each time.

NOTICE: FMAM will be closed to story submissions from June 1st to August 1st and November 1st to January 10th each year. This closure is for story submissions only and does not include contests.

FOR ALL WORK Submitted:

Don't rely on your spellchecker; proofread your work! Give your name, address, email address, word count, along with the genre or subgenre at the TOP (we realize it is difficult to categorize many stories, but we want to give YOUR STORY the best chance by assigning it to editors who enjoy the kind of writing you do—and later, if accepted, tempt the readers!). "Include a brief tagline (twenty words or less) telling what your story is about." List these things, one under the other like an address, not in paragraph formation.

Under the title of your story please put YOUR NAME as you would like to see it in print.

Include a short third person bio. Limit your bio to 50 words or less (count them). The bio is a flash synopsis of your writing career. For example:

"Mary Writer teaches Physics at Arizona State University and writes fantasy tales in her spare time. Her stories have been printed in many prestigious magazines, including…"

IN ADDITION:

Use single spaced lines. One space between sentences, not two.

After each paragraph, skip one line. This includes dialogue. To let us know that you would like a one line scene BREAK, leave two lines.

To indicate italics, use the asterisk, thus: *word/sentence*. Again, use plain text, no underlining, bold print, accent marks, etc. These look nice on paper, but we are not looking at paper. Type THE END at the end of your story. This enables us to verify that your entire manuscript was received.

Fiction: Send the entire story. We publish up to 10,000 words on a regular basis.

Non-fiction: We seldom print non-fiction. If you feel your article fits with the tone of the magazine, send a query telling us about your idea. An example of what we are not using would be how to articles about writing, remember that we want *readers* who are not writers to read your stories, too.

Poetry Submission Guidelines: Because our editors are scattered around the world, we can no longer accept submissions via regular mail. Please submit electronically to: RCHildebrant@mwsc.edu .Write Poetry Submission on the subject line and paste your poems into the message box. Mark line breaks with a slash / at the end of the line since email programs can distort line breaks. Double space between stanzas. If your formatting is somewhat complicated, please send the poem as an attached file in Rich Text Format. You can save most word processed documents as .rtf by choosing it from the "Save" menu. If I have trouble reading your attachment, I will let you know. See website for poetry guidelines.

Artist Guidelines: FMAM is constantly looking for new creative people to illustrate our great fiction. If that's you, submit samples of your artwork to: babs@suspenseunlimited.net

You may send hard copies to the address below. DO NOT SEND ORIGINALS. Please always send SASE with proper postage, send a note telling us what you are interested in doing. We can give you a story to illustrate as a trial, just ask if you'd like this opportunity to show us your work.

I will accept email jpeg's if you send me a letter first and I agree to it.

Cover Artwork Guidelines:

All artwork for covers must be done up as CMYK 300 dpi/ppi tif/tiff images only. (DO NOT use RGB at all as this creates a problem with the rich black part of the image). Since we will be using two color covers (RED and BLACK), it is recommended, (by the printer), that you place the design elements on the black and magenta channels only.

Please contact Ardy at ardy@fantaseeworks.net for more information on the process we require.

CARTOONIST Guidelines:

We are actively in search of cartoon artists. Political especially! Life in the modern world, anything to do with mystery. Those and other areas.

Send a query letter first to: babs@suspenseunlimited.net

We want cartoons in a small format: black and white; maximum 300 dpi/ppi jpg; no larger that 5 inches x 5 inches; we will generally want them with a border but there are exceptions; put the artist's name on the left outside vertical line of the border. Please do not use fancy fonts/text as they do not print well.

Ask Babs about payment when you query.

Categories: Fiction—African-American—Alternate Life-style—Arts—Asian-American—Cartoons—Crime—Drama—Entertainment—General Interest—Government—Graphics—Horror—Human Rights—Language—Lifestyle—Literature—Men's Fiction—Mystery—Native American—Paranormal—Poetry—Politics—Satire—Science Fiction—Senior Citizen—Short Stories—Theatre—True Crime—Women's Fiction

CONTACT: Babs Lakey, Publisher
Material: Cartoons
CONTACT: Earl Staggs Fiction Editor
Material: Fiction
CONTACT: Andy Scott, Art Director
Material: Illustrations
3039 38th Ave South
Minneapolis MN 55406
Phone: 612-724-4023
E-mail: babs@fmam.biz
Website: www.fmam.biz

FUTURIFIC

Futurific Magazine

Futurific Inc., Foundation for Optimism, is a not-for-profit research and educational organization reporting its findings every month in *Futurific Magazine*. We highlight positive developments in all subject areas—everything from international affairs, science, technology, and finance, to all aspects of human interest. Emphasis is on accurately forecasting the future. Material submitted, text and/or graphics, should provide realistic forecasts and/or analysis of what the future will be.

FUTURIFIC welcomes book, software, CD-ROM, hardware, news reviews, and interviews providing they follow the guidelines listed above. Copy should be appropriate to the subject. Art work accompanying the submission, graphics, cartoons and illustrations are all useful.

Typically, writers retain full rights to their work and receive a number of copies of the issue in which their work appears under their byline. Based on the importance of their story, writers occasionally receive payment for their expenses. These conditions are negotiable.

FUTURIFIC accepts no responsibility for unsolicited queries, articles, photographs, short stories or poetry.

Submissions accepted on floppy diskettes, CDs or hard copy.

Categories: Nonfiction—Agriculture—Architecture—Automobiles—Aviation—Business—Careers—Computers—Economics—Education—Electronics—Engineering—Internet—Money & Finances—New Age—Politics—Science—Society—Energy—Public Policy—Technology—Space—Medicine

CONTACT: Submissions Editor
Material: All
305 Madison Ave.
New York NY 10165
Phone: 212-297-0502
Fax: 212-297-0502
E-mail: Key To NYC@aol.com

The Gaited Horse

Thank you for your interest in *The Gaited Horse*: The ONE Magazine FOR ALL Gaited Horses. We appreciate your efforts and offer these tips to help you in preparing your work for publication. Our mission is to promote gaited horses to the 'rest of the horse world'. Your work is vital in accomplishing this goal, so know that you are important to us.

Since most of our 'writers' are horse people first, and not professional writers, we encourage you to participate in TGH on the basis that you have something valuable to offer your fellow horsemen, and not to worry about dotting the 'i's or crossing the 't's. That's our job!

Again, thank you for considering TGH for your work. We consider that an honor. Should we have to decline your work, we will be as frank and clear as possible in explaining why. Should we accept your story, we will work with you in polishing it to the very best version possible.

Follow these suggestions to present a clear and intriguing story and we will do the rest.

Warmest Regards, RjHart-Poe, Editor

Writers: All gaited horse enthusiasts are welcome to submit articles or ideas to *The Gaited Horse*. We are most concerned with accurate, lively content from those with first hand experience. If you have a good story to tell we can help you turn it into a great article!

Submission: We encourage you to query through e-mail (editor@thegaitedhorse.com). If you do not get an acknowledgment within three working days, please send us a brief note. Occasionally, e-mail messages wind up in space.

Include a brief overview and an outline of the article within the body of an e-mail. State availability of photos. Please do not send attachments. Full manuscripts are also considered. We do not return submissions (or photos) sent by regular mail unless accompanied by a S.A.S.E. (Self-addressed, stamped envelope) ALLOW 2 WEEKS FOR RESPONSE.

Focus: We are looking only for material that relates directly to GAITED horses. Submissions must deal exclusively with one aspect of gaited horses, i.e. adding toe-weight to correct paciness, or on a broader topic that involves gaited horses as the central focus, i.e. evaluating yearlings, including how to pre-determine their gait of choice once under saddle. If you have an idea that seems appropriate, we are happy to help you develop it to fit our needs.

Style: Articles should sound professional and authoritative, yet engaging and conversational. Since we expect you, the author, to be the authority, quotes from other sources are not usually necessary. (The obvious exceptions being profile type stories, or interviews.) Begin with a catchy lead. Divide your story into digestible segments, usually 3 - 4, that can be sub-headed, either chronologically, according to climaxes in the story, or by increments in training, medical treatment or other

natural breaks in the article. Conclude, with a paragraph or two that pulls it all together. It is very effective to enter a 'problem' in your opening lead, and show how the content of the article 'solves' it in the conclusion.

Length:
Newsbits /Short news flashes: Approximately 50-300 words.
Departments: 500 to 1000 words.
Features: Full-length features run from 1500 to 2500 words.
Fillers: Brief bits of interest, from one to a few lines.

Photos: Most articles require accompanying photos. Providing these often affects acceptance of a story. TGH requires EXCELLENT photos. Consider these tips:

Unless the story concerns dirt, mistreatment, or some other angle that warrants it, horses should not appear unkempt. Among other things, TGH promotes the BEAUTY of gaited horses, so bear that in mind when choosing or preparing a subject for photographs.

Be aware of the setting of the photo, the background, color and lighting contrasts. The photo must first be high quality and attractive, and secondarily, illustrate some point of the story. No fence posts emerging from the horses belly, no extra legs, no cutting off ears, tail ends, or feet.

If possible, send more photos than you anticipate being used. A good selection, utilizing different angles, backgrounds, etc. is preferable.

Obtain a written statement from anyone in your photos giving permission to reproduce their photo in TGH. Exceptions are shows, public places, public trail rides, etc. where a 'reasonable expectation' of privacy does not apply. *The following is adequate:*

I NAME OF SUBJECT give my permission for YOUR NAME to release my photo for publication in *The Gaited Horse* magazine. Be sure it is signed by the subject and dated.

PLEASE NOTE: TGH does not offer compensation for photo subjects. Rarely do we pay for photos separate from manuscripts. It is the author's responsibility to arrange with subjects any compensation for their photos. Except for professional models, it is very unusual for photo subjects to demand compensation.

Originals: Never, never, NEVER send your only copy of a manuscript or photo to any magazine or publisher for consideration! Sometimes they cannot be returned to you, they may even be lost in the mail. If you do require photos be returned, please enclose a S.A.S.E. and we will make every effort to get them back to you promptly.

Liability and compensation: Submission of material infers that you are the sole legal owner of the material with all inherent rights to it, including the right to allow us to publish it. TGH shall not be held liable for any material which is misrepresented to us. Since many writers are more concerned with promoting their ideas or horses, than in monetary profit for their articles, compensation varies. When payment is required, we offer between $50 and $300 for full manuscripts, including any accepted photos.

Thank you for your interest in *The Gaited Horse*. We look forward to seeing your work!

Categories: Nonfiction—Animals—Outdoors

CONTACT: Submissions Editor
Material: All
4 Cadence, LLC
PO Box 3070
Deer Park WA 99006-3070
Phone: 509-276-4930 -or- 866-320-2233
Website: www.gaitedhorse.com

Game Developer

Game Developer magazine is by game developers, for game developers. No one in this industry can afford to develop in a vacuum. When we share our individual knowledge and experience, the whole industry benefits. *Game Developer* is constantly seeking out articles on cutting-edge game development techniques in the areas of graphics, AI, or network programming, audio design and engineering, art and animation, game design, quality assurance, and project management, written by those who know your challenges best: professional game developers.

Feature articles

Features are generally technical, on subjects ranging from programming, design, project management, art/animation, quality assurance, sound effects, and so on. The length of these articles is approximately 4000 words. Submit an article idea to the editors.

Postmortem

The Postmortem column is a look at a recently finished game you just worked on. Like a real-life postmortem, you talk about the goals of the game, and explain what went right and wrong during the development and roll out of the game. The length of this column is approximately 4000 words.

Soapbox

The Soapbox column, on the last page of the magazine, is your chance to rant on a topic relevant to the game development industry. Don't mince words when you talk about broken technologies, harmful industry trends, bad business practices, and so on. Just remember that there are libel laws! The length of this column is approximately 800 words.

Product Reviews

Game Developer reviews game development tools on a regular basis. It does not review games. If you are interested in writing product reviews, follow this link to get more information. Important: we do not accept unsolicited product review submissions. The length of product reviews is approximately 600 (for short reviews) to 1300 (for long reviews) words.

Also we gladly accept Letters to the Editor

Any views or opinions are solely those of the author and do not necessarily represent those of CMP Media.

The information transmitted is intended only for the person or entity to which it is addressed and may contain confidential and/or privileged material. If you are not the intended recipient of this message please do not read, copy, use or disclose this communication and notify the sender immediately. It should be noted that any review, retransmission, dissemination or other use of, or taking action or reliance upon, this information by persons or entities other than the intended recipient is prohibited.

Categories: Nonfiction—Arts—Computers—Engineering—Games—Graphics—Technical

CONTACT: Jennifer Olsen, Editor in Chief
Material: All
600 Harrison St.
San Francisco CA 94107
Phone: 415-947-6000
Fax: 415-947-6090
E-mail: jolsen@cmp.com
Website: www.gdmag.com

Garden and Hearth

Monthly magazine embracing family, home and garden, fitness and family finance.

Rights: The writer shall retain all rights to the work granting Garden and Hearth unlimited use.

Needs: All departments

Length: 500-1000 words

Payment: Garden and Hearth will pay $10.00 upon acceptance of manuscript through Paypal. The writer must have an email account.

How to Submit: Do not send attachments. Send completed submission to editor@gardenandhearth.com

Response Time: 4 weeks

Writer's Guidelines

Garden and Hearth publishing is offering $15.00 per 750 (est.) word article. Articles should be written in a web friendly format with a one paragraph introduction leading directly into the body which should consist of 5-7 direct paragraphs with bold headings if applicable. Payment is made upon acceptance regardless the intended publishing date.

Topics and Themes

We are looking for articles that fit the home, garden and family theme. We purchase articles based on the popularity of the subject matter and its ability to bring in advertising revenue.

Subject matter that does well are short "how-to" articles such as: "Ten Steps to Selling Your Home" or "How to Arrange Flowers." To keep content timely and fresh year round, try to avoid seasonal themes or speaking of the time of the year.

We currently are not accepting articles with a poetry or essay format.

Publishing Rights

We purchase the rights to publish your works on one or more of the Garden and Hearth Publishing properties. The writer retains all other rights to their works.

Submission Guidelines

Paste your completed manuscript into the body of an email and mail to submissions@gardenandhearth.com with freelance submission in the subject line. Our mail system automatically deletes attachments.

Don't forget to add your 3 line byline following the article. Bios with business information or links to other websites are not accepted.

Due to the number of submissions received each week please allow up to 4 weeks for a response.

Categories: Garden

CONTACT: Kim Simonovitch, Editor
E-mail: articleseditor@gardenandhearth.com
Website: www.gardenandhearth.com

Garden Railways

These notes are for those of you who have asked about the requirements for writing an article for *Garden Railways*, and for those of you who haven't inquired but have something interesting to contribute. People often feel they are not qualified to write, don't know how to write, or don't have enough experience. This is too bad because their reluctance deprives the hobby of their special knowledge.

Garden Railways is not a literary magazine. If you are unsure of spelling and syntax, as many of us are, don't worry. It is the editor's job to straighten out the kinks. Moral: Don't be shy. If you have something to say, say it.

Query letters

We have a large backlog of articles, and it is a good idea to drop us a note to make sure that the article you have in mind is not already in our files.

Putting an article together

Wondering how to put an article together? You might appreciate a tip that was helpful to us. "Tell 'em what you're gonna tell 'em, then tell 'em, then tell 'em what you told 'em." In other words, briefly introduce your subject by telling the reader the topic of your article in general terms. Then continue with the body, or meat, of the article. Finally, finish up with a short summary or concluding statement. Don't be too wordy. Write as you speak (pretend you're chatting with a neighbor). When you have finished, give your article to someone to read. Pay close attention to the parts they don't understand. You might have to rephrase these sections to make them clearer. Chances are if your reader understands something, so will everyone else.

You should consider the probable experience level of the reader. If your knowledge is highly specialized, then the inclusion of some background information may be in order before you progress to the main body of the article. Don't risk boring your readers, though, by assuming they know nothing and explaining every detail.

Keep in mind that no one's work will be rejected because of style. The goal here is to disseminate information on our favorite topic. We believe that everyone has something to contribute, regardless of his or her level of experience; even sharing a bad experience can help others.

Suggestions for articles

All of us like to read about other garden railways, and the general How-I-Did-It sort of articles are among the most popular. The best ones cover the following ground: the general idea or philosophy behind the railway; how it was planned; how it was constructed; how any special problems were overcome; the line's rolling stock, locomotives, and structures; landscaping considerations and plants, including things of unusual interest; family and friends' involvement; and the melding of multiple hobby pursuits. Finish up with a few words about the future of the railway.

Dealing with plants

An aspect of the hobby that we'd like to print more information on is one people seem particularly timid to write about. The creation of a small-scale landscape is a very vital part of building any garden railway, and our readers are increasingly asking for your ideas, as regional-specific as you can make them. Include a few sentences about the climate you live in. People in your geographic area or similar climatic zone will take special interest in what you have to say.

When you list the name of a favorite plant you've used, give us as much information off of the nursery's identification marker as you can. Common names (such as monkey flower or pussytoes) are easier to remember but also easy to confuse with other—often very different—plants that share a common name. Every plant, like every animal, has a Latin name, and that nomenclature is what tells us precisely what we're working with. If you have no source of Latin identification, try to give us some kind of description to go on, and if at all possible, send clear photos (snapshots are fine) to help us do a little detective work. This extra trouble is greatly appreciated by staff and readers. Consider including a brief mention of what unique quality a little plant has, to earn and keep its place on your railway. Again, relating a story about an unfortunate choice can be helpful to your readers.

Submitted form

An article may be submitted in any form that can be read. Ideally it should be typewritten, double-spaced, on one side of the sheet. You can also submit a computer disk (floppy, ZIP, or CD). If you send your text this way, please also send a hard copy. We can also accept manuscripts online in Word, ASCII, Quark Xpress formats, or simply pasted into the body of an e-mail letter sent to mhorovitz@gardenrailways.com. We have the capability of reading files created on both Macintosh and IBM-compatible computers.

Product reviews

In general, we write product reviews in-house. If you have a product you'd like to review, though, let us know about it. Chances are, we'd like to see it reviewed too. Please don't send unsolicited product reviews. We may not want them, or you may be wasting your time by duplicating work that has already been done but has not yet been published.

We are pleased to have a healthy backlog of articles, and we certainly appreciate all that has been sent in to us. If there is a surplus of articles on the same topic as yours, they will sit in the files until their turns come up, which sometimes takes a while. On the other hand, if we receive something that is particularly timely, we try to get it in sooner. Also, as mentioned before, articles that take less preparation on our part may be given priority, depending on our workload.

Payment

Payment will be made upon publication, at the rate of $15 per column (including drawings and photos), with a minimum payment of $75. For the cover photo you will receive $100. Sorry, but we are not set up to trade subscriptions for magazine contributions.

Categories: Hobbies

CONTACT: Submissions
Garden Railways Magazine
PO Box 460222
Denver CO 80246

Phone: 303-377-7785
Fax: 303-377-7785
E-mail: mhorovitz@gardenrailways.com
Website: www.trains.com

Gardening How-To

About *Gardening How-To*

Gardening How-To is the bimonthly publication of the National Home Gardening Club, headquartered in Minnetonka, Minnesota. As the primary benefit of membership in the Club, the magazine is available by mail only to Club members. The magazine aims to provide timely, informative, and inspiring editorial content that will appeal to avid home gardeners across the United States and Canada. Our audience of more almost 700,000 paid subscribers is 78 percent female, average age 51, intermediate skill level.

Queries

Most GHT articles are written by staff or assigned to writers previously published in the magazine. However, we encourage potential first-time writers for *Gardening How-To* to submit strong story ideas with a broad, practical appeal to our readers and with an emphasis on the "how-to" approach to gardening. We do not accept simultaneous submissions or unsolicited manuscripts, and we do not encourage telephone queries. Please query first via e-mail.

Familiarize yourself with the content and focus of the magazine before querying. To obtain a copy of the magazine, write to Sample Copy, *Gardening How-To*, 12301 Whitewater Drive, Minnetonka, MN 55343.

When suggesting seasonal material, keep in mind that issues are planned approximately 9 months prior to publishing.

Submit a one-page query including: a brief summary describing the article idea, purpose of the piece, and its value to readers; your qualifications to write the piece and nonreturnable published clips when appropriate; suggested length and date it could be finished; scouting slides or snapshots (need not be publication quality) if applicable; your mailing address, daytime phone number, and e-mail address.

Manuscripts

All manuscript submissions from accepted queries are received on speculation. An accepted query does not guarantee purchase of the manuscript. We reserve the right to reject any manuscript at any stage.

We will respond to queries and manuscripts in four to six weeks. Please allow six to eight weeks for response. Include a self-addressed, stamped envelope (SASE) of correct size if you wish your manuscript returned.

Manuscript Format

We encourage submission of a text file via e-mail attachment (also pasted into the body of the e-mail). Include your Social Security number, address, daytime telephone number, and word count. Please include a list of all resources, sources, and interviewees, including telephone numbers and e-mail addresses, when available.

Payment Terms

We pay $500 to $1,000 for full-length features (750 to 1500 words); $300 to $500 for columns or departments (500 to 750 words). Fees are based on the nature of individual articles, assigned length, and amount of research required. Payment will be made upon acceptance of completed article and receipt of an invoice and signed purchase agreement.

Rights

Freelance writers are asked to sign a purchase agreement stating that North American Media Group, Inc., publisher of *Gardening How-To*, purchases First North American Rights for all works, unless both parties agree to alternate arrangements. No agreement will be considered final until a signed copy of the purchase agreement is returned to the attention of Mary Pestel, Senior Editor, *Gardening How-To*, 12301 Whitewater Drive, Minnetonka, MN 55343.

Photographs

In general, the *Gardening How-To* staff does not solicit photographs from story writers, as we regularly work with top professional photographers across the country. However, writers should mention the availability of photos they own the rights to at the time of their query or during discussion of story assignment with the editor. Photographers must include their Social Security or Federal Tax I.D. number, address, and daytime telephone number with all materials submitted to *Gardening How-To.*

Guidelines for Botanical Description

In dealing with plant names and descriptions, *Gardening How-To* expects writers to follow these guidelines: The American Horticulture Society's *Encyclopedia of Garden Plants* is the primary reference source for botanical (Latin) names and common names (as well as for plant heights and hardiness ratings). If a plant is not listed in AHS, cite which sources you use. If you prefer a source other than AHS, contact the assigning editor to discuss options.

Unless specified otherwise, include USDA Plant Hardiness Zone ratings for all plants mentioned, preferably stated in a range of Zones: (hardy in Zones 4 to 8). This and other descriptive information (color, height, bloom time, et al.) may be presented outside of text in a separate box, sidebar, or other listing, as determined by the assigning editor.

Following standard nomenclature, italicize the botanical name (*Acer ginnala*). Do not italicize parentheses. Use initial capitals for genus names. Use Roman type for cultivar or variety names, and enclose them in single quotation marks (*Acer ginnala* 'Flame'). Place all other punctuation marks outside of the single quotes.

When referring to a genus with multiple species, use plural: "A low-maintenance border of daylilies (*Hemerocallis* spp.)."

When providing sources for plants and seeds, list correct company name, address, customer phone number, Web site, and other pertinent information as needed. Include at least one Canadian source. Editors reserve the right to add or delete sources.

As much as possible, doublecheck that sources will carry the plants or seeds at issue date. Also, ascertain that plants or seeds will be readily available to consumers. Consult the assigning editor when you have any questions concerning botanical description or nomenclature.

Categories: Nonfiction—Gardening—Hobbies

CONTACT: Mary Pestel, Senior Editor
Material: Queries
North American Media Group
12301 Whitewater Dr.
Minnetonka MN 55343
Phone: 952-988-7474
Fax: 952-988-7486
E-mail: mpestel@namginc.com
Website: www.gardeningclub.com

Gateway Heritage

Thank you for your interest in *Gateway Heritage*, the quarterly magazine of the Missouri Historical Society. Please send one copy of your manuscript to the address below. A Macintosh or PC disk with your manuscript and the name of the word processing program you used to prepare it is also requested. Though the magazine no longer publishes endnotes, if notes are necessary they should be supplied and prepared in accordance with *The Chicago Manual of Style*, as we keep them on file and in our library for those who are interested.

Gateway Heritage publishes articles on St. Louis and Missouri cultural, social, and political issues, both historical and contemporary. Submissions for full-length essays ideally run 3,500 to 5,000 words (not including notes). Gateway also publishes shorter essays in its departments. Submissions for these departments should run approximately 1,500 to 2,500 words.

The Missouri Biographies department features essays focusing on individual Missourians. Submissions to this department often can not (and should not) cover a subject's entire life. Some of the most successful biographical sketches choose one particular aspect of their subject on which to focus.

Literary Landmarks includes sketches of literary figures with a Missouri background.

Our Gateway Album department features excerpts from diaries and journals from the Missouri Historical Society's collections and other collections.

Missouri Memories highlights firsthand accounts of Missouri's historical personalities and events.

In the Collections focuses on the Missouri Historical Society's artifacts.

Finally, At the Society spotlights events and the work of the staff at the Missouri Historical Society.

Not all articles submitted to *Gateway Heritage* are subject to a referee process, but some articles may be sent to scholars or other experts for advice and guidance. In addition, if you are affiliated with a university or college that requires your article be submitted for peer review, such review will be arranged. In any case, you will be notified if your article will be sent out for review.

In general, the editor will let you know within four weeks from the date your submission is received in the office if it will be accepted for publication; if there will be a delay longer than four weeks, you will be notified. Should you have any other questions on our submissions policy, feel free to contact us by mail or by telephone.

Categories: History—Regional

CONTACT: Josh Stevens, Editor
Material: All
PO Box 11940
St. Louis MO 63112-0040
Phone: 314-746-4557
Fax: 314-746-4548

Genealogical Computing

Formal guidelines not available. Please read a number of issues to ascertain the publication's style and needs.

Please query by mail with SASE or email to gceditor@ancestry.com.

Categories: Computers—Family—History—Genealogy

CONTACT: Elizabeth Kerstens, Managing Editor
Material: All
My Family.com, Inc
360 W. 4800 North
Provo UT 84604
E-mail: gceditor@ancestry.com
Website: www.myfamilyinc.com

General Aviation News
The Southern Aviator

Thank you for your interest in writing for *General Aviation News* and *The Southern Aviator*. We do accept freelance submissions for feature stories. All news stories are handled in house, except in rare instances. If you would like to send us news tips, that would be great. Queries for feature stories are preferred and will receive greater consideration than unsolicited manuscripts.

We prefer our writers to be pilots or in pursuit of their private pilot's license.

Stories that work best for us are features on pilots and aircraft owners, restoration articles, Living With Your Plane articles, interesting destinations for aircraft owners/pilots, different ways pilots are using their planes (business, personal, charity, etc.), careers in GA, etc.

What we don't want: Anything to do with airlines or military flying.

Format

We prefer stories to be submitted via email in a word document. Stories should be single spaced with no space between the paragraphs. Do not indent paragraphs. Also, do not double space between sentences.

Space is quite limited in our publication. We prefer stories to be between 700 and 1,000 words. Longer stories will be very difficult to schedule for publication. In that vein, we also prefer short sentences. For example: If you are in the habit of using semi-colons, just put the idea into two sentences. I will probably do it any way.

Put your name as you would like it to appear in a byline at the top of the story in all capitals:

example: By JANICE WOOD

If you have a nickname and would like to use it in the byline, you can put it in quotes:

example: By MARCIA 'SPARKY' BARNES

Do not put your address, word count or anything else on the top of the story. Instead, include your snail mail address in the email that accompanies the story. If the story is used, I will eventually need your Social Security Number for payment purposes. You can submit this to me in the email, or if you prefer, you can call me and give it to me in person or leave it on my voice mail: 888-333-5937.

Payment is around the 15th of the month, following publication (For example, if your story appears in the October 10 issue, you can expect payment to be sent about November 15). We do not pay per word. Each story is negotiated separately. Fees start at $75 and increase as the complexity of the story increases. For example, pilot reports start at $250. However, it is quite uncommon for us to assign a pirep to a writer we are unfamiliar with. I would have to have a track record with the writer before assigning one.

All feature stories require art. Please obtain the art yourself. We run into problems when the subject of the story is charged with sending us art. They usually don't understand the importance of art and/or meeting deadlines.

We prefer to receive digital photos at least 300 dpi. However, prints and slides are acceptable. They can be sent directly to our layout designer, Russell Kasselman, Flyer Media, P.O. Box 39099, Lakewood, WA 98439. Be sure you identify which story the photos go with. Also, if you want the photos returned, let Russell know. It would aid greatly if you send a stamped, self-addressed envelope for the return.

Obviously in the varied world that is GA there are going to be stories and circumstances that aren't covered by these guidelines. Feel free to call or email me at any time to discuss ideas. I will endeavor to get back to you as soon as I can. However, do NOT fax or mail me unsolicited manuscripts. I cannot guarantee a quick response on these.

It is acceptable to email me with a story idea. If I'm interested in reviewing the story, I'll let you know. Once I review it, I will try to give you an answer as to whether we'd like to publish it or not. If the answer is no, the most likely reason would be that the subject matter or style do not fit our publication. If the answer is yes, the story will go into a backlog and will be used as space is available.

Categories: Aviation

CONTACT: Janice Wood, Editor
Material: All
PO Box 39099
Lakewood, WA 98439
Phone: 253-471-9888
E-mail: janice@generalaviationnews.com
Website: www.flyermedia.com
Website: www.generalaviationnews.com
Website: www.southern-aviator.com

Genre

About us
Sexy, Stylish, Compelling Editorial.

The first glossy, mainstream gay publication, GENRE has led the industry by providing an upscale perspective on lifestyle for the gay consumer. Awarded numerous honors by mainstream and gay media outlets, GENRE continues to provide an editorial format of style and substance that is friendly to national advertisers. GENRE's loyal market base of affluent gay consumers has subscribed an average of 5+ years, according to MRI market research.

OUR Mission

GENRE is about how we live. It's a full perspective on living a better life for gay men everywhere, from those in the urban metropolis to those in small towns. Through exciting photography, interviews, fashion, fiction and design, we offer lifestyle choices and stories that encapsulate the options for today's gay consumer. GENRE is "an upfront, upscale and unashamed celebration of gay lifestyle" according to USA Today. We are committed to providing our readers with stylish editorial content as informative and entertaining to the world at large as it is to the broad range of gay men in America today.

Editorial Content

From home design to sports, we write about the things that matter to our unique and loyal readership. We cover celebrities – gay, straight and undecided - but we're much more than a star-chasing glossy. GENRE appeals to a niche segment of the community, the gay male consumer, and we are committed to connecting with that consumer on personal and aesthetic levels. Our focus is on the advance and celebration of the individual. In each issue we present fresh, stylish fashion as well as architecture and interior design through the homes and public spaces of gay men across the country. We cover media and entertainment, health and fitness, the latest gadgets and products, grooming and hot cars from informative, humorous and enlightening points of view. Our travel section features unparalleled coverage of not only exotic international destinations, but of U.S. cities and local regions of interest to the gay consumer. Along with portfolios on artists and photographers, we provide editorial fiction that has won 3 Maggie awards from the Western Publishers Association. GENRE's first rate design, photography and cutting-edge editorial content by the pacesetters in gay culture continues to appeal to a loyal gay readership interested in style, substance and better living.

Genre. Definitive culture and lifestyle for gay men.

Categories: Nonfiction—Alternate Life-style—Book Reviews—Fashion—Gay/Lesbian—Lifestyle—Men's Fiction—Men's Issues—Sexuality—Short Stories

CONTACT: John Mok, Associate Editor
Material: Any
CONTACT: Andy Towle, Editor-in-Chief
Material: Any
7080 Hollywood Blvd., Ste 818
Hollywood CA 90028
Phone: 323-467-8300

The Georgia Review

Published quarterly by The University of Georgia since 1947, The Georgia Review features an eclectic blend of essays, fiction, poetry, graphics, and book reviews. Appealing across disciplinary lines, The Review draws its material from a wide range of cultural interests-including, but not limited to, literature, history, philosophy, anthropology, politics, film, music, and the visual arts.

Essays: We are seeking informed essays that attempt to place their subjects against a broad perspective. For the most part we are not interested in scholarly articles that are narrow in focus and/or overly burdened with footnotes. The ideal essay for The Georgia Review is a provocative, thesis-oriented work that can engage both the intelligent general reader and the specialist.

Poetry & Fiction: We seek the very best work we can find, whether by Nobel laureates and Pulitzer Prize-winners or by little-known (or even previously unpublished) writers. All manuscripts receive serious, careful attention; we try to respond within two or three months, but sometimes the ebb and flow of manuscripts causes delays. We have published stories ranging in length from less than one of our pages to more than 60, and we have run poems of less than ten lines and more than 1,000. Ordinarily we do not publish novel excerpts or works translated into English, and we strongly discourage authors from submitting these. In recent years we have been able to accept less than one-half of one percent of the poetry and fiction manuscripts received.

Book Reviews: In most cases, selection of titles to be reviewed and assignments to specific reviewers are made by the editors, so unsolicited reviews should not be submitted without a prior query. However, we are quite willing to entertain proposals from reviewers concerning assignments they might like to undertake. (Separate, more detailed guidelines for book reviewing are available upon request.)

Artwork: We publish reproductions (color or black and white) of a wide range of artwork: paintings, photography, woodcuts, ink drawings, sculpture, and more. Usually we feature one work on the cover plus an interior layout of 6 to 16 additional works, and our editorial preference is for groupings that display an engaging variety within some overall thematic unity. Submissions should include 15 to 20 original slides or sharp, glossy, black-and-white 5" x 7" photographs.

SUBMISSION OF MANUSCRIPTS:

1. Every submission to The Georgia Review should be accompanied by a postage-paid and self-addressed return envelope. Work previously published in any form or submitted simultaneously to other journals will not be considered. Submissions should be limited (except under unusual circumstances) to one story or one essay or three to five poems. All prose manuscripts should be double spaced. We do not accept submissions via fax or e-mail. If a submission is known to be included in a book already accepted by a publisher, please notify us of this fact (and of the anticipated date of book publication) in a cover letter.

3. Unsolicited manuscripts will not be considered from 15 May through 15 August; all such submissions received during that period will be returned unread. (Our offices are open year around, but our staff is small and needs the summer months to complete evaluations of the manuscripts already received.)

4. Scholarly documentation, if appropriate, should adhere to the format outlined in the MLA Stylesheet (2nd edition).

5. The Georgia Review does not consider book manuscripts. Please direct all such works or queries about them to The University of Georgia Press, 330 Research Drive, Athens, GA 30602.

OTHER CONSIDERATIONS:

1. The Georgia Review pays all contributors; the current standard rates are $40 per printed page for prose and $3 per line for poetry.

2. We try to avoid having an extended backlog of accepted works awaiting publication; if accepted, your work would almost always be printed within a year-and often sooner.

3. We are capable of printing high-quality illustrations to accompany essays.

4. The Georgia Review buys first North American serial rights only. All other rights revert to the author at publication, but we offer formal, written reassignments upon request. We ask that whenever an author reprints a work that first appeared in our pages, The Georgia Review be given acknowledgment for the specific work(s) involved.

5. The Georgia Review is produced with the greatest care: we offer a well-designed format, printing on book-quality stock, and durable perfect binding of each issue's 200-plus pages. Our paid circulation is about 4,000, making The Review one of America's most widely read journals of arts and letters.

The best way to become acquainted with any publication is to read its recent issues. We invite you to enjoy and study our pages at your library or—even better—to subscribe yourself (for only $30 per year for four issues, with sample copies available for $8).

Recent contributors include: Lee K. Abbott, Rita Dove, Stephen Dunn, Albert Goldbarth, Mary Hood, Philip Levine, Barry Lopez, Pattiann Rogers, Reg Saner, Robert Wrigley.

Categories: Fiction—Nonfiction—Arts—Book Reviews—Poetry—Short Stories—Essays

CONTACT: Editors
Material: All
The University of Georgia
012 Gilbert Hall
Athens GA 30602-9009
Phone: 706-542-3481
Fax: 706-542-0047
E-mail: garev@uga.edu
Website: www.uga.edu/garev

German Life

German Life

German Life is a bimonthly magazine is written in English for all interested in the diversity of German culture, past and present, and in the various ways that the United States has been shaped by its German element. The magazine is dedicated to solid reporting on cultural and historical events as well as travel information.

Queries/Manuscripts

To suggest a story, send us a query letter (3 or 4 paragraphs) with backup clips of your idea. Keep in mind that we receive numerous solicited and unsolicited manuscripts. Due to the large volume of unsolicited materials received by the editorial office, only queries of interest will be acknowledged. If you wish to verify receipt of your materials, we suggest scheduling them via certified mail or other traceable means. We schedule articles for our editorial calendar approximately a year and a half in advance of publication. *German Life* assumes no responsibility for the return or condition of unsolicited manuscripts, photographs or art.

Each issue of *German Life* is bound by our editorial calendar and seasonal events. Given scheduling restraints, we prefer that you submit your work several months prior to the appropriate issue. Deadlines will be given when the article topic is accepted.

Manuscripts

Your manuscript should not exceed 1,200 words. Longer pieces will be considered solely at the Editor's discretion. Smaller pieces appropriate for a sidebar or one of the magazine's departments should range between 300 and 800 words. Book reviews average 250 to 300 words.

Please ensure that we are the sole recipients of your manuscript. Also, please guarantee your work's originality. Give proper credit for any other author's ideas that you may use. If your article recounts only firsthand experiences, references are seldom necessary. In all other cases, cite the direct source on a separate sheet of paper, following *The Chicago Manual of Style*. Check the accuracy of your items carefully!

Please include: author's name, mailing address, daytime telephone, fax number and e-mail address. Please submit manuscript both on disk (IBM-compatible 3.5 inch) and as hard copy or they can be e-mailed as a Word document attachment. Photographs may be sent in digital form They must be scanned at 300 dpi and can be TIFF or EPS files. We prefer them to be sent on a CD-R, but they can also be sent on a floppy, Zip or Jaz disk. Be sure to convert all colors to CMYK. Please check first before e-mailing any graphics, especially large files. Submit the original(s) (including photos, slides, and/or illustrations), to the address below.

Most manuscripts are published from nine months to two years after acceptance. Manuscripts requiring revision are either returned in original form or first edited and then sent to the author for approval.

Please be advised that all manuscripts at the acceptance stage, including solicited works, are considered on speculation. You will be duly alerted when your accepted manuscript/photo/illustration has been scheduled into an upcoming issue. Payment is upon publication and ranges from $300 to $500 for feature articles, from $100 to $130 for reviews and short pieces, and up to $80 for fillers. In exchange for remuneration, *German Life* retains first English/German language serial rights.

All manuscripts are edited for style, consistency, and clarity. The final title of the published article, subheads, captions, photographs and illustrations, and other elements that attract attention to an article or contribute to the tone and appearance of the magazine are the Editor's prerogative.

Photographs / Illustrations

With or without manuscript, feel free to submit photographs, transparencies, or illustrations that are in accordance with the magazine's direction and style. We look for pictures that capture and/or detail the diversity of German or German-American life and culture, including images of everyday life, landscapes, people, architecture, art, festivals, and so on.

Photos should be black-and-white or color glossy prints, 4x6 or larger, with excellent focus, fine grain, and clear contrasts. Label the back of each photo with your name and caption information. Do not write directly on the back of photos, or ink stamp, or paper clip labels to them. Identify slides by writing your name, the location, and the subject on the margins.

For illustrations, any medium is acceptable. With four-color art, please send 35 mm transparencies. Computer illustrators may submit four-color laser printouts of their work (e.g., maps, charts, and graphs) for consideration. In the case of black-and-white art, we prefer to first see photocopies. However, unless you are (have) a professional artist (available), submit only rough sketches for figures and diagrams. Type captions on a separate sheet of paper, along with any credit lines.

Please note that every photograph or illustration with an article must be credited. A release must be signed by the person or party responsible for object(s) not open to public photography such as special museum items. In addition, to avoid legal complications and embarrassing situations, please alert us to any purchase of your work by other publications.

Include with each submission all relevant contact information, such as the artist's name, mailing address, daytime telephone, fax number, and e-mail address if available. For each photograph, include a description and photo credit on a label on the back of the photo. Please do not submit more than 20 glossies or transparencies at a time. On a separate sheet of paper, include a description and photo credit for each and key to the slides/transparencies. Place slides in individual plastic protectors and in a plastic slide sleeve fit for 20 slides. Send all submissions to the address below.

We rarely purchase photographic material without manuscripts. Please inquire before sending any original materials. CDs or photocopies should be sent if unsolicited. With your permission, we will keep visual materials of appropriate quality and interest for our files. Photographs, slides, illustrations, and sketches are returned only upon request. (Please include a SASE.) Publication of photographs/illustrations depends on need and topic. Effective March 18, 2002.

Categories: Nonfiction—Culture—History—Travel—Special Interest (German)

CONTACT: Mark Slider, Editor
Material: All
1068 National Hwy
LaVale MD 21502
Fax: 301-729-1720
E-mail: editor@germanlife.com
Website: www.germanlife.com

Get in the Game

Please also refer to *Turkey Call.*

Get in the Game, published for members of the NWTF's Hunting Heritage Program, is targeted toward people with a passion for hunting and managing their acres for wildlife. *Get in the Game* feature articles average 1,500 words; articles in the 600- to 700-word range are also needed. The magazine helps readers learn how to improve habitat for deer, quail, wild turkeys, small game and other wildlife using layperson terminology. Readers will also learn about strategies that work for hunting deer, turkey and more. The articles range from secrets for locating your treestand in a whitetail hotspot, suggestions on how to improve your soil, tips to tune up your tractor, building a duck blind and more. *Get in the Game* emphasizes the importance of active forest management.

This 64-page magazine mails twice a year, in February and July. While a limited use of the author's own experience is acceptable, articles should feature advice from experts and not rely too heavily on biological terms to emphasize points. Preference centers on anecdotes about people besides the author. *Get in the Game* relies heavily on charts, tables and other graphic elements to quickly communicate concepts to a readership busy hunting and managing their land. Good research, reporting and fact checking are vital.

Editorial coverage for *Get in the Game* is prepared three months or more ahead of each issue's release date. We pay $100 for short pieces of 600 to 700 published words; $200 to $275 for articles of 700 to 1,100 words; $300 to $375 for up to 1,500 words; and $400 to $500 for up to 2,000 words. Individual queries or laundry lists are acceptable.

We accept images that illustrate wildlife, scenes depicting hunting deer, turkey, ducks, quail and more. In addition we are looking for photos that showcase wildlife management equipment and activities from plowing to planting to prescribed fire and beyond. Check with the editor for current photographic needs.

Rates for published photographs:
- Cover = $400
- Two-page spread = $175
- Full page = $125
- Half-page = $100
- One-third page or less = rate negotiated by editor

Categories: Nonfiction—Recreation—Sports—Hunting

CONTACT: P. J. Perea, Editor
pperea@nwtf.net
National Wild Turkey Federation
PO Box 530
770 Augusta Rd
Edgefield SC 29824
Phone: 803-637-3106
Fax: 803-637-0034
Web site: www.nwtf.org

Get Up & Go
A Magazine For Active & Involved Grandparents

Please refer to United Parenting Publications.

The Gettysburg Review

Guidelines for Submissions

Published quarterly, *The Gettysburg Review* considers unsolicited submissions of poetry, fiction, essays, and essay-reviews from September 1 through May 31 (postmark dates). New submissions received from June 1 through August 31 are returned unread. We welcome submissions of full-color graphics year round.

The main criterion for selection is quality, but the best way to determine what might be accepted by *The Gettysburg Review* is to read what has already been published. Sample copies are available at $7 each; one-year subscriptions (4 issues) are $24. We strongly encourage all potential contributors to read several issues before submitting.

In the genre of poetry, both short and long poems are of interest, including longer narrative poems. Fiction is generally in the form of short stories, although lengthier pieces are sometimes accepted and serialized, and excerpts from novels have been published. Essays can be on virtually any subject, so long as it is treated in a literary fashion—gracefully and in depth. *The Gettysburg Review* does not reprint previously published material.

Poetry submissions should be typed either single- or double-spaced on one side of the page. Prose manuscripts should be typed double-spaced on one side. Visual artists interested in having work considered should submit a selection of slides with a cover letter. Simultaneous submissions are tolerable so long as authors indicate in their cover letters that a manuscript is under concurrent consideration and notify us immediately upon acceptance elsewhere.

Address all submissions to Peter Stitt, Editor, *The Gettysburg Review*, Gettysburg College, Gettysburg, PA 17325-1491. *The Gettysburg Review* does not accept unsolicited submissions via fax or e-mail.

No manuscript or artwork will be returned, nor any query answered, unless accompanied by a self-addressed, stamped envelope. Expect three to six months for a decision. Please do not query us about a manuscript's status until five months have passed. If you do inquire, we prefer that you send us a note with an S.A.S.E. rather than contact us via phone or e-mail. *The Gettysburg Review* accepts no responsibility for the delay, damage, or loss of unsolicited manuscripts.

Payment is upon publication: $2.50 per line for poetry and $30 per printed page for prose. Published authors also receive two copies of the issue containing their work and a one-year subscription.

Categories: Fiction—Nonfiction—Arts—Book Reviews—Literature—Poetry—Short Stories—Writing

CONTACT: Peter Stitt, Editor
Material: All
Gettysburg College
Gettysburg PA 17325
Phone: 717-337-6770
Website: www.gettysburgreview.com

Girls' Life

1. *Girls' Life* does not accept unpublished fiction or poetry from adults.

2. *Girls' Life* accepts unsolicited manuscripts on a speculative basis only. Send query letters with descriptive story ideas. Please include a detailed resumé and published writing samples.

3. All stories will be assigned by the editors. Once assigned, a memorandum of agreement is to be executed by both parties before payment is made.

4. Every story should have a headline, by-line, introduction, lead, body and conclusion. Author's full name, address and phone number must be provided. Referrals for art sources are appreciated.

5. *Girls' Life* conforms to *The Associated Press Stylebook and Libel Manual.* Please submit in MS Word or similar program on disk. Manuscripts can also be e-mailed.

6. All research must rely on primary sources. Manuscripts must be accompanied by a complete list of sources, telephone numbers and reference materials.

7. Queries are responded to within 90 days if submitted with a self-addressed, stamped envelope. If material is not returned in due time, it has been placed in a file for possible future consideration. *Girls' Life* cannot be held responsible for the return of any unsolicited material.

8. Unless submission is stated to be a possible work for hire, submission will be considered property of *Girls' Life* magazine.

Categories: Children—Crafts/Hobbies—Ecology—Entertainment—Film/Video—Music—Outdoors—Relationships—Sports/Recreation—Teen—Young Adult

CONTACT: Sarah Cordi
Material: General
4517 Harford Rd.
Baltimore MD 21214
Phone: 410-426-9600
Fax: 410-254-0991
E-mail: sarah@girlslife.com

Gist Review

About *GIST Review*

GIST Review is a spin-off of *INK Literary Review*, which was published from September 1995 until September 1998. We decided to abandon traditional publishing in favor of electronic publishing because we believe that the latter allows us to reach more readers and it is also cheaper. Thus, *GIST Review* was born.

SUBMISSION GUIDELINES

GIST Review is a non-paying e-review and we are committed to promote electronic literary arts in America. *We publish all types of works including the following:*
- Book Reviews (between 500 - 2000 words)
- Fiction (between 1000 - 5000 words)
- Poems (maximum 100 verses per poem)
- Literary essays, critiques on culture/society/technology, academic or non-academic (between 1000 - 5000 words)
- Fresh interpretations of great works (between 1000 - 3000 words)
- Artwork/Photography
- Photographic journalism (maximum 1000 words)
- Non-English works are encouraged (especially in Spanish and French)... and whatever else you think we should publish!

We will only accept electronic submissions. Paper submissions will automatically be trashed.

If your works can be found in your personal webpage, we need your permission to copy and paste an accepted work into our own website. The same policy applies for artworks and photos.

Academic essays must follow the writing guidelines of *MLA Handbook for Writers of Research Papers* by Joseph Gibaldi (4th edition).

All submissions are subject to editorial trimming.

We will not publish unnecessary obscene, pornographic or unsavory material that we think may offend our readers.

Publication Frequency: *GIST Review* is published annually.

Send your comments, questions and submissions to: GISTREVIEW@aol.com

Categories: Fiction—Arts—Book Reviews—Literature—Photography—Poetry

CONTACT: Submissions Editor
Material: All
E-mail:GISTREVIEW@aol.com
Website: www.geocities.com/Broadway/Stage/8861/GIST/Home.htm

Glamour

Most of our readers are women between the ages of 18 and 45, and articles that are slanted to our older readers must work for the younger ones as well. As a rule, we do not publish unsolicited short stories or poems. Although we want timely articles, we steer away from subject matter that will seem dated by the time of publication: Stories generally take two to six months to get into print.

We do review manuscripts; however, we usually prefer to see a story proposal first, as we may already have assigned or published articles on the same subject.

"Hear Me Out," our opinion page, is approximately 1,000 words, for which we pay $500-$1000. As the name implies, "Hear Me Out" works best when the writer has a strong point to make about a newsworthy subject. Manuscripts or queries should be typed and double-spaced.

Categories: Nonfiction—Book Reviews—Careers—Cooking—Entertainment—Fashion—Food/Drink—Health—Lifestyle—Physical Fitness—Psychology—Relationships—Society—Travel—Women's Issues—Beauty—How-to

CONTACT: Manuscripts
Material: Queries and Manuscripts
Condé Nast
4 Times Square
New York NY 10036-6593
Phone: 212-880-8800
Fax: 212-880-6922
E-mail: glamourmag@aol.com
Website: www.glamour.com

Glimmer Train Stories

What will readers find in *Glimmer Train Stories*?

Great short stories by established and emerging writers, ten in every quarterly issue. A feast of fiction for the mind and heart, these stories are both beautifully written and emotionally affecting.

What We Are Looking For

Glimmer Train Stories welcomes the work of established and upcoming writers.

We especially appreciate work that is both well written and emotionally engaging. Please let us read yours! If it is chosen for publication in *Glimmer Train Stories*, you will be paid upon acceptance. Your story or poem will be prepared with care, and presented in a handsome, highly regarded literary journal to readers all over the country (even a few in Ireland, England, and Australia). If you've seen *Glimmer Train Stories*, you know that we go to some lengths to honor our contributors and their writing.

See our website for submissions categories (other than standard submissions), which provides specific details on when you can submit work for each category, when you can expect to hear results, how much (if any) is required for reading fees, how much we pay for accepted pieces, and if there are particular restrictions, such as word count limitations. *In all cases*: We are interested in original, unpublished pieces. We don't publish stories for children, and we don't publish novels. Multiple submissions are okay. (You can send more than one submission per competition, if you like, or submit the same story for different categories, if it qualifies). Simultaneous submissions are not okay, I'm sorry. (It breaks our hearts to fall for a story we can't publish.)

We are happy to consider your stories whether they are submitted as competition entries or standard submissions. There are no reading fees for standard story submissions. On the other hand, the monetary award paid to competition winners is more substantial than the already tidy $700 payment for accepted standard submissions. All stories are read and appreciated and considered for publication by the same diligent readers either way. So relax and choose the category that suits you.

Note: In an effort to save our backs from heavy mail buckets, we ask that you send all work via our online submission procedure (See our website). It's easy, and will save you postage and paper.

Standard Submissions

Welcome in January, April, July, and October.

We are interested in reading your original, unpublished stories.

(We don't publish stories for children, and we don't publish novels.) No simultaneous submissions, please. When we accept a story for publication, we are purchasing first-publication rights. (Once we've published your story, you are free to, for instance, include it in your own collection.)

Dates: January, April, July, and October. Response within 12 weeks.
Reading fee: None.
Payment for accepted stories: $700 for first-publication rights.
Other considerations:
• Open to all writers.
• Stories should not exceed 12,000 words.
• Okay to submit up to three stories per reading month.
We look forward to reading your work!
Categories: Literature—Short Stories

CONTACT: Submissions Editor
Material: All
Glimmer Train Press, Inc.
1211 NW Glisan St, #207
Portland OR 97209
Phone: 503-221-0836
Fax: 503-221-0837
E-mail: info@glimmertrain.org (for submission questions)
E-mail: eds@glimmertrain.org (for all other questions)
Website: www.glimmertrain.org

Go Magazine

Stories are submitted on spec and publication is not guaranteed. However, should we decide to use an article, our rates are $150 per story, paid after the story runs. There is no kill fee.

We prefer stories to be approximately 750-1,000 words, focusing on travel in North Carolina, South Carolina and surrounding states.

We also request that color photographs or slides accompany a story.

If you are interested, please send us your previously unpublished story to review.

Categories: Nonfiction—Automobiles—Consumer—Travel

CONTACT: Sarah Davis, Associate Editor
Material: All
Carolina Motor Club
6600 AAA Dr.
Charlotte NC 28212
Phone: 704-569-3600

Going Places
Magazine for Today's Traveler

Style: We prefer lively, upbeat stories that appeal to a well-traveled, sophisticated audience. Negative travel experiences are not acceptable. Articles must be original, accurate and up-to-date. An article should appeal both to readers who will travel to the destination and to those who will only "experience" it through reading the story. Only AAA-approved vendors may be mentioned in articles.

Inquiry: We will review your query letter or finished manuscript with equal interest. We cannot comment on each submission, but we will notify you if your material is being considered for future use. Please keep submissions to less than 1,300 words.

Art: Do not send original slides, unless we agree to publish your article, at which point, original, color slides of good quality are accepted. High-resolution digital images are also acceptable.

Payments and Rights: We pay upon publication, and publication is not guaranteed. There is no kill fee. AAA does not accept responsibility for unsolicited manuscripts and photography. Although we do not pay extra for photography, knowing that slides are available may help in the determination of using your story.

Please submit your articles or queries to the attention of Sarah Davis at the address below. If you have any questions, please direct them to the following email address: sbdavis@mailaaa.com.

Categories: Automobiles—Consumer—Travel—Group Publishing Services

CONTACT: **Sarah Davis, Associate Editor**
Material: All
AAA Carolinas
6600 AAA Dr
Charlotte NC 28212
Phone: 704-569-3600
E-mail: sbdavis@mailaaa.com

Golf Business Magazine

Writers Guidelines
Publication Overview

Golf Business is the official magazine of the National Golf Course Owners Association. Published monthly, Golf Business is designed to promote the exchange of information and ideas among course owners, operators, general managers, partners, directors, investors and senior industry executives. The publication"s mission is to help improve profits for course owners/operators. It is a four-color, high-quality, saddle-stitched publication. Currently, circulation is more than 19,000.

Golf Business provides readers timely and substantive information beneficial for course owners and operators. The magazine keeps the golf industry informed of current trends in areas such as legislation, agronomics, employment, marketing, design and business tips. Golf Business also offers fresh perspectives on ways to make a course more profitable.

Editorial Information

The readers of Golf Business are in the business of golf. Because this is a business publication, articles should be succinct and straightforward; avoid overloading articles with anecdotes or editorializing. Although readers are business men/women, a conversational tone is preferred to ensure articles are easy to read. Golf Business recommends articles be written in the third person rather than first person.

Before submitting any assignment, writers should edit articles to the best of their ability, adhering to AP Stylebook guidelines. If deemed unacceptable, articles may be returned to the writer for re-working. Keep in mind that all articles are subject to intense editorial scrutiny.

Terms

Payment for articles varies by length, location in the magazine and other factors, and is negotiated with the writer. Payment is made 30 days following publication. Golf Business will pay telephone and certain other expenses, if agreed-upon in advance. A 20% ""kill fee"" will be paid for articles assigned and completed but not published.

A formal invoice from the writer is required for payment. Invoices should be made to Golf Business with details of the assignment noted. Please include Social Security number on invoice.

The publisher is granted one-time editorial rights to the submitted article for publication in the print version of Golf Business. Once the submitted article is accepted for publication, it cannot be published elsewhere for 90 days from the publication release dates unless written permission is granted by the publisher.

Categories: Sports

CONTACT: **Ronnie Musselwhite, Editor**
Golf Business Magazine
291 Seven Farms Dr
Charleston SC 29492
Phone 800-933-4262 ext 224
Fax: 843-856-3288
E-mail: rmusselwhite@ngcoa.org
Website: www.golfbusinessmagazine.com

Golf Course Management

Most of GCM's articles deal with problems faced by superintendents or describe techniques that allow superintendents to do their jobs better. The magazine particularly welcomes contributions from superintendents.

Send a one-page synopsis of the article (or proposed article) to: Scott Hollister, Editor, at address below.

If you are a superintendent, a one-page synopsis is not necessary. Please contact: Angela Nitz, Senior Associate Editor, at address below.

The article synopsis should:

Detail the author's qualifications for writing the article. (Is the author a superintendent who has faced the problem or an industry-related participant who has specialized knowledge?)

Describe in detail the problem addressed by the article and the author's solution or technique.

Describe available artwork that could illustrate the article. GCM is a color magazine — good color illustrations, photos, graphs, etc., are a plus when the editors consider an article for publication.

Let the editors know if the article has already been prepared, or if it is yet to be written. If the article is not completed, include an estimate of the completion date.

Upon receipt, GCM editors will review the synopsis to determine if the suggested topic and treatment are appropriate. Editorial submissions on individual golf course operations, outstanding superintendents, special on-course projects, reconstruction, renovation and on-course applications of technology are always welcome for review. The greater the emphasis on the management role of the superintendent and the more effective the presentation of that role, the greater the likelihood of acceptance for publication. Notification of acceptance or rejection occurs as soon as possible.

General Submission Guidelines

Language: GCM generally employs a blend of Associated Press and magazine style for published feature articles. Even the most technically intricate articles often can be written in simple, conversational style, using verbal illustrations to make a point. Use short, precise words. Convey one thought per sentence. Construct brief paragraphs.

Editing: GCM will edit all published articles, and the editing staff can be ruthless. There is generally no author review after the editing process.

Industry submissions: GCM welcomes story submissions from companies within the golf course maintenance industry or public relations firms representing these companies. However, these stories should not be commercial in nature, should not be product specific and are subject to extremely strict editing by GCM staff members. Ideally, industry submissions will trade on the expertise of the submitting company in the discussion of a topic of general interest to golf course superintendents or focus on how a GCSAA member superintendent solved a problem or improved the management of the golf course.

Illustrations: GCM is a full-color magazine. An article's chance of publication is greatly enhanced if photographs or other illustrative material accompany the article.

Payment: GCM pays on acceptance of articles and receipt of a signed author's agreement.

Length requirements: Feature articles should be (in general) from 6 to 10 double-spaced pages (1,500 to 2,500 words).

Preferred electronic software: Current or recent versions of Microsoft Word for Windows are preferred. Contact the editors if an alternative submission is planned.

Preferred mode for submission: Please e-mail your article to the appropriate editor. If you do not have e-mail access, please contact the editor about an alternative submission format.

Photo requirements: Photographs and illustrations are vitally important to stories published in GCM, and authors are strongly encouraged to include an appropriate amount of these elements with their story submissions. GCM will accept color prints, slides, negatives and digital images. When taking digital photos for use in GCM, authors are strongly encouraged to use cameras that are at least 3.2 megapixels or higher and are set to produce the highest resolution file possible. Submitted digital photos should be high resolution (at least 300 dpi) JPG, TIFF or EPS files and their physical size should be at least 4 inches wide. Digital photos may be submitted on CD-ROM or by e-mail. Original low-resolution digital photos that have been altered into high-resolution files in Photoshop or other photo editing programs are discouraged. Slides, photographs and negatives will be returned to authors following publication.

Standard operating procedure for photographs:

Photographs are a key element in complementing articles and in illustrating advertisements in Golf Course Management and Newsline. It is the intention of both publications to show the physical appearance of superintendents in the most professional light possible. The GCSAA Board of Directors approved the following publication dress standards.

Superintendents will not be depicted in blue jeans.

Superintendents will not be depicted in shorts.

Superintendents will not be depicted in t-shirts or sweatshirts.

Hats are allowed, but discouraged. Superintendents will not be depicted in hats bearing seed, chemical, grounds equipment or other commercial logos. Hats bearing employer/facility, GCSAA, or chapter logos are acceptable.

Superintendents, including those with facial hair, must appear well-groomed.

Sunglasses, when feasible, should be removed before taking a photograph for publication.

Competition: GCM will not reprint articles if they have previously appeared in another national publication. Also, once an article has been accepted for publication in GCM, we ask that it not be submitted to other national golf/turf industry publications or other publications. An article may be reprinted in a GCSAA-affiliated chapter publication. However, we request that the article appear in GCM first.

Leo Feser Award: All superintendent-written articles are eligible for the Leo Feser Award, presented first in 1956, and then annually since 1977 to the author of the best superintendent-written article published in Golf Course Management magazine during the previous year. Winners receive an all-expenses paid trip to the annual conference and show, are recognized during the Opening Session and reception at conference and show, and have their names engraved on a plaque permanently displayed at GCSAA headquarters.

Categories: Nonfiction—Golf

CONTACT: Scott Hollister, Editor
Golf Course Management
Material: Synopses
1421 Research Park Dr
Lawrence KS 66049
Phone: 785-832-4456
Fax: 785-832-3665
E-mail: shollister@gcsaa.org
CONTACT: Angela Nitz
Senior Associate Editor
Golf Course Management
Material: Articles
1421 Research Park Dr
Lawrence KS 66049
Phone: 785-832-3647
Fax: 785-832-3665
E-mail: anitz@gcsaa.org

Golf Digest

Rarely accepts unsolicited manuscripts.
Categories: Nonfiction—Physical Fitness—Recreation—Sports/Recreation—Golf

CONTACT: Michael O'Malley, Exec. Editor
Material: All
PO Box 395
Trumbull CT 066113
Phone: 203-373-7240
Fax: 203-373-2162

Golf Journal Magazine

We appreciate your interest in Golf Journal, the official publication of the United States Golf Association. We purchase articles from freelance writers on a wide variety of subjects: history, players of the game (both past and present), course architecture, the environment, equipment (of a historic nature), profiles and humor. We do not generally publish instruction or equipment (new product) stories, nor can we publish any stories that could be construed as an endorsement by the USGA, one of the game's governing bodies. Fictional stories are also welcome.

Articles and stories should range from 1,200 to 2,800 words. Payment is negotiated on an individual basis at the editors' discretion.

All manuscripts are submitted on speculation at the author's risk. We accept no responsibility for unsolicited manuscripts, but will make every effort to return them. Stories must be typewritten and accompanied by a stamped, self-addressed envelope large enough to hold the manuscript. Queries should also include a stamped, self-addressed envelope. Manuscripts are usually read and processed within three to four weeks, although processing can take slightly longer during our busy championship season (summer months). If desired, writers may first send inquiries as to the suitability of their subject and approach.

Categories: Fiction—Nonfiction—Short Stories—Sports/Recreation—Golf

CONTACT: Brett Avery, Editor
Material: Any
CONTACT: Cathrine Wolf, Managing Editor
Material: Any
Golf House, PO Box 708
Far Hills NJ 07931-0708
Phone: 908-234-2300
Fax: 908-781-1112
E-mail: golfjournal@usga.org
Website: www.usga.org

Golf Tips Magazine

The following information should give you a general guide for preparation and submission of materials to Golf Tips for editorial consideration:

Submit a query letter to the editor. Be sure to include as much detailed information as possible on your idea, the proposed length of the article and the type of photography that you expect to provide.

All material, unless previously assigned in writing, is submitted on a speculation basis.

Obtain copies of the magazine from the newsstand to study the format. Or, send a check for $4.50 and $2.50 shipping and handling for a sample copy from our office.

Text must be double-spaced, typewritten and free from handwritten corrections. On a separate sheet of paper, include your suggested title, deck and byline, photo credits and social security number.

Submit suggested heads, decks and captions for all photos with each story.

Black & white photography material can be submitted in proof sheet form with negatives. If you wish to provide prints, we require 8x10 size with a glossy finish. Be sure that your prints and proof sheets have your name and address on the back.

Color photography: Material can be submitted in the form of transparencies. Size can be 2.25x2.25, 4x5 or 35mm. Transparencies must be protected in plastic sleeves and your name should be on each slide.

Use cardboard stiffeners to protect your photos and materials in shipping. We'll take every available measure to protect your work once it has arrived in our offices, but will not be responsible for its loss or damage in shipping.

Payment will be made during the middle of the issue's month in which your article appeared, unless otherwise stated in writing. Rates vary depending on the value of the material as judged by the editors.

The publisher buys all rights to the material as judged by the editors.

Categories: Sports

CONTACT: Editors
Golf Tips
E-mail: editors@golftipsmag.com
Website: www.golftipsmag.com

The Golfer

These departments are open to freelance contributions:

Sports Fitness: Written with an authority on some aspect of fitness. These stories are usually written with the "we" voice (i.e. We should avoid dehydration.), mixed with references to "players" or "athletes" and maybe the very occasional "you." The goal of this section is to inform, hopefully about something "cutting edge" while trying to avoid making things sound dry and scientific. Usually about 1,400 words.

Chip Shots: Personal experiences are great, but beware the fact that at one time or another most golf writers believe that they have written the first story about someone who has a real passion for the game. Look for the offbeat.

Destinations: First-person travel stories. Approximately 1,000 to 2,000 words.

Categories: Health—Physical Fitness—Sports/Recreation—Travel

CONTACT: Lisa Maxbauer, Editorial
Material: All
21 E. 40th St. 13th Floor
New York NY 10016
Phone: 212-696-2484
Fax: 212-696-1678
E-mail: thegolfer@walrus.com

Good Housekeeping

Good Housekeeping addresses 24 million married women, most of whom have children (anywhere from newborn to college age) and who work outside the home.

Areas of interest covered include consumer issues, human interest, social issues, health, nutrition, relationships, psychology and work/career.

Several sections are especially well suited to freelancers: Better Way, which is comprised of 300 to 500 word how-to pieces; Real Lives, 400 to 600 word features on people involved in inspiring, heroic or fascinating pursuits; and "My Story," a first person or as-told-to format, in which a woman (using her real name) relays how she overcame an especially difficult impasse in her life.

It's best to familiarize yourself with the tone and content of *Good*

Housekeeping before you query us. (Back issues will likely be available at your local library.) The most successful queries or manuscripts are those that are timely, appropriately researched, engagingly written, freshly angled, and tailored to *Good Housekeeping* readers in particular.

Manuscripts and queries submitted on speculation should be typed, and when possible, should have clips of previously published articles attached. Please allow 2 to 3 months for a response due to the large volume of unsolicited queries we get.

Categories: Fiction—Crime—Diet/Nutrition—Family—General Interest—Health—Lifestyle—Marriage—Short Stories—Women's Fiction—Women's Issues—Human Interest (dramatic narrative)—Humor—Profiles (inspirational, real people)

CONTACT: Submissions Editor
Material: All
959 - 8th Ave.
New York NY 10019
Phone: 212-649-2260
Fax: 212-265-3307

Good Old Boat

Our niche is cruising sailboats from the 1950s, '60s, '70s, '80s, and '90s. We publish articles focused on pride of ownership and articles that discuss upgrades, maintenance, refits, and restoration of good old boats. In addition to these core themes, we publish articles about vendors of good old boat products and services and histories of sailing industry companies and individuals who have influenced the industry.

Because these themes are well-covered by other magazines, we do not publish: destination articles, racing coverage.

What else do we publish? In addition to technical articles, we also welcome articles focused on sailors and their boats, reflections columns, cruising memories, and other features.

Photos

Illustrations and photographs are important. Thirty to forty percent of the page space can effectively be used with illustrations and photos. We prefer slides shot with Fujichrome Provia 100, Kodachrome 64, or similar films. Color prints are second best. Please turn off the date stamp. It is difficult to remove that from your photograph. It may render a photograph useless, in fact.

Digital cameras are out there. Electronic photo files must be high resolution—at least 300 dpi—to be usable for print reproduction. 4.2 to 6.2 megapixel cameras are generally up to the task. If you want to take digital photos for publication: 900x1500 pixels is the absolute minimum size that works for us. That image can be printed (at 300 dpi) as a 3x5-inch photo. No larger. To run an image as large as a 5x7, it needs to be 1500x1200 pixels and somewhere around 7 megs in file size. A full-page image is 2500x3500 pixels, often running 25 megs or more. If you give us a very small image, it limits our ability to do page layout. So larger images are better.

However, please don't send huge unsolicited images by email. Before sending those large high-resolution images, send small jpgs (900x1500 pixels. Just because you can put a lot of images on a CD doesn't mean you should. Choose the best shots, don't make us open and look at every shot you took. We have incredibly short attention spans.

Don't manipulate your images for us (using Photoshop and other image software). Send your files as .jpg or .tif files without doing any color management or sharpening. We'll do the conversions here. An image is degraded with each modification. So don't modify it in advance, please.

If the photo editor's comments (above) sound grumpy, wait until you hear from the technical editor (below). Understand that we've had to deal with a lot of problem files. Often the same problems over and over. Sometimes we get frustrated by the repetition.

Technical articles

There are some specific characteristics we prefer in technical articles. While we appreciate humor in any article, fluffy technical articles that do not thoroughly cover the topic are not appropriate for our niche, even though they work well and are popular with some publishers. We will publish much longer articles than are allowed by other magazines — up to 5,000 words — because we want technical writers to have enough space to be thorough.

After reading a technical article, the reader should have enough information to enable him or her to act. All necessary contacts and resources should be presented. The reader should know whether he or she would like to do this work and is capable of doing it. How to do it and advantages and disadvantages should be presented. The article should include what can be expected if one does this, both during the process of doing it and after the work is completed. The writer should present potential stumbling blocks and point out areas which are open for misinterpretation. (For example, during barrier coat applications, just how dry must the previous coat be before applying the next round? Might this differ from one side of the boat to the other if the sun shines on one side only? This is one issue that caught us "off guard" in the boatyard.)

Last, but not least, we prefer honesty to "apple pie and motherhood." We are not trying to appease advertisers, so if something doesn't work well, feel free to offer your opinion for the benefit of fellow readers. After all, we're all in this together.

Software

At this writing, we're using around a dozen Macs in our Good Old Boat home office and many other Macs in the offices of our associates. Electronic files you send us will be read on a Mac. If your material is published, it will have been translated through many software programs before it is finally put in print. We have learned to translate to and from most platforms, but the following file formats are preferred:

Microsoft Word
AppleWorks
.RTF file extensions
Word Perfect

Formatting

Please do not use fancy formatting. By the time your work has been translated from one computer software to another and through several word processors and page design programs, most formatting is gone anyway. The spaces between words will survive, as will the returns between paragraphs. Embedded graphics, bold and italic font changes, headers and footers, etc. will be lost. The more complicated your formatting, the more difficult it is for the editors to read your manuscript. There is absolutely no chance that we will use your formatting. It will be deleted through our process without ever being appreciated by the editors. Simple is good. Simpler is better.

Further advice from the technical editor

It is not uncommon for us to need to obtain clarification from an author because the materials used were not described in sufficient detail. In one case we even pulled a scheduled article at the last minute because we could not confirm, identify, and find sources for the materials used. In other cases we simply did not consider some articles for publication because such details were lacking.

Think of the work you are describing as a process involving specific materials and activities. Did you use epoxy resin or polyester resin? Instead of saying marine bondo, be specific about which product was used. Was the sealant RTV, urethane, or polysulfide? What kind of wood did you use? A process that worked well for you involving specific materials may not work at all if the materials involved are substituted for others that are not compatible with each other or not really suited to the task.

Try to give us more detail than we will need. If it breaks up the flow of words, include an appendix with materials and sources. We will publish as much of it as we think is appropriate to make certain that, if a reader attempts the project, there is a good chance of success. You can't give us too much detail about materials used.

While we're on the subject, a few tips

The technical editor is a curmudgeon. There is nothing we can do about that. He owns half the business. His notes follow.

Authors should avoid the following usages:

RPMs—(Revolutions per minutes?) Always use RPM, never RPMs. It is that simple.

Amps per hour, Amps/hr. and similar — Although actually published occasionally, these are meaningless terms which only confuse the well-informed reader and demonstrate the writer's lack of comprehension of basic electricity. If amps per hour does not grate on your sensibilities like fingernails on a blackboard, you probably should not write about electricity. If you do the algebra on this, you come out with the reciprocal of time (1/time) or charge divided by the square of time (T squared). Nonsense.

Electricity and water don't mix—Many writers eventually resort to some kind of water analogy to try to explain how electricity works. I have yet to see what I thought was a really good water analogy. If you want to explain electricity, talk about electricity. Hydraulics is another field entirely. Avoid this trap; it is already full.

ABYC — Marine technical writers often quote the ABYC (American Boat and Yacht Council) chapter and verse as though the quoted requirements came from the burning bush. This is not a popular practice with the Good Old Boat editors. The ABYC Standards and Recommended Practices for Small Craft documents are not available to the vast majority of our readers. Membership in the organization is quite expensive and is, therefore, not common among non-professionals. Although regulating agencies and insurance companies may adopt all or parts of the ABYC standards, the ABYC standards are otherwise completely voluntary having no inherent force in law. They also do not preclude good design and engineering alternatives.

Acceptance (or not)

Articles are submitted on speculation. Competition for space in Good Old Boat magazine is brisk. Our responsibility to our readers requires that we try to get the best and most appropriate material. Don't be discouraged if your submission is not accepted. A piece that is not accepted by one publication could easily be just what another publication is looking for.

Payment for articles

$700 Original new technical article (runs 3,000-5,000 words)

$500 Maintenance and upgrade articles and other sailing features. (1,500-3,000 words)

$100-300 Other short pieces along these lines

$250 Brief refit articles and photos (running from 1,000-2,000 words)

$500 Boating couple and boat feature with good photos. This can run 1,500-3,000 words.

$700 Boat reviews focused on sailing characteristics, layout and design, pros and cons when considering a purchase (possible trouble spots to watch for, and so on). This can run 1,500-3,000 words.

$100 Reflections. This is a short, philosophical statement. The kind of stuff that comes to us when we've been "out there" a while. (runs 350-750 words)

$500-700 History features. We'd also like stories about specific boat types (such as what's gone on with Ericsons over the years), profiles of designers (the career of Carl Alberg or George O'Day, and how the individual influenced what we're sailing today) or about other things such as sail shape and materials, hull shapes, keel shapes, etc. (runs 1,500-4,000 words)

$300-500 Good old vendor articles with good photos (1,000-2,500 words)

$150 Cruising memories (1500-2,000 words)

$50 Book reviews 375-450 words

$200 Simple solutions with photos (500-1,500 words)

$50 Quick and easy projects with illustrations or photos (300-600 words)

$50-75 Sidebars

$50 Photos (when purchased separately, not as a part of an article)

$75 Artwork (when purchased separately, not as a part of an article)

$100 Cover photos or art

$200 Center spreads (photos or art)

Categories: Nonfiction—Boating—Sailing

CONTACT: Good Old Boat Magazine
7340 Niagara Lane N
Maple Grove MN 55311-2655
Phone: 763-420-8923
Fax: 763-420-8921
Website: http://www.goodoldboat.com

Good Old Days
Good Old Days Specials

Guidelines:

Manuscripts should be typed (preferably double-spaced) with the author's name, address and phone number in the upper left-hand corner. We prefer to buy all rights, but will negotiate. If you cannot offer all rights, you must specify the type of rights you are offering when submitting your manuscript. Please submit only one manuscript at a time. We do accept e-submissions via e-mail, but treat them as unsolicited manuscripts without SASE; you will only hear from us if we offer a contract for your story.

Our preferred word length is 500-1500 words. Please indicate whether or not photos are available. You may include photocopies or duplicates of your photos with your manuscript, but please do not include your originals. If we need the originals or photographic copies, we will ask for them. Do not send scanned or laser-copied photos; the quality isn't high enough for use. Identify the backs of photos with your name, address and story title. Manuscripts should include captions of complete information concerning the photographic material you are submitting.

Payment

Payment generally ranges from $15-75 and is dependent on how much of the manuscript will actually be used (don't assume that your 3,000 word document will be paid on the basis of pre-edited weight), how much editing will be required and what photographic support you have. Please enclose an SASE if you want your material returned. Sample copies: $2.00 and a self-addressed stamped manila envelope.

Good Old Days tells the real stories of the people who lived and grew up in "the good old days" (about 1900-1955). We like stories to sound conversational, as if you're sitting around the fire and Grandpa's telling you about the time he and Grandma got shivareed. However, we are open to any way you choose to write your story, as long as it is true and falls within our targeted period of time.

Subject Matter

These regular departments are in each issue: *Good Old Days* on Wheels (transportation: auto, plane, horse-drawn, train, bicycle, trolley, etc.), *Good Old Days* in the Kitchen (favorite foods, appliances, ways of cooking, recipes), Home Remedies (herbs and poultices, hometown doctors, harrowing kitchen table operations) and Looking Hollywood Way (this feature is written by a regular columnist and pretty much fulfils the quota of movie related features).

If your story is about how you remember Mom boiling handkerchiefs with her homemade lye soap, include how she made the soap! If Grandma's secret recipe for baking powder biscuits made you drool at the very thought, include the recipe!

We accept seasonal stories year 'round, from holidays to harvest, shivarees to maple-sugaring. We look for real stories; happy, sad, the good, the bad. Humor is always a plus. Good, clear, interesting old photos are a definite plus. We also purchase interesting old photos alone, with about a paragraph of caption material describing what is pictured.

Most of our writers are not professionals. We prefer the author's individual voice, warmth, humor and honesty over technical ability. Successful stories tend to stick with one subject (i.e.: how my brother and I got caught skipping school one day and faced the consequences...how I love to cook on a wood-burning stove, etc.). We also publish an occasional biography, as well as stories on memorable events, fads, fashion, sports, music, literature, entertainment, etc. Many people write a story "as told to" by the person who actually experienced it. But never, never try to pull the wool over our eyes with fiction or non-authentic manuscripts.

Good Old Days Specials

Good Old Days Specials is a bimonthly publication with basically the same story requirements of *Good Old Days*.

We receive about 200 manuscripts a month and can only offer contracts on a limited number. Therefore, we must return a lot of good stories. The mark of a good free-lance writer is persistence; be sure to keep trying! Thank you for your interest in contributing material to *Good Old Days* and *Good Old Days Specials*.

Categories: Automobiles—Cooking—Film/Video—Food/Drink—Health

CONTACT: Ken Tate, Editor
Material: All
House of White Birches
306 East Parr Rd.
Berne IN 46711
Phone: 260-589-4000
Website: www.goodolddaysonline.com

GORP.com

Content on The Away Network (Away.com, GORP.com, OutsideOnline.com) comes from in-house writers, our stable of regular contributors, and Outside magazine. While there are opportunities to freelance for Away.com and GORP.com, we rarely assign articles to unsolicited queries. Please note there is a separate query process for Outside magazine (see Outside's Contributor's Guidelines).

Generally, we encourage professional writers and photographers to first query us with their proposals, and provide credentials, clips, and areas of interest/expertise. Please include the word "Query" in the subject heading and DO NOT send attachments. We will be in touch should we wish to pursue your proposal, and we'll add your information to our database of people to contact with details of upcoming assignments.

Unfortunately, due to the number of submissions we receive each week, we cannot respond to each of you individually. Please include an SASE for any material you send by mail that you want returned.

PAYMENT AND RIGHTS INFORMATION

The Away Network buys non-exclusive print and online rights to all material, to be featured on the appropriate Web site as long as we deem necessary. (You are quite free to sell the material elsewhere, however.) Once purchased, content may also be released for third-party syndication with The Away Network's affiliates and partners.

Payment is scaled to article length and subject matter.

CONTACT: Editorial Department [specify your site of interest: eg. Away or GORP]
c/o The Away Network
702 H Street NW Ste 200
Washington DC 20001
Fax 202-654-8081
E-mail: Editorial@away.com; Editorial.gorp@away.com

Gourmet

Formal guidelines not available. Please read a number of issues to ascertain the publication's style and needs.

Send queries to address below.

Categories: Nonfiction—Cooking—Entertainment

CONTACT: Shannon Rodgers, Editorial Dept.
Material: All
4 Tiems Square
New York NY 10036
Phone: 212-286-2860

Government Executive

Government Executive, a publication of National Journal Group Inc., is a monthly business magazine serving executives and managers in the federal government. Our 60,000 subscribers are high-ranking civilian and military officials who carry out the laws that define the government's role in our economy and society.

Government Executive aspires to serve the people who manage these huge agencies and programs much in the way that Fortune, Forbes and Business Week serve private-sector managers.

Editorial goals include:

Covering news and trends about the organization and management of the executive branch; Helping federal executives improve the quality of their agencies' services by reporting on management innovations; Explaining government problems and failures in ways that offer lessons about pitfalls to avoid; Creating a greater sense of community along the elite corps of public servants to whom the magazine circulates; Improving the image of the public service by teaching our non-government readers about the challenges federal officials confront.

Government Executive has twice won the Gerald R. Ford Prize for Distinguished Reporting on National Defense, in 1990 and 1995.

TYPES OF ARTICLES WE PUBLISH

Feature Stories

These usually range in length from 1,500 to 4,000 words. Any sidebars must be figured into the total word count. Feature stories fall into these general categories:

Management issues

These focus on topics of broad interest and include reporting from several agencies. Topics could include downsizing of agencies; reinventing government; recruitment and retention; ensuring that computers succeed in improving productivity; and upgrading training.

Agencies

These stories often focus on one agency with an eye toward finding generally applicable lessons for federal managers. For example, one story assessed the change in NASA's culture as the agency handed off operation of the space shuttle to a private firm.

Government people

Some articles are organized around certain professions within government. For example, we've written about the influence of economists on policy-making, how to make the best use of agency lawyers, and how to recruit and retain a good clerical work force.

Civil service issues

These include articles about pay, executive training, ethics, politicization of the civil service and the impact of technology on the workplace.

Guest Columns

Our Management and Viewpoint columns are good forums for members of our audience to share an opinion or their experiences. Management columns should include advice that would be useful to managers in a variety of fields. Viewpoint columns express opinions on issues relevant to civil servants. These columns are usually about 1,000 words long.

Other Departments

These are usually 1,000 words or 1,700 words, except as noted. Monthly departments for which we sometimes use freelance contributions include: Executive Memo: A series of short news items, 100-200 words each. Travel: On government/business travel. Information Technology: government applications of computer technologies.

OUR CONTRIBUTORS

Following are some guidelines for different categories of would-be contributors:

• Professional journalists

• These may be full-time freelance writers or employees of other publications. We look for people who have expertise in civil-service issues or the management of federal agencies.

• Current or former federal employees

• We publish personal reflections on the problems and opportunities of public service, as well as analytical articles on the causes and solutions of real-life agency problems. However, we often prefer to assign stories suggested by government officials to writers outside of government. We think independent reporting and analysis often lends credibility to an article.

• Consultants, corporate executives, public relations representatives

We shy away from articles that seem to be aimed at promoting the fortunes of any individual, product, or program. We almost never publish articles submitted by or on behalf of companies or trade associations.

HOW TO GET AN ASSIGNMENT

We prefer to receive queries about possible assignments in the form of a one- or two-page letter that lays out the subject you want to write about, the angle you will take and the sources you will interview. The letter should also detail any relevant experience you have. If you do send us a completed manuscript, be warned that deadline pressure often prevents us from considering or returning unsolicited manuscripts in a timely manner. We do not object if you submit a piece to other publications simultaneously. We do not return unsolicited manuscripts.

STORY SUBMISSION CHECKLIST

Stories may be submitted via e-mail or on floppy disk. Along with your manuscript, please include:

Art memo

Your written list of ideas for graphics may include portraits of your major sources, other photographs, cartoons and illustrations. We especially like to run charts, tables and graphs, so keep any eye out for information relevant to your story that could be presented that way. Please provide us with the contacts we need to arrange to shoot or obtain photographs.

Author bio

At the end of the story, please include a one to two sentence description of your professional background.

Contract

The first time you write for us, you must sign a contract stating that you will pay income taxes on your fees. If you have never signed such a contract, please request one when you submit your story.

WHAT HAPPENS NEXT?

Rewriting

We may ask for a second draft of a story, particularly if you haven't written for us before.

Accuracy checks

We expect you to check all names, titles, dates and facts for accuracy before your story is submitted. However, we always send an edited version of the story back to you so that you may check that no errors have crept in during the editing process.

Payment

We pay upon acceptance, which means after you have completed any requested rewriting or additional billtracker to our satisfaction. Please submit an invoice for the amount agreed upon at the time the story was assigned.

Copyright

Government Executive holds all rights for publication (including publication on the World Wide Web) and all reprint rights.

Categories: Nonfiction—Business—Government—Politics

CONTACT: Timothy Clark, Editor and Publisher
Material: All
1501 M St. NW Ste. 300
Washington DC 20005
Phone: 202-739-8500
Fax: 202-739-8511
E-mail: govexec@govexec.com
Website: www.govexec.com

Grading & Excavation Contractor

Please refer to Forester Communications.

Grain

A choice Canadian
literary magazine since 1973

Grain's Beginnings

Grain magazine published its first issue in June 1973, a gestetner edition with stapled, taped bindings, and with cover art on a card-stock cover by a then new artist Joe Fafard. The first edition, edited by Ken Mitchell, Anne Szumigalski, and Caroline Heath included writings by Robert Kroetsch, George Bowering, Robert Currie, and John V. Hicks, and cost $1.00. A subscription cost $2 a year, or $5 for three years. This was the first of a series of semi-annual issues.

Grain is a quarterly publications.

Throughout all these years, *Grain* has published the best new writing from Canada and abroad, approximately 2000 pieces of writing and over 220 art images, many of them from Saskatchewan. *Grain* editors over the years have been: Ken Mitchell, Caroline Heath, E.F. Dyck, Brenda Riches, Mick Burrs, Geoffrey Ursell, J. Jill Robinson, and currently, Kent Bruyneel.

Grain has grown up with a generation of literary magazines, and is proud to be alive and flourishing after nearly 30 years of life. This flourish is due to the readers, and contributors, but also to primary funding sponsors: Saskatchewan Writers Guild (publisher-in-chief), Sask Lotteries, Saskatchewan Arts Board, The Canada Council and The Canada Magazine Fund.

Submitting to *Grain*

Grain Magazine is an internationally acclaimed literary journal, publishing the freshest poetry and prose from Canada, the US, and abroad.

If you are interested in submitting your work to *Grain*, take a look at the following

Submission Guidelines. If possible, read back issues of our magazine before submitting. Sample issues of *Grain* are available for $9.95 (plus GST in Canada) or $12.00 US for American and International orders. If you'd like to order a copy, go to the go to the Subscription section of our web site.

Grain has a ten-month reading period. During June and July manuscripts will be automatically returned to writers.

E-mail submissions are not accepted. *Grain* will respond to submissions via e-mail, if submittors provide us with an e-mail address, but submissions must be sent via snail-mail.

The Manuscript

Send typed, unpublished material only. The simultaneous submission to *Grain* of material submitted to other publications is not acceptable.

Poetry: You may submit a maximum of 8 poems.

Fiction: Submit a maximum of 2 stories, or up to 30 pages of a novel-in-progress.

Other: Although fiction and poetry are the main focus of *Grain*, the editors will also consider creative non-fiction, and drama.

Do not send your only manuscript copy. A good quality, fully-legible duplicate copy is fine. Use 8 1/2 x 11 paper, one side only. Poetry may be single-spaced; fiction, double spaced; plays, standard play format. All copy must be typewritten.

Type your name and full address on the title page or first page of each work. On subsequent pages, type your last name and the abbreviated title of the piece.

Number every page of a poem or story other than the first page. Use paper clips only. No staples.

Please do not send a second submission until the *Grain* editors have completed consideration of your first one.

Grain receives more than 150 submissions a month. The editors need 2 to 4 months to consider your submission.

Submit Art Work

Artwork submissions should consist of:
• 12 to 20 slides, and black & white prints if available
• A short artist's statement (up to 200 words)
• A brief resume.

The Covering Letter

Indicate the number of poems, stories, or visual images submitted. Include your full address, postal code and phone number (with area code).

Mailing

A stamped, self-addressed envelope (SASE) is required for any response. We will not consider or return any material without this.

Submissions from outside Canada require sufficient International Reply Coupons to cover return postage. Foreign stamps are not valid in Canada for mailing out.

NEW: Save your IRC's and stamps! Provide an e-mail address, and we will respond to your submission electronically, as long as you don't need your manuscript returned. (But we still don't take e-mail submissions—sorry!)

Payment

Poetry: $40 to $175 (depending on number of pages published).

Fiction, and Other: $ 40 to $175.

Front Cover Art: $100.

Other Art: $30 per image.

Rights

Grain purchases first Canadian serial rights only. Copyright remains with the author or artist.

If you have any further questions about our Submission Guidelines, don't hesitate to contact us at: grainmag@sasktel.net.

Categories: Literature—Poetry

CONTACT: Kent Bruyneel, Editor
Material: Grain Submissions
CONTACT: Gerry Hill, Poetry Editor
Material: Poetry
CONTACT: Joanne Gerber, Prose Editor
Material: Prose
PO Box 67
Saskatoon Saskatchewan, Canada S7K 3K1
E-mail: grainmag@sasktel.net
Website: www.grainmagazine.ca

Granta

The main guideline for submitting work to Granta is simply to read the magazine thoroughly and ask yourself honestly if you feel your piece meets our criteria. We receive many submissions every day, many of which are completely unsuitable for Granta (however well written).

Here is a list of things that Granta does not publish:

Academic essays, or essays about writers.

Book reviews.

Straight reporting or feature articles whose primary interest is immediate, i.e., stories whose relevancy will not last the life span of the magazine. We have a three-month lead between going to press and being published. The pieces we publish should outlast that period by several years (as the issues themselves do).

Genre fiction. That means: no Romance, Crime, Science Fiction,

Fantasy Fiction, Historical.

Poetry.

Travel writing without a story. Then we went to X and a funny thing happened, then we went to Y and another funny thing happened, etc. There should be a narrative focus, a point, a reason for you to tell us the story.

Any issue of Granta magazine will reveal stories or non-fiction that breaks one or the other of these rules to some degree. That's why it's useful to take a look at a copy and try and work out what convinced us about a particular piece.

Here is a list of practical things that will help us to deal with your submission:

Do not send more than two stories at a time.

Submissions should be made by post only. Faxes and emails are not accepted. Please don't send computer discs.

Enclose either a current email address or an SAE and postage: International Reply Coupons if you are outside the UK (US stamps do not work from the UK. Sorry to state the obvious, but no one seems to be aware of this). Please indicate (and enclose sufficient postage) if you would like your ms returned, otherwise it will be recycled if unsuitable.

Layout: please type in a plain, legible font on one side of the page.

Cover letter: a brief intro is fine.

Length: we have no length guidelines.

Timing: we aim to respond in three months. However, we have regularly exceeded this timespan, unfortunately, just so you are prepared for a potentially long wait. We do respond to every manuscript eventually.

Photographs

Granta publishes at least one set of photographs per issue, in addition to the single pictures that run opposite the first pages of most pieces. In the past we have been restricted to black and white reproduction, but now (since Granta 76, Winter 2001) we have a colour facility.

Photographic stories do not have a statutory page allocation in the magazine. As a rough guide, however, thirty-plus pages would be considered a long section for a single story and we sometimes break up that allocation to allow us to publish two or even three shorter sets of pictures in one issue.

There are no rules about what kind of photographs we publish. We traditionally run photojournalism that tells a story—about current events, social issues, political conflict and history. We also—in keeping with the writing in the magazine—publish photographic memoirs, diaries, and more personal sets of pictures. We have, in recent issues, published photographs of Antony Gormley's sculptures (Granta 71, Shrinks), Martin Chambi's archive photographs from the 1920s to 1950s (Granta 74, Confessions of a Middle-aged Ecstasy Eater) and colour photographs of the sea (Granta 76, Music). In general we prefer there to be a narrative element to the pictures and although often we run sets of pictures which later appear in a book of their own, we do not run photographs that have been published elsewhere in the English-speaking world. (In some cases one or two photographs from a set may have been used as spot photos in a magazine and we would still, in this case, consider the full set from which they were taken.) If possible, we always prefer unpublished material.

An accompanying text is not necessary for new submissions, though a short paragraph usually helps. If a photographer has an existing text, or a preferred writer, then this should be included with the proposal. Granta does commission writers to provide texts for photographs, depending on what we feel is required.

How to submit photographs and photographic ideas:

Ideally we like to see submissions on CD-ROM (though we would always want to see a set of prints before making a final decision to publish). Before sending in your photographs, it is advisable to write in with your idea, and with a brief explanation of what visual form your idea takes.

You can email any of the magazine staff with a story idea, and make an appointment to show your work. Currently Liz Jobey is the best person to contact. Please do not send picture stories by email.

We cannot take any responsibility for the loss of unsolicited prints, transparencies or CD-ROMs sent to us, though of course we make absolutely every effort to look after material we receive and will, eventually, return it, provided an adequate self-addressed envelope or Jiffy bag is enclosed.

As with written submissions, there may be a long delay in being given a final decision on your work, so please be patient, and don't send us your only existing set of photographs.

And finally, if you remain undaunted, the address for submissions is listed below.

Categories: Fiction—Nonfiction

CONTACT: The Editor
Granta
2-3 Hanover Yard
Noel Rd
London N1 8BE
United Kingdom

Grave Tales

Current Needs: Authors and Artists

Grave Tales is a horror anthology comic book presented by the World Fantasy Award-winning publisher Cemetery Dance. Each issue is comic-sized (48 pages, color cover, B&W interior) and features three tales of terror from today's most popular authors. Previous contributors include Edward Lee, Richard Laymon, Al Sarrantonio, Nancy Collins, Thomas F. Monteleone, and others. As always, it is strongly suggested you read a copy of Grave Tales first to get a feel for the publication.

Author Submissions: We're looking for stories that can be adapted to comic format, in the tradition of Warren's Creepy and Eerie, Marvel and DC anthologies like The Witching Hour and Ghosts, and the EC's legendary Tales From the Crypt and The Vault of Horror. We are also in need of short prose stories, up to 1,000 words. Again, prose stories should have the pulp horror feel. What we don't want: anything modern or that doesn't fit the concepts described above. Query at address above with description of story and a short sample, or, if you prefer, the script. The ideal script will run no longer than 8 pages. Also include a bibliography. Samples cannot be returned without SASE.

Artist Submissions: We are looking for artwork in the tradition of Warren's Creepy and Eerie, Marvel and DC anthologies like The Witching Hour and Ghosts, and the EC's legendary Tales From the Crypt and The Vault of Horror. Think the retro look of Bernie Wrightson or Mike Ploog. No manga or other modern styles. We are in need of both interior and cover art. Send samples to the mailing address above. Samples cannot be returned without SASE. DO NOT send originals or your only copy!

Payment: Professional rates

Response Time: up to four months

Please do not send any email submissions, proposals, or pitches.

Categories: Fiction—Horror—Short Stories

CONTACT: Richard Chizmar, Editor
CONTACT: Brian Keene, Associate Editor
PO Box 623
Forest Hill MD 21050

Gray Areas

We do not print fiction, poetry or short stories. We have no word count limits and prefer depth to fluff.

We explore gray areas of law and morality in the fields of law, music, technology, sociology and popular culture.

We print all points of view and run articles by active criminals, academics, victims, law enforcement, psychiatrists and ordinary citizens.

We also review books, movies, computer software, video games, concerts, comics, catalogs, music CDs, small press magazines and more.

Categories: Alternate Life-style—Book Reviews—Crime—Culture—Film/Video—Internet—Law—Music—Society

CONTACT: Netta Gilboa, Publisher
Material: All
PO Box 808
Broomall PA 19008
Website: www.grayarea.com

The Green Hills Literary Lantern
Truman State University

Fiction

The *Green Hills Literary Lantern* is published annually, each summer, by Truman State University. Website: http://ll.truman.edu/ghllweb. It includes poetry, fiction, reviews, and interviews. The publication runs 200-300 pages. It is printed on good quality paper with a glossy 4-color cover. For the past several issues, it has received grants from the Missouri Arts Council.

We respond to work in 3-4 months. When submitting manuscripts, please send a short bio listing publications (50 - 100 words). We accept simultaneous submissions but discourage multiple submissions, though 2 - 3 "short shorts" are acceptable. Please send an SASE for return of manuscript or for reply only. Please include a phone number on manuscript where we can reach you.

This magazine is open to the work of new writers as well as more established writers. We are interested in stories that demonstrate a strong working knowledge of the craft. Avoid genre fiction or mainstream religious fiction. Otherwise, we are open to short stories of various settings, character conflicts, and styles, including experimental.

Above all, we demand that work be "striking." Language should be complex, with depths, through analogy, metaphor, simile, understatement, irony, etc. - but all this must not be overwrought, or self-consciously literary. This does not mean that in rare cases, style itself cannot be center stage, but if so, it must be interesting and provocative enough for the reader to focus on style alone. "Overdone" writing surely is not either.

We tend to be interested in stories with strong character, with conflicts that matter (where the stakes are fairly high), and with stories that do not have simple resolutions. Stories that go nowhere, that get blurred in focus, or that seem thin in idea have little chance of being accepted for publication.

We accept short stories, short shorts, and excerpts from novels. Our maximum length is 7,000 words. In rare cases, we'll accept a longer story. There is no absolute minimum.

If work is accepted, author will receive prepublication galleys. Publication is copyrighted. We purchase one-time rights.

Poetry

Submit 3-7 poems, typed, one poem per page. There are no restrictions on subject matter, though pornography and gratuitous violence will not be accepted. Obscurity for its own sake is also frowned upon. Both free and formal verse forms are fine, though we publish more free verse overall. Poems of under six lines or over two pages are unlikely to be published. A genuine attempt is made to publish the best poems available, no matter who the writer. First time poets, well-established poets, and those in-between, all can and have found a place in the GHLL. A cover letter is appreciated but not required. We try to respond within 3-4 months, if not sooner. We try to supply feedback, particularly to those we seek to encourage.

Categories: Fiction—Book Reviews—Interview—Poetry

CONTACT: Joe Benevento, Co-Editor
Material: All Poetry

Truman State University, Division of Language & Literature
Kirksville MO 63501
Phone: 660-785-4513
Fax: 660-359-2211
E-mail: Jbeneven@truman.edu
E-mail: JackGHLL@earthlink.net
CONTACT: Jack Smith, Co-Editor
Material: All Fiction
PO Box 375, Trenton, MO 64683
Website: ll.truman.edu/ghllweb

Green Mountains Review
Johnson State College

The GREEN MOUNTAINS REVIEW is an international journal publishing poems, stories, and creative nonfiction by both well-known authors and promising newcomers. The magazine also features interviews, literary criticism, and book reviews.

The editors are open to a wide range of styles and subject matter as is apparent from a look at the short list of writers who have published in its pages: Julia Alvarez, John Ashbery, Hayden Carruth, Billy Collins, Stephen Dobyns, Mark Doty, Stephen Dunn, Carol Emshwiller, Linda Gregg, Donald Hall, Maxine Kumin, Denise Levertov, Larry Levis, Phillip Lopate, Dionisio D. Martinez, William Matthews, Naomi Shihab Nye, Lynne Sharon Schwartz, Ntozake Shange, Reginald Shepard, Alix Kates Shulman, David St. John, Walter Wetherell, and Meredith Sue Willis.

Past issues have included interviews with writers such as Galway Kinnell, Grace Paley, and Derek Walcott, as well as literary essays such as David Wojahn's on memory narrative poetry and David Mura's on multicultural writing.

There have been several special issues: one devoted to Vermont fiction writers, a second called "Women, Community, and Narrative Voice" featuring short stories by women, a third filled with new writing from the People's Republic of China, a fourth devoted to multicultural writing in America, and another featuring contemporary comic poetry.

The editors read manuscripts between September 1 and March 1. During that period they will make every attempt to respond within three months. Manuscripts received outside the reading period will be returned unread.

Categories: Fiction—Nonfiction—Book Reviews—Interview—Poetry—Writing

CONTACT: Neil Shepard, General Editor
Material: Poetry, Essays, Interviews
CONTACT: Leslie Daniels, Fiction Editor
Material: Fiction
Johnson State College
Johnson VT 05656
Phone: 802-635-1350
E-mail: gmr@jsc.vsc.edu
Website: http://greenmountainsreview.jsc.vsc.edu

GreenPrints

GreenPrints shares the human side of gardening: the joy, humor, frustrations, and heart in fine prose and fine art.

Thanks for your interest! GreenPrints lives because people like you care about gardening—and about sharing with other gardeners. Without your contributions, the magazine simply would not exist. Still, it almost feels like a contradiction in terms to offer Writer's Guidelines for GreenPrints. (After all, what we want is special, exciting, provocative, sparkling, unordinary writing—and how do you prescribe that?) But people do ask, so I better be a good fellow and come up with something! To wit:

1) We want the best, personal (key word, that) garden writing we can find. Expressive, thoughtful, humorous, angry, contrite, flippant, searching, witty, observant, sad, inviting—whatever! We focus on the human, not the how-to side of gardening. On the people as well as the plants. After all, gardening is a relationship, not a recipe. GreenPrints explores that relationship, not by instructing, preaching, or lecturing about it. Instead, we celebrate it…by sharing the stories and experiences we all have trying (and sometimes failing) to get along with plants. I can put what we want in one word: Storytelling. Or maybe storyshowing. The most common shortcoming I see is people who forget the old high-school English-class dictum: Show, don't tell. Take us through the experiences with trenchant details and tight descriptions. Don't tell us how profound or funny or beautiful it was: make us experience the feeling.

2) We're not opposed to essays, but the good ones a) evolve directly from personal experience and b) offer new insights or at least new ways of expressing old insights. We're not opposed to fiction, either, but don't you agree that it should offer something special that the nonfiction stories we get wouldn't (i.e., don't just imitate reality).

3) One thing for sure, we don't want sappy, gooey writing. Tender, moving, poignant is wonderful. But syrupy is the biggest trap GreenPrints has to avoid. (Trap #2: preachy. We can all read lectures and sermons other places, n'est-ce pas?)

4) Strong endings. Many, many, many times I send pieces back to say, "This peters out. The ending is weak, obvious, trite. Give me a creative, witty, forceful conclusion. Stop the piece with a wham, not a whimper." A good ending (some of which make a clever reference back to the beginning) can lift the whole piece a notch and make it end with an exclamation point of strength, instead of, well…just… fading…away…forgettably…

5) Length? I don't know. Since we're digest-sized, most of our pieces are no more than 2,000 words. But write what you have to. If it's good, we'll work out length problems.

6) Payment? Did you have to ask? We pay miserably; top payment is $100 and we often pay less. I apologize. You deserve more. When GreenPrints starts paying me better than miserably, I will be only too glad to pay more. Right now, I'm working for peanuts to get this different little gardening gem to take off. We pay on acceptance, buy First North American Serial Rights (unless you've already published it somewhere else first; we're happy to reprint pieces-as long as they're good!).

7) SASE? Oh, yes, PLEASE!

8) In your cover letter, please tell me something clever/witty/appropriate about yourself that I can use for our "Contributor's Page" if we use your piece.

9) Poetry: Well, we run about 1 poem per issue. That's 4 per year, so let's admit there's not much chance I can accept your poem. The ones I do take tend to be a) not too hard to follow, b) not too saccharine, and c) rarely in rhyme, but most of all d) clever. Innovative. Offering well-expressed, detail-dressed new twists on this magazine's very old topic. Payment: $25.

10) E-mail submissions? I accept these very reluctantly. Easier for you? They're harder for me. I much prefer a printed manuscript mailed with a self-addressed stamped envelope. (Plus, I write personal responses on all the printed manuscripts I receive.)

11) One last thing: Are you a SUBSCRIBER? If not, would you please consider becoming one ($19.97 a year)? Not only does it get you a wonderful little magazine and the best possible feel for the type of writing we run, it also helps us survive so we can run your writing! Thanks again. Best to you with prose, plants, and life,

Pat Stone, Editor

P.S. Oh, one more thing: I generally can't find time to read submissions until the month after an issue deadline. So your submission is likely to lie fallow until Feb., May, Aug., or Nov. Sorry.

Categories: Garden

CONTACT: Pat Stone, Editor
PO Box 1355

Fairview NC 28730
E-mail: greenprints@cheta.net
Website: http://greenprints.com/

The Greensboro Review
University of North Carolina at Greensboro

• No previously published works, works accepted for publication, or dual submissions are eligible.

• Poetry may be any length; maximum length for fiction is 7,500 words.

• All manuscripts must be typed and accompanied by a self-addressed, stamped envelope for return.

• All manuscripts must arrive by September 15 to be considered for the Spring issue (acceptances in December) and February 15 to be considered for the Fall issue (acceptances in May). Manuscripts arriving after those dates will be held for the next consideration.

Categories: Fiction—Poetry

CONTACT: Poetry Editor
Material: Poetry
CONTACT: Fiction Editor
Material: Fiction
UNCG
3302 Hall for Humanities and Research Administration
PO Box 26170
Greensboro NC 27402-6170
Phone: 336-334-5459
Fax: 336-256-1470
E-mail: jlclark@uncg.edu

Grit Magazine

WHO WE ARE

Grit, America's family magazine since 1882, is dedicated to ringing the joy bells of life for its readers. We publish items about ordinary people doing extraordinary things, accounts of interesting places or events, and real-life stories about others in the GRIT family.

We tailor our magazine to provide an informative, yet entertaining, look at life in America, past and present. GRIT explores values, lifestyles and traditions important to those concerned about themselves, their families and their communities.

GRIT focuses not on age or abilities, but on attitude—taking a positive approach to the goodness of life. GRIT celebrates our readers' courage, dedication and determination to make a difference.

GRIT gladly accepts reader contributions and freelance materials appropriate for publication. See tips below. The best inside tip is to read several issues of GRIT. Copies are available by subscription, or by requesting a sample copy directly from GRIT at the address shown below.

The best inside tip is to read several issues of GRIT. Copies are available by subscription, 800-678-4883, or by requesting a sample copy from address below. For single copies, please enclose $4 for postage and handling, plus a stamped, self-addressed 9"x12" envelope. Writers guidelines are free with a SASE.

FEATURES

GRIT publishes feature-length articles (1,200-1,500 words) about topics important to today's families: American values and quality of life; outstanding people and interesting places; parenting and grandparenting; home and garden; arts and crafts; American history and traditions; family lifestyles; community involvement or service; family-oriented media and movies; Americana and nostalgia; antiques and collectibles, and travel. Submit manuscripts to the editor-in-chief on speculation, for review, color photos (original negatives and slides preferred) or black-and-white nostalgia photos. Photos are required for manuscripts to be considered. We buy only upon publication, therefore, no updates or advance commitments can be given.

PHOTOS

GRIT expects professional quality color and black-and-white negatives, slides, transparencies or prints. Original negatives and slides are preferred. Be sure to label each submission with your name, address and telephone number and include caption information. Photos are required for manuscripts to be considered.

SUBMISSIONS & PAYMENT

Payment is on publication. No assignments or guarantees of publication are expressed or implied. GRIT assumes no responsibility for any material that is not returned or is lost or damaged.

Generally, the standard rate of payment for nonfiction feature-length articles, upon publication, is 15 to 22 cents per published word and $35 to $50 per original published photograph. However, when articles are used in departments or department features, the author is paid a discretionary flat rate according to length, placement and overall value to the magazine.

TIPS FOR CONTRIBUTORS

The best education is reading several issues of GRIT for types and subjects of stories we use, and our style;

Include the names and telephone numbers of all sources for fact-checking. Identify sources fully, including their credentials, titles or reasons they are qualified to comment, and provide full references for any publications used as sources.

Articles should have national appeal. Information in sidebar or graph form is appropriate for many stories: lists of tips, resources or questions to help readers better understand the subject. For travel stories, include tips such as prices, how to get there, where to stay, etc.

HOW DO I SUBMIT SOMETHING TO GRIT?

• Include your full name, address, telephone number, social security number and submission title on each page. Also send a brief synopsis of your submission, a short personal biography and several clips of any previously published works in your dated cover letter.

• Manuscripts must be accompanied by suitable photos to be considered.

• Submit double-spaced, typed manuscripts. If possible, submit the same material on a 3.5-inch Macintosh disk. Keep a copy of your work and send only completed, proofread manuscripts, including photos. GRIT is not responsible for the return of any materials. GRIT does not consider submissions made simultaneously to other publications.

• Include a return envelope with adequate postage for acceptance/rejection correspondence and for possible return of unused photos. We usually do not return full manuscripts, only the front page.

• All material should be mailed to the editor-in-chief. If writing for a particular department, please note department's name on the envelope and in your cover letter.

• Volume prohibits individual acknowledgments and status updates. No advance commitments are made nor implied. No phone calls, please. Rejected submissions are returned immediately after reading; others may be held for further consideration.

• No calls or queries. E-mail submissions or queries will not be accepted.

Categories: Agriculture—Animals—Biography—Children—Col-lectibles—Conservation—Cooking—Crafts/Hobbies—Culture—Ecology—Family—Fishing—Folklore—Gardening—General Interest—Health—History—Hobbies—Lifestyle—Outdoors—Recreation—Recreation Vehicles—Regional—Rural America

CONTACT: Kathryn Compton, Editor-in-Chief
Material: All
1503 SW 42nd St.
Topeka KS 66609
Phone: 785-274-4300
Fax: 785-274-4305
E-mail: grit@cjnetworks.com (no submissions)
Website: www.grit.com

The Growing Edge

Guidelines for Writers/Photographers

The Growing Edge magazine and Web Site provide the latest news & information for indoor & outdoor growers, including hobbyists, educators, researchers, and commercial growers. A moderate to high level of experience and knowledge is necessary for successful articles. Some research may be necessary. The Growing Edge is actively seeking writers and photographers to cover hydroponics, aquaponics, greenhouse growing, and other related subject areas. Freelance article inquiries are encouraged.

Download:
Contract
FTP site instructions
Model release form

General Information
The Growing Edge magazine is published bimonthly, four color, and 96 pages.

Manuscript format: double-spaced typed or word-processed; final, accepted manuscript must be on computer disk (include hard copy); e-mail is acceptable.

The Growing Edge and New Moon Publishing, Inc., purchase first world serial ($0.10/word), first anthology ($0.05/word), and nonexclusive electronic rights ($0.05/word) for a total of $0.20/word.

The Growing Edge and New Moon Publishing, Inc., purchase print and nonexclusive electronic photography rights (see below for rates).

Editorial Guidelines
Articles should be directly related to high-tech indoor or outdoor soilless cultivation, including hydroponics, aquaponics, greenhouse growing, and other related subject areas. Traditional, soil-based gardening articles will not be considered for publication.

All content-related queries should be addressed to the editor. New contributors should include two writing samples (preferably published) and a resume.

Include an SASE with sufficient postage for return of unsolicited photos or manuscripts.

By-lines are given, except where extensive rewriting makes them inappropriate. Please include a suggested author biography of one to two sentences.

Payment for articles is based on published word count and is made upon publication ($0.20/word).

Photography Guidelines
Photos should be related in some way to the indicated general subject areas. Most photography is submitted by the author of accepted articles.

Color negatives, slides, and prints are preferred. Photos should be numbered. Include a brief suggested caption for each photo.

Include a photographer by-line if different than the author's by-line.

Include a model release for any included human subjects.

Picture-Taking Tips:
Check focus and depth of field carefully, especially in close-ups.
Photographing under artificial lighting can be difficult with auto-

matic cameras; use manual control and bracket exposures under and over the meter's setting.

Never write on the backs of prints in ink—it can rub onto other photos.

Payment for photos is based on published usage and is made upon publication. Payment for photos published in the interior of the magazine is $25 each. Payment for a photo published on the cover is $175.

High-quality, high-resolution color digital images are sometimes accepted. Digital images need to be at least 300 dpi at a reasonably large physical size.

Other Artwork

Diagrams and charts may be submitted but will not be purchased and will probably be redone.

The Growing Edge and New Moon Publishing, Inc., do not assume responsibility for unsolicited photos or manuscripts.

Digital Photos

Top 3 rules for digital photography:

You can always "size-down" an image, but you can never "size-up" an image without sacrificing image quality.

In digital cameras, as in most other products: You get what you pay for.

If you take poor pictures with a regular camera, you will probably take bad pictures with a digital one.

Digital cameras are still in their infancy. Even the most expensive models are just starting to be able to capture an 8.5 x 11 inch image at 300 dpi quality. Scanners follow along the same rule, but a mid-range priced scanner (with the right settings) should be able to scan your prints into digital form at an acceptable size and resolution.

For more information

There are many Web sites that offer basic tutorials on photography. Here are a few links to check out:

http://www.photocourse.com
http://www.shortcourses.com
http://scantips.com
http://www.google.com

Categories: Nonfiction—Crafts/Hobbies—Environment—Garden—Hobbies—Science—Hydroponics

CONTACT: Amy Knutson, Editor
E-mail: Amy_Knutson@growingedge.com
Website: www.growingedge.com

Gryphon Doubles

Please refer to Gryphon Books in the publisher's section.

Guide

Guide is a Christian story magazine geared for young people, ages 10-14. The 32-page four-color publication is published weekly by the Review and Herald Publishing Association. Our mission is (1) to point young people to Jesus and (2) to show Christian character-building principles in practice.

Stories

Each issue includes three to four true stories. Although adventure continues to be the staple product of *Guide*, we do need stories in all categories. Preferred word count is 800-1,200 words. Payment is 7-10 cents per word upon acceptance for first serial rights.

Adventure

Guide adventure stories allow the reader to vicariously experience the excitement of making new discoveries while seeing character-building principles in action. These stories can take place anywhere (outdoors or even in an urban setting). Try to incorporate mystery, action, and discovery (MAD).

Personal Growth

The *Guide*-age years (10-14) can be turbulent on many fronts.

Young people often struggle with friendships, self-esteem, family members, peer acceptance, body changes, etc. Stories in the personal growth category are aimed at providing guidance from a Christian perspective.

Christian Humor

Stories in this category use a lighthearted story line that goes beyond one-liners to expose a character-building principle. The key is to write what's funny to kids and keep it believable. Also let the reader decide if something's funny rather than tell that a character is "doubled over in laughter."

Inspiration

Possible topics in this category include answers to prayer, biblical narratives, mission stories, and Bible study. However, don't limit yourself to "traditional" themes. Show God at work in both the common and unusual circumstances of life.

Biography

In today's society, as much as ever, young people need good role models. Some stories we have printed in *Guide* feature Martin Luther King, Jr., Johannes Gutenberg, and Anne Frank.

Story Series

We also run continued stories (five to 12 parts, with each chapter about 1,200 words in length). The story line should maintain some degree of spirituality throughout. An adventurous slant always captures our interest—and the reader's. Please query first.

Nature

We suggest that you carefully study our bimonthly Creation Station feature and other nature stories before submitting. We are looking for creative approaches to nature, not an encyclopedia-style rendition of facts. Please include a spiritual application in the article or as a sidebar. Documentation necessary.

Games and Puzzles

We are interested in fresh game concepts for *Guide*-age readers. We see far too many word search and crossword puzzles, though of course we need some of those, too. Check out puzzles in current puzzle books and Web sites to find something new that could work for *Guide*. Payment is $35-40 for first serial rights.

Reprints

We accept submissions for reprints, but payment is less. Please let us know when and where the story or game first appeared.

10 Writing Tips

1. Be sure to study at least three issues of the magazine before submitting any of your work.

2. Before writing any *Guide* story, we encourage you to ask for the Holy Spirit's involvement.

3. Think true. We no longer use fiction.

4. Choose a story line that hasn't been beaten to death.

5. Keep your protagonists *Guide* age. Regularly spend time around 10- to 14-year-olds. This includes working to understand ethnic singularities.

6. Use lots of dialogue and word pictures. Show, don't tell.

7. Bring out a spiritual or character-building principle that the reader can put into practice in his or her life. Make the story make a difference.

8. Put a twist on the ending. Don't make the story line an exercise in predictability. Be creative.

9. Look for places to boost the energy level of your piece.

10. After you've finished your story, set it aside for at least a few days. Then give it a final editing before sending it to us. We prefer receiving final drafts.

Categories: Nonfiction—Children—Christian Interests—Inspirational—Juvenile—Religion—Spiritual

CONTACT: Randy Fishell, Editor
Material: All
Review and Herald Publishing Association
55 W. Oak Ridge Drive
Hagerstown MD 21740
Phone: 301-393-4037

Fax: 301-393-3209
Website: www.guidemagazine.org

Guideposts

Guideposts Editorial Guidelines

Guideposts magazine is a monthly inspirational, interfaith, non-profit publication written by people from all walks of life. Its articles present tested methods for developing courage, strength and positive attitudes through faith in God. Our writers express viewpoints from a variety of Protestant, Catholic and Jewish faith experiences.

A typical *Guideposts* story is a first-person narrative written in simple, dramatic, anecdotal style with a spiritual point that the reader can "take away" and apply to his or her own life. The story may be the writer's own or one written in the first person for someone else. Even our short features, such as "His Mysterious Ways," "What Prayer Can Do," "Angels Among Us" and "The Divine Touch" use this format Writing a short feature is often the easiest way of making a sale to *Guideposts*.

Please observe the following in writing your Guideposts story:

Don't try to tell an entire life story in a few pages. Focus on one specific happening in a person's life. The emphasis should be on one individual. Bring in as few people as possible so that the reader's interest stays with the dominant character.

Decide what your spiritual point, or "takeaway," will be. Everything in the story should be tied in with this specific theme.

Don't leave unanswered questions. Give enough facts so that the reader will know what happened. Use description and dialogue to let the reader feel as if he were there, seeing the characters, hearing them talk. Dramatize the situation, conflicts and struggle, and then tell how the person was changed for the better or the problem was solved.

Most important: Study the magazine.

Payments:

Full-length manuscripts (750-1500 words): $250 - $500, occasionally higher.

Shorter manuscripts (250- 750 words): $100 - $250.

Short features and fillers (under 250 words): $25 - $100. These include "What Prayer Can Do" and heavenly encounters such as "His Mysterious Ways," "Angels Among Us" and "The Divine Touch"

We do not use fiction, essays or sermons, and we rarely present stories about deceased or professional religious people. We do not evaluate book-length material.

We receive thousands of unsolicited manuscripts each month, so allow two months for a reply.

Submission@guideposts.org

Categories: Nonfiction—Christian Interests—Inspirational—Religion—Spiritual

CONTACT: The Editor
Material: All
16 E. 34th St.
New York NY 10016
Phone: 212-257-8100
Website: www.guideposts.com

Guideposts for Kids

About Your Manuscript: Make it good. Interactive, if possible. Relevant, playful, punchy. Tight, tight text, to reflect the quick click mentality of our Internet readers. Lots of links (at least possibilities) provided, lots of subheadings. And please, no preachy stories about Bible-toting children. *Guideposts for Kids* on the Web is not a beginner's market. Some areas of interest to freelancers:

Feature Stories: 700 words, including sidebar(s) that may include links to other cool stuff on the site, or other appropriate, reliable online materials or outside resources. Make it timely. Something kids not only need to know, but want to know as well. Recent examples include "Are You on Homework Overload?" (included sidebar linking kids to homework help sites) and "Is My Family Normal?" (included a quiz on "What is Normal?"). Topics for stories include animals, school issues, friendship, current events, sports, and any other creative, kid-friendly topic you may think of. Query.

Secondary Features: 350 words, including sidebar(s). More playful. Recent examples include "How Columbus Kept Track" (article on how Christopher Columbus measured the distance he sailed), "Dip, Dip, Goose" (story about the origin of ink pens, including a recipe for invisible ink and a sidebar on the gel pen craze), and "A Gooey New Pet," (piece on the popularity of jellyfish as pets in Japan, with a sidebar on jellyfish facts). Query.

Tips from the Top: 500 words, including "tips" (advice) from celebrity athletes who are also good role models for kids. Main piece should be a kid-friendly look at the sports star's background and rise to the top, and must include direct-from-the-source quotes. (In other words, make sure to interview the celebrity yourself!) Tips should include practical advice on how to play the game rather than simply intangible directives like "Reach for your dreams." Query.

Cool Kids: Profiles of kids (150-300 words) ages 6-11 doing great volunteer work in their communities. "Finder's fee" for clippings used. Include suggestions on how to get started helping others, point to sites and other resources that can offer kids volunteer opportunities. Query with lead/slant.

Fiction: 900 words maximum. Stories featuring conflicts our readers will respect, resolutions our readers will accept. Problematic. Tight. Filled with realistic dialogue and sharp imagery. No stories about "good" children always making the "right" decision. If present at all, adults are minor characters and do not solve kids' problems for them. Always interested in short short stories—500-700 words. Also stories that have a craft or recipe tie-in. If so, include.

Trivia: Amusing, unusual, informative. On animals, school, sports, holidays, books, music—whatever!

Quizzes: Humor works best. Be clever. No more than 10 questions, with scoring and feedback included. Can be true/false or multiple choice. Avoid sermonizing. Strive for copy that lets kids discover something about themselves.

Poetry: Original work only. Fresh language; strong imagery. (Every other line may rhyme just fine and it will still be less than a shineing piece of work.)

Crafts: Original work only. Creations should showcase easy-to-follow instructions that need minimal adult supervision. Include samples.

About the Money: There is some. We buy electronic and non-exclusive print rights and pay higher rates for stories exceptionally well-written or well-researched. Regular contributors get bigger bucks, too.

Closing Comments and Parting Advice: Study our Web site. Think like a kid! Neatness does count. So do creativity and professionalism. SASE essential.

Categories: Animals—Children—Christian Interests—Crafts/Hobbies—Education—Family—Games—General Interest—Inspirational—Juvenile—Poetry—Short Stories—Sports/Recreation

CONTACT: Submissions Editor
Material: All
1050 Broadway, Ste. 6
Chesterton IN 46304
E-mail: rtolin@guideposts.org
Website: www.gp4k.com

Guns & Ammo

Editorial Profile

GUNS & AMMO is edited for the sportsman with a keen interest in the practical applications of sporting firearms always emphasizing their safe and proper use. For more than 40 years, the magazine has met the needs of recreational shooters by reflecting every aspect of shooting and firearms. It is the primary source of information for shooters, hunters and collectors.

As active participants themselves, the editors of GUNS & AMMO share the interests of their readers, and each issue of the magazine delivers a well-balanced editorial mix that includes hunting, shooting, reloading, antique and modern arms, ballistics and arms legislation. Natural resource protection and environmental preservation issues, and new products and new trends also receive regular in-depth reporting.

GUNS & AMMO attracts an audience of 5.8 million readers every month, and our appeal covers a vast spectrum of gun owners and users from the competitive shooter of rifles, handguns or shotguns, to the weekend plinker, hunter, reloader and collector. Our readers are true shooting and outdoor enthusiasts and they consider their avocation to be of paramount importance.

Submissions

Guns and Ammo rarely accepts unsolicited submissions. It is mostly a staff written publication. Queries must be submitted by snail mail. Both hard copy and digital text (any format) must be provided upon submission. The Editor will contact you, if your submission is accepted for publication.

Photos: Must be color transparency.

Categories: Nonfiction—Consumer—History—Hobbies—Outdoors—Recreation—Sports/Recreation—Firearms/Hunting/Shooting—Profiles—Opinion

CONTACT: Kevin E. Steele, Editor
Material: All
6420 Wilshire Blvd.
Los Angeles CA 90048
Website: www.gunsandammomag.com

Handwoven

Handwoven is devoted to the interests of hand weavers at all skill levels. Material submitted for publication should display in-depth knowledge based on experience and research. Even when the material is technical, the tone of all articles should be informal and accessible. If you are not familiar with the content and style of *Handwoven*, please request a complimentary copy.

Manuscripts

If your article is already written, enclose a copy of the manuscript with relevant graphics (photographs, slides, drawings, drafts, etc.) and a brief, informal personal biography. Your article should be typewritten or computer- generated, double-spaced, on 8½" x 11" paper. Include your name, address, and telephone number (and fax number and e-mail address if available) at the top of the first page. Write your name on all remaining pages and number each page. Do not write any notes on the copy (other than name and page numbers). If you send your article on disk, send hard copy as well. If using Microsoft Word, save files in any format; if using other word-processing programs, save as "text only." Please do not use any bolds, all caps, bullets, tabs, multiple columns, or other desktop publishing goodies - just straight text. Do not embed graphics. Do not send articles by fax. If you e-mail text, also send hard copy by mail. If fractions appear in the text, write them as 1/2, 12 - 3/4, etc. not as a superscript/subscript (1½). Keep a copy of everything. Enclose a self-addressed envelope with sufficient return postage.

Photographs and drawings

Photographs must be sharp and clear with good contrast and a simple background (please do not send digital photos as e-mail attachments). Make sure each photo is numbered and identified with your name. Do not write on the back of the photo; type the identifying information on a separate piece of paper and tape to the back. Drawings and diagrams should be prepared in black ink on white paper (or on white graph paper with blue lines) ready for redrawing by a staff artist. Include a list of all graphics with explanatory information about each on a separate sheet.

All materials will be returned. We also request a photo of you to include with your biography as part of the article.

Projects

When project articles have been accepted for publication, we usually request that authors send the projects to Interweave for photography. You will not be reimbursed for these shipping costs. We will need to keep the items on hand during photography and production (usually about four months). All projects are returned after publication of the article.

Contracts and payment

A contract is sent when an article is accepted for publication in a designated issue of *Handwoven*. The contract indicates the fee paid for the article and specifies that Interweave Press is purchasing first serial rights (in North America) for publication in *Handwoven* and subsequent non-exclusive rights for use in other Interweave Press publications and promotions. The author verifies that the article is original work and that it has not been published previously. The author retains the publication rights for the original materials.

Interweave Press reserves the right to edit the material as necessary to fit the style, format, or other requirements of *Handwoven*. A copy of the edited manuscript is submitted to the author for corrections before publication.

Tips for preparing project articles

Easy-to-understand instructions are an important feature of the projects shown in *Handwoven* and the Design Collections. For clarity and continuity, we have standardized some of the calculations and methods we use. Before writing your project directions, familiarize yourself with the project format in a recent issue.

Measuring. Take accurate measurements throughout the project.

Take-up and shrinkage. Technically, take-up is loss due to the interlacement process and shrinkage is loss due to the finishing process, but handwoven combines them in calculations. Measure the finished width and length after the fabric has gone through the finishing process but before it has been cut or hemmed.

Steps for calculating width-wise shrinkage and take-up

Method:
a. subtract finished width from width in the reed
b. divide a. by width in the reed
c. multiply b. by 100

Example:
a. 40" width in reed - 36" finished width = 4"
b. 4" 40" width in the reed = .1
c. 100 x .1 = 10% shrinkage and take-up in width

Steps for calculating lengthwise shrinkage and take-up

Method:
a. subtract loom waste and finished length from warp length
b. divide a. by warp length minus loom waste
c. multiply b. by 100

Example:
a. 118" warp length - 36" loom waste - 73" finished length = 9"
b. 9"82" (82" is 118" warp length - 36" loom waste) = .10976"
c. 100 x .10976 = 11% shrinkage and take-up in length

Yarns. Use readily available yarns, not mill-ends or odd lots. If the project has already been woven using yarns that are no longer available, find a suitable substitute and list it in the project directions (and send the substitute for the yarn sample) instead of the original yarn. Give complete information about each yarn (yds/lb, color numbers, manufacturer's name, etc.) and exact amounts required. To calculate warp yardage, multiply the number of warp ends by the warp length and add 5%. To calculate weft yardage, multiply the number of picks per inch by the woven length in inches; multiply the result by the width in the reed; and add 10% for weft take-up. Include with your article a 10" sample of each yarn used, in white if possible. Include floating selvedges in the total warp ends required by the project.

Include in your text any special features of the project, your design process, how the project was inspired, and how it evolved. If you have ideas for changes, variations, or different color schemes, mention them also.

All project articles must be accompanied by a project information sheet (Project at-a-glance) that includes attached yarn samples (request a copy of this form from Liz or Madelyn).

When you receive a copy of the edited article prior to publication, check the copy for accuracy, completeness, and inclusion of all important details.

Categories: Nonfiction—Arts—Crafts/Hobbies—Trade—Textiles

CONTACT: Madelyn van der Hoogt, Editor-in=Chief
Material: Articles or proposals for Handwoven
Interweave Press
PO Box 1228
Coupeville WA 98239
Phone: 360-678-6225 (Questions for Madelyn)
E-mail: mvdh@whidbey.net
CONTACT: Liz Gipson, Managing Editor
Interweave Press
201 NE 4th St.
Loveland CO 80537
Phone: 800-272-2193, ext 629 (Questions for Liz)
E-mail: LizG@interweave.com
Website: www.interweave.com

Hanging Loose

About Us It doesn't sound flippant, we hope, if we say that the most meaningful guide is the magazine itself. We've published it continually since 1966 so, to some extent, past is prologue. While we hope we will always be open to new ideas, it seems unlikely that we will develop an interest in formula romance or sing-song verse. Sample copies may be ordered directly from us ($11.00 including postage) and are also available at many bookstores and libraries. Writers who send work to publications they've never seen are usually wasting time, money and effort, theirs and ours.

Magazine Submissions As a rule, send up to six poems or one story at a time. We rarely publish non-fiction, but there are exceptions. We do not publish reviews. Manuscripts must be legible and be sure that includes your name and address. Enclose a stamped, self-addressed envelope of adequate size or we cannot reply. If you don't want your work returned, please make that clear. Cover letters are welcome if they contain pertinent information, but they are hardly a requirement. Because we read all submissions carefully, please allow up to three months for an answer. That's also why we will not consider simultaneous submissions. We also cannot accept submissions by fax or e-mail. We never have contests or theme issues. We do have a regular section of work by high school writers: special guidelines for high school writers. All contributors receive checks on acceptance and copies of the issue containing their work.

Artwork and book manuscripts are by invitation only, without exception. We cannot be responsible for unsolicited work.

High School Submissions (Special Section) *Hanging Loose* magazine welcomes high school submissions. As with other writers, we reply within three months, and high school authors whose work we publish receive the same small fee and two copies of the issue in which their work appears. We feel a special responsibility to those young writers who look to us not only for possible publication but sometimes also for editorial advice, which we are always happy to give when asked. Our work as editors is of course time-consuming, but we feel a strong commitment to give as much time and attention as possible to the work we receive from high school age writers. We urge writers of high school age to follow these guidelines, in order to help us respond to their work.

Send all work to High School Editor, *Hanging Loose*, 231 Wyckoff Street, Brooklyn, NY 11217. Please also send us a note identifying yourself as a high school age writer, and telling us your age, and be sure to include a self-addressed stamped envelope with sufficient return post-

age. Send 3 to 6 poems, or 1 to 3 short stories, or an equivalent combination of poetry and prose. This enables us to get a good idea of what your work is like. All work should be neatly typed. High quality photocopies or readable computer-generated hard copies are acceptable. A brief biographical statement is welcome. We are always interested in knowing how you found out about us, what school you attend, and so forth.Please Note: We prefer to receive submissions from young writers themselves, rather than from their teachers. We strongly discourage teachers from submitting samples of work from members of their classes. Similarly, we discourage teachers from asking students to submit their work as a class assignment. We prefer teachers to encourage students who take themselves seriously as writers to write us directly.

Hanging Loose has long been known for its special interest in new writers. We read manuscripts throughout the year and we look forward to reading yours.

Categories: Fiction—Poetry

CONTACT: Editor
Material: All
231 Wyckoff St.
Brooklyn NY 11217
Phone: 212-243-7499
E-mail: print225@aol.com
Website: www.hangingloosepress.com

Happy Times Monthly
The Good News Newspaper

About Us
Brigitte Lang, Publisher
Amy O'Rourke, Office Manager
Jonathan Lederman, Production Coordinator

The Happy Times/Happy Herald was established in May of 1995 with the purpose of empowering and inspiring its readers with good, positive, and upbeat news. today with over 250,000 readers The Happy Times/Happy Herald continues to empower and inspire its readers through a myriad of upbeat stories.

Stories should be submitted to happyherald@aol.com by the 15th of the month 6 weeks prior to the publication month. Stories should be 500-600 words and accompanied by 4-6 high resolution color photos.

Florida Coverage: Delray Beach, Boca Raton, Deerfield Beach, Pompano Beach, Ft. Lauderdale, Jupiter, Tequesta, and Palm Beach Gardens.

The *Happy Times Monthly*, the good-news newspaper, is a forum to spread positive ideas everywhere, and contains what people like you send us or tell us about. It provides the community with education, humor, wisdom, inspiration, and awareness of what's good in the news, and highlights people, businesses, social groups and events that can give a positive lift to our readers.

Does one of these categories bring a Happy Times story to mind?
• What I'm thankful for
• Random Acts of Kindness
• Tribute to an amazing friend
• Successful people in business, life, health, or love
• People who care
• Good deed stories
• Positive events
• Everyday heroes
• People helping people

- Tragedy turned positive
- Outstanding students/teachers
- Funniest thing that ever happened to you
- The best time of your life
- Gratitude and thank you's
- Nature & environment stories
- Unusual, funny or cute pet or animal stories
- Humorous relative stories
- Someone that really inspired you!

Write about the person and the experience and send in one or two photos with it

Word Count: 150 to 500 word articles with 1 or 2 photos (place name and address on back of photos). Encourages human interest, feature-type articles about people, organizations, or animals on a good news theme. Stories need to be expressed from the heart. For more writer guidelines or information or suggestions on articles, go to our Web Site. Pays in copy. SASE for sample issues. Subscriptions $20.

The *Happy Times Monthly* pays $50 for Cover Pages stories accompanied by color pictures.

Categories: Nonfiction—Adventure—Animals—Business—Careers—Cartoons—Children—Comedy—Cooking—Entertainment—Environment—Family—Fishing—Games—Gardening—General Interest—Hobbies—Inspirational—Lifestyle—Marriage—Men's Issues—Outdoors—Parenting—Photography—Physical Fitness—Recreation—Relationships—Romance—Senior Citizen—Short Stories—Teen—Writing—Good Deeds—Good News—Heartfelt—Humor—Philosophy

CONTACT: Sue Elmore, Submissions Editor
Material: All
Star Publications, Inc.
PO Box 7253
Boca Raton FL 33431
Phone: 561-394-7466
Fax:E-mail: HappyHerald@aol.com
Website: www.thehappytimes.com

Hard Hat News

I am looking for two types of articles–1) original reporting of events (i.e. conferences, seminars, equipment promotional events, major legislation, 2) feature stories on heavy construction projects (i.e. roads, bridges, major structures, etc.) Where possible, articles should be 1200-2400 words and should include both facts AND human-interest elements.

However, if you have a story that justifies the space, break it into two (or more) sections, with pictures appropriate to each section.

If you think a story might be more suitable for one of the other publications, send it to me and I will see that it is delivered to the correct person.

I look forward to hearing from you.

Holly Rieser, Editor, *Hard Hat News*

General Freelance Information

We pay $2.50 per column inch (it works out to be about $.11 per word), $15.00 per photo used and $60.00 for a cover photo. A story printed in another publication (not another edition of the same publication) pays $1.25 per column inch and $7.50 per picture for each additional publication. Occasionally we will suggest an article. Should you choose to follow up, we will reimburse mileage, telephone, film and developing, and postage expenses as they relate to the article.

Lee Publications prints: Hard Hat News (heavy construction), Grower (greenhouse, turfgrass, nursery, vegetables and fruits), Farm Chronicle (general agriculture for mid-Atlantic states), Country Folks (general agriculture for the Northeast and Pennsylvania), Quarry News (quarry and mining, aggregates and asphalt), Waste Handling News (wood recycling/C+D).

If you have an idea for an article, you might speak with me before you begin. I'll guide you as to what we are looking for. I can be reached at 518-673-3237, ext. 231. Or, preferably, via email at the email address listed below

Stories should be emailed as attachments. Word documents are preferred.

Payment Policy for Photographs, Illustrations, Graphics and Artwork.

Payment is for original work only; specifically: photos, illustrations, graphics and artwork produced or created by the person submitting the work.

Payment DOES NOT include:

1. any form of photography, graphics, illustrations or artwork copied from any source such as books, manuals, clip art disks or other publications. If you feel your article needs these illustrations, obtain permission to use the materials (second sources are almost always copyrighted) and show proof of permission when submitting the materials with your article.

2. graphics, photos, illustrations or artwork copied from the Internet. If you feel your article needs these materials, obtain permission to use the work if it is from a copyrighted site and submit the website address for the graphics along with your article.

Please note: Photos, artwork, graphics and illustrations are very important to feature stories and we encourage all freelance writers to ask interviewees if those materials are available. To save time and expenses, whenever possible please have the person submitting materials send them directly to Lee Publications.

Categories: Nonfiction—Trade—Heavy Construction

CONTACT: Holly Rieser, Editor
Material: All
Lee Publications
PO Box 121
Palatine Bridge NY 13428
Phone: 518-673-3237
E-mail: hrieser@leepub.com
Website: www.leepub.com

Hardboiled

Please refer to Gryphon Books in the publisher's section.

Harper's Bazaar

Formal guidelines not available. Please read a number of issues to ascertain the publication's style and needs.

Send queries to address below.

Categories: Fiction—Nonfiction—Beauty—Fashion—Sexuality

CONTACT: Submissions Editor
Material: All
The Hearst Corp.
1700 Braodway, 37th Floor
New York NY 10019
Phone: 212-903-5000
Website: www.harpersbazaar.com

Harper's Magazine

Harper's Magazine welcomes reader response. Short letters are more likely to be published, and all letters are subject to editing. Volume precludes individual acknowledgment.

Harper's Magazine does not accept editorial submissions via e-mail (please see our submission guidelines for more information), though suggestions for the magazine's Readings section are welcome. Please send those to: readings@harpers.org.

Harper's Magazine will neither consider nor return unsolicited nonfiction manuscripts that have not been preceded by a written query. Harper's will consider unsolicited fiction. Unsolicited poetry will not be considered or returned. No queries or manuscripts will be considered unless they are accompanied by a self-addressed, stamped envelope. Submissions to the Readings section (readings@harpers.org) are welcome and are encouraged, though volume precludes individual acknowledgment.

Categories: Fiction—Nonfiction—Arts—Business—Crime—Culture—Literature—Poetry—Politics—Science—Society—News—Essay—International Affairs—Humor—Humanities—Memoirs

CONTACT: Submissions Editor
Material: Queries
CONTACT: Letters Editor
Material: Reader response letters
666 Broadway 11th Floor
New York NY 10012
Phone: 212-420-5720
Fax: 212-228-5889
E-mail: letters@harpers.org. (Reader response letters only)
E-mail: readings@harpers.org (Reading Section only)
Website: www.harpers.org

The Harvard Business Review

The Harvard Business Review has one goal: to be the source of the best new ideas for people creating, leading, and transforming business. Since its founding in 1922, HBR has had a proud tradition as the world's preeminent management magazine, publishing cutting-edge, authoritative thinking on the key issues facing executives.

HBR's articles cover a wide range of topics that are relevant to different industries, management functions, and geographic locations. They focus on such areas as leadership, organizational change, negotiation, strategy, operations, marketing, finance, and managing people. While the topics may vary, all HBR articles share certain characteristics. They are written for senior managers by experts whose authority comes from careful analysis, study, and experience. The ideas presented in these articles can be translated into action and have been tested in the real world of business. Proposals for articles demonstrating fresh thinking that advances previous knowledge—whose practical application has been thought through in clear, jargon-free language—are those most likely to meet our readers' needs. When evaluating an idea, our editors often look for two things first—what they call the "aha!"—How compelling is the insight?—and the "so what?"—How much does this idea benefit managers in practice?

The best way to inquire about HBR's potential interest in a topic is to prepare a proposal. It can be submitted by mail or electronically and should answer the following questions:

What is the central message of the article you propose to write (the "aha")? What is important, useful, new, or counterintuitive about your idea? Why do managers need to know about it?

1. What is the central message of the article you propose to write (the "aha")? What is important, useful, new, or counterintuitive about your idea? Why do managers need to know about it?

2. How can your idea be applied in business today (the "so what")?

3. For which kinds of companies would the idea NOT work well? For which kinds of companies would it work especially well? Why?

4. What research have you conducted to support the argument in your article?

5. On what previous work (either of your own or of others) does this idea build?

6. What is the source of your authority? What academic, professional, or personal experience will you draw on?

It need not be long and it certainly need not be written in question-and-answer format. The important point is to cover the topics the questions raise.

Then please write a two-to-three page (500–750 word) narrative outline laying out the structure of your article and describing each important point in a separate paragraph. Give us a sense not just of the ground you will cover but of how the logic will flow. Please illustrate your points with real-world examples or provide one extended, detailed example.

Some of the questions we will ask ourselves when evaluating your proposals are:

1. Is this idea new? If not, does it offer a new and useful perspective on an existing idea?
2. What is it based on? What are its antecedents?
3. Did it persuade me?
4. Did I find it interesting? Would HBR readers find it interesting?
5. Does it address an issue that matters to managers?
6. Could it be put into practice?
7. Is the author trying to sell the reader something? To use the insights in the article, would the reader need to consult the author?
8. Are there good illustrations? Have I seen the same company examples used to illustrate a multitude of other models, theses, or points of view?
9. Where are the holes in the thinking?

Each issue of HBR contains both feature articles and departments.

Each feature is an in-depth, rigorous presentation of a significant advance in management thinking and its application in the real world of business. These articles help business leaders establish an intellectual agenda for discussion—and change—within their companies.

Best Practice presents an in-depth description of the how and why behind a successful business practice.

Tool Kit provides a nuts-and-bolts explanation of a useful business tool that can be translated into action at many companies.

Forethought, the opening section of the magazine, surveys emerging ideas and trends, reports on provocative research, and spotlights interesting people and company practices. Each issue contains approximately a dozen Forethought pieces, which range in length from about 200 to 800 words. Each item may have no more than two authors. The section begins with an essay or similarly substantive, thoughtful article and usually includes a short opinion piece. Frequently recurring items include reports on cutting-edge technologies, short best-practice items, lessons from business history, and explications of new and important data.

The HBR Case Study is a fictional account of a business dilemma with advice from several experts suggesting how to solve that dilemma.

Managing Yourself explores new ideas about the personal development of managers and leaders.

First Person recounts a personal business story that contains lessons for executives.

HBR at Large presents reporting on business trends, phenomena, companies, or individuals.

Different Voice features people from outside business whose ideas hold salient lessons for those within.

Big Picture examines broad economic, social, political, or demographic trends affecting business.

A word on attributions: HBR has its roots in the world of academic journals, where detailed citations are de rigueur. HBR articles should be similarly punctilious about giving credit to all direct quotations, paraphrased statements, and borrowed ideas. To improve the flow of the prose, we prefer to incorporate attributions into the text whenever we can. In the meantime, please be sure we understand exactly which ideas, and what language, are yours and which ones are drawn from someone else. We would rather see source notes than not, for example. Then, if your submission is accepted for publication, we will work with you to determine which sources need to be cited and in what way.

In addition, please tell us about any financial relationship you may have with companies cited in the proposed article. We need to know if you have a consulting relationship, for example, or if you serve on a board of directors.

Nearly all HBR articles undergo extensive editing and rewriting, and HBR typically holds copyright on the finished product. Authors continue to own the underlying ideas in the article.

HBR deeply appreciates the time and energy required to prepare a proposal for our publication, and we are grateful to you for that investment. We are always looking for new sources of solid, useful ideas that can improve the practice of management. Because of the volume of submissions we receive, we are not able to respond substantively to every one, but we do read them all closely, and we will do our best to respond within six to eight weeks. We thank you again for your interest.

Categories: Nonfiction—Business

CONTACT: Siobhan Ford
60 Harvard Way
Boston MA 02163
E-mail: hbr_editorial@hbsp.harvard.edu

Harvard Magazine

We don't have formal guidelines. Our content is about Harvard University and the extended Harvard alumni community worldwide, and the best way to see what we do is to examine our contents at www.harvardmagazine.com. John Rosenberg, Editor

Having a Baby Today

Please refer to *Midwifery Today.*

Hawaii Review

Hawaii Review publishes all forms of literature, including–but not solely–works which focus on Hawaii and the Pacific. *Hawaii Review* accepts solicited and unsolicited works of poetry, fiction, literary nonfiction, and visual art; including plays, short-short stories, reviews, translations, essays, humor, songs, and chants.

All manuscript submissions must be typed, double-spaced, crisp originals/copies on 8½" x 11" paper and must include: the writer's name, address, phone number, and number of words (prose) or lines (poetry) at the top right-hand of the first page; numbered pages; and a SASE with proper postage for reply. Manuscripts may also be submitted as Microsoft Word documents on a Macintosh- or IBM-formatted diskette. Please indicate whether you would like the manuscript returned and include enough postage on the SASE for the manuscript.

Fiction: Please submit no more than one manuscript with a maximum length of 7,000 words (28 double-spaced pages) per submission. More than one manuscript for short-short fiction or chapters from novels are acceptable if they do not exceed 7,000 words total.

Poetry: Please submit no more than five double-spaced poems per submission. Longer poems, up to 500 lines (20 double-spaced pages) will be considered; however, space limitations are more likely to be taken into account.

Nonfiction: Please submit no more than one manuscript at a time, up to 7,000 words (28 double-spaced pages) per manuscript. All nonfiction manuscripts must include complete documentation conforming to the *MLA Handbook of Style.* For book reviews, please submit no more

than two manuscripts, each between 500 and 1,500 words (2 to 6 pages) long. Manuscript reviews must include at the top of the first page the title of the literary work being reviewed, the names of the authors and writers of introductions/forewords/afterwords, publisher's information, publication date, number of pages, and price of cloth/paper/hardcover copies.

Translations: Please include a copy of the original piece, and indicate the copyright status of the original.

Visual Art: Submissions of photography, and photographs of non-photographic artwork (paintings, three-dimensional art, etc.), must be printed on 8" x 10" glossy black-and-white photos. Black-and-white drawings and paintings may be submitted on 8½" by 11" paper. Artwork may also be submitted on slides. Artists may submit up to 10 pieces of art per submission. Include, in clear print, on the back of each piece: the artist's name, address, phone number, title, date, and medium. Include SASE with proper postage for return of art with response.

Allow two to three months response time.

Categories: Fiction—Nonfiction—Poetry

CONTACT: Submissions Editor
Material: All
University of Hawaii
c/o Board of Publications
1755 Pope Rd., Bldg. 31-D
Honolulu HI 96822
Phone: 808-956-3030
Fax: 808-956-9962
E-mail: hi-review@hawaii.edu
Website: www.hawaii.edu/bop/pubindex.html

Hawaii Westways

HAWAII WESTWAYS, the bimonthly member publication for AAA Hawaii, has a circulation of over 52,000 and is published by the Automobile Club of Southern California. In each issue we celebrate Hawaii's culture and traditions. We report on current Island happenings, and provide information about dining, car care, and financial matters. We also cover local, domestic, and international travel. Our lead time is four to six months. We create our editorial calendars in spring and early summer for2 the following calendar year.

Major features typically run 1,500-2,000 words, but we also run 300- to 500-word articles. We look for writers with sound research and reporting skills, a strong voice, and good storytelling ability.

Our departments include:

Holoholo (going on excursion): 700-word articles about places in the Islands that would make a good day-trip or weekend destination. These might be an entire neighborhood, such as Oahu's North Shore or Maui's Wailuku; a specific excursion or attraction; or even a specific hotel or resort.

Celebrity Secret Spots: 600-word stories about a noted Island resident and his or her favorite place in Hawaii. Recent stories have featured Honolulu Symphony conductor Samuel Wong, chef Sam Choy, and entertainer Jim Nabors.

We pay $1 a word, plus agreed-upon expenses, upon manuscript acceptance. We buy first North American rights. If we reuse an article in another of the six publications produced by the Auto Club, we pay up to 33 percent of the original fee for second-use rights.

Samples of previously published work must accompany your query. We do our best to respond within eight weeks. We do not accept queries by fax or phone, only by email or snail mail. We do not accept unsolicited or previously published manuscripts. We use professional, high-quality photographs or slides with our articles, so if you are also a published photographer, please let us know. Thanks for your interest in HAWAII WESTWAYS. We look forward to reading your proposal.

Categories: Nonfiction—Associations—Automobiles—Consumer—Regional—Travel

CONTACT: Robin Jones, Editor
Material: Queries and clips
3333 Fairview Rd., A-327
Costa Mesa CA 92626
Phone: 714-885-2376
Website: www.aaa-calif.com/westways

Hayden's Ferry Review
Arizona State University

Hayden's Ferry Review, Box 871502, Arizona State University, Tempe, AZ 85287-1502, (480) 965-1243. Sample issues are $7.50. Yearly subscriptions are $14.00 (two issues).

Hayden's Ferry Review is a nationally distributed magazine publishing quality literary and visual art. Produced twice a year at Arizona State University, *HFR* promotes the work of emerging and established visual artists and writers of fiction, poetry, and creative nonfiction. Writers are urged to read the magazine before submitting. Editors serve for two issues (Fall/Winter, Spring/Summer).

Deadlines (postmark):

Fall/Winter, February 28

Spring/Summer, September 30

Submissions received after the deadline will be held for the next issue. Response time is 8–12 weeks after the deadline. Payment is $25.00 per page/ maximum of $100.00 (cover art payment—$100.00), two copies of the magazine, and a one-year gift subscription to *HFR*. Authors/artists receive page proofs for review prior to publication.

Manuscripts must be typed or letter-quality printed; clean photocopies are acceptable. Prose must be double spaced and printed on one side of paper. Send poetry and prose separately, limiting submissions to six poems or one story or essay per submission. Please send one manuscript per genre at a time, and wait for response before you submit additional work. We do not respond to manuscripts unless they are accompanied by a SASE. **We are not able to accept electronic submissions.** Art submissions should be standard 2" x 2" slides, clearly labeled with title, artist, medium, size, date, and arrow or dot to indicate orientation. Submit slides (limit: ten per artist) in a clear slide sheet. No reading fee.

SPECIAL SECTION: "Metafiction": (n) fictional objects that self-consciously pose questions about the relationship between illusion and reality. *Hayden's Ferry Review* seeks groundbreaking prose for an upcoming special section highlighting experimental flights of the imagination. Postmark deadline: June 15, 2004.

Categories: Fiction—Poetry

CONTACT: Fiction Editor
Material: All Fiction
CONTACT: Poetry Editor
Material: All Poetry
Arizona State University, PO Box 871502
Tempe AZ 85287-1502
Phone: 480-965-1243
Fax: 480-965-2191
E-mail: HFR@asu.edu
Website: www.haydensferryreview.org

Health

Health's focus is not on illness, but rather on ideas, events, and people. Our stories are written to inform decisions and compel action-in effect, giving readers more control over their own health. Each issue of the magazine presents some of the most important developments in health in its broadest sense-physical, emotional, even spiritual-in readable stories written with warmth, wit, and authority.

The audience for *Health* is predominantly college-educated women, age 30 through 50, who, by reason of their intellectual curiosity or practical interest, want both a dependable source of useful health information and a perspective on the rapidly changing face of personal health.

Health is published 10 times a year, with a nationwide circulation of approximately 1.4 million. The magazine relies heavily on staff writers and contributing editors. We usually assign features to regular contributors or to experienced writers whose work we know-and only after extensive discussion. Departments are more open to freelance writers new to us. Practical, service-oriented ideas are more likely to receive consideration. First-time contributors should propose stories for our front-of-book departments.

Departments usually run about 1,200 words. Fees are paid on acceptance. We pay research and travel expenses that have been agreed upon with the assigning editor.

HOW TO QUERY

All writers must submit written proposals before sending manuscripts, regardless of the planned length or nature of the story. *Health* does not accept unsolicited manuscripts.

Proposals should be sharply focused with the style and sources clearly defined. Send proposals, along with a legal-sized, self-addressed stamped envelope, resume, and copies of no more than two published stories to:

Categories: Nonfiction—Cooking—Diet/Nutrition—Family—Food/Drink—Health—Marriage—Physical Fitness—Psychology—Relationships—Self Help—Medicine

CONTACT: Editorial Query
Material: All
2100 Lakeshore Dr.
Birmingham AL 35209
Phone: 205-445-5123
E-mail: health@timeinc.com
Website: www.health.com

HeartLand Boating

Readership description: HeartLand Boating magazine is devoted to both power and sailboating enthusiasts throughout the middle America. Primary geographic readership areas include Alabama, Arkansas, Florida, Georgia, Illinois, Indiana, Iowa, Kansas, Kentucky, Louisiana, Michigan, Minnesota, Mississippi, Missouri, Nebraska, North Carolina, Ohio, Pennsylvania, South Carolina, Tennessee, Texas, West Virginia and Wisconsin.

Publication description: HeartLand Boating reflects the lifestyle of the boater, the challenge, joy and excitement of life afloat. The content is informative and warm, with some personal observations and humor mixed in. We record some trips, especially to areas we don't see too often. We like profiles of unusual and noteworthy people along the waterways and places to visit, things to see and do, tips and hints. We rarely use poetry and strictly humorous articles and do not accept fiction.

Free-lance submissions: HeartLand Boating welcomes submissions of photographic, art and written material for possible publication. Our focus is on the freshwater inland rivers and lakes of the HeartLand, primarily the waters of the Tennessee, Cumberland, Ohio, Mississippi and Missouri rivers, the Tennessee-Tombigbee Waterway and the lakes along these rivers. The magazine caters to all kinds of boating: sailboats, houseboats, cruisers, runabouts, pontoons, etc. Writers not familiar with HeartLand Boating's style should write for a sample issue. Enclose $5. We are looking for materials with a fresh snap and a new angle on life afloat. Please be correct, concise, clear and colorful.

Regular features open to free-lance writers.

Marina Profile: A feature highlighting a marina in the coverage area. Writers should provide comprehensive information about facilities, restaurants, services, things to do, etc. - the kind of information traveling boaters want to know about marinas they might visit. Articles should be accompanied by a good selection of sharply focused color photos and a navigation chart showing the location of the marina. 1,000-1,200 words.

Near the Water: A regular department featuring shore-based, close-to-the-water places accessible to boaters. Articles should be knowledgeable and informative, with background about the area. Articles should be accompanied by a good selection of sharply focused color photos. 1,000-1,500 words.

Cruises: A description of a particularly interesting cruise. Topics should be anything out-of-the-ordinary and can be human interest pieces or purely descriptive. Articles should be accompanied by a good selection of sharply focused color photos. Side bar possibilities. 1,000-1,500 words.

Maintenance/nuts and bolts: Technical articles about boat maintenance/repair. Supply charts/graphics. 500-1,000 words.

Nature: Articles on flora and fauna along waterways. Sharply focused color photos. 500-1,000 words.

Electronics: Technical articles. 300-1,000 words, with art, if possible.

Books Aboard: Reviews of nautical books. Book reviews don't have to be dry and boring. Prove it. 600-800 words.

Miscellaneous: Query first.

Manuscript specifications: We prefer that prospective contributors query with an idea first, rather than submit an unsolicited manuscript. However, an unsolicited manuscript must be accompanied by a SASE to ensure return of the material. HeartLand Boating will not be responsible for the return of unsolicited material sent without a SASE. Manuscripts must be typed (dot matrix OK but not preferred) and double-spaced on 8½ x 11 paper. Please indicate the approximate number of words and mark all sheets with the page number, feature title and author's name. Those using Macintosh personal computers are asked to submit a Macintosh computer disk (MacWrite or Word OK or indicate what application you used) along with the hard copy. For IBM DOS, save as a text file.

Free-lance photographers: HeartLand Boating buys a limited number of photographs for each issue. Query first with samples of your work.

Black-and-white photos: 8 x 10 glossy prints preferred. High quality with moderate contrast and sharp focus. Contact sheets can be submitted for consideration.

Color: Good-quality transparencies are acceptable for editorial use. Color prints are preferred if submitted with negatives. Consideration will be given to 35 mm for possible use as covers, but large-format transparencies are preferred. Photo essays are occasionally awarded to an artistically outstanding series centered on a single facet of boating in our editorial area.

Free-lance illustration: HeartLand Boating has few requirements for illustration and works with illustrators on an assignment basis only. Professional illustrators interested in being considered for the magazine should have a well-developed style, be strong in line art and be familiar with the contents of the magazine. Non-returnable standard file-size samples of work should be accompanied by a brochure or résumé that can be kept on file. Illustrations requiring return of samples or other information must include a SASE.

Free-lance cartoons: HeartLand Boating occasionally uses free-standing single panel or gag cartoons. Submissions should be prepared in black line art on 8½ x 11 paper and must include a SASE for return of submission. Remember, send only material slanted for this specialty audience.

General: HeartLand Boating pays for contributors upon publication. We are especially looking for a core of free-lancers who also are boating on the inland waters of middle America.

Categories: Nonfiction—Boating—Regional: Mid-America

CONTACT: Lee Braff, Editor
Material: Editorial and Photography
HeartLand Boating

319 N Fourth St Ste 650
St Louis MO 63102
E-mail: lbraff@heartlandboating.com
CONTACT: John Cassady
Material: Illustrations or Cartoons
PO Box 310
Murphy NC 28609
E-mail: info@heartlandboating.com

Heartland USA

HEARTLAND USA is a general-interest, bi-monthly magazine with a BPA-guaranteed circulation of over 1,200,000 and a readership exceeding 2.7 million. Targeted primarily at active, outdoors-oriented blue-collar working men, the publication regularly includes an eclectic mix of short, easy-to-read articles on hunting and fishing, spectator sports (motorsports, football, basketball and baseball), how-to, country music, human interest, and wildlife.

Please keep in mind that our average reader is a high school graduate who sees himself as hard working, traditional, rugged, confident, uncompromising and daring. We have consciously chosen not to "write down" to our readers, but rather to pursue an editorial voice that reflects a relaxed, jocular, street-smart familiarity, with just a hint of attitude. The liberal use of anecdote or compelling quotations—anything to breathe some life into a piece—is looked upon favorably.

The target length for feature articles is 1,200 words, with payment varying from $250 to $950. Feature-length pieces must lend themselves to strong photographic support.

Department-length articles (generally 550-1,200 words) pay from $140 to $950.

We pay on final acceptance (i.e. when we're certain the piece will appear in an upcoming issue), offer a 20% kill fee on assigned work, purchase the first or second North American serial rights, and copyright our publication. Hard-copy submissions must be sharp, legible, and include an SASE. E-mail queries and submissions are welcome and should be sent to us at husaedit@att.net. Simultaneous, photocopied, and reprint submissions are okay. Response will usually be within 4-6 weeks. A free sample copy is available on request. Clips of published work should accompany hard-copy queries.

Categories: Nonfiction—Adventure—Animals—Automobiles—Aviation—Biography—Boating—Cartoons—Civil War—Conservation—Crime—Disabilities—Ecology—Environment—Fishing—Gardening—General Interest—Inspirational—Men's Issues—Military—Music—Outdoors—Recreation—Rural America—Sports/Recreation—HuntingMartial Arts—Technology

CONTACT: Brad Pearson, Editor
Material: All
100 W. Putnam Ave.
Greenwich CT 06830
Phone: 203-863-7279
E-mail: husaedit@att.net

Remember: Editors change jobs and publishers change addresses. It is wise to invest in a phone call for the current information before submitting.

The Hellenic Calendar

Tabloid newspaper (17"x11") presenting news and features of special interest to the Greek-Americans of Southern California and the Great Southwest. Circulation 10,000.

Needs: Articles on prominent Americans of Greek descent, also on trends or issues of special interest to Greek-Americans. 500-2,000 words. We're not interested in a story about your trip to Greece or the best gyro you ever ate. Mail or e-mail complete manuscript.

Reports in two weeks.

Payment: Varies, usually ranges from $25 to $100.

Categories: Nonfiction—Culture—Multicultural—Regional—Ethnic—Greek

CONTACT: Steve Pastis, Publisher/Editor
Material: All
2747 N. Grand Ave. PMB 250
PMB 250
Santa Ana CA 92705
Phone: 714-550-9933
Fax: 714-550-9696
E-mail: greekpaper@aol.com
Website: www.helleniccalendar.com

Her Sports

CONTRIBUTION GUIDELINES

Her Sports is for smart, active women who use sports and fitness to balance their busy lifestyles and who are looking for more in a magazine than the mainstream health and fitness publications offer. Our readers are strong, independent women who participate in a variety of active sports—including running, triathlon, mountain biking, skiing, surfing, snowboarding, hiking and other popular individual sports, or who are motivated to adopt an active lifestyle and are looking to Her Sports for the encouragement to get them out the door.

Following are guidelines to assist you in sending successful submissions our way:

Tone and Style
Features:
- Profiles
- Training Articles
Departments:
- Body & Mind
- Fit Foods
- Weekend Warrior
- Her Gear
- Discoveries
- Adventure Journal
- Her Story
Submission Requirements
Payment
Photography

Tone and Style: All accepted Her Sports articles are well-researched and well-crafted and appeal to intelligent, active women. The voice of Her Sports is one that is intelligent and lively while also motivational to women athletes of all ability levels and ages. Please keep in mind that creating a "motivational" tone can be tricky. Stories should encourage women to lead active sports lifestyles through compelling language and stories that avoids clichéd approaches to writing.

Features: Her Sports features generally fall within one of two distinct categories: profiles and training articles. Generally, feature stories range from 1,200 to 2,000 words and should include relevant sidebars that will be described in detail by the editor upon acceptance.

Profiles: Her Sports publishes stories on professional athletes whose stories will inspire the "average Jane" athlete to continue her active lifestyle and test herself further. Profiles should always have an interesting hook, and the subjects should not fit into a mold that's too typical. In general, professional athletes should have an element of depth to them beyond just excelling at their sport. We also profile amateur athletes who have fascinating lives or careers, as well as active women who are making a difference in their communities or elsewhere. Above all, we're looking for women who manage to lead exciting, active lifestyles in the face of many other commitments.

Typical word length: 1,100 to 1,500 words

Training articles: Training articles should always be written by experts in a given field, i.e., a certified instructor or coach. Unless otherwise stated by the editor, articles should include workout ranges for a variety of ability levels. For instance, if you are pitching an article on "How to PR in Your Next 10k" include ranges for the beginner runner as well as the runner looking to improve her fastest time. Training articles should include a persuasive introduction that will hook readers into wanting to follow the plan, as well as a detailed description of how each week of the plan will unfold. Appropriate sidebars will be assigned by the editor.

Typical word length: 1,400 to 2,000 words including training plans

DEPARTMENTS

Body + Mind: Her Sports recognizes that being fit goes far beyond working out. Body + Mind stories include more holistic approaches to well-being, including new information on yoga, Pilates, meditation, massage, sports psychology and general wellness. These articles are generally 800 to 1,200 words and should be written by experts in the related field, i.e., certified instructors or degreed professionals.

Typical word length: 800 to 1,200 words

Fit Foods: The latest research and information on nutrition as it relates to athletic performance and overall health can be found in our Fit Foods section. In general, stories are written by registered dietitians. Articles should be backed by scientific research. Her Sports does not advocate "fad diets" or weight loss trends. Sample article themes include eating for greater energy, dispelling nutrition myths, good fats vs. bad fats and the top protein sources for women,

Typical word length: 800 to 1,200 words

Weekend Warrior: Weekend Warrior stories are geared toward women with limited time during the week and who fit in their sporting moments where they can. Straightforward and practical stories such as "10 Tips for Kayaking" or "Shortcuts to Mastering Your First Snowboarding Lesson" are appropriate here. Gear sidebars may also be assigned for this section.

Typical word length: 1,000 to 1,200 words

Her Gear: The Her Gear section highlights the latest trends in gear and apparel for active women. Contributors to this section must have experience in product review writing and/or be an expert in the related product field, i.e., former product designer for running shoes or active apparel.

Typical word length: 800 to 1,200 words

Discoveries: We're looking for vivid, fact-filled, intelligent writing on active destinations in North America and beyond. In most all cases we work with only experienced travel writers for this section to write on any destination that would make for a great weekend getaway or active vacation.

Typical word length: 1,200 to 1,700 words

Adventure Journal: Tell us your adventure stories! Whether you've just returned from a month hiking through the South Island of New Zealand, adventure racing with your girlfriends through the Colorado mountains or attempting a brand new sport, we're looking for creative, well-written personal essays that will inspire other women to take on new adventures. Adventure Journal stories should NOT be a step-by-step or day-by-day account of what you did. Readers should come away with a strong sense of where you have been, what the experience meant to you, what lessons were learned, and how your perspective may have been changed by it. These stories may also include a sidebar detailing travel tips or "must sees" for others traveling to the area or tips for others wishing to attempt the same sport.

In almost all cases, we'll also be looking for quality photography from your trip to accompany these stories.

Typical word length: 1,200 to 1,400 words, including sidebars

Her Story: While we highlight compelling women throughout the pages of Her Sports, Her Story is reserved for our back page, and includes a one-page story on "everyday" athletes who are colorful, unique, inspiring or who remain active in the face of challenges or unusually busy lifestyles (remember, just because someone has three kids and still manages to exercise regularly doesn't mean her story is unique). We are inherently choosy about the women we feature in this section—they should be the exception, not the rule.

Typical word length: 600 to 650 words

SUBMISSION REQUIREMENTS

Submissions are preferred via e-mail as opposed to standard post. In general, query letters to the editor are preferred, although completed manuscripts will occasionally be accepted if they are in keeping with the magazine's tone, style and overall philosophy.

Send queries and submissions to:

Christina Gandolfo, Editor in Chief

christina@hersports.com

Submissions should adhere to standard AP Style and should be sent in a Microsoft Word e-mail attachment. Lead time for submissions is four months minimum, and six months is required for seasonal material.

Payment: Payment will be determined on a per-article basis based on the research requirements and story length, as well as the proven experience of the contributor. Her Sports buys all North American serial rights, and payment is made on publication. General fees range from $150 to $450.

PHOTOGRAPHY

Her Sports uses a variety of both stock and original photographic material. In general, we are always seeking dynamic stock images of women engaged in the sports we cover. If you have images you'd like to share with us, please e-mail a low-res image to:

Kristin Mayer, Creative Director, kristin@hersports.com

If you have slide transparencies without the ability to scan a digital version, please e-mail the creative director prior to sending them for consideration.

Additionally, each issue the creative director generates an e-mail detailing stock needs for that issue. If you feel your work fits these needs, please send a note to the e-mail address above. If your work meets our standards you will be included on the monthly call for images.

In most cases, Her Sports photography will be taken by proven professionals. We accept both slide transparencies and high-resolution (300 dpi or higher) digital images.

Our pay rates for photography vary based on how the photograph is used, and at what size:

General Photo Payment Guidelines: Cover images: $500 to $800

Photo used inside the magazine: $100 to 400 (depending on size and placement)

Day Rate Assignment: $500

PUBLISHING FREQUENCY

Her Sports is published six times annually

Categories: Nonfiction—Sports—Women

CONTACT: Christina Gandolfo, Editor in Chief
Materials: All
Her Sports Editorial
4480 33rd St
San Diego CA 92116
E-mail: christina@hersports.com
Website: www.hersports.com

HerbalGram

About Us

HerbalGram is a publication of the American Botanical Council and the Herb Research Foundation. ABC and HRF are non-profit, educational and research organizations which focus on herb and medicinal plant research, regulatory issues, market conditions, native plant conservation, and other general interest aspects of herb use.

All articles published in *HerbalGram* are peer reviewed by some of the leading authorities in the field of phytopharmaceutical research, including James A. Duke, Ph.D., U.S. Department of Agriculture, retired; Varro Tyler, Ph.D., Lilly Distinguished Professor of Pharmacognosy, Purdue University; Norman Farnsworth, Ph.D., Professor of Pharmacognosy, University of Illinois Medical School, and Dennis V. C. Awang, Ph.D., MediPlant, Ottawa, Canada.

Submissions

We welcome proposals and finished manuscripts in hard copy form, preferably accompanied by a computer disk. We prefer Microsoft Word for Macintosh, but can interpret from Word for Windows. If neither of these programs are possible, then please save your text in rich text format (.rtf), a universal style which retains any italics or other individual formatting. Do not send manuscripts formatted in WordPerfect. If you have any questions about rich text format, please contact the editorial office at the number below. You may also send articles to our e-mail address.

We also prefer that you send straight text, with little or no formatting except when necessary for presentation of charts or diagrams. The common name of all botanicals mentioned must be followed by the Latin binomial. References must be complete, with title of the article cited as well as author/s names, publication, pages, and dates. Example—Smith, Maurice I., and E. Elvove, with the cooperation of P.J. Valaer, Jr., William H. Frazier and G. E. Mallory, "Pharmacological and Chemical Studies of the Cause of So-Called Ginger Paralysis: A Preliminary Report," Pub. Health Rep., 45 (1930): 1703-1716 (especially p.1704).]

Our stylistic authority is *The Chicago Manual of Style* and our botanical reference is *The Plant Book* by D. J. Mabberly.

Photos

If you have excellent quality color or black and white slides or photographs to illustrate your article we are interested in seeing them and will, of course, return them to you. Please include a proper description of such materials and label your photos/slides with your name and the name of the subject.

Payment

We do not pay for manuscripts, but will send you six copies of the issue in which your material appears.

We strongly suggest that you obtain a sample copy of at least one of the latest issues in order to familiarize yourself with our subject matter, journalistic style, and general focus. If you have any questions, please contact Barbara Johnston, Managing Editor.

Categories: Nonfiction— Conservation—General Interest—Health—Nature—Science—Herbal Medicine —Herbs—Medicinal Plants

CONTACT: Submissions Editor
Material: All
Herb Research Foundation
1007 Pearl St. Ste 200
Boulder CO 80302
Phone: 303-449-2265
Fax: 303-449-7849
E-mail: info@herbs.org
Website: www.herbs.org

High Country News

High Country News, a nonprofit, every-other-week news magazine that focuses on environmental, cultural, and social issues in the Western United States, is always looking for new voices for our pages. The publication reaches over 24,000 subscribers, including grassroots activists, public land managers, educators, tribal leaders and government policy-makers. Our Web site is at hcn.org.

HCN will consider well-researched stories on any natural resource or environmental topic, as long as it concerns the West. We define "resources" to include people, culture and aesthetic values—not just coal, oil and timber. Keep in mind that we have an 11-state region to cover in a small news space—we want local stories that have significance across the entire region, that can be told in ways that go beyond what the daily newspapers report.

We welcome queries from writers familiar with HCN. Our ideal articles include strong storytelling, compelling characters, and a clear, jargon-free style. Though we are mainly an environmental publication, we strive to understand and communicate all points of view. We want writers who can view topics with a critical eye and dig deeply into issues. We also would like our writers to be as diverse as the region they cover, and encourage Native American, Hispanic, and other minority journalists to send us queries.

We divide submissions into several general categories: "Book Reviews," at 300-350 words; "Hotlines," 250-word news briefs; "Roundups," topical stories of about 800 words; features, generally up to 4,000 words, of which we print one per issue; and essays, of no standard length but generally under 1,000 words.

New writers should begin by sending a query for a Book Review, Hotline or Roundup. E-mail queries are preferred; send to editor@hcn.org and include "Story Query" in the subject line. Essay writers are also encouraged to contact Betsy Marston, the editor of our syndicated column service Writers on the Range.

Freelance rates begin at 25 cents a word, and are adjusted depending on the quality of work, the editing required and the writer's working relationship with the paper. The editing process is rigorous but productive. Regular contributors usually receive higher rates than occasional writers. Payment is made upon publication.

High Country News' purchase includes the right to publish your work in High Country News, to collect the work in an electronic archive (currently on the World Wide Web), and the right to authorize reprinting for classroom use or for publication in small non-profit newsletters. Other commercial uses of the work will be negotiated with the author.

PHOTOGRAPHIC GUIDELINES

Solicited work: High Country News accepts good quality color or black and white prints (8x10 preferred) and 35 mm negatives and slides. Electronic images are welcome, as well, and should be saved as JPEG files, at 300 dpi or higher at about 7 inches on the long side. E-mail as attached files to cindy@hcn.org.

All submissions should include the name of the photographer as it is to appear in the credit line and description of the place or name of the subject for the caption. Please also indicate whether HCN should return the photo after use or keep it for our files. We pay for each use. We also need your name, address and phone number for payment purposes and for our files.

Unsolicited work: HCN will not return unsolicited photographs without a self-addressed, stamped envelope.

Rates: Prices for individual photographs range from $35-$100 depending upon quality, published size, and location within the paper. HCN pays for work upon publication.

Contract: High Country News' purchase includes the right to publish the photograph/art in High Country News, to collect the work in an electronic archive (currently on the World Wide Web), as well as the right to authorize reprinting for classroom use or for publication in small nonprofit newsletters. Other commercial uses of the work will be negotiated with the photographer/artist.

Responsibility: HCN will take the best possible care of all submissions, but cannot assume responsibility for loss or damage. Please include your social security number with all submissions.

Categories: Nonfiction—Book Reviews—Culture—Environment—Social Issues—Regional: Western United States

CONTACT: Editors, High Country News
Material: Articles, Book Reviews
CONTACT: Cindy Wehling, Art Director
Material: Photos
High Country News
PO Box 1090
Paonia CO 81428
E-mail: editor@hcn.org
Website: hcn.org

Highlights for Children

We appreciate your interest in *Highlights for Children*. Highlights is published monthly for children 6 to 12. Circulation is more than 2 million.

Please note:
• We do not pay persons under age 16 for contributions.
• We buy all rights, including copyright, and do not consider material previously published.
• We prefer to see a manuscript rather than a query.
• All material is paid for on acceptance.
• We do not accept submissions by email or fax.
• We accept material year round, including seasonal material.

FICTION should have an engaging plot, strong characterization, and lively language. Stories for pre-readers and beginning readers should be 400 words or fewer. Stories for advanced readers should be 800 words or fewer and be appealing to younger readers if read aloud.
• We prefer stories that teach by positive example, rather than by preaching.
• Suggestions of crime and violence are taboo.
• Frequent needs include humor, mystery, sports, and adventure stories; retellings of traditional tales; stories in urban settings; and stories that feature world cultures.
• We seldom buy rhyming stories.
Payment: $150 and up.

REBUS STORIES are a monthly feature for beginning readers, featuring a variety of familiar words that can easily be shown as pictures. Rebuses should be 120 words or fewer.
Payment: $100 and up.

NONFICTION includes biography, autobiography, and various approaches to the arts, science, history, sports, adventure, and world cultures. All articles should be 800 words or fewer.
• Focused articles are more successful than broad factual surveys.
• We prefer research based on consultation with experts or first-hand experience.
• Writers with an extensive background in a particular field are encouraged to share their experiences and personal research.
• Articles about cultural traditions and ways of life should reflect a deep understanding of the subject.
• Biographies of individuals who have made significant artistic, scientific, or humanitarian contributions are strengthened by the inclusion of formative childhood experiences. We prefer biographies that

are rich in anecdotes and place the subject in a historical and cultural context.

• Nonfiction articles geared to pre-readers and younger readers are especially welcome. These should not exceed 500 words.

• References or sources of information must be included with submissions.

• Color 35mm slides, photos, or art reference materials are helpful and sometimes crucial in evaluating submissions.

Payment: $150 and up.

CRAFTS should appeal to a wide age range of boys and girls and should have clear, numbered directions, typically not more than five steps.

• A well-made sample should be submitted with each craft idea. If this is not feasible, then a photo or a detailed illustration would help.

• Projects must require only common household items or inexpensive, easy-to-obtain materials.

• Projects should result in attractive, useful gift items, decorations, toys, and games.

• Crafts that celebrate holidays or religious traditions are welcome. Crafts from world cultures are a frequent need, as are crafts that result in games and crafts that appeal to boys.

Payment: $25 and up.

FINGER PLAYS/ACTION RHYMES should have plenty of action and minimal text. They must be easy for very young children to act out, step-by-step, with hands, fingers, and body movements.

Payment: $25 and up.

GALLANT KIDS articles should be about kids who take an active role in making positive changes in their communities. Articles should be 350 words or fewer, and the child featured should be no older than 13. Query with idea before writing.

VERSE is purchased sparingly. It is rarely longer than 10 lines and should be meaningful for young readers.

Payment: $25 and up.

Categories: Fiction—Nonfiction—Children

CONTACT: Manuscript Submissions
Material: All
803 Church St.
Honesdale PA 18431
Phone: 570-253-1080
Fax: 570-251-7847
E-mail: eds@highlights-corp.com

Highways

Thank you for your interest in *Highways*, the official publication of the Good Sam Club. *Highways* is published 12 times a year by TL Enterprises Inc. and is a sister publication of *Trailer Life* and *MotorHome*.

Highways is a specialty magazine for RV enthusiasts and has a circulation of more than 960,000. We suggest that interested contributors study recent issues before sending us queries. All queries must be submitted via e-mail to goodsam@goodsamclub.com. **We do not accept unsolicited manuscript submissions.** The response time to queries is generally three weeks. Our staff works considerably with freelancers, but primarily on assignment. If you receive an assignment, the text of your story must be e-mailed to us. We do not accept disks or typed stories.

Payment is on acceptance for publication. *Highways* buys first North American serial rights and electronic rights. The editors reserve the right to edit and even rewrite any article in order to make it suit the theme or space limitations of a specific issue. Major alterations will be discussed with the author when possible.

TRAVEL FEATURES

The easiest way to sell your work to *Highways* is to query us on an interesting and tightly focused RV travel story. We need features that evoke the sights, sounds, smells and even tastes of specific travel destinations. Consequently, we d much rather have a tight 1,200 words

on traveling to Anchorage in the spring than on all of Alaska.

We are also looking for short 800 words first-person stories written in a smart and breezy style. These could be about your RV travels or about how a Good Sam Club benefit proved of particular value to you. Again, submit a query, not the entire feature. Fees for full-length travel features with photos start at $300. Higher fees are negotiable. Short travel features start at $75.

If you are assigned a story by the editorial staff, please keep in mind that you now represent the magazine. Be conscious that if you receive information or materials about the subject/area you are covering, you must still write an ethical, objective story.

MAINTENANCE AND TECHNICAL

Highways publishes several types of technical stories, all of which are assigned. If you have an idea for a technical feature maintenance, how-to, RV safety send a query.

VEHICLE TESTS

Highways does not publish vehicle tests, though we do print previews of new rigs. However, they are staff written.

SPECIAL INTEREST *Highways* editorial focus also includes hobbies, crafts and other recreational activities that are popular among RVers. Recent stories have covered dominoes, a shelter for cats that could be affixed to the outside of an RV, computers and other hobbies. Special-interest features should be 1,000 words. Please do not send a manuscript send a query.

RV HUMOR

In each issue of *Highways*, we try to include a humorous vignette on some aspect of the RV lifestyle. Humor stories should be directly related to the RV experience. Maximum length for humor stories is 1,000 words. Do not send photographs. All humor stories are illustrated by line drawings. Humor stories are the only genre that *Highways* will accept without first receiving a query

COLUMNS

All *Highways* columns are assigned. If you have a column idea, send us your idea along with several sample columns and we will consider them. Columns are a tough sale and we do not foresee a need to add any new columns to the magazine in the near future.

HUMAN INTEREST

Highways publishes personality features about Good Sam Club members. If you come across a good story and know that the person/couple is a member of the Good Sam Club, please send a query

POETRY AND FICTION

Highways does not publish poetry or fiction.

PHOTOGRAPHY

All stories (excluding humor) should be accompanied by a minimum of 15 color transparencies, all originals. All transparencies should be numbered with an accompanying caption sheet identifying each subject. Digital images are accepted in TIF format and sent via e-mail or on a CD. When possible, images should feature RVs against a scenic backdrop. Also, think cover shot (vertical) when taking these photos and remember lighting is crucial to the overall effect. Focus your photography on scenic or panoramic views for the opening layout and points of interest, local color and activity shots for the carryover pages. Photos and slides supplied by someone other than the manuscript author should be clearly identified for photo credit. All photos and slides will be returned after publication when possible. Please include a self-addressed, stamped envelope for this purpose.

Neither *Highways* nor TL Enterprises Inc. assumes any responsibility for unsolicited material. —*Revised 01/04*

Categories: Associations—Lifestyle—Outdoors—Recreation—Recreation Vehicles—Senior Citizen—Travel—Camping

CONTACT: Dee Reed, Managing Editor
Material: All
2575 Vista Del Mar Dr.
Ventura, CA 93001
Phone: 800-765-1912, Ext. 609
Fax: 805-667-4009

Hinduism Today

Writer's Guidelines

We welcome anyone to contribute to Hinduism Today. Over the years, our contributors have ranged from professional reporters to great Hindu religious leaders to lay Hindus and children. Together they have allowed us to produce an educational and informative magazine issue after issue. If you'd like to join this band who make Hinduism Today possible, please let us know.

Hinduism Today is a 86-page international quarterly magazine written for educated, English-speaking Hindus, the general public interested in Hinduism and to inform the scholastic community dedicated to Hindu-related studies. Now in its 26rd year of publication, our magazine is considered "the voice of Hinduism" and — many tell us — is the best Hindu newsjournal in the world both in content and design. We are published in North America and distributed worldwide. The magazine is posted regularly on the Web, with archives back to 1979, and also distributed digital form.

It is not necessary that contributing writers be Hindu, but that they empathize with Hindu thought, practices and culture.

Our interests range over timely events, human interest stories, profiles, interviews, trend analysis, social issues, lifestyle pieces, cultural explorations, travel-log and special feature reporting. We solely cover the spiritual, humanistic and cultural dimensions of Hinduism; we do not cover politics, with the exception of a political event that has a direct impact on Hindus or our faith. Writers should study Hinduism Today for an overview of our approach, writing style and typical subject matter. Articles need to be in English, that is, every Sanskrit or other non-English word needs to be defined (simply) in the text.

Types of stories we might cover include:

1.) Current news and events in Hinduism, or that impact Hindus.

2.) Profiles of individual Hindu gurus, swamis or lay leaders who are contributing in a dynamic or unusual way to the Hindu/yoga community. These are contemporary people, but on occasion can include those from recent past. Profiles are also sought for Hindu royalty, movie stars, sports stars, authors, businessmen, thinkers and unusual personalities.

3.) Investigative reports on Hindu or yoga-related institutions. This would include monastic, educational, specific research and academic institutions; and would include non-Hindu institutions that are studying or teaching Hindu-related areas.

4.) Investigative reports on ethical and social issues pertinent to and including the Hindu perspective: abortion, euthanasia, genetic engineering, vegetarianism, animal rights, global pollution, environment, nuclear arms and power, appropriate technology, agriculture, smoking, AIDS, mad-cow disease, etc.

5.) In-depth treatments of special facets of Hindu practice and knowledge: various sects or schools of Hinduism, systems of yoga, astrology, arts, sciences, social structure, diet, scriptures, architecture, etc.

6.) The interface, both positive and negative, between Hinduism and other faiths. Occasionally, we run feature pieces on Sikhism, Buddhism, Taoism, and other religions, with an effort to reveal links with Hindu history, knowledge or present-day concerns.

7.) The religious life of the indigenous tribals in India.

8.) The interface between Hinduism and science/technology; Hinduism in the 21st century.

9.) Specific concerns for women, adolescents and children: Hindu family customs, acculturation for immigrants, discrimination, education, lifestyle, helpful domestic and social hints. We have an on-going concern with wife and child beating, and the consequences of so many mothers working outside the home, breakup of the joint family, divorce, etc.

10.) First person accounts of journeys to exotic Hindu or formerly-Hindu locales.

11.) Reports on extraordinary events, projects and discoveries, such as magnificent new temples, huge Hindu religious statues, amazing archeological finds and Guiness Book of Records type events.

12.) Exploration of specific anti-Hindu activities, programs, publishing or other media efforts.

Queries on article proposals are desirable. We encourage a well-written query letter outlining your subject and describing its special characteristics and appeal. Though queries are preferred, unsolicited articles are accepted for consideration.

Article Guidelines:

Length for short pieces is 200-500 words. Features run 1,000-4,000 words. All manuscripts are edited prior to publication.

Good Professional Photos are necessary with every story. This is a critical area, and we will work with the writer to insure proper photos.

Presentation: Manuscript submissions should emailed. Submissions must be in English and include a two-sentence bio and a photograph of the author.

Payment is US.08 cents per word and $20.00 for each photo we publish. Rates for professional photographs are negotiated on a case by case basis. Payment is made upon publication. Sometimes we can pay for expenses.

Rights: Hinduism Today buys all rights of publication, unless other specific arrangements are worked out with the author. We also purchase second (reprint) rights. Everything published in the magazine (except photographs) goes on our web site.

The Fine Print: We consider everything except a direct assignment to be submitted on a speculative basis. If an article has been assigned, we reserve the right to reject it and agree to pay a maximum termination fee of $25.00 for features, pro-rated for shorter pieces. No such fee will be paid for articles which are delivered after deadline or if the author fails to comply with requests for revisions or additional research.

Categories: Nonfiction—Religion: Hinduism

CONTACT: Managing Editor
Hinduism Today
Kauai's Hindu Monastery
107 Kaholalele Rd
Kapaa Hawaii 96746
Phone: 808-822-7032, ext 227
Fax: 808-822-4351
Website: http://www.hinduismtoday.com

Hispanic Business®

Hispanic Business® is an independently owned publication focusing on news, trends, and information relevant to the U.S. Hispanic economy.

Readership includes business owners, executives, professionals, researchers, and marketers. We have readers in every state, with the greatest concentrations in California, Texas, Florida, New York/New Jersey, and Illinois.

Published continuously since April/May 1979, Hispanic Business is the nation's longest-running national Hispanic magazine. Current circulation is 225,000.

All editorial content is in English.

Hispanic Business Inc.® is a member of BPA International.

EDITORIAL COVERAGE

Hispanic Business magazine is a monthly publication for and about Hispanic entrepreneurs and professionals. Our feature stories highlight significant trends in the U.S. Hispanic market and include profiles of successful entrepreneurs, analysis of economic trends, and news and data on such topics as government procurement, workplace diversity, politics, advertising, entertainment, and events. Our editorial content also is useful to media and marketing professionals with an interest in trends in the Hispanic marketplace.

Our regularly featured research-based projects include the Hispanic Business 500®, the Hispanic Business Fastest-Growing 100®, the Hispanic Business 100 Most Influential Hispanics®, and the Hispanic Business 80 Elite Women list. Other special sections published annually include a media markets report, a technology report, and a list of the graduate and law schools considered best for Hispanic students.

Columns and departments appearing regularly in Hispanic Business include:

The Informant (news, trends, and numbers from the Hispanic economic sector)

Money Matters (useful information for sound financial planning)

TechPulse (high-tech trends, products, and players)

LegalEase (practical advice about legal matters)

RegionaLatitudes (regional reports of national interest)

ProActive (career and workplace news)

The Traveler (travel news and reviews)

Readers Write (opinions and comments from our readers)

ORIGINAL STORIES

All stories are assigned by Hispanic Business editors. We assign articles to staff editors, contributing editors, and freelance writers.

We do not assign articles to vendors or writers who work for advertisers.

If you have an idea for an article that you think we might be interested in publishing, please send us a concise outline, not a finished story. Please do not submit an article proposal without familiarizing yourself with the magazine and the editorial calendar. Abstracts may be submitted via our online form, selecting "editorial" from the dropdown menu. Please be patient and allow at least six weeks before following up on your submission.

We do not publish unsolicited manuscripts.

We plan cover stories and feature stories about three months in advance. In January, for example, we are editing the March issue, assigning the April issue, and planning the May issue.

Please refer to the Hispanic Business editorial calendar (www.hispanicbusiness.com/advertise/mediakits) for a summary of annual features.

If your article or story idea is accepted, you will be expected to provide the following:

Article submitted as an e-mail Word attachment.

Sources used in preparing the article, including interviews, books, other articles, websites, and any other resources.

Full contact information for each company mentioned and for each person interviewed, including name, title, company, address, phone, fax, e-mail, and URL. Your article will be fact-checked against the information you provide.

Suggested headlines, pull quotes, and callouts that may be used to emphasize key points.

Camera-ready artwork, when applicable, in either digital or hardcopy form. Digital photos must have resolution of at least 300 dpi at publication size (at least 3" by 5" in most cases).

STYLE GUIDELINES FOR WRITERS

Our style guide follows the U.S. News & World Report stylebook.

Use active voice and present tense. For example, write "she says" rather than "she said."

On first reference to a person, give his or her full name. On succeeding references, refer to the person as Mr. or Ms.

On first reference to a company, organization, or agency, give the full legal name.

Spell out state names except in mailing addresses.

Try to include financial information on companies or subjects profiled, including ownership, sales, and profits.

Information sources should reflect geographic diversity.

PRESS RELEASES

Your press release should tell us who you are, what your company does, and how you can be contacted. It should summarize briefly (in no more than two pages) what the news is about and why you think it

should be covered by Hispanic Business. The information should be relevant to our audience.

We do not guarantee publication of any information sent to us.

Please don't call us repeatedly about your press release. One follow-up call is enough.

Please contact us if you have questions about our editorial coverage.

Let us know right away if you believe we have printed any factual errors.

Categories: Nonfiction—Business—Hispanic

CONTACT: Hispanic Business Magazine
425 Pine Ave
Santa Barbara CA 93117
Phone: 805-964-4554
Fax: 805-964-6139 Attention: Editorial
Website: www.hispanicbusiness.com

Hispanic Career World

Please refer to Equal Opportunity Publications, Inc.

The Hollins Critic
Established in 1964

The Hollins Critic

Poetry editor Cathryn Hankla reads poetry from September 1 to December 15 only. Submissions received at other times will be returned unread.

Poetry submitted to The Hollins Critic should be typed or word processed. There are no rules about style or subject. One to five poems should be submitted to Cathryn Hankla, Poetry Editor, P.O. Box 9538, Hollins University, Roanoke, VA 24020. The Critic cannot reply without a self-addressed stamped envelope. We do not accept e-mail submissions.

The Critic pays $25.00 per poem, upon publication. All rights revert to the author following publication, but if the poem is reprinted elsewhere, the Critic should be credited.

Besides poetry, the Critic publishes an essay on a contemporary author in each issue, and book reviews as space permits. The Critic does not accept unsolicited essays. Rarely do we accept unsolicited book reviews. When a review is published, the author receives a copy of the issue, and two copies are sent to the book's publisher.

Categories: Nonfiction—Literature—Poetry

CONTACT: Cathryn Hankla, Poetry Editor
Material: Poetry
Hollins University
PO Box 9538
Roanoke VA 24020
Phone: 540-362-6275
Fax: 540-362-6642
E-mail: acockrell@hollins.edu (No Submissions)
Website: www.hollins.edu/grad/eng_writing/critic/critic.htm

Home Business Journal

HOME Business Journal's purpose is to arm the reader with the best advice available to help those in home business, or seriously interested in such work, thrive and enjoy working at home.

Articles must be submitted in conventional style, word-processed or typed, with title, contributor's name, address and telephone/fax number on first page. Approximate word count and rights offered should also be displayed on first page. Feature articles should be approximately 1000 words. Filler materials are items of 300 words or less. Articles may also be submitted via E-Mail to Kim@HOME BusinessJournal.net. Submissions made by E-Mail should be included in the text. Phone ideas are not acceptable.

Contributors must warrant that all work submitted is original and that no Copyrighted material is used within contribution without permission in writing. Such permission must accompany contribution. If article or contribution that has been requested does not meet editor's approval, contributor may or may not be asked to edit material and resubmit. No additional payment will be made for such re-submissions. All photos or illustrations that include persons must be accompanied by permission to use and complete captions to explain the artwork.

HOME Business Journal is not responsible for contributions submitted to the magazine and cannot be responsible for the return of such materials.

HOME Business Journal may provide contributing writers with a byline upon publication of article. *HOME Business Journal* welcomes the submission of quality articles and news pertaining to home based businesses. Gratis submissions are welcome. Base pay of $75 is offered upon acceptance to authors seeking compensation for their original article. All other requested submissions are negotiated by the editor on a per-piece basis. Payment for requested submission is made upon publication.

HOME Business Journal is able to issue payment only to writers in the United States and Canada at this time.

HOME Business Journal recently expanded what was formerly the Entrepreneur Spotlight section of the magazine. Now labeled "The Neighborhood CEO," there are four to six of these home biz profile articles in each issue. *The specs for these articles are as follows:*

1. The profile must be on a business that is currently home based.

2. I am looking for articles that provide the story behind the business owner as opposed to an "advertorial" for the home business. Articles written from a personal, inspirational angle are preferable: ie. a senior starting over, friends combining talents, young entrepreneur, unique business, unique reason business was begun, etc.

This column was designed to provide proof that home business opportunities are not limited to MLM's, franchises, or other Business-In-A-Box type deals. In essence, I am looking for articles that leave readers saying "I could do that."

3. Neighborhood CEO articles may not exceed 700 words.

4. The home business name, address, and phone number (if applicable) must be supplied. These will be published in an inset within the article. A clear, head-shot photo of the business owner is also required. Color photos sent electronically (TIF,EPS,JPG) need to be at least 300 DPI when viewed at a 2 x 2 size.

4. Writers will be paid $75 - payable upon publication - and will receive byline credit.

Categories: Nonfiction—Business—Money & Finances

CONTACT: Editor
Material: All
9584 Main Street Holland Patent
Holland Patent NY 13354
Phone: 315-865-4100 Ext: 223 (No queries by phone)
Fax: 315-865-4000
E-mail: Kim@HOMEBusinessJournal.net or
Kim@SteffenPublishing.com
Website: www.HOMEBusinessJournal.net

Home Business® Magazine

Writers' Guidelines

Home Business® Magazine is selecting press releases on new books, newsletters, and magazines for publicity in the magazine. These releases appear in the Bookshelf for your Home Office. Each publica-

tion receives approximately 1/4 page for the review that will include either a picture of the author, graphic, illustration, or document cover provided by the publisher or author. This is an excellent opportunity because the publications selected are screened for quality and for the readers of our magazine.

Please note that each publication submitted must be related to the subject of home business. Information on obtaining the publication and the price is to be provided at the end of the press release. The press release must provide good information on the contents of the publication and its benefit to readers. A copy of the publication must be provided to Home Business® Magazine for it to be considered for review. If your publication qualifies as a candidate, you may be contacted for follow-up on the review.

For serious review and consideration, please email all photos and editorial submissions (200-250 words) to henderso@ix.netcom.com with each editorial pasted into an email. We may change or rewrite the editorial as we deem necessary.

Please mail your publication to: Home Business Magazine, Attn: Editor.

Guidelines for Submitting Home Office Products for Review and Consideration in Home Business® Magazine

Home Business® Magazine spotlights home office products in most issues. Each home office product receives approximately 1/4 page for the review that will include a picture of the home office product provided by the company. This is an excellent opportunity, because the home office products selected are screened for quality and for the readers of our magazine.

Please note that each home office product submitted must be related to the subject of home business. Information on obtaining the home office product and the price is to be provided at the end of the press release. The press release must provide good information on the home office product and its benefits to readers. A sample of the home office product and all pertinent brochures and literature on the home office product must be provided to Home Business® Magazine for it to be considered for review. If your home office product qualifies as a candidate, you may be contacted for follow-up on the review.

For serious review and consideration, please email all photos and editorial submissions (200-250 words) to henderso@ix.netcom.com with each editorial pasted into an email. We may change or rewrite the editorial as we deem necessary.

Writers' Guidelines for Articles

We appreciate any articles you have to share with our readers on home business. Your submissions help HOME BUSINESS® MAGAZINE help others who want to learn more about working at or from home.

The following are notes on writing style for HOME BUSINESS® MAGAZINE (HBM):

1. Write short paragraphs with bullet headings for the paragraph(s).

2. Use headlines that catch people's eyes as they skim the editorial.

3. Good grammar is a must! Have someone proof your work before submitting. Editorial is expected to be "camera-ready" to drop into the magazine.

4. Avoid first-person experiences, commentary, and stories.

5. Provide good, quality, "how-to" content.

6. Use smooth-flowing syntax, parallel structure, and good sentence structure.

7. Recommend key phrases/sentences to put in pull quote boxes within the article.

8. Be prepared for a potential need to cut content or to add content. Fast turn-around is needed for last minute editing. HBM usually handles, however, the last minute editing in-house.

9. If desired, provide recommendations for stock photos or clip art to insert into your article. You can also provide sketches or recommendations for a graphical concept for the article.

We can then research our stock photo libraries to see if something similar is available.

Your name, address, phone number, fax number, and postal address must be on your emailed submission. If you are a new writer, please also include your resume describing your past writing experience and assignments, along with copies of your past published work.

You must also indicate, in writing, any publishing requirements or fees for your unsolicited submissions and queries. Omission of such will indicate you have none, and we will treat your unsolicited submissions and queries as such. Home Business® Magazine generally only monetarily compensates for new editorial assignments it gives to freelance writers who follow its explicit outlines and specifications to write new articles for Home Business® Magazine. All other submissions selected for publication in a particular issue of Home Business® Magazine are compensated in the way of the writers being given a 50-75 word resource box at the end of their articles to provide contact information and promote their products and services to readers of Home Business® Magazine.

All submissions are given serious review and consideration for approximately six months. Due to the enormous volume of submissions received, Home Business® Magazine cannot discuss submissions over the phone. Once submitted, please do not call the editorial staff for a status of your submission. If your submission is selected for publication in a future issue of the Home Business® Magazine, the editorial staff will contact you prior to publication.

Please email all submissions to henderso@ix.netcom.com with each article pasted into an email.

All submissions to Home Business® Magazine are deemed permission to print in full or part. The editorial staff reserves the right to edit submissions for publication due to space constraints, grammatical incorrectness, poor writing quality, lack of clarity, etc. Those views expressed in published submissions are not necessarily the views shared by the editorial staff. Home Business® Magazine assumes no responsibility for return of unsolicited submissions, which include manuscripts, photos, computer disks or artwork.

Categories: Nonfiction—Book Reviews—Business—Campus Life—Careers—Crafts/Hobbies—Family—General Interest—Lifestyle—Money and Finances—Self Help—Society—Women's Issues—Young Adult

CONTACT: Richard Henderson, Publisher
Material: Celebrity Interviews and Money and Finance
CONTACT: Stacy Henderson, Editor-in-Chief
Material: Home Office, Telecommunication, Business Growth
CONTACT: Sandy Larson, Managing Editor
Material: Work from Home Success Stories and Product/Book Reviews
9582 Hamilton Ave PMB 368
Huntington Beach CA 92646
Phone: 714-968-0331
E-mail: henderso@ix.netcom.com
Website: www.homebusinessmag.com

Home Cooking

General Information
House of White Birches publishes Home Cooking magazine, a 96-page, bimonthly, newsprint issue.

Submissions
1. Queries or manuscripts:
• Query and manuscript reviews are held approximately every eight weeks. Check the editorial calendar for themes and dates. Your query or manuscript must be in our office by this scheduled date to be considered for inclusion in the issue.

• Queries should include an opening or summarizing paragraph, along with a list of six to 10 recipes with brief descriptions (previously published recipes are not acceptable). Completed manuscripts may also be submitted. Keep a copy of all materials.

• We will contact you within three weeks after the review date if we accept your query or manuscript. Responses to accepted queries will request the complete manuscript on speculation; no articles will be

assigned. All others will be returned within four weeks after the review date when an appropriate SASE or e-mail address is provided.

2. Manuscript guidelines:
• Type and double-space all manuscripts on white paper in our magazine style, following a current publication.
• Pay special attention to ingredient lists. Spell out amounts, such as tablespoon, teaspoon, cup, ounce, etc. List ingredients in order used.
• Include temperatures, cooking times, container sizes and all other pertinent information in the directions.
• Give number of servings.
• Follow an introduction of 200 to 750 words with six to 10 recipes.
• Be certain that the subject matter has nationwide appeal.
• Include your name, address, telephone/fax number and e-mail address as appropriate in the upper left-hand corner of the first page. The upper right-hand corner must include the word count.
• Note a simultaneous submission as such. Simultaneous submissions are not encouraged.

3. Departments: Only "Kitchen Know-How" and "Pinch of Sage" are open to freelancers. Check current issues for style.

4. Photographs. Do not send.

5. Mailing address: Send queries and completed manuscripts to Shelly Vaughan James, Home Cooking, House of White Birches, 306 East Parr Road, Berne, IN 46711 or Editor@HomeCookingMagazine.com. If you e-mail, send a text message only; do not send attached files.

Contracts and payment
Following the manuscript deadline, we will send you a contract, a copy for your records and a business-reply envelope. Sign the contract and return it in the postage-paid envelope. Keep the copy of the contract for your records.

Payment will be made within 45 days of the time we receive your contract. Amount will be determined by length, overall quality, accuracy and adherence to guidelines. Average fees range from $25 to $250. HWB purchases all rights to manuscripts. Contributors should not sell the purchased manuscript or one very similar to it to another publisher.

If you have any questions, contact the editor. We look forward to working with you.

Categories: Nonfiction—Cooking—Entertainment—Food/Drink

CONTACT: Shelly Vaughan James, Editor
Material: Queries and completed manuscripts
House of White Birches
306 East Parr Rd
Berne IN 46711
Phone: 260-589-4000
E-mail: Editor@HomeCookingMagazine.com
Website: www.whitebirches.com

Home Education Magazine

Home Education Magazine is for families who enjoy living and learning together. If you're not familiar with homeschooling please study our publication before submitting. If you are familiar with homeschooling you might want to study it anyway, as we do take an active political stance for empowering individual families.

The current issue will be sent for $6.50 postpaid.

We offer selected articles and columns from each issue at our website.

There is also an excellent collection of reading from our magazine, sorted by topic, in the Homeschooling Information Library at our website.

TOPICS
Any topic of interest to homeschooling families will be considered. Please be aware that we have the most widely diverse readership in the homeschooling community, and our content reflects that diversity. We generally prefer completed articles to query letters. We welcome articles from inexperienced writers, especially mothers with

homeschooling experience. Regardless of what you were taught in high school English classes, writing is nothing particularly mysterious. It's only another form of communication. If you can clearly explain your ideas to a friend, you can write a good article for our magazine. Please see the article at the end of these guidelines for tips and information on writing for *Home Education Magazine.*

DEADLINES

Please feel free to submit an article on any topic at any time, and we'll schedule it appropriately. Please note that articles are often selected 4-6 months ahead of an issue.

SUBMISSIONS

Submissions via email are the preferred format (see Suggestions below), please send to Articles@homeedmag.com (when submitting via email please remember to include your postal mailing address). Our computers are Macintoshes, and we have many filters so we can read most submissions, but sometimes files will need to be reformatted and special formatting (bolds, italics, etc.) will be lost. Please refer to "Suggestions for E-mail Submissions" below.

We do accept typed or handwritten articles, which you can mail to Articles, *Home Education Magazine,* Post Office Box 1083, Tonasket, WA 98855-1083. When submitting articles via postal mail, please remember to include a self-addressed, stamped envelope with sufficient postage for the return of your work. If you don't need your article returned, a stamped reply postcard or an email address will be fine.

General article length is 900 to 1,500 words, but we do occasionally run longer articles.

Please include a 40-60 word biographical credit (in third person) with your submission. If you prefer, we can run only your name and city/state. We will also accept pen names.

SUGGESTIONS FOR EMAIL SUBMISSIONS (from our Articles Editor, Kim O'Hara)

1. Start your subject line with "HEM:" or include the word "article" or "submission" in the subject header to help me sort them out from other email.

2. Include the article in the text of your email so I can look it over quickly and send you a response.

3. Also attach the article as an RTF file, which seems to be the most universal format for all different computer systems, and retains bolding and italics.

4. If you have any footnotes, be aware that RTF files don't include those; make sure they are included in the email text.

5. Include your name, regular-mail address (where we can send payment and a copy of the magazine if your article is accepted), and a short 40-60 word bio (written in third person).

PHOTOS

We always need sharp, clear photos for inside editorial use. Regular B/W print sizes work fine for inside use (images are printed at 200 dpi, 100 lpi). Covers (133 lpi, 300 dpi) require a very sharp, clear image. Color enlargements are best (8 by 10 min.), but please sent an image for review first. We prefer photos showing children and families doing everyday things, not necessarily posed educational-type shots. We advise studying our magazine before attempting photo submissions. Please include information about the photo, including names of anyone in the pictures, and the name of the photographer. Please make sure photos are clearly marked with your name so if they become separated we can still tell whose they are. Also include a SASE with sufficient postage for the return of your photos. This should be a separate SASE from the SASE or postcard you send for return of your article or editorial response.

Electronic submissions of photos are accepted. Please arrange to send low resolution (72 dpi) for review. If your low resolution image is accepted, you can send the full-sized version at the resolutions noted above for inside and cover photos. For more information write to Mark Hegener at HEM@home-ed-magazine.com.

RIGHTS

Home Education Magazine buys First North American Serial Rights (print and electronic) to all articles, columns, artwork and photos.

We upload selected articles and columns from each issue to our website: http://www.home-ed-magazine.com/ Rights purchased include our right to reproduce your work in CD-ROM format as well as in any other formats of *Home Education Magazine* in which your work appears, or in an anthology or collection of articles, columns, artwork and photos which have appeared in *Home Education Magazine.* All rights not stated here, or not directly related to *Home Education Magazine,* including Second Serial, or reprint rights, remain yours.

PAYMENT

Feature articles — $50.00-$100.00 each. We occasionally pay more for articles we've requested, or which require special expenses or considerations. Photos for inside use $12.50 each. Cover color photos $100.00 each. Contributors always receive at least one free copy of the issue in which their work appears. Up to three additional copies are available free on request.

Categories: Children—Education—Family—General Interest—Parenting

CONTACT: Helen Hegener, Managing Editor
Material: All
PO Box 1083
Tonasket WA 98855-1083
Phone: 509-486-1351
E-mail: Articles@homeedmag.com
Website: www.homeedmag.com

Home Educator's Family Times

Print and online newspaper meeting the needs of today's homeschooling families. Topics covered include homeschooling, practical family life issues, parenting, research, legal issues, teaching and resources.

Rights: We seek one-time publishing rights and request the right for future inclusion in our online publication and in our archived back issues online. Rights revert back to the author. We also accept reprints.

Needs: Homeschooling Experiences, Education and Instruction of Children, Family Life and Homemaking, Fatherhood, Budgeting and Finances, Parenting, Teen Issues, Education Commentaries, Homeschool Commentaries, Family, Children, Homeschool Humor, Book Excerpts, Book Reviews, Curriculum Reviews, Educational Research, Educational Resources

Length: 900 - 1500 words

Art/Photo Needs: (Optional) Accompanying artwork or photos with article in a 200 dpi or above resolution (color) in EPS, TIF or PDF. Book cover photos same as above.

Payment: $0 - $35 depending on writer's experience and type of article compensation include the author's bio, publication history, pertinent published works, web link, contributor copies

How to Submit: Text file - attached text or RTF (Word, AppleWorks, Plain Text) or pasted into the body of an Email.

Response Time: 2 weeks

Tips for Writers: Suggest that writers visit our web site review content.

Sample Copies/Subscription Information: Subscription $12/year Available online: http://www.homeeducator.com/FamilyTimes/subscribe.htm

Categories: Education

CONTACT: Jane R. Boswell, Editor
PO Box 6442
Brunswick ME 04011
E-mail: famtimes@blazenetme.net
Website: www.homeeducator.com/FamilyTimes/current.htm

Home Furnishings Retailer

Home Furnishings Retailer is the official publication of National Home Furnishings Association (NHFA). NHFA is a national trade organization serving the interests of the nation's home furnishings retailers. Home Furnishings Retailer is published monthly with the exception of December. The magazine's primary audience comprises the top executives of retail stores specializing in furniture, decorative accessories and other products for the home.

Home Furnishings Retailer is owned by retailers, targeted to retailers and its editorial content focuses on issues that impact the retail community. On-going objective of all articles is to provide inrely heavily on home furnishings industry experts to author articles. Some freelance material is used. However, the NHFA Board of Directors, which provides direction for the publication, requires that writers have credentials that include specific knowledge of the industry and extensive experience in writing about it. Freelancers are compensated based on subject matter and the amount of research required.

Suggestions for freelance articles relating to the business interests of retailers will be reviewed. When submitting a query or requesting a writing assignment, include a resume, writing samples and credentials. Generally, only writers with experience within the home furnishings industry will be considered.

When articles are assigned, Home Furnishings Retailer will provide general direction along with suggestions for appropriate artwork. The author is responsible for obtaining photographs or other illustrative material.

Assigned articles should be submitted via email or on disc along with a list of sources with telephone numbers, fax numbers and email. Fees will be set upon assignment and payment made upon acceptance.

Categories: Nonfiction—Home—Woodworking

CONTACT: Submissions Editor
Material: All
3910 Tinsley Drive, Ste., 101
High Point, NC 27265
Phone: 336-886-6100
E-mail: info@nhfa.org
Website: www.nhfa.org

Home Improver Magazine

STYLE & POLICY GUIDELINES

The goal of *Home Improver* is to provide readers with concise information reported in a responsible manner. Individual style is encouraged, but not at the cost of good journalism techniques, proper word usage and grammar. Our purpose is to be informative, educational and entertaining.

It is strongly recommended that all writers read and consult *Strunk & White's Elements of Style* with particular regard for those sections detailing punctuation and sentence structure. Originally published in 1935, this small text is neither outdated nor a fundamental primer. Its contents are the foundation of skillful written communication. A writer's personal style develops from the proper creative use of the basic writing tools. It's inexpensive, a quick read and an invaluable writer's companion.

FREELANCE SUBMISSIONS

We want our editors to be known throughout the Home Improvement Industry and *Home Improver* encourages you to submit articles for publication in other periodicals. The only exceptions, of course, are submissions to our direct competitors. If possible, try to include your title of Contributing Editor, *Home Improver* as byline information.

FAX TRANSMISSIONS

Please double space all copy transmitted by fax service. Our fax machine is open 24 hours, 7 days a week.

As a backup, please have a printed copy available so it can be resent if possible.

E-MAIL TRANSMISSIONS

Files must be transmitted in ASCII.txt format. They should be sent to LouKojak@aol.com

FRACTIONS

You may write fractions in either decimal (1.75 pounds) or fraction (1 3/4 pounds) format. For modem transmissions only, please prefix fractions with a hyphen (-) as in 1 - 3/4 pounds. As with italic notations, this cues our computer to alter the printing style.

NUMBERS

Unless the reference is to a weight or measure (as above) numbers from zero to ninety-nine should be written. Numbers of 100 and above should be numerical.

JARGON

We face the use of slang and colloquialisms everywhere in the home improvement industry and we face the urge to emphasize such jargon words with quotes and italics. To do so tends to exclude the reader and makes it appear as if the reader is on the outside of a clique that knows better. Avoid emphasizing jargon words whenever possible.

PROPER NAMES

There are many ways individuals choose to spell their names and many ways to spell various location place names around our region. Without exception, we will defer to the spelling that you provide so double-check your copy.

BLOCK THAT METAPHOR

Be judicial in your use of metaphors and in your use of words that may be offensive to readers. When in doubt, don't write it.

©Home Improver Publications, Inc., 1998

Categories: Nonfiction—Architecture—Consumer—Gardening—Lifestyle—Home Improvement—Remodeling

CONTACT: Susan Luft, Editor
Material: All
©Home Improver Publications, Inc
11 Virginia Rd.
White Plains NY 10603
Phone: 914-328-1992
Fax: 914-328-1993
E-mail: himprover@aol.com
Website: www.himprover.com

Home Times Family Newspaper

Home Times is a monthly tabloid newspaper, distributed locally and nationally by U.S. Mail to paid subscribers, requestors, churches, and homes. We cover world & national news & views, home & family, arts & entertainment, religion, and people features—all with a Biblical world view.

We are a NEWSpaper. Content is generally related to current events and vital issues of the day. We aim squarely at the general public and write for them, (though we receive most of our support from Christian readers.) Features on family, education, parenting, and entertainment are positive, practical, not moralistic, related to issues and values.

SONLIGHT in particular, our special news section for the churches, has the mission to call churches to Prayer, Unity, Revival and Harvest.

HOME TIMES is non-denominational, non-doctrinal, free of religious cliches or churchy or preachiness. It tries not to moralize but just to be positive and Biblical in perspective. Our goal is to publish godly viewpoints in the marketplace, and to counteract the culturally elite of media and politics who reject Judeo-Christian values, traditional American values, and faith in God.

HOME TIMES is DIFFERENT from all other "Christian" publications. *We strongly suggest you read these guidelines AND sample issues.* Once you understand our slant, and if this is your kind of writing, you'll enjoy writing for us!

This is a prime opportunity for new writers (or old ones) who pursue the ministry of writing in "a world gone mad." To help you hone your skills, we have written a 12-chapter book entitled "101 Reasons Why I Reject Your Mss"—an effective training course for new or struggling freelancers, easy to understand and enjoyable, with the greatest focus on becoming marketable.

General Requirements: We want complete manuscripts—no queries please. Photos and illustrations may enhance a story if appropriate. No unsolicited slides, negatives, disks, faxes or e-mail *please.* Pay, on publication, ranges from $5 to $50 ($5 to $25 for reprints). PHOTOS $5 each.

Rights: We buy ONE-TIME RIGHTS ONLY. Mail SEASONAL materials 8 weeks in advance. Length: 500-1000 words. We reserve the right to shorten and edit to fit our slant and style. Replies: Holler if you don't hear in four weeks.

Special Opportunities: We want personal features in: **Faith, Heroes, Nostalgia, Religion, History, Holidays, Home & Family, Parenting, Arts & Entertainment, LifeWatch, Sports, Voices, Politics, Humor, People, Advice, Writing, etc.**—especially true-to-life stories, especially with photos, generally about ordinary people (ESPECIALLY LOCAL) who do extraordinary things; positive, about good people and the goodness of God in our lives. LENGTH: generally 500-1000 words works best.

Non-Cash Opportunities: We do not pay for the following (or with free issues if requested): **Briefs** of all sorts, **Anecdotes** in various categories such as: **Family Life** (funny stories from Parents & Kids); **Tales Out Of School** (funny incidents from teachers & students, all grades through college); **In The Pew** (funny things that happened in church or synagogue); **First Grade Jokes** (clean corny kid stuff); **America 101** (funny or poignant stories about Americans); **Great Shots** (photos of kids, family, pets, action, happenings that are cute, funny or unusual); and **OpEds** (up to 400 words). We welcome Letters to the Editor up to 200 words.

Do's/Don'ts:
• No preaching or devotionals.
• We accept some **poetry** (traditional or light verse to 16 lines, max. 3 per submission) and **short fiction (creative non-fiction)** (750-1,200 words).
• We like historical humor dealing with issue ("Tom Jefferson Meets the ACLU").
• **SONLIGHT** is more spiritual and wants articles on prayer, unity, revival and harvest.

Categories: Fiction—Nonfiction—Adventure—African-American—Arts—Book Reviews—Business—Cartoons—Children—Christian Interests—Comedy—Culture—Economics—Education—Entertainment—Family—Film/Video—General Interest—Government—Health—History—Human Rights—Inspirational—Interview—Jewish Interest—Lifestyle—Literature—Marriage—Money & Finances—Music—Parenting—Physical Fitness—Poetry—Politics—Psychology—Recreation—Relationships—Religion—Rural America—Satire—Science—Self Help—Senior Citizen—Short Stories—Singles—Society—Spiritual—Sports/Recreation—Teen—Television/Radio—Theatre—Women's Fiction—Women's Issues—Writing—Young Adult—Current Events—Current Issues

CONTACT: Dennis Lombard, Editor & Publisher
Material: All
3676 Collin Dr. Ste. 16
W. Palm Beach FL 33406
Phone: 561-439-3509
E-mail: hometimes2@aol.com

HomeLife

Thanks for your interest in writing for *HomeLife* magazine. We are always looking for qualified Christian writers who deliver professional Christian journalism. These guidelines will help you understand more about who we are, what we're looking for, and how we work with writers.

WHO WE ARE

The mission of *HomeLife* is to equip and challenge families to experience dynamic, healthy, Christ-centered lives.

All articles submitted should be consistent with the vision and doctrinal statements of our publisher, LifeWay Christian Resources:

• **LifeWay Vision:** As God works through us, we will help people and churches know Jesus Christ and seek His Kingdom by providing biblical solutions that spiritually transform individuals and cultures.

• **Doctrinal Statement:** We believe that the Bible has God for its author; salvation for its end; and truth, without any mixture of error, for its matter and that all Scripture is totally true and trustworthy. The 2000 statement of "The Baptist Faith and Message" is our doctrinal guideline (available online at www.sbc.net/toc.html).

FIRST CONTACT

HomeLife does not accept unsolicited queries or manuscripts. We do not accept reprints and offer nonexclusive license contracts.

In your initial contact with our editors, we ask that you provide the following:

1. **Resume.** Emphasize your formal writing training (such as a degree in journalism, communications, English, and so on); writing experience; and recent published works. List your qualifications as a writer (such as experience in researching and interviewing or particular areas of expertise).

2. **Clips.** Send recently published pieces, including your original drafts as available. Include articles that are similar to what you might write for our publication.

3. **Biographical Form.** Available upon request, this form allows you to tell us your areas of interest/expertise, as well as a brief description of your journey with Christ. (As a Christian magazine, we desire to have writers who are Christ followers and are growing spiritually.)

Please send the requested information to HomeLife, New Writer, One LifeWay Plaza, Nashville, TN 37234-0175 or fax them to HomeLife, New Writer at 615.277.8272.

Writers will be evaluated on their ability to produce articles that fit within the tone and mission of *HomeLife* and their ability to produce articles that offer our readers practical ways to live out their faith in everyday family life.

You may contact *HomeLife* with any questions through e-mail at homelife@lifeway.com.

WORKING WITH WRITERS

HomeLife's method of working with writers is by article assignment. Typically, the *HomeLife* team develops the concepts for articles in each issue. We then assign articles to freelance writers. Occasionally we accept queries from writers we have a working relationship with.

OUR EDITORIAL VOICE

In developing our editorial voice, we emphasize:

• **Practical help.** We want to offer our readers articles that offer takeaway value. As a Christian family magazine, we print articles that address matters of faith, marriage, parenting, and the practical issues of daily living.

• **Authenticity.** We want to address real-life needs and issues.

• **Quality research.** We want to offer readers information that is fresh, not stale. We look for research of primary sources and interesting slants that offer help unique to HomeLife.

• **Scriptural integrity.** Our goal is to help families experience Christ-centered life, so all of the articles in the magazine should line up with and be supported by the truths of Scripture. However, we are looking for practical magazine articles, not devotionals or Bible studies.

We follow The Associated Press Stylebook and Libel Manual. All

Scripture quotations should be from the Holman Christian Standard Bible (HCSB) or New International Version (NIV), unless you have a compelling reason to use a different translation.

Categories: Nonfiction—Health—Lifestyle—Parenting—Relationships

CONTACT: Submissions/Copy Editor
Material: All
One LifeWay Plaza
Nashville TN 37234-0175
Phone: 615-251-2011
Fax: 615-277-8272
Website: www.lifewayonline.ocm/mags

Homeschooling Companion

Rights: All rights. May consider previously published work.
Needs:
NONFICTION: This includes biographies and various other approaches to history, science, mathematics, geography and arts that pertain to the theme or topic in each issue.

LITERATURE STUDY: Literature study guides will also correspond to the historical theme. We are looking for guides to literature and verse that are appropriate for two age ranges: Ages 7-11 and Ages 12 and up.

ARTS & CRAFT PROJECTS: Arts and crafts submissions should appeal to either a (7-11) or (12 and up) age level or all ages and tie into the historical topic or theme of each issue.

Length: NONFICTION - 800-1400 words
LITERATURE STUDY GUIDE - no more than 1400 words.
Payment: NONFICTION - $50 per article
LITERATURE STUDY - $50 per study guide, $75 if study guide includes vocabulary/spelling lesson
ARTS & CRAFT PROJECTS - $25 per project
How to Submit: Submissions are via email in RTF or plain text format. Response Time: 6-8 weeks
Categories: Education

CONTACT: Rebecca Thompson, Editor
Material: All
E-mail: rebeccat@zbzoom.net

Hopscotch for Girls

Every HOPSCOTCH contributor must remember we publish only six issues a year, which means our editorial needs are extremely limited. An annual total, for instance, will include some 30 to 36 nonfiction pieces, 9 or 10 short stories, 18 or so poems, six cover illustrations, and a smattering of puzzles, crafts, and the like.

It is obvious that we must reject far more contributions than we accept, no matter how outstanding they may seem to you or to us.

With that said, we would point out that HOPSCOTCH is a magazine created for girls from 6 to 12 years, with youngsters 8, 9, and 10 the specific target age.

Our point of view is that every young girl deserves the right to be a young girl for a number of years before she becomes a young adult.

As a result, HOPSCOTCH looks for articles, fiction, nonfiction, and poetry that deal with timeless topics, such as pets, nature, hobbies, science, games, sports, careers, simple cooking, and anything else likely to interest a young girl. We leave dating, romance, human sexu-ality, cosmetics, fashion, and the like to other publications. Each issue revolves around a theme. You may request a theme list by sending in a self-addressed, stamped envelope, or check our website.

Writers

We are looking for lively writing, most of it from a young girl's point of view—with the girl or girls directly involved in an activity that is both wholesome and unusual. Examples have included girls in a sheep to shawl contest, girls raising puppies that are destined to guide the blind, and girls who take summer ballet lessons from members of the New York City Ballet.

While on the subject of nonfiction—remembering that we use it 3 to 1 over fiction—those pieces that are accompanied by black and white photos are far more likely to be accepted that those that need illustrations.

The ideal length of a HOPSCOTCH nonfiction piece is 500 words or less, although we are not about to turn down a truly exceptional piece if it is slightly longer than the ideal. We prefer fiction to not run over 1,000 words.

We will entertain simultaneous submissions as long as that fact is noted on the manuscript. Computer printouts are welcome if they are (as all submissions should be) double-spaced.

HOPSCOTCH prefers to receive complete manuscripts with cover letters, although we do not rule out query letters. We do not answer submissions sent in by fax or e-mail. All submissions must be accompanied by a self-addressed, stamped envelope, with sufficient postage.

We will pay a minimum of 5 cents a word for both fiction and nonfiction, with additional payment given if the piece is accompanied by appropriate photos or art. We will pay a minimum of $10 per poem or puzzle, with variable rates offered for games, crafts, cartoons, and the like.

HOPSCOTCH buys first American serial rights and pays upon publication. It welcomes the contributions of both published and unpublished writers.

Sample copies are available for $6.00 within the US & $7.00 outside the US. All payment must he in US. funds. A complimentary copy will be sent each writer who has contributed to a given issue.

Photographers

We use a number of black and white photos inside the magazine, most in support of articles used. Payment is $5-10 per photo, and $5 for color slides.

Artists

Most art will be by assignment, in support of features used. The magazine is anxious to find artists capable of illustrating stories and features and welcomes copies of sample work, which will remain on file. Payment is $25 for partial illustrations and $35 for full-page illustrations.

Incidentally

Although we are working far into the future, we occasionally have room for one or two pages.

One More Thing

We are always in need of cute and clever recipes, well-written and illustrated crafts, riddles, and jokes.

Categories: Fiction—Nonfiction—Animals—Cartoons—Children

CONTACT: Marilyn Edwards, Editor
Material: All
CONTACT: Bethany Sneed, Associate Editor
Material: All
PO Box 164
Bluffton OH 45817-0164
Phone: 419-358-4610
Fax: 419-358-5027
Website: www.hopscotchmagazine.com

Horror Tales
Short vampire-related horror fiction

Published: Annually

Book Formats: Anthology is a book-zine (eclectic like a magazine but in book form) and will be published in one or more of the following, traditional paper (either hardback or paperback), electronic (ebooks and/or audio).

Poetry, short fiction and other writings about the macabre (horror of all types), including ghost stories, spooky tales, ironic horror, etc.

Lengths: Open for all short fiction, poems, articles manuscripts of all lengths will be considered.

The deadline for submissions: Editor read submissions year-round.

Rights: One-time use in book form (all formats). Considers reprints if author owns rights.

Poets and writers should send a bio to accompany their writings in the anthology.

Please note: Writers with books and other publications or venues (i.e. a website) can submit information, website address, etc. for inclusion in the anthology to accompany their bio information. This will give writers added exposure for themselves and their books, websites, etc.

Contributors must send note (email or by regular mail) stating that he/she would like the writing(s) included in the published anthology. Submit up to 5 manuscripts, either by email or regular mail (see below). Please enclose SASE with regular mail submissions.

Contributors will receive one copy of the finished anthology.

Categories: Fiction—Entertainment—Horror—Short Stories

CONTACT: Eugene Boone
Material: All
RSVP Press
129 Thurman Lane
Clinton TN 37716
E-mail: rsvppress@yahoo.com

Horrorfind

Here at *Horrorfind*, we are willing to work with both new and seasoned authors. If you write horror stories, chances are that we're willing to look at it. We have published the latest from best-selling authors alongside the first story from high school students. We don't accept names. We accept stories. Our fiction section is updated regularly, and stories appearing here have gone on to be nominated or recommended for several genre awards, including the prestigious Bram Stoker Award and the Year's Best Fantasy & Horror.

We want horror fiction and all of its sub-genres. Quiet, extreme, dark fantasy, cross-genre (horror blended with sci-fi, sword & sorcery, etc.), weird western, dark crime, surreal, occult, splatterpunk, supernatural, magic realism, bizarre, erotic, HORROR. Yes, we will look at vampires, werewolves and serial killers. We love them. Just make sure you know your history and aren't repeating something that's already been done to death.

We don't want straight science fiction, fantasy or mystery. We won't consider stories without horror content. No gore for gore's sake. No sexual or extreme violence toward children. No poetry. No copyrighted characters (i.e. Jason, Freddy Krueger, Conan, etc.) unless you either own the copyright to those characters or have legal permission to be writing about them. Permission must be documented.

Fiction to 3,000 words. Anything longer, query first. We will accept reprints as long as you have obtained the rights. Simultaneous submissions okay, but please have the courtesy to inform us. Absolutely no multiple submissions at any time. Multiple submissions will be deleted unread. Include a brief bio.

Electronic submissions only. Send as either an attached Microsoft Word Document or pasted directly into the body of the email. You may also use the submission board here at Horrorfind and paste directly into that. If your story is accepted, you will be asked to follow it up with an attached Word Document or disc.

Horrorfind requires the assignment of Electronic Rights for a period of four (4) months. You retain all other rights. After 4 months, Electronic Rights revert back to you as well. You may choose to leave the story archived at the website, or may request to have it removed at any time, providing 24 hours notice is given. We reserve the right to remove the story from publication at any time after the 4 month period.

Payment for solicited submissions will vary on an individual basis, beginning at a professional rate of three (.03) cents per word. Payment for unsolicited submissions is in exposure. Stories published at Horrorfind may also be considered for future volumes of the *Best of Horrorfind* anthology. If selected, a separate contract would be negotiated for print rights.

Our response time will vary. We receive an average of 10 to 30 submissions a week. If you haven't received a response within 5 weeks, feel free to query.

Categories: Fiction—Erotica—Fantasy—Horror—Paranormal—Science Fiction—Short Stories—Western

CONTACT: Brian Keene, Fiction Editor
Material: All
E-mail: fiction@horrorfind.com

Horse Illustrated
The Magazine for Responsible Horse Owners

WRITER'S GUIDELINES

Thank you for your interest in HORSE ILLUSTRATED. We hope you find the following guidelines helpful in preparing any future submissions.

Magazine Focus: *Horse Illustrated* is directed to hands-on horse owners and riders of English and western disciplines. The magazine promotes responsible horse ownership, from providing tips to owners on better horse care and training, to alerting horse lovers about pertinent issues in the equine community. We direct our articles to the adult audience.

Suggested Articles: The best way to decide what type of article to submit is to look over a sample copy of the magazine, available at newsstands, tack stores or book stores nationwide. Look over more than one issue, if possible. The article index and back issue listings on our web site (www.horseillustrated.com) are also helpful guides to topics we have covered recently.

We need informative, in-depth, upbeat articles (limited to 2,000 words) that will help readers better care for and enjoy their horses. They may be about such topics as training (for both horse and rider), management or horse-related activities.

What NOT to Send:

Fiction

Personal essays

Tributes to deceased horses

Poetry

Book reviews

Please do not send breed profiles; this monthly feature is always assigned.

Series, columns and multi-part articles are assigned only to our established writers.

How to Submit: Address all correspondence to Moira C. Harris, Editor, HORSE ILLUSTRATED, P.O. Box 6050, Mission Viejo, CA 92690. Enclose a self-addressed stamped envelop with all materials, and please allow eight to twelve weeks for a response. If materials do not need to be returned, we appreciate knowing that.

While e-mail makes it easy to fire off those article proposals, it is harder for us to track, evaluate and respond to these submissions, not to mention concerns with opening attachments from unknown senders. In order to give your article proposal the best consideration, we prefer to receive queries via mail rather than e-mail.

HORSE ILLUSTRATED receives dozens of unsolicited manuscripts and queries every week. The magazine accepts only a small fraction of what is submitted. Due to the high volume of unsolicited work, we cannot review or respond to any material sent to us by fax, or material that isn't accompanied by a self-addressed stamped envelope.

Manuscript Requirements: Manuscripts should be double spaced with wide margins. If your article is accepted, we'll also need an electronic copy: a disk or CD containing the text as a Word document that can be opened on a PC. Accepted manuscripts may be sent via e-mail. Many great story ideas cannot be considered if we will be unable to find images to illustrate them. If specific photos will be essential to your manuscript, please indicate what photos are available to accompany your piece. It's a huge plus if you can include professional-quality color transparencies (preferred), or sharp, well-lit 35 mm color prints with these types of articles. Additional guidelines are available for artists and photographers.

Reviewing Material: We prefer to review **completed manuscripts** on speculation. However, if you would like to query us before preparing an article, you must include a detailed outline of what the proposed article will cover, including any expert resources, and sample paragraphs as well as clips that demonstrate your writing style. We do not accept simultaneous submissions, but may accept reprint material from noncompetitive publications. We require first North American serial rights in the equine industry.

Responsibility: We cannot assume responsibility for material submitted, but reasonable care will be taken in the handling of your work.

Payment: Articles are paid upon publication. Rates of payment are based on quality, not length. We pay between $200 and $400 for feature articles. Smaller items receive $50 to $100 per piece. Articles accompanied by high-quality photographs or illustrations earn the highest rates.

For new (and new to *HI*) writers:

The majority of our articles are assigned in advance to our regular writers. However, we are always looking to expand our "stable" of talented freelance equestrian journalists. The best way to get your foot in the door is to query with a completed manuscript demonstrating your writing ability, and just as important, an understanding of our tone and audience, and subject matter appropriate to our magazine. Once we have worked successfully with a writer on a manuscript or two, we will feel comfortable entertaining queries or assigning articles.

Because we have limited space to accept and publish queries, it can take up to a year to establich this type of relationship. We always appreciate your patience and professionalism throughout this process.

PHOTO GUIDELINES

Welcome to *Horse Illustrated*! *Horse Illustrated* is the nation's largest equine publication, and we pride ourselves on providing quality illustrative photos to our readership. We are pleased to offer our photographers some of the most competitive rates in the equine industry. *Horse Illustrated* strives to have images that are unique to its pages.

HORSE ILLUSTRATED is a magazine directed toward **adult** horse owners. Please study a copy of the magazine before making your submission. That way you won't be sending us photos that are inappropriate for our content.

Safety and responsible care are the keynotes of our editorial content. Therefore, photos must depict healthy horses (unless submitting photos for a particular article on unhealthy horses), well-appointed riders (no shorts, bare feet or other inappropriate riding attire) and horses, and handlers using safe practices.

Hunt-seat, show jumping riders and dressage riders schooling must be wearing safety helmets. Please learn the difference between an ASTM-SEI approved helmet and a "for apparel only" riding hat. Just because a hat has a harness and chinstrap does not make it safety headgear. We will not be accepting any photos of riding hats. There

are minor exceptions. 1) Dressage riders who are showing above 4th level normally wear top hats, so this is acceptable while showing; 2) international riders of all disciplines who may not choose to wear a helmet; 3) Western riders of any discipline. No BARE HEADED shots or photos of riders wearing BASEBALL CAPS will be accepted. Western riders must be wearing western hats. (NOTE: if setting up your own shoots, why not invest in a low-cost schooling helmet to put on your subject?)

YOUR PHOTOGRAPHIC SUBJECTS: Select individuals who are attractive, with well-groomed, fit horses wearing clean, up-to-date tack and equipment. We know that in the real world, a lot of riders grab their grubbiest clothes, whisk a little dirt off their pasture-kept horses, saddle up and go. Magazines, however, are not "reality TV." We want to show our readership how to put their best foot forward. We are reporting on trends. We do not want to show dated apparel, worn out tack and sloppy appearances.

Ditto for your location. Select an attractive, uncluttered background. Move the collection of broken jump standards out of your shot. Tidy up the barn aisle before shooting. Grab a pitchfork and get the manure out of your frame. These little details won't go unnoticed by the reader. Ask yourself if the horse, rider and background are worthy enough to be in YOUR shot.

STOCK: We are always on the lookout to update our files with sharp 4/C slides. We draw from this file for every issue. If you do not have anything to submit for a specific article or issue, you may still submit for our stock files. If you do so, please include a letter stating this purpose. If the photos meet our standards, you will be sent a contract detailing which shots we are holding. Stock photos are held for an indefinite period of time, and are usually not returned until after they are used or until you request their return, which you can do at any time. Photos not selected for the stock photography are returned.

We are constantly in need of quality photos of problem behaviors of horses for our training columns, and medical ailments for our veterinary column. If you are shooting "naughty horses" you must submit a model release with the photos for any taken on private property (i.e. not a show).

Rates:

$275 - cover photo (just increased!)

$200 - centerspread; two-page spread

$150 - partial page spread (photo that goes across gutter of magazine, but is less than 2 page bleed)

$90 - full page color

$60 - partial page color

$25 - if a photo used in a feature is also included on the Table of Contents

When photos are submitted for a particular use or article, they are reviewed during the production schedule for that issue. Contracts are written for the photos selected, and are usually sent to the photographer along with those photos not selected. Photos used in the magazine are returned during the month that the magazine appears in print.

Payment is made upon publication. Our rates are paid according to the format that the photo appears in the magazine, not the format in which the photo was submitted. For example, a 35mm color photo on the cover is paid $275, while a 35mm color photo used in a smaller format is paid $60. We buy first North American serial rights on an exclusive basis; the non-exclusive right to use the photos in electronic media; and the non-exclusive right to use the photos, as well as your name, image and biographical data in advertising and promotion.

What to Send

Color transparencies are our preferred format. We cannot accept duplicate slides, since we cannot reproduce a quality image from them. Even when photographers want to send dupes in "just to review the work" they are often doing themselves a disservice, because the images are so poor. Our magazine is produced "direct to plate," and all images are electronically drum scanned on high-end equipment. Therefore, it is extremely important that all photos be sharp, with well-balanced contrast.

Transparencies should be rich in color. No whites that are blown out, and no blacks that are muddy. Always review your film with a loupe. Only tack-sharp images will be considered. Horses in motion should have crisp hooves and detail in the mane.

FILM OR DIGITAL?: Digital photography is a Pandora's Box for us editors! The pros: Instantaneous results; no color separation necessary; affordable alternative to buying/storing film. The cons: Difficult to review, difficult to catalog, equipment quality varies, digital image quality varies, color is difficult to predict.

You can see why we do still prefer color transparencies over digital—hands down, the digital is going to appear slightly softer than the slide when it is color separated and printed. But there is an increasing desire for photographers to use digital, so we will accept them under these conditions:

1. CDs have only ONE subject per CD on them. If you are shooting a couple different topics, send one CD per topic.

2. Label each CD with your name, and the topic of each.

3. Each CD must be accompanied by a color thumbnail printout (digital contact sheet). No CDs will be reviewed without them.

4. Each CD must be accompanied by a caption list.

Digital images tend to go GREEN as well as have that softer focus. Know your white balance!!! And although your image looks color correct on your monitor or on a printout, it still has to be converted from an RGB file to CMYK. And then it needs to be calibrated to our printing press profile. So whatever you can do on your end (while setting your camera) to make it easier on our pre-press, so much the better.

Professional-grade equipment is a must to achieve the size and quality image we require. The highest setting on the camera should be used (for maximum resolution and file size), and *the less the digital file is manipulated, the better*. As much as possible, the images should be submitted direct from the camera (raw file). We have such a tight color model in our pre-press department that any photo manipulation/adjustment is best done here.

How and Where to Send It

With each submission, please include correspondence that details what article your work should be considered for. Please include your social security number (or taxpayer ID) on your correspondence to expedite payment. Each shot should be labeled with your name, address and phone number. Information about the subject (breed, event) should also be included.

Please mail submissions to us at:
HORSE ILLUSTRATED
PO Box 6050
Mission Viejo, CA 92690-6050
For UPS or overnight deliveries:
HORSE ILLUSTRATED
3 Burroughs Drive
Irvine, CA 92618

Always include a self-addressed stamped envelope with enough postage for return of your photos. We cannot be responsible for lost or misdirected mail.

Categories: Animals

CONTACT: Micaela Myers, Associate Editor
Material: All
PO Box 6050
Mission Viejo Ca 92690-6050
Phone: 949-855-8822 ext 3430

Horticulture

Published: 6 times per year
Circulation: 210,000
Query response time: 8 to 10 weeks
Number of articles purchased: About 10 a year from the approximately 400 unsolicited queries and manuscripts received
Rights purchased: One-time, first North American serial; all rights

purchased for some departments
Expenses: Reasonable expenses paid if previously arranged with editor
Kill fee: Depends on final fee
Rates:

Type of article	Word length	Payment
Features	1,200-2,000	$600-$1,000
Departments	200-1,500	$50-$600

The Magazine

Horticulture, the country's oldest gardening magazine, is designed for active amateur gardeners. Our goal is to offer a blend of text, photographs, and illustrations that will both instruct and inspire readers. While we place great emphasis on good writing, we also believe that every article must offer ideas or illustrate principles that our readers can apply in their own gardens. No matter what the subject, we want articles to help our readers become better, more creative gardeners.

We assume that our writers have an interest in and some experience with gardening. We look for and encourage personal experience, anecdote, and opinion. At the same time, an article should place its subject, to whatever degree appropriate, in the broader context of horticulture.

Query Letters

Tell us why—as succinctly as possible—you think your idea belongs in *Horticulture* and give us the general outline of your piece. Please let us know your personal involvement with the subject. If the article will require research or reporting, give us a brief description of the work you'll need to do.

We appreciate receiving any background material you may have that will help us assess the appropriateness of your idea. Proposals for garden profiles, in particular, should be accompanied by photographs or transparencies. We would also like to see a sample of your writing. Queries with a seasonal angle should be submitted at least ten months in advance of the proposed publication date.

Manuscript Submissions

We prefer that a query precede any manuscript. Manuscripts should be neatly typed and accompanied whenever possible by a computer disk. Include your name at the top of each page.

Categories: Nonfiction—Gardening

CONTACT: Thomas Fischer, Executive Editor
Material: All
98 N. Washington St.
Boston MA 02114
Phone: 617-742-5600
Fax: 617-637-6364
E-mail: horticulture_editorial@primediamags.com

House Beautiful

Thank you for your interest in *House Beautiful's* writer's guidelines.

We are primarily interested in service articles dealing strictly with the home. We use no fiction or poetry.

Be sure to study the style and contents of a few recent issues before submitting any proposals or articles. With your submission, please include some samples of your published work.

We prefer receiving queries rather than finished manuscripts. This will save you time. If we are interested in an idea, we will ask you to send in the article on speculation.

Rates, payable on acceptance, are determined by the length of the article. Most of our articles run 400 to 1000 words.

Please label with complete name and address every page, caption, photo, etc. that you submit. We receive many articles and queries and it is very easy for material to become separated.

Any submissions sent without a stamped, self-addressed envelope will not be returned.

Address all articles, queries and related correspondence to the address below. No phone calls or e-mails, please.

Thank you again for your interest in *House Beautiful*.

Categories: Architecture—Home—Lifestyle

CONTACT: Features department
Material: All
1700 Broadway, 29th Floor
New York NY 10019
Phone: 212-903-5084

House, Home and Garden

House, Home and Garden, a bimonthly publication, publishes articles related to the home, gardening, cooking and entertainment. We reach a diverse audience whose interests include various aspects of home life. We would like to see more submissions with information, new product, decorating and pet themes.

About three quarters of what we publish is written by non-staff writers (approximately 50 manuscripts per year). If you are new to us, please send for a sample copy of our magazine before submitting your work ($3.50 and 9" x 12" SASE with four first class stamps). Doing so will help you to better understand our style and content requirements.

We will accept queries or complete manuscripts. Computer printouts are fine.

Word length varies for both articles and department/columns. When thinking about an article for us, think about real estate, practical decorating ideas, house and home, antiques, travel, leisure and crafts. For departments/columns, think about home management, beauty, new products and travel.

We will negotiate rights and pay $0.10 per word up to 1,500 words on publication, plus one contributor's copy.

Thank you for your interest in writing for *House, Home and Garden*. We look forward to hearing from you.

Categories: Adventure—Animals—Antiques—Architecture—Arts—Children—Collectibles—Computers—Cooking—Crafts/Hobbies—Diet/Nutrition—Electronics—Entertainment—Family—Fashion—Feminism—Food/Drink—Gardening—Health—Hobbies—Money & Finances—Outdoors—Poetry—Real Estate—Self Help—Short Stories—Travel—Pets

CONTACT: Earl D. Unger, Editor
Material: All
809 Virginia Ave.
Martinsburg WV 25401-2131
Phone: 304-267-2673
Fax: 304-262-0676
Website: www.hhandgmag.us

Houseboat

Writer and Photographer Guidelines

Houseboat is a family-oriented publication for Houseboaters of all types across the United States and Canada. Readers of *Houseboat* includes houseboating families, couples, and retired couples; houseboat renters; houseboat manufacturers; boaters; full-time and part-time liveaboards; water-sport enthusiasts; fishermen; travel enthusiasts and so on.

Within our pages, readers will find features on new boats, destination pieces, new products, how-tos, service tips, industry news, houseboater profiles, special events and vintage houseboat articles. We also publish an annual buyer's guide and an annual Family Vacation Guide, as well as cover fishing and secondary water sports on occasion. If a topic can be tied into houseboating, there may be a place for it in our publication.

Queries: Query first with story ideas either by e-mail or snail mail to the addresses listed below. Include one or two paragraphs that briefly outline your idea and tell us why your story is timely, unique, new or of special interest. What qualifies you to write the story? Do you have photos to accompany the article?

Manuscripts: Features should run between 1,000 and 1,200 words. In addition, we like to run sidebars with features when appropriate that may run a few hundred words.

Use a third-person, reporter's viewpoint in how-to stories unless your experience in the boating industry qualifies you to write from a first-person perspective (please clear this with the editor beforehand). Our tone is a light and fun, as we want our readers to feel they can kick their feet up on their houseboats and enjoy the magazine from cover to cover.

Style: All submitted material should be consistent with the Associated Press style guide. Please pay particular attention to the use of numerals and measurements, as well as the abbreviations for states.

We prefer to receive manuscripts electronically as Microsoft Word attachments. Articles pasted into the body of the e-mail message are also acceptable if Word is not available. Include author's name, address and phone number on the top of the article. Harris Publishing reserves the right to edit submitted material as required.

Photos: We work with color slides or transparencies only. We prefer E100SW by Kodak, or Velvia by Fuji. Good contrast and sharp focus are a must. Submit 10 to 15 different photos to illustrate a feature thoroughly.

Involve people in every photo if possible. Show action and movement and attempt to do so from a fresh perspective. Utilize dawn and dusk lighting for dramatic photos.

Note: If you submit photos that belong to another person, you are responsible for splitting payment with him/her. We purchase manuscripts and photos as one package and pay only one fee.

Captions: All photo submissions must be keyed to a numbered caption sheet. Captions should be detailed enough to require little or no rewriting by our editorial staff.

Please identify people in your photos. Obtain a signed, model release if necessary and submit with the photos. Your name and address should be on each photo or transparency for proper credits, payment and photo returns.

Payment: Rates vary according to several factors including length, quality of the material, quality of the photos, and how much editing or rewriting is required. We work with professionals to maintain a certain level of quality for our readers. Therefore, we expect copy and photos to be of high quality.

Payment for features (including photos) range from $150 to $300. Columns, departments, mini-features and fillers (including photos) are worth $50 to $175. Payment is made after publication. *Houseboat* buys first North American serial rights to manuscripts and photos.

Revised 7/00

Categories: Nonfiction—Boating—Fishing—Lifestyle—Recreation

CONTACT: Steve Smede, Editor
Material: All
Harris Publishing
360 B St.
Idaho Falls ID 83402
Phone: 208-524-7000
Fax: 208-522-5241
E-mail: hbeditor@harrispublishing.com

HowStuffWorks

HowStuffWorks is a source for clear, reliable explanations of how everything around us actually works.

Find writer's guidelines information on website.

Categories: Education

CONTACT: Email: Authors@HowStuffWorks.com
Material: All
Website: www.howstuffworks.com

HR Magazine

Every year, HR Magazine receives more manuscripts—and offers to write manuscripts—than it can possibly publish. Only the best manuscripts—those that truly add to the fund of knowledge for HR professionals and advance the profession—are accepted.

Is your manuscript likely to be accepted for publication? By reading these guidelines, hopefully you can answer that question for yourself.

Mission statement: HR Magazine helps HR professionals perform their jobs more effectively. It offers practical solutions to current workplace problems, discusses new approaches and innovative best practices in all areas of HR management, and prompts readers to consider new models or ways of thinking.

Our audience: HR Magazine is the monthly flagship publication of the Society for Human Resource Management (SHRM). SHRM, the leading voice of the human resource profession, has more than 180,000 professional and student members in countries all over the world.

Our primary readers are HR generalists who hold positions as executives and managers in private-sector companies in the United States and Canada.

Our audience includes HR professionals from both large and small organizations. The largest concentration of readers works for firms that employ between 100 and 499 people. The next-largest group works for firms that employ 5,000 or more workers.

How to get an assignment: We prefer that potential authors send us article outlines before they begin writing. This helps us focus potential articles to our specific needs, and avoids repetition and wasted effort.

Outlines should summarize the main points of the article, as well as the evidence, potential sources and subtopics to be covered. Outlines should be submitted via the HR Magazine web site. (See the end of these guidelines for contact information.)

Due to the number of queries we receive, we are unable to respond to all queries that are rejected.

If your article idea is accepted, you will receive a letter or e-mail asking you to submit your manuscript; this does not guarantee that the completed manuscript will be accepted for publication.

HR Magazine also reviews unsolicited, completed manuscripts. These manuscripts may be accepted, rejected or tentatively accepted pending satisfactory alterations and rewrites. (Again, see the end of these guidelines for contact information.) Authors of completed manuscripts—or their representatives—will be notified of the status of their submissions within 45 days of receipt. Accepted authors must sign the standard HR Magazine copyright form.

What type of articles do we want?: HR Magazine accepts manuscripts and queries for three types of articles: features, certain departments and columns, and agendas. All three are explained below. All submitted articles, regardless of type, must be original, unpublished works.

FEATURES. These are in-depth articles—approximately 2,200 to 2,500 words in length—on a fairly narrow topic. The goal is to provide readers with enough information so they can deal adequately with an issue.

HR Magazine's goal is to investigate topics as fully as possible within our space constraints. As a result, we prefer articles that have a narrow focus, rather than those that take a broad overview. For example, an article on how to avoid age discrimination would probably be too broad; a better, more narrowly focused article would examine how to avoid age discrimination when conducting layoffs.

DEPARTMENTS AND COLUMNS. HR Magazine accepts freelance written manuscripts for the following departments: Legal Trends, Management Tools, HR Technology, Court Report and HR News.

Legal Trends articles should be written by experts—such as attorneys, regulatory experts and law professors. These articles analyze employment law issues and offer guidance to help readers better understand how to: comply with new laws and regulations; comply with existing laws and regulations that intersect in confusing ways (such as when multiple statutes create complex or even contradictory requirements for HR professionals); minimize liability for situations that are particularly sensitive or legally risky (such as conducting a mass layoff or reclassifying workers as exempt or nonexempt); or help readers better manage general HR practices that can affect legal risks (such as ways to conduct record keeping to avoid common legal problems). Legal Trends articles are 1,600 to 2,400 words long.

Management Tools columns offer practical, hands-on HR tips for front line managers. The goal is to provide information that HR professionals can share with supervisors to ensure that effective HR is practiced at all levels of an organization.

Tools columns are the only section in HR Magazine that offers general management advice.

A sample of potential Management Tools subjects includes: how to deal with conflict, how to run a meeting, interviewing tips for non-HR professionals and how to inspire and motivate subordinates.

Management Tools articles are approximately 1,800 words long.

HR Technology columns cover technology issues related to human resource management. These articles analyze significant industry trends and offer practical advice and solutions on technological problems.

Potential HR Technology subjects include: establishing and managing an HRIS system, selecting vendors, making the best use of intranets and protecting electronic privacy.

HR Technology articles are 1,800 to 2,100 words long.

HR News is primarily produced by staff reporters, but professional freelance writers may send queries to Managing Editor Steve Bates at sbates@shrm.org.

AGENDAS. Agendas are similar to features but are shorter and narrower in focus, with heavy emphasis on providing practical hands-on, how-to information.

For example, while a feature might deal with the new trend in consumer driven health care–discussing what it is, why it is becoming prevalent and how employers stand to gain from using it–an agenda might deal specifically with the ways HR professionals can help educate and prepare employees so they can make more informed decisions when purchasing health care services.

While agendas may include charts, they generally do not include photographs or sidebars. Agendas are 1,800 words long.

Criteria for accepting manuscripts

Articles have the best chance of being accepted for publication when they:

...provide new, cutting-edge information. Our readers are savvy, knowledgeable professionals. They already know the basics; they look to us for advanced information. Good articles give readers information they did not otherwise possess by, for example, making them aware of a new problem or showing them a new way of dealing with an old problem.

...are broadly applicable. Articles that deal with a situation or issue faced by most–or many–HR professionals stand the best chance of making it into print.

Articles that deal with a narrower aspect of human resource management or with a particular industry (such as manufacturing or hi-tech) are acceptable only if they apply to most readers within those areas. For example, an article that applies only to specific types of manufacturers is less valuable than one that applies to all manufacturers.

...are well focused. The best stories make one or two major points convincingly. Before writing you should be able to clearly describe your topic in a sentence or two. If you can't, you may need to rethink your topic.

For example, an unfocused description might be: This article will deal with the legal aspects of sexual harassment. (There are many legal aspects of sexual harassment–which ones will be discussed in the text?)

A better description would read: This article will help HR professionals create a program for eliminating retaliation in sexual harassment cases.

...provide information from a number of sources. The best stories quote many sources–both subject matter experts and HR practitioners–or discuss how several companies have approached the same problem. Case studies of individual organizations are acceptable, but they must offer information and insights that are broadly applicable to other organizations, and quote multiple sources within the organization.

...quote knowledgeable, credible sources. Quotes can come from experts in a field, HR professionals with special knowledge of the topic being discussed, and participants in events or case studies being written about. Quotes should be concise and should further the discussion of the main points of the story. Quotes should not be excerpted and repeated from other publications and books, with rare exceptions that should be clearly attributed.

...offer enough information. Articles must give readers enough information to come to a conclusion, take action or be able to intelligently conduct further research on the topic. No article will ever answer all of a reader's questions. Good texts, however, anticipate and answer readers' most important questions and suggest resources for additional guidance.

...add significantly to the information already published in HR Magazine and elsewhere. HR Magazine does not reprint material previously published elsewhere.

...can be easily illustrated. Articles that are accompanied by charts, graphs or photos are more likely to be accepted and given favorable placement in the magazine.

Avoiding promotional writing: Our readers expect articles that are unbiased, even-handed and non-promotional in nature. As a result, HR Magazine does not dedicate full-length articles to any single, specific product. Doing so would be a disservice to our readers, who want several objective options for solving their workday problems. Our desire to avoid self-promotional articles does not preclude us from accepting informative manuscripts from experts and knowledgeable practitioners in the field of human resource management–such as consultants, attorneys, vendors and service providers. We understand that such authors naturally will be inclined to write about the topics they are most familiar with. However, to be accepted in HR Magazine, articles must be objective, offer advice that is broadly applicable and include information about competing products or services.

Vendors and manufacturers who wish to share news of new products and services may submit them via the HR Magazine web site (contact information is listed at the end of these guidelines) to What's New–a special section dedicated exclusively to new products and services. Items for this section are chosen solely at the discretion of the section editor, and publication does not imply endorsement by SHRM or HR Magazine.

Suggestions on writing style

Write clearly and concisely. Use simple language; make your point in as few words as possible.

. Use the active voice, not the passive voice. For example, writing "it was decided" leaves questions in the readers' minds. (Who decided?) Writing "Smith decided" is stronger and more informative.

. Define terms that may not be well known. Avoid jargon and clichés that may confuse readers or send them running for the dictionary. On first reference, spell out abbreviations or acronyms. If in doubt, define.

. Make sure all direct quotes are accurate and are clearly attributed to a source. Be aware of what constitutes libel.

. Do not submit academic-style papers with footnotes and numerous references to other publications. Such articles are not appropriate for HR Magazine.

. Use subheads. Subheads can help you organize an article and can facilitate transitions from one idea to another.

. Whenever you name a company or organization in an article, include the city where that company is located or headquartered and a brief description of the nature of its business or mission.

. Follow the Associated Press Stylebook and Libel Manual.

Payment

Payment for articles is offered only to professional freelance writers commissioned by our editors. Experts in the field, such as attorneys, consultants and professors are not normally compensated for articles in which they share their expertise. Rates for paid freelancers vary, and payment is made upon acceptance of the final manuscript.

Formatting

Articles may be submitted in Microsoft Word or some other popular word processing format. Charts and illustrations should be included at the end of the article or on a separate file. Do not place charts and illustrations within the main text.

Final manuscript checklist

When writers submit a final manuscript they also should send:

Any sidebars. These are short, stand-alone items that appear in boxes next to the original story. These items offer information that is relevant and pertinent, but not central, to the main story.

Any relevant charts or graphics that help to illustrate the story. Let us know if photos or photo opportunities exist, and we will try to acquire the photos or arrange for a photographer to take the appropriate pictures. If interviewed sources are willing to have a photo taken for the article, send us this information with your manuscript.

The names, addresses and phone numbers of sources interviewed for the story. We will send each source a complimentary copy of the issue in which the article appears.

An invoice, if applicable, that includes your name, phone number, Social Security number, date and a brief description of the article.

Biographical information. Include the name, address and telephone number of the author(s), as well as a short biography (title, organization and city). The biography should include any information that illustrates an author's experience (especially in HR related matters) and credibility.

Queries and unsolicited articles must be sent to the HR Magazine web site at www.shrm.org/hrmagazine/contact.

This is the only mechanism for submitting manuscripts. This eliminates duplication, allows us to screen manuscripts by topic, and is the most efficient means available for us to provide potential authors with a rapid decision regarding their articles.

Articles and queries sent by any other means will not be entered in our article review system and will not be considered for publication.

To check on the status of an article or query 45 days after submission, contact Nicole Gauvin at e-mail address below.

Categories: Nonfiction—Business—Human Resources

CONTACT: Nicole Gauvin, Editorial Coordinator
Material: All
Society for Human Resource Management
1800 Duke St
Alexandria VA 22314
Phone US Only: 800-283-SHRM
Phone International: +1 703-548-3440
TTY/TDD 703-548-6999
Fax 703-535-6490
E-mail: ngauvin@shrm.org
Website: www.shrm.org/hrmagazine

The Hudson Review

The Hudson Review publishes fiction, poetry, essays, book reviews; criticism of literature, art, theatre, dance, film and music; and articles on contemporary cultural developments.

We read unsolicited submissions. Prose manuscripts should be under 10,000 words; if you have a novel, please make an excerpt of a section that stands well by itself. Please do not submit more than seven poems at one time; again, it is very helpful to us if you make a selection of your best work. We do not publish work that has already been printed elsewhere or that is due to appear in book form in the near future. We do not consider simultaneous submissions, and we do not accept electronic submissions.

If you are interested in writing reviews for our magazine, please note that we consider first-time review submissions on an "on approval" basis only.

Please allow up to three months for decisions on unsolicited manuscripts. Notification of decisions on manuscripts will be made only by postal mail; telephone and email inquiries cannot be answered. Manuscripts will not be returned, nor will inquiries be answered, unless accompanied by a stamped, self-addressed envelope. No responsibility is assumed for their loss or injury.

Unsolicited manuscripts are read according to the following schedule:
- Poetry: April 1 through June 30
- Fiction: September 1 through November 30
- Nonfiction: January 1 through March 31
- Unsolicited manuscripts received at other times will be returned unread. Manuscripts submitted by subscribers who so identify themselves will be read throughout the year.

As noted on the masthead, the Editors are responsible for the entire contents of the magazine. *The Hudson Review* does not have special "Poetry," "Fiction," "Articles," or "Book Review" editors. Unsolicited manuscripts should be addressed to: The Editors, *The Hudson Review*, 684 Park Avenue, New York, NY 10021.

We do not specialize in publishing any particular "type" of writing; our sole criterion for accepting unsolicited work is literary quality. The best way for you to get an idea of the range of work we publish is to read a current issue.

Thank you for your interest in *The Hudson Review*.

Categories: Fiction—Nonfiction—Arts—Book Reviews—Dance—Drama—Film/Video—General Interest—Literature—Poetry—Short Stories

CONTACT: The Editors
Material: All
684 Park Ave.
New York, NY 10021
Phone: 212-650-0020
Website: www.hudsonreview.com

Humpty Dumpty

Please refer to Children's Better Health Institute.

Hurricane Alice

Thank you for your support of Hurricane Alice. Unfortunately, we have suspended publication due to financial and time considerations. We feel very sad about this decision, but there is no way to avoid it at present. There has not been a new issue of the magazine mailed in two years, but we have delayed announcing the suspension of publication in the hope that a new collective would take over and continue the magazine. That has not yet happened; however, we are maintaining our subscription database and will turn it over to any future acquirer of the magazine. We cannot review any submissions, but hope you fina home for your work elsewhere.

The Hurricane Alice Collective
Dept. of English, Rhode Island College
Providence RI 02908
Phone: 401-456-8377

I Love Cats

We will not be accepting any new material in 2006.

I am always interested in new ideas for *I Love Cats* and request that you either send a paragraph or two about your idea or the finished piece. ALWAYS include a self-addressed, stamped envelope with a return address. If accepted, I will request the story be sent via e-mail or on a disc in a format compatible with Windows.

I am now accepting email queries and completed stories at yankee@izzy.net. If you prefer, completed manuscripts to be delivered by mail to *I Love Cats*, c/o Lisa Allmendinger, Editor, 16 Meadow Hill Lane, Armonk, NY 10504.

I do not want poetry (as I seldom publish it) but I am interested in feature stories about cats and their owners, (no talking cats, please), interesting or odd happenings with cats, tips for cat owners, health issues, nonfiction pieces, behavior problems, that sort of thing. Please do not send stories about cats that live outdoors.

I'm looking for a story—preferably with photos or drawings—that is 1,000 words, tops, ideally 500-700 words. I buy all rights, since we copyright all stories. You also must sign a consent form, which spells out all resale questions. I pay between $40-$100. **Payment is upon publication.**

Nonfiction pieces can be longer and the price varies, but starts at $50-$100. Color slides are always a plus as I am usually in need of color photos. Short fillers are also welcome and payment is $25.

I have quite a backlog at the moment and we go to press about four months ahead of the publication date. If your story were accepted today, the earliest publication date would be the end of 2004, so please keep that in mind when submitting stories, especially seasonal ones.

I am no longer returning photographs, so please do not send your only copy.

Please do not send any stories that have been published in other cat magazines or competing animal publications.

I will return any unused manuscripts provided there is a SASE with your submission. I do my best to report back in 1-2 months. I hope this answers all of your questions.

Sample copies are $4. If you would like one, please send a check or money order to *I Love Cats* Publishing c/o Hochman Associates, 900 Oak Tree Road, Suite C, South Plainfield, NJ 07080 and write sample copy of *I Love Cats* on the outside of the envelope. It may take up to 30 days to receive your copy.

PHOTO GUIDELINES FOR *I Love Cats*

We will not be accepting any new material in 2004.

I thank you for your letter regarding photo guidelines. I require 33 mm slides or color prints and buy all rights. I pay $50 for black-and-white or color inside photos, $150 for a cover. I will preview photos as .jpegs, but will need the actual print or slide for publication.

Covers may have props in them, but the cat must dominate the image. We love sweet eyes that beg the reader to "pet" the cover. To be considered for the cover, slides must be shot vertically.

Please send copies of your slides/photos to the above address and not the originals. Always include an SASE. Please do not send photos with a signature required as there is seldom anyone in the office to sign for a delivery.

Payment is upon publication and I am usually working 4-5

months ahead of the cover date. You will be required to sign a copyright contract.

Thank you for thinking of *I Love Cats*. Lisa M. Allmendinger Editor

Categories: Fiction—Nonfiction—Animals

CONTACT: Lisa Allmendinger, Editor
Material: All
16 Meadow Hill Lane
Armonk, NY 10504
E-mail: yankee@izzy.net
Website: www.iluvcats.com

ICONOCLast

The Iconoclast

Mission: To provide an imaginative alternative for readers and writers of original work bypassed by corporate and institutional publications. To ignore fads, movements, fashions, styles, current events, politics, the mass media, and agendas (except for the purposes of satire). To support reflection, emotion, thought, and humor. To search for wisdom, accept delight, smile at wit, and admire craft.

Appearance: Full-sized, with as many as 96 pages.

Needs: Poetry and Prose from writers interested in the creation, sharing, and transmission of ideas, imaginings, and experiences. Getting rich or famous from publication here is unlikely, but more people in more places actually read ICONOCLAST than the vast majority of other small press literary magazines.

Prose: To 3500 words (*occasionally* longer). Subjects and styles are completely open (within the standards of generally accepted tast—though exceptions, as always, can be made for unique and visionary works). We like work to have a point or more. We don't care for the *slice of life* type of story—or any other kind in which characters are unable or unwilling to change their own conditions. Most stories of alcoholism, incest, domestic and public violence are best left to the mass media. Anything topical has probably already been overdone. Simple storytelling usually wins out over slickness of style or the perfectly crafted workshop, MFA story about nothing or the author's neurosis. We never look down our noses at plot. Nor are we immune to the power of a literary stylist. With the possible exception of mysteries, most genres written well, sincerely, and conscientiously have a chance. Humor and science fiction are hard sells (too often these writers think an interesting concept can substitute for a plot or an original ending), but we do publish a fair amount of both. Politics and religion are best left to the demagogues and hypocrites. Killing a character(s) off in the end usually indicates a lazy or unimaginative beginner. Will we ever publish another bar room story? I don't think so.

Is a cover letter really necessary? We don't do bios (as iconclasts, we're not into personality cults or self-glorification). A good writer can make us interested in nearly any subject or person. Essays that are merely undocumented opinion or op-ed pieces have little chance.

Please don't send preliminary drafts—rewriting is half the job. If you're not sure about the story, don't truly believe in it, or are unenthusiastic about the subject (we will not recycle your term papers or thesis), then don't send it. This is not a lottery (luck has nothing to do with it).

One submission per person per month is all we can handle. We tried accepting simultaneous submissions: it didn't work. Our resopnse time is usually well within six weeks (which we think is a fair amount of time both to writers and editors serious about what they do). All submissions are seen by the editor-in-chief. There are no first readers, committees, grad students, interns, advisors or politics/favoritism (confession: in two stories of equal merit, the subscriber may have an edge).

Please include a sufficiently stamped self-addressed envelope with all submissions or correspondence from which you expect a reply—and make it clear whether or not you want the material returned. Everything counts.

Poetry: To 2 pages. Everything above applies. Try for originality; if not in thought, then expression. No greeting card verse or noble religious sentiments. Look for the unusual in the usual, parallels in opposites, the capturing of what is unique or often unnoticed in an ordinary or extraordinary moment. What makes us human—and the resultant glories and agonies. The universal usually wins out over the personal. Rhyme isn't as easy as it looks—especially for those unversed in its study.

Art: We're always looking for black and white drawings for the cover and spot illustrations.

Payment: Prose—2 copies and 1 cent a word for the First N.A. Serial Rights on publication. Art and Poetry, 1 copy per page or work–2 copies for cover art—$2-$6 per poem or artwork for First Rights on publication. All contributors get a 40% discount on extra copies.

Reality Check: People who buy, read, and subscribe to ICONOCLAST keep it alive and available to those who seek publication. This is not a government program. We don't apply for grants, nor do we have non-profit status. Our biggest resource is the curious, literate, general interest reader with a zest for life. Are you one? If ICONOCLAST is good enough to send your work to, is it good enough to buy and read?

Single/Sample copy: $5.

Subscription: $16/8 issues (Canada: $18, Rest of World: $20)

Categories: Fiction—Nonfiction—Adventure—Arts—Biography—Cartoons—Culture—Drama—General Interest—Humor—Interview—Literature—Poetry—Satire—Short Stories

CONTACT: Phil Wagner, Editor & Publisher
Material: All
1675 Amazon Rd
Mohegan Lake NY 10547-1804

IDEA Fitness Journal
IDEA Trainer Success
IDEA Fitness Manager

IDEA Fitness Journal is published 10 times per year. *IDEA Trainer Success* and *IDEA Fitness Manager* are published five times each per year on a rotational basis. Our readership includes personal trainers, health club and fitness staff, fitness instructors, program directors, business owners and managers, and other health and wellness professionals. These readers have a broad range of educational backgrounds, including many with advanced degrees in health- and fitness-related fields.

We encourage readers to submit articles for consideration by our editorial committee. If we are not able to accept your idea, we hope you will understand that the decision is a multifaceted one, not a negative judgment of your unique skills or talents. Each year, we receive hundreds of queries by mail, fax and email. We produce a limited number of issues, and we have a limited number of articles that we can assign. Current trends, previous or planned articles on related subjects, and numerous other factors also determine our ability to accept submitted ideas.

Whether or not we are able to accept your query, we appreciate your interest in IDEA and your initiative in submitting your idea to us.

Content

An article must be an original piece of work that has not been published elsewhere. In order to determine if an idea is appropriate for IDEA's publications, ask yourself the following questions:

1) Would this article directly address the needs of fitness and health

professionals (not just fitness and health consumers)?

2) Am I qualified to write this article? Why?

3) Would this article include practical, how-to application?

4) Would the general topic area and length of this article be appropriate for the IDEA newsletters, or would it work as a feature or column for *IDEA Fitness Journal*? Please review the following descriptions.

Publication - *IDEA Fitness Journal*

Mission: To inspire and educate fitness and health professionals with up-to-date industry information and comprehensive research on topics such as exercise physiology, weight management, nutrition, health promotion, wellness, sports conditioning, industry and programming trends, and personal and professional growth.

Features:

Each issue of *IDEA Fitness Journal* includes several feature articles, which are approximately 3,000-3,500 words in length (10 typed, double-spaced manuscript pages) and cover larger topics, such as industry issues and research reviews.

Sample topics include client motivation and counseling techniques, industry growth, health care integration, nutrition research, exercise technique and program design.

Columns:

In addition to features, the magazine includes the following rotating columns, which are approximately 1,200-1,400 words in length (6-8 typed, double-spaced manuscript pages):

Personal Training Section Columns:

PFT Profile – Each month, IDEA features a one-page profile of a PFT member who may be doing outstanding work on inspiring the world to fitness, has a unique business model or stands out among others through his/her contribution to the community.

Exercise Rx - This column emphasizes the application of exercise theory. These articles are geared to the intermediate/advanced trainer who is familiar with training variables and needs information on how to manipulate them. Target populations include clients with special conditions, such as diabetes or back injuries, or clients with special goals, such as running a 5K or conditioning for golf. The column also includes program design applications. Past articles in this category are: when to change sets, loads and reps; using manual resistance; eccentric training; and super slow resistance training.

Profit Center - Articles give specifics on marketing a PFT business, retaining clients, payment schemes, finance and administration, and career options. Profiles of operating businesses give information on the administration and best practice strategies that have helped them.

PFT 101 – This series can be used as a guidebook for the neophyte personal fitness trainer, a refresher course for the veteran trainer or as an education tool for PFT managers to share with staff. Topics covered in the past include scope of practice, client assessment, liability and safety, and working cooperatively through referrals and communication with the medical community.

Fine Anatomy – This ongoing series focuses on the basics and details of how joints and muscles in the human body work together for optimum performance. Each installment includes a detailed anatomy illustration of the area under discussion, a thorough description of origin insertion, and action and a list of step-by-step exercises with illustrations that can help strengthen the muscles and joints featured.

Tricks of the Trade – An IDEA editor interviews members in a Q & A format covering diverse areas of a personal trainer's career. Answers give readers a sampling of how others handle client situations, business issues, ongoing education, staffing challenges, communication and other related topics.

Nutrition:

"Food for Thought" Section

This comprehensive news section focuses on all aspects of nutrition from trends in food consumption and popular diets to research, legislation, nutrient specifics and recipes. Each column aims to cover the spectrum of client age groups from youth to seniors.

Columns:

Nutrition Research – This column may focus on a particular nutrient (such as iron) or food category (such as sports drinks), or describe eating behaviors, dietary plans or nutrition myths. Written by dietitians or nutritionists, articles are designed to help readers both personally and professionally.

Practical Nutrition – This "how to" column alternates with the research column and takes a more practical approach to food and eating issues. Topics may focus on how to prepare healthy meals and snacks in a flash, how to shop to keep your pantry stocked with essential items for healthy cooking, and cooking techniques for healthy eating.

Group Exercise Section

Columns:

Master Class – One-on-one interviews with past group fitness IDEA award winners on topics ranging from teaching skills to continuing education and participant interaction.

Buzz – Short list of progressive classes from around the world. "Bonus Buzz" signifies unique class ideas that successfully reach out to the deconditioned market.

Class Building Blocks – This brief column offers practical and effective ideas for the different sections of a group exercise class. Each "block" can be mixed and matched among different formats.

Ignite offers creative ideas for a warm-up

Ebb features a useful cool-down

Core succinctly presents a core or abdominals-focused training sequence

Pop Quiz – Small box on Group Exercise section opener that poses a teaching skills question. Answer appears later in the section.

Class Take Out – A one-page (front and back) choreographed class format, complete with diagrams, music suggestions, counts, injury prevention, etc. (Step, cycling, high-low, circuit, group strength, misc. dance).

Inner IDEA: Mind-Body Fitness Section

This comprehensive section opens with news items regarding all aspects of mind-body fitness including yoga, Pilates, tai chi, Feldenkrais and Alexander techniques, client motivation and compliance issues, wellness, coaching techniques, psychology of exercise, stress management and mindfulness in general. Look for a "Move of the Month" that illustratively or photographically breaks down how to do various yoga poses, Pilates and tai chi moves and other popular mind-body exercises.

Inner IDEA – This column provides guest columnists a chance to address any of the above areas in more depth. Each column is 1,200-1,400 words long. Authors must have credentials and expertise in the area they wish to explore.

Additional Columns

Your Membership – Articles in this column provide details on new IDEA member benefits, upcoming events, happenings at IDEA and a focus on 4 to 6 members per issue who are doing outstanding work toward our shared mission to Inspire the World to FitnessTM.

Making News – What's new on the fitness, health, business and international fronts. Brief items of interest about current research, companies, legislation and innovative programs are included.

Research – Authors review and report on relevant exercise and health literature and provide practical application suggestions for fitness professionals.

Career Path – This column offers practical career and business information for fitness and health professionals. Topics include current and future career opportunities, job skills and strategies, mentoring, start-up ventures, networking and developing successful specialty programs.

Just For You – Articles focus on personal enrichment outside the fitness arena. Topics are diverse and apply to lifestyle enhancement for busy fitness pros. Areas of focus may include everything from vacation planning and enjoying and exploring nature to having a spa experience and planning finances for retirement.

Publication — *IDEA Trainer Success*

Mission: To help personal trainers stay up to date with the robust growth and entrepreneurialism in personal training. Intended for PFTs who already own and operate businesses, those thinking of starting businesses and those who manage PFT departments in health clubs. Includes articles and tips from industry-leading personal trainers and business owners who offer insights, strategies and directions to help trainers carve a niche and conduct themselves as serious business persons in this burgeoning segment of fitness.

Columns:

(Each column is 1,200-1,400 words in length)

The Start Up – A series in which the author explores the path he took to launch his personal training business.

Reinvigoration Strategies – This column is focused on evaluating your existing business or PFT department and finding ways to refresh and revitalize it.

Training for Growth – Once you have your business or PFT department up and running the way you want it, how do you keep growing it? Topic discussion includes creative ways to add value to all aspects of your business or department with the ultimate goals of client and staff satisfaction and increased revenues.

Technology – There's a lot of great business technology and equipment out there that trainers aren't using yet. This column highlights specific product categories and provides practical advice on how to integrate these time savers into a business or department.

Liability/Risk Management – As the popularity of personal training grows, so does your liability and risk. This column raises issues on how to protect yourself and your business.

Staff Issues – This column addresses hiring, firing, problem employees, rewarding employees and recruitment and retention challenges.

Sales & Marketing – Topics in this column include increasing sales, proven sales techniques and how to market your business, yourself or your department for maximum return.

Publication — *IDEA Fitness Manager*

Mission: To provide the management information that program and fitness directors and club owners need to effectively plan program choices, supervise staff and attract and retain clients.

Features:

Focused on a theme, including program planning, personnel, time management, customer service, financial management

Columns:

People – Topic areas focus on Interpersonal communication, staffing issues, hiring and firing, rewarding employees, recruitment and retention.

Money – This column examines budgeting issues and metrics for success.

Sales & Marketing – Topics in this column include practical ideas for increasing sales, proven sales techniques and how to market your facility, department or program for success.

Programs – Programming experts provide examples from their experience arsenals on how to test, budget and introduce new programs.

Group Ex Director – Clients demand programs that are fun and exciting and want instructors who have high energy and charisma. This column examines all aspects of programming, staff management and client service for a successful group exercise department.

PFT Director – PFT directors must keep up with the rapid changes and high demand in facility-based PFT services. Authors look at all aspects of programming, staff management and client service for a successful personal training department.

Submission Procedure

Before you write an article, send us a query letter of one or two pages outlining the proposed topic and the questions you will try to answer, and tell us:

why this idea is important to fitness and health professionals

why you are the person to write the article (A resume or biography listing your credentials is helpful.)

the general topics or points you will cover with this article (List a few, or include a rough outline.)

how you will include practical how-to information in your article

The editorial committee will consider your idea on the basis of timeliness, relevance to our audience and your credentials or experience. Written queries are preferred.

Unsolicited material must be accompanied by a self-addressed, stamped envelope if you wish it returned.

All these written ideas, as well as those generated by the editors, circulate through an editorial board of instructors, exercise physiologists and business experts who determine the ideas' relevance and timeliness.

The review process takes six to eight weeks. After this time, you will receive notification as to whether or not your article may be used.

When an idea is tentatively approved but cannot be immediately slated for a specific issue, it may be held for a period of time for additional consideration. If an idea is approved, it is placed on the "go" list for inclusion in an upcoming issue. When the article is definitely placed in an issue, it is formally assigned to the author.

Preparing the Manuscript

Once your idea has been accepted for publication, the assigning editor will establish manuscript length and payment. Manuscripts vary in length from five to 12 double-spaced pages. We pay within 60 days of final acceptance and purchase all rights. Remember as you begin to write that submissions should be targeted toward the professional, not the consumer. Authors are responsible for the accuracy of all data and must be able to document their information with firsthand experience, interviews with experts and/or references to published sources. You will be required to include this backup documentation with your manuscript. Writing should be in a clear, concise and easy-to-understand style.

Categories: Nonfiction—Cooking—Food/Drink—Health—Physical Fitness

CONTACT: Sandy Todd Webster, Editor in Chief
Material: All
IDEA Publications
10455 Pacific Center Court
San Diego CA 92121-4339
Phone: 858-535-8979 ext 217
Fax: 858-535-8234
E-mail: websterS@IDEAfit.com
Website: www.ideafit.com

Illinois Beverage Guide
Michigan Beverage Journal
Wisconsin Beverage Guide

Submission Format: All articles must be submitted in typewritten form. All submissions should adhere to AP style. Articles should be based on in-depth, behind-the-scenes reporting. Material is subject to editing for length, style and format. Seasonal articles should be submitted three months in advance to allow for editorial planning. We pay after accepted work is printed in any of the magazines and purchase only one-time rights. We will respond to all submissions within 2 months.

What we are looking for: We are in need of a freelance writer for a monthly column about bartending. Freelance writers interested in taking up this 500 word column should contact the editor directly. We also are looking for articles about recent trends in employment, alcoholic beverages, and non-alcoholic beverages. We also need articles profiling successful or unique restaurants, bars, taverns or liquor stores and new items or promotions available in the industry. We have a strong need for writers to cover the legislative and grassroots scenes in all three states.

Tip: Our magazines are tailored to fit the needs for liquor licenses in the states of Illinois, Michigan, and Wisconsin. As you write, please keep in mind that bar and restaurant owners are your audience–not patrons. This is the biggest problem we face. If you are unsure of what we are looking for, please contact the editor for free copies of the magazine.

Categories: Nonfiction, Business, Food/Drink.

CONTACT: Submissions Editor
Material: All
Michigan Licensed Beverage Association
PO Box 4067
East Lansing MI 48823-4067
Phone: 877-292-2896 or 517-374-9612/9611
Fax: 517-374-1165
Website: www.mlba.org

In the Family
The Magazine for Queer People and Their Loved Ones

GUIDELINES FOR SUBMITTING WORK

Thank you for your interest in writing for In the Family, the award-winning magazine for queer couples, single people and families. We use a psychology lens to explore the variety and complexity of our intimate relationships. We strongly recommend that you read a copy of the magazine to get an idea of the kinds of pieces we publish. To order a copy, send $6.50 to the address below.

We invite submission of feature articles, personal essays and case presentations on all aspects of queer family life, and particularly seek submissions from mental health professionals on fresh, new aspects of their clinical work or research with lesbian, gay, trans and bisexual families, couples and individuals.

We also invite submissions of original, unpublished fiction and poetry that fits with our theme of queer life. No erotica and no harlequin romance stories, please.

Submit one double-spaced copy, including your name, phone number, email address and mailing address on the first page, and an SASE. Please do not submit work by fax or by email.

We pay on publication: $35 for essays, $35 for short stories and $35 for poetry. All contributors received 5 free copies of the issue in which their work appears.

Because of the volume of material we receive, we do not give detailed feedback on pieces we are not able to use.

If you have further questions about submitting your work, please email us at LMarkowitz@aol.com

Categories: Fiction—Nonfiction—Alternate Life-style—Family—Gay/Lesbian—Human Rights—Multicultural—Psychology—Relationships—Sexuality—Society

CONTACT: Laura Markowitz, Editor
Material: All
Family Magazine, Inc.
7850 N. Siverbell Rd., #114-188
Tucson AZ 85743
Phone: 520-579-8043
Website: inthefamily.com

In Touch
Indulge

Emphasis is on the light-hearted, romantic, erotic, provocative and entertaining. There are no limits on sexual content or explicitness in fiction, although safer sex must be depicted. Please refrain from submitting stories involving fantastical characters (i.e. vampires, ghosts, Tarzan).

All individuals must be 18 years of age or older whether they are models or characters in fiction. All submissions are subject to editing.

Sample issue is $6.95/postage paid. Please indicate which magazine (In Touch or Indulge) you are requesting a copy of.

Erotic fiction is between 3,200 to 3,800 words, typed, double-spaced. Fiction may also be submitted on Mac formatted computer disk or via e-mail to: michael@intouchformen.com. A requirement of acceptance is the ability to send a final version of the material electronically.

In Touch magazine features smooth, fresh young men between 18 to 24 years old. Indulge magazine features more mature, aggressive, muscular men in their late twenties and thirties. It is recommended that a writer create a story targeting the audience of the magazine they are submitting to. Serials, for either magazine, are not under consideration.

The fee paid is $75 for one-time usage, first North American rights and limited electronic rights (for use on the web site). Payment is issued upon publication. A copy of the magazine is sent with the payment.

Please include a SASE for response. Thank you.

Categories: Fiction—Erotica—Gay/Lesbian—Men's Fiction

CONTACT: Alan W. Mills, Editor
Material: All
13122 Saticoy St.
North Hollywood CA 91605
Phone: 818-764-2288
Fax: 818-764-2307
E-mail: alan@intouchformen.com
Website: www.intouchformen.com

Inc.

Formal guidelines not available. Please read a number of issues to ascertain the publication's style and needs.

Send queries to address below.

Categories: Nonfiction—Business—Lifestyle—Money & Finances—Technology

CONTACT: Micheal Hoffman, Submissions Editor
Material: All
38 Commercial Warf
Boston MA 02110
Website: www.inc.com

Independent Business

Please refer to Group IV Communications, Inc.

Indiana Review

Indiana Review is published semiannually in June and December. We read manuscripts year round, and reporting time is 2 - 4 months. IR accepts less than 1% of manuscripts submitted. Payment for publication is $5.00 per page ($10.00 minimum), two contributor's copies, and the remainder of a year's subscription. Rights revert to author upon publication.

Needs: IR publishes 6-10 stories, 40-60 pages of poetry, 1-2 nonfiction pieces, and 6-12 book reviews per issue, as well as art inserts when funding allows. All work must be previously unpublished. We look for poems, stories, and nonfiction that are well-crafted and lively, have an intelligent sense of form and language, assume a degree of risk, and have consequence beyond the world of their speakers or narrators. We also welcome interviews with established writers.

Stories: Send only one story per submission, up to 40 double-spaced pages. Translations are welcome.

Poems: Send only 4-6 poems per submission. Do not send more than 4 poems if longer than 3 pages each. Do not fold poems individually or staple poems together. Translations are welcome.

Nonfiction: Send only one essay per submission, up to 30 double-spaced pages.

Book Reviews: Reviews should be of recent fiction, poetry, nonfiction, and literary criticism (publication date within two years). Small press titles are preferred. Reviews must be 500 to 700 words, double-spaced, and include complete publication information (press, ISBN, price). Send a maximum of two reviews per submission.

Graphic Arts: Paintings, photographs, comics, and drawings are welcome. In lieu of originals, please send slides or digital images of work. DO NOT send only copy of work. Indiana artists are preferred. Send up to five pieces that are up to 6 x 9" in dimensions or may be later reduced to this size. Visual works must also be publishable in black and white, but, when funding allows, may be published in full color.

There is no need to query editors about submitting work. Submission status may be queried by mail or email, but please allow 4 months before querying.

All submissions and correspondence MUST include a self-addressed stamped envelope. We cannot respond to submissions otherwise. Include additional postage if work is to be returned. Simultaneous submissions are okay, but we must be promptly notified of acceptance elsewhere.

Clearly mark envelope to the appropriate genre editor's attention (e.g. "Fiction Editor"). Include cover letter listing work titles, previous publications and awards, and a SHORT bio. For receipt confirmation, please include email address. Explanations of manuscript meaning, theme, or technique are not necessary.

No handwritten, faxed, emailed, or poorly copied/printed manuscripts will be considered. Further, IR cannot consider work (other than book reviews) from anyone currently or recently affiliated with Indiana University.

Sample Issues: Sample copies of IR are available for $9. Add $6 per issue for postage outside of the United States ($3.50 for Canada).

Categories: Fiction—Nonfiction—Book Reviews—Literature—Poetry—Writing

CONTACT: Tracy Trueis, Editor
Material: All other
CONTACT: Kate Whetzel, Poetry Editor
Material: Poetry
CONTACT: Megan Savage, Fiction Editor
Material: Fiction
Indiana University
Ballantine Hall 465
1020 E. Kirkwood Ave
Bloomington IN 47405-7103
Website: www.indiana.edu/~inreview

Indulge

Please refer to *In Touch* magazine.

Industrial Engineer
Institute of Industrial Engineers

Industrial Engineer welcomes feature articles and letters to the editor. Please use the following guidelines to help you develop your article.

Feature Articles

Try to focus on the most current industrial engineering issues, problems, and solutions, or recent developments and research that may have a significant and positive impact on today's industrial engineer. While every submission will be considered for publication, emphasis will be placed on the article's practical value and analytical approach.

Highly theoretical or statistical articles are discouraged. Articles based on experience and actual "hands-on" operating situations, or those that have valuable applications in a working environment will be favored. Authors are encouraged to include supporting graphics and/or color photographs with articles.

Submission

Articles submitted to *Industrial Engineer* should be offered on an exclusive basis and limited to 3,500 words or less. In addition to printed copy, please include a Microsoft Word or ASCII version of the article on a PC-compatible or Macintosh disk. Charts, graphs, and other non-photo artwork should be sent separately or included as individual files (BMP, JPEG, or TIFF) on the same disk. Articles are subject to normal review and editing procedures by the editor.

Additional Tips
The following hints may also assist in preparing an article for publication:
• Number each page.
• Photographs: High-quality transparencies/slides or prints are best. Provide identification and caption material with all photos, and do not attach with paper clips or staples. Also, please don't write on the back of photos. Specify whether the photo should be returned.
• Include a short biographical paragraph about the author and co-authors of the article.

Industrial Engineer holds the copyright of all published articles. For permission to use the article for personal or educational purposes, please contact the Permissions Department at the Institute of Industrial Engineers (IIE).

Categories: Ergonomics—Facilities Planning—Logistics—Industrial Engineering—Management—Production & Inventory Control—Technology—Warehousing

CONTACT: Candi S. Cross, Managing Editor
Material: All
3577 Parkway Lane Ste 200
Norcross GA 30092
Phone: 770-449-0461
Fax: 770-263-8532
E-Mail: ccross@iienet.org
Website: www.iienet.org

Industrial Management

Industrial Management welcomes feature articles that focus on current management issues, developments, challenges, problems and solutions. The material should offer significant insight or assistance to the readers of *Industrial Management*, who are executives, department heads, operating managers, industrial engineers, and those aspiring to management positions.

While every submission will be considered for publication, articles based on experience and actual hands-on operating situations or case studies, or those that have valuable applications in a working environment will be favored. Highly theoretical or statistical articles are discouraged. Articles should be clearly written and readily understandable, though authors may assume that readers have some knowledge of basic industrial engineering concepts and have management experience.

Sample topic areas include:

Benchmarking—Budgeting—Change Management—Competitiveness—Concurrent Engineering—Continuous Improvement—Costing and Cost Control—Cycle Time Reduction—Ergonomics and Human Factors—Environmental Management—Facilities Management—Forecasting, Planning, and Scheduling—Human Resource Issues—Incentive Programs—Inventory Management—Labor Relations—Lean Manufacturing—Logistics Management—Maintenance Management—Management of Technology—Manufacturing Strategies—Materials Management—Organizational Behavior & Change—Performance Measurement—Product Development—

Production Control—Productivity—Quality—Reengineering—Return on Investment—Safety—Simulation—Statistical Process Control—Strategic Planning—Supply Chain Management—Systems Integration—Teams—Technology Transfer—Theory of Constraints—World Class Strategies.

Submission

Articles submitted to *Industrial Management* should be offered on an exclusive basis and limited to 3,500 words. Articles will be edited for publication, and all editorial changes will be made solely at the discretion of the editor. Members of the editorial staff may contact authors for clarifications of fact or intent. The editor makes the final decision about whether to accept or reject an article.

Please note that IIE publishes several other periodicals. If the editor determines that your submission is more appropriate for another of our periodicals, your article may be published in a periodical other than *Industrial Management*. Under these circumstances, the editor will attempt to obtain your permission before publication, though this is not always possible. Authors are encouraged to include supporting illustrations (graphs, charts, tables, and/or photographs) with articles.

Article Checklist

Include a suggested title for the article. You may give alternate titles, as well. Titles should not be overly wordy or technical.

Include a brief overview of the article. Summarize your article in two or three clear sentences.

Use subheads where appropriate. This will help organize and communicate your information.

Bulleted and numbered items or lists are acceptable, though excessive use is discouraged.

Do not include specific references within the body of the work. Do not include footnotes or endnotes. Vital material or appropriate references should be incorporated into the narrative of the article itself. An optional list of suggested reading or reference works should be included for the "For further reading" section at the end of your article.

Include a very brief biography (one paragraph) about the author or authors. Please indicate if you are a member of the Institute of Industrial Engineers or other professional societies and, if so, whether you are a senior member, Fellow, or other distinguished member. Indicate your professional title, employer and, if appropriate, the type of business, as well as your educational background.

Materials Checklist

Please include:

• A printed copy of your article.

• An electronic file of your article. If possible, save your file as a Microsoft Word document; otherwise, save it in ASCII format. You may send the file either on a 3.5" PC-compatible or Macintosh disk, or as an e-mail attachment to editor@iienet.org.

• Relevant charts, graphs, illustrations, and photographs. Photos should be submitted as color slides, prints, or transparencies rather than electronic images. If you must send photos electronically, the following formats are acceptable: EPS, PICT, GIF, TIFF, JPEG, Photoshop, BMP, PCX, and SCITEX CT. Electronic photos must be at least 300 DPI at actual size. Other artwork such as illustrations, charts, and graphs may be submitted electronically and accompanied by a hardcopy print out. These electronic images should be saved in separate files from the text of the article. Send the images in one of the following original program files, if possible: Macromedia Freehand, Adobe Illustrator, Microsoft Word, Microsoft PowerPoint, or Quark XPress.

• Identification and caption material for all illustrations and photos. Please do not attach items to photographs with paper clips or staples, as this may damage your material and render it unusable. Do not write on the back of photos. Specify if photos should be returned.

For each article we publish, we must have a signed copyright release form on file. One will be sent to you upon receipt of your article. *Industrial Management* holds the copyright of all published articles. For permission to use the article for personal or educational purposes,

please contact the Permissions Department at the Institute of Industrial Engineers.

If your article is an opinion or commentary piece, please submit a color photograph of yourself.

Categories: Technology—Industrial Engineering

CONTACT: Jane Gaboury, Editor
Material: All
CONTACT: Monica Elliot, Managing Editor
Material: All
IEE Solutions: Institute of Industrial Engineers
25 Technology Park/Atlanta
Norcross GA 30092
Phone: 770- 449-0461
Fax: 770-263-8532
Website: www.iienet.org

InnerCity

WRITERS' GUIDELINES:

Thank you for your interest in writing for INNERCITY, the only consumer urban entertainment magazine that people can hear on the radio and can read at home. INNERCITY Magazine is the promotional magazine for Inner City Broadcasting Corporation.

The new INNERCITY has the right formula for urban young-oriented celebrity and entertainment-driven reporting. The editorial [DNA] focus is 100% pure celebrity with action-oriented photography. The magazine will have 'A'-list guest feature contributors, music and journalism professionals including a team of correspondents filing reports plugged into what satisfies the readers' insatiable appetite for all-matters celebrity. Stories behind the lyrics/songs and fashion trends that cross-pollinate around the world as told by the artist, writers, producers, video directors and fashion designers. Plus reviews, releases, interactive contests, promotions, polls, quizzes, surveys and giveaways including fashion in entertainment spreads.

CATEGORIES REQUESTED

The primary editorial objectives of the magazine are: to provide an accounting of "All-Matters" happening throughout the world of urban entertainment in the areas of music, film/video, TV, theatre, dance, and fashion.

SUBMISSION GUIDELINES

Submissions must be lively, engaging, researched, and jargon-free. The general length or short profiles, standard articles and full manuscripts should range from 400 to 3,000 words. Photography submissions must be via email, on the form of a diskette (IBM/PC formatted) or via FTP. Writers must also provide a brief biography, i.e. "real life" experience or a resume along with sample articles.

PAYMENT

Payment for accepted work at this time for printed submissions, or if assigned (regardless of whether or not it's printed). Contribution amounts are paid based on item post print. Payment is based on quality of work, amount of editing or rewriting needed, length of work, and inclusion of photos or graphics. Contributors also receive up to five free copies of the issue in which their piece appears and may obtain additional copies at a minimal charge.

Categories: Entertainment

CONTACT: Editor
INNERCITY
67 Wall St, Ste 2212
New York NY 10005
E-mail: Editor@INNERCITYMagazine.com
Website: www.one2onemag.com/innercity/

Inside Texas Running

INSIDE TEXAS RUNNING is a tabloid magazine issued monthly, except June and August, and is published primarily for Texas runners. Each issue averages 40-52 pages and includes race reports, a "Texas Roundup" of news from around the State, in-house columns on sports medicine and nutrition, the over-40 runner ("Concerning Masters") and articles on unusual running events, training, etc. All but the columns require freelance input. We also are seeking good photos. General guidelines are as follows:

ARTICLES: We need profiles, travel tips, unusual races, historic pieces or almost anything that would interest our readers. If you are not sure about a subject, try us anyway—especially if it's Texas-related. General topics about running are usually handled by our columnists. Unique slants are wanted.

Our audience includes beginning runners as well as veteran marathoners, so the subject matter may reflect the varying abilities of our readers. Since ability varies so widely, we might be interested in a five-hour marathoner, for example, if there is something unique about that marathoner that would inspire or intrigue. Controversy is welcomed, but not faddish or dangerous nutritional or training pieces; observing the common sense rules of running, etc. is necessary. Training articles should be written by or with the help of experts such as reputable coaches (always state experience and background) and elite athletes.

Anecdotes, examples and quotes are very much appreciated.

Payment ranges from $25 for fillers of less than 500 words up to $75 for 1,000 to 1,500 words. Higher fees are available for established writers. Byline is provided.

RACE REPORTS: We contact race directors from around the state for race reports and results and cover many major races. Any unusual happening (odd weather, lost runners, unique course layout, etc.), along with a brief account of the race, will find eager acceptance here. Results listing the top finishers (minimum top 10 overall male and female, top 3 age division winners) should accompany the write-up. The report should include the proper name of the race, the date, the distance, weather conditions, number of participants, and, if possible, quotes from participants reacting to some aspect of the race. Payment: $25 for report, one usable photo and results. Length: 100-250 words max.

CORRESPONDENTS: We are looking for regular correspondents from around the state to cover races, do interviews, report races, take photos and keep us informed of upcoming races. These regulars will be listed on the masthead of the publication and receive the publication complimentary.

FICTION: Some fiction accepted. Please contact with article.

BEST WAY TO BREAK IN: Our Texas Roundup Section includes short items of one to several paragraphs long that include news about races-unusual themes, celebrity runners, prize money, and other information above and beyond its basic calendar listing-as well as human interest, records set, and miscellaneous tidbits. We are looking for items across the state, particularly outside the Houston area.

PHOTOS: We accept digital images and prints. Please don't send snapshots of runners where features are undefinable and figures are miles away.

Human interest subject matter is desired, as well as our always necessary race photos. Articles profiling runners should be accompanied by photos of the subject training, at work, with his family or whatever else will illustrate the piece appropriately. Similarly, travel pieces might have figures running past recognizable landmarks. Pay-ment: $15 per photo, $50 for color photo on cover. More for outstanding shots.

CARTOONS: Like everything else in INSIDE TEXAS RUNNING, cartoons are about runners, etc., but the subject matter might overlap into medical concerns, diet, non-running spouse, general fitness. Payment: Contact us to arrange.

ON SUBMISSIONS: Complete manuscripts only; no queries. Please do not send photo negatives. We will pay on publication and will report on all submissions received as above within several weeks. Please indicate whether ms is simultaneous submission.

THANK YOU FOR YOUR INTEREST IN INSIDE TEXAS RUNNING.

Lance Phegley, Editor

Categories: Outdoors—Physical Fitness—Recreation—Regional—Sports/Recreation—Travel

CONTACT: Lance Phegley, Editor
Material: All
PO Box 19909
Houston TX 77224
Phone: 281-759-0555
Fax: 281-759-7766
E-mail: lance@runningmags.com
Website: www.insidetexasrunning.com

Insider Magazine

Publication Definition:

INsider magazine is a national general interest publication published 5 times per year. *INsider* has a minimum 200,000 circulation and over 1.6 million readers every other month. It is distributed directly to 445 colleges and direct mailed to over 1,500 college newspapers and 600 college radio stations. There are over 15 individualized local editions of the magazine targeting various campuses and metropolitan markets. Our target audience is 18 to 34 year olds. *INsider* is also available as a national publication at many major newsstands and Borders & Barnes and Noble Bookstores.

Editorial Sections:

INsider magazine is a publication designed and written by twentysomethings from all over America. We have graduated, per se, from just focusing on the college market and your stories should reflect our new readership. Monthly surveys conducted in the magazine show that 18 to 34 year olds have tremendously varied habits and interests.

They love music and buy numerous CDs.

They are concerned about their health and appearance.

They are very active socially, going to nightclubs, bars and concerts several times a month and are constantly pursuing relationships and meeting new people.

They love to see movies both at the theater and at home on video tape.

They are very aware of current events, actively vote in major elections and are very active as volunteers for causes dealing with the environment, political issues, etc.

A majority have credit cards that they use on a regular basis.

INsider entertains our readers' interests while developing a unique editorial impression that celebrates the exclusivity of being a young adult today. One thing is true for all college-age consumers; they do NOT like to be referred or spoken to as college students. We want to emphasize what is unique about this demographic without exposing its limitations (ie: their age, where they are in their careers). Any quantitative observation makes students recoil from fear of being labelled a "member of the pack"!

ENTERTAINMENT:

Guest Editor — Each issue of INsider magazine is hosted by a guest editor that interacts with several of the on-going featured columns. Guest editors are featured on the cover of the magazine; there is a two page interview with the guest editor; we note their birthday on the horoscope page; the guest editor assists in reviewing music and products in the issue; and anything else we can think of related to our bi-monthly theme. The guest editor is generally a notable actor, actress or musician.

INmusic — Examines the hottest music and trends in the so-called alternative market. From Smashing Pumpkins to R.E.M. to the Dave Matthews Band, readers look to INsider first, to find out what they should be listening to.

In-depth features and interviews from the music industry should be from 1,000 to 1500 words. These may be considered for cover stories.

Shorter profile pieces or band reviews should be between 400 to 750 words.

CD or concert reviews should be no more than 400 words.

INsider will feature a guest entertainer (music, film, or TV), who will appear on the cover of his or her specific issue and will be tied-in to that issues' theme by way of product reviews, horoscopes, and a question and answer session focusing on the integral sections of the magazine (movies, TV, video, books, travel, careers, and sports).

INfilm — INsider focuses on up-and-coming actors and directors as well as established stars who appeal directly to our readership. Recent profiles include everyone from new faces such as Kevin Smith, the director of Clerks and Michael Rapaport, star of Kiss of Death, to Hollywood fixtures like Sara Jessica Parker and Ethan Hawke. INsider gets the celebrities to tell all about their lives, careers, and details of upcoming movies.

In-depth articles, usually featuring personality profiles or interviews, should be 750 to 1,500 words. These are often the cover story.

Movie reviews and guides featuring upcoming releases should be 300 to 500 words. Satirical or research-based retrospectives on a genre or person should be 500 to 1,200 words.

If Walls Could Talk — The movie editor writes a monthly movie-industry buzz column that tells all about soon to be released movies and the people who star in them.

INvideo — A round-up of the latest videos for rent. Readers look to INsider for the newest releases and the greatest classics on the market.

Video reviews and feature should be 250 to 350 words.

INtv — From MTV and cable access, to the latest Friends episode, television is a predominant source of entertainment for our readers. In TV features profile of today's TV stars like Friends' David Schwimmer, Seinfeld's Julia Louis-Dreyfuss, and JonStewart, or humorous articles on the latest trends in television. Profiles should be between 750 and 1500 words. Satirical or humor pieces should be between 600 to 750 words.

INbooks — INsider attracts a highly literate audience. They enjoy engaging stories about a wide and diverse range of authors and writers. Profiles should be 800 to 1500 words. Short reviews on books of interest to our readers, from fiction to career and travel guides should be 200-500 words.

FEATURES:

INsider brings readers the latest information about what is happening in the world and how it directly affects their lives. Bimonthly, INsider offers two to four national features covering current issues including alcohol/drug use, 'Aids and Sex in the 90s,' environmental issues and interviews with famous personalities. Features are 750 to 2500 words, often with accompanying sidebar. These are usually the cover stories with national slant.

CAREERS:

INsider gives our readers an edge on how to get ahead, from writing their r sum , to tips on how to interview and stories on workplace issues like sexual harassment. Past features have included advice from recent graduates, job and salary demographics and the do's and dont's of job interviews. INsider helps prepare readers for the job market with success. Informative/resource articles pertaining to job or career issues should be 400 to 750 words with a national slant.

THEMES:

Each issue of INsider revolves around a theme. Consider these themes when submitting:

November: Annual Travel Guide/Spring Break Issue

March: Automotive Issue/March Madness Preview

May: Outdoor Adventure Issue

September: Technology/ Computer Softwear/College Football Preview

October: Annual Ski Issue

LIFESTYLE:

INtravel — This section features stories on destinations popular with our readership. INsider will also consider humorous travel stories, travel tips and travel round-ups. Stories should be 500 to 1,500 words, often with accompanying sidebar.

INsports — This section features stories on participatory sports popular with our readership like ultimate frisbee or rugby. Also consider profiles of professional or amateur athletes. Stories and profiles should be 500 to 1,500 words. The reader that INsider is trying to capture is the active young adult who is interested in personal excellence and commitment to bettering their community. INsider wants to position itself as a proactive publication, deadicated to actve endeavors.

INteractive— The latest in happenings and issues on the info superhighway and in the world of technology. We also review the latest CD-ROMS and video game. Stories and profiles should be 500 to 1,500 words. Reviews should be 200 to 400 words.

IN View — In-depth explorations of political issues. Personal essays on issues effecting our generation. Profiles of leaders or people making a difference. Stories and profiles should be 500 to 1,500 words.

Relationships — Guest authors, specializing in relationship-counseling give advice on how to deal with the problems many readers face in their relationships. This section also features first person narratives and research based articles concerning relationships in '90s. Articles often take a humorous slant. Should be 500 to 1,200 words.

INsider Choice — Features the newest products on the market appealing to our readership. From mountain bikes to backpacks to beers, this section previews the latest trends. INsider is a key source of information for readers looking to buy the best products for the most reasonable price. INsider reviews the latest products on the market for quality, versatility and affordability. The top selections are given the INsider Choice Award.

Anywhere from four to eight products are previewed with graphics and accompanying descriptions including any outstanding qualities, where they can be found and the cost.

FORMAT:

Submissions — on Macintosh disk with Microsoft Word 5.0 or earlier version preferred, otherwise a clear, double-spaced copy that can be scanned is acceptable. Fax stories or queries to INsider at 847.329.0358 or e-mail to INsideread@aol.com

Computer Functions — Often, a great deal of our time is spent correcting minor formatting errors in the text that should, ideally, be fixed on your end. Please adhere to the following guidelines:

AP Punctuation Guide:

Space: MAKE SURE THERE IS ONLY ONE SPACE BETWEEN EACH WORD, INCLUDING THE BEGINNING OF SENTENCES. When copy editing, run the "Find" program. FIND every double-space and REPLACE it with a single space. THIS IS VERY IMPORTANT!

Brackets: cannot be transmitted over news wires. Use parenthesis. Colon: USE AT THE END OF A SENTENCE to introduce lists, text, etc.

: Can be used for EMPHASIS.

Comma: Do not use a comma before the final item in a series. When in doubt refer to an AP Style book.

Dash: Use dashes to denote an abrupt change in thought in a sentence or emphatic pause: Smith offered a plan — it was unprecedented — to raise revenues.

PUT A SPACE ON EITHER SIDE OF DASH. TO MAKE A DASH ON A MACINTOSH: HIT <opt> <shift> <->.

Ellipsis: An ellipsis is the "..." punctuation that indicates a break in thought or an omitted part of a direct quote. Instead of using the period key: to make an ellipsis on a Macintosh, hit <opt> <;>.. AN ELLIPSIS DOES NOT NEED A SPACE IN FRONT OF IT BUT IT DOES NEED A SPACE BEHIND IT.

Titles: A rule of thumb to decide if a title should be in italics or quotes: IF A WORK CAN STAND ALONE IT SHOULD BE IN ITALICS, IF IT IS A PART OF A LARGER WORK , IT SHOULD BE IN QUOTES. For example: use quotes around song titles, newspaper articles, chapter titles, article names, etc. Use italics for album names, poems, works of art, book titles, magazine names, newspapers, etc. Parentheses: USE AS SPARINGLY AS POSSIBLE! Parentheses are jarring to the reader and is often a clue that a sentence is becoming contorted. Try to write it another way. If a sentence must contain incidental material, commas or dashes are usually more effective.

Semicolon: In general, use a semicolon to indicate a greater separation in thought then a comma can convey but less then the separation that a period implies.

Indentation — The computer can automatically space and indent paragraphs, this is done by recognition of individual character returns. Therefore when typing, only put ONE RETURN at the end of every paragraph. Also, DO NOT PUT ANY SPACES OR TABS at the beginning of the next paragraph. Any marks of this nature have to be removed by us.

Smart Quotes — There are smart quotes and dumb quotes. Smart quotes curve toward the text, dumb quotes don't. Smart quotes are a preference setting on most word processing systems. If you don't have this option they can be typed manually: hit the (opt) and ([) key for opened quotes, and (shift) (opt) ([) for closed quotes.

To make single quotes: hit (opt) (]) for an opened single quote, and (shift) (opt) (]) for a closed single quote.

State Abbreviations — Are not the same as postal abbreviations. See AP stylebook.

Emphasis — to convey emphasis use italics, do not capitalize, bold or underline.

Numbers — Spell out through nine, use figures for 10 and above. Do not start a sentence with a figure. For years, use closed single quote ('94, mid-'70s). Do not make years possessive (the roaring 20s). Any Doubts? REFER TO AP STYLE GUIDELINES! It is imperative that you proof for these style errors before submitting articles.

Setting Story Headings:
Set text for SINGLE SPACE.
Set font on 12 point Helvetica.
PLACE TITLE on first line, capitalizing all principal words. Do not use all caps, bold, or underlining, and do not skip any extra spaces. Use no more then 25 characters.

Place sub-title on next line capitalizing all principal words. Use no more than 50 characters. BYLINE goes on the next line. Do not type the word "Byline," only the writer's full name should appear. SKIP ONE LINE.

DO NOT INDENT and start typing article.

If submission is on disk, write text in one block, do not skip lines between paragraphs. If hard copy only is submitted, text should be double spaced.

Hard copy should be submitted with or without a disk.
ALWAYS remember to spell check and proof all work!
Always use AP style guidelines!
ALWAYSmake sure your article is no longer than it is suppose to be!

Deadlines — 45 Days prior to issue unless otherwise specified by editorial director.

Compensation — There are several classes of writers and each is compensated differently. The associate publisher and editorial director are in charge of all class promotions.

Contributing writer: 1¢ per word
Staff Writer: 2¢ per word
Senior Writer: 3¢ per word
Featured Columnist: To Be Negotiated

Costs of article are included in payment. Any other costs associated with the production of an article must be approved in advance by the Editorial director.

Assignment

Most stories are by assignment, however suitable submissions are considered. Queries and story ideas are strongly encouraged. There is no guarantee that unsolicited articles will be returned, even with SASE. If interested in writing, please send a resume and writing samples, published or otherwise, with any story ideas or area of interest.

Categories: Nonfiction—Adventure—Arts—Automobiles—Careers—College—Computers—Conservation—Consumer—Culture—Economics—Entertainment—Environment—Feminism—Film/Video—Food/Drink—General Interest—Government—Internet—Interview—Law—Men's Issues—Music—Outdoors—Politics—Regional—Relationships—Sexuality—Society—Sports/Recreation—Theatre—Travel—Women's Issues—Public Policy—Technology

CONTACT: Jon Erchell, Senior Editor
Material: Entertainment
CONTACT: Rita Cook, Senior Editor
Material: Theme
CONTACT: Mark Jansen, Senior Editor
Material: Issues
4124 W. Oakton
Skokie IL 60076-3267
Phone: 847-673-3703
Fax: 847-329-0358
E-mail: info@incard.com

Insight

What's Insight?
• It's a weekly 24-page magazine for high school and college students.
• It's published by the Review and Herald Publishing Association and is a ministry of the North American Division of the Seventh-day Adventist Church.
• It's distributed to youth at church, at church schools, and through home subscriptions.

Who Reads Insight?
• Insight's audience is primarily American and Canadian youth and young adults of the Seventh-Day Adventist Church.
• The readers are diverse in gender, ethnicity, school experience (public school, private day school, boarding academy, home school, college), church experience (large, small, formal, informal, "liberal," "conservative"), interests, and spiritual maturity.

What to Write
• Insight needs: true inspirational stories, profiles of Adventist celebrities, profiles of outstanding Seventh-day Adventist youth and young adults, and general spiritual articles.
•Insight doesn't need: fiction, sermons, puzzles, and parables.

HOW TO WRITE - Writing a Story
A series of events doesn't make a story. A story has three basic elements:
1. a beginning, which provides factual details such as who, where, when;
2. a conflict or crisis, which builds suspense;
3. a resolution (physical or mental), which shows character growth.
All Insight stories must be true, and should be told from a high school or college student's point of view. They should include elements

of good storytelling, such as realistic dialogue, believable characters (not "perfect" or "terrible"), sensory impressions (show—don't tell), and a strong spiritual conclusion.

Writing a Profile: When interviewing an outstanding youth or adult, look for a current "story" (see previous section). Find a time of conflict or crisis they've encountered recently (or if an adult, in their younger years). Then describe the experience as well as how the subject has grown through it.

Profiles shouldn't be a resume of what a person has done. Rather, they should show how a person has faced tribulation and how God helped them persevere and grow. Profiles should also include quotations from the subject, but they should be only the most powerful statements and should be used sparingly. Some leading interview questions might be: "What was the most difficult time of your life? How did God help you? How did the experience change you? When did you first begin to trust Christ? When you blow out the candles on your eightieth birthday cake, what do you want to look back on?" Good profiles also benefit from interviewing other people who know the subject, such as parents, close friends, siblings, etc. After asking factual questions ("How did you meet the person? How long have you known him/her?"), ask such questions as: "How have you seen God work in this person's life? What hard times have they been through? What character growth have you observed? How has this person changed your life?"

Writing an Article

Articles should address topics of interest to today's teenagers and young adults from a Christian perspective. An article should begin with a story or several anecdotes to introduce the topic. The story or anecdotes should be true and involve youth or young adults. (See section "Writing a Story" for tips.)

The article should include a Biblical perspective. (We prefer Scriptural quotations in the New International Version.) Most articles benefit from one or two sidebars, which might provide "how to" steps, resources, definitions, a self-quiz, or other information related to the subject.

Editing Checklist

When checking over your piece, make sure it includes:
* an opening that will grab the reader
* active verbs rather than "be" (is, was, were, etc.) or passive verbs
* dialogue
* description that is concrete rather than abstract, specific rather than general
* true examples and anecdotes
* simple, current language in a conversational tone
* unpredictable details and fresh insights
* a strong spiritual message

How to Submit a Manuscript
* Manuscripts must be typed, doublespaced.
* With each manuscript please include: your name; mailing address; phone number; church name, city, and state; social security number (necessary for payment); gender and ethnicity(for illustrative accuracy); and biographical facts (such as age, job title, school attending, major, etc.).
* Include a stamped, self-addressed envelope for return of your manuscript.

Send manuscripts by mail or e-mail.

Categories: Nonfiction—Christian Interests—Religion—Teen

CONTACT: Editor
Material: All
Review & Herald Publishing Association
Insight Magazine
55 W. Oak Ridge Dr.
Hagerstown, MD 21740
Phone: 301-393-4038
Fax: 301-393-4055
E-mail: insight@rhpa.org
Website: www.insightmagazine.org

InSite

PURPOSE: *InSite*, the bimonthly flagship publication of Christian Camp and Conference Association (CCCA), seeks to inform and inspire professionals serving in the Christian camp and conference community.

FOCUS: The magazine primarily prints practical how-to pieces related to the following critical aspects of Christian camping ministries: outdoor setting; purpose and objectives; administration and organization; camper and guest needs; personnel development; programming; health and safety; foodservice; site, facilities, and maintenance; business and operations; marketing and public relations; and fund raising. In addition, it features profiles of influential camp and conference professionals and inspirational, in-depth features related to what God is doing in and through Christian camp and conference ministries.

APPROACH: In-depth articles in *InSite* show (rather than tell) what God is doing in and through Christian camp and conference ministries, and demonstrate how camping professionals can be most efficient and effective in their outreach efforts. *InSite* publishes first- and third-person articles.

FORMAT: *InSite* is published bimonthly on 8-3/8 by 10-7/8-inch matte stock with full color throughout. The article length for profiles and features is 1,200–1,500 words; how-to pieces are 1,000–1,200 words, and sidebars are 250–500 words. Please query first; electronic queries e-mailed to editor@ccca-us.org are preferred. Response to queries, photos, and manuscripts are sent within one month. *InSite* retains first rights.

PAYMENT: *InSite* offers 16 cents per published word for articles contributed by individuals outside CCCA. Payment is sent upon publication. Travel expenses are not compensated.

PHOTOS: *InSite* will generally arrange for photographs of individuals profiled in the magazine. For other photo contributions, sharp color glossy prints or high quality digital shots are acceptable. Mood/action shots covering the gamut of emotion and activity in camp, conference center, and retreat center ministries will be considered.

MISCELLANEOUS: Current circulation is nearly 9,000; *InSite* is distributed primarily to individuals involved in all aspects of Christian camp and conference ministries. Bylines and photo credits are given. Submit seasonal material queries six months in advance.

TIPS: Profiles/interviews are the best bet for newcomers and freelancers. It is crucial to study a sample copy first and then query. Send $4.95 for a recent copy (this will also cover shipping and handling).

Categories: Nonfiction—Christian Interests—Outdoors—Sports/Recreation—Camps

CONTACT: Alison Phillips, Editor
Material: All
PO Box 62189
Colorado Springs CO 80962-2189
E-mail: editor@ccca-us.org
Web Site: www.christiancampandconference.org

Instructor

Instructor Magazine's Writer's Guidelines for Teachers of Grades K–8

Instructor publishes more teachers' bylines each issue than any other educational magazine. We would love to hear from you!

Features: Feature stories of approximately 800 to 1,200 words on timely, relevant topics of interest to K–12 teachers. Articles may cover classroom management and practice, education trends and issues, and suggestions for professional development. Please send the completed article or a query letter in which you describe the article you'd like to write. To get a clear idea of the feature articles we publish, read the features found in three or more recent issues of Instructor.

Ready-to-Use Activities & Tips: Do you have an activity that's particularly effective with your students? A great tip for classroom management, organizing your time, or building classroom community? Please share it with us-we're always looking to hear about your classroom successes! Maximum 250 words; color snapshots or samples of students' work that clarify your ideas are helpful.

E-Activities: Tech-based activities for the classroom. The same information applies as for the Ready-to-Use Activities, above.

General Tips

• Read the magazine so you are familiar with our style and our needs. If you would like to order an issue, call 866-436-2455.

• As you write, think: How can I make this article most useful for teachers?

• Write in your natural voice. We shy away from wordy, academic prose.

• Let us know what grade/subject you teach and the name and location of your school.

• Send seasonal material at least six months in advance.

• Make sure your manuscript is typewritten and double-spaced; send only one copy to the appropriate department.

• Print your name and address on the manuscript and on all photos and samples. Include your phone number.

• Enclose a self-addressed stamped envelope.

• Please note that due to the volume of mail we receive, we regret that we cannot reply to submissions, and materials will not be returned. You will be contacted if we decide to use your activity or tip.

Thank you! We can't wait to hear from you.

Categories: Education

CONTACT: Manuscript Editor
Material: All
557 Broadway
New York NY 10012
Phone: 212-343-6100
Website: www.scholastic.com/instructor

Intelligent Enterprise

Thank you for your interest in writing for Intelligent Enterprise, the first and only information resource for IT and business leaders focusing on business-critical solutions that make organizations smarter, faster, and more profitable.

Unlike other publications covering technical subjects which rely heavily on freelance writers, Intelligent Enterprise content is written almost exclusively by independent experts: senior IT managers, system architects, consultants, and analysts. If you're such an expert and are interested in making a submission, the following guidelines will explain the entire process for you.

As you review these guidelines, please keep the following important points in mind:

To avoid conflicts of interest, we very rarely accept vendor-bylined submissions. However, we will review all submissions on a case-by-case basis.

We do not accept "canned" submissions written on generic subjects for a generic audience. All submissions must be written specifically for Intelligent Enterprise.

All submissions must be original (never before published in any form) as well as exclusive.

If you are making a submission on behalf of the author, please note that we will need to work with the author directly during editorial production.

Intelligent Enterprise routinely purchases all rights to published stories, meaning we reserve the right to reprint, republish, or post articles online. However, we do not deny authors the permission to repurpose their own work unnecessarily, provided we receive a written request.

Intelligent Enterprise reserves the right to reject an article at any time, even after it's been initially accepted.

Publication lead time is approximately 3 months. For example, manuscripts received in January will publish in a March issue.

Intelligent Enterprise and Its Readers

Intelligent Enterprise is a controlled subscription publication, with print editions distributed worldwide to 100,000 readers 18x per year. Most of these readers work within (or are consultants serving the needs of) corporate organizations, whether as IT-focused business leaders (CEOs, line-of-business managers, business analysts) or senior IT managers (CIOs, VPs of MIS, IT directors, senior IT analysts).

Our readers are educated, technically astute, and experienced; they use their knowledge to guide them through a dynamic, market-driven industry. They're exploring the powers and pitfalls of technology platforms that enable processes such as:

E-commerce

E-business-enabled enterprise resource planning (ERP)

Business intelligence and decision support

Enterprise application integration

Customer relationship management

Supply-chain management and analysis

To help them make key purchasing decisions, Intelligent Enterprise readers require strategic but technically-rich information about these technologies in a business context. Because these readers tend to be high-level managers focusing on business and IT strategy, they will leave most of the low-level implementation details to their staff.

Author Qualifications

We welcome proposals from qualified authors. You're considered qualified if:

You have at least three years of field experience.

You have a working knowledge of theories and techniques beyond your own personal experience.

You can communicate effectively in written English.

You can meet deadlines and follow through on assigned topics.

You are willing to accept criticism and are comfortable with the idea of editorial professionals helping you improve your work.

You are not accepting payment from a third party for writing the article (without our prior approval).

You are familiar with Intelligent Enterprise's style, content, and editorial focus.

You have a desire to share your personal experiences and expertise with other professionals.

Article Types

In general, five kinds of feature articles appear in Intelligent Enterprise:

Case studies might focus on how your shop has implemented a new information systems strategy, focusing on the challenges and advantages of the new environment. Interesting applications or interesting solutions to knotty problems are particularly desirable.

Industry analysis articles focus on the implications of recent news or technology developments. For example, what is the significance of a vendor's recently announced commitment to a particular standard?

Explanations of technology should describe new, different, or difficult solutions, taking care to cover why this technology is important to our readers. For example, what is the business significance of the emergence of enterprise information portals, how do the respective vendor architectures compare?

Business view stories should describe the intersection of business issues and technology, what business concerns our readers should consider when deciding what technology to use, and how IT can work together with business executives to implement successful systems.

Product reviews take an in-depth look at hot new products as well as at established products. New product reviews should include information received from beta testers as well as first-hand information. Reviews of established products (generally products that have been available for about a year) should pay attention to integration and implementation issues and how the product fits into the big picture; reviewers should speak to current users of the product and explain how these users worked the bugs out.

Core Topics

For detailed examples of the core topics covered in Intelligent Enterprise, review our Editorial Calendar and TOC Archive .

Submitting Your Idea

Prepare an abstract, outline, or summary of your proposed article idea (maximum one page) and send it to Editorial Director David Stodder. The abstract must include a brief bio about the author. Be sure to include your email address, phone and fax numbers, and your mailing address.

You're free to send in a completed manuscript. However, we receive a number of unsolicited manuscripts and proposals, and they take time to review. It may take us up to six weeks to accept or reject such an article. Please do not submit your proposal to any other publications while it is under review.

If your abstract is approved, we will contact you, set a tentative publication date, and determine a deadline for delivery of the manuscript. Keep in mind, however, that publishing schedules can change quickly.

In most cases, accepted manuscripts will be scheduled for publication within a 3-issue window.

Article Specifications

If your article proposal has been accepted, it's time for you to start writing! Feature article length is 2,000 words, with a maximum of 4 figures, tables, or screenshots (include captions). No need to worry about providing publication-quality figures; our production department will re-build your originals from scratch.

If your product review proposal has been accepted, we'll arrange to have a Product Review Guide and an evaluation copy sent to you. Product reviews should be a maximum of 2,000 words in length, with no more than 3 figures, tables, or screenshots.

If for any reason you are unable to meet your deadline, you must contact us as soon as possible. If you miss your deadline without informing us beforehand, your article will be withdrawn from the publication schedule and may not be published at all.

Author Payments

Intelligent Enterprise offers payment for the acquisition of publication rights; typically, first-time authors will receive $500 per article.

Payment is processed upon publication (not manuscript acceptance).

You will receive an author contract when your article is scheduled for publication. This contract must be signed and returned before we can process a payment.

Good luck! We look forward to seeing your submission.

Categories: Nonfiction—Business—Information Technology

CONTACT: David Stodder, Editorial Director
2800 Campus Dr
San Mateo CA 94403
Phone: 650-513-4300
Fax: 650-513-4613
E-mail: dstodder@cmp.com
Website: www.cmp.com

Interior Design

Needed for publication:

Set of original 4 x 5 transparencies illustrating the project.

Camera-ready floor plans and other drawings needed to explain the job. These should be 8 x 10 glossy prints of ruled ink drawings or high quality black and white laser prints. Please put all necessary legends, notes and dimensions on tracing paper overlay, not on the drawing; we will have them set in type. Please be sure your name and address are on all pieces submitted including the people biographies.

A brief professional biography of the principal team. A brief description of the project, noting the clients program, your design solution, total square footage and the project cost. If total project cost not available, give cost per square foot.

Please note that *INTERIOR DESIGN* is adamant about exclusivity; we make no publishing commitments without seeing original 4x5' transparencies (their quality being a factor in our decision) and that we look for photography in which the lighting detail is clear: fabric patterns, chair legs, etc. Some other magazines prefer dramatic shadows, but we prefer visual information.

The project submitted must not have been published in any magazine as a feature layout in the United States or Canada. It is acceptable that a project may have been mentioned as a news item.

We hope this information will help you and we look forward to seeing your presentation.

Categories: Arts—Home

CONTACT: Cindy Allen, Editor-in-Chief
Material: All
360 Park Ave. South, 17th floor
New York, NY 10010
Phone: 646-746-6400
Website: www.interiordesign.net

Internal Medicine World Report

Internal Medicine World Report is committed to the highest quality medical journalism. Any writer who wishes to contribute news articles to Internal Medicine World Report must agree to the conditions and guidelines below.

Queries

Writers should query editors before embarking on any assignment for Internal Medicine World Report.

Exclusivity

Articles must be written exclusively for Internal Medicine World Report, which will own all print and electronic (online) rights to the articles.

Acceptance

Authors are paid by the word on publication. If for some reason an article assigned by an editor cannot be published in a timely manner, authors will receive a $50 kill fee.

Pay Rate

Internal Medicine World Report pays 50 cents per published word.

Expenses

Internal Medicine World Report usually does not pay expenses.

Outside comment

Important topics in medical research almost always are the subject of debate. Researchers often have different perspectives on how to answer to a research question and invariably interpret with caution the study findings of other investigators. Criticism of a study's methodology and conclusions is common. Good medical journalism demands that articles that report on new study findings include comment from individuals who were not part of the study team and who are qualified to judge the study and its findings. All articles on new study findings (except really short articles) submitted to IMWR must include such independent comment. In addition, all articles dealing with controversial topics (e.g., physician-assisted suicide) must include opposing viewpoints.

Relevance

Articles about new medical findings must be written so that they are clinically relevant to IMWR readers. Use what a researcher has presented at a conference as a starting point to create an article that helps clinicians in their day-to-day practice. Readers should know right away why new findings are important to them, if not in the lead, then in the second or third paragraph.

Articles must be reader-friendly.

Timeliness

Timeliness is critical. You will be writing articles for one or two months ahead of when they will be published. It is important not to use references in the articles that will date the material. Be careful to word things so that they seem fresh.

Length

Watch the length of articles. Physicians are bombarded with information and have little time to read. Try to make your points with as few words as possible. Wordy or rambling articles could turn off readers.

Hit key points quickly and move on. If you feel a passage is particularly long and cumbersome, then it probably is. Always try to reduce or condense. A story may be brilliantly written and interesting, but a busy doctor will never know this if the article runs 1,500 to 2,000 words and beyond. He or she does not have the time to read the article to the end despite its interest or importance.

Generally, the length of a good article should be no more than 600 words. If need be, break a long story or column into two or three smaller stories, parts or sections.

Quotes

Whenever possible, quote what an individual has said rather than what he or she has written. When reporting on journal articles or scientific posters, make every effort to interview and quote a member of the study team, preferably the lead investigator.

Direct quotes taken from a journal report or a poster should be denoted clearly as such, using attributions like "the researchers concluded in their report" or "the report stated." Writers sometimes pull text from a journal article, put quotes around the words, and then report that the first author said those words. This can leave the impression that the writer interviewed the first author. Besides, the first author is not necessarily the person who wrote the paper. The objective is to be honest with the reader.

Study Numbers

When reporting on studies with comparison groups (e.g., one treatment versus another, or a treatment versus a placebo), be sure to include the number of persons involved in the study and the number of persons in each study arm. Also, give the number of persons in each study arm who achieve the endpoint or endpoints under consideration, and proportion of the study arm that this number represents. For example: Of the 100 patients in the treatment arm, 10 (10%) experienced a decline in glucose levels, compared with 42 (40%) of the 105 patients in the placebo group.

Also, be sure to describe differences among comparison groups as statistically significant or not statistically significant.

Press releases

Press releases can help in writing an article and can provide background information. They are not a substitute for original reporting, however. Avoid lifting quotes that appear in press releases. It is not unreasonable to expect medical writers to get their own interviews and quotes. If all attempts to interview a source fail, and you believe you must rely on press release quotes, then be clear about the attribution (e.g., "...Dr. Smith noted in a prepared statement").

Journal citations

When citing a journal, always provide full reference information: journal name, year, volume number and pages, e.g., "...the researchers reported in the Journal of the American Medical Association (1999;140:320-326)."

Sources, affiliations

When quoting sources, be sure to include their titles and affiliations, as well as the city of each institution (e.g., a professor of medicine at the Washington University School of Medicine in St. Louis).

Phone Numbers

Wherever possible, please provide phone numbers of all sources interviewed. IMWR editors may need them to check facts.

Drug Names

When mentioning drug names, please include the generic name, brand name and the drug's maker, e.g., lamivudine (Epivir, Glaxo Wellcome).

Categories: Nonfiction—Medicine

CONTACT: Jody A. Charnow, Editor
Material: All
241 Forsgate Dr
Jamesburg NJ 08831
Phone: 732-656-1140 ext 134
Fax: 732-656-9267
E-mail: jcharnow@mwc.com

The International Railway Traveler

The International Railway Traveler® (IRT) is the official magazine of The Society of International Railway Travelers®, an international organization of sophisticated travelers who prefer going first class by rail. (The International Railway Traveler® (IRT) and The Society of International Railway Travelers® (SIRT) both are registered trademarks of Hardy Publishing Co., Inc.)

Through generous use of superior color photos, graphics and design—as well as through the inclusion of evocative and entertaining stories—IRT conveys the romance, elegance and excitement of first-class railway travel worldwide. Wherever possible, IRT's editorial schedule emphasizes railways, trains and venues featured in The Society of International Railway Travelers' upcoming tour schedule.

IRT also features, on an occasional basis, amenities of interest to first-class international railway travelers, such as cruises, hotels and restaurants.

WRITERS

IRT needs writing that is timely, detailed and accurate. All story submissons must include superior, high-resolution color photos and, where appropriate, graphics (i.e., items with a railroad's logo, etc.)

IRT seeks the following kinds of stories:

1) **Short Travel Features** of around 300-500 words in length. These stories report on new equipment, services, routes, package deals, dining and sleeping car services, stations and anything else of interest to the first-class international railway traveler.

2) **Main Travel Features** consist of the main story and a detailed, informational ("If You Go...") sidebar, which together should run no more than 800-1,000 words. (Lengthier submissions will be returned.)

Main Travel Features

To reiterate: *IRT's editorial schedule emphasizes railways, trains and venues which are featured in The Society of International Railway Travelers' upcoming tour schedule. Please review our Tour Bro-*

chure or visit our web site to learn about the Society's plans for the coming year.

IRT's travel features should convey the romance, wonder and excitement of rail travel for the newsletter's sophisticated, well-traveled readership. The stories should be lively, personal and, above all, not dull.

Sidebar

The following information must be included in a separate sidebar.

a) Prices for major portions of trip described, such as air and rail fares, hotel, restaurant, public transit, major attractions, etc.

b) Specific advice on amenities from the rail traveler's point of view. This includes hotels, restaurants, museums, etc., accessible to the main railroad station or public transit.

c) Phone, fax, Internet address, Web page URL and mailing addresses of travel providers/attractions mentioned in story as well as contact information for the national tourism office in the U.S. of the country or countries described. The writer is responsible for the accuracy of this information. Please double-check these numbers and addresses.

d) Any other pertinent traveler's information, such as visa requirements, health news, political updates, etc.

e) Relevant Thomas Cook Timetable numbers.

f) Date the trip was taken.

In all cases, IRT retains the right to publish "The Society of International Railway Travelers" as the sole contact for more information and booking of travel connected with stories published in IRT.

Style: Unless otherwise noted, IRT follows the Associated Press Stylebook. See http://fredericksburg.com/FreeLanceStarCompany/Newsrooms/newsroom/FLSstyle/flsstyle.htm and click on "AP Stylebook."

Note: In IRT, train names are always italicized; train companies, routes or lines are not. Example: "The *Trans-Siberian Express* runs over most of the original route of the Trans-Siberian Railway."

PHOTOGRAPHS

IRT photos now are published in color.

Trains may be fascinating to look at and a joy to ride. But pictures of them tend towards monotony if they are taken from the same dull perspective (i.e., on the station platform, with the train describing an oblique, diminishing line). Include people with train shots wherever possible.

Also, IRT likes train photographs which include something of the country's native scenery, photographs that emphasize the word "international" in IRT's name. (The Japanese "Shinkansen" racing past Mt. Fuji is the classic example.) And, besides obvious panoramic shots, we appreciate several detail photos: i.e., a teacup with train logo resting on a table, a vase of flowers in dining car, a particularly attractive wall sconce, etc.

We prefer photos submitted digitally as TIFF files for Macintosh computers, via email, ZIP disk or CD-ROM at a resolution not below 300 dpi. Digital files should be submitted in a compressed format (i.e., as "zip" or "sit" files).

If digital submission is not possible, we prefer color glossy photos, although prints or transparencies are also acceptable (cost of conversion to digital format will be deducted from payment; see "payment" section). Photos should be high contrast, and in focus, preferably 8 x 10 inches, although 5 x 7's will be accepted.

SUBSIDIZED TRAVEL

IRT recognizes that professional travel writers must accept subsidized travel. However, writers for IRT must acknowledge receipt to us in writing of any subsidized travel and promise to remain scrupulously objective in their reporting. If a writer plans to request complimentary travel of any kind, with the intention of publishing a story and/or photos deriving from that travel in IRT, he or she must receive written permission from the IRT editor **in advance** of his or her request. Again, please note: IRT retains the right to publish "The Society of International Railway Travelers" as the sole contact for more information and booking of travel connected with stories in IRT.

PAYMENT

IRT pays for stories and photos within one month of the cover date of the issue in which a writer's or photographer's work appears. IRT buys first N. American serial rights and all electronic publishing rights to stories and photos. In addition, IRT buys all rights to republish photos, as well as short excerpts from stories, to promote and advertise its tours, whether in print, electronically or by other means.

Payment is $.03 per word plus $10 for each photo used ($20, if the photo is the main page-one art). Payment is in U.S. dollars. To receive full payment, photographers should submit photos as digital files with a resolution of at least 300 dpi. Digital files should be submitted in a compressed format (i.e., as "zip" or "sit" files). Costs associated with converting photographic material to digital format are deducted from payment.

In the event a story requested or accepted by IRT is unsuitable for publication, IRT will pay its author a "kill fee."

Sample copies of The International Railway Traveler cost $6 each within the United States. Elsewhere, a sample copy costs $10.

SUBMISSIONS

IRT encourages submissions by email. Submissions may also be made on CD-ROM or computer disk (3½-inch disks or zip disks for IBM or compatibles, or Macintosh, with Microsoft Word preferred. Use ASCII file format if Microsoft Word is not available.

Although IRT welcomes the submission of unsolicited material, it can assume no responsibility for its return unless a self-addressed envelope with sufficient postage is enclosed. Query letters with published clips are strongly encouraged.

Categories: Nonfiction—Travel—Rail Travel

CONTACT: Owen Hardy, Editor, IRT
Material: All
1810 Sils Ave, Ste 306B
Louisville KY 40205
Phone: 502-454-0277
Fax: 502-458-2250
E-mail: railtours@bellsouth.net
Website: www.irtsociety.com

International Sports Journal
University of West Haven

The *International Sports Journal* welcomes both empirical and theoretical articles that can be applied or be pertinent to current sports issues and practices or contribute to academic research in the international sports community.

Authors' articles should not exceed 25 double-spaced typewritten pages, and footnotes should appear on a separate page and follow A.P.A. style. References should be listed separately corresponding to the body of the manuscript. The author should send three copies of his/her manuscript plus a short biography. Include also an abstract of not more than 100 words summarizing the paper.

All articles are anonymously reviewed by the editorial board entirely in terms of scholarly content. Previously published articles cannot be accepted.

Categories: Nonfiction—Health—Physical Fitness—Recreation—Sports/Recreation

CONTACT: Thomas Katsaros, Ph.D., Editor
Material: All
University of New Haven
300 Orange Ave.
West Haven CT 06516
Phone: 203-932-7118
Fax: 203-931-6084
E-mail: mharvey@charger.newhaven.edu

The Internet Writing Journal

Award-Winning Monthly Online Writing Magazine with Articles, Interviews and Book Reviews

Submission Guidelines

The Internet Writing Journal® ("*The IWJ*") is seeking original articles. Please read the guidelines carefully before submitting. Remember, we only publish nonfiction articles—please do not submit poetry or fiction! We recommend that writers read articles published *The IWJ* to get an idea of our editorial style and the types of articles that we publish. Click here to see a list of links to prior articles. We look forward to seeing your submission!

Article Submissions

The IWJ is seeking articles on improving writing skills (any genre), the publishing industry, journalism, screenwriting, songwriting, business writing, playwriting, writing markets, Internet writing, and articles on writing-related topics. The articles should be between 1500-1750 words in length. If you have a proposal for an article that deviates from this length, please query first.

We are looking for how to, informational and journalistic articles. Personal experience articles should focus on a learning experience which would be of interest to other writers, or should describe how a particular writing technique has proven helpful.

Articles must be the work of the original author. *The IWJ* generally does not accept reprints; however, we will consider excerpts from published books or scholarly articles. For works which have already been published, please query first describing the piece and where and when it was published. *The IWJ* does not accept simultaneous submissions. *The IWJ* takes first worldwide electronic publishing rights with the right to archive the material indefinitely in any electronic medium and to publish the article in a possible print or electronic anthology in the future. Rights return to the author thirty (30) days after the first date of publication, subject to the archiving and anthology rights described above.

The *IWJ* does not offer monetary payment at this time. However, articles will be published on a separate webpage as part of *The IWJ* with an author bio and links to the author's webpage and novels, if applicable. All articles will be archived on the Web, when the next month's issue is uploaded.

Submissions should be sent to: journal@NOSPAMwriterswrite.com. Be sure to remove the NOSPAM when you send your email. Sorry, we only accept electronic submissions. If you cannot include the entire article in the body of your email, please attach the article to the email as a text document. If the document will not fit in the body of an email, please attach it to the email in either Microsoft Word, Corel Wordperfect or text format. Writers may also submit queries to the above email address. Please include a short author bio written in third person with any submission!

Product and Book Reviews

If you would like to submit your product or book for possible review in *The IWJ*, please submit it to our snail mail address below.

Writers Write, Inc
Attention: Reviews
8214 Westchester Ste 500
Dallas TX 75225
Important note: At this time, we do not review e-books.
Categories: Writing

CONTACT: Claire White, Editor
5930-E Royal Lane #106
Dallas TX 75230
Website: www.writerswrite.com/journal/

Interweave Knits

Interweave Knits is a quarterly publication of Interweave Press for all those who love to knit. In each issue we present beautifully finished projects accompanied by clear step-by-step instruction. The projects range from quick but intriguing projects that can be accomplished in a weekend, to complex patterns that may take months to complete. The magazine includes feature articles from around the country and around the world about people who knit. *Interweave Knits* readers want to know where each kind of knitting comes from, how it was and is done, who did and does it, and why. Striking examples of the technique are important.

Our knitters want to know how to employ any new techniques they encounter in our magazine today. Therefore, each article will have an associated knitting project that uses the technique to produce a high-quality item that they will want to keep or give away.

Submissions

We invite written queries and submissions of manuscripts, photographs, and artwork related to all aspects of hand knitting. Material submitted should display in-depth knowledge of the subject matter and, when appropriate, careful, documented research, with all sources acknowledged.

Keep a copy of everything. If the submission is unsolicited and/or you wish any part of it to be returned, include a self-addressed envelope with sufficient return postage. *Interweave Knits* is published quarterly-press dates are last week of January for Spring, first week of April for Summer, first week of June for Fall, and last week of September for Winter. Issues are planned six to twelve months in advance; if you have materials intended for a particular issue, please submit them six months before the month of publication.

Manuscripts

Technical accuracy is essential, but the tone should be personal and informal. If your article is historical, use primary resources, such as letters and diaries, wherever possible to make information accessible and arresting to the reader. Strive for clear organization as you convey information, including subheads where appropriate.

Please include a sketch and yarn sample for the project that will accompany your article. The project must include clear step-by-step directions and precise diagrams wherever the reader will need visual direction on where fingers, yarns, tools, or other materials go. Highlight techniques that the knitter will learn and/or employ to complete the project successfully. Include any information you have on where to get necessary supplies and what they will cost. A unique feature of *Interweave Knits* is that for each project, we will suggest yarn substitutions and alternate colorways. We aim to accommodate the knitter who needs to start your project today, so it is important to propose readily-available yarns.

We expect that the article you ask us to consider has not been published nor is it presently submitted elsewhere. If any part of your submission has been published previously, please let us know when and by whom. If the article is still in the idea stage, send a detailed proposal-complete outline, written description, sample pages, or sketches-sufficient to give us a clear idea of what to expect in the finished piece. Once we've made any adjustments to the project concept and agreed on the details, you would begin work on the project instructions. It is possible to provide the design and written instructions and have us outsource the actual knitting.

The manuscript should be computer-generated and submitted on a 3/12-inch disk. Include a hard-copy of the manuscript as well; it should be double-spaced, on 8 1/2-by-11-inch white bond paper with at least a 1-inch margin all around. Our production is done on MS-DOS computers with Microsoft Word software, but we can accept and convert generic (ASCII) text files created with other MS-DOS software and most Macintosh computers. Label the disk with your name and phone number as well as program used to create the manuscript. Any special instructions or charts may be included on a separate sheet of paper. We will accept typewritten manuscripts if you do not have access to a computer.

Visuals

When you submit a manuscript in which you plan to include photographs of historical or other items, please send photocopies of those items with your manuscript. When you are providing visuals for an accepted article, please send samples of finished, publication-quality photographs (color transparencies or black-and-white glossies, please) or artwork. On occasion, it may be best for you to send actual garments and tools for us to photograph. We will work together to choose what will best suit the story and make sure all pieces are transported safely. All photographs, artwork, and other materials will be returned promptly and appropriately insured. If you are knitting or supervising the knitting of the project that will accompany your article, please send the article to us for photographing. Projects will be photographed and retained by Interweave Press unless other arrangements are made.

Acceptance, Editing, and Payment

Receipt of your submission will be promptly acknowledged, but we may not be able to make a decision about its use right away. Please be patient.

When we pay for accepted material, we purchase first North American serial rights for publication in *Interweave Knits* and subsequent nonexclusive rights for use in other Interweave Press publications and promotions. The author retains the publication rights for the original materials. Payment for manuscripts is at the rate of approximately $100 per published page (approximately four manuscript pages or 1000 words) and is made upon publication unless other arrangements are made. Project instructions are contracted for separately. Before your work is published, we'll send you an agreement stating the terms of acceptance and payment for your approval.

We reserve the right to edit your material as necessary to fit the style, format, or other requirements of *Interweave Knits*. For feature articles and projects, a copy of the edited manuscript will be submitted to you for review before publication. Unfortunately, it is sometimes necessary to make further edits due to space limitations, and we may not always have the opportunity to appraise you of these changes.

Categories: Nonfiction—Crafts/Hobbies—Hobbies

CONTACT: Editors
Material: Queries or submissions
Interweave Press
201 East Fourth Street
Loveland CO 80537
Phone: 970-669-7672
Fax: 970-613-4667
E-mail: knits@interweave.com
Website: www.interweave.com

The Iowa Review

The Iowa Review comes out three times a year (April, August, and December), carrying stories, poems, essays, and reviews. We look for the best writing available and are often pleased to introduce new writers. We also sponsor The Iowa Awards, an annual contest in our three main genres.

Unsolicited manuscripts are welcome during the fall semester only—September, October, and November. Unsolicited work that arrives at any other time will be returned unread. Work without a SASE— even if the cover letter includes an e-mail address—will be discarded. We do not consider e-mail submissions.

Entries for The Iowa Awards, given in fiction, poetry, and literary

nonfiction, should arrive during January. Please look for our annual announcements. Reading those entries occupies the remainder of our year. Outside judges name the winners, who receive $1000 apiece and are published, along with a gathering of finalists, in our December issue.

We purchase first North American serial rights, non-exclusive rights for any later Iowa Review generated anthology, non-exclusive classroom copyrights, and non-exclusive electronic rights for our web site, if we choose. We pay $25 dollars for the first page and $15 for each additional page, whether of poetry or prose. Contributors also receive two free copies of the issue in which their work appears and the remainder of a year's subscription.

Sample copies are $8, as are back issues when available. Subscriptions are $24 for one year, $44 for two, and $64 for three. Call our order department at (800) 235-2665 to charge your order to VISA or MasterCard, or send a check to the address below.

Categories: College

CONTACT: Submissions
The Iowa Review
308 EPB
The University of Iowa
Iowa City IA 52242
Email: iowareview.org

Iris
A Journal about Women
University of Virginia

Submissions

iris offers feature stories, fiction, art and photography, poetry, book reviews, news, and personal essays focusing on feminist issues for young women. We appreciate the diversity and activism found in fine writing, whether it be critical or creative. We are a nonprofit organization, staffed by undergraduate student interns and women interested in making a difference in the world around them. The magazine appears twice yearly, and each issue has a particular theme.

Call for Submissions!

Spring 2005, Issue #50

Milestones: The 25th Anniversary Issue

Iris is celebrating 25 years in print-what's your excuse to party? Dig deep to your roots and reveal the tantalizing tales and amazing achievements that have grounded your feminism. How, when, and where did the "f" word enter your life? What are your milestones? Reminisce about a long sought graduation, an unorthodox wedding, a valiant act of social protest, or the birth of your child. These are and have always been your pages-join us in writing iris's next chapter.

Final Deadline: December 1, 2004

Directions for Submissions:

For all nonfiction submissions, please submit two typed, double-spaced, clean copies of all material, and use language inclusive of differences in gender, sexual orientation, and race. Use short endnotes as needed, and provide a short bibliography at the end of the article when it is appropriate. Please use MLA style. Send an SASE for response; if you'd like your submission returned, be sure to include sufficient postage.

Feature stories and personal essays should run between 1500 and 2500 words. We are looking for timely, well-written pieces of political import or intellectual concern. These pieces generally fit into an issue's theme, so determine upcoming themes before you submit. Address submissions to Abby Manzella, Coordinating Editor.

Short news items should run 500 to 1000 words. We seek coverage of issues not generally addressed in the mass media, that relate to our theme, and fit into our twice-yearly publishing schedule. Address submissions to Abby Manzella, Coordinating Editor.

Film, book, music, exhibit, and other reviews generally run about 900 words for a single item and 1500 for a combined review. Address submissions to Abby Manzella, Coordinating Editor.**Fiction submissions** should run between 2000 and 6500 words-we rarely publish long pieces-and be typed and double-spaced. Please submit only one story at a time unless they are "short shorts." We prefer a point of view that reflects the diversity of women's experiences. We are seeking fiction that takes risks and that is not necessarily of the sort found in mainstream publications. While we always keep the theme in mind while selecting pieces, it is not our deciding factor for acceptance. Above all, the writing must be fresh and imaginative. Please address submissions to the Fiction Editor.

Poetry decisions are made with the goal of showcasing quality work from a variety of women's viewpoints. We seek vivid and surprising poems that take risks and teach us to see things in a new way. Though we do keep the theme in mind when making final selections, it is not our deciding factor in acceptance. Send no more than three poems at once, and please be patient as turnaround times can be up to four months. Please address submissions to the Poetry Editor.

Art submissions can include line drawings, cartoons, photography, or slides of other media. All work will be returned with an SASE. We are looking for original pieces that reflect the many facets of women's lives and stories. Please address submissions to the Art Editor.

Upon acceptance, please submit a copy of your piece, preferably as an e-mail attachment, in a format able to be read by Word for Windows. We also may ask you to submit a copy on an IBM-formatted computer disk. Additionally, we require a brief biography (two or three sentences). Upon acceptance of artwork, we will provide specifications for scanned images to be submitted on zip disk. You will be paid with five copies of the magazine in which your work appears.

iris acquires one-time rights to the printed work we publish. Accepted pieces may also appear in iris online. If you subsequently sell the piece to a reprint publication, remind the editors to forward a standard permission form to us and to acknowledge that the piece first appeared in our journal.

send all submissions to the address below.

We do not accept e-mail submissions, but you may reach us at iris@virginia.edu if you need information.

Categories: Fiction—Nonfiction—Book Reviews—College—Feminism—Gay/Lesbian—Multicultural—Poetry—Short Stories—Women's Fiction—Women's Issues—Writing

CONTACT: Submission Editor (specify genre)
Material: All
The Women's Center, PO Box 800588, University of Virginia
Charlottesville VA 22908
Phone: 434-924-4500
Fax: 434-982-2901
E-mail: iris@virginia.edu

Islands

Thank you for your interest in ISLANDS. The most useful thing a prospective contributor can do is read the magazine, which is available on newsstands or in bookstores. If the magazine is not available locally, we'll mail you one for $6 ($11 for non U.S.). Subscriptions cost $24 per year ($33 for non U.S.).

ISLANDS (8 times a year) is a travel magazine that focuses on islands around the world: urban, rural, tropical or windswept, well-known or virtually undiscovered. We strive for geographical and topical diversity and encourage articles with a well-defined focus and point of view. Our purpose is, in effect, to take the reader to the island. To that end, we seek informative, insightful, personal pieces that reveal the essence of the place.

In every issue there are usually several feature articles, ranging from 2,500 to 4,000 words. There are also occasional shorter features of about 1,500 to 2,000 words.

Front-of-the-book sections include Art Beat (columns on the arts), with brief book and record reviews (staff written), short profiles, and Q & As with artists and writers, as well as short pieces on museums, films, and other arts topics. Crossroads includes regular columns by contributing editors on the Caribbean and Hawaii, as well as department-length pieces (750-1500 words) on slices of island life. These can be essays or narrative experiences - profiles or topics that range from sports to nature to encounters with islanders.

The Guide is our back-of-the-book section of service information. Within The Guide, Bearings relates specifically to the features and is staff-written. Insider (850 words) is a Top 10 list of not-to-be-missed (but not overly obvious) things to do in on-the-beaten track island destinations. IslandWise pieces (up to 500 words) showcase a great place to stay, eat, or hike; a tour to take or a new thing to do; even a whole island experience. For a hotels or restaurant to be an appropriate subject, it must be more than something new or luxurious. There must be a good story behind it, something that links it inherently to the island.

Prospective authors should submit material on speculation or send a detailed proposal of each article idea (no laundry lists, please), including an estimate of travel expenses (for features only) and samples of previously published work. Do not send query letters without samples of writing. In general, we look for accomplished feature writers with many assignments to their credit. Less experienced writers may have better luck submitting articles on speculation or proposing shorter pieces — Horizons, Crossroads, or IslandWise columns.

Be sure to enclose a self-addressed envelope with adequate postage to ensure the return of your material. Allow at least two months for a response. We receive a large volume of inquiries and need time to consider each thoughtfully. You may also send queries or articles on speculation via E-mail to editorial@islands.com. (We may request writing samples via regular mail.)

ISLANDS pays $.50 and up per word for articles. The fee is paid within 45 days of acceptance of the manuscript. If an assigned article is rejected, a kill fee of 25% is paid within 45 days of rejection. Contributors receive three complimentary copies of the magazine in which their article appears.

We hope you continue to enjoy the magazine.

HORIZONS Column

The "Horizons" section is great for writers and photographers with creative ideas, especially those relating to idiosyncratic events, people, activities, customs, news, oddities, etc. from islands anywhere. It's also a great place to break into the magazine.

This section is light, punchy, and varied. We often accompany the stories with humorous illustrations. Some pieces may be purely photographic.

Horizons is the place to use the stuff that didn't quite fit into a feature story; it's a home for intriguing and amusing items you happen to find. The scope is as wide as the horizon, so while the headings below are useful as guidelines let them be your outer limit.

Features: Solid short subjects of up to 200 words, with lively leads and headlines. *Sample subject:* The nation's top private security expert has moved to Fiji to study this peaceful society and bring its lessons home to the U.S. The headline could be: "Peace and Love Man." Subhead: "Why is the world's smartest bodyguard (Madonna, etc.) living in Fiji? To find out why a society needs no bodyguards."

Other elements: These range from creative visual presentations to text pieces of 25-150 words. You can submit ideas and concepts, and/or write the finished products. Imaginative graphic suggestions can "sell" an idea. Example: "Lipstick Sunset," an illustration of a tropical sunset done in hot shades of lipstick - with a chart showing the SPFs and skin-moisturizing benefits of various brands.

Reader Interaction: Designed to get readers involved. Examples: Contests (e.g., writing a caption for a desert-island cartoon). Island travel tips. Responses to editorial queries (the most romantic island you've visited?). All ideas welcome (and paid for if used).

Celebrity Connections: Film or TV star, director, writer, musician, architect, fashion designer, explorer, chef, journalist, politician, etc.

Formats Ideas: Q & A. On a Desert Island: What a celebrity castaway couldn't live without ? and could. Top-five list John LeCarre's favorite London bookstores, surfing champ Kelly Slater's top island surf spot. On location: about a movie or TV show being filmed on an island (note: should have genuine story value in addition to celebrity angle). We also want newsy leads; e.g., Don Johnson bought an island in Vietnam and recently honeymooned there (we'd need details) and a way to verify the facts. Or maybe a celebrated person was on an island you visited, and you can supply information, island contacts, and great quotes. Editorially, this might be fashioned into an "island postcard" with a photo and a quote.

Photo features: A photo that conveys an intriguing "visual factoid" about an island. Format might be a single illuminating photo with a caption. A small group of photos on a theme: Pacific islander tattoos, London clubgoers, Japanese Elvises. A photo quiz: What in the world is this? preferably offbeat and revealing of an island culture, not a scenic. Humor and the unexpected are welcome in all categories.

Island Classics: A single "iconic" product, such as the perfect beach chair. Arrows and blurbs point out its features (e.g., "alloy frame weighs less than a Tom Wolfe novel"). Or a text-and-graphic exploration of a classic island subject. Examples: The Pineapple. The Volcano A-Z. A Perfect Zombie (i.e., the tropical rum drink).

PEOPLE:

Island Character: Photo and text that create a brief encounter with a worthy, funny, offbeat, or colorful personality.

Culture-Gram: Manners, customs, etiquette in an island culture. Several factoids that can be illustrated. Example: When visiting a village in Fiji, bring the chief a gift. Usually it's yangona, the root used to make kava, the national drink.

Locals Rule: Insiders' tips from island residents. Examples: Beach where a Waikiki beachboy goes on his day off. This could be verbatim, capturing a local voice.

Island Health: Health issues, prevention, remedies for island travelers. Could be a short item (see Briefings, below) or a more developed piece. Better as positive tips than frightening hypotheticals.

Life's a Beach: Highlights of a great island beach, with highlight noted.

Short-shorts: Tidbits that multiply the information and entertainment value of Horizons: Web sites for island travelers (with a brief review of what's special). Lingo (how the locals talk; lingo translator). Jokes (heard any good ones lately? must be island oriented). Factoids (quirky, fun items). Statistics (illustrating or ironic, as in *Harper's*). Verbatim (quote from writer, comedian, island character, etc. From the sublime to the ridiculous, but must be memorable). How an island got its name (e.g., why "Santorini"? what does it mean?) Briefings: News and updates on islands around the world. Can be almost anything: environmental news, quirky museum or attraction opening, natural-history update, money saver, travel tip , health news, or…

PAY

Ideas and leads: $25. These are ideas, graphic concepts, or leads that Horizons develops and uses.

Short-shorts: $25. About 20-50 polished words. You can send finished ones on spec., or just the idea for a go-ahead.

Non-feature pieces: $50-150. These are developed midsize pieces of 50 to 200 words (such as a celebrity Q & A, Culture-Gram, Life's A Beach). Please send a brief query.

Features: $150-200 for 250 words. Please send a query.

Photos: Standard rates, plus $25 if suggested concept is used.

Categories: Nonfiction—Travel

CONTACT: Mancy Maul, Editorial Assistant
Material: All

CONTACT: Allison Joyce, Senior Editor
Material: Art Beat, Islandwise
Islands Media Corporation
PO Box 4728
Santa Barbara CA 93140-4728
Phone: 805-745-7100
CONTACT: Jerry Camarillo Dunn, Jr.
Material: Horizons Submissions
6309 Carpinteria Ave.
Carpinteria CA 93013
E-mail: jdunn@islands.com (for Jerry Camarillo Dunn, Jr.)
Website: www.islands.com

Italian Cooking and Living

General Guidelines

Italian Cooking & Living is aimed at an audience that is not necessarily well informed about Italian food and culture but is interested in learning more. Our readers have little time for cooking, but they want to glean all they can and learn easy tips for impressive entertaining and dining. IC&L is overall a "guide"-type magazine that provides a savvy introduction to Italian cuisine and culture for the busy professional.

We are looking for qualified contributing editors to submit articles and accompanying photographs on relevant subjects. We only seriously consider articles that include photographs.

Main Article Subjects

1. TRAVEL to various locations in Italy, highlighting their most distinctive and significant features: the mountains, lakes, rivers, big cities (one or more of their aspects), towns. We usually make a distinction between a city article and a region article.

    a. In 70-80% of the cases, the photos must contain people. We try to present Italian cuisine and culture with the people that make it interesting. In other words, if the article is about Herculaneum, the images should show people in front of the ruins, walking around, holding interesting objects, eating (even someone enjoying a sandwich if there is nothing else), and perhaps selling souvenirs. The rest of the pictures should show the surrounding places and perhaps some from your arrival and any typical modes of transportation. A personal voice in the article is encouraged.

2. Articles on an INGREDIENT such as a cheese, meat product, or other ingredient specific to Italy and Italian cooking. These articles should have some of the aspects of a trip article and some of a purely food feature. These articles are to be 1000-2000 words, with 12-16 images (3 or 4 of which must be of dishes). The recipes must be included.

3. Articles on a cellar or producer of WINE, or on a specific wine. In addition to the images outlined above, you must also provide images of vines, vineyards, cellars, bottles, and labels. These articles are to be of 1000-2000 words with 10-14 images. The article must refer to a production zone (or IGT wine).

Photographs

Pictures of food must have natural coloring and succeed in capturing the beauty of the dish and its composition. They should be done with a large-format camera, or if of very high quality, with 35 mm film (100 ASA). We do not accept postcard-type photos.

The publisher reserves the right to examine services not specifically requested, whether photographs or complete texts, and will return them only if requested and provided with a SASE.

Conditions and Procedures

Any agreement made will be confirmed in writing and will outline the topic, images, price, and deadline to be signed by both parties.

The articles must be sent either by mail, fax, or e-mail to the managing editor, accompanied or preceded by the photographic images. The material must be unpublished. The author will be informed of the outcome of the manuscript in the shortest time possible. For the first submission, we would like a short biography of the author as well.

If the submission is accepted, it will be edited (or edited, translated, and edited again) and when possible, sent to the author for approval before publication.

The images that are accepted will be held from when they are received until after the publication of the article.

The payment of a fixed price for the service will be sent immediately after publication.

Categories: Cooking—Culture—Food/Drink—Lifestyle—Travel

CONTACT: Editorial Office
Material: All
230 Fifth Ave., Ste 1100
New York NY 10001
Phone: 212-0725-8764, ext.24
Fax: 212-889-3907
E-mail: stella@italiancookingandliving.com

Jack and Jill

Please refer to Children's Better Health Institute.

Jakes/Xtreme JAKES Magazine

Please also refer to *Turkey Call.*

JAKES Magazine is the NWTF's publication for members of its youth program, JAKES (Juniors Acquiring Knowledge, Ethics and Sportsmanship). The magazine is dedicated to informing, educating and involving youth in wildlife conservation and the wise stewardship of our natural resources.

All stories need to be fun and keep the interest of our readers (mean age of 10 years old). Feature criteria for *JAKES Magazine* should be either documentary or fictional with the emphasis on the outdoors, conservation, hunting, hunter safety, hunting ethics or heritage. Historical fiction must be accurate, including cultural and social accuracy. Stories run between 800 and 1,200 words.

Xtreme JAKES is a special section of *JAKES Magazine* for teenagers. This section's focus is to attract young readers to outdoor pursuits and to help them better understand their role in natural resource conservation.

Article ideas for *Xtreme JAKES* must be outdoor-related with an emphasis on education and entertainment. Topics may include traditional outdoor pursuits including hunting, fishing, hiking, biking, camping, etc., and also popular extreme sports such as snowboarding, rock climbing, etc. Typical articles run between 800 and 1,200 words.

Editorial coverage for *JAKES Magazine* is prepared three months or more ahead of each issue's release date. Magazines are published seasonally, with winter, spring, summer and fall issues each year. Article payment is negotiable, up to 25 cents per published word. Individual queries or laundry lists are acceptable.

We accept images that illustrate wildlife, conservation, colorful scenics, families participating in hunting and outdoor pastimes together and youth and their involvement in hunting. Check with the editor for current photographic needs.

Rates for published photographs:
• Cover = $400
• Two-page spread = $175
• Full page = $125
• Half-page = $100
• One-third page or less = rate negotiated by editor

Categories: Nonfiction—Recreation—Sports—Hunting

CONTACT: Matt Lindler, Editor
mlindler@nwtf.net
CONTACT: P. J. Perea, Managing Editor
pperea@nwtf.net

National Wild Turkey Federation
PO Box 530
770 Augusta Rd
Edgefield SC 29824
Phone: 803-637-3106
Fax: 803-637-0034
Web site: www.nwtf.org

Jam Rag

MISSION STATEMENT

Jam Rag exists to promote our local community of independent, creative musicians. *Jam Rag* strives to foster a creative environment, draw attention to talented independent artists in our area, and invigorate our local music economy.

We are not interested in major label bands or artists, even from Detroit. *Jam Rag* is about independent musicians.

We are not interested in bands from other areas. *Jam Rag* is about the independent music being created in our own home town.

For the most part, we aren't interested in cover bands. *Jam Rag* is about creative artists.

As a *Jam Rag* writer, you are allowed to set your own pace and your own direction. You work as hard as you want, as much or as little as you like. You can turn in stories every week, every month, or once a year if you like. You set your own deadlines. You write when it's convenient for you and when you feel like it.

And you choose your own stories. Unless you request guidance, we will never give you assignments. You decide which bands you want to cover, and how you want to cover them. You (for the most part) decide how long your article needs to be, and how it should be written.

Not only is this approach intended to make the job more fun, we also want *Jam Rag* to reflect a wide variety of personalities and backgrounds. Thus, by giving our writers this freedom, each brings their own unique character to the mix.

We try to give our writers as much freedom as possible. However, at the same time, we try to stay closely focused on local independent, creative music.

We're looking for stories on local bands, musicians and songwriters. We're looking for bands with an interesting story to tell, bands who are particularly talented, bands who've played a key role in our local community, etc. Who decides if a band is interesting or talented enough to deserve story in *Jam Rag*? You do.

We're not interested in articles on music in general, musical instruments or stereo gear, etc. We're not looking for how-to articles. We're not trying to teach local musicians how to play their guitar or how to make it in the music business.

We don't want potential readers to pick up *Jam Rag* and think, "This is a magazine for wanna-be musicians." We want them to pick up the magazine and realize there is a huge and fascinating world of creativity blossoming right in their own back yard. We interview local bands as if they are already stars—because, in our eyes, if they are contributing something new and creative to our collective cultural stew they are stars.

We are also interested in articles about local music-related businesses: studios, music stores, labels, clubs, etc. However, these articles should not serve as a plat-form for the subject to pitch their business. These articles should not appear to be a glorified ad. Instead, you might want to cover things like how the person got into the business, their opinions about local music, predictions for the future, etc.

Call or write for a complete copy of our guidelines.

Categories: Arts—Entertainment—Music—Politics—Society

CONTACT: Tom Ness, Owner/Publisher
Material: All
PO Box 20076
22757 Woodward Ste 240
Ferndale MI 48220
Phone: 248-336-9243
E-mail: jamrag@glis.net

Japanophile
Evoking the old and the new Japan

CONSIDER:

Japanophile takes the culture of one country as its only subject. Other literary magazines try to cover everything, everywhere.

Japanophile covers not only Japan, but Japanese culture as it's found throughout the world. One article may be about zen in New York City, another about a Japanese garden in Vancouver.

WHO'S IT FOR?

It's not just for the initiated few who are studying Japanese or who like to write haiku or who are taking classes in Japanese flower arranging or in judo or karate or for those who wonder about travel in Japan ... or any of hundreds of other approaches that may bring one to an interest in Japan. It's for virtually everyone who is interested in Japan and isn't satisfied with the snippets given on television and the press during a Presidential visit or an Imperial wedding.

JAPAN'S CULTURE

Japan culture is not a narrow, limited subject. Here are lively articles about a wide range of subjects: education, sports, literature, religion, art, architecture, international relations, politics, economics, painting, crafts, flower arranging, science, technology; and not just as they affect Japan, but the world.

***Japanophile*'s GUIDELINES FOR WRITERS**

Short stories may be up to 5,000 words and should involve at least one Japanese and one non-Japanese. Most stories used in the magazine are only 3,000 words.

We need:

1) Color or b&w photos with good contrast. 5x7 is large enough. We need drawings and cartoons. These can be simple drawings. We also like to see sumi-e.

2) Articles about Americans or other non-Japanese who are interested in Japan and its culture. A Michigan naturalist who is also a haiku poet was the subject of one article. Other examples: an Ohio man who collects netsuke, a North Carolina woman who has become a bunraku performer in Osaka, a Virginia potter who was an apprentice potter in Japan.

3) Poems in a Japanese form such as haiku. These may be about America or any place in the world. If a poem is not in a Japanese form it must be about Japanese culture. For example: a comic poem about a Kentucky man who rides a Honda motorcycle, a serious poem about racism as it has affected Japanese-Americans. A haiku about New York City may work for *Japanophile*.

4) Scholarly articles with authoritative quotes or a first person account of living or traveling in Japan may be acceptable if it has literary merit.

If you can write a column about a particular part of the United States or some other country as it relates to Japanese culture, you can become a columnist for *Japanophile*. For example: Japanese culture in London or San Francisco or Chicago. We already have a column called TOKYO TOPICS. Your sources include your local newspapers.

Payment for stories is $20 and sometimes an article gets that much, usually less. We pay $1 for haiku and the same for a funny filler. Cartoons and other art fetch $15 and up. All are payment for one-time rights and rights revert to the author.

A reading fee of $5 must accompany short stories entered in our annual contest. Payment for each published short story is $25 and rights revert to the author. A prize of $100, plus an attractive certificate, is awarded to the author of the best short story each year. This is in addi-

tion to $25 paid for one-time publication of the story.

It's best to study the magazine. Subscriptions are $14 for four issues and a single issue is $4.00. Add one dollar for a single issue sent abroad; foreign subscriptions are $20.

Include a short bio, i.e., "Ralph Smith taught English to Tokyo businessmen for two years. His poems have appeared in *Ploughshares* and *The Iowa Review.*" (A list of credits is not required.) Also, a disk (DOS or Mac format) of a text file or MS Word file is greatly appreciated, but not required.

Categories: Fiction—Nonfiction—Asian-American—Book Reviews—Poetry—Short Stories

CONTACT: Submissions Editor
Material: All
PO Box 7977, 415 Main St.
Ann Arbor MI 48107
Phone: 734-930-1553
Fax: 734-930-9968
E-mail: jpnhand@japanophile.com
Website: www.japanophile.com

THE MAGAZINE OF THE ORTHODOX UNION
Jewish Action

Jewish Action

Thank you for expressing an interest in our publication.

Submissions should cover topics of interest to an international Orthodox Jewish audience. Articles related to current ongoing issues of Jewish life and experience, human-interest features, poetry, art, music and book reviews, historical pieces and humor are all acceptable. Because the magazine is a quarterly, we do not generally publish articles dealing with specific timely events.

Articles should be double spaced, typewritten and should average 1,000-3,000 words, including notes. If used, notes should follow the article as endnotes. E-mail submissions are preferred. Mailed or faxed submissions are also acceptable. The author's name, address and daytime telephone number should be enclosed with the article. If mailed, a self addressed, stamped envelope is appreciated.

Authors will be informed of a decision within six-eight weeks of submission.

Jewish Action is published by the Orthodox Union, a non-profit organization based in New York City. See our web site at www.ou.org. Nechama Carmel is the editor of Jewish Action. The assistant editor is Diane Chabbott.

Categories: Jewish Interest—Religion

CONTACT: Submissions Editor
Material: All
11 Broadway
New York NY 10004
Phone: 212-613-8146
Fax: 212-613-0646
E-mail: ja@ou.org

Jewish Currents

JEWISH CURRENTS prints articles, reviews, fiction and poetry pertaining to Jewish subjects or presenting a Jewish point of view on an issue of interest. Pieces submitted should ideally be about 3 magazine pages in length, but in any case, should not exceed 4 such pages. (A magazine page contains approximately 600 words.) Submissions must be typed and accompanied by a SASE and a brief biographical note including the author's publishing history.

Finally, JEWISH CURRENTS is unable to pay its contributors beyond a year's free subscription plus six copies of the issue in which they appear.

Categories: Fiction—Nonfiction—African-American—Alternate Lifestyles—Biography—Book Reviews—Cartoons—Ecology—Economics—Education—Environment—Feminism—Government—History—Human Rights—Jewish Interests—Literature—Poetry—Politics—Psychology—Society

CONTACT: Editorial Board
Material: All
45 E 33 st - 4th Flooor
New York NY 10016
Phone: 212-889-2523
Fax: 212-532-7518

Joiners' Quarterly

Thank you for thinking of *Joiners' Quarterly*. While our basic interest lies in timber framing, we also pursue several topics that are relevant to natural and traditional building. We look for new enclosure systems such as straw bales, straw/clay and wood chips/clay, rammed earth, wheat straw panels, or any other new products that would be suitable for enclosing a timber frame.

We also look for articles on mechanical systems such as heating, air conditioning, solar, plumbing and electrical and how they can be applied to timber frame structures, whether it is an article about new innovations, historical uses, or simply installation techniques and precautions. We're always looking for articles on joinery techniques, timber frame design, CAD programs compatible with timber framing, engineering aspects whether modern or historical. Natural house building and whole house building systems also appeal to us.

Other topics: historical building techniques (especially if they are still viable today), hand-hewing, thatch, historic paints, barns, outbuildings, boats, innovative projects, new materials or equipment that would pertain to any of the above, green building. We also desire book and video reviews on any of the above subjects. The more relevant your articles are to timber framing and sustainable construction, the more likely we are to be interested in publishing them.

Payment is generally $50 per published page including photos and/or diagrams.

Manuscripts should be typewritten. Each page should have a page number, title of article, and author's name. Photos should be developed "glossy" and should be labeled with a suggested caption and ID info on back. We do not pay for cover photos.

Diskettes need to be Mac formatted in Microsoft Word.

Call for e-mail submissions.

Thank you,

Editorial Staff at JQ—Steve Chappell, Laurie LaMountain, Jim Marks, and Janot Mendler

Categories: Nonfiction—Architecture—Engineering—Environment—Sustainable Building—Technology—Timber Framing

CONTACT: Steve Chappell, Editor/Publisher
Material: All
PO Box 249
Brownfield ME 04010
Phone: 207-935-3720
Fax: 207-935-4575
E-mail: foxmaple@foxmaple.com
Website: www.foxmaple.com

The Journal of Adventist Education

The *Journal of Adventist Education* is the professional publication of Seventh-day Adventist teachers and educational administrators, worldwide, and should address topics of interest to that group.

The target audience may be teachers: elementary, secondary, or college/university level; or educational administrators. The Journal's constituency is international, a fact writers should keep in mind as they explore the implications or applications of a given topic. Special attention, where applicable, should be given to the concerns of minorities and students with special needs. Writers should define their target group precisely and address its concerns in a specific manner.

Articles by free-lance authors are welcome. Please submit an inquiry or summary of the article before sending a finished manuscript. The *Journal of Adventist Education* purchases first North American rights for each article it prints. Authors are paid upon publication of their articles. Amount varies, depending on length and other factors. Authors also receive two copies of the finished magazine in which their article appears. Articles may be translated and printed in the international edition of the *Journal* (French, Spanish, and Portuguese), and/or posted on the *Journal's* Web site.

Articles may deal with educational theory or practice, although the *Journal* seeks to emphasize the practical. Articles dealing with the creative and effective use of methods to enhance teaching skills or learning in the classroom are especially welcome. Whether theoretical or practical, such essays should demonstrate the skillful integration of Seventh-day Adventist faith/values and learning.

Periodically, issues will deal extensively with a single topic or issue. Articles representing various approaches or the in-depth discussion of aspects of the issue will be welcome.

Topics Preferred for *Journal of Adventist Education*:

• Call for action on some problem (drug use, need for physical activity, lack of computer access, minority graduation rates, violence, sexual harassment, teacher burnout and morale, hazards at school); with suggestions about how to solve it

• Addressing the needs of students with special needs-learning disabilities, physical handicaps

• New methods and approaches; applying educational research in the classroom

• Church projects related to education

• Classroom climate, interpersonal skills; counseling; discipline

• New methods and approaches, such as cooperative learning, multiple intelligences, individualized instruction, thematic instruction, etc.

• Educational administration

• Extracurricular activities

• Ideas for professional enrichment, staff development, teacher training

• Ideas for worships, religious activities

• Inspirational articles related to the task of the teacher, goals of Adventist education

• Integration of faith and learning

• Issues relating to multigrade and multicultural classrooms

• Legal issues in schools

• Marketing, promoting Adventist education

F-L

• Personal experience or inspirational articles (school-related)
• Pro and con on a controversial topic
• Relations with boards, parents, administrators
• Reports on innovative programs and projects or research on Adventist education
• School libraries
• Service and outreach activities
• Teaching techniques, innovative and practical methods of presenting specific topics and subjects
• Testing and assessment
• Use of technology in the classroom
• Clear, sharp, black-and-white photographs and appropriate charts and graphs are a welcome adjunct. Photos can be submitted as prints, slides, or in electronic format such as high-resolution scans or digital photos (300 dpi).

The *Journal of Adventist Education* is published five times yearly, with approximately eight articles appearing in each issue. Due to space limitations, many articles will not be published immediately. Articles should be submitted at least five months before publication date. The editorial staff reserves the right to edit all manuscripts as they deem necessary.

Please call, fax, or write the Editor before submitting an article, to be sure that the topic is usable and that the *Journal* has not printed anything recently on the same subject.

If the article has already been printed elsewhere, please include information regarding publisher, source, and date of issue.

When sending materials to the *Journal*, include the following: your name, employer, position as an educator or status if a student; Social Security number and home address if employed in the United States; and other contact information such as E-mail address and fax number. Please include a photo of yourself.

The following manuscript form is preferred:
• Articles should be six to eight pages long, with a maximum of ten pages in length, including references.
• Two-part articles will be considered.
• Material should be double-spaced, using a 70-character line and standard paragraph indention.
• Subheads should be inserted at appropriate intervals.
• Articles submitted on disk or by E-mail as attached files are welcome.
• Please store in IBM WordPerfect or Word format.
• If you submit a disk, be sure to include a printed copy of the article with the disk.
• Quotations should be clearly indicated. Please follow the instructions in *The Chicago Manual of Style* for bibliography and endnotes. Endnotes, in numerical order, should include complete bibliographic information: full name of author, title of work, volume and number if applicable, city of publication, publisher, year of publication (include month if a periodical), and page number(s). Please enclose photocopies pages to verify facts and quotations. The information to be photocopied is as follows: the page(s) on which the fact or quotation occurs, the title page of the book or journal, and copyright information. Authors should obtain permission for reprints of charts, graphs, and photos.

Writers are paid upon publication of their articles. In addition to financial remuneration, they will receive two copies of the issue in which their article appears, and may purchase additional copies (a discount will be offered on orders of ten or more copies).

All of the magazine's articles are copyrighted, and may not be reproduced without permission of the editor.

The *Journal* purchases first North American rights to all articles published, unless other arrangements are made. Articles published in the English edition may be translated into French, Spanish, and Portuguese for the *Journal's* international edition, and may be featured on the *Journal's* Web site.

Categories: Nonfiction—Christian Interests—Education

CONTACT: Submission Editor
Material: All

12501 Old Columbia Pike
Silver Spring MD 20904-6600
Phone: 301- 680-5069/5075
Fax: 301-622-9627
E-mail: 74617.1231@compuserve.com
E-mail: CookeC@gc.adventist.org
Website: www.education.gc.adventist.org

The Journal of Asian Martial Arts

MESSAGE FROM THE EDITOR
There are more aspects related to Asian martial arts than commonly meet the eye. Most publications have focused on this subject only to satisfy the interests of the mass market, while other scholarly writings limit themselves to a highly specialized audience. Our journal spans both types of readership. *How?*—Although the journal treats the subject with academic accuracy, we believe that writing styles need not lose the reader! *The Journal of Asian Martial Arts* offers a mature, well-rounded view of this uniquely fascinating subject, attracting a readership that has a close affinity to Asian history and culture.

Our journal logo stylizes the tips of a sword and pen—symbolic of the martial and the cultured. Entwined, they represent an embodiment of balanced characteristics that is necessary for individual and social welfare. Viewed in this perspective, the field of Asian martial arts offers a broad range of interrelated material to cover. Therefore, being both general and specific, our journal offers a unique display case for works by artists and writers. We appreciate your interest and thank you for considering our journal as a medium for your work. Feel free to contact me personally, the editor, regarding any aspect of the journal.

EDITORIAL POLICY
The Journal of Asian Martial Arts is a cover perfect bound 8.5" x 11" quarterly journal. We publish three types of materials: (1) scholarly articles based on primary research in recognized scholarly disciplines, e.g., cultural anthropology, comparative religions, psychology, film theory, and criticism, etc.; (2) more informal, but nevertheless substantial interviews (with scholars, master practitioners, etc.) and reports on particular genres, techniques, etc.; and (3) reviews of books and audiovisual materials on the martial arts. These three types of materials are organized in separate sections of the journal. In order to ensure the quality of all submissions in terms of scholarship as well as writing, each submission will be reviewed by at least two members of our editorial board. We look forward to making the journal accessible to all readers while establishing and maintaining a high quality of scholarship, writing, and graphics.

EDITORIAL CONTENT
Interview/profile—art/aesthetics—philosophic—announcements—cross-cultural—translation—media—reviews—comparative—geographic—technique—scientific—legal—weaponry—reports—social—historical—literary—health.

Article length: 2,000 to 10,000 words for feature articles.

Review length: 1,000 or less for news items, reviews and reports.

Buys: First World Rights with Reprint Rights.

Pays: For articles, $150-500 on publication, plus 2 copies. Payment in copies for reviews.

Audience: Although the *Journal* is targeted for college-level readers, it is distributed to persons of varied backgrounds, ages and occupations. For this reason, articles are written in a clear style for those who may not be totally familiar with the subject and its particular vocabulary.

Internationally distributed: practitioners, scholars, schools, libraries, bookstores, and institutes.

Reports: 2-4 weeks on queries; 1-2 months on manuscripts.

Bionote: Given. Include a short summary of your background and credentials (academic and martial) in your cover letter.

STYLE DETAILS FOR WRITERS
Writers should have martial arts experience and be very knowledgable in Asian culture. Query letters should tell of the writer's quali-

fications, provide a clear outline of the intended article, and state if illustrations are available. We pull our hair out when submissions arrive that simply rehash old material or are geared to the wrong audience! Articles are published for knowledgeable readers and must offer special information and insights not available elsewhere.

It is not necessary to provide clips, but a self-addressed stamped envelope (SASE) is appreciated, especially if you want your materials returned. We like to work with writers and are happy to provide suggestions on how to improve any materials that do not meet all criteria the first time through our office door. If you decide to submit a manuscript, have a martial artist and/or Asian scholar critique it first. Of course, the best guide for suitability is the *Journal* itself.

Reviews all articles on speculation. Double-spaced typed manuscripts or letter-quality computer printout acceptable. If possible, also provide text on computer disk in any basic word-processing program (Macintosh formats preferred). Articles must be historically and technically accurate with a list of references at the end. Keep footnotes at a minimum.

Romanization: Provide Chinese and Japanese characters when possible for important names, terms, and places mentioned in the article. Give personal names in the Asian order with family name first. We use Pinyin Romanization for Chinese.

DETAILS FOR PHOTOGRAPHERS & ARTISTS

We expect the quality of article illustrations to be of equally high quality as the articles we publish. The talents of a professional photographer should be utilized in order to meet the proper standards for printing. Most photographs and other illustrations should emphasize what is important to the text.

Special note must be taken when photographs are used to illustrate technical aspects of a martial art. Please do not include distracting backgrounds, such as school insignia or busy geometric patterns! A simple, plain background works best in these cases. We want to view the martial art, not studio decor or geographic scenery. However, we do encourage photographers to be creative whenever appropriate. Photos showing movement, a mood enhancing environment, or a particular social aspect are welcome whenever they portray a significant insight, feeling, or thought that relates to martial arts.

Material Requirements: We will only consider good quality black-&-white glossy prints, negatives, and color transparencies. Color photography is reproduced in black-&-white inside the *Journal*, but in full color if used on the cover. Contact sheets and photocopies of hand art can be submitted for preliminary review purposes.

Acceptance & Payment: Reviews art work on speculation. In the case of computer generated art, we prefer Macintosh formats, such as Quark-Express, Adobe Illustrator, or Photoshop. Rates vary, but are competitive with other publications of similar standards.

Model Releases: Photo model releases and captions are required for all photos.

Categories: Nonfiction—Arts—Asian-American—Culture—Health—History—Literature—Mass Communications—Military—Multicultural—Philosophy—Physical Fitness—Science—Sports/Recreation—Martial Arts

CONTACT: Michael A. DeMarco, Publisher
Material: All
Via Media Publishing
941 Calle Mejia #822
Santa Fe NM 97501
Phone: 505-983-1919
E-mail: md@goviamedia.com
Website: www.goviamedia.com

Journal of Modern Literature
Temple University

The editors welcome submissions of research-based studies of modern literature as well as critical studies based on scholarship. Papers should conform to the 1977 MLA Style Sheet. See recent issues for House Style variations. We require a disk in WordPerfect format for accepted articles. Essays will not be returned unless they are received with return postage.

Submit two copies of your manuscript.
Categories: Literature—Academic

CONTACT: Dr. Morton Levitt, Editor-in-Chief
Material: All
Temple University
921 Anderson Hall
Philadelphia PA 19122
Phone: 215-204-8505
Fax: 215-204-9620
E-mail: dmcmanus@nimbus.temple.edu
Website: www.muse.jhu.edu/journals/jml

jubilat

jubilat welcomes submissions of poetry, as well as essays and other forms of writing on poetry, poetics or—especially—subjects that have nothing to do with "poetry" but capture, in some way, a quality of poetic thought. Past issues have included work by Dean Young, Caroline Knox, Michael Burkard, Mong-lan, Matthew Rohrer, Jane Miller, Nathaniel Mackey, Paul Celan, James Tate, Claudia Rankine, Killarney Clary and Odysseus Elytis among many others. Please visit www.jubilat.org for complete submission guidelines, features from recent issues and other information.

Mail three to five poems and/or one prose piece at a time (mail genres separately). Poems should be individually typed either single- or double-spaced on one side of the page. Prose should be typed double-spaced on one side and be no longer than twenty-five pages. We do not publish short stories. All manuscripts and correspondence regarding submissions should be accompanied by a self-addressed, stamped envelope (SASE) for a response.

jubilat considers manuscripts year around.
Categories: Poetry

CONTACT: Jedidiah Berry, Managing Editor
Material: All
Bartlett 482
Dept. of English
University of Massachusetts
Amherst MA 01003-0515
Website: www.jubilat.org

Junior Baseball

Writers Guidelines

JUNIOR BASEBALL addresses the needs and interests of the youth baseball player, parent, and coach. Covering the 7 to 17-year old age range (with emphasis on the 10-14 year old experience), Junior Baseball is the magazine for the kids who play the game. Youth baseball becomes a way of life for those families involved, and the family aspect is emphasized, along with such wholesome values as sportsmanship, teamwork, pride, responsibility, and respect for others.

Features: Writers interested in contributing to Junior Baseball must be well-versed in the subject matter, as the readers are intelligent, and know their sport! Most articles for youth readers should be written on a fifth to sixth grade reading level. When targeting the youngest segment, text should be written for the second and third grade levels. Subject for the parent"s section should be intelligent, well-researched (if applicable), and appropriate for the eyes of the children who also read the publication (although not written to their level). All articles should be composed in such a way as to not sound like something that has been said many times before. A well-detailed story, full of supporting facts, figures, and anecdotes, makes for a better feature.

Articles can run from one to four pages in the magazine, depending on topic, depth, and scope. The addition of excellent photographs with a feature greatly increases its potential for publication. Fiction and poetry are not used.

Technical, Skills, How-To - The author should have extensive experience in coaching. A query with an outline and introduction is acceptable for discussion prior to a completed manuscript. Step-by-step photos are, in most cases, recommended to accompany a manuscript. Note that there are specific columns by regular contributing editors covering skills in each issue, so check with editor to avoid redundancy. (Approx. 1000 - 1500 words)

Leagues, Tournaments - Spotlighting a particular youth baseball league or organization, event, tournament with action described, results, highlights, photos. (Approx.1000 - 1500 words)

Industry - Featuring businesses involved in baseball, i.e., how bats are made (a visit to a particular factory), testing balls, the baseball industry, etc. Also historical, museums or collections. (Approx. 1000 - 1500 words)

Parents Feature - Topics of interest to parents of youth ball players, i.e., dealing with coaches, other kids, school, attitudes, pros and cons, etc. (Approx. 1000 - 1500 words)

ADULT LEVEL
YOUTH WRITERS:
"Player's Story" - Written by the kids themselves. One player per issue will tell about his best day, worst game, a lesson learned, etc. Should include his opinion - what he thinks, as well as his description of the experience. Articles must be written by the child; the editors will correct grammar if necessary. (Approx. 500 words)

DEPARTMENTS:
Most departments are handled by staff; however, we do accept freelance submissions for the following:

"In The Spotlight "- News, events, etc. Submissions must be newsworthy, accurate, accompanied with one or two photos. (Approx. 50 - 100 words)

HOT PROSPECT - Written for the 14-and older competitive player. High school baseball is the level targeted, and the focus is on improving the finer points of the game to make the high school team, earn a college scholarship, or attract scouts. Written to an adult level, approx. 500-1000 words.

COACHES' CLINIC - We invite coaches to share their favorite coaching tips, drills, practice methods, etc. Can be a short (100 word) tip, or a 500-1000 word article on more depth. You"re speaking to other coaches here.

Payment: The standard rate for text is 20¢¢ per published word, unless other arrangements are made. For reprinted articles, or work that requires extensive re-editing, the payment is half standard rate. ""In The Spotlight"" articles accompanied by photos (when applicable) pay $25 - $50. "Player's Story" pays $50. Coaches" Clinic pays from $50 to $100.

Photos: Well-focused and uncluttered photos are essential. Captions and identification of subjects are required. For features, color transparencies (35mm slides or larger), or color glossy prints (preferably 4" x 5" or larger) reproduce best. Do not write on back of photos with ball point or felt tip pen as ink ruins photos piled below.

COLOR PHOTOS: full cover $150, cover inset $50, double page spread $150, full page $100, half page $50-75, under 1/2 page $25-50. BLACK & WHITE: Not used unless period or vintage photo only available in B&W.

All Submissions: Preferred method of submission of a manuscript is by email (either as Microsoft Word attachment or text in body copy area of email to editorial@juniorbaseball.com . Also acceptable by mail are Macintosh formatted floppy disks, zip disks or double-spaced computer printout. Preferred programs are Microsoft Word, QuarkXpress, or Simple Text. No faxes please. The publisher assumes no responsibility for material submitted, but will exercise reasonable care. Junior Baseball buys all worldwide rights to manuscripts published, and any accompanying photos and artwork unless other arrangements are made. The publisher reserves the right to edit for clarity and space.

Inquires are generally answered within two weeks. Submissions may be kept on file for any length of time pending appropriate use, or can be returned if SASE is enclosed.

Correspondence: Do not send anything with an unsolicited submission, such as original photographs that cannot be replaced. Please do not fax unsolicited manuscripts. All submissions must be accompanied by a self-addressed, stamped envelope or will not be returned. Please direct all correspondence to the address below.

Categories: Nonfiction—Sports

CONTACT: The Editor
JUNIOR BASEBALL
PO Box 909
Canoga Park CA 91309
Business & Editorial Offices: (818) 710-123
email: editorial@juniorbaseball.com

Junior Swimmer

Please refer to *Swimming World* magazine.

Just Between Us

Just Between Us is a quarterly magazine for ministry wives, youth workers, missionaries, Christian educators, seminary students, social workers, Sunday school teachers, leaders in parachurch organizations and any woman, married or single, who wants practical, biblical encouragement and inspiration. Each issue includes several major feature articles, a special section centered around a theme, a number of regular features, and ministry how-to's and resources. The emphasis is on practical help, encouragement, and inspiration.

Our Readers
Writers for *Just Between Us* should keep in mind that they are writing for a diverse audience of ministry wives and women in leadership. *JBU* readers include women in mega churches and small congregations; they live in large cities and rural areas; they are Baptist, Methodist, Presbyterian, Assemblies of God, Episcopal, Pentecostal, Lutheran, and many other denominations. They are married to a person in ministry or are themselves serving in various leadership roles with all the unique challenges and opportunities that involves. Our readership also includes single leaders and both married and single missionaries on the field.

Our Editorial Needs
JBU articles should be personal in tone and full of real-life anecdotes as well as quotes/advice from noted Christian professionals. Articles should be practical and have a distinct Christian and ministry person perspective throughout. *JBU* seeks to apply the truths of Scripture to everyday life and ministry situations.

Major sections of *JBU* include:
Feature Articles take a topic of interest to ministry wives and women in leadership and deal with it in a practical and enjoyable manner. Word Count: 1,200 to 1,500.

Special Section Articles focus in on the theme of the issue (click here for the themes list). These articles take the theme and teach, encourage, instruct and challenge through biblical principles and application and illustrations that women in ministry can relate to. Word count: 1,200 to 1,500.

What's My Story? This is a short testimonial focusing on the theme of the issue. It is the personal face of the theme—what you have learned about that particular subject, how God has met you in your circumstances, etc. Word Count: 450.

Consult back issues of *JBU* for examples.

We do not accept poetry, fiction or book reviews.

Articles should be double-spaced and all paragraphs indented three spaces. (Please do NOT use the tab key to indent new paragraphs.) Preferably, send your manuscripts e-mail in a Word document or on a disk. In addition to the author's address, the first page should include his/her phone number and the word length. Manuscripts cannot be returned unless requested and accompanied by a self-addressed return envelope with the correct postage. Please allow four to six weeks for a response. Along with your submission, please include brief autobiographical information, including your current place of service, vocation, family, special ministry experience, etc. *JBU* is unable to provide financial remuneration, but will provide up to five complimentary copies of the issue in which your article appears. *JBU* uses the *New International Version* for Scripture references.

Sample issues are available at a cost of $4.00 each. Send your check, payable to *Just Between Us*, to: *Just Between Us*, 777 S. Barker Road, Brookfield, WI 53045. Unless you request otherwise, the most recent issue will be sent.

Categories: Women

CONTACT: Shelly Esser, Editor
Just Between Us
777 South Barker Rd
Brookfield WI 53045
Phone: 262-786-6478
Fax: 262-796-5752
E-mail: jbu@elmbrook.org
Website: www.justbetweenus.org

Kaleidoscope
Exploring the Experience of Disability through Literature & Fine Arts

Kaleidoscope Magazine has a creative focus that examines the experiences of disability through literature and the fine arts. Unique to the field of disability studies, this award-winning publication is not an advocacy or rehabilitation journal. Rather, *Kaleidoscope* expresses the experiences of disability from the perspective of individuals, families, healthcare professionals, and society as a whole. The material chosen for *Kaleidoscope* avoids stereotypical, patronizing, and sentimental attitudes about disability. Although the content always focuses on a particular aspect of disability, writers with and without disabilities are welcome to submit their work

The criteria for good writing apply: effective technique, thought-provoking subject matter, and in general, a mature grasp of the art of story-telling. Works should not use stereotyping, patronizing, or offending language about disability ("uses a wheelchair" not "confined to a wheelchair" or "wheelchair bound"). *Kaleidoscope* uses person-first language ("person who has cerebral palsy" not "cerebral palsied").

Kaleidoscope is published twice a year, in January with a submission deadline of August 1, and in July with a submission deadline of March 1.

Kaleidoscope accepts:

Nonfiction—Articles relating to the arts, both literary and visual, interviews, or personal accounts.

Fiction—Short stories with a well-crafted plot and engaging characters—5,000 words maximum.

Poetry—Poems that have strong imagery, evocative language—six poems maximum.

Book reviews—Reviews that are substantive, timely, powerful works about publications in the field of disability and/or the arts. The writer's opinion of the work being reviewed should be clear. The review should be a literary work in its own right.

Visual arts—Art of all media, from watercolor and charcoals to collage and sculpture; three to six works maximum. We accept art in 5"x7" or 8"x10" black and white glossy photos or 35mm slides, or color photos. The photos should have minimal background with the art as the main focus. Include captions on the photos stating the size, medium, and title of work. Also accepts art on CD.

Publishing information

• Considers unsolicited material
• Accepts simultaneous submissions
• Publishes previously published work
• Acknowledges receipt in two weeks
• Rejects or accepts within six months
• Accepts photographs or illustrations complementing work
  Double space work and number pages
• Reserves right to minor editing without author's approval; substantive editing with approval

Payment information

• Payment is made upon publication, and varies from $10 to $125.
• Contributors receive two complimentary copies of the magazine.
• Copyright reverts to author upon publication.

Subscription rates:

Individual—$10 per year
Institutional—$15 per year
Sample copy—$6, prepaid
Single copy—$6
Add $8 for international, $5 for Canadian (U.S. funds only) for postage and handling.

Categories: Arts—Disabilities—Literature

CONTACT: Gail Willmot, Editor-in-Chief
Material: All
701 S. Main St.
Akron OH 44311
Phone: 330-762-9755
Fax: 330-762-0912
E-mail: mshiplett@udsakron.org
Website: www.udsakron.org

Kalliope
a journal of women's art
Kalliope
A Journal of Women's Literature and Art

Kalliope is recognized as one of the best women's literary journals in the U.S.A. 2006 marks *Kalliope*'s twenty-eighth anniversary, which makes us one of the oldest feminist literary journals in the U.S.! Please support *Kalliope* in our effort to ensure that women's works will continue to be seen and heard.

Kalliope publishes poetry, short fiction, interviews, reviews, and visual art by women. We are open to experimental forms. Please submit poems in groups of 3-5; submit short fiction under 3,500 words.

Visual art should be sent in groups of 4-10 works. We require B&W professional quality glossy prints made from negatives. Please supply photo credits, date of work, title, medium, and size on the back of each photo submitted. Include artist's resume and model releases where applicable. We welcome an artist's statement of 50-75 words.

Please include SASE and a short contributor's note with all submissions. Foreign contributors must send U.S. postage or International Reply Coupons. Manuscripts without SASE will be neither read nor returned. Payment is usually in copies; a grant sometimes permits a small stipend. Copyright reverts to the author upon request. Because each submission is reviewed by several member of the *Kalliope* Writers' Collective, response time may be 3-6 months.

Thank you, in advance, for your patience.

Categories: Fiction—Book Reviews—Poetry—Short Stories

CONTACT: Dr. Margaret L. Clark
Material: All
FCCJ South Campus
11901 Beach Blvd
Jacksonville FL 32246

Kentucky MONTHLY

Kentucky Monthly

1. Query first, either e-mail, mail or fax. We try to respond within one month to queries. E-mail query to Stephen M. Vest at Steve@kentuckymonthly.com or Michael Embry at membry @kentuckymonthly.com.

2. We publish stories about Kentucky and Kentuckians, including those who live elsewhere. Among the subjects are history, fashion, art, profiles, travel, politics, bed and breakfast, restaurants, religion, and humor. Most cover stories run in the 1,500-2,500 word range.

3. We prefer a minimum editorial lead time of three months, but chances for publication are enhanced with longer lead time.

4. We publish fiction and poetry by Kentucky writers or Kentucky-related subjects. Fiction usually runs from 1,000-3,000 words.

5. State availability of photos with query.

6. Sample copy available at www.kentuckymonthly.com.

7. *Kentucky Monthly* is also listed in *Writer's Market.*

Categories: Nonfiction—Arts—Biography—Book Reviews—Campus Life—Civil War—Collectibles—College—Conservation—Consumer—Cooking—Crafts/Hobbies—Crime—Culture—Dance—Drama—Ecology—Education—Entertainment—Environment—Fashion—General Interest—Government—Health—History—Inspirational—Lifestyle—Literature—Music—Outdoors—Poetry—Politics—Regional—Short Stories—Sports/Recreation—Television/Radio—Theatre—Travel—Women's Fiction—Women's Issues

CONTACT: Michael Embry, Editor
Material: All
CONTACT: Stephen Vest, Publisher
Material: All
PO Box 559
Frankfort KY 40602-0559
Phone: 502-227-0053

The Kenyon Review

The Kenyon Review

An online submissions program is now available on our web site. We no longer accept work via regular mail. All work must be submitted using the online program on our web site. **(It's free and saves you postage.)**

We urge all submitters to be thoughtful of others and submit no more than two works in a given genre during our reading period. Thank you!

We consider
• short fiction and essays (up to 7,500 words)
• poetry (up to 6 poems)
• plays (up to 35 pages)
• excerpts (up to 35 pages) from larger works
• translations of poetry and short prose
• only previously unpublished material is considered

We do not accept
• unsolicited reviews
• unsolicited interviews
• simultaneous submissions

• email submissions (please use the online program on this site)
Tips and other helpful information—please read!
• Read our FAQ for answers to frequently asked questions.
• Unsolicited work may be submitted for consideration September 1-January 31. Review of submissions takes up to four months.
• Regarding translations, the original language work must accompany translations and the translator is responsible for author permissions.
• We generally follow the *Chicago Manual of Style* and *Webster's Tenth New Collegiate Dictionary.* Authors planning to use end notes and/or citations should download our guidelines (Acrobat Reader is required) or send a stamped, self-addressed envelope for our citation style guide before submitting manuscripts.
• If you are submitting poetry via our online program, please group up to six poems in a single document and then upload your submission. You will not be able to submit your poems individually.
• If you are using our online submissions program, please be sure to add the *Kenyon Review*'s email address (kenyonreview @kenyon.edu) to your spam blocker software so that you can receive correspondence from us.
• Payment for accepted work is made upon publication. Authors retain their copyrights and will receive a contract upon acceptance.

Categories: Fiction—Nonfiction—Arts—Drama—General Interest—Language—Literature—Multicultural—Poetry—Short Stories—Writing

CONTACT: David H. Lynn, Editor-in-Chief
Material: All
Kenyon College
104 College Drive
Gambier OH 43022
Phone: 740 427-5208
Fax: 740 427-5417
E-mail: kenyonreview@kenyon.edu
Website: www.kenyonreview.org

Kids' Ministry Ideas

Managing Editor: Tamara Michalenko Terry. Contact: Editor. 95% freelance written. "A quarterly resource for those leading children to Jesus, *Kids' Ministry Ideas* provides affirmation, pertinent and informative articles, program ideas, resource suggestions, and answers to questions from a Seventh-day Adventist Christian perspective."

Estab. 1991. Circ. 5,000. Pays on acceptance. Publishes ms an average of 3 months after acceptance. Byline given. Offers variable kill fee. Buys first North American serial, electronic rights. Editorial lead time 3 months. Submit seasonal material 3 months in advance. Accepts queries by mail, e-mail, fax. Responds in 3 weeks to queries; 3 months to mss. Sample copy and writer's guidelines free.

Nonfiction: Inspirational, new product (related to children's ministry), articles fitting the mission of Kids' Ministry Ideas. Buys 40-60 mss/year. Send complete ms.

Length: 300-1,000 words. Pays $30-$100 for assigned articles; $30-$70 for unsolicited articles.

Photos: State availability with submission.

Buys one-time rights. Captions required.

Columns/Departments: Buys 20-30 mss/year. Query. Pays $30-$100.

Tips: "Request writers' guidelines and a sample issue."

Categories: Nonfiction, children, inspiration, religion, spiritual

CONTACT: Tamara Michalenko Terry, Managing Editor
Material: All
Review and Herald Publishing Association
55 W. Oak Ridge Dr.

Hagerstown MD 21740
Phone: 301-393-4115
Fax: 301-393-4055
E-mail: kidsmin@rhpa.org

Kitplanes

Welcome to KITPLANES magazine's website and the fascinating world of homebuilt aircraft, currently the most dynamic segment of sport aviation. (Compared to factory-built certified light airplanes, many times more homebuilt aircraft are registered with the Federal Aviation Administration [FAA] every year.)

Now in its 18th year, KITPLANES is the premier periodical for people interested in the most dynamic segment of sport aviation: homebuilt airplanes, rotorcraft, ultralights and other special-interest, do-it-yourself flying machines.

The magazine features pilot reports on the best kitbuilt and plansbuilt aircraft, builder surveys on the most popular projects and annual directories of hundreds of current kit aircraft, plus homebuilder supplies and aviation electronics.

Every issue contains a wide range of topics from understanding aerodynamics to humor. Our objective with this website is to introduce the subject of building your own aircraft and provide enough information to help you decide whether to investigate this possibility further.

Writers Guidelines

Read this first. Thank you for your interest in KITPLANES magazine. Before submitting material, we suggest that you obtain a copy to the magazine and acquaint yourself with its style and content. Back issues are $6 postpaid. Call 800/358-6327 or 413/662-2610 (International). Your queries and submissions are welcome, but they may be in our hands for several weeks before we can evaluate them. We cannot assume responsibility for material submitted, but be assured that reasonable care will be taken.

Submission Format

First choice: PC- or Mac-compatible ASCII (text) files on a 3.5-inch floppy with a hard copy included as a backup. We routinely use Microsoft Word, so files in this format are also acceptable. We encourage articles via e-mail (address to editorial@kitplanes.com). An attached text file works well.

Color photos are preferred, but black-and-white photos are acceptable. Do not send negatives. High-resolution digital images can be used in some cases, but those need to be discussed in advance. Please send only sharp, professional-quality photos.

Necessary artwork (usually photos) and captions must accompany manuscripts. Technical artwork must be sharp and clear, drawn with black ink or drafting pencils. Drawings may be submitted in EPS, PICT or TIF file formats. Include versions both with and without text.

Please include your daytime phone number.

Payment: Payment depends on the length of the article as published, including artwork. Thus the more and better the art, the more we pay. The budget for first-time KITPLANES writers is $70 per page as printed in the magazine (this includes illustrations/photos). Thus an average feature that runs four pages will pay about $280. After your first KITPLANES appearance, the rate increases to $100 per page.

A photo used on the cover brings an additional $300. For covers, 35mm slides, vertical format, are the usual medium.

Categories: Nonfiction—Aviation

CONTACT: Dave Martin, Editorial
Material: Submissions or queries
8745 Aero Dr., Ste. 105
San Diego CA 92123
Phone: 858-694-0491
E-mail: editorial@kitplanes.com
Website: www.kitplanes.com

Knitting Digest

Knitting Digest
Please refer to *Creative Knitting* magazine.

Knives Illustrated
The Premier Cutlery Magazine

As the title implies, what we are looking for at *Knives Illustrated* magazine are factual, well-researched, knowledgeable articles about knives-preferably leaning toward a large quantity of photos showcasing a large number of knives.

The most important item above everything else is that what you write about knives must be INTERESTING!

1. It must interest you in writing about it because that will show in the story.

2. It must interest me to the point that I believe it will interest our readers.

3. Most important it must have the potential to interest our readers.

If you have not read *Knives Illustrated* or other knife magazines and are not familiar with the desires of knife readers, then you're probably not going to sell us an article. If you have a different approach, we're eager to see it and eager to publish it-but you do have to understand the world of knives as a base from which to start your new approach.

How to contact us: If you have a story idea, query first. E-mail will get you the quickest response.

Technical stuff: We can take your article electronically, but we strongly prefer PC-based articles. Do not attach as an automatically opening file via E-mail. If you send it on a floppy disk, make sure you have the floppy within a rigid container, and be sure you print out a hard copy of the EXACT file on the floppy (and note on the hard copy the exact name of the file on the floppy). E-mail me first that you are sending an article and attach as a download. My E-mail address is bruce@jbrucevoyles.com

Article Length: Use every word it takes to tell the story and not one word extra. If you use a lot of adverbs that end in "ly" you can often find another word. Note: We have no place for words proclaiming any knifemaker as to their ranking among other knifemakers. Everyone is "one of the best" and "one of the top makers" in someone's opinion. We don't pay by the word, so don't get crazy with the keyboard thinking you'll get more money. It might actually get your story turned down completely.

Photos: I know you may have a scanner, but I prefer to see the photos themselves as hard copies rather than electronic for a number of reasons, most importantly I can spread them all out at one time on a table-which I can't do with a computer image. If I

have a hard copy print or transparency, I can control more aspects of the photos. Color photos are preferred. (If I want it in black and white I can convert it that way, if it's sent in as black and white I can only run it in black and white.) No Polaroids! We need clear, crisp, in focus photos of the knives in full frame (don't cut the tip off). We only want shots of the knife. It would be seriously worth your while to pick up a copy of KI and see the types of photos we use.

General articles: Choose strong, dramatic subjects with a lot of photos. When possible, if the article is centered around a group of knives based on older versions (such as Bowie reproductions), photos of original Bowies etc. included adds more interest. We can supply some of those and on vintage knives as well, but be aware of that as a potential sidebar when writing such an article.

Profiles/Shop Tours: What we do not want is to be Knife People Illustrated. We do publish three to four profiles/shop tours per issue, but understand that just because someone makes knives doesn't mean they will merit a profile.

Again, and I can't stress this enough-it has to be interesting. It is possible for a knifemaker who is not making the best knife in the world to be the subject of a published profile provided he and his approach to knifemaking is interesting. SPECIFICS: On any shop tour we want to know the equipment the makers uses: brand specifics, speed and types of, belts, anything special or a different approach, steels, etc. However, this information is boxed and should not be included in the text of the story; use the words in the story to say something interesting about the maker or his methods.

Ethics: Do not use a profile as an excuse to get free knives. If we find that was a condition of the article we will kill it automatically. If a maker gives you a knife that's his business. If a knife is a condition of a profile or your writing about him that is our business, and will end in a rejection if we find out about it.

Also in your selecting subjects for profiles, the fact that they advertise in *Knives Illustrated* is a minor factor in whether a profile is accepted or rejected. At KI we do appreciate our advertisers, they are one of the things that keep us in business. However, from the editorial side our first obligation is not to our advertisers but to our readers. We produce quality editorial that attracts and keeps readers. Advertisers pay us for access to those readers. If we let advertisers direct our editorial we are letting the tail wag the dog, and in the long term we lose readers because of it, because we are not producing the editorial that the readers want. Magazines are edited for readers not advertisers. We must always use that as the first criteria.

We can break down the decision to publish into a scale as follows:
Out of 100 points:

• Is the article interesting?	60 points
• Is the subject newsworthy or significant	25-30 points
• Advertiser	5 points
• Other intangibles	5-10 points

Payment: Payment is upon publication, as all article payment vouchers are submitted to bookkeeping on the same day and issued at one time. If your story is accepted for publication, you will be sent a contract to fill out. No payment can be sent to you until the contract is filled out completely, so it is very important that you provide, when submitting your story, your entire contact information (full name, address, phone number, fax number, E-mail address) so we can contact you later. If you do not provide adequate contact information, and we can't locate you, payment may be delayed or you may not receive payment at all.

Categories: Nonfiction—Collectibles—Consumer—Fishing—General Interest—Men's Issues—Outdoors—Hunting

CONTACT: Bruce Voyles, Editor
Material: All
CONTACT: Jeff Howe, Managing Editor (send to the California address)
Material: All
265 S. Anita Dr. Ste. 120
Orange CA 92868
Phone: 714-939-9991, ext. 202
Fax: 714-939-9909

Kung Fu Tai Chi

Thank you for your interest in submitting your work to *Kung Fu Tai Chi* magazine and KungFuMagazine.com. Much of the magazines' contents are freelance-written. All submissions are reviewed for publication for either media, print magazine or web 'e-zine', unless you specify that your work is designated only for one or the other. However, our editorial board may opt to accept any given piece for one specific media only, and not the other. On occasion, unabridged versions of longer print magazine articles are accepted for the e-zine.

In general, we accept more experimental 'edgy' submissions for the e-zine. First person narratives such as travel logs, tournament reviews, media reviews such as recent films and articles that are over 2500 words are also directed towards the e-zine. Many authors find the print magazine to be more prestigious, but in fact, a well-written article can find a larger readership on the web since it is free access and does not fall victim to shelf life.

Topics: Topics should be of interest to advanced, traditional Chinese Martial Arts aficionado as well as the rank beginner of any style. We welcome articles on martial arts history, weapons, training, techniques, philosophy, well-known martial artists, and notable individual experiences. We are not accepting any fiction, poetry, personality profiles, comics or cartoons, or articles for or about children at this time.

Query Letters: If you have not written your article already, it is advised that you call, write or email to discuss your topic. This will save your time of writing an article on a topic which may not be right for the magazine or has already been covered.

Simultaneous Submissions: Simultaneous article submissions are not accepted. You may submit simultaneous queries.

Focus: Rather than generalizing about a topic in a superficial way, narrow your subject, find an interesting angle, and write an in-depth, information-packed piece. For example, instead of trying to fit your style's entire history into an article, you might write about how one incident changed the course of your martial art. Rather than writing about various kicks, for instance, one writer angled a recent story to explain how kicks can set the opponent up for grappling maneuvers. General topics such as "What is martial arts?" have been narrowed to a more specific focus, such as "10 Questions to Determine if You're Learning True Wing Chun".

Point of View: Most articles should be written in the third person. The second person form is sometimes appropriate for instructional articles. Use the first person only if the focus of the whole article is an incident from your life.

Attribution: If quotes or information are attributable to other sources, cite them within the story; do not use footnotes or end notes. Do not add "thank you to..." at the end of the article; if another person was an integral part of writing or researching the story, you may share the byline either as "by Jane Smith and John Jones", or "by Jane Smith with John Jones".

Author Information: Please provide brief information about yourself for "About the Author" section at the end of the article. This could include your martial arts style and rank, education, profession, city of residence, school, and teacher. Contact information is permissible. This is subject to editing. If no material is provided, it will be determined by our editorial board without your consultation.

Foreign Words and Phrases: Please italicize all foreign words and phrases throughout the text. On the first reference place a concise definition in parenthesis following, such as jian (straight swords), and provide the Chinese characters. All mandarin words should use modern pinyin Romanization. Other dialects such as Cantonese, Hakka, etc., can be preserved in their original spelling along with the Chinese characters. Chinese characters are mandatory.

Capitalize proper names of systems, but not the martial art itself, such as Fut Gar, Bak Mei Pai, White Crane kung fu. Words that appear in the English dictionary such as "kung fu, "tai chi," "karate" need not be capitalized or italicized. Capitalize names of organizations, ie: United States Kung Fu Association. Do not capitalize the names of weapons such as guandao, gun, qiang.

These rules may be disregarded for organizations and names that have previously established spellings in English, such as Jun Fan Gung Fu, but do not change the spelling within the text of the article, such as "Gung Fu," instead of "kung fu."

Photo Quality:

All articles must be accompanied by at least eight photos or illustrations. Photos must be in sharp focus, well-lit, and composed so that the main subject is not too small or cut off. Shoot against a neutral, contrasting background such as wall for techniques shoot. Do not shoot subjects against a background of trees, mirrors, equipment, signs, etc. All photos must be done with a matte finish, no glossiness. Digital photos must be submitted at full size with a minimum of 300 dpi for print.

Letters, News and Promotional articles: Letters, News and Promotional articles are not contracted or compensated. They are subject to editing.

Captions: Please provide a separate caption for each photo or illustration, including a separate caption for each photo in a sequence. Clearly identify people present in the shots, and clearly mark the photo order and which captions go with which photos. Photo credit should be included for each photo as well, either "courtesy of ..." or "photo by...".

Physical Guidelines: Articles should be between 1500 to 2500 words for print. There is no limitation on the word count for web submissions. Insert subheads where appropriate. Please avoid using the subheads "introduction" and "conclusion" within your article. That may be fine for technical or scientific writing, but is inappropriate for a popular newsstand magazine.

Technical Guidelines: All text submissions must be sent in a format that is readable by Microsoft Word for IBM. All photo submissions must be sent in a format that is readable by Adobe Photoshop for IBM. Both text and photos may be submitted by email, however separate the photos into separate emails, or compress them appropriately. E-mail submission is highly recommended. If submitting via regular mail, please include a hard copy of the article and the photos. Digital submissions are preferred.

Categories: Nonfiction—Asian-American—Culture—Health—Physical Fitness—Sports/Recreation

CONTACT: Gene Ching, Associate Publisher
Material: All
40748 Encyclopedia Circle
Fremont, CA 94538
Phone: 510-656-5100
Fax: 510-656-8844
E-mail: gene@kungfumagazine.com
Website: www.kungfumagazine.com

Kungfu Qigong Magazine

Please refer to *Kung Fu Tai Chi* magazine.

Kuumba

POETRY: *Kuumba* seeks previously unpublished verse of the highest quality. Your work should be well written and feature themes related to the experience of being black and in the life. You may submit up to five original poems at one time, but no more than one poem per page. All poetry should be typed, with line and stanza breaks clearly delineated. Include your name and mailing address. Tell us if you wish to use a pseudonym.

ILLUSTRATIONS: *Kuumba* also seeks line-art illustrations related to the experience of being black and in the life. These are typically images of two women or two men, but we are open to other possibilities. Acceptable media include pen-and-ink, pencil line, linoleum cut, woodcut, and computer-generated or digital illustrations that mimic these styles. We are less interested in illustrations that include tonal graduations such as watercolor or airbrush. We are not accepting photographs at this time. Submit photocopies of your work. Do not send originals.

DEADLINES: While we accept submissions year-round, submissions should be postmarked no later than February 1 to be considered for publication in the spring/summer issue, October 1 for consideration in the fall/winter issue.

RIGHTS: *Kuumba* secures first North American rights and the right to anthologize accepted work. You retain all other rights to your work. Payment is in four copies of the issue in which accepted work appears.

DELIVERY: Submission may be mailed to Editor, *Kuumba*, PO Box 83912, Los Angeles, CA 90083-0912. Please include a self-addressed, stamped envelope with adequate postage if you want your work returned. Submissions may be faxed to the Editor at 310-410-9250. Submissions may be emailed to: reggieh@blk.com. We usually respond within a month.

ACCEPTANCE: Individuals whose works are accepted for publication must provide *Kuumba* with a brief biographical sketch. Accepted poetry should, whenever possible, be provided on diskette in either PC or Macintosh format. You should provide the original or a reproduction-quality duplicate of accepted artwork.

LEGALESE: The Editors do not assume responsibility for loss of or damage to submitted materials. Publication of the name, photograph or likeness of any person or organization in articles or advertising in *Kuumba* is not to be construed as any indication of the sexual orientation of such persons or organizations. The opinions of *Kuumba* are expressed only in editorials. Other opinions are those of the writers and do not necessarily represent the opinions of *Kuumba*.

Categories: African-American—Gay/Lesbian—Poetry

CONTACT: Reginald Harris, Editor
Material: All
PO Box 83912
Los Angeles CA 90083-0912
Phone: 310-410-0808
Fax: 310-410-9250
E-mail: reggieh@blk.com
Website: www.kuumba.net

LA Architect
The Magazine of Design in Southern California

LA Architect is interested in articles on art, architecture and design topics with a Southern California connection. This includes all design disciplines including architecture, graphics, interiors, set design, etc. Articles normally emphasize design innovation or culture as opposed to technical or how-to. Our focus is contemporary and modern design.

Submit proposals electronically to jennifer@balconypress.com or mail to address below.

Proposals should include the following:
• Brief summary of the content.
• Proposed length of mss. and approximate quantity of illustrations, photos, etc.
• What is unusual about the topic and has it been published previously (if published, what was the slant?)
• 100-word author bio.
• DO NOT SEND MATERIAL WITH THE PROPOSAL YOU WANT RETURNED.

In general:
• Authors are responsible for providing all photos and permissions to be used.
• No advances or expenses are offered.
• Payment varies by piece.
• Proposals will be responded to within 1 month.

Categories: Nonfiction—Architecture/Design—Arts—Careers—Culture—Environment—Interview—Real Estate—Regional—Technical

CONTACT: Jennifer Caterino, Editor-in-Chief
Material: All
512 E Wilson, Ste 213
Glendale CA 91206
Phone: 818-956-5313
E-mail: jennifer@balconypress.com

The Labor Paper
Serving Southern Wisconsin

Columns are 200-500 words.
Submit by email.
Payment varies by piece.
Categories: General Interest

CONTACT: Mark T. Onosko, Editor/Publisher
Material: All
Union-Cooperative Publishing
3030-39th Ave., Ste 110
Kenosha WI 53144
Phone: 262-657-6116
Fax: 262-657-6153

Lacunae

Lacunae publishes comics, fiction, poetry, prose, reviews of independent music, film, fiction, comics and web sites. We are always open to new ideas and pride ourselves on versatility.

Please pay attention to the guidelines. They are important. And, if you are not familiar with the publication, take the time to read a copy to see if your work suits our needs.

Lacunae offers some of the writing and comics industry's best information, art, reviews and fiction. *Lacunae* is a great market for professional and never-before-published writers and artists. Published bimonthly by CFD Productions, *Lacunae* is distributed internationally, features full color covers and at least 32 interior b/w pages. Standard cover price is $2.50 USA.

Lacunae is for mature readers (not adults only). We don't publish full nudity, but we do present some mature themes. There is no requirement to submit mature or provocative manuscripts or illustrations.

SUBMISSIONS: Short stories, poems, columns, reviews, comics, illustrations, photography, among other forms of work are generally considered for publication year-round.

Fiction and poetry may be almost any genre (humor, horror, sci-fi, etc.), except no romance. Lengths vary upon submission and space availability. Generally, the cap on word count is 3,500. Please Note: *Lacunae* is overwhelmed with poetry submissions and is cutting down on the amount of poetry featured each issue.

Illustrative submissions should consist of a clean photocopy, and should be mailed, not e-mailed.

Reviews (of old and new media) must always include price, ordering address (if applicable), ISBN or other identification and other standard information (page count, media type...)

Submissions must be typed in a serif font (preferably Courier). Usual response time is 3-6 weeks, but this time may vary during certain seasons, depending on the influx of submissions. If you have not received a response in 12 weeks, feel free to alert us.

When making a submission, be sure to include full name and address on the first page of any manuscript, name on subsequent pages; full name and address on each page of poetry or artwork. A cover letter is required. When making an e-mail submission, include text as an e-mail message. *Lacunae* does not accept uploads of submissions.

PAYMENT: *Lacunae* pays in copies according to work (usually 5 to 25 copies) and great recognition in the comics and writing markets. Copies of each issue are sent to major publishers and agents in the industries. Writers and artists retain all rights to their work and *Lacunae* contracts allow for creators to republish their work in other publications after such works appear in *Lacunae*. Previously published works are OK, provided there is no buying of second rights on *Lacunae*'s part. No work may be published in *Lacunae* without a contract (provided by *Lacunae*).

REVIEWS: *Lacunae* accepts other publications—magazines,

comics, books, albums, videos, etc. for review. These will not be returned, but offered as giveaways to our readers. The creators or publishers of reviewed works will receive a tearsheet, but will be required to purchase an entire issue at a discount cost if desired.

COPIES: If there are questions as to whether your work(s) meet our specifications, we, as all publishers, recommend you review a copy of our latest issue. Those requesting guidelines may purchase the latest issue at $3.25 (standard cost, includes postage).

Anyone published in *Lacunae* requesting additional copies will be able to purchase them at a discounted rate.

QUESTIONS? Just ask!

THE CFD E-MAIL LIST: CFD Productions periodically notifies those interested of upcoming projects, calls for submissions and publishing schedules. To be included on the CFD e-mail list, send us your e-mail address.

Categories: Fiction—Entertainment—Horror—Interview—Music—Mystery—Writing

CONTACT: Pamela Hazelton, Editor
Material: All
PO Box 827
Clifton Park NY 12065
E-mail: judy@mediasi.com
Website: www.mediasi.com

Ladies' Home Journal

Thank you for your interest in writing for the Journal. While we do not have specific guidelines about subject matter or writing style, we do offer these suggestions:

Read Back Issues: We do not publish an editorial calendar, so familiarizing yourself with our editorial content and style will help you decide if your work fits our needs. Back issues can be found in the periodicals section of your library or purchased from our customer service department for $3 each (Call 800-678-2699). Do not send payment to our editorial offices.

We Have a Four Month Lead Time and seasonal material is usually assigned six months in advance.

Submit Queries Rather than Manuscripts: Keep your query brief - one to two pages - citing your lead and describing how you will research and develop your story. Be specific, and always direct your query to the appropriate editor, as listed on the masthead of the magazine. If you have been published before, send clips, your credits and a resume.

Always Include a Self-Addressed, Stamped Envelope: We will not respond unless an SASE is enclosed (with adequate postage for return of the manuscript, if so desired). We are not responsible for returning unsolicited material, so do not send original copies or photographs.

Payment, Story Length and Deadlines are discussed upon assignment and writers are paid upon acceptance. Average story length is 2,000 words.

We particularly welcome reader submissions for the following column: "First Person": Submissions should be approximately 1,500 words, written in the first person and typed double spaced. These must be true, personal stories about dramatic events. Enclose a self-addressed, stamped envelope and mail to *Ladies' Home Journal* at our New York address.

Submit Fiction Only Through a Literary Agent
We Do Not Accept Poetry of Any Kind

Please Do Not Call to Query or Follow up on a Submission: We read every query carefully, and do our best to respond as promptly as we can. It may take up to three months to receive a response.

We Cannot Provide Comments on Unaccepted Material: Due to the large volume of manuscripts we receive, we are unable to evaluate each writer's work personally.

Categories: Fiction—Nonfiction—Arts—Biography—Children—Consumer—Cooking—Crafts/Hobbies—Diet/Nutrition—Education—

Entertainment—Family—Fashion—Food/Drink—Gardening—Health—Hobbies—Marriage—Parenting—Psychology—Relationships—Self Help—Sexuality—Society—Travel—Women's Issues—Beauty—Medicine—Interior Decorating—Celebrities—How-to

CONTACT: Editor
Material: All
125 Park Ave. 20th Floor
New York NY 0\10017-5516
Phone: 212-557-6600
Fax: 212-455-1313

Ladybug
The Magazine for Young Children

About Us
For a sample issue of Ladybug, please send $5.00 to: Ladybug Sample Copy • PO Box 300 • Peru, IL 61354. NOTE: Sample copy requests from foreign countries must be accompanied by International Postal Reply Coupons (IRCs) valued at US $5.00. Please do NOT send a check or money order.

Ladybug, a magazine for young children ages 2 to 6, is published by Cricket Magazine Group. *Ladybug* features original stories and poems written by the world's best children's authors, illustrated in full color by the best children's artists from around the world. *Ladybug* measures 8" x 10", is full color, contains 36 pages plus a 4-page activity pullout, and is staple-bound. We hope that the following information will be useful to prospective contributors.

Published 12 months a year. Price is $35.97 for 1-year subscription (12 issues).

Manuscripts
Fiction: read-aloud stories, picture stories, original retellings of folk and fairy tales, multicultural stories. Length: up to 800 words. Rebuses focus on concrete nouns. Length: up to 250 words.

Nonfiction: concepts, vocabulary, simple explanations of things in a young child's world. Length: up to 400 words. (Be prepared to send other backup materials and photo references—where applicable—upon request.)

Poetry: rhythmic, rhyming; serious, humorous, active. Length: up to 20 lines.

Other learning activities, games, crafts, songs, and finger games. See back issues for types, formats, and length.

An exact word count should be noted on each manuscript submitted. Word count includes every word, but does not include the title of the manuscript or the author's name.

Rates
Stories and articles: 25¢ per word; $25 minimum
Poems: $3.00 per line; $25 minimum
Payment upon publication

Art
• *By assignment only.* Artists should submit review samples of artwork to be kept in our illustrator files. We prefer to see tear sheets or photo prints/photocopies of art.

• If you wish to send an original art portfolio for review, package it carefully, insure the package, and be sure to include return packing materials and postage.

• Author-illustrators may submit a complete manuscript with art samples. The manuscript will be evaluated for quality of concept and text before the art is considered.

• *Rates:* $500/spread ($250/page)

• Payment within 60 days of acceptance. We purchase all rights; physical art remains the property of the illustrator and may be used for artist's self promotion.

Comments:
• *Ladybug* would like to reach as many children's authors and artists as possible for original contributions, but our standards are very high, and we will accept only top-quality material. Before attempting to write for *Ladybug*, be sure to familiarize yourself with this age child.

• In evaluating manuscripts, we look for beauty of language and a sense of joy or wonder.

• PLEASE DO NOT QUERY FIRST.

• We will consider any manuscripts or art samples sent on speculation and accompanied by a self-addressed, stamped envelope. Submissions without a SASE will be discarded.

• Please allow 6 months response time for manuscripts, 12 weeks for art samples.

• We do not distribute theme lists for upcoming issues.

Ladybug **normally purchases the following rights:**

For stories and poems previously unpublished, *Ladybug* purchases all rights. Payment is made upon publication. For stories and poems previously published, *Ladybug* purchases second North American publication rights. Fees vary, but are generally less than fees for first publication rights. Payment is made upon publication. Same applies to accompanying art.

For recurring features, *Ladybug* purchases the material outright. The work becomes the property of *Ladybug* and is copyrighted in the name of Carus Publishing Company. A flat fee per feature is usually negotiated. Payment is made upon publication.

For commissioned artwork, *Ladybug* purchases all rights plus promotional rights (promotions, advertising, or in any other form not offered for sale to the general public without payment of an additional fee) subject to the terms outlined below:

(a) Physical art remains the property of the illustrator,

(b) Illustrator may use artwork for self promotion.

Categories: Fiction—Children—Crafts/Hobbies—Fantasy—Games—Music—Poetry—Short Stories

CONTACT: Submissions Editor
Material: Manuscripts
CONTACT: Suzanne Beck, Art Director
Material: Art Samples
CONTACT: Mary Ann Hocking, Permissions Coordinator
Material: Questions about rights
Ladybug Magazine
PO Box 300
Peru IL 61354 (after Mar. 1, 2007: 70 E Lake St, Ste 300
Chicago IL 60601)
Website: www.cricketmag.com or www.cobblestonepub.com

Lake Country Journal

Lake Country is one of the fastest-growing areas in the midwest. Each bimonthly issue of Lake Country Journal Magazine captures the essence of why we work, play, and live in this area. Through a diverse blend of articles from features and fiction, to recreation, recipes, gardening, and nature, this quality lifestyle magazine promotes positive family and business endeavors, showcases our natural and cultural resources, and highlights the best of our people, places, and events.

READERS
Most of the people who will read your articles live in the north central Minnesota lakes area as well as many in the metro or outstate locations. All have some significant attachment to the area. We have readers of various ages, backgrounds, and lifestyles.

EDITORIAL STATEMENT
After reading your article, we hope to have a deeper understanding of some aspect of our community, our environment, ourselves, or humanity in general.

Tell us something new. Show us something we didn't see before. Help us grasp the significance of your topic. Use analogies, allusions, and other literary techniques to add color to your writing. Add breadth by making the subject relevant to all readers—especially those who aren't already interested in your subject. Add depth by connecting your subject with timeless insights.

FRONT PORCH

In 100–400 words, amuse our readers with amazing facts, hints, tips, advice for solving problems, true stories that happened in our region, funny or clever things you heard someone say, humorous photos with clever captions, lists of the best of something, or ways to do something, or service information.

PROMOTIONS

Tell us about a unique product, business, or service available in our area. Send us 100 words and several photos or drawings to choose from. We will select articles that we deem to be of interest to our readers. Preference will be given to well-written and amusing or clever articles.

There is no charge nor payment for this reader service.

FEATURE ARTICLES (Query first)

1,200–1,500 words, General categories:
* How to . . .
* Local business trends
* Lifestyle issues
* Photo essay
* Phenomena of nature/wildlife
* Gardening
* Humor
* Local heroes
* Festivities, celebrations, local color
* Businesses that are contributing
* Local artists of world-class caliber to the community
* Fascinating people who live or have lived here
* Food
* Remarkable things people are doing or have done
* Cultural events or opportunities for involvement
* History of something in the area/landmarks (especially if there is a current tie)
* Investigation or issue-oriented pieces: not to dig up dirt, but to thoroughly analyze a trend or movement and challenge readers to pay attention to the direction our community is moving

ESSAYS

Thoughtful prose or drawings about life—particularly life in our region. Humorous, inspirational, or philosophical. We're looking for significant ideas, cleverly, or beautifully expressed. Essays: 600–800 words.

DEPARTMENTS (Query first)

Profiles

800 words capturing the uniqueness of a local resident.

Recreation

Choose an activity that may interest our readers. Focus on one location, but you may want to mention other good places in the area to do the same kind of activity. Note details such as costs, suggestions for when to go, what to pack, how to get the most out of the experience, mistakes to avoid. 600–800 words.

Healthy Living

Choose a topic of interest to both men and women relating to finding balance, dealing with stress, being one's best—physically and psychologically. 600–800 words.

Poetry

We are looking for short poems on regional subjects or written by local poets. A related photo or artwork is nice but not necessary. We prefer free verse poems that are tightly written and have several levels of meaning—yet are easily accessible to a popular audience.

Short Fiction

We like short stories by local authors or those which are in some other way relevant to our readers and our region. 1,000–2,000 words.

SUBMISSIONS

Send hard copy in standard manuscript form: double-spaced; name, address, and telephone number (include FAX number if available) in top left-hand corner; word-count and rights offered in top right-hand corner. If you are offering second rights, please give the name and location of the publication in which the work first appeared. We prefer to receive all articles on digital file. If necessary, we will work with "hard copy" but will deduct the re-typing costs from the contributor's payment.

We can work with either PC or MAC Files. It is necessary that you save the file format as either "ASCI" or "txt". This option will usually be in your save dialog box, under file format options. It is also possible to export your file by going to a command called "Export". If you have difficulty establishing these two options call us with any questions

E-MAILING AN ARTICLE

When e-mailing an article (which is a very effective method of sending to us), do not send it as an attachment. Please call up your article, select all, copy, then paste it directly into your open e-mail document. Then just send it. Our e-mail address is jodi@lakecountryjournal.com.

We cannot be responsible for your manuscripts or photos, so don't send us your only copy. If you want them returned, include a stamped, self-addressed envelope.

Categories: Fiction—Nonfiction—Arts—Business—Culture—Food—Gardening—History—Humor—Poetry—Short Stories—Regional: North Central Minnesota

CONTACT: Editor, Lake Country Journal
Material: All
PO Box 465
Brainerd MN 56401
Fax: 218-825-7816
E-mail: jodi@lakecountryjournal.com
Website: lakecountryjournal.com

Lake Michigan Travel Guide

Who We Are

LAKE MICHIGAN TRAVEL GUIDE is an annual magazine focused on Lake Michigan and its bordering states: Wisconsin, Michigan, Indiana and Illinois. LMTG features articles on unique travel opportunities and the interesting destinations that await readers, as well as that which will enhance their travel experiences along the lakeshore. From history, nature and adventure to culture, events, family fun, unique lodgings and restaurants serving fine and regional cuisine, this is the ultimate Lake Michigan traveler's guide. LMTG is produced by the editors of *Wisconsin Trails* magazine, and owned and published by Trails Media Group Inc., publisher of regional magazines, guidebooks and other publications.

Subjects

We're interested in the out-of-the-way and the popular (even widely traveled destinations hold surprises). The articles are meant to entertain and provoke readers' desires to travel to the featured destinations. *The LMTG format:*

• an upfront department on various subjects (see "The Lake Effect" guidelines)

• a full-length feature per state, focused on some aspect of that state

• a short feature, map/attractions page, lodging department, dining department and events department for each tourism region.

*The tourism regions within each st*ate:

• **Michigan**
Upper Peninsula: Menominee to Mackinac Island
Northwest: Mackinaw City to Ludington
West Central: Pentwater to Grand Haven
Southwest: Holland to New Buffalo

• **Indiana**
Michigan City to Whiting

• **Illinois**
Chicago to Winthrop Harbor

• Wisconsin
Southeast: Kenosha to Milwaukee
East Central: Port Washington to Manitowoc
Northeast: Two Rivers to Marinette, including Door County

Style

We are committed to stories of the highest quality, and expect lyrical, engaging magazine-style writing that takes you beyond just the nuts 'n' bolts of an experience or place. First-person is appropriate only for essay submissions. We appreciate a moderate use of the verb "to be" and welcome fresh, descriptive approaches. It is important that you write in an engaging, active tense and style that lets the reader join you in the experience. We expect that a story convey a sense of place-history, geography, environment, which all help set the scene. After reading your story, readers should know what they can expect from a visit to the highlighted destination or event-and what they will come away with. For example, if you're camping by a stream, we'd like to hear about the last thing you saw at night or the first thing you heard in the morning. What kind of creatures inhabit this place? If you're visiting the dunes, tell us what sort of impact the area and setting have on a person, what makes it special enough to send your friends there. If it's a piece on canoeing, biking, hiking, etc., we want a sense of the action-not a dull blow-by-blow rundown, but a vital account of the experience that lets readers join in the adventure. If you're writing about people, ethnic festivals or community events, we're interested in the spirit and interaction of people, place and culture, and what makes these events unique and exciting.

Currently we prefer stories on specific destinations near the shoreline-a great sand dune or state park, as opposed to a roundup of several great dunes or state parks. Sidebars accompany each story. They serve two purposes: to share specific trip details-how readers can make the same trip-and share other great similar destinations (i.e., roundup sidebars).

Length, Contract and Payment

Features vary from 1,000 to 2,000 words.
Payments: $300-$650.
Departments range from 75 to 1,000 words.
Payments: $50-$350.

We expect and accept only original work. We purchase first, one-time rights that last through 160 days after publication (the magazine will be on newsstands April to September). Flat-fee and by word payments are based on $.30/word and story length and difficulty. Expenses as discussed with and approved by the editors are reimbursed upon submission; receipts and an invoice detailing the expenses are required. (Unfortunately, there are no reimbursable expenses for the 2003 issue).

Submissions One-page written queries, with enclosed SASE, are preferred over manuscripts. Writers new to the magazine should enclose a letter of introduction outlining their writing, editing and publishing backgrounds and topics of interest. Published writers should include a resume detailing their writing, editing and other pertinent backgrounds, as well as nonreturnable published clips of their work (photocopies are acceptable). Please: We prefer printed material, so no e-mailed clips or referrals to Web sites. SASE required for return of any submitted materials. No telephone queries; we prefer written materials and/or e-mails we can share at editorial planning meetings. Response time is one to three months. Accepted stories must be furnished on computer disk or via e-mail as attached files in Microsoft Word or RTF; a double-spaced hard copy must also be supplied. A source list including names, addresses and contact phone numbers for sources is required, as are copies of background material used to research and write about the assigned topic.

LMTG Departments

Lodging (100-200 words per locale)

We feature up to five unique lodgings per region. Text should describe the lodgings what's unique about it, its amenities and setting, and who it's best suited to (families vs. couples only). Include price ranges for room rates, address, phone and e-mail.

Events (100-200 words)

We highlight two to five major events per region, plus a calendar of other notable events. Events must occur some time from April through August. Unusual festivals, places, exhibits, classes, heritage events and sites are of particular interest. The writing should be lively, capture the spirit of the event and invite the readers into a fun experience.

Restaurants (100-300 words)

These minireviews offer a glimpse into up to five of the region's restaurants. From cafes and diners offering down-home or ethnic fare, to fine dining establishments, each offers readers a worthwhile dining opportunity-whether it's just about a place that's the spot for cherry pie or an establishment that's the perfect place for a special occasion. These reviews are tightly written; describe the setting, atmosphere and fare; and mention any other notable aspects about the restaurant (for example, an interesting owner or noteworthy chef). Include price ranges for entr es, phone number, address, credit cards accepted, and whether reservations are required and if the restaurant is wheelchair accessible.

Previous restaurant reviewing experience preferred.

"The Lake Effect"—the upfront department
(100-1000 words per item)

An upfront department about other general travel opportunities within each of the four states. *For example:*

• a piece on the history of lighthouses on Lake Michigan with a sidebar on those open to tourists in each of the four states.

• a short piece on a great scenic drive in each of the four states

• a short piece on cruising, ferry and sailing opportunities on Lake Michigan.

Categories: Nonfiction—Adventure—Culture—Food/Drink—Nature—Regional—Travel

CONTACT: Knick Wood, Editor
Material: All
LMTG Trails Media Group Inc.
PO BOX 317
1131 Mills St.
Black Earth WI 53515
E-mail: nwood@wistrails.com
Website: www.wistrails.com

Lake Superior Magazine

Lake Superior Magazine is a bimonthly full-color consumer magazine which focuses exclusively on the Lake Superior region — history, current events, life styles, environment, tourism. Our long suit is outstanding photography accompanied by well-written and relevant editorial. We like to surprise our readers, and therefore will try to present an unexpected slant to the stories they'll receive in each issue. The magazine was established in 1979 and has since become the authority on Lake Superior living and travel. All submissions should support that concept.

As a regionally focused publication with national distribution, we are highly selective, considering only quality material. However, each year we accept a number of offerings from new writers and photographers. The strongest advice we can give is to read the magazine to understand our approach before submitting. Sample copies are not free. Send cover price ($3.95) plus $4.00 shipping and handling.

Categories (not all inclusive):

• *Photographs* — Our hallmark! As a complete picture essay or as illustrations for articles.

• *Illustrations* — Normally assigned, although freelance submis-

F-L

sions will be considered.

• *Cartoons* — Must be pertinent to the region and humorous.

• *Nonfiction* — Persons, places and events in the Lake Superior region (contemporary; historic with current tie).

• *Fiction* — Pertinent to the region or theme of an issue. (Only about two published per year.)

• *Departments* — Shorter articles on specific topics of interest (Nature, Wilderness Living, Chronicle, I Remember, Superior Science, Wild Superior, Haunted Shores, Heritage).

• *About the Boat* — Short articles and photographs about boats, ships or watercraft of note, and their crews.

• *Around the Circle* — Significant short items and photographs of interest concerning the condition of Lake Superior and the events and highlights from the region.

• *Destinations* — Short articles or features about places of particular interest to travelers.

• *Life Lines, Lake Superior's Own, Making It In the North* — Short articles about individual people who work and play in our region, their life styles and impact. "People who make a difference in our lives."

• *Lake Superior Living* — Articles about homes, life styles and construction.

Written Submissions

Lake Superior Port Cities Inc. receives many queries on duplicate subject matter. We reserve the right to accept or reject a specific query based upon quality, appropriateness and editorial subjectivity. We prefer manuscripts, although short queries, naming possible sources, will be considered. Submissions must be in writing. Please do not FAX queries or unsolicited manuscripts. DO NOT CALL. Do not send queries or manuscripts. Send a sample of your work. We do not purchase from queries. Submissions will be acknowledged, expect an opinion in three to four months following review by our Editorial Review Board. Although we plan a year or more in advance, articles are not earmarked for a specific issue of the magazine until they have been accepted. We cannot return material that is not accompanied by a self-addressed, stamped return envelope. You should retain a copy of all submitted material.

Persons whose manuscripts are accepted for publication must be able to assume responsibility for permission to publish photos and names of individuals and places. Secure written permission to protect yourself when appropriate. Short biographical information on the writer should always accompany the submission. If accepted, a black-and-white photo of the writer may be requested. When accepted, we may edit, abridge and condense the material as we may consider appropriate. As a rule, Lake Superior Port Cities Inc. does not consider material previously published.

Payment for Writing — We may pay up to $600, according to length, importance of story and writer's experience. Top dollar is earned by a well-written and researched manuscript-photo package. The average feature runs 1,600 to 2,200 words. Departments and Columns average 900 to 1,400 words and usually pay from $65 to $125.

Assignment — Lake Superior Port Cities Inc. publications are copyrighted. You will be asked to sign a standard agreement assigning some rights to your work. We generally ask for First North American serial rights and electronic rights and some Second serial rights in the case of reprints of our special publications. You will be notified before reprinting. First serial rights are reserved for 90 days following the first month of the publication. Payment is made upon publication. You will receive at least one copy of the publication in which your work appears, with additional copies available at wholesale cost.

Submission Appearance — Please double space and leave reasonable one-inch margins! Dot matrix computer printouts are acceptable if dark ribbon is used. MS-DOS ASCII, Windows95/98 and MAC disk submissions are acceptable if they are submitted with a legible printout, preferred when a submission is accepted. Most word processing formats can be accommodated, although software neutral files are preferred. Disks cannot be returned unless accompanied by proper postage. Place name, address and telephone number in the upper left-hand corner of every page of your manuscript with the total number of

words on the first page in the upper right-hand corner. Social Security number is required prior to publication.

Photographic Submissions

When you query, we suggest you send duplicates of good quality, if available. Lake Superior Port Cities Inc. will assume a maximum insurance liability of $10,000 per submission, so we advise sending duplicates only for approval. Please identify these as duplicates. However, only originals are used for final publication. Full name of photographer must appear on each photo or slide, or they will be returned without consideration. We will not apply your name to your material for you. Complete photographic identification must be on each photo or on an accompanying cutsheet, which includes subject ID, location and date taken. Photos must be numbered to coincide.

Lake Superior Port Cities Inc. cannot accept responsibility for material damaged during transit to or from the publisher. Enclose a self-addressed, stamped return envelope or box. Unless specified, material will be returned by the mode received to the extent covered by your postage, or by an insured mode convenient to us.

Formats

• *Black and White* — 5" x 7" or 8" x 10" glossies.

• *Color* — 35mm, 2 1/4," 4" x 5" or 8" x 10" transparencies preferred, although color-corrected glossy prints are accepted.

• *Digital* — at this time, size, resolution and quality limit use of digital photography. Considered on a case-by-case basis. Photographer has sole responsibility for rights of accessibility and acquisition, proper attribution and release for use of each photograph. Written permission may be necessary from the subject of the photograph, and at the very least should be held by the photographer for personal protection.

• *Payment* — Payment is made to originators of photographic works. We pay $50 for each usage, not based on size of use or number of pages. Cover photo pays $150. Additional use within the same publication, such as on the title page, at no additional payment. Combination writer/photographer stories may be negotiated as a package. Payment is made upon publication.

• *Assignment* — As with editorial material, you will be asked to sign a standard agreement assigning some rights to your work. We prefer photography being published for the first time. We ask for 90-day protection and electronic rights for all photography and illustrations used in magazines, 18-month protection for use in calendars or books. To protect our investment in color separations, we also ask for pre-assignment of republication rights. You will be notified before reprinting. You will receive at least one copy of the publication in which your work appears, with additional copies available at wholesale cost.

• *Ancillary Categories* — Lake Superior Port Cities publishes many additional products which require photography and artwork. Although photographic material submitted to the magazine is primarily considered for that publication, we also look for other uses. Some of the other products we produce are calendars, note cards, Christmas cards and books. We accept submissions for all.

All submissions MUST include an address, daytime and evening phone numbers, fax number, website and e-mail address as applicable.

Categories: Nonfiction—Adventure—Consumer—Regional

CONTACT: Konnie LeMay, Editor
Material: All
Lake Superior Port Cities Inc.
P.O. Box 16417
Duluth MN 55816-0417
Phone: 218-722-5002
Fax: 218-722-4096
E-mail: edit@lakesuperior.com
Website: www.lakesuperior.com

> *Remember: Editors change jobs and publishers change addresses. It is wise to invest in a phone call for the current information before submitting.*

The Lane Report

WHO WE ARE, WHO READS US

The Lane Report is an intelligent, enterprising magazine that informs readers and drives a statewide dialogue by highlighting important business stories in Kentucky. Founded in 1985, the monthly magazine has over 50,000 readers who fill the ranks of top business leadership and policymakers. While some content is produced by The Lane Report's editorial staff, roughly 60 percent comes from freelance writers.

What Stories Does The Lane Report Publish?

The Lane Report is about businesses, what shapes them and the people who make them run. Each issue contains five or more features touching on issues including economics, policy, tourism, small business and business trends. The story selection is balanced to fairly represent each major region of Kentucky, though some extra attention is given to Louisville and Lexington.

The Lane Report's editors are interested in well-written, insightful stories that shed light on the way business works in Kentucky. The magazine also highlights partnerships and collaboration between the business world and schools, universities and other public institutions. We particularly look for stories that illustrate notable trends within Kentucky's economy and business community.

We also keep an eye out for quirky, dynamic businesspeople who are innovating and changing the way business is done in Kentucky.

Ideas for most of our sections are generated by both the Lane Report staff and by freelance contributors.

Sections

A proposed piece should fit into one of these sections of the magazine:

FAST LANE BRIEFS: (100-400 words) – Recent news and trends and how they might shape the future.

OPINION: (750 words) – Opinion on a business or economic issue about which you, the writer, feel passionate and qualified to write.

ENTREPRENEURS: (750-1,400 words) – Profile of a particularly interesting or quirky member of the business community.

FEATURES: (750-3,000 words) – Major trends shaping the state; noteworthy business and practices; stories with sweeping implications across industry sectors and state regions.The Lane Report pays upon publication and buys all rights to stories as they appear in print. Compensation varies depending on the type of feature or department but is competitive with other magazines in the state.

How to Query The Lane Report

Send a query letter outlining your proposal and story by e-mail or regular mail to the editor listed below. Provide a clear understanding of the angle and a sense of the tone your piece would take. Show us your key interviews and research sources. Please include a resume and two to three representative clips of your previous work.

Please do not send unsolicited manuscripts. Search www.lanereport.com to make sure we have not recently run a piece on the topic you are proposing.

The Lane Report prefers a news analysis style, similar to most newspaper writing. It should be lively and engaging, even in mundane stories. First-person narrative should be avoided except when appropriate in opinion pieces.

From the time of assignment, writers have between one and two months to complete a story. Shorter FAST LANE items may have less lead time. Stories typically appear in print about three weeks after their final editing – good to keep in mind when pitching ideas.

Categories: Nonfiction—Business—Economics—Regional: Kentucky

CONTACT: Andy Olsen, Managing Editor
210 E Main St 14th Fl
Lexington, KY 40507
E-mail: aolsen@lanereport.com
Website: www.lanereport.com

Law Office Computing

Law Office Computing (LOC) is geared toward the technological needs of the legal professional, with an emphasis on legal software reviews, profiles of prominent figures in legal technology and "how-to" articles for attorneys looking to increase their computing knowledge.

This is a general guide for LOC writers, and may be modified on a case-by-case basis. In addition to these general guidelines, we commission the following three types of software reviews:

Short Reviews: 400 to 500 words per reviewed product.

Software Shootouts: 1,200 to 1,500 words for a two-product (or more), head-to-head comparison.

Round-Ups/Buyer's Guides: Eight to 15 products, 300 to 400 words per product.

Each type of software review article has its own specific guidelines.

Authors

We seek authors who have an understanding of the legal technology field, who often (although not always) are attorneys working with technology and who have the expertise necessary to write authoritatively on this niche subject. News stories and features may be contracted to professional freelancers with a legal or technology background.

Process

While we do consider unsolicited manuscripts for publication, it is recommended that authors first submit a query (article idea) via fax or e-mail. An editor will respond to your query within 30 to 60 days, and if LOC is interested in your idea, will assist you in crafting the completed manuscript.

Copyright

Manuscripts are considered for publication with the understanding that they are original material and are offered exclusively to James Publishing Inc. James Publishing buys First North American Serial rights on an exclusive basis; the non-exclusive right to use the article in electronic media and the right to use the article, your name, image and biographical data in reprints, advertising and promotions. We also reserve the right to return the article to the author for the addition of material, editing or rewriting under the original agreement. The editorial staff may reject any story deemed, in our sole discretion, unacceptable for publication. We reserve the right to edit any article.

Editorial Policy

We do not accept vendor-generated articles. Any work authored or commissioned by a vendor or vendor's agent (e.g., PR rep.) will be rejected. Authors, especially review authors, may not have any financial or other ties to the software they cover.

Tips

Feature articles should run from 2,500 to 3,500 words in length.

E-mail text as a Microsoft Word or WordPerfect attachment.

Text should be broken down with subheads as needed.

Use active voice and keep sentences brief and to the point.

We encourage the inclusion of sidebars, charts and other article supplements.

We may require screen shots of products reviewed or photographs of interview subjects. Please do not imbed these images in the text. Images should be separate attachments.

Do not use footnotes—incorporate the information into the text.

We prefer a casual style—feel free to use "I" and "you." Please use contractions (e.g., "don't" instead of "do not.")

Submit a brief (50 words) biographical sketch for inclusion with your published article.

Names and phone numbers for all sources quoted in your article MUST be provided to the editorial staff for fact-checking. ALL submitted materials are fact checked for accuracy.

Accuracy

Authors are responsible for checking and verifying the accuracy of the information included in their articles. Product versions, prices and contact information MUST be verified with the company for any software discussed or reviewed.

Payment

Payments for all articles are decided on a case-by-case basis determined by the article's newsworthiness, content, author's track record and a variety of other factors. Agreed upon payments include the article and all attachments (charts, sidebars, etc.) unless otherwise specified upon negotiation, and address all issues listed in these and other referenced guidelines. These fees also include any rewriting or additional materials the editorial staff may ask the author to include in order to round out the story or clarify existing ambiguities as determined by the editor.

Thank you for your interest in Law Office Computing.

Categories: Nonfiction—Business—Computers—Law—Technology

CONTACT: Jamie Ann Tyo, Managing Editor
Material: All
Law Office Computing
Phone: 714-918-1603
Fax: 714-751-5508

Leadership Journal

Writer's Guidelines and Shopping List of Articles We'd Like to See

How do I submit a query?

What is *Leadership* looking for?

Who reads *Leadership*?

What is *Leadership*'s personality?

How do I write a "how to" article?

Does *Leadership* prefer a certain style of writing?

How To Submit A Query: *Leadership* is written by our readers, so we welcome your ideas. Please send a brief query letter describing your idea and how you plan to develop it. We will respond as quickly as possible—almost always within two weeks.

Send your query to:Marshall Shelley, Executive Editor, LJeditor@LeadershipJournal.net.

Put your name, address, and telephone numbers, and your church name and address, and your position at the top of the e-mail. Please put your query in the body of the e-mail. Please do not send a file attachment. We do not open attachments.

Or by mail: Leadership, 465 Gundersen Dr., Carol Stream, IL 60188.

Core Qualities of a *Leadership* Article: Each article describes real experiences, painting vivid scenes that those in ministry can identify with. Readers can see what went wrong and what went right—valuable lessons they won't have to learn the hard way. Writers must show they understand the complexities, joys, and pain of local-church ministry. Then they can offer right-to-the-point counsel on the practical issues: the conflicts, temptations, mistakes, and successes.

A fuller explanation of writing a "Leadership article" follows this list of article-starters. Be sure to read the Writer's Guidelines.

What Kinds Of Articles Is *Leadership* Looking For?

Leadership has two major sections and three departments.

Theme section. Half of each issue focuses on a single theme. Upcoming themes are listed below.

Non-theme section. Each issue has several non-theme articles of general interest. We look for articles on leading volunteers and staff, developing disciples, the pastor's personal life, solutions to church problems and problem people, true stories from personal experience.

Currents: a section on trends in ministry and ideas for ministering in the local church setting. We especially welcome "Ideas that Work," short accounts telling how a new idea worked in your church.

Sunday's Comin': a department on preaching and worship ideas, and illustrations. Short items are welcome.

Growing Edge: book reviews and new resources.

Upcoming Themes And Article Ideas: Half of each issue is de-

voted to a particular theme. Our upcoming themes include:

• Ministry in a Sexually Charged Culture

• State of the Leadership Art: How Can We Lead Today?

• Consumerism and the Ministry It Produces

• The Pastor's Family: Healthy Kids and Healthy Marriages in the Ministry Mix

• Going Global: Local Ministry with International Impact

• Preaching: Theology Is Back; Probing the Deep Things of God in a Postmodern Context

To spark your creativity, here are some ideas, but don't limit your thinking to these suggestions. Your experience and interests provide the best material for your article.

Non-Theme, Anytime Ideas

• Docudrama: the story you wouldn't believe if it hadn't happened to you. What happened? Tell it drama-style, and let the scenes tell us what you learned along the way.

• Homelife: Stories from the fishbowl. Tell the ministry episode that affected your family life and how you grew from it. Or, perhaps how your family life is affecting your ministry.

• Turning Point: A moment that changed my ministry. There was a moment when a relationship changed, an antagonist became a friend, the church grasped your vision, the momentum shifted. What was it? What did you do to bring it about? What have you learned from it?

• Learning to Lead: What I've learned about leadership recently. Did your latest plan work well or did it bomb? Is the vision you cast three years ago finally coming about? Tell us the transferable principles from your leadership experience that other pastors can use.

• Managing conflict. A church member blew up at you. She said she's just being honest. You said she's rude and out of control. Suddenly, everybody was taking sides. So what did you do?

• Team building: Training leaders and future leaders. How are you training deacons or team members or new staff members? What are you teaching them and in what setting. Tell how you're enabling others to use their spiritual gifts.

• The Pastor's Heart. Give us fresh insight into your ministry, something new you've discovered about preaching or pastoral care. What happened in a member's long illness or the crisis involving the youth department that made you love the calling even more?

Who reads *Leadership*? Who doesn't?!: Although a select group, *Leadership* readers represent a broad spectrum of denominations, degree of education, background, experience, and expertise. Pastors, church staff members, and lay leaders read *Leadership*.

What Is *Leadership*'s Personality? Practical, thoughtful, and (we hope) fun.

Every article in *Leadership* must provide practical help for problems that church leaders face. *Leadership* articles are not essays expounding a topic or editorials arguing a position or homilies explaining biblical principles. They are how-to articles, based on first-person accounts of real-life experiences in ministry. They allow our readers to see "over the shoulder" of a colleague in ministry who then reflects on those experiences and identifies the lessons learned.

As you know, a magazine's slant is a specific personality that readers expect (and it's what they've sent us their subscription money to provide). Our style is that of friendly conversation rather than directive discourse—"what I learned about local church ministry" rather than "what you need to do."

Our readers expect our articles to be fresh and candid, to reflect the honesty of the writer—describing disappointments and struggles as well as triumphs. Each article must balance "what went well" and "what didn't go so well." We find this allows our pastor/readers to identify more readily with the situation and gives the writer more credibility.

How Do I Write A "How To' Article?: Since *Leadership* articles help church leaders with pressing problems, they often take a how-to format. Here's how to structure the article in that format:

Select one problem that you and many church leaders have—and you've made progress in dealing with. You'll know you've gotten a topic defined when you can express it as "How to ..." For example, "How to help a congregation want to reach out" or "How to preach about hell to postmodern people" or "How to restore your soul on Monday morning."

Identify 2-7 principles, practices, and/or understandings that have helped you in addressing this problem.

For each principle, tell a story, from your experience or someone else's, that shows the principle at work.

Does *Leadership* Prefer A Particular Style?: Yes. Content makes an article worthwhile; style makes it readable. Unlike some journals that don't make the effort to develop compelling and lucid writing, we believe Leadership's impact is enhanced through fine and fascinating writing. We want to produce such a well-written, practical journal that the reader will always approach Leadership with a sense of anticipation.

Have you read *The Elements of Style* by Strunk and White? We recommend this widely read little paperback as a guide for style.

—Use action verbs. Forms of the verb "to be"—is, was, were, etc., make for dead writing. In every possible case, pick forceful verbs.

—Use anecdotes. Each point in a *Leadership* article needs a carefully chosen illustration, colorfully written. By basing principles in specific experiences, we show how to minister effectively amid the complexity and ambiguity of real life.

—Use short sentences whenever possible. Variety of length, of course, contributes to good style, but writers err more often with too many long sentences than short ones.

—Use long words only when necessary. Some critics claim scholars and professionals purposely write to obfuscate meaning, to cover fuzzy thinking, or to sound intellectual. Of this *Leadership* writers will never be guilty!

—Assume your reader bores easily. Remember, if he flips the page from lack of interest, you've lost! Keep asking yourself, "What grabs my attention? An illustration? A fresh insight? A well-turned phrase?" Keep the reader with you by introducing a constant stream of interesting material.

After writing your manuscript, go through it and see how many action verbs you have. Mark each noun you can taste, hear, see, smell, or feel. You can see hubcaps, handkerchiefs, coffee mugs, and lightning bugs. Good writers fill their prose with objects you literally see in your mind's eye. Be as specific as possible. For instance, "Toyota" is better than "car" for conjuring up an image.

We don't want to put a straitjacket on anyone; styles do differ. We are not looking for a formula type of writing in *Leadership*. But we are looking for a readable, commanding, and fluent style.

How Should I Submit A Manuscript?: After your query has been accepted, write the article. We welcome electronic submissions. When sending your manuscript electronically, you should include it as part of the body of your email and not as a separate attachment. Be sure to include full name, address, and phone number, plus church name, address and phone number, and your position.

If you submit a manuscript by mail, we prefer to read typed, double-spaced material submitted on 8½ x 11 inch paper (one side only). The full name, address, and phone number of the author should appear on the first page of the manuscript with the last name appearing near the number on each succeeding page. If we decide to publish your material, we will contact you for a copy of your article on disk.

Thanks for your interest in writing for *Leadership*. Send us a query, and let's get started.

Categories: Nonfiction—Christian Interests—Religion—Spiritual—Leadership

CONTACT: Marshall Shelley, Executive Editor
Material: Queries
Christianity Today Publications
465 Gundersen Dr.
Carol Stream IL 60188
Phone: 630-260-6200
Fax: 630-260-0114
E-mail: LJeditor@LeadershipJournal.net
Website: www.christianitytoday.com

Leading Edge Magazine

Rights: Leading Edge purchases First North American Serial Rights.

Needs: Leading Edge is a semi-professional magazine dedicated to the presentation of new and upcoming talent. We accept science fiction and fantasy short stories, novelettes, novellas, and poetry, as well as scholarly articles, book reviews, and interviews that deal with current popular authors. We do accept unsolicited submissions. We will not consider stories with sex, profanity, or excessive violence, or stories belittling traditional family values or religion.

No simultaneous submissions will be considered. No electronic submissions will be considered. All simultaneous submissions and submissions not containing a SASE will be recycled without reply.

Length: No longer than 17,000 words.

Art/Photo Needs: If you are interested in illustrating for the magazine, please send a disposable portfolio to our art director. To submit a piece for consideration as a cover, send a slide or print of the work along with a short explanation. Make sure to include a SASE with sufficient postage. Any questions can be e-mailed to us at tle@byu.edu. Do not send your art as attachments in e-mail, though feel free to send links to your artwork online.

Leading Edge will not accept material that contains nudity or vulgarity of any kind.

Payment: Fiction payment is 1 (one) cent per word, $10.00 minimum, $100.00 maximum, plus two contributor copies.

How to Submit: Send all fiction submissions to: Leading Edge Magazine, Attn: Fiction Director, 3146 JKHB, Provo, UT 84602.

Response Time: Response times vary, but generally fall between four and six months.

Sample Copies/Subscription Information: See the following page for detailed information: http://tle.byu.edu/subscribe.php

**Writer's Guidelines*: Leading Edge* is a semi-professional magazine dedicated to the presentation of new and upcoming talent. We accept science fiction and fantasy short stories, novelettes, novellas, and poetry, as well as scholarly articles, book reviews, and interviews that deal with current popular authors. We do accept unsolicited submissions. We will not consider stories with sex, profanity, or excessive violence, or stories belittling traditional family values or religion.

No simultaneous submissions will be considered. No electronic submissions will be considered. All simultaneous submissions and submissions not containing a SASE will be recycled without reply.

Because of our current backlog, expect processing time to be around two to four months. Any questions or comments can be e-mailed to our fiction director.

Manuscript Preparation: Your manuscript should be printed one-sided on white paper. Double-space and use an easily-read font, such as Courier New (12 point, please). Make sure that each page is numbered and has one-inch margins all around. The first page of your manuscript should include your name, street address, and e-mail address (if you have one). Include a cover letter that explains a bit about you and any publication credits you might have. Please always keep a copy of your manuscript for yourself! The postal system isn't perfect.

Include a SASE; if you don't, we have no way of responding to you. If your manuscript is disposable, just include a regular envelope with sufficient postage. If you would like your manuscript returned, include a manila envelope, again with sufficient postage. International submissions must be disposable due to difficulties presented by international postage.

Fiction: We buy First North American serial rights. We publish short-short to novella. Stories under 12,000 words are preferred, though we will consider up to 17,000 words. Because *Leading Edge* is interested in helping new authors to improve, each story is critiqued by at least two members of our staff; the "comment sheets" are returned to the author. If you do not want your story critiqued, let us know. Fiction payment is 1 (one) cent per word, $10.00 minimum, plus two contributor copies. Send all fiction submissions to: Leading Edge Magazine, Attn: Fiction Director , 4198 JFSB, Provo, UT 84602.

Scholarly Articles and Book Reviews: *Leading Edge* publishes nonfiction scholarly articles on such subjects as science fiction, science, fantasy, mythology, speculative anthropology, etc. Don't query to see if we're interested; we are. We're always in need of more nonfiction.

Scholarly articles should deal with real sciences, including physics, biology, chemistry, geology, or astronomy. We also welcome articles dealing with the social sciences, such as psychology and sociology. Literary reviews (such as issue 43's "Plato and The Matrix") are also encouraged. Basically, any well-written paper that explores science fiction or fantasy issues will be considered.

Book reviews (not book reports) should cover significant works published within the last year. Check out a back issue for sample book reviews.

Scholarly articles shouldn't run longer than 5,000 words. All sources must be documented using The Chicago Manual of Style. Book reviews should be between 500 and 1,000 words. *Leading Edge* pays two contributor copies for nonfiction prose. Send all nonfiction submissions to: Leading Edge Magazine, Attn: Nonfiction Director, 4198 JFSB, Provo, UT 84602.

Poetry: *Leading Edge* publishes two to four poems per issue. Poetry should reflect both literary value and popular appeal and should deal with science fiction- or fantasy-related themes. Payment is $10.00 for first 1 to 4 pages, $1.50 for each subsequent page of published poetry, plus two contributor copies. Send all poetry submissions to: Leading Edge Magazine, Attn: Poetry Director , 4198 JFSB , Provo, UT 84602.

Categories: Fantasy

CONTACT: Kristina Kugler
3146 JKHB
Provo UT 84602
Phone: 801-378-3553
E-mail: tle@byu.edu
Website: http://tle.byu.edu

Legacy

The National Association for Interpretation's premier publication, *Legacy* magazine offers a thoughtprovoking look at the field of heritage interpretation through articles about individuals who interpret natural and cultural history, biographies of important figures in or related to the field, discussions of interpretive sites, and trends in interpretation. The magazine, published six times a year, appeals to those interested in learning about natural and cultural heritage and interpretive sites around the world.

Freelance assignments for *Legacy* magazine must be approved through a query process. Please review the article descriptions below before submitting a query. Queries should be addressed to *Legacy* Managing Editor Paul Caputo at design@interpnet.com, or by mail at NAI's postal address. Manuscripts must be submitted as a hard copy and digitally as a Microsoft Word or Corel Wordperfect document. Manuscripts must include the full names, professional affiliations, and complete mailing addresses, telephone numbers and e-mail addresses for all authors. All necessary photo releases and permissions to use copyrighted material must accompany submission. Citations of other works should be incorporated into the running text rather than as a reference list at the end of the article. If you wish to include a reading list, provide it under the heading "For More Information" at the end of the story. *Legacy* follows *The Chicago Manual of Style*. *Legacy* will request copyright ownership (first North American rights) before publication. Final proofs of articles with multiple authors will be sent to the primary author only. *Legacy* does not maintain specific deadlines for receipt of materials for review.

WRITING

Feature (2,000–2,500 words) Subject matter for feature stories includes (but is not limited to) articles about sites or individuals that interpret natural and cultural history, interpretive themes (for example, comparing how various sites interpret similar subject matter), biographies, trends in interpretation, and the history of the field. Features should include quotes from a variety of sources. Authors must provide a minimum of six high-quality images in slide, print, or digital format. (Useable area of digital images must be at least 1350 pixels by 1350 pixels.) Freelance rate: $300.

Commentary (1,000 words) Takes a firm stance on thought-provoking, timely, or controversial subject matter relevant to the field of interpretation. Commentaries must address interpretive subject matter (i.e. interpreting religion, interpreting native cultures, etc.) rather than criticize a specific site. No images are required, but accompanying photographic or illustrative matter is welcome. Freelance rate: $150.

Profile (500 words) Focuses on an individual important to the interpretive field using a question-andanswer format (preceded by a one-paragraph introduction of the individual). Authors must provide at least one high-quality image of the profiled individual in slide, print, or digital format. (Useable area of digital images must be at least 1350 pixels by 1350 pixels.) Freelance rate: $75.

Visitor's View (500 words) Describes a visit to a specific interpretive site. Authors must provide at least one high-quality image in slide, print, or digital format. (Useable area of digital images must be at least 1350 pixels by 1350 pixels.) Freelance rate: $75.

Book Review (500 words) Offers a critical review of an interpretive publication. Authors must include bibliographic information in the following format: *Title*. Author. Year of publication. Publisher: City, State. Binding (softbound/hardbound), price, page count. Freelance rate: $75.

PHOTOGRAPHY/FINEART

Photo Essay Multiple-image series addresses the same subject matter as feature articles. Photographers and artists must provide a short blurb about each image. High-quality images must be provided in slide or digital format. (Digital images must be at least 1350 pixels by 1350 pixels, with at least one full-spread at 5250 by 3450 pixels.) Freelance rate: $300.

First Impressions (11" x 17") Full-spread photograph or other work of fine art addresses interpretive people, places, or events in an attractive and thought-provoking manner. Photographers and artists must provide a short blurb about the image. High-quality images must be provided in slide or digital format. (Digital images must be at least 5250 by 3450 pixels.) Images may orient horizontally or vertically. Freelance rate: $75.

Categories: Nonfiction—Culture—History—Nature

CONTACT: Editor, Legacy
PO Box 2246
Fort Collins CO 80522
Phone: 970-484-8283
Toll free: 888-900-8283
Fax: 970-484-8179
E-mail: www.interpnet.com

331 ANNETTE COURT • RHINELANDER, WI 54501-2902

The Leather Crafters & Saddlers Journal

We are always looking for how-to, step-by-step leather and saddle working articles of projects for all skill levels. Most of the details about the magazine are spelled out in *Writer's Market*, available at most libraries. We will not consider articles with religious symbolism, nudity, alcohol, controversial materials, or tobacco usage. Call for article project ideas and publishing information prior to submitting article.

Manuscript Prepartaion Includes:

1. Text: Please type text in upper and lower case *(not in all capital letters)* in MS word or simple text. Save text on disk or e-mail directly to projournal@mac.com and include the following:

    a. Short - 150 word autobiography regarding leatherwork.

    b. Title of article.

    c. List of toos and materials.

    d. A step-by-step description of what methods work best for completeing this project using Step 1, Step 2, etc.

2. Patterns: Draw pattern(s) using black ink on clean white paper with black type-set labels, or supply digital pattern in pdf, jpeg or tiff format at 100% actual size as an attachment along with the text to projournal@mac.com. *Include:*

    a. The pattern(s) sized at 100%.

    b. Carving designs and patterns.

    c. Alternative design pattern (where possible).

    d. Show sequence of tooling and/or coloring if applicable.

3. Photos: Digital photos need to be in pdf, jpeg or tiff format set at 300 dpi and files labeled according to reference within the textual body. Developed 35mm photos need to be labeled lightly on reverse side of photo. Paper photo print-outs are not accepted for publication but may be supplied as a hard copy to show labeling and captioning as a supplement to the digital or developed originals.

    a. Submit good contrast photos (slides are not accepted).

    b. Photos of project labeled as photo 1, photo 2, etc. that correspond with photo reference within the article text may be e-mailed or supplied on CD.

    c. Photos of project taken during construction must be clearly labeled.

    d. Photos of completed project numbered and captioned.

How to Send the Article: E-mailed articles are preferred. However, *call or e-mail to answer questions and we will work with you based on your resources.* Type article in MS Word or simple text only—do not type text in all capital letters. E-mail digital photos and pattern(s) as separate, jpeg, pdf or tiff attachments. Include your full name, phone number, fax, complete postal mailing address and e-mail address. *Note: All original photos need to be supplied separately. Photos embedded and laid within MS Word are not acceptable.* Please e-mail text, photos, and patterns together in one e-mail or send one complete package via postal mail.

The better the article is prepared and topic pre-approved, the better the consideration that it will be printed. We want only articles that include hands-on, how-to, step-by-step information of a project oriented nature. These pay up to $250.00, depending on several factors:

    • How complete and "digital-ready" is the article?

    • Are patterns labeled, type-set and finalized in black ink on clean white paper or supplied digitally?

    • Are text, photos, patterns, and print-outs supplied in an orderly, clearly understandable manner?

We buy first North American serial rights.

Postal mailed articles need to include appropriate postage and a SASE if article materials are to be returned. Otherwise, all article materials are recycled one year after publication.

Categories: Nonfiction—Consumer—Crafts/Hobbies—Hobbies—Trade—Leather

CONTACT: Rachel
Material: All
331 Annette Ct
Rhinelander WI 54501-2902
Phone: 715-362-5393
E-mail: projournal@mac.com

The Ledge Magazine

1. Reading period for regular submissions: September through May.

2. Submit 3-5 poems with SASE.

3. Reporting time: 3 months.

4. We recommend that you read a copy of *The Ledge* before submitting. The current issue is $8.95. A subscription is $15 for 2 issues, $28 for 4 issues.

5. No restrictions on form or content. We publish a wide range of work by poets of all backgrounds and persuasions. We seek exciting poems, compelling poems, poems with purpose, poems we can empathize with, powerful poems. Excellence is the ultimate criterion.

6. We consider simultaneous submissions but not previously published poems.

7. Contributors receive a copy of the issue in which their work appears. We send typeset copies of all poems to contributors for proofreading before going to press.

8. Send submissions, inquiries and orders to: *The Ledge*, 40 Maple Ave., Bellport, NY 11713.

9. Thank you for your interest in and support of *The Ledge*. We look forward to reading your work.

The Ledge **announces its 2005 and eleventh annual poetry awards competition.**

First prize: $1,000 and publication in *The Ledge*.

Second prize: $250 and publication in *The Ledge*.

Third prize: $100 and publication in *The Ledge*.

Complete guidelines:

1. No restrictions of form or content. Excellence is the only criterion. Unpublished poems only. Simultaneous submissions are acceptable.

2. Entry fee: $10 for the first three poems; $3 for each additional poem.

3. $15 subscription to *The Ledge* gains free entry for the first three poems.

4. All poems will be considered for publication in *The Ledge*.

5. Postmark deadline: April 30, 2005.

6. Include name and address on each poem. Include SASE for contest results or manuscript return. Winners will be announced.

7. Send entries to *The Ledge* 2005 Poetry Awards at address below.

The Ledge **announces its 2004 and eleventh annual poetry chapbook competition.** Winner will receive a cash award of $1,000, chapbook publication and 50 copies of typeset, perfect-bound, professionally printed chapbook.

Complete guidelines:

1. Submit 16-28 pages of original poetry with title page, bio and acknowledgments, if any. The title page should include name, mailing and e-mailing addresses (if applicable). Simultaneous submissions are acceptable and poets may enter as many manuscripts as they wish.

2. There are no restrictions on form or content. Excellence is the only criterion.

3. Entry fee: $15. All entrants will receive a copy of the winning chapbook upon its publication in the Fall of 2005. Sample chapbooks: $7 postpaid.

4. Please include a SASE for contest results or manuscript return. Winner will be announced in February 2005 and in the September/October issue of *Poets & Writers*.

5. Postmark deadline: November 1, 2004.

6. Send entries to: The Ledge 2004 Poetry Chapbook Contest, 40 Maple Ave., Bellport, NY 11713.

The Ledge **announces its 2005 fiction awards competition.**

First prize: $1,000 and publication in *The Ledge*.

Second prize: $250 and publication in *The Ledge*.
Third prize: $100 and publication in *The Ledge*.

Complete guidelines:

1. No restrictions of form or content. Excellence is the only criterion. Stories should not exceed 7,500 words Unpublished stories only. Simultaneous submissions are OK.

2. Entry fee: $10 for the first story; $6 for each additional story.

3. $15 subscription to *The Ledge* gains free entry for the first story.

4. All entries will be considered for publication in *The Ledge*.

5. Postmark deadline: February 28, 2005.

6. Include SASE for competition results or manuscript return. Winners will be announced in June.

7. Send entries to *The Ledge* 2005 Fiction Awards Competition at 40 Maple Ave., Bellport, NY 11713.

Categories: Poetry

CONTACT: Timothy Monaghan, Editor and Publisher
Material: All
40 Maple Ave.
Bellport, NY 11713

LEFT CURVE
Left Curve

Editorial Statement: *Left Curve* is an artist-produced critical journal that addresses the problem(s) of cultural forms, emerging from the crisis of modernity, that strive to be independent from the control of dominant institutions, and free from the shackles of instrumental rationality. In general we are interested in any form of work that can be readily reproduced within a 7"x9" format. We encourage open, critical, defetishized work that attempts to unravel, reveal contemporary (inner/outer) reality.

Articles: We publish fiction (traditional or experimental) and nonfiction texts (critical social, cultural, historical, philosophical essays, as well as reviews, interviews, journalistic pieces, etc.) that are concerned with issues that deal with our general editorial thrust. Length can be roughly up to 5,000 words, though most are about 2,500. Illustrations to accompany texts (photos, graphics, etc.) are welcomed.

Poetry: Most of our published poems are one page length, though we have published longer poems of up to 8 pages. We will look at any form of poetry, from experimental to traditional.

Visuals: We are interested in any form of visual work (reproducible painting, line drawings, traditional as well as electronic graphics, photography, visual/verbal art, etc.) that fit into our general editorial thrust.

Other Information: We make a serious attempt to personally respond to all submissions. Please allow at least 3 months response time. Our issues are published irregularly. For accepted work, we will let you individually know when to expect the work to appear. In general, payment for published work will be 5 copies of the issue in which the work appears for longer pieces, 3 copies for short works. In the event that we receive funding specifically for honorariums (which has happened once so far), payments will be determined on an individual basis depending on available funds. Sample copies of the current issue are $10, $10 for back issues. A list of published issues will be sent upon request with a SASE.

For accepted longer work we prefer submission of final draft on a floppy disk. E-mail submissions are also acceptable.

Categories: Arts—Culture—Literature—Multicultural—Poetry—Politics—Society—Cultural Critique

CONTACT: Csaba Polony, Editor/Publisher
Material: Fiction and Nonfiction
CONTACT: Jack Hirschman, Associate Editor
Material: Poetry

PO Box 472
Oakland Ca 94604
Phone: 510-763-7193
E-mail: editor@leftcurve.org

Legacy
A Journal of American Women Writers

Legacy is the official journal of the Society for the Study of American Women Writers. It is the only journal to focus specifically on American women's writings from the seventeenth through the early twentieth century. Each issue's articles cover a wide range of topics: examinations of the works of individual authors; genre studies; analyses of race, ethnicity, gender, class, and sexualities in women's literature; and historical and material cultural issues pertinent to women's lives and literary works. In addition, *Legacy: A Journal of American Women Writers* regularly publishes profiles of lesser-known or newly recovered authors, reprints of primary works in all genres, and book reviews covering current scholarship in the field. Periodically, the journal publishes conversations on provocative issues in the field and presentations of previously unpublished archival material.

Legacy: A Journal of American Women Writers is available electronically through Project MUSE.

Subscription Information
Semiannual
ISSN 0748-4321
Individuals $25.00
Institutions $40.00
Students $17.00
Single issue $13.00

For foreign subscriptions please add $15.00. Payment must accompany order. Make checks payable to University of Nebraska Press and mail to:

University of Nebraska Press
233 N 8th St
Lincoln, NE 68588-0255
or call: 1-800-755-1105 U.S. Orders and customer service.

Submission Information

Legacy: A Journal of American Women Writers welcomes essays on texts and contexts of U.S. women writers from the seventeenth through the early twentieth centuries. The journal seeks articles on individual authors' works; genre studies; implications of race, ethnicity, class, and sexualities in women's (con)texts; and historical and material culture issues pertinent to women's lives and literary productions. *Legacy: A Journal of American Women Writers* also publishes sections on "Profiles" of lesser-known authors and "Reprints" of notable works in all genres, as well as book reviews. The journal accepts articles for its "From the Archives" section, which focuses on letters and other previously unpublished archival materials.

Legacy: A Journal of American Women Writers accepts submissions that meet the following requirements:

• 10,000 words or less

• profiles no more than 2,500 words

• submit 2 copies accompanied by a self-addressed envelope with sufficient postage for return of the article

• prepare according to the latest *MLA Style Manual* .

Legacy observes a "blind reading" policy. The author's name should appear only on the title sheet, and references to the author's previous work in the text or the notes should be in the third person. Permissions and copyright fees, if any, are the responsibility of the author and should be arranged for and paid before submitting the article. Individuals whose works are accepted for publication must supply them in both paper and electronic form (IBM compatible, Microsoft Word, or WordPerfect).

Categories: Fiction—Nonfiction—Book Reviews—History—Literature—Multicultural—Society—Women's Fiction—Women's Issues

CONTACT: Prof. Sharon M. Harris (Texas Address)
Material: Manuscript
Department of English
Texas Christian University
TCU Box 297270
2800 South University Ave
Fort Worth TX 76129
CONTACT: Prof. Karen Dandurand (Pennsylvania Address)
Material: Profiles and Reprints
Dept. of English
Indiana University of Pennsylvania
Indiana PA 15705
CONTACT: Prof. Martha Cutter
Material: Book Reviews
Department of English
Kent State University
PO Box 5190
Kent, OH 44242-0001
Website: www.nebraskapress.unl.edu/journals.html

Leisure Group Travel

Please refer to Premier Tourism Marketing, Inc.

Leisure Travel Directories

Please refer to Premier Tourism Marketing, Inc.

Letter Arts Review

Letter Arts Review magazine (formerly *Calligraphy Review*) began publication in 1982 as a focal point for the exchange of calligraphic information. Published quarterly, *Letter Arts Review* has evolved into its current status as the primary international publication of record for the lettering arts. As such, *Letter Arts Review* actively encourages and welcomes submissions from practicing calligraphers, graphic designers, and lettering artists, as well as from professional writers, photographers and others with an interest in the related arts.

Audience
Letter Arts Review readers include calligraphers, lettering artists, graphic designers, teachers, students and individuals who appreciate the best in lettering.

Objectives
The only magazine in the field, *Letter Arts Review*'s objective is to serve the lettering community on many levels: *Letter Arts Review* offers the amateur and the professional informative articles on topics ranging from historical manuscripts to contemporary trends; *Letter Arts Review* presents thought-provoking viewpoints which stimulate inquiry into related topics; as well as quality reproductions which provide the serious student and the art lover with a valuable visual resource.

Format
Each 64 page issue (except for the Annual Review) has 4-6 feature articles plus up to 4 other columns.

Feature articles should be between 1,500 and 3,500 words unless otherwise agreed upon. Contents should be of lettering interest or related in nature. For instance, many of the book arts would be of interest to practicing calligraphers. Practical and conceptual treatments are welcomed, as are learning and teaching experiences. Third person is preferred, however first person will be considered if appropriate. Contributors should read current issues of *Letter Arts Review* prior to submitting queries or materials.

Topics of particular interest to our readers include:
• Profiles of past and present leaders in the field-this can be written in interview form, or third person. Several examples of the artist's work should be included;
• Manuscripts-reproductions of both contemporary and historical manuscripts appear in this section. Advanced and beginning calligraphers should be able to refer to this section as a resource. Color reproductions are often used;
• Creative process pieces;
• Ethical issues of specific interest to the lettering audience.
Columns should generally be between 500 and 1,000 words.
Topics include:
• Viewpoints: this department contains feedback from readers as well as input of new ideas and personal opinions on all aspects of lettering.
• Reviews: Reviews of books, exhibitions, or new type designs. Some reviews can be in-depth, others can be noteworthy.
• Other topics and new ideas will gladly be considered.
Guidelines for submitting work to be reproduced in full color in *Letter Arts Review*:
1. For best lighting and color-and to avoid the "Keystone" effect that usually results from using standard lenses and equipment—have your work shot by a professional.
2. When interviewing a photographer, look for one who is skilled not only in lighting and technology, but who also understands the limitations of printing. Look at their printed portfolio, not just their transparencies and color prints.
3. Whenever possible, submit transparencies (slide format, 2¼", 4"x5", etc.).
4. When shooting 35mm, use Kodachrome rather than Ektachrome for sharpness and color quality. When possible, use Kodachrome 25 because of its absence of grain.
5. When shooting 2¼" or 4"x5", use as low a speed Ektachrome film as possible—or Fujichrome films.
6. Open up dark shadow areas (even when shooting outdoors) by using fill-in flash.
7. Shoot at the correct exposure—as well as one f-stop underexposed and one-half and one f-stop overexposed. Indicate the one which best represents the color as you see it-but submit all transparencies to provide for the best reproduction at the separation and print stages.

Submission Requirements
Queries for all submissions are preferred. Unsolicited manuscripts and artwork will be considered.

Photography and artwork: Photographs and artwork/illustrations are an integral part of each issue. Considerable space is devoted to illustrative material. Black and white photographs, and color transparencies are preferred. Good quality 35mm slides are acceptable. Please arrange with our editor as to what would be required specifically. Captions indicating artist, title, medium, size and date must be included for each piece.

Payment: Manuscript rates range from $100-250 for feature articles depending on length and quality. Review rates are $50. Photography and artwork rates must be agreed upon.

All payments are mutually agreed upon in advance of commitment to publish. Payments are made upon publication.

Assignments: Assignments are made by written agreement. If for any reason *Letter Arts Review* does not accept an assigned feature after completion and submission on deadline, the contributor will be paid a "kill fee" of 25% of the mutually agreed upon payment. All materials will be returned to the contributor with all rights. When schedules permit, contributors will be given an opportunity to resubmit.

Sample Copies: A sample copy of *Letter Arts Review* is available upon request accompanied by a self-addressed 9"x12" mailing envelope with seven first class postage stamps.

Categories: Nonfiction—Arts—Graphics—Photography—Calligraphy—Lettering

CONTACT: Rose Folsom, Editor
Material: All
212 Hillsboro Dr.
Wheaton MD 20902
Phone: 336-272-6139
Fax: 336-272-9015
E-mail: lar@johnnealbooks.com
Website: www.johnnealbooks.com/lar

Libido
The Journal of Sex and Sensibility

Does not accept unsolicited submissions.

Life

Special Editions publication only. Does not accept unsolicited submissions.

Lifeglow

Will not be accepting additional manuscripts until 2009.

LifeWayonline.com

LifeWayonline.com will consider freelance articles, but does not pay for unsolicited content. If you are interested in having your work appear on *LifeWayonline*.com, please e-mail a brief summary to Lifeway@*LifeWayonline*.com. If we choose to use your submission, we can provide a hyperlink back to your Website, as well as a brief author bio. When *LifeWayonline*.com does pay for content, it is for specific assignments that we have commissioned.

About *LifeWayonline.com*

For many of you, the name *LifeWayonline* represents the brand name of our popular filtered Internet Service, and that will not change. You will still be able to find all the information you need at *LifeWayonline*.com to continue to benefit from our first class, family-safe Internet service provider. But, after listening to our customers, it became clear that there was so much more that we could offer. Thus, we are now offering our *LifeWayonline*.com subscribers and guests some of the best lifestyle content on the Web, in the form of articles from LifeWay's many family magazines, as well as in moderated on-line message boards and chats.

What makes *LifeWayonline*.com different from other online destinations? Unlike similiar Web sites, nearly all of the content you will read at *LifeWayonline*.com has been developed and published by the seasoned editorial teams here at LifeWay. When looking for "biblical solutions for life," it is important to find sources you can trust. LifeWay has been writing and publishing magazines, devotionals, and teaching guides for over 100 years. Where else on the Web will you be able to find over 100 years of trust? Nowhere else, but at *LifeWayonline*.com.

LifeWayonline.com is wholly owned by LifeWay Christian Resources.

Categories: Nonfiction—Christian Interests—Religion—Spiritual

CONTACT: Submissions Editor
Material: All
One LifeWay Plaza

Light

LIGHT is the only magazine available in this country devoted exclusively to light verse, satire, cartoons, parodies, and word-play. Published quarterly, each issue contains 64 pages of the best of well-known and new writers. (Our contributors include John Updike, William Stafford, Donald Hall, Michael Benedikt, J.F. Nims, Tom Disch, W.D. Snodgrass, and William Matthews, among others.)

• What's unique in this magazine is that it prints not only funny, topical, satiric and witty verse (both free-form and metrical), but that this verse is understandable by a literate reader, and enjoyable as well. Its pages are accessible, with large type-faces and elegant graphics. It also features light and literate essays and articles, gossip, prose satire and letters, and puzzles that are guaranteed to sharpen your mind and blunt your pencil.

Guidelines for contributors:

LIGHT seeks to continue the tradition established by the *Punch* of the 1890s, the *Vanity Fair* of the twenties, and the *New Yorker* of Ross and Shawn, of De Vries and Nabakov, of Thurber and E. B. White. While most of what we print will have meter, rhyme, or some combination of these, the ingredients we look for (apart from talent) are clarity, wit, humor, and understandability. A wide range of forms is welcome, from villanelles to rondeaux, triolets to sonnets, ballads to ballades, terza rima to ottava rima, as well as parodies, translations, pastiches, and occsional verse. *LIGHT* also prints essays and reviews; write for detials. Cartoons and line drawings are welcome. Dimensions should be less than 5" by 4". No washes or half-tones. Do not send your originals. Send only clean photocopies on good heavy-weight white paper with a 94 brightness or higher. Hammermill Laser Print #004640-4 is recommended. Submissions should be in black and white. Please note that almost no fiction is currently being accepted.

Please observe the following format *exactly:*

1. Poems should be printed on 8½ by 11 inch pages. Short poems may have more than one poem on a page.

2. In typescripts that extend beyond one page, your full name, mailing address, telephone number, and e-mail address (if you ahve one), should be on the first page. All pages that follow should have your name, the title of the piece, and a page number.

3. Poems of one page should have your name, address, telephone number, e-mail if available, and the title of the piece on the page.

4. Do not use exotic type fonts. Times Roman twelve-point is preferred; Courier (the "typewriter" font) is acceptable.

5. Put *one space only* between words, sentences, and after colons and semi-colons.

6. Include a self-addressed stamped envelope with all submissions and correspondence, making sure that there is sufficient postage to ensure your work's return. If you wish your rejected work to be recycled, please tell us so in a cover.

7. While we will request electronic copy of accepted work, please note that work should not be submitted via e-mail or fax.

8. Submit groups of 1-6 poems; longer submissions are discouraged.

Payment is in copies (two for domestic contributors, one for international) of the issue your original contribution appears in. International submissions shoujld include sufficient U.S. postage for their return or IRCs. Please allow up to six months for our response.

Subscriptions are $22/yr (4 issues), $34/2 yrs. (8 issues), international $38 (4 issues), single copies $6, and back issues/sample copies $5. For domestic First Class postage, add $2 per copy.

Send contributions, queries, subscriptions, correspondence to address below.

Categories: Fiction—Nonfiction—Cartoons—Comedy—Literature—Native American—New Age—Poetry—Short Stories—Writing—Humor

CONTACT: The Editors
Material: All

PO Box 7500
Chicago IL 60680
E-mail: lightquarterly@sbcglobal.net
Website: www.lightquarterly.com

Light of Consciousness
A Journal of Spiritual Awakening

Light of Consciousness is in its 17th year of publication. We welcome submissions of articles and poetry inspiring and interesting to spiritual seekers in today's world. A universal message or meaning is preferred but writing may derive from or illustrate a particular tradition. Contributions should be reader-friendly (non-academic), uplifting (not derogatory), and from the heart as well as the intellect. These can range from personal accounts to epic passages and include non-fiction, fiction, poetry and "how-to" in spiritual practice or living.

Departments include Featured Articles plus The Spiritual Journey, Spirit and Nature, Spiritual Practice, The Eternal Wisdom, Spirituality and Science, Saints and Sages, Spirituality and Art, Healing, "Lightlines," Poetry.

Please send clean documents (spell-punctuation checked), 1,000-4,500 words, if possible on a disk in MAC format. Photographs and artwork are also welcome.

Currently, *Light of Consciousness* has a national circulation of 20,000, appealing to readers interested in spiritual unfoldment, meditation, personal growth, music, books/magazines, healing, environment, nature, the arts and travel.

Light of Consciousness is a not-for-profit service; we make no profit on it nor do any of us take salaries. As such, we rely upon and are deeply grateful for the generosity of writers and artists; full credit to the contributor (and contact information if desired) is published; copyright remains with the creator of the work.

Categories: Fiction—Nonfiction—Inspirational—New Age—Poetry—Religion—Spiritual

CONTACT: Submissions Editor
Material: All
Desert Ashram
3403 W. Sweetwater Dr.
Tucson AZ 85745-9301
Phone: 520-743-8821

Ligourian

LIGUORIAN is a leading Catholic magazine written and edited for Catholics of all ages. Our purpose is to lead our readers to a fuller Christian life by helping them to better understand the teachings of the gospel and the Church, and by illustrating how these teachings apply to life and the problems confronting them as members of families, the Church, and society.

1. Articles and stories should not exceed 2,000 words. Style and vocabulary should be popular and readable. Use an interest-grabbing opening, state Wily the subject is important to readers, use examples, quotes, anecdotes, make practical applications, and end strongly.

2. LIGUORIAN does not consider simultaneous submissions or articles previously accepted or published.

3. Topical articles should be submitted six months in advance.

4. Manuscripts should be typewritten, double spaced, and should include name, address, and social security number. (No check may be issued without a SS#.)

5. Please allow six to eight weeks for our response.

6. We pay 10 to 12 cents a published word on acceptance.7. Authors are advised to read and study several issues of LIGUORIAN before submitting articles.

8. LIGUORIAN receives over two hundred manuscripts each month. Your manuscript stands a better chance of acceptance if it is neatly presented, carefully polished, and on a topic of special interest to our readers.

Good luck and we hope to be hearing from you soon.

The editors of Liguorian

Categories: Christian Interests—Family—General Interest—Parenting—Relationships—Religion—Senior Citizen—Spiritual—Young Adult

CONTACT: Allan Weinert, .SS.R., Editor-in-Chief
Material: All
One Ligouri Dr.
Ligouri MO 63057
Phone: 314-464-2500
Fax: 314-464-8449
E-mail: aweinert@liguori.org
Website: www.liguori.org

Lilith
The Independent Jewish Women's Magazine

Lilith, the independent Jewish women's magazine, publishing since 1976, welcomes high quality, lively writing: reportage, opinion pieces, memoirs, fiction, and poetry on people and issues of concern to Jewish women.

Content:

• Features (1000-2000 words approximately) can include: autobiography (testimony, letters, journals, memoirs); biographies of women living or dead; interviews; social analysis; sociological research; oral history; new rituals; reviews; investigative reporting; coverage of local, national, international conferences and grassroots projects; opinion pieces.

• *Lilith* welcomes: Letters to the Editor, news briefs (500 words or less), and resource listings of new organizations, projects or upcoming events.

Editorial Specifications:

• Author's bio: one to two sentences, written in the third person, should accompany the manuscript.

• Footnotes: None! Sources should be incorporated into the story, in parentheses if necessary. Larger digressionary remarks or information should be submitted on separate pages for use as possible "boxes" or "sidebars" (companion pieces to the main feature).

• Translations: All non-English (including Hebrew or Yiddish) words or phases must be followed by English translation the first time they are used in a non-fiction piece and should appear in italics.

• Form: Manuscripts should be submitted in hard copy, double spaced with author's name, address and phone number and e-mail address on the first page. Name and email address or phone number on each successive page. If an article is accepted for publication, author will usually then be asked to submit an electronic version, preferably in Word software. Queries may be sent by e-mail to Lilithmag@aol.com.

Procedures:

Receipt of manuscripts cannot be acknowledged unless a stamped self-addressed postcard is enclosed. Manuscripts will be returned only if *Lilith* receives a self-addressed envelope with sufficient postage. Allow 12-16 weeks for editorial decisions. All artwork and photographs accompanying articles that need to be returned should be labeled (lightly on back). Letters to the Editor cannot be acknowl-

F-L

edged or returned and must include the writer's name, address and daytime phone number, though these can be withheld from publication at the writer's request.

We encourage you to read our magazine to judge whether *Lilith* is the appropriate vehicle for your work. The enclosed subscription flyer gives examples of topics we have covered. You may order a sample copy of *Lilith* for $6.00 (includes postage). One-year subscriptions are $21. Orders accepted by mail, e-mail, fax or phone.

Categories: Fiction—Nonfiction—Biography—Drama—Film/Video—Jewish Interest—Lifestyle—Music—Poetry—Women's Issues

CONTACT: Submissions Editor
Material: All
250 W. 57th St., #2432
New York, NY 10107-0172
Phone: 212-757-0818
Fax: 212-757-5705
E-mail: lilithmag@aol.com
Website: www.lilithmag

Linn's Stamp News

General

The goal at *Linn's Stamp News* is to create a weekly publication that is indispensable to stamp collectors.

Everything we do, from the broadest editorial policy to the most trivial stylistic idiosyncrasy, is thought out in the light of this one overriding goal.

We try to achieve indispensability in various ways:

Every collector, from the beginner to the most sophisticated, wants to know the news. Our aim is to provide all the news, as conveniently and as accessibly as we can. In this regard, we feel we are the *New York Times* of philately.

In stamp collecting, the news is not just club and show announcements, new issues and auction realizations.

New discoveries are constantly being made, sometimes involving material that is decades or even centuries old. We cover this news too, relying on the worldwide network of columnists and correspondents who contribute to our pages.

Of course, we rely on these contributors for much more than hard news. Many of the feature items in *Linn's*, which make up the bulk of our editorial content, originate with free-lance contributors in the collector community.

Here *Linn's* performs an important educational function, by bringing to the attention of approximately 55,000 subscribers (and many more thousands of readers) a diverse selection of facts, thoughts and observations about stamps, postal markings, covers and stamp-related subjects.

Writing in *Linn's*, the free-lance contributor has the opportunity to share his specialized knowledge with the largest stamp collector audience of any periodical in the world.

It should go without saying, then, that *Linn's* features are aimed at a broad group of relatively novice collectors, whose average level of sophistication, on any given subject, is less than that of the specialist author.

Linn's writers should keep this general interest level of the audience uppermost in mind. Advanced or more sophisticated collectors, as many of our columnists tend to be, must also avoid writing down to the reader.

The goal in writing for the *Linn's* audience is to provide information that makes stamp collecting more interesting to more people. Ideally, every feature we run promotes the hobby.

A *Linn's* article is not the appropriate place to showcase everything the author knows, nor is it a lofty podium from which to speak over people's heads.

The *Linn's* writer must strive to reach out and embrace the reader, to invite him in, even to hold his hand along the path. This attitude of friendliness and openness in one's prose is difficult to articulate, but it's extremely important. It is very much a part of our desire to make *Linn's* accessible to all collectors, and to help them grow as philatelists.

Without condescending, the *Linn's* writer should assume that the reader knows little or nothing about the specific subject at hand. Complicated terms or unfamiliar words should be defined, even if they might be familiar to the more advanced philatelist.

The *Wall Street Journal* is a good model here: Every time its uses the phrase "short sale," it defines what a short sale is. *Linn's* strives to be similarly introductory in its approach to the jargon of philately.

The ideal *Linn's* feature would contain enough new (or newly presented) information to instruct even the specialist in the field, written in a way to capture the attention (and hold the interest) of the beginning collector.

While the scope of our editorial interest ranges as widely as philately itself, many of our features focus on U.S. and U.S.-related material. No matter what his collecting specialty, the *Linn's* reader still maintains an interest in the stamps and postal history of his own country. Week after week, *Linn's* offers the most complete coverage of the U.S. philatelic scene available anywhere.

This is not to say that we ignore the philately of the rest of the world—quite the contrary. We have regular columns in many non-U.S. areas; we record and notice the new issues of the entire world; and our feature writers routinely range the globe, writing on subjects from classic to contemporary.

Linn's is also big enough to accommodate a wide range of writing styles.

Many of our columnists have individual voices, and we don't discourage this.

We will always try to preserve a writer's style, if it is a style worth preserving.

Terms

We purchase first worldwide periodical rights plus a non-exclusive right to anthologize or otherwise reuse on a proportionate royalty basis, and to use the artwork online.

We want to be the first periodical to publish the work. The author is subsequently free to resell the work elsewhere, 60 days after we've published it; but here we'd like to be credited. We reserve the right to reuse all works published in *Linn's* (in our almanac or in an anthology, for instance), and we will pay an appropriate royalty for such print reuses.

The specific legal details of our purchase are spelled out in the "Standard terms governing acceptance of original material" section at the end of this guideline.

Articles submitted should be exclusive to *Linn's*. We are not interested in material that is simultaneously submitted to other publications (except press releases, of course, which are not part of this discussion).

Thus, we want to see original e-mail files, faxes or typescripts.

We reserve the right to edit, cut or reject anything submitted. Unsolicited materials will be returned only if accompanied by an addressed envelope, suitably franked.

Articles accepted may not appear immediately. Please be patient. The acceptance/rejection process is fairly quick (about four weeks), but accepted pieces sometimes sit for months before publication.

Payment for features and columns is made upon publication. Checks are mailed monthly, shortly after the 5th of the month. Thus, in the ordinary course of events, writers should have received, by the middle of the month, our check for whatever of their works was published in the issues of *Linn's* cover-dated the previous month.

Rates vary, generally between $25 and $100 per feature. We do strive to pay every contributor who produces original work for us. This is more by way of saying "thank you" than providing a livelihood, because the economics of newspaper publishing don't sustain magazine rates.

Payment varies according to quality, craft, degree of difficulty, previous work done for *Linn's*, number and quality of visuals, and length.

We do not pay by the word. Longer is not necessarily better. In fact, the longer a feature, the less likely we'll have room for it.

We usually have a large inventory of half- to full-page features (over 750 words) and a screaming need for shorter items (200-500 words).

Illustrations

Include illustrations wherever possible: stamps, covers, postmarks or whatever other visual material supports your text.

Many would-be contributors seem to break down here. For *Linn's*, a picture is indeed worth, if not 1,000 words, at least 250. More frequently than we would prefer, we find ourselves returning otherwise publishable work because it lacks the necessary visual support.

As a general rule, the best way to write an article on almost any philatelic subject is to have the photos, scans, stamps or covers in front of you before you begin. That way you are sure to properly illustrate your subject, and your text is fairly certain to explain what's in its pictures.

Conversely, an easy way to get into trouble is to write an article with no visual support, in the expectation of finding a photo after the article is done. Nine times out of 10, the result is a text that lacks illustrations or doesn't connect to them.

On the other hand, bear in mind that in final page make-up there must be a balance between illustrations and text. Too many illustrations can overpower a skimpy text and make it difficult (sometimes impossible) for us to lay out the words.

We prefer separate (not embedded) jpg or tif scans at 300dpi twice the size of the original item. Crisp, sharp-focus, high-contrast glossy black and white photos can still be used, but here no color is possible, of course. Each of our weekly issues includes approximately three to five pages with color editorial news or columns.

A few items that have no tonal gradations, postmarks or surcharges for instance, can be reproduced adequately from photocopies. Stamps and covers cannot.

If you can't provide decent photos, send us the stamps or covers and we'll make the scans or photos here. (Clear this with us first if the value is substantial.)

Please don't expect us to seek out your visuals for you; we don't have the time or the resources.

Our typical purchase includes the acquisition of the illustrations. If you want any photos returned, we should discuss this beforehand. Include your name and full address on the reverse of each photo.

Along with illustrations, we expect you to provide captions. Please provide captions on a separate sheet of paper, not embedded within your manuscript.

The ideal caption should explain what the picture shows and make the reader want to read the accompanying text. At the very least, a caption should explain what's in the picture. Identify all people and everything else that would provoke reader curiosity. "Figure 1" with no explanation is not an acceptable caption. All information in a caption must also be in the text of the article.

Don't paste visuals or captions onto your manuscript. Don't embed scans into a text document. Keep them separate.

Copy Preparation

Copy should be prepared in a standard electronic format, such as Microsoft Word or similar software, and submitted on a disk with a paper copy. With the managing editor's permission, it can be submitted by e-mail.

If typewritten, it should be double spaced with ample margins, on one side only of sheets of white 8 1/2-inch by 11-inch bond paper. Put your name and the page number in the upper-right corner of each page.

Those still using a typewriter should avoid typewritten strikeovers, especially with figures. Better to cross it out and say it again. Clarity is more important than neatness.

Footnotes and bibliographies are not appropriate to our newspaper style. If attribution or citation is essential, then it's important enough to be worked into the text.

Refer to illustrations as Figure 1, Figure 2, etc. Avoid eye directions such as above and below, which might be contradicted by page makeup.

For similar reasons, charts in the text should be avoided. They typically run wider than one column width, and cause difficult (sometimes impossible) make-up problems. If you must include a chart, prepare and discuss it separately, as if it were a photo.

Submit articles to Managing Editor, *Linn's Stamp News*, Box 29, Sidney, OH 45365.

Style: General

Linn's is a weekly magazine in newspaper format. Our editorial style is designed to communicate information as quickly and as clearly as possible.

Stylistic quirks that hinder rapid communication are discouraged. Our basic reference in matters of editorial style is *The Associated Press Stylebook*, available from AP at 50 Rockefeller Plaza, New York, N.Y. 10020.

Even though your subject might be specialized, write it understandably.

Always explain terms. Remember that *Linn's* is read by tens of thousands of readers who don't know your subject as well as you do. Reach out and help them.

Avoid lengthy paragraphs. One typewritten line makes two lines of type in *Linn's*. Our newspaper style calls for very short paragraphing. This also aids readership.

Don't use lengthy sentences. Two or three short sentences are easier to read than one long one. Never use parentheses or dashes when commas or separate sentences will serve the same end. Never use a comma when a period will do.

Avoid cliches. Don't try to be cute. Reread your sentences to see if you can express the same thoughts in fewer words.

Check and double check all facts, especially names, addresses, catalog numbers and other critical bits of information. We rely on you for the accuracy of your prose.

Don't be afraid of the first person. We'll be publishing your work under your name. "We" or "this writer" are pedantic and often confusing. Say "I" if it's appropriate. Use a dictionary or a spelling guide. Frequent misspellings suggest a lack of attention to detail that is inappropriate to the craft of journalism. The back pages of Webster are useful regarding punctuation and grammar. Avoid jarring repetition of the same words or phrase. There are many ways to say the same thing.

Style: *Linn's*

Never refer to a stamp by Scott number only. Describe it first and then add the Scott number if needed.

As an example: "The U.S. 10¢ 1869 stamp (Scott 116) . . ." In a series, it's Scott 51-58; 233-37.

Spell out numerals one through nine, then use figures for 10 and higher.

Don't use decimals after an even number of dollars (we say $20, not $20.00). For large numbers, insert the comma beginning with 1,000.

Generally, figures are used in ages; always in percentages.

No comma after a month without a day (March 1983); adding the day requires the comma (March 13, 1983). The reverse "13 March 1983" takes no comma, but is difficult to read and should be avoided.

We abbreviate months when used with days (Aug. 12, 1869) but not without days (August 1869). We never abbreviate the five short months: March, April, May, June, July.

We never use italics or quotation marks for emphasis. If you want to emphasize a word or a point, write emphatically. Don't use quotation marks to indicate anything other than a quotation. Periods and commas go inside the quotation marks; semicolons go outside.

Abbreviations: We use the old style state abbreviations. We don't abbreviate Alaska, Hawaii, Idaho, Iowa, Maine, Ohio, Texas, Utah. Two-word states are abbreviated with no space: W.Va. We only use the two-letter postal abbreviation when an address is given.

Mr. is used only with Mrs. or when the man is dead. Mrs. and Miss are generally unnecessary. We never use Ms.

We don't use periods with most well-known organizations: USSS, APS, UPU, USPS, UNPA, APO, GPO, etc. However, we do use periods with country initials as an adjective: U.S., U.N.

Postal administrations and other organizations take the singular: APS will stage its spring meeting, UNPA will announce its 2003 stamps.

Note the punctuation and separation of the following: American Stamp Dealers Association, Citizens' Stamp Advisory Committee, price list. The following are all one word: mailcoach, handcancel, handstamp, datestamp, semipostal, multicolor, steamship.

Our general style is lowercase. When in doubt over whether a word should be capitalized, leave it down.

STANDARD TERMS GOVERNING ACCEPTANCE OF ORIGINAL MATERIAL

Linn's Stamp News, a division of Amos Press Inc. (the publisher), accepts original copy and/or artwork subject to the following terms and conditions:

1. *First Worldwide Periodical Rights and Electronic Rights.* The contributor grants to publisher the exclusive right to be the first to publish the article and supporting artwork in whole or edited fashion (sometimes referred to collectively as the "work" in *Linn's Stamp News* and to use said work in advertising and/or promotion.

The contributor also grants to the publisher the non-exclusive right to publish in electronic form, on any Internet web site created or maintained by *Linn's Stamp News*, any and all stories and/or photos that *Linn's* has purchased, or will purchase, from the writer.

This authorization for electronic publishing may be terminated at any time by written notice to *Linn's Stamp News*, which notice shall be effective with respect to such stories and/or photos received by *Linn's* after receipt of the written notice.

2. *Subsequent Use.* The contributor retains the right to sell the work elsewhere provided such subsequent sale occurs no sooner than sixty (60) days after publication by *Linn's* Stamp News. The contributor agrees that any subsequent reprint will appropriately reference *Linn's Stamp News* copyright.

The contributor grants to publisher a right to reuse said work in any print publication of the publisher, subject to publisher's payment of an appropriate fee to the contributor.

3. *Copyright.* The contributor grants to the publisher the right to obtain copyright on the work in the publisher's name in the United States and any other country, subject to the contributor's retained non-exclusive right to reuse as set forth above.

4. *Indemnity.* The contributor warrants and guarantees that he is the sole proprietor of the work; that said work violates no existing copyright, in whole or part, that it contains no libelous or otherwise injurious matter; that the work has not heretofore been published; that he is the sole and exclusive owner of the rights granted herein to the publisher; and that he has not heretofore assigned, pledged, or otherwise encumbered said work. At his own expense, the contributor will protect and defend said work from any adverse claim of copyright infringement, and shall indemnify, defend and hold the publisher harmless from asserted claims of whatever nature, damages, costs and expenses that the publisher may incur as a result of the publication of said work and/or subsequent reuse.

5. *Payment.* The contributor accepts such amount as is tendered by separate check from the publisher as payment in full for the rights in the work granted herein to the publisher; provided, however, that it is agreed that additional monies may be due only as a result of subsequent reuse as set forth in paragraph 2 hereof.

6. *Rights Reserved.* All rights in the work not specifically granted to the publisher are expressly reserved to the contributor.

7. *Applicable Law.* The agreement between the contributor and publisher shall be governed by the law of Ohio and shall be deemed to have been entered into at Sidney, Ohio, as of the date of the issuance of publisher's check in payment of the amount due to the contributor pursuant to paragraph 5.

8. *Arbitration.* Any claim, dispute or controversy arising out of or in connection with the agreement between the contributor and publisher or any breach thereof, shall be arbitrated by the parties before the American Arbitration Association under the rules then applicable of that association. The arbitration shall be held in the city of Sidney, Ohio.

9. *Successors and Assigns.* The agreement of the contributor and publisher shall be binding upon, and inure to the benefit of each of their respective heirs, successors, administrators, and assigns.

10. *Entire Agreement.* It is understood by the contributor and publisher that these Standard Terms And Conditions and publisher's check tendered in payment in accordance with paragraph 5 set forth the parties' entire agreement regarding this work and may not be varied except by an additional writing signed by the contributor and the publisher. Copyright 2001

Categories: Nonfiction—Hobbies—Stamp collecting only

CONTACT: Michael Schreiber
Material: All
PO Box 29
Sidney OH 45373
Phone: 937-498-0801
Fax: 888-304-8388
E-mail: linns@linns.com
Website: www.linns.com

The Lion Magazine

The Lion Magazine welcomes freelance article and photo submissions that depict the service goals and projects of Lions clubs on the local, national and international level.

Contributors may also submit general interest articles that reflect the humanitarian, community betterment and service activism ideals of the worldwide association or family-oriented, humorous essays.

Lions Clubs International is the world's largest service club organization, with a membership composed of 1.35 million men and women in 199 countries and geographical areas. Lions are recognized globally for their commitment to projects that benefit the blind, visually handicapped and people in need.

The Headquarters Edition of *The Lion Magazine*, produced in Oak Brook, Illinois, is published 10 times yearly; December/January and July/August are combined issues. The circulation of the Headquarters Edition reaches approximately 500,000 readers.

Article length should not exceed 2,000 words, and is subject to editing. No gags, fillers, quizzes or poems are accepted. Photos should be at least 5"x7" glossies; color prints are preferred, or digital. *The Lion Magazine* pays upon acceptance of material.

Advance queries save your time and ours.

Categories: Nonfiction—Associations

CONTACT: Jay Copp, Senior Editor
Material: All
Lions Clubs International
300 W. 22nd. St.
Oak Brook IL 60523
Phone: 630-571-5466
E-mail: jay.copp@lionsclubs.org

Liquid Ohio

Format: Our format is 8.5 X 11, 32 pages, B&W.

Poetry: Try not to go over 60 lines, but a good epic is fine.

Short stories: Between 2000-3000 words.

Photography/artwork: Color or b/w, but they will appear in B&W.

Genre: The best idea is probably to order a sample copy and get a feel for what we're all about.

All written work sent in via e-mail should either be pasted into the letter itself or in MS *Word.* Any work sent via postal mail should include a SASE if you would like a response. If you would like your work returned, please indicate this with your submission.

Sample copies are available for $4.00. Subscription rates are $15.00/year for 4 issues. Please make checks payable to Amber Goddard.

Categories: Fiction—Arts—Cartoons—College—Feminism—General Interest—Photography—Poetry

CONTACT: Submissions Editor
Material: All
PO Box 60265
Bakersfield CA 93386
Phone: 661-871-0586
E-mail: info@liquidohio.net
Website: www.liquidohio.net

STIMULATING PROSE, POETRY & ART

Literal Latte

Literal Latte is the stimulating Literary Arts Magazine of fiction & Poems from known & emerging writers around the world

It's brewed in New York City and is brimming with stories, poetry, essays & art. *LL* is in its twelfth year of publishing the best words around.

LL features fiction, poetry and essays by established and emerging authors:

Ray Bradbury, Michael Brodsky, Robert Olen Butler, Stephen Dixon, Harlan Ellison, Allen Ginsberg, Daniel Harris, Phillip Lopate, Carole Maso, Nancy Milford, Carol Muske, Lynn Sharon Schwartz, Gloria Steinem, Frank Stella, John Updike, Jerry Uelsmann & exciting new talents.

MIND STIMULATING PROSE, POETRY & ART

It's Not Who You Know or Where You've Been...It's What You Write

98% of what we publish comes from the so-called slush pile.

We take submissions 365 days a year.

We accept work for publication on a continual basis, not just for the upcoming issue, and publish

within one year of acceptance.

Most issues contain someone who has not been published before.

GENERAL GUIDELINES

• Send unpublished stories or personal essays, up to 6,000 words.

• Short plays or poems up to 4,000 words.

• Art—from cover art to literary cartoons. Photographs, paintings, drawings in B&W or Color (slides or copies, not originals)

• Styles range from classical to experimental.

• Include biography and SASE or email for response or return of work. Or include email for response only.

• Simultaneous submissions welcome, let us know if a piece is accepted elsewhere.

• It takes us approximately 3-6 months to respond.

• E-mail submissions are NOT accepted.

Categories: Nonfiction—Arts—Poetry

CONTACT: Submissions Editor
Material: All
61 East 8th Street, Ste 240
New York NY 10003
Phone: 212-260-5532
E-mail: LitLatte@aol.com
Website: www.literal-latte.com

Literary Magazine Review

Literary Magazine Review is a twenty-five-year-old quarterly that reviews periodicals that publish mostly poetry and creative prose. LMR is an excellent resource for writers seeking publishing outlets and readers searching for the best contemporary literary magazines to read. Its audience includes writers, academic libraries, and the editors of literary magazines. Its reviews are often quoted in other national magazines such as *Poets and Writers* and *American Poetry Review,* as well as in advertisements for the literary magazines it reviews.

Jenny Brantley, Editor; Brian Fitch, Assistant Editor, Univ. of Wisconsin-River Falls, English Dept., 410 S. 3rd Street, River Falls, WI 54022, email: jennifer.s.brantley@uwrf.edu, web site: http://www.uwrf.edu/lmr/. Founded in 1981. Articles, criticism, reviews. LMR is devoted to providing critical appraisals of the specific contents of small, predominantly literary periodicals for the benefit of readers and writers. We print reviews of about 1.5M words that comment on the magazines' physical characteristics, on particular articles, stories, and poems featured, and on editorial preferences as evidenced in the selections. Recent contributors include John Pennington, D.E. Steward, Phil Miller, Kevin Prufer, Steve Heller, Maria Melendez, Stella Pope Duarte, and John McNally. We would be happy to entertain queries offering disinterested reviews and omnibus notices and pieces describing, explaining, or examining the current literary magazine scene. Subscription exchange inquiries are welcome. Circ. 300. 4/yr. Pub'd 4 issues 2005; expects 4 issues 2006, 4 issues 2007. Sub. price $16; per copy $5; sample $5. Back issues: $7 an issue. Discounts: 10% to subscription agencies. 48-52pp. Payment: copies. Copyrighted, rights revert on author's request. Pub's reviews: 70 in 2004. Literary magazines. We are interested in magazines that publish at least some fiction, poetry, literary nonfiction, or all three. Ads: none. Subjects: Criticism, Literary Review, Magazines, Reviews.

Categories: General Interest—Literature—Poetry—Reference—Short Stories—Writing

CONTACT: Dr. Jenny Brantley, Editor
Material: All
University of Wisconsin
English Department
410 S. Third St.
River Falls WI 54022
Phone: 319-273-2821
Fax: 319-273-5807
E-mail: jennifer.s.brantley@uwrf.edu
Website: www.uwrf.edu/lmr

The Literary Review
Fairleigh Dickinson University

MAJOR INTERESTS: TLR has an international focus and welcomes work in translation.

CONTENT: Original poetry, fiction, work in translation, essays, review essays on contemporary writers and literary issues. Review-essays should include a group of works of common interest rather than a single title.

LENGTH: We have no length restrictions for fiction or poetry; however, long works must meet an exceptionally high standard of excellence. In general, essays should be under 5,000 words and reviews from 1,500 to 2,500 words.

STYLE: We accept work in any format or style, ranging from traditional to experimental. We expect our contributors to have a strong understanding of technique and a wide familiarity of contemporary writing, but editorial decisions are based on quality alone.

NUMBER: We read only one story, essay, or review-essay by an author at one time, and no more than six poems.

PRESENTATION: Clear photocopies and dot-matrix printouts are permissible.

TIME: We try to advise of our decision within 12 to 16 weeks of receiving a manuscript. Accepted manuscripts usually appear within 18—24 months, often sooner, depending upon our commitment to special issues.

COMPENSATION: Contributors receive two copies of the issue in which their work appears, as well as a one-year free subscription, and are eligible to compete in our annual Charles Angoff cash award.

COPYRIGHT: All material appearing in TLR is copyrighted. Authors are granted reprint rights as TLR only holds one-time rights to their work.

SAMPLES: Sample copies are available for $7.00 U.S., $8.00 foreign, prepaid.

Categories: Fiction—Nonfiction—Literature—Short Stories

CONTACT: René Steinke, Editor-in-Chief
Material: All
285 Madison Ave.
Madison NJ 07940
Phone: 973-443-8564
Fax: 973-443-8364
E-mail: tlr@fdu.edu
Website: www.theliteraryreview.org/

The Living Church

Formal guidelines not available. Please read a number of issues to ascertain the publication's style and needs.

Send queries to address below.

Categories: Nonfiction—Christian Interests—Religion—The Episcopal Church

CONTACT: Submissions Editor
Materials: All
Living Church Foundation
PO Box 514036
Milwaukee WI 53203
Phone: 414-276-5420

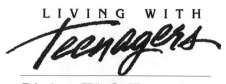

Living With Teenagers

Living With Teenagers is a Christian monthly magazine for parents of teenagers. It focuses on the practical aspects of parenting, as well as informs, educates, and inspires parents to be aware of issues and understand their teenagers as they grow into responsible young adults.

Content: The editorial staff will evaluate articles dealing with any subject of interest to parents of teenagers.

Preparation: Cover page should include suggested title and blurb, by-line, author's full name, address, social security number, and rights offered (all, first, one-time reprint).

Submit manuscripts 600-1,200 words in length.

Queries with writing sample are preferred.

Disk submissions must be accompanied by a hard copy. Prefer disk on a Macintosh word processing program, but can convert most IBM programs.

Writing Tips: Quoted material must be properly documented (publisher, location, date, and page numbers), along with permission verification.

Include Bible references and thoughts when appropriate.

Remember readers are parents of teenagers.

Use brief, clear sentences.

Construct paragraphs logically.

Sidebars helpful.

Payment: Payment is negotiable and on acceptance.

Publication: Writers will receive, without cost, 3 advance copies of the issue in which their manuscripts are published. Extra copies can be ordered from the Customer Service Center (MSN 113 at address below, or 800-458-BSSB).

• For a sample copy, send a 9"x12" manila envelope with your address and return postage.

• I have prayed about and reread my submission, and it reflects a Christian worldview that will help distinguish the magazine from other secular parenting magazines.

• I have included a cover page with this information: article title, a short writer bio; total word count; my full name, address, phone number, email address (if available), and Social Security number.

• I am submitting the manuscript in one of the following ways:

1. I am submitting the manuscript in hard-copy form through regular mail, and I agree to submit it electronically if it is purchased through a contract.

2. I am submitting the manuscript by disk, and I am also sending it in hard-copy form. I have indicated on the disk which word processing program was used. (Microsoft Word is preferred.)

3. I am submitting the manuscript by email. I am sending it to parentlife@lifeway.com or to lwt@lifeway.com. I am also sending this checklist by regular mail.

• I have secured necessary permission for quoted material and have properly documented all quotations (source, publisher, date, and page number). I have also enclosed a photocopy of the original quote as well as a photocopy of the title page and copyright page of the source from which the quote is taken.

• I have verified all statistics and factual information (anything that is not considered common knowledge among the general public). I have properly documented this information (source, publisher, date, and page number), and I have enclosed a photocopy of the source (including a copy of the title page and copyright page).

• I have verified any Scripture that I have quoted, and it is quoted from NIV. (LifeWay has permission to quote from the NIV, and photocopies are not necessary.)

• I have included at least two blurbs or pull quotes that will quickly draw the reader into the article.

• I have included at least one and possibly up to three sidebars. The sidebar provides valuable information for the reader (quick tips, ministry ideas, lists, Web sites, books, phone numbers, addresses, and so on).

• I have used headings and subheadings throughout the article, and they relate to the suggested title.

Please provide a two or three sentence writer bio that we can use as a standard for you.

Please check the topics or subjects which interest you most as a writer:

College—communication—cults—education—entertainment/media/music—exceptional teens—finance—food/nutrition—health issues—recreation—religion—technology—teen physical development—teen emotional development—teens and spiritual issues—discipline—siblings—sports—learning styles—sex education—peer pressure—drugs/alcohol—problem solving/conflict resolution—family issues (for example: single parent, blended family)—other

As a Christian parenting magazine, we desire to have writers who have a growing commitment and relationship to Jesus Christ. Please tell us briefly how you became a Christian and about your present journey with Christ.

Other biographical information we would like to have: birth date, current vocation (if retired, previous vocation), place of employment, church membership, current church or denominational leadership positions, educational background, spouse's name, children's names and ages, articles and books you have had published, special interests and hobbies.

Categories: Christian Interests— Teen—Young Adult

CONTACT: Editor
Material: All
One LifeWay Plaza
Nashville TN 37234-0140
Phone: 615-251-2229
Fax: 615-251-5008
E-mail: lwt@lifeway.com
Website: www.lifewayonline.com/mags

Llewellyn Journal

Thank you for your interest in *The Llewellyn Journal*. For more than 100 years Llewellyn has published books on metaphysics, astrology, magic, spirituality, alternative healing, and associated topics. *The Llewellyn Journal* is our on-line presentation of in-depth articles on these and similar subjects.The following Guidelines include the information you need to send us an article for consideration.Purpose:

There are two major purposes for *The Llewellyn Journal*:First, *The Llewellyn Journal* will give authors published (or soon to be published) by Llewellyn a chance to present practical ideas and concepts from their writings. *The Llewellyn Journal* also gives these authors a chance to share some of the results of working with those ideas and concepts. These may include new concepts based on their writings or expand upon ideas presented in one of their Llewellyn books. Second, *The Llewellyn Journal* will give voice to a selection of high-quality writers who have not yet been published by Llewellyn. If a submitted article is intelligent, well-written, has documentation for any references, and can be seen to comment upon, build interest in, or in some way add to a current Llewellyn title, it will be considered for publication.We are providing *The Llewellyn Journal* as a free service to the community. However, the costs of design, editing, maintenance, articles, artwork, etc. are considerable. Further, unlike magazines you might obtain by subscription or buy at a store, *The Llewellyn Journal* receives no money from outside advertisers and no money from subscriptions or newsstand sales. It's free. In return for this free service, we hope readers will support the Journal by purchasing Llewellyn books which they read about here. It is only through such reader support that we will be able to maintain *The Llewellyn Journal* as a free service. Articles that further this end are most likely to be published.

Length: We are seeking articles of 2,500 words or less.Subjects:

The Llewellyn Journal considers for publication substantive, in-depth articles that discuss metaphysical topics. For Llewellyn, the metaphysical category is broad and inclusive as can be seen in the wide subject range of books that we publish. If you have a topic in mind for *The Llewellyn Journal*, please email us and ask if it is appropriate before writing and submitting an actual article. *The Llewellyn Journal* seeks to publish powerful, practical, even life-changing techniques (including necessary background), based on Llewellyn books. *The Llewellyn Journal* may also carry articles that are thought provoking, philosophical, and theoretical as long as they are focused toward a specific Llewellyn book.*The Llewellyn Journal* will include articles that are between popular and academic styles. Including bibliographic references to concepts and ideas are encouraged but not required. References to any quoted material are required (see below). For an article to be accepted for publication in *The Llewellyn Journal*, it must be clear and unambiguous in content. We are not looking for beginners' guides. For example, if you are a Llewellyn author with a book on the Tarot, we would prefer to see an article on "Working with The Tower Card to Improve Your Life" as opposed to "Your First Tarot Deck."

How to Submit an Article to The Llewellyn Journal

Things to consider before you submit: 1) Are you sure we would be interested in your article's subject? Does it clearly and directly relate to a book published by Llewellyn? E-mail the editor (TLJEditor@llewellyn.com) and ask first. 2) We only accept new, previously unpublished articles. By that we mean your article cannot have previously appeared in a book, magazine, on a web site, on a CD, or in any printed form whatsoever.3) *The Llewellyn Journal* is an online only publiation. Therefore, we only accept email submissions.4) We accept complete articles only. We do not accept partial articles.5) Although we primarily support authors who are published by Llewellyn, we will also consider thoughtful, well-written articles by other writers if they discuss a Llewellyn title or focus on a Llewellyn topic. We do not work with agents.

Specifications: For the article itself, we require the following:1) If you send the article as an attachment, use a standard, easy-to-read font (Times, Palatino, Helvetica, Arial, etc.). 2) Do not justify the page. Right margin should be "ragged." 3) Do not use the return or enter key (or make a "hard break") at the end of each line. You should only use the return or enter key at the end of a paragraph. 4) Do not indent paragraphs. 5) Do add an extra line space between paragraphs. 6) Date your title page. 7) Include your name, address, email address, and phone number in the article. 8) Keep a copy of your article and all correspondence for reference and to protect against loss. NEVER SEND US YOUR ONLY COPY.

Submission: We accept email submissions only. They must be in one of two forms: 1) Within the body of the email. 2) As an attachment. Under no circumstances will we accept any "executable" file (.exe). No matter what word processor you use, please send us a "text only" (ASCII or .txt) file.2a) If you are sending an attachment be sure to include your name, address, email address, and phone number in the attachment as well as in the body of the email.

What is Unacceptable: 1) As mentioned above, if a topic does not fit our broad metaphysical field or support a Llewellyn title, it will not be considered. 2) We will not accept writing that is sexist or racist; writing that ""bashes"" any group; or writing that shows intolerance toward groups, organizations, or individuals. 3) Words that are popularly considered to be obscene or defamatory are unacceptable. Writing containing these words will not be considered for publication. 4) Decisions of the editors on what will be published are final.

Permissions and Fair Use: *The Llewellyn Journal* seeks fresh, original approaches to metaphysical topics; we don't want ""retreads"" of what's already out there. We strongly discourage quoting or paraphrasing of books or articles not published by Llewellyn.If you cite concepts from other sources, *The Llewellyn Journal* requires proper attribution and documentation. When citing an outside source in your text, include the complete publishing information for the reference (title, author(s), publisher, date and city of publication, and page number) in the body of the article or in your endnotes. For more information on citation and documentation, we recommend the Chicago Manual of Style.

Illustrations: As a journal that is focused on text, the use of illustrations and photographs is limited — and frankly discouraged. However, if you feel that an illustration or photo is necessary for your article, you may send a .gif, .jpg, or .tif attachment file along with your article. Indicate in ALL CAPITAL LETTERS where the image should be placed within the text of your article. Please be aware that *The Llewellyn Journal* reserves the right to omit any graphics.If you include a photo, you must either have taken the photo yourself or have written permission from the copyright holder to use the photo. If there are any people in the photo besides yourself, you must have written permission from them to use their image for any purpose.If you are using illustrations or photographs from other published sources, you must obtain permission and suitable reproductions from the copyright holder. Do not assume anything is public domain, no matter how old. You are responsible for obtaining all art clearances, and will be held responsible if permissions are infringed upon.

Llewellyn's Editing Process: If we decide to publish your article and you agree to the terms of the agreement, your article will be edited. *The Llewellyn Journal* reserves the right to edit all or any part of the article submitted by the author, and to make the final decisions in terms of editing.

Payment: 1) Payment for articles is $75 per article, regardless of length. 2) The Article is a Work For Hire. Llewellyn will own and copyright in its name. 3) You will be paid no more than 30 days after your article is posted on our site and during a regular Llewellyn payment cycle. 4) You will always receive credit as the author of the article.5) Llewellyn will grant the Author, as well as any other person, permission to post the first 250 words of your Article on their own websites so long as the following is printed with the article: "Permission to post this article granted by *The Llewellyn Journal*" followed by the Internet address of *The Llewellyn Journal* (www.llewellynjournal.com). 6) Llewellyn employees will not receive payment for Journal articles, unless they are written off the clock.

Policies: We want to keep *The Llewellyn Journal* free so as many people as possible can see it. We even encourage websites to post portions of our articles, including your name as author. In order to do these things, we maintain the following policies:1) Articles purchased for use by *The Llewellyn Journal* are considered ""Works for Hire."" This means that the payment you receive gives *The Llewellyn Journal* the right to use it in any way.2) If you are having a book published that includes material from an article you have published in *The Llewellyn Journal*, write to us at TLJEditor@llewellyn.com giving details, and we will send you written authorization to use the article at no charge as long as *The Llewellyn Journal* is credited as the original source.3) Neither *The Llewellyn Journal* nor Llewellyn Worldwide, Ltd. are responsible for any actions of the readers of *The Llewellyn Journal* or the Public at Large who may copy all or parts of your article or even make changes to it with or without your permission.4) If you have questions or concerns about this policy, please write to us with your specific question and we will send a detailed reply.

Personal Information: In order to publish your article in *The Llewellyn Journal* we must have the following information:
• Your name, mailing address, phone number, and email address.
• Your pseudonym, if you wish to use one.
• Your social security number or tax ID number.

If you are not comfortable sending this information to the Journal editor via e-mail, please send it via post to the address below:

Categories: Nonfiction—Health—Metaphysics—New Age—Spiritual

CONTACT: The Editor
Material: All
Llewellyn Worldwide
PO Box 64383
St. Paul, MN 55164-0383
Phone: 612-291-1970
E-mail: TLJEditor@llewellyn.com
Website: www.llewellynjournal.com

Log Home Living
Timber Frame Homes

Description
Log Home Living is a monthly magazine for people who own or are planning to build contemporary log homes. It is devoted almost exclusively to modern manufactured and handcrafted kit log homes. Our interest in historical or nostalgic stories of very old log cabins, reconstructed log homes, or one-of-a-kind owner-built homes is secondary and should be queried first.

Readership
Our audience comprises primarily married couples between 30 and 45 years old. They are generally well-educated and very individualistic do-it-yourselfers.

Specifications
Log Home Living welcomes new talent and strives to develop long-term relationships with those contributors who consistently deliver quality work. We buy two to four bylined feature articles of 1,000 to 2,000 words per issue. These articles should reflect readers' lifestyles and interest in log homes as follows:

• *Log Home Owner Profiles.* Articles about people who have built modern log homes from manufactured or handcrafted kits. In a conversational tone, describe the home as it is and tell how it came to be. Emphasize the elements that make this home special—intent, design, solutions to unique problems, features, furnishings, interior design and landscaping. Every story must include feature photos. Floor plans of the completed home, construction costs and schedules are a plus.

• *Design and Decor Features.* Photo stories on various architectural features of log homes. Stories can focus on a particular home or the same architectural feature on different homes.

• *Historical Features.* Articles about historical log structures in North America or abroad and restorations of same. As mentioned before, we have a limited need for this material.

• *Technical Articles.* How-to advice about specific aspects of log home construction or pre-construction. Examples are scheduling a construction project, selecting wood preservatives, installing flooring, decorating log homes, dealing with subcontractors and innovative financing programs. Writers of these articles should be experts or able to interview experts and convey the information for a lay audience.

Submissions
Manuscripts should be typed, double or triple spaced with wide margins, on white bond paper. Computer printouts are acceptable, but we prefer they be unjustified (ragged right) and letter quality. We will read unsolicited manuscripts but prefer an outline or a detailed query letter first. Enclose a SASE.

Photos
Stories must be accompanied by extensive professional-quality color photographs of log home interiors, exteriors or construction shots as appropriate. See our Photographers Guidelines for specific requirements. If you are not a professional photographer, advise us in your query. Also tell us if you know a professional photographer who can work with you on an assignment; otherwise, we will locate one to accompany you.

Payment & Rights
Payment for features ranges from $250 to $500 (without and with photos), depending on their length, the nature of the work and the amount of editing required. We acknowledge receipt of submissions immediately and try to provide an editor's response within thirty days. Payment is made within 30 days of acceptance.

Cancellations
If we determine that a submitted article requires substantial rewriting, we will pay a $100 research fee for the information supplied. If we decide not to use an assigned accepted article, we will pay a $100 kill fee.

Rights & Conditions

Log Home Living buys first North American rights and nonexclusive reprint rights. Upon publication, authors will receive two complimentary copies of the issue with their work.

We cannot accept responsibility for the personal safety or property of any freelancer while on assignment for the magazine. Writers and photographers are urged to have their own insurance in place while on assignment.

We assume that all contributed manuscripts are original and that all facts and quotes have been verified. Articles that have been published or submitted elsewhere must be so identified; in such cases, the author is responsible for obtaining permission to reprint previously published materials prior to submission to *Log Home Living*.

Expenses

Reasonable expenses will be covered, provided that travel plans and all anticipated costs are discussed beforehand with the editor. A complete expense report, including receipts for all claims, should accompany the contributor's work. Expense reimbursement is made with payment for an accepted article.

Sample Copy

If you would like a sample copy of *Log Home Living* magazine, please send your check or money order for $4.00 to HBPI, Attn: Sample Copy, PO Box 220039, Chantilly VA 20153.

Timber Frame Homes

Timber Frame Homes magazine uses the same guidelines as *Log Home Living*.

Categories: Nonfiction—Architecture—Lifestyle—Real Estate—Trade—Home Construction—Travel

CONTACT: Kevin Ireland, Executive Editor
Material: All
PO Box 220039
Chantilly VA 20153
Phone: 703-222-9411
Fax: 703-222-3209
E-mail: editor@loghomeliving.com
E-mail: editor@timberframehomes.com
Website: www.loghomeliving.com/loghomeliving
Website: www.loghomeliving.com/timberframehomes

Long Island Woman

About the Publication

We are a monthly tabloid magazine with a free distribution of 40,000 copies throughout Long Island, NY.

Types of Articles: Articles of special interest to women ages 35 and over. Topics would include news, lifestyles & family, mental & physical health, sports & fitness, nutrition & dining, fashion & beauty, business & finance, home decorating & gardening, entertainment & media, travel & leisure, books, interviews with interesting or inspiring women and women celebrities. No poetry or fiction, please.

Manuscripts

·Submissions and queries will be accepted via mail and email.
·*No submissions or queries will be accepted by telephone.*
·All manuscripts and queries should be typed and double-spaced.
·Please include suggested headlines, subheadlines, and a brief biography (up to 15 words) that may appear at the end of the article.
·Include any photographs or artwork that may enhance the presentation of your article.
·Include your name, address, telephone number, fax number, email address.
·Submissions will be returned only if accompanied by a self-addressed, stamped envelope.
·Articles that are chosen for publication will be notified within 8-10 weeks of being recieved.

Deadlines: Issues are planned 4-5 months in advance of issue date.

Rights: We buy one-time rights to articles that will appear in print and on our website (liwomanonline.com) and won't appear in other Long Island, NY publications, within one year of publication.

Payment: Invoice us for our agreed amount plus include your name, address and social security number. Payment will be made within 30 days of publishing of article. Our Kill Fee is 33%.

Reprint Rates		Assignment Rates	
501-750 words	...$40	501-750 words	...$70
751-1,000 words	...$50	751-1,000 words	...$90
1,001-1,250 words	...$60	1,001-1,250 words	...$110
1,251-1,500 words	...$70	1,251-1,500 words	...$130
1,501-1,750 words	...$80	1,501-1,750 words	...$150
1,751-2,000 words	...$90	1,751-2,000 words	...$170
2,001-2,250 words	...$100	2,001-2,250 words	...$200

Categories: Nonfiction—Antiques—Arts—Book Reviews—Business—Careers—Cooking—Crafts/Hobbies—Diet/Nutrition—Economics—Family—Fashion—Food/Drink—Gardening—Health—Law—Marriage—Money & Finances—Physical Fitness—Psychology—Relationships—Senior Citizen—Sexuality—Singles—Sports/Recreation—Women's Issues

CONTACT: A. Nadboy, Managing Editor
Material: All
PO Box 176
Malverne NY 11565
E-mail: editor@liwomanonline.com

Long Story Short, a Magazine for Writers

An ezine dedicated to the advancement of writers, showcasing fiction, non-fiction, flash fiction, inspirational stories and poetry.

Needs: Need articles about writing, poetry, short stories, non-fiction, we love international writers, would love to interview authors and editors; we have a teen writers page and a page just for teens. We need children's stories.

Length: No more than 2000 words on all submissions except flash fiction/non with a 1000 word maximum. Poetry no more than 32 lines.

Payment: Good exposure for emerging writers.

How to Submit: writingfriend6@gmail.com for everything but poetry: poetrysubmissions@usa.com for poetry. Please try to use a word format, pasted into an email. No indents, single space, no fancy formatting.

Response Time: No longer than 3-5 weeks. Electronic submissions only—no snail mail submissions accepted.

Tips for Writers: Proofread, check punctuation, spell check. We want crisp, clean writing, no profanity, no graphic sex, no pornographic material.

Copies/Subscription Information: www.alongstoryshort.net

Do you have a piece of writing you're proud of? Don't be shy! Send it to us! We'd love the chance to publish your work.

Long Story Short Submission Guideline

Please read and follow instructions carefully.

Thank you for your interest in LONG STORY SHORT, a monthly e-zine that encourages new and emerging writers by showcasing their best work. Although our primary focus is on promoting women writers, we've been receiving so many wonderful stories from men that we decided to include them too.

Each issue contains contests and stories in a wide range of genres including true life, mystery, fantasy, comedy, romance...We're open to anything your imagination has to offer!

We also publish poetry and non-fiction, "How-to's," tips for writers, essays and anything else topical and interesting. Ours is a publication prone to optimism and achievement, but well-written murder mysteries, bizarre stories, tales of infidelity or anything of the sort will be considered for publication.

If your style runs to darkness, misery and pain, we may not be the best publication for you—but who knows? An intriguing tale will capture our attention, no matter how gloomy.

GUIDELINES:

We will consider every submission for publication, but please follow the suggestions below to ensure your chances of acceptance:

1. No obscene language AT ALL, excessive violence and absolutely no pornography! We understand that fiction has to be realistic, but we won't consider graphic material, so please save your time and ours.

2. Short stories and non-fiction articles should have a 2,000-word maximum; flash fiction a 1,000 word maximum; and poetry should be no longer than 32 lines. We also have a page for short items under 500 words.

3. Please review and spell check carefully before submitting. We don't mind doing minor editing, but don't have the time or patience to consider correcting entire stories. It's easier to reject them instead. Don't let this happen to yours! Proofread, proofread, proofread!

Submissions should be in WORD FORMAT, SINGLE SPACED WITH A BLANK LINE BETWEEN PARAGRAPHS AND SEPARATING DIALOGUE. NO FANCY INDENTATIONS OR SPACING!! Submissions not complying often require complete reformatting which is time-consuming and tedious.

4. Unfortunately, we aren't able to pay for published material at this time. Be optimistic and consider the increased exposure our publication will give your writing!

5. The author always maintains complete rights to his/her work. Reprints are welcome, but please advise us where and when your story was previously published. Simultaneous submissions accepted.

6. All stories we publish will be archived for four months. If an author wishes to have his/her story removed from our archives, they will need to email us. The story will be deleted within five days of the author's request. If an author has specific reasons for needing a story archived longer, we will consider it.

Electronic submissions only, attachments will NOT be accepted. Paste your work onto the body of an e-mail and send to the following:

For poetry submissions, put "POETRY SUBMISSION" in the subject line, plus the title. For Fiction submissions, put "FICTION SUBMISSION" in the subject line, plus the title. For Non-Fiction, put "NON-FICTION" in the subject line, plus the title. SEND ALL POETRY SUBMISSIONS TO: poetrysubmissions @usa.com. ALL OTHER SUBMISSIONS TO: storysubmissions@usa.com.

8. Please make sure to include your name, e-mail address and word count on the top of the page! Include a brief biography along with permission to use your email address for reader contact should we publish your work.

9. Please, only send two submissions of any type per month per author!

10. We reserve the right to reject any submission without explanation. Some stories simply do not meet our standards or needs at any given time.

11. We're dedicated to responding within two weeks. We will provide critiques whenever possible. We encourage you to browse through the site to get a better idea of the types of stories we're looking for and to enjoy some great writing.

Thanks for sharing your work with us and our readers!

The Editors: Linda Barnett-Johnson, Denise Cassino, Sue Scott and Gloria Pimentel

Categories: Fiction—Nonfiction—Adventure—Book Reviews—Children—Fantasy—Feminism—General Interest—Horror—Internet—Language—Literature—Men's Fiction—Men's Issues—Mystery—Poetry—Short Stories—Women's Fiction—Women's Issues—Writing—Young Adult

CONTACT: poetrysubmissions@usa.com
Material: Poetry
CONTACT: storysubmissions@usa.com
Material: All other submissions
PO Box 1223

Conifer CO 80433
Phone: 303-670-1900
Fax: 303-670-1900
E-mail: d.cassino@att.net
Website: http://www.longstoryshort.us

The Long Term View
Massachusetts School of Law

Editorial Philosophy

The *Long Term View* is a public policy journal which devotes each issue to a balanced discussion of a single topic or question. We provide a forum where academics, professionals, and other knowledgeable persons can make their information available to lay persons in a direct and readable manner.

To achieve this objective, we welcome submissions in many forms, including essays and analytical articles. Whatever the format, we want unambiguous, economical prose. We discourage the extensive use of footnotes: main points should be made in the text. Authors are responsible for the accuracy of all citations and data.

Manuscripts will be edited for clarity, brevity, and style. Topics for future issues of LTV are printed at the end of each issue.

Manuscript Guidelines

Authors are asked to include an electronic version of their manuscript, via e-mail (vietzke@mslaw.edu) or disk.

Any footnotes should appear at the end of the manuscript.

Please include a separate cover page with your name, affiliation, title of manuscript, and a brief biographical note.

Categories: Nonfiction—Government—Law—Politics—Academia

CONTACT: Holly Vietzke, Editor
Material: All
500 Federal St.
Andover MA 01810
Phone: 508-681-0800
Fax: 508-681-6330
E-mail: vietzke@mslaw.edu

The Lookout
For Today's Growing Christian

Our Magazine

• THE LOOKOUT is a 16-page, full-color weekly magazine from Standard Publishing with a circulation of 80,000.

• THE LOOKOUT is written and designed to provide Christian adults with true-to-the-Bible teaching and current information that will help them fulfill their desire to mature as individual believers, develop godly homes, and live in the world as faithful witnesses of Christ. In short, we went to help our readers understand and respond to the world from a biblically based viewpoint.

• THE LOOKOUT publishes from a theologically conservative, nondenominational, and noncharismatic perspective. It is a member of the Evangelical Press Association.

Our Readers: • We have a diverse audience with readers in every adult age group, but we aim primarily for those aged 35 to 55. • Most readers are married and have older elementary to young adult children. But a large number come from other home situations as well. • Our emphasis is on the needs of ordinary Christians who want to grow in their faith, rather than on trained theologians or church leaders.

Our Needs: • As a Christian general-interest magazine, we cover a wide variety of topics—from individual discipleship to family concerns to social involvement. We value well-informed articles that offer lively and clear writing as well as strong application. We often address tough issues and seek to explore fresh ideas or recent developments affecting today's Christians.

• Our annual theme list is available on request (send a self-addressed stamped envelope). *Query for theme-related articles.* **Please note.** We publish strictly according to our theme for the year. All major articles we purchase will address one of the 52 themes we have scheduled for the year. We continue to purchase non-theme articles for occasional features (Salt & Light, Faith Around the World, and Outlook).

• Please do not submit poetry or fiction.

• Please do not submit previously published material.

We usually publish six kinds of nonfiction articles:

• *Teaching articles* (1,000-1,600 words): Help readers *practically* apply Scripture to present-day needs or show them fresh ways to grow in their Christian walk. Your article should provide either solid principles to help readers better understand your subject or skills to help them effectively respond.

• *Informational and journalistic articles* (1,200-1,600 words): We are looking for timely, well-researched articles, interviews, profiles, or essays dealing with topics of current concern. (List sources when applicable.)

• *Human-interest stories* (1,200-1,600 words): Let your unique experiences and observations help our readers see God at work in the world. Better yet, show us the experiences of others. Become a reporter and tell our readers about Christian individuals or families with extraordinary stories. Humor and inspiration articles are welcome.

• *"Outlook"* (500-800 words): We publish reader-written opinion essays addressing current issues that concern Christians. Address your submission to "Outlook."

• *"Salt & Light"* and *"Faith Around the World"* (500-800 words): These articles inform our readers about Christians—in America and other parts of the world—who are living out their faith and reaching out to their communities. We're looking for exciting true stories about people who are making a positive difference.

Your Submission

• Please query six to nine months in advance for theme-related articles and nine to 12 months in advance for seasonal articles. Your query letter should concisely describe the article you propose to write. Enclose a legal size, self-addressed, stamped envelope. If we are interested, we will ask for the article "on speculation," which means we are willing to examine the article, but cannot promise to publish it.

• Submit your typed manuscript, double-spaced, on one side of 8½" x 11" paper. Enclose a legal size, self-addressed, stamped envelope. (Self-addressed, stamped reply postcards are also acceptable.) Do not send more than one manuscript per SASE.

• Suggest a subhead for every 250-300 words of the article and a pull quote for every 500-600 words.

• Secure permission from the appropriate publishing house when quoting songs, hymns, or poetry in the article.

• Legible photocopies and letter-quality printouts are acceptable.

• We do not accept unsolicited submissions by fax.

• We accept queries by e-mail, but we do not accept unsolicited submissions by e-mail or on disks.

• With your submission, please provide your name, address, daytime telephone number, social security number, and word count.

• Allow up to 10 weeks for reply.

• THE LOOKOUT pays up to 11 cents per word for first rights on unsolicited articles and up to 17 cents per word for first rights on assigned articles. We pay on acceptance.

• Simultaneous submissions to non-competing markets are acceptable.

• THE LOOKOUT does not publish poetry or fiction.

• To receive a theme list, send a self-addressed stamped envelope with your request.

• To receive a sample issue, send $1.00 and your mailing address with your request.

Categories: Christian Interests—Inspirational—Religion—Spiritual

CONTACT: Submissions Editor
Material: All
8121 Hamilton Ave.
Cincinnati, OH 45231
Fax: 513-931-0950

E-mail: lookout@standardpub.com
Website: www.lookoutmag.com

Lost Treasure
Treasure Cache

Lost Treasure, Inc. reviews manuscript submissions for two treasure magazines as follows: 1) *Lost Treasure*, a monthly publication, accepts lost treasure, folklore, personal adventure stories; legends; and how-to articles. 2) *Treasure Cache*, an annual publication, accepts only documented treasure cache stories with a sidebar from the author telling the reader how-to search for the cache highlighted in the story. Additional tips and guidelines on writing for *Treasure Cache* are sent on request (be sure to include an SASE).

SUBMISSIONS

1. Original Stories with photos, maps, and documentation are what we want! No rehashes of well known treasure stories.

2. Queries: *Lost Treasure*—not required. *Treasure Cache* and *Treasure Facts*—required. Queries should be typed, one page or less, and may be faxed, mailed, or emailed. Queries are answered as quickly as possible, usually 2-4 weeks.

3. Source Documentation: *Lost Treasure, Treasure Cache* and *Treasure Facts*—require source documentation. Articles dealing primarily with personal how-to information does not require source documentation unless the author makes reference to information outside of the realm of his/her personal experience. Then documentation is required. For source documentation requirements, see Source Documentation, #15.

4. Format, Disk: Manuscripts must be typed, caps and lower case (not all capital letters) and accompanied by a readable 3½" floppy disk in ASCII or Microsoft Word. If a disk is not available, typewriter copy must be of scannable quality (clean, clear, sharp black ribbon). See #8 below.

5. Page Identification: Your name, address, telephone number (including area code) and social security number should appear on each manuscript page in the upper right hand corner, and on the backs of all slides, photos, maps, or other accompanying material. Photos should also be numbered on the back (see # 9 below).

NOTE: Do not rubber stamp nor write information on the backs of photos, maps, etc., as damage may result making them unusable.

TIP: Type information on a sticky back label and affix or, type on a piece of paper and tape to the back of the photo.

6. Word Count: An approximate word count should appear in the upper right hand corner on the first page of your manuscript.

7. Page Numbering: Manuscript pages should be page numbered.

8. Sequence: Manuscripts should be typed in the following sequence: 1) Article. 2) Sources. 3) Captions (photo, map, art) and should appear on your disk as well as hard copy.

9. Identification—Photos and Captions: All photos should be assigned an identification number (i.e., 1, 2, 3, etc.). Accompanying captions should be typed and numbered to correspond to photo I.D. numbers and, appear at the end of the article. If you are submitting a computer disk, captions must appear on the computer disk at the end of the article.

10. All or Nothing: All photos, maps, documentation, other pertinent information and floppy disk (if available) should accompany your manuscript at the time of submission.

11. Article Lengths: *Lost Treasure*—500-1,500 words. *Treasure Cache* and *Treasure Facts*—1,000-2,000 words. Occasionally two-part articles are published. These are accepted by query only.

12. Issue Themes: *Lost Treasure* articles should coordinate with an issue's theme if possible (editorial calendar available on request. Send SASE with [one first class stamp]). Stories deviating from the theme are always considered and used whenever possible. How-to articles are used in each issue. *Treasure Cache* is documented stories, and *Treasure Facts* is how-to articles, etc.

13. Caution: Stories should not read like ads for particular prod-

ucts. It is acceptable to name products in your story, but refrain from consistently repeating the detector's name or the name of other equipment unless you are submitting a field test story or the product did something unusual.

14. Don't Fold Them: Submissions should be mailed unfolded in 9"x12" (or larger) envelopes.

15. Source Documentation: At least two sources (preferably more) are required with each submission. Exception: personal experience stories.

• Newspapers: List newspaper name, issue date, article title. If newspaper clippings have no identification or date, note this fact in your sources.

• Magazines: List magazine title, publication date (month and year), article title, article's author.

• Books: List by author, title, publisher, publication date.

• National Archives, Library of Congress, etc.: List title, document number.

• Historical Societies, Museum Files, etc.: List organization name, location (city, state), and other identifying information as applicable.

• Personal experience stories:

• Yours: Identify yourself as the source, telling this is a personal experience, where it happened and when.

• Others: Identify whose experience it is, where it happened and when. Tell how you learned of the experience (examples: interview, letters, other).

TIP: Write down source information as you work. This insures accuracy and eliminates the necessity of backtracking.

16. PHOTOS: (Remember to identify them. See #'s 5 and 9 above.)

• Cover Photos: Accepted with or without accompanying story. Only 35mm color slides (vertical shots) are accepted.

• Article Photos: Black and white or color photos, any size smaller than 5"x7" accepted. No Polaroid shots. All photos must have sharp focus with good contrast.

17. MAPS: May be hand drawn or copied. They should indicate where the lost treasure is located and contain specific directions to lost treasure sites. (Remember to identify them. See #'s 5 and 9 above.)

18. PICTURES, BLACK AND WHITE LINE ART (not created by you): May be used only if you have received permission to do so and, credit is given to the source (museum, Library of Congress, illustrator's name, etc.). Exception: Newspapers—permission is not required but, credit must be given to the newspaper if a picture is copied. (Remember to identify them. See #'s 5 and 9 above.)

19. CARTOONS: As a rule we do not use cartoons in our magazines. Occasionally a cartoon accompanying a story is used.

20. SAMPLE ISSUES OF OUR MAGAZINE: Available on request. Write to: Managing Editor, Lost Treasure, Inc., at the address shown below. Enclose SASE with $1.47 postage.

21. NON ACCEPTANCE: We do not accept foreign manuscripts. Writers must reside in the U.S.A.

22. CONTRACT: We required a signed contract (our Magazine Rights Agreement form) from each writer giving us ALL rights to all material used (manuscripts, photos, art, etc.). No exceptions.

23. PAYMENT: Cover shots—$100.00. Articles—4¢ per word. Photos, hand-drawn maps, artwork—$5.00 each used. Payment is made on publication, not acceptance.

Categories: Nonfiction—Treasure Hunting

CONTACT: Carla Short, Managing Editor
Material: Metal Detecting/Treasure Hunting
PO Box 451589
Grove OK 74344
Phone: 918-786-2182
Fax: 918-786-2192
E-mail: Managingeditor@losttreasure.com

Lucky Magazine

Formal guidelines not available. Please read a number of issues to ascertain the publication's style and needs.

Send queries to address below.

Categories: Nonfiction—Beauty—Fashion—Literature

CONTACT: Submissions Editor
Material: All
4 Times Square, 8th Floor
New York NY 10036
Phone: 212-286-2860

The Lutheran Digest

The Lutheran Digest, published quarterly, accepts a limited number of original manuscripts. Approximately 70 percent of the magazine's content is reprinted from other publications. *The Digest*'s goal is twofold: To entertain and encourage believers and to subtly persuade nonbelievers to embrace the Lutheran-Christian faith. Distribution is free to participating Lutheran churches through the proceeds of business advertising.

ARTICLES WE WOULD LIKE TO SEE:

Articles should be no more than 7,000 characters in length. Articles of less than 3,000 characters are encouraged. Stories frequently reflect a Lutheran-Christian perspective, but are not intended to be "lecturing" sermonettes. Popular stories show how God has intervened in a person's life to help solve a problem. Also needed are seasonal and special interest stories and stories reflecting God's presence in nature. Seasonal stories should be submitted at least 6 months in advance of possible publication date. Please review the following schedule when submitting holiday pieces:

Issue	Topic	Submit By
Fall	Thanksgiving	April 15
Fall	Christmas	April 15
Winter	Easter	July 15

ARTICLES WE WOULD RATHER NOT SEE:

• Stories with premises such as: "I was walking my dog (watering the lawn, washing the dishes, etc.) when I suddenly thought about how God takes care of my daily needs (gives us nourishment, washes away our sins, etc.)" • Personal tributes to deceased relative or friend are seldom used unless the subject of the article is well known. • Stories about the moment when an individual personally accepted Christ.

STYLE FOR BIBLICAL QUOTATIONS: Scripture references, which should be included for any Biblical quotations, should be inside the final quotation mark. [Example: "God so loved…life (John 3:16)."] Also, the first letter of all pronoun references to God and/or Jesus should be capitalized.

MANUSCRIPT MECHANICS: Front page—In the upper-left corner include your name, address and phone number. In the upper-right corner, note the character count (not word count). Title should be centered and printed in upper- and lower-case lettering, 1/3 down the page, followed by your byline. Manuscripts should be typed, double-spaced, with paragraph indentations and spacing between paragraphs. A short, one-line biographic sketch should follow the article. ***Please do not submit more than three or four articles every three months.***

MANUSCRIPT RECEIPT PREFERENCES: *The Lutheran Digest* **prefers to receive manuscripts in hardcopy format via conventional mail.** Response to, and return of, manuscripts that are not accepted will occur only if accompanied by a self-addressed, stamped envelope. We take no responsibility for lost or damaged manuscripts.

Our preference is to not receive simultaneous submissions, but they will be considered. Please notify us of the manuscript's simultaneous submission status.

Manuscripts submitted by fax or email should comply with the Manuscript Mechanics section above. We regret that the number of unsolicited submissions we receive makes it impossible to respond to everyone. Therefore no responses to manuscripts submitted by fax or email will be made unless a manuscript is accepted for publication. Emailed manuscripts should come as separate attachments and not be included in the body of the email text. Acceptable email attachment formats are Microsoft Word documents or .pdf (portable document format) files suitable for viewing with Acrobat Reader.

PAYMENT: *The Lutheran Digest* generally pays $35 per article on acceptance, plus a complimentary copy upon publication.

REPRINTS: Authors are encouraged to submit previously published articles for which they have retained reprint rights. Content should be similar to that described in Article above. Payment is generally $35 on acceptance plus a complimentary copy upon publication. [Note: As a professional courtesy, the last publication to feature the article will be acknowledged via a credit line. Be sure to include the name/publication date of that publication.]

POETRY: *The Lutheran Digest* accepts a limited number of *short* poems each issue. We're most likely to accept poems of one or two stanzas that will fit into a single column of the magazine. Only two full-page poems are used each issue. Subject matter is open. There is no payment for poetry, however, a complimentary copy is sent when the poem is used. Each poem should be typewritten on a separate sheet of 8 ½" x 11" paper. We are interested also in seeing poems that can be sung to the melodies of familiar hymns. We do not publish poems that are depressing or express the poet's despair with life or with God. *Please do not submit more than three poems at a time.*

FILLERS: Items such as "Recipes Lutherans Digest" and jokes may be submitted. A complimentary copy of the magazine will be sent on publication.

RIGHTS PURCHASED: *The Lutheran Digest* buys one-time rights for original material or one-time reprint rights for previously published items. We also ask that authors allow us to grant limited reprint permission to individual churches for use in their congregations. (Commercial inquires are referred to the author.) Articles accepted for print may also be considered for our website: (www.lutherandigest.com). If we include your article on our website an additional payment will be made.

Categories: Nonfiction—Animals—Christian Interests—Comedy—Confession—Conservation—Consumer—Cooking—Diet/Nutrition—Family—Gardening—General Interest—Health—Hobbies—Inspirational—Marriage—Money & Finances—Music—Outdoors—Parenting—Poetry—Recreation—Relationships—Religion—Rural America—Senior Citizens—Spiritual—Teen

CONTACT: The Editor
Material: All
PO Box 4250
Hopkins MN 55343
Phone: 952-933-2820
Fax: 952-933-5708
E-mail: tldi@lutherandigest.com
Website: www.lutherandigest.com

Lynx Eye

LYNX EYE is a quarterly literary magazine of short stories, poetry, essays, social commentary, and black-and-white art. "Lynx-eyed" means sharp-sighted, and each issue showcases the work of visionary writers and artists. Familiar formats are combined with the experimental; experienced contributors appear alongside new voices. The opening feature, *Presenting*, introduces a previously unpublished artist.

The pages of LYNX EYE take you on imaginative journeys in the company of colorful characters. You may visit a Baltimore diner, the Indiana state fair, or a Tuscan village. Meet the world's greatest fishing dog, a forgetful vampire, and the queen of jingle junk. From pastoral odes to biting commentary, each issue of LYNX EYE offers thoughtful and thought-provoking reading.

Along with the pleasure of the written word, visual treats are plentiful. Original cover art invitingly presented—occasionally in eye-opening color—greets the LYNX EYE reader. Graphic designs, pen-and-ink drawings, and astute cartoons are scattered throughout the publication.

LYNX EYE is a journal-sized magazine; average page count is 120. It is published every February, May, August, and November. With a steadily growing readership, the lynx has been spotted worldwide: Paris, Kharkov, Bangkok...and Whidbey Island. Shouldn't your address be listed too?

In the U.S.
- One-year subscription (4 issues): $25.00
- Two-year subscription (8 issues): $48.00

Outside the U.S.
- One-year subscription (4 issues): $32.00
- Two-year subscription (8 issues): $60.00

Sample Issue: $7.95 within the US.
                  $10.95 outside the US

Please make checks payable to ScribbleFest Literary Group.

ScribbleFest Literary Group is a nonprofit organization dedicated to the promotion and development of the literary arts. With a mission to encourage excellence in writers and artists, founders Pam McCully and Kathryn Morrison began publishing LYNX EYE in November, 1994. ScribbleFest plans to expand its activities by sponsoring special events, readings, and support services vital to the development of the literary arts.

"From our humble beginnings over tepid cappuccino in a Westwood coffeehouse, our love of literature compelled us to provide a forum for uncommon ideas and unheard voices."

—Pam and Kathryn

Writer's Guidelines

Each issue of LYNX EYE includes fiction, essays, poetry and black-and-white artwork. Prose should be between 500 and 5,000 words, Poetry should be 30 lines or less. Our format is journal size; artwork should be 6"x4" (or something that will reduce to that size). If you have an excellent piece of work that falls outside of our requirements, send it.

Each issue opens with the feature, *Presenting*, in which a writer or artist makes his or her print debut.

LYNX EYE accepts never-before-published work only. We acquire first North American serial rights to your work. All other rights remain with you. We pay $10 per piece upon acceptance. You also receive three complimentary copies of the publication.

Manuscripts must be typed. Artwork should be camera-ready. We will respond within eight to twelve weeks.

Creativity is the antithesis of prejudice: having an open mind in the most complete sense of the word-non-judgmental, open to possibilities, open to new ideas, open to one's own feelings, open to others' feelings and needs.

Creativity is not-stopping too soon. How many creative ideas are squelched, and how many creative possibilities are never approached because someone gave up? But the creative person has to know when to "change gears": on arriving at an idea you really believe in, determination becomes necessary to follow through with it and to not be discouraged by others. Creative people work hard.

—From Cognition to Creativity
LYNX EYE

We are committed to the written word and eagerly await reading yours.

Categories: Arts—Poetry—Short Stories—Essays—Social Commentary

CONTACT: Pam McCully, Co-editor
Material: All
PO Box 6609
Los Osos CA 93412-6609

The MacGuffin

The MacGuffin publishes the best new work in contemporary poetry, prose, and visual art. Although the editorial staff of *The MacGuffin* pride themselves on the fact that every submission is considered, the following guidelines are highly suggested for a thorough examination and prompt reading of your material.

For All Submissions
· In general, we do not accept previously published work.
· Standard, easy to read, typeface are preferred.
· List titles and brief bio in cover letter. Do not staple work.
· Include name, email, address, and the page number on **each page**.
· Do not send revisions unless our editors have requested them.
· Allow 8 to 16 weeks for a response. We thank you in advance for your patience.

Postal Submissions
· All inquires about submissions must be made via electronic or US Mail.
· Please enclose a self-addressed, stamped envelope (SASE) or sufficient International Reply Coupons for reply only. No work will be returned unless specified with sufficient postage.

Email Submissions
· Submissions may be made electronically to macguffin @schoolcraft.edu
· Submissions made in the body of an email will not be considered. Please submit each work on a separate page as a Word document attachment.

Additional Information
· We do accept simultaneous submissions if informed. We expect prompt notification if the work is accepted elsewhere.
· Manuscripts may be withdrawn until issue enters the typesetting process.
· Authors and artists receive two copies of the issue in which their work appears.
· Additional copies may be purchased at substantial savings.
· Translations are welcome and should be accompanied by a copy of the original text. Translators are responsible for author's permission.
· *The MacGuffin* is copyrighted. Upon publication all rights revert to authors. We appreciate acknowledgement as first place of publication.

Poetry
· We consider traditional, formal, free verse, and experimental poetry.
· Poems can be up to 400 lines.
· There are no subject biases.
· Please do not submit more than **five** poems at one time.
· Poems should by typed, single-spaced, and one per page.

Fiction and Creative Non-Fiction
· We have no subject biases, though obvious pornographic material will not be published.
· Maximum length is 5,000 words. Please include word count. Portions of longer works are acceptable if they can stand-alone.
· All prose should be typed and double-spaced.
· One submission per envelope.

Images
· Submit the best quality image available; i.e., original photographs, slides, or artwork. Photocopies or laser output scan unevenly and leave streaks across the image.
· If you want an image cropped, indicate the cropping on a photocopy of the image. Do not crop photos or artwork. We size and crop the image on the computer.
· Electronic Images should be EPS or TIFF files saved at 300 dpi for photos and 600 dpi minimum – 1200 dpi maximum for line art.
· Embedded images are not accessible to the page layout software.

Categories: Fiction—Nonfiction—Literature—Poetry—Short Stories—Writing

CONTACT: Anne Hutchinson, Senior Editor
Material: All Other
CONTACT: Carol Was, Poetry Editor
Material: Poetry
CONTACT: Elizabeth Kircos, Fiction Editor
Material: Fiction
Schoolcraft College
18600 Haggerty Road
Livonia MI 48152-2696
Phone: 313-462-4400 ext. 5292
Fax: 313-462-4558
E-mail: macguffin@schoolcraft.edu
Website: www.schoolcraft.edu

Mad

We're actively looking to expand our pool of freelance comedy writers and there's more opportunity to join The Usual Gang Of Idiots than ever. If you have a twisted sense of humor, a peculiar way of looking at the world, or are simply eager to express your immature, strange or just plain silly side, then we want to see your stuff! Here's what we're looking for:

1. Material for The Fundalini Pages: Introduced in January 2004, this still-evolving front-of-the-book-section provides great outlet for topical, short form humor. Especially prized are biting social satire and outrageously funny quick takes. Throw the kitchen sink at us! This is an excellent place for first time writers to break in.

2. Comic strips: We want to add new comics to the magazine. Whether a strip is an ongoing, monthly feature, or a one-time-only, single or multi-panel gag, we'd love to see your ideas. While we are particularly interested in comics that reflect adolescent male sensibilities, feel free to let your mind roam. Got a really weird concept that you think belongs in an underground comic? Have an idea for an irresistibly irreverent character? Whatever it is, if you think it's funny, send it to us. (And, no, you don't have to be an artist.)

3. Hard Hitting Satire/Cutting Edge Yuks: Tackle ongoing cultural themes and fads, problems and issues, including controversial court cases, political blunders, celebrity and sports scandals and anything else ingrained (and sometimes senselessly beaten!) into the American consciousness. Good areas include: pop culture, sex/dating, politics, the Internet, the music and fashion scenes, and any topics of interest to teens. Especially prized are articles on video games, kid/parent and student/teacher relationships.

4. Media Parody: Poke fun at and lambaste your favorite (or least favorite) showbiz celebs, movies, TV programs and channels, radio shows, videos, commercials, magazines, books, catalogs, etc. Be audaciously original!

5. Utter Silliness: Pointless humor for humor's sake, which may include a heavy dose of stupidity, faulty logic, moronic conclusions and non-sequiturs. (Articles we've run in this category include Most Wanted Renegade Clowns and Sadistic Simon Says.)

6. MAD 20 Features: Our annual run-down of the 20 Dumbest People, Events & Things of the Year has become a reader favorite. Especially prized are full-page visual-impact pieces. (Take a look at one of our previous MAD 20 installments to familiarize yourself with the feature.)

Here's what we're NOT looking for:

1. Movie & TV Satires: Unless they're entirely different in format and approach from the ones we're currently using.

2. Rewritten MAD-Like Junk: Nothing will get you a rejection slip faster that an article with a title like "Other Uses For Your Old _____" or "Who's Who At A _____."

3. Your Take On Already Existing Features: Including Spy Vs Spy, A MAD Look At..., The MAD Fold-In, The MAD World Of..., etc.

4. AND PLEASE: No advice columns, short stories, book manuscripts, articles about Alfred E. Neuman, or Alfred E. Neuman cover gags.

HOW TO SUBMIT MATERIAL

Send us a paragraph or two explaining the premise of your article, with three or four examples of how you would carry it through. Be sure to include art notes describing the visual content of each example. Rough sketches are welcomed but not necessary. Be neat and to the point. No hand-written submissions.

IMPORTANT NOTES

1. Our preference is for you to submit via email. Send your material to submissions@madmagazine.com. Please note: We will respond only if we're interested. Fax submissions are not accepted.

2. If your material contains significant sketches or is otherwise art-intensive, you may submit via snail mail. Be sure to include a self-addressed stamped envelope with sufficient postage to send your submission back, or we will not be able to return your artwork. (Overseas contributors must include U.S. stamps or International Reply Coupons.) Send your submission to address below.

3. Before submitting become familiar with today's MAD, not the MAD you grew up with (although that helps). Don't be discouraged if the rejection slips pile up. Writing for MAD isn't a piece of cake. That's why we pay top rates—$500 per MAD page (for new contributors)—on acceptance (pieces that are less than a page—e.g. comic strips, Fundalini bits, etc.—are pro-rated accordingly).

Any other questions? See your spiritual advisor or write your Congressman! We've told you everything we know. Now it's time to sit down at your computer, word processor, typewriter, notebook, stone tablet (or whatever it is you use to record your idiotic brainstorms!) and exercise your funny bone. We're waiting to hear from you! Lots of luck!

Categories: Fiction—Humor

CONTACT: MAD Submissions Editor
1700 Broadway
New York NY 10019
E-mail: submissions@madmagazine.com

Madison Magazine

About us: *Madison Magazine* is a monthly lifestyle and business publication, which began in 1978. We are family-owned, and other holdings and affiliates include WISC-TV3 and the websites wisbusiness.com and Channel3000.com. We have a circulation of more than 18,500 and a total readership of 75,000.

Editorial content is divided into these main sections: Your Town, OverTones, Habitat, Fine Dining, the features section, Health Watch, and Madison Business. Your Town is a mixture of small articles, briefs and profiles of people, events, goods, arts, humor and entertainment. These items range from 50 to 300 words in length. Because our readers have a strong interest in arts and entertainment, our OverTones and Fine Dining sections are designed to give them a guide to the city, including a restaurant guide, an events calendar, and meatier articles on the arts, dining out and more. Habitat has its own cover and the design style is driven by spectacular photography of homes and gardens. The features section, or the "well," is where our longer (700 to 3,000 words) in-depth articles run. Subjects vary, but include personal and professional profiles, government, science, medicine, environment, education, family, travel, money and health. We also regularly publish service pieces, such as top lawyers, best doctors, suburbs ratings, Best of Madison readers' poll, Best of Madison Business and more.

The business section was conceived to lead the market in coverage of the New Economy – the high-tech and biotech industry that encompasses university science, research and education as well as industry trends, profiles, Q&As with area business leaders, general interest articles, columns, and a regular feature on the job market. We cover the traditional "old economy" stories, such as manufacturing, land use and development, agriculture and others, but the main focus is on new technology and how it drives today's marketplace.

Editors are open to any ideas as long as they relate to Madison and the surrounding area or would be of interest to readers in this area. Because of our two-month or longer lead time, articles must have a long-term perspective that is as readable several months from now as it is today. We have several columns: politics is written by former Capitol reporter Jeff Mayers, who now runs two online news services, WisPolitics.com and WisBusiness.com; John Roach, a native Madisonian and award-winning screenwriter, writes a monthly column called "Out There;" our business column rotates between business strategist Kay Plantes, futurist Rebecca Ryan and others; and Michael Kwas, wine director at the renowned L'Etoile Restaurant, provides advice on the best and most affordable wines for any and all occasions. Our most recent addition is a food column called "Genuine Articles." Written by former restaurateur Nancy Christy and her husband – and Madison Magazine editorial director – Neil Heinen, the column is designed not only to document the local food and dining scene but also to excite and inspire readers to think about how a thriving local food market can enhance a city's sense of pride and place because how we eat is a symbol of who we are. The food and wine columns are part of our dining section, which features a food or dining-related article each month as well as shorter pieces on food news, such as bar and restaurant openings, festivals and seasonal suggestions.

Writer's Guidelines/Updated: Oct. 2005

Queries and specs: Article queries are welcome. Please allow several weeks for the editors to review the query. In some cases, editors may ask the writer to keep the story on file and resubmit it at a later date. Stories may be written on spec, but because they are unsolicited, editors may not respond. All prospective writers must submit a resume and clips.

Contract: After a story is assigned, the writer will receive a contract in the mail within three working days. The original contract must be signed and returned within three working days. New writers are also asked to sign a W-9 form for tax purposes.

Story assignments: The writer will receive a one-page story brief (via e-mail, unless otherwise requested) that includes the article outline, sidebar assignments, due date, month of publication and freelance payment.

Word count: Content space is always tight, and editing time is limited, so please write to the assigned word count. If an article is too long, the writer may be asked to rework the article to the appropriate length. Editors reserve the right to edit for length, accuracy and tone. Final edits are routinely sent back for review.

List of sources: For editing and fact-checking purposes, all writers must include a list of sources and contact information with each article submission.

Deadlines: Writer's deadlines are generally scheduled at least one month in advance of the magazine issue for which they are assigned. They are firm and rarely negotiable. Missed deadlines interfere with the edit, arts and design staff, who strive to meet internal deadlines that are integral to the magazine's success. The magazine reserves the right to cancel a writer's article if it isn't turned in by the deadline. In extreme circumstances, the magazine reserves the right to refuse payment if a writer's tardiness severely affects the production of the magazine. In addition, please carefully review the writer's contract for more specific line items related to percentage decreases in fees for tardy work.

Payment: Payment varies with the length of the article, degree of difficulty, a writer's experience, and amount of research and interviews. Payment is issued on the 5th of the month in which the article appears.

Kill fee: If an assigned article is turned in on time and meets all other requirements, but fails to be published, the writer will receive a kill fee of 1/3 of the agreed upon writer's fee.

Expenses: The agreed upon fee for an article includes any expenses incurred in the reporting and writing process. Added expenses (excess mileage, photo development) require magazine preapproval.

On-line publication: Any story published in Madison Magazine will be considered for publication at madisonmagazine.com, Channel3000.com, or wisbusiness.com. For on-line rights, please refer to the writer's agreement. Please send a resume, cover letter and work samples to the address below.

Categories: Nonfiction—Arts—Education—Environment—Family—Food—Government—Health—Medicine—Money—Science—Travel—Regional: Madison, Wisconsin

CONTACT: Brennan Nardi, Editor
7025 W Raymond Rd
Madison WI 53719
Phone: 608-270-3624
E-mail: bnardi@madisonmagazine.com

Maelstrom

1. For poetry submissions please send no more than 4 pieces with name and address on each page.

2. Short Fiction must be 3,000 words or less.

3. Every submission should include address, cover letter, 2-3 line bio and a SASE or they will not be returned. While not required, submissions accompanied by a $1.00 donation will be answered immediately.

4. No attachments in e-mail submissions will be accepted. Please paste your text into the body of your e-mail.

5. Previously published and simultaneous submissions O.K.

6. Also seeking black and white art and book reviews.

7. Pay is 1 copy.

8. Pornography is not acceptable.

9. Staff writes short reviews of chapbooks and magazines, materials can not be returned.

10. Subscriptions are available for $20.00/4 issues or single copies may be purchased for $5.00 current or $4.00 sample. Check or money order made payable to *Maelstrom*. Copies also may be purchased online through Paypal at our web site, IMaelstrom@ aol.com

11. Response time at least 3 months*

*Submissions accompanied by a $1.00 donation will be answered immediately.

Categories: Fiction—Book Reviews—Cartoons—Poetry—B/W Art—Humor

CONTACT: Christine L. Reed, Editor
Material: All
PO Box 7
Tranquility NJ 07879
E-mail: IMaelstrom@aol.com
Website: www.geocities.com/~readmaelstrom

The Magazine of La Cucina Italiana

General Guidelines

The Magazine of La Cucina Italiana is unique in its authoritative approach to Italian cuisine, travel, wine, and culture. Readers rely on our publication to provide them with in-depth, accurate information concerning Italian regional foods, dining establishments, places and people of interest, and Italian specialty food shops in Italy and around the world. The *Magazine of La Cucina Italiana* is aimed at an audience that is well-to-do (with incomes around $150,000 per year) who "know" Italy, its food, and culture. They love cooking and good eating, as well as the cultural subjects that we write about. This magazine is fit for coffee table display.

Our editorial mission is to attract and educate the public about the many pleasures of Italian gastronomy, wine, culture, art, tradition, and tourism.

We are looking for qualified contributing editors to submit articles and accompanying photographs on relevant subjects. We only seriously consider articles that include photographs.

Main Article Subjects

1. TRAVEL to various locations in Italy, highlighting their most distinctive and significant features: the mountains, lakes, rivers, big cities (one or more of their aspects), towns. We usually make a distinction between a city article and a region article.

In 70-80% of the cases, the photos must contain people. We try to present Italian cuisine and culture with the people that make it interesting. In other words, if the article is about Herculaneum, the images should show people in front of the ruins, walking around, holding interesting objects, eating (even someone enjoying a sandwich if there is nothing else), and perhaps selling souvenirs. The rest of the pictures should show the surrounding places and perhaps some from your arrival and any typical modes of transportation. Every article must contain at least one element that suggests "luxury" or "richness" in the presentation of the object or items being sold. For example, a restaurant, café, or hotel that is clearly upscale and luxurious in appearance or a place that is open to the public (a monument or gallery) that has the same qualities. Stores that sell gifts or elegant items are also acceptable. It would be ideal to have enough pictures to contrast the typical with the luxurious. For our readers, this lavishness could be Baroque, Rococo, or contemporary, as long as it is obviously upscale.

2. CHEFS/RESTAURATEURS, their kitchens/restaurants, (inside and out), personalities, their context and training, two or three dishes, typical ingredients, and customers.

Occasional Topics for The *Magazine of La Cucina Italiana*:

1. Articles on an INGREDIENT such as a cheese, meat product, or other ingredient specific to Italy and Italian cooking. These articles should have some of the aspects of a trip article and some of a chef article (and must have some element of luxury). These articles are to be 1000-2000 words, with 12-16 images (3 or 4 of which must be of dishes). The recipes must be included.

2. Articles on a cellar or producer of WINE, or on a specific wine. In addition to the images outlined in points "a" and "b" above, you must also provide images of vines, vineyards, cellars, bottles, and labels. These articles are to be of 1000-2000 words with 10-14 images. The article must refer to a DOC or DOCG wine.

The Article Breakdown

For every issue, there are 2 or 3 travel articles (of which at least one must be on an urban environment) and 1 article about a famous chef or restaurateur. The breakdown is as follows:

• 1 travel article of 2500-3000 words and 12-14 images; and 2 travel articles of 1500-2000 words and 8-12 images.

• 1 chef article of 1500-2000 words and 12-16 images (more images and fewer words). Images of at least 2 or 3 dishes and their recipes.

The mix of articles in each issue showcases different regions of Italy.

Photographs

Pictures of food must have natural coloring and succeed in capturing the beauty of the dish and its composition. They should be done with a large-format camera, or if of very high quality, with 35 mm film (100 ASA). We do not accept postcard-type photos.

The publisher reserves the right to examine services not specifically requested, whether photographs or complete texts, and will return them only if requested and provided with a SASE.

Conditions and Procedures

Any agreement made will be confirmed in writing and will outline the topic, images, price, and deadline to be signed by both parties.

The articles must be sent either by mail, fax, or e-mail to the managing editor, accompanied or preceded by the photographic images. The material must be unpublished. The author will be informed of the outcome of the manuscript in the shortest time possible. For the first submission, we would like a short biography of the author as well.

If the submission is accepted, it will be edited (or edited, translated, and edited again) and when possible, sent to the author for approval before publication.

The images that are accepted will be held from when they are received until after the publication of the article.

The payment of a fixed price for the service will be sent immediately after publication.

Categories: Nonfiction—Cooking—Food/Drink—Life-style—Travel

CONTACT: Marie Dalby, Managing Editor
Material: All
230 Fifth Ave. Ste. 1100
New York NY 10001
Phone: 212-725-8764, Ext. 14
Fax: 212-889-3907
E-mail: piacere@earthlink.net
Website: www.italiancookingandliving.com

The Magazine of Fantasy & Science Fiction

Writer's Guidelines

We have no formula for fiction. We are looking for stories that will appeal to science fiction and fantasy readers. The SF element may be slight, but it should be present. We prefer character-oriented stories. We receive a lot of fantasy fiction, but never enough science fiction or humor. Do not query for fiction; send the entire manuscript. We publish fiction up to 25,000 words in length. Please read the magazine before submitting. A sample copy is available for $6 (to NJ address).

We do not accept simultaneous or electronic submissions. Please type your manuscript on clean white bond, double spaced, with one inch margins. Put your name on each page, and enclose a self-addressed, stamped envelope. Writers from abroad are encouraged to send recyclable manuscripts with a letter-sized SASE and an International Reply Coupon or 84 cents in US postage (63 cents to Canada and Mexico). You can obtain US postage online from www.usps.com.

We prefer not to see more than one submission from a writer at a time.

Allow 8 weeks for a response. Please write and enclose a self-addressed stamped envelope if you have any questions.

Payment is 6-9 cents per word on acceptance. We buy first North American and foreign serial rights and an option on anthology rights. All other rights are retained by the author.

Our columns and non-fiction articles are assigned in house. We do not accept freelance submissions in those areas.

Since we use so little art—just eleven covers a year, no interiors—we have no separate artist's guidelines. Please send art samples to Gordon Van Gelder at the address below.

Send story submissions and cartoon queries as well as orders for sample copies to Gordon Van Gelder, Fantasy & Science Fiction, P.O. Box 3447, Hoboken, NJ 07030.

Categories: Fiction—Fantasy—Horror—Satire—Science Fiction—Short Stories—Young Adult

CONTACT: Gordon Van Gelder
Fantasy & Science Fiction
PO Box 3447
Hoboken NJ 07030
Website: sfsite.com/fsf

The Magazine of Speculative Poetry

MSP was founded in 1984 by Mark Rich and Roger Dutcher. Mark published one the first speculative poetry magazines, "Treaders of Starlight." Roger published "Uranus," another speculative poetry magazine. Finding themselves in the same city, they naturally founded a new magazine. MSP went 13 issues with both as editors when Mark, having moved and found success in his writing, decided to "move on." MSP has been edited by Roger since then.

Basics:

3 cents a word, $7.00 minimum, $25.00 maximum on acceptance.

First North American rights.

All rights revert to the author(s) upon publication, except for permission to reprint in any "Best of" or compilation volume. Payment will be made for such publication.

Poets receive a copy of the issue in which their poem(s) appears.

Return time of 1 to 8 weeks. Usually 1 to 2 weeks.

No simultaneous submissions; we do not use reprints.

What MSP wants:

I want more than just images. I want a poem to take me someplace I haven't been before. Have a fresh look at an old trope. I am more concerned with a good poem first, then a speculative poem.

Speculative poetry: Speculative poetry may be described as the equivalent in poetry to speculative fiction, that interesting confluence of post modernism and science fiction in the late sixties and early seventies of Britain and America. Authors associated with this movement include: J.G. Ballard, James Sallis, Pamela Zoline, Keith Roberts, Brian Aldiss, Samuel Delaney, Thomas Disch, and the poets George MacBeth and D.M. Thomas.

Speculative poetry can result from several approaches. One might be called projection: we imagine ourselves viewing from other perspectives than our own or simply being another being—for instance, we might be a tree, an alien sentience, perhaps ourselves five years from now. A second approach is simply that of the extended metaphor: science fiction has created a rich vocabulary of images and ideas, many of which might be utilized in generating poetry. Other approaches may be used and the poems themselves may range from the meditative to the narrative to the lyric. What is most important to remember is that speculative poetry is a species of imaginative literature, and that it is a new species. Each poem in part defines the field as it is written.

I will leave it to others (or to another place) to argue whether speculative poetry is separate from or inclusive of, yet more than, science fiction poetry and the other identifiers we use, fantasy and horror. "Slipstream" seems to be a term that is similar. Literary has been used to describe the type of poetry we use.

Science fiction poetry: Based on science (soft or hard) and speculating on or exploring that science for an outcome we, in our current world, have not discovered yet. How do we react to, manage in, the world you have constructed. Was it Ray Bradbury who said SF doesn't predict the future, it tries to prevent it.

Science poetry: Read Diane Ackerman and Loren Eisley for an idea. The poem should still convey a sense of wonder. Not just nature poetry. Astronomical poetry with an edge perhaps. Speculation on contemporary science perhaps.

Fantasy poetry: I don't see enough fantasy poetry. What does MSP want? Fantasy from the realm of myth, fairy tales, and contemporary fantasy like Tolkien, Susan Cooper's "Dark is Rising" series, Le Guin's "Earthsea," McKillip's "Riddle Master" series, etc. Jim Dorr "Flight From the Tower" in a previous MSP fits the bill. I don't mean horror, dark fantasy or sword and sorcery. Once in awhile MSP sees Beowulf "like" poems, usually epic in length, no, I don't mean these, either, and not just because of the length. Just because there is an elf doesn't make it fantasy. I don't particularly like elves with motorcycles and assault weapons fantasy. In contemporary settings I enjoy the prose of James Blaylock and prose and poetry of Charles de Lint.

Horror or Dark Fantasy poetry: I am hard to please in this area. There is a lot of poetry written in this area. There are a lot of markets

M-Q

in this area. It is going to take a poem that grabs me to be accepted. It is not likely to be a vampire, werewolf or zombie poem. I do seem to have a penchant for mummies. It is most likely to be psychological horror that I will look at more closely. I am not likely so take a "splatter" poem.

Concrete and prose poetry: OK, I have not seen a lot of concrete poetry I have liked that was speculative, but then again, it seems the field should be able to produce some interesting visions. I would probably ask for a disc copy of any poem I might accept.

I won't try to define prose poetry. Shorter will be better. Have more than images.

Essays and reviews but query first with general idea/outline.

Not much help? If you feel it is a good poem and you want to spring for the postage, try me out. MSP would publish good poems in any of the areas above. I would rather read, enjoy and accept a poem than not have it sent because of any strictures inferred or implied above.

I have sent back good poems that are: mainstream, love, nature or political in content, but are not speculative. I have taken some I have liked because they are "on the edge."

Length, style, etc.:

A number of editors are very strict about how they want everything. You should pay attention to those details if you are submitting to them. Although we have always been pretty easy going, there are some general guidelines that make it easier for me.

We are a small magazine, we can't print epics, yet they still arrive now and again. We have printed some poems that run two or three pages, but it is rare to do anything longer. If you have something you feel is your best and it is longer, go ahead and send it.

No simultaneous submissions. We do not use reprints.

I am not persnickety about the number of poems you send. Send as many as you want to spring for postage on. Your acceptance is based on your poem, not on the number. Be reasonable though, not twenty or thirty. There does seem to be a correlation between a poet sending large numbers and my not liking the poetry, but that could be illusion. But, it seems a waste to send one, unless it is long, so send what you want. Three to five seems to be the most common number.

I have read poems that are hand written (usually prisoners or young people), single-spaced, double-spaced, with a regular font, with hard to read fonts, etc. I am not persnickety here either, but double-spaced (on smaller poems) is better, and a "regular old font" is best. I don't recall ever accepting a poem that was handwritten, in a hard to read font or something out of the ordinary. Not because of the handwriting but because of the poem; again, there seems to be a correlation. My eyes do seem to require more focusing of late, so double-spacing is best.

Cover letters: I like 'em. But they aren't necessary. If you do include a cover letter, make it more than "here are my poems, I hope you like them." A practical matter is to include the names of the poems you are submitting, if the poems get separated from your cover letter, then it helps to find them. Tell me where you have been published before (you don't have to have been) if you want, it may help trigger a memory of a poem you have done. You don't need to send a complete list of every poem you have ever published, just some high spots. Tell us where you have heard of us, it helps us know which market sources produce the best results. You can tell me a bit about yourself if you like.

Your name and your address should appear somewhere on each poem, your name on each page if it is a longer poem. This is practicality, if your poems get separated from your cover letter or return envelope, I am not likely to recall whose they are. Including the number of lines/words in each poem, usually in the corner opposite your name and address, is useful as well.

Postage: You should include an appropriate amount of postage for the return of your mss., if it cost you 37 cents to mail them to me it is going to cost you 37 cents to mail them back. If you are submitting from a country other than the US, remember, I can only use US stamps. Send loose US stamps (see USPS website for current rates to your country) or an IRC. I have yet to meet a USPS employee who has treated an IRC the same as another. Most of the time I have good luck

with them. However they do require you and me to stand in line and to have the employee figure out what to do with them. If you can arrange a stamp swap with someone, that is nice. In the case of non-US poets only, if you don't want your mss. returned, send me your e-mail address and I will let you know. My e-mail address is a work address and seriously limited re: non-work related mail.

If you send me your poems in an 8"x10" envelope and a #10 envelope for their return, I am going to stuff them all in the #10 envelope. This can result in an envelope which is overweight for the postage on it. I don't put on extra postage, you are liable to get a postage due return.

If you don't want your mss. returned, please state this clearly in your cover letter and/or on the mss. itself. If you don't, you will get your poems back in whatever envelope you send me.

If your submission comes to me postage due you are very likely to get it returned to you as "refused."

Submissions without an SASE or postage/IRC are held for about 2 to 3 months. If I haven't received an SASE in that time the poems are recycled.

Electronic submissions: Yes, it is the world of the Internet and e-mail, no, I don't have a computer (believe it or not.) I do have an e-mail address but it is for work and I have to limit the amount of non-work e-mail I receive. I am not open to electronic submissions. With the exception of non-US poets noted above, I can not e-mail a poet about their submission.

At the moment I am not requiring or requesting submissions on disk.

MSP does not want:

Prose. Plays. Art work.

Nature poetry, animal/pet poetry, religious poetry, love poetry unless they have some correlation to one of the genres we publish. We get a fair amount of the type of poetry completely unrelated to speculative poetry, some of it is good, most of it bad, but none of it accepted.

An Organization of interest:

Science Fiction Poetry Association, now in its 28th year. The SFPA publishes Star*Line, a newsletter, six times a year and the association administers the Rhysling Award for best science fiction poems of the year. You also receive the Rhysling Anthology, which publishes the nominated poems, with your membership. Membership information at www.sfpoetry.com.

Categories: Fantasy—Horror—Literature—Poetry—Science Fiction

CONTACT: Roger Dutcher, Editor
Material: All
PO Box 564
Beloit WI 53512

Magical Blend

Thank you for your interest in *Magical Blend* magazine. We are always interested in reviewing focused, well-written nonfiction articles and interviews. The best way of assessing our style is to look at copies of our magazines, which are available in most major bookstores and on the internet at www.magicalblend.com. Our Statement of Purpose, located in the beginning each issue, is a good places to start. You might also examine *A Magical Universe: The Best of Magical Blend Magazine* (Swan Raven, 1997) and *Solstice Shift: Magical Blend's Synergistic Guide to the Coming Age* (Hampton Roads, 1997) for samples of the kind of writing we publish in *Magical Blend*.

We do not respond to query letters, and we only consider final products.

We prefer that you submit your article by email. If you do submit a hard copy, please include a self-addressed, stamped envelope or email address for our reply. Allow up to six months for a response. We don't send back submissions, so do not send us your only copy. We no longer publish poetry or fiction. Writing in the form of a sermon is discouraged.

Submissions should not have already appeared in other publications or on the web.

Magical Blend is the leading magazine for metaphysics, cultural trends, indigenous spirituality, and more. Now in its third decade, Magical Blend tracks the changes in society, always holding true to the vision that, together, we can co-create the best possible reality for our world and ourselves. Our readers are primarily interested in personal and planetary growth and change, with an emphasis on spiritual and social subjects that are well researched. It is not news to our readers that alternatives to the Western medical paradigm or to conventional consciousness exist. They want innovative techniques for living life more fully, articles that show where magic, miraculous healing, and esoteric philosophy meet Main Street, and information that sheds light on the process of global and personal transformation. They are curious about alternative technologies, health, the environment, and the significance of the internet. Their musical tastes range from inspirational to world beat to fusion jazz. Light-hearted pieces with a point to make about the human condition are welcome.

FORMAT: Feature articles range in length from 1000 2000 words. E-mailed

versions are preferred (in Rich Text Format or text-only format, or in MSWord 98 or earlier), though hard copies can be mailed to Magical Blend, PO Box 600, Chico, CA 95927-0600. E-mail us at editor@magicalblend.com. Work that has been edited for length and clarity is more likely to be considered. Payment is considered strictly on an individual basis.

Artwork for our Creativity section or to accompany articles may be submitted digitally or on slides or color prints. Do not send us originals! SOME ARTICLE IDEAS *Magical Blend* MAGAZINE CONSIDERS:

- Sacred Travel
- Health & Alternative Healing
- Music
- Better Tomorrow
- Personal Transformation
- UFOs/Paranormal
- How-To
- Sexuality & Intimacy
- Celebrities
- Women's Empowerment
- Men s Empowerment
- Traditional Spirituality
- Notes & Quotes
- Money, Work, & Technology
- Culturally Diverse Spirituality Children s Spirituality
- Nature & Spirit
- New Ideas & Innovations
- Animals as Spiritual Teachers
- Humor
- Ancient Mysteries
- Practical Spirituality
- Astrology/Astronomy/The Stars
- Environmentalism/ Gaian Spirituality
- Fairies
- Conscious Death & Dying
- Divination
- Love
- Mythology/Archetypal Tales

We look forward to reading submissions that show your passion!

Categories: Nonfiction—Alternate Lifestyles—Animals—Book Reviews—Conservation—Culture—Diet/Nutrition—Ecology—Environment—Feminism—Health—Inspirational— Internet—Interview—Lifestyle—Men's Issues—Multicultural Music—Native Americans —New Age—Outdoors—Paranormal—Psychology—Relationships—Religion—Science—Self Help—Sexuality—Society—Spiritual—Travel—Women's Issues

CONTACT: Susan Dobra, Editorial Director
Material: All
PO Box 600
Chico, CA 95927-0600
E-mail: editor@magicalblend.com
Website: www.magicalblend.com

The Maine Organic Farmer & Gardener

The Maine Organic Farmer & Gardener is the newspaper of The Maine Organic Farmers and Gardeners Association (MOFGA). It is published four times a year (March-May, June-August, September-November, December-February) and accepts about three articles from freelancers per issue.

Some areas of concentration are:
- Rural skills and rural development
- Livestock care and management
- Farming, gardening and forestry practices and techniques
- Agricultural and biological research (soil-plant relationships, biochemical interactions...)
- Profiles of individual plants (edible and ornamental) and pests
- Agricultural economics, politics, and issues--international, national, regional, community
- Agricultural agencies, organizations and groups; influential individuals within agriculture
- Agricultural resources, their efficient use and ecological management
- Tools, equipment and machinery for small, diversified or organic farming and gardening
- Energy use, production and conservation
- Farmers and gardeners, preferably organic, with interesting farms, gardens, viewpoints or techniques. Also, first-person farming and gardening experiences
- Businesses related to agriculture, food or natural resources
- Agricultural marketing
- Environmental issues
- Nutrition

Sample copies of The MOF&G are available for $2 each from the MOFGA office at PO Box 170, Unity ME 04988; Phone (207) 568-4142; Fax (207) 568-4141; email: mofga@mofga.org. Some articles from our paper are on our website, www.mofga.org, as well. Unsolicited manuscripts are welcome when accompanied by SASE or sent by email. Queries are also welcome.

Accompanying photos and/or illustrations are a plus.

We pay about $25 to $250 for articles, depending on length (250 to 2500 words, usually) and quality. Payment is on publication. We buy first or one-time rights. We do not pay a kill fee. Deadlines for final drafts of articles are January 15, April 15, July 15 and October 15 for the respective issues.

We look forward to working with you on educational and entertaining, ecologically-oriented articles that will help people enjoy farming, gardening and healthful eating.

Categories: Nonfiction—Agriculture—Alternate Life-styles—Animals—Book Reviews—Conservation—Consumer—Cooking—Crafts/Hobbies—Diet/Nutrition—Environment—Food/Drink—Gardening—Health—Hobbies—Human Rights—Interview—Lifestyle—Regional—Rural America—Science

CONTACT: Jean English, Editor
Material: All
Maine Organic Farmers & Gardeners Association
662 Slab City Rd.
Lincolnville ME 04849
E-mail: jenglish@midcoast.com

Manoa
A Pacific Journal of International Writing

What We Are Looking For

Fiction, poetry, essays, and interviews need not be related to Asia, the Pacific, or Hawaii'i, nor be by writers from the region. We are not interested in genre or formalist writing for its own sake, or Pacific exotica and picturesque impressions of the region.

Translations are usually commissioned by a guest editor, who is responsible for the portion of the issue featuring writings from a country or region of Asia or the Pacific. The rest of the issue is usually reserved for North American writing. We may occasionally run translations other than those selected by the guest editor, but you might want to query us first.

Submissions

We do not have specific length, subject-matter, or style requirements. We do prefer to see five or six poems at a time, depending upon the length. Like most literary magazines, we suggest reading a copy of the magazine to get an idea of what we like to publish. To order a sample copy, please visit our ordering page.

Please also note that we do not accept submissions by e-mail.

MANOA is published twice a year, summer and winter, and accepts submissions throughout the year. Please include a self-addressed, stamped envelope with each submission for the return of the submission and/or our reply. Submissions should be originals or good photocopies; handwritten manuscripts, dot-matrix printouts, and originals typed on onion-skin sheets are not acceptable. Please allow about four weeks for reply on poetry manuscripts, essays, and reviews, and about six months for reply on fiction manuscripts.

Reviews

Reviews are on recent books in the arts, humanities, or natural sciences; usually, these books are related to Asia, the Pacific, or Hawaii, or are published in these places. Separate guidelines are available for reviews.

Questions

If you have further questions, we'll be glad to answer them. Just drop us a note. We try to reply promptly.

July 2002

Categories: Nonfiction—Asian-American—History—Literature—Multicultural—Nature—Poetry—Short Stories

CONTACT: Submissions Editor
Material: All
English Dept. University of Hawaii
Honolulu HI 96822
Phone: 808-956-3070
Fax: 808-956-3083
E-mail: mjournal-l@hawaii.edu
Website: www.hawaii.edu/mjournal

Marine Corps Gazette:
The Professional Journal of
U.S. Marines Since 1916

Writers' Guidelines:

Our basic policy is to fulfill the stated purpose of the *Marine Corps Gazette* by providing a forum for open discussion and a free exchange of ideas relating to the U.S. Marine Corps and military capabilities. The *Gazette* welcomes material in the following categories:

Commentary on Published Material: Submit promptly. Comments normally appear as letters (see below) 3 months after published material. **BE BRIEF**.

Feature Articles: Normally 2,000 to 3,000 words, dealing with topics of major significance. Manuscripts must be DOUBLE SPACED. Ideas must be backed up by hard facts. Evidence must be presented to support logical conclusions. In the case of articles that criticize, constructive suggestions are sought. Footnotes are not necessary, but a list of any source materials used is helpful.

Ideas and Issues: Short articles, normally 750 to 1,500 words. This section can include the full gamut of professional topics so long as treatment of the subject is brief and concise. Again, please DOUBLE SPACE all manuscripts.

Letters: E-mail submissions to gazette@mca-marines.org are preferred. Limited to 200 words or less and DOUBLE SPACED. As in most magazines, letters to the editor are an important clue as to how well or poorly ideas are being received. Letters are an excellent way to correct factual mistakes, reinforce ideas, outline opposing points of view, identify problems, and suggest factors or important considerations that have been overlooked in previous *Gazette* articles. The best letters are sharply focused on one or two specific points.

Book Reviews: Prefer 300 to 750 words and DOUBLE SPACED. It is a good idea to check with the editor in advance to determine if a review is desired. Please be sure to include the book's author, publisher (including city), year of publication, number of pages, and cost of the book.

The best advice is to write the way you talk. Organize your thoughts. Cut out excess words. Short is better than long.

Submissions: Submissions may be sent via regular mail and should include one hard copy of the manuscript and a disk with the manuscript in Microsoft Word format. Photographs and illustrations must be in TIFF, JPG, or EPS format (300 dpi, 5 x 7 inches, color preferred) and **must not be embedded in the article. Please attach photos and illustrations separately.** (You may indicate in the text of the article where the photos are to be placed.) Include the author's full name, mailing address, telephone number, and e-mail address. Articles may also be submitted via e-mail. Please follow the same instructions for format, photographs, and contact information when submitting by e-mail. Any queries may be directed to the editorial staff by calling 800–336-0291, ext. 344.

Categories: Military

CONTACT: *Marine Corps Gazette*
Material: All
PO Box 1775
Quantico VA 22134
Phone: 800–336-0291, ext. 344
Fax: 703–640–6161, ext. 344
E-mail: gazette@mca-marines.org

Marlin
The International Sports Fishing Magazine

1. *Marlin* accepts freelance-written articles on a query basis for both features and departments. Please send written queries for any articles you may have for *Marlin* with your name, address, phone number, social security number and an SASE. Queries should be concise and pertain to offshore fishing, destinations, personalities and related topics only. For detailed information regarding *Marlin*'s scope, direction and editorial needs, call editor David Ritchie at (407) 628-4802.

2. All features will be edited as necessary, usually to a length of 1,500 to 2,500 words. If an assigned article is unacceptable as submitted, the author may be given one opportunity at a rewrite. If an article is accepted by the editor, but is not used for reasons out of the author's control, a one-third kill fee will be paid to author.

3. *Marlin* gladly accepts "over the transom" submissions, but ac-

cepts no responsibility for the return of such materials. In all cases, though, the editors will attempt to respond to such materials in a timely fashion.

4. Very often, one of the key determining factors in our decision-making process regarding submitted queries and manuscripts is the amount and quality of available photography on the subject in question. See the Photographer's Guidelines in the following section for more information on this subject.

5. One of the easiest ways to begin publishing your material in *Marlin* is by contributing to the smaller departments:

Send short news items which directly relate to offshore fishing, fishery regulations, the boating industry or other related topics to the attention of "Blue Water Currents." Keep the items short and to the point, and provide photography or illustration support when possible.

The "Tips & Techniques" section is the place for you to submit short briefs on offshore fishing techniques, tackle innovations, boat handling advice, etc. Keep the items under 250 words, and provide photo or illustration support.

"Lines In" is *Marlin*'s section for tournament reports. Call editor David Ritchie at (407) 628-4802 to discuss possible event coverage. Keep "over the transom" reports short, make sure all names and boats are spelled correctly, detail the "Keys to Victory" that led to the winning catch, and provide a photo of the winners when possible. No hanging fish photos, please.

PHOTOGRAPHER'S GUIDELINES & POLICIES

Marlin continues to emphasize the finest saltwater fishing photography to be found in any magazine. Most of that comes from freelance professionals. *Marlin* provides bona fide international exposure for photographers' best work.

RETURN POLICY: It remains our fundamental goal to review and send out images not selected within a few days of receipt. We do NOT ordinarily hold photos at all unless we have a projected possible use. A tracking sheet will be included with images returned showing which slides are being kept and for what purpose.

SHIPPING: If we call and request photography quickly, we'll reimburse for shipping. Otherwise, the photographer pays to ship. We'll take care of returns, usually via Certified Mail unless otherwise specified.

OVER-THE-TRANSOM SUBMISSIONS: When in doubt, ship it out. We're always happy to review images, whether solicited or unsolicited (and since we won't hold those for which we see no specific, possible use, there's little to lose and much to gain).

WHAT TO SEND

FILM TYPE: We prefer Velvia 50 or equivalent for non-action shots in bright light; High shutter speeds for fast moving fish (1/1000+); Bracket where possible and try for both horizontals and verticals; Compose to keep fish main focus of most shots and to avoid extraneous objects in frame (also avoid clothing with nasty/racist/sexist inferences).

DUPES OR ORIGINALS?: We run originals, not dupes. You may send in duplicate slides for review purposes, but only if the originals are available. Also, there is always a better chance of selection for an original slide simply because it offers better definition and color than subsequent generations.

SUGGESTIONS

DON'T SEND US FUZZY SHOTS!!!

Instead, give us photos that are, by any measure, "tack sharp." Every day I see otherwise great shots precluded from use by being too "soft." There's just not much point in sending any images that are not crystal clear.

AVOID INANIMATE "GRIN & GRAB" SHOTS.

Send us images of people animated as they hold fresh (preferably lively) but not bloody fish. Counteract the dreaded Zombie Stare Syndrome. Have subject interacting with someone else if available. (Have 'em hold fish together and look at/talk to each other—while forgetting the camera even exists—anything to get subject loose, happy, natural.) If subject alone, suggest interaction with the fish—hook removal, lifting from deck, even admiring it (looking at it, not you). Avoid dead fish

in such photos—take 'em quick when the fish is in the boat and lively, before it's clubbed or languishes to a pale, glassy-eyed state of rigor mortis.

Finally, do keep the angler's tackle in the shot!

AVOID KILL SHOTS OF BILLFISH AND BLUEWATER SHARKS!

Send us exciting, in-focus shots of leaping, tailwalking, greyhounding fish; of fish being wired for tagging or being released or admired at the boat. Skip the traditional dead stuff— hanging at the dock, draped over the transom, bleeding on deck—or anything with a gaff in it.

"Kill" shots of other, food fish okay if—you should pardon the expression—tasteful. Sport, not carnage, is what we're after.

AVOID SHADOW-DARKENED SHOTS.

Give us shots liberal with use of fill flash under high sun or backlit conditions.

DON'T LIMIT SUBMISSIONS TO FISH/FISHING ALONE.

Have an eye to all things related to fish/fishing, viz: rigging, technique (gear/action), baits, lures, equipment, diving birds, weather, water (color/rips/ weedlines), feeding schools, schools of baitfish (and catching them), other boats fishing/running, Bimini starts, etc, etc. Also, don't hesitate to photograph any/all near shore/offshore species, gamefish or others, including those that are unusual.

COVERS

Marlin covers emphasize fish, boats and fish action—fish leaping, underwater, at the surface, on a line out of the water and so on. That may include anglers interacting with fish—fighting fish, releasing or tagging fish and the like. Other offshore pelagic gamefish may occasionally qualify. Remember: 35 mm focus must be laser-sharp to retain its quality when enlarged 1,200 percent. The dominant image must fill most of the frame to minimize blow-up necessary (e.g. a jumping fish that's a dot on the horizon won't make it).

WHEN PACKAGING SUBMISSIONS

1. Make sure that every image has—at the very least—your name on it. Otherwise, return can't be guaranteed. Words of description (area, species, etc.) written right on the slide can be of great help.

2. If sending slides/other images in one package targeting two or more articles, please places slides in a separate sheet (or sheets) for each different article and mark the sheet accordingly.

3. If brief captions are written on each image, a page with extended captions is helpful; if no information is written on images, a sheet of captions is essential.

4. Make sure your social security number is included somewhere, unless you are certain we have it (or unless you have no interest in remuneration).

5. Payment will be issued to the first name on the slide (stock agency or photographer) unless other payment arrangements are specified.

COMMUNICATIONS

Don't hesitate to call Editor David Ritchie or Managing Editor Scott Leon at (407) 628-4802 anytime you have any general or specific questions about photo needs, submissions or payment.

Categories: Nonfiction—Adventure—Boating—Conservation—Consumer—Fishing—Outdoors—Recreation—Sports/Recreation

CONTACT: David Ritchie, Editor
Material: All
PO Box 2456
Winter Park FL 32790
Phone: 407-628-4802
Fax: 407-628-7061
E-mail: editor@worldpub.net
Website: www.marlinmag.com

Marriage Partnership

Description & Philosophy

Marriage Partnership seeks to provide realistic, challenging, and practical insights into healthy Christian marriage. We offer hope and help to our readers through practical how-to pieces; interviews with experts; humorous articles; true-life, dramatic stories of couples dealing with major life challenges; thoughtful essays; and couple profiles.

We begin with the premise that marriage is a life-enhancing gift from God. We are solidly rooted in biblical truth, but our approach to sharing that truth is somewhat different from other Christian magazines. The principles we communicate—lifelong commitment, sexual fidelity, mutual sacrificial love, mutual respect—are taken from Scripture, but we use everyday language to communicate those principles. We recognize that there are a number of legitimate models for successful and God-honoring marriage; therefore, we avoid dogmatic, legalistic advice. While we want to show how God's grace and redemptive power can work in our readers' lives, we also recognize that staying married in today's culture can be a difficult and complex challenge. The answers aren't always easy—but God sees us through.

Our Readers

We want our readers to "see" themselves in the articles we publish. The majority of our readers are middle-class, college-educated Christians in their 20s, 30s, and 40s (median age 36). They are busy raising kids and juggling jobs (about two-thirds of our women readers work outside the home). Our readers are concerned with finances, communication, church involvement, time management, parenting, sex, conflict management–everyday, nitty-gritty issues. Rather than presenting an idealized portrait of marriage and family, we work hard to present a realistic image of life that makes our readers say, "Yes, that's how it is in my house!"

Our Writers

We do not accept unsolicited manuscripts or simultaneous submissions. Rather, we welcome well-thought-out and well-written query letters that include: a thorough summary of the article, the purpose of the piece and its value to readers, the author's qualifications to write the piece, suggested length and deadline, and a stamped, self-addressed envelope.

Writers who can communicate with freshness, clarity, and insight will receive serious consideration. We are looking for writers who are willing to candidly speak about their own marriages. We strongly urge writers who are interested in contributing to *Marriage Partnership* to read several issues to become thoroughly acquainted with our tone and slant.

With some exceptions, we pay on acceptance of completed articles and buy first rights. All submissions are received on speculation. An accepted query does not guarantee purchase of the manuscript. Editors reserve the right to reject any manuscript at any stage. We try to respond to queries and manuscripts within 8 to 10 weeks. Manuscripts should be typed double-spaced. Send queries and other editorial correspondence to the address below.

Categories: Nonfiction—Christian Interests—Consumer—Family—Lifestyle—Marriage—Relationships

CONTACT: Ginger Kolbaba, Managing Editor
Material: All
Christianity Today International
465 Gundersen Dr.
Carol Stream IL 60188
Phone: 630-260-6200
Fax: 630-260-0114
E-mail: mp@marriagepartnership.com
Website: www.marriagepartnership.com

The Massachusetts Review
University of Massachusetts

Thank you for your interest in *The Massachusetts Review*, a quarterly of literature, the arts and public affairs. We represent no stylistic or ideological coterie. The editors seek a balance between established writers and artists and promising new ones, and material of variety and vitality relevant to the intellectual and aesthetic life of our time. We aspire to have a broad appeal; our commitment, in part regional, is not provincial.

"Inspired pages are not written to fill a space, but for inevitable utterance; and to such our journal is freely and solicitously open." (Emerson)

ARTICLES & ESSAYS of breadth and depth are considered, as well as discussions of leading writers; of art, music, and drama; analyses of trends in literature, science, philosophy, and public affairs. No reviews of single books.

FICTION: We consider one short story per submission, usually up to 25-30 pp.

POETRY: A poetry submission may consist of up to six poems. There are no restrictions in terms of length, but generally our poems are less than 100 lines. Please write your name on every page.

Fiction and Poetry manuscripts should be submitted separately. No mixed submissions, please.

MR no longer considers plays for publication.

In addition:

Please include your name and address on first page of manuscript.

Please do not send mss. from June 1st through October 1st.

Please do read a copy of MR before sending work.

Include an SASE with all correspondence.

The Massachusetts Review is a nonprofit journal and it is impossible for us to acknowledge receipt of the many manuscripts we receive or to honor requests made for sample copies. You may order an issue for $9.00 (incl. Postage) or begin a subscription. Subscription rates:

Individuals, USA: 1 year, $25; 2 years, $40; 3 years, $55

Outside USA: 1 year, $30

Libraries: 1 year, $35

Categories: Fiction—Poetry—Essays/Articles—Memoirs

CONTACT: Ellen Watson
Material: Poetry
CONTACT: Editors
Material: Fiction
South College, University of Massachusetts
Amherst MA 01003
Phone: 413-545-2689
Website: www.massreview.org

Massage & Bodywork
Nurturing Body Mind & Spirit

Massage & Bodywork is a specialty magazine, published six times per year, for professional practitioners of massage, bodywork, and somatic therapies, as well as members of the general public with an interest in the field. Unsolicited submissions are accepted. We suggest that potential writers study recent issues before sending queries or manuscripts. All manuscripts should be submitted via e-mail.

If accepted, *Massage & Bodywork* negotiates for North American rights and electronic rights. The editor reserves the right to edit or rewrite any article in order to make it suit the theme, style or space limitations of a specific issue. Major alterations will be discussed with the author. It is always acceptable, even beneficial, to include photographs and/or illustrations with the submission. Authors are compensated on a case-by-case basis once submission is accepted.

Modality/Technique Articles

Massage & Bodywork looks for interesting, tightly-focused stories concerning a particular modality or technique of massage, bodywork, somatic and esthetic therapies. The editorial staff welcomes the opportunity to review manuscripts which may be relevant to the field of massage, bodywork and esthetic practices, in addition to more general pieces pertaining to complementary and alternative medicine. This would include the widely varying modalities of massage and bodywork (from Swedish massage to Polarity therapy), specific technique articles and ancillary therapies, including such topics as biomagnetics and aromatherapy. Reference lists relating to technical articles should include the author, title, publisher, and publication date of works cited. Word count: 1,500 to 4,000 words; longer articles negotiable.

Technical/Research Articles

For an audience eager to explore the scientific aspects of massage and bodywork, writers are encouraged to submit technical articles relating to the field. Pieces specific to anatomy, medical conditions, and contraindications are welcome. Research-related articles and accounts of formal and informal case studies are of interest. Word count: 1,500-4,000 words; longer articles negotiable.

Professional/Practice-building

Other articles of interest to *Massage & Bodywork* magazine include those relating to legalities/legislation, business or practice-building, success stories, politics of the profession, healthcare and insurance. Word count: 500-2,000 words; longer articles negotiable.

Travel Related to the Profession

Accounts of travel to places that help expand knowledge of techniques particular to certain areas of the world are welcome. Exploration of other cultures' views of the healing arts, historical considerations and similarities are areas of interest. Word count: 800 to 1,200 words.

Human Interest

Articles about people who have had an impact on the fields of massage, bodywork, or somatic therapies are welcome. The story should relate the person's connection with the particular field, why their contribution is important, how their students or clients have been affected by their work, etc. Photographs of the person in action or posed photos should accompany the article. Personal accounts, successful community interactions, volunteer events, etc. are also of interest. Word count: 800 to 1,200 words.

Columns

All *Massage & Bodywork* columns are assigned. If you have a column idea and wish to discuss it with us, explain your proposal, write a sample column and submit for consideration.

Fiction

We do not accept fiction.

Note: If your topic is not mentioned here, but you feel it would be of valid interest to the readers, please feel free to discuss it with our editor.

Photo Requirements

Features should be accompanied by color transparencies, high quality prints or slides, or high resolution electronic images. All photos should be accompanied by a caption sheet identifying each subject.

Artwork supplied by someone other than the manuscript author should be clearly identified for credit, along with necessary releases. All photos, slides and illustrations will be returned after publication. Please include a self-addressed, stamped envelope for this purpose, and allow 45 days after the mail date of the publication for return.

Lead Time

Because this is a bimonthly publication, it may be a matter of months before your article appears in print, although the decision as to whether or not the article will be used is generally made promptly. We assume no responsibility for material submitted, but every effort will be made to return original artwork. Please enclose a self-addressed stamped envelope if return of items is requested.

Liability

Neither *Massage & Bodywork* nor Associated Bodywork & Massage Professionals assumes any responsibility for unsolicited material.

Demographics

80% of our readers are female, average age of 42, with an average household annual income of $56,833.

Categories: Nonfiction—Health

CONTACT: Leslie A. Young, Editor
Material: All
Associated Bodywork & Massage Professionals
1271 Sugarbush Drive
Evergreen CO 80439-9766
Phone: 800-458-2267 x648
E-mail: leslie@abmp.com
Website: www.massageandbodywork.com

Massage Magazine

About Massage Magazine

Massage Magazine is an internationally circulated trade publication for massage therapists and allied health professionals. We have been in publication since 1985, have a readership of about 80,000, and publish six times per year.

We strive for comprehensive coverage of the art and science of massage therapy and related healing arts, with the goal of supporting our readers as they work to promote the benefits of healing touch.

About our readers

Most of our readers are professional therapists who have been in practice for several years. About 80 percent are self-employed; 95 percent live in the United States.

The vast majority of our readers have completed formal training in massage therapy. The techniques they practice include Swedish, sports and geriatric massage, energy work and myotherapy, among many others. Our readers work in settings ranging from home-based studios to spas to integrated clinics.

What we're looking for

Our readers seek practical information on how to help their clients, improve their techniques and/or make their businesses more successful, as well as feature articles that place massage therapy in a positive or inspiring light.

Since most of our readers are professional therapists, we do not publish articles on topics like "how massage can help you relax."

Before preparing a query or manuscript for us, read at least one issue of the magazine, as this is the best way to get a feel for the topics we cover and the tone they're presented in.

Types of articles

FEATURES. We publish six to 12 full-length feature articles per year. Topic examples: the use of massage in a particular setting (such as corporate or hospital); projects that provide massage therapy to disadvantaged populations; accounts of how massage helped a person overcome or deal with a physical condition; descriptions of types of massage used in non-Western cultures; and trends of national significance, such as the incorporation of complementary techniques into the mainstream medical system, among others. Submissions should be 1,500 to 3,000 words.

BUSINESS. We publish at least six articles per year that describe, in detail, to grow or improve a massage therapy practice. Topic examples: increasing or retaining clientele; setting goals; marketing techniques; new business ventures; and money management, among others. General business-related articles written for small-business owners will be considered. Submissions should be 500 to 3,000 words, depending on the complexity of the topic.

NEWS BRIEFS. We publish up to 15 news articles per issue. These articles must display concise, fact-checked reporting and direct or paraphrased quotes, and must focus on current events or trends in the massage and/or spa industries. News briefs can be on anything newsworthy, particularly those situations that impact therapists on a national or North American level. Submissions should be 200 to 800 words.

IMPRINTS. We publish one article per issue that details an experience which has left an imprint on the client and/or therapist: a new realization, a reason for entering the health care field, a poignant or humorous remembrance, etc. Submissions should be 500 to 1,000 words.

PROFILES. We publish two to six profiles per year. Profiles must highlight why a particular therapist's story is compelling; describe a particular clientele; or serve as an example of how the therapist solved an ongoing business- or clientele-related situation. Submissions should be 400 to 600 words.

MIND/BODY/SPIRIT. We publish two to six articles per year on the topic of the relationship(s) between mind, body and spirit, with a specific focus on how massage therapy impacts clients' emotions or spirituality, and how therapists can address or respond to this during sessions. Submissions should be 1,000 to 3,000 words.

SELF-CARE. We publish three to six articles per year which describe techniques that help the therapist care for her/himself. Topics range from exercises to relieve repetitive stress injuries, to ways to relax. How-to articles must be accompanied by photos or illustrations. Submissions should be 1,000 to 3,000 words.

GUEST EDITORIALS. We publish one guest editorial per issue. These may be written by either a practicing therapist or student of massage/bodywork who is passionate about a particular issue facing the field, who has a challenge to present to massage and bodywork practitioners, or who has a unique perspective on the role of massage/bodywork in the greater society. Guest editorials must be accompanied by a professional-quality head shot of the author. Submissions should be 750 to 1,500 words.

TECHNIQUE, GENERAL DESCRIPTION. We publish three to six articles per year that describe a particular, well-established system of bodywork. These articles must be written to a specific guideline, available by contacting our editorial department.

TECHNIQUE, HOW-TO. We publish three to six articles per year that tell readers, through both text and photos/illustrations, how to perform a massage technique or stroke. These articles must be written by a professional therapist with several years' proven experience in the application of the technique, and must be written to a specific guideline, available by contacting our editorial department.

Categories: Health—Physical Fitness

CONTACT: Karen Menehan, Editor
Material: Queries via e-mail only
200 Seventh Ave., #240
Santa Cruz CA 95062
Phone: 831-477-1176
Fax: 831-477-2918
E-mail: kmenehan@massagemag.com
Website: www.massagemag.com

Mature Living
Christian Magazine For Senior Adults

Mature Living, a Christian-oriented, leisure-reading magazine designed for senior adults, has a lead time of approximately 10 months. We are interested in unique, creative manuscripts that are characterized by human interest, Christian warmth, and humor. Manuscripts should be written with simplicity and clarity. Writers should provide documentation for quotations, titles, facts, figures, or other information taken from other sources for verification by the *Mature Living* staff.

Mature Living **only purchases all rights**. Writers who want to continue to sell a manuscript after publication in *Mature Living* can receive a non-exclusive perpetual license to publish the work in whole or in part, allow others to publish the work in whole or in part, and receive payment from other publishers. However, *Mature Living* retains all rights to the manuscript in these situations.

Mature Living claims the editorial privilege of editing, abridging, and condensing purchased manuscripts. Purchase of a manuscript is an intent, but not necessarily a commitment, to publish. The magazine staff further retains the right to illustrate manuscripts as deemed appropriate.

QUERIES

Do not send queries (letters, e-mail, or telephone).

GUIDELINES FOR SUBMITTING MANUSCRIPTS

• With the exception of manuscripts for "Grandparents' Brag Board" and "Cracker Barrel," all manuscripts must be accompanied by a self-addressed, stamped envelope (not just stamps). Allow 2 months for a reply from the editors. Writers who submit manuscripts without a self-addressed, stamped envelope will not receive a response. NOTE: Manuscripts for "Grandparents' Brag Board" and "Cracker Barrel" features are not returned.

• Although *Mature Living* does not accept responsibility for photos and slides that may get lost or damaged in the publication process, all reasonable care will be taken to ensure their safe return. If pictures are old and rare, please have them professionally reproduced locally and send the reproductions with the manuscript.

• Do not submit previously published manuscripts or simultaneous submissions.

• Keep a duplicate copy of the manuscript for your files.

• Do not write or call to inquire about which issue an accepted manuscript will appear. Manuscripts originally intended for one issue might be moved to another issue or, on rare occasions, discarded.

• Send manuscripts via postal mail to the address listed here. Do not send articles via e-mail. If your article is accepted for publication, you may be contacted to then send an electronic copy via e-mail.

SPECIFICATIONS

Manuscripts should be typed and double-spaced. Include word count, your name, address, telephone number, e-mail address, and Social Security number on the top of the first page and your name on every page. If you use a pen name, please indicate that clearly on the first page. Correct all spelling, document unique material, and conform to preferred lengths.

TYPES OF ARTICLES DESIRED

General: Articles may deal with a variety of subjects related to senior adult life, such as current issues, problems, and life adjustments; humor; or seasonal emphases. Preferred length is 600 to 1,000 words.

Nostalgia: Articles of 600 to 1,000 words may be about personal memories or historically based.

Travel: Articles should have general appeal to senior adults that includes descriptive information. Preferred length is 800 to 1,200 words with 4 to 8 color slides or photographs.

Fiction: High-quality fiction, relating to senior adults, should have a strong story line, underscore a biblical truth, and provide enjoyable leisure reading. Preferred length is 800 to 1,200 words.

Cartoons: Cartoons should relate to senior adults and their interests.

DEPARTMENT FEATURES

Cracker Barrel: Each issue includes a page of brief, humorous, original 4-line verses. Payment: $15 upon acceptance.

Crafts: A craft of interest to 55+ adults, describing step-by-step procedures, is used in most issues. Quality color photographs or slides are desired. Depending on size, writers may submit a sample of the craft. Payment: $40 upon acceptance.

Food: Recipes should be of special interest to senior adults. Include an introduction and 4 to 6 recipes. Payment: $50 upon acceptance.

Game Page: Crossword or word-search puzzles and a variety of quizzes are used. Please include solution. Payment: $40 upon acceptance.

Grandparents' Brag Board: Accounts of something said or done by your grandchild or great-grandchild (humorous or insightful) should be brief, accurate, and original. Payment: $15 upon acceptance.

Inspirational: Each issue includes devotional articles (125 words or less each) and poetry (12 lines our less) for "Communing with God" section. Items should be Bible-based, insightful, unique, and slanted to senior adults. Payment: $25 upon acceptance.

Over the Garden Fence: Informational articles of 300 to 350 words should relate to vegetable or flower gardening on a year-round basis. Payment: $40 upon acceptance.

Poetry: We accept a limited amount of brief (12 lines or less), quality poetry that has a direct relationship to senior adults. Payment: $25 upon acceptance.

PAYMENT

Except for Department Features (see above), the payment rate for all rights ranges from $75 to $105 per manuscript accepted. Exceptional quality may be rewarded above the base rate. Payments are made upon acceptance.

Payment of $25 for the use of each original photograph or slide is paid after publication. These will be returned after publication. Please include your name and address on the back of every photograph submitted.

Writers will receive, without cost, 3 copies of the issue in which their manuscripts are published. Extra copies can be purchased from LifeWay Church Resources Customer Service Center, One LifeWay Plaza, Nashville, TN 37234-0113; or call 1-800-458-2772.

Categories: Christian Interests—Senior Citizen

CONTACT: Editorial
Material: All
One LifeWay Plaza
Nashville TN 37234-0175
Phone: 615-251-2000
Fax: 615-277-8272
E-mail: matureliving@lifeway.com (no submissions)

Mature Years

So You Want Your Work in *Mature Years*

Mature Years magazine is published by Abingdon Press, an imprint of the United Methodist Church. The audience comprises persons of retirement age and beyond (55 years plus), and the magazine's purpose is to help persons understand and use the resources of the Christian faith in dealing with specific opportunities and problems related to aging.

We publish quarterly with 112 pages, trim size 8.5 x 11 inches, full-color, 12 point New Century Schoolbook typeface. Pages are two-column. The publication is perfect bound. Circulation is approximately 70,000, and is entirely paid subscription. The magazine is mailed throughout the United States, and through the Protestant Church-owned Publishers Association, it is available in some military base chapels around the world.

Writers are not restricted to being older adults. Unsolicited manuscripts are welcomed.

Reader Description

Our readers like to see themselves in what they read. Writers should acknowledge the readers' maturity and use illustrations that reflect older adult lifestyles, which are varied. Some older adults are employed; some are retired. Some of our readers are active; some are not. Some are married while others are widowed or never married. Housing arrangements may be in their own homes, living with adult children, or in congregate housing of varied types. Most older adults are in good health, but many are ill. They have a variety of educational backgrounds, but writers should assume that they are intelligent and not treat them as forgetful, mindless individuals. Financial status is also greatly varied among our readers.

Mature Years magazine readers do not want to see only older adults in their stories, poems, and articles. They are fearful of being shut up in an "old age ghetto." Inter-generational pieces score great successes with our audience.

Guidelines for General Editorial Content

Quoted Material—You must include photocopies of any material quoted from other sources and give a complete citation.

Subheads—You may include subheads in your text. The editor may or may not use them. If there are multiple levels of subhead, make them plainly distinguishable.

When we review manuscripts we look for the following:

Appropriate Subjects—Popular articles address current issues in aging; including health and fitness, housing, financial conditions, social and emotional needs, security, family life, self-help, and so on. Articles should provide practical aids for older adults: what to do, how to, when to, where to. Especially important are opportunities for older adults to read about service, adventure, fulfillment, and fun. Items of entertainment, like hobbies and crafts, are also popular.

Positive Approach—Articles should be upbeat, picturing older adults who are enjoying living and finding fulfillment in this period of their lives. If articles are about the problems of living as an older adult, they should demonstrate the power of faith for difficult times and offer possible solutions and/or sympathy and comfort.

Active Subjects—Persons featured in articles should be active, creative, involved with their family, church, community, nation, and world. While many of our readers are inactive, they do not want to read about people sitting and doing nothing with their lives.

Varieties of Approaches—Articles can be serious or humorous. They may be based on memories or current experiences. Fiction may be for the purpose of pure entertainment, or stories may explore a social justice issue or concern of aging.

Christian Orientation—When appropriate, articles should demonstrate faith in God as a resource for life in all circumstances, both good and bad. Persons featured should be older adults with a vital lifestyle. For instance, when they travel it will be for educational purposes or to engage in ministry or service to others. Articles and stories should reflect the joy of living out one's Christian faith.

Absence of Stereotypes—Older adults should be freed from the stereotypes of age, gender, nationality, and race. Examples of aging stereotypes are frailty, memory loss, illness, sedentary lifestyle, being socially inflexible, and being unstylish. Be supportive of persons and groups rather than poking fun at them.

Guidelines for Cartoons and Photographs

Cartoons—Cartoons may either have a religious theme or relate to aging as outlined in the "Guidelines for General Editorial Content" above. While bringing some humor to older adult situations, cartoons should never trivialize circumstances and should never demean anyone or their circumstance.

Photographs—If photographs accompany articles, color prints or transparencies are required. If photos are historical, black and white prints or negatives are accepted. Photographs of recognizable people must be accompanied with model releases.

Unsolicited professional studio photos are reviewed and returned. If the quality of the work is acceptable, the studio will be added to the approved list for future assignments.

Be certain that captions are clearly matched with photographs to guarantee proper placement with the photographs.

Guidelines for Poetry

Poetry—Poems are limited to sixteen lines of up to fifty characters. Content should conform to the "Guidelines for General Editorial Content" detailed above. Free verse is allowed. When using rhymes and meter, make sure they are accurate. Seasonal poems are accepted according to the "Seasonal Acceptance Schedule" below. Accompanying photography and graphic designs are never accepted.

Guidelines for Departments

Daily Meditations and Bible Study—This department is a part of the Uniform Series of the National Council of Churches of the USA and is written by invitation only to professional Bible study writers.

Fragments of Life—This department uses short glimpses of everyday life (cuddling with grandchildren, a humorous moment at church, a sweet memory) to inspire and to illustrate the joys, sorrows, and poignant moments of living. It may or may not overtly mention God, but it never preaches. (250 to 600 words)

Going Places—Travel articles must:

a) feature some location or travel aspect particularly appropriate to older adults, such as special activities or facilities planned for the age group. Seniors hiking or snorkeling are examples. Tours for grandparents and grandchildren is another.

Or, b) reflect the predominantly Christian character of the magazine by taking our readers to Bible lands or on a pilgrimage, discussing the historic sites of Christian believers, or showing the countryside or towns of different Christian groups. Typical articles might feature cathedrals of Europe, monasteries or retreats in the United States, Amish communities, or Roman Christian catacombs. (1,000 to 1,500 words)

Health Hints—Health problems and fitness opportunities for older adults are found in this department. Description of a health problem and solutions for alleviating or eliminating conditions should be discussed. Other articles might tell about exercises and activities designed to help older adults keep fit. We never promote pharmaceutical companies or their products. Medicare and Medicaid are not acceptable subjects. (900 to 1,500 words)

Media Shelf—This department reviews books, audio recordings, and computer software of special interest to older adults. Review copies of these items are welcome, but articles are by invitation only.

Merry-Go-Round—This page features cartoons, jokes, and 4-6 line humorous verses. The subject of all these items must conform to the "Guidelines for General Editorial Content" and "Cartoons" printed above. We publish two cartoons in every issue.

Modern Revelations—Overtly religious and inspirational, this department deals with contemporary understanding of the Christian faith. While it is often an essay relating the Bible to modern life and quotes Scripture, it is not a Bible study. It may give advice for spiritual living as an older adult. (900 to 1,500 words)

Money Matters—All economic issues of importance to older adults are acceptable; including banking, investing, wise purchasing, savings instruments, consumer frauds and scams, cost of health care, and insurance. All articles must be written with a personal finance point of view. (1,200 to 1,800 words)

Puzzle Time—Many different forms of puzzles and quizzes are published; including cross words, word-finds, anagrams, and unique formats. Subjects must either have biblical or religious themes or have older adult interest such as great dance bands, grandparenting, or reminiscence. Puzzles and quizzes must be challenging.

Social Security Questions and Answers—This department is furnished by a regional office of the Social Security Administration.

Seasonal Acceptance Schedule

Mature Years magazine closes manuscript purchases for individual issues approximately one year before publication. We are looking for seasonal articles and poems in the following time frames:

Spring—December, January, February

Summer—March, April, May

Fall—June, July, August

Winter—September, October, November

Because *Mature Years* has such a long lead-time, we are not able to publish hard news or anything with specific upcoming dates. The exception to this rule is annual events.

Several departments (Going Places, Health Hints, Media Shelf, and Money Matters) have a news briefs sidebar with a four-month deadline. Information about upcoming events and products and services introduction is included.

Guidelines for Manuscript Preparation

Maximum Word Limit—Specific departmental lengths are printed above. For all other articles no more than 2,000 words are published.

Electronic Submission—Electronic submissions are preferred. They may be sent as a Word attachment to an e-mail or the text may simply be printed in the e-mail. All submissions must be accompanied by your name, address, telephone number, and social security number. We automatically decline submissions without this essential information.

Our e-mail address is matureyears@umpublishing.org.

Hard Copy Format—All manuscripts must be typed double-spaced on 8.5 by 11 inch white paper. Do not send computer disks. Hand written manuscripts will be automatically returned.

Hard Copy Submission—Send manuscripts printed with your name, address, telephone number, and social security number along with a required SASE to the address below.

Rights

Mature Years requests a variety of rights depending upon the material offered. Our most common request is for one-time North American serial rights. We do accept a limited number of Reprint Rights. For work-for-hire we require All Rights.

Payment Schedule

Payment is made upon acceptance of any text or cartoon. We pay 5 cents per word for articles and $1.00 per line of poetry. Verses and fillers used in the Merry-Go-Round department are paid a flat $5.00.

Payment for photos accompanying stories is $20.00 for each one inside publication. Payment for cover publication is negotiable. Payment for photos follows final selection during the design stage. Payment for professional photography to accompany articles is negotiable.

Miscellaneous

Response Time—Replies to unsolicited manuscript submissions come within eight weeks of receipt. We do not acknowledge receipt of manuscripts at the time they are received. Because of the tremendous volume of submissions, it is not possible to make comments in the replies.

Letters of Inquiry—Inquiries are permissible with a required SASE; responses come within two weeks of receipt of the proposal. Permission to submit an article does not guarantee publication.

Samples—Sample copies are available for $5.00 each including shipping and handling.

Columns—*Mature Years* magazine is not interested in adding new regular columns.

Categories: Fiction—Nonfiction—Christian Interests—Family—Health—Inspirational—Money & Finances—Poetry—Relationships—Religion—Senior Citizen—Short Stories—Spiritual—Travel

CONTACT: Marvin W. Cropsey, Editor
Material: All
201 Eighth Ave. S
Nashville TN 37202
Phone: 615-749-6292
Fax: 615-749-6512

MB Media

Please refer to *Magical Blend, Natural Beauty & Health*, and *Transitions magazine*s.

The Meeting Professonal

Mission Statement

The Meeting Professional will deliver strategic editorial content on meetings industry trends, opportunities and items of importance with a commitment to compelling design and production that fosters superior professional development and career enhancement. It will serve as the official monthly publication of Meeting Professionals International, supporting the association's multiyear strategic plan, Pathways to Excellence.

Audience

The Meeting Professional is mailed monthly to approximately 20,000 MPI members as a membership benefit and to approximately 10,000 qualified non-member prospects and meetings industry planners. Although most MPI members reside in the United States, more than 10 percent live and work in Canada and 63 other countries around the world.

The Meeting Professional is produced primarily for meeting planners, but includes articles and columns relevant for hoteliers, airline personnel, caterers, audiovisual professionals, speakers, facility managers, production company personnel and others providing services or products to the meetings industry. Among those employing meeting planners are corporations, associations, educational institutions, government entities and independent firms. Many meeting planners are self-employed, operating independent firms and other service-related organizations.

Editorial Criteria

The Meeting Professional prefers not to publish unsolicited manuscripts. Writers are encouraged to submit detailed article queries or pitches and, if accepted, the editor will work with the writer to develop the required article.

The Meeting Professional strives to incorporate a variety of unique voices from MPI members and other industry experts. Article queries and pitches from active MPI members are given preference. From features and columns to news-oriented sections, the magazine aims to be the principal vehicle for educational value for meetings industry planners and suppliers.

Writers contributing to The Meeting Professional for the first time should peruse issues published since January 2003 to ascertain what types of news items, feature articles and columns have appeared. The Meeting Professional publishes only original, never-before-published material. Article queries and pitches are judged for suitability based on the following points:

1. Information: Does the article deliver the promised facts? Are those facts supported? Is it logical and convincing?

2. Analysis/Organization: Are facts examined and discussed in a cohesive, cogent fashion?

3. Balance: If there are several sides to an issue, are all of them presented? Is opinion presented as such?

4. Originality: Is the topic presented with a fresh, new perspective?

5. Audience appeal: Does the article capture and retain reader interest? Does it address the proper audience? Does it use examples and quote multiple sources in the industry?

6. Relevance: Does the editorial provide our readers with useful information? Does it address a topic of current interest?

7. Truth: Is statistical information correct? The responsibility for accuracy rests with the author.

8. Product or service endorsements: Does the editorial primarily promote or endorse a specific product or service? "Advertorial" copy is not encouraged in features or columns. Some news sections accept press releases about new products and services.

Editorial Submission and Acceptance

Before offering a complete feature story or column to The Meeting Professional for consideration, please submit a brief summary of the proposed subject matter. Such queries should be submitted to the managing editor at the address below.

When an article query or pitch is accepted for publication:

1. The editor will work with the writer to establish word count, deadline, requirements, specifications and date of publication.

2. Once the article is received, the editor has the right to edit the article for style, clarity and length and to make final selection on headlines, subheads and graphic treatment.

3. Writers may be asked to revise manuscripts or provide additional information for clarification.

4. MPI owns the copyright on all published material. You will be sent an Agreement for Publication, which further describes this requirement.

5. An invoice, including the author's Social Security number, must be submitted to receive payment. Invoices may be submitted via e-mail in attached Microsoft Word or Adobe Acrobat (PDF) documents. (Invoice guidelines will be provided.)

Manuscript Preparation

1. Length: Columns typically run 500 to 1,000 words; features typically run 2,000 to 3,000 words, including sidebars.

2. Editorial Style: The Meeting Professional generally adheres to The Associated Press Stylebook and Merriam Webster's Collegiate Dictionary.

Format

1. Send the manuscript in Microsoft Word (for Windows or Macintosh) via e-mail to Blair Potter at address below.

2. A list of sources and contact information should be provided for fact-checking purposes.

3. At the end of the article, include a brief author biography listing current position, background and contact information if needed. Columnists should also provide a color (preferred) or black-and-white head shot (at least 300 dpi, 2" x 3") via e-mail.

Categories: Nonfiction—Meetings

CONTACT: Blair Potter, Managing Editor
The Meeting Professional
Meeting Professionals International
3030 LBJ Freeway Ste 1700
Dallas TX 75234
E-mail: bpotter@mpiweb.org

Meetings East
Meetings South
Meetings West

Please refer to Stamats Meetings Media.

The Melic Review

The *Melic Review* seeks poems, essays, and fiction of the highest quality. To get a better idea of what we mean, read C.E. Chaffin's essay "On Modulation."

With accept previously print-published material, but not previous net publications as yet. We discourage simultaneous submissions, as we take our work as editors seriously. All work should be sent in the body of the e-mail. Attachments will be accepted for formatting reasons, but only if accompanied by plain text versions in the body of the e-mail.

Submissions are always open, but the cut-off date for inclusion in a new issue is the tenth of the month preceding the issue. Thus, for our March 1 issue, submissions received after February 10 will be carried over for consideration in the next issue. Our response time is less than or equal to three months. If you haven't heard by then, please write us.

We prefer fiction under a thousand words and poetry under fifty lines but will make exception for longer works of exceptional merit. 5000 words is the absolute limit for fiction of exceptional merit, two hundred lines for poetry. Only one fiction piece of this length has made it into the magazine, and no poems of this length have yet been accepted. Please send no more than five poems or one prose piece per submission.

We do not pay contributors, nor are we a publishing house for chapbooks or books. We are simply a literary e-zine.

Copyrights revert to the authors upon publication. All work published is with the express consent and permission of the author, who may withdraw it at anytime before we go online with a new issue.

We also offer a one-on-one online tutorial in poetry taught by Dr. Chaffin, including an extensive syllabus. Cost is $250 and the course lasts six weeks. Please send a query if interested.

All submissions and queries should be e-mailed to melicreview@hotmail.com. We do not accept snail submissions.

Categories: Fiction—Poetry—Short Stories

CONTACT: C.E. Chaffin M.D.
Material: All
700 E. Ocean Blvd. #2504
Long Beach CA 90802
E-mail: melicreview@hotmail.com
Website: www.melicreview.com

Memory Makers
The First Source for Scrapbooking Ideas

Dear prospective writer,

Thank you for your interest in *Memory Makers*. As a short introduction to our editorial content, let us explain that in addition to feature articles we have several departments that appear in each issue. These departments, including Keeping It Safe and Scrapbooking 101, deal with topics that are of continued importance and interest to our scrapbooking audience. The following editorial guidelines are offered to help you as you develop story ideas for us.

Our Writers

We have in-house writers who are responsible for many different features and departments. However, we are looking for talented freelance writers who possess knowledge or new insights on scrapbooking. Material is aimed at scrapbookers of all levels and age groups.

Our Content

Editorial content for *Memory Makers* features is typically driven by actual scrapbook page ideas submitted by our readers. However, we also consider article queries covering related topics (Pages That Heal, Scrapbooking Around the World). Editorial is finalized six months in advance of newsstand date, so plan appropriately for timely or seasonal article topics. Our "voice" is conversational and friendly. We look for detail-oriented writing that captures people's personalities and experiences. When applicable, we prefer articles that include at least two expert sources.

Features

We typically run five features in each issue. The two longest are usually about 1,500 words in length and deal with a scrapbook theme (such as scrapbooking about yourself or everyday inspiration for pages) or technique (such as using vellum). Our inspirational feature (1,000-1,200 words) tells the personal story of how someone's life has been impacted by scrapbooking. It is often written in the first person, from the perspective of the person featured in the article. The two other features (about 800 words each) are designed to motivate readers to try a new technique, craft or product in their albums. Our craft features include a short introduction and step-by-step instructions. Strong instructional writing skills are necessary. Material for these articles is typically generated from reader-submitted ideas.

Keeping It Safe

This section covers all issues surrounding the safe preservation of your albums and photographs. It includes one topic per issue. Previously published articles include The Safety of Computer Inks, The Stability of Color Copies, The Safety of Crayons. (500-700 words)

Scrapbooking 101

Here, we offer how-to instructions and tips for the beginning scrapbooker as well as a basic review of techniques for the pro on various scrapbook-related topics. Previous articles include Design Basics: Creating Focal Point and Five Things Every Scrapbook Page Should Have. (about 800 words)

Photojournaling

This department gives readers new and useful ideas for improving their journaling techniques. Past articles have dealt with calendar-style journaling, creative ideas for adding journaling to finished pages and self-esteem journaling. (600-800 words)

Modern Memories

In this department, we address computer and modern technology issues as they relate to scrapbooking. Past issues have included articles on sharing pages via Internet and e-mail, using your computer for scrapbook layouts and choosing genealogy software. (600-800 words)

Ask *Memory Makers*

This department is written in question/answer-style, based on questions our readers send us. If you are writing an Ask *Memory Makers* article, we will assign you one to three questions to research and write the response. Let us know if you'd like to be considered for this section of the magazine. (600 words)

Our Deadlines

Deadlines for articles will be assigned when the editor initially contacts the writer about an article. Articles can be submitted by e-mail or Macintosh-formatted disk (using Microsoft Word or Quark Xpress) on or before the deadline that the writer has been given. Computer disks should be clearly marked with the author's name (and address if they want the disk returned), magazine department and article's title. Along with the finished article, please include information for verifying all sources used in the article. Freelancers are responsible for providing some means of verification for names, titles and other pertinent information used, such as a phone number, business card or e-mail address.

Payment

Memory Makers purchases first world serial rights for the one-time use of articles. Payment will vary on a per-assignment basis. We will not reprint articles previously published in other scrapbooking publications. *Memory Makers* Writer's Contract outlines all agreement details. The contract must be signed and returned by the author, accompanied by a numbered invoice. Authors will be paid approximately 30 days after completion of the project.

Advice to New Writers

Familiarize yourself with *Memory Makers*. Then send or e-mail a query letter to the attention of our copy editor, Amy Partain, with the idea you feel may interest our readers. Include samples of your previous work and an outline of your writing experience. We are also willing to look at completed manuscripts. Be sure to include your phone number and enclose a stamped return-reply postcard. We are unable to return unsolicited manuscripts.

We look forward to working with you in the future!

Editorial Guidelines 2004

Categories: Nonfiction—Computers—Crafts/Hobbies—Hobbies—Inspirational—Internet—Interview—Photography—Software—Technical—Scrapbooking

CONTACT: Sarah Kelly, Editorial Assistant
Material: Any
F&W Publications
12365 Huron St., Ste. 500
Denver CO 80234
Phone: 303-452-1968
Fax: 303-452-2164

E-mail: editorial@memorymakersmagazine.com
Website: www.memorymakersmagazine.com

Men of Integrity

OUR PURPOSE

Men of Integrity is a pocket-sized daily bible devotional guide that encourages regular Scripture study and applies biblical truth to the specific gritty issues men face.

Men of Integrity, published in association with Promise Keepers, also seeks to encourage men in their Christian walk to better fulfill their commitment to godly service in Christ by reminding them of the Seven Promises of a Promise Keeper:

1. Commitment to honoring Jesus Christ through worship, prayer and obedience to God's Word in the power of the Holy Spirit.

2. Commitment to pursuing vital relationships with a few other men, understanding that he needs brothers to help him keep his promises.

3. Commitment to practicing spiritual, moral, ethical and sexual purity.

4. Commitment to building a strong marriage and family through love, protection and biblical values.

5. Commitment to supporting the mission of his church by honoring and praying for his pastor and by actively giving his time and resources (I Thessalonians 5:12-13).

6. Commitment to reaching beyond any racial and denominational barriers to demonstrate the power of biblical unity.

7. Commitment to influencing his world, being obedient to the great Commandment (Mark 12:30-31) and the Great Commission. (Matthew 28:19-20)

OUR READERS

Men of Integrity readers are usually men between the ages of 30 and 50 working in business, or a specialized trade, such as sales or engineering. They are not likely to be a pastor or teacher, and have attended at least some college. About 30 percent of our readers are using the guide as part of a men's group or Bible study. Often, they are new Christians and not readers of a "traditional" Bible devotional. *Men of Integrity* serves as an introduction to regular Bible study for these men.

OUR WRITERS

Typically, our writers are Christian men fairly established in their walk with Christ. We look for stories that illustrate biblical principles, written by men who draw from their everyday experiences and lives. Personal experiences that caused you to grow in your faith, or stories about areas of struggle where God has challenged your thinking and encouraged a change in behavior, are the types of stories that fit best into the *Men of Integrity* format.

Men of Integrity seeks to regularly publish African-American, Hispanic, Native American, and Messianic Jewish writers.

THE ARTICLES

Men of Integrity gets its point across by telling gripping stories rather than by exhorting or commenting on Scripture passages. We are looking for easy-to-read pieces built on narrative. The narrative should clearly illustrate a biblical principle around a certain theme.

Generally, we choose themes that will help men cultivate healthy "horizontal" (human) relationships—with their wives, children, co-workers, and friends. Themes also address the "vertical" relationship—relationship with God. Articles should offer practical advice and personal insights that support growth in both these areas.

Themes used in past issues include: caring for others, loving your wife, spiritual accountability, prayer, self-discipline, God's love, dealing with failure, sexual purity, spiritual warfare, handling anger, fatherhood, hearing God, loving Jesus, wise decisions, boldness, commitment, truthfulness, and enriching your wife. This is not meant to be an exhaustive list but to give you examples of what we have used in the past.

Men of Integrity seeks a mix of articles, from both individuals known in the evangelical community and from ordinary laymen.

Men of Integrity uses the New Living Translation for all Scripture References.

Should you wish to obtain a sample issue, please send $5.00 with your request to Men of Integrity, 465 Gundersen Drive, Carol Stream, IL 60188. *Men of Integrity* also appears in online form at www.christianity.net/menofintegrity.

MANUSCRIPTS

Men of Integrity accepts unsolicited manuscripts. They can be sent in hard copy format or via e-mail. Submissions should be sent to the attention of the editor, 465 Gundersen Drive, Carol Stream, IL 60188 or, via e-mail, to: moimail@christianitytoday. com.

Men of Integrity will report only on those manuscripts received via e-mail or sent with a self-addressed, stamped envelope (SASE). We will respond in 3-5 weeks. Please include your name, address and telephone number on all manuscripts.

Devotionals are no more than 200-300 words each. We will accept longer pieces, but you should expect them to be condensed to about 200 words. We like a tight, punchy style and prefer condensing a slightly longer piece to make it fit to receiving a more loosely constructed 200-word piece.

Men of Integrity will pay $50 for each original piece accepted ($25 for reprints and excerpts). (4/04/01)

Categories: Nonfiction—Christian Interests—Family—Lifestyle—Men's Issues—Parenting—Religion—Spiritual

CONTACT: Harry Genet, Editor
Material: All
Christianity Today International
465 Gundersen Dr.
Carol Stream IL 60188
Phone: 630-260-6200
Fax: 630-260-8428
E-mail: mail@menofintegrity.net;
moimail@christianitytoday.com
Website: www.christianitytoday.com

Men's Fitness

Men's Fitness magazine is a total-service publication for healthy, active men. It contains a wide range of features and monthly departments devoted to all areas of health, fitness and an overall active lifestyle.

Editorial fulfills two functions: entertainment and information, with special attention paid to accuracy.

Manuscript tone: The editorial voice must be friendly, speaking directly to the healthy, active man. Academic-journal composition is not acceptable. Please read the magazine for an understanding of its style.

Manuscript length: 1,000 to 1,250 words for departments; 1,500 to 1,800 words for features.

Response time: Four to six weeks.

Writers' contracts/kill fees: Contracts are required for all work. Kill fees (paid if we find the work unacceptable for any reason after a contract is signed) are 1/3 the original payment amount.

Payment rates: $500 (or less) for departments; $1,000 (or less) for features. All fees are negotiated individually. Payment made within six weeks of final acceptance.

Fact checking: Accuracy is the responsibility of the author. Manuscripts should be accompanied by the telephone numbers of sources quoted within the article, so editors can verify their names, titles and educational credentials. Products or services mentioned in the articles should also be accompanied with contract names and phone numbers. Books should be cited by complete title, publisher and price. Include photocopies of both covers and the title page in the article's backup. Include a copy of the abstract of any studies cited. If the information cited comes from a secondary source, include a copy of the newspaper or magazine article.

Queries: One-page summary of idea or ideas. Send recent clips with bylines. Please send only clips that reflect your own writing style along with a SASE.

Unsolicited manuscripts: We prefer queries. Please do not send manuscripts.

Sample copies: Unfortunately, we cannot offer sample issues.

Categories: Nonfiction—Consumer—Diet/Nutrition—Health—Inspirational—Physical Fitness—Psychology—Science—Self Help—Sexuality

CONTACT: Dean Brierly, Managing Editor
Material: All
21100 Erwin St.
Woodland Hills CA 91367
Phone: 818-884-6800
Fax: 818-704-5734

Men'sHealth.

Men's Health

It's not easy to break into *Men's Health.* Don't even try if you haven't been published in a major magazine. Still with us? Okay, study a back issue or two, then consider the following: Most unsolicited queries fail because they don't address the Men's Health reader.

The *Men's Health* Reader

Our circulation is 1,625,000+; 85 percent of our readers are men. Our average reader is 35 years old and is a well-educated urban or suburban professional. He's active in a number of sports and exercise pursuits.

What We Cover

As you'll see, we're an authoritative source of information on all aspects of men's physical and emotional health. We rely on writers to seek out the right experts, and to either tell a story from a first-person vantage or to get good anecdotes. We carefully fact-check all quotes and health information contained in the magazine.

Tone

Most of our articles have the tone of a peer who happens to have spoken to a few authorities on the issue at hand. Imagine you're relating that information to the reader, one on one, over a beer or at dinner.

Length, Payment, Rights

The best place to break into the magazine is "Malegrams" or one of our one-page columns. For "Malegrams," we seek submissions of about 200 words. We pay $25 to $50 upon completion of fact-checking. Other than that:

Departments run 1,500 words and pay $500-$2,000

Features run 1,200-4,000 words and pay $1,000-$5,000

We usually buy all rights, but this is negotiated on an individual basis. We will consider buying second rights, if your published piece has not appeared in another national magazine, in another health magazine, or in another magazine written primarily for men. When we pay: For departments and features, following acceptance, upon completion of the fact-checking process.

The Departments

Malegrams: Short takes relevant to men. Clinical and research advances in health, medicine, psychology, sports performance, work and relationship issues, the offbeat.

Training: We cover what's tried and needs to be tried again (i.e., calisthenics revisited), as well as the trends.

Nutrition: What to eat and when.

Working: How to succeed. How to fail. How to know the difference.

Couples: New takes on major relationship issues.

Self-Care: What to do so that you don't have to call a doctor.

Looks: Practical and health aspects of grooming, dressing, etc.

Man-to-Man: Simple, well-told stories about manhood, manliness, machismo, momentary lapses. The wiser you are, the more of a wiseguy you can be.

Mind/Body: The psychology of men, and how that relates to health, exercise, performance.

Clips

We don't assign anything without seeing published clips. Photocopies are a good idea, as we may not return clips. Send your best. One or two will do. They don't all have to be about health or medicine. We want to see how well you report, write and interpret stories.

How to Query *Men's Health*

Structure an article proposal this way:

• Start with the lead you expect to put on the piece.

• Write a summary of where you'll go from there.

• Give specifics on whom you plan to interview, what types of real-life anecdotes you'll include, what research sources you plan to go to and what conclusion the story might reach. Queries shouldn't run longer than one page, single-spaced. We'll get back to you in two-four weeks. (Be sure to enclose a SASE.)

Manuscripts

If you send a manuscript, it must be typed double- or triple-spaced, with margins of at least 1 inch. Send a copy of your original, just in case. We report on manuscripts in four to eight weeks.

Back Issues

Call our customer service department at (800) 666-2303 to order back issues.

Please send article submissions by regular mail to me at the address below. No phone calls please!

Categories: Nonfiction—Careers—Diet/Nutrition—Fashion—Health—Physical Fitness—Recreation—Relationships—Sports/Recreation—Travel

CONTACT: Pamela Brinar
Material: All
Rodale, Inc.
33 East Minor St.
Emmaus PA 18098-0099
Phone: 610-967-5171
Fax: 610-967-8963
Website:www.menshealth.com

Men's Journal

Men's Journal is a men's lifestyle magazine for 25- to 49-year-old active men. Its editorial emphasis is on travel, fitness, adventure and participatory sports, but it is also open to a wide range of topics of interest to contemporary American men.

Front-of-the-book articles cover a wide range of general interest topics and news, and are between 400-1,200 words. Feature articles and profiles run between 2,000-7,000 words. Articles for the equipment and fitness sections are 400-1,800 words. These are service-oriented articles meant to provide sporting and leisure reviews for the active man.

One-page queries, accompanied by one or two applicable clips, should be sent to the address below. Do not submit queries by fax.

Categories: Adventure—General Interest—Men's Issues—Physical Fitness—Sports/Recreation—Travel

CONTACT: Submissions Editor
Material: All
1290 Avenue of the Americas
New York NY 10104
Phone: 212-484-1616
Fax: 212-484-3434
E-mail: letters@mensjournal.com
Website:www.mensjournal.com

Mercury

Mercury
The Journal of the
Astronomical Society of the Pacific

Thank you for agreeing to write for *Mercury, the Journal of the Astronomical Society of the Pacific*. In its original incarnation, *Mercury* was first published by the ASP in 1925. It is now read by 5,200 ASP members and at 800 academic libraries, observatories, and other institutions in 71 countries. The ASP is the largest general astronomy society in the world. Our members include professional astronomers, amateurs, educators, and motivated lay people.

Fees

Alas, because the ASP is nonprofit and impoverished, we are unable to pay for submissions. Writing for *Mercury* is a labor of love and good exposure for your ideas. We do have a limited capacity to reimburse expenses, such as postage or photo reproduction. We send four free copies to all contributors and can provide more, within reason.

Queries

We are unequipped to review unsolicited manuscripts; if you have article ideas, please write or e-mail the editor. In your letter, please discuss the basic idea for the article, its general content, its relevance to our readership, and the relationship of the prospective writer to the subject matter. The editor tries to respond to all correspondence within two weeks, although it may take somewhat longer or shorter depending on other deadlines we must meet.

Level of Articles

We encourage writers to read past issues to get a sense of our style. *Mercury* assumes that its readers are motivated and informed about basic astronomy. In our 1994 survey of readers, 49 percent of the respondents said they were involved in amateur astronomy, 29 percent in astronomical research, and 86 percent in astronomy education at some level. *Mercury* articles are roughly at the same level as *The Sciences*: between a mass-market science magazine such as *Discover* and a more scholarly magazine such as *Scientific American*.

We think of *Mercury* as the *Atlantic Monthly* of astronomy, giving informed perspectives on salient issues in research, education, history, and public policy. An article should not focus solely on the research or history of any particular individual, unless it is of unusual importance. Articles should appeal to readers' personal experiences and draw broader conclusions about how science is conducted. We encourage writers to be innovative and forceful, to devise clever metaphors, to go out onto a limb. The ASP does not endorse anything our contributors say, but we believe in challenging readers and making *Mercury* a vigorous part of the marketplace of ideas.

Length of Articles

Regular departments are one magazine page, or 1,000 words. Book reviews are one page, 800 words. The standard feature is eight magazine pages, 3,000 words plus illustrations and a sidebar.

Rights

The ASP asks that contributors transfer their copyright to the ASP in order to facilitate electronic distribution and academic photocopying, which we allow free of charge. In return, we grant writers the non-exclusive right to reuse any part or all of their work. We have found that this arrangement avoids hassles, but if contributors prefer to retain copyright, we have no problem with that. Our concern is simply to protect ourselves legally. The minimum we can accept is worldwide first appearance, non-exclusive print and electronic rights.

Submission

To avoid transcription errors, we require electronic submission. We prefer rich text, (.rtf) or Microsoft Word 5.1 format, but will accept plain-text, MacWrite, or WordPerfect formats. You can e-mail the document to the address below or send us a 3½" low-density Macintosh diskette. If you send a plain text file, we ask that you fax or mail a formatted version as well.

Deadlines

First drafts are due 10 weeks before the cover date; final drafts, eight weeks before.

Editing

Mercury rarely rejects a manuscript. When you submit an article, we assume that you agree to work with the editor in preparing it for publication. The *Mercury* editor is an active one who enjoys bouncing ideas back and forth and who takes pain to ensure readability and interest. Most writers realize that every manuscript benefits from careful, respectful critiquing.

Editing occurs in two stages. First, the editor reads the submitted draft and makes suggestions for a revised draft. On occasion, the editor may ask an anonymous outside reviewer for advice. Typical issues include: making sure readers know where the article is heading and why they should be reading it; making sure that the article does not present readers with too much information too quickly; checking that concepts are defined as naturally as possible; identifying and highlighting particularly enlightening ideas; and anticipating and addressing readers' questions.

Second, the editor copy-edits the revised draft for grammar, spelling, flow, style, and so forth. We make every reasonable effort to show writers the final version of their articles while there is time to make changes. There is one exception: During layout, the editor sometimes must condense in order to fine-tune length, eliminate widows, or correct errors noticed at the last minute. Usually such changes are vanishingly minor. We cannot inform writers of such changes.

Titles, abstracts, subheads, and captions are our domain, although we generally work from writers' suggestions and include these elements in the drafts we return for writers' approval.

House Style

Mercury is somewhere between a magazine and an academic journal. In most cases, it adheres to Associated Press style, with concessions to Chicago style. Exceptions are detailed in the *Mercury* stylebook and are routinely made during copy-editing.

Mercury does not have footnotes or formal bibliographies. If acknowledgment has to be given, work it into the body of the article or the biography. Articles should not include a bibliography unless it is interesting in itself. Such bibliographies should be short and annotated.

Mercury uses SI units, with English equivalents given in parentheses. Spell out the names of measurement units. Take care not to overstate precision. Normally, two significant figures suffice.

Acronyms intimidate readers. Use only abbreviations likely to be recognized outside a specialty. Do not define an abbreviation in parentheses on first reference: If the abbreviation is not obvious enough to be recognized on second reference, it shouldn't be used to begin with.

Biography

Following every article is a one-paragraph biography of the writer, written in third-person, including research interests, a personal anecdote or factoid, and an e-mail address.

Illustrations

We ask the writer to obtain, help to obtain, or at least suggest illustrations. This ensures that the illustrations are what the writer intends; in any event, most writers have better access to illustrations than we do. We prefer photographs in print form and can reimburse reproduction expenses. We can also accept GIF, JPEG, and TIFF files. *Mercury* is published in two colors.

Categories: Education—Science

CONTACT: Submissions Editor
Material: All
390 Ashton Ave.
San Francisco CA 94112
Phone: 415-337-1100
Fax: 415-337-5205
E-mail: rnaeye@astrosociety.org

M-Q

Meridian

Currently, we accept electronic submissions year-round.

We continue to accept regular postal submissions (free, no reading fee) during the fall and spring semesters. We do not accept postal submissions postmarked during the summer (April 15 to August 15); these will be returned unread. We accept submissions sent over our winter break (December 12 to January 15), but we are unlikely to begin reading them until late January. Postal submissions should contain only one prose submission or up to four poems. Please also enclose an SASE for our reply.

We do not accept e-mail submissions.

Due to budget constraints, we can no longer pay all authors published in *Meridian*. The authors we publish receive two complimentary copies, a chance to purchase more at a reduced rate, and, funds permitting, one or two authors in each issue may receive a modest prize for outstanding work.

We do accept simultaneous submissions; however, if we accept your work for publication, it is your responsibility to immediately notify all other magazines it is no longer available. Similarly, if someone else accepts your work, please write or e-mail us as soon as possible.

We try to respond in 1-4 months.

We generally do not accept creative work by current University of Virginia students. University of Virginia students should not send unsolicited work.

Categories: Fiction—Nonfiction—Book Reviews—Poetry—Short Stories

CONTACT: Specific Editor (Fiction, Poetry, Nonfiction, or Book Review Editor)
Meridian
UVA
PO Box 400145
Charlottesville VA 22904-4145

Message Magazine

Thank you for your interest in MESSAGE Magazine. MESSAGE is the oldest and most widely circulated African-American religious journal addressing ethnic issues in the USA. We work hard to preserve our unique role interpreting current events through a Black Christian perspective. We're happy you want to be a part of this powerful ministry. Here is how you can participate in writing the message.

Getting to know MESSAGE

• Published: Bimonthly, in a 32-page format, by the Review and Herald Publishing Association. Sponsored by the Seventh-day Adventist Church. Circulation: 125,000; primary readership based in the United States.

• Audience: Predominantly Black, though increasingly multi-cultural. MESSAGE is a missionary journal tailored to the unchurched.

• Lead time: When submitting seasonal material, remember our production schedule requires us to work four to six months ahead.

• Payments: MESSAGE pays upon acceptance.

• Rights: MESSAGE purchases first North American publishing rights to all submissions. This also includes first electronic publishing rights. Each article published first in MESSAGE should carry a line attributing credit to MESSAGE magazine.

WHAT TO WRITE

• MESSAGE publishes: informational, devotional, inspirational, doctrinal, profile, interview and self-help articles that have wide appeal to people of many backgrounds. Feature articles should never exceed 1,200 words unless otherwise specified.

• MESSAGE does not accept: sermons, outlines, poetry, reprints, or anything that is not in an article format.

• Hot topics include: biblical exposition, celebrity and humanitarian profiles with distinct ministry perspectives, family, health, education, worship, news and current events, religious freedom and racial reconciliation. Feel free to query us by phone or e-mail about article ideas.

Departments

• MESSAGE also accepts freelance submissions for the following magazine departments:

Minding Your Business: This 600-word column addresses work-related issues such as personal development and finance, stress control, and workplace politics. Pieces should include a distinctive biblical Christian response or perspective on these issues.

HealthSpan: This 600-word column—sidebar excluded—covers a variety of health topics of interest to our audience. It is typically accompanied by a sidebar or chart.

Message Jr.: Our column for children, ages 5 to 8, is no longer than 500 words. We prefer Bible-based stories, but stories with a clear-cut moral are also accepted.

HOW TO GET PUBLISHED:

Here are Nine Ways to Woo Our Editors:

1. Make sure your article is biblically sound and offers spiritual perspective and insight.

2. Support your material with facts, statistics and quotes from experts.

3. Invite the reader to read your whole story by writing an interesting lead.

4. Sharpen your focus. Sometimes writing a title, subtitles and subheadings helps.

5. Look for interesting, fresh, insightful twists on old topics. Say something new.

6. Write about timely topics and events.

7. Answer the underlying, heartfelt questions a reader may have about your topic.

8. Include anecdotes or illustrations to make your writing come alive.

9. Carefully follow all directions you have read in these guidelines or those given by editors.

How to submit a manuscript

• Submit only typewritten, double-spaced articles no longer than 1,200 words, unless otherwise specified.

• Enclose your name, address, phone number, e-mail address, Social Security number, and a self-addressed, stamped envelope. Without this information your manuscript will not be reviewed.

• Enclose a one-sentence bio at the end of your article. Example: "Jane Doe is…"

• We prefer manuscripts on computer disk (MS Word for MAC or PC) or e-mailed (MS Word for MAC or PC) to Message@ rhpa.org. Articles submitted via regular mail should be accompanied by a typewritten, double-spaced copy.

• You will be notified by postcard that we have received your manuscript. If your article is accepted, you will be notified within six to eight weeks. If your manuscript is not accepted, we will return it to you only if you have enclosed a SASE.

Categories: Fiction—African-American—Christian Interests—Consumer—Inspirational—Religion—Spiritual

CONTACT: Ron Smith, Editor
Material: All
55 W. Oak Ridge Dr.
Hagerstown MD 21740
Phone: 301-393-4099
Fax: 301-393-4103
E-mail: Message@rhpa.org or ronsmith@rhpa.org
Website: www.Messagemagazine.com

Metro Baby

Please refer to *Metro Parent* magazine.

Metro Parent
Metro Baby
African American Family
Best of Times
Educators Edition
The Party Book

Guidelines - Query by email to: sdemaggio@metroparent.com
Feature stories are 1500-2500 words. Columns are 750 words.
Categories: African-American—Children—Culture—Education—Family—Parenting—Regional—Senior Citizens—Teen

CONTACT: Susan DeMaggio, Managing Editor
Material: Parenting, Women's Health, Family, Travel
CONTACT: Denise Crittendon, Editor
Material: Black lifestyle
Metro Parent Publishing Group
24567 Northwestern Hwy., Suite 150
Southfield MI 48075
Phone: 248-352-0990
E-mail: dcrittene@metroparent.com
Website: www.metroparent.com

MetroKids
MetroKids Pennsylvania, MetroKids
South Jersey, MetroKids Delaware

General Information: In business for more than 16 years, *MetroKids* Magazine has become an indispensable family tool. *MetroKids* distributes 130,000 copies of our magazines, *MetroKids Pennsylvania*, *MetroKids South Jersey* and most recently, *MetroKids Delaware*, each month to more than 1,500 locations in eleven counties throughout the Tri-State Area.

We distribute to public libraries, museums, schools, childcare centers, community centers, retail stores, malls, hospitals, doctor's offices, bookstores, tourist centers, and many other locations.

Mission statement: *MetroKids* is the resource for parents and children in the Delaware Valley. Our objective, in monthly publications, special issues, and special events, is to help Delaware Valley families take advantage of the vast resources—both educational and recreational—available in the culturally rich and diverse community in which we live.

MetroKids, through its editorial, advertising and promotional outreach offers options to Delaware Valley families.

Submissions: Submit at least 6 weeks ahead of publication. 800-1200 words. No first-person accounts. Delaware Valley (Philadelphia and suburbs, Delaware, Southern New Jersey) sources preferred. Send via e-mail.

Topics: Health, practical parenting, women's issues, technology for the family, children's fashion, home décor, special needs, education, nutrition and activities.

Categories: Family—Parenting

CONTACT: Tom Livingston, Executive Editor
Material: All
1080 Delaware Ave., Ste 102
Philadelphia PA 19125

Phone: 215-291-5560
Fax: 215-291-5563
E-mail: editor@metrokids.com
Website: www.Metrokids.com

METROPOLIS

Metropolis

WHAT IS METROPOLIS?
Metropolis examines contemporary life through design—architecture, interior design, product design, graphic design, crafts, planning, and preservation. Subjects range from the sprawling urban environment to intimate living spaces to small objects of everyday use. In looking for why design happens in a certain way, *Metropolis* explores the economic, environmental, social, cultural, political, and technological context. With its innovative graphic presentation and its provocative voice, *Metropolis* shows how richly designed our world can be.

EDITORIAL SUBMISSIONS
Send query letters—not complete manuscripts—describing your idea and why it would be good for our magazine. Be concise, specific, and clear. Also, please include clips and a resume. The ideal *Metropolis* story is based on strong reporting skills and includes an examination of current critical issues. A design firm's newest work isn't a story, but the issues that their work brings to light might be. We do not cover conferences or seminars. Please send these announcements to the general magazine address or email.

DESIGN WORK SUBMISSIONS
Design professionals: keep us apprised about projects as they are awarded, in progress, and completed. We are especially interested in projects that illustrate innovative design approaches or unconventional responses to typical problems in:
• Single-family (though we publish few in this category) and multi-family interiors and exteriors
• Public work, such as schools and health facilities
• Graphic design
• Product design
• Commercial work.
Each year we cover the evolving workplace, educational buildings, and new or forgotten materials or technologies.

Include a brief description of the goals of the project and snapshots, renderings, floorplans, color copies of professional photos, or digital images—tiffs, jpegs or other formats that can be opened on a Mac. Please do not send irreplaceable art.

Digital images intended for use in the magazine are best in jpeg, tif, or eps format in the final print size or larger, and with a resolution of at least 300 dpi. Zipped and stuffed files are fine; compressed images are unacceptable.

Categories: Nonfiction—Architecture—Arts—Consumer—Culture—Environment—General Interest

CONTACT: Julien Devereux
Material: All
61 West 23rd St. 4th Floor
New York NY 10010
Phone: 212-722-5050
Fax: 212-627-9988
E-mail: edit@metropolismag.com (queries); kira@metropolismag.com (submission questions)

M-Q

Metropolitan Home

Writing for *Metropolitan Home* requires expertise in the field of home design and associate lifestyle matters. It is not enough to be a good writer. You must be able to speak with authority about interior design, architecture, cooking, gardening, or whatever other subject you wish to cover. It is not a market for beginners or those new to the world of interior design.

In most cases, you must query before submitting. The only exception is the first-person experiential essay.

No previously published work will be considered. No home will be considered for publication if it has previously been published in a competing national magazine. If you are proposing a location that has appeared in local newspapers and/or magazines, we need to see copies of the articles to consider the story.

All queries and/or submissions must be written. We do not accept telephone calls or fax submissions. We prefer that you submit by mail or courier service.

Proposals should be approximately 250 words long and must include basic reportage. Remember: *MET HOME* is a timely journal of contemporary design. We do not generally cover antiques, restorations or anything that is not newsworthy. We do not generally use seasonal material (i.e. December holidays, Mothers Day, etc.); our lead time is six to twelve months. We are a consumer publication with a highly educated, affluent audience, not a "ladies magazine" or a "how-to" magazine. Forty percent of our readers are men.

Most proposals must be submitted with visuals: We prefer 35mm slides. We cannot consider any proposal about any aspect of design without seeing pictures.

If you have not already written for *MET HOME*, please include no more than three clips with your proposal. "Clips" means published stories in a related field.

We are not seeking travel stories of any kind. "My House" stories are normally written by widely published writers at the invitation of the editors of *MET HOME*. We generally do not accept unsolicited "My House" pieces.

What we need most are front-of-book stories about issues of contemporary housing, about "good works" relating to design and architecture, about ecological issues, financial aspects of home owning, apartment living, etc.—in other words, thought pieces that involve expertise and research.

Please know the magazine before submitting. We are not able to offer free copies of the magazine. If you cannot find *Metropolitan Home* on your local newsstand or in a nearby library, you may order back issues from 201-451-9420.

Categories: Architecture—Design

CONTACT: Megan O'Neill, Assistant Editor
Material: All
1633 Broadway
New York NY 10019
Phone: 212-767-6000

Michigan Beverage Guide

Please refer to *Illinois Beverage Guide*.

Michigan Historical Review
Central Michigan University

The *Michigan Historical Review* publishes articles on Michigan's political, economic, social, and cultural history, and those on American, Canadian, and Midwestern history that explore important themes related to Michigan's past. All manuscript submissions receive a double-blind peer review, but final decisions about publication rest with the editorial staff. The *MHR* does not accept manuscripts under consideration elsewhere.

Prospective authors are requested to use the following guidelines:

1. Manuscripts should not exceed 10,000 words; endnotes must be used and are to be double spaced.

2. Authors should submit electronically or send three paper copies of the manuscript and a copy on an IBM-compatible diskette (preferably in MS Word). To permit anonymous reviewing, the author's name should appear on a separate title page.

3. *The Chicago Manual of Style*, 15th edition, should be followed in matters of style and for endnote format. The *MHR* uses open punctuation and standardizes spelling of Native American tribal names.

4. Authors are requested to use bias-free language that is sensitive to race, ethnicity, gender, religion, age, ability, and sexual orientation. We recommend the *Task Force on Bias-Free Language of the Association of American University Presses* (Bloomington: Indiana University Press, 1995).

5. We encourage the inclusion of photographs, illustrations, and graphs within articles. Photographs should be in 5" x 7" black-and-white glossy format. It is the author's responsibility to secure permission to publish when necessary as well as to pay any fees.

6. For additional information, please contact the editorial staff via telephone or e-mail.

Categories: Michigan and Great Lakes History

CONTACT: Editor/Michigan Historical Review
Material: All
Clarke Historical Library, CMU
Mt. Pleasant MI 48859
Phone: 989-774-6567
Fax: 989-774-2160
E-mail: MIHISREV@cmich.edu

Mid-American Review
Bowling Green State University

Stories, poems, and articles will generally be returned or accepted within one to four months. Please include an SASE. Sample copies $5.00, current issue $7.00, rare back issues $10.00. Payment is $10.00 per page (pending funding) for fiction, poetry, translations, and nonfiction, with a maximum payment of $50.00; contributing authors receive two complimentary copies. All rights revert to the author upon publication. MAR does not consider work which has previously been published in any form..

Fiction Editor: Michael Czyzniejewski
Assistant Fiction Editor: Lisa DeCook

Mid-American Review considers work that is character- and/or language-oriented without sacrificing narrative. We are open to submissions from new and established authors, both traditional and experimental work, including short-shorts, but discourage genre fiction. Basically, we want to read something well written and original. MAR considers pieces up to 6,000 words; authors wishing to submit longer manuscripts or novel excerpts should query first with SASE.

Nonfiction Editor: Dustin Parsons

Mid-American Review seeks creative nonfiction, literary essays, and critical articles which focus on contemporary authors and topics of current literary interest. Contributions should generally not exceed 5,000 words and should follow standard MLA style. We also seek short (400-word) book reviews of current works of poetry, fiction, and nonfiction prose, published within six months of our publication (Apr. & Nov.).

Poetry Editor: Karen Craigo
Assistant Poetry Editor: Abigail Cloud

Poems should emanate from textured, evocative images, use language with an awareness of how words sound and mean, and have a definite sense of voice. Each line should help carry the poem, and an individual vision must be evident.

We encourage new as well as established writers. There is no length limit on individual poems, but please send no more than six at one time.

Translation Editor: George Looney

All submissions must include the original as well as the translated work. Chapbooks (approx. 10-15 poems) are designed to provide readers with an introduction to a single contemporary poet or a group of poets. An introductory essay of 300-500 words outlining the historical context of the poetry is encouraged.

Translations of contemporary fiction are also welcome and should follow these guidelines as well as those listed under Fiction.

Categories: Fiction—Nonfiction—Book Reviews—Poetry—Translations

CONTACT:
Karen Craigo, Assoc. & Poetry Editor
Material: Poetry
E-Mail: karenka@bgnet. bgsu.edu
CONTACT: Michael Czyzniejewski, Fiction Editor
Material: Fiction
E-Mail: mikeczy@bgnet.bgsu.edu
CONTACT: Dustin Parsons, Nonfiction Editor
Material: Non-fiction and reviews
E-Mail: djack@ bgnet.bgsu.edu
CONTACT: George Looney, Translation Editor
Material: Translation-related queries
E-Mail: gol1@psu. edu
Dept. of English
Bowling Green State University
Bowling Green OH 43403
Phone: 419-372-2725
Website: www.bgsu.edu/midamericanreview

MidWest Outdoors

MidWest Outdoors' Philosophy

MidWest Outdoors is in business to help people enjoy the outdoors, so we print only positive stories about outdoor experiences. MidWest Outdoors does not dwell on pollution, poaching, bad manners, etc. Please do not be critical of lakes, products or services. If you do mention a product, service or resort, please give us a contact name for possible advertising.

MidWest Outdoors' Editorial Requirements

MidWest Outdoors is interested in where to go and how to do it stories on outdoor recreation in the Midwest—an area encompassing a 10- to 15-hour drive from Chicago. Material should provide information the outdoorsman can use in his immediate vicinity and in areas he can travel to on weekends or a short vacation.

The accent in MidWest Outdoors is on:
• FISHING • HUNTING • CAMPING.

Related subjects are hunting dogs, archery, boats, snowmobiling, shooting, outdoor cooking or wild game cooking and canoeing.

Remember, you are writing for publication one or two months in advance, and your subject matter should reflect that time lapse. Spring fishing articles should be submitted in January, February and March; fall hunting articles in July and August. Illinois turkey hunting, for example, is in April, but turkey stories should be printed as early as February because that's when hunters must apply for permits. We never want to lose sight of our primary goal which is to provide useful information for the reader.

Any material accepted is subject to such revision as is necessary to meet the requirements of this publication. Manuscripts and photos not used will be returned if a stamped, self-addressed envelope is provided, but we assume no responsibility for lost materials.

Please include a title of the article on each page. Also include an overline or subtitle (example: Walleye Hotspot—Fox River Spring Madness). Include a byline and page number on each page and please include your social security number. If you submit a timely item, please indicate the month for suggested use.

Main Vs. State Section Requirements

Main section editorial should be general in tone, not area specific. The Main section is seen and read by people throughout the Midwest. Please keep facts such as fishing regulations or opening dates out of your material or specify the areas such rules are intended for. Example: readers in Iowa or Illinois would be confused by length requirements for Wisconsin northern pike. *MidWest Outdoors'* editors are particularly interested in where-to and how-to articles.

State section editorial should focus on one state exclusively or be written for one particular region. Example for a good state story: bass fishing on the Illinois River for the Illinois section. Example for a good regional story: fishing Wisconsin's southern lakes for the Wisconsin and Illinois sections. First time writers are encouraged to first write for state sections.

MidWest Outdoors' Special Sections

You are invited to submit material for any or all of these special sections:

• IceBreakers: The most comprehensive ice fishing annual in the Midwest. Deadlines: October 1st plus expanded ice fishing coverage in Nov., Dec., Jan. and Feb. issues.

• Canada Fever: The only two months *MidWest Outdoors* features Canadian editorial. Deadlines: Nov. 1st, Dec. 1st and Jan. 1st

• Cabin & Vacation Home Section: This section will be loaded with articles and tips on enjoying the cabin and vacation home experience. Deadline: March 1st

MidWest Outdoors' Acceptance Policy—PLEASE READ BEFORE CALLING

If you make an editorial submission to *MidWest Outdoors* and it is not returned in 30 days, you can assume we do plan to use it. However, we do keep some material for as long as 12 to 18 months before using it. Your best way of knowing if we have used your editorial is if you receive payment from *MidWest Outdoors*. Payment will be issued promptly after a submission has run in the magazine.

MidWest Outdoors Magazine receives a very large volume of editorial submissions daily. Therefore, a call to our office asking about the status of an article will not receive an immediate response. Again, your best check if you have made a submission that has not been returned is to wait for payment. After you receive payment, you know the article has been used.

MidWest Outdoors' Deadline Schedule

Main Section: 35 Days Preceding Publication. Example: April 25th for the June issue. Subscribers receive the issue the 28th and newsstand sales start the 1st.

STATE SECTIONS:

Illinois Sections (Southern/Northern): 5th of the Month Preceding Publication. Example: May 5th for the June issue.

Iowa, Michigan, Minnesota, Wisconsin, Indiana and Kentucky Sections: 1st of the Month Preceding Publication. Example: May 1st for the June issue.

Specific Requirements for *MidWest Outdoors* STORIES...

• Should be accompanied by black and white or color photos or slides.

• Should be between 600 and 1,500 words—with shorter stories preferred. The story's focus should be on where to and how to. Stories should impart information in an entertaining fashion, and not in a text book or preachy tone.

• Should be prepared with the top sheet as illustrated below.

• Can be submitted in the following forms:
  - via e-mail
  - e-mail address: info@midwestoutdoors.com

PHOTOS...

• *MidWest Outdoors* can accept color or black and white photos or color slides. Photos may also be e-mailed. A good photo is usually one that catches the action of some outdoor pursuit.

• Please send no more than 3 to 4 photos per story.

• You must place your return address on the back of the photo if you want it returned. Caption sheet, with the title of the story it accompanies should be taped to the back of the photo. There is no better way to insure that your photo will not be used with another writer's story.

E-MAILING PHOTOS:

This is what we need. Minimum 5" x 5"; 200 pixels per inch; 1000 pixels x 1000 pixels from input device—scanner, digital camera etc. and not from a graphics program. Any questions contact Jesse Saenz (our Graphic person) 888-666-8878 x116 or email jsaenz@midwest outdoors.com.

IMPORTANT CHECKLIST BEFORE SENDING IN MATERIAL

• Your name is on all pages and photos.

• You have included your social security number.

• You have indicated what month the material is for.

• You have written a headline and subheadline.

• You have written a caption for each photo.

PLEASE REMEMBER: If we do not plan on using your material, it will be returned to you within 10 days of receipt. The best check you have for knowing if we have used your material, is if you receive a check from *MidWest Outdoors*.

Categories: Nonfiction—Fishing—Outdoors—Recreation—Regional—Sports/Recreation—Travel

CONTACT: Submissions
Material: All
111 Shore Dr
Burr Ridge IL 60527
Phone: 630-887-7722
Fax: 630-887-1958
E-mail: info@midwestoutdoors.com

Midwest Traveler

About Us

Founded: April 1971. Name magazine changed from *The Midwest Motorist* to *AAA Midwest Traveler* in January 1999.

Frequency: Mailed bi-monthly, Jan./Feb. through Nov./Dec.

Circulation: 435,000. Mailed to AAA households in Missouri, southern Indiana, Southern Illinois and Eastern Kansas

Readership: 870,000

Source: Mediamark Research, Inc., New York, NY / February 2000

AAA Midwest Traveler features articles on regional, national and international travel opportunities. Area history, auto safety, highway and transportation news also are featured. The South is often the focus of travel articles.

As the official publication for AAA members in Missouri, southern Illinois southern Indiana and eastern Kansas, we reach an audience that travels throughout the year. AAA, America's premier travel organization, serves more than 40 million members nationally.

The magazine's goal is to provide members with a variety of useful information on travel, auto safety, and other topics that appeal to the motoring public. The magazine carries on average six articles per issue and buys 20-30 manuscripts per year.

How to contact us: Send queries rather than finished manuscripts. In addition, please send a list of credits or published clips when you query us for the first time. We will not take phone queries and prefer not to see a laundry list of story ideas. In general, we try to reply within four weeks of receipt. We will consider a previously published article if it appeared in a non-competing publication. Simultaneous queries are acceptable, but tell us the idea is being considered elsewhere.

Assignments: We work from an editorial schedule and assignments are usually made at least six months in advance. Sometimes the calendar is assigned by July for the following year. Usually purchase first North American rights. A story assignment is always made by letter. The writer signs an outline-agreement and returns one copy to the editor. We do not pay any expenses in conjunction with the article (travel expenses, phone bills, etc.). Payment for an article is made upon acceptance. Our rates range from $50 to $350. It helps to send photos/slides (color only) with manuscripts. While we do not pay for photos, we consider it in payment for the manuscript. To assist with fact-checking, please send copies of materials used to research the article.

Style: We use the *AP Stylebook*. Third-person voice usually works best, but in some cases first-person description is appropriate. A copy of a current magazine will be sent with assignment so our editing style can be observed. A story will not be drastically changed without discussing this with the writer. Send the manuscript on floppy disk, saved either in Microsoft Word 5.1 or a lower version, or as an ASCII text file. Always include hard copy with the disk.

Taboos: Humor, satire, fiction, poetry, cartoons. Technical and safety articles usually are written by staff. Departments (e.g. "Travel Treasures, Day Tours") also are written by staff.

Categories: Associations—Automobiles—Consumer—Travel

CONTACT: Deborah Reinhardt, Editor
Material: All
AAA Auto Club of Missouri, 12901 N. Forty Drive
St. Louis MO 63141
Phone: 314-523-7350
Fax: 314-523-6982
E-mail: dreinhardt@aaamissouri.com
Website: www.ouraaa.com/traveler

Midwifery Today

Mission Statement

Midwifery Today (a 72-page journal that includes International Midwife) and The Birthkit (a 12-page newsletter) are quarterly publications for birth practitioners. We emphasize natural childbirth, breastfeeding, networking and education. Our aim is to foster communication between practitioners and families, and to promote responsible midwifery and childbirth education around the world.

We seek a balance between scientific or technical material and "softer" personal and/or philosophical articles, including birth-related art, poetry and humor. We consider submissions on all aspects of pregnancy and childbirth. The professional and business aspects of midwifery and childbirth education are also of interest to our readers.

Concise material that clearly expresses your knowledge, experience, feelings or findings will receive consideration. If you are submitting an instructive article aimed at midwifery procedure or practice, please be accurate and factual. Identify and credit your sources of information. Proofread your work. We reserve the right to edit for clarity, content, and length, but whenever possible, we ask you to approve all edits.

E-mail your article, if possible, to: mgeditor@midwifery today.com, or include a disk if mailing. (See guidelines for e-mail at end of this document.) We prefer articles that are typed and double-spaced, although neatly written articles are also accepted. Include your name, address and telephone number, as well as your e-mail address on the opening page. Your name, article title, and page number should appear on each following page if you are mailing. Please include a biographical sketch of no more than 40 words. If you wish to withhold your name, please indicate this; instruct us whether you prefer an anonymous citing, your initials, or a pseudonym.

Photography and Artwork

Overall guidelines: We prefer that images come to us in the highest resolution format possible, closest to the original picture. Thus, it's best to have prints of film images and original digital files of digital camera output. We have difficulty working with digital versions of film images and printed versions of digital camera pictures. It is not impossible, in most cases, but it is substantially more difficult. The results are rarely the best they could be. In all cases, cameras and pictures should be handled with care. If you keep your lenses free from dust and scratches, handle prints gently to avoid fingerprints and dust, and avoid re-sampling digital files, we've got a better chance of being able to work easily with your pictures.

We generally pay $15 per inside shot, $25 for full bleed and $50 for MT cover. We will also trade for magazine subscriptions or advertising space in the magazine. Advertising space is generally only traded when we use a large number of photos over a long period of time or for special photos (for example, the cover of our conference program, book covers, etc.)

We like pictures of mothers and babies together, babies alone, siblings with babies, etc. We prefer pictures of babies for our cover, with or without parents/siblings/etc. Photos that involve midwives, doulas, midwifery students, and specific procedures/positions/equipment are also helpful.

Glossy prints are preferable. Color is fine. We can use either color or black and white easily. 5x7 is ideal, but we can work with smaller snapshots, too.

In general, we recommend the following when taking pictures:
• Make sure your lens is free from dust and grime.
• Take lots of photos
• Film is more likely to make it onto our cover than digital...only the newest digital cameras are capable of capturing enough information to present a quality 9x11 ½ print at 300 dpi (the resolution we need for our cover). Film is continuous tone, and so resolution is not such an issue. See the sections below on each type of photography for more information.

Take care to keep your focus on the important parts of a picture. It is easy to accidentally blur a face by setting focus on a collar, or blur a baby by focusing on a mama's breast.

• Get more information than less. That means that you shouldn't try to crop the picture before it's taken. For example, if you're shooting in a bathroom, don't try to eliminate the top of the shower curtain for style if that means also eliminating the top of the subject's head... We manipulate images heavily in production, which means that the entire shower curtain may be "digitally cut" from the image... but we can't put the top of someone's head back on very convincingly.

• At the same time, don't be afraid to get as close as your camera will tolerate and still be focused.

• Remember that we have great flexibility once a picture is taken to adjust colors, lighting and fix minor flaws and dust... If you're not sure about a picture, send it anyway.

Digital Manipulation
We're used to getting photos in all sorts of states of disrepair... we enhance, tweak, edit, etc. almost every photo that comes in. That said, we greatly prefer to do that enhancement in-house. We've got good eyes for "diamonds in the rough" and don't mind working with a rough print.

We generally do all digital artwork in house. I don't believe we've ever used a photographer's digital artwork, particularly not printer output of digital files. There is just no good way for us to get a high enough quality, high resolution scan of printer output. Printers are not "continuous tone" the way that photos are, and it just doesn't work well. Photoshop has nifty and neat filters, but they work best at 72 dpi. Because our output (halftoned greyscale) is so radically different from the format most pictures come to us (continuous tone color), many effects get lost completely in the translation. It is best, when filters are needed, for them to be applied with a mind to the end result, not just in overall appearance, but in terms of the printing process. This is why we prefer to do such manipulation in-house.

Film images
We can work with a wide variety of prints. Our preferred photo format is 5 x 7 glossy prints. We can work with just about any size print, but 5 x 7 seems to be the ideal compromise between detail and graininess for cover or full-page images. Larger film prints tend to be grainier than scanned enlargements, while smaller film prints can lose detail or get blurry on scanning enlargement. For anything smaller

than a full-bleed photo such as the cover or center image, size of the original photo is much less important. Anything from 2 x 3 up to 8 x 10 will usually work. Larger images get down sampled, improving sharpness, and smaller pictures are simply scanned at their original size, which avoids the problem of enlargement blur.

Please avoid sending matte photos. A glossy finish will scan much better, the irregular surface of a matte photo will cause distortions on a scanner. With many photos this is not terribly significant, but for anything that will be enlarged, glossy finish is vitally important.

Color or black and white images are acceptable. We have no preference in either direction. Although our final output is black and white, our photo-manipulation capabilities are such that we can convert a color photo into a higher-contrast black and white image with very little difficulty at all. We do occasionally have use for color images (such as on book covers, catalog, Web site).

About composition and picture quality:
Dust, lines, etc. are not a reason to scrap a photo. We have a lot of tools for "erasing" dust and lines without losing detail.

Background: Ditto. Half the time we don't use the background at all. Much of the time we will "blur out" the background. When we do leave it in, we edit liberally—we've been known to erase oddly placed light switches, remove the ring and bar from a shower curtain, etc. Cropping is trivially easy, so is vignetting.

Even poor lighting can be fixed. We've managed to pull shadows off of faces or out of the background when necessary. As long as there aren't overexposed places where all definition is lost, we can usually compensate for just about anything else.

Digital cameras
Digital photos will work with the following caveats:
• We will be altering resolution to make the photo 200 dpi in most cases, and we will do that without altering the total pixel resolution. That means that if a photo is designed to be viewed in a reasonable size on the screen, we'll probably reduce it down to a fairly small picture, less than half of the "screen size".

• There is no "lossy" compression. This means that image quality must be "best," not a compressed .jpg. Uncompressed .jpg is okay in most cases. Compression creates all manner of weirdness in a .jpg—fine for viewing on screen and absolutely rotten for printing. Otherwise we will have to make the photo much smaller to compensate and still get a good print.

To give you a sense of what we can do with different digital cameras:
• To print a cover photo at proper resolution, a photo must be 9 inches wide by 11.25 inches tall, at 266 dpi minimum resolution. That is the equivalent of an 8 MP camera. 8 MP cameras are not currently available at prices mere mortals can afford.

• To print a full-bleed image inside the magazine, a photo must be 9 inches wide by 11.25 inches tall, at 200 dpi minimum resolution. That is well within the range of a 5 MP camera.

For photos inside the magazine, digital cameras are much more practical. Even a 2 MP camera will make a reasonable sized photo which can be easily used in the magazine at 200 dpi. We often use a 1.3 MP camera to do small images within the magazine.

Another limitation of digital cameras is picture format. If pictures are taken with .jpg compression used, they will often have to be down sampled to smooth out the compression artifacts generated by the format. That is, when you save a jpeg, it averages out blocks of color to make a smaller save file, and those blocks can sometimes lead to distortions and "fuzzy" images. This can be minimized on most cameras by using "best quality" or "no compression." You will get fewer pictures per disk, but we're more likely to be able to use them. Some cameras will allow you to save in .tif format. This is preferred, because it does not degrade the image quality.

With any digital photo, we prefer that you send the photo without any alterations or edits. Every time you edit, re-save as a .jpg, rotate, adjust color, etc. you reduce the amount of information available in the picture. We edit photos as needed, but we can't usually put back information that isn't there. Repeat saving as a .jpg is a good way to trash a

M-Q

photo completely. The ideal is to keep your original photos as they come off the camera, and make edits and changes on copies of those photos for your own use. For our use, we want the originals, not even opened and re-saved. This allows us the greatest latitude for getting the end result we need.

Scanned pictures

We prefer that any picture we receive come to us as a copy of the original, in the same format. If your pictures are taken with a digital camera, we want you to copy the original files and send those to us. If your pictures are taken with a film camera, we want you to make duplicate prints from the original negatives and send the duplicates to us. We prefer that if at all possible, we be allowed to do the scanning from film. If you want to e-mail us low-resolution scans (72 dpi jpgs) before having prints made and snail mailed-to be sure we're interested in the photos-you may do that. But we try to avoid having other people do the scanning for our final output.

Photo Submission Guidelines

We prefer that prints be sent by post for all film-based photo submissions.

If you are sending a photograph or artwork via e-mail, it must be saved in the TIFF standard (.tif).

Send only one attachment per e-mail (.zip and .sit packages are okay.) E-mail all photos to layout@midwiferytoday.com ONLY.

• Do not send photos to jan@midwiferytoday.com.

We cannot guarantee return of material submitted.

Submit high quality copies of your work and retain a copy of your photography or artwork.

Editorial Columns and Features

Full Length Articles: All pregnancy, birth and postpartum subjects directed toward midwives, doulas, childbirth educators or their clients. Technical, objective (or journalistic reporting), or instructive, as well as personal experience. References are encouraged where appropriate, and suitable photographs, charts, diagrams and other graphics may clarify or enhance your article. Although quarterly themes are useful for our editorial plan, please do not feel constrained by them.

Please note the following topics *Midwifery Today* emphasizes in its publications: birth insights—birth stories told in a way that shares the author's insights or information learned; recipes for tinctures, hot packs, herbal treatments, salves, teas, as well as nutrition-packed recipes for pregnancy and labor; her story (hers, his and kids', too)—birth stories that are powerful, poignant, challenging, entertaining and educational, related by mothers or other family members, with the specific intent of helping birth practitioners gain knowledge and understanding; improving your practice—specific information, systems, and suggestions to help midwives and childbirth educators improve their practices; an autobiographical or biographical portrait: how and why did you or someone else enter the birthing field; your training, practice(s), goals, family, non-birthing interests and insights; midwifery and the law—news, litigation, information and advice, pending legislation, insurance issues concerning the practice of midwifery in your area; opinion pieces; evidence-based practice issues.

Media Reviews: Each publication features media reviews. Be sure to include the following information: authors/editors, name of book/video/cassette, cost, pages/length, format, publisher/producer name, address, phone. Keep in mind the item should be useful to birth practitioners or parents; explain why it is or isn't helpful and give readers a feel for what the product is like. Topics covered? Clearly covered? References included? Photos or illustrations included?

Networking: Air formal and informal comments and opinions, share news, ask questions, critique articles in past issues, and give technical advice or spiritual support. Two to five paragraphs, or in letter form.

Tricks of the Trade: Information you won't find in a textbook. Share practical wisdom and helpful hints from your practice.

We welcome additional contributions to any of the following columns:

International Midwife, a section of *Midwifery Today*: Midwifery from around the world:

All feature articles should emphasize pregnancy, birth and postpartum subjects, customs, traditions, remedies, cultural roles, legal issues, challenges and triumphs from a global perspective. How can midwives weave a global future? What are some opportunities for working abroad? Tell readers about your experience working in a country other than your own. Or, list current opportunities you are aware of. Explain how work abroad can be accomplished.

International Midwife will enable all readers to share and learn more about each other, and share ideas and practices for midwifery care from other countries. This is more than a cultural exchange; it's a place where we can explore and expand. Submission of photos is strongly encouraged.

Cards and Letters: We welcome your letters, opinions, updates on your international practice, submissions from midwives in all corners of the globe, descriptions of the joys and challenges as you practice in your own country, information on your country's midwifery organizations, etc. Limit length to two to five paragraphs.

The Birthkit

Full-length articles submitted to *Midwifery Today* are also considered for *The Birthkit*. We look for birth stories with an eye toward imparting midwifery knowledge; short practice articles; articles about the business of midwifery, childbirth education or doula practice; articles that can serve as handouts for midwifery clients; motivational pieces; pregnancy, birth and midwifery poetry; related line drawings; a day in the life of a midwife; nutrition; herbal remedies; pregnancy-related health care.

Midwifery Today E-News

A free bi-weekly online publication for all childbirth practitioners and interested parents. Our intention is to reach beyond our print capabilities as well as expand our already existing Internet capabilities by offering a modern, quick and timely way to inform, network and support those who work with women during their childbearing years. E-News features convenient links to other appropriate and helpful sites, and an eventual link to the *Midwifery Today* articles database. It is also a springboard to other *Midwifery Today* Internet projects.

E-News guidelines: All material must be e-mailed. Please send to this address: mtensubmit@midwiferytoday.com. Your e-mailed submission must be received in the form of a standard e-mail message, not an attachment. Include your full name and city/state or country.

We do not accept graphics at this time. Photography and art are always considered for our print publications, however.

We will not consider simutaneous submissions or previously published articles for publication in *Midwifery Today*. Exceptions are made for *The Birthkit*. We also reserve the right to publish articles in other forms, such as theme booklets and electronic sources, including World Wide Web pages. You will be required to sign a copyright transfer agreement.

Please Note: All submissions are reviewed by the editors and are considered for the upcoming editorial year.

Payment

Midwifery Today and *The Birthkit* are nonpaying markets. Contributors receive two copies, and authors of full-length feature articles also receive a complimentary one-year subscription to either *Midwifery Today* or *The Birthkit*, depending on placement.

How to Submit Via E-Mail

First, save your article in one of the following formats:

.rtf (Rich Text Format)

.doc (Microsoft Word)

.txt (Plain Text)

Send only one attachment per e-mail. E-mail your document to BOTH of the following addresses (using the "cc" function):

jan@midwiferytoday.com

mgeditor@midwiferytoday.com

We reserve the right to edit for clarity, content, and length, but whenever possible, we ask you to approve all edits.

Important: We reserve the right to refuse any advertisement.

Categories: Nonfiction—Health

CONTACT: Editor (mgeditor@midwiferytoday.com)
Material: Articles
CONTACT: Photo Editor (layout@midwiferytoday.com)
Material: Photos
PO Box 2672
Eugene OR 97402
Phone: 541-344-7438
Fax: 541-344-1422
E-mail: mgeditor@midwiferytoday.com
Website: www.midwiferytoday.com

Military History

Please refer to WEIDER History Group.

Military Officer

General
Publisher: Military Officers Association of America, a nonprofit organization.
Editor in Chief: COL Warren S. Lacy, USA-Ret.
Audience: Commissioned and warrant officers, families, and surviving spouses of the seven uniformed services: Army, Marine Corps, Navy, Air Force, Coast Guard, Public Health Service, and National Oceanic and Atmospheric Administration — both those in active components and members of the National Guard and Reserve.
Circulation: 370,000 monthly. Sample magazines available on request with 9x12 SASE.
Editorial Requirements
Topics: Current military/political affairs; recent military history, especially Vietnam and Korea; financial planning; health and fitness; military family; retirement lifestyles; travel; and general interest. No fiction, poetry, or fillers. Original material only; no reprints.
Format: MS Word-compatible file. No footnotes.
Deadlines: Feature articles normally are scheduled six months in advance.
Queries: Submit detailed query before sending manuscript. Enclose or attach copies of published clips and résumé. Unsolicited manuscripts are rarely accepted.
Style: Active voice, non-technical, with direct quotes. Optimistic, upbeat theme. Use *The Associated Press Stylebook and Libel Manual.*
Length: Features, up to 2,500 words; mini-features, up to 1,400 words.
Terms: First rights, to include Internet and reprint rights.
Payment: Features, up to $1,800; mini-features, up to $1,000. Payment on acceptance.
Submit to Managing Editor, Military Officers Association of America, 201 N. Washington St., Alexandria, VA 22314-2539 or e-mail editor@moaa.org. Enclose SASE for return of hard copy submissions.
Response time: Three months. No phone calls, please.
Photographs
Original color transparencies suitable for color separation preferred. Digital photos must be at highest image size and resolution supported by your camera. $75 for one-eighth page, $125 for one-fourth page, $175 for one-half page, $250 for full page. 5x7 or 8x10 black-and-white glossies occasionally acceptable. $20 for each black-and-white photo used. Prefer captions and credit line on separate sheet. Include SASE for return of photos.turn of photos.
Categories: Nonfiction—Military—Senior Citizens

CONTACT: Managing Editor
Material: All
MOAA
201 N. Washington St.
Alexandria VA 22314-2539
Phone: 800-234-6622 x105
E-mail: editor @ moaa.org
Website: www.moaa.org

Miniature Quilts

Please refer to *Traditional Quiltworks.*

Minnesota Memories

Minnesota Memories accepts prose stories from current and former Minnesota residents. The books, which are compilations of stories and accompanying photos, are published at least once a year and marketed mainly in Minnesota. Stories may be funny, sad, heroic, historical, mysterious, reflective, inspirational or unusual, but they must be true. *Minnesota Memories* will not accept commercial endorsements for products or services, nor will it accept self-congratulatory testimonials. Published stories usually range from 300-2000 words. Storytellers receive a copy of the book and a chance to become part of published Minnesota history via the *Minnesota Memories* project.
E-mail or snail mail stories. Include a 25 word bio of the writer, which will appear at the end of your published story.
Categories: Nonfiction—Biography—Regional History—Personal History

CONTACT: Submissions
Material: All
439 Lakeview Blvd.
Albert Lea, MN 56007
Phone: 507-377-1255
E-mail: Minnmemory@aol.com

the minnesota review
Carnegie Mellon University

Regarding submission guidelines for *the minnesota review*, please note the following:
We have a long tradition of publishing politically engaged work, whether it be Marxist, socialist, feminist, etc. In particular, we would like to publish the work of committed younger writers.
We will continue to publish poetry and fiction on a variety of topics that need not relate to our special topics. In each issue, our editor's aim is to present writing that is cutting-edge, both stylistically and conceptually.
As for technical matters, we ask that essays and reviews be submitted in duplicate and that they adhere to the form specified in the MLA Handbook. We also ask that your manuscript, whether poetry or fiction, be double-spaced. Clear photocopies are acceptable. Simultaneous submissions are also acceptable. Our reading period is usually about two to six months. Please enclose SASE; manuscripts submitted without postage will not be returned. If we do accept your work for publication, we will request the article as an MS Word file on a Macintosh-formatted disk. We will also need a few sentences for Contributors Notes.
Sample issues are available for $15 each. Past issues include n.s. 52-54 (Academostars); n.s. 50-51 (Activism and the Academy); n.s. 48-49 (The Academics of Publishing); and n.s. 47 (The White Issue). Send

check to the address below.

Categories: Fiction—Nonfiction—Book Reviews—Culture—Feminism—Film/Video—Gay/Lesbian—Human Rights—Literature—Multicultural—Poetry—Politics—Short Stories—Spiritual

CONTACT: Editorial Submissions
Material: Correspondence, submissions, and subscriptions
Department of English
Carnegie Mellon University
Baker Hall
Pittsburgh PA 15213
Phone: 412-268-9825
E-mail: editors@theminnesotareview.org
Website: www.theminnesotareview.org

Minnesota Technology®

If you are interested in writing for Minnesota Technology® magazine, we choose top-notch writers with an eye for business, and the ability to translate technology and business concepts into useful and fun-to-read information. Our readers are looking to be informed about people learning and prospering like themselves and, companies producing new and innovative ideas that are relevant to doing business in today's marketplace. We aim to help people gain knowledge that will apply to their own businesses in order to compete, advance and grow.

If you have an idea that may fit our needs, please submit a one-page written query along with several writing samples. Minnesota Technology, Inc. pays its writers upon final approval and publication of each issue (5 X annually). Article lengths range from 250-word pieces for our "Up Front" section to 2,000 words for our full-length features. We pay competitive rates that we determine on an individual basis by assignment.

Categories: Nonfiction—Business—Technology

CONTACT: Editor
Minnesota Technology® magazine
111 Third Ave S Ste 120
Minneapolis MN 55401
E-mail: editor@mntech.org

Minority Engineer

Please refer to Equal Opportunity Publications, Inc.

MISSISSIPPI
Magazine

Mississippi Magazine

Mississippi Magazine is a bimonthly publication that celebrates the positive points of our state—from interesting people and places to homes, gardens, food, history, culture, special events, and more. All topics that appear in the magazine must have a direct and obvious link to Mississippi.

Many of our articles are written by freelance contributors, and because our magazine is only published six times each year, we must choose each story very carefully. We often develop story ideas ourselves and assign them to freelancers. To be considered for such assignments, send at least three clips of your recent work, along with a letter detailing your writing specialities. We also welcome article proposals from freelance writers themselves. Follow these tips to ensure that your idea will be promptly considered.

Developing a Story Idea

Before submitting a query, study at least one recent issue of *Mis-sissippi Magazine*. Familiarize yourself with our editorial style and the types of articles we generally include. Sample copies are available for $6 each; mail a check (Memo: Sample Copy) to Mississippi Magazine, 5 Lakeland Circle, Jackson, MS 39216.

Consider whether your idea will fit well in our publication. Try to place your story within one of our current issues and see if you can visualize it, illustrations and all. Chances are, if you can't see the story in the magazine, you will have a hard time convincing the editorial staff to use it.

We are always looking for unusual subjects that still manage to fit within our editorial scope. Find a unique perspective that you can use to make your story out of the ordinary. A general story on a well-covered topic (like the Natchez Trace, the city of Oxford, or Eudora Welty) is not likely to be accepted. We are looking for unique topics or fresh angles on familiar ideas.

Keep in mind that we strive to be original, so don't propose an article on something you've recently seen in another statewide publication unless you have a very different perspective or new information.

We do not accept fiction; poetry; articles relating to politics, business news, or controversial topics; or previously published articles.

Suitable Topics

Subjects that we regularly cover include interesting people, places, or events; unique historical subjects; great gardens or gardening topics; beautiful and unique homes or interior design; and party or recipe ideas.

For new writers, departments—rather than features—are often the best places to break into our magazine. These include:

Southern Scrapbook—Short (100- to 600-word) articles on a variety of topics. See recent issues for examples. Due to the brevity of these articles, we prefer to consider **full manuscripts** instead of queries.

Culture Center—800-1,200-word articles on a specific artist or any aspect of the arts, culture, theater, or music in Mississippi.

Gardening—800-1,200-word articles on specific planting topics or profiles of individual gardens.

Home Pages—400-800-word reviews of new books that directly relate to Mississippi.

On Being Southern—The last page of each issue is a personal essay written by someone with a Mississippi connection. These essays may be humorous, are often nostalgic, may be related to a specific season, and should always have an upbeat, positive tone. Full manuscripts must be submitted for consideration and must be 500-800 words. Send these stories by email (no attachments, please) or by U.S. mail on a disk in text-only format, along with a printed hard copy and cover letter containing your name, address, social security number, daytime phone number, and a short biographical sentence.

Submitting a Query Letter

With a few exceptions (noted above), we prefer preliminary query letters to unsolicited full manuscripts. Queries allow us to more easily review your idea and potentially suggest how to tailor it for our audience before you begin writing. Due to the large volume of queries we receive, **we cannot accept story ideas by phone**. And no simultaneous submissions, please.

Because we are a bimonthly publication, keep in mind that we plan each issue several months in advance. Seasonal topics should be submitted well in advance of the intended issue date.

Query letters must be typed and must include the following information:

• Name, address, daytime phone number, and email address.

• The subject of story, along with (if applicable) the intended department or specific issue for which it would be appropriate.

• Your proposed lead, followed by a short but thorough summary of the story's content—noting potential interviewees, sources, and other highlights—and a conclusion. Also note any ideas for sidebars.

• Details about why you think this story would be of interest to the readers of *Mississippi Magazine*.

• Any photographs you have to illustrate the article. This is crucial for–this is crucial for home, garden, or art-related story ideas. For consideration purposes only, snapshots are fine. If you have strong photography skills and would like us to consider using your photographs along with the article, please submit high-quality prints or 35mm color transparencies. For articles on subjects other than home, garden, and art, it's okay if you don't have photos, but please briefly describe how the article will lend itself to visual presentation.

• Brief information about yourself and your writing experience.

• A few recent clips or samples of your work.

All queries must also include a self-addressed stamped envelope for a reply and for the return of any materials you would like to have back. Always make a copy of any original materials before submitting. *Mississippi Magazine* assumes no responsibility for the return of unsolicited materials.

Queries sent by U.S. mail are preferred, but emailed queries are acceptable if you follow a few special guidelines: Type or paste the entire text of the proposal in the body of the email rather than include an attached document. Compose an email query just as you would one that is sent by regular mail, being sure to include all of the details mentioned above. Please do not send large picture files as attachments. E-mail queries will not be answered any more quickly than those submitted by mail.

Our Response

The editor will respond to your letter within eight weeks in one of the following ways:

• Acceptance for publication. If your idea is accepted, you will receive a letter detailing word count, payment information, specifics of the article, deadline, and tentative publication date. You will also receive a writer's contract, which should be signed and returned immediately, and a format sheet, which you should follow carefully in preparing your article.

• Request for more information. Sometimes the staff needs photographs or more details about your idea in order to make a decision. If we request more information, we are still considering your idea.

• We would like to file your idea. Sometimes we have an overflow of ideas for a particular kind of story and need to wait a while to see if and when the story will fit into our editorial plans. With permission from contributors, we also like to keep selected "On Being Southern" essays on file indefinitely for potential use in future issues.

• This story does not fit into our magazine. We want each issue to possess a distinct style and continuity from story to story. Many good ideas simply do not fit into the current editorial plans, or a similar story may have recently been done.

While waiting for a response, your patience is appreciated. Please do not call to check on the status of your submission until at least eight weeks have passed. We receive hundreds of freelance queries each year, and with a small staff, it takes a while to go through each inquiry and respond accordingly.

Submitting an Article

After writing an article you have been assigned, take time to confirm and double-check all facts and figures, quotations, spellings of names and places, phone numbers, addresses, etc. Please consult *The Associated Press Stylebook* for all style questions.

Include two or three suggested headlines (usually 2-6 words) and subheads (can range from a short phrase to a couple of sentences), but please note that these elements are selected at our discretion.

Send the completed piece on a disk in text-only or Microsoft Word format. On the first page, include your name, address, phone number, social security number, and the number of words in the article. Also send a hard copy of the article, printed on high-quality paper by a laser or inkjet printer. Attached to your article, please include a list of references used and people interviewed or included in the article, along with their phone numbers. Articles may also be submitted by email if prior arrangement is made with the editor to do so.

Mississippi Magazine buys only previously unpublished manuscripts. We buy first publication rights and pay on publication. We assume no responsibility for unsolicited manuscripts, and we request a self-addressed stamped envelope for the return of any materials. We reserve the right to edit any article for space, grammar, and content. Author proofs are generally not provided. All articles submitted will remain in the custody of *Mississippi Magazine* until publication, unless a rewrite is necessary.

Payment
Feature articles: $250-$350
Southern Scrapbook: $25-75
On Being Southern: $150
Other department articles: $150-$250
Expenses: $35 limit
Categories: Nonfiction—Culture—Food—Gardening—History—Regional

CONTACT: Kelli L. Bozeman, Editor
Material: All
5 Lakeland Circle
Jackson, MS 39216
Phone: 601-982-8418
Fax: 601-982-8447
E-mail: editor@mismag.com
Website: www.mississippimagazine.com

The Mississippi Review
The Mississippi Review online
University of Southern Mississippi

The Mississippi Review online is posted quarterly. Each issue has a guest editor and to submit work you should contact the guest editors directly. The guest editors for upcoming issues will always be listed on the home page of the magazine. If you can find no editor and issue listed there, then the magazine is not reading new work for the moment. Usually, however, you will find the names of editors who have issues in progress, often with notes about what kinds of things these editors are looking for--please contact these editors directly with queries and submissions.

Submissions should be sent as attachments preferably in Microsoft Word or RTF format, or in ASCII text in the body of an email message.

Our so-called mission?

Mississippi Review is a national literary magazine published twice yearly in print, and quarterly on the web. Among the writers MR has published in recent years are Jamaica Kinkaid, Derek Wolcott, Tom Drury, John Barth, Rick Bass, Padgett Powell, Barry Hannah, Martin Amis, Roddy Doyle, Will Self, Margaret Atwood, Robert Olen Butler, Susan Minot, Thom Jones, Paul Auster, Kazuo Ishiguro, Tomaz Salamun, William Gibson, and hundreds of others. While we continue to publish well-known writers, we are also committed to finding new work in fiction and poetry by emerging writers.

Categories: Fiction—Poetry—Regional—Essay

CONTACT: Frederick Barthelme, Editor
Material: Fiction
CONTACT: Angela Ball, Poetry Editor
Material: Poetry
Center for Writers
The University of Southern Mississippi
Box 5144
Hattiesburg MS 39406-5144
Phone: 601-266-5600
Fax: 601-266-5757
E-mail: rief@netdoor.com
Website: www.mississippireview.com

Phone: 573-882-4474
Fax: 573-884-4671
Website: www.missourireview.org

The Missouri Review

The editors invite submissions of poetry, fiction and nonfiction of general interest (no literary criticism). Please clearly mark the outer envelope as fiction, poetry or essay. Do not mix genres in the same submission.

Previously unpublished material only. Manuscripts will not be returned unless accompanied by a stamped, self-addressed envelope. Standard response time is from 10-12 weeks. Manuscripts are read year round. Sample copies are available for $8.95.

Simultaneous submissions are okay as long as you notify us if accepted elsewhere.

POETRY

MR publishes poetry features only—6 to 14 pages of poems by each of 3 to 5 poets per issue. Please keep in mind the length of features when submitting poems.

The Tom McAfee Discovery Feature in poetry is an ongoing series, awarded at least once a year at the discretion of the editors, to showcase the work of an outstanding new poet who has not yet published a book. This award is chosen from among the regular submissions. There are no deadlines and no application process. This feature carrries an additional cash award beyond the regular payment schedule and has been funded by the family and friends of Tom McAfee.

FICTION

All fiction manuscripts should be double-spaced. While there are no length restrictions, "flash fictions" are rarely accepted. We recommend writers familiarize themselves with fiction from previous issues before submitting.

The William Peden Prize of $1,000 is awarded annually to the best piece of fiction to have appeared in the previous volume year. The winner is chosen by an outside judge from stories published in MR. There is no separate application process.

ESSAYS

Nonfiction of general interest only. All submissions should be double-spaced and addressed to "nonfiction editor." There are no restrictions on length or topic, but we suggest that writers familiarize themselves with nonfiction from previous issues. Queries are welcome. Excerpts from book-length nonfiction manuscripts will be considered, but must be able to stand alone.

EDITORS' PRIZE & LARRY LEVIS PRIZE

MR sponsors an annual Editors' Prize Contest in fiction and essay and the Larry Levis Editors' Prize in poetry, with a winner and 3 finalists named in each category. Length restrictions are 25 pages for fiction and essay, 10 pages for poetry. Winners will be published in the following spring issue plus each will receive a cash prize: $2,000 each for fiction, poetry, and essay. Postmark deadline is October 15. A $15 fee per submission includes a one-year subscription to MR.

The Larry Levis Editors' Prize is to honor the memory of MR co-founder and distinguished poet, Larry Levis and is partially funded by his family, friends, students and colleagues.

SUBMISSIONS

Send all submissions by snail mail.

Categories: Fiction—Nonfiction—Book Reviews—Interview—Poetry

CONTACT: Editor
Material: Indicate genre or contest category
1507 Hillcrest Hall, University of Missouri
Columbia MO 65211

Model Railroader

Thanks for your interest in contributing to MODEL RAILROADER. Before you prepare and submit any article, you should write us a short letter of inquiry describing what you want to do. We can then tell you if it fits our needs and save you from working on something we won't want.

We publish articles on all aspects of model railroading and on prototype (real) railroading as a subject for modeling. Here's a general list of our requirements:

TEXT: Present your subject simply and directly in plain English. Keep it brief-most of our articles are one-third text and two-thirds illustrations.

PHOTOGRAPHS: For color we need original 35mm slides or larger transparencies; or glossy color prints 5"x7" or larger. Be sure to include a caption for every photo.

Photography makes or breaks most of the articles we see, so here are six pointers on color photography:

1. Load your 35mm (or larger format) camera with slow-speed indoor color film such as Fujichrome 64T (RTP) or Kodak Ektachrome 64T (EPY).

2. Use at least three photo floods matched to your color film. Floodlights rated for 3200K match the Fuji RTP and Kodak EPY films.

3. Stop your camera down as far as it goes; f22 is good for a 35mm camera, f32 is best. Mount your camera on a tripod so you can make long exposures.

4. Position your lights for even lighting with no harsh shadows. Always light the background first, then the foreground.

5. Bracket your exposures by time, and make lots of bracket exposures over a wide range. You're bound to get a couple of good exposures.

6. Select what you think is the best exposure for each shot, along with one lighter and one darker for insurance. The best exposure for magazine reproduction is the "perfect" exposure.

DRAWINGS: Clean, neat pencil drawings are fine for how-to illustrations, electrical schematics, track plans, and maps-these will be redrawn by our art staff for publication. Track plans must be to scale. If you are a draftsman and want to contribute prototype drawings, write for information on our style and standards.

Send everything for one article at one time, if possible all in one package, and with your name and address on every item. Address your package to "TO THE EDITOR, MODEL RAILROADER MAGAZINE," and mark it "MANUSCRIPT ENCLOSED." We'll send you a card acknowledging receipt of your article, and try to review it within 60 to 90 days. We'll return articles that we can't use if you include return postage.

If we can use your article, we'll pay you for it upon acceptance. Our standard rate is $30 per column, or $90 per page, including drawings and photos. Our standard acceptance agreement specifies that we are buying all rights to the article.

The soonest an article can appear in MODEL RAILROADER is usually four months after acceptance, and we try to use most articles within a year. Our initial payment will be based on a space and color estimate, and we'll make an additional payment upon publication if the article exceeds our estimate. We'll return photos and other material that we don't publish, but we usually keep everything that is used in MODEL RAILROADER.

Thanks for your interest in MODEL RAILROADER.

How-to checklist

The how-to article you send to MODEL RAILROADER should include the following items:

1. TEXT: Tell how you did the project, or tell the reader how to do it, in simple, clear, and direct language. Keep it as brief as possible—most MODEL RAILROADER stories are no longer than six maga-

zine pages. Use photos and drawings extensively, and put details, dimensions, and part numbers in the illustrations. Use active description or instruction, such as "I painted the roof black" or "Paint the roof black," and avoid the passive, "The roof was painted black."

2. LEAD PHOTOGRAPH: Show the model or project at its best, to get the reader's attention and encourage him to read and follow the article. The lead photo should be in color. Usually it's best to show the subject of the article in a finished model scene, with the photo composed so the article subject is the dominant element. Alternately, show the subject against a plain, untextured backdrop of a neutral color-seamless photo backdrop paper is ideal.

3. HOW-TO ILLUSTRATIONS: Use drawings and photos to show the project under construction. Number each as a figure, i.e., fig. 3, and refer to them by the corresponding number in the text. Neat, legible pencil drawings are adequate, as our art staff will prepare finished ink drawings for publication. Drawings need not be to scale unless scale is important, as with exact-size templates, for example.

4. BILL OF MATERIALS: Give a detailed list of items needed to build the project. Include manufacturers' names, part numbers, part names or descriptions, and quantities required. Be sure your information is current. Explain if the reader will have to substitute for items which are no longer available. If you doubt that the reader will know where to find some item, include the manufacturer's address.

5. PROTOTYPE INFORMATION (where applicable): Use photos and/or drawings to show the reader the prototype you followed. Photos may be color, black-and-white, or both. If you have drafting skills and would like to prepare prototype drawings, write for information about our requirements.

Categories: Crafts/Hobbies—Hobbies

CONTACT: Submissions Editor
Material: All
PO Box 1612
Waukesha WI 53187-1612
Phone: 262-796-8776
Fax: 262-796-1142
E-mail: mrmag@mrmag.com
Website: www.modelrailroader.com

Model Retailer
Resources for Successful Hobby Retailing

The magazine pays for one-time print and electronic publication rights to freelance manuscripts and images. Freelance stories generally are assigned in advance, but we welcome proposals for feature articles and columns, or the submission of articles sent on speculation. Payment is made upon acceptance of the material for publication. Feature material generally should be limited to 1,500 or fewer words. Illustrative materials—including but not limited to photographs, graphics, charts and graphs—are welcome and will be judged on their own merit. The material must be original and, where needed, referenced as to the source.

Please send freelance material in hard copy or disk format.

You also may send the manuscript as a e-mail attachment to msavage@modelretailer.com, or fax it to 262-796-1383.

Categories: Business—Cartoons—Collectibles—Computers—Hobbies—Money & Finances—Retail

CONTACT: Mark Savage, Editor
Material: All
Kalmbach Publishing
21027 Crossroads Circle
PO BOX 1612
Waukesha WI 53187-1612
Phone: 262-796-8776
Fax: 262-796-1383

E-mail: msavage@modelretailer.com
Website: www.modelretailer.com

Modeler's Resource

No longer accepting submissions.

Modern Bride

1. We are a consumer bridal publication. All articles must be of direct interest to the engaged or newly married couple.

2. Send query letter with a brief outline of areas to be covered or complete manuscript. Enclose a stamped self-addressed envelope for response or return of material.

3. If you are a published author, send two clips with your query.

4. Queries usually are answered within four weeks of receipt.

5. Article lengths range from short features, 500 to 800 words, to main features, 1,500 to 2,000 words.

6. Prefer typed, double-spaced manuscript or computer letter-quality print-out.

7. Assignments may be made on speculation or with a 25 percent kill fee provision depending on circumstances.

8. Purchase first periodical publishing rights. Payment on acceptance.

Categories: Nonfiction—Consumer—Crafts/Hobbies—Family—Fashion—General Interest—Health—Hobbies—Marriage—Money & Finances—Physical Fitness—Psychology—Relationships—Self Help—Travel—Home-Beauty—How-to—Personal Experience

CONTACT: Susan Schneider, Executive Editor
Material: All
4 Times Square
New York NY 10036
Phone: 212-286-6285
Website: www.modernbride.com

Modern Drummer

Modern Drummer is dedicated to helping drummers in all areas of music, and at every level of ability. It is important to understand that MD is not a "fan magazine" for people who like drummers; it is a professional magazine for drummers themselves. In fact, many of our columns are written by top professional drummers and drum teachers. While it is not crucial that all of our writers be drummers, it is necessary that they know enough about drums and drumming to be able to write about such topics as technique, equipment, style, and musical philosophies.

A certain amount of biographical information is good, as long as it serves to provide background or put things into perspective. But remember: There are any number of magazines providing biographical and lifestyle information; MD is read by people who want information about drumming, so do not get too far away from our main focus.

Additionally, MD is looking for music journalists rather than music critics. Our aim is to provide information, not to make value judgements. Therefore, keep all articles as objective as possible. We are interested in how and why a drummer plays a certain way; the readers can make their own decisions about whether or not they like it.

Before you attempt to write an article for *Modern Drummer*, make sure you are familiar with the magazine. You should have read at least three recent issues to acquaint yourself with our general style and tone. (Sample copies are available upon request for $7 each at mdrm @kable.com.)

In addition, when considering writing an article, you should ask yourself the following questions: Will this article help a substantial group of drummers improve their abilities? Will it enlighten them on a particular phase of drumming? Will it save the reader time, money, or effort? Is the topic interesting enough to attract a large number of readers? Will the article help the reader arrive at a decision or draw a conclusion? Will the article help drummers do their jobs better? Not every article will do all of those things, but if the article does not do any of them, then MD will probably not be interested in it.

Please query us on lengthy material before you begin writing. This helps us avoid receiving articles we cannot use, and it will help you avoid having your article returned. Send us a brief outline of the subject matter and your angle on the story. The editors will then be able to guide you in tailoring the material to the exact needs of the magazine. Also, if your idea has already been assigned or covered, we can notify you before you begin working. If you are writing for MD for the first time, or if your idea is somewhat out of the ordinary, you will be asked to submit your piece on speculation.

The above information should guide you in submitting material to *Modern Drummer*. If you need any further information, please contact Bill Miller or Rick Van Horn at the address listed above. We are always interested in acquiring good editorial material, and in finding talented, competent writers.

PAYMENT - *Modern Drummer* pays upon publication. Rates vary depending upon length of the story after editing, whether the article will be used as a feature article or column, and, to some extent, the length of the writer's association with *Modern Drummer*.

General Rates

Feature article: $300: $500. Buys all rights.

Column: $75: $150. Buys all rights.

(Receipt of payment generally occurs three to six weeks after publication.)

OPEN COLUMNS - Music Columns: Column material can be technical, conceptual, or philosophical in nature. Topics should be very specific, and we encourage the use of musical examples where appropriate, as well as photos or illustrations.

Rock Perspectives: Mainstream or commercial rock

Rock 'N' Jazz Clinic: Progressive rock and fusion

Jazz Drummers' Workshop: Mainstream, bebop, or avant-garde jazz

Driver's Seat: Big band

Strictly Technique: Technical studies that could be applied to any area of drumming

Shop Talk: How-to's on maintaining, customizing, and restoring drums

Latin Symposium: Latin and reggae rhythms as applied to drumset

Teachers' Forum: Articles dealing with teaching and education

The Jobbing Drummer: Freelance drumming: casuals, weddings, etc.

In The Studio: All facets of recording

Show Drummers' Seminar: Broadway, Vegas, theater, resorts, circus, ice shows, etc.

Basics: Primarily beginner-oriented material

Rock Charts: Complete transcription of the drum part to a classic track or current hit

Drum Soloist: Transcriptions of current or classic drum solos

Health & Science: Health matters of importance to drummers

Rudimental Symposium: Technical material pertaining to rudimental technique, drum corps, etc.

Taking Care Of Business: Legal and/or business matters relevant to drummers

Profile Columns: These columns are similar to feature interviews, but shorter in length, and can include popular contemporary drummers, those who have recently come to national attention, or historical drummers from all areas of music (1,500 to 2,500 words).

EDITORIAL POLICY

Manuscripts are edited to conform with style policies, as well as for consistency and readability. This may involve condensing, rearranging, re-titling, and, to some extent, rewording the article. Please refer to the MD Stylesheet for specific style preferences. Final decisions regarding style, grammar, and presentation are the right of the editorial staff of *Modern Drummer*.

STYLESHEET

I. MANUSCRIPT LAYOUT

A. Margins

1. First Page: 3" margin at the top, 1" margin at bottom and sides

2. Subsequent Pages: 1" margin top, bottom, and sides

B. Type Specs

1. Copy must be double-spaced

2. Text must be typed as a Word document, and either emailed or printed & mailed to us. Type should be 12 point, double-spaced. Typewritten manuscripts are acceptable, as long as they are clean and easy to read.

3. Preferred font for computer-printed articles: Geneva

C. Page Numbering-consecutive

D. Paper

1. 8½ x 11 only

2. Original manuscript or clear Xerox copy

E. Bylines

1. Top of first page under title at left margin "by" (lowercase) followed by name of author.

2. Author's address, phone number, and social security number should also appear on manuscript

II. COPY LENGTHS

A. Feature material should range from 2,000 to 4,000 words

B. Column material should range from 350 to 1,500 words

III. PUNCTUATION

A. Album, film, book, and periodical titles should be underlined.

B. The initial letter of each word in album, song, book, and periodical titles should be capitalized.

C. Song titles should be in quotation marks.

D. Dashes should be typed as double hyphen with a space before and after (—).

E. Do not hyphenate words at ends of lines.

F. Periods and commas should be placed before quotes; colons and semi-colons come after quotes.

IV. MUSICAL GENRES: Preferred spellings (note capitalization)

Afro-Cuban

ambient; trance; chill-out; alternative rock; college rock; indie rock; alternative country; alt-country; Americana; y'alternative; avant-garde; avant-garde jazz; bebop; hard bop; big band; bluegrass; blues; the blues; blues-rock; Cajun; classic rock; classical; 20th-century classical; C&W or country & western; country; country-rock; dance music; disco; Dixieland; doo-wop; drum 'n' bass; dub; dub reggae; electronic music; electronica; emo; folk; funk fusion; jazz-rock; garage rock; glam; Gospel goth; goth rock; hard rock; heavy metal; metal; death metal; nüü metal; dark metal; grind; (grind-core); thrash; hip-hop; house; industrial; jam bands; jazz; jump blues; klezmer; Krautrock; laptop; glitch; Latin; Latin jazz; lite jazz; lo-fi; lounge; minimalism; new age; new wave; synth-pop; opera; pop; pop-rock; post-punk; power-pop; progressive rock; prog rock; psychedelia; psychedelic; pub rock; punk; punk rock; hardcore punk; hardcore; rap; rap-rock; reggae; R&B or rhythm & blues; rock 'n' roll; rockabilly; roots; contemporary roots music; ska; skiffle; soul; soundtrack music; southern rock; surf-rock; swing; techno; Tejano; Tex-Mex; world music (specific styles generally lower-case: samba, afro-pop,; polka, etc.); zydeco

V. STYLE NOTES

A. Spell out numbers one hundred and below. Use numerals for numbers over one hundred. Exceptions include: 8th note, 16th note, and 32nd note; dimensions of gear (drum sizes, shell plies, etc.); and instances where many numbers are used throughout an article that's technical in nature.

B. '60s, '70s, '80s when dealing with decades.

C. Twenties, thirties, forties, etc. when dealing with age.

D. LP (LPs), 45 (45s), CD (CDs).

E. A.M. and P.M. should be typed in small caps.

F. Specific times should be expressed in numerals, with minutes: "The gig ended at 2:00 A.M."

VI. PARAGRAPHING

The first paragraph of an article should be aligned entirely with the left margin. The first line of subsequent paragraphs should be indented with a standard tab, with subsequent lines aligning with the left margin. Make sure your preferences do not automatically indent the first line of paragraphs. New paragraphs should be manually tabbed in.

VII. INTERVIEWS

A. For question & answer format, introduction should follow paragraph format described in VII above. Uppercase MD (followed by a colon) should precede questions, and first name of interviewee (also followed by a colon) should precede responses. MD and interviewee's name should be boldfaced.

B. Interviews that follow narrative format should follow paragraph rules outlined in VI above.

VIII. MISCELLANEOUS PREFERRED SPELLINGS

musical terms; backbeat; bandleader; bandmember; barline; butt plate; China cymbal; China-type; drum & bugle corps; drumhead; drum key; drumkit; drum pad; drumset; drum shell; drum shop; drumstick; EQ; EQ'd (past-tense verb); footboard; freelancer (noun); freelance (verb, adjective); hi-hat; lineup; mic' (microphone) (noun); plural: mic's; midrange; miking, miked, mike (verb: I mike my drumset.); multitrack; odd time (noun); odd-time composition (adj); onstage; on stage (my onstage sound when I'm on stage); overdub; rimclick; rimshot; setup (noun), set up (verb); sight-read; single strokes; single-stroke roll; soundcheck; throwoff; timekeeper; timekeeping; tom-tom; upbeat

Miscellaneous terms alright; email; okay; T-shirt; Web site, World Wide Web; " (inch), for instance: 2"; x (by), for instance: 5x14

IX. LANGUAGE

A. Do not use gonna for going to, gotta for got to, or 'cause for; because. In general, stay away from contracting verbs by omitting the ending; "g," for instance: sayin' or playin'.

B. Language should be kept reasonably "clean." Profanities should be; kept to a minimum; obscenities should be avoided.

Categories: Nonfiction—Music

CONTACT: Submissions Editor
Material: All
Modern Drummer Publications
12 Old Bridge Rd.
Cedar Grove NJ 07009
Phone: 973-239-4140
Fax: 201-239-7139
E-mail: sueh@moderndrummer.com
Website: www.moderndrummer.com

Modern Haiku

Modern Haiku is a journal devoted to English-language haiku, book reviews, and articles on haiku. Publication is three times a year: February, June and October. Now in its 38th year of publication, it has an international circulation and is widely subscribed to by university, school, and public libraries. *Modern Haiku* has been cited by the International Division of the Museum of Haiku Literature in Tokyo as: "The best haiku magazine in North America." Issues have from 90 to 136 pages.

Material submitted to *Modern Haiku* should meet these guidelines:

1. Haiku should by typed or clearly printed. They may all be on one or two sheets of paper; each sheet must contain the contributor's name and full address in the upper left corner. Submissions are welcome at any time.

2. A self-addressed, stamped envelope must accompany each submission of material.

3. It is advisable to submit several haiku at a time.

4. All material submitted to *Modern Haiku* must be the original, previously unpublished work of the contributor, and no material may be currently under consideration by any other publication.

5. E-mail submissions are not accepted.

6. Please inquire before sending articles or reviews.

Normally, contributors will receive a report on their material in two to four weeks.

Modern Haiku does not give copies of the magazine to contributors whose work has been accepted, as it pays $1 for each haiku that is accepted and $5 a page for articles and reviews.

Since *Modern Haiku* refrains from carrying advertising and depends on subscriptions to meet costs, we would sincerely appreciate your subscription. If you enter a gift subscription a card in your name will be sent at your request to the recipient with the first issue.

A one-year subscription (three issues) is currently $26 bulk rate. Payment should be made in U.S. currency. A sample copy is $10.

Thank you for your support of *Modern Haiku*,
Charles Trumbull, Editor
Categories: Asian-American—Literature—Poetry

CONTACT: Charles Trumbull, Editor
Material: All
PO Box 7046
Evanston IL 60204-7046
E-mail: trumbull@comcast.net
Website: www.modernhaiku.org

Modern Maturity
AARP, The Magazine

Please Note:
Modern Maturity is now known as AARP, The Magazine.
General Editorial
Most *AARP, The Magazine* features are assigned to writers whose work is known to us and who have an established reputation in journalism. We rarely assign a major feature as the result of an unsolicited query.

The magazine does, however, encourage query letters for specific features and departments. These should be one-page in length and accompanied by recent writing samples. We expect proposers to be familiar with the magazine and its departments.

AARP, The Magazine discourages the submission of unsolicited manuscripts and assumes no responsibility for their return.

Features and departments cover the following categories:
- Finance, investments, legal matters
- Health
- Food (including recipes; emphasis on healthy eating)
- Items of regional interest - 150 to 300 words
- Travel (domestic and international)
- Consumerism (practical information and advice)
- General interest (new thinking, research, information on timely topics, etc.)

Rate of Payment
AARP, The Magazine pays on acceptance at the minimum rate of $1.00 per contracted word. A kill fee of 25% will be paid for assigned articles that are not accepted for publication.

Categories: Nonfiction—Careers—Cooking—Food/Drink—Health—Money & Finances—Relationships—Senior Citizen—Society—Travel—Retirement—Medicine

CONTACT: J. Henry Fenwick, Editor
Material: All
601 E St. NW
Washington DC 20049

Phone: 202-434-6880
Fax: 202-434-6883
E-mail: 310-496-4124

Mom Guess What Newspaper

CONTENT: General and Political News, Book, Film, Restaurant, Theater Reviews, Entertainment, Interviews, Art Profiles, Advertising, Sports, Features, and Financial.

AUDIENCE: A newspaper for gay men, lesbians and their straight friends in the State Capitol and the Sacramento Valley area. Founded in 1978. First and oldest gay newspaper in Sacramento.

FORMAT: Deadlines: 8th and 23rd. 60%, 40% advertising. Tabloid, 34". Newsprint. Trim size 17"x11¼". Body copy is 9/10 points. 85 line screen photographs. Free and/or 50¢ donation. Published every 2 weeks since 1978. 21,000 copies. $30 subscription. Sample issue $1.00. 32+ pages each issue.

NEEDS: Freelance articles on People, Politics, Trendsetters, Features, Health, Artists, Photography, Artwork. Material is not limited to the gay & lesbian lifestyle. 1,500-2,500 words. No Poetry.

TERMS: MGW is published primarily from volunteers. Payment is in copies. Byline appears with each published article; photos credited. Editors reserve right to edit, crop, touchup, revise, or otherwise alter manuscripts, and photos, but not to change theme or intent of the work. Enclose SASE postcard for acceptance or rejection.

MECHANICAL REQUIREMENTS: Author's name, address, phone should appear on first page with approximate word count. Photo captions should be typed on a separate page. Black & white glossy preferred. 5"x7" or 8"x10". No negatives or slides. Label all photos.

DISKS: Label each diskette with:
1. Headline/Filename
2. Your name
3. Program and version you used
4. Type of computer: PC-IBM compatible or Macintosh
5. Date you're submitting the disk
6. Your phone number
Send printed copy with disk. We use Quark.

CARTOONS: Pen & Ink. High contrast. PMT/stats, velox preferred. Do not send originals.

Categories: Computers—Feminism—Film—Food—Gay/Lesbian—Lifestyle—Men's Issues—Politics—Relationships—Sexuality—Sports

CONTACT: Submissions Editor
Material: All
1103 T St.
Sacramento CA 95814
Phone: 916-441-6397
Website: www.mgwnews.com

Moment
America's Premier Independent Jewish Magazine

Stories for MOMENT are usually commissioned, but unsolicited manuscripts are occasionally selected for publication. We look for analytical, colorful, thought-provoking features and essays on Jewish life in the United States, Israel, and elsewhere.

MOMENT's feature articles run from 2,500 to 4,000 words. Successful features offer our readers an in-depth journalistic treatment of an issue, phenomenon, institution, or individual-a treatment that is characterized by solid and accurate reporting, that draws upon multiple sources, that makes lively and abundant use of quotations, and that offers visual color through accurate observation. The more the writer can follow the principle of "show, don't tell," the better for our readers.

A fresh perspective on an issue, or a national or global take on an otherwise local affair, is also an important editorial consideration. Also, a writer must be familiar with other works on the same topic, and with articles published in previous issues of MOMENT.

In addition to major features, MOMENT runs regular departments. Olam (the Jewish world) contains a selection of first-person accounts, colorful reportage, and humor pieces of 800 to 1,500 words each. 5760 contains snappy pieces of not more than 300 words each, including news items, ideas to improve Jewish living, and coverage of quirky events in the Jewish community. MOMENT also reviews fiction and nonfiction books, but these 250- to 800-word pieces are generally assigned to regular contributors.

We receive many more articles than we are able to publish, particularly about certain subjects, such as the Holocaust and Israel. We're more likely to use an article if it is not on these subjects.

Payment for articles is determined on an individual basis, depending on the nature of the piece, its length and complexity, and the writer's experience.

Best of luck!

Categories: Nonfiction—Jewish Interest—Religion—Spiritual

CONTACT: Submissions Editor
Material: All
4710 41 St., NW
Washington DC 20016
Phone: 202-364-3300
Fax: 202-364-2636
Website: www.momentmag.com

Money

Does not accept unsolicited submissions.

Monitoring Times

Style and Content

Stories accepted for publication in *Monitoring Times* have two things in common: first, the story is a "good read" and second, it is of utility to the radio monitor.

This means that your story should have broad appeal in a *Reader's Digest* or *National Geographic* sort of way. Anyone, radio enthusiast or not, should find the story fascinating. Those that are radio enthusiasts, on the other hand, should find within the article information of value—especially specific frequencies—that they can use to participate in the topic you have addressed.

We encourage the use of vivid imagery and lively anecdotes, especially for the opening and closing paragraphs. It's important that you convey a sense of excitement and enthusiasm for the topic you are covering. You are, in effect, "selling" people on the radio monitoring hobby.

K-I-S

No matter what topic you've decided to write about, *Keep It Simple*. The vast majority of MT readers are beginners. Believe it or not, there are hundreds of millions of people out there to whom shortwave is a mystery and UTC absolutely mind-bending. Thus, it is unlikely they'll understand a passing mention of something like propagation or synchronous detection circuitry. K-I-S!

Always define abbreviations and acronyms on first use (FCC, NASA, USB, etc.) and always provide a source (company address or publisher) for any business, equipment, or book you recommend. Though writing on a basic level, if you explain your terms as you go along, your article will bring the beginner along with you.

If your article is a basic one, you can provide those who wish to pursue the topic further with suggestions of where to go for more information or experience. If your article is more complex or technical, it would be appropriate to suggest sources for more basic background information.

Keep in mind the time factor while writing; your article must still be valid six months from now. We appreciate your willingness to check the article for accuracy if significant time passes before publication.

Homework

We do not suggest topics for potential authors. Rather, we rely on your creativity and experience to suggest articles. We strongly advise prospective authors to review past copies of the magazine to get an idea of what kind of articles we generally run. While we hope you don't try to mimic what you see, it does give you some idea of where it is we are headed editorially.

The most general ideas include profiles of radio systems, "how-to" articles ranging from "how to hear a broadcast or transmission" to listening tips such as "how to make the best use of loggings, DX Latin America, where to find military communications, etc...."

Technical articles and reviews are hardest to place, so be sure to check first before investing a great deal of time. We do accept them, but our regular columnists also cover these topics, so check with us to avoid duplication.

Common Courtesies

Check your facts; don't expect the editor to catch errors. If they're someone else's facts, check for obvious mistakes.

Credit your sources and your graphics (individuals, publications, clubs). It's their only payment for making your material look good!

Provide a current contact address or phone number for any companies whose products or services are mentioned in your article.

Query Us

Although we do accept unsolicited manuscripts, if you have an idea for an article, we recommend you query us in advance of completing a manuscript. And when you do query us, do not be afraid to give us your best pitch. Give an overview of the article, highlight some of the things you want to cover, perhaps providing an anecdote or two from the article, and tell us why we would want to buy the article and how it might appeal to the reader. Don't hesitate to follow up the written query with a phone call to the editor after at least six weeks have passed.

All queries, questions and comments, along with manuscripts submitted on approval, must be accompanied by a self-addressed stamped envelope. Direct your query or manuscript to the editor, Rachel Baughn, at *Monitoring Times*, 7540 Hwy 64 West, Brasstown, NC 28902, e-mail mteditor@grove-ent.com, or you may fax your request to (828) 837-2216. The editor is not available by phone, but a call-back may be arranged by leaving a message at 828-837-9200.

The Next Step

If your idea sounds good and there is a reasonable chance the article will be published, you will be invited to submit a manuscript. We ask that in addition to submitting your manuscript in hard copy form that you also include it on IBM-formatted disk or via email, if possible. Be sure to include the following information at the top of your manuscript: Name, address, daytime phone number, date, and your social security number. Once received, the manuscript will be accepted, returned for modification, offered hold status, or rejected.

Payment and Rights

We receive more articles worthy of acceptance than we can publish or pay for in a month. Our practice is as follows: after an article is accepted, it remains in file, and payment is made when the manuscript is published. If this arrangement is not acceptable, other terms may occasionally be negotiated with the editor. If you live in the U.S., we must have your Social Security number on file before payment is made.

Payment for most full-length (1800-3000 words) feature articles accompanied by at least three suitable illustrations is around $50 per laid-out page: $i.e., $150-$200. A one-year subscription to the magazine is complimentary (limited to one per year). The inclusion of appropriate illustrations, in the form of photos, slides, or line art, and your proven reliability will help guarantee this payment.

On occasion, a manuscript will be offered "hold" status. These are manuscripts which, perhaps because of the writing, information, or subject matter, have less guarantee of being published. If you are offered hold status, your manuscript will remain at the editorial office

under the same conditions as "accepted" articles.

Monitoring Times purchases First North American Serial Rights (we will be the first to publish your article in North America), and limited reprint rights as follows: single photocopies of your article if the back issue is no longer available, its inclusion in single issue sales of the magazine in digital format, and inclusion in the yearly compilation of all twelve issues on a compact disk.

Until you receive payment, you may retract an article or *Monitoring Times* may return an article for any reason.

Once Published

Once published, you are welcome to give or resell your article elsewhere with the proviso that it contain the line "(Name of article) was previously published in *Monitoring Times*, Brass-town, NC 28902." It is your responsibility to ensure that this line appears in all subsequent publications.

Text Preparation Guidelines for *Monitoring Times*

STYLE

Type your article in a simple, straightforward style; do not do any formatting or layout on your disk. For example, long lists of frequencies should be typed in a single column, even though it may end up as three columns in a finished layout. If you wish to provide a suggested layout on your hard copy, that's okay.

Use subheads to break up your work; it helps you, the editor, and the reader to follow the flow of logic throughout the article. Type subheads in upper and lower case.

Indent paragraphs with a tab, not spaces

Do not insert blank line between paragraphs

Use one tab, not spaces, to separate columns in tables

Single space (hit space bar once only) between sentences.

Use upper and lower case, never all caps, even in tables, if possible

MT/ST customary usage of some commonly confusing punctuation/spellings:

• Hz / kHz / MHz / GHz / kW / am-pm / AM-FM

• Comma is used before and AFTER state when giving city and state .

• Periods and commas go inside ending quotation marks.

• Comma is used preceding the word "and" when used in a series (example: red, white, and blue).

WORD PROCESSOR

MS Word, Word Perfect, or Rich Text Format preferred.

Use minimal formatting, and NO TABLES.

Recommended: Provide file in ASCII as well in case it does not convert correctly.

MODE OF TRANSMISSION

Best: On disk (IBM 3½" HD disk), accompanied by graphics and hard copy.

OK: Sent as email attachment.

Typed, high contrast paper copy for scanning.

Worst: Faxed copy (okay as advance copy only).

Note: Unless this is a rush job, provide back up hard copy whenever possible.

Graphics

Best: Glossy prints, especially for cover art (Matte, velvet, or textured surfaces do not scan well); high quality line art (please avoid super thin lines and shading screens); digital vector graphics (anything that can be imported by Aldus PageMaker, such as Aldus -FreeHand EPS, Adobe Illustrator EPS, Corel Draw placeable EPS, etc.); and digital bitmap graphics (Tiff, jpg, gif and pcx with resolutions of at least 200 dpi at the approximate size of final reproduction).

OK: Pen and ink drawings; already published pictures if they are not copyright protected and exhibit good contrast and very fine dot screens.

Worst: Pencil sketches; dot matrix graphics; low resolution digital files that exhibit "stairstepping" or "jaggies"; no graphics at all!

Send digital illustrations in a separate file, not imbedded in text file.

Please provide photo captions on disk; a list of graphics and captions should appear at the head of your article. DO caption your pictures, even if it's just a simple identification.

CONTACT: Rachel Baughn, Editor
Material: All
7540 Hwy 64 West
Brasstown NC 28902-0098
Phone: 828-837-2216
E-mail: mteditor@grove-ent.com

The Montana Catholic

The Montana Catholic newspaper serves the Roman Catholic community residing in western Montana. Tabloid in format, it is published 16 times per year—usually every three weeks—and is mailed directly to some 9,200 homes for an estimated readership of 21,000. Some parishes and institutions make free copies available on their literature stands. Total printed circulation is 9,400.

Nearly all recipients of *The Montana Catholic* are paid subscribers. All contributors to the Diocesan Offertory Program—the annual appeal of the Catholic Diocese of Helena—receive a one-year subscription to the newspaper as part of their contribution. Individuals who do not contribute to the DOP may subscribe separately. Provision is made for free subscriptions for persons who wish to receive the paper but cannot afford it.

Our predominant editorial focus is to report news and develop feature stories which relate directly to the activities and concerns of the Catholic community in western Montana.

News and Feature Articles

We buy a limited number of news and feature articles from freelance writers. The majority of these are articles which originate with or are assigned to established freelance writers who reside in western Montana. However, several articles each year are purchased from freelance writers outside the area who write more general feature stories relating to seasonal or special supplement topics.

Seasonal topics include Thanksgiving, Advent, Christmas, Lent, and Easter. Supplement topics have been scaled back recently, but two that will remain will be Religious Vocations (January and early Spring) and Respect Life (October).

Submissions are also welcome for an ongoing series on the coming of the Third Millennium.

In general, however, our emphasis is on the local church; therefore, we look primarily for Catholic-oriented material with a tie-in to western Montana.

We buy one-time rights; reprint rights and simultaneous submissions are accepted. We prefer full disclosure of where else submitted or previously printed.

Commentaries

At present, our only regular columns are by local writers. However, we often allow space for occasional commentary by other local, non-local, or syndicated writers. Thoughtful commentaries on issues of current or seasonal concern to the Catholic church are welcome.

Photos/Illustrations

Original photos and illustrations which help highlight news and feature stories are encouraged. All pertinent subjects appearing in the photo must be identified and, where necessary, permission for use must be granted.

Poetry

Please do not submit poetry. We have published perhaps three poems in the last eight years, only one of which was written by a freelance writer.

Length

News and feature articles can range from 400 to 1,200 words, although most successful writers keep their work in the 600- to 900-word range. We reserve the right to edit all manuscripts accepted for publication.

Payment

For original news and feature articles assigned to local freelance writers, we pay up to $0.10 per word based on the final, edited word count, up to the maximum word count assigned.

For other news, features and commentaries, we generally pay $0.05 per word, based on the final, edited word count.

Rarely, a different fee or rate can be negotiated for first rights on a particularly outstanding piece.

We do not guarantee publication of assigned articles, and publication may be advanced or delayed for space or editorial reasons.

Kill fee on assigned articles is 50%. If writer has been informed that article is "accepted for publication" but the article is later killed, kill fee is 25%. No kill fee will be paid if articles are delivered after deadline or if the author fails to comply with requests for revisions or additional research.

Payment for photos varies from $5 to $20 per photo published.

Style

Please observe the following writing guidelines:

Although there are exceptions, avoid writing in the first person, except perhaps for commentary pieces.

Maintain a positive, uplifting tone—but avoid Pollyannaism.

Avoid "preachiness," including excessive quotation of scripture or other church documents. When scripture citation is appropriate, use the *New American Bible* or the *Revised Standard Version*.

Check all facts and quotations. One error will cast suspicion upon the accuracy of the entire manuscript.

Also check spelling and grammar carefully; leaving fundamental writing errors is the fastest way to make an editor lose interest in a writer.

Do not inject subjective language into news pieces; limit its use in feature stories.

We value strong leads, a body of the article which develops and delivers on the lead, and a definitive conclusion.

Manuscript Preparation

Please do not use a dot-matrix printer. For submissions on disk, IBM-compatible format is required, preferably using Microsoft Word or ASCII. Use a standard indent for paragraphs and a one-inch margin on every page.

Title page should include writer's name, address, and telephone number in the upper left corner; word count in the upper right corner; and article title with writer's byline centered in the middle of the page. Subsequent pages should have a running head in the upper right corner with the writer's surname, article title (abbreviated if necessary), and page number.

Underline titles, italicized words or phrases, and foreign words for emphasis.

Handwritten corrections and changes should be few and legible.

Queries and Submissions

For news and feature stories pertinent to the Catholic community in western Montana, query or send completed manuscripts. Writers should familiarize themselves with our style and format prior to submitting a query. Each query should include the primary focus of the proposed article, the main point of discussion, and a list of any authorities who would be consulted in the article. No phone calls except from freelance writers in western Montana who have an established relationship with us.

Categories: Regional—Religion—Rural America—Catholic—Montana

CONTACT: Editor
Material: All
Diocese of Helena, PO Box 1729
Helena MT 59624
Phone: 406-442-5820
Fax: 406-442-5191
E-mail: MontanaCatholic@DioceseHelena.org
Website: www.diocesehelena.org/pages/montanacatholic.htm

Montana Magazine

Montana Magazine is published bimonthly, in January, March, May, July, September, and November. Please read our publication so you have a good grasp of our style and content. Back issues are available for $5 each, postpaid. Subscriptions cost $23 per year. We assign work, and also consider freelance material. Please query in writing. We read every query and try to respond within two months. Queries by e-mail are accepted, but go into the queue along with all the snail-mail ones.

Overview

Montana Magazine varies from 92 pages to 140 pages. We are noted for excellent photographs and entertaining, informative writing about Montana. The magazine contains about five feature articles of 1,800 to 2,500 words, and four to six departments of 800 to 2,500 words. The issues are four-color throughout.

Focus

Montana Magazine subscribers include lifelong residents, first-time visitors, and "wanna-be" Montanans from around the nation and the world. Readership is estimated at 110,000. We publish articles on Montana recreation, contemporary issues, people, natural history, cities, small towns, humor, wildlife, real-life adventure, nostalgia, geography, history, byways and infrequently-explored countryside, made-in-Montana products, local businesses, and environment—in short, anything that will inform and entertain our readers. We avoid commonly-published topics so Montanans won't ho-hum through more of what they already know. If it's time to revisit a topic, we look for a unique slant. We are strictly a Montana-oriented magazine. Articles of generic Western flavor will not make it. We're ill-disposed toward stories of wild-animal trapping, gory hunting tales, or "me & Joe" adventures. No poetry or fiction, please.

Queries

We accept written queries and unsolicited manuscripts. Please be patient—eventually all submissions are reviewed and responded to. Telephone queries are heartily discouraged. If we like your proposal, we may ask to see it on speculation. Acceptance for review does not imply that the article will be published. Queries should include a thorough outline of the proposed article. Start with the lead, then write a short summary of content, including specifics on whom you plan to interview, research sources, highlights, anecdotal information, and conclusion. Provide several samples of your writing if we are unfamiliar with your style. Include a return envelope and postage. Manuscripts must be typed, double- or triple-spaced. Do not send your original copy. We can convert almost any commercial software word processing program from 3.5" or 5 1/4" disks. Include a return envelope and postage if you want your material returned. We are not responsible for unsolicited material of any kind.

Rates

Montana Magazine's basic rate is approximately 20¢ per published word. Higher payment for assignments involving extra expenses may be arranged before publication. Whenever possible, include illustrative material for the article, such as snapshots or portraits supplied by the subject of the article. Please identify all such artwork with the name of the photographer (if known) or studio. Artwork in that category is credited in the magazine as "Courtesy of XXXX." Payment for assigned, published photographs is additional. Full-page $125; larger than half-page $100; half-page or smaller $50. Payment, returnable materials, and a complimentary copy of the magazine are sent to each author within thirty days of publication.

Rights

Montana Magazine buys one-time-rights to your article, which may include both print and electronic versions. This does not require the written exchange of copyright from freelancers to the magazine. Occasionally, we are asked for permission to reprint an article. These requests are generally from an educational institution or a hobby club. We cannot grant permission, and will forward such requests to the author. Most material is purchased on a one-time-rights basis, which does not require the written exchange of copyright. We reserve the right to edit and rewrite to comply with our style. Author proofs are generally not provided.

Categories: Nonfiction—History—Outdoors—Recreation—Regional—Travel

CONTACT: Beverly Magley, Editor
Material: Queries
PO Box 5630
Helena MT 59604
Phone: 406-447-5100 (no phone queries)
Fax: 406-443-5480
E-mail: editor@montanamagazine.com
Website: www.montanamagazine.com

Montana
The Magazine of Western History

Submitting Your Manuscript

Montana: The Magazine of Western History, published quarterly by the Montana Historical Society, welcomes authentic articles on the history of Montana and the American and Canadian wests.

Montana is a scholarly journal, which means that articles are submitted to peer review and must show evidence of original research, through footnotes or bibliography, on significant facets of history or provide a new interpretation of historical events that changes the way we view a particular historical topic. A rewriting of standard incidents generally available in other sources will not be accepted.

Manuscript length should run between 3,500 and 6,500 words, or about 14 to 25 double-spaced pages, plus endnotes. Because we are an illustrated journal, photographs of acceptable quality assist in our judgments.

In reviewing articles, if your article is judged appropriate for *Montana*, we will submit it to anonymous review; that is, a blind copy of your manuscript will be sent out-of-house for evaluation, usually to two experts in the field. Upon receiving their comments, we will forward a summary of the readers' reports to you with our determination. The process usually takes six to eight weeks.

The best guide to style for *Montana* is a recent issue of our magazine, but generally we follow the latest revised edition of *Chicago Manual of Style*.

We prefer receiving two copies of your manuscript for review and end notes instead of footnotes. No computer disk is necessary at first, although we will request to have your manuscript on a 3.5 disk if accepted. At that time, endnotes should be made a separate document from the text.

Categories: Nonfiction—History—Regional—Western—Western History

CONTACT: Molly Holz, Associate Editor
Material: All
225 N Roberts St
PO Box 201201
Helena MT 59620-1201
Phone: 406-444-0090
Fax: 406-444-2696
E-mail: mholz@mt.gov
Website: www.montanahistoricalsociety.com/pub/magazine/default.asp

Moody Magazine

WHO WE ARE

Published six times a year, *MOODY* magazine exists to encourage and equip Christians to live biblically in a secular culture. *MOODY* seeks practical, popular-level articles that focus on the application of scriptural principles in daily life, as well as some that examine current events and issues from a scriptural perspective.

OUR READERS

Conservative, evangelical laity of all denominations, with a target age of 35-54 years. Most of our readers are married, college graduates, and active in their church. The male-female ratio is 41-59.

WRITING FOR MOODY

Because we assign each issue's package of cover articles—and because we seek to present a variety of topics in each issue—we do not offer an editorial theme list. Instead, we look for free-lancers to query us about individual article proposals.

FEATURE ARTICLES

Feature Articles cover a broad range of topics, but have one common goal: to foster application—by a broad readership—of specific scriptural principles. Many authors use a personal narrative style, but we are also open to articles that take an anecdotal reporting approach. Typical Length: 1,200 to 2,400 words.

MOODY especially seeks narrative accounts showing the process of one's realization and application of specific, scriptural principles in daily life—that others can also apply in their own situations. In generating ideas for such articles, we recommend a writer consider:

What have you been learning that Scripture calls you to do in some key area?

What difficulties have you encountered as you've sought to put those insights into practice?

What effect has this ongoing application had on you and those around you?

Looking beyond your own experience, what could others learn—and apply—from this?

SOME ARTICLE CATEGORIES

- discipleship
- innerlife
- church
- outreach
- issues/culutre/society
- family/marriage
- workplace/finances

DO's AND DON'Ts

How-To's: Rather than directive how-to's, we prefer articles that show how you (or other believers) have learned to approach a situation scriptural and the difference that has made.

Exhortations: Similarly, we do not seek articles declaring a certain issue is a problem Christians should address. We prefer a journalistic approach that shows examples of believers who are already taking a positive, scripturally based response.

Inspirationals: Our goal for narratives is not simply to describe a dramatic or inspirational event, but to show the process of one seeing the need to apply the truth of God's Word to an aspect of everyday life—and then following through with that application.

No biographies, historical articles, or studies of Bible figures.

COMPELLING WRITING

Remember the last time you glanced at an article—then flipped the page because it just wasn't interesting. Now remember that other article you couldn't stop reading. Afterward you clipped it out, made copies for a friend, and told others about it. That's the kind of writing MOODY seeks. An article has perhaps 10 seconds to grab a reader's attention. We want articles that grab readers—and then keep them grabbed all the way to the end. Great topics alone aren't enough. Ask yourself, "Would I want to read my article if someone else had written it?" We know your mom, your spouse, or your best friend would read it. We look for articles that everyone else wants to read, too. We want writing that breathes life into a topic—but not melodramatic or jargon-filled prose. We look for accounts that find the human dimension, apply God's Living Word, and then convey that information in simple, powerful, straightforward language.

OUR PROCEDURE

MOODY does not accept unsolicited manuscripts. Writers must first write a query letter and secure permission to forward their manuscripts. Our usual response time is eight weeks. Do not query by telephone, fax, or e-mail unless urgent subject matter requires an immediate editorial response.

QUERY LETTERS

In you letter, which should be only one page, include your article's:
- title
- topic (what it is about)
- takeaway/purpose/application/audience (what and whom it is for)
- treatment (its style of writing, such as narrative or journalistic) and length

It should also include types of support materials, such as:
- anecdotes
- personal observation
- interviews
- Scriptures
- statistics
- quotations/citations

If possible, include a representative sample paragraph. In addition, please let us know briefly about your writing experience and your qualifications to write on this subject. Always include a self-addressed stamped envelope. Please, no simultaneous or reprint queries.

DEADLINES

MOODY begins editing each issue five months prior to the date of publication and plans each issue several months in advance of that. For seasonal material, query nine months in advance.

POETRY AND FICTION

MOODY does not print poetry. Although we print little fiction, we will consider well-written contemporary stories. Rather than inspirational accounts, we seek one that, like our non-fiction, are rooted in biblical truth. Dialogue, action, and descriptions must be crisp and believable. Avoid clichéd salvation accounts, biblical fiction, parables, and allegories. Typical Length: 1,200 to 2,200 words.

MANUSCRIPT FORMAT

Print-outs must be double-spaced. Include a 3.5-inch floppy disk in any popular word-processing format. Include on the first page the approximate article length, your name, address, day phone, e-mail address, and Social Security number. Always include an SASE for the return of your materials should your manuscript not meet our needs.

PAYMENT AND RIGHTS

MOODY buys First North American Serial Rights. Once the work has been published in an issue of *MOODY* magazine, we retain the non-exclusive right to re-publish that work in electronic form, without further compensation. *MOODY* may authorize electronic "readers" worldwide to print a copy of the work for personal use; however all requests for commercial reprints shall be referred to the author. All other rights return to the author once the article has been published.

MANUSCRIPT POLICY

We examine all manuscripts on speculation. A positive response to a query does not guarantee purchase. The author grants *MOODY* the right to edit and abridge the manuscript and warrants that it has not already appeared in print and that it has not been simultaneously submitted to other publications. Further, the author warrants that nothing in the article infringes the copyright ownership of any person, firm, or corporation, and that he is its sole and true author.

Categories: Nonfiction—Christian Interests—Evangelical Christianity

CONTACT: Managing Editor
Material: All
820 N. La Salle Blvd.
Chicago IL 60610
Phone: 312-329-2164

Fax: 312-329-2149
E-mail: MoodyEdit@moody.edu
Website: www.moody.edu/MOODYMAG

Mopar Muscle

Formal guidelines not available. Please read a number of issues to ascertain the publication's style and needs.

Send queries to address below.

Circulation: 69,621

Frequency: monthly

Mopar Muscle is dedicated to Chrysler performance. Its primary emphasis is on musclecar-era Dodge, Plymouth and Chrysler vehicles, with technical and feature articles oriented toward functional restoration and street/race performance.

Categories: Nonfiction—Automobiles

CONTACT: Geoff Stunkard, Editor-in-Chief
Material: All
3816 Industry Blvd.
Lakeland FL 33811
Phone: 863-644-0449
Website: www.moparmusclemagazine.com

More

Thank you for your interest in writing for MORE. While we do not have specific guidelines about subject matter or writing style, we do offer these suggestions:

READ BACK ISSUES: We do not publish an editorial calendar, so familiarizing yourself with our editorial content and style will help you decide if your work fits our needs. Back issues can be found in the periodicals section of your library or purchased from our customer service department for $3 each (call 888-699-4036, then press #1). Do not send payment to our editorial offices.

WE HAVE FOUR MONTH LEAD TIME: Keep in mind that *MORE* is targeted at women ages 45-64, so we will be looking for stories that both involve and appeal to women in that age group. If we feel that a submission to *MORE* is more appropriate for *Ladies' Home Journal*, we will consider it for publication in that magazine. Please do not send simultaneous submissions to both magazines.

SUBMIT QUERIES RATHER THAN MANUSCRIPTS: Keep your query brief-one to two pages-citing your lead and describing how you will research and develop your story. Be specific, and always direct your query to the appropriate editor, as listed on the masthead of the magazine. If you have been published before, send clips, your credits and a resume.

ALWAYS INCLUDE A SELF-ADDRESSED, STAMPED ENVELOPE: We will not respond unless a SASE is enclosed (with adequate postage for return of the manuscript, if so desired). We are not responsible for returning unsolicited material, so do not send original copies or photographs. Our editorial offices are located at 125 Park Avenue, New York, NY 10017. We regret that we cannot reply to submissions sent by fax or E-mail.

PAYMENT, STORY LENGTH AND DEADLINES: are discussed upon assignment and writers are paid upon acceptance. Average story length is 2,000 words.

SUBMIT FICTION ONLY THROUGH A LITERARY AGENT. WE DO NOT ACCEPT POETRY OF ANY KIND.

PLEASE DO NOT CALL TO QUERY OR FOLLOW UP ON A SUBMISSION: We read every query carefully, and do our best to respond as promptly as we can. It may take up to three months to receive a response.

WE CANNOT PROVIDE COMMENTS ON UNACCEPTED MATERIAL: Due to the large volume of manuscripts we receive, we are unable to evaluate each writer's work personally.

Categories: Nonfiction—Culture—Entertainment—Fashion—General Interest—Health—Money & Finances—Travel—Women's Issues

CONTACT: Barbara Brody, Associate Editor
Material: All
Meredith Corp.
125 Park Ave
New York NY 10017
Phone: 212-455-1303
E-mail: bbrody@mdp.com

Mortgage Banking

• Feature articles should run between 2,500 and 3,000 words in length. Columns should run between 750 and 1,000 words.

• Please e-mail a Word (any version) or text file of the article and e-mail or fax hard copies of any accompanying charts/graphs in advance of sending the article (all graphics are recreated from scratch in Quark by a typesetter). Article should be in text-only format (no graphics embedded in text). The text-only file may be e-mailed to jhewitt@mortgagebankers.org. Hard copies of graphics can be faxed to (202) 721-0245.

• Do not use footnotes. Include subheads to help set off transitions from one subject to another throughout the article. Spell out acronyms and use trademark or service mark symbols on first reference ("Fannie Mae's Desktop Underwriter   (DU)," and thereafter, "DU"). Use full names/ titles of people being quoted and full names of companies/company locations on first reference.

• Clearly label the hard copies of accompanying charts/graphs (Figure 1, etc.), and be sure all graphics are referenced in text where appropriate ("see Figure 2," etc.). All charts and graphs must include a title and source, even if the source is the company submitting the article.

• Include brief biographical information for each author at the end of the article. This should include the author's name, title, company name and location and e-mail address. A brief description of the company is permitted. The editor reserves the right to condense biographical information as necessary.

• Should your article be selected for publication, an edited version will be e-mailed back to you prior to publication. This version will include, embedded in the text, queries from the editor. You will be asked to type your answers into the document and to then e-mail it back to us within a short period of time—generally one to two days.

• Two author's copies of the magazine will be mailed to you as soon as they are received from the printer. A reasonable number of additional copies may be requested by contacting the editor.

• Please submit your invoice as soon as possible after sending your article. Include your full name and address, Social Security No. or tax identification number and our full address on the invoice.

Please note that we can only accept an original hard copy or e-mailed invoice—faxed invoices are not acceptable. Payment will be mailed within 7-10 days of receipt of your invoice. Please send invoice to: Lesley Hall, Mortgage Banking magazine, 1919 Pennsylvania Ave. N.W., Washington, DC 20006, or e-mail it as a Word document to lhall@mortgagebankers.org.

Categories: Associations—Economics—Money & Finances—Real Estate

CONTACT: Janet Hewitt, Editor-in-Chief
Material: Real estate finance, mortgage banking
Mortgage Bankers Association of America
1919 Pennsylvania Ave, NW
Washington DC 20006
Phone: 202-557-2853

Mother Earth News

INFORMATION FOR POTENTIAL CONTRIBUTORS

Mother Earth News is a bimonthly magazine dedicated to presenting information which will help readers become more self-sufficient, financially independent and environmentally aware. Readership age ranges from the early teens to over 90. The magazine is distributed to 350,000 people across the United States and Canada.

WE USE ARTICLES ON:

Organic gardening—Renewable energy—Living well cheaply—Self-sufficiency—Building projects—Alternative Housing/Green Building—Holistic Health—Wild foods—Wildlife/Wildlands Conservation—Crafts—Herbal remedies—Energy conservation tips—Small farm livestock—House and garden tips—Hand tools—Homesteading techniques (If at all possible, accompany articles with diagrams and/or photos. Please include your return address on all materials, including slides and photos. As we cannot guarantee return of items submitted, please retain a copy of all materials you send.)

WE DO NOT USE: Poetry, memoirs or fiction.

MANUSCRIPT PREPARATION PRINCIPLES: Work should be double spaced, typed (or word processed) in a standard serif black font (e.g., Times New Roman, 12 pt.) on one side of white 8½" by 11" paper. We prefer manuscripts to be submitted via e-mail (in either Microsoft Word or WordPerfect) to the appropriate editor.

PAYMENT will be negotiated between writer and editor. The writer will receive payment upon publication.

Mostly written by staff and team of established freelancers. Bimonthly magazine emphasizing living wisely. Resourceful living and country skills for rural residents and for urbanites who aspire to a more independent lifestyle. *Mother Earth News* is dedicated to presenting information that helps readers be more self-sufficient, financially independent and environmentally aware. Circ: 400,000. Pays on publication. Byline given. Submit seasonal material 5 months in advance. No handwritten manuscripts. Responds within 6 months. Sample copy for $5. Writer's guidelines for #10 SASE with one first-class stamp.

Non-fiction: How-to, alternative energy systems, organic gardening, home building, home retro-fit and maintenance, energy-efficient structures, seasonal cooking, home business, living "off the grid." Buys 35-50 mss. a year.

Query: "A brief, focused paragraph or two will generally do the trick. If the idea intrigues us and seems appropriate for our readers, we'll ask to see the whole piece. No fiction and no telephone queries, please."

Length: 300 to 3,000 words. Payment negotiated. Publishes non-fiction book excerpts.

Photos: "Although not essential, we very much encourage contributors to send good, usable photos with their mss." Send prints or transparencies. Use 8 x 10 b&w glossies or any size color transparencies. Include type of film, speed and lighting used. Total purchase price for mss includes payment for photos. Captions and photo credits required.

Columns/Departments: For those with little writing experience, submissions to Country Lore or Reports from the Field (personal accounts of the *Mother Earth News* lifestyle) are a good entry point. Other departments include Natural Remedies and Mother's Natural Kitchen.

Tips: "Read our magazine. Read our magazine. Read our magazine. Readers of *Mother Earth News* comprise one of the most thoughtful, curious, industrious and engaging magazine audiences in the country. Since 1970, *Mother Earth News* has been an exemplary source of information about homesteading, rural skills, environmental consciousness and natural health. It is North America's leading publication for people interested in contemporary rural lifestyles, and we are committed to providing hands-on, useful information for real people who want to take charge of their own lives. Practicality is the key. Articles should be well-documented and tightly written."

Categories: Nonfiction—Agriculture—Conservation—Cooking—Crafts/Hobbies—Food/Drink—Gardening—Health—Home

CONTACT: Submissions Editor
Material: All
Ogden Publications Inc.
1503 SW 42nd St.
Topeka KS 66609-1265
Phone: 785-274-4300
E-mail: letters@motherearthnews.com
Website: www.motherearthnews.com

MOTHERJONES
Mother Jones

Who we are:
Mother Jones, with a paid circulation of 140,000, is one of the largest progressive publications in the country. The national bimonthly magazine is known for its investigative journalism and exposes, and its coverage of social issues, public affairs, and popular culture. Most of the articles we print are written by freelancers.

What we're looking for:
Hard-hitting, investigative reports exposing government cover-ups, corporate malfeasance, scientific myopia, institutional fraud or hypocrisy, etc.

Thoughtful, provocative articles which challenge the conventional wisdom (on the right or the left) concerning issues of national importance.

Timely, people-oriented stories on issues such as the environment, labor, the media, health care, consumer protection, and cultural trends.

How to query us:
Send a letter proposing your story idea(s).

Explain what you plan to cover and how you will proceed with the reporting. The query should convey your approach, tone, and style; and should answer the following: What are your specific qualifications to write on this topic? What "ins" do you have with your sources? Can you provide full documentation so that your story can be fact-checked?

Keep in mind that our lead time is three months and submissions should not be so time-bound that they will appear dated. If we, or another publication, have run a similar story in the last few years, explain how your story will differ.

If you have not contributed to *Mother Jones* before, please send two or three photocopies of previously published articles along with your query. We do not accept unsolicited manuscripts or fiction. Mother Jones assumes no responsibility for unsolicited queries or manuscripts and will only respond to those accompanied by a self-addressed, stamped envelope. Therefore, please do not query us by phone or fax.

Back issues are $6.00 and can be ordered through Reader Services at the address below.

Categories: Nonfiction—African-American—Asian-American—Culture—Economics—Environment—Film/Video—General Interest—Government—Interview—Money & Finances—Multicultural—Politics—Investigative Reporting

CONTACT: Queries and Manuscripts
Material: All
731 Market St. Ste. 600
San Francisco CA 94103
Phone: 415-665-6637
Fax: 415-665-6696
E-mail: query@motherjones.com
Website: www.motherjones.com

MotorHome

Please refer to *Highways magazine.*

Motor Trend

Formal guidelines not available. Please read a number of issues to ascertain the publication's style and needs.

Send queries to address below.

Categories: Nonfiction—Automobiles—

CONTACT: Matt Stone, Exec. Editor
Material: All
Petersen Publishing Co.
6420 Wilshire Blvd.
Los Angeles CA 90048
Phone: 323-782-2220
Website: www.motortrend.com

Mountain Living

Mountain Living

1. SUBJECT. Subject will be determined following discussion with editor, who will provide resource materials, contact names and suggestions for research when possible. Editor prefers written queries.

2. LENGTH. Department articles usually run 300-1,500 words. Feature articles run 1,200-2,000 words.

3. DEADLINES

All assignments are due on the morning of the date assigned. If an agreed-upon deadline can't be met, please contact the editor a minimum of two weeks beforehand to renegotiate an appropriate date.

4. SIDEBARS. As discussed with editor. Department articles may require a sidebar with information such as reference-book listing, ingredients, facts and figures, and addresses.

5. PHOTOGRAPHS. For all department articles and some features, we ask that you speak with your sources about obtaining photographs. Slides or transparencies are preferable. When possible, mail the photos with your completed article. Otherwise, include a list of photo resources. We will return all artwork after the issue has been published.

6. RESOURCE LIST. Each home feature must be accompanied by a list of interior designers, architects, landscape planners, contractors, builders, etc., who have contributed to the project, as well as their company names, addresses and phone numbers. Each feature must also be accompanied by a list of design resources, for all furnishings, fabrics and materials (available retail or wholesale) used in the project. Only antiques are excluded—custom pieces should be identified as such, with credit to the designer and manufacturer. The interior designer or other professionals who contributed to the project are usually willing to help put together this list.

7. COMPLIMENTARY COPIES. Include a list of photo, research and interview resources, their addresses and phone numbers, so we can send a complimentary copy of the magazine.

8. DELIVERY. Printed submissions should be accompanied by a disk. Speak with the editor about sending articles on-line.

9. PAYMENT. As discussed with the editor and stipulated in the contract. Checks are usually mailed two to three weeks after the material is accepted. A 15 percent kill fee is paid for unacceptable material.

Categories: Antiques—Architecture—Arts—Conservation—Cooking—Culture—Ecology—Environment—Fishing—Gardening—Lifestyle—Travel

CONTACT: Editor
Material: All

7009 S. Potomac St.
Englewood CO 80112
Phone: 303-397-7600
Fax: 303-397-7619
E-mail: irawlings@mountainliving.com
Website: www.mountainliving.com

MSW Management

Please refer to Forester Communications.

Muscle & Fitness

Thank you for your interest in writing for *Muscle & Fitness.*

Of note, we generally don't assign articles to new freelancers but rather ask that you pitch us a detailed query. Please try and narrow in on a specific topic(s) of interest and the points you will bring up. If relevant, cite research, experts you will speak with and any pro bodybuilders that will help fill out the article. As we are a bodybuilding publication, M&F likes to include quotes from exercise/nutrition researchers and bodybuilders whenever possible to bring in an "in the trenches" perspective.

Please contact me if you have any further questions.

Sincerely, Bill Geiger, Editor

Editorial Guidelines

MUSCLE & FITNESS is a bodybuilding and fitness publication for healthy, active men and women. It contains a wide range of features and monthly departments devoted to all areas of bodybuilding, health, fitness, injury prevention and treatment, and nutrition.

Editorial fulfills two functions: information and entertainment, with special attention to how-to advice and accuracy.

Assignments: All features and departments are written on assignment (including those written on speculation). Writers must be cognizant of deadlines, article length, outline approval and technical requirements. Writers should check assignment confirmation forms for details, and contact assigning editor if necessary.

Queries: Contact us in writing with your article ideas. Your query should be a short summary (one page or less) of your idea or ideas, along with potential sources and your own qualifications to write the article. Send recent clips with bylines. Please send only clips that reflect your own writing style.

Manuscript tone: The editorial voice must be friendly, speaking directly to the healthy, active man or woman. Academic journal composition is not acceptable. Please read the magazine for an understanding of its style.

Manuscript length: As specified with assignment. Generally 500-800 words for departments; 1,500-1,800 words for features.

Writer's contracts/kill fees: All manuscripts from first-time contributors are read on speculation only. Contracts specifying kill fees and author rights are available to repeat contributors.

Payment rates: $360 (or less) for departments; $400-800 (or less) for features. All fees are negotiated individually. Writer must sign M&F contract before any payment can be made.

Fact checking: Accuracy is the responsibility of the author. Manuscripts should be accompanied by the telephone numbers of sources quoted within the article, so editors can verify names and titles, professional associations and any related product prices. If a book is referred to in the article, you must include the author's name, the book publisher, year of publication and the book's price if it's still in print. For scientific journal citations, full references are required (and photocopies requested).

Unsolicited manuscripts: We require queries. Please do not send manuscripts.

8 STEPS TO WRITING A BETTER ARTICLE FOR M&F

The following guidelines are intended to remind all writers on those elements that make for great copy. They include:

1) Focus your article. What's your special angle? Why is it impor-

tant to readers? What new do you have to add to the volumes already printed on the subject?

2) Be clear on where you are going. What questions will you answer? What controversies are there? What research supports the question? What relevant bodybuilders and experts can provide insight? Get an outline together and talk to your assigning editor about it.

3) Get quotes. Unless you are THE one and only expert, it's better to quote those who really are. This adds credibility. Dissenting quotes also offer balance. Quotes from bodybuilders are also good because these are the people who've done it "in the trenches."

When you quote a "doctor," like a physician, dentist, chiropractor or university professor, do not precede the name with "Dr.," but rather give their degree after the name (like MD, DC, PhD, etc.) Also affiliation if applicable (i.e., from the University of Pittsburgh School of Medicine) and its location.

When you introduce anecdotal persons, provide more than just name. Also include city, state, age, maybe profession.

4) Leave out filler. Too many articles come in over 3,000 words that must be returned to be cut. (Or would you rather have a copy editor unfamiliar with your material cut it for you?) Make your points succinctly and don't repeat yourself.

5) Pull the reader into the article. Know why the reader is going to be interested in reading your piece. What's she learning that she can use? Provide solutions and how-to information. How-to articles work well in the second person: for example, "Keep your arms by your sides at all times as you curl the weight."

6) Use subheads to break up long sections of copy and to organize ideas. Use sidebars for background that slows the flow of the main copy, like tangential but relevant topics, technical information, a summary of tips, relevant diagrams or charts, background information, or related information that doesn't insert into the text well but is important to the article.

7) Make sure you're on schedule. Talk to your editor in advance if you need an extension. Don't turn in a half-baked article just to meet deadline; it will be coming back to you for a rewrite.

8) Review your article. Double check the spelling of all names, titles and facts. Also do a spell check.

How to send: Completed manuscript should be e-mailed, sent via dial-in modem connection to M&F at 818-348-1195 (we use PC Plus, 9600 baud, settings are N,8,1). By mail, send 3.5" disk. We prefer IBM Microsoft Word for Windows 6.0 (saved as a document); other software users should save as ASCII text files. Don't forget a clean manuscript as well.

Categories: Diet/Nutrition—Health—Men's Issues—Physical Fitness

CONTACT: Vince Scalisi, Editor
Material: All
21100 Erwin St.
Woodland Hills CA 91367
Phone: 818-884-6800
Fax: 818-595-0463
E-mail: vscalisi@earthlink.net

Muscle & Fitness Hers

Thank you for your interest in writing for *Muscle & Fitness Hers*.

Of note, we generally don't assign articles to new freelancers but rather ask that you pitch us a detailed query. Please try and narrow in on a specific topic(s) of interest and the points you will bring up. If relevant, cite research, experts you will use that will help fill out the article. As we are a fitness publication, *M&F Hers* likes to include quotes from exercise/nutrition researchers and fitness competitors whenever possible to bring in a "real world" perspective.

Please contact me if you have any further questions.

Sincerely,

Carey Rossi Walker, Executive Editor

Editorial Guidelines

Muscle & Fitness Hers is a publication for healthy, active women who are enthusiastic about the fitness lifestyle. It contains a wide range of features and monthly departments devoted to all areas of weight training, health, fitness, injury prevention and treatment, and nutrition.

Editorial fulfills two functions: information and entertainment, with special attention to how-to advice and accuracy.

Assignments: All features and departments are written on assignment (including those written on speculation). Writers must be cognizant of deadlines, article length, outline approval and technical requirements. Writers should check assignment confirmation forms for details, and contact assigning editor if necessary.

Queries: Contact us in writing with your article ideas. Your query should be a short summary (one page or less) of your idea or ideas, along with potential sources and your own qualifications to write the article. Send recent clips with bylines. Please send only clips that reflect your own writing style.

Manuscript tone: The editorial voice must be friendly, speaking directly to the healthy, active woman. Academic journal composition is not acceptable. Please read the magazine for an understanding of its style and its audience.

Manuscript length: As specified with assignment. Generally 750-1000 words for departments; 1,500-2,000 words for features.

Writer's contracts/kill fees: All manuscripts from first-time contributors are read on speculation only. Contracts specifying kill fees and author rights.

Payment rates: $400 (or less) for departments; $400-800 (or less) for features. All fees are negotiated individually. Writer must sign *M&F Hers* contract before any payment can be made.

Fact checking: Accuracy is the responsibility of the author. Manuscripts should be accompanied by all backup material and the telephone numbers of sources quoted within the article, so editors can verify names and titles, professional associations and any related product prices. If a book is referred to in the article, you must include the author's name, the book publisher, year of publication and the book's price if it's still in print. For scientific journal citations, full references and photocopies are required.

Unsolicited manuscripts: We require queries. Please do not send manuscripts.

8 STEPS TO WRITING A BETTER QUERY FOR M&F HERS

The following guidelines are intended to remind all writers on those elements that make for great copy. They include:

1) Focus your article query. What's your special angle? Why is it important to readers? What new do you have to add to the volumes already printed on the subject?

2) Be clear on where you are going. What questions will you answer? What controversies are there? What research supports the question? What relevant competitors and experts can provide insight?

3) How will you pull the reader into the article? Know why the reader is going to be interested in reading your piece. What's she learning that she can use? Provide solutions and how-to information.

4) Review your query. Double check the spelling of all names, titles and facts. Also do a spell check.

Categories: Physical Fitness

CONTACT: Carey Rossi Walker, Executive Editor
Material: All
21100 Erwin St.
Woodland Hills CA 91367
Phone: No phone calls please.
E-mail: Carey.Rossi-Walker@weiderpub.co
Website: www.muscleandfitnesshers.com

Remember: Editors change jobs and publishers change addresses. It is wise to invest in a phone call for the current information before submitting.

Muscle Mustang & Fast Fords

About Us

Circulation: 135,000

Frequency: 12 times per year

Published by the PRIMEDIA Enthusiast Group.

Muscle Mustangs & Fast Fords is written by and about enthusiasts of high performance Fords, with special emphasis on late-model 5.0L and 4.6L Mustangs. It features editorial on the latest factory aftermarket and performance parts and services for the street and strip, as well as how-to tech articles on making a great car even better. Regular features include inside stories on Ford racing, new car news, plus ways to make a Mustang run faster and handle better.

Ninety-three percent of *Muscle Mustangs & Fast Fords'* readers drive a late model Mustang. *Muscle Mustangs & Fast Fords* offers these enthusiasts a practical guide to making their vehicles perform at peak level. Superchargers, nitrous oxide systems, any and all aftermarket parts and accessories currently manufactured to increase performance are presented in the magazine, usually in the context of a highly readable tech piece. In addition, we bring to our avid readers the hottest industry news, the latest products and complete coverage of shootouts and races.

Submissions

Editorial submissions are welcomed, but the editor recommends that contributors query first. All contributions must be accompanied by a self-addressed, stamped envelope. Solicitations for editorial coverage, including car feature articles, should be submitted via US mail. Please include a photograph of the vehicle/project, a quick reference sheet and a few paragraphs detailing the editorial significance of your work. Due to busy travel and work schedules, the editor is not able to field calls related to potential editorial coverage. We assume no responsibility for loss or damage of any unsolicited materials.

For more information, visit the magazine's Web site at: www.musclemustangfastfords.com.

Categories: Nonfiction—Automobiles—Technical

CONTACT: Jim Campisano, Editor/Editorial Director
Material: Editorial Feedback, Submissions
299 Market St.
Saddle Brook NJ 076636
Phone: 201-712-9300 ext. 611
E-mail: jimc@mcmullenargus.com
Website: www.musclemustangfastfords.com

Muse Magazine

About Us: From the publishers of *Smithsonian* and *CRICKET* magazines.

In October 1996, the Cricket Magazine Group, in conjunction with *Smithsonian Magazine*, launched a new publication entitled MUSE, a nonfiction magazine for children ages 9 to 14. MUSE is published 10 times a year for a subscription price of $ 32.97. It is 48 pages long.

Mission: The goal of MUSE is to give as many children as possible access to the most important ideas and concepts underlying the principal areas of human knowledge. It takes children seriously as developing intellects by assuming that, if explained clearly, the ideas and concepts of an article will be of interest to them. Articles should meet the highest possible standard of clarity and transparency aided, wherever possible, by a tone of skepticism and humor.

Queries: Articles for MUSE are commissioned. Authors interested in being considered for commissioned work should send a resume, writing samples, and detailed story ideas. We cannot respond to a query that doesn't include story ideas. It is also important to describe any relevant areas of expertise. Please allow 16 weeks for a reply.

Terms: For commissioned articles, MUSE pays inexperienced writers 25 cents a word for all rights. Higher rates are negotiated on the basis of experience. Authors will receive three complimentary copies of the issue in which their article appears.

Commissioning Procedures: Once commissioned, authors are required to submit as many drafts as are necessary. Articles will be assigned at between 1,000 and 1,500 words, and drafts should be sent by e-mail. Authors are also required to provide MUSE with a bibliography that lists all resource material (including names, addresses, and telephone numbers of key persons interviewed for an article). Please note that because of the unique mission of MUSE, extensive rewrites are often necessary.

Criteria for an Acceptable Article: Each article must be about a topic that children can understand. The topic must be a large one that somehow connects with a fundamental tenet of some discipline or area of practical knowledge. The treatment of the topic must be of the competence one would expect of an expert in the field. On the other hand, MUSE does not want articles that could be mistaken for chapters in a textbook. Instead we prefer the author visit the scientist or research site and report on what he or she sees or hears there. An article must be interesting to children, who are under no obligation to read it.

Categories: Nonfiction—Children—Education—Juvenile—Teen

CONTACT: Submissions Editor
Material: Queries
CONTACT: Art Director
Material: Art Samples
332 S. Michigan Ave., Ste 1100
Chicago IL 60604
Website: www.cobblestonepub.com or www.cricketmag.com

Mushing
The Magazine of Dog-Powered Sports

CONTRIBUTOR GUIDELINES

Mushing works with experienced freelance writers and photojournalists as well as first-time authors and photographers. These guidelines are intended to provide an idea of the kinds of submissions we are looking for as well as how our submission process works. Please feel free to contact us if you have questions or if you would like to discuss an idea for submission.

Editorial Profile. *Mushing* is distributed in 49 states and 25 countries. Readers include both recreational and competitive mushers with a wide range of experience, from beginners to veterans. In addition, some of our readers are "armchair mushers," who enjoy reading about or watching the sport but are not mushers themselves.

We urge contributors to study the magazine before submitting material. Samples are $5 in the United States, $6 (U.S. funds) to Canada and $8 (U.S. funds) overseas.

ARTICLES

We prefer detailed queries but also consider unsolicited manuscripts. Please make proposals informative yet to the point. Spell out your qualifications for handling the topic. We like to see clips of previously published material but are eager to work with new and unpublished authors, too.

An affirmative response to a query proposal does not necessarily mean the resulting article will be accepted. Tentative scheduling does not necessary guarantee publication.

Content. Each issue of *Mushing* includes a mix of information, features and columns. We consider articles on canine health and nutrition, sled dog behavior and training, musher profiles and interviews, equipment how-to's, trail tips, expedition and race accounts, innovations, sled dog history, current issues, and humor, including cartoons. We consider personal experience when the experience illustrates information that is useful to mushers and generally do not when the focus is the personal experience itself. See Editorial Schedule below for current special issue focuses.

All articles should be well researched, logically organized and readable. Appropriate photo support and/or illustrations are encouraged.

Mushing also publishes news, stories, poems, artwork and puzzles by junior contributors. See Junior Mushers Page.

Style and Length. We prefer clear, informative, straightforward writing. We generally follow Associated Press style, although we have our own style guide as well. We reserve the right to edit all submissions.

Features generally run between 1,000 and 2,500 words. Longer articles are considered if well written and of particular interest. Columns and departments usually run from 500 to 1,000 words. Short news pieces run from 150 to 500 words.

Submission Format. Contributor phone number, social security number, name, address and the article's approximate word count should appear at the top. Include a two- to four-sentence author's biography. Do not send originals, and always keep a copy of your work. We treat submissions with care but cannot be responsible for loss or damage.

E-mail: Send as enclosures, as part of the message or both.

Computer Disks: Send Mac or IBM disks, but include a hard copy of the article.

Hard Copies: These need to be clearly typed/word-processed, doublespaced, with a minimum of 1-inch margins all around. Number pages. Photocopies OK if good quality.

PHOTOGRAPHS AND ARTWORK

Mushing uses both color and black-and-white photographs. All photos and slides to be considered must be clean, sharp and accurately exposed. Potential subjects include dogs working, playing and resting as well as expedition and racing events, recreational Mushing, skijoring, winter camping, freighting, mushing equipment and mushing personalities. We use a variety of horizontals and verticals.

We work at least three months ahead of each publication date, so we need summer photos beginning in February and winter photos in June. We are always looking for good cover photographs. These should be strong, sharp, uncluttered vertical photographs with enough open area at the top for the *Mushing* banner.

Black-and-white images account for about 50 to 80 percent of the art in any given issue. Contributors of color images agree to have their images published in black-and-white format unless a specific written agreement is made with *Mushing* in advance of submission.

All photos and artwork must be clearly marked with the contributor's name and address. If you are concerned about the safety of your work, keep the original and send prints, duplicate slides, digital images or photocopies of artwork as long as originals are available for final printing. All photos, slides and original artwork are returned after consideration or use unless other arrangements are specified.

Photo Prints. Black-and-white photos should ideally be 8-by-l0-inch glossy prints, or negatives accompanied by a contact sheet. High-quality prints on semi-matte paper are acceptable but not preferred.

Color prints should be high-quality and be submitted on glossy paper. We prefer slides.

Slides. Ideally submit color photos in 35-mm or 120-mm Kodachrome transparencies. Submit slides in protective slide sheets.

Digital Photos.Send by e-mail for preview at low resolution. JPEG format preferred. For final printing, we need high resolution digital images but prefer original slides or prints.

Artwork. *Mushing* occasionally uses black-and-white illustrations and drawings—mostly simple images of sled dogs running, howling, sleeping, eating, playing, etc. We have used color artwork on the cover. Sled dog-related cartoons are considered.

Artwork and cartoons can be sent digitally in TIFF or EPS formats. Some artists submit work that *Mushing* can keep on file and use as the need arises.

RATES, RIGHTS, AND PAYMENT

We purchase first serial rights and second (reprint) rights. Please advise us if submitted work has been published elsewhere, including on the Internet, and where and when that publication took place.

Article rates average $.09 per published word.

Photograph and artwork payment rates run from $15 (small black/white) up to $165 (cover).

We also purchase the right to publish some articles and photos on our Internet site for one year following the print publication date. An additional fee of $10 per photo and $20 per article is paid for work used in this way.

Payment within 60 days of publication. Unless a written agreement is made between *Mushing* and a writer or photographer, exact rate of payment for articles and photographs will be determined by the editorial staff of *Mushing*.

Categories: Nonfiction—Animals—Outdoors—Recreation—Sports/Recreation

CONTACT: Deirdre Helfferich, Managing Editor
Material: All
PO Box 149
Ester AK 99725-0149
Phone: 907-479-0454
Fax: 907-479-3137
E-mail: editor@mushing.com

Mustang & Fords

About Us
Circulation: 98,657
Frequency: bi-monthly

Mustang & Fords is dedicated to performance enthusiasts who have a passionate interest in vintage Fords, Mercurys and Lincolns. The primary editorial focus is on 1965-73 Mustangs with an emphasis on Ford musclecars like Fairlanes, Galaxies and Falcons.

Mustang & Fords does not have any written formal guidelines. For more information, visit *Mustang & Fords* on-line at www.mustangandfords.com.

Categories: Nonfiction—Automobiles—Technical

CONTACT: Submissions Editor
Material: All
3816 Industry Blvd.
Lakeland FL 33811
Website: www.mustangandfords.com

Mustang Monthly

About Us
Circulation: 58,122
Frequency: monthly

Mustang owners turn to *Mustang Monthly* for advice on making their distinct cars look and perform better. The title's specialized editorial package covers everything from do-it-yourself recommendations to the history of Mustang; it is the only magazine on the market that caters strictly to the Mustang hobby, from vintage to late-model vehicles.

Submissions

Mustang Monthly does not have formal guidelines. Send submissions to the address below.

For more information, visit *Mustang Monthly* on-line at www.mustangmonthly.com.

Categories: Nonfiction—Automobiles—Technical

CONTACT: Submissions Editor
Material: All
3816 Industry Blvd.
Lakeland FL 33811
Website: www.mustangmonthly.com

Muzzle Blasts

Thank you for your interest in our magazine. Enclosed is a set of writing guidelines to help you prepare your manuscript. If you have any further questions, please don't hesitate to call.

SELECTED TOPIC INFORMATION

Many of our members are knowledgeable in various fields of our muzzleloading sport and the era we represent. Our magazine publishes articles with topics on the history of the muzzleloading era, on hunting with a muzzleloading rifle, and on technical aspects of muzzleloading firearms. If you would like to write an article on any given topic related to muzzleloading, the following will provide needed information in submitting your manuscript.

If your article deals with the history of the muzzleloading era or a muzzleloading firearm, please include detailed information about all references used in developing the article. Articles will not be accepted without proper source documentation in footnote or endnote form. If quoting from a book, please include the author's name, title of book, city and state of publication, publisher's name, year of publication, and page references. If periodicals (such as magazines) are sources, include the author's name, title of periodical, volume and issue numbers, cover date, and page references. If extensive quotations are used, submit photocopies of the pages from which the quotations came.

If hunting is your forte, precede your article with a short descriptive background of the hunting area so the reader can better envision the hunt. Give full details of the firearm used-include the manufacturer or gunmaker, bullet make and caliber, and powder type and load. (Beware of blackpowder overloads; do not exceed manufacturer's recommended maximums.) Pay attention to the details of the hunt, and try to relay humorous situations that occurred, or the imminent danger that was present.

If your article is technical or instructional ("how-to"), be sure to mention the equipment used and describe the procedures step-by-step. Relate the reasons why the subject matter works. Be especially accurate in measurements. Include all charts, photographs, and tables necessary to give a complete description of the process. Remember to include all relevant manufacturer information, especially if the article involves a product evaluation.

In whatever topic you are writing, do not be wordy. Simple and direct writing enhances your subject matter. On the other hand, be sure you provide all necessary information.

TO SUBMIT AN ARTICLE

First, know your topic. Know that the subject matter conforms to the standards of our association and that it has been researched thoroughly.

Be aware of all safety measures (see photo requirements) when writing technical, instructive, or hunting articles.

Present a manuscript on DOS format computer diskette, preferably in one of the WordPerfectTM formats, MicrosoftTM Word©, LotusTM Ami Pro©, or in ASCII. If that is not possible, please submit the typewritten manuscript.

Six to eight typewritten pages, double-spaced, provide the editor with an average-sized article. Longer manuscripts will be considered if the topic warrants the length. Please number manuscript pages.

All manuscripts accepted for publication are subject to editing. This will ensure that they conform to *MUZZLE BLASTS*' format, style, and space limitations.

Be sure your name, address, telephone number, and social security number are included in a cover letter accompanying your manuscript. Please note: We require your social security number for payment and taxation purposes only.

Manuscripts will be acknowledged upon receipt.

ILLUSTRATIONS

All submissions should include high-contrast black-and-white or color photographs and/or well-defined diagrams. Black-and-white or color prints are preferred and must be of good quality. Photos will be reviewed and selected by the editor. On the back of the photo(s) submitted, print your name, address, and title of the article. Use a very soft lead pencil or a typed label. Ink pens, especially felt pens, can bleed through the backing paper. Include a separate sheet of paper with captions, and key the captions to the photos.

All mechanical art, line drawings, and tables must be submitted in black and white. If necessary, ink the drawings for clean-cut reproduction. Submit on a separate sheet of paper. Mechanical art and line drawings produced on IBM-compatible computers can be submitted on a diskette in PCX or TIFF formats, among others. Contact the editor for more information.

REQUIREMENTS FOR PHOTOS AND MECHANICAL ILLUSTRATIONS

Photos should be 5" x 7" or 8" x 10". However, a good, sharply contrasting 3" x 5" photograph is acceptable. All submissions should be black-and-white or color prints. The submission of color slides with a document may be the cause for its return.

Mechanical artwork, including charts, may be lettered in pencil; such text will be typeset and sized to fit the illustration. Identify the manuscript location of illustrative work on the back of the sheet.

When submitting cover art, recognize that 3" x 5" transparencies are preferred; sharply-contrasting 35mm color slides are acceptable if the subject is unusual or exceptionally deserving of attention, but acceptance is extremely rare. Submissions for cover art must be in portrait (vertical) format.

BE AWARE OF SAFETY WHEN SUBMITTING PHOTOS

Do not submit photos that depict firearms used in an unsafe manner (such as with a blocked muzzle, pointed in an unsafe direction, cocked or half-cocked, and so forth). When submitting photos for technical articles, be aware of and demonstrate all safety measures; for example, if the topic is a review of a new rifle, all shooters who are photographed should be wearing hearing and eye protection.

WRITER/ARTIST RESPONSIBILITIES

Liability for copyright-law compliance of submitted materials (such as artwork or text), as well as the procurement of all model-release forms, is the responsibility of the submitter and not the NMLRA or its affiliates. When submitting materials that have been reproduced whole or in part from other sources, include with the materials copies of permission letters from the appropriate person or persons.

Upon receipt, articles will be reviewed for MUZZLE BLASTS publication by the editor, the publications committee, and technical advisors as deemed necessary. Payments will be made for articles that deal with muzzleloading firearms or firearms with historical value, and for those that provide good instructive subject matter. If there are questions on an accepted article, the editor will contact the writer.

ELECTRONIC RIGHTS

The National Muzzle Loading Rifle Association also publishes on the World Wide Web. This electronic magazine is focused primarily for a nonmember audience. From time to time the editor will contact a writer if he feels that a submission is appropriate for the Web publication. Writers and photographers are free to accept or reject this use of their work, and statements regarding this issue can be enclosed with your submission. Payments for electronic rights are made in addition to regular rates for the paper publication.

M-Q

MUZZLE BLASTS Writers' Pay Schedule
(All payments made upon publication.)

Special Purchase Photos

Black and white, up to $30 maximum

Four-color (for covers), up to $300 maximum

All reviews, $100-$300, depending on the amount of research and tests necessary and the number of photos submitted.

Columns and Articles

All standing columns, $50-$150, depending on the amount of research and tests necessary and the number of photos or illustrations submitted (if any).

All features, $100-$400, depending on the amount of research and tests necessary and the number of photos or illustrations submitted.

Electronic Use

Standing columns, $50 paid in addition to standard scale above.

Feature articles, $100 paid in addition to standard scale above.

Categories: Nonfiction—Associations—Civil War—Crafts/Hobbies—History—Hobbies—Outdoors—Recreation—Rural America—Sports/Recreation—Shooting Sports—Hunting

CONTACT: Terri Trowbridge, Director of Publications
Material: Any
CONTACT: Eric A. Bye, Editor
Material: Any
PO Box 67
Friendship IN 47021
Phone: 812-667-5131
Fax: 812-667-5137

MyBusiness

Small business today is no longer merely a job or a business, but a movement, a cause, an adventure, a lifestyle. MyBusiness is a guide to survival and success in this new small-business economy. We seek to highlight and celebrate the people and ideas making this movement a reality. That's why the experiences of real small-business owners are essential to every story.

Our readers

MyBusiness is sent bimonthly to the 600,000 members of the National Federation of Independent Business. These small-business owners range from at-home sole proprietors to heads of companies with up to 500 employees. Our research shows our readers' companies average an annual sales volume of $454,100, and a mean number of 19 employees. Yet success for MyBusiness readers is not measured merely in year-to-year revenue growth, but also with such radical measures as year-to-year personal growth, health and happiness.

Review our editorial calendar for more details.

What we want

Cover stories are usually staff-written, but the following sections are open to freelance pitches:

Upfront is a section of short (200-600 words) stories offering insight into and ideas of the new small-business economy. Each issue, we will include some of the following departments: Idea network, management, human resources, legal, financial, lifestyle, travel, auto, technology.

MyBusiness Manual is an in-depth exploration of key issues affecting small business. See the editorial calendar for the topic for each issue. This section is made up of 6-12 stories, varying from 300-800 words.

MyAdvice is a first-person column written by a small-business owner on the topic of their choice. We are looking for writers with personality, who can inject some voice (possibly humor) into a 500-word column. We do not pay for these submissions, but feature a credit line with the author's business name and Web site.

Uncommon Enterprise celebrates businesses you never knew existed. We're looking for very unusual concepts. After hearing about an Uncommon Enterprise, our editors want to say, "Wow, I had no idea you could start a business doing that."

Submission policies

Please read this section carefully before submitting an idea.

Rather than unsolicited articles, we prefer to hear story ideas. It is strongly encouraged that writers check several recent issues of MyBusiness to find if their proposal is suitable. The most successful queries are tightly focused and contain unique information about the small-business experience.

Send proposals in writing to Editorial Department c/o MyBusiness magazine, 3322 West End Ave., Ste. 700, Nashville, TN 37203, or e-mail to feedback@mybusinessmag.com. Include your resume and two to four clips, preferably business-related.

Because of the large number of inquiries we receive, we accept written queries only. You can send your query by e-mail or regular mail. No phone calls please. We will contact you if your pitch is a fit.

Deadlines are usually 90 days before publication. Copy should be submitted as an e-mail or a Microsoft Word enclosure. We pay upon acceptance. Our rates vary and are not discussed until we agree to accept an article query for publication.

Writing standards

Keep these key points in mind as you write for MyBusiness: We're here to help small-business owners by giving them a range of how-to pieces that evaluate, analyze and lead to solutions.

We expect writers to double-check their facts and be able to vouch for every phone number, Web address and name spelling in a story. We also request a list of sources with contact phone numbers, for fact-checking purposes.

We follow The Associated Press style in most cases, with a few exceptions. Please, only a single space after periods.

Categories: Nonfiction—Automobiles—Business—Financial—Lifestyle—Technology—Travel

CONTACT: Editorial Department
3322 W End Ave Ste 700
Nashvillle TN 37203
E-mail: feedback@mybusinessmag.com
Website: mybusinessmag.com

My Daily Visitor

Who we are: A bimonthly publication of Our Sunday Visitor.

What we publish: Daily reflections/meditations based on the Scripture readings for the Roman Catholic Mass of the day.

Our mission: To promote personal spirituality by encouraging and inspiring a deeper appreciation of the Faith.

Our readers: Catholics, although the writing should be relevant to other Christians.

Our writers: We use **Catholic writers only.** Our writers have a full and up-to-date knowledge of Catholic practice and belief.

The nitty-gritty: — A writer is assigned for one complete month of material.

—Each day features a reflection/meditation and short prayer. The prayer can be no more than 15 words. The meditation must be between 125 and 135 words.

—We use the New American Bible for Catholics with Revised New Testament.

—A reflection/meditation is based on either a quote or theme from the Mass readings (with an emphasis on the Gospel), or on the saint's or liturgical feast celebrated that day. Either angle also gently challenges the reader to apply the lesson, suggestion or observation being presented.

If you are interested in writing for us: Please first review our publication before mailing a cover letter, one week's sample of meditations/reflections and prayers, and a S.A.S.E. to the above address.

No other freelance material is accepted.

We do NOT publish articles, features, profiles, poetry or fillers.
Categories: **Nonfiction**—Catholicism—Religion—Spirituality

CONTACT: **Our Sunday Visitor**
200 Noll Plaza
Huntington IN 46750

My Legacy

My Legacy is for short stories only, and the guidelines are short and sweet. Just remember 2,500 words maximum (sometimes a bit longer is OK). Please submit work in good taste…with no bad language (think of a better way to say it). Stories on any subject are read but must catch my eye to be accepted. The "Editor's Choice Award" of $5 goes to my favorite story in each issue.

USA Rates for Subscription/Single Copy: $16/4 issues; $4.50 next issue only.

Categories: Fiction—Adventure—Animals—Children—Christian Interests—Civil War—Crime—Culture—Family—Fantasy—Inspirational—Mystery—Native American—New Age—Rural America—Science Fiction—Senior Citizen—Short Stories—Spiritual—Western—Writing—Ethnic

CONTACT: **Kay Weems, Editor/Publisher**
Material: All
207 Willow Wind Dr.
Artemas PA 17211-9405
Phone: 814-458-3102

Nation

We are a weekly journal of left/liberal opinion, covering national and international affairs as well as the arts. The magazine goes to press on Wednesdays.

We run two types of news items: **comments** (approximately 750 words), which are brief analyses of news developments, e.g., a Supreme Court decision or a change of government in Mexico; and **articles** (typically 1500-2500 words), which combine reporting and analysis to provide in-depth looks at issues.

On the domestic front, we are particularly interested in civil liberties, civil rights, labor, economics, environmental and feminist issues and politics. Because we have readers all over the country, it's important that stories have national significance. In our foreign affairs coverage, we are interested in pieces on international political, economic and social developments. We are strongly committed to investigative reporting. Arts coverage includes book reviews, arts reviews, poetry and cultural essays. We are always interested in new writers; we published Ralph Nader's first piece.

Queries can be sent using our online form or sent by regular mail (the form is preferred). If sending by regular mail, please double-space and include a SASE.

Our standard payment for a comment is $150; for an article $350-$500 depending on length. Payment for arts pieces is dependent on length; generally $225 and up. In special cases, we will do all we can to assist writers in obtaining research grants to make ambitious projects possible.

Please do not phone with queries as we will only ask you in that case to submit a written query.

Categories: Nonfiction—Arts—Book Reviews—Culture—Foreign Affairs—Government—Politics

CONTACT: *The Nation*
33 Irving Pl 8th Fl
New York NY 10003
Fax: 212-982-9000

The National Enquirer

An *Enquirer* story requires fast, extremely detailed, accurate work. It's not particularly complex, but it has to be done. On the other hand, The *Enquirer* pays enough money to make the work worthwhile. A number of freelancers are making better than $1,500 a week right now and there is room for twenty more like them.

You get $360 or $180 just for providing a story idea, plus source information, even if you do nothing more on the story. If you go ahead and cover the story, you get another $720 or $450. So that's either $1,080 or $630 a story—the difference being whether it's used as a "T" (top page) or a "D" (down page). You should aim for twenty leads and one or two stories each week and don't worry about the high attrition rate of story suggestions. Everyone faces the same situation and it's worth it if you can get one out of ten.

The lead fees and story rates I've just mentioned are the best in the country for newspaper stories. What do you have to do to get them? Well, you have to do a couple of things differently from the way they are done on most newspapers.

First, the writing: the difference here is that we want you to over-write substantially. We want a basic magazine structure: lead, backup (with anecdotes), conclusion. But forget about stylistic tricks—everything is rewritten, you are supplying a basic file, like *Time* reporters do—and you write at least five to seven double-spaced pages. Just put on a straight introduction covering the points raised in the lead sheet and follow it mostly with quotes—the more that's in direct quotes the better, far more than you'll see in the finished story. And get this point clear in your mind—even a small story has to start out this big. We need to cover all the bases.

Your report will be read for the quality of the reporting, not the writing. I know this is frustrating, but it is an essential part of the system and you will be highly regarded for doing it. I might add that, since you don't have to worry about tight writing, style and paraphrasing, an *Enquirer* piece tends to go a lot quicker than a magazine yarn.

Second, there will be questions and call backs. Please don't feel put down if I come back and ask for clarifications. There are three levels of people beyond me whose job it is to nitpick—we strive not just for accuracy but for proof of accuracy. So almost everyone gets called back, though not on every story, and has to check back sources. Just do a thorough reporting job and callbacks will be minimal. We know it is tedious. One of the reasons we pay more than other publications is to compensate you for this occasional necessity.

Here's how to avoid callbacks:

1. Don't state anything in your copy unless you have it in quotes or have other adequate proof that it is true. Don't leave any unanswered questions.

2. Each assignment will have a story number. Mark this number on your copy and add a 'contact sheet' with names and phone numbers of interviewees (they won't be called back if you don't want it, but we need them for our files).

3. Get backup for any substantial claims from other reputable sources. A medical breakthrough, for instance, needs details of test results proving its efficacy, plus a statement by some other authority (often the original source will refer you to others in the file) that the discovery is valid and significant.

4. Avoid dull copy by including anecdotes where at all possible (and appropriate).

5. Follow the lead sheet exactly. If the lead says something is an incredible breakthrough, then you can't quote someone as saying it may be a breakthrough. *Enquirer* stories are black and white—there are no gray areas. We don't do balanced stories. If we decide to run a story, it's because we believe in it. Negative or questioning comments by anyone quoted—either in the file or in the tape recording of interview—will lead to the story being killed.

To ease the shock of all of this, think of this—you can get as much as $2,780 for one story in the *Enquirer*. That's $360 for the lead, $720 for the reporting—and $1,700 if your story makes Page 1. That bonus is paid twice every week and each week we use eighty to ninety stories about half from non-staffers.

Okay, so where do you get these stories? The basic starting points are the newspapers—all the newspapers. Next comes the TV and radio talk shows, then the magazines, general and special interest; then the trade papers and specialist journals, abstracts, and so on. Offbeat books also tend to be good sources. There are also your personal contacts in the various fields—show biz, the universities, hospitals, politics, newspapers and so forth. Also stories you have worked on, are now working on, often have aspects that make an Enquirer angle.

Here's how to recognize an *Enquirer* story and how to write a lead that'll grab us. First, you can pretty much rule out stories that have been picked up by the wire services, unless you find a completely fresh angle. Second, look for stories that have mass appeal to about half the population. Third, look for the significant things the daily press tends to miss—the story behind the story: a case in point was the disastrous Kentucky nightclub fire some years ago, where *Enquirer* reporters discovered that the reason so many people died was that the management was trying to collect customers' checks before opening the doors.

In writing your lead suggestion, try always to indicate a clear, fresh angle to the story. But be awfully careful you don't write anything in the lead that you can't back up. This is a major reason for stories being killed. In fact, it is a very good idea to do some investigation of your story before submitting it. This will enable you to spell it out with concise facts, figures and examples and give you a much better chance of getting it accepted.

Here's what happens to your idea when you submit it. If I like it, I send it to the Editor. He either okays the lead or kills it. He marks it a "T" or a "D" if approved. I have the approved ones typed on lead sheets. We then give it a story number and check the computer to see that we haven't already done the story in the last five years or that no one currently is working it. When I get the lead sheet back, I assign the story to you or someone else if you can't or don't want to do it.

When you send in your copy—always with the story number on it, I check that it's all there and then I send it to an evaluator. His job is to assess how big the story should finally run and he writes this opinion, along with a summary of your file for the writers to then re-write to the length decided. The written article then goes to the researchers, who check it. You can see that there are quite a few steps here and this is why it's important that your file be complete—otherwise any or all of these people will ask for clarification and this causes delays.

What kind of stories? Please read the paper. Browse through some back issues. They will tell you more than I could. The requirements haven't changed, except perhaps that stories pertaining directly to women are more popular now than before. A general test is—would this story interest 50% of our readers?

Here are some suggestions and reminders you should tape to the wall over your desk:

1. Scandals, big news breaks, exclusives of all kinds—especially untold angles on major stories.

2. Anything about major personalities, especially TV—romances, breakups, illnesses, interviews with them. Almost any interview is usable if the star is big enough but always look for a fresh angle.

3. Medical breakthroughs, especially concerning cancer, heart disease, arthritis, diabetes, and other maladies a broad spectrum of the public has or is worried about. Important scientific discoveries—especially involving common substances.

4. Interesting new diets.

5. Beauty ideas that people can use.

6. Dramatic new fashions, good news and self-help for women.

7. Success stories, people overcoming adversities.

8. Miracle escapes, great rescues, adventures, survival.

9. Ghosts, exorcisms, physics, ESP, UFOs.

10. New self-help ideas—five steps to a new you (especially getting smarter or more successful).

11. Great ripoffs.

12. New light on famous unsolved mysterious (e.g. Amelia Earhart,

Bermuda Triangle, etc.)

13. The Kennedys, Reagans, Clintons—their fads, dirty linens, new interests, etc.

14. New information on major controversies—saccharine and cancer, butter and cholesterol, etc.

15. 'Fringe Medicine'—acupuncture, graphology, reflexology, healing—studies that appear to show they have scientific validity. Dreams that come true. But there must be good backup on all these offbeat claims.

16. Governmental misbehavior—officials ripping off funds, unnecessary trips, putting relations on payrolls, misuse of government plans, FDA keeping valuable drugs off the market, CAB keeping airlines unsafe, etc.—major sources are government auditors, congressional committee staffs and investigators (and equivalents on state and city levels) and ambitious 'out' politicians. Also good are consumer and special interest groups and wayout publications.

17. Sins against the community by other major power blocks—business lobbying and ripoffs, oil depletion, unions costing people their jobs by feather-bedding that kills the firm, stealing pension funds. Labor rackets like the wholesale organized stealing on waterfronts.

18. Public health—good and bad news—e.g., plague still a threat, cancer 'epidemic' in Rutherford, New Jersey, polio is dead.

19. Where are they now? Film star Betty Hutton is a cook in a rectory, etc.

20. New info, especially with pics, on childhoods of famous people or hidden episodes in their lives.

21. Delicately handled sex stories like 'How to Put New Life Into Your Marriage,' 'Why Husbands Lose Interest,' etc.

22. Stories of great wealth—like the custom-made aircraft of the rich.

23. Every kind of 'How To' story especially ten ways to variety.

24. Significant new gadgets and scientific devices, like attaching magnets to your fuel line to increase gas mileage 30 to 40%.

25. News about computers—especially development of artificial intelligence, computer crimes and means of combatting the privacy issue, 'the government has your number' sort of thing.

26. Wacky stunts, such as those of having an *Enquirer* reporter check the waiting time in hospital emergency rooms across the country or taking the Encyclopedia Britannica sales course and reporting all the sales tricks they teach.

27. Human interest. This can be anything that people like to read and talk about. But it's got be good. If it's a dying child who miraculously survives, I want quotes that make me cry, ones that will really touch my heart. If it's a handicapped man who's climbed Mount Everest, I want quotes in the story that will make me cheer. Human interest stories are obviously 'people' stories, but don't forget their pets too.

28. Any happening or development that will cause readers to exclaim, 'Gee Whiz!' or 'How Dare They?' or similar expressions of amazement, joy or anger.

29. There is one other story source—a most important one. It's what we refer to here as 'off the top of your head.' This source can be tapped single-handedly by sitting back, putting your feet on the desk and just thinking in headlines. Think of the sort of headline you've seen on the front page of the *Enquirer*, on the cover blurb of *Reader's Digest*, on the TV ads for this and other publications. Then mentally write a few yourself. All you have to do then is figure out where and how and from whom you can get a story that would fit such a headline. And there you have it—the $1,700 front page bonus. Joint assaults on the top of the head also work; sit around with some of your favorite friends and favorite substances and bounce a few 'what-ifs' around. You'll be amazed how they blossom in mid air. As often as not, this sort of process is the source of our big 'production numbers,' and they're the stories we like best and that will score best for you.

Samples of the sort of thing I mean.
- What if there is one best diet?
- How to find your roots
- 100 easy ways to save money
- Harvard docs reveal simple plan to beat stress
- Lose weight on fast food diet

- TV shows that reduce stress
- Simple no-drug headache cure
- Live up to 20 years longer

Each one of these made a front-page banner headline. Of course, the slight catch to it is that the reporters who thought of those leads also came up with ideas on how to do them.

I am also sending along a couple of other idea ticklers: one is an alphabetical listing of *Enquirer*-type subjects, the other is a list of *Enquirer* 'category' stories.

You may choose to specialize in one or two of these areas; it can be a good strategy. But be aware of them all. There's money in every one. Good luck and stay in touch.

***Enquirer* Category Stories:**

- Card & Letter Appeal: for the very sick/lonely/courageous.
- Celebrity Fantasies: The *Enquirer* can make come true.
- Contests: see those we publish to spark your imagination.
- Court Watch: shocking examples of injustice.
- Diet
- Education
- *Enquirer* Impact: how an *Enquirer* article has changed a reader's life for the better.
- Escape From the Rat Race: focusing on somebody successful who's given it all up for a less stressful, preferably wayout, life.
- Good Samaritan Award
- Government Waste or Bureaucracy Run Wild: self-explanatory examples of red tape, incompetence, bureaucratic waste that will make our readers hot under the collar.
- Hero Award: potential recipient must have risked own life.
- Honest Person Award
- How To: self-improvement, etc.
- How To: improve your marriage.
- How To: beat loneliness.
- Incredible World of Animals: each feature concentrates on fascinating attributes of a particular creature.
- Medical: general—breakthrough, new treatments, techniques, etc. We have sub-categories recognizing readers' special interests in cancer, arthritis and heart problems.
- My Most Embarrassing Moment: (celeb)
- My Most Frightening Moment: (celeb)
- Occult
- Rags to Riches: subjects must have started in straitened circumstances and now be verifiably wealthy.
- Recipe for a Happy Marriage: (celeb)
- Reveal Personality: interesting how mannerisms, habits, etc. show us what we're really like.
- Success Without College: subject must be well-known or be associated with a well-known venture.
- Woman at the Top: must be well known.
- Women's Interest: fashion, beauty, etc.
- Young Achiever: kids, preferably under 20, who've achieved fame or fortune through their own endeavor (not showbiz).
- Quiz: relatively light—often psychological (such as "How Brave Are You?") or general knowledge ("How Much You Know About Such and Such?")

Categories: Nonfiction—Adventure—Alternate Lifestyles—Animals—Arts—Biography—Diet/Nutrition—Education—Entertainment—Fashion—Government—Health—New Age—Physical Fitness—Relationships—Science—Self Help—Sexuality—Women's Issues—Celebrities—Astrology—Medicine —UFO Experiences/Research—How-to—Human Interest

CONTACT: Charlie Montgomery, Articles Editor
Material: All
5401 Broken Sound Blvd.
Boca Raton FL 33487
Phone: 800-628-5697, ext. 2216
Fax: 800-336-3973
Website: www.nationalenquirer.com

National Geographic Traveler

Thank you for your interest in contributing to *National Geographic Traveler*, which is published eight times a year by the National Geographic Society. *Traveler*'s publishing goals are to find the new, to showcase fresh travel opportunities, to be an advocate for travelers. *Traveler*'s tag line is "Where the Journey Begins," and accordingly, a *Traveler* story must capture a place's essence in a way that inspires readers to follow in the writer's footsteps—and equip them to do so with useful destination information.

What Types Of Stories Does *Traveler* Publish?

Each issue of the magazine contains five or more features, roughly balanced between U.S. and foreign subjects. Generally, we are interested in places accessible to most travelers, not just the intrepid or wealthy. The types of destinations we cover vary widely, from mainstream to adventure travel.

Traveler features are usually narrow in scope; we do not cover whole states or countries. Subjects of particular interest to us are national and state parks, historic places, cities, little-known or undiscovered places, train trips, cruises, and driving trips. Service information is generally given separately at the end of each feature in a section that includes how to get to the destination, things to see and do there, and where to obtain more information. The writer is expected to send along as much service information as possible with the manuscript to help us prepare this section.

We also publish several regular service-oriented departments, with the emphasis on meaty, practical information. Subjects include photography, food, lodgings, ecotourism, adventurous learning experiences, and short getaways. Essays offering reflections on the travel experience round out the department mix.

What Kinds Of Proposals Is *Traveler* Looking For?

We accept freelance queries for most of our departments. Ideas for features are generated both by the *Traveler* staff and by freelance contributors. We do assign features to writers we have not used but only to those whose published clips demonstrate the highest level of writing skill. We do not accept phone queries from writers, and we discourage the submission of unsolicited manuscripts for feature articles. We do not accept proposals about trips that are subsidized in any way.

How Should An Idea Be Proposed?

If we have to sell readers to consume our magazine, then writers must sell us with more than just notions and place-names, so please do not send us any unfocused wish lists of multiple queries. Restrict each submission to one or two well-developed proposals that have been crafted especially for us. A carefully considered proposal combines support for doing a particular destination with some premise or hook. A good query has a headline that suggests what the story is, a deck that amplifies on that, a strong lead, and not much more than a page that clearly sets out the premise and approach of the piece. The query should represent the writer's style and should answer these questions about the story: Why now, and why in *Traveler*?

Check the *Traveler* index to make sure we have not recently run a piece on the topic you are proposing. Please include your credentials, relevant published clippings and a SASE to ensure that the requested materials are returned. Mail your proposal to Query Editor, *National Geographic Traveler*, 1145 17th St NW, Washington DC 20036. Prospective contributors doing preliminary research for a story must avoid giving the impression that they are representing the National Geographic Society or *Traveler*. They may use the name of the magazine only if they have a definite assignment. When *Traveler* gives an assignment, the terms are clearly stated in a written contract.

How Long Are Traveler Feature Stories And Departments?

Most *Traveler* features range from 1,500 to 2,500 words, depending on the subject. *Traveler* departments generally run from 750 to 1,500 words. Compensation varies depending on the type of feature or department but is competitive with other national magazines. Payment is made upon acceptance. We buy all rights to manuscripts, although copyright is returned to the author 90 days after publication.

What Does *Traveler* Look For In Writing Style?

There are no limitations on style, as long as the writing is lively and interesting, although a sense of discovery should be at the heart of every *Traveler* story. We want our writers to project a curious and knowing voice that captures the experience of travel—the places and personalities, the insights and idiosyncrasies. Writers who work for us must see destinations with fresh eyes and real insight. We place a premium on surprise and good storytelling—the compelling anecdote, the colorful character, the lively quote, the telling detail. And we prefer that our readers be allowed to experience a destination directly through the words and actions of people the writer encounters, not just through the writer's narrative.

Beyond being strongly evocative of place, our articles attempt to speak to the soul of traveling. Every traveler, no matter how seasoned, wonders what awaits at a new destination. This goes beyond weather and accommodations and language and scenics and museums. There's a certain frisson of expectation: How foreign is this destination? What new experience will I have? This is travel as texture—the feel of a place, its essential differentness, its look, its flavor. We seek that texture in every story we publish.

Categories: Nonfiction—Consumer—Ecology—Economics—Education—Food/Drink—Health—Money & Finances—Photography—Recreation—Regional—Sports/Recreation—Travel

CONTACT: Submissions Editor
Material: Queries
National Geographic Society
1145 17th Street N.W.
Washington DC 20036-4688
Phone: 202-775-6700
Fax: 202-828-6640
Website: www.nationalgeographictraveler.com

The National Pastime

Please refer to the Society of American Baseball Research.

National Review

NR isn't a likely place to break in; virtually all our contributors are established writers and/or experts in their fields. But if you wish to submit a manuscript, please do so at the below address.

Categories: Nonfiction—Politics—Public Policy

CONTACT: Submissions Desk
Material: All
215 Lexington Ave
New York NY 10016
Phone: 212-679-7330
E-mail: letter.nationalreview.com
Website: www.nationalreview.com

Native Peoples

Native Peoples strives to offer a sensitive portrayal of the arts and lifeways of the Native peoples of the Americas. We seek writers and photographers—Native and non-Native—who have a unique expertise about their subject. If you are Native, please let us know. Competition is stiff: The magazine receives numerous unsolicited manuscripts and hundreds of queries a year.

Native Peoples is a high quality, bimonthly magazine of nonfiction feature articles and departments. We do not publish fiction, photo es-

says or reprints. Poetry is only published in context with an accompanying nonfiction article. Most feature stories run 1,200 to 2,000 words, but the subject should dictate your story length. The only departments open to freelancers are our travel section, "Pathways," opinion section "Viewpoint" and "History."

The magazine seeks stories reflecting Native life throughout the Americas, from the Arctic Circle to the southern tip of Chile, though our prime focus is on subjects set in the United States. We strive to include a diverse mix of topics, from serious to entertaining, including artist and other personality profiles, events and issues reflecting today's Native peoples. We value stories that help bring an understanding of Native culture—its past, present and future. We write for a diverse audience—about one-third of our subscribers are Native and two-thirds are non-Native. Powerful, descriptive, clear and concise prose is essential. Accuracy and sensitivity are paramount. The readership wants to know and we want you to show them— not just tell them—the Native point of view on any given subject matter.

Stories need to be illustrated with high quality photography. Writers are asked to suggest, or work with, professional photographers.

To have a story considered for publication, please submit a brief outline of your proposed subject via mail or e-mail (e-mail is preferred). Please do not submit original manuscripts, art or photography unless solicited by the magazine. The magazine cannot accept responsibility for unsolicited original materials. A biography or resume, and writing sample(s) are encouraged. We try to respond to queries within 30 days. We work a minimum of six months in advance. We plan a year in advance, so the more lead time you give us about a time-sensitive story, the better the chances are that we will be able to respond and get it published in the most appropriate issue. If an unsolicited story is accepted, the editing process begins. Backup material and rewrites may be requested.

Our standard rate is 25 cents per published word, payable upon publication. (First publication rights only—you own the story).

Categories: Nonfiction—Arts—Biography—Book Reviews—Collectibles—Consumer—Cooking—Crafts/Hobbies—Culture—Dance—Drama—Entertainment—Environment—Fashion—Film/Video—History—Lifestyle—Multicultural—Native Americans—Travel

CONTACT: Daniel Gibson, Editor
Material: All
5333 North Seventh St, Ste 224
Phoenix AZ 85014-2804
E-mail: dgibson@nativepeoples.com

Natural Beauty and Health

Thank you for your interest in *Natural Beauty & Health*. We are always interested in reviewing focused, well-written nonfiction articles and interviews. The best way of assessing our style is to look at copies of our magazines, which are available in most major bookstores and on the internet at www.nbhonline.com. Our Statement of Purpose, located in the beginning each issue, is a good place to start.

We do not respond to query letters, and we only consider final products. We prefer that you submit your article by email. If you do submit a hard copy, please send a self-addressed, stamped envelope or email address for our reply. Allow up to six months for a response. We don't send back submissions, so do not send us your only copy. We no longer publish poetry or fiction. Writing in the form of a sermon is discouraged.

Submissions should not have already appeared in other publications or on the web.

Natural Beauty & Health inspires people who take personal responsibility for their mental, physical, and spiritual health and who seek alternatives to the standard paradigm such as yoga, meditation, nutritional discoveries, organic living, holistic healing, and an awareness that beauty comes from inside out. *Natural Beauty & Health* is almost fully devoted to holistic health issues and information. It is not news to our readers that alternatives to the Western medical paradigm exist. They respond to significant discoveries and research into alternative therapies, revised ideas of health and beauty, cultural mythologies, and spiritual disciplines.

FORMAT: Feature articles range in length from 1000 2000 words. E-mailed versions are preferred (in Rich Text Format or text-only format, or in MSWord 98 or earlier), though hard copies can be mailed to MB Media, PO Box 600, Chico, CA 95927-0600. E-mail us at editor@magicalblend.com. Work that has been edited for length and clarity is more likely to be considered. Payment is considered strictly on an individual basis.

Artwork to accompany articles may be submitted digitally or on slides or color prints. Please do not send us originals!

SOME ARTICLE IDEAS *Natural Beauty & Health* MAGAZINE CONSIDERS:
- Herbal Remedies
- Homeopathy
- Ayurveda
- Aromatherapy
- Flower Essences
- Nutrition
- Bodywork/Yoga
- Spiritual/Paranormal Healing
- Self-Improvement
- Alternative Ideas of Beauty Well-Known Health Experts/Celebrities
- Parenting
- Food/Healthy Recipes
- Detoxification/Cleanses
- Organic, non-GMO Foods
- Personal Transformation
- How-To
- Natural Childbirth/Pregnancy
- Men s/Women s Health
- Senior Health

We look forward to reading submissions that show your passion!

Categories: Nonfiction—Alternate Lifestyles—Careers—Children—Comedy—Conservation—Consumer—Cooking—Culture—Diet/Nutrition—Education—Family—Food/Drink—Gardening—General

Interest—Health—Interview—Lifestyle—Marriage—Men's Issues—Money and

Finances—Parenting—Physical Fitness—Politics—Psychology—Recreation—Relationships—Self Help—Sexuality— Society—Sports/Recreation—Spiritual—Travel—Womens Issues

CONTACT: Susan Dobra, Editorial Director
Material: All
PO Box 600
Chico, CA 95927-0600
E-mail: editor@magicalblend.com
Website: www.nbhonline.com

NATURAL HISTORY

Natural History

We are a magazine of nature, science, and culture published monthly. We are seeking new research on mammals, birds, invertebrates, reptiles, ocean life, anthropology, astronomy, preferably written by principal investigators in these fields. Articles for *Natural History* are written by scientists and scholars. Scientists may write about their own research findings or report upon new findings in their field. Straight environmental reportage is not in our purview, but related issues are. Our slant is toward unraveling problems in behavior, ecology, and evolution. In every case, the highest standards of writing and research apply. All submissions are subject to review by experts in the field and to rigorous fact-checking.

The most important thing to do before submitting a proposal to *Natural History* is to look closely at the magazine. We run a range of columns and features. While many are written by staff or regular contributors, we do welcome new submissions. Columns run from 800 to 1,500 words and include "Journal," a short piece of reporting from the field on a subject of scientific interest or debate; "Samplings," a summary of new or ongoing research that poses some new questions; "Naturalist at Large," a medium-length essay usually tied to field experience; and "Endpaper," a short essay. We also publish essays, profiles, and commentaries on current events in science.

Features run 1,500 to 2,500 words and are usually accompanied by photographs. Writers may submit photographs, but most photography for *Natural History* is obtained from professional photographers. Occasionally a photographer will be commissioned to work directly with a scientist or writer.

Article proposals may be submitted at any time via e-mail. Our article schedules are set at least six months in advance. Please consider this in proposing articles with a time-critical or seasonal connection. (We are glad to work with scientists who would like a general article on their research to appear in *Natural History* the same month their research paper appears in *Nature, Science,* or other peer-reviewed journal. We will develop the article ahead of time and, if necessary, hold it until the research paper appears.)

Article proposals should be brief. Scientists should accompany their proposals with samples of their published work in the field and/or in general publications. Unless arranged beforehand, we do not accept proposals or submissions by phone, fax, or email. Editorial decisions are usually made within six months. Because of the number of submissions we receive, we are unable to supply comments on the reasons for rejection. Payment for articles ranges from $300 to $2,500 depending upon length.

Categories: Nonfiction—Environment—Science—Anthropology—Natural History

CONTACT: Submit by e-mail
Phone: 646-356-6500
Fax: 646-356-6511
E-mail: nhmag@nhmag.com
Website: naturalhistory.com

Natural Home

Natural Home offers today's health-conscious, environmentally concerned homeowners the information they need to practice earth-inspired living. Since our first issue in May 1999, *Natural Home* has brought together the best in home design, earth-friendly décor and natural living. Our bimonthly magazine and dynamic website feature sustainable, healthy homes, decorating tips, and the latest green

M-Q

products and services.

Natural Home's readers are educated, eco-savvy home-owners whose values and purchasing patterns mirror the Cultural Creatives, a growing market of 50 million individuals who care deeply about healthy living, natural products, and a sustainable economy. Join us!

Writers' Guidelines

Natural Home is a bimonthly magazine devoted to health-conscious, earth-conscious readers who are concerned with the quality of their personal environment.

Natural Home is published six times a year in January, March, May, July, September, and November. Issues are planned six to twelve months in advance; queries should be sent at least eight months before an issue's publication date. Material submitted for publication should display in-depth knowledge of the subject matter based on experience and thorough research.

Keep a copy of everything. If the submission is unsolicited and/or you wish any part of it to be returned, include a self-addressed, stamped envelope with sufficient return postage.

Manuscripts

If you aren't familiar with the content, style, and tone of *Natural Home* magazine, we suggest you read a few issues.

Although we prefer to assign our own stories, if the article is already written, please enclose a copy of the manuscript, accompanying photos or drawings if any, and a brief informal personal biography. (These illustrations are for editing purposes and will not necessarily be published as part of the article.) If any part of your submission has been published previously, please tell us when and by whom. If the article is still in the idea stage, send a detailed proposal—complete outline, written description, sample page(s), or sketches—sufficient to give a clear idea of what to expect in the finished piece.

The manuscript should be computer generated and submitted on disk or via email. A hard copy of the manuscript should be double-spaced on 8½ x 11 white bond paper with at least one-inch margins. Manuscript length may range from three to sixteen typewritten pages depending on the subject matter. Put your name, address, and telephone number at the top of each page.

We will accept Microsoft Word documents or text files (.txt) created with MS-DOS or Windows-based software and most Macintosh software. Any special instructions may be included on a separate sheet of paper.

Visuals

If you wish to provide your own visuals, please send samples of finished publication-quality photographs (35mm, 2¼ or 4x5 transparencies, please) or artwork; we will determine what best suits the material and our design requirements. All artwork and photographs will be returned promptly and appropriately insured.

Acceptance and Payment

Receipt of your submission will be promptly acknowledged, but we may not be able to make an immediate decision about its use. Please be patient.

Natural Home pays on publication unless other arrangements are made with the editor. Articles range in length from 250 to 1,500 words. Fees are based on a rate varying from $.33 to $.50 per word.

We reserve the right to edit your material as necessary to fit the style, format, or other requirements of *Natural Home.*

Categories: Nonfiction—Environment—Health—Home

CONTACT: Maren Bzdek, Managing Editor
Material: Queries and submission
201 E. Fourth St.
Loveland CO 80537-5655
Phone: 970-613-4660
E-mail: editor@naturalhomemag.com
Website: www.naturalhomemagazine.com

Naturally

Please refer to Travel Naturally.

Nebo: A Literary Journal
Arkansas Polytechnic University

Submissions are preferred from August through February. Themes vary according to the current editor.

Please enclose a cover letter with author's name and address, brief bio, a short list of published works, and a SASE. Indicate for return of manuscript if necessary, and use the required amount of postage.

We do not accept simultaneous submissions or previously published material.

Poetry: We accept blank verse, free verse, sonnets, dramatic monologues, etc. No more than five poems per submission.

Fiction: Short-short (up to 750 words) and short stories are the stuff of life and we appreciate all such submissions. Due to space restraints, please limit stories to 2,000 words.

All works must be typed (single-spaced for poetry is acceptable). Please include an approximate word count for short prose fiction.

Advice to Writers

We are interested in quality poetry and fiction by new and established writers. In fiction we are open to a wide range of styles, but ask that the length be kept to 2,000 words (750 for short-shorts). We seek poems whose content is convincing and whose rhythms are as compelling and memorable as their diction and images.

Thank you for your interest in our journal!

Categories: Fiction—Poetry

CONTACT: Dr. Michael Karl Ritchie
Material: Any
English Dept. Arkansas Tech. University
Russellville AR 72801-2222
Phone: 501-968-0487

Nebraska Review
The University of Nebraska-Omaha

Quality, well-crafted literary fiction, creative nonfiction and poetry. No restrictions on content, style, or length, although fiction generally should not exceed 7,500 words. Longer pieces of exceptional merit will be considered. Response in 3 to 6 months, sometimes sooner.

Please note these submissions deadlines:
Open submission of original fiction and poetry
January 1 - April 30

Fiction manuscripts should include the writer's name and address on the first page.

Poetry may be single-spaced, and should include the writer's name and address on each poem. Standard submission is three to six poems.

Subscriptions: $15.00 per year (2 issues); $18 for two years. Individual copies: $8. Back issues and sample copies: $4.50 when available.

Categories: Fiction—Nonfiction—Literature—Poetry—Short Stories—Writing

CONTACT: Coreen Wees, Poetry Editor
Material: Poetry
CONTACT: James Reed, Fiction Editor
Material: Fiction
CONTACT: John Price, Nonfiction Editor
Material: Creative Nonfiction
Program in Creative Writing, University of Nebraska-Omaha
Omaha NE 68182-0324
Phone: 402-554-3159

Nevada Magazine

Submission Guidelines for Writers and Photographers 2006

Nevada Magazine is constantly searching for stories and photographs that tell the story of Nevada.

Nevada Magazine is designed to promote tourism in Nevada and educate the public about the state's recreation, people, places, history, events, entertainment, and other attractions. Since the state publication first appeared in 1936, readers have relied on Nevada Magazine for informative and entertaining features on the Silver State. The magazine's circulation (bimonthly) is approximately 70,000 (for the Nevada Events & Shows section, 170,000), and 70 percent of the magazine's readers are from out of state. Readers are active travelers and Nevada enthusiasts who take frequent Nevada vacations.

SUBMISSIONS: Stories and photos are accepted on speculation. Recommended subjects include Nevada's people, history, recreation, entertainment, events, towns, and scenery. If you have another Nevada topic you'd like to write about, we'd be happy to hear your suggestion. Keep in mind that the magazine's purpose is to promote tourism in Nevada and that the majority of readers live out of state.

Payment is on publication and varies with article length and the size and quality of photographs. Most stories range between 500 to 1,800 words. Fees range from 25 to 30 cents per word and $30 to $150 for photos and illustrations. The magazine buys first North American rights.

STORIES: Manuscripts can be sent by regular mail or email. Hard copies should be double-spaced with a suggested title, byline, and writer's credit. Your name, address, phone(s), and email address should be at the top of the story.

You can email queries and stories to Joyce Hollister, Editor, jhollister@nevadamagazine.com. We are Mac-based. Our software program, Microsoft Word, can convert most Macintosh and PC programs.

PHOTOS: Nevada Magazine uses transparencies, prints, and digital photos. You can email digital images to Art Director Denise Barr at denise@nevadamagazine.com. Send 72 dpi jpeg images for evaluation and 300 dpi (at least 5 inches wide) tiff or jpegs for publication. Please note the photo name in the subject line.

We prefer transparencies (35mm sides and larger) to color prints, although sharp color prints can be used. Label your name, address, and identification of the subject on each slide or photograph. To receive a copy of the magazine's bimonthly Photo Alert, which lists current photo needs, email Production Assistant Melissa Loomis at melissa@nevadamagazine.com.

The editors reserve the right to edit all material and cannot guarantee against damage to, or loss of, any materials. However, we will make every effort to handle submissions as if they were our own and to work with writers and photographers. You can help by sending a self-addressed, stamped envelope with your material to ensure its safe return. Please allow four or five weeks for reply.

We look forward to hearing from you.

Developing Story and Photo ideas

When developing your ideas, consider Nevada Magazine's audience and how your story would work in the magazine's format. For example, these kinds of stories appear in every issue:

Places and Travel

Destinations: Focusing on locales such as Wendover, Laughlin, Lake Tahoe.

Roadside Attractions: Intriguing things to do, places to go.

Side Trips: Excursions to unique places.

Dining Out: Unusual eateries.

Hotel-Casinos

People stories.

Trends in gaming, dining, and other hotel offerings.

Vacation Ideas.

Recreation

Guides to golf, fishing, skiing, boating, and other sports.

First-person stories on outdoor adventures.

History

People, places, and events in old-time Nevada.

People

Nevada Characters, Celebrities in Nevada.

Photography

Photo features.

Annual photo contest, the Great Nevada Picture Hunt.

Nevada Events & Shows (the magazine's statewide events section)

Lead stories on seasonal events or entertainment, show people, and show reviews in the Las Vegas, Reno-Tahoe, and rural areas.

Event and show listings.

Nevada Travel Update (newsletter to travel agents)

Hotels, destinations, sightseeing, adventure tours.

Submitting Items and Ideas to Nevada Magazine

Please write, email, or give us a call if you have a story or photo idea that you think might work in Nevada Magazine.

Categories: Nonfiction—History—Outdoors—Recreation—Regional—Travel

CONTACT: Joyce Hollister, Editor
Phone: 775-687-0603
E-mail: jhollister@nevadamagazine.com
Matt Brown, Associate Editor
E-mail: mbrown@nevadamagazine.com
Matt Smith, Art Director/Photo Editor
E-mail: matt@nevadamagazine.com
401 N Carson St
Carson City NV 89701
Phone: 775-687-0607
Fax: 775-687-6159
Ann Henderson, Nevada Events & Shows Editor
555 E Washington Ste 5600
Las Vegas NV 89101
Phone: 702-486-2433
Fax: 702-486-2789
E-mail: ann@nevadamagazine.com
Website: www.nevadamagazine.com

New Beginnings

NEW BEGINNINGS Writers' Guidelines

NEW BEGINNINGS is a bimonthly magazine for La Leche League members with a readership of 40,000 worldwide. It is published by La Leche League International, 1400 N. Meacham Rd., Schaumburg, IL 60173-4840.

Purpose: To inform and inspire LLL members worldwide through articles, stories, poems, and other information about breastfeeding and parenting that reflect LLL's philosophy and mission.

What We're Looking For: Narrative Features—Mothers' Stories, Focus On Fathers, Growing Families

Primary purpose: to tell a personal story

First person perspective

Conversational tone

Leave the reader with hope

Strike a balance between describing details and sharing feelings

Photos of your child and/or family add to the appeal of these stories. (Black and white photos are easiest to reproduce, but color photos are fine if they are sharp and clear. We will do our best to return photos after use; however, they are occasionally lost, so it is best not to send the only copy of a favorite photo. Please do not write on the back of the picture.)

Mothers' Stories: Focus on breastfeeding and/or mothering issues. Usually concerns children under the age of about one year, but may vary depending on the underlying theme of the story.

Focus On Fathers: A celebration of the father's unique role in the life of his breastfed baby.

Growing Families: How LLL philosophy can be applied as children grow older.

Informative Features—Lead Articles, Information Please, Eating Wisely

Primary purpose: to develop an idea or discuss a topic

Usually third person perspective; personal examples may add interest

More formal tone

Include references—to books from Group Libraries where possible

Balance general statements and claims with supporting evidence and examples

Lead Articles: Written with the first-time mother in mind and reflect LLL philosophy. References are helpful because they provide a way for mothers to find out more about a topic that interests them. References to books available from LLLI or through LLL Group Libraries are preferred.

Information Please: Current, referenced information about the benefits of human milk and other topics related to breastfeeding.

Eating Wisely: Thoughtful, creative stories designed to increase the readers' understanding about nutrition and provide practical information about feeding families.

Question-and-Answer columns—Toddler Tips, Staying Home Instead, and Making It Work.

Three question-and-answer columns pose hypothetical situations about different aspects of mothering and breastfeeding. Our readers send a variety of responses, which helps us to mimic the atmosphere at LLL meetings (both online and in person), where a mother can ask a question and gather ideas from others in similar situations.

Toddler Tips focuses on challenges with parenting toddlers and/or extended breastfeeding.

Staying Home Instead offers support for the mother who is staying home with her baby and/or young children by addressing concerns from the mother's point of view.

Making It Work offers tips for balancing breastfeeding with separation from baby due to school, work outside the home, or other reason. This column covers everything from concerns about pumping to engaging the support of caregivers and co-workers.

We appreciate submissions of real-life situations for these columns to help us meet the needs of our readers all over the world.

Things to Avoid

Broad generalizations: Ex: "No mother would . . ." or "All women feel. . . ." Very few things are true or false for every mother.

Brand names (except where it would add to the sense of the story)

Mixing causes: Avoid describing in detail experiences with causes that go beyond the general topic of mothering through breastfeeding (ex: circumcision, vaccinations, home schooling, alternative medicine, home birth, vegan/kosher/non-dairy diets).

Criticizing healthcare professionals

Length

Write what needs to be said—no more, no less.

A column inch is about 40 words.

One-page articles or columns are 800-900 words.

Lead articles may be 1500-2500 words.

Submitting Articles or Stories

All submissions will be acknowledged. Submissions may be held for a period of time before publication. Submissions that are accepted for publication become the property of LLLI and will be edited for clarity, grammatical usage, and adherence to LLL publishing guidelines. Authors whose submissions are published will receive two complimentary copies of the issue in which their work appears. We are unable to return unused submissions.

Categories: Children

CONTACT: Sharon Barsotti
Material: Mothers' Stories
1400 N Meacham Rd

Schaumburg IL 60173
CONTACT: Jo-Anne Elder-Gomes
Material: Focus on Fathers, Information Please
180 Liverpool St
Fredericton, New Brunswick
Canada E3B 4V5
E-mail: elder@nb.sympatico.ca
CONTACT: Patty Jacobs
Material: Growing Families
E-mail: jacobs15@alamedanet.net
CONTACT: Lesley Robinson
Material: Eating Wisely
377 Third Ave
Ottawa, Ontario
Canada K1S 2K4
E-mal: lesleyrobinson@rogers.com
CONTACT: Larissa Lee
Material: Toddler Tips
178 Maple Ave
Rahway NJ 07065
E-mail: larissalee@erols.com
CONTACT: Joylyn Fowler
Material: Making It Work
12970 Newhope St
Garden Grove CA 92840
E-mail: joylyn@earthlink.net
CONTACT: Dori Pelz-Sherman
Material: Staying Home Instead
21 Valleystone Dr
San Rafael CA 94903
E-mail: dpelzsherman@attbi.com
CONTACT: Kathleen Whitfield
Material: Lead Articles
4174 LaSalle Ave
Culver City CA 90232
E-mail: EditorNB@llli.org

The New Centennial Review
Interdisciplinary Perspective on the Americas

About CR (Formerly *The Centennial Review*)

CR: The New Centennial Review is devoted to comparative studies of the Americas. The journal's primary emphasis is on the opening up of the possibilities for a future Americas which does not amount to a mere reiteration of its past. We seek interventions, provocations, and, indeed, insurgencies which release futures for the Americas. In general, CR welcomes work which is inflected, informed, and driven by theoretical and philosophical concerns at the limits of the potentialities for the Americas..

Such work may be explicitly concerned with the Americas, or it may be broader, global and/or genealogical scholarship with implications for the Americas. CR recognizes that the language of the Americas is translation, and that therefore questions of translation, dialogue, and border crossings (linguistic, cultural, national, and the like) are necessary for rethinking the foundations and limits of the Americas.

For forty-five years, CR has been a journal committed to interdisciplinarity, and we continue to encourage work which goes beyond a simple performance of the strategies of various disciplines and interdisciplines, and which therefore interrogates them. This journal is a member of the Council of Editors of Learned Journals.

Submission Guidelines

CR is a refereed journal. We take approximately 2-3 months to read and comment on unsolicited manuscripts. When submitting an article for consideration, please enclose three (3) copies and an e-mail address where you may be reached.

In preparing your submission, use *The Chicago Manual of Style* with the following modification: you may cite page numbers interlinearly once a text has been referenced in the notes. Please use endnotes rather than footnotes.

We do not accept electronic submission of articles at this time. Unsolicited manuscripts are returned to authors only when accompanied by a stamped, self-addressed envelope.

Please e-mail one of the editors if you would like to write a book review for CR.

Categories: Nonfiction—African-American—Agriculture—Architecture—Arts—Biography—Careers—College—Culture—Drama—Ecology—Economics—Education—Electronics—Engineering—Feminism—Government—History—Language—Literature—Multicultural—Politics—Psychology—Society—Theatre—Philosophy—Public Policy—Technology

CONTACT: Scott Michaelsen (smichael@msu.edu)
Material: All
CONTACT: David E. Johnson (dj@acsu.buffalo.edu)
Material: All
Department of English
201 Morrill Hall, Michigan State University
East Lansing MI 48824-1036
Phone: 517-355-9543
Fax: 517-353-3755
E-mail: David E. Johnson (dj@acsu.buffalo.edu)
Website: www.msupress.msu.edu/journals/cr

New England Review
Middlebury College

New England Review is published four times a year: winter, spring, fall, and summer. However, our submissions period is September 1 through May 31 (postmark dates) only. Any submissions that arrive during the summer will be returned unread.

We suggest that you examine a copy of *NER* to see what our standards and preferences are. The current issue is available at better bookstores nationwide and can be purchased online and through our offices for $8, payable by check, money order, or Visa/Mastercard. Be sure to add $3 for foreign orders. Orders should be sent with payment to Order Department, New England Review, Middlebury College, Middlebury, VT 05753; or call our toll-free number (800-450-9571). Sample works from recent issues are also featured on our website at http://go.middlebury.edu/nereview.

We consider short stories, short-shorts, novellas, and self-contained extracts from novels; long and short poems; interpretive and personal essays; book reviews, screenplays, dramatic works, translations, critical reassessments, interviews, and letters from abroad. Please do not combine genres in the same envelope, and do not submit work that has been published previously elsewhere, whether in print or on the web.

Prose: maximum of 10,000 words (approx. thirty pages) in length, double-spaced. Novellas should not exceed 30,000 words (approx. ninety pages). Please send just one piece at a time, unless the pieces are very short.

Poems: send no more than six at once.

All manuscripts should be printed in standard type and should be clean and legible. Never send your only copy; we cannot be responsible for lost or damaged manuscripts. We do not accept electronic submissions. Please address your submission to Prose, Fiction, or Poetry Editor. If you don't need your manuscript returned, enclose a letter-size self-addressed, stamped envelope (SASE) for our reply only; we recycle unreturned manuscripts. If you would like your manuscript returned, enclose an SASE that is large enough and carries enough U.S. postage to return your manuscript and our reply. Overseas contributors should include international reply-paid coupons. Be sure to send an SASE with any query.

Please do not send another submission until you've received a response about the first. Additional manuscripts will be returned unread. We cannot accommodate revisions or forgotten SASEs. We will consider submissions that have been offered simultaneously to other publications, as long as you make it clease that this is a simultaneous submissions and withdraw your submission immediately upon acceptance elsewhere.

NER will respond to your submission within twelve weeks. After twelve weeks have passed, you may query as to the status of your submission by mail (include SASE), e-mail, or phone.

A contract is sent on acceptance, and payment is $10.00 per page, $20.00 minimum, upon publication, plus two free copies of the issue in which your work appears. Authors receive pre-publication galleys. Copyright reverts to the author upon publication, but *New England Review* retains the right to publish and reproduce the work in *NER*'s print and electronic or website publications, in the original format or as part of an anthology or compilation, and to authorize third-party online databases that reprint *NER* materials to publish and reproduce the work.

Categories: Fiction—Nonfiction—Literature—Poetry—Essays

CONTACT: Carolyn Kuebler, Managing Editor
Material: Fiction, Poetry, Literary Essays
Middlebury College
Middlebury VT 05753
Phone: 802-443-5075
E-mail: nereview@middlebury.edu
Website: http://go.middlebury.edu/nereview

New Letters

Thanks for your interest in *New Letters*. Although we do not have any formal writers' guidelines, here are a few suggestions:

• We prefer that you send no more than six poems or one short story per submission.

• We prefer shorter stories to longer ones. An average length is 3,000 to 5,000 words.

• We have no rigid preferences as to subject, style or genre, although "commercial" efforts tend to put us off. Even so, our only fixed requirement is on good writing.

• We discourage multiple submissions, but appreciate knowing if you're sending your work to us and someone else simultaneously.

• Like most literary magazines, our staff is small, so our reporting time varies from 6-18 weeks. Sorry.

• We do not read submissions between May 1 and October 15.

We require a self-addressed, stamped #10 envelope if you want notification of our decision only; if you want your entire manuscript returned, please send an apporpriately sized envelope with sufficient postage.

Sample copies are available from this office for $10.00. We pay the postage if you prepay.

I hope this information is helpful.

Cordially, Robert Stewart, Editor

Categories: Fiction—Nonfiction—Arts—Culture—Literature—Poetry—Short Stories

CONTACT: Robert Stewart, Editor
Material: All
University House, 5101 Rockhill Rd.
Kansas City MO 64110
Phone: 816-235-1168
Fax: 816-235-2611
Website: www.newletters.org

New Mexico Journey

Texas Journey and *New Mexico Journey* are the bimonthly magazines for members of AAA Texas and AAA New Mexico, with 608,000 and 80,000 readers respectively. Editorially focused on regional, travel, and automotive topics, we strive to present creative, intelligent, and helpful stories.

In each issue, we publish three to four feature articles between 1,000 and 2,000 words each. Items for our Travel News and Auto News columns are 75 to 250 words each. We assign stories based on writers' proposals, and, as a rule, do not accept already completed manuscripts. We assign most often to established writers with a solid knowledge of Texas, New Mexico, and the surrounding states, and value writers with a strong voice, storytelling ability, and sound research and reporting skills.

We pay $1 a word, plus agreed-upon expenses on acceptance of a manuscript, and $50 each for story ideas. We buy first North American rights.

We seek stories that uncover a fresh angle on the people and places in and around Texas and New Mexico. Generally speaking, we're most interested in features about the outdoors, cultural travel, consumer travel, and personality profiles. We periodically cover the states of Colorado, Arizona, Louisiana, and California. Non-U.S. destinations include Mexico, Europe, and Canada.

We usually respond to queries within two months. Phone and fax queries are not encouraged. To be considered for an assignment, please mail queries, clips, and a self-addressed stamped envelope to the address below. Thank you for your interest in our publications. We look forward to reading your proposal.

Categories: Nonfiction—Associations—Automobiles—Consumer—Regional—Travel

CONTACT: Nina Elder, Features Editor
Material:3333 Fairview Road, A-327
Costa Mesa CA 92626
Phone: 714-885-2376
E-mail: www.aaa-calif.com/westways

New Mexico Magazine

New Mexico Magazine covers the people, culture, arts, history and landscape of New Mexico for a highly educated readership from every corner of the world. Monthly magazine, 84 to 132 pages. Established 1923. Circulation: 117,000. Pays on acceptance for manuscripts, on publication for photos. Buys first North American serial or one-time rights for photos and artwork. Query first. Buys few manuscripts on speculation. Plans issue six to 12 months in advance. SASE. We reply in four to six weeks. Sample copy $3.95.

Articles

Profile, travel, archaeological, historical (examining little-known facets of New Mexico history or shedding new light on major events and personalities of the past), humor, Southwest lifestyles (food, fashion, homes, gardens), arts and crafts, cultural topics (traditional ways of life, customs, unusual celebrations, social trends), photo features, offbeat science, business stories—anything involving an aspect of New Mexico. Buys seven to 10 manuscripts/issue. Send published writing samples with query. Length: 250-2,000 words. Pays 30 cents a word, $100 minimum.

Style

Use AP style for writing guidelines. Type name, address (including E-mail if available) and phone number in the upper left corner of each page of correspondence and manuscript. Double- or triple-space text. Number pages. Prefer letter-quality printout, typed manuscript or computer diskette.

What We Need From You

Tag Line—Include a short paragraph about yourself and your experience for the end of the story. This lets the reader know who you are.

Contact Information—(A) If there is any way the public can contact and/or interact with the subject of your story, include it. Telephone numbers, addresses, locations to sites, galleries where art is shown or sold, etc.—we want to involve the reader if at all possible. (B) Though it may be the same as above, editors need the names and contact information for subjects interviewed or mentioned in your story. Sometimes we hold onto a story for up to a year and need to make sure nothing has changed in your story. If you interview a national park superintendent, we need to be able to easily call and confirm that person is still there. If not, we can easily edit the story to bring it up-to-date, saving us all embarrassment.

Think Art—We almost always run photos or artwork to illustrate stories. While you may not be a photographer, we encourage your suggestions as to what images would enhance your story or how to contact subjects regarding photos. Also, consider if your story is seasonal. If an outdoor story is scheduled to run next summer, we need to shoot images this summer. Shooting gardens in the winter doesn't work too well. If your story is a timely event, it is best to do the photography at that time. Let us know in advance so we can arrange for a photographer to cover these events as well.

Develop Queries—We sometimes receive the "shotgun" approach to queries, where the writer gives only a sentence or two of explanation for a story idea and then moves on to the next. We usually reject all the proposals, as we get 20 ideas with no good information. Your best bet is to pick one or two strong ideas and develop these into at least a half-page pitch. If the idea isn't interesting enough to at least write this much in a query, it's probably not interesting or detailed enough for a story. Always include your contact info on each page of the query. Often, pages of queries are separated. It's hard to make assignments if we can't get in touch with you. We do not accept e-mail or fax queries.

Be Familiar with the Magazine—This isn't a ploy to sell more magazines. The best way to find out what we're after is to read *New Mexico Magazine*, know the departments, style and what we have already covered. Many libraries catalog the magazine. With any writing, know your audience.

Makin' Tracks

Makin' Tracks focuses on outdoor recreation in New Mexico's backcountry. While all fitness and experience levels should be considered and addressed, the idea is these are places you can't just drive to—you have to get out, explore and enjoy. The text is 750 words. Two quality slides are needed, at least one horizontal. Relevant information such as ranger district contacts and maps to use are required. The text pays $300; photos are paid based on our stock rates. Query with writing samples first.

Makin' Tracks Notes:

• The point of the trips should be to have fun, learn about and enjoy New Mexico's backcountry, not to prove you can power hike 30 miles in a day.

• All destinations should be completely open to the general public. List all restrictions and necessary permits, if any.

• Be very clear and honest about the physical level needed for the trip. Can you be in average shape to do the hike or should you work up to it? Is altitude a factor to consider? If you have to be an Olympian athlete to make the hike, we're probably not interested.

• Avoid lingo without explanation. Write in such a way a general audience will understand you.

• List special considerations of the trip. Is water available? Are the trails marked? Where, if anywhere, can people go for help? Is the area open to hunting at certain times of the year?

• State what makes this trip unique. No generic strolls in the woods—there should be something special about this place. Note flora, fauna, archaeological sites, anything to look out for.

• Keep in mind the health of the environment. If a section of a trail is receiving too much pressure, make people aware so they can reroute.

Many people don't willingly harm areas, they're just unaware they're doing so. We want to tell people about these great areas, but we also want to help protect them. State the rules so people can follow them.

• Know your subject. Anyone can look at a map and some U.S. Forest Service brochures and get a general feeling for what's there. Write about the details you can only experience by going there.

Así Es Nuévo Mexico (This is New Mexico)

This department is a fun mixed-bag of short stories from all over the state with a strong New Mexico angle—things you can only find here. Text should not exceed 350 words. One quality slide or illustration to accompany the story is needed. Asis pay $100 upon acceptance; the photographer or artist is paid $60 upon publication of the story and artwork. Query with writing samples first. Así's cover, but are not limited to, these categories:

• **Human interest stories**—Examples: A grandmother who has sent homemade tamales to troops overseas during the holidays for the past 40 years; an individual who is for no pay helping communities restore their churches. We're looking for New Mexicans who inspire and deserve recognition.

• **Unique artists, crafts and business people**—New Mexico has no shortage of quality artists and it's impossible to feature them all, so we look for those who stand out, either in their work or in the way they live. This could mean they have donated work to the public, use an unusual process to create their work, use a cave as a studio—anything out of the ordinary. Artwork must be publicly displayed.

• **Quirky, fun subjects**—Anything of interest the public can visit or participate in that's out of the ordinary. If you enjoyed checking it out, readers may also.

Some Así requirements:

• **General public should be able to interact with the subject of the story.** Examples: An artist's work needs to be on public display or available in a gallery; an event needs to be open to the public; unique objects and places need to be accessible to the general public and not located on restricted property. Contact and additional information should be clearly noted in the Así story.

• **Short and Sweet.** Though many Así subjects could justify a book, we just don't have the space. The objective is to pique the readers' interest with fun, active, informative writing and tell them how to pursue learning more about or interacting with the subject.

• **Make sure it's interesting.** You should be able to express in a sentence or two why this subject stands out, even if you think it's obvious. Also, if it is boring to write, it's probably boring to read.

• **Make sure it's New Mexico.** Enough said.

Categories: Regional

CONTACT: Steve Larese, Assoc. Editor/Photo Editor
Material: All
495 Old Santa Fe Trail
Santa Fe NM 87501
Phone: 505-827-7447
Fax: 505-827-6496
E-mail: Submissions@NMMagazine.com (Proposals, articles and queries)
E-mail: Photos@NMMagazine.com (Photo submissions)
Website: NMMagazine.com

New Mexico Woman

Thank you for your interest in writing for *New Mexico WOMAN* magazine. Please see our Editorial Calendar for 2007. The calendar outlines the proposed theme and industry focus for each issue in 2007.

Our primary readership is working women between the ages of 25 and 55 who are interested in reading about successful New Mexico women and women-owned businesses. The majority of our readers are professionals, and many are business owners. (Detailed readership demographics are available from our advertising department.)

The editor currently accepts queries for article ideas via FAX, e-mail or mail only. Please request an Editorial Query Form to be sent to you by e-mail or by FAX if the form is not included in this packet. Duval Publications Inc., is not responsible for unsolicited manuscripts or photographs.

The majority of our contributors are experienced, professional writers. *New Mexico WOMAN* magazine currently pays writers new to the magazine a minimum of .05 per published word, unless otherwise negotiated. While all support the mission of our magazine, each writes for different reasons. Our magazine is an excellent way to break into the freelance market, or to have a continuing voice in women's activities.

Guidelines for manuscript submission:

1. Submit an Editorial Query Form to the editor.

2. Receive acceptance for your query and suggestions for story angle from the editor.

3. Submit your article by deadline to the editor via e-mail attachment in this format:

   a. Microsoft Word .doc file-OR-.rtf file (If a Mac user, please submit .rtf)

   b. Times New Roman or similar serif font in 12-point type.

   c. Single spaced. ALSO: Please only one space after a period.

   d. Each paragraph indented (NO double space between paragraphs).

   e. Writer's name, phone number, and e-mail address attached.

4. Please follow AP style (outlined in the Associated Press Stylebook) with this exception:

   Include the serial comma before the and in a series.

   Example: cats, dogs, and horses

   NOT: cats, dogs and horses

Guidelines for photograph submission:

1. Preference: e-mail photos. Compress file attachments (.zip) or send separately. Max file size: 800K.

2. If sending prints, include SASE for return. Send copies only; we cant guarantee return of originals.

3. Label on all prints (or include in all photo filenames) the article title for easy identification.

4. Always include captions/cutlines and photo credits for all photos.

5. Best formats for photos that are e-mailed as attachments: Highres JPEGs, PDFs, or TIFs.

Categories: Business—Women's Issues

CONTACT: M.T. Hyatt, Editor
Material: All
Duval Publications, Inc
PO Box 12955
Albuquerque, NM 87195
Phone: 505-247-9195
Fax: 505-842-5129
E-mail: heygals@nmwoman.com
Website: www.nmwoman.com

New Millennium Writings

Awards & Contests

$3,000 twice annually in prizes, plus publication in NMW and on the Website, newmillenniumwritings.com Final Deadlines are Nov. 17 and June 17, (twice annually.)

$1,000 for best Story; $1,000 for best Poem; $1,000 best Nonfiction (Nonfiction includes humor, memoir, creative nonfiction, essay, interview/profile, etc.).

Winners of NMW Awards are showcased along with interviews and profiles of famous writers such as Julia Glass, George Garrett, Ken Kesey, John Updike, Lee Smith, Cormac McCarthy, Lucille Clifton, Shelby Foote, Paul West, Norman Mailer, Sharyn McCrumb, William Kennedy and tributes to writers for the ages, including Faulkner, Hemingway, Dickinson, Keats, Percy, Warren and others; also, prize-winning stories, poems & articles, plus humor, graphic arts & writing advice; 200 pages plus.

To Enter, follow these Guidelines:

1. No restrictions on style or content.

2. Winners & selected finalists published in our annual anthology, which you will receive for entering, and also on the NMW Website, at www.newmillenniumwritings.com.

3. Send any time, entries applied to next applicable deadline. 4. Simultaneous & multiple submissions welcome. 5. Each Fiction or Nonfiction piece is counted as a separate entry and should total no more than 6,000 words. 6. Each Poetry entry may include up to three poems, not to exceed five pages total. 7. Include name, phone, address, email (if applicable) & category. 8. Manuscripts not returned. Send SASE for list of winners or await your book. 9. Include $17 check payable to NMW with each submission. 10. Send to: "NMW," Room M2, PO Box 2463, Knoxville, TN, 37901.

To order our latest issue, send $12; to sample a back-issue only, send $10.

Categories: Fiction—Nonfiction—Arts—College—Comedy—Education—Environment—Experimental Fiction—Literature—New Age—Poetry—Public Speaking—Sexuality—Short Stories—Spiritual—Women's Fiction—Writing—Trade - Writing/Publishing

CONTACT: Dan Williams, Editor
Material: All
NMW Contest Room 101, P. O. Box 2463
Knoxville TN 37901
Phone: 423-428-0389

New Moon
The Magazine for Girls and Their Dreams

Objectives of *New Moon*:

New Moon portrays girls and women as powerful, active and in charge of their own lives—not as passive beings who are acted upon by others. *New Moon* celebrates girls and their accomplishments. *New Moon* supports girls' efforts to hold onto their voices, strengths and dreams as they move from being girls to becoming women. *New Moon* is a tool for a girl to use as she builds resilience and resistance to our sexist society, moving confidently out into the world, pursuing her unique path in life.

***New Moon* strives to:**

• be an international, multicultural magazine which connects girls and celebrates diversity by providing a place for girls to express themselves and communicate with other girls around the world.

• portray strong female role models of all ages, backgrounds, and cultures now and in the past.

• encourage pursuit of interests in which girls are often discouraged, e.g. math, science, and physical activity.

• acknowledge the difficulties and celebrate the joys of being female in the world.

• understand that respecting girls, attending to their needs and giving them voice and power means upsetting the fabric of society.

Therefore, we seek high-quality literary and artistic work which has a diversity of cultural and stylistic influences, and represents real connection with girls.

General Guidelines:

All material should be pro-girl and focus on girls, women, or

female issues. *New Moon* was created by girls and women for girls who want their voices heard and their dreams taken seriously. It is edited by and for girls ages 8-14. *New Moon* takes girls very seriously; the publication is structured to give girls real power. The final product is a collaboration of girls and adults. An editorial board of girls aged 8-14 makes final decisions on all material appearing in the magazine.

Submissions:

Please read a copy of *New Moon* to understand the style and philosophy of the magazine. Writers and artists who comprehend our goals and philosophy have the best chance of publication.

Include your name, address and phone number on the title page of each submitted work or query.

New Moon is not able to acknowledge or return unsolicited manuscripts. Please do not send originals.

New Moon prints original works, except under special circumstances. If your work has been published previously, note the date and publication. If you are sending this work simultaneously to another publication, please let us know this, too.

For Writers:

New Moon edits manuscripts for style, length, clarity and philosophical considerations.

We prefer e-mail submissions. All other work must be typed, double spaced with one-inch margins. Your name and address should appear on each page.

Submit only copies of your work, not originals. We do not acknowledge or return unsolicited submissions.

Non-fiction articles are between 300 and 1,200 words. Non-fiction profiles of women are preferred. Feel free to send us ideas of girls to profile, but we will ask the girl herself to write the article. Non-fiction has better chance for publication when it focuses on one of our editorial themes. We regularly publish adult non-fiction in our Herstory and Women's Work sections.

New Moon publishes about three adult-written, short fiction pieces (1,200-1,600 words) annually.

Please keep the original of your work for your own files. Submissions from girls and women only, please.

For Artists:

New Moon has a four-color cover and four-color interior.

For cover guidelines, send us a SASE or go to www. newmoon.org. Proposals for covers should be sent as drafts, and include examples of earlier, finished artwork. Several drafts may be required in the multi-step process by which the Girls Editorial Board chooses a cover. Cover art submissions from girls and women only, please.

To be considered for editorial illustration work, please send samples to the address below. Samples will not be returned. New Moon Publishing, Inc. is not responsible for unsolicited material.

Categories: Fiction—Nonfiction—Children—Education—Feminism—Juvenile—Multicultural—Teen—Writing—Young Adult

CONTACT: Editorial Department
Material: All
2 W First St #101
Duluth MN 55802
Fax: 218-728-0314
E-mail: girl@newmoon.org
Website: www.newmoon.org

the new renaissance

At *the new renaissance* (**tnr**), we're looking for writing that has something to say, says it with style and grace, and, above all, speaks in a personal voice.

FICTION: Contemporary, literary, off-beat, translations, humor, satire, prose/poems and, occasionally, experimental fiction. We don't want to see popular or slick writing, overly academic or sentimental fiction, or strictly commercial pieces. No pornography. One story per submission unless stories are four pages or less, then two stories are allowed.

We are interested in fiction that offers a revelation or illumination on the human condition. Although we stress substance, style is important, and we pay close attention to diction, phrasing, and personal vision.

Approximations in language are not good enough. Since we accept only one ms out of every 125 submissions, we ask writers to read tnr closely and to send in stories that are at least as good, however different, as those we've been publishing. Mss. can be two to 36 pps. although we will occasionally accept a longer work. We are interested in translations (send originals). Allow 4-5 months for a decision.

POETRY: Contemporary, lyrical, narrative, humorous and satirical poems. No pornography or obscenity. Eroticism will be considered. We are especially interested in poetic imagery ground in experience, but accept all styles

Mss. of 3-6 one-page poems or 2-4 two-page poems are preferred,; we occasionally publish the long poem, but only one long poem per submission. We are especially interested in translations (send originals). Allow 3-4 months for a decision.

FICTION/NON-FICTION ONLY SUBMITTING PERIODS: [1997] January through May; and September and October.

HOW TO SUBMIT: All fiction and poetry submissions are tied to our award programs: The Louise E. Reynolds Memorial Fiction Award and the **tnr** Poetry Award. These awards have been established in order to honor **tnr**'s Founding Manager, Louise E. Reynolds, "to reward **tnr**'s writers," and to promote quality writing. Only writers published in a three-issue volume are eligible. Entry fee required.

Independent judges determine winners. All published writers will receive our regular, nominal rates of payment as well as a copy of the issue containing their work. There are three awards in each category: Fiction: $500.00, $250.00, and $125.00. Honorable Mention $50.00. Poetry: $250.00, $125.00, and $50.00, with three to four honorable mentions for poetry ($20.00 each).

Current subscribers: Send ms. with SASE or IRC, and $11.50 entry fee ($13.50 foreign). Each discipline and each submission requires an entry fee. You may extend your subscription or receive two back issues or a recent issue.

All others: Send ms. with SASE or IRC, and $16.50 entry fee ($18.00 foreign). You will receive two back issues or a recent issue. Each discipline and each submission requires an entry fee.

Categories: Fiction—Nonfiction—Culture—Film/Video—General Interest—Interview—Literature—Multicultural—Music—Poetry—Politics—Short Stories

CONTACT: Louise T. Reynolds, Editor-in-Chief
Material: All
26 Heath Rd. Ste. 11
Arlington MA 02474-3645
Website: www.tnrlitmag.net

▊ NEW TIMES

The New Times

We welcome your interest in contributing to *The New Times*, your monthly resource for authentic living. Our purpose is to provide inspiration and resources for wellness, personal growth, and spirituality and to empower positive choices for the natural and social environments, and we look for articles, interviews, news items, and art that support that purpose.

The New Times is distributed free to over 50,000 readers at 500 locations throughout the Pacific Northwest, and there are paid subscribers throughout the United States and Canada.

Please read and follow these guidelines before submitting your article.

CONTENT

Besides the quality of the writing, acceptance or rejection of an article submitted to *The New Times* is essentially based on the answers to four questions:

Will it benefit readers? Will the article provide our readers with new, unique, or relevant insights or information that will be useful to them regardless of whether they follow up by buying a book or CD, attending a workshop, etc.?

Does it stand alone? Will readers benefit from the material whether or not this is the only article by you or on your topic they ever read?

Is it original? We do not accept articles excerpted from published works or ones previously published in or simultaneously submitted to other publications.

Is it consistent with our purpose? Will the article encourage readers to be more spiritually aware, happy, and healthy, and to actively carry these values into the world?

We do not base our decisions on whether or not advertising is being placed, whether we like or dislike the author or whether she or he is famous, or whether we agree with the material.

We accept articles that analyze or disagree with issues, but do not print ones that attack, demean, or negate other people, organizations, philosophies, or systems. Unless the topic being discussed is gender-specific, articles must be written in gender-inclusive language. We do not print press releases or any other strictly promotional material.

APPEAL TO OUR READERS

Our readers have told us that they are looking for practical, grounded, and succinct editorial content; they look to us for useful, "how-to" information and inspiration they can apply to their own lives. Here are just a few examples of the types of articles we're looking for:

• Memoirs that follow the author from a vividly and artfully described concrete experience to a breakthrough or some other deeply significant—preferably life-changing—and universally appreciable insight.

• Pieces designed to awaken awareness of what Thomas Moore and others would call "the soulful approach to living," inspiring one to look at small details of life anew; fresh contemplations of "ordinary" daily tasks and personal exchanges.

• Articles that deal with difficult-to-talk-about or controversial subjects. You should be well versed in the subject and acknowledge and respectfully address at least one other side of the question.

• Pieces that give readers fresh, practical ways to renew their experience of relationships and communication.

• Articles on parenting targeted toward guiding the smallest among us to understanding, even as we seek to better understand our world and ourselves.

• Short, inspiring, hands-on pieces with one clear spiritual theme. Examples include pieces that inspire and uplift readers' experience of work as well as thoughtful pieces on aging and the elderly, beauty, health, and longevity, especially focusing on how spiritual disciplines support these, with compelling examples from ancient times to the present.

TAKE RESPONSIBILITY

Speak in "I" or "you," not "we," statements. Our readers are anxious to learn about—and from—your experiences, feelings, and thoughts, but are put off by generalizations like "When we experience such-and-such, we feel so-and-so."

We do not accept submissions consisting solely of channeled material.

All quotations must be accompanied by a cited source. Partial quotations, as a single word or phrase, must be treated according to the context in which they originated, and entire quotes (at least entire sentences) are preferable in every case.

WORD COUNT

The quality of the writing determines the maximum length we will accept: the longer the submission, the more stringent the acceptance criteria. We will consider outstanding articles of up to 1800 words if they need very little editing; otherwise, the absolute maximum word count is 1500 (and the recommended maximum 1200). Articles of fewer than 1200 words are adjudicated equally.

HOW TO SUBMIT

Always include a cover letter with your article submission. It should contain your name, address, and telephone number, a brief statement of how you feel your article supports our purpose, and your assurance that the article has not been and will not be submitted elsewhere unless we do not accept it.

Whenever possible, send your article as an e-mail attachment (doc, rtf, or wpd) to: editor@newtimes.org, using "article submission" as the subject line. We will send you a form letter indicating either that a) we successfully opened your attachment, b) we were unable to open it, or c) your article was in the body of your e-mail rather than in an attachment and therefore not eligible for review. If you don't receive one of these letters within a week, it means that we didn't get your message and that you should try again.

If you cannot e-mail your submission, we prefer it on disk, but ask that you enclose a hard copy of your article in case we are unable to open the electronic version. If you cannot supply a disk, make sure your paper copy is double-spaced and free of markings, and use a sans-serif font (such as Arial) 11 points in size or larger.

ADD GRAPHIC INTEREST

We encourage writers to send photos or relevant art with their articles. Your submission has a better chance of being considered for a feature position (front page or lead article in our "In Harmony" or "Education" section) if you provide a compelling and pertinent image to accompany it. We are especially interested in photos and illustrations that relate to the theme of the article, but are always happy to have a head shot of the author, too. Graphics can be e-mailed with your submission; if you mail them, they must be 8.5 by 14 inches or smaller, black and white or high-contrast color (no photocopies, please). We'll return your photo with the notification of your article's acceptance status.

We are also always looking for distinctive art and photos to use on our front page, and make every effort to correlate cover art and cover story. While we cannot pay for images selected, we will be happy to publish up to 150 words on the contributor and the work. Contact us for information on how to have your work considered.

DEADLINES, ACCEPTANCE, AND TIMING

Articles are generally due the last Friday of each month (see calendar for specific dates), and acceptance/rejection letters are sent out within a few days of the deadline. Articles received after one deadline will be held for the following one.

If you submit by mail, include a stamped, self-addressed envelope for notification of your article's acceptance status; if you submit by e-mail, you will be notified by return e-mail. These notifications usually go out within a week after the article deadline.

Because we routinely receive more material than we can print each month, we are not able to promise any particular publication date for articles accepted. Once an article is accepted for publication, we publish it in the timeliest manner possible, but articles are generally held over for several months before they appear in print.

EDITING

We edit every submission for punctuation, spelling, grammar, clarity, and compliance with our conventions. If substantial editing is required, we will either reject the article or return it with some suggestion as to what is needed.

Attention-grabbing headlines that convey the article's content are a must; we reserve the right to re-title accepted submissions as needed.

CHANGES

Any changes to an article must be made in writing prior to the deadline date. If changes are made after that date, we will hold the article until the next deadline.

PHONE CALLS

We do not discuss articles over the phone. If you have not heard back from us regarding your article, drop us a postcard or e-mail.

MULTIPLE SUBMISSIONS

Space restrictions preclude us from running more than one article by any one writer at a time. Do not submit again until one accepted article has been published.

COMPENSATION

You receive a free one-year subscription upon acceptance of your article (up to a maximum of three years from the one most recently accepted). We do not pay for articles, nor do we exchange advertising for them. At the end of the article, you may, if you wish, include a short (up to sixty-word) statement of who you are and how people can reach you.

RIGHTS

The New Times retains the rights to all articles published within its pages. There is an exception: we will consider excerpts from unpublished manuscripts. If we accept yours, we will return rights to you once we have published it, provided that you 1) specifically state that you are submitting an excerpt from a book scheduled for publication and are granting us first North American serial rights and 2) let us know when the book is due to be published.

If you would like to have your article reprinted elsewhere, contact us first for the wording of the short statement of acknowledgment to add at the end. If others request reprint rights from us, we will not grant them without first obtaining your permission and any revised closing paragraph about yourself you may wish to provide.

We reserve the right to publish your article as a reprint in response to readers' requests. Some articles also appear in *The New Times*' Internet edition. We assume that we have your permission to use accepted material on our Web site unless you specifically let us know when you submit that we do not.

Please note: While we have made our writers' guidelines as comprehensive as possible, we reserve the right to accept or reject submissions for any reason we deem appropriate.

Categories: Nonfiction—Diet/Nutrition—Ecology—Environment—Feminism—Gay/Lesbian—Health—Inspirational—Interview—Lifestyle—Men's Issues—Native American—New Age—Paranormal—Religion—Spiritual—Women's Issues

CONTACT: Charles Alkire, Editor
Material: All
PO Box 51186
Seattle WA 98115
Phone: 206-320-7788
Fax: 206-320-7717
E-mail: editor@newtimes.org
Website: www.newtimes.org

New Witch

Please refer to *SageWoman* magazine.

New York Runner

NEW YORK RUNNER is the official quarterly magazine of NYRR. The magazine is written by runners, for runners, with the strong belief that running is great exercise, great fun, and a good, healthy thing to do.

Consequently, we consider it our job to keep the magazine a perpetual source of interest and joy by:

1. Addressing current and topical issues in the sport

2. Reporting the interesting happenings at recent and upcoming NYRR events

3. Finding insights and information related to the sport that are useful, relevant, and entertaining

4. Finding ways for you to keep your running interesting and finding ways for you to use your running and fitness to keep your life interesting

5. Providing training, nutrition, and injury information that will keep you feeling and running your best

Categories: Nonfiction—Diet/Nutrition—Lifestyle—Recreation—Sports/Recreation

CONTACT: Gordon Bakoulis, Editor
Material: All
New York Road Runners
9 East 89th St
New York NY 10128
Phone: 212-423-2260

New York Spirit

All Submissions should be sent in this format:

Please include a one paragraph synopsis of the article, the article itself, contact information, and any other information you might like us to know about you.

Mail, E-mail or Fax to the attention of our editor. We are not able to make use of or return unsolicited manuscripts.

Categories: Nonfiction—Astrology—Metaphysical—New Age

CONTACT: New York Spirit
107 Sterling Pl
Brooklyn, NY 11217

New York Stories

Guidelines for Submission

New York Stories is seeking short fiction and non-fiction.

Stories should have strong characters, fresh voices and distinctive angles of vision. We are open to the best work we can find from around the world. The stories do not need to be set in New York, but we do welcome stories that explore the city's diversity. Stories above 5,000 words have less chance due to space constraints. We publish six to eight an issue.

Non-fiction pieces should focus on life in New York City—the magic moment, history unlayered, the familiar, the off-beat, the marginal illuminated. We've published pieces as diverse as a profile of Ludlow Street and an account of a job in a bagel factory. At least one appears in each issue.

We publish interviews with major literary figures or film directors: E.L. Doctorow, Grace Paley, James Gray. Query us on these.

Competition is intense. We pay for your work on publication at rates competitive with major literary magazines.

Please include a cover letter listing prior publications or relevant background and an SASE. No need to provide a synopsis of your story or reasons why we should publish it: the work will speak for itself. Multiple submissions okay.

We are keen to discover new talent and have published first-time stories as well as the John Updikes of the literary universe. We generally respond within two months. Stories that excite interest among our editors are, alas, occasionally held longer. We publish three times a year: March, June and November. Sample copies available at $5.95.

Categories: Interview—Literature—Regional—Short Stories

CONTACT: Daniel Caplice Lynch, Editor in Chief
Material: Manuscripts
English Dept. E-103, LaGuardia College
31-10 Thomson Avenue
Long Island NY 11101
Phone: 718 482-5673
E-mail: NYSTORIES@lagcc.cuny.edu
Website: www.newyorkstories.org

The New Yorker

Submissions should be sent by e-mail to the appropriate department, as indicated below. We cannot accept submissions that are sent as attachments, so please send your work as part of the body of an e-mail. No more than one story or six poems should be submitted at one time. We prefer to receive no more than two submissions per writer per year, and generally cannot reply to more.

The New Yorker does not accept unsolicited submissions by mail or by fax, and we cannot be responsible for the loss or return of unsolicited pieces. We do not consider simultaneous submissions or material that has been previously published. We try to respond to all submissions, but, due to volume, we may take up to eight weeks to respond.

Categories: Fiction—Antiques—Arts—Book Reviews—Cartoons—Culture—Entertainment—Film/Video—Food/Drink—Music—Poetry—Politics—Theatre—Travel

CONTACT: fiction@newyorker.com
Material: Fiction Submissions
CONTACT: talkofthetown@newyorker.com
Material: The Talk of the Town Submissions
CONTACT: shouts@newyorker.com
Material: Shouts & Murmurs Submissions
CONTACT: poetry@newyorker.com
Material: Poetry Submissions
The New Yorker, Inc., 4 Times Square
New York NY 100326-6592
Website: www.newyorker.com

Newsweek

My Turn Column

Submissions for *My Turn* columns must be original, unpublished essays, approximately 850 and 900 words. If your piece is a time sensitive subject, it's probably not appropriate for the column.

Please, do not submit any photographs, but be sure to include your full name, address and phone number.

Responses take 8-10 weeks. We receive about 500 essays a month. It takes time to read them and make decisions. We will send you a letter, if your piece is not accepted.

All submissions should be emailed to: myturn@ newsweek.com.

Do not send your essay as an attachment. The article *must* be included as text within the email.

Categories: Nonfiction—Current Affairs—Politics—News—Opinion

CONTACT: Submissions Editor
Material: All
Phone: 212-445-4000
E-mail: myturn@newsweek.com

Nimrod
International Journal of Prose and Poetry
(University of Tulsa)

Subject: High-quality, literary poetry, prose and short essays. Two issues annually. Spring issue: thematic, theme announced preceding fall. Previous themes have included Writers of Age, Range of Light: The Americas, Australia, From Time to Time, The City, and Islands. Nimrod has also devoted numerous issues to emerging writers from many countries.

What Nimrod Seeks:

Vigorous, fresh writing; characters should be well-developed and believable. Dialogue should be realistic without being banal. Poetry open to all styles and subjects. We seek poems that go beyond one word or image, honoe the impulse to reveal a truth about, or persuasive version of, the inner and outer worlds. Reading a sample issue before submitting a manuscript is recommended.

Over-the-Transom Submissions

Accepted all year. Send SASE for notification and/or return of manuscript. Turn-around time for over-the-transom submissions is one to three months. Nimrod does not accept e-mail transmission unless the writer lives overseas and has unreliable mail service. Send SASE for guidelines, upcoming themes and contest guidelines.

Manuscript Format:

Fiction: double spaced, 1" margins on all sides, word processed, one side of plain white paper only. Poetry: word processed.

Payment:

Always pays with two contributors' copies.

Annual Contest:

Annual contest begins January 1 and ends April 30 of each year. $2,000 first prize; $1,000 second prize in poetry and fiction. Send SASE for contest guidelines.

Categories: Fiction—Nonfiction—Arts—Culture—Poetry—Writing

CONTACT: Francine Ringold, Editor-in-Chief
Material: Poetry, Fiction, Essays
The University of Tulsa, 600 S. College
Tulsa OK 74104-3189
Phone: 918-631-3080
Fax: 918-631-3033
E-mail: nimrod@utulsa.edu
Website: www.utulsa.edu/nimrod

Nine
A Journal of Baseball History and Culture

NINE studies all historical aspects of baseball, centering on the societal and cultural implications of the game wherever in the world it is played. The journal features articles, essays, book reviews, biographies, oral history, and short fiction pieces.

NINE is available electronically through Project MUSE.

Subscription Information
Semiannual
ISSN 1188-9330
Individuals $50.00
Institutions $60.00
Single issue $25.00

For foreign subscriptions please add $15.00. Payment must accompany order. Make checks payable to University of Nebraska Press and mail to:

University of Nebraska Press
233 N 8th St
Lincoln, NE 68588-0255
or call: 1-800-755-1105 U.S. Orders and customer service.

Submission Information

NINE will seek to promote the study of all historical aspects of baseball and will center on the cultural implications of the game wherever in the world baseball is played. The journal will reflect an eclectic approach and will not foster a particular ideological bias. *NINE* accepts submissions that meet the following requirements:

- between 2,000-5,000 words
- submit 3 copies
- prepare according to *Chicago Manual of Style*, 14th edition
- include a short personal bio (no more than three sentences)
- footnotes and author date systems are not acceptable
- simultaneous submissions are not accepted
- accepted works must supply manuscripts in both paper and electronic form (RTF, Microsoft Word or Word Perfect)
- all figures and tables must be submitted in camera-ready format and will be printed as is
- book reviews are by invitation only

Authors will be asked to sign a declaration that the submitted work is not being considered for publication elsewhere. No major revisions will be allowed after acceptance. The editor will attempt to have all manuscripts reviewed by two umpires and will respond to the authors within three months of receiving the manuscript.

Submissions can be e-mailed to bkirwin@ualberta.ca or snail mailed.

Categories: Fiction—Nonfiction—Biography—Book Reviews—Culture—History—Short Stories—Society—Sports/Recreation

CONTACT: Bill Kirwin, Editor
Material: All
The University of Calgary in Edmonton
Faculty of Social Work
#444, 11044-82 Ave
Edmonton, Alberta
Canada T6G 0T2
E-mail: bkirwin@ualberta.ca
Website: www.nebraskapress.unl.edu
or **www.ninejournalofbaseball.com**

Nineteenth-Century French Studies

Nineteenth-Century French Studies provides scholars and students with the opportunity to examine new trends, review promising research findings, and become better acquainted with professional developments in the field. Scholarly articles on all aspects of nineteenth-century French literature and related fields are invited. Published articles are peer-reviewed to insure scholarly integrity. The journal has an extensive book review section covering a variety of disciplines.

Nineteenth-Century French Studies is published twice a year in two double issues, fall/winter and spring/summer.

Beginning with volume 29, *Nineteenth-Century French Studies* can be consulted on-line, by subscription, through Project MUSE of the Johns Hopkins University Press.

Subscription Information
Semiannual
ISSN 0146-7891
Individuals $45.00
Institutions $60.00
Single issue $18.00

For foreign subscriptions please add $15.00. Payment must accompany order. Make checks payable to University of Nebraska Press and mail to:

University of Nebraska Press
233 N 8th St
Lincoln, NE 68588-0255
or call: 1-800-755-1105 U.S. Orders and customer service.

1-800-526-2617 U.S. Fax orders and customer service.

1-402-472-3584 Foreign orders and customer service.

1-402-472-6214 Main fax line.

Telephone and fax orders must be prepaid.

Submission Information

Nineteenth-Century French Studies accepts submissions that meet the following requirements:

• should not exceed 5,000 words (20 pages, 25 lines per page, double-spacing, and ample margins), including endnotes

• submit 3 copies

• footnotes are not acceptable

• original typescript, plus an electronic copy in Word, will be requested for accepted works

• abstracts will be requested for accepted works

• book reviews need only be submitted in a single copy

• suggested length for book reviews is between two and three type-written pages (double-spaced) and without endnotes

Anonymous submission

NCFS subscribes to the policy of anonymous or "blind" submissions. Readers will not know the identity of the authors whose articles they are asked to evaluate. Authors must therefore omit references that would allow them to be identified. They should include a separate, unnumbered page giving the essay's title along with their name, postal and e-mail addresses, and telephone and fax numbers. The first page of the manuscript paper should be numbered and the title repeated one inch from the top of the page (in capitals). Articles not retained for publication will be destroyed.

For further information contact:

Professor Marshall Olds, Editor

molds2@unl.edu

Categories: Nonfiction—Biography—Culture—Literature—Poetry—Theatre—French studies

CONTACT: Editors
Material: Submissions in English or French
PO Box 880319
University of Nebraska-Lincoln
Lincoln NE 68588-0319
E-mail: molds2@unl.edu
Website: www.nebraskapress.unl.edu/journals.html
***or* www.unl.edu/ncfs/**

North Dakota Horizons

North Dakota Horizons is a quarterly, non-profit magazine with circulation in all 50 states and several foreign countries. The mission of *Horizons* is to discover and showcase North Dakota's resources and people. The magazine promotes North Dakota's many virtues: a clean environment, open spaces, friendly and creative people, and interesting things to see and do. Stories that encourage people to travel to state places and events are of prime importance.

Unsolicited contributions are welcome; however, written or e-mail inquiries are preferred. *Horizons* seeks short, nonfiction stories (1,000 to 1,500 words) and major in-depth feature articles (1,500 to 3,000 words). Whenever possible, manuscripts should be accompanied with illustrations, black and white photographs, color slides or color prints. *Horizons* strives to be a visual publication. Sketches, maps, artwork or illustrations available and appropriate should be submitted for ideas.

When submitting written material, please double space the manuscript. Work may be submitted on Macintosh or PC compatible discs, zip disks or 3½ inch diskettes. On the disk cover, please indicate your word processing software. Your name, address and telephone number

should be clearly marked. Identifications for illustrations and photos should be clearly marked and as complete as possible. Stories may also be submitted by e-mail to lyle_halvorson@gnda.com.

Horizons reserves the right to edit all material submitted. We cannot provide proofs to authors or photographers before publication. If you wish your material returned, please provide a self-addressed, stamped envelope of appropriate size. We are not liable for unsolicited materials sent to us. We cannot guarantee against loss or damage to any materials while in our possession, but we make every effort to handle the material carefully.

Short articles and essays average $50 to $150. Feature length articles average $150 to $300 depending on subject matter, timeliness and available illustrations.

Horizons also encourages the submission of photographs that relate to life in North Dakota, which may include people, places and events. Payment for a front cover photo ranges up to $150 and up to $50 for a back cover photo. Generally, photo rates are based on a one-time use. Photographs and original artwork are returned by mail to the photographer or illustrator after publication unless other arrangements are made with the editor in advance.

Horizons requires writers and photographers to sign an agreement specifying agreed upon compensation as well as deadlines. Payment will be made after publication unless other arrangements are negotiated with the editor in advance.

Categories: Nonfiction—Consumer—Culture—Regional—Rural America—Society—Travel

CONTACT: Lyle Halvorson, Editor
Material: All
PO Box 2639
Bismarck ND 58502
Phone: 701-222-0929
Fax: 701-222-1611
E-mail: lyle_halvorson@gnda.com
Website: www.ndhorizons.com

Northwest Baby & Child

Thank you for your interest in writing for *Northwest Baby & Child.* Our 20-page newspaper is published monthly by Baby Diaper Service. Our newspaper is also published online at nwbaby.com.

Our goal is to inform, entertain, inspire, and reassure expectant parents and parents of young children. We believe raising children is life's most challenging and satisfying work. All *Northwest Baby & Child* staff members are parents, who like helping families get off to a good start. Our editorial emphasis reflects these beliefs: There is no one right way to raise a child.

• Parents are the experts on their own children.

• If you don't know your options you don't have any.

Familiarize yourself with our publication. We have a theme for each issue (e.g. celebrating mothers, birth and postpartum, family vacations, holidays); articles throughout the paper reflect our theme.

We accept manuscripts for these topics: monthly themes, parenting, health and safety, and family activities. We assign reviews of books, cassettes, CDs, software, and videotapes. When sending a query by mail or email (editor@nwbaby.com), please include the article you wish us to consider. We do not accept attached files via email, so simply embed your manuscript in the text of an email query. If you wish to send a hard copy of an emailed article, you may fax it to us at 425-228-2503. Articles are usually 200-500 words. Articles for Page One are usually 1000-1500 words. Please double-space your manuscript, and put your name, address, email address, and phone number on the first page. If you are a BDS customer, please include your account number. You may wish to include a one- or two-sentence biographical sketch at the end of your submission.

We try to use an article within three months of receiving it. Submission of an article grants us the right to edit the work for publication and to convert it into digitized form for a one-time placement on our website (nwbaby.com), unless you specify in writing that your work is not to be used on the website. Upon publication, rights revert to the author, and you are free to sell it as a reprint. We respectfully ask you not to resell articles to parenting publications in the greater Puget Sound region of Washington State.

We also accept poetry and photographs. We often print color photos; however black and white photos reproduce better. We sometimes sacrifice the reproduction quality for the emotional quality of a picture. Photos must be at least 3" by 5" to clearly show the subject. Photos can be sent via email as well, in TIFF or PDF formats. No JPEGs, please.

Submit all queries, manuscripts, and photos to the editor at address below.

Contributors are compensated with certificates from Baby Diaper Service or we compensate monetarily if the writer is not in need of diaper service. A 500-word article usually pays $40 either in certificate form or check; shorter articles—$20, poetry and photos—$10 each. Payment is upon publication.

Thank you again for your interest in *Northwest Baby & Child*.

Categories: Nonfiction—Babies—Children—Family—Health—Parenting—Regional: Northwest

CONTACT: Betty Freeman, Editor
Material: All
4395 Rollinghill Rd
Clinton WA 98236
Phone: 360-341-1076
E-mail: editor@nwbaby.com
Website: www.nwbaby.com

Northwest Family News

Northwest Family News strives to provide its readers with informative, educational, entertaining and locally-focused articles which emphasize positive parenting. Our readership is largely comprised of educated parents, ages 25-45, with an upper-level income. The editorial emphasis is uplifting, positive and practical, focusing on the importance and pleasures of family life.

Our publication is tabloid-sized on newsprint with a circulation of 50,000. We are distributed at 1,200 locations from Seattle/Tacoma through the Puget Sound region to the Canadian border.

SPECIFICATIONS

Submitted articles via email to nwfamilysubmissions@earthlink.net as plain text in the body of the email. Submissions should include the authors name, address, phone number, email address for reply and word count. If you don't have email access, we request submissions be submitted on a Macintosh Compatible disk in Microsoft Word or plain text. Query via email or phone is appreciated, but not necessary for email or electronic submissions.

Submissions may also be on letter quality paper, typed (upper/lower case), double spaced, one side only, on 8-1/2 x 11 white paper with word count noted. Please query before submitting paper copy. We usually don't have time to consider unsolicited paper submissions. The first page should include the writer's name, address, phone number, email address (if applicable) and article word count. Subsequent pages should include the writer's name and page numbers.

Photos to accompany the article are encouraged and may be submitted for us to scan or as digital images. File size of digital images should be no smaller than 350Kb. Please indicate whether photos are available to accompany the article in your email or in your written or electronic submission. Photos submitted to us can be returned at your request at our expense if used in an issue. Unsolicited photos will not be returned unless sent with a stamped, self-addressed envelope or mailer.

Please advise as to whether you're offering electronic rights for our website at www.nwfamily.com.

Local content and local writers are given priority. Human interest stories of local families dealing successfully with challenges such as natural disasters, health or education.

We accept both previously unpublished articles and reprints (our standard rate is $25-40). Payment is made within 30 days after an article has been published. Reimbursement for photos is in addition to the rate for articles and reports and is based on the size of the image used. A tear sheet will be mailed to the writer along with a check. Please note, we do not use much poetry, even as filler. However, poetry by children will be considered if a query is sent.

Categories: Book Reviews—Children—Family—Juvenile—Parenting—Recreation—Teen—Travel

CONTACT: Rick Adair, Features Editor
Material: All
16 West Harrison St., Ste. 204
Seattle, WA 98119
Phone: 206-281-8015, 800-494-3025
E-mail: nwfamilysubmissions@earthlink.net
Website: www.nwfamily.com

Northwest Fly Fishing

Thanks for your interest in *Northwest Fly Fishing* magazine. To receive consideration for publication you should read and follow these guidelines closely.

ABOUT THE MAGAZINE

Northwest Fly Fishing magazine is a destination specific publication to be viewed as an inspiring, collectible reference of Northwest angling destinations. The staff at *Northwest Fly Fishing* takes pride in our editorial content. Our writing is refreshing, our photography, captivating. *Northwest Fly Fishing* is issued bimonthly.

FEATURE ARTICLES

Our goal is to give an inspiring and complete report on specific Northwest angling destinations. Angling destinations include both the famous and the lesser know waters, and include all species found in our diverse geographical region. If more than one species is found in any given water, writers should cover each species, as well as every season that water is fishable. In short, feature articles should be concise, and leave no holes. Our goal is to cover specific angling destinations as no other publication has done in the past. **The best way to get a feel for what we want is to study one of our magazines.**

Photography is very important. *Northwest Fly Fishing* has set high standards for all images used in our magazine. Writers have a much better chance of being published if articles are accompanied by stunning photography. We will not publish dead fish, poorly exposed or composed shots.

The area of coverage for our features includes Washington, Oregon, Northern California, Idaho, Montana, Wyoming, Alberta, British Columbia, Alaska, Yukon Territory, and Northwest Territories.

Feature Article Requirements

• Provide practical traveling and angling information to specific destinations, including personal anecdotes

• Included should be pertinent angling history and thorough description of the fishery

• Detailed description of angling techniques, tackle and flies, and local perspectives

• Articles should be thorough and specific so as to sufficiently inform and give the angler confidence to effectively fish the presented water

• Included with each article should be any applicable hatch chart and detailed map of the coverage area

• Conservation issues and future considerations should be addressed

• Selection of 35mm (or larger) slides (**captioned and placed at**

the end of the manuscript)

• A popular fly of the fishery should be included for us to photograph, as well as a material list for that fly

• Feature article length should be 2,500 to 3,500 words

DEPARTMENTS

Most department material is staff-written. Exceptions are as follows:

Northwest Fly Tying

This department covers one Northwest fly pattern each issue. New, unusual and exciting patterns are encouraged, but we will also represent the time-proven standards. Flies for any Northwest species can be considered. Articles should include a little history and use of the fly, as well as step-by-step photos of the tying sequence, shot against a neutral-colored background. Two finished flies should accompany the article for photographic purposes.

Notes, News & Reviews

This department covers news events, and mini destinations (200 to 500 words). As with all material submitted, query first.

Conservation

Any conservation issue concerning the Pacific Northwest. Maximum length 750 words.

Exposure

Photo essay of 12 images depicting Northwest angling.

Digital Image Submission Guidelines
Feature Articles/Exposure

1) We only accept files from digital SLR cameras with a minimum of 6-megapixels, 8-megapixel or higher are preferred! **Note:** A 35-megabyte file is needed for full page offset printing.

2) When making a submission please include 2 images per image file, the unedited RAW file and a processed JPEG.

3) Include a color contact sheet with file names of your images.

4) If the RAW file or contact sheet is not included, the submission will automatically be rejected.

5) Please do not submit images that are out of focus or overexposed.

Departments

1) Image files must be a minimum of 5-megabytes (11-megabyte files are preferred).

2) Files submitted for use in our departments may be sent in RAW, TIFF or JPEG format. If submitting files in JPEG, please use the maximum quality when saving images from your camera.

3) Please do not submit images that are out of focus or overexposed.

MANUSCRIPT SUBMISSIONS AND PAYMENTS

Initial contact with the editor by e-mail is preferred. A formal query letter, outlining the proposed article, should be sent to the editor before making a submission. A selection of slides **MUST** accompany the formal query. Unsolicited manuscripts must include a self-addressed, stamped envelope (S.A.S.E.) for their return. *Northwest Fly Fishing* is not responsible for submissions in transit to and from our editorial office.

Text and photos are purchased as a package. Manuscripts accepted without the appropriate photographic support will warrant less money for their use. *Northwest Fly Fishing* buys first North American serial publication rights. We reserve the option to edit all articles, however, we will make every effort to minimize editing to avoid changing the style or content of manuscripts.

All manuscripts should be submitted in typewritten form, double spaced. The author's name, address, phone number and manuscript word count should appear on the first page of the manuscript. A 3½" computer disk needs to be included, and your work saved in Microsoft Word. Manuscripts should also be e-mailed to the managing editor using a .doc or .rtf extension.

Payment is made approximately one month prior to publication, and the pay rate varies with the length and completeness of the submission. Inclusion of high-quality slides has a major impact in determining the pay rate for any given article. Our pay rate is as follows:

Feature Articles $400 to $600
Northwest Fly Tying $250
Notes, News & Reviews $100 to $125
Conservation $150

PHOTO SUBMISSIONS, ARTWORK AND PAYMENTS

Northwest Fly Fishing usually buys text and photos as a package. There are exceptions, however, and additional photography may be purchased on occasion. Contributors must query first.

We accept 35mm (or larger) transparencies only. Slides should be shipped in a clear sleeve, with concise captions. The photographer's name and address should appear on each slide mount. Payment varies for size used and impact. Our pay rate is as follows:

Cover $500
Exposure $600
Inside use $25 to $300
Illustrations and artwork $25 to $300

Categories: Nonfiction—Conservation—Fishing—Nature—Photography—Recreation—Sports/Recreation—Travel

CONTACT: Steve Probasco, Editor-in-Chief
Material: Queries
PO Box 708
Raymond WA 98577
Phone: 360-942-3589
E-mail: probasco@matchthehatch.com
John Shewey, Managing Editor
Material: All manuscripts/slides
PO Box 12275
Salem OR 97309
E-mail: shewey@matchthehatch.com

Northwest Palate

Our editorial mission

Founded in 1987, *Northwest Palate* is a bimonthly magazine devoted to food, wine, travel, and lifestyles in the Pacific Northwest. Our readers are well-read, well-traveled, and knowledgeable about food and wine. We strive to educate and entertain them by profiling the places, products, and people that exemplify this region's extraordinary bounty and quality of life.

Submitting a story

We rely on freelancers for the majority of our stories and departments. All wine reviews, special tastings, and book reviews are handled in-house or on assignment only. Please review these guidelines and recent issues of the magazine in order to familiarize yourself with our format and subject matter. Bear in mind that we plan our editorial calendar as much as a year in advance, and we follow the seasons closely.

Submit a written query before sending a finished piece. If you have not written for us before, please enclose samples of your writing, preferably work that has been published. Queries are accepted by mail at *Northwest Palate*, PO Box 10860, Portland, OR 97296, or email (you may call us first if you like) and will be answered within three months. Materials will be returned only if you provide a stamped, self-addressed envelope.

Departments

Our "Department" stories range from 650-1200 words. Our most frequently assigned departments include the following:

"Inns & Lodges"—Profiles of inns, lodges, resorts, hotels, and B&Bs in the Pacific Northwest. These are often accompanied by recipes from the inn's restaurant or chef.

"Wine"—Includes profiles of Northwest wineries, discussions of particular varietals, round-ups of good value wines, stories about wine and food pairing, and more.

"Artisans"—Profiles of artisans in the food and wine world, from bread-bakers to wine-label artists.

"Flavors"—Focusing on a particular cuisine, dish, or ingredient. Usually includes recipes.

"In Our Kitchen"—In which a rising or renowned Northwest chef visits our Portland kitchen and prepares a dish or demonstrates a technique. These stories include recipes.

"Excursions"—Outings in the Pacific Northwest that emphasize outdoor activities.

"Last Course" An essay or article of no more than 700 words, on any subject within our normal editorial scope. This is an opportunity to offer personal or humorous reflections, or to describe, with brevity and flair, an interesting phenomenon, person, activity, or place.

Features

Feature stories range from 2000-2500 words, and offer more in-depth treatment of the subjects mentioned above. Some of our most common topics are "destination" stories, in which the writer explores the lodgings, wineries, eateries, and other attractions of a Pacific Northwest destination.

More Specific Guidelines

For a complete set of writers' guidelines, including rates and rights, email or call us.

Categories: Nonfiction—Cooking—Entertainment—Food/Drink—Lifestyle—Regional—Travel

CONTACT: Submissions Editor
Material: All
PO Box 10860
Portland OR 97296-0860
Phone: 503-224-6039
E-mail: editorial@nwpalate.com

Northwest Regional Magazines

OUR PUBLICATIONS
Oregon Coast and *Northwest Travel* magazines
WRITERS:
We prefer a clear, crisp writing style. We publish family magazines—no four-letter words or off-color references. We do not want stories of limited interest or any that are exceedingly technical. We do not publish fiction or poetry.

Thoroughness, accuracy, and logical organization are crucial. We respond best to articles that are rich in anecdotes, quotations, and personal experiences. Be perceptive—but not flowery.

Writing must be accurate. Check and double-check spelling—especially proper names—and any numbers before submitting an article. Be wary of details that may change between writing and publication.

We cannot emphasize enough the importance of accuracy of all material submitted for publication. We subject manuscripts to a fact checking process, but it is the primary duty of the contributor to provide accurate, up-to-date information. Stories containing errors or out-of-date information may be returned, and stories that require excessive editing may receive less than the standard rate of pay.

Include current addresses and phone numbers of your key sources of information and photocopies of references to aid in editing and fact checking. Brochures are helpful.

Brief information, if applicable, should include how to get to a featured destination, places of interest nearby, opening and closing times of attractions, whether they are wheelchair-accessible, when roads are open and if they are suitable for RVs, and where to obtain more information.

In general we consider any article submitted to Northwest Regional Magazines for use in any of our magazines.

We buy first North American serial rights with an understanding that the article will not be offered to a similar publication for at least six months following its appearance in one of our magazines. Similar publications include *Cascades Fast*, *Western Living*, *Sunset*, *Travelin'*, and *Beautiful B.C.*

We don't want stories written from travel brochures. Bring your story alive with quotes and anecdotes.

QUERY LETTERS

Please do not telephone us about story proposals. Send us a query letter, with clips of your work, that briefly outlines the ideas (no more than three at once) being proposed. If we like your idea, we will ask to see your story on speculation, set a story length, and give you a deadline. A go-ahead on spec does not constitute an assignment or guarantee publication.

We prefer not to receive queries or manuscripts via fax.

ARTICLES SUBMITTED ON SPEC

Features, usually supported by some black-and-white or color photos, maps, or art, from 1,250 to 2,000 words (5 to 9 double-spaced typed pages): $100 to $250 total.

Features of special interest requiring special research or with heavy photo or art content, from 1,250 to 2,000 words (5 to 9 double-spaced typed pages): $200 to $350 total.

Restaurant reviews (*Oregon Coast*) should be about 1,000 words and include prices of foods mentioned and a recipe (if possible). A menu, brochure, or something with the restaurant's name or logo should accompany the review. Payment for restaurant reviews is $125, and we do not reimburse for the meal.

Do not announce you are doing a review or do anything that would obligate you to give a favorable review or create an expectation in a proprietor's mind that a story will be published. Interview a restaurant owner, resort manager, or B&B proprietor after your meal or stay or make a follow-up phone call.

ASSIGNED ARTICLES

We occasionally assign an article. Payment will be agreed upon at the time of assignment. Such assignments will be made in writing. If an assigned story is not run for any reason, a kill fee of 1/3 the agreed upon price will be made.

EDITING

We reserve the right to edit all material submitted for publication.

PAYMENT SCHEDULE

Payment is made after publication, and the amount is dependent on quality, not length. Most photos supporting submitted articles will be considered part of the editorial package.

You must return a completed W-9 form to us. Your name as shown on the form must exactly match the name on your federal income tax return. We cannot issue payment without this form.

Typical news-release items, such as chamber of commerce reports of coming events or local club news, will be accepted on a no-fee basis. We are pleased to receive such articles and will publish as many as space permits.

DEADLINES

Copy and accompanying photographs should be in our office at least four to five months prior to desired date of publication. Stand-alone color photographs should arrive at least three months prior to publication.

PHOTOGRAPHERS (COLOR SUBMISSIONS)

We prefer to work with positive transparencies 35mm to 4" x 5" but can use color negatives. It is sometimes necessary to cut negatives. If you object to this, please send duplicates.

We do not send out want lists but would be happy to review your work. Please send 20 to 40 seasonal scenic shots in mostly vertical format.

Payment for magazine cover photo, $325; for photos used in calendars (including the cover), $100; for full-page photos used inside the magazine, $75; for less than full-page $25-$55. Payment is for one-time rights, with the understanding that no pictures will be printed in any similar magazine within two months. We reserve the right to use photographs of the magazines and calendars in which your work has been published in our own promotional material. Unless we are informed otherwise, we reserve the right to use color photos in a black-and-white format to accompany editorial features.

We publish two annual four-color calendars. One calendar needs photos of the Oregon Coast and the other one needs photos of the Northwest. Submissions should be horizontal rather than vertical and be in slide or other transparency format. Any size up to 4" x 5" is acceptable. Deadline for calendars is May 15.

We prefer scenic photos for calendar and full-page use. We also have a need for humorous, unusual, or animal photos for features in both magazines.

We take every precaution with photographic submissions, but we cannot be responsible for damage in processing, loss in mailing, or normal wear. If a transparency is damaged beyond repair, we will pay up to three times our normal one-time use fee.

PLEASE NOTE: We do not sign personal delivery memos and agree only to the terms stated herein.

GENERAL INFORMATION

If your submission includes slides, negatives, or historical photos, add $1.90 (beyond the cost of postage) to cover cost of return by certified mail. We do not guarantee return of submissions unless you include return postage. Label all photographs with a number and your name and address.

Be sure to provide a complete caption and credit for each photo on a separate typed sheet. If your manuscript is on disk, include the captions on the disk also. Send slides or negatives in plastic sleeves or protectors, not loose or in plastic boxes. Check accuracy and spelling on captions. Advise us of any change in your address.

If art is needed for a story, send a photocopy. Usually color prints or slides are satisfactory.

We accept 5¼" or 3½" IBM-formatted diskettes in Word-Perfect 5.1 or ASCII text. Enclose a hard copy. Leave at least 1½" margins on all sides of copy. Your manuscript should be typed or printed using 10- or 12-point type with name, address, and phone number on the first page. Allow one character space between sentences. Don't use tabs. Use hard returns at ends of paragraphs only.

Portions of our magazines may be used on the Internet at www.northwestmagazines.com. Before any writer's or pho-tographer's work appears on the Internet, permission will be obtained. The fee will be negotiated and paid afterwards.

Oregon Coast and *Northwest Travel* magazines are published bi-monthly.

Sample copies are available for $4.50, which includes shipping and handling.

Send all mail to the address below.

OREGON COAST

Oregon Coast publishes articles of interest to residents, visitors, and anyone else who loves the coast. Some suggested topics to develop are:

- Historical items
- Beachcombing adventures
- Special happenings
- Backroads and byways
- Favorite camping and picnicking spots
- Nature and everyday science
- Popular one-day driving tours
- Community profiles
- Walking tours
- Restaurant reviews
- Profiles of notable coastal residents

NORTHWEST TRAVEL

Northwest Travel regularly covers Washington, Oregon, British Columbia, Idaho, and occasionally covers adjacent areas and Alaska.

Northwest Travel emphasizes places to visit. Some suggested topics to develop are:

- Special happenings in the Northwest
- Community profiles

- Popular one-day tours
- Profiles of notable Northwest residents
- Adventure stories
- Backroads and byways
- Restaurant features
- Weekend getaways
- Historical (prefer to have museum, park, or other present-day connection)
- Eye-catching photo (slide) and brief text (100 words) for back page (Include camera type and lens, film, and F/stop used.)
- B&Bs, country inns, or other small lodging establishments
- Photo essays
- Nature and wildlife stories (prefer to have travel connection)

The Worth a Stop department features bylined 300-500 word stories on unusual destinations that are worth a stop—$50 payment. Photos are occasionally used.

PROFILE FOR WRITERS AND PHOTOGRAPHERS

Please provide a 30- to 50-word summary of appropriate information. (Please note we reserve the right to edit.) See samples below for style.

Return of this form indicates that you have read and understood the writers and photographers guidelines.

Samples of typical profiles:
- Norman Hesseldahl is the Public Affairs Staff Officer for the Siuslaw National Forest. He and his family are regular visitors to the Oregon Coast, where they have discovered many special places.
- Melissa Livingston, a native Oregonian, has lived in France and traveled extensively throughout the United States. She returned to Oregon after living in New Jersey while attending Rutgers University. Currently she is writing a children's book.
- Karen Keltz is a nationally published poet, essayist, and freelance Writer-photographer. An English teacher at Tillamook High School, she has written a novel and accompanying writing textbook for the upper elementary grades.

Categories: Nonfiction—Outdoors—Regional—Travel

CONTACT: Submissions Editor
Material: All
4969 Hwy 101, North Ste #2
Florence OR 97439
Phone: 541-997-8401
Website: www.northwestmagazines.com

NORTHWEST REVIEW

Northwest Review
University of Oregon

NORTHWEST REVIEW is published tri-annually, and invites submissions of previously unpublished poetry, fiction, essays, interviews, book reviews and artwork. Artists are encouraged to query before sending their work. Manuscripts are considered year-round.

1. The only criterion for acceptance of material for publication is that of excellence.

2. No simultaneous submission will be considered.

3. If submitting both poetry and fiction, please send in separate envelopes.

4. There are no length restrictions.

5. The author's name and address should appear on each poem and on the cover page of each story submitted. The author's name

should appear on each page of his or her story.

6. We try to respond within ten weeks. Payment (unless grant money comes available for this purpose) is in contributor's copies. Potential contributors are encouraged to subscribe to any magazine that they admire enough to want their work to appear therein. Magazines such as *Northwest Review* depend for their survival on subscriptions.

7. We encourage you to study a recent issue of *Northwest Review*, available to authors at the discounted price of $4.00.

Subscriptions:

One year (three issues) at $22.00.

Two years (six issues) at $40.00.

Three years (nine issues) at $58.00.

Students: $20.00/year; $36.00/two years.

Foreign subscribers please add $5.00/year for handling.

Special Bonus: Subscribe for two years and receive free our 30-Year Retrospective issue, a $10.00 value.

Subscribe for three years and receive the Retrospective plus our six-color Morris Graves/Northwest Review poster, a $30.00 value.

Categories: Fiction—Arts—Literature—Poetry

CONTACT: John Witte, General Editor
Material: Essays, Artwork, Interviews, Book Reviews
CONTACT: John Witte, Poetry Editor
Material: Poetry
CONTACT: Jan MacRae, Fiction Editor
Material: Fiction
369 PLC, University of Oregon
Eugene OR 97403
Phone: 541-346-3957
Fax: 541-346-1509

Northwest Travel

Please refer to Northwest Regional Magazines.

Northwoods Journal

Please refer to The Conservatory of American Letters in the Book Publishers section.

Northwoods Press

Please refer to The Conservatory of American Letters, in the Book Publishers section.

Nostalgia
Nostalgically

Please refer to *Secondwind*.

Notre Dame Magazine

Notre Dame Magazine is published quarterly by the University of Notre Dame for more than 130,000 readers, most of whom are graduates of the university. The magazine reports on alumni activities, covers institutional events, people and trends, and examines a broad spectrum of cultural issues reflecting the university's wide-ranging discussion of science and the arts, society and its structures, the spiritual and the human. Because a large proportion of its readers are Catholic, the magazine often addresses topics of interest to a Catholic audience.

Departments: The magazine has four departments, including campus news and an alumni notes section. A third section, "Perspectives," contains three to four essays per issue. Often written in first-person, these pieces range in length from 750 to 1,500 words and deal with a wide array of issues—some topical, some personal, some serious, some light. Feature stories, typically 3,000 words or more, comprise the major part of the magazine. These, too, address a variety of issues appealing to college-educated readers who take an active interest in the contemporary world.

Submissions: Most of the magazine's editorial content is freelance-written. This is especially true of the Perspectives and Features sections. For features, the editors require a QUERY LETTER with clips of published articles. Less experienced writers may be asked to write on speculation. For Perspectives, it is appropriate to submit manuscripts. We buy first serial and electronic rights. Payment (comparable to fees paid by some national publications) is made upon acceptance. All copy is subjected to rigorous editing.

Mechanics: Generally we follow AP style. Manuscripts should be typed and double-spaced. Assigned stories also may be e-mailed to ndmag@nd.edu. The magazine's postal address is Notre Dame Magazine, 538 Grace Hall, Notre Dame, IN 46556.

Photographs and illustrations: The magazine seldom buys photos from writers. Photos and illustrations are assigned to professionals chosen by our art director.

Caveats: The editors are always looking for fresh story ideas. However, the caliber of the magazine and frequency of its publication dictate that the writing meet very high standards. The editors value articles strong in storytelling quality, journalistic technique, and substance. They do not encourage promotional or nostalgia pieces, stories on sports or essays that are sentimentally religious. Reprints are rarely used. Poetry and fiction are not accepted.

It is imperative that those interested in writing for Notre Dame Magazine actually read the magazine. You may view samples online by returning to our home page or request a sample copy by e-mailing the magazine at ndmag.1@nd.edu. A list of staff members is also online.

Categories: College

CONTACT: Submissions
Notre Dame Magazine
538 Grace Hall
Norte Dame IN 46556
E-mail: ndmag@nd.edu
Website: www.nd.edu\~ndnag

Now What? E-Zine

Please refer to the *Bible Advocate*.

Oblates

No longer accepting submissions.

Obsidian III
Literature in the African Diaspora

Obsidian III: Literature in the African Diaspora, a non-profit organization hosted by North Carolina State University, is a semiannual journal of contemporary poetry, fiction, drama, and non-fiction prose from within and concerning the African Diaspora. All bibliographies should follow the *MLA Handbook for Writers of Research Papers*. Manuscripts should be submitted in hard copy and on disk in PC compatible format. Files are preferred in Microsoft Word; otherwise, RTF.

Poetry should be single spaced. All other submissions should be double spaced. Poetry submissions are limited to five poems totaling no more than eight pages. Fiction and essays are limited to twenty pages. Playwrights should submit scenes or short plays of no more than twenty pages in the Samuel French format.

Reviews should be no more than 1500 words. All writers should include cover sheets bearing the author's name, contact information, and the contents of the submissions. All decisions of the editorial staff are final.

We do not accept simultaneous submissions or previously published works. Copyright reverts to authors upon publication. Poets and fiction writers should allow three months for a response. Scholars and critics should allow four months for a response.

Obsidian is published twice a year (Spring-Summer and Fall-Winter).

Subscription Information:

Individuals

One year: $22 (US); $25 (Outside US)

Two years: $37 (US); $40 (Outside US)

Institutions

One year: $28 (US); $30 (Outside US)

Two years: $45 (US); $48 (Outside US)

Send check or money order to:

Obsidian III

Department of English

Box 8105

North Carolina State University

Raleigh, NC 27695-8105

Categories: Fiction—Nonfiction—African-American—Book Reviews—Culture—Drama—Interview—Language—Literature—Men's Fiction—Multicultural—Poetry—Reference—Short Stories—Theatre—Women's Fiction—Writing—Ethnic

CONTACT: Submissions Editor
Material: All
North Carolina State University
Dept of English, Box 8105
Raleigh NC 27695-8105
Phone: 919-515-4153
Fax: 919-515-1836
E-mail: obsidian@social.chass.ncsu.edu
Website: www.ncsu.edu/chass/obsidian

Odyssey Magazine

General Information

ODYSSEY is interested in articles rich in scientific accuracy and lively approaches to the subject at hand. The inclusion of primary research (interviews with scientists focusing on current research) are of primary interest to the magazine. Keep in mind that this magazine is essentially written for 10- to 16-year-old children. Writers are encouraged to study recent back issues for content and style. (Sample issues are available at $4.95. Send 10" x 13" self addressed $2.00 stamped envelope.) All material must relate to the theme of a specific upcoming issue in order to be considered. *ODYSSEY* purchases all rights to material.

Procedure

A query must consist of all of the following information to be considered:

• a brief cover letter stating the subject and word length of the proposed article,

• a detailed one-page outline explaining the information to be presented in the article,

• a bibliography of sources (including interviews) the author intends to use in preparing the article,

• a self-addressed stamped envelope.

Writers new to ODYSSEY should send a writing sample with the query. If you would like to know if your query has been received, please also include a stamped postcard that requests acknowledgment of receipt. In all correspondence, please include your complete address as well as a telephone number and/or email address where you can be reached.

A writer may send as many queries for one issue as he or she wishes, but each query must have a separate outline, bibliography, and

self-addressed stamped envelope. Telephone queries are not accepted unless the material is extremely time-sensitive to a specific issue. Please type all queries.

Articles should be submitted via e-mail using a word processing program (preferably Microsoft Word-MAC). Text should be saved as ASCII text (in MS Word as "text only").

GUIDELINES

Feature Articles:

750 - 1200 words

Includes: in-depth nonfiction articles. (An interactive approach is a definite plus!) Q & A interviews, plays, and biographies are of interest, as well.

Supplemental Nonfiction:

200-500 words

Includes: subjects directly and indirectly related to the theme. Editors like little-known information but encourage writers not to overlook the obvious.

Fiction:

Up to 1,000 words

Includes: science-related stories, poems, science fiction, retold legends, etc., relating to the theme.

Department Features:

400-650 words

Includes: "Far out"; "Fantastic Journeys"; "Places, Media, People to Discover." Not a bad idea to consult back issues for direction of these departments that are also theme-related.

Activities:

Up to 750 words.

Includes: critical thinking activities, experiments, models, science fair projects, astro-photography projects, and any other science projects that can either be done by children alone, with adult supervision, or in a classroom setting. Query should be accompanied by sketches and description of how activity relates to theme. The above pays on an individual basis.

The above five pay 20 to 25 cents per printed word.

Photo Guidelines

To be considered for publication, photographs must relate to a specific theme. Writers are encouraged to submit available photos with their query or article. We buy one-time use.

Please note that fees for non-professional quality photographs are negotiated.

Cover fees are set on an individual basis for one-time use, plus promotional use. All cover images are color.

Prices set by museums, societies, stock photography houses, etc., are paid or negotiated.

Photographs that are promotional in nature (e.g., from tourist agencies, organizations, special events, etc.) are usually submitted at no charge.

If you have photographs pertaining to any upcoming theme, please contact the editor by mail or fax, or send them with your query. You may also send images on speculation.

Note

Queries may be submitted at any time, but queries sent well in advance of deadline MAY NOT BE ANSWERED FOR SEVERAL MONTHS. Go-aheads requesting material proposed in queries are usually sent four months prior to publication date.

Categories: Nonfiction—Children—Juvenile—Science—Teen

CONTACT: Elizabeth Lindstrom, Editorial Dept
Material: All
Cobblestone Publishing
30 Grove Street, Ste C
Peterborough 03458
Phone: 603-924-7209
Fax: 603-924-7380
E-mail: bethlindstrom2000@cobblestone.mv.com
Website: www.odysseymagazine.com

M-Q

Offshore
Northeast Boating at Its Best

Offshore is a monthly full-color magazine for boaters—both power and sail—in the Northeast. Our territory reaches from Maine to New Jersey. The majority of our readers own cruising and fishing boats from 20 to 40 feet.

With our features we cover destinations (both ports of call and narrowly defined regions), cruising trips, fishing, people involved in boating (from harbormasters to maritime artists), boat design, seamanship, maritime history and the environment. Most of our features are about things that take place in or are particular to the Northeast. Some topics, however, are universal (such as seamanship) and can be handled as such, but local references are desirable where appropriate. Every month we also publish two to three marina reviews (staff- and freelance-written), about six regular columns, and short news briefs.

Our typical reader is an experienced boater, so articles on the basics are usually not our fare. Freelance writers themselves need a certain level of boating knowledge to handle most assignments.

Our features range from 1,500 to 3,000 words. Our news briefs and marina reviews are shorter. We buy first-time North American publishing rights and pay on publication or within 60 days of acceptance, whichever is first. We pay between $100 and $500 for articles, with exceptions made for more involved work. We also pay extra (stock photo rates) for writer-submitted photography, but we need very high-quality slides.

Interested writers should submit a detailed, written query outlining the story, their angle on the story and why they are a good choice to write it. They should also submit a written summary of their writing experience, a writing sample and a photography sample (if applicable).

Categories: Nonfiction—Boating—Environment—Fishing—History—Travel

CONTACT: Editorial Dept.
Material: All
Offshore Communications Inc.
500 Victory Rd, Marina Bay
No. Quincy MA 02171
Phone: 617-221-1400

Ohio Magazine

Ohio Magazine Guidelines for Writers

Ohio Magazine is in the process of increasing its pool of freelance writers, and we are particularly looking for writers in Southeast, Southwest and Northwest Ohio. If interested, please send a resume, clips, an SASE and any story pitches to: *Ohio Magazine*, Attn: Nicole Gabriel, Managing Editor, 62 E. Broad St., Columbus, OH, 43215. In your cover letter please tell us where your writing interests and strengths lie (i.e. travel, profiles, living, general features, etc.). Please note: only those resumes that include writing samples—or a link to a web site with samples—will be considered. Also note: submitting great story pitches with your packet is another way to stand out of the crowd. Here's what we look for:

First and foremost, *Ohio* publishes stories that "celebrate Ohio"—stories that celebrate its people, its rich culture and heritage, and especially, its wonderful travel spots. Our audience is educated, active, affluent and very loyal to Ohio. We know they expect the best. Because our readership is drawn from the entire state, each of our stories must possess a statewide appeal.

Features

Feature stories in *Ohio* should meet all the above criteria. Typically, our feature well contains stories about interesting Ohioans, top travel destinations, Ohio's arts and cultural institutions, as well as trend pieces and service pieces that provide readers with a statewide set of options on a particular topic. All features should have the potential for wonderful art to accompany it, so the story has a strong visual impact on our readers.

Profile pieces typically focus on an individual who can claim an impact—large or small—on the entire state, or whose actions would be of interest to our statewide audience. A recent piece profiled the new ambassador to Switzerland who hails from Cincinnati. Similarly, emerging trends should be pitched with the same attention to statewide appeal. A story about a man with an impressive private wine collection is interesting, a story on Ohio's first master sommelier (professional wine taster) has much better appeal (this story was in our October, 2001, issue).

Trend stories can vary greatly, ranging from home decorating, gardening and food. But all must be proven emerging trends in our back yard. A trend toward massive renovations of old hotels was the cover story in the September issue of *Ohio Magazine*. Food trends are also important and in the last few months, we've covered an emerging taste for imported specialty cheese and blended teas.

We are often pitched service pieces, but choose very few. Service, or "roundup" stories typically cover one topic by providing localized, statewide information on the topic. A piece on Ohio's best colleges, or the state's best boutique shopping are good examples of excellent service pieces. A good service piece is one that provides hard-to-find information that readers would otherwise not have. So, while a guide to Ohio's biggest shopping malls isn't very crucial to readers—they could easily discover them on their own—a guide to Ohio's specialty clothing boutiques would be valuable.

Travel

While *Ohio* has evolved somewhat in recent years, we still remain dedicated to bringing our readers the best travel information in the state—where to go, what to do and what to see all over our great state. Each month, *Ohio* dedicates well over 50 percent of its pages to covering travel destinations in the state. *Ohio* readers are interested in discovering new inns and B&Bs in which to stay, finding off-the-beaten-path destinations where they can immerse themselves in local culture, and exploring excellent outdoor parks and recreation areas where they can relax and play. Almost every story provides readers with an itinerary that includes a place to stay, highlights a mixed variety of things to do and suggests local venues for dining and shopping. The key to the success of any travel pitch is the words "local" and "unique." We have files filled with information about museums and major attractions in every area of the state—we rely on contributors to tell us what's new, unique or different about each destination.

The travel section of *Ohio* contains a number of running features. Main Street stories profile a small town in Ohio that has big appeal. Typically, these are charming, old-fashioned downtown streetscapes where a reader could spend a day shopping, eating and perhaps taking in a local museum or attraction. Weekend Itinerary pieces provide readers with just that, an itinerary for an entire weekend in one location, complete with a locally owned inn or B&B, a series of options for what to do that include both well-known and not-so-well-known local attractions, and suggestions on the best locally-owned restaurants. Borderland departments cover a destination just outside of Ohio. Destination stories explore one specific destination—a new museum, a historic site, or a place worth visiting for a day or an overnight trip. These are all places that an Ohioan could drive to with ease, and have the same appeal described in the sections above.

Story Pitches

Too many writers send us pitches without ever having looked at a copy of the magazine. We encourage all potential freelance writers to do some research—go to the library, look at our archives on our web site, go to the bookstore and pick up this month's issue. Story pitches should be well thought out and offer, in a few paragraphs, a brief outline of the topic. Be specific about your subject and provide details on elements of the story that you plan to write about. Take care to note those elements of the story that you feel we might not know about—new destinations, updated attractions, and newly opened restaurants always help a pitch.

It is essential that you also provide a resume, at least three clips of your work and a SASE. Links to your web site are also welcome and e-mails with your resume and attached clips are also fine. Phone queries are discouraged. Pitches and clips should be forwarded to the address below.

Guidelines for Photographers

Send samples of your work in slides or as printed clips along with any proposed photo idea(s) to Rob McGarr, Art Director, 1422 Euclid Ave. Suite 730, Cleveland, 44115. If you have an electronic portfolio, e-mail a few examples to the attention of rmcgarr@glpublishing.com. If you're on the Web, even better. Point us in the direction of your site. If you do send samples via the mail and would like your materials returned to you, please include a self-addressed, stamped envelope and be sure to include your telephone number and e-mail address. Telephone queries are discouraged.

Please remember that our editorial calendar is established three to six months in advance. For queries related to a timely event or seasonal events, allow nine month's to a year's notice. If we're interested in your work, we'll contact you to discuss a potential assignment.

Payment

For writers and photographers, we pay on publication, buy first-time rights (and, sometimes, electronic rights), but may reassign second serial (reprint) or one-time rights.

Thanks for your interest in *Ohio Magazine.*

Categories: General Interest—Regional

CONTACT: Nicole Gabriel, Managing Editor
Material: Articles
CONTACT: Rob McGarr, Art Director,
E-mail: rmcgarr@glpublishing.com
Material: Photo samples and proposals
62 E. Broad St.
Columbus OH 43215-3522
Phone: 614-461-8723
Website: www.ohiomagazine.com

Ohio Writer

We are looking for nonfiction articles that deal with any area of writing, including how-to, profiles and interviews with Ohio writers, poets and journalists. *Ohio Writer* is read by both beginning and experienced writers and hopes to create a sense of community among writers of different genres, abilities and backgrounds. We want to hear a personal voice, one that engages the reader. We're looking for intelligent, literate prose that isn't stuffy.

Focus articles should be approximately 700–1,500 words. Payment: $25 on publication. Reprinted articles: $15 on publication.

Feature articles should be approximately 2,000-2,500 words. Payment: $25–$50 on publication.

Reviews are accepted of any publication or book by an Ohio writer or Ohio press. Include title, author, press, city where published, year of publication, number of pages and price. Occasionally we use reviews of events: conferences, readings, bookstores, etc. Length: 400-600 words. Payment: $5-$10.

Include short biographical statement with all submissions.

Unsolicited manuscripts and book reviews will be accepted.

Reporting time: Four to six weeks.

We suggest writers unfamiliar with the magazine order a sample copy. Back issues are available for $2.00 plus 50 cents postage.

We buy one-time rights, plus the right to reprint. Any editing, except copy editing, will be done with author's approval.

We also accept announcements or notes concerning writing, writing opportunities, and the writing life in Ohio for publication in our "Notes, Previews and Announcements" column. Suitable calendar listings are published without charge.

Categories: Fiction—Nonfiction—Literature—Poetry—Short Stories—Writing

CONTACT: Mark Kuhar, Editor
Material: All
c/o Poets' and Writers' League of Greater Cleveland
12200 Fairhill Rd, #3A
Cleveland OH 44120
Phone: 216-421-0403
Website: www.pwlgc.com

Oildom Publishing

Writer's guidelines for these Publications:
* *Underground Construction*
* *Pipeline & Gas Journal*
* *Power & Gas Marketing*
* *Pipeline News*
* *Rehab Technology*

Submissions
* Always query first—1200 to 1500 words per query.
* Article rate includes basic telephone work. However, extensive long distance phone work and/or faxes, along with other relevant expenses may be paid by Oildom Publishing.

Significant expenses (generally defined as over $25 per story) should be pre-approved. Payment upon final article approval by the magazines' editors. Always submit invoice with final story draft/disk.

* We prefer stories submitted on disk. Oildom Publishing is PC based. Sometimes stories written on a Mac can be imported via special programs we have; often times they can't. The word processing software we support for PC is WordPerfect Windows, Microsoft Word for Windows 6.0, or generally any program in ASCII or ANSI formats. To circumvent any software incompatibilities, a clean, clear hard copy should accompany all submissions. We can then scan the story into our system.

For specific questions on formats and compatibility issues, contact Maxine Witcher, in the Houston office, (713) 558-6930, ext. 221.

* Whenever possible, all stories should be accompanied by artwork: Slides, color photographs and/or graphics. For specific graphic formats and compatibility inquiries, contact Elizabeth Bailey, for *Underground Construction*, (713) 558-6930, ext. 216, or Sheri Biscardi, (713) 558-6930, ext. 214 for *Pipeline & Gas Journal.*

* We like to break out all significant manufacturers, vendors and/or contractors with reader service numbers so interested readers can easily obtain information. Please include contact names, address, phone and fax numbers whenever possible.

* We buy exclusive rights. We prefer story queries, but cold submissions are considered. We generally will respond within 30 days.

* As a rule, we follow the *Associated Press Stylebook*. Exceptions include certain industry-accepted terms and abbreviations, and two-letter state abbreviations.

* Our readers tend to be management personnel from both contractors and owning companies. Technical material is acceptable only to a moderate level. Our readers are responsible for dollars. Always try to include economic considerations when applicable and practical.

* Kill fees are addressed on a case-by-case basis.

Categories: Trade—Underground Construction (gas, sewer, water, cable)

CONTACT: Robert Carpenter, Editorial Director
Material: Underground Construction
CONTACT: Jeff Share, Editor
Material: Pipeline & Gas Journal
CONTACT: Rita Tubb, Managing Editor
Material: Underground Construction/Pipeline & Gas Journal and all other
Executive Offices
PO Box 941669
Houston TX 77094-8669

Phone: 281-558-6930
Fax: 281-558-7029
E-mail: rita@oildompublishing.com
1160 Dairy Ashford Rd., Suite 610
Houston TX 77079
Phone: 281-558-6930
Fax: 281-558-7029
Website: www.oildompublishing.com

Oklahoma
TODAY

Oklahoma Today Magazine

About *Oklahoma Today* Magazine

Oklahoma Today is a regional bi-monthly magazine with a circulation of 45,000 and an estimated readership of 153,000. Stories, essays, columns, etc. focus on Oklahoma's people and places. We strive to give our readers a sense of what Oklahoma is all about.

People figure strongly into all of our stories. We believe the best way to write a story is not to just tell it, but to show our readers through anecdotes, quotes, and experiences of past and present people.

The magazine likes to give the readers information on not only the regular "hot spots" to visit, but places that are "off the beaten track" as well.

About Your Story

When deciding on a subject, you need to think "Could the reader see or do what the article talks about?" or "Will the story expand the knowledge of the readers' Oklahoma cultural knowledge?"

The history behind the person or place also should be included. It lets the reader know why a particular thing is happening, but the focus needs to be on today.

Considering A Story For Publication

Some of the questions we ask when considering a story are, "Does the writer answer all the questions about the subject?," "Who and what are the source materials?," "Does the writer surprise the reader with something?," and "Could anything else be included in the story?"

Topics in *Oklahoma Today* have a wide range. Some of the successful stories from the past include: Oklahoma cowboy poet roundup, profiles—hamburger joints, and a photo essay on the Tallgrass Prairie.

Oklahoma Today is always looking for a fresh editorial perspective to complement the seasoned writers we already use. While we appreciate and encourage a distinct voice, we usually do not publish opinion pieces. The best way to get in is to send us a story with a fresh angle on an old subject or person, or a new idea that goes along with our style of covering Oklahoma's people and places.

How To Get In

Read our magazine. Read Oklahoma newspapers and any other Oklahoma publication you can get your hands on. Keeping up with what goes on in our state is the best way to write stories that we can use. Include a biography of yourself and clips of previous work, so we can see what experience you have. Realize that the editors receive many manuscripts and that yours will be reviewed as soon as time allows. Don't necessarily expect your first piece in the magazine to be a feature; start small and suggest items for departments such as Across the Range. Even Letters to the Editor are good ways to "get some ink."

1. Deadlines

Oklahoma Today is usually planned a year in advance, so stories submitted in March may not appear until next January. We produce an issue two months ahead of time (in September, we are in production for November/December), so submit timely stories well before the pro-

duction deadlines. *Oklahoma Today* is published seven times a year.

2. Story Guidelines

Stories will range in length from 250 words for regular department articles to 3,000 words for major features. We prefer to be queried in advance, but will review unsolicited manuscripts and photos "on spec."

Submission of transparencies and black-and-white photographs are welcome. We prefer scenic photographs that may or may not include people. However, we reserve the right to reject photographs submitted with the story, even if we accept the story itself.

3. Rates/Payments

Rates start at $50 for shorter pieces, $75 and up for department and feature stories, and $300 and up for major profiles or stories.

Payment will be upon publication.

We pay for quality, not quantity.

We do not pay for expenses, but do take into account the demands of story assignment when negotiating payment.

Terms of the agreement for stories on both assignment and bought "on spec" are confirmed with a standard editorial contract.

4. Policies and Procedures

Oklahoma Today takes no responsibility for unsolicited manuscripts, artwork, or photography.

Articles need to be e-mailed or submitted on disk, preferably in Microsoft Word, and with an accompanying printout.

Never send an original, uncopied manuscript.

Rejected material will not be returned unless sent with a SASE.

REPORTING STANDARDS

Oklahoma Today requires its writers to conduct their reporting according to the magazine's high standards of truth and accuracy. To that end, we have adopted the following guidelines. Of course, all stories are unique. Editorial judgment is always the final arbiter and will be exercised on a case-by-case basis by *Oklahoma Today*'s editors.

Our Guidelines

1. *Oklahoma Today* won't publish any statements that haven't been documented to its satisfaction.

2. *Oklahoma Today* requests primary sources for all previously unreported facts and for all other facts important to the story.

Any fact that might be contested should ideally have at least two primary sources.

Although *Oklahoma Today* typically does not publish controversial material, the more controversial a fact, the higher a standard of sourcing will be required. Countervailing opinions should be weighed by the writer and brought to the editor's attention if appropriate. An example of a primary source is a credible person in a position to know the fact in question. A properly filed public document is also a primary source. Other documents uncovered in reporting may be considered primary sources.

3. *Oklahoma Today* discourages reporting that relies too heavily on secondary sources.

However, we accept that certain facts—mostly, minor facts that serve as background for a story—may be established via secondary sources. Newspapers and magazines will be accepted as secondary sources on a case-by-case basis. Common sense and skepticism will be our guides. In the field of medicine, for example, the *New England Journal of Medicine* would likely be accepted as authoritative. In most cases, *Oklahoma Today* will regard the following publications as acceptable secondary sources:

- *Daily Oklahoman*
- *Tulsa World*
- State dailies (Lawton, Muskogee, Enid, Stillwater, Norman)
- *Dallas Morning News*
- *New York Times*
- *Washington Post*
- *Wall Street Journal*
- *Time*
- *Newsweek*

Why these particular publications? Because they're journals of record, widely available and widely read, with a good record for correcting mistakes. We don't necessarily believe they are more accurate than other publications. But we do believe it's reasonable to assume that if one of these publications reports something and it's not corrected, it's accurate. Reports in publications that aren't deemed acceptable secondary sources by your editors should be verified with a primary source—or more that one primary source, if appropriate.

4. *Oklahoma Today* believes in giving credit to other publications for original reporting

We don't think it's right to rely on other publication's work without acknowledging the debt. Even if we re-establish the facts first reported by another publication, we give credit if credit is due. The guidelines here are common sense and generosity.

5. *Oklahoma Today* expects its writers to take responsibility even for so-called common knowledge.

For matters of general and historical background, we rely on established encyclopedic reference and other general sources. But we will accept citation to any source that, in our opinion, can reasonably be called authoritative.

6. *Oklahoma Today* requires its writers and editors to keep unpublished drafts of assigned articles confidential.

We believe sharing any unpublished version of your article with the subject matter or a source—a big journalistic no-no—is inappropriate. Soliciting approval from your subject or source compromises the editorial integrity of the piece and thus the magazine. Many sources will ask you to share with them a printed version of your draft. Please explain the magazine's policy and refer those sources to your editor. If you feel you need feedback on a draft, please contact your assigning editor.

7. *Oklahoma Today* requires its writers to supply an annotated fact-checking manuscript that reflects these guidelines.

Writers and editors will work together to decide which sources should be cited in final copy and how they should be cited. Meanwhile, writers must submit material that provides appropriate documentation of their reporting. Usually, such material will be requested shortly after a story has been accepted.

8. Here's what we need, specifically:
- Any notes, transcripts, or tapes of interviews
- All magazine or newspaper stories used in reporting
- All other supporting material, with relevant parts clearly marked
- Phone numbers for sources
- The annotated manuscript

Please be understanding of the fact checkers' work and cooperate fully with their efforts. Highlighting quotes and supplying page numbers helps enormously—and reduces the amount of time you'll spend on the phone with a fact checker. Any questions about these guidelines? Ask your editor.

In keeping with the intent of these "Reporting Standards," *Oklahoma Today* would like to acknowledge Worth for creating the original version of this document.

Categories: Nonfiction—Consumer—History—Native American—Regional—Travel

CONTACT: Editor
Material: All
PO Box 53384
Oklahoma City OK 73152
Phone: 405-521-2496
Fax: 405-522-4588
Website: oklahomatoday.com

Remember: Editors change jobs and publishers change addresses. It is wise to invest in a phone call for the current information before submitting.

The Old Farmer's Almanac

The Old Farmer's Almanac is the oldest continuously published periodical in North America. Since 1792, it has provided useful information for people in all walks of life: tide tables for those who live near the ocean; sunrise tables and planting charts for those who live on the farm or simply enjoy gardening; recipes for those who like to cook; and forecasts for those who don't like the question of weather left up in the air. The words of the *Almanac*'s founder, Robert B. Thomas, guide us still: "Our main endeavor is to be useful, but with a pleasant degree of humor."

An almanac, by definition, records and predicts astronomical events (the rising and setting of the Sun, for instance), tides, weather, and other phenomena with respect to time. In recent years, we've expanded the *Almanac* content—but always with an eye on Mr. Thomas's wise words about keeping things fun and practical.

We encourage you to study back issues of our publication to gain an idea of what we publish. Some of our content is also available on our Web site, www.almanac.com. Keep in mind that we attempt to create a sort of time capsule with each issue: We cover the current year with articles that reflect current events, trends, and interests, and we commemorate past people and events with "anniversary" stories that shed new light on the subject and update the subject as is appropriate. (An anniversary year is typically one that is divisible by 5.) The "big picture" goal is to produce a "snapshot" of the issue year so that readers in 2, 20, or 200 years will understand and appreciate what is topical today.

These are among the general story categories we look for: pertinent articles on science and weather; nature, including insects, animals, and the outdoors (fishing, for example); plants, gardening, and farming; history, including events, people, and inventions; natural health, folklore, and traditional ways (herbal remedies, for example); geography and climate; amusements; food and recipes. We regularly feature a "special report" on a topic of broad general interest. Recently those have included romance, superstitions, and wedding traditions past and present. We especially encourage humor of all kinds: the fanciful, the bizarre, the ludicrous, and the offbeat.

Our readership spans the generations: In age, they range from 9 to 90; they live in the cities, the suburbs, and out in the country.

We publish both a U.S. and a Canadian edition. For the Canadian edition, we substitute six to eight stories that are uniquely and specifically about life in Canada, based on the topic areas cited above.

The *Almanac* comes out every year on the second Tuesday in September. Payment is made on acceptance; rates vary. We prefer to buy all rights.

If you have a story idea, send us a query with a brief outline via regular mail (email only if an editor has invited you to do so). Please include a self-addressed, stamped envelope for our reply. If you have been published—especially in the proposed topic area—a sample of clips would be appreciated (photocopies only, and an SASE if you would like clips returned).

Categories: Nonfiction—Agriculture—Animals—Associations—Biography—Cooking—Environment—Folklore—Gardening—General Interest—Outdoors—Reference

CONTACT: Janice Stillman, Editor
Material: All
PO Box 520
Dublin NH 03444
Phone: 603-563-8111
Website: www.almanac.com

Old West

Please refer to *True West* magazine.

M-Q

Omnific

Are you guilty of storing your poetry in the closet? Do you say that contests are not for you because you would waste your money? Do deadlines make you nervous? If you answered "yes" to any of these questions, then this publication is for you.

Get those poems out of the closet and dust them off because OMNIFIC is now accepting 4 poems per person, per year, for publication in this well-known quarterly. Just think of it. Each issue could feature one of your poems. This is your chance to become published and stay published.

Poems are attractively displayed in alphabetical order according to your state, along with complete address of author. Readers vote on their favorites, and for now we have small prizes to be awarded. The top three entries receiving the most votes receive the next issue free. There is also an "Editor's Choice Award" of $5, and the poem(s) in the "Lucky No. 7" spot will receive a small award. As interest builds and subscriptions come in, prizes will be increased. (Not to mention the contact and awards furnished by some of our readers.)

Each author's complete name and address will be published with his/her poem. This encourages reader/writer contact, and also the awards given by our readers may be mailed directly to YOU. (However, if you wish your address to remain anonymous, I will accept your awards and forward them on to you. But YOU must let me know this at the time you send in your poetry, or upon receiving your acceptance letter.)

You will be proud to see your work published here and I can also promise that you will enjoy reading each issue, along with voting for your favorites. And the excitement builds from one issue to the next, because after reading OMNIFIC and casting your vote, you will want to know who the winners will be—and that information will be disclosed in the next issue.

OMNIFIC means "all creating" and as poets and writers, isn't that what we're doing?

COME...join our family today. Don't you be the one to miss out on the fun that's in store for everyone.

Wouldn't YOU like to be published in this exciting, fun-filled quarterly and have your poem appear in the next issue?

There is no entry fee and due to the weight involved, no payment in copies. Poetry to 40 lines (sometimes over), and in any style or format. Submission does not guarantee publication. Only work in good taste is accepted.

1 Year Subscription (4 issues) $16.00/Overseas $20 (US Funds)

Single issue—$4.50/Overseas $5.00 (US Funds). Payable to Weems Concepts.

This publication is habit-forming and good for your morale. Read at your own risk.

Categories: Poetry

CONTACT: Kay Weems, Editor/Publisher
Material: Poetry
207 Willow Wind Dr.
Artemas PA 17211-9405
Phone: 814-458-3102

On Mission

Flagship magazine of the North American Mission Board, SBC.

On Mission's primary purpose is to help readers and churches become more on mission in the areas of personal evangelism and missions. Effective articles will always include elements that move readers toward spiritual growth, evangelism and missions. On Mission is approximately 50 percent freelance written. Articles are 600-1,200 words. Payment is 25 cents/word—35 cents/word for cover stories (usually assigned). On Mission's readership is 100,000.

Here is a checklist of some points to consider as you match your work with On Mission's objectives:

Spiritual – Each article should move readers toward a deeper walk with God and a commitment to sharing Christ with others. On Mission articles must maintain an eternal, "big picture" perspective.

Practical – Each article should include "take away" value readers will find helpful. Will they gain insights into how they can grow in sharing their faith or gain strength in their own relationship with Jesus Christ? Will they learn more effective ways of relationship building or communication? In what specific ways will your article encourage, provide hope or show "how to?"

Personal – On Mission wants readers to feel connected with the people featured on its pages. Articles should quote and describe the people in ways that not only convey meaning, but also give readers a glimpse into the hearts and minds of those being featured.

Approachable – Readers might be intimidated if those featured appear to be "super Christians" who seem to live on a higher spiritual plane. Try to introduce subjects as "three dimensional, real" people. Include anecdotes or examples of their fears and failures, including ways they overcame obstacles. In other words, take the reader inside the heart of the on mission Christian and reveal the inevitable humanness that makes that person not only believable, but also approachable. We want the reader to feel encouraged to become on mission by identifying with people like them who are featured in the magazine.

Believable – The Bible clearly explains the basics for the Christian walk. These points are non-negotiable. However, working out an approach to evangelism and missions can take many forms. On Mission will look for different insights on this topic, but we will not be afraid to admit that we don't know everything on the subjects of evangelism and missions.

Hopeful – Sharing Christ is an intimidating prospect for many readers. Without increasing fear, On Mission wants to acknowledge that reality while at the same time giving readers encouragement and hope. We can do this by holding up as models of the successful on mission lifestyle those people who are willing to share their struggles with the reader – as well as their success stories.

Knowledgeable – Without conflicting with these last two points, On Mission strives to be a source of information and knowledge, as well as a helpful resource. On Mission will help readers do their homework on these issues. We want to provide accurate information and up-to-date knowledge. Research your article. Document your sources. Depend on the most trustworthy, factual sources you can locate.

Submission Format:

Articles may be submitted by postal mail or email. If you send a document electronically, please ensure that your document is in a Microsoft Word format and double spaced. We prefer electronic submissions, with the article included as an attachment to the email or embedded into the body of the email. Material is subject to editing for length, style and format.

On Mission is primarily an "on assignment" magazine, meaning that editors first develop story ideas and then locate writers whose expertise and interests fit the articles. However, we do accept queries and manuscripts. If you have a story idea, please send a query letter and/or manuscript along with your resume and clips. It takes about 8-16 weeks to respond to query letters and manuscripts, so allow time for event-related and seasonal story ideas. Payment is made on acceptance. Send queries with SASE or manuscript.

Categories: Nonfiction—Christian Interests—Religion

CONTACT: Carol Pipes, Editor
Material: All
North American Mission Board
4200 North Point Pkwy.
Alpharetta GA 30022-4176
Phone: 770-410-6382
E-mail: cpipes@namb.net
Website: www.onmission.com

Onion World

Onion World is written for commercial onion growers, packers and shippers. Hence, any free-lance material accepted for publication must be informative and specifically addressed to this audience.

The following types of articles represent subject matter that normally would be acceptable:

Educational pieces: Articles focusing on various disease, insect and production challenges and what is being done to resolve them. Such articles must be based on solid research from reputable industry sources.

Feature articles: Focus should be on onion growers and/or onion packer/shippers, what they are doing, what kinds of equipment they are using, the benefits, etc.

Health-related articles: Articles pointing out the health benefits of eating onions. Again, solid research is a must.

Onion Meetings/Field Days: Reports on special onion educational meetings/seminars are acceptable and are encouraged.

Taboos:
1. General interest articles with no particular focus on onions.
2. Articles designed for the home gardener.
3. Fiction pieces.
4. Poetry

Length:
1. Articles should not exceed 1,200 to 1,500 words.
2. Shorter articles are acceptable and are often preferred.

Photos:
1. Avoid the canned pose.
2. Involve people.
3. Colored jps or prints preferred.
4. Color prints and/or jpgs considered for covers.
5. Writers should submit prints or jpgs, along with appropriate captions.

Remuneration:
Dependent upon length of and quality of submission. Price range: Up to $250, including photos.

Categories: Nonfiction—Agriculture—Business—Education—Health

CONTACT: Editor
Material: All
Columbia Publishing
413-B N 20th Ave
Yakima WA 98902
Phone: 509-248-2452
Fax: 509-248-4056
E-mail: dbrent@columbiapublications.com
Website: www.onionworld.net

ONLINE

ONLINE is written and edited for librarians and other professionals who routinely use online services for information delivery, research, and knowledge management. Articles are directed to the "hands on" searcher and to managers of information resources in business, professional, and educational environments. ONLINE stresses practical, how-to advice on the efficient and effective use of electronic information. The readership runs the gamut from novice to experienced researcher.

ONLINE covers the entire range of electronic information topics, including industry trends; new products and technologies; professional, business and consumer online services; the Internet; enterprise-wide information management; practical search and information management techniques; information professional roles and responsibilities, electronic content; quality issues; Web design from an information professional perspective; intranet/extranet creation and promotion; and search engines.

EDITORIAL PRACTICES

We stress original work (as opposed to a synthesis or overview based on previously published work).

Write in simple, straightforward English.

Short, pithy, fact-filled articles are much better than long, wordy pieces.

Write tersely, in popular magazine style, not in verbose, academic prose.

Begin the article with a paragraph or two to attract the reader's interest. Boring, background introductions are not appropriate.

Stress "dos and don'ts" and "tips and techniques" that can be applied to readers' situations.

Use examples to enhance the text; gather comments from colleagues or users when appropriate and include them.

Use subheads frequently to break up text (make them descriptive - not just a single word).

Provide photos and screen shots where appropriate, also diagrams, charts, tables, and graphs. Do not embed these in the text.

Do not capitalize database names, or use boldface or italics, unless the producer does; use the producer's preferred style and exact wording.

Keep cited references to a minimum, and follow our preferred style.

Identify references in the text [e.g., "Sally Smith, writing in the Nov. 2004 *ONLINE*, noted that..." then add a [1], [2], etc. for the full reference (Note: Use square brackets.)

The byline should include the author's full name, title, and affiliation.

Some preferred terms are as follows: online, database, offline , World Wide Web, printout, update, logoff, menu-driven, disk, e-mail, logon, host, end-user, CD-ROM, hardcopy, FTP, user-friendly, in-house, multimedia, URLs, MB (4MB), KB (24KB), U.S., U.K.

MECHANICAL REQUIREMENTS

Please use a spell checker.

All parts of an article must be submitted in electronic format, preferably via e-mail. This includes sidebars, tables, charts, printouts, etc. Discuss formats in advance with the editor.

Length should be from 1500 to 4000 words, according to your discussions with the editor. Use the word count feature of your word processor to determine length.

Use as little formatting as possible in the manuscript since it must be removed and revised to suit our production requirements. Do not use a word processor's "style sheets."

Use carriage returns only at the end of paragraphs, not after every line.

Do not indent at beginning of paragraphs, instead use a double linefeed between paragraphs.

The edited manuscript will be sent to the author for proofing. (Necessary corrections can be made at this point, but not extensive revisions or rewrites.)

SCREENSHOTS, CHARTS, GRAPHS, TABLES, PRINTOUTS, ILLUSTRATIONS

Submit all illustrations by e-mail if possible. Discuss file formats with the editor.

When making screen captures for illustrations, be sure to open your capture screen to the maximum monitor size.

Charts and tables should have tabs, not spaces, delineating the columns. Set the appropriate tabs on your word processor, using one tab per column. Do not use the Table feature in your word processor.

Submit screen captures and other graphics each in a separate file. Acceptable file formats include: TIF, PICT, BMP, PCX, JPG, GIF.

If you include search printouts or search examples, format them as separate figures.

Each printout and figure must have a descriptive title, and a line or two of explanation since it is possible it will appear elsewhere than near the part of the article where it is mentioned.

Keep the length of search printouts and screen captures to a minimum, using vertical ellipses where possible to eliminate repetitious parts.

Good photographs or other illustrations are welcome and encouraged. Use high resolution.

CITATION FORMAT

Journal citations: Cite the volume, the number, and the complete date of the journal article. All three elements are essential. (Example: Webster, Peter. "Breaking Down Information Silos: Integrating On-line Information." *ONLINE* 28, No. 6 (November/December 2004): pp.30-33.)

Book citations: Cite the author, title, place of publication, publisher, date of publication, and total page count. (Example: Bates, Mary Ellen. *Building and Running a Successful Research Business: A Guide for the Independent Information Professional.* Medford, NJ: CyberAge Books, 2003. 472 pp.)

URLs: Web sites referred to within the text of the article should be in brackets, where possible, e.g., [www.infotoday.com/online]. If the URL does not begin with www, include the http://; otherwise leave out the http://, e.g. [http://onlinemag.net]. When a number of sites are mentioned, these should be summarized in a separate list (including title and URL) that will be in a box or sidebar near the end of the article.

DEADLINES

Manuscript deadlines are set by the editor, and are staggered according to publication schedules and work flow. Missing the scheduled deadline may jeopardize publication of your article since timeliness is often of critical importance. Lead time for actual production is about three or four months due to the rigorous editing, proofing, art, and production efforts expended on each manuscript. If a manuscript needs fact checking or review by outside experts, database producers, Web site owners, or online services, additional time is required to complete the editorial process.

PAYMENT AND RIGHTS

Payment for a manuscript varies according to the article's complexity, length, quality, and original research. Payment is determined by the publisher, with a recommendation from the editor, after the manuscript has gone through the editorial process. All authors are paid except those whose employer does not permit payment and those employed by online suppliers (and consultants to suppliers) who are writing about their employers' products and services. Payment is made upon publication; a check and a complimentary copy of the issue are sent to the author on publication.

Authors will be asked to sign a publication agreement prior to the editing process, granting to Information Today, Inc. the right to publish the article in ONLINE magazine in print and electronic formats. (Information Today, Inc. will copyright the issue to protect the entire issue as an entity.) The agreement also stipulates that the author not publish any version or excerpt of the article prior to, or for 90 days following, its publication in *ONLINE*.

Unacceptable manuscripts will not be returned. Information Today, Inc. is not responsible for lost manuscripts or photos.

Categories: Computers

CONTACT: Marydee Ojala
Material: All
PO Box 78225
Indianapolis IN 46278
Phone: 317-870-1994
Fax: 317-870-1996
E-mail: marydee@infotoday.com
Website: onlinemag.net

Open Spaces

Open Spaces is a quarterly which gives voice to the Northwest on issues that are regional, national and international in scope. Our readership is thoughtful, intelligent, widely read and appreciative of ideas and writing of the highest quality. With that in mind, we seek thoughtful, well-researched articles and insightful fiction, reviews and poetry on a variety of subjects from a number of different viewpoints. Although we take ourselves seriously, we appreciate humor as well. We welcome your interest and provide the following submission guidelines.

Nonfiction: General interest, profiles, book excerpts (prior to publication), essays. Topics of interest include: public affairs, medicine, business, law, education, the family, economics, the environment, natural history, science, the arts, religion, culture and society. Preferred length is 1,500-4,000 words. Payment varies.

Columns/Departments: Personal experience and observation, humor, travel, etc. Please query with SASE. Payment varies.

Fiction: Send complete manuscript with SASE. Preferred length is 2,000 - 5,000 words. Payment varies.

Poetry: Submit maximum of 3 poems with SASE. No epics, please.

Book reviews: Our reviews go beyond summarizing and assessing the book; they provide thoughtful insight into the subject matter. Therefore, we seek reviews written by established authorities. Query with SASE and send samples of reviews written.

Interludes: Cartoons, interesting or amusing Northwest facts, expressions, etc.

Please Note: The surest way for a writer to determine whether his or her material is right for us is to look at our magazine. The cost of a sample copy is $10. All submissions must be accompanied by an SASE. No e-mail submissions will be reviewed.

For additional information including general submission guidelines, tables of contents and names of contributors to back and current issues see our web site at www.open-spaces.com.

Open Spaces is not responsible for the return or loss of submissions. Surface mail submissions must be accompanied by a self-addressed envelope bearing adequate return postage.

Categories: Fiction—Nonfiction—Arts—Business—Culture—Economics—Education—Environment—Family—General Interest—Law—Poetry—Science—Society

CONTACT: Open Spaces Publications, Inc.
PMB 134
6327 C SW Capitol Hwy
Portland, OR 97239-1937
Phone: 503-227-5764
Fax: 503-227-3401
E-mail: info@open-spaces.com

Orange Coast Magazine

Orange Coast Magazine and *Orange Coast Online* (www.orangecoastmagazine.com) are published for the educated and affluent residents of Orange County, California. Priority is given to well-told stories that have strong local interest, always with an emphasis on stylish writing and clear thinking.

GUIDELINES

To propose a story, writers should send a detailed query with published writing samples, or a completed manuscript. Proposals that arrive with a stamped, self-addressed envelope will be returned if the manuscript is not usable. Others will not be returned. Manuscripts should be saved in ASCII, or text-only, format and sent by e-mail. Writers should include their name, address, phone number and social security number.

WRITING TIPS

1. Read previous issues of *Orange Coast* to gauge the range of story ideas and how they were handled.

2. Give stories a hard, narrow focus. Rather than a story about the Pacific Symphony Orchestra, tell us the story of the lead cellist who scoured the world for the perfect cello, then mortgaged his house in order to buy it.

3. Once the story is focused, broaden the perspective. A story focused on our cellist should raise much larger questions: Why would a musician take a huge financial risk to get an instrument that to an

untrained ear sounds pretty much like any other cello? What does the musician hear that the rest of us don't?

4. Narrative stories work best, with scenes, characters and situations developed in the writer's own words. But the editors also encourage writers to experiment with style—there is no right formula. Ask yourself what's the best way to tell this particular story. The story should dictate the style and the style never should dominate or obscure the story.

5. Show, don't tell. Instead of telling readers the room was cold and drafty, give them the details that show the cold: a character puffing clouds of vapor, a flickering candle, the butler wearing mittens. Effective details let the reader see; useless details clutter the story.

6. Avoid newspaperese. In the economy of newspaper writing, a man who dedicated his life to police work, who built a career during weekends and midnight shifts and who faced countless dangers for inadequate pay becomes a "28-year police veteran." In magazine writing, you can create real characters for the reader. There is no need to boil the elements of a personality into such efficient language.

7. But don't overwrite. If the subject isn't compelling enough to carry the story without embellishment, the value of the story immediately comes into question.

8. When appropriate, draw conclusions and interpret what you have seen and learned. If the most powerful banker in town has a pencil-thin mustache and dresses in hand-painted Niagara Falls ties, white bucks and loud sports jackets, provide the reader with those details. Then, if you think he looks like a used-car salesman, you're certainly free to say so. Just make sure the image is precise and accurate.

9. Save your notes in case additional material is needed for the story.

10. Remember that you are writing for an audience that generally is literate, wealthy and sophisticated, but avoid dry intellectual discourse.

11. Write about real people in real situations; let their stories crystallize the broader issues.

RATES

• *Orange Coast* pays between $300 and $700 for main features, which generally range between 1,200 and 2,500 words. The amount of the payment ultimately depends on the amount of reporting involved and the quality of the writing, and it includes the writer's expenses. Monthly travel features pay $210. Short Cut stories pay between $50 and $75.

• Payment is made on publication. Editorial payments are processed on the 20th of each month and checks are mailed out within one week. No additional payments are made for photographs or accompanying artwork

• For stories done on speculation, no kill fee is paid if the submission is unsuitable for use. For stories assigned by the editors, the kill fee will not exceed 20 percent of the agreed-upon publication price.

• *Orange Coast* buys one-time rights. If the submitted article has appeared elsewhere, writers should let the editors know when and where, and verify in writing that they have not relinquished their rights to it.

Categories: Nonfiction—Regional

CONTACT: Nancy Cheever, Editor
Material: Any
CONTACT: Anastacia Grenda, Managing Editor
Material: Any
3701 Birch St. Ste. 100
Newport Beach CA 92660
Phone: 949-862-1133
Fax: 949-862-0133
E-mail: agrenda@orangecoastmagazine.com

Oregon Business

Dear Prospective Contributor:

Our purpose is to produce a useful, compelling and indispensable monthly magazine that will serve our business readers and help us earn our motto: "Indepth, intelligent, inspiring,." In addition we hope we can help you in your professional development. We understand that contributors are the editorial engine of Oregon Business.

Gillian Floren, Publisher

Readership

Our subscribers include owners of small and medium-sized businesses, government agencies, professional staffs of banks, insurance companies, ad agencies, attorneys and other service providers. The typical reader earns more than $100,000 a year, is college educated and owns a home. Circulation is 21,000, although readership reaches 53,000.

Coverage

About 50% of the magazine's content is written by freelancers, including standing section stories and cover features. Although freelancers most commonly pitch general profiles, we rarely cover a company just because it's there. An *Oregon Business* story must meet at least two of the following criteria:

• Size and location: The topic must be relevant to Northwest businesses. Companies (including franchises) must be based in Oregon or Southwest Washington with at least five employees and annual sales above $250,000.

• Service: Our sections (400-800 words) are reserved largely for service pieces focusing on finance, marketing, management or other general business topics. These stories are meant to be instructional, emphasizing problem-solving by example: "Building a Business Plan: Company X broke the rules and succeeded."

• Trends: These are sometimes covered in a section piece, or perhaps a feature story (2,000 to 4,000 words). We aim to be the state's leading business publication, so we want to be the first to spot trends that affect Oregon companies. If we can't be first, we'll be best. That means going deeper than the typical coverage, offering fresh perspectives and challenging assumptions: "Are Employee Incentives on Their Way Out?" "The New Oregonians: They came, they stayed, get used to it."

• Exclusivity or strategy: Usually a feature or cover story offering a insider's account of an event, whether it's a corporate merger, a dramatic turnaround, a marketing triumph or a PR disaster. The rare breaking news story will focus on the "what"; the more common piece analyzing strategy will talk about the whys and the hows: "Two CEOs. One Golf Game: How the courtship between U.S. Bank and West One led to marriage."

• Compelling figures: A personality profile of a business leader whose style or accomplishments merit an in-depth look. The subject must be interesting, complex, visionary or controversial: "High Volume, High Pressure. How Scott Thomason turned a single dealership into an auto empire."

Standards

Oregon Business adheres to the highest journalistic standards of fairness, diligence and accuracy and expects our contributors to do the same. Stories must be authoritative, which requires thorough reporting using several sources. They must be clearly organized with a well defined theme. And they must be illustrated with real-life examples, because, above all, business is composed of people.

We expect smart and elegant writing in the best of magazine traditions. This means telling—or more accurately, showing—the story from the players' perspectives: the executives who did the deal, the middle manager who got laid off, the line workers who changed the manufacturing process. Industry analysts and statistics are necessary to support a point, but they should be used sparingly.

Writers are responsible for making sure their submissions are error-free; this includes fact checking in final draft form. Editors will return for a rewrite stories that are sloppily put together or underreported. Poor rewrites requiring extensive editing may result in a fee reduction.

Submissions

We do not accept unsolicited material, but we're happy to receive query letters in writing (no phone calls). If we like your idea we'll give you a written assignment along with a word length and deadline, usually 45 days before publication.

• Format. Send material via e-mail with plain text attachments. Use fax or snail mail sparingly.

• Compensation. We pay an average of $360 for a section story and between $700 and $1,500 for a feature story, depending on length and complexity. Submissions should include an invoice. Payment is shortly after publication.

• Rights. We buy first publication rights, which include the contributor's agreement not to sell the story or photo to another publisher within four months after publication in *Oregon Business*.

Photography

Oregon Business is recognized for its artful and unusual pictures. A successful contributor will have an eye for turning the mundane into the interesting and the drab into the colorful. We encourage creativity, which sometimes means puffing together elements from disparate locations or asking subjects to travel off site. The more our magazine's reputation grows, the more our subjects are willing to go along with the photographer's vision.

We like candid shots as much as portraits, so please include both to give us a variety. We do not accept grip-and-grin shots, gimmicky set ups or "class picture" poses. If we receive photos that do not meet our standards, we may request a reshoot at no extra charge.

• Format: Color slides, either 2¼" or 35mm. To avoid confusion, stamp each frame with your name, address and phone number and encase the slides in plastic sleeves. Attach the subject's business card and always include written caption information.

Although we like a variety of shots, one roll of film is usually enough and not more than two.

• Compensation: We pay $125 plus film and processing for photos inside the magazine and a flat $450 for covers. Include an invoice with your submission. We return the slides along with a copy of the issue on publication. Payment is sent 30 days after invoicing.

• Loss/damage. We will not be liable for any lost or damaged slides, negatives or prints if the photo was assigned by the magazine. Photographers submitting stock photos must obtain written loss/damage protection in advance.

What you can expect from us

We will do our best to treat you fairly and professionally. If we need you to turn around work for us quickly, we will try to remember that you write or shoot for other publications, too. If your story requires substantive editing, we'll go over the changes with you before the piece goes to press.

We want to create steady, long-term relationships with our contributors. The best will be given frequent assignments and projects.

We look forward to working with you to make a good magazine even better.

Categories: Business—Regional

CONTACT: Mitchell Hartman, Editor
Material: All
CONTACT: Christina Williams, Managing Editor
Material: All
610 SW Broadway Ste. 200
Portland OR 97205
Phone: 503-223-0304
Fax: 503-221-6544
E-mail: Christinaw@oregonbusiness.com

Oregon Coast

Please refer to Northwest Regional Magazines.

Oregon Quarterly
The Magazine of the University of Oregon

Oregon Quarterly is the successor to *Old Oregon*, the University of Oregon's alumni magazine founded in 1919. Although our 90,000 readers consist predominantly of UO alumni, our editorial approach has evolved in the past few years from a traditional alumni magazine to a regional magazine of ideas. To highlight this change, we now describe ourselves as "The Northwest Perspective from the University of Oregon."

Unlike a traditional alumni magazine, the majority of our features are not about the UO as such. Instead, we generally address topics of state and regional interest (ideas, issues and personalities) using the resources of UO faculty and alumni. The UO benefits from its involvement in these stories, not as their subject matter. Our goal is to reach a broad, well-educated regional audience, whether or not they have ties to the UO.

As a magazine, we want to be recognized for the quality of our writing. Good magazine stories should have shape and depth. They are closer in conception and execution to a thoughtful essay than to a newspaper feature. They should involve the reader, awaken the imagination. They require some effort to write, but they are much more a pleasure to read.

A few of our department stories and most of our features and profiles are contributed by freelancers. If the topic has a contemporary regional interest, and if UO involvement can be demonstrated (through faculty or alumni participation), we'd like to hear about it. We prefer brief query letters (with SASE) that show the flavor of the proposed article and your writing style. Submit clips that demonstrate your ability. If you don't have a story idea but would like to be considered for assignments, submit clips with a cover letter explaining your interests and experience.

We invite queries for features and UO alumni profiles. Our features generally run 1,500–3,000 words; short subjects run about 400–1,000 words. Pay varies depending on subject matter and writer's experience, with department stories usually ranging from $100 to $350 and features significantly more. We pay on acceptance (after requested revisions), plus reasonable expenses (with receipts), provided they are cleared by us in advance. For contracted stories we do not accept, we pay a kill fee of 20 percent the contracted amount. We generally follow the *Chicago Manual of Style*.

Categories: Nonfiction—Education—Regional

CONTACT: Submissions Editor
Material: All
5228 University of Oregon
Eugene OR 97403
Phone: 541-346-5047
E-mail: rwest@oregon.uoregon.edu
Website: www.oregonquarterly.com

OReview

About OReview and Its Readers

OReview is brought to you by the publisher of *OReview*, *Database Programming & Design*, and *DBMS* magazine. It is a qualified subscription magazine distributed nationally and internationally to about 30,000 readers. Most of these readers work within (or are consultants serving the needs of) corporate IS organizations. *OReview* is the only independently published technical journal for Oracle product users and serves database professionals, working in Oracle shops, with technical, unbiased, solutions-oriented editorial written by experts in the field. The primary editorial focus is on the implementation and management of Oracle's database product, but *OReview* also covers development strategies and researches various application tools (both Oracle and third-party tools). *OReview* 's goal is to help Oracle DBAs and developers understand and manage their Oracle-based systems, and give them tools they need to solve their day-to-day problems. Our readers are educated, technically astute, and have been around the block a few times; they know how to use their experience to guide them through a dynamic, market-driven industry.

Article Types

We accept many different types of articles, including "how to" articles, explanations of technology, industry reports, case histories, and so forth.

"How to" articles explain, step-by-step, how to solve a problem using a product, procedure, technology, or methodology, describing the do's and don'ts involved with implementation. Explanations of technology should describe new, different, or difficult solutions (such as distributed or object-oriented database), taking special care to cover why this technology is important to our readers, and what it can do for them.

A case history might focus on how your shop has implemented a new database or information systems strategy, focusing on the challenges and advantages of the new environment. Examples from recent issues of the magazine include migration from old to new database systems, introduction of CASE and repository technology, and downsizing from mainframe systems.

Getting Started on an Article

Now that you've got the writer's guidelines and hopefully a copy of the magazine, the best way to start is to use the following procedure:

We ask that you first prepare a one- to two-page abstract, outline, or summary of your proposed article idea and fax it to (415) 655-4350, or email it to our editor Kathleen O'Connor via the Internet at koconnor@mfi.com or via CompuServe at 76711,466. Alternatively, you can mail it to *OReview* , Article Submissions, 411 Borel Ave., Ste. 100, San Mateo, CA 94402. This way, our editors have the chance to look over your idea and decide if it fits in with the magazine before you put a lot of hard work into it. It should take us three-to-four weeks to respond to an article idea in abstract form.

You're free to send in a completed manuscript. However, we receive a number of unsolicited manuscripts and proposals, and they take time to review. Because of their length, it will take us approximately 6 to 8 weeks to accept or reject an article. Our staff will notify you upon receipt of your article or abstract. Be sure to include your phone and fax numbers, as well as your address. However, if you fail to hear from our staff, feel free to call us at (415) 358-9500 to inquire about your proposal.

Because we spend a great deal of time going over the ideas and articles we receive, we would appreciate if you would not submit your proposal to any other publications while it is under consideration with us. Please call our offices and notify us, in advance, if you plan to submit the idea or article to another publication while we are reviewing it.

If your abstract is approved, we will contact you, set a tentative publication date, and determine a deadline for completion of the article. Keep in mind, however, that in the magazine business things can change quickly. An article originally scheduled for April may get bumped to September for space reasons or for stronger editorial positioning.

Deadlines for each issue are approximately 4 months before the cover date. For example, articles for the April issue enter production in the beginning of January. And if you're submitting an abstract, factor at least an extra month into the equation.

Just a note: Because the editors travel a great deal, their time is in high demand when they are in the office. Although they like to discuss article ideas and help you develop them, attempts at such discussions are often plagued by a vicious game of telephone tag. Therefore, your best bet is to approach the editors via email at 76711.466@compuserve.com or via fax at (415) 655-4350. Be sure to address your fax or email to Editor, *OReview* magazine.

Preparing Your Manuscript for Publication

If your article idea is accepted, it's time for you to start writing. Article lengths may range from 2,500 to 6,000 words (18,000 to 43,000 characters). All articles should include any cited references and any needed tables, code fragments, figures, graphs, or screen shots (including appropriate captions). Please be sure to include a short biographical paragraph. We do not need artwork; however, if you have an idea for the artwork, feel free to mention it in a cover letter. Also be sure to include a working title for your article.

Please adhere to the following style when using references, including all of the information listed in these examples:

Books: Date, C. An Introduction to Database Systems, Volume One. Addison-Wesley, 1990. **Magazines:** Melton, J. "SQL2 (The Sequel): An Emerging Standard," Database Programming & Design, Volume 3, Number 11, pages 24-34, November 1990. **Technical Publications:** IBM. "IBM Database 2 Version 2 SQL Reference," September 1989, IBM order number SC26-4380-1.

Getting Your Article to Us

When you complete your article, you can send it to us in one of the following two ways:

1. Send it by overnight mail to *OReview* , Article Submissions, 411 Borel Ave., Ste. 100, San Mateo, CA 94402. Be sure to enclose on a Word or DOS-formatted disk (or with a note telling us the type of program it was created with), a hard copy of the article, and hard copies of any diagrams or figures you wish to accompany the article. Remember to format the file as any Macintosh, Word for Windows, or DOS word-processor file.

2. Email the article to our Internet account, 76711.466@ compuserve.com, or Kathleen O'Connor's email account, koconnor@ mfi.com. If you use email, remember to format the file as any Macintosh, Word for Windows, or DOS word-processor file. And don't forget to include your name, telephone, and fax numbers, and address on the email version and follow up with a faxed copy of the article and any figures to (415) 655-4350.

Your article will undergo editing for content, form, and style, and will then be returned to you via email for a final error check. Your job will be to answer any questions the editors may have as well as to check for factual errors and any mistakes that might have crept in during editing and transmission.

The Fine Print

OReview offers payment for all printed articles. At the time you call in your galley corrections, we ask that you provide your social security or tax-ID number so we may process your payment.

OReview routinely purchases all rights to articles, which means that the editors reserve the right to reprint or republish the work at a later date. The editors will modify this standard practice upon written request; it is not *OReview*'s intention to deprive authors of rights to their work.

OReview reserves the right to reject an article at any time, even after it's been initially accepted. If we reject an article that we had formerly accepted, we will pay a "kill" fee of one third the rate promised for the article.

Categories: Computers

CONTACT: Article Submission
411 Borel Ave., Ste. 100
San Mateo, CA 94402
Fax: 415-655-4350
E-mail: 76711.466@compuserve.com
Website: www.oreview.xom

The Other Side

Our Mission and Focus:

The Other Side is an independent ecumenical magazine that seeks to advance a broad Christian vision that's biblical and compassionate, appreciative of the creative arts, and committed to the intimate intertwining of personal spirituality and social transformation. We weave together first-person essays, insightful analyses, biblical reflection, interviews, fiction, poetry, and an inviting mix of visual art. We strive to nurture, uplift, and challenge readers with personal, provocative writing that reflects the transformative, liberating Spirit of Jesus Christ.

How to Submit:

Articles should be sent with a stamped, self-addressed return envelope to the attention of our fiction, nonfiction, or poetry editor (as appropriate) at the address below. Articles without return postage will not be returned. Although we do not require queries or purchase articles on speculation, if you want to query about our potential interest in an article, you may call 215-849-2178 and ask to speak to someone on the editorial staff. We do not currently accept unsolicited manuscripts by fax or e-mail.

Prospective authors should review current issues of the magazine—or at least examine the material on our website at www.theotherside.org—before submitting. Sample issues are available for $6.00; Subscriptions are $27 per year. Send payment to Subscription Office, 300 W. Apsley St., Philadelphia, PA 19144—or order by credit card by calling 1-800-700-9280 or visiting our subscription page.

Submission Guidelines:

NONFICTION pieces range from 400 to 4,000 words, with most running 2,000 words or less. Payment for nonfiction ranges from $50 to $300, depending on the piece. Less than 3 percent of submitted manuscripts are accepted. We publish reflective essays, personal journeys, biblical analysis, spiritual explorations, interviews with unusual people, theological explorations, investigative reporting, and creative thinking.

We are looking for articles addressing contemporary social, political, and economic issues (especially those revealing an awareness of race, class, gender, and other dynamics). We have a strong interest in the arts, cultural change, and creative expression. And we are always interested in writing that makes connections between spiritual and social renewal, reflecting God's longing that our world—and each of our lives—might be made new. All authors should keep in mind *The Other Side*'s commitment to social and economic justice, peace and nonviolence, the liberating power of Scripture, and the compassionate, inclusive ways of Christ.

POETRY submissions should include strong imagery, fresh viewpoints, and lively language, while avoiding versifications of religious instruction or syrupy piety. Poems should be no more than 50 lines in length, and no more than three submissions will be considered at any one time from the same author. Payment for poems is generally $25. Less than one-half of 1 percent of all poems submitted are accepted.

FICTION should be between 500 and 5,000 words in length, the shorter the better. Payment is between $75 and $250. We're looking for strongly crafted fiction that deepens our readers' encounter with the mystery of God and the mystery of ourselves.

We normally report on submissions in four to eight weeks, depending on the timeliness of the piece. We buy first serial and additional associated rights. We will not consider previously published material.

In addition to financial payment, authors receive complimentary copies of the issue in which their material appears and a free two-year subscription (or subscription extension). Payment is on acceptance.

Categories: Fiction—Nonfiction—African-American—Arts—Christian Interests—Environment—Feminism—Gay/Lesbian—Human Rights—Inspirational—Poetry—Politics—Religion—Spiritual

CONTACT: Deborah Good, Editorial Associate
Material: Nonfiction, Fiction

CONTACT: Jeanne Minahan, Poetry Editor
Material: Poetry
300 W. Apsley St.
Philadelphia PA 19144-4285
Phone: 215-849-2178
Website: www.theotherside.org

Other Voices
University of Illinois-Chicago

Fiction Guidelines

1. OV reads unpublished, unsolicited manuscripts between October 1 and April 1, only.

2. Short stories and self-contained novel excerpts only

3. One story at a time, please!

4. 5,000 word maximum preferred, but not mandatory.

5. Writer's name on each page of mss.

6. Save a tree—the Editors suggest a letter-size SASE for reply only (and promise to recycle your mss.).

7. 10-12 week reply

8. No taboos, except ineptitude and murkiness.

Send Us Your Best Voice/Your Best Work/Your Best...

Categories: Literature

CONTACT: Gina Frangello, Executive Editor
Material: Fiction
CONTACT: Marina Lewis, Associate Editor
Material: Fiction
University of Illinois at Chicago
Dept. of English, 601 S. Morgan
Chicago IL 60607
Phone: 312-413-2209

Our Sunday Visitor

Our Sunday Visitor, our award-winning flagship publication, is by far the largest-circulating national Catholic weekly newspaper in the United States.

Our proud history began in 1912 in Huntington, Ind., when Father (later Archbishop) John F. Noll founded *Our Sunday Visitor* newspaper in response to a proliferation of anti-Catholic publications, most famously "The Menace." Father Noll's purpose was to educate Catholics in their faith so as to empower them to respond to questions about Catholic beliefs and practices as well as to live their faith as Catholics within the secular environment.

Anti-Catholic bigotry has become more subtle since Father Noll's early days, but OSV's aims remain generally the same: We help Catholics to understand the news, challenges and cultural trends of our day from an authentically Catholic perspective. Seeing the world through the eyes of the Catholic faith and in harmony with the magisterium of the Church ennobles us to serve as effective witnesses to our faith in the workplace, in the schools, in the public square, and within our own homes and families.

OSV thus serves as a kind of "defogging agent" — clarifying the confusion present in the mixed messages received amid the rapid changes in technology, shifting contemporary moral viewpoints and political rhetoric. This apostolate is summarized in our tagline as we strive to provide "Catholic Clarity in a Complex World."

Although the majority of our content is generated on assignment by our core contributors, we welcome and consider all freelance contributions, whether offered by query or unsolicited manuscript.

Here's a quick summary of what we are looking for:

* News analysis — not merely news reporting — pertaining to the Catholic Church in the United States and throughout the world.

* Features linked to the current events and trends of the day.

* Faith-based articles that take advantage of the "catechetical

moments" derived from the daily headlines and the liturgical year.

* Sound, reader-friendly, well-crafted presentation packages that engage and draw the reader more deeply into the text.

Here's what we generally are *not* looking for:

* Articles written in the first person.
* Long, academic or preachy commentaries.
* Features with no real link to Catholic faith or sensibilities.
* Straight news reporting, especially on strictly local events.
* Articles designed to publicize a future event.
* Short stories, whether fiction or non-fiction.
* Poetry.

Specific OSV submission categories

OSV's content is sectioned into several regular categories (News Analysis, News Briefings, In Focus, Faith, Perspectives) and several recurring categories (Trends, Family, Media, Heritage, Profile, Conversation, Essay).

NEWS ANALYSIS: Provides the "second-day" perspective on the critical events of the day. We get behind the news to examine its implications and applications from a Catholic point of view. The writer must exercise a degree of journalistic clairvoyance: What angle and developments will be relevant to the reader two weeks hence? These articles usually involve investigative interviews and prudent use of sources to get to the heart of the issue at hand. Generally 950-1,100 words (including sidebars), but occasionally run as short as 500 words or as long as 2,000 words.

NEWS BRIEFINGS: These items are edited from wire services and do not present an opportunity for freelance submissions.

IN FOCUS: This four-page pull-out section is at the heart of OSV. Planned many weeks in advance, the In Focus section takes a particular topic of contemporary interest and examines it thoroughly within a package of articles. One In Focus section each month is devoted to a series on "What the Church Teaches and Why." In Focus sections comprise a package of articles totaling 3,000-4,000 words written by one or several authors.

FAITH: An intentionally broad topic that can range from weighty issues of belief to methods of enhancing one's prayer life to a discussion of parish "best practices" in a given area of ministry. It should always result in a suggestion for further exploration through an "action plan" or sources for additional information. The package, including sidebars, can reach 1,100 to 1,300 words.

PERSPECTIVES: Primarily an outlet for comment by OSV's editors and columnists, there are no opportunities here for compensated submissions. Letters to the editors and responses to our OSV Reader Poll are always welcome, however.

TRENDS: Here we look at the observed religious, cultural or statistical swings and provide context from a faith perspective: What is behind this particular trend? What are its advantages and pitfalls? What are Catholics to make of it? What ought or can we do about it? What does it say about the direction of our culture as a whole? Aim for 600 to 750 words.

FAMILY: This topic area can explore issues involving parents, grandparents, children, marriage, couples, and the family as a whole. In practical terms, how should we apply our faith to family life, to the interpersonal relationships therein? Word count: 600 to 750 words.

MEDIA: Analysis of trends in the entertainment and news industry, book and film reviews, the Internet and related topics comprise the content for this recurring section. Word count: 600 to 750 words.

HERITAGE: Here we revisit key moments in Catholic history, recall the inspiring examples of holy men and women in the Church, or survey some of the grand sites and stories that reflect our Catholic past. Word count: 500 to 750 words.

CONVERSATION: This section takes two forms: Question-and-answer-format interviews with selected personalities and roundups of reader comment on topics of particular interest. Our interviews require an introductory paragraph or two that sets the background and the speaker's credentials for the discussion that follows. All told, these interviews can run 500 to 1,200 words in their edited form.

PROFILE: Here we examine a particular person, place or organization that serves as an example of Catholic faith in action. What benefit can readers draw from hearing this story? The purpose here is not so much to honor the individual or group as to inspire by its example. Word count: 500 to 750 words.

ESSAY: OSV does not have a "guest column" per se, but occasionally we use a reader's commentary under the Essay heading. This represents the very limited opportunity for a longer opinion piece or first-person narrative. It must have a point to make and succeed at making it succinctly, keeping the facts firmly in mind and avoiding a shrill, ranting or uncharitable tone. Word count: 500 to 750 words.

Characteristics of a viable OSV article

All OSV entries should be:

* **Tightly written.** We have limited space for editorial copy, so we don't need excessively breezy articles. Get to the point, express it clearly, and draw the necessary conclusions.

* **Cleanly written.** We have the best editors in the Catholic press, but we don't need to be spending our time correcting basic grammatical and spelling errors.

* **Timely.** Your story should be more than simply generically inspirational or informative. It should tie it in to some news or current trend that makes it more relevant today. In other words, have a reason for bringing up the subject.

* **Objective.** Follow basic journalistic ethics and exhibit professional skills. This doesn't mean we boil everything down to a "he said/she said" approach, however: The Church's teaching or official position must come through. However, we deal with all issues with a sense of charity, justice and a responsibility to proclaim the faith.

* **Instructive.** Generally, this must be done in a subtle, non-preachy way. Features particularly should inspire readers and motivate them to actively apply the faith to their daily lives.

* **Faithful.** The teachings of the Catholic Church as reflected in its catechism, as well as the statements and teachings of the popes and the bishops of the United States on doctrinal, moral and social-justice issues must be respected.

How to submit queries

A query—a solicitation or "pitch" to write a particular article on a particular topic and angle — can be sent to us via e-mail or postal mail. Clearly state your objective, outline the expected article and commit to how quickly you can have it in. You might attach clips of your past work for us to review as well if you have not written for OSV previously.

Writers with whom we are not familiar may be asked to produce article "on spec" ("on specification") — meaning that we'll be glad to read your finished product, but without any commitment to purchase it.

When submitting a query by e-mail, always put the word QUERY in the subject line. This will help us sort the story pitches from the daily flood of e-mail so that your query does not get lost and can be answered more promptly. We generally respond within 4-6 weeks, sooner when possible.

How to submit unsolicited manuscripts

You may send a manuscript without an advance query via either e-mail or postal mail to the attention of OSV Editor.

Include your name, mailing address, telephone number and e-mail address. Social Security Number is needed for U.S. citizens in case we purchase your article, but you can phone that in to us later if you have security concerns.

Always indicate what rights are being offered and whether the manuscript has been submitted or published in any other publication or website – even if it's just another version of the article.

Send a cover letter extolling the virtues of the article and its relevance as well as your qualifications to write it. Add a resume or other samples of your writing if you prefer. We request all documents be attached in Microsoft Word format, although rich text, plain text or even pasting the article directly into the e-mail message is also acceptable.

When submitting by e-mail, always include the word MANU-SCRIPT in the subject line. This will help us sort the manuscripts from the daily flood of e-mail so that your article does not get lost and can be answered more promptly.

We generally respond within 4-6 weeks, sooner when possible. Things we'd rather not spell out....

Because not all of our would-be freelance writers are trained journalists, we must state the following criteria more clearly:

* **Don't plagiarize.** All articles must be original work of the author. Its content must not have been previously published, in whole or in part, whether in print, broadcast, Internet or electronic form, even by the author himself. If a piece has been so published and there is a compelling reason to offer it to OSV, or if what is being offered is a version of a previously published article, this information must be divulged at the outset.

* **Familiarize yourself with OSV first.** Every publication has its own unique "flavor" and style. Even the best writers' guidelines can't fully express the kind of voice, flow and format the editors are seeking. Subscribe to OSV for several weeks to get a better feel for what we are trying to do.

* **Follow the submission guidelines closely.** If you don't write the subject line as we request, your e-mail risks getting lost in our system. Without an SASE or cover letter, we may not reply if the piece is not accepted. Lacking a clear statement that you are offering first rights, we may be led to believe it is a simultaneous submission and reject it out of hand. Take the time to provide the information and tools we require upfront.

POLICIES

* We respond to freelance queries and unsolicited manuscripts within 4 to 6 weeks of receipt.

* We pay writers within 4 weeks of acceptance.

* We generally follow the Catholic News Service 2005 Stylebook (available through www.cns.com) and the current Associated Press Stylebook. For scriptural citations, we generally use the New American Bible.

* We comply with the Fair Publishing Practices Code of the Catholic Press Association of the United States and Canada. We expect freelance writers to do the same. For a complete copy of this code, visit www.catholicpress.com.

* For a sample copy of OSV, send $2 (payable to OSV) and a 10-inch by 13-inch SASE with 93 cents in postage affixed.

Categories: Fiction—Nonfiction—Family—History—Poetry—Religion—Short Stories—Catholic Church

CONTACT: Our Sunday Visitor
200 Noll Plaza
Huntington IN 46750
Phone: 800-348-2440
E-mail: oursunvis@osv.com
Website: www.osv.com

Outdoor America

SUBMISSION GUIDELINES
ABOUT OUR MAGAZINE AND THE IZAAK WALTON LEAGUE OF AMERICA

Since 1923, Outdoor America has been the flagship publication of the Izaak Walton League, a conservation organization that works at the local, state, and national levels. The magazine is mailed quarterly to the League's 40,000 members. We also send copies to members of Congress and other national leaders who set conservation policy. Our mission is to provide readers with the information and inspiration to protect America's outdoors through grassroots action. The magazine is published in January, April, July, and October.

MANUSCRIPTS

Outdoor America is primarily staff written, however, we publish a handful of freelance articles per issue. These include 2,000–3,000 word features, 1,500–2,000 word essays, and shorter column and news pieces. Although we welcome queries and submissions from new writers, we strongly recommend that you read a recent copy of our magazine to get a feel for our subject matter and style.

What we want: Every story must have a direct connection to the League's members, activities, or policies. We rarely make exceptions. All stories should have two goals: to inform and to inspire. We prefer writing that has a conversational tone, speaks directly and concisely, and provides a fresh perspective. We encourage journalists to employ scene, characterization, narrative, and other tools of literary nonfiction.

What we don't want: We do not publish fiction, poetry, or unsubstantiated opinion pieces.

Audience: League members are community-based conservationists with strong interests in fishing, camping, boating, hunting, and other traditional forms of outdoor recreation. Most live in towns and small cities in the Great Lakes, Midwest, and Mid-Atlantic regions. About 85 percent belong to local chapters.

Tip: Our biggest pet peeve is receiving queries from writers who have never read our magazine or researched the Izaak Walton League's work. Most queries are rejected because they simply fail to demonstrate a connection to the League.

Queries: Letter queries should be one page and must include a self-addressed, stamped envelope. E-mail queries should be brief and without large attachments. Do not fax or phone queries. We do our best to respond within 60 days. We assume no responsibility for lost or damaged manuscripts. Send materials to Outdoor America Editor at address below.

PHOTOGRAPHY

The outdoor photography market is very saturated, and we usually find what we need from our regular pool of stock and assignment photographers. However, we do welcome new photographers into the mix. Please look at recent issues of our magazine to get a feel for our needs and style. If you think your work is right for us, send tearsheets or nonreturnable samples. We will contact you if we want to see more.

Tip: We look for creativity as much as quality.

Subjects: Our scope of coverage is broad, and it's best for photographers to check out our Web site for the latest issues we're working on. However, here are some subjects we regularly search for: stream restoration, litter, habitat loss, sprawl, human-wildlife conflicts, air pollution, wetland protection, agricultural conservation, clean and renewable energy, sustainable forestry, conservation on private lands, outdoor ethics, public land management, fisheries conservation, game species, and scenes of individuals and families enjoying the outdoors.

Submitting material: Do not send original material unless requested. Mail to Outdoor America Art Director, IWLA, 707 Conservation Lane, Gaithersburg, MD 20878-2983. Include SASE if you would like a response. We do our best to respond within 60 days.

PAYMENT

Articles: We generally pay between $1,000–$1,500 for feature stories (2,000–3,000 words). The fee grants Outdoor America first North American serial rights, exclusive to us for 30 days following publication. If the writer wishes to sell subsequent rights, we ask that he or she credit Outdoor America as the first publisher. Kill fees are determined at the editor's discretion, and are generally one-third of the original rate.

Photos:

Front cover: $500*

Inside pages: .... $100–$450*

(*Standard fees for stock photos. Assigned & exceptional work can receive more.)

Note: Front-cover fee grants IWLA the non-exclusive use of the photo in the Outdoor America cover format for publication on our Web site, media guide, and other promotional materials. Any other appearance of the photo in non-cover format would be considered an additional use and would be subject to an additional fee.

Contracts and invoices: When Outdoor America hires a writer or photographer, the magazine will send a contract outlining the terms of the assignment. To process payment, this contract must be signed and returned, and must be accompanied by an invoice noting the contractor's full name, mailing address, Social Security number, amount due, article or photo title, and publication date.

Sample copies are available for $2.50 each. Please make check out to "Outdoor America, c/o Izaak Walton League." Or you can purchase copies through our Web site, www.iwla.org.

Categories: Nonfiction—Conservation—Environment—Fishing—Outdoors—Sports/Recreation—Hunting

CONTACT: Jason McGarvey, Editor
Material: All
Izaak Walton League of America
707 Conservation Lane
Gaithersburg MD 20878
Phone: 301-548-0150 x228
Fax: 301-548-9409
E-mail: oa@iwla.org
Website: www.iwla.org

Outdoor Life

WHAT DOES *Outdoor Life* BUY?

Outdoor Life serves the active sportsman and his family with primary emphasis on hunting, fishing, outdoor adventures and game conservation.

• We do not buy: poetry, fiction, backpacking, kayaking, cycling or adventure travel stories. If you are interested in writing for *Outdoor Life*, study the magazine. What we publish is your best guide to the kinds of material we seek.

• We accept very few unsolicited manuscripts. The best advice is to query first. Write a crisp, concise (one-page) query letter that clearly outlines your idea in a few paragraphs. Include a few sentences about how the story might best be illustrated, e.g. with photographs, illustrations, technical drawings or cartoons. Please include a self-addressed, stamped envelope to expedite replies. Electronic queries are also acceptable (OLMagazine@ aol.com).

• Do you have something new to offer the reader that will help him or her enjoy hunting and fishing more? How do you think it will help? How would you present it? All of our columns and features include a wide use of interesting sidebars, charts, graphs, pull quotes, pictographs and subheads to provide multiple points of entry for readers into stories. How might you incorporate these to engage readers?

• Our Snap Shots, Private Lessons and Regional sections are three places where writers who have never worked with us before can break in. Please note the section in which you are interested on the outside of your envelope to ensure that your query reaches the right editor for that section.

You are better off being early—even considerably early—with a query than to be even a little late. Right now, we are thinking about what will be in *Outdoor Life* a year from now. Writers and photographers should be thinking the same way. Though we have millions of readers, we never forget that we reach them one at a time. A reader who picks up a copy of *Outdoor Life* is asking, "What's in it for me?" You are writing for intelligent readers who are eager to learn more about the sports they are most passionate about. Your job is to make it clear and interesting.

• Please be advised that we are free at any time to use story ideas that are the same or similar to yours and that we shall be under no obligation to you unless we enter into a written agreement with you with respect to your story.

• We pay on acceptance.

PREPARING MANUSCRIPTS AND PHOTOS

• Manuscripts must be typed, double-spaced and you must include a copy of your manuscript on a 3½-inch computer disk either as a Word document or MS-DOS file. Number the pages, and type your name and the story title at the top of every page. Leave wide margins. Do not staple or bind manuscript pages. Paper clips are fine.

• Please do not send photographs until your query has been accepted and a formal assignment made.

• Photographers desiring to make "photo-only" submissions should request our photographer's guidelines before sending photos.

We take every possible precaution in handling unsolicited materials. However, we are not responsible for their damage or loss. Submissions not accompanied by a properly stamped, self-addressed envelope WILL NOT be returned.

Categories: Nonfiction—Adventure—Animals—Book Reviews—Conservation—Consumer—Cooking—Crafts/Hobbies—Ecology—Fishing—Health—History—Hobbies—Interview—Outdoors—Photography—Physical Fitness—Recreation—Regional—Sports/Recreation—Travel—Hunting - How-to - Nostalgia—Essay—Personal Experience—Nature

CONTACT: Collin Moore, Exec. Editor/Manuscript Review
Material: All
CONTACT: Joi Harvey, Senior Assistant to the Editor-in-Chief
Material: All
Time4 Media, Inc. /Time, Inc.
Magazine and Publishing Division
Two Park Ave., 10th Floor
New York NY 10016-5695
Phone: 212-779-5257
Fax: 212-779-5366
E-mail: olmagazine@aol.com
Website: www.outdoorlife.com

Outdoor Photographer

Submission Guidelines

OUTDOOR PHOTOGRAPHER is a national magazine published 11 times per year for enthusiasts with a special passion for nature, travel and outdoor sports. We take a fresh look at the modern photographic world by encouraging photography as part of a lifestyle associated with outdoor recreation. Editorial is intended to demystify the use of modern equipment by emphasizing practical use of the camera in the field, highlighting the technique rather than the technical. OUTDOOR PHOTOGRAPHER is written and presented to accomplish two ends: to stimulate outdoor, sporting and nature enthusiasts to enhance their recreational and travel enjoyment through photography, and to satisfy the needs of amateur and professional photographers with a special interest in the outdoors.

Feature articles include:

1. Interviews and portfolio displays of accomplished professional and amateur photographers.

2. Non-technical equipment evaluations directed at outdoor use. Methods and techniques for using, transporting and maintaining photo equipment in the field.

3. Travel, destinations, photo tours, field courses, workshops. Submissions that OUTDOOR PHOTOGRAPHER publishes in the "Favorite Places" section of the magazine also will be archived on the Website as a service to our readers.

4. New technologies, from traditional to digital, that help readers make better images.

5. Photographic instruction as it relates to outdoor interests and activities, including wildlife viewing, landscape, close-ups, nature, adventure and scenic travel, and outdoor sports such as backpacking, camping, canoeing/kayaking/rafting, skiing, climbing, surfing, bicycle touring, etc.

GENERAL POLICY

The majority of the magazine's features and several departments are freelance-written and -photographed. We look for a variety of contributors from different backgrounds and geographic areas. Submitted manuscripts should be typewritten and double-spaced (a computer disk is fine, but we also need a hard copy for evaluation). Photographs (see Photographs for Submission guidelines below) must be protected for shipment and preferably sent by registered mail or other traceable means. We receive too many submissions to check if yours was received. If you need that information, use a verifiable delivery service. All submissions must be accompanied by an SASE. All work is submitted as speculation (see Terms and Conditions) unless specifically assigned in writing by an assignment letter. Return or notification of possible use can be expected in approximately two months. **OUTDOOR PHOTOG-RAPHER** buys one-time rights for publication in the magazine and on the magazine's Website as part of our permanent archives. Payment is initiated on date of publication.

PROCESS OF SUBMISSION

Since **OUTDOOR PHOTOGRAPHER** is a photography magazine, we must see photos before any decision can be made on an article, so phone queries are not appropriate. Ultimately, whether or not we can use a particular piece will depend greatly on the photographs and how they fit in with material already in our files.

1. For initial queries, we request photo submissions to be in the form of duplicate transparencies, photographic prints or high-quality inkjet printouts. Tear sheets from books or calendars also are acceptable. We do not accept original transparencies or negatives. Do not send photo submissions on disk or CD-ROM unless a hard copy index or proof sheet is included.

2. Your letter should include exactly what you wish to cover in your proposed article and a brief outline of the information or points you intend to include. The more specific you can be, the better we will be able to judge the merits of your idea.

3. If your story and photographs are selected for publication, we will decide whether or not to use the duplicates that you originally submitted or require new ones to be made for improved quality. Only on special occasions will we ask for original transparencies, and special arrangements will be made for their shipment and handling as well as insurance.

4. Often, we are overwhelmed by the great volume of submissions we receive for the limited number of pages available in any given issue of the magazine. We wish we could use all of the terrific work we receive. Unfortunately, we can't. We try to get materials returned within approximately eight weeks. While **OUTDOOR PHOTOGRAPHER** hopes to review and return unusable material as quickly as possible, our priority has to be producing each issue of the magazine. If photographs or manuscripts are deemed suitable for publication, they may be held for future consideration. Holding such materials does not automatically constitute an acceptance of terms and conditions printed on delivery memos, packing slips or similar correspondence.

PHOTOGRAPHS FOR SUBMISSION

Please limit submissions to approximately 20 photographs or less. We don't need more than that to see the merit in an article idea. In fact, we consider the initial submission of too many photographs to represent the lack of necessary editing to present a selection that succinctly supports the subject being queried.

1. We accept all film formats, preferring 35mm, medium format and 4x5 for transparencies and 5x7 or 8x10 for prints. In all cases, we work with digital files and duplicate transparencies. We do not accept original transparencies or negatives. If, of your own accord, you choose to send originals, you do so only at your own risk. Realize that while we try to protect images sent to us on speculation, **OUTDOOR PHO-TOGRAPHER** accepts no responsibility for lost or damaged photographic materials.

2. Since we do not accept original materials, **OUTDOOR PHO-TOGRAPHER** will not accept financial responsibility for lost or damaged original photographic materials, transparencies or negatives.

INSURANCE

Your photographs will be carried, shipped and mailed by messengers, couriers and mail services while in transit to and from **OUTDOOR PHOTOGRAPHER** and, in the case of use, by its vendors. All these carriers and vendors will decline coverage of "extraordinary value" for items like photographs. Under their policies (and in the case of mail services, no matter the amount of insurance purchased), photographs will be covered only for the replacement value of the film and processing. Therefore, it is impossible for **OUTDOOR PHOTOGRAPHER** to warrant against damage or loss while photographic or written materials are in our office or in transit. When returning materials to a contributor, the class of mail will be determined by the amount of postage provided for on the SASE enclosed with the submission.

TERMS AND CONDITIONS OUTDOOR PHOTOGRAPHER assumes no responsibility for solicited or unsolicited contribution materials unless otherwise agreed to in writing over our signature as detailed under Photographs for Submission in these guidelines. **OUT-DOOR PHOTOGRAPHER** does not automatically accept or agree to the conditions and stipulations printed on delivery memos, packing slips and related correspondence as they are presented without prior notice when accompanied by submission materials. **OUTDOOR PHO-TOGRAPHER** does not accept the premise that any and all transparencies or negatives are automatically worth a minimum of $1,500 as suggested by some photographic organizations, especially since we make a policy of not accepting original material and any original material sent to us is at the photographer's risk. Exceptions to this disclaimer of liability on the part of **OUTDOOR PHOTOGRAPHER** must be prearranged, executed in writing and signed by both parties prior to the shipment of materials in question. Again, this policy is for your protection as well as ours.

THANK YOU FOR THE CONTRIBUTIONS! We value your article ideas and photographic offerings. With your help, **OUTDOOR PHOTOGRAPHER** continues to be vital, informative and unpredictable.

Categories: Sports

CONTACT: Editor
Material: All
Phone: 310-820-1500
Fax: 310-826-5008
Website: www.outdoorphotographer.com

Outdoor World

Subjects. *Outdoor World* covers all aspects of hunting and fishing from spring gobbler hunting to trolling for walleyes to bow-hunting monster whitetails. It strives to keep readers aware of all aspects of the outdoors by mixing serious conservation issues with informational articles and light-hearted stories.

Length. Features range from 1,000 to 3,000 words.

Contract and Payment. We buy one-time rights, and a signed contract is required. Payment is $250 to $600 for features.

Submissions. Queries accompanied by a SASE are preferred over manuscripts. Published writers should include a resume and nonreturnable clips of their work. Other materials will not be returned without a SASE. Written queries are preferred over phone queries. E-mail is also acceptable. Response time is three to four months. Accepted stories should be sent by e-mail or on a computer disk, if possible, and should be accompanied by typed hard copy. Address correspondence to Brian Lovett, editor.

Photos. *Outdoor World* requires a variety of photography and is very dependent on contributions. We are always in need of good vertical shots with cover potential. Cover images are generally of animals, and should be sharp and vibrant. Each cover relates to the theme of the issue, i.e. white-tailed deer for the bow-hunting issue or elk or mule deer for the big-game issue. Inside photo possibilities are endless. A photography needs list is available upon request. Contact Jennifer Pillath, managing editor.

Outdoor World purchases one-time rights for photography, and payment varies according to the size of the photo used in the magazine.

Photography Rates:
- Front Cover - $500
- More than 1.5 pages - $250
- Full to 1.5 pages - $150
- Half-page to full - $100
- Less than half-page - $75
- Black and white - $50

Categories: Nonfiction—Fishing—Outdoors

CONTACT: Brian Lovett, Editor
Material: All
CONTACT: Jennifer Pillath, Managing Editor
Material: All
Krause Publications
700 E. State St.
Iola WI 54945
Phone: 715-445-2214
Fax: 715-445-4087
E-mail: lovettb@krause.com
Website: www.outdoorworldmag.com

Outside

Outside is a monthly national magazine dedicated to covering the people, sports and activities, politics, art, literature, and hardware of the outdoors. Although our features are usually assigned to a regular stable of experienced and proven writers, we're always interested in new authors and their ideas. In particular, we look for articles on outdoor events, regions, and activities; informative seasonal service pieces; sports and adventure travel pieces; profiles of engaging outdoor characters; and investigative stories on environmental issues.

Queries should present a clear, original, and provocative thesis, not merely a topic or idea, and should reflect familiarity with the magazine's content and tone. Features are generally 1,500 to 5,000 words in length. Dispatches articles (100 to 800 words) cover timely news, events, issues, and short profiles. Destinations pieces (300 to 1,000 words) include places, news, and advice for adventurous travelers. Review articles (200 to 1,500 words) examine and evaluate outdoor gear and equipment.

Separate guidelines are available for prospective photo and illustration contributors. Please request them directly from the photo or art departments.

Please send queries (not manuscripts) and two or three relevant clips along with a self-addressed stamped envelope to address below. Our response time is usually six to eight weeks.

Categories: Nonfiction—Adventure—Environment—Sports—Travel

CONTACT: Editorial Department
Material: All
Outside magazine
400 Market St
Santa Fe NM 87501

Over the BACK FENCE

Over the Back Fence

Writers' Rates and Guidelines

For written submissions used in *Over the Back Fence*, or in other publications produced by Long Point Media the following rates and guidelines apply:

Over the Back Fence is a regional magazine serving counties in southern Ohio. Our approach can be equated to a friendly and informative conversation with a neighbor about interesting people, places and events. Southern Ohio coverage includes: Adams, Athens, Brown, Clark, Clermont, Clinton, Coshocton, Darke, Delaware, Fairfield, Fayette, Franklin, Gallia, Greene, Guernsey, Hamilton, Highland, Hocking, Holmes, Jackson, Lawrence, Licking, Madison, Meigs, Miami, Montgomery, Morgan, Muskingum, Noble, Perry, Pickaway, Pike, Ross, Scioto, Vinton, Warren, Washington and Wayne counties.

Long Point Media purchases print publication and web rights from freelance writers as well as makes assignments for specific articles. We reserve the right to reprint written submissions and will make payment for any additional usage, not to exceed original payment. If a submission has been previously published elsewhere, the date and name of the other publication must accompany text.

QUERIES: Send queries for articles. This allows Long Point Media the opportunity to work with writers in developing the most appropriate stories for our publications. However, you may send samples of your writing style or you may send already published articles for consideration. A self-addressed, stamped envelope MUST be enclosed for a response to be sent or samples returned.

SUBMISSIONS: Your manuscript should be double spaced on 8 ½ X 11 inch white paper with your name, address and daytime phone number on the top right corner of the first page. Include an e-mail address, if possible. Your name must appear on every page thereafter. Always send a cover letter containing contact information. Responses will be sent only if a SASE is included. You may also submit the piece pasted within an e-mail message.

Feature stories are usually 1,000 to 1,200 words after editing. A byline will appear in the publication. Our magazine is published quarterly, each spring, summer, fall and winter. Please make submissions at least six months to one year in advance, and consider the season for which your submission is intended.

RATES: They begin at 10 cents per word, but are negotiable with experience. A minimum fee of $25 will be paid, and payment is upon publication, net 15 days. Writers receive a contributor copy.

ASSIGNMENTS: Writers may be selected to complete writing assignments that match their writing styles, interests and specialties.

TEXT / PHOTO PACKAGES: For writers who want to supply photographs or illustrations along with their submissions, please request our Photographers' and Illustrators' Rates and Guidelines. Rates and guidelines are subject to change without notice. Sample copies of the magazine may be obtained by sending $4.00. Subscriptions are $12.50 annually.

Categories: Fiction—Nonfiction—Arts—Family—General Interest—History—Outdoors—Recreation—Regional—Rural America—Short Stories—Travel

CONTACT: Sarah Williamson, Over the Back Fence Magazine
Material: All
PO Box 756
Chillicothe OH 45601
Phone: 1-800-718-5727
E-mail: backfenc@bright.net or sarahw@longpointmedia.com
Website: www.backfencemagazine.com

Overland Journal
Oregon-California Trails Association

The *Overland Journal* is always in need of articles, and all articles received are appreciated and given careful consideration. There are three general requirements for an *OJ* article:

(1) TOPIC: The focus of an article must be on some aspect of the emigrant trails or the overland migration in western America;

(2) ORIGINAL RESEARCH: An article must reflect some form of original research or interpretation. It should not be just a compilation of information from modern authors' articles or books (i.e., secondary sources.) Original research would include any one or combination of the following:

a) articles that are based substantially on primary written source material, both published and unpublished, such as diaries, journals, reminiscences, letters, contemporary newspapers, government reports and other archival materials. It is understood that articles of original research can and usually will make use of and have reference to secondary sources, but the main supporting evidence should be taken from primary sources. An exception to this requirement would include articles that interpret, evaluate or analyze secondary sources and published primary sources of published emigrant trail literature;

b) articles that are based on non-literary evidence drawn from areas of archaeology, technology, geology, geography, cartography, field research, statistics or personal interviews;

c) articles that are themselves primary sources and are supported by primary and secondary sources, such as an unpublished emigrant diary edited and annotated especially for the *Overland Journal*.

The requirements on documentation and original research are not to imply that the *OJ* is a scholarly publication primarily written for academic specialists. Quite the contrary, it is a history magazine primarily designed for the lay reader who is interested in the western overland trails and the migration experience. Nevertheless, even with this lay emphasis, there is a need for original ideas and interpretations that are convincingly documented.

Articles submitted for consideration must not be submitted to other publications concurrently;

(3) DOCUMENTATION: All significant evidence, references, assertions, data and facts not commonly known must be well documented. The appropriate form of documentation will depend on the type of evidence used.

The *OJ* uses endnotes rather than footnotes. Text and notes are based for the most part on *The Chicago Manual of Style*. However, the best reference to use when preparing a manuscript is a copy of the *OJ* itself. If you do not have a copy, please write to OCTA headquarters to obtain a sample copy.

Notes should include author of publication cited, editor if appropriate, exact title (including unusual spelling, capitalization or punctuation), city and state of publisher, publisher's name, date of publication *of the source you used* and page numbers of text to which you have referred. When quoting from a diary, please give the present location of the diary and whether it has been published. If it has been published, all of the above information about annotation of books would apply.

MANUSCRIPTS

Manuscripts, both text and footnotes, should be typed and double-spaced and average approximately 35 double-spaced pages in length. We also welcome shorter submissions for special use. Lengthy studies of more than 35 to 40 pages will be considered for serialization, but editorial contraction or re-writing to a more focused subject is preferred. We suggest authors give attention to illustration materials and maps to accompany their articles and advise the editor regarding same at the time of submission.

When directly quoting from another source, *please* triple check for exact accuracy of spelling, wording and punctuation as the author wrote it. Some sources are difficult for us to obtain for verification.

This is of utmost importance when quoting from a diary. When a diarist has not bothered with punctuation, we use four spaces to indicate we think this is the end of a sentence. We do not improve upon spelling, punctuation, etc.

COMPUTER DISKETTES

We prefer receiving both a printed copy and an electronic file in Microsoft Word (PC or Mac) or Rich Text Format. The electronic file can be sent on a CD or as an email attachment to the editor.

When submitting manuscripts in electronic format, please keep the copy as clean of codes, hidden or shown, as possible. Avoid any manual or automatic hyphenation of words. Do not use the paragraph return to break lines, only to end paragraphs.

BIOGRAPHY

Please include with your manuscript a brief biography, one to three sentences about yourself that can be used to accompany your article.

Categories: Nonfiction—History—Western

CONTACT: Ariane C. Smith, Editor
Material: All
1429 E Thirteenth Ave
Spokane WA 99202
Phone: 509-928-9540
Fax: 509-279-0832
E-mail: ariane@capitala.net

Oxendine Publishing, Inc.

The mission of Oxendine Publishing is to teach college and high school students to be more effective and ethical leaders of the future. We believe that it is vital to help students understand why it is important to be fair, conscientious, and moral leaders in their future careers in business, politics, and government.

Through magazines, related books, newsletters, seminars, and on-line services, Oxendine Publishing strives to be an information source with our staffers viewed as experts in the area of leadership development.

WRITER'S GUIDELINES—The Publications

Oxendine Publishing produces three four-color, glossy magazines for high school and college students, two of which are distributed in Florida and one nationally.

Florida Leader for college students, the company's flagship publication launched in 1983, is read by students at 86 colleges and universities around the Sunshine State. In 1990, Oxendine Publishing started an edition of *Florida Leader* for college-bound high school *Student Leaders*, which is now read at more than 550 public and private high schools statewide.

In October 1993, America's premier leadership-development magazine, *Student Leader*, was unveiled as a forum for the top five percent of active students at nearly 1,400 colleges and universities across the nation.

Primarily produced by Oxendine Publishing staff, *Florida Leader* for college students (see www.floridaleader.com) is published in March, April, and September with a circulation of 25,000. Each issue has a unique theme, and queries for general content are considered for the September issue only. Readers of the college version of *Florida Leader* are above-average college students who likely are involved in several campus activities and may hold one or more leadership positions.

In March, the "Best of Florida Schools" issue is a 48-page annual review that highlights more than 100 outstanding and unusual accomplishments by students and campus organizations. The issue also profiles the winners of the hotly contested "Best Student Government" and "Best College Newspaper" Awards.

The 24-page "Student of the Year" issue published in April features the profiles of the 20 winners of the annual Florida College Student of the Year Award, a scholarship and leadership-development program founded by *Florida Leader* (see www. floridaleader.com/soty).

Each fall, *Florida Leader* releases the results of the "What Florida Students Think" survey in the 24-page September issue. General content makes up about half of this issue, and queries from freelance writers are considered. Recent stories include "Nurturing Young Leaders" and "Homecoming Traditions."

The high school edition of *Florida Leader* is published in January, June, and October with a circulation of 44,000. Each 24-page issue includes the following departments: College Life, The Lead Role, Florida Forum, and In Every Issue (a pop quiz and brief "FYI" columns).

Student Leader, a national leadership-development magazine, is published in October, and March with a circulation of 50,000 per issue at 1,400 schools, most of which pay to get the magazine (see www.studentleader.com). *Student Leader* provides practical information and leadership news to help Student Government officers, Greek leaders, resident assistants, honor society leaders, volunteer coordinators, programming staffers, and other campus decision-makers lead more ethically and effectively. Queries are accepted for both issues. See www.studentleader. com for sample articles.

In addition to student readers, *Student Leader* and Oxendine's regional magazines are read by college and high school guidance counselors, career faculty, public relations directors, deans of students, directors of campus activities, college and corporate recruiters, as well as members of the media and legislators statewide.

EDITORIAL FOCUS

Both *Florida Leader* magazines feature academic-major and career articles, current financial aid and admissions information, and stories on other aspects of college life for current or prospective college students.

• Note: *Florida Leader: For High School Students* and *Florida Leader: For College Students* have the same guidelines.

Oxendine Publishing's national magazine *Student Leader* focuses on helping veteran and developing campus leaders become more effective and ethical campus decision-makers, and student government leaders. Typical articles include advice on motivating and organizing students, recent leadership and management strategies, how to balance school, work and extracurricular activities, and news about service and fund-raising projects and achievements nationwide.

WRITER'S TIPS FOR PRINT

Full-length articles (about 900 words) should include five to nine sources, quoting student and collegiate leaders, as well as appropriate sources. For the four Florida publications, primary sources, for the most part, should be from colleges, high schools and businesses within the state. For *Student Leader*, college and corporate sources should be varied geographically and demographically. Writers may query ideas for articles or discuss possible assignments already on the calendar. If possible, state availability of photos with query.

Longer stories (more than 1,000 words for 1-page article) can be placed in their entirety at the website and cut for print for the publication. Sidebar information can also be included at the web or in print.

Copy should be double-spaced and follow AP style. When students are mentioned by name, first reference should include year in school, institution they attend, and if relevant, their major. The full names, titles, addresses, and E-mail addresses of all interview subjects should be included separately with each submission. Articles may be edited for space and content. Writers are responsible for the accuracy of all information in the article. Articles by first-time writers may be used, but only experienced writers will receive payment, which varies from $35 to $75 per piece for Florida publications and from $50 to $200 for *Student Leader*. Payment is made within 30 days after publication. All writers will receive at least one full-color copy of their article. Unsolicited manuscripts or art will not be returned unless accompanied by sufficient postage. Send a SASE envelope to receive query response, writer's guidelines, or an editorial calendar, or $3.50 for guidelines and a sample issue.

WRITER'S TIPS FOR WEB

Articles for the *Student Leader* website fall under two categories, Featured Articles and Trendsetters. Featured Articles cover broad topics with a variety of different sources. Trendsetter articles cover outstanding groups and people on specific campuses and highlight their accomplishments. Often, Trendsetter articles are written by the person or group that is involved. Both Featured Articles and Trendsetters are exclusive to the web. Trend-setters should be 500-1,000 words and Featured Articles should be around 1,000.

WHAT SHOULD A QUERY INCLUDE?

A one-page query should include all personal contact information, such as a name, address, phone number, and E-mail address along with a SASE. Include a detailed idea for the article, demonstrating major themes and reader need, as well as key point the article will cover and types of sources to be used. Also, give past writing credits and one to two sample pieces of work. You may include suggestions for the article's format as well as information regarding photo options and artwork. Please include suggestions for titles and subheads also. Direct *Florida Leader* queries to Stephanie Reck and Student Leader queries to John Lamothe.

The query should give a sense of your writing style, not just important information.

Oxendine DOES NOT ACCEPT...

No previously published work will be accepted. Oxendine buys first rights only. Poetry, trivia, puzzles, or straight humor pieces are not accepted for publication. Focus on trends and how students are adapting them to their organizations. Current happenings are too timely for a magazine that publishes three times a year. The information should be practical, not philosophical.

HOW TO CONTACT US

For *Florida Leader*: Stephanie Reck, stephanie@student leader.com
For *Student Leader*: john@studentleader. com
Categories: Teen—Young Adult—College

CONTACT: Submissions Editor
Material: All
PO Box 14081
Gainesville FL 32604-2081
Phone: 352-373-6907
Fax: 352-373-8120
E-mail: info@studentleader.com

Pacific Fishing

GUIDELINES FOR WRITERS AND PHOTOGRAPHERS

For Writers: *Pacific Fishing* is a trade magazine for the U.S. and Canadian West Coast commercial fishing industry. Our audience is primarily commercial fishermen from San Diego to Alaska, and secondarily seafood processors, distributors and brokers. Circulation is around 10,000.

We view fishermen as small businessmen and professionals who are innovative and success-oriented. To appeal to this reader, *Pacific Fishing* offers four basic features:

1. Technical, how-to articles that give fishermen hands-on tips that will make their operation more efficient and profitable;

2. Practical, well-researched business articles discussing the dollars and cents of fishing, processing and marketing;

3. Profiles of a fisherman, processor or company with an emphasis on practical business and technical areas;

4. In-depth analysis of political, social, fisheries management and resource issues that have a direct bearing on West Coast commercial fishermen.

Features usually range between 2,000 and 3,000 words, specific length to be assigned by the editor. For most assignments, we pay $.10 to $.15 per word on publication.

Before sending unsolicited manuscripts, contributors should query the editor with a brief written proposal outlining the article idea and noting whether photographs are available. Contributors should also include samples of their writing unless it is already familiar to the editor. All first-time contributions are submitted on a speculative basis. All proposals will receive our immediate attentions, but please allow 2-3 weeks for a response. Note: Any expression of willingness to consider material from a freelancer does not constitute an assignment, nor does it in any way indicate that the contribution will be purchased. A kill fee of 10% will be paid for assigned articles that are deemed unsuitable.

Only original, previously unpublished manuscripts are solicited. Manuscripts may be submitted digitally; hard copy should be double-spaced on one side of the paper only. Unsolicited manuscripts, photographs or illustrations will not be returned unless accompanied by a self-addressed stamped envelope.

For Photographers: We need high-quality photography, especially color, of West Coast commercial fishing. In general, shots showing people and action (e.g. fishing activity, running boats) are more useful than scenics. We prefer 35mm color slides and usually consider prints for inside use only. Our rates, payable on publication, are:

- Cover: $200
- Inside Color: $100 for full page and larger
- $75 for one-half page up to full page
- $50 for spot photo less than one-half page
- Black and White: 75 for full page and larger
- $50 for one-half page up to full page
- $25 for spot photo less than one-half page
- Table of Contents: $10

Unsolicited photos can be sent to the attention of the art director if they are for general use and not accompanying a written submission. Salient information should be included with the photos, including: location of shot, fishery, year, vessel name, and, if possible, names of people featured prominently in the photo. Name of photographer should be printed on each individual slide.

Clear indication of how to contact the photographer should be included in the submission.

Unless otherwise stipulated by the photographer, photos will be kept on file here if it is perceived that they may be useful within the year to illustrate relevant stories; photos deemed not usable will be returned. A self-addressed stamped envelope is appreciated for this purpose. Photos on file will be returned anytime upon request from the photographer. If preferred, dupe slides or scans may be submitted for our files with the understanding that the original photo could be obtained from the photographer when needed.

Pacific Fishing is the prestige publication of the fishing industry and our editorial and photographic standards are high.

Further inquiries are welcome.

Categories: Nonfiction—Fishing—Recreation—Sports/Recreation

Salmon Bay Communications
4209 21st Ave W, Ste 402
Seattle WA 98199
Phone: 206-216-0111
Fax: 206-216-0222
Website: www.pfmag.com

Pacific News Service

Provides news, articles and writing focused on young people, ethnic media and the "literati" of California's ethnic communities.

Newspapers and other publications can obtain PNS's daily wire over AP Data Features at a monthly subscription rate or per piece based on circulation.

Writer's Guidelines

Please familiarize yourself with PNS stories, especially recent stories on the topic you are considering.

Exclusive submissions only, please.

All stories are considered on an "on spec" basis.

Maximum length: 800 words.

PNS pays $125 for each story run on the wire.

PNS retains all copyright, print and electronic distribution rights to articles published on the PNS wire or www.pacificnews.org.

Please email stories as indicated below. Include your telephone number and how you wish to be described in the editor's note.

We welcome your comments, suggestions and contributions.

Categories: Young Adult

CONTACT: Brain Shott
Material: All
E-mail: brian@pacificnews.org
CONTACT: Andrew Lam
Material: All
E-mail: lam@pacificnews.org
Pacific News Service
275 9th St
San Francisco CA 94103
Phone: 415-503-4170
Fax: 415-503-0970
Website: www.pacificnews.org

Pack-o-Fun

If you would like to submit a craft idea for possible publication, we ask that you follow these guidelines:

- Send us a photo of the item or items and a telephone number where you can be reached during the day.
- Write complete, accurate instructions (typed and double-spaced, please). Explain everything someone would need to know to complete the project. Use a current issue of the magazine as a guide.
- Include all patterns. Suggest any illustrations you feel necessary to make things clear. A quick line drawing may save many words of instruction.
- If drawing a cross-stitch or needlepoint chart, draw one symbol for each color, using a black grid and black ink. DO NOT color in chart squares.
- Please include a source for hard-to-find supplies. if a brand name is given, indicate whether a ™ or ® is used with the name. (Look on the packaging.)

We will contact you if we are interested in your project. If the design is accepted for publication, you will be asked to send the item to be photographed.

We are looking forward to seeing your original designs and hope that we will be able to work with you sometime soon!

POLICIES

Final Acceptance

- When you are notified that your design has been accepted for publication, you will be asked to send the completed design to us. We reserve the right to ask you to rework your design or the right to return it if we do not feel that your completed design meets our necessary standard for publication.

Contracts

- Contracts are sent to the designer on the Design-In date, provided the completed design and instructions are in our office. Check the schedule card. The design and instructions must be in our office before we send the contract.
- Payment will be sent 30 days after Design-In date, provided the signed contract is in our office by the due date stated on the contract. Otherwise, payment will be sent within 30 days of the date contract is received.
- You may send your completed design to us earlier than the Design-In date; however, the contract will not be sent until the Design-In date.

Design Fees

• The design fees we pay are based on quality, originality, craftsmanship, complexity, and appeal of the design. We also consider the accuracy and completeness of the instructions.

• All fees quoted are for all rights to the design. Fees are discounted 10% for first rights.

• Six complimentary copies of the issue in which your design appears will be sent to you shortly after the On-Sale date. Additional copies are available to designers at a discounted rate.

Rights

• We buy all rights to the design, which means that you grant us all rights to the design/article, including the right to publish the article in printed form and to publish video productions and other derivative works.

• If you would like to print your original article in another publication after we have purchased all rights, please let us know which publication and the publication date; we will be happy to grant you permission whenever possible.

• You must warrant that you are the sole owner of the design/article, that it is original and does not infringe upon the copyrights or rights of anyone else, and that it has never been published in any form.

• We will buy first rights upon special request, paying 10% less than the originally quoted design fee.

Issue of Publication

• When a design is accepted, we will notify you of the magazine issue in which your design is scheduled to appear. If we move your design to another issue before the Design-In date, we will let you know the new deadline. If we move your design after the Design-In date (after the contract has been signed and payment processed), we will let you know that it has been held-over for another issue, and we will keep you informed of its status.

Manufacturer/Product Names

• We will list manufacturers' names only when use of their specific products are vital to the successful completion of the design.

Completed Designs

• We ask that you send us your completed design so we can photograph it in our studio; the completed design also helps us edit instructions accurately. We will keep your design until the magazine is published. We will return the design to you shortly after the On-Sale date. If for some reason you need your design returned before then, please let us know in advance, and we will try our best to comply.

Categories: Children—Crafts/Hobbies—Recreation—Skits

CONTACT: Billie Ciancio, Editor
Material: All
2400 Devon Ste. 375
Des Plaines IL 60018
Phone: 847-635-5800
Fax: 847-635-6311

Paddler
World's No. 1 Canoeing,
Kayaking and Rafting Magazine

So you want to write for *Paddler*? Great. We'd love to have you. Here's all we ask: Send us stories that are both informative and entertaining. If your article only has one of these two ingredients, then try again before sending it to us. For example, if your destination piece tells us everything there is to know about a particular place to paddle, but does so in a boring manner, then you've only achieved half your goal. Also, to paraphrase Steve Martin (In Planes, Trains and Automobiles): "If you're going to tell a story, have a point—it makes it so much more interesting for the reader."

Paddler is published six times a year and is written by and for knowledgeable paddlers. We cover the whole spectrum—whitewater, flatwater, canoeing, sea kayaking, rafting, sit-on-tops—if you do it with a paddle in your hand, we're all over it. Our core audience is the intermediate to advanced paddler, yet we strive to cover the entire range from beginners to experts. If you're the type of contributor we're looking for, you already know this because our first requirement is that you be familiar with *Paddler* magazine. We ask that you not just read the magazine before querying us, but that you know it. Check out a few issues and think about querying for one of the departments first—that's the easiest way to break into the magazine and those are often the stories we are most in need of—particularly the Hotlines department. Being able to include photos with the piece is also a huge plus, as it means one less step for us.

After sending in your query, please allow up to an eternity for a response, but feel free to bug us along the way—email is best. A SASE must accompany all material if it is to be returned. We assume no responsibility for unsolicited manuscripts, photographs or other material or for loss due to postal negligence, natural disasters or dogs carrying envelopes off to parts unknown. We prefer to receive queries by e-mail or snail mail and we prefer to receive manuscripts by e-mail or 3.5-inch, IBM-compatible disks. Include typed, double-spaced hard copy with each submission, as well as your name, address, telephone number, e-mail and a word count.

We prefer queries, but will look at manuscripts on speculation. No phone queries please. Make your ideas unique. Think creative—not outlandish but original. Remember, we don't know exactly what we're looking for—if we did, we'd simply assign it or write it ourselves. Show us something we haven't seen, not a boring, "Me and Joe" story.

Features: *Paddler* publishes at least three features per issue, trying to give equal representation to all disciplines. They should be between 2,000 and 3,000 words and be accompanied by high-quality photos—preferably slides.

Departments: Submissions should include photos or other art. Again, consider submitting to departments first, especially as a first-time contributor, and be creative.

• *Hotlines*—timely news, exciting developments or humorous happenings relating to the paddling community. Stories should be lively and newsworthy. (150-800 words)

• *Paddle People*—unique individuals involved in the sport. (600-800 words)

• *Destinations*—places to paddle, plain and simple. We often follow regional themes and cover all paddling disciplines. Submissions should include map, photos and all pertinent information. (800-1000 words) Marketplace Review—new boats, paddles, clothing, etc. Paddling Schwag includes gadgets, Into the Wild includes other equipment paddlers use—like headlamps, tents and water purifiers. (250-800 words)

• *Paddle Tales*—short, generally humorous anecdotes. (75-300 words)

• *Different Strokes*—two opposing viewpoints from the world of paddling. Must be first-person and opinionated—no fence-sitting. (600-800 words)

• *Skills*—a "how-to" forum for experts to share their knowledge, from playboating techniques to backcountry safety. (250-1,000 words)

• *Eco*—issues related to the paddling environment, from dam updates to pollution and access issues. (150-800 words)

• *First Descents*—doesn't have to be a river. Any exploratory journey qualifies. But remember, we don't just want good stories, we want good story-telling. Include photos and a map if possible. (700-1,500 words)

• *Innuendos*—essays, generally first-person. Can be humorous or serious and introspective. But should be non-fiction. (800-1,500 words)

• *Book and Video Reviews*—current reviews of interest to a large number of Paddlers—'nuff said. (500-700 words)

Paddler pays 15 to 25 cents per published word 30 days after publication. Rates are based on the experience of the writer and the amount of work we put into the piece. Letters to the Editor ("Eddylines") are unpaid. *Paddler* buys First North American Serial Rights and one-time electronic rights. All subsequent rights revert back to the author.

Photographer's Guidelines: Photo submissions should be 35mm transparencies and/or glossy prints. Dupes are acceptable. Call for details about digital submissions. Photos for "Frames" can be scenic or action but need to be exceptional; photos for "Ender" and "Flip Side" are humorous. Originality and quality count. Feel free to suggest captions. Place name, address, phone number or e-mail on each image. We give one photo credit per image and pay 30 days after publication. Please allow eight weeks for return of photos. Photo Rates: $200-$300 for cover; $100 for full page; $50-$75 for a half-page to full-page; $35-$50 for less than a half-page.

Correspondence: Address all submissions to appropriate department or e-mail.

Categories: Nonfiction—Adventure—Associations—Boating—Conservation—Environment—Fishing—Lifestyle—Outdoors—Physical Fitness—Recreation—Regional—Short Stories—Sports/Recreation—Travel—Paddlesports

CONTACT: Editorial
Material: All
PO Box 775450 • 735 Oak St.
Steamboat Springs CO 80477
Phone: 970-879-1450
Fax: 970-879-1450
E-mail: bieline@paddlermagazine.com
Website: www.paddlermagazine.com

Pakn Treger

Pakn Treger publishes original work of high quality that explores aspects of modern Jewish experience and sensibility.

Needs: Pakn Treger publishes original work of high quality that explores aspects of modern Jewish experience and sensibility. Our interests are in Jewish cultural identity and history, with an emphasis on Yiddish culture. Nonfiction, fiction, essays, translations from Yiddish literature, photographs, and artwork are welcome. We do not accept poetry at this time. Articles typically run from 2,000 to 4,000 words. Multiple submissions are acceptable, if so indicated. Allow three to four months for a response. Be sure to send a self-addressed stamped envelope.

Sample Copies/Subscription Information: Sample issues available for $6.50.

Categories: Culture

CONTACT: Nancy Sherman, Editor
Pakn Treger
National Yiddish Book Center
1021 West St
Amherst MA 01002
Website: www.yiddishbookcenter.org

PanGaia
Creating an Earthwise Spirituality

PanGaia is a magazine for all people who share a deep love and commitment to the Earth. If you live here, this is the magazine for you! Our readership includes Gaians, Pagans, Scientific Pantheists, Quakers, Christians, atheists, and others. The one thing they all have in common is a desire to express their spirituality in harmony with the natural world. We hope to reach not just people already involved in such things, but also those who would love to join in if only they knew

we existed. We are particularly interested in developing resources for the Pagan/Gaian community. *PanGaia* gladly accepts contributions of essays, factual articles, fiction, poetry, rituals, interviews, artwork, and photographs relevant to our subject matter and goals. (Separate guidelines are available upon request for members of the reviewers' circle, interviewers' circle, and debators' circle, and for those wishing to submit review copies; we also have a stylesheet for punctuation/usage.) **Please include** your preferred contact information and a brief bio with all submissions. At minimum, we need your pen name and email address or phone number; preferably your check-cashing name, pen name if you use one, postal address, email address (if you have one), phone number, and a brief bio. Put it on the manuscript itself, not just the email message to which the file is attached. *We cannot accept submissions without a way to reach you!* See below for details about anonymity.

General Parameters: *PanGaia* is dedicated to helping explore our spiritual, emotional, and practical lives in a way that respects all persons, creatures, and the Earth while offering immediate application to our everyday lives. Folks of all paths may send their work, but our focus falls on material expressing an Earth-centered spirituality. We refuse to accept material that demeans persons or practices; we do not publish personal attacks, gossip, or diatribes: *PanGaia* is a tool, not a weapon. Check out a previous issue of our magazine or visit our Website to see what kind of material we like to buy.

All submissions must be the original work of the author/artist. If you collaborate with other folks, we need to hear from all parties concerned or else be assured that you have the legal authority to assign rights to the work. *PanGaia* valiantly supports and defends the rights of creative people to control their own material; we do not condone plagiarism or copyright infringement of any kind and will take action in that regard if necessary. This also means that we require citations for factual submissions – if you quote someone, mention a specific theory or argument, etc. then you must give its origin. Please double-check your sources; when writing about historical examples, always refer back to ancestral traditions and original documents, not to modern literature or coven texts alone. See our stylesheet for examples of how to format footnotes and so forth.

We do not accept simultaneous submissions within the Pagan/Gaian market. This is due to the difficulty in obtaining first rights to manuscripts that are in what amounts to the public domain. Several times recently we've run into problems where a work we bought or planned to buy has appeared in another magazine in our market in advance of our publication of the piece. Although we understand that the policy of not accepting simultaneous submissions is new in the Pagan/Gaian market, it is fairly standard practice for professional-level magazines in other fields. It keeps magazines from duplicating each other, and we feel that's a good idea, so we're encouraging the trend in our market as well. *However*: if you feel that your material is appropriate to more than one market (for example some "nature" articles might be appropriate for magazines such as *Sierra* as well as *PanGaia*) we may be able to make an exception to this rule. If you feel such an exception may apply to your piece, please inform us of where else you have submitted it when you send it to us, so we can make a decision at the time we evaluate your work.

We are aware that you have worked hard on your writing, it is personal and special to you, and contains your unique voice. Nonetheless, we usually find it necessary to edit for length, clarity, and grammar – sometimes at the last minute before publication. Therefore, we *cannot* guarantee that your article will appear precisely as you submitted it. If you do not want your material edited in any way, please do not submit your writing to us. (Also, please inform us of deliberate uses of non-traditional spelling so the tone of your work does not get accidentally altered.)

If you have previously contacted any *PanGaia* staff regarding a particular manuscript – i.e. sent us a query letter and we asked to see the proposed article, or met the Managing Editor at an event, or talked to the Editor-in-Chief on the phone – please reference that prior contact in the cover letter accompanying your manuscript! We deal with dozens, sometimes hundreds, of people every month and, as much as we'd like to, we just can't remember everyone off the top of our heads. So tell us when and how you made contact before, and whom you spoke with, and approximately what was said regarding your manuscript; then we should know what you're talking about. Yes, you can ask us if we think a given idea would appeal to our readers *before* you invest all that time and effort actually writing it!

PanGaia maintains contact with a number of regular contributors, but happily accepts freelance submissions. The easiest way to get your foot in the door is by writing letters to the editor, short articles, essays, or reviews; you can work up from there, so don't feel that you have to begin with a huge feature piece. On the other hand, if you have a longer piece, go ahead and send it in; there is no prerequisite for writing for us. Don't be shy if you do not consider yourself a "professional" writer or artist. *PanGaia* depends upon the contributions of our readers to make this magazine a reflection of the Earth-loving community as a whole. *PanGaia* is you!

Compensation: *PanGaia* is proud to be a paying market. We offer a standard range of about $.03 to $.05 per word for all written works except letters to the editor, as well as a contributor's copy of the issue in which your work appears. Occasionally we accept reprints (almost always solicited by us) at a rate of $.01 per word. New authors or anyone requiring substantial editing should expect the $.03 per word rate; established authors should normally expect $.04 per word; the $.05 a word rate is reserved for work of unusual quality and will be offered only with authorization of the Editor-in-Chief. The new rates are *inclusive* of non-exclusive reprint and electronic rights. We have a minimum payment of $11 per piece, so short works such as poems and reviews typically get a flat fee of $11. Payment for artwork, photography, and other visual works is negotiated individually; the Editor-in-Chief also handles our design/layout work and you should contact her with any questions regarding visual works. Other exchanges, such as subscriptions or advertising space, may be discussed with the staff and may be much more generous than cash payments.

Length: Features (articles, essays, sidebars, fiction, interviews, and rituals) should range between 500 and 5000 words. We most often publish items between 1000 and 3000 words; we prefer in-depth coverage to tidbits in most cases, and the upper ranges are usually reserved for lead pieces assigned to specific writers. For poetry, we suggest a maximum length of 100 lines per poem; please bear in mind that we are more likely to publish shorter rather than longer poems, as *PanGaia* does not specialize in this type of writing.

Format: Submit all written material in electronic format. Our first choice is Microsoft Word file attachments emailed directly to the Managing Editor at: ysabet@worthlink.net with a second copy to the Editor-in-Chief at editor@pangaia.com. Other acceptable file attachment formats include text files and commonly used word processing programs; you may also paste the text of your manuscript directly into an email message. Use a plain, legible font or typeface large enough to read easily.

We no longer accept hardcopy submissions of written material. The small number of manuscripts we have accepted in this format does not justify the large amount of time we have spent processing these submissions. It makes more sense to save everyone's time, paper, and postage by adapting our policies. Therefore we only take email submissions now.

Diversity: *PanGaia* seeks to represent the whole fascinating spectrum of humanity as relevant to our subject matter. Therefore we want to publish material by members of all different ethnic traditions, racial heritage, sexes and sexual orientations, religions, ages, body shapes and sizes, levels of physical ability, lifestyles, degrees of experience, geographic locations, and so forth. If you belong to a minority and you'd like us to know about it, you can put that information in your bio or cover letter when you contact us. At this time, we are particularly interested in increasing participation by men and by people of color.

Topics: Ecology, gardening, herbalism; activism, current issues, and political concerns; scientific mysticism, magic, shamanism, liturgy, and ritual; personal development, prayer, and insight experiences; leadership, organization, techniques, and infrastructure in the Pagan/Gaian community; spiritual fiction (including science fiction and fantasy); scholarly research, history, anthropology, and mimetic engineering; legends, folklore, mythology, God and Goddess lore; recipes; health, interpersonal relations, and sexuality; celebrations of Nature, love, birth, death and other transitions; humor; interviews/profiles of individuals, groups, or sacred sites.

In selecting an angle, consider some basic points. First, the above topics are general – you need something more specific before you start writing. Narrow down the broad subject area to a single incident or argument, or to a set of related ones. Second, say something new and interesting. If you have seen a given subtopic covered more than once in a Gaian/Pagan magazine within the last year or two, think twice before trotting it out yet again. Third, follow through on what you present – never just complain about some awful problem and then conclude your piece without suggesting a response or solution. Tell readers what they can go *do* about it. The same holds true for more positive articles where readers may want to learn more about your subject. Fourth, no advertorials! If you want to recommend a product, write a review, and not for your own product. (We need an objective opinion on your product, so please contact us if you'd like something you make or sell to be reviewed and if we are interested, we'll find a contributor to review it.)

There are some things we *always* love to see because we don't get enough of them: anything that includes an innovative and effective solution to a ecological/theological problem; humor, particularly if it pokes fun at religion or government in a lighthearted rather than snide way; and serious scholarship which is delightful instead of dry. We'd like to see more high-quality fiction and poetry too. Then there's a nebulous category of stuff that defies description but which immediately grabs our attention, particularly if it seems likely to have the same effect on people browsing the newsstands. Upcoming focus topics for 2006 are:

Issue #46 "Dreams and Visions" (Feb. 1, 2006)

Issue #47 "Words of Power" May 1, 2006)

Issue #48 "Science and Magic" (Aug. 1, 2006)

Columns: The regular columns are each written by a specific author. Occasionally a columnist retires and we have an opening for a new column. Most of our columnists began as feature writers. If you have been writing features for us and want to write a column, please submit a proposal complete with column title, proposed topic, length per installment, and outline of the first eight installments. (We typically sign new columnists for eight issues, after which we may choose to renew the contract.) Should we approve the proposal, you will be asked to submit the first installment, and we will make our final decision based on that sample.

Debates: We invite you to participate in "Toe to Toe," a forum for the expression of strong and opposing opinions. Here we present both sides of hot topics so that our readers can make an informed decision. See the current issue, or email or send SASE for upcoming topics. Writing for this department requires a firm grasp of debate technique; you must know how to establish an effective argument without ranting, preaching to the choir, falling into logical fallacies, or otherwise boring your audience with soapbox brouhaha. A skilled debator also addresses the opposing side's main points to refute them. If you don't want to write a whole essay yourself, we accept topic proposals as well. Finally, we have introduced a debators' circle similar to our reviewers' circle; here we post calls for specific essays when we have half a set and need to find a matching counter-argument for it. If you wish to join the debators' circle, send your request and credentials to the Managing Editor. Specialized guidelines are available.

Fiction: Exercise your imagination. Show us the kind of world you'd like to live in, or the kind that scares you silly. Stories may deal with any aspect of nature, sustainable technology, magic, Earth-centered spirituality, etc. They may take place in consensus reality, or they may add speculative elements. For a good example of realistic fiction we like, see John Broussard's "You Can't Stop Progress" in issue #27; for speculative fiction, see Alexander Bledsoe's "Croaked" in issue #25.

We are especially interested in stories which depict science solving problems, people using their own talents to make a difference, what it means to live as a Gaian/Pagan in today's world, hopeful but not gooey futures, potential drawbacks of shortsighted actions, or a healthy respect for diversity. Please, no "fantasy" or "Dungeons and Dragons" material about ancient matriarchal warriors or large-breasted sorceresses; if it is appropriate for *Fantasy and Science Fiction*, send it there; *PanGaia's* forte is magic in the modern world. (We've been known to make exceptions to this rule, but not often!) Retellings of myths or fairy tales are also unlikely to succeed. The story you send us needs to link closely to our magazine's overall field of interest.

Poetry: We accept poetry in a wide range of forms and styles. The Managing Editor has considerable experience in this field and is very selective. (We have to be; we receive more bad poetry than any other genre.) If you use forms, the technical aspects of your work must be flawless; if you can't handle rhyme or meter well, try free verse instead. Make sure you send us material relevant to our scope; we get a lot of fluffy Christian, feminist, and random literary poems that we can't use. Submit 3-5 poems at a time, up to about 100 lines per poem.

Reviews: *PanGaia* prints reviews of books, music, movies, videos, and other relevant products. These typically range from 200-700 words. We accept unsolicited reviews and a copy of our review guidelines is available upon request. However, a substantial portion of our reviews come from a group of regular reviewers organized by the Managing Editor; if you would like to join this group, please send an email message (or a snailmail letter with SASE) to the editor outlining your interests. If you are a writer, musician, artist, producer, publisher, etc. and would like us to review your product(s), then you may request our review copy submission guidelines.

Art/Photography: We seek portfolios from artists/photographers who wish to place their work in *PanGaia*. We commission most of the visual art featured in our pages. Please send a hardcopy portfolio that we can keep on file for you; it does not need to be of reproduction quality, but should give a substantial indication of the subject matter and style in which you work and should be on white paper. Size is not crucial here; in general, images should be large enough to see clearly (preferably at least snapshot size instead of thumbnails) but not so large as to cause storage problems (8" x 10" is a good upper limit). You may submit material in color, black-and-white, or a combination but we only use color work on the cover. It is much easier to get published with B/W work in the interior. Do not send originals! Indicate availability of works in your portfolio; if we decide to use anything we will contact you for a better copy/original. If we ask you to send us an electronic image, the preferred format is .JPG but .TIF or .PDF are also acceptable. (Yes, this is opposite from our policy on written materials; we're choosing from available technology based on which works better for specific uses.)

PanGaia has a distinct style and tone that is not always easy to grasp. We like fresh, crisp images that convey a sleek professionalism *without* coming across as cold or modernist. Aim to instill a sense of reverence, or whimsy, or joy – you want to pull viewers into the world you depict. Our rules about fantasy material (see above, under fiction) apply to artwork as well; if it has wings, pointed ears, cloven hooves, or an impossible physique, then it's probably not a *PanGaia* image. (Rules are meant to be broken, but you've been warned, so don't be disappointed if your drawing of Astarte as a Xena-lookalike with long red fingernails is rejected out of hand.) Certain types of written material (interviews, event reports, travelogues, how-to articles, etc.) have a better chance of acceptance if you can provide high-quality photographs or artwork to match the text. We do pay extra for such visual aids if the writer can provide them. (If the accompanying photos come from an interview subject or the like, we usually barter for them instead; our standard offer is a ¼-page ad of the photographer's choice in the following two issues.) Questions regarding artwork or photographs should be directed to the Editor-in-Chief, who also handles design/layout work

for our magazine.

Reprints: We very rarely accept reprints, and the few we print are usually solicited by the magazine staff. We recommend against submitting unsolicited reprints. Absolutely do not send us reprints off the Web; if the material is on the Web, everyone who wants to see it has seen it. Materials that originally appeared in a tiny hardcopy market or with no overlap in our audience may be acceptable for reprint.

Names and Anonymity: 1) If being published under your real name would cause *irrevocable* harm to your life (real, not imagined, danger of custody or job loss, physical harm etc.) we recommend that you *don't* submit material to any paper publication, Pagan or mundane, on Pagan subjects. Please don't submit anything to us; please don't put your life in our hands. We call this the RED ALERT level of anonymity. 2) If being published under your legal name would cause you major embarrassment, but no permanent harm, submit material *only* under your byline, and include a email address and phone number ONLY. This will force us to contact you via phone or email in order to get a copy of the magazine to you or to pay you for your work. We call this the YELLOW ALERT level of anonymity. Please put the words "YELLOW ALERT" after your pen name so that we know you have deliberately decided to leave out your legal name and snailmail address. 3) If you'd *rather* be published under your Craft name, but it won't really get your dander up if we goof, put your legal name *and* your Craft name on your submissions, along with your email and snail mail addresses as well as your phone number. We will try *very* hard to always print your Craft name, but accidents happen. We call this the GREEN LIGHT level of anonymity. 4) If you always publish under your legal name, we will prostrate ourselves in your general direction and kiss your feet but we know that not everyone is fortunate enough to be able to afford this level of transparency in their lives. We look forward to a world in which no one would ever need a Craft name (though some may want to have one anyway). We call this the ANGELIC level of anonymity.

For those of you really concerned with anonymity, we recommend that you stick with publishing under Craft names with ezines that don't need to know who you are in order to acquire legal rights to material, pay authors, or deliver contributor copies using U.S. mail. Those are the things that require us to know your legal name, and once we have that information, even our best efforts can't *guarantee* that the information won't slip out of our hands.

Categories: Fiction—Nonfiction—Interview—Spirituality—Travel

CONTACT: Elizabeth Barrette, Managing Editor
Material: All
PanGaia
PO Box 641
Point Arena CA 95468
Phone: 707-882-2052
Fax: 707-882-2793
E-mail: ysabet@worthlink.net
Website: www.pangaia.com

Paperback Parade

Please refer to Gryphon Books in the publisher's section.

Parabola
The Magazine of Myth and Tradition

Parabola is a quarterly journal devoted to the exploration of the quest for meaning as it is expressed in the myths, symbols, and teachings of the world's religious traditions, with particular emphasis on the relationship between this store of wisdom and modern life.

Each issue of *Parabola* is organized around a theme. Examples of themes we have explored in the past include Rites of Passage, Sacred Space, Dreams and Seeing, Ceremonies, Addiction, The Sense of Humor, Language and Meaning, The Hunter, and Prayer and Meditation.

TYPES OF SUBMISSIONS

• Articles and Translations

Parabola welcomes original essays and translations. We look for lively, penetrating material unencumbered by jargon or academic argument. We prefer well-researched, objective, and unsentimental pieces that are grounded in one or more religious or cultural tradition; articles that focus on dreams, visions, or other very personal experiences are unlikely to be accepted. All articles must be directly related to the theme of an issue.

All material should be written in clear, grammatical, and fluent English. We are willing to consider submissions by authors for whom English is not a primary language, but they should be checked carefully by a reader who is fluent in English before they are sent to us.

• Poetry and Short Fiction

We rarely consider original fiction, and then only if directly related to the theme of an issue. We do not accept submissions of poetry.

• Book Reviews and Epicycles

Separate guidelines for book, video, and audio reviews and for retellings of traditional stories are available upon request.

• Readers Forum

The Forum is an expansion of our letters column, in which we invite readers to share their thoughts about the topic of the forthcoming issue (Forum contributions on past issue themes are also welcome, but will only appear on our web site). Contributions to the Forum should be brief, but can be more personal and informal than article submissions. There is no payment for Readers Forum contributions.

SUBMISSION GUIDELINES

1. Length

• Articles run 1000-3000 words

• Book Reviews run 500-1500 words

• Retellings of traditional stories run 500-1500 words

Forum contributions should be no longer than 500 words

2. Query Letter: Please send us a one-page letter describing what you propose to write about and how it relates to a given theme. We will let you know if we are interested, or we may suggest a different approach or subject. If the idea fits into our editorial plans, you will be given a deadline to submit a finished manuscript. Assignment of a deadline does not guarantee acceptance or publication of the article; it only means that we are interested in your idea and would like to pursue it.

Brief queries may be sent via e-mail to editors@Parabola.org. We prefer electronic queries to be included in the body of the message, rather than as attachments.

Our acceptance of a query serves as permission to submit material electronically.

3. Preparation of copy: Typewritten, double-spaced, on standard white letter-size paper (8 ½" x 11"), with wide margins at top and bottom. No onionskin or erasable bond. In the upper left-hand corner of the first page of your article, please type the following information:

1. Your Name
2. Your Address and Telephone Number
3. Your Social Security Number
4. Word Count

If endnotes are used, they should be as complete as possible: include the author's name, book or article title, translator or editor (if applicable), city of publication, name of publisher, date, and page numbers.

4. Electronic submissions: *Parabola* will accept material submitted on disk or via email, providing we responded positively to a prior query. *Our acceptance of a query serves as permission to submit material electronically.* We prefer to receive attached documents, and can open most Macintosh and IBM-compatible applications. If you include your article in the body of an email message, please use only ASCII text. Your biographical information should be included in the same document as the article; do not send it as a separate attachment. It is very easy for bios to get lost or mixed up if sent as separate attachments. Include your last name in the file name (ie, "smith.doc"), not our name (ie, "parabola.doc").

Do not use "netspeak" either in your query or submission. Upon acceptance we will request your disk or transmission. *Parabola* will not accept any articles via e-mail without a prior query. If you are sending us a word processing file or disk copy, please try to keep the formatting as simple as possible. In particular, we prefer manually created endnotes to automatic footers.

5. Biographical Information: On a separate page, include a brief (2-3 sentence) biographical description of yourself. Fit the description to the subject matter of the article, e.g., for an article on Tibetan Buddhism, "Smith spent three years travelling in Tibet." Or, a publication credit: "Smith is the author of Pilgrimage in Tibet (W. W. Norton, 1987)." Always include your publisher. When submitting material electronically, please note that "separate page" does NOT mean "separate document."

6. Return Envelope/Postage: All submissions must be accompanied by a stamped, self-addressed return envelope, #10 or larger. Manuscripts without SASE will not be returned.

7. Rights: *Parabola* purchases the right to use an article in all substantially complete versions (including non-print versions) of a single issue of our journal. We also request the right to use the piece in the promotion of *Parabola*, and to authorize single-copy reproductions for academic purposes. All other rights are retained by the author.

8. Payment: We do not have a fixed pay rate for articles, but pay each author a portion of a set issue budget, depending on the length of each article and the number of total articles accepted. If an issue includes a few long articles, each author will receive a larger payment; if there are a larger number of shorter articles, each author will receive a smaller amount. Article payment generally ranges from $150 to $400. The payment for epicycles and book reviews is $75. Forum contributions are unpaid. Payment is made upon publication. Publication is not guaranteed.

Categories: Nonfiction—Folklore—Religion—Spiritual—Philosophy

CONTACT: The Editors
Material: All
656 Broadway
New York, NY 10012
Phone: 800-560-MYTH
E-mail: parabola@panix.com
Website: www.parabola.org/

Parade

Thank you for your interest in *Parade*. The following guidelines should help prospective writers tailor and present article ideas for editorial consideration.

Give us a unique perspective on the news.

Parade covers topics as diverse as the 81 million readers we reach each Sunday. Many stories involve news, social issues, common health concerns, sports, community problem-solving or extraordinary achievements of ordinary people. We seek unique angles on all topics-this is especially important for subjects that have already received national attention in newspapers and other media.

Topics must appeal to a broad audience.

• Your subject must have national scope or implications. For example, a story about first-year interns at a Dubuque hospital might have limited appeal, but the subject of job opportunities or work conditions in hospitals across the nation would be of widespread concern.

• Reporting must be authoritative and original, based on interviews that you conduct yourself. Health for example, should quote medical experts rather than simply relating a personal tale.

• Choose a topic that you care about deeply. If your story does not make you happy or sad, angry or elated, excited or curious, chances are that *Parade* readers won't care that much either.

Do not propose spot news, fiction or poetry, cartoons, regular columns, nostalgia or history, quizzes, puzzles or compilations of quotes or trivia. We almost never assign unsolicited technical-science queries or unsolicited queries for interviews with entertainment celebrities, politicians or sports figures.

You should be able to write your article concisely.

Parade has room to publish only the most tightly focused story. Topics that will be compelling and complete at 1,200 to 1,500 words are the only ones worth proposing.

How to submit your proposal to *Parade*:

Assignments are based on query letters of one page-three or four paragraphs should be sufficient. Propose only one topic per query.

The query should include:

• Your central theme or point in no more than a few sentences. If you cannot state the theme in this way the article surely lacks focus.

• Your sources on all sides of the issue. Whom will you interview?

• The story's general trajectory. Briefly, how will you organize it?

• A summary of your most important writing credits.

• Attach one or two writing samples and a self-addressed, stamped envelope and send to the address below.

Parade is not responsible for unsolicited materials. Do not send any valuable or irreplaceable items. Though many queries have merit, because of great volume we can only assign those few that precisely meet our needs and standards.

Again, thank you for your interest, and best of luck in your efforts.

Categories: Nonfiction—General Interest

CONTACT: Sharon Male, Articles Editor
Material: All
711 Third Ave., 7th Floor
New York NY 10017
Phone: 212-450-7000
Fax: 212-450-7284

Parameters
US Army War College Quarterly

Subject: *Parameters* is a refereed journal of ideas and issues, providing a forum for mature thought on the art and science of land warfare, joint and combined matters, national and international security affairs, military strategy, military leadership and management, military history, military ethics, and other topics of significant and current interest to the US Army and the Department of Defense. It serves as a vehicle for continuing the education and professional development of USAWC graduates and other senior military officers, as well as members of government and academia concerned with national security affairs.

Style: Write clearly and simply. Clarity, directness, and economy of expression are the main traits of professional writing, and they should never be sacrificed in a misguided effort to appear scholarly. Avoid especially Pentagonese and bureaucratic jargon. Humdrum dullness of style is not synonymous with learnedness; readers appreciate writing that is lively and engaging. Theses, military studies, and academic course papers should be adapted to article form before submission. In the interests of length, security, clarity, and conformity with the stylistic standards of *Parameters*, the editor reserves the right to edit all manuscripts; however, substantive changes are provided to the author for approval.

Length: Articles of 4,500-5,000 words (18-20 double-spaced pages) are preferred.

Concurrent Submissions: Do not submit a manuscript to *Parameters* while it is being considered elsewhere. Also, do not submit a manuscript if it has been published elsewhere or if it is available on the internet.

Submitting Your Manuscript: Unsolicited article manuscripts are welcome; book reviews are by assignment only. Authors are encouraged to submit their manuscript by e-mail, as an attachment, to Parameters@carlisle.army.mil. Manuscripts also may be mailed to the address below; in that case include one paper copy and a disk containing the computer file. Paper copies should be double-spaced and printed on one side of the sheet only. Carefully edit your text before submitting it. Include your name, address, daytime phone number, and e-mail address. Indicate whether the disk is Windows or Mac format, and tell us what word processing program you used. Do not submit your manuscript by fax.

Documentation: Documentation is placed in endnotes; a bibliography is not necessary. Indicate all quoted material by quotation marks or indentation. Reduce the number of endnotes to the minimum consistent with honest acknowledgment of indebtedness, consolidating notes where possible. Lengthy explanatory endnotes are discouraged. Endnotes must contain complete citation of publication data; for internet citations, include the date accessed. *Parameters* generally uses the conventions prescribed in Kate L. Turabian, *A Manual for Writers*, 4th ed. (Chicago: Univ. of Chicago Press, 1973).

Biographical Sketch: Include a brief biographical sketch of four to six lines, highlighting your expertise.

Illustrations: Charts and graphs should be used only if they are absolutely essential to clarify or amplify the text. Photos are seldom used, but illustrative black-and-white photos (preferably 5" x 7") are considered.

Clearance: Manuscripts by US military personnel on active duty and civilian employees of the Defense or service departments may require official clearance (see AR 360-1, ch. 6). *Parameters* will assist authors on request.

Honoraria: Upon publication, *Parameters* extends a modest honorarium to eligible contributors.

Review Process: We send an acknowledgment to the author when the manuscript is received. Submissions not forwarded to our referees for further consideration are generally returned to the author within three to four weeks. For submissions sent to our referees, the review process can take from six to eight weeks from date of receipt, sometimes longer.

Our Website: To familiarize yourself with our journal, and to gain a better understanding of our current editorial scope, visit our website.

Categories: Nonfiction—Military—Politics—Public Policy

CONTACT: Col Robert H. Taylor (USA Ret.), Editor
Material: All
US Army War College
122 Forbes Ave.
Carlisle PA 17013-5238
Phone: 717-245-4943/DSN 242-4943
Fax: 717-245-4233
E-mail: Parameters@carlisle.army.mil.
Website: www.carlisle.army.mil/usawc/Parameters

Parent & Child

Scholastic Parent & Child enhances the learning link between home and school. Guided by experts in child development and education, the most current and important research is translated into everyday language to help parents understand their children's emotional, physical, and intellectual growth. Imagine the best early childhood teacher in the world as your personal guide to raising a smart, well-adjusted, happy child; that's Scholastic Parent & Child.

Most of our articles are written by professionals in the field of childhood education and members of our staff. Please send submissions addressing appropriate subjects via regular mail or email. Due to the number of manuscripts we receive, we cannot guarantee that you will receive a response to your submission.

Categories: Nonfiction—Children—Education—Parenting

CONTACT: Samantha Brody, Assistant Editor
555 Brodaway 5th Fl
New York NY 10012
E-mail: sbrody@scholastic.com

Parenting

Parenting addresses readers who are considering pregnancy or expecting a child, as well as parents of children from birth through age 12. The magazine covers both the psychological and practical aspects of parenting.

The magazine is largely freelance written. Fees for articles depend on length, degree of difficulty, and the writer's previous experience. Generally, feature articles run between 1,000 and 3,000 words in published form.

For writers new to *Parenting*, the best opportunities are the departments, which are comprised of pieces that range from 100 to 800 words. Queries for each of these departments should be addressed to the appropriate editor (such as Parenting Reporter Editor, or Ages & Stages Editor).

Put all queries in writing (no phone calls, please), and enclose a stamped, self-addressed envelope for a reply and the return of any materials you submit. Allow about two months for a response, due to the large volume of unsolicited queries we receive. We will not consider simultaneous submissions. In addition, we do not publish poetry.

The best guide for writers is the magazine itself. Please familiarize yourself with it before submitting a query—read several issues if possible. The most successful queries and manuscripts are timely, appropriately researched, well-written, and geared to PARENTING in particular.

Categories: Nonfiction—Book Reviews—Children—Consumer—Education—Family—Folklore—Health—Marriage—Parenting—Physical Fitness—Psychology—Relationships—Humor—Personal Experience

CONTACT: Submissions Editor (Specify Dept.)
Material:All
530 5th Ave., 4th Floor
New York NY 10036
Phone: 212-522-8989
Fax: 212-522-8699
Website: www.parenting.com

Parenting Today's Teen

Our readers are mostly parents, professionals, educators, and some teens. Therefore, we welcome any original articles on parenting teens that are written by parents, professionals, educators, and teens. However, we do not claim to offer any kind of professional advice so please remember that in your writing.

Please send your article via email to Lezlee@parentingteens.com, Attn. Lezlee Shaw, with "Article Submission" in the subject line.

What Are We Looking For?

All topics related to parenting teens are welcome. Keep in mind that the tough issues are the ones that get the most viewers. This is important mainly to professionals as they may be able to generate business by submitting articles.

Tips

No fiction or poetry.

Make sure your content is original.

Include your e-mail address, postal address and telephone number on all submissions and related correspondence.

Columns and Articles

Payment: $15

Word Count: Columns — 250-500 (approximately)

Copyrights

We buy First North American Rights for previously unpublished pieces for inclusion on our Web site. Ninety days after publication, rights revert back to the author, but we will retain all articles in our archives indefinitely.

References

Always attribute the sources of statistics, studies and all quoted or paraphrased material. Use complete references at the end of the manuscript and include the first three authors. Use the following format:

For magazine articles: Author's last name, initial (x 3 if applicable): "Article title in quotations," Magazine Name (in italics). Volume (Number): pages, year.

For books: Author's last name, initial (x 3 if applicable): Book Title (in italics). City: Publisher, year.

Review Process

All articles undergo an editorial review, which may take from one to three weeks. If needed, you will be contacted during the review process to discuss any comments or questions.

Categories: Nonfiction—Children—Parenting—Teens

CONTACT: Lezlee Shaw
E-mail: lezlee@parentingteens.com

ParentLife
BabyLife

Thank you for your interest in writing for *ParentLife*. We are interested in finding Christian writers who are able to deliver professional journalism. By following these guidelines, you enable us to get to know you, your writing style, and how carefully you can craft an article that will impact parents. At the same time you will have less frustration trying to figure out what our editorial team is really looking for when we evaluate manuscripts.

WHO WE ARE

Our Vision

All articles submitted should be consistent with the vision for our publisher, LifeWay Christian Resources, as well as our magazine.

ParentLife vision: To encourage and equip parents with biblical solutions that will transform families.

LifeWay vision: As God works through us ... we will help people and churches know Jesus Christ and seek His kingdom by providing biblical solutions that spiritually transform individuals and cultures.

Our Audience

Our readers are primarily parents of babies through 12-year-olds. Most of our readers are women, although we are making a concentrated effort to impact more fathers throughout our entire magazine. Our audience is a mixture of stay-at-home moms and dual income families. We also have a mixture of home school, Christian school, and public school families. We also are sensitive to the needs of single parents, adoptive families, blended families, grandparents, and families with special needs.

HOW TO ESTABLISH A WRITING RELATIONSHIP

We currently accept few unsolicited manuscripts. At the same time, we know that God may have a message that we might overlook if we don't at least glance at the submissions that do come into our office. In your initial contact, we suggest the following:

1. Guidelines

Be familiar with our writer's guidelines and our magazine. If necessary, request a current issue of our magazine by sending us a 10-by-13-inch manila SASE.

2. Bio Form and Resume

In the writer packet we also will send a bio form that must be completed and returned with the rest of the requested information. We will ask you to share about your personal salvation experience and how you are currently serving in your church or community. A current resume is not required, but it will help us identify your formal writing training, experience in feature writing, and recent publishing credits. You will be able to identify topics and subjects which interest you most as a writer on your writer bio form. We do accept Christian writers from various denominational backgrounds. Return the bio form to William Summey, MSN 172, One LifeWay Plaza, Nashville, TN 37234-0172.

3. Clips, Published Pieces, Queries, and Manuscripts

We prefer writers to submit queries you believe of value to parents rather than articles or completed manuscripts. Articles are not returned without a SASE. Journalists will be evaluated on their ability to convey the tone and editorial voice of our magazine and on their ability to write in a clear, concise, and grammatically correct manner. Please submit these at any time to william.summey@lifeway.com or when you return your bio form.

4. Contracts and Payment

Be patient. We have been known to keep an article for 6 to 12 months before stepping out to invite a new writer to write for us. If you want an immediate yes or no as soon as we receive the article, the answer will be no in most cases. If we decide to accept your article, we will contact you to discuss payment and ask you to sign a non-exclusive rights contract. To process your payment, you will need to verify your social security number, address, and phone number on your contract. You will receive, without cost, one complimentary copy of the issue in which your article is printed. The complimentary copies are processed outside our department, so if you do not receive your copy, you can contact our editorial team and we will be happy to send you some copies.

5. Extra Copies of Magazines

You can order extra copies of the magazines by writing LifeWay Customer Service Center, MSN 113, One LifeWay Plaza, Nashville, TN 37234-0113, sending a fax to Customer Service at (615) 251-5818, or e-mailing customerservice@lifeway.com. Churches can buy our magazine in bulk (five or more copies to one address) for $1.40 per issue by calling (800) 458-2772. Please encourage your church or parenting groups to order our magazines.

6. The Quick Tips

You will find an enclosed tip sheet that will give you an overview of what we are looking for when your article arrives. We suggest that you use this sheet as your guide and make sure that you are writing to our specifications with our mission and target audience in mind.

The Quick-Tip Reference Page For Queries and Submissions

(Please use this sheet as a reminder when sending in your manuscript.)

• I have prayed about and reread my submission, and it reflects a Christian worldview that will distinguish the magazine from other secular parenting magazines.

• Cover page includes title of article; a short writer bio; total word count; writer's full name, phone number, e-mail address (if available), and social security number.

• The article is being submitted in one of the following ways:

1. If the article is being submitted in hard copy form through regular mail, the writer agrees to submit it electronically at the time of contract.

2. If the article is being submitted by e-mail. The attachment can be sent to William Summey at william.summey@lifeway.com.

• Quoted material must be properly documented (source, publisher, date, and page numbers) along with permission verification and a photocopy of the original quote.

• Statistics or factual information which the public would not normally know need to be properly documented along with a photocopy of the information.

• Quoted Bible references must be from the Holman Christian Standard Bible® (HCSB) and do not need to be photocopied.

• Include two blurbs or pull quotes that will quickly draw the reader into your article.

• Include at least one and possibly up to three sidebars that could impact the reader. The sidebar provides helpful information that the reader will value (quick tips, ministries, suggestions, Web sites, books, phone numbers, addresses, and so on).

• Headings and subheading are used throughout the article and relate to the suggested title.

The Quick-Tip Reference Page For Contracted Assignments

(Please use this sheet as a reminder when sending in your manuscript.)

• I have prayed about and reread my submission, and it reflects a Christian worldview that will distinguish the magazine from other secular parenting magazines.

• Cover page includes title of article; a short writer bio; total word count; writer's full name, phone number, e-mail address (if available), and social security number.

• The article is being submitted in one of the following ways:

1. By disk. (If the article is being submitted by disk, a hard copy must also accompany submission. Indicate word processing program on the disk. Microsoft Word is preferred.)

2. By e-mail. (If the article is being submitted by email. *ParentLife* articles may be sent to William Summey at william.summey@lifeway.com. Editors will verify receipt of articles through e-mail.)

• Quoted material must be properly documented (source, publisher, date, and page numbers) along with permission verification and a photocopy of the original quote.

• Statistics or factual information which the public would not normally know need to be properly documented along with a photocopy of the information.

• Quoted Bible references must be from the Holman Christian Standard Bible® (HCSB) and do not need to be photocopied.

• Include two blurbs or pull quotes that will quickly draw the reader into your article.

• Include at least one and possibly up to three sidebars that could impact the reader. The sidebar provides helpful information that the reader will value (quick tips, ministries, suggestions, Web sites, books, phone numbers, addresses, and so on).

• Headings and subheadings are used throughout the article and relate to the suggested title.

Categories: Nonfiction—Christian Interest— Diet/Nutrition—Education—Family—Parenting—Spiritual

CONTACT: William Summey, Editor in Chief
Material: All
One LifeWay Plaza
Nashville, TN 37234
Phone: 615-251-2021
Fax: 615-277-8142
E-mail: william.summey@lifeway.com.
Website: www.lifeway.com

Parents Magazine

We are interested in:
- Articles which offer professional and/or personal insights into family and marriage relationships.
- Articles that help women to cope with our rapidly changing world.
- Well-documented articles on the problems and successes of pre-school, school-age, and adolescent children-and their parents.
- Good, practical guides to the routines of baby care.
- Reports of new trends and significant research findings in education and in mental and physical health.
- Articles encouraging informed citizen action on matters of social concern.

We prefer a warm, colloquial style of writing, one which avoids the extremes of either slanginess or technical jargon. Anecdotes and examples should be used to illustrate points which can then be summed up by straight exposition.

Articles vary in length from 1,500 to 3,000 words. Payment is on acceptance.

We recommend that writers query us by mail, fax or email (no phone calls please) about the article idea before submitting a completed manuscript. Manuscripts should be typed, double-spaced, and must be accompanied by a stamped, self-addressed envelope.

Please allow three to four weeks for a reply.

The Editors/*Parents Magazine*

Categories: Nonfiction—Beauty—Children—Family—Fashion—Health—Marriage—Physical Fitness—Relationships—Women's Issues—Retirement

CONTACT: Wendy Schuman, Executive Editor
Material: All
375 Lexington Ave.
New York NY 10017
Phone: 212-499-2083
Fax: 212-867-4583
Website: www.parents.com

Parents' Press

Who We Are

Parents' Press is a monthly newspaper for parents and expectant parents in the San Francisco Bay Area counties of Alameda, Contra Costa, Marin, San Francisco and Solano. Our circulation is 75,000. Our readers have children ranging from infancy to high school.

What We Buy

Our focus is on practical, down-to-earth articles. We use very little academic, theoretical or personal-experience pieces. No political material, fiction or poetry. Please study the newspaper before submitting ideas. We do not mail out sample copies, but free copies are available at most Bay Area Albertson's stores, libraries and children's stores. Back issues are available at some local libraries, or by mail from us for $3 per issue.

Writers

We use up to 3 freelance articles per issue. All manuscripts must be typed, double-spaced and accompanied by a stamped, self-addressed envelope. (If you do not accompany your manuscript with an SASE, we will not return it. We do not respond to query letters that are not accompanied by an SASE.) You may e-mail queries and/or submissions to us at parentsprs@aol.com. Please include material in the body of the e-mail; we do not download attachments. We do not download or review unsolicited e-mail manuscripts.

Articles on health, education and child development are usually written by professionals in those fields. Good possibilities for non-specialist writers include interviews with well-known Bay Area figures who have young children; places to go with children; parent resources (e.g., crisis hotlines): "how-to" articles on every day aspects of childrearing (e.g., giving a birthday party, buying play equipment, dealing with peer pressure). We seldom use articles that focus on a single

organization. Round-up articles should cover the five counties named above. Popular past articles by freelances have included: "Skates and Blades: Bay Area Youths' Hot New Pastimes," "How To Set Up A Parent Co-op," "Air Travel with Children," "Choosing the Right School for Your Child" and "Are You Spoiling Your Child?"

Parents' Press generally buys all rights, including web/electronic publishing (certain rights may be assigned back to the author upon written request). Other rights we occasionally purchase include First North American Serial Rights with a provision for perpetual exclusivity in Northern and Central California. This means that an article that appears in *Parents' Press* cannot be sold without our written permission to any publication whose primary circulation area is in Northern or Central California. We will occasionally buy reprint rights or simultaneous submissions, but pay considerably less for such material and require the same territorial exclusivity. We do not buy material that has been simultaneously submitted to other Northern or Central California publications. You must accompany previously printed or syndicated submissions with a statement of their publishing history.

Payment

Payment ranges from $50 to $500, depending upon the complexity of the material, quality of writing, amount of research and length. Articles generally run from 300 to 1,500 words, occasionally up to 2,500 words. We usually pay within 45 days of publication. If we accept an article that we think may be delayed in getting published, we will pay on acceptance. If you accompany an article with photos, the fee we negotiate with you will include payment for them.

Photographers

We use 10 to 20 black-and-white photos of children per issue. Preferred form is glossy, professional quality 5x7 or 8x10 prints. We encourage the submission of photos of children of different ethnicities, abilities and ages. We require written parental permission for any child whose face is identifiable in a photo, as well as model releases for similarly identifiable adults.

Payment is $15 per photo, paid within 6 weeks of publication; one-time rights. Call Ann Skram at 510/524-1602 to show photos. (You may submit photos by mail, accompanied by an SASE, but we cannot guarantee a quick response.)

We usually purchase one-time rights to one full-color photo for our cover each month. Contact Ann Skram to discuss rates and requirements and to show photos. Slides accompanied by prints or color photocopies are preferred. Model releases are required. Photos showing professional models are seldom used and require special arrangements.

Expenses

Parents' Press will pay certain expenses (mileage, phone, photocopies, film) within limits stated in writing at the time we commission an article. No expenses are paid for articles submitted on spec.

Categories: Nonfiction—Children—Juvenile—Parenting—Teen

CONTACT: Dixie Jordan, Editor
Material: All
1454 Sixth St.
Berkeley CA 94710
Phone: 510-524-1602
Fax: 510-524-0912
E-mail: ParentsPrs@aol.com
Websites: www.parentspress.com & www.parent-teen.com

Parnassus
Poetry in Review

Thank you for your interest in *Parnassus*. We consider unsolicited poetry and prose year round, and usually respond within two months. However, you should know that virtually all our material is solicited; while we try to give unsolicited work close scrutiny, we almost never publish it. On poetry, we place few restrictions of length, form, or style. As for prose, though, we have no interest in reading academic or "theoretical" work, only criticism that is colorful, idiosyncratic, and written with verve.

Categories: Literature—Poetry

CONTACT: Ben Downing, Managing Editor
Material: Poetry, Poetry Criticism
205 W. 89th St. Apt. 8F
New York NY 10024-1835
Phone: 212-362-3492
Fax: 212-875-0148
Website: www.parnassuspoetry.com/about.htm

Parnassus Literary Journal

Parnassus Literary Journal is a tri-yearly (spring, summer, fall-winter).

We welcome well constructed poetry in any form, but ask that you keep it uplifting and free of language that might offend one of our readers. We have no regularly scheduled contests, but a contest is sometimes sponsored by one of our subscribers. All rights are returned to our authors after publication.

Due to the ever increasing expense of publishing and mailing, we are now asking our subscribers to either subscribe or purchase a copy of the issue in which their work appears. Subscribers are guaranteed a by-line in each issue. I regret this change in our procedure, but it is necessary for survival. We receive no grants and we sell no advertising.

Type your poems on a single sheet of 8½x11 bond (haiku excepted) and enter your name and address at the upper left corner of each page. No carbon copies or onion skin. Clear xerox ok, simultaneous submissions and previously published ok. Haiku on a single sheet of bond, please. No poetry on half-sheets, 3 x 5 cards, and never more than 3 poems at one time. We do not publish stories, reviews, or articles.

Submit your work in a number 10 envelope with an SASE of like size folded in thirds and sufficient postage for return if necessary. If you do not wish your work returned, so state.

Important: *I do not acknowledge submissions, request for guidelines, or queries unless accompanied by a SASE. Nor do I accept work that arrives here with postage due.*

Our last issue contained over 145 poets from the beginner to the well known, including Eugene Botelho, Matthew Louviere, David Hay, and many others. Ours is one of the oldest and most respected literary journals in the business. We recommend you purchase a sample copy.

Categories: Poetry

CONTACT: Denver Stull, Editor
Material: All
PO Box 1384
Forest Park GA 30298-1384
Phone: 404-366-3177

The Party Book
Celebrations Magazine
Please refer to Metro Parent/Metro Baby.

Parting Gifts

Please refer to March Street Press, in the Book Publishers section.

Party & Paper Retailer

Formal guidelines not available. Please read a number of issues to ascertain the publication's style and needs.

Send queries to address below.

Categories: Trade—Parties & Paper—Retail

CONTACT: Submissions Editor
Material: All
107 Mill Plain Rd., Ste. 107
Danbury CT 06811-6100
E-mail: editor@partypaper.com

Passages North
Northern Michigan University

Passages North, a biannual literary journal, has been publishing since 1979. The journal features poetry, short fiction, creative nonfiction, and interviews.

General Guidelines
All work submitted should:
• Include your name and address on the top right corner of each page.

Additional Poetry Guidelines
• Poems need not be double-spaced.
• Please submit 3-6 poems only.

Additional Prose Guidelines
• We accept prose up to 5,000 words.

Hints for Writers
• Brief cover notes help.
• Editors review work only from the beginning of September through April.
• Simultaneous submissions are considered.
• If you wish, please include your phone number and/or e-mail address.
• We seldom publish poems over 100 lines.

Payment for accepted work is one copy of *Passages North*.

Subscriptions
Passages North, a voice of the nation from the shores of the Great Lakes, publishes one issue annually. Like all literary journals, *Passages North* is entirely dependent upon its subscribers, occasional grants, and donations. We invite you to take this opportunity to subscribe or renew your subscription. Please make checks payable to *Passages North*.

2 years (2 issues): $23/US, $30/Foreign
1 year (1 issues): $13/US, $16/Foreign
Sample (current issue): $7/US, $9/Foreign
Back issue: $3/US, $5/Foreign

Categories: Fiction—Nonfiction—Arts—General Interest—Interview—Literature—Poetry—Short Stories—Writing

CONTACT: Jennifer A. Howard
Material: All
Dept. of English, Northern Michigan University, 1401
Presque Isle Ave.
Marquette MI 49855-5363
Website: www.myweb.nmu.edu/~passages

Passport

Passport

Passport is no longer accepting freelance submissions. We will begin accepting them again in 2008.

Categories: Fiction—Nonfiction—Adventure—African-American—Asian-American—Cartoons—Children—Christian Interests—Crafts/Hobbies—Family—Games—Jewish Interest—Juvenile—Multicultural—Mystery—Religion—Short Stories—Teen—Humor

CONTACT: Submissions Editor
Material: All
6401 The Paseo
Kansas City KS 64131-1284
Phone: 816-333-7000
Fax: 816-333-4439
E-mail: mwonch@nazarene.org
Website: www.nazarene.org

Paste Magazine

About the Magazine

Paste Magazine is a bi-monthly publication focusing on music, film, books and other forms arts and entertainment. We focus on what we call Organic & Eclectic music—encompassing rock, singer/songwriters, alt.country, Americana, indie rock, world music and whatever else we think will grab music-lovers seeking something a little deeper. Paste hopes to cover the best music in this eclectic mix, devoting space to independent musicians alongside more established artists. The tagline, "Signs of Life in Music, Film and Culture," refers to the growing demand for depth and meaning.

With a focus on songcraft and an emphasis on good writing, *Paste* has featured artists such as Wilco, Patty Griffin, Tom Waits, Lucinda Williams, Death Cab for Cutie, Coldplay, Aimee Mann and Ben Folds. Our film coverage has included features on filmmakers Wes Anderson, Gus Van Sant, Jim Jarmusch and Cameron Crowe. The magazine also delves into other areas such as film, books, visual arts and cultural commentary. One of the best opportunities for writers is to come up with article ideas we wouldn't have thought of—like the article we published on a radio station in Louisiana run by prison inmates or the trash dump art series in San Francisco.

Paste Magazine can be found most every Barnes & Noble and Borders, along with independent book and record stores, airports and newsstands. We print approximately 250,000 copies of each issue, and each comes bundled with a compilation CD (featuring many of the above artists) and a DVD sampler with music videos and short films.

Submissions

Solicitations & Assignments:

· *Paste Magazine* welcomes unsolicited articles from anyone that believes the piece to be appropriate to *Paste* and its readers. (Hint: Best way to figure out what is appropriate is to read the magazine.)

· Queries soliciting approval of an idea may be submitted. Queries should include proposed subject, length, applicability and writer samples.

· Please do not simultaneously submit the same material to another publication.

· *Paste* will assist in obtaining interviews, attending events, etc. as needed. *Paste* will provide complimentary CDs for assignment when possible

· **NOTE:** Solicitation of record labels, promoters, artists, and publicists on behalf of *Paste* must be done in coordination with *Paste* editors. If you want to pursue a story and need to use the name of our publication for access, please authorize it with Paste staff directly.

· Submissions may be edited and may be published at any time. Writers will be paid upon publication.

· Paste retains the right to also publish everything that appears in our magazine on the PasteMagazine.com website and other sites that use our content.

Writer Payment:

Payment is issued within one month of publication.

· Print Features: $0.25/word (as edited) for features and scrapbook.

· Print Reviews: Lead (800 words) - $160, Featured (500 words) - $100, Breakout (250 words) - $60, Long (150 words) - $35, Short (100 words) - $25, Dischord (200 words) - $60, Book reviews - $70 - $200.

· Online: We don't currently pay for online features.

· Photos & Illustrations: negotiable. Contact art director José Reyes (photos@pastemagazine.com or illustrations@pastemagazine.com)

Issues & Deadlines:

· Print: Published bi-monthly; submissions due 8 weeks prior to issue date.

· Online: Published on a rolling basis.

Submission Format:

Electronic submissions (email, text files, MS Word files, or Rich Text Format files) preferred. Send review submissions to Jason Killingsworth (reviews@pastemagazine.com), web submissions to Steve LaBate (web@pastemagazine.com), scrapbook submissions to Reid Davis (scrapbook@pastemagazine.com), film submissions to Tim Porter (film@pastemagazine.com), book submissions to Charles McNair (books@pastemagazine.com) and feature and essay submissions to Josh Jackson (features@pastemagazine.com). Additional material may be mailed to the appropriate editor at Paste Magazine, PO Box 1606, Decatur, GA 30031.

· On the first page, include your name (as you want it to appear in the magazine), e-mail address, phone number, mailing address, the artist, title and label of the piece, and any notes for the editors. Suggested headlines and sub-headlines are also welcome.

Writing Guidelines:

Personal Style. Develop your voice, express your opinion, but be concrete in how you formed that opinion and distinguish the subjective from the objective. Your writing should display maturity and emphasize substance over attitude. But do personalize your writing; inject your life into your writing as appropriate (see http://eserver.org/bs/44/bertsch.html). Search for a sense of place or a narrative. After all, cultural criticism is not an objective, quantifiable science.

Fact-Checking. Be thorough. Never do an interview without a tape recorder, and save the tapes in case there's an alleged discrepancy. If you are unsure of any facts in the article, please call this to our attention at the beginning of the article. We can help you verify the facts or remove them from the article.

Length. Cover stories – 3000 to 4500 words; Features – 1500 to 4000 words; Scrapbook features – 50 to 800 words; Film Reviews – 200-500 words; Book Reviews – 200-500 words; CD reviews – 100 to 800 words.

Style

· Use italics for titles of recordings, videos, books, films, and television programs.

· Song titles, chapters titles, and article titles should be placed in quotations; punctuation goes inside the quotation marks.

· Write out numbers nine and under and numbers that begin a sentence (if necessary); otherwise use numerals.

· Use numerals for decades, except at the beginning of a sentence. Use 4 digits for the first reference, with no apostrophe, and then 2 digits with an initial apostrophe (e.g., 1990s then '90s).

· Write-out the complete title of a song or album on first use; it may be abbreviated subsequently. Generally, credit songwriters rather than performers (e.g., unless you're commenting on something specific to Hendrix' or U2's version, it's Dylan's "All Along the Watchtower").

Tips

·Shy away from statements like, "In a just world, Artist X would be getting more attention, mainstream attention, etc." We believe that this could be said about most of the artists we cover. That's why we exist.

· There is a definite spiritual/philosophical/socially conscious bent to the magazine. But don't feel like you need to force this angle. We don't have an agenda, and we place a higher value on art that has depth and meaning rather than platitudes and propaganda.

· KNOW THE MAGAZINE. Buy one on the newsstand or at pastemagazine.com.

What we're looking for ...

Feature Profiles

Each feature needs to involve contact with the artist (we will help set these up for you). These need to be well-researched, well-written pieces from an original angle. We'll work with you to get these just right. We'd like these to be more than just articles about artists, their careers and their label problems and hopes for a bigger audience. We want these to be explorations into the art of an individual. Incorporate song lyrics. Use narrative structures. Appeal to a variety of the reader's senses—place them in the room with the artist. Make it relevant to the reader's life—why should they care about this person's art?

Essays. We generally publish one long-form essay each issue. These can be humorous, personal, opinionated or all three.

Film and Book Features. These include profiles of filmmakers and authors, coverage of new films and other articles on writing.

Trend Stories. We also generally publish one trend story or historical article each issue. Topics have included rock festivals, the new Americana music, the Brill Building Sound, independent films and music videos. Trend stories don't necessarily have to be related to music and film.

Music Reviews. We're a little more wide-open on reviews. We've got some ideas of what we want but also want you to write on the artists whose music is having an impact on you. Don't be afraid to personalize these or come at them from a different approach. Music reviews are notoriously boring to read, and while they serve a utilitarian purpose, they should also be creative. I'd rather read a well-written review of an artist I know I won't like than a shoddy review of someone interesting.

Film Reviews. In addition to music, we cover films that dig a little deeper. These include upcoming art-house films, foreign films and movies with a broader release. Think of the next *Amélie, Kandahar, Chelsea Walls, Lost in Translation, No Man's Land*.

Other Reviews. We also cover books, television shows, radio programs, music DVDs, video games, etc. addressing the music and culture from a Paste-y perspective. If you have suggestions, we'd love to hear them.

Scrapbook. Our front-of-book section includes profiles of up-and-coming artists (4 to watch), news blurbs, trend stories, smaller artist profiles with specific angles, articles on food and beverage (Taste) and a page devoted to either visual art, theatre, comedy or some other non-music/film/books category (... And Culture). Film Clips includes smaller stories about new films, film trends and filmmakers.

PasteMagazine.com. In addition to most of the content that appears in the magazine, PasteMagazine.com publishes several concert reviews each month and a new artist profile called "Artist of the Week." While these are typically unpaid, it's the easiest way to begin writing for Paste.

Categories: Nonfiction—Arts—Book Reviews—Entertainment—Essays—Film—Humor—Music

CONTACT: Jason Killingsworth
Material: Reviews
E-mail: reviews@pastemagazine.com
CONTACT: Steve LaBate
Material: Web Submission
E-mail: web@pastemagazine.com
CONTACT: Charles McNair
Material: Books
E-mail: books@pastemagazine.com
CONTACT: Reid Davis
Material: Scrapbook Submissions
E-mail: scrapbook@pastemagazine.com
CONTACT: Tim Porter
Material: Film
E-mail: film@pastemagazine.com
CONTACT: art director José Reyes, Art Director
Material: Photos/Illustrations
E-mail: photos@pastemagazine.com
or illustrations@pastemagazine.com

Paste Magazine
PO Box 1606
Decatur GA 30031

Pastoral Life
Magazine for Today's Ministry

Purpose
Pastoral Life is a religious monthly review designed to focus on the current issues, needs and practical activities related to pastoral ministry and life. It avoids merely academic treatments on abstract and too controversial subjects. It features pastoral homilies for Sundays and Holydays.

Manuscript Requirements
Articles average between 1600-2000 words and shouldn't be longer than 3,500 words. Articles for our Reflections section are between 600-1000 words. Articles should be typed single-spaced and enclosed with a self-addressed return envelope. Articles submitted be e-mail or disk using or translating into Microsoft Word. Long articles should be broken with proper subheadings. Queries are appreciated before submitting manuscripts. New contributors are expected to accompany their material with a few lines of personal data.

Additional Information
Payment of four cents per word. Receipt of manuscripts acknowledged within 14 days. Rejected manuscripts are returned unless otherwise specified. Publishers retain exclusive rights between acceptance and publication. Contributors receive 50% of honoraria when their material is reprinted. Free copies available to contributors.

The editors of *Pastoral Life* invite you to submit manuscripts on any topic similar to the following suggestions (simply meant to be a basis for a wider development of ideas):

Communications
• Parish Outreach through a Media Approach
• Impact of TV/Movies on Faith Values
• Communication within the Diocese/Parish
• New Approach in Home Visitation
• Providing Reading Material for Parishioners
• Liturgy and the New Media
• Improving Public Relations in Your Parish
• How do Parents and Children Communicate?

Counseling
• Counseling the Alcoholic
• Premarital Counseling
• Counseling Victims of an Addiction
• Counseling Youth
• Counseling Servicemen and Veterans
• Counseling Single Parents
• Counseling Divorced, Singles or Widowed
• Counseling the Aged/Homeless
• Counseling Vocations
• Counseling the Depressed
• Counseling in Hospitals
• Counseling in Jails/Detention Centers
• Counseling Victims of Tragedy

Education
• School Crisis— Old and New
• Adult Education
• Continuing Pastoral Education
• Teaching the Catechism
• Sex Education
• OCD Programs

Liturgy and Sacraments
• Options in Sacramental Rights
• Effective Paraliturgies
• Conducting Funeral Services
• Role of Music in Liturgies
• How the Choir Saves the Parish

• Power of the Word in Liturgies
Categories: Education—Inspirational—Religion—Spiritual

CONTACT: Bro. Joshua Seidl, SSP, Managing Editor
Material: Religion
CONTACT: Fr. Arthur J. Palisada, SSP, Associate Editor
Material: Religion
Society of St. Paul, PO Box 595
Canfield OH 44406-0595
Phone: 330-533-5503
Fax: 330-533-1076
E-mail: plmagazine@hotmail.com

PC Magazine

Formal guidelines not available. Please read a number of issues to ascertain the publication's style and needs.

Send queries to address below.

Categories: Computers, Technology

CONTACT: Submissions Editor
Material: All
28 E. 28th St.
New York NY 10016
Phone: 212-503-5100

PCPHOTO

PCPHOTO is a national magazine published 8 times per year (6 bimonthly regular issues plus 2 special issues) for people who want to explore and expand their application of photography by making good use of the computer. **We take a fresh look at the modern photographic world by encouraging photography and the use of new technologies.** Editorial is intended to demystify the use of modern equipment by emphasizing practical use of the camera and the computer, highlighting the technique rather than the technical. **PCPHOTO** is written and presented for photographers of any computer persuasion—we use the PC to mean personal computer in its classic, original meaning. It also features and highlights both traditional, film-based photography and image-making with a digital camera.

Feature articles include:

Interview and portfolio displays of accomplished professional and amateur photographers.

How-to articles on highly photographic subjects and imagery to help the photographer better understand how the computer can be used to affect, adjust and control the image.

Non-technical equipment evaluations directed at all photographic enthusiasts. Methods and techniques for using, transporting and maintaining photo and computer equipment.

Reviews of new technology that can help readers make better images.

GENERAL POLICY

The majority of the magazine's features and several departments are written and photographed by assignment. However, we do search for a variety of contributors from different backgrounds and geographic areas. Manuscripts submitted on speculation should be typewritten and double-spaced (a computer disk is fine, but we also need a hard copy for evaluation). *Original photographs should never be sent to us. We will accept digital files of images only if a hard copy printout is included, and e-mail submissions will not be accepted.* We receive too many submissions to check if yours was received. If you need that information, use a verifiable delivery service. All submissions must be accompanied by a SASE. All work is submitted as speculation (**see Terms and Conditions**) unless specifically assigned in writing by an assignment letter. Return or notification of possible use can be expected in approximately six to eight weeks. **PCPHOTO** buys one-time rights for publication in the magazine and on the magazine's Website as part of our permanent archives. **Payment is initiated on date of publication.**

PROCESS OF SUBMISSION

Since **PCPHOTO** is a photography magazine, we must see photos before any decision can be made on an article, so phone queries are not appropriate. Ultimately, whether we can use a particular piece or not will depend greatly on the photographs and how they fit in with material already in our files.

For initial queries, we request photo submissions to be in the form of high-quality inkjet printouts or duplicate transparencies (including transparencies made from digital files). Tear sheets from previously published material such as books or calendars are also acceptable. *We do not want to see original transparencies or negatives.* We will accept digital files of images, but *only* if a hard copy printout is included, and e-mail submissions will *not* be accepted. Your letter should include exactly what you wish to cover in your proposed article and a brief outline of the information or points you intend to include. The more specific you can be, the better we will be able to judge the merits of your idea.

Often, we are overwhelmed by the volume of submissions we receive for the limited number of pages available in any given issue of the magazine. We wish we could use all of the terrific work we receive. Unfortunately, we can't. We try to get materials returned within approximately six to eight weeks. While **PCPHOTO** hopes to review and return unusable material as quickly as possible, our priority has to be producing each issue of the magazine. If images or manuscripts are deemed suitable for publication, they may be held for future consideration. Holding such materials does not automatically constitute an acceptance of terms and conditions printed on delivery memos, packing slips or similar correspondence.

PHOTOGRAPHS FOR SUBMISSION

Please limit submissions to approximately 20 photographs or less. We don't need more than that to judge the merit in an article idea. In fact, we consider the initial submission of too many photographs to represent the lack of necessary editing to present a selection that succinctly supports the subject being queried.

The original image can come from any film formats or a digital camera. Do not send original transparencies or negatives as we will not accept them (transparencies or negatives made from a digital file are okay). Realize that while we try to protect images sent to us on speculation, **PCPHOTO** accepts no responsibility for lost or damaged photographic materials.

Since **PCPHOTO** does not accept original negatives or transparencies, we accept no financial responsibility for lost or damaged materials sent to the magazine on speculation.

SHIPPING AND HANDLING

As mentioned, your images and associated materials will be carried, shipped and mailed by messengers, couriers and mail services while in transit to and from **PCPHOTO** and—in the case of use—by its vendors. All these carriers and vendors will decline coverage of "extraordinary value" for items like photographs. Under their policies (and in the case of mail services, no matter the amount of insurance purchased), photographs will be covered only for the replacement value of the film and processing. Therefore, it is impossible for **PCPHOTO** to warrant against damage or loss while photographic, digital or written materials are in our office or in transit. When returning materials to a contributor, the class of mail will be determined by the amount of postage provided for on the SASE enclosed with the submission.

TERMS AND CONDITIONS

PCPHOTO assumes no responsibility for solicited or unsolicited contribution materials unless otherwise agreed to in writing over the signature of the publisher, editor or managing editor. **PCPHOTO** does not automatically accept or agree to the conditions and stipulations printed on delivery memos, packing slips and related correspondence as they are presented without prior notice when accompanied by submission materials. Since **PCPHOTO** does not accept original negatives or transparencies, the magazine can't be responsible for the loss or damage of photographic materials and does not accept the premise that any and all transparencies or negatives are automatically worth a set minimum as suggested by some photographic organizations. This policy is for your protection as well as ours.

THANK YOU FOR THE CONTRIBUTIONS!

We value your article ideas and photographic offerings. With your help, **PCPHOTO** continues to be vital, informative and unpredictable.

Categories: Computers

CONTACT: www.pcphotomag.com

PC World

What kind of magazine is *PC World*?

PC World is a monthly magazine providing real-world reviews, advice, feature stories, news, and how-to support to people who buy manage, and use IBM and compatible computer systems for professional productivity. It is geared to a consumer audience of business decision makers who are responsible for making their personal computers work on the job. *PC World*'s circulation exceeds 1,000,000 copies per month.

Who Writes for *PC World*?

We look for writers who have a clear writing style and a degree of technical knowledge appropriate to a knowledgeable PC user audience. This combination of talents can make it difficult to break into our pages. Freelance writers contribute to all sections of the magazine.

We pay varying amounts depending on the author's experience, the quality of the writing, and the length of the piece. The fee is negotiated with a staff editor whose specialties include the subject area under consideration. At every stage of every article, editors work closely with writers to generate the best work possible.

Though most of our regular writers are people we're familiar with, we do welcome queries from those who are new to us. One way we discover new talent is by assigning short tips and how-to pieces.

What's the Best Way to Proceed?

Our first suggestion is to be familiar with the magazine. Read some issues, understand the editorial focus (why particular topics are covered, what level of knowledge is imparted), and learn what the magazine's sections are and what goes into each one.

Once you're familiar with *PC World*, you can write us a query letter if you have an idea for a review, how-to, news item, or feature. Your letter should answer the following questions as specifically and concisely as possible:

- What is the problem, technique, or product you want to discuss?
- Why will *PC World* readers be interested in it?
- Which section of the magazine do you think it best fits?
- What is the specific audience for the piece (e.g. database or LAN users, desktop publishers, and so on)?

PC World editors ask these questions when considering ideas for every piece in the magazine, and we expect you to do the same. So send us a letter with your ideas, but please do not send unsolicited manuscripts, clips, or any disks: We will not be able to return them. If we're interested in your query, we'll contact you for more information and proceed from there.

Thanks again for your interest in *PC World* magazine.

We hope this information is useful. Feel free to write us.

Categories: Nonfiction—Computers—Technology

CONTACT: Proposals
Material: Queries
501 - 2nd Ave.
San Francisco CA 94107
Phone: 415-243-0500
Fax: 415-442-1891
E-mail: letters@pcworld.com
Website: www.pcworld.com

Pearl
A Literary Magazine

SUBMISSION GUIDELINES

Pearl is a 96-128 page, perfect-bound magazine featuring poetry, short fiction, and black & white artwork. We also sponsor the Pearl Poetry Prize, an annual contest for a full-length book, as well as the Pearl Short Story Prize, an annual ficiton contest. Our annual poetry issue contains a 12-15 page section featuring the work of a single poet, and our annual fiction issue features the winner of our short story contest, as well prose poems, "short-shorts," and some of the longer stories submitted to our contest. Submissions are accepted September through May only. Manuscripts received in June, July or August will be returned unread. We do not read email submissions. We report back in 6-8 weeks. Work accepted for publication appears 6-12 months from date of acceptance. Please send submissions and correspondence to:

POETRY

Send 3-5 previously unpublished poems with cover letter and SASE. Simultaneous submissions must be acknowledged as such. We prefer poems no longer than 40 lines, though we occasionally consider longer ones. Our format and page size, however, will not accommodate lines of more than 10-12 words. So unless you're Walt Whitman or Allen Ginsberg, please consider your line breaks.

FICTION

Send previously unpublished stories with cover letter and SASE. We only consider short-short stories up to 1200 words (about 5 manuscript pages). Longer stories (up to 4000 words) may be submitted to our short story contest only. All contest entries are considered for publication.

ARTWORK

Send camera-ready, black & white spot-art (either photocopies or originals) and SASE. Accepted artwork is kept on file and used as needed.

BOOK-LENGTH MANUSCRIPTS

We do not consider unsolicited book and chapbook manuscripts for publication.

PAYMENT

Contributors receive a copy of the magazine as payment. Additional copies may be purchased at a 50% discount.

SAMPLES

We recommend reading our magazine before submitting. For a sample copy, send $8 check or money order payable to: *Pearl*, 3030 E. Second St., Long Beach, CA 90803. If you wish to receive a copy of the all-fiction issue, please specify.

Categories: Fiction—Poetry—Short Stories

CONTACT: Joan Jobe Smith or Barbara Hauk, Poetry Editors
Material: Poetry
CONTACT: Marilyn Johnson, Fiction Editor
Material: Short Fiction
3030 E. Second St.
Long Beach CA 90803
Phone: 562-434-4523
Fax: 562-434-4523
E-mail: PearlMag@aol.com
Website: www.pearlmag.com

The Pedestal Magazine

As editors of *The Pedestal Magazine*, we intend to support both established and burgeoning writers. We are committed to promoting diversity and celebrating the voice of the individual. We are currently receiving submissions in the following areas:

• **Poetry:** We are open to a wide variety of poetry, ranging from the highly experimental to the traditionally formal.

• **Pay Rate:** $30-$60 per poem

• **Fiction:** We are receptive to fiction of all sorts, including literary, experimental, science fiction, and fantasy; however our interests do lean towards works that cross genres, works that do not readily fall into one specific category.

• **Pay Rate:** $.05 per word

• **Non-Fiction:** We are open to academic/scholarly works, as well as works that focus on issues of aesthetics, psychology, philosophy, and religion.

• **Pay Rate:** $.05 per word

• **Length:** up to 6,000 words

The Pedestal Magazine does not accept previously published work, unless specifically requested; however, we will accept simultaneous submissions. At the time of publication, all rights revert back to the author/artist; however, *The Pedestal Magazine* retains the right to publish your piece in any subsequent issue or anthology, whether in print or online, without additional payment. Should you decide to republish the piece elsewhere, we ask that you cite *The Pedestal Magazine* as a place of previous publication and provide *The Pedestal Magazine*'s web address.

Due to the number of submissions we are currently receiving, *The Pedestal Magazine* has implemented reading periods. We accept submissions according to the following schedule: Our new issues are released bimonthly on the (give or take a day or two) 21st of the month. During a month in which an issue of the magazine is released (February, April, June, August, October, and December), we close submissions beginning a week prior to the release date, and reopen submissions a week after the release date; for example, we close submissions on August 14 and reopen them on August 28. In addition, during the odd month (January, March, May, July, September, and November), we close submissions for one week, from the 12th to the 19th. We will receive submissions at all other times. Here is a clear breakdown of our submission cycle:

Closed

January 12-19	July 12-19
February 14-28	August 14-28
March 12-19	September 12-19
April 14-28	October 14-28
May 12-19	November 12-19
June 14-28	December 14-28

Submissions

Online submissions only at: www.thepedestalmagazine.com

We will be open to submissions at all times other than those periods listed above.

We thank you for your incredible support of *The Pedestal Magazine* and look forward to receiving your work.

Categories: Fiction—Nonfiction—Poetry

Website: www.thepedestalmagazine.com

Pediatrics For Parents

Pediatrics For Parents emphasizes an informed, common-sense approach to childhood health care. We stress preventative action, accident prevention, when to call the doctor and when and how to handle a situation at home. We are also looking for articles that describe general, medical and pediatric problems, advances, new treatments, etc. All articles must be medically accurate and useful to parents with children—prenatal to adolescence. *Pediatrics For Parents* is not a general parenting magazine and will not consider such material.

Professional Submissions by Medical and Dental Authorities: We will consider articles previously published in professional journals if rewritten for our lay audience. All articles must be in an active voice, avoiding medical language while adhering to our strict standards of factual accuracy. Explanatory articles on body functions, disease processes and treatment approaches would be on target. We are also looking for articles on wellness, prevention, and modes of interaction between children, parents and medical and dental professionals.

Submissions by Non-Medical and Dental Authorities: We are interested in original, well researched, factual, and informative articles on topics described above. Articles must be authoritative and specific with reference citations accompanying each article. We are not particularly interested in "first person stories" unless they are extremely moving or contain a large amount of information.

Submission Requirements: All articles must be typed, single spaced, and have 1 inch margins. Use block paragraph style. Don't use proportional spacing or full justification. Capitalize the first letter of titles, subtitles, etc. Use single space to separate sentences, etc. Put your name, address and phone number on a title page only and not on subsequent pages. Don't number your pages.

Submission Format-Electronic: We only accept articles via email. We can read most formats, but prefer Word. We do not publish photographs, although drawings and diagrams may be used. Articles will be returned within 6-8 weeks if not accepted. We will consider reprints.

Fillers and Short Articles: We do not accept these items.

Length: 1500-3000 words.

Payment: Our pay schedule varies depending on the type of article, its length, and our needs. Payment is also influenced by the quality of expression, importance of topics, amount of research and/or expertise involved. We generally pay between $5 and $50 per article. Payment is on publication.

Sample Copy: We strongly recommend you read a couple issues of the newsletter the get a flavor for our publication. Sample copies are available free for downloading on our website at www.pedsforparents.com or for $3 each, postage paid.

Categories: Nonfiction—Children—Health

CONTACT: Submissions Editor
Material: All
Pediatrics For Parents, Inc.
120 Western Ave
Gloucester MA 01930
Website: www.pedsforparents.com

Pen America
A Journal for Writers and Readers

Unfortunately, due to extremely limited staff and other resources, at present we are unable to review unsolicited submissions except from members of PEN.

As you may have noticed, almost all of the content to date has been drawn from PEN events or from books that received awards from the organization. We hope that as the journal's circulation and reputation grow, we will soon be able to attract enough funding to sustain a more inclusive editorial process. Until then, however, I'm afraid it's PEN all the way. Our calls for submissions are distributed as needed via e-mail or membership mailings, so we have no prepared guidelines for you to include.

Categories: Nonfiction—Politics—Writing

CONTACT: Bridget Cross, Managing Editor
Material: All
568 Broadway, Ste 401
New York NY 10012
Phone: 212-334-1660 Ext.115
E-mail: journal@pen.org
Website: www.pen.org/journal

Pennsylvania Magazine

WHO ARE WE? *Pennsylvania Magazine* is a privately owned, bimonthly publication produced by a team—our staff and people like you, the freelance contributors throughout the state who have contact with the topics that our subscribers will enjoy. Since our name is Pennsylvania, all topics we cover must have an obvious link to someone, something, or some event within our borders. And, since our subscribers live in all parts of the state, your topic must also have an interest to this widespread audience.

THE SUBSCRIBERS OF *Pennsylvania Magazine* expect the magazine to be a source of timely articles about interesting people, unique places, fun festivals, and fascinating history. When our readers exclaim, "I didn't know that about Pennsylvania," we have succeeded and they are likely to renew their subscription.

WE RELY ON FREELANCERS. Therefore, we've included more advice and comments in our guidelines than you may find in others'. We've found that when we begin with a contributor who knows how we work, much time is saved in queries, rewrites, photographs, and other aspects of the publishing routine. So please take the time to review these guidelines thoroughly.

Begin With a Query Letter

WE LIKE TO WORK FROM QUERIES. This simple letter that briefly explains your idea saves time and effort for both of us. Within four weeks of our receipt of your query, you'll receive one of the following responses:

1. Go ahead with your idea. Guidance as necessary for completion of your article will be provided.

2. We need more information to make a decision. You will be asked to supply illustration samples for your topic, provide more information about your topic, or supply something else so that we can determine if our subscribers will find your topic of interest.

3. Send this idea to another publication. This idea is not what our subscribers look for in our magazine. If possible, we will direct you to another publication that may be interested in your topic.

Hints for Your Query

1. If you are sending a multiple query, use a separate sheet of paper for each topic. This helps us respond faster.

2. Explain how you would cover the topic and give an estimated word count.

3. Consider these topics first:
- Historical events (past).
- Travel with a historical interest (specific theme, i.e. hex signs, steeples or geographic area—county, region).
- Vacation/weekend trip ideas within the state.
- People/family success stories—see Panorama.
- General interest subjects that are related to happenings in Pennsylvania.
- Statewide roundups of attractions, resources, happen-ings, etc.

4. We usually avoid these topics: Hunting, skiing, fashions, exposes and scandals, film and product reviews, government/church/borough/institution anniversary-related events.

Template for Your Query Letter to *Pennsylvania Magazine*

Today's date
Your name/address
City/State/Zip Department/Feature
Phone Number Estimated word count
If seasonal, when the article should run
RE: Article subject

Introduction paragraph—who you are, why you suggest this topic now to *Pennsylvania Magazine*, why the subject would be of interest to our readers.

Explain what types of photos you can supply to illustrate your subject. Enclose photocopies of existing illustrations for your topic, or of photos similar to the ones you will supply.

What is your expected timeline for completion? Is this a simultaneous submission? Has this been printed previously elsewhere? Have you seen coverage of this topic in other publications?

Your name
List any enclosures

Tips

1. In your query, send photocopies of available illustrations or tell how you will provide them.

2. Do not send original slides at any time.

3. Do not send originals or anything valued by you or the owner (such as an old photo or certificate). Send a photocopy when you query.

4. We want people-related photos. With few exceptions, we do not want photos of building/structures (such as, "This is the house William Penn built.") or rooms/an empty field/etc. as the only illustration.

5. We prefer to begin with a written query, but if you already have a ms, you can send us a photocopy (include how you will handle illustrations).

6. Tell us if your material has been printed or is being considered elsewhere.

7. Do not send samples of previously published work.

8. Send your ideas often. The wider the choice, the more likely of a go-ahead.

9. We strongly suggest you send for a sample copy ($2.95 prepaid) if you are not already familiar with the magazine.

When an Article Is Submitted

SUBMITTING MATERIALS: Send your article and its illustrations together. Do not have an illustrator or photographer send illustrations to us under separate cover. We can wait for you to assemble all components of an article package before sending it to us. Provide names and addresses of photographers or artists whose work is used. You will need to supply written permission for our use of photos/illustrations from owners/copyright owners) and their names so we can provide credit.

EDITING: All written materials submitted to us are subject to editing for style, clarity, flow, and organization. This editing is intended to keep a cohesive, familiar style for readers of the magazine.

STYLE NOTES: We use the Associated Press Stylebook. Do not use the terms first, only, or unique unless you can prove it. Include a citation with your text.

Write in the active voice. Location of a person, place or event should usually be cited in the first paragraph and include the county—Terry Smith of Camp Hill in Cumberland County. Omit county references for the following: Erie, Harrisburg, Lancaster, Philadelphia, Pittsburgh, Scranton, Allentown, Bethlehem, and York.

DEADLINES: We operate without rigid deadlines for most stories. If your item is appropriate for an upcoming issue, and we expect that you are able to complete it for that issue, we'll give you a deadline. Otherwise, articles are scheduled in the magazine when we have a suitable text/illustration package and the subject/geographical location fits a niche in the content of a specific issue.

ASSIGNMENTS: When we respond favorably to a query from a potential contributor who has not worked with us before, this does not constitute an assignment (and we will not pay a kill fee if the materials are not acceptable).

A contributor new to us submits only on speculation.

Payment for accepted materials is usually made upon acceptance. It may sometimes follow editing if the writer has exceeded the word limit.

Unless we specify otherwise, we purchase first, one-time use rights of your original materials. We then own our edited, published version. You can resell your original copy elsewhere after our publication of your material.

Payment Information
RATES: We pay 10 to 15 cents a word, depending on the amount of editing required. (Payment for reprinted articles is five cents per word.)

We pay $15 to $25 for each photo we use. For a cover, we pay up to $100. Photos you obtain from a subject's file: $5 each. We may suggest a flat package fee for an article with illustrations.

MINIMUM RATES: We pay a minimum of $50 for each item (copy and one photo) appearing in the Roundup or Town and Country departments—more if two photos and/or copy exceeding 350 words are used.

EXPENSES: We seldom pay expenses. The only expense that we usually pay is for the reasonable fee for reproduction of a photo or illustration provided by a museum, library or historical society.

Quick Reference
CREDITS: In the author credit at the end of the article, we like to mention your hometown, county, and any related interest you may have in the subject of your article.

COPIES: Upon publication, we will return your materials with five copies of that issue. Additional copies are provided free of charge.

COPYRIGHT: We copyright each edition of the magazine with the Library of Congress.

Specifics Regarding Content Features
GENERAL: Usually range between 1,000 to 2,500 words in edited form and cover historical items (places, people, and events), travel with a people focus, and topics of current interest. GENERAL FEATURES must be illustrated with a majority of color photos; HISTORICAL ITEMS should have period photos or appropriate illustrations. Published articles range from two to eight pages.

Departments: Usually range between 250 to 900 words.

ROUNDUP items cover people and organizations involved in noteworthy projects/festivals, unusual activities, or significant achievement.

Other items usually cover collections in the state that are open to the general public on a regular (not appointment) basis.

PHOTOGRAPHY ESSAY highlights our annual Photo Contest entries. The contest is announced in the first two issues of the year, and winners are announced/published in the fourth.

Details on Photography
WE ALWAYS ASK OUR CONTRIBUTORS TO supply photographs with articles. If you don't own or are not familiar/comfortable with a camera, we suggest that you join a photography club in your area to refine your skills. We believe that you will sell more material to us and other publications when you can supply the illustrations as a package.

We prefer people to be in photographs for articles and department items. This is for scale and personality. In close-up shots, we should have people's names and addresses (if their photo is used, we'll send a copy of that magazine).

People should be doing something or talking to one another to give the photograph vitality. Objects important to the article can be in the foreground or background, and people can also be shown looking slightly off camera. The best way to show people in a natural setting is to ask them questions and shoot as they respond, remembering to direct their attention away from you and the camera. A flash on the camera should not be used unless the background wall is at least 10 feet away.

We do not want original slides and will not be responsible for them. We prefer color prints (4" x 6" to 5" x 7") or duplicate slides. We have found that Kodacolor, if shot in a contrasting setting (sunshine and dark areas in the same scene) will result in either over- or under-exposure. Seek shade or all sun in a scene. If faces are in shade or backlit, use flash for fill-in.

Articles about resorts, parks, etc. should have a people focus, with them in the fore- or background of shots. We don't need model releases. But if a person notices you taking a picture and objects, do not take or use it. Do not send us photos of Amish people. We need to identify people when appropriate. For example, staff in a museum or attraction photo.

We may hold your submission for some time, so do not send us your only copies of original illustrations. Make and send a copy.

Categories: Nonfiction—History—Regional

CONTACT: Matthew K. Holliday, Editor
Material: All
PO Box 755
Camp Hill PA 17001-0755
Phone: 717-697-4660

Penthouse

1. The best way to discern the material *Penthouse* might be interested in is to look at the magazine. Articles are usually related to current affairs or topics that would appeal to our readers (predominately male, aged 18-49). Subjects might include celebrity or sports figure profiles, exposes on government or corporate affairs, and analyses of trends in lifestyle or sexuality. Interviews should be exclusive queries on personalities who are obviously of interest to a diverse audience.

2. Queries should include a detailed description of your article, who or what your sources will be, and how you plan to present the material. Queries should demonstrate an in-depth knowledge of the subject. Proposals for photo essays should be accompanied by slides or suggestions for sources of art.

3. Please submit any credits, clips or other examples of your published writings, if available. A stamped, self-addressed envelope is essential for a reply or return of material.

4. Features run 3500 to 5000 words and shorter articles for our "View From The Top" section are 600-700 words.

5. Writer's fees and expenses are negotiated when an assignment is made. Features pay from $2,500 to $5,000, depending on length and complexity of subject. Shorter pieces pay $250. Payment is made on acceptance. There is a 25% kill fee on assigned articles.

6. Forum letters should carry name and address, though these will be changed by the editor. All letters become the property of *Penthouse*. We do not pay for letters but your submissions are welcome.

7. All letters should be sent to address below. Designate Editorial Department and appropriate editor (i.e., features, fiction, sports, forum).

Bedtime Stories, Women's Erotic Fiction Section Writer's Guidelines: Thank you for your interest in "Bedtime Stories," *Penthouse*'s women's erotic fiction section. Stories for the column should be well-developed, well-plotted, erotic in nature, written by a woman, and between 2,000-2,500 words in length. The main character or voice should be female. We request that the stories contain no bondage/discipline, S/M, painful anal sex, fist fucking, excessive come on the face, or minors (which includes reflections on adolescence—no one even thinking about being younger than 19). We also request that the material be unpublished, and that it not be submitted to any of our associate publications during the time we are reviewing it. If it is being considered elsewhere, please make note of that in your cover letter.

The manuscript should be double spaced, with 1" margins, on white paper. Please make sure the pages are numbered, and that your name, address, phone number, and social security number appear on the first page. The fees vary per author and individual story. We do request that writers use their own names, not pseudonyms; if this is a problem for you, please consider it before submitting material.

We will return submissions which arrive with envelopes large enough to accommodate them. If not, they will be discarded.

We look forward to hearing from you soon.

Categories: Fiction—Nonfiction—Entertainment—Erotica—Fashion—Food/Drink—Government—Humor—Interview—Lifestyle—Recreation—Sexuality—Society—Sports/Recreation

CONTACT: Barbara Rice
Material: Bedtime Stories
CONTACT: Peter Bloch
Material: All
1110 Pen Plaza Floor 12
New York NY 10001
Phone: 212-702-6000
Fax: 212-702-6279
Website: www.penthouse.com

Penthouse Variations

Thank you for expressing interest in *Penthouse Variations* magazine.

Contributions to *Variations* should be neatly typed and double-spaced with one-inch margins. Proper grammar should be used as well as the kind of language you would be proud to share with a good friend. If you are making a professional freelance submission to be published as one of our featured stories, be sure to clearly indicate this in a cover letter to the editor. *Variations* publishes 3000-word, first-person narratives of credible erotic experience, squarely focused within a specific category. *Variations* does not accept electronic story submissions or pay for material sent to the editorial office via e-mail. For your material to be considered for publication as a lead story, you must send a manuscript to the editorial office with your legal name and mailing address printed on the first page. Payment for an accepted, fully revised manuscript is up to $400.00. One contributor's copy is mailed to each author of a featured story upon publication. *Variations* does not publish poetry of any kind.

Manuscripts take six to eight weeks to be read. They are rejected usually because of the quality of the writing or because the category described is unsuitable or oversold to us. We strongly recommend that you read several issues of the magazine to become familiar with our categories, style and vocabulary.

Variations is proud of its reader-generated letter sections and less experienced writers should feel free to make submissions to the editor on this basis, either by surface mail or e-mail. Letters to *Variations* magazine are assumed intended for publication and republication in all media, in whole or in part, edited or unedited. All letters become the property of *Variations*. We do not make payments for letter material. We guarantee confidentiality of all material, both letters and articles. In fact, we choose pseudonyms in order to avoid writers libeling themselves in choosing their own.

Categories: Fiction—Alternate Life-style—Erotica—Gay/Lesbian—Sexuality

CONTACT: Submissions Editor
Material: All
11 Penn Plaza, 12th Floor
New York NY 10001
Phone: 212-702-6000
E-mail: variations@generalmedia.com
Website: penthouse.com

Perdido
Leadership with a Conscience

Editorial description & audience. *Perdido* is a magazine devoted to examining organizational life in all its forms. "Leadership with a Conscience" means that we are concerned with what's happening in organizations that are mission-oriented—as opposed to merely profit-oriented. *Perdido* is focused on helping conscientious leaders put innovative ideas into practice. We seek articles on management techniques as well as essays on social issues. Perdido publishes feature articles, interviews/profiles, book excerpts, and book reviews. The common thread is being the questioning of easy answers and examining issues from a socially-aware, progressive perspective.

Our readers are managers, CEOs, executive directors, vice presidents, and program directors of nonprofit and for-profit organizations. We try to make the content of *Perdido* accessible to all decision-makers, whether in the nonprofit or for-profit world, government, or academia. *Perdido* actively pursues diverse opinions and authors from many different fields.

Writer's guidelines. In general, follow *Associated Press Stylebook and Libel Manual* guidelines. Humor, opinion, and innovative insights into management, leadership, and organizational issues are sought-after qualities in writers. *Perdido* is interested in new management trends, concepts, practices, philosophies, business leaders, and authors. Articles should use stories and anecdotes to put these ideas into a useful context.

Any article submitted to *Perdido* should possess a strong (i.e., humorous, compelling, shocking, thought-provoking, perplexing, enigmatic) lead.

In terms of writing style, *Perdido* favors clear, concise, active writing that tries to entertain the reader. Jargon, unnecessarily big words, passive constructions, and italicized, foreign phrases like zeitgeist or mise en scène (unless used ironically) are heartily discouraged. Journal articles belong in journals and research papers belong wherever it is they are published. Dry, excessively technical, or just plain dull articles will be handled with steel tongs and placed in the appropriate receptacle. Strunk and White's *The Elements of Style* and William Zinsser's *On Writing Well* are excellent guides to the kind of engaging, accessible prose we strive for at *Perdido*.

Offensive speech is a particular no-no for *Perdido* in that many of our readers work in human services. Sexist, bigoted, and stereotypical language is obviously not welcome—nor is speech offensive or insensitive to minority groups and people with disabilities. The *Publication Manual of the American Psychological Association* is a good reference for using language that is not unnecessarily offensive. Common sense is probably the best guide.

Queries and submissions... We accept queries with published clips for feature articles. If you are interested in writing a book review, please send a sample book review (published or unpublished) and your resume. We usually respond in about four weeks to queries and submitted manuscripts. Articles should be submitted via mail or e-mail. If submitting the article by mail, please include a double-spaced printout of the file. If an article is accepted for publication, you will be required to provide a digital file. Files in Microsoft Word for Mac or Windows, WordPerfect for Mac or DOS/Windows, or any word processing application are acceptable.

Every article should include a title, author, submission date, and word count.

Deadlines... *Perdido* is published quarterly—Winter, Spring, Summer, and Fall. Deadline for copy, photographs, and artwork is always 45 days prior to the publication date, i.e.; Winter: Nov. 15; Spring: Feb. 15; Summer: May 15; Fall: Aug. 15.

Articles and queries should be directed to: Mary Rundell-Holmes, Editor, at address below. E-mail and computer files can be sent to: editor1@hightidepress.com.

DEPARTMENTS...

Fast Foreword. This one-page (500-750 words) article comes at the beginning of the magazine and usually relates a story from personal experience that imparts some insight or lesson in leadership or management. It is always written by *Perdido*'s editor-in-chief, Art Dykstra.

Points of Interest/Voices Carry. News items/quotes, culled from a variety of sources by *Perdido* editorial staff.

Book Reviews. *Perdido* always features one main and one alternate book review per issue. This is normally two pages (750-850 words) and covers a new or recently-published book important to the fields of management, leadership, business, technology, trends, self-improvement, or psychology. Usually this a book that we want to recommend to our readers. However, if the book warrants a negative review and it's an important title, we will run it.

One alternate book is usually reviewed following the main selection. These are shorter (650-700 word) reviews of similar books that are determined to be less significant than the main selection.

***Perdido* Puzzler.** Usually a crossword puzzle written by staff, the Puzzler is open to anyone who can originate a good management/leadership-related puzzle (not necessarily a crossword puzzle, but something challenging).

Rewind. A companion to Fast Foreword, Rewind is usually on the last page or two pages of the magazine and is similar in form to Fast Foreword. It is created by *Perdido* staff.

Features... 1500-3500 word articles on a wide variety of subjects. Investigative reports, interviews, and profiles of businesses, programs, and individuals in a variety of fields are all desirable story formats for *Perdido*. The focus of any article should always relate in some way to the issues surrounding leadership, management, human resources, current events that impact organizational life, technology as it applies to the workplace, and/or psychology. Current trends in business, new ways of doing things, new concepts and models should always be sought out.

Pay rates for submissions... Features of 1500-3500 words are paid at the rate of between $0.05 and $0.07 per word upon publication. Book reviews are paid a flat rate of $75.00 upon publication.

For samples of *Perdido*'s content, visit us on the Web at: www.perdidomagazine.com.

E-mail us at editor1@hightidepress.com to request a sample issue.

Categories: Nonfiction—Book Reviews—Business—Careers—Disabilities—Leadership Management

CONTACT: Mary Rundell-Holmes, Editor
Material: All
High Tide Press, 3650 W. 183rd St.
Homewood IL 60430-2603
Phone: 708-206-2054
Fax: 708-206-2044
E-mail: editor@hightidepress.com

PEREGRINE
The Journal of Amherst Writers & Artists

Peregrine
The Journal of Amherst Writers & Artists

Peregrine has provided a forum for national and international writers since 1981, and is committed to finding exceptional work by beginning as well as established writers. We seek work that is unpretentious and memorable. No work by or for children. Peregrine features poetry and fiction. Each work is read by several readers. Final decisions are made by the editors. Published annually, designed by Janet Sadler, cover art by Barry Moser, Peregrine is professionally printed, perfect-bound with glossy cover. No unsolicited manuscripts for our

AWA Chapbook Series.

FICTION: 3,000 word limit. Double space. Indicate word count on first page.

POETRY: 3-5 poems, each poem limited to 50 lines (and spaces). Indicate line count for each poem.

- we accept manuscripts postmarked January 1 to June 1
- original, typed/word processed, unpublished work
- no electronic submissions
- up to 3 manuscripts a year; simultaneous submissions OK.
- cover letter with name, address, day/evening phone numbers, 40 word bio (max).
- If you use a pseudonym, provide legal name for mailing purposes.
- #10 self-addressed stamped envelope (SASE) for our response.
- for manuscript return: affix sufficient postage. (otherwise, we'll recycle)
- for acknowledgment of manuscript receipt: self-addressed stamped postcard (SASP)

Submission Deadline: June 1 (postmark)

The editors make decisions after reading ALL incoming manuscripts. Send submissions and all other correspondence to the address below.

Current copy of Peregrine: $12. Sample copy, $10 (ppd). Check payable to AWAPress

3-year subscription $25, 5-year subscription $35, Lifetime Subscription $250.

- Subscriptions and Gifts are fully tax deductible. Friends of Peregrine ($100 or more).

Categories: Fiction—Poetry—Short Stories—Writing

CONTACT: Nancy Rose
Material: All
Amherst Writers & Artists Press
190 University Dr.
Amherst, MA 01002
E-mail: awapress@aol.com (e-mail contact preferred)
Website: www.amherstwriters.com
Phone: 413-253-3307
E-mail: awapress@aol.com
Website: www.amherstwriters.com

Persimmon Hill

Persimmon Hill magazine is published quarterly by the National Cowboy and Western Heritage Museum for an audience interested in western art, history, ranching, and rodeo. Circulation approximately 15,000. Buys first North American rights; byline given. Accepts no reprints. Pays on publication. Query with clips and self-addressed, stamped envelope. No phone or fax queries are accepted. Allow a minimum of six weeks for a response from the editor and editorial board. Sample copy $10.50, including postage and handling. Annual subscription $30.00.

Non-fiction:
Historical and contemporary articles on notable persons connected with pioneering the American West; western art, rodeo, cowboys, western flora, animal life, or other phenomena of the West of today or yesterday. Articles must be historically accurate. Sources must be documented. We require lively, top-notch writing for a popular audience. Length: no more than 1,500 words. Pay ranges from $100 to $250, including illustrations.

Regular Departments:
- Around the Western States—Short features (500 to 750 words) on events in the West or interesting places to visit.
- Great Hotels of the West—historic lodges, hotels or inns, 1000 words or less.
- Western Entrepreneurs—contemporary craftsmen who are keeping traditional western gear and trappings alive, 1000 words or less.

• Western Personalities—contemporary western men/women who are making a positive contribution to the western lifestyle, 1,000 words or less.

Photos:

Black and white glossy prints or color transparencies, submitted and purchased with the manuscript. Captions required. *Persimmon Hill* will not be responsible for any loss or damage to original or historic photographs or documents. If materials are of heirloom quality, copies should be made.

Format for Submissions:

All manuscripts must be typed, double spaced, using front side of paper only. Computer discs accompanied by a letter quality print-out are required. Discs must be in a software program that is compatible with Word Perfect 6.1. Software program information must be provided with the manuscript. Discs will not be returned. We prefer not to receive E-mail manuscripts.

Tips:

Send us a story that captures the spirit of adventure and individualism that typifies the Old West or reveals a facet of the western lifestyle in contemporary society. The availability of superior illustrations or photographs strongly influences the sale of an article to us.

Categories: Nonfiction—Adventure—Animals—Antiques—Architecture—Arts—Biography—Book Reviews—Careers—Collectibles—Conservation—Cooking—Entertainment—Environment—Fashion—Folklore—History—Lifestyle—Literature—Native American—Outdoors—Regional—Rural America—Travel—Western

CONTACT: M. J. Deventer, Editor and Director of Publications
Material: Western Themes
National Cowboy and Western Heritage Museum
1700 NE 63rd St
Oklahoma City OK 73111
Phone: 405-478-6404
Fax: 405-478-4714
E-mail: editor@nationalcowboymuseum.org

Personal Branding Magazine

The only publication on Personal Branding.

Peter Montoya's *Personal Branding* magazine is the only source for the critical secrets you need to become a Personal Branding scholar and develop the skills to achieve the success you desire.

• Each full color issue is a power-packed user's manual of insights, how-to tips and real-world branding stories:
• Profiles of some of today's hottest Personal Brands
• Personal Branding basics
• Practical brand strategies for entrepreneurs
• Career advancement tactics for corporate professionals
• Ideas on using Personal Branding in sales, financial services and more

Personal Branding Press

For Personal Branding Press, please refer to their listing in the Book Publisher section of this directory.

Categories: Business—Careers—Money & Finances—Advertising, Sales

CONTACT: Peter Montoya, Publisher
Material: All
Personal Branding Press
1540 S. Lyon St.
Santa Ana CA 92705
Phone: 714-285-0900
Fax: 714-285-0929
E-mail: info@petermontoya.com
Website: www.petermontoya.com

Petals Magazine

An online magazine and retreat for women of all ages
Submission Guidelines

Petals Magazine is broken into various sections to cater to women of every age and every situation in life. Each portion of Petals includes fiction, poetry, and articles about the related topic.

For those of you who enjoy writing and using words to define yourself, see "Inspirations." Every issue will include a writing prompt. The next issue will announce the winners of the previous contest and address a new prompt.

Sections of Petals Magazine:
• **Looking Back:** Childhood experiences and defining moments
• **College and Beyond:** Breaking out into the real world.
• **The Working Woman:** Careers and the daily grind.
• **Dating and Relationships:** The ups and downs of the meat market.
• **The Married Life:** Keeping the peace, and the sparks!
• **Motherhood:** First moms, first words, and first days of school.
•**Inspirations:** For the writing woman. ~not accepting submissions~

Feel free to send your submissions via email to submissions@amyjamie.com. If sending multiple submissions, please send in separate emails. I prefer attached Word documents. Do not send more than three pieces of work. If I am interested in seeing more, I will let you know. (Currently I am having "issues" with my email, so if yours bounces back when sending to the above address, feel free to use the questions email below or email to aj@amyjamie.com. Thank you!) We accept work from women only, being it's a "for women, by women" magazine. Allow up to one month response time on your work.

Petals Magazine currently does not pay for accepted materials. Petals Magazine owns no rights to your work, but we prefer that it is not published elsewhere on the web while appearing in publication here. Any questions, email Sara at petalsquestions@amyjamie.com.

Categories: Women

CONTACT: Sara Jamison, Publisher
E-mail: petals@amyjamie.com
Website: www.amyjamie.com/petals

Phantasmagoria

Guidelines for Submission

1. Send previously unpublished short stories or poems of literary merit, and include SASE for return of your work.

2. Fiction—typed and double-spaced short stories of 4,000 words or less. Send only one story at a time.

3. Poetry—typed poems of 100 lines or fewer. Send no more than six poems at a time.

4. Faxed or emailed submissions will not be read.

5. As payment, contributors will receive two copies of the issues in which their work appears.

6. *Phantasmagoria* acquires First North American Serial Rights. All other rights revert to the author upon publication.

Categories: Fiction—Literature—Poetry—Short Stories

CONTACT: Abigail Allen, Editor
Material: All
English Dept.
Century Community and Technical College
3300 Century Ave. North
White Bear Lake MN 55110

Phi Delta Kappan

Phi Delta Kappan, the professional journal for education, addresses policy issues for educators at all levels. An advocate for research-based school reform, the Kappan provides a forum for debate on controversial subjects. The annual PDK/Gallup Poll is published in September. Published since 1915, the journal appears monthly September through June. The Kappan is indexed in Education Index and in Current Index to Journals in Education; available in microform, ProQuest Information and Learning Company, Ann Arbor, Mich.

Following are brief answers to the more common questions asked by persons interested in publishing in the *Phi Delta Kappan*.

What makes an article acceptable to the editors?

We look primarily for two qualities: educational significance and readability. There is no easy formula for achieving these goals, since there are many kinds of significance and many different styles that are readable. However, we believe that to be significant an article must in some way be usable by our readers — to enlarge their knowledge, to improve their practice, to influence their decisions. We want it to deal with real problems. We want it to be factual, logical, and well focused. To be readable, it should avoid the use of jargon, it should include concrete examples, it should not waste words, and it should display — if at all possible — some wit and erudition.

What are the procedures for submission of manuscripts?

Manuscripts may be submitted either by U.S. mail or by e-mail. Please use double-spaced format.

Hard copy: Send one copy to the editor. If you want your manuscript to be returned if it cannot be published, enclose a stamped, self-addressed envelope. In your cover letter, give us sufficient information about yourself for a standard author-identification paragraph.

E-mail: Send an e-mail "cover letter" to manuscripts@pdkintl.org, including sufficient information about yourself for a standard author-identification paragraph, and attach file of manuscript (Microsoft Word preferred).

If you wish, send or e-mail a letter of inquiry first, describing the article and perhaps including an outline. We must balance our coverage; sometimes we can tell you, on the basis of an outline, whether an article will fit in with our editorial plans.

Who makes the decision to publish?

The editor. Usually he will consult with the other editors or with other members of the Phi Delta Kappa International professional staff. Sometimes, if he is undecided, he will solicit the opinions of one or more of the editorial consultants listed on the Kappan masthead.

What is the ideal length?

Feature articles run between 1,500 and 5,000 words. Certain types of articles—usually more personal reflections or humorous pieces—tend to be shorter, 1,000 words or less.

What editorial style is used?

Kappan style is based largely on the University of Chicago Manual of Style. For footnote style, see past issues of the Kappan.

What about diagrams, tables, graphs, photographs?

We use graphic material quite sparingly. The rare diagram, table, or graph that we find indispensable will be re-created to our specifications. We will consider photographs, either black and white or in color, but they should be of professional quality. Amateur photography is seldom usable.

Do you pay for manuscripts?

Very seldom. Usually we pay an honorarium only when we solicit an article from a well-known authority or from a professional writer.

How can I contribute to one of the special sections?

Special sections are generally planned by the editors and/or a guest editor many months in advance, and most of the articles are solicited from individuals who have published original work on the topic. We do not announce special sections in advance, largely because we wish to preserve some flexibility. But special sections never fill entire issues; thus we are always seeking good manuscripts on a variety of topics.

Who holds copyright on Kappan articles?

Phi Delta Kappa International generally does. Each issue is fully copyrighted by Phi Delta Kappa. Authors may choose to retain the general copyright in their own name, but, as a condition of publication, Phi Delta Kappa requires authors who hold copyright to grant permission to post the full text of the article on the PDK website for the use of Phi Delta Kappa members and Kappan magazine subscribers.

How long does it take for the editors to make a decision?

We acknowledge all unsolicited manuscripts immediately upon receipt. We try not to hold a manuscript longer than two months without returning it, accepting it, or in some way communicating with the author. But in the months when more than 100 unsolicited manuscripts come in, we sometimes fall behind schedule. If two months pass and you have not heard from us, please feel free to phone our office.

Categories: Nonfiction—Education

CONTACT: Bruce M. Smith, Editor
Material: All
408 N Union
PO Box 789
Bloomington IN 47402-0789
Phone: 812-339-1156
Fax: 812-339-0018
E-mail: manuscripts@pdkintl.org
Website: www.pdkintl.org

PHOEBE
A JOURNAL OF LITERATURE & ART

Phoebe
A Journal of Literature & Art

Phoebe seeks to publish quality writing. Do not send formulaic writing, romance fiction, or greeting card poetry. We welcome experimental writing.

All submissions must be typed. Address submissions to Poetry or Fiction Editor. Enclose an SASE with sufficient postage for return of manuscript. Submissions without an SASE will not be returned. If you want your manuscript to be recycled, please tell us. Keep a copy of your work, as *Phoebe* cannot be responsible for lost or damaged manuscripts.

Reporting time can be up to three months, though it is usually sooner. We do not read during June, July, and August.

Contributors receive two copies of the journal upon publication.

Phoebe also sponsors poetry and fiction contests each year.

Categories: Fiction—Literature—Poetry—Short Stories—Writing

CONTACT: Poetry Editor
Material: Poetry
CONTACT: Fiction Editor
Material: Fiction
MSN 2D6
George Mason University

M-Q

4400 University Dr.
Fairfax VA 22030-4444
E-mail: phoebe@gmu.edu
Website: www.gmu.edu/pubs/phoebe

PieceWork
Needlework and History, Hand in Hand

PieceWork is a bimonthly magazine with high visual impact focusing on the historical aspects of needlework around the world. *PieceWork* readers are passionate about and do needlework; they value the role needlework has played, and plays, in the ongoing human story. Well-researched feature stories explore the historical traditions of needlework, including needlepoint, embroidery, cross-stitch, quilting, knitting, crocheting, basketry, beadwork, lace making, and surface design. *PieceWork* readers want to know the origin of the various needlework techniques, how they were done, who did them, and why. Striking examples of the technique are important. Readers also want to know how they might use a technique today. Therefore, several articles in each issue have associated projects that use the technique to produce a high-quality finished item that readers will want to keep or present as a gift.

SUBMISSIONS

Features: We invite submissions of complete manuscripts related to most aspects of historic needlework, textiles, and fiber arts. Stories focusing on a particular person in needlework history are encouraged. Material submitted for publication should display in-depth knowledge of the subject matter and carefully documented research with all sources acknowledged. Visuals are critical; manuscripts should include a list of appropriate visuals and where each may be obtained.

Projects: We invite submissions of design sketches and/or color charts for hands-on projects in any of the techniques mentioned above. Projects should display technical expertise in the technique. Include an outline for the instructions, along with a list of diagrams and/or illustrations, necessary to complete the project.

Keep a copy of everything. If the submission is unsolicited and/or you wish any part of it to be returned, include a self-addressed envelope with sufficient return postage. *PieceWork* is published six times a year in January, March, May, July, September, and November. Issues are planned six to twelve months in advance, and we prefer to have materials intended for a particular issue at least six months before the month of publication.

MANUSCRIPTS

If you are not already familiar with the content, style, and tone of the magazine, we suggest you read a few issues. Historical and technical accuracy are essential but the tone should be personal. Use primary resources such as letters and diaries whenever possible to make the story arresting to the reader. Strive for clear organization as you convey information, but also include vivid detail and engaging quotations to give readers a sense of people, place, and meaning: you are telling a story. Please include a brief informal personal biography. A list of sources for "Further Reading" is very helpful.

We expect that the article you ask us to consider has not been published nor is it presently submitted elsewhere. If any part of your submission has been published previously, please let us know when and by whom. If possible, submit copies of the manuscript electronically either via email (piecework@interweave.com) or on a disk in addition to sending a hardcopy. All manuscripts not produced on a computer should be typewritten and double-spaced. Manuscript length may vary from 1,000 to 5,000 words depending on the subject matter.

VISUALS

Please include all the information you have about supporting visual materials you think will enhance the story. Museum photographs are preferable; if citing a piece in a museum collection as a supporting visual, please include the accession number of the object whenever possible. Some visuals (such as a family photograph showing a vintage piece of clothing) can only be provided by you. When you submit your manuscript, however, photocopies of such will be acceptable. If an article is accepted, arrangements for receiving publication-quality color transparencies, black-and-white glossies, color prints, or color slides will be made by the *PieceWork* staff. You also may be required to ship actual pieces and tools to the *PieceWork* office for photography. We will work together to choose what will best suit the story and make sure all pieces are transported safely. All photographs and other materials will be returned promptly and appropriately insured.

ACCEPTANCE, EDITING, AND PAYMENT

Receipt of your submission will be promptly acknowledged, but we may not be able to make a decision about its use right away. Please be patient. We are primarily looking for manuscripts that fit within the issue themes outlined on the editorial calendar. All unrelated manuscripts are considered on an issue-by-issue basis depending on the available space in the magazine. When we pay for accepted material we purchase first North American serial rights for publication in *PieceWork* and subsequent non-exclusive rights for use in other Interweave Press publications and promotions. The author retains the publication rights for the original materials. Payment rate is $100 per printed page based on a two-column galley of the edited text without visuals or illustrations (approximately four manuscript pages or 800 words) and is made upon publication unless other arrangements are made. Projects are contracted for separately. If a project design is accepted, most materials for completing the project will be supplied to you and the finished item will be retained by *PieceWork*. Before your work is published, we will send you an agreement stating the terms of acceptance and payment for your approval. We reserve the right to edit your material as necessary to fit the style, format, or other requirements of *PieceWork*. Thank you for your interest in *PieceWork*. We look forward to hearing from you.—Jeane Hutchins

Categories: Nonfiction—Crafts/Hobbies—History—Hobbies

CONTACT: Editor
Material: All
Interweave Press
201 East 4th St.
Loveland CO 80537-5655
E-mail: piecework@interweave.com
Website: www.interweave.com

Pig Iron Series

Guidelines for Writers and Artists
The *Pig Iron* Series

The *Pig Iron* Series was established in 1975. The series reviews and considers Poetry, Fiction, Literary Nonfiction, Living History, Articles, Scholarship, Art, Design, Photography, and Cartoons for publication in the *Pig Iron* Series of Thematic Popular Cultural, Literary, and Social Commentary free-lance authored collections. Published irregularly. Traditional and experimental forms considered.

Format
Vinyl, square-back bound at 8.5 x 11 inches. 60 lb. text. 150+ pages. 1,000 copies. Retail list varies; Number 19 at cloth, $24.95 and paper, $14.95. Number of pages varies. Buys 50+ poems; 20+ articles; 30+ graphics per edition. No advertising. Designed by Jim Villani.

Content
The editor adopts, for each edition in the Pig Iron series, an editorial and content theme that investigates specific political, moral, or cultural imperatives. A variety of genres, styles, viewpoints and conclusions are included.

Terms
Purchases first North American Serial Right or one-time Reprint Right. Will consider previously published works. Payment is $5 per poem or $5 per published page for prose & three copies. Additional copies at 50% list price. Reports eventually. Not responsible for submissions not containing sufficient return postage or for materials lost in the mail.

Deliver by mail to P.O. Box 237, Youngstown, Ohio 44501.

Mechanical Requirements

Submission must not be under consideration by another publisher. Will consider previously published works if notified on the manuscript when and where the material was published. Include a self-addressed, stamped envelope (SASE) for return of work or decision. No stapled manuscripts; no bound manuscripts. Photocopied manuscripts O.K. Does not accept submissions by Fax or email.

No more than 10 poems, or 6,000 words prose. Include number of words for prose.

Reads for themes only. A variety or viewpoints, styles, forms, and media are included. Unusual or contrary interpretations encouraged.

For themes and deadines query with SASE.

Art, Design, Sketches, Cartoons, and Photography limited to black & white. Media include ink, marker, pencil, rubbings, and prints. Submit graphic materials at 11x17 inches maximum.

Forthcoming Titles and Deadlines

Family: The Possibility of Endearment, Number 21

Jazz Tradition, Number 22

Frontier: Custom & Archetype, Number 23

Years of Rage: 1960s, Number 24

Religion & Modernity, Number 25

Twentieth Century, Number 26

Categories: Fiction—Nonfiction—Alternate Lifestyles—Arts—Family—General Interest—Graphics—History—Literature—New Age—Photography—Poetry—Writing

CONTACT: Jim Villani, Managing Editor
Material: All
Pig Iron Press
PO Box 237
Youngstown OH 44501
Phone: 330-747-6932
Fax: 330-747-0599
E-mail: pigironpress@cboss.com
Website: www.pigironpress.com

Pipeline & Gas Journal

Please refer to Oildom Publishing.

Pipeline News

Please refer to Oildom Publishing.

PITTSBURGH

Pittsburgh

It's your town. Make the most of it.

Mission: PITTSBURGH magazine is the monthly community publication for Western Pennsylvania, Eastern Ohio, Northern West Virginia and Western Maryland. PITTSBURGH presents issues, analyzes problems and strives to encourage a better understanding of today's community to more than 75,000 readers.

Style: Each issue features a mix of stories that includes a "people" profile, in-depth news and a service piece, plus feature and lifestyle stories for our target reader: primarily 30ish, professional, with children. Without exception-whether the topic is business, travel, the arts or lifestyle—each story is clearly oriented to Pittsburghers today and the greater Pittsburgh region of today. We have minimal interest in historical articles. PITTSBURGH does not publish fiction, poetry, advocacy pieces or personal reminiscences.

Scheduling: Seasonal story ideas should be submitted at least six months in advance. Each issue is fully scheduled at least four months in advance; feature ideas that do not fit that timeframe cannot be considered. Short (under 200 words) timely items for UpFront can be considered as late as six weeks before publication.

Payment & rights: Features vary from $300 up, depending upon length and complexity of story, and experience of writer. Feature fees are negotiated separately. UpFront items start at $50, up to $150. Most feature stories and service pieces range from 1,200 to 4,000 words, in-depth news features up to 4,000. We purchase first North American serial rights; second rights, only when the article has not appeared in the same geographic market.

Submission: Address all queries to the executive editor. PITTSBURGH prefers to receive a brief query with a sample lead and one-page outline, not completed manuscripts. We will, however, review manuscripts on spec. Writers should enclose samples of their writing when submitting queries. We do not assign stories to new freelancers. All queries will be answered within two months. We do not respond to unsolicited email, fax, or phone queries. Manuscripts and other materials will be returned only if the writer includes a self-addressed stamped envelope, or can be picked up at the office. The writer guarantees that the piece is his or her own work and is not plagiarized.

After acceptance: Once a story is accepted, we will review the first draft and, possibly, ask for changes and a second draft. The writer is responsible for completing all research deemed necessary by the editors. We also need a list of sources and their phone numbers for fact-checking.

Categories: Regional

CONTACT: Michelle Pilecki, Executive Editor
Material: All
4802 Fifth Ave.
Pittsburgh PA 15213-2918
Phone: 412-622-1360
Fax: 412-622-7066

Plane&Pilot

The following information should give you a general guide for preparation and submission of materials to Plane&Pilot for editorial consideration:

Submit a query letter to the editor. Be sure to include as much detailed information as possible on your idea, the proposed length of the article and the type of photography that you expect to provide.

All material, unless previously assigned in writing, is submitted on a speculation basis.

Obtain copies of the magazine from the newsstand to study the format. Or, send a check for $3.99 and $2.50 shipping and handling for a sample copy from our office.

Text must be double-spaced, typewritten and free from handwritten corrections. On a separate sheet of paper, include your suggested title, deck and byline, photo credits and social security number.

Submit suggested heads, decks and captions for all photos with each story.

Black & white photography material can be submitted in proof sheet form with negatives. If you wish to provide prints, we require 8x10 size with a glossy finish. Be sure that your prints and proof sheets have your name and address on the back.

Color photography: Material can be submitted in the form of transparencies. Size can be 2.25x2.25, 4x5 or 35mm. Transparencies must be protected in plastic sleeves and your name should be on each slide.

Use cardboard stiffeners to protect your photos and materials in shipping. We'll take every available measure to protect your work once it has arrived in our offices, but will not be responsible for its loss or damage in shipping.

Payment will be made during the middle of the issue's month in which your article appeared, unless otherwise stated in writing. Rates vary depending on the value of the material as judged by the editors.

The publisher buys all rights to the material as judged by the editors.

Categories: Nonfiction—Aviation

CONTACT: Werner Publishing Corporation
12121 Wilshire Blvd 12th Fl
Los Angeles CA 90025-1176
Telephone: 310-820-1500
Fax: 310-826-5008
E-mail: editor@planeandpilotmag.com (Editorial questions only)

Plastic Canvas Today

GENERAL INFORMATION

Plastic Canvas Today is a full-color, 32-page, bimonthly, House of White Birches plastic canvas publication. *Plastic Canvas Today* features innovative plastic canvas designs worked in a variety of styles and on 7-count, 10-count, 14-count and 5-count plastic canvas.

SUBMISSIONS

Project submissions or manuscripts:

Your completed project or photo.

Typed, double-spaced, step-by-step instructions following our format.

Complete and labeled graphs, diagrams and color keys.

Materials list including types of materials, quantities used and ordering information if unavailable at most craft stores. If design materials were supplied free of charge, please indicate which materials should be credited and to whom.

Your name (as you would like published), address, telephone number.

Accepted projects or manuscripts:

We will review submissions on the dates given on our editorial calendar, after which we will issue agreements and return all designs we are unable to use. Please see our Editorial Calendar for specific deadlines.

Published projects will be returned to the designer (unless otherwise arranged) after all photography is complete. All manuscripts, diagrams, etc. remain our property.

Since we purchase all rights to designs unless otherwise arranged, designers should not sell the purchased design or one very similar to it to another publication.

Mailing Address: Send submissions and completed projects to *Plastic Canvas Today*, 306 East Parr Rd., Berne, IN 46711.

CONTRACTS & PAYMENT

If your project is accepted for publication, we will send you an agreement with our payment offer and a pre-addressed envelope. If the agreement is acceptable, you should complete it with your signature, phone number and Social Security number. Please sign and keep the photocopy of the agreement in your records and return the original to us in the pre-addressed envelope. Payment will be made within 45 days of acceptance. Amount will be determined by creativity, workmanship, skill level and overall quality.

If you have any questions, contact Vicki Blizzard or Kelly Keim.

Categories: Nonfiction—Crafts/Hobbies—Hobbies

CONTACT: Submissions Editor
Material: Submissions and completed projects
House of White Birches
306 East Parr Rd.
Berne IN 46711
Phone: 260-589-4000
Website: www.whitebirches.com

Playboy

Playboy regularly publishes nonfiction articles on a wide range of topics—sports, politics, music, topical humor, personality profiles, business and finance, science and technology—and other topics that have a bearing on our readers' lifestyles.

You can best determine what we're looking for by becoming familiar with the nonfiction we are currently publishing. We frequently reject ideas and articles—many of high quality—simply because they are inappropriate to our publication. We have a six-month lead time, so timing is very important.

Your brief query should outline your idea, explain why it's right for *Playboy* and tell us something about yourself. Handwritten submissions will be returned unread. Manuscripts should be typed, double-spaced and accompanied by a self-addressed, stamped envelope. Writers who submit manuscripts without a stamped, self-addressed return envelope will receive neither the manuscript nor a printed rejection.

The average length for nonfiction pieces is 4,000 to 5,000 words, and minimum payment for an article of this length is $3,000. We do not accept unsolicited poetry. *Playboy* buys first North American serial rights only—no second serial rights are considered. *Playboy* does not accept simultaneous submissions.

A bit of advice for writers: Please bear in mind that *Playboy* is not a venue where beginning writers should expect to be published. Nearly all of our writers have long publication histories, working their way up through newspapers and regional publications. Aspiring writers should gain experience, and an extensive file of by-lined features, before approaching *Playboy*. Please don't call our offices to ask how to submit a story or to explain a story. Don't ask for sample copies, a statement of editorial policy, a reaction to an idea for a story, or a detailed critique. We are unable to provide these, as we receive dozens of submissions daily. Our response time is approximately four weeks.

We appreciate your interest in *Playboy*. We hope these guidelines will assist you in submitting work that is suited to *Playboy*'s high standards.

Categories: Nonfiction—Business—Culture—Entertainment—Fashion—General Interest—Interview—Money & Finances—Music—Politics—Recreation—Science—Sexuality—Sports/Recreation—HumorProfiles—Technology

CONTACT: Articles Editor
Material: Nonfiction
680 North Lake Shore Dr.
Chicago IL 60611
Phone: 312-751-8000
Fax: 312-751-2818
E-mail: articles@la.playboy.com
Website: www.playboy.com

Playgirl

Playgirl addresses the needs, interests and desires of women 18 years of age and older. We provide something that no other American women's magazine provides: an uninhibited approach to exploring sexuality and fantasy that empowers, enlightens, and entertains.

We publish feature articles of all sorts: interviews with top celebrities, articles on sex, love, and romance and dating, how-to features, and erotic fantasies. Playgirl's common editorial thread, besides being good, lively writing and having scrupulous research, is a fresh, open-minded, irreverent, inquisitive attitude.

Freelancers MUST read a few issues before submitting their article ideas. Query letters with published clips are preferred, but completed, unsolicited manuscripts will be considered. Payment rates vary. All submissions must include a self-addressed, stamped envelope, and a telephone number at which you can be contacted.

Freelance writers may contribute to any of the following Playgirl departments:

Nonfiction features are 1600-2500 word (may vary) articles. we ask that you send us outlines and descriptions of projects (with documentation) rather than completed pieces.

Celebrity features are in-depth interviews with today's hottest stars that ask questions that only Playgirl can get away with asking. If you have a professional relationship with a celebrity that you know you can approach, we'd love to hear about it. You MUST supply a transcript and a tape recording of these interviews.

Q&A is a quick, 500-word question and answer interview with a celebrity or a well-known entertainer. You must include documentation (tape recording and transcript).

Erotic Encounters features first person, steamy erotic fiction. This column is devoted to female pleasures of the flesh, must be written from a female perspective and is the best opportunity for unpublished writers to write for Playgirl. Please mark envelopes with "Erotic Encounters." All submissions become Playgirl's property and will not be returned.

Playgirl does not publish poetry, jokes (or short humorous blurbs), or features that do not pertain to women's issues.

We regret that all submissions cannot be acknowledged or returned.

Entries must include your name, address, telephone number (e-mail address is optional).

Categories: Fiction—Nonfiction—Comedy—Consumer—Culture—Entertainment—Feminism—Health—Lifestyle—Sexuality—Singles—Travel—Women's Fiction—Women's Issues

CONTACT: Jill Sierzcki, Editor-in-Chief
Material: All
Playgirl Magazine
801 Second Ave, 9ᵗʰ Floor
New York, NY 10017
Phone: 212-661-7878
Fax: 212-697-6343
E-mail: editorial@playgirlmag.com
Website: www.playgirl.com

Pleiades
A Journal of New Writing
Central Missouri State University

Pleiades publishes fiction, poetry, essays and reviews by writers from around the world. The editors read manuscripts year-round. When submitting to *Pleiades*, please observe the following guidelines:

• Submit manuscripts with a SASE for response or manuscript return.

• Prose should be double spaced with reasonable margins. Poetry should be single spaced, with the author's name on each page.

• Do not send your only copy of any manuscript.

• *Pleiades* accepts simultaneous submissions. We ask, however, that you note if a piece has been sent to another magazine.

• Do not fax or email submissions.

• Submit in only one genre at a time.

• Poetry should be addressed to Kevin Prufer and Wayne Miller.

• Fiction should be addressed to Susan Steinberg.

• Non-fiction should be addressed to Eric Miles Williamson.

• We accept queries for book reviews. Please send query and clips of previously published reviews to Kevin Prufer. No unsolicited reviews will be accepted.

• Cover art is solicited directly from artists. We do not accept unsolicited submissions of art.

• Send submissions to the appropriate editor.

Categories: Fiction—Nonfiction—Book Reviews—Drama—Literature—Poetry—Short Stories—Personal Essays

CONTACT: Kevin Prufer, Editor-in-Chief
E-mail: kdp8106@cmsu2. cmsu.edu
Material: Poetry
CONTACT: Susan Steinberg, Fiction Editor
E-mail: ssteinberg@ usfca.edu
Material: Fiction
CONTACT: Eric Miles Williamson, Essays Editor
E-mail: guniter@ earthlink.net
Material: Essays
Dept. of English, Central Missouri State University
Warrensburg MO 64093
Phone: 660-543-4425/8106
Fax: 660-543-8544
E-mail: kdp8106@cmsu2.cmsu.edu
Website: www.cmsu.edu/englphil/pleiades

Ploughshares
The Literary Journal of Emerson College

Ploughshares welcomes unsolicited submissions of fiction, poetry, and a limited amount of nonfiction. We are planning to launch a beta version of an online submissions system on August 15.

GUEST EDITOR POLICY: *Ploughshares* is published three times a year: mixed issues of poetry and fiction in the Spring and Winter and a fiction issue in the Fall, with each guest-edited by a different writer of prominence, usually one whose early work was published in the journal. Guest editors are invited to solicit up to half of their issues, with the other half selected from unsolicited manuscripts screened for them by staff editors. This guest-editor policy is designed to introduce readers to different literary circles and tastes, and to offer a fuller representation of the range and diversity of contemporary letters than would be possible with a single editorship. Yet, at the same time, we expect every issue to reflect our overall standards of literary excellence. We strongly suggest that you examine one or two issues of *Ploughshares* or, at the very least, some of the work displayed on this site before submitting.

NEEDS: We seek work of the highest literary quality, but otherwise do not have any specific guidelines for style or subject matter. We no longer arrange issues with thematic topics. On occasion, we do publish issues that feature emerging writers; always look at our website before submitting for announcements. Although we look primarily for short stories, we occasionally publish personal essays/memoirs. Novel excerpts are acceptable if self-contained. Unsolicited book reviews and criticism are not considered. Translations are welcome if permission has been granted.

GENERAL FORMAT: Submit one prose piece or one to three poems. A citation of publications and awards, if any, is helpful. Poems should be individually typed either single- or double-spaced on one side of the page. Prose should be typed double-spaced on one side and be no longer than thirty pages. There are no preferences in regards to names in headers or footers, or to staples or paper clips; we do like margins to be flushed left, however, instead of justified.

DEADLINES AND ADDRESSES: Our reading period is August 1 to March 31 (postmark dates). All submissions sent from April through July are returned unread. We adhere very strictly to these dates. Since we operate on a first-received, first-read basis, we cannot make exceptions or hold work. Submit your work at any time during our reading period; if a manuscript is not timely for one issue, it will be considered for another. We do not recommend trying to target specific guest editors. Our backlog is unpredictable, and staff editors ultimately have the responsibility of determining for which editor a work is most appropriate. Mail submissions to: *Ploughshares*, Emerson College, 120 Boylston St., Boston, MA 02116-4624. Our online submission system may be accessed at http://www.pshares.org/submit.

RESTRICTIONS: Send only one manuscript at a time, either by mail or online. Do not send duplicate or multiple submissions. There is a limit of two total submissions per writer per reading period, regardless of genre, whether it is by mail or online. Do not send a second submission until you have heard about the first. We will cross-reference our databases periodically, and if we find more than one active submission, or a third submission (or more) during the reading period, all submissions will be immediately and summarily rejected unread. Simultaneous submissions to other journals are amenable as long as they are indicated as such and we are notified immediately upon acceptance elsewhere. We do not reprint previously published work.

SUBMISSIONS BY MAIL: Mail your manuscript in a page-size manila envelope, your full name and address written on the outside. In general, address submissions to the "Fiction Editor," "Poetry Editor," or "Nonfiction Editor," not to the guest or staff editors by name, unless you have a legitimate association with them or have been previously published in the magazine. Unsolicited work sent directly to a guest editor's home or office will be ignored and discarded; guest editors are formally instructed not to read such work. All manuscripts and correspondence regarding submissions should be accompanied by a self-addressed, 39¢-stamped #10 envelope (S.A.S.E.) for a response; no replies will be given to domestic addresses by e-mail or postcard. For international submissions, please include a stamped International Reply Coupon (I.R.C.) with your self-addressed envelope, or provide a valid email address for us to respond with. Send a recyclable copy of your manuscript; manuscript copies will not be returned.

SUBMISSIONS ONLINE: Go to our home page: http://www.pshares.org/. Upload only one file, containing one prose piece or one to three poems. If you have a legitimate association with a guest or staff editor or have been previously published in the magazine, you may address that editor by name in the "Comments" box. You should also paste a brief citation of publications and awards (less than 50 words), if any, into the "Comments" box. A longer citation of credits or a cover letter may be included as the first page of your submission file. We recommend saving files as rich-text format (.rtf). If you are not familiar with this format, simply do a Google search for "Saving files in rich text format." Mac users, please be sure you save your file so the filename includes the ".rtf" file extension. More instructions are on the first login page. In general, you will receive a faster response online versus by regular mail. However, please be advised that, depending on volume, we may shorten the reading period for online submissions at any time. Announcements will be made on our website. The reading period for submissions by mail will not change.

NOTIFICATIONS AND QUERIES: Expect three to five months for a decision (our backlog is heaviest during the fall). We now receive well over a thousand manuscripts a month, so please be patient. Do not query us until five months have passed, and if you do, please write to us, including an S.A.S.E. and indicating the postmark date of submission, instead of calling or e-mailing. If you submit online, you will be able to track the status of your submission yourself. We cannot accommodate revisions, changes of return address, or forgotten S.A.S.E.'s after the fact. We cannot be responsible for delay, loss, or damage.

PAYMENT: Payment is upon publication: $25/printed page, $50

minimum per title, $250 maximum per author, with two copies of the issue and a one-year subscription. For more information about literary magazines, consult directories such as CLMP's *Literary Presses and Magazine Direcotry, The Writer's Market*, and *The International Directory of Literary Magazines and Small Presses.*

Please read our usage policy.
Categories: Fiction—Poetry

CONTACT: Submissions Editor
Material: All
120 Boylston St., Emerson College
Boston MA 02116
Phone: 617-824-8753
E-mail: Pshares@emerson.edu
Website: www.pshares.org

We Weren't Born Yesterday

Plus Magazine

PLUS welcomes submissions from freelance writers.
Our ideal story or article length is 900-1,200 words.

We are interested in profiles of unusual or notable people, nostalgia, unique hobbies, men and women in second careers, health, physical fitness, humor (if handled deftly, not heavy-handed), travel and reviews of current books.

We pay $1.50 per published column inch and $10-$15 for photos we use with the article or story. We prefer black and white photos.

We receive many more submissions than we can publish. If you would like a query answered or an article returned if we can't use it, enclose a stamped, self-addressed envelope with the query or submission.

For a sample copy of the magazine send $2.00 in postage and a large self-addressed stamped envelope.

We try to respond to queries and submissions within two weeks after receiving them.

Categories: Nonfiction—Biography—Collectibles—Comedy—Diet/Nutrition—Entertainment—Gardening—Health—Recreation Vehicles—Television/Radio—Travel

CONTACT: Anne Stubbs, Health Editor
Material: Health & Fitness
CONTACT: George Brand, Editor
Material: All Other Submissions
3565 S. Higuera
San Luis Obispo CA 93401
Phone: 805-544-8711
Fax: 805-544-4450

FROM THE UPPER ROOM

Pockets
A Devotional Magazine for Children

What is *Pockets*?
Designed for 6- to 11-year-olds, *Pockets* magazine offers wholesome devotional readings that teach about God's love and presence in life. Each page of *Pockets* affirms a child's self-worth. Included are fun

and exciting puzzles, games, stories, poems, recipes, colorful pictures, and scripture readings. The magazine is published monthly (except in February) and includes a wide variety of materials.

The purpose of *Pockets* is to open up the fullness of the gospel of Jesus Christ to children. It is written and produced for children and designed to help children pray and be in relationship to God. The magazine emphasizes that we are loved by God and that God's grace calls us into community. It is through the community of God's people that we experience that love in our daily lives.

What should I write about?

Each issue is built around a specific theme with material that can be used by children in a variety of ways. Scripture stories, fiction, poetry, prayers, art, graphics, puzzles, and activities are included. Submissions do not need to be overtly religious. They should help children experience a Christian lifestyle that is not always a neatly wrapped moral package but is open to the continuing revelation of God's will. Seasonal material, both secular and liturgical, is appropriate. We welcome submissions from children.

Themes are set each year in December. They are available with an SASE or online.

Pockets is ecumenical, and our readers include persons of many cultures and ethnic backgrounds. These differences should be reflected in the references that are made to lifestyles, living environments (suburban, urban, rural, reservation), families (extended families, single-parent homes), and individual names. Stories should show appreciation of cultural differences and not leave the impression that one way is better than another.

What ages are *Pockets* readers?

The magazine is for children of ages six through eleven, with a target reading age of eight through eleven. Though some may share it with their families, it is designed primarily for the personal use of children.

What type of material should I write?

Fiction and scripture stories should be 600 to 1400 words. Our primary interest is in stories that can help children deal with real-life situations. We prefer real-life settings, but we occasionally use fables. We do not accept stories about talking animals or inanimate objects. Fictional characters and some elaboration may be included in scripture stories, but the writer must remain faithful to the story.

Stories should contain lots of action, use believable dialogue, be simply written, and be relevant to the problems faced by this age group in everyday life. Children need to be able to see themselves in the pages of the magazine. It is important that the tone not be "preachy" or didactic. Use short sentences and paragraphs. When possible, use concrete words instead of abstractions. However, do not "write down" to children.

It is no longer common practice to use such terms as "man," "mankind," "men," in the familiar generic sense. Substitute non-sexist terms that are inclusive of everyone (e.g., "humankind," "persons," "human beings," "everyone").

Poems should be short, not more than 24 lines.

Non-fiction articles should be 400 to 1,000 words. These should be related to a particular theme which has been projected (a list of themes and due dates is available with an SASE or online at www.pockets.org). We also seek biographical sketches of persons, famous or unknown, whose lives reflect their Christian commitments and values. These may be either short vignettes (a single incident) or longer and more complete biographies. Articles about various holidays and about other cultures are included.

We particularly desire articles about children involved in environmental, community, and peace/justice issues.

How should I submit my writing?

Contributions should be double-spaced, on 8½" x 11" paper, accompanied by a SASE for return. Writers who wish to save postage and are concerned about paper conservation may send a SASP for notification of unaccepted manuscripts. We will recycle the submission. Please list the name of the submission(s) on the card. We do not accept manuscripts by FAX or e-mail.

Will *Pockets* pay to use my writing?

Yes, payment will be made at the time of acceptance. We will make an initial response within six weeks of receiving the manuscript. We often place manuscripts on long-term hold for specific issues. Authors are free to request that their manuscripts be returned at any time during the long-term hold. We purchase newspaper, periodical, and electronic rights, and we accept one-time previously published material.

Stories and articles: 14 cents a word

Poetry: $25.00 and up

Activities, games: $15.00 and up

Categories: Children—Christian Interests—Family—Religion—Spiritual—Devotional

CONTACT: Lynn W. Gilliam, Editor
Material: Manuscripts
The Upper Room
PO Box 340004
Nashville TN 37203-0004
Phone: 615-340-7333
E-mail: pockets@upperroom.org
Website: www.pockets.org

Podiatry Management

Podiatry Management is the national practice management magazine for podiatrists.

A sample of the current issue is posted at the Internet address shown below.

We invite articles to be submitted via e-mail. Articles can also be mailed along with an IBM formatted disk to the address below.

You may telephone us.

Articles should be of interest to the practicing podiatrist. Articles which feature quotes from podiatrists or are about DPMs are preferred.

Categories: Nonfiction—Business—Health—Management—Podiatry

CONTACT: Barry Block, Editor
Material: All
PO Box 750129
Forest Hills NY 11375
Phone: 718-897-9700
E-mail: bblock@prodigy.net; copy to: bblock@prodigy.net
Website: www.podiatrym.com

Poem
Huntsville Literary Association

Poem, published in spring and fall, has been in continuous publication since 1967.

We equally welcome submissions from established poets as well as from less known and beginning poets. We publish both traditional forms and free verse. We want poems characterized by compression, rich vocabulary, significant content, and evidence of "a tuned ear and practiced pen." We want coherent work that moves through the particulars of the poem to make a point. We do not want "greeting card verse" or proselytizing or didactic poems.

The editor and two assistant editors individually read all submissions. At each editorial conference, all preliminary selections are read aloud and discussed. Then final selections are made. We sometimes accept a poem upon the condition that the poet agree to a suggested change. We do not comment on rejections.

We do not accept translations, previously published works, or simultaneous submissions.

Poem is perfect bound, digest-sized, professionally printed on good stock paper with a clean design and a matte cover. It is about 90 pages and contains over 60 poems and notes on contributors. Press run is 500. Copies go to all Huntsville Literary Association members, to individual out-of-town subscribers, to subscribing libraries throughout the United States and in Canada, and to the contributors.

Poem is a member of CLMP and indexed in the Index of American Periodical Verse.

Submissions: Submit 3-5 poems, preferably with a cover letter. Include a self-addressed envelope with sufficient postage. Submissions are read throughout the year. We generally respond in 1-3 months. We normally wait several issues before again publishing a contributor, especially if several poems were accepted for an issue.

Copyright and payment: *Poem* acquires first serial rights. Because we are a non-profit organization, we can pay only in copy to contributors. We pay 2 copies to each contributor.

Subscriptions and sample copies: Subscriptions for out-of-towners are $20 per year. Sample copies and back issues are $7. Send to *Poem*, Huntsville Literary Association, P.O. Box 919, Huntsville, AL 35804.

Categories: Poetry.

CONTACT: Rebecca Harbor, Editor
Material: All
PO Box 2006
Huntsville, AL 35804

Poetic Realm

Poetic Realm is for poetry only. The guidelines are easy. Poems to 36 lines on any subject, in good taste. No reading fee...and my favorite poem in each issue will receive the "Editor's Choice Award" of $5.00.

Please help keep this publication afloat by either becoming a subscriber or purchasing the copy you are published in.

Thank you.

Rates: $16/yr; $14 for a single issue

Categories: Poetry

CONTACT: Kay Weems, Editor/Publisher
Material: All
207 Willow Wind Dr.
Artemas PA 17211
Phone: 814-458-3102

Poetry

SUBMISSION GUIDELINES

All submissions and inquiries regarding submissions must be made by mail. Your return address must appear on the outside of the envelope. Always include a self-addressed return envelope for our reply. We do not consider, and will not respond to submissions made by email and fax.

Poetry has no special manuscript needs, no special requirements as to form or genre: we examine in turn all work received and accept that which seems best. We can not consider anything which has been previously published or accepted for publication, anywhere, in any form, either in the United States or abroad. We do not consider simultaneous submissions. We regret that the volume of submissions received and the small size of our staff do not permit us to give individual criticism.

Submissions should be limited to four poems or fewer, typed single-space. Manuscripts are usually reported on within 16 to 20 weeks from the day of receipt. All manuscripts must be accompanied by a stamped, self-addressed envelope. Stamps alone are not sufficient. Writers living abroad must enclose a self-addressed envelope together with enough postage in validated international reply coupons for air mail return.

Manuscripts should have the author's name and address on every page. Avoid oversized envelopes. Do not send revisions unless they have been specifically requested by the editors. Inquiries about the status of a manuscript should be avoided, but when necessary must be made in writing and should include a self-addressed stamped return envelope for our reply.

Payment is made on publication at the rate of $10.00 per line, $150.00 per page of prose. All prose contributions are commissioned.

Poetry is copyrighted for the protection of its contributors. The author, the author's agents or heirs, and no one else, will be given transfer of copyright when they request it for purposes of republication in book form.

Several prizes, awarded annually, are announced each December for the best work printed in *Poetry* during the preceding year. Only poems already published in the magazine are eligible for consideration, and no formal application is necessary.

The Ruth Lilly Poetry Prize is also given each year to a poet whose published work merits special recognition. The selection is made by a panel of judges and no applications are accepted.

Two Ruth Lilly Poetry Fellowships are awarded annually to students who have not yet received the M.A. or M.F.A. degree, based on work submitted. Students must be nominated by their program directors or department chairs.

Anyone contemplating a submission is encouraged to examine the magazine before sending a manuscript. Sample copies cost $3.75 plus $1.75 for postage and handling.

Categories: Nonfiction—Book Reviews—Poetry

CONTACT: The Editor
Material: All
444 N Michigan Ave Ste 1850
Chicago IL 60611
Phone: 312-787-7070
Fax: 312-787-6650
Website: poetrymagazine.org

Poets & Writers Magazine

Thank you for your interest in *Poets & Writers Magazine,* a bimonthly trade publication for writers of poetry, fiction, and creative nonfiction. Before you send us your submission, please read the following.

Our Audience

Available by subscription and on newsstands of most major bookstores, *Poets & Writers Magazine* reaches a national audience of 60,000 readers—from emerging to established literary writers. The magazine has a strong following among both students and faculty in creative writing programs across the country. In addition, many of its readers pursue creative writing as an avocation, often pairing their literary lives with other careers.

What We Publish

We recommend that you read *Poets & Writers Magazine* before sending us a query or an article for consideration. You may also visit our online Archive, which contains a selection of articles from past issues. Our editorial content is divided into the following four sections.

• *News & Trends*: brief articles (500-1,200 words) that keep our readers abreast of pertinent information in the writing and publishing industries.

• *The Literary Life*: essays (1,500-2,500 words) on the more contemplative aspects of writing, ranging from creative process to the art of reading.

• *The Practical Writer*: advice and how-to articles (1,500-2,500 words) that offer nuts and bolts information about the business of creative writing.

• *Features*: profiles of and interviews with (2,000-3,000 words) contemporary writers who reflect the rich diversity of current American literature. Recent featured authors include Anne Carson, Sandra Cisneros, Jonathan Franzen, Li-Young Lee, Chuck Palahniuk, Colson

Whitehead, and C.D. Wright. Other features include articles and essays (2,000-3,000 words), frequently grouped into special sections, that provide an in-depth look at subjects of interest to creative writers, such as writers conferences and residencies, small presses, regional writing, and the distinctions of genre.

Submission Information

All correspondence should be addressed to The Editors, *Poets & Writers Magazine*, 72 Spring Street, New York, NY 10012 and should include an SASE with appropriate postage, or sent via e-mail to editor@pw.org.

For those articles we publish, we buy First North American Serial Rights and non-exclusive reprint rights shared 50/50 thereafter. We pay when the piece is scheduled for production.

If you plan to query us with a story proposal, please include two samples of your journalistic writing.

For articles submitted on spec, manuscripts should be typed, double-spaced, and no more than 3,000 words in length.

E-mail queries must be fully developed and must include two samples of your journalistic writing.

It usually takes four to six weeks for us to respond to your query or manuscript.

We do not publish original fiction or poetry.

We do not publish book reviews.

We do not accept queries made over the phone.

We do not cover genre fiction, such as mysteries, mainstream science fiction, romance novels, and children's literature, nor do we cover screenwriting and playwriting.

Photography

If you are a professional photographer and would like to be considered for commissioned work (or have existing photography of authors), please send a sample and contact information to Suzanne Pettypiece, Managing Editor, at address below, or send a link to your Web site via e-mail to editor@pw.org. No phone calls please.

General Information

We are published by Poets & Writers, Inc., a nonprofit literary service organization that has been the central source of practical information for the literary community in the United States since 1970.

Categories: Fiction—Literature—Writing

CONTACT: Suzanne Pettypiece, Managing Editor
Material: All
72 Spring St
New York NY 10012
E-mail: editor@pw.org

Points North
Serving Atlanta's Stylish Northside

Points North was created to provide a first-class lifestyle magazine for affluent residents of suburban communities in north metro Atlanta. We place editorial emphasis on leisure activities for our readers, with articles that cover travel, dining and shopping; interior and landscape design; cultural, community and sporting events; as well as profiles of interesting people and places with ties to Atlanta's north side.

Our magazine currently runs three to four features (including a profile) per issue, along with one or two travel and recreation pieces, one or two home and garden articles, a shopping column, and a wine column. We also print three to five short restaurant reviews each month, which are substituted once a quarter for a full-length feature on a "special occasion" restaurant. Currently, we are accepting articles in all areas of the magazine except the wine column. (Please see article specifications for more information.)

Points North, a free publication with a circulation of 50,000 copies per month, is distributed to many of the Atlanta area's most prestigious ZIP codes including Buckhead, Dunwoody, Sandy Springs, East Cobb, Roswell, Alpharetta, Windward, South Forsyth, John's Creek, Duluth and other neighboring areas at more than 400 retail businesses. *Points North* is also available at several locations within North Point Mall, Perimeter Mall and Phipps Plaza, and is distributed via direct-mail each month to 15,000 north Atlanta homeowners with properties valued in excess of $400,000.

Submitting Queries

If you are interested in submitting an existing article, or if you have an idea for an article, please submit a written, one-page Query Letter to include:

• **Personal information.** Your name, address, an e-mail address and a daytime phone number (or a number where you can be reached in the evenings if you cannot be contacted during the day).

• **Article description.** Describe the subject of your article or the story idea in enough detail for us to get a clear picture. If it's an existing piece, you might want to include the opening paragraph(s) to show us how this article will grab our readers' interest. How many words is or will the article be? What direction did or will you take with it (e.g., a humorous look at average commute times for morning rush hour in Atlanta, filled with anecdotes and quotes from north side residents). Tell us where in the magazine you think the article should appear (as a feature or profile, or in Food & Entertainment, Travel & Recreation, North-side Shopper or Grand Designs).

• **Article relevance.** Explain why you think *Points North* readers will find this article interesting, or why it's specifically significant to them. What elements does or will your piece contain that makes it relevant to the north side of Atlanta or its residents? What questions that our readers might have about the subject does or will your article answer? Why is now (or at a certain time in the future) a good time to publish this story?

• **Writer's sources.** What sources have you used or will you use for the article? What are their connections to our readership or to Atlanta's north side? If the article is not yet written, how do you know your sources are available to you? In addition, let us know if you have photographs available for an existing story, but please do not send photos with your Query Letter.

• **Writer's qualifications.** Why are you qualified to write about this subject? What experience or particular interest do you have in the subject matter, or what contacts do you have available to you that make this a subject that "fits" you? We prefer that Queries and/or existing articles be sent via e-mail (as attachments only please—not within the body of an e-mail message) to managingeditor@ptsnorth.com.

If you're not Internet-active, you can mail your Query and articles to Managing Editor, *Points North*, 568 Peachtree Pkwy, Cumming, GA 30041.

Important:

Please do not send originals of any kind, including manuscripts, photographs, etc., to our offices. We assume no responsibility for any materials sent unsolicited to *Points North*. Copies sent by mail to our offices will not be returned unless accompanied by a written request and a self-addressed envelope suitable for mailing the materials in, with proper postage affixed.

We will respond to your submission, normally within six to eight weeks of receipt, by e-mail or form letter. Due to time constraints we regret that we cannot respond individually to questions about materials or Query Letters sent to the editor.

If your article is one we intend to pursue further, or if we are interested in talking with you about writing a story for an idea you've submitted, we'll be in touch by telephone within six to eight weeks.

Editorial Content

Popular regular columns appearing in *Points North* include:

• **Travel and Recreation.** Most issues include our "Here" column, which highlights day trips or weekend getaways within a few hours of north metro Atlanta by car. Past columns have included Calloway Gardens, Big Canoe, Lake Hartwell and the Asheville area. The column "There" includes destinations for three-or four-day weekend getaways within a few hours by car or less than three hours away by plane, such as Charleston, The Cloister at Sea Island, Colonial Williamsburg and The Greenbrier in Virginia. Length of articles: 1500-2000 words.

• **Food and Entertainment.** Three issues per quarter include short reviews on three to five restaurants, usually done with a style, theme or location in mind. We've spotlighted groups of restaurants specializing in Italian and southern cooking; pubs and sushi bars; as well as establishments in Duluth, Roswell and the Perimeter Mall areas.

We are looking for restaurants in or close to north Atlanta that demonstrate a passion for pleasing their clientele through preparation, presentation and outstanding service.

Length of articles: 500-750 words.

Once per quarter we present a more in-depth overview of a "special occasion" restaurant. These pieces contain not only a review of the food and the restaurant in general, but might also include topics such as banquet facilities, an interview with the chefs and/or owners, and highlights of special amenities the restaurants have to offer when the reader is looking for that very special place to celebrate. Length of articles: 1500- 2000 words.

• **Grand Designs.** This department consists of one or two articles each month; "Home" covers interior matters such as painting, decorating and basement remodeling, while "Garden" spotlights exterior subjects like garden pests, spring planting and coping with summer droughts. Some of the north side's best interior, exterior and landscape designers have demonstrated and discussed aesthetic improvements for both the dwelling and the yard including Feng Shui, grand landscaping and home wine storage.

Length of articles: 1500-2000 words.

• **Northside Shopper.** Added in August 2001, each month this column will look at a particular shopping area or a specific group of specialty stores or unusual items. We've featured the North Georgia Premium Outlet Mall in Dawsonville, Ga. and The Avenue shopping center in East Cobb, along with Halloween costumes for our October issue and holiday shopping for December. Some brainstorming from our editorial staff came up with suggestions for 2002 such as china, crystal and silver, elegant linens for bed and bath, and high-end children's clothing as examples of group items; one-of-a-kind art pieces, unusual collectibles and rare book sellers; jewelry stores, Christmas boutiques and those great places where you can design your own gift baskets. Come up with your own ideas! Length of articles: 1200-1500 words.

• **Indulgence.** Added in January 2002, Indulgence is a column that will provide readers with options for fulfilling desires (or maybe just dreams!) for that perfect larger-than-life experience: The Perfect Valentine's Day, the Essential Guy's Weekend, Learning to Race at Panoz Racing School or a Truly Romantic Anniversary.

The focus of these columns should be experiences people have always wanted to have but have hesitated to spend the time and money to indulge themselves. Length of articles: 1200-1500 words.

The best way for a freelance writer who is interested in being published in *Points North* to get a sense of the types of articles we're looking for is to read the magazine. The current issue is available in many locations free of charge, and we will mail one or more back issues to you upon receipt of your check for $3.00 per issue (to cover shipping and handling).

Additionally, most features from each issue published to date are available for viewing at our Web site: ptsnorth.com.

ARTICLE SPECIFICATIONS

In general, successful articles will be clear, concise and well organized, with an effective introduction, sufficient information presented in a way that's easy to understand and makes us want to read more, and a strong conclusion to the piece that leaves us satisfied or eager to find out more on our own. Basically, when you're deciding if an existing or proposed article achieves a "fit" with *Points North* magazine, please keep these things in mind:

• **Composition.** Your piece should have just one central theme and an effective lead-in which attracts our attention, then lets us know what the article is about and piques our curiosity regarding what's to come and why we're going to be interested.

The body of the article should give us the information we need about the subject—in a logical order—and be organized in a few individual sections (with appropriate sub-headings) which together present, support and substantiate the theme. The summary and conclusion should close the article, bringing the readers full-circle and, hopefully, leaving them happy that they read to the end.

• **North Atlanta connections:** anecdotes, quotes and details. *Points North* readers pick up our magazine because they know the articles will have relevance to them as north side residents. We feel that the use of as many anecdotal stories and details related directly to the people, places and things in our circulation area, as well as quotes from experts on the subject being written about or from North Atlanta residents and businesses, is crucial to a successful *Points North* article. Whenever possible the article should have a connection with the people, places and businesses in north metro Atlanta, or relate to issues of concern to our readership.

• **Personal observations.** As we read your article, we want to know your opinion about why the topic is something we should be interested in; why you liked what you wrote about and why the readers won't be sorry if they take the time to read the piece. That being said, remember that most articles should have more than just the author's voice. That can be done with quotes, anecdotes and descriptive details as mentioned above, written in a narrative style that allows us to picture in our mind's eye what you are writing about.

• **Negative and controversial elements.** Articles don't have to be 100% objective; however, negativity in any form has no place in an article published in *Points North*. This will generally be a stopper to the article getting published, as will a subject considered to be controversial. (At the very least, negative and controversial elements will be edited out.) We realize this makes an article about a subject such as out-of-control development or the traffic in north Atlanta a bit difficult, but you are a writer after all!

• **Summary/conclusion.** Leave the readers with a lasting impression of your topic. For example, why did you find this subject interesting or worth writing about, and how did the points you made, along with the examples and expert quotes you used, fit together to bring you to this conclusion? Give the readers something to think about—perhaps challenge them to redirect their thought processes regarding the topic by posing a question, or answer a question you posed in your introduction. Offer a strong opinion, use a significant quote, or include something from the intro to bring the topic full circle.

• **General information.** Before submitting your article, please take a moment to spell-check and self-edit to the best of your ability; then re-read what you've written with a mind toward the following things:

—**Using Web sites as resources.** Research pulled from a Web site should be incorporated into the article, in the author's voice, and not submitted as a "listing" of items (and of course, cutting and pasting information directly from a Web site is not acceptable). As with all facts, information and statements presented within an article, the author is responsible for insuring that the Web information is current and accurate.

—**Sidebars.** We like the use of sidebars in an article if they genuinely enhance the presentation. The information presented in this manner should be a definite highlight to your story, as opposed to being simply pieces of data pulled from the article for the sake of a sidebar. Sidebars shouldn't contain information on how a reader can contact a source or listings of local events; these go in that issue's Resource Guide or Calendar of Events.

—**Advertorial.** The current policy of *Points North* is that we don't do paid "advertorial." What is or isn't advertorial is subjective—so we let our publisher decide.

We do like to support our advertisers and the merchants in our distribution area with a plug when we can—this is a lifestyle magazine and we don't take ourselves too seriously (and our salespeople gratefully accept all the help they can get!). So any time you can use a current or prospective advertiser for *Points North* as a resource or as an expert reference in your article, you should certainly do so.

—**Sources.** We generally require a minimum of three sources for each feature article. A writer's first choice for all sources should be, as much as is possible, people, businesses and experts with a connection to our circulation area.

In addition to information required for the Resource Guide (see below), the author is responsible for submitting a full name and phone number for any person quoted or referred to within the article so the editor can contact sources when the author is unavailable. When a book, article, professional paper, etc. is referred to, please provide the name of the source and the author's name. We'll also need addresses for all sources used in each article who would like a copy of the magazine mailed to them.

—**Resource Guide**. In lieu of resources detailed within an article itself or in sidebars, *Points North* includes a monthly Resource Guide to provide a central place for all information contained in that issue. Information for the Resource Guide must be complete on all sources including correct business names and addresses, local (and if available, toll-free) telephone numbers, along with e-mail addresses and Web site information when applicable.

—**Fact-checking requirements**. Authors are responsible for the accuracy of all information used within their articles. Submission of any printed materials available about your subject (e.g., brochures or other advertising materials, business cards, etc.) are extremely helpful, and we require menus or business cards to be submitted for all restaurants reviewed.

—**Photographs**. We do not expect our authors to provide photographs for the articles they submit. Please do, however, ask your sources if they have professional-quality photos that might be used in the article. 35mm color slides are preferred; we also may be able to use 4"x6" color prints and digital images of 270 dpi or better (TIF or EPS format) submitted on CDs, JAZ or ZIP disks. (CDs must be formatted for Macintosh; all other disks accepted in PC or Mac format.)

FINANCIAL AND LEGAL INFORMATION

• **Story rights.** In most cases, terms for story rights can be negotiated with the publisher but generally, *Points North* buys first serial rights in the Southeast with a six month moratorium, along with electronic rights. That means your article hasn't been previously published anywhere in the southeastern US, and that you will not sell it for publication in the southeastern US for a period of 6 months after its *Points North* publication. Electronic rights enable us to publish your article as part of the issue it originally appeared in on our Web site for an indeterminate period of time, and are not normally negotiable.

• **Bylines.** Our authors receive a byline for all published articles.

• **Fees and payment for articles.** Fees for unsolicited articles and assigned features begin at $350, and may be negotiable at the publisher's discretion depending upon such factors as the author's experience with *Points North*, article content and the complexity of research required, the amount of editing required after submission, and other circumstances. Fees for assigned restaurant reviews are $75.00 plus reimbursement for the cost of the meal up to but not exceeding $100.00 and, for legal liability reasons, exclusive of alcohol. Receipts with menu items detailed are required for all meals before payment will be made.

Points North does not pay expenses, and writers are encouraged to consider this before accepting an assignment.

Once an article is accepted for publication, payment will be processed on the first of the month after the deadline date for the current month's issue, regardless of whether the article is actually published in that issue or not. For example, an article accepted for the October issue, with a deadline date of August 1 will be paid on September 1.

Categories: Nonfiction—Culture—Food/Drink—Gardening—Home—Lifestyle—Regional—Sports/Recreation—Travel

CONTACT: Submsissions Editor
Material: All
568 Peachtree Pkwy .
Cumming GA 30041
E-mail: managingeditor@ptsnorth.com
Website: www.ptsnorth.com

Police and Security News

The target audience for *Police and Security News* consists of middle and upper management, including top administration, in a variety of law enforcement entities comprised of city, county, state and federal agencies. Our goal is to provide information of a contemporary, educational and/or entertaining nature. We strive to offer our readers information that can be of assistance by explaining how to do their jobs better or easier, how to save money (very important), how to avoid problems, etc. Basically, we try to provide "news they can use." We also endeavor to present subjects that can be, at times, complex in nature in a manner that is easily understood, but not oversimplified. In other words, we try to edit for the expert in a way the nonexpert can understand. Articles that are directed towards helping the smaller municipal department or agency are especially desirable, since nearly eighty percent of the municipal departments in this country have ten or fewer employees.

In terms of article length, they can run anywhere from 500 to 3000 words. Past that limit, please advise me regarding specific plans.

We typically pay ten cents per published word for articles and ten to twenty dollars per published photo or illustration. Payment is issued upon publication of your material.

Categories: Nonfiction—Law—Trade—Law Enforcement

CONTACT: Al Menear, Assoc. Publisher
Material: All
CONTACT: James Devery, Editor
Material: All
DAYS Communications, Inc
1208 Juniper St.
Quakertown PA 18951
Phone: 215-538-1240
Fax: 215-538-1208
Website: www.policeandsecuritynews.com

Police Times
The Voice of Professional American Law Enforcement
The Chief of Police Magazine

Dear Writer/Photographer:

Police Times is the official journal of the American Federation of Police and Concerned Citizens. We seek articles on speculation regarding all areas of law enforcement, with special emphasis on stories involving smaller police departments or individuals who have made a special place in law enforcement…past or present. *Police Times* is published quarterly. *The Chief of Police Magazine*, published bi-monthly, is the official journal of the National Association of Chiefs of Police. For *The Chief of Police Magazine* we seek articles that would be of particular interest to command rank American law enforcement personnel. If accepted, we may elect to publish a particularly interesting piece in both publications. Allow 90-180 days for publication, which is

M-Q

at the editor's discretion, and may include publication on our website as part of our magazine's contents.

We pay from $25 to $100 for articles including photographs. Photos may be submitted in b&w or color. Fillers and short articles are also considered. Length of articles may vary, but usually range up to 2,500 words for *Police Times*; 5,000 words for *The Chief of Police Magazine*. Payment is made upon acceptance. A complimentary copy of the issue in which the article appears is provided to the writer.

If you are using a personal computer for typing articles, please send them on IBM compatible 3½" disks as well as a hard copy.

Sample copies: For *Police Times* $2.50, for *The Chief of Police Magazine* $3.00. Include SASE with all submissions.

Assigned Articles: Articles specifically assigned by the editors are paid at double scale. These are reserved for writers who we have previously published in our publications.

Faxed proposals: Accepted by faxing short proposal to: Jim Gordon, Executive Editor, *Police Times* (321) 294-0033. Allow ample time for reply. If corresponding via E-Mail, please provide hard copy address for reply.

Categories: Law Enforcement

CONTACT: Jim Gordon, Executive Editor
Material: All
6350 Horizon Dr
Miami FL 33137
Phone: 321-264-0911
Fax: 321-264-0033
E-mail: policeinfo@aphf.org
Website: www.aphf.org

Polo Players' Edition

About The Magazine

POLO Players' Edition is an approximately 6,000-circulation magazine published 12 times a year by Rizzo Management Corp. for Westchester Media. Our readers are polo players and fans from the United States and abroad who come from diverse social and economic backgrounds and share a passion for polo.

First and foremost, *POLO Players' Edition* is a sports magazine that offers readers profiles of the game's personalities, professional advice on everything from horse care to playing techniques and strategy, and coverage of important tournaments. It is also an "insider's" magazine for those who want to follow polo people and their lifestyles. We go behind the scenes at Palm Springs, West Palm Beach, Boca Raton, Saratoga, Dallas, St. Moritz, Buenos Aires, Windsor Park and other places where polo people live and play.

Our readers are an affluent group. Most are well educated, well read and highly sophisticated. They're well enough established in the business world to be able to afford the game. A general knowledge of polo and of horses is necessary for some of the more technical stories in *POLO Players' Edition*. For profiles and other features, we don't demand that you know what an offside foreshot means or how long a chukker lasts, but you'll find it helpful in communicating with people who are devoted to the game.

Writing Opportunities with *POLO Players' Edition*

The best entree for a first-time writer in POLO Players' Edition is to query us on a personality profile or a general-interest feature. Full-length features run from about 1,500 to 4,000 words; short profiles, columns and departments run from 800 to 1,200 words. *POLO Players' Edition* pays on acceptance a minimum of $200 for full-length features and a minimum of $50 for columns, departments or short profiles. Some expenses are paid if arranged at the time of assignment. A 10 percent bonus is offered to writers who can provide visuals to accompany their articles. While we prefer to receive submissions by computer modem in ASCII format, legible typed manuscripts, computer printouts and Apple Macintosh or IBM-compatible disks are acceptable.

Submitting A Manuscript

In addition to staff-written articles, *POLO Players' Edition* publishes work by freelance contributors who have been assigned or who have suggested articles are submitted on speculation, which means the author is guaranteed payment only if the material is accepted for publication. Fees and rights purchased are specified at the time of acceptance and all acceptances are made in writing.

In the case of manuscripts or queried articles assigned in writing by the magazine, *POLO Players' Edition* will pay all fees stipulated at the time of assignment if the manuscripts is accepted and published. If an assigned manuscript is not accepted for publication, the author will be paid a percentage of the agree-upon fee as compensation for his time and effort. Unless otherwise specified, the magazine purchases first North American rights..

Categories: Animals—Hobbies—Recreation—Sports/Recreation

CONTACT: Gwen D. Rizzo, Editor and Associate Publisher
Material: All
Rizzo Management Corp.
3500 Fairlane Farms Rd, Ste 9
Wellington FL 33414
Phone: 561-793-9524
Fax: 561-793-9576

Poptronics

Dear Author: If you have a story or a story idea centered around electronics, I'd like to have the chance to read it, and consider it for purchase and use in *Poptronics*. To improve the probability of your story being published, I have placed some suggestions in this guide to help you prepare your article.

What type of article is *Poptronics* seeking? I've always sought first-rate stories covering communications, computers, test equipment, audio, video and virtually every other electronics subject. Good construction, tutorial, informational, and how-to articles are always in demand. If they are timely, their appeal and chances of acceptance are further enhanced.

Articles about new technology or the theory behind new devices are particularly valuable and make for interesting reading. The key to writing such an article with authority is thorough research and accuracy. A poorly researched article can lose its author some respect among the editors, as well as lose the sale. Make sure of your facts, and make them complete.

How-to-do-it features are among the most interesting types of articles that you can write. Show a reader ten new ways to use his oscilloscope or sweep generator or an easy way to make printed-circuit boards, and your story will be enjoyed by our readers.

Troubleshooting and service manuscripts, on the other hand, require an experienced author. Nothing falls apart as thoroughly as a troubleshooting article written by someone who knows little about the subject.

Construction articles must show readers how to build electronic projects. The devices discussed must be of practical use in the field of electronics, in hobby pursuits, or around the house or in the car. The cost of parts is important; the cost of assembling a project should be justified by what it does. I seek construction stories at different levels, some for neophytes and some for those who have the training to carry out complex building instructions. In general, easier projects take preference.

Construction manuscripts need special care. Schematics must be complete and detailed. Show all IC pinouts, power connections, bypass capacitors, parts designations and values, etc. If a printed-circuit board is used, a clear, reproducible, full-size foil pattern must be included. Parts-placement diagrams should be shown from the component side of the board and the parts should be identified by part number, not values. Completely describe all construction methods and techniques that are not common knowledge.

Include calibration and adjustment instructions in all construction articles that require them. Include debugging information: How long did it take to get the device working? To build it? The reader may experience some of the same difficulties. Place critical voltages on schematic diagrams; those help the project builder check the operation of the finished project.

Include a complete list of parts, manufacturers, type numbers, and electrical/electronic specifications and ratings where appropriate. Make sure that the list agrees with the information presented in the text and on schematic diagrams. Accuracy is absolutely necessary! Avoid hard-to-get items or those that are one-of-a-kind. If you must use an uncommon part, you must give two sources for that part. Where values are not critical, say so and give approximate tolerances. Where special parts are required, be precise in the Parts List by including all the specifications. Do not merely say "5,000-ohm relay" if contact spacing or armature tension is critical. Tell us (in the text) why a particular part is chosen over others like it. Failure to make the parts list complete may mean some reader can't make the project work and will blame the magazine or author.

Check and double check your work. Be sure that the schematic agrees with the Parts List, the parts-placement diagram, other illustrations, and the text. Your reputation as an author, as well as the reputation of this magazine, can be damaged by inaccurate or sloppy work.

Commonly used abbreviations such as AC, DC, IC, Hz, etc., may be used freely. However, the use of less common abbreviations should be limited except when their use promotes clarity. All such abbreviations must be defined in the article the first time they are used.

Do not dismantle your equipment or change it after sending us your manuscript. Before the article is finally accepted, the editors must compare it to its description to check for accuracy.

Finish the job! Don't send half-done manuscripts. "Photos to come" or "material to be added here" are flags of incompleteness. I can't judge the manuscript without seeing all of it. Incomplete articles will be rejected as they cannot be properly evaluated.

MECHANICS:

Use standard 8½-inch by 11-inch paper. Print on one side only. Double-space between lines. You must have your name and address in the top left corner of the first page; some authors use a rubber stamp to put their name and address on the back of each succeeding page. Also include a telephone number where you can be reached during the day in case my editors have a question that requires immediate attention.

If you are working on a computer, submit your story with text pages printed on a letter-quality, laser, inkjet or dot-matrix printer and include a floppy disk of the manuscript in the following IBM-compatible formats: ASCII, WordPerfect, or MS Word (the latter is preferred). Label the disk, indicating what word processor you used. Please include photographs and images for the article on the disk. Photographs should be saved as JPEGs. Resolution should be at least 300 dpi. A disk of your article will save input time and eliminate typing errors at this end.

Mail the manuscript flat. Include a self-addressed envelope and return postage. Save a copy of your manuscript until you see it in print. It is often necessary for us to ask questions about it so having access to a copy is important. Furthermore, a copy helps protect your work should it get lost in the mail. Do not send Xerox copies of the manuscript or the illustrations. Send the original and keep the copy for your own files.

ILLUSTRATIONS:

If any of your illustrations are smaller than 8 by 10 inches, fasten them to standard-size sheet of paper.

Photographs should be 5 by 7 inches, or larger, black-and-white glossy prints, and in good focus all over. Avoid using color prints. All details should be easy to see, not hidden in dark areas or "washed out" in overexposed or too-bright areas. Don't mark or write on prints; you simply spoil them for reproduction. If you need to identify sections of a photograph, put a piece of tracing paper over the print and make the

identification on it, or send an extra print.

Put an asterisk or the figure number in the margin of your text when you refer to an illustration or figure. Try to scatter illustrations throughout the story so they're not all bunched.

Diagrams must be clearly drawn in pencil or ink, but need not be finished artwork, as all art is redrawn here in Poptronics style. To enhance accuracy, we request that you adopt *Poptronics* parts designations and symbol conventions where possible. Contact us for a sample issue if needed.

Draw each diagram on a separate page. Use standard-size paper or sheets that can be folded to standard size. Drawings must be accurate. Check each one carefully; it is almost impossible for the editors to catch all errors.

RATE OF PAYMENT:

My payment calculations are more complex than a simple page rate, since I consider such variables as reader interest, illustrations, text, photography, how much editing my staff will have to do, accuracy of research, and originality of approach.

The payment rate currently ranges from $100 to $500. Manuscripts that need practically no editing, are complete, that hit precisely the slant we want, that are written in the easy-reading style of *Poptronics*, and that are thoughtfully and imaginatively illustrated will command the highest payment rate. Payment is issued upon publication of the manuscript.

The staff members are trained in writing, researching, and editing. As you are developing your story, I will gladly work with you. After I buy your manuscript, your help is often needed to fill gaps in your story, check a doubtful connection on a schematic diagram. etc. The editors take every possible step and precaution to make sure that your article is authoritative, easy-to-read, and interesting, but much of the responsibility must, of course, rest with the author.

I'll look forward to reviewing your manuscripts.

Chris La Morte, Managing Editor

Categories: Nonfiction—Automobiles—Electronics—Engineering—Internet—Science—Software—Technical—Television/Radio—Robotics

CONTACT: Chris La Morte, Managing Editor
Material: All
Gernsback Publications, Inc.
275-G Marcus Blvd.
Hauppauge NY 11788
Phone: 631-592-6720

Popular Mechanics

We are always in the market for good free-lance articles, and invite your queries. Because our magazine is divided into departments according to subject matter, you should direct editorial queries to the departmental editor m your area of interest. The editors are listed at the end of this guide. Since we do not print fiction, please don't submit any fiction articles. Because of the workload of our editors, queries are best handled by a short paragraph and perhaps a photo or drawing, via mail. Before you submit a query, do a little homework. Check with the *Reader's Guide To Periodic Literature* and/or our own indexes to editorial features. Chances are, we've already published an article similar to the one you are about to propose. Don't waste your time unless you can give us something new that we haven't run before. Our typical reader is male, about 37 years old, married with a couple of kids, owns his own home and several cars, makes a good salary and probably works in a technically oriented profession. Keep this in mind before proposing articles. In any article query, you should be specific as to what makes the development new, different, better, interesting or less expensive.

Submission Format: All articles must be submitted to us typewritten, double spaced on one side of the page only. All manuscripts must include a self-addressed, stamped envelope with sufficient return postage in case we do not accept your submission. All how-to articles must be accompanied by well-lit, clear, black-and-white photos or rough artwork that we can use to produce finished art for publication. Photos should be either 5x7 or 8x10 in size, glossy finish. If we like an idea, we may also ask you to supply color photos. These should be 35mm or larger transparencies. We pay anywhere from $300 to $1000 and more for features. We pay on acceptance and purchase all rights. If we pay for your submission, we are under no legal obligation to run the piece, but will make our best effort to get it into print. Material is subject to editing for length, style and format Here is some specific information from each of our areas of editorial interest:

Automotive: We do all of our own road testing and conduct our own owner surveys. Please don't query us about submitting driving reports on specific models, or articles about what it's like to own a specific car.

Home Improvement: We buy how-to-do-it articles on home improvement, home maintenance, energy-saving techniques, and shop and craft projects. These must be well illustrated with drawings and photos. Finished drawings suitable for publication are not necessary. Rough, but accurate, pencil drawings are adequate for artist's copy. Topnotch photos are a must, shot during construction of the project as well as after construction. Photos should be taken with a background that is not cluttered or distracting from the main action.

Science/Technology/Aerospace: We are interested in long and short pieces that cover the latest developments in science, technology, aerospace, industry and discovery. We stress newsworthy items here. An old subject can be interesting if new facts have recently become known. Accuracy is paramount. Check your facts and sources before submitting queries. As a rule, we are not interested in machines or inventions applicable to a very limited field or industry, ordinary industrial processes, informative material without a news angle as found in textbooks or encyclopedias, or items that deal with accidents or freaks of nature. We publish articles on sport aviation, homebuilt aircraft, net commercial aircraft, new combat aircraft, etc. Also, we are interested in restoration projects on older collectible aircraft and other hands-on type articles that involve planes.

Boating/Outdoors: Testing of new boats, recreational vehicles or outdoor gear is conducted by our own staff. We publish articles on new equipment in the boating and outdoors areas, as well as articles on how to maintain and/or repair boats, boat engines, camping equipment, motorcycles, recreational vehicles, etc. We are interested in articles covering new types of outdoor recreational devices, such as paraplanes, balloons, all-terrain vehicles and campers.

Electronics/Photography/Telecommunications: We publish articles on new types of equipment in the audio, video, computer, telecommunications, photographic and optical fields, but our staff does most of these. We also publish technique articles, such as how to take trick photos, new developing techniques, how to hook up stereo equipment and telephones in the home, etc. Check some back issues for specific areas of our coverage.

General Interest Articles: We occasionally publish general interest articles. We look for pieces with a strong science, exploration or adventure emphasis.

Departmental Editors: If your query doesn't fit into any of the department, send it to the editor-in-chief.

Categories: Nonfiction—Automobiles—Aviation—Boating—Business—Computers—Consumer—Crafts/Hobbies—Electronics—Engineering—Environment—Military—Outdoors—Photography—Recreation—Science—Home—Technology—How-to—Audio—Telecommunications

CONTACT: Don Chaikin
Material: Automotive
CONTACT: Steven Willson
Material: Home Improvement
CONTACT: Tobey Gumet, Tech Editor
Material: Electronics/Photography/Telecommunications
CONTACT: Jim Wilson
Material: Science Editor

CONTACT: Cliff Gromer
Material: Boating/Outdoors
CONTACT: Joe Oldham, Editor-In-Chief
Material: All other material
810 7th Ave. 6th Floor
New York NY 10019
Phone: 212-649-2000
E-mail: popularmechanics@hearst.com
Website: www.popularmechanics.com

Popular Photography & Imaging

Do you have a story idea or photos that you think are perfect for *Pop Photo*? Here's how to submit your ideas to us.

We are primarily interested in articles on new or unusual phases of photography which we have not covered recently or in recent years. We do not want general articles on photography which could just as easily be written by our staff. We reserve the right to rewrite, edit, or revise any material we are interested in publishing.

Anyone wishing to write for us is advised to send a query letter, not a finished manuscript. The query should briefly describe the purpose of the proposed article, and give a sense of your writing style.

Queries should be accompanied by a sampling of how-to pictures (particularly when equipment is to be constructed or a process is involved), or by photographs which support the text. Please send duplicates only; do not send negatives or original slides. We are not responsible for the loss of original work.

All written materials should be typed double-spaced. The sender's name and address should be clearly written on the back of each print, on the mount of each slide, watermarked on digitally sent sample images, and on the first and last pages of all written material, including the accompanying letter.

Technical data should accompany all pictures, including the camera used, lens, film (or image format if digital), shutter speed, aerture, lighting, and any other points of special interest on how the picture was made.

Material mailed to us should be carefully wrapped or packaged to avoid damage. All submissions must be accompanied by a stamped, self-addressed return envelope. We assume no responsibility for safe return, but will make every effort to handle and return it with care.

The rate of payment depends upon the importance of the feature, quality of the photographs, and our presentation of it. Upon acceptance, fees will be negotiated by the author/photographer and the editors of the magazine.

E-mail submissions are also welcome. Samples of your work in attached Microsoft Word files are OK (sorry, no other word processing formats can be accepted). A small selection of sample photos under 75K each in JPG format are OK. If we are interested we will request high-resolution files and hard copy versions of prints for color matching purposes.

Please note: we are unable to accept individual portfolios for review. However, we do welcome samples of your work in the form of promotional mailers, press kits, or tear sheets for our files. These shoud be sent to the attention of Mason Resnick, Managing Editor, at the above address or via email at mresnick@hfmus.com.

Categories: Arts—Photography

CONTACT: Jason Schneider, Editor-in-Chief
Material: All
1633 Broadway
New York, NY 10019
E-mail: popeditor@aol.com
Website: www.popphoto.com

Popular Science

Submitting article ideas or product information :
What's New
What's New Editors: Suzanne Kantra Kirschner and Jenny Everett
The following information is required for consideration:
• Color photograph, transparency, or slide(unsolicited materials will not be returned).
• Date when product will be available to the public or date when product was first sold if available.
• Description of the product's unique features and how the product works Suggested retail price of the product.

Newsfronts
Newsfronts are broken down into content areas. Article queries should be addressed to the appropriate editor.
Computers & Software Newsfront Editor: John Quain / john.quain@time4.com@popsci.com
Electronics Newsfront Editor: Suzanne Kantra Kirschner / kantra@popsci.com
Home Technology Newsfront Editor: Charles Wardell / charles.wardell@time4.com
Sci-Tech Newsfront Editor: Dawn Stover / stover@popsci. com
Medicine & Health Newsfront Editor: Gunjan Sinha / gunjan.sinha@time4.com

Feature Story Proposals
Please send your short (one- to two-page) pitch to: features@popsci.com . Proposals should include the story's suggested angle, timing, and length. Ideas about illustrations and a short list of potential sources are also helpful. If you have not written for *Popular Science* before, please also include two or three clips. Due to the volume of queries,only materials accompanied by a SASE can be returned.

WRITER'S GUIDELINES
Popular Science covers new and emerging technology in the areas of science, automobiles, the environment, recreation, electronics, the home, photography, aviation and space, and computers and software. Our mission is to provide service to our readers by reporting on how these technologies work and what difference they will make in our readers' lives. Our readers are well-educated professionals who are vitally interested in the technologies we cover.

We seek stories that are up-to-the-minute in information and accuracy. We expect the writer to interview all sources who are essential to the story, as well as experts who can provide analysis and perspective. If a hands-on approach is called for, the writer should visit critical sites to see the technology first-hand—including trying it out when appropriate.

We publish stories ranging from hands-on product reviews to investigative feature stories, on everything from black holes to black-budget airplanes. We expect submissions to be, above all else, well written: that is, distinguished by good story-telling, human interest, anecdotes, analogies, and humor, among other traits of good writing. Stories should be free of jargon, vague statements, and unconfirmed facts and figures.

We seek publishable stories written to an agreed-upon length, with text for agreed-upon components such as sidebars or how-to boxes. The writer is responsible for the factual content of the story and is expected to have made a systematic checking of facts. We require that the writer file with his story contact numbers for all important sources and subjects in the story.

We expect our authors to deliver a complete package. The *Popular Science* Art department requires illustrations, photographs, and diagrams/sketches pertaining to stories submitted. These may be in the form of copies, but we prefer camera-ready artwork. We accept the following formats: four-color or black and white photography, illustration and digital files (tiff or eps). We track and log all artwork and, if indicated on the original, we will return artwork. We also require more than one piece of reference material. This allows for more accurate and original artistic interpretations.

A story should come with a headline for each story element and captions for photos. The complete package will include background material and documentation used by the author.

Freelance contributions to *Popular Science* range from feature-length stories to shorter "newsfront pieces" and shorter-yet stories to accompany What's New products.

We respond promptly to queries, which should be a single page or less and include an SASE. The writer should submit a tight summary of the proposed article and provide some indication of the plan of execution. Samples of the writer's past work and clips concerning the emerging story are helpful.

Categories: Nonfiction—Automobiles—Aviation—Computers—Electronics—Environment—General Interest—Photography—Science—Technology—Home

CONTACT: features@popsci.com
Material: Feature Story Proposals
CONTACT: John Quain, Computers & Software Editor
E-mail: john. quain@time4.com@popsci.com
Material: Computers & Software
CONTACT: Suzanne Kantra Kirschner, Electronics Editor
E-mail: kantra@popsci.com
Material: Electronics
CONTACT: Charles Wardell, Home Technology Editor
E-mail: charles.wardell@time4.com
Material: Home Technology
CONTACT: Dawn Stover, Sci-Tech Editor
E-mail: stover@ popsci. com
Material: Sci-Tech
CONTACT: Gunjan Sinha, Medicine & Health Editor
E-mail: gunjan. sinha@time4.com
Material: Medicine & Health
2 Park Ave.
New York NY 10016
Phone: 212-779-5000
Fax: 212-481-8062
Website: www.popsci.com

Popular Woodworking
Woodworking Magazine

Writer's Guidelines
Popular Woodworking is published seven times a year. This magazine invites woodworkers of all levels into a community of experts who share their hard-won shop experience through in-depth projects and technique articles, which helps the readers hone their existing skills and develop new ones. Related stories increase the readers' understanding and enjoyment of their craft. Any project submitted must be aesthetically pleasing, of sound construction and offer a challenge to readers.

Features
On the average, we use four features per issue that are written by freelancers, usually professional woodworkers. Our primary needs are

"how-to" articles on woodworking projects, and instructional features dealing with woodworking and techniques. We do not publish features about woodworkers and their particular work. The tone of articles should be conversational and informal, as if the writer is speaking directly to the reader. Word length ranges from 1,200 to 2,500. Payment for features starts at $150 per published page, depending on the total package submitted, including its quality, and the writer's level of woodworking and writing experience. Submit your best work. Submissions must include three-view construction drawings and professional slides or digital images to be considered (see "Illustrations"). We receive and look at many great submissions each month. If you want your work to be considered for publication, you must put your best foot forward.

Columns

• Out of The Woodwork: This one-page article, averaging about 700 words, reflects on the writer's thoughts about woodworking as a profession or hobby. The article can be either humorous or serious. Payment starts at $150. This is a good entry-point for first-time freelancers. We purchase six of these columns a year. The writer does not need to be a professional woodworker.

• Tricks of the Trade: Each issue we publish woodworking tips and tricks from our readers that we think are useful. Tricks should be two to three paragraphs long. Brevity is important. Sketches are helpful. In each issue, the author of the best trick receives a prize. All other tricks' authors each receive a check for $75. Send your tricks to David Thiel at david.thiel@fwpubs.com or Tricks of the Trade, *Popular Woodworking*, 4700 E. Galbraith Road, Cincinnati, OH 45236.

Queries

All submissions, except Out of the Woodwork columns and Tricks of the Trade, should be preceded by a query. We will accept unsolicited manuscripts and artwork, although they must be accompanied by a self-addressed stamped envelope to be returned. We will try to respond to all queries within 60 days.

Queries must include:

• A brief outline of the proposed article.

• A summary of the techniques used to complete the project. Include step-by-step illustrations if possible.

• A short biographical sketch, including both your woodworking and writing experience and accomplishments. Also provide your address and daytime telephone number.

• A color photo or transparency of the completed project.

• A list of all materials needed.

Manuscript Submissions

Send your manuscript via U.S. mail or e-mail to Megan Fitzpatrick, *Popular Woodworking*, 4700 E. Galbraith Road, Cincinnati, OH 45236 or megan.fitzpatrick@fwpubs.com.

For project articles, include the following:

1. Introduction: Describe an important point about your project or subject. What made you develop or design it? Also note any unusual qualities.

2. Preparation: Explain any work needed to be done before starting the project.

3. Instructions: Go step-by-step through the process, explaining each point without excessive detail. Include only necessary information, and write in a conversational style. When writing, keep in mind that there may be multiple ways to do any one step. Offering these options to the reader makes your manuscript more flexible and appealing. Clarify any technical words. NOTE: Brand names should only be included when they are critical to the construction or finishing process.

4. Finishing: Give complete instructions on how to finish the project.

5. Closing: Close your article with a brief paragraph that ties everything together.

6. Materials: Please provide the list of all materials used in the project, including types and sizes (thickness, width & length). Also, if materials are hard to find, include the supplier's address and telephone number (with the price of the product & shipping, if available).

7. About the Writer: Provide a brief biography on your experience and interests.

Illustrations

Visual aids are a vital part of instruction, and essential to both projects and articles. Whenever possible, PW prefers to show through photography and diagrams how a step is done rather than tell through text. Many queries are rejected on photo quality alone.

• All projects must include professional photos. We only accept slides and digital images. We don't accept prints. The opening photo for the article is almost always shot in medium (2-1/4") format to account for the enlargement in the magazine.

• All projects must include a fully detailed three-view construction drawing with an accurate cut list.

• If a complex technique is necessary for the project, make a suggestion for a special "sidebar" demonstrating it. Sidebars also can be used as an important source of additional information, such as suggesting alternative methods or tools.

• All artwork, photographs and drawings will be returned upon request.

Originality and Rights

All material submitted must be original and unpublished. *Popular Woodworking* purchases first world rights for one-time use in the magazine, and all rights for use of the article (both text and illustrations) in any F+W Publications Inc. promotional material/product or reprint, and in non-fee paying areas of our web site. You always retain the copyright to your work, and are free to use it in any way after it appears in the magazine. We request, however, that you do not publish the same material for at least six months from the time it appears in our publication.

Popular Woodworking's Guide to Writing and Style

• Write as if you're standing beside the readers as they follow your instruction. Use second person (ex: Cut the wood size). Only use first person when talking specifically about yourself (ex: I chose oak, but any wood will do.).

• Writing should be concise and straightforward.

• Watch redundancies and get rid of unnecessary words, such as that, all, rather, in order, very, etc.

• Avoid repeating the same word within the sentence or in the following one. For example: The board should be sanded on the board's right side. Include a pronoun instead: The board should be sanded on its right side. Don't be afraid to use pronouns, unless they hinder comprehension.

• Replace passive voice with active voice to avoid redundancies and increase clarity. Hint: Watch for words like was, were, is and are—they usually indicate passive voice. Passive: The project was a success. Active: The project succeeded.

• Possessive apostrophes also can cut back on your word count. For example, the side of the board can become the board's side. As a side note, remember it's is a contraction of it is, while its shows possession.

• For measurements, *Popular Woodworking*'s style is: 7" x 8", 7", 7"-thick board. Take note of the difference between measurements: The 7"-thick board should be cut 2" wide. The hyphenated version is used as an adjective of an object, while no hyphen denotes a measurement itself.

• Generally, a comma does not separate the last series member from a verb. For example: You will need shellac, sandpaper and wood. However, if the omission of commas becomes too confusing, leave them in: You will need shellac and stain, sandpaper and steel, and pine and maple wood.

• When using and, but, so, nor, or, remember the comma precedes them when it introduces a complete sentence. Never use the phrase and then. Only then is necessary.

• Parentheses should be used sparingly and only for information that needs understatement. For example, note the distinction between the use of dashes and parentheses in this sentence: For 10 hours—but only 10 hours—let the glue dry (yellow carpenter's glue works best) so your project will not come apart while you are working.

• Always have punctuation follow parentheses, unless a complete sentence is within it: This book is excellent for beginners (zero to one year experience), but only a handy guide for more advanced levels.

I cut the wood according to size. (I later found out I had used the wrong materials.)

Final Checklist

Although the following reminders are simple, they've been neglected by writers in the past. So make sure your manuscript meets these requirements when you read it over a final time:

• Make sure you're getting your point across to the readers. Look at the article through their eyes—not your own experienced ones.

• Double check all measurements and facts to make sure they're correct. Error-plagued manuscripts will not be published.

• Watch the overuse of you and I. It does make the piece more personable, but use sparingly. Often you can get the same point across after omitting them.

• Make sure all punctuation is used correctly.

Categories: Nonfiction—Crafts/Hobbies—Hobbies—Technical

CONTACT: Megan Fitzpatrick
Material: All manuscripts
Contact: David Thiel
Material: Tricks of the Trade articles
F+W Publications Inc.
4700 E. Galbraith Rd.
Cincinnati, OH 45236
Phone: 513-531-2690 ext. 1348
Fax: 513-891-7196
E-mail: megan.fitzpatrick@fwpubs.com
E-mail: david.thiel@fwpubs.com
Website: www.popularwoodworking.com

Potluck Children's Literary Magazine

The magazine for the serious young writer

Potluck is an international, not-for-profit, quarterly magazine for and by writers/artists 8 to 16, though we have published works from writers as young as four. Young writers from around the world fill each issue with an array of poetry, short stories, book reviews and artwork. *Potluck* provides informative articles to expand one's writing abilities and knowledge on the business of being a writer. We want your experience with *Potluck* to be one of accomplishment and new understanding. Welcome to the world of *Potluck*.

Guidelines

1. Work should be typed Roman or Arial, and in black ink.

2. Your name, age, address, email address, and word or line count should be in an upper corner.

3. #10 (large) self-addressed stamped envelope (SASE) must be included for reply. E-mailed work will receive reply by email. Work without a SASE or an email address will not be considered.

4. Do not send your only copy, it will not be returned. Proper postage and envelope must be included for return of original artwork.

5. Profane, sexual, or violent works are not accepted.

Poetry (30 line max.) All forms; double space between stanzas.

Short Stories (1500 word max.) Any subject. Double space between paragraphs.

Book Reviews (250 word max.) Title, author, awards the book may have received. Tell us about the book, what made it worth reading, do you recommend it, and for what age level.

Artwork (8½" x 11"). All styles. A color photocopy is acceptable.

Potluck pays one copy and responds 3 weeks after deadline. All work must be original, unpublished, and not submitted elsewhere.

By submitting to *Potluck* you give *Potluck* permission to publish your work online as well as in print format. Work will remain online for 3 months. *Potluck* acquires first rights. All rights return to author/artist upon publication.

Submission Deadlines (Work received after deadline will be considered for the next issue.)

Spring Issue - December 1
Summer Issue - March 1
Fall Issue - June 1
Winter Issue - September 1

Subscriptions: US: $21.99 one year (4 issues), single issue $5.80 prepaid

Canada: $31.99 one year, single issue $7.80 prepaid (US dollars)

Elsewhere: $41.99 one year; single issue $14.80 prepaid (US dollars)

Visa and MasterCard accepted.

Categories: Book Reviews—Children—Education—Juvenile—Literature—Poetry—Short Stories—Teen—Writing—Young Adult

CONTACT: Susan Napoli Picchletti, Editor-in-Chief
Material: All
Box 546
Deerfield, IL 60015-0546
Phone: 847-948-1139
Fax: 847-317-9492
E-mail: submissions@potluckmagazine.org
Website: www.potluckmagazine.org

Potomac Review

A Journal of Arts & Humanities
SUBMISSION GUIDELINES

—Poetry: up to three poems/five pages at a time.
—Prose: (fiction/nonfiction) up to 5,000 words.
—Art: bookplates/line art/photographs; inquire first.

Please send by regular mail to: Potomac Review, Montgomery College, 51 Mannakee St., Rockville, MD 20850. Include SASE, brief bio, e-mail address. Response within six months. Fall/winter issue due out in October. Simultaneous submissions accepted, but not for contests. Two complimentary copies for contributors; 40% discount for extra copies.

Deadline for submission: Reading period September 1st–May 1st; only one submission per genre per reading period.

Subscriber Information: Sample issue $6. One-year subscription $10 (1 issue), two years $15 (2 issues). For more information, please see our Web site: www.montgomerycollege.edu/potomacreview.

Categories: Fiction—Nonfiction—Arts—Children—Culture—Ecology—Environment—Literature—Poetry—Regional—Short Stories—Writing

CONTACT: Potomac Review Editor
Material: All
Montgomery College
51 Mannakee St
Rockville MD 20850
Email for inquiries: PotomacReviewEditor@montgomerycollege.edu
Website: www.montgomerycollege.edu/potomacreview

M-Q

Power & Gas Marketing

Please refer to Oildom Publishing.

POWER & MOTORYACHT

Power & Motoryacht

EDITORIAL PROFILE

Power & Motoryacht is edited and designed to meet the needs and pleasures of owners of powerboats 24 feet and larger, with special emphasis on the 35-foot-plus market. Launched in 1985, the magazine gives readers accurate advice on how to choose, operate, and maintain their boats as well as what electronics and gear will help them pursue their favorite pastime. In addition, since powerboating is truly a lifestyle and not just a hobby for these experienced readers, PMY reports on a host of other topics that affect their enjoyment of the water: chartering, sportfishing, and the environment, among others.

Some of the regular article themes are:

• CRUISING—places readers can take their own boats for a few days' enjoyment

• PROFILES—stories about interesting and even quirky boaters, craftsmen, etc.

• MAINTENANCE—tips on upkeep and repair

• TECHNOLOGY—advances that are improving construction/ engineering and performances

WRITING STYLE

Since PMY readers have an average of 35 years' experience boating, articles must be clear, concise, and authoritative; knowledge of the marine industry is mandatory. Include personal experience and information from marine industry experts where appropriate. Also include a list of the people and organizations (with phone numbers) contacted during your research.

All manuscripts must be e-mailed (Microsoft Word). Articles should run between 800 and 1,400 words. If a travel story is being submitted, original 35-mm color slides must accompany the manuscript.

PAYMENT POLICY

Depending on article length, compensation is between $500 and $1,200; this fee includes photography if it is part of an assignment. Payment is upon acceptance; if an assigned article does not meet with our guidelines, a one-third kill fee will be given.

SUBMISSIONS

Query first; unsolicited manuscripts and photography are not accepted and will not be returned.

Send a one-page query with a self-addressed, stamped envelope to the address below or via email. No phone inquiries.

Categories: Boating—Environment—Fishing—Outdoors— Sports/Recreation—Travel

CONTACT: Diane M. Byrne, Executive Editor
Material: All
260 Madison Ave., 8th Floor
New York NY 10016
E-mail: diane.byrne@primedia.com
Website: www.powerandmotoryacht.com

Prairie Schooner
University of Nebraska Press

Thank you for your interest in our magazine. *Prairie Schooner* publishes short stories, poems, interviews, imaginative essays of general interest, and reviews of current books of poetry and fiction. Scholarly articles requiring footnote references should be submitted to journals of literary scholarship.

Prairie Schooner's intention is to publish the best writing available, both from beginning and established writers. In our 80 years of publication, we have printed the work of Eudora Welty, Octavio Paz, Tennessee Williams, Weldon Kees, Joyce Carol Oates, and Rita Dove, Richard Russo, Reynolds Price, Julia Alvarez, Sharon Olds, Cornelius Eady, plus scores of others.

All submissions to *Prairie Schooner* should be typed, double-spaced (except for poetry), and on one side of the paper only. Use margins of at least one inch, and be sure to put your name on each page of the manuscript. A self-addressed envelope, with adequate return postage on it, must accompany the submission. For poetry, we prefer a selection of 5-7 poems; for fiction, essays, and reviews, we prefer you send only one selection at at time. Send submissions to the attention of the editor at the address below.

Please allow 3-4 months for reply. *Prairie Schooner* does not read simultaneous submissions, and submissions must be received between September 1 and May 1. All manuscripts published by *Prairie Schooner* will be automatically considered for our annual prizes.

Subscription Information

We encourage you to read *Prairie Schooner* before submitting work.

Subscribe now to one of the oldest and most prestigious of the campus literary magazines in America. *Prairie Schooner* is published quarterly by the University of Nebraska Press.

Subscription rates
$28.00 for one year
$45.00 for two years
$65.00 for three years
Prairie Schooner accepts Visa and Mastercard.
Please send a check or money order to:
Prairie Schooner
201 Andrews Hall
Lincoln NE 68588-0334 or call 1-800-715-2387

The *Prairie Schooner* Prize Series

The *Prairie Schooner* Prize Series, an annual book series competition publishing one book of short fiction and one book of poetry each year through the University of Nebraska Press.

The *Prairie Schooner* Prize Series welcomes manuscripts from all writers, including non-US citizens writing in English, and is open to all writers, including those who have previously published volumes of short fiction and poetry.

Award winning manuscripts will be published by the University of Nebraska Press under the Press's standard contract. Winning authors will receive $3000 (including a $500 advance from UNP). The submission period is from January 15 to March 15 each year.

Guidelines:

Stories and poems previously published in periodicals are eligible for inclusion. Novels are not considered. Xeroxed copies are acceptable. Writers are welcome to enter both contests. No application forms are necessary. All entries will be read anonymously. Please send two cover pages: one listing only the title of the manuscript, and the other listing the author's name, address, telephone number and email address. The author's name should not appear on the manuscript. A $25 processing fee must accompany each submission, payable to *Prairie Schooner*. No past or present paid employee of *Prairie Schooner* or University of Nebraska Press or current faculty or students at University of Nebraska will be eligible for the prizes. Please include a self-addressed postage-paid postcard for confirmation of manuscript receipt. A stamped, self addressed business size envelope must accompany the submission; the manuscript will be recycled.

Any questions, please contact Kelly Grey Carlisle, Managing Editor (kgrey2@unl.edu).

Categories: Fiction—Nonfiction—Poetry

CONTACT: Hilda Raz, Editor
Material: All, except Prairie Schooner Prize Series

CONTACT: Kelly Grey Carlisle, Managing Editor
Material: Prairie Schooner Prize Series
201 Andrews Hall
University of Nebraska
Lincoln NE 68588-0334
Phone: 402-472-0911
Fax: 402-472-9771
E-mail: kgrey2@unl.edu
Website: www.nebraskapress.unl.edu/schooner.html

Premier Tourism Marketing, Inc.

WRITERS' AGREEMENT FOR PREMIER TOURISM MARKETING PUBLI-CATIONS

Premier Tourism Marketing Inc. publishes three publications: Leisure Group Travel, Group Travel Directory and Prep Traveler. Group Travel Directory is published as a supplement to Leisure Group Travel, which comes out seven times per year. Prep Traveler is twice annually. Leisure Group Travel usually contains four to five feature stories per edition. Story lengths are typically 1500-2500 words, although regional features can run as high as 7000 words. Prep Traveler always contains six regional features and several columns.

All stories are specifically aimed at helping our readership, travel planners for group travelers, who use the information when planning and booking trips for their groups. We include details about attractions and festivals, events, cultural attractions, historic and scenic spots, etc. We include information and details about seasonality, distances between destinations, suggested gateways or hubs and transportation options. Local convention and visitors bureaus or other travel information sources are included, **always with phone numbers and URLs.** The demographics of the travelers skew toward the more mature traveler (50+ years) in Leisure Group Travel and elementary school through college level in Prep Traveler. Therefore, stories should include age-appropriate information. Also, Prep Traveler is specific to the amateur sports and performing arts market.

Leisure Group Travel Article Content: While we're always looking for interesting sidebars and other interesting related material, here's what we are always looking for with respect to each article type:

What We Cover: Given that our audience is group travel organizers, we would not typically cover something that could not accommodate groups, such as a two-bedroom B & B. Adult travel groups tend to be comprised of mature adults, so activities mentioned should be appropriate to them. When covering events or dated items, we will not include ones that occur within three months of publication. Our August issue, then, would only cover features occurring after Nov. 1. When covering international events, they must be no sooner than six months after publication. If the event is annual, it can be covered by referring to the following year's dates or general timeframe.

When describing an attraction, we do not include driving directions, hours, prices, contact person or street addresses. If an attraction is seasonal or has operating hours that one would not expect, however, that should be mentioned.

Photos: We ask writers to request CDs or emailed photos from contacts during story research and we credit photos as noted. We also use maps or other illustrations. Stories will not be accepted without ample accompanying photographs.

Contacts: We will provide some contacts that writers should use while researching a story and expect the writer to find other appropriate contacts and verify information for accuracy.

Rights & Payments: We pay upon publication (generally $.12 per assigned word) or as agreed upon. We will pay for the greater of the contracted number of words or the actual number of words used. Kill fee is usually $25. It is mutually agreed that one revision is included in the contract, not including any revisions necessitated by the word count varying more than 10% from the contracted story length. It is further agreed that Premier Tourism Marketing Inc., by making

payment to writer, has the unlimited right to republish all stories in print and electronic format. Writers will be paid one half the original fee for any stories republished in any other of its print magazines.

Format: We ask that stories be submitted via e-mail attachment in Microsoft Word for Windows format. Alternatively, we can accept a Word diskette.

Time: Feature stories are assigned to writers at least one month in advance. Premier Tourism Marketing Inc. reserves the right to kill stories without payment if the copy deadline is missed.

Note to writers: We welcome query letters and are willing to consider story ideas and angles, but rarely accept stories directly from queries, as our editorial calendar is prepared a year in advance. We like to see writing samples and are happy to send a sample issue upon request.

Categories: Regional—Travel

CONTACT: Editorial Coordinator
Material: All
621 Plainfield Road Ste 406
Willowbrook IL 60527
Phone: 630-794-0696
Fax: 630-794-0652
Email: kelley@ptmgroups.com

Presbyterians Today

Presbyterians Today is a magazine for members of the Presbyterian Church (U.S.A.). It is published 10 times a year, with combined January/February and June/July or July/August issues. Circulation is about 52,000.

The target audience for *Presbyterians Today* is laypeople. Readers are quite diverse in age, sex, education, theological viewpoints, and involvement in the life of the church.

Presbyterians Today seeks to:

• Report in a fair, accurate and balanced way on the activities of the Presbyterian Church (U.S.A.) and of its members, leaders and mission partners.

• Uphold the mission of the Presbyterian Church (U.S.A.).

• Illuminate the faith and heritage that bind Presbyterians together.

• Express the rich diversity within the denomination.

• Challenge readers to grow in their commitment to Jesus Christ as Lord.

• Provide a Christian perspective on contemporary issues.

• Be a source of inspiration, spiritual direction and practical tools for life and ministry.

• Reflect the denomination's priorities: evangelism, justice, spiritual information and leadership development.

FEATURE ARTICLES

Presbyterians Today welcomes contributions from free-lance writers. Stories vary in length (800-2,000 words; preferred, 1,000-1,500). Appropriate subjects: profiles of interesting Presbyterians and of Presbyterian programs and activities; issues of current concern to the church; ways in which individuals and families express their Christian faith in significant ways or relate their faith to the problems of society. Most articles have some direct relevance to a Presbyterian audience; however, Presbyterians Today also seeks well informed articles written for a general audience that can help individuals and families cope with the stresses of daily living from a Christian perspective.

Presbyterians Today almost never uses fiction or short fillers, and poetry only occasionally. Original manuscripts are preferred. Reprints are occasionally used, but submission of reprints and multiple submissions are not encouraged.

Authors are asked to submit only one article at a time. Manuscripts are read by at least one editor, and a reply given normally within one month after receipt.

Presbyterians Today pays for articles upon acceptance. With the author's permission, the magazine may hold a manuscript for future consideration (which does not preclude the author from submitting the article elsewhere), and payment will be offered at the time the article is scheduled for publication—if publication rights are available to Presbyterians Today at that time. Authors receive complimentary copies of issues in which their articles appear.

SHORT FEATURES

Presbyterians Today also accepts short features (250-600 words) about interesting people, programs, events and congregations related to the Presbyterian Church (U.S.A.), for the "SpotLight" department. The editors may suggest that a full-length feature article, because of timeliness, space limitations or content, would be more appropriate as a "SpotLight" feature.

HUMOR

Presbyterians Today uses jokes or short humorous stories for the "LaughLines" department. Credit will be given to contributors, but the material should be in the public domain, not copyrighted. Preferred length: 150 words or less. No payment is offered.

"AS I SEE IT"

Presbyterians Today's op-ed department, "As I See It," on its Web site (www.pcusa.org/today), is primarily for *Presbyterians Today* readers—an opportunity for them to express views or opinions on current topics of interest to Presbyterians. Normally only one submission will be posted each issue. Preferred maximum length, 500 words. No payment is offered for "As I See It" articles. Because of planning and production schedules, specific responses to material in previous issues of Presbyterians Today should be made in shorter form as letters to the editor for the "Readers Write" department.

QUERIES

Queries are not required, but may save effort and postage if a subject proposed is clearly inappropriate or if similar articles have fairly recently been used or are currently in the works. Manuscripts are received on speculation.

SUBMISSIONS

Manuscripts should be typed, double-spaced, on 8 1/2" X 11" paper. The author's name and address, including zip code, and Social Security number should be typed on the manuscript as well as the cover letter. Postage or a self-addressed, stamped envelope should be enclosed for the return of a manuscript if it is not accepted. Manuscripts may also be submitted by E-mail.

Photos accompanying a manuscript should be of good quality for reproduction. Black-and-white or color prints, transparencies, or contact sheets are acceptable. They should be identified as to content and credit line. Photos may be sent after an article is accepted, but it is helpful to know whether or not they are or could be available.

Facts, quotations and the spelling of proper names should always be checked for accuracy. *Presbyterians Today* normally uses the New Revised Standard Version for Biblical quotations; if another version of Scripture is used, this should be indicated. If copyrighted material is quoted, the author should secure permission in writing from the copyright holder and cite the work, author, publisher and date of copyright.

RULES FOR WRITING

Writer's Digest has suggested 20 rules for good writing:
1. Prefer the plain word to the fancy.
2. Prefer the familiar word to the unfamiliar.
3. Prefer the Saxon word to the Romance.
4. Prefer nouns and verbs to adjectives and adverbs.
5. Prefer picture nouns and action verbs.
6. Never use a long word when a short one will do as well.
7. Master the simple declarative sentence.
8. Prefer the simple sentence to the complicated.
9. Vary the sentence length.
10. Put the word you want to emphasize at the beginning or end of your sentence.
11. Use the active voice.
12. Put the statements in a positive form.
13. Use short paragraphs.
14. Cut needless words, sentences and paragraphs.
15. Use plain, conversational language.
16. Avoid imitation. Write in your natural style.
17. Write clearly.
18. Avoid gobbledygook and jargon.
19. Write to be understood, not to impress.
20. Revise and rewrite. Improvement is always possible.

To these *Presbyterians Today* adds one more:

Reporting is preferred to reflection. Your chances of having your article accepted for publication increase to the extent that you write in the third person, not the first person. Most stories can be told better without the use of "I."

Before you begin to write, ask yourself: "What do I want to say?" "Why?" "To whom?" "How do I plan to say it?" If your article is geared to a Presbyterian audience, make sure it is clear how and why the subject relates to that audience. Assemble and organize your material. An outline may help. After you have written your first draft, it is good practice to leave it for a time. When you return to it, read it aloud, making sure its language flows freely and comfortably.

Categories that pertain to our publication: Non-fiction relevant to the Presbyterian Church (U.S.A.)—not essays, but articles about unusual Presbyterian individuals, creative ministries.

Categories: Nonfiction—Christian Interests—Religion

CONTACT: Eva Stimson, Editor
Material: All
100 Witherspoon St.
Louisville KY 40202-1396
Phone: 502-569-5637
Fax: 502-569-8632
E-mail: today@pcusa.org
Web site: www.pcusa.org/today

Presentations

TECHNOLOGY AND TECHNIQUES FOR EFFECTIVE COMMUNICATION

Presentations
Technology and Techniques for Effective Communication

Presentations Magazine accepts three kinds of articles for publication: columns, product reviews, and features. Many of our contributors are unpaid. As a rule, we pay only for pieces by professionals with whom we have contracted ahead of time, and with whom the fee is negotiated in advance.

For all manuscripts, it will increase your chances of acceptance if you bear the following stylistic guidelines in mind:

• We generally use the present tense ("say," not "said"), the active voice, and the familiar "you" when appropriate ("you find," not "it is found"). We discourage unsolicited first-person pieces.

• We do not describe situations or scenarios that did not happen without explaining to the reader that the event is fictional.

• We use the Associated Press stylebook as our chief reference in matters of editorial style.

• We encourage writers to interview end users of technology (not just vendors and manufacturers) whenever possible.

• Word counts in our magazine amount to about 800 words (just over three double-spaced typed pages) per printed page. Thus 800 words is the target length for "Speaker's Notes" and other one-page columns.

• For features, we expect writers to interview four to eight sources, chosen with an eye to their geographical disbursement as well as their expertise. We are a national magazine, not a regional one, and we expect our sources to reflect this.

• Most of our stories are accompanied by pictures of products, which we generally expect the writer to supply via the manufacturer. Many columns—"Speaker's Notes," for example—also require a head shot of the author. We welcome high-quality photographs, which we are happy to get electronically (by diskette or e-mail), although good prints, 35mm slides or 4 x 5 transparencies are also acceptable. Our software supports a variety of file formats, including EPS and TIF (300 dpi or higher); digital files are accepted on Iomega Zip and Jaz disks, as well as floppies, CDs and via e-mail. *JPEG and GIF file formats tend to degrade image quality and are strongly discouraged.* If your article is illustrated with screen captures, they should be 640 x 480 in the highest color resolution possible.

• Your manuscript should include a headline and subhead (with the understanding that editors may choose another one for the article once it appears in print). You should also provide captions for any pictures or images you submit with your story. Any book or article you cite should have a complete bibliographic reference (author, publication date, publisher); any product you mention should include the exact product name and number, together with the full company name and location (including the manufacturer's phone number and e-mail address). Please also provide a list of the names and phone numbers for all your article's sources. (This last information won't be printed, but it will be very helpful to your editors.)

• We insist on exclusive, first-time publication rights to all accepted manuscripts, which means we don't reprint articles that have appeared in other publications. We may consider an author's original adaptation of material from a previously published (or about-to-be-published) book, however.

Queries from writers new to our magazine are considered for feature articles only, not for columns (excluding Speakers Notes submissions). For full manuscripts, we accept paper copies, but we encourage writers to submit articles electronically—by diskette or e-mail. Allow 30-60 days for response. Special formatting (other than bold, italic and underline) is strongly discouraged. **E-mailed articles *must* include the contributor's snail-mail address and telephone number.**

E-mail **features or columns** to: jhill@presentations.com

(If you are submitting an article that has been previously assigned to you, please e-mail it to your assigning editor—and call to tell him or her you sent it.)

Categories: Nonfiction—Business—Computers—Education—Government—Internet—Presentations—Technology

CONTACT: Julie Hill, Managing Editor
Material: All
VNU Business Media Inc.
50 South Ninth St.
Minneapolis MN 55402
Phone: 612-333-0471
Fax: 612-333-6526
E-mail: jhill@presentations.com
Website: www.presentations.com

Prevention Magazine

Dear Writer:

Thank you for your recent request. Unfortunately, we do not have writers' guidelines to send you because we use very little freelance material. If you are interested in submitting material, we suggest sending a query with full details.

If the piece is already written, you may send a nonreturnable copy if you wish.

We appreciate your interest in our publication.
Best wishes!
Sincerely yours,
Readers' Service

Categories: Nonfiction—Cooking—Diet/Nutrition—Food/Drink—Health—Physical Fitness—Medicine

CONTACT: Denise Foley, Features Editor
Material: All
33 E. Minor St.
Emmaus PA 18098
Phone: 610-967-7650
Fax: 610-967-7654
Website: www.prevention.com

The Priest

Monthly magazine.
Pays on acceptance.
Byline given.
Not copyrighted.
Editorial lead time is three months.
Responds in five weeks to queries; three months on manuscripts.
Sample copy free.

We publish articles that will aid priests in their day-to-day parish ministry. Includes items on spirituality, counseling, administration, theology, personalities, the saints, etc.

Nonfiction: Essays, historical/nostalgic, humor, inspirational, interview/profile, opinion, personal experience, photo feature, religious. Send complete manuscripts; length: 1,500 words maximum.

Photos: Send photos with submissions; reviews prints; buys one-time rights; negotiates payment individually; captions and identification of subjects required.

Columns/Departments: *Viewpoints* (whatever applies to priests and the Church); 1,000 words or less; send complete manuscript.

Tips: Say what you have to say in an interesting and informative manner and stop. Freelancers are most often published in *Viewpoints*. Please do not stray from the magisterium of the Catholic Church.

For a sample copy, send a check for $4, payable to The Priest, with a 10-by-13-inch SASE with $1.52 in postage affixed.

Categories: Nonfiction—Essays—History—Humor—Inspirational—Religion—Catholic Church

CONTACT: The Priest, Editorial Department
200 Noll Plaza
Huntington IN 46750
Phone: 800-348-2440
Fax: 260-359-9117
E-mail: tpriest@osv.com.

Primavera

IN GENERAL

Primavera publishes original fiction, poetry, and art that reflects the experiences of women. We interpret this theme as broadly as possible. We select works that encompass the lives of women of different ages, races, sexual orientations, social classes, and locations. We will consider work by male writers but it must not require a male perspective to be understood or enjoyed.

Address all submissions to the editors at the address below. All submissions without an SASE will be discarded—illustration or manuscript.

Primavera pays both writers and artists in contributors' copies: two for each published item. If your work is accepted, we will send you a form to assign us the first rights to its publication. After publication, the copyright reverts to you, and you may reprint your work as long as *Primavera* is credited with its initial publication.

Do not send previously published work or simultaneous submissions.

We are happy to offer artists and writers a special discount on copies of *Primavera*! Back issues, usually $7.00 each, are only $5.00 when you mention this offer; current issues, usually $9.00, cost only $7.00. We pay for shipping.

WRITING

Poetry should be single-spaced, with stanza and line breaks clearly indicated. Computer printouts are fine, as long as the type is legible.

Primavera is published by a small staff of volunteers who meet biweekly (less often in summer), and it often takes several weeks, even months, before a manuscript completes the review process. Please be patient with us! We will respond to you, although unfortunately our staff is too small, and the volume of manuscripts we receive too large, for us to comment on each submission.

We edit poetry and fiction. If your work is selected, we may write to you with proposed changes, or ask you to rewrite troublesome sections. We always send you the edited version for your approval before publication.

We are interested in all writers, published and unpublished. We judge each work on its merit and not on the author's reputation (or lack of one).

ART

Primavera publishes black-and-white art inside the magazine: line and continuous-tone drawings, paintings, and photographs. Infrequently, we publish color illustration. We accept submissions on approval and do not commission work. We review work by women artists only.

For review, please send slides or photocopies. If we select your work for publication, we will ask you to send us the original or a professional-quality transparency. Write us if you aren't sure of the best way to represent your work

Categories: Fiction—Literature—Poetry—Women's Fiction

CONTACT: Board of Editors
Material: All
PO Box 37-7547
Chicago IL 60637
Phone: 733-324-5920

Presstime

Presstime provides newspaper executives with accurate information about issues that affect their daily operations and their futures.

HOW TO WRITE FOR PRESSTIME

Presstime, the four-color flagship magazine of the Newspaper Association of America, reaches 144,500 executives from all departments with definitive news and timely business analyses affecting this $51 billion industry. Twelve times per year, top newspaper executives rely on Presstime for accurate information about issues that affect their daily operations and their futures—in advertising, editorial, education, finance, marketing, management, new media, personnel, production and printing technology, and public policy.

THE AUDIENCE

Presstime is read by more newspaper professionals than any other newspaper trade publication. Eighty-nine percent of Presstime readers have read the last issue; 94 percent have read at least one of the last four issues. Presstime's 17,000-plus subscribers pass their copies of Presstime along to an average 7.5 additional readers, according to the 1999 Presstime Survey of Readers conducted by MORI Research of Minneapolis.

Presstime readers include group managers, publishers and senior executives in departments from the newsroom and advertising to circulation and production. They manage staffs numbering from one to thousands. And their readers number from hundreds to millions.

The primary purpose of the magazine is to provide its readers with useful information and ideas today, along with perspectives to guide their decisions about tomorrow.

"We strive to present newspaper managers with all the tools they need to compete in the expanding and increasingly competitive media world," notes Editor Terence Poltrack. "We also aim to help publishers better serve their communities and more effectively execute their critical role in the democratic process."

THE MIND-SET

If you are a newspaper employee, personal experience is probably your best source of article ideas. As a practitioner, you have encountered problems, developed solutions and corrected mistakes—and your colleagues want to hear about them. Has your newspaper created a product or designed a method or a policy that works? Do you have a cost-effective remedy to an industrywide problem? Then you should join the hundreds of other newspaper folks—accountants, administrators, ad reps, journalists, lawyers, new-media techies, printers, and publishers—who have found that the time and effort required to write for Presstime pays off tenfold. As an author, you gain industry recognition, public airing of issues and ideas, and the satisfaction of knowing you've given back to your profession.

Focus on your newspaper as an example, but frame the problem and solutions in terms of the lessons learned:

How can other newspapers adapt what you've done?

What kinds of pitfalls might they run into?

What costs are involved?

Try to anticipate readers' questions, then answer them. *Presstime* features keep a sharp focus. Many profile a single newspaper or newspaper owner or study a single management issue, technology or profession while still citing several points of view. They almost always feature interviews with at least five sources, unless they are commentaries or essays. The goal: View newspapers' problems and successes through the eyes of the people who run newspapers.

Presstime also contracts with free-lance writers for a limited number of department stories. Such contributors are often members of the working press, particularly those with special knowledge of advertising, business, computer technology, finance, human resources, newspaper readership, new media or public policy. To be considered, please send the editor a letter explaining why you would like to write for *Presstime* and include a resume and three clips.

If you receive an assignment, you will be asked to sign a contract that defines the task and sets a fee for your services as an independent contractor. Therefore, your fee must cover all your expenses. The contract assigns all print and electronic rights to NAA, as *Presstime* often posts articles on the Association's Internet site. *Presstime* pays on acceptance.

If you write for the magazine regularly, you will want to ask for copies of three electronic files: a list of U.S. newspaper names; a list of cities that do not require state names; and Presstime's style book.

To receive free sample copies of the magazine, contact Managing Editor Nancy M. Davis. E-mail, davin@naa.org; phone, (703) 902-1679.

THE PLAN

Send a 150-word outline or proposal addressed to the editor. If you have questions about how to orient a feature idea for the newspaper industry, call one of our staff members. Types of features include five- or six-page, 3,000-word cover stories; one- to three-page, 1,500-word features; and one-page, 750-word commentary or personal-opinion columns.

Some ideas find their way into *Presstime* departments including Education, Marketing to Advertisers, Marketing to Readers, New Media, Newsbeat, Public Policy, Operations and Workforce. The Ideas department offers successful ways that newspaper staffs have overcome common problems. Overset, a "brites" page, highlights amusing or unusual events that take place in and around newspaper offices or plants and the interesting people who reside therein.

Backtalk features 600-to-800-word, personal-opinion essays on topics ranging from how to buy a flexo press to the pros and cons of public journalism. These are submitted pro bono to encourage industry discussion and debate.

If your topic is not suitable for Presstime, NAA's family of publications also presents alternatives. NAA newsletters include Big Ideas for Smaller-Market Newspapers; People & Product, a newsletter about diversity; and updates for NAA's Circulation, Classified, Cooperative Advertising, Display, Market Development & Promotion, New Media, and Research Federations.

After receiving your inquiry, an editor might contact you to discuss your idea. If approved, the editor will provide direction for developing the manuscript.

Common reasons why articles are turned down:

Topics are elementary or irrelevant to running a newspaper.

They lack insight.

They offer too few examples from newspapers.

They are self-promotional or market a product or service available only from select vendors.

Presstime does not publish speeches in their entirety, articles that have appeared or will appear in other publications, or straight press releases or other such communications. A manuscript must be submitted by the person who wrote it.

Editors prefer well-constructed query letters to completed manuscripts. Submit only original ideas that have not been submitted elsewhere. If your idea is not suitable for publication in Presstime, you will be notified.

THE EXECUTION

Should you receive an assignment, here are some guidelines for your submission.

1. Review your outline or proposal.

2. Create a working title.

3. Write a compelling lead.

4. In the first five or six paragraphs, try to fashion a "nut graph," a statement that tells readers what they are going to learn by reading the remainder of the piece.

5. Research. Call the NAA Information Resource Center at (703) 902-1692 for facts, figures and case histories; after identifying yourself as a writer working for the magazine, you can also make generous use of NAA staff who are conducting experiments in your subject area.

6. Draft.

7. Once you have a draft, reorganize and insert subheads to shape the story. Be generous with bullets, numbers and other organizational tools. Pull related material into sidebars, tables, time lines and charts. List other ideas for illustrations.

8. Rewrite and tighten, paying close attention to meaning, style and tone. Writing coaches often say, "Show, don't tell," so avoid a lecture when explaining your ideas to colleagues. Avoid jargon and acronyms. Use detail to add clarity. Write as you speak, choosing active rather than passive verbs.

In addition:

Use the full, formal name of newspapers as they appear on Page One nameplates. For instance, The Sun in Baltimore, not the Baltimore Sun; the St. Louis Post-Dispatch, except on Sunday, when it becomes the Sunday Post-Dispatch.

List full company names and headquarters cities.

Refer to The Associated Press Stylebook and Webster's New World Dictionary.

Give full names, middle initials and titles.

Use past tense when referring to statements made at a specific time and place or in a public record. Use "says" and other present-tense verbs with quotes from interviews.

9. Fashion a conclusion that summarizes the main points of your story and brings the reader back to the lead.

10. Prepare a sources list containing the following information for each person interviewed: name, employer, office street address, city, state, ZIP code. Internet and/or e-mail addresses, phone and fax numbers. Refer to the format in the magazine. And please note: After publication, a copy of the magazine will be sent to each of your sources with a letter asking for further comments on the topic.

11. Edit your article by deleting unnecessary words, turning passive phrases into active ones, and linking paragraphs so readers move easily from thought to thought

12. Select tables and graphs that complement your work and list possible photos and other suggestions for art. Photos should be scanned to 300 dots per inch. If compression is required, please do not use Stuffit. Photos should have captions listing full names, middle initials and titles, left to right; photographer credits should include full names and employers' full formal names.

13. Double check accuracy of your facts by using the ""red-check"" method: Consult your original interview notes and other research. Verify every fact, figure, name. Place a red check over each in your manuscript. Accuracy is the authors" responsibility

14. You can file your story on a 3 1/2-inch disk in almost any word-processing program. However, a relatively current version of Microsoft Word is preferred. Mail to Managing Editor Rebecca Ross Albers, Presstime, 1921 Gallows Road, Vienna, Va. 22182. You can also e-mail stories, photographs or other computer files to alber@naa.org, or to an assignment editor.

THE ACCEPTANCE

Manuscripts are evaluated on originality, readability, content, timeliness and focus on the newspaper industry.

Your work may be accepted as is or contingent on your revision or a staff rewrite. Editors invariably work with authors through at least one or two revisions, carefully editing for style, content, clarity, appropriate language and length.

You will receive a copy of your article in page proofs for a final accuracy check. Then, you're done.

Sit back and wait for the accolades!

Categories: Writing

CONTACT: Nancy M. Davis, Managing Editor
Presstime
1921 Gallows Rd
Vienna VA 22182
E-mail: davin@naa.org
Website: www.naa.org/presstime/

Progressive Engineer

Progressive Engineer celebrates the accomplishments of forward-thinking engineers using a journalistic style that goes beyond describing the technology they work with and delves into their personal background. Published monthly on the Internet, the online magazine reaches engineers of all disciplines in all types of jobs.

How to Approach Us

The best way to to get a feel for our editorial style and content is to read a sample issue of the magazine on our website. Then send us a query letter outlining your idea.

Types of Articles We Use

Features: These cover projects that entail significant amounts of engineering with broad implications and describe the technology used and profile the engineers involved. Length: Approximately 2000 words (including sidebars). Payment: $300.

Short Profiles: These describe engineers or inventors who accomplish something significant in the course of their jobs and careers and tell of engineers applying their skills in unusual and innovative ways. These are often average people who do something out of the ordinary either on the job or off. Length: 1000-1500 words. Payment: $150.

Company Profiles: Describe companies that employ engineers, such as engineering firms, manufacturing companies, and construction companies, focusing on engineering work the company does as well as its scenario for hiring engineers. The latter includes the types of engineers the company uses, current hiring status, and what they look for in engineers. 1000-1500 words. Payment: $150-$175

Style

Progressive Engineer covers engineering in an easy-to-read style devoid of equations, jargon, and long words found in many technical journals. When applicable, we expect authors to use several sources in researching an article to maintain balance and objectivity. Obtain quotes from experts, principles involved in projects, and subjects of profiles. Feel free to use first person if appropriate. Features often use sidebars (generally 300-500 words) to complement the main body, often covering the technical content involved. Profiles should be written around a theme, such as a particular development or characteristic of the individual, and shouldn¹t just list credentials and accomplishments.

Manuscript Requirements

All manuscripts should include name, address, phone number, social security number, e-mail address, and word count at the top of the first page. Submit them by e-mail.

Photos

When possible, supply photos (and diagrams, if helpful) with your manuscript or tell us where we can obtain them. We can use digital images as well as B&W and color prints and 35mm or larger transparencies—originals or duplicates. Include a list of captions keyed to numbers on the photos. If you didn't take a photo you send us, tell us who did so we can give proper credit. We accept photos from companies and PR firms but don¹t pay for them. Payment: $25 per photo used in an article.

Rights and Payments

We consider reprints and simultaneous submissions if the markets don¹t compete; for reprints, payment is 50 percent of normal rates. Many times, we can use previously published material modified for our slant, in which case we pay full rate. Payment for all work is on publication.

Categories: Nonfiction—Engineering—Technical

CONTACT: Tom Gibson, Editor
Material: All
2049 Crossroads Dr.
Lewisburg PA 17837
Phone: 570-568-8444
E-mail: Tom@ProgressiveEngineer.com
Website: www.ProgressiveEngineer.com

Psychology Today
MIND BODY SPIRIT

Psychology Today

Thanks for your interest in *Psychology Today*! As you know, PT explores every aspect of human behavior, from the cultural trends that shape the way we think and feel to the intricacies of modern neuroscience. Although many psychologists and mental health professionals read PT, most of our readers are simply intelligent and curious people interested in the psyche and the self. Think of us as a health magazine for the mind!

WHAT WE NEED: Good, clearly articulated feature ideas and writers with the talent to bring those ideas to life. Nearly any subject related to psychology is fair game. We value originality, insight, and good reporting; we're not interested in stories or topics that have already been covered ad nauseam by other magazines unless you can provide a fresh new twist and much more depth. Although our articles are aimed at an intelligent mainstream audience, rather than specifically at psychologists, the ideas and claims made in the stories should be backed up where appropriate by good, solid scientific research. We're not interested in simple-minded "pop psychology."

While our readership is two-thirds female and largely college-educated, it is also diverse. There is no typical PT reader—and no typical PT story.

HOW TO GET AN ASSIGNMENT: Please don't send us complete manuscripts—our desks are already overflowing with journals, faxes, books, and articles awaiting editing. Instead, send a one- to two-page query letter explaining:

• what you want to write,
• why you want to write it now, and
• why you should be the one to write it.

Tell us why and how your story will affect people's lives, if applicable, and mention sources you might contact. If your work has been published before, feel free to attach a clip or two. Address the query to executive editor Lybi Ma or senior editor Carin Gorrell. We greatly appreciate an enclosed SASE.

We highly recommend that you read some recent back issues of the magazine to get a feel for what we publish and what topics we've covered lately. If we've written about topic X in a recent issue, chances are we won't want to run another feature on that subject for at least a year or two.

Many of the news stories in our Insights section are written in-house, but we do run pieces by freelancers. Topics include work, education, health, nutrition, relationships and neuropsychology and are directly linked to the most recent scientific findings. Address your queries to news editor Kaja Perina.

WE DON'T PUBLISH poems or short stories; we do consider first-person accounts of facing and overcoming psychological adversity for the one-page "My Story" column.

PLEASE NOTE: that we receive a lot of queries, and sorting through all that mail takes time, particularly for a tiny staff. We usually answer queries within six to eight weeks, but if your letter arrives as deadlines approach we may not get to it for awhile. Please be patient.

MISCELLANY: We pay on publication and payment will be negotiated between the writer and editor. We'll also reimburse you for minor necessary expenses (phone calls, yes; plane tickets, no). Of course you'll also receive some contributor's copies.

If your article has a seasonal or timely aspect, keep in mind our production schedule: our editorial deadline for an issue is nearly three months before the issue hits newsstands. Count on a five-month lead-time to get an assignment.

If you have any further questions, feel free to call executive editor Lybi Ma (ext. 130).

Thanks again for your interest, and we look forward to hearing from you!

Categories: Nonfiction—Health—Psychology—Science

CONTACT: Carin Gorrell, Senior Editor
Material: All
49 E. 21st St. 11th Floor New York NY 10010
Phone: 212-260-7210, ext. 105
Fax: 212-260-7445

Pyramid Magazine

Pyramid Magazine is a general-interest gaming magazine published on the World Wide Web by Steve Jackson Games in Austin, TX. At one time, we printed our magazine the old-fashioned way — on paper (30 issues!). But in 1998 we began publishing entirely on the Internet, becoming the first electronic publication to first be nominated for— and then win—an Origins Award for Best Professional Game Periodical. *Pyramid's* URL is http://www.sjgames.com/pyramid/

Pyramid covers all aspects of adventure gaming — roleplaying (of course), but also boardgames, card games, strategy games, miniatures, wargames, and even play-by-mail. And while some of what we put up each week is written by SJ Games staffers, most of it comes from freelancers. *Pyramid* provides an excellent opportunity to get some exposure in the game business, and to establish a professional relationship with Steve Jackson Games.

We get many submissions, more than we could ever use, so a lot of perfectly good articles get rejected. If this happens to you (and it will...) please don't take it personally. If the editor has any comments or suggestions, take them to heart. If he suggests that you resubmit the article after making certain changes, do it—editors love perseverance and a willingness to take directions. But let's get to the important stuff:

What We Want

What kind of articles do we publish? Well, a quick look at the *Pyramid* archives (or back issues of the paper magazine) will answer that question. In fact, if you don't have at least a passing familiarity with our magazine, you have no business trying to sell us an article. No, you don't have to be a devoted reader with a complete run of slipcovered back issues and a hard drive full of downloaded files, but you should know what kind of magazine we are. Our "want list," in no particular order, is something like this:

Something that surprises us. This is our favorite. Come up with something that isn't on this list, that makes us want to stop working and play games. If we knew exactly what we wanted, we wouldn't need freelancers.

Roleplaying Material. This means articles on better GMing and playing, complete adventure scenarios, new monsters, new equipment, articles adapting real-world ideas to a game, new magic, essays on campaign-building...anything relating directly to roleplaying games. A tip, though: "seed" items like creatures, characters, and magic objects need to have context—give them an interesting back story, adventure seeds, ideas on how to work them into a game. Just sending us the stats for your favorite character (or a random list of magic swords) won't do.

Game Variants and Strategy Articles. If you have an interesting variant or strategy for your favorite wargame, boardgame, card game, CCG, computer game, or strategy game, send it in! We prefer that the game in question be currently available — we're more likely to buy an article for *Kill Doctor Lucky* than one for *Junta*. On the other hand, some currently unavailable games (like *Talisman*) are sufficiently "classic" that we might assume that enough of our readers will like your article, anyway.

Entire Games. If the components can be found around the house or printed onto a website, and the game is simple and fun, we want it. "Magazine-scale" games are often more whimsical than entirely serious, but again, feel free to surprise us! Games submitted for publication in this way should, above all else, be *fun*, ideally strategic or combining strategic with random elements; entirely random games are almost always unsatisfying. If your game boils down to a game with the depth and playability of the card game War, we probably aren't interested.

The Gaming Life. Articles on how to keep your gaming group together, articles on teaching games to newcomers, articles on integrating your gaming schedule with your real-life schedule, articles on cross-media gaming and on how gamers relate to each other . . . Our readers are game players, and many are serious hobbyists. Although these articles can be difficult to write (since it takes more than random observations to make these type of articles satisfying), *Pyramid* is very interested in any articles about the gaming life.

While some portion of *Pyramid* will be always be devoted to SJ Games products, we are by no means a house organ. So yes, send us those *GURPS* and *Car Wars* and *Toon* and *Ogre* and *In Nomine* articles, but don't forget *d20, Champions, Kult, Call of Cthulhu, Magic: The Gathering, Vampire, Kingmaker, Empire Builder, Third Reich, Star Wars CCG, Trinity,* or anything else that interests you.

Features

Pyramid publishes a number of features. The information here is a collection of information on each one, and tips for what we're looking for; read previously accepted articles of these types to get an idea of what each feature is like.

Supporting Cast: This feature details non-player characters, with game stats and background. Supporting Cast members are the most common feature to submit; as such, we need to be choosy with what we accept. To increase your chances of acceptance, we recommend mak-

ing sure your NPC is different and interesting. Stats and background for a generic police officer probably aren't that interesting; an FBI agent who's working undercover to bring the mob down while double-crossing both to the Yakuza is a lot more likely to catch our eyes.

By the same token, avoid making characters *too* weird or interesting. Resist the urge to make the double-crossing police officer a psychic, for example, without a very good reason. (As a general rule, more than one plot twist in a character is usually too much to be believed.)

It is acceptable to make Supporting Cast members with more than one set of stats; for example, a medieval thief might be detailed in both *GURPS* and *d20.*

Terra Incognita: Articles of this type describe an unusual place, whether it's a fantasy temple, a modern horror hotel, or the mysterious moon of a planet deep in space. They are usually generic (and without game statistics), although they are usually tied to a certain genre (fantasy, horror, science fiction). This type of feature details the history, geography, and features of the place. Again, make sure the place is *interesting;* a standard hotel isn't terribly likely to spark our interest, although a hotel that travels through time might.

Warehouse 23: This feature details strange objects from any campaign type and genre. An ancient goblet that allows the user to communicate with people he's killed, a sentient car that wants to tour the world, or a computer that contains all the world's information as of 1977 are all equally weird for Warehouse 23. Again, they are usually generic, although if they are tied to a game world they can contain rules for use in that campaign. The history, effects, and consequences of the artifact are detailed in the article. Yet again, make sure the object is interesting and unique. Armor that magically protects someone from damage is commonplace; armor that transfers all damage to the wearer a week in the future is special—especially if the background story is compelling!

Supporting Cast, Terra Incognita, and Warehouse 23 submissions should generally have adventure seeds—mini-adventure ideas that give the reader some ideas how the person, place, or thing can be used in a game.

Adventure Pizza: This is our generic adventure feature. It's designed to be open-ended and applicable to many campaigns (although, again, it's common to tie them to one genre). These are, generally, looser than more formal adventures; ideally, the core idea, conflict, and/or story are all applicable to many different games. Formally, this feature consists of an "Ingredients" section, detailing the setting and opening action through a narrative that fits within the given genre, including a few details suggesting useful NPCs, items, and the like; the "Cooking Tips" section, offering at least three different plot directions, each with multiple "Extra Spice" entries that elaborate on the theme; and the "Side Salad" section, reminding the GM of any areas in the narrative that he may wish to develop further. These designations are, however, fairly loose; see previously accepted Adventure Pizzas for guidance.

Appendix Z: This is a catch-all category of articles, usually 1,000 words or less, that contain new rules, game aids, or other short information. They can be generic ("Complications While Gathering Information") or game specific ("Jumpgate Encounters for *Fading Suns*"). These articles are ideal for us to fill in small holes in our issues, and good for writers who have an idea that's difficult to write a larger article around.

Pyramid Reviews

Pyramid publishes reviews of new products in our "Pyramid Reviews" section. We run reviews across the spectrum — love it, hate it, or somewhere in between, we want to see it. We will choose a special few products as "Pyramid Picks," spotlighting the very best in gaming (the section subtitle is, "Gee, We Wish We'd Done That"). *Pyramid* reviews are typically 750 to 1,000 words in length. **With almost no exceptions, reviews shorter than 750 words are automatically rejected.** It simply isn't possible to provide the depth we require from our reviews with less. Longer pieces are perfectly fine . . . but don't overdo it. If your review is more than 2,000 words, then the game is either gargantuan in depth and scope, or you're writing too much.

Pyramid also publishes reviews of non-gaming material, provided it has *direct* roleplaying relevance. For example, we have in the past reviewed the *Howdunnit* series of mystery-writer reference books and a compact disc with music from a ***Fading Suns***-based computer game. Such reviews must directly tie to roleplaying. It's not enough to simply review a book about inventions of the 1920s; you should mention how the book can be used by GMs and/or players for ***Cliffhangers*** or other historical games. We're looking for insights and observations not available from your standard Amazon.com review. Any such reviews should be useful and positive; if a product doesn't have gaming relevance, *and* it isn't any good, why should we care?

We will also consider reviews of computer games and products. These reviews must, again, have direct roleplaying or gaming relevance. There are a thousand sources for standard computer game reviews — especially most mainstream multimillion-selling computer games — so we try to be distinct and focused. Thus we might be interested in a review about how faithful and satisfying the latest ***Dungeons & Dragons*** computer RPG is, compared to the tabletop game, or a review of an ***Axis & Allies*** computer game from a fan of the original wargame. (Of course, products that are originally designed for gamers — like the latest ***Campaign Cartographer 2*** expansion — need no special focus.) Utilities of possible interest for gamers are also acceptable to review; for example, we have published a review of the *Faces* utility, designed originally as a mug shot generator for police departments, suggesting it as an aid for GMs looking to generate NPC faces.

Tips for Reviews

For non-roleplaying material, make sure you give a sense of *how* the game plays. For a boardgame, it's not enough to explain how the game is set up, what pieces are moved where, or the like . . . you should also describe what choices a player has, how fast the game plays, how replayable it is, what strategy (or lack thereof) the game encourages, and so on. You might even give a brief example of a turn.

For roleplaying material, you may want to include a note about how the book might be of use for people who don't play that game. (For example, if a ***Vampire: The Dark Ages*** supplement would be particularly useful for people who play other historical medieval games, you may want to mention that.)

For that matter, anything you can do to avoid giving the sense of "Those who are fans of this roleplaying game world will like this game world supplement" is a good thing.

Avoid a methodical inventory list of a book's contents; if a book has nine chapters detailing nine regions of a game world, it's not necessary to have nine paragraphs each saying, "Chapter one gives the history, geography, and important NPCs of this region. Chapter two gives the history, geography, and important NPCs of this region . . ."

Try to determine who the audience is for a review, and determine how well the review targets that audience. For example, if a roleplaying supplement is designed for story-heavy games, it's appropriate to mention that the book won't be of much use for those who like hard game information, and to say how well (or poorly) it provides story-building possibilities for its target audience.

Please include all information traditionally included in the header of our published reviews. This includes the product name, the game line it supports, the publishing company and its website, the writer(s) and artist(s), the page count (and whether it is color or black & white), and the cost of the product.

What We Don't Want

Articles that aren't game-related. While our readers are often fans of science fiction, fantasy, anime, and comics, *Pyramid* doesn't cover those things.

We can't publish articles that give game stats for characters we don't own or have license to use — this means there's no point in sending us ***GURPS*** stats for Spider-Man or James Bond, or adventures that include them.

We don't accept submissions of fiction or poetry.

We're very picky about articles of any kind that exceed 5,000 words. Frankly, most articles that long are overwritten. There are exceptions, though, and if you've written something Big and Brilliant, we do want to see it. (If you do submit something this big, you may want to include a suggestion as to how the article can be logically split into two or more articles.)

Articles for games based on licensed properties can be problematic. For example, at this time we cannot publish any support articles for the ***Star Wars RPG***. Articles for such games generally require a bit of additional checking around to make sure we can publish them; before you write such an article, you may want to contact the company that publishes the licensed game to see what their policy is, to avoid writing a piece no one can use. (As a general rule, if we have published an article for that game in the past year or so, it's probably safe to submit. Also, properties that SJ Games has licensed — like ***Planet Krishna*** or ***Alpha Centauri*** — are fine.)

Checklist: Before You Submit Your Article

Every *Pyramid* submission sent to us via the Internet should be mailed to pyramid@sjgames.com, and must include the following elements. **If your submission doesn't conform to this checklist, we're likely to either bounce it back to you with a request to fix it, or simply reject it.** Please, follow directions . . . it makes our lives so much easier.

A proper subject line. If you're sending us an article called "Pain Magic for d20," the subject line of the e-mail should look like this:

[SUBMISSION]: Pain Magic for d20

A cover letter. Keep it brief, but describe (in one or two paragraphs) what your article is like, and what part of our audience it's written for. If you like, you can also include a brief history of your published work; this helps us get to know you, but it's optional.

Your contact information. We want your full legal name, your phone number, your e-mail address, and your physical (snail mail) address. If you have a Social Security Number, we want that, too. We can't pay you without it. If you are not a citizen of the United States, there's a form we'll send you, if your article is accepted, to allow us to pay you. Also include how you want to be paid, either in cash or SJ Games credit. (If you want a *Pyramid* subscription, this is where you should mention it, too.)

An article! The article should be spell-checked and proofread before we ever see it. Failure to do so *seriously* harms your chances of a sale. The article should have a title; under the title should be your name as you want it to appear in the magazine (many writers forget this part! Don't!). The article should be in plain text in the body of your e-mail; please set your email program to send plain, unformatted ASCII text. (Turn off HTML, "Smart Quotes," etc.) **Do not send articles as file attachments.** The article should be written in American English; do not use British/Canadian spellings of words like armor and authorize.

Footnotes and References. If your article is a factual essay (an article on the history of WWI firearms, for instance), you should include a reading list at the end of your article, preferably a mix of in-print books that the reader might enjoy and web links. Suggested reading lists are also appropriate for some other kinds of articles — if you think you've written one that would benefit from one, include it! When referring to fictional works, keep in mind that novels often have different titles in other countries, even English-speaking ones. If you are aware of these alternates, include them.

Things You Should Have, But Not Send

There are two things (specifically: graphics and WYSIWYG documents) you should have ready for us when you submit your article that should not be included in the e-mail (because we don't like spending an hour downloading our mail any more than you do).

Graphics: If your adventure needs maps or diagrams (or photographs) of any kind, you need to be able to provide them. At this time we are generally unable to redraw these illustrations; as such, if your graphics are unsuitable for publication and your article requires them, we'll probably be forced to reject the article. We do pay for these illustrations, as per SJ Games' standard *Pyramid* ·   art rates. Please don't e-mail us graphic files with your submission! Rather, include a note in your cover letter that you have such things waiting for us, should we ask to see them. (Internet-savvy contributors might put illustrations in a hidden part of their websites and submit the relevant URLs with their contributions.)

The exception to this rule is if, in essence, your article *is* a graphic file. For example, if you are submitting a printable, foldable tank compatible with **Cardboard Heroes,** then there isn't much to evaluate without the graphic. In that case, feel free to send the file in a common format (GIF, JPG, or PDF) with your submission. Just *please* make sure your files are fairly small. A needlessly huge file will assuredly be rejected.

WYSIWYG: We don't accept submissions from new writers in WYSIWYG formats of any kind (including HTML); as stated above, we want them in plain text. If the italics and bolds are so vital to your article that you feel it can't be evaluated properly without them, then feel free to use your own system to denote such items; for example, -this- might be italics and *this* might be bold. (Describe your system in your cover letter.) Alternately, you can use the HTML tags of <B>, <I>, </B>, and </I>. Just make sure your email program isn't converting those to HTML!

In some rare cases we may ask for a formatted version of your article in an alternate format — usually HTML or RTF. This is most common if your article contains complex tables that we can't figure out.

Where To Send It

All submissions must be sent via e-mail; send them to pyramid@sjgames.com. In the event that you absolutely cannot submit via e-mail, you may contact us via e-mail at this same address for how to submit via paper. (Yes, we require you to have e-mail access to tell us you don't have e-mail access.) Since *Pyramid* is an electronic publication, paper submissions are problematic for us, and will delay evaluation of your article by at *least* six to twelve months. And, ultimately, we will still require an electronic version of your article if it's accepted.

Queries and Follow-Ups

How often should you write to find out if your article is accepted? Should you e-mail us with an idea before committing yourself to writing an article?

The short answers to both: never, and no. The long answers are:

We do our best to evaluate any new submission within eight weeks of receiving it. If you haven't received a reply in three months, drop us a polite note to make sure we received it. Do not write us three hours after e-mailing it! If you didn't receive a bounce message, then odds are we got it, and will respond to it in turn. We get a lot of e-mail — sometimes hundreds a day.

Query letters (where you ask us "are you interested in an article on Giant Wombats?") are a reasonable idea, but the reality of it is this: our answer will always be the same. If it's game-related, and it doesn't violate any of the other rules here, we want to see your submission. If it's not, we don't. We can't tell if we want your article until we read it, so please don't expect any hints or revelations if you send us a query, and just because we want to see your submission is never a guarantee that we'll buy it.

What We Pay

Pyramid pays 3 cents a word, shortly after the article appears online (we do the word count ourselves based on the final, edited article). Pyramid Reviews pay a flat $25 each. If you prefer, we can pay in SJ Games merchandise credit instead of money. If that's your choice, the pay is doubled (in other words, we'll pay $50 in merchandise credit for an article we'd normally pay $25 cash for). We generally just cut checks; if you want merchandise instead, let us know with your submission. (It's always a good idea to say how you want to be paid, just to be on the safe side.)

Merchandise credit is paid in the form of a voucher mailed to you via post. (International customers have the option of having the voucher mailed directly to SJ Games, saving the two-way international trip.) Once you receive it, you can redeem it when purchasing any product directly from us, either via Warehouse 23 or at an official SJ Games convention booth. Merchandise vouchers cannot be redeemed through retailers. Please read the Voucher FAQ before redeeming. Contribu-

tors do not get automatic access to *Pyramid*. Non-subscribers may choose to be sent an electronic version of their HTML document (complete with graphics, if any), for their own personal use *only*. If you wish to receive a *Pyramid* subscription as part of your payment, we'll be happy to do that (deducting $20 from your check before any doubling for merchandise credit). Just let us know you want a subscription as part of your payment with your submission.

What Rights We Purchase

Pyramid buys all electronic rights to any original article we publish; if it appears in *Pyramid*, it may not appear in electronic form anywhere else without permission or license from Steve Jackson Games. We reserve the right to take the first crack at paper publication of any article purchased for *Pyramid* — we may eventually publish anthologies of electronic *Pyramid* articles in book form, for instance. If there are other parties interested in buying paper rights to an article we own the electronic rights to, contact us immediately to let us know. We reserve two months from that time to make a counter-offer. *Pyramid* is also interested in purchasing second serial rights to articles that have already been published (as first serial purchases) in other magazines. We pay half our normal rates (1.5 cents instead of 3) for second serial rights.

Alternate arrangements to these can be made in special cases; ask us.

Reasonable permission is granted in advance to authors who wish to include *Pyramid* articles in a writing portfolio. We would prefer not to have to define "reasonable"; in general, if you think you're skirting (or over) the line, you probably are.

Some Tips for Writers

Not all of these are not hard and fast rules, but they are some of the points we keep in mind while evaluating an article. If you're brilliant, feel free to deviate from these points if you think it makes for a better article . . . but it's always better to break a rule knowingly than to do so from ignorance.

Style: Although *Pyramid* can be a bit looser in style than, say, your average **GURPS** book, we still generally prefer to be professional. Unless your writing style is very confident and sharp, it's generally best to remain detached yet interesting; don't feel the need to include slang, pop culture allusions, or other "kewl" lingo in your piece. You *can* use first person language if appropriate ("In my modern horror campaign, I had the vampire prince take control of the newspapers in order to sway the city council . . ."), but often it is better to rewrite such pieces into the third person ("For example, in a modern horror campaign, a vampire prince may take control of the newspapers in order to sway the city council . . .") This is especially true for reviews; although it's easy to get emotional about particularly good (or bad) games, too much emotion makes it difficult for readers to discern if a product would be of interest to them.

Generally Avoid Absolutes: *Pyramid* has, arguably, the most diverse readership of any gaming magazine. We have those who love heavy number-crunching articles, those who love story ideas, those who love campaign settings, those who love one particular genre or game, those who hate one particular genre, and so on. As such, it's *very* difficult to make statements that are universally true. To that end, we generally frown on any blanket statements . . . especially those that are unfounded or likely untrue. For example, a statement like "No one likes to have their characters die . . ." is probably better written "Many players don't like to have their characters die . . ." Remember that there are all manner of gamers; blanket statements are likely to alienate someone.

Avoid Overly Broad Articles: Articles with too wide a scope are almost always too meandering to be satisfying. "How to Be a Better GM" is perhaps the most common article title we get . . . and with few exceptions, these are rejected. Why? Because even 5,000 words isn't enough to do justice to such a huge concept. Try to focus big concepts into something more manageable; articles like "How to Use Audio to Be a More Atmospheric GM" or "How to Avoid Plot Holes as a GM" are more likely to cover their topics effectively than "How to Be a Better GM."

Length Vs. Audience: *Pyramid* only has a limited number of words per week we can print, yet we have a wide and varied audience. As such, we are constantly trying to balance between articles that are of interest to a wide group, while also having pieces that will appeal greatly to a smaller audience. We need to be aware of how big an article is, versus how much of our audience will be able to use it; as such, a long article will need to appeal to a larger audience, or be of greater interest to a smaller audience.

For example, we'll almost always have room for good 2,000-word articles we like, even for an obscure game. If that article is 3,000-4,000 words, we need to look at it a bit more closely, particularly if it's for a game without many fans. One 5,000-word article will take up most of a week's issue; it will either need to appeal to a large number of people, or be the best darn article for an obscure game we've ever seen.

What does all this mean? Well, a longer article for a little-used game may be rejected, with advice to either shorten it or make it more general-purpose. As such, it is often helpful to plan your article toward one of those two goals in the first place. (On the other hand, if a long article for a less-popular system is brilliant, we may well accept it anyway.)

As an aside, crossover games are especially tricky; if you want to write an article about crossing over **Call of Cthulhu** with **Bunnies and Burrows,** then it will generally only be of interest to those who are fans of both games…which will obviously be a smaller group than fans of either game individually. Again, such articles will need to be short and focused, appeal to a broader audience, or be *brilliant.*

Read all the guidelines. Steve Jackson Games has a lot of authors' guidelines; read the SJ Games style guide, and if you're writing for a specific SJ Games product, read the guidelines for that game. Yes, it can take a while to read all those pages, but it takes longer to write an article that will be rejected because you didn't follow the rules.

Of particular note are the rules against libel. *Pyramid* tries to avoid *any* mention of real living people, including celebrities, political figures, and anyone else. Articles that contain such references will probably be rejected, with instructions to rewrite without mentioning real people. Articles mentioning real companies and organizations are likewise problematic; it's bad to, say, describe how the real company GloboMediCo is, in fact, controlled by undead monsters. Try to avoid the headache altogether; don't say "GloboMediCo," say "a large pharmaceutical company."

Don't plagiarize. Although this is covered elsewhere, it bears mentioning again. Plagiarizing is the taking of anyone else's work and passing it off as your own. This is especially important with "real world" articles; if you find a website detailing a list of 100 medieval plants, it is *not* acceptable to simply reiterate that list in your own article . . . especially if your article has a title like "100 Medieval Plants." In the event you plagiarize, we will (of course) reject your article, and we will *never* work with you again.

Tie articles to gaming. Although it may be obvious that articles should be tied to gaming, many people seem to forget . . . especially with historical or factual articles. For example, you might submit an article about the history of communication innovations in the last millennium. It might be entirely accurate and well-written, but you may forget to include any context for how it can be used in a roleplaying game. Without that tie, the article might well seem like one that could be found in *Time, Discover,* or *National Geographic.* Probably the easiest way to connect an article to gaming is to give adventure seeds or possibilities using the ideas presented in the article.

It must be fun. Consider this the canonical rule of *Pyramid* submissions. All aspects of gaming are, ultimately, hobbies—which are supposed to be fun. And as a gaming magazine, *Pyramid* strives to make sure its articles are fun.

Of course, "fun" is entirely subjective, and difficult to describe. Generally, though, it's easier to determine what *isn't* fun: Overly academic or formal writing, needlessly complex or pointless rules, and topics so esoteric that only a select few would care . . . these are all examples of "un-fun" mistakes that writers make. If we doze off while

reading your article, its chances of acceptance aren't very good.

GURPS books are generally great examples of writing that is factual and well-researched while still fun.

Make it as flawless as you can. Perfection is probably impossible, but dumb mistakes are avoidable. Spell-check, proofread, go over it. Have a friend read it. *Pyramid* publishes over 750,000 words a year …everything you can do to make sure *your* words require as little editing as possible increases its chances of acceptance.

If you discover your article has a significant mistake after submitting it, feel free to resubmit it. (Include a note in the cover letter that it's a resubmission.) Of course, issuing too many corrections in this way shows us that you may not know how to make it right the first time…

Include full contact and payment information, including how you want to be paid. If you don't, there may be months between when we print your article and when we finally sort out everything necessary to pay you.

Further Reading?

We've said it before, but every *Pyramid* submission should make it plain to us that you've read these guidelines and are willing to follow them. You should also show a familiarity with our "house style" and other details described in the general Steve Jackson Games Authors' Guidelines. These guidelines are a supplement to those; treat both as gospel. *Exception:* don't bother with a Game Evaluation Waiver. Those are for manuscripts that you hope to sell to SJ Games for publication as a game product, not for magazine articles.

Where to Get the Document You're Already Reading

Our guidelines change occasionally as the magazine matures; you should be working from the most current version of these guidelines. If you're reading a hardcopy that you feel might be out of date, you can always find the most current version on our website.

Categories: Hobbies

**CONTACT: Website: www.sjgames.com/pyramid/writing.html
Material: All**

Quarterly West
University of Utah

Thank you for your interest in our magazine.

Quarterly West is a semiannual publication. Sponsors a biennial award for novellas. Work published in *Quarterly West* has been selected for inclusion in *Best American Short Stories, Best American Poetry, Best American Travel Writing,* and the Pushcart Prize anthology. QW publishes literary, experimental, and formal poetry, fiction and creative nonfiction as well as translations and reviews. Submit 3-6 poems, 2-3 short shorts, or 1 short story/essay/book review. Brief cover letters welcome. Send SASE for reply or return of ms. No fax or email submissions. Responds in up to 8 months; sooner when possible. Sample copies are available for $7.50. Pays $15-50 and two contributors copies on publication for all rights.

You may wish to know the following information:

1. *Quarterly West* expects the standard format for fiction or essays: typed, double-spaced, author's name and title on the first page. Poetry should be single-spaced.

2. Each manuscript must be accompanied by an SASE for response and return.

3. Editors will consider simultaneous submissions, but expect to be informed. Authors must notify editors immediately of simultaneously submitted work accepted elsewhere.

4. We read submissions between September 1 and May 1 only. Submissions received between May 2 and August 31 will be returned unread.

5. Submit only one story or essay, or three to five poems at a time. Writers may submit up to two short-shorts (less than five pages each).

6. Contributors receive two copies of the issue in which their work appears, as well as a small honorarium.

7. *Quarterly West* sponsors a biennial novella competition. Please send an SASE for complete guidelines.

8. We ask that former contributors wait at least one year after publication before submitting new work to *Quarterly West*.

Categories: Fiction—Nonfiction—Book Reviews—Interview—Literature—Poetry—Short Stories—Writing

CONTACT: David C. Hawkins, Editor
Material: All, except poetry
CONTACT: Poetry Editor
Material: Poetry
200 S. Central Campus Dr., Rm 317
University of Utah
Salt Lake City UT 84112-9109
Phone: 801-585-5167
Website: www.utah.edu.quarterlywest
or www.webdelsol.com/Quarterly_West

Quick & Easy Quilting
Quilt World

General Information

House of White Birches publishes *Quick & Easy Quilting* and *Quilt World* magazines, two quilting hardcover books a year, patterns for e-PatternsCentral.com and quilt pattern books.

Project submissions or manuscripts:

Begin each submission with a sentence or two about the topic/project (a personal anecdote or historical information about the project).

Each publication has its own style. Look through recent copies of each one to familiarize yourself with that style and the type of project that has been published recently. Pattern your submissions after those in the publication to which you are submitting your designs.

Quilt World is a general quilting publication. We accept articles about special quilters, techniques, coverage of unusual quilts at quilt shows, special interest quilts and patterns. We include 5–8 patterns in every issue.

Quick & Easy Quilting fills the need of the quilter wanting to make quality quilts in less time. We print patterns (traditional or contemporary) and technical articles on machine piecing, quilting and quick-cutting techniques.

Quilt Pattern Books feature the work of one quilter and include several projects with a specific theme. They are usually 8 to 32 pages in length.

Quilt Hardcover Books feature the work of many quilters. They include 30 to 60 projects around a general theme. Designer suggestions for specific hardcover books are sent to quilters in our database, but can also be requested.

Include a list of materials needed to complete the project using generic names. Brand names can be listed beneath the Materials List in the form of a credit. If you do so, provide exact names of products and a current address for the company.

Mark whether patterns/templates are with or without seam allowances both on templates and in cutting instructions.

Be sure the instructions are accurate.

Diagrams/drawings should be numbered (using Figure 1, Figure 2) and clear and easy to understand.

Mailing address: Send submissions and completed projects to Sandra Hatch, Magazine Name, RR #3 Box 930, Sweet Rd., Lincoln, ME 04457, or for books and pattern books to Jeanne Stauffer, Book Name, House of White Birches, 306 East Parr Road, Berne, IN 46711.

Writing guidelines:

Query letters with photos are encouraged. Unsolicited manuscripts should be typewritten, easy to read and accompanied by return postage.

The author/designer's name and complete address and page number should appear in the upper left-hand corner of all pages.

Submissions may be made on disk. We use Macintosh computers with Microsoft Word. We also need a hard copy of the manuscript.

Photos

Color slides or clear photographs are accepted. Please provide photo captions for all photographs.

Label each slide/photograph with your name and address and a number. List the numbers with photo captions as part of your manuscript.

Return of published projects: Projects will be returned to you after publication with your complimentary copy. This may be 6–8 months for magazines or 10–12 months for hardcover books and pattern books.

Contracts and Payment

When we receive the completed project, instructions and all related materials, we will send you an agreement and a business-reply envelope. Sign the agreement and return it in the postage-paid envelope. Keep the photocopy of the agreement for your records and return the original to us.

Payment will be made within 45 days of the time we receive your contract. Amount will be determined by accuracy, creativity, workmanship, skill level, overall quality and instruction format. Average fees range from $50 to $550. Because HWB purchases all rights to designs unless otherwise arranged, designers should not sell the purchased design or one very similar to it to another publisher.

If you have any questions, contact Jeanne Stauffer or Sandra Hatch. If you have a question about the status of a book design, contact Dianne Schmidt, Associate Editor, (260) 589-4000, Dianne_Schmidt@whitebirches.com.

We look forward to working with you in the coming months!

Categories: Nonfiction—Crafts—Hobbies

CONTACT: Sandra Hatch, Editor, hatch@link.net
Material: Submissions and completed projects (Send to Maine address)
RR #3 Box 930
Sweet Rd.
Lincoln ME 04457
Phone: 260-589-4000
CONTACT: Jeanne Stauffer
Material: Books and pattern books
House of White Birches
306 East Parr Rd.
Berne IN 46711
Website: www.quilt-world.com

Quilt World

Please refer to *Quick & Easy Quilting*.

Quilting Arts Magazine®

***Quilting Arts Magazine*® is actively seeking the following queries for publication:**

- Art Quilt and Mixed Media Artists to be profiled
- Fiber-altered books
- Quilts with a landscape theme
- Unique embellishment and surface design techniques
- Quilting with mixed media including found objects
- Pictorial quilts
- Art dolls made of cloth
- Narrative quilts (quilts that depict a story)
- Working with interesting mixed media
- Quilts with image transfers
- Beaded embellishments
- Interesting uses of silk ribbon
- Bobbin thread embroidery
- Wearable art techniques
- One-of-a-kind garments
- Abstract quilts
- Fiber journals

M-Q

- Working with transfer inks
- Embossing on fabric
- Unique fabric painting and dyeing methods

Guidelines for Submissions: *Quilting Arts Magazine*® is interested in articles concerning contemporary art quilting, wearable arts, embellished quilting, mixed media, surface design, and crazy quilting.

Copyright Issues: No submissions which may violate copyright laws will be accepted. If your artwork could be perceived by Quilting Arts, LLC as a potential copyright violation, please provide written consent by the party which may have standing with regard to the copyright issue. Thank you for cooperation.

Query first, please. Editors will consider articles submitted on speculation, but prefer that you query first MAIL ONLY (no emails, please) with an idea or brief proposal describing the idea, explaining how you'd handle the story, and summarizing your writing experience. If you'd like to see sample queries, click here.

What we are looking for? We like an enthusiastic, inspiring and elegant approach whenever possible. For how-to articles, we ask that they be user-friendly.

The length of the articles we publish varies greatly depending on subject and treatment. Feature articles range from 800-2500 words; briefer articles are usually 400-1,000 words.

Quilting Arts Magazine is most interested in receiving queries regarding the following:

Previously unpublished how-to articles that cover unique embellishing, quilting, and wearable arts techniques geared for either the beginner or advanced quilter.

Feature articles that explore motifs and methods of interest to art and embellished quilters; for example, different types of threads and their common (or uncommon) uses.

"In the Spotlight" pieces — Quilts with brief explanations of how the work was accomplished.

Rates of Pay: *Quilting Arts Magazine*® pays for feature articles only. Rates of pay depend on length of article, depth of subject matter, and quality of writing. Payment occurs within 45 days after publication.

For All Submissions: Please include your address, telephone number and a brief biographical paragraph that specifies the way you prefer your byline to appear, your title, your affiliation, and/or any relevant experience.

Materials submitted—written or photographed—cannot be returned unless a SASE (Self Addressed Stamped Envelope) is provided.

Categories: Arts—Crafts/Hobbies—Hobbies

CONTACT: Patricia Bolton, Editor in Chief
Material: All
PO Box 685
Stow, MA 01775
Phone: 978-897-7750
E-mail: editorial@quiltingartsllc.com (no submissions please)
Website: www.quiltingartsllc.com

Quilting Today

Please refer to *Traditional Quiltworks*.

Rack
Adventures in Trophy Hunting

Rack magazine is published six times a year, from July through December, and is available only by subscription. Inside each issue are between 20 and 25 stories (averaging 1,000 words apiece) detailing the hunts behind world-class big game animals. Approximately 75 percent of the stories concern white-tailed deer, which MUST be scored on the Buckmasters (BTR) measuring system. By this yardstick, whitetails must score at least 160 as "typicals" or a minimum of 175 as "irregulars" to qualify. Other big game animals must simply qualify for any of the record books (B&C, P&Y, SCI, Rowland Ward or Longhunter).

Two-thirds of the stories that appear in *Rack* are either first-person accounts furnished by the hunters or written by the editors. The rest are bought from freelancers. An unpublished 1,000-word article with at least two accompanying photographs will fetch between $175-$325 upon publication; half that for second-time rights. A cover photo (always hunters with their whitetails) could garner an extra $500.

Queries and/or manuscripts should be sent to the managing editor via e-mail (mhandley@buckmasters.com). We prefer color prints or slides to be sent by regular mail. Please do not bother submitting queries or stories that stray beyond actual hunting tales. We do not publish how-to or destination stories; no gear-related features; no columns; and no personal profiles or human interest pieces.

Categories: Nonfiction—Adventure—Outdoors—Hunting

CONTACT: Mike Handley, Managing Editor
Material: All
Buckmasters Ltd., PO Box 244022
Montgomery AL 36124-4022
Phone: 800-240-3337

Radio World
The Newspaper for Radio Managers & Engineers

Why should I contribute to *Radio World*?
Radio World is the newspaper for U.S. radio station managers and engineers, with more than 12,000 readers. Our readers are the people who own, manage and operate FM and AM stations as well as the suppliers and other organizations that serve this audience. These readers are radio professionals: engineers, corporate managers, general managers, owners, production people, IT managers, news reporters, show hosts, educators, regulators and more. We have a technical pedigree but have evolved into a publication covering a broad range of news and feature topics.

Your article will reach a nationwide audience of important radio people. Exposure in *Radio World* can increase your stature in the industry and help you build a valuable network in our business. In addition to the satisfaction they feel in taking part in this forum, many of our contributors benefit professionally from the exposure that their articles give them.

What topics does *Radio World* seek?
Our readers want to know about radio in the United States: how to use new technology, how to keep or find a job, what the latest business trends are. We write about books, education, industry news, public radio, satellite radio, the Internet and more. You can help them by

bringing your expertise on a given topic to an article, or by writing about other people involved in these trends. Our sister publication, *Radio World International*, pursues a similar mission abroad.

Radio World is divided into sections: News, Features, GM Journal, Studio Sessions, Buyer's Guide, Reader's Forum.

News: Goal: to provide news and in-depth analysis. *Radio World* articles are more in-depth than those found in other trade publications, many of which are not devoted strictly to radio. Radio World articles also address the important technical side of these issues, which is lacking in other trades. This section includes breaking industry developments, regulation, important technology, convention coverage, obituaries, format trends.

Features: Goal: to provide a broad range of engineering and general-interest articles, including technical how-to tips, personality interviews, history of radio, unusual new programming, ideas on finding or keeping a job, product news, humor.

GM Journal: Goal: to help the radio manager understand our medium and make his or her station more profitable or successful at meeting its mission. Station promotional ideas, radio business trends, station profiles, advertiser profiles, station services. This section also looks at Internet radio: how to stream, how to run a profitable Web site and more.

Studio Sessions: Goal: to provide a resource for on-air and production personnel. Product reviews, how-to articles, profiles of successful production people and voice-over talent, humor.

Buyer's Guide: User Reports by consumers of these products. Goal: to assist equipment buyers in making their decisions. Every other issue of RW contains a Buyers Guide category (e.g., Microphones, FM Transmitters, Live Assist and Automation).

Reader's Forum: Goal: to give readers a place to air their views. Letters to the editor and Guest Commentaries.

How should I submit my article?

Submit your article in electronic form, preferably in MS WORD, via e-mail to radioworld@imaspub.com; or if typed, mail to the address at the top of this document. Your editor will specify the story length (usually between 600 and 1,200 words).

On questions of style, refer to the *Associated Press Stylebook and Libel Manual* (published by The Associated Press, 50 Rockefeller Plaza, New York, N.Y. 10020). From time to time, *Radio World* will provide a list of industry-specific style points to complement the AP Stylebook.

If sending hard copy, mail text and photographs so that they reach us by the deadline. If possible, please send a floppy disk or CD with the story saved in MS WORD or as an ASCII file.

Although headlines frequently are reworked to comply with our format and to fit the allotted space, please give your article a title of 28 to 32 characters, using a clearly defined subject and an active verb.

Include your name as you want it to appear in the byline. Include your title, address and phone number.

Radio World often includes a brief bio at the end of stories, usually a sentence or two. ("The author is a freelance writer and former production manager for Smith Broadcasting. Reach her at (703) 998-7600 or via e-mail at carrot@aol.com.") Please let us know whether we can print your phone number for use by our readers.

Should I submit photographs? In what format?

Writers are responsible for providing artwork to illustrate articles. Please do not overlook this important part of your story. Visual elements help pull the reader into your story and make it more informative.

Artwork can be a picture of a piece of equipment, a studio snapshot, a "headshot" photo of your subject, company logos, a copy of the book you are reviewing, charts and graphs, or any other visually interesting art that pertains to the story. Use your imagination. No one knows the topic like you do.

We can accept a print, slide or electronic file of the image. Electronic JPG or TIF images should have resolution of at least 300 dots per inch for publication at 5 inches wide. The most common mistake made by contributors is that electronic images sent to us are of insufficient resolution.

RW publishes images in both color and black-and-white.

If you wish to have artwork returned to you, please include a note to that effect with your article.

Most RW writers find that they can obtain artwork for their stories at no cost. For example, if you are writing about AM antenna monitors, call manufacturers of such equipment and request photos to illustrate your story. Most will be happy to oblige you and will ask only that you include a photo credit. If you are writing about a radio station group owner, ask for a headshot of the company president, a photo of their headquarters, a studio picture, a logo, a copy of the company's annual report, or any creative photos from recent station events. With the spread of digital cameras, many subjects now can take photographs at your request and e-mail them to you.

If you expect to incur expenses related to artwork (for instance, if you plan to shoot your own pictures), please call your editor first to make arrangements.

I need more info. I still have questions.

Call your editor with any questions. We would rather hear from you ahead of time, than discover later that we and you had different expectations about your article.

Each section of our newspaper has its own demands and guidelines. If you are uncertain where your article will appear and would like help in targeting your article, don't hesitate to call your editor.

Categories: Nonfiction—Business—Education—Engineering—Internet—Mass Communications—Technology—Television/Radio

CONTACT: Paul McLane, Managing Editor
Material: All
PO Box 1214
5827 Columbia Pike, First Floor
Falls Church VA 22041
Phone: 703-998-7600
Fax: 703-820-3245
E-mail: radioworld@imaspub.com

The Ragged Edge

What we publish:

The Ragged Edge examines current and emerging public issues from a disability perspective: civil rights, politics, culture, humor, sexuality, art, technology. We publish freelance journalism, essays, poetry and fiction.

Nonfiction:

The Ragged Edge accepts very few new freelance submissions. Nonfiction essays and articles should be between 750 and 1500 words and must focus on issues of interest to the disability rights movement. Analysis, criticism and journalism are acceptable approaches; we publish very few first-person accounts. We are not interested in inspirational accounts. Freelancers are urged to familiarize themselves with the subjects we cover and our style and approach by reading back issues, available in the archives on our website at http://www.raggededgemagazine.com.

Fiction/poetry:

We seek work of high literary quality which explores the social and political aspects of disability. We'd love to see work from writers exploring the intersections of ethnicity and disability, sexual identity and disability, writing that's experimental; work in which it's clear that the writer has thought about disability culture and aesthetic practice. Since space is limited, short poems and short pieces of fiction have a better shot at getting published.

Terms/Rights purchased:

We do not pay freelancers; we provide two copies of issue with your article. We also publish your article online at http://www.raggededgemagazine.com.

Query first for nonfiction, please!

Please send a short (2-3 paragraphs) query first that opens with a possible lead for your story. Send your query by e-mail only to: editor@raggededgemagazine.com.

Submitting your article: formats

Once we accept your query, you will need to submit your article by e-mail. Our e-mail address is: editor@raggededge magazine.com..

ALL Submissions by e-mail only, to: editor@raggededge magazine.com.

Also, please note that we expect queries first for nonfiction.

Sample issues:

A sample issue of *The Ragged Edge* is available for $4 . Or browse our website at http://www.raggededgemagazine.com to read our archives.

Categories: Disabilities

CONTACT: Mary Johnson, Editor
Material: General
CONTACT: Anne Finger, Poetry/Fiction Editor
Material: Poetry and Fiction
PO Box 15
Louisville KY 40201
Website: www.raggededgemagazine.com

Rainbow Review
gay & lesbian poetry, fiction, and nonfiction

Poetry, fiction and articles about being gay, experiences, coming out, reactions of family and others, love, relationships, abuses, rights, discrimination, anything that is important, influences or affects gay and lesbian people today.

Published: Annually

Book Formats: Anthology is a book-zine (eclectic like a magazine but in book form) and will be published in one or more of the following, traditional paper (either hardback or paperback), electronic (ebooks and/or audio).

Publishes: Poems, short fiction, and nonfiction.

Lengths: Open for all manuscripts - poetry, short fiction, nonfiction. Manuscripts of all lengths will be considered.

The deadline: We read manuscripts all year for this annual anthology publication in book-zine format.

Rights: One-time use in book form (all formats). Considers reprints if author owns rights.

Poets and writers should send a bio to accompany their writings in the anthology.

Please note: Writers and poets with books and other publications or venues (i.e. a website) can submit information, website address, etc. for inclusion in the anthology to accompany their bio information. This will give writers added exposure for themselves and their books, websites, etc.

Contributors must send note (email or by regular mail) stating that he/she would like the writing(s) included in the published anthology.

Submit up to 5 manuscripts, either by email or regular mail (see below). Please enclose SASE with regular mail submissions.

Contributors will receive one copy of the finished anthology.

Categories: Alternate Life-style—Gay/Lesbian—Lifestyle

CONTACT: Eugene Boone
Material: All
RSVP Press
129 Thurman Lane
Clinton TN 37716
E-mail: rsvppress@yahoo.com

Reader's Digest

Reader's Digest, headquartered in Pleasantville, N.Y., 45 minutes north of Manhattan, has been published monthly since February 1922. From that first issue, founders DeWitt Wallace and Lila Acheson Wallace built a mass-interest magazine that is now bought by more than 16 million people in the United States and nearly 31 million around the world—reaching 100 million readers every month.

What is the market for original material at *The Digest*? Roughly half the 30-odd articles we publish every month are reprinted from magazines, newspapers, books and other sources. The remaining 15 or so articles are original—most of them assigned, some submitted on speculation. While many of these are written by regular contributors—on salary or on contract—we're always looking for new talent and for offbeat subjects that help give our magazine variety, freshness and originality. Payment, on acceptance, is $3,000, plus reasonable expenses. For a "Drama in Real Life" or "Unforgettable Character," we pay $3,500. This rate covers all world-wide periodical rights—including condensation, adaptation, compilation and anthology rights—for all forms of print and electronic publishing media. *Reader's Digest* also reserves the right of first refusal on all remaining rights. For assigned articles that don't work out, our kill fee is $500. There's one other important market: fillers and short department items. We pay up to $400 for true, unpublished stories used in our departments; for original material that runs as a filler, we pay $30 per *Reader's Digest*, two-column line, with a minimum payment of $50. To the first contributor of an item we use from TV, radio or a published source, we pay $35. For more on this market, check the front of the magazine, where we solicit reader contributions each month.

How should an original article be proposed to *The Digest*? Don't send us unsolicited manuscripts. We no longer read them. Just send a letter to *The Digest*, briefly describing the article you'd like to do and, if you're new to us, listing your writing credits. If the idea sounds right for us, we'll check our article index, our assignment list and our inventory of original and reprint material for overlaps. If there are none, we'll ask to see a manuscript on speculation, or, if the idea is assignable, we'll request a detailed outline—not a formal A-B-C outline, but a structured, reasonably polished piece of writing that sells not only the article but also you-the-writer and what you bring to your subject. In three or four double-spaced pages, give us a lead that could sit on top of your finished article, and show us where you plan to go from there. Above all, we want a sharp, crisp focus and viewpoint. Here is how Patricia Skalka opened a proposal about a flood that threatened Fort Wayne, Ind., and how Fort Wayne's children helped save the city:

"'I can't feel my fingers anymore,' the young girl sobbed. 'Don't stop. Don't stop,' the others cried. With hands bloody, backs sore and eyes bloodshot from exhaustion, they continued to pass bag after bag of heavy sand down the line. Nearby someone told a joke. In the distance, a rhythmic chant began. The lines of volunteers knew the words from days of marching with schools bands to victory, from evenings spent sitting around Scout camp fires. 'One-two. Sound off. Three-four. Once more…' Now in the eerie dark, rain-soaked from head to foot and mired ankle-deep in mud, they joined the chant.

"Along a 32-mile network of water-logged earthen dams, they sang. They sang to keep going, to keep the sand bags moving. They sang for themselves, for their city. They sang to protect the lives and homes of total strangers. They sang because it is the nature of youth to face danger with bravado, innocence and good spirit. They sang to win one of the country's most awesome battles against the forces of nature. This is the story of Fort Wayne, Ind., and last month's 'Great Flood,' a disaster of such proportions that it literally threatened to destroy the city. Nearly one third of Fort Wayne's populace fought to save the city from the flood waters that poured over the banks of the St. Mary, St. Joseph and Maumee Rivers. Of the estimated 50,000 volunteers who joined in the effort, 30,000 were students. Some were as young as eight years old. Some were in college. Most of them were teenagers. When it was all over, their valor reduced Fort Wayne's mayor to tears and brought them credit for saving the city."

How soon, after assignment, does *The Digest* expect to see a completed manuscript? We seldom set deadlines, because our magazine is geared toward articles of lasting, rather than passing or topical, interest. Such material can usually run anytime. But as a rule, writers deliver two to three months after assignment.

How long should a manuscript run? Only as long as it take to tell your story. The average manuscript length on straight, reportorial journalism is 3,000 to 3,500 words. Some manuscripts run much longer, some shorter. Only after an article is purchased and scheduled do we start thinking about its final length in the magazine. So don't try to write to *The Digest* length—almost certainly, you'd exclude some top-notch material. Leave the condensation to us. This is a meticulous process in which article length is reduced by a third to a half or more—while preserving the style, flavor and integrity of the original manuscript and, more often than not, heightening the effect. The author, of course, reviews the edited version before publication.

How does a writer get his previously published material reprinted in *The Digest*? If your article has appeared in a major American magazine or newspaper, the chances are it's already been considered. In our search for article pickups, fillers and department items, our reading staff screens more than 140 publications each month, along with 2,000 books a year. If in doubt, simply submit tear sheets of your article. For reprinted articles, we pay $1,200 per *Reader's Digest* page for world periodical rights. This is split 50-50 between the original publication and the writer.

What kinds of articles is *The Digest* looking for? The best advice: read and study the magazine. You'll find our subject matter as varied as all human experience. Here are some titles from a single typical issue: "Beirut Under Siege," "Why Our Weather Is Going Wild," "Help Keep Your Teen-Age Driver Alive," "Are You a Man or a Wimp?", "The Real 'Lessons of Vietnam,'" "The Day Jessica Was Born," "Troubled Waters for Our Coast Guard," "Dancing Ground of the Sun," "Top Secret: Is There Sex in Russia?," "Trapped in a Sunken Ship," "New Ways to Buy and Sell Houses," "From Cuba With Hate: The Crime Wave Castro Sent to America." The common thread that weaves through all these articles is reader involvement. When we deal with major concerns—child abuse, government waste, Mideast tensions, breast cancer—we want a constructive approach that goes beyond the problem itself and points the way toward solution or hope. In the same way, we want profiles that go beyond merely "interesting" or "successful" people; we want to celebrate those who inspire by their example. "Chi Chi Rodriguez: Golf's Ace with Heart" was typical. Here's how Jolee Edmondson opened her article:

"It was another tournament town, another cardboard hotel room, another evening spent staring at the too blue, too orange TV images atop the Formica-covered bureau. Juan 'Chi Chi' Rodriguez, vying for the lead at the 1967 Texas Open in San Antonio, was practicing putts on the carpet and thinking about the birdies that had got away that afternoon. The drone of the evening news suddenly riveted his attention: a reporter was interviewing a distraught woman whose home in Illinois had been destroyed by a tornado. All she had left were the clothes she had on. Rodriguez was so moved that he made a pact with himself. If he bagged the trophy the following day, he would send the tornado relief fund $5,000. The next day he won—and so did the tornado victims."

A prime article category is the personal happening or awakening. In "Lure of the Winter Beach," Jean George stumbled onto one of nature's many magical surprises and had an experience everyone can readily share and appreciate. She opened her article this way:

"After a storm several winters ago, a friend asked me to check on her Long Island beach house. So one bright, windy day I bundled against the cold and drove out to the edge of the Atlantic Ocean. I imagined a dreary scene—an abandoned cottage set among pines, stirred by mournful winds. But the instant I climbed from my car my senses came awake. The air smelled clean as I looked out on a brilliant waterscape. The sea was a violet-blue, the sky turquoise, and the beach, which last summer had sloped gently, was no steep, scooped-out and luminous. Crabs scurried for burros and gulls spiraled down on them, like paper airplanes against the sky. At the water's edge, empty shells that whisper when summer waves turn them now made shrill, whistling sounds."

What does *The Digest* look for in writing? Clarity. Straight, simple sentences in simple, direct language. We also want the writer to show us, through solid example or anecdote—not just tell us—through gen-

eral statements without anything to back them up. The best writing evokes an emotion and gets the reader to experience what the writer experienced—whether shock, affection, amusement. When he wrote his hard-hitting article on "Auto Theft Turns Pro," Thomas R. Brooks combined fact, viewpoint, emotion and anecdote in a deceptively simple, straightforward lead:

"Every 28 seconds, somewhere in the United States, a car is stolen. That's 1.1 million vehicles a year. If your turn is next, chances are you will never get your car back. If you do, it possibly will have been stripped for parts. When Connecticut police showed a West Hartford owner his new Buick Riviera—minus fenders, hood, doors and wheels—he wept."

Above all, in the writing we publish, *The Digest* demands accuracy—down to the smallest detail. Our team of 83 researchers scattered through 19 cities around the world scrutinizes every line of type, checking every fact and examining every opinion. For an average issue, they will check 3,500 facts with 1500 sources. So watch your accuracy. There's nothing worse than having an article fall apart in our research checking because an author was a little careless with his reporting. We make this commitment routinely, as it guarantees that the millions of readers who believe something simply because they saw it in *Reader's Digest* have not misplaced their trust.

How to Submit Brief Anecdotes to *Reader's Digest*: Have you read—or heard—something interesting or amusing you would like to share? Although *Readers' Digest* does not read unsolicited article-length manuscripts, it welcomes short contributions. Payment is made on publication:

$400 for Life in These United States. Contributions must be true, unpublished stories from your own experience, revealing adult human nature and providing appealing or humorous sidelights on the American scene. Maximum length: 300 words. Address: Life in U.S. Editor.

$400 for true, unpublished stories used in Humor in Uniform (experiences in the armed services), Campus Comedy (life at college), Tales Out of School (highschool anecdotes), and All in a Day's Work (humor on the job). $35 to the first contributor of each item from a published source used in any of these departments. Maximum length: 300 words. Address: Humor in Uniform, Campus Comedy, Tales Out of School or All in a Day's Work Editor.

$50 for an original item for Toward More Picturesque Speech. $35 for the first contributor of a published item. Address: Picturesque Speech Editor.

For items used in Laughter, the Best Medicine, Notes From All Over, Personal Glimpses, Points to Ponder, Quotable Quotes and elsewhere: $35 to the first contributor of an item from print or electronic media; $30 per *Reader's Digest* two-column line for original material. Original poetry is not solicited. Address: Excerpt Editor.

Original contributions—which become our property upon acceptance and payment by *Reader's Digest*—should be typewritten. Previously published material must have the source's name, date and page number. Please address your submission to the appropriate features editor; for electronic mail, put feature name under Subject. Include your name, address, phone number and date; in e-mail, make this part of your Message.

Contributions Cannot Be Acknowledged or Returned

Categories: Nonfiction—Education—General Interest—Health—Inspirational—Interview—Physical Fitness—Society—Medicine—HumorHuman Interest—Profiles—Opinion—Personal Experience

CONTACT: (Appropriate Feature) Editor
Material: All
Reader's Digest Rd.
Pleasantville NY 10570-7000
Phone: 914-238-1000
Fax: 914-238-6390
E-mail: readersdigest@notes.compuserve.com
Website: www.readersdigest.com

Rearview

Rearview is constantly looking for submissions of all styles of poetry, black and white artwork and photography, and very short stories and vignettes. We suggest before you submit that you read these guidelines carefully and look over back issues of *Rearview* to get the feel of what we're looking for. All contributors receive one complimentary copy. Accepted work will appear in the print edition and may appear in the edition highlights online as well.

Poetry: We are currently looking for poetry of all styles, with a special emphasis on narrative poetry. We acquire First North American Serial Rights. We accept simultaneous submissions and previously published works, if the situation is noted in the submission.

All submissions should be made via email to rearview quarterly@yahoo.com. Submissions should include three to seven poems in the body of the email, along with your name and e-mail address. A cover letter is optional. We will respond within three months. If accepted, you will be asked for a brief biography.

Short Stories: We will occasionally publish very short stories of exceptional quality. Short stories must be less than 1.000 words and relate to our central theme of memoir and narrative works.

All submissions should be sent in the body of an email to rearviewquarterly@yahoo.com. Please include your name and email address, along with a cover letter if you wish. We will respond within three months, but if accepted the work may be held for publication in future issues.

Art and Photography: We accept black and white photography and line drawings for the front and back covers, as well as several places within, *Rearview Magazine*. We acquire One Time Rights on artwork. Submissions should be fairly small in size. Please send submissions to rearviewquarterly@yahoo.com; we accept attachments or urls. In your email, please include a title to your artwork, your name, and your email address.

Individual authors retain all rights to their work.

Categories: Arts—Photography—Poetry—Writing

CONTACT: rearviewquarterly@yahoo.com
Material: All
PO Box 486
Sudbury MA 01776
E-mail: rearviewquarterly@yahoo.com
Website: rearview.domynoes.net

Recreation News

Recreation News

Most feature articles in *Recreation News* come from freelance writers or outside contractors. Although we have many fine writers whose work consistently appears on our pages, you can increase your chances of breaking into the lineup if your story meets certain criteria. The following guidelines can help you tilt the odds in your favor.

What We Want

Your article must fit our publication. Our target readership is government and corporate employees working in the National Capital Region. They want to know about relaxing, stimulating, and interesting activities for their leisure time. Your story must address that need. Most articles we reject are turned down because they have little to do with recreation or are too far out of our geographical region.

Most of our features cover destinations and activities within a day or weekend drive of Baltimore/Washington, D.C. (i.e. Maryland, Virginia, West Virginia, Delaware, Pennsylvania, New Jersey and North Carolina.) Yes, our readers do travel out of the region, but most of our readers' leisure time is spent near home. We rarely cover foreign travel. We purchase rights for one-time and electronic use and will accept certain reprints.

Mechanics

Recreation News stories are relatively short. Our longest pieces—those featured on our cover—seldom exceed 1,500 words. Long features run up to 1,100 words. Short features about daytrips, activities, or destinations around the Baltimore/Washington-area run about 750 words. A sidebar, or information box, listing pertinent contact information, hours, rates, etc. is required.

We prefer electronic submissons. An MS Word .doc file is best; a flat .txt file is second best. We prefer that you submit your stories via e-mail. If you chose to submit hard copy, it must be scanable.

Photos are important to selling and telling your story. We prefer .jpg files at 150 dpi or better resolution. If you send actual photos or slides, **send an SASE if you want the materials back**. We cannot be responsible for their condition.

A word to the wise: Appropriate standard spelling and grammar always count!

Approach and Style

Recreation News strives for a lively, informal style. That does not mean wordiness or endless tangents. It does mean a lean and brisk conversational tone. Try to give your article a fresh point of view and, if possible, cover some out-of-the-ordinary subject matter. Your article must go beyond the self-serving listing of information doled out by visitors' bureaus, travel agencies, DMOs or PR firms. Use quotes from visitors to the sites or the participants in a particular activity, and let them express their thoughts about how they feel. If they happen to be federal employees and/or from around Baltimore or Washington, even better! Additionally, particularly with destination pieces, comments from colorful locals spice up a story. Remember, you can catch our eye faster with a piece about a little-known location or activity rather than with one about a subject everyone already knows about.

We don't use "pans." We aim to present the best opportunities, not criticize poor ones. We are "investment counselors," helping our readers to wisely invest their precious leisure time. If a location or experience is poor, we don't want the story.

Avoid writing in the first person and present tense. Only use the first person or present tense if it is **demonstrably** the best way to tell the story.

Rarely do we accept pieces focusing on a single resort, hotel, inn, or restaurant or lodge. You stand a much better chance of scoring with us by expanding your coverage to a wider scope. Do give passing mention to available lodging and dining facilities, but only as sidebar material. Remember, no blatant puffery.

Recreation News does not accept poetry, "my best/worst experiences," religious, sectarian, political, or "reflection" articles.

Our Editorial Calendar

We plan and assign articles anywhere from six months to a year in advance; plan accordingly. In other words, do not wait until the snow falls to query us about a skiing or ice-fishing piece.

December is always the ski issue, April is golf, July is theme parks. **Article deadling is always the first of the month previous to publication**. For example, stories for the July issue are due June 1.

Acceptance and Payment

If we accept your article, we will contact you.

Recreation News pays on publication. Rates vary, depending on length, placement, previous publication and other factors negotiated between the author and the editor or publisher. As a general rule, rates range from $50 (reprint) to a ceiling of $300 for a first North American printing of an original cover story. All articles are submitted on speculation.

Please Note: Submissions from first-time contributors are **always** taken "on spec," no exceptions. Regardless whether we asked for the story or it is a blind submission, *Recreation News* reserves the right to reject a first timer's submission **without benefit of a kill fee** if we feel it does not meet our requirements.

If you have any questions, contact Reed Hellman, Editor, at the address below.

Categories: Nonfiction—Adventure—Recreation—Sports—Regional: Baltimore/Washington, D.C. area

CONTACT: Reed Hellman, Editor
8109 Dogwood Rd
Windsor Mill MD 21244
Phone 410-944-4852
E-mail: editor@recreationnews.com
Website: www.recreationnews.com

Red Rock Review

Manuscripts must be mailed flat in a large manila (clasp-style) envelope. Do not fold pages into a letter-sized envelope.

Submissions must include a cover letter and a self-addressed, stamped envelope for return of manuscripts.

Manuscripts must be legibly typed or computer-generated on 8½" x 11" white bonded paper. Use standard fonts or typefaces (Courier, Helvetica, or Times) and standard font sizes (10 point for typing, 12 point on computers).

Freshly typed or printed manuscripts or clear, fresh photocopies are required.

Fiction must be no more than 7,500 words; essays must be no more than 5,000 words; poems must be no more than 80 lines.

Short Fiction and Essay Submissions (Suggested):

One-inch margins all around each page. Indent new paragraphs five spaces or ½"; justify left margin. Justification of right margin is not necessary.

Name, address, and phone number appear single-spaced in the top left corner of page one.

Approximate word count appears in the top right corner of page one.

Title (in CAPS) and byline (including name) appear single-spaced and centered 1/3 of the way down the first page.

A header including last name, key word from title, and page number appears on subsequent pages. The header appears in the left corner ½" down from the top of the page and 1" in from the left edge.

Text is double-spaced. Do not add extra blank lines between paragraphs unless creating section breaks.

Poetry Submissions (Suggested):

Left and right margins are set at the discretion of the poet; top margin (and bottom if necessary) should be 1".

Name, address, and phone number appear single-spaced in the left corner of every page.

Include key word from title and page numbers (top right corner of page) if a poem goes over one page.

Lines of text may be single- or double-spaced.

Send all correspondence and submissions to *Red Rock Review*, Richard Logsdon, Editor, Department of English J2A, Community College Southern Nevada, 3200 East Cheyenne Avenue, North Las Vegas, Nevada 89030.

We do not consider general submissions between June 1 and August 31.

The *Red Rock Review*, a literary journal published twice annually by the Community College of Southern Nevada and edited by Dr. Richard Logsdon, is dedicated to the publication of fine contemporary literature. We invite submissions of poetry, fiction, and creative non-fiction as well as book reviews. We do not publish literary criticism.

Red Rock Review Homepage:

If you have questions about the material on this web page, please contact Todd Moffett at todd_moffett@ccsn.nevada.edu.

Categories: Fiction—Poetry—Short Stories

CONTACT: Dr. Richard Logsdon
Material: All
English Dept. J2A
Community College of Southern Nevada
3200 East Cheyenne Ave.
North Las Vegas NV 89030

Redbook

Redbook is targeted to young married women between 25 and 44 who define themselves as smart, capable and happy with their lives. Each issue is a provocative mix of features geared to entertain and inform them, including:

• News stories on contemporary social issues that strike a universal chord and reveal the emotional ramifications; • First person essays about dramatic pivotal moments in a woman's life; • Marriage articles with an emphasis on strengthening the relationship; • Short parenting features on how to deal with universal health and behavioral issues; • Reporting exciting trends in women's lives.

Writers are advised to read at least the last six issues of the magazine (available in most libraries) to get a better understanding of appropriate subject matter and treatment.

We prefer to see detailed queries, rather than completed manuscripts, and suggest that you provide us with some sources/experts. Please enclose two or more samples of your writing, as well as a stamped, self-addressed envelope.

The *Redbook* Short Story Contest has been discontinued, but we continue to welcome high quality, accessible short stories.

Writer's Guidelines for Fiction: Thank you for your interest in *Redbook*. We publish approximately 15 short stories a year, and we welcome unsolicited short story manuscripts. Our fiction has received such prestigious honors as the National Magazine Award for Fiction and inclusion in *Prize Stories/The O. Henry Awards* and *The Best American Short Stories*.

Redbook's target reader is a woman between the ages of 25 and 45 who is or was married, has children, and generally is employed outside the home. Because she's a bright, well-informed individual with varied interests, she's not solely concerned with fiction that reflects her own life—although most of our stories deal with topics of specific interest to women: relationships, marriage, parenthood, relatives, friendships, career situations, financial problems, and so forth.

All submissions should be typed and double-spaced and accompanied by a self-addressed, stamped envelope. (If you do not send an SASE, you will not hear from us unless we are interested in buying the story.) Our reply time is usually 8 to 10 weeks. We receive approximately thirty-five thousand submissions per year and take every care in handling them, but we cannot be responsible for the receipt or the condition of the manuscript. (In the interest of protecting the original manuscript, you may submit a legible photocopy.)

Redbook publishes short stories 25 manuscript pages or fewer; the average length is 15 pages. Payment for a short story begins at $1,000. *Redbook* buys First North American Serial Rights and pays on acceptance. Most stories are scheduled within a year of purchase, and prior to publication, short story galleys are sent to the author. Please note that we do not consider unsolicited poetry and novels.

Sorry, but we are unable to provide complimentary copies.

Categories: Fiction—Nonfiction—Arts—Beauty—Biography—Book Reviews—Business—Children—Cooking—Crime—Entertainment—Fashion—Food/Drink—Health—Interview—Marriage—Mass Communications—Money & Finances—Parenting—Psychology—Sexuality—Society—Women's Fiction—Women's Issues

CONTACT: Lisa Lombardi, Fiction Editor
Material: Fiction
CONTACT: Patty Curtis, Health Editor
Material: Health
CONTACT: Andrea Bauman
Material: All except fiction and health
224 W. 57th St.
New York NY 10019
Phone: 212-649-3450
Fax: 212-581-8114
Website: www.Redbookmag.com

R-U

Referee

The Style Guide is developed for the convenience of our writers and editors. When we receive an article from a freelance writer, the editor will consider it for publication.

Rates vary from five to 10 cents per published word, depending on how we use the text. We may decide to hold your submission on file until space opens up or we will pick a month to run it. Scheduled articles need standard contracts that will be sent to the writer to sign and return for payment.

We accept submissions on speculation, but appreciate direct queries, either by mail or e-mail. No phone calls, please.

Thanks again for your interest.

WHAT WE ARE LOOKING FOR

Referee publishes three main types of articles: features, sport specific columns and regularly appearing articles ("Profiles," "Law," "Back To Basics," etc.).

Features

We want articles that speak to our readership—sports officials. The content must focus on officiating. We are interested in articles that help our readers improve an aspect of their officiating, articles about unique or very successful officials, articles dissecting the major issues that officials face and articles that delve into certain officiating "philosophies." *Referee* also publishes several "Banner Features." Examples of these are:

• **You Are There**: Two-page features that focus on a famous sporting event through the eyes of an official. It is almost always necessary to interview one or more of the officials from whatever game or event is being covered.

• **Basic Training**: Two-page features that focus on a single aspect of officiating and give a "basic" how-to lesson on that topic, including tips and expert opinions from several officials in a variety of sports and levels.

Sport-Specific Columns

Sport-specific columns may pertain to rules, mechanics or officiating philosophy. Rules columns must include parenthetical rulebook, casebook or approved ruling references to the pertinent rules. In all cases, the NFHS reference should be listed first, followed by the NCAA reference. Other rulebook references may follow in any order. Use semicolons to separate codes. Here is and example of correct referencing: (NFHS 6-3-1A, 7-4-1 THROUGH 3, 6.2.2C; NCAA 6-2-1; Pro 6-5).

Following are the required references for each sport: Basketball—NFHS, NCAA men's and NCAA women's; Baseball—NFHS, NCAA, pro; Football—NFHS, NCAA; Soccer—NFHS, NCAA, FIFA; Softball—NFHS, NCAA, ASA, USSSA.

Regular Appearing Articles: To get a better feel of articles that appear monthly in *Referee* and that are not sport specific, request a sample issue at submissions@referee.com.

PAYMENT

You will receive a contract soon after your article is received, accepted and edited. Payment will be sent within 30 days of the date we received the signed contract or the completed writing effort. Our standard rate varies from 5 to 10 cents per published word. Return your contract as soon as possible.

SCHEDULES

The due dates have been carefully selected, so we need your help in staying on the schedule provided. Obviously, we work well ahead of the publication date in this business. Early due dates allow us ample time to edit your work and work with you on any potential changes. **We welcome early submissions!** If you feel like cranking out two or three articles, go ahead and do so. If an emergency threatens a deadline, let us know immediately. Adjustments can be made if we know early enough.

SIZE AND SPECULATIONS

All sport-specific articles should be around 500-1,000 words; features vary from 1,000-3,000 words. Items must be typed and double-spaced. Please use our on-line style sheet, found at submissions@referee.com, when writing your material.

SUBMITTING MATERIAL

The best way to submit your work is via e-mail. Our e-mail address is submissions@referee.com.

We also accept mailed articles on high-density computer disks.

Categories: Nonfiction—Law—Sports/Recreation—Sports Officiating

CONTACT: Jim Arehart, Senior Managing Editor
Material: All
Referee Enterprises, Inc.
PO Box 161
Franksville WI 53126
Phone: 262-632-8855
Fax: 262-632-5460
E-mail: jarehart@referee.com
Website: www.referee.com

Rehab Technology

Please refer to Oildom Publishing.

Remembrance
A Celebration of Life

REMEMBRANCE ANTHOLOGY GUIDELINES:

A tribute to lives lived well—people who are so memorable, they will never be forgotten.

Publication date: Anthology in book-zine format, published annually.

Book Formats: one or more of the following, traditional paper (either hardback or paperback), electronic (ebooks and/or audio).

Poetry and other writings (articles, prayers, etc.) about loved ones, their lives, and how they touched us and others while they were alive.

Lengths: Open for all poems, articles, prayers, etc. Manuscripts of all lengths will be considered.

Contact us for the next deadline for submissions for *Remembrance*.

Rights: One-time use in book form (all formats). Considers reprints if author owns rights.

Poets and writers should send a bio to accompany their writings in the anthology.

Contributors must send note (email or by regular mail) stating that he/she would like the writing(s) included in the published anthology. Submit up to 5 manuscripts, either by email or regular mail (see below).

Contributors will receive one copy of the finished anthology.

Categories: Family—Lifestyle

CONTACT: Eugene Boone
Material: All
RSVP Press
129 Thurman Lane
Clinton TN 37716
E-mail: rsvppress@yahoo.com

Reminisce Magazine

Reminisce helps readers "bring back the good times" through true stories and vintage photographs. Any appropriate photo or memory is welcome, as long as it originated from 1900 through the 1960s.

We also publish a sister magazine to *Reminisce* called *Reminisce EXTRA*. It's similar in format and is available by a separate bimonthly subscription—mailed on alternating months. This lets subscribers choose whether to receive a magazine every month or every other month. Neither magazine contains any paid advertising.

Our editorial style is relaxed and conversational, so please write your memory the way you'd relate it to a friend. We invite "regular" people like you to tell their own stories. As a result, most of the issue is written by our readers who are eager to share their memories. We rarely use freelance-written material.

Because our features don't often run more than 700 words, we cannot take the time to read lengthy submissions or books. We especially like short items with a first-person "I remember when" angle. An exception is an interesting article describing the origin of a certain product or business with a nostalgic tie.

Before you send anything:
Be sure the first page of your submission contains your name, mailing address, phone number and E-mail address, if available. Don't forget to include the year or decade (can be approximate) in which your memory took place.

Write your name and address on the back of each photo, preferably with soft pencil or marker, and identify any information you know regarding who, what and when. You're welcome to send a photocopy of an original photo (for reference only, since photocopies cannot be reproduced for publication). Or, we recommend that you first have a reprint made of cherished family photos before sending them. If we're able to use the story, we'll ask to borrow the original or a sharp reprint. We are also able to use high-resolution scans sent via E-mail. Photos are returned upon publication.

We do not publish fiction. Instead, we invite folks to tell their own true-life stories—personal reminiscences of years gone by...memorable people who affected their lives...interesting descriptions of trips, adventures and family anecdotes...seasonal or holiday memories (these may be submitted at any time of the year)...recollections of now-famous people they knew "back when"...little-known historical items, etc. We're especially glad to get humorous anecdotes. We will accept previously published material, as long as the story had minimal exposure and appeared in a "non-nostalgia" publication.

• Due to the high volume of submissions we receive, and in an effort to involve as many contributors as possible in this "reader-written" magazine, we often edit or excerpt longer stories to fit within one of our "short memory" departments.

Any submission may also be considered for publication in a *Reminisce* or Reiman Publications book or related product, promotional piece or on our web-site.

Reminisce pays only for "feature" stories. Photos and shorter memories earn contributors a unique gift they can display on a bookshelf or coffee table—a Classic Red '57 Chevy car bank. This popular keepsake car identifies them as a "Reminisce Staffer." We normally pay $50 per full-page feature, plus the tabletop Chevy.

If you would like a response regarding your submission, or if you're sending photos you'd like to have returned, be sure to enclose a self-addressed return envelope, with the proper return postage. Due to postage costs and our limited amount of staff, we cannot respond to submissions that do not have an SASE.

After you send us photos or articles, and if you've included an SASE for a response, please be patient. We receive an awful lot of material, and often it takes us a while to catch up.

Professional/stock photos: Separate guidelines and payment rates are available upon request. Write to Trudi Bellin at the address below.—Revised Jan 2001

Categories: Nonfiction—Photography—Short Stories

CONTACT: Submissions Editor
Material: All
5927 Memory Lane
Greendale WI 53129
E-mail: editors@reminisce.com
Website: www.reminisce.com

Renaissance Magazine

Renaissance Magazine accepts unsolicited manuscripts related to the Renaissance and Middle Ages, including but not limited to: historical articles, martial arts, recipes/culinary arts, travel, interviews with artisans, articles on the SCA and related re-enactment groups, etc. Before pursuing any topic, please query first to confirm our need for it.

Average article is approx. 3,000 words in length although longer work will be considered. Sidebar information is also encouraged, as well as graphics, including copyright-free logos, illustrations and photographs (finder's fee: $7.50/image). *Renaissance Magazine* takes full North American serial rights on all work accepted.

Those interested in writing for *Renaissance Magazine* on a regular basis as a staff writer must query first, and include a brief bio/resume and sample article. If accepted, a writing contract will be mailed to that individual and this person will be expected to contribute articles on a regular basis.

All submissions should be set up in the standard manuscript format (title, name, address, phone number, approx. word count on title page, and every subsequent page fully numbered). Cover letter should include a brief bio and credits, where you heard of *Renaissance Magazine*, and any other pertinent information. An SASE must be included with your submission to be considered. We encourage writers to e-mail their articles directly, to save on mailing and paper costs. E-mail all queries and submissions to the address below.

Work may receive a written critique and editorial suggestions. All work will be edited to some degree, to match our editorial format. No one need submit articles who is not willing to have their work edited. Allow 3-6 weeks for a response.

Although all writers will be notified of acceptance within a few weeks of submission, we cannot guarantee a publication date. However when the article is scheduled for an upcoming issue, we will attempt to notify the writer before publication. We reserve the right to reject previously accepted work at any time and for any reason.

Book Reviews: We accept unsolicited reviews of Renaissance and Medieval-related books, including fiction and nonfiction (500 words max.). Please include the original cover of the book or a GOOD photocopy of the book jacket along with review. Authors of Renaissance and Medieval-related books (fiction or nonfiction) are encouraged to submit a review copy of their book to Kim Guarnaccia, Editor, at the address below.

Editorial Suggestions: We encourage all readers and writer to make suggestions on what kind of articles should be published in *Renaissance Magazine*. To do so, call, write or e-mail Kim Guarnaccia, Editor.

PAYMENT
Payment of $.08 per published word is made upon publication. Two (2) contributor copies will also be given to each contributor, and more copies are available upon request. Direct your queries to Kim Guarnaccia, Editor.

SAMPLE ISSUES
Sample issue: $9; 1 year subscription (6 issues) $29; 2 year subscription (12 issues) $56. To order, make checks payable to Renaissance Magazine and mail to SFS, PO Box 82, Vandalia, OH 45377, Attn. Renaissance. US funds only. Overseas orders, please add an additional $4 per year to order. Back issues are available; please query first for prices.

Categories: History

CONTACT: Kim Guarnaccia, Editor
Material: As Above
13 Appleton Rd.
Nantucket MA 02554
Phone: 508-825-8864
Fax: 508-325-5992
E-mail: editor@renaissancemagazine.com
Website: www.renaissancemagazine.com

R-U

Reptiles Magazine

So you want to write for REPTILES magazine? That's great, provided you know your subject. REPTILES publishes articles about a wide variety of reptile- and amphibian-related topics, and all of our authors are experts on what they write about.

Who qualifies as an expert? If you have some experience with the animals you wish to write about, or a particular type of setup, that's the best place to start. Long-term success with keeping reptiles and/or amphibians is great, and a track record of successful breeding efforts is even better. This type of experience is much preferred over an author who simply scans a book or does some brief research on the Internet before churning out an article.

What should you write about? Topics could include a particular reptile or amphibian species or group of animals, herp-hunting trips you've experienced, breeding tales, interviews with "name" people in the reptile world, humorous accounts, etc. Articles about disease are typically assigned to our veterinarian authors, but if you're a vet with expertise in treating herps, you are welcome to send health-related articles.

Articles about a particular species of herp, or family of herps, should contain a bit of natural history as well as, and this is most important, detailed care and husbandry of the animal(s) in captivity. Include info about tank size, food, temperature, tank setup, potential cagemates, temperament, lighting, potential lifespan, breeding info, etc. Reptiles is mostly intended for the beginner to intermediate enthusiast, so include as much basic info as you can.

You are welcome to send any article to us for review. Submissions are sent "on spec." This means "on speculation," which translates as, "You send, we read, we either accept or we don't." We're under no obligation to accept your article. It may be a while (few weeks to a month... maybe even longer) before you hear back from us. Please be patient. Contacting us once to make sure we received your materials is fine. Pestering us repeatedly could result in your article being returned just to get you off our backs. You may query first, by letter, e-mail or phone. But even if we listen to your idea and tell you to go ahead and write the article, the submission will still be on spec. Our telling you to go ahead with your article idea does not guarantee acceptance once we receive it.

General comments about writing style. Articles should be easy for beginner hobbyists to understand. For the most part, we prefer a somewhat folksy tone to our articles, and some humor is always great, of course. Break the text up using subheads for specific sections. Show some pizzazz in your opening comments. Avoid beginning your article with a comment such as, "The Uromastyx lizards have grown tremendously in popularity." We know that. Jazz up your opening comments, and grab the reader immediately.

Regarding references: It is fine to send us a list of references, and you should because we sometimes use them to fact check information in articles. But you should not expect a lengthy list of references to appear at the end of your article. While we may run a short references list on occasion, we don't have the room or the inclination to run an exhaustive references section. References may appeal to some of our readers, but if the references are out of print, obscure papers or foreign publications that our readers cannot get hold of, they are of little use. Occasionally, if an article really warrants a lengthy list of references, we may decide to list them on our Web site, and reference that in the article. But for the most part, we are not trying to present technical papers or dissertations that need a large reference backup.

Regarding charts and diagrams: These should be used sparingly. If you send a chart or diagram that you did not create yourself, you need to let us know the source. We cannot simply reprint one that has already appeared elsewhere. Detailed charts with a mind-numbing glut of figures typically turn off our readers, so keep charts to a minimum, please. Include them only if their information cannot be condensed and included in the article proper.

Regarding acknowledgments: Even though it's a nice gesture, we prefer that you thank the people who helped you with your article in person or with a personal letter, not in print. Acknowledgments are nice for those receiving them, but they have zero benefit for our readers and take up valuable space that could otherwise be used for text/photos.

When mailing us materials that you want back, such as articles, computer disks or photos, be sure to provide a self-addressed, stamped envelope with sufficient postage to cover their return in case we choose not to keep them (or for return after we're done using them). You can e-mail articles to us as text-only attachments. You can also send articles using regular mail; include a hard copy as well as a copy on disk, if possible.

Got photos to go with your article? Many of our writers supply their own photos, and you can, too, if you have some you'd like to include in your article. Be forewarned, however: Even though you send photos specifically for your articles, we may still use other photographers' photos to illustrate your article. As for format, we prefer 35mm slides. Good-quality prints can work, too, but slides are best. As for digital photos: We prefer not to work with them. However, if you must send digitals they need to be sized at least 5x7 inches at 300 dpi, tif or eps. Remember to include captions.

If we like your article, we will send you a contract telling you we want to purchase it for potential future use in the magazine. You'll need to sign the contract and return a copy to us before we can use the article. It is unlikely that we will be able to tell you exactly when the article will appear in the magazine. You will be provided two contributor copies upon publication.

Of course, anything that appears in the magazines is subject to editing by our staff.

Pay rates. Prices can vary, depending on length and level of technicality. We generally pay $300 for a 2,500 to 3,000-word article; less for shorter pieces. If you include good photos with your article, the price will increase. For a 3,000-word article with a good selection of usable photos, you could receive between $500 and $700. We do not pay for Table of Contents photos or cover insets if they appear elsewhere in the magazine. Payment is made upon publication, during the cover month of the issue in which your work appears (e.g., you will be paid in May for an article that appears in the May issue).

What rights do we purchase? We buy only first-time North American rights. All rights revert back to you after we publish your article/photos. Do not send articles that have been published elsewhere. We also do not accept simultaneous submissions.

Where to send your stuff. Our mailing address is Reptiles, P.O. Box 6050, Mission Viejo, CA 92690. E-mail can be sent to reptiles@bowtieinc.com. If you have further questions, phone us at (949) 855-8822.

We make every effort to handle materials with the utmost care and respect. However, we cannot be held responsible for lost or damaged materials.

Categories: Animals

CONTACT: Editor
Reptiles
PO Box 6050
Mission Viejo CA 92690
Phone: 949-855-8822
E-mail: reptiles@bowtieinc.com
Website: www.reptilesmagazine.com

The Retired Officer Magazine

Audience: Commissioned and warrant officers, families, and surviving spouses of the seven uniformed services: Army, Marine Corps, Navy, Air Force, Coast Guard, Public Health Service, and National Oceanic and Atmospheric Administration—both those in active components and members of the National Guard and Reserve.

Sample magazine on request with 9x12 SASE.

Editorial Requirements

Topics: Current military/political affairs; recent military history, especially Vietnam and Korea; financial planning; health and fitness; military family; retirement lifestyles; travel; and general interest. No fiction, poetry, or fillers. Original material only; no reprints.

Format: MS Word-compatible file. No footnotes.

Deadlines: Feature articles normally are scheduled six months in advance.

Queries: Submit detailed query before sending manuscript. Enclose or attach copies of published clips and résumé. Unsolicited manuscripts are rarely accepted.

Style: Active voice, nontechnical, with direct quotes. Optimistic, upbeat theme. Use The Associated Press Stylebook and Libel Manual.

Length: Features, up to 2,500 words; mini-features, up to 1,400 words.

Terms: First rights, to include Internet and reprint rights.

Payment: Features, up to $1,800; mini-features, up to $1,000. Payment on acceptance.

Submit to: Managing Editor, Military Officers Association of America, at address below or e-mail editor@moaa.org. Enclose SASE for return of hard copy submissions.

Response time: Three months. No phone calls, please.

Photographs: Original color transparencies suitable for color separation preferred. Digital photos must be at highest pixel size and resolution supported by your camera. $75 for one-eighth page, $125 for one-fourth page, $175 for one-half page, $250 for full page. 5x7 or 8x10 black-and-white glossies occasionally acceptable. $20 for each black-and-white photo used. Prefer captions and credit line on separate sheet. Include SASE for return of photos.

Categories: Nonfiction—Military

CONTACT: Col. Warren S. Lacy, USA-Ret., Managing Editor
201 N Washington St
Alexandria VA 22314-2539
Website: www.troa.org

Reunions Magazine

American mobility intensifies a desire to reunite with people/places to recapture what seem to be simpler times. Reunions touch everyone and can be with family, friends, classmates, associates, buddies, neighbors, survivors.

Reunions magazine is primarily for those actively involved in organizing reunions. Readers refer to us for practical ideas about searching, researching, planning, organizing and attending reunions, along with good stories.

Read *Reunions* magazine to discover our tastes. We welcome your queries.

Please address our readers. They are people organizing family, class, military and other reunions; or are searching (lost loves, friends, ancestors).

Give our readers what they want. They want to learn the nitty gritty of organizing successful reunions. Give help, suggestions, smashingly fresh new ideas, reunion advice and inspiration. What's special about your reunion? Where was it and why? Who was invited and why? What made attendees happy and wanting to come back?

Ease organizers' challenges, answer questions they don't know how to ask, solve problems before they know about them. Our readers ideas about getting people engaged, involved, enchanted by the idea of being part of a special group.

We highlight and examine ways to be a savvy reunion consumer. We point readers to wonderful places to stay and why they're special for reunions. They want products and services that make reunions special. Family reunions want ways to entertain kids, not just theme parks and video games but active play and exploring, involving all genera-

tions, grounding them with family, history, pride, strength, and fun.

Titles. Please be creative. Avoid using: Reunion, Reunions, The Reunion, A Reunion, Our Reunion, My Reunion. In fact anything with any of the foregoing titles is rarely read with eagerness.

Say it with "humor, expertise, passion, perseverance, creativity, a fresh approach"

Comments. We appreciate constructive feedback. If you have a complaint, tell us. If you have praise, tell others—though we'd not mind hearing praise too!

CONTENT GUIDELINES

Features are written mainly by readers and roughly fall into these categories.

• How-to articles about organizing reunions usually address single issues of relevance to many reunion groups. Examples include early decisions, how to formulate and follow through with plans, how to use convention and visitors bureaus, document reunions, plan games, make invitations and newsletters, etc.

• Personal stories. These articles encourage and inspire others initiating similar reunions. Articles elaborating on the reunion organizing process or search are preferred. We're partial to triumph stories. Many readers have similar stories to share, so unusual or heartwarming stories with unique aspects, twists or universal insights are more likely to be published. Topics include family, class and military reunion stories with humorous or poignant narratives, military buddies returning to the scene or genealogical searches with surprising results. When appropriate, feature articles should include additional sources, names, addresses, emails, websites, publication title, author, publisher, etc.

Departments

Reviews. Reunion books, movies, TV programs, computer software, videos or plays to be reviewed by persons with proven subject-matter expertise. Bio must accompany reviews. We welcome materials with requests for review.

RSVP: Inviting Examples. Share reunion invitations, include original sample (flat), its use, distribution and why it was effective.

Scrapbook. We accept clipped articles (recipes, cartoons, fliers) about reunions. Sources and dates must be identified. Credit is given (and a small fee paid) to the first contributor of material that is used.

Photos can accompany articles or be independent with a caption. They must be well-focused, tell a reunion story and identify name, address, phone number of owner, names of persons in the picture (unless it's a large group) and a signed publication permission release. Vertical photos are all considered for covers. Self-addressed, stamped envelopes (SASE) must accompany photos you wish returned.

Hot Spots. Tell us about exciting or unusual reunions places. Tell us where, how to get there, what's special, what they did for your reunion and why you'd go back.

Regular columns highlight single issues or current trends and must educate reunion organizers. Submissions about 1,000 words with universal and timeless appeal.

SPECIFICATIONS. E-mail is our preference. Please attach it in Microsoft Word and send to reunions@execpc.com. All mailed submissions must be typed and double-spaced. Send articles and queries to address below.

Payment. We are able to pay very little for unassigned work but are generous with extra copies of the issue.

Replies in up to two years. Possible 12-month delay between acceptance and publication.

Categories: Nonfiction—African-American—Children—Family—Games—General Interest—History—Lifestyle—Recreation—Relationships—Senior Citizens—Travel—Reunions

CONTACT: Submissions Editor
Material: All
PO Box 11727
Milwaukee WI 53211-0727
Phone: 414-263-4567
Fax: 414-263-6331
E-mail: reunions@execpc.com

Rhino

Annual Reading Period: April 1-October 1

Sorry, no electronic submissions at this time!

Basic Guidelines. Send 3-5 poems, typed, single-spaced, along with a short cover letter telling us a little bit about you, how you heard about *RHINO*, and/or your past publications, if you have any. Always include a SASE (self-addressed stamped envelope), and let us know whether we should use it for return of the poems or just for our response. (We can recycle unused poems, if you prefer. If you want them returned, be sure to put sufficient postage on the SASE.) Please also include your name, address, and phone number on each poem, for ease in contacting you. Send submission by first-class mail to RHINO, PO Box 591, Evanston, IL 60204.

Etiquette Note: Please do not send more than one submission during our reading period, April 1 to October 1, unless we request to see more via your first SASE. We will return extra submissions unread.

Sample Copy. As with any literary publication, it is always best to read the magazine first. You can read sample poems here at our website, and you can obtain a hard copy by sending a check or money order for $10 for the current issue or $5 for a back issue before 2001 and $8 for a back issue from 2001 on to RHINO, PO Box 591, Evanston, IL 60204. You can also purchase copies of RHINO at our workshops, readings, and at some bookstores and galleries in Chicago, its suburbs, and in central Illinois. We are our own distributors for now.

RHINO is looking for excellent poetry, translations, and short short fiction in any style. Send 3-5 poems OR 1-3 short prose pieces. Please note that we only read very short prose—pieces of 250-650 words—no novel excerpts, no long academic essays.

Submissions are read by multiple editors with various tastes, all looking for quality work. We have published formal poems, free verse, very accessible poems, wild experimentations with language, visual poems, prose poems, poems of stark beauty, and even funny poems. Sometimes we call ourselves "eclectic" in the best sense of the word. We are very proud of the content of RHINO and of the variety of the work we publish.

Annual Awards. Modest cash prizes are now awarded annually through our Editors' Prizes (no special application necessary) and through our READERS-WRITERS Contest, open to readers of RHINO. Details about the latter appear on the website when the new issue is pending or available, and on the inside back cover of the magazine.

Art: We occasionally print photos. (See RHINO 2000 for the photographs of Roger Pfingston and RHINO 2002 for the photographs of Liz Chilsen and Joanne Warfield.) Interested photographers should submit a group of 8x10 black and white photos for distribution throughout the magazine, or a possible center section. Again, enclose a SASE with sufficient postage for return of the photographs.

Acceptances: If we accept your work, we will ask you to sign a contract allowing us to publish it and ensuring that it is not previously published. We want first serial publication rights only, and the copyright reverts to you. Please credit RHINO with first publication if you republish your work in a book or anthology or on a website. On our contract, you can say yes or no about electronic publication of your work (or an excerpt of it) here on our website. We will also ask for a brief bio, a contributor's note, and a list, if you like, of people who might want to hear about the issue you are in. These names will not be added to our general mailing list. We will request a new clean copy of the accepted work and a diskette with your work in both MS Word and ASCII format for ease in typesetting. The diskette helps avoid typesetting errors, but please send it in appropriate packing to avoid damage, or we can't use it, anyway. We do not permit any revision of accepted work after this stage, though we may suggest slight revisions upon acceptance or during the proofreading process. We generally provide you with a proofing copy in late fall or early winter.

Rejections: When we reject submissions, please know that we have read your work with care. If we have brief comments that we think could help you, we will write them on the rejection slip. If you don't receive comments, then perhaps this particular work just wasn't right for us. Just do more market research, revise, write something new, and move on! Don't let it get you down! Occasionally we make pencil notations to alert you to typos or glitches in the manuscript you sent us. Etiquette Note: Such errors are a turn-off for some editors, and not a big deal for others, but do realize that errors can damage your credibility as an artist. Readers, like writers, do pay attention to small details; what if you get them wrong? So it's best to send us a carefully proofread manuscript, but don't worry too much if a small error slipped by your personal or technological spell check or grammar check. It happens. We'll do our best to edit/proofread your work if we publish it! Because of the volume of submissions, we cannot respond personally to most writers, but we do wish you well! Keep writing, and keep trying!

Categories: Poetry—Short Stories

CONTACT: Alice George, Editor
Material: Any
CONTACT: Alice George, Deborah or Nodler Rosen, Editors
Material: Any
PO Box 591
Evanston IL 60204
Website: www.rhinopoetry.org

River Town Gazette
Rockland County's Lifestyle Publication

At the *River Town Gazette*, our focus is on Entertainment and Information of interest to residents and tourists in the Historic River Towns of New York's Hudson Valley area.

Featuring Columns and Articles about: Automotive, Boating, Restaurants and Food, Home Improvement, Real Estate, Personal Improvement, Alternative Healing, Commuter Information, Cultural Events, Social Events, Style and more.

Categories: Nonfiction—Antiques—Architecture—Arts—Automobiles—Boating—Book Reviews—Business—Campus Life—Cartoons—Children—Collectibles—Comedy—Computers—Consumer—Crafts/Hobbies—Culture—Diet/Nutrition—Disabilities—Ecology—Entertainment—Family—Fashion—Film/Video—Fishing—Folklore—Food/Drink—Games—Gardening—General Interest—Health—Hobbies—Internet—Jewish Interest—Juvenile—Lifestyle—Marriage—Men's Issues—Money & Finances—Music—Mystery—Native American—New Age—Outdoors—Parenting—Photography—Politics—Psychology—Real Estate—Recreation—Regional—Relationships—Self Help—Senior Citizen—Singles—Society—Sports/Recreation—Teen—Television/Radio—Travel

CONTACT: Mark Kalan, Publisher
Material: All
PO Box 808
Nyack NY 10960
Phone: 845-353-0000
E-mail: info@rivertowngazette.com
Website: www.rivertowngazette.com

RiverSedge
The University of Texas-Pan American

RiverSedge is published twice yearly by The University of Texas-Pan American Press. The contents of the journal do not necessarily represent the viewpoints of the University.

RiverSedge welcomes submissions of art, photography, poetry, short stories and essays. Works may be submitted in either traditional or electronic media, but must be accompanied by postage and packaging if return is desired. Artwork should be reproducible in black and white. Please include telephone number. Payment is in copies. Rights revert to artists and writers.

Submission deadlines: Fall issue, November 15; Spring issue, April 15. Please remember to include a short bio with each submission. Address submissions to the address below or contact the editors by e-mail.

FICTION GUIDELINES

RiverSedge, a journal of arts and literature, seeks quality mainstream literary and experimental fiction, emphasizing that prose which has a regional Southwestern flavor or locale, but not excluding voices from other areas. Characters should be memorable and plots believable within the story's setting and context.

Our audience is educated and largely academic, but we are interested in work that transcends the campus and explores the real world in language and contexts accessible to lay readers.

Because of limited space, stories should not exceed 2,500 words. Payment is two copies upon publication. Short biographical sketch should accompany submission.

Submissions should be accompanied by SASE, or clear instructions not to return. Simultaneous submissions should be identified, although they are not prohibited. Computer disks in Macintosh format preferred.

Notification time is usually within 3 to 4 months, but may be sooner.

POETRY GUIDELINES

RiverSedge seeks quality mainstream literary and experimental poetry, emphasizing regional Southwestern flavor or locale, but not excluding voices from other areas. Any variety is welcomed, although most of the poetry we print is modern free verse. There are really no limitations on themes, topics, or language.

Our audience is educated and largely academic, but we are interested in work that transcends the campus and explores the real world in language and contexts accessible to lay readers. Poetry should be foolishly simple, but divinely insightful.

Because of limited space, poems of 25 or fewer lines are preferable, although longer ones are used on occasion, since quality and interest are more important than length.

Payment is two copies upon publication. Short biographical sketch should accompany submission.

Submissions should be accompanied by SASE, or clear instructions not to return. Simultaneous submissions should be identified, although they are not prohibited.

Notification time is usually within 3 to 4 months, but may be sooner.

Subscriptions: $12.00

Categories: Poetry—Short Stories

CONTACT: Director
Material: All
The University of Texas-Pan American
1201 W University Dr
Lamar Bldg Rm 9A
Edinburg TX 78539
Phone: 956-381-3638
Fax: 956-381-3697
E-mail: Bookworm@panam.edu

The Roanoker

The *Roanoker* magazine is a city magazine accepting stories relating to the Roanoke and New River Valley areas of Virginia. The magazine covers lifestyles, dining, history, homes, events, arts/culture

and business and is geared towards an upscale readership. Queries are accepted for feature-length stories in these topics and also for departmental shorts (150-300 words); contact the editorial department for more information.

Special annual features and issues:
- Education and schools (fall)
- Retirement in western Virginia (Sept/Oct)
- Roanoke-area Almanac/visitor and newcomer guide (Jan/Feb): Education, retirement, technology, real estate, arts and culture

Every-issue sections: • Dining in Roanoke area; • Festivals and special events; • Short news/cultural/human interest pieces (The Skinny)

Categories: Nonfiction—Consumer—Diet/Nutrition—Education—Food/Drink—Real Estate

CONTACT: Kurt Rheinheimer, Editor in Chief
Material: Lifestyle, Profile, Dining, Business
CONTACT: Jeffrey K. Wood, Associate Editor
Material: Events/Arts/New Business
Leisure Publishing
PO Box 21538
Roanoke VA
Phone: 540-989-6138
Fax: 540-989-7603

Rock and Ice

Rock and Ice, established in 1984, celebrates the high-energy sports of rock climbing, bouldering, mountaineering, ice climbing, and aid climbing. We are proud to be the industry's leading venue for world-class adventure writing, training and technical tips for climbers of all levels, hard-hitting gear reviews, and stunning photography. Our readers look to *Rock and Ice* as the authentic source of climbing information and inspiration, so their expectations for accuracy, detail and talent from our contributors are very high. Below are some suggestions on crafting your work to fit our needs.

Editorial Submissions

Rock and Ice is published nine times a year, or roughly every six weeks. Please submit all article proposals in a one-page query letter, preferably via email, to editor@bigstonepub.com. If this is your first time submitting to *Rock and Ice*, it's helpful if you can include clips of previously published work. Please be sure to read several issues of *Rock and Ice* to familiarize yourself with the voice and content of the magazine before submitting queries.

We pay $.35/word for published work.

Features: *Rock and Ice* features focus primarily on: profiles, destinations, current outdoor/climbing-related issues, survival stories and, occasionally, fiction. Features are 1200 to 3500 words in length, and require in-depth research, quotes, and talented writing. We do not publish trip reports.

Departments: These are good places for writers to begin a relationship with *Rock and Ice*. The departments have a specific focus and format, and are generally shorter than features.

Breaking News—short (100 to 500 words) write-ups of the latest feats, events, controversies, and access issues in the climbing world. Strong photos are a big plus when we are considering a piece for publication.

Spotlight—a 700-word profile or Q&A featuring an up-and-coming climber, or noteworthy person in the news.

Milestones—obituaries, generally 250 to 300 words in length, of well-known climbers.

Road Trips—covering the finest destinations in North America for rock and ice climbing. This department currently includes

SuperTopos, highly accurate and featured topos by SuperTopo.com founder Chris McNamara.

Famous Faces—a 500- to 800-word article opening with a stunning photo of a legendary North American alpine face (e.g. the North Face of the Grand Teton, the North Ridge of Mount Assiniboine) and highlighting a memorable story or adventure from the peak's history. A sidebar includes detailed Nuts and Bolts information, including a topo of the route(s) mentioned. You don't have to supply the photo, we can solicit that separately.

Performance—the latest training tips and techniques, presented in a detailed, easy-to-digest format for beginner and advanced climbers alike. We like to see the article focused around one or two top climbers and their training strategies. This section also includes Nutrition, dedicated to eating strategies for more power, endurance, etc, and generally ties into the training tips. Alternating positions with Nutrition every other issue is Field Medicine, focusing on, for example, how to treat a sprained ankle in the field or preventing heat stroke.

Scene—photos and brief, 100-word accounts of the latest gatherings, festivals, and events. This department also includes our Happenings calendar of upcoming events.

Field Tested Gear—our equipment reviews are a signature item of the magazine, and require expert (and exhaustive) field testing of gear in a certain category (i.e. two-person portaledges, ultra-light waterproof/breathable shell jackets). Writer/testers must be objective, honest, hard-working, and capable of writing catchy, detailed reviews.

What's New—our new-products section, featuring field-tested reviews of the latest gear and cragwear. Reviews are roughly 200 words long, sometimes only 100 words. Our reviews section also include Book of the Month, a 150-words review of a book or video.

PHOTOGRAPHY

Rock and Ice places a strong emphasis on stunning, cutting-edge photography. Please feel free to submit photos for any of the above departments as well as for our Exposed section, featuring the staff's picks of their favorite images each issue.

Rock and Ice is not responsible for unsolicited submissions. Please address all submissions to photo editor David Clifford, Big Stone Publishing, 1101 Village Road Ste UL D4, Carbondale CO 81623 USA. You must include a self-addressed, stamped envelope for their return. We accept original slides and black-and-white prints; color prints are NOT acceptable for our Exposed section. You can also email David Clifford low-res samples at: dclifford@bigstonepub.com.

Below are *Rock and Ice*'s photo rates:

Cover:	$700
Two-page spread:	$400
Full Page (and Exposed):	$300
2/3 Page:	$200
1/2 Page:	$150
1/3 Page:	$100
1/4 Page and Spot:	$75

Table of Contents: paid at standard space rates, or $50 per photo as a second use if published elsewhere in a department.

Categories: Nonfiction—Health—Photography—Physical Fitness—Recreation—Sports/Recreation—Rock Climbing

CONTACT: Tyler Stableford, Editor-in-Chief
Material: All
BIG STONE PUBLISHING
1101 Village Rd., Ste UL D4
Carbondale CO 81623
Phone: 970-963-4965
Fax: 970-704-1442
E-mail: editor@bigstonepub.com
Website: www.rockandice.com

Rockford Review

The Rockford Writers' Guild was formed originally in 1947 and now has over 130 members nationwide. A non-profit corporation, the Rockford Writers' Guild exists to encourage, develop and nurture writers and good writing of all kinds and to promote the art of writing in the Rockford area.

The Guild provides an environment for writers to develop ideas, improve their craft, and share their writing experiences and marketing techniques. We seek to increase community interest, support and appreciation for the literary arts by providing a forum for discussion, conducting workshops and encouraging local talent.

Two times a year, we publish the *Rockford Review*, which has been praised for the quality of its content and its production values. Its poetry, short stories, essays, art and photography represent the best works submitted from all parts of the world.

The *Rockford Review* is a 100-page perfectbound literary arts magazine published by the Rockford Writers' Guild each winter and summer. The summer issue is devoted to Guild members who are invited to publish any one piece of their choice.

Review seeks experimental or traditional poetry of up to 50 lines (shorter works are preferred). Short fiction, essays, and satire are welcome in the 250 to 1,300-word range. We also publish one-acts and other dramatic forms (1,300 words). *Review* prefers genuine or satirical human dilemmas with coping or non-coping outcomes that ring the reader's bell. We are always on the lookout for black and white illustrations and glossy photos in a vertical format.

If your work is accepted, you will receive an invitation to be a guest of honor at a Contributors' Reading and Reception in the summer and a complimentary copy of the *Review*. Your work also will be considered for the $25 Editor's Choice Prizes.

Try us with up to three pieces of your best unpublished work at a time. We read year-round and try to report within eight to 12 weeks. There is no reading fee. Simultaneous submissions are okay.

Good luck!

Categories: Fiction—Drama—Poetry—Satire

CONTACT: David Ross, Editor
Material: All
Rockford Writer's Guild
PO Box 858
Rockford IL 61105
Website: http://writersguild1.tripod.com

Rocky Mountain Rider

RMR is looking for positive, human interest stories that appeal to an audience of horsepeople, ranchers, seniors, and folks who live in the West. Pieces may include profiles of unusual people or animals, history, humor, anecdotes, coverage of regional events and new products. We occasionally excerpt books by regional authors. We aren't looking for many "how to" or training articles, and are not currently looking at any fiction. We sometimes run cowboy poetry, and we always need clean jokes and short humorous pieces with a western theme.

LENGTH: Feature articles generally run between 500-2,000 words in length. Fillers should run about 100-500 words. Cowboy poetry should be no more than 4-5 stanzas.

FORMAT: Please submit articles typed and double-spaced on 8-1/2 x 11 paper.

RIGHTS: RMR buys first serial rights, one-time rights, as well as some reprint rights, if material has NOT been published in a competing publication in Montana, Idaho, Wyoming, Washington, Oregon, Colorado, or Utah.

PHOTOS: We need photos of Western scenes and people. Photos accompanying articles may be either black-and-white or color (as long as the contrasts are good). We also need humorous and action shots from various events in the northern Rockies. Send only photos (no slides, contact sheets or negatives).

PAYMENT: RMR pays on publication. Written material pays approximately $30 per 1,000 words. Photos pay $5.00 per photo.

Be sure to enclose a self-addressed, stamped envelope or your submission cannot be returned.

Categories: Nonfiction—Horses—Seniors—Regional: West

CONTACT: Editors
PO Box 995
Hamilton MT 59840
Phone: 888-747-1000/406-363-4085

Rocky Mountain Sports

Thank you for your interest in *Rocky Mountain Sports*. rocky is about the cutting-edge attitudes and athletic lifestyles that thrive in the Rocky Mountain region. Our mission is to inspire, inform and entertain through provocative profiles, reviews and where-to/how-to writing. Blow-by-blow news reporting applies only if it has an angle, a twist, an insight that a newspaper wouldn't dream of printing.

There are several hard and fast rules for prospective ROCKY writers:

• QUERY ALL stories in writing or via e-mail; don't submit a manuscript.

• DON'T send us a query without first reading ROCKY.

• DON'T send us a personal essay—we use "how-to, where-to" guides, profiles and news formats almost exclusively.

• DON'T ask for your own column—we don't have the space.

Your best bet for getting published with us is to target one of these sports: running, mountain biking, road racing, snowboarding, both alpine and nordic skiing, kayaking, hiking, climbing, mountaineering or other individual sports.

Incorporate humor but avoid cornball. Think fun. On a final note, feel free to go ballistic, be weird or provocative. Don't be afraid to try something new. We like new.

The following goes into more detail on what we're looking for.

Here are some general rules of writing for *Rocky Mountain Sports*:

• You should try to make it fun. We like to see anecdotes, great quotes and vivid descriptions.

• We try to keep a conversational tone to most of the stories in the magazine. You can get away with using the first person if it works in your story. For the most part, we follow the Associated Press Stylebook, although we use the present tense in attribution. ("People want to be like me," Michael Jordan says.)

• Your story should be thoroughly edited, spell-checked and fact-checked when submitted.

• Stay away from technical jargon. Keep the tone conversational.

• Quote Colorado people as often as possible. If that's not possible, try to stick to the Rocky Mountain region or people with Rocky Mountain connections.

• Avoid relying too heavily on PR people and manufacturers. They obviously have a bias for their product or company. Getting their input is fine, just make sure you have others to confirm what they say.

• Whenever you quote someone, get their age, where they live and the correct spelling of their name. You should never invent quotes, but it is legitimate to clean up people's grammar or put in a word for clarity's sake.

• Every story should have multiple sources. If you need additional sources, please ask.

• Make sure that your story isn't quote heavy. Quotes are vital to a good story, but they shouldn't dominate it.

• All claims involving statistics or scientific research should be attributed to a source, such as the League of American Bicyclists, The Environmental Protection Agency or a professional (doctor, nutritionist, personal trainer).

Include the following with your copy:

• A headline. If you can't write a good, concise headline, your story may lack focus. It's a good test to be sure that your story accomplishes what you set out to do.

• Photos. Always try to include a graphic element with your story. Ask your subjects for photos. (We can convert color photos to black and white, and we can use slides. We will return them if asked.) Also interesting with stories are graphs, charts and cartoons—keep your eyes open. If you are unable to come up with any photo ideas, let your editor know early.

• A bio. In about three sentences, tell our readers about yourself, including your involvement in sports or anything relevant to the subject of the article.

• A bill. Send the editor an invoice with your name, address, telephone number and social security number. Payment will follow upon publication.

Categories: Nonfiction—Adventure—Diet/Nutrition—Health—Outdoors—Physical Fitness—Recreation—Sports/Recreation

CONTACT: Rebecca Heaton, Editor
Material: All
Windy City Publishing
2525 15th Street, #1A
Denver CO 80211
Phone: 303-477-9770
Fax: 303-477-9747
E-mail: rheaton@rockymountainsports.com
Website: www.rockymountainsports.com

Rosebud

Thank you for your interest in *Rosebud*. We are open to outside submissions and we review material throughout the year. Although there are a few pointers below, the best way to get a feeling of what we do is to read an issue or two. You can either visit your local bookstore (we are available in Borders and Barnes & Noble), or better yet—subscribe or buy a sample copy directly from us at www.rsbd.net.

***ROSEBUD*'S SUBMISSION POLICY:** Rosebud, Inc. is a nonprofit organization staffed by volunteers. To handle the growing thousands of submissions we receive every year, we are launching the Rosebud Fast-track Initiative (RFI) to streamline submission processing. To achieve this we will be charging a handling fee of one dollar. For a guaranteed response to your submission in 30 days from the date of receipt, along with some reasons for our response, please:

• Put the letters RFI on the outside of the envelope, and circle it!

• Include a one-dollar fee or check for $1 made out to ROSEBUD.

• Include no more than three stories or five poems per envelope.

• Include a self-addressed stamped envelope for our reply and manuscript return (or, if you specify, we will recycle the manuscripts).

• Send fiction, essays, and/or poetry with SASE and $1.00 handling fee included.

The Rosebud Fast-track Initiative (RFI) offers advantages to authors at a reasonable cost:

• Approximate 40 day response from date of manuscript receipt.

• An acceptance notice or, where appropriate, some indication of why a given piece was not a match for *Rosebud*, and/or how you might better target future work (for prose pieces only).

• Periodic reports on *Rosebud* writing contests with $1000 prizes.

A $1 handling fee (cash or check) must be included with all mailed submissions. Unsolicited materials unaccompanied by a $1 fee will no longer be considered for *Rosebud*.

We must be able to easily contact you by phone, e-mail or regular mail. Fiction and non-fiction submissions must be typed, double-spaced; poetry must be typed, single spaced. The writer's name should be at the top of each page. Send only hardcopy at this time. If your piece is accepted be prepared to send an electronic file by e-mail or on disk. We use *The Chicago Manual of Style* and *Webster's Dictionary* (10th Edition) as editorial guides.

WHAT WE ARE LOOKING FOR IN PROSE: We publish short stories and an occasional essay. The ideal length for prose is 1,200 to 1,800 words. Send one to three of your strongest pieces. We like good storytelling, real emotion and authentic voice. On rare occasions we publish essays, but we do not publish conventional travel, political, or religious material, sentimentality, "inspirational" essays or nostalgia. Most of the stories we receive read like stories submitted to journals 50 years ago, and often are too generic and predictable to publish. Many start too slow and spend too much time up front telling us what the story is about. Get us interested first, then weave in exposition as you go.

WHAT WE ARE LOOKING FOR IN POETRY:

Send three to five one-page poems representing your best work. If you send an SASE and sufficient postage we will return the poems. Otherwise the paper will be recycled. You should be well-read in contemporary poetry and criticism. Avoid excessive or well-worn abstractions, not to mention clichés. Present a unique and convincing world (you can do this in a few words!) by means of fresh and exact imagery, and by interesting use of syntax. Explore the deep reaches of metaphor. But don't forget to be playful and have fun with words. Never tell the reader what to think.

IF WE PUBLISH...

Rosebud purchases one time rights of original or previously published pieces; this means you are free to sell that same piece to another publication. Selected writers may be contacted later for publication in *Rosebud* anthologies. For stories or articles, *Rosebud* currently pays a flat fee of $25.00, and three issues. *Rosebud* pays for poems in issues only: the amount is generally three, depending on supply. (For those published, the RFI fee will be returned.) Aside from compensation, however, the benefit of publishing in *Rosebud* can be enormous. Your piece will be read across the U.S., Canada, and to some extent, around the world. Literary agents often ask us about writers they have seen in *Rosebud*, and sometimes we can make connections. A significant number of *Rosebud* writers later publish collections or novels elsewhere.

HOW TO SUBSCRIBE:

Subscribe or purchase issues online at The Rosebud Store. Or you can send a check or money order payable to *Rosebud*. A 3-issue subscription is $20; a 6-issue subscription is $35. Sample copies are $7.95 each + $2 shipping/handling. For subscriptions, renewals, and sample copies contact us at the address below.

WHY YOUR SUBSCRIPTIONS AND SUBMISSIONS ARE IMPORTANT:

As writers, all of us are dependent upon magazines which publish our work. And, these magazines depend upon us. If we don't buy, read and promote them, they cease to exist. This is particularly true of periodicals like *Rosebud* that are open to submissions from new voices. We are a non-profit organization with no outside affiliation, grants or subsidies. Send in your manuscripts, but also send in your subscription. Let us work together to create a new kind of writing/publishing success.

Categories: Fiction—Nonfiction—Arts—Biography—Consumer—Drama—Erotica—Family—Fantasy—Feminism—General Interest—Humor—Language—Literature—Men's Fiction—Men's Issues—Music—Mystery—Native American—New Age—Poetry—Rural America—Science Fiction—Short Stories—Theatre—Women's Fiction—Women's Issues—Writing

CONTACT: Roderick Clark, Editor
Material: Prose
CONTACT: R. Virgil Ellis, Poetry Editor
Material: Poetry
Send Prose to: N3310 Asje Rd.
Cambridge WI 53523
Phone: 608-423-9609
Send Poetry to: PO Box 614
Cambridge WI 53523
Website: rsbd.net

Rug Hooking

Make your *Rug Hooking* article the best it can be by following these guidelines. Adhering to them will save time and eliminate frustration for both you and the editorial staff.

1. To help you with the arrangement of information in your article, begin with an outline and refer to it often throughout the writing of the story.

2. Please use complete sentences.

3. Use proper punctuation.

4. Answer within your article all the questions listed in your contract.

5. Double-space your article.

6. Make sure your article contains the number of words that are stipulated in your contract. Your word processing software should include a word counting feature. If you do not have this feature, do a rough estimate by counting the average number of words per line of type and multiplying it by the number of lines on a page. Then multiply that figure by the number of pages you have written.

7. Check your spelling. Refer to a dictionary and use the spellcheck feature included in your computer's word processing software.

8. Double check the spelling of all names, addresses, phone numbers, and any other piece of information that you incorporate into your article.

9. When you have finished your story, read it aloud—hearing your story often alerts you to poorly constructed sentences or sections that don't make sense.

10. If you are including art, such as slides of rugs, list for each image the following caption information: the name of the rug, its dimensions, its cut of wool and backing, the designer's name, the hooker's name, the location of the hooker, and the year the rug was hooked.

11. Submit your article on a computer disk as well as on paper. Let us know which word processing software you used to create the file.

Categories: Nonfiction—Antiques—Arts—Crafts—Hobbies

CONTACT: Virginia P. Stimmel, Editor
Material: All
Rug Hooking Magazine
5067 Ritter Rd
Mechanicsburg PA 17055
Phone: 717-796-0411
Fax: 717-796-0412

Ruminator Review

As a theme-based magazine, we are rarely able to use unsolicited essays and reviews. If you are interested in joining our group of reviewers and want to grab our attention, the best way to do so is by sending a query letter that outlines your writing experience and reviewing interest, along with three or four published clips (book reviews preferred.) If it looks like your writing and interests are a good fit, we'll try and assign a review your way.

What to Expect

We're a very small staff, so it usually takes us a month or two to respond to queries. (Don't worry, though, we will.) Writers are paid on publication; queries and other unsolicited material will not be returned unless sufficient postage is included.

Where to Go to Find Out More

If you'd like a sample issue to see for yourself the quality and style of writing in *Ruminator Review*, e-mail review@ruminator.com to find out how to obtain one. General questions and queries can be addressed to mjk@ruminator.com or mailed to:

CONTACT: Matt
Material: All
1648 Grand Ave.
St. Paul, MN 55105
Phone: 651-699-2610
Fax: 651-699-7190
E-mail: review@ruminator.com
Website: www.ruminator.com

Runner's World

We're providing the following information to help you tailor materials for publication in *Runner's World*. It should go without saying that the best way to understand RW, and what we're looking for from freelancers, is to read several recent issues of the magazine closely.

In addition, you should understand that most RW articles are written by staffers, senior writers or experts (podiatrists, nutritionists, etc.). In other words, it's not easy to be published in *Runner's World*. We have little interest in general articles on the benefits of running, fitness and the like. We may agree with your sentiments and advice, but that alone isn't enough to make an article publishable.

These departments offer the best opportunities for freelancers: Real Runners, Race Roundup, Rave Run and Personal Record. It's not necessary to query when contributing to these sections of the magazine; all submissions are on speculation. Because of the large number of submissions received, we cannot acknowledge receipt, and we do not send out rejection letters or return the original materials. Therefore, please keep copies of everything you send us. You will hear from us only if we are interested in publishing your materials.

We encourage electronic submissions. These should be sent to rwedit@rodale.com. Do not send your story as an attachment. Please paste it directly into the body of your e-mail. We appreciate your attention to this detail.

Here's some additional information on submitting materials to *Runner's World*.

Real Runners tells the everyday, inspirational and humorous stories of regular people doing amazing things. Almost anyone can be a Real Runner as long as you find out something interesting about the person's running or lifestyle. Photos essential. Address all materials to "Real Runner."

Race Roundups are printed in each issue from readers who have run a fun, unique, or inspiring race that stands out from the pack. If you recently ran a race that deserves coverage in Runner's World, we want to hear about it. Please tell us about it by filling out our brief survey (it will only take a few minutes). If we publish your report in the magazine, you'll receive a Runner's World T-shirt.

http://survey1.rodale.com/rodale-2way-v56/2w5Q6P/2WAY.html

(Some computers may have difficulty processing the survey. If you have trouble, e-mail Katie Neitz at Katie.Neitz@Rodale.com and the questions will be provided to you.)

Rave Run requires a simple descriptive letter. Briefly describe your Rave Run…where it is located, what you see while running, why it is meaningful to you, etc. It is also important that you include details like distance of the run and the name of the road or trail on which you run. If you think you have awesome publication-quality photos, send them in a 35mm horizontal slide format. Naturally, we can only publish a small number of Rave Run nominations we receive. But, don't let this discourage you! If you meet the qualifications please send to: Runner's World, Attn: Don Kinsella, Photo Editor, 135 N Sixth St., Emmaus, PA 18098-0009.

Personal Record is a column featuring first-person essays about running-related experiences. Topics can be personal in nature, of course, but should appeal to a wide range of readers. We look for a variety of voices to contribute to this column; the tone can vary from humorous to sentimental to reflective. Essays are reviewed on speculation.

OTHER DEPARTMENTS AND FEATURES: Most other departments are written by experts or professionals with whom we have ongoing relationships. There are few freelance opportunities.

We receive hundreds of first-person stories each month, many from people describing how they ran their first marathon. These are nearly always inspirational, but they are rarely publishable, because we don't have magazine-quality photos to accompany the stories. Still, the occasional first-person story is so unique and emotional that we decide to publish it. So, give us your best. Remember, however: We can't acknowledge receipt or return materials. Keep copies of everything.

We are always looking for "Adventure Runs" from readers—runs in wild, remote, beautiful and interesting places. These are rarely race stories but more like backtracking/running adventures. Great color slides are extremely helpful, and often crucial in the decision to publish or not. We suggest sending us your story first, and letting us know if you have color photos to accompany it.

Photos. Nearly all our photos are taken by professionals. The exception would be the photo that you managed to capture that no one else in the world got, i.e., Madonna running in Central Park, a scenic wilderness photo, a photo of an elephant chasing a runner in India.

RUNNER'S WORLD ONLINE: Our Web sites, which include runnersworld.com and kidsrunning.com, are not currently paying for materials. However, they have many interactive sections, including bulletin boards, where you can make quick, valuable contributions. They will also consider stories submitted on a not-for-payment basis. We hope the above answers many of your questions.

Happy writing and running.

The Editors

Categories: Nonfiction—Health—Physical Fitness—Recreation—Sports/Recreation

CONTACT: Adam Bean, Managing Editor
Material: All
33 E Minor St.
Emmaus PA 18098
Phone: 610-967-5171
Fax: 610-967-7725
Website: www.runnersworld.com

Running Times
The Runner's Best Resource

Running Times, The Runner's Best Resource, is the national magazine for the experienced running participant and fan. Our audience is knowledgeable about the sport and actively participates in running and racing. All editorial relates specifically to running: improving performance, enhancing enjoyment, or exploring events, places, and people in the sport. Please read recent issues to learn the type of material we seek.

Three principles that guide our editorial section are:

1) We go beyond basic, beginner information: presenting the "why" as well as "how-to," digging for principles, exploring contexts, analyzing and drawing conclusions from the facts.

2) We present honest content that accurately reflects the runner's experience and inspires trust.

3) Good writing is a priority; writing aimed at an intelligent, informed and discriminating audience.

We assign approximately 40% of our editorial material to freelance writers. We are willing to work with unpublished writers. Although we consider unsolicited manuscripts, we prefer to see a written query which describes in two or three paragraphs your idea, the article's proposed length and scope, why *Running Times*' readers would find the material interesting, and what qualifies you to write about it.

We close each issue three months ahead of on-sale date, and assign well in advance of our printing deadlines. Payment is made upon publication.

We publish editorial material in the following categories:

• Features (1,500 to 3,000 words). Training, Athlete Profiles, Travel, Current Events and Issues

• Columns (400 to 1,000 words). Nutrition, Sports Medicine, Training.

• Fiction (1,500 to 3,500 words). Any genre, related to running and runners.

We request that all writers submit their articles via e-mail. Send your proposal via email or with an SASE.

Categories: Fiction—Nonfiction—Health—Recreation—Sports

CONTACT: Jonathan Beverly, Editor
Material: All
CONTACT: Marc Chalufour, Managing Editor
Material: All
Fitness Publishing, Inc.
213 Danbury Rd.
Wilton CT 06897-4006
Phone: 203-761-1113
Fax: 203-761-9933
E-mail: editor@runningtimes.com
Website: www.runningtimes.com

RURAL HERITAGE

Rural Heritage

RURAL HERITAGE was established in 1975 as a link with the past, not for nostalgic reasons, but to help preserve a way of life for future generations. Our readers are commonsense country folks who enjoy doing things for themselves. Many of them have always farmed with horses, mules, or oxen; others are returning to the practice for economic and/or environmental reasons. Our editorial policy is guided by the philosophy that the past holds the key to the future.

Subjects: We publish hands-on how-to stories covering the broad spectrum of rural skills and creative problem solving, with emphasis on draft animals used in the field or wood lot. We are especially seeking technical details on specific pieces of horse-drawn equipment, how it was obtained/restored, how much it cost, how it's put together, how it works, problems encountered, and how they were solved. We do not publish religious material or non-relevant political or social topics.

Submission: If you are unknown to us, please either submit your material on speculation or else query (outline what you intend to cover and how you'll handle it) and if possible include clips of three previously published pieces. Be sure you know your subject—our savvy readers are quick to notice errors in terminology, breed identification, and similar details.

Format: Disk, CD, or via email. Please include a two or three sentence bionote describing your non-writing interests and qualifications for your subject.

Length: Minimum is 650 words with at least one illustration (850 words without illustration); features run 1,200 to 1,500 words; special subjects occasionally run longer.

Illustrations: Please include detailed captions identifying breed(s), equipment, and visible people, and indicate the name of the photographer or artist to whom we should give credit. Put your name and address on the back of each piece and send a self-addressed stamped envelope for the return of your material.

Payment: Payment for first English language rights is 5 cents per published word and $10 per illustration, paid on publication, and

two copies of the issue bearing your work.

Sample copy: If you are not familiar with RURAL HERITAGE and would like a sample issue, please send $8.00 (US $10.00 to Canada or overseas). Subscriptions to the bimonthly are $29.00 per year (US $35.00 to Canada, US $40.00 overseas).

Categories: Nonfiction—Rural America—Draft Animals—Farming—Livestock—Logging

CONTACT: Gail Damerow, Editor
Material: All
281 Dean Ridge Ln.
Gainesboro TN 38562-5039
Phone: 931-268-0655
E-mail: editor@ruralheritage.com
Website: www.ruralheritage.com

Russian Life

Russian Life has as its fundamental editorial mission telling the story of Russia. It is a primary looking glass into Russia for some 40,000+ Americans and covers Russian culture, travel, history, politics, art, business and society. As a bimonthly magazine, *Russian Life* focuses on current issues and events facing Russia and Russians. The majority of *Russian Life* content is feature articles, most of which are not time-sensitive, but all of which are current.

The majority of *Russian Life* articles are also written by freelance Russian journalists and writers. The role of contributions by freelance Western or expat writers is to provide a unique "outsider" perspective. While no one knows Russia like Russians, sometimes it takes the view of foreigners to help shape a message that resonates with foreign readers.

Russian Life's writing style is frank, terse and incisive. The model is good American journalism style (and spelling) on the lines of the AP Stylebook—i.e. third person reportage. We seek to provide coverage of Russia that is free of illusions (but not blemishes) and full of hope (but not ideology or agendas). We adhere to the belief that Russia is a land of endless fascination and opportunity, but a place that, like many others, is fraught with its own problems, risks and dangers. Our job is to present a realistic, truthful and independent view that balances these realities, providing enjoyable, insightful reading. It is also helpful to remember that *Russian Life* is a very visual magazine; few stories do not include photographs.

Persons interested in either submitting articles (or photos) to *Russian Life* or being assigned stringer work should first contact *Russian Life* editorial offices to discuss the parameters of such work with our editors. While we welcome unsolicited manuscripts, we feel that it is most productive to work with writers ahead of time—to hone story ideas to fit the *Russian Life* mold. Manuscripts are returned only if accompanied by a self-addressed stamped envelope. Submissions may also be made electronically, with prior approval. Fees for freelance work is agreed upon on a individual basis, depending on the scope, difficulty and nature of the story being written. Payment is upon publication. Most stories will be between 2000-4000 words in length.

Categories: Nonfiction—Culture—History—Travel—Russian Topics

CONTACT: Paul Richardson, Editor
Material: All
RIS Publications
PO Box 567
Montpelier VT 05601
Phone: 802-223-4955
Fax: 802-223-6105
E-mail: editorial@russianlife.net
Website: www.russian-life.com

Rutgers

We are a 48-page magazine, published three times a year, that is dedicated to developing and maintaining in readers an active interest in Rutgers, the State University of New Jersey.

Our goal is: To make the magazine's readers feel that, no matter where they are or what they're doing, they are an integral part of an active and vital university community. Our audience is: 70,000 alumni, faculty, and friends of Rutgers University as well as important members of the New Jersey government, education, corporate and community-affairs sectors.

Our approach is: Unlike that of traditional alumni magazines, Rutgers Magazine seeks to tie Rutgers to its community through insightful, thought-provoking feature articles that explore the way Rutgers shapes and is shaped by current trends and ideas. The magazine explores the many ways in which the university and its alumni help shape life in New Jersey, around the nation and the world. Its stories illuminate the professional and personal lives of alumni, faculty, staff and students; explore new research taking place on campus; offer commentary, opinions and analysis of current trends by members of the university; and, because Rutgers is the state university, examine trends and issues affecting New Jersey.

We expect articles to: Have a direct and obvious tie to Rutgers issues and to Rutgers alumni, faculty, staff and students; to exhibit shape, depth and imagination; and to be thoughtful, informed, well-researched and well-organized.

We expect writers to: Have experience in magazine writing as evidenced by published clips; conduct background research; find, read and understand relevant materials; conduct interviews; write skillfully and creatively; accept editor revisions; and rewrite and reinterview as directed by the editor.

Assignment Procedures

Please keep in mind that we do not accept:

• Fillers or shorts
• Motivational or how-to articles
• Unsolicited manuscripts
• Articles with no or scant ties to Rutgers University
• Reprints or revised versions of articles published elsewhere
• Newspaper-style writing
• Poorly executed contacted articles Query letters
• No unsolicited manuscripts accepted or read. Unsolicited manuscripts will not be returned unless accompanied by SASE.

If you have a story idea, write a brief cover letter demonstrating the flavor of the proposed article and your writing style. Supply brief relevant background materials if available.

If you do not have a story idea but want to be considered for future assignments, write a brief cover letter about your experience and interests that demonstrates your writing style.

Assignments

• The editor will assign articles to an appropriate writer, who will be supplied with assignment sheet, contact persons, available background materials, writer's guidelines, and summary of expected content and angle of the story.
• Assignments given to writers who have never written for Rutgers Magazine may be assigned on spec.
• Deadline is usually one month from assignment.
• Editor reserves the right to pay a 30% kill fee for a contracted article deemed unpublishable.
• Editor reserves the right to pay no kill fee for an article assigned on spec.
• Payment varies with writer's experience, article length, extent of research and interviews and difficulty of subject matter.
• Expenses directly incurred in writing article will be reimbursed if original receipts are supplied.
• Writers must sign a standard university contractor's agreement.
• Articles range in length from 1,000 words to 4,000 words. Editor will supply expected word count.

• We adhere to the Chicago Manual of Style and Webster's Dictionary.

Submissions

• Articles should be submitted via e-mail or on disk. Please double space between lines.
• We can translate copy from most word-processing programs, Mac and PC, but prefer Word for Macintosh.
• Article must be submitted with paper invoice that includes Social Security number.
• Articles will be edited and resubmitted to writer with expectations for rewriting and reinterviewing if and as necessary.
• Editor will assign due date for revisions.
• Editor retains the right to a 30% kill fee at any point before final acceptance.

Acceptances

• Stories appear in print at the editor's discretion.
• Payment generally is mailed 6 to 8 weeks after acceptance.
• Editor retains the right to cut or alter article after acceptance. Content revisions will be cleared with writer; copyfitting revisions will not.
• Writers will be supplied with two copies of the issue in which it appears.
• Writers can request additional copies depending on availability of overruns.

Categories: Nonfiction—Career—College—Rutgers Alumni

CONTACT: Rutgers Magazine
Rutgers, The State University of New Jersey
Department of University Relations
96 Davidson RD
Piscataway NJ 08854
Phone: 732-445-3710
Fax: 732-445-5925
E-mail: rutgersmagazine@ur.rutgers.edu

S & T Magazine

Please refer to *Space & Time Publishing*.

Safari

SAFARI Magazine was founded in 1971 as the official publication of Safari Club International. SAFARI Magazine is bi-monthly; is focused on big game hunting and conservation; and, includes editorials, feature stories and columns about SCI national, international and chapter activities, affiliated organizations and members' hunting reports from around the world. Circulation is 27,000-30,000, mailed nationally and internationally to the SCI membership list and to selected other individuals or organizations. Send submissions to SCI, at the address shown below.

EDITORIAL CONTENT

The magazine scope of interest is:

• Outdoor recreation with special emphasis on big game hunting around the world
• Ethnic and traditional hunts of particular regions around the world
• Current or historical hunting and conservation
• Philosophy and heritage of hunting
• Background on a particular species
• Conservation and environmental affairs relevant to big game or hunters

We buy first rights manuscripts. Queries prior to submissions are encouraged; no fiction or poetry accepted. Avoid sending simple hunting narratives that lack new approaches. Features run 2,000-2,500 words and should be informative, accurate, designed to appeal to sportsmen and women as well as others who enjoy out-of-doors. Rate for a full-length story with illustrations submit-

R-U

ted by a professional writer is $300 paid upon publication. Short stories or non-pro contributions by SCI members rate an honorarium of $25. (Professional photographers are paid up to $100 for each color photo used, depending on size, up to $45 each B&W-all on if published/when published basis.)

News briefs are welcomed and will include bylines, but are not bought by SAFARI.

MANUSCRIPT PREPARATION

Submitted manuscripts should fit these specifications in order to be reviewed.

- Original: typed or laser jet printout, no photocopies.
- Consecutive-number all manuscript pages.
- Computer disks: ASCII language accepted with hard copy. (Mac 3½" or IBM 5¼")
- Double-spaced or 1½-spaced text OK.
- All pages: 1½" left margin, 1" right and base.
- Title page (first page): Author name, address, telephone in upper right corner, title halfway down first page, followed by text. Author name on all pages following.
- Pica-sized, sans-serif type preferred.
- Spell-check for proper names, animals, places.
- Do not staple manuscript pages.
- We have prepared an editorial style sheet for information and use on any manuscript.

PHOTOGRAPHY SUBMISSION

We are interested only in huntable big game subjects of trophy quality in a natural setting.

Color photographs, slides or transparencies are preferred. (Prints accepted for color or black-and-white uses. In all cases, use will depend on the reproduction quality of submitted materials.)

All photos must be captioned. Type caption information on a separate sheet of paper and number to match slide or print being described. We prefer to receive more photos than we may be able to use, in order to have a choice. Send SASE. All photos will be returned following publication unless otherwise directed.

- Color Slides: use plastic sheets to hold slides or transparencies; do not ship unprotected. Label each slide with name stamp or label.
- Black-and-White: 35mm contacts, glossy or semi-gloss prints; added minimum of ½" white border on four sides preferred.
- Slides or transparencies preferred for color and should be sharp and well-exposed. (Prints are OK, glossy preferred. If 35mm: double-sized, or 5"x7" or larger).
- Print sizes 5"x7" or 8"x10" preferred; others considered based on quality and story needs.
- Do not write on prints. Attach label with pre-typed information or use grease-pencil only.

Categories: Conservation—Outdoors—Hunting

CONTACT: Steve Comu, Director of Publications
Material: All
Safari Club International
4800 W. Gates Pass Rd.
Tucson AZ 85745
Phone: 520-620-1220
Fax: 520-618-3555
E-mail: scomus@safariclub.org
Website: www.safariclub.org

SageWoman

SageWoman is a quarterly magazine of women's spirituality. Our readers are people who identify positively with the term "Goddess." Our readership includes women of a variety of religious faiths, ranging from Roman Catholic to Lesbian Separatist Witch and everywhere in between. What our readers have in common is summed up in the statement "Celebrating the Goddess in every woman." If you feel a connec-

tion with our subject matter, we welcome your contributions to our pages. The majority of every issue is created from the contributions of our readers, so your creativity and willingness to share is vital to *SageWoman*'s existence! We welcome material from women of all races, ages, sexual orientations, and socio-economic backgrounds. Our editorial staff is English-speaking only, so we ask that written contributions and letters to us be submitted in English, but we encourage submissions from non-American women and women for whom English may be a second language. We also strongly encourage contributions from women of color. SageWoman offers the following guidelines to help you in submitting your work to us.

1. Subject matter

a. All submissions should focus on issues of concern to Pagan and other Goddess-friendly women. We accept non-fiction prose related to women's spiritual experience. We accept very modest amounts of poetry and receive far more poetry than we can publish. We also accept photographs and graphic artwork (drawings, painting, prints, etc.) suitable for publishing in a magazine format. We do not accept fiction, screenplays, long narrative poems, erotica, or press releases/advertorial.

b. *SageWoman* is dedicated to helping women explore their spiritual, emotional, and mundane lives in a way that respects all persons, creatures, and the Earth. We encourage women of all spiritual paths to send writings and artwork, but our focus is on material, which expresses an Earth-centered spirituality. Our editorial style focuses on personal experience; please write in the first person! Please don't limit yourself because you aren't a "professional" writer or artist—most of our published material is from previously unpublished writers. If you haven't seen a copy of *SageWoman*, please send for a sample copy ($7) or look at our sample articles at our website before submitting material; this will enable you to understand the kind of material we publish and will save both you and us a lot of time!

c. *SageWoman* accepts material created by women only. (Male contributors are encouraged to contact our co-ed publications *Pan Gaia*, *The Blessed Bee*, or *New Witch*, at the same address; these titles accept submissions from both men and women.)

2. Written Submissions

a. All written submissions should be the original work of the author. We prefer receiving submissions via email sent to editor@sagewoman.com or on computer disk accompanied by a double-spaced paper manuscript. (Please don't just send a disk—sometimes compatibility problems prevent us from reading disks which are submitted to us, and without a manuscript, we won't be able to evaluate your submission!) We are Windows based and prefer ASCII compatible or Word files attached to your email or if email is not an option by 3.5" or Zipdisks. We may be able to translate Macintosh based disks as well. Disks sent to us will not be returned unless you send an SASE with adequate postage with the submission. If computer-based submission is not possible, typed, double-spaced manuscripts are also acceptable, as well as neatly handwritten pieces if no other method is possible. Please do not send us your only copy of your manuscript; accidents can happen and material sent to us is occasionally lost or damaged.

b. Articles should be between 800 and 5000 words in length, and written manuscripts should contain the author's name, pen name (if appropriate), address and phone number on each page.

c. We are aware that you have worked hard on your writing, it is personal and special to you, and contains your unique voice. Nonetheless, we often find it necessary to edit for length, clarity and grammar, sometimes at the last minute before publication. Therefore, we CANNOT guarantee that your article will appear precisely as you submitted it. If you do not want your material edited in any way, please do not submit your writing to us. (Also, please inform us of deliberate uses of non-traditional spelling so the tone of your work will not be accidentally altered.)

3. Graphic Art

a. All graphic art submissions should be the original work of the artist. Clear, black and white drawings are best, but penciled or colored works may be acceptable in some cases. Please be aware that all artwork will be reproduced in black and white only, except for pieces used on our outside covers. Our covers are usually commissioned works, but you may feel free to submit color photocopies or slides of your color work for possible use on the cover. Please send us clean copies of your artwork only—we cannot be responsible for your original artwork! We encourage the submission of artwork which celebrates the Goddess and women in all of our many guises; different skin colors, cultures, ages, sexual orientations, body types, sizes, and shapes, and levels of ableness.

b. We are always looking for new artists to share their creativity in our pages. If you have a portfolio of your work, feel free to send it; when sending a body of work, please inform us if any of the pieces have been previously published or are not available for publication. We do commission special pieces of artwork for the magazine; however, the majority of artwork we publish has been sent by artists on spec. We keep files of artwork, by artist, and when an issue is in production we find the pieces of artwork on file that fit each article, and then inform the artist in question that we have decided to publish their work. For this reason, your artwork maybe on file for months, or years, without being used—if this is a problem for you, please inform us so we can work out other arrangements with you.

4. Photography

a. All photographic submissions should be the original work of the photographer. If persons other than the photographer are shown, a signed release from said person(s) must be included in order for us to publish the photo. Please send standard black and white or color prints, negatives or slides.

All photographs will be reproduced in black and white only. Our use of photography is similar to that of graphic art; please see guidelines above.

5. General Information

a. Please send a self-addressed, stamped envelope with your submission. If you wish for us to return your submission, please ensure that the SASE has adequate postage to return your manuscript, artwork, or other submission. If you do not wish for your submission to be returned,please write "Do not return" on it, and simply send an SASE or stamped postcard for us to respond to your submission. Please put your name, address and phone number with area code on each page of your manuscript.

b. Your submission will be acknowledged when we receive your material; we cannot guarantee exact publishing dates but will attempt to keep you up-to-date on the status of your work. We prefer to accept material which has not been previously seen or published—please inform us of multiple submissions or previous publications.

c. *SageWoman* publishes quarterly. All material should be sent to the attention of the Editor at the address (either e-mail or U.S. mail) given below.

6. Compensation and Rights

a. *SageWoman* offers modest cash payments for unsolicited artwork, photography, and articles.

Articles are compensated at approximately $.02 per word for unsolicited material, with a minimum of $10. (No payment is made for *Rattle* letters or networking information printed in W*eaving the Web*.) Artwork and photography are compensated on a piece-by-piece basis, depending on the size, complexity and usefulness of the piece. Artists and photographers are paid a minimum of $15 per piece for their work. We are often able to pay more in cases where the article, artwork, illustration or photograph is commissioned especially for *SageWoman*; please contact us if you are interested in working with us on commission. We realize how very modest these payments are; we offer them not as full compensation for your creativity, but as a "thank-you" for sharing your gifts with us. If you are a business or craftsperson who would benefit from advertising in our pages, please inform us that you are interested in trading advertising for your contributions; we are able to be substantially more generous in trading for advertising space than we can be in our cash payments!

b. If your material is accepted, you will also receive a free copy of the issue in which your work appears. Payment will be sent to you within 30 days of your return of our contributor's form, which is sent

out to all contributors shortly after an issue goes to press. *SageWoman* requires first worldwide serial rights, and prefers (but does not require) all rights for one year, and the right to reprint in future *SageWoman* collections as well as non-exclusive electronic rights (for use on the "sample" page of the *SageWoman* Website.) All remaining rights will revert to you.

When you submit work to us, we will assume your work is available for the purchase of these rights at the compensation level specified above, unless you state otherwise.

If there are any questions that these guidelines do not answer, please feel free e-mail, call or write to us for more information, or simply to try out your ideas on us! Our usual office hours are 9-4 Pacific Time, Monday-Friday, but feel free to leave a message if you don't reach us.

We will return your call! Thanks again for your interest in *SageWoman*. We look forward to hearing from you soon. Submissions may be sent by e-mail, fax or postal mail. An FTP site is available for graphics files call for details, 707-882-2052.

Categories: Lifestyle—New Age—Occult—Religion—Spiritual—Women's Issues—Pagan

CONTACT: Submissions Editor
Material: All
PO Box 641
Point Arena CA 95468-0641
Phone: 707-882-2052
Fax: 707-882-2793
E-mail: editor@sagewoman.com
Website: www.sagewoman.com

SAIL

A popular article length is 1,500-3,000 words, though it takes a strong concept to merit maximum length. Most stories in SAIL are shorter, and very, very short pieces are prized. Developing writers should pay attention to sections at the front of the magazine and be alert to our search for small stories with punch.

FORM: We prefer to receive material via email or on disk (include hardcopy). Please add a brief sailing biography. Hard-copy manuscripts should be typed, double-spaced, with wide margins. All submissions by mail should include a self-addressed, stamped envelope large enough to enclose your material so that we may return it to you should it not meet our editorial needs.

SAIL will not consider articles that have been submitted simultaneously to another publication. Payments vary depending upon the type of article. We pay upon acceptance. Articles that have been published elsewhere are occasionally considered. We usually buy first North American and e-magazine rights.

We strongly suggest that writers query SAIL about specific ideas. Although we cannot make a decision without seeing the article, we can tell you whether or not your idea is appropriate for SAIL. We attempt to read, consider, and reply to your query or article within 60 days.

SUBJECT MATTER: We look for unique views of sailing. Read recent issues of SAIL to see the sort of articles we publish. Remember that SAIL teaches sailors of all abilities, beginner to expert, how to improve their sailing skills, equip their boats for more effective sailing, and enjoy sailing more. Think constructively; write about how to avoid common problems.

Here are hints for different sections of the magazine.

FEATURES: Select specific actions or events and build your article around them. Focus on a theme or choose a specific aspect of sailing and discuss perhaps a personal attitude or philosophic approach. Notice that we devote certain issues to special themes: chartering, electronics, commissioning. Stay away from pieces that chronicle your journey in the day-to-day style of a logbook (these have rarely been successful). And keep in mind that you want to take readers onboard to share your sailing experience. We repeat: Many of our favorite features are simultaneously entertaining, practical and instructive.

Think locally. SAIL will continue to publish stories about sailing among the exotic islands of the Caribbean (for example), but we receive more of these than we can use. Meanwhile we are always on the hunt for good material about sailing the lakes, rivers and coastlines of America.

HOW-TO, TECHNICAL ARTICLES: We want clear and concise articles of 1,000 to 2,000 words written for the intelligent layman. Discuss systems or techniques for navigation, sail trim, or seamanship that have worked for you. Don't bounce over a wide range of topics superficially; instead, deal with one subject in detail, with precision.

SAILING MEMORIES: These short essays are reminiscences of the author's sailing life, including favorite boats, learning experiences, people encountered, places visited. It's an opportunity to let the writer in you have rein.

SAILING NEWS: We give CRUISERS news-you-can-use. Any change or development that a cruiser might benefit from knowing is news-your-can-use. We give RACERS news-with-added-value. We cover very little "regatta news" in the magazine; given a ubiquitous internet, it is pointless to print a story that merely tells the winners and winning moves of a regatta that happened two months prior. But the racing scene is always changing, or experiencing new pressures, or developing new players; there are many opportunities to identify the story behind the story. And we cover relevant industry, legal, political, and environmental matters. We usually assign news reporting in advance; it is best to query SAIL at least one month ahead of any scheduled event you want to cover. Accuracy and clarity are demanded.

VOICE OF EXPERIENCE: If it happened to you, and you learned something from it, you are a candidate to write a Voice of Experience piece. These stories generally run about 1,800 words and focus upon a particular situation, an evolving set of events, and consequences. A sidebar of 250-350 words, included in the total wordcount, presents the lessons learned as "Hindsight."

Categories: Nonfiction—Sailing

CONTACT: Managing Editor
Material: All
SAIL Magazine
98 N Washington St 2nd Fl
Boston MA 02114

Sailing Magazine

20% freelance. Sailing Magazine *is for the sailor committed to the sport. All kinds of sailing are featured on big pages full of pictures and text complemented by technical articles. Welcomes new writers. Circ. 40K. Monthly.*

Pays on publication. Publishes ms 6 months after acceptance. Buys one-time rights. Rarely accepts reprints. Responds 2 months. Sample for written request and $5.

Needs: Features with pictures. Pays $250-500 for 800-2,500 words. Submit complete ms with cover letter by mail with SASE.

Photos/Art: Pays $50-800.

Categories: Nonfiction—Boating—History—Outdoors—Recreation—Sports/Recreation

CONTACT: Greta Schanen, Managing Editor
Material: All
PO Box 249, 125 E. Main St.
Port Washington WI 53074
Phone: 262-284-3494
Fax: 262-284-7764
E-mail: editorial@sailingmagazine.net
Website: www.sailingonline.com

Sailing World

Guidelines for Writers

Prospective contributors to *Sailing World* should study recent issues of the magazine to determine appropriate subject matter. The emphasis here is on performance sailing: keep in mind that the *Sailing World* readership is relatively educated about the sport. Unless you are dealing with a totally new aspect of sailing, you can and should discuss ideas on an advanced technical level; however, extensive formulae and graphs don't play well to our audience. When in doubt as to the suitability of an article or idea, submit a written query before time and energy are misdirected. (Because of the volume of queries received, editors cannot accept phone calls.)

All mss. should be typewritten and double-spaced. Unless specific arrangements have been made ahead of time with *Sailing World*, submissions must include all necessary artwork and photos. (See SW's Photographer's Guidelines.) Materials should bear the contributor's name, address and phone number. Unsolicited articles should be sent as queries via e-mail. If the article idea is accepted, the full text can then be sent as a text or Microsoft Word document on a floppy disk (Mac or Windows format). The disk should be sent with a self-addressed, stamped envelope.

Most writing for *Sailing World* falls into one of several categories. Articles on one-design or offshore sailing can be presented as any of the following:

1. Feature (B&W or color)
   - Instructional
   - Event-oriented
   - Personality profiles
2. Race Report
3. Starting Line
4. Finish Line

Non-racing features may be either instructional or narrative; in the latter case, suitability for SW will be determined by the quality of writing and ideas, or by the value of lessons learned.

"Gee-whiz" impressions from beginning sailors are generally not accepted.

Payment for article is upon publication, and varies with the type of article, its placement in the magazine, and the amount of editing required. Average payment is $400 for up to 2000 plus words.

Thank you for your interest in contributing to *Sailing World*.

Guidelines for Photographers

Prospective contributors should study recent issues of the magazine to determine photographic style. Preference is given to color slides; our Art Department recommends shooting with Fuji VELVIA film. Other submissions should be 5x7 or larger B&W or color glossy prints—no negatives, please. Name and address of contributor should be attached to each submission or slide, and the delivery should be accompanied by a memo covering the details of the submission. Return method should be specified if other than Certified Mail. Please also include a street address for Express return services, as well as any account information with FedEx or other courier services. Returns typically take 3 months, unless an expedited return is requested by the photographer. Payment for photos is upon publication, and varies with photo size and type according to *Sailing World* rates.

Generally, all photos are story related. While *Sailing World* does not discourage the submission of other photos, it is unlikely that they will be used in feature stories. We do, however, encourage submissions of competitive, current events taking place throughout the world for use in our monthly columns which examine the local and global racing scene. In addition, we will enter your name in our contributors file to receive periodic mailings regarding our needs.

Photos usually fall into one of the following categories:

1. Cover: Always color, usually related to an inside story. Preferably vertical. Feature Or Photo 2. Feature: Color slides. Usually covers a specific topic (instructional or technical) or event. Most is commissioned work. Assignment ideas accepted in writing only (or fax).

3. Finish Line: One shot per story. Exciting event action preferred.

4. General: General sailing photography welcomed (new boats, interesting people, spectacular wipe-outs, unusual rigs). Please send all photos to the attention of Elizabeth Carroll. Thank you for your interest in contributing to *Sailing World*.

Digital Photo Guidelines

Digital photos must be 300 dpi: 6 by 8 inches for standard (half-page or less) photos, 11 by 16 inches for spreads. Please include a labeled contact sheet or an additional folder containing 72 dpi thumbnails of your photos.

Please send files in one of these formats, listed in preference order:

- Photoshop compressed TIFF
- Photoshop EPS
- Photoshop BMP
- Photoshop JPEG

We cannot accept these formats: GIF, PCX, PDF, PNG, PIXAR, RAW, SCITEX, EXE.

Please send a disc, again in order of preference:

- CD
- Zip
- floppy

Categories: Boating—Outdoors—Sports/Recreation

CONTACT:
David Rud, Managing Editor
Material: All
5 John Clarke Rd.
PO Box 3400
Newport RI 02840-0992
Phone: 401-847-1588
Fax: 401-848-5048
E-mail: editor@sailingworld.com
Website: www.sailingworld.com

Saint Raphael's Better Health

Writers' Guidelines:

Better Health is a bimonthly health and wellness magazine that offers its 500,000 readers perceptive articles on health, medicine, fitness, nutrition and personal well-being. Our aim is to help people live smarter, longer and make better-informed healthcare decisions. The magazine is published by the Hospital of Saint Raphael in New Haven, Conn. Although it has subscribers in all 50 states and parts of Canada, its primary circulation area is Southern Connecticut. Thus, Connecticut health professionals and people are featured along with national experts in all our stories. Established in 1979, Better Health is always looking for exceptional writers who accept nothing but the best from themselves and the publications they work for.

Please observe the following guidelines, so you can be considered seriously for publication:

1. Always query in writing. Never submit a finished article. In your query, be sure to describe not just your story idea, but the approach you will take and possible sources. All articles published in Better Health must contain some quotes and narrative from Saint Raphael health professionals, or affiliates of the Saint Raphael Healthcare System. Include 4-5 published clips with your query, as well as a SASE so we can respond to your idea. Mail to: Better Health magazine, Hospital of Saint Raphael, 1450 Chapel St., New Haven, CT 06511.

Do not fax or e-mail your query and clips.

2. We buy 30 feature articles a year. Each piece runs between 1,500 and 3,000 words, as determined by the editor. We do not run essays, poems, fiction, cartoons, filler material, or book or product reviews.

3. We do not accept reprints or simultaneous submissions. Also, since we are part of a Catholic healthcare system, we do not accept material advocating birth control, abortion, or any other issues at odds with Catholic church doctrine.

4. If we ask to see your proposed article on speculation, submit it doubled-spaced in black ink on white paper. Be sure to include your name, address, phone number and e-mail address. Your name should be on the top of the first page, as well as every page that follows. Also include a SASE. Our asking to see your article does not guarantee its publication.

5. Your manuscript should be written in an up-beat, lively, active voice, observing the highest standards of writing and grammar. It should be error-free in spelling and syntax and—most importantly—in facts. We reserve the right to edit all material and to add or substitute our own material, as needed.

6. Final versions of all assigned/accepted stories must be submitted in a text only format on a 3.5-inch IBM disk or via e-mail, along with a mailed or faxed hard copy.

7. We pay on acceptance, $250 to $700 depending on the article size, and purchase First North American Serial Rights. We pay some expenses, which are agreed upon in advance. If we accept an article but then decide not to publish it, we pay a 20% kill fee. All stories must be received on, or before, the assigned deadline date to be considered for acceptance.

8. Please give us at least one month to review, and respond to, your query. Do not call our office. We will contact you with our decision within a reasonable period of time.

Thank you for your interest in Better Health, and good luck! If you have not seen a recent issue of the magazine, we suggest sending a $2.50 check for a sample copy.

Categories: Health

CONTACT: Editor
Better Health Magazine
Hospital of Saint Raphael
1450 Chapel St
New Haven CT 06511
Website: www.srhs.org

Salmon-Trout-Steelheader

No formal guidelines. However, we do accept unsolicited articles. Our general focus is on fishing and the out-of-doors.

Categories: Fishing—Outdoors—Recreation—Sports/Recreation

CONTACT: Nick Amato
Material: All
PO Box 82112
Portland OR 97282
Phone: 503-653-8108
Website: www.amatobooks.com

Salon

Salon welcomes article queries and submissions. The best way to submit articles and story pitches is via e-mail.

We ask that you please send the text of your query or submission in plain text in the body of your e-mail, rather than as an attached file, as we may not be able to read the format of your file. If you wish to contribute, please spend some time familiarizing yourself with *Salon*'s various sites and features. Please put the words "EDITORIAL SUBMISSIONS" in the subject line of the e-mail. You can find the editor's name on our *Salon* Staff page. And please tell us a little about yourself

— your experience and background as a writer and qualifications for writing a particular story. If you have clips you can send us via e-mail, or Web addresses of pages that contain your work, please send us a representative sampling (no more than three or four, please).

We do our best to respond to all inquiries, but be aware that we are sometimes inundated. If you have not heard back from us after three weeks, please assume that we will not be able to use your idea or submission.

Also please note that *Salon* does not solicit fiction or poetry submissions and will not be able to respond to such submissions

Categories: Nonfiction—Arts—Book Reviews—Business—Current Affairs— Entertainment—Lifestyle—Politics—Sexuality—Technology

CONTACT: Kerry Lauerman, Editor
E-mail: klauerman@Salon.com
Material: Arts & Entertainment
CONTACT: Andrew O'Hehir, Editor
E-mail:aoh@Salon.com
Material: Books
CONTACT: The Editor, Life
E-mail: life@Salon.com
Material: Life
CONTACT: Geraldine Sealey, Senior Editor
E-mail: gsealey@Salon.com
Material: News/Politics
CONTACT: Karen Croft, Editor
E-mail: kcroft@Salon.com
Material: Sex
CONTACT: Andrew Leonard, Editor
E-mail: aleonard@Salon.com
Material: Technology & Business
22 4th St., 11th Floor,
San Francisco, CA 94103
Phone: 415-645-9200
Fax: 415-645-9204
Website: www.*Salon*.com

San Francisco

We do not have formal writer's guidelines. We accept queries. Ouor advice to new writers: First, read a few back issues of *San Francisco* to get a feel for what we publish. Then send us a query letter.

Categories: Culture—General Interest—Lifestyle—Regional
CONTACT: Lisa Trottier, Managing Editor
Material: All
243 Vallejo St.
San Francisco CA 94111
Phone: 415-398-2800

San Francisco Chronicle Magazine

LETTERS TO THE EDITOR: Send letters to: Letters Editor, ChronicleMagazine, 901 Mission St., San Francisco, CA 94103. E-mail letters to magazine@sfchronicle.com; fax 415-543-6956. Include name, city and phone number. Unsolicited contributions must be accompanied by a stamped, self-addressed envelope.

The San Francisco Chronicle Magazine does not accept responsibility for any unsolicited items. To respond to Facetime or Neighborhood, or if you have an idea for a future column, e-mail Sam Whiting at swhiting@sfchronicle.com.

WRITERS: The Magazine is looking for general interest features and profiles with a Bay Area connection. To pitch a story or idea, e-mail Alison Biggar at abiggar@sfchronicle.com.

FREELANCE OPPORTUNITIES: We don't have strict guide-

lines, but familiarity with The Chronicle is important. We are a weekly Sunday Magazine. All stories MUST have a local (Bay Area) angle. We do not run syndicated columns, comics, poetry or op-eds, arts previews, listings or event-related stories. We do not cover breaking news. If you're not sure whether we've covered a particular topic, please check www.sfgate.com.

The Magazine also plans coverage at least 6 to 8 weeks in advance. Rates vary by individual, and payment is upon publication.

MY WORD: Our back-page personal essay is 900 words. We're looking for writers who have a distinctive voice and a compelling story to tell. Some of our favorites: "The Way of the Bus" by Dashka Slater (August 3, 2003), "Finding Mrs. Experience" by Douglas Cruickshank (March 23, 2003), "At One With the Market" by Rodes Fishburne (February 23, 2003).

Topics we're not so interested in include bouts with illness, death of a parent or loved one (unless you're Dave Eggers), childhood memories of Playland-at-the-Beach, children's charming antics, special pet stories and childhood sports memories. E-mail essays to Alison Biggar at abiggar@sfchronicle.com.

PHOTOS AND ILLUSTRATIONS: We use a limited number of freelance photographers and illustrators. Send information to Joey Rigg at jrigg@sfchronicle.com.

THEMED ISSUES: We publish a number of themed issues each year. See our website.

Categories: Nonfiction—San Francisco Bay Area

CONTACT: Alison Biggar, Editor
Material: Stories
E-mail: abiggar@sfchronicle.com
CONTACT: Joey Rigg, Art Director
Material: Photos and Illustrations
E-mail: jrigg@sfchronicle.com
CONTACT: Sam Whiting
Material: Facetime or Neighborhood
E-mail: swhiting@sfchronicle.com
San Francisco Chronicle Magazine
901 Mission St
San Francisco CA 94103
Website: www.sfgate.com

Sandlapper®

Sandlapper
The Magazine of South Carolina

Editorial Philosophy

Sandlapper is a quarterly magazine focusing on the positive aspects of South Carolina. We look for articles and phot-essays about South Carolina's interesting people, places, activities, heritage and cuisine. No political/controversial issues, except as they relate to history. *Sandlapper* is intended to be read at those times when people want to relax with an attractive, high-quality magazine that entertains and informs them about their state.

Article Content & Style

We consider for publication nonfiction articles and photo-essays. No fiction or poetry, at this time. We occasionally buy reprints.

Simultaneous submissions are not accepted; we presume an article submittal is for our exclusive consideration, subject to terms under the "Payment & Rights Acquisition" section, below.

The editors consider articles of variable length, from approximately one to six magazine pages (500-3,000 words). Any approach the author chooses to take—standard third-person, first-person, Q&A format, impressionistic, etc.—may be accepted, provided it works. We look for top-quality literature. Humor is encouraged. Profanity is discouraged. Good taste is a standard. Unique angles are critical for acceptance. Dare to be bold. But not too bold. ! (Napoleon, or whoever)

Topics to avoid:
- Politics
- Topical/controversial issues
- R-rated subjects
- Commercial enterprises
- First-person nostalgia

Articles should not be submitted incomplete or subject to change/correction/addition. Late changes can create major problems. If you elect to let your sources review your m;anscrtipt draft, then YOU deal with them; please complete all discourse with them before submitting the manuscript for publication.

The editors reserve the right to change the title of a submitted article and to alter, condense, expand and otherwise edit the text of the article without approval by the author.

Photographs & Illustrations

Sandlapper buys black-and-white prints, color transparencies and art. Digital photography will be accepted in the following format only: JPEGS at minimum 300 dpi, at 8½ x 11-inch size. Please provide digital images on CD or IBM-compatible disk, accompanied by proof or laser print. Photographers should submit working cutlines for each photograph. Unused photos will be returned to the photographer if adequate return postage is provided. Photographs for accepted articles will be returned after publication. Please put your name on each slide or print so they can be properly credited and returned.

Our guidelines for accepting digital photography:

- First and foremost, all digital photos used by *Sandlapper* have to have been taken in South Carolina.
- Next, if you are simply submitting in hopes of being published, rather than for an assignment we have handed out, consider this: There are four issues a year—Spring, Summer, Fall and Winter—so we shoot photos that represent those seasons and you might just find your photo on the cover. A date reference on your submissions would help. In the past we have selected what we thought was a beautiful spring flower shot, but upon further research found that the plant actually blooms in fall. If we had only known we might have used that photo two issues earlier. But we missed that chance, as well as the Spring issue!
- Always take pictures on the highest settings your camera allows. The higher the resolution the sharper and clearer the image will reproduce. The larger the file, the less photos you can get on your camera's disc—invest in a 64 MB or larger disk for your camera!
- When taking photos remember that magazines are vertical. Do you want to get the cover shot? Do you want to see your photo as a full page in an article? Remember to take some vertical shots!
- Please do not direct us to Ofoto or a similar internet site to review your submissions—we need a CD or Zip disk containing your photos and a printout of each photo to do our job effectively. The printout of each photo should be *100% size*. This can be as simple as a black and white laser printout. Only digital photos *with* printouts will be considered! If you sorted through thousands of great images each issue, you would understand how important it is to keep each article and its corresponding images together in one envelope! The internet doesn't fit in an envelope.
- Please be sure that your Zip disk or CD is not formatted exclusively for PCs. Our photo editors work on Macs and you may get bumped out of the photo selection if we can't open your submissions. Want to submit your photo on a floppy disk? Think twice! A general rule is that if the photo will fit on a floppy, it's probably not a large enough file!
- JPG or TIF formats are preferred.
- RGB color modes is preferred.
- Please submit lo-resolution files as well as hi-resolution files—and label them as such. We handle thousands of photos each issue and it would be wonderful if your hi-res and lo-res files were named exactly the same name, but with the addition of LO on the lo-res files and HI on the hi-res files names. For example: RedBarnLO.jpg and RedBarnHI.jpg.

- Do not try to make the file sizes or image sizes larger AFTER you have taken the digital image. The information is not there—don't force it or the images will look pixilated.
- Before submitting photos, please do a little editing. We trust that you can edit from the 300 shots you took last week down to 10 you are really, really proud of! Please send your best, not your entire portfolio. Please give us a call of email if you have any questions about *Sandlapper* digital image submissions: Elaine Gillespie, 803-779-2126, elaine@thegillespieagency.com.

Queries, Assignments & Article Submittals

Unsolicited manuscripts will be considered, but we strongly recommend that you query in writing with a brief description of the article topic you have in mind. Several ideas maybe described in one query. (Please don't send further query letters until we've responded to your first one.) One or two (maximum) clips of your previously published work would be helpful. Telephone queries are DISCOURAGED; we will not be able to give you an immediate decision on the phone, and we prefer that you submit your own typed description rather than make us scribble a description based on telephone notations.

Seasonal article ideas should be suggested at least six months in advance.

Article topics are discussed at regular editorial staff meetings. We try to report on queries withn one month. If we like an idea, we will invite the author to submit the article ON SPECULATION; we will not guarantee purchase of an article in advance of submittal. No kill fees.

Text should be TYPED, DOUBLE-SPACED, on standard 8½ x 11-inch white paper. Article submittals on microcomputer diskette are STRONGLY encouraged but not required. Acceptable disk systems are PC Windows or DOS. The diskette should be accompanied by a hard-copy print-out of the text, double-spaced. Electronic submissions encouraged.

DO NOT submit an article that is incomplete, is pending approval or revision by your sources, or is otherwise subject to change before we go to press.

All correspondence, including query letters and article/photography submittals, should be accompanied by an SASE with adequate return postage. *Sandlapper* accepts no responsibility for unsolicited material.

Payment & Rights Acquisition

Payment for articles and photographs varies, based on a freelance budget of approximately $50-$100 per published magazine page (including combined text and photography/art). We typically pay $25-$75 per photograph and artwork; maximum $100 for a cover or centerspread photo.

Payment normally is made approximately one month after publication.

The author/photographer will retain the copyright. *Sandlapper* will acquire a) the right of first publication of the article and photographs (in the magazine and in the on-line editions of *Sandlapper*), b) subsequent, multiple reprint rights, including electronic media of the article and photographs in *Sandlapper*-related reprints, and c) the right to grant access to the article, photographs, and other bibliographic citation material stored electronically in public databases, and to furnish printed copies thereof requested through such public databases. If the author/photographer subsequently grants reprint rights to another publication, *Sandlapper* requests but does not require that the subsequent publication include credit to *Sandlapper* as the original publisher. *Sandlapper* requires a current issue embargo on subsequent publication; the article must not appear in print elsewhere until after the dateline period of its *Sandlapper* appearance has ended.

By submitting an article, the author warrants and represents that a) the author has included no material in the article in violation of any rights of any person or entity, and b) the author has disclosed to *Sandlapper* all relationships of the author to any person or entity featured in the article, and all relationships to any person or entity producing or marketing any product or providing any service referred to in the article.

A Note about Idea Submittals...

Before the start-up of the magazine was announced formally, the editors began building a database of article ideas (several hundred, initially). Most of these were the editors' ideas; some came from prospective freelance writers. we immediately discovered many suggestions were duplicates—as many as five different writers suggested the same article topic almost simultaneously. In the ensuing weeks, as more freelancers got word of pending publication, the duplicity of certain article topics quickly became a *multiplicity*.

We try to be fair. Whenever we receive a good article suggestion, we enter a brief description of it in a computer database, noting the name of the original proposer. However, we make no pledges. If you suggest an article idea to us and you see an article on the subject published later in the magazine under another writer's byline, it probably will be because a) that writer submitted the idea first or b) we believed that writer had better credentials to prepare that particular article.

Where to Send Queries, Articles and Photographs

Please correspond to: Aïda Rogers, editor. Please enclose a self-addressed, stamped envelope. Or, E-mail her at aida@sandlapper.org.

Thank you for your interest in *Sandlapper*! We wish you the best with your writing, photography and art, and we hope to work with you in the future.

Categories: Nonfiction—Adventure—Arts—Biography—Business—Children—Civil War—College—Conservation—Cooking—Culture—Education—Entertainment—Environment—Family—Fishing—Folklore—Food/Drink—Gardening—General Interest—History—Hobbies—Humor—Interview—Lifestyle—Outdoors—Photography—Recreation—Regional—Rural America—Senior Citizen—Sports/Recreation—Travel

CONTACT: Aïda Rogers, Editor
Material: All
PO Box 1108
Lexington, SC 29071
Phone: 803-359-9941
Fax: 803-359-0629
E-mail: aida@sandlapper.org
Website: www.sandlapper.org

The Saturday Evening Post

Guidelines for Submitting Work Writers & Cartoonists

Before submitting work to *The Saturday Evening Post*, please take the time to read our guidelines

For Writers

Before sending us a manuscript or query, we hope you will look over past issues of the *Post* to get an idea of the range and style of articles we publish. You will discover that our main emphasis is health and fitness. Although there are many specialty publications in this field, the *Post*'s goal is to remain unique by presenting not only cutting-edge news but by combining this with information of practical use to our readers.

Major freelance contributions in recent years include: "Hats On For Health: A Skin-Cancer Warning from Down Under," about the advanced skin-cancer-prevention program in Australia, and "Munchausen by Proxy: The Deadly Game," about a little-understood but prevalent psychological disorder that can be devastating to children.

In addition to health-related articles, the *Post* buys humor and anecdotes suitable for "Post Scripts," as well as cartoons, illustrations, and photos. Payment ranges from $15 for Post Scripts to $25-$400 for most feature articles.

Our nonfiction needs include how-to, useful articles on gardening, pet care and training, financial planning, and subjects of interest to a family-oriented readership. For nonfiction articles, indicate any special qualifications you have for writing about the subject, especially for technical or scientific material. Include one or two published clips with your query. We prefer typed manuscripts between 2,500 and 3,000 words in length. We generally buy all rights.

Although we seldom publish new fiction, our readers enjoy upbeat stories that stress traditional relationships and family values. A light, humorous touch is appreciated. We are also always in need of straight humor articles. Make us laugh and we'll buy it.

We respond quickly to queries, normally within three weeks. If you do send the whole manuscript, either (1) include a sufficiently stamped and sized SASE for its return should we decide not to use it; or (2) indicate you do not want the material returned and include an SASE with appropriate postage for a reply. Please send typed, double-spaced copy. We normally respond to manuscript submissions within six weeks. You are free to submit the article simultaneously elsewhere.

Feature articles average about 2,000 words. We like positive, fresh angles to *Post* articles, and we ask that they be thoroughly researched.

For Cartoonists

Objective: We aim to please all readers and insult or offend none.

Audience: All ages, average age 50+, male/female evenly split.

Payment: The Post buys all rights for $125, payable upon publication.

Size Requirements: 8 1/2" x 11" or half that size is fine.

SASE: Return envelopes are required because you will get a response letter; business envelopes are OK if you send in Xerox copies that don't need to be returned. Response postcards are not helpful.

Copies or Originals: Either is acceptable. We are careful with originals, and they are easier for us to pick.

Lines: We tend to only use cartoons we can typeset captions at the bottom. Avoid dialogue balloons. Please print or type your captions in dark blue or black ink only.

How Many?: Feel free to send up to a dozen submissions per mailing. Please submit one mailing to The Post at one time. The Post publishes every two months, so expect an 8-10 week turnaround.

Original Ideas Only: We like to buy never-published material. That's what our readers expect.

Ideas to Avoid: Vices, such as smoking, drinking, adultery. People you would not like or trust. Don't ridicule doctors, lawyers, or politicians.

Ideas that Work: Kids, pets, family, twists of fate. Doctor and medical situations are always needed.

Categories: Fiction—Nonfiction—Animals—Cartoons—Family—Gardening—Health—Humor—Money and Finances—Physical Fitness—Travel

CONTACT: Cory SerVaas, M.D.
Material: Medical/Fitness
CONTACT: Holly Miller
Material: Travel
CONTACT: Fiction Editor
Material: Fiction
CONTACT: Steve Pettinga
Material: Post Scripts
Saturday Evening Post
1100 Waterway Blvd
Indianapolis IN 46202
CONTACT: Post Toons
Material: Cartoons
Post Toons
Box 567
Indianapolis, IN 46202
Phone: 317-634-1100
Website: www.satevepost.org

Saveur
Savor a World of Authentic Cuisine

Formal guidelines not available. Please read a number of issues to ascertain the publication's style and needs.

Send queries to address below.

Categories: Nonfiction—Cooking—Food/Drink

CONTACT: Submissions Editor
Material: All
World Publications
304 Park Ave, South
New York NY 10010
Phone: 212-219-7400
E-mail: saveur@worldpub.com
Website: www.saveur.com

School Mates

Please refer to *Chess Life* magazine.

SchoolArts

SchoolArts is a national magazine for elementary and secondary art and classroom teachers as well as for others who are active or interested in art education. We encourage anyone involved in the field of art education to submit articles for publication.

What our readers want:

Art educators look to *SchoolArts* for inspiration, information, and ideas. Think about what excites them, what worries them, and what they need to know in order to do what they do better. We're most interested in articles on:

• successful and meaningful units, lessons, or activities
• safe and economical applications of art techniques, equipment, or materials; low-budget tips
• how to integrate art with other subjects
• how to organize artrooms or classrooms; tips for teaching from a cart
• exemplary art programs (in school, after school, museum, summer or community)
• how to teach, and assess learning in, art history, art production, art criticism and aesthetics
• teaching art to special populations
• effective public relations efforts related to art (exhibitions, open houses, newsletters, advocacy)
• art curriculum development (pre-K-college)
• staff development programs for art teachers
• parent involvement and community partnerships

Writing your article

1. Before you begin, review recent issues of *SchoolArts*. Notice the balance of photographs and text in feature articles. Remember that teachers spend about an hour reading an issue. Try to keep your ideas focused and your article concise.

2. Outline your ideas. If your article describes an activity or process, think about these questions:

• How and why was the activity developed? What will students learn?
• What equipment, materials, and resources are needed?
• For what grade level(s) is the activity intended?
• What skills, concepts or attitudes can be improved by the activity?
• How is learning assessed?
• Can other disciplines be incorporated?
• What problems might teachers encounter when attempting this activity?

3. When you begin to write, remember to:

• Tell more than just the facts. Share the human element in your experiences: sights, sounds, unexpected events, humorous situations. Don't be afraid to mention the hard parts or disasters.
• Take a friendly, casual tone.
• Break complex processes into simple steps.

Special reminders

Avoid presentations of school projects that trivialize the sacred arts of cultural groups.

If you use hazardous, volatile, or toxic materials in your activity, say so. Explain what precautions and safety measures teachers and students must take while using these materials.

Include suggestions to adapt your article for different grade levels.

Include references and helpful resources.

Submitting your Manuscript

Electronic submission along with a hard copy is preferable. Submit a double-spaced, typed manuscript, preferably using Helvetica (Mac) or Arial (PC) fonts, with one-inch margins on all sides. Number each page. Please avoid using any script-type fonts and or all capital letters. On a cover page, suggest a title and type your name, position, school, home mailing address, home telephone number, and e-mail address. All but your home mailing address and home phone number will be included in your credit line, so that readers can contact you if they have questions or comments about your article. Most manuscripts are about four pages, not counting the title or captions.

Captions

Provide captions for each photograph on a separate captions page. Number each caption with a corresponding number marked on the back of the photograph or on the top of the slide. If the photograph is of student artwork, the caption should, at least, identify the name of the student, grade level, age, school, media, and title. If the student has described the work or made a personal statement about the work, include that as part of the caption.

Electronic Submissions

We accept digital files on:

• 1.44MB HD floppy disks (3 1/2")
• Zip disks--100MB or 250MB
• CD ROM
• Jaz disks--1GB
• Imation SuperDrive 120MB disks
• E-mail attachments—stuffed or zipped only.

Photographs and artwork

Let your illustrations tell your story! Illustrations are as important as the text of an article, and they should accompany any submission to *SchoolArts*. Include as many illustrations as necessary. If your article describes a process or technique, photograph each step. Submit slides and photographs in plastic sleeves. Do not mount prints. Do not write directly on front or back of photographs: Use self-adhesive labels on backs. Number each illustration and provide the student's name, your name, and any other relevant information on a separate caption sheet. Indicate the top of image. Supply photographs that are in focus and carefully composed. Avoid busy backgrounds or foregrounds. Photograph sculptures or three-dimensional works against a plain background. If the subject is colorful, use color slide film. Slides reproduce best. Color prints and digital files are also acceptable. We cannot use digital print-outs without the actual digital files or color photocopies. Note: Turn off the date mode on your camera. If photographing under fluorescent lighting, use a flash or Tungsten 160 film. If black-and-white film suits the subject, send high contrast black-and-white prints.

Permissions:

If students appear in the photographs, send signed permission forms for each student.

When submitting electronic images, please remember:

• Images must be scanned at 300 dpi or higher. Any image less than 300 dpi will not print well. Please do not convert images from a lower resolution to 300 dpi; it does not change the poor quality of the image.

• In order to be able to provide you with the best designed article, scan images to approximately 4 x 6" or larger.

• Save images in the following formats: TIFF (.tiff) EPS (.eps) Quark 3.3 or greater* Illustrator 6.0 or greater* Photoshop 5.0 or greater* (*Mac applications only)

• All images should be submitted as CMYK or grayscale.

• Always submit laser copies of all images on the disk. If you are concerned about color, please submit color copies for color correction.

We prefer:

• clear photographs of finished artwork.

• step-by-step photographs illustrating a process.

• photographs of individual students or small groups creating art, especially views that focus on the artwork.

• photographs of teachers working with students.

We prefer not to use:

• photocopies of drawings.

• photographs of students holding their artwork.

• Polaroid™ photographs.

• color photocopies or low resolution computer printouts

Line Drawings

If line drawings best illustrate your article, label, caption, and number them as you would photographs. Line art should be drawn with black ink or felt-tip markers. Protect art with a tissue overlay and pack between cardboard for protection.

Return of your submissions:

For return of your submissions, please enclose a self-addressed stamped envelope with sufficient postage. If you submit original artwork, *SchoolArts* cannot be responsible for its return.

Categories: Nonfiction—Arts—Children—Education—Juvenile—Teen

CONTACT: Nancy Walkup, Editor
Material: All
Davis Publications, Inc.
2223 Parkside Dr
Denton TX 76201
Website: www.davis-art.com/schoolarts/index.asp

Science Fiction Chronicle

Needs op-ed pieces on subjects of relevance to the genre publishing market place; feature articles about the future of genre publishing from both the perspective of those involved in the publishing end and those involved in the retail end. Also needs interviews and retrospectives on prominent writer's careers. NO fiction submissions. Pays 4 cents/word on acceptance. No e-mail subs. Please mark clearly as being for *SFC.*

Categories: Nonfiction—Writing—Genre Publishing

CONTACT:
PO Box 2988
Radford VA 24143-2988

Science of Mind

Science of Mind magazine accepts query letters and manuscripts only. Include a brief description/outline and word count. We publish several types of articles that teach, inspire, motivate, and inform. Editorial content addresses the concerns, interests, and problems of readers, offering thoughtful perspectives on how they can experience greater self-acceptance, empowerment, and meaningful living. Achieving wholeness through applying Science of Mind principles is the primary focus.

The basic requirements of good, clear writing apply to all material used in the magazine. In addition, these special guidelines should also be noted:

First-Person Articles—These articles concern individuals who have experienced a significant, often dramatic, event in their lives. The theme of the article should inspire readers to make a similar change in their own lives. The article may also recount a deep spiritual experience or the way in which Science of Mind principles have been applied to create a positive inner change. Queries only. Length: 2,500-2,000 words. Payment: negotiable.

Interview—Each month an interview with a notable spiritual leader is featured. These articles are usually assigned, but queries are welcome. Refer to previous issues of *Science of Mind* for typical interview subjects and style to be followed. Bio, lead-in and photo required. Length: 2,500 words. Payment: negotiable.

1. Carefully check punctuation, spelling, and sentence structure before submitting your article. ELEMENTS OF STYLE by William Strunk is an excellent source book for basic writing practices.

2. Make a concerted effort to use language that is inclusive and gender neutral.

3. All accepted articles should be typed and preferably accompanied by Macintosh or IBM disc.

4. Type the number of words in the upper right corner of the first page. Be sure to include your name, address, and telephone number.

REMINDERS

• Ensure quality printout.

• Double-space everything, including quotations.

• Do not try to imitate the typeset copy using different styles of type. Simply type everything normally using lower-case letters, capitalizing in accordance with standard practice.

• Represent the quotations accurately and be sure they are sourced correctly.

• Be sincere.

Payment will be made within 30 days of the masthead date. We buy one-time rights unless otherwise specified. Simultaneous submissions and previously published work are accepted.

Categories: Nonfiction—Inspirational—Religion—Spiritual—New Age

CONTACT: Amanda Pisani, Editor-in-Chief
Material: All
2600 W Magnolia Blvd
Burbank CA 91505
E-mail: apisani@scienceofmind.com
Website: www.scienceofmind.com

SCI FICTION

Fiction Writer's Guidelines

SCIFICTION is looking for literate, strongly plotted science fiction and fantasy stories between 2,000 and 17,500 words—on a variety of subjects and themes. We want to intrigue our readers with mind-broadening, thought-provoking stories. Characterization is crucial. Stories must be written in clear, understandable prose. Payment is 20 cents a word up to $3,500. Originals only; no reprints.

It is impossible for us to judge a story's quality without seeing the complete manuscript. If you have a story you think fits our requirements, submit it for consideration. But please do not send more than one story at a time; wait for a response on one before submitting another.

Note: we do not publish sword-and-sorcery or space opera. And we do not accept unsolicited poetry or simultaneous submissions. We will consider a self-contained story that is part of a novel, or may later be developed into one.

All stories must be typed, double-spaced, and on only one side of each page. Each page should be numbered and include title and author's last name. The author's full name and address should appear in the upper left-hand corner of page one; an approximate word count should appear in the upper right-hand corner. Do not staple and do not use unusual fonts. All italics must be shown by underlining. Please paper clip your manuscript. If you choose to submit photocopies, they must be clear and readable. We do not accept any form of electronic submission.

Please include an appropriately sized, self-addressed, stamped envelope (SASE). Contributors residing outside the United States should include one (1) international reply coupon and a letter-sized envelope for reply. Foreign manuscripts will no longer be returned under any circumstances.

We usually respond within five to eight weeks after receiving a submission. Depending on numerous variables, however, it can sometimes take longer. Please give us ample time before inquiring about a submission's status.

Categories: Fantasy

CONTACT: Ellen Datlow, Fiction Editor
SCIFI.COM
PMB 391
511 Avenue of the Americas
New York NY 10011-8436
Website: www.scifi.com

Scouting

The magazine is published by the Boy Scouts of America six times a year. It is mailed to about one million adult volunteer and professional Scout leaders (Scouters). Subscription is included as part of each Scouter's annual registration fee.

Scouting magazine articles are mainly about successful program activities conducted by or for Cub Scout packs, Boy Scout troops and venturing crews. We also include features on winning leadership techniques and styles, profiles of outstanding individual leaders, and inspirational accounts (usually first person) of Scouting's impact on an individual, either as a youth or while serving as a volunteer adult leader.

Because most volunteer Scout leaders are also parents of children of Scout age, *Scouting* is also considered a family magazine. We publish material we feel will help parents in strengthening families. (Because they often deal with communicating and interacting with young people, many of these features are useful to a reader in both roles as parent and Scout leader).

We also feature an occasional general-interest article geared to our adult audience. These include subjects such as nature, social issues and trends, historical topics and humor.

Many of our best article ideas come from volunteer and professional Scouters, but most stories are written by staff members or professional writers assigned by us. We seldom publish unsolicited manuscripts (the exception being inspirational accounts or successful program ideas by individual Scouters). We rely heavily on regional writers to cover an event or activity in a particular part of the country.

A query with a synopsis or outline of a proposed story is essential. Include a SASE to insure a reply. We respond to queries within three weeks. We buy short features of 500 to 700 words; some longer features, up to 1,200 words, usually the result of a definite assignment to a professional writer. We do not buy fiction or poetry.

We pay on acceptance. We purchase first rights unless otherwise specified (purchase does not necessarily guarantee publication). Photos, if of acceptable quality, are usually included in payment for certain assignments. (We normally assign a professional photographer to take photographs for major story assignments). Payment rates depend on the professional quality of the article. Payment is from $300 to $500 for a short feature, $500 to $800 for a major article.

Writers or photographers should be familiar with the Scouting program and *Scouting* magazine. A sample copy will be sent if you provide a SASE and $2.50.

Categories: Nonfiction—Children—Conservation—Crafts/Hobbies—Ecology—Education—Environment—Family—Fishing—Health—Outdoors—Parenting—Physical Fitness—Recreation—Sports/Recreation—Teen—Travel—Young Adult

CONTACT: Magazine Division—Editorial
Material: All
Boy Scouts of America
1325 W. Walnut Hill Lane
PO Box 15207
Irving TX 75015-2079
Phone: 972-580-2367
Fax: 972-580-2079
Website: www.bsa.scouting.org

Scr(i)pt Magazine

scr(i)pt magazine is a bi-monthly publication that examines the film industry through the eyes of the screenwriter. The magazine serves as both a resource for the craft of screenwriting and source of inspiration from professionals in the field. We have featured interviews with such talented screenwriters as: Ron Bass, Frank Darabont, Robert Duvall, Randall Wallace, Les and Glen Charles and Richard LaGravenese. Each issue of *scr(i)pt* offers writers information about writing, marketing and selling screenplays throughout the industry. Having been established in the industry since 1989, *scr(i)pt* magazine offers writers the edge they need to break into the screenwriting community.

EDITORIAL GUIDELINES

scr(i)pt is currently seeking writers presently working in the industry to contribute meaningful articles on the craft and business of screenwriting.

SUBMISSION GUIDELINES
TYPES OF ARTICLES

We are interested in articles written by or dealing with currently working screenwriters, agents and producers. Any articles submitted should be timely, in-depth and of interest to screenwriters in particular. We accept articles about both the craft and business of screenwriting, with an emphasis on writing excellent screenplays and managing a successful career. We are interested in both feature articles and interviews. We do not accept comparative book or software reviews, or film or festival reviews in the print magazine. We do, however, consider those types of pieces for the web site. Please do not submit fiction, poetry, cartoons or reviews. We publish only original, previously unpublished material. IF YOUR ARTICLE PERTAINS TO OR PROMOTES SOMETHING YOU ARE SELLING—WE WILL NOT PUBLISH IT. NO EXCEPTIONS.

SENDING A QUERY

We ask that all potential writers send a query letter proposing your article before sending a complete manuscript. Please do not telephone our editors, as we only accept proposals in writing. All unsolicited and assigned articles are on speculation unless prior arrangement is made. You should receive a response in four to six weeks (please enclose a SASE). For a faster response, feel free to send queries via e-mail , being sure to supply a return e-mail address.

ARTICLES AND STYLE

All articles must be between 2,000 and 3,000 words unless other arrangements are made with the editors. Please consult the General Style Guidelines for further information.

SUBMISSION FORMAT

Accepted articles can be either e-mailed or sent on a Macintosh compatible disk in Microsoft Word, RTF or Text Only format. All submissions should be neatly typed and double spaced, include a title, your byline and a suggested deck. Please place an asterisk around any italicized words or movie titles, (i.e. *Raging Bull*). For interviews, please list contact information for the interviewee(s). Additionally, a list of any photo stills or illustrations that you feel would best illustrate your article would be helpful. Please check with the editors before submitting photos.

REVISIONS

Depending on the number of revisions that need to be made, we may either return the article to you with suggestions for changes, or make minor changes before publication. Any articles which are significantly longer than the assigned length will be returned to the sender

R-U

to be edited. Writers who provide us with a fax number will be faxed a designed copy of his article.

PAYMENT

An invoice must accompany all articles accepted for publication. Writers are responsible for submitting invoices! Payment will be made 30 days from receipt of the article and invoice (no exceptions). Rate is $0.05 to $0.08 cents per word based on edited word count, amount of research and style of the article and is for first-time reprint rights. An additional $25 may be paid should the editors decide to print all or part of the article on the web site. Invoices must be submitted on a separate piece of paper, hard copy, and must include the date, your name, address, contact information, social security number, article title, intended print issue and amount due. A kill fee of 50% of the agreed upon fee may be paid for materials originally solicited by the editors.

ISSUES

Sample issues of *scr(i)pt* are available for $8 per issue plus postage. Send check or money order to: *scr(i)pt* magazine, 5638 Sweet Air Road, Baldwin, Maryland, 21013. Issues are also available at most major bookstore chains, or purchase a back issue or subscription online.

ONLINE ARTICLES

Scriptmag.com accepts a wide range of articles for the e-articles. Film, book, software, video, and seminar reviews are accepted. Payment is between $25 and $50 per article. Please contact editor@scriptmag.com with your article ideas.

Categories: Nonfiction—Business—Screenwriting—Writing

CONTACT: Editor-in-Chief
Material: All
5638 Sweet Air Rd.
Baldwin, MD 21013-0007
Phone: 888-245-2228, ext. 202
Fax: 410-592-8062
E-mail: editor@scriptmag.com
Website: www.scriptmag.com

America's Western Boating Magazine

Sea
The Magazine of Western Boating

Sea is four-color, monthly publication for active West Coast boat owners. It was founded in 1908, and is published by the Duncan McIntosh Co. Circulation is approximately 50,000.

Sea is read by power boaters and sportfishing enthusiasts from Alaska to Mexico, and across the Pacific to Hawaii. *Sea* contains articles on Western cruising and fishing destinations, new boats and marine electronics, safety, navigation, seamanship, maintenance how-to, consumer guides to boating services, marine news and product buyer's guides.

Readers of *Sea* are experienced boaters: • 89.4% own a boat • 91.5% own a power boat • 58.8% have been boating 20+ years • 63% sportfish from their boat. —Source: Simmons Market Research

EDITORIAL FOCUS

Feature articles generally are between 1,200 and 1,600 words. Other articles range between 250 and 750 words. First-time contributors are encouraged to pitch articles on:

• West Coast cruising destinations—especially those in Baja California, Southern California, Puget Sound and British Columbia.

• Boating news from your Western home port.
• Western boating trends and issues.
• Seamanship (power boating only).
• Boat maintenance and repair.

Another good avenue for freelancers is *Sea*'s West Coast Focus section. It is comprised of brief news stories or isolated bits of information about Western boating and sportfishing. Focus stories are about 250 words each, and stand the best chance of running if they are accompanied by a color slide.

Focus story topics include: new marinas and boating projects; new fishing regulations; boat parades, festivals or owner rendezvous; and boating legislation updates. Preview stories are preferred over post-event reports, so readers who wish to participate may do so.

WHAT NOT TO SEND

Sea is not the market for stories about: boardsailing, canoeing, kayaking or surfing; power boat racing; wetlands restoration; party boat fishing; commercial fishing; boating accident reports; fiction; poetry; yacht club-oriented social activities; marine mammals; ferry boats, steamships, military ships, cruise ships, river boats or any boat or ship that is not a pleasureboat; and boating events on the East Coast of the United States or abroad.

SUBMISSION GUIDELINES

Submit written queries.

• Please allow 4 weeks for review of unsolicited manuscripts.

• Assigned stories should be sent via e-mail or on 3.5" computer disk, single spaced in ASCII format or Microsoft Word. Enclose a hard copy of the story with the disk.

• Include your address, daytime phone number and social security number on the first page of the manuscript.

• *Sea* buys first-time North American rights. Please notify us if your query or manuscript is a simultaneous submission or has been previously published.

PAYMENT

• Rates are based on length of the article, amount of research required and complexity of the assignment. A rate will be quoted by the assigning editor prior to commencement of work.

• Payment for articles and photographs used is made on publication. Checks are sent out in the first week of the issue month.

• Quoted rates may change if a story does not meet the criteria of the assignment. If major revisions are required, we will return the manuscript to the author to revise prior to final editing or rate adjustment.

• Some expenses, such as telephone calls or mileage, may be reimbursed by the assigning editor only if approval for such expenses is requested in advance. An invoice itemizing the expenses must be submitted within 10 days of the article.

• Approved overnight mail charges are reimbursed. We do not accept C.O.D. packages and do not have an account with a mailing service.

• *Sea* retains reprint rights via print and electronic media. The contributor retains all other rights for resale, re-publication, etc.

• It may be necessary to reschedule the publication date of the author's accepted work as editorial space dictates.

FOR MORE INFORMATION

Individual guidelines are available upon request for:

• West Coast Focus, SoCal Focus, Boat Reports and Cruising Destination Features.

Thank you for your interest.

Categories: Nonfiction—Boating—Recreation—Sports/Recreation—Travel

CONTACT: Eston Ellis, Managing Editor
Material: Any
17782 Cowan
Irvine CA 92614
Phone: 949-660-6150
Fax: 949-660-6172
E-mail: editorial@goboatingamerica.com

Sea Kayaker

We prefer contributions from experienced kayakers with some writing experience. You may submit articles on speculation or contact our editorial department for feedback before you begin work on an article.

Submission Requirements: Contributions may be submitted via email with text pasted into the body of the email message or as an attachment using one of the following formats: plain text (.txt), rich-text (.rtf), or Microsoft Word (.doc). Please include complete contact info (name, address, phone number and alternate email address, if applicable). Submissions may also be sent via regular mail to our office on CD (previously listed file formats are acceptable) with a hard-copy print-out. Clearly label all materials with your name, address, phone number and email address (if applicable).

Features: We recommend submitting an outline of your proposed feature along with a short writing sample from the story (approx. 500 words) to give us an idea of your writing style, ability and story direction (see our Writer's Tips for additional suggestions).

Destination Articles: Destination articles provide our readers with information about interesting places to paddle. They are usually based in North America, as the majority of our readership resides in this area. The area described should be large enough to provide several paddling itineraries and numerous overnight options.

If you'd like to write a Destination piece, you should have longstanding experience with the area: numerous trips and experiences throughout the location's paddling season. One or two trips to an area will not provide enough personal knowledge of the place.

Destination authors are required to provide information about launch sites, camping/overnight options, permits and other requirements for the area, along with tips on weather and water conditions to advise paddlers on paddling safely.

Destination articles include a map of the area (original provided by the author) and a short "Trip Planner" sidebar listing contact information for outfitters and other resources that our readers would find useful. Word count for Destination articles should be in the range of 2,500-3,000 words. See our Photography Guidelines for information about Destination photography.

Journey Articles: These are narratives about kayaking trips that take place over a minimum of 4 or 5 days. (Articles about trips organized by a 3rd-party touring company pose some special challenges and should be discussed with the editorial department.) The focus and length of Journey articles vary, but you'll need to do more than recount your trip: You must create an experience for the reader.

To give Journey continuity and a sense of progress, it helps to develop a theme or relate a personal goal or expectation specific to the trip. Whether your experience was a harrowing adventure, a trip to an exotic or unique setting, or a journey during which you experienced some transformation or learned something valuable, a theme will help drive your story.

Journey stories usually range from 2,500 to 5,000 words. See Photography Guidelines for information about Journey images.

Other Features: Other acceptable feature formats include essays, race stories, event coverage (from a non-commercial standpoint) and more. We will consider short-format Journey stories (if the duration of the trip is too short for a regular Journey) or narratives of kayaking experiences that don't fall into Destinations or Journeys. This category is flexible. Contact the editorial staff for feedback.

Departments

We recommend that all Department ideas are approved by the editor before articles are written. Regular Departments include:

• **Daytrippers**—These are "mini-Destinations" that provide information on one-day paddling itineraries in urban, densely populated, or frequently visited areas. Authors must be well-versed in the area. Contact the editors for complete guidelines.

• **Technique**—Techniques cover a wide range of topics: paddles strokes and braces, rolling, navigation, group dynamics, rescues, etc.

We prefer authors to be experienced paddlers or instructors. Articles include: a brief intro explaining the technique's usefulness and, if relevant, history; instruction in an appropriate order; precautions about any risks; and images, usually photos, illustrating each step and demonstrating the technique in a "realistic" setting. Length varies from 500 words for a single technique to 3,000 words for a range of techniques.

• **Do-It-Yourself**—D-I-Y articles are complete sets of instructions for projects useful to kayakers. Supplied instructions must be clear and complete, and materials must be available from independent sources. Projects must be within an average skill range and require tools that readers are likely to own or can easily afford to purchase. We require photos of the finished project as well as photos or drawings of the parts and critical phases of the work in progress. A list of materials, sources and costs should be supplied. D-I-Y articles lengths vary in relation to the complexity of the project.

• **Off the Water**— Short tips (200 words or less) for the workshop or on shore that enhance kayaking-related experiences or solve problems typically encountered while camping or maintaining kayaking equipment.

• **Gear Reviews**— Equipment reviews are usually assigned articles. Reviewers must be free of any relationship with the manufacturer that would compromise an objective review or suggest a conflict of interest. Authors must have experience or credentials to make a thorough and fair evaluation of the gear.

• **Safety**— Safety articles primarily cover kayaking accidents. Their main purpose is education to enable readers to learn from and avoid the misfortunes of others. Safety articles have two sections: a description of the incident and an analysis underscoring the significant factors and discussing how to better handle similar situations. We encourage readers to inform us about accidents they've heard of or been involved in, and we make every effort to be sensitive to the needs of those involved.

• **History**— Our History section covers everything from Aboriginal kayaking to events in past decades. Articles must reflect a thorough knowledge of the topic or extensive research. Old photographs or drawings are useful. Image sources must be identified, as we may need permission to publish them.

Submitting Content to Sea Kayaker All content submitted should be previously unpublished unless special permission is given from Sea Kayaker's editor. For examples of acceptable writing style, see our current issue, available through many bookstores and newsstands. To obtain a current or back issue, click here, or phone 206-789-9536. Please contact Sea Kayaker's editorial department with questions or for more information at 206-789-1326. Materials can be sent via USPS to: Sea Kayaker Editorial Dept.; P.O. Box 17029; Seattle, WA, 98127 (if a physical address is needed, send to: 7001 Seaview Ave. NW, Suite 135; Seattle, WA 98117), or emailed to: gretchen@seakayakermag.com Sea Kayaker magazine is not responsible for any unsolicited materials received. To ensure return of your materials, enclose a self-addressed envelope with correct postage.

Photography Guidelines

Feature Articles

For Journey and Destination articles, we prefer approximately 40 images to choose from. If you have significantly more, we suggest eliminating those of poor or questionable quality. A minimum of 20 images will be considered if the shots are directly in keeping with the guidelines below. Requirements for "Other" features vary. Sea Kayaker will assign accompanying illustrations as necessary. If interested, keep our Cover Photography Guidelines in mind while taking photos for feature articles.

Accepted Image Formats 1. High-quality 35mm film color slides (SK's preferred format) or negatives (larger format transparencies OK) NOTE: Duplicate slides may be submitted initially for approval, but we'll request originals for final scanning 2. High-resolution digital photographs (TIFF format on CD preferred; JPEG acceptable for email) 3. High-quality print photographs

Image Quality/Composition • Sharp focus and good, clear composition—subjects should be attractively framed and easy to "read" by viewers • Good contrast with rich, vivid color • Proper exposure (no overexposed or underexposed images) • Interesting subject matter • A dynamic quality (for example, an active paddler versus one who appears to be posing) • An interesting perspective or angle (we rarely use bow shots; often, the best photos are taken from a different eye level than that of sitting in a kayak or standing on shore) • Photos that support the article (there should be a good selection of images to match locations mentioned in the text) • A portrayal of safe, correct kayaking practices (PFDs should be worn in most cases)

Destination Articles

In order of importance (meaning, the categories from which we'd like the most photos to choose from), here is what we look for in Destination photography:

1. On-the-water shots of paddlers actively paddling, with a scenic backdrop unique to the paddling location.

2. Panoramic or scenic shots that don't necessarily show paddlers, but that give a feel for the geography of the area.

3. Medium-focal-length shots of paddlers doing things like reading charts, setting up camp, launching, fishing, exploring caves, or something specific to the area.

4. Shots of flora, fauna or scenery particular to the area paddled.

Journey Articles

Same guidelines as for Destination articles but including shots that capture moments in the narrative and any images describing an area's unique culture as discussed in the text: the people, their dwellings, handicrafts, etc.

Departments

See Writer's Guidelines for descriptions of individual Departments. General photo quality should be good and easy to "read." Contact editorial staff for more information.

Last Glance

The last page of Sea Kayaker magazine features a single photo or photo series providing an unusual perspective, along with a text-based description. Send your unique, humorous and/or thought-provoking sea kayak–related images in the following formats: 35mm slide or negative, good-quality print photo, print-resolution digital image.

Cover Guidelines

Vertical orientation required for cover images

Accepted Image Formats

1. High-quality 35mm color slides (SK's preferred format) or negatives (larger format transparency OK)

2. Digital images: • Most consumer-quality digital cameras cannot achieve a high enough resolution for a cover image. If you have a professional-quality digital camera (6 megapixels or higher), the following specs must be met for digital files: High-quality digital images must be a minimum size of 9" x 12" at 300 dpi • Large-format digital photography is still a new area for us, so please feel free to educate or enlighten us as necessary.

General Comments

Following are general guidelines for Sea Kayaker cover images; however, we are always willing to consider other possibilities. Be creative!

1. Cover theme should tie into kayaking; images should include a striking central subject that is very clear, well-lit and easy to "read" by the viewer.

2. Color and contrast should be rich and well-defined.

3. Pictures taken from unique angles or perspectives are generally more visually interesting than standard eye-level "landscape" images taken with a mid-frame horizon line.

4. Faces are good. Not all potential cover images have to include faces, but readers like being able to "connect" with a cover subject.

5. A cover image should include background area simple enough that the magazine logo and cover text can be clearly read over it (not too much texture and/or color variation). Keep this in mind when framing your pictures—it's always a good idea to include some space around your subject.

Note: The Sea Kayaker logo always appears on the top portion of the cover, covering approximately the top 1/5 of the image; cover text generally appears in the area below the logo, particularly on the left side, but is not limited to this space. We may also put additional text over the bottom of the image or elsewhere on the page.(Cover images must not appear to endorse a particular product or products by way of including company logos or product names. To comply with this policy, our production department may alter final digital files as necessary to remove logos appearing on kayaks, clothing and equipment.)

Submitting Images to Sea Kayaker All images should be previously unpublished unless special permission is given by Sea Kayaker's editor. For examples of appropriate images, see our current issue, available through many bookstores and newsstands. To obtain a current or back issue, visit our website or phone 206-789-9536.

Please contact Sea Kayaker's editorial department with questions or for more information at 206-789-1326. Images can be sent via USPS to: Sea Kayaker Editorial Dept.; P.O. Box 17029; Seattle, WA, 98127 (if a physical address is needed, send to: 7001 Seaview Ave. NW, Suite 135; Seattle, WA 98117). Low-resolution sample digital files can be sent in JPEG format via email to: gretchen@seakayakermag.com.

Sea Kayaker is not responsible for any unsolicited materials received. To ensure return of your materials, enclose a self-addressed envelope with correct postage.

Top 10 Tips for Writers—Feature Articles

1. Appeal to the senses. During your paddling experience, the world around you came to you through your eyes and ears. To put the reader in that same place, focus the writing on the same sensory information. For example, "The wind was blowing very hard," doesn't describe the scene, it only analyzes it. Write vividly, describing what you saw in enough detail for the reader to picture the same image: "The waves crested in white streaks of foam, and the spray coming over the bow stung my skin and eyes. I shouted to John, who was no more than a boat length ahead of me, but he never even turned his head." The readers can feel that they are a part of the scene and will come to the same conclusion: It's blowing hard.

2. Avoid unnecessary language. Avoid vague descriptors: Words like "glorious," "incredible," "awesome" and "magnificent" have no real content. What is an enormous wave? Is it as big as a boxcar? A split-level house? What color is the "colorful" fish?Avoid words you wouldn't use in conversation: An "ursine interloper" is still just a bear that wandered into your camp. If you interrupt the flow of the story to send a reader to the dictionary, the word should be worth the trip.Avoid pathetic fallacy/anthropomorphism: The sea may seem cruel, but it's just a bunch of waves, none of them malicious. In describing animal behavior, focus on what you see and hear, and steer clear of what you think the animal is thinking or feeling.

3. Write economically and selectively. William Faulker said, "Writing consists of killing your little darlings." In other words, be your own editor, and be ruthless. The writing should not draw undue attention to the writer. We want articles filled with great description, yet short enough to be read in one sitting. Eliminate extraneous words and passages.

4. Develop a theme. It helps to develop a theme or relate a personal goal or expectation specific to your paddling experience. Whether your story was a harrowing adventure, a trip to an exotic or unique setting, or a journey during which you experienced some transformation or learned something valuable, a theme will help drive your story.

5. Cover the important stuff. Focus on the highlights and the most significant moments of your story. We can include section breaks in the article to signify gaps in time. If it's important to describe regular routines, pick a specific representative instance. Describe events as they unfold, not as you are looking back on them.

6. Keep to the point. Tangents must take readers somewhere worth going. If you need to take a detour to bring some interesting information to readers, make sure you bring them back to the story. Don't lead them down a dead end, only to pick up the narrative again where you left off.

7. Maintain flow. Read your story aloud. Better yet, have someone read it aloud to you. You'll get winded if your sentences are consistently too long and hyperventilate if they're too short. Vary the length and structure of sentences as the content dictates to keep the pace of the story lively.

8. Use the appropriate tense. Although there are exceptions, the past tense is the best choice for most narrative stories. Don't confuse readers by switching back and forth between present and past tense.

9. Create an interesting chronology. Nothing puts readers to sleep faster than a story that starts at Day One of a trip and trudges on through Day Two, Day Three, etc. If your story is a harrowing adventure, you may want to start with the most harrowing moment, whether it's in the middle or at the end of your trip, then take the reader back through the events leading up to that point. If your story is more reflective, lead off with your central theme and follow it through to the end.

10. Be clear. Put yourself in the reader's seat. Be aware that others will not be as familiar with your subject as you are, and write accordingly. Develop a sense of continuity throughout. We (editors and readers) don't want to work too hard at deciphering your meaning.

Categories: Nonfiction—Boating—Kayaking—Recreation—Sea Kayaking—Sports

CONTACT: Connie Chaplan, Editorial Assistant
Material: All
PO Box 17029
Seattle WA 98107-0729
Phone: 206-789-1326
Fax: 206-781-1141
E-mail: editorial@seakayakermag.com
Website: www.seakayakermag.com

SEATTLE HOMES
AND LIFESTYLES™

Seattle Homes and Lifestyles

Seattle Homes and Lifestyles is published eight times a year. Sixty percent of the content is written by freelance writers on assignment for the magazine. Writers are paid between $125 and $375 per article, depending on the assignment.

We always welcome inquiries from experienced freelance writers, with special consideration given to those living in the Puget Sound area. Interested parties should submit a resume and photocopies of three published articles to Fred Albert, Editor, at the address below. Please do not e-mail or fax your submission, or follow up with a phone call. We regret we cannot return writing samples or unsolicited photos.

Although we will review story proposals, such queries are not encouraged, and should be limited to Seattle-focused lifestyle topics, consumer pieces and personality profiles, or stories on US or international travel. (Travel stories should focus on a region, not a hotel or resort.) Food, wine and garden stories are written by regular columnists and are not assigned to outside freelancers.

Thank you for your interest in *Seattle Homes and Lifestyles*. We look forward to hearing from you.

Categories: Nonfiction—Architecture—Gardening—Lifestyle—Regional

CONTACT: Fred Albert, Editor
Material: All
Wiesner Publishing LLC, 1221 East Pike St., Ste. 204
Seattle WA 98122-3930
Phone: 206-322-6699

Seaways' Ships in Scale

Writer's Guidelines
Thank you for your interest in writing for *Seaways' Ships in Scale*. Our magazine is dedicated to the integration of ship modeling and nautical research into a powerful tool for the ship modeler.

TECHNICAL REQUIREMENTS FOR MANUSCRIPTS
Articles should be submitted on an IBM compatible diskette, accompanied by a double-spaced printed hard copy. Please indicate the name of the word processing program on the label. Typed manuscripts (double-spaced) can be used, but are compensated at a lower rate. We encourage the citing of sources and the use of bibliographies in each article. Ships' names should be in italics. We do not guarantee the publishing date for any article. Please do not include return envelopes and postage with your submissions. We will package and post manuscripts and materials for return at cost; the amount will be deducted from your last payment check.

A title page should be included with the author's name, address, phone, fax numbers, as well as e-mail address. A brief biography of the author is also encouraged. (Include past articles, appointments, related jobs or positions, past accomplishments, etc.)

Copyright clearance and payment for all materials used photographs, plans, drawings, and paintings is the sole responsibility of the author. Please include copies of these releases and payments.

Seaways Publishing, Inc. purchases from the writer the right to publish each article in both print and electronic media, the right to reprint articles and/or photographs and drawings, the right to use portions of the article in advertising publications and the right to produce archival reproductions of the magazine issues in physical or electronic formats. The author retains copyright privileges.

Payment is eight cents a word for original material on hard copy with floppy diskette six cents a word for material on manuscript only. Payment for articles is made on publication, not acceptance. Checks are mailed within approximately two weeks of the cover date of the issue in which the article appears.

Illustrations, including drawings, sketches, and original plans, are compensated at the rate of $5 to $15 each (editors discretion). They must be clearly and/or professionally drawn and lettered, and should be self-explanatory. All illustrations should have identifying captions or legends.

TECHNICAL REQUIREMENTS FOR PHOTOGRAPHS
Photographs must be of good quality. Color or black-and-white are acceptable. Please send prints only; no negatives. Photos must include captions on the back and be numbered. The number of the accompanying negative should also be written on the back. An accompanying legend sheet is also required. For photos that contribute to rather than detract from the article, we recommend using a manual 35mm SLR camera with a shutter release cable, on a tripod. The lens should be set to the fastest f-stop, f28 or f32, to get maximum depth of field; please- no photos for us at less than f22. Film should be no faster than ASA 100. Long duration timed exposures should be expected. For indoor photos, please use at least two photo-blue light bulbs in reflectors to illuminate the model and light blue or light gray seamless photo backdrop paper under and behind the model. Payment is $5 per photograph.

Digital images must meet certain criteria:
The camera resolution must be at least 4 megapixels in capacity.
The camera must have a macro function for close-ups.
The camera must save images in either the tagged image file format (tiff) or as raw data files (RAW).
The prints need to be edited (eg in PhotoShop or a similar program) to the form in which you want them to appear.
You must supply maximum size (for your CCD capacity) black and white photo prints with your manuscript. If you are doing a color photo for the cover, a full-color print of the file needs to be supplied with the digital file.

Your computer must have a CD burner to deliver the images on compact discs.

For a more complete explanation, please read the article "Digital Photography for Magazine Publication" on our website.

Authors of major articles or article series may be required to submit a high-quality full-model color photograph for cover illustration consideration. Seaways Publishing, Inc.may compensate the author a certain amount if a studio session is required. Please check with the Editor before committing yourself. These, and all other photos submitted, must have no copyright restrictions prohibiting us from using them in magazine production, limited reprint servicing, archival reproduction in any medium and advertising.

Illustrations, including drawings, sketches, and original plans, are compensated at the rate of $5 to $15 each (editor's discretion). They must be clearly and/or professionally drawn and lettered, and should be self-explanatory. All illustrations should have identifying captions or legends.

CATEGORIES OF ARTICLES

Ship Modeling: Single, self-contained, and multi-part series articles with basic research and detailed construction instructions. Photos, drawings, and plans are necessary and should be of very high quality. All eras and types are welcome, both static and operational, kit, and scratch-built. Articles may be directed to any level of modeling or skill status, but must be from competent author-modelers.

Nautical Research: Histories, plans, and photos should include as many details relative to the appearance and structure of the vessel under consideration as possible. Dimensions, materials, coloring, flags, and peculiarities are featured anything that will help the marine historian or ship modeler understand exactly what she looked like.

Shop Hints: Detailed discussion of workshop techniques, materials, and tools. Shop-made tools and jigs are welcome, as are the selection of materials, adhesives, and coloring agents.

Nautical Archaeology: Studies of significant historical vessels which help us understand their construction, design, equipment and function are sought here. Photographs in abundance are necessary; reconstruction plans and models are highly desirable.

It's always a good idea to contact the Editor in advance of sending articles to get a clear idea of the magazine's needs.

Finally, a signed copy of this guideline must be submitted with your article, indicating your having read and understood them and complied with the necessary requirements. Thank you for your participation.

Categories: Hobbies

CONTACT: Jim Raines, Editor
Material: All
Seaways' Ships in Scale
1750 W Stardust Dr
Taylorsville UT 84118
Phone/Fax: 801-964-2077
E-mail: fourwindspublishing@juno.com
Website: www.seaways.com

Second Wind

Formerly *Nostalgia*.

Poetry: Modern prose poetry preferred. Payment in copies. Submissions returned if SASE included. Author retains all rights. If material previously published, please advise. Please do not e-mail submissions.

Categories: Poetry

CONTACT: Connie L. Martin, Editor
Material: All
Nostalgia Press
2003 Broughton St.
Orangeburg SC 29115
E-mail: secondwind@sc.rr.com

The Secret Place

The Secret Place was begun over sixty years ago by a woman who wanted to provide a way to draw Christians closer to Christ and to one another. It's now a quarterly devotional magazine with a worldwide readership of over 150,000 and editions in regular print, large print, Braille, and cassette. Produced by National Ministries of the American Baptist Churches in the U.S.A. and the Christian Church (Disciples of Christ), Christian Board of Publication.

How to Submit Devotions, Poems, and Photographs

The Secret Place is written solely by freelance writers, and anyone may submit original, unpublished meditations for consideration. Each submission should be typed (if possible), double-spaced, and contain:

• your name, address, and phone number in the upper left-hand corner of each devotion.
• a title.
• a suggested Scripture passage to be read.
• a "Thought for Today," usually a Scripture verse (cite full reference and Bible version) but may also be a pertinent thought. We use the New Revised Standard Version unless you specify otherwise.
• an original meditation of 100 to 200 words that relates to your Scripture reading and "Thought for Today." (Do not quote others at length unless you include written permission to do so.)
• a brief concluding prayer.
• your name, city, and state as you would like them to appear in print.
We are especially interested in devotional meditations that:
• are original, creative, and spiritually insightful.
• are concise and focused on one theme.
• explore less familiar biblical passages and themes.
• address urban/suburban as well as rural/nature experience.
• appeal to young adults as well as older adults.
• encourage outreach, mission, and service.
• are written by men as well as women, young adults as well as older adults.
• reflect racial and cultural diversity and use inclusive language.

We retain the right to edit submissions as necessary for clarity, brevity, and inclusivity of language. Original poems (thirty lines maximum) and clear, high-quality photographs (eight-by-ten-inch color prints for the cover, four-by-six-inch or larger black/white or color prints for inside, verticals preferred) are also welcome. We pay $15 for each submission printed and purchase first rights to the use of original, unpublished material in *The Secret Place* and on our website (www.judsonpress.com). We work nine to twelve months ahead of schedule, so please plan any seasonal submissions (maximum six at a time) accordingly. Include a stamped, self-addressed envelope for the return of your submissions and notification of any rejections. Due to the volume of material we receive, we are unable to give updates on the status of individual submissions. Please allow up to nine months for notification of publication. Send your meditations, poems, and photographs to the address below.

Categories: Nonfiction—Poetry—Religion—Spiritual—Devotional

CONTACT: Kathleen Hayes, Senior Editor
Material: All
PO Box 851
Valley Forge PA 19482-0851

Seek®

Seek® is an illustrated weekly take-home or pass-along paper designed to appeal to adults. Seek® first appeared in its present form in 1970, expanding a four-page Sunday school lesson leaflet that was published for 95 years into a new concept for personal spiritual enrichment. It can be used in a Sunday morning Bible class, in a weekly small group discussion, or as light inspirational reading for individuals and the family.

Materials Accepted for Publication

Articles—400 to 1,200 words in length. We do not accept poetry. Usual rate of payment is $.07 per word for first rights and $.05 per word for reprint rights. No simultaneous submissions, please! Articles written for publication in Seek® should be on theme in one of the following categories: inspirational, devotional, personal, human interest, first-person testimonies of Christian life or experiences, true-to-life happenings, vignettes, emotional situations or problems, examples of answered prayer. All Scripture quotes are from the King James Version of the Bible. The theme list is attached below. Please download or print a copy for your files.

The stories must be wholesome, vibrant, and relevant to today's reader. They should be uplifting rather than preachy and have a title that demands the article be read.

Articles for Seek® must be submitted according to dates on the theme list. Expect to hear a response within three months of the deadline date. A complimentary copy of the article is mailed to the writer following publication.

Photographs—The need for general photos is currently being met. But writers may send specific, professional-quality photos to accompany articles.

Instructions

On the first page of each article, please include your name, address, telephone number, and e-mail address. This information will be placed on the contract that is signed by the writer. first or reprint rights, and word count. Also note the issue number and date (from the theme list) for which the article is intended.

REGULAR MAIL SUBMISSIONS: Submit manuscripts on 8 1/2 x 11-inch paper, printed on one side only, double-spaced, with generous margins. Enclose a SASE for each manuscript.

E-MAIL SUBMISSIONS: Send your article as a Word document or in Rich Text Format e-mail attachment to: seek@standardpub.com. In the subject line include: "submission: title of article."

We are unable to critique or offer suggestions in regard to contributions that are not accepted. Feel free to write for a free copy of Seek: enclose a 6 x 9-inch self-addressed stamped envelope for return of the sample copy.

Categories: Fiction—Nonfiction—Christian Interests—Inspirational—Religion—Short Stories—Devotional

CONTACT: Eileen Wilmoth, Senior Editor
Material: All
8121 Hamilton Ave
Cincinnati OH 45231-2396
Phone: 513-931-4050
E-mail: seek@standardpub.com
Website: www.standardpub.com

Self

Formal guidelines not available. Please read a number of issues to ascertain the publication's style and needs.

Send queries to address below.

Categories: Beauty—Food/Drink—Health—Physical Fitness

CONTACT: Submissions Editor
Material: All
4 Times Square
New York NY 10036
Phone: 212-286-2860

Self-Help & Psychology Magazine

SUBMISSION GUIDELINES

SelfhelpMagazine is a service-oriented, educational magazine published to promote the understanding of how research-based psychology can benefit human welfare. Opinion pieces are also invited. Please read this entire file to make the process easy for yourself. Your feedback about our submission process is also invited.

Opinion pieces are occasionally reviewed from professionals for specialized topic areas. All such pieces must be clearly identified upon submission. Opinion pieces and reviews from non-professionals are welcomed, and will be posted in clearly identified areas of the magazine, such as the Interactive Department. Please specify whether or not you are a professional, and if your submission is research-based, send at least three references for your work.

Categories: Self Help

CONTACT: Miryam E. Williamson, Editor
E-mail: drm@cybertowers.com
Website: www.cybertowers.com/selfhelp/

Seneca Review

Seneca Review reads manuscripts of poetry, translations, essays on contemporary poetry, and lyric essays between September 1 and May 1 annually. We do not publish fiction. Manuscripts received during the summer months are returned unread. We recommend submissions of 3-5 poems and essays up to 20 pages. We generally respond to submissions within twelve weeks.

Due to the great number of manuscripts we receive, we ask that you limit yourself to just one submission during our annual reading period (September 1-May 1). We can then give all submissions the attention they deserve.

Please note that we do not accept manuscripts electronically and that we do not wish to receive simultaneous submissions. All submissions must be accompanied by a self-addressed, stamped envelope in order to be returned. If you don't wish to have your manuscript returned, please indicate that in a cover letter and supply a stamped envelope or postcard for our reply.

Although we cannot pay authors for work published, we provide two copies of the issue in which your work appears and a complimentary two-year subscription. Copyright is held by Hobart and William Smith Colleges until publication, at which time rights revert to the author.

To get a sense of our editorial interests, we suggest you read a recent issue of the magazine. Sample copies are available for $7 each on our website or at the address below.

Seneca Review is published twice yearly, spring and fall.

Categories: Poetry—Lyric Essay
CONTACT: Deborah Tall, Editor
Material: All
Hobart and William Smith Colleges
Geneva NY 14456
Website: www.hws.edu/SenecaReview

Senior Living

About *Senior Living* newspapers: *Senior Living* newspapers has a circulation of 50,000 plus. Papers are published monthly with distribution in Arkansas, Missouri, Kansas, and Oklahoma. Editorial slant is directed to mid-life and retirement lifestyles and offers a positive and upbeat look at the 50 + reader.

Senior Living readers are primarily well-educated and affluent retirees, homemakers, and career professionals—most of whom enjoy a very active lifestyle.

Topics: *Senior Living* publishes feature articles, personality profiles, and timely articles on travel, health, finance, relationships, nostalgia, consumer issues and retirement. We do very little poetry and no fiction. Staff writers and columnists do most of our writing, but we welcome queries and unsolicited manuscripts.

Query & Cover Letters: A query letter is not necessary, but should you choose to send one, make it short and to the point. Indicate the focus and tone of your proposed article. We prefer that you send a cover letter with your manuscript informing us about your experience or qualifications as a writer. If you don't have any experience, tell us that too. Perhaps we will be able to help you get a much needed byline. No need to tell us what the article is about, we'll know that when we read it.

Manuscripts: Preferred length is 400-600 words. They should be typewritten and double-spaced on 8 1/2 X 11 inch paper, with 1 inch margins. Place name, address and Social Security number in upper left corner and word count in upper right corner. Computer discs are acceptable, but you still need to send hard copy. Absolutely no manuscripts or photographs will be returned without a SASE with ample postage to cover their return.

Style: Keep it clear, simple and to the point. Originality, concrete details, short paragraphs and strong words are essential. Avoid flowery prose in articles. Accuracy is a must.

All articles are submitted on a speculative basis unless assigned.

Payment of ($5 to $35) will be decided according to timeliness of article, content, clarity and neatness. Fillers and Poetry, if accepted pays $1 to $5. Checks are mailed 30-45 days post publication. Beginning writers who need a byline may stand a chance with *Senior Living*. We welcome articles and poems that require no compensation. Please state if payment is, or is not required. Unpaid writers may obtain a paper containing their work by request.

Categories: Nonfiction—General Interest—Health—History—Inspirational—Physical Fitness—Poetry—Recreation—Senior Citizen—Sports/Recreation—Retirement—Essay—Nostalgia—Personal Experience—Humor

CONTACT: Joyce O'Neal, Managing Editor
Material: All
2010 S Stewart
Springfield MO 65804
Phone/Fax: 417-862-9079
Website: www.seniorlivingnewspaper.org

Seventeen

Seventeen accepts articles of interest to teens and young adults, roughly ages 13-21. Please read 6-12 back issues of the magazine (not just the fiction) before submitting your work. Include a SASE for our response. Correspondence should include the writer's name, address and phone number. We regret that we cannot offer individual comments or criticism. We read all stories and will respond as quickly as possible. Generally, allow six to eight weeks for consideration of your manuscript. No follow-up phone calls, please.

GUIDELINES

My Story and Real Deal Stories

Do you have an experience you'd like to share? Tell us what you're thinking. Real Deal and My Story sections of the magazine are devoted to first-person essays, and we welcome all original contributions. We are looking for true stories on interesting, unusual, life-altering or inspiring events, struggles or challenges overcome, and reflective essays on significant personal decisions.

Real Deal and My Story is a chance for you to speak about what matters to you in your individual style and voice.

Your article should be typed, double-spaced, and about 1,200 words. Be sure to include a brief cover letter with your name, age, address and telephone number (with area code), as well as a SASE for our reply. With few exceptions, authors should be 23 or younger.

Fiction Stories

We're looking for great short fiction. The stories we want should deal with issues that are familiar and important to our readers (roughly ages 13-21), but they should also challenge the reader and make them think.

Seventeen publishes between six and twelve short stories each year that run from 1,000 to 3,500 words and possess the quality and integrity of today's very best literary short fiction.

Aspiring writers, especially those in M.F.A. programs, are encouraged to submit. We also hold an annual Fiction Contest for writers between 13-21 years old; guidelines appear in the December issue.

All fiction submissions should include a brief cover letter listing prior fiction publication credits, if any. Only completed manuscripts will be considered.

Non-Fiction Stories

Seventeen gives assignments and guarantees a fee only to writers who have been published in the magazine or whose work is known to the editors. Writers whose work has not appeared in *Seventeen* should include published clips when submitting. Inexperienced writers may be asked to write on speculation, with no guarantee of payment. Work is paid for on publication, and rates vary depending on quality, length and placement in the magazine.

Queries are preferred for all sections, except Voice, Fiction and Quizzes, where only complete manuscripts are considered. Please read the additional guidelines for Voice and Fiction, and see past issues for the tone and style of Quizzes. Simultaneous submissions are considered, although not preferred. Seasonal material should be submitted at least six months in advance. *Seventeen* does not accept filler.

We recommend that writers target queries to the appropriate section to speed the consideration process:

• Features: Tamara Glenny, Deputy Editor. Maximum 2,500 words.
• Quiz: Margaret Magnarelli, Assistant Editor. See past issues.

Categories: Nonfiction—Beauty—Fashion—Health—Relationships—Sexuality—Women's Issues—Young Adult

CONTACT: Real Deal Editor
Material: Real Deal submissions
CONTACT: My Story Editor
Material: My Story submissions
CONTACT: Darcy Jacobs, Fiction Editor
Material: Fiction
CONTACT: Tamara Glenny, Deputy Editor
Material: Non-Fiction Features
CONTACT: Margaret Magnarelli, Assistant Editor
Material: Non-Fiction,Quiz
1440 Broadway, 13th Floor
New York NY 10018
Phone: 212-204-4300
Website: www.seventeen.com

Sew News

Who We Are

Sew News magazine is a monthly, national consumer magazine for the sewing enthusiast, whether novice, expert or somewhere in between. The magazine expresses the fun, creativity, excitement and rewards of sewing though "how-to" and feature articles, as well as monthly columns. It is sold by subscription, in retail fabric and sewing machine stores and on many newsstands.

What We Want

Articles should teach a specific technique; inspire the reader to try a project; introduce the reader to a new product or company related to sewing, textiles or fashion.

Although *Sew News'* primary emphasis is fashion-sewing for women, secondary interests include home decor sewing, sewing for children and men, and sewing for specialty groups like senior citizens,

R-U

large sizes, petites and the handicapped. In addition to sewing, *Sew News* also peripherally covers the areas of machine embroidery, monogramming and fabric painting. *Sew News* does not normally cover "artisan" areas like hand weaving and hand needlecrafts or "crafty" areas like cross stitch, crochet, macrame and tole painting.

Acceptance/Payment

At the time an article is assigned, you will be sent a succinct form letter detailing what is expected of you for the assignment and the intended payment (from $50 to $1,000, depending on the length and complexity of the subject, and the garment(s), photography, illustrations or sources to be supplied).

However, all articles, including those specifically assigned, are written "on speculation." Payment will be made only on acceptance. To be accepted at the full payment suggested in the assignment letter, the article must:

- be submitted by the deadline specified.
- include all elements detailed in the assignment letter.
- be of acceptable quality (to be determined by the *Sew News* editorial staff).

Payment may be decreased for late arrival, missing elements or poor quality. *Sew News* reserves the right to return articles for rewriting or clarification of information and, in extreme cases, to return them without payment.

In all cases, *Sew News* reserves the right to edit, rewrite and cut articles where necessary.

Any extraordinary writing expenses (fabric, notions, travel, telephone bills, etc.) will be reimbursed only by previous agreement between you and *Sew News*.

The Contract

Sew News, as part of the Primedia Enthusiasts Group, requires an "all rights" contract to be signed before publication of any article. "All rights" means *Sew News* purchases complete rights to the manuscript and art covered in the contract and that they may not be used in conjunction with any other article in another publication.

These rights apply to specific projects, but not to individual techniques. For example, when a writer signs a *Sew News* "all rights" contract for an article on a machine-embroidered jacket, he/she may not allow the particulars (step-by-step how-tos) of that project to be published anywhere else. However, he/she may publish another article on machine embroidery, including an article on a machine-embroidered jacket, as long as it's neither the same jacket nor the same embroidery designs.

Submissions

We would appreciate receiving your work via e-mail or CD-Rom.
To submit by e-mail:

- Attach a text file to your e-mail and send it to Ellen Marchant@primedia.com.
- You may also include the text in the body of your e-mail.
- Send how-tos separately via regular mail.

To submit by CD Rom:

- If you use Microsoft Word 5.5 or higher software, simply print a hard copy, save the article on the disk as you normally would and send us both the hard copy and the disk.
- If you use any other software program, print a hard copy, save the article on the disk as a text file (in ASCII; see your manual for details) and send us the hard copy, the disk and a note telling us which software you used. We'll take it from there.

Please do:

- Computer-generate or type your article on 8½"x11" nonerasable paper.
Use approximately 1" top and bottom margins and a 55-character line, and double-space between lines.
- Begin your article approximately halfway down the first page.
- Keep an article under eight pages, unless otherwise specified.
- Include your name, address, phone number(s) and social security numbers on the last page and paper clip all pages together. Mail together with your disk (in the disk mailer for protection).
- Follow the *Sew News* Style Guide (sent to new writers upon

acceptance of a query) for style matters and specific punctuation preferences, referring to *The Associated Press Stylebook* (revised edition), *Webster's New Collegiate Dictionary* and Chilton's *Grammar For Journalists* for matters not covered in the guide.

- Submit sources and resources of products and publications noted in your article, as well as information on how *Sew News* readers can contact the businesses of people interviewed. Be sure all information is current.
- Submit sketches of how-to drawings to accompany your article, drawing only one or two on one page and supplying appropriate cutline and label information. Label the illustrations Figure 1, Figure 2, etc. and refer to them as such within the copy.
- Label all photographs submitted with an article with descriptions and information on where they should be returned.
- Assume nothing. Check and double-check all spellings (especially those of proper names) and all facts. In the case of how-to articles, the writer bears responsibility for testing techniques.
- Include a short biography and high resolution photo for use with your story.
- Submit your article on or before the due date, allowing time for mailing to: Ellen Marchant, *Sew News*, 741 Corporate Circle, Suite A, Golden, CO 80401.
- If mailing projects, please pack them carefully and send via UPS, keeping the appropriate information for tracing in the event of loss. Second-day air and overnight mail also are acceptable, but not required unless necessary for your project to arrive on time. Send projects (with the related article enclosed, if possible) to: *Sew News* Editor, 741 Corporate Circle, Suite A, Golden, CO 80401. If agreed in advance, *Sew News* will return the project via UPS after publication. *Sew News* does not reimburse your shipping expense.
- Keep a copy of your completed article and all of your notes for at least six months after the date of the article's publication.
- Read your published articles and compare them to your originals for feedback.

Please don't:

- Deviate from the *Sew News* style.
- Change an article's focus without approving it with *Sew News* first.
- Submit any article containing facts or techniques of which you are unsure.
- Copy material directly from any other source.
- Make excuses about missed deadlines. Legitimate reasons will be accommodated if possible. Questionable and recurring ones will not.
- Hesitate to give *Sew News* feedback. A better product is always our goal!

Sample query

Ours is a small staff. Therefore, we request you query by letter; do not send finished manuscripts. Your query should consist of a brief outline of the article, a list of the types of illustrations or photographs you envision with it, an explanation of why your proposed article would be of interest to the *Sew News* reader and, when applicable, why you are qualified to write it. Consider the season and timeliness of your suggestions, keeping in mind *Sew News* works on a six-month lead time.

The *Sew News* staff considers queries and makes story assignments quarterly. At that time, all queries are considered and, within a few days, you will either receive an assignment, a request to hold the query for further consideration, or a rejection. If more than three months have passed without a reply to your query, feel free to write a note requesting its status.

Categories: Nonfiction—Accessories—Crafts/Hobbies—Education—Fashion—General Interest—Home Decor—Lifestyle

CONTACT: Ellen Marchant
Material: Sew News
741 Corporate Circle, Ste A
Golden CO 80401
Phone: 303-278-1010

Sewanee Review

The *Sewanee Review* is America's oldest continuously published literary quarterly. Only erudite work representing depth of knowledge and skill of expression is published here. We urge you to read at least one issue of the magazine before submitting any work. Sample copies cost $8.50 ($9.50 foreign). Individual subscriptions cost $25 per year ($32 foreign). MasterCard and VISA are accepted, as well as checks payable in U.S. dollars drawn on U.S. banks. Further information about the magazine is available on our Web site: www.sewanee.edu/sewanee_review

For matters of spelling and usage, consult the *The Chicago Manual of Style*, 15th edition; *Merriam-Webster's Collegiate Dictionary*, 11th edition; and *Webster's Third New International Dictionary*. Unsolicited submissions should be original double-spaced typescripts mailed to the editor at 735 University Avenue, Sewanee TN 37383-1000. No electronic submissions are accepted at this time. A self-addressed stamped envelope must be supplied for reply. Rejected submissions without sufficient return postage will be discarded. No responsibility can be assumed for loss or damage. Only unpublished original work (no translations) can be considered.

Queries are suitable for essays (7500 words or less) and reviews (unsolicited reviews are rarely accepted). Send fiction and poetry without writing in advance. Poems (40 lines or less) should not exceed 6 per submission; stories (3500-7500 words; no short short stories, please) should be sent individually. For each poem published, roughly 250 poems are considered here; for each story, 150 stories.

The average time to reply to a submission is four to six weeks. We do not accept simultaneous submissions. When you have sent one submission, please do not send another before you have received a reply to the first. Unsolicited works should not be submitted between June 1st and August 31st. A response to any submission received during that period may be greatly delayed.

The *Sewanee Review* awards four prizes annually to the best short fiction, poetry, essay, and book reviewing of the previous year. The Aiken Taylor Award in Modern American Poetry is presented annually to established poets. Winners of these awards are determined by the board of editors and a prize committee; one cannot apply for any of them.

For information about literary magazines see the current editions of the *International Directory of Little Magazines and Small Presses*, *Literary Market Place*, *Magazine Industry Market Place*, and *Ulrich's International Periodicals Directory*.

Thank you for your interest in the *Sewanee Review*.

Categories: Fiction—Nonfiction—Arts—Biography—Book Reviews—Culture—Drama—General Interest—Language—Literature—Poetry—Short Stories

CONTACT: The Editors
Material: All
University of the South
735 University Ave.
Sewanee TN 37383-1000
Website: www.sewanee.edu/sewanee_review

Shaman's Drum

Shaman's Drum is a quarterly journal on experiential shamanism with a paid circulation of about 14,000 copies reaching approximately 40,000 readers. We seek contributions directed to a general but well-informed audience. Past contributors have included Jeanne Achterberg, Paula Gunn Allen, Hal Zina Bennett, Doug Boyd, Wade Davis, Richard Erdoes, Felicitas Goodman, Peter Gorman, Lee Irwin, Stanley Krippner, Luis Eduardo Luna, Thomas Mails, Ralph Metzner, Larry G. Peters, Donald Sandner, Janet Siskind, Jeremy Taylor, Edith Turner, and others.

The primary purpose of *Shaman's Drum* is to educate our readers about shamanism. We see *Shaman's Drum* as an ongoing effort to expand, challenge, and refine our readers' and our own understanding of shamanism in practice. In the process, we cover a wide range of related topics—from indigenous medicineway practices to contemporary shamanic psychotherapies, from transpersonal healing ceremonies to ecstatic spiritual practices. Our focus is on experiential shamanism.

We prefer original material that is based on, or illustrated with, firsthand knowledge and personal experience. Articles should be well documented with descriptive examples and pertinent background information. Photographs and illustrations are always welcomed and can help sell articles. Our overall focus is cross-cultural, but our editorial approach is culture-specific. Authors may write about particular practices from a cross-cultural, comparison-contrast perspective, but we often prefer they focus on specific ethnic traditions or personal practices about which they have significant firsthand knowledge. While we do not expect our authors to be credentialed experts, we do expect them to be thoroughly knowledgeable about their subject. Our intent is to inspire people to explore shamanism in greater depth. We do not want to become a journal of "armchair shamanism." We are looking for examples of not only how shamanism has transformed individual lives but also practical ways it can help ensure the survival of life on this planet. We want material that captures the heart and feeling of shamanism and that can inspire people to direct action and participation. accepted for publication, however, every effort is made to publish it in as timely a manner as possible.

Publication Rights

We prefer original, previously unpublished work and generally purchase First North American Serial Rights only. Copyright reverts to the author after publication; however, we do ask to be credited if you subsequently reprint the article. We will also consider pre-publication book excerpts. Occasionally we will consider Secondary Serial Rights, but authors must clearly indicate where and when the work was published previously, who possesses the copyright, and if other permissions are required.

Submission Deadlines

Please keep in mind that we tend to work several issues ahead, so the sooner you submit materials for consideration the better. The dates listed below indicate when we make final selections for each issue: September 15 for Winter; December 15 for Spring; March 15 for Summer; June 15 for Fall. We prefer to review completed manuscripts. However, article ideas may be suggested to the editors by query letter or outline (please do not call). For a prompt response, please include an SASE (self-addressed, stamped envelope). Please be advised that a positive response to a query should not be viewed as a contract to publish. It only means that we're interested in your idea and hope you will pursue it. Our editorial staff does its best to notify authors within two months of the acceptance or rejection of their manuscript. Authors may also be asked to revise an article for further consideration. The *Shaman's Drum* editorial staff reserves the right to edit material to meet our standards. Authors will be offered an opportunity to review edited copy if changes other than simple grammatical or stylistic alterations are made. Once a manuscript has been reviewed and accepted, it will be scheduled for publication. Please keep in mind that publication schedules are subject to change for various reasons. The lead time (the time from receipt to final publication) for *Shaman's Drum* articles can be as short as three months or as long as one year.

Reviews: We print reviews of books, magazines, movies, records, and tapes about shamanism or closely related subjects such as medicineways, indigenous lifeways, ethnobotany, transpersonal healing, and ecstatic spirituality. Must include all publishing or cataloging information with mss. See examples in latest issues of *Shaman's Drum*. Buys 20 or more mss./year. Length: 500 to 1,500 words, longer if subject merits it.

Open Dialogue: Our guest editorial column is designed to initiate discussion of important or controversial questions and topics of interest to our readers. The aim of *Open Dialogue* is to provide a catalyst, challenging readers to examine and take responsibility for their personal and/or collective practice of shamanism. Buys up to 4/year. Length: 1,000 to 2,000 words.

Letters to the Editor: These provide an opportunity to freely discuss matters which pertain to shamanism or which relate to articles and letters published in the magazine. We cannot guarantee that all letters will be printed, but we welcome them. We reserve the right to edit for style and length. Length: 100 to 250 words, occasionally longer. No payment, but the satisfaction of seeing one's views in print.

Photos and Artwork: We purchase one-time rights on b&w and color photos, transparencies, and illustrations, either with manuscripts or as separate works. The availability of high-quality photos or artwork can greatly enhance the chances of an article being accepted. For color covers and Arts Gallery, we prefer professional quality 120 mm or 4x5 color transparencies of previously unpublished works. Please include a b&w photo of yourself with Arts Gallery submissions. Please send copies and *not* original art and irreplaceable photos; if needed, we will request originals on acceptance. Make sure all illustrations are marked with titles. Please provide brief descriptive captions and identify primary subjects of your photos; include credit lines for the artists or photographers.

PAYMENT POLICIES

Shaman's Drum accepts submissions on speculation only and pays for material on publication: $300 and up for feature-length articles and interviews; $100 and up for short articles, reprints, and fiction; $40 and up for poems and reviews; $40 and up for interior photographs and illustrations; $50 and up for Arts Gallery; and **$150 and up for front cover art.** (Payments for texts are calculated at approximately 5 cents per word.) If an article is accepted for publication but not published within one year, a 50% kill fee will be offered.

Non-Fiction: All articles must have a clear relationship to shamanism, but they may be on topics which have not traditionally been defined as shamanic. When dealing with related fields—such as indigenous lifeways, transpersonal healing, or sacred places—it is important to explicitly point out their relationship to shamanism. We will consider pre-publication book excerpts. Buys about 12- 20 mss./year. Length: 4,000 to 8,000 words. Personal Experience: We accept first-person accounts of shamanic or medicineway experiences. Subjects may include trance or dream excursions, spirit contacts, journeys to power places, cases of curings, experiences with ecstatic music and/or dance, etc. No fiction or embellished fact, but truthful narratives convincingly reported. Buys about 4 mss./year. Length: 3,000 to 6,000 words.

Interviews: It is usually best to query us before initiating a question-and-answer type interview. We are looking for well-focused, in-depth interviews with practicing shamans and medicinepersons—not promotional, public relation pieces or long rambling interviews. In a field that has previously been dominated by male anthropologists reporting primarily on male practitioners, we enthusiastically welcome quality interviews with women shamans. Buys 3 to 5/year. Length: 4,000 to 8,000 words.

Classical Reprints: We publish articles and excerpts on shamanism or medicineways from old books, periodicals, etc., published prior to 1930, particularly if they are out-of-print. If you submit selections for this section, please include full bibliographic information (author, publisher, title, date and place of publication, etc.). Buys about 4 mss./year. Length: 2,000 to 4,000 words.

Fiction: We occasionally publish original stories or retellings of traditional myths with shamanic themes. Buys 1-4 mss./year. Length: 1,000 to 3,000 words.

Poetry: We occasionally publish poems, but only ones that speak directly about shamanic experience. All styles of poetry considered. Buys about 2 poems/year.

Earth Circles: This section includes news about events, issues, and organizations related to shamanism, indigenous peoples, caretaking the Earth, and protecting religious freedom. Length: 500 to 2000 words. Please address submissions to *Shaman's Drum*—Earth Circles. Buys 4-6 mss./year.

We also encourage the submission of relevant clippings from newspapers and periodicals worldwide on the above subjects. Please indicate author (if any), date of publication, and title of source (e.g., "James Reston, *New York Times*, Oct. 2, 1987"). No payment for clippings, but contributors will be credited by name.

A CHECKLIST FOR BEGINNING WRITERS

Many of our authors are not professional writers or scholars, but rather amateur researchers, enthusiastic students, and active practitioners. We welcome submissions from non-professional writers, but we like to remind them that good writing is usually 10% inspiration and 90% hard work. The chances of getting an article published in *Shaman's Drum* are greatly increased if most of the hard work is already done before we receive it. We therefore suggest you submit your article to the following checklist before submitting it to us:

1. The first paragraph (or two) should clearly communicate what the article is about and at the same time capture the attention, imagination, and interest of the readers. If it doesn't, try to identify one paragraph in your article that does and consider moving it to the start of your article. Often a personal anecdote, quote, or short example can do this job better than a scholarly extract.

2. Keep your article focused on one theme. Identify the central theme and consider cutting out all unrelated parts. Sometimes the "outs" can be turned into an informative sidebar, or even into a separate article, but don't let them sidetrack the reader into leaving your article.

3. Limit yourself to your areas of experience and knowledge. Avoid trying to write "the definitive work" on a particular culture or tradition unless you have the extensive research background or experiential base from which to do so. Overgeneralizations such as "Native Americans believe or practice..." should be avoided by identifying as closely as possible the source (individual, tribe, etc.) of the belief or practice you are describing.

4. Support your hypotheses with documentation. If you claim "shamans from all over the world use sexual terminology to describe their ecstatic states," give some examples, case studies, references, or other evidence for your conclusion. When you expound theories, particularly when they are contrary to prevailing viewpoints and paradigms, support your theories with ample corroborating evidence and references.

5. Explain your examples. Even when you know what you are talking about, don't presume others do. If you mention a particular ceremony or practice in passing, it is probably worth taking a sentence or two to describe what it's about and how it is relevant to the discussion.

6. Be careful how you use specialized or technical terms. When discussing traditional cultures or particular practices, it is often informative to use their own special vocabularies. However, if you do find it productive to use specialized vocabularies, take the time to succinctly define your terms.

7. Avoid taking pot-shots at your favorite pet peeves, such as the superficiality of workshop shamanism, the blind ignorance of Western medicine, and the destructiveness of capitalistic technology, unless of course they are truly relevant to your article and you can take the time to document and substantiate your statements.

8. Proofread your manuscript carefully for sentence fragments, spelling, punctuation, accuracy of facts, subject- verb agreement, number and person agreement, and excessive repetition of a word or an idea, etc. Pay special attention to the overall flow and readability of the article. Akward phrasing and poor grammar may jeopardize the chances of an article being accepted.

9. In general, material laced with inaccurate facts, hasty conclusions, and superficial generalizations is likely to be summarily rejected,

whereas a simple topic that is well documented and enhanced with personal anecdotes and direct observations may be accepted for publication.

1. All submissions should be clearly identified by title, author's name, address, phone number, and social security number, and they should be accompanied by a selfaddressed stamped envelope (with sufficient postage). We are not responsible for submissions sent without SASEs.

2. All manuscripts should be neatly typewritten or wordprocessed and double-spaced with at least one-inch margins on all sides. No email submissions, please. All pages must be numbered consecutively, preferably at the bottom center. Please include accurate word-counts on articles and fiction.

3. Submissions should include a short biographical sketch on a separate page that specifies the writer's name as it should appear on the byline, and which gives pertinent experience, current work, etc., and, *if desired*, an address and telephone number where the writer may be contacted by readers for additional information or communication.

4. Titles and subtitles may be suggested, but Shaman's Drum assumes final responsibility for the wording and placement of these elements. Send manuscripts, art, and queries, with SASEs, to: *Shaman's Drum* Editor P.O. Box 270, Williams, OR 97544.

Please do not send via email. Sample copies of *Shaman's Drum* are available at $6 each, including postage and handling. We look forward to hearing from you.

MANUSCRIPT PREPARATION AND SUBMISSION

The following quotations are offered to provoke potential contributors to consider whether the subjects they are writing about fall somewhere firmly within the field of shamanism. If uncertain, contributors should query the editors of *Shaman's Drum* or—perhaps more appropriately—study the field of shamanism more thoroughly before sending us material.

"Healer and psychopomp, the shaman is these because he commands the techniques of ecstasy—that is, because his soul can safely abandon his body and roam at vast distances, can penetrate the underworld and rise to the sky. Through his own ecstatic experience he knows the roads of the extraterrestrial regions. He can go below and above because he has already been there. The danger of losing his way in these forbidden regions is still great; but sanctified by his initiation and furnished with his guardian spirits, the shaman is the only human being able to challenge the danger and venture into mystical geography." —Mircea Eliade, *Shamanism: Archaic Techniques of Ecstasy*

"Every Indian can obtain a 'tutelary spirit' or a 'power' of some sort that makes him capable of 'visions' and augments his reserves of the sacred; but only the shaman, by virtue of his relations with the spirits, is able to enter deeply into the supernatural world; in other words, he alone succeeds in acquiring a technique that enables him to undertake ecstatic journeys at will." —Eliade, *Shamanism*

"At the center of shamanistic religion stands the personality of the shaman and the ecstatic experience that is uniquely his, in his crucial role as diviner, seer, magician, poet, singer, artist, prophet of game and weather, keeper of the traditions, and healer of bodily and spiritual ills." —Peter Furst, *Hallucinogens & Culture*

"The shaman in all cases is one who has direct relationships with spirit powers in contrast to the priest who fills his office largely by virtue of his knowledge of ritual. Among peoples, however, there is a certain overlapping of the functions belonging to the two offices." — Willard Park, *Shamanism in Western North America*

"A shaman is a man or woman who enters an altered state of consciousness—at will—to contract and utilize an ordinarily hidden reality in order to acquire knowledge, power, and to help other persons." —Michael Harner, *The Way of the Shaman*

"Shamanism is a complex system of beliefs which includes the knowledge of and belief in the names of helping spirits in the shamanic pantheon, the memory of certain texts (sermons, shaman songs, legends, myths, etc.), the rules for activities (rituals, sacrifices, the technique of ecstasy, etc.), and the objects, tools and paraphernalia used by shamans (drum, stick, bow, mirror, costumes, etc.)." —Mihály Hoppál,

"Shamanism: An Archaic and/ or Recent System of Beliefs," in *Shamanism: An Expanded View of Reality*

"Among tribal peoples the shaman is the person, male or female, who experiences, absorbs, and communicates a special mode of sustaining, healing power … this power presence is evoked by a shaman in ritual prayer and sacrifice to guide tribal hunts, perpetuate sacred crafts, and sustain human life in its confrontations with the destructive aspects of the surrounding world." —John A. Grim, *The Shaman: Patterns of Siberian and Ojibway Healing*

"Shamans are healers, seers, and visionaries who have mastered death. They are in communication with the world of gods and spirits. Their bodies can be left behind while they fly to unearthly realms. They are poets and singers. They dance and create works of art. They are not only spiritual leaders but also judges and politicians, the repositories of the knowledge of the culture's history, both sacred and secular. They are familiar with cosmic as well as physical geography; the ways of plants, animals and the elements are known to them. They are psychologists, entertainers, and food finders. Above all, however, shamans are technicians of the sacred and masters of ecstasy." —Joan Halifax, *Shamanic Voices*

"Typical of the shaman, in any case, is the repeated inducement of a state of trance, the experience of being called, the continual reactivation of the images of the tribe's mythology, considerable artistic activity, the selfcure of a psychosis through this activity, and therapeutic activity performed in a state of trance." —Andreas Lommel, *Shamanism: The Beginnings of Art*

"There is no consensus among scholars as to exactly what a shaman is." —Lowell John Bean and Sylvia Brakke Vane, **"Shamanism: An Introduction,"** in *Art of the Huichol Indians*

Categories: Fiction—Nonfiction—Interviews—Poetry—Shamanism

CONTACT: Editor, *Shaman's Drum*
Material: All
PO Box 270
Williams OR 97544

Shape Magazine

Queries/Pitches/Story Ideas: When submitting a query or pitch to *Shape*, please follow the guidelines below regarding tone and style. For further information, see a recent issue of the magazine. *Shape* is not responsible for and does not accept unsolicited material. Story ideas and query letters should be on suitable topics and reflect *Shape*'s philosophy (see below).

***Shape*'s Mission Statement**: We seek to help women 18-34 years old create better lives. Each issue provides immediately useful information in the areas of exercise, nutrition, psychology, beauty and more — to help the reader improve her health and to stimulate a deeper understanding of fitness.

Submissions: We recommend that writers who haven't been previously published in the magazine submit story ideas in the form of a one-page letter. We do not accept completed, "spec" articles.

Please identify your story pitch as either a feature or column. If you are suggesting a story for a particular column, please tell us which one.

When pitching a story, please be sure to include the names and qualifications of your resources, the reasons they are viewed as experts in their fields and/or why you chose them for your direct quotes.

Be sure to include your contact information with your pitch, including your e-mail address, if you have one.

If you want your materials returned, please include a stamped return envelope.

Tone: The "voice" of a story should always reflect *Shape*'s service role and embody the magazine's mission as a positive, empowering force in its readers' lives. Toward that end, we eschew derogatory physical descriptions or characterizations of women's bodies. The desired tone is affirming and helpful.

We do not publish: Celebrity question and answer stories

Celebrity profiles

Profiles of anyone (other than Success Stories that have a specific format)

Menopausal or hormone replacement therapy stories

Categories: Nonfiction—Cooking—Diet/Nutrition—Fashion—Food/Drink—Health—Interview—Physical Fitness—Recreation—Sports/Recreation—Travel—Women's Issues—How-to —Profiles—Medicine—Beauty

CONTACT: Anne Russell, Editorial Dept.
Material: All
21100 Erwin St.
Woodland Hills CA 91367
Phone: 818-595-0593
Fax: 818-704-7620
Website: www.shapemag.com

Shenandoah
The Washington and Lee University Review

For over half a century *Shenandoah* has been publishing splendid poems, stories, essays and reviews which display passionate understanding, formal accomplishment and serious mischief.

Founded in 1950 by a group of Washington and Lee University faculty members and students, including Tom Wolfe and William Hoffman, *Shenandoah* has achieved a wide reputation as one of the country's premier literary quarterlies and has been praised by *USA Today* as "a 'little' magazine notable for not being little in its aspirations." Recent issues have featured work by Stephen Dunn, Mary Oliver, Rodney Jones, Alyson Hagy, Erin McGraw and Chris Offutt.

Please type (double space for prose) your manuscript on one side of the page only. Number pages consecutively and use margins of at least one inch. Place your name and address in an upper corner of the first page. Address the outer envelope to the Editor and write your name and address on the upper left corner of the envelope. Enclose a self-addressed stamped envelope (SASE) with your manuscript; we will not return manuscripts or disks not accompanied by an SASE. E-mail and simultaneous submissions are not considered.

We read previously unpublished poetry, fiction and critical as well as personal essays, and we prefer that work submitted to us not be simultaneously submitted elsewhere. Manuscripts are read between September 1 and May 30. We adhere strictly to postmark dates; manuscripts received outside that period will be returned unread provided an SASE accompanies the manuscript.

You are encouraged to read *Shenandoah* to acquaint yourself with the material we publish. Single copies are $8.00 each and are available from this office or your local bookstore. Subscription rates are 1 year (4 issues) / $22; 2 years / $40; 3 years / $54.

Contests
• THE JEANNE CHARPIOT GOODHEART PRIZE FOR FICTION—$1,000
• THE JAMES BOATWRIGHT III PRIZE FOR POETRY—$1,000
• THE THOMAS H. CARTER PRIZE FOR THE ESSAY—$500

Each prize is awarded annually to the author of the best story, poem and essay published in *Shenandoah* during a volume year.

Categories: Nonfiction—Book Reviews—Poetry—Short Stories

CONTACT: Lynn L. Leech, Managing Editor
Material: All
Troubadour Theater, 2nd Floor
Washington and Lee University
Lexington VA 24450-0303
Phone: 540-458-8765
Fax: 540-458-8461
Website: shenandoah.wlu.edu

Shofar

Shofar, an interdisciplinary journal of Jewish Studies, is the official journal of the Midwest and Western Jewish Studies Associations. *Shofar* ranges far and wide thematically in a multi-disciplinary world that spans four thousand years. It publishes scholarly articles, opinion pieces, readers' forums, pedagogical essays, and book reviews. Articles are peer reviewed for scholarly rigor but at the same time are written with a minimum of professional jargon and are accessible to a diverse and general readership.

Frequent special thematic issues are also published under guest editorships. Topics for recent and forthcoming special issues include Jewish feminism, Jewish-Christian dialogue after the Shoah, Judaism and Asian religions, Jewish music, Jewish studies in Latin America, and Jewish studies in Germany.

Shofar is available electronically through Project MUSE.

Subscription Information
Quarterly
ISSN 0882-8539
Volume 23 (2004-2005) Pricing

Domestic Institutions:	$75.00/volume
Foreign Institutions:	$95.00/volume
Domestic Individuals:	$50.00/volume
Foreign Individuals:	$70.00/volume
Single Issues Domestic:	$18.00
Single Issues Foreign:	$28.00

Note: domestic subscription rates only apply to shipping addresses within the 50 US states. All other subscriptions must use the foreign rate.

All orders should be sent to: SHOFAR, Purdue University Press, PO Box 388, Ashland, OH 44805, or call 1-800-247-6553, or fax 1-419-281-6883, or e-mail order@bookmasters.com. Please make all checks payable to Purdue University. Credit cards also accepted.

Submission Information
The aim of *Shofar* is to promote the exchange of ideas and information among teachers and scholars in the area of Jewish Studies. *Shofar* favors material written for the general reader rather than a subgroup of specialists. Of particular interest is the area of teaching Jewish Studies at colleges and universities. *Shofar* publishes scholarly papers (5,000-15,000 words), book reviews, and review essays. All papers are reviewed by invited readers; other materials are evaluated by the editorial board. *Shofar* accepts submissions that meet the following requirements:

Papers must be submitted via e-mail to the Managing Editor (nlein@purdue.edu).

Include a brief bio (5-10 lines).

Include a brief abstract (100-150 words).

Categories: Items of Jewish interest in all fields

CONTACT: nlein@purdue.edu
Material: All
Jewish Studies Program
Purdue University
Beering Hall
100 N University St
W. Lafayette IN 47907-2098
Phone: 765-494-3633
Fax: 765-496-3633
1363 Liberal Arts & Education Bldg.
West Lafayette IN 47907-1363
E-mail: nlein@purdue.edu
Website: www.case.edu/artsci/rosenthal/shofar.htm

Short Stuff Magazine

Short Stuff Magazine (for grown-ups) is 8½" x 11", 32-40 pages, bond paper, enamel cover, black & white illustrations and photographs.

Fiction and humor can be any genre, any subject. We are designed to be a *Reader's Digest* of fiction. Nonfiction must be regional, pertaining to Colorado and the adjacent states (Wyoming, Nebraska, Kansas, New Mexico, Arizona, Utah). We are found in professional waiting rooms (doctors', dentists', lawyers' offices, etc.) Bimonthly.

Needs: We are not considering any essays at this time. Adventure, contemporary, historical (general), humor/satire, mainstream, regional, romance (contemporary/historical), science fiction, senior citizen/retirement, suspense/mystery. Some poetry accepted, preferably humorous. We always need clean jokes. We receive 300 mss/month, but use 9-12 mss/2 months. Length: 1,500 words maximum (no exceptions).

How to Contact: Send complete manuscript with cover letter telling about the author. Put full name, title of submission, address and telephone number on the first page. Must include self-addressed stamped envelope–otherwise the manuscript will be destroyed. If the manuscript is dated, indicate this on the envelope (e.g., if the story is related to the Christmas holiday season, put CHRISTMAS). We are seasonal. We report in roughly three to six months. Photocopied submissions OK. We do accept computer printouts. For a sample copy send $1.50 plus a self-addressed, 9" x 12" envelope with $1.85 postage (or five 37-cent stamps).

Payment: We pay $10-$50, at our discretion, with free subscription to magazine for stories. Fillers (500 words or less) $1-$5. We do not pay for single jokes or poetry but do give free subscriptions.

Terms: Acceptance and pay at publication for first North American serial rights.

Advice: We seek a potpourri of subjects each issue. A new slant, a different approach, fresh viewpoint. Prefer third person, past tense. Be sure it is an actual story with a beginning, middle and end. It must have dialogue!

Categories: Fiction—Adventure—Drama—Family—History—Romance—Short Stories

CONTACT: Donnalee Bowman, Editor
Material: Fiction
CONTACT: Rick Bowman, Copy Editor
Material: Non-Fiction
Bowman Publications
712 West 10th St.
Loveland CO 80537
Phone: 970-669-9139
E-mail: shortstf89@aol.com

Shuttle Spindle & Dyepot
Handweavers Guild of America, Inc.

Background

Published by the Handweavers Guild of America, Inc., *Shuttle Spindle & Dyepot* magazine features emerging artists and craftspeople, highlights innovative techniques and events, and honors established fiber artists and textile traditions. SS&D is a magazine for artists and craftspeople. As an international forum for weavers, spinners, dyers, basketmakers and felters, it is a visually appealing, in-depth publication that promotes excellence in fiber art through articles that inform, enlighten, instruct and inspire.

Articles

We are interested in articles that present ideas and concepts related to textile arts; articles on textile history and preservation, artists' profiles and guild related projects. We feature in-depth reviews of museum, gallery and textile shows, as well as examine current issues relative to textiles.

Targeting all levels of experience, we look for articles on weaving, spinning, dyeing, felting, weaving with beads and basketmaking that examine a technique or tradition. Our emphasis is on developing design skills, understanding techniques, marketing and craftsmanship.

Manuscripts

We invite written proposals that summarize the subject and point of view of the article. Complete articles, not exceeding 1200 words, are also welcomed.

Please present your article or ideas in the following format:
• Use 8½" x 11" white bond paper.
• Type and double space.
• Provide a disk with the hard copy. Indicate Macintosh or IBM format.

Save the document:
1. in Microsoft Word (as Word 2)
2. in Word Perfect (as WP 5.1)
3. or as an ASCII file
Label disk with your name, file name, and indicate MAC or IBM disk format.

• Place your name, address and phone number in the upper right hand corner of each page.
• Indent paragraphs.
• Use two inch margins at the top and bottom and one inch on the sides.
• If the article is unsolicited, please include a brief outline of the article, hard copy only (no longer than one page).
• Include the bibliography at the end of the manuscript on the hard copy and disk.
• Include photo captions on the hard copy and disk.
• Include a list (hard copy) of enclosed illustrations (photographs, slides, drawdowns, graphs, line drawings) with an accompanying descriptive note of each illustration.
• Include a brief autobiographical note.

Illustrations

Use clear, good quality original slides, 4" x 5" transparencies and/or black and white glossy prints to illustrate articles. All slides and photographs should be sharp and clear without background clutter.

Photographs should be included on the list of illustrations with a brief description. All illustrations/photograhs/samples should be keyed to the text and captioned. Do not write on the back of photographs but tape a piece of paper on the back of the photo. People in the photograph should be identified.

All illustrations should be labeled with the following information:
• Name of artist and/or author
• Address of author (or artist if different)
• Name of piece, dimensions, fiber content and other pertinent information
• Name of photographer to be given photo credit
• How the piece is keyed to the text for example (Illustration 1)
• An arrow on the right side indicating the top of the slide/photograph/sample

When it is necessary for the author/artist to send in the actual piece for in-house photography, the item must be tagged with:
• Owner's name and shipping address
• Title of the piece
• An indication of the right side
• Insurance value
• The piece must be keyed to the text

We will return the piece/s postage paid, insured via the same transport service used for delivery.

Drafts

In order to keep drafts uniform all drafts will be redone on a computer software program to our specifications.

- Draw drafts on graph paper.
- Use numbers to mark the threading draft.
- For the rising shed (jack loom) tie-up draft, number the harnesses, with the highest number on top and the lowest on the bottom, and indicate it as a rising shed.
- For the sinking shed (counter balance) tie-up draft, use X.
- Use short vertical dashes for the treadling draft.
- For the drawdown, fill in the squares where appropriate.
- Be sure to label the threading and the treadling.
- Indicate tabby by using a and b.

The publication process

Once a manuscript is chosen for publication, the copy is read for content, clarity, conflicts and duplications. Then it is sent to the copy-editor.

The copy-editor checks spelling, punctuation and grammar. She also corrects awkward sentence structure. She edits and checks that names and places are spelled correctly. Whatever appears on the original copy from the author is considered correct. For example, if a person's last name is Smith and the author spells it Smythe, we have no way of knowing that it should be Smith.

The copy is then set in a three column format and a draft or galley proof is printed. The galley proof or draft copy is returned to the author for verification and author comments. It is extremely important to check the spelling of names and places at this time.

Authors, members and guilds love to see their name in print, especially in their national organization's magazine, but only if it is spelled correctly!

Check: photo, illustration and diagram captions; author's biographical note, illustrations and diagrams.

Comments from the author should be forwarded (faxed, if possible) to the editor as quickly as possible with errors, misspelled names or misplaced diagrams noted on the returned copy.

Review

The manuscript will also be reviewed by a specialist. For example, an article that includes formulas for mixing dyes will be reviewed by a chemist. Once the consultant's and author's comments have been implemented, the page layouts are designed.

Proofreader

The proofreader inspects all final copy and photo captions.

Honoraria and Publication Agreement

The Handweavers Guild of America, Inc., provides a small honorarium, upon publication of an article. In exchange, the author agrees to convey First English Language publication rights, Anthology (reprint) rights, electronic publication rights, and rights to photocopy or otherwise reproduce the work to the Handweavers Guild of America, Inc./*Shuttle Spindle & Dyepot*. In addition, the author agrees not to sell, assign or transfer any remaining rights in and to the article until six months after publication in SS&D, unless otherwise agreed with the editor.

Occasionally we may request electronic publication rights—work will be watermark protected—to include on HGA's Web site: www.weavespindye.org.

References

All references must be documented.

Bibliography:

Please use this format for a book:

Atwater, Mary M. *The Shuttlecraft Book of American Hand-Weaving*. New York: Macmillan Publishers, 1928.

Use this format for a magazine article:

Guy, Sallie. "Twill 2-Double Width Afghans." *Shuttle Spindle & Dyepot*, Winter 1983, 34.

Citations:

Parenthetical references are used to clarify (in the body of the text) when documenting research or when reference should be made to a particular book, page or section of a book. For examples see below.

Example 1: author date method (Atwater 1928) or

Example 2: author, date, page method (Atwater 1928, p. 178)

An example of citations used in an article can be found in the following:

Duncan, Kate. "The Kutchin Baby Carrying Strap." *Shuttle Spindle & Dyepot*. Spring 1992, 38.

Book reviews

Book reviews follow general manuscript instructions. Please begin your book review with this format:

BOOK TITLE IN CAPITALS, by Author's Name. Publishing Company, Street, City, State, Zip. Year of Publication. Soft or Hard Cover. Number of pages. Price.

Do not exceed 500 words.

Suggestions for discussion:

- general description
- to whom it would appeal
- author's purpose in writing the book
- author's qualifications
- merits of the book
- any weakness
- quality of illustrations and/or diagrams

Reviewed by Your Name, City and State or Province

Categories: Arts—Associations—Crafts/Hobbies—Culture—Education—Fashion—General Interest—Hobbies—Reference—Trade—Textile & Fiber Arts

CONTACT: **Submissions Editor**
Material: **All**
Two Executive Concourse, Ste. 201
3327 Duluth Hwy.
Duluth GA 30096-3301
Phone: 770-495-7702
Fax: 770-495-7703
E-mail: weavespindy@compuserve.com
Website: www.weavespindye.org

SIERRA

Sierra
The Magazine of the Sierra Club

Sierra is a bimonthly national magazine publishing writing, photography, and art about the natural world. Our readers are environmentally concerned and politically diverse; most are active in the outdoors. We are looking for fine writing that will provoke, entertain, and enlighten this readership.

Though open to new writers, we find ourselves most often working with authors we have sought out or who have worked with us for some time. We ask writers who would like to publish in Sierra to submit written queries; no email queries please. Phone calls are strongly discouraged. If you would like a reply to your query or need your manuscript returned to you, please include a self-addressed stamped envelope. Prospective Sierra writers should familiarize themselves with recent issues of the magazine; for a sample copy, send a self-addressed envelope and a check for $3 payable to Sierra; back issues are included on the Sierra Club's Web site, www.sierraclub.org/sierra/.

Please be patient: Though the editors meet weekly to discuss recently received queries, a response time of from six to eight weeks is usual.

Please do not send slides, prints, or other art work. If photos or illustrations are required for your submission, we will request them when your work is accepted for publication.

FEATURES

Sierra is looking for strong, well-researched, literate writing on significant environmental and conservation issues. Features often focus on aspects of the Sierra Club's work. For more information about issues the Club is currently working on, visit our Web site at www.sierraclub.org. Writers should look for ways to cast new light on well-established issues. We look for stories of national or international significance; local issues, while sometimes useful as examples of broader trends, are seldom of interest in themselves. We are always looking for adventure travel pieces that weave events, discoveries, and environmental insights into the narrative. We are more interested in showcasing environmental solutions than adding to the list of environmental problems. We publish dramatic investigative stories that have the potential to reach a broad audience. Nonfiction essays on the natural world are welcome, too.

We do not want descriptive wildlife articles, unless larger conservation issues figure strongly in the story. We are not interested in editorials, general essays about environmentalism, or in highly technical writing. We do not publish unsolicited cartoons, poetry, or fiction; please do not submit works in these genres.

Recent feature articles that display the special qualities we look for are "Beneath Wyoming Stars" by Geoffrey O'Gara (March/April 2004), "Lessons in Granite" by Daniel Duane (March/April 2005), "Dangerous Liaisons" by Marilyn Berlin Snell (May/June 2005), "Earth's Innovators" by Dashka Slater (July/August 2005).

Feature length ranges from 1,000 to 3,000 words; payment is from $800 to $3,000, plus negotiated reimbursement for expenses.

DEPARTMENTS

Much of the material in *Sierra*'s departments is written by staff editors and contributing writers. The following sections of the magazine, however, are open to freelancers. Articles are 100-1500 words in length; payment is $100 to $1500 unless otherwise noted. Expenses up to $50 may be paid in some cases.

"Lifestyle" is a new section, debuting in our November/December 2005 issue, that provides a colorful, upbeat take on green living. At turns practical and whimsical, this lavishly illustrated section informs readers about the latest (and best) trends, products, and tips in food, fashion, housing, transportation, and other areas of their everyday lives. The section also includes brief Q+As with green innovators in the lifestyle field, and short takes about the books, music, movies, art, and other media that should be on any well-rounded environmentalist's radar. Writers are encouraged to submit queries on light, positive, inspiring topics that will help readers add more value to their lives, not more work—or more guilt. We especially welcome ideas that incorporate lists, factoids, photos, how-tos, recipes, quotes, statistics, tips, and other quick-hit presentations. Items should generally be 50 to 200 words in length; payment will vary depending on length and complexity.

"Good Going" succinctly describes a superlative place, including fascinating natural and cultural facts, in about 300 words.

"Lay of the Land" focuses on environmental issues of national or international concern. Regional issues are considered when they have national implications. At 500 to 700 words, "Lay of the Land" articles are not sweeping surveys, but tightly focused, provocative, well-researched investigations of environmental issues. Payment varies according to length.

"Profile" is a 3,000-word biographical sketch of a person doing important work to protect the environment. We try to broaden our readers' understanding of the environmental movement with subjects they haven't read about elsewhere: for instance, a pig farmer in Mississippi or an outfitter in Wyoming.

"One Small Step" features the first-person accounts of ordinary folks doing extraordinary things. We publish a 100-150 word quotation from an interview that explains the person's actions, motivations, and impact. Payment for all articles is on acceptance, which is contingent on a favorable review of the manuscript by our editorial staff, and by knowledgeable outside reviewers, where appropriate. Kill fees are ne-

gotiated when a story is assigned.

Categories: Conservation—Ecology—Environment—Travel

CONTACT: Managing Editor
Material: All
85 Second St, 2nd Floor
San Francisco CA 94105-3441
Phone: 415-977-5572
Fax: 415-977-5794
E-mail: sierra.letters@sierraclub.org
Website: www.sierraclub.org/sierra

Skating Magazine

Thank you for your interest in writing for SKATING magazine. Without your help, we would not have the informative, interesting and compelling articles that make up SKATING magazine. This is a list of guidelines that we like to follow in SKATING magazine.

Who We Are:

SKATING magazine, with a paid circulation of about 45,000, is the official publication for the United States Figures Skating Association, the national governing body for the sport of figure skating. The magazine is published 10 times a year (June/July and August/September issues are combined), and freelancers write the majority of articles. The magazine's mission is to communicate information about the sport to the USFSA membership and figure skating fans, promoting USFSA programs, personalities, events and trends that affect the sport. Over half of our membership is under 17 and active in the sport of figure skating and the vast majority is female.

What We're Looking For

There are three main types of stories that we usually run in *SKATING* Magazine:

Competition Reviews.

Features: (on athletes of all levels—elite, adult, synchronized skaters; also judges and other USFSA members).

Remember that SKATING focuses on U.S. eligible athletes. We occasionally print an article on a foreign skater(s) or coach.

Columns: i.e. sports medicine; On the Lookout (dealing with young athletes working their way up the ranks); Athlete Programs (showcasing USFSA athletes who have succeeded due to USFSA programs).

Stories for SKATING magazine are evaluated on an individual basis, but in general, should fit more than one of the following criteria:

1. Accurate
2. Interesting and entertainin—appeals to the majority of our readers
3. Newsworthy—should have value and affect and/or impact our readers
4. Representative of the USFSA
5. Timely
6. Relevant to the figure skating audience
7. Educational
8. Has not appeared in any other publication

How to Query Us:

Send a letter or e-mail proposing your story idea to the address below.

Explain what you plan to cover and how you plan to proceeding with the reporting. The query letter should discuss your qualifications and knowledge of figure skating and convey the tone and style you plan to use for the story. If you are a first-time writer for SKATING, copies of published samples would be appreciated. If you are an unpublished writer, any sample of your writing would help. SKATING magazine wants quality writers with an imaginative style and the courage to seek out the interesting and unusual in a story, regardless of how often a writer has been published.

SKATING Magazine will occasionally accept unsolicited manuscripts, but a query is preferred. SKATING assumes no responsibility for unsolicited queries or manuscripts and will only respond to those accompanied by a self-addressed, stamped envelope. SKATING does not accept articles and stories that have appeared in other skating publications.

Photos are an important part of submitting a story idea. In your query, please note what kind of photos you plan to provide for the article.

Submitting an Article

• As you go through and edit your article, it is important to do a fact check. Consult second sources and make sure everything in your article is verified.

• If you are writing a sports medicine article, please clearly state your qualifications for writing the article. All outside sports medicine articles will be reviewed by the USFSA Sports Medicine Committee for accuracy before publication.

• Under no circumstances should you feel compelled to advance a copy of the entire story to your sources.

• Before submitting an article, make sure it has been spell-checked and edited for grammatical errors.

• SKATING also has a style guide for writers for the magazine. Please adhere to this guide when you are writing for SKATING. It makes our editing work much easier!

• E-mail submissions are preferred. Payment upon publication. Payment varies.

Photography

SKATING pays $35 per color photo used; $15 for black and white. A color photo on the cover is paid $50. All payment is on publication. SKATING will accept prints, slides and transparencies or electronic images. Electronic images must be scanned at 300 dpi, at least 100 percent of the original image, if the image is scanned from a print. Other details about electronic images can be determined when a photo is "purchased."

Quality prints and high quality scans are preferred.

For more details about photography, please contact Laura Fawcett at lfawcett@usfsa.org.

Categories: Diet/Nutrition—Physical Fitness—Sports/Recreation

CONTACT: Amy Partain
Material: All
20 First Street
Colorado Springs CO 80906
Phone: 719-635-5200
Fax: 719-635-9548
E-mail: apartain@usfigureskating.org
Website: www.usfigureskating.org

Ski
The Magazine of the Ski Life

SKI focuses on accuracy and timeliness. And we need your help. SKI's authority is contingent on the accuracy of your submission. While we do as much fact-checking as possible, you must provide us with accurate information. That includes everything from general facts to quotes to spellings.

Writers are paid upon acceptance. They will not be paid until manuscripts are complete—and that includes all TKs.

Please review the following list of guidelines. If you have any questions, contact your assigning editor.

Thank you.

WRITER GUIDELINES
I. SOURCES AND FACT CHECKING

You are responsible for providing a source list A) names and phone numbers of all your contacts and B) phone numbers for each individual quoted.

Hold onto your notes and research materials. If we have questions during the editing process, we will come back to you for clarification or more information.

II. TRAVEL INFORMATION

Authors submitting travel/feature stories that focus on particular resorts or regions must provide a standard information box with the following information: Contact address and phone and fax numbers (including tourist boards and airlines when applicable); Acres of skiable terrain (including off-piste for European destinations); Ticket prices—weekday and weekend; Snow report number; Nearest city; How to get there.

Lodging and dining information must offer at least two options in three categories—budget, moderate, luxury. If a resort has SKIwee or NASTAR programs, these should be mentioned as well.

III. STYLE

For grammar, please follow *The Associated Press Stylebook*. You are responsible for correct spellings (names included) and word usage.

IV. FORMAT

All stories must be submitted by the deadline indicated, on computer disk (please specify what software) or via e-mail and in hard copy format. NOTE: *SKI* will not pay for overnight delivery of stories or materials.

V. WORD COUNT

Stories that are grossly above (or under) the specified word count will be returned to the writer and considered incomplete.

VI. EXPENSES

An itemized list of expenses, with receipts attached must be received no later than 45 days after the assignment is completed. Expenses received later than this may not be reimbursable.

Categories: Nonfiction—Adventure—Lifestyle—Recreation—Sports

CONTACT: Submissions Editor
Material: All
Times Mirror Magazine
929 Pear St.
Boulder CO 80302
Phone: 303-448-7600
Fax: 303-448-7638
Website: skimag.com

Skiing Magazine

SKIING readers are smart, curious and passionate about the sport. For them, every ski trip is a modern adventure. They might ski, snowboard, or telemark; they will seek out the best clubs, parties, and restaurants. They want to know about the biggest expeditions, the most exotic locations, the latest first descents. Studying several past issues of the magazine should help you determine whether a query is appropriate, and whether we've covered a given subject before. While a large portion of SKIING is written by regular contributors and staff members, including nearly all features, we welcome freelance writers to send us your ideas. Scene, the Hot List, and Trail Run are all good entry-level sections for your first assignment.

In general, we look for the following attributes:

• Skiing. Although we cover other winter sports, such as snowshoeing, mountaineering, and nordic skiing, SKIING primarily sticks to its title—with some exploration into resort telemarking, backcountry, AT, and even snowboarding.

• Trends. Whether it's new gear, an up-and-coming resort, or a hot destination, we want to be the first to reveal it.

• Service. Virtually every SKIING story contains useful information, something practical that the reader can learn.

FEATURES: Most SKIING features focus on gear, instruction, destinations—both nearby and far-flung, big and small—and personalities. The voice can range from objective reporting and service to humorous first-person narrative, but it needs to be unique and descriptive. All stories have some component of service (how to get there, where to stay, what to buy), whether it's a sidebar, a box, or a more central focus of the piece. Our regular contributors usually pitch fantastic stories (China, Morocco, Iran, Turkey) and popular destinations (heli-skiing in Alaska, Chamonix, summer in Chile), so it may help to consider less obvious subjects: smaller ski areas, local ski cultures, and colorful personalities.

Every year, we publish a Best Of, a gear guide/ski test, a travel guide, and regular Private Lessons (instruction). These are generally written and produced in-house with the participation of experienced testers and skiers.

DEPARTMENTS

Scene: Often defined by art, these are short snapshots that inspire readers and reveal what's really going on in skiing: rumors, weirdness, athletes, trends, techniques. It's our most timely section. 70-150 words per item.

Hot List: Hottest new innovative products, techniques, books, trends, with a quick description about why it's the latest, greatest thing on the market, and price/contact info.

The Inside Line: These are essentially pocket guides to skiing resorts with a map and short paragraphs that deliver hardcore service.

Face Shot: A profile of someone in the ski world, with a range from an Olympic downhill racer to an up-and-coming freeskier to a world-class mountaineer, who has recently done something notable.

Outfitter: This section shows readers how to outfit themselves for adventure, whether it's a comprehensive look at the basics, a rundown of techie accessories, or the gear you need for hut trips or preseason training. We try to uncover trends in the industry and give round-ups on products in categories. Examples: soft shells, AT gear, helmets, hydration packs.

Trial Run: We rank a certain gear category (glasses, altimeter watches, packs) for three price points—Race Stock, Retail, and BroDeal—with brief descriptions of the product and its functionality.

Be Strong: Legitimate, scientific and timely information about how to get and stay strong and fit. Each issue includes a 3-5 page short feature about a certain exercise program or trend, smaller boxes that highlight recent studies and charts to compare new products, and a sidebar or two with short new/product/website blurbs.

East/California Regional: We publish an extra section in these two regions with limited distribution, and each one has an Inside Line section, a Deal Monitor, and short news items. (The Underground, Deep Thoughts, and Dropping In are written by our columnists.)

ACCURACY: We are committed to providing reliable information, so it is important that all contributors check facts and figures, provide contact information for sources, and provide extra copies of maps, catalogs, brochures, or other primary sources when the story is submitted.

QUERIES: We prefer queries to completed works. With your initial query, please send examples of your published work and a brief cover letter explaining your background and past experience. Include a SASE if you would like your materials returned. We're not responsible for returning unsolicited artwork, photos, and manuscripts, so don't send originals.

ASSIGNMENTS AND PAYMENT: SKIING assignments require a signed contract, which specifies rights, payments, and deadline in order to be valid. We pay $.75-$1.00 a word, depending on the experience of the writer.

Categories: Nonfiction—Adventure—Consumer—Outdoors—Recreation—Sports—Travel

CONTACT: Perkins Miller, Editor-in-Chief
Material: All
929 Pear St., Ste 200
Boulder CO 80302
Phone: 303-448-7600
Fax: 303-448-7676
E-mail: editors@skiingmag.com
Website: www.skiingmag.com

Skin Inc. Magazine:
The Complete Business Guide for Face & Body Care

Manuscripts are considered for publication that contain original and new information in the general fields of skin care and makeup, dermatological, plastic and reconstructive surgical techniques. The subject may cover the science of skin, the business of skin care and makeup establishments or of an individual esthetician, or treatments performed by estheticians, dermatologists and plastic surgeons on healthy (i.e., non-diseased) skin. Subjects may also deal with raw materials, formulations and regulations governing claims for products and equipment.

A manuscript must be written exclusively for this publication, that is, not submitted to any other publication, and contain significant material not previously published elsewhere. Publication rights for reprints and other republication purposes is normally granted on request.

Acceptance for publication is in the hands of our Editorial Committee. A decision will be given to an author within one month.

TECHNICAL DETAILS

A manuscript must be submitted in English, although perfect grammar and style are not required. We reserve the right to edit all manuscripts accepted for publication. Any editing required will be done by our editorial staff. Whenever possible, please submit your manuscript to us on a 3E" DS/DD PC disk. Manuscript file must be submitted in Microsoft Word or ASCII format. Manuscripts also can be e-mailed.

All product trade names for product lines, drugs, equipment, etc. must be credited to their manufacturers including the city and state of manufacture. All facts quoted or used in the manuscript text from other literature sources must be properly referenced. References must be submitted according to the style sheet below.

Illustrations should be provided as color glossy photographs or via e-mail, 300 dpi in size. Original charts and graphs should be in black ink on white paper. They will be returned at the author's request. Photocopies of illustrations are most often not clear enough to be reproduced in a publication.

Two copies of the manuscript should be supplied.

The usual scheduling of manuscripts is done four to eight months in advance of publication. This will be the usual time between acceptance of a manuscript for publication and its appearance in the magazine.

In the case of original material written exclusively for this magazine, an honorarium will paid to the author upon publication.

Style Sheet for References and Footnotes
Magazines, Journals, and Periodicals

Please number the references. Start with the author's name(s), article title, journal or magazine name, volume number, issue number, starting page number, month and year of publication.

1. Science of beauty: High tech products: form meets function. Elle IV (2), 252 (October 1988)

2. C Duhe, Powder is back: The return of delicate dustings. Elle IV (2), 276 (October 1988)

Please note that the author's initials precede the surname, that there is very little punctuation, that only the first letter of the article title is capitalized, that the first number is the volume number, followed by the issue number, followed by the page numbers, followed by the year. The page number and issue month and year must be included with each reference.

Books

Start with the book's author(s), chapter name and number if appropriate, book name, editor's name(s) if any, publisher's city and state, publisher name, year of publication, and page number(s)

2. L Schorr and SM Sims, The need for skin care, Ch 6, in Lia Schorr's *Seasonal Skin Care*, New York, NY: Prentice Hall Press (1988) p 87

FOOTNOTES

Retin-A (Ortho Pharmaceutical Corporation, Raritan, NJ)

Please footnote all trade names (e.g. drugs, product lines) used in the text. Include the full name of the manufacturer, its city and state.

Please contact the editor if you have any questions on this style sheet.

Categories: Diet/Nutrition—Education—Health—Lifestyle—Physical Fitness—Spa and Skin Care—Women's Issues

CONTACT: Melinda Taschetta-Millane, Editor
Material: All
362 S. Schmale Rd.
Carol Stream IL 60188
Phone: 630-653-2155
Fax: 630-653-2192
E-mail: skininc@allured.com

Slipstream

For Magazine

Submit poetry, black & white or color photographs, graphics, and illustrations (better to send photocopies of artwork rather than originals).

We prefer contemporary urban themes—writing from the gut that is not afraid to bark or bite—and shy away from pastoral, religious, and rhyming verse.

If you're unsure, the editors strongly recommend that you sample a current or back issue of *Slipstream*. Submitting blindly to any magazine may result in wasting your time, money, and effort.

If you desire a response, please include a SASE. Payment is in copies.

For Annual Chapbook Contest

$1,000 prize plus 50 professionally printed copies of your chapbook.

Deadline for entries: Dec. 1 every year.

Send up to 40 pages of poetry—any style, format, theme (or no theme), plus a SASE with correct postage for the return of your manuscript, and a $15 check, bank draft, or money order for reading fee.

Simultaneous submissions are okay as long as you keep us informed of status. Previously published poems with proper acknowledgement and photocopies which are easy on the eyes are also acceptable.

All entrants receive a copy of the winning chapbook plus one issue of *Slipstream* magazine.

A winner is selected in the spring, at which time manuscripts are returned.

The winner may be featured on the Grants & Awards page of *Poets & Writers Magazine* as well as *Slipstream*'s web site, and will also receive exposure in *Slipstream* catalogues, press releases, and promotional materials.

Past winners include: Gerald Locklin, Kurt Nimmo, Sherman Alexie, Serena Fusek, Matt Buys, Robert Cooperman, Richard Amidon, Katharine Harer, David Chorlton, Leslie Anne Mcilroy, Renny Christopher, Alison Pelegrin, Laurie Mazzaferro, Ronald Wardall, J.P. Dancing Bear, Nikki Roszko, Beth Anne Royer, and Jason Irwin.

Categories: Literature—Poetry

CONTACT: Editor
Material: Poetry and chapbook entries
Box 2071
Niagara Falls NY 14301
Website: www.slipstreampress.org

Small Farm Today

Small Farm Today magazine is dedicated to preserving and promoting small farming, rural living, community and agri-preneurship. We use a "can-do," upbeat, positive approach and all articles submitted should reflect this attitude.

We need "how-to" articles (how to grow, raise, market, build, etc.), as well as articles about small farmers who are experiencing success through diversification, specialty/alternative crops and livestock, and direct marketing. *Small Farm Today* is especially interested in articles that explain how to do something from start to finish citing specific examples involved in the process or operation being discussed. It is important to include data on production costs, budgets, potential profits, etc. See the list of topics at the end of these guidelines for ideas. We do not usually use fiction, poetry or political pieces.

REPRINTS: If your manuscript has been printed in another publication, please list the publications and dates published. We prefer to publish original articles.

WE PREFER:

• 1,400-2600+ word articles, typed or on a 3.5" disk in text format.

• Accompanying captioned photographs with SASE for photo return.

• The article should be "how-to," describing how to raise the crop or animal and how it is marketed. It should list the address of the farm examined or other resources to contact for more information.

• Please include data on production costs, budgets, profit information, and marketing methods.

• Articles which meet these preferences and the other standards listed herein (in the opinion of the editors) will be paid a half-cent bonus per word published. Contact the Managing Editor for more information.

MANUSCRIPTS: We welcome both completed manuscripts and queries, but recommend you query your idea before sending in a manuscript.

Manuscripts submitted for consideration become the property of Missouri Farm Publishing, Inc. and will NOT be returned unless accompanied by a self-addressed, stamped envelope. Please type manuscripts, allowing at least 1/3 page at the top of the first page for editing notes. We also accept articles on disks compatible with a Macintosh computer. Length, depending on subject, should probably be between 800 and 3,000 words (we usually prefer 1,200-2,600 words). We prefer manuscripts with accompanying photos (see Photos, below).

Because we use an image scanner to transfer most hard copies of manuscripts onto the computer, we would prefer an original copy of your manuscript or a very clean photocopy.

It is important to include the addresses and phone numbers of your primary sources/interviewees. We usually include this information at the end of the article so the readers can contact them for more information. Please specify if the source or interviewee does not wish to have their phone number or address listed at the end of the article.

If you have charts, diagrams or sources for additional information on your subject matter, we will try to use them as sidebars with the article.

ALTERATIONS: *Small Farm Today* reserves the right to alter your manuscript for readability or space considerations. There will be no deliberate changes in the meaning of the text. Although every effort is made to avoid error, *Small Farm Today* does limit its responsibility for any errors, inaccuracies, misprints, omissions, or other mistakes in the article content.

SPECIAL SECTION: OUR PLACE

R-U

Small Farm Today features a special section called Our Place. This section is written by farmers/landowners about their own property. We prefer it to be written in first person form (I, we, our). It should include a description of your farm and what you raise. Some "how-to" tips on what you have learned from dealing with your crops/livestock would be appreciated. Other things that can be mentioned are: how you got started, plans for the future, what makes your property unique, and marketing strategies you employ.

Several people have expressed concern about their writing abilities—don't worry. The story will be edited for publication, but will still contain your own unique voice. Payment for Our Place is a box of magazines of the issue featuring your story. You can pass it out to family, friend, and customers.

HOLDING POLICY: After the article is received, it is submitted to the editor for review. If approved, it will be slated for publication. There is a long waiting period for articles to be published, often close to a year. This is due to limited space (only 6 issues) and a multitude of interested writers. Please bear with our slow publishing times. If we have not published the issue after one year, we will return the story to you (if you included an SASE). If you would prefer not to have your story held, please send notification of this with your manuscript.

PAYMENT: Unless otherwise arranged with the publisher, Missouri Farm Publishing, Inc. buys first serial rights and nonexclusive reprint rights (the right to reprint article in an anthology) for both manuscripts and photos. Missouri Farm Publishing, Inc. reserves the right to edit the story for publication. (See Alterations.) Rate of pay for reprints may be less than our standard rate of pay.

Payment for articles: • 3.5 cents per word for each word published (see above paragraph) for first serial rights and nonexclusive reprint rights. • There is a half-cent per word bonus for quality articles. (See We Prefer, above.) • 2 cents per word for each word published for reprinted articles. • We do not pay for book reviews

Payment for photos: $6.00 each for b&w or color prints • $10.00 for photo used on cover • $4.00 each for negatives or slides

Payment for line art, graphs, charts, and cartoons: • $5.00 each Payment is made 30-60 days after publication. Sorry, no exceptions.

PHOTOS, LINE ART, GRAPHS, CHARTS, & CARTOONS

Please send color or black and white prints of photos and include information about each photo for use in captions. Only color photos can be used on the cover. If you do not have prints, we can use negatives or slides. All photos sent to us will be returned if you include a SASE for photo return. Cartoons, line art, graphs and charts are also welcome.

SUBJECT MATTER

Here is a list of some of the topics we cover regularly:
• Money-making alternatives for the small farm
• Exotic animals (ostriches, buffalo and elk are some we have covered)
• Minor breeds (Jacob sheep, Dexter cattle and red wattle hogs are some we have covered)
• Draft horses (using them on a small farm; also other draft animals)
• Small stock (sheep, goats, rabbits, poultry)
• Direct marketing (farmers markets, subscription marketing, roadside stands, U-pick)
• Gardening
• Wool and other fibers (production, processing, and marketing)
• Specialty crops
• New uses for traditional crops (ethanol and plastic from corn, for example)
• New sustainable farming methods
• Rural living (particularly how-to)
• Small fruits (grapes, berries, exotic new fruits)
• Tree fruits
• Sustainable agriculture (organic, reduced-input, agro-ecology)
• Horticulture (herbs, ornamentals, wild flowers, vegetables, other opportunities)
• Aquaculture (catfish, crawfish, fee fishing, tropical fish)
• Home-based business (crafts, food processing)

• Small-scale production of livestock (cattle, hogs, poultry)
• Equipment appropriate to small-scale acreage work

Be warned that stories may have a long lead time. As of this writing, we have 80 stories in stock. We do not limit ourselves to the topics on this list. If you have an idea for a story, drop us a note outlining your idea. If you are not familiar with *Small Farm Today*, we can send you a sample copy for $3.00.

If you have any other questions, please write or call.

Categories: Nonfiction—Agriculture

CONTACT: Paul Berg, Managing Editor
Material: All
3903 W. Ridge Trail Rd.
Clark MO 65243-9525
Phone: 573-687-3525
Fax: 573-687-3148
E-mail: smallfarm@socket.net
Website: www.smallfarmtoday.com

Smithsonian Magazine

Smithsonian Magazine accepts unsolicited proposals on our website: www.smithsonianmag.com. To access the web submissions form, select "contact us" and then "Submissions." The web page contains Writer's Guidelines and the answers to Frequently Asked Questions. We no longer accept unsolicited e-mail or postal mail article proposals.

Categories: Nonfiction—Arts—Conservation—Culture—Ecology—History—Humor—Nature—Science—Society—Technology—Travel—Archaeology

CONTACT: www.smithsonianmag.com
Material: All

Smoke Magazine
Life'sBurning Desires

Formal guidelines not available. Please read a number of issues to ascertain the publication's style and needs.

Send queries to address below.

Categories: Nonfiction—Automobiles—Crime—Fishing—Food/Drink—Men's Issues—Recreation—Recreation Vehicles—Sports

CONTACT: Allyson Boxman Levine, Editor-in-Chief
Material: All
Lockwood Publications, 26 Broadway, Floor 9M
New York NY 10004
Phone: 212-391-2060

Snake Nation Review

Snake Nation Review appears four times a year:
We welcome submissions throughout the year.
Fiction: 5,000 word limit
Poetry: 60 line limit
Essays: 5,000 word limit
Art: pen & ink drawings, photographs,
Payment $100 for art
Subscriptions are $20; sample copy $6 (includes mailing)

Institutions $30

Subscription includes the contest poetry book.

All well-written submissions on any topic in any form will be considered.

Simultaneous submissions are allowed with prompt notification if the piece places elsewhere.

Editors' Choice wins $100 for each category.

Categories: Fiction—Arts—Culture—Poetry—Science Fiction—Sexuality—Writing

CONTACT: Jean Arambula, Editor
Material: Poetry
110 West Force St.
Valdosta GA 31601
Phone: 229-244-0752

Society of American Baseball Research

The Baseball Research Journal
The National Pastime

SABR's membership publications are written mainly for members. We're interested in hearing from any member who wants to share a piece of research on any baseball topic that would interest a portion of the membership. If you're interested in working up a piece for a SABR publication, here's some information that should help.

Queries

For your own sake, don't go to all the trouble of writing an article before you touch base with the Publications Director, who is the editor of most SABR publications. Query first. E-mail your proposal, an outline or both, setting out your idea for an article to Publications Director Jim Charlton at binswanger@aol.com. SABR will give you an honest appraisal of your idea, perhaps some suggestions, and will tell you whether or not we'd like to see a complete manuscript.

This doesn't necessarily mean that your article will be published. We may find that it doesn't stick to the point that your query advertised, or even (heaven forbid) that it is just poorly written. But querying does prevent you from doing a lot of work on something that we simply don't think will work for the publication in question.

Computers

You don't have to submit your manuscript on a computer disk, but if you do, you save SABR both time and the expense of having your article keyboarded.

We produce SABR publications on a MAC, using Microsoft Word and PageMaker. We can handle most Mac or MS-DOS word-processing programs, but not CP/M, Apple II, Amiga, Atari, et al.

Even if you do submit your article on disk, please send along a hard copy as well. It's easier to read that way, so we can make a judgment on it and get back to you more quickly.

Format (For Hard Copy)

Please double-space your manuscript. Please give us a word count. Leave generous margins all around—a roughly 60 character line (if using Pica or Courier type) and 25 lines or so per page is about right. This makes your manuscript easy to read and leaves room for notes in the margins.

Start typing manuscript about halfway down the first page. This leaves space for even more notes at the top of your copy. Make sure the top of every page carries your last name and the page number. If you are using a computer, please don't set your word processing program to justify text (this means making every line the same length as in a book). Your manuscript should be ragged right, as in standard type-written documents. The reason? It's much easier for the editor working with the hard copy to roughly verify your word count for a non-justified manuscript.

Photos, Graphics, Tables, and Charts

If you have photos, sent them (or copies of them) along, so we know what we've got to work with. Sometimes, researchers come up with wonderful cartoons or drawings. We'd like to see those, too. If your article requires tables or charts, build them carefully, and make sure they make their point clearly (A surprising number don't). Tables will be re-keyboarded and set up to fit the publication. Charts, on the other hand, should be "camera ready"—clear enough to be shot and printed.

Copyright

If we accept your article, we will send you a letter of agreement, which will make a few points clear. the two main ones are these: (1) you retain copyright, (2) you grant us First Serial Rights and the right to use the article in any future SABR compendiums.

How Long Should You Wait For Response?

We try to get back to you within a few days of receiving any sort of communication. But, the office is small, the work is large, and occasionally something falls through the cracks. If you don't hear from us in three weeks or a month, give a call or write an indignant note.

Authors' Galleys

We will send you an edited, typeset of your article before it goes in press. If you have any serious problems with it, you must get back to your editor by phone within two weeks so we can work them out.

Which Publication

SABR puts out four membership publications a year. Not meant to be commercial publications, these are for the most part by SABR members, for SABR members.

Of these four publications, *The Baseball Research Journal* (BRJ) and *The National Pastime* (TNP) are annuals, and the two others are "specials" often created by one of SABR's committees. The two annuals are open to all SABR members, but there's often some confusion over how they differ. Here's a short description that might help you decide which one your article best suites.

The Baseball Research Journal is the repository for SABR members' "hard" research. Virtually all statistical studies belong here, and although we don't want to turn it into an academic journal, you should include notes, bibliographies, etc., where appropriate. Short articles focused on long-passed historical figures or events are okay here, but they must have a strong analytical approach. This is also the place for articles focusing technically (as opposed to historically) on the business of baseball, or on playing techniques.

The National Pastime is just what John Thorn's original subtitle calls it—"A review of baseball history." Articles don't require that strong analytical edge, and are usually more anecdotal than those in BRJ. This doesn't mean that we don't require solid research on historical subjects for TNP, just that there's more room here for speculation, opinion, nostalgia, humor, poetry and a certain amount of writing culled from non-SABR resources.

There's some overlap between the two publications. Some articles can go either way, and if that's the case with yours, your editor will make a suggestion.

Timely Publication

When we accept an article for publication, we usually tell you where and when we want it to run. Sometimes we get so much good material that we're forced to tell you when we accept it that we may have to hold onto you manuscript until the next year's edition.

Occasionally, we learn as we get into the editorial process and start assembling an issue that we have to roll one or more articles out and over to the next years' edition. This is sometimes a matter of space, and it's sometimes a matter of editorial balance (too much National League 1950's, not enough 19th Century). It's never a signal to you that we really don't like your article. (If we accepted it, we want to run it!) We never do this casually, because we know how hard you've worked and how eager you are to see your article in print. And we never do it without notifying you apologizing for the disappointment we know we're causing, and offering to free you from your Letter of Agreement (although we hope you stick with us).

Categories: Nonfiction—History—Humor—Poetry—Sports/Recreation

CONTACT: Jim Charlton, Publications Director
Material: Queries
James Charlton Associates
680 Washington St.
New York NY 10014
Phone: 212-691-4951
E-mail: binswanger@aol.com
Website: www.sabr.org

South American Explorer

South American Explorers is a non-profit organization. With clubhouses in Quito, Ecuador, and Lima and Cusco, Peru and U.S. headquarters in Ithaca, New York, the SAE collects and makes available to its members up-to-date, reliable information about Latin America.

Aims and Purposes

South American Explorers is dedicated to:

• Furthering the exchange of information among travelers and researchers

• Promoting responsible travel through the publication of pamphlets, information packets, the internet, and our magazine, the *South American Explorer*

• Publicizing projects aimed at improving social and environmental conditions in Latin America and collecting funds for their activities

• Awakening greater interest and appreciation for the welfare of endangered peoples, wildlife protection, and wilderness conservation

• Collecting information on volunteer and research opportunities

• Fostering ties between non-profit organizations, NGO'S, and conservation groups

General Membership Services:

Members of the South American Explorers receive:

• A one-year subscription (four issues) to the *South American Explorer* magazine.

• Access to our clubhouses in Quito, Lima and Cusco—trip reports, luggage storage, book exchange, mail and e-mail service etc.

• Discounts at a number of lodges, hotels, travel agencies, language schools, and guides in Peru and Ecuador.

• Help and advice from the friendly, knowledgeable club staff when planning trips and expeditions. Members can do their own information searches at any one of our clubhouses or solicit information by phone, mail, e-mail. It helps if we know when you plan to travel, the size of your budget, your interests, the number of people in your group, your preferred type of transportation, and anything else that will guide us in providing you with the most useful and detailed information possible. As a rule, the more specific your questions, the better our answers.

• Discounts on books, tapes, maps, and other goods available from the club's store.

• Access to the club's libraries, map collections, scientific reports, magazine and newspaper articles, theses, and books.

• Networking, the art of bringing like-minded people together. Members looking for travel companions or who wish to contact experts in various fields can post notices to the SAE electronic bulletin board, or on the bulletin boards in the Lima, Quito and Cusco clubhouses. They can also place classified ads in the *South American Explorer* (For the first 25 words: Members—(noncommercial) $10, (commercial) $30. Non-members—(noncommercial) $20, (commercial) $40. Each additional word is 50 cents).

• Additionally, members can call upon the SAE staff for help when emergencies or other problems arise.

The club will receive donations of money or goods for research and allocate these to worthy projects. Gifts by donors are tax deductible.

SAE Membership Categories

• Regular ($50 individual, $80 couple): Benefits include a subscription to the *South American Explorer*, the quarterly journal of the club, discounts on items in our catalog, a laminated rabid-bat-spittle-proof membership card, use of our information and trip planning services, storage for equipment and supplies at the Lima and Quito lubhouses, and much more. A complete list of membership services is available upon request.

• Contributing ($80): Contributing Members, as the name indicates, contribute immeasurably to the general cheer and goodwill of their club. In addition, they receive a free t-shirt.

• Supporting ($150): As the name implies, these Members are virtual pillars, generously supporting their club in its heroic efforts. Our honored Supporting Members receive a free t-shirt. And, because we know that Supporting Members always welcome a thoughtful token of our appreciation, we offer these discerning individuals a book from the catalog. Finally, a Supporting Member may also bestow two free gift subscriptions to the *South American Explorer* at any time during the period of their Membership.

• Life ($750): Our most worthy Life Members receive all the benefits of club Membership during their mortal tour of this planet. These esteemed Life Members are encouraged to choose any one of the large selection of items from our catalog. As a final gesture of gratitude, Life Members will be sent a complete set of South American Explorers still in print, and ten free gift subscriptions upon request.

• Afterlife ($7,500): As an Afterlife Member you will, of course, receive all the benefits bestowed upon Regular, Contributing, Supporting, and Life Members. In addition, when you pass into the realm beyond, you will face eternity with serenity, assured of your club's perpetual gratitude. You will know the true meaning of immortality as you return each year to preside at the annual club bacchanal held in your honor. Imagine the envy of your fellow spirits when they witness this outpouring of affection and devotion to your revered memory, a blessed dividend of immortality that might have been theirs had they but followed your sublime example and shown but a mote of your greatness of heart during their brief and pointless jigs upon the stage of life.

Rough Writer's Guidelines for the *South American Explorer*

If you're a famous, frequently published writer commanding tens of thousands of dollars for your breathless prose, calmly disregard the following. On the other hand, if you're a humble quill-pusher like the rest of us, peruse these not necessarily hard-and-fast guidelines.

Generally we like pieces that run about 3-5,000 words.

Even wretched and awful submissions are greeted with cries of joy and read in the most favorable light if they arrive on an IBM-compatible diskette. Preferably in WordPerfect 6.1. However we can read any IBM-compatible word-processing program. Please put your diskette in a protective mailer. If mailing from abroad, inscribe "Do Not X-Ray" on the package. Yes, we know it's not a photographic plate, but do it anyway.

The inclusion of dramatic photographs in focus is appreciated. Ideally we like color or black-and-white glossy photographs. If you send copyrighted slides, include a release so we can have them made into prints. Please label (your name and address) and caption all photos and slides. Also include biographical info on yourself, and a sketch map (it can be rough, we'll redraw it anyway) where appropriate.

Content and style? Ay, there's the rub. Need we say the article should be readable. This is a magazine, after all. Style helps. Lengthy extracts from a dreary diary don't hack it. "Got up at 7:00, breakfast ham & eggs, boat in at 7:30, blah, blah." No Inca trail articles unless they're fantastic. Personal accounts fine, provided they reveal the wonderful and fascinating you. Best of all are articles by knowledgeable authors about their specialty.

To get a better idea of what we want, read Mark Mardon's *In Search of Elusive Metaphors: The Art of Travel Writing*.

Remuneration? Ah yes, well…Best of all, there's vanity indulged. Then too, the Club pays, albeit reluctantly, a munificent (if you happen to live in Bangladesh) $50, and even sweetens the deal by conferring a one-year membership, or extending your existing membership one year. You also get any amount (within reason) of free magazines featuring your article, a free T-shirt (we choose the color), and if you visit us briefly in Ithaca, we will treat you to a sumptuous, though modest, meal at a local beanery.

Boot up and write on.

Categories: Nonfiction—Associations—Conservation—Ecology—Nature—Travel

CONTACT: Don Montague, Editor
Material: All
126 Indian Creek Rd.
Ithaca NY 14850
Phone: 607-277-0488
Fax: 800-274-0568
E-mail: explorer@saexplorers.org (digital format is preferred)
Website: www.saexplorers.org

South Florida History

South Florida History

Purpose of the Magazine : To engage readers in stories about the history of South Florida and the Caribbean in a manner that is both educational and entertaining and is illustrated with both historic and contemporary images.

History: The Historical Museum of Southern Florida began publication of the magazine in 1974. In 1988, the name was changed to *South Florida History Magazine*, and in 2000 it became *South Florida History*.

Presentation Style: Articles should be suitable for general audiences with interest—but not necessarily with a great deal of background—in our region's history. The editors strive for variety and balance so that each issue contains at least one article of interest to each reader.

Style Authority: *The Associated Press Stylebook and Libel Manual* should be consulted on matters of style as this is the guide used by the editors of the magazine. Webster's first choice is used when multiple spellings of a word are acceptable. Exceptions are made when the presentation form warrants.

Content: Articles should recall, retell and explore historic events, people, places and themes pertaining to southern Florida and the Caribbean. The magazine covers Florida south of Lake Okeechobee, coast to coast, and all countries in the Caribbean. Articles are generally presented as non-annotated narratives in third person or first person, and can include quotations from historic records, diaries and other documents. Exceptions are made when material warrants. Bibliographies and footnotes will not be published.

Book reviews are also accepted. Reviews are encouraged for publications relating to southern Florida and the Caribbean. It is suggested that potential reviewers inquire about a specific book they would like to cover to see if a review is already in the works.

Photographs : Photographic illustration is very important in *South Florida History*; authors are encouraged to identify available accompanying visual material whenever possible and provide copies of such images when submitting manuscripts. Original documents and photographs that must be returned to their owners will be copied by the Historical Museum of Southern Florida and handled according to the highest level of curatorial standards. Materials will be returned via certified delivery systems after publication of the magazine.

Submission of Articles and Book Reviews

• Articles should be 2,500 to 5,000 words, and book reviews should be approximately 300 words in length. Submissions may be edited for clarity or to meet space requirements.

• Articles may be submitted via e-mail or on a disk or cd (IBM or Macintosh), saved in a word processing format. Label disk/cd with author's name and article's title.

• Photographs and other illustrative materials, if identified, should be submitted with the manuscript (copies acceptable). Scanned photographs and images may be sent electronically as well, but prints will be required upon acceptance of the article for production.

• A brief biographical sketch of the author should accompany the article.

• Articles related to the published editorial calendar must be submitted prior to the submission deadline; any other articles may be submitted at any time.

• All articles are subject to review by *South Florida History* editorial staff. Submission of an article does not guarantee publication. Articles will be accepted based on appropriateness of subject and quality of writing.

The editorial staff of *South Florida History* strives to respond in a timely fashion to writers who have submitted manuscripts. When we receive your article we will notify you that it is under consideration for publication. If acceptable, the article becomes part of the pool of material undergoing production steps to ready them for publication. Articles are pulled from the pool and assigned to specific issues on an ongoing basis. The editors at the Historical Museum of Southern Florida maintain the right for flexibility in deciding publication dates as geographical, thematic and seasonal concerns are considered.

Due to our non-profit status, we cannot pay our contributors, but the Historical Museum of Southern Florida will send you our most sincere appreciation and ten (10) copies of the magazine.

Standards: The editorial staff of *South Florida History* strives for the highest level of accuracy and fairness possible when presenting the past. Standard journalistic and research practices and principles should be adhered to at all times.

The Historical Museum of Southern Florida disclaims any responsibility for errors in factual material or statements of opinions expressed by contributors.

A Word to Contributors: You are the lifeblood of *South Florida History*. Your time, energy and thoughtfulness in submitting a contribution are sincerely appreciated as we strive to spread interest in and understanding of our region's rich past.

Thank you. Editor, *South Florida History*

Categories: Nonfiction—African-American—Arts—Asian-American—Biography—Conservation—Culture—Hispanic—History—Jewish Interest—Lifestyle—Multicultural—Native American—Regional—Ethnic

CONTACT: Editor
Material: Any
Historical Museum of Southern Florida
101 W. Flagler Street
Miami FL 33130
Phone: 305-375-1492
Fax: 305-375-1609
E-mail: publications@historical-museum.org
Website: www.historical-museum.org

Southern Accents

No formal guidelines.
Categories: Antiques—Architecture—Arts—Book Reviews

CONTACT: Dawn Cannon, Managing Editor
Material: All
Southern Progress Corp., 2100 Lakeshore Dr.
Birmingham AL 35209
Phone: 205-445-6000

The Southern Aviator

Please refer to *General Aviation News.*

The Southern California Anthology
University of Southern California

We read all fiction and poetry that comes to us, whether traditional or non-traditional, and publish a variety of forms and styles. The *Southern California Anthology* selects manuscripts for publication using literary merit as the sole criteria.

All manuscripts should be typed. Poetry should be single-spaced within stanzas; double-spaced between stanzas.

Fiction submissions and interviews should be no longer than twenty-five pages. Please limit prose submissions to one.

Please limit poetry submissions to no more than five. Place only one poem per page.

We appreciate cover letters. They give us not only a sense of the writer, but are also helpful if they include sufficient information for the editors to compose a brief biography in the event of acceptance.

Categories: Fiction—Poetry—Short Stories

CONTACT: Dr. James Ragan
Material: All
Master of Professional Writing Program
University of Southern California
WPH 404
Los Angeles, CA 90089-4034
Phone: 213-740-3252
Fax: 213-740-5775
E-mail: mpw@usc.edu
Website: www.usc.edu/dept/LAS/mpw

SHR Southern Humanities Review

Southern Humanities Review
Auburn University

Always include a self-addressed stamped envelope, or a self-addressed envelope with international reply coupons, even for a reply only. Queries are welcome. Simultaneous submissions are NOT accepted. E-mail submissions are NOT accepted. Submit poetry, fiction, and essays separately, as different editors will consider them. Do not submit a second manuscript if we already have one from you under consideration. With the exception of translations, we do not consider material that has been published elsewhere. In prose submissions use one-inch margins and double line spacing. Prepare manuscripts using the MLA Handbook. Use at least a 10-pt. font. If you use an ink printer, make sure the print is dark. Payment is two contributors' copies; copyright reverts to author upon publication. Response time usually varies from two weeks to three months, depending on the editors' other responsibilities, but might be a bit slower in summer. Please do not assume from our name that we're interested in Southern literature or research topics only; any setting or subject matter is acceptable, but do avoid excessive vulgarity, profanity, and jargon (medical or military, for example).

Poetry Send three to five poems at a time. It is wise to submit no more than four times per year unless the editors ask to see more of your work. We rarely print a poem longer than two pages. Translations are encouraged, but please include the original AND written permission from the copyright holder for you to publish a translation.

Fiction Send only one story per submission. Manuscripts should be between 3,500 and 15,000 words, double-spaced. It is wise to submit no more than four times per year unless the editors ask to see more of your work. Translations are encouraged, but please include the original AND written permission from the copyright holder for you to publish a translation.

Essays Send only one essay per submission. Manuscripts should be between 3,500 and 15,000 words, double-spaced (including notes). Be sure to direct your essay to a general humanities audience, avoiding specialist jargon. Translations are encouraged, but please include the original AND written permission from the copyright holder for you to publish a translation.

Book Reviews The review should be no more than 1200 words in length. About two thirds of the review should be devoted to a summary of the content of the book, and about one third to your evaluation. Please pay particular attention to the forms illustrated below for the heading and closing of your review. Do not use footnotes or cite page numbers in your review.

A SAMPLE REVIEW HEADING:
Your Name
Your Address
Contemporary Literary Theory. Edited by G. Douglas Atkins and Laura Morrow. Amherst: University of Massachusetts Press, 1989. xiv + 249 pp. $40.00, cloth; $12.95, paper.

(If the price of the book is not listed, please use the abbreviation "Npl." as follows: xiv + 249 pp. Npl. For non-university presses in unfamiliar cities use the city and state as follows: Port Townsend, Washington: Copper Canyon Press, 1994.)

A SAMPLE REVIEW ENDING:
Your University or Your City and State   Your Name
                                        (Please note italics here.)

Categories: Fiction—Nonfiction—Arts—History—Literature—Music—Poetry—Short Stories—Criticism—Humanities—Philosophy

CONTACT: Editors
Material: All
9088 Haley Center
Auburn University, AL 36849-5202
Phone: 334-844-9088
Fax: 334-844-9027
E-mail: shrengl@auburn.edu
Website: www.auburn.edu

Southern Living

Thank you for your interest in submitting articles to *Southern Living*. However, with the exception of our Southern Journal column, the articles and photography are produced by members of our staff.

For Southern Journal, we don't have a rigid set of guidelines; however, there are some characteristics of a typical Journal that you might find interesting. Above all, it must be Southern. We need comments on life in this region—written from the standpoint of a person who is intimately familiar with this part of the world. It's personal, almost always involving something that happened to the writer or someone he or she knows very well. We take special note of stories that are contemporary in their point of view.

We require that the piece be original and not published. We need about 600 words, typed and double spaced. The writing must have an essay quality—as opposed to a reporting, interpretive, or editorial approach. Finally, it must be of exceptionally high quality.

We can't guarantee acceptance of any piece for publication, but if we do decide to use it, we require complete ownership rights. If interested, send your manuscript to the address below. If we are interested, we will contact you directly.

Again, thanks for considering *Southern Living*. Good luck in placing your work.

Categories: Nonfiction—Book Reviews—Cooking—Diet/Nutrition—Food/Drink—Gardening—Regional—Travel—Home

CONTACT: Sara Askew Jones, Associate Features Editor
Material: All
2100 Lakeshore Dr.
Birmingham AL 35209
Phone: 205-445-6000

Southern Lumberman:
The Sawmill Magazine

A leading forest industry trade publication, *Southern Lumberman* appeals to owners, managers and supervisors at sawmills, lumber remanufacturing plants, log/lumber concentration yards, flooring plants, dimension plants, lumber drying entities and manufacturers of lumber processing equipment.

The magaine's editorial menu includes profiles on these companies, technology application articles, business management information, news about lumber firms and expert columns on lumber drying, saw filing and hydraulics.

Southern Lumberman is primarily interested in article about the foregoing types of businesses. Examples include newly established or expanded operations, new equipment/systems applications that improve performance, operational milestones (multi-generation family companies, employee-owned businesses, special anniversaries, etc.) and human interest pieces. Payment varies with the type and quality of such articles. All articles must be accompanied by quality digital or film photography and consist of no more than 1200-1500 words.

A monthly, *Southern Lumberman* is distributed by request to lumber interests in the eastern half of the U.S. Circulation hovers around 15,000.

Categories: Sawmills

CONTACT: DK Knight (dk@hattonbrown.com)
or Rich Donnell (rich@hattonbrown.com)
Material: All
Phone: 334-834-1170
Website: southernlumberman.com

The Southern Review
Louisiana State University

The Southern Review publishes fiction, poetry, nonfiction, and excerpts from novels in progress. We subscribe to the set of standards for good art staked out by John Gardner in his book *On Becoming a Novelist*: the work must (1) create a vivid and continuous dream; (2) demonstrate authorial generosity; (3) reveal intellectual and emotional signifcance; (4) be rendered with elegance and efficiency; and (5) exhibit an element of strangeness. Although we are willing to publish experimental writing that appears to have a valid artistic purpose, *The Southern Review* also agrees with Flannery O'Connor's observation that a writer is free to try and get away with whatever he wants, but that it had been her experience that there wasn't much one could get away with. We are, finally, looking to publish the best work that arrives in the mail. Poetry lengths preferred are one to four pages; fiction and nonfiction, four hundred to eight thousand words. Manuscripts must be typewritten—fiction and nonfiction double-spaced—and accompanied by self-addressed, stamped envelopes with sufficient postage to cover return. Queries are not necessary. Only previously unpublished works will be considered. Allow at least two months for editorial decisions.

Contributors are paid thirty dollars a printed page for both prose and poetry. Payment is made upon publication. Two complimentary copies of the issue in which the work appears are sent to each contributor; we also give a one-year subscription beginning with the issue after the one in which the work appears. No reprints are available. First American serial rights only are purchased. We cannot accept e-mail submissions, nor can we respond to manuscripts unaccompanied by self-addressed, stamped envelopes. Manuscripts will not be returned without adequate return postage. We recommend using regular post or, if you must send your manuscript by guaranteed post, using Federal Express. Sample copies are $8.00 payable in advance. Manuscripts will not be considered during the months of June, July, and August.

Categories: Fiction—Poetry—Nonfiction—Interview—Literature—Short Stories

CONTACT: The Editors
Material: All
The Southern Review
Old President's House
Louisiana State University
Baton Rouge LA 70803-5005
Phone: 225-578-5108
Fax: 225-578-5098
E-mail: southernreview@lsu.edu
Website: www.lsu.edu/tsr

Southern Traveler

Founded: January 1998
Frequency: Mailed bi-monthly, Jan./Feb. through Nov./Dec.
Circulation: 175,000. Mailed to AAA households in Arkansas, Louisiana and Mississippi
Readership: 350,000
Source: Mediamark Research, Inc., New York, NY / February 2000

AAA Southern Traveler features articles on regional, national and international travel opportunities. Area history, auto safety, highway and transportation news also are featured. The South is often the focus of travel articles. As the official publication for AAA members in Arkansas, Louisiana and Mississippi, we reach an audience that travels throughout the year. AAA, America's premier travel organization, serves more than 40 million members nationally.

The *Southern Traveler* magazine's goal is to provide members with a variety of useful information on travel, auto safety, and other topics that appeal to the motoring public. The magazine carries on average six articles per issue and buys 20-30 manuscripts per year.

How to contact us: Send queries rather than finished manuscripts. In addition, please send a list of credits or published clips when you query us for the first time. We will not take phone queries and prefer not to see a laundry list of story ideas. In general, we try to reply within four weeks of receipt. We will consider a previously published article if it appeared in a non-competing publication. Simultaneous queries are acceptable, but tell us the idea is being considered elsewhere.

Assignments: We work from an editorial schedule and assignments are usually made at least six months in advance. Sometimes the calendar is assigned by July for the following year. Usually purchase first North American rights. A story assignment is always made by letter. The writer signs an outline-agreement and returns one copy to the editor. We do not pay any expenses in conjunction with the article (travel expenses, phone bills, etc.). Payment for an article is made upon acceptance. Our rates range from $50 to $350. It helps to send photos/slides (color only) with manuscripts. While we do not pay for photos, we consider it in payment for the manuscript. To assist with fact-checking, please send copies of materials used to research the article.

Style: We use the AP Stylebook. Third-person voice usually works best, but in some cases first-person description is appropriate. A copy of a current magazine will be sent with assignment so our editing style can be observed. A story will not be drastically changed without discussing this with the writer. Send the manuscript on floppy disk, saved either in Microsoft Word 5.1 or a lower version, or as an ASCII text file. Always include hard copy with the disk.

Taboos: Humor, satire, fiction, poetry, cartoons. Technical and safety articles usually are written by staff. Departments (e.g. "Travel Treasures, Day Tours") also are written by staff.

Categories: Nonfiction—Associations—Automobiles—Consumer—Culture—History—Regional—Travel

CONTACT: Robin Jones, Editor
Material: All

12901 N. Forty Drive
St. Louis MO 63141
Phone: 314-523-7350
Fax: 314-523-6982
Website: www.ouraaa.com/traveler

Southwest Fly Fishing

Thanks for your interest in *Southwest Fly Fishing* magazine. To receive consideration for publication you should read and follow these guidelines closely.

ABOUT THE MAGAZINE

Southwest Fly Fishing magazine is a destination specific publication to be viewed as an inspiring, collectible reference of Southwest angling destinations. The staff at *Southwest Fly Fishing* takes pride in our editorial content. Our writing is refreshing, our photography, captivating. *Southwest Fly Fishing* is issued bimonthly.

FEATURE ARTICLES

Our goal is to give an inspiring and complete report on specific Southwest angling destinations. Angling destinations include both the famous and the lesser know waters, and include all species found in our diverse geographical region. If more than one species is found in any given water, writers should cover each species, as well as every season that water is fishable. In short, feature articles should be concise, and leave no holes. Our goal is to cover specific angling destinations as no other publication has done in the past. The best way to get a feel for what we want is to study one of our magazines.

Photography is very important. *Southwest Fly Fishing* has set high standards for all images used in our magazine. Writers have a much better chance of being published if articles are accompanied by stunning photography. We will not publish dead fish, poorly exposed or composed shots.

The area of coverage for our features includes Colorado, Utah, Nevada, New Mexico, Arizona, Texas, Central to Southern California, Mexico, and Central America.

Feature Article Requirements

• Provide practical traveling and angling information to specific destinations, including personal anecdotes

• Included should be pertinent angling history and thorough description of the fishery

• Current regulations for the fishery

• Detailed description of angling techniques, tackle and flies, and local perspectives

• Articles should be thorough and specific so as to sufficiently inform and give the angler confidence to effectively fish the presented water

• Included with each article should be any applicable hatch chart and detailed map of the coverage area

• Conservation issues and future considerations should be addressed

• **Selection of 35mm (or larger) slides** (captioned and placed at the end of the manuscript)

• A popular fly of the fishery should be included for us to photograph, as well as a material list for the pattern.

• Feature article length should be 2,500 to 3,500 words

DEPARTMENTS

Most department material is staff-written. Exceptions are as follows:

Southwest Fly Tying

This department covers one Southwest fly pattern each issue. New, unusual and exciting patterns are encouraged, but we will also represent the time-proven standards. Flies for any Southwest species can be considered. Articles should include a little history and use of the fly, as well as step-by-step photos of the tying sequence, shot against a neutral-colored background. Two finished flies should accompany the article for photographic purposes.

Notes, News & Reviews

This department covers news events, and mini destinations (200 to 500 words). As with all material submitted, query first.

Conservation

Any conservation issue concerning the Southwest. Maximum length 750 words.

Exposure

Photo essay of 8 to 10 images depicting Southwest angling.

Digital Image Submission Guidelines

Feature Articles/Exposure

1) We only except files from digital SLR cameras with a minimum of 6-megapixels, 8-megapixel or higher are preferred! Note: A 35-megabyte file is needed for full page offset printing.

2) When making a submission please include 2 images per image file, the unedited RAW file and a processed JPEG.

3) Include a color contact sheet with file names of your images.

4) If the RAW file or contact sheet is not included, the submission will automatically be rejected.

5) Please do not submit images that are out of focus or overexposed.

Departments

1) Image files must be a minimum of 5-megabytes (11-megabyte files are preferred).

2) Files submitted for use in our departments may be sent in RAW, TIFF or JPEG format. If submitting files in JPEG, please use the maximum quality when saving images from your camera.

3) Please do not submit images that are out of focus or overexposed.

MANUSCRIPT SUBMISSIONS AND PAYMENTS

Initial contact with the editor by e-mail is preferred. A formal query letter, outlining the proposed article, should be sent to the editor before making a submission. A selection of slides MUST accompany the formal query. Unsolicited manuscripts must include a self-addressed, stamped envelope (S.A.S.E.) for their return. *Southwest Fly Fishing* is not responsible for submissions in transit to and from our editorial office.

Text and photos are purchased as a package. Manuscripts accepted without the appropriate photographic support will warrant less money for their use. *Southwest Fly Fishing* buys first North American serial publication rights. We reserve the option to edit all articles, however, we will make every effort to minimize editing to avoid changing the style or content of manuscripts.

All manuscripts should be submitted in typewritten form, double spaced. The author's name, address, phone number and manuscript word count should appear on the first page of the manuscript. A 3½" computer disk needs to be included, and your work saved in Microsoft Word. Manuscripts should also be e-mailed to the managing editor using a .doc or .rtf extension.

Payment is made approximately one month prior to publication, and the pay rate varies with the length and completeness of the submission. Inclusion of high-quality slides has a major impact in determining the pay rate for any given article. Our pay rate is as follows:

Feature Articles $400 to $600
Southwest Fly Tying $250
Notes, News & Reviews $100 to $125
Conservation $150

PHOTO SUBMISSIONS, ARTWORK AND PAYMENTS

Southwest Fly Fishing usually buys text and photos as a package. There are exceptions, however, and additional photography may be purchased on occasion. Contributors must query first.

We accept 35mm (or larger) transparencies only. Slides should be shipped in a clear sleeve, with concise captions. The photographer's name and address should appear on each slide mount. Payment varies for size used and impact. Our pay rate is as follows:

Cover $500
Exposure $600
Inside use $25 to $300

Illustrations and artwork $25 to $300

Categories: Nonfiction—Conservation—Fishing—Nature—Photography—Recreation—Sports—Travel

CONTACT: Steve Probasco, Editor-in-Chief
Material: Queries
PO Box 708
Raymond WA 98577
E-mail: probasco@matchthehatch.com
John Shewey, Managing Editor
Material: All manuscripts/slides
PO Box 12276
Salem OR 97309
E-mail: shewey@matchthehatch.com

Southwest Review
Southern Methodist University

Published: Quarterly.

Subscriptions: 1 yr. $24; 2 yrs. $42; 3 yrs. $65; sample issue $6. VISA and Mastercard accepted on our secure web site. (Please add $6 per year for each subscription outside of the U.S.)

Begun in 1915 and with a circulation of approximately 1500, the *Southwest Review* is the fourth oldest, continuously published literary quarterly in the U.S. We try to discover new writers and publish them beside those of more established authors. All submissions should be typed neatly, on white paper. Manuscripts must be accompanied by a stamped, self-addressed envelope for reply, and will not be returned unless SASE includes sufficient postage. *SWR* prefers not to receive simultaneous, email, or fax submissions, and does not consider work that has been published previously. If you so choose to submit simultaneous submissions, we must be informed immediately if the work is accepted elsewhere. Manuscripts will not be accepted during the months of June, July, and August.

Our articles embrace almost every area of adult interest: contemporary affairs, history, folklore, fiction, poetry, literary criticism, art, music, and the theatre. Material should be presented in a fashion suited to a quarterly that is not journalistic and not terribly overloaded with academic apparatus or jargon. It should not be too specialized, after the manner of papers that appear in learned journals of different fields of study.

In each issue the *Southwest Review* publishes two or three stories, which must be of high literary quality. We have published fiction in widely varying styles. We prefer stories of character development, of psychological penetration, to those depending chiefly on plot. We have no specific requirements as to subject matter. Some of our stories have a southwestern background, but even more are not regional. We prefer, however, that stories not be too strongly regional if the region with which they deal is not our own.

The preferred length for articles and fiction is 3,500 to 7,000 words.

It is hard to describe *SWR*'s preference in poetry in a few words. We always suggest that potential contributors read several issues of the magazine to see for themselves what we like. But some things may be said: We demand very high quality in our poems; we accept both traditional and experimental writing; we place no arbitrary limits on length; we have no specific limitations as to theme.

The McGinnis-Ritchie Memorial award is given to the best works of fiction and non-fiction that appeared in the magazine in the previous year. The two awards consist of cash prizes of $500 each. Robert F. Ritchie, who died in 1997, was a long-time generous supporter. In 1960 he established the John H. McGinnis Memorial Award to honor the man who edited the Review from 1927 to 1943. With a bequest in his will, Mr. Ritchie enabled us to maintain the tradition of his generosity. Please note that manuscripts are submitted for publication, not for the prizes themselves.

The Elizabeth Matchett Stover Memorial award was established in 1978 by Jerry S. Stover of Dallas in memory of his mother, who was

for many years a key member of the *Southwest Review*. The award consists of a $250 cash prize and is given to the author of the best poem or group of poems published in the magazine during the preceding year. Please note that manuscripts are submitted for publication, not for the prizes themselves.

Thanks to the generosity of Marilyn Klepak of Dallas, the *Southwest Review* gives an annual award of $1000 to a poem by a writer who has not yet published a first book. Ms. Klepak has endowed the prize in honor of her father, Morton Marr. Owing to a generous supplemental donation by Mr. and Mrs. David T. Searls, Jr., we are now able to offer a second place prize of $500. Contestants may submit no more than six poems in a traditional form (e.g., sonnet, sestina, villanelle, rhymed stanzas, blank verse, et al.). A cover letter with name, address, and other relevant information may accompany the poems which must be printed without any identifying information. Contest entry fee is $5 per poem. Submissions will not be returned. Entry deadline is November 30, 2006. The poem (or poems) will be published in the *Southwest Review*.

The *SWR* is published quarterly. We make a nominal payment upon publication and send author three gratis copies of the issue in which the work appears.

Categories: Fiction—Nonfiction—Arts—Culture—Interview—Literature—Multicultural—Poetry—Short Stories—Essays

CONTACT: Submissions Editor
Material: All
Southern Methodist University
PO Box 750374
Dallas TX 75275-0374
Phone: 214-768-1037
Fax: 214-768-1408
E-mail: swr@mail.smu.edu
Website: www.southwestreview.org

Space and Time

We are currently reading, very selectively, for #94. Because of our cash flow situation, even if we love your stuff, we can't pay until just before publication.

Space & Time is a bi-annual magazine of science-fiction and fantasy. We publish supernatural horror, hard s-f, swords and sorcery, and our favorite: that-which-defies-categorization. If you're not sure your manuscript is right for us, send it in and let us decide.

For fiction, we prefer under 10,000 words; more than that has to be very good indeed. Poetry of any type is fine, as long as it falls within the sf/fantasy genre; strong narrative poems are welcome here. We're generating pretty much all the non-fiction we want right now, so hold off on that. Payment is 1 cent per word ($5.00 minimum) for First North American Serial Rights, with a non-exclusive option on subsidiary rights, plus two copies on publication and a 40% discount on additional copies. Normally we pay on acceptance; because of our current cash-flow problems, though, we probably can't issue checks until we're ready to start work on the issue for which you are scheduled.

Manuscripts must be typed double-spaced, with your full name and address in an upper corner of the first page. Legible photocopies are okay; also dot-matrix of near-letter quality with a dark ribbon. We prefer no simultaneous submissions.

We do not take electronic submissions at present, although if we accept your work we will ask if it is available in that form. You must include a self-addressed envelope with sufficient return postage (or IRCs outside of the U.S.), or use disposable manuscripts and a stamped business-size envelope for our response. Address fiction to Gerard Houarner (or any associate editor), and poetry to Linda D. Addison. Mixing poems and stories delays our response.

You needn't read our magazine before submitting material, but we're not about to discourage you from trying to psyche us out or ingratiate yourselves. We could use the sale, especially now. A sample issue is $5.00 plus $1.50 handling charge (Canada $2.00; all other countries $3.00). Order from: *Space & Time*, 138 West 70th Street (4B), New York NY 10023-4468. Outside U.S., please use U.S. postal money order or check payable against any U.S. bank.

Categories: Fiction—Fantasy—Horror—Science Fiction

CONTACT: Gerard Mouarner, Fiction Editor
Material: Fiction
CONTACT: Linda D. Addison, Poetry Editor
Material: Poetry
CONTACT: Faith L. Justice, Features Editor
Material: Nonfiction
Space & Time Publishing
138 West 70th Street, 4B
New York NY 10023-4468
Website: www.cith.org/space&time.html

SpecialLiving

We do not have any written guidelines.

SpecialLiving is a quarterly publication for mobility impaired individuals. Each issue has information about travel, medical issues, accessibility, inspirational people, products, etc. Photos are very important to the content of the magazine. Writers are paid 10 cents/word (800 words max.) and $10 per photo upon publication.

Query first with an article idea.

Categories: Nonfiction—Health—Inspirational—Travel

CONTACT: Betty Garee
Phone: 309-820-9277

Specialty Retail Report

Specialty Retail Report is a full-color, quarterly trade magazine that serves the specialty-retail industry. We're an established, quality publication with a strong and growing readership.

Our readers

Independent specialty-retail entrepreneurs (including temporary and seasonal retailers) selling from carts, kiosks and stores in malls and other shopping venues; mall management and developers; product entrepreneurs (manufacturers, distributors, turnkey companies).

Our editorial

Features (three to five per issue; 2,500 words and up, depending on subject): Topics include new products/product categories, market profiles, location opportunities/profiles, consumer trends. Recent features include "The Power of Color" (color trends), "A New Sense of Calm" (massage/spa products), "Shades of Cool" (sunglasses), "Show Time! 12 Top Gift Shows"; **Entrepreneur Profile** (two per issue; 1,800-2,000 words): The success stories of individual specialty-retail entrepreneurs; **Departments** (include Money Matters, Business Builders, Marketing Matters, Selling Points; three or four per issue; 1,200-1,500 words): Retail business strategies, management and how-to on topics such advertising, hiring, visual merchandising, purchasing. Recent articles include "Nine Secrets of Yellow Pages Ads," "Finding a Bank You Can Bank On" and "Merry Ideas for Great Holiday Sales."

Nearly all of our editorial is freelance-written. All of our features and Entrepreneur Profiles are by assignment only. We do buy reprints for Department articles.

Note to writers

Always query first, and include your bio or résumé with clips and/or links to your work online. We're an upbeat publication that speaks to a unique, knowledgeable audience, so please become familiar with SRR's scope and target readers before querying. Feel free to visit our Web site for more about us, and call or e-mail to request a sample copy of the magazine plus our "Writers' Guide to Formatting."

Categories: Business—Trade—Retail/Gifts

CONTACT: Gerard Mouarner, Fiction Editor
Material: Fiction
293 Washington Street
Norwell MA 02061
Phone: 800-936-6297 or 781-659-7675
Fax: 781-659-4394
E-mail: info@specialtyretail.com
Website: www.specialtyretail.com

Specialty Travel Index

Specialty Travel Index (STI) is the number one magazine and web site about worldwide adventure travel. Our readership is a combination of consumers and travel trade professionals (travel agents, etc). Our print circulation is 50,000 (45,000 travel agents, 5,000 consumers). The accompanying web site is mainly accessed by consumers and is receiving up to 30,000 hits a day.

The magazine is semi-annual, published in January (Spring/Summer issue) and August (Fall/Winter issue). The web site is updated frequently with home page articles on a weekly rotation. In addition to a directory-type listing of over 600 adventure tour operators, the magazine and web site run approximately 11 special-interest travel stories per issue.

Our editorial requirements are:

• Length—1,250 words
• Rate—$300 (payable upon receipt of completed manuscript)
• Lead time—Six months
• Web site use—Writers receive 10% of the Original Fee when story appears on the STI web site.

We consider both written queries (accompanied by clips and writer bio) plus finished manuscripts ON SPEC. ABSOLUTELY NO SUBMISSIONS BY PHONE OR FAX. Story may not be written by employee of tour operator being featured in the piece. STI will not accept articles that have been picked up by any major wire service (i.e. Copley, AP).

Stories should deal with special-interest, adventure-type travel—from soft adventures (cycling through French wine country) to daring exploits (an exploratory river-rafting run in Pakistan). A variety of styles work for us: first-person, descriptive, etc. In general, STI does not like articles written in the present tense.

Articles should have a lively immediacy, not just relate facts that readers might know already. Since the readership includes both travel agents and consumers, avoid using "you" in the articles (i.e "You'll walk through flower-filled meadows..."). Instead, say: "Travelers (or trekkers or participants) can walk through..."

For submission of materials, we require:

• Hard copy and 3.5" disk--IBM compatible (ASCII) or Word document sent via e-mail plus color transparencies or digital images (high-rez--at least 300 dpi). We pay $25 per contributor photo used.
• Upon assignment or acceptance of story, writers will receive a contract which must be signed and returned to *Specialty Travel Index*.

Categories: Nonfiction—Travel—Specialty Travel

CONTACT: Submissions
Material: All
CONTACT: Risa Wyatt, Editor
Material: Any

PO Box 458
San Anselmo CA 94979-6458
Phone: 415-455-1643
Fax: 415-455-1648
E-mail: info@specialtytravel.com
Website: www.specialtytravel.com

Speedway Illustrated

Speedway Illustrated is a monthly, full-color magazine sold at newsstands and by subscription. It covers stock car racing exclusively. Our audience is deeply committed to the sport. Many own, drive or crew race cars. Typical readers attend 30 or more races per year. Therefore, stories we buy must be written for the relatively sophisticated.

Story Needs:

Study the magazine before attempting to write for us. We want the story behind the story in stock car racing, from backyard street stock garages to the biggest events in the sport. We buy interesting technical articles, offbeat features and shorts, interviews, personality pieces and issues-oriented features. Most of the stories we run are short. Most issues have no more than four full length features but carry many one- or two-page items. We buy dozens of photos that have one or two paragraphs of support copy, but very few 10-page articles.

Support Graphics:

A separate photo guideline sheet is available. In some cases, we can provide support photography. However, it's always wise to be sure that if we can't provide pictures, you can. If the story's about an active big-league racer, or if we can illustrate it with generic images, we can probably help. But if the story is about a weekend racer from your area, you must be able to supply quality support photography (snapshots won't do) or we can't publish it.

Rights:

We purchase first-time rights. Material purchased for the magazine may also be used on our internet site but without additional payment.

Credentials/Press Cards:

We do not issue credentials–only speedways can do that. We can, however, write to speedways requesting credentials for those working on stories and shorts for *Speedway Illustrated*.

Payment:

We pay on publication. Tech features pay most. Photos are paid separately. Payment varies with story quality, length, and interest value.

Method of Submission:

We prefer receiving work on computer disc with a hard copy backup, or via e-mail. If an SASE is included with a submission, we'll do our best to return your submission if we fail to accept it. However, we can take no responsibility for lost or damaged manuscripts, art, photography, etc. It's always best to include support photography with written submissions since judging is always based not only on the story but its support art as well.

Exclusivity:

We expect that all materials submitted to us are exclusive and have not been previously published. In some cases, we will publish material that has already been published or will be published elsewhere. If you are making a simultaneous submission here and elsewhere, please tell us.

Story Ideas:

The most important part of any story is the idea behind it. Our goal is to publish stories that are so interesting that people will buy the magazine to read them. Therefore, interest value—the story behind your story—is absolutely critical. We rarely call an author to offer a story idea. Editor Rob Sneddon prefers that you query story ideas either by e-mail, conventional mail or by fax. Phone queries are our least favorite method, since it's difficult to judge a person's writing ability based on a phone call. Interest value counts. If a short or feature is of high interest value to people deeply involved in stock car racing, it appeals to us.

Categories: Nonfiction—Automobiles—Recreation—Sports/Recreation

CONTACT: Karl Fredrickson, Technical Editor
Material: Technical Material, New Products
CONTACT: Rob Sneddon, Editor-in-Chief
Material: All other materials
Performance Media, LLC
107 Elm St.
Salisbury MA 01952
Phone: 978-465-9099
Fax: 978-465-9033
E-mail: rsneddon@speedwayillustrated.com

Spider
The Magazine for Children

About Us: For a sample issue of SPIDER, please send $5.00 with a 9 x 12 SASE to: SPIDER Sample Copy, PO Box 300, Peru, IL 61354.

NOTE: Sample copy requests from foreign countries must be accompanied by International Postal Reply Coupons (IRCs) valued at US $5.00. Please do NOT send a check or money order.

In January 1994, Cricket Magazine Group of Carus Publishing Company launched SPIDER, a magazine for children ages 6 to 9. SPIDER publishes original stories, poems, and articles written by the world's best children's authors. Occasionally, SPIDER publishes reprints of high-quality selections. SPIDER is full color, 8" x 10", with 34 pages and a 4-page activity pullout. It is staple bound. We hope that the following information will be useful to prospective contributors.

Published: 12 months a year

Price: $35.97 for 1-year subscription (12 issues)

Categories

Fiction: realistic fiction, easy-to-read stories, humorous tales, fantasy, folk and fairy tales, science fiction, fables, myths.

Nonfiction: nature, animals, science, technology, environment, foreign culture, history.

(A bibliography is required for all nonfiction articles, and copies of research material will be required for all accepted articles. Be prepared to send other backup materials and photo references—where applicable—upon request.)

Poetry: serious, humorous, nonsense rhymes.

Other: recipes, crafts, puzzles, games, brainteasers, math and word activities

Length

Stories: 300 to 1,000 words. Poems: not longer than 20 lines

Articles: 300 to 800 words

Puzzles/Activities/Games: 1 to 4 pages. An exact word count should be noted on each manuscript submitted. Word count includes every word, but does not include the title of the manuscript or the author's name.

Rates

Stories and articles up to 25¢ per word

Poems up to $3.00 per line

Payment upon publication

Themes

There is no theme list for upcoming issues. Submissions on all appropriate topics will be considered at any time during the year.

Comments

SPIDER would like to reach as many children's authors and artists as possible for original contributions, but our standards are very high and we will accept only top-quality material. PLEASE DO NOT QUERY FIRST. SPIDER will consider any manuscripts or art samples sent on speculation and accompanied by a self-addressed, stamped envelope. For art samples, it is especially helpful to see pieces showing children, animals, action scenes, and several scenes from a narrative showing a character in different situations. SPIDER prefers to see tear sheets or photo prints/photocopies of art. If you must send original art as part of a portfolio, package it carefully and insure the package. SPIDER will also consider submissions of photography, either in the form of photo essays or as illustrations for specific nonfiction articles. Photographs should accompany the manuscript. Color photography is preferred, but black-and-white submissions will be considered depending on subject matter. Photocopies or prints may be submitted with the manuscript, but original transparencies for color or good quality black-and-white prints (preferably glossy finish) must be available upon acceptance. Please allow 12 weeks to receive a reply to submissions.

SPIDER normally purchases the following rights: For stories and poems previously unpublished, SPIDER purchases all rights. Payment is made upon publication.

For stories and poems previously published, SPIDER purchases second North American publication rights. Fees vary, but are generally less than fees for first publication rights. Payment is made upon publication. Same applies to accompanying art.

For recurring features, SPIDER purchases the material outright. The work becomes the property of SPIDER and is copyrighted in the name of Carus Publishing Company. A flat fee per feature is usually negotiated. Payment is made upon publication.

For commissioned artwork, SPIDER purchases all rights plus promotional rights (promotions, advertising, or in any other form not offered for sale to the general public without payment of an additional fee) subject to the terms outlined below.

(a) Physical art remains the property of the illustrator.

(b) Illustrator may use artwork for self promotion.

Categories: Fiction—Nonfiction—Animals—Arts—Children—Crafts/Hobbies—Family—Folklore—Games—Literature—Multicultural—Poetry—Science—Science Fiction—Short Stories

CONTACT: May-May Sugihara, Editor
Material: Manuscripts
CONTACT: Sue Beck, Art Director
Material: Art Samples
CONTACT: Mary Ann Hocking, Permissions Coordinator
Material: Questions about rights
Spider Magazine
PO Box 300
Peru IL 61354
Website: www.cricketmag.com

Spin-Off

Thank you for requesting contributor's guidelines from *Spin-Off* magazine.

Spin-Off is a quarterly magazine devoted to the interests of handspinners at all skill levels.

Informative articles in each issue aim to encourage the novice, challenge the expert, and increase every spinner's working knowledge of this ancient and complex craft. If you are not already familiar with the style and tone of the magazine, please read a few issues before submitting a proposal. We review both proposals and full manuscripts. If you'd like to get our thoughts before you start, please write us a letter and tell us about your project or idea.

• If you are not a spinner, it will be difficult for you to write effectively for this magazine.

• If you are a spinner whose idea interests us, but you're an inex-

perienced writer, we will work with you on presenting your thoughts.

• Your projects and/or samples must contain handspun yarns as an essential component; commercial yarns may be used only in supporting roles.

• *Spin-Off* is many things—as a contributor think of it as a forum where you can share your experiences and knowledge with your community. Consider how your contribution will serve the reader.

Articles in a typical issue may include the following subjects.
• Spinning and preparation techniques
• Tools for spinning and preparing fibers
• Information on fibers: how to choose them, how to use them
• Ideas for using handspun yarn in a variety of techniques (knitting, weaving, rug hooking, lace—anything spinners can think of)
• Profiles of people who spin: why and how
• A gallery of contemporary work, complete with instructions or just as inspiration
• Tips on blending fibers
• The history and/or cultural role of spinning
• Something a little bit surprising
• Methods of dyeing, with natural and chemical dyes
New approaches to familiar topics are welcome.

Technical matters
You should display a thorough command of your topic—technical accuracy is a must. Make your information accessible to the reader. Strive for a personal and informal style of presentation. We prefer double-spaced computer-generated manuscripts presented both as hard copy and disk, but we read everything that's legible.

If you include references to other published sources or if your idea is based on or was inspired by someone else's work, please provide a complete bibliography. You can photocopy the title and copyright pages of each book for us, or make a list. For a book, we need full title and subtitle, complete names of author(s), publisher's name, place of publication, date of publication, and pertinent page numbers. For a magazine article, we need full title and subtitle, complete names of author(s), magazine title, volume number, issue number, and pertinent page numbers.

We reserve the right to edit material as necessary to fit the magazine's style and available space.

Submitting manuscripts or ideas
If you have already written an article, enclose a copy of the manuscript, supportive photos or drawings, and a brief personal biography. If you are at the idea stage, send a detailed proposal of your subject, with any sketches or photos you have. Clear snapshots are always useful. If you send the actual handspun item(s), we like to see them but may need to keep them for longer than you'd wish. Keep a copy of everything you send. Please include your name, address, e-mail address, and telephone and fax numbers in your cover letter.

Rights, scheduling, and payment
We purchase first North American serial rights, paid upon publication, and we give byline credit.

We occasionally arrange to reprint an article that has appeared in a local or regional publication.

You retain all other rights to your material.

We schedule articles several issues in advance, and we'll let you know the issue your article is scheduled for as soon as we know. Before we go to press, we will send you a copy of your edited article for review. About a month before the publication date, we'll send you an Author Agreement form to sign.

Payment for articles is $50 per published page, based on the edited version. If you provide images, we pay you $10 per published photograph.

Deadlines
Spin-Off is published four times a year, in March, June, September, and December.

Once we have scheduled your article, we will contact you to make sure that the deadlines for the completed manuscript, projects, and photography are agreeable to you.

Format

Ideally, your article will be computer generated, double spaced, and printed on 8½" x 11" white paper. Please include hard copy and a disk labeled with the program you used to create the file.

Titles, headings, and subheadings, if appropriate, should be included in your article.

Captions for photos, with all people clearly identified, are very useful.

Simultaneous submissions

Simultaneous submissions are generally not acceptable. Please tell us if you are submitting your material elsewhere.

Length

Length depends on the subject; most articles contain between 200 to 2,700 words.

Visuals

Good, solid visual information is an important feature of *Spin-Off*. If you can provide clear photos or drawings, we may be able to use them directly; even if we choose not to use them, they will help us produce finished artwork. Snapshots and sketches are wonderful resources. Feel free to send us several versions.

Photographs: Please send color transparencies (slides) or color prints for your article.

Photographs must be sharp and clear, with good contrast, clear focus, and a simple background.

Make sure to include the photographer's name with the image.

Put captions on a separate sheet of paper, with a sticky note on the back of each photo number-coded to the caption list. Include your name on each photo or slide. Do not write on the back of any photograph. Sticky notes or taped strips of paper will not harm the image. All photographs will be returned to you.

In many instances, we photograph items, materials, and tools here. We'll schedule photography sessions and then ask you to send the objects. We will usually need to have them on hand for between four and twelve weeks, although we will do our best to get them back to you as quickly as possible. If you need an item at a particular time, call us before shipping it to make special arrangements.

Drawings and diagrams should be created in black ink on white paper; use white paper with blue graph lines if the grid is helpful. We nearly always re-render drawings here to be sure they will reproduce consistently. Any type of sketch is helpful, even if it's not in the ideal format.

Please provide any necessary labels, captions, or explanations.

Swatches, yarn, and fiber samples should be included whenever possible.

Swatches should be a minimum of 4" x 4" (10 x 10 cm), and yarn samples at least two yards (2m) long.

Remember: Handspun yarns should be the critical part of your samples.

Please enclose a self-addressed, stamped envelope to return your materials.

Receipt of your submission will be promptly acknowledged with a postcard that lists everything we received.

You may also email your submission to SpinOff@ Interweave.com. Visuals can be submitted electronically as jpeg, tiff, or GIF files. Expect a response to your submission within two months.

Please call us if you have any questions about the submission process or the status of your submission at (970) 669-7672. Thank you for your interest in contributing to *Spin-Off.*

We look forward to hearing from you.

Categories: Nonfiction—Crafts—Hobbies

CONTACT: Amy Clarke Moore, Editor
Material: All
Interweave Press
201 East Fourth St.
Loveland CO 80537-5655
Phone: 970-669-7672
E-mail: SpinOff@interweave.com
Website: www.interweave.com

Spoon River Poetry Review

The Spoon River Poetry Review is a journal of fine poetry from both established and emerging poets from the United States and around the world (in translation). Its publication base is located in the heart of the midwest but its soul aspires toward something more transcendent, having, like Borges' circular book, everywhere for its center and nowhere for its circumference. Each issue features a selected Ilinois poet alongside others from around the nation and the world. In both open and closed forms, from the traditional to the avant-garde, the journal publishes poems written on the edge, in language that takes risks. The journal has been published without a break since 1974 and features review articles that engage some of the most compelling poetry you'll read.

The Spoon River Poetry Review is published twice a year by the Spoon River Poetry Association. The editors read submissions of fine poetry from all over the nation and the world from September 1 to May 1 each year. Manuscripts postmarked between May 1 and September 1 are returned unread. Send 3-5 poems to the address below. Submissions to *The Spoon River Poetry Review* Illinois Poet feature should contain 12-18 pages of mostly unpublished poems by poets who have an Illinois connection. Reviews of contemporary poetry and poetic theory should address texts and issues in a balanced and intelligent way. All submissions should be accompanied by a SASE (self-addressed stamped envelope).

Categories: Poetry

CONTACT: Dr. Lucia Getsi
Material: All
4240 English Dept., Illinois State University
Normal, IL 61790-4240
Website: www.litline.org/Spoon/

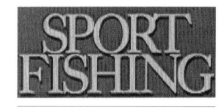

Sport Fishing Magazine

BACKGROUND: *Sport Fishing* is geared to serious saltwater fishing around North America. That means bluewater, reefs, inlets and inshore (bays, flats and backcountry). It's published nine times per year (monthly January-June; bimonthly July-December). Our readers: several-hundred thousand (over 130,000 paid circ nationally) are generally well-educated and quite affluent. Nearly all are men who own boats, often both a large offshore boat and skiff as well.

EDITORIAL CONTENT: Material in *Sport Fishing* should provide useful information about saltwater fishing which is (1) new/fresh/different; (2) specific/in-depth and (3) accurate. Concepts behind all queries should meet these criteria. Please don't submit an idea which has been written about by us and/or similar publications. FIND A FRESH IDEA OR A FRESH ANGLE TO AN OLD IDEA; like most publications, we too are looking for subjects that will have our readers saying, "I never knew that!" Examples of material that could be of interest: a new, effective technique for a species or type of fishing that has wide applicability; an area recently opened up to sport fishing; or a new look at conservation concerns regarding a particular fishery or species/group. As with any magazine, our very specific needs are best understood by studying recent issues.

FEATURES: We strive for a mix of genres including fishing how-to, where-to and conservation. Remember that our readers are not beginners; they're seeking to advance their knowledge, not rehash basic saltwater fishing. We cannot use material related to pier/jetty/

surf fishing; a boat must be involved if an idea is to work for *Sport Fishing*.

DEPARTMENTS: We're always looking for good material for several departments, particularly Sportfishing News, Rigging and Techniques and Fish Tales. Unlike short items that fit the format of the first two departments, Fish Tales can be 800 to 1,200 words. Except for the humorous Fish Tales (for which a cartoonist draws art), these columns are illustrated. Clear photos or even a good hand sketch from you will do; we'll have it professionally drawn for publication.

QUERIES & SUBMISSIONS: We'll look at over-the-transom submissions, but your efforts are much more likely to bear fruit if you query us first. First choice is e-mail, but we'll accept queries sent via fax or (with SASE) via post. They should be directed to the attention of Jason Cannon. He'll will pass along queries to the appropriate editor. "Laundry list" written queries are a welcome initial step. If a query warrants a speculative submission, then communication between editor and writer becomes the key to making things work. The editor will send a feature proposal to reiterate exactly what we expect in terms of substance, slant, style, length, sidebars, maps/charts and of course deadlines and request a written/emailed response. Most *Sport Fishing* editors request some sort of outline from the writer. Generally, this step is an invaluable way to (1) make sure the writer doesn't waste his/her time on something not right for us and (2) in general maintain close communication between writer and editor to make sure what the writer thinks the editor wants is in fact what the editor really wants. Often the outline will be reworked; so when the writer actually begins writing the feature he'll be on the right track. Finally, if questions develop as you work, give the editor a call to discuss it. We welcome the opportunity to work with new/unestablished writers who know their stuff—and how to say it.

SUBMITTING FEATURES/DEPARTMENTS: Most features, after editing as necessary, run 1,500 to 2,500 words including sidebars; rarely longer. Payment (see below) is for edited length. Please try to keep length of your features under 3,000 words; avoid submitting rambling 8,000-word manuscripts. If extensive rewriting is necessary, we like to work with the writer to resubmit the feature rewritten to meet our needs. However, again, writer-editor communication before and during the time the feature's written should minimize the chances of any major rewrites.

TIPS FOR *Sport Fishing* CONTRIBUTORS:

1. Meet or beat deadline dates. We like to work regularly with writers we can count on. Also that gives us time to ask you to rewrite if necessary.

2. Send photos. They may be yours or those of other photographers (remember: photo payment is additional to payment for manuscript. Separate photo guidelines are available upon request).

3. Quotes the experts. When possible, interviewing one or more professionals (skippers, mates, tournament experts or the like gives a subject great credibility. Also, wherever appropriate, contact fishery managers/biologists regarding status of species/fisheries. (Often they can provide tables, graphs, charts, etc. to help illustrate a topic.)

4. Balance information with readability. Anecdotes can impart information while lending human interest. These are safest in third person but there are times when first-person narrative, if not overdone, is useful. Avoid talking down to our informed readership, but also avoid sounding ponderous or using $10 words when 5-cents' worth says it clearly.

5. Include sidebars where appropriate. In any feature that has to do with a destination include information on travel, lodging, charters/guides etc. We also like to see a seasonal availability chart for species (a hand sketch is acceptable). See recent issues for examples of required format. If a feature has to do with a genre of product, include a sidebar listing manufacturers.

FORMAT FOR SUBMISSIONS: These days, it's generally unnecessary to bother with hardcopy or floppy disks; simply email your text as Word, ASCII or text files. Of course you need to make sure your header contains your address (email, post), phone and social security numbers. Send maps, illustrations, charts/diagrams as well as photos separately.

PAYMENT: Payment is initated once the manuscript has been reviewed for acceptability. All features and columns are submitted on speculation. For features we pay $500. You'll be paid $75 to $300 for each of your photos used to illustrate a manuscript. Other payment schedules: Rigging/Techniques or Sportfishing News shorts, $25-75; Fishtales, $250.

Categories: Nonfiction—Boating—Conservation—Fishing—Recreation—Sports

CONTACT: Jason Cannon, Managing Editor
Material: All
460 N. Orlando Ave., Ste. 200
Winter Park FL 32789
Phone: 407-628-4802
Fax: 407-628-7061
E-mail: do1@worldzine.com
Website: www.sportfishingmag.com

Sporting Kid

From training tips to its feature stories that analyze youth sports trends and products, the publication is a valuable resource for parents whose kids play sports—enabling them to take a more active role in their children's lives.

Writer's Guildelines
Queries and Articles

E-mail Queries to: editor@sportingkid.com. All queries (and/or article submissions) must be formatted in a Microsoft Word document. SportingKid will contact you within four weeks if we are interested in the query and/or article you submitted. Queries can be pasted within an e-mail message; please limit to no more than 50 words.

Manuscripts must be attached in a Microsoft Word document.

Payments and Contracts

Fees are negotiated when the article is assigned.

All contributors must sign a contract when the article is assigned.

SportingKid does not pay on a 'per word' basis. Assignment fees will be determined by the editor based on factors such as number of sources, research, number of sidebars, etc.

SportingKid pays upon publication of articles commissioned.

All articles and photographs become the property of Sporting Kid, LLC and may be used in print or electronically.

Categories: Nonfiction—Sports—Young Adult

CONTACT: Michael Pallerino, Editor
240 Prospect Pl, Unit E1
Alpharetta GA 30005
E-mail: editor@sportingkid.com
Website: www.sportingkid.com

Sports Afield

Sports Afield is America's original outdoor magazine, founded in 1887. The magazine is devoted to people who share a passion for high-end sporting pursuits, especially North American and African big-game hunting. Our focus is on species such as sheep, elk, caribou, moose, trophy whitetails and mule deer, bears, African plains game, and dangerous species such as Cape buffalo, lion, and leopard. Coverage of fine guns, optics, clothing, and equipment is an essential part of the magazine. To a more limited extent, we also feature stories on upland hunting and big-game hunts outside North America and Africa.

While most of our departments are written by regular contributors, we are continually looking for fresh feature ideas. The majority of our coverage consists of big-game hunting destination pieces and exciting, well-written hunting adventure stories. Please do not send "hunt-payback" pieces; we do not run stories that are blatant advertisements for a particular outfitter. We are interested in stories about guns and gear that are appropriate to the type of hunting we cover. Features should be no more than 2,500 words in length. We also accept short items (100-400 words) for our Almanac section. These items can include hunting tips, travel tips, and unusual facts about wildlife or outdoor lore.

The best way to sell to *Sports Afield* is to first query the editor. Queries should clearly explain what you'd like to write about, show the editor why the subject is relevant, and why you're qualified to write the piece. Each feature concept should be accompanied by sidebar suggestions that support the main subject of the feature.

Specific Guidelines

All manuscripts should be submitted on 3.5-inch disk or CD-ROM; both Mac and PC disks are acceptable. Microsoft Word files are preferred; otherwise, save your article as a text-only file. Please include a hard copy of the article. Please include a self-addressed, stamped envelope with all queries or manuscript submissions. Articles should not be submitted via email unless requested in that format by the editor. We will not review any simultaneous submissions or stories that have been previously published elsewhere.

Photographic support is very important. Every article submission should be accompanied by a good selection of high-quality color slides. Package slides and transparencies carefully, for the magazine will not be responsible for photos damaged or lost in shipment. All editorial submissions should be accompanied by a variety of supporting images ranging from scenic/landscapes to action and portraits. Photos of hunters posing with their trophies should be tasteful, free of blood, and show the animal to best advantage. We cannot accept black-and-white photos or color prints. In some cases we can accept digital photos, but they must be of exceptionally high quality, with a resolution of 300 dpi at the size they will be used in the magazine, and taken with a camera of not less than 4 megapixels.

Include a photo release form for all recognizable people pictured in your photographs, and submit clear captions for each photograph that include: names of people depicted, location, date, activity, and relevance to the story subject.

Unless they were assigned by the editor, all submissions are reviewed "on speculation." If your work is accepted for publication, you will be sent a freelance contract. We purchase first worldwide rights for all features and departments; we buy all rights to Almanac items. Payment will be made after we receive your signed copy of the contract.

Categories: Nonfiction—Adventure—Environment—Outdoors—Recreation—Sports—Travel

CONTACT: Diana Rupp, Editor in Chief
Material: All
15621 Chemical Ln.
Huntington Beach, CA 92649-1506
E-mail: Editorinchief@sportsafield.com
Website: sportsafield.com

Sports Illustrated for Kids

Freelance writers may query *Sports Illustrated For Kids* with specific story ideas. Completed articles, submitted on the basis of speculation, will be read. But such articles are not encouraged. Be advised that most *SI For Kids* articles are staff written. Fewer than 20 freelance proposals are accepted each year.

Sports Illustrated For Kids reaches sports fans ages 8 to 15. The

magazine strives to be informative and fun, presenting exciting personalities and insightful stories from the world of sports. Freelance writers should note that editors expect extensive reporting and research on all stories. The following are categories in which the editors might accept freelance material:

• Cover/Bonus Stories—Articles about interesting topics and trends in sports, 1,000-1,500 words, $1,000-$2,000.

• Athlete Profiles—Articles about top pro, college, high school, or kid athletes, 400-1,500 words, $500-$1,500.

• Puzzles and Games, $500-$700.

Kids are encouraged to submit letters, drawings, and poems to *SI For Kids*. These submissions are unpaid.

Please note that *SI For Kids* does not run general fiction or fillers.

Categories: Nonfiction—Children—Games—General Interest—Inspirational—Interview—Juvenile—Recreation—Sports/Recreation—How-to—Humor—Profiles

CONTACT: Bob Der
Material: Pro Football
CONTACT: John Rolfe
Material: Pro Baseball
CONTACT: Erin Egan, Ellen Cosgrove or Andrea Whittaker
Material: Pro Basketball
CONTACT: Nick Friedman
Material: Action Sports, Kid Sports, Pro Hockey
CONTACT: Ellen Cosgrove
Material: College Sports
CONTACT: Andrea Whittaker
Material: Puzzles and Games
135 West 50th St., 4th floor
New York NY 10020-1393
Phone: 212-522-1212
Fax: 212-467-4247

Springfield! Magazine

Springfield! Magazine is a monthly publication now in its 28th year. The magazine is 85% free-lance written, and the magazine works with talented but unpublished writers along with veteran writers from a variety of backgrounds. The best approach to selling material to this magazine is to study copies of the magazine to determine its style and approach before submitting material for publication. A sample copy of the magazine is available by mail for $5.30, and a one-year subscription is only $16.99.

Springfield! Magazine is very provincial. Query in writing first, and be sure that the query includes a clear "hook" to Springfield, Missouri, to be sure that the article will fit in with the magazine's local slant. If the query includes a Springfield "peg" the query will be answered within two weeks.

Springfield! Magazine buys approximately 150 manuscripts each year. Payment ranges between $35 and $250 for manuscripts and payment is made upon publication. Both by-line and photo credits are given. Magazine buys only first serial rights. Publication ranges from three months to three years after acceptance. Photos of subjects and subject's family should accompany the manuscript and originals will be returned after publication. Captions, model releases and full identification of persons appearing in photos are required.

Springfield! Magazine publishes no fiction, and non-fiction material sought includes in-depth profiles (with more quotes from others than subject) on men and women of distinction, personal experiences, local photo features, travel within a day's drive of Springfield for most part, humor (if strong local angle), historical/nostalgic pieces (if photos available) and book reviews and/or excerpts (by Springfield authors only). Features on Springfield couples are a strong priority right now.

Springfield! Magazine prefers both queries and manuscripts be typewritten, double spaced, with your full name and address (plus social security number) on first page. Editors will read unsolicited manuscripts (allow six months). Unsolicited manuscripts should be accompanied by stamped, self-addressed envelopes if return is expected.

Categories: Nonfiction—Adventure—African-American—Animals—Architecture—Arts—Asian-American—Associations—Biography—Book Reviews—Careers—Children—Civil War—College—Comedy—Confession—Crime—Culture—Drama—Directories—Ecology—Education—Environment—Erotica—Family—Fashion—Feminism—Film/Video—Fishing—Folklore—Food/Drink—Gardening—Government—Health—Human Rights—Inspirational—Interview—Jewish Interest—Juvenile—Language—Law—Lifestyle—Literature—Marriage—Mass Communications—Men's Issues—Military—Money & Finances—Multicultural—Music—Native American—Outdoors—Parenting—Photography—Psychology—Real Estate—Reference—Relationships—Religion—Romance—Satire—Science—Self Help—Sexuality—Singles—Sports/Recreation—Teen—Television/Radio—Textbooks—Theatre—Travel—Women's Issues—Writing—Young Adult

CONTACT: Robert C. Glazier, Editor & Publisher
Material: All
Springfield Communications, Inc.
PO Box 4749
Springfield MO 65808-4749
E-mail: pub@sgfmag.com

St. Anthony Messenger

St. Anthony Messenger is a general-interest, family-oriented Catholic magazine. It is written and edited largely for people living in families or the family-like situations of Church and community. We want to help our readers better understand the teachings of the gospel and Catholic Church, and how they apply to life and the full range of problems confronting us as members of families, the Church and society.

Examples of articles we have published:

Church/Sacraments: "L.A.'s New Cathedral: A Tour With Cardinal Mahony"; "Confirmation: What's a Parent to Do?"; "Truths Jews, Christians and Muslims Hold in Common"; "'Opening the Door': Black Catholics in the U.S."

Education/Spiritual Growth: "Bioethics and Faith"; "Project Rachel: Vicki Thorn's Post-abortion Ministry"; "God's Photo Album"; "Hope for Family-friendly TV"; "Washington's New Pope John Paul II Center"

Family/Marriage: "September 11: Finding My Son Alive"; "When Our Son Told Us He Was Gay"; "Elizabeth Ministry: Helping Moms"; "Marriage: Forgiving and Being Forgiven"

Profile/Celebrity/Saints: "Sister Mary Rose McGeady: Rebuilding Covenant House"; "The Real St. Nicholas"; "Calm Amid the Storm: An Interview With Bishop Wilton D. Gregory"; "Artist John August Swanson and His Images of Francis of Assisi"; "Ronald Rolheiser on The Holy Longing"; "She Opens Doors: Marie Wilkinson"; "Bil Keane's

Family Circus" (won CPA 1st-place award for Best Personality Profile); "St. Anthony: Portugal's Favorite Son"

Scripture/Theology: "Mark My Words"; "Biblical Laments: Prayer out of Pain"

Social Issues/Foreign: "The Bethlehem Siege: An Insider's Account"; "Renewing the Face of the Earth: Jesuit Al Fritsch"; "Praying for Peace in Assisi"; "Haitian Children in Bondage"; "El Salvador: Climbing up From the Rubble"; "Globalization: Friend or Foe?"

Spirituality/Inspirational Stories: "The New Mysteries of the Rosary"; "Friends of the Creche"; "Roamin' Catholic: The Spirituality of Travel"; "Finding God in Life's Transitions"; "An Irish Journey Into Celtic Spirituality"

All of the articles listed above are available at www.American Catholic.org.

Fiction: We do not have examples of fiction on our Web site. Consult our Writer's Guidelines about fiction and see recently published stories.

The best way to know what we publish is to read and study several recent issues of St. Anthony Messenger.

GUIDELINES FOR WRITING, PREPARING AND SUBMITTING AN ARTICLE

Query in advance. State proposed topic, sources, authorities and your qualifications to do the article. Library research does not suffice. Fresh sources and interviews with experts or people in the field will be necessary. Reporting articles are more needed than opinion pieces. Seasonal material (Mother's Day, Lent, Christmas, etc.) should be submitted six or more months in advance.

We do not publish filler material—anecdotes, jokes, thoughts to ponder.

We do not publish articles or stories in installments or serial form. And we very rarely reprint materials first published by other publishers.

We do not use essays or personal reminiscences. Articles about historical events or people no longer living need a current news peg.

We do not consider articles submitted simultaneously to other magazines.

Manuscripts should be typed double spaced. Mark your submission fact or fiction. Place your name, address, phone number and Social Security number on the first page. Number the pages. Address manuscript to Pat McCloskey, O.F.M., editor, St. Anthony Messenger, 28 W. Liberty St., Cincinnati, OH 45202.

Articles should not exceed 3,000 words. Preferred length is 2000-2500 words.

Keep the vocabulary simple. Avoid jargon, technical and theological language. Keep sentences short. Ask, "Would my grandmother understand this?"

An attention-getting introduction is important! Use anecdotes, examples, quotes from real people. Make practical applications. End strongly.

For return of manuscripts, enclose a self-addressed stamped envelope.

We assume no responsibility for lost manuscripts, accompanying photos or slides. Keep copies or insure against loss. Protect photos against cracking.

Please allow up to eight weeks for return or purchase of publication rights. Hardly any manuscript is published without review by eight or more staff members. Phoning the editor for a progress report invites aborting review process and returning the manuscript immediately to avoid more phone calls.

Payment for articles and fiction is 16 cents a published word—upon acceptance and return of signed author-publisher agreement form. Authors receive 2 copies of published work.

Payment for photos accompanying an article is $25 for each photo used. Photos should be documented with any necessary releases from photographers or persons in the photos. Payment for photos is made after photos have been selected and the issue laid out and printed.

Articles sent after a positive response to a query are received on a speculation basis.

If no article is received within two months after a positive response to a query, we feel free to consider a query on the same subject from another author.

We buy first worldwide serial rights to publish and republish "the work" in any and all forms or formats, including all electronic formats.

INFORMATION FOR FICTION AUTHORS

Besides these guidelines, freelance authors submitting fiction pieces should read our general information sheet for all freelance writers. Note the audience for whom we publish and the purpose of St. Anthony Messenger. Most of our readers live in families. The greater part are women between 40 and 70 years old.

Preferred word length for short stories is 2,000 to 2,500 words.

Manuscripts must be typed and should be double-spaced with wide margins.

We cannot accept responsibility for undelivered, lost or damaged manuscripts. Authors should always keep a copy of their stories.

Please do not phone to ask if your manuscript has been received. Allow six to eight weeks for response or return of your manuscript. Any story that is accepted will have had at least six or eight readers. And many that are returned may also have had as many readers.

We receive over 1,000 short story submissions a year. We publish 12 at the most—one an issue. Man: stories must be returned—even stories that may be well written and have merit.

In submitting a short story please clearly label it as fiction. Number the pages. Include a self-addressed, stamped envelope and your Social Security number (information we must supply the I.R.S. when issuing a purchase check). Address manuscripts to: Pat McCloskey, O.F.M., St. Anthony Messenger, 28 W. Liberty St., Cincinnati, OH 45202.

We pay 16 cents a word on acceptance for first Worldwide Serial Rights and do not consider stories submitted to other publications at the same time or reprints.

We are interested in stories about family relationships, people struggling and coping with the same problems of life our readers face. Stories that show people triumphing in adversity, persevering in faith, overcoming doubt or despair, coming to spiritual insights. Stories about people that offer hope. Characters and resolutions must be real and believable. Sudden realizations, instant conversions and miracle solutions won't do.

Stories that sound more like essays or monologues, stories that are straight narratives with no dialogue or interaction on the part of characters will not succeed.

Dialogue should contribute to moving the story forward, It should sound real—the way people talk to each other in real life. Conversation should not be artificial or sound stilted.

We are not interested in retold Bible stories or stories overly sentimental or pietistic.

Seasonal stories (Christmas, Easter, etc.) should be submitted at least six months in advance.

INFORMATION FOR POETRY WRITERS

St. Anthony Messenger is a general-interest, family-oriented Catholic magazine. It is written and edited largely for people living in family situations or the family-like situations of Church and community. We want to help our readers better understand the teachings of the gospel and Catholic Church, and how they apply to life and the full range of problems confronting us as members of families, the Church and society.

The poetry we publish attempts to reflect the philosophy stated above. Poetry is subjective, for the most part, but we do require that the poems we publish have most or all of these characteristics: originality; creativity in word choice, images and overall thought/idea; each section of the poem fitting together well with other sections; subject matter somewhat universal in nature; a religious (in a broad sense, not theological) or family dimension.

Both rhyming and non-rhyming materials are considered. We do not consider previously published poetry, or poetry submitted at the same time to other publications.

Each poetry submission should be typed, double-spaced on a separate piece of paper. Your name, address and Social Security number should be typed at the top. Address poetry to: Poetry Editor, St. Anthony Messenger (see address below).

PLEASE DO NOT SUBMIT POEMS LONGER THAN 20-25 LINES—the shorter, the better. Due to space limitations, the poetry section does not appear every month. When space is available for it, there is room for only one page of poetry (four to five poems at the most). Therefore, OUR POETRY NEEDS ARE VERY LIMITED.

As we like to give as many people as possible the chance to be published poets, we do not buy "collections" of poems for publication (that is the role of a poetry book publisher), nor do we usually buy more than a few works from each poet a year. And while we pay on acceptance, publication may not follow for a considerable length of time. When a poem is published the poet receives two complimentary copies of the issue it appears in.

WE PAY $2 (two dollars) PER LINE for each poem purchased. We try to return poems not accepted within FOUR TO SIX WEEKS. Please do not write or phone to ask if your poem has been received until that amount of time has passed. Poetry WILL NOT BE RETURNED UNLESS ACCOMPANIED BY A SELF-ADDRESSED STAMPED ENVELOPE. We assume no responsibility for material damaged or lost, and advise poets to keep a copy of any poem submitted. Due to the poetry editor's time constraints, poetry critiques will not be given. Thank you very much for your interest!

Categories: Nonfiction—Religion—Short Stories

CONTACT: Pat McCloskey, O.F.M., Editor
Material: Articles, Fiction
CONTACT: Poetry Editor
Material: Poetry
28 W. Liberty St
Cincinnati OH 45210
Phone: 513-241-5615
Fax: 513-241-0399
E-mail: St.Anthony@AmericanCatholic.org
Website: www.americancatholic.org

Stamats Meetings Media
Meetings West, Meetings South and Meetings East

Stamats Meetings Media publishes three regional monthly trade magazines—*Meetings West, Meetings South,* and *Meetings East*—targeted at a controlled circulation audience of meeting and convention planners. All three magazines focus on the meeting, convention, conference, tradeshow, and retreat industry.

Freelance coverage includes: features and site inspections (4 to 6 full-length city/state/regional roundups per issue)

We RARELY take stories on query; the vast majority of our assignments are based on our editorial calendar.

(Editorial calendars are available at: www.meetings411.com/editorialcal_main.asp)

If you're interested in writing for us, please send a resume and two or three "relevant" clips covering meetings/conventions topics to the address below, along with the list of localities in which you are expert. We typically pencil in story assignments in the fall for our upcoming calendar year's coverage, although some last-minute assignments may occur.

We strongly favor writers who are local to their subject matter.
Categories: Nonfiction, Business

CONTACT: Tyler Davidson, Editor
Material: All
Stamats Meetings Media
550 Montgomery St. #750
San Francisco CA 94111
Phone: (no calls, please)

Standard

Thank you for considering *Standard* for your free-lance submissions.

Standard is published 52 times a year by Beacon Hill Press of Kansas City and has a circulation of more than 150,000. Based on biblical truth and the Wesleyan-Arminian tradition, *Standard* seeks to present quality Christian material for a diverse audience of adults.

Standard uses about 200 manuscripts and 30 poems per year (during Advent/Christmas and Lent/Easter only, and only on those themes. We publish a variety of material, including:

- Short stories (1200 words maximum)
- Christian poetry (30 lines maximum)
- Puzzles

In *Standard* we want to show Christianity in action, and we prefer to do that through stories that hold the reader's attention. We seldom use how-to articles, sermons, and devotionals, unless they are written in our preferred style.

Standard purchases the right to publish material one time, either first rights or reprint rights. After publication, copyrights to the material revert to the author. *Standard* does not purchase first rights on simultaneous submissions. Due to our lead time, we assume that the story will appear elsewhere before *Standard* goes to press. Payment is made on acceptance as follows:

- First Rights: 3½ cents per word
- Reprint and simultaneous submissions: 2 cents per word
- Poetry: 25 cents per line (minimum payment $5.00)

Manuscripts can be submitted by e-mail.

(We can only work with Microsoft Word or WordPerfect attached documents in PC formats. If you use any other word-processing programs or a Mac computer, please put your manuscript in the body of the e-mail.)

We will respond within 90 days. Material accepted for publication will appear in *Standard* approximately 18 months after acceptance. Contributors will receive three complimentary copies at time of publication.

- Include a SASE with every mailed submission, and please indicate if the manuscript is disposable. If you submit via e-mail, we will respond within our usual review time frame (90 days) to the e-mail address on your submission.
- We need the following information on the first page of the manuscript:
  1. Your name
  2. Mailing address (and e-mail address, if available)
  3. Telephone number
  4. Social Security number
  5. Number of words in manuscript or number of lines of poem
  6. Whether first or reprint rights are being offered
  7. If reprint, where previously published
- Please put your name on second and subsequent pages you send via regular postal service, because sometimes pages get separated during handling.
- Do not submit any manuscript which has been submitted to or published in any of the following: *Vista, Wesleyan Advocate, Holiness Today, Preacher's Magazine, World Mission, Women Alive,* or various teen and children's publications produced by WordAction Publishing Company. These are overlapping markets.
- Since we accept unsolicited manuscripts, query letters are unnecessary. Please submit only complete manuscripts.
- Be conscientious in your use of Scripture; don't overload your story with quotations. When you quote the Bible, quote it exactly and cite chapter, verse, and version used. (We prefer the NIV.) *Standard* will handle copyright matters for Scripture. Except for quotations from the Bible, written permission for the use of any other copyrighted material (especially song lyrics) is the responsibility of the writer.
- Keep in mind the international audience of *Standard* with regard to geographic references and holidays. We cannot use stories about cultural, national, or secular holidays.
- Do not mention specific church affiliations. *Standard* is read in a variety of denominations.

Categories: Nonfiction—Christian Interests—Poetry—Religion—Short Stories—Spiritual

CONTACT: Submissions Editor
Material: All
6401 The Paseo
Kansas City MO 64131
E-mail: Evlead@nazarene.org
E-mail: Cyourdon@nazarene.org

Stock Car Racing

Circulation: 257,296
Frequency: monthly

Stock Car Racing remains the largest and best-selling automotive racing magazine in the United States. From NASCAR to the local dirt track scene, the title's respected journalists and photographers mix inside stories of special interest with basic how-to technical information for racing fans, enthusiasts and competitors.

Formal guidelines not available. Please read a number of issues to ascertain the publication's style and needs. Or visit *Stock Car Racing* on-line at www.stockcarracing.com

Send queries to address below.
Categories: Automobiles

CONTACT: David Bourne, Editor-in-Chief
Material: All
3816 Industry Blvd.
Lakeland FL 33811
Phone: 863-644-0449
Website: www.stockcarracing.com

Stone Soup
The Magazine by Young Writers and Artists

Stone Soup welcomes submissions by young people through age 13!

What to Include: Include your name, age, home address, phone number, and e-mail address if you have one. Please do not include a self-addressed stamped envelope. Send copies of your work, not originals. If we need the original, we will request it. You do not need to include a photo of yourself.

Please send your work by regular mail; do not send it by Certified Mail or Registered Mail. Thank you.)

E-mail Address: (for foreign contributors only) editor@ stonesoup.com

A Word About E-mail Submissions: We do not accept e-mail submissions from the U.S. or Canada. Because we are a very small company we're concerned that if we allowed e-mail submissions, we'd be flooded with material and we wouldn't be able to handle it all. We like to think that serious young authors would be more than willing to polish their work, print it out in a nice format, and mail it to us. We hope you'll understand.

What Happens Next: We only respond to those submissions we are considering for possible publication. If we are considering your work, you will hear from us in four to six weeks. If you do not hear from us, it means we were not able to use your work. Don't be discouraged! Try again!

General Information: Stone Soup is made up of stories, poems, book reviews, and art by young people through age 13. Although all the writing we publish is in English, we accept work from all over the world. To get an idea of the kind of writing and art we like, please look through our highlights from past issues.

Writers: Send us stories and poems about the things you feel most strongly about! Whether your work is about imaginary situations or real ones, use your own experiences and observations to give your work depth and a sense of reality. Writing need not be typed, as long as it is legible. If you type your work, please type it double-spaced in a plain, medium-sized font. We can consider writing in languages other than English; include a translation if possible. The maximum length we can publish is about 2500 words; we have no minimum length. It's OK to send more than one piece of writing in the same envelope. Please don't send us work you are also sending to other magazines. Send your work to one magazine at a time.

Illustrators: If you would like to illustrate for Stone Soup, send editor Gerry Mandel some samples of your art work, along with a letter saying what kinds of stories you would like to illustrate. Although we sometimes use simple line drawings in Stone Soup, we are especially interested in artists who can draw or paint complete scenes. Send us samples that fill the entire page with detail, including the background. Please include your name, age, birthdate, address, telephone number, and a self-addressed stamped envelope for our response to you.

Book Reviewers: If you are interested in reviewing books for Stone Soup, write Ms. Mandel for more information. Tell her a little about yourself, why you want to be a book reviewer, and what kinds of books you like to read. Be sure to include your name, age, birthdate, address, telephone number, and a self-addressed stamped envelope for our response to you.

Payment: All contributors whose work is accepted for publication receive a certificate, two complimentary copies, and discounts on other purchases. In addition, contributors of stories, poems and book reviews are paid $40 each; illustrators are paid $25 per illustration.

Note: We're always looking for new writers and artists, and we really want to encourage all our young readers to send us their work. However, please keep in mind that we receive an average of 250 submissions a week; we are only able to publish a small percentage of the work we receive. Send us your work with a spirit of adventure, and try not to be too disappointed if we can't use it.

Categories: Arts—Book Reviews—Children—Education—Juvenile—Literature—Poetry—Short Stories—Writing—Young Adult

CONTACT: Submissions Dept.
Material: All
PO Box 83
Santa Cruz, CA 95063 USA
Phone: 831-426-5557
Fax: 831-426-1161
E-mail: (for foreign contributors only)
editor@stonesoup.com
Website: www.stonesoup.com

Stormwater
The Journal for Surface Water Quality Professionals

Please refer to Forester Communications.

Strategic Health Care Marketing

Editorial Profile

Twelve-page monthly newsletter, covering all areas of marketing and business development in a wide range of health care settings—hospitals, medical group practices, home health services, HMOs. Editorial focus is on strategies and techniques employed within the health care field and on relevant applications from other service industries.

No photos or artwork. Byline on longer articles.

Kinds of Articles/Style

News, interviews, profiles, opinion and commentary, advice and how-to. Preferred format for feature articles is the case history approach to solving marketing problems. Crisp, almost telegraphic style...most articles range from 500 to 2,000 words in length.

Reader Profile

Directors/Vice Presidents of Marketing, Public Relations, Planning in hospitals. Administrators in small hospitals, medical groups, and in other types of delivery systems. Marketing and advertising consultants and agencies serving the service sector of the health care industry. Pharmaceutical and medical device sectors are not represented.

Rights

All articles must represent original unpublished work. First North American serial rights; Publisher also retains rights to use work in subsequent editorial reprints, collections, advertising and promotion, and in any other Health Care Communications publications.

Payment

Upon publication. Payment runs $100-$400+, depending on complexity of assignment, length, and writer's credentials. Articles normally published within two months of manuscript acceptance. Two revisions if necessary.

Kill Fee

25% for specifically commissioned material.

Out-of-Pocket Expenses

For commissioned material will reimburse long-distance telephone and out-of-pocket travel expenses, provided documentation submitted. Prior approval required for expenses (individual or in total per article) that will exceed $50.

Query First!

Many articles are written by marketing authorities and practitioners in the health care field. You should be familiar with either marketing or the industry—preferably both.

Categories: Health Care Marketing

CONTACT: Submissions Editor
Material: All
11 Heritage Ln.
Rye NY 10580
Phone: 914-967-6741
Fax: 914-967-3054
E-mail: healthcomm@aol.com

Student Lawyer
The Magazine of the Law Student Division

INFORMATION FOR AUTHORS

Award-winning *Student Lawyer* magazine is published each month from September through May by the American Bar Association's Law Student Division. It circulates to approximately 38,000 readers, most of whom are law student members of the ABA.

Student Lawyer is a legal-affairs features magazine, not a legal journal, that competes for a share of law students' limited spare time. The articles we publish, therefore, must be informative, lively, well-researched good reads. We do not accept poetry, fiction, or footnoted academic articles or briefs. These guidelines are for paid submissions only. For letters to the editor, reviews, opinion essays, and student/school news, please refer to our guidelines for unpaid submissions.

Each issue of *Student Lawyer* includes feature articles by paid freelance writers that range in length from 2,500 to 4,000 words apiece. We are looking for features on societal trends that affect the law, trends in the legal profession or law of interest to law students and young practitioners, possible careers—legal or otherwise—for lawyers, and legal education issues. Writers should provide thorough reporting, lively writing, and insightful analysis. They should expect to work extensively with the magazine's editor to provide missing or additional information, to clear up the unclear, and to polish any rough edges.

Columns also offer publication possibilities for freelance writers. Most are prepared by regular columnists, but we're open to new talent. "Briefly" consists of short news items of interest to law students. "Coping" helps law students deal with the unique challenges of law school. "Legal-ease" offers tips for readers to improve their writing and communications skills. "Jobs" helps readers market themselves to potential legal employers. "Online" is *Student Lawyer's* computers-and-the-law column. And "Esq." profiles lawyers who are doing something out of the ordinary with their careers. Columns should be about 1,500 words. If you'd like to propose a new column on a topic that would serve law students, please send us your résumé, three clips, and your ideas for possible columns.

We don't make assignments to writers with whom we're unfamiliar. If you're interested in writing for us, mail us a double-spaced hard copy of an actual story or a detailed query with three previously published clips. We are always willing to look at material on spec, but we don't accept such material via e-mail or fax. Sorry, we don't return manuscripts. Please include your e-mail address if you'd like a quick response.

The best way to find out what *Student Lawyer* is all about is to read an issue. They're available for $8 apiece (plus postage and handling) from the ABA Service Center, 800-285-2221.

Questions? Call editor Ira Pilchen at 312-988-6048 or e-mail studentlawyer@abanet.org.

Submissions

Student Lawyer welcomes unpaid submissions from readers as well as paid features and columns from professional writers. *Student Lawyer* is a legal-affairs features magazine, not a legal journal. We do not accept footnoted academic articles or briefs, poetry, or fiction. For feature articles and columns that require lively writing and extensive reporting and analysis, please see our guidelines for paid submissions.

• Letters to the editor. Brief, to-the-point letters that respond directly to a *Student Lawyer* article are preferred.

• Opinion essays. Readers may submit 600-word essays for *Student Lawyer's* Opinion department. To be accepted for publication, Opinions should pertain to issues relevant to our nationwide readership and have a clear introduction, body, and conclusion. We can accept an essay previously published (for instance, in a law school newspaper) if the writer provides contact information for the previous publisher and if we're able to secure reprint permission.

• Reviews. *Student Lawyer* accepts 600- 1,500-word reviews of books, films, and other media that have a connection with the law or unique perspective of law students. Submissions will be evaluated for writing quality and relevance to our readers.

• Student/school news. Please keep *Student Lawyer* and our Division Dialogue section in mind when issuing news releases, photos, and other material about student bar association events and accomplishments. We also want to know about interesting students to profile in our Spotlight department—all we need are their name, phone number, and brief description of why they deserve to be featured. Photos, preferably, should be in color and clearly shot. (For digital submissions, we require 266 dpi resolution.)

• General submission requirements. Editorial contributions are evaluated by the editor and student editor and are subject to review by a committee of the Law Student Division. We reserve the right to edit for clarity and space, and to reject any unsolicited item. Because of our production schedules, an item may not appear until several months after submission.

We cannot guarantee publication of any particular contribution, but we will acknowledge receipt upon request if an e-mail address is provided. You may enhance your chance at publication by discussing approaches beforehand with the editor, by e-mail (studentlawyer@abanet.org) or phone (312-988-6048).

All contributions must include the writer's name, school and year, address, daytime phone number, and, if available, an e-mail address.

E-mail submissions should have "Letter to the Editor," "Opin-

ion," "Review," or "Student News" in the subject line. *Student Lawyer's* e-mail address is abastulawyer@abanet.org. Word or WordPerfect attachments are preferred.

You may also mail or fax your submissions.

Authors of accepted Opinion essays, reviews, and other bylined articles will be required to sign a standard publication agreement granting copyright to the American Bar Association.

Categories: Nonfiction—Careers—Education—Law

CONTACT: Ira Pilchen, Editor
Material: All
American Bar Association—ABA Publishing
321 N. Clark St.
Chicago IL 06010
Phone: 312-988-6048
Fax: 312-988-6081
E-mail: studentlawyer@abanet.org
Website: www.abanet.org/lsd/studentlawyer

Student LEADER

Student Leader
The Forum for America's Emerging Leaders

Please refer to Oxendine Publishing.

Studies in American Jewish Literature

Studies in American Jewish Literature (SAJL), the official journal of the Society for the Study of American Jewish Literature, publishes peer-reviewed scholarly articles, book reviews, occasional poetry, and short stories dealing with aspects of the Jewish experience in literature. Published annually, SAJL has issues featuring one writer, such as "Bernard Malamud: In Memoriam" and "The World of Cynthia Ozick," and issues that cut across various authors, subjects, and themes, such as "New Voices in an Old Tradition." Future issues will focus on new American Jewish voices, including Myla Goldberg, Thane Rosenbaum and Allegra Goodman.

Subscription Information
Annual
ISSN 0271-9274

Individuals $22.00/volume; $32.00/volume outside of the United States. Institutions $45.00/volume; $55.00/volume outside of the United States. To order this publication, please call our toll-free number, 1-800-247-6553. For other questions, contact the Subscription Manager at pupress@purdue.edu.

Submission Information
Studies in American Jewish Literature accepts submissions that meet the following requirements:

• between 10-20 pages
• prepare according to the MLA Style Manual
• should contain endnotes rather than footnotes

Categories: Nonfiction—Jewish Interests—Literature

CONTACT: Daniel Walden, Editor
Material: All
116 Burrowes Building
Penn State University
University Park PA 16802
Website: www.thepress.purdue.edu

Succeed
The Magazine for Continuing Education

SUCCEED Magazine is designed to provide its readers with information about postgraduate and continuing education programs. The magazine's editorial content includes information of interest to adults recommitting themselves to education and provides insight on making such a transition easier.

Published four times a year to coincide with the fall, winter, spring, and summer academic semesters, SUCCEED Magazine is distributed to colleges and universities, career and planning centers, corporations, and public library branches throughout the New York, New Jersey, and Connecticut area.

SUCCEED Magazine is comprised of both regular departments and full-length feature articles. We typically pay $50 to $75 for department inclusions and $75 to $125 for feature articles. Departments run approximately 300-600 words. Features should be 1,500-2,000 words in length. We usually buy first rights to a piece. We will consider buying second rights if your published piece has not appeared in a national magazine, continuing education-oriented publication, or any other magazine written primarily for adults returning to the classroom. For all departments and features, you will receive payment upon publication.

Please query us by structuring an article proposal in the following matter:

• Begin with the lead you expect to put on the article—grab our attention!

• Write a summary of your intended areas of coverage.

• Give specifics about who you plan to interview, what types of real-life anecdotes you'll include, which resources you plan to utilize, and what conclusion the story might reach.

(With your query, please send us two or three published clips. Please send photocopies; we do not return writing samples.)

Familiarize yourself with SUCCEED Magazine. Get to know what kinds of articles interest our readership of over 155,000 professionals.

Departments:

• Memo Pad—Consists of short, newsworthy items about cutting-edge trends and tips that relate to today's changing job market and continuing education endeavors. (100-225 words)

• To Be…—Profiles career-changers and lifelong learners with captivating stories. How were they inspired? What sorts of contacts did they utilize to "get where they are now?" What advice do they have to offer others interested in pursuing careers or study in a similar field? (500-700 words)

• Financial Fitness—Advises readers how to keep their money in tip-top shape—even after they've signed their tuition check! Consists of interviews with financial experts, explorations of money-saving strategies and suggestions, etc. (200-350 words)

• Job Talk—Provides cutting-edge career resource news, often in the form of short feature articles. Recent issues have included an in-depth look at on-line job sites, tips for managing a bad boss, a "job search refresher," etc. (700-900 words)

• Tech Zone—Offers objective reviews of software, CD-ROMs, Web sites, and other techno-advancements that assist with educational and professional advancement endeavors. (200-450 words)

• Sold Success—Includes entrepreneurial advice for readers who've chosen to "do it on their own," including professional profiles and recommendations of related resources. (200-400 words)

• School@Home—Features a cutting-edge look at news and advances affecting adults' capabilities to advance their education via distance learning and technology-enhanced academic and career services. (200-500 words)

Recent Feature Topics:

• Finding A Career That Fits
• A Week in the Life of an Online Learner
• Sharpening Your Emotional Intelligence
• Preparation Is the Cure to Exam Anxiety
• Turning Techie: Clicking Into E-Commerce
• Submit your intelligent, thought-provoking ideas. To us, a winning article presents useful information with creativity!

• Keep in mind that our response time to manuscripts and queries is approximately four to five weeks.

Categories: Nonfiction—Business—Careers—Education

CONTACT: Gina LaGuardia, Editor-in-Chief
Material: All
1200 South Ave., Ste. 202
Staten Island NY 10314
Phone: 718-761-4800
Fax: 718-273-2539
E-mail: editorial@collegebound.net
Website: www.classearch.com

The Sun

We publish essays, fiction, and poetry. We tend to favor personal writing, but we're also looking for thoughtful, well-written essays on policitical, cultural, and philosophical themes. Please, no journalistic features, academic works, or opinion pieces. Other than that, we're open to just about anything. Surprise us; we often don't know what we'll like until we read it.

We pay from $300 to $1,500 for essays and interviews, $300 to $1,000 for fiction, and $50 to $250 for poetry, the amount being determined by length and quality. We may pay less for very short works. We also give contributors a complimentary one-year subscription to *The Sun*.

We're willing to read previously published works, though for reprints we pay only half our usual fee. We discourage simultaneous submissions. We rarely run anything longer than seven thousand words; there's no minimum word length. Don't bother with a query letter, except perhaps on interviews; the subject matter isn't as important to us as what you do with it.

We try to respond within six months. With nearly a thousand submissions a month, however, our backlog of unread manuscripts is often substantial. Don't let a longer wait surprise you.

Submissions should be typed, double-spaced, and accompanied by a self-addressed, stamped envelope. Your work will not be returned without sufficient postage, and we cannot respond unless a return envelope is provided. Do not send your only copy. Do not submit work by e-mail or fax; submissions received this way will not be acknowledged.

Thanks for your interest in *The Sun*.

Sy Safransky, Editor

P.S. To save your time and ours, we suggest you take a look at *The Sun* before submitting. Sample issues are $5 each, which includes shipping and handling.

Categories: Interview—Literature—Photography—Poetry—Short Stories—Creative Nonfiction

CONTACT: Sy Sanfransky, Editor
Material: All
107 N Roberson St
Chapel Hill NC 27516
Phone: 919-942-5282
Website: www.thesunmagazine.org

R-U

Sun Valley Magazine

Articles should relate specifically to the Wood River Valley, Idaho, or environmental in nature. Almost all stories are assigned to local authors. We will consider articles of a more general nature as they relate to life in the mountains.

Query with article

(Departments average 1,200-1,500 words), or fully developed idea (including opening paragraph, brief outline, and conclusion).

We begin developing our storyline a year in advance. Send SASE with $2.50 postage for sample copy of magazine.

Categories: Nonfiction—Environment—Nature—Outdoors—Recreation—Regional

CONTACT: Deb Gelet, Managing Editor
Material: All
12 E. Bullion St., Ste. B
Hailey ID 83333
Phone: 208-788-0770
Fax: 208-788-3881
E-mail: info@sunvalleymag.com
Website: sunvalleymag.com

Sunset Magazine

Freelance travel articles

Sunset is Western America's largest-circulation regional magazine, with monthly issues devoted to four subject areas: travel and recreation; garden and outdoor living; food and entertaining; home design, remodeling, and projects.

Sunset is looking for well-written travel stories that offer our readers reliably satisfying travel experiences that can be successfully accomplished in a day or weekend outing, or included as part of a vacation.

Submission Procedures: No responsibility is assumed for unsolicited manuscripts. Writers must submit a query letter to the editor in advance. The letter should explain and outline the proposed story idea, and suggest an appropriate month or season. E-mail queries are preferred. Send them to travelquery@sunset.com. You also may send your query letter along with a return SASE to Editorial Services, *Sunset*, 80 Willow Rd, Menlo Park, CA 94025. It will be forwarded to the appropriate editor.

Once an editor approves an idea for a story, the writer will be issued a Story Contract assigning an approximate word length and due date for the text. The contract specifies the terms of the agreement between the writer and *Sunset* Publishing Corporation.

Writers must have computer capabilities to submit stories by e-mail. The assigned text should be submitted with the resource material specified in the contract.

Following submission of the text, the writer may be asked to revise the manuscript for publication or to supply further information or answer questions posed by the editor.

Payment will be made upon acceptance of the text with submission of an invoice in the amount specified in the contract.

After acceptance, the text will then be processed by staff copy editors and fact checkers. Writers will be credited with a byline if the manuscript is not substantially altered before publication in *Sunset Magazine*.

Word Length: One-page stories usually run from 300 to 400 words, depending on the number of color photographs or other illustrations such as maps.

Regional Editions: Some of *Sunset*'s travel stories offer close-to-home outings for readers in *Sunset*'s five regional editions: Northern California; Southern California (Los Angeles, Santa Barbara, Ventura, San Diego, and western parts of Riverside and San Bernardino counties, and also, Hawaii); Northwest (Oregon, Washington, Alaska, and British Columbia); Southwest (Arizona, New Mexico, and Clark County, Nevada); Mountain (Colorado, Idaho, Montana, Nevada

except Clark County, Utah, and Wyoming).

Take-action Magazine: *Sunset* is not an armchair magazine. While each story ought to be entertaining to read, it must also take a how-to approach so that readers can actually participate.

Accuracy & Readability: Every story must be correct, clear, and interesting. *Sunset* is proud of its reputation for accuracy and dependability.

Style: Stories should be written using the active voice. The tone should be informative but friendly, intelligent but not intimidating. Write as if you were giving travel guidance to a friend or family member. Writers may want to address the reader in the familiar (you) form ("You've probably never heard of a calf blabber, a chain-gang persuader, or a frozen Charlotte. Even if you have, you'll enjoy a stop at the Frontier Relic Museum.").

Sense of Place: Travel writers should strive to convey a sense of place: the characteristics that set a place apart and make it a worthwhile destination.

The writer's personal insight into a place or event can help the reader to more thoroughly enjoy a travel experience ("Upon arrival, honk your horn") or to avoid an unpleasant one (crowds, sunburn, dangerous terrain, etc.).

Insight and local flavor also can be expressed through the judicious use of a quote or two from an expert source ("I've traveled the world, and always come back. There's a lot of hype about Malibu but also an intangible magic.").

Logical Order: Establish a logical order for topics, categories, and listings: alphabetical, chronological, geographical (north to south, near to far, etc.). Begin with an arresting lead that clearly establishes a reason for reading on.

Straight Facts: Basic travel facts are essential—directions for getting to a destination, distances, addresses, dates, hours of operation, costs, and telephone numbers for further information.

Freshness: Look for news pegs and fresh angles on familiar destinations or events. Often a single destination offers multiple opportunities for readers to visit related attractions such as art galleries, specialty shops, or restaurants.

Variety: Look for activities that would appeal to a wide range of readers, from families to empty-nesters. Here are some subjects regularly treated in *Sunset*'s stories:

OUTDOOR RECREATION: Bike tours; bird-watching spots; camping and hiking in state and national parks; cruising; fishing; hiking; skiing (downhill and cross-country); walking or driving tours of historic districts, fruit- or wine-producing areas.

INDOOR ADVENTURES: New museums and displays; art exhibits with unique Western themes; living history programs dealing with Western lore; hands-on science programs at institutions such as aquariums or planetariums; specialty shopping (Western art, crafts, antiques).

SPECIAL EVENTS: Festivals that celebrate a region's unique social, cultural, or agricultural heritage (examples: Oktoberfest, jazz festival, strawberry festival).

SURPRISE US: Look for great weekend getaways, backroad drives, urban adventures, culinary discoveries (ethnic dining enclaves).

Photography: Writers are encouraged to submit the names of prospective sources of color photographs (35mm or medium-format transparencies preferred) to illustrate stories. However, *Sunset* will arrange for all photo submissions and/or assignments to photographers.

Freelance garden articles

Sunset is Western America's largest-circulation regional magazine, with monthly issues devoted to four subject areas: travel and recreation; gardening and outdoor living; food and entertaining; and home design and decorating.

Sunset is looking for thoroughly researched, well-written stories and Garden Guide items that describe home gardening projects that can be successfully accomplished in a day or over a weekend or growing season.

Submission Procedures: No responsibility is assumed for unsolicited manuscripts. Writers must submit a query letter to the editor in advance. The query letter should explain and outline the proposed story idea, and suggest an appropriate month or season and the intended edition. Snapshots showing gardens or plants may be submitted with the query letter; include a self-addressed, stamped envelope for their return. Send query to Editorial Services, *Sunset*, 80 Willow Rd., Menlo Park, CA 94025. It will be forwarded to the appropriate editor.

Once an editor approves an idea for a Garden Guide item or story, the writer will be issued a Story Contract assigning an approximate word length and due date for the text. The contract specifies the terms of the agreement between the writer and *Sunset* Publishing Corporation.

Writers must have computer capabilities to submit stories by e-mail. The assigned text should be submitted with the resource material specified in the contract.

Following submission of the text, the writer may be asked to revise the manuscript for publication or to supply further information or answer questions posed by the editor.

Payment will be made upon acceptance of the text with submission of an invoice in the amount specified in the contract.

After acceptance, the text will then be processed by staff copy editors and fact checkers. Writers will be credited with a byline if the manuscript is not substantially altered before publication in *Sunset Magazine*.

Word Length: One-page stories usually run from 300 to 400 words, depending on the number of color photographs or illustrations such as charts or drawings.

Items for *Sunset's Garden Guide* currently run from 150 to 300 words.

Take-action Magazine: *Sunset* is not an armchair magazine. While each item or story ought to be interesting to read, it must also take a how-to approach so that readers can use the information to duplicate the activity in their own home gardens.

Climate Zones: In the West, the kinds of gardening people do, and the seasons in which they garden, are determined by the climate and topography of the area in which they live. The *Sunset Western Garden Book* identifies 24 different plant climate zones in the West, and it is to these zones (not USDA zones) that stories in *Sunset Magazine* refer. These climate zones dictate different planting times, gardening seasons of varying lengths, and, in most cases, different plants. For this reason, *Sunset's Garden Guide* items and many of the garden stories are published in regional editions.

Regional Editions: Garden Guide items are tailored to meet the home gardening needs of readers of *Sunset*'s five regional editions: Northern California; Southern California (Santa Barbara to San Diego; also Hawaii); Pacific Northwest (Alaska, Oregon, Washington, and British Columbia); Southwest (Arizona, New Mexico, Clark County, Nevada/Las Vegas) and West Texas (Amarillo to El Paso); Mountain (Colorado, Idaho, Montana, Nevada except Clark County, Utah, and Wyoming).

Seasonality: *Sunset* times the publication of its garden stories to coincide with the periods during which plants are planted, in bloom, or ready for harvest.

Plant Availability: Every plant *Sunset* describes must be readily available in nurseries or from mail-order suppliers of plants or seeds. For plants not commonly available, be sure to list sources, including complete mailing addresses, telephone numbers, and prices for plants or seeds.

Accuracy: Every *Sunset* article must be correct. *Sunset* is proud of its reputation for accuracy and dependability. Writers are urged to verify their information by consulting with several expert sources such as botanists, horticulturists, Certified Nurserymen, extension agents, commercial growers, Master Gardeners, and landscape architects and designers. Writers are also urged to check botanical and common names for plants as listed in The *Sunset Western Garden Book* or another widely respected reference such as Hortus Third.

Style: Stories should be written using the active voice. The tone should be informative but friendly, intelligent but not intimidating. Write as if you were giving gardening guidance to a friend or family member visiting your backyard. Writers may want to address the reader in the familiar (you) form. Begin with an arresting lead that clearly establishes a reason for reading on.

Logical Order: Establish a logical order for topics, categories and listings: alphabetical (by common name), chronological (step-by-step technique), physical characteristics (plant size or flower color), sun to shade, etc.

Straight Facts: Basic gardening facts are essential: plant form and size; leaf color and shape; flower color, shape, size, and scent; fruit or vegetable size, flavor, and texture. Give clear directions for planting, fertilizing, harvesting, pruning, etc.

Variety: *Sunset* publishes Garden Guide items and stories that address a wide range of gardening subjects, including the following:

PLANTS: Flowering plants (annuals, bulbs, perennials); landscape plants (deciduous and evergreen trees, shrubs, vines, ground covers, ornamental grasses); fruits (berries, citrus, grapes, nuts, pome and stone fruits); vegetables and herbs. Emphasis is on what's new, rediscovered, or otherwise noteworthy.

GARDENS: Borders (mixed and formal); containers (pots, hanging baskets, window boxes); country-style (informal or old-fashioned Western look); raised beds; small spaces (narrow yards, rooftops); specialty gardens (antique roses, cooks' gardens, herbs, native plants, rock gardens, wildflowers).

LANDSCAPING: Drought-tolerant landscapes; garden remodels; outdoor "rooms" (spaces defined by plants, decks); privacy screens using plants; steep-slope landscaping solutions; water features (ponds). Timeliness is important: for example, a story on landscaping in fire-prone areas of California might be most appropriate for summer when there is the greatest chance of wildfires.

INDOOR GARDENING: Houseplant care, culture, and display; greenhouses, lighting techniques.

TIPS AND TECHNIQUES: *Sunset* looks for new and better solutions for familiar gardening problems, including soil preparation, planting, transplanting, propagation (cuttings, grafting), irrigation, mulching, fertilizing, harvesting, composting, pruning, plant disease and pest control using environmentally safe methods, lawn care, and flower arrangement (fresh and dry).

HOMEMADE DEVICES: Tools and other devices that help gardeners achieve success while saving time and effort. These devices must be tested and their usefulness proven.

PHOTOGRAPHY: Writers are encouraged to submit the names of prospective sources of color photographs (35mm or medium-format transparencies preferred) to illustrate stories. However, *Sunset* will arrange for all photo submissions and/or assignments to photographers.

Categories: Nonfiction—Architecture—Cooking—Crafts/Hobbies—Family—Food/Drink—Gardening—Outdoors—Recreation—Reference—Regional—Travel—Western

CONTACT: Editorial Services
Material: All
80 Willow Rd.
Menlo Park CA 94025
Phone: 650-321-3600

Supervision

Supervision is a monthly magazine for supervisory and middle management personnel. Its primary objective is to provide informative articles which develop the attitudes, skills, personal and professional qualities of the supervisory staff, enabling them to use more of their potential to increase productivity, reduce operating costs and achieve personal and company goals.

CONTENT: *Supervision* usually contains five or six feature articles each month, plus several regular columns prepared by our contributing editors. Most of the articles are contributed by people with practical experience in business and industry. We will also use question-and-answer interviews with people in industry and in-depth third-person features about how foremen and supervisors are doing their jobs in innovative ways. No advertising is used in this publication.

NEEDS: We are interested in articles addressing the following: time management, planning, delegating authority and assigning responsibility, building morale, empowering their staff, goal setting, quality management, motivating staff, teamwork, discipline, safety/accident prevention, cost cutting and new innovative management concepts.

We can use articles that deal with human relations and communication, such as specific ways in which people in business and industry can deal with each other more effectively; ways the supervisor can aid in the development of an individual employee; specific methods of supervision that produce results such as improved morale, lowered turnover, reduced absenteeism; ways to improve the communication of facts and feelings both upward and downward. How product costs and product quality affect the company's competitive position; topics that will stimulate the supervisor to broaden his/her perspective, develop personally and thus make an increasing contribution to a company.

SUBMISSION OF ARTICLES: We work in advance. Therefore, articles may be retained over a year. NRB buys all rights. A signed release is required before publication. Finished articles should contain from 1,500 to 1,800 words. We pay 4 cents a word. Payment is made according to the release date of the issue in which the manuscript appears. A sample is mailed to the free-lancer.

Manuscripts should be high quality typed (suitable for scanning—do not submit articles on low quality dot-matrix printers), double-spaced and on only one side of the paper. *The Associated Press Stylebook* is followed for editing. Please list the approximate number of words on each manuscript. The author should indicate address, current by-line containing background employment, company affiliation and educational degrees listing alma mater. Send a black-and-white glossy author photo to accompany credit line upon acceptance.

Your experience and your ideas are valuable. Through the pages of *Supervision*, your message may become helpful to thousands of supervisors.

Categories: Business—Careers—Cartoons—Money & Finances—Relationships—Personnel

CONTACT: Teresa Levinson, Editor
Material: All
320 Valley St.
Burlington IA 52601-5513
Phone: 319-752-5415

Supply Chain Systems Magazine

About Us

Supply Chain Systems Magazine, the automation/collaboration resource, is published 12 times a year. This publication was formerly known as *ID Systems: The Magazine of Automated Data Collection*. *Supply Chain Systems Magazine* writes about the software and hardware used by companies to improve efficiencies and cut costs in their business. These products include extended ERP, Warehouse Management Software, Advanced Planning and Scheduling, Customer Relationship, distribution, e-business, and bar code labeling on the software side. On the hardware side, we cover RFID, wireless local and wide area networks, mobile handheld devices, portable data terminals, ruggedized PCs, printers, media, smart cards, biometrics, and bar code scanners and readers. In addition to the magazine, ID Systems also publishes an annual hardcopy Buyer's Guide, which is also available in an online, interactive format on the Web at www.idsystems.com. We also publish news on our Website, and a weekly email with headline links called Supply Chain NewsLink.

Supply Chain Systems Magazine's readers are professionals involved in the design, specification, and approval of supply chain and asset management solutions. According to *Supply Chain Systems Magazine*'s June 2000 BPA statement, 29 percent of readers' primary function is IT professional, 23 percent corporate management, 18 percent warehouse or manufacturing, 15 percent engineer, and 15 percent, Other Supply Chain management.

Submissions

If you write a feature story for *Supply Chain Systems Magazine*, you are required to submit a source list with contact information of each person interviewed for the story, and a summary of attempted contacts with sources that the author and editor deemed appropriate for the story.

Supply Chain Systems Magazine has several types of feature stores. Most of our features require the author to interview multiple (at least 10) sources. For example, the Vertical Industry Overview requires the author to interview vendors and users in a given industry about a wide variety of new and emerging technologies and practices used in that industry's supply chain. The same is true for our TechEdge (focus on a particular emerging technology) and TechFocus (focus on a particular product category such as CRM) feature tracks. Additionally, the author needs to work with the editor to help provide ideas for and sources for graphical artwork.

Graphics & Photos

Supply Chain Systems Magazine's graphics are often technical diagrams that show the relationships and data flow between various integrated systems. We will also accept screen shots, photos, and other types of graphics, provided they advance the text of the article by relaying additional information. The author doesn't need to create these graphics, but instead should work closely with the editor to provide ideas or rough drafts of graphics that *Supply Chain Systems Magazine*'s professional designers can re-do in a professional format. We can accept Illustrator, PhotoShop, PowerPoint, JPG, EPS, TIFF, GIF, and PDF file formats. Electronic images must be at 266 Dots Per inch at 100 percent size to be used in the magazine.

Solutions Focus

Supply Chain Systems Magazine also publishes every month a case study on manufacturing and one on warehousing called Solutions Focus. If you are writing a case study for a vendor, and submit it to *Supply Chain Systems Magazine*, you should expect the article to be rewritten, and that the *Supply Chain Systems Magazine* editor will need to follow up with a source who works for the customer to ask additional questions. We also require technical figures to show data flow between various integrated systems in the particular solutions focus.

For information visit this year's editorial calendar in our Media Kit on our website.

Categories: Nonfiction—Business—Computers—Technology

CONTACT: David Andrews, Publisher
Material: All
PO Box 874
174 Concord St.
Peterborough NH 03458
Phone: 603-924-9631
Fax: 603-924-7408
E-mail: editors@idsystems.com
Website: www.idsystems.com

Surfer

Surfer gives surfers of all levels spectacular photos, informative and impassioned articles, insightful interviews and ground-breaking travel features. For more than four decades, it has been internationally recognized as a leading publication and trendsetter for the surfing community.

We do not have formal writer's guidelines, but we do accept unsolicited material on a highly discriminatory basis. This publication is very subject specific, therefore, few freelance articles are published in our magazine. Please read a number of issues or visit us online to ascertain the publication's style and needs.

Send queries to address below.

Categories: Nonfiction—Interview—Lifestyle—Photography—Recreation—Sports—Travel

CONTACT: Sam George, Editor-in-Chief
Material: All
33046 Calle Aviador
San Juan Capistrano CA 92675
Website: www.surfermag.com

Swank
Erotic Fiction

All of the fiction currently used by SWANK is erotic in some sense—that is, both theme and content are sexual. Most of the stories (The Mysterious Stranger, The Bawdy Birthday Present) have been done before, so familiarity with previous tales of this type—in SWANK and elsewhere—is recommended. New angles are always welcome.

• Canadian restrictions: SWANK is distributed in Canada and the censors there practice their own strict standards regarding sexual material. To avoid problems, we generally shy away from material we know they'll object to or edit out any offensive references. Thus, we cannot consider stories about, or containing, the following: 1) S&M (including light bondage and mild humiliation); 2) Sex involving, or between, minors; 3) Unconscious, or dead, participants in sex; 4) Incest; 5) Bestiality.

Other Fiction

The magazine's format is currently flexible, and we will consider stories that are not strictly sexual in theme (humor, adventure, detective stories, etc.). However, these types of stories are much more likely to be considered if they portray some sexual element, or scene, within their content.

Nonfiction

1) Sex-related: Although dealing with sex and sexually related topics, these articles should be serious and well researched without being overwritten. Examples: "Sexaholics Anonymous," "Dream Programming," and "Voyeurism." Advice-type articles are also regularly featured. Examples: "How To Pick Up Girls At The Beach," and "How To Make The Man Shortage Work For You."

2) Action-oriented: We will consider non-sexual articles on topics dealing with action and adventure. The availability of photos to illustrate the articles is crucial to their acceptance—frequently, we will buy a package that includes both the article and transparencies. Recent features include such diverse topics as mercenaries, dangerous occupations and off-road racing. Automotive features run monthly.

3) Interviews: Although SWANK has not been running interviews lately, we will consider conversations with entertainment, sports and sex-industry celebrities.

Procedure

In most cases we respond to article queries within three weeks and manuscripts within five weeks. Due to the volume of material we receive, we discourage phone calls.

Terms

Payment is upon publication. You will be notified of the publication date after acceptance. A sample copy is available for $7.99 postpaid; please make checks or money orders payable to Swank Publications.

Categories: Fiction—Nonfiction—Adventure—Entertainment—Erotica—Horror—Men's Issues—Paranormal

CONTACT: Jeremy McSandal, Editor
Material: All
210 Rt. 4E, Ste. 401
Paramus NJ 07652
Phone: 201-843-4004
Fax: 201-843-8636

Swim Magazine

Established 1984. *SWIM Magazine*, "the world's foremost authority on adult swimming," is an internationally recognized swimming magazine dedicated to adult fitness and competitive swimmers. *SWIM Magazine* has a circulation of over 50,000 subscribers and is the official magazine of United States Masters Swimming (USMS). Subscribers are about 50% male and 50% female. The average reader is a college-educated professional in his or her mid-30's to mid-40's; almost 17% of our readers have "terminal" (i.e., professional) degrees, such as M.D., Ph.D., etc. Swimmers subscribe to our magazine for entertainment, instruction and inspiration. Masters swimmers range in age from 19 to 103+. Articles must be well written and appeal to a broad audience. Query first.

SPECIFICS

Bimonthly. Pays approximately within one month after publication, generally 12 cents per word. Publishes ms. an average of four months after acceptance. Buys all rights. Byline given. Negotiates payment for artwork and photos. Photo credit given. Query first. Reports in two months on queries. Sample copy for $3.95 prepaid and 9" x12" SASE with $1.67 for postage.

EDITORIAL

Training Tips, Interview profiles, inspirational stories, new products, medical advice, dryland exercise, swim drills, nutrition, fitness, competition and exercise physiology make *SWIM Magazine* the #1 source worldwide of information for adults about the sport of swimming.

COPY

All submissions must include a brief background about the author. If possible, send a disk or an e-mail attachment as well (Word preferred). *SWIM Magazine* accepts freelance articles on a continuing basis. Articles range in length from 500-3,500 words. *SWIM Magazine* reserves the right to make any editorial changes.

Categories: Nonfiction—Diet/Nutrition—Health—Lifestyle—Physical Fitness—Recreation—Sports—Swimming

CONTACT: Phillip Whitten/Editor-in-Chief
Material: All
90 Bell Rock Plaza, Ste 200
Sedona AZ 86351
Phone: 928-284-4005
Fax: 928-284-2477
E-mail: swimworld@aol.com
Website: www.swiminfo.com

Swimming Technique

Established 1964. *Swimming Technique* magazine is the leading magazine for coaches and self-coached adult swimmers. Subscribers are primarily swim coaches, technical directors and self-coached adult swimmers. Articles must be well written and authoritative. Query first.

Specifics

Quarterly. Pays approximately one month after publication, generally 12 cents per word. Publishes mss an average of two months after acceptance. Buys all rights. Byline given. Negotiates payment for artwork and photos. Photo credit given. Query first. Reports in two months on queries. Sample copy for $5.50 prepaid and 9x12 SAE with $1.80 for postage.

Editorial

Technique, stroke analysis (especially through the use of underwater photography), training methods and tips, training programs of leading swimmers and swim clubs, interview profiles, new products, medical advice, dryland exercise, swim drills, nutrition, exercise physiology and discussion of new ideas, techniques and theories make *Swimming Technique* the #1 source worldwide for swimming coaches and self-coached adult swimmers.

Copy

All submissions must be typed, double-spaced and include a brief bio of the author. If possible, send a disk or an e-mail attachment as well (Word preferred). *Swimming Technique* accepts freelance articles on a continuing basis. Articles range in length from 500-3,500 words. *Swimming Technique* reserves the right to make any editorial changes.

Categories: Nonfiction—Health—Interview—Sports/Recreation

CONTACT: Dr. Phillip Whitten, Editor-in-Chief
Material: All
CONTACT: Bob Ingram, Managing Editor
Material: All
Sports Publications, Inc., 90 Bell Rock Plaza, Ste. 200
Sedona AZ 86351
Phone: 928-284-4005
Fax: 928-284-2477
E-mail: swimworld@aol.com

Swimming World
Junior Swimmer

Established 1960. *Swimming World* magazine, acknowledged as "the Bible" of competitive swimming, is internationally recognized as the foremost authority on all aspects of competitive swimming. Circulation is 59,000. Subscribers are about 60% female and 40% male. Though readers include top competitive swimmers in their teens and twenties, and coaches, technical directors and officials from around the world. However, the average reader is a 14 year-old American girl. Swimmers subscribe to our magazine for information, instruction and inspiration. Articles must be well written and appeal to at least one (and preferably, several) of the major segments of our readership. Query first.

Specifics

Monthly. Pays approximately one month after publication, generally 12 cents per word. Publishes mss an average of two months after acceptance. Buys all rights. Byline given. Negotiates payment for artwork and photos. Photo credit given. Query first. Reports in two months on queries. Sample copy for $4.50 prepaid and 9x12 SAE with $1.80 for postage.

Editorial

Training and technique tips, meet stories and results, insider information, interview profiles, inspirational stories, new products, medical advice, dryland exercise, swim drills, interview profiles, inspirational stories, new products, medical advice, dryland exercise, swim drills, nutrition, fitness, competition and exercise physiology make *Swimming World* the #1 source worldwide of information for competitive swimmers. The "Junior Swimmer" section of each issue includes articles and interactive features written by and for kids.

Copy

All submissions must be typed, double-spaced and include a brief bio of the author. If possible, send disk or e-mail attachment as well (Word preferred). *Swimming World* accepts freelance articles on a continuing basis. Articles range in length from 500-3,500 words. *Swimming World* reserves the right to make any editorial changes.

Categories: Nonfiction—Children—Health—Physical Fitness—Recreation—Sports/Recreation—Teen—Young Adult—Swimming

CONTACT: Phillip Whitten, Editor-in-Chief
Material: All
Sports Publications Inc
90 Bell Rock Plaza, Ste 200
Sedona AZ 86351
Phone: 928-284-4005
Fax: 928-284-2477
E-mail: swimworld@aol.com

> *Remember: Editors change jobs and publishers change addresses. It is wise to invest in a phone call for the current information before submitting.*

Sycamore Review
Purdue University

Submission Guidelines
Reading Period: August 1 - March 31
Sycamore Review is looking for quality, original poetry, fiction, non-fiction and art. The most successful work is exciting, new, fresh, creative, carefully-wrought. We accept unsolicited submissions of fiction, poetry, personal essays and art. Please query for other non-fiction, including book reviews, brief critical essays, etc. as well as all art. We are interested in expanding our non-fiction content. At this time we are not able to accept outside interviews, previously published works (except for translations) or genre pieces (conventional science fiction, romance, horror, etc.).

We do accept simultaneous submissions, but request prompt notification if the work is accepted elsewhere. Please note simultaneous submissions in your cover letter.

Poetry manuscripts should be typed single-spaced, one poem to a page. Please send no more than 4-5 poems in one envelope. Wait until you have recieved a response to submit again.

Fiction, Non-Fiction, and all other manuscripts should be typed double-spaced, with numbered pages and the author's name and title of the work easily visible on each page. Please send only one story or essay at a time.

All manuscripts must be accompanied by a self-addressed, stamped envelope. At this time SR cannot accept submissions by email: please do not request an exception.

Art: If you are interested in submitting art for either our print issue or online art gallery, please send a query email describing your work (Is it black and white? Photos of installations?) and introducing yourself to rsilverm(@)purdue.edu. Do NOT send unsolicited images attached to emails. Your email will be deleted without being opened (we fear viruses). To submit work, please send via snail-mail as slides or CD-ROM (no prints!) or note in your emailed query a web address where your work can be viewed. For web pages, please indicate which pieces you would like considered. We are interested in serious, original work.

We read manuscripts from August 1 - March 31. Manuscripts sent at other times will be returned unread.

Purdue University acquires first-time North American rights to work published in *Sycamore Review*. After publication, all rights revert to the author. *Sycamore Review* does not publish creative work by any student currently attending Purdue University. Former students should wait one calendar year before submitting.

Sycamore Review pays two contributor's copies for printed work. Unfortunately, we are unable to pay money at this time.

Categories: Fiction—Nonfiction—Arts—Book Reviews—Poetry—Writing

CONTACT: Poetry Editor
Material: Poetry
CONTACT: Fiction Editor
Material: Fiction
CONTACT: Editor-in-Chief
Material: All other submissions
Purdue University Department of English
500 Oval Dr
W Lafayette IN 47907
Phone: 765-494-3783
Fax: 765-494-3780
E-mail: Sycamore@purdue.edu
Website: www.sycamorereview.com

symploke

symploke supports new and developing notions of comparative theory and literature, and is committed to interdisciplinary studies, intellectual pluralism, and open discussion. The editors are particularly interested in scholarship on the interrelations among philosophy, literature, culture criticism and intellectual history, though we will consider articles on any aspect of the intermingling of discourses and disciplines.

The journal takes its name from the Greek word *symploke* which has among its various meanings interweaving, interlacing, connection and struggle. The journal's editors believe that continuing change in the humanities is contingent upon the interweaving, connection, and struggle between traditionally independent domains of discourse. One of our broader goals is to contribute to the opening of alternative academic frontiers by providing a forum for scholars of varying disciplines to engage in the intermingling of ideas in innovative ways.

symploke is published and distributed in association with the University of Nebraska Press.

Submissions

Submissions of any length which are appropriate to the aims of *symploke* will be considered, although those between 4,000 and 6,500 words (approximately 16-26 typed, double-spaced pages) are preferred. Please keep in mind that submitted manuscripts need not be intended for an upcoming special issue; general submissions of high quality are encouraged. The editors reserve the right to make stylistic alterations in the interest of clarity. Authors will receive two complementary issues of the journal. All submissions must strictly follow the guidelines for copy preparation listed below. Articles not conforming to these guidelines may be sent back to the author for revision.

Preparation of Copy

1. All submissions must provide a complete listing of references and use footnotes rather than endnotes.

2. Footnotes should generally consist only of references and are to be consecutively numbered throughout the manuscript.

3. References must include the names of publishers as well as places of publication. Also include full names and a complete listing of translators and editors.

4. The format of the manuscript must conform to the current *MLA Style Manual.*

5. All manuscripts must be submitted in duplicate. If the manuscript was word-processed, include a copy of your IBM- or Macintosh-compatible disk. Microsoft word or ASCII files are preferable.

6. All quotations, titles, names and dates must be checked for accuracy.

7. All articles must be written in English.

8. This journal has a policy of blind peer reviewing; thus the author's name should not appear on the manuscript and a separate title page must be provided.

9. Material not kept for publication will be returned if accompanied by a stamped, self-addressed envelope.

All materials published in this journal are copyrighted by *symploke*. Submission of an article to this journal entails the author's agreement to assign copyright to *symploke*. Articles appearing in *symploke* may be reproduced for research purposes, personal reference, and classroom use without special permission and without fee payment. This permission does not extend to other kinds of reproduction such as copying for general distribution, for the creation of collected works or anthologies, for advertising or promotional purposes, or for resale. These and all other rights are reserved.

Categories: Culture, History, Literature, Philosophy

CONTACT: **Jeffrey R. Di Leo, Editor-in-Chief**
Material: All
University of Houston—Victoria
3007 N. Ben Wilson
Victoria TX 77901

E-mail: editor@symploke.org (send submissions as attachments)
Website: www.symploke.org

Syracuse New Times

Every year more than half the editorial matter published in the *Syracuse New Times* comes from people not on our full-time staff. Cover stories, interviews, What's Shakin' items, arts and entertainment features, sports stories, book reviews and cartoons are all occasionally generated by free-lancers. It's fair to say *The New Times* would have a tough time surviving without them.

As a result, we look forward to reading, editing and eventually publishing free-lance material.

This being said, you should be aware that for every 10 unsolicited manuscripts we receive, only one is likely to be published in *The New Times*. To ensure that you waste neither our time nor yours, here are some guidelines.

Substance

Generally speaking, what most impresses us is thoughtful, clear writing. The subject matter is almost secondary. It is crucial that the piece be lively, interesting and appealing to the uninterested reader—in the way that a well-written piece on boxing can appeal to a reader who hates the subject. We tend to avoid journalism that is abstract and generalized and to favor writing that deals with specifics and, in so doing, suggests the universal. We generally turn down stories written in the first person.

With good writing of paramount importance, we then give preference to the stories that fit our format. Take a look at recent copy of *The New Times* to see what we make room for and what we don't really have. Cover stories are often news stories or features of considerable length. The What's Shakin' section is shorter, newsier items; other sections contain art and entertainment stories, human-interest pieces, food and lifestyle articles and reviews.

Since *The New Times* is a Syracuse newspaper, we generally run stories that are about the metropolitan area, or at least relevant to Central New York readers.

Now that we've laid down the rules, remember that rules are made to be broken. A story, no matter how it may deviate from these guidelines, may be published in *The New Times* if it is well written and strikes our fancy.

Process

If you have an idea for an article, send us a brief explanation of the story and how you expect to put it together, including possible sources and key questions. If this is your first query to us, please include some kind of resumé. (Sorry about the formality, but we like to know with whom we're dealing.)

Generally speaking, the shorter the better, but you should write what you're comfortable with. We can always adjust it later.

Odds and Ends

The New Times purchases first publication rights only; all other rights revert to you.

The New Times' libel insurance does not cover free-lance writers. You must assume full responsibility for the legal consequences that may occur as the result of your reporting.

NEVER say you are writing a story for this newspaper without first getting permission from the editor.

Please e-mail manuscripts in Word or Word Perfect format.

Do not send us your only copy. We do not return manuscripts unless they are accompanied by a stamped, self-addressed envelope. Please allow us up to a month to respond to your submissions.

A Final Note : You may mail, e-mail or fax your query to us or leave it in person at our front desk. Please don't make an editor's life any more difficult by asking to see him or her. The time to discuss a story is after we have read it, not when you first bring it in.

Categories: Nonfiction—Alternate Life-style—Arts—Book Reviews—Campus Life—Culture—Entertainment—Food/Drink—Human Rights

CONTACT: Molly English, Editor-in-Chief
Material: All
A. Zimmer, Ltd.
1415 W. Genesee St.
Syracuse NY 13204-2156
Phone: 315-422-7011
Fax: 315-422-1721
E-mail: menglish@syracusenewtimes.com
Website: www.syracusenewtimes.rway.com

T'ai Chi

Types of Articles

Generally speaking, an article should take into account the special needs and desires of the readers of T'ai Chi. Many are beginners or thinking about starting classes. Many are serious students, and have studied and even taught for years.

They are interested in many aspects: self-defense, internal skills, health, meditation, fitness, self-improvement, ch'i cultivation, Traditional Chinese Medicine (acupuncture, herbs, massage, etc.) and spiritual growth.

More specifically, articles may be a feature or interview about a style, self-defense techniques, principles and philosophy, training methods, weapons, case histories of benefits, or new or unusual uses for T'ai Chi Ch'uan. Try to avoid profiles of teachers that focus just on their many skills and accomplishments. Interviews with teachers or personalities should focus on their unique or individual insight into T'ai Chi Ch'uan, internal martial arts, qigong, or Traditional Chinese Medicine rather than on their personal achievement or ability, although their background can be woven into the article.

Examples of the uses could be teaching the disabled, teaching of T'ai Chi Ch'uan in a corporate or medical environment, or martial techniques. New approaches to teaching or practice or the basic principles are almost always of interest as long as it doesn't promote a particular teacher or school. When planning and writing the article ask yourself: Is the material new or fresh? Is it useful to practitioners? Is it interesting?

An examination of past issues is one of your best guides to what we publish.

Present the information clearly, fairly, and objectively. Quotations, anecdotes, examples, and parallel references help make an article more readable and interesting. Writing that is simple and direct is understood best. If organization of the article is a problem, try a question and answer format.

Send e-mail inquiries to Marvin Smalheiser at taichi@tai-chi.com. If you want to discuss a story possibility first, please feel free to contact me by phone or with a note or by e-mail at taichi@ tai-chi.com.

Please do not send articles that are simultaneously sent to other publications, unless it specifies on the first page that it is a news release or that it has been submitted elsewhere, too.

Also, please do not send articles that you have put on your web site or plan to put on your web site. We pay for articles and do not want to have to pay for an article that you are giving away free on your website. Our subscribers should not have to pay to read articles that are available free on a website.

We appreciate that many people now have their own websites and want to include good articles to attract visitors. But it is best that you create your own material for your website that is distinct from whatever you submit to us.

Manuscript Specifications

Manuscripts should be typed, double-spaced, with a margin not more than 80 characters wide. Put a tentative title on the front page. Put the title abbreviated on each subsequent page with a page number. At the end of the article write "-30-" to indicate it is complete. Include your name, address, and phone number on the first page and the best times to reach you by phone. Include a paragraph about yourself and also about the subject if it is an interview with someone else. Articles can be from 500 to 3500 words long or more. Payment can range from $75.00 to $500.00, depending on the length and quality of the article. This includes payment for photos. Payment is for first North American Serial rights only. Payment is on publication. Payment is usually within 30 days of publication.

If possible, include one or more 4 x 6, 5 x 7 or 8 x 10 glossy black and white prints. Color photos can be used but may print a little dark, red colors in particular. Indicate if you want them returned.

If you plan to send them on a CD or over the Internet, they should be scanned as RGB at 300 dpi and saved as Tiff files. If they are digital they should be Tiff, PDF or Jpeg at 300 dpi.

The photos should have identification of the individuals in the photo written on a separate piece of paper sent with the photos or on a post-it on the photo. If the photo is of a posture, the name of the style and posture should be given. Don't write on the back of the photo. Model releases are required. Releases authorizing use of the photos should be dated and witnessed.

Categories: Nonfiction—Asian-American—Health—Physical Fitness—Sports/Recreation—Martial Arts

CONTACT: Marvin Smalheiser, Editor/Publisher
Material: All
PO Box 39938
Los Angeles CA 90039
Phone: 323-665-7773
Fax: 323-665-1627
E-mail: taichi@tai-chi.com
Website: www.tai-chi.com

Take Pride! Community

Take Pride! Community is a weekly publication that promotes education and economic empowerment for all people. Topics must pertain to the following categories: Education, Economics/Finance, Business, Technology, Health Arts/Culture, Politics, Religion, Family/Society, History, or Seasonal pieces. Article length: 250-800 words. Writers are paid upon publication of their articles, which must be submitted one month in advance of publication. Byline given. All paid articles must be requested and approved by the president/CEO. Responds in two weeks on queries. (Include SASE for postal response.) Every article must include photograph(s); exceptions within discretion of the editor. Photo payment negotiated individually. Model releases and identification of subjects required. Take Pride! Community buys unlimited rights, makes work-for-hire assignments and accepts queries by mail and e-mail.

Categories: Arts—Business—Culture—Economics—Education—Family—Health—History—Money & Finances—Politics—Religion—Society

CONTACT: Ryan D. Arnold
Material: All
1014 Franklin St SE, Ste. 4969
Grand Rapids MI 49507-1327
Phone: 616-243-4114
E-mail: gdesigns@oneblood-onerace.org
Website: www.oneblood-onerace.org/TakePride/Contact.html

Tales of the Talisman

Writer's Guidelines

Tales of the Talisman (formerly *Hadrosaur Tales*) is a literary journal published quarterly by Hadrosaur Productions and LBF Books. The format is an 86-page, perfect-bound, printed magazine.

The hadrosaur talisman logo is inspired by a duckbilled dinosaur called a tsintaosaurus. These dinosaurs looked remarkably like early depictions of unicorns. We chose this blending of the creature of science and fantasy as the symbol of our magazine and press devoted to publishing the finest quality speculative fiction.

Needs: Science Fiction, fantasy, and horror short stories to 6000 words and poems to 50 lines. Send only complete manuscripts. Postal submissions should be prepared in standard manuscript format as described in most writer reference books. Detailed guidelines for preparing and sending electronic mail submissions are at the bottom of this document. We do not assign themes.

Artwork: If you are interested in doing artwork for *Tales of the Talisman*, contact our art director, Laura Givens via e-mail at: lauragive@msn.com.

Submission periods: Reading periods are May 1 - June 15 and November 1 - December 15. You may submit material up to one month in advance of the reading periods, but please do not send unsolicited material otherwise.

Tips: Let your imagination soar to its greatest heights and write down the results. Above all we are looking for thought-provoking ideas and good writing. Speculative fiction set in the past, present, and future is welcome. Admittedly, science fiction, fantasy, and horror are broad genres that overlap many other genres. We welcome cross-genre stories, but they must include some element of science fiction or fantasy. Examples of cross genre stories we have published: A western story with fairies and a vampire story set in virtual reality.

Do not send: Works with excessively graphic/gory violence (good horror is about atmosphere, not cheap gross outs, and absolutely no violence to children). Please avoid clichéd or overdone ideas. I really like stories that take the conventions of fantasy, horror, and science fiction and turn them on their head—exploring them seriously and intelligently from new perspectives. Do not send stories or poems with essentially no science fictional or fantasy elements—that includes the horror stories; I can read about serial killers in the newspaper. Do not send stories or poems with copyrighted characters unless you are the copyright holder. Sex and erotica in submissions is OK, as long as its necessary to the work and tastefully presented.

Simultaneous and Multiple Submissions: We do not accept simultaneous or multiple submissions. A submission is one short story or a packet of five (or fewer) poems.

Reprints: We will consider reprints. However, be aware that we prefer to publish original fiction. If given the choice between unpublished fiction and previously published fiction of equal quality, we will go with the unpublished fiction. However, if your reprint is fabulous,

feel free to send it to us and we'll have a look.

Rights: We buy one-time rights for all material. Please inform us if the story would be a reprint.

Payment: We pay $10.00 per original published story and $4.00 per original published poem or the equivalent in trade. Though we consider reprints, we reserve the right to pay less for them. Contributors also receive one copy of the issue in which their work appears.

Response time: Our goal is to respond to submissions within 4 weeks of receipt. We respond to all submissions received during or prior to a reading period no later than 4 weeks after the reading period ends.

Sample copies and Subscriptions: Sample copies of *Tales of the Talisman* are available for $8.00 (includes shipping and handling). A one-year subscription (four issues) is available for $24.00. Make checks payable to "Hadrosaur Productions." Sample issues may also be purchased on-line at The Genre Mall: http://www.genremall.com, and Clarkesworld Books: http://www.clarkesworldbooks.com

Unfortunately, spam advertisers and hackers who propagate viruses have forced us to implement the following guidelines for e-mail submissions: No attachments—embed your work in the body of the e-mail. Format stories so that there is a blank line between paragraphs. Submissions must be formatted as plain text—no HTML formatting and absolutely no scripts. E-mail submissions should include a physical address and an e-mail address in the body of the message. If the message looks like spam, there's a good chance we will delete it unread—not because we're being draconian, but because it looked like one of the dozens of junk e-mails we receive every day. Please include the words "Talisman submission" in the subject line to help us recognize your mail as a submission. Like postal mail, e-mail can be misrouted or lost. E-mail submissions are done at the author's risk.

Categories: Fiction—Fantasy—Horror—Literature—Poetry—Science Fiction—Short Stories

CONTACT: David L. Summers, Editor
Material: All
Hadrosaur Productions
PO Box 2194
Mesilla Park NM 88047-2194
E-mail: hadrosaur@zianet.com
Websites: http://hadrosaur.com and http://www.zianet.com/hadrosaur

Tampa Review
Literary Journal of the
University of Tampa

1. *Tampa Review* is the faculty-edited literary journal of the University of Tampa. We publish two issues a year, one in the Fall and one in the Spring. Our editorial staff considers submissions between September and December for publication in the following year. Manuscripts received prior to August will be returned unread. We maintain this policy so that works submitted to us are not held for an unduly long time.

2. We suggest you submit 3 to 6 poems and/or one or more prose manuscripts of up to 5,000 words. We do not print book-length poetry, and rarely publish excerpts from larger works of either poetry or prose.

3. Poetry may be submitted single-spaced. Clearly indicate any space breaks within stories, and stanza breaks in poetry, especially when they occur at the end of a page, so that these breaks will be obvious to our editors.

4. Please do not send us work which is also being submitted elsewhere. We do not consider simultaneous submissions. This policy saves our editors from reading work which is not actually available for first North American publication, and it saves authors the embarrassment of having to withdraw a manuscript.

5. The writer's name and complete address should appear on the first page of each manuscript. For multiple-page submissions, subsequent pages should be numbered and should include the author's name and short title at the top of each page. We also appreciate receiving a telephone number and/or e-mail address.

6. Fiction and nonfiction submissions should state a total word count at the top of the first page (upper right-hand corner). For poetry manuscripts, a line count is useful.

7. Translations must be submitted in original language as well as translated versions. Please also include a short biographical note on the translated author and the author's permission to translate.

8. A reporting time of approximately 12 weeks can be expected.

9. Our payment is ten dollars per page for both prose and poetry, payable upon publication, one free copy of the review in which the work(s) appears, and a 40% discount on additional copies.

Suggestion: It is sometimes helpful to get an idea of the kinds of work a magazine is publishing; sample copies are available for that purpose. *Tampa Review* sample copies are $5.00, including postage.

Categories: Fiction—Nonfiction—Literature—Poetry—Creative Nonfiction

CONTACT: Donald Morrill/Martha Serpas, Poetry Editors
Material: Poetry
CONTACT: Lisa Birnbaum/Kathleen Ochshorn, Fiction Editors
Material: Fiction Editor
CONTACT: Elizabeth Winston, Nonfiction Editor
Material: Nonfiction
University of Tampa Press, 401 W. Kennedy Blvd.
Tampa FL 33606
Phone: 813-253-6266

Teacher Magazine

Teacher Magazine was founded in 1989 by Editorial Projects in Education, which also publishes Education Week. Teacher is an independent, nonprofit publication that covers education issues, school culture, and the profession in general. It is published eight times a year and goes to about 130,000 readers nationwide.

Guidelines for submitting STORY IDEAS:

Articles in *Teacher Magazine* are split into several sections: Current Events, which are shorter and newsier; Front of the Book, mid-length features about different facets of educational life; and full-length features, which run 3,000 to 6,000 words and are more narrative in style.

The editors of Teacher welcome ideas from new sources, though the large number of unsolicited pitches received makes it impossible to respond personally to each one. An editor will be in touch if an article is to be considered for an upcoming issue. Please do not follow up with phone calls, e-mails, or letters to check the status of a submission. Future submissions will be considered independently.

Guidelines for submitting COMMENT PIECES:

The editors of Teacher encourage submissions for the magazine's "Comment" section. The magazine aims to challenge, provoke, connect, and entertain teachers. To do this, we must hear from a variety of voices in "Comment."

Articles generally fall under two headings. "Viewpoint" submissions should address issues in pre-collegiate education that are of particular interest to classroom teachers. In organization and tone, these articles should take the form of opinion essays rather than scholarly papers, research reports, or lesson plans. The essays may touch on local or state issues, but they must not solely focus on regional matters.

"First Person" submissions should describe a particularly meaningful or moving personal experience. These articles are generally school-related, and they are often lighter in tone than "Viewpoint" essays.

Submissions should run at most about 1,200 words (roughly four to five double-spaced pages). Shorter stories are also accepted and often run under a separate heading, "Voices." If your submission is accepted for publication, you will be contacted about its publication date by phone or mail. An honorarium will be paid upon publication.

Essays can be submitted at any time. Note clearly on your submission your name, phone number, fax number, address, and e-mail address.

Categories: Nonfiction—Education

CONTACT: Features Editor
Material: Story Ideas
CONTACT: Comment Editor
Material: Comment Section
6935 Arlington Rd., Ste. 100
Bethesda, MD 20814
Phone: 301-280-3100
Website: www.teachermagazine.org

Teachers of Vision
A Publication of Christian Educators Association International

Teachers of Vision is a magazine for Christian educators in public and private education. Its articles inspire, inform and equip teachers and administrators in the educational arena. In the words of Forrest Turpen, executive director of CEAI, "It is an extended faculty room, a place of refreshment, dialogue, encouragement and guidance." The guidance often deals with the legality of living out one's faith in the workplace.

Our Readers

Teachers of Vision is a membership and limited subscription publication. Readers look for educational articles that inspire and provide practical ideas they can use in their profession. Our audience is primarily public school educators.

Our writers are:
• Able to integrate secular and spiritual insights
• Faithful to the teachings of Scripture
• Up-to-date on trends in contemporary education

Our Editorial Needs

We invite writers to submit the following types of manuscripts:

Feature articles between 1000-2500 words, dealing with specific issues of interest to Christian educators. These may be written as how-to articles, personal experience pieces, educational philosophy, methodology, or documented reports.

Our Editorial Needs

Mini-features between 400-750 words that: highlight a holiday or special event and its classroom relevance; describe a successful teaching technique; or update readers on newsworthy happenings in education; or share an inspirational personal experience.

Interviews of 500-750 words with outstanding Christian educators.

Classroom resource reviews between 100-200 words. These may be on books, curriculum, videos, visual aids, games or other items related to teaching.

Payment issued upon publication $20-$40 and copies.

IMPORTANT: Please submit articles via email to: judy@ ceai.org or send a floppy disk (WordPerfect 6.1 , WORD or RTF format) to the mailing address below. Request permission to send photographs.

When you submit manuscripts, remember:
• Include a 2-3 sentence byline with your article (we may also request a color photo if your work is accepted for publication).
• Due to limited staff, it may take several weeks to respond to your submission. You are welcome to inquire about the status of your manuscript after four weeks.

- We cannot guarantee your article will be accepted.
- We reserve the right to edit material for length and content.
- We maintain the right to reprint your article in other CEAI publications and CEAI's website.
- We accept previously published articles, provided you inform us of where the article appeared and verify ownership of reprint rights.
- You are welcome to query us with article ideas to avoid submitting material we cannot use (send a brief description of the article, detailing its main points).
- Seasonal material must be received at least four months in advance.
- If you wish to have your manuscript returned, you must enclose a self- addressed, first-class stamped envelope.
- If your article is accepted for submission, it may take 4-6 issues before final publication. We do appreciate your patience.
- For a hard copy of these guidelines and samples of our publications, please send a 9x12 SASE with five first class postage stamps.

Teachers of Vision Magazine Theme:

Keep in mind that our articles need a distinctively Christian viewpoint. However, please avoid even the appearance of preaching and cut all religious jargon! We need writers who are able to present topics naturally and who portray issues of faith as an integrated part of teaching.

Categories: Nonfiction—Education—Religion

CONTACT: Judy Turpen, Contributing Editor
Material: All
Christian Educators Association Int'l
PO Box 41300
Pasadena CA 91114
Phone: 626-798-1124
Fax: 626-798-2346
E-mail: judy@ceai.org

Teaching Theatre

Teaching Theatre is a quarterly educational theatre journal published by the Educational Theatre Association, a professional association for theatre educators and artists. *Teaching Theatre*, available to EdTA members and libraries only, has a circulation of approximately 3,200. The majority of the journal's readers are high school theatre teachers. Subscribers also include elementary, middle school, and college theatre teachers, school administrators, libraries, and others interested in educational theatre.

Opportunities for contributors

Teaching Theatre is an even blend of advocacy, how-to, and theory. If an article can be of use to a theatre teacher—either by presenting a model, an innovative idea, or a specific teaching methodology—we're going to be interested in taking a look at it. *Teaching Theatre*'s readers are a well-educated and experienced group, for the most part; general interest essays on the value of educational theatre aren't going to be of much interest to them and, therefore, not to us either.

We buy twelve to fifteen articles a year, general length 750-4,000 words. A typical issue might include an article on theatre curriculum development, a profile of an exemplary theatre education program, a how-to teach piece on acting, directing, or play writing, and a news story or two about pertinent educational theatre issues and events.

Graphics

Photos and illustrations to accompany articles are welcomed, and when available, should be submitted at the same time as the manuscript. Acceptable forms: black and white prints, 5 x 7 or larger; line art. Unless other arrangements are made, payment for articles includes payment for the photos and illustrations.

Rights and returns

We buy first publication rights (unless we make other arrangements with an author), pay on acceptance, report in four to six weeks, and return all material that is accompanied by a self-addressed stamped envelope.

Queries and sample copies

We prefer to see a finished manuscript but will respond to query letters. Sample copies are available for $2.

Payment

Honorariums of $50 to $350 are paid for accepted work. Payment is based on quality of work, amount of editing and rewriting needed, length of work, and inclusion of photos or graphics.

Manuscript specifications

We edit manuscripts to conform to *The Chicago Manual of Style*. Manuscripts should be typed double spaced on a sixty-character line. Photocopies are acceptable as long as they are clearly legible. Contributors should keep an exact copy or computer file of any manuscript submitted.

Once articles are accepted, authors are asked to supply their work electronically via e-mail (jpalmarini@edta.org) or on IBM compatible diskettes, sent to Teaching Theatre, 2343 Auburn Avenue, Cincinnati, OH 45219.

All submissions are subject to editing, and we try to involve authors in that process as much as possible.

Whenever time allows, we send galley proofs to authors for review—usually by fax.

A Contributor's Cheat Sheet:

What makes us cranky

- Writers who are too lazy or careless to do basic reporting and research. Very few articles are complete with only one quoted source.
- Writers who misrepresent themselves as experts, or are not up front about if and where a piece has been previously published.
- Submissions that ignore or misunderstand our audience; articles that either talk down to our readers or are way over their heads. (If a piece has footnotes, it's probably too academic for us.)
- Contributors who create an impression of conflict of interest by writing about an organization in which they themselves are involved—although we do sometimes publish first-person accounts.
- Writers who are impossible to get a hold of, or who do not return messages.

What makes us happy

- Writers who really understand our audience.
- Writers who bring lots of strong, specific article ideas to the table, and keep abreast of topics recently covered by the journal.
- Contributors who submit written queries or complete articles, rather than interrupting our work to make a sales pitch by phone.
- Writers who understand the need for editorial input, and can make and/or accept necessary changes gracefully.
- Writers who can provide publishable photography to go along with their pieces (snapshots are not publishable).

Illustration ideas are also appreciated.

- Writers who include student voices in their pieces when appropriate, as well as a variety of other sources.
- Writers whose work is well organized, factual, and clean.

Categories: Drama, Education

CONTACT: James Palmarini, Editor
Material: All
Educational Theatre Association
2343 Auburn Ave.
Cincinnati OH 45219
Phone: 513-421-3900
E-mail: jpalmarini@edta.org
Website: www.edta.org

R-U

Remember: Editors change jobs and publishers change addresses. It is wise to invest in a phone call for the current information before submitting.

Teaching Tolerance

The semiannual magazine *Teaching Tolerance* is dedicated to helping preschool, elementary, and secondary teachers promote tolerance and understanding between widely diverse groups of students. It includes articles, teaching ideas, and reviews of other resources available to educators. Our interpretation of "tolerance" follows the definition of American Heritage Dictionary: The capacity for or the practice of recognizing and respecting the beliefs or practices of others.

In general, we want lively, simple, concise writing. The writing style should be descriptive and reflective. Writers should show the strength of programs dealing successfully with diversity by employing clear descriptions of real scenes and interactions, and by using quotes from teachers and students. We cannot accept articles that employ jargon, rhetoric, or academic analysis. We ask that prospective writers study previous issues of the magazine to see our style and content. Then submit a query letter and writing samples.

Features: 1,000-3,500 words. Should have a strong classroom focus, with national perspective where appropriate. Usually accompanied by sidebars of helpful information such as resources, how-to steps, short profiles. Writers are typically free-lance journalists with knowledge of issues in education or educators with experience writing for national non-academic publications. Fees range from $500 to $3,500 depending on length and complexity. The freelance fee and reasonable expenses are paid on acceptance. If a solicited story is unacceptable as submitted, we may assist in preparing a publishable manuscript, but sometimes, despite the best intentions of both author and editor, a manuscript will be judged unacceptable. In such instances, a kill fee in the amount equal to one-half of the agreed-upon fee will be paid to the writer.

Essays: 400-800 words. Personal reflection, description of school program, community-school program, classroom activity, how-to. Writers are typically teachers, counselors, parents or other educators. "Between the Lines" essays describe how literature can be used to teach tolerance. Fees range from $300-$800 upon publication.

Idea Exchange: 250-500 words. Brief descriptions of classroom lesson plans, special projects, or other school activities that promote tolerance. These are usually submitted by teachers, administrators or parents who have successfully used the technique or program. Fee: $100-$200 upon publication.

Student Writing: Poems and short essays dealing with diversity, tolerance and justice. Printed when appropriate to magazine content. Fee: $50 upon publication.

If you have any questions concerning submissions, please contact Cynthia Pon.

Categories: African-American—Arts—Asian-American—Associations—Book Reviews—Cartoons—Children—Christian Interests—College—Crime—Culture—Dance—Drama—Directories—Disabilities—Education—Entertainment—Family—Feminism—Film/Video—Folklore—Gay/Lesbian—General Interest—Government—Hispanic—History—Human Rights—Internet—Jewish Interest—Juvenile—Language—Law—Lifestyle—Men's Issues—Multicultural—Music—Native American—Parenting—Poetry—Psychology—Reference—Relationships—Religion—Rural America—Short Stories—Society—Spiritual—Teen—Television/Radio—Textbooks—Theatre—Women's Issues—Writing—Young Adult

CONTACT: Submissions Editor
Material: All

400 Washington Ave.
Montgomery AL 36104
Phone: 334-956-8200
Fax: 334-956-8484
E-mail: cpon@splcenter.org
Website: www.teachingtolerance.org

Technical Analysis of Stocks & Commodities

These guidelines are provided to acquaint you, as a *Technical Analysis of Stocks & Commodities* artist or prospective artist, with our needs and requirements, as well as to provide you with some basic information about submitting art to STOCKS & COMMODITIES for publication.

WHAT IS TECHNICAL ANALYSIS?

Technical analysis is a form of financial market analysis that studies demand and supply for securities and commodities. This analysis is based on studies of price and trading volume. Using charts and modeling techniques, technicians attempt to identify price trends in a market.

Charting is the most common method of analysis for technical analysts. Traders chart price movement in various markets either by hand or by computer. Because charts are such a basic component of technical analysis, most illustrations for articles will incorporate some chart elements. Below is a typical price chart that a technical analyst or investor might study:

Technical Analysis of Stocks & Commodities is a monthly magazine for traders and investors who trade or invest in securities, commodities, options, mutual funds or other tradables. Our readers include institutional as well as individual investors. The magazine is an educational, how-to publication that covers a variety of subject categories in each issue. Some of those categories are trading techniques and methods, computerized techniques, statistical and mathematical analysis, artificial intelligence, psychology of trading, and product reviews.

ART CONTENT, STYLE & USE OF COLOR

We are looking for art that is relevant to technical analysis and trading as well as to the article for which the art piece is assigned. The Art Director, Christine Morrison, assigns art monthly for an upcoming issue. Each art order will list the specifications and other important information about each art assignment, including art dimensions, deadlines and ideas for content. A summary of an article scheduled to be published is sent with an art assignment to help establish a theme for the art. However, because the editorial content of any issue may change without notice at any time, art submitted may be used with another article in the same issue instead.

COVER ART

For cover art, we require two elements to be present: first, that the content of the art is generically representational of technical analysis and trading; and second, that colors used are bright enough to stand out on the newsstand.

The cover art for any given issue is usually used inside the magazine as well to introduce one of our articles. Therefore, the concept used for the cover art will usually be based on an article.

COPYRIGHTS

Upon acceptance, Technical Analysis, Inc. acquires one-time rights to the artwork plus reprint rights. Reprint rights include the right to reuse an image whenever a page of the magazine or magazine cover is reprinted, such as in book form, on computer disk or other media. Your material must be an original work that has not been previously published and is not currently under consideration by any other publication.

PAYMENT

Payment is made upon publication. Payment for art varies depending on the art budget for that issue and art specifications, such as whether the piece will be color or black and white and whether the piece is for the cover or inside the magazine. Payment information for each art assignment will be included in the art order.

To receive payment, we need the following information: Artist's name, address, telephone number and Social Security Number (SSN). You can include all this information in an invoice sent to us based on your art order.

Payment is mailed along with a tearsheet or copy of the STOCKS & COMMODITIES issue in which the art appears. Artists wishing additional copies of the issue in which their work appears may order them from the main office (currently $3.50 per copy). Large quantity orders should be arranged prior to publication. Reprint rates are available for quantities of 100 or more.

Categories: Nonfiction—Money & Finances

CONTACT: Jayanthi Gopalakrishnan, Editor
Material: All
4757 California Ave. SW
Seattle WA 98126
Phone: 206-938-0570
Fax: 206-938-1307
E-mail: www.traders.com
Website: www.traders.com

Technology & Learning Magazine

Editorial Guidelines

Technology & Learning publishes articles that encourage educators to think about new approaches to teaching and new ways to use technology in the classroom. *Technology & Learning* magazine is circulated to over 80,000 elementary, middle, and high school teachers, technology coordinators, and administrators at the building, district, and state levels. We publish articles that encourage educators to think about new approaches to teaching and new ways to use technology in the classroom. We cover all aspects of educational technology: hardware, software, and the Web.

There are three sections of the magazine to which you might contribute.

Feature Articles

These articles are assigned by our editors. They are of general interest, appealing to a broad audience of K-12 educators (covering a range of grade levels, subject areas, etc.). Manuscripts are generally between 1,200 to 2,500 words in length. Payment varies from $400 or more on publication. If you are interested in authoring feature articles for *Technology & Learning* your best approach is to send a query letter with specific article ideas and clips of your previously published work.

Software Evaluations

Evaluations are assigned through our editorial offices. If you have regular access to a school setting and would like to review educational or administrative products, let us know your areas of interest and expertise as well as the computer(s) and other hardware you have available to you. You may also want to suggest specific software programs you feel qualified to review. We will send you specific evaluation guidelines when we assign a review to you. Payment varies depending on the assignment.

What Works

In addition, we are always looking for "success stories" from schools/districts that are using technology in innovative ways to help students, teachers and community members. Although our What Works department is written in-house and does not involve payment or bylines for the individuals and schools mentioned, it is a way for educators to get the word out about what's happening in their districts.

General Guidelines for Writers

Submissions and queries may be e-mailed to techlearning_editors@cmp.com. Please place query or article abstract in the body of the message. Articles may be attached to the e-mail in Microsoft Word or plain-text format.

Queries should be accompanied by a writing sample or published clips.

Hard-copy submissions without the author's e-mail address or a self-addressed, stamped envelope will receive no response. Manuscripts will not be returned unless requested and accompanied by an SASE.

Leave wide margins and space at the top and bottom of the paper. Double-space all text.

Place name, title and page numbers on all pages of your manuscript.

Include a work/home phone number and e-mail address on the manuscript or cover letter.

Do not send simultaneous submissions.

Allow at least 8 weeks for a response. Then if you have not heard from us, e-mail techlearning_editors@cmp.com and ask for the status of the manuscript.

Categories: Education

CONTACT: Editor
Technology & Learning
600 Harrison St
San Francisco CA 94107
E-mail: techlearning_editors@cmp.com
Website: www.techlearning.com

Tennis Magazine

Formal guidelines not available. Please read a number of issues to ascertain the publication's style and needs.

Send queries to address below.

Categories: Nonfiction—Physical Fitness—Recreation—Sports—Travel

CONTACT: Submissions Editor
Material: All
79 Madison Ave., 8th Fl.
New York NY 10016
Phone: 212-636-2700
Fax: 212-636-2730
E-mail: editors@tennis.com
Website: www.tennis.com

Tequesta

Purpose of the Journal

To present articles about our region's past in a scholarly format that is informative and, when possible, illustrated with historic images.

Distribution

3,000 copies of the journal are printed, reaching an estimated readership of 7,700, not including users in libraries and at other institutions receiving the journal in their collections.

History

The Historical Association of Southern Florida began publication of the journal in 1941, and it has been published annually since its beginning. *Tequesta* has become one of the most authoritative journals on Florida's history.

Presentation Style

Articles should be suitable for academic audiences with interest in our region's history. The editors strive for variety and balance so that each issue contains at least one article of interest to each reader.

Style Authority

The Chicago Manual of Style should be consulted on matters of style as this is the guide used by the editors of the journal. Webster's first choice is used when multiple spellings of a word are acceptable. Exceptions are made when the presentation form warrants.

Content

Articles should recall, retell and explore historic events, people, places and themes pertaining to southern Florida and the Caribbean. The journal covers Florida from about Lake Okee-chobee on down, coast to coast, and all countries in the Caribbean. Articles are generally presented as annotated narratives in third person or first person, and must include citations from primary research material, such as historic records, diaries and other documents. Exceptions are made when material warrants. Footnotes are required; bibliographies are optional.

Photographs

Photographic illustration is helpful but not necessary in *Tequesta*. Authors are encouraged to identify available accompanying visual material whenever possible and provide copies of such images when submitting manuscripts. Original documents and photographs that must be returned to their owners will be copied by the historical Museum of Southern Florida and handled according to the highest level of curatorial standards. Materials will be returned via certified delivery systems after publication of the journal.

Submission of Articles

A typed manuscript is requested with accompanying computer disk or CD copy of the article whenever possible. Manuscripts are also accepted via e-mail. Photographs and other illustrative materials, if identified, should be submitted with the manuscript (copies acceptable). Scanned photographs and images may be sent electronically as well, but prints will be required upon acceptance of the article for production. Articles may be submitted at any time throughout the year and should be 2,500 to 6,000 words in length.

The editorial staff of *Tequesta* strives to respond to writers who have submitted manuscripts in a timely fashion. Writers are asked to call if a timely response has not been made. The first response back will generally be an indication of whether the material is of interest for the publication and subsequent correspondence will indicate whether any additional research or writing is requested. If acceptable, the article becomes part of the pool of material undergoing production steps to ready them for publication. Articles are pulled from the pool and assigned to specific issues on an ongoing basis. The Editors at the Historical Museum of Southern Florida maintain the right for flexibility in deciding publication dates as geographical, thematic and seasonal concerns are considered.

Payment to authors for articles used includes the Historical Museum of Southern Florida's most sincere appreciation and 10 copies of the journal.

Standards

The editorial staff of *Tequesta* strives for the highest level of accuracy and fairness possible when presenting the past. Standard journalistic and research practices and principles should be adhered to at all times. Please refer to the *Associated Press Stylebook and Libel Manual* and *The Chicago Manual of Style* for any questions or doubt.

The Historical Association of Southern Florida disclaims any responsibility for errors in factual material or statements of opinions expressed by contributors.

A Word to Contributors

You are the lifeblood of *Tequesta*. Your time, energy and thoughtfulness in submitting a contribution are sincerely appreciated as we strive to spread interest in and understanding of our region's rich past.

Thank you. The Editors, *Tequesta*

Categories: Nonfiction—African-American—Arts—Asian-American—Biography—Civil War—Culture—Hispanic—History—Jewish Interest—Multicultural—Native American—Regional—Ethnic

CONTACT: Managing Editor
Material: Any
CONTACT: Dr. Paul S. George, Editor
Material: Any

101 W. Flagler St.
Miami FL 33130
Phone: 305-375-1492
Fax: 305-375-1609
E-mail: publications@historical-museum.org

Texas Gardener

TEXAS GARDENER is interested in articles containing practical, how-to information on gardening in Texas. Our readers want to know specific information on how to make gardening succeed in Texas' unique growing conditions. All articles must reflect this slant.

Our bimonthly magazine reaches over 25,000 home gardeners and covers vegetable and fruit production, flowers and ornamentals, landscape and trees, technique and features on gardeners.

We will accept both technical and feature articles. Technical articles should explain how to do some aspect of gardening (like graft pecans or plant bulbs) in a clear, easy-to-follow manner, and must be accurate. All technical articles should refer to experts in the field. Accompanying artwork such as photographs, illustrations or diagrams are essential.

Feature articles, including interviews or profiles of Texas gardeners, new gardening techniques or photo features should relate specifically to Texas. We will not publish general gardening essays. Personality profiles may be on hobby gardeners or professional horticulturists who are doing something unique.

In-depth articles should run 8 to 10 double-spaced type pages (approximately 1,400 to 1,750 words) though we encourage shorter, concise articles that run 4 to 6 typed pages (700 to 1,050 words). All articles are reviewed on speculation. Writers should submit a query and outline of a proposed article first, unless they wish to send a manuscript they have already completed. We accept articles on PC disks written in Microsoft Word for Windows or WordPerfect 5.0. Writers should include a list of areas of expertise and a writing sample or copy of published work.

Rights negotiable. We pay $25 for submission to Between Neighbors and $50 to $200 for feature articles. Payment is made upon publication and includes two copies of the issue in which the author's article appears. We respond to queries within 6 weeks. Please—no duplicate submissions.

We accept only high-quality color and clear black-and-white photographs. Slides are preferable, but prints, transparencies and contact sheets may be acceptable. Model releases and identification of subjects are required. Rights negotiable.

Categories: Nonfiction—Gardening

CONTACT: Chris S. Corby, Publisher, Editor
Material: Any
CONTACT: Michael Bracken, Managing Editor
Material: Any
PO Box 9005
Waco TX 76714
Phone: 254-848-9393
Fax: 254-848-9779
E-mail: suntex@aenbb.net
Website: www.texasgardener.com

Texas Highways,
The Travel Magazine of Texas

Subscribe to *Texas Highways*...Discover the Lone Star State!

Take a monthly page-by-page journey with Texas' top travel writers and photographers as they explore the best of Texas. A one-year subscription includes 12 issues of *Texas Highways* magazine. As a special gift, you'll receive the Texas Highways Travel Discount Card

FREE with your paid order. You can use it for travel savings around the state.

There's not another magazine like it anywhere. It's *Texas Highways*—the state's official travel magazine.

FREELANCE PHOTOGRAPHY PROCEDURES AND RATES

Submission Guidelines

Want to write or photograph for *Texas Highways*? The magazine always seeks new creative talent, and the links below will download guidelines that spell out how we work.

For a copy of our photographic wants list, please write, call or email Mike Murphy, photo editor, at PO Box 141009, Austin, TX 78714-1009.

Freelance Photographer's Guidelines:

The Travel Publications Section publishes all travel literature distributed by the Texas Department of Transportation. This includes *Texas Highways* magazine; the Texas State Travel Guide, state maps, various brochures; and ancillary products such as posters, calendars, and cards. Photographers submitting photography to the magazine automatically have the work considered for ancillary products as well. The following guidelines should help you understand how the travel publications section utilizes photographs.

Magazine Guidelines

Submit a query letter outlining your suggested picture-story topic or theme before sending actual photographs and captions, unless you're submitting work in response to our photographic wants list. The magazine is not responsible for unsolicited photographic materials! The magazine works at least three months in advance, and generally has an editorial calendar planned 18 to 24 months ahead.

1. After being notified of our interest, submit original color slides or transparencies (no color prints, negatives, or digital files) in 35mm or larger format. There should be enough images to fully illustrate the topic.

2. Photographs should depict an interesting Texas event, theme, site or activity. They also may depict interesting shopping, dining, or entertainment in the border areas of Mexico adjacent to Texas.

3. Your name and an identification number must be printed clearly on the mount of each slide or on the sleeve of each transparency. Each photograph must have its own unique number (not number 1, sheet 4 or top right, sheet 10). If you submit 100 slides in five sheets, they should be numbered from 1 to 100. If they have been numbered differently for some other purpose, they will be acceptable if each has a unique number keyed to the caption information. (Slides with neatly labeled mounts are okay, too.)

4. Include a caption sheet with the photographs, listing by identification number the location of each image, names of objects, identities of recognizable people (unless crowd or distance shots) and date taken. Send us the telephone number where we can reach you during office hours in case we have questions. The more information you send us the better. (Accuracy is very important, too.)

5. All photographs are submitted for speculation only. The magazine may choose to retain certain images for publication at a future date. In this case we would return the photographs in two parts—the "outtakes" right away, and the "selects" after publication.

6. If you include a delivery memo with your submission, please note we do not accept work "for examination only," nor do we pay holding fees. If you use a standard ASMP-style delivery memo that specifies holding fees, "for examination only," "negotiated fees," "payment before use," or other similar clauses, please alter and initial each one. If you can't do this, we can't consider your work.

Space Rates (Paid upon publication)

- $60 for individual photograph used less than 1/4 page.
- $80 for individual photograph used 1/4 to 1/2 page.
- $120 for individual photograph used 1/2 to 3/4 page.
- $150 for individual photograph used 3/4 to full page.
- $170 for individual photograph used full page.
- $300 for back cover
- $350 for two-page spread
- $400 for front cover

- $550 for wrap-around cover
- $15 additional for electronic usage on TexasHighways.com (low-res)
- $25 additional for use in Table of Contents

Usage Rights

Texas Highways purchases one-time use of photographs for the magazine, but reserves the right to use the same images for promotional purposes and/or reprints without additional compensation. Re-use of images for other purposes such as prints or calendars will be compensated separately—see rates below. *Texas Highways* expects six months' exclusivity for all work. (This means the same or like images must not appear in other publications distributed in Texas for six months—three months before magazine publication and three months after.)

Should we electronically reproduce an image we used in the magazine on our *Texas Highways* website, we'll pay $15 in addition to our normal space rates.

Ancillary Products Guidelines

Ancillary Products include calendars, posters, greeting cards, and other items. All of the guidelines stated above apply, with the exception of exclusivity. All work must come with 12 months of exclusivity—six months before scheduled publication and six months after.

Image Format

Transparencies submitted for *Texas Highways'* calendar must be horizontal. We prefer medium and large format images. Vertical and horizontal images will be considered for print and greeting card use.

Rates

(The following rates apply for each individual photograph)

Item	Rate	Quantity	Reprint Rate:
• Calendar cover	$350	20,000	
• Calendar, full page	$250		
• Poster	$250	1,000	$125
• Greeting card	$200	1,000	$100
• Other products are negotiated on an individual basis.			

Photographers must agree to reprints or work submitted will not be accepted. (Reprinting means printing additional copies in excess of the original quantity.) Photography used in producing ancillary products will be paid for upon publication.

All photographs will be returned after publication. The above rates include the right to reproduce the photograph in any related promotions. (Photographs will be used to advertise the products for sale.)

Image Content Considerations

1. All of the department's publications are meant to showcase Texas as a premier travel destination. Consequently, we are seeking photography taken under the best possible circumstances, whatever the topic. Given the choice of two images of the Alamo, one taken on a nice, sunny day, the other shot in gloomy, overcast weather; the sunny day image will have a greater chance of being used.

2. Litter (discarded cups, bottles, cans, scraps of paper) is unacceptable in any photo.

3. Models—when and where possible, involve people in photographs meant for use in travel literature. This generally enhances travel aspect of the imagery, allowing viewers to think "That could be me." Find and utilize people, of all races, that represent an American family image, including children and senior citizens. Models should be engaged in activity appropriate to the subject, and definitely not posing for the camera. Smiles are important—the people should look like they are enjoying themselves. Spontaneity is what we're seeking, not stilted, posed shots of someone pointing at some distant attraction. Model (and property) releases are not required, but are always good protection for any photographer.

4. When automobiles are in a scene, attempt to use late-model vehicles. Older cars, unless antiques or classic cars, make fresh photos seem dated. Avoid large trucks, but pickups, RVs, and trailers are fine.

5. Technique should be appropriate for the subject. For landscapes, use the largest format and/or slowest film available. When shooting indoors, light areas so they will look natural; and balance your light with existing light. On-camera flash by itself won't do the job. High-speed film is okay for dimly lit events with lots of action, but

otherwise we prefer the slower films such as Fuji Velvia and Provia, Kodachrome, and Kodak's newest E-6 films. Film should be balanced to the light to render natural appearing color—don't shoot daylight film under tungsten lights and expect natural color. Also, when shooting under overcast conditions it is appropriate to use a warming filter on daylight film.

6. Regional diversity—for travel promotion purposes, Texas is divided into seven regions: Big Bend Country, Panhandle Plains, Prairies and Lakes, Piney Woods, Gulf Coast, South Texas Plains, and Hill Country. We seek images that showcase the best of each region, and take care not to over-emphasize any one region. When we select images for the calendar, we include at least one photo from each region and won't use more than three photos from any one region. Please help us highlight the state's geographic diversity by sending us compelling images from every region.

Work will be reviewed promptly for potential usage in any of the department's travel publications. All photographs will be returned by Certified Mail.

WRITERS' GUIDELINES AND RATE INFORMATION

Texas Highways, the official travel magazine of Texas by designation of the Texas Legislature in 1974, "encourages travel within the state and tells the Texas story to readers around the world." The magazine, which is published by the Travel Division of the Texas Department of Transportation, has gained wide respect, as well as numerous awards, for its stories and outstanding photography. The magazine has a circulation of approximately 250,000, with subscribers in every state in the nation and more than 80 countries. Surveys tell us that a majority of our readers are 60 and older, and that they especially like coverage of Texas scenery, history, small towns, and out-of-the-way places.

Approximately 80% of our stories and photographs come from freelance contributors.

Query Guidelines:

1. Submit a query letter outlining your proposed feature with a brief description of the scope and slant. The letter should give us some idea of the style and tone you propose to take in the story. Do not send the completed story until requested to do so. It helps to include copies of previously published articles to show your writing style. Keep in mind, however, that *Texas Highways* never approves a story idea based on how much or where you may have published. The subject matter, slant, and style must be right for us.

We are not responsible for unsolicited material. We do not accept queries over the telephone or by email. We do not publish poetry or fiction.

2. Before you query, review the indexes found in the December issues of the magazine and online at www.texashighways.com. You can find back issues of *Texas Highways* at most libraries. Since we do not publish two features on the same subject within five years, the indexes are useful in identifying previously published subjects.

3. Subjects should focus on things to do or places to see in Texas. Include historical, cultural, and geographic aspects if appropriate. Text should be meticulously researched. Include anecdotes, historical references, quotations, and, where relevant, geologic, botanical, and zoological information.

4. We do not commission articles. Material is submitted on speculation only. The author warrants that the work is his or her original creation.

5. *Texas Highways* purchases first North American serial rights, and may reproduce the work in printed and/or electronic form.

6. Include a SASE, and allow up to eight weeks for a reply.

Manuscript Guidelines:

1. After we notify you of our interest, submit manuscripts typed, double-spaced, standard six-inch line on white paper. Length will vary according to topic (generally about 1,200 words), but we prefer too much rather than not enough. Again, material is submitted on speculation only.

2. Good research is imperative. Get everything right the first time. Check and doublecheck facts, dates, spellings, directions, distances, heights, all matters of historical record, telephone numbers—check and recheck everything. Assume nothing: Ask individuals how to spell their names. Do not rely on friends, relatives, telephone books, newspaper articles, or programs for an event. Put a small check mark in ink over names, addresses, times, numbers, etc. (first occurrence only), so that we know that you have verified them beyond a doubt.

3. Read a few back issues of *Texas Highways* before submitting your story. The approach should be informal, with a polished, readable quality. Write a strong lead and ending. Use active constructions and strong verbs. Avoid the passive voice. Avoid the "to be" verb form as much as possible. We welcome a sense of humor when and if appropriate.

4. Include the names and phone numbers of all persons quoted or used as information sources for your article. Check the spelling of all names in your story, then check again. Include a list of published sources, as well. *Texas Highways* customarily fact-checks all aspects of every story. We need a telephone number where we can reach you between 8 am and 5 pm.

5. If, in the course of researching an article, you find interesting illustrations on the subject such as old photographs, period engravings, maps, or paintings, please make a note of what they are, what publication they're in, and who owns the copyright, if any. Please include this information with your feature.

6. If you write about a place, please send us the most recent descriptive literature. If you write about an event, send us the latest program.

7. Send information for the Essentials box with your manuscript. Include dates, times, locations, prices, and instructions on how to get to a place or event. Be sure to include information on facilities for the handicapped. If you prepare a historical feature, furnish names or descriptions of sources (books, old letters, museum displays, etc.). Refer to recent issues of the magazine for the format and type of facts needed.

8. Please submit a brief biographical sketch that we might edit and use with your story.

9. Please submit two or three title suggestions with your story.

10. We expect you to write to the editors' specifications. When necessary, we expect you to rewrite an article at least once.

11. Except for certain in-house preferences, we use *The Random House Dictionary of the English Language*, Second Edition Unabridged as our standard reference.

12. When your article is scheduled, an editor will work with you to resolve ambiguities and answer questions. The editor may request that you add material or rewrite portions of the text to prepare the story for publication. We cannot promise that an article will be published when scheduled.

Rates (We pay on acceptance.):

1. *Texas Highways* pays approximately 40 to 50 cents per word. After we accept your manuscript, we will ask you to send us an invoice that includes the subject matter of your article, and your name, address, a unique invoice number, and social security number. Payment takes about four weeks.

2. Please type your name, address, and telephone number on the front of your manuscript. Let us know immediately if your address or phone number changes.

Remember:

—Submit a list of your sources, including names, addresses, and telephone numbers. If you have used published sources, provide that information as well. *Texas Highways* customarily fact-checks every aspect of every story.

—Submit brochures, maps, charts, or other information that will help us verify what you have written or help us in illustrating your material.

—Keep a copy of your article. Manuscripts may get lost in the mail or in our office.

—Always check and double-check your information. *Texas Highways* strives to be accurate on all counts, including spelling of names, historical facts, highway numbers, directions, place names, and caption details. Because we do not have the staff to retrace the steps of every author, we depend on YOU for much of that accuracy. Please take the time to ensure that you have included all the information we need to keep your feature correct. Thank you.

Writing for Texas Highways
By Jack Lowry, Editor

The first thing we think of when we review a query is our readership: Is the proposed subject of interest to our readers? Familiarize yourself with the magazine, with the kinds of stories we publish, and with topics we have covered recently.

Work on your writing. We like strong leads that draw in the reader immediately. We look for writing that is accurate, clear, and concise. Think about ways to tighten your writing.

For example, use adjectives and adverbs sparingly; opt for nouns instead. Favor the concrete over the abstract. Get to the point. Specify. Avoid passive constructions and the "to be" form as much as possible. When appropriate, use anecdotes, quotes, wordplay, examples, and contrast. In general, your writing should help information and ideas flow smoothly for the reader.

Keep our production cycle in mind. Queries frequently arrive too late for us to consider. For most features, we must work at least a year in advance, primarily because we schedule seasonal photography one year for publication the following year.

Expect anything you send us to be edited and possibly returned (at least once) for a rewrite.

What do we not want? Avoid superlatives that sound like advertising copy. Don't use words whose meanings you don't really understand. Avoid words whose meanings have become distorted through general (over)usage: "Unique" is perhaps the most common example in travel writing.

Don't forget the basics—who, what, when, where, why, and how.

Categories: Nonfiction—History—Outdoors—Recreation—Regional—Travel

CONTACT: Jack Lowry, Editor
Material: All
CONTACT: Jill Lawless, Managing Editor
Material: All
CONTACT: Michael A. Murphy, Photo Editor
E-mail: mmurph1@ dot.state.tx.us
Material: Photos
PO Box 141009
Austin TX 78714-1009
Phone: 512-486-5858
Fax: 512-486-5879
E-mail: letters07@texashighways.com
Courier: 150 E. Riverside Drive
Austin TX 78704
Website: www.texashighways.com

Texas Journey

Please refer to *New Mexico Journey*.

Texas Parks & Wildlife

Texas Parks & Wildlife, the Outdoor Magazine of Texas, is a monthly magazine published by Texas Parks and Wildlife. We are looking for strong, well-researched and eloquently written stories on all aspects of the Texas outdoors. *Texas Parks & Wildlife* covers state park destinations, conservation issues, trends, and such outdoor activities as fishing, hunting, camping, bicycling, canoeing and hiking. Keep in mind that we publish many features that don't necessarily fit into the categories listed below.

Departments
• Scout—This front-of-the-book department is a collection of short (100-700 words), lively articles covering news and trends in the outdoors across the state. We particularly welcome submissions from freelancers for this department.
• Skill Builder—How do you tie fishing knots? Train your dog to avoid rattlesnakes? Pack a first-aid kit? These authoritative how-to lessons (700 words) brief readers on a variety of outdoor skills.
• Legend, Lore and Legacy—As the title indicates, this award-winning department (1,000 words) encompasses a wide range of stories. We've run profiles of people who've left a legacy on the Texas outdoors (wildlife artist Orville Rice, duck hunting guide and conservationist Jimmy Reel); legends (tales of the Big Thicket), and Lore (the horned lizard and other natural history pieces).

Features
• State Parks—These destination pieces (1,500-2,500 words) cover a Texas state park in a compelling way that would make readers consider visiting it. Recent stories have included "Glorious Goliad," bass fishing at Possum Kingdom and hiking in Pedernales. Stories should convey a strong sense of place, weave in the natural history of the park and describe the primary activities. Include a sidebar on facilities, how to get there, and reservations phone number.

Hunting and Fishing stories
• Conservation stories—Recent assignments have included "Crabbers Sing the Blues: A Losing Season for Blue Crab" and a feature on the fate of the prairie dog. These pieces must be informed by good science and reflect a balanced approach. Include quotes from experts at TPW, reliable research universities or elsewhere.

General Tips
• We prefer that stories be written in an active rather than passive voice.
• Use present tense when possible.
• Use good quotes. Quotes from experts, whether from inside or outside TPW, add much to the reliability of a story. A pithy quote is also an excellent way to help paint a picture for the reader. Sidebars, subheads and other devices for breaking up copy are welcome.

Hunting/Fishing Writers' Guidelines
Be aware of the magazine's audience. Hunting and fishing stories should emphasize the challenges, pleasures and rewards of the entire outdoor experience rather than simply the taking of game. Many of our readers are neither hunters nor anti-hunters, and we want to build as many bridges as we can with that group, showing them that hunters share many of their interests. Readers love to learn about a hunter or fisher who is passionately interested in wildlife-viewing, wildflowers or other outdoor-related activities. Such experiences can be included either in the main body of the story or in a sidebar, as appropriate. If you enjoy watching neotropical migratory birds while spring turkey hunting, you could do a sidebar on what species you saw and that can probably be seen in the area covered in the story, and give birding tips. Other ideas for sidebars include:
• Information about requirements for hunting or fishing on public lands the best places to hunt or fish for a particular species on public or private lands tips on the best hunting or fishing methods (unless that is the main thrust of the story) conservation programs or successes related to the species in the article (TPW and others) threats to the continued survival of the species in the article and what is being done about them, especially if hunter/fisher groups or funds generated by hunters and fishers are helping fund the effort experiences related to introducing someone to the outdoors recipes for preparing wild game or fish.

Harvesting of Game—Since TPW magazine is a general-interest, family-oriented magazine, hunting and fishing stories, while dealing honestly and matter-of-factly, with the fact that game is harvested, should take care to avoid emphasizing body count and killing. It is usually not necessary to give details on the methods used to harvest animals. It is sufficient to say that the animal was shot, or boated, or released or that the hunt ended with the successful taking of the game (or not). Naturally, articles dealing with specific hunting or fishing techniques will go into considerable detail of this type, but it should be done tastefully. If you provide photos, no pictures of mounted animals, please see photo guidelines.

Use care in dealing with issues that affect conservation. Hunters and fishers are as concerned as anyone with caring for game and the habitat where it lives, and this needs to come through in articles in the way we show respect for game and the environment, not to mention the sensibilities of our readers. Avoid graphic descriptions of blood and gore while being honest about the fact that game is harvested. Show respect for the game in both text and photographs. Some examples of ways to handle this follow:

• Example 1:

No: Among the five of us, we had 50 dead geese piled up on the ground.

Yes: Each of us took our limit of geese.

(The body count is not important, but the way you treat harvested game is.)

• Example 2:

No: On the way to my blind, I killed a rattlesnake.

Yes: On the way to my blind, I was startled by a rattlesnake.

(You may indeed kill a rattlesnake while hunting, but we don't want to hear about it, nor do we want to rile readers who object to such behavior.)

• Example 3:

No: I cut a limb from a tree to probe for hidden obstacles in the water.

Yes: I used a stick to probe for hidden obstacles in the water.

(Harming vegetation is forbidden on most public land, and many private landowners don't appreciate it, either.)

Photography/Artwork Guidelines

Transparencies in any format 35mm or larger are acceptable. Photographers may submit duplicate transparencies for consideration, provided that originals can be furnished on request. Each transparency must be labeled, stamped or marked with the photographer's name and address. A caption or description of each transparency must be included with every submission. All transparencies will be returned if this is not done.

Properly exposed transparencies are preferred. One-half stop overexposed is better than underexposure. Do not underexpose for deep color saturation.

Make it your goal to submit transparencies that are as good or better than those you see in our magazine. Edit your photos carefully before submitting. More is not better. Submit no more than 80 transparencies per story. Use separate slide file pages for each story submission so slides can be reviewed and those selected can be placed in the respective story folder. Those rejected will be returned.

Photographs of a location such as a state park should evoke a sense of place. Photos should show an intelligent selection of subject and time of day. For hunting stories, no pictures of mounted animals, please.

Artwork to be published will be on assignment to illustrate a specific story. Contact the magazine art director for size and medium limitations. Payment to be determined. We occasionally use previously published photos in departments such as the letters page. Payment for use of the photos will be one-half the original payment.

Payment photo schedule:

• Front cover: $500
• Wraparound and gatefold: $400
• Other covers: $250
• Inside color—rate per individual picture
• More than a full page: $180
• Three-quarters to a full page: $165
• One-half to three-quarters of a page: $125
• Less than one-half page: $80
• Black and white: $50 for all sizes

Payment is upon publication. The magazine retains possession of color separations for all photos and art published. No original separations leave the magazine, but duplicates are available at cost. Occasionally, other publications request the use of *Texas Parks & Wildlife* separations. No freelance material will be released without the permission of the contributor, but it will be the responsibility of the contributor to arrange for compensation from the requesting publication.

Texas Parks & Wildlife will exercise care in the handling of all material received, but the department will not be responsible for loss or damage. Color separator is responsible for the care of color photos and art while in his possession.

Submitting

Please submit assigned articles typed and double-spaced. Submit e-mailed as an attachment or pasted in as text. Or submit on a 3 1/2-inch disk, either Mac or DOS format. Be sure your name, address, and phone number are on your manuscript. Please submit queries with published clips.

Please address your submissions to the appropriate editor, listed below:

Categories: Nonfiction—Adventure—Boating—Conservation—Environment—Fishing—Outdoors—Regional—Travel—Camping—Hiking—Hunting—State Parks—Wildlife

CONTACT: Robert Macias, Editorial Director
Material: All
CONTACT: Andres Carrasco, Photo Editor
Material: All Photos
CONTACT: Randy Brunicki, Publisher
Material: All Other
CONTACT: Charles Lohrmann, Managing Editor
Material: All Other
3000 S. IH-35, Ste. 120
Austin TX 78704
Phone: 512-912-7000
Fax: 512-707-1913
E-mail: magazine@tpwd.state.tx.us
Website: www.tpwmagazine.com

THEMA

Thema

SUBMISSIONS

Schedule: See our website for upcoming premises and deadlines for submission.

The premise must be an integral part of the plot, not necessarily the central theme but not merely incidental. Fewer than 20 double-spaced pages preferred. Indicate premise on title page.

Because manuscripts are evaluated in blind review, do NOT put author's name on any page beyond the title page. Indicate target theme in cover letter or on first page of manuscript. Include self-addressed, stamped envelope (SASE) with each submission. Rejected manuscripts unaccompanied by an SASE will not be returned. Response time: 3 months after premise deadline.

Payment: short story, $25; short-short piece (up to 1000 words), $10; poem, $10; artwork, $10. Copyright reverts to author after publication.

SHORT STORIES

All types welcome, both traditional and experimental.

What we like: A carefully constructed plot; good character delineation; clever plot twists.

What we don't like: bedroom/bathroom profanity.

Why we object to bedroom/bathroom profanity: It's boring! Writers should be more creative than to depend on the same tired and dubious language crutches to express surprise, disdain, shock, bemusement, anger, sadness, and other emotions.

Such profanity, used in excess, often serves as a camouflage for a weak plot. If the plot is good, the story can be told much more effectively in nonscatologic language even though a character in the story may be sleazy. Stories of lasting quality rarely need it.

POETRY

All types of poetic form welcome. Submit no more than three poems per theme, please.

What we like: poems that are thoughtfully constructed and carefully distilled.

What we don't like: sexually explicit wording. Subtlety is more creative.

ART

MUST FIT THEME—Cover: color illustration/photograph; inside art: black and white (pen and ink; computer-generated; photograph) Submit xerographic copy or 5" x 7" photograph of artwork.

SAMPLE COPIES

Sample copies of THEMA are available at $8.00 per copy. Subscription rate: $16.00 per year for three issues ($20.00, foreign addresses). Make check payable to "THEMA Literary Society" and mail to the address below.

NOTE: For all submissions, include SASE and indicate premise.

Categories: Fiction—Arts—Cartoons—Literature—Poetry—Short Stories

CONTACT: Virginia Howard, Editor
Material: Short Stories and/or Art
CONTACT: Gail Howard, Poetry Editor
Material: Poetry
PO Box 8747
Metairie LA 70011-8747
Phone: 504-887-1263
Website: members.cox.net/thema

Thoughts For All Seasons
The Magazine of Epigrams

Thoughts for All Seasons:
The Magazine of Epigrams

The guidelines for writing epigrams published in Vol. 5 of TFAS (2000 issue) are still applicable.

1) Is the statement (or question) original, or have we heard it somewhere before?

2) If the stem of the statement (question) is an old saw, has the author put an interesting twist on it?

3) Is the statement (question) intelligible, or are we uncertain about the author's intentions?

4) Is the statement (question) succinct, or is it overly wordy?

5) Is the statement (question) funny, or is it preachy?

6) If it is not funny, is it a profound and original truth?

7) If the statement (question) is silly, is it at least a good play on words?

8) Is it a dancing thought, or a sinking thought?

9) Is it sour grapes, or is it wine?

10) Is it outrageous, or is merely tasteless?

Volume 6 (2006) will mark the centennial of *Devil's Dictionary* by Abrose Bierce. Other themes (volume 6) will include satirical tips for good health, and new lyrics for old songs.

Poetry Guidelines

Suggestions: rhymed quatrains, original limericks, and longer poems including nonsense verse with good imagery. Tone may be serious or humorous. (We do not accept Haiku.) For more detail, consult any back issue of TFAS.

Readers who are interested in a more technical analysis may wish to refer to "A Taxonomy of Epigrams" by M. P. Richard in the Autumn 1989 issue of *Verbatim: The Language Quarterly.*

Categories: Humor—Language—Poetry—Satire—Society—Writing

CONTACT: Prof. Michel P. Richard, Editor
Material: All
86 Leland Rd.
Becket, MA 01223
Phone: 413-623-0174

Threads

Threads is a bimonthly, how-to magazine celebrating garment sewing, design and embellishment, machine and hand embroidery, and related crafts. We're always looking for new authors to help us bring fresh, exciting ideas, techniques, and information to our readers. If you've never written anything before, don't worry. We work with many first-time authors and are far more interested in your excellence in your craft and your innovative ideas than in your ability to spell or punctuate a sentence (that's where our editors come in).

We're interested in articles about construction and embellishment techniques, materials, tools, and design. We want the magazine to include both classic and innovative techniques, which produce the best results in the most streamlined manner possible. In particular, we're interested in articles on dressmaking, tailoring, patternmaking and alteration, fabrics, fitting, and embellishment. We're also looking for related articles on making interesting closures and buttons, and making unusual fabrics, as well as on intriguing ways of finishing edges and hems.

Our readers span the gamut of skill levels, from those just turning—or returning—to sewing, to those with advanced skills who may even be earning a living at their craft. To accommodate this broad range of readers, as well as those who work in or outside the home and have very little time for their favorite pastime, *Threads* includes articles geared toward several skill levels and degrees of complexity.

Threads has a paid circulation of about 150,000 readers. The magazine is four-color throughout, and its feature articles are uninterrupted by advertising.

Our Point of View: Our emphasis is on teaching techniques, developing skills, understanding finishing details, and providing ample inspiration to help readers begin to create their own uses for this information. We focus on providing the basic information readers need in order to sew successfully.

We are a reader-written magazine (we don't use freelance writers) that looks at techniques and processes from the viewpoint of the curious, practical craftsperson who wants to know how and why things work. We want to know, for example, how and why you make a bound buttonhole or set in a sleeve the way you do, whether or not your method conforms to a classic technique. We're interested in the full range of technical information, from what you've discovered in your own workroom to the methods used in the garment industry to produce high-end, ready-to-wear and couture clothing. Our goal is to give home sewers the knowledge they need to create professional-looking garments and projects and have fun in the process.

Threads presents casually elegant, beautifully constructed, wearable garments and accessories. We're interested in exceptional examples of the techniques we present, whether their design is classic or cutting-edge. Because we feel that inspiring our readers is key, we work hard to create lively photography, illustrations, and layouts that enhance the technical information presented and make the magazine both accessible and a pleasure to read.

Article Proposals: If you would like to write an article for *Threads*, start by sending us a proposal. Here's what to include: a brief one- or two-paragraph summary of the article you have in mind; an outline of the ideas and points you'll cover; sample photographs of work illustrating the topic (quick snapshots are fine) or supporting fabric swatches if you have them. The idea is to give us an overview of what you're proposing with enough details and supporting information to help us carefully consider your proposal.

Manuscripts: When we decide to pursue the article you're proposing, we'll contact you by phone or mail to clarify any questions and further explore the outline that you provided and discuss a timeline for the article delivery. Authors are not expected to provide photography or illustrations.

Payment: Once we accept your article and have all of the necessary materials in hand, we'll agree upon a fee and send you a contract. We are buying exclusive first publication rights, the right to republish all or part of the article in print, electronic or other media, the right to use it on the *Threads'* Web site if we choose, and the right to excerpt it in promotional pieces for The Taunton Press. We have the right to edit, revise, and adapt the article as we deem appropriate. Once the contract has been signed and we receive your manuscript, we usually advance a partial payment to you. We pay the balance when we've completed the editorial process, and you have sent us all samples (if they were agreed upon in initial discussions). We'll also send you two complimentary copies of the issue when it has been published.

We would be happy to discuss article ideas with you. If you have questions, feel free to call us at 800-309-9262 (from outside the United States, call 203-426-8171). If you are ready to submit a proposal, you may send it via postal mail or email, whichever you prefer, using the addresses printed on the reverse.

We appreciate your interest in *Threads.*

Categories: Nonfiction—Crafts/Hobbies

CONTACT: Articles Editor
Material: All
The Taunton Press
63 South Main St.
PO Box 5506
Newtown, CT 06470-5506
Phone: 203-426-8171
Fax: 203-270-6753
E-mail: th@taunton.com
Website: www.taunton.com

The Threepenny Review

1. At present *The Threepenny Review* is paying $400 per story or article, $200 per poem or Table Talk piece. In addition, each writer gets a year's free subscription and may buy extra copies of the issue in which his or her item appears at a discounted rate ($3.00 each, including postage).

2. All manuscripts should be submitted with a stamped, self-addressed envelope.

3. All articles should be double-spaced, with at least one-inch margins. Critical articles should be about 1500 to 3000 words, stories and memoirs 4000 words or less, and poetry 100 lines or less. Exceptions are possible.

4. Xeroxes and computer-printed copies are acceptable (letter quality preferred to dot matrix). We will not, however, consider simultaneous submissions.

5. Critical articles that deal with books, theater, films, etc., should cite these occasions at the front of the article in the following form:
• Theater Piece by Playwright.
• Theater, City
• Season 20_ _
• Book Title
• by Author's Name, Publisher, Year Published, Price (cloth) (paper).

Remember that *The Threepenny Review* is quarterly and national; therefore each "review" should actually be an essay, broader than the specific event it covers and of interest to people who cannot see the event.

6. Writers will be consulted on all significant editing done on their articles, and will have the opportunity to proofread galleys for typographical errors.

7. Response time for unsolicited manuscripts ranges from three weeks to two months.

8. It is recommended that those submitting work for the first time to *The Threepenny Review* take a look at a sample copy beforehand. Individual copies are available from the publisher for $12.00 each (cover price plus $5.00 postage/handling).

9. We do not review manuscripts September through December.

Categories: Fiction—Nonfiction—Arts—Book Reviews—Dance—Drama—Film/Video—General Interest—History—Literature—Music—Poetry—Politics—Short Stories—Essay—Personal Experience—Memoirs

CONTACT: Wendy Lesser, Editor
Material: All
PO Box 9131
Berkeley CA 94709
Phone: 510-849-4545

Tikkun

Bimonthly magazine covering politics, culture and society. 95% freelance written. Established in 1986. Circulation 20,000. Publishes manuscripts an average of six months after acceptance. Byline given. Kill fee varies, buys first North American serial rights. Editorial lead time two months. Submit seasonal material four months in advance. Reports in six months. Sample copy for $8.00.

Nonfiction: Book excerpts, essays, general interest, historic/nostalgic, humor, opinion, personal experience, photo feature, religious, political analysis, media and cultural analysis. Prints 25 manuscripts/yr. Send complete manuscript. Length: 2,000 words maximum.

Photos: State availability of photos with submissions. Reviews contact sheets or prints. Negotiates payment individually. Buys one-time rights.

Fiction: Contact Thane Rosenbaum, fiction editor, 60 W 87th, NY, NY 10024. Ethnic, historical, humorous, novel excerpts, religious, romance, slice-of-life vignettes. Prints 6 manuscripts/yr.

Poetry: Avant-garde, free verse, Haiku, light verse traditional. Submit a maximum of five poems. Long poems cannot be considered. *Tikkun* does not pay for poetry.

Tips: Internships are available. Write to *Tikkun* for information. Enclose a résumé and a self-revealing letter. Read magazine as writer's guidelines.

Telephone Contact: Jodi Perelman, Assistant to the Editor
Categories: Fiction—Nonfiction—Culture—Economics—Education—Environment—Feminism—Government—Jewish Interest—Literature—Poetry—Politics—Psychology—Religion—Sexuality—Society—Spiritual—Writing—Humor

CONTACT: Michael Lerner, Editor
Material: All
CONTACT: Thane Rosenbaum, Fiction Editor
Material: Fiction (to address above)
CONTACT: Josh Weiner, Assistant Poetry Editor
Material: Poetry
2107 Van Ness Ave. Ste. 302
San Francisco CA 94109
Phone: 415-575-1200
Fax: 415-575-1434
E-mail: magazine@tikkun.org

Timber Frame Homes

Please refer to *Log Home Living* magazine

TimBookTu

Submission Guidelines

The TimBookTu Web Page is a non-paying web site provided for writers, poets, and essayists to publish their work on the World Wide Web. All works should be by or of interest to African-Americans. While the work featured on the site is geared towards African-American writing and culture, TimBookTu will accept work from other cultures as long as the work has an Afrocentric nature to it.

Stories and poems published by TimBookTu should be suitable for the general public. While TimBookTu does not attempt to censor any work, works using strong language or strong sexual content will be considered and a message such as: Advisory. Contains strong language will be added in the table of contents. Submissions deemed to be too explicit, pornographic, too violent, racist or hate-filled, or any work considered distasteful by the Advisory Committee, will be refused for publication.

Due to volume of submissions, only three (3) works from each author will be published each month and they should reach the editor at least two (2) months prior to the posting date as indicated on the main page of the website. This will allow adequate time for the submissions to be prepared and for any adjustments to the selections. You are welcome to send more than three pieces at a time but the other pieces will be held and published the following months.

Emphasis should always be on content and not form. If the writing submitted does not translate well into HTML code, TimBookTu will contact the writer with suggestions for changes. TimBookTu will not correct for grammar but will make only minor spelling corrections primarily in essays and fiction. Since poets often use poetic license for effect, spelling will be left as is unless it is an obvious misspelling. SO, PLEASE SPELL CHECK YOUR WORK AND HAVE SOMEONE PROOF IT BEFORE SUBMITTING. Please refrain from using all capital letters in your submissions. Submissions with too many syntax or spelling errors, will be returned to the author for correction and revision.

If upon viewing your work you wish to make corrections, please contact the editor (editor@timbooktu.com).

TimBookTu is copyrighted. Submitted work remains the property of the creator and is self-copyrighted. To find out more about copyrights, visit the U.S. Copyright's Office FAQ Page. While work submitted remains the property of the writer, the design and layout of the web pages are the property of TimBookTu.

Before submitting, please review TimBookTu's Disclaimer.

How to Prepare Your Work to be Published.

Send your story, poem, or essay to TimBookTu and the required HTML codes will be added by the editor to make your work readable on the World Wide Web. Or you can send it as an HTML document. We will make every attempt to print it in the same style as submitted.

We will add your title, byline, and sometimes a brief description of the work to the TimBookTu Table of Contents page. Your work(s) will remain on the TimBookTu for at least 90 days. After that time the works will be archived. Your work can be removed from TimBookTu at any time upon request of the author.

Using the TimBookTu Submission Form

You can submit your submission(s) via the TimBookTu Submission Form, available on the website. This form will prompt you for the necessary information and send your work to the editor automatically. This is the preferred method of sending your submissions. If you have very long submissions, such as an essay or fictional piece, use the E-Mail Submission information below. However, you can use the other methods indicated below for all submissions. If you choose to use the submission form, disregard the following information and go straight to the form.

E-Mail Submission

Please send your work(s) in ascii text format or Microsoft Word format. Your work(s) can be sent as an attachment to your e-mail or within the body of the e-mail. If problems occur sending it, please let the editor (editor@timbooktu.com) know and an alternative method will be suggested.

The format of your work is important:

The subject line of the E-Mail should specify "TimBookTu Submission."

The message should show:
Your full name
Pen name or name to be used on work
Your e-mail address and your mailing address
City, State, Zip Code
Home Phone (optional)
Work Phone (optional)
Then:
Title of Work
Type of Work (i.e. Poetry, Essay, Fiction, Book Excerpt, etc)
Name of author or whatever name you want to accompany work.
Start your work with: "Start of work."
Two blank lines.
Then begin the story or poem.
Two blank lines.
End your work with the words "End of Work."
Copyright date or date of creation.

Please make sure to indicate whether your work is poetry, a short story, an essay, or other types of work. This will help the editor to place it under the right category. If untitled, please so indicate. If any of the above is omitted, it may delay posting of your work.

Please provide a brief biographical sketch and a photograph to be included with work. The photo is optional and if you do not wish to have one included, please indicate that in your submittal. If your photo is not in electronic form (jpeg, gif, or bmp), you can send it via regular mail and TimBookTu will scan the photo and return it to you. Be sure to include a self-addressed, stamped envelope, if you would like the photo returned.

Note: No personal info such as address, phone number, etc. will be displayed on the author's bio page unless you request it. Only the e-mail address will be used to allow readers to contact you.

See mailing info below.

Regular Mail Submission

If you do not have a way to e-mail your work, you can send a 3-1/4" floppy disk with your submissions saved in the Microsoft Word or Ascii text format. If a disk is not possible, typed submissions will be accepted. However, typed submissions may take longer to be posted. Send all submissions via regular mail to the following:

TimBookTu, PO Box 933, Mobile, Alabama 36601-0933.

Please do not send your original manuscripts as they cannot be returned. Photos will be returned if accompanied by a self-addressed, stamped envelope.

Categories: African-American—Culture

CONTACT: Editor
E-mail: editor@timbooktu.com
Website: www.timbooktu.com

Timeline

TIMELINE is an illustrated magazine published quarterly by the Ohio Historical Society. TIMELINE's editorial content embraces the fields of history, prehistory, and the natural sciences, and is directed towards readers located in the Midwest.

Each issue features lively, authoritative, and well-illustrated articles, photo essays, and occasional reviews, and special departments.

Since its inception in 1984, TIMELINE has received numerous

local, state, and national awards. Among them are Printing and Publishing Executive's Gold Ink Award, American Association of Museums Award of Merit, Ohio Museums Association Award of Excellence, Ohioana Award for Editorial Excellence, Printing Association of America Award of Merit, and American Association for State and Local History Award of Merit.

TIMELINE is distributed to members of the Ohio Historical Society and to public libraries throughout Ohio. Single copies may be obtained from the Ohio Historical Society or from selected retail outlets.

Manuscripts

The editors are accepting manuscripts of 1,500 to 6,000 words related to the history; prehistory; and natural history of Ohio and to the broader cultural and natural environments of which Ohio is a part. Articles with a regional or national focus also will be considered. Suitable topics include the traditional fields of political, economic, military, and social history; biography; the history of science and technology; archaeology and anthropology; architecture; the fine and decorative arts; and the natural sciences including botany, geology, zoology, ecology and paleontology.

In addition to full-length feature articles, shorter, more sharply focused vignettes of 500 to 1,000 words will be considered.

Both feature-length manuscripts and short submissions should be susceptible to high-quality black-and-white or color illustrations and will be evaluated, in part, on that basis. Authors are encouraged to include photographic prints, transparencies, or photocopies concurrently with submission of manuscripts and will be expected to supply the editors with suggestions for supplementary illustration.

Unless otherwise specified, the publishers will purchase one-time North American serial rights to both manuscripts and illustrations. Manuscript fees are negotiable and will be paid upon acceptance. Photographs and transparencies will be purchased separately. The editors reserve the right to edit all accepted manuscripts to conform to the style and usages of TIMELINE. For further information in this regard, please refer to the guidelines.

Manuscript Guidelines

• Articles are intended for the lay person, not the specialist.

• Writing style should be simple and direct. Vary the arrangements of sentence elements, paragraph length, and sentence length. Avoid one-sentence paragraphs.

• Avoid jargon and non-standard English. Limit use of technical terms to those necessary for clarity and accuracy.

• Although formal documentation will not be reproduced, manuscripts should be accompanied by a list of sources and suggestions for further reading. Limit internal documentation.

• Graphics should be accompanied by captions that do not duplicate textual information. Authors are expected to provide suggestions for illustrations.

• Avoid first-person narratives except in special cases where the first-person point-of-view is an essential element of the manuscript.

• Avoid extended direct quotations and parenthetical materials. TIMELINE does not accept fiction, fictionalizations, or poetry.

• Where questions of style or usage arise, refer to *The Chicago Manual of Style*.

• Manuscripts should be 1,500 to 6,000 words in length. Longer manuscripts will be considered if suitable for serialization.

• If unsure of a manuscript's suitability, authors are encouraged to submit outlines in advance.

• If your manuscript is prepared on an IBM-compatible, Apple II, or Macintosh computer system, please indicate this in your submission letter.

Illustrations

TIMELINE features photo essays related to the subject areas described. In addition, some freelance photographic contracts for article illustration may be offered from time to time. Photographers and illustrators are encouraged to submit portfolios to the editors for consideration. Proposals for photo essays should be submitted in advance. Appropriate model releases are required.

Categories: History—Regional

CONTACT: David A. Simmon, Editor
Material: All
1982 Velma Ave.
Columbus OH 43211-2497
Phone: 614-297-2360
Fax: 614-297-2367

Times News Service

Thank you for your interest in writing for the *Times News Service*, which serves Army Times, Navy Times, Marine Corps Times and Air Force Times, with a combined worldwide circulation of approximately 250,000. We are always interested in receiving freelance articles that are informative, helpful, entertaining and stimulating to a military audience. We prefer that you first send a query, describing your purpose and goal. If you have an idea with a military angle and aren't sure whether we would be interested, don't hesitate to write us.

WHAT WE WANT: We are looking for articles about military life, its problems and how to handle them. Keep in mind that our readers come from all of the military services. For instance, a story can focus on an Army family, but may need to include families or sources from other services as well. You do not have to be in the military, or part of a military family, to write for us. But the stories we publish reflect a detailed understanding of military life. We also buy articles dealing with hunting and fishing, automobiles and motorcycles, and travel.

WHAT WE DON'T WANT: We don't publish fiction or poetry. We cannot use historical essays or unit histories. We don't want articles that have nothing to do with the military. They are our audience, and it must affect their lives in one way or another.

RIGHTS: Articles will be a work made for hire under the U.S. copyright laws. That means we buy exclusive publication rights in our newspapers, as well as the exclusive rights to reproduce, edit, adapt, modify, perform, transmit and otherwise use the work, including any derivative works created therefrom, in any manner or medium throughout the world in perpetuity without additional compensation.

PAYMENT: Payment for articles is made upon acceptance. Remember that once we purchase an article, it might be several months before we publish it. When we do publish it, the article will appear simultaneously on the electronic service Military City Online, a division of Army Times Publishing Co. Your acceptance of payment is acceptance of these conditions.

PHOTOS: We pay for use of original photographs. Color slides or prints are acceptable. By original, we mean photos that you own either because you took them or because you bought the rights to them. We do not pay for photos bought at a souvenir stand, for example. Fees are negotiable.

SPECIAL SECTIONS: The *Times News Service* also publishes regular supplements to *Army Times, Navy Times, Marine Corps Times* and *Air Force Times.* Topics include careers after military service, travel, personal finance and education. Stories generally should include military people.

Categories: Nonfiction—Adventure—Careers—Civil War—Entertainment—Film/Video—Military—Money & Finances—Television/Radio—Travel

CONTACT: Phillip Thompson, Editor
Material: All material except material for supplements
CONTACT: Donna Peterson
Material: Material for Supplements
Army Times Publishing Co.
6883 Commercial Dr.
Springfield VA 22159
Phone: 703-750-7479
Fax: 703-750-8781

Tiny Lights
A Journal of Personal Essay

Since 1995, *Tiny Lights* has been celebrating the power of personal voice with a biannual journal devoted to short essay. The annual essay contest, which offers $1000 in prizes, provides the material for the summer issue, while the winter issue is by invitation only.

Regarding unsolicited manuscripts: At present, we are only considering material submitted to the annual essay contest and to two Lights Online columns mentioned below. See also: www.tiny-lights.com.

Guidelines for our annual Essay Contest:

We can only consider unpublished work, or previously published material for which the author holds rights. Rights revert to author after publication in *Tiny Lights*.

Each essay must be accompanied by an entry fee. $15 for first essay, $10 each additional essay.

SASE (self-addressed, stamped envelope) with sufficient postage required for contest notification and/or manuscript return. Multiple submissions OK.

Essays must be no longer than 2,000 words.

Entries should be typed and double-spaced.

Cover letters are optional, but the first page of the manuscript should include author's name, complete address, e-mail (if one exists), phone number, and essay word count.

Personal essay requires writers to communicate the truth of their experiences to the best of their abilities. While no theme restrictions apply to this contest, we will not consider essays that celebrate brutality or pornography in any form. *Tiny Lights* does not accept poetry, short stories, or material written for children. Entry fees for inappropriate submissions may not be returned.

Entries must be postmarked by deadline date in February (see website.)

Prizes are awarded as follows:

First Place: $400 // Second Place: $200 // Third Place: $150 // Two Honorable Mention Prizes: $100. Awards will be determined by a panel of judges. Final authority rests with the Editor-in-Chief.

Winners will be posted at www.tiny-lights.com by April following contest deadline.

Winning essays may be edited before publication. Final copy must be approved by writer. No essays published without author's permission.

All contestants will receive *Tiny Lights*' contest publication featuring the winning entries.

The online component of *Tiny Lights* (www.tiny-lights.com) is designed to catch what can't be contained in the pages of the newsstand editions. Lights Online provides a venue for additional voices, information about *Tiny Lights* and resources for writers of personal essay.

Lights Online has two columns of particular interest to writers seeking publication. Searchlights & Signal Flares is a monthly writer's exchange which features answers to questions like, "What inspires you?" and "What's the best writing advice you ever got?" Flash in the Pan, for those brief bursts of first person genius, is posted quarterly. Detailed guidelines are posted at www.tiny-lights.com. All business with Lights Online is conducted via email.

Subscriptions to *Tiny Lights*: $10 per year (3 issues)

Current issues: $5 each; Back issues: $3 each. Checks payable to *Tiny Lights* Publications, P.O. Box 928, Petaluma, CA 94953

Categories: Nonfiction—Autobiography—Personal Essay—Memoir

CONTACT: Susan Bono, Editor
Material: All
PO Box 928
Petaluma, CA 94953
Website: www.tiny-lights.com

The Toastmaster

Circulation

Toastmasters International, a nonprofit educational organization, publishes *The Toastmaster* monthly for approximately 180,000 members in 9,000 clubs worldwide.

Toastmasters are people who recognize the need for self-improvement in communication, especially in their own oral presentations, and for developing their leadership potential. Members give at least one speech each month. An average Toastmaster will stay with his or her club for about eighteen months and completes the basic educational manuals. But many remain members longer to take advantage of more specialized programs, such as advanced speaking and leadership programs, community involvement and leadership development. The average member is 35 years old and has a college degree.

Payment

Toastmasters International will buy all serial rights for $100 to $250; payment is on acceptance. Payment for reprint rights depends on how valuable the material is to us. One-time and/or first serial rights are available on request.

Article Guidelines

Send a query letter first. Article length should be from 600 to 2000 words, double-spaced. Include a brief author biography and a word count.

To speed up publication of your article, send it on a 3.5" disk in either Microsoft Word or ASCII text. (Please do not format the text of the article.) If you do not have access to the above programs, send your article in a text only format and we will try and convert it. Please include a typed, double-spaced manuscript along with your disk and indicate the article's word count. Please note: We prefer not to receive unsolicited article submissions via e-mail.

We need articles related to the fields of communication and leadership, on topics members can use in their self-improvement efforts. Use anecdotes and examples to present your ideas and write with a "how to" approach, giving readers practical tips for improving their communication and leadership skills. Appropriate topics include speaking techniques, leadership development, language use, club management principles, and profiles of famous speakers in history.

Book reviews, exposes, personality profiles, articles with obvious political and religious slants, poems and speeches will not be accepted for publication.

Categories: Nonfiction—Associations—General Interest—Trade—Public Speaking

CONTACT: Submissions Editor
Material: All
Toastmasters International
PO Box 9052
Mission Viejo CA 92690-9052
Phone: 949-858-8255
Fax: 949-858-1207
E-mail: pubs@toastmasters.org
Website: www.toastmasters.org

Today's Catholic Teacher

Today's Catholic Teacher is a nationally circulated magazine for K-12 educators concerned with private education in general and Catholic education in particular. Issued six times during the school year, it has a circulation of about 50,000 copies and an estimated total readership of about 200,000. Although that readership is primarily classroom teachers, *Today's Catholic Teacher* is read also by principals, supervisors, superintendents, boards of education, pastors, and parents.

Articles: *Today's Catholic Teacher* aims to be for Catholic educators a source of information not available elsewhere. Subject matter may be any topic of practical help, concern, or interest to educators in Catholic schools. Examples include:

• Developments in curriculum, testing, technology, school rela-

R-U

tionships, creative teaching, school and community needs, classroom management, and administration as it affects the classroom

• National issues and trends which are of concern to Catholic educators

• Suggestions on the teaching of curricular subjects, including all academic areas as well as religion

Audience: The focus of articles should span the interests of teachers from early childhood through junior high. Articles may be directed to just one age group yet have wider implications. Preference is given to material directed to teachers in grades 4 through 8.

Style: The desired magazine style is direct, concise, informative, and accurate. Writing should be enjoyable to read, informal rather than scholarly, lively, and free of educational jargon.

Length: Feature articles fall into three general categories: 600-800 words, 1,000-1,200 words, and 1,200-1,500 words. Photographs: Prints or digital images in color or black and white are helpful. Photos will not be returned unless requested.

Payment: Paid on publication, payment for features is generally $100 to $250, depending on length and quality of writing. Photos or other illustrations may increase payment.

Sample Issue: Send $3 for mailing and handling.

Contact: Query letters are encouraged. Write, call, fax, or e-mail the editor for editorial calendar, current editorial plans, and specifications for computer submissions.

Categories: Nonfiction—Education—Religion

CONTACT: Mary C. Noschang, Editor
Material: All
2621 Dryden Rd., Ste. 300
Dayton OH 45439
Phone: 937-293-1415
Fax: 937-293-1310
E-mail: mnoschang@peterli.com

Today's Christian

Today's Christian accepts fewer freelance articles than many other magazines since most of our articles are reprints or staff-written. But in each issue (6 per year), we feature several outstanding original pieces. While competition is keen (we receive an average of 40 unsolicited manuscripts a week), you can tailor your submissions to meet our needs by observing the following guidelines.

The *Today's Christian* audience is truly a general interest one, including men and women, urban professionals and rural homemakers, adults of every age and marital status, and Christians of every church affiliation. We seek to publish a magazine that people from the variety of ethnic groups in North America will find interesting and relevant.

We welcome both original and reprint materials on a wide range of subjects (see topics below), though first-person nonfiction stories are our staple. We do not accept juvenile material. Fiction is almost never used. Payment is made upon acceptance for original material; upon publication for reprint material. *Today's Christian* retains the right to edit material for length or content.

While query letters are accepted, article manuscripts are preferred. In general, they should be no longer than 1,300 words and should be computer-generated (no disks, please) or typed. *A cover letter or entry at the top of the manuscript should provide the following information:*

• Your name
• Date
• Phone number (day and evening)
• Fax number (if available)
• Rights offered (first rights preferred; if reprint, give publication and date)
• Type of submission (non-simultaneous strongly preferred)

Note: Enclose a self-addressed, stamped envelope if you wish to receive an acceptance/rejection letter. (If you want the manuscript returned, indicate that and enclose appropriate return postage and envelope size.) Or, you can send your manuscript by e-mail. We respond to most submissions within 4-6 weeks, but please allow up to two months processing time. E-mail: TCeditor@christianitytoday.com.

TYPES OF ARTICLES SOUGHT BY *Christian Reader*
Stories

• *Action Drama:* real-life; also missionary; first or third person
• *Character Drama:* conversions, recovery, relationships, etc.
• *Lessons from Life:* winsome, poignant, but not moralistic
• *Real-Life Parable:* a short true story with an implicit moral lesson
• *Fiction:* TC almost never uses fiction
• *Humor:* quality humor is hard to write and highly valued by TC editors
• *Celebrity Profile:* Christian and "cross-over" personalities
• *Seasonal:* Christmas, Easter, Mother's/Father's day, etc.; best if submitted at least nine months in advance.

Interesting & Artsy Stuff

• *History/Archaeology/Science:* written factually and popularly with a Christian angle
• *Trivia:* fun, quirky, or interesting facts about life and Christian culture

Topics

• *Family:* stories, how-to's
• *Romance & Marriage:* stories, how-to's
• *Sex:* Christians' perspectives and benefits of purity
• *Social Issues:* compelling, informative, and fresh perspectives on cultural, moral, social issues such as gambling, euthanasia, abortion, racial injustice, etc.–written for the popular audience, usually with statistics or personal accounts that illustrate the subject

Spiritual Reflection

• *Church Life:* no yawners, please
• *Evangelism/Missions:* stories, how-to's
• *Meditation/Devotional:* shorter than most articles; must be fresh, contemporary, personable
• *Prayer:* stories, how-to's
• *Personal Growth:* stories, how-to's
• *Other:* general articles on spiritual living

Categories: Nonfiction—Christian Interests—Drama—General Interest—Inspirational—Religion—Spiritual

CONTACT: Editor
Material: All
465 Gundersen Dr.
Carol Stream IL 60188
Phone: 630-260-6200
Fax: 630-480-2004
Website: www.todays-christian.com

Today's Christian Preacher

The focus and frequency of these magazines will be changing in the near future in response to changing marketplace conditions. For this reason, we will no longer be accepting unsolicited submissions.

We apologize for any inconvenience these changes may cause you. Of course, we wish you all the best as you submit your material to other publishers.

Sincerely,

Elaine Williams, Asst. Editor

Today's Christian Teen

The focus and frequency of these magazines will be changing in the near future in response to changing marketplace conditions. For this reason, we will no longer be accepting unsolicited submissions. We apologize for any inconvenience these changes may cause you. Of course, we wish you all the best as you submit your material to other publishers.

Sincerely,

Elaine Williams, Asst. Editor

TODAY'S CHRISTIAN
woman

Today's Christian Woman

Our Purpose

Today's Christian Woman is a practical magazine geared for women in their 20s, 30s, and 40s. It seeks to help women deal with the contemporary issues and hot topics that impact their lives, as well as provide depth, balance, and a biblical perspective to the relationships they grapple with daily in the following arenas: family, friendship, faith, marriage, single life, self, work, finances, and health.

Our Readers

The TCW reader represents a broad spectrum of familiarity with what it means to have a vital faith in Jesus Christ. Readership includes those who are knowledgeable about the Bible and are involved in a church, as well as those who either are still investigating Christianity or are relatively new believers.

Almost 83 percent of TCW readers are married; 17 percent are single, widowed, divorced, or separated; 66 percent are employed (49 percent full-time), and 57 percent have children living at home.

Our Tone

TCW articles should be personal in tone and utilize real-life anecdotes as well as quotes/advice from noted Christian professionals or related resources. Articles should be practical and contain a distinct evangelical Christian perspective. While TCW adheres strictly to this underlying perspective in all its editorial content, articles should refrain from using language that assumes a reader's familiarity with Christian or church-oriented terminology. Bible quotes and references should be used selectively. All Bible quotes should be taken from the New International Version if possible.

Our Writers

• TCW does not accept unsolicited manuscripts. Please query first (see below).

• TCW will report on queries and manuscripts in 8 weeks. Include a SASE of correct size, if you wish your manuscript returned.

• All submissions are received on speculation. An accepted query does not guarantee purchase of the manuscript. Editors reserve the right to reject any manuscript at any stage.

• Payment on acceptance of completed articles, 20 cents per printed word, first rights.

• TCW does not accept simultaneous submissions.

• TCW does not issue kill fees.

Query letters should include:

1. A summary describing the article idea
2. The purpose of the piece and its value to readers
3. The author's qualifications to write the piece
4. Suggested length and date it could be finished
5. A self-addressed stamped envelope for reply

Address query letters to The Aquisitions Editor, at the address below. Include your mailing address and daytime phone number. No query should be sent without a thorough knowledge of TCW's audience.

For a sample copy, writers' guidelines, or subscription information, write:

Today's Christian Woman
PO Box 37060
Boone, IA 50037-0060.
Please include a self-addressed, stamped #10 envelope for writ-

ers' guidelines.

For a sample copy, please send $5.00.

Manuscripts

Manuscripts should be typed double-spaced. In addition to the author's address, the first page should include his/her phone number, social security number, and the word length. Also include a SASE for possible return of the manuscript. Manuscripts may also be e-mailed (but not as attached files) to: tcwedit@ christianitytoday.com.

Our Editorial Needs

Freelance submissions are accepted for the following: 1,000- to 1,800-word articles that help women grow in their relationship to God as well as provide practical help and a biblical perspective on these topics: family/parenting, friendship, marriage, health, self life, single life, finances, and work. TCW is also interested in practical spiritual living articles.

We do not accept poetry, fiction, or Bible studies.

Our magazine is also always on the lookout for:

• **Humor:** light, first-person pieces that exaggerate a real-life occurrence instead of focus on a hypothetical situation, giving a fresh twist and a subtle spiritual distinctive to topics the majority of women can relate to. Length: 1,000-1,500 words.

• **Issues/Hot Topics:** reports that tackle the topics that impact women's lives today, such as infertility, homosexuality, ADHD, or pornography. These articles need to avoid a preachy or clinical tone; fully develop the scope of the specific issue and provide authoritative research and/or up-to-date statistics; incorporate real-life illustrations from women our readers can relate to; present a distinct Christian perspective. Sidebars of accompanying first-person stories and/or resources are welcome. Length: 1,800-2000 words.

• **My Story:** a first-person, true-life dramatic narrative that describes how you worked through a difficult situation, event, or traumatic turning point in your life (can be written as an as-told-to).

• **Length:** 1,500 words. Payment: $300 upon purchase.

Regular Features

We pay $25 for the following features, and regret submissions cannot be acknowledged or returned:

• Readers' Picks—a short review of your current favorite cd or book, and why. Length: 200 words.

Categories: Christian Interests—Family—General Interest—Inspirational—Interview—Marriage—Relationships—Self Help—Spiritual

CONTACT: Lisa Ann Cockrel, Associate Editor
Material: Queries
CONTACT: Camerin Courtney, Managing Editor
Material: "My Story" submissions
Christianity Today International
465 Gunderson Dr.
Carol Stream IL 60188-2498
Phone: 630-260-6200
Fax: 630-260-0114
E-mail: tcwedit@christianitytoday.com
Website: www.todayschristianwoman.com

Today's Florida Woman

Today's Florida Woman is a bi-monthly business-lifestyle magazine for and about accomplished women, whose mission is to inform, support, and inspire women by focusing on their success—both personally and professionally; individually & collectively.

Needs: The editorial staff is interested in articles, 500-2,000 words, on career strategies, personal, family and business development, entertainment, health and fitness, finance, politics, and travel. Photographs encouraged. Poetry, essays, excerpts, and reprints also considered. Payment varies, on publication, with complimentary copy of publication issue. Query with resume, clips and SASE.

R-U

Length: 500-2,000 words

Payment: Payment varies, on publication, with complimentary copy of publication issue.

How to Submit: Query with resume, clips and SASE to:

Today's Florida Woman P.O. Box 358461 Gainesville, Florida 32635-8461

Final submissions required on 3.5 diskette or Zip disk (100mb) with hardcopy printout.

Response Time: Allow 4 weeks for response.

Categories: Women

CONTACT: Linette Singleton, Editor
PO Box 369461
Gainesville FL 32635
Phone: 352-374-6863
Fax: 419-821-3980
E-mail: flgawomg@bellsouth.net

Today's Pentecostal Evangel

Please note: About 95 percent of our material is done by assignment. Only a small percentage of free-lance articles are accepted. Before submitting an article, please adhere to the guidelines below.

ARTICLES WE USE

1. **Christian Living**. How to better understand the Bible, develop a richer prayer life, live more victoriously, overcome personal problems, etc.

2. **Soul winning, conversions and answers to prayer**. Often written in the first person or "as told to."

3. **Doctrinal**. The baptism in the Holy Spirit, the Second Coming (premillennial in viewpoint) and divine healing. Physical healings must be endorsed by a minister acquainted with the case.

4. **Salvation appeal**. Strong evangelistic appeal targeted to the unsaved (250 to 500 words).

5. **Home and family**. Helps for building Christian homes. Include illustrations from life. Avoid preachiness.

6. **Seasonal**. New Year's, Easter, Pentecost Sunday, Mother's Day, Father's Day, Thanksgiving, Christmas. Submit at least six months in advance, preferably longer.

7. **Current issues**. Adhere to doctrinal positions of the Assemblies of God.

8. **News**. News pieces and photographs from freelancers are printed in the World view section occasionally. If you can report on a major event connected in some way with the Assemblies of God or with religious issues, please call our news office. Generally, stories written about a church, Bible college or some religious institution do not receive payment. If the story requires independent research, payment can be negotiated.

9. **Human interest**. To glorify God for what He is accomplishing through individuals, groups or churches. People like to read stories about sacrifice, courage, victory, etc.

10. **Regular features**. Material for "Living it " and "Letters."

11. **Testimonies**. Healings and stories of God's provision. These are unpaid and may be edited for content.

12. *Poetry or fiction is not being accepted at this time.*

TO HELP YOU MEET THESE NEEDS

1. Be familiar with Today's Pentecostal Evangel. Read the magazine regularly to understand our approach. Study current issues for slant, content and style.

2. Be thorough. Give attention to sentence structure, spelling and word selection in your article. When quoting a Scripture passage, check the Bible for wording, spelling and punctuation. Please indicate which version is used.

3. Keep the reader in mind. Today's Pentecostal Evangel is the voice of the Assemblies of God and is read by both Christians and non-Christians.

4. Pray. The Evangel goes into homes, prisons, public libraries and many other places. Pray that your article, if published, will bless many.

If your manuscript is returned, it does not mean the work is of poor quality; it may mean we already have similar material or your article would be more appropriate in another publication. We are unable to give reasons for rejection of manuscripts; however, each manuscript is carefully reviewed and appraised.

MECHANICS OF PREPARATION

Manuscripts. E-mailed manuscripts are preferred and should be sent to tpe@ag.org. They should be sent as attachments, not in the body of the E-mail. They should be double spaced, with your name, address and Social Security number in the upper left-hand corner of the first page. The approximate number of words should be in the upper right-hand corner. Hard copies should be typewritten or printed on a letter-quality or near-letter quality printer (preferably not dot matrix). Be sure to keep a copy; we cannot be responsible for safe-keeping of manuscripts.

1. **Postage**. Mail to: Today's Pentecostal Evangel, 1445 N. Boonville Avenue, Springfield, MO, 65802. Your manuscript must be accompanied by a self-addressed envelope and sufficient postage if you wish it returned. It will be discarded six weeks after rejection.

2. **Article length**. From 500 to 1,200 words. Testimonies. 200-300 words.

3. **No multiple submissions**. We do not accept manuscripts submitted to other publications at the same time. We do purchase second rights on some previously published material.

4. **Personal information required**. In a cover letter, please tell about yourself, including your current occupation. Please tell us what church you are a member of and who your pastor is. Assemblies of God affiliation not necessary.

5. **Queries**. Submit your manuscript without query. We accept queries only from authors who have written for us on assignment.

6. **Rate of payment**. We pay 6 cents a word for first-rights articles by freelance writers. Payment is made upon acceptance. Writers will receive complimentary copies of the Evangel in which the article appears. Second rights are paid at approximately half of first-rights material. We do not offer payments for testimonies.

7. **Rights**. We purchase first or second North American serial rights, plus nonexclusive reprint rights, which includes electronic reproduction. We reserve the right to publish inspiring excerpts from testimonies. Please inform us if the article has been printed before or if you are offering first rights.

8. *No handwritten manuscripts accepted.*

Categories: Nonfiction—Christian Interests—Family—Home—Religion—Spiritual

CONACT: Submissions Editor
Material: All
1445 N. Boonville Ave.
Springfield MO 65802
Phone: 417-862-2781 ext 4109
Fax: 417-862-0416
E-mail: pe@ag.org
Website: www.pe.ag.org

Town&Country

Town & Country

If you are interested in proposing an article for *Town & Country*, please send a query letter and samples of your published work to the appropriate editor and department at the address below. Be sure to include an e-mail address or self-addressed stamped envelope so we may reply. Please do not submit article queries by e-mail.

Send query letters to *Town & Country* at address below.

Regarding writer's guidelines, we do no make available any such listings. The magazine itself serves as the best guide possible to the kinds of stories we're looking for, so please consult recent issues for content and style before making your submission.

Also, in the case of already completed manuscripts, please keep in mind that we rarely publish work we have not originally commissioned.

Thank you for your interest in *Town & Country*.

Categories: Nonfiction—Antiques—Architecture—Arts—Beauty—Fashion—General Interest—Health—Home—Literature—Society—Travel—Women's Issues

CONTACT: Melissa Biggs Bradley, Travel Editor
Material: Travel
CONTACT: Sarah Medford, Director of Design & Architecture
Material: Luxury Homes, Estates
CONTACT: Janet Carlson Freed, Director of Beauty & Health
Material: Health & Beauty
CONTACT: Tom Farley
Material: "On the Town" and "Social Graces"
CONTACT: Tony Freund
Material: "In the Country" and "Connoisseur's World"
The Hearst Corp.
1700 Broadway, 30th Floor
New York NY 10019
Phone: 212-903-5000

Toy Cars & Models

Unsolicited manuscripts are welcome but should include a self-addressed, stamped envelope (SASE) with sufficient return postage. Query letters are appreciated with samples of the author's writing.

Content: *Toy Cars & Models* is published monthly and includes feature stories, news items and columns in each issue. Articles are of general interest to toy car and model car collectors, focusing mainly (but not exclusively) on newer items from the 1960s-present. Stories should focus on the collectibility of specific toys or manufacturers' lines. Features should not be too narrow but rather hit the highlights of a particular line or type of toy/model. Smaller features may focus on more specific topics.

Features generally run 750-900 words for a short piece and 1,000-1,250 for a longer feature. All stories are subject to editing for accuracy, clarity, conciseness and space considerations. Current values of toys/models and other pricing information should be incorporated into features or placed in an accompanying sidebar. Readers want to know not only the historical information about toys/models, but also what is available and how much the items are worth.

Other ideas for stories may include histories of prominent toy/model companies, interviews with collectors, model reviews of new or old releases and features on topics that affect and interest those in the toy car and model hobby.

Rights and Payment: Krause Publications purchases exclusive rights. Krause Publications also maintains a license to reproduce the material and distribute it by all means and media now known or hereafter discovered, including, without limitation, print, microfilm and electronic media as well as the right to display and transmit the work publicly online.

Authors must warrant that each contribution is original work that has not been in the public domain or previously published, unless noted otherwise, and that each is free of unauthorized extractions from other sources, copyrighted or otherwise. Payment for accepted articles is decided on a per-story basis at the editor's discretion. Payment is upon publication. Contact editor Merry Dudley for specific and current rates.

Manuscript Format: Hard copy submitted must be typewritten on white paper with the author's name, address and phone number at the top. Please leave at least a one-inch margin on all sides of the page. Computer submissions should be in Microsoft Word format to be followed by hard copy.

Electronic submissions are accepted only for solicited or assigned stories. No unsolicited manuscripts via e-mail, please. Send e-mail submissions to editor Merry Dudley.

Style: We follow the basic journalistic style guidelines in *The Associated Press Stylebook*. Consult Strunk & White's *The Elements of Style* for additional considerations.

Photographs: Authors are encouraged to submit color photographs (slides, prints or transparencies) to accompany their submissions. Photos should be identified on a separate sheet or with a Post-It note on the back of the photo. Do NOT use ink on the backs of photos. If desired, photo credits will be given, and photos will be returned upon publication if requested.

High-resolution images sent via e-mail or on disk in TIFF format are acceptable, but please call for more information if you choose to use this method.

Publication: Authors will not be notified prior to publication and will be sent one copy of the issue containing their story.

Please note: Publication time may be anywhere from 3 months to 12 months following acceptance.

Sample Copy: For a sample copy of *Toy Cars & Models* or other titles published by Krause, call 800-258-0929.

Categories: Automobiles—Hobbies

CONTACT: Merry Dudley, Editor
Material: Query
Krause Publications
700 East State St.
Iola WI 54990-0001
E-mail: dudleyMCkrause.com (no manuscripts)
Website: www.collect.com

Toy Farmer

Monthly magazine covering the farm toy hobby. Collectors turn to this magazine for information on toy shows, profiles of collectors, hobby trends, historical data, company reports, youth in the hobby, worldwide news and expert columnists. Each year one month is devoted to themes of custom-built and scratch-built stories, pedal tractors and farm layout displays.

Established 1978, family owned, with a circulation of 25,000, approximately 98 pages. Feature stories are between 900-1,500 words. Photographs are responsibility of writer. Need writer on the East Coast, West Coast, and Southwest. Pay on publication. Byline given. Editorial lead time of three months. Accept queries by mail, e-mail, fax or phone. Accepts previously published material. Writer's guidelines available upon request.

Categories: Nonfiction—Agriculture—Crafts/Hobbies—Hobbies

CONTACT: Cheryl Hegrik, Editorial Assistant
Material: All
Toy Farmer Publications
7496 - 106th Ave. SE
LaMoure ND 58461
Phone: 800-533-8293
Fax: 701-883-5209
E-mail: chegvik@toyfarmer.com

Toy Shop

Submissions

Unsolicited manuscripts are welcome, but should include a self-addressed, stamped envelope (SASE) with sufficient return postage. Query letters are appreciated with samples of the author's writing.

Content

Toy Shop is published bi-weekly (twice a month) and includes feature stories, news items and columns in alternating issues. Articles are of general interest to toy collectors, focusing mainly (but not exclusively) on toys from the 1940s to present. Stories should focus on the collectibility of specific toys or manufacturers' lines. Features should not be too narrow, but rather hit the highlights of a particular type of toy—such as board games, Marx play sets, action figures, Barbie dolls or construction sets. Smaller features may focus on more specific topics. Auction coverage is also welcome.

Features generally run around 500 to 750 for a short piece to 1,000 to 1,500 for a longer feature. All stories are subject to editing and rewriting for accuracy, clarity, conciseness and space considerations.

Current values of toys and other pricing information should be incorporated into features or placed in an accompanying sidebar. Readers want to know not only the historical information about toys, but also what is available and how much it's worth.

Other ideas for stories may include histories of prominent toy companies, interviews with collectors or features on particularly unique, unusual, or large toy collections.

Rights and Payment

Krause Publications purchases exclusive rights to manuscripts for *Toy Shop*. For more details on our editorial contract, contact Editorial Director Sharon Korbeck.

Authors must warrant that each contribution is original work that has not been in the public domain or previously published, unless noted otherwise, and that each is free of unauthorized extractions from other sources, copyrighted or otherwise.

Payment for articles accepted is based on a per-story basis at the editor's discretion.

Payment is upon publication, unless other arrangements have been agreed upon. Contact Editorial Director Sharon Korbeck for specific, current rates.

Manuscript Format

Hard copy submitted must be typewritten and double-spaced on white paper with the author's name, address and phone number at the top. Please leave at least one-inch margins on all sides of the page. Computer submissions should be on a DS/HD disk in ASCII (text) format with accompanying hard copy.

Electronic submissions are accepted only for solicited or assigned stories. No unsolicited manuscripts via e-mail, please. Send e-mail submissions to korbecks@krause.com.

Style

We follow the basic journalistic style guidelines in *The Associated Press Stylebook*. Consult Strunk & White's *The Elements of Style* for additional considerations. Please proofread stories carefully before submitting them.

Photographs

Authors are encouraged to submit color or black-and-white photographs (slides, prints or transparencies) to accompany their submissions. Photos should be identified on a separate sheet or on a Post-It note on the back of the photo. Do NOT use ink on the backs of photos. If desired, photo credits will be given, and photos will be returned upon publication.

Photos sent via in TIFF or JPG format electronically or on disk are acceptable. Resolution must be 170 dpi or greater.

Publication

Authors will not be notified prior to publication and will be sent one copy of the issue containing their story.

Please note: Publication time may be anywhere from two months to 24 months following acceptance.

Contact

Interested free-lance writers should query Editorial Director Sharon Korbeck at 715-445-2214, ext. #468, via mail at 700 E. State St., Iola, WI 54990-0001 or or via e-mail at korbecks@ krause.com.

For a sample copy of *Toy Shop* magazine or other Krause publications, call 800-258-0929.

For more information about our company's books and magazines, visit our Web site at www.collect.com.

Categories: Collectibles—Consumer—Hobbies

CONTACT: Sharon Korbeck, Editorial Director
Material: All
700 E. State St.
Iola WI 54990-0001
Phone: 715-445-2214, ext. 468
Fax: 715-445-4087
E-mail: korbecks@krause.com
Website: www.collect.com

Toy Trucker & Contractor

Please refer to *Toy Farmer*.

Tradition

Only accepts articles that deal with traditional, acoustic music. Pays in copies of our publication. Otherwise, there are no formal guidelines.

Categories: Nonfiction—Arts—Dance—Entertainment—Folklore—Music—Recreation—Rural America

CONTACT: Robert Everhart, Editor
Material: All
Nat. Trad. C.M.A.
PO Box 492
Anita IA 50020
Phone: 712-762-4363

Trail Runner
The Magazine of Running Adventure

Author Submissions

First, be sure to read about *Trail Runner* on our website. When pitching story ideas to *Trail Runner*, please include information regarding the availability of images to illustrate the article. Send your queries with published clips.

Photo and Art Guidelines

Trail Runner pays $250 per page with a minimum of $50 per spot usage. A two-page spread pays $375 and covers pay $500. A submission of images to *Trail Runner* implies acceptance of these rates. We also ask that you notify us when making simultaneous submissions to other magazines. If we decide to publish one of your images, we request that you do not submit the image to any other publication for six months from the on-sale date.

We are happy to consider original art—photos, illustrations, cartoons, etc.—with or without accompanying text. For photos, we prefer original color slides or black-and-white prints. We are also willing to review a representative sample of your work; a stock list would be a useful reference. All slides should be clearly labeled with the photographer's name, address and telephone number. Include a caption sheet that indicates the location of the photo and, if applicable, the trail name and names of the people in the photo.

Shooting Trail Running: A few notes for photographers planning to shoot images for *Trail Runner*. Trail running is a fun activity, but most people aren't smiling with perfectly clean clothes and looking directly at a camera out on the trail. Please do not shoot runners wearing brand-new clothes and shoes with smiling faces looking right at the camera. Even if shots are staged, there are ways to get more authentic shots. Use real runners, not pretty models. Also, let the runners run for 30 to 45 minutes before shooting. (Sweat, mud, blood and other elements of trail running make good pictures.) And, make sure runners have proper hydration equipment (either water bottle pouches or proper hydration reservoir packs), especially if photos are taken in the mountains or in the desert.

Off the Beaten Path: The last editorial page of *Trail Runner* will feature an Off the Beaten Path photo. This will consist of a stunning photo (in crispness, color, subject matter, location) and run at least two-thirds of the page. A brief caption will be included, as well as details of the photographer, camera and film.

SUBMISSIONS

All materials sent to *Trail Runner* should be accompanied by a self-addressed, stamped envelope suitable for return of all of your submitted work. If you would like your work returned certified or registered, please include sufficient postage. Please include your name, address, telephone number, Social Security number and email address for billing purposes.

Categories: Nonfiction—Health—Physical Fitness—Sports/Recreation

CONTACT: Brian Metzler, Editor/Associate Publisher
Material: Features and departments, except Wanderings,
Off the Beaten Path and Training
E-mail: editor@trailrunnermag.com
CONTACT: Monique Cole, Senior Editor
Material: Training, Wanderings
E-mail: monique@ trailrunnermag.com
CONTACT: Jeff Cloud, Photo Editor
Material: Photo submissions and queries, plus
Off the Beaten Path
E-mail: photo@rockandice. com
North South Publications
5455 Spine Rd., Mezzanine A
Boulder CO 80301
Phone: 303-499-8410
Fax: 303-530-3729
E-mail: www.trailrunnermag.com

Trailer Boats

EDITORIAL PROFILE: As the name implies, *Trailer Boats* is written for owners and prospective buyers of trailerable powerboats—generally under 30' with no more than an 8'6" beam (no sailboats). Most of our readers are seasoned boating veterans who use their boats and equipment frequently.

Regular features include reports and evaluations of products useful to trailerboaters, including boat tests on current-model cruisers, runabouts, skiboats, fishing boats, pontoon/deck boats, etc. Related topics such as maintenance, seamanship, towing, navigation, electronics, repairs, watersports, etc., are also regularly covered, often in either a technical or how-to format. Each issue also includes travel destinations and a high-performance (racing oriented) article.

SPECIFICS: Boat tests, comparisons, and product evaluations are generally staff written. Technical articles are always in demand, wherein experts in the field either write them or are consulted for accuracy. When consulting "experts" it is best to go to more than one source—our readers catch errors. How-to articles should be explained in simple, easy-to-follow terms, but should not be superficial in content. Travel articles on trailer boating destinations in and around the continental U.S. and its Canadian and Mexican borders, as well as Alaska, are welcome.

We prefer a hands-on boating approach to travel pieces, rather than a simple travelogue. The boating theme must permeate the story.

We don't want redone news releases from local chambers of commerce. The high-performance story in each issue is generally presented as race coverage, a personality profile, or a how-to, although general-interest pieces on new developments run occasionally.

Fishing articles should center around the boat—its special design, equipment and accessories, etc.—more than on fishing techniques. How to install downriggers or how to choose the right electronics are examples. An occasional fishing oriented destination story is also acceptable.

SUBMISSIONS: Queries are welcome. We prefer submissions on computer disk (Microsoft Word), accompanied by a type written hard copy of the manuscript. We desire complete packages, including headline, subhead, photos (and/or artwork) and captions, along with a self-addressed stamped envelope. Travel articles should also include a map of the area.

PHOTOGRAPHY: *Trailer Boats* is a visually oriented magazine that uses photos with virtually all stories. We want sharp—no dupes, please—color slides, medium-format transparencies, or high resolution digital images (300 dpi). First-time travel articles are usually assigned after we've seen the quality of photos. Please identify all photos with a tag line or caption. Photos are usually included as part of the editorial package, but when submitted separately, we will negotiate price. That includes the cover.

PAYMENT: We pay on acceptance except for departments, which are paid on publication. Payment ranges from $100 for short fill pieces, to between $300 and $700 for features, depending on length, nature of assignment and quality of product.

Categories: Automobiles—Boating—Outdoors—Recreation Vehicles—Travel

CONTACT: Rebecca Stone, Managing Editor
Material: Any
CONTACT: Ron Eldridge, Editor
Material: Any
20700 Belshaw Ave.
Carson CA 90746-3510
Phone: 310-537-6322

Trailer Life

Please refer to *Highways* magazine.

Transaction Publishers Rutgers
The State University of New Jersey

Please see this listing in the book publishing section.

Transitions

Thank you for your interest in *Transitions*. We are always interested in reviewing focused, well-written nonfiction articles and interviews. The best way of assessing our style is to look at copies of our magazines, which are available in most major bookstores and on the internet at www.transitionsmag.com. Our Statement of Purpose, located in the beginning each issue, is a good place to start.

We do not respond to query letters, and we only consider final products. We prefer that you submit your article by email. If you do submit a hard copy, please include a self-addressed stamped envelope or email address for our reply. Allow up to six months for a response. We don't send back submissions, so do not send us your only copy. We do not longer publish poetry or fiction. Writing in the form of a sermon, research paper, or personal narrative is discouraged. Submissions should not have already appeared in other publications or on the web.

Transitions reassures readers over the age of 50 that "It s still our time!" *Transitions* addresses the wide range of issues that confront society today politics and aging, sex and entertainment, and everything in between. It s fun, challenging, thought provoking, sometimes controversial...but never boring!

FORMAT: Feature articles range in length from 1000 2000 words. E-mailed versions are preferred (in Rich Text Format or text-only format, or in MSWord 98 or earlier), though hard copies can be mailed to MB Media, PO Box 600, Chico, CA 95927-0600. E-mail us at editor@magicalblend.com. Work that has been edited for length and clarity is more likely to be considered. Payment is considered strictly on an individual basis.

Artwork to accompany articles may be submitted digitally or on slides or color prints. Please do not send us originals!

Some article Ideas *Transitions* magazine considers:
- Health & Fitness over 50
- Retirement
- Estate Planning
- Aging
- Travel
- Celebrities
- Humor
- Families & Grandchildren
- Eating for Longevity
- Optimism and Quality of Life
- Dealing with the Loss of Loved Ones Dating/Sex after 50
- Interviews
- Health and Life Insurance
- Gardening/Pets
- Assisted Living/Home Care
- Volunteering
- Leisure
- Learning New Things Late in Life
- Anecdotes
- Age-Related Mental Illness and Depression
- Book Reviews

Categories: Nonfiction—Animals— Biography—Book Reviews—Careers—Comedy—Culture—Crafts/Hobbies—Disabilities—Education—Entertainment—Environment—Family Food/Drink—Gardening—General Interest —Health—History—Hobbies—Inspirational—Interview—Lifestyle—Marriage—Men's Issues—Money and Finances—Outdoors—Parenting—Physical Fitness—Politics—Psychology—Real Estate—Recreation—Relationships—Religion—Science—Self Help—Senior Citizens—Sexuality—Society—Sports/Recreation—Spiritual—Travel—Women's Issues

CONTACT: Editorial Director
Material: All
PO Box 600
Chico, CA 95927-0600
E-mail: editor@magicalblend.com
Website: www.transitionsmag.com

Transitions Abroad

Transitions Abroad is a bimonthly magazine guide to practical information on the alternatives to mass tourism: living, working, studying, volunteering abroad, and vacationing alongside the people of the host country. The emphasis is on enriching, informed, affordable, and responsible travel. Circ. 12K , 95% freelance. Editorial Calendar is available on the Transitions Abroad website under "Join Us/Write Ar-

ticles" (see URL below). Lead-time is six months prior to issue date. Pay is $2.00 per column inch. Photography $25 per use ($10 each if part of an accompanying article.) Read a copy of the magazine. *Transitions Abroad* is the "alternative" to standard travel magazines for traditional kinds of travel. Readers like to think of themselves as travelers and not tourists. Preferred method of query is e-mail.

Who We Are

After over a quarter of a century of publication, Transitions Abroad remains the premier magazine for independent travelers, especially for those seeking to extend their time abroad through employment, study, and/or finding the best bargains. (It's also great for those of us who want to keep our overseas experiences alive by discovering and sharing ways that overseas culture can be maintained in our lives at home through food, music, literature, and other creative arts and activities.) The magazine's title, *Transitions*, suggests the personal discoveries and changes in perception and understanding—not just in place—that result from immersion in another culture, even for a short time. Its purpose is to provide readers with the practical information and ideas they need to make their own plans. Readers are most interested in learning about the culture by meeting the people and value for money, in a responsible, fair, respectful way.

Features and Departments Overview
What We Are Looking For

The magazine's five major departments—Immersion Travel, Work, Volunteering, Study, and Living abroad—are all devoted to immediately usable practical information and ideas (the "nuts and bolts"). Contributors write from personal knowledge, usually from first-hand experience, and stress ways to avoid the cultural isolation of a tourist. The more useable information presented in a concise manner, the greater the likelihood of publication. As the editors are unable to check sources, current and accurate information is essential. Sidebars include details that are not in the body of the article: relevant names and addresses, web sites and email addresses, telephone numbers, costs, and other options similar to the ones described in you submission. Well-researched supporting material in sidebars greatly increases the likelihood of publication.

Information Exchange Departments

Since Transitions Abroad is primarily a place for travelers to share information, your contribution need not take the form of a full-length article. Be as brief as possible (250 words maximum). The editors will sometimes shorten material submitted for other departments for inclusion in Information Exchange, which leads off each issue. Payment is a free one-year subscription or subscription extension.

Submissions that otherwise fit our guidelines but are simply too lengthy to include in the magazine (or to shorten for Information Exchange) may be published on our web site. Please tell us if you do not wish your material to be considered for web publication.

What We Do Not Want in Features or Departments

Sightseeing or "destination" pieces that focus exclusively on what to see rather than on the people and culture;

Personal travelogues or lengthy descriptions of personal experiences (unless readers can use the practical details in your account to make their own travel plans);

Articles that represent travel as a form of consumption and objectify the people of other countries;

Information that is readily available in guidebooks or from government tourist offices.

Featured Articles

Length and Format of Feature Articles

Maximum length: 1,500 words. Average length: 1,000 words. For the magazine we must edit tightly because of space limitations. Four feature-length articles are used in each issue: one each on Travel, Work, Study, and Living. Their content, which must be information-based and not a travelogue or narrative description of a personal, should correspond to those of the shorter articles for departments described below.

Departments
Immersion Travel

In this major section of the magazine the emphasis is on avoiding superficial tourist routines, and engaging with local people and culture. Articles may involve finding and selecting such things as a homestay or a rural bed and breakfast, a 1- or 2-week language study course, or pursuing a hobby or activity like cooking, music or mountain hiking. The length of the articles vary: If you have a lot of useful information to share, put it all in (1,000 words maximum if possible). The editors will decide whether your submission can run as a full-length feature or under the heading of one of the shorter features described below.

(Note: Because of space limitations in the magazine an abbreviated version may sometimes run in print and an extended version on the web site. This is true of all submissions.)

Responsible Travel, Community-Based Travel, Eco-Travel

600-1000 words. Current information on how to travel in a manner that respects and supports local people and their culture and travel that helps preserve and protect the environment. First-hand reports are typically preferred, providing information on how local communities abroad organize and profit from eco-tourism, plus details on responsible travel organizers. Short-term vacations or long-term travel opportunities are published. Be specific about dates, contacts, etc. either in the text or in sidebars.

Best Travel Bargains

500 words maximum. Current information on good value for money options (not necessarily the cheapest). Be specific about dates, contacts, etc. in the text (no sidebars). Several used each issue.

The Learning Traveler

500 words maximum (longer pieces will be considered for the Education Abroad section). Usually first-hand reports on a travel-study program or an independently organized learning experience such as a language-learning vacation.

Itineraries

500 words maximum. Readers who travel on their own like to learn about detailed itineraries that will take them off the tourist trail—whether to the less-visited areas of Europe or to remote regions of the rest of the world.

Alternative Tours and Activities

500 words maximum. Ways to combine a vacation abroad with a rewarding activity that travelers would find difficult to organize on their own. Several used each issue.

Solo Woman Traveler

500 words maximum. More and more women are traveling solo or with other women. Submissions should emphasize the advantages of independent solo travel and precautions regarding health and safety.

The Gay or Lesbian Traveler

500 words maximum. The increasing numbers of our gay and lesbian readers are seeking details on gay-friendly destinations abroad.

Travel to Eat

500 words maximum, excluding recipe. Travelers who explore the gastronomic side of travel are encouraged to send articles that explore new lands, new cultures, and new cuisines through culinary experiences. Cooking schools, culinary tours, or independent culinary travel reports are accepted. Include up-to-date contact information, resources, and one recipe.

Travel Tips

500 words maximum. Seasoned and novice travelers alike submit their best practices and insiders' tips to help others have a smoother, more rewarding and educational experience.

The Working Traveler
International Careers

1,000 words maximum. Submissions should focus on securing long term jobs abroad and discuss the experience. Emphasize practical information and insights based on experience in an international career (which may include international work in the U.S.).

Short-Term Work

1,000 words maximum. Your experience in finding and maintaining a short-term job abroad (from crewing a yacht to teaching English) is of great interest to our readers, especially as a way to extend your stay. You should include resources and practical information for how readers can find a similar work experience. Working Traveler Editor Susan Griffith, an authority on short-term work abroad, supplements your own articles with her own expert reports on topics such as the pros and cons of particular jobs around the world, and tips on how to make the most of your job abroad. Several used each issue.

Volunteering

1,000 words maximum. Another very popular, fascinating and rewarding way to extend a trip abroad is to exchange work for free room and board (and sometimes a stipend). First-hand reports on how to do this are welcome. Several used each issue.

Living Abroad

1,000 words maximum. The best way to learn about a country and its culture is to live there (or short of that to travel like a local). For longer stays nothing beats exchanging your home for a comparable home abroad or renting or buying a vacation home. Share your first-hand experience and practical information on assimilating into the local culture and getting to know the people.

Abroad at Home

1,000 words maximum. The opening of borders between people and cultures through art and other forms of expression (music, film, literature, art, craft work, cuisine, etc.) is a bridge to other countries and cultures. Submissions should provide insights on the creative arts of another culture that may be embraced in our day-to-day life while not physically abroad. Resource sidebars may include web sites related to the subject and contact information for relevant groups, clubs, and organizations.

Education Abroad

Articles in this department provide practical information and advice for readers planning a Òstudy abroadÓ experience, travel abroad for specifically academic purposes, or travel to gain experience in preparation for an international career. Columns include: Study Abroad Adviser, Student to Student, Work Abroad Adviser, and Disability Travel Adviser. (See Education Abroad Guidelines and Student Writers Guidelines. Columnists appreciate your feedback and suggestions, and guest columnists are welcome. 1,500 words maximum.

Program Notes

250 words maximum. News of newly organized programs and tours—work, study, or study/travel—or changes in existing programs. Several used each issue.

Submission Procedures
Articles

Maximum length: 1,500 words. Average length: 1,000 words. We edit tightly for length. Manuscripts should be sent electronically and addressed to editor@transitionsabroad.com. Include your contact information. Please attach only Microsoft Word documents: if you use another format, please cut and paste your article into the text portion of your email message. We prefer that you do not send photos electronically until your article has been accepted for publication. If you do not submit your article via email (not recommended), you must provide an electronic version of your manuscript on disk (Macintosh platform) via regular mail. The author's name, address, phone and fax number, and email address should appear on at least the first page of the manuscript.

Photos

We strongly recommend that you let us know whether photos are available with your article. However, if you are submitting an article electronically, please do not submit photos electronically until your article has been accepted for publication. It is fine to send prints or digital photos on disc or standalone photos via postal mail at any time. It is also fine to send electronic standalone photos at anytime. See Photographic Guidelines for all information on sending photos.

Other Submissions Considerations

Regular mail should be accompanied by a business-size SASE. If sending by mail please include your email address! All material is submitted on speculation. We purchase one-time rights only; rights revert to writers upon publication. However, we reserve the right to reprint published articles in part or whole on our web site. We will consider reprinted material from publications outside our primary circulation area. Since ours is not the usual travel publication, writers may want to browse the back issues of our web site or review a recent issue of Transitions Abroad for style and content (See order form).

Contact Information

Electronic Submissions: Editor@TransitionsAbroad.com.

Our postal address is below.

Include a short biographical note at the end of each submission, including your email address. We include these on all published articles so that readers can contact you directly with their feedback.

Include your name, address, telephone numbers (day and evening), and email address on at least the first page of your manuscript.

If sending the manuscript in postal mail, include an envelope of adequate size and with the correct postage for return. We do not return material unaccompanied by SASEs.

Initial response time to manuscripts is about six to eight weeks. We often request permission to hold a submission longer pending final decision shortly before publication. We record and file each submission and take great care with material Òon holdÓ awaiting the appropriate issue. Unless you need your manuscript or photographs returned immediately, please do not telephone. We cannot provide status reports by phone.

Payment

Payment is on publication, approximately $2 per column inch (50-55 words), sometimes more for repeat contributors. For the most part our contributors are not professional travel writers but people with information and ideas to share; we are much more interested in usable first-hand information than in polished prose. Two copies of the issue in which your story appears will be included with payment.

Categories: Nonfiction—Adventure—Conservation—Education—Language—Multicultural—Travel

CONTACT: Ms. Sherry Schwarz, Editor
Material: All
PO Box 745
Bennington VT 05201
Phone/Fax: 802-442-4827
E-mail: editor@transitionsabroad.com
Website: www.TransitionsAbroad.com

Travel & Leisure

Editorial Submissions

If you'd like to pitch a story to Travel & Leisure magazine, please first review the writers' guidelines below.

Travel + Leisure is published monthly has a ratebase of 950,000—including subscribers & newsstand buyers. Our readers are sophisticated, active travelers who look to us for planning both pleasure and business trips.

About 95 percent of the magazine is written by freelance writers on assignment . Every assignment is confirmed by a contract. We pay upon acceptance of the article. Neither editors nor contributors may accept free travel.

How to Proceed:

Look at several issues of the magazine and become familiar with the types of articles published in the various sections.

Please note that a place is not an idea, and that editors are looking for a compelling reason to assign an article: a specific angle, news that makes the subject fresh, a writer's enthusiasm for and familiarity with the topic.

Service information is important to every destination article: when to go, how to get there, where to stay, where to eat, what to see and do. The reader must be able to follow in the author's footsteps, and the articles are scheduled with that in mind.

Please do not telephone us about story proposals. Instead send a query letter that briefly outline the ideas (no more than three at once) being proposed. Please enclose recent clips of your work and a SASE. Query letters can also be sent by filling out the form here. In most cases, these queries will receive the fastest responses.

It is rare that we will assign a feature article to a writer with whom we have not worked. The best section to start with are those in the front of the magazine.

Photography Submissions

Photography portfolios may be sent to address below. If mailing a portfolio, include a self-addressed stamped package for its safe return. You may also send it by messenger Monday through Friday between 11 A.M. and 5 P.M. We accept work in book form exclusively—no transparencies, loose prints, nor scans on cd, disk or email. Send Xerox copies or photo prints, not originals, as we are not responsible for lost or damaged images in unsolicited portfolios. We do not meet with photographers if we haven't seen their book. However, please include a promo card in your portfolio with contact information, so we may get in touch with you if necessary.

If you are sending a messenger to retrieve your portfolio, please call ahead to notify us, and send him to the building's loading dock on 43rd Street. If you are coming personally, you do not need to call ahead. Simply come to the 10th Floor reception area at Travel + Leisure Monday through Friday between 11 A.M. and 5 P.M. and the receptionist will notify the Photo Department to bring out your book. You may also get this information by calling 212-382-5856. Thank you.

Categories: Nonfiction—Leisure—Travel

CONTACT: Travel + Leisure Magazine
Material: Queries
CONTACT: Travel + Leisure Magazine Photo Deptartment
Material: Photography
1120 Avenue of the Americas 10th Fl
New York NY 10036
Phone: 212-382-5600

Travel Naturally
(Formerly known as Naturally)

Overview: For the average American, a vacation is a period of travel and relaxation when you take twice the clothes and half the money you need. And for nude vacationers? Well, the latter may still hold true, but the places where you spend that money can be oh-so-different! *Travel Naturally* looks at why millions of people believe that removing clothes in public is a good idea, and at places specifically created for that purpose with good humor, but also in earnest. *Travel Naturally* takes you to places where your personal freedom is the only agenda, and to places where textile-free living is a serious commitment. *Travel Naturally* invokes the philosophies of naturism and nudism, but also activities and beliefs in the mainstream that invoke nudity: spiritual awareness, New Age customs, pagan and religious rites, alternative and fringe lifestyle beliefs, artistic expressions and many individual nude interests. Our higher purpose is to help restore our sense of self. *Travel Naturally*'s parent company, Internaturally, Inc., is a marketing-publishing firm that came out of the naturist movement — a non-membership-based organization with distribution access to the public. Internaturally, Inc. also publishes and distributes other educational materials about nude recreation; its attractive Internaturally catalog is known worldwide and on the Internet at www.Internaturally.com. *Travel Naturally* seeks mainly informational articles that showcase nude resorts, nude parks, and other nude recreation organizations. Their success assures future clothes-free vacations for everyone. We support public nude beaches, volunteer groups and even private nude homes, because their successes increase public awareness and participation. It's obvious that nudity or nude activities are not philosophies in themselves but, rather, the products of certain philosophies and ideologies some of which are deeply rooted in history and social ritual like nude public bathing and skinny-dipping, meditation and celebration through dance. For most nudist and naturist organizations social nudity, and its benefits, is a serious philosophy and lifestyle commitment that is their main purpose for existence. Other alternative lifestyle groups include nudity ritually, peripherally, or spontaneously, as one of many ways to express cleansing, a celebration of life, and personal freedom. Although the term "nude recreation" may, for some, conjure up visions of sexual frivolities inappropriate for youngsters which can also be technically true these topics are outside the scope of *Travel Naturally* magazine. Here the emphasis is on the many varieties of human beings, of all ages and backgrounds, recreating in their most natural state, at extraordinary places, their reasons for doing so, and the benefits they derive. *Travel Naturally* exists to explore these notions of higher personal freedom and recreational possibilities, worldwide. This is our purpose and your invitation to submit your story, articles and pictures.

Photography: Travel Naturally's photo policy is liberal. We encourage photography at all clothes-free events by courteous and considerate photographers. Although Travel Naturally publishes primarily the work of nudist and naturist (amateur and professional) photographers, we believe strongly that all who are interested in taking pictures at nude events should be free to do so without extraneous restrictions for purposes of protecting anonymity. Unreasonable photo restrictions discourage openness and sabotage the depiction of genuine, and sincere nude recreation. Of course, we do respect the rights of nudist and naturist clubs to set the rules as hosts. Travel Naturally will honor imposed publishing restrictions placed upon some photos by a host. Photographs taken on public land or in establishments open to the public, do not require photo releases unless intended for commercial use (e.g., in an advertisement, to sell something). However, common courtesy and consideration prevails. Photographs acquired surreptitiously or by insensitive methods are not accepted for publication. Photographs taken in closed private areas, not generally thought of as public should have releases from all recognizable persons when the photo is not of a newsworthy situation. For a legitimate newsworthy photograph, Travel Naturally magazine does not require photo releases, even when the picture is taken on private property. Again, common courtesy and consideration prevails, and photographs acquired by insensitive methods are not accepted for publication. Photo releases are the responsibility of the photographer. Photographs may be submitted in color or b & w, as prints, negatives, or slides. Slides or negatives yield the highest reproduction quality. It is preferred, but not required, that selected photos for publication are retained as file copies for possible future use. Unpublished photos are returned as a matter of procedure, unless there is a likelihood for future publication in Travel Naturally magazine or other books and magazines published by Events Unlimited.

Illustrations and Poetry: Thematic renderings, paintings, poems, and other art submissions are welcomed. We document the theme of all submissions and attempt to combine the art with relevant articles, poems, and stories, which are available to the magazine. Please submit only copies or photos of the art so that they can be filed. Do not send originals.

Cartoons: Cartoon illustrations can generally stand on their own, although we may combine them with relevant editorials or other text. The topics are wide open, but the cartoonist should avoid any sexual connotation or innuendo. Payment ranges from $15 per small spot, to $70 per full page. Compensation for full-color cartoons and more elaborately illustrated plates are negotiable.

Organizations: We support most naturist and nudist groups and organizations in their endeavor to educate the mainstream about nude recreation. Toward this endeavor, we have chosen a less political and more lighthearted approach. However, articles and/or photos submitted by nudist/naturist organizations, to inform, to promote an event or political agenda, are accepted and appreciated. Fund-raising appeals are accepted for publication from naturist and nudist organizations. Brevity is requested. We accept event schedules for publication if open to all-comers and dated sufficiently ahead (preferably 5-6 months) to be useful to our readers for at least up to one month after publication.

Paid Participation (at time of publication): All contributors receive copies of Travel Naturally magazine in which their material appears. Travel Naturally pays $70 per published page (text and/or visuals). Fractional pages or fillers are pro-rated. Frequent contributors and regular columnists, who develop a following through Travel Naturally, are paid from the Frequent Contributors Budget. Payments increase on the basis of frequency of participation, and the budget is adjusted quarterly as Travel Naturally grows. We purchase news items that are creatively combined and submitted as one major news article. Blurbs or short news write-ups are graciously accepted as contributions to the cause (see unpaid participation).

Unpaid Participation & Contributions: Published materials, submitted with a commercial agenda, such as product releases, news releases, resort news, etc. are not paid. Published articles intended to promote a commercial entity, resort or nudist park, organization, group, etc. are not paid. It is generally understood that Travel Naturally publishes this material as free promotional/publicity support. Short news (current events) items and clippings are also appreciated as contributions to the cause of promoting the benefits of clothes-optional freedom. Opinion pieces are accepted as contributions only when adequately researched.

Exclusivity: We accept articles and photos that have been previously published elsewhere, when submitted by the original authors or photographers. However, the value of the material is diminished as a non-exclusive submission. We deduct 50% from previously published submissions if accepted for publication.

Assignments: When all-expense-paid assignments are awarded, Travel Naturally magazine will provide paid travel and accommodation expenses. Food and other routine daily living expenses are not paid for. Additional payments are made for the published article(s) and/or photo(s), based upon the above-stated "Paid Participation" criteria. Articles and photos resulting from assignments are for Travel Naturally magazine's exclusive use.

Categories: Nonfiction—Alternate Life-style—Lifestyle—Travel

CONTACT: Submissions Editor
Material: All
PO Box 317
Newfoundland NJ 07435
Phone: 973-697-3552
Fax: 973-697-8313
E-mail: naturally@internaturally.com
Website: www.internaturally.com

Travel Tips

Please refer to Premier Tourism Marketing, Inc.

Treasure Cache

Please refer to *Lost Treasure*.

Troika Magazine

Formal guidelines not available. Please read a number of issues to ascertain the publication's style and needs.

To submit your work to *Troika* for consideration please e-mail your submissions to submit@troikamagazine.com.

You will be contacted by the editors within approximately 90 days.

Categories: Nonfiction—General Interest—Lifestyle—Literature

CONTACT: Submissions Editor
Material: All
PO Box 1006
Weston CT 06883
Phone: 203-227-5377
Fax: 203-222-9332
E-mail: submit@troikamagazine.com
Website: www.troikamagazine.com/home.html

True Romance

True Romance was formerly *Modern Romance*. *True Romance* features first-person narratives written for the average, high school educated woman. She is juggling family and work responsibilities, but family comes first. After a long day, she wants to read compelling, realistic stories about other women and how they have overcome obstacles. Stories must be set in towns, cities, and neighborhoods where hardworking Americans live.

Emotionally charged stories with a strong emphasis on characterization and well-defined plots are preferred. Our suspenseful stories deal with romance, families, marital problems, tragedy, peril, mystery, and Americana. The plots and characters should reflect the average American's values and desires.

Do not send query letters. Send completed manuscripts. Seasonal material should be sent six months in advance. Mark the outside of the envelope: seasonal material. We do not accept simultaneous submissions. We buy all rights of our published materials.

Manuscripts should be double-spaced. Typewritten and letter-quality inkjet or laser printer manuscripts are acceptable. A dot-matrix manuscript is only acceptable if it is letter quality. Please send your submission on disk, along with a paper copy. If you want your manuscript and/or disk returned, you must send a self-addressed, stamped envelope. Unfortunately, the editorial staff cannot critique each manuscript.

Tips: Writers should read three or four issues of *True Romance* before sending submissions. Do not talk down to our readers. Timely, first-person stories told by a sympathetic narrator are appreciated. Dramatic stories and stories featuring ethnic characters are always needed, but stay away from stereotypical plots and characteristics.

Greatest Needs: Stories between 5,000 and 10,000 words.

Terms: We receive a vast number of submissions, and each one is given careful consideration; therefore, we ask for your patience in receiving replies. *True Romance* reports back to writers in eight to twelve months. The editor reads all stories. We pay three cents per word a month after publication. Again, please do not send simultaneous submissions.

Columns: "Loving Pets" pays $50 for a photo and up to 50 words about your pet. Photos must be in focus and no other people should be in the picture. "Love Letter" pays $50. "Family Recipe" pays $50. "Let It Out" pays $50. "Happily Ever After" pays $50.

Poetry: Look at poetry published in three or four issues before submitting. Poetry should be no longer than twenty-four lines. Payment is $10 to $50.

Good luck with your writing,
The Editors

Categories: Fiction—Relationship—Romance—Rural America—Short Stories—Women's Fiction

CONTACT: Nell Miller, Editor
Material: All
Dorchester Media
333 Seventh Ave., 11th Floor
New York NY 10001
Phone: 212-979-4894
Fax: 212-979-7342

True Story

Thank you for your interest in True Story magazine.

If you would like to send us your story on speculation, we'd be glad to read it. The best way to learn about our editorial style is to read several issues and get a feel for the types of stories we publish.

Subject matter can range from light romances to sizzling passion, from all-out tearjerkers to happily-ever-after endings, and everything in between. True Story is unique because all of our stories are written from the hearts of real people and deal with all of the issues that affect us today—parenthood, relationships, careers, family affairs, and social concerns.

All of our stories are written in the first person, just as if you were talking to a friend and should be no less than 2,000 words and no more than 10,000. If you have access to a computer, we require you to send your submission on a disk, along with a clean hard copy of the story. Please keep in mind that when sending stories to us, all files must be saved as rich text format (RTF). Stories should be typed and double-spaced. If you don't have a computer, please use a typewriter.

If we publish your story, we will buy all world rights and pay you at our regular rate—five cents a word. We cannot accept stories that are simultaneous submissions.

We receive a vast number of manuscripts, and each one is given careful consideration, so it usually takes twelve months for a response. Please include a stamped, self-addressed envelope with your story so that we may return it to you if it doesn't meet our needs. It is advisable for you to keep a copy of your story in case anything should happen to the original.

We look forward to reading your story. Good luck!

Categories: Fiction—Nonfiction—Career—Family—General Interest—Parenting—Relationships

CONTACT: Tina Pappalardo
Material: All
True Story
The Sterling/Macfadden Partnership
333 Seventh Ave 11th Fl
New York NY 10001-5004

True West

TRUE WEST magazine publishes nonfiction articles on the history of the American West from 1800 to the early 20th Century. More recent topics may be used if they have a historical angle or retain the Old West flavor of trail dust and saddle leather.

Our readers are predominantly male, forty-five years of age or older, from rural areas and small towns. Nearly all have graduated from high school, and slightly more than half have attended college. They are knowledgeable about Western history and ranching and want articles to be informative and entertaining.

We cover all states west of the Mississippi and all areas of western history—Native Americans, trappers, miners, cowboys, ranchers, farmers, pioneers, the military, ghost towns, lost mines, women, and minorities. We especially need good western humor and stories on lesser-known people and events. If widely-known topics are used, the article should include newly discovered information or take a fresh approach to the subject.

Historical accuracy and strict adherence to the facts are essential. We much prefer material based on primary sources (archives, court records, documents, contemporary newspapers, and first person accounts) to those that rely mainly on secondary sources (published books, magazines, and journals). We occasionally use first person reminiscences, but proper names and dates must be accurate and double-checked by the author. We do not want dialogue unless it can be documented, and we do not use fictionalized treatments of historical subjects. Manuscripts other than first person recollections should be accompanied by a bibliographic list of sources.

TRUE WEST prefers one-page queries with one subject per query. Please provide information regarding the availability of photographs and/or illustrations. We usually need from four to eight photos for each story, and we rely on writers to provide them. We respond to submissions in a timely manner.

To judge our needs, consult our 2003 back issues.

TRUE WEST is published 10 issues per year. 2004 is the 51st anniversary of the magazine.

Categories: Nonfiction—History—Lifestyle—Western

CONTACT: R.G. Robertson, Editor
Material: All
True West Publishing, LLC
PO Box 8008
Cave Creek AZ 85327
Phone: 888-687-1881
E-mail: editor@truewestmagazine.com
Website: www.truewestmagazine.com

Turkey Call

NWTF Editorial Contributor Guidelines

The NWTF publishes six magazines—*Turkey Call, Women In The Outdoors, Wheelin' Sportsmen, Get in the Game, JAKES Magazine* and *The Caller*—that are available through membership.

Articles submitted for publication fulfill the promise of the author's query and, more importantly, the editor's assignment. Familiarize yourself with our publications to ensure your material is compatible with the magazine's format or needs. Articles must be free of spelling errors, grammatically correct and accurate.

Failure to follow these guidelines may result in the rejection of your manuscript or photographs. We purchase first North American serial rights to articles. All written material should be original and unpublished and must consist of accurate information that appeals to our special-interest readership. While most feature stories deal with non-fiction subjects, we do accept fiction that contributes to the education, enlightenment or entertainment of our readers. We pay upon publication. Kill fees are 20 percent of contracted payment.

Our readers enjoy articles that are easy to read. Feature stories are typically supplemented with sidebars, bulleted lists, subheads, pull quotes and other graphic-friendly elements.

Queries

Written queries may be submitted via conventional or electronic mail and must fully explain a proposed article and its main points. Queries should include ideas for potential graphic aids and sidebars. Because queries exemplify an author's writing talent, verbal queries are not acceptable.

Check each magazine's section below to see whether laundry lists are accepted.

Queries allow us to assign specific articles according to our needs. Even though you may have a fantastic article idea, we may have recently published a similar story or have one in our files.

We typically respond to queries within 14 business days. However, we may ask to hold certain queries for review at a later date. An editor will contact you with assignment specifications if your idea is accepted, or a rejection if it is not. Provide e-mail (preferred), telephone or other contact information with each query.

Assigned Articles

Articles, sidebars and photo captions must be submitted in one of the following methods:

- Microsoft Word (file ends with .doc suffix)
- Rich-Text Format (file ends with .rtf suffix)
- Text-only format (file ends with .txt suffix)
- On paper

All text must be single-spaced, with only one space after periods, no tabs or indentions on the first line of paragraphs, and only one "hard return" at the end of each paragraph.

For e-mail submissions: Paste all text within the body of an e-mail message and send as an attachment in one of the formats listed above. Ask the editor if e-mail is appropriate for sending a particular assignment. We follow the Associated Press (AP) Stylebook and Libel Manual.

Unsolicited Articles

Though we accept unsolicited manuscripts, they are not preferred. Such speculative submissions may remain in our files for a long time before being reviewed. If an unsolicited manuscript is accepted, an editor or publishing assistant will contact you. If rejected, all materials will be returned to you. (Enclose a SASE for return; the NWTF does not pay shipping costs for the return of unsolicited material.)

Photographic Submissions

All photographers making submissions to the NWTF and its publications must agree and comply with the terms listed in the following guidelines. These terms supersede any terms submitted or offered by the contributor at the time of submission.

Terms

- All submissions, unless approved otherwise by the editor, are sent at the expense of the contributor.
- The NWTF does not pay agency research fees.
- The NWTF will negotiate the replacement cost of damaged or lost slides at the time of the incident based on fair market values, and does not agree to any contracts, delivery notices or statements of value included in a submission.
- The NWTF does not return digital submissions, nor does it hold any liability to replace discarded or lost CDs, DVDs, digital files or any prints from these digital files that may accompany a submission.
- The NWTF agrees to one-time North American rights for each image selected for publication or additional rights as negotiated with the contributor.

We look for quality—clarity, sharpness, composition and correct exposure. Each photo should have a written caption with a description of the shot and the names of any people shown.

Images are accepted on speculation as well as to accompany specific assignments. It is best to limit the number of images to less than 20 on any one submission unless directed otherwise by the editor. Rather than sending near-duplicates and similar images, state in a cover letter whether you have more images similar to images submitted.

Slides and Photographs

For color photo submissions, the NWTF accepts only original (not duplicate) transparencies; 35mm is the most common, although medium formats are also acceptable.

Prints must be silver-process photographic enlargements, not inkjet or laser-printed copies. Minimum size for prints is 4x6 inches; maximum size is 8½x14 inches.

Images must be in focus and well exposed.

Each photo should have the contributor's name, address and phone number on it, and a code number for identification.

Each photo should have a written caption with a description of the shot and the names of any people shown. Photos including people must have a model release on file with the contributor for each of the subjects in the photo.

Carefully package your photographs and use a traceable shipping system. Remember that those who handle the mail may not have our same consideration for the value of your photographs; if not packaged correctly, your photos risk being damaged. The NWTF is not responsible for photos not received or photos damaged while in transit to the NWTF.

Return of your photos is important to us. Provide ground-shipping instructions at the time of submission to ensure delivery by traceable shipping method (Federal Express, UPS, etc.).

Digital Images

The NWTF and its publications follow the specifications set forth by the Digital Image Submission Criteria working group (www.disc-info.org) for Category A publications. Digital photos submitted to the NWTF publications must pass these criteria before being considered for publication:

• The minimum allowable resolution for photos in all NWTF publications is 2,000x1,500 pixels. If your camera will not take photographs at this resolution or higher, do not submit digital photos from that camera.

• Always shoot in the digital camera's highest quality, lowest compression mode.

• The camera's colorspace (color matrix, color setting) must be set to ADOBE RGB (1998). We do not accept images with a colorspace of sRGB (optimized for Web).

• Images that have been cropped, sharpened, brightened, color-adjusted or manipulated in any way will not be accepted.

• Do not submit scanned prints or slides. Submit the original prints or slides and let us scan them to our printing specifications.

• Photos scanned from another magazine or newspaper are not acceptable.

• Images must be in either uncompressed TIFF or low compression JPEG format. We also accept RAW files.

Digital images must be embedded with ownership metadata, the photographer's name and contact information, as well as caption and credit information.

A printed contact sheet that includes image names must accompany digital images submitted on CD-ROM or DVD.

E-mailed submissions must not exceed 18mb and must be approved by the editor prior to transmission. It is best to send low-resolution thumbnails at 3x5 inches/72dpi in an initial e-mail. The editor may then ask you to send specific high-resolution files as needed.

Turkey Call

As the flagship publication of the NWTF, *Turkey Call* is dedicated to the interests and entertainment of wild turkey enthusiasts everywhere—people who hunt, study and actively support the restoration and conservation of the North American wild turkey. It is published bi-monthly with issues in January/February, March/April, May/June, July/August, September/October and November/December. *Turkey Call* feature articles focus on the restoration, management, biology, distribution, history and hunting of wild turkeys. Features typically run 1,500 words, and are accompanied by graphics, sidebars, bulleted text, pull quotes, fast facts and other reader-friendly shortcuts. We also publish short features on unusual hunting experiences, historical vignettes, the wild turkey in art or literature, biographical sketches, tips, anecdotes, humor or other appropriate outdoor subjects.

While limited use of the author's experience is acceptable, articles should feature advice from experts and not rely too heavily on biological terms to emphasize points. Preference centers on anecdotes about people besides the author.

Send individual queries; no laundry lists. Articles should:
• Be written for wild turkey experts, except when specifically addressing neophytes
• Appeal to a national readership
• Be meticulously researched
• Be accurate; dates, figures and the names and titles of agencies and people involved must be correct
• Provide documentation and contact information for all sources, including people interviewed and quoted within the story

Turkey Call works four months to a year ahead of each issue. Most feature story material is planned a year in advance.

We pay $100 for short pieces of 600 to 700 published words; $200 to $275 for articles of 700 to 1,100 words; and $300 to $500 for up to 1,800 words.

We publish images of various wild turkey subspecies in their natural habitats, turkey hunting scenes, colorful scenics of wild turkey habitat and vintage turkey hunting scenes. Images may be submitted to accompany specific assignments or on speculation. See photograph submission information and send speculative images to the photo editor at the NWTF shipping address.

Rates for published photographs:
• Cover = $400
• Two-page spread = $175
• Full page = $125
• Half-page = $100
• One-third page or less = $75

Categories: Fiction—Nonfiction—Recreation—Sports—Hunting

CONTACT: Burt Carey, Editor
bcarey@nwtf.net
CONTACT: Jake Fagan, Managing Editor
jfagan@nwtf.net
CONTACT: Matt Lindler, Photo Editor
mlindler@nwtf.net
National Wild Turkey Federation
PO Box 530
770 Augusta Rd
Edgefield SC 29824
Phone: 803-637-3106
Fax: 803-637-0034
Web site: www.nwtf.org

Turtle

Please refer to Children's Better Health Institute.

Twins
The Magazine for Parents of Multiples

TWINS, *The Magazine for Parents of Multiples*, is a bimonthly, international publication that provides informational and educational articles regarding parenting twins, triplets and more.

TWINS magazine consists of four to six features and 10 departments per issue. Features are 1,100 to 1,500 words and departments are 750 to 950 words including sidebars and additional materials. Please limit your manuscripts to these lengths.

Because our readers are very busy, articles must be written in an easy, conversational style. Please study our format before starting an article. To make articles more readable, please break up long copy with subheads. TWINS conforms to AP style.

All department articles must have a happy ending, as well as teach a lesson or provide a moral that parents of multiples can learn from.

TWINS accepts queries for feature articles. For departments, we accept either queries or manuscripts sent on speculation. Submissions must tell stories that teach lessons about family life with multiples. Subjects of interest include perspectives on being or parenting multiples, as well as child-rearing, family and social issues.

Please send queries by mail or e-mail to the contact listed below, along with a resume and samples of your work. Please indicate if you are interested in us contacting you for feature assignments.

Submit assigned articles by mail or e-mail. When mailing assigned articles, please include a hard copy as well as the file saved on a 3.5" floppy disk. To ensure our computers can read the file, save it as an ASCII or "text only" file. If you would like your disk back, please enclose a self-addressed, stamped envelope. When e-mailing articles, please embed the story in the body of the message and attach the word processing file at the end of the message.

Please also include your signed contract, an invoice and a two-sentence biography for the story tag line. We cannot publish an article without a signed contract and cannot pay a you without an invoice. The invoice must have your name, address, payment amount and social security number.

Fees are negotiated prior to publication and payment is made within 30 days following publication. A contract is sent after assignment is made.

A byline is supplied, and one complimentary copy of the magazine is sent to each contributor following publication.

TWINS magazine purchases first North American serial rights.

Categories: Family—Parenting

CONTACT: Sharon Withers, Managing Editor
Material: All
5350 S. Roslyn St. Ste. 400
Englewood CO 80111
Phone: 303-290-8500
Fax: 303-290-9025
E-mail: twins.editor@businessword.com
11211 E. Arapahoe Rd., #101
Centennial CO 80111

Two Rivers Review

Founded in 1998, *Two Rivers Review* is a biannual journal of quality contemporary poetry and fiction. Our goal is to present the best writing we can find, with a special interest in writing that gives pleasure to the reader. To that end, we have published authors as respected as Billy Collins, Lee Upton and Naomi Shihab Nye, alongside lesser-known but equally astonishing poets like Robert Bense, Myrna Stone and Daniel Donaghy. Each issue of TRR is 40-48 pages long. Work is printed in a clear, easy-on-the-eyes format. TRR mostly prints contemporary poetry, along with a small amount of short fiction, and occasional translations. TRR also publishes an annual poetry chapbook, selected through a national competition.

Poetry Guidelines

TRR welcomes submissions of original, unpublished poetry. Please follow the following guidelines when sending your work.
• All submissions must include an SASE.
• Submit no more than four poems per submission.
• All poems must be previously unpublished.
• No handwritten submissions.
• No e-mail submissions, please.
• Please do not submit more than three times per calendar year.

Poets should keep in mind that TRR is extremely competitive. We receive approximately 5,000 poems per year, and accept about 25 per issue. Of those 25, 5-10 are from manuscripts solicited by the editor. This is not to discourage anyone, of course; merely a reminder that all poets, regardless of reputation or prior publication, should submit only their best work for consideration at TRR. We strongly suggest that poets read an issue of *Two Rivers Review* before submitting work.

All poetry submissions (as well as subscriptions and other business correspondence) should be sent to:
Two Rivers Review
PO Box 158
Clinton, NY 13323

Fiction Guidelines

Beginning with issue #7, TRR will print short fiction along with poetry. Please follow the following guidelines when submitting fiction.
• All submissions must include an SASE.
• Submit no more than one story per submission.
• All stories must be previously unpublished.
• Simultaneous submissions acceptable, provided that you tell us

in your cover letter.
• All submissions must be typed and double-spaced.
• No e-mail submissions, please.
• Stories may be submitted ONLY during the following reading periods: June 1 - July 15, and January 1 - February 15. Fiction received outside of these reading periods may be returned unread.

Categories: Fiction—Poetry

CONTACT: Carole Burns
Material: Fiction
CONTACT: Submissions Editor
Material: Poetry
PO Box 158
Clinton NY 13323
Website: trrpoetry.tripod.com

THE UKRAINIAN WEEKLY
Published by the Ukrainian National Association

The Ukrainian Weekly

We greatly appreciate the materials—feature articles, news stories, press clippings, letters to the editor, and the like—we receive from our readers. In order to facilitate preparation of *The Ukrainian Weekly*, we ask that the guidelines listed below be followed.
• News stories should be sent in not later than 10 days after the occurrence of a given event.
• All materials must be typed and double-spaced.
• Photographs (originals only, no photocopies or computer printouts) submitted for publication must be accompanied by captions. Photos will be returned only when so requested and accompanied by a stamped, addressed envelope.
• Full names (i.e., no initials) and their correct English spellings must be provided.
• Newspaper and magazine clippings must be accompanied by the name of the publication and the date of the edition.
• Information about upcoming events must be received one week before the date of *The Weekly* edition in which the information is to be published.
• Persons who submit any materials must provide a daytime phone number where they may be reached if any additional information is required.
• Unsolicited materials submitted for publication will be returned only when so requested and accompanied by a stamped, addressed envelope.

Categories: Ethnic newspaper
CONTACT: Roma Hadzewycz, Editor-in-Chief
Material:Ukrainian National Association
2200 Route 10
PO Box 280
Parsippany NJ 07054
Phone: 973-292-9800

Underground Construction

Please refer to Oildom Publishing.

Unique Opportunities

EDITORIAL PHILOSOPHY

Unique Opportunities is a national bimonthly magazine for physicians looking for their first or next practice opportunity. Its goal is to educate the reader about how to evaluate career opportunities, negotiate the benefits offered, and plan career moves. It also provides information on the legal and economic aspects of accepting a position and running a practice.

AUDIENCE: *Unique Opportunities* is distributed to 80,000 physicians who are interested in new practice opportunities or who are in their final years of residency.

QUERY: Submit article ideas via mail or e-mail. The editors prefer to assign articles from queries rather than receive complete article submissions.

TYPES OF ARTICLES

Unique Opportunities publishes feature articles that cover the economic, business, and career-related issues of interest to physicians who would like to relocate or change practices. Feature articles range in length from 1,500 to 3,500 words. Previously run stories include:

- Paving the Way for Employee Terminations—Firing the smart way.
- Logged on to the Future—On-line CME gets easier and better.
- The Road to Private Practice—A roadmap to entering private practice.
- What's That, Doc?—Physician-inventors.

FORMAT FOR SUBMISSIONS: Submit articles via e-mail as ASCII text file attachments or as the body of an e-mail message. Articles may also be submitted on a 3.5" diskette as ASCII text or other files compatible with Microsoft Word from either a Macintosh or MS-DOS computer.

PAYMENT: *Unique Opportunities* pays within 30 days of acceptance and receipt of an invoice. Standard rate for feature articles is $.75 a word plus expenses up to $75. (Any expenses incurred over $75 must be approved at the Louisville office, 502-589-8250.)

Rights: First North American print rights, exclusive for 90 days after publication, and rights to publish electronically on UO's Web site with no time limit. Will not consider duplicate submissions.

Categories: Nonfiction—Careers—Trade—Physicians Career Opportunities

CONTACT: Bett Coffman, Associate Editor
Material: All
214 S. 8th St., Ste 502
Louisville KY 40202
Phone: 502-589-8250
Fax: 502-587-0848
E-mail: tellus@uoworks.com
Website: www.uoworks.com

United Parenting Publications

United Parenting Publications publishes these periodicals in the San Francisco Bay Area:

- *Bay Area Parent* magazine is a regional monthly parenting magazine with distribution of 180,000 copies through four zoned editions, covering San Francisco, Silicon Valley, the East Bay, and the North Bay, including Sonoma and Marin Counties.
- *Get Up & Go, A Magazine For Active & Involved Grandparents*, is published in March, June and October.
- *Bay Area Parent's B.A.B.Y.* (The Best Advice For Baby & You) is published two times a year, with distribution of 60,000 copies to new and expectant parents all over the Greater San Francisco Bay Area.
- *Bay Area Parent of Teens* is no longer published.

To receive a free copy of one of these magazines, please send a self-addressed envelope (at least 8½ x 11) stamped with ten stamps. Indicate which publication you want to receive.

Most of the editorial for these publications is written by freelance writers on assignment. A few unsolicited articles are run. The information most likely to BE used is local, well-researched and geared to parents of newborns to early teens.

Poetry or fiction is not accepted. Timeliness is critical, e.g., swimming in June and snow skiing in December. Editorial content is planned 3 to 6 months in advance, so articles pertinent to a particular season should be proposed or submitted well in advance.

We appreciate submission of appropriate photographs with a story. We pay upon acceptance. Rates are based on the nature and scope of the piece.

United Parenting Publications was formerly known as Bay Area Publishing Group.

Categories: Children—Family—Juvenile—Parenting—Teen

CONTACT: Regional Editor
Material: All
11076 Coloma Rd., Ste. 7
Rancho Cordova CA 95670
Phone: 916-635-1655
Fax: 916-635-4262
Website: parenthood.com

The Upper Room

The meditations in each issue are written by people just like you, people who are listening to God and trying to live by what they hear. *The Upper Room* is built on a worldwide community of Christians who share their faith with one another.

The Upper Room is meant for an international, interdenominational audience. We want to encourage Christians in their personal life of prayer and discipleship. We seek to build on what unites us as believers and to link believers together in prayer around the world.

Literally millions of people use the magazine each day. Your meditation will be sent around the world, to be translated into more than 44 languages and printed in over 73 editions. Those who read the day's meditation and pray the prayer join with others in over 100 countries around the world, reading the same passage of scripture and bringing the same concerns before God.

Have God's care and presence become real for you in your interaction with others? Has the Bible given you guidance and helped you see God at work? Has the meaning of scripture become personal for you as you reflected on it? Then you have something to share in a meditation.

Where do I begin?

You begin in your own relationship with God. Christians believe God speaks to us and guides us as we study the Bible and pray. Good meditations are closely tied to scripture and show how it has shed light on a specific situation. Good meditations make the message of the Bible come alive.

Good devotional writing is first of all authentic. It connects real events of daily life with the ongoing activity of God. It comes across as the direct, honest statement of personal faith in Christ and how that faith grows. It is one believer sharing with another an insight or struggle about what it means to live faithfully.

Second, good devotional writing uses sensory details — what color it was, how high it bounced, what it smelled like. The more sensory details the writing includes, the better. Though the events of daily life may seem mundane, actually they provide the richest store of sensory details. And when we connect God's activity to common things, each encounter with them can serve as a reminder of God's work.

Finally, good devotional writing is exploratory. It searches and considers and asks questions. It examines the faith without knowing in advance what all the answers will be. It is open to God's continuing self-revelation through scripture, people, and events. Good writing chronicles growth and change, seeing God behind both.

How do I get started writing a meditation?

When you find yourself in the middle of some situation thinking, "Why—that's how God is, too!" or, "That's like that story in the Bible...," that can become a meditation. Excellent ideas come from reading and meditating on scripture, looking for connections between it and daily life. When you see such a helpful connection, here's a simple formula for getting it on paper:

Retell the Bible teaching or summarize the passage briefly.

Describe the situation that you link to the Bible passage, using a specific incident. Write down as many details of the real-life situation as you can. For example, if you write about an incident when people were talking, write down what each person said.

Tell how you can apply this spiritual truth in days to come.

After a few days, look carefully at what you have written. Decide which details best convey your message, and delete the others. Ask yourself whether this insight will be helpful to believers in other countries and other situations. If you feel that it will, add any elements that are necessary to *The Upper Room's* format. Then you are ready to submit your meditation for consideration for possible use in *The Upper Room.*

Tips to keep in mind

· Begin with studying and meditating on the Bible so its power supports your words.

· Connect scripture with your own life. Your experience is unique.

· Each day's meditation includes a title, suggested Bible reading, quoted scripture verse, personal witness or reflection on scripture, prayer, a "thought for the day" (a pithy, summarizing statement), and a "prayer focus" (suggested subject for further prayer).

· Meditations should be about 250 words long.

· Remember that what you write will be translated for use around the world, so use clear, direct language. Hymns, poems, and word plays such as acrostics or homonyms ("God's presence/presents", "the light of the sun/Son") make meditations unusable.

· Poetry and quoted lines from poems cannot be used.

· Previously published material cannot be used. Use of material that cannot be verified (such as quotes) will hinder publication.

· Very familiar illustrations have little impact and should not be used.

· Avoid preaching ("you should ...," "you need to ...," "we must ...," etc.)

· Use language and examples that appeal to the five senses. Tell what you heard, saw touched, smelled tasted. When appropriate, use dialogue to tell your story.

· Make only one point. Think snapshot, not movie.

· Focus on how you can deepen the Christian commitment of readers and nurture their spiritual growth.

· Indicate the version of the Bible quoted in the text, and give references for any scripture passages mentioned.

· Seek always to encourage readers to deeper engagement with the Bible.

· Include your name and address on each page you submit. Please include a guide for pronouncing your name as our meditations are recorded for an audio edition. If possible, please type your meditation, double-spaced. Always give the original source of any materials you quote. Meditations containing quotes or other secondary material that cannot be verified will not be used.

When are the deadlines?

We continually need meditations, and you can submit a meditation at any time. However, seasonal material should reach us fifteen months before use date. Below are the due dates and special emphases for the various issues.

January - February Issue: Deadline: August 1 of second year preceding. (For example, 2008 should reach us by Aug. 1, 2006) Special emphases: New Year, Epiphany, Ash Wednesday

March - April Issue: Deadline: Oct. 1 of second year preceding. Special emphases: Lent, Palm Sunday, Maundy Thursday, Good Friday, Easter, World Day of Prayer

May - June Issue: Deadline: Dec. 1 of second year preceding. Special emphases: Mother's Day, Father's Day, Ascension Day, Pentecost, Trinity Sunday

July - August Issue: Deadline: Feb. 1 of preceding year. Special emphases: Creative uses of leisure

September - October Issue: Deadline: April 1 of preceding year. Special emphases: World Communion Sunday, God and our daily work

November - December Issue: Deadline: June 1 of preceding year. Special emphases: Bible Sunday, All Saints' Day, Thanksgiving, Advent, Christmas

Special emphases

January-February issue: New Year, Epiphany, Ash Wednesday

March-April issue: Lent, Palm Sunday, Maundy Thursday, Good Friday, Easter, World Day of Prayer

May-June issue: Festival of the Chrisian home, Ascension Day, Pentecost, Trinity Sunday

July-August issue: Creative uses of leisure

September-October issue: World Communion Sunday, God and our daily work. Tithing/Stewardship

November-December issue: Bible Sunday, All Saints' Day, Day of Prayer for Persecuted Christians, Thanksgiving, Advent, Christmas

Our response to your work

If your work is being considered for publication, we will send you a postcard, usually within six weeks. Later, if your meditation is chosen for publication, you will receive a copyright release form to return to us. It may be as much as a year before a final decision is made. If you wish to be notified if your work is eliminated from consideration, include a stamped, self-addressed postcard for each meditation.

We buy the right to translate meditations for one-time use in our editions around the world, including electronic and software-driven formats, and to include them in future anthologies of Upper Room material should we choose. We pay $25.00 for each meditation, on publication.

We are unable to give updates on the status of submitted material or to offer critiques. All published meditations are edited.

Please be sure to include your postal address with each meditation, since we must send a form to be signed if your work is chosen for publication. If you submit by email, send your meditation as the body of the message, not as an attachment.

Meditations cannot be returned, so keep copies of what you submit. Please send no more than three meditations at a time. If you wish to know we have received your work, include a stamped, self-addressed postcard in addition to the one(s) previously mentioned. We will use the postcard to notify you that your work has reached us.

We look forward to receiving meditations from you to be considered for possible use in future editions of *The Upper Room.*

Categories: Nonfiction—Christian Interests—Inspirational—Religion—Spiritual

CONTACT: Managing Editor
Material: All
PO Box 340004
Nashville TN 37203-0004
Phone: 615-340-7200
E-mail: TheUpperRoomMagazine@upperroom.org
Website: www.upperroom.org

The Urbanite
Surreal & Lively & Bizarre

First of all, my apologies to anyone who has been waiting longer than usual for a reply from *The Urbanite: Surreal & Lively & Bizarre.* For some time now, I have been trying to figure out the next step in the magazine's evolution. I considered many possibilities—Webzine? CD? Some sort of electronic book? I did some research and discussed the various options with different folks.

Eventually talks began with an exciting new publishing firm, and I am happy to state that *The Urbanite: Surreal & Lively & Bizarre* has been reborn as an annual paperback anthology, published by Catalyst Books. I'll still be editing it, so manuscripts should still be sent to the usual Urbanite address. Still snail-mail only—I do most of my manuscript reading in coffee shops.

The Urbanite will be an annual paperback anthology of dark fiction. There will be no themes—except of course, quality. I'll still consider poetry, but probably won't be accepting as much. Payment for fiction: three cents a word. Payment for poetry: $10 per poem.

Categories: Fiction—Poetry

CONTACT: Mark McLaughlin, Editor
Material: All
PO Box 4737
Davenport IA 52808

U.S. Kids

Please refer to Children's Better Health Institute.

USA Cycling

Please send summary of your article to Kelly Walker by fax, email, or snail mail with a SASE. Editor will respond within 2 weeks. Articles will run no sooner than two months of acceptance. Feature articles are at least 1,000 words. Payment depends on length and quality and usually ranges from $50-$100.

Categories: Nonfiction—Outdoors—Sports/Recreation

CONTACT: Kelly Walker, Editor
Material: All
TPG Sports, Inc.
One Olympic Plaza
Colorado Springs CO 80909
Phone: 719-866-3360, Ext 3360
Fax: 719-866-4628
E-mail: kwalker@usacycling.org
Website: www.usacycling.org

Utne

Writers' Guidelines

Thank you for your interest in *Utne*. Most of the articles that run in our magazine are reprinted from the thousands of magazines, newsweeklies, newsletters, and literary journals we receive regularly. We will consider your article for *Utne* only if it has been published recently in another alternative publication. We do not accept fiction or poetry.

Our Gleanings department, which features short (250 to 1,000 words), eclectic, often personal, occasionally humorous pieces, offers the best odds. You might also submit shorter articles for our View section, which covers new developments in social, political and cultural issues, but relies mostly on assigned articles.

Submitting an Article

To submit your already published article for consideration, send a high-quality photocopy (no reductions or two-sided copies, please). Include information about the publication (description, address, phone number) and the publication date your article originally appeared. If you do not hold the rights to the article, also include the name, address, and phone number of the party who does. Include a self-stamped, self-addressed envelope (SASE) if you want a response or your article returned.

Via E-mail

If you choose to submit a previously published article via e-mail (editor@utne.com), please include your address and phone number and the publication information described above.

Because we are primarily a reprint magazine, we are of course open to receiving simultaneous submissions; make sure other publications know we are also considering your work. Our staff is small, so we may take a number of months to reply to unsolicited manuscripts. Thanks again for your interest.—The Editors of *Utne*

Art Submissions

First, we'd like to make this clear (if it isn't already): We love visual artists! In every issue of *Utne* magazine, we seek to present a lively range of illustrative and photographic "voices." We are always on the lookout for skilled artists with a talent for interpreting editorial content, and welcome examples of your work for consideration. Because of our small staff, busy production schedule, and the volume of samples we receive, however, we ask that you read and keep in mind the following guidelines.

We also kindly ask that you not call or e-mail seeking feedback or to check if your package has arrived. We wish we could be more generous in this regard, but we simply don't have the staff or the memory capacity to recall what has come in. (SASE's and reply cards will be honored.)

Be assured, if your art strikes us as a good fit for the magazine, we want to talk to you as much as you may want to talk to us. It just might take a while.

Make seeing your art easy for us! Send samples that can be quickly viewed and tacked to a bulletin board. Single-sided postcards, color or black & white photocopies, printed agency/rep samples, and small posters are all good.

Show us that you are consistent in your ability to execute high-quality work. We are highly unlikely to give you an assignment based on only one sample, and we strongly prefer that you send several samples in one package rather than single pieces in separate mailings.

DO NOT SEND cover letters, resumes, and gallery or exhibition lists.

DO NOT SEND e-mails, CD's, disks, links to Web sites, etc. We do not have the staff capacity to follow-up and your messages and samples will be deleted or thrown away.

IMPORTANT: Clearly mark your full name, address, phone number, fax number, and e-mail address on EVERYTHING you send. (PHOTOGRAPHERS: Tell us where you are!)

PLEASE DO NOT EVER SEND ORIGINAL ARTWORK OR ORIGINAL PHOTOGRAPHS OF ANY KIND.

Send your samples to: (Samples cannot be returned.)

Artwork, *Utne* magazine, 1624 Harmon Place, Suite 330, Minneapolis, MN 55403.

Cartoon Submissions

Size matters. Most of the cartoons we run are single panel, and must reproduce well at approximately 3x3 inches. Please limit submissions of multi-frame cartoons. REMEMBER: We are a bi-monthly! Cartoons submitted will not potentially be published for at least 2 months.

Send camera-ready drawings or high-quality photocopies to the "Artwork" address above. Comic books may be directed to our librarian, Chris Dodge.

Categories: Culture

CONTACT: Editor
Material: All
Utne Magazine
1624 Harmon Pl, Ste 330
Minneapolis MN 55403
E-mail: editor@utne.com
Website: www.utne.com

Remember: Editors change jobs and publishers change addresses. It is wise to invest in a phone call for the current information before submitting.

Vacation Industry Review

Editorial Policy: *Vacation Industry Review* is a quarterly trade magazine published by Interval International, a global vacation-exchange company. The readership of VIR consists of people who develop, finance, market, sell, and manage timeshare resorts and mixed-use projects such as hotels, resorts, and second-home communities with a vacation-ownership component; and suppliers of products and services to the vacation-ownership industry. Interval International operates The Quality Vacation Exchange Network, and resorts featured in VIR should be part of that network.

We assign practically every article in VIR. Most ideas originate with us, although we make some assignments based on detailed queries. We accept practically nothing "over the transom" because few such submissions meet our very specific and specialized needs. VIR is not a consumer travel magazine.

We want articles about the business aspects of the vacation-ownership industry: entrepreneurship, project financing, design and construction, marketing and sales, operations, management—in short, anything that will help our readers plan, build, sell, and run a quality vacation-ownership property that satisfies the owners/guests and earns a profit for the developer, marketer, and management entity. We're also interested in owners associations at vacation-ownership resorts (but not residential condos).

Articles in VIR typically range in length from 800 to 1,500 words. Queries should include a suggested length.

To Break In: By way of introduction, write a letter to tell us about yourself and enclose two or three (non-returnable) samples of published work that show you can meet our specialized needs.

Photo Requirements: We don't pay extra for photos, but we may require them as a condition of purchase. Resort and destination photos must be in color (transparencies 35mm or larger, or prints 5" x 7" or larger). We prefer people photos in color, though black-and-white prints are acceptable. Images must be esthetically effective and must reproduce well in print. We will reject photos that are grainy or poorly focused.

Rights and Payment: Unless otherwise specified, we buy all rights to original material, on a work-for-hire basis. When we accept an article, we will ask you to sign a letter of agreement that confirms your understanding of these terms.

Upon written request, we may allow you to reprint your material without compensation to us, providing that you require any subsequent user to identify this material as having been reproduced from *Vacation Industry Review.*

We pay on acceptance at the rate of 30 cents a word (calculated at a flat rate on assignment).

Categories: Timeshare—Timeshare Resorts

CONTACT: Matthew McDaniel, Editor-in-Chief
Material: All
6262 Sunset Dr.
Miami FL 33143
Website: ResortDeveloper.com

Vampire Tales

Short vampire-related horror fiction
VAMPIRE ANTHOLOGY PUBLICATION GUIDELINES:
Publication date: Published annually. Manuscripts are read year-round.

Book Formats: *Anthology* is a book-zine (eclectic like a magazine but in book form) and will be published in one or more of the following, traditional paper (either hardback or paperback), electronic (ebooks and/or audio). Poetry, short fiction and other writings about vampires.

Lengths: Open for all short fiction, poems, articles Manuscripts of all lengths will be considered. The deadline for submissions: Editor read submissions year-round.

Rights: One-time use in book form (all formats).Considers reprints if author owns rights. Poets and writers should send a bio to accompany their writings in the anthology.

Please note: Writers with books and other publications or venues (i.e. a website) cansubmit information, website address, etc. for inclusion in the anthology to accompany their bio information. This will give writers added exposure for themselves and their books, websites, etc.

Contributors must send note (email or by regular mail) stating that he/she would like the writing(s) included in the published anthology.

Submit up to 5 manuscripts, either by email or regular mail (see below). Please enclose SASE with regular mail submissions.

Contributors will receive one copy of the finished anthology.
Categories: Fiction—Entertainment—Horror—Short Stories

CONTACT: Eugene Boone
Material: All
RSVP Press
129 Thurman Lane
Clinton TN 37716
E-mail: rsvppress@yahoo.com

Vanity Fair

Formal guidelines not available. Please read a number of issues to ascertain the publication's style and needs.

Send queries to address below.
Categories: Arts—Biography—Culture—Film/Video—Literature—Politics—Society—Theatre

CONTACT: Submissions Editor
Material: All
4 Times Square
New York NY 10036
Phone: 212-286-2860

Veggie Life

GENERAL REQUIREMENTS

• All articles must be credible and authoritatively written. We're not interested in personal opinion (product/company bashing), dogma, or religious beliefs. Provide us with clear, upbeat, concisely written information and you'll have our attention. Writing resume and related published clips are a plus! Please do not send us any articles on why you became vegetarian or any related spin-off on the subject.

• All articles making specific health claims for foods and ingredients must be accompanied by pertinent reference material for our verification. Reference information must include full names, phone numbers, email, and any other necessary information. No article will be considered without sufficient fact-verification information.

• Queries are preferred to completed manuscripts. If possible, send us a couple of clips or copies of previously published work. We do not accept phone queries. Materials will not be returned unless accompanied by a self-addressed envelope with sufficient return postage. Allow at least 12 weeks for response–no phone calls please. E-mail OK (VeggieEd@egw.com).

• Manuscripts should be submitted in a typed format with proper

V-Z

identification. Include a few sentences about yourself for your author bio. For Macintosh or PC users, you may include a digital copy of the manuscript on a 3½" disk, along with a hard copy of the file. For online writers, e-mail text to VeggieEd@ egw.com.

• Payment rate is per article, at approx. $.35/ed, $35.00/recipe, $25.00/photo (if applicable). Payment is made half upon acceptance of the completed manuscript, and half upon publication. EGW Publishing buys all rights to manuscripts and art on a work-for-hire basis only. One-time unpaid photographic agreements are also made in certain cases.

FEATURES

• Food features include a 200 to 300-word article land 7 to 8 recipes, each with a short introduction. Please observe the *Veggie Life* recipe style and write your recipe in that manner. (See below.)

• We're looking for a wide variety of delicious seasonal vegetarian recipes. Exciting regional, ethnic, special occasion, everyday, and down-home cooking are our favorites, but we're open to your original ideas. Quick and tasty recipes are always welcome. We do not publish food travel articles.

• All recipes accepted for publication will undergo editing, testing, and nutritional analysis. With some exceptions, most recipes in *Veggie Life* should have 30% or fewer calories from fat—ideally no more than 10 grams of fat per serving. Some of our meatless recipes may contain dairy and/or eggs, but vegan options are regularly included.

DEPARTMENTS

• Healing Foods—A 1000-word article followed by 3 to 5 recipes focusing on improving health and preventing disease by eating certain known health-enhancing whole foods (like garlic, nuts, tomatoes, beans, olive oil, etc.).

• Readers' Recipes—Send us your favorite vegetarian recipes. Please include a few words about why the recipe is special to you, along with your name, address, and telephone number. Readers whose recipes are selected for publication will receive a $50 honorarium.

• On the Table—An 1800 to 2500-word comparison article on nutritious plant-based packaged foods. This article needs to provide the reader with a descriptive analysis of the nutritional components of a particular packaged food group. We're looking for nutritional analyses, comparison charts, and solid scientific information written in a lively and dynamic style. For example, past articles have included a descriptive analysis of the nutritional characteristics of different types and brands of flours, alternative sweeteners, tofus, soy yogurts, and veggie meats, giving readers valuable information for making informed buying decisions. Articles must include 4 to 5 recipes using the featured packaged food.

• People Profile—1800-2500 word feature on a pioneering, exuberant individual or group who has made a difference in the world of vegetarian cooking, natural healing, responsible farming, and public awareness. This may include a vegetarian chef, writer, responsible farmer, natural healer, artist, or an inspirational person who has made a difference in the community. The article involves an interview but should not be written in a question and answer format. Celebrity profiles are welcome but not necessarily preferred. Examples of people profiled in *Veggie Life*: Mollie Katzen, Deborah Madison, Sarah McLachlan, Dean Ornish, and Bradley Ogden. Profile articles generally include 2 to 4 recipes.

VEGGIE LIFE RECIPE GUIDE

RECIPE TITLE: The recipe title should be descriptive and creative.

RECIPE INTRO: This is a good place to mention variations, special tips, or food facts. Give one or two descriptive phrases about the recipe's taste, compatibility with other foods, etc.

INGREDIENTS:

• The ingredients should be listed in the order in which the steps refer to them, larger amounts first.

• For clarity, preparation method should follow whole ingredients (i.e., 1 large onion, chopped; 1 16-oz. can kidney beans, drained). They should precede prepared ingredients (i.e., ½ cup chopped onions; 1 cup cooked kidney beans).

• Spell out measurements (i.e., tablespoon or ounce, not Tbs or oz.).

• List ingredients in the easiest unit of measure (i.e., ¼ cup, not 4 tablespoons).

• When possible, use the entire unit (can, package, carrot, or apple) in the recipe.

• Provide can and package sizes–(1 15½ ounce can kidney beans).

• If an ingredient is optional, follow the ingredient with the word (optional) in parentheses.

INSTRUCTIONS:

• Instructions for preheating the oven generally should be the first step.

• Keep the steps simple. Be sure to note the size and type of mixing bowls, cookware, and bakeware used (In a large skillet; a 9x13-inch baking pan).

• Use phrases that create a picture of the procedure or result in the reader's mind (Chill until syrupy; beat until frothy; mixture thickens to the consistency of sour cream).

• Name each ingredient as it is to be combined saying, for example, "Add parsley, thyme, salt, and pepper," rather than just saying, "Add spices."

• Try to foresee questions, problems, or doubts. For example, if you have developed a cake recipe and the batter is unusually thin, say so.

• Give specific and descriptive cooking or baking times. For example, "Bake 20 minutes, or until puffed and golden."

SERVINGS:

List how many cups, cookies, slices, etc. per recipe and/or state how many servings per recipe.

WATCH THOSE FATS:

Our definition of a low-fat recipe is one that derives 30% or less of its total calories from fat or has no more than 10 grams of fat per serving. While we strive to keep fats to a minimum, we are mindful that using the right fat is even more important. When possible, keep to healthy fats like olive and canola oils and avoid saturated fats.

All of our recipes undergo a nutritional analysis and will be tested for this criteria before they are accepted. There are some exceptions, however. Optional ingredients are not included in analyses.

Low-fat cooking tips:

• Cut back on nuts, oils, cheese, and eggs.

• Sauté vegetables in vegetable stock, wine, or water instead of oil.

• Use pan sprays instead of oils or margarines.

• In many recipes, 2 egg whites can be substituted for one whole egg.

• Use non- or low-fat dairy and soy products.

SAMPLE RECIPE:

Pasta Fagioli Soup

Makes 6 servings

"Fagioli" is the Italian word for beans—and there are plenty more good things to be found in this hearty meal-in-a-pot.

1 large onion, chopped
6 cups vegetable stock or water
1 28-ounce can crushed tomatoes
1 15-ounce can cannelloni or navy beans, drained
1 cup diced carrots
1 cup sliced celery
2 cloves garlic, chopped
1 teaspoon each, dried oregano and basil
4 ounces ziti or penne pasta
6 ounces prepared veggie burgers, crumbled
Salt and pepper
Chopped parsley (optional)
Parmesan cheese (optional)

1. In a large pot over medium heat, cook onion in ½ cup vegetable stock or water until softened, about 4 minutes. Add tomatoes, beans, carrots, celery, garlic, oregano, basil, and remaining vegetable stock or water. Bring to a boil, reduce heat to low, and simmer, partially covered, until vegetables are tender, about 15 minutes.

2. Add pasta and cook until almost tender, 7 to 10 minutes. Stir in crumbled burgers. Add salt and pepper to taste. Cook until heated through, about 3 minutes. Sprinkle with chopped parsley and grated

Parmesan cheese, if desired.

Categories: Nonfiction—Consumer—Cooking—Diet/Nutrition—Gardening—Health—Physical Fitness—Herbs—Remedies

CONTACT: Shanna Masters, Editor
Material: All
1041 Shary Circle
Concord CA 94518
Phone: 925-671-0692
Fax: 510-671-0692
E-mail: VeggieEd@egw.com

Verses Magazine

Verses Magazine is a quarterly publication dedicated to publishing both new and experienced poets, essayists and short-story writers. *Verses* is designed as a learning, teaching and publishing tool for writers, students and teachers alike.

In each issue of *Verses* we include poetry, prose and short stories from authors all around the world. We will also include information on poetry competitions, awards programs, workshops, seminars, writing groups and other educational programs. We will publish book reviews, articles on copyright, publication, etc. Receive a sample back issue of *Verses* be sending a 9" x 12" self-addressed envelope and $2.00/issue to cover shipping and handling. A one-year (4 issue) subscription is only $21.00.

THE LAUREATES PROGRAM
QUARTERLY LITERARY COMPETITIONS
General Guidelines

The *Verses Magazine* competition, the Laureates Program, is running continuously. There are three (3) categories of competition: Poetry, Short Prose and Short Story. Each issue will feature a "Poet Laureate," "Prose Laureate," and "Short Story Laureate."

• Each quarter, a winner will be picked in each of the categories and awarded one (1) complimentary copy of the issue of *Verses* in which he/she was published.

• In addition, the winners will receive a handsome, personalized "Laureate" award certificate.

• In consideration of publication, each published writer will receive one complimentary copy of *Verses*.

• All published contributors in the magazine can purchase additional copies of the magazine at $3 while supplies last.

Judging

Entries will be judged by the editorial staff appropriate to each genre, based upon content, style, clarity, meter, ability to hold the reader's interest, aesthetic appeal and subject matter. All decisions are final.

Poetry Competition

• There are no line-limits or style limitations for the Laureates Program.

• Selected, non-winning entries will be published in *Verses*.

Prose Competition

• Prose pieces arc limited to 575 words.

• Selected, non-winning prose will be published in *Verses* at the discretion of the editors.

Short Story Competition

• Short stories may range from 600 to 2,500 words.

• Selected, non-winning short stories will be published in *Verses* at the discretion of the editors.

Submission Procedures

• Please send entries with the entry form below. Use a separate entry form for each of the three categories, (i.e., do not send both prose and poetry on the same form).

• Be sure to put your name and address in the upper right-hand corner of each entry. Write the name of the contest below your name and address, (i.e., "Poet Laureate," "Prose Laureate," "Short Story Laureate"). Improperly addressed and/or labeled entries will be disqualified.

• Send only copies of your works, not originals. Entries cannot be returned.

• If you would like confirmation that your entry has been received, either send your submission certified mail, return receipt requested, or enclose a self-addressed, stamped post card, and we'll drop the post card in the mail when we receive your submission(s).

• Submit with the appropriate reading fees if necessary.

Reading Fees & Number of Allowable Submissions

• Lifetime Members of the National Authors Registry may submit an unlimited number of Laureates Program entries in any combination of categories.

• Regular NAR members and Associate Members may submit up to 10 entries per quarter.

• Subscribers to *Verses* may submit up to three (3) entries per quarter.

• Contestants who are neither subscribers nor members must submit a reading fee of $2 per entry with every entry.

• Entries submitted may be in any single category, or any combination of categories.

• The fourth and subsequent entries in a calendar quarter must be accompanied by a $2 reading fee per entry.

ARTICLE/BOOK/REVIEW/FILLER GUIDELINES

There are no reading or submission fees for articles, book reviews or fillers. We pay on publication at the rate of 2 cents per word for articles and book reviews. Other fillers, quotes and comics may be published at the editors' discretion. All published authors will receive as consideration, a complimentary copy of the issue of *Verses* containing his/her work. We do not pay kill fees.

Submission Guidelines

• Send copies and not originals. Your submissions cannot be returned.

• Send your submissions certified, return receipt requested, or, include two self-addressed, stamped post cards with your submission. We will drop the first post card in the mail upon receipt to confirm that we have, in fact, received your submission. We will return the second post card when your work has been accepted or rejected. Please do not call to inquire whether or not we have received your submissions. Please allow three to six months for notification of acceptance/rejection.

• Be sure to put your name and address in the upper left-hand corner of page 1 of each article/review. Write "Article," "Book Review," or "Filler" below your name and address. Improperly addressed and/or labeled submissions cannot be considered for publication.

This form may he reproduced.

VERSES LAUREATES ENTRY FORM

Please enter the attached poems/essays/stories in the Laureates Program. I grant Cader Publishing, Ltd permission to print all listed/attached entries in *Verses*. If my entry(ies) are selected for publication, I will receive one (1) complimentary copy of Verses.

Name
*Age
Address
City
State, Zip
*If you are under age 21 and your work appears in the "Youthful Voices" section, your age will be published.

[ ] Yes, include my name and full address in Verses if I am published.

Check category of work submitted. One entry form required per category.

[ ] POETRY [ ] PROSE [ ] SHORT STORY

Check one of the following:

[ ] I am a subscriber to *Verses* [limit 3 entries]
[ ] I am an Assoc. NAR member [limit 10 entries]
[ ] I am a regular NAR member [limit 10 entries]
[ ] I am not a subscriber or member. I have enclosed $2.00 per entry as a reading fee.

I have read, understood and agreed to the guidelines for regular submission to *Verses*.

Contestant's Signature

Parent or guardian must sign if author is under 18 years of age.

All entries must be accompanied with this form. The Verses Laureates Entry Form may be reproduced. Failure to submit entries with this form properly filled out will result in disqualification of entries.

Categories: Fiction—Poetry—Short Stories—Writing

CONTACT: Sharon Derderian, Executive Editor
Material: Poetry, Prose, Short Stories, Articles
36923 Ryan Rd.
Sterling Hts. MI 48310
Phone: 810-795-3635
Fax: 810-795-9875

VFW Magazine

VFW Magazine is published by the Veterans of Foreign Wars at national headquarters in Kansas City, Mo. *VFW* is the nation's 48th largest magazine in circulation. It is published 11 times a year and has a readership of some 1.7 million.

Subscription is largely through VFW membership, which is restricted to honorably discharged veterans who received an officially recognized campaign medal. Founded in 1899, the VFW is the oldest major veterans organization in America.

TOPICS: Recognition of veterans and military service is paramount at the VFW. Articles related to current foreign policy and defense along with all veterans issues are of prime interest. Topics pertaining to American armed forces abroad and international events affecting U.S. national security are particularly in demand.

Some national political and social issues also qualify for inclusion in the magazine, especially if covered by VFW resolutions. New resolutions are passed each August at the VFW national convention and priority goals are subsequently established, based on these formal issue positions.

And, of course, we are always looking for up-to-date stories on veterans' concerns. Insight into how recent legislation affects the average veteran is always welcome. Anything that contributes to a better understanding of how the Department of Veterans Affairs operates is useful to fellow veterans. Positive, upbeat stories on successful veterans who have made significant contributions to their communities make for good reading, too.

Also, interviews with prominent figures are of interest if professionally done. No first-person accounts or personality profiles accepted.

We do not accept poetry , fiction, reprints or book reviews.

MANUSCRIPTS: Manuscripts should be no longer than five double-spaced typewritten pages (or about 1,000 words), depending on the subject. Simultaneous submissions and reprints are not considered. Changes are often required to make copy conform to editorial requirements. Absolute accuracy is a must. If little-known facts or statistics and quotes are used, please cite a reference.

Quotes from relevant individuals are a must. Bibliographies are useful if the subject required extensive research and/or is open to dispute. E-mail submissions are acceptable.

STYLE: Clarity and simplicity are the two cardinal virtues of good writing. Originality, concrete detail, short paragraphs and strong words are essential. Write in the active voice, and avoid flowery prose and military jargon. Please feel free to suggest descriptive decks (sub-titles) and use sub-heads in the body of the copy. Consult *The Associated Press Stylebook* for correct grammar and punctuation.

PHOTOGRAPHS: Photos of exceptional interest are considered for publication. Payment is arranged in advance. Captions must accompany photos, including a separate caption sheet. Pictures accompanying manuscripts are generally for one-time use only. Please send along all relevant sketches, maps, charts and photos. Sources of additional artwork are also most helpful. Color transparencies (35mm slides or 2¼"x2¼") are preferred. But we can always use color as well as black and white prints (5" x 7" or 8" x 10").

PAYMENT: Payment generally ranges up to $500 per article, depending on length and writing quality. Commissioned articles are negotiable. Payment is made upon acceptance, and entitles *VFW Magazine* to first North American serial rights. Kill fees are paid if the writer is working on assignment and the article is not published.

QUERIES: Do not query over the telephone. A one-page outline (theme, scope, organization) of the proposed article will save the author and editor valuable time and effort in determining the suitability of a piece for *VFW Magazine*. Articles are submitted on a speculative basis for first-time contributors unless commissioned. Topics that coincide with an anniversary should be submitted at least four months in advance.

Use the query letter to demonstrate your knowledge and writing ability. Send along published examples of your work. Familiarize yourself with *VFW Magazine* before writing full-length features.

BIOGRAPHIES: Finally, please enclose a brief biography describing your military service and expertise in the field in which you are writing. Three sentences is generally sufficient. If you are a VFW member, let us know.

VFW Magazine looks forward to receiving submissions from members and freelancers alike.

Categories: Nonfiction—Associations—History—Military—Current Events

CONTACT: Richard K. Kolb, Editor-in-Chief
Material: Any
CONTACT: Tim Dyhouse, Senior Editor
Material: Any
CONTACT: Robert Widener, Art Director
Material: Any
406 W. 34th St. Ste. 523
Kansas City MO 64111
Phone: 816-756-3390
Fax: 816-968-1169
E-mail: kpetrovic@vfw.org

Via

Via (formerly *Motorland*) is the magazine of the California State Automobile Association (AAA). It is published bimonthly and goes to almost 2.5 million members in northern and central California, Nevada, and Utah. It is primarily a service magazine, with articles on travel, events, leisure activities, and matters of interest to the motoring public—car care, insurance issues, consumer information, legislation, and transportation.

Although most of our content is staff-written, we do buy a few freelance articles each year, almost all of them on travel. The purpose of our travel stories is two-fold: first, to encourage members to use the free-with-membership services of the CSAA, such as maps, trip-planning, reservations for hotels, tours, car rental, air and train travel. Second, we also consider the magazine a service in itself, and giving our readers ideas about places to go is part of that service. Our emphasis is on close-to-home travel in our territory and nearby western states, although we do occasional stories on foreign travel.

Competition is very keen; we receive between 1,200 and 1,500 freelance queries and manuscripts each year, and can buy only 12 to 20 of these (in other words, a little over one percent of stories submitted). Because our small staff is perpetually occupied with writing and editing, it may take us a very long time to respond to queries. In fact, most of our freelance stories are purchased from, or assigned to, writers already known to us for excellent, accurate, and dependable work.

If you are still interested, here are some guidelines: We are always looking for excellent writing. We like our stories to be personal, original, and literary, not the usual dry guidebook recounting of where-and-what. We want to sense the magic and wonder—or even squalor—of a place, to know what it means to go there, to know how the visitor might be changed by the journey. We urge you to read our magazine to get a sense of what we're looking for. We also need the service details which will help our readers go, too.

At this time, we are not giving firm assignments for features to writers new to us—even if they have an impressive portfolio of clippings. We prefer to see a finished manuscript. You may, of course, query to see whether we'd consider a story on a certain subject.

Our articles are short—between 250 words for our travel columns and 1,500 words for a feature. We pay from $150 to $700, depending on the research required, length and quality of the writing. We illustrate our articles with freelance photography, and you're welcome to submit your finest color transparencies with your story. We pay separately for any photography published.

We are unhappy with writers who get their facts wrong. Because of our small staff, we don't have the facilities for extensive fact-checking. We are also unhappy with writers who do not send SASE's with their queries and manuscripts. Also, we do not buy stories from writers who do any kind of public relations work with travel, automotive, or other suppliers which might be covered in the magazine.

Thank you for your interest in *Via.*

Bruce Anderson, Editor

Categories: Nonfiction—Automobiles—Consumer—Travel

CONTACT: Bruce Anderson, Editor
Material: All
150 Van Ness Ave.
San Francisco CA 94102-5292
Phone: 415-565-2451
Fax: 415-863-4726

Vibe

Formal guidelines not available. Please read a number of issues to ascertain the publication's style and needs.

Send queries to address below.

Categories: African-American—Arts—Culture—Entertainment—Fashion—Lifestyle—Multicultural—Music—Politics—Society

CONTACT: Writer's Submissions
Material: All
215 Lexington Ave., 6th Floor
New York NY 10016
Website: www.vibe.com

Victory In Grace

Our Purpose

Victory In Grace exists to clearly share the message of God's grace to those who do not believe and to draw believers into a deeper relationship with Jesus Christ by encouraging a daily walk and involvement in their local church. *Victory In Grace* is a ministry of the radio and television broadcasts of Dr. James A. Scudder.

Content

The articles published fall into three basic categories:

1. Daily Reflections which combine relevant illustrations, current news items, and/or Biblical stories with a specific Scriptural teaching, applying them to the everyday life of the believer. Most Daily Reflections come directly from Dr. Scudder's sermons and messages but occasionally we will do a small series on a relevant topic from a freelance writer.

2. How-to articles on all areas of the Christian life, including marriage, child-raising, workplace issues, relationships, evangelism or church life. We generally accept only short articles with numbered lists and the articles must avoid a preachy tone.

3. Profiles of individuals who have experienced the power of God in their life in overcoming loss, hardships, or illness or Christian warriors who, through the Holy Spirit, have overcome tremendous odds to fulfill their God-given calling. Articles can be personal testimonies, as-

told-to's or human-interest feature stories. This is the type of article that is most likely to be published in *VIG*.

4. Teaching on a Scriptural topic or passage of relevance to the Christian believer. Articles may address questions of doctrine or may point believers to a better understanding of difficult Scriptural passages. Such articles must reflect the beliefs and mission of *Victory In Grace*. Most of the time, these articles are written by Dr. James A. Scudder or assigned to an in-house writer.

5. News articles on the work and outreach of *Victory In Grace* in the lives of Christians both in overseas missions and as a result of television, radio, or print ministries. We welcome these types of personal testimonies or stories.

6. Informative pieces on issues facing the Christian believer and families, reflection the breakdown of traditional values in American society or threats to religious freedom by local or federal government. These are almost always assigned in-house, usually to our featured culture columnist, Rev. Robert Vanden Bosch. It is rare that we publish an issue-oriented piece.

Topics

Articles in *Victory In Grace* usually, but not always, follow a general monthly theme. However, we encourage writers to write nontheme articles which can touch on any aspect of Christian living.

Currently, we'd like to see more personal narratives. Recently we published a story on a husband and wife's difficulty in coping with the loss of a child. Another article shared a couple's year-long struggle to adopt a child from Mexico.

Our Readers

Victory In Grace is primarily to viewers and listeners of Victory In Grace the international teaching ministry of Dr. James A. Scudder. Readers are primarily looking to the magazine as a supplement for their devotional time. Our readers could also be divided as follows:

1. The bulk of our audience is viewers and listeners of Dr. Scudder's broadcasts.

2. We ship many magazines to churches who offer *Victory In Grace* to their members as a devotional supplement.

3. Many readers tell us that what they read in the Daily Reflections devotional that particular day really spoke to their heart.

4. We have a large percentage of pastors and Christian leaders who glean sermon ideas or illustrations from a particular article.

5. We ship many magazines to inmates in correctional facilities around the United States.

6. Many of our readers are elderly and/or physically limited. They use Victory In Grace television, radio, and magazine as their church.

How to Submit a Query

We prefer a query letter, but will accept unsolicited manuscripts. Your query letter should include: 1) the working title, 2) a clear statement of purpose, 3) a tentative outline, 4) some indication of the style and approach you plan to use and 5) the prospective length (500 to 2,000 words) 6) a short description of your background and biographical information.

1. Before you submit a query, study several issues of *Victory In Grace*. Look at the style and format of the types of articles we publish. You can contact us at 1-800-78-GRACE and request back issues.

2. We prefer to be queried by email (ddarling@victoryingrace.org), but we also accept mail queries. Please send them to the address below.

3. Response time is typically between 3 and 6 weeks. Feel free to drop a note or email reminder if you haven't heard from us within that time frame. If you receive a positive response to your article, you will be invited to send your article on speculation.

Categories: Nonfiction—Christian Interests—Spiritual

CONTACT: Daniel Darling
Victory In Grace Magazine
60 Quentin Road
Lake Zurich, IL 60047

Vietnam

Please refer to WEIDER History Group.

Virginia Quarterly Review

1. For results only, include a #10 SASE. You will not be notified otherwise.

2. No simultaneous submissions are accepted.

3. Submissions per envelope are limited to two stories or five poems.

4. Articles, essays, memoirs, and short stories are usually reviewed within three weeks, but, due to the large number of poems we receive, results for these may be delayed three months or longer.

The Emily Clark Balch awards for fiction and poetry are made annually for the best short story and best poem published in the *Virginia Quarterly Review* during the calendar year. There are no specific guidelines except that submissions be of reasonable length (fiction: 2,000-7,000 words; no length restrictions on poetry).

Categories: Fiction—Nonfiction—Literature—Poetry—Politics

CONTACT: Submissions Editor
Material: All
One W. Range
Charlottesville VA 22903
Phone: 434-924-3124
Fax: 434-924-1397

Vision E-Mazine
A Resource for Writers

A magazine by writers for writers—live writing workshop, general and genre-specific articles on writing, discussions, a large and supportive linked community—all free. HTML, Adobe.pdf and PalmOS versions.

Needs: We will happily consider manuscripts from either unpublished or published writers—we prefer to be queried (all queries and manuscript submissions are handled by e-mail). We are interested in all facets of writing, from first-person experience articles to genre-specific how-to's to informational articles about your area of specialization—whether it be history or science or nursing or long-distance running—and how and where your specialty can be used correctly by writers. Write something that will help other writers write better, and we'll be interested in taking a look.

Length: 500-2000 words (May run longer, but not shorter.)

Art/Photo Needs: none

Payment: Contributors copies, author bio with links in future editions (current editions have webpage links to bios).

Response Time: 3 days to one month.

Tips for Writers: You must be a member of the Writers' Community. Membership is free. To join the community, obtain a Network54 login: http://network54.com/Create/Signup

Join the community at: http://network54.com/Hide/Group/3188

Sample Copies/Subscription Information: http://hollylisle.com/community/Downloads.html

Both PalmOS and Adobe.pdf formats are available, as well as the live HTML version at http://www.lazette.net/vision/

Guidelines

We will happily consider writing-related manuscripts from either unpublished or published writers. We are interested in all facets of writing, from first-person experience articles to genre-specific how-to's and informational articles about your area of specialization—whether it be history or science or nursing or long-distance running—and how and where your specialty can be used correctly by writers. Write something that will help other writers, and we'll be interested in taking a look.

Starting in 2004 Vision will pay half a cent per word for articles. That's not much money, and we're going to be asking a lot for that half cent—both ezine rights as well as the right to publish anything we choose in a POD 'Best of' Anthology at the end of the year. By printing the anthology, we hope to make back the funds that I will be putting into Vision to buy the articles and perhaps even make enough to fund the following year's article acquisitions.

We will be limiting the number of articles bought, and 2000 words ($10) will be the cut off point for payment. All the other guidelines remain the same. I will be looking for articles on theme-related, general writing and genre topics. If you have some suggestion that you think might help another writer, consider writing it into an article and submitting it to Vision.

We strive to maintain professional standards. Manuscripts must be professionally formatted, as free from spelling and grammatical errors as you can make them, and in what you perceive to be final draft form. We will not welcome massive rewrites of a piece after we have accepted it—when we accept it, we consider it pretty close to finished, and will only edit it to our standards. If we feel that it needs massive rewrites, we won't accept it.

If you have any questions, or wish to query about an article, email Lazette Gifford.

We look forward to hearing from you. Holly Lisle and Lazette Gifford, Publishers, Vision

Expanded Submission Guidelines:

Articles must be at least 500 words with 2000 words as the 'soft' top. I'm willing to go over that count if the article needs it, but payment stops at 2000 words.

Check your spelling and grammar! Also, if you are from a country that does not use US spelling conventions, let me know in the email. That will stop me from making several 'corrections' before I realize they aren't mistakes.

Place your Title AND YOUR NAME at the top of the document. I hate having to go search through emails, checking attachments, to figure whose article I'm actually reading.

Use one of these fonts: Courier, Courier New, Times New Roman, Verdana or Arial, 12pt.

Double space your manuscript.

Do not indent.

I would like submissions to be made in either Word Doc files, or .rtf files, and as attachments to the email. (I believe that WordPerfect allows .rtf saves, doesn't it?) If you use Works, a regular file will do, although (at least in the 4.5 version I have), this program also allows for an .rtf file save.

A plain text copy (.txt) can be sent, but be certain to mark any italics like this: *before and after the section in italics*, and bold likes this: _before and after anything in bold._ If you cannot do attachments, use the body of the letter as the last resort.

Indicate book titles with italics. And yes, that means if you are doing a Word doc or rtf that you can use actual italics and not an underline to indicate italics. (This is not common submission procedure, but it's far easier for me since I can cut and paste to my wysiwyg web page editor.)

Do not use an underline for emphasis. Underline on websites indicates a link, and people often send emails to say the link is not working. Use italics or bold.

NO HTML code except for links, and those written in this fashion: http://www.whatever.com/this.htm

Provide the ISBN #s and publishers for all books mentioned or reviewed. Do this by adding the title, author, publisher and ISBN# at the bottom of the file. The same is true for articles—be certain to cite them.

An additional note to Word users: You should turn off the 'smart quotes' option in Word which can be found under Tools-AutoCorrect and then the tabs AutoFormat while you type AND Autoformat. Also uncheck the symbol replacement for —. While Smart Quotes look really neat on the screen, they sometimes translate to funny little squares that cannot be taken out with the 'find-replace' feature, but have to be hunted down by hand. If you are submitting anything electronically, you will very likely hear back from the editor on these. And remember—a lot of print publishers are now asking for electronic copy for their end as well.

We've been receiving very good articles, and I hope that all of you look at the list of upcoming issues at the bottom of this page and choose something you feel comfortable with writing about.

We are also still looking for general genre-related articles. If you would like to write an article on how to research romantic settings, the proper use of codes in spy thrillers, etc., let us know. The genres we like to cover in each issue are:

And we are always interested in articles about the act and art of writing.

Categories: Writing

CONTACT: Holly Lisle and Lazette Gifford, Publishers
Materials: All
E-mail: webmaster@hollylisle.com
Website: www.lazette.net/Vision/

Vogue

Thank you for inquiring about *Vogue*'s writers' guidelines.

Articles for *Vogue* are written in an upbeat, engaging manner to appeal to a broad-based, well-educated audience. Ranging in length from 500 to 2,500 words, stories are informative and thoroughly researched. Payment depends on source, length and use.

Writers are welcome to direct article ideas and writing samples for consideration to the appropriate editor listed on the masthead.

We appreciate your interest in *Vogue* and hope that this brief outline of *Vogue*'s editorial standards is helpful.

The Editors
Categories: Culture—Fashion

CONTACT: Laurie Jones, Managing Editor
Material: All
4 Times Square, 12th Floor
New York NY 10036
Phone: 212-886-6910
Fax: 212-880-8169
E-mail: talkingback@vogue.com
E-mail: stylefeedbac@CONDENT.com
Website: condenet.com

Volleyball Magazine

Formal guidelines not available. Please read a number of issues to ascertain the publication's style and needs.

Send queries to address below.

Categories: Nonfiction—Health—Physical Fitness—Recreation—Sports

CONTACT: Dennis Steers, Editor
Material: All
774 Marsh St., Ste. C
San Luis Obispo CA 93401
Phone: 805-541-2438
E-mail: letters@volleyballmag.com
Website: www.volleyballmag.com

> **Remember: Editors change jobs and publishers change addresses. It is wise to invest in a phone call for the current information before submitting.**

VOYAGEUR

Voyageur
Northeast Wisconsin's Historical Review

Voyageur: Northeast Wisconsin's Historical Review is a nonprofit magazine about the history and prehistory of a twenty-six-county region of greater Northeast Wisconsin. Its coverage area extends from the Sheboygan and Fond du Lac areas northward to the Michigan border and westward from Lake Michigan to the Wausau and Stevens Point areas.

Voyageur is cosponsored by the Brown County Historical Society, University of Wisconsin-Green Bay, and St. Norbert College in De Pere. Submissions may focus on social, economic, political, technological, institutional, religious, environmental, educational, legal, archeological, architectural, transportation, health, sports, recreational, or other historical issues and themes.

Manuscripts are blind-reviewed by *Voyageur*'s Editorial Committee and will be returned upon request. Authors will be notified within three months of submission whether a manuscript has been accepted for publication. *Voyageur* does not accept creative nonfiction or fictional accounts of people, places or events based on the historical record.

Submissions

1. Format & Length. *Voyageur* is produced on Macintosh computers using Microsoft Word 5.1. Authors are encouraged to submit their works on a DOS-based or Macintosh disk and specify the word-processing program used. Authors should also submit at least one typed or computer-processed, double-spaced copy of their manuscripts.

Manuscripts should be no longer than 5,000 words, not including notes and tables. Only with the author's approval, longer manuscripts may be edited down or split into parts as a multi-part series. Please indicate word count on your manuscript. Original manuscripts are preferred, although exceptions on occasion are made to publish previously published works in Voyageur if appropriate permission is given.

2. Style. Use *The Chicago Manual of Style* (14th edition) guidelines for all manuscripts. Do not use in-text references, i.e., (Weston, 1972). In ordinary text, whole numbers from one through ninety-nine are spelled out. However, when normally spelled numbers cluster in a sentence or paragraph, use figures. Use % instead of percent in reference to statistics; for rounded percentages write the words. Underline or italicize names of cities when using newspaper names, i.e., New York Times.

3. Sources. *Voyageur* strongly urges endnotes and/or a bibliography or sources consulted list to help readers evaluate information presented in a manuscript. See the *The Chicago Manual of Style*.

4. Photographs and Other Images. Voyageur also urges authors to submit images or photocopies of images that could be used with their texts. Images may include photographs, drawings, maps, artwork, and reproductions of documents.

5. Tables. Do not duplicate material in text and tables. Tables and figures are helpful when they aid the reader in clarifying complicated or voluminous information or data.

6. Headings. The use of headings is encouraged to organize information and to break up long blocks of text. First-level headings should be typed in bold and centered. Second-level headings, if used, should be flush left and typed in bold italic. Third-level headings, if used, should be flush left and typed in italic.

7. Abstract. Please include an abstract of no more than 150 words.

8. Deadlines. Deadlines for manuscripts submitted to Voyageur are June 1 and November 1 of each year.

9. Copyright. The contents of *Voyageur* are protected by copyright in the name of the Brown County Historical Society. Permission is freely granted by Voyageur and the Society for authors to have their submissions published elsewhere if proper credit is given to *Voyageur*.

10. Remuneration. It is not possible at this time for the nonprofit Voyageur to pay authors or other contributors for publishing their work.

V-Z

However, *Voyageur* does pay image reproduction fees.

If your manuscript is accepted, please submit the final copy on a 3½-inch disk in WordPerfect or Microsoft Word for IBM Compatible or in Microsoft Word 5.1 for Macintosh. Please submit images to accompany the story and include appropriate captions on a separate piece of paper.

Also indicate the source of your images on the same sheet. Finally, please write a 100-word biography and include a photograph of yourself (head shot).

Book & Video Reviews. Anyone who wishes to review books or videos for *Voyageur* or to propose a book or video review should contact *Voyageur* at the address below hereafter.

Categories: Nonfiction—History—Regional

CONTACT: Victoria Goff, Editor
Material: All
PO Box 8085
Green Bay WI 54308-8085
Phone: 920-465-2446
Fax: 920-465-2890
E-mail: voyageur@uwgb.edu
Website: www.uwgb.edu/voyageur

Wall Fashions

Formal guidelines not available. Please read a number of issues to ascertain the publication's style and needs.

Send queries to address below.

Categories: Fashion—Reference—Trade—Wall Products

CONTACT: Kate Lundquist, Managing Editor
Material: All
G & W McNamara Publishing
4215 White Bear Parkway, Ste. 100
St. Paul MN 55110-7635
Phone: 651-293-1544

Washington Monthly

Writers' Guidelines

The *Washington Monthly* is a DC-based publication covering politics, government, culture and the media. Before you pitch a story to us, we recommend you read through a few of our back issues online or in print to get a feel for the type of investigative, system-analysis journalism we value and promote.

The magazine is published 10 times a year and includes investigative and opinion-based feature articles (2,000 to 5,000 words), occasional short news items and humorous sidebars (500 to 1,000 words), and book reviews of recent political and cultural titles (usually about 800 words). We occasionally print excerpts from forthcoming political books. We never publish fiction, poetry, or celebrity profiles.

Our editors welcome story pitches that suit our editorial mix. We ask freelancers to submit query letters or articles in writing by either emailing us at: editors@washingtonmonthly.com or mailing submissions to 1319 F St. NW, Suite 710, Washington, DC 20004.

All freelance pieces are submitted "on spec"; we don't pay kill fees. The pay rate for published articles is 10 cents per word.

Complimentary copies of the magazine in which their articles appears are mailed to freelancers. Published articles are also available online.

Thank you for your interest in *The Washington Monthly*.

Categories: Nonfiction—Culture—Government—Politics—Media

CONTACT: Submissions Editor
Material: All
1319 F St NW Ste 710
Washington DC 20004

Phone: 202-393-5155
Fax: 202-393-2444
E-mail: editors@washingtonmonthly.com
Website: www.washingtonmonthly.com

Watercolor

Please refer to *American Artist* magazine.

Watercolor Magic

If you'd like to see your work featured in a national magazine specializing in watermedia, here are a few secrets from the editors of *Watercolor Magic*:

CHOOSE THE TYPE OF ARTICLE

Watercolor Magic is open to submissions for feature articles. Features, which typically amount to four to six pages, should focus on teaching a watermedia technique (many artists showcase a signature technique), and most often will include a step-by-step demonstration.

SEND A QUERY LETTER

Submitting your work for an article in *Watercolor Magic* is much like entering a juried show, but with a few extra steps. The first thing you should do is send a query letter to the editorial staff. This letter should explain what you are interested in writing about and why it would appeal to *Watercolor Magic*'s readers. Your query letter also should explain your background in watermedia, including any awards or instructional experience you have. Most importantly, include at least eight samples of your work by photographing them on slides or larger transparencies.

WAIT FOR A RESPONSE

If the editorial staff is interested in publishing your work, you will receive an assignment letter that outlines how your article should be structured. While taking your ideas and information into account, the editor will suggest a theme, introduction, body and conclusion for your article, as well as work out the details such as your deadline, payment and the issue your work is scheduled to appear. (Please note this may change due to space limitations.) Once you have your assignment, keep in mind that you should stay focused on the technique you are teaching. We'll supply more details on how to put your article together at this point.

SUPPLY FIRST-RATE PHOTOGRAPHY

Photography is a very important element in your article. Please remember that your color slide or transparency will be magnified in size, so any flaws in color or lighting from the photography will also increase. You may want to put your slides in a projector to see how they will look. You also can get photo tips from "Photographing Your Paintings," a reprint from *The Artist's Magazine*. (To order with your Visa or Master Card, call 513-531-2690, ext. 1328, or you can write to Photographing Your Paintings, F&W Publications Inc., Attn: Terri Boes, 4700 E. Galbraith Rd., Cincinnati, OH 45236.) Remember, the better the photography, the better your work will reproduce.

Once your article and photography has been sent to us, an editor will make it fit the magazine's style and "clean it up." After it is edited, you will be sent an author's galley, which is a copy of the article that you can review before publication. You will also receive your payment (negotiated individually) around the same time. Then your article will be ready for the magazine.

You can expect a reply within four to six weeks. Good luck!

Categories: Arts—Painting—Watermedia

CONTACT: Submissions Editor
Material: All
4700 E. Galbraith Rd.
Cincinnati OH 45236
Phone: 513-531-2690
Fax: 513-531-2902
E-mail: wcmedit@fwpubs.com
Website: www.watercolormagic.com

Weatherwise Magazine
The Magazine about the Weather

Guidelines for writers and photographers

Weather is one of the common denominators of our lives. It helps shape our culture, character, conduct, and health. It frequents the pages of our history and can change its course. It colors our conversations, folklore, and literature; it rains on our parades, awes us with its power and beauty, frightens us, and sometimes kills us. *Weatherwise* magazine shares this force of nature with engaging features and breathtaking photography. *Weatherwise* articles are anecdotal, analytical, and illuminating. They take a creative look at everyday occurrences and are accurate, authoritative, and easily understood by a large, non-technical audience that includes teachers, students, and farmers.

Generally

Please initiate your interest in writing for *Weatherwise* by sending a query letter and SASE (or e-mail) to Lynn Elsey, Managing Editor, Weatherwise, 1319 18th St. NW, Washington, DC 20036-1802.

Your letter should outline the direction of the article, give an indication of your writing style and perspective, tell us why or how you're qualified to write the article, list potential sources and illustration possibilities, and include clips of your published work. (If you have not been published, please send a sample of your writing suitable for magazine-style work.) We will consider research topics, but do not publish academic papers. Authors are expected to write (or rewrite) in a conversational, magazine style suitable for a popular audience. Look for the story within the story, and emphasize the human element. Tell us about the triumphs, failures, and other anecdotes of the people you meet while researching your article.

Be aware of the *Weatherwise* production schedule and submit your story ideas and photos accordingly. We begin planning an issue at least six months before the cover date (i.e. September/October in March). In other words, think hurricanes in January and blizzards in July. We try to respond to queries within two months.

Unsolicited manuscripts are discouraged, and may be held indefinitely without response. Please remember that queries and manuscripts under consideration at *Weatherwise* should not be submitted to other publications concurrently.

Payments to established authors are at the discretion of the managing editor and are made upon publication.

Manuscripts

Feature articles are relatively short (900 to 2,000 words) and well-illustrated. Departments—including software, video, and book reviews; and essays on topics ranging from folklore to personal experiences—should be between 600 and 1,000 words. Short news fillers (200 to 500 words) about noteworthy people, events, or trends will also be considered. Where appropriate, include a list of sources, both published materials and personal interviews.

Include your name and phone number on everything you submit. Also, include other ways we can contact you—preferable an e-mail address—and a SASE large enough for the return of your materials if necessary. Once an article is accepted, it must be submitted in an electronic format, as a word file. On the first page, include a word count. Our preferred format is Microsoft Word 5.1 for Macintosh.

Illustrations

Published articles are often chosen as much for the quality and impact of the photographs as for editorial excellence. Authors must at least provide sources, leads, or ideas on illustrating an article. We will gladly research photo leads or commission artwork for an author whose article is worthy of publication. On the other hand, photos are rarely accepted without supporting text, even if that's just a short but enlightening discussion of the circumstances under which the photos were taken. We maintain a file of stock weather photos and prefer photos of recent events or unique treatments of familiar sights. Great photos that stand alone may be considered for our annual Photo Contest with permission and a signed entry form from the photographer.

We do not publish cartoons.

Photographs may be submitted as prints, slides, or electronic files. Color is preferred. Please provide captions on a separate sheet of paper. Do not write on the backs of photos. Other illustrations (i.e. maps, graphs, charts, tables, etc.) should be submitted as finished, camera-ready art or on disk with hard-copy back-up that need not be camera-ready. Many software formats are acceptable.

Categories: Environment—Hobbies—Science—Meteorology

CONTACT: Lynn Elsey, Managing Editor
Material: All
1319 - 18th St. NW
Washington DC 20036-1802
Phone: 202-296-6267
Website: www.weatherwise.org

Weavings

General Guidelines

Weavings seeks to promote informed, committed spiritual growth with attention to the corporate dimension of the spiritual life. Such growth, to which laity and clergy alike are called, embraces all those expressions of discipline and discipleship that mark the Christian's response to God's work of weaving together the torn fabric of life.

Weavings invites participation in the spiritual life, seeking to provide a forum in which our life in the world and the spiritual resources of the Christian heritage can encounter and illuminate one another. The journal strives to create a space in which contributors and readers can converse on important matters of common concern. Published bi-monthly and organized by themes, each issue presents a broad range of materials dealing with:

• significant topics in Christian spirituality visible in personal, congregational, and public life;
• practicing spiritual disciplines;
• the role of non-discursive communication in spiritual formation (e.g. art, music, architecture, dance);
• linking individual and corporate renewal in the church;
• relating personal and social transformation;
• integrating contemporary experience and classical wisdom.
• These and similar themes may be explored through articles, stories (fiction and non-fiction), meditations on scripture, sermons, or poetry.

Readership

The journal is for clergy, lay leaders, and all thoughtful seekers who want to deepen their understanding of, and response to, how God's life and human lives are being woven together in the world. The journal seeks to move beyond the dichotomy between pulpit and pew by probing the depths of the spiritual life in ordinary language common to both clergy and laity.

Format and Length

Articles should be 1250 to 2500 words in length. Our main interest is in writing that perceptively examines the spiritual issues that arise when Christian faith and present-day cultures meet. Articles should help readers see that the spiritual life leads to the very heart of the world, and that there is no issue in the personal, congregational, or political sphere that is without spiritual significance.

Sermons and meditations on scripture may vary in length from 500 to 2500 words. At the center of the Christian spiritual life is the practice of listening attentively to God's word in scripture. Contributions should exemplify the rich variety of insights and incentives to action that flourish when we begin to see the connections between the biblical story of God's redemptive love and our own life story. These guidelines also apply to spiritual autobiographies and biographies.

Stories (fiction or non-fiction) in the form of short vignettes or longer narratives (up to 2500 words) should strive to depict the movements of God's Spirit in the very midst of ordinary human life. Humor is welcome, as are poems and profiles of "ordinary saints."

Book reviews should be approximately 750 words.

Style

Contributions may take several forms. Hard copy should be typed, double-spaced, on 8.5" x 11" paper and should be accompanied by a self-addressed stamped envelope (SASE). Electronic files should be compatible with Microsoft Word 6.0 or higher or Word for Mac 6.1.0. Please include proper documentation for all direct quotations or other references to published works. Copyright law allows for quoting up to two lines of poetry. If more than two lines are quoted, we ask that an author secure permission to do so. When citing passages from the Bible, kindly indicate which translation is being used. Writers should include their Social Security number.

Weavings is neither a popular devotional guide nor a technical scholarly journal. We are looking for material that has spiritual depth expressed in simple, even poetic, prose. We hope authors will show our readers the subject rather than simply describe or explain it. That is to say, we encourage authors to offer readers an experience of the subject itself. For example, we would hope that an article on prayer would be prayerful in style, and that readers would be likely to experience reading this article as a prayerful event. Reading the article might even lead a reader into a time of prayer. We seek material for *Weavings* that is meditative in tone, drawing on the rich metaphors of scripture and everyday life to help readers see and respond to God at work in their lives and in the world.

Weavings readers may be assumed to share a real interest in the spiritual life, while differing significantly in their knowledge and experience of Christian tradition. Therefore, writing should be simple, authentic, and inclusive.

Simplicity in the structure and language of contributions places the spiritual life where it belongs—at the center of life as such. Simplicity shows that spirituality is not only for the select few.

Authenticity accents the integrity of the spiritual life. Authentic writing expresses what the writers themselves have sought, experienced, and struggled with in their own lives. The best guidance for authentic spiritual writing is still to be found in the First Letter of John: "It was there from the beginning; we have heard it; we have seen it with our own eyes; we looked upon it, and felt it with our own hands; and it is of this we tell. Our theme is the word of life" (1:1, NEB).

Inclusiveness means, among other things, sensitivity to gender-specific language, openness to the many traditions of historic Christianity, and attention to the manifold wisdom of various cultures and ethnic groups. Such inclusiveness affirms that the spiritual life is not merely a special province of life, but the whole of life lived under the authority of the One whose claim upon humanity is universal in scope.

Payment

We buy first periodical rights for a variety of media, including print, electronic, software-driven, and other media formats. We accept previously published material.

Payment is made when the final content of an issue is determined.

Articles, stories, sermons, book reviews, and reports: 11 cents a word and up.

Poetry: $75 and up.

We will notify contributors of manuscript status within three months of receipt. Unusable material will be returned if an SASE was sent with the manuscript.

Additional copies of our writer's guidelines and a list of themes for future issues will be sent free upon receipt of SASE. If you would like a sample copy of *Weavings*, please send SASE of at least 7.5" x 10.5" with postage (approximate weight is 5 oz.).

Categories: Fiction—Nonfiction—Arts—Christian Interests—Poetry—Religion—Spiritual

CONTACT: Editor
Material: All
1908 Grand Ave., PO Box 340004
Nashville TN 37203-0004
E-mail: weavings@upperroom.org
Website: www.upperroom.org/weavings

Weekend Adventures Magazine

Freelance Writer Information

Weekend Adventures Magazine is a regional travel magazine—its focus is almost exclusively on vacation destinations in Western Maryland, The Potomac Highlands of West Virginia, The Laurel Highlands of Pennsylvania. The magazine was launched in January 1997, and attracts over 100,000 readers annually. 15,000 copies are printed quarterly on newsprint, and are distributed free at visitor centers, resorts, businesses, state parks, and events.

More than half of our readers are visitors from nearby metropolitan areas Washington DC, Pittsburgh, Baltimore. Local residents make up the other half. They are an educated and affluent audience. Our readers travel, dine out, enjoy the outdoors, entertain, read, and on average spend more.

Writers come in all ages and types and backgrounds. Some make their living as writers; others are teachers, counselors, entrepreneurs, and government officials. More important than journalism experience is knowledge of a subject very well and being able to write clearly about it. We are very open-minded as long as the article idea is interesting and relates to the magazine's overall theme.

Send us a written query about your article idea. Tell us who you (in resume form) are and what kind of article you'd like to write. We'll let you know if the idea has possibilities. If your article is already written, mail it to us. We'll respond as soon as possible. If you want your article returned, include a stamped, self-addressed envelope.

Past Articles have included: Fallingwater: The House On The Waterfall, Backpacking in Dolly Sods Wilderness Area, Johnstown Flood Museum Examines Causes, Consequences, Laurel Highlands Scenic Drives, Brilliant Colors of Autumn Leaves Explained, Battle of Antietam Revisited-135 Year Later, Discovering Victorian Architecture. Check out our Back Issues to get a better idea.

Subjects of articles include outdoor adventures, historical places, dining out, getaways, day trips, equipment, attractions, etc.

In general, we try to help our readers understand the outdoors better, to help our readers relax, and live better, and to make our mountain communities a better place to live.

The magazine is published usually the first week of June, September, December and April. We need completed manuscripts six weeks before publication. Thus, an article for the autumn issue should be submitted by mid July. Include your name, address, and telephone number on the first page of the manuscript. We prefer 8½"x11" paper, with copy typed and double-spaced, and with a margin of at least an inch. Copy does not have to be perfectly typed, but it should be easily readable.

It is helpful if, in addition to the typed or printed manuscript, we receive the article in digital form—either on a computer disk or via e-mail. Articles submitted on disk should be in text-only or in Microsoft Word.

The length of articles varies. We don't like to specify length, we'd like each piece to run at its optimum length. When in doubt, ask us about it.

Our regular payment is $50.00 for features (pieces over 1,000 words). We pay on publication. Again, if you have any doubts or questions, talk to us. We normally don't pay expenses, but sometimes do when an unusual amount of travel or long-distance calls are involved: Please talk to us first!

Basically, we buy first North American serial rights, including rights for publication on our Internet website: wamonline.com as well as any websites owned or operated by Away Media.

Categories: Nonfiction—Regional—Travel

CONTACT: Editor
PO Box 1895
Cumberland MD 21501-1895
Phone: 301-722-3533, 1-888-805-5235
Fax: 301-722-8020
E-mail: info@wamonline.com
Web site: www.wamonline.com

Weight Watchers Magazine

Weight Watchers Magazine has no formal guidelines.

Weight Watchers Magazine is the proven authority on motivating self-improvement, self-image, nutrition, fitness and healthy, active living with an emphasis on weight loss and weight maintenance. Our readers are affluent, sophisticated, well educated, professional, and interested in living healthy lives.

Send submissions/queries with a SASE. Be sure to include a your resume and clips.

Categories: Nonfiction—Diet/Nutrition—Fashion—Health—Inspirational—Physical Fitness—Self Help

CONTACT: Editor
Material: All
747 Third Ave
New York NY 10017
Phone: 212-207-8800
Website: www.weightwatchers.com

WEIDER History Group

Guidelines apply to the following periodicals:

American History	*America's Civil War*
Aviation History	*British Heritage*
Civil War Times	*Military History*
Vietnam	*Wild West*
World War II	

WEIDER History Group, located in Leesburg, Va., publishes nine historical magazines: *American History, America's Civil War, Aviation History, British Heritage, Civil War Times, Military History, Vietnam, Wild West,* and *World War II.* All are bimonthly with the exception of *World War II,* which is published 10 times a year. Prospective contributors should be familiar with the individual magazines before querying. *America's Civil War, World War II* and *Vietnam* cover strategy, tactics, personalities, arms and equipment for the applicable period. *Military History* deals with war throughout human history. *Aviation History* covers military and civilian aviation from man's first attempts at flight to the jet age. *American History* provides insight into the cultural, military, political and social forces that have shaped our nation and is aimed at a general audience. *British Heritage* explores the cultural legacy and historical impact of the British Isles. *Civil War Times* examines the war and its personalities, but also the social and material context of the era. *Wild West* covers the American frontier, from earliest times through its westward expansion.

Historical accuracy is imperative. We do not use fiction or poetry. We do not publish reprints.

STYLE: The two paramount considerations in all **WEIDER** History Group publications are absolute accuracy and highly readable style. Give proper attribution in the manuscript when using another author's work and cite your major sources for our review. We like to see action and quotes where possible to heighten reader interest.

QUERY: Submit a short, self-explanatory query summarizing the story and its highlights. Also state your sources and expertise. Cite any color and black-and-white illustrations and primary sources of illustrations (museums, historical societies, private collections, etc.) you can provide. Please put complete name on **every** photo submitted. Pho-

tocopies of suggested illustrations are extremely helpful. Illustration ideas are an absolute must. The likelihood that articles can be effectively illustrated **often determines the ultimate fate of manuscripts.** Many otherwise excellent articles have been rejected due to a lack of suitable art. **All submissions are on speculation and must be accompanied by an SASE if you want your submission returned. Sample copies cost $6 each. Xerox copies of articles cost $2 each.**

FORMAT: We strongly urge authors to submit computer disks (3½ x 5 floppies or compact disks) with their manuscripts. These must be IBM or Macintosh compatible. Disc or e-mail copies of the manuscripts should be text only (without imbedded images or graphics). Manuscripts must be typed, double-spaced on one side of standard white 8½ x 11, 16- to 30-pound paper. Name, address, telephone number and Social Security number must be on the first page of your article. Indicate sources and suggested further reading at the end of your manuscript. Include a 1-2 paragraph autobiography. Address your submission to the appropriate magazine, Attention: Editor, c/o WEIDER History Group at the address listed below.

LENGTH: Feature articles should be 3,000-4,000 words in length and should include a 500-word sidebar. Departments should be 2,000 words or less. **WEIDER** History Group retains the right to edit, condense or rewrite for style.

PAYMENT: Payment, which is made 30 days after publication, varies by magazine and ranges from $300 for *World War II* features to $400 for *Military History* features (including sidebar) and $150 to $200 for departments. We also use book reviews, payable at a per-published-word rate, with a minimum payment of $40. WEIDER History Group buys exclusive worldwide publication rights, and the right to reprint the article in all languages, in hard copy or through electronic means, at no additional cost. Payment for Web site only article usage is set at 50% of the applicable magazine rate. We do not pay for Web site reprint use.

REPORTING TIME: Please allow six months' response time for queries and manuscripts. If you want immediate verification that a submission has been received and is being considered, please enclose a stamped, self-addressed postcard containing the title of your submission. Be forewarned that in some cases we have a 2-year backlog of scheduled manuscripts.

WEIDER History Group Editorial Philosophy

WEIDER History Group is committed to creating accurate, entertaining, and informative magazines, books, and products. It is our responsibility to ensure the loyalty and confidence of our customers by maintaining the highest editorial standards. To this end, our editorial content is never used as a sounding board for political partisanship, religious points of view, or social agendas. Our mission is to present an undistorted view of history and to encourage understanding and appreciation for the events, personalities, and artifacts of the past.

Just as writer's guidelines provide the mechanical requirements for submission of a manuscript, the following tips are intended to provide more subjective guidance for the preparation of copy that is editorially "clean" and enjoyable to read.

• Please give the reader a little excitement, some sense of being there, with lively—**but always factual,** anecdotes. Lead with one of these, if possible, to foster the reader's interest in seeing more of your story and to let him or her know that here is an article that is worth reading.

• Know what the reader expects from the publication in terms of subject matter and style of writing. Be very careful to keep technical terminology in the proper context.

• Start most paragraphs with a simple, active sentence—so many begin with As, When, Because, After, or other passive openers. Active writing keeps readers' eyes open. Our aim is to bring life to history, not to use it as a bedtime soporific. The same goes for "...ing" verbs; use them sparingly, as you do sleeping pills, to which their effects are related.

• Provide each paragraph with more than one sentence, except to make an occasional emphatic point. Break a paragraph before it runs on and takes up half a page.

V-Z

• Keep to your story, and tell one story at a time. If there is a related aside, put it into a sidebar rather than break the flow of the main story.

• Maintain a smooth flow of information. It's fine to begin with an attention-getting action lead and a flashback, but from then on proceed straight through the story rather than jump around chronologically. If you make it difficult for the reader to follow your story, he will desert you; if you do that to the editor, he will protect his readers from a similar experience.

• Watch your spelling and grammar. You may be an expert in your subject, but your credibility can be shattered by sloppy copy.

• When you—either in exhaustion or exultation—finish the last keystroke, never, never rush the manuscript into the mail in an I'm-so-glad-to-be-finished dismissal. Put the manuscript aside and out of your mind at least overnight; then get back to it in a day or two and play editor. Go through the entire manuscript slowly, thoroughly and critically and correct all spelling errors. **Question the spelling of every name—person, thing, company—all of them**. Make sure you have included full name and rank/title for every person mentioned. Read through the manuscript as if you were the reader who has never seen it before and does not know what you are trying to get across. Does it flow smoothly? Does it say what you want it to say? Does it proceed logically through a basic beginning, middle and end? Is it simple and clear rather than flowery and hobbled by descriptive adjectives? **Are your facts straight?** Check how presentable the final, assembled package is. Make it professional, not pretty. Do not dress it in fancy folders or tie it with ribbons. Keep your manuscript straight, neat and clean.

• What you are doing here is just what the editor will do when he receives your material. His job is to select quality material that will hold the interest of his readers. If your submission is unprofessional, it may be returned unread with a standard rejection letter. A professional presentation of a well written and researched manuscript has a better chance of being reviewed and seriously considered. From then on, the appropriateness of the subject, the writing and the facts will influence whether the editor believes your manuscript will please the reader—and will determine its acceptance.

• Keep your facts straight.

Categories: Nonficton—History—Military

CONTACT: Editors, WEIDER History Group
Material: All
741 Miller Dr SE Ste D-2
Leesburg VA 20175
Web site: www.thehistorynet.com

Weird Tales

Some of what follows may be terribly basic to you — but will be new to someone else. And some of what you already know (especially in matters of format) may be wrong, and you may have been irritating various editors for years by — for example — using italics in on-paper manuscripts instead of underlining or even *gasp* leaving your snail-mail address off the first page of manuscripts. So:

There are only three **Rules** for writing; all else is commentary.

Rule One: You must seize, then hold, your readers' and your editor's interest and attention, then repay the readers' time and the editor's money by having something to say.

...and the Awful Truth of the matter is (as Rear Admiral Pinney once put it) "If you don't get the reader's attention in the first para-

graph, the rest of your message is lost." This applies even more to fiction than to U.S. Navy correspondence; you must capture the reader's attention on the first page (or better, in the first few words).

These **Rules** apply both to poetry (discussed throughout these Guidelines) and to prose.

Rudyard Kipling wrote: "There are nine and sixty ways/ of constructing tribal lays,/ and every single one of them is right!"

What follows is commentary, not rules. These suggestions may help, but what's important is the result — your selling an *interesting* story to our magazine.

The archetypical plot consists of a *Situation* (the protagonist meets a problem), *Complication* (the problem makes the protagonist do something about it in a series of actions/reactions of rising intensity), *Climax* (the protagonist must solve the problem or be broken by it), *Resolution* (the problem unwinds, the protagonist succeeds or fails), and an *Anticlimax* (left-overs are carted off or explained away). Many (but not all) stories follow this pattern.

One of those nine and sixty ways to construct your story is based on suggestions from the science-fiction writer and teacher, James Gunn:

• Begin with an idea: What would happen if...? And then work out its logical, believable consequences.

• Create a background, colorful enough to hold interest; but don't overwhelm the story. Remember background is *back*-ground; write a story, not a gazetteer nor a history text.

• Select characters who will best dramatize the conflict you've plotted. Observe real people, and model your cast on them. show them in action from the start; show their characters by what they say and do. Write a story, not a set of résumés.

• Pick the best viewpoint for telling this story (almost always the most important decision made when writing fiction). Put the reader so firmly into that viewpoint that as he reads, he *is* that character. Do not pull the reader out of a viewpoint character to describe what he looks like or to present his biography. Get on with the story. If your protagonist's appearance is important to him, he'll think about it or act on it soon enough, showing the reader that facet of character without telling the reader about it; if it's not that important, get on with the story.

• Begin your story where and when things become interesting. Homer began the Iliad right in the middle of a war ("Sing, Godless, of the anger of Achilles...") and Homer sings to us still! Backtrack to explanation or flashback only when it's so relevant to the story that the viewpoint character and the reader, still *being* that character, remember what happened before this story began. You'll be surprised how few flashbacks you really need!

• Write in scenes, dramatizing everything possible. In every scene, put your characters — and readers — firmly into the time and place of that scene. Appeal to the senses — go beyond how things look, go on to the sound and smell and *feel* of the setting. But don't overdo it; omit everything that doesn't advance the story.

• Don't lecture; exposition is all dead matter. Avoid clichés like the plague! Learning to avoid triteness in word and phrase and in ideas, plots, characters, and backgrounds is easily half of becoming a good writer.

Mark Twain wrote, in his famous essay, "Fenimore Cooper's Literary Offenses," that:

1. A tale shall accomplish something and arrive somewhere.

2. The episodes of a tale shall be necessary part of the tale, and shall help to develop it.

3. The personages in a tale shall be alive, except in the case of corpses, and always the reader shall be able to tell the corpses from the others.

4. The personages in a tale, both dead and alive, shall exhibit a sufficient excuse for being there.

5. When the personages of a tale deal in conversation, the talk shall sound like human talk, and be talk such as human beings would be likely to talk in the given circumstances, and have a discoverable meaning, also a discoverable purpose, and a show of relevancy, and remain in the neighborhood of the subject in hand, and be interesting

to the reader, and help out the tale, and stop when the people cannot think of anything more to say.

6. When the author describes the character of a personage in his tale, the conduct and conversation of that personage shall justify said description.

7. When a personage talks like an illustrated, gilt-edged, tree-calf, hand-tooled, seven-dollar Friendship's Offering in the beginning of a paragraph, he shall not talk like a Negro minstrel in the end of it.

8. Crass stupidities shall not be played upon the reader by either the author or the people in the tale.

9. The personages of a tale shall confine themselves to possibilities and let miracles alone; or, if they venture a miracle, the author must so plausibly set it forth as to make it look possible and reasonable.

10. The author shall make the reader feel a deep interest in the personages of his tale and in their fate; and shall make the reader love the good people in the tale and hate the bad ones.

11. The characters in a tale shall be so clearly defined that the reader can tell beforehand what each will do in a given emergency.

12. The author shall *say* what he proposing to say, not merely come near it.

13. He shall use the right word, not its second cousin.

14. He shall eschew surplusage.

15. He shall not omit necessary details.

16. He shall avoid slovenliness of form.

17. He shall use good grammar.

18. He shall employ a simple, straightforward style.

Elsewhere, he wrote: "The difference between the right word and the almost-right word is the difference between the lightning and the lightning bug." Also: "Truth *is* stranger than fiction, because fiction is obliged to stick to possibilities. Truth isn't."

But these just are commentary, not **Rules**.

Rule Two: You must put your story into a format the editor can read, the copy-editor can edit, and the compositor can set into type.

Ursula Le Guin, in her *The Language of the Night*, writes: "Your story may begin in longhand on the backs of old shopping lists; but when it goes to an editor, it should be typed, double-spaced, on one side of the paper only; with generous margins — especially the left-hand one — and not too many grotty corrections per page.

"Your name and its name and the page number should be on the top [right corner] of every single page; and when you mail it to the editor it should have enclosed with it a stamped, self-addressed envelope."

Typed (or **machine-printed**) means just that. If you use ribbons, have a supply of new ones on hand; change to a new ribbon when you start the final draft of a story. When you make a xerographic copy, make sure that all pages are copied clearly. The printing must be black, not grey. But do not overdo that; be sure no letter looks like a black blob. The typesetter must follow copy to the letter. To do this, he must be able to read, without guessing, every letter on every page. It's best to use a simple font that looks like the output of a typewriter, like 12-point Courier type, which is ideal; the closer to that, the better. Never change typefaces within your manuscript; if you want the editor to make such a change, say so in a penciled, marginal note. Avoid typefaces that confuse "i," "I," "1," and "l," or which confuse the comma "," with the period "."

Modern computers offer an astonishing variety of type-faces and type-sizes. Keep in mind, however, that editors are not asking you to typeset your stories; we merely want to see which words you picked, which punctuation you picked, and the order that you put them on paper. Do not use all-italic, all-capital, or script or other fancy fonts. We strongly prefer what's called a "mono-spaced" font, like 12-point Courier.

Do not use type smaller than 12-point. This should give you about 10 letters, spaces, and punctuation marks per horizontal inch of text.

Double-spaced means double-*line*-spacing: leaving a full, blank line after every typed line; it does not mean putting extra space between words! On a typewriter, set the line-feed control to advance the

paper two full lines at a time; on a printer, set the line spacing at 24 points. Either should give you about three typed lines per vertical inch. Do not use the on-&-a-half-line setting some typewriters have; do not reduce the line spacing anywhere in the manuscript.

Indent every paragraph five spaces, including every paragraph of dialog. (And remember that it is customary to start a new paragraph wherever the speaker changes from one character to another.) Leave extra space between paragraphs only where you want to mark a shift in scene or a lapse of time.

On one side of the paper, which should be white, 8.5 by 11 inches (or European equivalent), inexpensive 16 or 20 pound bond. Do not use "erasable" paper.

With generous margins, about an inch, all the way around. Margins much larger than one inch waste paper and postage. If you use a word processor, check its manual, and then turn *off* the right-justification and the hyphenation; do *not* let it suppress "widows & orphans" (that is, do *not* let the word-processing program keep the first line of a paragraph from appearing at the end of a page nor keep the last line of a paragraph from appearing at the top of a page.) Do *not* break words at the end of lines. Editors (all editors!) Prefer ragged right margins with even spacing between words, and we prefer the same number of lines on every page but the first and the last. Keep in mind that the people who write word-processing programs do not have the remotest idea what proper manuscript format is.

And not too many grotty corrections per page. Neither editors nor compositors are grading for neatness; we don't demand letter-perfect-the-first-time typing. We *do* object to erasures. If you use a typewriter, XXX-out or line out your deletions, and type or legibly hand-print any corrections above the place each is to be inserted. If you are using a word-processor and printer, proofread, proofread, and proofread again before you print the submission copy. Watch out for mistakes that spell-check programs are blind to, like "it's" for "its," "breath" for "breathe," "hoard" for "horde," and all the many possible mistakes involving "lie" and "lay."

Identify your story. Type (or machine-print) your full real name, yur social security number, **and your address** (make it easy for us to send you money!) At the upper left-hand corner of the first page, an inch inside the top and left edges of the page. If you use a cover letter, put your address on that too. Your story's title is *your* responsibility (editors don't buy nameless stories) goes about a quarter of the way down the first page, with your name (or your pen name, if you use one) directly under that title. (Two suggestions: Avoid cutesy pen names; your own real name, especially an unusual one, is far better. But if a well-known writer has the same name as yours, change yours in some say, such as spelling out your middle name instead of an initial, or the like.) Use paper clips, not staples, to hold manuscripts together.

Pages sometimes do go astray in an editor's office. Therefore, a glance at any page in the manuscript should reveal the story title, its author, and the page number. So: type or print your last name (plus initials if your name is a common one), a word or two from the title, and the page number on the upper right-hand corner of every page, starting with page 2, like: **XmasCarol/Dickens/pg 26**, or **Cujo/S. King/7**. (If you use a separate title page, page numbering starts with the first page of text.)

And when you mail it to the editor, it should have enclosed with it a stamped, self-addressed envelope. Editors much prefer a new, 9-by-12, *non*-clasp envelope to carry the story to the editor, with a second envelope of the same size, folded once, paper-clipped to the back of the manuscript. (The Post Office and editors do not like clasps, those brass things that stick through holes in envelope flaps; and non-clasp envelopes are cheaper.) Please do not use padded envelopes or envelopes larger than 9 by 12. Address the return envelope to yourself. Both the outgoing and return envelopes should be addressed by typewriter or printer; if the envelope won't fit, type or print addresses on labels. Please *affix* U.S. postage stamps (foreign postage is useless to us, and you do us no favors by sending loose stamps!); do not use binders or stiffeners; do not use registered or certified mail, because these make editors go to the post office and stand in line, which makes them grumpy and eager to reject you and all your works. Your only protection against loss is to keep a good copy of anything you send out. need U.S. postage? See below.

The more standard your format, the less editors are distracted from what is really important: *the story itself*. Manuscript format is not a place to innovate.

To find out how long the story is, do not actually count the words. Instead, take an average-length, mid-paragraph line. Count the letters and spaces and punctuation in that line (with 12-point monospace type, this will be around 60; if it's much large, you are using type that is too small). Divide by six. Multiply by lines per page. Multiply by pages (correcting for partly blank pages at beginning and end). Put this "word" count in the upper right corner of the first page.

Call for italics by underlining; do not use an italic typeface in the manuscript itself (but it is okay to use underlined italics); do not use the e-mail convention of putting one underline before and one after the "underlined" word. Distinguish between the hyphen, as in "mother-in-law" and the dash — which should be typed like this — with a space before and a space after.

Proofread: Spell-check programs do not catch errors like its for it's; remember that you're responsible for proofreading your manuscripts.

We say, "You must punctuate, paragraph, and indent carefully and correctly."

"How about in dialog? You ask.

"Especially in dialog," we say. "If in doubt, you must look up how to do it properly. Note that when two or more consecutive paragraphs are spoken by the same speaker, all have quote marks at the beginning, but only the last has quote marks at the end.

"Also," we suddenly, excitedly expostulate unto thee, "when you're writing dialog, do not reach for substitutes for 'say' or 'said,' as we did in this paragraph, nor hang unnecessary adverbs on 'say.' doing so will soon get silly; worse, it distracts from the story. Notice how we punctuated and capitalized all through this conversation."

You look puzzled. "Can I identify the speaker without using 'said' or a synonym for 'said'?"

"You just did." We smile reassuringly. "Just don't overdo it. Identify the speaker often enough that the reader always knows who is speaking. Don't let pronouns run wild as in: 'He saw him look at him.' Since 'ten foot long sticks' can mean 'ten sticks a foot long' or 'sticks ten feet long,' use commas or hyphens ('ten foot-long sticks' or 'ten-foot-long sticks') to tell the reader which."

Cover letter? No more than one page long, and only if you really want to; remember that editors don't buy cover letters; they buy stories. Don't spoil the suspense with a synopsis; and don't include your bibliography or resume. You may cite two or three earlier sales, especially if they are to markets as good or better than our own (do mention if you've sold something to *The New Yorker*. Don't bother to mention selling something to *The Bee-Keeper's Gazette* unless your story involves bees); then get out of the way and let the story sell itself.

However, if the editor has seen the story before, a cover letter is necessary, to remind her what she said about the story before and to tell her exactly what you've done about her suggestions. Use a cover letter to explain anything unusual about the rights offered — for example, if the story is part of a novel to be published by [insert name] on [insert date]. Put your typed name and address, and your story's title on every cover letter. But if you don't need a cover letter, omit it.

If it's cheaper to send a disposable copy (and it usually is), mark the manuscript "disposable" so the editor can throw it away if she doesn't buy it. Provide a business-letter-sized return envelope, what stationers call a number 10 envelope (not a postcard!), with letter-postage affixed, for the editor's reply.

If you are sending us stories from outside the U.S., remember that only U.S. stamps can be used for return postage. Since international postage is so expensive, we strongly recommend that you send a disposable manuscript (so marked0 and a return envelope at least 10 by 230 centimeters in size, for the editor's reply. You can send International Postal Reply Coupons to pay for the return postage; each is worth about U.S. $0.84 to us. To send a one-ounce (28 gram) letter to Canada costs us U.S. $0.63; to an overseas address, U.S. $0.80. Reply Coupons cost you a lot, but you can buy U.S. postage by sending a postal money order, payable in U.S. funds, to cover the cost of 10 stamps or more, to Postmaster, Bridgeport, PA 19405, U.S.A. (or to the Postmaster of any other U.S. city). Include your own address. Explain what stamps you want, and how many of each.

When a reply envelope is to be mailed in the U.S. for delivery to another country, put the name of that country at the *end* of the *last* line of the address.

Dot-matrix printing is acceptable only if one cannot tell at a glance that the print is dot-matrix. Do not use draft mode, do not use seven- or nine-pin dot-matrix machines.

Submissions to us must be on paper in the format described above, not on disk and not by e-mail. (We have a system for handling on-paper submissions; having two systems — one for snail-mail and another for e-mail — is more than we can cope with.) Unless an editor announces otherwise, assume this is so for all publications. an editor who buys your story will almost certainly want to know if you can supply it by disk — and if so, which word processor and which kind of computer: PC, Apple, or MacIntosh — or by e-mail. Put these data on the manuscript's first page. (We use a PC, XyWrite, and Ventura; we can also cope with Word, plain-text, and .rtf formats.)

Again: format is not the place to innovate; do not divert the editor's attention from the story! Instead, your format should be as invisible as possible.

Rule Three: You must put your story before an editor who might buy it.

Parents, siblings, spouses, offspring, teachers, and friends don't count; neither do closets or desk drawers. You simply must send your story to editors (one editor at a time). Remember that editors do not reject people, nor do they predict careers. At worst, editors reject pieces of paper that you typed on; at best, editors send you money. The only opinion that really counts is that of someone who might pay to publish your story.

We call your attention to the chorus in the opening song of The Music Man: "But ya gotta know the territory!" Read your target publications. See what kind of stories they use; note what kinds of stories they use. Ask for guidelines, always including a return envelope (with postage affixed) for the reply.

In the short-story market, it is almost always better to send a complete manuscript rather than a "would you like to see?" letter. If you fear that a particular market might not be open for submissions at all, write to the editor and ask if it's open now; and if it's not open, when will it be, with a postcard (addressed to you, with postage affixed) for the editor's reply.

How does the "who might buy it" part of the Rule apply to *Weird Tales*? Please keep in mind our magazine's title. We almost never buy a story or a poem which has no fantasy content; we hardly ever buy science fiction which lacks fantasy elements; we never buy stories in which the weird elements turn out to be nothing but a dream. But this leaves room for an extraordinary range of fiction — and poetry: Robert E. Howard's Conan the Cimmerian and modern swordplay-&-sorcery were born in Weird Tales. H. P. Lovecraft's Cthulhu Mythos, Miskatonic University and all, are welcome to our pages, as are stories set in fantasy-worlds of your own invention. We're looking for the best in fantasy-based horror, heroic fantasy, and exotic mood pieces, plus the occasional "odd" story that won't fit anywhere else. We want to please our readers with superior writing and to surprise them with new ideas. To this end, we will occasionally publish a story in which the ominous, eldritch, and/or squamous horrors waiting to pounce turn out to be quite harmless. We almost never use material already published in the U.S.

Most stories we buy are shorter than 7,000 words. We may serialize novellas in two parts; we do not serialize novels. We have no minimum length. Short-short stories (less than 1,000 words or so) are very hard to write, but they are easy to sell.

WT does use humor, but the humor should touch on fantasy or horror themes. We find that humor works best when structured like other fiction, with high points and low, tension and relief, building to a climax and (usually) a very quick anticlimax or none at all. Do not try to make every line screamingly funny.

Remember that printed fantasy stories (and science fiction, for that matter) are usually years — even decades — ahead of movie and TV versions of the same themes. Especially beware of building a story (*any* kind of story) on current newspaper headlines, which may well be forgotten by the time the story could be printed. As an example: spousal and child abuse, and schoolyard shootings are real-life problems, yes — but they're perhaps too familiar to our readers to work as fiction just now.

To know our territory ("…ya gotta know the territory!"), look at what we publish in *Weird Tales*. Then try to do even better. (Back issue of Weird Tales ((and *Worlds of Fantasy & Horror*, our title for four issues)) are available from the address below: single copies, $6 each, including postage; in Canada & Mexico, $7; and elsewhere, $10. Make back-issue and single-copy payments by checks or money orders payable to Weird Tales, all prices in U.S. dollars.)

We respond as fast as we can, and we write an individual letter almost every tme. In return, we expect that your submission is not now being seen by any other editor (that is, no simultaneous submissions), and we hope you will not get too upset if we tell you why *we* don't want to use it. Ours is only one opinion, but it *is* possible for us to be right, and our comments might help you to do better with your next story. Again: we reject pieces of paper; we cannot and will not reject *you*. We pay about 3¢ per word on publication.

Problems we see too often:

No return address on the first page of the manuscript, and no return address on the cover letter. Do you really want to make it hard for editors to send you money?

No return envelope with postage affixed. We couldn't possible afford to pay postage to return comments on all the manuscripts we get — and why put editors in a bad mood before they even start reading?

Format so far removed from professional standards that we did not or could not read your story at all.

Writing which is simply not of professional quality — which includes awkward writing, using not-quite-right words, using too many adjectives (there isn't an adjective built that is as effective as the exactly right noun!), or failing to stay in a chosen viewpoint character for the duration of a scene.

Stories that don't catch the reader's attention by the middle of the first page.

Stories and poems which have no supernatural or fantasy content. (Remember, though, that some of our best stories have been about apparently supernatural elements that turn out to have a non-supernatural explanation; we don't use many like that, but will run a few such stories that have exceptional merit.)

Stories with characters we cannot bring ourselves to care about.

Stories and poetry which try to make up for uninteresting content by "going for the gross-out," as by using shock-value instead of real story-telling and innovation.

Stories with disappointing endings, or whose resolution is too obvious too soon (some as early as half-way through the first sentence!), or that do not resolve at all. We don't object to corpses nor to tragic endings, but protagonists who exist only to wallow in mundane woes and then succumb quietly to an undeserved doom really don't belong in *Weird Tales*. Your protagonists must at least *try* to cope, and must try to change *some*thing, even if the outcome is tragic.

Stories whose only point is that the world is a dreadful, dreadful place tell our readers what they already know; people read *Weird Tales* to escape everyday futility, not to be splattered with more.

More description of a horror is not as effective as telling a story about people trying to cope with one, successfully or not. Believable, often sympathetic people make horror stories scary; but standard-is-

sue, cardboard villains rented by the yard from Central Casting and who come to a (usually predictable) bad end do not.

The pseudo-Medieval never-never land, overrun with generic swords-persons, wizards, and dragons has been sword-played (and ensorcelled) into the ground by now. But *your* imaginary-world setting, characters, and plot elements can be fresh, and new, and *interesting*. Look at real histories; get a feel for just how complex the pre-industrial world was. Don't base your characters or your magic on a role-playing game; invent your own.

Although there's nothing inherently wrong with stories about classical vampires, deals with the Devil, formalities of the Hereafter, and people eating people (or vice versa), our readers have already read stories based on these ideas. If you wrap a story around an old, familiar idea, then add something new and different! A story seldom surprises readers if all it does is reveal, as "surprise" ending, that the protagonist is a vampire, or that he just noticed he's been dead snce page 1.

Please remember that *Weird Tales* is a fiction magazine; the Real Inside Truth About The Occult belongs elsewhere, as do real-life ghost sightings and anything about airborne crockery and alien abductions.

To sum up:

Most manuscripts rejected by any fiction editor are rejected for one or more of these flaws:

Text that is too hard to read comfortably.

Lack of a clear, consistent point of view.

Failure to establish the characters' identity (including gender) and setting, in both time and place, early in the story.

Too much exposition and too little narration, especially at the beginning.

Characters so uninteresting, unpleasant, or unconvincing that the readers don't *care* whether or not those characters get eaten alive (or worse) on stage.

Characters who don't even try to cope with their problems (your protagonists should protag!)

Plots that fail to resolve (tragically, happily, or otherwise) their problems or conflicts, but just present them. Plots with neither problems nor conflicts. Plots based on ideas so old and tired that the ending is obvious half-way down page 1. Plots that cheat readers by holding back information for a "surprise" ending.

Writing so flowery and so filled with sesquipedalian prose that the basic story is lost under too many adjectives, adverbs, and not-quite-right words.

Writing which feels as if the author were being paid by the word (well, you are, but don't let the readers notice that).

Writing too murky or opaque to decipher and decode.

Writing so filled with errors in spelling, punctuation, and grammar that no editor wants to wade through the mess.

Something you must read:

The Elements of Style by William Strunk, Jr., and E. B. White, third edition, published by Macmillan, is widely available from good bookstores in hard covers and soft. Absolutely essential. Get hold of a copy, and you better believe it!

Something we'd merely *like* for you to read:

On Writing Science Fiction: The Editors Stroke Back! By Scithers, Schweitzer, and Ford — we wrote it, so of course we recommend it. In it, we discuss fantasy as well as science fiction; you can order it from Owlswick Press, 123 Crooked Lane, King of Prussia, PA 19406-2570, for $19.50, postpaid. (In Pennsylvania, please add 6% sales tax.)

Categories: Fiction—Fantasy—Horror—Short Stories

CONTACT: Submissions Editor
Material: All
9710 Traville Gateway Dr #234
Rockville MD 20850-7408
PO Box 4001
Rockville MD 20849-4001
E-mail: weirdtales@comcast.net

V-Z

Westchester Magazine

Westchester and lower Fairfield's premier upscale lifestyle publication, *Westchester Magazine* focuses on the hot issues, the innovative trends, the people on the scene, what to do and where to go in two of the wealthiest counties in the U.S. Departments focus on area people in the news, regional events, travel, gift ideas, education, shopping, restaurants and theater, health and fitness, among others.

Editorially, *Westchester Magazine* tries to reflect the values of the strongest magazine journalism: objective reporting, lively writing and trenchant analysis. We are interested in the news of the area—the creative idea, happening, the important concern, the entertainment the unusual place or "find"—delivered in sophisticated, crisp and punchy fashion.

Westchester Magazine accepts queries and clips from all writers. Manuscripts should be accompanied by a self-addressed stamped envelope, cover letter, resume and any applicable clips. The annual subscription rate for writers is $15, the professional rate.

Articles are accepted on speculation as well as assigned. Optimum length for articles is 800-2,000 words. If you have photographs relating to your story, please include them.

Thank you for your interest in our magazine.

Categories: Lifestyle—Regional

CONTACT: Esther Davidowitz, Editor-in-Chief
Material: All
100 Clearbrook Rd.
Elmsford NY 10523
Phone: 914-345-0601
Fax: 914-345-8123

WestCoast Magazine

Thank you for your interest in submitting articles to *WestCoast Magazine*.

We receive articles from seven cities, crossing three county lines every month. So that we may process your submission in a timely manner, articles are due no later than the 10th of each month for consideration in the upcoming issue. To be considered for publication, articles will be accepted in the following format:

- Name and phone number on front page, upper left hand corner
- Typed, double-spaced
- Preferred font: Times Roman, 12 point
- Length: 375 words maximum
- Preferred method of submission:
E-mail to editorial.wcmedia@mindspring.com
- May fax to: 909-390-9590
- Hard copy or computer disk may be walked in or mailed to address listed below

WestCoast Media strives to uphold excellent standards to educate, entertain and inform our readers with a balance of local and general articles in our community magazine. We are always looking for fresh, innovative and inspiring articles of interest for our readers; however, publication is not always guaranteed. Publication is based on appropriateness of the article, quality of writing and available space in the magazine.

Your ideas are always welcome. We look forward to hearing from you.

Categories: Book Reviews—Cooking—Diet/Nutrition—Education—Entertainment—Family—Fashion—General Interest—Health—Inspirational—Money and Finances—Parenting—Physical Fitness—Psychology—Real Estate—Relationships—Self Help—Short Stories

CONTACT: Elizabeth Cohn, Publisher
Material: All

800 S Rochester Ste. B.
Ontario, CA 91761
Phone: 909-390-5727
Fax: 909-390-9590
E-mail: editorial.wcmedia@mindspring.com

Western Humanities Review

We do not publish specific writers' guidelines, because we feel that the magazine itself conveys the most accurate picture of our requirements.

Writers may wish to obtain a sample copy from us or to look for a recent copy at their local university or college library. (Poets may want to check out a recent issue of the more widely distributed *Paris Review*, with which we share our poetry editor, Richard Howard.)

Submissions

Submissions are read from September 1 through May 1 of every year. Submissions received outside of this time frame may be returned unread. Electronic submissions or queries are not accepted. Please be sure to include an SASE, or we will not respond to your submission. We accept simultaneous submissions with notification of such.

Categories: Fiction—Nonfiction—Literature—Poetry

CONTACT: David McGlynn, Managing Editor
Material: Fiction, Non-Fiction
CONTACT: Richard Howard, Poetry Editor
Material: Poetry
Dept. of English
The University of Utah
255 S. Central Campus Dr., Rm. 3500
Salt Lake City UT 84112-0494
Phone: 801-581-6070
Fax: 801-585-5167
Website: www.hum.utah.edu/whr

Western Publications

Please refer to *True West* magazine.

Western RV News & Recreation

Submission Guidelines
Submit Your Press Releases and Photos

To proceed as a contributor to submit an article, press release and/or photos you must have subscriber privileges and access to the submission forms. We prefer to receive all materials via the appropriate submission forms on our web site. We prefer you do not send us a hard copy in the mail or via an email. All submissions must come through our website. If you have additional questions or comments regarding submitting an article, press release or photo please use the Contact Us form. Remember editorial submissions must be sent using our submission forms only.

Photos and images can be submitted as digital files, CD or as photographic prints. Digital files must be TIFF or EPS at a resolution of 300 dpi and submitted via email or on a CD (PC format). If you submit an article or press release via our online article/news submission form only jpeg images should be uploaded.

All rules outlined below in our writer's guidelines apply.

Writers' Guidelines

Due to the volume of article submissions we receive each day, *Western RV News & Recreation* does not accept phone calls regarding submissions. If we are interested in your query or submission we will contact you.

Sincerely, Tom & Darlene O'Connor, Publishers & Editors

Content:

Western RV News & Recreation is celebrating its 40th year in publication. During that time *Western RV News & Recreation* has established a loyal readership and is devoted to the promotion of the recreational vehicle enthusiast. Published monthly, our editorial mix strives to provide full-color travel features and destinations, useful repair and technical articles, how-to advice, and product reviews. Regular columns written by on-the-road RVers share the back-roads and first-hand experiences of the part-time and full-time RV lifestyle. Our readers say that generations of their families have subscribed to *Western RV News & Recreation* for many years, and they continue to enjoy *Western RV News & Recreation* from cover to cover.

Submissions:

We publish a very respected and followed RV newspaper. A healthy number of regular columns appear each month and other "feature" articles on RV travel and RV news, as the primary focus. Please do not query us before you spend some quality time with our publication. We expect our writers to know our readers and help them solve problems, suggest quality destinations and events, and give them news and editorial content which is appropriate and interesting to the RV lifestyle.

• Upon publication, *Western RV News* will pay 8 cents per published word and $5 per image for original articles.

• Feature articles are (800-1,200 words) and are generally assigned.

• We are currently accepting short stories (300 words or less) on subjects such as readying your RV for the road, and "Just Off I-5" a series which shows RVers events, destinations, and "finds" right off the freeway on their way to where they are going.

• We are always on the lookout for NEWS but we avoid running press releases that sell. Our "Product Spotlight" is a regular feature that showcases a product or resource which is truly helpful to the RVer and tent-camper. Submissions in this catagory are always accepted.

The Rules:

• We only accept first rights articles—we do not accept reprint submissions at all.

• We only accept submissions via email—we do not accept submissions by regular mail.

• We receive a huge number of submissions daily so please show patience in awaiting our response.

• Our editorial lead time is typically 9 to 12 months, although this varies.

• If we are interested in your query, we will ask to see tearsheets of your previous work.

• All submissions should include word count, author's name, address, phone number, and email.

• We do expect the submission to include images—we do not accept transparencies or slides.

• Images must be sumitted as (in order of preference) digital files, CD or as photographic prints.

• Digital files must be TIFF or EPS at a resolution of 300 dpi and submitted via email or on a CD (PC format).

• Author warrants copyright ownership and unconditional rights to reproduce/publish and must have model and/or property releases available upon request for each image, where applicable.

• Editors and graphic designers reserve the right to retouch, crop, or alter images for layout purposes.

• Materials will be returned after publication if requested.

• Accepted article submissions will be edited, shortened, or trimmed down to meet space requirements.

• All submitted work must be grammatically clean and well documented with an emphasis on accuracy.

• Authors warrant that material submitted is their original work and that they are sole owners of publishing rights.

• By submitting articles to Western RV News & Recreation, it is understood that the author has read and agrees to the terms detailed in these guidelines.

Send us your submissions via our submission forms only. If you have any questions please feel free to contact us.

Categories: Nonfiction—Adventure—Automobiles—Lifestyle—Outdoors—Recreation—Recreation Vehicles—Senior Citizen—Travel

CONTACT: Darlene G. O'Connor, Managing Editor

Material: All
21821 Cole Lane NE
Aurora OR 97702
Phone: 503-629-8323; 1-888-978-6397
E-mail: editor@westernrvnews.com
Website: www.westernrvnews.com

Westways
Southern California Lifestyle Magazine

Westways, the bimonthly magazine for Auto Club of Southern California members, has a circulation of 3.2 million. Our editorial focus is Southern California popular culture, travel, and automotive topics.

In each issue, we publish several feature articles ranging from 1,000 to 2,500 words in length. We assign stories based on writers' proposals and rarely accept completed manuscripts. We look for writers with sound research and reporting skills, a strong voice, and good storytelling ability. In early summer, we create our editorial calendars for the following calendar year.

Before you submit article ideas, we strongly encourage you to read several issues of *Westways* to familiarize yourself with our requirements. Please send samples of your published work with your proposal; otherwise, we will not make an assignment.

Sections that are most open to new writers include: What's New (Travel, Automotive, and Lifestyle), Day-Tripping, and Quick Escapes. What's New items are typically between 150 and 250 words in length; the other departments vary from 750 to 1,500 words.

We pay $1 a word upon acceptance, plus agreed-upon expenses, for first North American rights. We use high-quality photographs or slides with our articles, so if you are a published photographer, please let us know. (Photographers may submit their books to the Art Director.)

We usually respond to queries within two months, but do not respond to queries submitted without an SASE, nor do we respond to follow-up calls regarding queries. In addition, we do not accept queries via fax or phone.

To be considered for an assignment, mail queries and clips to the address below. We look forward to reading your proposal. Thank you for your interest in *Westways*.

Categories: Nonfiction—Associations—Automobiles—Consumer—Regional—Travel

CONTACT: Linda Volman, Editorial Assistant
Material: All
PO Box 25222
Santa Ana CA 92799-5222
Phone: 714-885-2376
E-mail: westways@aaa-calif.com
Website: www.aaa-calif.com/westways

Wheelin' Sportmen

Please also refer to *Turkey Call.*

Wheelin' Sportsmen is the quarterly magazine of the Wheelin' Sportsmen NWTF program, which delivers, and in some cases re-introduces, the beauty and excitement of the outdoors, including hunting, fishing and recreational shooting, to thousands of people with disabilities. The publication is also a tool for able-bodied sportsmen and women to learn more about sharing the outdoors with their disabled peers and relays information about the Wheelin' Sportsmen NWTF program and the NWTF. *Wheelin' Sportsmen* feature articles average 1,500 words. Most articles deal with concepts and ideas on "how to enjoy" to "where to enjoy" the outdoors. We're also interested in stories about disabled people who enjoy the outdoors and ways able-bodied individuals can help people with disabilities participate in outdoor fun. Articles should depict outdoor activities in a positive/encouraging manner and appeal to a national audience. Editorial coverage for Wheelin' Sportsmen is prepared three months or more ahead of each issue's release date. Magazines are published seasonally, with winter, spring, summer and fall issues each year. Send individual queries; no laundry lists.

We pay $100 for short pieces of 600 to 700 words; $200 to $275 for articles of 700 to 1,100 words; $300 to $375 for up to 1,500 words; and $400 to $500 for up to 2,000 words. We accept images that illustrate wildlife, conservation, colorful scenics, individuals with a variety of disabilities participating in hunting, shooting, fishing and other outdoor pastimes, as well as able-bodied and disabled people enjoying the outdoors together. Check with the editor for current photographic needs.

Rates for published photographs:
- Cover = $400
- Two-page spread = $175
- Full page = $125
- Half-page = $100
- One-third page or less = rate negotiated by editor

Categories: Nonfiction—Recreation—Sports—Hunting

CONTACT: Karen Lee, Editor
klee@nwtf.net
CONTACT: Chasiti Kirkland, Managing Editor
ckirkland@nwtf.net
National Wild Turkey Federation
PO Box 530
770 Augusta Rd
Edgefield SC 29824
Phone: 803-637-3106
Fax: 803-637-0034
Web site: www.nwtf.org

Whole Life Times

Calling All Freelancers!

Whole Life Times relies almost entirely on freelance material to fill its pages every month. We have only a few "regulars," so the field is wide open to all who wish to submit. We depend on freelancers like you!

What Kind of Articles Should I Submit?

As a Cultural Creative lifestyle publication, *Whole Life Times* is open to articles on a wide variety of topics. Our main focus of coverage includes new approaches to: health, food, social justice and social responsibility, conscious business, the environment, spirituality and personal growth; in short, anything that deals with a progressive lifestyle. The important words to remember when writing for WLT are information and narrative style: We strive to provide leading-edge editorial that is not only entertaining, but also directly usable by our readers—information that the mainstream media often abridges, is unaware of or is unwilling to print.

Whole Life Times' content is predominantly local. We publish stories about issues, events and people in southern California. In generic stories (e.g. health-related), we use local sources for quotes and back-up information.

Whole Life Times accepts up to five long (1,500-2,200 words) and short features (800-1,000 words) per issue, covering the areas mentioned above.

In addition, we have several short features we run regularly:

Spotlight focuses on an individual in our community who is generously giving of self to those less fortunate in some way. Subjects of this feature are our local heroes and sheroes.

Conscious Business highlights a local business that is operating with a consciousness of the triple bottom line: In addition to being a profit-making venture, it has environmentally-friendly business practices and treats its employees and customers with integrity.

BackWords is a short feature that highlights a personal event or moment in the life of the writer. It could be characterized as an "aha" moment or event. Ideally it inspires, educates or informs our readers.

Uncommon Healer profiles a health provider in our community.

Manuscript Format

Typed, double-spaced submissions are best, and we also accept in MicrosoftWord format via email. For best results with completed stories, please attach a Word file, and also copy and paste in the message section of your email. Queries may be sent via e-mail to Editor@wholelifetimes.com.

If including graphs, charts or other original art, please send a hard copy in addition to a disk, or e-mail us for digital art submission guidelines. Original photos and illustrations are welcome and may be submitted along with your article for consideration.

Notification of Acceptance or Rejection

Ah, the life of an editor—deadlines, deadlines and more deadlines! Every time we look up from our desks, it seems there's another deadline to meet. So, we set aside time to look at submissions during our precious, limited "quiet time," that late time of the month just after we've completed the last issue. Sometimes our response rate to submissions is probably not as rapid as you'd like it to be.

If we do not immediately accept or reject your article or pitch, we may set it aside for a rainy day. If you are uncomfortable with ambiguity or are in a hurry because you want to submit it to other publications, be sure to make note of it on your submission.

No matter what, be sure to include a self-addressed, stamped envelope for notification of acceptance or rejection. Articles will not be returned unless specifically requested, so be sure to keep a duplicate.

Query Letters

If you have not written for us before, please be sure to include your bio and up to three published clips. Alternatively, you may submit a completed manuscript. If your article addresses the categories described above, your treatment of the issue, the timeliness of the article and the quality of your writing are the main keys to getting published.

General tip: Keep in mind that *Whole Life Times* readers are more sophisticated than the average Joe or Joan when it comes to health, personal growth, social justice and metaphysical issues. We prefer thoughtful, well-researched articles with an informed and upbeat tone. We favor a narrative approach in which "story-telling" is emphasized. We welcome investigative reports and personal interviews, but outside of BackWords, rarely publish pov. Please include reference material for fact verification, and avoid using anecdotal claims to support your thesis or argument.

Deadlines

We accept articles any time. If you want your article to be considered for a specific issue, we should have it in hand three to five months before the month of publication.

Pay

Our rates vary dramatically from $35-$800 based on our experience with the writer, the writer's professional experience, and type and length of story.

In the event that the magazine decides not to publish your assigned story, a kill fee of 50 percent of the original fee is offered. However, no kill fee is offered if this is your first assignment with *Whole Life Times*; you are free to publish the work elsewhere. If we do print your work, we customarily pay within 30 days of publication.

We ask for one-time print rights and non-exclusive perpetual Web site publishing rights. In addition, we request the right to reprint your article in other Dragonfly Media publications at the rate of 33% of the original fee.

AlterNet (www.alternet.org) also picks up our articles, and we pay the writer a fee equal to half of any payment we receive.

Please join *Whole Life Times* in our endeavor to make our world a healthier, happier place!

Categories: Nonfiction—Adventure—African-American—Agriculture—Animals—Architecture—Arts—Asian-American—Comedy—Conservation—Cooking—Culture—Diet/Nutrition—Ecology—Education—Environment—Fashion—Feminism—Food/Drink—General Interest—Health—Inspirational—Interview—Lifestyle—Men's Issues—Money & Finances—Multicultural—Music—Native Americans—New Age—Outdoors—Parenting—Physical Fitness—Relationships—Religion—Science—Self-Help—Society—Spiritual—Travel—Women's Issues

CONTACT: Eliza Thomas, Senior Editor
Material: All
6464 Sunset Blvd Ste 1080
Los Angeles CA 90028
Phone: 323-464-8848 x 212
Fax: 323-464-8838
E-mail: editor@wholelifetimes.com
Website: www.wholelifetimes.com

The Wild Foods Forum

The Wild Foods Forum is a quarterly publication with articles on wild edible foods, rare or poisonous plants, book reviews, upcoming events, trip reports, forager feature stories, herbal folklore, and survival skills. Articles are accepted from large pool of contributing writers. A few are regular, but most are occasional. Informative or unusual topics based on personal experiences are preferred.

Articles

Length: Recipes-24-50 words. Book reviews: 50-100 words. Trip reports: 200-5 words. Informative or How-to Articles: 500-1,200 words.

Format: E-mail or as an attached document in Microsoft Word preferred; otherwise, Typed, single spaced. Each page should contain author's name, address, phone number.

Subject: See topics listed above.

Deadline: Articles should be submitted at least 2 months before the publications date.

If it is an article that would be better suited for another time period, it will be held until that time.

Art, Illustrations, Photography

Original line drawings with captions and artist's name, address, and phone number. Color or black-and-white photos or slides are accepted. Identification, including scientific names, should accompany each photo or slide. Duplicates should be used for irreplaceable slides, photo, or artwork. All artwork and photos or slides will be returned to the contributing artist or photographer.

Payment

Contributing writers and artists receive a free subscription. Additional payments are not always possible and depend on the length, amount of research and uniqueness of the article.

Editing

All work is subject to editing, depending on space and the quality of writing. When possible, editing is reviewed with the author. Please indicate with your submission if you wish to be notified of editorial changes or if you feel strongly about keeping the article intact.

Categories: Alternate Lifestyles—Cooking—Diet/Nutrition—Gardening—Outdoors

CONTACT: Vickie Shufer
Material: All
PO Box 61413
Virginia Beach VA 23466-1413
Phone: 757-421-3929
Fax: 757-421-3929
E-mail: wildfood@infionline.net
Website: wildfood.home.infionline.net

Remember: Editors change jobs and publishers change addresses. It is wise to invest in a phone call for the current information before submitting.

Wild West

Please refer to WEIDER History Group.

Wildlife Art
The World's Foremost Wildlife Art Magazine

Wildlife Art is the recognized journal about contemporary and historical art and artists, depicting wildlife and nature. *Wildlife Art* strives to present informative, thought-provoking features on wildlife and art topics, while providing a forum for news and events of the wildlife art industry. We also include articles about conservation, as habitat preservation is essential to the survival of wildlife. Themes (e.g., sporting art, conservation, landscapes, Western) provide special writing opportunities. *Wildlife Art* has more than 33,000 subscribers worldwide and about 18,000 copies of each issue are sold on newsstands, at art shows and in galleries in the United States and Canada. Our target audience includes art collectors, wildlife art enthusiasts, publishers, galleries and artists.

Topics of Articles

Many of our feature stories spotlight artists. These articles define artists' skills and techniques, share details of artists' personalities and experience, and provide insight into their art. We also publish authoritative and thematic pieces in art history or current art trends, and about groups of artists who share similar medium, location, style, nationality, etc. Read a current issue of the magazine and scan back issues to learn about the range of subjects we cover, what we have addressed recently and typical topics and lengths of articles.

Writing for *Wildlife Art*

You must query us to gain an assignment. Articles must be original, accurate, timely, educational, memorable and entertaining to our readers. We seek dynamic articles that cover new artistic treatments or familiar issues from a new angle. Good writing is essential. We want to take our readers on a journey of words and images that reveals the thoughts, techniques, and styles of present-day and historical artists who depict nature.

You should be able to describe works of art with clarity and perception, and use insight to assess the place of the artists in the field—but we don't want academic criticism. We want lively, knowledgeable writing that places art and artists in context and helps readers judge for themselves. Biographical highlights can be included, but should not be overemphasized—the art should be core. In-depth articles should examine what artists are communicating and their techniques. When possible, include appropriate assessment and evaluation from recognized experts.

Query and Assignment Procedure

The best way to query is with a letter containing:

A title and topic heading for your article.

A one- or two-paragraph outline of the content, and structure, indicating why *Wildlife Art* should publish it.

Several sentences about your qualifications to write this article. Send photocopies of writing samples (writing samples will not be returned).

Examples of the artist's/artists' work(s) in the form of photographs, slides, or transparencies—we must see the art to give proper consideration to the idea.

Mail or e-mail your query to the editor—if you elect to fax it, send your art samples by mail. Allow a minimum of 8-10 weeks to hear from us. If accepted, you may be asked to sign a writer's agreement. Deadlines are arranged at the time of story assignment, but the general editorial deadline is four months in advance of the publication month (e.g., March 1 for the July/August issue). *Wildlife Art* magazine assumes no liability for unsolicited material.

Submissions

Articles must be typed, double-spaced, with wide margins, on numbered pages. Final page should include a brief biographical statement about the writer (see samples in magazine), an artwork courtesy line, if possible, and a listing of the captions for the accompanying artwork. Feel free to make headline and subhead suggestions when appropriate. Send the article by e-mail to mnelson@wildlifeartmag.com as a text or Word file. Include full contact information. All submitted manuscripts are subject to approval/acceptance.

Fundamentals that increase your article's chances of acceptance: A snappy, creative lead, a well-crafted structure and a strong close.

Incorporate specific examples, descriptive details and quotations.

The ability to capture the artist's vision and to elicit anecdotes about experiences.

Verify accuracy, especially of quotations and proper names. Do your research thoroughly.

Judicious use of expert opinions from gallery owners, collectors, museum curators, other artists, etc., will bolster the credibility of your evaluation. (*Wildlife Art* may be able to assist you with contacts.)

Assure that you have checked with the artist(s) about art availability. (Do not focus your article on one or two works without being certain that reproduction-quality transparencies or slides are available for possible use in the article.)

Use the *Associated Press Stylebook* and *Webster's New World College Dictionary* (fourth edition) as authorities.

All articles are edited by the magazine's editorial staff. We reserve the right to edit the manuscript as necessary for our publication. Manuscript acceptance does not guarantee publication.

Submit background materials and a source/contact list with your article(s) to aid us in checking facts. This material may also be used to create a "Read More About It" sidebar. Authors are responsible for obtaining any necessary permission to quote from other publications and to reproduce copyrighted photographs or artwork. Enclose permission letters with submitted materials (see *The Chicago Manual of Style* for sample permission requests).

Artwork and Captions

Do not send original art. Photographs are adequate for querying, but unacceptable for reproduction. Professionally photographed medium- or large-format transparencies (preferred) or high-quality, professional 35mm slides will provide the best four-color reproduction. Send us the transparencies or a source/phone number where we can obtain them. Captions must accompany art submissions, including complete and accurate title, dimensions in inches (height x width x depth), medium(s), year completed, and artist's name. Be sure to code the slides or transparencies to the caption list and label all slides and transparencies with title, artist, "top," and "front." Artwork will be returned only if you request it at the time of submittal and only if accompanied by a self-addressed envelope large enough to accommodate the art and sufficient postage. Delays in requested returns can result from the review process and/or the production process.

Rights and Requirements

All articles must be exclusive to *Wildlife Art* magazine as submitted, and the content must be original and essentially exclusive. A manuscript (or parts of a manuscript) that appeared in other, noncompeting publications may be considered, but only if the author makes *Wildlife Art* magazine aware of this previous publication at the time of submittal. By submission, contributing artists, writers and advertisers agree to indemnify and protect the publisher from any claim or action based on unauthorized use of any person's name, photography or copyrighted material.

Wildlife Art magazine purchases rights to the article for a period of ninety (90) days from the date of publication and has an unlimited right to use the article for other purposes (reuse in special issues) and to authorize reprints. If *Wildlife Art* magazine authorizes a reprint of the article, writer will receive $100 for reprint rights. If *Wildlife Art* magazine is able to negotiate a "larger press run" or if the reprint is for special purposes, every effort will be made to obtain a larger fee. After 90 days, all rights to the article, except for use by *Wildlife Art*

magazine for promotional, advertising (including our Internet Web page), historical, anthology or reprint purposes, revert to the writer. Any subsequent appearances of the article elsewhere must indicate the article first appeared in *Wildlife Art* magazine. If *Wildlife Art* magazine reprints the article in a separate magazine or book published by Pothole Publications, a flat $150 fee will be paid to the writer.

Payment

Material submitted for publication is considered on speculation; we are not obligated to buy an article until we have approved it, even if we assigned it. Payment is made upon acceptance. If your story is accepted, submit an invoice that includes your Social Security number. We do not usually pay a kill fee, although this can be negotiated at the time of assignment. Basic phone expenses are reimbursed. Other expenses must be authorized prior to expenditure.

How to Reach Us

Submit written queries by mailing.

Categories: Animals—Arts—Collectibles—Conservation—Environment—Outdoors

CONTACT: Mary Nelson, Editor
Material: All
PO Box 22439
Eagan MN 55122-9439
Phone: 952-736-1020 (Writers on assignment only)
Fax: 952-736-1030
E-mail: Publisher@winternet.com
Website: www.wildlifeartmag.com

William and Mary Review
College of William and Mary

The *William and Mary Review* is published annually by the College of William and Mary. The *Review* is dedicated to publishing visual arts, fiction, nonfiction, poetry and innovative literary works by established artists and authors in addition to introducing those by new and vital talents.

When submitting, it is best to send no more than one or two fiction or nonfiction works, unless they are under 1,000 words; length should not exceed 7,000 words in any case. For poetry, five to eight poems is a good size selection. All work must be typed; visual arts must be submitted in color slide format. We do not acknowledge receipt of work, and decisions are usually reached within four months. Please note that staff members are not available during the summer months; all material received then will be considered beginning in September.

As the *Review* is published in April of each year, the deadline for each issue is January 15. Back issues of the *Review* are available from the above address at $5.50 including postage. Direct all inquires to Fiction, Poetry, Nonfiction, Art or Managing Editors, whichever is most applicable.

PAST CONTRIBUTORS TO THE REVIEW INCLUDE

Douglas Crase, Amy Clampitt, Julie Agoos, W.S. Penn, Debbie Lee Wesselmann, John Allmann, Dana Gioia, W.D. Snod-grass, David Ignatow, Cornelius Eady, A.R. Ammons, Barnie K. Day, Paul Wood, Carolyn Harris, Geneva Beavers, Michael Mott, William Logan, Debora Greger, Ron Smith, David Acker, Jane Hirschfield, Judson Jerome, and Richard Kostelanetz.

Categories: Fiction—Nonfiction—Arts—Literature—Poetry—Short Stories

CONTACT: The Editor
Material: All
CONTACT: Elizabeth Lathrop, Fiction Editor
Material: All
Campus Center, PO Box 8795
Williamsburg VA 23187
Phone: 757-221-3290

Willow Springs

Willow Springs is published twice a year, in spring and fall. We accept manuscripts year-round, though you should expect delays in response time between June and September. In most cases, we respond within eight weeks, though we ask that you do not follow up on a submission unless it has been longer than four months since you sent it. We offer a year's subscription and two complimentary copies for work we publish.

We publish poetry, fiction, and non-fiction of literary merit. We also interview authors of note, but we do not accept unsolicited interviews. We suggest you familiarize yourself with our journal before submitting. We're open to experimental work in all genres. Translations are welcome if publication permission has been acquired from the author of the original work.

Please submit prose and poetry in separate envelopes. No electronic submissions please. All manuscripts must be accompanied by an SASE with postage sufficient to return the submission or a response. We accept simultaneous submissions.

Categories: Fiction—Nonfiction—Adventure—African-American—Alternate Life-style—Arts—Asian-American—Book Reviews—Civil War—Culture—Dance—Drama—Entertainment—Environment—Experimental Fiction—Folklore—General Interest—Hispanic—History—Human Rights—Interview—Literature—Men's Fiction—Multicultural—Music—Native American—Outdoors—Poetry—Regional—Satire—Short Stories—Society—Theatre—Women's Fiction—Writing

CONTACT: Christopher Howell, Editor
Material: All
Eastern Washington University
705 W. 1st Ave.
Spokane WA 99201
Phone: 509-623-4349

Wines & Vines

About Us

Since 1919, *Wines & Vines* has been the Authoritative Voice of the Wine and Grape Industry. From prohibition to phylloxera, we have covered it all and our paid circulation reaches all 50 states and 40 foreign countries. Because we are intended for the trade, including growers, winemakers, winery owners, retailers, wholesalers, restaurateurs and serious amateurs, we do not accept "gee whiz" type articles on the "wonders of wine," the romance of the grape, etc.

Wines & Vines magazine has been published every month since December, 1919. Issues include the latest industry news, editorial columns on politics, legal and regulatory opinions, the world wine market, health, vineyard management, a variety of pertinent articles, profiles of industry people and businesses and a calendar of upcoming events. Each month we also devote a portion of the magazine to one particular focus.

Submissions

All articles should be summated on typed pages (e-mail is fine too) and the cover page should include your name, address, phone and fax. We encourage you to send photos with your article but we cannot guarantee the return of unsolicited manuscripts and photos.

Our January issue is our trade show issue. In February, we focus on the Vineyard: An overview of last year's harvest; crop size; quality by regions and by states. Other editorial covers pest control, vineyard

management and much more. In March we zero in on International issues. April is our Hot Topics issue. In May we focus on Packaging. Wine Marketing. June is the Annual Open Meeting of the Society for Enology and Viticulture (ASEV) and Enology issue. We supply our readers with extensive convention information and the most accurate floor plan available. Exhibitors are given an opportunity to tell our readers what they will be displaying at the show. This issue is given out at the convention so our advertisers are seen even if they can't attend. July is our Import/Export issue. August is the Wine Marketing issue, in which we cover such things as electronic wine marketing, the top retail players and their markets, interviews with marketers, designers, those who create the new campaigns and those who pay for them.

September, our State-of-the-Art issue, is just that. It covers the new, the innovative and the future, throughout the grape and wine industry. October is set aside for what we term Management. It's a compilation of what is going on within the industry; how companies are being run; how problems are being tackled and solved. In this issue we focus on the business of wine. November is primarily reserved for Equipment, Supplies and Services. In this big issue we list the suppliers, contact information and descriptions of new products and services.

In the December issue we look at Champagne. We visit wineries and cover the new and the not so new but always fun side of champagne.

Payment

Our current rate for articles accepted for publication is $.15 per word and $10 per photo.

If you have any questions please call me.

Categories: Nonfiction—Agriculture—Business—Careers—Diet/Nutrition—Food/Drink—Government—Health—Interview

CONTACT: Tina Caputo, Managing Editor
Material: All
1800 Lincoln Ave.
San Rafael CA 94901
Phone: 415-453-9700
Fax: 415-453-2517
E-mail: tina@winesandvines.com
Website: www.winesandvines.com

WIN-Informer

Writers Information Network is celebrating 25 years of providing a link for professional writers, editors, publicists, and others trying to keep in touch with the expanding and changing climate of the Christian publishing industry.

Articles We'd Love to Receive

• UP-TO-DATE MARKET INFORMATION: Anything that is news-worthy telling our writers what today's religious editors seek.

• INDUSTRY NEWS AND TRENDS: hot tips, trends, announcements of CBA magazines and book publishers. If you can quote editors/publishers, agents or other industry insiders, all the better.

• WRITING HELPS, CONNECTIONS, HOW-TO ADVICE and CHALLENGING ARTICLES: short, pithy ideas of what works; the best suggestions that you've picked up at conferences; practical advice to advance writing/speaking careers; devotional/inspirational material and quotes with "take-away value" from successful Christian authors. Subjects we'd love to see: working with your agent, hot tips for the "business" end, keeping tax records, effective radio or TV appearance, contract negotiation, and more.

• WRITERS CLUBS/FELLOWSHIP GROUPS/AND CONFERENCE ANNOUNCEMENTS: news of conferences, meetings, events of interest to Christian writers and speakers. Send a press release.

• BOOK REVIEWS: Books of special writing/speaking interest; books by WIN members; bestselling books that show popular trends, current issues, what people are talking about, what's important in our world; books by authors writers should be reading.

Your Submission

Your article must encourage and challenge professional Christian writers, editors, and publicists. Give us btye-sized information in reader friendly 800 words or less. For longer feature articles, interviews, personality profiles, query first via e-mail. Please submit all news, press releases, and articles in the body of an e-mail. No attachments! Articles received any other way will not be considered. Payment varies, $20–$50 depending on length and quality, or often a one-year subscription ($49.95) to WIN. Accepts first rights only.

Sample copies: $5.00. Send 9" x 12" envelope with 6-stamps, and check payable to WIN.

Categories: Associations—Book Reviews—Christian Interests—Inspirational—Religion—Writing

CONTACT: Elaine Wright Colvin, Editor/Publisher
Material: All
Writers Information Network
PO Box 11337
Bainbridge Island WA 98110
Phone: 206-842-9103
Fax: 206-842-0536
E-mail: WritersInfoNetwork@juno.com
Website: www.ChristianWritersinfo.net

Wired

The purpose of *Wired* is to illuminate the roots, issues and possible destiny of the emerging digital culture. *If you want to write for us, here are some things to keep in mind:*

Amaze us.

• We know a lot about digital computers and we are bored with them. Tell us something about them we've never heard before, in a way we've never seen before. If it challenges our assumptions, so much the better. *Wired* is a multimedia event on paper. Fiction, non-fiction, semi-fiction; essay, how-to, expose; picture story, profile, interview—all in one issue.

• We seek young and new voices—voices that are passionate and involved.

• Events drive the news of television and newspapers. "Ideas"—conceptual reporting—drive the news in *Wired*. It shouldn't matter too much if someone rereads your piece next month or next year. Poet Ezra Pound calls this kind of information "news that stays news." It's rare. We'll go out of our way to find it and publish it.

• If you care deeply about something that's inextricably tied to digital technologies, chances are we cover it. If the topic is just cresting the digital horizon, it's perfect.

• Write it well—long, if the material demands. Take chances. Sweep, color, scene, and strong character anecdotes are imperative. If there's no conflict—moral, institutional, cultural—there's no story.

• The piece must be definitive.

• We are re-inventing paper as a communication tool for the digital era. Send us an example of what a re-invented magazine article would be like.

• We don't want anything that duplicates what you can read elsewhere.

• We print complaints.

• How to review a product, book, or item: Write your review. Then write us a letter explaining why we should devote space to your item. Throw away your review and send us the letter.

• Give it to us in digital, or analog form. We'd prefer you send it on Mac diskette, Word ready. Don't send us the only copy of anything. Via E-Mail—send it to (submissions@wired.com). If it's a long piece, (over 7500 words) we'd prefer you first send an under-300 word synopsis of what it's about.

Thanks for your interest in *Wired.*

Categories: Fiction—Nonfiction—Computers—Electronics—Interview—Lifestyle—Software—Technology—Communication—Essay—Opinion—How-to—Profiles

CONTACT: Editor
Material: All
520 Third St. 3rd Floor
San Francisco CA 94107-1815
Phone: 415-276-5000
Fax: 415-276-5150
E-mail: editpress@wiredmag.com
Website: www.wired.com

Wired News

Please submit story ideas to **pitches@wired.com.**

Generally, if you have seen a story on Boing Boing or Slashdot, you should have a compelling new angle or slant on it to pitch it to us. We read these sites too, and usually once a story has appeared there, it's probably a little late to be pitching us on it.

We encourage you to pitch your idea in terms of one of the three categories below: (bear in mind folks these aren't set in stone—if you submit a 600 word story we won't cop a fit).

1: 350-500 word dailies—breaking news quickies. These usually require no more than 2 sources and should be a quick turnaround.

2: 800-1,200 word features—the meatier story. These should involve more research, so more time, and 3 or more sources.

3: Multi-day special reports—an idea with legs that can run to several stories. These require authoritative editorial voice based on in-depth research, high level sources and a thorough understanding of the material.

If you are not sure which category your story idea falls into, feel free to bend your editor's ear for advice.

Stories:

Once your story idea has been given the go ahead please be sure to follow the Wired News style when composing the article (see below). Submit the finished article to stories@wired.com. This e-mail address will deliver your story to all the appropriate parties. You will not have to submit additional copies to individual editors. Attach the story as a Word document.

Sources:

If a quote came from an e-mail interview or a written statement, you must identify that, rather than presenting it as a spoken quote.

Please be sure to include a **list of sources** and their contact information along with the finished story.

You must **disclose any and all potential conflicts of interest before submitting a story**. These include investments, litigation past or present with subjects or sources, financial or other relationships with subjects/sources etc. etc. In short, anything that could create the appearance of a conflict of interest.

If we find you have submitted an article without first declaring a potential conflict of interest you will not be asked to write for us again.

If in doubt please contact your editor for advice.

Submit **photos, graphics or video** to art@wired.com. Give a brief description of the story in the subject line. Please include captions and photo credits. This e-mail address will deliver your images directly to the multimedia desk. You can also give this address to sources so they can directly send images to us.

Wired News Style:

When submitting stories to Wired News please follow these style points:

Links: Please add your own links. The correct html code for links, whether to an external site or to another Wired News article is:

<a href="http://yourlink.com/">linking text</a>.

Please check that there is no spaces anywhere in the URL, always include the quotation marks around the URL, and leave any punctuation outside the brackets. For example:

The futures market, ugly as it may sound, doesn't involve any of those moral compromises, said <a href="http://hanson.gmu.edu/">Robin Hanson</a>.

If the link is a PDF file please indicate it like so: (.pdf) after the link.

Please change all curly quotation marks (" or ') to straight quotation marks (" and '). (You can turn curly, or "smart" quotation marks off in Word, under Tools, AutoCorrect, AutoFormat.)

Italics:

Avoid using italics to emphasize words. Do italicize foreign words that have not yet entered mainstream English (consult the dictionary for help). (Use the <em> tag in this instance.)

We italicize the following, using the <cite> tag):

album, CD titles

book titles

comic-strip names

lyrics, poetry

movie titles

names of museum exhibits

newspaper, magazine names (also see online publications)

play titles

radio, TV programs

sculptures, paintings, performance art titles

ship names

space shuttles, rockets that carry humans

symphony, opera, ballet titles

video games, metaverses

It is not necessary to leave two spaces between sentences.

Don't use brackets — { } or [ ] use parenthesis ( ). Even in quotes.

Said vs. says—use either says or said, as long as you are consistent and don't switch back and forth.

Message Boards

Some of you may not be aware of our message boards allowing readers to comment on our articles—comments can be found at the bottom of each story. It is your responsibility to monitor the message boards and respond when appropriate.

Most importantly—if you see a comment on one of your articles pointing out an error you must address the comment.

If the reader is correct please be sure to email us (copydesk@wired.com) pointing out the error. Once we have made the fix you need to write a comment on the message boards owning to the mistake and pointing out it has been fixed.

If, on the other hand, you stand by your article, you need to post a response to the comment laying out your reasoning.

Registering for the Message Boards:

To register with Lycos—an easy procedure, just go to this page and fill out the required fields: http://ldbreg.lycos.com/cgi-bin/mayaLogin?m_PR=49&m_CBURL=http://www.wired.com/news/technology/0,70093-0.html?tw=wn_index_2

If this link doesn't work for you, go to the home page (www.wired.com), select a Wired News article, scroll to the bottom of the page and hit the Login / Register link. Sign up from here.

Make sure you go through all the steps in the sign up process. The last page asks you to sign up for newsletters—if you don't want any hit the No Thanks button. At this point you are all set.

Once you have registered, let me know your user name so I can tag it with the Wired News logo—this way readers will recognize you as a Wired News writer.

We recommend you register your name using various configurations—*eg* lknapp, l_knapp, louiseknapp—to avoid anyone masquerading as you.

If you have any questions please feel free to shoot me an e-mail or call.

Expenses:

Before you incur any expenses connected to an article you have to get the expenses OK'ed by the assigning editor.

To invoice for expenses you need to fill out an expense form and send to me along with receipts for the expenses.

Categories: Nonfiction—Arts—General Interest

CONTACT: Louise Knapp
Material: All
Phone: 415-276-8424
E-mail: pitches@wired.com
CONTACT: Art Editor
Material: Photos/Art
E-mail: art@wired.com

Wisconsin Beverage Guide

Please refer to *Illinois Beverage Guide*.

Wisconsin Trails

Who We Are *Wisconsin Trails*, a privately owned bimonthly magazine, turned 45 in 2005. As the "Magazine of Life in Wisconsin," it features articles on Wisconsin people, history, nature, adventure, lifestyle, arts, sports, recreation and business. We're interested in the out-of-the-way (ever been to Blueberry Bog, known for its bluegills and blueberries?) and the popular (even widely traveled places hold surprises). Nearly 80 percent of our readers are Wisconsin residents, while most of the other 20 percent are frequent visitors here.

Subjects *Wisconsin Trails* magazine gives readers experiences of all kinds. Some articles are meant to entertain, some to provoke readers' desires to participate in an adventure, others to educate or enlighten. It is important that you write in a style that lets the reader join you in the experience and conveys a sense of place. If you're camping by a North Woods stream, we'd like to hear about the last thing you saw at night or the first thing you heard in the morning. What kind of creatures inhabit this place? Tell us what sort of impact the area has on a person, what makes it special enough to send your friends there. If it's a piece on canoeing, biking, hiking, etc., we want a sense of the action—not a blow-by-blow rundown, but a vital account of the experience that lets readers join you in the adventure. If you're writing about people, ethnic festivals or community events, we're interested in the spirit and interaction and what makes them unique and exciting.

Style Many *Trails* stories have a strong sense of voice and place. We always appreciate a moderate use of the verb "to be" and we welcome fresh, descriptive approaches. Typically, our stories are written in the present tense, and published in the appropriate season.

Length Departments range from 75 to 300 words. Features vary from 800 to 2,500 words.

Contract and Payment We expect original work. We buy one-time rights that last through 60 days after publication. Payment, made upon publication, is 25 cents a word, based on assigned word count.

Submissions One-page written queries via snail mail, with a SASE, are preferred over manuscripts, with one exception: we need to see a complete manuscript of a "My Wisconsin" essay submission. Please include two or three nonreturnable writing clips that showcase stories and/or approaches similar to the one you're pitching. Other materials will not be returned without a SASE. No phone queries, please; we prefer written materials we can share at editorial planning meetings. Response time is three to four months. Accepted stories must be furnished via e-mail. We do not subscribe to clipping services or pay for clippings.

Tips

Familiarize yourself with the magazine: We publish only six issues each year, so we choose our stories carefully. We also prepare our stories carefully, so be ready to work with the editorial staff. Please direct department submissions to the appropriate editor.

General Wisconsin stories we're always looking for:
- outdoor activities; family-oriented travel; romantic couples getaways; adventure travel
- history
- natural history and environmental pieces—our readers love both
- hidden or out-of-the-way places
- unknown and quirky people for profiles
- unique homes, gardens, vacation homes and cottages
- suggestions for the photography portfolio in each issue
- the offbeat—we're looking to fun things up
- unique Wisconsin businesses
- new happenings—in everything from the arts to medicine

Wisconsin Trails *Departments*

Editors' Finds

Editor: Laura Kearney

"Editors' Finds" should share with readers new places they might like to visit while traveling around the state, or items they might like to purchase. The spectrum is pretty broad: "Editors' Finds" includes everything from reviews of books written about Wisconsin subjects or by Wisconsin authors to Wisconsin-made products. Maybe you've found a new adventure outfitter, specialty garden store or even an antiques shop, bakery, art gallery or jumpin' swing club. If you have, our readers would like to hear about them.

What doesn't fit: theater or other performance reviews; events and happenings; items that do not have a Wisconsin connection.

Style: These are minireviews that capture the charms of the item reviewed, tell readers what the item offers them and make clear why the place or item is worth a visit or their money. We prefer that quotes from owners, authors, etc. not be included, as they often make the copy seem promotional. We do not run negative reviews.

Each issue, we feature approximately four finds. Word count: 100 to 150 words. Payment: $40, flat fee. Send in written reviews for consideration. Also let us know if a visual is available.

Profile

Editor: Harriet Brown. Wisconsin is filled with interesting people of all ages, and not all of them are high-profile. They may be business or community leaders, artists, craftsmen, educators, entrepreneurs, athletes. We'd like to know more about these individuals, from the award-winning 80-year-old gardener to cutting-edge artist to the innovative business leader. Who are they? What makes them interesting to a wider audience? Word count: 500 to 750 words. Payment: $0.25/word.

My Wisconsin

Editor: Harriet Brown. Each issue we spotlight a personal essay—a first-person vignette or slice of life in Wisconsin. "My Wisconsin" is an opportunity to recollect, philosophize, be humorous about a wide range of topics: people, places, events, nature, history, the environment, seasonal reflections—just about any Wisconsin subject is an opportunity for "My Wisconsin." As with any well-written essay, "My Wisconsin" submissions should transcend the experience and take the reader somewhere beyond—the meaning behind the experience, lessons learned, etc. Simple recountings or regurgitations will not do; we want essays that are poignant, intelligent, probing, observant or just plain fun. Word count: 800 to 1,000 words. Payment: $0.25/word.

News & Views

Editor: Harriet Brown. This department is a compendium of news, quips, quotes, facts and quirks from across Wisconsin that is fun, intelligent and sometimes, slightly irreverent. Word count: 50 to 125 words. Payment: $40, flat fee.

Discover / Calendar

Editor: Laura Kearney. Each issue we highlight about 10 events or places for readers to attend or visit. They must fall within the two calendar months the issue covers. We are always looking for unusual festivals, places, exhibits, classes or other events. The writing should be lively and invite the readers into a fun experience. Word count: 75-125 words. Payment: $40, flat fee.

Gone for the Weekend

Editor: Harriet Brown

"Gone for the Weekend" is a standing department of 1,200 to 1,500 words that appears in each issue of Wisconsin Trails. Your mission, when writing a "Gone for the Weekend," is to give the reader a "you are there" feel while offering fun suggestions for making an enjoyable weekend escape to the destination you're writing about. Weekend adventures come in many shapes and forms—think of the many ways a visit to Milwaukee can be cast. Though each piece must satisfy a basic formula, each trip should have its own unique flavor. Good travel pieces convey a sense of place. They are immediate, intimate without being too personal, and rich with details, and are written in a flowing (but not long-winded) style that focuses on the writer's actual experiences while visiting the destination. Keep in mind during your weekend and as you write:
- Unique people who made your visit memorable.
- Unexpected places worth visiting. Don't overlook the obvious, but don't dwell on it either. You've probably encountered the unusual along the way—include those remarkable people, places and things in your story.
- Information for the "details" sidebar at the end of the piece: necessary phone numbers, addresses and other details that would get in the way if placed in your story. (Some appropriate sidebar subheads include: "Lodging," "Special Events" and "Eating Well."
- Are you able to photograph your weekend?

You should not:
- write a blow-by-blow of your weekend.
- make your piece so personal readers can't glean helpful information for their own trip-planning needs.

The bottom line: Show us, don't tell us. Have fun! Payment: $0.25/word, plus pre-approved expenses.

Echoes: Wisconsin History

Editor: Harriet Brown. Every issue includes at least one substantial story devoted to the people, places, and events that have enriched our past, shaped our present, and continue to influence our future. We're interested in stories that we haven't heard before: the lost, the forgotten, the overshadowed, the unrevealed. It could be an individual whose name is unfamiliar but whose deeds had a lasting impact. It could just as easily be a little-known episode in the life of a famous person, or an obscure aspect of a pivotal event. It might be a place that seems unremarkable today, but was once a prominent landmark; it might be a contribution to art, science, commerce, or culture that Wisconsinites would be proud of—if they only knew about it. All realms of human endeavor are fair game, as are all the men and women who, for better or worse, made their marks on the Badger State. We want your best ideas, the ones that will grab the reader's attention and keep it, the ones that are the most fascinating, the most compelling, the most surprising. Keep your queries short and sweet, and be sure to indicate how and where we can access photographs, artwork, or other materials for illustration purposes.

Payment: $0.25/word.

Categories: Nonfiction—Environment—Food/Drink—Regional—Travel—Wisconsin

CONTACT: Harriet Brown, Editor
Material: All
Trails Media Group, Inc.
PO Box 317
Black Earth WI 53515
Phone: 608-767-8000
Fax: 608-767-5444
E-mail: hbrown@wisconsintrails.com
Website: www.wisconsintrails.com

With
The Magazine for Radical Christian Youth

With is published six times a year for Mennonite and other Christian youth, ages 15 to 18, in the U.S. and Canada. Each issue focuses on a theme such as peer pressure, peacemaking, or devotional life. A list of upcoming themes is available for a #10 SASE. *With* has a reputation for tackling tough social issues other Christian magazines won't touch.

WHAT WE NEED

FIRST-PERSON STORIES: (800 to 1,800 words): We like to lead off with a Christian teen's first-person story of a life-changing experience. Such a story usually involves the teen's faith, and the lesson the teen learned must be one readers can apply in their lives. We sometimes use a how-to sidebar (100 to 600 words) with a personal experience article.

These stories are usually written on an as-told-to basis. You interview the teen then write his/her story in first-person. You receive an as-told-to byline unless you prefer not to. We also welcome stories from adults describing such experiences from their own teen years. We consider stories of any Christian youth, but give preference to stories of youth involved in Mennonite, Mennonite Brethren, or Church of the Brethren congregations.

We prefer a query on this kind of story. Detailed guidelines for first-person stories available for a #10 SASE. We pay $100 for first rights on first-person stories written on assignment and pay extra for photos. Usual rates for reprints.

HUMOR: (prose 100 to 1,500 words; poetry up to 50 lines): We're hungry for more well-written humor—fiction, nonfiction, light verse, or cartoons. When it comes to humor, it doesn't have to be religious, just wholesome. If your writing makes teens laugh, we want to hear from you.

REALISTIC FICTION: (800 to 2,000 words): Most issues include a short story with many of the same elements we look for in the first-person stories described above, except that fiction can be either first- or third-person. Fiction must have strong elements of conflict and change, and the message must be one readers can apply to their lives. We look for fiction that is believable and engages the readers' emotions. We're interested in occasional fiction with an "unreliable narrator."

HOW-TO ARTICLES: (800 to 1,500 words): Most issues include a how-to article with practical teaching on the issue's theme. Examples: "How to Help a Friend Who's Suffering" and "How Not to Be a Witless Witness." How-to articles need a strong opening hook (usually a true anecdote from the author's teen years), a clear step-by-step outline, anecdotes to illustrate at least most outline points, and a satisfying conclusion. To avoid sounding preachy, tell how you learned through your mistakes or from another's example. Detailed how-to guidelines available for a #10 SASE. We pay $75 for first rights on an assigned how-to. Query to receive an assignment.

SPECULATIVE FICTION: (500 to 1,800 words): We like parables, allegories, and fantasy that communicate spiritual truth with symbolism, but the symbolism must be clear. Subtle writing goes right by some of our younger readers.

POETRY: (up to 50 lines): We consider poetry of any style. While most poetry has a spiritual theme, we also use short nature poems (often seasonal), and light verse (just because it's funny). We look for strong sensory images, fresh insight or perspective, and language that pleases the ear. We use about six poems a year.

MEDITATIONS: (100 to 1,200 words): We use meditations that inspire wonder, awe, or reflection in the reader. These can be based on personal experience, a biblical event or symbol, or even a dream or imagined scene. We occasionally publish prayers (up to 200 words).

PHOTOS, CARTOONS, ILLUSTRATIONS: Photographers' guidelines available for #10 SASE. For cartoons, see "HUMOR" above and check recent issues for samples. If you wish to illustrate on assignment, send samples of your work.

OUR WRITER-FRIENDLY APPROACH

Because we have a small circulation (about 6,000), we can't pay top dollar, yet we expect top-quality writing. So we try to make it worthwhile for good writers to work with us through favorable policies on rights, prompt replies and payments—in general, lots of TLC. Here are the specifics:

RIGHTS AND PAYMENT: We pay on acceptance 5 cents a word for simultaneous rights (unpublished manuscripts you are free to submit elsewhere simultaneously) and 3 cents a word for reprint rights. We pay $10 to $25 for poetry (one-time rights) depending on length and how it is used. We pay more for first rights to assigned work (see "First-Person" and "How-To" articles). We sometimes offer a 30%-50% kill fee for assigned articles. You get two author's copies upon publication.

REPLY TIME: We respond to most submissions within four to six weeks. If we want to hold a manuscript longer, we'll ask your permission.

SAMPLES: For a sample copy, send a self-addressed stamped 9"x12" envelope ($1.24 postage). For two issues, affix $1.93 postage. For three, $2.62.

SUBMISSIONS AND QUERIES: Make seasonal and theme-specific submissions at least 6 months before publication date. All manuscripts except poetry should be double-spaced. Type your name, address and phone in the upper left corner of the first page, and the approximate word count and rights offered in the upper right corner.

Queries should be no more than a page and a half, accompanied by published clips if you haven't written for us before. Include your phone number. Don't phone us with a query without prior invitation from an editor.

Categories: Fiction—Nonfiction—Cartoons—Christian Interests—Fantasy—Inspirational—Religion—Teen—Humor

CONTACT: Carol Duerksen, Editor
Material: All
PO Box 347
Newton KS 67114
Phone: 316-283-5100

WittenburgDoor
The Wittenburg Door

OK, this is serious. That's because *The Wittenburg Door*, at its most basic, is serious. Beneath the brilliant humor, the wicked satire, the jaw-dropping interviews, the witty bon mots, we've got an actual purpose for putting out the magazine. We're the guys and gals who shout, "The emperor's got no clothes!" We're the people who are all about busting idols. We're folks who are interested in holding a mirror before the Church.

Why? Because we love the Church of Jesus Christ. We expose venal televangelists not because we're opposed to Christians, but because we're opposed to people who make a mockery of the Cross. We do it because we're called to do it.

That means we generally don't run straight-ahead slapstick humor. We like our humor to reflect one of those points. And that's why we don't do attack-styled ambush interviews OR softball touchy-feely interviews — because we're trying to make a point.

The absolute best place to see what we're trying to do is in past issues of *The Door*. (Sample issues are $5.95 from 5634 Columbia Avenue, Dallas, Tex, 75214.) We have a very definite style, a distinctive approach, a certain elan that belies the fact that our editor lives in Waco, Texas.

We love hearing from freelance writers. We're still 90% freelance written and proud of it — proud in a modest, life-affirming sort of way, of course. Alas, we rarely commission articles or interviews. But if you'd like to tackle former President Jimmy Carter or Stone Cold Steve Austin, by all means go for it. Just let us know ahead of time so you won't waste your time interviewing someone we've already interviewed (Steve Allen or Garrison Keillor) or someone we've already interviewed who is dead (Sam Kinison or Anton LaVey).

As for the legendary *Door* humor articles, they too are written on spec.

Here are some dos and don'ts for the prospective Door writer:

• Don't send us first person, mildly humorous essays or re-hashed sermons.

• Don't send us poetry, unless it is in the form of a howlingly funny song or hymn parody.

• Don't send us funny true-life stories, jokes, funny filler, articles with a moral to the story type ending. Aesop we ain't.

• Don't send us satire without humor.

• Don't send us humor without satire.

• Don't send us humor that's not somehow redemptive (and we can be very subtle on the redemptive stuff if we need to be).

• Don't send us articles that are only mildly amusing in a Steve Canyon suck on your pipe and gently smile sort of way. Be bold. Be funny.

• Do ... Well, I can't think of any dos.

If you've got an article or interview (or even a cartoon — and we pay $50 for each published 'toon) that meets the above criteria, then by all means send it.

If you want to e-mail an article, send it in WORD format to dooreditor@earthlink.net

We look forward to hearing from you, oh Keeper of the Faith!

Categories: Nonfiction—Christian Interests—Religion—Spiritual—Humor—Satire

CONTACT: Robert Darden, Editor
Material: Religious Humor & Satire
PO Box 1444
Waco TX 76703-1444
E-mail: dooreditor@earthlink.net
Website: www.wittenburgdoor.com

Woman Engineer
An Equal Opportunity Career Publication for Women and Experienced Professionals

Please refer to Equal Opportunity Publications, Inc.

Woman's Day

Woman's Day publishes articles from freelance writers on a broad range of subjects of special interest to women, including marriage, health, diet and exercise, spirituality, saving and managing money, interpersonal relationships, careers, lifestyle issues, etc. The editors are primarily interested in practical, service-oriented pieces that will help millions of readers improve their lives. Look at WD Solutions and the YOU section of the magazine for examples.

The magazine is also in the market for dramatic narratives about women or families who have experienced a medical triumph, survived a disaster or achieved something special or significant in their lives. Look for stories that will inspire readers. A dramatic narrative should have a happy ending or at least a clear resolution.

We do not publish fiction or poetry, so please do not submit this material.

Article lengths range from 650 to 1,600 words. *Woman's Day* pays top rates upon acceptance. Please send us a query first, not the entire manuscript. The editors regret they cannot accept unsolicited manuscripts or offer individual comments on submissions. The magazine is not responsible for unsolicited material and cannot return anything

that is not accompanied by a self-addressed, stamped envelope. Any publication of an essay or article is at the sole discretion of *Woman's Day*.

Submissions should be sent to Reader Service, *Woman's Day*, 1633 Broadway, New York, NY 10019. We appreciate your interest in *Woman's Day*.

Essay Submission Guidelines

Woman's Day regularly publishes personal essays in the YOU section of the magazine. These essays are always based on the writer's personal experience and written in the first person. We like to cover significant issues that concern a large number of women and families, rather than subjects that impact only a few. The sentiments expressed should strike a chord with readers.

For example, a writer may share a strong opinion or point of view. These essays are usually thought-provoking and may have an edgy, even somewhat controversial tone. Other essays have a softer, more reflective tone, and focus on how women can improve the quality of their lives.

We accept no queries for essays. They must be submitted in their entirety and on speculation.

Essays run about 650 words. *Woman's Day* pays $2,000 on acceptance. The editors regret they cannot offer individual comments on submissions. The magazine is not responsible for unsolicited material and cannot return anything that is not accompanied by a self-addressed, stamped envelope. Any publication of an essay or article is at the sole discretion of *Woman's Day*.

Categories: Children—Food—Health—Fashion—Family—Women

CONTACT: Reader Service
Woman's Day
1633 Broadway
New York NY 10019
Website: www.womansday.com

woman's touch

Woman's Touch
An Inspirational Magazine for Women

Do You Write?

Woman's Touch is looking for submissions!

About *Woman's Touch*

Woman's Touch is a bimonthly inspirational magazine for women published by the Women's Ministries Department of the Assemblies of God. We are committed to providing help and inspiration for Christian women, strengthening family life, and reaching out in witness to others. *Woman's Touch* is the voice of Women's Ministries across the nation.

The editors of *Woman's Touch* seek original articles written from a perspective that includes God or spiritual laws and is geared specifically for women. The following is a list of topics that may be covered in upcoming issues.

• Aging gracefully—inner beauty / outer beauty / character / health / wisdom / planning ahead

• Blended families

• Careers—your life in the workplace or in the home

• Character—the goal of our Christian walk

• Compassion—developing true compassion like Jesus had

• Crafts/décor—unique, relatively simple ideas for home décor

• Depression—combating on spiritual/mental/emotional/physical levels

• Forgiveness

• Health / fitness / exercise—informative, practical advice

• Humor

• Kindness—making the world a better, friendly place by our behavior and presence

• Knowing God intimately and discerning His will

• Loving our neighbors—unchurched around us/those hit by disaster; etc.

• Marriage/family—Positive testimonies as well as dealing with various difficulties

• Ministering to others—personal ministry to various groups/needs

• Profiles of born-again women who are leaders or entrepreneurs in their own particular sphere: Finance, education, research, medicine, politics, music, finance, law, the arts, journalism, etc.

• Recipes—tested, well-loved recipes for food features

• Staying committed to Christ through all kinds of trials/good times/hard times

• Temptation—avoiding/being victorious in

• Volunteering—touching those around you with practical love and godly lifestyle

• Witnessing—through relationships with unchurched; methods for, etc.

Query Letters

• *Woman's Touch* does not accept manuscripts.

• *Woman's Touch* does welcome query letters. We prefer queries sent via e-mail to womanstouch@ag.org. Writers who have no access to e-mail can mail queries to: Woman's Touch, 1445 North Boonville Avenue, Springfield, MO 65802-1894.

• Do not enclose a self-addressed stamped envelope or postage-paid postcard.

• All queries will be evaluated.

• Specify whether you own photographs related to your proposed article, but do not send photographs. E-mail queries may include scans.

• Due to the large volume of materials received, writers are urged to refrain from contacting *Woman's Touch* for status reports regarding queries. If your query is of interest to our editorial team, you will be contacted.

• A request to see your manuscript does not guarantee that *Woman's Touch* will accept or print the article.

• Study our style and content to learn what type of articles we use. Subscribe to the magazine or purchase a single copy of *Woman's Touch* by contacting Gospel Publishing House at GPH@ ag.org or 800-641-4310.

• Seasonal queries should reach us 9 to 12 months prior to the holiday or season described.

Important Details

• We purchase electronic rights and one-time print rights. Payment will be made on publication. You will receive two complimentary copies of the issue in which it appears.

• The editors of *Woman's Touch* reserve the right to edit your manuscript for clarity and space, and to reject any article at any stage of our editing/production process.

Thank you for considering *Woman's Touch*!

Categories: Nonfiction—Christian Interests—Inspirational—Women's Issues

CONTACT: Submissions Editor
Material: Queries
1445 North Boonville Ave.
Springfield MO 65802-1894
Phone: 417-862-1447, Ext. 4066
E-mail: womanstouch@ag.org
Website: www.womanstouch.ag.org

> *Remember: Editors change jobs and publishers change addresses. It is wise to invest in a phone call for the current information before submitting.*

Woman's World
The Woman's Weekly

V-Z

Fiction Guidelines
Romance Guidelines:

We buy contemporary romances of 1,000 words. Stories must revolve around a compelling, true-to-life relationship dilemma; may feature either a female or male protagonist; and may be written in either the first or third person. Characters may be married, single, divorced or widowed; should be down-to-earth (no yuppies or jet-setters); and their dilemma should be poignantly or humorously conveyed. Please think carefully about a story's setting, mood and plot, and tell the story with interesting action and dialogue. (Every sentence, paragraph, and scene of the story should deliver more information about your characters and their situation and/or briskly advance the storyline.)

We are not interested in stories involving life-or-death matters, nor are we interested in fluffy, flyaway-style romance. When we say romance, what we really mean is relationship—whether it's just beginning or is about to celebrate its 50th anniversary. The emphasis in our stories is on real life—which is why we do not buy science fiction, fantasy or historical romance.

We pay $1,000 per romance and retain First North American Serial Rights for six months after publication.

Mini Mystery Guidelines:

We purchase short "solve-it-yourself" mysteries of 1,000 words—a count that includes the narrative and the solution. Stories should be cleverly plotted, entertaining cliffhangers that end with a challenge to the reader to figure out whodunnit or howdunnit. The solution to the mystery is provided in a separate box.

Robbery, burglary, fraud and murder are acceptable subjects, but no excessive violence or gory detail, please! We are also not interested in ghost stores, science fiction or fantasy.

Important Notes!

Manuscripts should be double spaced in legible size type.

Where to send manuscripts: Fiction Editor at 270 Sylvan Ave., Englewood Cliffs, NJ 07632. Indicate Mini Mystery or Romance on the envelope.

How to send manuscripts: (1) You must include a Self-Addressed Stamped Envelope to receive a reply. Manuscripts not accompanied by a SASE will be discarded. Note: A #10 SASE is necessary not just for a response, but for your contract if we purchase your story.

(2) Please DO NOT fax or e-mail manuscripts—because such submissions do not include SASEs, we have no means of responding to your submission.

Get to know us: Please familiarize yourself thoroughly with our romances and mini mysteries before submitting your work.

Be patient: Because we receive a tremendous volume of manuscripts, our turnaround time may range from one to six months. If you still have not heard from us after that time, feel free to re-submit your manuscript. Please do not call or write us to inquire about a manuscript's status.

Our feature articles are divided into categories. A brief description of each is listed below. Keep in mind that some of the categories overlap and that a story may fit into more than one classification. Don't worry if you're not sure which category would suit a particular story or even if it doesn't fit an established category—we always have room for a compelling story.

Emergency!: Gripping, minute-by-minute accounts of heart-pounding dramas are told as they unfold, so the reader can feel as if she is an actual witness to the event. Written in the third person, dramatic quotes and splashes of colorful detail (but no gore!) should give the reader a vivid mental picture of what occurred. The focus is on a true story of a woman (or child) overcoming a life-threatening crisis, such as a disaster or a dangerous situation.

• Examples: (1) A four-year-old girl calls 911 and saves her diabetic mother. (2) Three strangers appear as if by fate to save a woman's life. (3) When a teenager falls through the ice, a woman braves frigid water temperatures to save him. (4) When a sudden storm overturns their boat, a couple spends seven terrifying hours in the water until they're rescued. (5) While walking to school one morning, a teenager notices smoke billowing out of an apartment building. She heroically risks her life to save the 13 elderly people living there. (6) When a little boy wanders into the woods and gets lost, his dog saves his life by keeping him warm through the night until searchers find him. (7) When flood waters reach her doorstep, a grandmother risks her life to save her grandchild.

Happy Ending: These third-person stories may resemble those in other categories, but here the emphasis is on the joyous resolution, which comes almost as a surprise considering how bleak the situation appeared.

• Examples: (1) After he finds his birth mother, a young man asks her to help him find his birth father. She does, and after they reunite, love blossoms again. They marry and live happily ever after. (2) A 40-year-old woman wants to have a baby but is told she's in the early stages of cervical cancer and must have a hysterectomy. By chance, she finds a woman who wants to give a baby up for adoption—two weeks after the surgery, she's holding a baby in her arms. (3) A handicapped man nobody really notices discovers a town full of friends after his bike is stolen. (4) After an on-again, off-again romance, a cop at last recognizes true love in his girlfriend as she helps him recover from a gunshot wound.

Helping Each Other: Heartwarming tales of good Samaritans who reach out to someone in need. These are third-person stories, told from a female point of view—either the good Samaritan, the person in need or someone (spouse, daughter, or the like) close to the story. Lots of emotion, vivid descriptions and strong quotes are needed. We need to know how grateful the recipients are, and how terrific the do-gooders are.

• Examples: (1) When a young mom gives birth to triplets, 25 members of her church volunteer to change, feed and play with the babies. (2) When they learn a little boy needs a bone-marrow transplant, friends, neighbors and even caring strangers turn out in droves to become possible donors—and one is found. (3) A young man's dreams are shattered when his 20-year-old fiancee is diagnosed with terminal cancer. Friends and neighbors give the couple a wedding. The rings, gown, cake—even the reception—are all gifts to the couple, who can't believe so many people care. (4) When a four-year-old girl suddenly goes into kidney failure and isn't expected to live, the people in her hometown start a prayer chain. Almost as suddenly as she was stricken, the little girl recovers. Her doctors can't explain why—but everyone else knows it's a miracle. (5) A homeless family of six gets a fairy godmother when a woman reads a newspaper article about their plight. She moves them into her own home until they can get back on their feet.

Medical Miracle: A third-person retelling of a recovery, birth or the like that defied all odds or was made possible by a new medical procedure.

• Examples: (1) Almost seven months into her pregnancy a woman suffers two heart attacks. An emergency angioplasty saves her and her unborn child. (2) When a brain aneurysm nearly kills a 22-year-old student, her doctors worry, is her identical twin in danger too? They find that she, too, has an aneurysm, and clamp it before it bursts. (3) After battling cystic fibrosis her whole life, a 29-year-old mom is told only a lung transplant can save her life. She's put on a transplant list, but when her condition worsens, her sister donates a lobe from one of her own lungs, giving her a second chance at life. (4) After trying for 10 years to have a baby, in vitro fertilization makes a couple's dream of conceiving come true. They feel triply blessed to learn they're having three babies, but when she goes into premature labor the woman fears for the lives of her unborn children. After delivering one baby, her doc-

tors are able to stop her labor, giving the other two more time to grow. Sixteen days later, the other two are born. All are healthy.

My Guardian Angel: Told in either the first or third person, My Guardian Angel tells the story of a woman facing a crisis or situation she doesn't think she can overcome. At her darkest moment, help appears. It can be a good Samaritan in the form of a friend, family member or perfect stranger. Or fate can step in, leaving the woman with a strong feeling that someone is watching over her.

• Examples: (1) Although she was never able to have a child, a woman loves her teenage nephew as her own. When he dies in a car accident, she thinks she'll never get over her grief. Then one day, she hears a bluebird chirping in her yard. She remembers that, as a young boy, her nephew promised that if he died before her, he'd come back as a bluebird and sing to her. Realizing that the love they shared could never die, her heart begins to heal. (2) A young mom is struggling to raise her two young children when her four-year-old is diagnosed with a brain tumor. She wonders how she'll cope with a sick child and pay the mounting hospital bills. Just when she feels she's all alone, a friend offers her a job that allows her to work from her daughter's hospital room. (3) After her abusive husband's beating leaves a woman visually impaired, she leaves him. But she feels worthless and alone until a service dog helps her reclaim her life and her happiness. (4) While in a coma, a young woman waits for death until she's "visited" by her deceased sister. Told it isn't her time to die, the young woman finds the will to live again and makes a full recovery. (5) A mother is heartbroken over her daughter's infertility. Desiring her child to know the happiness she's known as a mom, she prays that her daughter will have a baby. Miraculously, the daughter and son-in-law are soon blessed with an adopted baby. A few years later, knowing her daughter aches for another adopted baby, she prays again. It works! Sure that God hears her prayers, the mom asks once more for a blessing of a child for her daughter. This time—against all odds—the daughter finally conceives! (6) After years in an abusive marriage, a woman feels so trapped and alone she doesn't think there's a way out. But one night, a stranger in a parking lot sees the pain in her eyes and hands her a card with her name and phone number on it. Telling her she isn't alone, the stranger asks the woman to call if she needs to talk. She does, and the kind stranger becomes her lifeline, helping her find the strength to leave her abusive marriage and build a new life for herself and her children.

My Story: A first-person narrative that reveals one woman's thoughts and emotions as she comes to terms with a major life problem. We must be able to sympathize with the woman and her plight: Her hopes, fears and aspirations must be candidly exposed. On occasion a man's story is told, but only as it relates to his wife's, daughter's or girlfriend's situation. Sometimes a child's story is told. No matter what the age or gender of the subject, the story must be moving.

• Examples: (1) When her baby girl tragically dies, a young mother's grief is so deep it tears her marriage apart. Just when all seems lost, she realizes she's pregnant. Although she could never forget her firstborn child, the new life growing inside her helps her realize life must go on. Her heart and her marriage are healed. (2) When an 18-year-old girl is diagnosed with breast cancer and undergoes a mastectomy, she faces a mountain of fear. Afraid she'll feel like a victim for the rest of her life, she takes on the challenge of joining a mountain-climbing expedition to raise money for breast cancer research. The grueling 19,000-foot hike teaches her she's stronger than she realized. At the end of the climb she realizes she's no longer a victim but a survivor. (3) After living her whole life hiding the fact that she has AIDS, an 11-year-old girl wants to share her secret in the hopes that her teachers, friends and the kids at school will understand why she's often tired and sick. She bravely stands before her class and tells her story. To her great joy, she wins understanding and acceptance. (4) A young mother's life turns into a nightmare when, just days after giving birth, she experiences severe mood swings that have her laughing one minute and crying the next. Things go from bad to worse when she becomes obsessed with cleanliness and begins hallucinating. She's diagnosed with postpartum psychosis and is hospitalized. Medication, therapy and her desire to be a mother to her child help her reclaim her life. (5) When her teenage daughter is diagnosed with anorexia, a heart-broken mother is determined to make her well. But her loving intentions turn their home into a battleground. As her daughter withers away before her eyes, the mom realizes her daughter will only get better when and if she decides she wants to live. She lets go, and the daughter chooses life and makes a full recovery. (6) After battling her weight all her life, a wife and mother decides that being happy and healthy is more important than being thin. Once she stops hating her reflection in the mirror, she feels freer and happier than she imagined possible.

One Woman's Battle: (runs in the magazine as Courage, Triumph, Victory, Justice or Success) One Woman's Battle is a third-person account of how a woman meets a challenge, injustice, poverty or other setback. The cause she takes up can be her own or one taken up on behalf or in memory of a loved one. Whenever possible, the piece should have strong quotes reflecting both sides of the story, and some sort of resolution. Take care not to approach it like a newspaper account—we don't want a list of facts. If legal proceedings are part of the story, include them as a springboard that gives us insight into how the situation has affected the woman and her family. As with any Woman's World story, we need to share her experience.

• Examples: (1) A teenager beseeches a high school to posthumously award an honorary diploma to her younger sister who, at the time of her death, was just a few credits short of graduation. (2) A woman sues her ex-husband on behalf of her young children because he's a deadbeat dad. (3) An emergency room nurse fights to get a law passed enabling doctors and nurses to notify the police when drivers responsible for DWI accidents are brought in for medical treatment. (4) A mom fights for anti-stalking laws after her teenage daughter is stalked. (5) Told she'll never walk again, a stroke victim refuses to give up hope for a complete recovery. With nothing but faith and her family's love to sustain her, she undergoes painful physical therapy for 10 years until, one day on the beach; she realizes she can wriggle her toes in the sand! Eventually she regains the use of her legs. (6) After her hairdresser gives her a bad perm, a woman sues the salon. (7) After she's told her pet pig must go, a woman fights her condominium association and wins the right to keep her beloved pet. (8) A woman whose little boy is diagnosed as learning disabled designs computer programs to help him—and winds up starting a successful business helping kids learn. (9) A woman left struggling after a layoff decides to become her own boss and launches her own construction business.

A Woman's Story: A third-person account of real, undying love—a moving piece about the bond that exists between a parent and child, a husband and wife or friends, or even a pet and owner. It can also be about the love that blossoms between a man and woman. The story should leave the reader with a warm, wonderful feeling. It has to be filled with tender, loving quotes and anecdotes.

• Examples: (1) An 11-year-old is in a coma after a car accident and nothing can rouse him until his dog Rusty gives him a kiss, waking his young master. (2) Although she's never had a child of her own, a single woman keeps a promise to her dying friend and raises her teenage daughter. (3) When their stepdad is diagnosed with terminal cancer, the kids he selflessly helped raise return his love a hundred fold. Telling their mom to quit her job so she can spend all her time with Dad, they make sacrifices to pay the bills—moving back home to pay rent, getting second jobs to cover the mortgage payments. They cook meals, cut the grass and take care of repairs. He tearfully thanks them—but they tell him he's the one who deserves the thanks for giving them the fatherly love, understanding and guidance they needed growing up. (4) A grandma donates her kidney to her critically ill granddaughter and saves the little girl's life. (5) An adoptive mom finds her son's birth mother to fill an empty place in his heart. (6) A dying dad leaves his two-year-old daughter a legacy of love by writing her letters for her to open on all the important days of her life—the first day of school, her graduation, wedding, birthdays, days when she's feeling sad.

Woman's Best Friend: We run real-life stories in our pets column.
• Examples: (1) A family's cat wakes a mom just in time for her to get help for her son, who was having seizures while the family slept. (2) An ailing cat receives a kidney transplant, and the owners adopt the donor cat, a stray who would have been euthanized at the shelter. (3) A family is heartbroken when their dog has a stroke. They can't bear to put her to sleep, so they give her lots of tender loving care, and against all odds, she walks again and makes a full recovery.

Send your story idea/synopsis typed and double-spaced, with the original newspaper clip, if any, along with a self-addressed, stamped envelope (SASE) and your name, address and day and evening phone numbers to the address below. Please be sure to include which category you think your article is appropriate for and write it on the envelope. Or fax to Features. Sorry, we can only return your submission if you provide an SASE.

Categories: Nonfiction—Beauty—Business—Children—Consumer—Cooking—Crafts/Hobbies—Diet/Nutrition—Economics—Entertainment—Family—Fashion—Food/Drink—Gardening—Health—Hobbies—Home—Marriage—Mystery—Nature—Physical Fitness—Romance—Short Stories—Women's Issues—How-to

CONTACT: Fiction Editor
Material: Fiction
CONTACT: Fred Gioffre, Research Editor
270 Sylvan Ave.
Englewood Cliffs, NJ 07632
Phone: 201-569-6699
Fax: 201-569-3584
E-mail: DearWW@aol.com

Women Alive!

We are especially interested in articles which encourage spiritual growth such as those on prayer, praise, and Bible reading.
Other topics of interest to our readers:
• Living as a Christian in the workplace
• Mothering—helps in discipline and in rearing spiritual children
• Improving marriage
• Discouragement—especially in ministry
• Self-consciousness/shyness—relating to new people
• Improve communication in family and marriage
• Help with handling finances
• Do retired women still have a place of service?
• Temptations known only to the singles
• Reinforcement techniques for single mothers
• How can I reach the unsaved?

We are interested in articles which show Scripture applied to daily living. Most Christian women understand what they should do but need godly role models, so we prefer that you use examples of your obedience rather than your failures.

To receive a sample magazine please send $1.25 or a 9 x 12 envelope with four first-class stamps.

Editors of Women Alive! *evaluate a manuscript using the following criteria:*
1. Can the focus of the article be supported by Scripture?
2. Does it meet our purpose of helping women who are intent on spiritual growth?
3. Is the focus maintained throughout the article?
4. Is it well developed and illustrated?
5. Does it have a unique approach to the subject?
6. Is it written in a natural style (avoiding triteness and clichés)?
7. Will it have impact?
8. Will the reader's interest be maintained throughout the article?
Women Alive! pays from $15 to $50 for each article depending on length and quality of article. *Women Alive!* purchases either first rights or reprints but with payment we purchase the right to allow the articles to be translated into other languages by nonprofit missionary organizations.

We look forward to receiving your articles!
Categories: Nonfiction—Christian Interests

CONTACT: Aletha Hinthorn, Editor
Material: All
PO Box 480052
Kansas City KS 64148
Phone/Fax: 913-402-1369
E-mail: ahinthornAkc.rr.com

Women and Music

Women and Music, an annual journal of scholarship about women, music, and culture, is a publication of the International Alliance for Women in Music. Drawing on a wide range of disciplines and approaches, the refereed journal seeks to further the understanding of the relationships among gender, music, and culture, with special attention being given to the concerns of women.

Subscription Information

Annual

ISSN 1090-7505

Individuals $55.00; Institutions $55.00; Single issue $40.00

For foreign subscriptions please add $6.00. Payment must accompany order. Make checks payable to University of Nebraska Press and mail to:

University of Nebraska Press

233 N 8th St, Lincoln, NE 68588-0255

or call: 1-800-755-1105 U.S. Orders and customer service.

1-800-526-2617 U.S. Fax orders and customer service.

Submission Information

Women and Music *accepts submissions that meet the following requirements:*

- submit a brief abstract
- submit 3 copies, two without identifying information and one with
- prepare according to *The Chicago Manual of Style*, 14th edition
- typed double-spaced (including quotations and endnotes)
- 8½" x 11" paper
- footnotes are not acceptable
- Microsoft Word and Word Perfect formats accepted
- obtain and provide necessary copyright permission

Authors whose articles are accepted will be asked to provide camera-ready, publication-quality musical examples. Submissions received after 30 November will be considered for the following year's issue.

Categories: Nonfiction—Culture—Music—Women's Issues

CONTACT: Catherine J. Pickar, Editor (The George Washington University)
Material: Manuscript
CONTACT: Fred Everett Maus (University of Virginia)
Material: Books for review
The George Washington University
Washington DC 20052
CONTACT: Department of Music
Material: For Book Submission
University of Virginia
Charlottesville VA 22903
Website: www.nebraskapress.unl.edu/journals.html

Women Artists News Book Review

Please refer to Midmarch Arts Press, in the Book Publishers Section.

Categories: Arts—Literature—Poetry—Women's Issues—Women Artists

CONTACT: Submissions Editor
Material: All
300 Riverside Dr.
New York NY 10025

Women In Business

Women in Business, the American Business Women's Association bimonthly national magazine, updates members on Association events and members' activities and accomplishments, in addition to featuring informative articles covering a range of topics of interest to business women. Besides previous articles about appropriate office gift giving and the health benefits of chocolate, past articles also have featured job hunting hints in the new millennium, considerations in starting a business, tax relief for women business owners, how to motivate your employees and hints on managing a career with motherhood. *Women in Business* also includes excerpts from today's powerful business books, which can be used by members for credits in the ABWA contact hours program. Magazine subscription is free for members (dues include a one-year subscription), non-member subscriptions are $20 a year; $24 foreign, plus taxes.

Categories: Nonfiction—Associations—Business—Careers—Computers—Consumer—Diet/Nutrition—Government—Health—History—Internet—Self Help—Women's Issues

CONTACT: Kathleen Isaacson, Editor
Material: All
American Business Women's Association
9100 Ward Pkwy.
Kansas City, MO 64114
Phone: 816-361-6621
Fax: 816-361-4991
Website: www.abwahq.org

Women in the Outdoors

Please also refer to *Turkey Call*.

Women In The Outdoors magazine informs and entertains outdoorswomen of all skill levels who aspire to become more involved in outdoor sports and activities, including camping, fishing, hiking, shooting, hunting, canoeing, boating and bird watching.

It is the quarterly magazine of the NWTF's Women in the Outdoors program, which provides exciting, hands-on outdoor learning opportunities for women ages 14 and up. *Women In The Outdoors* is prepared three months or more ahead of each issue's release date. Magazines are published seasonally, with winter, spring, summer and fall issues each year.

An average feature/sidebar mix runs about 1,800 words. We also publish shorter articles that average 800 words, depending on the specific department. Regular departments include:

- Outdoor-related book reviews
- Game and fish recipes
- Wildlife profiles
- Stories of notable outdoorswomen
- Outdoor health issues
- Outdoor gear
- Backyard habitat enhancement

Most articles are geared toward novice outdoors enthusiasts, including information on where to go, necessary equipment and how to find out more on a specific activity. We prefer stories quoting experts over narrative treatments. Articles should treat women as independent outdoors enthusiasts, depict outdoor activities in a positive/encouraging manner and appeal to a national audience.

Send individual queries; no laundry lists.

We pay $200 to $275 for articles having up to 1,100 words; $300 to $375 for up to 1,500 words; and $400 to $500 for up to 2,000 words.

We accept shots that illustrate wildlife, conservation, colorful scenics, women participating in various outdoor activities and families participating in hunting and outdoor pastimes together. Check with the editor for current photographic needs.

Rates for published photographs:

- Cover = $400
- Two-page spread = $175
- Full page = $125
- Half-page = $100
- One-third page or less = rate negotiated by editor

Categories: Nonfiction—Recreation—Sports—Hunting—Women

CONTACT: Karen Lee, Editor
klee@nwtf.net
CONTACT: Chasiti Kirkland, Managing Editor
ckirkland@nwtf.net
National Wild Turkey Federation
PO Box 530
770 Augusta Rd
Edgefield SC 29824
Phone: 803-637-3106
Fax: 803-637-0034
Web site: www.nwtf.org

Women Today

Women Today Magazine offers the women of the world information about the issues that affect us every day: relationships, career, health and beauty, spirituality, fitness, parenting, marriage, finances, and more. This information, while broad-based, is offered from a Christian perspective.

Seeking

We select articles that will appeal to a global audience. These articles must be uplifting, informative and pertinent to modern women. With the exception of Life Stories, articles do not need to have specific Christian content; however, the tone and content of every story will reflect a Christian viewpoint. We believe that every woman's life is a gift from God and that a personal relationship with Him will provide them with meaning, purpose and significance.

We publish journalistic, nonfiction items only and therefore do not accept photography, cover art, poetry, short stories, or product endorsements. We welcome unpublished and first time writers. Excerpts from books that can stand alone are considered.

Readership

Statistics indicate that our visitors tend to be engaged in a career, are moderately to highly computer-literate and are usually over the age of eighteen. Many of our visitors log on from the workplace and many find us as a result of commercial women's networks and search engines.

Publishing

Women Today Magazine is published monthly online. We are currently seeing over 1.5 million hits a month with an impressive average user session of just over 8 minutes. Close to 60% of the magazine is free-lanced.

NB: There is also a print magazine called *Women Today* that is loosely associated with the online version. The print version is printed annually, published in- house and does not accept submissions.

Rights & Compensation

We are seeking One Time Rights. All copyright remains with the author. Any reprint requests we receive will be directed to the author if a contact address has been provded for this purpose. The copyright you designate will accompany all text online. *Women Today Magazine* is part of a non-profit organization and as such cannot offer compensation for articles. We also do not carry advertising for revenue. Publication on our site offers contributors international exposure and we are always happy to add a link to the website of your choice along with author contact information.

Queries & Submissions

E-mail queries and submissions are preferred. Queries sent by email receive a response approximately three times faster than those sent by mail. Please do not fax queries or submissions. All submissions must be preceded by a query letter that states the title of the article, a brief synopsis, the department you are submitting it to, length (approx) and author contact info (an email address is sufficient). The departments are as listed below. Simultaneous submissions are permitted within reason.

E-mail submissions should be in standard manuscript format (exactly the same as the format for print submissions) and sent as an attachment. WordPerfect 8 or higher is preferred, however most word processing programs are accepted. Please do not cut and paste submissions into the body of your email as we do not have time to format your submission for you. Use the subject line of the email carefully. Do not label it "submission" – make it easy for me to find you. Last name and abbreviated title of the article is preferred. HTML coding is not required as we will format the final version to meet our specifications.

Departments & Columns

Departments

Articles for the different departments should range 1000 to 1200 words (approx) and be in a format suitable for Internet readers. Again, we are seeking non-fiction journalistic articles. Assignments are occasionally given to writers we have worked with previously. If you wish to be considered for further assignments, please indicate this in your query. Writing for the Internet audience entails the use of subtitles, bulleted lists where possible and concise writing. Paragraphs are usually shorter than those in a print article and must not contain more than one idea. Simply submitting the same article as written for print is not effective. If you need assistance to format for an Internet audience we can help you, however articles in the proper format will always be given precedence.

Career Focuses on any aspect of the working woman in the new millennium. Includes, but not limited to, using technology, office protocol, stress, working moms, tele-commuting, career switching, continuing education, the glass ceiling, balancing home and office, effective interviewing and goal setting.

Family Seeks to provide women with the information they need to nurture and maintain positive, meaningful family relationships. Includes parenting, children of all ages, schooling, step-families, dealing with bereavement, home management, stress, spending quality time and the ever changing role of women in the modern household. Does not include marriage (see Relationships below).

Life Stories Life Stories are the true autobiographical account of one woman's personal encounter with Jesus Christ and the resulting positive changes in her life. All life stories will be edited to include a sample prayer and invitation. Please not that the same word count applies for life stories. We receive many life story submissions that far exceed the length guidelines. We are unable to use these lifestories as we do not have the time to edit them down for you.

Money Approaches finance from an international perspective. Articles must be applicable outside of North America. Sample topics include household budgeting, use of credit, starting your own business, insurance, investing, the need for retirement savings, and teaching kids about responsible use of resources.

Relationships Focuses on healthy relations between the sexes. Sample topics include marriage, couples, dating, singleness, online dating, marriage building, dating your spouse, mutual devotion, encouraging your spouse, dealing with stress, marital expectations and heartbreak.

Columns

All columns should range 600 to 1000 words and deal with a practical application of the topic. Columns tend toward, but are not limited to, "how-to" articles.

Beauty Any aspect of fashion, make up, hair, nails, spa treatments, bath necessities or personal grooming.

Health and Fitness Nutrition, (please note that we rarely print diets) exercise, healthy living, well being are all covered.

Food and Cooking Recipes, kitchen tips, exotic food, preparation tips, seasonal, time savers, plan ahead and freezer meals. For recipes nutritional information including Food Exchange values are appreciated, but not mandatory.

Advice The advice column is written by a professional, licensed therapist and does not accept submissions.

Specifics

All articles will be accompanied by the byline and the biography specified by the author. Author bios should be one to three lines of type (approximately 50 words). A contact email and / or URL will be included if provided and deemed appropriate. *Women Today* reserves the right to refuse URLs that link to sites that are in conflict with the mandate of the magazine. A photograph of the author is not necessary. Published clips are also optional. If all the requested information appears in your query a cover letter is not necessary.

Lead time is at least one month in advance of publication date (publication date is the last week of the previous month) for regular submissions, two months in advance for seasonal pieces.

Reviewing takes approximately four to six weeks – please do not inquire about your work before this time as it slows down the process for everyone. If we have not responded to you by the end of the fifth week, feel free to send an email enquiry. Please note that we are unable answer phone enquiries in regard to submissions.

Categories: Nonfiction—Beauty—Biograohy—Career—Christian Interest—Cooking—Family—Food/Drink—Health—Marriage—Money and Finances—Parenting—Physical Fitness—Relationships—Spiritual

CONTACT: Claire Colvin, Editor
Material: All
Campus Crusade for Christ
Women Today Magazine
Box 300 Stn A
Vancouver, BC V6C 2X3
E-mail: editor@womentodaymagazine.com (preferred)
Website: www.womentodaymagazine.com

Wonderful Ideas
for Teaching, Learning,
and Enjoying Mathematics!

1. Manuscripts should focus on a successful teaching idea, lesson, strategy, project, problem, or program for teaching, learning, and enjoying mathematics. While the readers of WI cover a wide range of ages and abilities, we generally publish ideas geared to grades 2 through 8. We prefer hands-on, classroom-tested ideas.

2. Manuscripts should be typed and not more than 900 words in length. Manuscripts submitted on 3.5" Macintosh format (Microsoft Word preferred) are welcome and appreciated. If sending a disk, please also send a printout of your article.

3. There are different types of articles that appear in *Wonderful Ideas*:

• Puzzlers: double-sided, problem-solving cards to be passed out directly to students. Featured every month.

• Kids' Corner: monthly "brain teaser" problems for students to solve. Each month, we include at least six problems and solutions.

• Wonderful Materials: occasional feature reviewing worthwhile math materials of many kinds, such as manipulatives, books, or games. In the past, reviews have included Fraction Bars and NCTM's Addenda Series.

• Make-It Math: occasional feature showcasing a puzzle or activity that requires students to make something. Past Make-It Math articles have included tessellations, Tangrams, and Pentominoes.

• Wonderful Ideas: general category for all other activities, games, and lessons.

4. Manuscripts should include the following information: topics involved, appropriate grade levels, materials needed, type of activity, description of the idea, and extensions or variations. If appropriate, include discussion questions, student responses, or samples of student work. Also, include author's name, address, phone number, current position, and school name.

5. Oftentimes in WI, text is accompanied by a reproducible page featuring worksheets, charts, game boards, problems or other graphics. We encourage you to include graphics with your article. Graphics must be black and white. Photographs are not acceptable. Examples of student work are welcome.

6. We reserve the right to edit and rewrite articles without prior author approval.

7. Payment is rendered upon publication. Rates of pay are modest and vary according to the material sent. Authors receive one copy of the newsletter in which the material is published.

8. Manuscripts are normally evaluated within ten weeks of receipt.

9. If you have an idea, but dislike writing, we will be happy to talk to you about your idea. If it matches our needs, we will write it up for publication and credit you for the idea. However, no payment is offered.

10. All submissions must be original and not previously published.

11. Samples of previously published articles are available upon request.

WI is always pleased to receive manuscripts and to talk to teachers about their ideas. Please call us with any questions you might have.

Note: Payment is not provided for students and/or teachers who send in names and solutions for Kids' Corner Problem Solvers. In addition, payment is not provided for contest entries that are published.

Multiple authors share the standard pay.

Categories: Nonfiction—Children—Education—Juvenile—Mathematics

CONTACT: Julie Wilder
Material: All
235 McCullough Hill Rd.
Mont Pellier VT 05602
Phone: 800-924-3327
Fax: 973-376-9386
E-mail: jwilder@math.tv

Woodall Publications, Corp.

Thank you for your interest in Woodall Publications, Corp. We publish five regional titles, which are distributed at RV campgrounds, dealerships, tourism centers and Camping World stores across the United States.

Following is a list of our publications and the states in which they are distributed:

• *Woodall's CamperWays* (Delaware, Maryland, New Jersey, Central and Northern New York, Pennsylvania and Virginia)

• *Woodall's Northeast Outdoors* (Connecticut, Maine, Massachusetts, New Hampshire, Central New York, Rhode Island and Vermont)

• *Woodall's Midwest RV Traveler* (Illinois, Minnesota, Indiana, Michigan, Ohio and Wisconsin)

• *Woodall's Southern RV* (Northern Florida, Georgia, North Carolina, South Carolina and Alabama)

• *Woodall's Florida RV Traveler* (Florida)

Each Woodall publication is a specialty magazine for RV and camping enthusiasts. Articles may appear in only one title, in multiple titles or in all titles at the discretion of the editorial staff. We suggest that interested contributors study recent issues before sending us queries.

You should hear from a member of our staff within four to six weeks for queries. We do not encourage unsolicited manuscript submissions. Our staff works considerably with freelancers, as well as on assignment. Manuscripts must be submitted electronically, via e-mail, or on disk (most word processing programs are acceptable) and typed on standard white paper. We accept queries via email at editor@woodallpub.com.

Payment is on acceptance for publication and ranges between $100 and $400. Woodall Publications Corp. buys first North American serial rights and electronic rights. The editors reserve the right to edit and even rewrite any article in order to make it suit the theme or space limitations of a specific issue. Major alterations will be discussed with the author when possible.

Travel Features

The easiest way to sell your work to Woodall's is to query us on an interesting and tightly focused RV travel story. Please do not send us travel logs of attraction lists. We need features that evoke the sights, sounds, smells and even tastes of specific travel destinations. We are looking for articles that have a unique approach, provide history and are relevant to RV travel or camping in the regions we serve. Articles should run about 1,500 words in length. The maximum length for travel features, unless cleared by the editorial staff, is 2,000 words.

All stories (excluding humor) should be accompanied by a comprehensive selection of clear, color transparencies with interesting captions and credits. Digital images are not accepted. Think cover shot when taking these photos and remember lighting is crucial to the overall effect. Focus your photography on scenic or panoramic views for the opening layout and points of interest, local color and activity shots for the carryover pages.

Campground Spotlights

Each issue highlights a campground in our "Stopping Points" department. These articles run between 800 and 1,000 words and should include information on location, facilities, recreation, local attractions and camping fees. Interviews with campers and campground personnel, as well as transparencies or photos of the grounds are essential. Articles submitted by campground personnel will not be considered. "Stopping Points" articles pay $150.

RV Humor

We accept humorous vignettes on some aspect of the RV lifestyle. Humor stories should be directly related to the RV experience. Maximum length for humor stories is 1,200 words; minimum, 800 words. Do not send photographs. Pay range is between $75 and $150.

Maintenance and Technical

Woodalls publishes a variety of technical stories. It is important that we maintain a balance of articles for both the novice and the veteran RVer.

• Maintenance: RV maintenance stories should be 1,100 to 1,500 words long. Color images showing the maintenance procedure are essential.

• How-to: These features for handy RVers should be 1,100 to 1,500 words and include step-by-step instructions, diagrams and transparencies.

• RV Safety: Stories should be 800 to 1,200 words and be accompanied by a selection of images.

• Gadgets & Gear: This department highlights RV accessories and maintenance products, as well as products that are pertinent to the RV lifestyle.

• Product Evaluations: Woodall's does not cover product evaluations.

Vehicle Tests

The editorial staff assigns Road Test articles. If you are interested in writing such a story, query the editorial staff and include published clips of similar work. Evaluations must be fair and unbiased. Queries by any representative of the product's manufacturer or distributor will be rejected and all product claims must be independently substantiated. No writer is to contact a manufacturer or distributor as a representative of Woodall's Publication, without explicit permission

from the editorial staff.

If you are assigned a story by the editorial staff, please keep in mind that you now represent the magazine. Be conscious that if you receive information or materials about the subject/area you are covering, you must still write an ethical, objective story.

Special Interest

Woodall's editorial focus also includes hobbies, crafts and other recreational activities that are popular among RV-ers. Special-interest features should be 800 to 1,500 words.

Columns

All Woodall's column are assigned. If you have a column idea, send us your idea along with several columns and we well consider them. Columns are a tough sale and we do not foresee a need to add any new columns to the magazine in the near future.

Poetry and Fiction

Woodall's does not publish poetry or fiction.

Photo Requirements

Travel features should be accompanied by a minimum of 10 color images, all originals. All images should be numbered with an accompanying caption sheet identifying each subject. Photos and slides supplied by someone other than the manuscript author should be clearly identified for photo credit. Photos and slides will be returned after publication when possible. Please include a self-addressed, stamped envelope for this purpose.

Revised 10/06

Categories: Recreation Vehicles—Travel

CONTACT: Maryanne Sullivan, Managing Editor
Material: All
2575 Vista Del Mar Dr.
Ventura CA 93001
Phone: 805-667-4204
Fax: 805-667-4122
E-mail: editor@woodallpub.com
Website: www.woodallspub.com

Woodworking Magazine

Please refer to Popular Woodworking.

The Worcester Review

The Worcester County Poetry Association, Inc. was founded in 1971 and incorporated as a non-profit organization in 1972. Over the years it has sponsored readings by nationally and internationally-known writers, providing a forum for local poets and students, and celebrating the rich literary history of Central Massachusetts.

The Association prints and distributes original poetry broadsides and publishes *The Worcester Review*, an annual literary magazine.

SUBMISSIONS

The Worcester Review invites submission of previously unpublished poetry, fiction, literary articles, photography, and graphic art.

Guidelines are as follows:

POETRY: Submit 3 poems, typed on 8½"x11" paper. The author's name should appear in the upper left-hand corner of each page.

FICTION: Submit 4,000 words maximum on 8½"x11" paper. Author's name should appear in the upper left-hand corner of each page. Pages must be numbered in sequence.

LITERARY ARTICLES: Submit scholarly and critical articles with a New England connection (10 typed, double-spaced pages maximum using MLA guidelines) on 8½"x11" paper.

PHOTOGRAPHY: Submit black and white glossy prints (minimum size 5"x7").

GRAPHIC ART: Submit black and white graphic art on white paper (5"x7").

All submissions must be accompanied by a cover letter indicating author, materials submitted, and return address.

The Worcester Review reserves first publication rights for all submissions chosen for publication. Payment will be two copies upon publication plus a small honorarium.

Response time is six-12 months so multiple submissions are acceptable if you note that.

Categories: Fiction—Poetry—Short Stories—Writing

CONTACT: Rodger Martin, Editor
Material: All
1 Ekman St
Worcester MA 01607
Phone: 508-797-4770
Website: www.geocities.com/paris/wreview

Workforce Diversity For Engineering and IT Professionals

Please refer to Equal Opportunity Publications, Inc.

Workforce Management

Workforce readers and users are human resources professionals who are moving beyond their traditional roles as policy police and picnic planners.

Guidelines for Writers and Contributors

Find out what *Workforce Management* is looking for when it comes to freelance articles and story ideas.

Mission Statement:

Workforce Management is a monthly business magazine for senior level human resources executive as well as other C-level leaders who make key decisions—for better and for worse—on people management issues in the 20,000 largest corporations in America. We believe that there is no more critical element to a business than its employees. The focus of Workforce Management is really about managing a major corporate asset—the company's people—to maximize the contribution to the bottom line. This is not HR for HR's sake. It's about results, not programs.

What We Want:

Whether the issue is staffing, recruitment, compensation, training, motivation or benefits, the Workforce Management story focuses on corporate employee and employment issues through the prism of senior management. Thought about in that way, and written about in that way, many stories ought to engage the interest of human resource executives, CEOs, COOs, and CFOs.

We want our features and departments to be the material that a senior VP of HR could take to his CFO and say, "These are the issues we need to address now." And ideally, it will be content that the CFO might read first, and flag for the VP of HR. While we want to focus on recognizable, larger (2,500 employees and up) organizations in our stories, we want to be read by workforce management leaders in companies with as few as 350 or 400 employees.

Key question for every story: Is this the smartest way to run a company? The story must clearly tie workforce issues into the well being of companies, and demonstrate how astute workforce management practices (or the lack of them) affect business results. For-profit companies, of course, strive for greater profitability (non-profits, which we also write about, have different goals, but the key concepts cross over). But there are myriad ways to achieve that result. What we want to see in each story is a demonstration of how smart, innovative workforce management affects the bottom line: Gordon Bethune and his turnaround team at Continental employed renewed pride and teamwork to make the planes arrive and leave on time—leading to a more profitable airline. Starbucks' enlightened approach to training and benefits connects directly to the productivity and attitude of its workforce—who in turn make coffee-buying and drinking an essential daily experience, thus making the company more profitable. And so on.

Cover stories in the printed magazine run 2,500 to 3,500 words. We also want secondary stories (1,500-2,000 words, perhaps not as grand in scope or in company size), dealing with issues such as diversity, management, legal issues and implications, outstanding and outrageous performance. These too generally will be close-up portraits of leaders on the way up…and on the way out.

We also want stories that cover the vendor side of this industry, noting that major advancement—as well as major problems—oftentimes originates with vendor activity. We want people stories on sellers of products, suppliers in compensation, heroes on the supply side, CEOs in outsourcing, technology, inventors of products and services used, people who do things on the sell side of the field. Note: these stories will not work if they are perceived as pandering or puffery!

Stories should show the financial implications and impacts whenever possible. Stories should be developed with an eye to the expected payoff derived from management decisions and the costs inherent in these decisions. Management always wants to know this information.

What did it cost XYZ Corporation to put in that Web-based employee portal system? What savings did it get them? If we're writing about training fads, and a company is the latest to present the wildly popular FISH! program to its troops, what did the program cost to implement? What were the hard-dollar outcomes in productivity, or sales, or reduced use of Prozac by the employees? And if the HR leaders in the company didn't bother to figure out the ROI, that's a story, too.

Stories should be written and edited as "news" features (see especially the page 1 Wall Street Journal news features. Also the New York Times, Business Week, and Forbes as role models). Further, these features need to be written in an active voice. Major Workforce Management stories react to news events and trends, explaining the how and whys, and what the developments mean for readers, through examples of people affected. And because we're not a general business publication, the workforce management implications should be the focus of every story.

Stories should be timely. Although we are a monthly publication, we seek to peg our feature stories to events in news. United Airlines' bankruptcy, for example, was the peg for a story about its workforce management woes, and how they must be addressed if the carrier is to survive. As the U.S. Treasury revised its advice about conversions to cash-balance pension plans, Workforce Management showed how some companies have successfully made the switch—and how some botched it. When the Space Shuttle Columbia was destroyed, we wrote a story about the aging of the NASA workforce, and how the agency must address the loss of key personnel and critical knowledge in the years to come. It's Workforce Management's job to show readers the workplace implications in stories, and provide breadth, depth, context and meaning.

Stories should be about people. Stories should incorporate "people behind the scenes" who are making things happen. The writing should be story-driven, more anecdotal than it has been in earlier times when the magazine was more service-driven. Stories should be told through the actions of heroes and villains (and many mixtures of the two). Change doesn't happen by itself. When a company introduces a revolutionary new consumer-driven health-care plan, it's because someone recognized a problem (out-of-control health care costs), and found a solution. Perhaps the employees revolted when they got the news about the new plan, and that should be part of the story, too. *Workforce Management* stories have players and actors—men and women who did something to make a difference (good or bad). Some stories will be profiles of prime movers in the world of workforce management. An example would be SAS's CEO Jim Goodnight, who set in motion innovative workplace programs that have helped the company save $60 to $80 million annually.

Some other examples:

Cyrus Mehri, Bringer of Lawsuits: By filing huge class-action discrimination lawsuits, this Washington, D.C. attorney has become the person HR hates most. But could he win so often if something wasn't terribly wrong in those companies? This profiles talks about who he is, where he came from, and why he's so feared by corporate HR.

Who is Bob Nelson, and How Did He Become the Rewards and Recognition King? His books sell in the millions. He's a fixture at HR conferences. Companies turn to him for ideas on how to make employees productive and happy—at minimal costs. We profile Nelson, explain his approach, and see whether it's really the answer to having happy, productive employees, or if it's just another warm and fuzzy program whose impact is impossible to measure.

Out Front: We sometimes commission and invite timely, news-pegged stories of 300-500 words to add variety to our front-of-the-book section. Examples of the kinds of stories include: "Like It or Not, Golf Can Drive Careers," on the link between the sport and business ascension; "Workforce Problems Imperil NASA," on the aging of that workforce, and the gaps in knowledge that will open as engineers retire; and "Tearing Down the 'Maternal Wall'" on a study that documented how parents are the victims of workplace bias and as a result are increasingly suing their employers for job discrimination due to their status as parents.

The Insider: We also want stories of 1,000 to 1,200 words for the back of the book departments—vignettes about developments and trends of interest, or people who did or attempted something of interest and value in categories including:

Benefits
Compensation
Recruitment
Rewards and Recognition
Training
Security
HRMS
Retirement Planning
Investment Education
Technology
Legal issues
Regulation
Relocation
Online Guidelines

Features. Online features should have all the characteristics described above in the "what we want" section. They should be newsy, timely, and people-oriented. They should be geared to a high-level audience, and should cover high-level executives. They should demonstrate how smart, innovative workforce management affects the bottom line. Past features have covered the vice-president of American Standard, the president of a hospital, and the CEO of Exult. They tend to run about 900-1,500 words, a bit shorter than print features.

Tools. In addition to online-only feature stories as mentioned we're always looking for "tools." These could be interesting analyst reports that cover workforce-management issues, interesting annual reports, conference-call transcripts, CEO speeches, recruiting radio ads, assessments, policies, forms, checklists, memos, mission statements, and other corporate information highlighting something about workforce management.

Opinion. Online editorials of about 700-900 words about topics in news, sports, entertainment, culture, society, and business affecting workplaces appear in the "Work Views" section of the Web site. We accept submissions. Write about the stuff you talk about at the kitchen table—your passions. Don't write about "why diversity is important" or "why employees deserve good benefits." Most everyone agrees; what we want to hear about is what you talk about behind closed doors.

Payment: Fees are negotiated with each writer, depending on the complexity and length of the story. The general range is 75 cents to $1.50 per word. The exceptions are the online opinion pieces and tools. These are most often contributed articles, or are purchased for a more nominal fee.

Rights purchased: All rights.

Special note to vendors: We don't accept articles from vendors of workforce management products and services (also known as byliners).

We are, however, always interested in hearing about interesting story ideas, and we want to develop our roster of experts in every aspect of workforce management. We're also eager to hear of any high-level workforce-management professionals you think would make good interviewees. Your ideas and your expertise help us develop great stories.

How to get in touch: Contact editor Carroll Lachnit at carroll @workforce.com or Online Editor Todd Raphael at (949) 255-5344.

Categories: Careers

CONTACT: Carroll Lachnit, Content Managing Editor
E-mail: carroll@workforce.com
CONTACT: Todd Raphael, Online Editor
Phone: 949-255-5344
Website: www.workforce.com

Working Mother Magazine

Thank you for your interest in *Working Mother*. The magazine is looking for articles (700 to 1500 words in length) that help women in their task of juggling job, home, and family. We like tightly focused pieces that sensibly solve or illuminate a problem unique to our readers. Topics of particular interest include: time, home, and money management; family relationships; and job-related (work/family) issues. Pieces dealing with travel, food, beauty, and fashion are usually staff-written.

It's best to familiarize yourself with the tone and content of *Working Mother* before you query us. The most successful queries are those that are timely, appropriately researched, engagingly written, and tailored to *Working Mother* readers.

Manuscripts and queries should be typewritten and double-spaced. If possible, please enclose clips of your previously published materials. Materials will not be returned. We prefer to receive proposals for pieces rather than completed work. Then, if we find the subject suitable, we can discuss the best way to handle the material. Due to the large volume of unsolicited queries we receive, we are, unfortunately, unable to respond to every proposal. Therefore, if you don't hear from us within three months, please assume that we are not interested in that particular idea.

Categories: Nonfiction—Beauty—Careers—Children—Cooking—Diet/Nutrition—Family—Fashion—Food/Drink—Home—Humor—Marriage—Money & Finances—Parenting—Relationships—Travel—Women's Issues

CONTACT: Editorial Dept.
Material: All
60 E 42nd St, 27th Fl
New York NY 10165
Phone: 212-351-6400
Fax: 212-351-6487
E-mail: editors@workingmother.com
Website: www.workingmother.com

The World & I Online

The World & I Online is intended primarily for a thoughtful, educated audience composed of middle school, high school and university students.

Below is a list of guidelines pertaining to all writers submitting manuscripts to *The World & I Online*.

Brief Article Proposal

• All initial inquiries should be a one- or two-paragraph proposal, hard copy or preferably email, which outlines the idea. Completed articles will be considered on speculation only. (While photographs are welcome as part of the article, and we often accept photos on a courtesy basis, we are not responsible for unsolicited images and cannot return them.) If your proposal is accepted, please adhere to the following guidelines.

Format

• Please submit the article by e-mail in Microsoft Word or text format, or in the body of the email, to Stephanie Wilson, Managing Editor, at editors@worldandi.com.

• If you don't have access to a computer or e-mail, please send us a clean, double-spaced manuscript on white, standard 8.5" by 11" paper of normal weight (i.e., not "onion skin" paper).

• Information for sidebars should **not** be included in the body of the text but should be in a separate manuscript, clearly identified.

• The manuscript should be headed by a short literary title and should include short subheadings at appropriate intervals (preferably every 1.5 pages).

• Please include a bibliography or an additional reading list when appropriate.

• Footnotes, where needed, should follow Style A (also called the Humanities Style) in the *Chicago Manual of Style*.

Style

• *The World & I Online* generally follows the *Chicago Manual of Style* (and *Merriam Webster's Tenth New Collegiate Dictionary* for spelling).

• The first reference to an organization or any other term with an abbreviation should give the full name followed by the abbreviation in parentheses. Subsequently, you may use the abbreviation alone.

• Because *The World & I Online* is read in many nations, the article should be clear from any reader's perspective (e.g. "the government" may need to read "the U.S. government" or "the French government").

• Be sure to write such that the article is comprehensible to people outside your area of expertise (don't use technical jargon that's not clearly explained).

Content

• We encourage articles that make an original contribution to the subject area.

• The content should be representative of current trends in the subject area.

• The information should be accurate, and the scholarship and research must be sound and verifiable.

• The overall coverage of the topic should be adequate; be sure that no important points are omitted.

• As our readers are mainly educators and students, submissions containing any profanity, gratuitous sex and/or violence are NOT ACCEPTED.

Miscellaneous

• Please double-check facts obtained from primary or secondary sources; do not rely on the research of others.

• Include your home address when signing the contract (if you are an American citizen, also include your Social Security number).

• For the length of the article or other particulars, please refer to the contract accompanying the assignment.

Photographs

• If you wish to submit photographs with your article, you may send high-resolution images by e-mail or mail prints or slides.

Items to Accompany the Manuscript

• Writer's name as it should appear in the byline.

• An author's biography indicating qualifications—including academic background, published works, and any special life experience—for writing in the subject area.

Payment

• *The World & I Online* pays generally $100 per article. Articles are usually a **minimum** 2,000 words in length and can be longer.

***The World & I Online* consists of eight colorful editorial sections:**

Current Issues

Covers national and world affairs—through analysis, commentary, and special reports—and presents foreign perspectives on timely issues through its "World Views" and "Global Forum" subsections.

The Arts

Presents current and lasting achievements in art, poetry, music, dance, film, design, architecture, theater, and more.

Natural Science

Illuminates the world of science from its historical underpinnings to the latest cutting-edge discoveries.

Life

Focuses on the enrichment of our daily lives by highlighting personalities, food, travel, health, sports, humor, and more.

Book World

Excerpts recent releases, with insightful commentary, and reviews important new fiction and nonfiction, including some foreign-language titles.

Culture

Surveys the world through a historical and an anthropological perspective.

Modern Thought

Presents diverse points of view on education, philosophy, history, political science, sociology, and economics by leading authorities throughout the world.

Categories: Nonfiction—Arts—Book Reviews—Culture—Current Affairs—Economics— Education—Lifestyle—Literature—Philosophy—Politics—Science

CONTACT: Submissiosn Editor
Material: All
The Washington Times Corporation
3600 New York Ave., NE
Washington, DC 20002
Phone: 202-635-4000
Fax: 202-269-9353
E-mail: editor@worldandimag.com
Website: www.worldandimag.com

World War II

Please refer to WEIDER History Group.

The Writer

SUBMISSION GUIDELINES

The Writer is dedicated to helping and inspiring professional and aspiring writers. We do this by producing a magazine that provides information, instruction and motivation. We hope to foster the idea of a writers' community in which writers share their experiences, expertise, struggles, successes and suggestions on our pages.

About 80 percent of our articles are by freelance writers. The best way to get an assignment is to send a query letter with clips of previously published work. It helps to include the lead and an outline of the proposed article. We do not accept fiction or poetry.

Feature articles run 1,600-3,000 words, including how-to articles that address issues of interest to writers in the areas of fiction, nonfiction, poetry, and children's and young adult literature. Recent articles include: "The role of fact in fiction," "Tips for writing a humorous mystery," "Mining family gold for fiction," "What makes a good short story?," "In whose voice should you write?," "Is it good enough for children?," "Adventures in travel writing" and "Writing issue-oriented articles."

We encourage a roundup approach for articles on market or publishing trends, such as the changing youth market, the growing interest in inspirational writing, the best of the small presses, how to get your manuscript past the first reading, what small press editors want, and how to find an agent. In addition, we run profiles of writers who have a unique story to tell—a first-time author, an unusual background, a unique approach to marketing, someone who breaks new ground in style or content.

Columns and departments run 800 to 1,200 words. Our columns and departments include:

Bottom line: How-to articles on the business of writing. Recent articles include: Organizing your accounts for taxes, balancing your assignments, tools that help writers make the most of their time.

Ethics: Ethical questions related to writing or freelance business.

Market focus: Reports on specific market areas such as trade journals, alumni magazines, parenting, sports and travel.

Net//working: The Internet and e-publishing.

Off the cuff: Personal essay on the writing life.

Poet to poet: Specific aspects of writing poetry, such as imagery, revision or poetic forms. Contributors are asked to include hands-on exercises for readers.

Syntax: Language and grammar usage. Should be light but informative.

WriteStuff: Reviews of books and other products of interest to writers.

Breakthrough: Short, formatted first-person articles about a writer's experience in "breaking through" to publication (with an article, book, etc.).

Get started: Short articles specifically angled toward instructing the beginning writer. Most of these are assigned by an editor but queries are accepted.

Basics

All queries should be submitted in writing. Include a SASE for a response and the return of materials. We do not take queries by telephone but we do accept electronic queries. You may electronically e-mail your submission to queries@writermag.com. Query for features about six months in advance; columns and departments, four months.

Assignments are acknowledged by a contract. Generally, we buy first rights. Payment varies, depending on length and complexity of the material covered. In general, our rates for articles range from $50 for book reviews to $200 to $400 for columns and $300 to $500 for features, depending on length, complexity and the research required. We are also looking for writing-related cartoons ($50) and photos ($50 to $100). Payment is made on acceptance. We pay only those expenses agreed upon in advance.

We prefer articles to be submitted electronically as a Word attachment or on a Mac disk. Otherwise, send a double-spaced printed manuscript (and a SASE, if you want it returned). Be sure to include your name, address, phone number, e-mail address and a list of contacts used for the article, along with their phone numbers. To help us fact-check, we ask that you include any printed background materials you used for the piece. Photo suggestions are appreciated. Be sure your name appears on each page of the manuscript. Please do not send original manuscripts, artwork or slides, as we cannot be responsible for their return. You may e-mail your submission to e-mail address below..

Categories: Writing

CONTACT: Ronald Kovach, Senior Editor
The Writer magazine
Kalmbach Publishing Co.
21027 Crossroads Circle
P.O. Box 1612
Waukesha, WI 53187-1612
Phone: 262-796-8776, ext. 275
Fax: 262-798-6468
E-mail: queries@writermag.com
Website: www.writermag.com

The Writer Gazette

The Writer Gazette is a writer's resource site that provides tips, techniques, resources, articles, job postings, and more to help induce, improve, and promote your writing career. We've also got online Writer Statistics, Freebies for Writers, and more!

We provide a free weekly newsletter that is sent out every Thursday and includes the following:
- Articles and Interviews
- Courses for Writers
- Resources for Writers
- Freebies for Writers
- Writer-Related Classified Ads
- Call for Submissions Listings
- Freelance Job Listings
- Contest Listings for Writers
- Books and Software for Writers...and more!

Submission Guidelines

Writer Gazette welcomes submissions from experienced and/or new writers. *We look for:*
- Informative articles pertaining to the craft of writing
- Tips & Techniques on the craft of writing
- Book Reviews on the craft of writing
- Product Reviews (such as writing programs, etc.)
- Course Reviews (Such as writers conferences, classes, etc.)

We are not looking for personal experience stories at this time. We want how-to or step-by-step, informative articles that will teach writers how to enhance and increase their writing skills. Articles are to be between 300-1,500 words. At this time we can offer you a full byline, bio, photo, two links to the website(s) of your choice, and a contact email address (optional).

All stories must be true and about you or someone you know. Reprints are acceptable but please tell us when and where your story was printed.

Submissions must be between 750-1,500 words. Any submissions that do not meet the word count requirement will be deleted immediately.

Please include the following with your submission:
- your full name (or pen name—please specify)
- address
- email address
- phone number
- story title
- word count
- your bio
- the book title you are submitting to

Send your submissions to: *writersguide@yahoo.com.*

Please make the subject line match the book title that you are submitting to. All submissions must be pasted into the body of your email—absolutely no attachments. E-mails with attachments will be immediately deleted.

Please note: it may take up to 2-3 months for us to respond to your submission. Thank you for your patience with us as we review submissions. There is no deadline to submit for these books at this time.

Payment Upon Acceptance:

At this time we can pay $10 (Canadian) per submission with full bio and a free copy of the book. It is our desire to raise the payment amount in the future.

Rights:

We require one time rights and editing rights (if needed). You retain all copyrights. Upon acceptance of your submission, we will send you an agreement form. This form will include the final proof of your submission and must be signed and returned in order for your submission to be published in our series. Upon acceptance of your submission, you hereby grant Topzone Publishing the right to publish and reproduce your submission in book form or any other media form that

V-Z

may result from publication worldwide.

Disclaimer:

We have the right to refuse any and all submissions that we believe will not fit with the theme of our books.

About Us:

Krista Barrett and Michelle Froese are the running force behind this new book series. Books will be published through Topzone Publishing and will be available in electronic format and POD.

Our Mission for this book series:

• To provide encouragement and inspiration to writers worldwide.

• To provide a new market for writers worldwide.

Special Call for Submissions:

Writer Gazette is currently seeking 750-1500 word submissions for the following upcoming writing inspiration books: Rejection Lessons, Writer Calamities, and Writer Inspiration. Payment upon acceptance. Online guidelines: http://www.writer gazette.com/insidewritersguide.shtml

Categories: Nonfiction—Computers—Interview—Writing

CONTACT: Submissions Editor
Material: All
E-mail: writersguide@yahoo.com
Website: www.writergazette.com/insidewritersguide.shtml

The Writer's Chronicle

The Writer's Chronicle, published six times a year, presents essays, articles, news, and information designed to enlighten, inform, and entertain writers, editors, students, and teachers of writing.

The Writer's Chronicle strives to accomplish the following:

• to present the best essays on the craft and art of writing poetry, fiction, and nonfiction;

• to help overcome the over-specialization and balkanization of the literary arts by presenting a public forum for the appreciation, debate, and analysis of contemporary literature;

• to present the diversity of accomplishments and points of view within contemporary literature;

• to provide serious and committed writers and students of writing the best advice on how to manage their professional lives;

• to provide writers who teach with new pedagogical approaches for their classrooms;

• to provide the members and subscribers with a literary community as a compensation for a devotion to a difficult and lonely art;

• to provide members and subscribers with information on publishing opportunities, grants, and awards;

• to promote the good works of AWP, its programs, and its individual members.

In general, the editors look for articles that demonstrate an excellent working knowledge of literary issues and a generosity of spirit that esteems the arguments of other writers on similar topics. In writing essays on craft, writers are often tempted to use their own work as an example. This is a bad idea, and such articles are not welcomed by the editors. Please keep in mind that 11,000 of our 21,000 readers are students or just-emerging writers. They must become good readers before they can become good writers, and we therefore expect essays on craft to show exemplary close readings of a variety of contemporary and older works. Essays must embody generosity, curiosity, and discernment rather than self-promotion. Writers may refer to their own travails and successes if they do so modestly, in small proportion to the other examples. Again, we look for a generosity of spirit—a general love and command of literature as well as an expert, writerly viewpoint—in the essays we publish.

We buy first serial rights and electronic rights for all manuscripts accepted for publication. We pay $10 per 100 words for accepted manuscripts. Regretfully, we do not pay kill fees. Authors are paid upon publication. AWP reserves the right to publish excerpts of pieces published in the *Writer's Chronicle* on the World Wide Web.

General Manuscript Guidelines

Manuscripts must be double-spaced, laser- or ink-jet printed, on 8½" x 11" white paper. Please, on the first page of your manuscript, include the word count of the article, your name, address, and phone number. All manuscripts must include an SASE for reply and a short author's biographical note of no more than three sentences. Essays longer than 7,000 words are generally not accepted.

Simultaneous submissions are *not* encouraged and must be noted as such on the cover letter. If we do not respond to your submission within three months, you are free to send your work elsewhere.

Electronic queries are okay, but no electronic submissions will be considered. Unsolicited works must be submitted only as a hard copy via U.S.P.S. mail.

Please do not follow the MLA style, which is well-designed for professional readers, but annoying to general readers, in whom we still have great faith. Acknowledge your sources by using endnotes and follow *The Chicago Manual of Style.*

If you quote a poem, song, or short-short story in its entirety, it is your responsibility to secure permission and pay for that permission.

We recommend that you limit quotes to fair use and avoid quoting whole works, as many trade publishers charge absurdly high fees for permissions; they would rather see their authors fade from public view than have their work reprinted often for a reasonable fee.

Submissions to *The Writer's Chronicle* may fall into one of the following categories:

1. Interviews. *The Writer's Chronicle* features interviews with well-published or up-and-coming authors of note in the genres of fiction, short fiction, poetry, creative nonfiction, and other forms of creative writing. In the past, we have published interviews with such authors as Jane Smiley, Donald Hall, Lynn Emanuel, Ron Carlson, Sonia Sanchez, Ernest Gaines, Marilyn Chin, and many others.

We especially appreciate interviews that include discussions of writing craft, the evolution of the author's own work, and literary influences and inspirations. Please query before submitting an interview. We publish interviews between 4,000 and 7,000 words.

Interviews should include a two paragraph introduction to the author, including all pertinent biographical information.

This document is also available online at www.awpwriter.org

Writer's Chronicle Guidelines for Submissions

The introduction should be mainly factual. We are not interested in how friendly you are with the subject, or what the subject was wearing that day, or when and where the interview was conducted, etc. We prefer interviews that have been revised heavily in the interest of accuracy, concision, and style. We are not interested in an interviews that is faithful to an actual spoken event. We are interested in an interview that represent a writer as well as possible in a *somewhat* personable and discursive manner. We do not publish interviews unless the subject has had an opportunity to revise his or her comments, and we encourage the interviewers and their subjects to revise their transcripts of the interviews extensively. We only publish interviews that have been approved in proofs by their subjects.

2. Lectures, Talks, & Panel Discussions do not appear in our pages, but we do ofen publish essays that are adapted from lectures and discussions. Many panel discussions, though engaging in person, are disappointing in the cool medium of print. As with interviews, we are not interested in transcripts of actual spoken events; we prefer articles that acknowledge sources and the other writers who have pondered the same topic (which one may sometimes overlook when one speaks informally); we prefer articles that are more elegantly organized and concisely written than the somewhat improvisatory ruminations of a panel discussion. We seldom publish all the presentations of any given panel discussion, so you should adapt your discussion to read well as a free-standing essay.

3. Essays on Pedagogy. Often, the Writer's Chronicle will publish essays concerning creative writing pedagogy. The most successful pedagogy pieces combine research, interviews, and teaching experience. Pedagogy pieces are not diatribes about the quality of a writer's own education or an argument against a specific teacher's methodology.

The pedagogy essay is an opportunity to inform and educate your peers about different methodologies of teaching, and should always be directed towards the writing community-at-large. Pedagogy pieces are generally between 2,500 and 6,000 words.

4. **Appreciations.** A writerly appreciation is our favorite kind of article. *The Writer's Chronicle* publishes appreciations of contemporary writers whose work came into prominence after 1965. Appreciations are not profiles or memoirs; instead, we seek close readings of an important author's work and an analysis of the author's contributions to our culture and mastery of craft. You may include some personal anecdotes to portray the author more vividly, but mostly self-referential or sentimental appreciations, of course, are not acceptable. The appreciation should answer the questions: What can I as a writer learn from this writer? What has this writer contributed to our culture? Appreciations are generally between 2,000 and 5,000 words.

5. **Craft Essays.** All craft essays must analyze an element of creative writing. Articles should not overlap with topics covered in recent issues of the *Chronicle*. Craft essays should contain concrete examples to illustrate the writerly advice they offer. Many of our published essays combine appreciations (as described above) with a study of elements of craft. A query on a specific topic is always welcome. Craft essays run between 2,000 and 6,000 words, depending on the topic.

6. **News/Features.** *The Writer's Chronicle* often runs stories of interest for creative writing teachers and students. These include hard news, such as coverage of public funding for the arts and education, unions for adjunct faculty, First Amendment issues, and developments in publishing or in other literary organizations. News articles and features should not run longer than 3,000 words.

7. **Essays on Academic Careers & Non-Academic Careers for Writers** no longer appear in the Writer's Chronicle, as AWP now features these essays in *AWP Job List*. *AWP Job List* publishes articles about academia and job opportunities for MFA graduates. We are always seeking well-researched articles regarding opportunities for our members to succeed in the corporate or non-profit sectors.

Payment rates are the same as those of *The Writer's Chronicle*. *Job List* articles are also published on the Web. These articles should not run longer than 3,000 words, and they should include the elements of good investigative reporting. They should not rely on personal anecdotes alone.

8. **Book Reviews.** Periodically, *The Writer's Chronicle* will run reviews of important books for creative writing teachers, students, or literary professionals. Generally, AWP solicits reviews. Please query before considering AWP for any book reviews; these books must be current nonfiction and of interest to our readers. Books selected for review are limited to nonfiction or critical works: biographies on writers and publishers, books on craft, essays on the writing life, etc. We do not review contemporary poetry or fiction. Reviews may run no longer than 1,200 words, and most reviews are brief, 250 words or less.

Thank you for your interest in *The Writer's Chronicle*.

Categories: Arts—Education—Interview—Literature—Writing

CONTACT: D. W. Fenza, Editor-in-Chief
Material: All
c/o AWP
Carty House, Mail Stop 1E3
George Mason University
Fairfax VA 22030-4444
Phone: 703-993-4308
Fax: 703-993-4302
E-mail: awpchron@gmu.edu
Website: http://awpwriter.org/magazine/

Writer's Digest

General Focus

Writer's Digest is a monthly magazine for writers who want to get more out of their writing. That means every word we publish must inform, instruct or inspire the reader. Our readers want specific ideas and tips that will help them succeed, whether success means getting into print, finding personal fulfillment through writing or building and maintaining a thriving freelance career.

Our style is informal and personal. We try to speak with the voice of a compassionate colleague, a friend as well as a teacher. But that doesn't mean we shy away from explaining the difficulties of getting published today. To the contrary, keeping informed on industry trends is essential to our readers' success, so it's essential for our editorial to address timely issues. *WD* is infused with a belief in anyone's potential to succeed as a writer. Our goal is to provide our readers with the inspiration, how-to instruction and insider information to fulfill their writing potential.

Our Readership

You can best understand our philosophy by being intimately familiar with *Writer's Digest*. Reading several issues of the magazine will help you understand the types and tone of the articles we publish.

We are a monthly publication founded in 1920 with a circulation of more than 150,000. Our readers are of all ages and are scattered throughout the US, Canada and several other countries. Each year we buy about 60 major articles and about 75 shorter items. Be aware that at least one-third of those articles are assigned by staff, and seldom result from unsolicited queries.

To obtain sample issues of *Writer's Digest*, send $5.25 per copy to Lyn Menke, *Writer's Digest*, 4700 E. Galbraith Road, Cincinnati, Ohio 45236. You also may purchase copies via our Web site, www.writers digest.com. A helpful index of each year's contents is published in the December issue. You can also turn to our Web site for issue previews and the current table of contents.

How to Submit

Freelance submissions are accepted for features and Markets. For features, *Writer's Digest* editors prefer queries over unsolicited manuscripts. Queries allow us to review your article ideas and to suggest how to tailor them for our audience before you begin writing. Queries also save you time and energy should we reject your idea.

Queries should include a thorough outline that introduces your article proposal and highlights each of the points you intend to make. Your query should discuss how the article will benefit our readers, why the topic is timely today and why you are the appropriate writer to discuss the topic.

Although we welcome the work of new writers, we respect success and believe the selling writer can instruct our reader better and establish more credibility. Make sure to include your publishing credentials related to your topic with your submission. We like to see published clips. For writers with whom we haven't previously worked, we prefer fully developed queries sent by mail with clips. Writers who have been published in the magazine may contact their previous assigning editor via e-mail.

Please submit only one query at a time and allow us 6-8 weeks to review your proposal. If we like your proposal, we may either assign the article to you or ask to see a more detailed query before we make a final decision. Each submission must include your name, address, daytime telephone number and e-mail address. Please wait for a response before sending another submission.

All submissions must include SASE—self-addressed, stamped envelope. We are not responsible for, and will not respond to, queries and manuscripts not accompanied by SASE—unless an e-mail address is included. If an unsolicited query or manuscript is rejected and an e-mail address is included, a rejection note will be sent via e-mail and the submission will be destroyed. If you don't enclose SASE or an e-mail address and we aren't interested in your query, it will be destroyed without acknowledgment; calls to check on the status of such queries will not be returned. E-mail queries should be addressed to wdsubmissions@fwpubs.com; again, give us 6-8 weeks to review your proposal and respond.

All accepted freelance articles must be submitted in electronic form, either by e-mail or on disk, in text-only or Microsoft Word 6.0.

Finally, we expect writers to double-check all facts included in their stories and to submit documentation to support the information included in their stories.

Submission Don'ts

If you want us to read your query—and take it seriously—then here are a few pointers to keep in mind:

We do not accept queries made over the phone or via fax.

We do not accept unsolicited illustrations, artwork, cartoons or photos.

We do not use poetry, fiction or scripts; we do not buy newspaper clippings and we handle book and software reviews in-house.

We do not buy reprints of articles previously published in other writing magazines.

We do not accept unsolicited proposals for columns.

We do not accept simultaneous submissions.

We do not accept freelance submissions for Assignment columns and departments. For information on how to submit a manuscript for a Writing Clinic critique, please go to the end of these guidelines.

Payment and General Terms

For manuscripts, we pay 30-50 cents per word, on acceptance, for first world rights for one-time use and non-commercial electronic use. Should we want to reprint anything we've purchased from you, in other than electronic format, we'll pay you 25% of the original purchase price for each use. Contributor copies are sent to writers and artists whose work appears in that issue.

Tone

In general, don't shy away from the word I in your articles. The first-person perspective is important to establishing your credibility. But don't overdo it. We want instructive articles, not articles based solely on your own writing experience (what we call "And then I wrote..." articles). Round out your experiences with those of other writers and with information from editors, when appropriate.

We use a friendly, informal—but not lackadaisical or cutesy—style. We demand lively writing. Use anecdotes, examples, samples and quotes to strengthen the message of the article. Also consider using sidebars and subheads in your writing. Look at the magazine for clues on how to do this effectively.

WHAT WE WANT—LONG STUFF

How-To Articles

How-to articles are our mainstay: How to write better, enjoy your writing life more, market successfully, recycle and resell ideas, maintain records and more. These articles present a common problem or goal, offer the appropriate solution, and give an example of how that solution has worked. Articles generally run 800-1,200 words. Pieces that can cover a topic completely in 500 words or fewer are of particular interest to us. Actual length will be discussed when the article is assigned.

In general, we're looking for timely articles, and we work on a five-month lead time. That's why, if you send us a proposal for a topic that was just covered on Oprah, it's too late.

Topics for features vary widely. Categories for which we seek material include writing inspiration and technique, trends in publishing, and how to write for specific genres. We're also interested in marketing opportunities and money-making ideas; tools, equipment and supplies; and marketing mechanics.

Writing Technique Articles

These pieces highlight an often misunderstood or poorly utilized writing method and detail how to use it precisely, appropriately and successfully. Examples include how to write an effective lead, how to use dialogue to establish character, how to brighten your prose or how to use suspense effectively.

Articles may cover fiction, nonfiction, poetry or script writing techniques, but must be accessible to all writers and offer advice that can be applied directly or indirectly to all forms of writing. Writers should

have a proven track record of publication in the area about which they are writing. How a particular piece is structured depends on the complexity of the subject, but every piece will need to:

• Define the technique and its importance.

• Outline how to use the technique. The best explanations break the technique down into distinct parts and deal with each part individually. When appropriate, use a step-by-step explanation.

• Give recent examples of its usage. Be in touch with current literature relevant to your topic and apply it. Using examples is a vital part of your article; give us more than you think necessary—and then add two more. Illustrate every point with examples—either from your own writing or from well-known works. On major points, readers can benefit from "right" and "wrong" or "before" and "after" examples, showing writing before the technique is applied or when it is used inappropriately, followed by the corrected version.

• If appropriate, give readers tips on incorporating the technique into their writing. For example, an article on using anecdotes might give tips on how to collect anecdotes to use.

As with all how-to articles, instruction is the key to making the article work. Analyze your own writing to determine what gives it power, what makes it successful. Then give our readers a thorough guide to using that technique powerfully and successfully, too.

WHAT WE WANT—SHORT STUFF

Breaking In

These pieces are very timely. Market reports are generally 750 words, highlight general article or book trends and offer instruction on how any writer might break into a particular market.

You'll want to cover several essential elements in genre and market reports. This isn't a formula—only a checklist. Remember, anecdotes, specific examples and quotes are important here, too. Establish the market. It must be current and have a growing need for manuscripts. Quote editors. Emphasize specific sales and payments, either your own or other writers'.

Describe the market. Detail the differences from and similarities to other markets and types of writing. Give an idea of the people who read these types of articles so readers will know if this is a market that appeals to them.

Explain how to find ideas for the market. What kinds of topics and treatments does the market use most? Point out how writers can generate ideas that are salable. Provide tips on matching ideas to publications.

Explain how to write for the market. Detail the process of turning ideas into salable stories. What are the special requirements of writing for this market or writing this type of article or book? Point out common pitfalls and how to avoid them.

Chronicle

Writer's Digest accepts submissions to the online-only monthly contest, Chronicle. Read the complete rules found at www.writersdigest.com/contests/your_chronicle_display.asp before submitting. Chronicle submissions should be personal essays on any aspect of writing. Entries must be no more than 500 words, including title and byline, and may not have appeared elsewhere in print or online. Submissions will be accepted until the 25th of each month. Each month the winning entry will be posted for 30 days beginning the business day closest to the 5th of the following month. All winners will be contacted in advance to sign a contract giving F&W Publications first world electronic rights and non-exclusive electronic archiving rights. More than one entry by the same author may be entered for the same month and essays may be re-entered in different months. Send entries only via e-mail to wdchronicle@fwpubs.com with Chronicle-Month as the subject line. Paste the entry directly into the e-mail message (no attachments) and include your name, e-mail address, and daytime phone number at the end so we may contact you if your essay is selected. All winners receive $125.

Writing Clinic

Each month, *Writer's Digest* offers an expert critique of an unpublished manuscript or poem. If you have a manuscript you'd like to submit, please print a copy of our release agreement, available at our

Web site (www.writersdigest.com) and mail it along with your work to Writing Clinic, *Writer's Digest*, 4700 E. Galbraith Road, Cincinnati, OH 45236. Alternatively, send SASE requesting a release to our address before submitting your manuscript. Manuscripts are not accepted by e-mail or by fax; any manuscript submitted without a signed release will be destroyed. All critiqued manuscripts also appear in our online discussion forum for moderated public critique; we also post additional manuscripts each month for online critique that do not appear in the magazine. The writer of the work being critiqued receives no payment. Visit www.writersdigest.com/forum/clinicrelease_text.asp.

Categories: Writing

CONTACT: Maria Schneider, Submissions Editor
Material: All
4700 E. Galbraith Rd
Cincinnati OH 45236
Phone: 513-531-2690, ext. 1431
E-mail: wdsubmissions@fwpubs.com
Website: www.writersdigest.com

Writers' Journal
The Complete Writer's Magazine

ABOUT US
Writers' Journal (originally named "The Inkling") was founded in 1980 as a four-page newsletter for writers. Through a period of several owners, it has been transformed into a full-fledged, professional writers' journal. We are a bi-monthly publication, with a circulation of around 26,000 aspiring writers whose love of writing has prompted them to take the next step—attempting to become published.

We try to give such writers the tools and information necessary to get their work in shape for publication. Articles are geared to those at all levels of experience, from beginning writers to those who are already professionals. We cover techniques for improving writing style—punctuation, grammar, structure, vocabulary, etc.—as well as helpful advice on how to develop various types of writing, in both fiction and nonfiction categories.

We offer writers guidance in selling and publishing their work and advice on desktop publishing, E-publishing, and publishing-on-demand. Our columnists deal with various creative forms, such as photography, poetry, and screenwriting.

Our readers also get the chance to put into practice what they learn by entering our short story, poetry and photography contests. We publish the winners of these contests.

The scope of *Writers' Journal* information makes the magazine a valuable tool for all types of writers, freelancers, screenwriter, editors, teachers and poets.

GUIDELINES
Although most of the columns in the *Writers' Journal* are staff written, articles from freelance writers are always welcome. Send either complete manuscripts or query with clips. Several feature articles, running 1200-2200 words, are published in each issue. Some of the topics we are looking for include:

• *The Business Side of Writing:* Tips, techniques, record keeping tactics on how to increase writing production, taxes, financial matters.

• *Self/Independent Publishing:* Practical advice on all aspects of independent publishing. Particularly wanted are success stories that impart solid information on book design and production, distribution costs, marketing, profits, etc.

• *Skills of Writing:* The how-to of writing style, punctuation, sentence structure, story composition, interviewing, and research.

• *Income Venues:* Unique and unusual income-producing methods. Past articles include: Juvenile craft writing, ghostwriting, church/business histories, technical manual writing, city web site writing, and specialty dictionaries.

• *Other Nonfiction Topics:* Photography, travel writing, screenwriting, technical writing, newspaper, corporate/business writing.

• *Fiction:* Although we publish staff-written articles on writing fiction, we welcome articles on the subject, covering technique, plotting, marketing, character development, or any of the other aspects of writing fiction. We do not publish fiction except for the winning entries of our various contests.

• *Poetry:* This is adequately covered by the *Writers' Journal*'s poetry editor, although an authoritative "guest editorial" may be considered.

• *Poetry Submissions:* The *Writers' Journal* buys about 25 poems a year, which we use for fillers. We welcome light verse, preferably about writing. Short, lively, exciting, witty and imaginatively written poems will stand a better chance of acceptance than "run-of-the-mill" pieces. We do not respond to submissions without a SASE. Author will be notified by mail if a poem is accepted. Unpublished poems only. (No vulgarity or pornographically explicit pieces considered.) Maximum length—15 lines. All other poetry submissions must follow poetry contest guidelines available with SASE or see our web site.

• *Style and Focus:* We want to see highly informative articles of an advisory nature that feature a positive and practical approach to the topic being covered, with a narrow focus, in a tightly written style, and with good use of basic elements of article construction. No dull writing, please. Appropriate touches of humor are always appreciated.

Mail submissions with SASE for editor's response, however, manuscripts will not be returned. Submissions may also be emailed—Text only. For overseas contributors, this option is welcomed.

Pay Rates and Rights:
• *Articles and Columns:* Writers' Journal pays on a variable scale, depending on budget. We ask for one-time rights. We print previously unpublished work only.

• *Poetry:* $5.00 per poem, for one-time rights.

• *Contest:* Writers' Journal sponsors a short story contest, a travel article contest, a romance contest, two photo contests and three poetry contests each year. *Writers' Journal* pays cash for first, second and third place. These and selected honorable mentions are published. All winners will be kept for possible future publication. Send SASE for current contest guidelines or see our web site.

A sample issue of the *Writers' Journal* is available for $6.00. Annual subscription is $19.97. Canada—$34.97. Europe—$49.97. Others—$54.97.

Categories: Nonfiction—Writing

CONTACT: Leon Ogroske, Editor
Material: All
Val-Tech Media
PO Box 394
Perham MN 56573
Phone: 218-346-7921
Fax: 218-346-7924
E-mail: writersjournal@writersjournal.com
Website: www.writersjournal.com

Yachting

Overview
Yachting is edited for experienced, affluent boat owners—power and sail—who don't have the time or the inclination to read sub-standard stories. They love carefully crafted stories about places they've never been or a different spin on places they have, meticulously reported pieces on issues that affect their yachting lives, personal accounts of yachting experiences from which they can learn, engaging profiles of people who share their passion for boats, insightful essays that evoke the history and traditions of the sport and compelling photographs of others enjoying the game as much as they do.

They love to know what to buy and how things work. They love to be surprised. They don't mind getting their hands dirty or saving a buck here and there, but they're not interested in learning how to make a masthead light out of a mayonnaise jar.

If you love what they love and can communicate like a pro (that means meeting deadlines, writing tight, being obsessively accurate and never misspelling a proper name), we'd love to hear from you. We prefer written queries. Include a self-addressed, stamped envelope.

A few pointers: Don't bother sending us anything about sailboarding or hydroplane racing. Translation: Read the magazine. We have a great desire for good powerboat stories and we kill for great first-person stuff, especially when our readers can learn something from it. Don't bother us with queries about sailboat racing. We have the scene covered. Send your fiction and poetry to *The New Yorker.*

If you have an idea you want to pitch to us, make sure it is focused and well-evolved. For instance, don't send us a query for a piece on "Cruising the Virgin Islands." Propose a lead. Make us love it. Share your enthusiasm. It wouldn't hurt to send some clips with your query.

Boat reviews and technical articles on navigation, electronics, engines, materials, etc., are mostly written by experts we know. However, if you have expertise in these areas, we'd be happy to review a resume and sample manuscript—submitted on speculation.

Payments

Generally, we pay $300-$500 for short pieces (columns) and $750-$1000 or more for longer stories (features).

Photos

Most photographs in *Yachting* are shot on assignment by professionals we know. However, we would be happy to review your portfolio. We can't be responsible for unsolicited material.

For photos we pay:
• Cover: $500
• Four-color inside $350/page; $200 1/2 page;
• Black and white $75 for spot art. Up to $250 for full page (rarely used).

For assignments we pay $450 a day against page rate (whichever is greater). In most cases a cap is agreed upon beforehand. We pay all reasonable expenses (to be discussed beforehand).

Whom to query:

Art Director: Rana Bernhardt
Executive Editor: Kim Kavin

If You Have an Assignment From Us

This is a guide written for the *Yachting* contributor or freelancer who has received an assignment from the magazine or is sending in an article on spec. All queries and copy submissions should follow these forms unless negotiated with the editor in charge beforehand.

Columns

These should contribute much toward defining the personality and authority of the magazine. They should inform, entertain and stimulate the reader to think beyond the surface of an issue, product, event, personality or how-to concept.

Whenever possible, columns should build upon, or launch from a news event, new product or emerging trend. They should have a narrow subject focus—not be "a column about sails" or "a column about depth sounders"—and should reveal the unique perspective of the writer.

They should be meticulously factual and the writer should indicate somewhere in the text that his point of view is based on experience or interviews with other experts in the field.

While *Yachting* hires columnists and contributors more for their expertise in a given field, we expect copy that is tight and reasonably polished. Word count is important. If we ask for 350 words, we expect 350, not 600.

The editing process often involves queries to authors and may sometimes include requests for rewrites. We may send unsatisfactory material back to the author for rewrites, more than once if necessary.

Columnists and contributors are expected to be our eyes and ears in the field. We expect them to provide briefs each month and keep us informed on developments in the field.

Features

Features are the heart of the magazine. They generally contain the greatest amount of space for copy and visual elements.

They should follow the classic feature model: they should have a beginning, preferably an anecdote involving someone using a boat or equipment that illuminates the "theme" or lead of the story which follows close behind; a middle that contains evidence to back up the lead; and an end that ties back into the lead.

Because we are a four-color magazine and visually driven, writers should work to obtain the best possible photos to accompany the story. Whenever possible, photos should illustrate the "theme" of the story, not just be a running shot of the boat and a shot of the interior. As with columns, writers should expect queries from editors and editors may request rewrites.

Categories: Boating

CONTACT: Refer to Guidelines
18 Marshall St., Ste. 114
Norwalk CT 06854
Phone: 203-299-5900
Fax: 203-299-5901
E-mail: editor@yachtingnet.com
Website: www.yachtingnet.com

The Yalobusha Review

The Yalobusha Review, founded in 1995, is an annual journal of fiction, poetry, creative non-fiction, and black-and-white artwork and photography.

We are open to submissions from students, writers in the Oxford community, the region, and across the country. Its sixth issue in 2002 featured a new story from Dan Chaon, an interview with Tom Franklin, and an introductory essay from Barry Hannah. It is published in April of each year by the University of Mississippi with an approximate distribution of 500 copies.

Single issue copies are available for $10.00 including postage.

Multiple-year subscriptions are available for $8.00 per year.

Send checks made payable to The Yalobusha Review to the address below.

Submission Guidelines:

We are looking for primarily short prose (up to 25 pages), poetry, and black-and-white artwork.

There is no preferred or restricted subject matter or theme; we just want work.

Submit a maximum of one piece of prose, 10 poems, or 5 pieces of 8"x10" artwork.

Submit only previously unpublished work.

We do not accept simultaneous submissions.

We pay two contributor's copies.

Cover letters and SASE are required.

Submit by regular mail only.

No submissions will be returned.

Categories: Fiction—Nonfiction—Literature—Poetry—Writing

CONTACT: Non-fiction Editor
Material: Non-fiction
CONTACT: Fiction Editor
Material: Fiction
CONTACT: Poetry Editor
Material: Poetry
CONTACT: Art Editor
Material: Art
The University of Mississippi
PO Box 1848
University MS 38677-0186
Phone: 601-232-7103

E-mail: yalobush@olemiss.edu (inquiries only)
Website: www.olemiss.edu/depts/english/pubs/
yalobusha_review.html

Yankee
The Magazine of New England Living

Guidelines for Writers and Photographers

It is to your advantage to read several current issues of *Yankee* before sending us a query or a manuscript. We prefer to receive queries and manuscripts by U.S. mail, with SASE. Manuscripts will not be returned without an SASE.

The editors are always open to receiving story ideas and reviewing short nonfiction manuscripts from established writers. Freelancers are welcome to query us on ideas; please send recent clips of your published work. Our staff and well-established freelancers who have worked with us before write most of our stories and articles, and provide photography and art.

We are no longer accepting submissions for fiction, poetry, cartoons, or book reviews. We do not use fillers or serial articles/stories.

New England Today: Every issue includes 6 pages of very short, factual, and sometimes humorous stories up front. Our editors write these stories but occasionally accept an item from freelance writers.

Submissions should be no longer than 400 words, and in most cases much shorter. We enjoy the occasional submission in the form of charts or graphs.

Home, Food, and Garden including House for Sale: Staff-written or assigned to established writers who have worked with us. If you would like us to consider writing about your house, send a letter describing the house, with the selling price and including photocopies of photographs, if available, to House for Sale at the address above.

Feature Articles: This is the most difficult kind of story for a first-timer to sell to us, but it is not without precedent. Study the magazine and query us first. Payment based on content and length. Send to Editorial.

Photography and Art: Assigned to experienced professionals. If you would like to work with us, show us a portfolio of your best work. We prefer 35 mm 2-1/4" or 4"x5" color transparencies.

Before sending work, please contact Leonard Loria, Art Director, at extension 115.

Travel: We may purchase short stories about favorite inns, restaurants, tourist attractions, historical sites, or an area of natural beauty in New England. Articles should not exceed 500 words, and you should query us first. Send query to Travel Editor.

Rights, deadlines, etc.: We buy all rights and pay upon acceptance by an editor. If a story relates to a holiday or season (e.g., Christmas, baseball season), ideas or manuscripts should be submitted one year earlier, so that there is time to get seasonal photographs. Our normal editorial deadline is 6 months prior to publication.

Payments: Upon acceptance of the editor, based on the length of the piece.

A self-addressed envelope with appropriate postage must accompany unsolicited manuscripts, art, or photos. We do not assume responsibility for the return of unsolicited material, so if it is priceless or irreplaceable, don't send it! It is always a good idea to query us first and send clips of previous work. Allow at least 8 weeks for reply or return of manuscripts.

E-mail note: Please always include at least your name and phone number. We have found that our server cannot always locate your sender address.

"Dear Yankee": Letters to the editor can be e-mailed to dearyank@yankeepub.com (please include your name, address, and phone number).

Categories: Nonfiction—Cooking—Food/Drink—Gardening—General Interest—Interview—Travel—Essay—Personal Experience—Home

CONTACT: Mel Allen, Interim Editor
Material: Manuscripts, Travel
CONTACT: Annie B. Copps, Food Editor
Material: Food
Yankee Publishing Inc.
PO Box 520
1121 Main St.
Dublin NH 03444-0520
Phone: 603-563-8118
Fax: 603-563-8252
E-mail: queries@yankeepub.com
Website: www.yankeemagazine.com
www.almanac.com

YES!

YES! Magazine documents how people are creating a more just, sustainable, and compassionate world. We describe a global society in the process of change, and we craft our issues to reflect that dynamic, creative process. We welcome submissions that relate directly to this focus.

Each issue of YES! focuses on a single theme, which means that there is a bit of luck involved in submitting a timely article. Articles that relate to the theme of the upcoming issue have the greatest chance of publication. We tend not to project these themes too far into the future to ensure their relevance, but we announce the next issue's theme on the back of the current issue. Check the back of YES! to find out what we are looking for in submissions now. If you cannot obtain YES! in print, write our office at the address listed below and ask about the current theme.

In the interest of avoiding redundancy, articles that fall within the scope of recently released issues of YES! have almost no chance of publication. Please see our back issues page for a complete list of past themes. We do allocate a small portion of our magazine to non-themed pieces. The best way to ensure that your article fits within our magazine is to submit a query instead of a full article.

YES! is a quarterly publication with a tiny staff. Please allow at least three months for a response.

CONTENT - Although we do not wish to minimize the problems that face us, YES! is not interested in bemoaning them. (There are plenty of publications covering that ground.) Instead, we highlight promising solutions, particularly those that address the structures behind our deepest ecological, social, and political problems. We do not accept submissions that simply state the author's opinion of what needs to be fixed and why. Our readers know why we need to move towards sustainability—they want to know what people are doing that is transformational.

We do not accept poetry, fiction, unsolicited book reviews or interview transcripts. Personal essays are considered only if they are especially timely or illuminate a relevant political or cultural issue. We will not endorse any candidate or party. In general, we are looking for groundbreaking articles that bring particularly innovative efforts to light and tell an interesting story.

STYLE - Authors should write in a conversational tone for a general, well-informed audience. We emphasize personal authenticity, factual accuracy, and telling an engaging story. The best way to familiarize yourself with our editorial tone is to look at previous articles from YES!, nearly all of which are posted on our website: www.futurenet.org.

COMPENSATION - We provide all our writers and artists with a one-year subscription to the magazine and two additional copies of the issue in which their work appears. Because we are a nonprofit organization and accept no advertisements, we are able to offer only a modest honorarium. Occasionally, we commission articles from professional freelance authors at a higher rate.

RIGHTS - We regularly grant editors, teachers, and others permission to reprint articles from YES! for free, and we distribute our

V-Z

articles and images for free via electronic services, including our website. Because we are eager to spread the message of YES! as widely as we can, we include in our contracts permission to allow reprinting of authors' work in these ways.

FORMAT - We do not accept electronic submissions unless the author is working from overseas. Please mail hard copies of submissions and queries to the address listed below. We recommend that you send queries and proposals rather than completed submissions, but please accompany queries with a writing sample.

Features are generally 1,500-2,500 words in length, and sidebars usually 100-250. Photos are encouraged. Illustrations must be reproducible in a single color. Please do not send any original images or artwork.

Categories: Nonfiction—Agriculture—Arts—Culture—Economics—Environment—Health—Human Rights—Politics—Science—Youth

CONTACT: Submissions Editor
YES! Magazine
P.O. Box 10818
Bainbridge Island, WA 98110

Yoga for EveryBody

Yoga for EveryBody is a quarterly publication dedicated to the encouragement and practice of yoga. We encourage descriptions of postures and asanas in detailed step-by-step instructions. We are also interested in the various schools of yoga.

Needs: We are especially interested in how yoga relates to ones day-to-day life; how the practice of yoga influences one's daily circumstances; how the attention to detail in asanas and awareness of the breath assist us during life's challenging and stressful times.

We are also interested in articles describing the various schools of yoga, such as Hatha, Vinyasa, Ashtanga, etc.

We are interested in holistic healing modalities and stress reduction techniques.

We have an interest in where yoga has been incorporated into the workplace, any corporate or business programs that encourage yoga and stress reduction through wellness programs or workplace classes.

We do not accept music reviews or unsolicited poetry and cartoons. We are interested in book reviews and tips on websites that encourage well being.

We would like to cover a diversity of views from many yogic traditions. How does the practice of yoga engender a wholeness of mind, body and spirit while deepening our connections to the world?

Length: Features are generally 1,500-2,500 words in length. Departments run 1,000–2000 words and Columns run 500-800 words Payment is determined on a case-by-case basis, .

Art/Photo Needs: We encourage descriptions of postures and asanas in detailed description along with useable professional quality photos (black & white and color).

Payment: When an article has been assigned, payment is made half upon acceptance of the completed manuscripts and half upon publication. If an article has been accepted and is never published your "kill fee" is the initial payment received.

How to Submit: Queries are preferred to completed manuscripts. We prefer electronic proposals via email. Please describe what you are proposing in a clear, well written outline. Indicate whether you intend to include accompanying photos or illustrations in your article. If possible, send along a couple of clips or copies of previously published work. Send to editor@yoga4everybody.com. If it is necessary to send your queries and clips via postal mail, send to: Editor, Yoga For EveryBody, 1041 Shary Circle, Concord, CA 94518. Materials will not be returned unless accompanied with an SASE with sufficient postage. We do not accept phone queries. Assigned manuscripts are best submitted electronically via email attachment or CD. Macintosh Word format is preferred. Contact us via email to discuss other formats. Include your name,

telephone number, email and mailing addresses at the top of the document. Include word count in the top right corner. It is also helpful to include a short two-three line bio/description of yourself.

Response Time: Allow twelve weeks for response. It is possible that an assigned article could be published anywhere from three months to one year from the date of acceptance. Yoga for Every Body reserves the right not to publish an accepted article.

Writers' Guidelines: Magazine Intention: Yoga 4 EveryBody is a quarterly publication dedicated to the encouragement and practice of yoga for all types of individuals. We encourage descriptions of asanas in detailed description along with professional quality photos when available. We would like descriptions of how particular asanas affect the body in healing. We are especially interested in the way yoga relates to ones day-to-day life; how the practice of yoga influences one's daily circumstances; how the attention to detail in asanas and awareness of breath assist us during life's challenging moments. Yoga 4 EveryBody encourages an accessible, personal writing style.

Queries: Queries are preferred to completed manuscripts. We prefer electronic proposals via email. Please describe what you are proposing in a clear, well written outline. Indicate whether you intend to include accompanying photos or illustrations in your article. If possible, send along a couple of clips or copies of previously published work. Send to editor@yoga4everybody.com. If it is necessary to send your queries and clips via postal mail, send to: Editor, Yoga 4 EveryBody, 1041 Shary Circle, Concord, CA 94518. Materials will not be returned unless accompanied with an SASE with sufficient postage. We do not accept phone queries.

Manuscripts: Assigned manuscripts are best submitted electronically via email attachment (Word format is preferred), email text or CD. Contact us via email to discuss other formats. Include your name, telephone number, email and mailing addresses at the top of the document. Include word count in the top right corner. It is also helpful to include a short bio/description of yourself. Features are generally 1,500-2,000 words in length. Columns and Departments can range from 500-1,000 words. Short Briefs range from 300-500 words.

Rights: Contributor grants Yoga 4 EveryBody all rights of purchased manuscripts with the exclusion for writer to publish article in later book and/or personal website.

Payment: When an article has been assigned, payment is made half upon acceptance of the completed manuscripts and half upon publication. If an article has been accepted and is never published your "kill fee" is the initial payment received. It is possible that an assigned article could be published anywhere from three months to one year from the date of acceptance. Yoga 4 EveryBody reserves the right not to publish an accepted article.

Subjects of Interest: Asana Basic & Intermediate Descriptions—How would you address particular parts of the body, such as shoulders, hips and lower back? Is there a particular theme you would like to write about, such as asanas for lower back or neck and shoulders? Please include step-by-step descriptions for asanas and professional quality photos when available.

Yoga Solutions: How has the practice of yoga and in particular which asanas have helped with physical and emotional disorders such as lower back pain, stiff neck, headaches, insomnia, depression and stress.

Health Notes: What are current and late breaking studies that are proving yoga and meditation to be beneficial to health and well-being? Health Notes are 300-500 words each.

Yoga Briefs: Late breaking news stories and activities involving the yoga community at large. Yoga Briefs are 300-500 words each.

Working Wisdom: Where is yoga being incorporated into the workplace and business world? Where are Wellness Programs that encourage stress reduction & yoga classes springing up and where are these ideas encouraged in our work environment?

Millennial Wisdom: What teachers are on the leading edge in the yoga and meditation field? What is your personal experience with them? Did you conduct an interview? We gladly accept narrative accounts of your impressions.

Yoga Fun • Retreats, Conferences and Workshops

Where are some favorite getaways that include yoga as amenities such as spas and yoga vacations? Which retreat facilities have you gone to that you can recommend and why? Was it over-the-top and exclusive, or down-to-earth and accessible?

Yoga Products: What new yoga props improve your yoga practice? Do you prefer a certain material "sticky mat" to another kind? Tell us about new props and paraphernalia that enchance your yoga practice.

Rights: Contributor grants Yoga for EveryBody all rights of purchased manuscripts with the exclusion for writer to publish article in later book and/or personal website.

Categories: Nonfiction—Health

CONTACT: Kelly Townsend, Editor
Material: All
1041 Shary Circle
Concord CA 94518
Phone: 925-671-9852 ext. 1311
Fax: 925-671-5573
E-mail: editor@yoga4everybody.com
Website: www.yoga4everybody.com

Yoga Journal

Yoga Journal covers the practice and philosophy of yoga. We define yoga broadly to encompass practices that aspire to union or communion with some higher power, greater truth, or deeper source of wisdom, as well as practices that tend to increase harmony of body, mind, and spirit.

In particular we welcome articles on the following themes:

1. Leaders, spokespersons, and visionaries in the yoga community
2. The practice of hatha yoga
3. Applications of yoga to everyday life (e.g., relationships, social issues, livelihood, etc.)
4. Hatha yoga anatomy and kinesiology and therapeutic yoga
5. Nutrition and diet, cooking, and natural skin and body care.

We encourage a well-written query letter outlining your subject and describing its appeal. Query before submitting an article, and please include a SASE (self-addressed, stamped envelope).

We encourage you to read an issue of *Yoga Journal* carefully before submitting a query. Please keep in mind our editorial department's three E's: Articles should be enlightening, educational, and entertaining. Please avoid New Age jargon and in-house buzz-words as much as possible. Features run approximately 3,000 to 5,000 words. Departments run 1,000 to 2,500 words. Centering runs about 750 words. We do not print unsolicited poetry or cartoons. We consider everything except a direct assignment to be submitted on a speculative basis. When an article has been assigned, we will send you a contract specifying terms, kill fee, and deadline.

Remember to indicate the availability of photos or artwork in your query letter or with your article. (Pertinent, high quality photos or illustrations can greatly enhance an article's desirability.)

Payment varies, depending on length, depth of research, etc. We pay within 90 days of final acceptance: $800 to $2000 for features, $400 to $800 for departments, $25 to $100 for Om Page and Well-Being, and $200 to $250 for book reviews.

All manuscripts should be typed, double spaced, and clean. Include your name, address, phone number, and word count on the title page, and your name and page number on each subsequent page. Also include a concise, two-sentence tagline identifying yourself to our readers. Always keep a copy of your work, and include a SASE with your submission if you want it returned.

If possible, please also send your work on a computer floppy disc. We strongly prefer submissions in Microsoft Word 5.1 for Macintosh. However, we may also be able to translate files from the following applications: (for Mac) ClarisWorks, FrameMaker, MacWrite, Macwrite II, MacWrite Pro, Nisus, Microsoft Works, RTF; Text,

WordPerfect, WriteNow; (for PCs) Ami Pro, ClarisWorks, DCA-RFT, FrameMaker, Microsoft Word, Microsoft Works, MultiMate, OfficeWriter, Professional Write, RTF, Text, WordPerfect, WordPerfect Works, WordStar, XYWrite. Please do not send us files written in other applications.

We cannot be held responsible for loss or damage to unsolicited manuscripts or artwork. We do not accept unsolicited manuscripts by e-mail or fax. Make sure all photos are marked with a brief descriptive caption and the photographer's name and address.

Categories: Health—New Age—Philosophy—Physical Fitness—Spiritual

CONTACT: Editor
Material: All
2054 University Ave., Ste. 600
Berkeley CA 94704
Website: www.hogajournal.com

Young & Alive

Will not be accepting addtional manuscripts until 2009.

Your Stepfamily Magazine

Your Stepfamily is a new bi-monthly magazine created just for moms, dads and kids who want to learn from and enjoy the relationships they're creating as they evolve as a stepfamily.

Editorial Guidelines

MISSION STATEMENT: *Your Stepfamily* aims to be the handbook for the men, women and children of today's stepfamilies. It chronicles the changes and challenges that over 9.2 million stepfamilies face, and highlights the new practices they can employ to strengthen family members from within. *Your Stepfamily* equips family members with tools, techniques and problem-solving strategies they can employ as they navigate through the unchartered territory of creating their healthy family unit. *Your Stepfamily* embraces the journey.

PLEASE SEND YOUR ARTICLE TO:

Editor, Karen Adolphson, Your Stepfamily Online, 10314 Tanager Trail, Brecksville OH 44141; Fax: 440-526-3395; E-mail: karen@your stepfamily.com

Your Stepfamily Online is always looking for feature articles that will be of value to our readers. Our editorial guidelines are clear and simple. We are also flexible; please contact us with your questions.

Your Stepfamily is a bi-monthly online publication that gathers credible content from a variety of sources and shares it with our readers. The editors work on a model of content aggregation. Associations and others who work with stepfamilies are not viewed as competition, but instead as potential authorities who can offer useful information to our readers.

WHAT WE NEED

We are interested in research-based, credible articles, case histories, and advice that help stepfamilies address the challenges they face each day. In short, we want articles to help the reader in his or her every day life.

HOW TO SUBMIT AN ARTICLE

1. Send an abstract of your article to the editor at least two(2) months in advance of your targeted issue month. The abstract should be at least one (1) paragraph outlining the focus and main points of your article. Also include a closing paragraph listing the benefit(s) to the reader. Send your abstract via e-mail to: karen@yourstepfamily.com

2. In general, our articles consist of Features, Short Reads, and Sidebars. Please choose one of these length criteria, and print your word count at the beginning of your article.

Word Counts
Feature 1,500-2,200
Short Read (Dept.) 750-1,500
Sidebar 500 - 750

3. You can submit an article via e-mail; send it as a Word, text only, or rich text document to: karen@yourstepfamily.com. If you send the article on a CD; please send a print-out with it.

4. The editor contacts you regarding your article. In general, abstracts and articles are read within two (2) weeks of submission.

5. Submit your final article text to the editor at least two (2) months before the intended date of publication. The editor will ascertain the final publication date; publication dates may be changed at the editor?s discretion.

6. THINGS TO KEEP IN MIND: Your Stepfamily Online reserves the right to edit all submissions for clarity and length, and according to the magazine's editorial guidelines and publications policies.

7. It is understood that, once your article is accepted, and you sign and return the Author's Release form for that article, your article (or sections of it) may be published, at Your Stepfamily Online's discretion, in the online magazine (www.yourstepfamily.com)

VOCABULARY USAGE GUIDE
Does Your Stepfamily Online and the Stepfamily Association of America (SAA) have a standard spelling and vocabulary usage guide?

Yes. The SAA has a standard spelling and vocabulary usage guide for stepfamily-related words, which you are encouraged to use. Submissions that do not use the recommended language may still be evaluated by Your Stepfamily Magazine and the SAA, and an appropriate language disclaimer may be published with your article. All materials submitted are evaluated according to content, style, source of materials, and disclaimers used.

View the Your Stepfamily Online and Stepfamily Association of America (SAA) Vocabulary Guidelines on our website.

Categories: Family

CONTACT: Sharon Stober, Editorial Director
Material: All
Your Stepfamily Magazine
2615 Three Oaks Rd, Ste 1-B
Cary IL 60013
Phone: 847-639-2200 ext. 247
Fax: 847-629-8148
E-mail: sharson@yourstepfamily.com
Website: www.yourstepfamily.com

Zoetrope: All-Story

Zoetrope: All-Story is a quarterly literary publication founded by Francis Ford Coppola in 1997 to explore the intersection of story and art, fiction and film.

Submission Guidelines

Zoetrope: All-Story considers unsolicited submissions of short stories and one-act plays no longer than 7,000 words. Excerpts from larger works, screenplays, treatments, and poetry will be returned unread.

Simultaneous submissions are accepted, and first serial rights are required. Please do not submit more than one story or one-act play at a time for consideration.

Only submissions with a return address clearly marked on the outside envelope will be opened. Submissions accompanied by a self-addressed stamped envelope (SASE) will receive a response within five months. We regret that we are unable to respond to submissions without a SASE.

Zoetrope: All-Story does not accept submissions via email. We do, however, provide the Virtual Studio as a way to submit online.

Categories: Fiction—Arts—Film/Video—Short Stories

CONTACT: Tamara Straus, Editor-in-Chief
Material: Any
CONTACT: Michael Ray, Senior Editor
Material: Any
916 Kearny St.
San Francisco CA 94133
Phone: 415-788-7500
Website: all-story.com

ZYZZYVA

ZYZZYVA

the journal of west coast writers & artists

West Coast writers and artists only. This means currently living in AK, HI, WA, OR, or CA.

Submissions by mail only; do not phone. O.K. to query by e-mail. Do not submit manuscripts by e-mail. Snail mail only. Double-spaced. Self-addressed stamped envelope required for a reply.

We respond promptly, but do not offer comments or suggestions. We do not read simultaneous submissions, that is, material submitted at the same time to other editors.

We pay on acceptance an honorarium of $50, plus two author's copies, for first North American serial rights (and *ZYZZYVA* anthology rights) only. We reserve the right to put your piece up on our Web page.

We do not commission work.

We are committed to reflecting the full range of talent in our neighborhood—many genres, many generations, many schools. We have published a wide range of poetry, fiction, and nonfiction. Take your best shot.

We do not do interviews, reviews, or criticism. We do do translations, especially of Latin American and Asian writers.

ZYZZYVA is published in March, August, and November.

Photographers and graphic artists: submit scans 5½" wide, 300 dpi, with caption information. Only of work originally done in black & white on paper. No photos of paintings or sculpture, please. Self-addressed stamped envelope required.

If you would like to volunteer to work on ad sales, circulation, distribution, or editorial, please send a cover note and resume.

If you would like a sample copy, send us a check for $7 ($4 off the cover price).

Categories: Fiction—Nonfiction—Poetry—Short Stories—Nostalgia—Humor—Personal Experience

CONTACT: Howard Junker, Editor
Material: All
Po Box 590069
San Francisco CA 94159-0069
Phone: 415-752-4393
E-mail: editor@zyzzyva.org
Website: www.zyzzyva.org

Book Publishers' Guidelines

29th Press

Duke Communications International, publisher of 29th Press books, *Windows NT Magazine*, NEWS/400, and *Controller Magazine*, maintains its corporate headquarters in Loveland, Colorado, with regional sales offices in New York, Chicago, and San Francisco. Duke Communications currently employs about 100 people in Colorado, plus a staff of technical editors and reporters throughout the U.S. Duke Communications began publishing a newsletter, NEWS 34/38, in 1982 when founder and president David A. Duke, a former IBMer, recognized the need for information about the proliferating IBM midrange systems entering the market.

About 29th Press

In January 1991, the 29th Press division of Duke Communications published its first book for 3X/400 professionals. Currently, 29th Press maintains a list of about 50 titles in print, including reference books and textbooks. Target audiences are AS/400 professionals, and Windows NT users, administrators, and developers.

29th Press strives to publish practical, easy-to-read books that present clear, complete explanations of underlying concepts needed by readers. Practitioners who can communicate their technological expertise in a down-to-earth manner are the mainstays of the 29th Press publishing tradition. Many of our authors are technical editors for or contributors to leading technology journals, as well as pioneers and entrepreneurs in their respective fields.

Check our Web site for new Windows NT and AS/400 books, as well as an online catalog of our entire product line.

How to Submit a Proposal

If you are interested in submitting a proposal to 29th Press, you should send us the following information about your project and yourself:

• An overview that describes the type of book, its approximate length, and any special features or accompanying materials (diskette, CD, and so forth)

• A description of the intended audience
• A content outline or proposed Table of Contents
• A sample chapter or several pages from a typical chapter
• An estimate of the length of time to complete the final manuscript
• Information about competing products and market potential

• Personal information about your background and writing experience, including such items as a resume, a list of previously published works, and a writing sample.

Categories: Nonfiction—Computers—IBM AS/400—Windows NT

CONTACT: Katie Tipton, Acquisitions Editor
Material: All
CONTACT: Dave Bernard, Publisher
Material: AS/400
221 E. 29th St.
Loveland CO 80538
Phone: 970-663-4700
Fax: 970-203-2756
E-mail: kmptipton@aol.com
Website: www.iseriesnetwork.com/store

Abbott, Langer & Associates

We do not have a formal set of guidelines for manuscripts. Initially, just the title and table of contents would help us decide whether to reject a manuscript or investigate further.

Categories: Nonfiction—Associations—Business—Computers—Reference—Security & Loss Prevention—Human Resources Management

CONTACT: Dr. Steven Langer, President
Material: All
548 First St.

Crete IL 60417
Phone: 708-672-4200
Fax: 708-672-4674
E-mail: slanger@abbott-langer.com
Website: www.abbott-langer.com

Abingdon Press

Abingdon Press provides resources that meet the needs of all those who seek and would serve God. We produce and deliver hundreds of thousands of resources that people want and use for their ministries. Among these products are books, supply items, music resources, curriculum resources, and a host of other print and non-print media, including audio and video cassettes, computer software, and periodicals such as Circuit Rider and Newscope.

Most of our book publishing is done on a royalty basis: The author is paid a percentage of the retail price of copies sold. We assume the expense of editing, printing, binding, advertising, and promotion and in most cases, we arrange for illustration. Through our own sales personnel, we distribute to retail bookstores those books published under our imprint. We also handle subsidiary rights as well as foreign sales and translation rights.

All curriculum writing is done by assignment. Curriculum writers are active members of The United Methodist Church and are often involved in the age level for which they write.

We suggest that an author first submit for consideration an outline or description of the writing plan together with one or two sample chapters. Because of the time and expense involved in the appraisal process, manuscripts should be submitted to only one publisher at a time.

The author should retain a copy of any unsolicited material submitted, since Abingdon Press cannot assume responsibility for the receipt, security, or return of such material. Correct postage should accompany the manuscript in the event it must be returned. The author should provide only one address—the one to which correspondence regarding the submission is to be sent.

Careful attention is given to every project submitted, and every attempt is made to reach a decision within eight weeks of receipt of a manuscript unless further consultation is necessary. All editorial considerations take place at 201 Eighth Avenue South, P.O. Box 801, Nashville, TN 37202-0801

Categories: Christian Interest

CONTACT: Submissions
Material: All
201 Eighth Acenue South
PO Box 801
Nashville, TN 37202-0801
Website: www.abingdonpress.com

ACTA Publications

1. If you are not familiar with our products, please request our current catalog or go on-line at www.actapublications.com. (Hint: People who do not do this often waste their time submitting manuscripts to us.)
2. If you truly feel we would be the best publisher for you, then send a proposal with three parts:
   a. A cover letter that explains your proposal and tells a little bit about yourself and why

Books A-L

your proposed work fits our product line, and exactly whom you see as the audience. (Hint: If your book is for "everyone," then it probably is not for us. We need to know the kind of person who will buy it and why.)

  b. A table of contents for your proposed work.

  c. An introduction and one chapter. We will not read entire manuscripts. (Hint: Send us your best writing. It does no good for you to tell us that something is "just a draft" or that you are "still working on it." We are going to judge it as if it is your final product.)

3. Be sure to enclose a self-addressed, stamped envelope with your proposal, indicating whether you want the entire proposal returned or just our answer. Your proposal will not receive a response without this SASE.

4. We do not accept electronic submissions.

5. Upon receipt of your proposal we will contact you with a rejection letter or a request for additional information or samples. (Hint: Wait four weeks for a response, and then send us an e-mail to inquire about your submission.)

6. Upon receipt of the requested material, we will contact you with a rejection or an offer of a contract.

7. If contract is signed, then a timetable will be set up for the completion and publication of your work.

8. We do not offer advances to any of our first-time authors.

9. We will accept proposals that have been sent to other publishers simultaneously. You must, however, indicate this on your initial proposal. If not, your proposal will be automatically rejected at the point this fact becomes known—no matter how far along we are in the process.

Categories: Religion—Spiritual

CONTACT: Andrew Yankech, Acquisitions Editor
Material: All
5559 W. Howard Street
Skokie IL 60077
Phone: 847-676-2282
Fax: 847-616-2287
E-mail: actapublications@aol.com

Absey & Co., Inc

We appreciate your interest in **Absey & Co.**, Inc. Please adhere to the following guidelines when submitting manuscripts. We accept mainstream fiction and nonfiction, poetry, educational books, especially those dealing in language arts. We do not accept e-mail submissions of manuscripts.

1.   Submit:

1. A brief cover letter

2. A chapter by chapter outline

3. An author's information sheet (please focus on relevant qualifications and previous publishing experience)

4. Two or three sample chapters

5. A self-addressed, stamped envelope
We prefer not to receive simultaneous submissions. Response time for manuscripts is six to nine months. Thank you again for your interest in Absey & Co., Inc.

Categories: Fiction—Nonfiction—Education—Poetry

CONTACT: Edward Wilson, Editor-in-Chief

23011 Northcrest
Spring, TX 77389
Phone: 888-412-2739
Fax: 281-251-4676
Website: www.absey.com

Adams-Blake

Adams-Blake Company is the parent of Adams-Blake Publishing. We have been publishing books since 1990 and been in the software business for the past TWENTY years. We are a technology driven company believe that the "future" in software is with server-side applications, not with downloadable software... which will occur when more people have fast connections.

We are a small company located in the Sacramento, California area. We pride ourselves on our superior customer service as well as the quality of our books, software, and consulting work.

CONSULTING AND PROGRAMMING

We've had a long history of providing programming services to state, local, and federal government agencies over the past ten years. We've worked directly with agencies via the CA Small Business Certification program or the CMAS infrastructure. We've also sub-contracted to many of the regional and national consulting firms that have contracts with the State.

In addition to State work, we've done a number of projects for local companies and the branches of national companies located in the Sacramento area.

PUBLISHING

Adams-Blake Publishing has published both trade (i.e. bookstore) and niche market books. However, we are getting away from doing trade titles and are doing more short run/high priced specialized publications targeted to corporations, law, medicine, engineering, computers, etc.

We are looking for industry how-to, training material, directories, policy and procedure manuals, etc. that run between 200-500 pages and which we can Docutech (huge Xerox machine with computer front-end), print in short quantities (100 copies) and sell for high prices: $89 - $150; or which would lend themselves to a database engine (not multi-media...too expensive to produce) and put on CD to sell for $399+.

We are NOT looking for things that are already out on the bookshelves. We WANT specialized products that we can sell via direct mail or with card deck advertising.

If you have written a manual, directory, training guide (our favorite type of publication) or anything that you think "your" specific industry sector might need, please let us know. You can send the ms. (by US MAIL, not e-mail) or just a query, whatever you prefer.

Our deal is simple. We do not pay an advance. We pay a straight 15% (on titles at or above $59) on all cash received. We pay our authors monthly. We do not hold a reserve against returns. Our contract is "author friendly." You do not need an agent, but we will be happy to work with agents.

We do not publish fiction, so please do not query us about it.

We urge you to NOT send a manuscript, but instead a query letter that details the subject matter of your book. There is no need to send a stamped, self-addressed envelope (SASE) as we will not reply unless we want to buy your property. (We get hundreds of offers each month and even just stuffing SASEs with a rejection slip takes resources we can better utilize elsewhere.)

SOFTWARE

If you are a software author and would be interested in us publishing your product, contact us with the details of your program. But do NOT send us the program itself as we will not run it unless we ask for it in advance. We are NOT interested in any games. We WOULD like to find software programs that are industry specific... for example... a chip manufacturing forecasting system for the semi-conductor industry, or perhaps a program used by doctors who do laser eye surgery. <u>Please do not call, visit, or fax. You can E-mail us a query.</u> **DO NOT E-MAIL US AN ATTACHED DOCUMENT OF ANY KIND. WE WILL NOT OPEN IT!**

Categories: Nonfiction—Software—Trade

CONTACT: Monica Blane, Senior Editor
8041 Sierra Street #321
Fair Oaks, CA 95628
Website: www.adams-blake.com

Addicus Books, Inc.

Addicus Books, Inc. is based in Omaha, Nebraska. An independent publisher, we publish ten quality nonfiction titles a year. Our focus is consumer health. We publish only nonfiction; we do not publish poetry or fiction.) We're seeking titles on: health, self-help, and psychology, however will also look at titles on, how-to, business, economics, investing, and books of regional interest — true crime, histories, and profiles.

Submission Guidelines

We prefer first a one-page query, outlining the nature of your work, who your market is and information about your background. If we're interested in taking a closer look at your book, we'll ask for a proposal.

Note: when querying electronically, send only a one-page email, giving an overview of your book and its market. Please do not send attachments unless invited to do so.

Book Proposals should include:
• A one-page overview of the book
• Two or three sample chapters
• A chapter-by-chapter outline
• Number of photos or illustrations
• Author's background/credentials
• Target completion date
• Market/audience information
• Word count/number of pages
Audience / Market information should include:
• Who is the audience?
• What is the market for your book and how many potential buyers?
• Who wants this book? Why do they want it? Why do they need it?
• Do you have specific marketing ideas in mind?
• Does your book help the reader?
• How will this book benefit the buyer? How will it help them?
• What need does it fill for your target market?
• What makes your book special?
• What makes your book different from other such books? (Are there other such books?)
• Does your book have more information? Is it more comprehensive, easier to use? What advantages does it have over the competition? Why will people buy it instead of something else? Note: Please do

a data base search for competing titles through Amazon.com—the largest online book store with more than one million titles in its data base. Report your findings in your proposal.
• Market niches/ Special markets (Please be thorough here.)
• List any special markets your book may have outside regular trade book channels (book stores).
• Could sales result from your contacts— associations, organizations, corporations, groups, hospitals, treatment centers, workshops, seminars or speaking engagements?
• Which magazines or professional/trade journals may review your book or print articles by you which in turn promotes the book?
• Do you have specific ideas for marketing your book?
• How willing are you to be active in marketing your book?

True Crime Submissions

We'd like a synopsis with a clear layout of the story line, how the plot unfolds. Also, give us a sense of the book's structure as well as its scope. Why does this book need to be written?

Note: We are seeking manuscripts that have good stories behind the crimes. Unfortunately, heinous crimes happen everyday, but crimes alone do not make a book. We're looking for twists and turns in the story behind the crime — a plot with rising action. And, we want the author to get us inside the minds of the main characters so we know what makes them tick. Characters' motivation must be established. As you can see, we're looking for many of the devices used in fiction. We also prefer fairly recent, high-profile cases. We publish high quality, trade paperbacks and do extensive promotion within the given region.

Submission of Text (for all genres)
• All materials should be clearly printed on white, 8 1/2 x 11 paper, double-spaced, with at least 1" margins on all sides.
• No more than 250-300 words per page.
• Do not staple, clip or otherwise bind pages in the submission.
• All submissions should include an SASE. Materials will not be returned unless accompanied by an SASE.

NOTE: Do not send by Certified Mail or Return Receipt Requested.
Categories: Nonfiction—Business—General Interest—Health—True Crime—Health Relationships

CONTACT: Acquisitions Editor, Addicus Books
Material: All
PO Box 45327
Omaha, NE 68145
Phone: 402 330-7493
Fax: 402 330-1707
E-mail: Addicusbks@aol.com

Aegis Publishing Group, Ltd.

We specialize in telecommunications books for non-technical end users such as small businesses (small office/home office) and entrepreneurs. We do not publish anything that does not fit this niche.

Categories: Nonfiction—Business—Technology—Small Business—Telecommunications

CONTACT: Robert Mastin, President
Material: All
796 Aquidneck Ave.
Newport RI 02842
Phone: 401-849-4200
Fax: 401-849-4231
E-mail: Aegis@aegisbooks.com
Website: www.aegisbooks.com

Aeronautical Publishers

Our Mission

"Our mission is to help people learn more about aviation and model

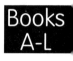

aviation through the written word. We want to help youth get started and enhance everyone's enjoyment of the hobby." Guidelines for #10 SASE with 2 first-class stamps.

Nonfiction: How-to and historical. Subjects include radio control, free flight, indoor models, electric flight, rubber powered flying models, micro radio control, aviation history, homebuilt aircraft, ultralights and hang gliders.

Recent Non-fiction Title: *Those First Magnificent Flying Machines.*

Tips: Our focus is on books of short to medium length that will serve the emerging needs of the hobby.

Categories: Nonfiction—Aviation—History—Hobbies

CONTACT: Michael A. Markowski, Publisher
Material: All
One Oakglade Circle
Hummelstown PA 17036-9525
Phone: 717-566-0468
Fax: 717-566-6423

Alaska Northwest Books

Please refer to Graphic Arts Center Publishing Company.

Alba House

Alba House is the North American publishing division of the Society of St. Paul, an International Roman Catholic Missionary Religious Congregation dedicated to spreading the Gospel message via the media of communications.

As such it welcomes for consideration manuscripts which contribute, from a Roman Catholic perspective, to the personal, intellectual and spiritual growth of individuals in the following area:

- Scripture
- Theology and the Church
- Saints–Their Lives and Teachings
- Spirituality and Prayer
- Religious Life
- Marriage and Family Life
- Liturgy and Homily Preparation
- Pastoral Concerns
- Religious Education
- Bereavement
- Moral and Ethical Concerns
- Philosophy
- Psychology
- No fiction
- No children's books
- No poetry
- No simultaneous submissions
- No personal testimonials or autobiographies

We prefer that manuscripts be submitted in full, typewritten and double-spaced along with a brief curriculum vitae of the author. Please include a self-addressed stamped envelope for the return of the manuscript if you wish to have it sent back to you in case it is not accepted.

If accepted for publication, we find it helpful if the work can then be submitted on floppy disk (IBM or Macintosh) from any of the more popular Word Processing programs: e.g., Word Perfect, Microsoft Word, Word for Windows, Wordstar, Ami Pro, etc.

We thank you for considering Alba House and look forward to reviewing your work with an eye to its possible publication. You can expect to hear from us within six weeks or less of our submission.

Categories: Nonfiction—Family—Marriage—Philosophy—Psychology—Religion—Spiritual

CONTACT: Father Edmund C. Lane S.S.P., Aquisitions Editor
Material: All

2187 Victory Blvd.
Staten Island NY 10314-6603
Phone: 718-761-0047
Fax: 718-761-0057

Algora Publishing
Imprint: Agathon Press

Algora Publishing is an independent publisher of serious nonfiction books featuring top American and international authors on questions of global scope. The perspectives our authors bring can help readers sharpen their own analyses of issues in the areas of international relations as well as human relations, politics, history, philosophy, sociology, economics, current events, mind & spirit, literature, and education and reference topics. No children's books, no fiction or poetry, self help, religious works or personal memoirs. Please visit our website at www.algora.com to familiarize yourself with the type of books that Algora publishes.

Proposals and manuscripts may now be submitted via our website, thus avboiding delays and inconvenience due to our email spamblocker. Go to www.algora.com, click on the yellow bar (upper right) "Submitting Your Manuscript" and familiarize yourself with our guidelines. Then click on "Submit Your Manuscript," fill in the blanks, and "browse" to select your computer file with the manuscript you wish to send us. Be sure to include your email address and descriptive information as listed below. Upload!

We also accept proposals by mail to the address below, with a stamped self-addressed return envelope/email address. We aim to respond with in 1-3 months.

Due to the large volume of inquiries we receive, Algora Publishing is unable to respond to queries by telephone and cannot answer or acknowledge receipt of query letters. Materials cannot be returned unless accompanied by a stamped, self-addressed envelope. Do not send original manuscripts, artwork, photographs or documents, as we cannot be responsible for their return.

First-time authors are welcome. We can sometimes offer guidance in the final shaping of a work, and we sometimes provide considerable editing, but we give preference to authors with professional qualifications, academic credentials, endorsements by established professionals in the field, and to works that reflect an extensive level of research.

Suitable manuscript length is generally 75,000-125,000 words.

What to submit:

• Include a one-page synopsis of the book (the subject matter and the approach taken), and an outline or table of contents, and a sample chapter or two

• Describe your qualifications for writing this book.

• Identify your intended audience: for what readers is the book written?

• Explain how your book is different from others on related topics. What unmet need does your book fill?

• Indicate how your position, circumstances, skills, abilities, or commitments would help to market the book.

Categories: Nonfiction—Business—Culture—Economics—Government—History—Philosophy—Politics—Relationships—Society

CONTACT: Martin DeMers, Editor
Material: All
222 Riverside Dr., 16th Floor
New York NY 10025-6809
Phone: 212-678-0232
Fax: 212-666-3682
E-mail: Editors@algora.com
Website: www.algora.com

Allworth Press

Manuscript Submission Guidelines

Allworth Press publishes business and self-help books for artists, designers, photographers, film and performing artists. The press also publishes classic and contemporary critical writing on art and graphic design.

Please review our catalog of books on our Web site, which should give you an idea of the kind of titles we are accustomed to publishing. We do not publish picture books, fiction, poetry, or full-color books.

We prefer to see a one- or two-page outline of a proposed book, even if the book has already been written. The outline should give a chapter-by-chapter summary of the book's contents. It should also indicate the author's background, the intended audience for the book, any books that might be considered competitive, and why this book will compete successfully with those books. If the book has been written, please include two sample chapters with the outline.

Categories: Nonfiction—Arts—Drama—Film/Video—Graphics—Music—Photography—Theatre

CONTACT: Nicole Potter-Talliy, Senior Editor
Material: All
10 East 23rd Street, Ste. 510
New York, NY 10010
Phone: 212-777-8395
Fax: 212-777-8395
E-mail: PUB@allworth.com
Website: allworth.com

Alpine Publications

If you excel in breeding, training or other aspects of dog or horse care, you may have something to write about and there is an audience thirsty for your knowledge. If you are searching for a publisher, let us help you decide whether Alpine Publications is right for your book.

We Offer:
As a small, specialized publisher concentrating on nonfiction animal books, you can count on us for:
• Personalized attention during both writing and production stages
• Targeted, specialized marketing plan
• Quality production resulting in a book you can take pride in
• Guidance and supervision that leads to award winning titles whether you are a professional author or writing your first book
We Are Interested In:
• Training or behavior books with a unique approach
• Semi-technical subjects for professionals or breeders
• Animal stories for youth.
We Favor These Approaches:
• Subjects covered in depth and well documented
• An unbiased, well-researched presentation of facts and opinions
• Inclusion of numerous photos or illustrations
• Breed books.
We Are Not Interested In:
• Fiction
• Books on small pets, fish, birds, or reptiles
• Books of poetry
• Photographic essays
We Create These Types Of Products:
• Hardbound books in various formats
• Trade paperbacks
• Workbooks
• Video or audio tapes
Our Audiences Are:
• Purebred owners, breeders, trainers, exhibitors
• Pet owners
• Students

We Sell Via These Channels:
• Direct to the consumer through magazine advertisements and direct mail
• Book, pet, tack and specialty retail stores
• Book and pet supply wholesalers in the U.S., Canada, Europe, Scandinavia, Britain, Australia, and other foreign markets
Should You Query First?
Yes, queries with an outline are encouraged. Queries are accepted by mail and by email to alpinepubl@aol.com
With All Submissions Include:
• Outline and up to three complete sample chapters
• Your credentials for doing this book
• Who is the intended audience?
• What your work will offer that audience
• What other books are available on the subject
• Why your work is unique
Complete manuscripts are also accepted. Specify if manuscript is being submitted simultaneously to other publishers. Submit only by mail; email submissions will not be accepted
What Writing Style Should You Use?
Use *The Chicago Manual of Style* (13th Edition).
Manuscript Requirements:
• Double-spaced on 8 1/2 x 11 white paper with margins of at least one inch on all sides pages numbered consecutively
• Photocopies are accepted
• Average length is 45,000 to 80,000 words
Photographs and Art
• Send samples only with initial query
Proper Submission Speeds Response Time
• Query first
• Include all materials mentioned above
• Enclose an SASE or adequate postage if you want the manuscript returned. Allow 12 weeks for a reply
Categories: Nonfiction—Animals

CONTACT: Betty McKinney, Publisher
Material: All
38262 Linman Rd
Crawford, CO 81415
Phone: 970-921-5005
E-mail: alpinepubl@aol.com

Alyson Publications, Inc.

QUERY SUBMISSIONS

Alyson Publications is the leading publisher of books by, for, and about lesbians, gay men, and bisexuals from all economic and social segments of society and of all ages, from children to adults. In fiction and nonfiction format, Alyson books explore the political, legal, financial, medical, spiritual, social, and sexual aspects of gay, lesbian, and bisexual life and the contributions to and experiences in society of our community.

We are happy to consider book queries. We only consider solicited manuscripts. Please note the following before submitting a query:

INQUIRY: Please send a query letter detailing your novel's plot or your nonfiction idea. Give a summary of the book, a chapter outline if you have it, approximately how many words, and what qualifies you to write this particular book. We do NOT want to see sample chapters at this stage.

MANUSCRIPT: Unsolicited manuscripts will not be considered and will be returned if accompanied by appropriate SASE. They will be destroyed if not accompanied by appropriate SASE.

OTHER: Nonfiction should be written in a popular (i.e., nonacademic) style. We do not consider individual short stories or poetry. At this time, we do not have a service referring individual short stories to any anthologies we will be publishing. We prefer manuscript length to be around 100,000 words. If you would like to see what Alyson has previously published, our books are available at all gay and lesbian bookstores as well as larger chains.

Books
A-L

DECISION TIME: We try to give serious consideration to each query we receive. Each query mill be reviewed and a response sent to you within one month of its receipt. Please do not call to check on the status of your submission.

Categories: Fiction—Nonfiction—Alternate Life-style—Gay/Lesbian

CONTACT: Acquisitions Editor
Material: All
PO Box 4371
Los Angeles CA 90078-4371
Phone: 213-871-1225
Fax: 213-467-6805
E-mail: alyson@advocate.com
Website: www.advocate.com

American Book Publishing

American Book Publishing's mission is to support, document, and disseminate, through book publication, great works and teachings of talented authors, scholars, and professionals. We publish both nonfiction and wholesome fiction books. We prefer books with an identifiable target market that has a reachable audience. We do not publish cookbooks, coffee table books, poetry, erotica, hate or books with obscenities or disrespectful use of the names of deity, or children's books with color illustrations.

We review unsolicited manuscripts within 30 days of submission, when submitted by e-mail to acqeditor@american-book.com when accompanied by answers to our submission questionnaire (ask info@american-book.com for that info and then send it with the manuscript as an attachment to e-mail. (No snail mail submissions).

We favor proposals that best fit the imprints of American Book Publishing. These imprints are divided into five distinct divisions, each

focusing on a particular genres. American Book Classics, American University & Colleges Press, American Book Business Press, Millennial Mind Publishing, and Bedside Books.

For more information please read our web site at www.american-book.com we keep it updated and have daily book publishing news and about a hundred articles for writers about publishing.

Categories: Fiction—Nonfiction

CONTACT: Submissions Editor
Material: All
E-mail: acqeditor@american-book.com
Website: www.american-book.com

American Correctional Association (ACA) Book Publishing

Publishing With ACA

Enhance Your Contribution to the Field of Corrections by Publishing Your Book with the American Correctional Association For more than 135 years, the American Correctional Association has been serving the needs of corrections professionals by providing them with the resources, support, and services they need to excel in the fields of corrections and criminal justice.

Whether you come from professional work in a prison, jail, probation, parole, juvenile, or from a counseling background, our members need your

expertise. We are seeking submissions on topics that would enhance and contribute to the field of corrections.

What better way to contribute your knowledge, research, and insight to this dynamic field than by authoring a publication which can be used by your colleagues.

Our current titles discuss the following topics:
- Anger Management
- Boot Camps
- Law/Legal Issues
- Career Development
- Management Issues
- Cognitive Behavioral Therapy
- Community Corrections
- Restorative Justice
- Counseling
- Security
- Facility Design
- Sex Offenders
- Female Offenders
- Special Needs Offenders
- Gangs
- Staff Training and Education
- Health Care
- Substance Abuse
- History Suicide
- Issues, Policy, and Research
- Women Working in Corrections
- Jails
- Youthful Offenders

Where Do I Start?

If you are interested in publishing a book with the American Correctional Association, please start by completing the Author Proposal Form (see our website). *Send the completed form to:*

Alice Heiserman, Manager of Publications and Research
American Correctional Association
4380 Forbes Boulevard
Lanham, MD 20706-4322
Phone 301-918-1894; Fax 301-918-1886
e-mail: aliceh@aca.org

We are seeking practical, how-to books based on professional experience. Our audience includes correctional practitioners. We also have texts suitable for college students taking courses in corrections, criminal justice and social work. If your proposal appears to have potential for inclusion in our publishing program, we will ask you to submit a full proposal. A full proposal includes an outline and a summary plus one or two sample chapters. You may submit a full proposal along with your Author Proposal Form. Full manuscripts also may be submitted.

Information About Our Authors

Many of our authors are first-time writers. Others have been published with major publishing houses but choose to work with ACA because of the personal attention we provide. Other authors choose ACA because they see an opportunity to make a significant contribution to corrections through our books.

We do not publish fiction, poetry or materials from offenders.

The Review Process

Your proposal will be reviewed by the core management of ACA. It also will be sent out for a blind review to your peers for their opinion. If the submission is deemed to have merit, and market potential, we then will ask you to submit your entire manuscript for review. At this point, you will need to submit one paper copy of the full manuscript plus an electronic copy in WordPerfect or Microsoft Word format. The review process usually takes four months.

As a result of the review process, ACA may make suggestions for modification of the original manuscript, or we may accept it as is. If you agree to make the revisions or changes, we will review your changes to see if they meet the recommendations of the reviewers. If they do, ACA will extend a contract. Once we have your signed contract and your manuscript, we can begin the processes of editing and typesetting your manuscript into a book. This stage generally takes between four and seven months.

The ACA Publishing Team

Our editorial department will review your manuscript to ensure that it meets our standards for clarity, punctuation, grammar, and style. We work closely with our authors to insure our books are readable and look inviting. During this time, we select a title and in conjunction with our graphics team, design the cover and interior pages.

Throughout this process, the marketing department will meet to discuss the format, price, and marketing strategies for your book. We will ask you to complete an Author Questionnaire. This will give us additional information on how and where to market your book. Marketing will include announcements to the criminal justice media, direct mailings, exposure at annual and regional ACA meetings, and at other criminal justice conferences and meetings. We are happy to provide you with materials to self-promote your book.

Additionally, we will look for partnerships outside the organization as ways to promote your book. These may include bulk sales to bookstores or other organizations that wish to distribute your title. We look forward to your active participation in the promotion of your book.

The American Correctional Association also publishes *Corrections Today* and *Corrections Compendium* magazines. Refer to the magazine section of this directory, for their writer's guidelines.

Categories: Crime—Disabilities—Juveniles—Psychology—Self Help—Textbooks—Corrections—Criminal Justice—Sociology—Women's Issues

CONTACT: Alice Heiserman, Manager
Material: Book submissions
CONTACT: Susan Clayton, Editor, Corrections Today and Corrections Compendium
Material: Magazine submissions
ACA Book Publishing
4380 Forbes Boulevard
Lanham MD 20706-4322
Phone: 301-918-1894
Fax: 301-918-1886
E-mail: aliceh@aca.org
Website: www.aca.org

American Literary Press
Noble House

Typed or laser printed, unbound 8.5"x11" pages, upper and lower case letters. Title page should include authors name, address, work and phone numbers with complete page count. Forwarding a 2-3 paragraph synopsis of your manuscript would be helpful to our staff. Please be aware that we will keep your work in our files for three months only.

Categories: Fiction—Adventure—Children—Cooking—Feminism—Health—History—Horror—Juvenile—New Age—Poetry—Religion—Romance—Science Fiction—Short Stories—Sports/Recreation—Western—Women's Fiction—Young Adult—Humor

CONTACT: Acquisitions Editor

Material: All
8019 Belair Rd. Ste. 10
Baltimore MD 21236
Phone: 410-882-7700
Fax: 410-882-7703
E-mail: amerlit@americanliterarypress.com

The Americas Group

The Americas Group has no specific guidelines for writers submitting manuscripts for possible publication. While not wishing to restrict writers as to style or format, it does not accept any material to review outside of the field of public policy or that exceeds 350 pages. It also always ask authors to identify the specific audience they think will not only be interested in their writing, but are likely to spend money to buy and own an authors work.

Categories: Business—Government—Politics

CONTACT: Godfrey Harris, Director
Material: All
9200 Sunset Blvd., Ste 404
Los Angeles CA 90069-3506
Phone: 310 278 8037
Fax: 310 271 3649
E-mail: hrmg@aol.com
Website: www.americasgroup.com

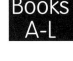

AMG Publishers

Before an actual book proposal is submitted, I would like to see, via e-mail a query letter for your manuscript.

This letter should:
• Be one page in length, no longer
• Include a brief, tantalizing description of the book that you propose
• State who and how large the market or audience is for your book-be specific
• Give the proposed page count of your book
• Include a few words about yourself, the author-why you are expertly qualified to write the book.

Then, at that point, I can inform you if your proposed book fits into our current publishing plan. If your query letter indicates a possible fit with AMG Publisher's focus, we will then ask you to submit an actual book proposal following the guidelines that I will then send you.

Please note:

AMG Publisher's focus is on books that:
1. Help the reader get into the Bible, directly or indirectly.
2. Facilitate confrontation and interaction with Scripture toward a positive change in thought or action.
3. Give a hunger to studying, understanding, and applying Scripture.
4. Encourage and facilitate one's personal growth in such areas as personal devotion and a skillful use of the Bible.

We have a broad interest in biblically oriented books, including Biblical Reference, Applied Theology and Apologetics, Christian Ministry, Bible Study Books, Christian Living, Women/Men/Family Issues, Single/Divorce Issues, Devotionals, Inspirational, Prayer, Contemporary Issues, and so on.

Our interests, though, do not include Fiction, Poetry, Children/Youth books, Personal-experience stories, and Autobiographical stories.

Categories: Nonfiction—Religion—Spiritual

CONTACT: Dan Penwell, Director of Product Development/ Acquisitions
Material: All
6815 Shallowford Rd.
Chattanooga TN 37421-1755
Phone: 423-894-6060

Amherst Media

Amherst Media is always looking for photographers interested in sharing their vision and experience with others. If you feel that there is a book inside of you, please contact us.

Keep in mind that Amherst Media only publishes instructional books on photography, but don't let that discourage you if you're interested in seeing your images in print. Our books are distributed across the globe and have been translated into three different languages. Most Amherst Media titles run up to 128 pages, with 15,000 to 30,000 words and anywhere from 25 to 300 images.

Please send an outline, small sample of your photographic work and contact information.

Categories: Photography

CONTACT: Submissions Department
Material: All
Amherst Media, Inc.
155 Rano St., Ste. 300
Buffalo, NY 14207
Phone: 716-874-4450
Fax: 716-874-4508
E-mail: submissions@amherstmedia.com.
Website: www.amherstmedia.com

Anchorage Press Plays, Inc.
International Agency of Plays for Young People

Anchorage Press Plays, Inc. (formerly Anchorage Press) publishes theatrical plays for a youth and family audience. Submissions should be appropriate in subject, theme and language to a universal norm of juveniles and adolescents: fantasy, fable, adventure, quest, journey, unfolding maturity, self discovery, etc.

1) Manuscripts must be typed or computer printed,

2) Submitted by mail with a SASE adequate for the postage return of the manuscript. No email or fax submissions accepted.

3) Please send play script only after it has gone through testing of productions and rewrites. We cannot accept play scripts for consideration that have not been produced.

4) Adaptations of books beloved by young people require proof of authorization to create a dramatic adaptation, and permission to submit for publication.

Several months are required for response to a submission.

Creative Education/Theatrical text books: Anchorage publishes a limited number of text books relating to theatrical design, production, education for the youth drama teaching field and producing plays.

Send one page inquiry describing text proposal, plus biographical/professional credentials relating to the specialty of the text. Initial inquiry in this short format is accepted by mail or email.

Categories: Fiction—Nonfiction—Arts—Children—Drama—Juvenile—Theatre

CONTACT: Submissions Editor
Material: All
617 Baxter Ave
Louisville KY 40204-1105
Phone: 502-583-2288
E-mail: applays@bellsouth.net (inquiries only)
Website: www.applays.com

Angel Bea Publishing

Mission Statement: Angel Bea Publishing produces top-quality books featuring true stories about real animals. Through full color illustrations and factual text Angel Bea delivers compelling information with an artistic flare.

Angel Bea is only interested in nonfiction for ages 8-12.

Categories: Nonfiction—Animals—Children—Christian Interests—Short Stories

CONTACT: Kat Shehata, Publisher
Material: All
9504 Bainbrook Court
Cincinnati, OH 45249
Phone: 513-683-8592
Fax: 513-683-9523
Website: www.angelbea.com

Anhinga Press

Anhinga Press publishes full-length volumes of poetry. For thirty years we have sought out the best writing available and brought it to the public in attractive and reasonably-priced editions. The Anhinga Prize for Poetry contest, which runs from February 15th through May 1st, draws about six hundred entries each year from around the world.

Interested in publishing your work with Anhinga? The best place to start may be the Contest page mentioned above; entries are blind-judged, which (at least in theory) puts relatively unknown and beginning poets on an equal footing with those who have been publishing their work for years. For non-contest entries, please first visit our GUIDELINES page.

Anhinga Press publishes only full-length collections of poetry (usually 60-80 pages), no individual poems or chapbooks. We are always open to reading manuscripts. There is nothing that we are inherently prejudiced toward or against; we are looking for the best poetry out there.

However, for the sake of your peace of mind (and perhaps your sanity), you should do some homework first. Start by reading some of the poems from the books here on our Web site to see if your work is comparable in quality, and perhaps style, to some of the poetry we have published. Read the biographical and other notes about each poet, and compare that information with your own. We are probably not a press for beginners (in the sense of "never had any poetry published before," regardless of how long you may have been writing it), for subjects of local or limited interest, or for private and/or overly sentimental work.

You should know that the odds are not good. We usually publish five books a year:

one is the winner of the Anhinga Prize for Poetry;

one is a volume of the Florida Poetry Series; and

For this reason, we reject far, far more unsolicited manuscripts than we accept. In fact, we reject about 98% of the work that is submitted to us.

If all of these dire warnings have not daunted your spirit, and if after looking at some of the poems on our Web site, you think that Anhinga Press might be interested in your manuscript, please send us a query letter and a ten-page sample (not the full manuscript!). No e-mail samples please.

CONTACT: Submission Editor
Material: All
PO Box 10595
Tallahasse, FL 32302
Phone: 850-442-1408
Fax: 850-442-6323
E-mail: info@anhinga.org (no submissions)
Website: www.anhinga.org

Apage4You Book Publishing

We accept all submissions (except those in the children's genre) without reading fees. Our primary interest is in Non-Fiction, Controversial and religious books, although each manuscript is carefully reviewed and considered for mainstream publication.

Additionally, unlike most other publishers, we also offer subsidy, self and e-book publication.

Many have inquired of Apage4You Book Publishing which genres have the best chance of receiving mainstream publication. *While each and every manuscript submitted is considered, we have extreme interest in the following:*

- Non-Fiction
- Fiction
- Novels
- Religious
- Political
- Lifestyle
- Historic
- Controversial
- Current Events

Reason being, mainstream publication is usually reserved for works appealing to a wide market. Works with limited public appeal are rarely accepted for mainstream publication, while many are offered alternative publishing options.

NOTE: submissions in the children's genre will not be accepted for mainstream publication until further notice. Children's books will however be evaluated for subsidy, self and e-book publishing if requested.

Submit Your Manuscript to Apage4You Book Publishing.

We've made it very easy to get you started. Just follow the instructions below and you'll be well on your way to seeing your book in print.

Step by Step Instructions:

1. Make certain your work is complete, fully edited, and ready for publication

2. Submit your manuscript for evaluation .

STEP ONE - Submit your Manuscript/Standard Submission FREE

Use your book title in subject line

1. Do NOT embed photos within your manuscript - Submit each photo as a separate file and advise page, paragraph and line where photo should appear.

2. Submit Manuscript as an attachment in RTF or Microsoft Word, or if unable to provide your manuscript as an attached file using your e-mail system, you may:

    a. Copy and paste the entire document into the body of your e-mail, and e-mail to acquisitions@apage4youpublishing.com

    -or-

    b. Send Complete Manuscript together with photos, graphs, illustrations, etc (remember do not embed in manuscript) by postal service to the address below.

Categories: Fiction—Nonfiction—History—Lifestyle—Religion

CONTACT: Manuscript Submissions
Material: All
2025 Balla Way, Ste 200
Grand Prairie TX 75051-3907
E-mail: info@apage4youpublishing.com
Website: www.apage4youpublishing.com

Arbenteuer Books

Please refer to Black Forest Press.

Arden Press, Inc.

Arden Press publishes nonfiction books, including women's titles (women's history, biography, general guides), popular how-to books, directories, guides, and film titles. We sell primarily to bookstores and to public and academic libraries. Many of our titles are adopted as texts for college courses. We do not publish fiction, poetry, or personal memoirs.

We prefer to receive manuscript proposals rather than complete manuscripts. If we believe that your project might fit our publication profile, we will request the manuscript.

What To Include In Your Manuscript Proposal

1.) Tentative Title: A descriptive title for the purpose of identifying the particular manuscript.

2.) Scope/Purpose: Describe in one paragraph the intended purpose of the book, the scope of coverage, and primary and secondary audience.

3.) Outline: A preliminary outline should show all chapters and key subsections. The outline should be accompanied by written chapter summaries that explain the main theme and scope of each chapter.

4.) Methodology & Presentation: Summarize the search plan that is to be used in locating necessary data. List the types of sources to be consulted. Indicate the need for illustrations, maps, appendixes, indexes, etc.

5.) Sample Section: A sample chapter or section in preliminary form should be submitted to demonstrate the organization, content, writing style, and documentation to be used.

6.) Similar or Related Works: Identify books on the same topic or on similar or related topics. Explain the need for the proposed book and how it will fill a specific gap in coverage or take a unique approach to the subject.

Thank you for your interest in Arden Press.

Categories: Nonfiction—Biography—Film/Video—General Interest—History—Reference—Women's Issues—College Course Adoptions

CONTACT: Susan Conley, Publisher/Editor
Material: All
PO Box 418
Denver CO 80201
Phone: 303-697-6766
Fax: 303-697-3443

Art Direction Book Company, Inc.

Want to see a Table of Contents and a chapter; not an introduction. Please list your various positions.

Categories: Arts—Advertising Art

CONTACT: Don Barron, Publisher
Material: Ad Art
456 Glenbrook Rd.
Glenbrook CT 06906
Phone: 203-353-1441
Fax: 203-353-1371

Arte Público Press
The University of Houston

Arte Público Press, affiliated with the University of Houston, specializes in publishing contemporary novels, short stories, poetry, and drama based on U.S. Hispanic, Cuban American, Mexican American, Puerto Rican, and other themes and cultural issues. Arte Público also is interested in reference works, non-fiction studies, especially of Hispanic civil rights, women's issues and history.

Manuscripts, queries, synopses, outlines, proposals, introductory chapters, etc. are accepted in either English or Spanish; the majority of our publications are in English. All submissions must be typed, double-spaced, and include a self-addressed, stamped envelope (SASE) to return those not selected for publication. Address all submissions to: Arte Público Press, SUBMISSIONS, University of Houston, 452 Cullen Performance Hall Houston, Texas, 77204-2004. *Manuscripts not accompanied by an appropriately sized SASE will not be returned. Queries and proposals take 2-4 months and manuscripts take 3-6 months to respond. We are NOT responsible for any damages or loss of any manuscript.*

Please be advised that we do NOT accept, review or respond to any submissions via Internet. Please take time to familiarize yourself with our current and previous titles, as well as specialized fields, and send only the material relevant to our publishing needs. Due to the overwhelming amount of submissions we get each year, we would advise that the writer take time to distinguish whether or not his/her work is appropriate for APP so that response time is diminished. We recommend that writers include a one-page cover letter specifying relevant information and brief description of the manuscript, and an introductory sample of the manuscript instead of sending the manuscript in its entirety first. We do not accept digital files of the work until it has been accepted for publication. For further information of our previous publications, please visit our website.

Accepted manuscripts should be accompanied by a digital file of the work on disk. (Microsoft Word v.6.0 or later, for Macintosh or Windows.)

Piñata Books

Piñata Books is Arte Público Press' imprint for children's and young adult literature. It seeks to authentically and realistically portray themes, characters, and customs unique to U.S. Hispanic culture. Submissions and manuscript formalities are the same as for Arte Público Press.

Illustrators

Guidelines for illustration submissions, for the most part, remain the same as stipulated above for Arte Público Press' and Piñata Books with the following exceptions: we will not return any submissions; so please do **NOT** send originals. All artworks, photos, slides, etc. will be kept in separate illustrator files for future consideration. These files may be updated by submitting new art samples. Our Managing Editor will contact you once it is determined that your work is suitable for our publishing needs; so please be sure to include your current address, phone number(s) and e-mail address.

Recovering the U.S. Hispanic Literary Heritage

The Recovering the U.S. Hispanic Literary Heritage series publishes recovered literature written by Hispanics between the colonial period and 1960 in the geographic area that has become the United States. For further details, contact Dr. Nicolás Kanellos, Director, at this address.

Categories: Fiction—Nonfiction—Hispanic—Juvenile—Literature—Multicultural—Women's Issues—Young Adult

CONTACT: Marina Tristán, Assistant Director
Material: All
University of Houston
452 Cullen Performance
Houston, TX 77204-2004
Phone: 713-743-2846
Fax: 713-743-3080
E-mail: submapp@mail.uh.edu
Website: www.artepublicopress.com

Aslan Publishing

Our Mission

Aslan Publishing offers readers a window to the soul via well-crafted and practical self-help books, inspirational books, and modern day parables. Our mission is to publish books that uplift one's mind, body, and spirit.

Living one's spirituality in business, relationships, and personal growth is the underlying purpose of our publishing company, and the meaning behind our name Aslan Publishing. We see the word "Aslan" as a metaphor for living spiritually in a physical world.

Aslan means "lion" in several Middle Eastern languages. The most famous "Aslan" is a lion in *The Chronicles of Narnia* by C. S. Lewis. In these stories, Aslan is the Messiah, the One who appears at critical points in the story in order to point human beings in the right direction. Aslan doesn't preach, he acts. His actions are an inherent expression of who he is.

We point the way toward joyful, satisfying and healthy relationships with oneself and with others. Our purpose is to make a difference in our reader's everyday lives.

Submit a query of 1-3 pages for any book related to our mission statement including; self-help; relationship; business-related, humor, autobiographical and so on. No full proposals only query letters.

We are not interested in text books, poetry books, or channeled books. Include your full name, mailing address, email address, and phone numbers and bio information.

Please Do Not send query letters via email. Please include a letter-sized, self-addressed stamped return envelope.

Categories: Nonfiction

CONTACT: Barbara Q. Levine, Publisher
Material: All
2490 Black Rock Turnpike, #342Q
Fairfield CT 06825
E-mail: barbara@aslanpublishing.com (no submissions)
Website: www.aslanpublishing.com

Aspect

Please refer to Time Warner Book Group.

ATHENEUM
BOOKS FOR YOUNG READERS

Atheneum Books

Atheneum Books publishes original hardcover trade books for children from pre-school age through young adult. Our list includes picture books, chapter books, mysteries, science fiction and fantasy, and middle grade young adult fiction and nonfiction. The style and subject matter of the books we publish is almost unlimited. We do not, however, publish textbooks, coloring or activity books, greeting cards, magazines or pamphlets or religious publications. Anne Schwartz Books and Richard Jackson Books is a highly selective line of books that are part of the Atheneum imprint. The lists of Charles Scribner's Sons Books for Young Readers have been folded into the Atheneum program.

General Submission Guidelines

Atheneum accepts only letters of inquiry describing your work, regardless of length or type (picture books, novels, non-fiction). Should the work seem to be in line with our current publishing needs, we will then request the complete picture book manuscripts or outlines and sample chapters of longer works.

With your submission, you may also wish to include a brief resume of your previous publishing credits.

Please allow twelve weeks for your material to be considered. Although it often takes less time, it can take even longer than we would like because of the many thousands of submissions we receive and because every submission is carefully considered.

Picture Book Submissions

Atheneum publishes 15-20 picture books each year. You may include illustrations with your manuscript submission. It is the prerogative of the publisher to choose illustrators. If you yourself are a professional artist, you might wish to send samples (no larger than 8½"x11") to our art director, Ann Bobco. Drop-off portfolios are accepted only on Thursdays at 10 a.m. and will be left at the reception desk for pick up at noon. No manuscripts will be read or considered at this time.

Questions frequently asked:

"What are you looking for?"

The most common answer each editor gives to this question is simply, "Nothing specific—just good writing." Atheneum puts less emphasis on particular trends, fads and gimmicks and more on quality of craftsmanship— fine writing and artwork. This and originality are the most important things we look for in a manuscript.

"Why did you turn my manuscript down?"

Although it is easy to understand a writer's desire for a critique of his work, the constant heavy influx of submissions makes it impossible to offer evaluations of work that has been declined. Form rejection letters are not meant as an insult, but simply are the only way publishers can handle the number of submissions received. A writer can expect feed-back on his work by taking one of the many excellent writing courses offered by local colleges and universities—some of them specifically geared to children's books. Another source of evaluation can be found in oining a local writers group. Such groups commonly critique members' work in progress. THE SUBJECT GUIDE TO BOOKS IN PRINT by R.R. Bowker Company also lists helpful books on writing for children and the Children's Book Council (568 BROADWAY, NEW YORK NY 10003) has a pamphlet on the subject available on request. But perhaps the simplest and cheapest way of finding out what publishers look for is to go to your local public or school library and read.

Categories: Fiction—Nonfiction—Children—Juvenile—Literature—Teen—Young Adult

CONTACT: Ginee Seo, Editorial Director
Material: Any not assigned below
CONTACT: Anne Schwartz, V.P., Editorial Director
Material: Anne Schwartz Books
CONTACT: Richard Jackson, Editor
Material: Richard Jackson Books
CONTACT: Caitlyn Dlouhy, Executive Editor.
Material: All other material
1230 Avenue of the Americas
New York NY 10020
Phone: 212-698-2715
Fax: 212-698-2796

ATL Press
Science Technology

1. We are interested in many science and non-fiction areas, including astronomy, biochemistry, biomedicine, biotechnology, chemistry, computers, earth science, foods, medicine, nutraceuticals, pharmaceuticals and polymers. We publish monographs, edited volumes and conference proceedings. However, ATL Press also welcomes submissions on other topics, including fiction titles. Our interests include non-book products, such as software, CDs, audiovisual materials, etc. Your submission will be particularly appealing to us, if it is unique or of special topical interest. Examples of such titles include leading edge research results, topics with broad public appeal, and areas of major scientific discoveries with notable impact on society.

2. Before you send us the completed manuscript or work, we prefer to receive an introductory letter that describes your proposed project, together with an outline, estimated length, expected completion date, nature (that is, line drawings, color, B&W photos, etc.) and number of any illustrations, and, if available, perhaps a few sample chapters (please include a SASE with your submission).

3. A very essential point to consider in your submission is the ultimate customer: who are your target readers, why should they be interested in your book, what makes your book unique, which other titles do you know of on your topic, and how does your book differ from these? A visit to one of the major bookstores or libraries in your neighborhood may help you answer some of these questions, if you look up the section that is most relevant to your topic.

4. Can you suggest individuals who can review and comment on your manuscript? If so, please provide a list with the relevant contact information.

5. Please tell us also about yourself: your educational background, professional credentials, any achievements, awards, etc. (a resume and a list of publications—if applicable—are acceptable).

6. We generally accept only manuscripts prepared with word processing software. Please indicate in your submission the word processor used, and the platform (PC or Mac). Detailed information on submitting camera-ready manuscripts is available upon request.

7. Last, and not least: if you have not embarked on this venture yet, be prepared to spend a substantial amount of time and effort. At the same time, it can be an extremely enjoyable undertaking. On our part, we work very closely with our authors to produce and market their projects.

Categories: Business—Computers—Juvenile—Science—Technology

CONTACT: Editorial Office
Material: All
PO Box 4563 T Stn.
Shrewsbury MA 01545
Website: www.atlpress.com

Avalon Books

Under its Avalon Books imprint, Thomas Bouregy & Co., Inc. publishes hardcover secular romances, mysteries, and westerns for the library market. Our books are wholesome adult ficiton, suitable for family reading. There is no graphic or premarital sex in any of our novels; kisses and embraces are as far as our characters go. It is the author's responsibility to heighten the romantic atmosphere by developing love scenes with tenderness and emotion. There is never any profanity in any of our books.

We publish sixty books a year in bimonthly cycles of ten. A cycle consists of: four contemporary romances, two historical romances, two mysteries, and two westerns. The mysteries and contemporary romances are all set in the present day; all the westerns are historical. Books range in length from a minimum of 45,000 words to a maximum of 60,000 words (usually about 160 to 210 manuscript pages.) However, if the manuscript is exceptional, we will accept somewhat larger books.

Romances

We do not want old-fashioned, predictable, formulaic books. We are looking for contemporary characters, fresh plots, and story lines. Supporting characters and subplots should be interesting and realistic, and they should add an extra and interesting dimension to the book.

Heroines: She should be an independent young woman with an interesting profession or career. She is equal to the stresses of today's world and can take care of herself, yet she remains feminine and loyal to traditional values; when he comes along, the man she loves will take priority in her life, just as she will be a priority in his.

Heroes: He should be warm, likable, realistic, sympathetic, and understanding. He should treat the heroine as an equal. With respect for her intelligence and individuality. The rude, overbearing, patronizing, egotistical, brooding, macho men are not welcome in our romances; they make very poor role models for husbands—and men—in today's world.

Historical Romances

The manuscripts should be between 50,000 and 70,000 words. Time period can range from medieval times to World War I. No time travel romances. Period, place and cultural events are vital to creating a historical feel. The historical romances will maintain the high level of reading expected by our readers.

Mysteries

The element of suspense is very important, but it is equally important to have a tight, well-researched, believable story line. Avoid contrived, predictable, mechanical plots and clichés. We are now looking for longer (50,000 to 70,000 words), gritty, more mainstream mysteries. Murders, of course, is often a necessary part of a mystery, but avoid gory descriptions. Sexual violence of any kind is not acceptable. The protagonists should not be drinkers, although it is acceptable if the villains drink. The occasional profanity is fine as well.

Westerns

All westerns are historical novels, and it is important that they be placed in the past and that the background be carefully researched. Avoid using words and phrases that were not part of the language at the time your western is set. Plots should be suspenseful and action-packed, but vivid descriptions of the gory details of violence should be avoided.

It is fine to you the occasional "hell" or "damn", but limit the use of profanity. Though it is important for flavor and authenticity to use some westernisms in dialogue ("pardner" and the dropping of the final "g" in present particles, for example), overuse of the dialect is to be avoided; it slows down the reader's pace and, as a result, the narrative pace too. The use of alcohol is allowed, but should not be overdone.

General Submission Guidelines

You must include with you submission:
• Query letter addressed to: The Editors (no specific editor's name is required)
• Synopsis (2-3 pgs.)
• First three chapters
• Self-Addressed, Stamped Envelope

S.A.S.E. (See requirements below*) Or note in your query letter that you do not want the partial returned.

Keep in mind, we do accept unagented work and multiple submissions. Multiple submissions are when authors send their manuscript to multiple publishing houses. Please indicate if it is a multiple submission in your query letter.

You should hear back from us anywhere between two weeks and a month from when we receive your submission. If we think that your novel may be suitable for our list, we will contact you and request that you submit the entire manuscript. After we receive your manuscript, the response time is typically 4- 6 months.

• The envelope must be large enough for the partial, with sufficient postage for its weight. Only first class and priority stamps allowed. No media mail, Fed Ex, or metered mail. Also, we cannot return partials or manuscripts to areas outside the U.S. No international Reply Coupons, please, except for letter-sized SASE's. Any material that does not meet these requirements will be recycled.

Categories: Fiction—Mystery—Romance—Western

CONTACT: The Editors
Material: All
Thomas Bouregy & Co. Inc.
160 Madison Ave.
New York, NY 10016
Phone: 212-598-0222
Fax: 212-979-1862
E-mail: editorial@avalonbooks.com
Website: www.avalonbooks.com

B. Klein Publications

Formal guidelines not available.
Send queries or book proposals to the below address.
Categories: Nonfiction—Business—Directories—Military—Money & Finances—Native American—Psychology—Reference

CONTACT: Submissions Editor
Material: All
PO Box 6578
Delray Beach FL 33482
Phone: 561-496-3316
Fax: 561-496-5546

Back Bay Books

Please refer to Time Warner Book Group.

The Backwaters Press

The Backwaters Press is pleased to announce that, effective December 1st, 2004, we will be accepting submissions year-around with no deadline.

Is this a contest? This is not a contest. Your manuscripts will not be competing with hundreds of other submissions at once.

What's the difference between open submissions and a contest? 1) a The press will read open submissions all year long and these submissions are n ot compared to other maunscripts submitted at the same time. 2) There is not submission deadline for open submissions. 3) Your manuscript is not competing head-to-head with other manuscripts, in the sense that when the editors read for the open submissions your manuscript will not be compared to several others and possibly culled out in comparison to a set of contest entrants.

Do I need to protect my identity from the readers/editors? No, since, this is not a contest, it will not constitute a conflict of interest for the editors to know the identity of the submitting poets.

Is there a fee? The press will charge an administrative fee of $25 per manuscript to read and evaluate for possible publication.

What about Publication? As the Editors find manuscripts they deem publishable, they will accept for publication. There will be no cutoff dates or release dates at a specific time of year. Rather, the press will publish in order of acceptance as time and money permit.

What's the turn around time when I send in a manuscript? The Editors will make every possible effort to respond to your submission within four weeks. Inquiries regarding the status of your submission are welcom at gkosm62735@aol.com.

How will I be notified if my manuscript is accepted for publication through open submissions? The press will use the self-addressed, stamped envelope (SASE) that you sent in with your submission for both acceptances and rejections.

Is the Open Submissions category for first books only? No. The editor will be happy to read any submission that falls within the guidelines. You may submit as many manuscripts for consideration as many times as you would each year.

What do I send? What are the guidelines for open submissions? Please address all submissions to: "Open Submissions"
The Backwaters Press
3502 N 52nd St
Omaha, NE 68104-3506
We will read only submissions that:
Meet the page length guidelines,
Meet the poems per page guidelines,
Have the reading fee submitted with the manuscript,
Have a self-addressed, stamped envelope for reply included.

How Many Pages? How many poems per page? We will read manuscripts that are between 50 and 70 pages in length, single, spaced, (double-spaced between stanzas) that have no more thatn one poem per page. This means that if you have numerous short poems, place only one poem per page, not 5 or 6. But you may also submit a long poem that spans the length of the entire book, or several poems that are longer than one page. Though we enjoy haiku and the other short forms, the press does not want to receive manuscripts with numerous haiku or short poems per manuscripts with one haiku or shor poem per page.

What if my manuscript does not meet those guidelines? Sorry, but we will recycle your manuscript without reading it. We will cash your reading fee check if you enclosed it, because the fee is to help us meet the administrative costs of running the press, and taking care of inappropriate submissions consumes administrative time.

What styles does the press like to see? The Backwaters Press is open to all forms of peotry. The criteria are: good writing. Our bias is toward the contemporary "prose lyric" but we like well written "formal" style poetry as well as experimental writing in the surrealist and the abstract modes, and are open to concrete and L=A=N=G=U=A=G=E poems. There is no restriction on content, though we will probaby not accept maunscripts for publication that are filled with gratuitous sex and violence.

Are they are guarantees that my manuscript will be published if I submit through open submissions category? No. Your manuscript will get a thoughtful evaluation by our editors, and each manuscript received by the press will be considered for possible publication by the press. We cannot guarantee that your manuscript will be accepted for publication.

Will the editors offer critical or editorial advice to the poets who submit manuscripts to the open submissions category? No. Time and staffing do not allow for The Backwaters Press to offer editorial services routinely. If the press accepts your manuscript for publication, then we will work with the poet to help shape the manuscript, give suggestions and comments, etc.

CONTACT: Greg Kosmicki
Material: All
3502 North 52nd Street
Omaha NE 68104-3506
E-mail: Gkosm62735@aol.com
Website: www.thebackwaterspress.homestead.com

Baen Books

Dear Author:

We publish only science fiction and fantasy. Writers familiar with what we have published in the past will know what sort of material we are most likely to publish in the future: powerful plots with solid scientific and philosophical underpinnings are the sine qua non for consideration for science fiction submissions. As for fantasy, any magical system must be both rigorously coherent and integral to the plot, and overall the work must at least strive for originality.

Those manuscripts which survive the "first cut" as outlined above are then judged primarily on plot and characterization.

Style: Simple is generally better; in our opinion good style, like good breeding, never calls attention to itself.

Payment rates: very competitive.

Preferred length: 100,000 - 130,000 words Generally we are uncomfortable with manuscripts under 100,000 words, but if your novel is really wonderful send it along regardless of length.

SUBMISSION PROCEDURES:

> *Remember: Editors change jobs and publishers change addresses. It is wise to invest in a phone call for the current information before submitting.*

Query letters are not necessary. We prefer to see complete manuscripts accompanied by a synopsis. We prefer not to see simultaneous submissions.

Electronic Submissions: Electronic submissions are strongly preferred.

Send to slush@baen.com . No disks unless requested.

Attach the manuscript as a Rich Text Format (.rtf) file. Any other format will not be considered.

Send the manuscript as a single file (do not break it into separate chapter files).

Your submission must include your name, email address*, postal mailing address, and telephone number. *[If you have an alternate permanent email address, please include it, in case your primary account goes out of service.] Include a plot outline if possible.

Minimal formatting, please. Indent paragraphs; center chapter headers and scene break indicators (###, ***, etc.); use page breaks only at the end of chapters. For emphasis, choose underline or italics and use it throughout. Try to avoid bold face, as it tends not to show up. Also avoid non-standard fonts, and unnecessary changes in font face, size, etc. Make it readable, or we won't read it. If something needs special formatting—e.g., small caps for a certain entity's dialog—explain it in a cover letter.

Include, if you like, your ideal cover treatment, including cover copy, a teaser page, and whatever else you would like. (But don't try to "sell" the story in a cover letter. It will stand or fall on its own merits.)

NOTE: Any viruses attached to your submission will send your manuscript straight into the bit-bucket.

Hardcopy Submissions: (for those who cannot submit electronically)

Standard manuscript format only: double-spaced, one side of the page only, 1 1/2" margins on all four sides of the page. We will consider photocopies if they are dark and clear.

Font must be readable, or we won't read it. This means seriphed or at least semi-seriphed, 12-point or greater. Publisher likes Omega and Lucida. Typesetter likes any standard bookface, Times Roman or Courier.

Title, author (last name only is okay), and page number at the top of each page are mandatory. Include your name, mailing address, and telephone number on the first page.

All submissions should be accompanied by a stamped return envelope. Submissions from outside the U.S. should be accompanied by sufficient International Reply Coupons.

Reporting time: usually within 9 to 12 Months. (Sorry, we get lots of manuscripts.)

Thank you for thinking of Baen Books.

The Editors

P.S. Baen will be maintaining offices in New York after the move so continue to use this address.

Categories: Fiction—Fantasy—Science Fiction

CONTACT: Submissions Editor
Material: All
PO Box 1403
Riverdale NY 10471
E-mail: jimbaen@baen.com
Website: www.baen.com

Baker Academic

Baker Academic welcomes book proposals from prospective authors holding relevant academic credentials (which usually means a Ph.D. or similar degree in the field of the proposed book and a teaching position at a recognized institution of higher learning). Proposals vary in form from a one-page description to an extensive prospectus including sample chapters.

We prefer to see a proposal before you complete the manuscript. This enables you to obtain feedback from us that may make the project more publishable.

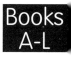

Even if you finish your manuscript before approaching us, we ask that you submit a proposal instead of the manuscript.

A fully developed proposal consists of the following:

a. The proposed book's topic, thesis (unless it's a textbook or reference book), and methodology or subdiscipline.

b. The primary audience for the book and its secondary audiences. If it has potential as a textbook in institutions of higher education, identify: (i) specific courses for which it might be used as a primary text (if any), then those for which it could serve as a supplementary text; (ii) the educational level of the book; and (iii) pedagogical aids, such as exercises, discussion questions, glossaries, and bibliographies, to be included in it.

c. Books with which it will compete, and the uniquenesses and strengths that set it apart from them; or reasons why no book of its kind exists.

d. The estimated date for the manuscript's completion.

e. An annotated outline, with a one-paragraph summary or a brief outline of each chapter.

f. The approximate length of each chapter, in words.

g. Kinds and quantities of illustrative material (such as photographs, line drawings, maps, charts, tables) that need to be included.

h. A sample chapter that represents the book's distinctive contribution or an introduction that explains such things as the book's background, purpose, distinctives, approach, thesis, and contents.

i. A full vita, one that shows your qualifications to write the proposed volume.

j. Letters from others in your field who testify to the need for such a volume and, if you are new to publishing, your ability to write it. We prefer to have the letters submitted at the same time the proposal is submitted and by the same method.

5. Put your proposal in the most refined form you can. We will judge your ability to craft a well-written manuscript by the quality of your proposal.

6. We naturally prefer that you submit your proposal to us first. If you choose to submit it simultaneously to other publishers as well, we only ask that you say as much in your cover letter.

7. After evaluating your proposal, we will advise you of our level of interest. If we have interest in publishing the project, an acquisitions editor will follow up with you.

8. If you have been in previous conversation with a Baker Academic editor, you may send your proposal to that editor. Otherwise, your proposal may be sent by post or email.

Categories:: Christian Interest

CONTACT: The Writers Edge
Po Box 1266
Wheaton, IL 60189
Email: info@Writers Edge Service.com
Website: www.writersedgeservice.com

Baker Books

Baker Books, Fleming H. Revell, and Chosen Books do not accept unsolicited manuscripts. All manuscripts received will be returned to the sender without review.

We will consider unsolicited work only through one of the following avenues. Materials sent to our editorial staff through a professional literary agent will be considered. In addition, our staff attend various writers' conferences in which prospective authors can develop relationships with those in the publishing industry.

If you are interested in having an editor view your work, we recommend submitting it to one of two writing services: The Writer's Edge, available both online and in print, or First Edition, an online service of the Evangelical Christian Publishers Association. We subscribe to both these services and regularly review the proposals which appear there, as do many other Christian publishers.

Categories: Fiction—Nonfiction

CONTACT:Baker Academic Submissions Editor
PO Box 6287
Grand Rapids MI 49516
Email: submissions@bakeracademic.com
Website: www.bakeracademic.com

Baker Publishing Group

About Us
Baker Publishing Group is a leading evangelical publisher offering more than 200 releases per year in its six separate divisions.

Mission Statement
The mission of Baker Publishing Group is to publish writings that promote historic Christianity, irenically express the concerns of evangelicalism, and reflect the diversity of this movement. Its books are well conceived, competently written, and handsomely produced. They furnish resources to all—from individuals to families, from laypeople to pastors, from collegians to seminarians—who seek to live for the Lord and worship him.

Submission Policy
Baker Books, Fleming H. Revell, Chosen Books, and Brazos Press (imprints of Baker Publishing Group) do not accept unsolicited manuscripts. All manuscripts received will be returned to the sender without review.

We will consider unsolicited work only through one of the following avenues: Materials sent to our editorial staff through a professional literary agent will be considered. In addition, our staff attend various writers' conferences in which prospective authors can develop relationships with those in the publishing industry.

If you are interested in having an editor at Baker view your work, we recommend submitting it to one of two writing services: The Writer's Edge, available both online and in print, or First Edition, an online service of the Evangelical Christian Publishers Association. We subscribe to both these services and regularly review the proposals which appear there, as do many other Christian publishers. *These organizations can be reached at the following addresses:*

• First Edition
On the web: www.ecpa.org/FE
E-mail: FirstEdition@ECPA.org
• The Writer's Edge:
On the web: www.writersedgeservice.com
E-mail: info@WritersEdgeService.om
Mailing address: P.O. Box 1266
Wheaton, IL 60189

Preparing a Proposal — Baker Academic Books Only
1. Book proposals, which are always welcome at Baker Academic, vary in form from a one-page description to an extensive prospectus including sample chapters.

2. We prefer to see a proposal before you complete the manuscript. This enables you to obtain from us guidelines for the project, which increases the likelihood that we will publish the manuscript.

3. Even if you finish your manuscript before approaching us, we ask that you submit a proposal instead of the manuscript. This helps us to control the flow of manuscripts, knowing that we can conscientiously review only so many at one time. We do not promise to examine unsolicited manuscripts; we return them only if you have sent return postage.

4. The proposal you submit initially may range from a brief query letter to an extensive proposal. As a rule, the shorter it is, the more quickly we answer; the longer and more promising it is, the more definitive our response.

5. A fully developed proposal consists of the following:

a. The proposed book's purpose.

b. The primary audience for the book; its secondary audiences. If it has potential as a textbook in institutions of higher education, identify: (i) specific courses for which it might be used as a primary text (if any), then those for which it could serve as a supplementary text; (ii) the educational level of the book; and (iii) pedagogical aids, such as exercises, discussion questions, glossaries, and bibliographies, to be included in it.

c. Books with which it will compete, and the uniquenesses and strengths that set it apart from them; or reasons why no book of its kind exists.

d. The estimated date for the manuscript's completion.

e. An annotated outline, with paragraph summaries or brief outlines of each chapter.

f. The approximate length of each chapter, in words. (See appendix below.)

g. Kinds and quantities of illustrative material (such as photographs, line drawings, maps, charts, tables) that need to be included. (Remember that, on the one hand, illustrations can make a good book a great one; and on the other, they can increase the book's price to the point of inhibiting its sale.)

h. Some sample chapters. These should include a chapter that represents the book's distinctive contribution and, if possible, an introduction that explains such things as the book's background, purpose, distinctives, approach, thesis, and contents.

i. A full vita, one that shows your qualifications to write the proposed volume.

j. Letters from others in your field who testify to the need for such a volume and, if you are new to publishing, your ability to write it.

6. Put your proposal in the most refined form you can. We will judge your ability to craft a well-written and accurate manuscript by the quality of your proposal.

7. We naturally prefer that you submit your proposal to us first. If you choose to submit it simultaneously to other publishers as well, we only ask that you say as much in your cover letter.

8. After evaluating your proposal, we will either advise you to send it elsewhere or we will commit to publishing your project and issue a contract.

Appendix: Estimating Length

Word processing programs make it easy to estimate the length of a project. Using the word count feature you can obtain an accurate word or character count.

As a rule of thumb, our standard trim-size academic book has 2700 characters (including spaces) or 450 words per typeset page. Footnotes are included in the character/word counts.

Add an additional 10-25 pages for front matter and indexes.

Thank you!

Categories: Fiction—Nonfiction

CONTACT:Baker Academic Submissions Editor
PO Box 6287
Grand Rapids MI 49516
Phone: 616-676-9185
Fax: 616-676-9573
Website: www.bakeracademic.com

Baker Books

Please refer to Baker Publishing Group.

Balcony Press

Balcony Press is interested in manuscripts on art, architecture and design topics with a preference for west coast or southwest subject matter. Books normally take a historic or cultural slant as opposed to technical, biographical or how-to.

If you are planning to submit an idea for a photography book please be sure there is a strong cohesive idea, that it is unique, and that you have a qualified writer lined up to do accompanying text.

Submit proposals via e-mail or snail mail.

Proposals should include the following:
• Book title and brief summary of the book's content
• Proposed length of manuscript and approximate quantity of illustrations, photos, etc.
• Description of the audience for the book and any ideas you have for promoting it
• What is unusual about the book and what is the competition?
• Author biography or resume
• Suggested table of contents
• Sample chapter and introduction
• SASE for anything you want returned—MANDATORY
In general:
• Authors are responsible for providing all photos, illustrations and permissions to be used in the book
• No royalty advances or expenses are offered
• Royalties are 10% of net revenues from book sales
• Proposals will be responded to within 1 month
• Full manuscript will be responded to in 3 months.
Categories: Nonfiction—Architecture—Arts

CONTACT: Ann Gray
Material: All
512 E. Wilson St., Ste. 213
Glendale CA 91206
Phone: 818 956-5313
Fax: 818 956-5904
E-mail: editor@balconypress.com (submissions)
Website: www.balconypress.com

Ballantine Books

We do not accept unsolicited submissions, proposals, manuscripts or submission queries at this time.

If you would like to have your work or manuscript considered for publication, we recommend that you work with an established literary agent.

Barbed Wire Publishing

Barbed Wire Publishing is a regional publisher that prefers to publish Southwestern, children's, and bi-lingual books. However, almost any subject that strikes our fancy is a potential candidate for publication. Novels, histories, political and religious manuscripts have been published by the company. Yucca Tree Press is an imprint of Barbed Wire Publishing.

The company has three publishing tracts: traditional publishing, Keepsake Publishing, and Pardner Publishing. Because we are a small company, our traditionally published books are limited (25% to 30% of our books). Keepsake Publishing is a process that is designed for family histories, generational stories and mementos where a limited number of copies (25-50 books) are produced reasonably for distribution to family and friends. Pardner Publishing is our form of vanity publishing in which the author participates finan-

Books A-L

cially in the production process, Barbed Wire provides full editorial, design, composition, and printing/binding services as well as sales, marketing, and distribution of the books. The author can expect 50% of net book sales after full return of his/her investment.

We aggressively market all of our books and distribute through B&T, Books West, Amazon.com, Borders.com, and BN.com. We submit all of our books to the major bookstore chains' Small Press Divisions and we actively sell into independent bookstores and defined niche markets.

E-mail query letters are encouraged. Manuscripts can be submitted electronically or as hard copy. A synopsis, a few representative chapters, a potential market analysis, and a brief author bio will help our evaluation of the MS.

Categories: Nonfiction—Children—History—Language—Politics—Regional—Religion—Southwestern

CONTACT: George Stein, Publisher
Material: All
400 South Compress Road
Las Cruces NM 88005
Phone: 505-525-9707
888-817-1990 (toll free)
Fax: 505-525-9711 (fax)
E-mail: thefolks@barbed-wire.net
Website: www.barbed-wire.net

Barnaby Books

Manuscript Guidelines for Prospective Authors

Barnaby Books, Inc. focuses on children's literature with Hawaiian and Pacific Rim themes. We are a small press, publishing no more than one title per year.

Format for Manuscripts
Please submit a double-spaced, hard copy of your manuscript and a self-addressed stamped return envelope.

Illustrations are not necessary, but if you do wish to include them, please send photocopies.

Response time
We try to respond within 3-4 weeks.

Categories: Children

Barnavy Books, Inc.
3290 Pacific Heights Road
Honolulu, HI 96813
Fax: 808-531-0089
E-mail: publisher@barnabybooks.com
Website: www.barnabybooks.com

Barricade Books

For starters, Barricade Books publish no fiction. Furthermore, we do not publish poetry or children's books.

We do look for non-fiction, mostly of the controversial type. We look for books that we can promote with authors who can talk about their topics on radio and television, and to the press.

Please review the books on our web site. Given the above stipulations, if you believe your material fits our list send an outline and one or two chapters together with a self-addressed, stamped envelope to Carole Stuart. We will not respond to email addresses or if a SASE is not enclosed. Please let us know if you want your material returned.

As of now, we do not accept proposals on disk, nor do we accept them via email.

Categories: Nonfiction—African-American—Biography—Enter-tainment—Gay/Lesbian—Mass Communications—Regional—Relation-ships—Sexuality—Martial Arts

CONTACT: Carole Stuart, Publisher
Material: All
185 Bridge Plaza North Ste 308-A
Fort Lee NJ 07024
Phone: 201-944-7600
Fax: 201-944-6363
E-mail: customerservice@barricadebooks.com (no submissions)
Website: www.barricadebooks.com

Barrons Educational Series, Inc.

Publishers of Elementary, High School, College and General Books.
Submission Guidelines
For initial consideration of your project, query letters are recommended.

NOTE: We do not accept e-mailed or faxed proposals.

Include a self-addressed postcard if you desire notification of receipt of material.

Include a large, ***self-addressed, stamped envelope*** to accommodate the return of your material should it be determined unsuitable for our needs.

Indicate if the material being submitted is in response to a positive reply to a query letter previously sent to Barron's; also, write **"Requested Material"** on the package.

Simultaneous submissions are welcomed.

It is not necessary to have a literary agent in order to submit material.

Due to the large volume of unsolicited submissions received, complete evaluation of a proposal may take up to eight months. A system for tracking the status of unsolicited material does not exist. Therefore, ***we do not accept telephone inquiries regarding the status of individual proposals.***

When submitting a work of juvenile fiction:
• Include the manuscript in its entirety.
• Artwork is not necessary. If artwork is available, include a sample.
• Include author's credentials.

When submitting a work of adult or juvenile nonfiction:
• Include a table of contents and two sample chapters.
• Include a brief description of the work. This overview should cite the market being targeted (e.g., children, ages 2-4; secondary school teachers; etc.).

• Include author's credentials.

We will contact you if additional information or material is needed in order to properly evaluate your project. ***Do not send additional material unless specifically requested to do so. It will be discarded.***

Thank you for your adherence to the above guidelines.

Categories: Nonfiction—Animals—Business—Careers—Children—College—Cooking—Crafts/Hobbies—Diet/Nutrition—Education—Gardening—Health—Juvenile—Language—Parenting—Reference—Text-books—Young Adult

CONTACT: Mr. Wayne Barr, Acquisitions Editor

Material: All
250 Wireless Blvd.
Hauppauge, NY 11788-3917
Phone: 631-434-3311
Fax: 631-434-3723
E-mail: info@barronseduc.com (no submissions)
Website: barronseduc.com

Battelle Press

Battelle Press publishes both science and management books for engineers, scientists, and researchers. Battelle Press is looking for management, project management, and communication titles specifically targeted to these technical readers. To review current Battelle Press titles, visit our web bookstore at battelle.org/bookstore.

Categories: Management

CONTACT: Joe Sheldrick, Aquisitions Editor
Material: All
505 King Ave.
Columbus OH 43201-2693
Phone: 614-424-6393
E-mail: press@battelle.org
Website: battelle.org/bookstore

Bay Tree Publishing

Bay Tree is an independent publisher of business, psychology,and current affairs. We are looking for manuscripts that appeal to an educated but nonprofessional audience. We do not publish fiction, poetry or personal memoirs. Recent titles include, *The Case for Affirmative Action in University Admissions, Get Hired Now! Taking the War Out of Our Words, Get Slightly Famous, and Them and Us: Cult Thing and the Terrorist Threat.* More information about Bay Tree is availble at www.baytreepublish.com.

Please do not send entire manuscripts. Query with a short synopsis (1-3pages), table of contents, author bio, competitive analysis, (competing books and how your book differs), and marketing plan (wht you would do to promote the book).

Categories: Nonfiction—Business—Psychology—Science

CONTACT: Acquisitions Editor
Material: All
721 Creston Road
Berkeley CA 94708

Baywood Publishing Company, Inc.

Baywood Publishing invites authors to forward proposals for publications in counseling, death & bereavement, psychology, and gerontology, health policy and technical communication. We welcome submissions in these areas from authors who desire to publish with a scholarly professional press. These guidelines are provided to expedite the submission process.

The Proposal Package:

1. Cover Letter introducing yourself, the title of your proposed publication, a concise description of the purpose and scope of the book, and an indication of whom the audience will be.

2. Curriculum Vita for each author(s)/editor(s) involved. This should include: Names, titles, addresses, and phone/fax numbers.

3. List of Contributors, if applicable. Please indicate the total number of contributors and provide their names, titles addresses, and phone/fax numbers.

4. Table of Contents, to include chapter titles and paragraphs describing those chapters.

5. Introduction or Preface, and at least one chapter for the proposed publication.

6. The primary specialty and any areas of subspecialization for the author/editor.

7. Status of the manuscript: Is it in the idea stage? Is it less than 50% complete? More than 50% complete? Has any of the material been previously published?

8. Probable date that the manuscript will be completed.

9. Mechanical dimensions including: Number of typed double-spaced pages; number of charts; number of tables.

10. Potential Markets. Describe the primary and any secondary professional and/or student markets for which this book is intended and the level of readership at which it is aimed.

11. Timeliness. Please try to estimate how long, in years, the content of the book will remain current and useful.

12. List of Competing Titles. Please include the author, title, publisher, year, pages, price of each competing publication.

13. Uniqueness. How does this book differ from competing titles? List any special or unique features your work contains

Categories: Nonfiction—Counseling—Health—Psychology—Technical—Textbooks—Gerontology—Public Health—Death & Bereavement

CONTACT: Stuart Cohen, Managing Editor
Material: Proposals
26 Austin Ave
P.O Box 337
Amityville NY 11701
Phone: 631-691-1270
Fax: 631-691-1770
E-mail: baywood@baywood.com
Website: www.baywood.com

Bear & Company

Books on ancient wisdom, new science, Western thought, indigenous traditions, Maya studies, extraterrestrial consciousness, and complementary medicine.

In order to make the review process more efficient for prospective authors and for our editorial staff, we have prepared a list of requirements for authors and for our editorial staff, we have prepared a list of requirements for authors who are submitting work. Please include the following when presenting a proposal:

1. A BRIEF LETTER THAT INCLUDES A SHORT SYNOPSIS OF THE BOOK

a) The letter should be no more than two pages long and should tell how your manuscript contributes to its field and what make is unique.

b) As specifically as you can, tell us who the audience is for your book.

c) Give a brief biography of yourself, noting especially any specific qualifications for writing your subject.

2. A TABLE OF CONTENTS, INTRODUCTION, AND SAMPLE CHAPTER(S)

There is no need to send a complete manuscripts unless it is specifically asked for. Proposals including the above materials are reviewed much faster than thick manuscripts sent unsolicited.

3. WE CANNOT RETURN PROPOSALS OR MANUSCRIPTS UNLESS THEY ARE ACCOMPANIED BY A SELF-ADDRESSED ENVELOPE STAMPED WITH SUFFICIENT POSTAGE.

Some prospective authors write or e-mail a query letter before sending a proposal. This is a good idea and can save time and postage, especially when you are not familiar with the books we publish. A list of our seven imprints follows, please read these before sending us a query letter or proposal.

If you have questions that have not been addressed above regarding our submission guidelines, please DO NO call the acquisitions editor; send a query letter to our submissions department at the address listed below. Your query letter should provide enough information about your work that the acquisitions editor can make an informed decision and contact you for further details.

Categories: Nonfiction—New Age—Science—Ancient Wisdom—Indigenous Taditions—Maya Studies

Contact: Submissions
Bear & Company
PO Box 388
Rochester, VT 05767-0388 USA
Phone: 802-767-3174
Website: www.InnerTraditions.com

Bear Club Books

Books for kids that feed the growing mind, body and spirit. **Note:** Bear Cub Books publishes illustrated traditional myths and stories from non-Western cultures for Western children ages 6 to 9, not fictional illustrated children's stories.

In order to make the review process more efficient for prospective authors and for our editorial staff, we have prepared a list of requirements for authors and for our editorial staff, we have prepared a list of requirements for authors who are submitting work. Please include the following when presenting a proposal:

1. A BRIEF LETTER THAT INCLUDES A SHORT SYNOPSIS OF THE BOOK

a) The letter should be no more than two pages long and should tell how your manuscript contributes to its field and what make is unique.

b) As specifically as you can, tell us who the audience is for your book.

c) Give a brief biography of yourself, noting especially any specific qualifications for writing your subject.

2. A TABLE OF CONTENTS, INTRODUCTION, AND SAMPLE CHAPTER(S)

There is no need to send a complete manuscripts unless it is specifically asked for. Proposals including the above materials are reviewed much faster than thick manuscripts sent unsolicited.

3. WE CANNOT RETURN PROPOSALS OR MANUSCRIPTS UNLESS THEY ARE ACCOMPANIED BY A SELF-ADDRESSED ENVELOPE STAMPED WITH SUFFICIENT POSTAGE.

Some prospective authors write or e-mail a query letter before sending a proposal. This is a good idea and can save time and postage, especially when you are not familiar with the books we publish. A list of our seven imprints follows, please read these before sending us a query letter or proposal.

If you have questions that have not been addressed above regarding our submission guidelines, please DO NO call the acquisitions editor; send a query letter to our submissions department at the address listed below. Your query letter should provide enough information about your work that the acquisitions editor can make an informed decision and contact you for further details.

Categories: Nonfiction—Children—Folklore—Juvenile—Multicultural—Native Americans—

Contact: Submissions
Bear Cub Books
PO Box 388
Rochester, VT 05767-0388 USA
Phone: 802-767-3174
Website: www.InnerTraditions.com

Bee-Con Books

BEE-CON BOOKS is a new publishing company (est. 2001) that concentrates on fiction. It has published *The Parcel Express Murders and Damaged!* by author Bernadette Y. Connor. Romance, mystery, children's fiction

and general fiction submissions will be considered. Submit a query letter and synopsis. Manuscripts will be returned only if self-addressed-stamped mailers are included.

Categories: Fiction—Children's—Mystery—Romance—Teen

CONTACT: Erica L. Watts
Material: All Submissions
PO BOX 27708
Philadelphia PA 19118
Website: www.bee-conbooks.com

Bella Books

Bella Books specializes in fiction by and about lesbians. We publish general lesbian fiction, romance, mystery/thriller, some sci-fi/fantasy, and some erotica. Bella is interested in novels with a solid plot and engaging, fully-realized characters. The main characters must be lesbians and the story must be credible. The manuscript should be between 50,000 and 80,000 words.

Bella Books does NOT accept unsolicited manuscripts. Your manuscript should be completed before sending your query to us. We are not interested in manuscripts that have been submitted simultaneously to multiple publishers.

To make sure that your manuscript is considered, please follow these instructions carefully. Send a cover letter, précis and a self-addressed, stamped envelope to:

Bella Books
P.O. Box 10543
Tallahassee, FL 32302

The cover letter should very briefly describe your book, including the title and word count. It should also include a brief biographical sketch of the author.

Make sure you include your address, phone numbers where you can be reached, and your email address. The précis should include an outline of the plot (please keep this to one or two pages) and some information about all of the main characters.

If we are interested in reading the manuscript, we will contact you. Please understand that we receive many queries each day, and it may take up to 30 days for us to contact you.

If we ask to see your manuscript, please send it typed (double-spaced) with one-inch margins. Remember that you are trying to woo a publisher for your book. Make it as clean (no typos, pages in correct order, etc.) as you can to the best of your ability. Your manuscript must be available by email or on disk if we need it. (Microsoft Word preferred.)

For more information on Bella's Manuscript Formatting Mechanics and the books we publish, please visit our website at www.bellabooks.com. Thank you for your interest in Bella Books.

Categories: Fiction—Erotica—Gay/Lesbian—Myster—Romance—Science Fiction

CONTACT: Acquisitions Editor
Material: All
PO Box 10543
Tallahassee, FL 32302
Phone: 800-539-5965
Website: www.bellabooks.com

BenBella Books

BenBella specializes in science fiction and pop culture. In the area of science fiction and fantasy, BenBella publishes both original works and classics. For our line of original science fiction and fantasy, BenBella is looking first and foremost for "great reads" - exciting plots, engaging characters and mind-blowing ideas. For our line of science fiction and fantasy classics, BenBella is looking for great works of fiction that should never have fallen out print, that remain accessible and relevant to today's readers.

In the area of popular culture, BenBella will be publishing a broad range of titles, from smart celebrity biographies to current trends to critical analyses of hit movies. The books in this line, however different, will share a common intelligence, accessibility and sense of fun.

BenBella will occasionally publish works of exceptional potential outside of our specialization. Please note that we do not accept works of fiction.

SUBMISSION GUIDELINES:

BenBella Books welcomes submissions from authors and their agents. *Our guidelines are as follows:*

Pop Culture

Have you written or are planning a non-fiction work that you'd like to submit to us, please send the following information:

• Description of the book — Describe, in a page or two, the essence of the book. This description should give us a good understanding of the book and should position the book as favorably as possible — think of this as the back cover/inside flap description of the book.

• High-level table of contents — Provide your thinking on the overall flow of the book. This should be only a page or two.

• Target market for the book — Who is the target market for this book? "Everyone" is not a good answer. The target market should be specific and clear. Explain why this book will have great appeal to the target market.

• Relationship of the book to the competition — What are the main competitors to this book and how will this book distinguish itself from the competition? Every book has competitors, so you will need to do the legwork to find your competition, review the books, and assess how you will effectively differentiate your book against theirs.

• Useful endorsements — If you have personal relationships that are likely to result in endorsements for the book from qualified/well-known individuals, please let us know.

• Resume and qualifications — Your expertise is a critical selling point for the book. So tell us why you are uniquely qualified to write this book. Also list your publishing credits, if any.

This entire package should just be 5-10 pages. If we like what we see we'll ask for a detailed table of contents and a sample chapter. Please do not send a manuscript until we ask for one. We prefer exclusive submissions and will respond quickly to them.

Science Fiction

BenBella publishes original works and republishes great sci-fi works that never should have fallen out of print.

To submit an original work, please send the manuscript to us, along with a 1-2 page letter describing the work.

To submit a great work for republication, please send a manuscript or copy of the published book, along with a 1-2 page letter describing the work.

The proposal should be printed in 12-point type, double-spaced on letter-sized unlined white paper. The Internet is great, but we prefer to review crisp proposals on paper so, please, no fax or e-mail submissions. We get a lot of these and they need to be easy to read and take notes on.

Please send only copies of your materials, no original manuscripts or artwork. We will not be held liable for materials lost or destroyed in the mail.

If you want your work returned, please enclose a properly sized self-addressed, stamped envelope with your proposal. If you don't include a self-addressed, stamped envelope, we'll assume you want us to keep your proposal on file.

Categories: Non-Fiction—Culture—Fantasy—Science Fiction—Televisioni/Radio

CONTACT: Editorial Submissions
Material: All
P.O Box 601389
Dallas TX 75360
Phone: 214-750-3600
Fax: 214-750-3645
E-mail: info@benbellabooks.co
Website: www.benbellabooks.com

Books A-L

Berkshire House Publishers

We specialize in a series of guides, the Great DestinationsTM Series, about specific destinations around the U.S. that are of unusual charm and cultural importance—destinations such as Berkshire County, Santa Fe and Taos, Napa and Sonoma, the coast of Maine, the Adirondacks, the Chesapeake Bay area, the Hamptons on Long Island, Newport and Narragansett Bay in Rhode Island, the central coast of California, Aspen, the Gulf Coast of Florida, and the Texas Hill Country. Our greatest interest would be in writers who reside in U.S. destinations that are particularly attractive to upscale visitors. Writers must be willing to write in the Great Destinations format—comprising chapters on the history, lodging, dining, culture, recreation, shopping, etc., of each area.

We also specialize in books about our own region (the Berkshires in Western Massachusetts) and the various recreational activities that can be enjoyed here. We occasionally publish cookbooks that are related to New England or to country living/country inns in general. We have a line of books on Shaker crafts and artifacts, but we are not currently seeking to add to it. We offer books of historical interest in our American ClassicsTM series, notably books by Alice Morse Earle—*Home Life in Colonial Days* and *Child Life in Colonial Days*—but have no immediate plans to add to this series.

Categories: Nonfiction—Cooking—History—Travel

CONTACT: Jean Rousseau, Publisher
Material: All
CONTACT: Philip Rich, Managing Editor
Material: All
480 Pleasant St. Ste. 5
Lee MA 01238
Phone: 413-243-0303
Fax: 413-243-4737
E-mail: Berkhouse@aol.com

Berrett-Koehler Publishers

Berrett-Koehler Publishers' publishing mission is to publish books that support the movement toward a more enlightened world of work and more free, open, humane, effective, and globally sustainable organizations. *With this in mind, please prepare a proposal that covers the following topics:*

• Need: Why is a new publication on this topic needed at this time?

• Purpose: How is the publication designed to meet the need? What are the primary and secondary purposes of the publication?

• New Contribution: What new does the publication offer? What are the five to ten most competitive or similar publications, and how—specifically—does the proposed publication differ from and go beyond each of them? Please describe the publication's new contribution in considerable detail—this is a central issue.

• Audiences and Uses: Who are the intended audiences and how will they be able to use the publication? Be specific and realistic, rather than claiming that people or managers in general will be interested. Distinguish between primary and secondary audiences. Identify specific professional associations that are audiences.

• Knowledge Base: Describe the publication's knowledge base of experience, research, theory, and/or literature review. Attach your vita or other biographical information.

• Outline: Attach a detailed chapter-by-chapter outline of the publication's planned contents.

• Manuscript Length and Special Materials: How many pages (assuming 250 words per page) do you expect that the manuscript (not the book) will be? What special materials (drawings, tables, figures, exhibits, and so on) do you anticipate will be included?

• Timetable: What is your schedule for completing the manuscript?

• Sample Chapters: Please submit two to four sample chapters with the publication proposal. Indicate if more of the draft manuscript is available, or when it might be available.

• Marketing Support: In what ways (speaking, articles, media contacts, etc.) will you as author be able to support the publisher's marketing of the book? Attach any interviews with you, stories about you, or articles by you that have already appeared in local or national media.

Categories: Nonfiction—Business—Careers—Consumer—Economics—Government—Human Rights—Inspirational—Self Help—Spiritual

CONTACT: Jeevan Sivasubramaniam, Managing Editor
Material: All
235 Montgomery St., Ste. 650
San Francisco, CA 94104
Phone: 415-288-0260
Fax: 415-362-2512
E-mail: bkpub@bkpub.com
Website: www.bkconnections.com

Bethany House Publishers

WRITER'S GUIDELINES FOR ADULT NONFICTION

Bethany House is an evangelical publisher of books in a broad range of categories. Non-fiction bestsellers include *Becoming A Vessel God Can Use* by Donna Partow, *I'm Too Young To Be This Old* by Poppy Smith, *The Subtle Power of Spiritual Abuse* by David Johnson & Jeff VanVonderen, *Telling Yourself the Truth* by William Backus & Marie Chapian, *Where Does A Mother Go to Resign?* by Barbara Johnson and *The Kingdom of the Cults* by Walter Martin. (BHP publishes no poetry or music.) *We are seeking unique, well-targeted, and thought-provoking books in the following categories:*

Christian Living

Books which help the lay person apply biblical truths to everyday life. (e.g. *Walking in Total God-Confidence* by Donna Partow, *12 Steps for the Recovering Pharisee* by John Fischer)

Devotional

Unique, stimulating approaches geared to specific audiences. (e.g. *The Perfect Catch* by H. Norman Wright, *Sweet Persecution* by Ron Brackin, *Becoming Friends with God* by Leith Anderson)

Contemporary Issues

Information and answers on cults, abortion, euthanasia, evolution, humanism, divorce, etc. (e.g. *Legislating Morality* by Dr. Norman Geisler & Frank Turek, *The New Absolutes* by William Watkins, *When Someone You Love is Dying* by David Clark & Peter Emmett, *Truth About Rock* by Steve Peters & Mark Littleton, *The Death of Truth* by Dennis McCullum)

Marriage and Family

Biblical principles for roles and relationships which will nurture love and communication. (e.g. *The Power of Believing in Your Child* by Miles McPherson, *Daze of Our Wives* by Dave Meurer, *Coaching Your Kids in the Game of Life* by Ricky Byrdsong & Dave and Neta Jackson)

Women's Issues

Books written by women, for women on various topics of concern to today's Christian woman. (e.g. *Where Does a Mother Go to Resign* by Barbara Johnson, *Sanctuary* by Marsha Crockett, *Be Still* by Elizabeth Hoekstra, *Shop, Save and Share* by Ellie Kay)

Spirituality

Experiencing a deeper walk with God through quiet time, Bible reading, and prayer. (e.g. *Contemplating the Cross* by Tricia Rhodes, *Quiet Places* by Jane Rubietta, *Into the Depths of God* by Calvin Miller)

Cults

Information and answers on cults and world religions. (e.g. *The Compact Guide to World Religions* by Dean Halverson, *Is The Mormon My Brother?* by James White, *The Dark Side of the Supernatural* by Bill Myers & Dave Wimbish)

Applied Theology

Theological topics investigated and explained for the lay person with practical application. (e.g. *The King James Only Controversy* by James White, *Chosen But Free* by Dr. Norman Geisler, *The Forgotten Trinity* by James White)

Once a contracted manuscript satisfies our editorial requirements, we assume all costs of production and distribution (the author is responsible for expenses incurred on inside art or photos, indexing, etc.). The author receives a royalty on each book sold, comparable with rates from other publishers in the CBA industry.

Our books are promoted through our trade catalog, dealer mailings, and ads in booksellers' journals and leading Christian magazines. The books are sold to bookstores, both Christian and general-market outlets, by a nationwide network of sales representatives, by major American and Canadian distributors, and by distributors in over twenty foreign countries.

WRITER'S GUIDELINES FOR ADULT GENERAL FICTION

Bethany House is the leading publisher of Christian fiction. Bestsellers include *The Meeting Place* by Janette Oke and T. Davis Bunn, *The Shunning* by Beverly Lewis, and *Legend of the Celtic Stone* by Michael Phillips. *We are seeking unique, carefully developed books in the following categories:*

Historical Fiction

This category features stories in any historical setting prior to 1950. Some examples include *The Widow of Larkspur Inn* by Lawana Blackwell, *Texas Angel* by Judith Pella and *The Dark Sun Rises* by Denise Williamson. Most of our historical fiction is developed in series.

Contemporary Fiction

This category features both stand-alone novels and series whose primary setting falls within the past 50 years. Examples include *The Redemption of Sarah Cain* by Beverly Lewis, *Some Wildflower in My Heart* by Jamie Langston Turner, and *A Son Comes Home* by Joseph Bentz.

Successful Bethany House fiction will generally include the following characteristics:

• An intriguing, well-written story with well-developed characters, a compelling plot and authentic description.

• A coherent, identifiable theme and/or particular characters who reflect biblical values or teachings.

• Historical/geographical/social accuracy.

• Relationships that portray the true meaning of love-commitment and responsibility rather than merely emotional and physical attraction.

• Adult manuscripts should be 75,000 words or longer. Typical Bethany House novels range up to 125,000 words.

WRITER'S GUIDELINES FOR CHILDREN'S AND TEEN BOOKS FICTION

Bethany House is an evangelical publisher of books in a broad range of categories, from preschool to adult. As the premier publisher of youth fiction in the Christian market, our list contains many bestselling series, including Three Cousins Detective Club, Mandie Books, Girls Only, and Bloodhounds, Inc. We also partner with Focus on the Family to bring their KidWitness Tales, The Christy Miller Series, and other youth books to the marketplace.

We do not accept unsolicited proposals for full-color picture books, nor do we publish cartoons, biographies, poetry, or short stories. Also, please note that we publish only series fiction, no stand-alones.

Bethany Backyard (imprint for ages 0-10)

Bethany Backyard comprises a variety of fun-to-read fiction and non-fiction books for young children ages 0-10. Some examples include Janette Oke's Animal Friends, *The Wonderful Way Babies Are Made*, *Glow-in-the-Dark Fish and 59 More Ways to See God Through His Creation*, and the For Me! Books. (For more information on our nonfiction books, please see the reverse side of this page.)

Early reader and first chapter book series are designed for children who are ready for the challenge of reading books divided into short chapters on their own. Books for early readers should be written for 5- to 8-year-olds and be about 3,000 words long. First chapter books are aimed at 7- to 10-year-olds and should be between 6,000 and 7,500 words in length. Stories should be exciting and fun, with a kid's view of the world. Each should integrate easy-to-understand biblical lessons that develop children's Christian faith. Examples: AstroKids, Three Cousins Detective Club, The Cul-de-sac Kids.

Middle-Grade Readers (ages 8-13)

Bethany has several strong-selling series for middle readers. Although our list is full, we will consider unique, imaginative stories (20,000 to 40,000 words) with believable characters who grow and change as a result of the events in the story. A Christian theme should be delicately woven into each book. Examples: Girls Only (GO!), Promise of Zion, and Bloodhounds, Inc.

Teens (ages 12 and up)

Fiction manuscripts for preteens and teens should be at least 50,000 words and should contain believable characters with real-life appeal; contemporary issues woven into a strong plot; and circumstances with which young adults identify. Scriptural themes should be skillfully crafted into the story in a way that is not preachy or tacked on. We are looking for suspenseful stories with strong take-away value. Successful series include Passport to Danger, Jennie McGrady Mysteries, SummerHill Secrets, and High Hurdles.

Before You Send Your Fiction Manuscript:

• Is the language appropriate for the intended age group?

• Have you checked your facts?

• Is the plot too complex? too simplistic?

• Is the theme realistic and meaningful to today's youth?

• Are there books in the market similar to your idea? If so, what makes yours unique?

• Does your main character have a clearly defined goal he or she is trying to achieve?

• Does your story build to a natural, effective climax?

Nonfiction

Bethany House has a history of publishing strong, relevant nonfiction for children and teens of all ages. A sampling of bestselling titles includes *Could Someone Wake Me Up Before I Drool on the Desk?*; *Hero Tales*; and *God's Will, God's Best*. We are seeking well-planned and thoughtfully developed books with an outstanding ability to communicate with youth.

Bethany Backyard

Backyard nonfiction includes a variety of books to be used for personal and family devotions, homeschooling, Christian education, and Sunday school. Books should teach key faith lessons in a way that is accessible to children. Representative titles are *Christmas Is...For Me!*; *The Wonderful Way Babies Are Made*; *Glow-in-the-Dark Fish and 59 More Ways to See God Through His Creation*; and *Fins, Feathers, and Faith*.

Devotional/Personal Growth

We're looking for unique, stimulating tools for middle readers and early and late teens to use in their personal quiet times or in youth group settings. Titles include *You're Worth More Than You Think!*; *Wise Up*; *Bad to the Bone*; and *Was That a Balloon or Did Your Head Just Pop*?

Contemporary Issues

Information on and answers to the issues most relevant to today's youth. *What Children Need to Know When Parents Get Divorced*; *What's With the Mutant in the Microscope?*; *If I Could Ask God One Question*; and *Find Your Fit* are examples of topics we've published in the past.

Nonfiction manuscripts should fall between 20,000 and 40,000 words for middle readers, and 30,000 and 40,000 words for teens.

FOR ALL SUBMISSIONS

(Adult Fiction, Non-Fiction, and Children and Teen Fiction)

Do your homework: Familiarize yourself with our company and what types of books we publish. Study our catalog and your local Christian bookstore shelves to determine where there might be a need. (To obtain a copy of our catalog, send an 11" x 14" self-addressed envelope with five first-class stamps affixed.)

Submitting Your Fiction or Nonfiction Proposal:

In light of current security concerns, Bethany House Publishers is no longer able to accept unsolicited manuscripts and book proposals. Material that does not come from a recognized source will be stamped Refused/Return to Sender when there is a return address.

We will accept one-page only facsimile proposals directed to Adult Nonfiction, Adult Fiction, or YA/Children editors. Faxes of interest will be responderd to in 4 to 6 weeks. Check our website for the current number.

Bethany House Publishers will continue to accept queries, proposals, and manuscripts through established literary agents, recognized manuscript services, and writers' conferences attended by BHP editorial staff.

Literary agents

Sally Stuart's annual publication, *The Christian Writers' Market Guide* (Harold Shaw) provides a list of literary agents who work with Christian publishers.

Manuscript services

First-time authors may find the following services valuable:

First Edition, a service of Evangelical Christian Publishers Association (www.ECPA.org), posts proposals on its Web site for review by ECPA member publishers.

Writer's Edge Manuscript Service (see information at www.writersedgeservice.com) evaluates manuscripts and provides information to subscriber publishers.

Writers' Conferences

Representatives of BHP and other Christian publishers attend various writers' conferences throughout the U.S. For a conference near you, consult The Christian Writers' Market Guide or www.billyates.com/cww/links.html.

Categories: Fiction—Nonfiction—Children—Family—Juvenile—Parenting—Relationships—Religion—Sexuality

CONTACT: Editorial
Material: All
11400 Hampshire Ave. South
Minneapolis MN 55438
Fax: 952-996-1304 (one-page queries)
Website: www.bethanyhouse.com

Beyond Words Publishing

Beyond Words is no longer accepting any new children's titles at this time. Please do not send queries or submissions. Thank you.

CONTACT: Acquisitions Editor
Material: Mind, Body, and Spirit
20827 NW Cornell Rd. Ste. 500
Hillsboro OR 97124
Phone: 503-531-8700
Fax: 503-531-8773
Website: www.beyondword.com

Bindu Books

Book on spirituality and self-transformation especially for young adults.

In order to make the review process more efficient for prospective authors and for our editorial staff, we have prepared a list of requirements for authors and for our editorial staff, we have prepared a list of requirements for authors who are submitting work. Please include the following when presenting a proposal:

1. A BRIEF LETTER THAT INCLUDES A SHORT SYNOPSIS

OF THE BOOK

a) The letter should be no more than two pages long and should tell how your manuscript contributes to its field and what make is unique.

b) As specifically as you can, tell us who the audience is for your book.

c) Give a brief biography of yourself, noting especially any specific qualifications for writing your subject.

2. A TABLE OF CONTENTS, INTRODUCTION, AND SAMPLE CHAPTER(S)

There is no need to send a complete manuscripts unless it is specifically asked for. Proposals including the above materials are reviewed much faster than thick manuscripts sent unsolicited.

3. WE CANNOT RETURN PROPOSALS OR MANUSCRIPTS UNLESS THEY ARE ACCOMPANIED BY A SELF-ADDRESSED ENVELOPE STAMPED WITH SUFFICIENT POSTAGE.

Some prospective authors write or e-mail a query letter before sending a proposal. This is a good idea and can save time and postage, especially when you are not familiar with the books we publish. A list of our seven imprints follows, please read these before sending us a query letter or proposal.

If you have questions that have not been addressed above regarding our submission guidelines, please DO NO call the acquisitions editor; send a query letter to our submissions department at the address listed below. Your query letter should provide enough information about your work that the acquisitions editor can make an informed decision and contact you for further details. .

Categories: Nonfiction—Teen—Young Adult—Spirituality—Self-transformation

Contact: Submissions
Bindu Books
PO Box 388
Rochester, VT 05767-0388 USA
Phone: 802-767-3174
Website: www.InnerTraditions.com

BkMk Press
University of Missouri-Kansas City

1. Send a sample of your work: approximately 10 pp. poetry; or 50 pp. prose.

2. Typed and paginated. Prose should be double-spaced.

3. Please include a cover letter indicating your name and address and the title of your submission.

4. Please also send a self addressed stamped envelope for our reply (with sufficient postage for the manuscript's return, if applicable). Please indicate whether you want your manuscript returned or recycled.

5. BkMk publishes quality poetry, short fiction collections, and creative non-fiction essays. We do not currently publish novels.

5. DO NOT SUBMIT MANUSCRIPTS VIA E-MAIL OR OTHERWISE THROUGH THE INTERNET

7. We try to reply to your submission in two to six months.

Note: It is highly unusual for us to accept a novella or anything aspiring to novel-hood, preferring instead to publish short fiction collections. We will not consider mystery, western, or romance novels.

Categories: Fiction—Nonfiction—Literature—Poetry—Regional—Short Stories—Creative Nonfiction

CONTACT: Ben Furnish, Managing Editor
Material: Poetry, Short Fiction, Creative Nonfiction
University of Missouri-Kansas City
5101 Rockhill Road
Kansas City MO 64110-2499
Phone: 816-235-2558
Fax: 816-235-2611
E-mail: bkmk@umkc.edu (no submissions)
Website: www.umkc.edu/bkmk

Black Forest Press
Arbenteuer Books, Dichter Books, Sonnenchen Books, and Kinder Books

Black Forest Press is a self-publisher. What we do is of interest to authors who want to see their book in print, but cannot get traditional publishing editors to read their manuscript. Black Forest Press is for authors who have considered the alternative to traditional or subsidy publishing and have decided to financially invest in their own work. These authors maintain 100% of their profit, and pay no book sale royalties to the publisher. That right! All profits and book sale royalties belong 100% to the author (that's you). Self-publishing with the experts makes much better sense.

Black Forest Press is now pleased to offer Print on Demand (POD). Black Forest Press (BFP) offers author's special terms, pricing and printing options with our Print on Demand (POD) Program. The POD option has different parameters than our traditional publishing program, and part of those parameters are limitations which many prevent some authors from choosing the POD approach to successful and quick publishing. Let's look at the benefits and drawbacks.

Drawbacks (Not for every book published; limited by size dimensions and short runs)

1. All POD books must meet a minimum of 108 pages and cannot go over 350 pages.

2. All books can only be 5 X 8, 5½ X 8½, 6 X 9, 7½ X 9¼, or 8¼ X 11.

3. Only a maximum of 500 books can be printed. POD is almost exclusively short runs, for small length books.

4. Only two options of marketing are available: The almost nonexistent plan, or the plan which covers considerable and significant basic features. Option two is the best choice. See Benefits below. Email us to discuss our POD Marketing package.

5. Books are listed in all important book availability data bases as POD books. This carries an unfair stigma of being not as good or acceptable as most standard published books. Yet POD books are as good as any book we've seen printed. The only difference is that POD books are digitally generated...and that is technology at its best. You won't believe how good the quality really is. We defy you to tell us the difference.

6. An author is limited to only so much production time: copy and online editing, a couple of covers, proofs or manuscript (book form) galleys and other individual needs are outlined in the POD Publishing Contract. Call BFP for an opportunity to find out exactly what the contract spells out.

Benefits (Save thousands of dollars if a book qualifies and meets the correct criteria)

1. The cost is terrific! Call us for a quote, each book has to be figured differently; however, the difference in publishing costs is affordable to almost everyone.

2. There is no set amount for how many books you want to publish. Publish and print one copy, ten copies, 100 copies or whatever amount you desire and the price of your publishing is mostly predicated on the size of the printing run plus production work. Marketing is separate.

3. The marketing plan is designed to meet all of the most necessary features for getting a POD book in front of the eyes of the book buyers, as well as notifying all the right book entities about the existence of a POD book.

4. All books are digitally generated and digitally stored. This means there are no warehousing fees and no chance of a book getting damaged. Why? Because a book is not printed until there is a need to print it. For example: no orders, no printing. If we get an order for five books, the books will be printed, bound and shipped within 48-72 hours! If the order is for one book or 330 books, it doesn't matter, they all get printed and shipped as they are requested or sold.

5. We also do hardback books with or without stamped covers. For example: a Kivar cloth-style cover with gold foil or a four color cover, or a dust jacketed cover is available. Unit prices for hardback books are more expen-

sive, but not by much. Request a specific quote.

6. All books are drop shipped as orders come in; handling and shipping prices are very low.

7. If an author decides to revise his or her book, all we need are the changes or revisions to do the production work and make a new set up for print.

8. Most books can be finished within six weeks; sometimes certain books take longer due to unexpected or unscheduled author delays in the publishing process.

Note: There are no discounts when doing POD publishing with Black Forest Press.

POD Publishing Contract and POD Marketing Contract

Both of these contracts may be discussed or reviewed by another, prior to an agreement for publishing an author's book. A review may be requested by simply contacting BFP and asking for the contract of interest, Publishing, Marketing or both, to be emailed with a contract attachment. BFP does not send out hard copies of contracts until a publishing agreement has been reached and a serious negotiation has been decided upon.

Most vanity/ subsidy presses will charge an author thousands of dollars to publish his or her work. The break down is simple: production, printing and promotion equal MEGA- dollars; at Black Forest Press we've learned how to cut costs throughout the publishing process. This includes all phases of production and printing. Lastly, our book-marketing efforts to sell and promote an author's work are separate. Black Forest Press has a special contract, which covers several significant items which are done in marketing an author's book. The cost of this contract is low, while getting an author started on the right foot towards a successful sales endeavor. There are a few good book marketing companies in the United States and each of these companies has their own cut on what should be done in marketing and what should have to be done. An author must carefully choose the book marketing company to handle his or her work. Black Forest Press will coordinate and/ or assist with the efforts of the marketing professionals hired by the author.

Our book publishing process is very easy to understand. Initially an author sends his or her non-returnable manuscript, which must be double spaced typed, preferably a laser printed copy, and a 3.5 inch MAC or PC computer disk or CD with the manuscript in Word Perfect 6.1 or a newer version. If there are difficulties in converting the text sent to Black Forest Press, the author will be contacted and arrangements will be made to secure a workable copy of the book. We then copy edit, line edit, and proofread the manuscript. During the entire publishing process, the author's manuscript will be edited and proofed between 12 and 14 times. Galley prints are then sent to the author for changes and approval. When the galleys are returned, they are typeset into Quark Xpress 4.1 and then once again the text is proofed and necessary content or format changes are made. An author can see his or her blue lines, but that takes more time and any new changes are additional charges. The author is sent and Authorization to Print form to be signed and returned giving approval to go to press.

Early in the editing process, Black Forest Press graphic cover designers begin working on the author's book cover. The author will receive drafts of the covers for approval. Authors do have input as to the design of their covers. An author is assigned an artist who will design the cover or dust jacket. Each author will see his or her cover design prior to Black Forest Press printing it. If an author desires his or her picture on the back cover, it will be necessary to send either a black and white or color picture and a short personal biographical sketch. Any endorsements will be placed inside or on the back of the book cover; they must come from the author. An author can have a color portrait printed on the back cover instead of a black and white one, because all book covers are full color, unless specified otherwise by the author. Any special artwork requested, like metallic ink, colored foils, or embossed lettering will be an additional charge. All these charges are totaled and a final figure is given to the author by Black Forest Press, and agreed upon in the formal written author contract.

Unlike most subsidy or vanity presses, Black Forest Press will provide an author open and ongoing communication with production and printing staff members working on his or her book. You'll be one telephone call away, eight hours a day, five days a week; from knowing how your book is maturing and progressing on schedule. This is a plus when an author self-publishes

with guidance, direction, instruction, awareness and confidence.

As previously mentioned, the promotion of an author's book is also done by Black Forest Press. Although we do have several marketing packages we can also give authors choices of various book-marketing companies that will package, distribute, and sell their books. Promotion is a separate cost from publishing (production and printing). When and author's book is printed, the majority of the books (along with 150 free copies of the author's book cover) will be shipped directly to the promoter, or a specified amount to the author's residence with the remainder of the books, perhaps, going to the promoters warehousing facility. If BFP is the promoter, a specified amount of books will be kept with BFP. If BFP is the promoter, a predetermined and specified amount of author books will be kept in the BFP storage unit. Black Forest Press will only stock or warehouse books for up to three months at no extra cost. We do, however, request a sample copy of an author's book for each contributing member of our production team. This should never exceed ten copies; two of those copies go into our archives and two copies go the Registrar of Copyrights.

Indexing is also available for an extra modest, reasonable fee. Most authors who desire indexing will provide Black Forest Press with a list of the subjects, names or various entries they wish to have indexed. This is also true of a working Bibliography and a Footnote section. Black Forest Press recommends an author use either The Chicago Manual of Style or Form and Style to properly construct these sections.

The normal time for book production is 90 to 110 days. Much of that time depends on how long the author takes to review the galley copies and return them to Black Forest Press. On occasion, some extra requested author changes may also hold up the production schedule of the book, such time delays are not the responsibility of Black Forest Press. Once the author's book goes to press, an author should allow no more than four weeks

Books A-L

for perfect bound books, or two to three months for hardback/case bound books, to be printed and packaged for shipment. Color page inserts are very expensive and are usually done in groups of four pictures. Full color books, especially children's books, will take about three to four months for printing, because the printing department brokers color printing with the Hong Kong facility. This is fairly standard printing time for any reputable quality color printer. Printing overruns are not calculated into the contract cost, nor are they an extra charge to the author: Overage charges: if an author requests a desire to purchase the overruns, the overages will be offered at Black Forest Press cost. Overruns can be used by promoters to effectively market an author's book along with or inside of press kits or promo packages, etc. To reiterate, Black Forest Press provides each author with an additional 150 covers, for promotional purposes, at no extra cost. This is a service where a necessary product is supplied to the author for free.

Common sizes for books are 5 ½ x 8 ½ and 8 ½ x 11 inches. Books which are

6 x 9 or 4 ½ x 6 inches are considered special cuts which cost the same as the next larger size. Printing runs of 1,000, 2,000, 2,500 or 3,000 books are usual for an author. Remember: although the cost of printing more books goes up, the unit cost per book will decrease drastically. For example, 1,000 books may have a unit cost of $3.00 per copy, but 2,000 books may drop the price to $2.00 or less per book. The unit price goes down with larger printing runs and prices vary with the size and page count of each book. With full color insides, the prices may vary or increase. Unless an author sells most of his or her books directly, without any middle men, distributors, wholesalers or libraries being involved in the sales process and/or taking a healthy percentage out of the actual sales price, an author may possibly clear a respectable profit from printing 1,000 books. Otherwise, depending upon the cost of publishing, the retail price at which the book is sold, and including the calculations of third party percentages, and author should consider printing upwards of over 1,350 to break even or make only a negligible profit. Serious profits begin with a minimum printing of 1,500 or 2,000 books, if the book is promoted properly and sells. Early in the publishing process, the marketability of each book should be discussed with the publisher and the promoter. Presale fliers would also be a wise decision to consider. Such fliers are designed and sent out early in the publishing process in order to get a feel for the potential sales of a book. A healthy result in presales may well deter-

mine the amount of extra books an author might want to have printed. An author may then want to consider increasing the amount of books to be printed for which he or she initially contracted. Black Forest Press will gladly renegotiate the printing amount with an author. The publishing process must be a win-win effort. There are no losers when working with Black Forest Press.

If you are interested in self-publishing with Black Forest Press, please write us and let us know the specifics of your book. You may also view our price graph. Only then can we give you a realistic cost for the publishing of your book. Read the Black Forest Press Production Procedure Steps for Processing Author Manuscripts very carefully. It details the most important specifics of the Black Forest Press publishing process. Personal inquiry should give a prospective author a good idea of what it costs to self-publish with Black Forest Press. If another publisher will not furnish you with similar detailed information, you should carefully consider what they may be keeping from you, like hidden cost or not so comprehensive work. For authors who are serious about publishing with Black Forest Press, the names and telephone numbers of other Black Forest Press authors can be provided, upon request, prior to contract signing, for your convenience. Call them and chat about their publishing experiences with Black Forest Press and the published product they each received. Because Black Forest Press does the job right, we are proud of our publications, all of them. You select authors with whom you wish to speak; we will not provide a prescreened list of authors. Individual choices are yours without Black Forest Press input or suggestion.

Payments are usually made in two parts: one payment is to be made at the beginning of production; the second payment must be made just prior to press time. An author may also pay everything down, or divide his or her payments into three parts: one third down, one third due at the time the first galleys are returned, and the last one third, prior to press time. No book will be printed until all author payments have been made in full. Black Forest Press does not do co-op publishing, nor does it sponsor and subsidize books for authors who suggest that Black Forest Press receive their manuscript for free, publish it at our cost and then take the first profits as repayment after the book sells. Black Forest Press will subsidize select books, which are felt to be within our realm of financial capability. However, we solicit those types of books and we only schedule them at our publishing convenience.

Personal blue line changes will result in an extra cost to the author who will be billed separately for his or her blue line changes. All payments should be a cashier's check or money order and made out to Black Forest Press Productions. We accept credit cards, however there is an additional charge. Black Forest Press will wait until your check clears our bank before we begin production or printing work. When you receive our contract, you may have an attorney review it for approval. You will feel better and have less worry. An author's trust and cooperation are paramount to us. This process can't be made much easier than what it is already.

We accept only good books worthy of being sold and read by the public. No obscene, racist, sexist, overly violent, blasphemous or discriminating manuscripts will be accepted by Black Forest Press. The materials we accept are totally at our own discretion; decisions are made without prejudice or bias. We reserve the right to refuse work. Black Forest Press chooses only works of good taste, offensive to no one.

If an author has suffered permanent physical disabilities, is 65 years of age or older, a United States Armed Forces veteran, ore receives social security benefits, a 5% deduction of production costs will be given. However, Black Forest Press request substantiating evidence or legal documentation for that claim. Keep claim submissions simple. Send no original documents or personal paperwork, only photocopies. This information must be presented to Black Forest Press prior to negotiating the contract or receiving the initial cost work up. We will not be surprising you, so please extend us the same courtesy and don't surprise us by expecting a discount after you've been give the contract amount.

Black Forest Press will serve you in a timely, efficient, and friendly manner. Prior to considering Black Forest Press as your publisher, we do suggest that you get at least four or five vanity/subsidy press or other self-publishing quotes for publishing your book. You will see the difference we make when the bucks hit the table. Black Forest Press will show you where we can save you money and probably time. Keep in mind, most vanity presses will only do a limited marketing or promotional campaign for your book; a book marketing company will cost you extra, but it should get the job done correctly. You can judge for yourself what they do. Black Forest Press has no ownership in any book marketing companies we recommend, we prefer our own. We can only direct you and give your our best advice. You will know a good deal when you see it. For further information, call or fax us your questions. If you do not choose Black Forest Press to do your work, we wish you good fortune and success elsewhere. There are many decent, fair and honest publishers around.

Black Forest Press hours of operation are Monday through Friday, 9:00am to 5:30pm Eastern Standard Time. No telephone calls are accepted. You can E-mail Black Forest Press at the following:blackforestpress@yahoo.com.

Categories: Fiction—Nonfiction—Adventure—Biography—Business—Careers—Children—Christian Interests—Civil War—College—Cooking—Culture—Drama—Disabilities—Education—Family—Fantasy—General Interest—Government—Health—Hispanic—History—Inspirational—Literature—Military—Multicultural—Mystery—Native American—Poetry—Politics—Psychology—Reference—Religion—Romance—Science Fiction—Short Stories—Society—Spiritual—Sports/Recreation—Textbooks—Western—Writing—Ethnic—Philosophy

CONTACT: Julie Knox, Chief Administrative Acquisitions Officer
Material: All
BFP
Belle Arden Run
490 Mt. View Dr
Mosheim TN 37818
E-mail: blackforestpress@yahoo.com
Website: www.blackforestpresspod.com

Bloomberg Press

Bloomberg Press publishes basic and advanced investing books, books for financial professionals and planners, and money-related books for the general public. We seek leading authors and experts recognized in their professional circles.

Overview: Bloomberg Press publishes topical books focused essentially on finance and business, written by experts in their fields. Books for:

• Financial Professionals
• Topics for money-makers and money-movers
• Guides to basic investing techniques and specialized interests for more sophisticated investors

Books Published: 15 to 20 books published annually domestically

Marketing: Bloomberg Press books are sold and distributed to the book trade by W.W. Norton, one of the leading independent publishers in America, and works with leading distributors worldwide. Bloomberg Press has won numerous design awards for its catalogues, as well as awards for its books. We can give our authors worldwide exposure through various media, including but not limited to our own TV, radio, magazines, international news service, and the BLOOMBERG PROFESSIONAL service (the company's proprietary global network of business news and financial information terminals).

Global Presence: Books available in countries throughout the world and many are published in multiple languages, including: Complex and Simplified Chinese, Japanese, Italian, German, Spanish, Portuguese, Korean, Arabic, Thai, Bulgarian, Polish, and Russian.

Categories: Business—Investing—Institutional Investing—Professional Finance

CONTACT: Acquisitions Editor
Material: All
100 Business Park Dr.

PO Box 888
Princeton NJ 08542-0888
E-mail: kpeterson@bloomberg.net
Website: www.bloomberg.com/books

Blue Mountain Arts®

We are interested in reviewing poetry and writings suitable for publication on greeting cards and in books. We are looking for original, heartfelt poetry and prose on love, friendship, family, special occasions, positive living, aspirations, self-help, and other similar topics. We strongly suggest that you familiarize yourself with Blue Mountain Arts products before submitting material. The following guidelines are for our books and poetry card lines and do not apply to card lines created specifically for niche or specialized markets.1. Greeting card submissions should communicate a message that one person would want to express to or share with another person. Writings on special occasions (birthday, anniversary, graduation, etc.) as well as the themes listed above are also considered. Poetry and writings should be about real emotions and feelings written from your personal experience. We suggest that you have someone in mind (a friend, relative, etc.) as you write. The majority of the poetry we publish DOES NOT RHYME. *Important note: Because of the large volume of poetry we receive written to mothers, sons, and daughters, we are accepting only highly original and creative poetry that expresses new thoughts and sentiments on these themes.*

2. Book manuscripts and proposals in typewritten form are also accepted. We are particularly interested in receiving books that fall under the self-help, family, gift, inspiring young adults, relationships, self-improvement, and motivational categories. We do not wish to receive poetry chap books.

3. Your work need not be copyrighted prior to submission. However, to obtain a copyright, you may contact the Copyright Office (address: United States Copyright Office, Library of Congress, Washington, DC 20559).

4. If you are submitting via postal mail, we prefer that manuscripts be typewritten; one greeting card submission per page please. Your name should appear on every page. You may submit as many poems at one time as you wish.

5. If you are submitting your work by postal mail and would like a response and/or to have your work returned, you must enclose a self-addressed, stamped envelope (SASE) of adequate size, with the correct postage. While we always try to respond to your submission as quickly as possible, please allow 2 to 4 months for a reply. Please be sure to include your name, address, and telephone number with your submission, and please keep us informed of all address and telephone number changes.

6. E-mail greeting card submissions are welcome. Send to editorial@spsstudios.com. PLEASE DO NOT SEND ATTACHMENTS. Type or paste the text of your work into the body of the e-mail. If you are submitting more than one poem at a time, please include all of them in one e-mail message. Be sure to include your name, address, and telephone number. Please do not submit book proposals or manuscripts by e-mail.

7. E-mail submissions will receive a reply only if the work is selected for further review for possible publication. Selected submissions will receive a response by postal mail within 2 to 3 months. We are unable to respond to e-mail submissions that are not selected for further review.

8. We pay $300 per poem for the worldwide, exclusive rights to publish it on a greeting card and other products, and $50 per poem for one-time use in a book. Book submissions are negotiated on an individual basis. Publication procedures will be explained in detail prior to actually publishing your work. 9. Manuscript submissions and questions concerning your work may be directed in writing to the addresses below. Please do not telephone.

Categories: Family—Poetry—Relationships—Self Help—Teen

CONTACT: Editorial Department

Material: All
PO Box 1007
Boulder, CO 80306
E-mail: editorial@sps.com
Website: www.sps.com

Blue Poppy Press, Inc.

If I had an idea for a book, what would I need to send in the way of a proposal?

First of all, Blue Poppy Press only publish books about acupuncture and Chinese medicine. Secondly, we only publish books by professional practitioners who have been in practice A) not less than five (5) years, and B) read at least one Asian language. We prefer our authors to be native English-speakers, but this is not a hard and fast rule.

What we like to see in the way of a proposal are the following:

• A query letter stating the concept of the book, why its needed, and identifying its target audience.

• The book's outline or Table of Contents

• At least two sample chapters, usually the introduction and at least one technical chapter.

• The author's resume or curriculum vitae

If the book is a translation, then we also need:

• The name and author of the source text

• Date and place of publication and original publisher's name

• Some description of copyright status, e.g. public domain

• Several sample pages of the original language text for comparison

• A description of translational methodology, whether denotative, connotative, or functional.

Categories: Nonfiction—Health—Acupuncture—Chinese Medicine

CONTACT: Bob Flaws, Editor in Chief
Material: All

5441 Western Ave, #2
Boulder CO 80301
Phone: 303-447-8372
Fax: 303-245-8362
E-mail: bob@bluepoppy.com
Website: www.bluepoppy.com

BLUE WATER

Blue Water Publishing, LLC

Please refer to Granite Publishing Group.

BNA Books

Discover the advantages of teaming up with a highly respected leader in legal publishing. *BNA Books welcomes inquiries from established, talented professionals who seek a publisher for their manuscripts in the following subject areas:*

• Labor and Employment Law

• Labor Relations

• Legal Practice

• Health Law

• Employee Benefits Law

• Arbitration and ADR

• Intellectual Property Law

• Occupational Safety and Health Law

BNA Books gives its authors an extraordinary combination of editorial support and marketing resources, backed by The Bureau of National

Affairs, Inc., one of the largest private information-gathering organizations in the world.

If you have an idea, outline, or manuscript that would complement the BNA Books publishing program, we would like to hear from you.

Please use the form below to describe your project's subject, purpose, content, intended market, and estimated length. An outline or table of contents will show us how the subject matter is organized. In addition, please send us a current curriculum vitae or description of your credentials. Be sure to include your current telephone and fax numbers.

ll suggestions you send will be kept in confidence and given our full consideration. We will contact you in three to six weeks to discuss your proposal.

If you prefer to submit your proposal by mail.

Categories: Nonfiction—Law

CONTACT: Acquisitions Manager
Material: All
BNA Books Editorial Offices
1231 25th St. NW
Washington DC 20037
Phone: 202-452-4110

Bonus Books, Inc.

We publish primarily nonfiction trade books.

If you would like to submit a manuscript or proposal for our review, please follow these guidelines.

1. The material must be typed and double-spaced.

2. Please include a self addressed, stamped business-size envelope for a reply. Because of the large volume of submissions we receive, if you don't include an SASE, you will not receive a reply. If you would like any of your material returned, please enclose an SASE large enough to do so.

3. If you are submitting your work electronically, please send it as an attachment in either Word or Rich Text Format.

4. If you are submitting a proposal, please include an outline or summary of your book and a few sample chapters.

5. Allow six to eight weeks for a response.

Thank you for the opportunity to consider your work.

Categories: Nonfiction—Business—Cooking—Games—Sports/Recreation—Textbooks—Textbooks (Medical, Health)

CONTACT: Erin Kahl, Acquisitions Editor
Material: All
160 East Illinois St.
Chicago IL 60611
Phone: 312-467-0580
Fax: 312-467-9271
E-mail: Webmaster@bonus-books.com
Website: www.bonus-books.com

Book Peddlers

No longer accepting submissions.

Bookhaven Press LLC

Bookhaven Press LLC, founded in 1985, is an independent publishing house dedicated to producing award winning business and career books. Owned and operated by Dennis V. Damp, the author of the Benjamin

Franklin Awards finalist for "Best Career Book" The Book of U.S. Government Jobs - 9th edition, 2005.

Bookhaven publishes for a select group of experts and our titles include:
• The Book of U.S. Government Jobs - 9th edition
• Post Office Jobs - 4th edition
• Health Care Job Explosion, 4th edition
• Dollars and Sense
• How to Raise A Family and a Career Under One Roof
• Applying For Federal Jobs
• Air Conditioning & Refrigeration Technician's EPA Certification Guide

Manuscript Submission Guidelines:

Writers must send a query with SASE. The query must include the following:

1) A comprehensive outline of the book

2) A draft table of contents

3) A copy of the first chapter

4) Detailed author bio, credentials, affiliations, etc.

5) Computer system that you work with, wordprocessor, IBM/Apple, etc.

6) Target marketing perspective (who would buy this book)

All authors that we publish are computer literate and submit the final manuscript on IBM formatted disks in WordPerfect or Microsoft Word.

Bookhaven replies within 8 weeks if an SASE is included with your material or via email if an email address is provided.

We do not accept files via the internet. Submit copies as noted above by snail mail.

Categories: Nonfiction—Business—Careers—Reference

CONTACT: Submissions
Material: All
PO Box 1243
Moon Township PA 15108
Phone: 412-494-6926
Fax: 412-494-5749
E-mail: Bookhaven@aol.com
Website: members.aol.com/bookhaven

Branden Publishing Company (Branden Books)

Branden Publishing Company is always interested in publishing new books and finding new authors. If you wish to contact Branden regarding the publishing of your work, please mail your query (one or two paragraphs) with a self-addressed, stamped envelope to the address below; no other form accepted.

Due to the high volume of publishing requests, we will not accept phone calls, e-mails, or faxes.

Categories: Fiction—Nonfiction—African-American—Arts—Aviation—Biography—Business—Children—Civil War—Consumer—Culture—Drama—Disabilities—Education—Entertainment—Family—General Interest—Government—Health—History—Internet—Jewish Interest—Language—Law—Literature—Military—Multicultural—Poetry—Politics—Regional—Religion—Society—Sports/Recreation—Teen—Textbooks—Theatre—True Crime—Western—Women's Issues—Young Adult—Ethnic

CONTACT: Adolph Caso, Editor
Material: All
PO Box 812094
Wellesley MA 02482
E-mail: Branden@brandenbooks.com
Website: www.branden.com

Brassey's Sports

Please refer to Potomac Books, Inc. Sports

Brazos Press

Please refer to Baker Publishing Group.

Bridge Works

Bridge Works is a small house, an affiliate of Rowman & Littlefield Publishers.

We publish very few titles each year (3-4) and, accordingly do not read unagented material. Our titles are usually trade fiction with occasional non-fiction in biography or public policy. We do not publish poetry or any genre fiction except mysteries.

An SASE or e-mail address is necessary for a reply to a submission. We do no read computer disks or attachments, only hard copies.

Categories: Fiction—Nonfiction—Adventure—Asian-American—Civil War—Comedy—Crime—Drama—Feminism—General Interest

CONTACT: Barbara Phillips, Editorial Director
Material: All
PO Box 1798
Bridgehampton NY 11932

Bright Mountain Books, Inc.

Bright Mountain Books welcomes adult, nonfiction manuscripts with Southern Appalachian or North and South Carolina content. We especially solicit new manuscripts by area writers and will consider relevant self-published or out-of-print books for republication.

Our emphasis is on nonfiction, though we also publish creative nonfiction — i.e., fictionalized histories based on factual events or historical novels with strong factual bases. We *do not* publish poetry, children's books, textbooks, self-help manuals, religious texts, family histories, or novels not based on true-life experiences.

As a traditional publisher, Bright Mountain Books

- is interested in seeing what you want your book to *say*, not how you think it should *look*.

- will convert your words and/or illustrations into a professionally produced book and market it successfully.

- produces books at no cost to the author, who then receives royalties based on sales.

- edits, designs, and typesets in-house, then sends books to be manufactured by quality book printers in the United States.

- offers a contract typical of traditional publishing policies.

Submission Instructions and Policies

If you have a manuscript to submit, please keep these points in mind:

- Manuscripts should be submitted in digital form if possible, preferably on CD-ROM or 3.5" floppy disks, along with a printed version of the first several pages.

- Submissions do not need to conform to a prescribed format.

- If the manuscript exists only in printed form, *do not* send the entire manuscript. Instead, send only a content outline along with three sample chapters. If we feel that we have a definite interest in publishing your book, we will request the entire manuscript.

- Send only photocopies or printouts of photographs and artwork. *Do not* send originals.

- Bright Mountain Books, Inc., cannot be held liable for any materials submitted, though we are committed to handling your submissions with care and respect.

- Please include a stamped, self-addressed postcard or envelope so we can acknowledge receipt of your submission.

- At least two readers will evaluate each relevant manuscript, which can take from one day to several weeks, depending on the nature of the submission. Please be patient during our evaluation.

- We will return your manuscript to you only if you supply a postage-paid envelope of suitable size.

Categories: Nonfiction—General Interest—Native American—Outdoors—Regional

CONTACT: Submissions
Material: All
206 Riva Ridge Dr.
Fairview NC 28730
Phone: 828-628-1768
Fax: 828-628-1755
Website: www.brightmountainbooks.com

Bristol Fashion Publications, Inc.
The World's Largest Nautical Publishing House

You will find we are very cooperative when dealing with freelance contributors. Our CEO and Publisher, John Kaufman, and our COO and Editor-in-Chief, Bob Lollo, were both freelance photographers and writers long before Bristol Fashion Publications, Inc. came to be in 1993. They still retain the memories of the "difficult years" getting started. This is one of the reasons we are interested in submissions from new authors and photographers.

All of our titles are nautical themes, aimed at the new or seasoned boater. All our titles cover restoration, repair, maintenance, cruising, living aboard, cruising, etc.

Boating is a fast changing industry. Therefore, we rarely project more than six months in advance. Always include a SASE for any submissions you would like returned. Include your telephone number with any correspondence or submissions. Sample books are available at a 40% discount.

Photography Submissions

COVERS: Color glossy prints. Prints should be 3-1/2 x 5 to 5 x 7. Digitized images (300 DPI) in a JPG or GIF file are preferred for final use.

All covers depict the theme of the book. Use deep saturation, vivid colors and good contrast to bring out the main subject matter. This is NOT the type of cover you will see on a boating magazine. Send several sample copies of your work for consideration. Mark each copy with your name, address and phone number.

INTERIOR: Digitized images (300 DPI) in a GIF or JPG file are the only images we consider for use.

Presently, we use line drawings for the bulk of the interior art work. We would rather use photos if more were available for our use. Photos should show hands using tools, when appropriate, the steps involved in completing a project and the finished results. These are the photos we most often need, however, other photos of boats and boating may be needed for a current title. Good contrast, lighting and subject matter is necessary. Send several hard copy samples of your work for consideration. Mark each copy with your name, address and phone number.

Simultaneous submissions are fine. Notify us if a photo we have on file becomes unavailable. Model and property releases are preferred if the person or vessel is identifiable. All submissions should be non-returnable disks or prints. If we can keep copies of your work on file, we are more likely to call you when the need arises. We will notify you within one month, whether or not we feel we can use your work. Assignments may be given at the same rate of pay, as noted below.

We purchase book/reprint rights as a one time buy. Cover prices range from $50.00 to $300.00 depending on the project. Interior B & W prices range from $10.00 to $25.00. Credit line given. One copy of the book will be given to each contributor.

Writer's Guidelines

Considering what we have read on the shelves, it appears we are the only publishing company that writes for the non-handy boater. Our books use simple to understand and follow processes, for the person who knows which end of the wrench to hold, but little else about boating. Each subject should take the reader from the very basics, through each step, until the complete subject matter is discussed.

As an example: Start by describing the steps involved in replacing a damaged receptacle and work up to wiring an entire boat. As the project expands and becomes more complicated, each new phase or technique should be described. If a friend, who knows nothing about boats, can read, understand and feel comfortable doing the work you have described, you have written what we want to publish.

Non-How-To titles should be extremely interesting to read. Cruising related books should speak of the culture and events more than the "what I did" topics. Live aboard topics are always well received. How-To topics are the most marketable with a wider audience. We are always seeking new ideas and topics for our books.

Simultaneous submissions are not accepted. Submit a few chapters for review, along with the table of contents. All submissions must be hard copy. Include your past credits, tear sheets, state if photos or line art is available and the state of completion of your manuscript. We will report in two weeks of receipt, often sooner.

If you have never been published or have not yet stated the manuscript submit a short sample (1000 words), outline, completion date and photo/line art availability.

We pay royalty of 8% to 11% based on the retail price of the book. Average retail price is $20.00 to $30.00. Photos and line art submitted by the author will be considered as part of the manuscript and the percentage adjusted accordingly. Follow the photography submission guideline above. We will purchase worldwide book/reprint rights.

WRITERS TIPS: Know or research the industry, boat owners and technical knowledge. Use the proper nautical language and terms. A well-written manuscript is useless if the knowledge of the writer is lacking. If you are not familiar with a given subject, talk to a tradesman who has been around boats for many years. Do not use unwarranted technical jargon to explain a subject. Use simple terms and an easy to understand and follow, step-by-step writing style. When we have to choose, we are more likely to use poor writing and good knowledge, than good writing and poor knowledge.

PREPARING YOUR MANUSCRIPT: Never use an exclamation point for emphasis except in a direct quotation. We! and! the! reader! don't! care! what! startles! you!

Don't double-space, regardless of what you were taught in typing class.

Don't use the Tab key or Space bar to indent a paragraph.

Boat names should be in italics, not quotation marks.

A boat's name is a proper name, therefore, the word The should not precede the name. It is not The Sea Cow it is Sea Cow. They don't call you The Bob, do they?

Don't attempt to make your manuscript look as you'd like your book to appear. Just write. Converting your manuscript into a book is what we do.

Don't use "Captain Bob," Captain Bob, Capt. Bob and CAPTAIN BOB—pick one and stay consistent.

Trust us. We have a combined experience of more than 300 years in the boating and publishing industries. We will edit your manuscript to suit its intended market. The better your work reads, the better it sells, and that benefits all of us.

Please understand this—You will not retire from the book sales of any single nautical title. Specialty titles simply do not sell that well in any market. A very successful nautical title may sell 20,000 copies over a five year run. A very few sell more. Most sell one quarter or less of that number and are considered a successful book. Our successful boating authors often have three or more books published with us and they started by reading this very same letter.

After preparing your submission, following the above guidelines, you may submit it by land mail (hard copy only, do not include a disk) or by email. To submit by email, attach an ASCII text or MSWord file to the email—DO NOT paste the text into the body of the email or include graphic files with this submission. Send the email to jpk@bfpbooks.com. Include only one manuscript with each email submission. Our best tip—Visit our web site to view our current titles.

Imprints

Motorcycling and Railroading are listed alphabetically in the book publisher section.

Categories: Nonfiction—Boating—Recreation—Sports/Recreation

CONTACT: Submissions
Material: All
P. O. Box 560989
Rockledge, FL 32956
Phone: 772-559-1379
Fax: 800-543-9030
E-mail: jpk@bfpbooks.com
Website: www.bfpbooks.com

Bristol Publishing Enterprises
Nitty Gritty Cookbooks

Greetings: We currently have no specific manuscript guidelines but are primarily interested in cookbooks.

Our Nitty Gritty cookbooks are 5¼"x8¼", bound on the short side, and include approximately 100 to 120 recipes. We are looking for authors with a proven history of success in the food industry: dietitians, professional chefs or bakers, teachers or others. Topics must be of interest to the mass market and must have an expected term of interest of at least 5 years.

Rather than submit an entire manuscript, we prefer that you send an initial proposal (an outline is also recommended), a resume and a sample of your published writing.

Sincerely,

Aidan Wylde, Managing Editor & President

Categories: Cooking—Food/Drink—Gardening—Home—Trade—Cookbooks

CONTACT: Aidan Wylde, President
Material: All
2714 McCone Ave
Hayward, CA 94541
Phone: 510-783-5472
Fax: 510-783-5492
Website: www.bristolpublishing.com

Broadman & Holman Publishers

Broadman & Holman actively seeks to enlist both new and established authors to work with us in producing the finest books in Christian publishing. We have been publishing books since 1934, and we bring a commitment to traditional Christian values and beliefs to everything we do.

OPPORTUNITIES

Broadman & Holman publishes books for adults, youth, pastors, church staff, and lay ministers. *We are currently accepting submissions in these general categories:*

• Bible Study Helps—Books in the Bible Study Helps Series help ministers and lay leaders communicate biblical truths to others.

• Christian Living—Books in the Christian Living Series are designed for adults ages twenty-five and older. These books apply sound, biblical principles to issues and concerns that face Christians, enabling them to grow in their faith.

• Inspirational—Books in the Inspirational Series are designed to inspire adults to grow in their Christian faith and relationships with others. Biographies, inspiring stories of faith and courage, and devotional books are included in this series.

• Ministry—Books in the Ministry Series are designed to equip laypersons with ministry and relational skills.

• Parenting/Leadership—Books in the Parenting/Leadership Series are designed for parents or adult leaders of children from birth through college. These books assist readers in dealing with children, teenagers, and college students as they face issues and develop as persons and Christians.

• Practical Theology—Books in the Practical Theology Series are designed for adults, ages twenty-five and older. These books apply timeless truths from the Bible, Christian theology, and church history to real-life situations, enabling believers to understand their faith and communicate the gospel clearly.

• Professional—Books in the Professional Series are designed to equip ministers for their work.

• Youth/Juvenile—Books in the Youth/Juvenile Series are designed for older children through college students. These books introduce readers to a relationship with Christ in an age-appropriate manner; offer guidance as they face questions, issues, and decisions; and encourage them to grow in their Christian faith and share that faith with others.

Please Do Not Send:

• Poetry
• Articles or short stories
• Adult fiction or Juvenile fiction
• Tracts or Pamphlets
• Exposés of prominent persons or organizations
• Art books
• Children's picture books

GETTING OUR ATTENTION

One of the secrets to catching our attention is helping us see the marketability of your idea. The following questions are commonly asked by our editorial, sales, and marketing staffs as we consider products.

• What other books or articles have you published?

• Have you read other books in your subject category? What makes your idea unique? What features or reader benefits have you included to make your book attractive to potential customers?

• Is your topic timely?

• How can you help market your book? Do you lead conferences or speak frequently in public? Do you have access to radio or television? Are you a recognized authority in your field?

• Are there prominent people who could give endorsements for this book?

OUR PROPOSAL FORMAT

While Broadman & Holman accepts ideas in several forms, we prefer that you query first. If sample chapters are available, please include at least two with your submission. *We ask that you use this format for your query:*

I. Content

A. Premise: a one-paragraph description of what the book is about.

B. The manuscript:

1. Status (Is it complete? When do you expect to complete it?)
2. Special features (epigraphs, charts, illustrations, lists, index, bibliography, etc.)
3. Anticipated length
4. Outline
5. Competition. List other recent titles in your subject area and compare the features and benefits of your manuscript to each title.

II. Audience

A. Target audience: age, sex, special interests or needs

B. Motivation: Why will readers want to purchase this book?

III. Author

A. Background

B. Previous writing

C. Resumé: include address, phone number, birth date, and social security number

D. Opportunities you have to market and promote the book

IV. Chapter synopsis: a one paragraph summary of the premise of each chapter.

V. Sample chapters (two)

Broadman & Holman receives over fifteen hundred unsolicited trade book submissions each year. We try to respond within two months. If you haven't heard from us within that time, please feel free to ask about your submission.

GENERAL GUIDELINES

• Do not bind or staple your submission.

• If you're submitting to several publishers, please tell us.

• Be open to editorial guidance.

• Provide suggestions for charts, graphs, photographs, illustrations, or other features that would make your idea attractive to readers.

• Final proposal submissions and finished manuscripts must be available on computer disk.

A FINAL WORD

Thanks for thinking of Broadman & Holman Publishers. If you're as committed as we are to being a leader in Christian publishing, you may be the type of author we're looking for; we may be the kind of publisher you need. If you have an idea for a book that will meet needs and change lives, we want to hear from you. Please write to the address below.

We look forward to hearing from you!

Sincerely,

Broadman & Holman Editorial Staff

Categories: Nonfiction—Christian Interests—Family—Inspirational—Humor

CONTACT: Acquisitions Editor
Material: All
127 - 9th Ave. N
Nashville TN 37234
Phone: 615-251-2644

Books
A-L

BROOK
LINE
BOOKS

Brookline Books

The trade and professional lines of Brookline Books publish titles in education, disabilities, psychology, parenting, and other related topics. Our selection includes workbooks for teachers and students, scholarly texts for teachers and health professionals, and trade books for students, parents, and a general audience. Please call and request a catalogue to get a better sense of our selection.

We look for well-written, well-organized manuscripts with a clear and original focus. We primarily consider texts based on solid research or professional experience. Books based solely on personal (vs. professional) experience are considered only if they display exceptional writing quality, provide original insights, and offer advice on parenting, self-help or education.

Categories: Fiction—Nonfiction—Animals—Disabilities—Education—Hispanic—Jewish Interest—Literature—Parenting—Poetry—Psychology—Short Stories—Travel—Writing

CONTACT: Michael Beattie, Assistant to the Publisher
Material: All
34 University Rd
Brookline MA 02445
Phone: 617-734-6772
Fax: 617-734-3952
E-mail:brbooks@yahoo.com

Bulfinch Press

Please refer to Time Warner Book Group.

Burford Books

Burford Books welcomes proposals on new projects, especially in the subject areas in which we specialize: sports, the outdoors, golf, nature, gardening, food and wine, travel, and military history. We are not currently considering fiction or children's books. In general it's sufficient to send a brief proposal letter that outlines your idea, which can be mailed, faxed, or emailed as you prefer. If you would like to send a sample chapter or two, please do so by mail. In all cases where you would like material returned, you must include a SASE.

We try to respond to all proposals within two to four weeks, but feel free to follow up with us if you have not heard after this period of time.

Categories: Nonfiction—Adventure—Civil War—Crafts/Hobbies—Crime—Environment—Fishing—Food/Drink—Games—Gardening—History—Hobbies—Military—Outdoors—Recreation—Rural America—Sports/Recreation—True Crime

Contact us at:
Burford Books—Editorial Dept.
32 Morris Avenue
Springfield, N.J. 07081
Phone: 973-258-0960
Fax: 973-258-0113
Email: Info@burfordbooks.com
Website: www.burfordbooks.com

The Business Group

We publish for the small business market. My cornerstone book is *How to Grow Your Business without Driving Yourself Crazy*—just out.
Other titles include:
- *Success Tips From Small Business Owners*
- *The Magic Chain of Marketing*
- *Pay Yourself First*
- *Finding and Keeping Good Employees*
- *Hiring Your First Employee*
- *Promote Yourself to CEO*
- *Recapture Your Time*

Up to now we have distributed exclusively through our own seminars and workshops, but are now entering the wider book market—via Amazon, Baker&Taylor, Publisher's Marketing Assn.

We will consider manuscripts with the following qualities:
- "How to" books for owners of small businesses. Practical, useful, nuts and bolts topics, like our titles above.
- Tested on real people; not just good ideas.
- Friendly, easy to read style; not academic or pedantic. Lots of examples and illustrations. All our materials are judged by one of the world's toughest audiences—small business owners.
- Short. Our workbooks are a max of 96 pages. Our "big book" is 304 pages.
- Has a demonstrable market.

I will consider products that include computer templates for CDs or electronic distribution. For example, a book on how small business owners can ever afford to retire that includes a CD template with a spreadsheet that helps readers calculate how much they need and how they will generate it, using different scenarios.

We cannot take on the role of a standard publisher; however, for the right submission, we will work with the author to help produce and distribute an excellent book.

An interested author should contact us via email with a proposal, table of contents, and sample chapter, along with the author's background and a marketing plan for the book. Send via Word (Office 98) or PDF. Mailed material will be returned only with SASE.

Contact info is below. My personal email is mvh@businessgroup.biz.
Problem solving groups for business owners.
Mike Van Horn
Categories: Nonfiction—Business—Money & Finances

CONTACT: Mike Van Horn, President
Material: All
135 Paul Drive, Ste. 300
San Rafael CA 94903
Phone: 415-491-1896
Fax: 415-491-1855
E-mail: mvh@businessgroup.biz.
Website: www.businessgroup.biz

Bye Publishing

Established 1996. We publish books by authors whose writings might otherwise be missed by many readers. We seek manuscripts from writers who write about experiences that will assist readers with achieving a higher level of awareness. We publish books that focus on self-development, empowerment, spirituality, ethnic studies, education, male and female relationships, and some specialized ethnic poetry. We publish 1-2 novels a year. No author advances. Pays royalty on retail price. Report in 30 days on queries.

Submit query letters only, which describe the project briefly, the author's writing and professional credentials, and promotional ideas.

Recent nonfiction title(s): *Super Sistahs, by Morrie Turner, the creator of Wee Pals cartoon.*

Categories: Nonfiction—Education—Inspirational—Poetry—Relationships—Religion—Self Help—Spiritual

CONTACT: Malcolm Kelly, Publisher
Material: All
BYE PUBLISHING SERVICES
5245 College Avenue Ste 333
Oakland CA 94618
Phone: 510-272-0101
Fax: 510-336-3230

CALYX Books

CALYX Books is a nonprofit feminist publisher particularly interested in fine literature by women. We are committed to publishing work by women of color, working class women, lesbians, and other women whose voices need to be heard. We publish one to two books each year: novels, collections of short fiction, poetry, translations of writers (poetry and fiction), nonfiction works of exceptional literary merit, and special anthologies.

CALYX Books is closed for submissions until further notice.

Categories: Fiction—Nonfiction—African-American—Asian-American—Feminism—Hispanic—Humor—Jewish Interest—Literature—Native American—Poetry—Self Help—Senior Citizen—Women's Fiction—Women's Issues

CONTACT: Margarita Donnelly, Director
Material: Any
PO Box B
Corvallis OR 97339
Phone: 541-753-9384
Fax: 541-753-0515
E-mail: Calyx@proaxis.com
Website: www.calyspress.org

Capital Books

Capital Books publishes non-fiction titles in the following areas of interest: self-help, personal and career development, business, lifestyles, travel, and parenting and family,.

We seek authors who are, or who have the potential to become, the preeminent spokesperson in the field and whose professional affiliations can provide a potentially large additional distribution channel to augment the traditional bookstore and retail channels.

We expect to collaborate with our authors in actively marketing their books using their contacts as well as those our marketing team provides. We offer a substantial author discount for the authors affiliated organizational sales.

We evaluate proposals using the following criteria:
• The subject matter is in one of our core areas
• The writing and literary style is compelling
• The author will actively participate in the marketing process
• The project is financially viable for both parties

While we prefer to review a finished manuscript, we will accept proposals that contain sample chapters. *All submissions should include:*

1. *A one page synopsis of the project comprised of:*
• Description of the book
• Definition of the target audience
• Statement of why you are uniquely qualified to write this book
2. Table of Contents or an outline of the structure of the book
3. One or two sample chapters or a manuscript (double spaced)
4. Biographical sketch or resume

Categories: Business—Careers—Family—Lifestyle—Parenting—Self Help—Travel

CONTACT: Acquisitions Editor
Material: All
22841 Quicksilver Drive

Sterling VA 20166
Phone: 703-996-1020
Fax: 703-661-1547
Website: www.capital-books.com

Carolrhoda Books
A division of Lerner Publishing Group

Please note: Our submission policy has changed. Effective immediately, we will only accept submissions during the month of November. Submissions received in any other month will be returned to the sender unopened. Thank you for abiding by our policy and please be patient—it can take up to 8 months to read and respond to each submission.

All submissions must contain a sufficiently posted SASE (we will not respond to or return manuscripts that do not have a SASE) and a one-page cover letter that briefly describes the project and includes the writer's name and previous publications, if any.

For nonfiction, we prefer to receive a complete manuscript. Please send a brief outline/synopsis and a recently updated résumé. Nonfiction submissions should be clearly marked as such.

For picture book submissions, we prefer to receive the whole manuscript. Dummy books are not necessary. For longer fiction, please send a brief outline/synopsis and a few sample chapters not exceeding fifty pages.

Our fiction department publishes about ten picture books each year geared to ages 5 to 8. We also publish longer fiction for ages 7 and up, including chapter books and middle-grade and YA novels. We like to see unique, honest stories that stay away from unoriginal plots, moralizing, and religious themes. We're also interested in seeing science fiction/fantasy for young readers.

In both fiction and nonfiction, we are especially interested in new ideas, fresh topics, and well-crafted, polished writing. Make sure your manuscript avoids racial and sexual stereotypes. The best way to know whether your work fits our company is to familiarize yourself with our books. Study our catalog, find our books in the library, or browse our website. For a catalog, send a self-addressed 9x12 envelope with $3.85 in postage. Address the request to CATALOG REQUEST. We do not publish alphabet books, textbooks, workbooks, songbooks, puzzles, plays, or religious material.

Thank you for your interest in Carolrhoda Books—and good luck!

Categories: Fiction—Nonfiction—Biography—Children—Fantasy—History—Juvenile— Science Fiction—Young Adult

CONTACT: Jennifer Zimian
Material: Nonfiction
CONTACT: Zelda Wagner
Material: Fiction
241 First Ave., North
Minneapolis, MN 55401
Phone: 612-332-3344
Fax: 612-332-7615
Website: www.lernerbooks.com or www.carolrhodabooks.com

Career Press, Inc.
New Page Books

Thank you for your interest in Career Press/New Page Books. Following are our editorial guidelines. If you determine that your proposal or manuscript meets these criteria, we welcome your submission.

Editorial Mission Statement

It is our mission to publish and distribute quality, nonfiction books for adult readers seeking practical information to improve themselves in careers, college, finance, parenting, retirement, spirituality, and other related topics. We strive to deliver well-written, comprehensive books that inform, advise, and educate the reader.

Readers

Our readers are a diverse group, representing many age, job, and demo-

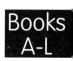

graphic categories. Yet they all demand the same high level of quality in the books they buy from Career Press/New Page Books; these characteristics will be identified below under Content Standards. Our primary markets include:

Students working through school and/or toward a career. Adults seeking to improve themselves in their work environment. Adults-singles, couples, families, seniors-seeking to improve their financial situation. Parents striving to enhance their role as parents and maximize their children's opportunities. Seniors, as well as adults approaching retirement, seeking help in meeting their financial and lifestyle needs. Anyone seeking information, a fun read, or interested in somehow bettering their lives

Book Categories

Book categories published by Career Press include:

Career Job Search College Preparation Small Business/Entrepreneurship Financial Planning Retirement Attitude Motivation Education Internet Self-help Sales Negotiation Research Study Aids Reference And more.

Categories published by New Page Books include:

Parenting New Age Wicca Alternative Health Gambling African-American Nutrition/Health/Wellness Pop Culture Judaica Weddings Parties/Entertaining Relationships and more.

This list is by no means comprehensive and, depending upon the project's tone, approach, and perceived sales potential, we publish other categories. To get a good feel for the kinds of books we represent, take a look at our Web site (www.careerpress.com or www.newpagebooks.com), or check out our current catalog.

Among the categories NOT currently published by Career Press are childrens' books, fiction, cookbooks, humor, picture books, photography books, and coffee-table publications.

Content Standards

Titles are written at an adult-minimum high school-level.

Titles are targeted to defined Career Press/New Page Books audiences. Copy is written in a helpful, practical, how-to-often step-by-step-style. Subjects are current, not faddish or trendy; style is not highly technical. Titles include directories, listings, web sites, and references as appropriate.

Author Standards

Authors must be proficient at communicating in writing.

Authors must have strong credentials to write on their topic. Authors should have some experience with publicity, such as speaking to groups and/or interviewing with broadcast or print media.

How to Submit Book Proposals

1. We prefer completed manuscripts.

2. We will also consider a proposal. For us to properly evaluate your proposal and its potential, please include:

Complete, detailed outline/table of contents of proposed book, with well-defined subject - what distinguishes your book from the thousands of other books published each year? Estimated length of book and approximate manuscript delivery date. Resources to be used. At least two complete sample chapters and introduction/thesis. 3. In addition, please submit the following: Author information/biography/credentials in light of the subject matter: why are you the perfect person to write this book? Sample copies of published articles and other materials you've written, and a complete list of your prior publications. Brief outline of marketing plan, including competitive titles known (and how your book will be better), primary markets (who will buy your book and why), and promotional opportunities you may be able to take advantage of (such as seminars, contacts with media, etc.). If you're the head of an organization that will commit to buy copies, you've gotten such commitments from major (i.e. credible) companies, or your last book sold exceedingly well, say so in your proposal. In your cover letter, please be sure to include your phone number during business hours, your street address, and your e-mail address. 4. If you want your materials returned, please include a self-addressed, stamped envelope whether you submit a manuscript or a proposal.

Proposals should be addressed to the attention of the Acquisitions Editor.

INSIDER TIPS ON PROPOSAL DEVELOPMENT

First Impressions We are deluged with submissions. We have seen a lot in the past 15 years, and we're admittedly a bit pressed for time. We are inclined to reject proposals that: (a) Don't sell us on the book in the first few paragraphs; (b) Don't anticipate and answer basic questions or allay obvious concerns; (c) Require us to do work the author should have done; (d) Raise any doubts about the author's commitment to the project or his/her ability and resolve to deliver a well-written manuscript on schedule and in the proper format.

A proposal is a sales document. It forms our first impression of you. If the proposal is top-drawer, you will be seen as a pro. If it's inadequate, you probably won't get a chance to make a second impression - there's simply not enough time, and too much else to do. Occasionally, an idea is so compelling it can overcome a weak proposal. Strong proposals raise your credibility; weak ones undermine it.

The process of writing a good proposal is as important to you as the finished product is to your editor. Writing a strong proposal forces you to think out what you want to say, how you're going to research the book, how to organize the material, and, most importantly, to decide if the subject really holds your interest - if you're not really interested in the subject, you'd be hard-pressed to convince a reader. To deliver a good proposal, an author must think deeply about the needs of the book's audience, which is exactly what determines whether the book succeeds after publication.

Agents?

If you get a literary agent, it can be to your advantage. We tend to take proposals a little more seriously if they come via an agent, because we know the proposal has been vetted by that agent and is now presented in the best possible style and form. An agent may also be helpful to you in contract negotiations.

However, we do publish a tremendous amount of unagented books, so agent representation is not necessarily required to get us to publish your book. We recommend you at least discuss your proposal/idea with several agents to see if their representation is right for you.

Format & Presentation

Appearances are important. Your proposal's presentation will be seen as indicative of the form in which your entire manuscript will be delivered. A clean, easy-to-read proposal encourages an editor to put it on the top of the "to do" pile. Here are some tips:

• Barring exceptional circumstances, your entire proposal (excluding sample chapters) should be no more than 20-30 pages long.

• Double-space and use reasonable margins on 8½ x 11 paper. Don't handwrite or use markers or crayons (you'd be surprised what people send us!).

• Unformatted proposals with many typos are taken less seriously than more well-prepared ones.

• Before turning in your proposal, we suggest you put it aside for a period of time. Then, take a good, hard, objective look at what you're about to submit. Is it a topic that someone will be interested in? Are people waiting for this book? Will someone read it? Have you presented the proposal in a professional manner? Are you qualified to write it? Sometimes it helps to have someone else read your proposal, whose detachment and objectivity may shed light on something you're too close to see.

• Make sure you keep an original copy of what you've sent us. We can't be held responsible if something is lost in the mail or, worse yet, by us.

Once you've submitted your manuscript or proposal, you should receive some word from us -pro or con - usually within 30 days. Please do not call us; if we're interested, we'll track you down. Should we decide to publish your book, we will contact you regarding contract terms.

Categories: Nonfiction—Alternate Lifestyles—Business—Careers—College—Folklore—Gay/Lesbian—History—Interview—Law—New Age—Occult—Paranormal—Reference—Science—Spirtual

Contact: Michael Pye, Director of Product Development
Materials: All
Po Box 687
Franklin Lakes NJ 07417
Phone: 800-227-3371

Fax: 201-848-0310
Website: www.careerpress.com/guidelines.html

Carson-Dellosa Publishing Co., Inc.

SUBMISSION GUIDELINES FOR MANUSCRIPTS

Carson-Dellosa Publishing Company, Inc. welcomes manuscripts and book proposals from teachers and writers. We accept submissions for PK–8th grades, including teacher resource books, activity books, and student workbooks. Works of fiction, including children's storybooks, are not considered for publication. **We do not accept submissions of non-book product ideas.** Please understand that we are only able to utilize a small percentage of the many submisssions we receive each year and that we also develop bok ideas in-house. Thus, we may already have projects similar in nature or in content to yours in development or production.

By sending in a submission, you agree and acknowlege that your submission of a manuscript and any related materials is of your own choice and without any promises by Carson-Dellosa, and that Carson-Dellosa will have no liability or obligation of any kind due to its review of your materials. In the event that Carson-Dellosa will be obligated only under the terms described in that agreement.

If you are interested in having Carson-Dellosa review your work, please observe the following guidelines:

PROPOSAL FORMAT:

A proposal for a manuscript should consist of:

• A brief cover letter introducing yourself.

• A summary of the manuscript containing its objectives, how it compares to other products on the market, how it would stand out from the competition, how it would fit in the Carson-Dellosa product line, and the intended audience/grade level for the product.

• A tentative table of contents including chapter titles and a three- to four-sentence summary of each chapter.

• The status of the manuscript explaining how much of the manuscript is complete, how long you think it will take to complete, and what length the book should be.

• 1–3 sample chapters to provide us with an introduction to the material and a representation of your writing style.

• The status of the manuscript explaining how much of the manuscript is complete, how long you think it will take to complete, and what length the book should be.

NO ORIGINALS: Do not send us the only copy of your manuscript or book proposal. Do not send us original artwork. We cannot be responsible for lost or damaged materials. If you wish to have your materials returned, please include a Self-Addressed Stamped Envelope or the appropriate postage for shipping.

DURATION OF REVIEW: Carson-Dellosa's editorial staff reviews proposals and we also send some proposals to appropriate outside reviewers. Due to the quantity of submissions and reviewers' schedules, the duration of review varies. On average, it takes 10-12 weeks for materials to be reviewed.

IF WE FEEL WE CAN USE YOUR MATERIAL, WE WILL CONTACT YOU. PLEASE NOTE THE FOLLOWING:

Carson-Dellosa Publishing prefers to purchase the manuscript and all rights to it from you for a flat fee, except in unusual circumstances.

Once your manuscript is purchased, the copyright to it becomes the property of Carson-Dellosa Publishing Company, Inc.

All artwork will be the responsibility and at the discretion of Carson-Dellosa unless agreed upon otherwise.

IF WE CANNOT USE YOUR MATERIALS, WE WILL NOTIFY YOU. PLEASE NOTE THE FOLLOWING:

We are unable to provide a critique of materials we do not plan to publish.

Materials sent without a Self-Addressed Stamped Evelope or appropriate postage will not be returned.

Please send all proposals to:

Book Acquisitions
Carson-Dellosa Publishing Company, Inc
P.O. Box 35665
Greensboro, NC 27425-5665
Categories: vEducation

CONTACT: Liz Halsch, Book Acquisitions Coordinator
Material: All
PO Box 35665
Greensboro NC 27425-5665
Phone: 336-632-0084
Fax: 336-632-0087

Caxton Press

CAXTON PRESS has a long tradition of publishing Western works of timeless appeal. We always are looking for new material. We ask that you follow our guidelines when submitting so that we may give your manuscript the attention it deserves.

Suggested Topics: Caxton publishes nonfiction trade books for general audiences. Although we may consider a manuscript on any subject, we prefer to publish western or frontier history, travel, pictorials, or narratives: nonfiction with a western theme. We will consider historical fiction if it deals with the West. We do not publish poetry.

Topics to avoid: "How I spent my years on the farm, on the mountain, in the city, etc." or "My family history."

Standards: We prefer to receive a query letter first that outlines your topic. If we feel it has possibilities, we'll usually request some sample chapters and an outline before requesting the complete manuscript.

We only accept manuscripts that are typewritten on one side of the page. Everything must be double-spaced: text, notes, bibliography, etc. Do not bind, staple, paper clip, or attach the pages together in any way. Send the pages loose and numbered, preferably in a box. We will accept sample chapters, and in some cases complete manuscripts, via e-mail. Please check in advance on format requirements.

Use active rather than passive verbs, and vibrant, colorful prose.

The piece must be responsibly researched. Your sources must be thoroughly documented and not infringe on existing copyrights. It is your responsibility to provide all photographs, illustrations, and graphics for your book. If your manuscript is accepted, the final version must be delivered to us on computer disk or via e-mail (WordPerfect or Microsoft Word format preferred). Some of our books include indexes, and we may ask the author to assemble the index at the appropriate time.

Style: We request our authors to follow *The Chicago Manual of Style* (14th edition).

Equipment: If possible, prepare your manuscript on Macintosh, Windows or MS Word documents preferred. No MS Works documents. Letter quality is required —dot matrix is not acceptable. Do not send your disk unless we ask for it.

Proposals: Submit a cover letter addressed to the editorial department with your proposal. Introduce yourself and the theme of your manuscript. Tell us about your target audience, and why you think Caxton should publish your book. Include either an outline or a table of contents, a sample of the manuscript (usually one or two chapters), photocopies of artwork samples, and a SASE for return of your materials.

We handle every manuscript we receive carefully. But prudence dictates that you keep a copy of everything you send us. Don't send original documents, photos or artwork unless we request them.

Please allow 8-12 weeks for our response. We receive many manuscripts every year and evaluate each for readability, literary merit, accuracy, research, and sale-ability.

Categories: Nonfiction—History—Native American—Western

CONTACT: C. W. Cornell, Editor
Material: All
312 Main St.

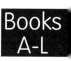
Books A-L

Caldwell ID 83605-3299
Phone: 208-459-7421
E-mail: wcornell@Caxtonpress.com
Website: Caxtonpress.com

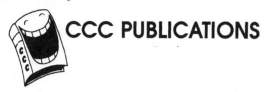

CCC Publications, LLC

1. CCC Publications is currently interested in reviewing Humor and How-to.

2. Our decision to publish a book is based on two criteria: the quality of writing and marketability. Both qualifications must be met before we will offer a contract.

3. For best results, send a query letter first, briefly explaining your book idea and your background (if it relates to the book). If we then solicit your ms. it has a much better chance of receiving priority in getting reviewed by an editor.

4. We prefer to see a complete manuscript—not chapter samples or outlines—submit photocopy or good quality computer printout.

5. Most of the books we do require some cartoon art or illustrations. Providing art or illustrations is the responsibility of the author. We will make an exception only in the case of an unusually well-written ms. If your book requires illustrations and you do not have them available at this time, include a list of your "proposed art" (short description and placement in the text).

6. As we receive approximately 200-300 submissions per month, our response time may be up to three months (shorter for query letters). Feel free after sixty days to inquire about the status of your submissions.

7. All manuscripts and correspondence that do not include a SASE receive low priority.

We thank you for your interest in CCC Publications and look forward to reviewing your manuscript for possible publication.

—Editorial Department

Categories: Fiction—Nonfiction—Comedy—Humor—Self Help—How-to

CONTACT: Mark Chutick, Publisher
Material: Humor
9725 Lurline Ave.
Chatsworth CA 91311
Phone: 818-718-0507

Celestial Arts

Please refer to Ten Speed Press.

Centerstream Publishing

Hello Writers,

We really don't have any formal guidelines. Since we only publish music history, music instructional books, and videos, our guidelines are simple: Just send it in.

We use Macs and request a hard copy and disk if we decide to do the project.

Thanks for considering Centerstream Publishing.

Ron Middlebrook

Categories: Music—Music History

CONTACT: Ron Middlebrook
Material: All
PO Box 17878
Anaheim Hills CA 92807
Phone: 714-779-9390
Fax: 714-779-9390
E-mail: Centerstrm@aol.com
Website: centerstream-usa.com

Century Press

Please refer to The Conservatory of American Letters, which can be found in the Book Publishers section.

Champion Press, Ltd.

Champion Press, Ltd. was established in 1997 in response to a need. With consolidation, change of ownership and attrition thinning the ranks of large publishing houses in New York and elsewhere, too many good books were going unpublished. Books providing valuable information, books telling stories that transport readers, books filled with imagery and imagination borne of the soul and capable of touching that in readers all of these works representing talented voices that would not be heard were it left to publishers dependent on minimum sales figures to cover overhead allocations and returns on equity. These books need to be published. They need to be printed and shipped and sold so that they may find their audiences, and do so without the added weight of supporting a corporate infrastructure so elaborate that product must constantly flow outward in massive quantities just to keep the lights on. We ask many things of our stable of authors at Champion Press, Ltd., but we demand only one: write a good book. When they do so (and they do with remarkable consistency), we'll work to get that book to its audience. No good book should fall like a tree in the forest, with no one there to hear its sound. Of our readers, we ask only that they trust our intent. The tastes of our editorial staff will not always mesh with their own, but our readers can rest assured that if a book bears the Champion Press, Ltd. imprint, it was deemed to be of quality, to be of value and to be deserving of presentation. We would rather work harder to find new sales for our existing books of quality than release a marginal title for financial requirements. Take a chance with our books. Try something that may not normally be your cup of tea. If we published it, it captured our fancy and it might just do the same for you. Then, if you like one of our books, let us know. Let us know if you didn't. We're easy to find, by both e-mail and traditional mail. If you keep letting us know who our audience is, we'll keep finding authors and titles that push you, thrill you, inform you and uplift you. Champion Press, Ltd. has been founded on these goals. We look forward to this century as one of the most exciting and challenging times in the history of humankind fully aware in the knowledge that no matter where peoples of this planet may reach, succeed, fail and endeavor; there will always exist the human need to occasionally look inward. There, we can hone improvement of self and mind. We can lose ourselves in lands and stories distant from our own existence. We can let our spirits dance with words and images. We can meet the very needs that make us human. Current Guidelines for Writers: NEEDS: Nonfiction: We are looking for cookbooks and fitness titles that are especially geared toward a busy woman's lifestyle. We are also interested in new and innovating home management topics. We publishing a limited number of education and homeschooling titles. We also publish self-help titles. We are no longer seeking submission in fiction, poetry or parenting. Please send ONLY a proposal, including market analysis, marketing plan and ideas (VERY IMPORTANT), your credential and bio, first 3 chapters and a SASE. Submissions without a SASE will not be returned. DO

NOT PHONE OR E-MAIL. We get too many solicitations this way and thus do not reply. Please follow our guidelines and be familiar with the types of books we publishing prior to sending your project our way. WHAT TO SEND: Submission guidelines: A query letter summarizing the project. o A detailed proposal including an overview, a summary of market competition, a chapter by chapter outline, author bio and marketing approaches (for nonfiction); for fiction—send the first three chapters instead of the chapter by chapter outline and market summary. o A self-addressed, stamped envelope with sufficient postage to ensure the return of all materials desired by author, or explicit instructions informing that author does not wish the return of materials. Submissions made without sufficient return postage will not be returned or acknowledge. Under no circumstances should an entire manuscript be submitted without express written request from Champion Press, Ltd. All manuscripts submitted without request by Champion Press, Ltd. will be discarded. Submissions should be made to the following: The Editors Champion Press, Ltd. 4308 Blueberry Road Fredonia WI 53021 WHEN WILL I HEAR BACK? Champion Press holds four editorial meetings per year for manuscript submissions. These occur in early January, April, July and October. If you would like your proposal considered at these sessions, please make sure it arrives by the 15th of the previous month. You can expect to hear back within 8 weeks of the meeting. I.e. for the January meeting, you would have a response by end of February—if proper postage or reply is enclosed. We will not response otherwise. Please do not e-mail queries or materials. Please follow the procedures outlined above. Any deviation from these procedures and the material will not be considered for publication.

Categories: Nonfiction—Cooking—Education—Health—Lifestyle—Self Help—Women's Issues

CONTACT: The Editors
Material: All
4308 Blueberry Rd.
Fredonia WI 53021

E-mail: info@championpress.com
Website: www.championpress.com

Charles River Media

WHAT IS THE BOOK OR CD-ROM ABOUT? (Be as descriptive as possible.)

The proposal should convey the ideas that motivate your work and present the essential features that will set your book or CD-ROM apart. Describe in two or three paragraphs the purpose and importance of the project.

Include an outline of topics to be covered or a tentative table of contents.

WHAT TECHNOLOGIES WILL BE COVERED?

What product or technology is discussed and why. Where do you think the technology is headed in the next 12-18 months, or what is the schedule for new releases of the product?

AUDIENCE

Describe as specifically as possible the primary audience(s) for your project, e.g. graphics programmers, multimedia developers. Are there any secondary audiences for the project? What topics in your project will be of the greatest interest to each of these audiences?

Would your project be appropriate for professional-level short courses? If so, please describe.

Optional: Would your project be appropriate as a textbook or as a supplement for a course? If so, please list the name of the course(s) which could use it.

DESCRIBE WHAT IS ON THE CD-ROM.

If your book includes a CD, please describe what will be included on it. If your project is a standalone, this will be covered above.

LIST 5 TO 10 SIGNIFICANT SELLING POINTS.

Please list the selling points that you think are the strengths of your

books on its own and as it compares to the competition.

COMPETITION

With which other products will your project most closely compete in terms of style, level and coverage? How will yours be better or different? Please be specific.

PRODUCTION CONCERNS

Please provide a rough estimate of the page length of the book and an estimated completion/delivery date. How many illustrations do you expect to include (roughly)? Will any of the illustrations need to be redrawn by Charles River Media?

Please provide the exact hardware and software used to prepare the manuscript. If this is for a CD-ROM, please list any software/authoring tools necessary to create the product and any licensing fees which may be necessary.

THE AUTHORS

Have you ever written a book or magazine article? Please include a current resume with your proposal.

Categories: Nonfiction—Technical

CONTACT: Aquisition Editor
Material: All
20 Downer Ave., Ste. 3
Hingham MA 02043
Fax: 781-740-8816
E-mail: info@charlesriver.com
Website: www.charlesriver.com

Charlesbridge Publishing

The Charlesbridge Trade Department publishes high-quality books for children, with a goal of creating lifelong readers and learners. We believe that books for children should offer accurate information, promote a positive worldview, and embrace a child's innate sense of wonder and fun. To this end, we continually strive to seek new voices, new visions, and new directions in children's literature.

Charlesbridge publishes both picture books and transitional "bridge books," books ranging from early readers to middle-grade chapter books. Our nonfiction books focus on nature, science, social studies, and multicultural topics. Our fiction titles include lively, plot-driven stories with strong, engaging characters.

EXCLUSIVE SUBMISSIONS POLICY
1 Charlesbridge accepts unsolicited manuscripts submitted exclusively to us. "Exclusive Submission" should be written on all envelopes and cover letters.
2 We make every effort to respond in three months but cannot guarantee that we will be able to do so, due to the volume of submissions we receive. If after three months you have not recieved a reply, you may send us a status query. Include the author's name, the title of the manuscript, and the date it was sent. No phone calls, please.
WHAT TO SEND
1 Please submit only one or two manuscript(s) at a time.
2 Please send complete manuscripts, rather than query letters. We are not actively seeking alphabet books, board books, coloring books, activity books, or books with audiotapes or CD-ROMS.
3 Manuscripts should be typed and double-spaced. Please do not submit material by email, by fax, or on a computer disk. Illustrations are not necessary.
4 Please make a copy of your manuscript, as we cannot be responsible for submissions lost in the mail.
5 Please include your name and address on the first page of your manuscript and in you cover letter. Be sure to list any previously published work or relevant writing experience.
6 Enclose a self-addressed, stamped envelope (SASE) large enough and with sufficient postage (not a check or cash) to return all submitted material, or a small SASE if the work need not be returned.
7 To find out if your project reached us, enclose a self-addressed, stamped

postcard for us to return upon receipt of your submisson.

WHERE TO SEND IT

1 Please send your work to the attention of Submissions Editor, Trade Division, Charlesbridge, 85 Main Street, Watertown, MA 02472.

GET TO KNOW US

1 To become acquainted with our publishing program, we encourage you to review our books and visit our website (www.charlesbridge.com), where you will find our catalog. To request a printed catalog, please send a 9"X12" SASE with $2.44 in postage.

Categories: Fiction—Nonfiction—Adventure—Arts—Biography—Children—Culture—Ecology—Environment—Family—Folklore—Food/Drink—History—Juvenile—Multicultural—Music—Outdoors—Poetry—Science

CONTACT: Submissions Editor, Trade Editorial Department
Material: All
85 Main St.
Watertown MA 02472
Phone: 617-926-0329
Fax: 617-926-5720
Website: www.charlesbridge.com

Chatoyant

Chatoyant publishes high quality poetry and literature. We presently do not accept unsolicited submissions. All unsolicited materials will be re-cycled. Please see our website for more information: www.chatoyant.com.

Thanks,

Susana Wessling

Categories: Literature—Poetry

CONTACT: Submissions Editor
Material: All
PO Box 832
Aptos CA 95001
Website: www.chatoyant.com or www.poetrysantacruz.org

Chelsea Green Publishing Company

Chelsea Green is an independent publisher located in Vermont. We specialize in nonfiction books that promote the "politics and practice of sustainable living" and that are suitable for a general audience. Some of our books are used in educational settings, but our books are not written with an academic audience in mind.

Before contacting us with a query letter or proposal for your book, please read these guidelines. We receive more than 800 submissions a year, and publish only around fifteen new titles a year. At least half of the submissions we receive are declined out of hand, because they fit neither Chelsea Green's mission nor the topics in which we specialize. Examples of our subject areas are:

Local agricultural movements and healthy food supplies

- : Organic gardening and market farming
- : Local agricultural movents and healthy food supplies

- Environmentally friendly building techniques

- Renewable energy sources and energy conservation

- Lifestyles that are simpler and require less consumption

- Economic systems that account for environmental and social needs

- Political activism that promotes sustainable economies

- Philosophical writing/social commentary that promotes sustainable living

The rules about what we do and do not publish are a little fuzzy, but if your work does not fit into the categories above, you will have to overcome an extra large hurdle. In short, before submitting a query or proposal to us, please spend some time reviewing our recent publications on our website (www.chelseagreen.com). If you think it is unlikely that your work will fit into our pattern of publishing, we will certainly think so as well. That does not mean that your book has no merit; it only means that we are the wrong publisher for you. If you don't want to use a literary agent, the best way to find an appropriate publisher is to see what other books are similar to yours. Contact the publishers of those books.

We avoid books that:

- Are fiction or poetry

- Have a regional focus (i.e., that only appeal to a regional readership; we do publish books on particular places when the approach and quality of writing will be of interest to readers from near and far, e.g., in the tradition of *A Sand County Almanac*)

- Are for an academic audience

- Are cookbooks, though we do publish many books on the culture, politics, and ecology of food

- Deal with agriculture/gardening and fail to promote organic methods

- Are New-Agey

- Cover material that has been dealt with in many other books (e.g., a summary of why George W. Bush has been a bad president)

- Offer top-down political policy prescriptions

We prefer to receive query letters via email (to jteller@chelseagreen.com), and we ask that you send full proposals through the mail. Please don't go to the expense of paying for Priority or Express mail services. It usually takes us several weeks to review incoming proposals, so you will not be saving any time. Submitted materials will only be returned if accompanied by a self-addressed, stamped envelope.

A query letter should be one or two pages long and give an overview of your book's topic, along with information about you as an author (who you are, why you are the right person to write this book, evidence that you will be able to complete a high-quality manuscript in a timely fashion).

If we think that there is a reasonable chance that we might pursue your book, we will request a full proposal. A full proposal should include most or all of the following:

- A cover letter summarizing the book

- A preliminary table of contents

- An expanded table of contents with one- or two-paragraph summaries of each chapter

- Marketing research such as

    - descriptions of other books on the same or similar topic (with sales history if possible) and an explanation of why your book is different

    - any special sales potential (organizations that might want to buy large numbers of your book; specialty catalogs or stores that don't usually sell books but might be interested in yours; events where attendees will be interested in your book)

    - your target audience (who they are, why they will be interested in your book. Be specific and realistic, for example, "readers of The Nation magazine" or "fans of Gertrude Stein." Do not say things like "all women should like my book because I write about problems women face," or "every American must read my book because we all face the danger of global warming together." Also, please do not refer to "cultural creatives." This mythical group is referenced in very many of the proposals we get, and carries no weight with us.)

- Biographical material about you (expanded from that in the query letter)

- Two sample chapters

Please feel free to print your materials single-spaced and double-sided, to save paper.

Categories: Nonfiction—Ecology—Environment—Agriculture—Gardening—Food—Energy—Politics—Economics

CONTACT: Ben Watson
Material: All
PO Box 428
White River Junction VT 05001
Phone: 802-295-6300
Fax: 802-295-6444
E-mail: bwatson@chelseagreen.com

Chess Enterprises

Chess Enterprises only publishes books on the game of chess: instruction, game collections, analysis.
Categories: Nonfiction—Games—Chess

CONTACT: Submissions Editor
Material: All
107 Crosstree Red.
Moon Township PA 15108-2607
Phone: 412-262-2138
E-mail: bgdudley@compuserve.com

Chosen Books

Please refer to Baker Publishing Group.

Christian Ed. Publishers

All writing is on assignment only. Please review guidelines carefully.
1. When submitting a manuscript to us:
a) That is a sample assignment—write SAMPLE ASSIGNMENT in lower left-hand corner of mailing envelope
b) That is by assignment—write ASSIGNMENT in lower left-hand corner of envelope.
2. The Kinds of Material We Publish
(all handled by our assigned free-lance writers only)
• Curriculum for children and youth, including program and student books
• Church-wide special event program kits
• Bible-teaching craft kits
3. The Kinds of Writers We Seek
• Those who love the Lord
• Those who relate well to the age group written for
• Those who have hands-on experience with the children or youth they want to write for
• Those who are active members of a Bible-believing church
• Those who write well, whether published or unpublished
• Those who are able to meet deadlines, and consistently submit manuscripts on time
4. How to Contact Us
If interested in writing by assignment for us, request a free-lance writer application. Include a SASE. Address all submissions to Carol Rogers, Managing Editor, at address below.
5. The Assignment Process
a) Contact us to receive a free-lance writer application. Include a SASE.
b) Return the completed application and a resume of your Christian experience with the age group you want to write for, and your writing background (including clips).
c) We send you a sample assignment for the age group you indicated.
d) After reviewing and accepting your returned sample assignment, we add you to our list of available writers.
e) We make an assignment to you based on our scheduled needs.
6. Payment Policy
a) Our payments are made upon acceptance within 90 days after an assignment is submitted, reviewed, and approved. We do not pay for sample assignments unless we are able to publish them.
b) Regular assignments receive 100% of the agreed rate of payment, upon acceptance, whether we are able to use the assignment for the particular project assigned, or use it in a future project.
c) We pay 3¢ a printed word, or a fixed amount for certain projects.
7. Additional Information for Writers
Make sure your typewriter ribbon or printer cartridge is not worn. Do not submit on onion skin or erasable paper. Always make a copy of anything you submit to us. Include a computer disk, if possible. (Let us know which software you use.) Neatness and legibility is a must. Carefully proofread before submitting anything.

We are always eager to locate writers of top quality who can have a part in our ministry for Christ. If interested in requesting an application, please include a SASE.

Christian Ed. Publishers is an independent, non-denominational, evangelical publishing company. We produce Christ-centered curriculum based on the Word of God. We provide these curriculum materials to thousands of churches of different denominations throughout the world. Our mission is to introduce children, teens, and adults to a personal faith in Jesus Christ and to help them grow in their faith and service to the Lord. We publish materials that teach moral and spiritual values while training individuals for a lifetime of Christian service. Spiritually dedicated writers and employees assist in this ministry.
Categories: Fiction—Nonfiction—Children—Bible Curriculum

CONTACT: Janet Ackelson, Editor
Material: All

PO Box 26639
San Diego CA 92196
Phone: 858-578-4700, ext.119
E-mail: jackeson@cehouse.com
Website: www.ChristianEdWarehouse.com

Christian Publications, Inc.

OWNERSHIP AND DOCTRINAL POSITION OF THE PUBLISHING HOUSE:

Christian Publications, Inc. (CPI) adheres to an evangelical doctrinal position. A copy of the leaflet, "Statement of Faith," is available free of charge to all who request it.

BOOK SUBJECTS CONSIDERED:

Christian Publications, Inc. publishes for the general Christian public. CPI will consider book manuscripts dealing with theology, the church, pastoral helps, Bible studies, the Christian home, devotional studies, Christian living and deeper life. Manuscripts NOT accepted are: poetry, short stories, children's, fiction, unsolicited Bible commentaries and reference works. A proposal must be submitted, as detailed below. Proposals will not be returned unless accompanied by sufficient return postage.

PREPARATION OF MANUSCRIPTS:

A proposal should include the following:

1. A query/cover letter explaining what you envision for the manuscript

2. An overview of the concept for the book, including a description of the intended audience

3. A biographical sheet or resume of the author(s), spelling out why you are qualified to write this book and/or what your unique perspective is.

An alternative submission method is to fill out the submission form on our web site: www.christianpublications.com.

All submissions should meet the standards of *The Chicago Manual of Style*. All submissions must be a copy of your original materials. We will not accept responsibility for lost text or artwork.

FINANCIAL ARRANGEMENTS FOR BOOK MANUSCRIPTS:

Contract arrangements are made upon final acceptance of the book by the publisher. While a flat rate is paid for some books, most are contracted on a royalty basis.

Please note that although we will consider ONE-PAGE queries by mail or email, we DO NOT appreciate receiving sales pitches for a manuscript over the phone.

Categories: Nonficiton—Christian Interests—Inspirational—Marriage—Religion—Spiritual—Trade—Christian

CONTACT: Editorial Department
Material: All
3825 Hartzdale Dr.
Camp Hill PA 17011
Phone: 717-761-7044
E-mail: editorial @christianpublications.com
Website: www.christianpublications.com

Chronicle Books LLC

Adult Trade Division—Submission Guidelines

Chronicle Books LLC publishes approximately 175 books a year. We specialize in high-quality, reasonably priced books for adults and children. Our titles include best-selling cookbooks; fine art, design, photography, and architecture titles; full-color nature books; award-winning poetry and literary fiction; regional and international travel guides; and gift and stationery items. We will accept unsolicited manuscripts in each of these subject areas. To gain a better understanding of our publishing program, please examine our books in a bookstore, library, a Chronicle Books catalog, or visit our web site: www.chroniclebooks.com.

When submitting a proposal, initial query letter, or completed manuscript, please remember that it may take up to three months for the editors to review it. (Please note, we do not accept proposals on disks, over the Internet, or by fax.) Outlined below is the basic procedure for submitting manuscripts and proposals. While by no means are all of the steps mandatory, bear in mind that it is your vision you are presenting to us, so the more information you give us to visualize your project, the better. Please send us copies of your material and keep the original for your records.

A nonfiction proposal could include:

1. Cover letter giving a brief description of the project and what is included in the package.

2. Proposal, including outline, introduction, illustrations list, sample captions, and text/sample chapters (approximately 30 pages of text). If you are submitting a cookbook proposal, include a list of recipes plus at least ten sample recipes with headnotes in addition to the information described above.

3. Sample illustrations or photographs (duplicates rather than originals).

4. A market analysis of the potential readership for the book, including title, publisher, and date of all similar books, with an explanation of how your book differs from each.

5. Author/illustrator/photographer biography, including publishing credits and credentials in the field.

6. A self-addressed, stamped envelope for return of the material. If desired, include a self-addressed, stamped blank postcard for acknowledgment of receipt of manuscript.

If you are submitting fiction (a novel or a short story collection), submit the complete manuscript to Adult Trade — Fiction and include a self-addressed, stamped envelope for its return. Please note that Chronicle Books does not publish romances, science fiction, fantasy, westerns, or other genre fiction.

Do not submit original material (either art or manuscript) and please keep a copy of your project. Please note that material unaccompanied by a SASE will not be returned. Also, please do not contact President Jack Jensen or Chairman/CEO Nion McEvoy directly with your query. Instead, direct your proposal to our editorial department at the address below.

Thank you for your interest in Chronicle Books.

Children's Division—Submission Guidelines

Chronicle Books LLC publishes an eclectic mixture of traditional and innovative children's books. We are interested in projects that have a unique bent to them — be it in subject matter, writing style, or illustrative technique. We are looking for books that will contribute to our lists a distinctive flair. Primarily we are interested in fiction and non-fiction picture books for children ages up to eight years and non-fiction books for children ages eight to twelve years. We are also interested in early chapter books, middle grade fiction, and young adult projects. To gain a better understanding of our publishing program, please examine our books in a bookstore, library, a Chronicle Books catalog, or visit our web site: www.chroniclebooks.com.

Picture books may be submitted without query first. Projects for older children and/or young adult, should be submitted by query (synopsis and three sample chapters) and SASE first. When submitting, please be sure to include a self-addressed, stamped envelope large enough to hold your materials. Projects submitted without an appropriate self-addressed, stamped envelope will be recycled. Do not send checks or cash for postage; only US postage and international reply coupons will be accepted. If you would like confirmation that your materials have been received, please include a self-addressed, stamped postcard. (Such confirmation cannot be given over the telephone. Also note that we do not accept proposals by fax, via e-mail, or on disk.) If your proposal is a simultaneous submission, please indicate this in your cover letter.

When submitting artwork, either as a part of a project or as samples for review, do not send originals. If you would like your work kept on file, please indicate which work we may keep. And please, always keep a copy of your project because we will not be responsible for the loss or damage of unsolicited material.

All materials received are reviewed and will get an official response, but due to the enormous number of children's projects Chronicle Books receives each year, we are unable to respond to each project personally. Our response time varies, but generally you should expect to wait from four to eighteen weeks.

Please note that due to postal regulations, SASE packages weighing a pound or more require special handling and therefore will be delayed by as much as 30 days.

Thank you for your interest in Chronicle Books.

Gift Division—Submission Guidelines

Chronicle Books LLC publishes approximately 175 books a year. We specialize in high-quality, reasonably priced books for adults and children. Our titles include best-selling cookbooks; fine art, design, photography, and architecture titles; full-color nature books; award-winning poetry and literary fiction; regional and international travel guides; and gift & stationary items.

The Gift Division of Chronicle Books publishes a wide assortment of quality gift items, including calendars, note cards, address books, journals, and postcard collections. We will consider unsolicited proposals and manuscripts.

To gain a better understanding of our publishing program, please examine our books in a bookstore, library, a Chronicle Books catalog, or on our web site at www.chroniclebooks.com.

When submitting a proposal, initial query letter, or completed project, please remember that it may take the editors up to three months to review it. (Please note that we do not accept proposals on disk, by fax, or via email.) The deadline for calendar submissions is 18 months prior to the year you wish to publish. Outlined below is the basic procedure for submitting proposals and manuscripts. While by no means are all of the steps mandatory, bear in mind that it is your vision you are presenting to us, so the more information you give us to visualize your project, the better.

A proposal could include:

1. Cover letter giving a brief description of the project and what is included in the package.

2. Samples of illustrations or photographs (i.e., duplicates rather than originals).

3. Where appropriate, a proposal including outline, introduction, illustrations list, sample captions, and text/chapter samples.

4. An analysis of the potential market for the project, including title, publisher, and date of all similar projects, with an explanation of how your proposal differs from each.

5. Author/illustrator/photographer biography that includes publishing credits and credentials in the field.

6. A self-addressed, stamped envelope for return of the materials. If desired, include a self-addressed, stamped blank postcard for acknowledgment of receipt of the materials

Do not submit original material (either art of manuscript) and please keep a copy of your project. Please note that material unaccompanied by a SASE will be recycled. Direct your submission to our Gift Department at the address below.

Note

These guidelines are for informational purposes only and do not constitute a solicitation of any manuscript, artwork, transparencies, or other material. Submission of any unsolicited materials shall be done at the author/illustrator's own risk of loss or damage.

Thank you for your interest in Chronicle Books.

Categories: Fiction—Nonfiction—Animals—Architecture—Arts—Cooking—Crafts/Hobbies—Culture—Entertainment—Film/Video—Food/Drink—Gay/Lesbian—General Interest—Lifestyle—Literature—Music—New Age—Parenting—Photography—Travel—Young Adult

CONTACT: Gift Division
Material: Gift Division Submissions
CONTACT: Editorial Dept, Adult Trade Division
Material: Adult Trade Division Submissions
CONTACT: Children's Division
Material: Children's Division Submissions
85 Second St., 6th Floor
San Francisco CA 94105
Phone: 415-537-4200

Website: www.chroniclebooks.com

Chrysalis Books

Please refer to the Swedenborg Foundation, Inc.

Clarity Press, Inc.

Human rights and social justice issues viewed in the context of universally recognized human rights norms.

Dear Writer:

Clarity's writer's guidelines are as follows:

Nonfiction only: visit Website for editorial purview. Please send query letter first, with brief bio, table of contents, synopsis and endorsements. SASE unnecessary; due to volume of queries, we will respond only if interested. Manuscript should be available on disk in Microsoft Word.

Sincerely,

Diana G. Collier, Editorial Director

Categories: Nonfiction—African-American—Asian-American—Economics—Government—Human Rights—Law—Multicultural—Native American—Politics—Society

CONTACT: Diana G. Collier, Editorial Director
Material: All
3277 Roswell Rd. NE., Ste 469
Atlanta GA 30305
Phone: 877-613-1495
Fax: 877-613-7868
E-mail: claritypress@usa.net
Website: www.claritypress.com

Books A-L

Clover Park Press

Clover Park Press, publisher of great books about life's wonders and wanderings, is seeking book-length manuscripts for its current publishing interests. We are looking for fresh ideas and superior writing in the following categories:

Non-Fiction in the areas of:

• California (history, natural history, travel, culture or the arts).

• Biography of extraordinary women.

• Acts of Courage (Please request further information before submitting in this category.)

• Nature, the environment or place.

• Other cultures.

• Travel, exploration, adventure.

• Scientific/medical discovery.

No fiction, poetry, children's, photography, true crime, diaries or journals, new age, or books about alcoholism or addiction.

Submission guidelines:

• Query with letter summary of one page; author's prior publications and background relevant to the subject; outline; and two strong sample chapters including the first chapter.

• Manuscript should have font between 10-12 pt, be paginated and secured with a clip (not stapled).

• If you have any questions, do inquire by mail or e-mail (preferred) before sending submission. Because of our heavy volume of e-mail, begin your subject line with "A-Query."

• No phone calls.

• Include your phone and e-mail address.

Categories: Nonfiction—Adventure—Biography—History—Multicultural—Regional—Travel—Women's Issues

CONTACT: Martha Grant, Acquisitions Editor
Material: All
PO Box 5067

Santa Monica CA 90409
E-mail: cloverparkpr@earthlink.net
Website: home.earthlink.net/~cloverparkpr/

Collectors Press, Inc.

Thank you for your interest in Collectors Press, Inc. Please note we do not publish novels, poems, children's books, or short stories.

To expedite a response to your inquiry, please send the following:
• A clean, typed, completed manuscript or three sample chapters clipped together or in booklet form. Do not send computer diskette.
• A table of contents (without page numbers).
• If illustrations/photographs are used, send high-quality examples, with an estimate of total images in the completed work.
• Include a post-paid mailer with your mailing label affixed if you want your manuscript returned. Include a SASE (self addressed stamped envelope) if you only want a reply.

Please help us learn more about you and your book by providing the following (if applicable):
• Brief explanation of the book.
• Why the subject is worthy of a book.
• What other published books does your work compare to?
• What will you do to promote the book on an on-going basis?
• Have you written other books?
• Do you have other books planned or in the works?
• Any media experience and/or contacts?
• Quotes of recognized authorities for your work. Do you have a published author or celebrity to write an introduction/foreword?

Please allow one to two months (including mailing time) for us to review your material and reply back to you. If you would like to know the date your submission was received, include a post-paid postcard or SASE with the request.

We look forward to reviewing your submission!
Categories: Nonfiction—Arts—Collectibles—Cooking—Food/Drink—Science Fiction

CONTACT: Lindsay Burt, Acquisitions Editor
Material: All
PO Box 230986
Portland, OR 97281
Phone: 503-684-3030x 107
Fax: 503-684-3777
Website: www.collectorspress.com
Email: lburt@collectorspress.com

Commonwealth Editions

Commonwealth Editions publishes nonfiction books about the history and beauty of New England. We do not publish fiction or poetry.

If you have a manuscript or book idea that fits this description, please feel free to send a short e-mail to publisher Webster Bull, explaining the book you have in mind.

If you like, instead, you may send a proposal and a writing sample of no more than twenty pages to the address below.

If you do send an outline and writing sample, please provide a stamped self-addressed envelope to assure the return of these materials.
Categories: Nonfiction—History—Regional—New England

CONTACT: Webster Bull, Publisher
Material: All
266 Cabot St.
Beverly, MA 01915
Phone: 978-921-0747
Fax: 978-927-8195
E-mail: websterb@commonwealtheditions.com
Website: www.commonwealtheditions.com
E-mail: sstewart@companionpress.com
Website: www.companionpress.com

The Conservatory of American Letters
Dan River Press, Northwoods Press and Century Press

The Conservatory of American Letters is a non profit tax exempt literary educational foundation. *The IRS requires we publish our purpose:*
• To conserve and make public literary works of exceptional merit without regard to commercial potential.
• To encourage and develop literary talent.
• To offer the reading public an alternative to mass marketing mediocrity.

In order to accomplish this objective, we own and operate the following companies and plans. Northwoods Press, the poet's press, publishes poetry, local and family histories and works about them. It does offer a teacher's custom publishing arm. Northwoods Press also publishes the quarterly *Northwoods Journal*, a magazine for writers.

Dan River Press publishes only fiction and biography. Dan River Press also publishes the annual (since 1984) Dan River Anthology.

Century Press publishes in all areas.

Perhaps most importantly (at least used by more writers than any other service) is our Personal Publishing Program (PPP) where you act as your own publisher. We believe that if you can't get a royalty contract this is the best way to go for most writers.

Notes to Authors: Don't waste time and postage by submitting before you've read guidelines. If you want to submit a book length work, query first with SASE. Do not send complete manuscript until query has been answered. There is a lot of money being wasted on postage. Do not send anything express mail, or overnight, it is a waste of perfectly good money. I recently received an express mail piece ($3.50 postage) that could have been sent for .60 postage (or maybe .37) for a deadline that is eight weeks away. If you've that kind of money to throw away, throw some at the Conservatory. It's deductible on all tax forms. Believe me, there is nothing we're that eager to see. When submitting your work, please adhere to the appropriate submission guidelines. To receive guidelines through the mail, send us a #10 self-addressed stamped envelope and tell us which guidelines you want. Do not submit anything electronically or on disk unless requested to do so.

Dan River Press
Dan River Press was created in 1976 in Meadows of Dan, Virginia. It has become the fiction and biography arm of the Conservatory and publishes the ever popular (since 1984) Dan River Anthology.

Guidelines For Submissions: Dan River Press
As always, we suggest writers read our books to determine if Dan River Press is an appropriate place for your work.

We pay royalties of 10% of the amount we receive on the first 2,500 copies, 15% of the amount we receive on all additional copies. Royalties are paid each March for the prior year, or by request. Quality book production is in hardcover and paperback with a guarantee of in-print status for two full years and as long thereafter as our sales total only $200 annually.

Everyone gets the same discount: 1-p copies none; 5-10 copies, 2% X number of books ordered. (10 books X 2%=20%); Per book max 20%. Hardcovers are usually produced in extremely limited numbers. Multiple copy discounts are on hardcover books.

Send self addressed stamped envelope for return of materials and additional SASEs for answers to questions, confirmation, and so forth.

Do not submit electronically, by fax, or by e-mail. Submit with disk and hard copy. Simultaneous submissions are not encouraged, but they are not forbidden. Because we are a conservatory, and publishing = conserving, we don't consider previously published work.

Dan River Press considers work from all. Membership in the Conservatory is not required. If accepted, however, membership will be required over the life of the publication. Members always receive preference when all else is equal, as we seek to support those who support us.

Dan River Anthology, 2006

You are not required to buy a copy!

We pay a non-refundable advance on acceptance and offer opportunities to earn more.

The anthology is not overpriced and is actually sold (Multiple Copy Discounts up to 50%).

Nothing is required of the author except proofing his/her own galleys.

Listed in the top 50 fiction markets in the land by *Writer's Digest*. (In spite of the fact that we consider our small advance but token payment.)

Nothing previously published can be considered. We can not accept simultaneous submissions. Do not submit anything electronically, on disk, or by fax, unless specifically requested. All rights returned to author on publication.

Guidelines: We can only consider submissions by disk. Do not justify. Avoid strange spacing in poetry. It usually only detracts from the poem anyway, and it's a good way to guarantee rejection. Titles of entires are bold and italic. Titles of parts are only italic. Foreign words should be italicized. We can produce most accented letters, but are not multi-lingual, so we can accept no responsibility for errors. Stanza break, or paragraph break, at the end of a page must say so.

We only receive work from January 1 to March 31 each year. We accept work by May 15 of each year and send proofs by June 15. Assuming all proofs returned in 24 hours we release the paperback and hardcovers about the first of December.

There is a reading fee of $1 per poem and $3 per 2,500 words, or any part, of fiction. Reading fee must be paid in cash, no checks, no money orders, no credit cards. The reading fee goes directly to the first reader of your work, the company gets none of it and bookkeeping such small amounts would be impractical, and costly.

SASE if you want your work returned. Others if you want acknowledgement or other correspondence.

Paperbacks sell for $16.95 and are subject to all discounts.

Hardcovers sell for $39.95 and are not subject to smaller copy discounts, they do qualify for CAL member discounts and do earn royalties. Normally only as many hardcovers as are sold in advance are produced. Almost always fewer than 50. Last year we produced 54 full-color dust jackets.

The only possible charge to authors is for Author's Alterations. If you change something from your original you will be billed at $52 per hour with a $25 minimum. Any change, even a comma to a period, will activate the charge. Proofreading after typesetting can be very expensive. Of course all errors that we make are corrected without charge of any kind.

The Dan River Anthology, 2006 will feature a full color cover and professional production.

Order a recent copy, see what we're like, then submit. Order from our bookstore or call us with a credit card at 207/354-0998.

Northwoods Press

The Poet's Press

Northwoods Press was created in Bigfork, Minnesota in 1972.

Any excellent poet with even a very small following may be able to have her/his book published with royalty contract. We may actually be able to publish with prospects of as few as 25-50 sales.

Over the years the company has changed and evolved. Currently it publishes poetry, local and family histories, and plays. Northwoods Press is available to academia for custom publishing books for classroom use under its University Press division. Northwoods Press seeks to provide a companion CD for every book published. The CD is usually recorded by the author and may/should include readings, and/or other comment deemed appropriate by author and publisher.

The University Press division requires advance sales of only 80 books. Books for classroom use are limited to poetry, local histories and related themes.

Northwoods Press publishes the annual Northwoods Anthology. Use the same guidelines as Dan River Anthology. Deadline is October 30th.

Northwoods Press is a royalty publisher and may pay an advance against royalties.

American History Press, a division of Northwoods Press, publishes histories, including family and church histories, and geneology.

You should send poetry manuscript exactly as you would have your book to appear, including all front matter (front matter means: title page, copyright page, dedication, acknowledgements, contents, forward, and whatever else you feel appropriate.) front and back covers (We want full color covers, or at least a clear idea as to what you want if you can't provide the artwork or photography.). If you have no cover design, we can acquire one, using color photography, for a $250.00 charge. You should paginate, using not more than 44 lines per page (40 is better) (remember, a line is a line is a line, no matter what is/isn't written in it). Include an SASE or clear instructions to discard manuscript if rejected. We regret we will not be able to comment on rejected manuscripts. Because we are tax exempt and a conservatory, we can not spend money on already conserved works (Published = Conserved), therefore no more than 10% (by line count) of any book or chapbook can be previously published in any form. You may submit in any hard-copy form, but prior to publication you will be required to provide a compatible disk.

Rhymed poetry has little chance.

Typewriter poetry has even less.

We have bias against poetry about poetry, and poetry about writing poetry.

We offer royalties of 10% of the amount received on the first 2,500 copies sold, and 15% on all copies sold after 2,500. Royalties are payable each March for the prior year.

We provide bar codes, ISBN, a listing in *Amazon.com, Baker & Taylor, Ingram, Books In Print, Small Press* record of books in print, the copyright, and so forth.

Most books of 4 pages or larger are produced in hardcover and paperback.

Books are promoted to libraries, bookstores, individual poetry buyers, and areas where the author has influence.

We don't accept simultaneous submissions, electronic submissions, faxed submissions, or previously published material.

Include an SASE for return of material, plus a #10 SASE or SASP for receipt confirmation or for other correspondence. Writers who are interested in submitting to Northwoods Press should check out our current offerings.

Northwoods Journal: *A Magazine for Writers*

Northwoods Journal, a magazine for writers, has been listed in *Writer's Digest's* Best 50 Fiction Markets.

Northwoods Journal offers writers an excellent chance to be published. We receive a small number of submissions. Publication "credits" help build a writer's career. We have lots of room in our pages for career building. If you submit good work, you're likely to sell to the Journal. More than 90% of work submitted to major publishers is never read by anyone, but this small press publisher reads every submission.

Most small presses pay nothing, but a couple of copies they can't sell anyway. We, on the other hand, do not pay in copies. We actually sell what we print. Our circulation runs 200 to 250—SOLD each issue. Most small-press magazines don't sell half that many. Many don't actually "sell" any.

Submit to the Journal. Your manuscript will actually be read by an editor with the authority to accept. While the *Northwoods Journal* is a magazine for writers, it is not a how to (though it may contain a few how to elements), it is a showcase. Writers get to show off their finest works through legitimate, paid publication. Everything published in the *Northwoods Journal*, a magazine for writers, is paid for on acceptance.

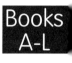

The Journal does not require any purchase, subscription, or membership. Send an SASE.

Century Press

Century Press was formed in 1997. Its purpose is to offer writers an outlet for other than fiction or poetry.

Century Press accepts any type of book.

Personal Publishing Program

In keeping with its purpose to encourage and develop literary talent, CAL offers a Personal Publishing Program (PPP) where the author becomes his/her own publisher.

This program is designed to make authors of writers. No acceptance is needed. (We don't even read the manuscripts.) All profits accrue to the author.

CAL will serve as your printer, your typesetter, your cover artist, your editor, your fulfillment office, your bookkeeper, your webmaster, anything you wish. All on a fee-for-services basis. We can provide things like bar codes, copyright services, and more.

Most writers hire us as printers and/or typesetters. A smaller number buy other services of creation or promotion. We've printed more than 2,000 (and counting) titles for writers. References on request.

Cost of printing is $200, plus cost of books ordered.

Categories: Fiction—Nonfiction—Adventure—Biography—Civil War—Conservation—Drama—Erotica—Fantasy—Fishing—History—Literature—Men's Fiction—Mystery—Outdoors—Paranormal—Romance—Rural America—Science Fiction—Short Stories—Sports/Recreation—Textbooks—Western—Writing—Hunting

CONTACT: Century Press
Material: Century Press submissions
CONTACT: Dan River Press
Material: Dan River Press submissions
CONTACT: Dan River Anthology
Material: Dan River Anthology submissions
CONTACT: Northwoods Press
Material: Northwoods Press submissions
CONTACT: Northwoods Journal
Material: Northwoods Journal submissions
CONTACT: Northwoods Anthology
Material: Northwoods Anthology submissions
PO Box 298
Thomaston ME 04861
Phone: 207-354-0998
E-mail: cal@americanletters.org
Website: www.americanletters.org

Contemporary Books
A Division of McGraw-Hill Companies

Project Submission Guidelines

McGraw-Hill is committed to maintaining the highest standards of quality in all areas in which we publish. If you have an idea for a book that you would like us to consider, please simply provide the information requested below. This will assist us in evaluating your proposal. Summarize your material concisely and accurately, being as specific as possible. Remember, the quality of the proposal you submit may be our only guide to the quality of the book that you plan to write.

Rationale

Why do you feel compelled to write this book? Why will someone want to read it? Is there a particularly timely nature of the subject area? What are the specific benefits of your book? These will be key selling points, so be precise.

Subject

Describe the contents of your book in commonly understood language. Be as precise as possible, providing both a general overview and a rundown of subjects treated in detail. Indicate how in-depth your coverage will be.

Market

Who will be the audience for this title? Try to avoid falling into the "all things for all people" trap. Specify who will need to read this book, citing job titles, and identifying industries. Include information on professional associations, potential courses, and any other items that may help us reach your audience.

Competition

List other books on the same or related subjects that have been written for the same market. Include all pertinent information (author, title, publisher, date published, price, and number of pages). Then provide a sentence or two to explain how your book is different from (and of course, better than) each.

The Book

Describe your ideas about the physical book: How many pages do you estimate it being? Approximately how many illustrations will be included? Can these be black and white, or is color necessary? How long will it take you to complete the entire manuscript? Is this tied to any software release? Will the work require any add-ons such as a disk or CD-ROM?

Your Curriculum Vitae

We'd like to get to know you. Please include a recent resume, as well as a list of professional affiliations. Are you a member of any Associations related to the subject matter of the book?

Suggested Reviewers

While we may not use them, at times we find it helpful to have the names of one or two people whose expertise or reputation in your field will facilitate our evaluation process. These should not be close colleagues or friends, but peers whose opinions you would appreciate having. Please provide names, addresses, and phone numbers if possible.

Rough Outline, Book Materials

Ideally, we'd love to see a finished manuscript. Therefore, please include as much material as you have already prepared, including Table of Contents and any Chapters you may have. If pertinent, it's also a good idea to enclose some illustrations if you can.

Thank you for your time and effort in compiling this information. We hope that the preparation of this proposal has helped you think about your book, and increased your awareness of publishing requirements.

Categories: Nonfiction—Business—Careers—Diet/Nutrition—Education—Health—Language—Money & Finances—Parenting—Physical Fitness—Recreation—Reference—Relationships—Self Help—Sports/Recreation

CONTACT: Submissions Editor
Material: All
130 E. Randolph St., Ste. 900
Chicago IL 60601
Phone: 312-233-7500
Fax: 312-233-7570
Website: books.mcgraw-hill.com

Contemporary Drama Services

Please refer to Meriwether Publishing Ltd., in the Book Publishers section.

Cornell Maritime Press, Inc.

Proposals must follow our submission guidelines, which are also posted on our website at www.cmptp.com No email submissions are accepted. A Self-Addressed, Stamped Envelope must be included if materials are to be returned.

Categories: Boating—Cooking—Fishing—Gardening—Outdoors—

Regional—Textbooks

CONTACT: Managing Editor
Material: All
PO Box 456
Centreville, MD 21617
Phone: 410-758-1075
Fax: 410-758-6849
E-mail: cornell@crosslink.net
Website: www.cimptp.com

Cottonwood Press, Inc.

Cottonwood Press is always looking for fresh material for our customers—English and language arts teachers, grades 5 - 12.

We like to use material that is clever, requiring thought and creativity from students—not mindless busy work. Many of our books have both ideas for teachers as well as ready-to-use activities designed for the teacher to photocopy and pass out to his or her students.

We are not interested in variations of the same old games and ideas you see everywhere. (If we see one more game on homonyms, for example, we may scream.) We also do not use word search (word find) puzzles. We love to use materials with a humorous, light-hearted, offbeat or down-to-earth approach, the kind of material that real teachers can use with real kids.

A careful look through our catalog will help you better understand our products. We strongly suggest that you also familiarize yourself with some of the activities in our books. It is impossible to write for Cottonwood Press without understanding how our books are different from similar products on the market.

We try to get a response to the author within two to four weeks after receiving a manuscript.

Sincerely,
Cheryl Thurston, Editor
Categories: Education—Juvenile

CONTACT: Acquisitions Editor
Material: All
109-B Cameron Dr.
Fort Collins CO 80525
Phone: 970-204-0715
Fax: 970-204-0761
Website: www.cottonwoodpress.com

Countrysport Press

Please refer to Down East Books.

Craftsman Book Company

Books on the following subjects would sell well to Craftsman customers. The book should be loaded with step-by-step instructions, illustrations, charts, reference data, diagrams, forms, pictures, samples, cost estimates, rules of thumb, man-hour estimates and examples that show how work should be done on the construction site or that solve actual problems in the builder's office. The book must cover the subject completely, become the owner's primary reference on the subject, and have a high utility-to-cost ratio. This list is by no means complete, and is subject to changing trends in the marketplace. Any reference manual that will help construction tradespersons, builders, remodelers, construction estimators or adjusters make a better living in their profession is a good candidate for publication by Craftsman Book Company.

• How to Estimate Sitework (or Concrete, Steel, Masonry, Roofing, HVAC, Demoliton, Mold Remediation)
• Man-hour Estimates for Residential, Commercial, and Industrial Con-

struction
• Cost Estimates for Commercial and Industrial Construction
• Estimating Remodeling and Renovation Costs (With Man-hour Estimates)
• Demolition Methods & Estimating (With Man-hour Estimates)
• How to Take-off Construction Material Quantities
• Estimating Building Losses and Damage Repair Costs (With Man-hours)
• Construction Scheduling, CPM and Project Control
• Set Up and Run Your Subcontracting Business
• How to Design and Build Homes and Apartments
• How to Get the Insurance and Bonds You Need at the Right Price
• Field Supervision for Construction Contractors
• How to Get Lucrative Government Construction Projects
• How to Remodel and Renovate Commercial and Industrial Buildings
• Operating Excavation and Grading Equipment (all types)
• Start and Run an Excavation and Grading Contracting Business
• General Excavation Methods (Earth, Rock, Hauling, Placing, Banks)
• Concrete Formwork: Designing, Installing and Estimating
• Simplified Design of Reinforced Concrete for Builders
• Installing and Estimating Concrete Reinforcing
• Modern Masonry (Block, Brick, Tile, Terrazzo—With Man-hour Estimates)
• Estimating and Erecting Structural Steel and Fabricated Metals
• Modern Cabinet Making and Installation Manual
• The Complete Manual of Roof and Stair Layout
• How to Install and Replace Flooring: Hardwood, Resilient, Carpet, and Tile
• Painting and Decorating Commercial and Industrial Buildings
• Plumbing Repair and Renovation Manual (With Troubleshooting Guide)
• Practical Guide to the Uniform Mechanical Code
• Plumber's Vest Pocket Reference Book
• Low Voltage Electrical Guide: Design, Installation, Estimating
• Electrician's Vest Pocket Reference Book
• Footing & Foundation Construction & Estimating
• Construction Estimating for Beginners
• How to Get Insurance Repair Work
• Specifications for Construction Plans
Categories: Business—Engineering—Reference—Construction

CONTACT: Laurence Jacobs, Managing Editor
Material: Professional Building Books
PO Box 6500
Carlsbad CA 92011
Phone: 760-438-7828
Fax: 740-438-0398
Website: www.craftsman-book.com

Creative Publishing International, Inc.
NorthWord Press

As an imprint of Creative Publishing International, NorthWord Press is a publisher whose primary commitment is to wildlife, habitat, and natural history topics of the world for adults and children.

The following topics may be considered, but generally stand little chance of acceptance: "how-to" titles, collections of magazine stories or articles, journal memoirs, essays about travel, and manuscripts dealing with limited regional subject matter.

We publish: Non-fiction wildlife and nature topics, including substantial species natural history information.

Our books generally focus on the species with little human interac-

**Books
A-L**

tion; we typically do not publish stories involving animals in domestic situations.

We do not publish these kinds of books: fantasy, adventure novel, rhyme/poetry, biography, memoir/journal books.

We do not publish books with ecology or "green" themes. Nor do we particularly emphasize endangered species.

Our children's list does not include "relationship" or growing-up stories.

Please include the following details when submitting a book proposal:
• Author background, credentials, writing experience
• Brief synopsis of the book being proposed
• Detailed outline or table of contents
• Sample chapters (generally 2 or 3 on hard copy)
• Samples of art, photos, or transparencies intended for use in the book (duplicate photos or transparencies only, please)
• Bibliography (if appropriate)

If the proposal is accepted, manuscripts should be submitted on 3½" floppy disks or CDs formatted in Macintosh or DOS word processing program. A hard copy (double spaced) should accompany the disk.

Proposals submitted to NorthWord Press are reviewed for style, content, appropriateness, conceptual integrity, author expertise, and marketability. Therefore, a rejection does not necessarily reflect any judgment regarding the literary merit of an author's work.

NorthWord uses a standard author contract, which may be modified upon mutual agreement by the author and publisher. Advances against royalties are negotiable, and royalties are paid semi-annually.

Categories: Nonfiction—Animals—Outdoors—Nature—Wildlife

CONTACT: Submissions Editor, Adult Books
Material: All
CONTACT: Submissions Editor, Juvenile Books
Material: All
18705 Lake Drive East
Chanhassen MN 55317
Phone: 952-936-4700
Fax: 952-933-1456

Cross Cultural Publications, Inc.

Submit book proposal in summary, with table of contents and resumé of author. If we are interested we will invite the author for more details and completed manuscript.

Categories: Asian-American—Biography—Christian Interests—College—Conservation—Culture—Ecology—Economics—Education—Entertainment—Environment—Family—Feminism—General Interest—Government—History—Inspirational—Jewish Interest—Literature—Multicultural—Native American—New Age—Politics—Religion—Society—Spiritual—Women's Issues—Ethnic—Philosophy—Public Policy

CONTACT: Acquisitions Editor
Material: All
PO Box 506
Notre Dame IN 46556
Phone: 219-273-6526
Fax: 219-273-5973

The Crossing Press

The Crossing Press is accepting book proposals in the following areas: Natural health; Spirituality; and Empowerment/self-help. We no longer publish fiction, poetry or calendars.

Please submit as much of the following information as possible in your book proposal. We find this information essential in evaluating the project for publication consideration.

Description of the book. Includes text content, style, number of manuscript pages, and how you envision the published book (physical attributes).

Definition of the market. Who is the intended audience? What need is this book fulfilling? What is the book designed to accomplish? How is the topic of increasing rather than declining or passing interest? How does it compare with other books on the market (please list)?

Outline and description of contents. Provide a few sentences about the purpose and contents of each chapter, giving specific details and examples as well as general statements. Explain the logic of the book's organization.

Introduction and sample chapters. If complete, please submit 1-2 sample chapters as well as an introduction to the manuscript.

Timetable. Is the manuscript complete? If not, provide a schedule for submitting sample chapters (if not already included), and the complete manuscript.

Author information. Include your resume, vita, or biography detailing your professional and educational background, including prior publications and publicity materials, and any other relevant information.

We look forward to reviewing your proposal.

Categories: Nonfiction—Cooking—Diet/Nutrition—Health—New Age—Spiritual—Empowerment—Natural Healing

CONTACT: Acquisitions Editor
Material: All
1201 Shaffer Rd. Ste B
Santa Cruz CA 95060
Phone: 408-722-0711
E-mail: Crossing@aol.com
Website: www.crossingpress.com

Crossway Books
A Division of Good News Publications

Crossway Books does not accept unsolicited submissions. Items sent without permission will not be returned. This policy went into effect June 1, 2003.

Crossway Books does review selected manuscripts submitted to:
First Edition
www.ecpa.org/FE
9633 S. 48th St. Ste:140
Phoeniz, AZ 85044
(800) 600-4592
The Writer's Edge
www.writersedgeservice.com
PO Box 1266
Wheaton, IL 60189
No phone number is available.

Both these organizations offer very fine services at modest rates that allow your work to be reviewed simultaneously by more than forty-five other Christian publishers. We will contact the author if we see a proposal that will fit within our publishing program. Proposals sent by agents will still be considered.

We do not accept or respond to e-mail queries or proposals.

We are interested only in books written from an evangelical Christian perspective. The best way to understand what type of books we publish is to review our current catalog. We provide the following information as a general reference.

Areas of Interest

We are interested in reviewing submissions in the areas listed in Category A, and are not accepting submissions for anything from Category B and Category C.

Category A—Of Interest

Nonfiction

• Issues Books. These books typically address the critical issues facing Christians today in our personal lives, families, communities and the wider culture.

• Books on the deeper Christian life. In general, these books seek to provide a deeper understanding of Christian truth and its application to daily life. Many of these involve the exposition of Scripture; others are more topical and systematic. Books in this category could include biblical teaching, the application of the Bible to Christian growth, evangelism, devotions, and so on.

• A select number of academic and professional volumes. These books tend to reflect the same general approach mentioned above under issues books and books on the deeper Christian life, but are directed more toward the academic and professional audience. These would include books in theology, biblical studies, church history, preaching, critical issues in specific academic disciplines, and so on.

Nonfiction

• End-time or prophecy books
• Collected sermons
• Missionary biographies
• Contemporary/popular biographies
• Exposés of well-known Christians
• Personal experience stories
• Art books

Fiction

• Children's picture books
• End-time or prophecy novels
• Short stories or anthologies
• Biblical novels (set in Bible times)
• Fantasy/science fiction
• Horror novels
• Romance

The following information is ONLY for those who have been given permission to submit a manuscript to Crossway Books.

Format

Please do as thorough a job of research and writing as possible before submitting your manuscript. If possible, have a professional proofreading service look over your manuscript for grammar, punctuation and spelling errors.

Requirements for a submission are: A synopsis of one or two pages as well as a chapter-by-chapter synopsis and two sample chapters. Please do not send outlines or tables of contents only. These will tell the reviewer little about the manuscript's content, nor will it give the reviewer any knowledge of your writing skills.

All submissions must be neatly typed and double-spaced. Send a photocopy, not the original. On the first page of the submission, please include your name, address, telephone number, and an approximate total word count for your entire manuscript.

We do not accept submissions of entire manuscripts. We are not accepting submissions on disk or by e-mail at this time.

Categories: Nonfiction—Christisn Interest—Education—History—Juvenile—Religion— Western—Young Adult

CONTACT: Jill Carter, Editorial Administrator
Material: All
1300 Crescent St.
Wheaton, IL 60187

Daily Guideposts

Guideposts Books creates inspirational, faith-filled books to help our family of readers live fuller, richer lives. Our devotional, *Daily Guideposts*, published annually since 1977, now brings more than a million readers closer to God through prayerfully sharing in the personal experiences of its writers. If you'd like to audition for Daily Guideposts, please read the guidelines below.

Auditioning for *Daily Guideposts*

Daily Guideposts devotionals are first-person anecdotes, told in an informal, conversational style, which make a single spiritual point. They open with a Bible verse related to the theme of the devotional, and end with a prayer. At their best, they are like short-short stories, using vivid description and dialogue to draw the reader into the spiritual insight the writer has gained from the experience described.

The challenge of writing a *Daily Guideposts* devotional is to tell a compelling story, convey something of your personality to the reader, and communicate an uplifting spiritual insight, all in the space of 200 to 350 words. *The following do's and don'ts should help you get started:*

• *Be concise.* A devotional should be no more than 350 words, including Scripture and prayer. One typewritten page, double-spaced, is preferable.

• *Make a point.* Each devotional should have one clear spiritual point to convey, a point that grows naturally out of the story.

• *Tell a story.* Use setting, dialogue, and a dramatic situation to get the reader involved.

• *Be specific.* Tell us the names of the people and places in your story. Use the senses: give the reader sights, sounds, smells, and tastes. Concrete details make the story live.

• *Be practical.* Show us how you were changed in some specific way. Giving examples of how you changed or did something differently will help the reader to identify with you, and give him or her something to apply in his or her own life.

• *Show us how your faith is part of your daily life.* Your story should be an occasion of spiritual growth for yourself and your reader. Although showing your faith in action may involve worship, prayer, and talking about spiritual things in the context of the everyday aspects of your life, it's not necessary to confine yourself to explicitly religious topics. Find a unique angle of vision. Look for a point or application that isn't obvious, that takes the story or situation out of the realm of the routine and provides new insight for the reader.

• *Tell us about yourself.* We are looking for writing that has personality, so the more your devotionals reveal about your lifestyle, work, family and hobbies, the better. Be selective—you can't tell us everything in only a few devotionals, so consider what details will be most revealing.

How to Audition for *Daily Guideposts*

Please submit three to five sample devotionals for consideration. Previously published material is not acceptable. Submissions should be typed, double-spaced, and accompanied by a stamped, self-addressed envelope. Please include your name, telephone number, and Social Security number. Please allow two months for our reply.

Categories: Nonfiction—Christian Interests—Inspirational—Religion—Spiritual

CONTACT: Daily Guideposts Editor
Material: All
Guideposts Book Division
16 East 34th Street
New York NY 10016
E-mail: www.guideposts.org

Dalkey Archive Press

Although we have returned to publishing original fiction, we are only publishing 2-4 original works each year, and our main focus is still on reprints. If you would like to submit a manuscript, you should be familiar with our list and the types of books we publish in order to determine whether your book is appropriate for our list. Please keep in mind we publish primarily literary fiction, and rarely publish poetry, criticism, or non-fiction. Additionally, we place a heavy emphasis upon fiction that belongs to the experimental tradition of Sterne, Joyce, Rabelais, Flann O'Brien, Beckett, Gertrude Stein and Djuna Barnes.

Also, keep in mind:

A query letter with contact information should accompany your submission.

Without an SASE we can't respond to or return unsolicited submissions.

In general, we respond within 2-4 months of receiving a submission.

We do not accept queries or submissions via e-mail.

Categories: Fiction—Experimental Fiction

CONTACT: Acquisitions Editor
Material: All
Dalkey Archive Press
ISU Campus Box 8905
Normal, IL 61790-8905
Phone: 309-438-7555
Fax: fax: 309-438-7422
E-mail: contact@dalkeyarchive.com
Website: www.centerforbookculture.org

Dan River Press
Dan River Anthology

Please refer to The Conservatory of American Letters, in the Book Publishers section.

David R. Godine, Inc.

David R. Godine, Inc., is a small publishing house located in Boston, Massachusetts, producing between twenty and thirty titles per year and maintaining an active reprint program. The company is independent (a rarity these days) and its list tends to reflect the individual tastes and interests of its president and founder, David Godine.

At Godine, quality has remained foremost. Our aim is to identify the best work and to produce it in the best way possible. All of our hardcover and softcover books are printed on acid-free paper. Many hardcovers are still bound in full cloth. The list is deliberately eclectic and features works that many other publishers can't or won't support, books that won't necessarily become bestsellers but that still deserve publication. In a world of spin-offs and commercial "product," Godine's list stands apart by offering original fiction and non-fiction of the highest rank, rediscovered masterworks, translations of outstanding world literature, poetry, art, photography, and beautifully designed books for children.

Our submissions policy:

Authors should note that Godine does not accept unsolicited manuscripts or proposals. Due to the large number of submissions, we will not be able to return any materials not accompanied by a self-addressed, stamped envelope. Any materials sent that do not include sufficient postage to cover the expense of their return will be held for 90 days and then destroyed. Please note that while we do reply to queries via email that we prefer queries and submission to be submitted by regular mail. Authors are advised to have their agent contact us if they would like us to consider a project. We strongly advise against sending original artwork or unreplacable documents; while all reasonable care will be taken with such materials, we cannnot be held responsible in the event of damage or loss.

Editorial, Publicity, Marketing, and Production are handled through our Boston office.

Categories: Fiction—Nonfiction—Architecture—Arts—Biogra-

phy—Boating—Children—Cooking—Crime—Feminism—Food/Drink—Gardening—Gay/Lesbian—History—Jewish Interest—Juvenile—Literature—Men's Fiction—Mystery—Outdoors—Photography—Poetry—Religion—Rural America—Short Stories—Women's Fiction—Writing—Young Adult

CONTACT: David R. Godine, Publisher
Material: All
9 Hamilton Place
Boston MA 02108-4715
Phone: 617-451-9600
Fax: 617-350-0250
E-mail: info@godine.com
Website: www.godine.com

DAW Books

Thank you for your inquiry concerning our requirements. We hope the following information will answer your questions:

We publish science fiction and fantasy novels. We do not want short stories, short story collections, novellas, or poetry. The average length of the novels we publish varies but is almost never less than 80,000 words. (To estimate the length of your manuscript, you may want to use the technique mentioned below.)

Please do not submit handwritten material. Manuscripts must be typewritten or letter-quality computer generated. Use a dark ribbon. Clear photocopies are acceptable. The manuscript should be on 8" x 11" good white paper, double-spaced, with at least 1" wide margins all around. Please use only one side of the page, number your pages consecutively, and put the title of your novel at the top of each page.

Very important: Please type your name, address and phone number in the upper right hand corner of the first page of your manuscript. Right under this, please put the length of your manuscript in number of words.

We publish first novels if they are of professional quality. A literary agent is not required for submission. We will not consider manuscripts that are currently on submission to another publisher.

Be sure to include a postage paid envelope for the return of the manuscript, if it is not found acceptable. You are entitled to Fourth Class rates for literary manuscripts—ask at your local post office. If you prefer to send your work by First Class Mail and wish it returned the same way, be sure to include sufficient postage, or a check or money order to cover the postage costs. Canadian return postage can only be sent via Canadian Postal Money Order in US$. If you are mailing your manuscript from outside the U.S.A. or Canada, postage payment may only be made via American Express Money Order in US$, or by a check in US$ payable from a New York City bank. (Please do not enclose International Postal Coupons, except as postage for a single letter. IPCs cost approximately $3.50 each, but are only valid for 55 cents postage). Never send cash through the mail.

It may require up to three months or more for our editors to review a submission and come to a decision. If you want to be sure we have received your manuscript, please enclose a stamped, self-addressed postcard which we will return when your manuscript is logged-in.

It is not necessary for you to register or copyright your work before publication—it is protected by law as long as it has not been published. When published, we will copyright the book in the author's name and register that copyright with the Library of Congress.

ADDITIONAL INFORMATION FOR NEW WRITERS:
HOW TO GET THE WORD COUNT OF A MANUSCRIPT

1. Count the words in 10 lines and divide the total number of words by ten.

2. Count the lines on an average page.

3. Multiply the total number of lines for the sample full page by the approximate word count for one line. This gives you the word count for one page.

4. Then multiply this total count for the words on one page by the total number of pages in your manuscript. This is the total length of your manu-

script in words. Please put this number on page one of your manuscript, right under your name address.

5. To check the accuracy of your count, please repeat this process twice.

6. Please send manuscripts to Peter Stampfel, Submission Editor.

7. Free DAW Books catalog available upon request.

Categories: Fiction—Fantasy—Science Fiction

CONTACT: Peter Stampfel, Submission Editor.
Material: All
DAW Books
375 Hudson St.
New York, NY 10014
Website: us.penguingroup.com/

Dawn Publications

Thank you for your interest in Dawn Publications. We accept unsolicited manuscripts. DAWN is primarily a nature awareness publisher for adults and children. In part the company grew out of the enthusiastic public response to the now-classic *Sharing Nature With Children* by Joseph Cornell, the eminent naturalist and nature educator. Increasingly our goal is to teach children the wonders of nature and of themselves through high-quality picture books, including trade books suitable for use in the classroom.

Dawn generally does not publish material which:

• contains animal dialogue or other highly anthropomorphic material;

• merely explains nature;

• is a fantasy;

• is a retelling of a legend with supernatural elements;

• is centered primarily on human situations or foibles.

The best way to get a sense of Dawn's publishing mission is to examine some of our books. Our complete catalog is available online at www.dawnpub.com.

Many of our publications come from unsolicited submissions and first-time authors. Please be aware, however, that we are a small company: we receive thousands of queries or manuscripts annually and accept only half a dozen or fewer for publication. Please observe the following mechanics of submission:

Please enclose a cover letter with the manuscript describing your work, the intended age of the audience, your other publications if any, your motivation for writing, and relevant background.

Be aware that most picture books are 32 pages. Indicate where you want your page breaks to be-don't send 32 separate sheets. (However, if you have a mockup that meaningfully enhances appreciation of the work, send it. Be sure to enclose an SASE if you want it returned.)

If you are presenting us with artwork, please let us know whether the art and text are a package. Usually we want to retain the option of selecting the artist.

Always enclose an SASE! If an SASE is not enclosed, we will not necessarily respond.

Address manuscript submissions to the attention of the editor, Glenn J. Hovemann. Although we try to be reasonably prompt, please allow at least two months for response.

If you are an illustrator please address your work to the art director, Muffy Weaver.

Categories: Nonfiction—Children—Nature—Science

CONTACT: Glenn Hovemann, Editor
Material: Manuscripts
CONTACT: Muffy Weaver, Art Director
Material: Illustrations Samples
12402 Bitney Springs Rd.
Nevada City, CA 95959
Phone: 530-274-7775
Website: www.dawnpub.com

The Denali Press

The Denali Press publishes books on multiculturalism. We emphasize reference and scholarly books with a strong appeal to the library and institutional market. Selected titles include: *Hispanic Resource Directory*; *Refugee and Immigrant Resource Directory*; *Judaica Reference Sources*; and *Lives Between Cultures: A Study of Human Nature, Identity and Culture*.

The Denali Press would like to see queries, proposals, summaries, and outlines rather than full manuscripts. If the substance of the work cannot be fully communicated in this manner, a couple of chapters may be included. We encourage queries with full descriptions both of the proposed work and of the author's background and interests, since from them we may be able to identify ideas for books other than the one proposed. *Specifically, proposals should discuss:*

• the book's subject matter and approach

• the audience, i.e., the size of the market and how it can be reached

• how the book differs from similar books currently in print, and

• author qualifications

We are pleased to sponsor the American Library Association's The Denali Press Award. This award is presented to recognize achievement in creating reference works, outstanding in quality and significance, that provide information specifically about ethnic and minority groups in the United States.

Categories: Nonfiction—College—Culture—Directories—Environment—Hispanic—Human Rights—Jewish Interest—Multicultural—Native American—Politics—Reference

CONTACT: Sally Silvas-Ottumwa, Editorial Associate
Material: All
PO Box 021535
Juneau AK 99802
Phone: 907-586-6014
Fax: 907-463-6780
E-mail: denalipress@alaska.net

Denlinger's Publishers, Ltd.

SUBMISSIONS AND RETURNS

Genre: We do not publish poetry, illustrated works, erotica or textbooks.

Length: Maximum: 100,000 words. Prefer: 70,000 to 80,000 words. Minimum 100 pages.

Note: All authors are required to read our contract BEFORE submission:

Go to: thebookden.com/agree.html. We DO NOT change the contract.

Query - Please use from.

Query should contain the following:

• Title of Manuscript.

• Genre(s).

• Target audience, add age range for Juvenile and Young Adult.

• Estimated number of words.

• Brief synopsis (single paragraph).

• Author's statement that they have read and agree to our contract if the work is accepted.

All forms & gudieline available at www.thebookden.com/guide.html

• **Manuscript via email attachment or on disk:**

Disks must be a standard 3.5 inch floppy disk in a PC, NOT Mac or ASCII, word processing format. HTML format is OK, but view it first utilizing latest versions of Internet browsers. View it on several computer monitors to verify correct format.

Do not zip (AOL does that automatically if multiple attachments).

Word processing software should be equal to or less than Microsoft Word 2000 or Word Perfect 8. MS Works 4.0 or Lotus

Books A-L

WordPro 96 are acceptable, but less desirable.

Word processing format must be single spaced - 1" margins without visible headers, footers, or page numbers.

Manuscript must be formatted as a single running file, not multiple files, i.e. by pages or by chapters.

Spell and grammar check is a necessity, possibly an outside edit. Over 5% errors equals reject, no matter how good a book.

Scene breaks must be marked by two or more asterisks.

Optional

If you wish verification that we have received your material via regular mail, ship your materials with a return receipt requested.

Inquiries regarding the status of your manuscript may be made by email only. Note: Please be patient. We handle hundreds of manuscripts and it can easily be six months or longer before yours is reviewed.

Returns: Since we no longer request hard copy submission during the evaluation phase, no return postage is required. If you do send any hard copy material or disks and wish to have them returned, you must send adequate postage and packaging for return shipping.

Categories: Fiction—Nonfiction—Adventure—History—Horror—Mystery—Memoirs—Self Help—Western

CONTACT: Cecelia Peters
Material: All
PO Box 1030
Edgewater, FL 32132-1030
Phone: 386-416-0009
Fax: 386-236-0517
E-mail: editor@thebookden.com
Website: www.thebookden.com

Destiny Books

Books on popular occult topics with original, substantive content that the reader can readily apply to his or her own life.

In order to make the review process more efficient for prospective authors and for our editorial staff, we have prepared a list of requirements for authors and for our editorial staff, we have prepared a list of requirements for authors who are submitting work. Please include the following when presenting a proposal:

1. A BRIEF LETTER THAT INCLUDES A SHORT SYNOPSIS OF THE BOOK

a) The letter should be no more than two pages long and should tell how your manuscript contributes to its field and what make is unique.

b) As specifically as you can, tell us who the audience is for your book.

c) Give a brief biography of yourself, noting especially any specific qualifications for writing your subject.

2. A TABLE OF CONTENTS, INTRODUCTION, AND SAMPLE CHAPTER(S)

There is no need to send a complete manuscripts unless it is specifically asked for. Proposals including the above materials are reviewed much faster than thick manuscripts sent unsolicited.

3. WE CANNOT RETURN PROPOSALS OR MANUSCRIPTS UNLESS THEY ARE ACCOMPANIED BY A SELF-ADDRESSED ENVELOPE STAMPED WITH SUFFICIENT POSTAGE.

Some prospective authors write or e-mail a query letter before sending a proposal. This is a good idea and can save time and postage, especially when you are not familiar with the books we publish. A list of our seven imprints follows, please read these before sending us a query letter or proposal.

> **Remember: Editors change jobs and publishers change addresses. It is wise to invest in a phone call for the current information before submitting.**

If you have questions that have not been addressed above regarding our submission guidelines, please DO NO call the acquisitions editor; send a query letter to our submissions department at the address listed below. Your query letter should provide enough information about your work that the acquisitions editor can make an informed decision and contact you for further details.

Categories: Nonfiction—New Age—Occult

Contact: Submissions
Destiny Books
PO Box 388
Rochester, VT 05767-0388 USA
Phone: 802-767-3174
Website: www.InnerTraditions.com

Dial Books for Young Readers
A Division of Penguin Putnam Books for Young Readers

Owing to the overwhelming number of unsolicited manuscripts we recieve, we at Dial Books for Young Readers have had to change our submissions policy:

As of August 1, 2005, Dial will no longer respond to your unsolicited submissions unless interested in publishing it. **Please *do not* include a self-addressed stamped envelope with your submission.** Submissions postmarked August 1, 2005, or later will be recycled. You will not hear from Dial regarding the status of your submission unless we are interested, in which case you can expect a reply from us withing four months. We regret that we cannot respond personally to each submission, but rest assured that we do consider each and every one we receive.

We at Dial accept entire picture book manuscripts and a maximum of 10 pages for longer works (novels, easy-to-reads). When submitting a portion of a longer work, please provide an accompanying query letter that briefly describes your manuscript's plot, genre (i.e. easy-to-read, middle grade or YA novel), the intended age group, and your publishing credits, if any.

Because confirmation postcards are easily separated from or hidden within the manuscript, we do not encourage you to include them with your submisson. Please send only one manuscript at a time. Never send cassettes, original artwork, marketing plans, or faxes, and do not send submissions by email. Please know that we only keep track of requested manuscripts; we cannot track unsolicited submissions due to the volume we receive each day, so kindly refrain from calling, faxing, or emailing to inquire after the status of an unsolicited submission as we will be unable to assist you. If you have not received a reply from us after four months, you can safely assume that we are not presently interested in publishing your work.

We do not supply specific guidelines, be we will send you a recent catalogs if you send us a 9x12 envelope with four 37-cent stamps attached (do not send cash or checks). This is one way to become informed as to the style, subject matter, and format of our books.

Art samples should be sent to Attn: Dial Design and will not be returned without a self-addressed stamped envelope. Never send original art. Please do not phone, fax, or email to inquire after your art submission.

Categories: Fiction—Nonfiction—Adventure—African-American—Biography—Family—Children—Family—Folklore—Juvenile—Teen

CONTACT: Submissions Coordinator
Material: Manuscripts
CONTACT: Dial Design

Material: Art Samples
Dial Books for Young Readers
345 Hudson St., 14th Floor
New York NY 10014

Dimi Press

No longer accepting submissions.

Dichter Books

Please refer to Black Forest Press.

Diogenes Publishing

As an alternative press, we are primarily interested in nonfiction pieces that challenge mainstream views. We will consider a variety of genres, including satire, humor, psychology, philosophy, and social criticism. Please do NOT send us self-help, spiritual, and inspirational material. We do not publish books with these themes.

If you believe your word fits our list, send a query letter or outline and one chapter with an SASE to Mary Gillissie. Please let us know if you want your submission returned. Currently, we are not accepting proposals on disk, though we are accepting them by email (Microsoft Word).

Categories: Nonfiction—Comedy—Culture—Family—Psychology—Satire—Society

CONTACT: Mary Gillissie, Editor-in-Chief
Material: All
PO Box 40
Sutter Creek CA 95685
Phone: 209-296-6082

Dixon-Price Publishing

Current Wants
We are looking for books about outdoor recreation on or by the water, about daily life next to an ocean, lake, or river, or about home-based businesses or professions that can be conducted within close proximity to a beach even if the business is not necessarily beach-related (freelance writing is one obvious example). Our publishing schedule is already full for the next year, so we would prefer that you send a brief query first outlining your book's subject, it's "slant," and its potential market.

For non-fiction books — If your idea is intriguing and fits our needs, we will contact you and ask you to provide a proposal with these sections:

> *Overview*—a description of the book that makes it sound like a "must have."

> *Comparison*—your analysis of competitive books on the subject and an explanation of why your book offers the reader a benefit by being different.

> *Target*—a description of your target audience.

> *Market*—an explanation of where and how your book can be sold in addition to the traditional bookstore and library outlets.

> *Promotion*—a preliminary list of potential free promotion and publicity venues. We will enlist your help to develop this

list more fully once the book is accepted, but need to have some idea of where to start looking.

> *Estimated Completion*—when could the completed manuscript be delivered?

> *Specs*—How many double-spaced manuscript pages or an estimated word length. Illustrations, including photos, charts, diagrams, etc., needed for the book. Note that we are unlikely to accept a book that is heavily illustrated, requires much four-color work, or needs special types of illustration such as maps.

> *About the Author*—details on why your previous experiences and accomplishments guarantee this book will be high quality.

> *Samples*—A sample chapter if you have one, or clips of previously published materials you've written.

For works of fiction—We are **only** interested in historical or mystery fiction with a tie-in to a beach, island, or waterfront setting. Perhaps one day we will expand into science fiction, fantasy, romance, etc., but for now, we ask you to please send those manuscripts to someone else.

Historical novels—To help you narrow consideration of us even more, we are unlikely to consider war stories, but would be very open to action and adventure within the context of the historical setting. We're not against pirate stories *per se*, but would be more interested in what the inhabitants of the old town of Brunswick in North Carolina might have worried about as Blackbeard sailed the coast than in what Blackbeard's exploits were. We would be more interested in the daring-do of an early 1800s shrimp fisherman in the Gulf of Mexico who is in conflict with Lafitte than in Lafitte as the central character.

Mystery fiction—Again, our interest is dominated by the setting of the novel as well as the interesting character of the detective. If your detective and story roam the plains of Nebraska, another publisher would be better for you. If your story takes place on South Padre Island, or Vanuatu, or on a small boat making for the Maldives, you might want to consider us. An excellent example of a book that would be right for us is Margaret Maron's *Shooting at Loons*. An excellent example of one that would be wrong—although it's one of our personal favorites by a family friend—is Tony Hillerman's *Dance Hall of the Dead*. We also will not consider publishing a mystery taking place in New York, Los Angeles, Chicago, or any "national" locale even though it may be by the ocean. Reasons in a moment.

Mystery series—We realize a popular detective is a popular detective. If you have an idea for a series but the detective will not always be located on beach, island, dock, or boat, we will still consider such a series provided the main thrust of the series is to keep the detective occupied in one of those settings. But after all, Travis McGee wasn't *always* in Fort Lauderdale.

CURRENT NEEDS—We do not plan to start publishing any fiction until at least 2001. As with our non-fiction requirements, it is best to send a two-page synopsis of your novel idea first. **DO NOT SEND FULL MANUSCRIPTS! IF YOU DO AND WE HAVE NOT ASKED FOR IT, THE MANUSCRIPT WILL BE THROWN AWAY IMMEDIATELY UNOPENED!**

If we like the premise shown by the synopsis, we will contact you and ask for:

> A 20-25 page treatment. This forces you to outline and carefully consider the plot points and dramatic rise of the novel.

Books A-L

Three sample chapters, preferably the opening chapter, the midway turn in the novel, and the final turn (called "plot point two" by Robert Ray) as the detective realizes who the perp is.

A promotion and publicity outline listing potential free promotion venues we can build on. If we accept the novel for publication, we will ask you to be closely involved with us in developing plans to market the book. We are a small company whose marketing budget is limited, so we look for creative ways to publicize and market inexpensively, thinking outside the traditional "box" of bookstores and libraries.

Since we are small, it is unlikely we will offer an advance for your book. However, we will pay either a royalty based on cover, not net, price, or a flat dollar amount per book. If you are looking for an advance, however, you should search elsewhere first.

A Brief Note On Our Approach To Fiction Publishing

We are looking for the type of novel which is well plotted and *can* be tightly written (even if it isn't yet), but would not necessarily appeal to a major publisher. When we build a marketing plan for the novel, we will concentrate primarily on making it a successful novel within the region where the story takes place or based on some other "hook" to a specialized audience, i.e., if the story takes place on Bainbridge Island, we will concentrate our marketing and sales efforts in Seattle, Vancouver, Portland and their surrounding areas. If our hero is based in Puerto Rico, then we would look at marketing to Puerto Ricans, travelers to Puerto Rico, and to Puerto Ricans living on the mainland U.S. In such a case, we might also look into translation to reach a Spanish-speaking audience as well.

If a book can gain a devoted following within a region or niche, then we will assist the author in trying to interest a major publishing house to purchase the novel and develop a national market for it, as well as assist him or her and their agent in seeking a movie company connection if they so desire. Most well-paid novelists make more money from movie rights than from their books.

We are interested, though, in working with authors who want to develop a lifelong career, not necessarily overnight riches. We are also interested in reprinting good novels that have gone out of print, providing the author has maintained the rights to the property and understands we are looking more for regional "stars" than national celebrities.

If this narrow focus applies to your work and you would like to explore the possibilities with us, please send your initial inquiries "Attn: Editor" to the address below or via email.

Categories: Fiction—Non-Fiction—History—Mystery

CONTACT: Submissions
9105 Leprechaun Lane
Kingston, WA 98346
Phone: 360-297-8702
Fax: 360-297-8952
Email: editor@dixonprice.com
Website: www.dixonprice.com

DLSIJ Press

Established in 1998, DLSIJ Press is committed to being a women's press in the truest sense: We publish *all* women, regardless of political leanings, belief system, genre, sexual orientation, etc.

DLSIJ Press publishes ebooks with an optional contract for paperbacks.

In all our endeavors, we strive to uphold the mores of traditional publishing, while returning a higher royalty to the author.

· No reading or set-up fees
· Rigorous review process
· Professional editing and book design
· 45% royalty (net) on ebooks
· 11% royalty on paperbacks (optional contract)
· Royalties paid monthly via PayPal
· Ongoing marketing strategies
· Private online community for our contracted authors

We invite you to explore our site and get to know us and our authors.

Book-Length Submissions

We will be open for new book-length submssions on July 17th, 2006. We are willing to entertain any genre except for Children's.

Per our Submission Guidelines, we are asking for a query letter (including a marketing plan and blurb), a short bio, and the first three chapters, or fair representation of collection. The sample chapters should be in Word or RTF and attached to an email.

The submission email is subs16@dlsijpress.com. (Note that the email will not work until July 17th.) If you submit to us, **please add subs16@dlsijpress.com to your address book** so that our correspondence will not be guzzled by your Junk Mail folder. We promise not to spam, and besides, if you end up with the dreaded 'rejection letter' from us, you at least will be able to enjoy the experience of deleting us.

During this submission cycle, we'll be giving the Submission Status a try. Once we receive your submission, we will acknowledge it by email and then add you/your work to the Submission Status. The status will change as your work goes through the queue. We are hoping that this will avert the frustrating unknowns for you, and that it will save us the wondering whether our emails got through or if you've just moved on. All that said... Come on and dazzle us!

When we are open for book submissions, we are seeking book-length works, both fiction and non-fiction, (35,000+ for prose) by women authors for inclusion in our catalog. We do not publish children's literature. Our taboos: hate, pornography, the "objectification" of women.

While we publish *only* women authors, we are open to *all* women, regardless of shade of skin, faith or lack there of, sexual orientation, over the hill, on the hill, still on the way up...you get the idea.

Due to the volume of submissions we receive, we ask that authors query, rather than sending an entire work. Please email the following to the

acquisitions email address listed in the Call for Submissions on the front page. (There is a different email address for each submission period.)

· query letter (to include marketing plan and blurb)
· short biographical statement
· first three chapters, or fair representation of collection

Please name your files so that they reflect author name and title. Examples:

· V_Woolf_Lighthouse.doc
· V_Woolf_bio.doc
· V_Woolf_query.doc

Format: We are a Mac office and can best deal with PC documents that are in MS Word, standard manuscript format. If you do not have Word, please supply your documents as RTF to preserve your formatting.

Please follow these guidelines! Submissions that willfully disregard our guidelines or submission periods will be neither acknowledged nor reviewed.

We will acknowledge receipt of your material and then contact you after our initial review. Completed work will be reviewed again. If it meets our standards, our editorial staff will decide upon the feasibility of a contract. All contracted work will be edited prior to public availability. We will publish in ebook with or without the optional paperback contract, but we will *not* publish in paperback without the ebook contract.

Note: We *are* dependable; we *do* follow through. If you utilize strict junk mail filters, especially if you only accept email from those in your address book, our email may not get through to you. If you do not receive an acknowledgement of receipt from us in a reasonable period of time, please email us again or use another email account if you have one (especially if you are on AOL or Earthlink).

At the time of this writing, we are implementing a project board on this site—the Submission Status link in the Menu. To protect author privacy, submissions will be noted by author initials coupled with the intials of the work. Example, Virginia Woolf's *To The Lighthouse* would be entered on the date received as VWttl. This example should allow you to identify your submission, monitor its status, and have a general idea of where you fall in the queue. If it is marked as completed and you have received no email from us, please let us know.

Categories: Fiction—Non-fiction—Women's Interest

CONTACT: Submissions Editor
Material: All
Email: subs16@dlsinpress.com

Do-It-Yourself Legal Publishers

We publish general, non-academic, non-fiction. The proposed work should address some aspect of American law—should have a simplistic, practical, self-help, how-to orientation.

Send the following:
1. A brief letter of inquiry
2. An outline of the proposed book
3. One or two complete sample chapters
4. One paragraph synopsis of each of the other chapters.

In the letter, include the following information:
What is the book's subject matter? For whom is the book primarily written and for what segments of society would it appeal? What needs or purposes do your book fulfill? Your general background and qualifications for writing the book? Why is your book appropriate for the kinds of books done by Do-It-Yourself Legal Publishers? Are you familiar with other books previously published on the same subject? And what distinguishes your work from others previously published or in the market today?

Provide us with a brief (1 or 2 pages), separate summary of the work, namely, the substance of the work and its' essential theme and essences.

Proposals should be submitted in this format: Unbound book (paper) format.

Thank you for your cooperation in respect to our above-outlined general policies for submission to Do-It-Yourself Legal Publishers, as we receive scores and scores of proposals each year.

Categories: Nonfiction—Law—Self Help

CONTACT: Submissions Editor
Material: All
Law Press of America
27 Edgerton Terrace
East Orange, NJ 07017

Phone: 973-675-0502

Dorchester Publishing Co., Inc.

THE FOLLOWING ARE THE ONLY CATEGORIES OF ORIGINAL FICTION WE ARE CURRENTLY ACQUIRING.

HISTORICAL ROMANCE—Sensual romances with strong plots and carefully thought out characterizations. Spunky heroine whose love for the hero never wavers; he's the only one she makes love with and she's as passionate as he, although he may have to instruct her in the ways of love, since she's almost invariably untouched before she falls in love with the hero. Hero is often arrogant, overbearing; heroine often can't stand him at first, but discovers that beneath the surface lies a tender, virile, and experienced lover. It helps if both the heroine and hero have a sense of humor—a certain amount of wit leavens the heavy-breathing passion. Hero and heroine are separated by emotional conflict or the twists and turns of the plot, but in the end they overcome the barriers between them and live happily ever after.

We don't want a heroine who sleeps around, or a hero who's sadistic, although if there's a villain or villainess, he or she can be as nasty as possible.

Historical background, details of costume, etc., should be accurate; however, we don't want endless descriptions of battles, the political climate of the period, or a treatise on contemporary social history. Our readers are much more interested in the trials, tribulations, and love life of the heroine than in how many men Napoleon lost at the Battle of Waterloo.

Historical Romances should be approximately 120,000 words.

FUTURISTIC ROMANCE—Futuristic Romances contain all the elements of Historical Romances—beautiful heroine, dashing hero, some conflict that separates them, a happy ending, etc.—but they are set in lavish lands on distant worlds.

Avoid science-fiction-type hardware, technology, etc.

Finished manuscripts should be 120,000 words.

TIME-TRAVEL ROMANCE—A modern-day hero or heroine goes back in time and falls in love. Traditional guidelines for Historical Romances apply. The challenge here is to maintain credibility during the transition between the present and the past. The fun is seeing history and another way of life through the eyes of someone from our own time. The conflict and resolution of the romance arise from the fact that the hero and heroine are from different eras.

Beware of a lot of philosophizing about fate, the meaning of time, and how the past affects the present. No time machines please.

Finished manuscripts should be 120,000 words.

PARANORMAL ROMANCE—Either historical or contemporary romance with magic, witches, ghosts, vampires, etc., as a subsidiary element. Must have a happy ending.

Finished manuscripts should be 120,000 words.

OTHER CATEGORIES

WESTERNS—Exciting novels set in the Old West (before 1900 and west of the Mississippi River) with three-dimensional characters and strong plots. Historical accuracy is important, but should not eclipse the story. In addition to traditional heroes, Native Americans, women, African Americans, etc. are fine as protagonists.

Finished manuscripts should be 70,000 - 90,000 words.

HISTORICAL FICTION—Sweeping sagas set primarily in the Old West, containing all of the general elements of Westerns, but with a larger scope and greater cast of characters.

Finished manuscripts should be 90,000 to 115,000 words.

HORROR—Suspenseful, terrifying novels in a contemporary setting. Supernatural horrors (ghosts, vampires, demons, monsters, etc.) are strongly preferred, although psychological suspense and killers on the loose can work if well-handled and original. Please avoid science fiction.

Finished manuscripts should be 80,000 – 115,000 words.

TECHNOTHRILLERS—Action-filled, contemporary or near-future thrillers with emphasis on cutting-edge technology, frequently featuring advanced jets, submarines, weaponry, etc. Conflict should be on a large, usually international, scale.

Books
A-L

Finished manuscripts should be 90,000 - 115,000 words.

GUIDELINES FOR SUBMITTING MATERIAL TO LEISURE BOOKS AND LOVE SPELL

Please query or submit synopsis and first three chapters only—no complete manuscripts unless specifically requested.

Synopsis, sample chapters (and manuscript if requested) must be typed, double-spaced. Word processors are okay, but letter quality only.

For a free catalogue of Leisure Books, please send a self-addressed, stamped envelope (#10) to the address below.

The best way to learn to write a Leisure or a Love Spell romance is to read a Leisure or a Love Spell romance.

Categories: Fiction—Horror—Romance—Western

CONTACT: Ashley Kuehl, Editorial Assistant
Material: Romance, Horror, Western
CONTACT: Leah Hultenschmidt, Editorial Assistant
Material: Romance, Horror, Western
276 Fifth Ave. Ste. 1008
New York NY 10001
Phone: 212-725-8811
Fax: 212-532-1054
Website: dorchesterpub.com

Down East Books

Imprint: Countrysport Press

Although Down East Books is the largest book publisher in Maine, we are still a relatively small, regional publisher specializing in books with a strong Maine or New England theme. Current subject areas include general interest nonfiction, art and photography, regional attractions and travel guides, biography and memoir, gardening, cooking, crafts, history, nature and ecology, nautical books, and fiction. Please note that a fully developed regional connection is critical in our fiction titles, too, and we do not as a rule publish collections of family lore or family recipes.

We also publish children's books, and here also the regional subject and setting are highly desirable. Note that the New England setting must be integral to the work; a story that with little or no change could be set in another region would not meet our requirements. We are not interested in stories about a writer's own children or pets.

Under the Countrysport Press imprint, we publish sporting titles on hunting, fishing, target shooting, dog training, cooking, and fine guns and fishing tackle. These titles include both "how-to" books and memoir and sporting literature.

New Media

Down East Books also distributes CD-Roms, videos, DVDs, and tapes. If you are looking for a distributor, contact us if you have a title that would fit well with our subject preferences. Please note that we distribute only professionally produced videos/CDs/DVDs/cassettes.

We have not yet published e-books, but we are always open to new ideas! If you'd like to discuss Web publishing on our sites or reprinting an article from one of our books or yours, send an email to: info@downeastbooks.com.

The Manuscript Submission Process

If you believe your project meets our requirements, we will be glad to evaluate its potential for our list. A query letter is a good place to start. Your letter should describe the subject and theme of the book and specify its intended audience. It should also include some information about your knowledge of the subject and your previous publications, if any. Providing a synopsis of the book is critical, as is including a sample chapter. A table of contents is helpful, too. There is no need to send the entire text at this stage, unless your manuscript is very short. If the synopsis and sample chapter look promising, we will ask to see the rest of the text (see Preparing Your Manuscript for Submission). Do keep a copy of anything you send us. We handle all submissions with care, of course, but accidents can happen, particularly when your manuscript is in transit.

If you wish to recommend a particular illustrator or photographer, please include samples of his or her work. Do not, however, go to the trouble and expense of having an artist or photographer prepare an art program until you know what your publisher wants. And unless you are a professional artist or photographer, it is best not to attempt to illustrate your book yourself. Keep in mind, too, that many of our books are not illustrated.

Please note: We do not accept electronic submission of proposals or manuscripts due to the large number we receive and difficulties tracking them and printing them out to be circulated.

What Happens Next?

A book proposal that is a good candidate for Down East Books's list will be reviewed by our editorial board, who will discuss your proposal's merits and marketability. From time to time, we will ask an outside authority to read and comment on a manuscript. (If you are a novice author, it's a good idea to have a professional in your field critique your work before submitting it to a publisher. Doing so could prove to be extremely valuable to you.)

Remember that sometimes a genuinely interesting title just isn't suitable for the markets we serve or would be too expensive to publish. Occasionally we partner with an organization or author who bears part of the costs or guarantees a certain number sold in order to publish a title we are interested in but that doesn't work financially. In general this is not the case, however; we are not a "vanity publisher."

If we accept your manuscript for publication, we will contact you about drawing up a contract. If we decide that your proposed book doesn't fit our current needs, we will let you know. With almost a thousand manuscript submissions every year between Down East Books and Countrysport Press, we obviously have to say no to most of them. Sometimes it is difficult to turn down a particular book idea, but please, unless we request that you revise a manuscript and resubmit it to us, consider our answer to be final. Sometimes we offer suggestions that might help you place the manuscript with another publisher, but if we want you to make revisions specifically for us, we will make that clear.

Allow up to eight weeks for a reply, and be sure to enclose a sufficiently large, self-addressed, stamped envelope for return of your materials in case we decide that your manuscript does not fit needs.

Categories: Fiction—Nonfiction—Arts—Biography—Children—Cooking—Crafts/Hobbies—Ecology—Fishing—Gardening—General Interest—History—Outdoors—Photography—Recreational—Regional (New England)—Sports/Recreation—Travel

CONTACT: Michael Steere, Editor
Material: All
PO Box 679
Camden, ME 04843
Street Address for delivery:
680 Commercial St.
Rockport, Maine 04856
Phone: 207-594-9544
Fax: 207-594-0147
E-mail: msteere@downeast.com
Website: www.downeastbooks.com/

Dutton Children's Books

Please include a self-addressed stamped envelope (SASE) to cover the full weight of all materials submitted or a business-sized SASE for a reply only.

Please supply a cover letter with the following information:

• Titles and publishers of any published children's books• names of magazines and/or newspapers in which any work has appeared

• Whether manuscript is simultaneous submission (will not disqualify)

Picture books may be sent in their entirety. Unless author is also the illustrator, publishers usually select suitable illustrators for manuscripts chosen for publication. We do not require or encourage authors to seek out illustrators for materials they plan to submit.

For longer manuscripts, please send synopsis and up to 10 pages. Author's full name and address must appear on title page of manuscript. Last name should be typed on each page of manuscript.

Authors who wish to confirm that Dutton has received their materials may include a "return receipt requested" (available at the post office) or a self-addressed stamped postcard with the work's title on it.

We recommend that authors send their materials via first class or fourth class manuscript rate. Costly overnight letters draw no attention to manuscripts.

Manuscripts are read as soon as possible and are returned to the author (if a SASE is enclosed) or discarded. Some are held for further consideration.

Unfortunately, the volume of manuscripts makes it impossible for us to write a critique of every submission. We do, however, give all materials a fair and extensive reading.

While we take reasonable care of all items we receive, we can assume no responsibility for loss of or damage to submissions. We discourage the submission of costly or irreplaceable items.

Categories: Fiction—Nonfiction—Adventure—Animals—Children—Literature—Middle Grade Fiction—Picture Books—Young Adult Novels

CONTACT: Submissions Editor
Material: All
345 Hudson St.
New York NY 10014
Phone: 212-414-3495

Eclipse Press

Non-Fiction: We are looking for prospective books on all equine and equine-related subjects, including Thoroughbred racing, breeding, handicapping; English sport horses and disciplines; Western sport horses and disciplines; horse health care and management; and horse people.

Fiction

Eclipse Press does not yet publish fiction.

To consider your non-fiction book for publication, we need your proposal to include the following:

- A brief synopsis of your book
- Author resume or bio
- Detailed outline or table of contents
- Sample chapters
- A list of competing or comparable titles and how your book differs

Do Nots

Do not send queries or proposals to the editor via e-mail. Please allow sufficient time for proper review of your proposal. If it is not accepted, we will return your materials to you. It could take longer to hear from us if your book comes under consideration for publication.

Do not send original materials or artwork. Eclipse Press will not be held liable for any materials lost or destroyed in the mail.

Categories: Nonfiction—Animals—Lifestyle—Sports/Recreation—Western

CONTACT: Jacqueline Duke, Editor
Material: All
PO Box 4038
Lexington KY 40544-4038
Phone: 800-866-2361
Fax: 859-276-6868
E-mail: editorial@eclipsepress.com

Edupress, Inc.

1. Manuscript submissions and all rights are purchased outright by Edupress, Inc. Edupress, Inc. does not pay royalties. Manuscript must not include any material that has been previously copyrighted.

2. Manuscript may be presented in any reasonable form. It does not have to be complete; outlines and sample pages are acceptable. Proposals are also acceptable; good ideas often generate usable products.

3. Original manuscripts should not be sent; send photocopies or other facsimile. If you would like your manuscript returned, please enclose a self-addressed, stamped envelope.

4. Receipt of the manuscript will be acknowledged immediately, but expect that a response to the submitted materials may take 3 to 5 months.

5. Manuscript must be accompanied by a cover letter that includes an outline or synopsis, as well as the author's name, address, and any curriculum information that is relevant. Please provide a résumé, if available.

6. Information regarding knowledge of different formats (Microsoft Word, Quark Xpress, etc.) should be included.

7. Edupress, Inc. uses its own staff of artists, but will consider any artwork that accompanies the manuscript.

Categories: Fiction—Nonfiction—Children—Education

CONTACT: Amanda Meinke
Material: All
208 Avenida Fabricante, Ste 200
San Clemente CA 92672-7536

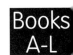

Elderberry Press, LLC

Remember when publishers considered more than profit? …fiction had a moral dimension? ...books had something real, something vital to say? ...agents and editors actually read submissions and made it their goal to encourage writers in their craft? We do.

At Elderberry we judge each submission by one standard:

Either a MS leaves the reader a better person and the world a better place, or we don't publish it. Period.

Tough standard...Does your writing meet it? If so, we'd like to read your MS.

Submission Guidelines

There's nothing new here, and nothing that's not common sense. Editors are just people, after all, and those of us who actually read what is sent us must be able to read it.

Submit your MS in hard copy printed on a single side, large enough to read, unbound, double spaced, with name, and page number on each page. I read in a leather chair by the fire, not at my monitor, so please don't send me a disk to read.

Please include a short author bio and one page synopsis. (Nothing formal, just for my information. And don't spend more than ten minutes writing the synopsis as I am well aware how frustrating it can be to try and condense 500 pages into one and make it sound anything but a Danielle Steel novel. And Dear God, we don't need any more of those, do we.

Don't bother sending your MS express or overnight. I'm stacked up two weeks out with submissions anyway. Save your money and send it MEDIA MAIL. I'll get it in a week anyway.

I'm looking forward to seeing your MS.

What We Publish

We Publish politically incorrect, Christian, conservative/progressive, iconoclastic fiction and nonfiction off all genres including memoir, military history, political, scripture and satire.

Categories: Fiction—Nonfiction—Cartoons—History—Military—Politics—Satire

CONTACT: David W. St.John, Executive Editor
Material: All Queries
1393 Old Homestead Dr, 2nd Floor
Oakland OR 97462

Phone: 541-459.6043
Fax: 541-459-6043
E-mail: editor@elderberrypress.com
Website: www.elderberrypress.com

Electron Press

Electron Press is interested in quality fiction (novels and short story collections) and non-fiction (politics, current events, history, ecology, popular science, essays, etc.). Electron Press does not publish romance, fantasy, or science fiction novels, new age books, how-to books, technical books or text books.

Electron Press never takes commercial considerations into account when evaluating a book for publication. If we like your work we will publish it. We pay substantial royalties.

If you would like Electron Press to consider your book, please submit an email query to . Please attach a separate word processing file that contains the first two or three chapters (maximum 25 to 30 manuscript pages) of your book, preferably in Microsoft Word, Wordperfect, or RTF-format. We will review your proposal and sample, and let you know whether we would like you to send a printout of the entire manuscript.

We are committed to providing a prompt response to submissions. In most cases we will respond within 2 weeks of the date we receive your query. Please include your telephone number if you would like a voice response.

If Electron Press decides to publish your book, we will send you a contract to review. When the contract signing is complete, you will have to provide the following items to Electron Press: The complete text of your book in a computer file (word processing or text file) on a standard 3.5 inch diskette

A one paragraph author's biography and (optional) a portrait photo

If no editorial revisions are required, Electron Press will immediately convert the file to the format used to download the book to customers. The book will appear for sale on the Electron Press web site within 3 to 6 weeks. If substantial copy editing or other revisions are required, publication may be delayed in proportion to the work required.

Categories: Fiction—Non-Fiction—Ecology—History—Politics—Short Stories

CONTACT: Submissions
101-A Shadow Lane
West Hartford, CT 06110
Website: www.electronpress.com

Emerald Ink Publishing

Dear Author,
Our submission guidelines are fairly simple.
We prefer electronic submission or on disk, PC readable (simply access our Website to begin communications, or send files). You should not send files larger than 300-400KB by attaching to e-mail. If files are larger, arrange transmission via ftp. Word, WordPerfect, text or ASCII files, .pdf or .rtf file formats are fine. However, if you wish to send us a manuscript, query first with a stamped, self-addressed envelope or include a return postage postcard.
We always answer inquiries.
Sincerely,

Chris Carson
Categories: Nonfiction—Business—Health—Inspirational—Energy

CONTACT: Chris Carson, Owner
Material: Business, Energy
CONTACT: Patrick Zale, Editor
Material: Health, Inspirational
16630 Imperial Valley Dr., Ste 149
Houston, TX 77060
Phone: 832-598-9808
E-mail: emerald@emeraldink.com
Website: www.emeraldink.com

Empire Publishing Service

Send query letter with SASE—ONLY—for response. Gaslight—Sherlock Holmes, only. Health Watch—Health and Nutrition, only. Empire—Entertainment, History.
Categories: Diet/Nutrition—Entertainment—Mystery

CONTACT: Submissions Editor
Material: All
PO Box 1344
Studio City CA 91614-0344
Phone: 818-784-8918

□ EMQUAD
INTERNATIONAL, LTD.

Emquad International, Ltd.

EMQUAD was founded in 1988 as a publisher of specialty advertising and has more recently turned to books. In September we shall publish "Ao Dai: My War, My Country, My Vietnam" by Xuan Phuong and Daniele Mazingarbe, which Robert MacNeil, author and former coanchor of The NewsHour on PBS, calls "one of the most extraordinary memoirs I have ever read." ISBN 0-9718406-2-8. More at www.emquad.com/aodai.html.

In general, we shall be pleased to consider any book of exceptional merit, regardless of category. Any book considered for publication will be in good taste.

Unsolicited manuscripts will not be returned without an SASE.
Categories: Fiction—Nonfiction

CONTACT: Jon Myers, Publisher
Material: All
PO Box 60
Great Neck, NY 11022
Phone: 516-829-3456
E-mail: emquad@att.net
Website: www.emquad.com

ETC Publications

Our guidelines are *The Chicago Manual of Style* (the book).
Categories: Nonfiction—Christian Interests—Education—Textbooks

CONTACT: Acquisitions Editor
Material: All
700 E. Vereda Del Sur
Palm Springs CA 92262
Phone: 760-325-5352
Fax: 760-325-8844

Evergreen Press

Please refer to Genesis Communications, Inc., in the Book Publishers section.

Excelsior Cee Publishing

Publishes nonfiction, general interest books. Simultaneous submissions accepted. Reports in one month. Does not accept electronic submissions.

Categories: Nonfiction—Biography—Family—General Interest—Inspirational—Writing—Genealogy—How-to

CONTACT: Acquisitions Editor
Material: All
PO Box 5861
Norman OK 73070
Phone: 405-329-3909
Fax: 405-329-6886

Faber & Faber, Inc. Publishers

Please refer to Farrar, Straus and Giroux, Publishers, Inc.

Face to Face Press

About Us

FACE to FACE is a community independent press devoted to publishing all genres of written works that explore the mixed race, interracial, transracial and, more broadly, the multi cultural experience. Founded in 1999, F2F Press published its flagship book *Voices of Brooklyn: Writings from The Women of Color Writer's Workshop,* an anthology of 14 women of color writers, in September 2000. F2F Press seeks to build ties and coalitions across marginalized communities; give under-represented writers a forum for expression and access into the publishing industry; and advocate that communities of color create and maintain their own media.

Submissions

Preparing a proposal is the first important stage in developing a project. In order for us to assess the merits of the idea and arrive at a careful publishing decision, *we recommend your proposal include the following key elements:*

• THE MARKET—Describe the market, customers, any relevant organizations, academic segments, etc.

• UNIQUE SELLING PROPOSITION—How is the book unique and different from other books in the same market?

• COMPETITION—What are the competing books? What are their strengths and weaknesses?

• CONTENT—Describe the project in as much detail as possible, with a description of the book's key features.

• FORMAT—Provide an estimate on the number of manuscript pages and illustrations and in what format. Please specify any design considerations.

• SAMPLE MATERIAL—Please submit 1-2 sample chapters and table of contents, if applicable.

• BIOGRAPHY—Please include your biography or resume.

If you have any questions, contact us by mail, phone or email.

Categories: African-American—Alternate Life-style—Lifestyle—Multicultural—Relationships—Society

CONTACT: Editorial Dept.
Material: All
16 West 32nd St., Ste 10A
New York NY 10001
Phone: 212-494-9143
Fax: 419-828-4684
E-mail: publisher@face2facepress.com
Website: www.face2facepress.com

Fairleigh Dickinson University Press

Established in 1967, Fairleigh Dickinson University Press has published over 1,400 titles in a variety of scholarly fields, including literature, history, art, and the social sciences.

Authors wishing to submit work to FDU Press should write a query letter that describes the manuscript and the contribution it will make to its scholarly field. If the Director and Editorial Committee believe the project is suitable for us, we will ask that the manuscript be submitted. Because of the costs associated with evaluation, FDU Press requires that we be the only press considering the work during the time we have it under review.

Manuscripts considered for publication by FDU Press are subject to internal review and external evaluation by specialist readers. The identity of evaluators is kept confidential, unless they specifically permit us to reveal their names. Authors may suggest possible evaluators, but should note any previous connection they may have had to the project.

The editorial committee of FDU Press, composed of university faculty in a variety of disciplines, meets every two months to select manuscripts for publication.

The typical run for FDU Press is 400-800 copies. Time from delivery of the final manuscript to publication averages between 14-18 months.

FDU Press discourages submission of unrevised dissertations. It does not publish textbooks or original fiction, poetry, or plays. It does, however, publish scholarly editions of literary works, in English or in translation.

FDU Press welcomes inquiries about essay collections. It requires, however, that the majority of the material in a collection be previously unpublished; that the essays have a unifying and consistent theme; and that the editor provides a substantial scholarly introduction. The press holds festschrifts to the same standards we would any other collection of essays.

Decisions of the Editorial Committee of FDU Press are based on the scholarly merit and value of manuscripts under consideration. FDU does not require subsidies or subventions for publication. Where such support is available, it will be employed in a manner mutually acceptable to the author, the press, and the subsidizing organization or individual.

Manuscripts must be submitted in "hard" copy for evaluation. However, once a manuscript has been accepted for publication, the press requests authors send a disk of the work.

Books accepted for publication by the FDU Press Editorial Committee are published by Associated University Presses, 2010 Eastpark Boulevard, Cranbury, NJ 08512, which has similar arrangements with the University of Delaware, Bucknell University, Lehigh University, and Susquahanna University. Only in exceptional cases will manuscripts rejected by one of the above mentioned presses be considered by one of the others.

For documentation, FDU Press books follow *The University of Chicago Stylebook,* 15th edition. MLA format is not accepted. Bibliographies are required. For spelling, the press follows *Webster's Third New International Dictionary* and the *Tenth New Collegiate Dictionary.* The press very strongly recommends that translations be provided for all foreign language extracts. As stated in *The Chicago Manual of Style,* the original language quotations should be retained only when the original language itself is of scholarly significance. For example, in a work of Racine, quotations from Racine's plays should be given in French, followed by English translations. Quotations from critical works on the plays, however, should be given in English translation only.

Fairleigh Dickinson University, founded in 1942, has campuses in Florham-Madison, NJ, Teaneck-Hackensack, NJ, and Wroxton, England.

Members of the Editorial Committee of FDU Press are: René Steinke, Walter Cummins, Kalman Goldstein, Martin Green, Samuel Raphalides, Irene Taviss-Thomson. Ex Officio member: J. Michael Adams.

A complete catalogue of FDU Press books is available online at www.fdu.edu/newspub.

Categories: African-American—Agriculture—Architecture—Arts— Asian-American—Biography—Civil War—Culture—Drama—Film/ Videl—Government—History—Jewish Interest—Native American— Psychology—Theatre—Women's Issues

CONTACT: Harry Keyishian, Director
Material: All
Fairleigh Dickinson University, 285 Madison Ave.
M-GH2-01
Madison NJ 07940
Phone: 973-443-8564
Fax: 973-443-8364
E-mail: fdupress@fdu.edu
www.fdu.edu/newspub

Fairview Press

At this time we are particularly interested in acquiring manuscripts on the following topics: grief and bereavement; aging and seniors; caregiving; palliative and end-of-life care; health, medicine (including complementary medicine), and patient education. But we will also consider proposals on other topics of broad interest to families.

We do not publish fiction, and, although our audiences include adults, teens, and children, we are not currently acquiring children's picture books.

Please take the time to study our catalog and the guidelines before submitting a proposal. We request that you mail your proposal rather than submit it by phone, fax, or e-mail.

Fairview Press is not responsible for lost or damaged submissions and will not respond to any submissions that do not include a self-addressed, stamped envelope (SASE).

Submissions should include:
• Cover letter
• Outline of book
• Sample chapter(s)
• Marketing plan for the book
• Self-addressed, stamped envelope

Categories: Nonfiction—Diet/Nutrition—Disabilities—Family—Health—Physical Fitness—Psychology—Reference

CONTACT: Stephanie Billecke, Editor
Material: All
2450 Riverside Ave. South
Minneapolis MN 55454
Phone: 612-672-4180
Fax: 612-672-4980

Falcon Guides

Please refer to Falcon Publishing.

Falcon Publishing
Falcon Guides, Two Dot, Three Forks

About *Falcon*

Falcon Publishing, an imprint of The Globe Pequot Press, specializes in outdoor guides, high-quality photographic gift books on regional or natural history themes, general interest nonfiction books with Western Americana or environmental themes, and regional cookbooks.

We publish about sixty new titles a year and have more than three hundred titles currently in print.

Imprint of The Globe Pequot Press
Falcon Guides, Two Dot, Three Forks

We Publish:
Outdoor recreation guidebooks (FalconGuides):
• Birding
• Camping
• Fishing
• Hiking (regions and statewide)
• Mountain Biking (cities and statewide)
• Rock climbing
• Rockhounding
• Paddling
• Scenic Driving
• Touring/Historic Traveling
• Walking
• Wild Areas
• How-to camping/wilderness/outdoor guides
• Field guides (wildflowers, wildlife, etc.)
• TwoDot Books: Western Americana, History, Biography,
• General non-fiction with Western/wilderness/Rocky Mountain regional themes
• Large format photo gift books (coffee table books)
• Cookbooks (with outdoor or regional themes)
• Some children's and young adult books (with environmental education or historical themes)

We Don't Publish:
• Poetry
• Coloring books
• New Age texts
• Religious texts
• Self-help books
• Scientific treatises

Submitting a Book Proposal to Falcon Publishing

Do not send us a complete manuscript. Instead, your proposal should include the following materials only:

• A letter explaining your proposal, its sales potential, and a description of its competition.
• A resume and/or list of publishing credits.
• An outline or annotated table of contents.
• One, or at most two, sample chapters.
• Sample copies of any illustrations or photographs. Do not send original materials (transparencies, original art, original copy of manuscript)!

The above materials should be organized, self-explanatory, and succinct. Address all queries to the Acquisitions Editor.

Considering Your Book

Our primary criteria are accuracy, lively and readable prose, and a new angle on natural history, regional, or environmental topics. We will analyze your proposal for editorial value, marketability, and projected costs, as well as for how well it fits with our existing line and publishing plan.

We will respond to queries within eight to ten weeks of their receipt. If your proposal is a likely candidate for a Falcon book, one of our editors may contact you for further writing samples or other materials. Once again, do not submit original materials-clear and readable photocopies are acceptable and preferred.

What You Can Expect From Falcon

Should Falcon decide to publish your book, you will be contracted and paid on a negotiated royalty basis, although we occasionally pay a flat fee. Once we have a contract with an author, we will invest in every necessary resource to produce an attractive, high-quality product and market it effectively.

Thank you for considering Falcon as a possible publisher for your book.

Categories: Nonfiction—Cooking—Environment—Fishing—History—Outdoors—Recreation—Regional—Rural America—Sports/Recreation—Travel

CONTACT: Acquisitions Editor: Falcon
Material: All
The Globe Pequot Press
246 Goose Lane
Guilford CT 06437
Phone: 203-458-4500
Fax: 203-458-4604
E-mail: info@globe-pequot.com

Farrar, Straus and Giroux, Publishers, Inc

Books for Young Readers
North Point Press
Hill and Wang
Faber & Faber, Inc

TRADE PUBLISHING

Farrar, Straus and Giroux was founded in 1946 by Roger W. Straus. The firm is renowned for its international list of literary fiction, nonfiction, poetry and children's books. Farrar, Straus and Giroux authors have won extraordinary acclaim over the years, including numerous National Book Awards, Pulitzer Prizes, and twenty-one Nobel Prizes in literature. Nobel Prize–winners include Knut Hamsun, Hermann Hesse, T. S. Eliot, Pär Lagerkvist, François Mauriac, Juan Ramón Jiménez, Salvatore Quasimodo, Nelly Sachs, Aleksandr Solzhenitsyn, Pablo Neruda, Eugenio Montale, Isaac Bashevis Singer, Czeslaw Milosz, Elias Canetti, William Golding, Wole Soyinka, Joseph Brodsky, Camilo José Cela, Nadine Gordimer, Derek Walcott, and Seamus Heaney.

Poetry has always played a pivotal role on the Farrar, Straus and Giroux list, which boasts some of the greatest names in modern verse, ranging from Elizabeth Bishop, Ted Hughes, and Philip Larkin to John Ashbery, Thom Gunn, and Les Murray.

Fiction has an even greater international reach, distinguished by Rosellen Brown, Jim Crace, Michael Cunningham, Jonathan Franzen, Carlos Fuentes, Peter Høeg, Jamaica Kincaid, Bernard Malamud, Alice McDermott, Péter Nádas, Walker Percy, Richard Powers, Susan Sontag, Scott Turow, Mario Vargas Llosa, Tom Wolfe, and Lois-Ann Yamanaka.

History, art history, natural history, current affairs and science round out a strong list in nonfiction represented by Thomas Friedman, Philip Gourevitch, Roy Jenkins, Gina Kolata, Ben Macintyre, Louis Menand, Giles Milton, and John McPhee, among others.

IMPRINTS of FARRAR, STRAUS and GIROUX:

North Point Press, Hill and Wang, Faber & Faber, Inc, FSG Juvenile Program.

Guidelines for Submission

Query letters should be approximately one page long. Fiction submissions should include one chapter and a synopsis or summary of the book. Authors of nonfiction books should send a proposal which includes a rationale for the book, and a description of proposed chapters. We do not encourage the submission of unsolicited poetry manuscripts due to the size of our list. All submissions must be accompanied by a stamped, self-addressed envelope; manuscripts will not be returned without one. The review process will take approximately three months.

We recommend that an author considering submitting his or her work to us look in a bookstore or library to see which publishers produce what kinds of books and then submit to houses that publish books with some similarity to their own. Narrowing down the field of potential publishers this way can save both the author and the publisher a great deal of time and work.

Books For Young Readers (FSG Juvenile Program)
Guidelines for Submission

Especially in the case of longer manuscripts, it is a good idea to send a letter of inquiry before submitting the entire manuscript.

Manuscripts should be typed, double-spaced. Make sure to keep a copy of your submission-publishers make every effort to safeguard a manuscript, but they cannot be held responsible in the event of its loss.

If you would like confirmation of the receipt of your submission, include a self-addressed, stamped postcard.

Include a cover letter containing any pertinent information about yourself, your writing, your manuscript, etc.

Be sure that your name and address are on the manuscript itself, as well as on the cover letter. ALWAYS include the right-sized, self-addressed, stamped envelope for reply and the return of your material. Clearly indicate the mail class by which you would like your manuscript returned.

If you have illustrations, please send only two or three samples. Do NOT send original artwork.

The length of story depends on the age of the reader for whom it is intended; there are no fixed lengths. Do not expect an editor to give you specific comments. We receive far too many manuscripts for this to happen.

We suggest familiarizing yourself with various children's publishers to get a sense of which company would be most receptive to your type of work. Most publishers will send their catalogue if you write a letter requesting it and provide a self-addressed, stamped manila envelope for it. (Please send us a 9 X 12 envelope, with $1.87 postage.)

THE LITERARY MARKETPLACE, published by R.R. Bowker, contains a list of all publishers; a list of children's book publishers can be obtained from the Children's Book Council, 568 Broadway, New York, NY 10012.

Send submissions to: Children's Editorial Department, Farrar, Straus & Giroux, 19 Union Square West, New York, NY 10003.

• Please do not submit more than one manuscript at a time.

• Please note: Response time for queries and manuscripts is generally within three months.

• Please do not call to query about the status of your manuscript before three months have passed, at which point we may ask that you write us regarding your submission.

Categories: Fiction—Children—Juvenile—Young Adult—Hardcover fiction

CONTACT: Children's Editorial Department
Material: Children's Literature
CONTACT: Editors
Material: All other
19 Union Square West
New York NY 10003
Phone: 212-741-6900
Fax: 212-633-9385
E-mail: fsg.editorial@fsgeebooks.com
Website: www.fsgbooks.com

Fiesta City Publishers

Before submitting material send a query letter.

Query should include brief description of work to be submitted.

With music or song submissions 1.) a lead sheet or complete manuscript and 2.) a cassette must be included.

Fiesta City Publishers will consider unique, unusual and well-constructed material in the fields of fiction, nonfiction (how-to books especially) and music and/or songs.

Categories: Fiction—Nonfiction—Music—How-to—Songs

CONTACT: Frank E. Cooke, President
Material: all
PO Box 5861
Santa Barbara CA 93110
Phone: 805-681-9199

Fleming H. Revell
A Division of Baker Publishing Group.

Please refer to Baker Publishing Group.

Fordham University Press

About Us

2002 marks the 95th anniversary of Fordham University Press, making it one of the oldest presses in the nation.

Fordham University Press, a member the Association of American University Presses (AAUP) since 1938, was established in 1907 not only to represent and uphold the values and traditions of the University itself, but also to further those values and traditions through the dissemination of scholarly research and ideas.

The press publishes primarily in the humanities and the social sciences, with an emphasis on the fields of philosophy, theology, history, classics, communications, economics, sociology, business, political science, and law, as well as literature and the fine arts. Additionally, the press publishes books focusing on the metropolitan New York region and books of interest to the general public.

Guidelines

Formal guidelines not available.

Send queries or book proposals to below address.

Categories: Nonfiction—Civil War—Economics—Education—Film/Video—Government—History—Law—Regional—Religion—Television/Radio—Philosophy—Theology

CONTACT: Anthony Chiffolo, Managing Editor
Material: All
University Box L
2546 Belmont Ave.
Bronx NY 10458-5172
Website: www.fordhampress.com

Forge Books

Please refer to Tom Doherty Associate, LLC, in the Book Publishers section.

Forum Publishing Company

Established in 1981, *Forum Publishing Company* specializes in business-related titles of all types. We are especially interested in 'how-to' start & run business books. We openly welcome unsolicited manuscripts. SASE for return of manuscript.

Categories: Nonfiction—Business—Trade

CONTACT: Submissions Editor
Material: All Directories
383 E. Main St.
Centerport NY 11721
Phone: 631-754-5000
Website: www.bizbooks.org

Frank Amato Publications, Inc.

No formal guidelines. However, we do accept unsolicited manuscripts. Our general focus is on fishing and the out-of-doors, but we are also looking for Non-fiction manuscripts. *Please send non-fiction only.*

Categories: Fishing—Outdoors—Recreation

CONTACT: Frank Amato, Publisher
Material: All
PO Box 82112
Portland OR 97282
Phone: 503-653-8108
Website: www.amatobooks.com

Franklin, Beedle & Associates, Inc.
Publishing for the Computer Sciences

We seek proposals for books and online products. The primary areas of interest are operating systems, computer programming, software applications, and the Internet and the World Wide Web. The intended market for your project should be either professionals in these fields or undergraduate students majoring in one of these disciplines.

Your submission should include the following: a prospectus, a topical outline, a sample of the proposed work, and a personal resume. The prospectus should identify the market the project is intended for, explain why it is unique, identify any existing competitors, cover any special features, provide a brief description of the end result, and offer an estimate of the schedule for completing it. The topical outline should explain the coverage and organization. If your publication will be a book, provide chapter titles and any important subtopics covered in the chapters. Sample material should be two to three chapters for books, or a runtime demo for online products.

Categories: Nonfiction—Computers—Internet—Software—Technology

CONTACT: The Editor
Material: All
Franklin, Beedle & Associates, Inc.
8536 SW St. Helens Dr., Ste. D,
Wilsonville, OR 97070
Phone: 800-322-2665
E-mail: jimleisy@fbeedle.com
Website: www.fbeedle.com

> **Remember: Editors change jobs and publishers change addresses. It is wise to invest in a phone call for the current information before submitting.**

Frederick Fell Publishers, Inc.

Frederick Fell Publishers, Inc is formerly known as Lifetime Books, Inc.

Thank you for your interest in Frederick Fell Publishers, Inc. *Our submission guidelines are as follows:*

1. Proposal Letter
2. Two sample chapters (optional)
3. A Table of Contents for the book
4. Author Bio/Credentials
5. Market Analysis: Tell us what books are your competition and why yours is better than the others. What makes it unique?

SASE for return of manuscript.

Good Luck and Good Writing!

Categories: Nonfiction—Business—College—Cooking—Diet/Nutrition—Entertainment—Food/Drink—Health—Hobbies—Inspirational—Jewish Interest—New Age—Sexuality

CONTACT: Don Lessne, Senior Editor
Material: All
2131 Hollywood Blvd. Ste. 303
Hollywood FL 33020
Phone: 954-925-5242
Fax: 954-925-5244
E-mail: info@fellpub.com
Website: www.fellpub.com

Free Spirit Pubishing

Our mission is to provide children and teens with the tools they need to succeed in life and to make a difference in the world. We publish high-quality nonfiction books and learning materials for children and teens, parents, educators, counselors, and others who live and work with young people.

Founded in 1983 by author and educator Judy Galbraith, Free Spirit Publishing produces award-winning books that are recognized and respected for their creative, practical, jargon-free, and solution-based focus. A contract and royalty publisher, we produce 20-25 new titles each year.

Free Spirit's books and learning materials are of the highest quality. They are widely and positively reviewed in major publishing, educational, and parenting publications (including Publishers Weekly, School Library Journal, Youth Today, and KLIATT), and winners of many awards. Each title we publish receives the close, careful attention of our editors and publicity and sales departments. Additonally, our strong backlist ensures that our books experience a long life in print.

Our titles are availble through major trade and library distributors (including Ingram, Levy Home Entertainment, and Baker & Taylor) and can be found in independent and national book stores (including Barnes & Noble and Borders), at Amazon.com and other online booksellers, and in select catalogs. Free Spirit books and learning materials are also availble through our own widely distributed mail order catalog and at our Web site. In additon, we attend and sell our books at about 50 regional and national conferences each year. Our books have been translated into more than 20 languages around the world.

Determining Whether Your Work Is a Fit for Free Spirit Publishing

If you are interested in working with Free Spirit, is is essential to familiarize yourself with our books. you may request a copy of our catatlog or review our titles online. We also recommend that you check out our books at your local library or bookstore to get a feel for our tone and style.

We do not publish the following:

• Fiction or picture storybooks
• Books with animal or mythical characters
• Books with religious or New Age content
• Single biographies, autobiographies, or memoirs

If your project is in any of the above formats, is is not right for us—even if content themes overlap with those we publish on. We are looking for strong nonfiction proposals in the following catagories:

Early Childhood: Board books for ages baby-preschool and picture books for ages 4 -8 that focus on social skills and getting along, early learning, self-esteem, and other topics related to positive early childhood development.

Self-Help for Kids®: Titles for ages 8-13 on school success, social skills, conflict resoultion, bullying, character development, conflict resolution, service learning, self-esteem, and other topics related to p ositive social and emotional health.

Self-Help for Teens®: Titles for ages 13 and up on life skills, conflict resolution, school success, positive decision making, family issues, character development, social action and civics education , and other topics related to positive social and emotional health.

Gifted & Talented: Books on academic, social, and emotional development for gifted youth of all ages, as well as resources for parents, educators, and other adults who live and work with them.

Learning Differences: Books on academic, social, and emotional development for youth with learning differences, as well as resources for parnets, educators, and other adults who live and work with them.

Parenting: Practical, pro-kid books for parents on specific issues related to youth development. We do not publish general parenting titles.

Teaching: Practical, jargon-free materials for educators, counselors, and youth workers that focus on positive youth development, creative teaching strategies, and a wide range of social and emotional needs.

Wondering if your work is a fit for Free Spirit? Send a query to acquisitions@freespirit.com. You may save yourself considerable time and mailing expenses.

Submitting a Proposal

If-after looking through our catalog and familarizing yourself with our list—your confident your work is a fit, we welcome reviewing a proposal. Proposals to be considered must be sent by mail (not by fax or email). Include the following:

1. A cover letter briefly outlining your project, the intended audience (including age ranges), and your relevant expertise.

2. A current résumé.

3. A detailed chapter-by-chapter outline.

4. At least two sample chapters. (If a full manuscript is available, you may send it.)

5. A market analysis with comprehensive listing of similar titles and detailed explanation of how your project differs from available products.

Note: For early childhood submissions, the entire text is required for evaluation. Bracketed art suggestions are also appreciated, though illustration samples should not be sent unless professionally competent.

Send copies, not originals. Free Spirit is not liable for work lost in the mail. If you want your work returned after evaluation, include a self-addressed returned envelope with sufficient postage.

As you prepare a proposal, it may help to keep a few of our main considerations in mind:

Need: Why is the book needed? How is it different from similar available titles?

Purpose: Who will u se the book? How will they use it?

Quality: Is the project well written and researched? Is the style similar to that of our other award-winning, jargon-free, solution-focused titles?

Relevance: Is the subject matter appropriate for our list? Does it compete with or complement other availble titles from Free Spirit?

Send proposals to:

Free Spirit Publishing

Attn: Acquisitions
217 Fifth Avenue North, Suite 200
Minneapolis, MN 55401-1299

We'll let you know when we receive your materials, generally by email. You may also include a self-addressed, stamped reply postcard which we will return upon receipt. While we do out best to offer timely feedback on your project, the high volume of proposals we receive dictates a reply time of 2-6 months.

Categories: Nonfiction—Children—Disabilities—Education—Family—Health—Juvenile—Parenting—Psychology—Self Help—Teen—Young Adult

CONTACT: Acquisitions
Material: All
217 Fifth Ave North, Ste. 200
Minneapolis, MN 55401-1299
Phone: 800-735-7323, 612-338-2068
Fax: 612-337-5050
E-mail: help4kids@freespirit.com
Website: www.freespirit.com

Front Row Experience

Perceptual-Motor Development Movement Education

We are only interested in "Movement Education" activities for preschool to sixth grade teachers. Send a one-page letter of inquiry with proposal. If we are interested, we will request more information, sample activities, manuscript, etc. Do not send unsolicited manuscripts! Call us for more information.

Categories: Physical Fitness—Movement Education

CONTACT: Frank Alexander, Editor
Material: All
540 Discovery Bay Blvd.
Discovery Bay CA 94514
Phone: 800-524-9091

Front Street
An Imprint of Boyds Mills Press, Inc.

Front Street is a publisher of books for children and young adults. Please review our online catalog to see the types of books that we publish before you submit your work to us.

Policy: Front Street will consider unsolicited manuscripts. It is our policy to consider submissions in the order they are received. This is a time consuming practice and we ask you to be patient in awaiting our response. Our usual response time is three months, but sometimes it takes longer. We regret that due to the large quantity of submissions, we are unable to acknowledge receipt of manuscripts or to give status reports over the phone. Please do not call for status reports. If you have not received a reply after four months, send a status query to Joy Neaves, Editor, at the address below. We understand the reasons for multiple submissions, although we discourage them. We feel it is important for you to know in advance that if our decision is negative, you will receive a form rejection letter. This procedure enables us to reduce the time it takes to respond to submissions, time we can devote to reviewing more submissions.

Picture Books: We publish few pictures books at this time and we cannot encourage you to send a picture book text only. If you are an illustrator, or are working with an illustrator, please include the manuscript, a dummy, and a sample reproduction of artwork rendered in the manner and style representative of the final artowrk.

Do not send original artwork-we cannot be held responsible for it damage or loss.

Fiction: Submit the first three sample chapters, and plot a summary.

We will request the balance of the manuscript if we are interested. Please enclose a dated cover letter with your contract information.

Poetry: Please send a selection of no more than 25 poems that are representative of your work. We will request more if we are interested.

Anthologies: We will only consider anthologies of work by various authors if accompanied by a detailed proposal and permissions budget.

Non-fiction: A detailed proposal and sample chapter will suffice.

Other: Whatever it takes to give us a sense of the project.

We prefer to receive submissions by e-mail. E-mail your query to **Neaves@frontstreetbooks.com.** Put the word SUBMISSIONS in the subject line, include your query letter in the body of the e-mail, and attach a synopsis and sample chapters (preferably in Microsoft Word document that has been scanned by virus protection software) to the e-mail.

We will accept manuscripts through reqular mail. Enclose a dated cover letter with your name and return address. Include any credentials relevant to the submission, particularly publications, in your cover letter. Provide a self-addressed, stamped envelope with appropriate postage for the return of your materials or for a reply. If there is no SASE included, the materials will be discarded. We regret that we are unable to return manuscripts to destinations outside the U.S. Thank you for giving us the opportunity to consider your work. Please send submissions to the attention of: **Joy Neaves, Editor, Front Street, Inc., 862 Haywood Road, Asheville, NC 28806.** Please do not send manuscripts to both our physical address and our e-mail address.

Categories: Fiction—Nonfiction—Children—Juvenile—Literature—Poetry—Teen—Writing—Young Adult

CONTACT: Joy Neaves, Editor
Material: All
862 Haywood Road
Asheville NC 28806
Phone: 828-236-5940
Fax: 828-236-5935
E-mail: neaves@frontstreetbooks.com
Website: www.frontstreetbooks.com

FSG Juvenile Program

Please refer to Farrar, Straus and Giroux, Publishers, Inc.

Future Horizons

Future Horizons, Inc., relies on a combination of personal relationships within the autism community and unsolicited manuscripts in order to offer unique, quality books and products that serve the autism community. Our goal is to offer parents, professionals, caregivers, and individuals with the disability fun, creative, practical information that will help them focus on the ability rather than the disability in autism, Asperger's Syndrome and other related disorders. We welcome all submissions written with this goal in mind, but due to limited time and the great number of manuscripts we receive, please do not submit proposals that are not related to the subject of autism and other pervasive developmental disorders.

In order to properly evaluate a publication proposal we need to receive certain essential information. All works are carefully reviewed for their quality, suitability, originality, and current information. Please include a cover letter, author resume, book synopsis, chapter-by-chapter outline, and at least three consecutive chapters. We do not accept hand-written manuscripts. We encourage authors to provide any relevant artwork, tables, charts or graphs that will enhance the quality of your submission. Please refer to the following guidelines for more information on our expectations.

Cover Letter
Be sure to include the following:
• Your name
• Your current mailing address
• The titles, publishers, and publication dates of any previous books, journal articles or presentations you have authored or co-authored
• A suggested book title

- The estimated length of the book
- Proposed artwork, tables, charts and/or figures
- A description of any special features of the book. For example, each chapter contains suggested readings or a "Coping Strategies" section.
- Your assessment of the book's main selling points
- A description of the book's unique qualities (how it differs from other books in its category and why there is a need for a book of its nature)
- An explanation of your intended readership

Author Resume

Be sure to include the following:

- Educational credentials, including degrees earned, awards, research projects and other information that would lend to your credibility and an expert on your chosen topic.
- Positions held within the autism community and a short description of your duties (Outreach centers, schools, medical practices, volunteer organizations)
- Speaking experience (if any), including a list of specific engagements
- General career timeline
- Interests and activities

Book Synopsis

Please include a typed summary of your book not to exceed 750 words.

Chapter Outline

This is a brief summary of each chapter. Please keep it to less than 500 words per chapter.

Three Consecutive Chapters

Send three chapters that express your originality, subject matter, and writing quality. You may send us a complete manuscript, but we ask that you recommend three chapters.

Keep a copy of your manuscript for your files as we may not return submissions. We know that you have spent months and possibly years crafting your work and we will do our utmost to do your submission justice by reviewing it thoroughly. However, please be aware that we receive many proposals and that it is not unusual for the process to take many months. We appreciate your patience in this lengthy process.

We notify all authors upon receipt of material, so there is no need to follow up.

Categories: Nonfiction—Disabilities

CONTACT: Kelly Gilpin, Editor Coordinator
Material: All
721 W. Abram St.
Arlington TX 76013
Phone: 817-277-0727
Fax: 817-277-2270
E-mail: Kelly@FHautism.com
Website: www.FHautism.com

Garth Gardner Company

For Authors: How to Submit a Book Proposal

GGC/Publishing is always looking for great book proposals! We accept submissions directly from authors (including first time authors) and also from literary agents.

Your book proposal should include the following:

- A description of the intended market for the book
- An explanation of why someone would want to buy the book
- A summary of the author's background
- A table of contents, as detailed as possible
- A sample chapter. Do not send in the whole manuscript.

We are not accepting electronic submissions at this time. We will contact you only if we are interested in your proposal. If you wish to have any material returned, include a self-addressed and stamped envelope.

We accept no responsibility for proposals and manuscripts. The volume of submissions does not allow us to accept phone calls or e-mail or other inquiries, or to provide comments or feedback on unsolicited manuscripts.

Thank you for your interest in Garth Gardner Company.

Categories: Nonfiction—Careers—Cartoons—College—Computers—Film/Video—Graphics—Reference—Textbooks

CONTACT: Anthony Mason, VP of Marketing
Material: Animation, Computer Graphics
GGC/ Publishing
5107 13th St. NW
Washington, DC 20011
Phone: 202-541-9700
Fax: 202-541-9750
E-mail: anthony@ggcinc.com
Website: www.gogardner.com

GATFPress

Please refer to Graphic Arts Technical Foundation (GATF).

Gazelle Press

Please refer to Genesis Communications, Inc., in the Book Publishers section.

Gem Guides Book Company

Gem Guides requests a book outline including Table of Contents and two or three sample chapters, along with examples of photos and illustrations that would accompany text. Please include information about the market for the book, how it is differentiated from competitive titles in print on the same topic, and your qualifications to produce a book on the subject.

Categories: Nonfiction—Crafts/Hobbies—Hobbies—Native American—Outdoors—Regional—Travel—Bead Crafts—Lapidary—Prospecting—Rocks and Minerals

CONTACT: Kathy Mayerski, Editorial Assistant
Material: All
315 Cloverleaf Dr. Ste. F
Baldwin Park CA 91706
Phone: 626-855-1611
Fax: 626-855-1610
E-mail: gembooks@aol.com
Website: www.gemguidesbooks.com

Genesis Communications, Inc.
Imprints: Evergreen Press, Gazelle Press, & Axiom Press

We publish books written from a biblical world view. We publish both hardcover and softcover books written from a Christian viewpoint. Our main categories of interest are: Christian business, Christian personal growth, Christian living, inspirational, true short stories, deeper life, Bible study, Christian health, Christian finance, Christian success and motivation, prayer. Above all, we are interested in books that empower people for breakthroughs in their lives.

We prefer to see the entire manuscript. We will send out author information packets and catalogs upon request.

We publish approximately 50 books per year. We have our own distribution company, plus our books are carried at Spring Arbor, and other major distributors.

Categories: Fiction—Nonfiction—Christian Interests—Health—Inspirational—Lifestyle—Marriage—Money & Finances—Parenting—Religon—Self Help—Spirtual—Christian Books

CONTACT: Kathy Banashak, Senior Editor
Material: All
PO Box 191540
Mobile AL 36619

Phone: 251-973-0680
Fax: 251-973-0682
E-mail: info@evergreenpress.com
Website: www.evergreenpress.com

The Globe Pequot Press

Guidelines for Globe Pequot Press titles

Thank you for your interest in The Globe Pequot Press! By perusing our website, you can see if your book idea is right for our list. You will note that our Globe Pequot line primarily publishes travel guides, with some select nature titles, cookbooks, and home-based business books. Our Falcon line specializes in outdoor recreation, both how-to and where-to, with hiking, biking, climbing, and other specialized lines, including regional history.

We welcome submissions appropriate to our publishing list. *When submitting a book proposal, please include the following:*

1. A brief synopsis of the proposed work.

2. A definition of the book's projected target audience/market and an analysis of competing titles, if any. (The latter can be found by researching *Books in Print.*) Who is the book for, and why is it better than what is already on the bookshelves?

3. A table of contents or outline of the entire book, plus a sample chapter to give us a sense of your writing style.

4. A biographical statement of your credentials. This statement should explain why you are particularly qualified to undertake the proposed project.

5. A self-addressed, stamped envelope large enough to return submitted materials. If this is not enclosed, we will not return your materials. Never send the only copy of anything!

6. To expedite the process, be sure to address your proposal to the Submissions Editor of the particular book category appropriate to your idea. For example, a proposal for a travel guide should go to Submissions Editor - Travel. A book about kayaking should be sent to the attention of Submissions Editor - Kayaking. You get the idea!

We wish you the best of luck. Please allow six to eight weeks for a response to your proposal. Again, thank you for your interest in The Globe Pequot Press.

Categories: Nonfiction—Business—Careers—Cooking—Family—Gardening—History—Outdoors—Recreation—Rural America—Sports/Recreation—Travel

CONTACT: Submissions Editor
Material: All (Specify subject category)
246 Goose Lane
PO Box 480
Guilford CT 06437
Phone: 203-458-4500
Fax: 203-458-4604
Website: www.GlobePequot.com

God Allows U-Turns Book Series

SEND US YOUR TRUE SHORT STORY

Published by Promise Press, an imprint of Barbour Publishing, Inc., in association with Alive Communications, Inc. This is a Christian inspirational book series. Each book in the series will contain up to one hundred uplifting, encouraging and inspirational true short stories written by contributors from all over the world. Stories go into a book. Multiple volumes are planned. Volumes are available in bookstores now. We are currently accepting true short stories for multiple future volumes, see web site for future volume topics. 100% freelance. Pays $50 honorarium upon publication (plus 1 copy of book). By-line and short bio. Send complete manuscript with full contact information. We will respond only if your story is selected for submission. Accepts simultaneous submissions & reprints (tell when/where appeared). Prefers submission via web site. Accepts e-mail submission (copied into message, NO attachments). Sample story appears on web site. Read a current volume in the series to understand our needs and story format. Thoroughly review web site if possible.

SPECIAL NEEDS

Open to well written, personal inspirational pieces showing how faith in God can inspire, encourage and heal. Hope should prevail. Human-interest stories with a spiritual application, affirming ways in which faith is expressed in daily life. These true stories MUST touch the emotions. Our contributors are a diverse group with no limits on age or denomination. When possible, show how a change of heart, attitude, thought, and/or behavior occurred that clearly describes a u-turn toward God. Using a "u-turn" lesson/analogy within the story is a plus.

TIPS

Read a current volume, or see the web site for a sample story. Keep it real. Ordinary people doing extraordinary things with God's help. Focus on timeless, universal themes like love, forgiveness, salvation, healing, hope, faith, etc. Be able to tell a good story with drama, description and dialogue. Avoid moralisms and preachy tone. The point of the story should be some practical spiritual help the reader receives from what the author learned through his experience. Remember our "u-turn toward God" theme.

DEADLINES

Deadlines vary and are open for future volumes, see our "Future Volumes" page on our website for specific niche titles and various deadlines. www.godallowsuturns.com.

THREE WAYS TO SUBMIT YOUR STORY

1. Via our Web Site at http://www.godallowsuturns.com (submit story directly from the site)

2. Via email at editor@godallowsuturns.com (write STORY SUBMISSION in subject line.)

3. Via the United States Post Office (aka: "snail mail") See snail mail guidelines on reverse side.)

STORY FORMAT

Submissions must be from 500-1,500 words. No formatting needed if sent via web site or email. If submitting via snail mail, you must send your story on a PC formatted disk, typed, double-spaced, one-inch margins, and 12 point "Times" font. Sorry, but we cannot accept handwritten stories.

RIGHTS

One time non-exclusive rights. Reprint rights. No returns. We will reserve full editorial rights. You will be sent a Permissions Form (contract) in the event your story is chosen for publication. This form must be signed and returned promptly.

TIMELINE

Due to the volume of material we are now receiving, we truly regret that we can no longer respond personally to every contributor. However, you can rest assured you will be contacted in the event your submission is selected for publication. Our professional team of editors is taking considerable time reading, rating and discussing all stories before final decisions are made. Feel free to submit your story elsewhere during this review process. In the event your work is chosen for inclusion in a future volume, you will be notified by mail to see if your story is still available for our use, and to obtain your written permission to edit and print your story.

SNAIL MAIL SUBMISSIONS

If you send your true short-story by good old-fashioned snail-mail, please include your contact information and send your typed submission along with a copy on a PC formatted disk.

CONTACT INFORMATION TO INCLUDE WITH YOUR STORY

• First and Last Name
• Day and Evening Telephone & FAX
• Mailing Address/City/State/Zip and Country
• E-Mail Address (if you have an email address, please send your story via email)

Triumphant Teens:
True Stories of Hope and Healing for Teens

We are in the process of compiling the fifth book in the popular God Allows U-Turns book series compiled by Allison Gappa Bottke and published by Promise Press, an imprint of Barbour Publishing in association with

Alive Communications, Inc.

While this book is being developed for Christian teens, it is our prayer that it will also be read by teens at the beginning of their U-Turn journey toward God. Stories in the God Allows U-Turns books are changing lives. People around the world tell us how the stories in previous volumes of God Allows U-Turns have touched their lives and helped them turn toward God - now the time has come to develop a collection that will impact and influence teenagers around the globe.

Please pray about writing a story that will make a difference in the lives of teenagers.

Our writers can be any age or denomination - but the story theme must involve a teenager and a teen topic. Perhaps you know a teen whose story is perfect but they choose not to write it - you may want to write that teen's story using the byline, "as told to." Here are some guidelines to help you in the process. Please read them carefully and prayerfully.

OUR AUDIENCE

The broad audience for this book is ages 12-18, but most readers will fall in the 13-15, possibly 16, age range.

TEEN VOLUME SPECIAL NEEDS

These TRUE stories MUST touch the emotions of teens. Open to well written, personal inspirational pieces showing how faith in God can inspire, encourage and heal. Hope should prevail. We want human-interest stories with a spiritual application, affirming ways in which faith is expressed in the daily life of a teen. When possible, show how a change of heart, attitude, thought, and/or behavior occurred that clearly describes a u-turn toward God. Using a "u-turn" lesson/analogy within the story is a plus.

TIPS

The God Allows U-Turns book series dares to go where many short story collections fear to tread. We touch on hard-hitting, real life topics in today's world. Read a current volume, or see the web site for a sample story. Keep it real. Ordinary teens doing extraordinary things with God's help. Focus on timeless, universal themes like love, forgiveness, salvation, healing, hope, faith, etc. Be able to tell a good story with drama, description and dialogue. Your story must have a clear beginning, middle and end. Use strong verbs - show us, don't tell us. Avoid moralisms and preachy tone. The point of the story should be some practical spiritual help the teen reader receives from what the author learned through his experience. Remember our "u-turn toward God" theme.

We are currently developing the chapter topics for this teen book and we are open to hearing feedback from you for possible chapter topics. (Join our TEEN TROUPE to help select stories - see web site.)

Perhaps the topics below will help trigger some story ideas for you.

- God's Love & God's Plan
- Faith and Forgiveness
- Prayer
- Peer Pressure
- Tales of Triumph
- Hope and Healing
- Courage
- Dare to Dream
- Heroes & Mentors
- New Direction U-Turns
- Life Lessons
- Virtue
- Trends VS Tradition
- Music & Movies
- Thankfulness
- Relationships
- Family & Friends
- Memories
- Ethics & Integrity
- Trust

DEADLINES

Deadlines change and vary and we are always open for future volumes. See our "Future Volumes" page on our website for future volume titles and various deadlines. www.godallowsuturns.com.

STORY FORMAT

Submissions must be from 500-1,500 words with a few exceptions for longer ones. No formatting needed if sent via web site or email. If submitting via snail mail, you must send your story on a PC formatted disk. Sorry, but we cannot accept handwritten stories.

RIGHTS and FEES PAID

One time non-exclusive rights. Reprint rights. No returns. We will reserve full editorial rights. You will be sent a Permissions Form (contract) in the event your story is chosen for publication. This form must be signed and returned promptly. The payment rate for non-exclusive rights varies from $50-$100, depending on word count and if the story was previously published.

TIMELINE

Due to the volume of material we are now receiving, we truly regret that we can no longer respond personally to every contributor. However, you can rest assured you will be contacted in the event your submission is selected for publication. Feel free to submit your story elsewhere during this review process. In the event your work is chosen for inclusion in a future volume, you will be notified by mail or email to see if your story is still available for our use.

CONTACT INFORMATION TO INCLUDE WITH YOUR STORY

First and Last Name— Day and Evening Telephone & FAX — Mailing Address/City/State/Zip and Country — EMail Address (if you have an email address, please send your story via email)

THREE WAYS TO SUBMIT YOUR STORY

1. Via our Web Site at http://www.godallowsuturns.com (submit story directly from the site)

2. Via email at editor@godallowsuturns.com (write STORY SUBMISSION in subject line.)

3. Via the United States Post Office (aka: "snail mail") See snail mail guidelines below.)

SNAIL MAIL SUBMISSIONS

If you send your true short-story by good old-fashioned snail-mail, please include your contact information and send your typed submission along with a copy on a PC formatted disk to:

Attention Editor, The GOD ALLOWS U-TURNS Project, STORY SUBMISSION, Post Office Box 717, Faribault, MN 55021-0717 (This is the God Allows U-Turns business address.)

Thanks so much, and we look forward to hearing from you! Please share this with other writers.

Categories: Nonfiction—Christian Interests—Family—General Interest—Inspirational—Lifestyle—Marriage—Men's Issues—Parenting—Religion—Self Help—Short Stories—Singles—Spiritual—Teen—Women's Issues—Young Adult

CONTACT: Allison Gappa Bottke, Compiler/Editor
Material: True Short Stories
The God Allows U-Turns Project
PO Box 717
Faribault MN 55021-0717
Phone: 507-334-6464
E-mail: godallowsuturns.com
Website: www.godallowsuturns.com

Golden West Publishers

Golden West Publishers specializes in cookbooks and books about outdoor recreation (Southwest). Currently we are expanding our cookbook line and are interested in regional titles. We are creating a cookbook for each state as part of our Cooking Across America series and we also want to add regional titles of interest. We prefer buyouts as opposed to royalties. We require a query letter with sample Table of Contents and sample chapter, if possible.

Categories: Cooking—Regional—Cookbooks

CONTACT: Hal Mitchell, Editor
Material: Cookbooks
4113 N. Longview
Phoenix AZ 85014
Phone: 602-265-4392
Fax: 602-279-6901

G. P. Putnam's Sons
Books for Young Readers

Picture Books

We accept full picture book manuscripts for review. Art should not be sent until specifically requested.

Fiction (middle-grade, chapter books, young adult)

Please send a query letter before submitting fiction. Please include a synopsis and one to three sample chapters. Your query letter and sample chapters will be circulated among the editors and the entire work will be requested upon interest.

Nonfiction

Please send a query letter before submitting nonfiction. Please include a synopsis and one or two sample chapters, as well as a table of contents. Your query letter and sample chapters will be circulated among the editors and the entire work will be requested upon interest.

Submissions must include a SASE (self-addressed, stamped envelope) for our reply. If you wish to have your materials returned, your SASE must have the correct postage.

If you would like to receive a catalog, you must send a 9x12 envelope with the appropriate postage.

Categories: Fiction—Nonfiction—Children's—Young Adult

CONTACT: Putnam Children's Editorial
Manuscript Editor
Material: All
345 Hudson St., 14th floor
New York, NY 10014
Website: us.penguingroup.com

Grace Abraham Publishing

GRACE ABRAHAM PUBLISHING - WRITERS' GUIDELINES
DARK-N-STORMIES: Fiction Imprint of Grace Abraham Publishing

We are currently seeking book-length fiction in the mystery/suspense, psychological thriller, cozy mystery, romantic suspense and procedural mystery categories. We are seeking family-friendly books that avoid graphic sex, violence and profanity.

If you have a completed manuscript you would like Dark-N-Stormies to consider, please send a cover letter, synopsis, and first two chapters only via snail mail (with SASE) to the address listed on our contact page or via e-mail (posted in the body of your message—attachments will NOT be opened) to gd830@hotmail.com.

Grace Abraham Publishing/Dark-N-Stormies is currently a royalty-paying publisher of works for sale in electronic format and trade paperback.

*Please do not send full manuscript unless it is requested.

Non-fiction: Grace Abraham Imprint

Do you have a compelling story to tell? Do you have the solution to a problem plaguing moms, dads, families or children? Are you a survivor who wants to share a tale of hope?

If you have a non-fiction, book-length manuscript you'd like Grace Abraham Publishing to consider publishing, please send us a proposal. Manuscript must be completed. Multiple submissions are okay provided you inform us of that at time of submission.

Please answer the following questions in your proposal (besides word count, synopsis, chapter headings, etc.):

- Is there enough interest to provide an audience large enough to justify our publishing your book?
- Is there enough material to justify a book on this topic?
- What's different or better about your book than similar books on the market?
- What qualifies you to write this book?
- How do you plan to market and promote this book?

Grace Abraham Publishing is currently a royalty-paying publisher of works for sale in electronic format and trade paperback.

*Please do not send full manuscript unless it is requested.

Categories: Ficiton—Nonfiction—Mystery—Romance Suspense

Contact: Editor
Grace Abraham Publishing
13335 Holbrook Street, Suite 10
Bristol, VA 24202
Phone: 276-645-0301
Email: gd830@hotmail.com
Website: www.graceabraham.com

The Graduate Group

We look for manuscripts that will be helpful to high school, college and graduate students in their attempt to establish themselves in a career, manuscripts which alert students to opportunities and ways to become more effective.

Graduate Group books are distributed exclusively to career planning offices and libraries in the U.S. and abroad.

Authors are provided a liberal royalty.

Categories: Nonfiction—Business—Careers—College—Computers—Crime—Education—Environment—General Interest—Government—Health—Internet—Interview—Law—Military—Money & Finances—Reference—Law Enforcement—Nursing

CONTACT: Robert Whitman, Vice President
Material: Any
CONTACT: Mara Whitman, President
Material: Any
PO Box 370351
West Hartford CT 06137-0351
Phone: 860-233-2330

Granite Publishing Group, LLC
Imprints: Wild Flower Press and Swan-Raven & Co.

Granite Publishing through its two primary imprints, Wild Flower Press and Swan-Raven & Co., accepts only a few manuscripts per year, and those that are accepted must follow the following guidelines:

Wild Flower Press prefers work that deals with some aspect of the UFO/ET phenomena and earth changes. Swan-Raven & Co. prefers material related to, spirituality, shamanism, societal change, or a related area. All work must be non-fiction. We do not do stories, fiction, novels, novellas or poetry.

The work must demonstrate high scholarship. The work must demonstrate coherent thinking and novel insights; it must break new ground and be significantly different from other works on the market.

Writing style must be clear, interesting and effective. Spelling must be exact as specified in *Webster's Ninth Collegiate Dictionary*, and grammar must follow the *Chicago Manual of Style*. Submissions should include a chapter outline, some representative chapters and a cover letter about yourself and about why the book will be of interest to a wide audience. See *Non-Fiction Book Proposals Anybody Can Write* by Elizabeth Lyon.

Categories: Nonfiction—Environment—Inspirational—Native American—New Age—Paranormal—Spiritual—UFO Experiences—UFO Research

CONTACT: Pam Meyer, Granite Publishing Group
Material: All
PO Box 1429
Columbus, NC 28722
Phone: 828-894-8444
Fax: 828-894-8454
E-mail: Pam@5thworld.com
Website: www.5thworld.com

Graphic Arts Center Publishing Company
Graphic Arts Books
Alaska Northwest Books
WestWinds Press

Graphic Arts Center Publishing Company publishes and distributes national and regional titles through its three imprints: Graphic Arts Books, Alaska Northwest Books, and WestWinds Press. GAB is known for its excellence in publishing high-end photo-essay books. Alaska Northwest Books, established in 1959, is the premier publisher of non-fiction Alaska books on subjects ranging from cooking, Alaska Native culture, memoir, history, natural history, reference, biography, humor, and children's books. WestWinds Press, established in 1999, echoes those themes with content that focuses on the Western States.

Categories We Publish
The rule of thumb is this: If you are proposing a photo-driven book, it would be published under the Graphic Arts Books imprint. Text-driven books that are supported with photos or illustrations–and all children's books–are published under Alaska Northwest Books or WestWinds Press. To familiarize yourself with the books that we publish, browse our website.
Editors look for the following:
• Non-fiction material that reflects life as it is or was in Alaska, the Northwest, adjacent Canada, and the Western states
• Authoritative material about the region's wildlife, plants, or other natural resources
• Material about people and places in history, especially that which provides unpublished information and fresh insights
• Arts and crafts of the region both aboriginal and contemporary
• Practical guides to cooking, gardening, travel, and recreation in Alaska and in the West
• Regionally focused children's books, non-fiction and fiction (with themes related to Alaska, the Northwest, or Western States)
• Occasional out-of-region subjects for which there is a demonstrable reader interest and market
Submission Basics
Submissions should be typewritten from a computer or typewriter,

double-spaced. Author should retain a copy of the submission.
Along with your manuscript, or sample chapters, please include the following with your submission:
• A cover letter describing the project
• A complete outline of your idea/concept (include your thoughts about what would be the ideal book specifications: trim size, number of pages, number of photos, text size)
• A table of contents detailing the areas/regions/themes to be covered
• An individual bio with examples of work previously published, if any
• Discussion of the potential market for the book–i.e.: what other books similar to this book exist and how this differs in quality, style, breadth, and timelines; who the potential buyers of this book are and what access you have to any of these markets through mailing lists, membership in professional societies, media contacts; trends that lend support to your project; relevant demographics; etc.

If you are enclosing samples of art and/or photography, do not send originals. Duplicate slides and color photocopies are acceptable.

Please package all materials securely, enclose return postage, and include cost of certification if material is to be returned certified mail. We do not guarantee the return of unsolicited material. We do, however, take all possible precautions against loss or damage.

Response to Submission
Upon receiving your submission, we will send you a letter of receipt. After you have received this, please allow ample time (up to 6 months) for careful consideration of your work. We will let you know as soon as we have made a decision.

Please remember that editors base their final decisions upon numerous considerations, such as books previously published by GACPC, material already accepted and scheduled for publication, and what appears to be current reader interest.

Further Reading
We highly recommend Judith Applebaum's *How to Get Happily Published* (Fourth Edition, 1992: Harper Collins) for additional information on preparing a successful proposal for consideration by a publisher.
About Graphic Arts Center Publishing Company
We publish scenic calendars and photographic essay books that cover topic, region, state, sort, or specialty. The following is a list of guideline specification.

We use only full-time, professional photographers and/or *well established* photographic businesses.

Transparencies, in any format, are acceptable. They must be tack sharp and possess high reproductive quality. If you prefer, you may submit equivalent digital files.

Our books and calendars usually represent one photographer

New calendar or book proposals must have large market appeal and/or have corporate sale possibilities, as well as, fit our company's present focus.
Obtaining Permission to Submit
Contact the Editorial Department to receive permission to send a submission. An unsolicited submission will be returned unopened, with postage due.

Once permission is granted to send in a submission, please include the following: (1) an individual biography (2) samples of your work (3) 20-40 transparencies that are numbered, labeled with descriptions, and verified in a delivery memo (4) return postage or a filled-out Fed Ex form.

You will receive a confirmation note upon arrival of your submission. Please allow 3-6 months for us to review a book proposal.

All transparencies wil be kept in our fire-proof vault, protected by a Halon fire protected system.

We will make every effort to handle your transparencies with the utmost of care. *However, we are not liable for any loss or damage of transparencies submitted with a book proposal. In addition, we do not pay pull, research, or holding fees to preview your transparencies.*

Thank you for your interest in Graphic Arts Books.
Categories: Nonfiction—Adventure—Children—Cooking—Culture—Native American—Outdoors—Photography—Reference—Re-

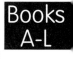

Remember: Editors change jobs and publishers change addresses. It is wise to invest in a phone call for the current information before submitting.

gional

CONTACT: Timothy W. Frew, Executive Editor
Material: Submissions for Graphic Arts Books
(photo-essay books)
Alaska Northwest Books or WestWinds
Press submissions
PO Box 10306
Portland OR 97296-0306
Phone: 503-226-2402
Fax: 503-223-1410
website: www.gacpc.com

Graphic Arts Technical Foundation
GATFPress

Please refer to Printing Industries of America.

Great Quotations Publishing

Great Quotations seeks original material for the following general categories:
• Humor
• Inspiration
• Motivation
• Success
• Romance
• Tributes to mom/dad/grandma/grandpa, etc.
Generally speaking we do not currently publish:
• Children's books and others requiring multi-color illustration on the inside
• Novels and other such fiction, or text that is extremely narrative and detailed
• Manuscripts substantially consisting of poetry
• Highly controversial subject matter
Our books are often purchased on impulse. Therefore the material must be simple, concise and a light read. *They are also physically small and short in length, and comprise five different formats:*
• Paperback Books 6"x4½", 168 pp., Retail $5.95
• Comb Bound Books 4½"x6", 78 pp., Retail $7.95
• Mini-Perpetual Calendars 4"x3¾", 365 pp., Retail $6.50
• Large Perpetual Calendars 5½"x4½", 365 pp., Retail $8.95
• Hard Cover Books 4"x5½", 64 pp., Retail $6.50
The ideal submission consists of a cover letter explaining the idea and a few sample pages of text. Include two SASEs for both a response and for the return of materials if such is desired. Submissions sent without a SASE are subject to disposal without consideration. We do not respond initially by phone.
We publish new books twice a year, in January and July. Submissions are usually reviewed approximately six months prior to publishing deadlines.
As an aside, we do not hire freelance readers/editors.
Thank you, and Good Luck!
Categories: African-American—Animals—Comedy—Diet?Nutrition—Education—Inspirational—Language—Marriage—New Age—Romance

CONTACT: Ringo Suek, Editor

Material: All
8102 Lemont Road, #300
Woodridge IL 60517
Phone: 630-390 3580
Fax: 630-390 3585
E-mail: greatquotations@yahoo.com

Green Nature Books

Our guidelines are simple!
1. Inquire first with small sample;
2. We want specialty "how-to" grow and breed exotics–written by experts; and
4. Writers who promote themselves increase their royalty checks.
Categories: Nonfiction—Agriculture—Animals—Conservation—Ecology—Environment—Tortoise Care

CONTACT: Submissions Editor
Material: All
PO Box 105
Sumterville FL 33585
Phone: 352-793-5496
Fax: 352-793-6075
Website: www.greennaturebooks.com

Gryphon Books

Small press publishing is a labor of love but it is also fraught with risk and very expensive. Therefore we must be selective in the work we choose for magazines or imprints of Gryphon Books. We receive dozens of stories and proposals each week, many are fine and quite publishable, however most are not compatible with our present publishing program. Please keep in mind that the rejection of a work can be for many reasons but is never intended to be a rejection of you as an author or of your talent.

What are we looking for? Quality material that will interest our readers.

The specifics are listed individually by publication below. Publishing today means a small outfit such as Gryphon Books must be very selective. That aside, if your work shows promise or is something that we think our readers will like, we'll work with you. We often comment on short stories that are sent for *Hardboiled* and have worked with writers to make their story publishable. In other cases, while we've rejected some stories, authors have told us that our comments allowed them to fix the story and send it to another market where it was published. We're very proud of any help we are able to give newer writers, especially when it results in that author being published.

A few things to remember before submitting any work to Gryphon Books:
• Absolutely NO submissions through email. Only hard copies to the PO Box address below will be considered. All email submissions or queries will be deleted unopened.
• We can NOT consider any work by anyone incarcerated in any prison facility. Manuscripts will be returned to sender unopened.
• We have a one-a-month rule: because of time constraints and ms volume, we can only look at one ms or query letter per month. So make it your best!
• NO multiple submissions. Only one story at a time (per envelope) and not more than one submission (envelope) per month. We don't want to open any more unsolicited envelopes with 10 or 20 stories in them. Or receive 10 separate envelopes with a story in each. That's not professional. You'll just be wasting time and postage as these will be returned unread.
• NO reprints, unless we request it. However, you may query about a reprint.
• We will look at simultaneous submissions, BUT they must be so labeled.
• Always remember to send in your ms in the standard format, which

MUST be double-spaced, also don't put it in a binder or folder.

Below is a general overview of what we are interested in for Gryphon Books.

Novels: Right now we are NOT actively looking at any novels from agents or any unsolicited manuscripts for any genres of fiction. DO NOT send any complete ms or chapters. However, if you want to take a chance and run a query idea by us we will look at a short one-page query letter, and if you want an answer you must enclose an SASE. The market is tough. We do mostly classic and pulp novels in various genres, not much contemporary material in the longer lengths.

Non-fiction: We are looking for finely written and detailed articles and book-length material on any aspect of books or book collecting, especially in the paperbacks, the pulps, hard-boiled crime fiction, authors, artists, or interviews with same; articles about science fiction, fantasy, horror, pulp-related books, bibliographic material, paperback book publishers. Your best bet is to query with a short ONE-PAGE letter about yourself and your work, and qualifications, if necessary. For shorter articles see *Paperback Parade.*

Paperback Parade: For this magazine we are looking for finely written and detailed non-fiction articles from 1,000 to 5,000 words (sometimes longer) on any aspect of paperbacks; including publishing, collecting, art, authors, runs of books, much more. We're open to different types of things but it is best to query first about your idea as many topics have been done in previous articles. This way we can better direct you to our specific needs. It is also a good idea to send for a sample copy or subscribe to *Paperback Parade* (subscriptions are $35 for 4 issues; a sample is $10 + $2.00 Media postage), and it just might open up a whole new world for your writing career. Nonfiction is a large and lucrative field. It offers many avenues for publication. *Paperback Parade* is also an excellent venue to have your work and byline seen by our many author, publisher, and editor readers. We've been publishing this magazine since 1986 and we still feel we've only scratched the surface in what this field has to offer. Payment is in copies or other arrangement depending on length and quality of your article.

Longer Stories: The *Gryphon Doubles* series contains tow short novels or novellas (generally 15,000 to 30,000 words each) published back-to-back in the format of the classic Ace Doubles. They have two illustrated covers (one for each story) and sell for $12 each. Some of the authors who have appeared include: William F. Nolan, Mike Avalione, Jack Williamson, E. C. Tubb, Jesse Sublett, Richard S. Prather. We are extremely selective here and at present the series is on hiatus, but there are new books in the hopper yet to appear and they will soon. We are looking for unique genre fiction, it can have a pulp flavor; exciting, hard-hitting stories, in all genres, but especially hard-boiled crime and noir, science fiction, pulp reprints. Pays nominal advance. ONLY query letters with an SASE considered at this time.

Short Stories: We are always looking for original short crime stories for *Hardboiled* magazine. Keep it short, hard, intense and to the point. You should become a fan of the genre you want to write in and of the magazine. Become familiar with the type of story by subscribing. No Chandler clones or cliches unless you can put a new spin on an old idea. We want quality writing, great ideas and interesting characters, mixed with hard-hitting realism. Competition is tight. We can offer only a minimal payment but your work will be published alongside giants like Mickey Spillane (latest issue #31), or Andrew Vachss, Joe Lansdale, Richard S. Prather, Ed Gorman, Richard Lupoff, Edward Hoch, Lawrence Block, Vin Packer and many other classic and contemporary crime masters. Just make it your best story and keep it under 3,000 words (longer would have to be extraordinary; anything over 4,000 words query with SASE).

Support: Lastly, as writers we need to keep our markets alive and viable and that means supporting the publishers and magazines in our field. I fervently believe that everyone who wants to sell to *Hardboiled* should subscribe to *Hardboiled* ($35 brings you 4 hard-hitting issues). Or for nonfiction writers, you should subscribe to *Paperback Parade* ($35 for 4 issues). Of course, not subscribing in no way hinders your chances for consideration. For longer fiction check out books in the *Gryphon Doubles* series ($12 each + postage). Your support keeps your markets strong. That support will also give you the opportunity to read a lot of great crime fiction or non-fiction,

better than the boring newsstand magazines. You'll also get an excellent idea of the type of fiction we're looking for in the pages of *Hardboiled* and the articles we want for *Paperback Parade*. So support the magazines you want to write for with a subscription, support the publishers you want to publish your book, *by buying one of our books*. The publishing world is very competitive and you need to make your voice heard. Small publishers need your support so there will be more venues for the work *you* write, and the work we all want to read.

Submissions and Subscriptions: All story or query submissions should be sent as hard copy only (NO disks, CDs, emails) with an SASE if your want a response. International ms must use 2 IRCs. All book orders or subscriptions to *Hardboiled* or *Paperback Parade* should be sent to this address only. Send to: Gryphon Books, PO Box 209, Brooklyn, NY 11228-0209, USA.

Final Advice: What do you think is the most important quality that a writer must have? That's a tough one. Could it be great dialog? Excellent plotting? A talent for fine characterization? Friends in high places? That's all well and good but the most important quality really is *professionalism*. Remember that in all your dealings with publishers and editors, even if they may not always be professional themselves. Sometimes especially if they're not professional. You will always need to be professional in all your actions and dealings. You never know when a submission will be accepted down the line or what can come of a small seed planted months or even years before. *Now get writing!*

Categories: Fiction—Nonfiction—Book Reviews—Crime, Interviews—Fantasy—Horror—Pulp—Science Fiction—Short Stories

CONTACT: Submissions Editor
Material: All
PO Box 209
Brooklyn, NY 11228-0209

Gryphon House, Inc.

We're Always Looking for New Book Ideas!

If you have an idea for a book, we'd like to hear about it. At Gryphon House, our goal is to publish books that help teachers and parents enrich the lives of children from birth through age eight. We strive to make our books useful for teachers at all levels of experience, as well as for parents, caregivers, and anyone interested in working with children. The staff at Gryphon House cares deeply about children and about teaching them appropriately and positively. We also believe that spending time with children is a valuable and fun thing to do. Our books reflect these beliefs.

We look for books that are developmentally appropriate for the intended age group, are well researched and based on current trends in the field, and include creative, participatory learning experiences with a common conceptual theme to tie them together. Our books are essential tools for teachers. As such, the books should be ones that teachers will want to use every day. Books that cater to a particular market beyond teachers are also appealing.

We are not interested in books of paper and pencil activities, or activities that involve cutting out patterns and pasting them on paper, or ditto books, or books about computers (or worse, television) and young children. We do not publish children's books at all.

Things to Consider Before Submitting a Proposal
Competition
Find and review books similar to yours. You can find books in the li-

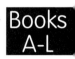

brary, in a book called *Books In Print*, retail bookstores, and teacher and school supply stores. Familiarize yourself with the books on your topic and then tell us how your book is different.

Market

Is there a need for another book on your topic? What makes your book unique? Is this a book that teachers will want to use every day?

Other Important Issues

Who has reviewed or tested your book? Have you led classes or workshops on the topic? What is your background? Have you published other books, articles, or other materials? If so, please tell us. How will you be able to promote your book? Can you conduct workshops at professional meetings, or do demonstrations at bookstores? Include this information in your letter of inquiry, outlined below.

Submitting a Proposal

We prefer to receive a letter of inquiry and/or a proposal, rather than the entire manuscript. That means you don't have to wait until you've completed your book to send it to us. *Your proposal should include:*

- The proposed title
- The purpose of the book
- Table of contents
- Introductory material
- 20-40 sample pages of the actual book

In addition, please describe the book, including the intended audience, why teachers will want to buy it, how it is different from other similar books already published, and what qualifications you possess that make you the appropriate person to write the book. If you have a writing sample that demonstrates that you write clear, compelling prose, please include it with your letter.

Categories: Nonfiction—Education—New Age—Paranormal—Parenting

CONTACT: Acquisitions
Material: All
PO Box 207
Beltsville MD 20704
Phone: 301-595-9500
Fax: 301-595-0051
E-mail: info@ghbooks.com
Website: www.gryphonhouse.com

Gürze Books

Dear Author,

Thank you for your interest in Gurze Books. We are a small company which publishes between 2-3 trade paperback books per year on eating disorders and related issues, including body image, size-acceptance, and self esteem. At this time, we do not publish personal stories, fiction, or poetry. Our books are sold through bookstores, our website (www.bulimia.com) and eating disorder resource catalogue, as well as other specialty markets. We have been in business since 1976.

In order to consider publishing your book, we need the following:

- Cover letter including the title.
- Table of Contents
- Provide an outline of your book, with optional 1-2 paragraph summaries of each chapter.
- The Concept Statement: In 150 words or less, explain what is unique about your book and how the reader will benefit from reading it.
- About the Author: Detail your qualifications to write the book.
- About the Market, the Competition, and Promotion: Describe your targeted reader, your market and how to reach them. Summarize the competition. Outline a plan for promoting your book.
- Sample Chapters: Send two edited chapters that best showcase the contribution your book offers to make in our field.

Please note: Allow for 1-2 months for us to get back to you. If you would like your manuscript returned, please send adequate postage.

Categories: Nonfiction—Food/Drink—Health—Self Help

CONTACT: Lindsey Hall/Cohn
Material: Manuscripts
5145-B Avenida Encinas
Carlsbad CA 92008
Phone: 760-434-7533
E-mail: gurze@aol.com
Website: www.bulimia.com

Hachai Publishing

Subject: Children Jewish Interests Religion.

Hachai Publishing welcomes unsolicited manuscripts. Children's books for the very young (2-4) and slightly older children (3-6) are our specialty.

We are looking for stories that convey:
- The traditional Jewish experience in modern times or long ago.
- Traditional Jewish observance such as Holidays and year-round mitzvos such as mezuzah, tzitzis, honoring parents etc.
- Positive character traits (middos) such as honesty, charity, respect, sharing etc.

We are also interested in:
- Biographies of spiritually great men and women in Jewish history.
- Historical fiction adventure novels for beginning readers (ages 7-10) that highlight devotion to faith and the relevance of Torah in making important choices.

Please, no fantasy, animal stories, romance, violence, preachy sermonizing.

We do not produce games, textbooks, workbooks, or books for adults.

All submissions must be typed or neatly printed, double spaced on opaque white paper - one side only.

Please include your name, address and phone number on title page of your manuscript.

You must include a self addressed stamped envelope (SASE). We will not respond to or return manuscripts sent without a SASE.

We are always looking for new artists with skill in children's book illustration. Please do not send original art. Color photocopies and tear sheets are best. Make sure your samples include a human character. SASE necessary for any response.

Categories: Nonfiction—Children—Jewish Interest—Religion—Spiritual

CONTACT: Submissions Editor
Material: All
762 Park Place
Brooklyn NY 11216
E-mail: yossi@hachai.com
Website: www.hachai.com

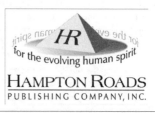

Hampton Roads Publishing

Please send a proposal only (a synopsis, a chapter-by-chapter outline and one or two sample chapters), not a full manuscript. Please, typed or computer-printed only; we cannot and will not read handwritten manuscripts, faxed, disk, web-based or e-mail submissions. Enclose SASE with sufficient first class postage if you wish to have your submission returned. (Note that prepaid postage strips from your post office are only good for that location; our post office will not accept them for outgoing mail.) If you do not enclose postage, we will recycle your proposal after we consider it.

At the moment we are not accepting submissions for our Young Spirit Line for children.

We welcome artwork submissions, but send a small sample of your work, and please send copies, not originals.

Your cover letter should contain your complete contact information (including phone number, address, and email).

Finally, be aware that we and all publishers have an enormous number of proposals to read and that it is not unusual for the process to take many months. Your patience is appreciated

Categories: Fiction—Nonfiction—Health—Inspirational—New Age—Occult—Paranormal—Psychology—Self Help—Spiritual

CONTACT: Frank DeMarco, Chief Editor
Material: All
1125 Stoney Ridge Rd.
Charlottesville, VA 22902
Phone: 434-296-2772
Website: www.hrpub.com

Hancock House

Hancock House requires the following for reviewing prospective manuscripts:

• A brief (one or two page) synopsis of the proposed manuscript.
• An account of any miscellaneous support information, such as the writer's expertise, or any marketing advantage inherent to the manuscript.
• A sample of the writer's work, such as a chapter from the work in question.
• Enclose your phone number as well as address.

Hancock House Titles
Our titles are predominantly as follows: Pacific Northwest history and biography, nature guides, and native culture; and international natural history, biological science, and conservation biology including aviculture and animal husbandry.

Manuscript Format
We require both a computer disc, PC format, and a hard copy.
Categories: Nonfiction—Animals—Aviation—Biography—Conservation—Cooking—Ecology—Fishing—History—Native Americans—Outdoors—Birds—Pacific Northwest

CONTACT: Editor
Material: All
1431 Harrison Ave.
Blaine WA 98230
Phone: 604-538-1114
Fax: 604-538-2262
Website: hancockhouse.com

Hannover House

Hannover House is a multimedia company with operating activities in both the publishing and film industries. As a publisher of books, Hannover releases about six titles per year. As a distributor of feature films and videos, the Company releases about ten titles per year, to theaters, video outlets and television broadcasters. The Company is currently seeking submissions of quality manuscripts, and prefers fiction or nonfiction works that may lend themselves to production as motion pictures.

Editorial inquiries should be to the Fayetteville, Arkansas office. Please do not send fax or e-mail submissions.

Categories: Fiction—Nonfiction—Entertainment—Film/Video

CONTACT: Samantha Nichols, Director of Editorial
Material: All
1722 N. College Ave., # C-303
Fayetteville AR 72703
Phone: 479-587-0857
Website: www.HannoverHouse.com

Harbor Press

Harbor Press publishes nonfiction books only. We are best known for our self-help and health titles, especially in the area of holistic health and healing, but we have recently begun branching out into other areas of interest in non-fiction. Recent publications include *Yes, Your Teen Is Crazy!–Loving Your Kid Without Losing Your Mind* by Michael J. Bradley, Ed.D., and *Healing Back Pain Naturally* by Art Brownstein, M.D.

We consider only titles which are, in our opinion, highly promotable, written by an appropriately credentialed author, and likely to appeal to a mass audience. If your nonfiction project meets these criteria, we welcome your submission. *Please include the following:*

I. Query letter
  A. Subject
  B. Audience
  C. Need/purpose
  D. Unique approach
  E. Qualifications for writing
II. Book proposal
  A. Title page
  B. Your contact information
  C. Overview
  D. Author background
  E. Competition section–What else is out there?
  F. Marketing analysis–Who will buy your book?
  G. Promotions section–What will you do to help market your book?
  H. Table of contents
  I. Two sample chapters

For detailed information on how to write a successful query and proposal, please consult any number of good books on writing proposals for nonfiction literature, such as *Write the Perfect Book Proposal: 10 Proposals That Sold and Why* by Jeff Herman and Deborah M. Adams (John Wiley & Sons, Inc. $15.95), or *The Fast-Track Course on How to Write a Nonfiction Book Proposal* by Stephen Blake Mettee (Word Dancer Press, $12.95).

We are also interested in hearing from professional, versatile, published writers who are interested in freelance writing and ghostwriting assignments. Please send a résumé and samples of your work.

Please address submissions to Debby Young at the address below. We review and consider all submissions that we receive. You will hear from us only if we find that your project is a good fit for us. Otherwise, we are unable to respond to submissions and to follow-up inquiries, so please do not call, write, or e-mail. We will be able to return your book proposal only if it is accompanied by a stamped, self-addressed envelope.

We are able to publish only a small percentage of the book projects submitted to us, so please keep in mind, if we do not respond to your submission, it is because it does not fit our objectives and requirement at that particular time. It does not mean that your project is without merit, or that it cannot be sold to another publisher.

Thank you for your interest in Harbor Press. We wish you well!

Categories: Nonfiction—Health—Inspirational—New Age—Parenting—Psychology—Relationships—Self Help—Spiritual—Teen—Young Adult

CONTACT: Debby Young, Acquisitions Editor
Material: All
5 Glen Drive
Plainview NY 11803
Phone: 253-851-5190
Fax: 253-851-5191
Website: harborpress.com

Books
A-L

Harlequin

Imprints of Harlequin
Harlequin American Romance
Harlequin Blaze
Harlequin Flipside
Harlequin Historicals
Harlequin Intrigue
Harlequin Presents (Mills & Boon Modern Romance)
Harlequin Romance (Mills & Boon Tender Romance)
Harlequin Superromance
Harlequin Temptation
Mills & Boon Historical Romance
Mills & Boon Medical Romance
Silhouette Desire
Silhouette Intimate Moments
Silhouette Romance
Silhouette Special Edition
Steeple Hill Women's Fiction
Love Inspired
MIRA
Red Dress Ink
HQN Books
Luna
Silhouette Bombshell

Please find below the editorial guidelines for Mills & Boon, Harlequin, Silhouette, MIRA, Steeple Hill and Red Dress Ink books. These pages are designed to be a guide, not a substitute for extensive reading. There is no formula for writing a publishable romance or mainstream women's fiction novel. The editors for each of the series have written guidelines that reflect their requirements. As a result, each set of guidelines "reads" differently as some are more specific than others, depending on the degree of focus the editors would like submissions to have.

What are some other things you can do to help sell your manuscript? First, we expect you to enjoy reading romance fiction. If you are already a fan, your appreciation for this type of book will be apparent in the writing. If you have not done so already, we encourage you to read many, many books from each series. The series that emerges as your favorite is probably where you should submit your manuscript.

Second, remember reading is an emotional experience. We hope you will write from the heart and we will feel touched by what you have to say. When you put pen to paper (or finger to keyboard), do so because you have something to share with other readers.

You will also find answers to some frequently asked questions. Should you require further information don't hesitate to write to us. The appropriate addresses have been included following the submission instructions for your convenience. Good luck!

Harlequin American Romance
Length: 70,000-75,000 words
Executive Editor: Paula Eykelhof
Editorial Office: Toronto
Upbeat and lively, fast-paced and well plotted, American Romance celebrates the pursuit of love in the backyards, big cities and wide-open spaces of America. These all-American stories have a range of emotional and sensual content and are supported by a colorful secondary cast, creating a sense of community within the plot's framework. In the confident and caring heroine, the tough but tender hero and their dynamic relationship that is at the center of this series, showcasing real-life love as the best fantasy of all!

Harlequin Blaze
Length: 70,000-75,000 words
Executive Editor: Birgit Davis-Todd
Editorial Office: Toronto
Harlequin Blaze is an exciting new series that has evolved out of the very successful Temptation line. It will showcase the very best writers and stars from the original Blaze program. It is also a vehicle to build and promote new authors who have a strong sexual edge to their stories. Finally, it is *the* place to be for seasoned authors who want to create a sexy, sizzling, longer contemporary story.

Blaze will feature sensuous, highly romantic, innovative plots that are sexy in premise and execution. The tone of the books can run from fun and flirtatious to dark and sensual. Submissions should have a very contemporary feel—what it's like to be young and single in the new millennium. We are looking for heroes and heroines in their early 20s and up. There should be an emphasis on the physical relationship developing between the couple: fully described love scenes along with a high level of fantasy and playfulness. The hero and heroine should make a commitment at the end.

Are you a *Cosmo* girl at heart? A fan of *Sex and the City*, *Ally McBeal* or *Friends*? Or maybe you just have an adventurous spirit. If so, then Blaze is the series for you! New authors should send a query and/or submit chapters and a synopsis. Agented and unagented submissions are welcome.

Harlequin Flipside
Length: 50,000-55,000 words
Editor: Wanda Ottewell
Editorial Office: Toronto
Harlequin Flipside are a delightful combination of romance and comedy. Fast-paced and plot driven, these novels depend upon the comedy building from the relationship between the hero and heroine. We are looking for a comic premise, a strong humorous voice and a great romance. A high degree of sexual tension is a must and while we encourage love scenes, they are not a requirement. So whether your story is a screwball comedy, a comedy of errors or simply the lighter side of love, we are looking for entertaining romance that would bring a smile to the face of every reader.

Harlequin Historicals
Length: 95,000-105,000 words
Editor: Ann Leslie Tuttle
Editorial Office: New York
The primary element of a Harlequin Historicals novel is romance. The story should focus on the heroine and how her love for one man changes her life forever. For this reason it is very important that you have an appealing and believable hero and heroine, and that their relationship if a compelling one. The conflicts they must overcome and the situations they face can be as varied as the setting you have chosen; but there must be romantic tension, some spark between your hero and heroine that keeps your reader interested.

We will not accept books set after 1950. We're looking primarily for books set in North America, England or France between 1100 and 1950 AD. We do not buy many novels set during the American Civil War. We are, however, flexible, and will consider most periods and settings. We are not looking for gothics or family sagas, nor are we interested in the kind of comedy of manners typified by straight Regencies. Historical romances set during the Regency period, however, will definitely be considered.

Harlequin Intrigue
Length: 70,000-75,000 words
Senior Editor: Denise O'Sullivan
Editorial Office: New York
Taut, edge-of-the-seat contemporary romantic suspense tales of intrigue and desire. Kidnappings, stalkings, women in jeopardy coupled with best-selling romantic themes are examples of story lines we love most. Whether a murder mystery, psychological suspense or thriller, the love story must be inextricably bound to the resolution where all loose ends are tied up neatly…and shared dangers lead right to shared passions. As long as they're in jeopardy and falling in love, our heroes and heroines may traverse a landscape as wide as the world itself. Their lives are on the line…and so are their hearts!

Harlequin Presents

(Mills & Boon Modern Romance)
Length: 50,000-55,000 words
Senior Editor: Tessa Shapcott
Editorial Office: London

Pick up a Harlequin Presents novel and you enter a world full of spine-tingling passion and provocative, tantalizing romantic excitement! Although grounded in reality, these stories offer compelling modern fantasies to readers all around the world, and there is scope within this line to develop relevant, contemporary issues, which touch the lives of today's women. Each novel is written in the third person and features spirited, independent heroines who aren't afraid to take the initiative, and breathtakingly attractive, larger-than-life heroes. The conflict between these characters should be lively and evenly matched, but always balanced by a developing romance that may include explicit lovemaking. Harlequin Presents novels capture the drama and intensity of a powerful, sensual love affair.

Harlequin Romance

(Mills & Boon Tender Romance)
Length: 50,000-55,000 words
Associate Senior Editor: Bryony Green
Editorial Office: London

Written in third person, from the heroine's point of view, each book should focus almost exclusively on the developing relationship between the main protagonists. The emphasis should be on warm and tender emotions, with no sexual explicitness; lovemaking should only take place when the emotional commitment between the characters justifies it. These heart-warming stories must be written with freshness and sincerity, featuring spirited, engaging heroines portrayed with depth and affection—as well as heroes who are charismatic enough to fulfill every woman's dreams! Readers should be thrilled by the tenderness of their developing relationship, and gripped by romantic suspense as the couple strives to overcome the emotional barriers between them and find true happiness in the romance of a lifetime!

Harlequin Superromance

Length: 85,000 words
Senior Editor: Laura Shin
Editorial Office: Toronto

The aim of a Superromance novel is to produce a contemporary, involving read with a mainstream lore in its situations and characters, using romance as the major theme. To achieve this, emphasis should be placed on individual writing styles and unique and topical ideas.

The criteria for Superromance books are flexible. Aside from length, the determining factor for publication will always be quality. Authors should strive to break free of stereotypes, clichés and worn plot devices to create strong believable stories with depth and emotional intensity. Superromance novels are intended to appeal to a wide range of romance readers.

A general familiarity with current Superromance books is advisable to keep abreast of ever-changing trends and overall scope. But we don't want imitations and we are open to innovation. We look for sincere, heartfelt writing based on true-to-life experiences and fantasies the reader can identify with.

Harlequin Temptation

Length: 60,000 words
Associate Senior Editor: Brenda Chin
Editorial Office: Toronto

Temptation is sexy, sassy and seductive! This is Harlequin's boldest, most sensuous series, focusing on men and women living—and—loving-today! Almost anything goes in Temptation; the stories may be humorous, topical, adventurous or glitzy, but at heart, they are pure romantic fantasy. Think fast-paced, use the desires and language of women today, add a high level of sexual tension, along with strong conflicts and then throw in a good dash of "what if…" The results should sizzle!

Mills & Boon Historical Romance

Length: 75,000-85,000 words
Senior Editor: Linda Fildew
Editorial Office: London

This series covers a wide range of British and European historical periods from 1066 to approximately the Second World War. The romance should take priority, with all the emotional impact of a growing love, and should be developed over a relatively short space of time. The historical detail should be accurate, without sounding like a textbook, and should help to create a true sense of the chosen setting, so that the reader becomes immersed in that time. A query letter with a synopsis and first three chapters are advised.

Mills & Boon Medical Romance

Length: 50,000-55,000 words
Senior Editor: Sheila Hodgson
Editorial Office: London

These are present day romances in a medical setting. There should be a good balance between the romance, the medicine and the underlying story. At least one of the main characters should be a medical professional, and developing the romance is easier if the hero and heroine work together. Medical detail should be accurate but preferably without using technical language. An exploration of patients and their illnesses is permitted, but not in such numbers as to overwhelm the growing love story. Settings can be anywhere in the world. More detailed guidelines are available on request with a stamped, addressed envelope.

Silhouette Desire

Length: 55,000-60,000 words
Senior Editor: Melissa Jeglinski
Editorial Office: New York

Sensual, believable, compelling, these books are written for today's woman. Innocent or experienced, the heroine is someone we identify with; the hero is irresistible. The conflict should be an emotional one, springing naturally from the unique characters you've chosen. The focus is on the developing relationship, set in a believable plot. Sensuality is key, but lovemaking is never taken lightly. Secondary characters and subplots need to blend with the core story. Innovative new directions in storytelling and fresh approaches to classic romantic plots are welcome.

Silhouette Intimate Moments

Length: 80,000 words
Executive Editor: Leslie Wainger
Editorial Office: New York

Believable characters swept into a world of larger-than-life romance are the hallmark of Silhouette Intimate Moments books. These books offer you the freedom to combine the universally appealing elements of a category romance with the flash and excitement of mainstream fiction. Adventure, suspense, melodrama, glamour—let your imagination be your guide as you blend old and new to create a novel with emotional depth and tantalizing complexity. The novels explore new directions in romantic fiction, or mine classic plots in contemporary ways, always with the goal of tempting today's demanding reader.

Silhouette Romance

Length: 53,000-58,000 words
Associate Senior Editor: Mavis Allen
Editorial Office: New York

Silhouette Romance books require talented authors able to portray modern relationships in the context of romantic love. Although the hero and heroine don't actually make love unless married, sexual tension is vitally important. Writers are encouraged to try creative new approaches to classic romantic and contemporary fairy-tale plots. Our ultimate goal is to give readers vibrant love stories with heightened emotional impact—books that touch readers' hearts and celebrate their values, including the traditional ideals of love, marriage and family.

Silhouette Special Edition

Length: 75,000-80,000 words
Senior Editor: Gail Chasan
Editorial Office: New York

Sophisticated, substantial and packed with emotion, Special Edition demands writers eager to probe characters deeply, to explore issues that heighten the drama of living and loving, to create compelling romantic

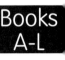

plots. Whether the sensuality is sizzling or subtle, whether the plot is wildly innovative or satisfyingly traditional, the novel's emotional vividness, its depth and dimension, should clearly label it a very special contemporary romance. Subplots are welcome, but must further or parallel the developing romantic relationship in a meaningful way.

Steeple Hill
Women's Fiction
Length: 80,000-125,000 words
Senior Editor: Joan Marlow Golan
Editorial Office: New York

This new Steeple Hill program will be dedicated to publishing inspirational Christian women's fiction that depicts the struggles the characters encounter as they learn important lessons about trust and the power of faith.

We are looking for compelling and thoughtfully developed stories that promote strong family values and high moral standards. These complex stories are character driven. They should provide readers with an uplifting and satisfying ending, and they can be written in the first or third-person narrative and can be single or multiple point of view.

The program is open to a variety of genres, ranging from contemporary women's fiction (family dramas, romance, suspense, romantic suspense) to historicals and thrillers. There should be no explicit sex in these stories, and a minimum of sensuality and sexual desire. And unless it is part of the struggle the protagonists face, there should be no premarital sex or graphic violence.

Although the faith element is central to these stories, the degree of religiousness can vary. We would prefer that specific Christian denominations not be named unless the story requires it, e.g., we prefer "Good Shepherd Christian Church" to "Good Shepherd Baptist (or Presbyterian, Methodist, etc.) Church."

Love Inspired
Length: 70,000-75,000 words
Senior Editor: Joan Marlow Golan
Editorial Office: New York

The Love Inspired line is a series of contemporary, inspirational romances that feature Christian characters facing the many challenges of life and love in today's world.

Each story should have an emotional, satisfying and mature romance; however, the characters should not make love unless they are married. These are "sweet" romances. Any physical interactions (i.e. kissing, hugging) should emphasize emotional tenderness rather than sexual desire.

Drama, humor, and even a touch of mystery all have a place in the series. Foul language, swearing and scenes containing violent content do not. Any subplots should come directly from the main story. Secondary characters (children, family, friends, neighbors, fellow church members, etc.) can also help contribute to a substantial and gratifying story.

Although an element of faith should be present in the books, it should be well integrated into the plot. And the conflict between the main characters should be an emotional one, arising naturally from the characters you've created.

Manuscript length is 70,000 to 75,000 words. The word count we are looking for is an approximate one which you can get by multiplying (the average number of words in a full line) x (the number of lines on a full page) x (the number of pages). Please don't go by the exact word count from your computer because it doesn't count the spaces in time breaks, conversation or chapter and time breaks.

MIRA
Length: 100,000-150,000 words
Senior Editor: Amy Moore-Benson
Editorial Office: Toronto

MIRA Books is proud to publish outstanding mainstream fiction for readers around the world.

As a result of the broad range of fiction published under the MIRA imprint, there are no tip sheets. MIRA publishes mainstream contemporary and historical romance, romantic suspense, thrillers, family sagas and relationship novels.

We recommend that you familiarize yourself with the wide range of books published by MIRA. Our authors include Mary Lynn Baxter, Rebecca Brandewyne, Stella Cameron, Candace Camp, Diane Chamberlain, Jasmine Cresswell, Margot Dalton, Karen Harper, Christiane Heggan, Penny Jordan, R. J. Kaiser, Debbie Macomber, Curtis Ann Matlock, Carla Neggers, Diana Palmer, Emilie Richards, Rosemary Rogers, Nan Ryan, Sharon Sala, Taylor Smith, Erica Spindler, Anne Stuart, Laura Van Wormer and Susan Wiggs.

Agented submissions only.

Red Dress Ink
Length: 90,000-110,000 words
Senior Editor: Margaret Marbury
Editorial Office: New York
We're looking for a few good women…

Women who are ready to start a new chapter in their lives by writing strong, sassy Red Dress Ink books.

Red Dress Ink books are about City Girls—urban women twenty-something and up who are discovering themselves, sharing apartments, meeting men, struggling with jobs. These books are pragmatic, relevant and have a unique tone: they show life as it is, but with a strong touch of humor, hipness and energy. Red Dress Ink books are about how single urban females *really are*. We see life in all its messy details—meddling moms, rivalries at work, unfaithful boyfriends. But driving the story is the heroine's development into a strong woman, supported by close friends. And if she finds love along the way, what a bonus! The style of writing is light, highly accessible, clever, funny and full of witty observations. The dialogue is sharp and true-to-life. These are characters you can immediately identify with in a story you just can't put down!

These books are *Ally McBeal* meets *Sex and the City*, *Bridget Jones's Diary* meets *The Girls' Guide to Hunting and Fishing*.

HQN Books
Length: 100,000-150,000 words
Executive Editor: Tracy Farrell
Editorial Office: New York

HQN Books is proud to publish outstanding romance fiction for readers around the world.

Debuting August 1, 2004, the new imprint will publish a broad range of romantic fiction. Because HQN Books is a mainstream imprint, there are no tip sheets.

While actual HQN Books titles will not be available until August 2004, perspective authors can familiarize themselves with the wide range of books we will be publishing by reading other books by the authors who will be writing for the imprint. These authors include Carly Phillips, Diana Palmer, Kasey Michaels, Beverly Barton, Gayle Wilson, Geralyn Dawson, Margaret Moore, Candace Mann and Rita Herron, among others.

The imprint is looking for a wide range of authors from know romance stars to first time authors. Both agented and slush submissions are welcome. Please send your projects to our New York Editorial Office.

LUNA
Length: 100,000-150,000 words
Executive Editor: Mary-Theresa Hussey
Editorial Office: New York
Editor: Kate Paice
Editorial Office: London
Powerful, alluring, mythic, elemental—magical.

Luna Books delivers a compelling, female-focused fantasy with vivid characters, rich worlds, strong, sympathetic women and romantic subplots.

Luna Books wants emotionally complex, sweeping stories that highlight the inner female power. Whether the heroine is on a quest to save the world—or someone or something important to her—discover her past or develop her own abilities, these stories are involving, gripping and sweep the reader away into a detailed, convincing world. They also contain romantic subplots that enhance the main story, but don't become the focus of the novel. They can be set in alternate historical worlds containing magic, a fantasy world or a contemporary location. Point of view can vary, but should be predominantly female. Read authors such as Mercedes Lackey, Catherine Asaro, Sarah Zettel, Barbara Hambly and Tanith Lee.

Silhouette Bombshell

Length: 80,000-90,000 words

Associate Senior Editor: Lynda Curnyn

Editorial Office: New York

Each Silhouette Bombshell book is a fast-paced action adventure story featuring a heroine often in high-stakes situations. It is the heroine's ability to get out of that situation that drives the plot and ultimately provides the thrilling and unpredictable reading experience. Each book will also contain an exciting romance subplot. Though not every book needs to end in marriage, in every book there should be a commitment at the story's end to take the relationship to the next level, whether that be a first kiss or a new emotional and/or sensual awareness between the couple. First and third points of view are acceptable, however the story should be mostly from the heroine's point of view. Settings can be urban, rural, international. Time period is contemporary but we will also consider futuristic stories.

How to Prepare Your Submission to Harlequin, Silhouette, MIRA

Unless otherwise noted, we do not accept unsolicited complete or partial manuscripts, but ask instead that you submit a query letter. The query letter should include a word count and pertinent facts about yourself as a writer including your familiarity with the romance genre. Please indicate what series you think your project is appropriate for, if it is completed, what you think makes it special and previous publishing experience (if any). Also include a synopsis of your story that gives a clear idea of both your plot and characters and is no more than two single-spaced pages. A self-addressed envelope and return international postage coupons will ensure a reply. Should your manuscript be requested, please note the following information.

1. Harlequin, Silhouette, Mills & Boon and Steeple Hill publishes only category/series romance (and inspirational romance under Steeple Hill). Please do not submit any other type of fiction or non-fiction. Your manuscript should be told in the third person, primarily from the heroine's point of view. However, the hero's perspective may be used to enhance tension, plot or character development. Please see the guidelines for each series for details.

2. All material should be the author's own original work. Stories that contain scenes or plot lines that bear a striking resemblance to previously published work are in breach of copyright law and are not acceptable.

3. All material must be typewritten, double-spaced and on a reasonably heavy bond paper. No disk submissions. Computer-generated material is acceptable, but must be letter quality, and pages must be separated. Any material received on computer reams will be returned without evaluation.

4. Do not submit your material bound in binders, boxes or containers of any kind. Secure material by rubber bands. Cover sheets must have your complete name, address and phone number. Each page should be numbered sequentially thereafter. Please type your name and title in the upper left-hand corner of each page. If we ask to see your manuscript, please include a complete synopsis. Enclose a self-addressed, stamped postcard if you require acknowledgment of receipt.

5. All material will be evaluated in as timely a fashion as volume allows. Please do not call regarding the status of your manuscript. You will be notified by mail as soon as your work has been reviewed.

6. Do no send any material that is being considered by another publisher. Multiple submissions are not acceptable. A literary agent is not required in order to submit.

7. You must enclose a stamped, self-addressed envelope with all material you send in. This will ensure the return of your material. Please send an envelope large enough to accommodate your work and adequate postage in the form of international postage coupons or an international money order, where appropriate.

8. This sheet is designed as a guide to aid you in understanding our requirements and standards. However, there is no better way to determine what we are looking for than reading our books.

9. We enter into discussions about payment only when a contract is offered. This information is confidential.

10. We take every reasonable care of manuscripts while they are with us and will return any which prove unsuitable (provided return postage is supplied), but we cannot take responsibility for the vagaries of the post office, so please be sure to retain a photocopy of your manuscript against unfortunate losses.

Submitting to Mills & Boon

Mills & Boon prefer to receive partial submissions. These should include the first three chapters and synopsis of the rest of the story.

Submitting to MIRA

At this time, MIRA Books is only accepting agented submissions. Harlequin and Silhouette published authors should contact their editor is interested in submitting to MIRA.

Submitting to Red Dress Ink

Point of view: first person/third person, as well as multiple viewpoints, if needed.

Settings: urban locales in North America or well-known international settings such as London or Paris.

Tone: fun, up-to-the-minute, clever, appealing, realistic.

If you are a city girl at heart, please submit a detailed synopsis and three sample chapters or a complete manuscript.

EDITORIAL OFFICES

• **Toronto**

Harlequin Books/MIRA Books

225 Duncan Mill Road

Don Mills, Ontario

M3B 3K9

Canada

• **New York**

Silhouette/Harlequin Books/Steeple Hill Books/Red Dress Ink

Harlequin New York

233 Broadway, Suite 1001

New York, NY 10279

• **London**

Harlequin Mills & Boon Ltd.

Eton House, 18-24 Paradise Road

Richmond, Surrey, United Kingdom

TW9 1SR

Check bookstores and your library for information about writers' organizations and writing. For updated submission guidelines, information about writing and tips, visit www.eHarlequin.com.

Categories: Fiction—Romance

CONTACT: Submissions Editor

Material: Submissions for Silhouette/Harlequin Books/ Steeple Hill Books (Send to New York address, listed above)

CONTACT: Submissions Editor

Material: Submissions for Harlequin Books/MIRA Books (Send to the Toronto address, listed above)

CONTACT: Submissions Editor

Material: Submissions for Harlequin Mills & Boon Ltd (Send to the London address, listed above)

Website: www.eharlequin.com

Harvard Common Press

The Harvard Common Press is a small independent publisher of quality trade books. We specialize in cookbooks, parenting and childcare books, and the occasional health and beauty book, though our backlist includes career, business, and nature titles.

Authors interested in publishing with The Harvard Common Press are asked to submit the following:

- a chapter-by-chapter outline of the proposed book
- two complete sample chapters
- a résumé or brief personal history
- an evaluation of other books available on the subject

Submissions should be typed, double-spaced, on a standard typewriter, word processor, or computer, but please avoid dot-matrix printers. We will return submissions not suited for our list if a stamped, self-addressed envelope is provided.

Categories: Nonfiction—Beauty—Busines—Career—Cooking—Health—Nature—Parenting

CONTACT: Publisher
Material: All
The Harvard Common Press
535 Albany St.
Boston, MA 02118
Website: www.harvardcommonpress.com

Hatherleigh Press

Hatherleigh Press is a small, independent publisher focusing on health, fitness and self-help titles, with a few other titles in general non-fiction. Submissions in the fields of health and fitness are welcome; however, most of the books we publish are written by trained doctors, trainers, psychologists, and other professionals, so please be sure to include a C.V. along with the manuscript.

Please use the following guidelines when submitting your proposal:

1. Cover letter
2. Complete table of contents
3. Chapter-by-chapter summary
4. One to three sample chapters

5. Author's C.V. and qualifications (especially important for health/fitness titles)
6. SASE

Please do not send complete manuscripts.
No memoirs or personal accounts, please.

Categories: Nonfiction—Health—Outdoors—Psychology—Recreation—Relationships—Self Help—Sports/Recreation

CONTACT: Submissions Editor
Material: All
5-22 46th Ave., Ste 200
Long Island City NY 11101-5215
Phone: 718-786-5338
Website: www.hatherleighpress.com

Hay House, Inc.

Hay House publishes hardcover and trade paperback originals, and trade paperback reprints. We average 60 titles a year. Agented submissions only. Free book catalog. SASE required for return material from agents. No response of any kind without an SASE.

NONFICTION: Self-help, New Age, Sociology, Philosophy, Psychology, Health, Men's/Women's Issues. Subjects include social issues, current events, ecology, business, food and nutrition, education, the environment, alternative health/medicine, money/finance, nature, recreation, religion, and men's/women's issues/studies. We also publish gift books in the above subject areas.

BEST SELLING NONFICTION TITLES: *You Can Heal Your Life*, by Louise L. Hay; *Left to Tell, by Immoculée Ilibagiza;* Secrets & Mysteries by Sylvia Browne; *Goddesse Virtue & Angels, By Doreen; The Power of Intention, by Dr. Waye W. Dyer.*

TIPS: Our audience is concerned with our planet, the healing properties of love, and self-help principles. Hay House has noticed that our readers are interested in taking more control of their lives. If I were a writer trying to market a book today, I would research the market thoroughly to make sure that there weren't already too many books on the subject I was interested in writing about. Then I would make sure that I had a unique slant on my idea.

Categories: Nonfiction—Cooking—Diet/Nutrition—Environment—Feminism—General Interest—Health—Inspirational—Marriage—Men's Issues—New Age—Psychology—Relationships—Self Help—Spiritual—Women's Issues—Astrology—Philosophy

CONTACT: Jessica Vermooten, Assistant Editor
Material: All
PO Box 5100
Carlsbad CA 92018-5100
Phone: 760-431-7695 x139
Fax: 760-431-6948

Hazelden Publishing

If you have an idea, a proposal, or a manuscript that you would like Hazelden to publish, these author guidelines will help you get started.

About Hazelden

Hazelden publishes information that helps build recovery in the lives of individuals, families and communities affected by alcoholism, drug dependency and related diseases. Hazelden publications and services are intended to meet a full range of chemical health issues for alcoholics, drug addicts, families, counselors, educators, doctors, and other professionals. Hazelden publications support Twelve Step philosophy and a holistic approach that addresses the needs of the mind, body, and spirit.

What We Publish

Hazelden publishes content in several formats: print (books, pamphlets, workbooks, leaflets, curricula), multi-media (video, audio, electronic), and live trainings. Our publications are sold to bookstores, treatment programs, hospitals, schools, churches, correctional facilities, government and military agencies, mental health and counseling agencies, and private corporations' employee-related programs.

Hazelden editors look for innovative materials that address issues relevant to substance abuse, prevention, treatment, recovery, and chronic illness. Our publications address topics related to chemical dependency, family and relationship issues, spirituality, eating disorders, gambling, nicotine cessation, mental health, and historical information on the Twelve Step movement.

What We Don't Publish

Hazelden discourages submissions of poetry, fiction, personal stories, dissertations, and art.

How to Submit a Proposal

It is not necessary to send an entire manuscript. *A complete proposal should include information on the following:*

- Overview: What is the general content and objective of your work? What do you intend to accomplish?
- Audience: Who or, what type of organization, is most likely to purchase your work?
- Market: Who, or what type of organization, is most likely to purchase

your work?

• Competition: What competing publications are on the market? How is your work different?

• Contents: Include with your proposal a table of contents, a detailed chapter outline, an introduction, and two or three sample chapters.

• Author information: Provide information on yourself and your qualifications, including previous writing or relevant experience, and previously published works.

All submissions must be typed double-spaced. Photocopies are acceptable. If you want your submission returned, please include a self-addressed envelope with correct postage. Otherwise, your submission will not be returned.

We encourage you to review our publication catalog for information on our current titles. You may request a catalog by calling our toll-free number: 1-800-328-0098.

Manuscript Evaluation

Once received, your proposal will be screened and either forwarded to an editor or immediately rejected. If it is not immediately rejected, a card will be sent to you to inform you it has been forwarded to an editor for review.

The review process may take up to twelve weeks, during which time an editor will evaluate your proposal based on editorial, marketing, and philosophical criteria. The purpose of such evaluation is to determine whether your proposal fits with our editorial mission, market niche, and product plans.

During this period, if conditions warrant, you might be asked to submit a complete manuscript for editorial review. As soon as a final decision has been made, you will be notified by mail or phone.

Literary Agencies

Having a literary agent represent your work is not necessary; however, our editors work with a wide network of agents.

Accepted Manuscripts

Authors are offered either a royalty contract or a work-for-hire agreement, according to the type of work and the market it serves. All manuscripts are subject to editing.

Thank you for your attention to these author guidelines.

Categories: Nonfiction—Counseling—Family—Philosophy—Relationships—Self Help—Spiritual

CONTACT: Editorial Department
Material: All
Hazelden Information and Education
PO Box 176
Center City MN 55012

Healing Arts Press

Books on alternative medicine and holistic health, including titles on natural foods, cooking, and self-help. **Note:** We no longer publish cookbooks.

In order to make the review process more efficient for prospective authors and for our editorial staff, we have prepared a list of requirements for authors and for our editorial staff, we have prepared a list of requirements for authors who are submitting work. Please include the following when presenting a proposal:

1. A BRIEF LETTER THAT INCLUDES A SHORT SYNOPSIS OF THE BOOK

a) The letter should be no more than two pages long and should tell how your manuscript contributes to its field and what make is unique.

b) As specifically as you can, tell us who the audience is for your book.

c) Give a brief biography of yourself, noting especially any specific qualifications for writing your subject.

2. A TABLE OF CONTENTS, INTRODUCTION, AND SAMPLE CHAPTER(S)

There is no need to send a complete manuscripts unless it is specifically asked for. Proposals including the above materials are reviewed much faster than thick manuscripts sent unsolicited.

3. WE CANNOT RETURN PROPOSALS OR MANUSCRIPTS UNLESS THEY ARE ACCOMPANIED BY A SELF-ADDRESSED ENVELOPE STAMPED WITH SUFFICIENT POSTAGE.

Some prospective authors write or e-mail a query letter before sending a proposal. This is a good idea and can save time and postage, especially when you are not familiar with the books we publish. A list of our seven imprints follows, please read these before sending us a query letter or proposal.

If you have questions that have not been addressed above regarding our submission guidelines, please DO NO call the acquisitions editor; send a query letter to our submissions department at the address listed below. Your query letter should provide enough information about your work that the acquisitions editor can make an informed decision and contact you for further details.

Categories: Nonfiction—Health—Physical Fitness—Self Help—Alternative medicine—Holistic Health—Yoga

Contact: Submissions
Healing Arts Press
PO Box 388
Rochester, VT 05767-0388 USA
Phone: 802-767-3174
Website: www.InnerTraditions.com

Health Communications, Inc.

Health Communications, Inc.

Dear Prospective Author:

Thank you for your interest in Health Communications, Inc. For over two decades, we have enhanced our readers' lives through top-quality books promoting recovery, personal growth, and the enrichment of mind, body and soul. In that time, we have become one of the nation's leading life-issues publishers.

Seven of our over 30 national bestsellers have appeared on the New York Times bestsellers list: *Healing the Shame That Binds You* by John Bradshaw; *Adult Children of Alcoholics* by Janet G. Woititz; and five books in the Chicken Soup for the Soul series by Jack Canfield and Mark Victor Hansen—*Chicken Soup for the Soul, A 2nd Helping of Chicken So up for the Soul, A 3rd Serving of Chicken Soup for the Soul, Chicken Soup for the Woman's Soul* (co-authored by Jennifer Read Hawthorne and Marci Shimoff) and *Chicken Soup for the Soul at Work* (co-authored by Maida Rogerson, Martin Rutte and Tim Clauss).

Although we have been a forerunner in recovery publishing, we have grown in new directions. Today, recovery/addiction is only one of several categories that comprise our title base. In addition, we now publish in the following areas: self-help/psychology, health/wellness, soul/spirituality, inspiration, women's issues, relationships, and the family.

To continue our tradition of excellence in publishing, we seek high-caliber authors who produce original material that appeals to a broad readership. We are interested in nonfiction books that emphasize self-improvement, personal motivation, psychological health, overall wellness or mind/body/spirit integration. We do not publish biographies, autobiographies, poetry, children's books or fiction of any kind.

Most of our authors are established experts in their fields and, in some cases, already enjoy national recognition. Many of the authors we publish are professional speakers and consultants who conduct workshops, seminars, or training classes regionally or nationwide. Therefore, these authors are well prepared to promote their books successfully.

The publishing process at HCI begins with a book proposal, which is evaluated by our editorial department. To ensure that book proposals are evaluated on an equal basis and that all necessary information is provided, we require prospective authors to follow our submission guidelines in preparing their proposals. Material that does not conform to our guidelines is rejected.

SUBMISSION GUIDELINES

In order to consider publishing a book, we need a book proposal consisting of the elements outlined below. Do not send a complete manuscript unless asked to do so. All submissions are evaluated on the basis of content, author credentials and marketability. Submissions that do not conform to these guidelines are rejected.

I. AUTHOR INFORMATION

Send us your bio or curriculum vitae. Include information on professional credentials, current occupation, previously published works, any public speaking or promotional experience you have, and any television or radio appearances you have made.

II. MARKETING DATA

• Supply detailed information on the marketability of your book, including:

• Target Audience

• Who is it? How big is it? How do you know it exists?

• Competing Titles

• What other books on the same or a similar topic have already been published? How popular are they?

• Uniqueness Value

• What makes your book interesting and different from others already on the market? Why would readers choose your book over others currently available?

• Marketing Plan

• How do you intend to promote the book? What marketing channels can you propose? Do you have access to any special avenues for marketing the book?

III. MANUSCRIPT SAMPLE

Please send no more or less than the following:

A. Detailed outline of the book.

B. Table of contents.

C. Introduction.

D. Two sample chapters.

In preparing the manuscript sample, please observe our format requirements (these also apply if you are asked to send a complete manuscript):

• Spacing and Type Size: All text, tables and caption material must be double spaced. Use at least 12-point type.

• Chapter and Section Titles: All words in these titles should be upper- and lowercase.

• Spelling: Use the first spelling listed in the most recent edition of *Webster's New International Dictionary* or *Webster's Collegiate Dictionary.*

• Punctuation and Style: Do not use the serial comma. In running text, numbers below 10 should be spelled out; all others should be written as numerals. Otherwise, refer to the most recent edition of *The Chicago Manual of Style.*

• Pagination (applies to complete manuscript only): Pages should be numbered continuously throughout a manuscript, not chapter by chapter.

IV. SASE

Due to new postal regulations, we can no longer use a SASE to return parcels weighing 16 ounces or more. Therefore, we no longer return any submissions weighing 16 ounces or over—even if a SASE is included. If your parcel weighs 16 ounces or more, neither your submission nor your SASE will be returned.

We are not responsible for submissions that exceed the returnable weight limit. Include a cover letter containing your name, return address and daytime phone number with your proposal. The cover letter is for our records and will not be returned to you. Send book proposals to the address below.

You should allow a minimum of six to eight weeks for a response. During periods when we receive a large number of submissions, response time can be two to three times longer. We consider all book proposals in the order received. We will notify you of our decision by mail. No phone calls, please. Calling to check the status of your submission will not expedite consideration of your proposal.

Categories: Nonfiction—Family—Health—Inspirational—Men's Issues—Psychology—Relationships—Spiritual—Women's Issues

CONTACT: Editorial Committee
Material: All
3201 SW 15th St.
Deerfield Beach FL 33442
Phone: 954-360-0909 x404
Fax: 954-360-0034.

HEARTS & TUMMIES COOKBOOK COMPANY
-a Dinky Division of Quixote Press

Hearts 'N Tummies
Cookbook Company

Regional cookbooks, fun cookbooks, cookbooks re specific geographic areas or historical periods, special interest cookbooks, offbeat cookbooks and cookbooks particularly suitable for sale at farmers' markets and tourist traps.

Vary in size from 120 to 500 recipes.

We would want the product, in final form, to be camera-ready...illustrated, clip art okay.

Categories: Children—Cooking—Fishing—Food/Drink—Gardening—Native American—Outdoors—Regional—Cookbooks—Hunting

CONTACT: Bruce Carlson, President
Material: All
1854 - 345th Ave.
Wever IA 52658
Phone: 319-372-7480
Fax: 319-372-7485

Hellgate Press

Please refer to PSI Research.

Heritage Books, Inc.

Heritage Books, Inc. was founded in 1978 to help Americans celebrate life by exploring various aspects of their heritage. We interpret heritage broadly to include history, biography, genealogy and related topics. Many of our publications deal with some aspect of history at the local or regional level, while others deal with some aspect of the various ethnic groups which constitute the American people. We also publish many reference works which contain the raw data used by historians, social scientists, and family historians, such as vital statistics and record abstracts.

The resources we publish are produced in traditional book format, as books and databases on CD-ROM, and/or in e-book format. In the past twenty-five years we have published over 2,500 titles and have over 1,800 in print at present. For a number of years we have published 20-30 new titles each month year round.

A free paper copy of a recent catalog describing many of our publications is available on request, and all our publications are listed on our web site: http://www.heritagebooks.com. An author information flyer is also available on request.

Submissions should include the following: 1) A cover letter which describes the nature and content of your compilation, the audience for whom it is intended and what you see as the market for it, the need that it fills and how it compares with other works on the topic, etc. Be sure to describe your experience and education as it relates to the project., i.e., your qualifications for writing the work. Also include your name, address, phone number, and email address. 2) A detailed outline or synopsis of the work and at least several sample chapters; a complete draft is preferred.

Submissions should be printed on standard bond typewriter paper; a single copy in either single or double spaced format is acceptable. Do not submit electronic media; if we decide to publish your work, we will request that later. Do not submit any originals of text or illustrations for which you do not have masters. We will not be responsible for lost materials, and will not return any materials submitted unless you provide adequate return postage. Submissions are normally accepted or rejected within four weeks of receipt by us.

Topics of interest include, but are not limited to: local and regional histories; accounts of various wars from the early Indian wars down to the present; compilations of source records of interest to historical and/or genealogical researchers; descriptions of the early settlements of various areas; studies of various aspects of the many ethnic groups found in America; biographical dictionaries, noteworthy memoirs, and family histories.

Categories: Nonfiction—Biography—Civil War—History—Native American—Reference—Regional

CONTACT: Editorial Director
Material: All
1540-E Pointer Ridge Place
Bowie MD 20716-7708
Phone: 301-390-7708
E-mail: submissions@heritagebooks.com
Website: www.heritagebooks.com

HiddenSpring

HiddenSpring, the general trade imprint of Paulist Press, publishes a broad range of non-fiction "with a spiritual twist." HiddenSpring publishes hardcover and both trade paperback originals and reprints. HiddenSpring publishes 8-10 titles a year, accepts manuscripts from both unagented and first-time authors, and offers variable advances. Please submit proposal package including outline, one (1) sample chapter, SASE; do not send complete manuscripts.

Categories: Nonfiction—Alternate Life-style—Biography—Culture—Ecology—Gardening—General Interest—History—Inspirational—Lifestyle—Multicultural—Religion—Science—Self Help—Spiritual—Travel

CONTACT: Jan-Erik Guerth, Editorial Director
Material: All
997 Macarthur Blvd.
Mahwah NJ 07430
Phone: 201-825-7300

High Tide Press

We're seeking titles on: mental health/psychology, disabilities, business, marketing, nonprofit leadership, and management. You should send us a one-page query with SASE, giving a brief overview of the book, its market, and your background. If we are interested, we will request a Book Proposal.

The Book Proposal (as described below) outlines the nature of your work, who your market is, and information about your background. If we're interested in taking a closer look at your book, we'll contact you. Please do not send a complete manuscript unless we request one.

Note: When querying via e-mail, please just give an overview of your book, its market, and your background.

Please do not send attachments unless invited to do so.

Book Proposals Should Include:
• A One-Page Overview of the Book
• Two (2) or Three (3) Sample Chapters
• A Chapter-by-Chapter Outline
• Number of Photos or Illustrations
• Author's Background / Credentials
• Target Completion Date
• Word Count / Number of Pages
• Audience / Market Information

Audience / Market Information Should Include:
1. Who Is the Audience?

What is the market for your book and how many potential buyers? Who wants this book? Why do they want it? Why do they need it? Do you have specific marketing ideas in mind?

2. Does Your Book Help the Reader?

How will this book benefit the buyer? How will it help them? What need does it fill for your target market?

3. What Makes Your Book Special?

What makes your book different from other such books? (Are there other such books?) Does your book have more information? Is it more comprehensive, easier to use? What advantages does it have over the competition? Why will people buy your book instead of something else? What existing or forthcoming titles compete with your book?

Note: Please do a database search for competing titles through Amazon.com, the largest online book store with more than four million titles in its database. Report your findings in your proposal.

4. Marketing Niches / Special Markets (please be thorough here)

List any special markets your book may have outside regular trade book channels (book stores).

Could sales result from your contacts—associations, organizations, corporations, groups, hospitals, treatment centers, workshops, seminars, or speaking engagements?

Which magazines or professional/trade journals may review your book or print articles by you which in turn promotes the book?

Do you have specific ideas for marketing your book? How willing are you to be active in marketing your book?

Submission of Text

All materials should be clearly printed on white, 8 1/2 x 11 paper, with at least 1" margins on all sides.

No more than 250-300 words per page.

Categories: Nonfiction—Disabilities—Intellectual—Psychology

CONTACT: Monica Regan, Managing Editor

Material: All
3650 W. 183rd St.
Homewood IL 60430-2603
Phone: 708-206-2054
Fax: 708-206-2044
E-mail: managing.editor@hightidepress.com
Website: www.hightidepress.com

Highlands Keep Publishing

Highlands Keep Publishing is an e-book and trade paperback press. At present, we are a niche market, and every effort will be made to acquire manuscripts with a military theme. Manuscripts should be well written and can include fantasy, science fiction, romance, history and alternative history. A major consideration for acceptance is that the manuscript must be "believable." Authors should be zealous in the accuracy of their descriptions of battle scenes, strategies, weapons, etc.

Books published by Highlands Keep Publishing include the Ragnarok Series "Song of the Valkyrie," Book 1, Episodes I and II by C. R. MacPhadrick.

Publishes three manuscripts per year. Responds within four weeks. Send a detailed synopsis and the first three chapters of your manuscript.

Categories: Fantasy—Military

CONTACT: Janet Musick, Senior Editor
Material: All
PO Box 157
Amherst VA 24521
E-mail: janetm1943@aol.com

Highsmith Press

Please refer to UpstartBooks.

Hikoki Publications

Please refer to Howell Press, Inc.

Hill and Wang

Please refer to Farrar, Straus and Giroux, Publishers, Inc.

Hillbrook Publishing Company

We focus on high quality books in spirituality, afterlife, channeled information, after-death communications, and out-of-body experiences. While we prefer nonfiction books, we will consider fiction in any of these categories.

Please send your query letter and book proposal to the attention of the Senior Editor by postal mail only. We cannot accept faxed, disk, web-based, or email submissions. Enclose a self-addressed-stamped-envelope (SASE) with sufficient postage if you wish to hear from us or want your manuscript returned. Your cover letter should contain complete contact information, including telephone number, mailing guddress, and email.

The chances of having your proposal considered for publication will be greatly enhanced if you include an analysis of competing books and show us how your book is different and better than others already in the market. Please be aware that we receive a large number of proposals and it may take us many months to respond. We realize it can be frustrating for an author to wait so long for a response. Therefore, we encourage you to submit your proposal simultaneously to other publishers or to consider self-publishing your work if you are turned down by several publishers.

Categories: Fiction—Nonfiction—Paranormal—Spiritual—Afterlife—After-Death Communications—Channeled Information

CONTACT: Senior Editor
Material: All
13190 Calle Caballeros, Ste. 201
San Diego, CA 92129-2916
Phone: 858-484-9850
Fax: 858-777-5459
E-mail: info@HillbrookPublishing.com
Website: www.hillbrookpublishing.com/

Hilliard & Harris

Initial Submissions for review:

Please submit a query letter identifying your manuscript and the genre that it is in. Include One (1) copy of the first 5 chapters of your manuscript or 100 pages whichever is greater. (Do not break a chapter to meet the 100 page limit.) Include a brief synopsis of your novel (as if for a jacket liner) and brief bio of the author. Also include a self-addressed, stamped mailing envelope large enough for the return of manuscript documents. If you prefer for us to shred the submission documents, please include written instructions to do so with signature.

If interested we will notify the author and request the entire manuscript. *The guidelines for submitting the entire manuscript are as follows:*

• All manuscripts must be typed, double spaced, 12 point type, in a standard font (for example, Arial or Courier New). No script fonts, please.

• Please calculate the word content of your manuscript with your word processing software and include on the upper left hand corner of the cover page. If you are submitting a manuscript from a typewriter, please estimate 250 words per page.

• Please include your name, mailing address, email address (if applicable), and phone number on the lower right hand side of your cover page. Please include your complete name, manuscript title, and page number on each page of the manuscript.

• Please include a self addressed stamped postcard for acknowledgment of receipt and return postage for the entire manuscript or instructions to shred it with signature in the event it is not accepted for publication.

Hilliard & Harris will notify authors of our progress in the evaluation process. We will correspond by mail and email as appropriate.

Hilliard & Harris will provide support from our editors for authors who are accepted for publication for final manuscript preparation, but manuscripts submitted requiring substantial mechanical or line editing will be rejected.

Categories: Fiction—NonFiction—Mystery—Young Adult

CONTACT: Shawn E. Reilly, Editor-in-Chief
Material: All
PO Box 275
Boonsboro MD 21713-0275
Phone: 301-432-7080
Fax: 301-432-7505
E-mail: info@hilliardandharris.com
Website: www.hilliardandharris.com

Historical Resources Press

We are a Small Press specializing in Publishing HISTORY Made

YESTERDAY and TODAY as RESOURCES for TOMORROW.

Our Mission:

Encouraging people of all ages to write, preserve and share history in published documents, small booklets and sometimes full-size books.

Our Guidelines:

Non-Fiction only, determined by the client to be accurate, true and important to those who are submitting it.

If you do not preserve this Non-Fiction, who will? What will be forever lost?

We are here to help anyone interested in Publishing HISTORY made YESTERDAY and TODAY as RESOURCES for TOMORROW.

Karin K. Ramsay, Owner & Sole Proprietor.

Categories: Nonfiction—History

CONTACT: Submissions Editor
Material: All
2104 Post Oak Court
Corinth/Denton TX 76210-1900
Phone: 940-321-1066
Fax: 940-497-1313
E-mail: historybuffs@worldnet.att.net
Website: www.booksonhistory.com

Hobby House Press, Inc.

Formal guidelines not available.
Send queries or book proposals to below address.
Categories: Nonfiction—Collectibles—Crafts/Hobbies—Hobbies

CONTACT: Editor
Material: All
1 Corporate Dr.
Grantsville MD 21536
Phone: 800-554-1447
Website: www.hobbyhouse.com

Hohm Press

Thank you for considering Hohm Press for your book proposal. Since 1975, Hohm Press has provided a venue for pioneering authors whose work promotes intellectual, emotional, physical and spiritual integrity. In response to the growing need for such work in contemporary culture, we publish books in the areas of transpersonal psychology and religious studies, herbistry, alternative health methods and nutrition. At present we are not accepting any poetry, fiction or children's books. *Please include the following in your submission:*

1. Cover letter—*start with a one or two page cover letter.*
   a. Summarize the topic of your book.
   b. State what qualifies you to write this book. Include applicable experience, education and other materials previously published.
   c. Briefly outline how you think your book could be most effectively promoted. Would you be willing to promote your book?

2. Outline and sample chapter—Provide a detailed outline and include a sample chapter. Please use white paper, double-spaced text.

3. SASE—If you would like us to return the materials that you send, please include a self-addressed return envelope large enough to hold the materials with the appropriate amount of postage.

4. Remember to be patient and allow us enough time to carefully review your proposal. We have a very small staff, and therefore this can take from eight to twelve weeks. Thank you.

Categories: Nonfiction—Diet/Nutrition—Health—Religion—Spiritual

CONTACT: Regina Sara Ryan, Senior Editor

Material: All
PO Box 31
Prescott AZ 86302
Phone: 928-778-9189
Website: hohmpress.com

Holiday House, Inc.

Holiday House is a small independent publisher of children's books only. We specialize in quality trade hardcovers from picture books to young adult, both fiction and nonfiction, primarily targeting the school and library market.

We are now especially interested in acquiring picture books, short chapter books, both humorous and serious middle-grade novels, multicultural stories, historical fiction, fantasy for ages 8-12, and exciting nonfiction books for all ages. We are not currently seeking easy reeaders, folktales or fairy tales, picture books for the preschool market, or books with a religious theme other than some limited Judaica.

We do not accept unsolicited manuscripts or simultaneous submissions. We do accept query letters. However, we do request that if you are making multiple submissions, you state this in your cover letter.

If you do not include a SASE, your manuscript will be discarded. This policy is strictly enforced.

We do not accept certified or registered mail.

Picture Books: Please send a complete manuscript. We do not respond to picture book queries. We do accept artwork with the text as each long as may be considered separately.

Novels: Please send a synopsis and the first three chapters.

Artwork: Please do not submit original artwork or slides; color photocopies or printed samples are preferred. Please send samples that can be kept on file.

Allow 8-10 weeks for a response. A manuscript under serious consideration may require more time. If 10 weeks have passed and you have not received an answer, follow up with a written query, including an SASE. No phone calls please.

Thank you for your interest in Holiday House.

Categories: Fiction—Nonfiction—Children—Young Adult

CONTACT: Acquisitions Editor
Material: All
425 Madison Ave.
New York NY 10017
Phone: 212-688-0085
Website: www.holidayhouse.com

Holloway House Publishing Company

Holloway House publishes African American crime, mystery, and street genre novels, along with highly provocative nonfiction such as Hollywood exposes and true crime. We welcome unsolicited submissions: please send us at least three chapters (or 30 pages) or your manuscript accompanied by a 1-3 page story synopsis. Include a SASE large enough to contain your manuscript, if you want the option of having it returned.

Categories: Fiction—Nonfiction—African-American—Crime—Mystery—Biography

CONTACT: Leonard King, Editor
Material: All
CONTACT: Neal Colgrass, Editor
Material: All
8060 Melrose Ave.
Los Angeles, CA 90046-7082
Phone: 323-653-8060
Fax: 323-655-9452
Website: www.hollowayhousebooks.com
www.hhbookstore.com

Horizon Books

Please refer to Christian Publications, Inc.

Howell Press, Inc.

About Us

Howell Press, Inc is a book publishing company located in Charlottesville, Virginia. We specialize in books about history, aviation, transportation, food and wine, quilts, and Mid-Atlantic and Southeastern regional subjects. Selected gift items and calendars are also available.

Our books are available in retail bookstores, museum shops, and specialty stores nationwide. Retail stores interested in carrying Howell Press books should call us at our toll-free number below to discuss establishing an account.

Howell Press publishes and distributes books featuring high-quality photography and artwork. Photographers who are not familiar with Howell Press are encouraged to request a free catalog before contacting us regarding assignments. Those who request catalogs should enclose a self-addressed, 8½ x 11-inch envelope and return postage with their request.

Please use the following guidelines to help make the review process as efficient as possible. Because we receive such a high volume of materials, we cannot review submissions that do not conform to these guidelines.

Author's Guidelines

Limit query letters to a concise one- or two-page description of your proposed project, its unique qualities, and its intended audience. Be sure to include your name and address on the first page of any correspondence. Your query should be accompanied by a proposal that provides a general overview of your idea and offers a chapter-by-chapter outline of the book. Please include three to five sample chapters (including the first two chapters) to familiarize us with your writing style and the development of your ideas. State your qualifications for handling this topic, including a brief summary of your writing experience.

If the proposed title is to be heavily illustrated, please outline the content and source of the photographs and/or artwork. It is also helpful to provide sample illustrations. For color illustrations, please send 8 x 10-inch prints. Send only transparencies or prints-no originals. While we will take every precaution in the handling and safe return of transparencies and prints, we assume no financial responsibility for them.

Offer a marketing plan for your book. How would you suggest your book's publisher reach the potential audience? Are there magazines, clubs, or radio and television shows that target the same market? Be specific. If you cite a magazine or club, tell us its circulation or size.

Be sure to check *Books in Print* (available at most public libraries) to see if someone has already published a book similar to the one you propose. Include an analysis of the competition in your proposal-let us know what similar titles are out there and how your book will be different.

For those who have queried Howell Press and have been asked to submit manuscripts, we ask that you include a cover letter with your manuscript. On the front page, include your name, address, telephone number,

and an accurate word count of the manuscript's length. The manuscript should be typed double spaced on 8½ x 11-inch white paper and have page numbers and at least one-inch margins on all sides. On the left margin, alongside key quotations, dates, figures, or other pertinent information, pencil in brief citations (author, book, and page) to direct us to the references for fact-checking purposes. If a source is not commonly available, please photocopy the relevant material and submit it with the manuscript.

Use *The Chicago Manual of Style* as a guide for proper punctuation, capitalization, and style. Tune your presentation to the popular reader rather than the scholarly one. Because quality illustrations and photography are a hallmark of our products, suggestions for obtaining illustrations to accompany your manuscript should be included.

All book proposals should be addressed to Ross A. Howell, Jr., President. No matter what materials you send, be sure to include sufficient return postage and a self-addressed envelope large enough to contain your materials if you want them to be returned. Manuscripts not accompanied by an SASE will not be returned. Do not send a check or cash for postage. If you do not wish to have your materials returned, please include a self-addressed No. 10 envelope with $.37 return postage for our response.

We will be in touch with you as soon as possible, but please keep in mind that it could take eight weeks or longer for us to adequately assess your submission and reach a decision.

Thank you for your interest.

Photographer's Guidelines

We work individually with photographers on book-length projects. Photographers who have proposals for book projects or wish to be considered for assignments should submit a written query.

Please limit queries to a concise one- or two-page letter describing your proposed project, its unique qualities, and its intended audience. Type your query/cover letter on 8½ x 11-inch white paper. Be sure to include your name and address on the first page of any correspondence. Photography samples must accompany your queries. For color illustrations, send 35 mm color transparencies; for black-and-white illustrations, please send 8 x 10-inch prints. Send only transparencies or prints-not originals. While we will take great care to ensure the safe return of your materials, we assume no financial responsibility for them.

State your qualifications for handling this topic, and be sure to include a brief summary of your photographic experience. Offer a marketing plan for your book. How would you suggest your publisher reach the potential audience? Are there magazines, radio and television shows, or clubs that target that market? Be specific. If you cite a magazine or club, tell us its circulation or size.

All proposals should be addressed to Ross A. Howell, Jr., President. No matter what size manuscript you're mailing, always include sufficient return postage and a self-addressed, stamped envelope large enough to contain your work should you want it to be returned. Work not accompanied by an SASE will not be returned. Please do not send a check or cash for postage. If you do not wish to have your materials returned, please include a self-addressed, No. 10 envelope with return postage for our response.

We will be in touch with you as soon as possible, but please keep in mind that it could take eight weeks or longer to make a decision.

Thank you for your interest.

Categories: Nonfiction—Automobiles—Aviation—Boating—Cooking—Crafts/Hobbies—History—Regional—Regional: Virginia

CONTACT: Ross A. Howell, President
Material: All
1713-2D Allied Lane
Charlottesville VA 22903
Phone: 434-977-4006 or 800-868-4512
Fax: 888-971-7204
E-mail: custserv@howellpress.com
Website: www.howellpress.com

Howells House, Inc.

We have no formal, written guidelines. Instead, we ask for a query letter giving a synopsis and description of the work and the qualifications and experience of the author. If we think we might be interested, we will request more information or samples. Ultimately, we will need sample chapters or the entire ms. on 3½" disk formatted in WordPerfect 6.0. Any necessary permissions will be the responsibility of the author.

Thank you for your interest.

Categories: Biography—Crime—General Interest—History—Military—Politics—Public Policy

CONTACT: Acquisitions Editor
Material: All
PO Box 9546
Washington DC 20016
Phone: 202-333-2182
Fax: 202-333-2184

HUMAN KINETICS

Human Kinetics

Do you have an idea for a book?

Human Kinetics publishes approximately 100 books a year. We do review unsolicited manuscript proposals, if prepared according to our book prospectus form.

If you are interested in submitting a book proposal, you can find prospectus forms available online for both trade (Consumer) books and academic/professional books.

Human Kinetics also publishes more than 20 journals for the physical activity field. Submission guidelines for articles are found on the Human Kinetics journals Web pages.

More Information about Submitting Manuscripts to HK

How long does it take for a manuscript to become a book?

Most trade books take about one year, often less, from the time the first draft is written by the author to the time the book is in print. Academic titles, such as textbooks and large reference books, may take longer to develop. Time frames for publication vary depending on the book's complexity, length, and the timeliness of the topic. At least half of the publication time involves careful review of your manuscript by our editorial staff, author revisions of the manuscript, design of the book's interior and cover, and planning for the marketing of your book.

How many products does HK release in one year?

About 100 books

23 journals (80+ issues)

Numerous other products including kits, videos, and software

Categories: Nonfiction—Nutrition—Education—General Interest—Health—Physical Fitness—Reference—Sports/Recreation—Trade-Coaching, Sports, Fitness

CONTACT: Academic Book Division or Trade Book Division
Material: All
Human Kinetics
PO Box 5076
Champaign, IL, 61825-5076
E-mail: webmaster@hkusa.com
Website: www.humankinetics.com

Hunter House Publishers

The guidelines below are in two parts: (a) the subject areas we publish in and the kind of books we do; and (1) the kind of proposals we like to see. They reflect our tag line, which is Books for health, family and community, although sometimes it is difficult to keep a clear separation between these three areas.

SUBJECT AREAS

Health and wellness, especially women's health

Our health books focus on emerging or current health issues that may be inadequately covered for the general population. We look for comprehensive, balanced and up-to-date information presented in a clear and accessible manner. The book should describe causes, symptoms, medical theories, current and possible treatments, complementary and alternative therapies, successful strategies for coping, prevention, and so on. Illustrations, sidebars, reading lists, and resource sections that provide additional information or enhance the content are desirable. We specialize in women's health, with sublists on cancer; pregnancy & childbirth; women's health reference; and women's health as a women's issue. We are currently interested in books about aging and complementary therapies. At the top of our health list are Menopause *Without Medicine*; *Women's Cancers*; *Running on Empty: The Complete Guide to Chronic Fatigue Syndrome (CFIDS)*; and *The Cortisol Connection*.

Family: Personal growth, lifestyles, relationships, sexuality

Personal growth topics that we are currently interested in are sexuality; partner and family relationships; and changing, evolutionary lifestyles. Successful titles provide step-by-step aids or a program to help readers understand and approach new perspectives on family issues or dynamics, celebrate their sexuality, and establish healthy, fulfilling lives that incorporate a planetary perspective. Examples include: *Sexual Healing: How Good Loving is Good for You* and *Your Relationship*; *Helping Your Child Through Your Divorce*; and *The Pleasure Prescription—A New Way to Well-being*.

Violence prevention and intervention, social justice

We have a small but growing line of books and workbooks, often done in collaboration with nonprofits, which address community issues such as violence prevention, access for people with disabilities, and human rights. They should include clear reviews and explanations, new activities and exercises, provocative insights, and practical theory. Examples are: *Violent No More: Helping Men End Domestic Abuse*; *Helping Teens Stop Violence: A Practical Guide for Counselors, Educators, and Parents*; *Computer Resources for People With Disabilities*; and *The Amnesty International Handbook*.

Resources for counselors and educators

Resources for educators are generally specialized curricula that address violence prevention and social justice issues, including *The Uprooted: Refugees and the United States*; *Human Rights for Children*; and *Making the Peace: A Violence Prevention Curriculum for Young People*.

Books for counselors and helping professionals tend to offer information in new and underexplored fields, such as trauma and crisis in children. Titles include *Trauma in the Lives of Children: Crisis and Stress Management Techniques for Counselors and Other Professionals*.

Audience

Our health and family books are meant to appeal to both the general reading public and health care and mental health professionals. They should be written clearly to the general reader, but include enough background explanation, theory, and resources so that they are good references for professionals. This comprehensive approach also ensures that readers can trust the authors as authorities on the topic. It is important that author have credentials and experience within the field. If you do not have this background, it is important that you have a co-author who does. It also helps if a reputable and well-known expert contributes a foreword or the introduction.

Our social issues books should be accessible to lay readers but should speak clearly to the specialized groups involved with the subject on a professional, volunteer, or community basis. Again, we look for credentialed authors with experience and a resource network in their field.

Books
A-L

It is crucial that the authors of educational or professional books have credentials and experience within the specific areas they address. We look for a need for information within these areas, and networks through which we can reach the professionals who will use these materials. Endorsements and a preface or foreword from noted individuals within the field are important and helpful.

We do not publish fiction or illustrated books for children.

PREPARING A BOOK PROPOSAL FOR US

A good non-fiction book proposal is made up of the following components: an overview; a chapter-by-chapter outline; about the author(s); and marketing considerations.

The Overview should be a two- to three-page summary of the work: the content, and your presentation and approach. *It should include the following:*

1. The subject hook, which creates interest in the book, including the title, subtitle, the book's angle on the current market, and approximate length of the book.

2. An anecdote or example that illustrates your theme and its significance.

3. Discussion of the book's other essential ingredients—illustrations, exercises, etc.

4. A foreword, preface, or endorsements for the book written by authorities or celebrities.

The final page of your proposal should discuss the markets for your work, your experience and credibility as an author, and any other information that makes the book unique. Our editors and salespeople must understand why your book should be written. Specify the audience your book will address (women, professionals, tradespeople). Include marketing or promotional ideas you have for getting the book known to your audience. Lastly, list current books that compete with and complement yours.

The Chapter-by-chapter Outline is a 3-6 page outline, including all chapter titles and itemized lists of the major topics or contents of each chapter. Significant illustrations, appendices, and recommended reading should be listed. Work from a table of contents. You should have enough chapters to break up the topic in digestible pieces for the reader, but not so many that the material is scattered. Most books flow from an overall organizing subject or theme—the subject "hook" we ask for in the overview. For example, a book on breast cancer can be organized according to risks and detection, operations and choices involved, and recovery processes. After you complete your table of contents, go on to outline each chapter. Make a brief listing of topics which will be discussed in each chapter, or summarize each chapter in a paragraph.

About the Author: your credentials as evidence you are qualified to write on the subject, and any experience or training that qualifies you especially well for this project. A resume or short biography that includes other publishing experience and media experience is helpful. The more you can tell us about yourself, the more we understand your proposal as a whole.

Marketing and Promotion Information: We look for authors who are positive about and have access to publicity. Explain what you will do to help promote the book. Describe your speaking, mass media, TV, radio, or promotional experience and include a plan of how your work can be promoted. Do you lecture, do seminars, tour, or travel for training and business; do you belong to active organizations and have strong networks; do you teach classes or write a newspaper column; are you prepared to market your materials?

The Review Process

If we are interested in pursuing your project further, we will request sample chapters. Please send only two to three sample chapters—not the whole manuscript. Each chapter should have one concept, subject, skill, or technique. Use main headings and subheads so a reader can know at a glance where the chapter is going.

In a chapter that explains a process or teaches a technique, explain the process step-by-step in exactly the order a reader should follow to understand the process. The general and most important concepts come first, while the exceptions and special considerations come last. Any background information can be explained first or in a separate chapter.

To effectively teach an individual step of a process or technique, follow this sequence: state the rule or instruction first. Be clear and to the point. Then give an example of how someone else did this step. Finally, provide an exercise for the reader to perform. This gives the reader three ways to learn the technique: intellectually by precept, emotionally by example, and experientially by doing.

Sending Us Your Manuscript

After you have done your marketing research and written your chapter outlines, consider whether Hunter House is the right publisher for you. We do not publish fiction, autobiography, or general children's books, so those types of works get returned right away. If you do have what we are looking for, then send it on. Proposals received without an SASE that are not accepted for publication will not be returned or responded to.

We do accept simultaneous submissions and look for computer printouts of good quality, or e-mail. Please inform us if a manuscript is available on computer disk (IBM format is preferable).

Categories: Nonfiction—African-American—Architecture—Biography—Boating—Business—Children—Christian Interests—Civil War—Collectibles—Cooking—Family—Hispanic—History—Inspirational—Jewish Interests—Politics—Regional—Self Help—Western

CONTACT: Kiran Rana, Publisher
Material: Any
CONTACT: Jeanne Brondino, Acquisitions Editor
Material: Any
PO Box 2914
Alameda CA 94501
Phone: 510-865-5282
Fax: 510-865-4295
E-mail: acquisitions@hunterhouse.com
Website: www.hunterhouse.com

Hyperion

We regret to inform you that Hyperion does not accept unsolicited manuscripts for review, as per our Legal Department:

"Note to authors: please do not send unsolicited submissions. As a matter of long-standing policy, The Walt Disney Company does not accept unsolicited creative submissions. Please understand that the policy's purpose is to prevent any confusion over the ownership of ideas that the company is working on or considering. Unsolicited submissions will be deleted without being reviewed or retained in our files."

Hyperion, like most major publishing houses will only accept manuscripts for review that have been submitted via a literary agent.

Website: www.hyperionbooks.com

Iconografix, Inc.

Iconografix is a publishing company specializing in books for transportation enthusiasts. We publish in a number of different areas, including Automobiles, Auto Racing, Buses, Construction Equipment, Emergency Equipment, Farming Equipment, Railroads and Trucks. The Iconografix imprint is constantly growing and expanding into new subject areas.

Authors, editors, and knowledgeable enthusiasts in the field of transportation history are invited to contact the Editorial Department at the address below.

Categories: Nonfiction—Automobiles—Recreation Vehicles—Transportation—Railroads

CONTACT: Editorial Department

Remember: Editors change jobs and publishers change addresses. It is wise to invest in a phone call for the current information before submitting.

Material: All
PO Box 446
Hudson WI 54016
Phone: 715-381-9755
Website: www.iconografixinc.com

IHS Press

Background and Editorial Philosophy: IHS Press is the only publisher dedicated exclusively to the Social Doctrine of the Catholic Church. As such IHS Press specializes in works of Catholic Social Thought which are faithful to the Traditional Teaching of the Roman Catholic Church. As a publisher in Social Thought, IHS Press is interested in considering for publication manuscripts which apply the Social Doctrine of the Church to any and all problems within the social science disciplines: history, sociology, economics, economic thought, history of economic thought, political theory; as well as works of a generally cultural, philosophical, or literary nature.

We are also seeking manuscripts by journalists, academics, scholars, and culturalists which explore various aspects of the numerous problems, both practical and philosophical, that plague modernity (as an ideology) and the modern world (in practice). We prefer analysis of those problems from the standpoint of the Social Doctrine of the Church, but we are happy to consider any analysis of those problems which speaks from a genuinely alternative viewpoint - that is to say a viewpoint that takes the true common good of society into account, and does not speak from the sterile categories of "right" and "left," or "communist/socialist" and "capitalist."

We intend, therefore, to be a publisher which is unique for its willingness to foster frank discussions, research, and intellectual exchanges about the issues that lie at the root of the problems of the modern world, and to contribute to their solution.

Submission procedure: Before considering a manuscript, the IHS editors prefer to have an opportunity to review and discuss the topic proposed for development in a full-length manuscript. This saves both the author and the editors time and energy.

The first step is to send us via fax, e-mail, or regular mail a one-page prospectus, sketching the general topic that a manuscript would potentially cover and the manner and extent to which the manuscript will cover it. Be sure to include an extensive author's biography and detailed and correct contact information. Including a stamped, self-addressed envelope will facilitate the process of our correspondence with you.

Additionally, include with the submitted prospectus the following supplemental information: (1) author's credentials and qualifications for writing on the proposed topic, (2) potential market(s) for the proposed book, (3) suggested contacts to approach for testimonials, blurbs, and endorsements (to include professionals, academics, individuals, and associations qualified to comment on the topic in question), (4) a list of the author's access to normal channels of book publicity including contacts with relevant special or mainstream media who would be interested in reviewing the book or interviewing the author on the subject of the proposed book (include a summary of the author's previous exposure in print or other media if applicable), and (5) the author's proposals, supplemental to the publisher's standard marketing efforts, for marketing the book.

In summary: In addition to considering manuscripts that correspond with our editorial vision, we insist upon manuscripts that are well written, to the point, and accessible. No manuscript, on no matter how interesting a subject, will be considered that is poorly written.

Categories: Nonfiction, Culture, History, Philosophy, Politics, Religion, Spiritual

CONTACT: John Sharpe
Material: All
222. W. 21st St., Ste F-122
Norfolk VA 23517
Phone/Fax: 877-IHS-PRESS (447-7737)
E-mail: editor@ihspress.com
Website: www.ihspress.com

Illumination Arts Publishing Co., Inc.

Mission Statement: Illumination Arts publishes high quality, enlightening children's picture books with enduring, inspirational and spiritual values. Our aim is to touch people's lives, with illumination and transformation. We are currently seeking fiction and non-fiction stories that are 500 to 1,500 words.

MANUSCRIPTS
All manuscripts must be typed, double-spaced. Please keep a copy of your work. Be sure your name and address are on your manuscript.

Manuscripts must be accompanied by a cover letter, including author's name, address, phone number, and the word count of the story.

Please enclose a short author's bio with personal and professional background and a list of previously published material, if any.

Include a description of what makes your book special or different from others currently on the market in the same category.

Tell us how you will be able to assist in the promotion of this book.

Sample illustrations are accepted but not necessary.

Please proofread the manuscript for spelling and grammatical errors.

We make every effort to respond in one month, but because of the volume of submissions received, we may be very late responding to authors.

We suggest that you review our books, and visit our website at www.illumin.com, to determine if your manuscript is appropriate for our company.

SUBMISSIONS
We do not accept chapter books or submissions on disc or video.

You *must* include SASE for reply, with sufficient postage, if you wish to have your manuscript returned. Submissions without SASE are not reviewed at all.

ARTWORK
Send resume, and samples of printed artwork, or photocopies. (Do not send original artwork or slides.)

Include SASE, with sufficient postage, if you wish to have your artwork returned. Electronic submission, discs, or video tapes are not accepted for stories.

Categories: Fiction—Children—Inspirational

CONTACT: Ruth Thompson, Editorial Director
Material: All
PO Box 1865
Bellevue WA 98009
Website: www.illumin.com

ImaJinn Books
Romance, Urban Fantacy, and Silk and Magic Erotica

NOTE: We are **NOT** an electronic publisher. We publish Trade-size paperback books.

• **Romance Guidelines:** ImaJinn (pronounced Imagine) Books publishes supernatural, paranormal, fantasy, and futuristic romances. We are looking for fast-paced, action-packed romances involving ghosts, psychics or psychic phenomena, witches, vampires, werewolves, shape shifters, and futuristic in space or on other planet. All novels should be atmospheric according to the chosen subject. Make sure the supernatural, paranormal, fantasy or futuristic element is strong enough to carry the story. If the element can be lifted out of the story and a publishable story still exists, the element is not strong enough. Also, in the case of vampires, werewolves, witches, or shape shifters, the hero or heroine must be the vampire, werewolf, etc., and these storylines should have a dark, eerie overtone.

The developing romantic relationship between the hero and the heroine is the focus of the story. The stories may be told from both points of view, and the hero may be the lead character of the story. Although books written in the third person are preferred, first person will be considered. Sensuality may range from sweet to highly sensual.

The heroine must be a strong woman, capable of confronting and conquering any threats of physical and/or psychological danger she faces in the story. She is always a match for the hero who should be bold and brash—an Alpha male—and he may or may not represent danger. The ending must be a happy one, with everlasting romance the reward for triumphing over the darkness or evil faced in the story. Although we prefer Alpha male heroes, we will consider Beta heroes, but they must still be bold and a match for the heroine. However, we do not want Beta vampires, werewolves, etc. We feel these types of heroes must have a dark, dangerous edge for survival purposes, and although they may have some Beta traits, their main personality should be Alpha.

• **Urban Fantasy Guidelines:** We are also considering Urban Fantasy storylines along the order of Laurell K. Hamilton's Anita Blake series. We do expect a romance or a blossoming romance in the story, although the romance does not have to be the main focus of the story. We expect these storylines to be set up for a continuing series with the same characters, although we will consider single book storylines. The main protagonist must be a "kick ass" heroine with the same traits as our romance heroines, as listed above.

LENGTH: 70,000 to 90,000 words

SUBMISSION: You do not need an agent to submit, but you **must** query us first. All query letters should include a synopsis no longer than six double-spaced pages and may be submitted by regular mail or e-mail, although we prefer e-mail queries and submissions. If you mail your query, please include an SASE if you want the material returned. If there is no enclosed SASE, we will dispose of the material. It is recommended that you either check our web site (http://www.imajinnbooks.com) or write or call us to see what storylines we're currently looking for. We do not accept simultaneous submissions. We only consider queries with story lines that meet our current needs.

We will **not** consider previously e-published books because of print-on-demand rights conflicts. If your book has been published by an e-publisher, please do **not** query us.

Copyright 2004 by ImaJinn Books

• **Silk and Magic Erotica Guidelines:** In keeping with the nature of all books ImaJinn publishes, a story or novel appropriate for our erotica line will be, first and foremost, a romance. The main plot of the story should be the sensual development of an intimate relationship between one man and one woman, who are both heroic in stature (i.e., possessing high moral standards) and who ultimately make a commitment to each other. In general, we are not looking for multiple partner relationships, although multiple partnerships are acceptable in some storylines, such as societies where there are more men than women or vice versa, but again, these multiple partners must ultimately make a commitment to each other.

We will accept any type of erotica storyline, from contemporary to historical to paranormal, futuristic and fantasy. A successful story will be highly erotic but not pornographic. The difference is usually one of focus; erotica, like romance, seeks to involve the reader's emotions, while pornography focuses almost entirely on the physical. We expect there to be sex involved—lots of it—but it must be part of the plot, not gratuitous. Authors are encouraged to begin with a premise that, by its nature, will put the hero and heroine in sexually charged circumstances from the beginning of the story. We don't expect the couple to make love in the first chapter, although it is acceptable to have it in chapter one, but we do expect some lovemaking

or sexually charged foreplay by chapter two. We expect that sexual scenes will be at least half or more of the story.

In general, we're looking for stories that turn us on, not off. We want to be excited—not disgusted or bored. We don't want stories about heavy BDSM, torture, bestiality (dogs, horses, snakes, and other real-world critters), non-sexual bodily functions ("golden showers"), pedophilia, necrophilia, cannibalism, weapons or other deadly implements being shoved into orifices, rape or anything else so kinky that it will offend our core readership. On the other hand, we understand that writing erotic stories about werewolves and aliens could lead to some interesting situations. Indeed, the paranormal element you choose could provide exactly the sort of sexual tension and eroticism these stories will require.

Regarding language, authors should think carefully about the words they use. A story doesn't automatically become erotic when "manhood" gets changed to "cock" or "feminine core" is replaced by "pussy." They're all still euphemisms, and the way they're used is what matters; indeed, it can mean the difference between erotica and pornography. So authors may use whatever words they wish to name body parts and to describe actions, but keep in mind that the goal is turn the readers on—not jar them out of the story or make them laugh at inappropriate moments. (By the way, it's perfectly acceptable to use real, official words for body parts and sex acts, too.)

LENGTH: We'd like the word count for these stories to be at least 30,000 words, and we have no limitation on word counts above 30,000, but lengthy stories must remain highly erotic from beginning to end. We will consider novellas between 15,000 to 30,000 words. However, we emphasize that even in the shorter format, it's essential that the story primarily be a romance.

Our erotica line will be available in e-book and CD format and as print-on-demand books. E-books and CDs will be sold exclusively by ImaJinn Books. Royalties will be paid at 50% of the net receipts for e-books and CD format, and royalties will be paid monthly on these sales. We will routinely combine novellas and books under 40,000-45,000 words into anthologies and offer them in print-on-demand books. Royalties on print-on-demand books will be split among authors, based on the number of stories in a book, and single title royalties will range from 6-10%. Royalties on books will be paid on a semi-annual basis.

These guidelines are subject to change as we refine this new line.

SUBMISSION: You do not need an agent to submit, but you must query us first. All query letters should include a synopsis no longer than six double-spaced pages and may be submitted by regular mail or e-mail, although we prefer e-mail queries. If you mail your query, please include an SASE if you want the material returned. We do not accept simultaneous submissions. Copyright 2004 by ImaJinn Books

Query letters or inquiries should be sent to the address below.

Categories: Fiction—Adventure—Fantasy—Juvenile—Paranormal—Romance—Science Fiction—Teen

CONTACT: Editorial Staff
Material: Silk and Magic Erotica
PO Box 545
Canon City, CO 81215-0545
CONTACT: Editorial Staff
Material: Romance and Urban Fantasy Submissions
PO Box 162
Hickory Corners, MI 49060-0162
Phone: 719-275-0060
Fax: 719-276-0741
E-mail: editors@editors@imajinnbooks.com
Website: www.imajinnbooks.com

Impact ✍ Publishers®, Inc.

Impact Publishers, Inc.

We believe an author-publisher relationship should be collaborative, not adversarial.

The author's job -- and it's hard work -- is to prepare the best possible presentation on a subject of interest to a definable audience, and to make that material available in every manner at his/her disposal. One part of that job is to find a publisher who can help.

The publisher's job -- it's not easy either -- is to help the author "polish" that work for the marketplace, to produce it attractively and appropriately for its audiences, and to place it in the hands of as many buyers as possible through effective marketing.

Impact, like all legitimate publishers, pays royalties to authors; we do not ask authors to subsidize their books. A modest advance and a royalty of 10 to 15 percent of sales receipts are typical.

Active authors (those who do workshops, make public and professional presentations, write articles, get media exposure) almost always have the most successful books.

You need not have a literary agent. We're happy to work with your agent if you have one, but we frequently contract directly with authors.

If you're writing now, keep your audience in mind, and remember that writing self-help is like talking to clients, but it's not the same. In a book, you must spell everything out clearly, simply, and completely. You won't be there for your readers to ask questions.

Manuscript Submission Procedures

We look at all submitted material.

Your chances of hearing from us promptly are greatly enhanced by the inclusion of a self-addressed stamped envelope.

We love to see initial inquiries which look like this:

(1) a brief letter of introduction, telling us:

a. what your book is about,

b. the audience to whom you've addressed it,

c. why you're the right person to have written it,

d. why Impact is the right house to publish it, and

e. why it's outstanding enough to have a chance when 50,000 other books will be published that year.

(2) an annotated table of contents (with a paragraph summarizing each chapter)

(3) a couple of sample chapters

(4) a short resume or curriculum vita (we don't need your lists of publications in refereed journals and/or presentations at professional meetings -- yet).

It'll take us a few weeks (from four to twelve, on average) to respond. Please don't telephone. If you want to be sure we got the manuscript, include a simple response device (postcard, or check-off letter & SASE) with your submission. (Please do not send entire manuscripts via email, unless specifically requested to do so; a brief proposal is usually sufficient.)

We rarely select manuscripts from prospective authors outside the U.S. If you wish to submit a proposal from abroad, please provide an email address or International Reply Coupon for our response

Criteria for Manuscript Selection

Since its founding in 1970, Impact Publishers has elected to publish only books which serve human development. A manuscript we select for publication will exhibit a strong combination of the following characteristics:

it will present a message we believe in.

it will be a work which, in our opinion, needs to be published.

it will present practical ideas which an individual, family, group, organization, or community may use to improve its well being in one or more of the following realms: emotional, intellectual, interpersonal/social, physical, political.

it will fit well into the Impact Publishers catalog of books.

it will honor the principles set forth in the Universal Declaration of Human Rights (although it need not be a work devoted to human rights per se).

it will be written in non-academic readable style. We're fond of the saying "The language of truth is unadorned, and always simple."

it will be written by person(s) whom we believe to be qualified to speak with authority on the subject.

it will be more likely to present an integrative perspective than one

which reflects a single school of thought regarding human behavior.

it will be marketable within our means. We have an assertive and effective marketing program which emphasizes publicity, direct mail, limited advertising, and energetic author activity. We do not send authors on extensive personal appearance tours.

it will have promise of selling enough copies -- at a fair price -- to pay its own way.

About "The Practical Therapist Series™"

For more than a quarter century, Impact Publishers has produced a quality line of popular psychology/self-help books and audiotapes. All of our materials are written by qualified professionals in the human services -- the population which has always been our strongest core of support.

In 1998 Impact launched a new line of select books for practicing professionals themselves. Each book in "The Practical Therapist Series™" will reflect a strong combination of the following characteristics: The Practical Therapist Series™" will reflect a strong combination of the following characteristics:

significant and timely topic in psychotherapy (issue, procedure, approach)

innovative concept, procedures, presentation

integrative -- rather than ideological -- approach

addressed to practicing professionals

(may also be appropriate for advanced graduate students)

specific therapeutic procedures

plain language style (technical terms as needed)

plentiful case examples

empirical research foundation

complete literature citations

experienced professional psychotherapist author(s)

theoretical assumptions identified

200-250 manuscript pages (75,000-100,000 words)

(Please do not send entire manuscripts via email, unless specifically requested to do so; a brief proposal is usually sufficient.)

Categories: Nonfiction—Careers—Family—Marriage—Parenting—Psychology—Relationships—Self Help—Senior Citizen—Women's Issues—Human Services—Divorce

CONTACT: Acquisitions Editor
Material: All
PO Box 6016
Atascadero CA 93423
Phone: 805-466-5917
Fax: 805-466-5919
E-mail: info@impactpublishers.com
Website: www.impactpublishers.com

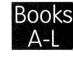

In Print Publishing

In Print publishes nonfiction books for a general sophisticated audience.

In these most difficult times of change the manuscript must be able to leave a reader with a positive message of HOPE or have impact for timely issues.

In Print does consider some metaphysical books but we will not consider any personal journey to awakening or any channeled material. Our editorial staff will only consider how-to books and other general manuscripts in the metaphysical genre.

At the present time there is no reading fee.

Submit letters of query or submissions with synopsis, three chapters and a bio of the author. In Print will respond in eight to ten weeks.

I wish you every bit of success in finding a publisher for your work.

Sincerely,

Tomi Keitlen, Publisher

Categories: Book Reviews—Disabilities—Ecology—Education—Entertainment—Environment—General Interest—Inspirational—

Law—Literature—Native Americans—New Age—Occult—Politics—Psychology—Reference—Spiritual

CONTACT: Tomi Keitlen, Publisher
Material: General Interest - Eclectic
PO Box 20765
Sedona AZ 86341
Phone: 928-284-5298
Fax: 928-284-5283
E-mail: inprintpub.@aol.com

Incentive Publications, Inc.

Manuscripts
Incentive Publications, Inc. publishes middle school reproducible resources and teaching strategy books for all levels. We publish no fiction or nonfiction storybooks.

If you have a manuscript that you think would be suitable for our needs, you may send: a letter of introduction; a table of contents; a sample chapter; and a self-addressed stamped envelope. If you would like your materials returned to you, please include an envelope large enough to hold the materials and with sufficient return postage. We make every effort to reply within 6–8 weeks.

Categories: Nonfiction—Children—Education

CONTACT: Jill Norris, Director of Development and Production
Material: All Manuscripts
CONTACT: Art Department
Material: Art Samples
2400 Crestmoor Road, Suite 211
Nashville TN 37215-2532
Phone: 615-385-2934
E-mail: jilln@incentivepublications.com
Website: www.incentivepublications.com

Intercontinental Publishing
New Amsterdam Publishing

In order to be considered, please submit the following:
1. Synopsis (about 2 pages maximum) of your book.
2. At least one (1), but no more than 3 sample chapters.

Additional suggestions:
Additional material may, or may not be requested, but final manuscript should be on disk in either WordPerfect 5.1 or ASCII. Text should contain no codes other than Tab [TAB], Underline [UND][und] to indicate italics and [RETURN]. Do not load any (unnecessary) parameters at beginning of manuscript, or repeat a lot of "macros" throughout text. Do not paginate, and do NOT add "headers" and/or "footers."

Material should be original and above all, should be entertaining. Use proper English and grammar. Do not use slang, vulgarisms or contractions (I'll, you'd, we're, etc.) in narrative and/or descriptive text unless book is written in the first person.

For spoken text (i.e. text within quotation marks ("/") almost anything goes, but Publisher frowns on the gratuitous use of vulgarisms, unless it is clearly a characteristic of the person (or character) speaking (being quoted).

We (me, myself and I) are a very small publisher and we will respond to all inquiries as soon as possible, but are not bound by a specific time frame. We only publish books in the spring of each year, therefore only submissions made (and accepted) before the 4th of July, will be published the next spring.

Our books are manufactured in the United States.

Thank You and Good Luck!
Categories: Fiction—Mystery

CONTACT: H. G. Smittenaar, Publisher

Material: All
11681 Bacon Race Rd.
Woodbridge VA 22192
Phone: 703-583-4800
Fax: 703-670-7825
E-mail: icpub@worldnet.att.net

Intercultural Press

Submitting a Proposal for Publication
Intercultural Press welcomes fresh ideas and new insights in the ways people live and work with each other across cultures. If you would like to submit a proposal for consideration, please follow the guidelines below.

Note that our review process may take several weeks, and we are not able to return your materials unless you send a self-addressed, stamped envelope for that purpose. Please do not send complete manuscripts.

Guidelines for a Book Proposal
The proposal is one of the most important parts of the publishing process, designed to clarify your thoughts and the viability of your project. We find the following key pieces of information helpful in making our publishing decisions. Please include:

Working title: Suggest a title that clearly expresses the essence of your work. Include possible alternatives as well.

Estimated length: Estimate the number of double-spaced pages, in your typewritten or word-processed manuscript.

Estimated delivery date and format

Synopsis: Provide a paragraph or two that describes the subject and overall content of the work.

Need: Explain what the work intends to do for the reader and how it will accomplish that goal.

Knowledge base: What unique features of the book contribute to the field? What new insights, models or research add to current thinking and practice?

Audience: Describe the primary and secondary audiences for the book. Is the project designed for consumers, travelers, trainers, students, educators, businesspeople, government agencies or NGO's? Is the audience global, North American? European? Regional?

Competing and related works: Please list the primary competition for your work and any titles that are similar to yours. What are the major differences? How is your work useful or authoritative?

Table of contents: Provide an outline of the contents with a sentence or two summarizing each chapter or section.

Sample chapters are helpful, but not essential at the proposal stage. A single chapter that is indicative of the content and shows your writing style is extremely useful in our decision process. Please, no complete manuscripts at this stage.

Author information: Your biography, vita or resume should include relevant professional experience and your qualifications for writing this book.

Marketing opportunities: How would you be able to promote your work: within your community or professional organization, through speaking engagements, through your own mailing lists and connections, at your training sessions? Publishing is a partnership, and we would like to understand your ability to help us market the book.

Other publishers: It is helpful to know if you have submitted this work to other publishers for consideration.

Topics of interest to Intercultural Press today

These are some, but not all, of the areas of interest to our readers: Intercultural communication, specific country and culture guides, organizational culture and diversity, diversity training, multicultural issues, intercultural training, business and culture, coaching and culture, international business-negotiation-mediation and conflict resolution, culture and counseling, culture and health care, culture and education, religion and culture, gender and culture, leadership across cultures, teams—virtual and real, across cultures.

You can get a good idea of our publishing program by viewing our complete catalogue at this website. Go to www.interculturalpress.com.

Categories: Nonfiction—African-American—Asian-American—Business—College—Culture—Education—Film/Video—Health—Multicultural—Religion—Textbooks

CONTACT: Judy Carl-Hendrick, Managing Editor
Material: All
Intercultural Press—A Nicholas Brealey Company
374 U.S. Rte. One
PO Box 700
Yarmouth, ME 04096
Phone: 866-372-2665 (toll free in U.S.), 207-846-5168
Fax: 207-846-5181
E-mail: judy@interculturalpress.com
Website: www.interculturalpress.com

Inner Traditions

Books on Eastern and Western philosophy, psychology, and metaphysics—particularly works that draw from the world's spiritual traditions.

In order to make the review process more efficient for prospective authors and for our editorial staff, we have prepared a list of requirements for authors and for our editorial staff, we have prepared a list of requirements for authors who are submitting work. Please include the following when presenting a proposal:

1. A BRIEF LETTER THAT INCLUDES A SHORT SYNOPSIS OF THE BOOK

a) The letter should be no more than two pages long and should tell how your manuscript contributes to its field and what make is unique.

b) As specifically as you can, tell us who the audience is for your book.

c) Give a brief biography of yourself, noting especially any specific qualifications for writing your subject.

2. A TABLE OF CONTENTS, INTRODUCTION, AND SAMPLE CHAPTER(S)

There is no need to send a complete manuscripts unless it is specifically asked for. Proposals including the above materials are reviewed much faster than thick manuscripts sent unsolicited.

3. WE CANNOT RETURN PROPOSALS OR MANUSCRIPTS UNLESS THEY ARE ACCOMPANIED BY A SELF-ADDRESSED ENVELOPE STAMPED WITH SUFFICIENT POSTAGE.

Some prospective authors write or e-mail a query letter before sending a proposal. This is a good idea and can save time and postage, especially when you are not familiar with the books we publish. A list of our seven imprints follows, please read these before sending us a query letter or proposal.

If you have questions that have not been addressed above regarding our submission guidelines, please DO NO call the acquisitions editor; send a query letter to our submissions department at the address listed below. Your query letter should provide enough information about your work that the acquisitions editor can make an informed decision and contact you for further details.

Categories: Nonfiction—Psychology—Religion—Eastern Philosophy— Metaphysics—World Spiritual Traditions

Contact: Submissions
Inner Traditions

PO Box 388
Rochester, VT 05767-0388 USA
Phone: 802-767-3174
Website: www.InnerTraditions.com

International Foundation of Employee Benefit Plans

The International Foundation Publications Department is looking for authors to write articles on the newest and most relevant employee benefits and compensation topics. We are looking for U.S. and Canadian articles on health care, pensions, retirement, and general benefits and compensation topics. If you would like to write an article for our publications, please see the following guidelines and suggested topics.

General Information

The guidelines are intended to make the writing process easier and more enjoyable for you. Please do not hesitate to call the Foundation editorial staff at any time. We're looking forward to working with you.

Articles covering new or developing topics are particularly appropriate. We welcome queries or outlines of proposed articles. The editors will respond promptly.

We assume all material submitted is the original work of the listed authors and has not been accepted for publication elsewhere. In the event of any potential conflict, it is the author's responsibility to notify the editor prior to publication. We will ask you to sign a copyright transfer agreement.

Article Length and Content

The recommended length for a printed article is 2,000 to 3,200 words. In addition, we are accepting longer, in-depth articles of more than 3,200 words. We will post these longer article on our Web site in a special online showcase called Web Exclusives. The full text of new articles, plus a permanent online archive of past articles, is available to all on the Foundation Web site at www.ifebp.org. Follow the article submission guidelines included in this flier.

Articles should be educational in nature. Pieces promoting a specific product, service or company will not be accepted.

You will be notified whether you article has been accepted within approximately two weeks.

How To Submit Your Ideas for Publication

1. Send your proposal

Please send proposals for both articles and books to the Publications Department. We make our initial decisions based on brief outlines. If you are interested in writing a book, please submit a one-to-four page typed outline. Indicate the nature and scope of each chapter as well as significant appendixes. Also tell us:

• Your proposed title
• Anticipated length of manuscript
• Titles of any previous books or articles
• Briefly why your treatment of the subject will be unique
• Briefly where/how you will collect and verify the factual information that you will be including
• Briefly why you are particularly qualified to write a book on this subject.

Be sure to include your complete address and telephone number.

2. What happens next?

You may anticipate our initial response to your proposal within one month. We will tell you if we feel that the proposed book is appropriate for our audience. If we are potentially interested in publishing the book, we will send you an autobiographical questionnaire that will help us in preparing future promotional material. At that time, we may request samples of your previous work.

Next, we will begin our formal review process. One step of the process is to submit the proposal to our Executive Committee for final approval. We will inform you of their decision as soon as possible after their review.

3. Sign a book agreement

Our basic agreement gives the author a standard royalty from our net receipts (after discounts and refunds) from all of our sales of the book. There is also a standard royalty paid for each copy of the work distributed without charge (excluding those distributed for advertising/promotional purposes and the copies provided to the author).

We will also require you to sign a copyright transfer agreement that will enable us to disseminate the work to the fullest extent.

4. What about the manuscript?

A completion date for the final version of your manuscript will be specified in your contract. Failure to meet this deadline could result in delays in publication or production.

Please submit your manuscript as a Word document. Charts and figures should be submited as tif, eps or jpg files.

After the book agreement has been signed, we will send a more detailed list of suggestions for submitting your manuscript.

5. Work with us

We will keep you informed of the schedule for publication of your book. An editor assigned to the project will keep you informed of our progress, give you suggestions for possible improvements, clear any major revisions with you, and seek your input for possible ideas for marketing and promotion of the book.

Learn about the Foundation

Since 1954 the International Foundation of Employee Benefit Plans has been recognized as the foremost educational association in the employee benefits field. The International Foundation is a nonprofit organization offering educational programs, publications, information services, and the Certified Employee Benefit Specialist (CEBS) Program.

The International Foundation continuously examines the latest issues and trends in the employee benefits field, and publishes in-depth reports, studies, survey results, periodicals and books for both the benefits professional and the general consumer.

Categories: Nonfiction—Associations—Business—Education

CONTACT: Dee Birschel, Senior Director of Publications
Material: All
18700 W Bluemound Rd
Brookfield WI 53045
Phone: 414-786-6710 option 4
Fax: 414-786-8780
E-mail: books@ifebp.org
Website: www.ifebp.org

International Marine

Thank you for requesting manuscript guidelines for International Marine. Our slogan is "Books that take you off the beaten path."

We publish a variety of books on outdoor sports, recreation, and fitness in several categories. First, we are interested in beginning-to-intermediate level how-to manuscripts about non-competitive sports or fitness. This could include anything from archery to sport diving. We have a special interest in paddlesports, including sea kayaking, whitewater paddling, and canoeing.

We are also interested in big, serious reference books and small, gift books for outdoor enthusiasts, including adventure narratives.

To help your proposal move swiftly through our review process, please address your materials to Tristram Coburn, Acquisitions Editor, and include the following:

• Cover letter with your contact information (address, telephone and fax numbers, email address)

• Table of Contents with brief summaries of each chapter

• One or two sample chapters

• Sample photographs and/or illustrations if these are central to your proposal

• Competition analysis (a listing of similar books in print, copies of recent supporting magazine articles and newspaper clippings, etc.)

• A personal or professional biography or resume (if you feel it is relevant)

• A self-addressed stamped envelope (if you want your materials returned)

Please anticipate a four- to six-week waiting period for a response from us. Thanks again for your interest in Ragged Mountain Press. We look forward to receiving your proposal.

Categories: Nonfiction—Biography—Boating—History—Outdoors—Physical Fitness—Recreation—Reference—Sports/Recreation

CONTACT: Jonathan Eaton, Editorial Director
Material: All
CONTACT: Tristram Coburn, Acquisitions Editor
Material: All
The McGraw-Hill Companies
PO Box 220
Camden ME 04843-0220

Interweave Press
Craft Books

We at Interweave Press produce genuinely useful, informative, and aesthetically pleasing literature and related products that nurture and extend the special interests of our communities of readers. We specialize in books about handweaving, knitting, beading, handspinning, needlework, and traditional textile processes. Most of our publications have a strong emphasis on technique, including general information on how to make and do things. We publish about twenty books each year, selecting material that will instruct and inspire our readers and will not duplicate available material.

Our authors are very special to us. They tend to become friends and colleagues as we work together to produce a new book, and we do everything within our power to foster good communications and positive working relationships during this process.

We have prepared this booklet to answer some major questions that you might have as an author dealing with us. Included is information on proposal preparation and submission, general contractual terms, manuscript preparation, and the publication process. Throughout, we have tried to make clear how author and publisher interact during the joint venture of producing a book.

Of course, we cannot possibly anticipate everything. Do let us know if you have additional questions or problems that we have not addressed. We look forward to hearing from you.

—Betsy Armstrong, editorial director

SUBMITTING a PROPOSAL
Topic

A subject with which you are thoroughly familiar, perhaps through doing, teaching, or writing about, will naturally be easiest for you to develop into a book.

Of great interest to both readers and publishers will be new topics not currently in print, or a fresh approach to a particular subject. Give serious thought to the niche you hope to fill with your book. What unique contribution could your book make to the knitting, weaving, spinning, or general textile world?

When you are developing an idea for a book, be sure to research the existing literature. If, for instance, a successful inkle weaving book is currently on the market, there may not be room for another one, even if you could write about the subject better.

Keep your audience in mind. For whom are you writing? Readers at different levels of expertise will require different approaches as well as different amounts and types of information. A very narrow topic likely will have a restricted audience; a broader subject may draw a larger, less homogeneous readership.

When and What to Submit

It is perfectly acceptable to approach us with the germ of an idea. A brief statement of your intent and an outline of the information you would like to cover will give us enough common ground to begin a dialogue about the possibilities for publication, and can save both you and us time if your idea is clearly not one we can use.

However, we cannot make a definite commitment to publish a manuscript until we have seen a fairly comprehensive proposal. It should include:

• Detailed outline
• Introduction
• Sample chapter or two
• Examples of illustrative material (to show both content and technical quality of photos and drawings, if applicable.)
• Estimated number of manuscript pages and illustrations

A cover letter summarizing why you think this book should be published can be very helpful. Put yourself in our shoes, and muster facts to convince us that your idea meets our criteria for publication.

Publisher's Considerations

First, we look at the concept of the book. Does it fit within the general area of textile related information which is the specialty of Interweave Press? Does it complement our current roster of books? Is the subject matter fresh, and not currently available in print? Is the approach to the topic positive and encouraging?

Further, what is the potential audience for this topic? Will enough people be interested in buying a book on this subject to make publishing it feasible? Are any other books currently available on similar topics which afford significant potential competition for this audience?

We must also take into account the quality of writing and illustrations submitted in a proposal. Even the best ideas may never find an audience if they are not well expressed. Not only words and pictures but also general organization are important here. Even if we like an idea very much we can not undertake projects that will require major rewriting. We can sometimes provide illustrations and photographs.

Finally, what would be the estimated production costs? Would they allow a reasonable return on our investment at a reasonable retail price for the volume?

As you can see, many of these factors have nothing to do with your particular manuscript. Keep in mind that even if Interweave Press cannot publish your work at this time, it may be appropriate for another publisher or for self-publication.

Response Time

Responses to book proposals may take several months. Don't expect quick decisions from any publisher, large or small. Manuscripts are often read by several editors who then engage in a wide-ranging discussion of world affairs and the effect of your proposed book on the twenty-first century before a decision is reached. Putting out a book represents a very large investment of time, money, and personal energy on the part of both author and publisher—so commitments cannot be made hastily.

If you'd like to know what's happening, you may follow your proposal with a letter or phone call inquiring about its status. Please wait at least a month before doing this, and have patience as we thoroughly evaluate your material.

THE CONTRACT

Timing

As publisher, we generally would offer a contract to you, as author, at whatever time we feel you have created a marketable product with which we can work. Both author and publisher must also be comfortable with setting schedules for manuscript delivery and publication before a contract can be written. If you have a proven track record, we might write a contract at the outline stage; if not, we might take this step after the complete manuscript is submitted.

Terms

Our standard contract provides a negotiated royalty based on the amount received by the publisher less returns. Royalties are paid semiannually.

An advance against future earned royalties can be negotiated to help an author cover up-front costs, such as photography, illustrations, supplies, etc. Advances from Interweave Press usually fall within the range of $500-$1,500.

Sometimes Interweave Press handles color photography, or all photography and/or illustrations. Once you have a contract in hand, please read its terms carefully, and don't hesitate to ask questions or get a legal opinion on it. Note the author's responsibility in the matter of obtaining permission to use copyrighted material from other sources. If you are quoting extensively from other material, modeling illustrative material after the work of others, or using someone else's photography, you must obtain written permission from the copyright holder and give appropriate credit.

After the book is published the author receives ten courtesy copies; additional copies can be purchased at our standard retail discount schedule. However, authors should not expect resale privileges except in special cases in agreement; Interweave Press is committed to supporting its existing retail dealers.

Manuscript Preparation

These guidelines for manuscript preparation have been devised to make life easier both for you, the author, and for the staff of Interweave Press. We hope that standardization of the format for manuscripts and accompanying illustrations will allow you to concentrate on words and pictures rather than on logistics. Editing, typesetting, layout, and associated duties all go more smoothly with such a format.

Included below is information pertaining to text, captions, photos, slides, drawings, drafts, projects, permissions and acknowledgments, bibliographies and references, indices, bibliographical material, and shipping. We hope we have covered everything that you will need to know, but if we have failed to anticipate your questions, please ask.

Text

Format. Interweave Press requires submitted material to be computer generated. Print a hard copy to include with the disk. Double-spaced on 8 1/2" x 11" white paper, one side only. Indent paragraphs. Include 2" margins at top and left side of each page and 1" margins on remaining sides. Set the line spacing for double-space—do not use hard returns at the end of each line. Do not right justify the lines. Use only one space after periods.

Please do not use erasable paper or onionskin. If necessary, a paragraph can be printed on an additional full-sized sheet, clearly marked, and clipped to the appropriate page.

Number all manuscript pages consecutively, including all front and back matter such as title, page, contents, bibliography, glossary, etc.

Put name, address, and telephone number at the top of page 1, and last name at top of all subsequent pages.

Headings. Type all headings flush left. Do not underline or type in all capitals. Indicate the comparative value of each heading by keying it with a number in pencil, in the left margin, as follows:

1-Major heading (chapter title)
2-Minor heading (sub-chapter)
3-Sub-heading

Make a hard return between sections.

Style, spelling, and measurements. Interweave Press uses Webster's New Collegiate Dictionary (and Webster's International Unabridged as necessary) or The American Heritage Dictionary for spelling and hyphenation, and the Chicago Manual of Style, in general, for style and grammar. At present, Interweave Press uses both English and metric units with English being dominant and metric following in parentheses.

In editing, we work to retain the author's own wording and individual style, but it is important that whatever style is used be consistent throughout the manuscript.

Please note that we work to make Interweave Press books approachable and readable, regardless of the subject. We strive for a friendly, reasonably informal style without passive verbs, tortuous pronouns, or outlandish prepositional constructions. We also ask you to eliminate any gender-specific pronouns which do not refer to individuals; use alternative sentence constructions instead.

Captions for Illustrations. Copy for captions should be typed separately from text, with color illustrations listed separately from other illustrations. Double space captions. Number caption pages consecutively (separately for each caption list). Do not attach captions to illustrations.

Number the illustrations and captions consecutively within each chapter. Prefix the illustration number with the caption number; for instance, the illustrations in Chapter 2 would be labeled 2-1, 2-2, 2-3, etc. If there are several parts to an illustration, label them a, b, c, etc.; for instance 2-1a, 2-1b, etc. Type the illustration number, followed by a period, before each caption.

Obtain permission from and give credit to all artists/craftspeople whose works are illustrated.

For each photo include the photographer's name, unless you give a blanket credit or acknowledgment at the beginning of the book. Examples: "Photo by John Jones", or "Photographer, Jane Smith".

Illustrations

Label all artwork with author's name, a number corresponding to the caption number, and an arrow indicating the top of the illustration. See below for specific directions on label placement.

If you have two illustrations of the same item and cannot decide between them, send both. Final choice can be based on page layout and actual size of the illustration in the book. If one or the other is your first choice, please indicate this.

Black-and-white halftones. Black-and-white photography should be submitted as 5" x 7" or 8" x 10" glossy prints. Include at least a 1/2" white margin for marking purposes. Do not crop or mount photos. If you want to indicate cropping, use tracing paper overlays. Do not send negatives.

Label all photos on the back. Do not press down heavily on the photo when labeling; use a felt-tipped marker or soft pencil, pressing lightly, or use previously marked adhesive labels.

Color illustrations. Color slides (35mm) or color transparencies (2 1/4" x 2 1/4" or larger) may be used for color illustrations. Except in special circumstances, these should be originals. Color prints are not useable. Transparencies are easily damaged—be careful not to scratch or soil them. Plastic pocket sheets will protect them in shipping and handling.

Label slides on their mounts, indicating viewing side and direction. It will also help us if you put your name and a brief identification of the subject on the slide.

Label transparencies by using adhesive labels on their protective envelopes. Do not handle transparencies any more than is absolutely necessary, and never write over them.

Line drawings. If possible, make drawings actual size or larger. Size reduction will hide flaws, while enlargement will exaggerate them. Line drawings should be rendered in India or similar black ink on heavy, smooth paper, with a separate sheet for each drawing. Protect them with tissue overlays; label them in pencil on the front.

Weaving drafts. Drafts will be typeset by Interweave Press. Write drafts clearly in dark ink on graph paper. Somewhere in your book, in text or appendix, clearly explain the format you have chosen for the drafts, then be consistent in using this format. For instance, HANDWOVEN magazine employs the following format: shaft numbers are used in the threading draft, which is at the bottom of the diagram; "O"s are used for the tie-up (indicating rising shed), which is at the bottom of the diagram; and slash marks are used for the treadling sequence (unless there are multiple repeats of that treadle in which case numbers are used, or multiple weft colors in which case symbols are used) which is above the tie-up. Threadings are to be read right to left; treadlings, bottom to top. If drawdowns are included, make completely black squares rather than using "X"s or other symbols, and note whether warp threads or weft threads are blackened.

Tables. Type tables or print very clearly in dark ink. Number tables separately within chapters (Table 2-1, Table 2-2, etc.). Include caption with each table. Consider placing large tables in appendices at the end of the manuscript. Use only one tab between column entries.

Tips on taking photographs. In general, photos and transparencies should be sharp and clear, with good contrast. If you are uncertain what film to use, check a photography book or consult your local photography shop. Indoor versus outdoor film or slow speed versus fast speed film are decisions you will have to make based on the conditions under which you will be working. (Slower speed films generally have finer grain structure, which produces better enlargements. This is particularly important when using 35mm film.)

Plain backgrounds are usually best, in a color which will set off the item being photographed. You should be careful to get a good value contrast (dark versus light) between the background and the item. This is especially important when you work in black-and-white. Watch out for small anomalous items such as electric light switches and cats, which you might not notice

until they magically appear in the processed photo!

Take care to avoid distracting shadows on the surface of the item. When photographing outside on a sunny day, a good placement of the item would be completely within the shadow of a building. Inside, position your lighting to eliminate or substantially reduce shadow. An exception would be if you want to highlight the texture of a fabric; side-lighting can help to bring it into prominence.

Generally, smaller apertures (higher f-stops) with correspondingly longer exposure times will give better depth of field. In photographing textiles, this can help bring out their texture. Of course, good depth of field is particularly important for three-dimensional pieces.

Particularly when shooting at slower speeds, set your camera on a tripod or solid object and use a cable release.

Film is relatively inexpensive compared to time wasted by having to retake botched photos. To be sure you get the right exposure, take at least three shots of a given item, including one "correct" exposure, one overexposed by an f-stop, and one underexposed by an f-stop. Consider photographing the item in several different positions or settings, so that you can choose the best one. (Note that you do not have to make full-size prints from all your negatives. Even if you are not doing your own darkroom work you can request that a "contact sheet" of negatives be printed without enlargement. From this, you can choose the best negatives for full-sized prints—or we can.)

Last, and perhaps most important, unless you have a good deal of experience, consider using a professional photographer. Authors who have done so have frequently found it to be a good investment in the quality of the final product. It's important to realize that photographers can only *lose* quality in the printing process.

Permissions and Acknowledgments

It will be necessary for you to obtain written permission from the owners of items illustrated in your book. (Specify that they are giving rights only for photographic reproduction of their work). Written permission from the copyright owner is also required for the use of written material or illustrations from a copyrighted work. In addition, you will need to obtain written releases from people (such as models) who appear in photographs.

A simple form can be used for this purpose, for example:

The undersigned authorizes Interweave Press, 201 East Fourth Street, Loveland, Colorado 80537 to include the following material in any and all editions of the forthcoming book tentatively entitled:

_____

by _____, to be published _____
Description(s):
Signature_____Date_____
Authority of Signator (author, owner, etc.) _____

Credits for permission to use material may appear in an "acknowledgments" section. Photographic and artistic credits related to items in photographs should be included in captions.

Bibliographic and References

A "Selected Bibliography" includes only articles and books directly referred to in your manuscript; a more general bibliography may include all titles which may help the reader pursue your topic further. You may or many not choose to categorize or annotate the entries.

Double-space the bibliography, indenting every line after the first entry. Arrange entries alphabetically by author. If entries are categorized, follow the same format for these section headings as for sub-chapter headings.

For each entry include author, title, place of publication and publisher (in the case of books), or magazine title, and publication date. Italicize titles of books and magazines; put titles of articles in quotation marks. Be consistent in the format you choose. Here are two examples of a possible format, one for a book or pamphlet and the other for a magazine article:

Collingwood, Peter, The Techniques of Rug Weaving. New York: Watson-Guptill, 1969.

Scorgie, Jean. "A Double Weave Jacket," Handwoven IV: 4:48-49 (September-October 1983).

Except in special circumstances (such as scholarly works incorporating significant book research), do not use footnotes or numbered references.

Publication usually can be cited by author within the text, avoiding the need for an additional formal system. If you do need to set up a formal reference system, choose a format and be consistent throughout the book.

Index

Indexing may be done by either the author or the publisher; this is a negotiable task. Though it may seem a daunting undertaking, indexing may be accomplished in a relatively straightforward manner.

One method is to go through the book page by page, noting key words and writing each one on a file card. Then the cards can be alphabetized and further annotated with page numbers on which these words appear. If you use a word processing program, you can key in the words with the page numbers, then sort alphabetically, and fine tune. Several decisions do have to be made; for instance, what level of detail to include (e.g., just "warping," or "warping—front to back," "warping—back to front," "warping—sectional beam," etc.), and what words are truly key (e.g. "herringbone twill" versus "twill, herringbone"). When in doubt, think of what would help you if you were looking up a topic in this book. Indexing is best done working with page proofs (see below, "The Publication Process").

Biographical Information

For the book jacket or cover, for marketing, and for Library of Congress cataloging, we will need a brief biographical sketch and a color photo of you, the author. A form will be provided with the contract. You may use other materials you have already prepared instead, if they cover the same territory.

You may send your photo(s) along with the completed manuscript.

Shipping

Be sure to keep a copy of your manuscript, including illustrations if possible.

With your manuscript, please include a summary count of all illustrations enclosed, listing black-and-white photographs, color transparencies, and line drawings and diagrams separately. All illustrations will be returned to you after your book has been published. (This will probably be around nine months to a year after submission of the completed manuscript.)

To forestall damage or loss in the mail, wrap everything very securely (include stiffening to keep the photographs from being creased) and send it Registered or Certified mail, UPS, or Federal Express.

Categories: Nonfiction—Crafts/Hobbies

CONTACT: Submissions Editor
Material: All
201 E. Fourth St.
Loveland, CO 80537
Phone: 970-669-7672
Website: www.interweave.com

Iron Horse Free Press

Formal guidelines not available.
Send queries or book proposals to below address.
Categories: Nonfiction—Biography—History

CONTACT: George R. Dreher, Publisher
Material: All
PO Box 10746
Midland TX 79702
Phone: 915-686-0397
Fax: 915-570-0397
E-mail: ihfp@aol.com
Website: www.georgedreher.com/Book_Publisher.html

Island Press

THE FOLLOWING INFORMATION will help both first-time and seasoned authors understand how Island Press's publishing process works. Please read it carefully, and remember that your editor is always available for questions.

Submitting Your Idea

Island Press will be happy to consider a book at any stage of development. The earlier in the writing process we receive your proposal, the more in-depth market research we can perform and the better able we are to guide you so that your manuscript addresses the major concerns of potential readers.

In order to consider a proposal, we should have the following:

A detailed table of contents with a brief paragraph or annotation describing the topics that will be covered in each chapter.

Two sample chapters. Please be sure that your sample chapters are as typical of your writing as possible. If illustrations, graphs, or charts are important elements of your manuscript, you should provide samples of those as well. Chapters must be typed double-spaced with one-inch margins on all sides.

A detailed curriculum vitae or resume of the author(s). If you are proposing a contributed volume, please include resumes or, at least, full identifications for all chapter authors.

A prospectus. The prospectus for the book gives you a chance to explain why you are writing your book, and for whom. It explains the logic behind the project: what need the book will address, and why it should be published. It enables you to communicate the goals and function of the book to the acquisitions editor, who can then make an informed decision on how the project is to progress.

The Prospectus

The following section lists questions that your prospectus should answer:

THESE QUESTIONS are intended to help you write a prospectus that will help us make a publishing decision. Please answer all questions that apply to your book and provide any additional information that will help us in our evaluation.

• Describe the contents of the book. What is its thesis? What do you hope to accomplish in writing this book? What need does it fill? (Be very specific on this point.) Why is the subject important?

• How would you characterize the book? Is it policy analysis or practical how-to information? • • • Does it develop a theory? Is it a practical tool that professionals will use? Does it shed new light on current controversies? Does it provide historical or analytical information? On what level is it written? Does the reader require specialized knowledge to understand it? What is unique about this book?

• Who is your audience? Be as specific as possible and identify both primary and secondary markets. For professional audiences, please give job titles (city planners, wetland managers, for example). Is the book likely to be used as a primary or supplemental text for college courses? If so, please provide course titles for which it would be appropriate. (If you know how many such courses are taught nationally or how many students they involve, please include that information.) If you think it will be of interest to citizen activists, list names of organizations and membership numbers. Also provide names of newsletters or other publications that reach that audience. Are there any other groups or associations that may have a particular interest in this book? If you know of possibilities for bulk sales, through organizations or conferences, include that information.

• What topics does your book cover? Are there any topics that have not been covered before?

If you are proposing a contributed volume, please discuss the origin of the project (is it based on a conference, for example?), how much (if any) of the material has been previously published, and what you as editor plan to do to make the book cohere. How will you work with the contributors? Will the contributors see other chapters? How much editing and/or rewriting will you do? What level of consistency of style and quality do you plan to achieve?

What other books have been published on this subject? (Include author, publisher, and date of publication.) What are their strengths and weaknesses? How will your book differ in organization, level, approach, and content? How will your book relate to other books in the field?

• What is the approximate length of the final typed manuscript? Assume 8-1/2-x-11 double-spaced pages with one-inch margins.

• *What elements will the manuscript include:* charts, graphs, tables,

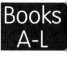

Books A-L

photographs, glossary, index, bibliography, and so on? Please be as specific as possible.

• Do you have any particular conception of the production, design, or marketing of the manuscript that we should know about?

• Has your proposal (or manuscript) been read by anyone else whose opinions would be of value to us? Can you suggest the names of three persons who would be competent to read and review your proposal or manuscript?

• When will the manuscript be complete?

Manuscript Development

MANUSCRIPT DEVELOPMENT encompasses the period of writing, reviewing, and rewriting necessary to ensure a well-organized, complete work that is attuned to the needs of its potential audience.

All proposals and manuscripts are carefully reviewed in-house. In addition, when appropriate, manuscripts are sent to several experts in the field. Reviews are conducted for two reasons. First, they help us ensure that the book offers the most complete, well-argued, and current information on the subject. Second, comments, suggestions, and quotations from the reviewers are used by our marketing department to help reach the greatest number of readers possible. In today's highly competitive marketplace, we realize that only a thoughtfully developed book can reach the highest level of success.

Expert reviewers are asked to critique the style, level of writing, organization, comprehensiveness, accuracy, and structure of the text. They evaluate the author's development of his or her argument and the thoroughness of the research. They are asked to cite strengths and weaknesses of the material and to offer suggestions for changes. They comment on the possible audiences for the book and how the book might best meet the needs of those audiences. Those comments are used to guide the authors in manuscript revision. The reviewers' comments help us to determine whether the manuscript requires further work or if it is in acceptable final form, as discussed in the publishing agreement.

We realize that if you are preparing your manuscript in collaboration with an organization you may be conducting your own reviews. In that case, we ask that you send us the names and addresses of reviewers, as well as copies of relevant correspondence. That information will help us in our marketing efforts as well as editorially.

Throughout the review process, our common goal is kept foremost in mind: to develop a book that meets the needs of its audience with cogent, well-presented information that will make a contribution to the environmental literature.

Production

ONCE YOUR EDITOR has an acceptable draft of the manuscript that includes all elements of the book-artwork, glossaries, introduction-it is ready to go into production. The production process and schedule vary for each book, depending on the format, number of pages, illustrations, complexity, and other considerations. What follows is a brief overview of the process.

Copyediting is the first step in the production process. The copyeditor edits the manuscript for grammar, typographical errors, style, consistency, and punctuation, and "marks up" the manuscript for the typesetter. The copyeditor will frequently raise questions regarding ambiguities in content, will point out or clear up discrepancies, and will make minor revisions as necessary.

You will see the copyedited manuscript for your final approval before it is typeset. We want you to review the entire copyedited manuscript to ensure that your meaning has not been inadvertently altered in the copyediting process. This is your last opportunity to make corrections.

The internal text and cover design of the book are done by professional designers who consider all elements of the text and illustrations, as well as the purpose and market of the book. The design process includes input from the editorial, production, and marketing staff.

After copyediting and design are completed, the book goes to the typesetter. The first set of proofs, either galleys or page proofs, will go to you for review, and although a copy will also be sent to a professional proofreader, you are expected to ensure the accuracy of the proofs.

Preparing Your Manuscript

ISLAND PRESS requires that final manuscripts be submitted in duplicate, accompanied by a disk of the same material. All text, including references and extracts, should be double-spaced, and paragraphs should be indented, with no extra lines of space between them. Pages must be numbered consecutively from the first page to the last. If you cannot provide a disk, Island Press can still produce your book, but your editor should be made aware that you will not submit a disk. More-detailed instructions on how to prepare your disk, organize art material, and secure permission to use previously published material can be provided by Island Press staff.

Marketing

AT ISLAND PRESS, we realize that producing a high-quality book is only the first part of a successful publication. Without proper marketing, even the best work in the field may go unnoticed.

We also recognize that you, as an expert in your field, can contribute to the marketing effort, and we encourage you to do so. Your suggestions and advice will be carefully considered, for we share the goal of reaching the largest market for your book.

Once your proposal has been accepted for publication, you will be asked to fill out an author information sheet that will help the marketing department begin its marketing plan. The information you provide will be used throughout the marketing effort.

Our individually tailored marketing plan is designed to capitalize on the strengths and uniqueness of each book and its intended market. Your editor will work closely with the marketing department to provide information and suggestions. Because we have positioned ourselves as the publisher of books for the environmental community, we have a specialized and in-depth understanding of the market for your book.

Our marketing program employs several different strategies in order to ensure that the information we develop and distribute is available to the interdisciplinary and disparate audiences that are working to solve our myriad environmental problems.

Direct mail, especially the Annual Environmental Sourcebook, is the principal marketing mechanism for our books and those of other nonprofit organizations whose work we distribute. The Sourcebook is a unique resource, distributed biannually to more than 150,000 federal, state, and local public officials, businesses, libraries, organizations, community leaders, colleges, and universities. Since 1985 we have marketed and distributed more than 150 titles published by 60 conservation and environmental organizations. The Island Press Sourcebook offers a selection of books available nowhere else. Publishers whose books are represented include nonprofit policy and research organizations, university presses, and commercial and professional publishing houses. The subjects covered include toxics, water, federal lands, wildlife, forestry, tropical forests, agriculture, community issues, business and the environment, population, and sustainable development. The books are used as manuals for citizen action, for technical training in college classrooms, for congressional and corporate offices, for environmental professionals, and for libraries. Books are selected by our editorial and marketing staff, taking into account recommendations of our Editorial Advisory Committee and other key individuals and organizations in the environmental community. The same criteria that we use to evaluate manuscripts submbitted to Island Press for publication are applied to our "client line" titles.

Our direct-mail program includes not only the Sourcebook, but other targeted direct-mail pieces about books that would be of interest to particular audiences. The direct-mail program ensures that Island Press books reach key groups of environmental professionals, planners, and state and local officials.

Journals and magazines are important marketing vehicles for Island Press books. Not only do we place advertising in specialized magazines and journals, but also our books are widely reviewed. Reviews are a major source of information on these books to key audiences. In our books are widely reviewed. Reviews are a major last two years, Island Press books have been reviewed in every major environmental periodical, and in many of the most important environmental newspapers and magazines. Reviews in Choice, Publishers Weekly, The New York Times, Library Journal, The Washington Post, Science News, Booklist, E Magazine, Environment, Garbage, Sierra, and others, including the more technical environmental periodicals, ensure that professors, professionals, librarians, and the public are made aware of Island Press books.

Course adoption. Special direct-mail promotions to professors have been extremely successful for Island Press. This is a crucial market for us because it means our information is being used for two critical purposes: to train the environmental professionals and public policymakers of the future, and to assist in current research and policy analysis.

Bookstores. Since 1988 our sales to bookstores have steadily increased, reflecting the growing interest among the general public in environmental issues. In 1989 we contracted with twenty-eight regional sales representatives; the result is that Island Press books are now marketed to bookstores throughout the United States, giving us the capacity to reach concerned citizens throughout the country.

Conference exhibitions. Our editorial and marketing staffs exhibit at professional conferences such as the North American Wildlife and Natural Resources Conference and the annual meetings of the American Institute of Biological Sciences, the American Association for the Advancement of Sciences, the American Planning Association, and the Society for Ecological Restoration. This is one of the most productive methods of introducing new titles to targeted groups of faculty and professionals.

Bulk sales. Selling books to organizations for distribution to their membership is an important channel of distribution for Island Press books. This is an effective way to reach key market segments efficiently and quickly.

Publicity and promotion. In addition to providing our authors with materials for speaking engagements, we conduct publicity campaigns to generate media coverage such as interviews on radio and television, articles in magazines and newspapers, and coverage by organizational newsletters. For selected books, we also arrange bookstore appearances by authors.

Categories: Nonfiction—Agriculture—Conservation—Ecology—Environment—Science

CONTACT: Acquisitions Editor
Material: All
1718 Connecticut Ave., N.W., Ste. 300
Washington, DC 20009-1148
Phone: 202-232-7933
Fax: 202-234-1328
E-mail: info@islandpress.org
Website: www.islandpress.org

Ivan R. Dee, Inc., Publisher

If you wish to inquire about our interest in a book manuscript you have prepared or are preparing, please send a query letter along with a brief description of the work, if possible a listing of contents or chapters, and at least two sample chapters. If you simply have an idea for a book, write us about it in detail.

Ordinarily you will hear from us within thirty days–sooner if the manuscript is clearly not for us, occasionally later if the work presents a difficult publishing decision.

We are publishers of serious nonfiction, in both hardcover and paperback, in history, politics, literature, biography, and theatre.

Categories: Nonfiction—Biography—History—Literature—Politics—Theatre

CONTACT: Ivan R. Dee, President
Material: All
1332 N. Halsted St.

Chicago IL 60622
Phone: 312-787-6262
Fax: 312-787-6269

Jewish Lights Publishing

Guidelines for Manuscript Submissions

Jewish Lights publishes books for people of all faiths and all backgrounds. Our authors are at the forefront of spiritual thought. They draw on the Jewish wisdom tradition to deal with the quest for the self and for finding meaning in life. Our books are non-fiction almost exclusively, covering topics including religion, Jewish life cycle, theology, philosophy, history, and spirituality. We do not publish biography, haggadot, or poetry. At this point we plan to do only two books for children annually.

Because of the tremendous number of manuscript submissions we receive, we cannot correspond individually with authors until we receive a proposal of what they would like to submit for publication.

A proposal includes:
• A cover letter
• A table of contents
• The introduction to the book
• Two sample chapters (do not send the entire book)

A self-addressed stamped envelope if the material is to be returned to the author. (Please note that without a self-addressed stamped envelope, your material will not be returned.)

If your project is a short (under 40 pages) children's picture book, you should send the entire text.

Send the material (on paper, no computer disks and no e-mail please) to the Submissions Editor at Jewish Lights at Sunset Farm Offices, Route 4, P.O. Box 237, Woodstock, Vermont 05091. Please note that we cannot accept submissions via the internet.

After sending your material, please allow approximately three months for a reply. We are very sorry that this process is slow, but it is the only way we can that all material receives proper consideration.

Thank you for considering Jewish Lights Publishing.

Categories: Nonfiction—Biography—Cooking—Crafts/Hobbies—Culture—Ecology—Family—History—Inspirational—Jewish Interest—Parenting—Religion—Spiritual—Travel—Women's Issues—Children's Picture Books—Healing/Recovery—Life Cycle—Mysticism—Philosophy—Theology

CONTACT: Submissions Editor
Material: All
Sunset Farm Offices, Route 4
PO Box 237
Woodstock VT 05091
Phone: 802-457-4000
Fax: 802-457-4004
E-mail: everyone@longhillpartners.com

JIST Works

Book Proposal Guidelines

Thank you for your interest in being a JIST author. We are proud of our hundreds of products that help people help themselves find good jobs and make their lives better. If you have an idea for a book that fits with JIST's core values and markets, we will be glad to review it for possible publication. To give your proposal the best chance of being selected for publication, please make sure that it includes everything we need to determine whether your book is right for JIST.

Before You Send Your Proposal

Before sending your proposal, you need to do a little homework to make sure your book is right for us and that we completely understand what your book is about, who it is for, and how it will sell.

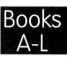
Books A-L

Familiarize yourself with JIST. Browse our Web site at www.JIST.com or request a catalog. Look at the types of books we publish and the subjects we cover. We are currently publishing books and other media (videos, software, assessment inventories, workbooks, and instructors' guides) on job search and careers. We are especially interested in products that appeal to institutional markets such as schools, colleges and universities, government agencies, and workforce-development programs. We occasionally publish books on education and training, as well as business topics; however, career and job search books get top consideration. Your book must fit our niche but not compete directly with any of our current products.

Research the competition. Go to bookstores or Amazon.com and see what other books have already been published on the subject. Think of how your book is different and better than existing books. Does it approach the subject from a different angle, include new coverage of the topic, or have some other element that will be irresistible to buyers?

Research the audience and market. Know who your book is for and how a publisher can best make these people aware of your book so that they will buy it.

Compile your formal book proposal. Put together all the items that we will need to determine whether will publish your book. See the next section for details.

Please don't call! We regret that the volume of submissions prevents us from discussing proposals over the telephone.

What Your Proposal Must Include

Your proposal should be clear and concise. It should be three to seven pages in length, not including the sample chapters and your resume or CV. Crucial elements to include are the following:

Working Title

What title do you propose for this book? Please include your first choice as well as a few alternatives. List the keywords that the title should definitely include—words that convey the essence of the book and appeal to the target audience.

Summary

Answer as many of the following questions as possible:
• In a nutshell, what is the book about?
• What led you to write it?
• What need does the book fill? What problems does it solve? Why is the information important?
• How is the topic increasing in importance rather than declining?
• How do you envision the finished product? What are its dimensions, page count, and other physical specifics? Does it include charts, worksheets, illustrations, or other special features?

Target Audience

Who is going to buy your book? Provide demographic information for your target audience, such as:
• Age
• Reading level
• Gender (if applicable)
• Education level
• Place in career (entry level, mid-career, advanced)
• Vocation or industry (blue collar, professional, clerical, etc.)
• Specific fields (medical, legal, computers, teachers, etc.)
• What magazines or professional journals do they read?
• What associations do they belong to and what conferences do they attend?

Target Markets

Besides bookstores, where is this book going to sell? Identify institutions and organizations that are likely to purchase the book. Identify the primary market and at least two secondary markets.

Competitive Analysis

Determine which existing books are the most similar to your proposed

> **Remember: Editors change jobs and publishers change addresses. It is wise to invest in a phone call for the current information before submitting.**

book in terms of audience, scope, and coverage. List the top 5 or more most relevant competing books and include the following information for each:
• Book title
• Year published
• Publisher
• Page count
• Price
• Trim size (6 x 9, 8½ x 11, etc.)
• Amazon.com sales ranking
• How your book is different and better than each book

Sales and Marketing Analysis

• Research the potential market for your book and give facts and figures that support the notion that significant numbers of people will buy it.
• Are there factors, such as government spending, that will affect the demand for information in this area?
• Demonstrate your ability and willingness to help promote and sell the book after it is published. Suggest ways that your publisher can partner with you to market and sell the book.
• If you have contacts within companies or organizations that would be interested in buying the book in quantity, describe them here.
• If you have previously published other books, please provide sales figures for them.

Outline

Include a full, detailed outline of the topics that your book will cover. The outline should include chapter titles, chapter subtopics, and synopses of what each chapter covers.

Sample Chapters

Include the book's Introduction, which should explain the questions the book addresses and what answers it gives. Also send at least one full chapter (preferably not the first chapter) that is representative of your writing and organizational skills as well as your knowledge of the subject.

Your Bio and Qualifications as an Author

Please send a copy of your current resume or CV. Include information on previous writing and publications you have done. Demonstrate why you are an authority on your subject and why you are the right person to write this book. Include any affiliations or associations you belong to that will enable you to help promote the book after it is published. Do you regularly speak to large audiences on topics related to your book's subject? Do you have access to specific, relevant mailing lists? Do you write a regular column for a newspaper or magazine? Are you an instructor who will use your own book as required reading in your classes?

Project Status

Is your book already written? If not, when do you expect to finish it? Have you proposed it to other publishers previously or simultaneously? Has it been previously published and the rights have reverted to you? What type of software are you using to prepare the manuscript?

Self-addressed, Stamped Envelope

If you would like your materials returned to you, please include a self-addressed, stamped envelope. Otherwise, they will be filed or discarded after a period of time.

Where to Send Your Proposal

We accept submissions through the mail and by e-mail.

Categories: Nonfiction—Business—Careers—Interview—Reference

CONTACT: Susan Pines, Associate Publisher
Material: All
8902 Otis Ave.
Indianapolis, IN 46216-1033
E-mail: spines@jist.com

J.N. Townsend Publishing

J. N. Townsend Publishing has been bringing you classic animal books since 1986. We will continue to bring out reprints of past classics, as well as occasional new books that catch our fancy and will delight our readers.

No formal guidelines available
Categories: Fiction—Nonfiction—Animals

CONTACT: Jeremy Townsend, Publisher
Material: All
4 Franklin St.
Exeter, NH 03833
Phone: 603-778-9883
Website: www.jntownsendpublishing.com

Jodere Group

Jodere Group was created as a unique publishing and multimedia avenue for individuals whose mission it is to positively impact the lives of others.

Jodere Group recognizes the strength of an original thought, a kind word and a selfless act — and the power of the individuals who possess them. Jodere Group is committed to providing the support, passion and creativity necessary for these individuals to achieve their goals and their dreams.

The Jodere Group is driven by our mission statement. If you and your book fall under the umbrella of our mission statement, then we would consider publishing you. Beyond that, we are looking for creative works that push the reader to explore new areas of life or of themselves. We don't shy away from controversy — so long as it serves a higher purpose. The Jodere Group team is happiest when our work provokes good conversation, stimulates thought and, ultimately, changes lives.

The best way to submit to us is by adhering to the following loose guidelines. We're only human, so queries that are thoughtful, well written, typed and proof read make a better impression. We want to know who you are, what you've done before, and what your project is about. In terms of length, we need enough detail to be interested, but it is not necessarily a bad thing to leave us wanting more.

A good guideline to follow is a cover letter, outline or brief synopsis of the work (with word count if possible), a sample chapter or two and a stamped, self-addressed envelope for our response. Please double-space.

Since we read all submissions, it does take us a little time to get back to you. We make every effort to respond no later than four weeks from receipt.

You're welcome to call and confirm that we've received your submission, but then if you could be patient we'll get back to you when we've had a chance to give it appropriate time and consideration.

If you include a SASE we will return your materials, however, we learned a long time ago not to assume responsibility for acts of God or the Post Office. If it doesn't make it back to you once it is mailed — we apologize.

We respect your work and would never deliberately lose or damage it.

We look forward to reading your work. Again, thank you for your consideration.

Categories: Nonfiction—Business—Children—Health—Inspirational—Psychology—Relationships—Self Help—Spiritual—Women's Issues

CONTACT: Submissions Editor
Material: All
PO Box 910147
San Diego CA 92191
Phone: 800-569-1002
Fax: 858-638-8170
E-mail: info@joderegroup.com

Website: www.jodere.com

John Daniel & Company
P U B L I S H E R S

John Daniel & Company

About the Press.
John Daniel and Company is a small press publisher of belles lettres. We publish only four titles a year, with print runs averaging 1,000-2,000. Our books are distributed to the trade by SCB Distributors. In addition to trade sales, we rely heavily on direct-mail sales from our website and from announcements we send out for each book we publish.

Editorial focus.
"Belles lettres" is a fuzzy term that allows us a lot of leeway, but it does exclude children's books, genre fiction, cookbooks, photography books, how-to books, and a number of other categories that are better published by the major-league publishing establishment. "Belles lettres," for us, means stylish and elegant writing; beyond that definition I should mention that we are particularly interested in essays, literary memoirs, and short fiction dealing with social issues. We publish only one poetry title a year. For economic reasons almost all our books are under 200 pages long.

Royalties.
We do not pay advances, and our royalties are based on 10 percent of the net receipts (cover price minus discount allowed to the customer).

Submission requirements.
To submit material, send synopsis plus 50 sample pages. Allow six to eight weeks for response. Manuscripts received without SASE will be discarded. We do not accept submissions in the form of disks, e-mail, fax, or phone calls.

Some free advice.
We receive over five thousand unsolicited manuscripts and query letters a year. We publish four manuscripts a year, of which fewer than half were received unsolicited. Obviously the odds are not with you. For this reason we encourage you to send out multiple submissions and we do not expect you to tie up your chances while waiting for our response.

Categories: Fiction—Nonfiction—Literature—Poetry—Short Stories—Essays—Memoir

CONTACT: John Daniel, Publisher
Material: All
PO Box 2790
McKinleyville, CA 95519
Phone: 707-839-3495
Fax: 707-839-3242
E-mail: dandd@danielpublishing.com
Website: www.danielpublishing.com

Johnston Associates International

JASI publishes nonfiction trade-format regional travel books. *The following guidelines are designed to assist you in submitting a book proposal:*

Submission Guidelines

Your proposal should consist of seven sections:

1. Important and unique features of the topic

Explain what your book is about and why it is needed. Also describe the unique features of your book and anything that makes it different from all other books of the same topic.

2. Market

Describe the audience for your book. Who are the most likely readers to buy your book? Why should they buy it, keep it or talk about it?

3. Competition

List the books that directly compete with the project you are proposing. How do they compare with your book subject in length, scope, format and visual appeal? Explain why they are not adequate to meet the need you have identified. If no such book is available for the market you're addressing, cite any books that seem even remotely comparable and explain the difference between your approach and theirs.

4. Outline or annotated table of contents

The outline of your book should be similar to a table of contents. It should include chapter titles and subheads, if any. For each chapter, include a paragraph of about 100 words summarizing the chapter's contents.

5. Publishing details

Give an estimate of how long your book will be. Do you plan to have photographs or illustrations? Maps? How many? How long will you need to complete the manuscript?

6. Author background

Please include a resume or information sheet detailing your background and areas of expertise and/or interest, including prior publications.

7. Promotion

How will you help promote your book? Do you have databases, lists of contacts?

Additional Tips

If you submit to other publishers simultaneously, please let us know.

Be sure to include phone and fax numbers and an e-mail address (if you have one) where you may be reached.

Allow 4 weeks for initial response.

Please include sample chapters. If you don't have these, the outline will suffice.

Thank you for thinking of JASI!

Categories: Nonfiction—Regional—Travel

CONTACT: Priscilla Johnston or Rebecca Johnston,, Publishers
Material: All
PO Box 313
Medina WA 98039
Phone: 425-454-3490
Fax: 425-462-1335
E-mail: JasiBooks@aol.com

Jona Books

GENERAL INFORMATION:

Submit an introductory letter, two sample chapters and synopsis for the rest of the book. All manuscripts should be on white paper and double-spaced. Please allow two months for a reply. Floppy or CD preferred.

- Queries/proposals — please allow two weeks for a reply.
- Simultaneous submissions are ok.
- Electronic queries accepted (please put Book Submission in subject line; attachments are in Microsoft Word).
- We publish 18 months after acceptance.

GENRE

Nonfiction:
- Biographies
- Native American history
- Old West
- True crime
- Military history
- Americana

Fiction:
- Alternate history
- Science Fiction
- Military Science fiction
- Historical fiction
- Humor

Payment:
- Negotiated on an individual basis with writer.
- No advance offered at this time.

Categories: Fiction—Nonfiction—Biography—History—Humor—Military—Science Fiction—True Crime—Western

CONTACT: Tim Baker, Senior Editor
Material: Queries
Po Box 336
Bedford IN 74721
Phone: 812-278-9512
Fax: 812-278-9518

Judson Press

Judson Press Guidelines for Unsolicited Book Proposals
First Things

Because the competition is so great, getting a book published is extremely difficult. Judson Press publishes only a very small percentage of books from the unsolicited proposals it receives. Thus it is important to consider carefully the elements that go into a successful book before submitting your proposal. For writers aspiring to publication, the primary ingredients for success are (1) content that is unique and compelling, (2) identification of an appropriate target market, and (3) high-quality writing that is inviting, well organized, and grammatically sound.

Content: Is It Unique and Compelling?

Do your research before submitting a proposal. It is your responsibility as writer to be aware of published resources related to the topic you have in mind and to ensure that the proposed book will be unique—substantially different from resources currently available—and compelling—offering some combination of information, analysis, perspective, or insight that a substantial number of readers will find valuable and to which they will be drawn.

Market: Who Is Your Target Audience?

Be clear about your target audience and become intimately familiar with the character traits, needs, and wants of the individuals who form that target market. Avoid an audience that is too broad by considering gender, age, race, profession, experience, special interest, and specific need. Too broad an audience suggests that you have not given sufficient consideration to the content or purpose of the book; too specific or narrow an audience limits the publisher's ability to promote and sell the project in sufficient quantities to warrant the expense of production. Keep both factors in mind as you consider who should or would buy your book.

Quality: How Well Do You Write?

Good writing involves strong organization, correct and coherent sentence structure, and a "voice" that is appropriate to the topic and audience. How you express your ideas is as important as the ideas themselves. Consider following these tips:

Ø **CREATE AN OUTLINE**, even if after the fact, to ensure a logical progression of concepts and to avoid redundancy

Ø **PROOFREAD YOUR WORK** because typos, grammatical errors, and spelling mistakes will be noticed and taken into consideration

Ø **CHOOSE A VOICE**, the perspective from which you will address your audience—formal or casual, "we" or "you," meditative or practical—and stick with it

All three of these elements are as important in the development of a proposal as they are in the writing of the actual book. If writing isn't your strong suit but you have something worth saying, consider partnering with a friend, colleague, or freelance editor who can help you.

Finding the Right Publisher

Successful publishers have developed specific "niches," or areas of specialty. These niches are based on such related factors as the content and style of books, as well as their target audience(s). It is your responsibility to research and identify the publisher(s) best suited for the book you have in mind.

Ø Consult publications as *The Writer's Market* and *Literary Marketplace*, both of which can be found in most public libraries

Ø Browse publishers' catalogs, either in printed form or online

Ø Visit local bookstores to determine which companies publish books similar to the one you have in mind

Ø **DO NOT** call publishers for this information

If you are submitting your book proposal to more than one publisher simultaneously, it is a professional courtesy to acknowledge that fact in your cover letter.

Judson's Publishing Niches

Judson Press is a Christian publishing house; all of our publications are explicitly Christian in content. Theologically, we hold a moderate position. Judson's primary areas of interest are:

Ø Practical resources for pastors, including preaching and program resources

Ø Practical resources for laity and lay leaders, including spiritual formation, discipleship, Christian education, evangelism, missions, leadership, Bible study, transformation and renewal, family ministry

Ø Resources for the African American church

Ø Baptist heritage and identity resources

Currently, Judson Press does NOT publish fiction, poetry, children's books, doctoral dissertations (in academic form), or personal memoirs, whether autobiographical or biographical.

Submitting a Book Proposal

Please **DO NOT** send a complete manuscript. As with most publishers, Judson Press prefers to receive a proposal that includes the following six elements:

1. WORKING TITLE—Choose a title and subtitle that convey the book's tone and essential content and that reflect careful consideration about the book's focus and target market. (Note: The final title for an accepted project will be determined by the publisher.)

2. SUMMARY AND TARGET AUDIENCE—Begin with two or three paragraphs summarizing the book's content and purposes, as well as a description of the book's intended readership.

3. MARKET ANALYSIS—Provide information on other books in print that relate to the proposed topic and that might compete with your project. How is your book distinctive? What makes it unique and compelling?

4. CHAPTER DESCRIPTIONS—Outline the book's proposed chapters, including a 2–3 sentence description of each chapter to demonstrate clear and logical organization and how the book will unfold.

4. SAMPLE CONTENT—Submit 20 to 30 pages of sample material from the proposed book, which typically means two or three sample chapters. This sample content will illustrate your writing style, skill, and the voice of

the book.

5. RÉSUMÉ OR CURRICULUM VITAE—Include any relevant qualifications (experiences, vocation, education, and publication history) for writing the proposed book.

Sample chapters should be double-spaced with 1-inch margins and in 12-point Times New Roman font. When writing your sample chapters, follow the general style established by *The Chicago Manual of Style, 15th edition*. You may send proposals via e-mail or in hard copy to the Acquisitions Editor at the addresses below. ***Please include a postage-paid envelope if you would like to have your materials returned to you.***

Categories: Nonfiction—African-American—Children—Christian Interests—Family—Inspirational—Multicultural—Religion—Senior Citizen—Spiritual—Women's Issues

CONTACT: Acquisitions Editor
Material: All
PO Box 851
Valley Forge PA 19482-0851
Phone: 610-768-2109
Fax: 610-768-2441
Website: www.judsonpress.com

Jupiter Scientific Publishing

Company Description

Jupiter Scientific is dedicated to the promotion of science and scientific education through books, the internet, and other means of communication.

Author Submissions

Jupiter Scientific Publishing will only consider non-fiction books of the highest scientific standards. No metaphysical or philosophical books should be submitted. Historical discussions of science, if present, should play a secondary role in the book.

Authors should first send a query letter no longer than two pages, providing the subject matter for the book, the qualifications of the author(s) and the targeted market. Authors should point out features that are unique and how their book is different from those currently available. The query letter may be sent by ordinary mail or by e-mail.

Multiple submissions are permitted but must be indicated in the query letter.

Jupiter Scientific Publishing responds to query letters within 30 days. Approximately 1% of the proposals submitted to JSP are accepted for publication.

After Submitting Your Proposal

Typically, Judson Press will respond to unsolicited book proposals in six to eight weeks. Generally, there is no relationship between Judson's interest in a manuscript and the amount of time it takes to respond.

Should your book proposal be approved by Judson Press, you will be contacted by the acquisitions editor and receive a contract offer. The contract specifies details pertaining to the length of the book, royalty payments to the author, and the author's deadline for turning in the completed manuscript.

As a royalty publisher, Judson Press holds all rights and pays all costs associated with editing, designing, manufacturing, marketing, and distributing the book, and the author receives a royalty—a percentage of the publisher's net proceeds on sales of the book.

The staff of Judson Press hope the best for you as you explore the possibility of writing a book for publication.

Categories: Nonfiction—Education—Science

CONTACT: Stewart Allen
Material: Popular Science Books

415 Moraga Ave
Piedmont CA 94611
E-mail: admin@jupiterscientific.org
Website: www.jupiterscientific.org/science/authors.html

Just Us Books

Thank you for your interest in Just Us Books. A premier, independent publisher of Black-interest books for young people, Just Us Books has an active publishing program that produces eight to twelve new titles per year.

Just Us Books is happy to announce that we are now accepting manuscript queries. We are currently looking for chapter-book manuscripts targeted to middle readers ages 8-12 and novels for young adult readers ages 13-16.

Writers: To submit a manuscript please mail a query letter with a 1-2 page synopsis of your manuscript, a short bio or description of previously published work or writing experience, and a self addressed stamped envelope (SASE) for our reply. If we wish to review your manuscript, we will request in writing that you forward it to us for consideration. All queries that are accompanied by a SASE will receive a response, generally within 8-10 weeks. Queries that are not accompanied by a SASE will not receive a response.

Please do not send unsolicited manuscripts. Just Us Books does not accept nor will we be held responsible for unsolicited manuscripts. Just Us Books also does not respond to queries sent via e-mail, fax or phone. All queries must be sent by mail only. Due to the volume of submissions we receive, our editorial department is unable to verify receipt of a query. Receipt verification must be done via certified mail, Federal Express, or other similar services.

Artists: Please send non-returnable samples or tearsheets only. Do not send original art. All submissions will be reviewed and filed for consideration.

We encourage authors and illustrators to familiarize themselves with Just Us Books publishing program before submitting a query. Information about the company, its focus, and editorial needs is available at www.justusbooks.com. Additionally, a wealth of information about the publishing industry is available through Internet resources and trade journals such as Publishers Weekly, Quarterly Black Review and Black Issues Books Review. You may also find helpful information through the MultiCultural Education and Publishing Council's web site, www.mpec.org, the Small Press Center, www.smallpress.org, and the Children's Book Council, www.cbcbooks.org.

Please also take advantage of continuing education courses, writing workshops, and publishing seminars offered by local colleges and professional literary organizations. Just Us Books founders, Wade and Cheryl Hudson are also available for customized writing workshops. For more information, visit www.justusbooks.com.

Again, thank you for your interest in Just Us Books.

Categories: African-American—Biography—Christian Interests—Culture—Family—Juvenile—Multicultural—Teen—Trade: Children's—Young Adult

CONTACT: The Editor
Material: All
356 Glenwood Ave.
East Orange, NJ 07017
Phone: 973-672-7701
Fax: 973-677-7570
E-mail: justusbooks@aol.com
Website: www.justusbooks.com

Kids Books By Kids

Dear Kid Writer,

Thanks for your interest in sending your book idea to Beyond Words Publishing. We do publish books written by kids like you in our "Kids Books

By Kids" series. We only publish nonfiction book ideas by kids—no fiction stories or poetry.

So far, we've published three "Kids Books By Kids": *Better Than A Lemonade Stand*, written by a 15-year-old, describes *50 Small Business Ideas for Kids*; *100 Excuses For Kids*, co-written by 10 and 11-year-old best friends, gives excuses for everything from escaping vegetables to avoiding chores; and *Girls Know Best* was written by 38 girls, ages 7-16, and gives advice and activities for girls. We are looking for unusual, practical, nonfiction book ideas for kids. If you can look at any of these three books (at a bookstore or library), they'll give you a better idea of what we're looking for.

When you send us your book idea, here's what we'd like you to include: 1 page about you, 1 page summarizing your book idea, 2-3 pages of writing from your book, 1 self-addressed stamped envelope (we call it a "SASE") so we can send back your story if we decide not to publish it. Also include 1 page of "market research" about your book idea. "Market research" is when you go to the library or a big bookstore and see if there are any other books like yours. If there are, tell us why yours is different and better. Also, tell us who you think will buy your book and why. Can you think of any places besides bookstores that will buy it?

It may take us a while to read and return your book idea, because we get so many every day. It can take up to six months. Thank you for being patient.

Thank you for thinking of us. By following these guidelines, it really helps us to see if your book idea is right for us.

We can't wait to see what you send us!

Submissions Department/Beyond Words Publishing, Inc.

Categories: Nonfiction—Children—Juvenile—Teen

CONTACT: Summer Steele, Manager Editor
Material: All
Beyond Words Publishing, Inc.
20827 NW Cornell Rd. Ste 500
Hillsboro OR 97124
Phone: 503-531-8700
Fax: 503-531-8773
Website: www.beyondword.com

Kinder Books

Please refer to Black Forest Press.

Lake Claremont Press

Where the Second City is second to none . . .
- Preserving the past
- Exploring the present
- Ensuring a future sense of place for our corner of the globe

In a highly-mobile, rootless world where places can easily lose their individual character, Lake Claremont Press books foster and reveal Chicago's special identity by sharing what's distinctive about our city's history, culture, geography, built environment, spirit, people, and lore.

In an age of giant media mergers at one end of the spectrum, Lake Claremont Press represents the alternative at the other end: a small, independent, niche publisher specializing in a subject that we know better than anyone. As such, we stand shoulder-to-shoulder with the publishing houses of that other big city.

Founded by Sharon Woodhouse in 1994, Lake Claremont Press has published over 30 titles, including local bestsellers *Chicago Haunts: Ghostlore of the Windy City* and *A Cook's Guide to Chicago* as well as award-winners *Hollywood on Lake Michigan: 100 Years of*

Chicago and the Movies, The Chicago River: A Natural and Unnatural History, Near West Side Stories: Struggles for Community in Chicago's Maxwell Street Neighborhood, The Streets & San Man's Guide to Chicago Eats, and *Finding Your Chicago Ancestors: A Beginner's Guide to Family History in the City and Cook County.* We will release seven new books in 2007 and are working on our first Spanish translation, two new product lines, and titles that cover aspects of Chicago social history, police culture, maritime history, music, and African-American neighborhoods.

We welcome new and established authors to submit book proposals and finished manuscripts on all things Chicago. We publish nonfiction trade paperbacks only at this time; we do not publish memoirs, coffee table books, photography, fiction, or poetry. If you have a query that fits these qualifications, we ask that you submit the following:

1. Complete proposal/cover letter
2. Book outline
3. Author credentials
4. Brief marketing analysis
5. 1–2 sample chapters (if not available send samples of previous writing)

Please do not send a full manuscript until it is requested.

Categories: Nonfiction-History-Regional-Travel

CONTACT:
Sharon Woodhouse, Publisher
Material: All
P.O. Box 25291
Chicago, IL 60625
Phone: 773/583-7800
E-mail: lcp@lakeclaremont.com
Website: www.lakeclaremont.com

Latin American Literary Review Press

The Latin American Literary Review Press is a non-profit publishing house dedicated to bringing the fiction and poetry of Latin American, Spanish, Brazilian and Portuguese authors to the English-speaking public.

Publications focus on works that were originally written in Spanish or Portuguese and translated into English.

Manuscripts are considered for publication only after the translations have been completed and received by us in their entirety.

Unsolicited manuscripts are considered.

Categories: Fiction—Hispanic—Jewish Interest—Literature—Poetry—Short Stories—Women's Fiction

CONTACT: Yvette E. Miller, Editor
Material: Any
CONTACT: Leanne Longwill, Assist. Editor
Material: Any
PO Box 17660
Pittsburgh PA 15235
Phone: 412-824-7903
Fax: 412-824-7909
E-mail: Latin@angstrom.net
Website: www.Lalrp.org

Legacy Press

Our Objective:
New acquisitions for Legacy Press are now focused on non-fiction books for children ages 2-12. Our books are evangelical Christian (non-denominational) and marketed primarily through Christian bookstores.

These books may include but are not limited to:
• Additions to our non-fiction books for boys or girls ages 2-12
• Devotionals
• Journals
• Activity ideas
• Books that encourage or promote Christian values
• Books that teach the Bible

We do not publish:
• Books for adults
• Academic work
• Poetry
• Curricula

The kinds of writers we are looking for:
• Have accepted Jesus as Savior and are dedicated to serving Him and leading others to Him
• Relate well to the needs of the evangelical Christian market
• Are active participants in a Bible-believing church
• Write creatively, either published or unpublished

To submit your proposal:
• Send a table of contents and 2-5 chapters for our evaluation
• Enclose a resumé or statement explaining your qualifications for writing the book
• Explain the audience for your book and how your book differs from those already on the market
• Enclose a SASE for return of your material if you want it returned
• Type on 8½" x 11" paper, one-sided and double-spaced
• Keep copies of everything you submit to us
• Address to Christy Scannell, Editorial Director. We normally respond in three to six months.

After evaluating your proposal/manuscript, we will do one of the following:
• Offer you a contract. We issue both royalty and full-rights contracts, depending on the type of book.
• Seek expanded material from you
• Ask for revisions and resubmittal

Categories: Nonfiction—Children—Christian Interests—Crafts/Hobbies—Games—Hobbies—Inspirational—Juvenile—Religion—Spiritual

CONTACT: Christy Scannell, Editorial Director
Material: All
PO Box 261129
San Diego CA 92196
Phone: 858-668-3260

Lehigh University Press

The Lehigh University Press is a conduit for nonfiction works of scholarly interest not appropriate for the popular market. Less constrained by demands for profit than a commercial publisher, LUP bases its selection criteria on a manuscript's contribution to the world of ideas. The Press does

Books
A-L

not publish fiction, poetry, or textbooks.

Our Ever Widening Publication List

Established in 1985 and initially publishing in areas of Lehigh's established strengths in technology and society and eighteenth century studies, LUP today is moving beyond these areas in pursuing its mission to provide high quality monographs for the academic community.

The Press's increasingly wide-ranging publication list includes titles on local, national, and international history; foreign affairs, biography, film, politics, philosophy, East Asian studies, and works for bibliographical reference.

Goals

The director and editorial board have recently made the commitment to publish an increasing amount of primary source material. Titles in our current catalogue include a memoir of the holocaust, an immigrant woman's frontier diary, and the autobiography of a noted scientist. Forthcoming publications will expand the list.

How We Work

Lehigh University Press is an affiliate of Associated University Presses, Cranbury, NJ. LUP's director acquires manuscripts through submission, has them reviewed, and gives his recommendation to the editorial board, which makes the final decision to publish. Approved manuscripts are forwarded to Associated University Presses, which handles the entire production and distribution process.

Inquiries are Encouraged

The Press welcomes for submission any manuscript (or synopsis and sample text of an unfinished manuscript) which is nonfiction, intellectually substantive, and whose format conforms to *The Chicago Manual of Style*, 15th ed. A current resume should accompany all submissions.

The Road to Publication

All manuscripts must be read by one or more scholarly reviewers, and it is rare that some degree of revision is not called for. Once favorably reviewed and revised, a manuscript must be approved by the editorial board, composed of Lehigh faculty members, which meets two or three times a year. To shorten a journey that extensive revision could make lengthy, it is wise to submit as polished a manuscript as possible. A clearly conceived, sharply focused, thoroughly researched, logically organized, fully documented, and crisply written manuscript sets the author well on the road to publication.

One Last Note

A very important point that scholars seeking to publish dissertations must remember is that dissertations and monographs address rather different audiences. Significant revision or reorganization is usually necessary before a dissertation can make the transition from research piece to scholarly publication.

For information or assistance please write or call Dr. Philip A. Metzger, Director, at the addresses given below.

Manuscript Information Sheet

• Author
• Current Position
• Title of Book

1. Has any part of this manuscript been published previously? If so, where?

2. Is this work a doctoral dissertation? From what University? Date If so, has it been revised? How?

3. Please list any previous publications.

4. Is the manuscript under consideration by any other publisher? (Please list)

5. How long is the manuscript?
Number of chapters or sections?

6. Please supply an abstract (ca. 500 words).

7. Has this manuscript been previously considered by another Associated Universities Presses member? *These include:*

Balch Institute Press
Bucknell University Press
Corning Museum of Glass Press
University of Delaware Press
Fairleigh Dickinson University Press
Folger Shakespeare Library
Lehigh University Press
Moravian Music Foundation Press
University of Scranton Press
Susquehanna University Press
Virginia Center for the Creative Arts
Western Reserve Historical Society

Categories: Nonfiction—Asian-American—Biography—Business—Film/Video—Government—History—Jewish Interest—Music—Reference—Regional—Academic—Philosophy—Public Policy—Technology

CONTACT: Dr. Philip H. Metzger, Director, LUP
Material: All
30 Library Dr.
Bethlehem PA 18015-3067
Phone: 610-758-3933
Fax: 610-758-6331
E-mail: inlup@lehigh.edu
Website: is1.cc.lehigh.edu/inlup/

Lerner Publishing Group
Imprints: Lerner Publications, Carolrhoda Books, Kar-Ben Publishing, LernerSports, First Avenue Editions, Lerner Classroom

Author Submission Policy

Please note: Our submission policy has changed. Effective immediately, we will only accept submissions during the month of November. Submissions received in any other month will be returned to the sender unopened. Thank you for abiding by our policy—it allows us the time to give each submission adequate attention.

The nonfiction submissions editor is Jennifer Zimian; the fiction submissions editor is Zelda Wagner. A SASE, addressed to either Ms. Zimian or Ms. Wagner, is required for all submissions. Allow 8 months for a response. No phone calls please.

Lerner Publishing Group does not publish alphabet books, puzzle books, song books, textbooks, workbooks, religious subject matter, or plays. We accept request for guidelines and catalogs year-round. Do not address these requests to Ms. Zimian or Ma. Wagner. For guidelines please address to GUIDELINE REQUEST and send a business-sized SASE. To receive both a catalog and guidelines, write to CATALOG REQUEST and send a 9"x12" SASE with $3.85 for postage.

Thank you for your interest in Lerner Publishing Group.

Categories: Nonfiction—African-American—Animals—Arts—Asian-American—Biography—Children—Culture—Education—Food/Drink—Government—History—Language—Mulitcultural—Science—Young Adult

CONTACT: Jennifer Zimian
Material: Nonfiction
CONTACT: Zelda Wagner
Material: Fiction
241 First Ave., North
Minneapolis, MN 55401-1607
Phone: 612-332-3344
Fax: 612-332-7615
Website: www.lernerbooks.com

Limelight Editions

To be considered by our editors, both previously published books and manuscripts must be submitted to the address shown below.

Although every proposal is reviewed, we cannot acknowledge any submission or return any material that does not include a self-addressed stamped envelope.

Responses are generally sent within three months.

We are unable to acknowledge receipt of submissions or give status reports.

We cannot be responsible for original copies of manuscripts, photos, artwork, etc. Send only photocopies of such material.

Limelight Editions, an imprint of Proscenium Publishers Inc., is an independent publisher specializing exclusively in nonfiction related to the performing arts–primarily theater, film, music and dance–that includes biographies and autobiographies, instructional books, histories, criticism, collections of interviews, and occasionally play scripts (for adults and children), screenplays and collections of lyrics. While many of our books are adopted for college course, we publish for a general audience and do not publish textbooks as such. Nor do we publish booklets, dissertations or art books.

Submissions must include a covering letter and/or a proposal that describes the book's subject matter and approach, identifies its audience, distinguishes it from other books on the subject and explains what qualifies the author to write the book.

Submissions may include up to four double-spaced chapters, representative of the book as a whole, that are not bound in any way (no staples, no looseleaf binders) and that are numbered consecutively within each chapter or throughout all the chapters.

Submissions must not include audio cassettes, computer disks or video tapes.

A proposal for a reprint of a previously published book should include a copy of that book.

Categories: Arts—Drama—History—Music—Theatre

CONTACT: Submissions Editor
Material: All
Proscenium Publishers Inc.
118 East 30th St.
New York NY 10016
Phone: 212-532-5525
Fax: 212-532-5526
E-mail: info@limelighteditions.com (for letters only)

LionHearted Publishing, Inc.

New Submission Guidelines

We no longer accept, review, or consider any unsolicited materials without a signed release. Check our website to see if submissions are open or temporarily closed.

Print, complete and return by email, fax, or mail the PDF Release Form or HTML Release Form (available on our website).

ALL SUBMISSIONS MUST FIRST BE EMAILED to Editor@LionHearted.com. Include:

1. A query letter with a 1 paragraph brief story synopsis
2. A 1-2 page full story synopsis.
3. An optional first chapter in the body of the email, or as an attachment, as a sample of your writing style.

An editor will respond by email, phone or mail. Please allow 2-4 weeks.

Any materials submitted without a Release Form will be held without review for 30 days pending arrival of the Release Form, then discarded, or returned if postage is provided.

We realize not everyone has email, but libraries and office supply stores are everywhere offering email, fax, and other electronic services.

Open PDF files with Adobe Acrobat Reader available for free from Adobe's web site.

If you are not able to view or print the Release Form, a PDF verson can be emailed or faxed to you.

Query Letter

E-mail submissions to: Editor@LionHearted.com. PLEASE include:

The manuscript sub-genere (ie: contemporary, historical, time-travel, paranormal, etc.)

Word count.

A one paragraph synopsis (thumbnail sketch) of the story line MUST be included.

A pseudonym if applicable.

Your phone, fax, mail and email addresses.

Synopsis

Synopsis must be included with every submission. It should be a 1-2 page, clear, concise rendering of the complete story line.

Format

Typewritten, double-spaced, minimum one inch (1") margins. Title page must include the author's real name, address, phone/fax numbers, email address, title and word count. Indicate if a pseudonym will be used. In the upper left hand corner include the author's last name and the first major word in the title, e.g., Mitchell/Gone; Woodiwiss/Flame. Include page numbering. Start chapters a third to halfway down the page to allow room for editor comments.

Agents

Unsolicited and non-agent manuscripts are welcome to follow the Submission Policy above. All manuscripts are evaluated equally at LionHearted. The contract is standard.

Postage

For manuscript return, include sufficient stamps (avoid dated postage), International Reply Coupons, or a check with a manuscript size self-addressed envelope.

Requested Manuscripts

Manuscripts must have a cover letter and a synopsis. Turnaround is aprox 4-12 weeks. Simultaneous submissions are discouraged.

Payment

LionHearted is not a vanity or subsidy press. Royalties are paid on paperbacks and ebooks. A market competitive advance is paid to contracted authors. LionHearted employs many avenues of distribution on a national level. No author funds are withheld for reserve against returns. All authors should promote their books.

Copyright

Copyright is in the author's name.

We Recommend:

Use two or three rubber bands in both directions to secure your pages.

Include a #10 SASE for editor's comments even if you include a large return envelope.

Send a self-addressed/stamped post card with requested manuscript if confirmation of receipt is desired.

For ease in handling we prefer return envelopes to be Priority Mail envelopes — free from any US post office. Self-address and attach return postage (if metered it must be without a date).

Mail is not delivered to the street address at Lake Tahoe.

Thank you in advance for your cooperation. We look forward to reviewing your submission.

Categories: Fiction—Nonfiction—Romance—Spirtual

CONTACT: Acquisitions Editor
Material: All
PO Box 618
Zephyr Cove NV 89448
Phone: 888-546-6478
E-mail: Editor@LionHearted.com
Website: www.lionhearted.com

Little Simon

An imprint of Simon & Schuster.

We are a novelty imprint that specializes in board books, pop-up books, life-the-flap books, sticker books, touch-and-feel books, and cloth books.

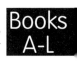

Books
A-L

The main focus of our list is children 6 months to age 8, and we do not publish picture books. All picture book queries should be directed to Atheneum Books for Young Readers or Simon & Schuster Books for Young Readers, attention of the Submissions Editor.

Because of the volume of submissions we receive, we ask that you follow a few guidelines when sending us a proposal. Please type all query letters and manuscripts, and be sure to include a copy of your manuscript along with your query letter. As we cannot be responsible for manuscripts that are misplaced or lost in the mail, it is advisable to always keep an original copy of your manuscript. Also, please include a self-addressed stamped envelope along with your submission. This helps us respond to you more quickly.

Categories: Children

CONTACT: Submissions Editor
Material: All
Simon & Schuster Children's Publishing Division
1230 Ave of the Americas
New York NY 10020-1295

Little, Brown Children's Books

Please refer to Time Warner Book Group.

Llewellyn Publications

Thank you for your interest in Llewellyn Publications. Llewellyn is the oldest and one of the largest publishers specializing in the New Age Sciences, and we always welcome new writers.

To save you time and effort, we have prepared these Guidelines. They explain both our subject areas and the information we need to consider a manuscript for publication. Please read the Guidelines carefully before submitting anything.

Llewellyn's subject areas include the following:

• *Alternative Realities and Technologies.* Whole food farming, organic gardening, moon gardening, herb gardening and preparation, alternative energy sources, pyramid energies, chaos theory.

• *Alternative Health and Healing.* Diet and nutrition, inner body awareness, longevity, massage and movement, herbalism, aromatherapy, visualization, energy and body work, tai chi, chi gong.

• *Astrology.* Any popular or professional aspect of astrology including natal, relationship, electional, predictive, mundane, horary, financial, medical, historical, magickal, etc.

• *Crafts.* Construction of magical tools, instruments, and objects; cookbooks.

• *Divination.* Tarot, I Ching, runes, dowsing, geomancy, numerology, cards, palmistry, graphology, and body language.

• *Fiction.* Educational and entertaining topics reflecting true "occult" principles: astrology, parapsychology, Witchcraft/Wicca, Pagan lifestyles. No "supernatural horror."

• *Magick and Shamanism.* World and folk magick; mysticism; ceremonial and high magick; use of incense, oils, candles, crystals; spells, ceremonies, and charms; invocation, evocation, and worship; animal magick; the Kabbalah.

• *Men's and Women's Studies.* New issues and approaches to gender-related spiritual, psychic, and physical concerns and needs.

• *Nature Religions and Lifestyles.* Certain aspects of mythology and folklore, solar and lunar related festivals, Paganism, Wicca, rituals, meditations, Earth energies, and ecology.

• *Paranormal.* Hauntings, psychic phenomena, mysteries, UFOs, lost continents.

• *Self-Awareness.* Dream recall, regression and past life recall, personality analysis, consciousness exploration, and occult anatomy (chakras, psychic energies, etc.).

• *Self-Development.* Meditation, personal programming, guided imagery, yoga and some martial arts, development of psychic abilities, past life therapy.

• *Self-Improvement.* Creative visualization, self-hypnosis; success principles; use of color, music, sound, dance; magick for better living; feng shui.

• *Spiritist and Mystery Religions.* Voudoun, Macumba, Huna, Shamanism, Candomble, techniques of trance, drumming, the use of masks, and body magic.

• *Spiritual Science.* Techniques for spiritual growth, prayer, mantra, worship, and the esoteric side of religious and ritual drama.

• *Tantra.* Sex magick, bio-energies, body awareness, Taoism, esoteric dance, Goddess worship, sensual enhancement.

In addition to books, we publish calendars, datebooks, almanacs, magazines, card deck kits, and audio and video cassettes. We prefer books and products that have strong mail-order potential as well as general bookstore and specialty store appeal, and we actively promote our publications, via mail order and direct mail.

Our emphasis is always on the practical: how it works, how to do it, and self-help material. We aim our products at a general audience and do not assume our readers possess previous specialist knowledge. We do not publish "about" books, collections of poetry, or biographies. We are not an academic or scholarly publisher.

PREPARING YOUR MANUSCRIPT FOR SUBMISSION

General Approach. Seeing your book in print is the reward for a long, arduous creative effort, and publishers understand and respect that. But publishing is a business, and you must regard potential publishers as you would any other professional contact. That is, be prepared, well-informed, and realistic. Use your library and any good bookstore for "How to Get Published" guides. *The Writer's Market,* updated annually, also has excellent general guidelines on preparing a submission, and there are some good FAQ (frequently asked questions) sites on the Internet.

Patience is another publishing virtue. Given the volume of submissions Llewellyn now receives, it can take six months for us to respond. If a manuscript requires a second read, it may take even longer.

Submission Package. Llewellyn accepts entire manuscripts for submission or proposals (cover letter, outline, and sample chapters). In either case, we ask you to observe some simple submission rules. *In general:*

• Inform us if this is a multiple submission, and include the number of current submissions.

• We welcome unagented authors (and actually prefer to work directly with authors), but if you do have a literary agent, provide the agent's name, address, and phone number.

• Date and sign all materials, including correspondence, manuscript title page, and diskettes.

• Complete and include the Author Questionnaire and Biographical Data & Book Info Form included with these Guidelines. These forms are essential for our acquisitions, production, marketing, and publicity departments, and your submission will not be reviewed without them.

Please see our website (www.Llewellyn.com) for more specific information on preferred formatting for submissions, marketing, etc.

Categories: Fiction—Nonfiction—Cooking—Diet/Nutrition—Gardening—Health—Inspirational—New Age—Paranormal—Psychology—Religion—Spiritual

CONTACT: Acquisitions Department
Material: All
Llewellyn Worldwide
PO Box 64383
St. Paul MN 55164-0383
Phone: 612-291-1970
Fax: 612-291-1908
E-mail: lwlpc@llewellyn.com
Website: www.Llewellyn.com

Remember: Editors change jobs and publishers change addresses. It is wise to invest in a phone call for the current information before submitting.

Lobster Press ™

Lobster Press

Fiction: Picture books, young readers, middle readers, young adults: adventure, animal, contemporary, health, history, multicultural, nature/environment, counting, special needs, sports, suspense/mystery, sci-fi, historical fiction, teen angst. Recently published THE WAY TO SLUMBERTOWN, written by L.M. Montgomery, illustrated by Rachel Bécdard (picture book); STOLEN VOICES, by Ellen Dee Davidson (Young Adult novel).

Nonfiction: Young readers, middle readers and adults/teens: animal, biography, Canadian history/culture, careers, geography, hobbies, how-to, multicultural, nature/environment, technology, health, references, science, self-help, social issues, sports, travel. Recently published Our Game, by Dave Stubbs, illustrated by Neal Portnoy, illustrated by Kun-Sung Chung.

How to Contact/Writers: Please address all submissions to: Lobster Press, 1620 Sherbrooke Street West, Suites C & D, Montreal, QC, H3H 1C9; Emailed or faxed submissions will not be considered.

Illustration: Uses line drawings as well as digital and color artwork. Reviews illustration packages from artists. Illustrations only: query with samples. Samples not returned; samples kept on file.

Terms: Pays authors 5-10% royalty based on type of book. Offers advances. Pays illustrators by the project or 2-5% royalty based on retail price. Originals returned to artist at job's completion. Writer's and artist's guidelines available on website.

Categories: Fiction—Nonfiction—Adventure—Animals—Biography—Careers—Environment—Health—History—Hobbies—Multicultural—Mystery—Nature—Reference—Science Fiction—Self Help—Sports/Recreation—Teen—Travel—Young Adult

Contact: Acquisitions Editor
Lobster Press
1620 Sherbrooke St. W., Suites C&D,
Montreal QC H3H 1C9 Canada.
Phone: 514 904-1100
Fax: 514 904-1101
E-mail: editorial@lobsterpress.com
Website: www.lobsterpress.com

Loyola Press

Loyola Press is a not-for-profit publisher, owned and operated since 1912 by the Chicago Province of the Society of Jesus. Our mission is "to help people find God in all things." In that tradition, we publish books about finding God's presence in every aspect of life.

Spirituality books have grown increasingly popular in bookstores over the last five or six years. With our 1997 publication of Cardinal Bernardin's nationally best-selling memoir, *The Gift of Peace*, trade books became our growing product line.

If you are interested in submitting your book proposal to our trade department, please take a few moments to read the following frequently asked questions. Our editorial staff has provided answers. We hope this information helps you decide whether or not to submit your materials to Loyola Press.

What kinds of books does Loyola Press publish?

Loyola Press publishes religion books for the general trade. Our books are about Catholic spirituality—how to live and pray as a Catholic Christian at the turn of the millennium.

Loyola books are practical, focusing on everyday life. Their tone is conversational, not scholarly. They are written for people who live in a fast-paced, bottom-line-driven, technology-focused world—and who long for a welcoming community, deep personal relationships, and time for solitude and reflection.

What kinds of authors write for Loyola Press?

We publish only about two dozen Loyola books a year, so we are highly selective. We are looking for authors who are experts in their fields, yet who can communicate their knowledge to beginners without "talking down." We need authors who love the Catholic spiritual tradition and can open up its riches to others, not in a pedantic way, but in an adult-to-adult manner. We want authors who write simply and clearly—and with style. The winning combination, then, is expertise + experience + style. If you have all three characteristics, please come to us!

What types of manuscripts are you currently interested in?

Loyola Press is a Catholic publisher, and we develop religion books for the general trade. Within the broad areas of religion, spirituality, and Catholicism, here are some specific categories we are developing:

• *Catholic spirituality:* books that integrate spiritual wisdom with various aspects of everyday life. We have a particular interest in Ignatian spirituality for lay people

• *Catholic tradition:* books that explore the time-honored traditions of the church and show what significance they have to our lives today

• *Personal relationships:* books that recognize the spirituality of human connections and help families, friends, and colleagues relate to one another in loving and healthy ways

• *Prayer and meditation:* books of short meditations or books that explain and illustrate how to pray

• *The Seeker Series:* short, popular introductions to various aspects of Christian living

• *Scripture study:* books for nonspecialists on how to pray with or gain wisdom from the Scriptures

• *Jesuit Way:* books that focus on Jesuit life and history as well as on Ignatian spirituality and ministry

What are some of the most recent titles published by Loyola Press?

Loyola books you may have recently seen in a bookstore include *Visions, The Book of Catholic Prayer, Inner Compass, spirituality@work*, and *Bumping into God Again*.

What types of books do not interest Loyola Press?

We also do not consider proposals for academic monographs or dissertations, textbooks, multiauthored collections of essays or symposium papers, fiction, poetry, drama, music, manuscripts with no spiritual applications, or any other category not mentioned in the list under "What types of manuscripts are you currently interested in?" Please also avoid sending us argumentative, ideologically driven books.

How do I interest Loyola Press in my manuscript?

Send a copy of your proposal, not your entire manuscript, to the editorial department. *Your proposal should include the following:*

• A one-paragraph description of the book's theme

• A description of the book's intended audience. Be specific. For example: "young Catholics (aged 18–35) seeking an understanding of Catholic traditions of prayer and devotional practices" instead of "everyone who is interested in prayer"

• A summary of your book's unique features. In other words, explain what your book offers that other books do not. What does it give a reader that he or she cannot get anywhere else?

• An extended outline or chapter summary showing how you develop the theme

• One or two sample chapters

• A summary of your qualifications for writing this book

• A stamped, self-addressed mailer if you wish your materials returned

If you send materials on disk, please:

• Use a fresh 3.5" disk, straight out of the box

• Save your files in MS-Word, Word Perfect, Rich Text Format, or text

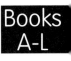

Books
A-L

only

Please do not send us originals of manuscripts, disks, photographs, illustrations, or anything else. We cannot accept responsibility for irreplaceable materials.

When can I expect a reply from Loyola Press?

Proposals are often read by several people, any of whom may be facing deadline pressure or a heavy travel schedule. Thus it can take anywhere from two weeks to three months for us to respond to your proposal. If you wish verification that your proposal was received, please include a stamped, self-addressed postcard, which an editorial assistant will return to you without comment.

Will Loyola Press return my materials?

Yes, if you include a stamped, self-addressed mailer. Otherwise we assume that you have saved the materials on your computer and do not wish us to return them.

What is your main reason for rejecting a manuscript?

In most cases, we turn down manuscripts because they are unsuitable for our list. Loyola Press serves it mission, its readers, and its authors by concentrating on those books that we know we can publish successfully. In general, these are books in the categories described elsewhere in these guidelines. We turn down many proposals not because they are unsound but because we do not think we could publish them well.

Where can I reach you?

Please do not phone. You may contact us by letter, fax, or e-mail.

Thank you for your interest in Loyola Press.

Categories: Nonfiction—Christian Interests—History—Relationships—Religion—Spiritual

CONTACT: Daniel Connor
Material: All
3441 N. Ashland Ave.
Chicago IL 60657-1397
Fax: 773-281-0152
E-mail: editors@loyolapress.com
Website: www.lionhearted.com

Lumen Editions

All manuscripts submitted to Lumen Editions should be typed. We do not publish genre writing, i.e., science fiction, fantasy, horror, romance. We look for intelligent fiction and nonfiction that is original and that is, most importantly, memorable and evocative of the senses. We do accept multiple submissions, but writers should note in their cover letter that the book is under consideration at other houses. It is suggested that before submitting any manuscript to Lumen, that you telephone and request a catalogue to get a sense of what we do publish. For a catalogue, please send an SASE with two first class stamps.

Categories: Fiction—Nonfiction—Hispanic—Jewish Interest—Literature—Travel—Writing

CONTACT: Milt Budoff, Series Editor
Material: All
PO Box 1209
Brookline MA 02445
Phone: 617-734-6772

E-mail: brbooks@yahoo.com

Luna Rising
A bilingual imprint of Rising Moon

Our multicultural mission is to create books for children that preserve Latino culture in the United States, value the strong language heritage brought to our country by children from Latin America, promote bilingualism, and expand a child's knowledge and perspective.

Luna Rising is currently seeking:

Agented and unsolicited bilingual Spanish/English picture book manuscripts for children ages 4-8.

We are especially interested in stories featuring:

• Contemporary bicultural experiences of living in the U.S.
• An understanding of diversity of the Hispanic experience in the U.S.
• Vivid, multidimensional characters
• Stories with wide, national appeal or regional southwest themes
• Biographies and important Hispanic figures

Examples from our current list are:

My Name is Celia: The Life of Celia Curz / Me llamo Celia: La vida de Celia Cruz

Playing Lotería / El juego de la lotería

Carlos and the Squash Plant / Carlos y la planta de calabaza

We are seeking samples of multicultural / Latino Artwork

Guidelines for Writers

• We accept submissions by mail only (no phone, fax, or email, please).
• Please submit the entire manuscript for children's picture books in English. Spanish translation is optional.
• Please include a cover letter with information regarding any previously published work.
• Please provide a self-addressed, stamped envelope (SASE) of adequate size and postage for our reply and your manuscript, should you want it returned.
• Please allow at least three months for out initial evaluation.

See below for submissions address.

Categories: Children

Contract: Theresa Howell, Managing Editor
Luna Rising
2900 N. Fort Valley Road
Flagstaff AZ 86001
Phone: 928-774-5251

The Lyons Press
An imprint of The Globe Pequot Press

Associate Publisher: Gene Brissie (*gene.brissie@lyonspress.com*)
Acquisitions: Lyons Imprint Core Categories (fishing, hunting, sports, health & fitness, outdoor skills, animals/pets, equestrian, history/current affairs, military history, self-reliant living, nature, games reference;

Tom McCarthy, senior editor (tom.mccarthy@lyonspress.com), (Americana, current events, health & fitness, history/military history, nautical, popular culture, sports).

Mary Norris, executive editor (*mary.norris@globepequot.com*), (women's interest, local interest, self-help).

Rob Kirkpatrick, senior editor (*rob.kirkpatrick@lyonspress.com*), (history, sports, military history, current events).

Scott Bowen, editor (fly fishing and fly tying techniques, hunting).

Holly Rubino, associate editor (*holly.rubino@lyonspress.com*), (adventure/survival, narrative nonfiction, nature, self-reliant living).

Steve Price, editor-at-large (works from NYC) (equestrian).

Lilly Golden, editor-at-large (works from upstate NY) (dogs & pets, animals, literary nonfiction, nature, wildlife, outdoors).

Ken Samelson, editor-at-large (works from NYC) (sports)

Established 1984: (Lyons & Burford), 1997 (The Lyons Press), Publishes hardcover and trade paperback originals and reprints. Publishes 270 titles per year: 50% of books from first-time authors; 30% from unagented writers. Pays 6-10% royalty of retail price. Publishes book one year after acceptance of ms. Accepts simultaneous submissions. Responds in 30 days to queries, proposals, and mss. Book catalog is available online.

The Lyons Press has teamed up to develop books with Orvis®, L.L. Bean, *Field & Stream*, *Outward Bound*, Buckmasters, *Golf Magazine* and many others. The Lyons Press publishes practical and literary books, chiefly centered on outdoor subjects-natural history, all sports, horses, fishing, and hunting. Currently emphasizing adventure sports, history and others, while de-emphasizing gardening, fiction, hobbies, travel.

Nonfiction: Biography, cookbook, how-to, reference. Subjects include agriculture/horticulture, Americana, animals, anthropology/archeology, cooking/foods/nutrition, health/medicine, history, military/war, nature/environment, recreation, science, sports, and travel. "Visit our website and note the featured categories." Query with SASE or submit proposal package including outline, three sample chapters (or 30-50 sample pages), and marketing description. Reviews artwork/photos as part of ms package. Send photocopies or non-original prints

Recent Titles: *From Baghdad With Love* by Lt. Col. Jay Kopelman (pets/current events), *Second Acts, Presidential Lives and Legacies After the White House*, by Mark Updegrove (history), *300 Pounds of Attitude* by Jonathan Rand (sports), *In the Company of Wild Bears* by Howard Smith (nature), *The L.L. Bean Fly Fishing Handbook*, Second Edition by Dave Whitlock (fishing), *Believe, A Horseman's Journey* by Buck Brannaman (equestrian), *Second Chances, More Tales of Found Dogs* by Elise Lufkin (pets)

Categories: Nonfiction—Adventure—Americana—Boating—Cooking—Fishing—Food/Drink—Health/Fitness/—History—Hunting—Literature—Military—Outdoors—Pets—Recreation—Science—Sports—Travel—Horses

CONTACT: Submissions Editor
Material: All
The Lyons Press
Box 480
246 Goose Lane
Guilford, CT 06437
Phone: 203-458-4500
Fax: 203-458-4668
Website: www.lyonspress.com

Mage Publishers

Mage Publishers publishes high-quality English-language books about Persian culture, including: cookbooks, translations of literature, history, children's tales, biography and autobiography, architectural studies, and books on music and poetry. Only books relating to Persian culture are considered by the editors.

Authors interested in submitting work for consideration should send a letter or email outlining their work and a brief biographical statement to the attention of Amin Sepehri at the following address: Mage Publishers, 1032 29th St. NW Washington, DC 20007. We will usually respond to your letter within 2-4 weeks.

Categories: Fiction—Nonfiction—Architecture—Cooking—Culture—Gardening—History—Literature—Multicultural—Music—Short Stories—Ethnic

CONTACT: Amin Sepehri
Material: All
1032 - 29th St. NW
Washington DC 20007
Phone: 202-342-1642
Fax: 202-342-9269
E-mail: as@mage.com
Website: www.mage.com

The Magni Group, Inc.

Formal guidelines not available.
Send queries or book proposals to below address.
Categories: Nonfiction—Animals—Cooking—Crafts/Hobbies—Health

CONTACT: E.B. Reynolds, President
Material: All
Magnico Publishing
7106 Wellington Point Rd.
McKinney TX 75070
Phone: 972-540-2050
Website: www.magnico.com

MAISONNEUVE PRESS

Maisonneuve Press

About Maisonneuve Press: We are the publishing division of the non-profit, educational organization, the Institute for Advanced Cultural Studies. The Institute defines itself as a progressive or left-wing group and intends to promote cultural studies from that radical perspective.

Subject Areas We Publish: The Institute seeks to bring the traditional university based scholar to the forefront of political activism and likewise bring the agenda of radical politics to the university classroom and research. We are interested in books in the general areas of critical cultural studies, the arts, politics, philosophy/theory, international relations, intellectual history, and history. These may be newly written works by a single or group of authors. They may be edited collections of new or old essays. MP does not publish poetry, novels, personal narratives, crime, police, or war stories (though we are interested in anti-war materials), or self-help books.

Currently two book series are active and we are especially interested in adding books in these areas:
   • Post Modern Positions
   • Critical Studies in Community Development and Architecture

Audience and Market: Our books are aimed somewhere between the academic market and progressive/activist politics. When we review manuscripts, we consider what they contribute to that readership group. The research must fulfill the best of academic standards while the style and rhetoric may address a more informal audience.

Submission Process: MP is interested in relationships with authors at any stage of manuscript development. Ideally, an author would send a letter of inquiry or a proposal for publication, describing the book project and telling something about the author. These initial contacts may range from a single page to about a dozen pages. We will respond to the proposal to let you know if your project appears to be appropriate for MP. If we feel it is appropriate, we will ask you to send the whole manuscript. If your manuscript is finished (or a near-final draft), you can send it or some sample chapters and we will read and report to you. In-house editors first evaluate every manuscript. If a work is judged to be appropriate for the press and to be of significant merit, it will be sent to an outside expert for review and commentary. While we encourage letters and proposals via e-mail, we do not take whole manuscripts electronically (i.e., by e-mail or on a floppy that we must print out to read).

Length and Etc.: Ideally we seek to publish books that have a finished length of 175-300 pages (75,000 to 125,000 words). We encourage the use of photographs, illustrations, or other visual materials. Inside the book, all illustrative material will be printed in black and white, but the cover will be in full color. We follow the MLA style of documentation and manuscript formatting. We appreciate your sending return postage if you wish to have your manuscript returned. We will help you secure rights to publish photos or illustrations.

Manuscript Selection: MP is a small publisher, producing about six titles per year. For that reason, we have to be very selective. We typically receive about 200-300 book proposals each year. The selection of which book to publish is entirely the responsibility of the editors, but each decision is supported by recommendations from outside, expert readers.

Contracts and Royalties: Normally, we issue a contract on finished books. In our contract, we seek exclusive rights to publish and distribute the work all over the world. We actively seek foreign translations and/or publications in other countries. The exclusive rights extend to all formats, including the Internet or CD, but all points in the contract are negotiable. Generally, we pay a royalty of about 5% of the cover price twice each year on actual sales, but on collections of previously published essays we generally pay a flat fee rather than a royalty. We do not pay advances. We pay 50% to the author on any fees we receive from translations or foreign publications. Typically, we publish books in both hardcover for libraries and paperback for the mass market.

Categories: Fiction—Nonfiction—Arts—Culture—Feminism—Film/Video—Human Rights—Law—Literature—Politics

CONTACT: Robert Merrill, Editor
Material: All
PO Box 2980
Washington D.C 20013-2980
Phone: 301-277-7505
Fax: 301-277-2467
Website: www.maisonneuvepress.co

Marcato Books

Please refer to Cricket Books.

Remember: *Editors change jobs and publishers change addresses. It is wise to invest in a phone call for the current information before submitting.*

March Street Press

March Street Press
Parting Gifts

About Us

We are publisher of ground-breaking poetry and fiction in chapbooks and the semiannual magazine, *Parting Gifts*.

Guidelines for *Parting Gifts* and March Street Press

The editorial vision of *Parting Gifts* and March Street Press relies entirely on a deeply entrenched collection of prejudices. We are highly suspicious of work that turns too heavily on rhyme or meter. Look for the work of Kelly Cherry, Janet Kauffman, C.K. Williams, Jim Harrison, Charles Baxter, and Amy Hempel if you want to see the kind of writing we most enjoy and want to foster. All of these authors are published widely, so you should have no trouble finding their work.

Poetry of the kind that can be found in Ann Landers, Hallmark cards, church bulletins, or high school haiku magazines will probably never appear in our publications. We occasionally receive poems that sound like recycled song lyrics. They are always returned immediately. Even though our semiannual literary magazine has what might be considered a sad title (*Parting Gifts*), that doesn't mean that we specialize in poems written on the deaths of parents, siblings, spouses, children, or pets. Come to think of it, we've covered all those bases over the past ten years—which means that we've paid our dues, so don't send us any more of those, thank you very much.

We publish more poetry than fiction, but fiction is actually our first love. The problem is that we have such high standards and peculiar preferences that it's hard to find fiction to publish. We prefer very short fiction, between 500 and 1000 words. The language in the fiction we publish has to be as strong as the language in poetry—not a misplaced word. And it has to tell a story. No slices of life, please. We've published more than our share of "mad girl" stories—stories about neurasthenic women with cruel boyfriends and outlandish ideas about the world they're muddling through. We're tired of them. Please don't send any more.

Chapbooks should be 25–50 pages. When we accept a chapbook, we often make suggestions—sometimes strong ones—involving inclusion and exclusion of poems or specific lines or stanzas that don't work for one reason or another. That's what real editors do. If you don't think that your work needs an editor, you shouldn't be sending it to one.

We usually accept 5–7 book manuscripts per year. Selection is always made on the basis of quality, so please don't write a letter promising to buy 100 (or 200 or 1000) copies if we accept the book. We aren't a vanity press and that sort of promise doesn't sway us in the slightest. In fact, we find it somewhat insulting. We accept no government grants or loans. For that reason, we occasionally, with deep regret, have to turn away excellent manuscripts for lack of resources to publish at a particular time. We wish we could publish everything of quality that we receive. Generally, when we reject a manuscript (if it is accompanied by a full-sized SASE) we include something of value (usually a book) so you won't feel you've wasted your $20 reading fee. We can't guarantee that, but it's something we try to do as funds permit. When we accept a manuscript, we send the author ten copies of the finished book free (a $90 value at retail) and we are open to providing a limited number of review copies and promotional materials (such as postcards or posters for readings) on request, so long as the privilege isn't abused.

Now we come to an issue that has confused many people: We don't consider book manuscripts from within North Carolina. This is a political statement against the peculiar arts policies of Senator Jesse Helms. We urge North Carolina artists to work against his re-election and we will not publish books by North Carolina artists or sell our books or magazines within North Carolina or accept money from the state arts councils until this man (and we use the term loosely) has have been replaced in the United States Senate by someone who more accurately represents the views of the citizens of North Carolina with regard to freedom of expression. Some feel this is a misguided policy that hurts artists in some way, but we reject that notion because there are plenty of other publishers both inside and outside North Carolina that don't have this policy. If you need a referral, we will be glad to provide it.

Sample copies: $9.00. Subscriptions: $18.00 per year. Checks and money orders (U.S. currency only) should be made out to March Street Press. First rights are all that is claimed by March Street Press for work that appears in *Parting Gifts*. Once the magazine is published, the rights revert to the author. March Street Press requests that publication elsewhere be accompanied by a mention of *Parting Gifts*.

March Street Press is actively seeking chapbook manuscripts. Economic pressures have forced a $20 reading fee. We are sorry for this, but the expenses of this operation are incredible and even at this, we are just breaking even. We encourage authors to submit a computer disk with the manuscript in electronic form along with the paper manuscript. Include a SASE with your submission. We can't seriously consider a submission unless it is accompanied by SASE and reading fee. Please don't bother sending a selection of poems and asking us to make a decision about the book based on them.

And now a word about a writer's responsibility to his or her constitution. Currently the ACLU is involved in a desperate fight to protect our First Amendment rights. While the late Ayatollah attempted to silence one author's voice, the spirit of Ed Meese rose from the sleaze to silence a whole generation of writers. If you thought Jesse Helms as art critic was chilling, the Justice Department as literary critic will put you in the deep freeze. Literally. In the words of Kurt Vonnegut, "The Justice Department has found yet another devastating legal weapon to misuse in its war on our…right to say, show, hear, read, or see whatever we please without fear of punishment." The facts are far too complicated to cover here, but I urge you to contact Ira Glasser of the ACLU at 132 West 43rd Street, New York, New York 10036 for details. And if your right to free expression is important to you, send a check as well. Tell as many people as you can about this situation. Motivate them to contribute, too.

Another worthy cause is the National Coalition Against Censorship. The kind of harassment you might have thought only happened in Nazi Germany is commonplace in America today. Teachers, librarians, booksellers, and others to whom we owe much of our culture and education (what little of it survives) inspire fringe religious and political groups to follow their basest instincts. Write for details: National Coalition Against Censorship, 2 E. 64th St., New York, NY 10023.

Any questions? Please send email to March Street Press.

Categories: Erotica—Literature—Men's Fiction—Poetry—Sexuality—Short Stories—Women's Fiction

CONTACT: Submissions Editor
Material: All
3413 Wilshire Dr.
Greensboro NC 27408-2923
Website: www.marchstreetpress.com

Books
M-Z

Margaret K. McElderry Books
An Imprint of Simon & Schuster

Margaret K. McElderry Books publishes original hardcover trade books for children from pre-school age through young adult. The list includes picture books, middle grade fiction, poetry, fantasy and young adult fiction. The style and subject matter of the books we publish is almost unlimited. We do not publish textbooks, coloring and activity books, greeting cards, magazines and pamphlets or religious publications.

General Submission Guidelines

Margaret K. McElderry Books is not currently evaluating unsolicited manuscripts. You may send a query letter. The letter should briefly describe the nature of the book. You may also include a very brief resumé of your previous publishing credits. Query letters may be addressed to Emma D. Dryden, VP Associate Publisher or Karen Woityla, Executive Editor.

If we ask to see your manuscript

All submissions must be typed on standard 8-1/2" x 11" white paper, double-spaced and typed on one side of the page only. We do not consider submissions sent by fax or on computer disk. If you would like

dressed, stamped postcard which we will date and send back to you. A self-addressed, stamped envelope must accompany each submission.

Please note: Margaret K. McElderry Books publishes a limited number of picture books each year. It is the prerogative of the publisher to choose illustrators and the art director regularly interviews professional artists for this purpose.

Categories: Children's Trade—Young Adult

CONTACT: Emma D. Dryden, VP Associate Publisher
Material: Query Letters
1230 - 6th Ave.
New York NY 10020

Marion Street Press, Inc.

Marion Street Press, Inc. publishes books of interest to writers and journalists. We are known for practical, professional titles that help writers and journalists do their jobs better. Our books are narrow in focus - how to cover a particular beat, how to write in a particular fashion, etc. We also publish reference works of interest to writers.

Recent titles have included *The Dictionary of Concise Writing, Championship Writing, Math Tools for Journalists* and *Pen & Sword: A Journalist's Guide to Covering the Military*. Please visit our website, www.marionstreetpress.com, for more information.

Please query publisher Ed Avis at edavis@marionstreetpress.com before sending a manuscript.

Thank you.

Ed Avis, Publisher—Marion Street Press, Inc.

Categories: Reference—Writing

CONTACT: Ed Avis, Publisher
Material: All
PO Box 2249
Oak Park IL 60303
Phone: 866-443-7987, 708-488-8820
Fax: 708-448-0101
E-mail: edavis@marionstreetpress.com
Website: www.marionstreetpress.com

Markowski International Publishers, Possibility Press

Established in 1976. Publishes trade paperback originals. Publishes 10 titles/year. Receives 1,000+ submissions/year. 95% of books from first time authors; 100% from unagented authors. Average print order for a first book is 5,000-50,000. Pays on royalty basis. Usually publishes book 24 months from acceptance. Accepts simultaneous submissions. Reports within 2 months. Books catalog and ms. guidelines at www.possibilitypress.com.

Nonfiction: Primary focus on personal development, self-help, sales and marketing, leadership training, network marketing, entrepreneurship, motivation and success topics. We are interested in how-to, motivational and instructional books of short to medium length that will serve recognized and emerging needs of focus topics. Query or submit outline, table of contents, and entire ms.

Recent Nonfiction Title: The Power of Having Desire?

Tips: We're intensifying our search for best-selling manuscripts. We're looking for authors who are dedicated to their message and want to make a difference in the world. We especially like to work with authors who speak and consult.

Categories: NonFiction—Psychology—Public Speaking—Self Help

CONTACT: Marjorie L. Markowski, Editor-in-Chief
Material: All
Hummelstown PA 17036
Phone: 717-566-0468
Fax: 717-566-6423
Website: www.possibilitypress.com

Maupin House

Maupin House publishes innovative and practical supplemental professional resources for K-12 educators. Our special focus is writing workshop. Other areas of interest are language arts; reading; research; and some K-5 math. All our resources are standards-based and are founded in solid research; however, they are not theoretical advice, but instead focus on the "how to do it" aspect of instruction. Many of the resources are written by teachers, or people who have taught and now are educational consultants. Please look at our web site to first to familiarize yourself with the Maupin House publishing philosophy.

All Maupin House books reinforce our basic publishing premise of empowering teachers to do a better job in the classroom. We do not accept, or espouse formula approaches to teaching. We believe in the power of the teacher to effect classroom learning. We are always looking for the "next great thing" in instruction for our target topics. Classroom-proven techniques always score higher with us than ideas that have not been tested. Our initial response to your email will be within a week. Upon submission of an outline or other supporting materials, expect a response in about two weeks to two months.

We are not interested in poetry, general non-fiction, children's picture books, or other non-target topics. We cannot be responsible for original copies of unsolicited art, photos, or manuscript copies.

Do not submit a finished manuscript. Query by email first with your idea. If we are interested, we will reply and ask you for more specifics regarding your credentials, the marketability and positioning of the work, the competition, and the need for or purpose of the book. Maupin House authors are enthusiastic partners in publishing. They are interested in actively working to market their books through speaking engagements and/or consulting.

Categories: Education—Language

CONTACT: Julia Graddy, Publisher
Material: All
PO Box 90148
Gainesville FL 32607-0148
Phone: 352-373-5588
E-mail: jgraddy@maupinhouse.com
Website: www.maupinhouse.com

Mayhaven Publishing

When Considering a Manuscript for Mayhaven or our Co-op option: For each manuscript we require one hard copy.

ACCEPTING A MANUSCRIPT IS BASED ON A NUMBER OF FACTORS:
- The subject
- The slant
- Writing style
- Marketing Considerations

Our Schedule

If the manuscript is a nonfiction work, we require the author's credentials and a summary of the research.

Children's books have special considerations in regard to the type of artwork required.

If a manuscript is accepted, we offer the appropriate Mayhaven or Wild Rose Agreement.

We also offer annual awards for fiction. Categories are adult fiction and children's fiction. Submissions must be in English; must be full manuscript; must not have been previously published; will be accepted from authors or their authorized agents; will not be returned. There is an entry fee of $50.

Thank you for your interest in Mayhaven/Wild Rose Publishing.
Newest Title: Misuse of Power Co-authors: Ed Asner and Burt Hall.

Categories: Fiction—Nonfiction—Adventure—Animals—Asian-American—Biography—Children—Civil War—Cooking—Crime—Drama—Disabilities—Family—Fishing—Folklore—Food/Drink—General Interest—Health—History—Inspirational—Juvenile—Literature—Military—Mystery—Native American—Paranormal—Poetry—Politics—Regional—Relationships—Rural America—Satire—Science Fiction—Short Stories—Spiritual—Teen—True Crime—Western—Young Adult—Awards

CONTACT: Doris Wenzel, Editor
Material: All
PO Box 557
Mahomet IL 61853
Phone: 217-586-4493
Fax: 217-586-6330
E-mail: mayhavenpublishing@mchsi.com
Website: www.mayhavenpublishing.com

MacAdam/Cage Publishing

MacAdam/Cage Publishing was founded as an independent trade publisher in 1998 by David Poindexter with the aim of publishing books of quality fiction and non-fiction and committed to bringing new and talented voices to the literary marketplace.

In 1999 MacAdam/Cage Publishing acquired MacMurray & Beck, another independent press, well known in the industry for launching authors such as Patricia Henley (Hummingbird House), William Gay (The Long Home) and Susan Vreeland (Girl in Hyacinth Blue) and heavily supported by the bookselling trade with many BookSense 76 picks as well as appearances in chainstore fiction programs aimed at highlighting new authors.

Having joined forces, and now with operations in both San Francisco and Denver, MacAdam/Cage Publishing represents independent publishing at its best. Innovative in its approach to marketing and yet committed to the time-honored style of publishing, MacAdam/Cage Publishing will continue to introduce new and exciting authors from across the nation and beyond.

We are not accepting unsolicited submissions at this time. Any materials received will be recycled. Please check our website for updates.

Categories: Fiction—Nonfiction

CONTACT: Editorial Staff
Material: All
MacAdam/Cage Publishing
155 Sansome St., Ste. 550
San Francisco, CA 94104-3615
Phone: 866-986-7470, 415-986-7502
Fax: 415-986-7414
Website: www.macadamcage.com

McBooks Press

We publish roughly 70% fiction and 30% non-fiction, but we are currently seeking to increase our non-fiction titles. In non-fiction, we are actively seeking manuscripts in the categories of nutrition/health, vegetarianism, sports (especially lesser-known sports), and regional (upstate New York). In fiction, our emphasis is on adventure-oriented historical fiction that appeals primarily to men, with a secondary appeal to women. While we have emphasized nautical fiction in the past, we are now moving away from that sub-genre toward other historical settings; the time-period of the story matters less than that the plot is exciting, the time-period accurate, and the characters well-developed and believable.

Books M-Z

Non-fiction: Query with outline.

Fiction: Query with synopsis and either with or without first three chapters.

Include a SASE if you wish your submission returned and/or expect a response via snail mail.

Electronic submissions OK.

We respond to queries and submissions in 3 months.

Categories: Fiction—Nonfiction—Diet/Nutrition—Food/Drink—Health—Men's Fiction—Parenting—Regiona—Spoort/Recreation—Historical Fiction—Vegtarian

Contact: Jackie Swift, Editorial Director
Material: All
ID Booth Building
520 N. Meadow Street, I.D. Booth Blgd.
Ithaca, NY 14850
Phone: 607-272-2114.
Fax: 607-273-6068
email: jackie@mcbooks.com

The McDonald & Woodward Publishing Company

Publishing Program

The McDonald & Woodward Publishing Company publishes nonfiction adult trade and semi-scholarly books in the areas of natural and cultural history, as broadly defined. The primary audience for these publications is the relatively curious and well informed sector of the general population. Our publishing program falls into three divisions, as described below. We rarely consider proposals which fall outside these divisions.

Manuscripts submitted for consideration should be authoritative, substantive, well organized, and written clearly at the semi-popular or sub-technical level. We are especially attracted to work by scholars or amateur authorities on their subjects that is written in a style which is accessible to the curious, informed reader. We may have any submission reviewed by at least two authorities in the subject area before a manuscript is accepted for publication.

We recommend that authors who are interested in having us consider a manuscript for publication:

a. visit our Web site at www.mwpubco.com to review our complete list of titles and

b. review a sample of titles that we have published recently. Doing so will suggest the scope of subject matter that we are interested in publishing and will demonstrate the style and level of writing that we have found acceptable.

We welcome inquiries from authors wishing to explore our interest in considering manuscripts for publication. Please feel free to contact us by telephone, fax, e-mail, or mail to discuss projects completed, under way, or contemplated. A final decision about our interest in publishing any manuscript will, however, be made only when a completed manuscript is submitted for our consideration; a complete manuscript includes text and front matter, back matter, and illustrations as appropriate.

I. General Titles

M&W will consider for publication as a general title any manuscript that deals with a subject within natural and cultural history, as broadly defined. The length and format of general titles will vary widely.

Representative examples of published and forthcoming general titles include:

• *A Guide to Common Freshwater Invertebrates of North America*, by J. Reese Voshell, Illustrations by Amy Bartlett Wright
• *Vernal Pools: Natural History and Conservation*, by Elizabeth A. Colburn
• *A Mile Deep and Black as Pitch: An Oral History of the Franklin and Sterling Hill Mines*, by Carrie Papa
• *The New Patterns in the Sky: Myths and Legends of the Stars* by Julius Staal
• *The Stone Canoe and other stories* by John L. Peyton (Ojibway tales)
• *Sweetwater Sea Saga* by Virginia Soetebier (45 years of sailing on Lake Superior)
• *The Other Side of the Medal: A Paleobiologist Reflects on the Art and Serendipity of Science* by Everett C. Olson
• *The Snowflake Man: A Biography of Wilson A. Bentley* by Duncan C. Blanchard
• *Ponce de Leon and the Spanish Discovery of Puerto Rico and Florida* by Robert Fuson

II. Guides to the American Landscape

Guides to the American Landscape are specialty guides that identify, describe, and interpret themes and places of significance on the landscape of Canada, Mexico, and the United States. Each title in the series is devoted to a specific place or set of places representing a well defined theme in the natural and/or cultural heritage of North America. Books in the Guides series are designed to facilitate the reader's awareness of, visitation to, and understanding of publicly accessible sites that represent or document the theme. Our guides typically are organized into three sections which provide (1) a narrative review of the content and temporal and spatial patterns of the subject theme which provides a conceptual framework by which the subject theme can be understood clearly; (2) detailed descriptive, interpretive, and access information about publicly accessible sites related to the theme; and (3) sources of additional information about the theme, including books, articles in periodicals, maps, museum exhibits, web sites, etc. The detailed organization of each guide will vary according to the nature of the subject; a guide to a national park, for example, will differ in the details of organization from a guide to archeological sites.

Books in the Guides series are written by persons with either scholarly training or authoritative amateur experience in the subject and for that part of the general public with a defined interest in the theme. The audience is broad, ranging from interested lay persons to professionals. Representative consumer groups include tourists, students, librarians, teachers, planners, resource managers, scholars, and various special interest groups.

Manuscripts submitted for the Guides series are expected to be authoritative, versatile, up-to-date, well organized, clearly written, and extensively illustrated with tables, line drawings, maps, and photographs. Book length can vary from about 75 to about 300 printed pages. Final book format is 6" x 9", perfect bound, paperback with full color cover, and, increasingly, with color inserts.

Titles in the Guides to the American Landscape series already published or forthcoming include:
• *Indian Mounds of the Middle Ohio Valley* by Susan L. Woodward and Jerry N. McDonald
• *Indian Mounds of the Atlantic Coast* by Jerry N. McDonald and Susan L. Woodward
• *Shenandoah National Park: An Interpretive Guide* by John A. Conners
• *Old Bones and Serpent Stones: A Guide to Interpreted Fossil Localities in Canada and the United States-Western Sites* by T. Skwara
• *Homes and Libraries of the Presidents* by William Clotworthy
• *Maryland's Catoctin Mountain Parks: A Guide to Catoctin Mountain Park and Cunningham Falls State Park* by John Means
• *In the Footsteps of George Washington* by William G. Clotworthy

III. Essays on a Changing Planet

Essays on a Changing Planet is a forum by which scholarly or other professional or learned opinions and perspectives can be disseminated to a broader audience than is normally available to specialists. The Essays should be addressed to the informed sector of the general public in a style convenient to both writer and reader.

Essays should deal with ideas of current or future significance relative to mankind's impacts on and adjustments to a changing Earth. The topics addressed may be large or small, simple or complex, global or regional, but the perspective must be that of a specialist addressing a general audience about an issue or issues of current or future importance.

As the name of the series implies, an essay format should be followed. Books may range from about 50 to about 200 pages in length. Illustrations are optional, but recommended.

Final book format is 6" x 9", paperback, perfect bound.

At present we have three titles in the Essays series:
• *Ownership and Productivity of Marine Fishery Resources* by Elmer A Keen
• *Taking Stock: The North American Livestock Census* by Donald E. Bixby and others.

Preparing and Submitting Manuscripts to McDonald & Woodward

1. Please submit inquiries, proposals, or manuscripts only for titles that fit within the scope of our publishing program. Whatever form the initial submission takes, it should be addressed to Acquisitions Editor, The McDonald & Woodward Publishing Company, 431-B E. College St., Granville, OH 43023.

2. Typically, no decision will be made as to the acceptability of a manuscript until it is complete; a complete manuscript contains all text and front, back, and illustrative matter, as appropriate. The manuscript will be first reviewed in-house by the Acquisitions Department. If interest remains high, the manuscript and background survey will then be passed to a) the Pre-press Department, which will determine feasibility of production in terms of copy editing and formatting and b) the Marketing Department, which will determine sales potential. The recommendations of all three departments will be considered by the Publisher before a final determination is made. Please allow a minimum of two to three months for this process to be completed.

In general, a project will be evaluated according to the following criteria:

• How well it fits within our publishing program

• How well it fits with our publishing schedule and existing commitments

• How substantive and authoritative it appears

• How appropriate it appears in subject, style, and content to the general, well informed audience to which we cater

• How well its sales potential fits within our marketing plan

3. We will try to notify you within 2-4 weeks of receipt of your submission whether or not McDonald & Woodward has further interest in your project. If you have not heard from us in that amount of time, please feel free to inquire by telephone, letter, fax, or e-mail.

4. If you initially submit a letter of inquiry or a proposal, and if the Acquisitions Editor deems your proposal of definite potential interest to McDonald & Woodward, you will be asked to submit a complete manuscript for review.

5. If the Publisher decides to accept your manuscript for publication, you will be sent a contract which stipulates our terms. In general we provide royalties to authors of 10% of gross receipts. We do not pay advances on royalties.

6. Upon signing the contract, you should be prepared to work initially with the Acquisitions Editor in finalizing the development of the project in terms of content and basic organization. All materials for completion of the book-illustrations, tables, appendices, bibliographies, etc. - must be assembled before the manuscript is considered final and can be referred to Pre-press for copy editing, text and page formatting, and cover design. Publication averages 6 months after the final manuscript is received.

7. The complete manuscript must be submitted as hard copy and on diskettes in PC-compatible format. DO NOT FORMAT your manuscript electronically other than to provide adequate margins, paragraph indentations, chapter breaks, and sub-heading breaks, and do not place or embed supportive materials (tables, figures, etc.) in the text. Text and page format is the responsibility of our Pre-press Department, and they will only have to spend valuable time removing unnecessary format commands and embedded elements. Please refer to our (a) Digital Manuscript Format and Content Guidelines and (b) Final Check-Off for Submitting Manuscript below for more specific guidance.

8. Generally speaking, illustrations which support a manuscript are part of the manuscript and hence the responsibility of the author. You will be expected to acquire and provide appropriate illustrative materials. The Acquisitions Editor may also recommend specific illustrations.

9. The single most important variable influencing the speed with which a manuscript can move through the review and production processes is the state of the submitted mansucript. Manuscripts which are (a) well organized and well written, (b) complete, and (c) properly formatted will become books much more quickly than will manuscripts that do not meet these criteria. We strongly advise authors to consider having their work reviewed by at least one critical reviewer or editor before submitting the final manuscript to us. Many manuscripts that we receive for consideration could benefit from more extensive presubmission review and constructive editing.

Presubmission Checklist

Digital Manuscript Format Specifications and Content Guidelines

• Page size is formatted at 8.5" x 11".

• Text proper is submitted as a single file.

• All files have been spell-checked.

• Supporting textual material, such as captions, tables, etc., is at end of text proper or as separate files.

• Body text is set in 11- or 12-point serif font in normal face (no sans serif or cursive fonts).

• Paragraphs are formatted to indent first line, to double-space all text, and to layout as left-justified (i.e., "ragged right").

• Chapter titles, subheads, and other titles and labels are not in all-caps and not in bold or italic face.

• All necessary indents and special line positioning are achieved by formatting commands (indents, tabs, center, justify right, etc.) and not by using the space bar. Unnecessary line formatting should be avoided.

• All double spaces between sentences and after colons or semicolons have been reduced to a single space.

• All spaces preceding a hard return at the end of paragraphs have been removed. The hard return should follow immediately the final number, letter, or punctuation sign at the end of a paragraph or paragraph equivalent.

• The manuscript has been checked further for any extraneous unnecessary "noise" such as, but not limited to, consecutive hard returns, consecutive quotation marks, underlines/rules linked to hard returns, unused section and/or page breaks, etc.

• All pages are numbered, and numbering is consecutive from the beginning to the end of the manuscript.

• All headers and footers - other than page numbers, if they are inserted as headers or footers - have been removed.

• The manuscript has not been coded for computerized indexing.

• No figures, tables, footnotes, or other supportive or decorative matter has been placed in (i.e., embedded in) the manuscript.

• Automatic hyphenation has not been used, and no words have been manually hyphenated.

• Bold and italic formatting has been kept to a minimum; italic formatting has been used, where necessary, instead of underlines.

• Letters have never been used as numbers, and numbers have never been used as letters - never use "ell" for "one," and never use "oh" for "zero," and vice-versa.

• All diacritical marks have been either included during word processing or clearly marked on the hard copy of the manuscript.

• Em-dashes, preceded and followed with a single space, have been used instead of single or multiple hyphens where a "dash" is intended. But, hyphens have been used where hyphens are necessary.

• The use of parentheses has been kept to a minimum. If something is worth saying, it can usually be stated as a part of the primary narrative, not as an aside.

• Abbreviations have been kept to a bare minimum; in most cases, either spell out the word completely (Figure, not Fig.) or use its acronym equivalent (VA, not Va.; US, not U.S.). The elimination of all abbreviations is, of course, not practicable, but if an abbreviation can be eliminated without increasing the awkwardness of the presentation, then it should be eliminated.

• Sources for specific information and supportive material, such as quotations, blocks of statistical data, tables, etc., have been provided.

• Permissions for the use of copyrighted material have been obtained and are being submitted herewith.

• All illustrations are in a form suitable for publication, or for conversion to a publishable form.

• Captions are included for all supportive material, and all supportive material is clearly identified (numbered, lettered, etc.) and cross-referenced with its caption and its suggested location in the text.

• Credits for the use of illustrations have been provided.

• All supportive material is necessary and directly relevant to the text of the book.

• All captions clearly and effectively relate the captioned matter and the text of the book to each other.

• No photograph is included in which: Resolution and/or color quality are poor; The central subject is cropped - buildings without roofs, people without heads or feet, etc.; The central subject is obscured by visual distractions such as light reflections or utility lines.

• My car, family, pets, etc., are featured as adornments to the subject.

• Parallax is extreme.

• All references in the bibliography or its equivalent are presented using the same format, and all necessary information for each entry is present.

• I have made and retained a copy of the final version of the manuscript being submitted.

Final Check-Off for Submitting Manuscript

1. The author should submit two hard copies (i.e., paper copies) of each manuscript, one copy on floppy disk, and supporting graphics (preferably more than will be required in the finished book). These materials should be submitted to the Acquisitions Editor. Authors who submit a complete, well-organized package will see their manuscript processed more quickly than those manuscripts that are only partly complete or poorly organized.

2. The two hard copies of the manuscript should be double-spaced throughout and produced directly from the disk version that you submit (i.e., do not print the hard copies, then make editorial changes on the disk) - the manuscript will be edited using the hard copy, but design will be done using the disk copy. Figure captions, tables, computer graphics, boxes, and all other supplemental matter should be separated from the main text and either placed at the end of the text portion of the manuscript or as separate files. One hard copy of the manuscript should contain no markings. On the other copy indicate the preferred location of figures, tables, boxes, etc.

3. The disk copy should be complete, contain the various categories of material (main text, tables, captions, etc.), be nondefective, and be submitted in PC-compatible format in a major word processing software. M&W uses Microsoft Word as its basic word processing software.

4. Figures may be submitted either as hard copy or digital copy. Where photographs are involved, we prefer prints to color transparencies in most cases.

What to Submit

• One disk copy of all word-processed files in PC-compatible format on 3.5" floppy or 100 M ZIP portable hard drive.

• Two paper copies of manuscript produced from final version of digital text. One of the 2 paper copies should be marked with the suggested locations of tables, maps, and other supporting material.

• One complete set of non-text supporting materials (maps, photographs, etc.) in either hard copy or digital format.

Categories: Nonfiction—Biography—Conservation—Ecology—Environment—History—Travel

CONTACT: Submissions Editor
Material: All
431-B E. College St.
Granville OH 43023
Phone: 740-321-1140
Fax: 740-321-1141
E-mail: mwpubco@mwpubco.com
Website: www.mwpubco.com

McFarland & Company, Inc.

McFarland is what has traditionally been known as a scholarly and reference publisher (no fiction, poetry, etc.). Our market has seen more libraries (of all kinds, including academic, public, corporate, etc.) than bookstores, though direct-mail sales to individuals are prominent in our overall marketing picture, particularly in certain specialty lines. We publish around 295 books a year.

We welcome nonfiction manuscripts on a wide range of subjects, not limited to the following: performing arts (especially film, television, and radio), pop culture, history, women's studies, black studies, sports (especially baseball), chess, philately, art, music, international studies, automotive history, librarianship, military history, and literature. Reference books are one of our specialties.

We do not publish fiction, poetry, children's books, inspirational works, cookbooks, diet or self-help books, religious or political tracts, exposés, stories of personal triumph over adversity, or occult or New Age works.

What We Need to See

Authors may contact us with a query letter, a full proposal, or even (if the manuscript is complete and you're confident it could fit in among the books we've already published) a finished manuscript with cover letter. In a query letter you should describe the manuscript, tell us how far along you are, estimate its final length (in either word count or double-spaced typescript pages), and tell us what is unique about the manuscript (or about you!).

We answer most queries within a few days; if we're interested we'll invite you to send either the complete manuscript or a full proposal, consisting usually of the following elements: an outline or table of contents, estimates of length and completion date, a preface or introduction, comments on how the book differs from any competing works on the same topic, a summary of what you might offer in the way of photographs or other illustrations, and some samples of the manuscript (1-2 chapters or the equivalent, plus representative pages of any special parts).

How to Present the Work

The most important thing is that it be typed and submitted on paper rather than disk (though if we accept the manuscript we will later be interested in your disks for possible use in typesetting). Manuscripts must have pages numbered consecutively, and we prefer that they not be bound in any way. Valuable documents or photographs need not be sent at the proposal stage, though photocopies of them are helpful.

Because of the nature of manuscripts and of reading, we prefer to operate via old-fashioned mail (or UPS) as opposed to phone, fax, or e-mail. We won't summarily turn you down if you come to us through electronic means, but (a) you won't get a faster reply that way, and (b) a hard copy makes a better impression. Please do not send copies to two or more of our editorial staff. Do not send e-mail attachments.

Be sure to put your name and return address on your cover letter, and on the top page of the proposal or manuscript.

What to Expect from Us

We usually respond to proposals quickly—within two to three weeks. Our decisions are based largely on the freshness of the topic, how well it fits in with our list, how thoroughly and authoritatively you cover it, the quality of the research and writing, and the likely marketability of the book.

When we do accept a book, publication cannot occur immediately. Because we can handle only a certain number of books in a year, and publication entails time-consuming processes (editing, design, typesetting, proofreading, promotion, printing and binding, and so forth), as well as considerable advance planning, a manuscript generally must reach us complete in every way no later than fall in order to be a candidate for publication in the following calendar year.

Categories: African-American—Asian-American—Civil War—Environment—Film/Video—History—Multicultural—Reference—Sports/Recreation—Television/Radio—Theatre—Scholarly—Automotive

CONTACT: Gary Mitchem, Acquisitions Editor
Material: Any
CONTACT: Steve Wilson, Executive Editor
Material: Any
CONTACT: Virginia Tobiassen, Editorial Development Chief
Material: Any
UPS: 960 Hwy. 88 W
PO box 611
Jefferson NC 28640
Phone: 336-246-4460
Fax: 336-246-5018
E-mail: info@mcfarlandpub.com
Website: www.mcfarlandpub.com

McGavick Field Publishing Co.

We are receiving about one hundred proposals a year, which is great for a small press. This leads us to ask for queries, which we will respond to within 90 days. It is not necessary to send a SASE because we feel that any author contacting us is worth a stamp.

We do accept proposals. We do not accept pictures.

Categories: E-mail: fhernan@prodigy.net for categories.

CONTACT: Anne Field
Material: All
118 N Cherry
Olathe KS 66061
Phone: 913-780-1973
Fax: 913-782-1765
E-mail: fhernan@prodigy.net

McKenna Publishing Group

Looking for nonfiction.

Send email query to: Mckennapubgrp@aol.com with a simple email query letter (no attachments please—we do not open attachments unless the author is under contract) addressed to Eric Bollinger, Publisher, McKenna Publishing Group. In your initial email query, please provide the following:

• Your name, address and email address.

• A brief synopsis of your work. Note: We do not publish children's books or poetry.

• Its length. We prefer works under 275 double-spaced pages. The reason? Book sellers provide publishers limited shelf space, and would prefer to offer two books from the publisher in that shelf space rather than one longer book. It gives them twice the opportunity for a sale. Also, shorter books keep our cost to print and the price of the book down, and that helps sell it to the book buyer.

• Your qualifications for writing this work.

• The market and audience for it.

• Other books you know written on the subject.

• Your ability to promote the work if published. We expect our authors to actively promote their works at book signings, on the radio, television and other unique events. We do not accept submissions from authors who reside outside of the United States, and who cannot actively promote their work in the United States.

If you receive an email back from us indicating we would like to give your work a read, we ask that you follow these guidelines:

• Include a cover letter to the publisher describing our email correspondence and our acceptance of your submission.

• Mail it in a US Priority pouch mailer (not a box) if possible.

• Put your name and the title of the work on the outside of the mailer.

• Include a SASE with postage affixed if you wish the work returned to you should that be necessary. Note: Do not use metered mail that is good only on the date of purchase. We will not return your ms to you if there is not sufficient and good postage included.

• Double-space the ms, and print on one side of the page only. Do not bind the ms.

• Put your last name and a key word from the title top left, and page numbers from one to the end top right.

• Always include its synopsis.

• Always include your email address with your cover letter

Categories: Nonfiction

CONTACT: Eric Bollinger, Publisher
Material: All
74-923 Hwy. 111, Ste. 173
Indian Wells, CA 92210
E-mail: Mckennapubgrp@aol.com
Website: www.mckennapubgrp.com

 Meadowbrook

Meadowbrook Press

General Author Guidelines

Meadowbrook has been in business since 1975 and has grown to become one of the leading Midwest publishers of books sold nationally through bookstores and other retail outlets. We specialize in pregnancy, baby care, child care, humorous poetry for children, and children's activities. Please note that we are not currently accepting unsolicited manuscripts or queries for the following genres: adult fiction, adult poetry, humor, and children's fiction. Also note that we do not currently publish picture books for children, travel titles, scholarly, or literary works.

We take great pride in our ability to edit, design, and promote books so that they achieve their full commercial potential. Four of our books have sold more than a million copies, three books have been New York Times best-sellers, two have been #1 bestsellers, and over twenty have been on B. Dalton's and Waldenbooks's bestseller lists.

Guidelines for Submitting Manuscripts to Meadowbrook Press

Manuscripts that lack an SASE will not be returned.

Summarize your manuscript in a cover letter. (What is it about? How is it organized? Does it have or require illustrations, charts, graphs, or photographs?)

Tell us why your book will sell. (Why do you think there is a need for this book? How large is the market? What is the precise market? What potential secondary distribution channels—outside of bookstores—exist?)

State the competition and why your book is better. Share any knowledge of the sales history of competing books.

Tell us what qualifies you to write this book. Also, if you have any promotional experience, or would be willing to promote the book, say so.

Please state your publishing history, if any. State what books you have written, when, and who published them. Please include sales figures for your books.

Be neat! Typos and sloppiness have a great negative impact.

We respond to submissinos and queries only if interested. All other submissions and queries will be recycled.

Categories: Parenting

CONTACT: Submissions Editor
Material: All
5451 Smetana Dr.
Minnetonka MN 55343
Phone: 800-338-2232
Fax: 952-930-1940
Website: www.meadowbrookpress.com

Medical Physics Publishing

Medical Physics Publishing is a small, nonprofit publishing company designed to publish books by and for medical physicists. We only publish books written by authors working in the fields of medical physics, diagnostic radiology, oncology, and related areas.

We welcome manuscript proposals for technical books written by professionals working in medical physics, mammography, radiation oncology, diagnostic radiology, and related areas. We do not accept general trade manuscripts.

—Betsey Phelps, Managing Editor

Categories: Technical—Medical

CONTACT: Acquisitions Editor

Material: All
4513 Vernon Blvd.
Madison WI 53705
Phone: 608-262-4021
Fax: 608-265-2121
E-mail: betsey@medicalphysics.org
Website: www.medicalphysics.org

Mel Bay Publications, Inc.

Before submitting a work for consideration, we recommend that you examine Mel Bay's full product line as presented on our web site and in our print catalogs to get a clear idea of the type of books we publish. Please note that traditionally we have not published individual pieces of sheet music, contemporary pop vocal music, or band or orchestra music, but rather method books and solo anthologies of historically, stylistically or thematically related material. Due to high print licensing costs, our primary focus has been on original and public domain material arranged for solo instruments.

To avoid duplicating areas that we have already addressed thoroughly, we strongly recommend that you examine our catalog before mailing your submission.

To evaluate projects and manuscripts for possible publication, we require that the following materials be sent by mail:

1.) A copy, not originals, of your manuscript or proposal. It is not necessary to send a completed work, although you may if you wish. Three or four pieces from a collection or a table of contents and a couple of chapters from an instructional book will usually suffice depending on the nature of the work. (We may request a more complete submission for clarification if necessary. This does not imply acceptance of the manuscript for publication.) A professional-looking submission, printed from a one of the products in the Finale® family from Coda Music if possible, is preferred. If this is not possible, send an orderly, clean and neatly handwritten manuscript. Do not send submissions in electronic format or on disk. While we appreciate an author's ability to provide computer files once a project is accepted, we cannot evaluate submissions in this format.

2). A detailed statement of purpose showing:
> a. what the book proposes to do;
> b. what makes it unique or different from other publications;
> c. and what the author views as the market or marketability of the item.

3). A demo CD or cassette if possible

4). A bio of the author.

We do not discuss submissions until they have been received and evaluated.

Finally, we suggest that you approach a music publisher as a freelance journalist might approach a magazine editor. Don't spend a year preparing a complete manuscript only to find out that your subject matter has already been thoroughly addressed in an existing publication. Rather, send the materials listed above. These are really all we need to evaluate a project. While Mel Bay Publications, Inc. is not currently soliciting new manuscripts, we are always open to an original music publishing concept.

Categories: Nonfiction—Music

CONTACT: William A. Bay
Material: All
#4 Industrial Dr.
Pacific, MO 63069
E-mail: email@melbay.com
Website: www.melbay.com

Menasha Ridge Press

Menasha Ridge Press publishes distinctive books about the outdoors, wilderness sport, wildlife, cooking, history, dining, and travel worldwide. Before you submit a book proposal, browse our website to see if your book idea matches what we publish. If you have a book idea you think would fit our book list, *follow the directions below:*

Provide a brief synopsis of the book

Describe the book's target audience and why would they buy it. Also, note any potential competition and describe how your book brings something new and exciting to the arena.

Table of contents for the book as well as 1 or 2 sample chapters.

A short, biographical statement noting your qualifications for writing this book.

How to Submit

Manuscripts can either be submitted via e-mail attachment or by mail. A cover letter should accompany the submission, including name, address, phone number, and e-mail address of the contributor.

If sent via mail, please include a self-addressed, stamped envelope large enough to return submitted materials. If this is not enclosed, we will not return your materials. Never send the only copy of anything!

Categories: Nature—Outdoors—Recreation—Sports—Travel

CONTACT: Acquisitions Editor
Material: All
2204 1st Ave, Suite 102
Birmingham AL 35233
E-mail: rhelms@menasharidge.com
Website: www.menasharidge.com

Mental Floss

So, you think you got what it takes to enter the Floss Factory? Well, bring it on! But before you write in with your brilliant ideas, here are some tips that might help you "wow" us.

A. Just Pitch It

Here at the Floss Factory, we don't dig people who write in to say, "Hey, look at all my clips. Can I write for you guys?" Clips don't tell us enough. We want to know that interested writers just "get it" – that they get the concept, style and wacky sense of humor that is *mental_floss*. In order to prove that to us, try pitching us an article idea that you think is quintessentially *mental_floss*. If we think you "get it," then we'll ask for clips/resumes and see if you're qualified to write it.

B. Give It to Us Straight

A lot of people have written into

mental_floss with really fascinating article ideas that look at new theories or perspectives on old themes. And while we like these ideas on a personal level,

mental_floss long ago made an editorial decision not to publish articles that "theorize." We are in the business of reporting facts — and straight facts only — in an entertaining and original way.

C. Complete the Mission

When *mental_floss* first started out, we wrote up some fancy, schmancy mission statement, but I won't bore you with that now. If you want to know what we look for in our articles, all you have to know is what we want to share with our readers. Here's a quick run-down:

> • What you SHOULD have learned in school but were too hung-over to remember.
> • What they WON'T TEACH YOU in school, but you've always wanted to know.
> • What you were too INTIMIDATED to learn about because it seemed too complex.

D. Know the Editor's Pet Peeves

> 1. No satire! (See #2 for reason)
> 2. Have a column or feature spot in mind for your article: Often, submitted facts or subjects are interesting, but they are only that: short facts or topics not necessarily suitable for a 1500-word article. If you send in an article idea, include where you envision the article being published in the maga-

zine: right_brain, left_brain, spinning_the globe, etc. Keep in mind that our scatter_brained section and cover stories are written in-house.

3. Stay out of politics:

mental_floss likes to stay as "controversy-free" as possible, so please avoid submissions dealing with political beliefs or current politicians.

4. Avoid current events:

mental_floss is one of the few magazines in the world that actually avoids "timely" topics. We try to present educational information that is more timeless, so submissions focusing on current trends or social situations may be hard sells here.

E. Just Do It!

Categories: Nonfiction—Book Reviews—Education—History—Philosophy—Science

CONTACT: Neely Harris, Editor-in-Chief
Material: All
PO Box 528
Novelty, OH 44072
Phone: 440-338-1816
Fax: 440-338-6315
E-mail: neely@mentalfloss.com.
Website: www.mentalfloss.com

Meriwether Publishing Ltd Contemporary Drama Service

School Guidelines
DRAMA:

Please include cast list, and (if required) prop list, costume information, set specifications, etc., with all play manuscripts.

Following are the types of drama we publish:

• One-act non-royalty plays — originals or adaptations, comedies, parodies, social commentary and novelty drama. Plays with large casts and with many parts for women.

• Full length (90 minutes) Musical Comedies — Large cast, 20 or more participants: soloists, chorus, dancers and comics. Author/composer must provide a cassette or CD of the music. Book and performance royalties paid.

• Speech contest materials — monologs for women and men, dialogs, short playlets addressing the high school experience with honest feelings and real situations of current importance.

• Full-length royalty plays — comedy, large casts.

• Adaptations — Shakespeare, the classics, and popular modern works (with original author's permission).

• Oral interpretations — folktales and storytelling.

• Prevention plays — drama as a teaching tool about drug abuse, pregnancy, gangs, etc.

• Readers Theatre — adaptations or originals.

BOOKS:

Our books cover a wide variety of theatre subjects from play anthologies to theatre craft. We publish books on monologs, duologs, short one-act plays, scenes for students, acting textbooks, how-to speech and theatre textbooks, improvisation and theatre games.

Send sample chapters or an outline — no complete manuscripts.

QUERY LETTER SPECIFICATIONS:

• Include a synopsis or brief statement of objectives.

• Tell us why you believe your work deserves publication. Define the market you see as the potential audience.

• Please include a list of your publishing credits and/or experience and your payment expectations.

• Include a self-addressed, stamped envelope for our response.

• Allow 4-6 weeks for response.

Church Guidelines

DRAMA:

Please include cast list, and (if required) prop list, costume information, set specifications, etc., with all plays and musicals. *Following are the types of drama we publish:*

• One-act non-royalty plays on religious themes up to 30 pages.

• Christmas and Easter chancel drama or liturgy — length 30 minutes maximum — for children's Sunday school departments and also for adults.

• Collection of short sketches on a central theme — five per collection — humorous, entertaining, Christian.

• Religious musicals for Christmas and Easter — one hour maximum. (Computer generated musical accompaniment score and cassette of performance preferred.)

• Readers Theatre scripts — 30 minutes maximum.

• Monologs.

BOOKS:

Our Christian books cover creative worship on such topics as clown ministry, storytelling, banner-making, drama ministry, children's worship, and more. We also publish anthologies of Christian sketches. We do not publish works of fiction or devotionals.

Send sample chapters or an outline — no complete manuscripts.

QUERY LETTER SPECIFICATIONS:

• Include a synopsis or brief statement of objectives.

• Tell us why you believe your work deserves publication. Define the market you see as the potential audience.

• Please include a list of your publishing credits and/or experience and your payment expectations.

• Include a self-addressed, stamped envelope for our response.

• Allow 4-6 weeks for response.

Categories: Fiction—Arts—Dance—Drama—Music—Religion—Spiritual—Theatre

CONTACT: Editor
Material: Manuscripts
CONTACT: Editor, Contemporary Drama Service
Material: Drama Scripts
885 Elkton Dr.
Colorado Springs CO 80907-3557
Phone: 800-937-5297
Fax: 888-594-4436
E-mail: MerPCDS@aol.com
Website: www.meriwetherpublishing.com

Metamorphous Press

Dear Writer:

Thank you for inquiring about our manuscript guidelines for new works. Since we receive from 2,500-3,000 unsolicited submissions each year, we ask that you first submit a query letter with an outline of your work, and a sufficient sample of your writing style for our acquisitions staff to determine if your work fits within our editorial policy. From there, we can decide whether we need to request a complete manuscript for further review.

We cannot be responsible for returning manuscripts due to the large quantity we receive. *We encourage you to submit your work for consideration at this time:*

• It may be considered (budget allowing) for publication by

Metamorphous Press
- We may offer subsidy publishing
- Or we can assist you with the details of self-publishing

In any case, we are always excited about being involved in projects that can make a positive difference.

Thank you for your interest in Metamorphous Press.

Sincerely,

Nancy Wyatt-Kelsey, Acquisitions Editor

Categories: Nonfiction—Business—Education—Health—Psychology—Self Help—Sexuality—Enneagram—Ericksonian Hypnosis—N.L.P.—Personal Development

CONTACT: Nancy Wyatt-Kelsey, Acquisitions Editor
Material: All
PO Box 10616
Portland OR 97296-0616
Phone: 503-228-4972
Fax: 503-223-9117
E-mail: metabooks@metamodels.com

Metropolis Ink

There are only two requirements to become an author published by Metropolis Ink:

- First, we have to like your book and believe in it as much as you do. We accept only well-written manuscripts with broad appeal. In fiction, we want excellence in narrative, dialogue, and plotting. In nonfiction, we want clear, distinctive, well-researched material on popular, helpful topics.

- Second, we accept only authors committed to working hard to promote their own books. We'll work hard to sell your books, but we need the assurance of your help.

We do not charge to publish the MSS we accept; neither do we offer an advance for those books.

To have your work considered by Metropolis Ink, attach at least the first several chapters of your manuscript to an email as an MS Word or Adobe PDF file and send it to the address below. In the body of your email, include a brief synopsis, and tell us something about yourself. What is your writing experience? Have you been published? What? Where? Are you able, willing and eager to promote your published book?

We'll evaluate your submission and tell you whether we are interested.

We especially encourage submission of nonfiction works, but are always open to high-quality fiction.

Thank you.

Categories: Fiction—Nonfiction

CONTACT: Kurt Florman, Partner/Editorial Manager
Material: All
PO Box 682
Yarnell AZ 85367
Phone: 928-427-0329
Fax: 928-427-9488
E-mail: submissions@metropolisink.com
Website: www.MetropolisInk.com

Michael Wiese Productions

MWP publishes a best-selling line of books for independent filmmakers and university film students around the world. Our how-to books are used in 500 film schools throughout the world and have been translated into ten different languages.

Submission

To submit a proposal, please send a Table of Contents, and two sample chapters.

Categories: Nonfiction—Arts—Education—Film/Video

CONTACT: Ken Lee (206-283-2948)
Material: All
11288 Ventura Blvd, Ste 621
Studio City CA 91604
Phone: 818-379-8799
Fax: 818-986-3408
E-mail: kenlee@mwp.com
Website: www.mwp.com

Midmarch Arts Press

Midmarch Arts Press publishes four books a year. Our books until 2001, are mostly on the arts and poetry of the 20th century.

- Include name, address and telephone number on all manuscripts and pictures.
- Book manuscripts should be queried before submission.
- Subjects: Our focus is on art, women artists, literature and poetry.
- Style: Avoid wordiness. Art doesn't have to be the best thing since Da Vinci to be worth writing and reading about. Gushing praise, rhetorical clichés, and overblown jargon are not interesting to read. Personal, social, historical, political, and artistic particulars are interesting—that is, information and explication.

Categories: Arts—Poetry—

CONTACT: Acquisitions Editor
Material: All
300 Riverside Dr.
New York NY 10025
Phone: 212-666-6990
Fax: 212-865-5509

Milkweed Editions
Milkweeds for Young Readers

The mission of the press

Milkweed Editions is a nonprofit literary press, publishing between 15 and 20 books a year. Founded in 1979, we have published over 200 titles and are dedicated to keeping our books in print. We read and consider each manuscript for publication according to our mission statement. We believe that literature is a transformative art, and that each book bears a responsibility to convey the essential experiences of the human heart and spirit.

We're proud to be the publisher of many outstanding authors: Ken Kalfus, Susan Straight, Marilyn Chin, Larry Watson, Bill Holm, Paul Gruchow, Janisse Ray, Pattiann Rogers, and many others, including emerging and mid-career authors. If you aren't familiar with our books, please visit our Web site (www.milkweed.org) to read about upcoming and past titles.

What we publish

Milkweed Editions publishes literary fiction, nonfiction about the natural world, poetry, and novels for young readers. We are looking for:

Works of fiction (novels, novellas, and short story collections) between 150 and 400 pages. We do not publish genre fiction, by which we mean we are not interested in romance, science fiction, mystery, crime, or westerns.

Works of literary nonfiction that focus on the relationships between human and natural communities. We are not interested in manuscripts written for an academic or scientific audience.

Collections of poetry (single-author collections only, please) that are at least 60 pages long. Please review our previous poetry titles to get a sense for what we're looking for in a poetry collection. We read poetry manuscripts biannually, in the months of January and June;

manuscripts received outside of those months will be held for the next reading period.

Books for young readers (readers between the ages of 8 and 13) that are full-length novels between 90 and 200 pages. We do not consider picture books or poetry collections for young readers

How to submit a manuscript

Please include a cover letter, complete manuscript, SASE for response, and a stamped mailer if you'd prefer to receive the manuscript back after consideration. If you do not provide a way to return the manuscript, we will recycle the manuscript.

If you prefer to send a proposal or query to Milkweed's editors, please include a cover letter, manuscript outline, sample chapter(s), and SASE for response (or a stamped mailer should you prefer to receive the material back). We are only interested in proposals that include writing samples (i.e., sample chapters). Queries that do not include an SASE will not receive a response. Queries and proposals can be sent to the same address as complete manuscripts.

Please address submissions to:

Fiction Reader (or Nonfiction, Poetry, Children's, as appropriate)
Milkweed Editions
1011 Washington Avenue South
Open Book, Suite 300
Minneapolis, MN 55415

We do our best to respond to submissions within six months of receipt. Due to our staff size and the steady flow of manuscript submissions, our review time may occasionally take a little longer. Please be patient while we give your manuscript our full consideration. We cannot respond to letters, phone calls, or emails requesting manuscript status. If you'd like to verify manuscript receipt, please include a stamped postcard or purchase delivery confirmation from the post office.

Milkweed does not accept submissions on disc or via email or fax.

Final thoughts

Milkweed Editions is happy to accept unsolicited manuscripts from authors of all backgrounds (previously published or not). In return, we ask that you take the time to familiarize yourself with our list in order to determine whether or not Milkweed Editions is a good fit for your manuscript. Many of the unsolicited manuscripts we receive are inappropriate for our press. This includes books that don't meet our manuscript page requirements, books that fall outside our publishing list (picture books, for example, or literary biographies), and works that are clearly not ready for publication. You can ensure that your manuscript will be fully read and considered by taking a little time before submission and making sure it's appropriate for Milkweed Editions.

Categories: Fiction—Nonfiction—Children—Conservation—Environment—Literature—Poetry—Short Stories

CONTACT: Fiction Reader
Material: Fiction
CONTACT: Children's Book Reader
Material: Children's
CONTACT: Poetry Reader
Material: Poetry
CONTACT: Nonfiction Reader
Material: Nonfiction
1011 Washington Ave. South, Ste. 300
Minneapolis MN 55415
Phone: 612-332-3192
Fax: 612-215-2550
Website: www.milkweed.org

Milkweeds for Young Readers

Please refer to Milkweed Editions.

Millbrook Press

Imprints: Twenty-First Century Books, Roaring Brook Press, Copper Beach Books

The Millbrook Press is a curriculum-oriented children's book publisher with a concentration on quality non-fiction for the school and library market. We publish approximately 130 new titles a year. Our imprints include Millbrook Press, Twenty-First Century Books, Roaring Brook Press, and Copper Beach Books.

ROARING BOOK PRESS

Roaring Brook Press is the new fiction and picture book division of Millbrook. We do not accept any unsolicited manuscripts or submissions.

Copper Beach Books

Copper Beach Books publishes works created by our affiliate in the United Kingdom. We do not accept any unsolicited manuscripts or submissions.

The Millbrook Press and Twenty-First Century Books

The Millbrook Press and Twenty-First Century Books accept only agented submissions. We do not accept unsolicited manuscripts. We are interested in works that have a strong, relevant tie to a school curriculum, such as math, science, American history, social studies, biography, etc. Proposals aimed at teachers or parents are not appropriate for us. We do not accept fiction, picture books, activity books, or other novelty submissions.

Please have your agent send a sample chapter, query letter, and outline, rather than a completed manuscript. Include a self-addressed, stamped envelope with all submissions, and allow at least six to eight weeks for our response. Manuscripts will be returned if not selected for further review by our editors—please send an appropriate-sized envelope with enough postage to handle the entire package—or you will not receive an answer of any kind.

We do not accept manuscripts over the Internet.

Categories: Nonfiction—Children—Education—History—Science

CONTACT: Editorial Assistant
Material: All
2 Old New Milford Rd .
Brookfield, CT 06804
Website: www.millbrookpress.com

Millennium Publishing Company

Established in 1998, MPC strives to produce quality literature that assists and serves a purpose that would otherwise go unnoticed by the publishing giants.

Facts

Publishes nonfiction only. Short, usually 200-400 pages. paperback only.

Publishes up to 5 titles per year.

90% first time authors. 100% unagented writers.

Responds in 1-2 months on queries, proposals and manuscripts.

Subjects

Nonfiction only. *Prefers the following:*

How To, Small Business Subjects, Career, General Reference, Travel, Medical Reference, Technical Manuals, Computer Subjects and Teen Subjects.

We consider any well-written nonfiction short book, that has a definable target market and that have not been done to death.

For example, in 2003 will publish: *Piece of Paradise: A Country by Country Guide to Foreign Ownership.* And *Entrepreneur's Guide to the Financial Section of a Business Plan.*

Does not want

Fiction, Poetry, cookbooks, personal stories and novels.

Pays

Usually buys all rights. Pays up to 30% royalty on net profits. Markets books with major retail bookstore chains and over the Internet.

How to submit

Prefers query (informal is okay) via email. State if book is already written or in progress. If written for a particular audience, explain potential market. If we are interest we will request sample chapter. E-mails can have attachments of .doc and .pdf only. Otherwise, paste directly into the body of the email.

Categories: Nonfiction—Business—Careers—Computers—General Interest—Health—Technical—Teen—Travel

CONTACT: Michele Hahn
Material: All
2307 Monaco
Mission TX 78574
E-mail: Michele@MillPubCo.com
E-mail: Submissions@MillPubCo.com (Send Queries)

Mills & Boon Historical Romance

Mills & Boon Medical Romance

Please refer to Harlequin, in the Book Publishers section.

Mira

Please refer to Harlequin, in the Book Publishers section.

Mississippi
University Press of Mississippi

The University Press of Mississippi is a nonprofit publisher that serves chiefly an academic audience. We receive approximately 600 submissions and publish an average of 60 manuscripts a year. Our editorial program focuses on the following areas:

Scholarly and trade titles in African American studies; American studies, literature, history, and culture; art and architecture; biography and memoir; ethnic studies; film studies; folklife; health; music; natural sciences; photography; popular culture; reference; serious nonfiction of general interest; Southern studies; women's studies; other liberal arts. Special series: American Made Music; Chancellor's Symposium in Southern History; Conversations with

Comic Artists; Conversations with Filmmakers; Faulkner and Yoknapatawpha; Hollywood Legends; Literary Conversations; Margaret Walker Alexander Series in African American Studies; Studies in Popular Culture; Understanding Health and Sickness; Willie Morris Books in Memoir and Biography

If you have a manuscript appropriate to our publishing program that you would like us to consider, we ask that you first submit a proposal. *Your proposal should include the following:*

- A description of the work
- A chapter outline

- One or two completed chapters
- The total number of words in the manuscript
- The number and type of illustrations, if any
- The anticipated date of completion

It normally takes 10-12 weeks for the editorial staff to review proposals and respond.

Thank you for your interest in the University Press of Mississippi.

Categories: Nonfiction—African American—Architecture—Arts—Biography—Civil War—Culture—Feminism—Film/Video—Gardening—General Interest—Health—History—Literature—Music—Native American—Photography—Reference—Regional—Theatre—Ethnic—Scholarly

CONTACT: Craig Gill, Editor-in-Chief
Material: Scholarly Books, Trade Books
3825 Ridgewood Rd.
Jackson MS 39211-6492
Phone: 601-432-6205
Fax: 601432-6217
E-mail: press@ihl.state.ms.us
Website: www.upress.state.ms.us

Moondance Publishing

Moondance Publishing, a company founded by Author/Lecturer Barry McKeown & Associates has positioned itself on the cutting edge of this revolution.

Moondance will continue to be very selective about what is published. If you have written what you feel is a work that will stand up to the high standards established by the associated network that makes up the Moondance Publishing Company we would be happy to hear from you. Please review the accompanying information and feel free to contact us about your manuscript.

Created by writers for writers, Moondance is an upscale publishing house with the highest regard for professionalism.

Submissions

Submission information and the submission form can found on our web site.

We publish mostly fiction but are not held to just that genre. Some humor and informational and if it's something really good we'll publish poetry.

Categories: Fiction—Humor—Poetry

CONTACT: Submissions Editor
Material: All
P O Box 16
Upper Black Eddy PA 18972
Phone: 610-982-5331
Fax: 610-982-5227
E-mail: caravan@moondancepublishing.com
Website: www.moondancepublishing.com

MORGAN REYNOLDS PUBLISHING

Morgan Reynolds Publishing

JUST THE FACTS

Morgan Reynolds publishes serious-minded nonfiction books for Juvenile and Young Adult readers. Our titles complement elementary and secondary school curriculums for young readers ages 10 to 18. We avoid obscure figures and "pop culture" icons (rock stars, movie stars, and sports figures). We prefer lively, well-written biographies of interesting figures for our biography series and insightful, exciting looks at critical periods for our events series. Subjects may be contemporary or historical. Past series have included: Civil Rights Leaders, Feminist Voices, Notable Americans, World Writers, Great Scientists, Masters of Music, American Business Leaders, and Great Events. We do not publish fiction, memoirs, pictures books, poetry, etc.

The burden is on the writer to convince us their idea is viable. To that effect, we suggest that writers wishing to make a submission first familiarize themselves with our books. Go to our website, your local public library, or favorite bookstore to obtain one or two of our books. Read our books!

A WORD ON FORM

We are looking for well-crafted biographies that present the subject's personality and development as a human being. Historical events should be treated with equal attention to detail and context. Thorough research of a subject is a prerequisite of any successful submission. The manuscript should draw from a variety of sources. Primary source quotations are a necessity. (However, secondary source quotations, such as what another biographer has written about the subject, are inappropriate.) Writers are urged to maintain chronology and to include information about the subject's childhood, youth, middle age, etc. Also important are the subject's family life, personal interests, and idiosyncrasies. Overall, manuscripts should bring the subject's PERSONALITY to the FOREFRONT, while providing a VIVID BACKDROP of CONTEXT.

Required text length is 25,000 words (exclusive of end matter) with 8-10 chapters of 2,500 to 3,000 words each. Writers provide contact information for illustration sources, a bibliography, source notes, glossary, and appendices (to be specified by the editor). Style sheets for end matter will be made available upon signing of a contract.

CHAPTERS, AN OVERVIEW

Chapter One

We prefer the first chapter to utilize a "hook," which gives the reader an idea of the subject's personality and legacy. The hook is generally a scene taken from adulthood of a particularly crucial point in the subject's life. For instance, a biography of Martin Luther King, Jr. may begin with his "I Have a Dream Speech."

Following the hook, there should be a brief discussion of the book's major theme. This theme is largely up to the writer, although it should incorporate the most notable aspect of the subject's life. The theme can be discovered by asking a few questions, such as: Why is this person or event worth writing about? What is the dominating characteristic of this person or event? Using King as an example, the theme of his biography could be: King fought to further the lives of black people in America using the tenents of nonviolence and direct action. Throughout the book, the writer should focus on the theme that is established in the first chapter.

Following the discussion of theme, the writer should begin a chronological biography starting with the subject's birth and family infor-mation, childhood, and education. In most cases, the first chapter should conclude with the subject's reaching maturity.

For books on historical events, the hook should reveal the players and circumstances at an exciting moment central to the event. The discussion of theme should isolate the focus of the book, and from there, the writer should begin a chronological discussion of the event.

Chapters Two and on

Each chapter can be thought of as mini-books, each with a beginning, middle, and end, that reflect the theme introduced in chapter one. Subsequent chapters should be centered around one or two central events, and care should be taken that the events are clearly explained with attention to their root causes and their influence. Conclude with a suggestion of what's to come.

At certain points in the book, it will be necessary to stop the chronological narrative for a discussion of historical context. Describing context will add interest and dynamism to the story. It will help young readers understand the world in which the subject lived and provide a framework for the choices the subject made. Using King as an example, a discussion of Jim Crow laws would help young readers understand segregation in the South. Pausing to discuss of the passage of the Civil Rights Act of 1964 will help young readers understand the impact of the Civil Rights movement. These discussions of context should provide enough information to embody the subject without overshadowing him.

In general, avoid ending with a summary chapter that lists why the subject was important. In some cases, a "legacy" chapter will be needed. For instance, in a biography of Martin Luther King, a short chapter at the end of the book discussing events after his assassination would be appropriate.

A WORD ON STYLE

Be concrete-use dates and outside events as yardsticks.

Although the audience is younger readers, the narrative voice should never be patronizing. Avoid speaking directly to the reader or asking rhetorical questions. Language should be concise and to the point. Strive to create reader interest by presenting the story in an exciting manner. Do not try to generate excitement with an elaborate or "cute" writing style.

COMMON STYLE CHOICES TO AVOID

- Rhetorical questions
- Subjunctive mood
- Overly-familiar tone
- Flowery language
- Extended metaphors
- Exclamation points
- Tentative language, such as "Probably," or "Perhaps"
- Passive voice

SUBMISSIONS

We suggest first-time writers query with a full manuscript. Sample chapter and an outline is admissible for experienced writers only. Mail submissions with a SASE to: Morgan Reynolds, Inc., Acquisitions, 620 South Elm Street, Suite 223, Greensboro, NC 27406. Please do not use any delivery service that requires a signature, such as registered or certified mail. Include daytime telephone number and email address on cover letter. If you would like your manuscript returned, include correct postage and envelope. A complete listing of our books is available at our website: www.morganreynolds.com or send us $1.06 postage to receive a printed catalog.

Categories: Nonfiction—Biography—History—Young adult.

CONTACT: Acquisitions
Material: All
620 South Elm St., Ste 223
Greensboro, NC 27406
336-275-1311
www.morganreynolds.com

Books
M-Z

Motorcycling
An Imprint of
Bristol Fashion Publications, Inc.

Dear Colleague,

Thank you for requesting our Writer & Photographer submission guidelines. You will find we are very cooperative when dealing with freelance contributors. Our Chairman and Publisher, John Kaufman, and our COO and Editor-in-Chief, Bob Lollo, were both freelance photographers and writers long before Bristol Fashion Publications, Inc. came to be in 1993. They still retain the memories of the "difficult years" getting started. This is one of the reasons we are interested in submissions from new authors and photographers.

All of our titles are motorcycle themes, aimed at the new or seasoned rider. All our titles cover restoration, repair, maintenance, touring, etc.

We rarely project more than six months in advance. Always include a SASE for any submissions you would like returned. Include your telephone number with any correspondence or submissions.

Photography Submissions

COVERS: Color glossy prints. Prints should be 3-1/2 x 5 to 5 x 7. Digitized images (300 DPI) in a JPG or GIF file are preferred for final use.

All covers depict the theme of the book. Use deep saturation, vivid colors and good contrast to bring out the main subject matter. This is NOT the type of cover you will see on a magazine. Send several sample copies of your work for consideration. Mark each copy with your name, address and phone number.

INTERIOR: Digitized images (300 DPI) in a GIF or JPG file are the only images we consider for use.

Photos should show hands using tools, when appropriate, the steps involved in completing a project and the finished results. These are the photos we most often need, however, other photos may be needed for a current title. Good contrast, lighting and subject matter is necessary. Send several hard copy or jpg/gif (on disk) samples of your work for consideration. Mark each copy with your name, address and phone number. We will not consider e-mailed images—please do not send them.

Simultaneous submissions are fine. Notify us if a photo we have on file becomes unavailable. Model and property releases are preferred if the person is identifiable. All submissions should be non-returnable disks or prints. If we can keep copies of your work on file, we are more likely to call you when the need arises. We will notify you within one month, whether or not we feel we can use your work. Assignments may be given at the same rate of pay, as noted below.

We purchase book/reprint rights as a one time buy. Cover prices range from $50.00 to $300.00 depending on the project. Interior B & W prices range from $10.00 to $25.00. Credit line given. One copy of the book will be given to each contributor.

Writer's Guidelines

Considering what we have read on the shelves, it appears we are the only publishing company that publishes for the non-handy riders. Our books use simple to understand and follow processes, for the person who knows which end of the wrench to hold, but little else. Each subject should take the reader from the very basics, through each step, until the complete subject matter is discussed. As the project expands and becomes more complicated, each new phase or technique should be described. If a friend, who knows nothing about bikes, can read, understand and feel comfortable doing the work you have described, you have written what we want to publish.

Non-How-To titles should be extremely interesting to read. Touring related books should speak of the community, to-do's, camping, culture and events not the "what I did" topics.

How-To topics are the most marketable with a wider audience. We are always seeking new ideas and topics for our books.

Simultaneous submissions are not accepted. Submit a few chapters for review, along with the table of contents. All submissions must be hard copy with a SASE. Include your past credits, tear sheets, state if photos or line art is available and the state of completion of your manuscript. We will report in two weeks of receipt, often sooner.

If you have never been published or have not yet started the manuscript submit a short sample (1000 words), outline, completion date and photo/line art availability.

We pay royalty of 8% to 11% based on the retail price of the book. Average retail price is $20.00 to $30.00. Photos and line art submitted by the author will be considered as part of the manuscript and the percentage adjusted accordingly. Follow the photography submission guidelines above. We will purchase worldwide book/reprint rights.

WRITERS TIPS: Know or research the industry, owners and technical knowledge. Use the proper motorcycle language and terms. A well-written manuscript is useless if the knowledge of the writer is lacking. If you are not familiar with a given subject, talk to people who has been around bikes for many years. Do not use unwarranted technical jargon to explain a subject. Use simple terms and an easy to understand and follow, step-by-step writing style. When we have to choose, we are more likely to use poor writing and good knowledge, than good writing and poor knowledge.

Preparing Your Manuscript

Never use an exclamation point for emphasis except in a direct quotation. We! and! the! reader! don't! care! what! startles! you!

Don't double-space, regardless of what you were taught in typing class.

Don't use the Tab key or Space bar to indent a paragraph.

Don't attempt to make your manuscript look as you'd like your book to appear. Just write. Converting your manuscript into a book is what we do.

Trust us. We have a combined experience of more than 200 years in the publishing industries. We will edit your manuscript to suit its intended market. The better your work reads, the better it sells, and that benefits all of us.

Please understand this—You will not retire from the book sales of any single specialty title. Specialty titles simply do not sell that well in any market. A very successful specialty title may sell 20,000 copies over a five year run. A very few sell more. Most sell one quarter or less of that number and are considered a successful book. Our successful authors often have three or more books published with us and they started by reading these very same guidelines.

After preparing your submission, following the above guidelines, you may submit it by land mail (hard copy only, do not include a disk) or by email. To submit by email, attach an ASCII text or MSWord file to the email—DO NOT paste the text into the body of the email or include graphic files with this submission. Send the email to jpk@bfpbooks.com. Include only one manuscript with each email submission.

Categories: Automobiles—Lifestyle—Mechanics—Travel

CONTACT: Submissions
Material: All
Bristol Fashion Publications, Inc.
PO Box 4676
Harrisburg, PA 17111
Phone: 772-559-1379

Fax: 800-543-9030
E-mail: jpk@bfpbooks.com
Website: www.bfpbooks.com

Mountain N' Air Books

1. Forms of Submissions
• By electronic means.
• Use major word processor, or ASCII format. Store it on a Zip 100-drive, or CD-ROM.
2. Subjects
• Non-fiction.
• Personal account on outdoor activities (climbing, biking, hiking, backpacking, etc)
• Adventure Travel, Armchair Travel, or Wilderness Travel Accounts.
• How to on cooking, outdoor activities, and travel tips.
3. Photos, Illustrations
• Prefer color slides, glossy black and white
• Illustrations, drawings and charts in 8" x10" or smaller.
• If submitting by electronic means all photographs, drawings and illustrations should be set at 300dpi (150 lpi)
• Must have model release from any identifiable person appearing on any photograph, or recognizable facsimile on drawings or illustrations.
4. Miscellaneous
• Any quotes contained must have permission to print from the author of the quote or publication from which the quote came from.
• Word count not necessary.
• No simultaneous submissions please.
• All materials should be sent to Mountain N' Air Books accompanied of a signed release authorizing Muntain N' Air Books and its agents to review the materials, without any obligation or commitment to publish or distribute any or all the materials.

Materials submitted will not be returned unless requested otherwise. If some or all the materials are to be returned to sender, or forwarded to others, please enclose a correctly addressed SASE.

Categories: Nonfiction—Adventure—Cooking—Outdoors—Recreation—Sports/Recreation—Travel—Western Writing

CONTACT: Gilberto Urso, Publisher
Material: All
PO Box 12540
La Crescenta CA 91224
Phone: 800-446-9696
Fax: 800-303-5578
Website: www.mountain-n-air.com

Mountain Press Publishing Company

Mountain Press publishes nonfiction trade books for general audiences, both adults and children. We will consider proposals for projects in natural history (including field guides for birds, wildlife, plants, etc.), western U.S. history, and earth science. Mountain Press is probably best known for its state-by-state series on Roadside Geology Roadside History, and Geology Underfoot; extended guidelines are available for these. Other than reprints of the works of Will James, we do not publish fiction, including historical fiction. We do not publish memoirs or personal stories. Children's books must be factual, without anthropomorphizing or storytelling.

STANDARDS. We accept only well-written, responsibly researched manuscripts. Your book must be both informative and engaging to the reader, written in lively, lucid prose. The topic must have broad, long-term appeal. The sources you rely on must be thoroughly documented and not infringe on any existing copyrights. You are responsible for supplying all photographs, maps, and other graphics your book may need.

STYLE. We urge authors to follow the tenets set forth in *The Chicago Manual of Style* (15th edition) and Strunk and White's *The Elements of Style*.

PROPOSALS. We accept unsolicited proposals from authors and literary agents. Please do not send your entire manuscript unless we ask for it. Submit a cover letter telling us who you are (including your credentials and publishing history), what your manuscript is about, who your target audience is, how your book differs from competing works, why you think Mountain Press should publish your book, and what you could do to help market it. Indicate the length of the book as well as the number of illustrations or photographs, whether they are color or black and white, and who owns the rights. Please do not send original photographs, illustrations, or artwork. Include an outline or table of contents, a sample of the manuscript (one or two chapters, double spaced), a core bibliography, photocopied examples of the artwork you plan to use, and an SASE to ensure safe return of your materials. Please do not send your submission by email or on electronic media. Normally we can respond to your proposal within six to eight weeks. Please call or email first if you have any questions.

Categories: Nonfiction—Biography—Ecology—History—Native American—Outdoors—Regional—Science—Geology

CONTACT: Acquisitions Editor
Material: All
PO Box 2399
Missoula MT 59806
Phone: 406-728-1900
Fax: 406-728-1635
E-mail: info@mtnpress.com
Website: www.mountain-press.com

Mountaineers Books

The Mountaineers Books produces guidebooks, instructional texts, historical works, adventure narratives, natural history guides, and works on environmental conservation. More than 450 titles from The Mountaineers are now in print. All of the books we publish are aimed at fulfilling the club's mission—to explore, study, preserve and enjoy the natural beauty of the outdoors—and, by extension, addressing the needs and concerns of like-minded outdoor enthusiasts throughout the world.

Mountaineers authors come from all over the world. Some are professional writers, while others are people who just want to share their specialized knowledge of some aspect of the outdoors.

Subject Matter:
The Mountaineers Books publishes nonfiction material about the outdoors. This includes non-competitive, non-motorized, self-propelled sports such as mountain climbing, hiking, walking, skiing, snowshoeing, and adventure travel. We also publish works on environmental and conservation subjects, narratives of mountaineering expeditions and adventure travel, outdoor guidebooks to specific areas, nature field guides, mountaineering history, safety/first aid, and books on skills and techniques for the above sports. If you plan to submit an adventure narrative, please request information about the Barbara Savage Miles From Nowhere Memorial Award. We do not publish fiction, general tourist guides, or guides dealing with hunting, fishing, snowmobiling, RV travel, horseback riding, or team sports.

Submission Procedures:
The Mountaineers is a non-profit outdoor activity club that publishes books via a paid staff. The review and approval process for a book we want to publish can take up to three months. We will make no commitment to any author until a project is approved. If you have something you think would fit in our line of books, we'd be happy to have a look and respond. If you aren't sure whether the subject of your proposal matches our interests, please send a query letter and SASE. *If*

you feel your proposal or manuscript fits the criteria above, then please supply the following:

- A statement that explains the proposed project's purpose, focus, scope, and significance, including a brief summary of the text
- A detailed chapter/subject outline or a detailed table of contents.
- At least five pages of introductory material and a complete table of contents
- For narratives, at least two sample chapters (not necessarily the first in the book) or for guidebooks, two to three trip write-ups, written in the style and length of the proposed book
- Information on the number and type of any photos, artwork, maps, or other illustrations proposed, along with samples (or good photocopies) of each type
- Information on the author's background and credentials to do this particular project
- Samples of other previously published writings by this author, if any
- Three editorial references
- Data on the size and scope of the intended market/audience of the project
- Description of what you would do to promote and market your book
- Information on any competitive books now in print (list and comment on specific titles) and how the proposed book is different and better than each

Mechanics:

All manuscript materials (reading text) must be double spaced, whether typewritten or word-processed. Please do not send disks. Do not send original manuscript materials; send only legible photocopies. When sending original art or photos, use UPS or Registered Mail to prevent loss in shipping. Include your name and address on all submitted materials-not just the outside envelope!

Categories: Nonfiction—Adventure—Conservation—Outdoors—Recreation—Hiking

CONTACT: Acquisitions Editor
Material: All
1001 SW Klickitat Way, Ste. 201
Seattle WA 98134
Phone: 206-223-6303
Fax: 206-223-6306
Website: www.mountaineersbooks.org

Munchweiler Press
Quality Books for Young Readers

(when we are accepting)

1. Submissions must be typewritten and double-spaced.

2. Enclose a brief cover letter with an introduction to the submission and a short bio of the author. Mention if you have anything published and by whom.

3. Enclose a self-addressed stamped envelope for feedback.

4. If you want the manuscript returned (if it's rejected), enclose a large enough envelope with sufficient postage for its return.

5. When we are accepting we are only open to picture book manuscripts for ages 4-8. No Young Readers, Middle Readers, chapter books, young adult or adult material will be considered. Stay tuned, we'll begin accepting again as soon as we can.

We normally respond within one to two months.

ARTIST'S SUBMISSION GUIDELINES

(Still accepting art samples.)

1. Artists may submit samples of their work for consideration in future projects.

2. Only copies should be sent. Please never send original art.

3. We are open to all styles, and all submissions will be acknowledged. We acknowledge receipt of materials within one to two weeks.

Categories: Nonfiction—Careers—College—Consumer—Culture—Entertainment—Family—Food/Drink—Games—General Interest—Hobbies—Lifestyle—Parenting—Recreation—Reference—Sports/Recreation—Travel—Humor

CONTACT: Rollin Riggs, President
Material: All
PO Box 770426
Memphis TN 38177
Phone: 901-684-1200
Fax: 901-684-1256
E-mail: MustangPub@aol.com

Music Sales Publishing Group

Please refer to Schirmer Trade Book.

The Mysterious Press

Please refer to Time Warner Book Group.

Naturegraph Publishers

Please approach us first with a query letter, outline of your work, and a sample chapter or two of your manuscript.

Your query letter should tell us what is unique about your book, your qualifications to write it, how it compares and contrasts with similar books on the same subject, why there is a need for your book, and how you can help us to make it a marketing success. We will acknowledge receipt of your proposal immediately.

If we are interested in your proposal, we will send you an author questionnaire to fill out and request to see the rest of your work. Authors whose work is accepted for publication will receive a contract specifying author responsibilities, royalties, expected publication date, etc.

Proposals submitted to us for consideration by our reviewing committee should belong to one of the following general categories: natural history, Native Americans, outdoor subjects, and natural crafts. Look at our catalog on our website or write to request our free catalog to get an idea of the types of books we publish.

Thank you for considering Naturegraph Publishers.

Categories: NonFiction—Crafts/Hobbies—Ecology—Environment—Gardening—Hobbies—Multicultural—Native American—Outdoors

CONTACT: Barbara Brown, Editor
Material: All
3543 Indian Creek Rd., PO Box 1047
Happy Camp CA 96039
Phone: 530-493-5353
Fax: 530-493-5240
E-mail: nature@sisqtel.net
Website: www.naturegraph.com

Naval Institute Press

Joint and general military subjects; naval biography; naval history; oceanography; navigation; military law; naval science textbooks; seapower; shipbuilding; professional guides; nautical arts and lore; technical guides. Limited military fiction.

Submissions require a minimum of two sample chapters, chapter outline, list of sources used, and authors biography. Include a cover letter.

All submissions must be typed, unbound, and accompanied by a cover letter. Only photocopies of artwork and photographs should be sent, not originals. Do not send disks with your submission. No manuscripts in binders!

Receipt of your manuscript will be acknowledged. Evaluation may take as long as twelve weeks.

Thank you for your interest in the Naval Institute Press.

Categories: Fiction—Nonfiction—Aviation—Boating—History—Military—Reference

CONTACT: Sara Sprinkle, Acquisitions Coordinator
Material: All
291 Wood Rd.
Annapolis MD 21402-5034
Phone: 410-295-4004
Fax: 410-295-1084

Neal-Schuman Publishers

A **general description of the book**, including: why such a book is needed, how it will be written or compiled, the audience and market to which the book is directed, any possible secondary audiences and markets, and comparisons with other similar books.

1 A **table of contents**, even tentative, including an estimate of the length or number of pages for each chapter, as well as the length of the total manuscript. Please specify types and approximate sizes of indexes.

2. A **tentative outline** describing in detail the main topics to be dealt with (this will go into more detail than the table of contents).

3. Any **chapter or sample pages** available in draft form, which are representative of the elements of the book, including tabular material, illustrations, entries, etc.

4. A draft **preface** that tells your potential readers: who the book is for, the purpose of the book, how it was compiled or written, your reasons for writing the book, how the book is organized, (if applicable) how it can be used. (This differs from item 1 above in that you're speaking here to your potential reader whereas item 1 speaks to us as a publisher.)

5. The **projected date** of manuscript completion.

6. A **brief resume**, including other publications, related activities, etc.

Categories: Test books

CONTACT: Charles Harmon, Director of Publishing
100 William Street
Suite 2004
New York, NY 10038
Phone: 212-925-8650
Fax: 212-219-8916
Email: charles@neal-schuman.com
Website: www.neal-schuman.com

Nelson Reference & Electronic Publishing

We welcome proposals for reference books that promise to serve readers well. We want to review a book proposal before receiving a completed manuscript. Reviewing and making initial publishing decisions on the basis of a proposal, rather than a completed manuscript, is almost always in the best interests of both the author and the publisher. Even if you have completed a manuscript you wish us to review, please prepare and submit a proposal first. Write the proposal as well as you can; in deciding whether or not to pursue publication, we will consider not only the merits of your proposal, but also the quality of your writing.

Do the following in your proposal:

1. State the books purpose and scope. Usually one paragraph is sufficient. The purpose statement should identify what your proposed work enables readers to do; and the statement of scope should identify your works range or depth of treatment. Keep in mind that we publish almost exclusively for the lay and general audience. We rarely publish works primarily for an academic audience. However, we do publish works that have special value for ministers and other church leaders when those works are also clearly useable by lay and general readers.

2. Describe the primary audience of the book and any secondary audiences. For us, the formula to publishing success requires books to have both merit and marketability. To determine marketability, we need to know who are the target buyers and who are the secondary ones.

Think carefully about who would benefit the most from what your work offers. Think about the situations in which your work would be used and what it assumes the target reader will already know, be able to do, and desire.

Sometimes the primary audience may be truly general. For example, the primary audience for a desktop or collegiate dictionary of American English includes all truly literate Americans—all who want help with words they find in their reading or use in their writing or speaking. But often the primary audience of a book is smaller. For example, the primary audience of our academically oriented Word Biblical Commentary differs greatly from the primary audience of our Communicators Commentary, which aims at helping preachers and teachers move from the biblical text to their contemporary listeners.

Describe your works primary and secondary audience(s) as realistically and precisely as you can.

3. Demonstrate the need for the book by analyzing the books already on the market with which it will compete. Research all books on the market that are at all similar to the work you propose. Identify and list in a comparative table the features and benefits to the reader for each; then list the features and benefits of your work. Indicate how your book will surpass what is now available. If no other books do what you propose to do, explain why that is the case. Do not overlook the importance of this step. Your proposal is your attempt to make a strong case for our publishing your work, and we need you to show us that you know what is already available and why the target audience for your work would buy it over another book.

4. Summarize the main points of each chapter with an annotated Table of Contents. Two to five sentences per chapter is usually enough. State concisely what each chapter does, as well as how each chapter benefits the reader. Some reference books are not, of course, divided into chapters. For such a work, treat each major section as a chapter.

5. Provide two or three complete chapters (or representative samples of major sections if the work is not organized in chapters). Provide an introductory chapter that sets the task of the rest of the book, the chapter you believe provides the most helpful or distinctive information, and a chapter that summarizes and concludes the work. For works not divided into chapters, provide a full introduction and representative samples of each major section. For these representative samplings, include a group of continuous pages that shows all the features of that section.

6. Estimate the length of the complete manuscript (in double-spaced pages and in total words) and the date by which you could complete it.

7. Describe the kinds and quantity of non-text material to be included in the work. Such items include photographs, line art, charts, tables, graphs, and maps. Indicate which you can provide and which you expect the publisher to provide. Keep in mind that properly illustrating a book enhances its value greatly but that such illustrations usually also raise the cost of its production. Be judicious in specifying non-text material that will not be provided in camera-ready form. (For example, photographs are not camera ready, while line drawings are.)

8. Identify authorities in the subject field of your work who you

believe will endorse or contribute a Foreword to your work. Especially if you are a new author, the marketability of your work increases at least partly to the extent to which you can solicit good endorsements. At the proposal stage, we must have only a list of potential endorsers. Depending on the work and the extent to which you are known as an author, we may agree to publish your work contingent on your getting enough satisfactory endorsements.

9. Indicate if you are submitting this proposal to other publishers at the same time. We prefer that you propose your work only to us; however, if you have proposed it to other publishers also, please tell us.

10. Provide information about you—the contents of a resume or vita (although not necessarily that formal), along with an emphasis on the education and/or experience that qualifies you as somewhat of an authority on the topic your work covers.

11. Allow us twelve weeks after receipt of your proposal before you call to ask about its review. We will acknowledge receipt of your proposal by letter.

Categories: Christian Interests—Reference—Religion—Spiritual

CONTACT: Nelson Reference & Electronic Publishing
Material: All
501 Nelson Pl., PO Box 141000
Nashville TN 37214(-1000)
Phone: 615-889-9000
Fax: 615-391-5225

New Concepts Publishing

New Concepts Publishing, the first totally electronic romance publishing house, was established in the spring of 1996. NCP went on-line with their first four novels, Amber Moment, Lord of Chaos, Liar's Poker, and Shattered Dreams, in October of 1996. At first publishing only 2 to 4 novels a month, NCP is now publishing 8 to 20 novels and short stories every month. NCP paved the way for many current independent e-publishers' success with innovative author contracts, royalty percentages, and by taking chances on fresh and original books. E-publishing is now a force to be reckoned with—it has changed the way major NY publishers deal with authors—and we are proud to have been on the forefront of this burgeoning market!

NCP currently receives between 25,000 and 45,000 hits to their website every day. We have numerous authors making between $1,000 and $10,000 in royalties every pay period, with that number growing exponentially each month. It is our goal to have all of our authors making a comfortable living exclusively by writing within the next several years if they can work full time as with any other career. Since 2003 our sales have doubled—and sometimes tripled—every quarter, and we are well on our way to becoming a multi-million dollar company by 2006.

Our print books are widely distributed through Ingram's, Baker & Taylor, Bertram's, and many other distributors, and our Trade Paperbacks are sold throughout Waldenbooks across the country as well as a growing number of fine independent bookstores. Our e-books consistently hold many of the top 25 best-selling e-book positions on Fictionwise.com, the leading retailer of e-books.

The primary goal of New Concepts Publishing, from its inception, was to bring high quality fiction to book lovers. By offering our authors generous royalty percentages and creative freedom, we've not only attracted many fine authors, but can offer work 'written from the heart', fresh, excitingly different stories stringent guidelines would not allow.

HARMONY™ Submission Guidelines

Authors should know that the Harmony™ line is all about romance and the harmonious blending of races and cultures. These are MULTI-RACIAL romances, not simply interracial romances, and race issues should NOT hang over the storyline like a dark thundercloud. The conflict, as with any other romance, should arise from the characters themselves and should be strong enough to carry the story, and yet resolvable. Bringing together racists is not resolvable conflict within the confines of a book and therefore not desirable as the primary conflict of the story. The hero and heroine can be of the same race, or of two different races. The main difference between the romances written for the Harmony line and other romances is that Harmony will bring color and intriguing cultures together so that readers of many backgrounds and races will have characters to fall in love with and identify with. Authors should keep in mind when they sit down to develop a storyline for Harmony that, regardless of race, creed, color, or religious background, women are women, the world over, all searching for that special someone to love who will give them love and passion in *return*.

Authors should always remember that romances are stories designed to fulfill every woman's fantasy, and Harmony™ is no exception.

Stories for the Harmony™ line should follow the general guidelines of any good futuristic, fantasy, historical, or paranormal romance. We are primarily seeking stories in these genres that are spicy or erotic in sensuality. These novels should be a minimum of 60,000 words and no more than 120,000 words long. A query letter and synopsis should be emailed to submissions@newconceptspublishing.com.

Please note: We will continue to consider multi-racial romances for our NCP romance line if it does not meet our goals for the Harmony™ line.

We are *actively* seeking top-notch:

Historical Romance
Contemporary Romance
Romantic Suspense
Fantasy Romance
Paranormal Romance
Futuristic/S.F. Romance

We're receiving a fair amount of good quality paranormals in old favorites like vampires. This is good, however, there are worlds beyond vampires and werewolves. NY is getting into this market in a serious way. Vampires and werewolves are going to get old fast, so it's up to us to keep the paranormal market fresh and alive. Ghosts, fairies, psychics, fire starters, superheroes, skin walkers, mystery, unexplained phenomenon (i.e. X Files) etc. The only limit to this genre is your imagination. Believe me, we have readers dying to get their hands on something different from the norm. Draw inspiration from classic TV like Outer Limits, Twilight Zone, X Files. There's no doubt that this genre is hot right now. You can see it everywhere on TV and in movies. Books should keep up with the times and go beyond.

We still have a need for original contemporary, historical, fantasy, and futuristic, so keep this in mind when you're brainstorming your next project. We want "big" contemporaries—not necessarily Harlequin type books, but along the lines of Jaycee Clark, Linda Howard, Susanne Brockman, Cherry Adair, etc. Romantic suspense, chick lit, and some romantic comedy would be great! Just remember, if you've seen the plot a thousand times by Harlequin, chances are it's not going to go over well with small press readers. NY publishers dominate this market. It's going to be extremely tough to build up sales in the small press industry, but it is possible to have good sales with readers-we've done it before. Sexy characters and situations are good. What can you do that's different? Take your story somewhere exotic, introduce elements of the forbidden or taboo in your story like domination/submission, voyeurism, fetishes, or have an adventure like Romancing the Stone or Treasure Hunt.

In the historical market, we want something other than what's being published in the NY arena. This means no Avon historical type plots that revolve around catching a husband. Unfortunately, this plot has been done to death. I'd love to see darker historical romance with a lot of "meat" to the plot, tormented/flawed characters, emotionally drenched, gothic, or epic adventures of the type that used to be published. Highland warriors, pirates, highwaymen, spies, clan wars, Vikings, Tudor, Celtic, American Indian, revolutionary period—the list goes on and on, and the possibilities are endless. We need fresh sexy plots, time periods, and exciting characters to revitalize this market. I'd hate to see it die off because it's headed that way right now. I think NY won't take chances, and it's up to us to do it. With the right books we can get the readers back to loving the historical romance genre.

Futuristic Romance-the world we live in is changing rapidly. Use it to plot your books. Scientists are discovering new worlds and galaxies right now. The first android has just been introduced in Japan. Nanotechnology is not far from practical use. Read science magazines and visit their websites. There is tons of stuff out there just waiting to be written about.

Fantasy Romance-again, good plots and characters are key to this. Chances are, if a reader likes historicals and paranormals, they're just steps away from loving this genre too. Dragons, manticore, centaur, unicorns-add interesting creatures and magical abilities to your characters. Take them on an epic adventure, or deal with social issues like racism, overpopulation, etc. We'd love to see more in this genre, and I know we've only scratched the surface here.

Also, keep in mind that your audience is mostly women, 25 years old and up. They want the men in these books to be different than what they see every day in their lives: romantic, cultured, strong, capable, take charge, witty. NO nerds or wimps. If they wanted that, there are plenty of NY books to satisfy that need. Heroes shouldn't demean the heroine or humiliate her and vice versa. Strong heroines are very good. Bitches are not. Learn to recognize the difference between spunky/sassy, and bitchy.

Elements strongly desired in any novel or short story include: edgy, unique plots; strong, believable conflict between the hero and heroine; heavy sexual tension; concise story-telling; combinations of dark, sexy heroes with sassy, humorous heroines, inter-racial, and characters that reflect the spectrum of the world such as East-Indian, Asian, African American, etc. We have readers of all colors and would love to publish romance representative of different cultures and races.

REGARDING SEX:

Why do readers read romance? For the experience of "seeing" two people fall desperately in love. Sex is a huge part of a relationship. Your romance should fully explore just how fantastic sex is between SOUL MATES. In the real world, would you continue dating someone that didn't excite you sexually? The most likely answer is no. Keep this in mind when writing your romance.

What we like to see in our CARNAL rated books are explicit love scenes that relate the FULL spectrum of making love/having sex between characters who are obviously meant for each other. Readers want explosive chemistry between the characters, with a heated buildup of sexual tension. What we want in all of our romances are love scenes that deliver exciting emotion once the characters come together sexually.

Vary your language and style in your love scenes to keep them fresh. Explore emotional aspects. Dialogue within a love scene is also good. But take note, overuse of any word, most particularly the more graphic or crude, can become tedious to anyone as well as desensitizing. As a writer, your imagination is key. Euphemisms are acceptable as long as they are not ridiculous or take away from the story. Love scenes should be earthy and frank, sensual and real.

Explicit language is perfectly acceptable as long as it not overused and is appropriate for what you've established with your characters. A medieval lady would never say "Eat my p*ssy, my lord"—this would most likely conjure up laughs because of its inaccuracy and lack of realism—something you should always bear in mind.

We do NOT publish, nor will we consider, pornography. We publish romance for romance readers. All books should have a fresh PLOT with intriguing characters as well as frank love scenes that make the story line progress and have bearing on the plot. If your love scene can be removed and it doesn't affect the plot, it shouldn't be there.

Now, aside from the technicalities of language, we prefer all books to have a strong plot and compelling characters. Romance is also a major focus of these types of books (CARNAL rated). Books with nothing but sex and little or no plot will not be considered. While personally, we have no problem with homosexuality, we cater to a specific audience, and so are not accepting books that focuse on homosexuality, however, this can be a subplot if the book is long enough. Other elements that will not be tolerated: bestiality, incest, underage sex, extreme S/M or D/S to the point of injury and humiliation. If you're unsure about something, please email us and we'd be happy to answer your questions.

NEW PROJECTS!

Anthologies:

Bound - Erotic or spicy BDSM romance in any setting, time period, or sub-genre. Stories should be 20,000 to 30,000 words in length. Bondage, domination, and submission preferred, with heroes being the dominant partner. First and foremost, the stories should be romances with BDSM as an integral part of the story-line along with heavy sexual tension. Captive fantasies, bondage clubs, suspense, and suspense are just some of the examples of what can be done for this anthology. Email submissions@newconceptspublishing.com with your query. Currently no deadline for submissions.

Tempting the Beast - Erotic or spicy Shape-shifter romance in any setting, time period, or sub-genre, such as Futuristic or Fantasy. Stories should be 20,000 to 30,000 words in length. Animal shifters such as wolf, lion, tiger, panther, etc. are ideal as well as shifting into winged men/women, centaurs, dragons, griffins, and other fantasy type creatures. We also prefer for the hero to be the shifter, alpha, sexy, and powerful. Email submissions@newconceptspublishing.com with your query. Currently no deadline for submissions.

The Eternal - Erotic or spicy Vampire romance in any setting, time period, or sub-genre, such as Futuristic or Fantasy. Stories should be 20,000 to 30,000 words in length. Email submissions@newconceptspublishing.com with your query. Currently no deadline for submissions.

Special Projects:

Legends and Lore - Another project on the drawing board are stories based on legends and lore. Every culture has them and there are any number of sites on the web devoted to different regions and the legends and lore of their culture. These projects should be BASED on lesser known legends and lore for the 'fairy tale' like atmosphere and the paranormal elements. Writers should avoid those that have already been done ad nauseum—such as the legend of King Author or Robin Hood. These stories can be any length, but novel length is preferred, from category length and up. They should also be at least spicy.

Romancing the Classics - Spicy or Carnal preferred, though we will consider Sensual. Classic stories and novels like Dracula, Pride and Prejudice, Beauty and the Beast, etc. are retold in a variety of romantic subgenres, i.e. suspense, futuristic, paranormal, comedy, etc. We want to be surprised with your ingenuity! Stories can range anywhere from 10,000 to 100,000 words.

NCP also accepts short stories (**10,000 - 15,000 words**) for our LOVE BITES series. This is a great way for interested authors to break into a new market and target new readers eager for erotic fiction. We also feel stories can be written fairly quickly for a good return on royalties and will be priced $2.00 - $2.99, download only. Stories can take place in any setting or subgenre but must include romance elements as well as fall under the SPICY or CARNAL rating system.

Andrea DePasture, Editor in Chief

Email Andrea DePasture

There are certain things we all look for when selecting a book to read, I, as an editor, am no different. What I look for in a book is an unusual plot, interesting twists, characters and situations that wring out every emotion, writing that is clear and concise, easily read or for high reading levels. We all want the thrill of discovering a new talent, and that's what I'm looking for. The beginning should have a powerful hook that leaves the reader breathless, filled with questions they simply MUST have answered. From there, however, you can't let them become bogged down with back story. Reveal just enough to leave them wanting more, enough to keep them reading. Pacing should be tight, no matter the genre, and there should be a balanced blend of narrative and dialogue. It is extremely important to have your book grammatically correct and to run a spelling check (you'd be surprised how many authors neglect this step). As for sexual content—it can range from sensual to erotic as long as whatever level it is, it is tastefully done. I do NOT want pornography, but erotica is highly welcomed.

I am currently acquiring all genres to round out my list:

HISTORICAL ROMANCE AND HISTORICAL EROTIC ROMANCE: I have a love of history and would like to publish books that vibrantly bring the past to life for readers. I am interested in all time periods, including the shorter Regency romances (Regency period is a long time favorite for me). I always enjoy a good medieval and am particularly interested in books set during time periods not frequently written about or set in unusual locales such as Russia, Germany, France, Caribbean, etc. It is my belief that readers of historical romance enjoy being immersed back in time, and every country and island has its own interesting history that I think would fascinate any reader. I am disturbed to see that the historical genre is dwindling down to only a few time periods. I do not want this to happen. Whatever time period is selected, the history and locale should, naturally, be vital to the story—your plot and characters should not be able to survive in another period. They should be products of their surroundings and time period, authentic to minute detail. Sexual tension should be taut throughout the book, teasing and teasing until the culmination. If sex happens early in the book, you still need tension, regardless, though it is more difficult once done. I also do not want to see stereotypical characters.

PARANORMAL ROMANCE (CONTEMPORARY AND HISTORICAL), THRILLERS, and PARANORMAL EROTICA: I love all things supernatural, having cut my teeth on horror when I first began reading as a child. Time travel, ghosts, reincarnation, vampires, shapeshifters, fairies, anything otherwordly—it's all vastly fascinating for me and for many a person, hence the rise of paranormal television shows, movies, and more. Erotic and sexually charged books in the vein of Laurell K. Hamilton are something I am on the particular lookout for.

FUTURISTIC/SCIENCE FICTION ROMANCE: These would include earth, space, other worlds, and altiverse as well. Futuristic romance is always a good seller for us, in particular captive scenarios, which seem to be a fantasy many readers have. If you have a plot that has been done many times before, that's fine, but what makes yours different? What makes it outstanding? Something that readers will pick up?

FANTASY ROMANCE: I've seen it done many times, but I still like epic fantasy, where good triumphs over evil despite the odds stacked against them. Lord of the Rings has brought back fantasy in a big way, and I think it will continue to rise in popularity over the next several years. The Dragonlance series was what I began with, and I still enjoy seeing books with fantastical creatures as an integral part of the action. Give me characters to care about, a villain to despise, magic, strife, sword fighting, even a touch of romance. Fairy tale type fantasy or books based on fairy tales (what about Russian fairy tales? German? Japanese? Indian? Etc.) are another I will look at, but please, no Robin Hood or Camelot. These have been done to death.

CONTEMPORARY ROMANCE: I enjoy most contemporaries, including suspense, multicultural, and ethnic. What I don't want to see are plots that have been overused ie. Secret baby, cowboy and city girl, etc.

WHAT I'M NOT INTERESTED IN: I have no interest in religious/inspiration/new age, politics or espionage, organized crime, poetry, or the drug trade.

PEEVES: Overuse of semicolons (really, they don't need to be there at all), incorrect grammar and spelling, wimpy heroines and heroes, telling instead of showing, not following submission instructions.

For submissions, I prefer the cover letter to be one to two pages long detailing what the book is about, what the genre is, what other works you have finished or sold, and your current email address. The synopsis should let me know, in more detail, the plot of the book and character development, but it should not be more that four or five pages long.

Jeri Smith Youness, Editor

Jeri Smith Youness is a former acquisitions editor and cover copywriter for Macmillan, Berkley, Silhouette and Penguin USA in New York City. She has taught romance writing at the Loft Literary Center in Minneapolis and has worked as an evaluation editor for Romantic Times in New York for over ten years. She is the author of three gothic novels, LEGACY OF HUNTER HOUSE, WITCH TREE INN and THE HAUNTING OF VICTORIA, which won the Bookrak Best-selling Gothic award. She conducts writing workshops at annual romance writing conferences where she leads authors in creating rough drafts of their story ideas. Under her mentoring, Jeri has helped many first-time writers get published. She recently attended the first Historical Novel Society in Salt Lake City where she critiqued historical romance novels for first-time novelists. Today, Jeri is an editor for New Concepts Publishing and is currently looking for Paranormal, Fantasy, Sci-fi/ Futuristic that are spicy or erotic, Historical romance (not Western). She will consider Romantic Suspense and Contemporary Romance, as long as they are well researched and well written.

All submissions should include a letter which briefly describes your publishing history or writing credits (contests, etc.) and/or any organizations you're affiliated with, the genre and story idea you're submitting.
2) a brief synopsis (one or two pages) or outline (we're looking for conflict and plot development)
3) a printout of the entire manuscript
4) a SASE large enough to accommodate the return of the manuscript
5) the book on PC DISK in either RTF or MsWord
6) Due to excessive postage expenses, Authors outside the US are not required to ship the printed manuscript. Authors outside the US should ship the book on disk, synopsis and SASE.

We do NOT publish non-fiction, pornography, literary works, or gay/lesbian fiction.
We DO publish popular romance in most every sub-genre. We rarely publish short story collections, but occasionally will accept stories

with a common theme and wide reader appeal.

Markets: New Concepts Publishing was the first, continuously operating romance electronic publisher in the world. Regardless, ebooks are still the new kid on the block and authors submitting should be aware that, although we offer the best royalty percentages possible, royalties at this time are not comparable to royalties paid by the megacorporation print publishers, who have been establishing their markets for 50 years or more. We are still building our markets, but are probably best established in the Romance Market (single title), which is where we began. Regardless, we're interested in building across the board, and are acquiring most genres. Since we are building markets, we require a minimum commitment of 2 years for exclusive electronic rights. Also, we do print publication, but books will be offered exclusively as ebooks for six months to the first year, so you should not look to see the book in print until after the book is released as an ebook.

Word count requirements/limitations - minimum word count for single publication is 60,000 for most genres. Currently, we are accepting some erotic romance novellas 20,000 to 39,000 words, but only those novellas with a SPICY or CARNAL sensuality rating. Maximum for any genre should be no more than 120,000. None of these word counts are set in stone. However, a story should be no longer than it needs to be.

Please do NOT decide to make major changes on the book after you have submitted and/or contracted with NCP. When we contract on the submission, we expect to publish the book we have contracted on.

The best way to determine whether your book is right for us is to thoroughly research our company by buying NCP books. However, the list below should help also.

What we look for:
1) A unique writing voice
2) Popular themes with new twists
3) Innovative story ideas
4) Mastery of writing skills
5) Tight pacing
6) Strong conflict (this can include both internal and external so long as the internal conflict is strong)
7) Strong motivations
8) Good, believable dialogue
9) A good balance between description and dialogue
10) Historical accuracy(accurate research)
11) Books that leap immediately into 'the problem'
12) Books that have an element of romance (love makes the world go 'round and is one of the most powerful (attractive) motivations a character can have. This is not a MUST and, in fact, the motivation of love could apply to love of family, or self etc. in genres other than romance. Self preservation is a perfectly acceptable motive. However revenge is far less appealing in a hero/heroine and greed belongs under villain motivations.

What we don't like to see:
1) Books that use the first two or three chapters to give us an in-depth background history of the characters.
2) Weak conflict
3) Little or no believable motivation
4) Poor grammar/spelling/punctuation
5) Well worn story plots that offer no new twists
6) Fad story lines
7) Too much technical or historical detail8) Not enough, or accurate, detail to attain the 'flavor' of the period
9) Stories that wander aimlessly and/or come to a stop while the author ventures off in another direction to give us background or character history or background history of minor character or subplots
10) Storylines with limited audience appeal

11) Dog tired politically correct themes and/or sterotypical characters - people are people, regardless of race, religion, sex, etc., etc. and behave according to upbringing, personality traits and economic situation... all fat people aren't jolly gluttons, gay people are no more likely to be evil than anyone else and so forth, not everyone during the civil war was against slavery, or involved in the underground railroad...all Africans were not Uncle Remus/Aunt Jemima.....Please do not send materials which include insulting/sterotypical behavior. Strive for accuracy and open-mindedness.

BOOK LENGTH:

Full Novel = 90,000 words and up; 360 pages and up (double-spaced)
Mid Novel = 61,000-89,000 words; 244-356 pages (double-spaced)
Category = 40,000-60,000 words; 160-240 pages (double-spaced)
Novella = 20,000-39,000 words; 80-156 pages (double-spaced)

SENSUALITY RATING:

SWEET: behind-closed-doors sex and/or very mild love scenes and sexual encounters
SENSUAL: love scenes comparative to most romance novels published today
SPICY: heavy sexual tension; graphic details and more sexual encounters
CARNAL: graphic sex and language; may be offensive to delicate readers; contains many sexual encounters and can include unconventional sex not normally found in romance; may or may not be romance; typically known as erotica

Response times vary, but we try to get back to authors on emailed queries within a month unless we are overwhelmed by submissions.

Categories: Romance

CONTACT: Submissions
5202 Humphreys Rd
Lake Park, GA 31636
Website: www.newconceptspublishing.com

New Harbinger Publications

We have an ongoing need for book-length manuscripts on how readers can best deal with specific psychological and health care challenges. We're looking for books that appeal to both lay and professional audiences, offering theory, step-by-step techniques, and examples.

Recent titles that we have published include:
1) Five Good Minutes: 100 Morning Practices to Help You Stay Calm & Focused All Day Long
2) Get Out of Your Mind and Into Your Life: The New Acceptance & Commitment Therapy
3) Parenting a Bipolar Child: What To Do and Why
4) Going Home without Going Crazy: How to Get Along with Your Parents and Family (Even When They Push Your Buttons)

If you have any further questions, please feel free to email me anytime. Thanks for including us in your directory.
Categories: Nonfiction—Health—Psychology

CONTACT: Acquisitions
Material: All
5674 Shattuck Ave.
Oakland, CA 94609
Phone: 510-652-0215, 800-748-6273
Fax: 510-652-5472
Website: www.newharbinger.com

New Horizons Press
Small Horizons Imprint

We are continuing the Tradition of True Stories of Uncommon Heroes. We are always looking for manuscripts about true-life heroes. If you have one, we welcome unsolicited manuscripts.

Topics and Types of Stories We Are Looking For

Topics: Manuscripts which fit into our :60 Second Series, such as grief aid and other "bandage" topics for quick remedy pain relief (*:60 Second Anger Management/:60 Second Sleep-Ease/:60 Second Stress Relief*).

• Targeted self-help topics for general and specialty audiences written by mental health and other professionals (*Older Women, Younger Men, I'm Grieving As Fast As I Can, Red Hot Relationships*).

• Hard-hitting issues with news impact and publicity value (*Swallowing A Bitter Pill Sweet Poison, Woman to Woman 2000*).

• Topics which fit into our *Small Horizons* imprint, such as those which teach crisis, coping and service skills, and which are written by mental health professionals or educators (*My Stick, Family, I Am So Angry, I Could Scream, The Empty Place*).

Types of Stories: People who change the system. The courageous individual must be one of the characters in the story and has to be the author or co-author.

• Redemption/True Crime Stories: A person goes wrong, repents and then does something incredibly good for others. Crime oriented accounts are welcome, as long as there is a hero advancing justice, but no child abuse or incest stories (*Grave Accusations, Legacy of Courage, Murder In Memphis*).

• Exploring New Frontiers Stories: People who break or dismantle social or personal barriers (*Klan-destine Relationships, A Mountain Too Far, Edgewalkers*).

• Victim Stories: Victims who fight back and refuse to be victimized and then fight for the rights of others or a good cause (*Tainted Roses, Whispers of Romance, Threats of Death, Run Jane Run*).

IF YOU HAVE A NONFICTION MANUSCRIPT THAT FITS OUR FOCUS, WE WOULD LOVE TO SEE IT.

Be Sure to Include:

• Cover letter with your name, address, phone and fax numbers and E-mail address
• Book Proposal, which includes:
• Title page
• Table of contents
• Overview
• Chapter-by-chapter outline
• Photograph of author(s)
• Bio or CV of author(s)
• Marketing or commercial outlook
• Competition
• Promotion outlets
• Full or partial manuscript (If you have been previously published in nonfiction, a partial is acceptable)
• SASE.

Categories: Nonfiction—Alternate Life-style—Children—Crime—Family—Health—Human Rights—Inspirational—Lifestyle—Multicultural—New Age—Relationships—Self Help—True Crime—Women's Issues

CONTACT: Ms. P. Patty, Editor
Material: All
US Mail—PO Box 669
Far Hills NJ 07931
Phone: 908-604-6311
E-mail: nhp@newhorizonpressbook.com
Package Delivery: PO Box 218
34 Church St.
Liberty Corner NJ 07938
Website: www.newhorizonpressbooks.com

New Society Publishers

New Society Publishers is a progressive publishing company that specializes in books for activists, books that contribute in fundamental ways to building an ecologically sustainable and just society. We sell our books to a North America-wide market, using trade distributors in both Canada and the United States, as well as through direct mail and the Internet. We also have distribution channels overseas.

A large majority of the books we publish we either initiate ourselves or acquire through previous contact with the author, or with an organization with which the author works. We sometimes publish manuscripts that are wholly unsolicited, and we welcome queries from authors, potential authors, agents, or organizations seeking a publisher or co-publisher. For a better sense of what we like to publish, please either request a catalog, or check out our on-line catalog at: www.newsociety.com.

Editorial Objectives

Our mandate is to work for broad social transformation toward sustainability, through nonviolent means. We specialize in providing the understanding, the tools and the skills for enabling such a transformation to occur. Our editorial focus on sustainable living includes a broad subject area ranging from globalization, through green building and renewable energy, to conscientious commerce, conflict education, and more. We aim to help build an alternative infrastructure to that of the mainstream—books to build a new society.

NSP also sees itself as a solutions publisher, providing 'good news' most of the time as well as clear analysis of the major issues we face in the struggle to create a more just and equitable world. Our emphasis is always inspirational, motivational, and skill-oriented. We don't publish books that merely catalog what is wrong in the world; we *do* publish books that show that we can take control over our lives and change the way things are - and which suggest how we can accomplish this. Although we believe that fiction and poetry can play an important role in social change, they require different expertise and different marketing, neither of which we can provide; *please do not submit such works*.

While we will consider any proposal that fits our broad editorial goals outlined above, we are particularly interested in books that fall into these major (and overlapping) areas:

Globalization, Current Affairs and Activism: Increasingly, we live in a globalized world dominated by large corporate and government interests. These books analyze key current affairs of global importance and focus on ways in which people are organizing and acting to resist the worst excesses.

Sustainable Living: books that contribute in original ways to achieving ecological, social, and cultural sustainability - from growing food to cooking it, to housing ourselves, moving ourselves around, changing our behaviors and facing a future with fewer resources.

Environment & Economy: these books address key issues ranging from climate change through the rapid demise of our oceans, the end of cheap oil and the 'nature' of economic growth.

Ecological Design: There are alternatives to slums, sprawl and suburbs. These books provide tools and methods for designing our towns and cities so that we may live more within the ecological limits of our home places and more in harmony with our neighbors.

Natural & Green Building: Shelter is one of our primary needs. Yet our dwellings have become so complex that most of us can no longer build them and they are now often bad for your health. The Natural and Green building movements are changing all this, as the highly practical books in this category demonstrate.

Renewable Energy: As the world runs out of oil, we need to learn how to live from the abundance provided from the sun, the wind, from water and from human ingenuity crafted carefully to place.

Resistance and Community: books that help break the vicious cycle of environmental exploitation and the cultural, economic, political, and social dislocation of communities - and books that help people reestablish the bonds of community, both with humankind and with nature.

Progressive Leadership: resources and training manuals devoted to nonhierarchical group dynamics and democratic decision making, nonviolent action strategies and tactics, support and empowerment for leaders, activists, and organizations, etc.

'Conscientious Commerce:' books that focus on the 'new business' - the ways in which business is transforming itself to take responsibility for environmental and social concerns, etc.

Education & Parenting: books that analyze our educational systems and propose alternatives; that explore nonviolent forms of child-rearing and play; and books that encourage conflict resolution, social responsibility, and democratic behavior in young people; books on environmental education.

For further information, please see "Key Topics" on our website.

What to Submit

The number of manuscripts we are actually able to read is finite. In order to increase the chance that your proposal will receive good attention and hence increase the chance that we'll publish it, we ask that you do not submit the entire manuscript until we ask for it, but rather send us the following:

a table of contents
a sample chapter
a proposal which answers the following questions:

1. In 75 words or less, what is the book about?

2. What qualifies you, or gives you authority, to write such a book? (We are interested as much in experience as in formal degrees.)

3. What other books in the field exist, when were they published, and how is yours similar or different? Trees are valuable and increasingly scarce: will the world really benefit from decreasing the number of trees in order to add another book on this subject?

4. Out of over 4,000 trade book publishers in the United States and Canada, why are you sending your proposal to New Society Publishers? How did you learn of us?

5. Whom do you imagine to be the audience for the book? What do you think are the best ways to reach them? If you could have the book serialized or reviewed, what are the 5 or 10 most important publications in which it could appear?

6. What help can you be in the promotion of the book? Organizational connections? Mailing lists? Workshops? Tours? (We are primarily interested in publishing authors who are prepared to help substantially with the promotion of their own books.)

7. We sell books back to authors at a deep discount. How many of your own books do you think you might need initially, if any?

8. Manuscripts *must* be submitted on disk. What platform do you work on (Mac or Windows)? What make and model of computer do you have? What word-processor and version?

9. What is the length of your manuscript? Provide a word count (many word processing programs can calculate this automatically).

10. When do you expect your book to be completed? How much do you currently have written?

How to Submit a Proposal

We cannot guarantee serious consideration of a proposal that does not include all of the elements above. If you want a response and/or your manuscript returned, include a self-addressed stamped envelope (or international stamp coupon of sufficient value, if you are outside Canada); we cannot either acknowledge receipt of, nor return, materials for projects we reject that come without a SASE or equivalent. Please be patient; we are reading as fast as we can! We will ask for the whole manuscript if we wish to see it. Please understand that decisions to publish are complex and require much more time than do refusals. Please *do not call us* once you have sent us your proposal; we'll contact you as appropriate. Thanks very much indeed for thinking of us!

Categories: Nonfiction—Business—Conservation—Ecology—Feminism—Lifestyle—Parenting

CONTACT: Submissions Editor

Material: All
PO Box 189
Gabriola Island
BC, Canada V0R 1X0
Phone: 250-247-9737
Fax: 250-247-7471
E-mail: editor@newsociety.com
Website: www.newsociety.com

New World Library

Manuscripts should be neatly typed and double-spaced. Please send two or three sample chapters, an outline or table of contents, a market assessment (a listing of competing books and how your book is different), and a detailed statement of author credentials/biographical information. Please do not send original artwork as we cannot be responsible for it. Instead, we recommend you only send copies of artwork, when appropriate. We do not accept email submissions. Sorry we are no longer accepting unsolicited children's book manuscripts at this time.

We presently focus on high quality books in the following categories: spirituality, self-improvement, parenting, women's studies, alternative health, religion, enlightened business, animal spirituality, and multicultural studies. Our works appeal to a large, general audience.

VERY IMPORTANT: Please include a self-addressed stamped envelope (SASE) if you wish to hear from us, and especially if you want your manuscript returned. Due to the number of queries and manuscripts we receive, we can respond only if a SASE is enclosed. Be sure the envelope is large enough to contain the manuscript and that you include sufficient postage.

Please allow us twelve weeks to respond.

Thank you.

Categories: Business—Health—Multicultural—New Age—Parenting—Religion—Spiritual— Women's Issues

CONTACT: Submissions Editor
Material: All
14 Pamaron Way
Novato, CA 94949
Phone: 800-972-6657, 415-884-2100
Fax: 415-884-2199
Website: www.newworldlibrary.com

No Starch Press

Your Book Proposal

Description. Describe your book. What makes it compelling and unique? Why will it make a difference?

Audience. Who is your target audience and how will your book meet their

needs? Who will buy your book and why?

Competition. List any competing titles. How do they compare with your book? How will your work compete?

Market. Discuss the market for your book. How is it changing? How large is

it? How will your book meet its current and future needs?

Outline and schedule. Provide a detailed outline of your book including parts, chapters, subheadings, illustrations, and any appendixes or additional material.

Describe each chapter, focusing both on its content and fit within the book.

Estimate the length of each chapter and your anticipated completion date.

Non-book features. Will your book contain a CD-ROM or be supported by a

web site? If so, what will these contain?

You. Who are you? What are your goals in writing this book? Do you have

any affiliations that will help us to market your book?

Please include your resume, vita, or a brief biography, as well as a writing sample, with your proposal. Also, list any previously published titles and their sales figures (if available).

Email submissions to: editors@nostarch.com

Categories: Technical

Contact: No Starch Press
555 DeHaro St., Suite 250
San Francisco, CA 94107
Phone: 800-420-7240
Fax: 415-863-9950
Email: info@nostarch.com
Website: www.nostarch.com

North Point Press

Please refer to Farrar, Straus and Giroux, Publishers, Inc.

North Ridge Books

North Ridge Books will consider manuscripts in the following categories:

If you have a manuscript ready to be published, e-mail us a book proposal—which must include a detailed marketing plan—at info@nrbooks.com.

Explain to us why your book fills a need. And remember: Publishing a book requires a considerable investment. Consider North Ridge Books only if you are a top-notch writer, have something fresh and original to say, and are able to heavily promote it on radio and TV.

We are not in a position to offer advances, but we will consider new talent. We are also open to co-publishing arrangements in which we package and promote the book for you, while you keep all rights. No phone calls and no faxes please. Please, no fiction or poetry or fiction—no matter how brilliant you are. We will only consider manuscripts we know how to market.

Categories: Biography—Current Events—History—Humor—Reference—Travel

CONTACT: Submissions Editor
Material: All
PO Box 1463
Lake Forest, CA 92609
E-mail: info@nrbooks.com
Website: www.nrbooks.com

North Street Publishers

We publish fiction, nonfiction, mysteries, biographies and memoirs.

To know me better, please go to our website. Also read the first chapter of *Hard Boiled Eggs and Other Psychiatric Tales*.

Categories: Health—Psychology

CONTACT: Albert Honig
Material: All
616 North St.
Doylestown PA 18901
Phone: 215-348-2134
Fax: 215-348-3266
E-mail: albhon@comcast.net
Website: www.alberthonig.net

Northern Publishing

We publish mostly Alaskan titles about hunting or other Alaska outdoor topics. Other similar topics are accepted depending on their merit. We do not publish fiction, how-to manuals are our preference. We accept manuscripts or detailed proposals targeting a specific audience. Titles with unique ideas or written by recognized authorities or experts on a subject are preferred.

Some of our titles are:

Sheep Hunting in Alaska: The Dall Sheep Hunters Guide, The Manual for Successful Hunters: Why 10% of the Hunters take 90% of the Game, The Quest for Dall Sheep: A Historic Guide's Memories of Alaskan Hunting, Bear Hunting in Alaska, Moose Hunting in Alaska.

Tony Russ, Owner, Northern Publishing

Categories: Nonfiction—History—Outdoors—Recreation—Sports/Recreation

CONTACT: Tony Russ
Material: All
PO Box 871803
Wasilla AK 99687
Fax: 907-373-6474
E-mail: tony@TonyRuss.com
Website: www.TonyRuss.com

Nova Press

We publish only books and software for, or closely related to, test preparation for college entrance exams: LSAT, GRE, SAT, GMAT, MCAT.

Categories: Nonfiction—College—Education

CONTACT: Acquisitions Editor
Material: All
11659 Mayfield Ave., Ste. 1
Los Angeles CA 90049
Phone: 310-207-4078
Fax: 310-571-0908
E-mail: NovaPress@aol.com

The Oasis Press

Please refer to PSI Research.

Oberlin College Press

Due to limited resources and space in our poetry series, we are unable to accept unsolicited manuscripts of original poetry in English. We encourage poets with book-length manuscripts to enter our annual contest, the **FIELD Poetry Series.** Manuscripts for this prize are submitted each May. The winning manuscript is published in our **FIELD Poetry Prize.** To obtain complete contest guidelines, visit our web site (or send a stamped, self-addressed envelope.

Oberlin College Press will consider works of poetry in translation for the **FILED Translation Series.** Please send sample poems and a letter of inquiry describing the work and indicating that you have the author's permission, where appropriate, to seek publication for your translations. Please enclose a self-addressed, stamped envelope for response. If the editors are interested in reading the complete manuscript, you will receive notification.

Categories: Poetry

Contact: Editors
Oberlin College Press

50 N. Professor Street
Oberlin, OH 44074
Phone: 440-775-8408
Fax: 440-775-8124
Email:
Website: www.oberlin.edu/ocpress

Omnibus Press

Omnibus Press is an imprint of Music Sales Corporation. Founded in 1935 by the Wise family, Music Sales is an international family of companies with interests in four main areas of music publishing: Copyright ownership and promotion of standard and popular music, classical music, printed music, and book publishing. Music Sales maintains offices in New York, London, Sydney, Copenhagen, Madrid, Tokyo, Helsinki, and Paris.

Omnibus is a leading publisher of musician biographies, with a special focus on rock & roll and pop. Most Omnibus books are commissioned in our U.K. headquarters, but the U.S. office is always interested in seeing your proposals.

We're especially keen on unofficial musician biographies (high-profile entertainers with large fan bases, as well as up-and-coming), as well as graphic novels. (See Godspeed: The Kurt Cobain Graphic and In My Skin: The Eminen Graphic.) We rarely publish books about classical music. We prefer rock & roll, folk, blues, and pop.

Send full book proposals, including: Cover letter, overview of the book, target audience, author bio, competitive titles, marketing and promotion ideas, detailed chapter-by-chapter table of contents, and a sample chapter (if available).

Categories: Nonfiction—Biography—History—Music—Reference—Performing Arts

CONTACT: Andrea Rotondo, Managing Editor
Material: All
257 Park Ave. South
New York, NY 10010
Phone: 212-254-2100
Fax: 212-254-2013
Website: www.musicsales.com

Orange Frazer Press, Inc.

In a nutshell, we specialize in highly designed, well-produced books on Ohio information, education, entertainment and sports—and every so often, cross over the borders (of Ohio) just for fun.

We cannot acknowledge any submission or return any material that does not include a self-addressed, stamped envelope.

Responses are generally sent within three months.

We are unable to acknowledge receipt of your submission or give status reports.

We cannot be responsible for original copies of manuscripts, photos, artwork, etc. Do not send these materials.

Orange Frazer Press is a small press that publishes books about Ohio that we have commissioned authors to write for us, or the authors have brought to us as finished manuscripts, that we feel suit our mission for providing lively, knowledgeable, entertaining and educational material about Ohio and famous Ohioans.

Submissions Should Include:
1. *A cover letter.*
2. An outline and a sample chapter or two.
3. A brief synopsis of each of the other chapters.

The Cover Letter Should Explain
1. The book's subject matter and approach.

2. Anticipated audience.
3. What distinguishes your book from others on the matter.
4. Your qualifications for writing this book.
5. Why do you think your book is appropriate for Orange Frazer?

Audio cassettes, computer disks, or videotapes in lieu of typed manuscripts are not acceptable. *All proposals must be submitted in the following format:*

• Unbound and without staples, paste-ups, or anything that will interfere with photocopying should multiple copies be necessary for editorial staff review.

• Consecutively numbered throughout–clean photocopies are acceptable.

• It is helpful if your name and address are on the first page of the document.

Although Orange Frazer Press does do extensive editing on many manuscripts, we do not have the staff for re-writing, so-called "ghost writing," or to serve as o-authors. (You may want to contact local universities or colleges, writers guilds, or editorial services for help.)

Additionally, we create, write, edit, design, format, and print books for companies, corporations, municipalities and organizations who wish to have a book made for one reason or another.

Categories: Nonfiction—Education—Entertainment—Regional—Sports/Recreation

CONTACT: Tammy McKay, Acquisitions
Material: All
CONTACT: John Baskins, Editor
Material: All
PO Box 214
Wilmington OH 45177
Phone: 937-382-3196
Fax: 937-382-3159

Books
M-Z

Orb

Please refer to Tom Doherty Associate, LLC, in the Book Publishers section.

Orchises Press

Orchises Press is a small literary and general publisher located outside of Washington, D. C. It publishes five to eight books a year and has a list of one hunded titles, many of them original poetry, a love of the editor, Roger Lathbury. Unlike many other presses, small and large, Orchises reads unsolicited manuscripts and tries to publish books on their merit, both literary and commercial. It prides itself on the attractiveness of its volumes, both paperback and hardcover.

MANUSCRIPT SUBMISSION GUIDELINES
Orchises is one of the few publishers that reads unsolicited freelance submissions. If a manuscript is presented in a reasonable manner, well look at it. "Reasonable" means:

1. Typed, preferably double-spaced. Photocopies are OK; they're indistinguishable from laser print anyhow.

2. A return envelope is enclosed-a self-addressed stamped envelope large enough to accommodate the manuscript if you want the manuscript returned, a size 10 or 6 3/4 envelope if a response is all that's needed. While understanding that such is not the fate writers most want, Orchises recycles all unreturnable manuscripts. In general, mail with no materials for a response will not receive a response nor will it be retained pending the arrival of a forgotten envelope.

3. A phone number is helpful for those rare occasions when we accept.

OTHER REMARKS
1. Orchises does not publish original fiction, children's books or cookbooks.

2. If you submit poetry, you may be interested to know that in one

year Orchises receives 200-300 poetry manuscripts or queries accompanied by poems. Two or three such may be accepted; one year four were, another none was. Usually poetry Orchises publishes has appeared previously in magazines of national repute, e.g., *American Poetry Review, The Atlantic Monthly, Harpers, The New Republic, The New Yorker*, Poetry—as well as respected literary magazines (e.g., The Paris Review, Shenandoah, The Southern Review). These places build audiences. Of course, publication in those magazines is not an absolute criterion. All readers, I expect, have read poems in those venues that are quite fine but also others that seem less good than poems in less prominent places. The only way to judge is to read; we'll read.

3. Reporting times vary but usually are within 1 month. Longer means closer.

4. The volume of submissions makes it impossible to provide commentary.

With thanks and good wishes,
Roger Lathbury, Orchises Press
Categories: Nonfiction—Poetry—Textbooks

CONTACT: Acquisitions Editor
Material: All
PO Box 20602
Alexandria VA 22320-1602
E-mail: lathbury@gmu.edu

Origin Media, Inc.
"Books for the Integral Age"

IMPRINTS
Origin Press—www.originpress.com
Wisdom Editions—www.wisdomeditions.com
Celestia—www.celestiapress.org

OUR APPROACH TO PUBLISHING:

Origin has won three national awards for its books, and currently enters into traditional publisher-author agreements only with previously published authors. Agents should know that we pay very low advances. We only publish a few commercial titles each year. We also have a unique arrangement for first-time authors or writers with specialized non-commercial titles who are willing to subsidize their first title—but only if their title meets high editorial standards. We also consult to self-publishers and small presses.

ORIGIN'S IMPRINTS:

The Origin Press and Wisdom Editions imprints work with authors of books on practical spirituality, psychology, self-help, global religion, philosophy, integral studies, progressive business and politics, ufology, visionary fiction, and related subjects. Celestia publishes works with authors in Urantia Book studies, esoterica, paranormal, and metaphysics. Please study the website for each imprint.

SUBMISSIONS

Prefer emails of short queries to: byron@originpress.com.
Categories: Fiction—Business—Politics—Psychology—Self Help—Spiritual

CONTACT: Submissions Editor
Material: All
PO Box 151117
San Rafael CA 94915-1117
E-mail: byron@originpress.com

Osborne/McGraw-Hill

McGraw-Hill/Osborne Media, a unit of McGraw-Hill Education, is a leading publisher of self-paced computer training materials, including user and reference guides, best-selling series on computer certification, titles on business & technology, and high-level but practical titles on networking, programming, and Web development tools. McGraw-Hill/Osborne Media is the official press of Oracle, Corel, Global Knowledge, J.D. Edwards, Intuit, and RSA Security Inc., and has a strategic publishing relationship with ComputerWorld. McGraw-Hill/Osborne Media is focusing on consumer support, emerging technologies, and innovative applications for developing future computer books.

McGraw-Hill Education is a division of The McGraw-Hill Companies (NYSE: MHP), a global information services provider meeting worldwide needs in financial services, education, and business-to-business information through leading brands such as Standard & Poor's and BusinessWeek. The Corporation has more than 300 offices in 32 countries. Sales in 2000 were $4.3 billion.

How to Prepare Your Manuscript Proposal

The following guidelines outline the major areas that you should cover in your proposal. Please be as complete as possible, as it will help us make a decision more quickly. Also, feel free to add relevant information even if we haven't specifically asked for it below.

The most important elements are:
• Why we should publish this book
• What specific skills do you bring to this book/topic
• Why will this book sell better than other similar books (or if there is no competition, what are the market conditions that make you believe that this is a book worth publishing.)

Your proposal should include the following information:
• Brief description of the book.
• Brief description of the product or technology.
• Audience: Who is the major audience for your book; for whom is your book intended? At what level is your book written; what technical background will the reader of your book need?
• Outstanding features: List what you consider to be the outstanding or unique features of your work.
• Outline: Provide a detailed outline of your book. This will give reviewers an idea of what topics you are including and how your material is organized. Your outline should include part titles, chapter headings, subheadings, and appendixes, with explanations as necessary. It should also include your estimate of the length in manuscript pages of each chapter.
• Competition: List the existing books, if any, with which yours will compete and discuss specifically their strengths and weaknesses. Spell out how your work will be similar to and different from competing books.
• The Market: Mention any factors that might have an impact (positive or negative) on the market for your work. How is the market changing? If your work focuses on particular hardware or software, and you have sales figures for the product, include these.
• Schedule: What is your timetable for completing your book? What portion of the material is now complete? When do you expect to have a complete manuscript?
• Size: What do you estimate to be the size of the complete book? (Double-spaced typewritten pages normally reduce by about one-third when set into type: for example, 300 typewritten pages equal approximately 200 printed pages).
• Resume: Include a copy of your vita, or a paragraph or two of relevant biographical information. Please include a list of hardware and software for which you have expertise.
• Writing Sample: Please include a magazine article or the introduction or chapter of the book, or other writing samples.

You can send your proposal directly to members of our Acquisitions team either through regular mail or e-mail.

Categories: Computers—Internet

CONTACT: Manuscript Proposal
Material: All
2600 10th St.
Berkeley CA 94710
Phone: 510-549-6600
Fax: 510-549-6603

E-mail: srogers@mcgraw-hill.com
Website: www.osborne.com

The Overmountain Press

If you are searching for a publisher and are considering The Overmountain Press, you need to know a few things about what we publish. Along with these guidelines, we will include our list of titles so that you may become more familiar with the type of books we publish, some of the authors we work with, and the retail prices of our books.

We are primarily a publisher of regional-interest books. Some of our titles are reprints of older historical accounts that have gone out-of-print. Below we will list some guidelines for manuscripts from different literary genres. This will list what you should provide when submitting a proposal.

In addition to these items, we would like for you to include the following: brief description of the book, your background and qualifications for writing this book, prospective market for selling the book, any other marketing suggestions you may have, and a self-addressed stamped envelope for returning. We will not return your manuscript without the self-addressed stamped envelope.

Categories of Publication

Children We have recently begun to publish titles for children. Although we have published a few exceptions, we are now accepting regional (Southern Appalachian) titles ONLY. In reviewing a children's manuscript for publication, we prefer to have copies of the illustrations at the same time we review the text. Very few publishers review in this way. Most of the larger companies with hundreds of titles prefer to find the illustrator from their database.

At an author's request we can send a list of illustrators and graphic artists who can be hired out or collaborated with in producing a children's book. At present this list is small, and we are looking for illustrators who wish to be added. This is a list of artists who have approached us. We do not recommend one over another. You can pay the artist a flat fee, or you can choose to split the royalties from book sales. This decision is between you and the illustrator. Again, please do not send the original artwork. Copies are fine, but please include a couple of color copies so we can get a feel for the artist's use of color.

The Overmountain History Series for Young Readers is a new series of books teaching Southern Appalachian history to readers on a 3rd-8th grade reading level. Books will need to have many photos or drawings - all historical. These books are strictly non-fiction. Books will have anywhere from 5000-15,000 words depending on subject matter and illustrations. Please submit the entire manuscript.

Cookbooks When accepting cookbook manuscripts, we look for a new and interesting way of cooking or organizing the recipes. A regular cookbook is hard to market without some sort of characteristic to set it apart from the others on the shelves. Your book should have a unique setup that is distinctive and obvious to the consumer.

Ghost Lore We have published several stories of "true" ghost lore. We have been successful in selling these titles and will consider manuscripts of this type. They must be Appalachian in nature and be "true" stories. For example, *The Infamous Bell Witch of Tennessee* is a "true" ghost story passed through generations and put into book form. This is extremely marketable.

Guidebooks We have published a few guide/hiking books, and we are interested in looking at others. It should be Appalachian in nature and include plenty of photographs, maps, drawings, etc.

Mystery Our new Silver Dagger Mystery series has its own set of guidelines for submission. They are available on our website at www.silverdaggermysteries.com.

Regional History / Nonfiction We would like to see either a complete manuscript or an outline plus three chapters. If the manuscript is very large, we can look at an outline with sample chapters to determine whether it will fit within our scope of titles. If, at that point, we decide to take a closer look, we will request the complete manuscript. We do not accept titles without looking at the entire work.

We like photographs! Illustrations, slides, photos, maps, etc., all enhance nonfiction works. When submitting your proposal, please send samples of illustrations for the book. PLEASE DO NOT SEND ORIGINALS! Photocopies are fine for review. Each photo should include a brief description. You do not need to send every photo that you plan to include in the book - just a few to let us get a feel for your collection.

Tall Tales / Folklore We have published several compilations of *Appalachian Tall Tales and Folklore*. Some of the works of Charles Edwin Price and Denvil Mullins fit into this category. In submitting, please send a proposal and a couple of sample tales along with any illustrations you may be planning.

We may have left some other categories off this list. Please do not hesitate to call with questions regarding the types of books we publish.

Categories Not Published by The Overmountain Press
- Biography
- General Fiction / Novels
- Inspirational
- Poetry
- Reminiscences

Timelines We generally take anywhere from one to three months to review manuscripts. Several people are involved in the decision-making process, and it sometimes takes time to read these manuscripts. Please do not call to find the status of your manuscript. It may take us a few weeks, but we will get back to you! After acceptance we generally plan a production schedule of approximately six months to one year. This is a huge variable depending upon what your book needs to be perfect. If your book will be hardback, this will typically add one month to the production schedule. This is annoying, but it is a fact that we cannot change. *Following is a list of pointers to take significant amounts of time off the production schedule:*

- Have the manuscript on a computer disk. Call us to see if your program is compatible with ours.
- Have several people offer editorial advice to reduce Overmountain editorial time
- Place your illustrations, photos, etc., where you want them before you submit the manuscript
- Devise some marketing strategies to share with our marketing department
- Obtain all permissions for using photos, quotes, excerpts, etc.
- Think of some possible cover ideas to share with our graphic designers
- Be receptive to changes concerning your manuscript

Questions If you are not sure of your project's suitability to our list, please call at 423-926-2691 before spending the time and postage to send it in for review.

PLEASE DO NOT EMAIL QUERIES. THEY WILL NOT BE ANSWERED!

Categories: Nonfiction—Biography—History—Native American—Regional

CONTACT: Jason Weems, Editor
Material: All
PO Box 1261
Johnson City TN 37605
Phone: 423-926-2691
Website: www.overmountainpress.com

Pacific Press

Pacific Press® is a Christian denominational publisher owned and operated by the Seventh-day Adventist Church. The publishing and printing company was established in Oakland, California in 1874 and moved to its current location in Nampa, Idaho in 1984.

Each year, Pacific Press® book division publishes 35 to 40 new

English book titles and 5 to 10 Spanish titles. The books are distributed mostly to Adventist Book Center® stores and Seventh-day Adventist ministry organizations in North America.

We would love to have you join our family of published authors. Please read on to find out how it's done.

Do you want to publish a book, or print a book?

Pacific Press® offers both publishing and printing as separate services. Most authors wish to have their manuscript published, which means the publishing house takes full responsibility for producing and selling the book and pays royalties to the author. Authors who wish to have their work published on this basis are invited to send submissions according to the information and guidelines given below.

A small number of authors wish to have their work printed so they can sell it themselves or request distribution through the publishing house. Authors who need **printing services only** should check the Pacific Press Graphic Services website or call for a FREE quote: 1-888-465-1350. Ask for Clare Woods or Bill Legg.

What does Pacific Press® publish?

The mission of the Pacific Press® book division is to provide readers with a wide variety of books that connect them with God and help them develop a relationship with Him; provide information about God and His character and His ways; and encourage and uplift them in the struggles of life. Pacific Press® books serve to bring individuals to salvation and to prepare them for eternal life with God, in complete harmony with the Bible.

Pacific Press® publishes Christian books with a Seventh-day Adventist perspective in the following categories:

What does Pacific Press® publish?

The mission of the Pacific Press® book division is to provide readers with a wide variety of books that connect them with God and help them develop a relationship with Him; provide information about God and His character and His ways; and encourage and uplift them in the struggles of life. Pacific Press® books serve to bring individuals to salvation and to prepare them for eternal life with God, in complete harmony with the Bible.

Pacific Press® publishes Christian books with a Seventh-day Adventist perspective in the following categories:

Recent examples:

Inspiration: **A Place in God's Heart** *(by Kay Rizzo)*

Doctrine: *Graffiti in the Holy of Holies* (by Clifford Goldstein)

Topics: *We Can Keep Them in the Church*

Biographies: *Set Free* (by James Ponder)

Practical Christianity: *Cooking With the Micheff Sisters*

Books for sharing: *Broken Chains* (by Doug Batchelor)

For children:

> Picture books illustrating a distinctive Adventist belief for ages 1–3

True or based-on-truth, contemporary or historical stories with Christian themes in the following age categories (usually in a series): 3–5; 6–8; 9–12

Sets of Bible stories for ages 8–108

Typical page lengths: 16–128
Typical word lengths: 1,000–20,000

Recent examples:

Picture book: *I Miss Grandpa* (by Karen Holford)

Contemporary story: *The Secret of Scarlett Cove* (by Charles Mills)

Historical story: An Adventist Girl, Set Three (by Jean Boonstra)

Bible stories: Shoebox Kids Bible Stories - Book 6 (by Jerry Thomas)

Before you send anything to Pacific Press®

Check the competition so you know if you're duplicating books in print. First examine the current products available from Pacific Press® at AdventistBookCenter.com. Next, do searches on bookstore sites such as ChristianBook.com, Amazon.com, and Barnes and Noble. Browse your local ABC or Christian bookstore. Also check subject listings at the library to find books on your topic published in the last five to ten years. Read similar books that you find through research, especially Pacific Press® titles if any exist in your subject area.

The submission process

First time: If you're sending material to Pacific Press® for the first time, please start with a **query letter**. It should contain these elements:

> A one-sentence thesis of the book's main idea.

> A summary of the book.

> The intended audience.

> Your qualifications for writing on the topic.

> A sentence making clear whether you have written the book or are in the planning stage.

> A chapter outline if it's available.

For help with a query letter, check the following site:
Can't Write a Query Letter?

Second time or more: If you've had a book published by Pacific Press® before, skip the query stage and submit a proposal. Be sure to include all the information that goes into a typical query letter in your proposal cover letter.

How to submit a proposal

If a book editor responds to your query with a request for a proposal, or, if you have been published by Pacific Press® before and wish to submit a new proposal:

> send **three** chapters and a chapter outline or annotated contents page

> write a cover letter and include the main thesis, the purpose of the book, the potential audience, and proposed length

> indicate whether you have submitted simultaneously to other

publishers

Email submissions sent to Book Submissions are preferred. For a postal mailing address, see How to submit a query above. If you wish to have a mail submission returned, please include an adequately sized SASE. Submissions without a SASE that are rejected will be stored for a short time and then recycled.

For help with writing a proposal, consult reference books such as Michael Larson's *How to Write a Book Proposal* (Writer's Digest Books) or find tips on the Internet, such as How to Write a Book Proposal.

Typical response time for a proposal: 3–4 months

About submitting manuscripts

Please do not send a complete manuscript unless an editor asks for it. Authors who skip over the proposal and submit a complete unsolicited manuscript can expect to wait up to **one year** for a response. Unsolicited manuscripts receive the lowest priority because they are time-consuming to review.

To ensure a prompt response, please use a query letter or proposal, even if your manuscript is already completed.

How to submit a finished manuscript

If a Pacific Press® editor asks to see a completed manuscript, please follow these requirements.

Format requirements:

Include complete contents page, plus any dedication, acknowledgments, foreword, or preface you wish to include.

Perform a spelling and grammar check with your word processor before sending a manuscript.

VERY IMPORTANT: Consult the Pacific Press® Manuscript Format Guidelines for the manuscript format.

Delivery of manuscript:

Email attachments sent to Book Submissions are preferred.

All word processing formats are acceptable (Microsoft Word, WordPerfect, etc.).

Mail delivery is acceptable. Send a diskette and hard copy. Hard copy alone is not acceptable. For a postal mailing address, see How to submit a query above. *About contracts, advances, and royalties*

After Pacific Press® has accepted a manuscript, the author receives a letter of acceptance and two copies of a **book contract**. Upon signing and returning both copies of the contract to Pacific Press®, the author receives an **advance** of $1,500 and an original copy of the contract signed by a Pacific Press® representative. The $1,500 payment is an advance on future royalties. The advance is deducted from earned royalties before royalty payments are made to the author. Royalty payments are made once a year, usually just after the close of the calendar year.

Pacific Press® is responsible for all editing, proofreading, formatting, cover design, and title and back cover copy. After editing and formatting work is completed, the formatted manuscript is sent to the author for review. This last step is guaranteed by a clause in the contract.

If your book is accepted for publication and you foresee an issue with international rights or rights to republish outside the Adventist market, please mention this issue to the book editor so that rights clauses can be included in the book contract.

Royalty rates are set by the General Conference of Seventh-day Adventists. The current rates are:

Paperback books: 12% of wholesale price up to 15,000 copies sold, 16% thereafter.

Hardcover books: 14% of wholesale price up to 15,000 copies sold, 16% thereafter.

About rejections

Your manuscript may not fit the needs of Pacific Press® at the time you submit it for a number of reasons. The book editors use 14 rejection form letters, each of which gives a clear indication of the reason for rejection.

What books will be rejected?

Here are the top reasons books or proposals are rejected:

1. Submitted to the wrong publisher (i.e., not the type of book we publish)
2. Not a topic of interest to our readers
3. Boring—didn't grab attention
4. Not a large enough audience to make a viable book
5. Nothing new or original in the manuscript
6. Focus of the topic is too narrow or specialized
7. Pacific Press® already has enough material on the topic
8. Unacceptable theology
9. Poor writing (frequently, good topic and poor writing)
10. More appropriate to general Christian market (not distinctive to Adventists)

Note the following reasons for rejection in particular categories:

1. Fiction Pacific Press® has published a small number of fiction titles, mostly end-time stories and a few historical fiction titles. We don't publish science fiction or fantasy or secular fiction.

2. Secular topics Pacific Press® publishes material related to Adventist Christianity. Practical books such as cookbooks must have an Adventist connection. Secular treatments of any topic are not considered.

3. Children's picture books We don't publish picture books that deal with general Christian topics, since other Christian publishers have taken care of most generally acceptable topics.

4. Daily devotional books Pacific Press® does not publish devotional books.

5. Unacceptable theology All Pacific Press® books reflect the spectrum of Adventist theology.

6. Poetry Pacific Press® **does not** publish poetry.

What not to expect with a rejection:

With a small staff and high volume of submissions, editors cannot provide feedback beyond a rejection letter. What not to expect from Pacific Press® editors:

Detailed critique of a manuscript.

A judgment on the quality of writing.

Revision suggestions, except in cases where an editor suggests or requests a rewrite.

Help with submitting to other publishers.

Help in finding a co-author, unless the editor suggests that this would be appropriate.

What is Pacific Press® looking for?

Fresh, original treatments of Seventh-day Adventist beliefs and doctrines.

Fresh material on inspirational and general biblical/spiritual topics.

Practical, original books on Christian living, including cookbooks and lifestyle guides.

Dramatic or moving life stories of Adventist individuals.

Bible-based, imaginative, and edifying children's books on specifically Adventist topics, including animal stories, mysteries, adventures, and Bible stories.

Categories: Children—History

CONTACT:Book Submissions
PO Box 5353
Nampa, ID 83653-5353
Fax: 208-465-2531
Email: booksubmissions@pacificpress.com
Website: www.pacificpress.com

Pacific View Press

Dear Author,

We apologize for this form letter, but we receive many queries, and cannot personally respond to those which are not within our area of publication interest.

We are a small press focusing on the Pacific Rim and its unique, growing interplay of economic and cultural forces. *We publish titles in three series:*

Contemporary Affairs, on Pacific Rim topics only, including guides for Asia-related international business; Books for a Multicultural Society; nonfiction on Asia and Asian-American themes, primarily for children [see guidelines below]; Traditional Chinese Medicine, primarily texts, for practitioners.

We do not publish travel books or travelogues, autobiographies or biographies, photojournalism, literature or fiction.

If you feel your project fits our publishing interests, you are welcome to submit a proposal, accompanied by a sample chapter, and an outline or table of contents. Please include autobiographical information. We prefer not to receive manuscripts. We do not accept typewritten material. You may wish to request a current catalog first or visit our website.

If we are interested in your proposal we will respond within 6 weeks, after your proposal has been evaluated by our editorial committee. Your material is assumed to be copyrighted and will be kept confidential.

Thank you for your interest, and good luck.
Regards,

Pacific View Press
Guidelines for Children's Book Authors and Artists
Our children's books focus on hardcover illustrated nonfiction for readers aged eight to twelve. We look for titles on aspects of the history and culture of the countries and peoples of the Pacific Rim, especially China, presented in an engaging, informative and respectful manner. We are interested in books that all children will enjoy reading and using, and that parents and teachers will want to buy. Our titles are available nationally through quality trade bookstores, museum stores, multicultural specialty catalogs, and the leading library and trade distributors. Recent titles have included *Exploring Chinatown: A Children's Guide to Chinese Culture* and *A Thousand Peaks: Poems from China.*

We welcome proposals from persons with expertise, either academic or personal, in their area of interest. While we do accept proposals from previously unpublished authors, we would expect submitters to have considerable experience presenting their interests to children in classroom or other public settings, and to have skill in writing for children.

We do not publish fiction, picture stories, or photo-picture books. At this time we are not considering natural history or biographies.

Our finished books are usually 48-96 pages, 8½"x11", with full-color illustration throughout.

You are welcome to submit proposals, accompanied by a sample chapter or unit and an outline for the entire book. Please include autobiographical information. We would prefer not to receive completed manuscripts.

If we are interested in your proposal we will respond within 6 weeks, after your proposal has been evaluated by our editorial committee. Our contracts with authors are fairly standard for small publishers and cover finances, time frames and obligations of both author and publisher. We pay royalties based on net sales, with a small advance against royalties paid upon acceptance of the final manuscript.

Categories: Nonfiction—Asian-American—Children—Multicultural—Asia—Contemporary Affairs

CONTACT: Acquisitions Editor
Material: All
PO Box 2897
Berkeley CA 94702
Phone: 510-849-4213
Website: www.pacificviewpress.com

Padlock Mystery Press

Hello! Padlock Mystery Press has published ten books since 1997 and plans to publish at least two books a year in the future. We are interested in mystery novels of 50 to 60 thousand words. No graphic sex scenes or torture. Our preference is for cozy novels, especially if they include locksmiths, key or lock themes whether present day forensic locksmiths or historical. KEY DECEPTIONS and KEY CONFRONTATIONS is an example. Query by email is preferred. If we are interested, we'll ask to see the entire novel.

Categories: Fiction—Mystery

CONTACT: Mary Ellen Cooper
Material: All
412 E. 9th
Stillwater, OK 74074
Phone: 405-372-2254
Fax: 405-372-8338
E-mail: Padlockmystery@aol.com
Website: www.mecooper.com

Paladin Press
Sycamore Island Books
Flying Machines Press

Paladin Press primarily publishes original nonfiction manuscripts on military science, self-defense, personal privacy, espionage, police science, action careers, guerilla warfare, and other action topics. Submissions may be outlines with 1-3 sample chapters or complete manuscripts. Allow 4 - 6 weeks from receipt for a reply. Paladin also produces videos on the above topics.

Categories: Nonfiction—Adventure—History—Military—Outdoors—Martial Arts—Personal Freedom—Weaponry

CONTACT: Editorial Department
Material: All
7707 Winchester Circle
Boulder CO 80301
Phone: 303-443-7250
Fax: 303-442-8741
E-mail: editorial@paladin-press.com
Website: www.palatin-press.com

Paradise Cay Publications

Paradise Cay is a small independent publisher specializing in nautical books, video, and art prints. Our major market is the United States; however, we have distributors in many other countries. Our primary interest is in manuscripts that deal with the instructional and technical aspect of ocean sailing and motorboating. We also publish and will consider fiction if it has a strong nautical theme.

All submitted manuscripts will be personally considered by the publisher, Matt Morehouse. He will usually contact the author by phone or e-mail. To present in the best possible way, submissions should include a cover letter containing a story synopsis and a short biography of the author, including any plans the author may have to promote the work. The cover letter should describe the book's subject matter, approach, distinguishing characteristics, intended audience, author's qualifications, and why the author thinks this book is appropriate for Paradise Cay.

Although Paradise Cay does do extensive editing on many manuscripts, it is the responsibility of first-time or little-known authors to pay for editing. We can refer authors to an independent editing service we use and highly recommend, www.we-edit.com, or the author may secure these services locally. We emphasize that any manuscript accepted for publication must be complete and ready for print production. Manuscripts must be double-spaced on 8.5" x 11" paper. Each page should be numbered consecutively and should carry a header with the author's name and the manuscript's title. Do not send the entire manuscript unless the publisher requests it; sixty pages should be sufficient. If the author wants these pages returned, a self-addressed, stamped envelope should be included.

Paradise Cay does not normally pay advances to first-time or little-known authors. If your manuscript is accepted for publication, Paradise Cay pays all costs of printing, binding, warehousing, shipping, advertising, marketing, billing, and collection. The author has no cost beyond manuscript preparation. The author is paid a semiannual royalty, usually ten percent.

Categories: Nonfiction—Boating—Cooking—Fishing—Recreation—Regional—Sports/Recreation—Trade—Nautical—Travel

CONTACT: Matt Morehouse, Publisher
Material: All
PO Box 29
Arcata, CA 95518-0029
Phone: 707-822-7038
E-mail: mattm@humboldt1.com
Website: www.paracay.com

Paragon House

Paragon House publishes reference and scholarly titles, in the areas of Biography, History, Philosophy, Psychology, Religion, Spiritual Health, Reference, Political Science, and International Relations.

Please include the following items to help us make a prompt decision on your project:

• An abstract of your project, which must include a summary of your premise, main arguments, and conclusions.
• A table of contents.
• A sample chapter.
• Your current curriculum vitae.
• An estimated number of diagrams, figures, pictures or drawings.
• An estimated number of double-spaced manuscript pages, in your completed project, along with the computer format (for example: PC compatible in Word Perfect).
• A tentative schedule for completion of your project.
• A list of competing books, if any, and a brief note telling how your book compares to each. Please include publisher, date of publication, page count and price, if possible.
• Any endorsements you have received.
• No email submissions
• A stamped, self-addressed, return envelope, of adequate size, and with enough postage to return your manuscript, in case of rejection. Materials submitted without adequate postage will not be returned.

Categories: Economics—Human Rights—New Age—Philosophy—Psychology—Religion—Spiritual—Textbooks

CONTACT: Rosemary Yokoi, Acquisitions Editor
Material: All
1925 Oakcrest Avenue, Suite 7
St. Paul MN 55113-2619
Phone: 651-644-3087
Fax: 651-644-0997
E-mail: paragon@paragonhouse.com
Website: www.paragonhouse.com

Parenting Press, Inc.

Categories that we publish:
1. Skill building books for parents
2. Personal safety for kids
3. Emotions and social problem solving for kids
We publish:
Books that teach practical life skills to parents, children, and the people who care for them. The books are nonjudgmental in attitude, useful to people with many different value systems, and full of options rather than "shoulds." They are short, easily understood, and present material in a fresh way.

We do NOT publish:

Books with animals as main characters

Fairy tales, autobiographies, biographies

Children's illustrated story books

Religious books

Parenting books based on an author's experience with one child or one family

Academic or theoretical works

Craft or activity books, workbooks

Poetry

Illness-or disability-based books

Submission guidelines:

Please tell us about you . . .

What uniquely qualifies you to write on your subject.

What you would like to accomplish by having this material published.

What experience you have writing other books or materials and their sales history.

What kinds of book promotion you are ready to undertake.

Tell us about your idea . . .

Who is the primary audience for your material? Secondary?

In what ways will your material be helpful to the audiences you identified?

Comparing your manuscript to the competition among published books, how and why is your idea different and better?

What kinds of promotion do you think will be particularly effective for you and your book?

What we need to see in writing . . .

Send a letter of inquiry to us in which you respond to the questions above and relate any other information you think will help us make a decision about the suitability of your manuscript.

Send a paper copy, double spaced, of all or as much of the manuscript as you have ready with your letter. At a minimum, we need a detailed outline showing the organization of the manuscript, a table of contents, an introduction, and two chapters showing your best and truest writing style.

If you would like your material returned to you in the event it is not suitable for Parenting Press, also send a postage-paid reply envelope large enough to hold it.

Do NOT send your material via e-mail.

Categories: Nonfiction—Parenting

CONTACT: Carolyn Threadgill, Acquisitions
Material: All
PO Box 75267
Seattle, WA 98175-0267
Phone: 800-992-6657
Website: www.ParentingPress.c

Parkway Publishers, Inc.

We are primarily interested in regional non-fiction books. The region of our interest is Western North Carolina in particular and North Carolina and Appalachian region in general. We like to receive completed manuscripts with self-addressed, stamped envelopes. We prefer manuscripts of about 200 double-spaced pages.

Thank you.

Sincerely,

Rao Aluri

Categories: Nonfiction—Regional

CONTACT: Rao Aluri, Ph.D.
Material: All
Box 3678
Boone NC 28607
Phone: 828-265-3993 (Ph & Fax)
E-mail: parkwaypub@hotmail.com
Website: www.parkwaypublishers.com

Park Street Press

Books on travel, psychology, consumer and environmental issues, women's and men's studies, and New Science. While this imprint is directed to a wider audience than are the other three imprints, it focuses on subjects that enhance our understanding o the world in which we live and that improve our quality of life.

In order to make the review process more efficient for prospective authors and for our editorial staff, we have prepared a list of requirements for authors and for our editorial staff, we have prepared a list of requirements for authors who are submitting work. Please include the following when presenting a proposal:

1. A BRIEF LETTER THAT INCLUDES A SHORT SYNOPSIS OF THE BOOK

a) The letter should be no more than two pages long and should tell how your manuscript contributes to its field and what make is unique.

b) As specifically as you can, tell us who the audience is for your book.

c) Give a brief biography of yourself, noting especially any specific qualifications for writing your subject.

2. A TABLE OF CONTENTS, INTRODUCTION, AND SAMPLE CHAPTER(S)

There is no need to send a complete manuscripts unless it is specifically asked for. Proposals including the above materials are reviewed much faster than thick manuscripts sent unsolicited.

3. WE CANNOT RETURN PROPOSALS OR MANUSCRIPTS UNLESS THEY ARE ACCOMPANIED BY A SELF-ADDRESSED ENVELOPE STAMPED WITH SUFFICIENT POSTAGE.

Some prospective authors write or e-mail a query letter before sending a proposal. This is a good idea and can save time and postage, especially when you are not familiar with the books we publish. A list of our seven imprints follows, please read these before sending us a query letter or proposal.

If you have questions that have not been addressed above regarding our submission guidelines, please DO NO call the acquisitions editor; send a query letter to our submissions department at the address listed below. Your query letter should provide enough information about your work that the acquisitions editor can make an informed decision and contact you for further details. .

Categories: Nonfiction—Ecology—Environment—Men's Issues—Psychology—Women's Issues—Psychedelics—Drug Use

Contact: Submissions
Park Street Press
PO Box 388
Rochester, VT 05767-0388 USA
Phone: 802-767-3174
Website: www.InnerTraditions.com

Pathfinder Publishing of California

Formal guidelines not available.

Send queries or book proposals to below address.

Categories: Nonfiction—Careers—Computers—Disabilities—Family—Health—Men's Issues—Self Help—Society

CONTACT: Bill Mosbrook, CEO

Material: All
3600 Harbor Blvd., #82
Oxnard CA 93035
Phone: 805-984-7756
E-mail: bmosbrook@earthlink.net

Pauline Books & Media

Pauline Books and Media publishes in the following areas:

For adults: spirituality (prayer/holiness of life/biblical), religious faith formation (adults/children), family life (parenting, activities...), teacher resources (reproducibles, activities, games, crafts...), biographies of the saints, mariology, Faith & Culture, and prayer books. Submissions are evaluated on adherence to Gospel values, harmony with the Catholic tradition, relevance of topic and quality of writing. Does not publish fiction for adults, autobiographical works poetry. No strictly non-religious works considered.

Requirments for incoming adults submissions: Submission by mail or e-mail only. Query letter accompanied by a one-paragraph abstract, proposed outline for the volume, estimated number of words, estimated date of completion, sample chapter, author description. SASE required, submissions will not be returned. Response in 6-8 weeks. For more information, see website.

For children: prayer books, lives of the saints, coloring books, Bible stories, Christmas and Easter stories, seasonal activity books and religious instruction titles at picture book, easy-to-read and middle reader levels. Submissions are evaluated on adherence to Gospel values, harmony with the Catholic tradition, relevance of topic and quality of writing. No strictly non-religious works considered.

Requirments for incoming children's submissions: Submission by mail or e-mail only. Query letter accompanied by a synopsis, outline or two or three sample chapters where applies. SASE required, submissions will not be returned. Response in 6-8 weeks. For more information, see website.

Categories: Nonficiton—Children—Christian Interest—Family—Religion—Spiritual

CONTACT:
Manuscripts for adults: Madonna Ratcliff, FSP, Aquisitions Editor
Manuscripts for children: Patricia Edward Jablonski, FSP, Children's Acquisitions Editor
Material: All
Daughters of St. Paul
50 Saint Paul Ave
Boston MA 02130-3491
Phone: 617-522-8911
Website: www.pauline.org

Paulist Press
HiddenSpring

HiddenSpring, the general trade imprint of Paulist Press, publishes a broad range of non-fiction spirituality. HiddenSpring publishes hardcover and both trade paperback originals and reprints. HiddenSpring publishes 8-10 titles a year. Accepts manuscripts from both unagented and first-time authors, and offers variable advances. Please submit proposal package including outline, one (1) sample chapter, SASE; do not send complete manuscripts.

Categories: Nonfiction—Biography—Culture—General Interest—History—Inspirational—Lifestyle—Multicultural—Religion—Spiritual

CONTACT: Paul McMahon, Managing Editor
Material: All
997 MacArthur Blvd.

Mahwah NJ 07430
Phone: 201-825-7300

Peachtree Publishers
Peachtree Jr., Freestone

Peachtree currently publishes the following categories: children's picture and illustrated chapter books, young adult books, parenting, self-help, health books, and travel and recreational guides about the southeast.

Peachtree does not publish: poetry, plays, science fiction, fantasy, romance, westerns, horror, historical novels, scientific or technical reference, or books intended specifically as textbooks. We do not publish adult fiction of any kind. We also do not publish CDs tapes, or videos.

If you would like to submit your manuscript, please send one of the following:
• For children's picture books, send full manuscript;
• For all others, send either the full manuscript or a Table of Contents plus three sample chapters.
Plus:
• Biographical material on the author(s) and
• A stamped, self addressed #10 envelope for a response.

Please do not send original artwork or original copies of manuscripts. Artwork in general is not required. The publisher reserves the right to select the illustrator.

Please do not fax or e-mail queries or manuscripts. We will not review any submission received this way. All queries and manuscripts must be sent by U.S. Mail.

Peachtree receives approximately 15,000 submissions each year, so please do not call regarding the status of your submission for at least four months. If you wish to receive a copy of our catalog, please send a self-addressed 10 x 12-1/2 envelope with $1.98 in postage attached.

Categories: Fiction—Nonfiction

CONTACT: Helen Harriss, Submissions Editor
Material: All
1700 Chattahoochee Ave.
Atlanta GA 30318-2112
Phone: 404-876-8761
Fax: 404-875-2578
Website: www.peachtree-online.com

Pelican Publishing Company

Pelican Publishing Company does not accept unsolicited manuscripts. All writers should send us a query letter and SASE, describing the project briefly and concisely. This letter should include a complete address and telephone number. Pelican Publishing Company does not accept queries or any other submissions by e-mail. All queries must be submitted by mail according to the following guidelines. Multiple (or "simultaneous") queries are not considered.

A query letter should discuss the following: the book's content, its anticipated length (in double-spaced pages, not in words), its intended audience, the author's writing and professional background, and any promotional ideas and contacts the author may have. If the author has previously been published by another firm, please specify why a change is being sought. A formal synopsis, chapter outline, and/or one or two sample chapters may be sent with a query letter, but these are not required. Never send the original copy of any material.

Be advised that we have certain expectations in the length of a proposed manuscript. Most young children's books are 32 illustrated pages when published; their manuscripts cover about 7 pages when typed continuously. Proposed books for middle readers (ages 8 and up) should be at least 150 pages. Adult books should be more than this. For cookbooks, we require at least 200 proposed recipes.

If necessary, brief children's books (for readers under nine) may be submitted in their entirety. Photocopies of any accompanying artwork are welcome, but again, NEVER send any original artwork.

We will respond as promptly as possible (usually one month), letting you know whether or not we feel the project is worth pursuing further. If we feel that it is worthy of consideration, we will request a partial or full manuscript. Following this procedure ensures the most expeditious treatment of all inquiries.

We do not require that writers contacting us have a literary agent representing them.

A phone call to the editor or secretary or an in-person drop off of unrequested material does not automatically imply that a project has been solicited. For this and other obvious reasons, we discourage phone inquiries and in-person drop offs. If an author we have requested additional material from is unclear as to what we're asking for, a phone call to clarify the matter is acceptable.

Solicited manuscripts are carefully scrutinized by the editor(s). On occasion, they may be examined by our sales and/or promotions departments to gauge their marketability. They are then passed on to the publisher for preliminary and final consideration. The submissions are reported on as soon as possible, but this process may take up to three months (12 weeks). If acceptance is recommended, the author(s) will be asked to sign a contract with Pelican Publishing Company.

If the three-month period for solicited manuscripts passes without the author being informed of a decision, a polite note of reminder from the author is not out of order. Phone calls on the status of manuscripts are very strongly discouraged. Never badger the editor for an instant decision or make demands or threats; this can only hurt the author's chances of acceptance. Authors who feel unsatisfied with our procedures or the amount of time being taken to reach a decision are free to request the manuscript's return at any time.

Pelican Publishing requires exclusive submission for all solicited manuscripts during the 12-week period mentioned above. This is for obvious reasons. We can only give full attention to those manuscripts which we are likely to be able to publish if accepted by us.

We also ask that authors who have solicited works under consideration please refrain from sending us other works or proposals during this time unless they are specifically requested to do so. Agreement on our part to look at a particular work does not imply blanket authorization to send unrelated materials and doing so could hurt, rather than help, an author. Materials related to the requested submission, such as favorable newspaper clippings, endorsements by qualified professionals in the field the author is writing about, or other amended data may be sent and added to the material already on file. Use careful judgment in selecting these items and be certain that they enhance the material and its chances of being accepted. Sending in later data that refutes or calls into question points made in the earlier submission may cast doubts on the whole project's veracity and damage its chances of acceptance. Always be certain to refer to the work's title, the author name under which it was submitted, and the date the original query was mailed.

Materials will not be returned unless they are accompanied by sufficient postage. Policies regarding SASE's apply to all submissions from foreign countries, including Canada. Return postage must be in stamps, checks on U.S. banks, or International Money Orders in U.S. money.

We require all submissions, including outlines, resumes, sample chapters, etc., be neatly typed on 8 ½ by 11 inch paper and double-spaced with sufficient margins (1 inch on all sides). Query letters are customarily single-spaced. Be sure that your typewriter has a well-inked ribbon and, if corrections are made, they should be "whited-out" as inconspicuously as possible. Submissions with numerous misspellings, typographical errors, and handwritten corrections reflect unfavorably on the author and may contribute heavily toward a rejection. Writers are cautioned not to rely on editors to clean up after them or interpret unclear information, regardless of how good they think their material may be. A sloppy submission is often indicative of worse problems—the type editors and publishers prefer not to deal with.

Handwritten submissions and/or queries, unless neatly printed in the absence of a typewriter, do not make favorable impressions on editors and could jeopardize your chances of acceptance. For those using computers, we strongly advise you to send us your submissions in letter-quality or near-letter-quality type—not dot matrix. Electronic submissions (discs) are not accepted. These would only be needed once a contract was signed. Never send discs, videotapes, or audio tapes without inquiring beforehand.

We accept no responsibility for original and only-copies of material. We require that all writers send us copies of their work and to retain the originals at home. We will not be responsible for misplaced or lost material.

Authors should avoid undue "hype-ing" of their work. Materials submitted with author projections of it being a "blockbuster" or "the next *Gone With the Wind*" rarely live up to these pretensions. The publisher and editor(s) are professionals who can make up their own minds on the quality and potential of a proposal without the "self-hype." Comments and/or reviews from qualified professionals or publications, as stated earlier, can be desirable in many cases. Likewise for rejection letters from other publishing companies that acknowledge a project's potential value and which base their rejections on other factors unrelated to quality of author workmanship.

We look for clarity and conciseness of expression and presentation in a synopsis/outline and we ask to see those that will most likely yield proposals fitting our list and that we feel we can market successfully. We turn down thousands of adequate proposals every year just because they have no clear "hooks" or well-defined audiences. The author should present a strong case as to why we should take on the book and who would buy it. Saying that "all children would love it" is very vague, but saying "libraries and schools in Tennessee would like this" is more informative.

All work submitted to us must be in good taste, nonlibelous, and consistent with the level of quality we have established for our company. Although many of our titles are specialized, they are all suitable for general readership and are free of gratuitous, off-color words, phrases, or references.

If an author seeking to publish an illustrated work plans to use artwork copyrighted by an author, illustrator, publication, or syndicate, permission must be obtained in writing from that source. Permission in writing must also be obtained by any author seeking to use quotes or other materials from previously copyrighted publications. We will not publish illustrations or portions of another copyrighted work without written authorization to do so.

Authors seeking to have previously published books reprinted must have, in writing from their previous publisher, a signed letter transferring all rights (including copyright) to them. This is required under the 1978 Copyright Law and must be adhered to in all such cases.

Under the revisions contained in the 1978 Copyright Law, a work is automatically copyrighted at the time of creation. If we agree to accept the work for publication, we will apply for the copyright in the author's name on publication.

TYPES OF BOOK PUBLISHED

Hardcover and trade paperback originals (90%) and reprints (10%) including hardcover, trade paperback, and mass market. We publish an average of 50 to 60 titles a year and have about 800 currently in print.

Specialties are art/architecture books, cooking/cookbooks, motivational, travel guides, history (especially Louisiana/regional), nonfiction, children's books (illustrated and otherwise), inspirational and religious, humor, social commentary, folklore, and textbooks. A very limited number of fictional works are accepted for publication, but we will consider fiction if well written and/or timely.

We seek writers on the cutting edge of ideas who do not write in cliches, or take the old, tired, unimaginative way of foul language and sex scenes to pad a poor writing effort. We strongly urge writers to be aware of ideas gaining currency. We believe ideas have consequences. One of the consequences is that they lead to best-selling books.

We do publish a limited number of posters, cards, giftware, and similar works of art. Consideration of submission of this type is based on consistency with other motifs we are marketing at the present time.

Finally, we would ask you to study Pelican's books and lists. Our latest catalog is available for free on request, and a look through it will help you understand where our interests lie. We have been called "innovative" by the *New York Times*. We will consider almost any well-written work by an author who understands promotion.

PAYMENT POLICY

Pelican pays its authors a royalty based on sales. The rate depends on the type of material and the format.

All terms are specified in the contract all authors publishing under our imprint(s) are required to sign. No book will be published by Pelican without a contract signed beforehand.

All guidelines listed above are subject to revision at any time by Pelican Publishing Company and its editorial board.

Categories: Fiction—Nonfiction—African-American—Architecture—Arts—Asian-American—Biography—Boating—Business—Cartoons—Children—Civil War—Cooking—Family—Hispanic—History—Inspirational—Jewish Interest—Multicultural—Music—Native American—Outdoors—Regional—Religion—Sports/Recreation—Textbooks—Travel—Western

CONTACT: Editorial Department
Material: All
PO Box 3110
Gretna LA 70054-3110
Phone: 504-368-1175
Website: www.pelicanpub.com

THE PERMANENT PRESS
SECOND CHANCE PRESS

The Permanent Press Second Chance Press

Dear Writer:

We are looking for material of a high literary quality; material that is original and stimulating with an authentic point of view and a unique voice.

If you are interested in submitting a manuscript, we would prefer the first 25 pages. We will get back to you as soon as possible.

Please note that we publish novel-length fiction, and occasionally nonfiction. We no longer publish cookbooks, children's stories, story collections, novellas, or poetry.

The above criteria is used for both Second Chance Press and The Permanent Press. Books submitted for reprint by Second Chance Press must be at least twenty years old.

Sincerely,
Judith Shepard, Editor and Co-Publisher
Categories: Fiction

CONTACT: Acquisitions Editor
Material: All
4170 Noyac Rd.
Sag Harbor NY 11963
Phone: 516-725-1101

Perron Press

Statement of Purpose

Perron Press is a relatively new imprint at the Stellar Attractions Network specializing in non-fiction from first time or little know authors who need a professional start for their good ideas and quality manuscripts. Unlike its sister imprint, the Enneagram Consortium's narrow editorial policy, Perron Press is seeking to publish and disseminate how-to and self-helpful works that assist people in becoming more personally and professionally effective, more fulfilled, healthier, and active in life.

Perron Press works with the author to present quality titles to the trade using its network of non-exclusive distributors, trade marketing lists, and promotional channels that may be individually tailored to the type and content of the work. Books are produced in quality trade editions with traditional front and back pages and bar-codes for trade outlets.

The publishing process is a cooperative effort with the author to produce a quality edition optimized for the target audience of the work. Perron Press' mission is to give overlooked quality works a professional first opportunity at being appreciated by the buying public.

Manuscript Submission Guidelines

Thank you for inquiring about our manuscript guidelines for new works. We receive thousands of unsolicited submissions each year. To save us both time, paper, and postage we ask that you first submit a query letter, instead of the whole manuscript, along with an outline of your work, your assessment of the target audience, and a sufficient sample of your writing style for our acquisitions staff to determine if your work fits within our editorial policy. From there, we can decide whether we need to request a complete manuscript for further review.

If you want a response from us either way, please send your query along with a SASE or a working e-mail address. We cannot be responsible for returning manuscripts due to the large quantity we receive, but we make every effort to do so with what you include for that purpose.

We are actively reviewing manuscripts again and we are eager to find manuscripts we can be excited about and get behind. Unagented and first time authors, simultaneous and email submissions are all okay. We encourage you to submit your work for consideration at this time:

• it may be considered (budget allowing) for publication by Perron Press

• we may offer subsidy publishing

• or we can assist you with the details of self-publishing

In any case, we are always excited about being involved in projects that can contribute positively to people's lives. Thank you for your interest in Perron Press.

Categories: Nonfiction—Education—Psychology—Relationships

CONTACT: Nancy Wyatt-Kelsey, Acquisitions Editor
Material: All
PO Box 10826
Portland, OR 97296-0826
Phone: 503-228-4972
Fax: 503-223-9117
E-mail: perron@sa-inc.net
Website: www.sa-inc.net/perron/pr.html

Personal Branding Press

What we are looking for

Non-fiction, Personal Branding disciplines only;

1. Personal Branding Development: (Collateral: brochures, web sites, direct mail etc.), Personal Marketing: Advertising (Print & Broadcast), Database Development, Direct Response, Networking, Outdoor Advertising, Professional & Client Referrals, Sales, Seminars, Web site development & marketing, Customer Service, Public Relations, Personal Presentation, Image, Speaking.

Will accept manuscripts or proposals. Books published include The Personal Branding Phenomenon, The Brand Called You and The Brand Called You for Financial Advisors.

Peter Montoya's *Personal Branding* magazine

For Peter Montoya's *Personal Branding* magazine, please refer to the their listing in the Magazine section of this directory.

Categories: Business—Public Speaking—Advertising—Marketing

CONTACT: Peter Montoya, Publisher
Material: All
1540 S. Lyon St.
Santa Ana Ca 92705
Phone: 714-285-0900
E-mail: 714-285-0929
E-mail: info@petermontoya.com
Website: www.petermontoya.com

Perspectives Press, Inc.
The Infertility and Adoption Publisher

Perspectives Press, Inc. is a small publisher focusing narrowly on infertility issues and alternatives, and on adoption and closely related child welfare issues such as interim (foster) care or psychological services. Our purpose is to promote understanding of these issues and to educate and sensitize those personally experiencing these life situations, professionals who work with such clients, and the public at large. We invite authors whose philosophy concerning these issues agrees with ours to follow our process for submitting manuscripts for consideration, beginning with a careful examination of the many pages on our web site, followed by writing a query letter. (All communications should contain a stamped, self addressed envelope. Please refrain from querying by telephone!)

OUR POINT OF VIEW Regarding infertility and alternatives, Perspectives Press takes the position that we live in the best and worst of times to be infertile. Though research daily provides new treatment options, it has become increasingly difficult for couples to know when to stop treatment, and alternatives are becoming more and more complex: infant adoption is a shrinking alternative, surrogate parenting is in legal limbo, donor insemination's traditional secrecy is being questioned, some technical alternatives provide for as many as five "parents" for a single child, and rising costs of testing and treatment and family building alternatives stifle the dreams of many families. We believe in and actively promote adoption as a positive option for family planning and family building. We do not accept the philosophy that adoption should be eliminated, nor are we accepting of the absolutist idea that any one form of adoption is the only appropriate approach. We agree that adoption is a service designed first to benefit children, not adults, and that every adoption should be child-centered. But we believe that it is incumbent upon professionals working in this arena to treat birthfamilies and prospective adoptors with respect and sensitivity and with objective regard for their needs, which will vary widely, as each set of birthparents and each set of adoptors is unique. We believe that children deserve the permanency of family as quickly as possible after the disruption of a birth family. We believe that any societal institution, including adoption, must meet the

needs of a current society, and to that end we are open to discussion and debate of a variety of approaches to and issues in adoption. Perspectives works actively to promote understanding between adoptees, adoptive parents, and birthparents. We feel that it is important that manuscripts respect the variety of feelings of and the decisions made by those who are members of the adoption triad and that they be written using realistic and neutral adoption language.

OUR EDITORIAL POLICIES Perspectives Press titles are never duplicative. We seek out and publish materials that are currently unavailable through other sources. Furthermore, because our company is small and our list of titles is kept short, we will not consider manuscripts that seriously overlap or compete with titles already on our list. After over ten years in business, we know our own subject matter and its audience very well, but we also know our limitations! We are not a general publisher. Please do not ask us to consider stretching our focus beyond infertility- or adoption-related issues or to change our stated decisions about what topics and genres we will consider as described here. Manuscripts outside our specific field are returned unread if SASE is supplied; without SASE, they are discarded. When submitting (see adult-specific and childrens-specific query/submission information which follows) we respectfully request that you NOT use registered, certified or other signature-required mail to send a manuscript to our post office box address. This necessitates a long and irritating wait in a post office line during "rush hour" or a trip back later in the day! If you would like notification of the arrival of your packet, we are indeed happy to accommodate. Simply enclose a stamped, self addressed postcard, which will be filled out and returned to you the day we open your package.

OUR AUTHORS While we do consider manuscripts from writers who are not personally or professionally involved in our field, we are more inclined to accept a manuscript submitted by an infertile person, an adoptee, a birthparent, an adoptive parent, or a professional working with these clients. Because we work most frequently with never-before-published authors, we make it a policy not to offer a contract based simply on a proposal. At a minimum we require a completed first draft. Authors are oriented before a contract is signed so that they have realistic expectations about the realities and complexities of marketing in our niche. We expect our authors to be closely involved in an ongoing way in their own title's promotion and in the full line of books from Perspectives Press, seeking opportunities to speak and write on the issue, distributing our catalog broadly, etc.

OUR NEEDS For adults we are looking for non-fiction in the form of decision-making materials, books dealing with issue-related parenting concerns, books to share with others to help explain infertility or adoption issues, special programming or training manuals. Our audience is made up of both consumers and professionals in our field. We are not an academic publisher and are disinclined toward research-oriented materials, though we are favorable toward research-based perspectives presented in consumer style. We insist that the books we publish be written in an open, engaging, and user-friendly style, free of jargon.

Manuscripts must be book length—a minimum of 40,000 words. We will not consider pamphlets or singly submitted essays, short stories, or poems.

Because in general first person, autobiographical, and journal-style books in this field have not sold well (no matter what size the publisher) we are not accepting "our infertility experience" or "how we got our child" or "the story of my search" manuscripts. The exception would be books in which the personal materials are included only to provide anecdotal color in a manuscript whose larger purpose is to offer decision-making materials or advice on developing coping skills.

We are not currently publishing novels or other adult fiction. We are a secular publisher and do not publish books rooted in a specific religious view.

After first carefully exploring our web site in order to get a sense of the kinds of books that have appealed to us for publication, writers of adult materials should *schedule a reading by querying* first with a proposal packet before sending a completed manuscript, enclosing a stamped, self addressed envelope for reply— which will follow within about two weeks. (Unsolicited manuscripts arriving without having scheduled a reading will usually be returned unread.) Please do not query electronically. Your proposal should fully describe your topic and should include an outline and/or a table of contents. Tell us the number of typed, double-spaced pages in the full manuscript and the approximate word count. We expect those who write in this field to be familiar with the literature already being marketed. Your query should mention similarly-themed books both in and out of print and discuss how your book would differ from and be superior to them. Also include a careful description of your book's potential audience, including a researched estimate of the realistic size of that audience and a marketing proposal discussing how you think your audience could best be located and reached out to. Tell us about yourself and your qualifications for writing your proposed book. If we are interested in your concept we will give you a date for sending the full manuscript (typed, double spaced, on standard size paper, with margins at least one inch all around, SASE for return) for a scheduled reading. We will respond within two months of the scheduled reading date.

Our *children's books* are primarily fiction and non-fiction manuscripts appropriate for preschoolers and elementary aged youngsters. We encourage writers to carefully examine materials that are already available for children about the issues which we address and to avoid developing materials which compete with or overlap well regarded books already in print from any publisher. Currently we see few glaring gaps in the children's market in our field. The exceptions may be in books for families built by donor egg and embryo and all forms of surrogacy, and for the children of birthparents who have made an adoption plan for another of their children, about families in open adoptions. We are looking for manuscripts to fill these gaps, but we are picky, picky, picky!...

We encourage authors to familiarize themselves with Piagetan theories about children's cognitive development before trying to write for a particular audience. We see far too many manuscripts which really deal with parents' issues rather than childrens'. We will read non-fiction, but not fiction, for middle schoolers and young adults. Unless you are an author/illustrator submitting your own art work, we would prefer that you NOT find your own illustrator before submitting your manuscript. We ask you to recall that because this market is narrow, it is important to make such materials as inclusive as possible. We are not likely to accept, for example, international adoption stories which are country-specific. Make stories racially and ethnically inclusive, remember that some adoptees join their families as infants and some at an older age, keep in mind that not all adoptive parents adopt for reasons of infertility and that many are single parents, and speak respectfully of birthparents.

Because our children's publication program is very small, writers of children's picture books, too, should *query first before submitting*. Your submission packet should include your writing resume and pertinent information about your personal or professional connections to the field about which you are writing. It should include information which indicates that you have familiarized yourself thoroughly enough with available materials in the field to understand how and why your book fills a heretofore empty niche. Include SASE for the reply. We will reply within one month.

I look forward to hearing from you!
Patricia Irwin Johnston, Publisher

Categories: Nonfiction—Children—Family—Health—Parenting—Psychology—Infertility and Adoption

CONTACT: Acquisitions Editor
Material: All
PO Box 90318
Indianapolis IN 46290-0318
Phone: 317-872-3055
E-mail: info@perspectivepress.com
Website: www.perspectivepress.com

Perugia Press

Perugia Press publishes one collection of poetry each year, by a woman at the beginning of her publishing career. Our books appeal to people who have been reading poetry for decades, as well as those who might be picking up a book of poetry for the first time.

Awards
Perugia Press Prize for a First or Second Book of Poetry by a Woman
Prize: $1000 and publication

Guidelines
Manuscript Requirements
• Send between 48 and 72 pages, on white, 8.5 x 11-inch paper, with legible typeface, pagination, and fastened with a removable clip.
• Include two cover pages: one with title of manuscript, name, address, telephone number, and e-mail address, and one with just title of manuscript. No cover letter or bio required. Include a table of contents and an acknowledgments page.
• No electronic submissions.

Terms
An entry fee of $20 must accompany each submission, made payable to Perugia Press. You may submit more than one manuscript; each is considered a separate submission and must include a separate entry fee.

Simultaneous submissions are permitted. Notify Perugia Press if manuscript is accepted elsewhere.

Individual poems may have been published previously in magazines, journals, chapbooks of fewer than 48 pages, or anthologies, but the collection as a whole must be unpublished.

Translations and previously self-published books are not eligible, nor are revisions; the winning manuscript may undergo revisions before publication.

Judging
A judging panel made up of published poets, previous Perugia authors, longtime poetry lovers, booksellers, and scholars will screen and choose the winner.

Notification
Enclose SASE or email address for notification of winner. Notification will be by April 1.

Do not enclose SASE for return of manuscript; all manuscripts will be recycled at the conclusion of the competition. Please do not send your only copy.

Deadline
Annual submission period: August 1 to November 15. Check our website for current information.

Mail Manuscript and Entry Fee to: (No FedEx or UPS)
Categories: Poetry

CONTACT: Submissions Editor
Material: All
Perugia Press Prize
PO Box 60364
Florence MA 01062
Website: www.perugiapress.com

Books M-Z

The Phi Delta Kappa Educational Foundation

And the Center for Evaluation, Development, and Research

Special Publications is the name given to the *Phi Delta Kappa Educational Foundation*'s publications department. When George H. Reavis established the Foundation in 1966, he expressed a vision:

The purpose of the Phi Delta Kappa Educational Foundation is to contribute to a better understanding of 1) the nature of the educative process, and 2) the relation of education to human welfare.

This vision guides the selection of manuscripts for Special Publications.

The Maynard R. Bemis Center for Evaluation, Development, and Research (CEDR), also founded in 1966, has two primary missions: 1) dissemination of research information and 2) improvement of understanding about processes of education research and evaluation. CEDR places a special emphasis on the practical applications of research, especially those findings that help teachers and administrators improve their professional skills.

The best way to understand the scope and character of works published by the PDK Educational Foundation and the Center for Evaluation, Development, and Research is to examine the annual PDK International catalog and to peruse individual publications.

Books

The books published by Special Publications and CEDR reflect a broad range of professional interests and topics. Some are sweeping in scope; a good example is John I. Goodlad's classic, *What Schools Are For*, now in its second edition. Others are more narrowly focused, such as Kenneth Chuska's *Improving Classroom Questions* and Jack Lyne's *Schoolhouse Dreams Deferred*. The principal topic areas include: education policy, philosophy, and history; curriculum and instruction; school administration; school law; international and comparative education; and education research.

Manuscript length: 40,000-70,000 words
Honorarium: $3,000-$5,000

Short Monographs

Like the books, PDK's short monographs cover a broad range of topics. Examples include: *Values on Which We Agree* (38 pages), *Your Future Career in Education* (62 pages), and the *S.A.F.E. Handbook on School Security* (53 pages). Works tend to be highly focused and practical.

Manuscript length: 20,000-30,000 words
Honorarium: $1,000-$2,000

Fastbacks

The Special Publications fastbacks were initiated in 1972 as a series of short, authoritative publications for educators at all levels. Twelve new titles are published annually, six each fall and spring. Of more than 500 titles, some 150 are currently in print. More than 8 million copies of the various titles have been disseminated.

The fastbacks have been characterized as "sophisticated primers." Many are practitioner-oriented, but the series also has room for program profiles and occasional philosophical pieces.

Manuscript length: 10,000 words
Honorarium: $500

From Inquiry to Practice

The CEDR booklets in the From Inquiry to Practice series are condensations of research on timely issues. They are designed to help educators make decisions about school management and student learning.

Manuscript length: 8,000-10,000 words
Honorarium: $500

Proposals and manuscripts for these four types of publications are accepted year-round.

SUBMISSION GUIDELINES

1. Initially, a query letter is preferred. This letter should succinctly state the purpose and audience for the publication, a proposed manuscript length, and a suggested writing timeline. Consider: Is the issue or topic "hot"? Is interest in the topic likely to be enduring? The editor responds to queries usually within 2-3 weeks.

2. The prospective author should be prepared to submit a well-developed outline, including chapter or section headings and basic content descriptions. For longer works, the editor may request a sample chapter. The editor responds to such proposals usually within two months, often sooner.

3. In most instances, an author-publisher agreement (contract) is issued on the basis of a successful proposal. However, in some cases, the editor may require a complete manuscript prior to issuing a contract to publish.

4. The editor will assist the author in developing a successful manuscript. However, in spite of the best intentions of both author and editor, sometimes a manuscript will be judged unacceptable. Authors should be aware that PDK editors reserve the right to edit extensively and, on occasion, to rewrite poorly written materials. But substantive changes are not made without the author's permission.

5. Authors are advised to avoid education jargon. Simple, straightforward prose that makes ample use of examples, anecdotes, and case studies is preferred. Any citations must be complete. The PDK style is based on *The Chicago Manual of Style*.

6. Tables, charts, and graphs should be used only when they are necessary to understand the text. Large figures are discouraged, particularly for the fastbacks, which are printed in a small format.

7. Photographs may be submitted with a manuscript. Clear, 5x7-inch (or larger) black-and-white prints are preferred. All photos must include captions. A model release must be provided for all persons who can be identified in a photograph.

8. Manuscripts must be submitted on standard size paper using a type that can be electronically scanned. CEDR also requires that manuscripts be submitted on disk and unformatted. A disk version is optional for Special Publications.

9. PDK purchases all rights by contract. Payment is made in the form of a one-time honorarium, which is paid about one month prior to publication. Royalty contracts are not provided at the present time.

10. PDK reserves the right to select the manner of publication — for example, paperback or hardcover — and how the work will be promoted and distributed. All costs of production, promotion, and distribution are borne by PDK.

Categories: Nonfiction—Education

CONTACT: Donovan R. Walling, Director of Publications & Research
Material: Queries, proposals, and other correspondence
PO Box 789
Bloomington IN 47402-0789
Phone: 812-339-1156
Fax: 812-339-0018
E-mail: information@pdkintl.org
Website: www.pdkintl.org

Piano Press

Piano Press is currently considering submissions of children's songs, holiday songs, and piano instrumentals for our piano songbooks and CD projects. Children's and/or holiday songs and piano instrumentals may be submitted on a CD or a cassette tape. Please include accompanying lyric sheets and lead sheets or piano scores if available. Please do not send MP3s or web links.

Piano Press is also considering submissions of short stories and essays ON MUSIC-RELATED TOPICS ONLY. Short stories and essays should be no longer than five double-spaced, typewritten pages. Please note, all music-related poems must be entered in The Art of Music Annual Writing Contest to be considered for our anthology.

Piano Press publishes *The Art of Music—A Collection of Writings*, an anthology of music-related poems and writings. The next edition will be published in 2007. Submissions placing first, second, or third in The Art of Music Annual Writing Contest and the top 75 entries will be included in the next edition.

Illustrators may submit samples of their work and contact information for our files. Please do not send samples, postcards, etc., more than once as we already have you on file.

Please do not send any non-music related short stories or essays, or songs other than children's or holiday songs or piano instrumentals.

Please include a SASE with sufficient postage for return of your materials (if you want them returned) and/or our reply.

Please note, we accept only electronic QUERIES at PianoPress@aol.com. We no longer accept electronic submissions of manuscripts or illustrations.

No phone calls please.

All written queries and postal submissions should be sent to:

Piano Press Submissions Dept., PO Box 85, Del Mar, CA 92014-0085. You can expect a reply within 2-3 months of receipt of your query or manuscript.

Categories: Children—Music—Poetry—Short Stories

CONTACT: Elizabeth C. Axford, Editor
Material: All
PO Box 85
Del Mar CA 92014-0085
Phone: 619-884-1401
Fax: 858-755-1104
E-mail: pianopress@pianopress.com
Website: www.pianopress.com

 PICCADILLY BOOKS

Piccadilly Books, Ltd.

Piccadilly Books specializes in the publication of books within two general subject categories (1) Theater & Entertainment and (2) Nutrition and Health.

THEATER AND ENTERTAINMENT

In this category we are looking for nonfiction, how-to, and activity topics suitable for children and adults. We have a strong interest in family entertainment—magic, clowning, puppetry, etc. Comedy skits, games, unique fun activities and any business topics related to these subjects are also of interest. *Samples of the type of titles we publish are:*

- Creative Clowning
- Ventriloquism Made Easy
- Clown Magic
- Tricks and Stunts to Fool Your Friends
- Humorous Dialogs
- The Birthday Party Business

NUTRITION AND HEALTH

Books in this category are published under our imprint name HealthWise Publications. We are interested in nonfiction books on any aspect of health, diet, exercise, and bodywork. Must be written from a holistic or natural health viewpoint. *Samples of the type of titles we publish are:*

- *The Detox Book*
- *The Healing Crisis*
- *The Healing Power of Rebounding*

We do not accept children's picture books, novels, or any subject outside those described above. Material from unagented and first-time authors are welcomed and encouraged.

Submissions should consist of a query letter and sample chapters of your manuscript. You may submit a full manuscript if it is completed along with a cover letter describing the contents of the manuscript. We do not return manuscripts or sample chapters, if rejected they are discarded. We review all submissions within a few days of their arrival and send responses as soon as we have made a decision. The most promising submissions take several weeks to thoroughly evaluate. Please allow up to two months for a response.

All manuscripts should include the title, your name, and your address on the first page. Following pages should be numbered consecutively.

Computer printout submissions are acceptable. Letter quality printouts are highly preferred over dot-matrix. Hand written manuscripts are not acceptable.

Be sure to obtain permission to use any quotation, illustration, or other copyrighted material. Contact the house which published the material and get their written permission.

Categories: Nonfiction—Comedy—Diet/Nutrition—Entertainment—Health—Theatre—Humor

CONTACT: Submissions Department
Material: All
PO Box 25203
Colorado Springs CO 80936
Phone: 719-550-9887

 PICTON PRESS

Picton Press

Our guidelines for submissions, in our categories of history and genealogy:

Picton Press publishes top quality scholarly works in these two fields, with emphasis on the 17th and 18th centuries.

Manuscripts to be submitted should show:

- 17th or 18th century subjects preferred; 19th century acceptable
- highest quality technical expertise
- comprehensive grasp of the subject matter
- new subject matter or a new approach to well-established subject matter

We will publish works with relatively limited markets, and even books which are unlikely to break even, so long as they demonstrate the items above. On a common-sense basis we give priority to works which are camera-ready and/or require only limited editing.

Categories: History—Genealogy

CONTACT: Acquisitions Editor
Material: All
PO Box 250
Rockport ME 04856-0250
Phone: 207-236-6565
Fax: 207-236-6713
E-mail: sales@pictonpress.com

Pineapple Press, Inc.

Most of our books are Florida nonfiction. We also publish a few literary novels, some nonfiction on other southern states, and some general nonfiction. Almost all of our fiction is set in Florida. We also publish books about lighthouses.

Our only children's books are on Florida topics for Florida schools. We publish a few Florida-related cookbooks. We do not publish genre fiction (mysteries, romances, science fiction, action/adventure, Westerns) unless they are strongly Florida-related.

Send submissions via US mail to our post office box. Do not send registered or certified or in any way requiring a signature. These packages will not be picked up as they require waiting in long lines at the post office. If you want confirmation of receipt, enclosed a self-addressed, stamped postcard with a place for marking that the submission was received.

Fiction

Please send:

1. query letter describing your manuscript and yourself (any previous publications, etc.). It should be brief and state specifically what you have to offer in the first paragraph (e.g., a historical novel, a mainstream love story, an experimental novel). Also please give the title. Though you may prefer not to categorize your work, please try.

2. brief (one-page) synopsis

3. sample chapters, including first

4. Self-addressed stamped envelope (SASE) for anything you want returned. Many writers are now sending SASE for the reply letter only. Paper is recycled.

Nonfiction

Please send:

1. query letter describing your manuscript and why you are qualified to write it. Please give the title.

2. table of contents

3. sample chapters, including introduction

4. proposed market for this book

5. listing of other books on or near this topic, with an explanation of how yours is different, better, targeted to a specific group, etc.

6. SASE (as above)

Please make sure that your manuscript is easy on the eyes. Manuscripts in all caps or single-spaced will not be read. We prefer manuscripts available on disk, but we do not read from computer disks until quite far into the editorial process. Please tape rather than staple your mailer. Again, please do not send anything via registered or certified mail.

We accept simultaneous submissions. We usually reply within eight weeks.

Thanks for your interest in Pineapple Press.

June Cussen, Editor

Categories: Fiction—Nonfiction—Associations—Cooking—Education—Regional

CONTACT: Submissions Editor
Material: All
PO Box 3889
Sarasota FL 34230
Website: www.pineapplepress.com

Players Press, Inc.

Players Press is continually looking for new works to publish. Send a clearly typed copy of your play, musical, or performing arts book to:

Players Press, Inc.
PO Box 1132
Studio City, CA 91614-0132
USA

Remember to enclose the following:

1. A stamped, self-addressed envelope for the return of your manuscript.

2. Two (2) stamped, self-addressed #10 envelopes for correspondence.

3. A brief biography and/or resumé of the writer.

For Plays and Musicals:

1. A copy of the flyer and program with production dates on it. **No manuscript will be considered unless it has been produced.** (Produced means: One professional production, or two amateur productions, or one award-winning amateur production. A *reading is* **not** *considered a production.*)

2. Reviews, when available. (Specify if no reviews are available.)

3. If a musical, supply a copy of the music, in text and audio cassette(s).

Performing Arts Books:

Send a query letter with synopsis, chapter contents and author's bio. We will advise if we can review the manuscript.

If accepted for publication, the script must be made available on computer disk. We prefer Mac-compatible in either Microsoft Word or PageMaker. Please advise.

Our editors will try to read your work and return it to you within 90 days (our normal reading is 30 to 365 days).

Categories: Nonfiction—Arts—Dance—Drama—Education—Entertainment—Fashion—Film/Video—Mass Communications—Military—Music—Television/Radio—Theatre—Writing

CONTACT: Robert W. Gordon, Senior Editor
Material: All
PO Box 1132
Studio City CA 91614-0132
Phone: 818-789-4980
Fax: 818-990-2477

Potomac Books, Inc.

If you are interested in submitting a manuscript for publication, please refer to the following guidelines:

Proposals should consist of a half-page synopsis, a table of contents or rough outline of the book's structure, 1-2 sample chapters (double-spaced), reviews of any previous books, and a biographical sketch or vita.

No email submissions, please.

Please include a self-addressed, stamped envelope so we can respond and return the materials if we decide not to proceed.

Categories: Nonfiction—Aviation—Biography—Civil War—Government—History—Human Rights—Military—Politics—Regional—Sports/Recreation—Textbooks—Defense—Foreign Policy—Intelligence—International Affairs

CONTACT: Donald Jacobs, Aquisitions Editor
Material: Proposals
22841 Quicksilver Drive
Dulles VA 20166
Phone: 703-661-1548
Website: www.potomacbooksinc.com

Possibility Press

Established 1995. Publishes trade paperback originals. Publishes 5-10 titles/year. Receives 1,000 submissions/year. 90% of books from first-time authors; 95% from unagented writers. Royalties vary. Publishes book approximately 18-24 months after acceptance of ms. Responds in 2 months to queries. For response you need to send a SASE. Manuscript guidelines are obtainable from website. Imprints: Aeronautical Publishers, American Aeronautical Archives, and Possibility

Press.

Nonfiction

How-to, business, self-help, inspirational. Subjects include business/economics, pop psychology, success/motivation, inspiration, entrepreneurship, sales, marketing, network marketing, and homebased business topics, success parables, and human interest success stories. Submissions need to include a one-page summary of book, contents, introduction, chapter-by-chapter synopsis, comparison with competitive books, marketing plans, and photo of author. Author needs to have completed manuscript before submission.

Recent Titles

The Power of Meeting New People by Debra Fine, The Power of Talking Out Loud to Yourself by Bill Wayne, The Millionaire Mentor by Greg Reid, Leading Leaders to Leadership by John Fuhrman, The Power of Having Desire by Bruce Garrabrandt.

Tips

"Our focus is on creating and publishing short-to-medium length (12,000-36,000 words) bestsellers written by authors who speak and consult. We're looking for authors who are serious about making a difference in the world."

Categories: Fiction—Nonfiction—Psychology—Self Help

CONTACT: Marjorie L. Markowski, Editor-in-Chief
Material: All
Markowski Int'l. Publishers
One Oakglade Circle
Hummelstown PA 17036
Phone: 717-566-0468
Fax: 717-566-6423
E-mail: posspress@aol.com
Website: www.possibilitypress.com

The Post-Apollo Press

Thank you for your interest in The Post-Apollo Press. We accept all manuscripts but are mostly interested in experimental poetry and fiction by new writers. We only ask that people send a SASE if they would like their manuscript returned to them.

The Post Apollo Press was founded in Sausalito, California in 1982, specializing in writing by women. Writers published on Post Apollo include internationally-known poets Etel Adnan and Anne-Marie Albiach, and novelists Marguerite Duras and Ulla Berke'wicz. Post Apollo books have received wide acclaim by noted writers in reviews in The New York Times Review of Books, the San Francisco Chronicle, The Nation, The American Book Review, P.M.L.A. Journal, the New England Review of Books, among others.

Categories: Fiction—Poetry

CONTACT: Simone Fattal, Editor
Material: All
35 Marie St.
Sausalito CA 94965
Phone: 415-332-7018
Fax: 415-332-8045
E-mail: tpapress@dnai.com
Website: www.dnai.com/~tpapress

PREP PUBLISHING

Prep Publishing

Established in 1994, PREP Publishing is the publishing division of a company, PREP, Inc., founded in 1981 by graduates of Harvard Business School and Yale University. The parent company is a diversified writing/editing organization and is the country's largest resume writing organization.

The company's first title was published in 1995: Second Time Around is a mystery/romance and literary fiction by Southern writer Patty Sleem. Library Journal described Patty Sleem's second book, Back In Time, as "an engrossing look at the discrimination faced by female ministers."

In 1996 PREP Publishing launched its line of career titles with the publication of Resumes and Cover Letters That Have Worked for Military Professionals, a how-to guide to resume and cover letter preparation for veterans and military professionals leaving active duty. Praised by the highly respected Booklist as "A guide that significantly translates Veterans' experience into viable repertoires of achievement," that 256-page book contains resumes and cover letters of "real people" who used those resumes and cover letters to transition into civilian jobs. The second title in PREP's line of career titles was Resumes and Cover Letters That Have Worked, a 272-page how-to book containing more than 100 resumes and cover letters of "civilians" with special sections devoted to Experienced Professionals, People Changing Careers, and Recent College Graduates.

PREP's publishing interests include mysteries and other fiction and nonfiction, including biographies of famous people, business books, self-help and how-to books, and career titles. We are also developing a line of Christian fiction. Our mission is to publish quality materials, both for children and adults, that enrich people's lives and help them optimize their human experience.

PREP Publishing is listed in Literary Marketplace and our titles are listed in Books in Print and in Forthcoming Books in Print. PREP Publishing is a member of the American Booksellers Association, Southeast Booksellers Association, Publishers Association of the South, Publishers Marketing Association, the Christian Booksellers Association, and the Council of Literary Magazines and Small Presses. Our titles are distributed by Seven Hills Book Distributors and by Ingram Book Company, Baker & Taylor Books, Quality Books, Unique Books, and others.

There are two ways to make submissions to PREP Publishing:

1. One way is to send a cover letter and synopsis of your book. Published authors may prefer this query-first method. Address cover-letter-and-synopsis submissions to Frances Sweeney at the address below. Limit your total submission to three pages! Try to sell us on your concept; if we are interested, we will get in touch with you.

2. The other way to make a submission to PREP is to send your complete manuscript with a non-refundable reading fee of one hundred dollars payable to PREP. Because of the volume of mail received, it has become impossible for our existing staff to read all the manuscripts which authors wish to submit to us and we now employ outside readers to evaluate the book's suitability for publication and write a written "Reader's Report" which the author gets a copy of. Pre-published authors or published authors writing in a new genre may find this professional evaluation helpful.

If you wish to submit your complete manuscript, please send a hard copy (not an electronic submission) of the entire manuscript along with a check for $100 to PREP and an SASE with sufficient postage for the manuscript's return to you. Our readers are professional editors, "book doctors," and respected librarians, and our turn-around time is two weeks. Please bear in mind that our professional readers do try to identify the areas in plot, characterization, etc. which need to be "fixed" if it is the reader's opinion that author revisions are necessary. Address such submissions to Janet Abernethy at the address below.

Once a manuscript is selected for publication, payment to authors is through a royalty schedule based on final sales. Once a manuscript is accepted, publication usually takes 18 months.

Thank you for your interest in PREP Publishing.

Categories: Fiction—Nonfiction—Adventure—Biography—Business—Careers—Christian Interests—Crime—Family—Inspirational—Literature—Military—Mystery—Relationships—Religion—Romance—Spiritual—Women's Issues—Writing—Young Adult—Humor

CONTACT: Anne McKinney, Editor-in-Chief
Material: All
110½ Hay St.
Fayetteville NC 28305
Phone: 910-483-8049
Fax: 910-483-2439

Prima Publishing

PRIMA PUBLISHING, founded in 1984, publishes hardcovers and trade paperbacks in nonfiction categories including popular culture, current affairs and international events, travel, business, careers, legal topics, sports, cooking, health, lifestyle, self-help, and music. Prima is an imprint of the Crown Publishing Group, a division of Random House, and maintains a solid backlist.

The following Prima titles reflect the varied interests of the company: *Churchill on Leadership* by Steven F. Hayward, *The Wave 3 Way to Building Your Downline* by Richard Poe, *Positive Discipline A-Z* by Jane Nelsen, Lynn Lott, and H. Stephen Glenn, *The Wealthy Barber* by David Chilton, *Encyclopedia of Natural Medicine* by Michael Murry, N. D. and Joseph Pizzorno, N.D.

Please include the following when sending a proposal to Prima Publishing:

1. Brief explanation of the book. What is the manuscript about, and why would someone buy it? Like the short text written on the back cover of a book, the explanation should describe the contents of the book while also enticing the reader to know more about it. The overview is also an opportunity for the author to display his or her unique writing style. To prepare for an overview, it may be a worthwhile practice to read the back covers of several books in a local bookstore, noting the way the publisher tries to catch and hold the reader's interest.

2. Detailed table of contents and chapter outlines. Breaking the manuscript down into individual chapters, write a paragraph discussing the information in each chapter.

3. Sample chapter. The editor will need to see your best chapter in order to evaluate your writing.

4. Anticipated market for the book. Who is the target audience? Publishers are looking for profitable books, and especially if it is a new area for Prima, we need to know the size of the market and the likelihood of reaching it. What makes your book unique from others already on the market? How will you promote the book? Will it have appeal outside the usual trade bookstore channels? are there books currently on the bestseller lists that reach the same type of market?

5. Competition for the book. Are there other books currently on the market that address the same or similar subjects? How and why is your book different? Does your proposed book fill a niche presently open? Identify the competition but tell us how your book will surpass that competition because of the added material or new slant it offers.

6. Author's Qualifications. What makes you the right person to write this book? Tell us about your career experience and educational credentials as well as your experience in the area of your subject and with the media, for example, speaking and teaching experience. Also of interest is your publishing history and why you came to write this book. Do you have periodical, journal, or book writing experience?

Prima does not publish original fiction, personal narrative, or poetry.

If you are a first-time author, the book should be completed before the proposal is sent. Please do not send a manuscript unless specifically requested.

For help in preparing a proposal, refer to Prim's *The Writer's Guide to Book Editors*, Publishers, and Literary Agents by Jeff Herman.

Please allow four to six weeks for an answer.

Categories: Nonfiction—Business—Careers—Computers—Cooking—Health—Lifestyle—Self Help—Sports/Recreation

CONTACT: Acquisitions Editor
Material: All
3000 Lava Ridge Ct.
Roseville CA 95661
Phone: 916-787-7000
Fax: 916-787-7005

Primer Publishers

Authors wishing to submit manuscripts should first send a brief letter stating purpose, qualifications of author on subject, and why Primer should be the publisher. We also ask that no more than 10 pages of sample text be sent at that time. Please be sure your subject matches our niche.

We publish book about the Southwestern United States, including Colorado, California, and Arizona. Our subjects are primarily about the outdoors, nature, and history of the West.

Primer Publishers imprints are Renaissance House Publishers and American Traveler Press.

Categories: History—Nature—Outdoors—Regional

CONTACT: Bill Fessler
Material: All
5738 N Central Ave.
Phoenix AZ 85012
Phone: 602-234-1574
Fax: 602-234-3062
E-mail: info@primerpublishers.com
Website: www.primerpublishers.com

Printing Industries of America Graphic Arts Technical Foundation
PIA/GATFPress

PIA/GATF's strong commitment to research and education drives its publications program—PIA/GATF*Press*—which includes textbooks, primers, reference books, training modules, and CD-ROMs. Many PIA/GATF publications are adopted as required texts at the high-school, college, and university levels across the country.

PIA/GATF*Press* publishes nonfiction books on most aspects of the graphic communications industry and the ancillary processes prevalent in today's rapidly changing technologies. Some of the manuscript topics in which GATF*Press* is interested include: graphic design, color management, safety, estimating, printing management, print buying, sales and marketing, desktop publishing, prepress, variable-data, job costing, press maintaince, digital asset management, print production workflow, aspects of lithographic production, and the printer's compliance with OSHA/EPA regulations. PIA/GATF*Press* does not publish "coffee table" art books.

PIA/GATF books are not product-specific; therefore, manuscripts on specific software programs or products are not accepted. In order to gain acceptance, content must not appreciably overlap with any other PIA/GATF books in print or production.

Book proposals from both veteran and first-time authors are welcome.

Submissions Should Include:

• *A cover letter:*

This serves as your sales proposal in which you convince PIA/GATF's editorial group that your manuscript is a marketable product and that you are the right author for them.

• *A comprehensive outline/synopsis, covering:*

1. The rationale behind the book: Include a summary of what the book is about, what it will and will not cover, how it compares to similar books, why it is unique, and why it is necessary.

2. The focus of the book: Define who the target audience is

and what readers will learn or gain from the text.

3. Your background: Explain why you are qualified to write this book—your professional background, expertise, and experience as a professional writer.

4. The book itself: Provide a chapter-by-chapter outline with a detailed explanation of the material to be covered in each segment. Identify chapter titles, heads, and subheads; explain each topic and segment division; and include a separate section on possible illustrations.

5. Writing samples: If you've already begun writing, include no more than two sample chapters from the manuscript.

Include a self-addressed stamped envelope (large enough and containing the proper postage) to return the materials to you. PIA/GATF is not responsible for unsolicited materials received without adequate return postage and packaging.

You can expect a response acknowledging receipt of your proposal within two weeks. Submissions are then reviewed by PIA/GATF's editorial staff, consultants, and a product planning committee for final approval. If your manuscript is accepted, it also will go through more in-depth technical review ("peer review") prior to publication. Responses are generally sent within four months. Interest in an outline does not guarantee publication of your manuscript. PIA/GATF does not pay kill fees for manuscripts for which there is no signed contract.

Categories: Nonfiction—Associations—Graphics—Technical—Textbooks—Trade—Printing

CONTACT: Amy Woodall, Managing Editor
Material: All
CONTACT: Thomas Desree, Editor in Chief
Material: Technical Information
200 Deer Run Rd.
Sewickley PA 15143-2600
Phone: 412-741-6860

Pruett Publishing Company

Pruett Publishing Company specializes in, but is not limited to, nonfiction books and guides for the Rocky Mountain West. Our subject areas include: outdoor recreation and hiking, flyfishing, travel, western history, and nature and the environment. We welcome proposals for books in any of these areas from both authors and agents. We encourage you to review our catalog to help determine whether your book is appropriate for our publishing program. First-time authors are welcome. If you are uncertain whether your topic will interest us, feel free to send a letter of inquiry.

Book Proposals should include the following:

1. A brief summary of the proposed book

2. An outline or table of contents

3. One or two sample chapters

4. Examples (or discussion about) artwork you plan to include

5. A discussion of the market you envision for the book

6. A list of other published books you know of on the topic that may compete with yours and comments on how they differ from yours

7. A biography or resume of the author

If you send a complete manuscript double-spacing will make it easier to read and comment on. If you prefer, you can query us via e-mail at pruettbks@pruettpublishing.com.

Categories: Nonfiction—Environment—Nature—Outdoors—Recreation—Regional—Sports/Recreation—Travel

CONTACT: Jim Pruett
Material: All
PO Box 2140
Boulder CO 80306
Website: www.pruettpublishing.com

PSI Research
The Oasis Press
Hellgate Press

Originally established in 1975 as publisher of Oasis Press (books and resources for small businesses and entrepreneurs), a second imprint, Hellgate Press, was added in 1997. Oasis Press was sold to Entrepreneur Media, Inc. in 2001 and no longer exists. Hellgate Press (military history, memoirs and travel adventure),however, is still going strong with more than 60 titles in print. We accept submissions from authors and agents; first-time authors are welcome. Please no fiction, historical or otherwise. We do not pay advances and royalties start at 10%.

Please send either a query letter or proposal only. DO NOT send an entire manuscript. If your proposal gets our attention, we will request a manuscript. Allow 4-6 weeks for response. You may query by email at harley@hellgatepress.com.

Proposals should include the following:

1. A brief synopsis of the book

2. An outline or table of contents

3. Three or four sample chapters

4. A brief discussion of the market for your book

5. An overview of your willingness/ability/ideas to promote the book

6. A brief biography of the author

7. Author contact information including e-mail address

8. SASE if you wish your materials returned

Categories: Nonfiction—Business—History—Military

CONTACT: Harley B Patrick
Material: All
Hellgate Press
PO Box 3531
Ashland, OR 97520
Phone: 800-795-4059
E-mail: harley@hellgatepress.com
Website: www.hellgatepress.com

Puget Sound Books

Here is the simple page...no fancy type, no guarantees, no hype. We are currently searching for quality, book-length manuscripts of 70,000 words or more. We are NOT currently looking for Romance, Westerns, Religious text, science fiction, children's books or political manifestos. Poetry we accept only for our Puget Sound Stories publication.

Short stories are also only accepted for our Puget Sound Stories publication.

What we ARE looking for is the finest in:

• Action Adventure

• Mystery

• Suspense manuscripts.

We will also consider other types of general interest fiction if the story is strong and your characters are bold, complex and fascinating.

Author Guidelines:

Manuscripts must be complete-no partial works. Don't send a query - send your complete manuscript along with a self-addressed, stamped envelope. If you want your manuscript returned, enclose an envelope and postage for it also.

• Hard Copy Only - No disc or email submissions.

• Print should be double spaced, printed on one side only, 11 or 12 point type - black ink.

• Please, no fancy typestyles- simple block or Times New Roman is appreciated.

• Do not send your only copy. We are not responsible for lost items.

• Manuscripts that do not have a return envelope and have not been considered for publication will be destroyed. Allow 4 to 6 weeks for our response. We are looking at many new manuscripts, but publish only 1 book per quarter - 4 per year.

Categories: Fiction—Adventure—Mystery

CONTACT: Editor
Material: All
P. O. Box 220
Gig Harbor WA 98335
Website: www.pugetsoundbooks.com

QED Press

QED Press is a small, award-winning west coast publishing house whose vision is to publish nonfiction and fiction that inspires readers to transcend national, racial and ethnic boundaries through an appreciation of the humanities, world literature, art, and poetry.

Submission Guidelines

Manuscripts must be typed or output on a letter-quality or laser printer, double-spaced and with ample margins. A self-addressed envelope with sufficient postage to return materials should accompany all manuscripts and queries.

We do not charge a reading fee and receive too many submissions to be able to comment on any but the most striking manuscripts. We generally respond between thirty and ninety days to queries and submissions and prefer to receive completed manuscripts. Electronic submissions are not welcome.

We are interested in books for readers over the age of thirty-five, preferably non-fiction, although we will publish strong, non-formulaic fiction. Previous credits are not necessary, although we hold to high writing standards. We are also very interested in publishing paper airplane books (we are currently working on our third), and welcome any serious folder to reply. Our royalties are as high as any mainstream publisher, but since we are not a large press, we do not pay advances against royalties.

Thank you for your interest in our company and we look forward to hearing from you.

—Stephanie Rosencrans for QED Press
Categories: Fiction—Nonfiction—Arts—Human Rights—Literature—Poetry

CONTACT: Stephanie Rosencrans
Material: All
155 Cypress St.
Fort Bragg CA 95437
Phone: 707-964-9520
Fax: 707-964-7531
E-mail: qedpress@mcn.org
E-mail: stephanie@cypresshouse.com
Website: www.qedpress.com

Quality Words In Print

No longer accepting submission.

Quill Driver Books
Word Dancer Press

We publish nonfiction books only and if you have one that has a large, identifiable and reachable audience, we'd like to hear from you. We do not publish poetry, children's books, or fiction.

We prefer to receive a query letter along with a book proposal. Please submit to us by snail mail. We consider simultaneous submissions. Naturally, if we are interested, we will contact you; however, if you wish to hear from us in the event we are not interested, please enclose an SASE. Keep in mind that every publisher turns down projects for reasons that have nothing to do with the merit or publishability of the book. Even if we aren't interested, we encourage you to keep trying with other publishers.

We suggest you read the book *The Fast Track Course on How to Write a Nonfiction Book Proposal* by Stephen Blake Mettee, available at bookstores and libraries, and follow Mettee's instructions in preparing your book proposal. While this isn't absolutely necessary, a properly prepared book proposal will increase your chances with us as well as with other publishers. It will also help you think your project through completely.

Recent titles we have published include *The California Wine Country Diet* by Haven Logan, Ph.D. and *Could It Be B12?* by Sally M. Pacholok, R.N. and Jeffrey J. Stuart, D.O.

We are particularly interested in seeing proposals that fit the following four areas:

The Best Half of Life ™ series

The Best Half of Life books are practical, upbeat, encouraging how-to or self-help books that enhance the lives of people in their 50s and over. These titles help the reader to improve and to better enjoy his or her life. We want sound, well-thought-out, positive, focused writing. No personal How-I-Survived (-Cancer, -Caring for a Spouse Afflicted with Alzheimer's, etc.) essays. The book must offer something distinctly helpful to the reader. Books with the greatest chance of being published as a part of The Best Half of Life series will have life-changing potential.

Text should be for the popular market rather than the academic market. The inclusion of checklists, sidebars, real-life anecdotes, exercises and similar elements is encouraged.

Subjects may include the whole gamut of human experience, from cooking to creativity, sex to careers, recreation to finances. A recent Best Half of Life book is *Sex After 50: Revving Up the Romance, Passion & Excitement* by Dr, Ruth K. Westheimer

Writing and Getting Published

We are always interested in seeing proposals on books for writers. Here the credentials of the author are very important. If you have never published a novel, it is doubtful that we would be interested in a book from you on how to write a novel.

There are quite a number of everything-an-author-needs-to-know-about-writing books out there. Try to focus your project to a specific aspect of writing or getting published. This focus is shown in our titles *Damn! Why Didn't I Write That? How Ordinary People are Raking in $100,000 or More Writing Nonfiction Books & How You Can Too!* by Marc McCutcheon and *Emotional Structure: A Guide for Screenwriters* by Peter Dunne.

California

We publish one or two regional California titles each year. Titles with a narrow focus, yet a broad appeal have the best chance of catching our interest. Examples are our *Black Bart Boulevardier Bandit* by George Hoeper, about the 1880s stagecoach robber; *California's Geographic Names* by David Durham, California's definitive gazetteer, and *From Mud-Flat Cove to Gold to Statehood: California 1840–1850* by Irving Stone. Titles may be on the history or the recreation of California, or on any other subject distinctive to the state. The availability of illustrations is often a necessity.

The Fast Track Course™ series

The Fast Track Course series features concise, clear, interestingly written books that present 90% of what a reader needs to know on the subject. FTC books can be on virtually any subject. They may be how-to or self-help, or simply informative. Word count should be 30,000 to 50,000.

Thank you for your interest, we look forward to hearing from you.

Categories: Nonfiction—Aging—Biography—Californiana—Celebrities—Directories—Health—History, Western—How-to—Lifestyles—Reference—Regional—Self-help—Senior Citizens—True Crime—Western—Writing

Contact: Stephen Blake Mettee
Material: All
1254 Commerce Way
Sanger, CA 93657
Phone: 559-875-2170
Fax: 559-876-2180
E-mail: Info@QuillDriverBooks.com
Website: QuillDriverBooks.com

Quilt in a Day Publications

Please refer to Howell Press, Inc.

Ragged Mountain Press

Thank you for requesting manuscript guidelines for Ragged Mountain Press. Our slogan is "Books that take you off the beaten path."

We publish a variety of books on outdoor sports, recreation, and fitness in several categories. First, we are interested in beginning-to-intermediate level how-to manuscripts about non-competitive sports or fitness. This could include anything from archery to sport diving. We have a special interest in paddlesports, including sea kayaking, whitewater paddling, and canoeing.

We are also interested in big, serious reference books and small, gift books for outdoor enthusiasts, including adventure narratives.

To help your proposal move swiftly through our review process, please include the following:
• Cover letter with your contact information (address, telephone and fax numbers, email address)
• Table of Contents with brief summaries of each chapter
• One or two sample chapters
• Sample photographs and/or illustrations if these are central to your proposal
• Competition analysis (a listing of similar books in print, copies of recent supporting magazine articles and newspaper clippings, etc.)
• A personal or professional biography or resume (if you feel it is relevant)
• A self-addressed stamped envelope (if you want your materials returned)

Please anticipate a four- to six-week waiting period for a response from us. Thanks again for your interest in Ragged Mountain Press. We look forward to receiving your proposal.

Categories: Nonfiction—Adventure—Boating—Conservation—Environment—Fishing—Outdoors—Physical Fitness—Recreation—Recreational Vehicles—Sports/Recreation—

CONTACT: Bob Holtzman, Acquisitions Editor
Material: All
CONTACT: Jonathan Eaton, Editorial Director
Material: All
PO Box 220
Camden ME 04843-0220

Railroading
An Imprint of Bristol Fashion Publications, Inc.

You will find we are very cooperative when dealing with freelance contributors. Our Chairman and Publisher, John Kaufman, and our COO and Editor-in-Chief, Bob Lollo, were both freelance photographers and writers long before Bristol Fashion Publications, Inc. came to be in 1993. They still retain the memories of the "difficult years" getting started. This is one of the reasons we are interested in submissions from new authors and photographers.

We rarely project more than six months in advance. Always include a SASE. Include your telephone number with any correspondence or submissions.

Photography Submissions

COVERS: Color glossy prints. Prints should be 3-1/2 x 5 to 5 x 7. Digitized images (300 DPI) in a JPG or GIF file are preferred for final use.

All covers depict the theme of the book. Use deep saturation, vivid colors and good contrast to bring out the main subject matter. This is NOT the type of cover you will see on a magazine. Send several sample copies of your work for consideration. Mark each copy with your name, address and phone number.

INTERIOR: Digitized images (300 DPI) in a GIF or JPG file are the only images we consider for use.

Photos should show hands using tools, when appropriate, the steps involved in completing a project and the finished results. These are the photos we most often need.

The railroad history books' photographic needs center around railroading from the beginning of railroading to the late 1960's.

Good contrast, lighting and subject matter is necessary. Send several hard copy or jpg/gif (on disk) samples of your work for consideration. Mark each copy with your name, address and phone number. We will not consider e-mailed images—please do not send them.

Simultaneous submissions are fine. Notify us if a photo we have on file becomes unavailable. Model and property releases are preferred if the person is identifiable. All submissions should be non-returnable disks or prints. If we can keep copies of your work on file, we are more likely to call you when the need arises. We will notify you within one month, whether or not we feel we can use your work. Assignments may be given at the same rate of pay, as noted below.

We purchase book/reprint rights as a one time buy. Cover prices range from $50.00 to $300.00 depending on the project. Interior B & W prices range from $10.00 to $25.00. Credit line given. One copy of the book will be given to each contributor.

Writer's Guidelines

Our books use simple to understand and follow processes, for the person who knows little about model railroading. Each subject should take the reader from the very basics, through each step, until the complete, advanced subject matter is discussed. As the project expands and becomes more complicated, each new phase or technique should be described. If a friend, who knows nothing about model railroading, can read, understand and feel comfortable doing the work you have described, you have written what we want to publish.

Non-How-To and History related titles should be extremely interesting to read. Photographic history books should be well captioned with a paragraph or two on each photo subject. These same guidelines apply to prototype photographic reference books.

How-To topics are the most marketable with a wider audience. We are always seeking new ideas and topics for our books.

Simultaneous submissions are not accepted. Submit a few chapters for review, along with the table of contents. All submissions must be hard copy with a SASE. Include your past credits, tear sheets, state if photos or line art is available and the state of completion of your manuscript. We will report in two weeks of receipt, often sooner.

If you have never been published or have not yet started the manuscript submit a short sample (1000 words), outline, completion date and photo/line art availability.

We pay royalty of 8% to 11% based on the retail price of the book. Average retail price is $20.00 to $30.00. Photos and line art submitted by the author will be considered as part of the manuscript and the percentage adjusted accordingly. Follow the photography submission guidelines above. We will purchase worldwide book/reprint rights.

WRITERS TIPS: Know or research the industry, owners and technical knowledge. Use the proper railroading language and terms. A well-written manuscript is useless if the knowledge of the writer is lacking. If you are not familiar with a given subject, talk to people who has been around trains/modeling for many years. Do not use unwarranted technical jargon to explain a subject. Use simple terms and an easy to understand and follow, step-by-step writing style. When we have to choose, we are more likely to use poor writing and good knowledge, than good writing and poor knowledge.

Preparing Your Manuscript

Never use an exclamation point for emphasis except in a direct quotation. We! and! the! reader! don't! care! what! startles! you!

Don't double-space, regardless of what you were taught in typing class.

Don't use the Tab key or Space bar to indent a paragraph.

Don't attempt to make your manuscript look as you'd like your book to appear. Just write. Converting your manuscript into a book is what we do.

Trust us. We have a combined experience of more than 200 years in the publishing industries. We will edit your manuscript to suit its intended market. The better your work reads, the better it sells, and that benefits all of us.

Please understand this—You will not retire from the book sales of any single specialty title. Specialty titles simply do not sell that well in any market. A very successful specialty title may sell 20,000 copies over a five year run. A very few sell more. Most sell one quarter or less of that number and are considered a successful book. Our successful authors often have three or more books published with us and they started by reading these very same guidelines.

After preparing your submission, following the above guidelines, you may submit it by land mail (hard copy only, do not include a disk) or by email. To submit by email, attach an ASCII text or MSWord file to the email—DO NOT paste the text into the body of the email or include graphic files with this submission. Send the email to jpk@bfpbooks.com. Include only one manuscript with each email submission.

We look forward to hearing from you.

Categories: Crafts/Hobbies—History—Model Railroads—Technical

CONTACT: Submissions
Material: All
Bristol Fashion Publications, Inc.

PO Box 4676
Harrisburg, PA 17111
Phone: 772-559-1379, 800-478-7147
Fax: 800-543-9030
E-mail: jpk@bfpbooks.com
Website: www.bfpbooks.com

Rainbow Publishers
Book for Children's Ministries

Our objective:
We publish helpful how-to books, activity books and "teaching tips" for leaders of children in both the church and home settings. Generally, our children's ministries products are reproducible books issued in series for ages 2 through grade 6. All are Bible-based and at least 64 pages.

We specifically seek:
• Classroom resources for Christian educators, such as crafts, activities and worksheets, bulletin boards and games
• Proposals for our existing series
• Manuscripts or queries for other teacher help books. All materials must be designed to help Christian educators lead ministries to children.

We do not publish:
• Poetry
• Picture books
• Fiction
• Symbolic stories
• Books that require full-color illustrations

The kinds of writers we are looking for:
• Have accepted Jesus as Savior and are dedicated to serving Him and leading others to Him
• Relate well to children and teachers
• Have hands-on experience working with children
• Are active participants in a Bible-believing church
• Write creatively, either published or unpublished

To submit your proposal:
• Send a table of contents and 2-5 chapters for our evaluation
• Enclose a resumé or statement explaining your qualifications for writing the book
• Explain the audience for your book and how your book differs from those already on the market
• Enclose a SASE for return of your material if you want it returned
• Type on 8½" x 11" paper, one-sided and double-spaced
• Keep copies of everything you submit to us
• Address to Christy Allen, Editor. We normally respond in two to eight weeks.
• If your proposal includes crafts, be prepared to send the completed crafts, if requested.

After evaluating your proposal/manuscript we will do one of the following:
• Offer you a contract
• Seek expanded material from you
• Ask for revisions and resubmittal
• Suggest you contact another publisher

Categories: Nonfiction—Children—Christian Interests—Crafts/Hobbies—Education—Games—Inspirational

CONTACT: Christy Allen, Editor

Material: All
PO Box 261129
San Diego CA 92196
Phone: 619-271-7600
E-mail: rainbowed@earthlink.net

Really Great Books

We are not accepting submissions at this time.
—Petra Frank, Acquisitions Editor
Categories: Nonfiction

CONTACT: Petra Frank, Acquisitions Editor
Material: All
548 S. Spring St., Ste. 320
Los Angeles CA 90013
Phone: 213-624-8555
E-mail: petra@reallygreatbooks.com
Website: www.reallygreatbooks.com

Red Wheel/Weiser
Imprints: Red Wheel, Weiser Books, Conari Press

Red Wheel/Weiser publishes three imprints: Red Wheel, Weiser Books, and Conari Press. Red Wheel publishes Spunky Self-Help, Self-Help/Inspiration, and Spirituality/Self-Help.

Weiser Books are esoteric by nature. Categories include Magic, Wicca, Tarot, Astrology, and Qabalah.

Conari Press topics include spirituality, personal growth, parenting, and social issues.

Before submitting any materials to Red Wheel, Weiser Books, or Conari Press, please study our books in a bookstore, a library, a Red Wheel/Weiser or Conari Press catalog, and visit our web sites at www.redwheelweiser.com and www.conari.com.

When submitting a proposal, initial query letter, or completed manuscript, please remember that it may take up to three months for your material to be reviewed. Please also note that we do not accept proposals on disc, over the Internet, or by fax. Only send copies of your material and keep the original for your records.

Include a self-addressed stamped envelope with your submission. Submissions will be recycled if ample postage is not included. Canadian and any other foreign submissions must included U.S. postage— we can't use international postage coupons.

A submission in the form of a proposal could include:
• Cover letter including author information and brief description of proposal.
• Proposal, including a table of contents, three sample chapters, and a synopsis of the entire manuscript.
• Sample illustrations or photographs (duplicates, please! Not originals.)
• A market analysis including similar books and how yours differs from each.
• A self-addressed stamped envelope for a response and/or return of materials. Please include ample postage if you would like to have your materials returned.

Good luck and thank you for your interest in Red Wheel, Weiser Books, and Conari Press.

Categories: Nonfiction—Inspirational—New Age—Parenting—Self Help—Society—Spiritual

CONTACT: Ms. Pat Bryce, Editor
Material: All
368 Congress St.
Boston, MA 02210

Phone: 617-542-1234
Fax: 617-482-9676
Website: www.redwheelweiser.com

Redleaf Press

Do you have a book idea?

Whether you have an entire manuscript or just a good idea, submitting a proposal to Redleaf Press is easier than you might think. We acquire most of our books as proposals rather than as manuscripts, which means that you don't have to write the whole book before sending it to us to be considered for publication.

To submit a book proposal, just send us the following:

• A cover letter describing your book idea. As well as the content, we need to know the audience it is intended for (family child care providers, staff in child care centers, trainers, directors); how it compares to books that are already available on the same topic; and the experience that makes you the right author for the subject.

• An outline or table of contents to show us what you think the book would include and how you would organize it.

• A writing sample that shows your ability to write clear, coherent prose. Ideally, this will be 2-3 sample chapters of your proposed work, but also be previously published material such as article, staff or parent handbook, brochure, or newsletter.

• A resume showing your relevant experience and education.

Your proposal will first be considered by our editorial department. If it meets our Acquisitions Standards , it will be sent to our full acquisitions committee for review. This group considers the following questions, among others:

• Is the content original and authoritative?

• Is the book needed in the field? Does it duplicate work that is already available?

• Does the content address our audience (primarily professionals in early childhood care and education)?

• Does the book fit into our editorial plan? Does it complement or compete with books we have already published or have already committed to publishing?

• Is Redleaf Press the best publisher for the book?

You can expect a response from the acquisitions committee within three months of submitting a proposal. If the proposal is accepted based on its content, we then have to determine that it is financially feasible for us to publish the book. This analysis takes an additional four to six weeks. If the proposal passes feasibility, we negotiate a contract with the author, and work on the project begins. We usually allow at least a year for an author to write a first draft and an additional three to four months for revisions before a final draft is expected. During this time, the author works closely with a development editor to shape the content and the writing style. Once we have the final draft in hand, publication takes from six to nine months.

Acquisition Standards

The mission of Redleaf Press is to improve the lives of children by strengthening and supporting the people who care for them. We publish and distribute resources to make best practice in the early childhood field accessible to people who work directly with young children. In order to be considered for publication or distribution by Redleaf Press, a resource must meet the following content standards:

1. The material must be developmentally appropriate for the age group for which it is intended. If it is intended for children from birth to eight years of age, it must take into account the Developmentally Appropriate Practice standards published by the National Association for the Education of Young Children (Bredekamp et al., Developmentally Appropriate Practice in Early Childhood Programs , revised edition [Washington, DC: NAEYC, 1997]). If the authors take issue with these standards for cultural or other reasons, the proposal or manuscript should explicitly address this difference.

2. The material must be based on sound theory and research in

Books
M-Z

child development. It should demonstrate an awareness of recent developments within the early childhood field, including the work that is being done on brain development, but should be grounded in theory that has proven durable over time. If the research of others is cited to support arguments made in the material, it must be documented thoroughly and used responsibly.

3. The material must take cultural differences in child development and childrearing practices into account. Examples, stories, curriculum activities, and training exercises must give an accurate picture of human differences and must not further stereotypes or bias based on gender, race, culture, economic class, age, family structure, sexual orientation, disability, or any other facet of identity. In addition, materials must actively contribute to welcoming all children and adults in early childhood programs and must address the issue of bias wherever appropriate.

4. Materials must reflect an active, learner-centered approach to education. Curriculum materials should acknowledge that each child has his or her own pattern of development and should recognize that firsthand and hands-on experiences are vital to young children's learning. For this reason, books that contain primarily dittos, patterns, or handouts that support teacher-directed early childhood education will not be considered. Materials for trainers and on professional development must demonstrate and an awareness of different learning styles.

Additional Guidelines

We also publish and distribute resources resources about the management of child care centers and family child care businesses. The material must be based on sound business practice, and the legal and financial information contained in these resources must be current.

We do not publish or distribute parenting or childrens books, unless they foster communication between parents and caregivers.

Categories: Nonfiction—Education—Child Development

CONTACT: Acquisitions Committee
Material: All
10 Yorktown Court
St. Paul, MN 55117-1065
Phone: 800-423-8309
Fax: 800-641-0115
Website: www.redleafpress.org

Renders Wellness Publishing

Renders Wellness Publishing only publishes non-fiction and would be interested in seeing manuscripts that include topics such as: Nutrition, alternative medicine and Weight loss. All manuscripts must include SASE for return, or will be unreturend. Publisher will give priority to manuscripts that include clinical research, and includes those references. Publisher pays 10% of Net Sales to author.

Allow 6 to 8 weeks for response, no phone calls please!

Categories: Nonfiction—Alternative Medicine—Diet/Nutrition

CONTACT: Editorial
Material: All
1540 Mays Landing Rd.
Egg Harbor Township, N. J. 08234

Republic of Texas Press

Republic of Texas Press was formed in 1987 to publish non-fiction books with a Texas theme. We are very interested in any book that relates to the history, humor, music, travel, especially with children, regional guidebooks and some specialized cookbooks. Please be familiar with our current book line. We will be happy to look at any idea as long as it fits our state-specific criteria. We do not, at this time, publish any fiction, poetry or novels.

To submit a proposal please include the following:

1. Proposed title and subject
2. Table of contents and a brief outline
3. Two or three sample chapters
4. Estimated number of words and/or pages
5. Manuscript completion date
6. Similar and/or competing books currently in the market
7. Target audience, author availability
8. Author experience, prior published works, subject expertise

Categories: Nonfiction—Regional—Texas related topics only

CONTACT: Ginnie Siena Bivona, Acquisitions Editor
Material: All
2320 Los Rios Blvd., Ste. 200
Plano TX 75040
Phone: 972-423-0090
Website: www.republicoftexaspress.com

Resurrection Press, Ltd.

For Catholic Book Publishing Co., which publishes mainly Liturgical Books, Bibles, Missals, and Prayerbooks, prospective authors should be mindful of the following information:

1. Most publications are composed in house or by direct commission with specific guidelines. We thus strongly prefer that query letters be sent in place of full manuscripts. These can be sent to Anthony Buono, Catholic Book Publishing Co., 77 West End Rd., Totowa, NJ 07512. PLEASE DO NOT SUBMIT QUERIES BY PHONE, FAX, OR E-MAIL.

2. We ask that neither simultaneous submissions nor submissions through agents be made.

3. Anticipate a response time of two to three months.

Please note that manuscripts are purchased outright; there are no royalties and no advances. Publication is generally within 12–15 months.

For **Resurrection Press**, which publishes affordable and readable nonfiction titles for popular Catholic and general Christian markets in the areas of prayer, healing and spirituality, as well as pastoral and liturgical resources, prospective authors should observe the following guidelines:

1. Send a summary proposal and two sample chapters typed double spaced with wide margins c/o Editor, Resurrection Press, 77 West End Rd., Totowa, NJ 07512. PLEASE DO NOT SEND FULL MANUSCRIPTS.

2. Include the focus and description of the contents, the intended audience, length of the completed manuscript, a listing of previously published works, and your ability to promote it.

3. Provide an SASE if you wish your material to be returned.

4. Anticipate a response time of four to six weeks.

Please note that royalties are negotiable and publication is generally within 12–18 months of contract signing.

Categories: Nonfiction—Religion—Spiritual

CONTACT: Emilie Cerar, Editor
Material: All
Catholic Book Publishing Co.
77 West End Rd
Totowa NJ 07512-1405
Phone: 973-890-2400, ext.118
Website: www.catholicpublishing.com

Richard C. Owen Publishers, Inc.
Books for Young Learners

Richard C. Owen Publishers, Inc. seeks brief, bright, fresh stories with charm, magic, meaning, and appeal for five, six, and seven year old children that they can read by themselves. We want stories that interest, inform, entertain, and inspire children.

We are interested in publishing a variety of themes **in different styles and genres.**

Fiction: includes original, realistic, contemporary stories, as well as tall tales, legends, myths, and folktales of all cultures.

Nonfiction: fascinating subjects presented as a story in language accessible to five-, six- and seven-year olds. No dry facts, or encyclopedia type pieces, please.

Structure: well-developed stories with captivating beginnings, clear and energetic middles, that end with a fresh, humorous, or unexpected twist or flourish. Length: between 45 and 100 words is best.

Storyline: fresh, strong, focused, lively, and interesting to today's children.

Characters: vivid, believable, and child-appealing, whom children can relate to, identify with, and care about. Animals in stories must act authentically and not be humanized or "cute."

Sentences: complete and grammatically correct.

Language: a mix of both natural and book language. If dialog is used it must sound natural and realistic.

Please do not submit:

• Holiday or religious themes

• Lessons, morals, vocabulary lists, or language skills

• Manuscripts that stereotype or demean individuals or groups, or present violence, or hopelessness

• Stories with talking, humanized, personified animals or objects

• Stories that have been previously published, unoriginal, or imitative stories or characters

• List stories

BOOKS FOR OLDER LEARNERS

Richard C. Owen Publishers, Inc. seeks short, easy to read, high-interest pieces that will fascinate, inspire, entertain and inform eight, nine, and ten year old children in the third grade.

We want short, strong, snappy, exciting pieces that will capture a child's imagination and hold a child's interest.

Please write clearly and simply, yet with richness, and style about topics, and events that have meaning for this age group. We want tight, concise, well-structured, and well-developed strong pieces in different genres about a variety of themes.

All submissions should have the economy of words, and the vitality, freshness, energy, and impact of high quality magazine or newspaper articles.

We will publish prose and poetry, fiction and nonfiction in a variety of styles, and formats.

We seek: adventure, action, mysteries, humor, science, science-fiction, journals, diaries, photo essays current trends, sports, music, how-to, letters, nature and the environment, careers, technology, geography, architecture, travel, myths and legends, and wordless pieces.

Word length: 250—750 words is best.

Our response time is 4—8 months.

Submission procedures:

1. Manuscripts should include your name, phone number, and the page number on each page.

2. Include a short cover letter with your name, address, and the manuscript title.

3. Send photocopies, no originals please.

Requests for revisions do not in any way imply, suggest, or guarantee acceptance or publication of a manuscript.

Categories: Fiction—Nonfiction—Children

CONTACT: Janice Boland, Director of Children's Books
Material: All
PO Box 585
Katonah NY 10536
Phone: 914-232-3903
Fax: 914-232-3977

RLN & Company

Accepting any genre, any category. (Non-fiction preferred.) Query first recommended.

Electronic submissions preferred in Microsoft Word (.doc) or Acrobat (.pdf) or plain text (.txt) files. Send electronic submissions or queries to submissions@rlnonline.com

Hardcopy submissions accepted with the provision that the manuscript cannot be returned without return postage included. Partial submission accepted only if complete manuscript is immediately available.

Expect up to 8 weeks for a response.

Categories: Nonfiction

CONTACT: Submissions
Material: All
PO Box 61219
Seattle WA 98121
E-mail: submissions@rlnonline.com
Website: www.rlnonline.com

Roadman Press
Eurail & Train Travel Guides

Are you a rail traveler? Roadman Press would like your stories for two rail guides, the "Eurail & Train Travel Guide to Europe" and the "Eurail & Train Travel Guide to the World." The books are updated annually and submissions are due in our office by August 31 for the next year's edition.

The two types of articles we want are (1) short, first-person rail experiences and tips for traveling by rail around the world, and (2) luxury train evaluations.

RAIL EXPERIENCES/RAIL-TRAVEL TIPS

Eurail & Train Travel Guides

We are seeking short (200-500-word) first-person musings about rail travel around the globe as well as tips for taking a smooth, trouble-free rail journey. Topics may include a favorite scenic trip, or an adventure-filled journey like a wild ride on a South American local train. Or it could be a fantastic dining car meal or an interesting night-train experience, or tips for making reservations and buying tickets. We're especially looking for off-beat "finds," rail trips not listed in other travel guides. Feel free to mention meeting interesting people on the rails, too. We want to give readers snapshots of the rail-riding experience and show them the infinite possibilities rail travel presents for a civilized, stress-free way to see the world. Your experiences should be current, within the last six months.

We buy one-time rights and payment is $0.07 per word. Please query first. E-mail submissions are OK, preferably pasted into an e-mail message. If you send a disk or printout, please include an SASE if you want your materials returned.

LUXURY TRAIN INSPECTIONS AND EVALUATIONS

Eurail & Train Travel Guides

For the first time, the "Eurail & Train Travel Guide to Europe" and the "Eurail & Train Travel Guide to the World," will include comprehensive information about luxury trains around the globe. The luxury train section will appear in both editions. We know of no other publication that offers this detailed level of information. To bring this information to our readers, we rely on travel writers and travel industry experts to provide us with the latest information about these luxury trains. Because our evaluation form is so complete, all you have to do is jot down notes while traveling and you'll be ready to write the short report. It's a perfect way to earn a few extra dollars while already on an assignment!

QUERY FIRST

Assignments are made upon review of a query letter. Writers should send a résumé, clips of published work highlighting relevant experience, and a self addressed stamped envelope. New reviewers submit work on spec. We will forward you an evaluation form by e-mail or by post.

ASSIGNMENTS

When you accept an assignment, you agree to cover the assigned luxury train. If you have any questions while on assignment, please contact the editor at 619.260.1332 or by e-mail, editors@roadmanpress.com. It is permissible to accept concurrent assignments on luxury trains. You may also accept complimentary transportation, meals, and accommodations if offered, but you must not enter an agreement with any train operator regarding the content of any review.

INSPECTIONS

You may identify yourself as a travel writer to railway personnel, and usually they will be accommodating. Your attire should be professional and fit in with the train's clientele. Speaking discreetly with guests can yield an unbiased opinion of the train. Also, talk with employees such as waiters or cabin attendants; they may be willing to point out the good and bad aspects of the operation. Ask the train manager if you can view a variety of compartments and suites, and obtain any pertinent printed information such as menus and gift catalogues.

You must inspect all public areas, and at least one accommodation of each type offered. On trip-related tours ask local tourism representatives or others connected with the train and the tour about the train's reputation and service, whether it's consistently excellent, good, fair or poor.

PRESS KITS

Unless advised otherwise, you should obtain the latest press kit for the train and forward it to us with your completed review. The press kit should include a fact sheet, brochure, fares, schedules and the public relation contact's business card.

WRITING THE REVIEW

When writing the review keep these things in mind:

• Give us a clear picture of the character of the train and its clientele: This is the kind of information available only from a firsthand visit. What stands out or is unique about the train? What are its strong and weak points? To whom is the train likely to appeal, and to whom will it be a turn-off? How does this train compare with other luxury rail services?

• Write in complete sentences and use strong, concrete, colorful prose. Skip vague terms like nice, pretty, some, there are, etc. Use active voice! Be creative! But also provide as much specific detail as possible.

• As you write your review please follow the order on the evaluation form. Every category is important, and failure to address even one can result in an incomplete review. Assume the editor is clueless about the train!

• Describe the reader precisely what the train is like, not just what it provides. Paint a word picture! Show us the condition and appearance of what you see. Give us a feel about the ambience of the train and the intangibles that contribute to its strengths and weaknesses.

• Tell it like it is! Don't sidestep when criticizing any aspect of an operation. Even the best luxury trains have flaws, and they must be included in your review. On the other hand, if your experience warrants praise, don't hesitate to report it.

• Reviews should run 200 to 500 words.

Please send your review by disk (MS Word, WordPerfect or text format for Mac) or by e-mail to editors@roadmanpress.com, preferably pasted into an e-mail message.

PAYMENT

Payment is $30 per review (this includes a postage allowance for sending us press kits, brochures, etc.). Please submit an invoice to the above address with your review, press kit and other related materials. U.S. citizens should submit their social security number. You are responsible for all your travel expenses connected with the inspection. You will receive a byline for your review, if you wish. We buy one-time rights.

Categories: Nonfiction—Travel

CONTACT: Eurail & Train Travel Editor
Material: Rail Travel
CONTACT: Luxury Train Evaluation Editor
Material: Rail Travel
PO Box 3747
San Diego CA 92163
Phone: 619-260-1332
Fax: 619-296-4220
E-mail: editors@roadmanpress.com
Website: www.roadmanpress.com

Roberts Rinehart
Imprint: Court Wayne Press

Roberts Rinehart publishes in the areas of Irish studies, National Parks, Nature, Native America, the West, and general non fiction and fiction (adult and children's works).

Submissions Guidelines

If you would like to submit a proposal, please include:

• A description of the book, what makes it unique, and why are you qualified to write it

• An analysis of competing or similar titles (include publisher and dates)

• A description of your target audience

• An indication of whether any of the material in the book has been previously published and if so, when and where

• The names of other publishers to whom you have submitted a proposal (if relevant)

• The length of the manuscript on 12 point type on double-spaced 8 ½ x 11 paper

• And, if the manuscript is not complete, an estimate of when you expect to finish

• Please also send a detailed table of contents

• Include one or two sample chapters

• If an introduction or overview is available, please include it as well

Categories: Fiction—Nonfiction—Children—General Interest—Irish Studies—National Parks—Native America—Nature

CONTACT: Rick Rinehart, Publisher
Material: All
5360 Manhattan Circle #101
Boulder, CO 80303
Phone: 303-543-7835
Fax: 303-543-0043
E-mail: No electronic submissions please.
Website: www.taylor-trade.com

Rockbridge Publishing

Now an Imprint of Howell Press, Inc. Please refer to Howell Press.

Rodnik Publishing Co.

Areas of publishing interest:
• Foreign language phrasebooks
• Foreign language dictionaries
• Language learning materials
• Vocational ESL materials

Titles currently in print:

"English-Dari Phrasebook for Aid Workers", 536 pp, C 2006

"Making Friends in Italy; An Italian Phrasebook", 424 pp, C 2005

"Making Friends in Mexico; A Spanish Phrasebook", 432 pp, C 2003

"English-Russian Dictionary-Phrasebook of Love", 800 pp, C 2000

Guidelines for manuscripts:

Paper manuscripts for foreign-language phrasebooks, foreign-language dictionaries, and textbooks and materials for learning foreign languages and ESL may be submitted at any time for consideration. If return of the manuscript is desired, please include a stamped self-addressed envelope of suitable size.

Authors wishing to submit manuscripts on computer disks should first contact Rodnik Publishing by telephone or e-mail to discuss and arrange the submittal.

Synopses of projects may be submitted by e-mail or e-mail attachment, but please do not submit full manuscripts as e-mail attachments.

We will endeavor to review your manuscript and give you a decision on it within two weeks of receiving it. If it appears that we need more time to assess it, we will notify you.

Authors and translators with native expertise in Albanian, Amharic, Armenian, Bahasa Indonesian, Bantu, Bengali, Kinyanwanda, Somali, Swahili, Urdu and tribal languages of Africa are especially encouraged to contact us.

Categories: Nonfiction—Education—Language

CONTACT: Bob Powers, Director
Material: All
PO Box 46956
Seattle WA 98146-0956
Phone: 206-937-5189
Fax: 206-937-3554
E-mail: rodnik2@comcast.net
Website: www.rodnikpublishing.com

Ronin Publishing, Inc.

Formal guidelines not available.

Send queries or book proposals to below address.

Categories: Careers—Culture—Health—Lifestyle—Religion—Self Help—Spiritual

CONTACT: Beverly Potter, Publisher
Material: All
PO Box 22900
Oakland CA 94609
Phone: No Phone Calls

Running Press

Children's Proposals

For our Running Press Kids list, we specialize in publishing innovative, hands-on, educational products for children from birth through ninth grade. Our industry-leading book-plus products encourage kids to enjoy learning about the world around them. Books bearing our Kinesthetic Learning Tools™ logo help preschoolers master basic concepts through movement and activity. And our high-quality picture books include fiction from award-winning authors and illustrators.

If you would like to submit a proposal for interactive nonfiction (see our Discovery Kit™ line for examples), basic concepts books (such as letters, numbers, opposites, or shapes), or beginning reading projects, we would be happy to respond to a query letter accompanied by a brief outline or table of contents.

When submitting a picture-book proposal please send the entire manuscript. Please note that at this time we are not publishing novels or any fiction longer than picture-book length.

General Audience (All Ages) Proposals

For our general-interest lists (Running Press, Courage Books), we specialize in publishing illustrated nonfiction. We very rarely publish any new fiction or poetry and are not seeking submissions in those categories at this time. We also do not accept proposals for Miniature Editions™ of any kind.

To submit a proposal for an appropriate work of nonfiction, please send a query letter accompanied by a brief outline or table of contents to the address below.

How to Submit Your Proposal

When submitting a proposal to Running Press, please note:

We do not accept submissions or query letters via e-mail.

We are not responsible for materials sent with your proposal that become lost or damaged.

Please do not send original photographs, slides, or artwork, one-of-a-kind dummies or mock-ups, or irreplaceable items of any kind with your proposal. Running Press is not responsible for the return of such materials.

Please include a self-addressed, stamped envelop (SASE) with your submission so that we may send you a reply.

If you send materials you would like us to return to you, we ask that you enclose sufficient return postage. Once again, please do not send any original or irreplaceable materials—we receive dozens of submissions each week and cannot guarantee the return of materials, even when postage is provided.

We try to respond to all submissions within six to eight weeks.

Categories: Fiction—Nonfiction—Children—Education

CONTACT: Submissions Editor, Running Press Kids
Material: Children
CONTACT: Assistant to the Editorial Director, Running Press Book Publishers
Material: General-Interest
125 South 22nd St.
Philadelphia, PA 19103-4399
Phone: 215-567-5080
Fax: 215-568-2919
Website: www.runningpress.com

Books M-Z

Rutledge Hill Press

No longer accepting submissions.

Safari Press, Inc.

Safari Press accepts manuscripts only on big-game hunting, firearms, and wingshooting. Always send a copy of your manuscript (MS), not the original, just in case it gets lost in the mail. Please state if the work is original or if it has been published previously. If previously published, we will need a written statement from the publisher giving you permission to reprint the work. Make sure to state if there is a co-author. We discourage autobiographies, unless the life of the hunter or firearms maker has been exceptional. We routinely reject MS along the lines of "me and my buddies went hunting for . . . and a good time was had by all."

Please do not offer a MS that is full of obscene, vulgar, or offensive language. We believe ethical hunting is sound conservation. Hunters have a duty to preserve their sport for future generations, and this will only happen if the general public has a positive view of hunting. Although we recognize that game laws were nonexistent or widely ignored in the past, we believe that all modern-day hunters should uphold the game laws of the country in which the game was shot.

Initial Submission of Manuscript for Consideration

If you are considering submitting a manuscript (MS) to Safari Press, please read the information on this sheet carefully. Make sure the following points are included when you submit your MS to us. (This will help you get your book published by either us or other publishers.

1. Cover letter that includes the subject matter and scope of book.

2. Approximate number of words.

3. Complete table of contents, annotated if you are submitting sample chapters and not a complete MS.

4. Author information (full name, address, phone, and fax numbers). Any other relevant background information on yourself. This might include a list of books you have previously published.

5. Approximate number of photos you can provide. We like to have 10 photos for every 10,000 words. Send us photocopies of some of the photos you plan to submit, if possible.

Normally, only MS over 60,000 words (we prefer 75,000) will be considered. We make exceptions for guidebooks and "how-to" books. (Almost all word-processing programs have a "word count" feature.)

While we will review a sample of chapters, we prefer the whole MS. Send only completed sample chapters or a complete MS.

Printout

Initial submission must be in hard copy (on paper) for all MS from North America. We accept printouts on 8.5x11 inch paper or the A4 (210 x 297mm) format. (If your MS is accepted, you will need to put it on a PC-compatible disk in MS Word for Windows (preferred), Word Prefect for Windows, or MS Works. MS tables should be converted to tab delimited or Excel format. If you don't understand, contact the production coordinator.) It is imperative that you follow the electronic guidelines noted below.

MS Submission from outside North America

We recognize the cost of courier services is high. Please send us a CD or DVD via standard airmail. Otherwise please adhere to the guidelines as listed herein. If you want to send us images on a CD for initial evaluation you may do so as well.

Book Title and Subtitle

Readers relate to a short, catchy title that gives a general sense about the book's topic and a subtitle that is specific to the content. Please give us your suggestions.

Chapter Titles

We prefer chapters with titles for all books. If you are writing a reference book or something of the sort, chapter titles are a must, so please be sure to include chapter titles and a table of contents with your submission. Please make the chapter titles concise and have them reflect the topic of the chapter.

Photos and Artwork

Manuscripts should have photos or appropriate artwork. Submit a list of pictures or illustrations you own or a general idea of what kind of images you have available. Better yet, make good clear Xerox copies of your photos and send these in. Be sure to include whether they are b/w photos, color photos, slides, or drawings and how many you have. As a general rule, we like to have at least one picture/illustration per 1,000 words.

Do not send any original art or photos unless there is an agreement to publish.

Manuscripts That Have Been Accepted for Publication by Safari Press

Unless instructed otherwise, final submission must be in hard copy (on paper) **and** in electronic format.

Once your MS is accepted, you will need to put it on a PC-compatible disk in MS Word for Windows (preferred), Word Prefect for Windows, or MS Works. It is imperative that you follow the electronic guidelines noted below. Please do not submit a MS in a page graphics layout

program such as Page Maker, InDesign or Quark Express.

Please do not e-mail the MS to us; there are all sorts of problems with e-mailed MS. Space prevents us from listing them all. In case you cannot submit a MS any way other than via e-mail, please contact us first for instructions before sending.

If you use a Macintosh computer and are unsure how to submit your MS in PC format, please contact us.

Please do not use the word processing program to generate a table of contents, index, or photo-locators as the automatic links will disappear when the book is edited.

Printout and Electronic Files

We accept paper printouts on 8.5x11-inch paper or the A4 (210mm x 297mm) format; however, please set up your **electronic** files for letter-page size of 8.5x11 inches. Leave at least one-inch (25-millimeter) margins all around, and use the space in the footer to NUMBER ALL PAGES. We prefer you to use Courier New (font) in size 12.

Spacing

When typing your MS, do not hit the Enter Key at the end of a sentence. Your word-processing program will automatically wrap sentences. Every time you use the "Enter" key, you create hidden paragraph marks in the MS that we have to eliminate. (We spend an inordinate amount of time stripping paragraph marks from manuscripts. In most cases, we will return the MS to you and ask you to do the work. Believe us, it is time consuming! Save yourself hours of work; let the program wrap the sentence!) Place two spaces between each sentence and two paragraph returns after each paragraph. Double space the entire ms.

Fractions

Type out the entire fraction as in the following example "the shotgun has a 2 1 / 2 inch chamber." Place a space between each digit and the slash. Some word processors will make "2 1/2" into "2½" if the numbers are typed without spaces in between them. We find that the typesetting program does not translate these reduced-size fractions, which makes for mistakes in the typeset version.

Tables

If your MS contains data with extensive tables, please use MS Excel or an equivalent spreadsheet program to input your information. If your tables are already prepared in MS Word. Please contact us if you are not sure what to do.

Naming and Saving Files

Name your chapters clearly so that they may be put in the correct order. It is a must to make a separate document for each chapter. Make sure your Dedication, Foreword, Introduction, Acknowledgments, Captions, et al. are labeled. Please note that it the word used in the frontal material of a book is Foreword (not forward, which is a movement in a forward direction); also note that Acknowledgments has no "e" between the word acknowledge and the suffix -ment, so it is acknowledgment not acknowledg(e)ment.

Photos and Artwork

Once we have signed a contract, please submit your original photos or slides. The first rule is always send the best image, no matter if it is a slide, black and white, or color picture. If you have a good slide but a bad black and white print, send the good slide and keep the bad black and white print!

Choosing the Right Image

Select your pictures with quality and variety of images in mind. A good, sharp, well-balanced image, via ANY media is ALWAYS preferred over a bad, out-of-focus image, from ANY media. If you have line drawings, advertisements, or other art that you want to submit, always send the original. As a rule, color copies or digital prints are not acceptable.

OK, so you have excellent photos and slides; what do we prefer? All other things being equal, slides reproduce better than anything else. Next to slides we prefer photos. We DO NOT want to take negatives UNLESS you can also send photos from the negatives. Why? With negatives alone it is impossible to see the quality of the image; therefore, we cannot choose the best image from a selection.

Do not send dozens and dozens of pictures with a note "please select the best." We are not nearly as qualified as the author to select the best picture, and we will invariably not use pictures you want in!

Marking of Photos and Art

USE A SHARPIE! We will provide a Sharpie free of charge to all authors with a contract!

We cannot tell you how many countless good pictures we have received over the years that were ruined with ink smudges and marks all over them! All ballpoints, felt tips, or fountain pens have ink that takes hours to dry on photo paper and even then will smudge. The result is ink smudging on the face of the next photo when the photos get stacked. We have also seen that the wrong type of pen can cause photos to stick together. USE A SHARPIE! We will provide a Sharpie free of charge to all authors with a contract!

Also, if you are taking your images out of a scrapbook or photo album, be sure all glue or tape has been removed from the back so your images will not stick together.

Once you have the right number of images together, please mark each one on the back with a number, which, in reality, is a code that lets us determine which image we have in front of us at all times. **It is imperative that you follow this system:** For picture 1 in chapter 1 by Ernest Hemingway, the label would read: EHCH0101. This is EH (Ernest Hemingway), CH01 (Chapter 1), 01 (picture 1). Use only a pen from a graphic supply store (such as a "Sharpie" by Stanford Manufacturing) made for marking photos. Also, write with light pressure so you do not damage the emulsion on the photograph. **USE A SHARPIE! We will provide a Sharpie free of charge to all authors with a contract!**

Scanning Your Own Photos

Please DO NOT attempt to scan your own photos to be sent to us on a CD. However appealing this may sound, the quality of the image (for all sorts of reasons) is always less than if we are in charge of getting the photos scanned by a very high-grade scanner. Our photos are scanned by professionals on professional scanning machines that render the quality of an image five to eight times better than a regular scanner attached to a home PC.

Digital Camera Images

We GREATLY prefer NOT to take digital camera images. Why? In most cases the quality cannot hold a candle to a regular slide or photo and the pixel resolution does not meet publication standards. In most cases the lighter shades (such as fog or smoke, etc.) do not show up well at all on a digital image.

Color Printouts

Please do not send us color printouts of scans that you have made. Again, because of the limitations of all normal PC scanners and color printers, the results are mediocre at best and most of the time a lot worse. Please send us the original slides or photos, and we will return these once we are finished.

Captions and Photo Placement in Text

Place the captions in a separate computer file entitled "Captions," and place the caption number above each caption. Number the photo captions with the same number as the photo (see below) to which it corresponds. Allow one blank line between each caption.

It is imperative that you follow these rules: Some authors think that if he/she marks the page number where each photo is to go in the ms, that it should be sufficient. This is NOT correct. Remember that when an author sends in a ms, the ms must be edited and then typeset; consequently, the typeset version will look nothing like the raw material in the original version. So, if the author labeled a picture or slide to go on page 240 of his original raw text, that information is absolutely useless to us since the typeset and edited version will not remotely reflect the author's original page 240.

What do we want you to do? We ask our authors to use the system described in the section on "Marking of Photos and Art." This means that you will decide which pictures are to go in which chapter and then label each with the Safari Press system. Say you have twenty chapters and ten pictures in each chapter, this is what chapter 15 would

look like: EHCH1501 through EHCH1510. What does this mean? Using Ernest Hemingway as the writer, the code means: Ernest Hemingway, chapter 15, photo 1 through photo 10.

Not only have you, as the author, determined which pictures go in which chapter, but you have also labeled the pictures in such a way that they won't get lost and they won't be put in a chapter where you don't want them to be. This doesn't mean that you can't indicate in the tex where you would like the picture to go.

If you do that, please do the following. Determine the text that relates to a particular photograph. Then type the number of the photograph directly into the manuscript using square brackets. For example, a paragraph in your manuscript could end with [photo EHCH0101 here]. No matter what happens to the text in typesetting, and no matter how it is rearranged, the photo-locator note will stay with the correct text. Even if chapter one later becomes chapter nine, the photo will still end up where it should. This will ensure that your photos go with text you intend and your Kenya photos don't end up in the Tanzania chapter.

Checklist for Submitting Your Final Manuscript

When your manuscript has been accepted for publication by Safari Press and a contract has been signed, we will be ready to receive all your materials. **We cannot begin the project until we have received ALL of the following:**

1. The MS in hard copy (on paper)
2. The MS on diskette or CD (not in Quark Xpress)
3. All original photographs and illustrations, numbered and with captions. Do not send color photocopies or computer printouts. Please review guidelines noted above to remind yourself how to label and mark images. Due to the production process of publishing, please appreciate that we will need to keep your images until the book is published. We realize that your original photos/slides/artwork are important to you, and we will handle them with the utmost care.
4. All tables
5. All frontal material (dedication, acknowledgments, introduction, table of contents, etc.)
6. Bibliography and index

Conclusion

Finally, we are not nearly as grumpy as this paper sounds! Please believe us when we say that in these few pages are the cumulative experiences of sixty years of publishing. By sharing this, we hope to help you avoid the most common mistakes made in writing a book. The instructions are not very difficult to follow, and you will have a better book for it.

Categories: Nonfiction—African-American—Animals—Book Reviews—Short Stories

CONTACT: Susan Appleby, Officer Manager
Material: All
15621 Chemical Lane, Bldg. B
Huntington Beach CA 92649-1506
Phone: 714-894-9080
Fax: 714-894-4949
E-mail: info@safaripress.com
Website: safaripress.com

Safer Society Press

Safer Society Foundation is a nonprofit organization dedicated to the prevention and treatment of sexual abuse. Safer Society Press, a program of the Foundation, publishes books, audio and video tapes that assist clinicians and professionals in the treatment of their clients and titles of interest to families, victims, survivors and organizations dealing with sexual abuse. We do not publish poetry or fiction.

Please use the following guidelines:

• Your proposal should include a brief description of the work, a complete outline of the book and 2 sample chapters. You will be contacted if additional information is needed.

• Include author's credentials.

• Enclose a stamped, self-addressed envelope for the return of your materials.

Please note evaluations can take up to three months. An acceptance or rejection letter will be sent once a decision is reached.

Thank you for following these guidelines.

Categories: Nonfiction—Health—Psychology—Self Help—Sexuality

CONTACT: Press Committee
Material: All
Safer Society Foundation, Inc.
PO Box 340
Brandon VT 05733

Santa Monica Press

Santa Monica Press is not shackled by a narrow publishing niche. Instead, we publish books across a wide variety of categories. For instance, our Arts & Entertainment titles include the critically acclaimed Silent Traces: Discovering Early Hollywood Through the Films of Charlie Chaplin and Footsteps in the Fog: Alfred Hitchcock's San Francisco; the cutting-edge L.A. Noir: The City as Character; and the wildly divergent photography books Childish Things, American Hydrant, and My So-Called Digital Life.

Chris Epting's trilogy of pop culture location books, *James Dean Died Here, Marilyn Monroe Dyed Here,* and *Elvis Presley Passed Here* leads off our best-selling Popular Culture titles, which also include the now-classic *Offbeat Museums* and the eye-opening *The Ruby Slippers, Madonna's Bra, and Einstein's Brain.*

Along the same lines, we have published some terrific travel books with a pop culture theme, including *Route 66 Adventure Handbook, Haunted Hikes: Spine-Tingling Tales and Trails from North America's National Parks,* and *Creepy Crawls: A Horror Fiend's Travel Guide.*

We also love humor, as evidenced by *The Bad Driver's Handbook; Things You Can Do While You're Naked, Atomic Wedgies, Wet Willies, and Other Acts of Roguery; Redneck Haiku: Double-Wide Edition;* and, of course, the infamous *The Butt Hello.*

Finally, we also specialize in "How-To" and Reference titles. Our "How-To" books provide readers with practical guidance in a wide variety of subjects, from the two volumes of *Letter Writing Made Easy!* (nearly 200,000 copies sold!) to *French for Le Snob* to *How to Speak Shakespeare.* On the reference side, we have published such titles as *Calculated Risk: The Extraordinary Life of Jimmy Doolittle, Loving Through Bars: Children with Parents in Prison,* and *The Largest U.S. Cities Named After a Food: And Other Mind-Boggling Geography Lists from Around the World.*

At Santa Monica Press, our goal is to inspire, inform, and entertain.

Look for the shell!

We love to receive book proposals from authors! You do not need an agent to submit a proposal to Santa Monica Press. Please send us the following information:

* A brief summary of the book, including its length (i.e., the approximate number of words in the manuscript).

* A table of contents

* Two sample chapters

* Photocopies of any photographs or illustrations you believe might assist us in evaluating your proposal (do not send originals!)

* A brief list of similar or competitive books, including title, author, publisher, ISBN number, and date of publication-all readily available on Amazon.com and other on-line booksellers. Tell us what makes your book unique. How does it differ from your competition? Please do not treat this request lightly; this is extremely important information!

* Marketing and publicity plans or ideas

* A description of your book's audience

* A brief autobiographical summary or resume. What do you, as the author,

bring to the project?

* Your mailing address, daytime phone number, and e-mail address

Please note that we do not accept proposals or submissions via e-mail or fax. If you would like a response, you must include a self-addressed, stamped #10 business envelope. If you would like your material returned, you must include a self-addressed, stamped envelope of the appropriate size with sufficient return postage. Note to authors who reside outside of the U.S. and Canada: We do not accept International Response Coupons and therefore cannot return your material. You may, however, include your e-mail address with your material, and we will send you a response.

You can expect a reply within two months of our receipt of your proposal.

No phone calls please!!

Categories: Nonfiction—Arts—Biography—Consumer—Culture—Drama—Entertainment—Film/Video—Folklore—General Interest—Mass Communications—Music—Photography—Reference—Television/Radio—Theatre—Travel

CONTACT: Acquisitions Editor
Material: All
Santa Monica Press LLC
PO Box 1076
Santa Monica, CA 90406
E-mail: books@santamonicapress.com

Sarabande Books

As a small press, Sarabande Books can accept unsolicited manuscripts only once a year, during its annual contest season.

Sarabande holds two national contests: The Kathryn A. Morton Prize in Poetry and the Mary McCarthy Prize in Short Fiction, judged by well-established writers. Guidelines and required entry form are available year round. You can get these guidelines and entry form by sending a business-sized, self-addressed, stamped envelope to us, or printing out everything you'll need from our Website at www.sarabandebooks.org.

Sarabande Books publishes complete manuscripts of poetry of 48 pages minimum.

We also publish collections of short stories, novellas, short novels, and literary essays that fall between 150-250 pages. We do not consider longer novels, mysteries, westerns, children's books, chapbooks, adventure or science fiction, nor do we publish single poems or stories.

Manuscripts written by Kentucky authors (current or former residents) or with a Kentucky setting, may be submitted during July for out Series in Kentucky Literature.

Sarabande Books looks for poetry and short fiction that offer originality of voice and subject matter, uniqueness of vision, and a language that startles because of the careful attention paid to language that goes beyond the merely competent or functional. We recommend that you request our catalog and familiarize yourself with our books. Our complete list shows a variety of style and subject matter.

Categories: Fiction—Nonfiction—Poetry—Creative Nonfiction

CONTACT: Submissions Editor
Material: All
2234 Dundee Rd., Ste 200
Louisville KY 40205
Phone: 502-458-4028
Fax: 502-458-4065
Website: www.sarabandebooks.org

Sasquatch Books

Sasquatch Books is happy to consider queries and proposals from authors and agents for new projects that fit into our West Coast regional publishing program. We can evaluate query letters, proposals, and complete manuscripts.

When you submit to Sasquatch Books, please remember that the editors want to know about you and your project, along with a sense of who will want to read your book.

Categories: Nonfiction—Children—Food/Drink—Gardening—Nature—Regional—Travel

CONTACT: The Editors
Material: All
119 South Main, Ste. 400
Seattle, WA 98104

Scarecrow Press, Inc.

Scarecrow Press publishes scholarly, professional and academic reference books on a variety of subjects. We seek proposals that represent new treatments of traditional topics, original scholarship in developing areas, and cogent syntheses of existing research. While we accept unsolicited submissions, we prefer that you submit a proposal rather than a completed manuscript. Please note that our review process normally takes between two and four months.

Guidelines for submitting a book proposal
1. Please provide a tentative descriptive title.
2. Tell us the subject matter, scope, and intended purpose of your manuscript. Include an introduction, table of contents, and chapter summaries. A completed sample chapter (so that we can gauge your writing style, organizational techniques, and documentation) would also be helpful.
3. What research methods or data sources will you use?

4. When do you estimate the work will be completed? How long do you think it will be?
5. Whom do you see as your audience? What other books exist in your subject area?

Please send your proposal, including a recent c.v., to the appropriate editor. Be sure to enclose a self-addressed envelope, stamped with sufficient postage, if you would like us to return the materials you sent in.

Categories: Nonfiction—African-American—Arts—Biography—Computers—Culture—Education—Feminism—Film/Video—Gay/Lesbian—Hispanic—History—Internet—Military—Multicultural—Music—Reference—Teen—Textbooks—Young Adult—Library Science

CONTACT: Editorial Department
Material: All
4501 Forbes Blvd., Ste 200
Lanham MD 20706
Phone: 301-459-3366
Fax: 301-459-2118
Website: www.scarecrowpress.com

Schirmer Trade Books

Schirmer Trade Books is an imprint of Music Sales Corporation. Founded in 1925 by the Wise family, Music Sales is an international family of companies with interests in four main areas of music publishing. Copyright ownership and promotion of standard and popular music, classical music, printed music, and book publishing. Music Sales maintains offices in New York, London, Sydney, Copenhagen, Madrid, Tokyo, Helsinki, and Paris.

Schirmer is committed to intelligent, educational, and entertaining books about all aspects of popular music, especially the recording arts, music business, and genre histories.

We're especially interested in books about songwriting (music and/or lyrics), musician biographies (high-profile entertainers with large fan bases, as well as up-and-coming), and gift books. We rarely publish books about classical music. We prefer rock & roll, folk, blues, and pop. We do NOT publish fiction.

Send full book proposals, including: Cover letter, overview of the book, target audience, author bio, competitive titles, marketing and promotion ideas, detailed chapter-by-chapter table of contents, and a sample chapter (if available).

Categories: Nonfiction—Biography—History—Music—Reference—Performing Arts

CONTACT: Andrea Rotondo, Managing Editor
Material: All
257 Park Ave. South
New York, NY 10010
Phone: 212-254-2100
Fax: 212-254-2013
Website: www.schirmertradebooks.com

Second Chance Press

Please refer to The Permanent Press.

Serendipity Systems
Books-on-disks

NOTE: E-mail with attachments from unknown sources will be dumped without being read or opened! Writers who violate this rule will have all their future e-mail automatically put in the trash unread.

Serendipity Systems publishes fiction and reference works related to literature, writing, and publishing.

We are only interested in seeing works which can take advantage of computer-enhanced features such as hypertext or multimedia. Except in rare cases, we do not publish works which are straight prose (no hypertext or multimedia.) We can NOT use manuscripts on paper. We may be able to use Macintosh files if they have been saved as ASCII under System 7 or higher, however, we only publish IBM-PC compatible disks. Royalties for books published under the BOOKS-ON-DISKS (tm) imprint are thirty-three percent of the retail or wholesale sales, less shipping. No advance is offered. Serendipity Systems only contracts for the electronic rights; all on-paper, movie, and similar rights are retained by the author.

We do NOT want to see:
- romance novels
- religious tracts
- sword and sorcery fantasy
- occult works
- anything "new age"
- political diatribes
- imitations of Stephen King or Tom Clancy
- "Penthouse Forum" quality materials
- children's literature (pre-teenage)
- "Academic" novels *
- non-fiction works not related to literature, writing, or publishing

We ARE interested in seeing:
- hypertext novels
- mixed-media works
- new computer-enhanced genres
- interactive fiction
- experimental works
- reference works on literature, writing, and publishing
- Windows-compatible works
- manuscripts written in HTML

Submissions should:
- be on IBM-PC compatible disks (160K, 5.25" to 1.44MB, 3.5"; 100MB ZIP disks; CD-ROMs)
- be in ASCII (unless the author has already added hypertext/ multimedia features)
- have margins of 1 and less than 80 (WordPerfect users note this!)
- include the complete manuscript
- include an SASE or return postage
- include a cover letter describing the work and the author's qualifications
- send the complete manuscript by postal mail (Postal address below;) send ONLY queries by e-mail

NOTE: E-mail with attachments from unknown sources will be dumped without being read or opened!

UPDATE: December 22, 1999

Things change very rapidly in the world of electronic publishing, and we have again changed our focus to meet the new conditions.

We are now publishing Rocket Editions—electronic books that run on NuvoMedia's Rocket eBook portable "reader" device. (See our Rocket Page.)

As a result of our survey of What do Rocket eBook users want? (See the results under "Survey" at EPF29.) we will be most interested in seeing science fiction manuscripts. As always, we are looking for believable plots, credible characters, and a strong story line.

For Rocket Editions we need manuscripts in ASCII or plain HTML. Do not submit manuscripts with complex HTML—Rocket eBooks can not display tables, color illustrations, or many of the common features of the versions of HTML used on the Internet. We will also be publishing windows-compatible versions of our Rocket eBooks— same source code; different display engine.

Submit manuscripts on disk via postal mail only. E-mail with an attached file from an unknown source will be automatically dumped.

We will continue to be interested in new genres, interactive fiction, etc., however, you should keep in mind that there isn't yet much of a market for such material.

UPDATE

September 8, 2000

Existing books and future publications will be converted into Microsoft Reader format. Other formats will continue be supported as long as they are viable. (The "source code" will continue to be HTML; files will be converted to .lit format.)

UPDATE: September 27, 2001

Serendipity Systems will publish general non-fiction books (primarily reference books) under the TheInfiniteBook imprint and will launch a www.TheInfiniteBook.com Internet site.

Before submitting a manuscript, see our Writers' Manuscript Help section on our website.

If you are getting rejection slips from publishers, see this file.

Categories: Fiction—Nonfiction—Internet—Literature—Writing

CONTACT: John Galuszka, Publisher
Material: All
PO Box 140
San Simeon CA 93452
E-mail: bookware@thegrid.net

Shambhala Publications, Inc.
Imprint: Trumpeter Books, New Seals Books, Weatherhill

Shambhala Publications publishes books of quality that express the potential of inner evolution and the values and aspirations of individuals and society, with special interest in philosophy, religion, art, literature, cultural studiex, psychology, health, and global concerns. Shambhala also has an audio program that publishes books on tape, workshops, and so forth. For a better idea of what we publish, please visit www.shambhala.com

Imprints include Trumpeter Books, New Seeds Books, and Wetherhill.

Trumpeter Books offers a line of books covering a broad range of genres and topics, all aimed at nourishing and celebrating our positive houman potential. New Seeds Books presents the wisdon of the Chiristian tradition with a special emphasis on prayer and contemplative practices. Weatherhill has published fine books on Japan and Asia for more than thress decades on a wide variety of subjects, including arts, culture, religion, martial arts, and travel.

If you are interested in submitting a book query, proposal, or manuscript to Shambhala for consideration, please read the following guidelines:

We suggest that you send a book proposal including a synopsis of the book, a table of contents or outline, a copy of the author's résumé or some other description of him or her, and two or three sample chapters. Be advised that we publish very few poetry, art, or children's books. Be sure to include a self-addressed envelope with sufficient postage (or an international postal money order) if you want your materials returned. We cannot be held responsible for lost or misplaced materials if you do not include a self-addressed, stamped envelope. The manuscript should be double-spaced, in upper and lower case letters. The review process of a manuscript can take two to four months. Please send your materials to:

We do not review materials submitted via e-mail.

Categories: Fiction—Nonfiction—Arts—Asian American—Biography— Christian-Interest—Health—Healing—Jewish Interests—Multicultural—Parenting—Psychology—Relationships—Religion—Self Help—Spiritual

CONTACT: Editorial Assistant
Material: All
Shambhala Publications
300 Massachusetts Ave.
Boston, MA 02115
Phone: 617-424-0030
Fax: 617-236-1563
E-mail: editors@shambhala.com
Website: www.shambhala.com

Sierra Club Books

Sierra Club Books is seeking nonfiction projects intended for the general reader. We are interested in great nature writing first-person narratives, and all subjects relating to ecology and the environment. Please send an outline and a sample chapter of your proposed book and sufficient postage if you would like your material returned. We are currently not accepting any unsolicited manuscripts or proposals for children's books. For additional information, current titles, and a list of FAQ's, please visit our website at www.sierraclub.org/books. Sierra Club Books is co-published and distributed by University of California Press.

Categories: Nonfiction—Conservation—Environment—Outdoors

CONTACT: Editorial Department
Material: All
85 Second St., Second Floor
San Francisco, CA 94105
Phone: 415-977-5500
Fax: 415-977-5792
Website: www.sierraclub.org/books

Silhouette Desire
Silhouette Intimate Moments
Silhouette Romance
Silhouette Special Edition

Please refer to Harlequin, in the Book Publishers section.

Silver Dagger Mysteries

Silver Dagger is an imprint of The Overmountain Press.
Please review the following guidelines before submitting manuscripts to us:

1. Subject matter. We publish Southern mysteries. Sub-genres such as cozies, police procedural, hardboiled, etc. will all be considered. We will consider romantic suspense only if the book is a true mystery first, and the romance is a subplot only. Young reader (3rd-9th grade) books are published as well. The book should be set in the South or the author should have very strong ties to the South. We define "The South" as the following states: Texas, Alabama, Arkansas, Mississippi, Georgia, Tennessee, Kentucky, Virginia, North Carolina, South Carolina, Florida. Manuscripts set in states which border these MAY be considered if the author lives in a Southern state.

2. Content. We do not publish books with graphic content. This includes graphic violence, graphic sex, horror, or heavy supernatural lines. Foul language must be at a minimum and not gratuitous. Basically, if the networks get away with it on prime time television, that's fine. Most books with dead bodies tend to have police, and police tend to use hard language. No problem! Just don't go overboard. Young reader books should have NO foul language at all.

3. Length. We are currently accepting books with a 60,000 to 80,000 word count for adult novels, and 30,000 to 60,000 word count for young reader editions.

4. Authors. Silver Dagger publishes only committed, strong, active authors. As you will realize with publication, your sales depend very heavily upon your promotional activity. As you may know, Silver Dagger is not your typical publishing house; we are a consortium of authors. Everyone knows each other and talks to each other regardless of geography. Our veteran authors hand down suggestions and pointers for our first-timers. Silver Dagger is committed to the first-time author; we plan to stock our publication list with half veterans and half first-timers. Each author is carefully selected not only for his or her writing, but also for his or her willingness to promote, speak to groups, serve on panels, attend book signings, etc. If your book is selected as a candidate for publication, we will contact you with details about contracts, the publication process, and a few more details about our promotional and marketing plans.

5. The submission package. *For your initial query, include the following:*
• Cover Letter — describing you, your background, your qualifications for writing this book
• Brief Synopsis — just a couple of paragraphs about your book. Write the blurb that will be on the back of your cover. NO more than a page.
• First three chapters — send this in hard copy format. We don't care about fonts, line spacing, point size, and all that. Just put it on plain white paper and make it readable. Please do not send in computer disks.
• Marketing Outline—Put together a sample marketing plan for your book. Include the following (if applicable): any contacts in the mystery field, contacts in the media, previous publications, and (realistically) how many copies of your book do you think you can sell? We ask for this outline for a number of reasons, most notably because we want ACTIVE authors to join our consortium. Each author on the 2000 list was very carefully selected not only on the basis of the manuscript but also for his/her track record and enthusiasm for promotion. If you have published before (even if it wasn't a mystery) tell us what you did that worked. If you are a first—time author, don't worry! We have a marketing department to assist you! Just give us some ideas as to what you think will work for you and your book.

6. Manuscripts. Do not send a manuscript unsolicited. It will be returned immediately. If our reviewing editors like your first three chapters and want to read the rest of the book, we will inform you of manuscript submission guidelines and addresses.

7. PLEASE DO NOT EMAIL SUBMISSION QUERIES.

8. Timelines. Due to possible overload of submissions, we cannot guarantee these times. We hope to adhere to the following schedule:
• Initial query — 2-4 weeks response time
• Manuscript request — 1-3 months
Please do not call to check on the status of your submission. If you

have not heard anything at all from us 3 months after your initial query, send an email to bethw@overmtn.com. We will check our records for your package and let you know if we have received it, and estimate a response date.

Categories: Fiction—Mystery

CONTACT: Alex Foster, Acquisitions Editor
Material: Mystery
The Overmountain Press
PO Box 1261
Johnson City TN 37605
Phone: 423-926-2691
Website: www.silverdaggermysteries.com

Skinner House Books

Skinner House Books is an imprint of The Unitarian Universalist Association.

Skinner House Books is currently seeking proposals on these topics:
- how to nurture tolerance in our children
- how to talk to children about spiritual subjects
- spirituality in the workplace
- spirituality and/or spiritual practice in everyday life
- aging and spirituality
- young adulthood and spirituality
- prayer collections
- how to become a social justice activist
- nature and spirituality
- interconnectedness; living the values consistent with our "small planet"
  - collected stories for children
  - cultural appropriation vs. cultural diversity: how to strike a balance
  - stories about congregational life that focus on a particular theme, such as welcoming blended families, nurturing diversity, nurturing social activism, managing grief, managing conflict, nurturing intergenerational contact

To submit a proposal to Skinner House or to contact us for more information, send an email to skinner_info@uua.org.

Proposals and Queries

Skinner House Books accepts query letters and proposal packages from interested writers. A query should be 1-3 pages long. In addition to a concise summary of the proposed manuscript, it should include an explanation of why the author is qualified to write such a work and why the manuscript is appropriate for the Skinner House audience. A proposal package should include an outline or summary (2-10 pages), table of contents, introduction, and two sample chapters.

Due to the large number of submissions we receive, Skinner House is unable to comment in detail on manuscripts or proposals that are declined.

Manuscript Guidelines

The Skinner House editorial style is based on *The Chicago Manual of Style*. Please consult it for questions regarding style and manuscript preparation.

All submissions should be typed on a word-processor or computer and printed double-spaced by a laser-quality printer. Please submit manuscript in one file on a PC disk if possible. Do not set manuscripts in all caps. Serial commas should be used. Subheads should be set off from text by a line space above and below. Pages should be numbered and held by binder clips or paper clips, not stapled. Please provide a table of contents identifying manuscript pages for each chapter/unit. Manuscripts will not be returned unless a self-addressed stamped envelope is enclosed with the submission.

Skinner House Books prefers numbered endnotes, divided by chapter. Do not use footnotes, as they will require extra time and money to convert to endnotes.

The Unitarian Universalist Association is committed to gender-inclusive language. Generic use of the words "man" or "he" are widely perceived as sexist and should be avoided. We also recommend using inclusive terms for occupations or roles (i.e., salesperson, police officer, chair) and "it" not "she" for ships, cities, and countries. Advice on avoiding sexist language can be found in *The Bias-Free Word Finder* by Rosalie Maggio (Beacon Press, 1992).

Categories: Nonfiction—General Interest—Inspirational—Religion

CONTACT: Ari McCarthy
Material: All
The Unitarian Universalist Association
25 Beacon St.
Boston MA 02108
Phone: 617-948-4603
Website: www.uua.org/skinner

Smithsonian Oceanic Collection
Smithsonian Backyard
Smithsonian Let's Go to the Zoo!

Please refer to Soundprints.

Soho Press Inc
Imprints: Soho & Soho Crime

Soho Press primarily publishes fiction, with the occasional autobiography or cultural historical account. Completed manuscripts should be 60,000 words or more. While many of our published works arrive here through agents, we place a high priority on publishing quality unsolicited materials from new writers.

Though eager to accept a wide range of literary fiction, we are generally unenthusiastic about publishing formula fiction, young adult dramas, stock romances, juvenile literature, cookbooks, self-help, fantasy, westerns, and anything that might recommend itself as a "quick read." Further, we do not consider electronic submissions.

Writers may submit completed manuscripts at any time, however, a query letter accompanied by three chapters of the work (preferably the first three) and a brief outline of plot events should precede the submission of an entire novel. A cover letter listing previous publishing credits should be included with your work. Please accompany all submissions with postage and packing materials sufficient for their return.

Write well!

Laura Hruska, Publisher

Categories: African-American—Asian-American—Crime—Literature—Mystery—Memoir

CONTACT: Laura Hruska, Editor-in-Chief
Material: Fiction, Nonfiction, Mystery
CONTACT: Katharine Herman, Editor
Material: Fiction, Nonfiction, Mystery
853 Broadway
New York NY 10003
Phone: 212-260-1900
Website: www.sohopress.com

Solas Press

SUBMITTING A QUERY
1. INTRODUCTION
The following is a brief outline of the publishing process. It will serve as guideline for authors who think Solas Press may be of assistance to them. Just as every author is different so each publisher is different. The

ideal relationship for publishing a book is when the author and publisher complement each other. However, an author should surely look for a publisher that will do a splendid job of editing his manuscript and has the resources and desire to promote the finished book.

2. WHAT IS A BOOK?

This question may sound somewhat outlandish. Does not everyone know what a book is? Six hundred years ago a book might have been so large that a person would have difficulty in removing from the shelf, where it was chained. Such a book likely took more than one manyear to copy, and consumed many expensive parchments. In Irish monasteries where the copyist art achieved a high level of perfection, the completed works were often stored in leather cases that hung from the rafters. Technology has brought a wide variety of physical types of books. This variety relates to the size and type of binding that is important in deciding on the design of a book.

More important than the physical unity of the book is the conceptual idea behind the work. Even works which are a compendium of materials must have a unifying concept.

3. WHAT IS A PUBLISHER?

The publishing industry is made up of some very large well known companies and a very large number of small entities. The basic functions of these publishers is to:

1 Acquire manuscripts suitable to the company's mission through contracts with authors.

2. Develop the manuscripts in conjunction with authors into viable products, through editing, rewrites and conceptual development.

3. Design the physical aspects of the books for production and distribution using service vendors and artists.

4. Prepare for the acceptance of the final product through galleys, press releases, opinion makers, peers, authorities in the subject area, official and semi official agencies.

5. Deal with vendors of binding, packaging, and printing.

6. Place the books into the distribution channels.

In addition the publisher needs to conduct the work as business which includes financial and fiscal responsibilities.

4. POLICIES OF SOLAS PRESS

Solas Press by the mission it has accepted works to meet two basic requirements:

1. To publish worthwhile ideas not otherwise available to the public.

2. To operate the business for profit.

To meet these two necessary conditions we follow these guidelines in working with authors

1 Initial inquiry

2. Sample materials

3. Manuscript evaluation

4.1 Initial inquiry

The initial inquiry is a short description of what the author intends to achieve. It should first describe the concept and uniqueness of the ideas. Secondly it should delineate the audience that will find the ideas interesting. Finally it should give the qualifications of the author in the area of interest. This final point is most important if there are any autobiographical elements.

Solas Press will respond within about a month to this initial query. A simultaneous submission of the initial query is acceptable to Solas Press.

4.2 Sample materials

If after the initial inquiry we mutually agree there is interest in proceeding the next step can be an evaluation of sample materials which shows the end quality that can be achieved.

4.3 Manuscript evaluation

Before submitting a manuscript for evaluation, the author(s) and Solas Press will complete an agreement dealing with the ownership of the materials, copyright protection, indemnity, and performance within a timeframe

One hard copy of the manuscript is required. The text should also,

if possible, be submitted in electronic form. A mock-up or a description of the proposed layout of the work will generally not be needed unless it is significant for some reason.

If during the editing of the manuscript Solas Press decides that it will not proceed to publish the work it will, if requested, return all the materials supplied by the author, and not retain copies of the materials. It may retain notes generated by Solas Press.

Categories: Nonfiction—History—Religion—Spiritual

CONTACT: Acquisitions Editor
Material: All
PO Box 4066
Antioch, CA 94531
Phone: 925-978-9781

Soundprints
A Division of Trudy Corporation

Soundprints currently publishes the following series:
• Smithsonian's Backyard
• Smithsonian's Let's Go to the Zoo!
• Smithsonian Oceanic Collection
• Soundprints' Wild Habitats
• Soundprints' Read-and-Discover (early reading chapter books)
• Soundprints' Make Friends Around the World

Soundprints is primarily a publisher of wildlife picture books for children that educate as they entertain. Soundprints' stories are fiction based on fact and are rigorously reviewed for accuracy by wildlife experts. Because of the review processes, all authors are responsible for the thorough and careful research of their subject matter. None of the animals in our stories are portrayed in an anthropomorphic light. As a publisher with very specific guidelines for our well-defined series, we are not able to accept unsolicited manuscripts for publication. All of our authors are contracted on a "work for hire basis," and create manuscripts to our specifications, depending on our need. We are always interested in reviewing the published work of new potential authors. If you would like to submit some samples of your published work, we would be happy to review them and keep them on file for future reference. Please send all writing samples to the address listed.

Categories: Animals—Children—Education—Nature—Outdoors

CONTACT: Chelsea Shriver, Assistant Editor
Material: All
353 Main Ave.
Norwalk CT 06851
Phone: 203-846-2274
Fax: 203-846-1776
Website: www.soundprints.com

Sourcebooks, Inc.
Sourcebooks Casablanca
Sourcebooks Hysteria
Sourcebooks Landmark
Sourcebooks MediaFusion
Sphinx Publishing

Sourcebooks has strong distribution into the retail market—bookstores, gift stores and specialty shops whose primary product is something other than books—and provides tremendous editorial, sales, marketing and publicity support for our authors.

We follow a somewhat out-of-date model for book publishing that makes our passion for books central. In short, we believe in authorship. We work with our authors to develop great books that find and inspire a wide audience. We believe in helping develop our authors' careers, and recognize that a well-published, successful book is often a cornerstone. We seek authors who are as committed to success as we are.

Fiction:

Our fiction imprint, Sourcebooks Landmark, publishes a variety of titles. We are interested first and foremost in books that have a story to tell. We are currently only reviewing agented fiction manuscripts.

Nonfiction:

We are interested in books that will establish a unique standard in their subject area. We look for books with a well-defined, strong target market. Our Sourcebooks publishing list includes most nonfiction categories, including entertainment, history, sports, general self-help/psychology, business (particularly small business, marketing and management), parenting, health and beauty, reference, biography, gift books and women's issues.

In addition, we have several imprints focused on publishing great books into specific categories:

• Sourcebooks Casablanca publishes titles related to love and relationships

• Sourcebooks Hysteria publishes humor books

• Sourcebooks MediaFusion publishes titles that uniquely mix traditional books with integrated new media

• Sphinx Publishing is a leading consumer self-help law publisher

We are not currently publishing children's books, but we do keep an active file of artists and illustrators.

In order to consider your nonfiction book for potential publication, we will need to see a proposal that includes the following items:

• A brief synopsis in 1-2 paragraphs

• Author bio or resume specifying credentials and publication credits, if any

• A complete table of contents, plus estimated length of manuscript in words and pages

• Two to three sample chapters (not the first)

• A description of the target audience

• One page/paragraph on your book's unique advantages

• A list of competing or comparable titles and how your book differs

• Please do not send complete manuscripts unless a specific request is made for one. Queries only and simultaneous submissions are OK. We advise against the expense of sending your proposal via overnight delivery or certified mail.

While we love talking to authors, we're a bit bookish, meaning we need to actually read your proposal. That's the long way of saying it's best not to call or personally email us. If you follow the directions above (or if you even come close), your proposal will be given a fair and thorough review. For more hints, try books like *The Writer's Market*, or any number of books and magazines like it, available in bookstores and libraries. Finally, receiving proposals via email or fax may seem convenient, but isn't for us, and may actually cause manuscripts to miss the review process other proposals receive. Therefore, we advise against it.

Please send only copies of your materials. Do not send us any original manuscripts or artwork. We will not be held liable for materials lost or destroyed in the mail. Please enclose a correct size (depending on what you want returned) self-addressed, stamped envelope with your proposal. We will not return manuscripts without appropriate postage. Canadian and foreign postage coupons will not be accepted.

We usually return rejections within six to eight weeks. We may take longer if your book is being considered for publication.

Thank you again for thinking of Sourcebooks for your book. We look forward to reviewing your materials and considering your book for publication.

Categories: Fiction—Nonfiction—Biography—Careers—College—Diet/Nutrition—General Interest—Health—History—Law—Marriage—Money & Finances—Music—New Age—Parenting—Relationships—Self Help—Singles—Sports/Recreation—Women's Fiction—Women's Issues

CONTACT: Editorial Submissions
Material: All

PO Box 4410
Naperville IL 60567-4410
Phone: 630-961-3900
Website: www.sourcebooks.com

Southern Illinois University Press

Southern Illinois University Press welcomes book proposals in the fields in which we publish. To ensure timely consideration of your proposed work, please provide the information outlined below. Do not submit unsolicited complete manuscripts. Your proposal should be about 750 to 1,000 words. This statement, which can take the form of a letter, should cover:

1. the names of the author(s) or editor(s).

2. the complete title and subtitle.

3. the length or proposed length.

4. the content of the book including your aims in writing it, your primary findings or arguments, the sources used in your research, and the relationship your work has to previous studies in the field.

5. the intended audience or markets for your book, including courses for which the book might be used as a text or collateral reading and organizations or groups that might be interested in purchasing copies of your book.

6. any features in the proposed manuscript that will require special attention in the design and production of your book, such as photographs, line drawings, or other illustrations; charts, graphs, or tables; technical or foreign languages; complex mathematical or scientific data.

7. the status of your manuscript-including how much of it has been written and when you expect to finish writing it.

Please include with your proposal a copy of your current vita and those of the other author(s) or editor(s). Also enclose a copy of the table of contents of the proposed work, preferably annotated. If available, please include a sample chapter from the manuscript-please double-space the text in all sample chapters.

Your proposal will be referred to one of several acquiring editors who specialize in the fields in which we publish. Your editor may follow a variety of procedures in evaluating your proposal, but in most cases, you will hear an indication of our decision from him or her within two months.

If you have additional questions about our publishing program, please write to the acquisitions department. You may also contact the acquisitions department by phone, fax, or by email.

Thank you.

Categories: Nonfiction—African American—Civil War—Drama—Film/Video—History—Language—Literature—Poetry—Regional—Television/Radio—Theatre

CONTACT: Acquisitions Department
Material: All
1915 University Press Dr Mc 6806
Carbondale, IL 62901
Phone: 618-453-2281
Fax: 618-453-1221
E-mail: kageff@siu.edu
Website: www.siu.edu/~siupress

Spellmount Publishers

Please refer to Howell Press, Inc.

Sphinx Publishing

Please refer to Sourcebooks, Inc.

Spinsters Ink

Spinsters Ink is primarily interested in full-length novels and nonfiction works that deal with significant issues in women's lives from a feminist perspective: books that not only name crucial issues in women's lives, but—more important—encourage change and growth. We are particularly interested in creative works by women writing from the periphery: fat women, Jewish women, lesbians, old women, women examining classism, women of color, women with disabilities, women who are writing books that help make the best in our lives possible. We want well-told stories that exhibit fine writing, are lively and engaging, and treat our lives with the honesty and complexity they deserve. The main characters and/or narrators must be women or address social justice issues.

Submission requirements and procedures:

If you wish to be read, your manuscript first must reach a holder, including a synopsis of the work for our review, by e-mail only (spinster@spinstersink.com). If we want to review the work in greater depth, we will send you a letter asking for two to five chapters (depending on length-should not exceed 50 pages or five chapters) of the work itself. Include a self-addressed, stamped postcard which we will return to you, letting you know that we received the material. Also, include a self-addressed, stamped envelope in which we'll respond to you when we've finished reading your materials. If the preliminary work looks suitable to us, we will ask you to send us the entire manuscript.

Please do not send anything—neither the query materials or the manuscript itself—by certified mail or return receipt requested.

Do allow at least three months to review your manuscript. Depending on our workload and availability of staff, we will get to your submission as quickly as possible and give it the thorough attention it deserves.

At the top of each manuscript page should be written the chapter number, the page number, and your last name.

If you have submitted your work to other publishers, please do us the courtesy of informing us of this and notifying us immediately if another publisher begins to give the manuscript serious consideration. We have no intention of "competing" with our publishing colleagues, so please don't put us in this position.

If you are offered a contract:

If you are offered a contract, we will go through it in detail with you. We can recommend reading resources to help you understand publishing contracts, and we encourage you to check with an attorney if you desire.

Spinsters Ink pays for all production costs of the books we publish. Because we are a small press, we cannot afford to pay advances or provide travel allowances for promoting your book. However, we do extensive publicity both prior to and after publication. Your royalties are a percentage of the sales of the books and of the sale of subsidiary rights, such as foreign translations and television and film rights.

When your contract is signed, we will determine a publication schedule for your book. This includes editing, text design, cover design, proofreading, and marketing. Generally, a book is published about 12 to 18 months after the contract is signed.

Call us with any questions you may have.

Categories: Fiction—Nonfiction—Feminism—Lesbian—Mystery—Women's Fiction—Women's Issues—Social Justice

CONTACT: Acquisitions Editor
Material: All
191 University Blvd., #300
Denver CO 80206
Phone: 303-761-5552
E-mail: spinster@spinsters-ink.com

SPS Studios, Inc.,

Please refer to Blue Mountain Arts, Inc.

Square One Publishers

Square One is an independent Long Island-based publisher of adult nonfiction trade books. Our books are aimed at people who are looking for the best place to start. We focus on providing titles that are accessible, accurate, and interesting. We look for intelligently written, informative titles that have a strong point of view, and that are authored by people who know their subjects well.

To submit your manuscript proposal to us, we ask that you include the following:

• a cover letter telling us about your book, its market, and your own background.

• a table of contents detailing each chapter in one or two paragraph summary.

• a two- or three-page introduction that provides an overview of your book's topic, its approach, and its goal(s).

• a self-addressed stamped envelope. If you wish the proposal returned, make sure the envelope is big enough to accommodate your material and that you have included sufficient return postage. If you wish nothing returned and you want a speedy reply, provide us with your email address.

Responses to submissions are generally sent within two weeks of receipt.

Before submitting your proposal, we strongly suggest you peruse our website (squareonepublishers.com) to determine if our house is truly right for your book.

Categories: Nonfiction—Collectibles—Cooking—Crafts/Hobbies—Games—Money & Finances—New Age—Paranormal—Parenting—Reference—Self Help—Singles—Writing

CONTACT: Acquisitions Editor
Material: All
115 Herricks Rd.
Garden City Park NY 11040
Phone: 516-535-2010
Fax: 516-535-2014

St. Bede's Publications

We are a small Roman Catholic publishing company owned and operated by a monastery of Benedictine nuns. Our major interests are in the areas of monastic sources and spirituality and patristics. Most of

Books M-Z

our books are in the areas of theology and philosophy, prayer and spirituality. We do not publish fiction and only rarely do we publish poetry.

Please do not send your entire manuscript unless requested. We prefer to receive an inquiry first, at which time you may submit a summary of your book, table of contents and a few sample chapters. If we are interested, we will request the full manuscript. Faxed proposals will not be considered.

Manuscripts should be formatted with at least 1½" margins on all four sides. Please use the same typewriter or printer font for the entire manuscript. All pages should be numbered consecutively. The first line of each paragraph should be indented one-half inch. Sketches, photographs and other art that is to be included must be submitted with the manuscript. Authors should submit a short biographical sketch and a précis of their book. If we accept the manuscript for publication, we will require two copies.

We prefer *The Chicago Manual of Style*, but any major style manual is acceptable as long as the manuscript is consistent. If your manuscript is accepted, we can accept, along with the hard copy, computer disks in IBM-compatible format. The computer files must be exactly the same as the printed copy.

If your manuscript is accepted, the final copy must be in perfect condition before it goes into production. Any alterations made in the text after page proofs will be charged against author royalties.

Categories: Religon—

CONTACT: Mother Mary Clare Vincent, President
Material: All
PO Box 545
Petersham MA 01366-0545
Phone: 978-724-3213
Website: www.fordhampress.com

Stackpole Books

Thank you for requesting our submission guidelines. Authors send us ideas for books in lots of forms, but we especially appreciate the query, and here's why:

For you, it's a quick way to find out whether we're interested in your idea before you take the time to write a book about it. For us, it's a quick way to decide whether your idea fits among the other books already on our list and those we've planned for the future, and whether what you have in mind and what we're looking for are similar.

Even if the idea you send isn't a book for Stackpole, your query might spark one that you and we could develop together, or it could show us that you'd be able to do another book for which we've been trying to find the right author. We hope that following the suggestions we've made below not only can help you convince the editor who looks over your proposal that it's worth pursuing but also will help you hone your thoughts about your subject.

First of all, send your query to an individual editor by name rather than to the Stackpole offices or to the editors in general. Describe briefly and clearly what the book is about, who and how large your target audience is, what qualifies you to write the book (including samples of previously published work if you have them), what other books are on the market that will compete with yours, and how yours differs from them. Include a sentence outline describing the contents of the book, and describe the physical book as you envision it. We also like to see sample photographs and illustrations if you have them. If you've already written the manuscript, send only a sample chapter or two, along with the other information.

Of course, when you submit a query, you may not have all of that information. However, the more you can supply, the better, because you must sell your idea to the editor, who, if she's convinced, must in turn sell it to the other editors and the sales department.

No, it's not a simple process, for you or for us. But one of the most pleasant aspects of our jobs as editors is opening the daily mail, antici-

pating potential books. So we look forward to hearing from you and to seeing your work.

Categories: Nonfiction—Fishing—History—Military—Outdoors—Regional—Sports/Recreation

CONTACT: Judith Schnell
Material: Outdoor Sports and Fly Fishing
CONTACT: Mark Allison
Material: Nature
CONTACT: Christopher Evans
Material: History
CONTACT: Col. Edward Skender
Material: Military Reference
CONTACT: Kyle Weaver
Material: Pennsylvania
5067 Ritter Rd.
Mechanicsburg, PA 17055
Phone: 717-796-0411
Fax: 717-796-0412
Website: www.stackpolebooks.com

Starscape

Please refer to Tom Doherty Associate, LLC, in the Book Publishers section.

Steeple Hill™

Steeple Hill Love Inspired

Please refer to Harlequin, in the Book Publishers section.

Stenhouse Publishers

As you're thinking about writing a book for publication by Stenhouse Publishers, this information is designed to encourage you, and help you proceed in a manner that will increase your chances of being published.

If you've never before written a book - or even submitted a proposal to publish a book - the process and prospects may seem daunting, if not downright frightening. In fact, while you are reading this, you may be thinking of a dozen other things you need to do before you start writing. Well, washing the dishes, mowing the lawn and paying the bills can wait. This is the time to start writing. You are in fact risking rejection, but rejection isn't the worst fate in life. Even if your proposal isn't accepted or your manuscript isn't published, you will have learned some valuable lessons that you can carry forward to your next attempt. And if your proposal and manuscript are accepted, you will have accomplished something to be proud of. Linda Rief knew it was time to start writing when she found herself vacuuming her pocket book. The outcome was *Seeking Diversity*, a wonderful book about teaching language arts with adolescents.

So, where to begin? A logical starting place is the proposal. The point of the proposal is to help you figure out what you want your book to be, to say, to accomplish, and you probably will be surprised by some of the ideas that emerge. There's nothing like writing to find out what you want to say.

The proposal also has a second purpose - and a second audience.

You are writing to answer basic questions likely to be asked by any publisher reviewing the proposal. *These questions include the following:*

- What is this book to be about?
- What is its intended audience?
- What writing style will you use?
- How will your book be organized?
- What books have been written on this subject, and how will yours differ?
- Who are you?
- How long do you anticipate the manuscript will be?
- How much have you already written?
- When do you expect to finish the manuscript - or a first draft?
- Will your book include samples of student writing, drawing or other work?

Of course, we understand that every proposal has its own wrinkles and specific questions; try to anticipate and pre-empt as many of these as you can. Remember that your proposal may be our first exposure to the idea you're offering. You can't assume that we understand very much. For example, you may submit a journal article that forms the basis of your manuscript; or, the article may be written in an academic style and you are intending to rewrite it as Chapter 4 of your book. We don't know; so explain exactly what you plan to do to any writing you submit, including stylistic changes you will make.

Here are a few other considerations in preparing your proposal and manuscript:

- Print everything double spaced. Your submission should be readable, not fancy. And please number the pages, either by hand or computer.
- Don't worry about submitting computer disks at this point. However, we will be interested in them later.
- If your project is accepted, you will need written permission for any student work that appears in the book. Photographs of students also require signed releases. And, if you are planning to reproduce extracts, poems, or illustrations from published books, you will need written permission from the copyright holder.
- Finally, if you are writing in detail about the classroom practices of other teachers, it is both courteous and prudent to show them what you plan to publish.
- We hope you will write the most complete proposal you can. If we are interested in your proposal but still have questions, we'll ask. For instance, if you haven't yet written any of the manuscript, we would ask to see a sample chapter or two if we think the proposal looks promising.
- Which brings us to the next step. After you've submitted your proposal you can expect first to receive a brief acknowledgment notice. We may call or write with questions, or we may notify you that we've decided, regretfully, that your book is not what we're looking for.
- On the other hand, we may decide to send your proposal directly to one or more readers for their responses. These readers may be teachers who are familiar with your topic and/or target audience, or they may be other professionals with experience and expertise that qualifies them to assess your ideas. This stage of the process almost always takes longer than you would wish; like you, these people are trying to squeeze this project into their busy lives.
- After we receive the readers' responses, we must decide whether any particular project is a "yes," a "yes, if . . . ," a "maybe," or a "no." A request for more material is an encouraging response that falls into the "maybe" category. On the other hand, please don't consider "no" as an indication that we judge your work unsuitable; it only means that it doesn't meet our present needs as publishers. Don't give up - on us or on writing.
- Which brings us back to the beginning: Relax, give this project your best effort and get it done. The only proposals we will never accept are the ones we don't receive.
- The rest of the material in this packet consists of a sample cover letter and a sample proposal. We've included these as examples of how one author has chosen to present her material. You will see that she has written a rather detailed cover letter and a detailed chapter outline; a

brief cover letter, overview, and chapter outline would also be an acceptable way to fashion a proposal. We did not want this packet to deter you with its sheer size, so we didn't include a sample chapter or vita; a brief vita can be helpful.

Enough. Now, start writing and good luck. We hope to hear from you soon.

Best wishes,
Philippa Stratton, Editorial Director, Stenhouse Publishers
Categories: Education

CONTACT: William Varner, Senior Editor
Material: All
477 Congress St Ste 4B
Portland ME 04101-3417
Phone: 207-253-1600
Website: www.stenhouse.com

Sterling Publishing Company

At present, our list is composed primarily of reference and "how-to" books with step-by-step instructions on practical subjects including: Art; body, mind, and spirit; business; ceramics; crafts, including paper crafts; culinary arts, including wine and drink; fiber arts, including knitting, crochet, sewing, and embroidery; games and puzzles (especially crosswords, logic puzzles, and I.Q. builders); gardening; hobbies; health and fitness; house building and construction; language; lettering, including calligraphy, lifestyle, magic, natural history, new age, reference, science, sports, pets, and woodworking.

Sterling does not publish any fiction and very few non-illustrated books.

CHILDREN'S BOOKS
Sterling's juvenile list focuses primarily on non-fiction, including: Crafts; hobbies; games; activities; origami; optical illusions; mazes; dot-to-dots; science experiments; puzzles (math/word/picture/logic); chess; card games and tricks; sports; and magic. We also publish fiction in the following categories: riddles and jokes; ghost stories; mystery and detective short stories; board books; and picture books.

We are not, at this time, accepting any children's fiction except in those categories listed above.

SUBMISSION GUIDELINES:
Please write to us explaining your idea and enclose an outline and a sample chapter of the proposed book (typed and double-spaced, please) along with sample illustrations where applicable. We do not accept electronic (e-mail) submissions. Be sure to include information about yourself with particular regard to your skills and qualifications in the subject area of your submission. It is helpful for us to know your publishing history - whether or not you've written other books and, if so, the name of the publisher and whether those books are currently in print.

Be sure to include your name, address, telephone number, and e-mail address. We will not return any materials submitted to us unless you specifically request that materials be returned and include, along with your submission, a stamped, self-addressed envelope. **Please note that, due to the volume of mail received, we cannot guarantee the return of unsolicited material. Please do not send original art or irreplaceable work of any kind; while we will make every effort to return your submissions, we are not responsible for any loss or damage.**

Submissions should be sent to the attention of the category editor, e.g., the material on a woodworking book should be addressed to the "Woodworking Editor"; a craft book proposal should be addressed to the "Craft Editor"; and so on. All children's book submissions should be sent to the attention of the "Children's Book Editor." Submissions should be sent to:
Category Editor
Sterling Publishing Co., Inc.
387 Park Avenue South, 10th floor

New York, NY 10016-8810

We will contact you as soon as we are able via either letter or telephone. Please do not attempt to call us regarding your submission. Given the volume of submissions we receive, it may take several months for us to reply.

Thank you for your interest in Sterling.

Additional Details:

In addition to the above guidelines, the following addenda can be downloaded in Microsoft Word format from our website.

ADDENDUM 2A: INSTRUCTIONS FOR AUTHORS

Manuscript. Please furnish a disk—preferably MS Word—and a hard copy of your book. Enter your text as simply as possible. Don't use tabs or extra letter spacing to position anything except table columns. Use enter only at the end of paragraphs, **never for line breaks**. If you need to present tabular material, use the table tools in your word processing equipment. If you don't have table tools, you can set up tables using one tab for each column. **DO NOT use your column tool for anything**, especially not for tables. You should use formatting such as italics, bold and small caps where appropriate. Don't insert art or box framing.

Heads. Type all heads flush left. Indicate the level of each heading by entering an @ sign, followed by a letter and a colon. Use A for major beads (chapter titles), B for minor heads, C for subheads. Don't apply any formatting to heads.

Style. Since we frequently sell our books in Canada, England, South Africa, New Zealand, and Australia, be careful to avoid using brand names, slang expressions, or references that will be meaningful only to American readers.

Art labels. Do not add labels to art. Place them on an overlay or photocopy for position and prepare as a separate double-spaced manuscript.

Captions. Copy for captions must be prepared as a separate manuscript. If you are using MS Word you can key in the placement in the main manuscript as an annotation. Number each caption to correspond to the illustration (1-1, 1-2, 2-1, etc.), but do not attach the caption to the illustration.

If you are not working on a computer, type your manuscript on standard 8-1/2 x 11 white typing paper (no onionskin or erasable paper). Double-space all lines and leave a one-inch margin on all sides. Indent all paragraphs except those that follow a head. Key illustrations by hand in the margin away from the text.

Line art. Line art may be prepared electronically or inked. Electronic preparation must contain **NO TEXT** and should be produced in a vector format. These EPS images must contain TIFF previews. Most of the good art programs will offer this option. Be sure that you have removed all color from such files. Do not use a CAD program. Inked line art should be protected by tissue overlay and numbered in pencil on the front. Use heavy, smooth drawing paper. Key each illustration to the text with a pencil notation in the margin.

Halftone art. Be sure that you know whether your book will be produced in full color, black and white, or a mixture of both. If you plan to supply art digitally make sure that you are supplying a TIFF image of at least 300-350 dpi Do not supply art produced on low-end programs that have a maximum dpi in the hundreds. Your program should be capable of producing images at least in the 600 dpi range. We must see and approve any scanned line art, which should be in the 900-1200 dpi range, so send us some samples before you produce something we can't use. Kodak Photo CDs are acceptable if they can be produced in CYMK, but they must be high resolution scans that offer at least five resolutions. Beware, not all photo CDs are the same.

Photographs. Most live art will be scanned and not reproduced photographically. If your book is black and white, we can convert color photos. **We cannot convert black and white to color**. For black and white you may send us negatives and contact prints. Color can be slides or transparencies. Color prints are acceptable, but **do not send printed images**. The larger the transparency, usually the better the quality. Best results occur when originals are roughly the same size as the final printed image. Be sure that your photos are developed by a professional developer and not by a high-volume commercial house. Tell the developer to give you good contrast.

Please arrange your photos in order of use and note the number on the slide casing, contact sheet, or transparency sleeve. Key prints with a soft, dull pencil on the back.

Our books sell in many languages. Try not to show English words on products, or brand names.

Taking Photographs. All photographs should be taken against a plain, neutral background. Do not use gray. Light them to bring out the contrast and to avoid shadows. Shoot each picture at several different exposures, so that we can pick out the best one.

If you are photographing people, please make sure to have an ethnic mix and to obtain model releases.

If you are photographing children, be sure that the children pictured are slightly older than the children who are the market for the book.

Be sure to avoid clothing or hair styles that will date the book.

Avoid trade names or words appearing in the photo: these could make the book unsuitable for foreign sales.

Inventory. Please give us a simple summary inventory of what you have sent: the quantity and kind of art, the length of your manuscript and its components, etc.

Finally, if you are in any doubt about the acceptability of what you are producing, please send us a sample here for evaluation before you invest time and money in something that we will not be able to use.

Materials Sources and Acknowledgments. Because we sell into many special accounts and foreign markets we always try to minimize the use of such lists. If a source must be acknowledged, it is best to do so in the text and not in a separate list. Any such acknowledgment should just give the source name and avoid any contact information.

If your subject requires you to specify sources, then the list must be international and include sources for all English-speaking markets and some foreign markets.

Contributors may, of course, be listed.

ADDENDUM 2B: INSTRUCTIONS FOR AUTHORS

Supplied Electronic Files and High Resolution Images:

If it is agreed to accept application electronic files and/or high resolution images for reproduction use, please contact the publisher to clarify acceptable software, platform for electronic files, line screen for images, and show a sample chapter or sample spreads containing representative elements used throughout the book for approval prior to completing the body of the work. Once sample material is approved, then supply completed files with a complete set of laser printouts plus acceptable color guidance to use when matching color on press.

4 color Images must be CMYK and a minimum 150 line screen must be used for color reproduction. If RGB files are used in the work, do not attempt to convert RGB to CMYK. RGB files will be supplied to our printers to color convert to correct color.

Use only Adobe Type 1 fonts, no TrueType or designer created fonts. Do not use applications to create bold and italic fonts; make sure they are true italic and bold fonts.

Categories: Fiction—Architecture—Arts—Crafts/Hobbies—Cooking—Games—Gardening—Health—History—Hobbies—Home—Juvenile—Lifestyle—Literature—Photography—Reference—Religion—Science—Sports/Recreation—Travel

Contact: Category Editor
Sterling Publishing Co., Inc.
387 Park Avenue South, 10th floor
New York, NY 10016-8810
Phone: 212-532-7160
Email: online@Sterlingpub.com
Website: www.sterlingpub.com

Stipes Publishing, LLC

Frequently Asked Questions

1. Does Stipes finance the publication? Yes. We pay all costs involved. The author has no financial obligation. Our obligation extends for all costs involved in the manufacture and distribution of the book. All of the risk involved is ours. We also pay a royalty twice a year.

2. Does Stipes market books nationally? Yes. Our books are sold through over 2,500 bookstores throughout the world. Four of our books have over 300 college adoptions and dozens of our books have from 20 to 250 adoptions.

3. Is Stipes interested in publications which are not for national distribution? Yes. Many of our publications are designed for use by an author for a specific course at his or her school. Some of these publications are course outlines, syllabi, or specialized materials developed for a particular course. The feasibility of such an arrangement depends upon the number of students involved. It would normally require over 150 students per year. If enough students are involved, revisions can be made from year to year and in some cases even more frequently.

4. Will Stipes work with material in its developmental stage? Yes. We frequently work with an author on a preliminary edition. Our requirements for the size of a printing are small enough that such an arrangement allows for revisions and additions after a short period of time. Until the book is in final form, it is usually used at only the author's own campus or possibly a few others. After it has evolved into a final publication, it can be marketed nationally.

5. Would Stipes be interested in working on a publication which is under contract to another publisher? With the approval of the other publisher, we have worked on preliminary editions of another publisher's book. In such a case, the author is enabled to use the material in the classroom for a few years before it is released for publication in a final edition.

6. What types of formats and bindings does Stipes offer? We are in no way limited in this sense. The economy involved is the only limitation. Some of our publications are cloth, some with standard wraparound paperback binding (perfect binding), some with spiral wire and plastic binding, and some with a specially designed binding that allows for tearout sheets.

7. Will Stipes permit photographs and other illustrations? Yes. All types can be used, including 4-color illustrations. Here again, economy is the only limitation.

8. Will my publication be reasonably priced? Yes. Very few publishers have their own printing facilities. We do have our own complete facilities. On occasion, we will farm out work the way most publishers do for all of their publications. However, our prices are based on our normal costs, which do not include a "middleman" mark-up that many publishers must include.

9. What sort of manuscript preparation is required? We have no magic formula. All we require is that the manuscript is legible. We can work directly from any type of computer disk. We usually request that the author supply us with a hard copy in addition to the disk. We also frequently work from camera-ready copy provided by the author.

10. Will I get help in the preparation of my manuscript? Yes. We work closely with our authors. We are not a giant corporation, and we feel that our personal working relationship with our authors is the essence of our business. We do not presume to be expert in each of our authors' fields. However, we can give some editorial assistance and arrange for critical evaluations if the author desires us to do so.

11. Can disks or CD's be included with my book? Yes, we include these media. We usually insert them in a pocket attached to the inside front or back cover and shrinkwrap the book.

12. Will Stipes take care of obtaining permissions to use copyrighted materials which I have included in my manuscript? Yes. We will contact the copyright holder and obtain all necessary permissions. We also pay any required permission fees. When we are faced with unusually high permission fees, we consult with the author before proceeding.

13. Will my publication be copyrighted? Yes. It can be copyrighted either in our name or that of the author. In addition, all books that are marketed nationally are listed in the various publications such as Books in Print that are used throughout the country to facilitate finding and ordering a book.

14. Can I obtain references regarding Stipes? Yes. We are more than happy to refer you to any of our authors. We have authors on campuses from coast to coast and in Canada. We feel that the goodwill we have with our authors is our greatest asset. Please do ask us for references.

15. Will I lose control over my manuscript once it is turned over to Stipes? No. We do not presume to make reprintings, revisions, editorial changes, or other changes without the author's consent. No decision regarding the handling of your book, manual, syllabus, or outline will be made without your consent.

16. How quickly can my book be produced? Because we have our own facilities, we are able to rush books through our plant. Sometimes we have been able to get a book out in a matter of two to three weeks. However, normal scheduling requires that we have two to four months. This is flexible, and we will be happy to do our best to accommodate your needs.

17. How long has Stipes been in the publishing business? We have been in business for over 70 years.

18. How many titles does Stipes have? We have more than 300 titles.

19. What is the standard Stipes royalty? Our standard royalty is 15% of the list price.

20. How will my book be distributed? Stipes publications are sold through all normal publishing outlets, including your local campus bookstores.

21. What kind of information can I furnish Stipes for evaluation of the commercial potential of the material? See the "Prospectus Guideline" below.

Prospectus Guidelines

This outline is intended to provide a general frame of reference for evaluation of the commercial potential of your material. Please discuss with us any questions it may arouse, or any concerns you may have about preparing material for review.

I. MARKET CONSIDERATIONS
A. General Market
    1. What course is the text intended for?
    2. What are the prerequisites for the course?
B. Market Segment
    1. What segment of the market is your text designed for?
    2. Discuss which competing books will be closest to your text in level and appeal.

II. THE TEXT
A. Brief Description
    1. In one or two paragraphs describe the work, its rationale, approach, and point of view.
B. Outstanding Features
    1. List briefly what you consider to be the outstanding features of the work.
C. Apparatus
    1. Please outline the pedagogical elements of a typical chapter.
    2. Please discuss all the ancillary items you feel will be needed to publish a competitive text.
D. Competition
    1. Identify the leading texts and briefly discuss their main strengths and weaknesses compared to your text.
    2. What aspects of your topical coverage are similar to or different from the competition?

III. STATUS OF THE TEXT
A. Schedule for completing the text

Books M-Z

1. When do you expect to have a completed manuscript?

B. Length

    1. What is the goal for the page length of a bound text?

    2. What is the estimate of the length of text in manuscript pages?

C. Competition

    1. Do you intend to class-test the material?

IV. STATUS OF THE GRAPHICS

A. Layout features

    1. What special layout features (spot color, shadings, gradients, bleeds) do you plan to employ?

B. Illustrations

    1. How many illustrations, photos and line-drawings (graphs and diagrams) do you plan to include? C. How are these illustrations generated, and in what form will they be submitted?

V. ADDITIONAL MATERIALS

A. Annotated Table of Contents

    1. A detailed outline provides reviewers with a sense of how the material will be organized and developed.

B. Vita

    1. We would appreciate a current vita.

C. Sample chapters

    1. Sample chapters need not be chronological – it would be advisable to prepare the chapters you feel initially most comfortable in writing.

Categories: Nonfiction—Agriculture—Architecture—Business—Ecology—Engineering—Gardening—Music—Sports/Recreation—Technical—Textbooks

CONTACT: Robert Watts, Partner
Material: Music, Ag, Business, Horticulture
CONTACT: Benjamin H. Watts, Partner
Material: Technical, Architecture, Sports, Ecology
PO Box 526
Champaign IL 61824-0526
Phone: 217-356-8391
E-mail: stipes@sbcglobal.net
Website: www.stipes.com

Stone Bridge Press

General guidelines for submitting proposals and manuscripts to Stone Bridge Press are listed below. These guidelines may not apply to every project; please use your best judgment as to which items are appropriate to include with your submission. If there is any question as to the suitability of your book for Stone Bridge Press, please consider sending us a detailed letter of inquiry first. If you want to make an electronic submission via e-mail, read this important information first!

Proposals for publication ideally should include items from the following checklist:

___(1) A one-page cover letter summarizing what the book is, who it's for, and why it's useful, important, necessary, or unique.

___(2) An expanded table of contents, chapter by chapter with summaries. Indicate what will be included in the front- and backmatter (introduction, preface, bibliography, glossary, index, etc.).

___(3) For fiction or translation, at least two sample chapters. For non-fiction, an introduction and one sample chapter, or two sample chapters.

___(4) Estimated manuscript length and completion date (if it's still incomplete). Indicate how the manuscript is being prepared (typewriter? word processor? If you're using a computer, what platform and what program?).

___(5) Number of illustrations and what kind (line drawings, black and white photographs, color, etc.). Are there any special production requirements? Please provide representative samples so we can judge for quality: use high-grade photocopies for samples of line drawings,

glossy prints for black and white photos, and transparencies for color photos (always send dupes, not originals, unless requested otherwise).

___(6) Information about you. Include a c.v. if you have one, and indicate your qualifications to write on your subject.

___(7) A discussion of the size of the market for your book and how the book compares to its competition. What makes it different/better? What are you prepared to do to promote the book (very important!)? Do you know others in your field who will provide reviews or testimonials?

___(8) Your financial and scheduling requirements, if any.

Mail your submission to P.O. Box 8208, Berkeley, CA 94707.

IMPORTANT!!!! If you require a certificate of delivery or are using Express Mail or a delivery service like UPS, DO NOT USE THE POST OFFICE BOX ADDRESS AND MAKE THE EDITOR STAND IN LINE; instead PLEASE use our street address: 1393 Solano Avenue, Suite C, Albany, CA 94706.

ELECTRONIC SUBMISSIONS: In principle we support use of the Internet for correspondence and submissions. However, we do NOT accept attachments from people unknown to us. So if you've got an idea you think we might be interested in, send a simple email query to us first. If you want us to see some of your work, embed a short sample within your e-mail message (that is, do not include it as an attachment). Detailed proposals with supporting information are welcome. If we do invite you to send an attached manuscript sample, you should send it as either ASCII text or as MS Word. WordPerfect? Fuggedaboutit! We prefer Macintosh files.

Please note that we are primarily interested in books with a Japan connection (however tenuous). If you have genre fiction, like science fiction, war stories, mysteries, and romances, or commercial fiction, you probably shouldn't be talking to us at all.

No materials can be returned to you unless you provide us with sufficient return postage.

Thanks for writing. We look forward to hearing from you.

Categories: Fiction(in translation)—Arts—Asian-American—Business—Culture—Film/Video—Language—Japan—Travel—Asia

CONTACT: The Editors
Material: All
PO Box 8208
Berkeley, CA 94707
For Deliveries:
1393 Solano Ave, Ste. C
Albany, CA 94706
Phone: 510-524-8732
Fax: 510-524-8711
E-mail: sbpedit@stonebridge.com
Website: www.stonebridge.com

Storey Publishing, LCC

The mission of Storey Publishing is to serve our customers by publishing practical information that encourages personal independence in harmony with the environment. We seek to do this in a positive atmosphere that promotes editorial quality, team spirit, and profitability.

The books we select to carry out this mission include titles on gardening, small-scale farming, building, homebrewing, crafts, part-time business, home improvement, woodworking, animals, nature, natural living, personal care, and country living.

We are always pleased to review new proposals, which we try to process expeditiously. We offer both work-for-hire and standard royalty contracts.

If you have ideas for a book on any of the subjects in our line, and if you are intrigued by the philosophy expressed in our mission statement, we hope you will think of Storey Publishing.

Please include the following information:
• A Letter of Introduction.

• A one-paragraph description of your book idea. What is the "hook" for your book? Why is it unique? Examples: "Finally, a natural health-oriented body care and personal grooming book focused on the particular needs and interests of men" (*Body Care Just for Men*); "Hands-on birding: How you can attract wild birds to come and feed right from your hand?" (*Hand-Feeding Backyard Birds*).

• A brief statement explaining why you think your book is needed and describing the potential readers of the book. Answer the question, "Who will buy this book and why?"

• A list of recent books (if any) that are similar to your own, with an explanation of how yours will be different and better. Give the competition for your book by listing books published within the last three years. Include title, author, page count, retail price, publisher, and description.

• A paragraph about yourself and your credentials for writing the book you are proposing, (you may also wish to include your resume).

• A table of contents, including a brief description of each chapter. Some of your thoughts about the length, general appearance, and photographic and illustrative requirements of the book.

• A sample of your writing from previous books or magazines.

• A sample chapter from the proposed book.

Storey is also looking for authors of our popular *Country Wisdom Bulletins*. Each 32-page bulletin provides valuable, in-depth, how-to coverage on a single topic with in-depth information and illustrations. We have over 150 widespread topics available now, and are always pleased to review proposals for new *Country Wisdom Bulletins*. Please address inquiries and proposals to: Nancy Ringer, Bulletin Program Manager.

Categories: Nonfiction—Agriculture—Animals—Architecture—Arts—Cooking—Crafts/Hobbies—Gardening—Hobbies—How-to

CONTACT: Deborah Balmuth
Material: Building and mind/body/spirit
CONTACT: Deborah Burns
Material: Equine
CONTACT: Gwen Steege
Material: Gardening
CONTACT: Dianne Cutillo
Material: Cooking, wine, and beer
CONTACT: Nancy Ringer
Material: Animals, nature, natural health and beauty, home reference and crafts
210 Mass MoCA Way
North Adams MA 01247
Phone: 802-823-5200
Fax: 802-823-5819
Website: www.storey.com

Stylus Publishing, LLC

Stylus is an independent publisher, and the distributor of independent publishers. *We meet the needs of:*

• Teachers, faculty developers and administrators in higher education

A clear, well thought out proposal is the key to getting a project considered by a publisher. We recommend taking time over your proposal, to think through the guidelines and questions that follow, and to give yourself the opportunity for reflection and second thoughts. The process of refining your focus and ideas will also help smooth the writing process.

Bear in mind that the market for books and information is highly competitive, and that as authors and publishers we need to focus on filling real needs, or developing new ideas, information, solutions or concepts which have real value for our audiences.

THE PROPOSAL

The proposal should cover all the following issues, many of which overlap, in the sequence that's most logical for your project.

1. Title

A good title sends a clear signal to your intended audience about your goals. It is also a vital element in marketing and differentiating your book from others. A good final title may only emerge during the writing process, so we're happy to begin with a "working" title.

2. Description, scope and purpose

Explain your subject matter and provide a rationale for why your project is timely and why it will appeal to your intended audience. Describe the scope and topics which will be covered. What are you contributing to the subject, and how broad an interest do you envisage?

If the project is an edited collection, a coherent focus is important. Discuss how you propose to achieve the cohesion and describe individual contributors' chapters in this light.

3. Audience

Be as specific as possible in terms of academic discipline or job title, level, type of institution/company. Distinguish between primary and secondary audiences, and consider specific geographical appeal if relevant (e.g. likely interest in specific regional or national markets). If you're proposing a textbook, specify level and courses, and give an estimate of market size.

4. Need

Define the need your book will meet or create. Why will people buy it? What does it do, or do in a new way, that meets the need of your intended audience? Will it significantly add to a body of knowledge, or significantly improve practices?

5. Competition

List competing and related works (giving author, title, publisher, year and price) and explain specifically how your book differs or improves upon the competition. Bear in mind that competition may include materials available in journal form or available electronically. State whether price, timing or format issues are critical.

6. Qualifications & related activities

Although this may duplicate information in your resume / curriculum vitae, highlight the work you've done which is relevant to this project. Also let us know if you lecture outside your institution, give presentations at meetings, are otherwise involved with information media related to the subject of your book (are you on the board of a journal; an owner of a listserv?), or active in a relevant organization or association. If you have plans to present at meetings in the next 12 months, let us know. Do you have influential contacts in your field you might be willing to give a pre-publication endorsement? Do you have contacts in relevant media?

In an environment where so much information competes for our limited time, an author's participation in publicizing his or her book can make a major difference to sales. With an edited volume, provide similar key information on contributors.

7. Table of contents

Provide a line or two of description with each chapter title. Your comments on sequence and organization may be helpful.

8. Format, length, special features

Let us know if you have specific ideas about format: traditional book? binder product? electronic component? Provide an estimate of length in terms of printed pages (approx. 360 words to a printed page). Does the book need illustrations? Are there any unusual features?

9. Timetable

Give an estimate for completion of manuscript. Are there any factors which should influence publication date? Do you have commitments which may delay delivery?

ACCOMPANYING MATERIAL

We ideally like to see proposals accompanied by:

1. A writing sample

A draft chapter or introduction, or recent article by you on the topic, but not a complete manuscript. With an edited work, are you familiar with the contributors' writings, and are you confident they will follow your guidelines as editor?

2. Resume / curriculum vitae

We look forward to hearing from you.

Categories: Education

CONTACT: John Von Knorring, Publisher
Material: Higher Education
22883 Quicksilver Dr.
Sterling VA 20166
Phone: 703-661-1504
Fax: 703-661-1501
Website: www.styluspub.com

Success Publishing

Formal guidelines not available.
Send queries or book proposals to below address.
Categories: Nonfiction—Business—Cartoons—Comedy—Consumer—Crafts/Hobbies—Diet/Nutrition—Directories—Entertainment—Family—Hobbies—Lifestyle—Public Speaking—Relationships—Self Help—Singles—Teen—Young Adult

CONTACT: Allan Smith
Material: All
3419 Dunham Rd.
Warsaw NY 14569
Phone: 585-786-5663

Sulgrave Press

Please refer to Howell Press, Inc.

Sunbelt Publications

Sunbelt Publications, incorporated in 1988 with roots in the book business since 1973, produces and distributes publications about "Adventures in Natural History and Cultural Heritage of The Californias." These include multi-language pictorials, natural science and outdoor guidebooks, histories and regional references, and stories that celebrate the land and its people.

Our publishing program focuses on the Californias, today three states in two nations sharing one Pacific shore. Sunbelt books help to discover and conserve the natural and historical heritage of unique regions on the frontiers of adventure and learning.

GUIDELINES FOR PROSPECTIVE SUNBELT AUTHORS

Thank you for your interest in publishing with us. Please review the following information, and call for clarification or further information.

Categories and Content

We specialize in regional travel and reference, guidebooks, natural science, and outdoor adventure in California, Baja California, and the Southwest U.S. Our publishing program focuses on "Adventure in the Natural History and Cultural Heritage of the Californias." A marketable non-fiction title generally includes photos and illustrations (e.g., maps, artwork, diagrams, tables), all with captions that enhance understanding of the text. Natural history and guidebooks require substantial map work.

A goal of our publishing program is to contribute to the body of knowledge about selected disciplines or topics (e.g., San Diego region, Baja California, introductory earth science). To this end, we highly encourage you to review Sunbelt books related to your topic and cite them as appropriate in your manuscript. We will loan copies of these books to local authors or you may purchase them for research purposes at 40% off retail prices.

Quantitative Guidelines

Sunbelt titles generally have about 200 pages of main text with approximately 400 words per formatted page, not including front matter (e.g. table of contents, title page) or back matter (e.g. bibliography, index). A design guideline is to have a photo, illustration, or chapter heading every three pages.

Query Letter

Authors are advised to query first with their idea/concept before submitting the initial proposal. Queries should be short, succinct, and focus on what makes the proposed work unique, as well as publishable and marketable. Authors may query via email to jredmond@sunbeltpub.com or send a single-page query letter to Jennifer Redmond, Editor-in-Chief, Sunbelt Publications, 1250 Fayette Street, El Cajon, CA 92020. Please do not query, or follow up on queries already sent, by telephone. Queries may be followed up by email or U.S. mail, if no answer has been received within 60 days. **Materials submitted will not be returned unless accompanied by SASE with sufficient postage.**

Initial Proposal

Once contacted, the author shall send the proposal. This includes the General Outline (see below), a brief discussion of the target market for the title and the author's qualifications, comments on complementary or competing titles currently on the market, and sample illustrations and/or photographs (if applicable). Include comments on author's commitment to promotion as noted below under "Teamwork." Proposals may be followed up by email or U.S. mail, if no answer has been received within 60 days. **Materials submitted will not be returned unless accompanied by SASE with sufficient postage.**

General Outline (for natural history, guidebooks, and histories)
Foreword—by the publisher or a topical authority.
Preface—to the book, its genesis, authorship and contributors, and niche.
Introduction—to the subject matter, geared to the target market.
Text—including illustrations and photos with captions.
• Natural history chapters (e.g. biology)
   b. Cultural history chapters (e.g. pioneers)
• Outdoor recreation chapters (e.g. trail logs)
References—geared to the target market (including related Sunbelt books).
Appendices—supplementary or technical material.
Glossary—May also be integrated into index or as "sidebars."
Index—every occurrence of proper names, key words and concepts (author's responsibility after final page proof).
General Outline (for literary non-fiction)
Text—synopsis and 2 sample chapters mandatory for all works of literary non-fiction and applicable fictional works (e.g. memoirs, historical fiction, regional short story collections).

Teamwork in Title Development and Marketing

The appropriate and profitable relationship between author and publisher is "teamwork" whereby both contribute to the production and promotion process. Promotional opportunities include written and online reviews, bookstore signings, author lectures, field trips (if applicable), media features and interviews (newspapers, magazines, radio and television), and brochure mailings to selected lists. Authors are expected to actively promote their book by following guidelines established for author signings and interviews, especially during the crucial 6 months after release. Authors are also encouraged to write articles for publication that will stimulate interest in the sale of their book, and to suggest promotional ideas or events. An active partnership is key to a successful sell-through of your book.

Materials Received from Author

• Once instructed to submit their full manuscript for evaluation, author supplies final text electronically together with identical hard copy. The preferred format for electronic files is Microsoft Word (Courier font). Hard copy should be double-spaced, single sided, in 11 point text. Author supplies camera-ready artwork, illustrations, and photographs at or above minimum standards of the appropriate profession (e.g. cartography).

Rights and Permissions

• Copyright is assigned to the publisher with exclusive permission to publish and distribute the work in all media and in all formats. Publisher will edit, title, price, and package the work to maximize its marketability, consistent with maintaining the essential content of the work. Excerpts printed in other Sunbelt books, with full credit to the author, facilitate promotion of the original work. Author is fully responsible for the accuracy of information presented in the work.

• Author is responsible to procure and provide written permission for use of all non-owned material including photographs and illustrations and to pay for same if required. Owners of such material are often willing to grant permission gratis if credit is given. There is generally no fee for material published by public entities although written permission is required for all but U.S. government agencies (e.g. USGS). Sunbelt-owned photo files and other materials are generally available at no cost but with full credit. Permission to reprint material from periodicals must generally be granted by original author.

Price and Royalty

• Retail price is determined by the cost of production, marketing and royalty plus the publisher's best judgement of a title's price point with respect to similar titles in the market. Royalty is a percentage of net sale receipts (less returns and promotional copies) and is paid semi-annually with a statement of sales. Typical examples of the margins for a $14.95 retail book are:

High margin direct sale to consumer (e.g. direct mail/website sales):

Retail price to consumer (100%)	$14.95
Price to buyer (100%)	$14.95
Royalty to author (10% of $12.95)	$ 1.50

Medium margin sale to bookstores:

Retail price to consumer (100%)	$14.95
Publisher price to bookstore (60% of $12.95)	$11.22
Royalty to author (10% of $7.77)	$ 1.12

Low margin sale from publisher to wholesaler for resale to bookstores:

Retail price to consumer (100%)	$14.95
Publisher price to wholesaler (45% of $12.95)	$ 8.42
Royalty to author (10% of $5.83)	$ .84

AUTHOR COPIES

Ten complimentary copes are provided to the author. The author may purchase additional copies at 60% OF or 40% OFF the retail price (same as for bookstores) plus sales tax, unless author's valid certificate of resale is on file with Sunbelt. These copies may be resold in compliance with legal requirements and not-to-compete with Sunbelt bookseller customers. Additional copies are available to the author on consignment for lectures and other sales opportunities.

PUBLISHING PROCESS

• After submission of proposal and request to submit full manuscript, author submits manuscript and accompanying materials to publisher, who may accept it finally or conditionally. Acquisition committee considers content (which may include a technical review process), marketing, and financial aspects of proposed project.

• Author is contacted and informed of Publisher interest, and signs memorandum of understanding (MOU), and/or publishing agreement.

• If conditional, author revises work until final acceptance by publisher, which will be established by written memo, and submits hard copy and disk of approved manuscript and camera-ready supplementary materials (e.g. photos, illustrations, maps). Author changes are not accepted beyond this point.

• Publisher copyedits, designs, and typesets the work including interior, cover, and title. Author reviews copyedited version.

• Publisher develops and initiates marketing plan in collaboration with author.

• Galley proof (text and layout w/o illustrations) is shared with author for comments, time permitting.

• Page proof is produced including total interior and cover. Final total proofreading.

• Printer produces blue-line for publisher approval; delivers final bound product by ship date.

• Publisher commences distribution to booksellers.

• Official publication date is peak of launch marketing campaign, several months after ship date.

• Commence on-going marketing process.

• Reprint if successful.

MARKETING MATERIALS:

• Author will complete an "Author Questionnaire" once the contract is signed.

• Author will provide the publisher a photograph and negative that can be used for promotional   purposes.

• Author will follow "Book Signing Tips" and "Interview Tips" while promoting his book. (to be supplied by Sunbelt)

• Author provides a paragraph "About the Author" and "About the Book", suitable for marketing use.

Categories: Nonfiction—History—Outdoors—Recreation—Regional—Travel—Regional History

CONTACT: Jennifer Redmond, Editor-in-Chief
1250 Fayette St.
El Cajon CA 92020
Phone: 619-258-4911
Website: www.sunbeltbooks.com

Swan-Raven & Co.

Please refer to Granite Publishing Group, LLC

Swedenborg Foundation, Inc
Chrysalis Books

A. Publishing History and Mission

The Swedenborg Foundation, Inc., was organized in 1849 and incorporated in 1850 as the American Swedenborg Printing and Publishing Company. Its original purpose was to print and distribute books by Emanuel Swedenborg (1688-1772), eighteenth-century scientist and visionary.

The Foundation operates as a nonprofit, educational, literary, and charitable organization, dependent on public support. Its mission is to make available materials that "foster an affirmative and increasingly broad engagement with the theological thought of Emanuel Swedenborg, especially among persons desiring to apply spiritual principles to life." To accomplish this mission, the Foundation has established two imprints : the Swedenborg Foundation imprint, for books written by or about Emanuel Swedenborg and his philosophy, and the Chrysalis Books imprint, for books intended for the general trade market; these work also incorporate Swedenborgian philosophy. Our publications are intended for three primary audiences:

1. Serious readers of Swedenborg. These books are published under the Swedenborg Foundation imprint.

2. Thoughtful persons seeking to broaden their spiritual insights and development, who may or may not identify with traditional religious organizations. These titles are intended for the general trade audience and are published under the Chrysalis Books imprint.

3. Scholars and teachers in the fields of Bible, theology, psychology and personal transformation studies, literature, and philosophy. These books are part of the "Swedenborg Studies" series and are published under the Swedenborg Foundation imprint.

B. Publication Program

The Foundation acquires quality manuscripts written for each of its audiences.

1. Books intended for either audience 1 (serious readers of Swedenborg) or audience 3 (scholars) must directly address the works of Emanuel Swedenborg. Audience 1 books should explain the philosophy of Emanuel Swedenborg and should show how that philosophy applies to living an ethical life. Books intended for audience 3 should analyze Swedenborg's writings from a comparative, historical, biographical, religious, or philosophical standpoint and should incorporate

existing and up-to-date scholarship.

2. Books intended for audience 2 (general trade) should also incorporate the philosophy of Emanuel Swedenborg in an integral way but may also include the philosophy of other spiritual traditions and may fall into one of the following categories:

a.Social concerns (such as stewardship of the earth, service to others)

b. Personal growth and spirituality (self-help, recovery, meditation, or lifestyle issues)

c. The spiritual dimension of reality from the perspective of art, nature, philosophy, or natural science.

C. The Book Proposal

A first step toward publication is the development of a book proposal. The proposal, in two to three pages, addresses several important questions:

1. What is the book about? A paragraph or two should describe the subject matter and the author's approach to writing about it.

2.How is the treatment of the subject different or unique from other books available in its field? Why was the manuscript written? In what ways does it incorporate a Swedenborgian theme or perspective?

3. For what audience or market is the book directed? Is there a special-interest group or market for whom the book might have appeal?

4. What is the anticipated or finished length of the book in manuscript pages and in approximate words? When will the completed manuscript be available for review?

5. What is the author's background or credentials for writing the book?

Academic or religious professionals may wish to send a resume. Include a list of publishing credits. The Foundation is open to publishing an author's first book, so lack of publishing experience is not a serious drawback.

In addition, the proposal should include an introductory letter, a detailed chapter-by-chapter outline (another two or three pages), a completed chapter or other sample of writing, and a stamped, self-addressed envelope (for the return of materials). It may also be sent via email. The author will receive an initial response from the senior editor on whether we are declining or interested in proceeding within a month of the proposal's arriving at our office. A final decision on whether the Foundation's Publication Committee wishes to read the completed manuscript may take as long as three months. Should the manuscript be requested, the Foundation asks for exclusive reviewer privileges.

D. Manuscript Format and Evaluation

If the Foundation is interested in evaluating the manuscript, the form for submitting copy is fairly standard. Submit two, unbound manuscripts. They should be typewritten, double-spaced (including any notes, bibliography, appendices, or other matter) on good-quality 8-1/2 x 11-inch white paper, with margins of at least one inch on all sides. Sending high-quality photocopies is acceptable, as are minor, neat corrections within the text. Experienced writers keep an extra copy of the entire manuscript in the unlikely event that it may be lost in handling. The Foundation assumes no liability for any materials submitted to it. Again, please include sufficient return postage.

The Foundation follows The Chicago Manual of Style, 14th ed. (University of Chicago Press) regarding questions of style and format. In preparing the manuscript, keep these points in mind:

1. The completed manuscript includes:

a. title page (with the author's name exactly as desired in print)

b. dedication page, if appropriate

c. table of contents

d. accompanying charts, tables, maps, photos or artwork, appendices, bibliography, and other matter

2. Number pages consecutively

3. Mark and fully document all quotations

4. Place notes (endnotes) in a separate section rather than on the page where the citation occurs

5. Clearly identify all biblical references, extracts from other sa-

cred literature, or the writings of Swedenborg

Use inclusive language in the body of the text.

Once the manuscript is received, several types of evaluations must be made. This process can be quite lengthy, typically six to eight months, sometimes longer. Generally, the Foundation asks one or more readers familiar with the subject matter to read and critique the manuscript. Financial and marketing studies are also made to determine the expected cost for producing the book, a projected retail price, and the number of copies which must be sold over a given period to break even. Sometimes a reviewer or editor may suggest that certain structural changes or redrafted passages will make the book stronger. Favorably reviewed manuscripts are accepted according to the overall quality of the book, the suitability for the publishing program of the Foundation, and anticipated market needs over the next several publishing seasons.

If, after reviewing the entire manuscript and on the advice of its readers, the Publications Committee accepts the book for publication, authors must also submit the draft manuscript in an electronic file. For transmission of an approved manuscript, the Foundation is best prepared to received text files using the Windows 95 version of Corel WordPerfect 8.

E. The Published Book

If the Foundation accepts the manuscript, the author will be asked to sign a formal agreement, or contract. This agreement gives the Foundation the exclusive right to publish and distribute the book. Book manuscripts designed to compete in the general religious trade are usually published on a royalty basis. In royalty contracts, the author is paid a percentage of the net income from the sale of the book, typically 10 percent. Sometimes an author might be paid a cash advance against future royalty earnings. The agreement also covers when the final manuscript is due, any special formatting requirements, copyright and subsidiary rights information, the number of free copies due the author, and other such matters.

Authors are responsible for obtaining the necessary permissions to quote at length from copyright-protected materials. Permissions must be obtained in writing, usually from a publisher, and submitted with the final draft of the manuscript. Photocopies of printed material from which quotes are taken may later be used for verification. The author is also asked to proofread galleys (typeset pages), and may be asked to prepare an index. Authors may also be asked to secure appropriate illustrative materials. On occasion, the author may be asked to contact agreed-upon persons to write a foreword or promotional statement.

Categories: Nonfiction—Lifestyle—Philosophy—Psychology—Religion—Spiritual

CONTACT: Mary Lou Bertucci, Senior Editor
Material:320 North Church St.
West Chester PA 19380
Phone: 610-430-3222, ext. 11
E-mail: editor@swedenborg.com
Fax: 610-430-7982
Website: www.swedenborg.com

Sycamore Island Books

Please refer to Paladin Press.

Talewinds

Please refer to Charlesbridge Publishing.

Taylor Trade

Imprints: Cooper Square Press,

Derrydale Press, Madison Books

Proposals should be limited to a query letter; an email will generate the quickest response. If querying by email, please note in the memo box "book proposal." Send no attachments unless requested. What we look for at this stage is suitability of the proposed book to our publishing program (see categories below) as well as the author's unique qualifications for writing his or her book.

Taylor Trade Publishing is especially interested in regional gardening, nature, field guides, cooking, sports, nature, self-help, Texana/Western history, general history and entertainment. We do not publish fiction or poetry. However, proposals from institutions such as museums or galleries pertaining to their collections are strongly encouraged.

Categories: Nonfiction—Cooking—Entertainment—Field Guides—Gardening—History—Nature—Self Help—Sports/Recreation—Texana/Western History

CONTACT: Editorial Assistant
Material: All
5360 Manhattan Circle, #100
Boulder, CO 80303
Phone: 303-543-7835
Fax: 303-543-0043
E-mail: aphillips@rowman.com
Website: www.taylor-trade.com

Temple University Press

Temple University Press invites inquiries and proposals that include a project overview, a tentative table of contents, and the author/editor's resume. Proposals might also include sample chapters or writing samples, but they are not required for an initial inquiry. Prospective authors are encouraged to contact the Editor-in-Chief by phone, e-mail or letter before sending completed manuscripts. Editors prefer to see double-spaced copy with no justification on the right margin and unbound pages. We do not accept electronic versions of proposals or manuscripts.

What Should You Send?

Apart from the cover letter and collateral material, editors strongly prefer to have all material typed and double-spaced. We do not accept project inquiries or proposed manuscripts on disk, and we prefer not to have extensive proposals sent by email. Please send only photocopies of art work; the Press cannot be responsible for one-of-a-kind materials.

For projects in the early stages of development, you might begin with a written inquiry or phone call to determine whether the topic is suited to Temple's editorial program. If you decide to send the proposal you have prepared, you should include a project overview, table of contents (with contributors' names, if appropriate), your c.v. or resume, and any available sample materials (e.g., abstracts, draft chapters, previously published work on a related topic, copies of illustrations).

If you would like to submit a completed or nearly completed manuscript, you should send a brief inquiry (by mail or email) or speak with an editor first to discuss the book's appropriateness for our list. When you send the manuscript, you should include your c.v. or resume as well as a cover letter that tells us whether you are also submitting it to other publishers. Manuscripts should come in the form of unbound pages so that we can easily photocopy them if we decide to send them out for review.

You are welcome to suggest possible readers for your proposal or manuscript; if you do, please supply their current affiliations. Please do not, however, contact the potential reviewers yourself. The editor will discuss your work and review process with you before deciding whether to send the project out for further evaluation.

An envelope with return postage is customary if you would like your materials returned to you in the event that we do not pursue the project.

To Which Editor?

If you have a project that you would like to submit to the Press, you can send an inquiry to Janet Francendese, Editor-in-Chief, or directly to the editor who seems to be responsible for acquisitions in your field. Our list is highly interdisciplinary, so the right choice is not always obvious. Be assured, though, that your project will soon find its way to the appropriate person.

Categories: Nonfiction—African-American—Animals—Asian-American—Biography—Culture—Dance—Drama—Disabilities—Ecology—Education—Family—Feminism—Film/Video—Gay/Lesbian—General Interest—Health—Hispanic—History—Jewish Interest—Law—Multicultural—Music—Politics—Psychology—Regional—Religion—Sexuality—Sports/Recreation—Television/Radio—Theatre—Women's Issues—Ethnic—Public Policy

CONTACT: Janet M. Francendese, Editor-in-Chief
Material: History, American Studies, Asian American Studies, African American Studies, Film, Music, Disability Studies, Animals and Culture
E-mail: janet@temple.edu
CONTACT: Micah Kleit, Executive Editor
Material: American Studies, Media & Television Studies, Political & Social Theory, Sociology, Education, Religion.
E-mail: mkleit@temple.edu
CONTACT: Mick Gusinde-Duffy, Senior Acquisitions Editor
Material: Labor Studies/International Political Economy, Urban Studies, Geography, Sociology, Political Science, and Information.
E-mail: gusinde@temple.edu
University Services 083-42
1601 North Broad St., USB 306
Philadelphia PA 191212-6099
Phone: 215-204-8787
Fax: 215-204-4719
Website: www.temple.edu/tempress

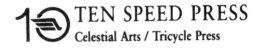

Ten Speed Press
Celestial Arts & Tricycle Press

Adult Trade Book Proposal Submissions

If you wish to send us your book proposal for consideration, please read our submission guidelines below. Before submitting your manuscript, you should first familiarize yourself with our publishing areas and imprints. Note that we do not consider certain genres, including fiction, poetry, memoir, and most photography.

Ten Speed Press

Genres include how-to, cooking, business/career, relationships, crafts, gardening, gift, humor, and pop culture. Please read the submission guidelines below and address your submission to:

Celestial Arts

Genres include alternative medicine, health, nutrition, parenting, spirituality, inspiration, and self-help. Please read the submission guidelines below and address your submission to:

Crossing Press

Genres include metaphysics, alternative therapies (chakras, color healing, herbs), mysticism, and feminism. Please read the submission guidelines below and address your submission to:

Tricycle Press
Children's books. Please read their submission guidelines here.

If you're not sure which publisher would be best for your proposal, there are resources available. A particularly good one is *Writer's Market*, available at most libraries and bookstores.

Submission Guidelines

If you wish to send us your book proposal, please include:

- A cover letter detailing the work as a whole. Include all information that you think we should have in order to make a decision about your project. In particular, tell us who your target audience is and provide a rationale for why we are the best publisher for your work.

- A chapter-by-chapter outline of the entire work.

- One or two sample chapters. It is not necessary to send the entire manuscript, just enough material to give us a sense of the work as a whole.

- A brief bio or a note describing who you are and why you are the right person to write this book. This doesn't need to be a formal resume.

- A self-addressed, stamped envelope with sufficient postage for the return of all of your material. Without this, we cannot return your materials to you. If you do not need your materials returned, please include an envelope with a 39-cent stamp for our reply.

Please do NOT send originals of anything. We are not liable for artwork or manuscript submissions.

We not accept unsolicited proposals through the web or email.

Thank you for your interest in Ten Speed Press, Celestial Arts, and Crossing Press. We look forward to reading your proposal soon. Be prepared to wait about six to eight weeks for a reply.

Children's Book Proposal Submissions

We intend the following to provide an informative, encouraging note aimed at getting your submission read and appreciated by an editor. All Tricycle Press submissions are considered on an individual basis, although a personalized response is often not possible due to the volume of submissions we receive. Please note that we do accept simultaneous submissions.

- DO NOT SEND ORIGINALS OR YOUR ONLY COPY OF ANYTHING. We are not responsible for lost submissions.

- Include an SASE of appropriate size and postage.

- Allow up to 24 weeks for a reply.

- Be sure your work is appropriate for us. Familiarize yourself with our list by going to bookstores, libraries, or right here on our website (www.tenspeed.com). We encourage you to request our catalog by mailing a 9 x 12 envelope with three first-class stamps (no checks or cash, please).

- Correspondence regarding status of manuscripts should

be conducted by mail-no email or phone calls, please.

- We do not accept electronic or faxed proposals.

- Read this article by Harold Underdown, formerly of Macmillan, for further information.

Board Books: Infant to 3
Complete text required. Include illustration ideas only if necessary for understanding text.

Picturebooks: Ages 3 and up
Complete text required. Include illustration ideas only if necessary for understanding text. Both fiction and non-fiction accepted.

Novels for Young Readers: Ages 8 to 12
If your manuscript is in chapters, please submit two to three sample chapters; otherwise one-third to one-half of the manuscript is usually sufficient. Also submit a table of contents or outline.

Real-Life Books: Ages 3 to 12
(to help kids understand themselves and their world)
Depending on length, one-third to one-half of the manuscript is usually sufficient. If written in chapters, please submit two to three, along with a table of contents or outline

Categories: Nonfiction—Agriculture—Animals—Business—Careers—Children—College—Cooking—Crafts/Hobbies—Diet/Nutrition—Food/Drink—Gardening—General Interest—Humor—Interview—Juvenile—Money & Finances—Outdoors—Recreation—Reference—Regional—Travel

CONTACT: The Editors
Material: All
PO Box 7123-S
Berkeley CA 94707
Phone: 510-559-1600
Fax: 510-559-1629
Website: www.tenspeed.com

Texas A&M University Press

We're interested in...

- Regional (Texas and Southwest) history
- Military history
- Business history, especially Texas and Southwest, and especially that related to the oil industry
- Natural history and natural sciences
- Agriculture and range ecology
- Presidential studies
- Anthropology and nautical archaeology
- Borderlands, multicultural, and women's studies
- For other topics, inquiries may be addressed to our acquisitions assistant:

We don't publish...

- Poetry
- Family memoirs or genealogy
- Fiction
- Children's books

· Cookbooks

How do I submit a proposal?

1. If one of our editors requested your manuscript, click here. If not, go to the next step.

2. Make sure your manuscript fits an area we're interested in (see , above).

3. Send us a query letter including the following:

   · What your book is about, why it's important, or what issues, questions, or problems it addresses.

   · How your book differs from others in the same subject area, or why your book is unique.

   · The audience for your book. Be as specific as possible.

   · Why you are uniquely qualified to write this book.

   · Names, addresses, and telephone numbers of esteemed experts in your field.

   · When you expect to have the completed manuscript ready (unless it is already completed).

4. Send a synopsis of your book that includes

   · A table of contents.

   · A description (length; illustrations, if any; format).

   · A chapter summary.

5. Send us a vita or brief professional summary, including previous publishing experience, if any.

6. Send at least one sample chapter of your book, if possible.

7. If you wish your materials returned to you, please include a stamped, self-addressed envelope with sufficient postage for the materials we are returning. Due to the volume of unsolicited manuscripts we receive, we cannot be responsible for packages without return postage included. DO NOT SEND US THE ONLY COPY OF YOUR MATERIALS; ALWAYS KEEP YOUR ORIGINALS.

Are multiple submissions acceptable?

The answer to this question depends on what stage your proposal has reached. If this is an initial proposal, prior to the submission of the complete manuscript, we will accept your submission even if it is currently being made to other publishers. However, once we have requested a full manuscript for evaluation, we do not accept multiple submissions due to the expense—in money and time—of soliciting peer reviews and performing the editorial preparation and other labor involved. Full disclosure is the best policy at this stage.

How will I know if my manuscript has been accepted? How long does it take?

We try to respond within three to four weeks. If the project looks promising, we will then arrange to have the manuscript reviewed by at least two readers outside the Press—people qualified to evaluate the contribution of the manuscript to its field. This part of the process typically takes two to four months but can take longer.

May I pay to have my book published by A&M Press?

Even if you or someone you know is willing to completely fund the publication of your book (a process sometimes called "subsidy publishing"), the Press does not accept works unless they meet the standards and criteria we have established. Some of our authors do obtain underwriting for their publishing projects, and while the Press encourages this and is happy to work with individuals and organizations interested in supporting our overall program or one of our areas of interest, we do not consider or approve any manuscript for publication unless it contains material of scholarly, historic, scientific, regional, or other interest in one or more of our targeted subject categories .

Will you show my manuscript to the rest of your consortium?

The Texas A&M University Press consortium is a distribution group. Each member press has its own, independent editorial program. Consult the relevant press for its submission interests and requirements.

To Submit a Manuscript for Review

Preparation of Manuscript:

   · Double-spaced on 8.5 by 11 inch paper

   · One side of the paper only

   · One-inch margins on all sides

   · Flat, loose sheets in a box—unfolded, unbound, and unstapled

   · Use standard fonts and MINIMAL FORMATTING

   · Include a title page and table of contents

   · Make sure pages are numbered systematically, either by chapter or consecutively through the entire manuscript

What happens next:

When you send the manuscript, a staff editor will read it, reviewing it for its appropriateness to our list. We try to respond within three to four weeks. If the project looks promising, we will then arrange to have it reviewed by at least two readers outside the Press—people qualified to evaluate the contribution of the manuscript to its field. This part of the process typically takes two to four months, but can take longer. With two positive outside readers' reports, we will propose the project to our faculty advisory committee, which must approve all manuscripts for publication.

Categories: Nonfiction—African-American—Agriculture—Architecture—Aviation—Business—Culture—Enviroment—Government—Hispanic—History—Military—Multicultural—Native American—Politics—Regional

CONTACT: Mary Lenn Dison, Editor-in-Cheif
E-mail: mary-dixon@tamu@edu
Material: Regional (Texas, Western, and Southern) history; Borderland studies; military and aviation history; presidential studies; anthropology and nautical archaeology
CONTACT: Shannon Davies, Louise Lindsey Merrick Editor for the Natural Environment
Email: shannondavies@austin.rr.com
Material: natural history and natural sciences; agriculture
Lindsey Building
Lewis St. 4354 TAMU
College Station TX 77843-4354
Phone: 979-845-1436
Fax: 979-847-8752
E-mail:d-vance@tamu.edu

Books M-Z

Texas Western Press

Before submitting a manuscript, check our mission statement to see whether your manuscript fits the literary focus of our press:

The mission of Texas Western Press of the University of Texas at El Paso is the publication of books on the history and cultures of the American Southwest, including particularly, historical and biographical works about West Texas, New Mexico, northern Mexico and the U.S.-Mexico borderlands. The Press has also published books in the areas of regional art, photography, Native American studies, demographics, border issues, and natural history. Texas Western Press also publishes two series: Southwestern Studies, short books on personalities and events of the American southwest; and The Border/La Frontera, a series based on current research directed at enhancing understanding of the diversity of conditions and experiences represented in the United States-Mexico borderlands. Texas Western Press is a member of the Association of American University Presses.

Texas Western Press follows the guidelines of *The Chicago Manual of Style*.

A manuscript proposal should include the following:
• cover letter
• prospectus to include analysis of current market competition and what place your book will have within it
• curriculum vitae
• potential audience for work
• table of contents
• sample chapter
• estimated length of manuscript
• examples or descriptions of artwork, including number of illustrations. Do not send originals
• self-addressed, stamped envelope for reply. If you want your materials returned, make sure to include an envelope that is large enough to hold the materials and include sufficient postage. Otherwise, your material will be recycled.
• If the manuscript is not a completed work, give estimated date of completion.
• Do not send irreplaceable materials.

For more information, contact Bobbi Gonzales at bobbi@utep.edu.

Categories: Nonfiction—Biography—Civil War—Culture—Hispanic—Military

CONTACT: Bobbi Gonzales, Assistant to Director
Material: All
500 W. University Ave.
El Paso TX 79968-0633
Phone: 915-747-5688
E-mail: bobbi@utep.edu
Website: www.utep.edu/twp

Third World Press

Thank you for your interest in publishing with THIRD WORLD PRESS. Third World Press is an African-centered publishing house dedicated to the creation and dissemination of written work of the highest quality.

A progressive publisher of Black and African-centered material for more than thirty years, our goal is to be the best provider of material to expand the mind and reach to all backgrounds especially the African-American community, and other African communities in the Diaspora. Third World Press promotes maximum effect of creative expression and cultural enlightenment in all the written genres, including fiction, nonfiction, poetry, drama, young adult and children's books which otherwise may not have an outlet.

Third World Press has published poetry works from noted writers including Gwendolyn Brooks, Sterling Plump, Haki R. Madhubuti, and Amiri Baraka. We value and support the talents of poets who wish to contribute to the literary world and showcase their poetics.

Third World Press welcomes the opportunity to review both solicited and unsolicited POETRY manuscripts that explore African-centered life and thought. When submitting poetry manuscripts for consideration, please adhere to the following guidelines.

POETRY MANUSCRIPTS MUST BE:
• At least fifty pages to be considered
• Typed and double-spaced
• Do not include more than one poem on a page
• Proofread for typographical and grammatical errors unless otherwise noted

SEND ONLY COPIES of any related artwork, photographs or layout boards. KEEP ALL ORIGINALS.

SEND ONLY COPIES of any other manuscripts-related materials. KEEP ALL ORIGINALS.

PLEASE INCLUDE THE FOLLOWING MATERIAL WITH THE SUBMITTED MANUSCRIPT:
• The subject of the manuscript, in a one-page synopsis form.
• Reasons why you, the author, are best qualified to write a book and why it needs to be published (what unmet needs in the literary market the book meets.)

Identify competition for your prospective book, and how your manuscript differs from those already existing.

• An identified market, and at least a preliminary outline of how your manuscript can be marketed to this segment.

Along with your manuscript, please attach one copy of these guidelines, as well as a self-address stamped envelope with correct postage and package size relative to your submissions. MANUSCRIPTS WILL ONLY BE ACCEPTED IN JULY OF EACH YEAR.

PLEASE REMEMBER THE FOLLOWING:

UNACCEPTED MANUSCRIPTS MAILED WITHOUT PROPER POSTAGE AND PACKAGING WILL BE DISCARDED.

FAILURE TO ADHERE TO SUBMISSION GUIDELINES WILL RESULT IN THE IMMEDIATE RETURN OR ELMINATION OF YOUR MANUSCRIPT.

Once your manuscript has been mailed, allow anywhere from four to six months for a written response. THE staff will not accept telephone calls regarding the status or review of a manuscript.

Categories: African-American—Poetry

CONTACT: Assistant to the Publisher
Material: All
PO Box 19730
Chicago, IL. 60619
Phone: 773-651-0700
E-mail: TWPress3@aol.com
Website: www.thirdworldpressinc.com

Three Forks

Please refer to Falcon Publishing.

Thriller Press

WHAT WE WILL CONSIDER

Thriller Press is a small publisher specializing in a narrow niche of fiction. We are not looking for new authors at this time. Please keep this in mind if you send us a submission and don't get a response from us.

Having said that, in the interest of our long term goals we will consider submissions in the following format.

You may send us ten pages in the body of an email. We will not open attachments. The email address to submit to is submissions@thrillerpress.com.

Your ten pages should consist of a one page letter with the remaining nine pages the opening of your novel. In your letter, please summarize your novel in 2 or 3 sentences. Also include any information about how you could help sell your book. (A critical part of selling books in today's market is author's own marketing efforts. i.e., if your job is being a Talk Show Host, let us know!) Please do not submit more than ten pages. If we're not hooked on your story by then, we won't respond anyway, no matter how great the rest of your novel may be.

We pay small advances, preferring to concentrate our resources on fantastic cover design, website marketing and direct contact with bookstores. If a book is successful it will earn royalties.

If, after reading our novels, you believe you have an intelligent, action-based thriller or mystery that would suit us, then please submit as described above.

Thank you,
—Tyler Larsson

CAVEATS

Please take a moment to consider that the typical successful fiction writer has done all of the following BEFORE submitting their work to agents and publishing companies:

• Taken multiple creative writing courses with a focus on fiction. You will find a range of courses at your local community college or through a university's extension program.

• Enthusiastically read and studied an enormous volume of work in the genre, i.e. mysteries and thrillers. If you don't read them consciously, don't try to write them.

• Had their work scrutinized by a professional in the writing/editing field whether a writing teacher, a friend in the business or an editor hired from an ad in *Publishers Weekly*. Ask for referrals and check them out.• When you find one who comes well recommended, pay the few hundred dollars and see what you learn. Remember, you don't want someone who flatters you, you want someone who will pick apart every aspect of your writing, plot line, character development, dialogue, syntax, grammar, the works.

• Attended several writing conferences and submitted his or her work to multiple critiques. There are hundreds of writing conferences available throughout the year. You can find them on the internet, or advertised in *Writer's Digest* and other writing magazines. Pick three or four one week conferences and sign up for all of them. Bring your completed novel to the first one. After the conference is over you will have a thousand ideas of how to improve your work. Rewrite accordingly, then take the result to the second conference. At each stage you will see improvement that you didn't think was possible. After taking your novel through four conferences, four complete rewrites, a dozen minor rewrites and a year or two of extra polishing, you'll be amazed at what you learned. Furthermore, you'll be glad you were spared the embarrassment of sending your work out earlier.

WHY WORK IS REJECTED

Every editor can tell you a thousand stories about writers who weren't prepared. Here are some telltale signs that immediately show an editor that the writer is not a professional.

1. The writer's cover letter calls their work a fiction novel, an embarrassing redundancy.

2. The writer makes mistakes in grammar and spelling.

3. The writer's novel lacks a compelling hook or setup.

4. The writer's work has "purple prose" (excessively fancy writing) and does not demonstrate economy of words. Mark Twain said, "Never use a quarter word when a nickel word will do the job." E.B. White said, "Cross out any word or sentence that doesn't develop character or advance the plot. And eliminate all adverbs." Study Hemingway for writing economy.

5. The novel doesn't start off with an immediate problem. Fiction is all about conflict and resolution. Read any good novel, whether a commercial "beach read" or a serious literary work or a fairy tale and you'll find that the story starts with a problem.

Here is a short, very simplified example of typical rising plot curve. Note that these characteristics apply to most fiction, be it *Moby Dick* or *Jurassic Park* or *The Old Man In The Sea* or Harry Potter or *Star Wars*.

The novel starts with a problem. Our hero (the protagonist) tries to solve the initial problem, but the problem gets worse. The protagonist takes a different approach, but the difficulties multiply until the problem is overwhelming. Eventually, our hero has an epiphany about how to solve the dilemma. He or she gears up to take on the problem in a final do-or-die climactic battle, engaging the antagonist/bad guy on his own turf. The climax is followed by a short wrap-up/resolution.

Note that the "problem" can be Captain Ahab's whale or genetic manipulation of extinct dinosaurs which are now running amok or the old man's fish or the evil professor or Darth Vader. Also, every aspect of the novel can be literal or metaphorical.

Categories: Fiction

CONTACT: Submissions Editor
Material: All
E-mail: submissions@thrillerpress.com
Website: thrillerpress.com

Tilbury House Publishers

Tilbury House narrowed its editorial focus several years ago, and we would appreciate receiving only queries and manuscripts that fit within our current areas of interest. We receive hundreds of unsolicited manuscripts each year; it's a time-consuming task to read and answer them all-although we sometimes find a gem! If you are connected to the Internet, please take a moment to visit our web site at www.tilburyhouse.com to familiarize yourself with our catalog and the kinds of books we publish. We look forward to seeing your manuscript and appreciate your interest in Tilbury House.

Children's Books

We are primarily interested in children's picture books (for ages 7-12) that:

1. Deal with issues of cultural diversity (global), nature, or the environment (we don't publish "general" children's books about animals, fables, or fantasy);

2. Appeal to children and parents and offer enough learning content so that they will also appeal to the educational market;

3. Will sell to the national (not just regional) market; and

4. Offer possibilities for developing a separate teacher's guide (written by an educator) that will expand the focus of the book, offer additional information, and suggest learning activities and approaches.

Adult Books

1. Much of our effort goes into our children's books, and it was difficult in the past to effectively market a diverse adult list. As a result, we decided to limit our new adult books to non-fiction about Maine or the Northeast, particularly books that are documentary or about Maine's history. Because the market for these books is small, we often seek out co-publishing arrangements with museums, historical societies, or other organizations; this helps us produce high-quality books that might not otherwise be published, and benefits both parties.

2. Please do not send us fiction, short stories, memoirs, or poetry. Our current catalog will give you a good idea of the kinds of books that interest us. You'll find our complete catalog, excerpts from our books, and more on this web site. If your manuscript doesn't seem like a good fit for Tilbury, you'll find guidance in books like Writer's Market or Children's Writers and Illustrator's Market to help you locate a more likely publisher.

What to Send

1. A query letter (a short, concise letter about your project), is a good start, or send a partial manuscript and outline, unless you feel we must see the entire manuscript to adequately assess it. For children's books, we prefer to see a complete manuscript. If you query us by email,

Books
M-Z

please put "Book Query" in the subject line, and do not send an attachment. We will not open attachments. Please do not send us large files over the Internet.

2. Work not accompanied by a self-addressed, stamped envelope will not be answered. If you want your materials returned, please be sure to enclose adequate postage, otherwise they will be recycled.

3. If you are making simultaneous submissions to other publishers, please note this in your query letter.

4. Please be patient with us; it usually takes us a month or so to respond.

We appreciate the opportunity to read your work. Thank you for your interest in Tilbury House, and for considering us as a possible publisher.

Categories: Fiction—Nonfiction—Children—Mulitcultural—Outdoors—Science

CONTACT: Audrey Maynard
Material: Children's Books Editor
2 Mechanic St., Ste. 3
Gardiner, ME 04345
Phone: 207-582-1899
E-mail: tilbury@tilburyhouse.com
Website: www.tilburyhouse.com

Time Warner Book Group

Time Warner Book Group, formerly known as Time Warner Trade Publishing, came into existence when Time Inc. and Warner Communications merged in 1990. Domestically, it consists of Warner Books and its various imprints: The Mysterious Press, Warner Vision, Warner Business Books, Aspect, Warner Faith, Warner Forever, and Little, Brown and Company and its various imprints: Little, Brown Adult Trade, Little, Brown Children's Books, Back Bay and Bulfinch Press. In addition, TWBG distributes publishing lines for Hyperion, Arcade, Disney, Harry Abrams, Time Life Books, and Microsoft. In 1996, Little, Brown opened a 750,000-square foot, state-of-the-art warehouse in Lebanon, Indiana. In addition to its New York and Indiana based companies, most of TWBG's back office operations are based in Boston.

Manuscript Submissions and Unsolicited Queries

Publishers in the Time Warner Book Group (including Warner Books, Warner Business Books, Warner Faith, Mysterious Press, Aspect, Little, Brown and Company, Back Bay Books, Bulfinch Press, Little, Brown Children's Books) are not able to consider unsolicited manuscript submissions and unsolicited queries. Many major publishers have a similar policy. Unfamiliar packages and letters mailed to our offices will be returned to sender unopened.

If you are interested in having a manuscript considered for publication, we recommend that you first enlist the services of an established literary agent. Many literary agencies can be located in Bowker's *Literary MarketPlace* (commonly known as the "LMP"), an annual reference publication which can be found in most major libraries. These literary agencies, in turn, have guidelines for submitting manuscripts. You can find out more about the LMP at *Literary MarketPlace.*

Categories: Fiction—Nonfiction

CONTACT: Submissions Editor
Material: All
1271 Ave of the Americas
New York NY 10020

Tom Doherty Associate, LLC
Tor Books, Forge Books, Orb, Starscape

About Tor Books

Tor Books, an imprint of Tom Doherty Associates, LLC, is a New York-based publisher of hardcover and softcover books, founded in 1980 and committed (although not limited) to SF and fantasy literature. Between our extensive hardcover and trade-softcover line, our Orb backlist program, and our stronghold in mass-market paperback, we annually publish what is arguably the largest and most diverse line of SF and fantasy ever produced by a single English-language publisher. Books from Tor have won every major award in the SF and fantasy fields, and for the last fourteen years in a row we have been named Best Publisher in the Locus Poll, the largest consumer poll in SF.

About Forge Books

Forge Books is an imprint of Tom Doherty Associates, and publishes fiction and nonfiction in a wide variety of genres and categories. Its sister imprint Tor Books, while famous for its science fiction and fantasy, also publishes books in other genres.

Here are some good rules to follow when submitting your work to us:

• Do not submit work on disk, tape, or other electronic media; do not submit work by email.

Submit only the first three chapters of your book, and a synopsis of the entire book. (We're not big on query letters, since we can't tell whether we'll like the book until we see a chunk of the manuscript.) And please make sure you send the first three chapters. No matter how good your synopsis is, it's difficult for us to get a good sense of the book from chapters 4, 17, and 32.

• Your cover letter should state the genre of the submission, and previous sales or publications if relevant.

• Never send us the only copy of your book. The U.S. Post Office is no more perfect than the rest of us, and things do get lost in the mail. Always put your name and address on the manuscript. In addition, your name, the manuscript title, and the page number should appear on every page of the manuscript. If you wish your manuscript to be returned, enclose a stamped, self-addressed envelope large enough to hold your submission; publishers are not responsible for returning submissions unaccompanied by return postage. If you do not wish your manuscript to be returned, please say so on the cover letter, and enclose a stamped, self-addressed, business-sized envelope for our reply. If you enclose a stamped, self-addressed postcard, we will return it to verify receipt of the manuscript.

• Type your manuscript on plain white paper, double-spaced, using only one side of the page. Do not staple or otherwise bind your manuscript; a paper clip will suffice. If you use a computer and printer, do not submit low-resolution dot matrix printouts; they will not be read. Please do not use a fancy font (this is almost as difficult to read as the palest dot-matrix), and please make sure you use a font large enough to read easily. Please turn off margin justification and proportional spacing; pages with ragged right margins are easier for us to read, and easier for our production department to set.

• Please indicate italics by underlining and indicate boldface by drawing a wavy line beneath the affected characters. Copy to be typeset needs to be marked in very specific ways, and if you use italics or boldface in the manuscript, they will still need to be marked up by production.

• Please allow at least four to six months for your manuscript to be considered. If you haven't heard from us after four months, and wish to make sure your manuscript got here, please write a letter stating the genre, the date of submission, and the title of the manuscript, rather than calling. We will respond promptly.

• We do not accept simultaneous submissions.

Good luck!

Categories: Fiction—Civil War—Crime—Fantasy—Horror—

Mystery—Occult—Paranormal—Science Fiction—Western

CONTACT: William Smith, Editorial Asst.
Material: General fiction
CONTACT: Fred Herman, Editorial Asst.
Material: Science fiction and fantasy
175 Fifth Ave.
New York NY 10010
Website: www.tor.com

Tor Books

Please refer to Tom Doherty Associate, LLC, in the Book Publishers section.

Tower Publishing

Tower specializes in legal and professional business publications. Submittals should take the form of a listing of chapters offered and at least three sample chapters. The market should be business or legal.
Categories: Nonfiction—Business—Law—Reference

CONTACT: Michael Lyons, Publishers
Material: All
588 Saco Rd.
Standish ME 04084
Phone: 800-969-8693
Fax: 207-642-5463
Website: www.towerpub.com

Towlehouse Publishing Co.

I don't have proposal guidelines per se. Just send me a proposal, period. A cover letter, outline, two sample chapters, and SASE.
Categories: Nonfiction—Sports/Recreation—Golf

CONTACT: Mike Towle, President
Material: All
1312 Bell Grimes Ln.
Nashville TN 37207
Phone: 615-366-9120

Transaction Publishers Rutgers
The State University of New Jersey

Transaction Publishers is widely acknowledged as a major independent publisher of social scientific books, periodicals and serials. Transaction's mission is scholarly and professional inquiry into the nature of society. Transaction offers publications in older, established disciplines such as economics, political science, history, sociology, anthropology, psychology, as well as recently established disciplines ranging from area research to urban studies, policy analysis, philosophy of social science, organizational behavior, and criminology. Located on the campus of Rutgers University in Piscataway, New Jersey, Transaction has strong ties to the traditional mission of American university life as a center of learning, and to applied needs of public and private institutions in social research. Through its many publications, Transaction promotes mutually beneficial exchanges between academic and professional life.
Guidelines
Formal guidelines not available.
Send queries or book proposals to below address.
Categories: Nonfiction—Society—International Criminal Law

CONTACT: Heike Fenton

Material: All
35 Berrue Circle
Piscataway NJ 08854
Phone: 732-445-2280
E-mail: ihorowitz@transactionpub.com
Website: www.transactionpub.com

Transnational Publishers, Inc.

Transnational is an independent publishing firm that has been producing material for the international community for over twenty years. We are distinguished for our well-crafted publications written by leading authorities on human rights law, public and private international law, international organizations, criminal law, dispute resolution, trade law, legal research, comparative law, taxation, foreign affairs, and political theory.

Transnational publications are innovative and thought provoking, provide need-to know information for legal practice, and explore the cutting edge of contemporary affairs. Scholars, students, and practitioners examining and working in the international arena will find Transnational publications significant resources.

For authors who wish to investigate publishing their work with Transnational, we offer a thorough review of proposed projects with a decision to publish within a month of submission. If we do agree to collaborate, authors will experience an open and cooperative atmosphere where they will be asked to be involved in all stages of production and marketing.

Our production process is set up to assure quality publications. Manuscripts are evaluated upon receipt and assigned to appropriate editors for copy editing. Once the edits have been approved by an author projects are sent to composition. The resulting page proof is sent to the author for review. When all corrections have been made and index completed, the book goes to press. In most cases a book will be published six weeks after going to the printer. We expedite the production of all projects but will work closely with authors who need to have a work available by a certain date.

The marketing of publications is of great concern to authors. As a publisher focused on the issues of international law and global affairs, Transnational is experienced in reaching those worldwide audiences seeking resources in these areas. We employ direct mail campaigns, an e-commerce enabled web site, internet booksellers, and an international network of agents and distributors to assure Transnational publications receive maximum exposure.

All Transnational books are sent out for review by major journals.
Categories: Anthropology,—African-American, Criminology, Environment—Economics—Political Science—Policy and Evaluation Research—Management and Organization—Penology—Psychology—Sociology—Reference—Urban Studies

CONTACT: Submissions Editor
Material: All
410 Saw Mill River Rd.
Ardsley NY 10503
Phone: 914-693-5100
Website: www.transnationalpubs.com

Tricycle Press

Please refer to Ten Speed Press.

The Trinity Foundation

No formal guidelines, but publishes only books consistent with Westminster Confession of Faith.
Categories: Nonfiction—Book Reviews—Christian Interests—Culture—Economics—Education—Government—History—Human

Books
M-Z

Rights—Law—Politics—Religion—Science—Textbooks

CONTACT: Dr. John Robbins
Material: All
PO Box 68
Unicoi TN 37692
Phone: 423-743-0199
Fax: 423-743-2005
Website: www.trinityfoundation.org

Trinity Press International

Profile
Academic and trade religion titles. Titles: 30 per year, many from first time authors. Hardcover and paperback publisher. Accepts unsolicited mss. Response time: 2-6 weeks.

Editorial Focus
Trinity Press International publishes serious books on Bible and theology for a broad range of readers. Its books offer enlightening perspectives of biblical, cultural, ethical, theological, and religious issues. Trinity Press International publishes books that address many of humanity's deepest questions. Specific categories include biblical studies, theology, religion and science, religion and culture, and ethics. Trinity Press International seeks to publish books that express diverse biblical and theological views.

Submission and Payment Policy
Submit query with one page synopsis of the book, an annotated table of contents, one page comparing the book to others like it on the market, a resume, an introduction to the book, and one sample chapter to Henry L. Carrigan, Jr. More detailed submission guidelines are available from Henry L. Carrigan, Jr. Include a self-addressed mailer with adequate postage so the proposal can be returned at a later date. Manuscripts originating outside the USA will not be returned. Simultaneous submissions should be identified. Advances on royalties are negotiable and paid on signing of contract and final ms. submission.

Book Catalog
Call 1-800-877-0012 for a free copy.

Guidelines for Submitting a Book Proposal
Author Information. Name, mailing address, and daytime phone number. Enclose a current vita which indicates your present position, educational background, previous publications, and why you are qualified to write the book you are proposing.

Title of the Book. Indicate the tentative title of the book with possible alternative titles.

Description of the Book. In 250-500 words, summarize the book you are proposing. What is the nature, focus, purpose, or argument of the book? What is its thesis? Write the summary as if it were on the back cover of the book convincing a potential reader to buy this book. What unique contributions to the subject does this manuscript provide?

Audience. For what audience, specifically, is the book written: lay person? pastors, or other religious professionals? college students? seminary/graduate school students? professors? Why does someone need to read this book? Does the book have potential for textbook adoption? If so, in what courses?

Competition. Are there competing titles? If so, what are they? What does your book offer that these competing titles do not? How will your book be superior to or different from them?

Table of Contents. Give a tentative table of contents of the book by chapters. Beneath each chapter title, give a brief outline of the chapter and a brief summary of its contents. This summary should explain the focus and development of the chapter and indicate how the chapter advances the argument of the whole book.

Manuscript Length. What is the estimated length of the proposed manuscript, printed double-spaced on 8½" x 11" paper with 1" margins and 12-point type size?

Sample Pages. Enclose a sample of 15-25 pages, perhaps of the introduction or first chapter, which illustrates your writing style. These should be pages that are typical of the book as a whole, especially critical to your argument, potentially controversial, or that give an overview of the book.

Manuscript Submission. If your proposal is accepted and a complete manuscript requested, you should plan to submit a hard copy of the manuscript together with a 3½" disk in IBM or MAC compatible text files. Indicate what program and version you have used.

Completion Date. Indicate the date your would expect to submit a completed manuscript.

Categories: Nonfiction—Biography—Christian Interests—Culture—Religion—Spiritual

CONTACT: Henry Carrigan, Editorial Director
Material: All
4775 Linglestown Rd
Harrisburg PA 17112
Phone: 717-541-8130

Truman State University Press

TSUP specializes in sixteenth century/early modern studies; American Studies, focusing on environmental history, regional/Midwest studies, and presidential histories; and poetry. Within American studies we publish both for the scholarly audience and the more general reader.

TSUP holds an annual poetry competition, the T. S. Eliot Prize, for the best unpublished book-length collection of poetry in English, in honor of native MissourianT. S. Eliot's considerable intellectual and artistic legacy. A $2,000 award and publication is given to the winner.

For nonfiction manuscripts, please submit a short, informative letter of inquiry with:
- a clear and concise description of your book and its notable features
- your intended audience for the book
- the current status of the manuscript and expected completion date
- the length, number of illustrations, tables, appendices
- a table of contents
- a preface, introduction, or other brief sample of your manuscript
- your curriculum vitae or biographical notes

If the press is interested, you will be invited to submit the complete manuscript. All manuscripts considered for publication are peer reviewed.

T. S. Eliot Prize manuscripts should be between 60 and 100 typed pages of original poetry in English. Each poem should begin on a separate page. Include two title pages: one with name, address, phone number, and manuscript title; one with only the manuscript title.

(Your name must not appear in the manuscript, since the poet's identity should not be known to the judge.) Include a table of contents and a list of acknowledgments for previously published individual poems, if applicable. Enclose a self-addressed, stamped envelope to be notified when we receive your manuscript. (No other postage-paid envelopes are necessary.) All entrants will receive notice of the results. Manuscripts will not be returned. Please do not send your only copy. Include $25 for the reading fee. Make checks payable to Truman State University Press. If you prefer to pay by Visa or MasterCard include your credit card number, expiration date, cardholder name, and signature. Manuscripts should be unbound, placed in manila file folder and mailer.

Categories: Nonfiction—History—Poetry—Regional—Religion

CONTACT: Nancy Rediger, Director
Material: All

100 E. Normal St.
Kirksville MO 63501-4221
Phone: 660-785-7336, 800-916-6802
Fax: 660-785-4480
E-mail: tsup@truman.edu
Website: tsup.truman.edu

Turtle Press

Turtle Press publishes a wide variety of books in the areas of sports, martial arts, Eastern philosophy, and self-improvement. While we are open to a broad range of topics, we prefer that a manuscript be tightly focused and give thorough coverage to its subject.

Please query with a self-addressed stamped envelope before submitting a proposal. Your query letter will be answered within two to three weeks.

If requested to submit a proposal, please send the following:
a. outline or summary
b. table of contents
c. two to four sample chapters, including chapter one
d. market potential for the proposed manuscript
e. author credentials
f. sample photos or artwork
g. availability of manuscript on disk, including format
h. postage paid return envelope

Materials should be submitted on 8½" x 11" white paper, double spaced. Please allow two to four weeks for a response. Materials sent without a postage paid return envelope will not be returned.

Thank you for your interest in Turtle Press.

Categories: Nonfiction—Asian-American—New Age—Physical Fitness—Sports/Recreation

CONTACT: Cynthia Kim, Acquisitions Editor
Material: All
Turtle Press 91 Holmes Rd
Newington CT 06111

Two Dot

Please refer to Falcon Publishing.

Unity House

Unity House is a publishing imprint of Unity School of Christianity, a nondenominational religious organization founded more than one hundred years ago. It publishes books, cassettes and CDs both for and beyond the churches and congregants of the worldwide Unity movement.

Unity teachings are based on metaphysical interpretation of scriptures with an emphasis on practical application, and the demonstration of the spiritual Truth of life as taught by Jesus Christ as well as other spiritual masters. If you would like further information about Unity's teachings and beliefs, please contact Customer Service at the address on the last page of this brochure, or call 1-800-669-0282, 7:30-4:30 CST, Monday thru Thursday.

WHAT WE'RE LOOKING FOR

We publish spiritual books based on Unity principles, as well as inspirational books on self-help psychology and practical spirituality. All manuscripts must reflect a spiritual foundation and express the Unity philosophy of practical Christianity using universal principles, and/or metaphysics. We're looking for complete manuscripts.

In reviewing manuscripts, one of the first things we consider is whether or not the subject would be appropriate for a person on a path of enlightenment and wholeness. The subject should be dealt with in such a way as to inform and uplift the reader, give hope, and assist with practical advice on meeting life's challenges creatively and positively. Emphasis should be on practical application of spiritual principles in everyday living. The following will give you an idea of a few of our editorial interests:

Nonfiction: Bible interpretation, biblical studies, comparative religion, Eastern thought, family, finances, holistic health, humor, inspiration, leadership, meditation, marriage, mythology, New Thought, philosophy, parenting, personal experience, prayer, recovery, renewal, spirituality, transpersonal psychology, and young adult issues

Fiction: Visionary fiction for adults based on Unity principles

Some of our current titles and authors include: *Looking in for Number One* by Alan Cohen; *The Quest for Wholeness* by Robert Brumet; *The Vortex Shift* by Mario De Ferrari; *That's Just How My Spirit Travels* by Rosemary Fillmore Rhea; *Henrietta the Homely Duckling* by Phil Hahn and illustrated by Joe Coker, Jr.; *Angels Sing in Me* by James Dillet Freeman.

WHAT YOU SHOULD INCLUDE IN A PROPOSAL

Please send full manuscript only

• A brief cover letter introducing yourself and a brief biographical resume describing your writing, education, and religious background

• A summary highlighting your proposal and its compelling, unique features–include suggested sales and publicity strategies

• Complete manuscript.

• Self-addressed, stamped envelope (necessary for returns)

WHEN WE APPROVE FOR YOUR MANUSCRIPT

If you quote an individual source more than casually (roughly more that 200 words in 200 pages of manuscript–less than this will usually constitute "fair use"), then you must seek formal permission from the publisher of your source. Furthermore, this guideline is not a legal guarantee of fair use nor a protection that we are offer as the publisher. Receiving permission to quote copyrighted material is your responsibility, and you are responsible for paying any fees (usually minimal) for this. Your manuscript draft will not be considered final until we have received a copy of each permission for our files.

All quotes must be verified by sending us a photocopy of the page on which the quote appears as well as a photocopy of the work's title and copyright page. If we cannot verify your quote, then we cannot use it. Please be sure all quoted material is quoted exactly.

If in your text you are referring to facts or statistics that are not easily verifiable with a good encyclopedia, world almanac, or unabridged dictionary, we require that you send us a copy of your source reference. This will help us assure that your book will be accurate.

We prefer to have Bible quotations conform to the *New Revised Standard Version*, but we will accept other translations if their version better makes your textual point. Please identify which version you are using.

We do not solicit artwork or graphic design. However, if your manuscript requires specific photographs that you can furnish, we will be happy to consider them. You are also responsible for providing an index or illustrations if you wish the book to have them.

IF WE PUBLISH YOUR MANUSCRIPT

After substantive editing is complete, expect publication in nine months. Payment contracts vary for the individual author. Copyrights are registered in the author's name.

Thank you for your interest in publishing through Unity House. If you have further questions regarding book publishing, please feel free to contact us.

Categories: Fiction—Nonfiction—New Age—Religion—Spiritual—New Thought/Metaphysical

CONTACT: BOOKS ACQUISITIONS
Material: All
Unity House
1901 NW Blue Parkway
Unity Village MO 64065-0001
Phone: 816-524-3550, ext. 3300
Fax: 816-251-3552
Website: www.unityonline.org

University of Idaho Press

The University of Idaho Press publishes titles in history and regional studies, Native American studies, folklore, western literature and literary criticism, natural sciences, and resource and policy studies. Individuals wishing to submit manuscripts should first request a current catalog to determine if the work fits the publishing program. If an author feels his or her work is appropriate for the UI Press, a cover letter explaining the purpose of the manuscript and the audience for which the book is intended should be sent along with a contents page, an introduction or preliminary chapter, and a bibliography indicating sources used.

When the director requests the entire manuscript for review, it should be prepared according to recommendations in *The Chicago Manual of Style*, Fourteenth Edition, *The Essential Guide for Writers, Editors, and Publishers* (Chicago and London: The University of Chicago Press, 1993) in all respects, including notes and bibliography. If you have followed another style guide in preparing the manuscript, please include that information when you submit the manuscript.

Please adhere to the following general guidelines:

1. Submit your manuscript on white 8 1/2 by 11 inch paper with all copy double spaced, including bibliographies, notes, and extracts (to distinguish extracts from text, draw a line next to the quoted material or use a second level of indent).

2. Include photocopies of all photographs or illustrations and indicate their approximate location in the text by numbering them consecutively and writing or circling the numbers in the left margin of the text.

3. Include all tables and indicate their location by using call-outs in the text (see *The Chicago Manual of Style*).

4. Hand number all pages consecutively in the upper right corner beginning with the first page and ending with the last page of the manuscript.

5. Use default settings and keep all special formatting to a minimum (i.e., chapter titles should be flush left in the upper and lowercase with bold or italic; subheads within chapters should be presented the same way and level of importance indicated by writing A, B, C circled in the left margin next to the headings).

6. Have the text unjustified.

7. Have no running heads or embedded page numbers.

8. Have consistent use of the tab key for paragraph indents.

9. Use one underlining command (not the italic code) for all words in a phrase (i.e., underline at the beginning of the first word and turn off the underline at the end of the last word).

10. Use the numeral 1, not the letter l, in all numbering.

11. Have notes grouped together in one or more files, numbered by chapter, double-spaced and paragraph indented, with no extra space between notes. Do not use on-page footnotes even if your software has this feature.

12. Please include a list of accented letters or special characters and hand-marked diacriticals instead of embedded diacritical marks.

The manuscript will be reviewed in-house. If the work seems a likely candidate for publication, it will be submitted to two or more readers. The readers may suggest the need for revisions and subsequent readings prior to the manuscript being presented to the editorial board, or the manuscript may be rejected at this stage. The editorial board provides final approval for all titles published by the UI Press.

Thank you for your interest in the University of Idaho Press. Please contact us if you have any questions.

Categories: Nonfiction—Folklore—History—Human Rights—Literature—Native American—Regional—Science

CONTACT: Candace J. Akins, Managing Editor
Material: All
PO Box 444416
Moscow ID 83844-4416
Phone: 208-885-3300
E-mail: candacea@uidaho.edu
Website: www.uidaho.edu/uipress

University of Maine Press

The University of Maine Press publishes scholarly books and original writing which focus on the intellectual concerns of the Maine region. Although the press occasionally publishes works of regional fiction (and works of nonfiction which are outside of its regional focus) the press is primarily interested in publishing scholarly studies in the sciences, the social sciences, and the humanities.

An author who is considering the University of Maine Press should send a letter of inquiry, a synopsis, and—if appropriate—a few representative chapters or sections from the manuscript of the proposed book. The entire manuscript should not be sent to the press with the initial inquiry. An author should not send the only copy of anything to the press. Although the press will make every effort to safeguard what it receives, it cannot be held responsible for lost manuscripts. A stamped envelope should be included with the letter and supportive material.

Since proposals for books need to be considered by the Director of the Press, the Board of Directors and outside expert readers, a thorough consideration of the initial manuscript material may take several months. The Director of the Press will make every attempt to expedite this process.

Inquires should be sent to Michael Alpert, Director of the Press. Correspondence about the status of a proposal should also be sent to the Director of the Press at the address below.

All manuscript material should be presented in a legible typeface, with ample margins and double line-spacing, to facilitate reading and annotation. Manuscript material in obvious need of basic copy-editing will not be considered by the press. In general, authors should prepare manuscript material by following the guidelines in *The Chicago Manual of Style* or a comparable standard style-manual in the author's discipline. Approved manuscripts must be submitted in hardcopy form and in Microsoft Word or a comparable electronic file that can be imported into commonly-used publishing software. AUG. 2002

Categories: Nonfiction—Agriculture—Arts—Biography—Civil War—History—Regional

CONTACT: Michael Alpert, Director of the Press
Material: All
126A College Ave.
Orono ME 04473
Phone: 207-866-0573
Fax: 207-866-2084

University of Nebraska Press

The University of Nebraska Press publishes in the following areas:

· Fiction (in series only: Flyover Fiction, *Prairie Schooner Book Prize in Fiction, Native Storiers*)
· Food and wine
· French colonial history
· Great Plains studies
· Native peoples of North America
· Histories and literatures of the U.S. West
· History of anthropology, archaeology, and comparative anthropology
· History of space flight
· Jewish studies
· Latin American studies
· Literature in translation
· Literary nonfiction
· Military history
· Reprints of classic science fiction and fantasy
· Sports history and culture
· U.S. Civil War studies

Submitting a Proposal

Why do a proposal?

1. An editor is intrigued by your cover letter but does not want to commit to reading an entire manuscript. She or he asks for a proposal, sometimes also a chapter sample.

2. You are a published author trying to nail down a contract for a new book before committing the time (and sometimes getting grant money) to write it. After discussions with an editor, you send a proposal in the hopes that the proposal will prove acceptable to the Press, be supported by outside readers, and become the basis of an advance contract.

3. You are an editor of a contributed volume trying to nail down a contract for the volume before asking your contributors to either write their chapters or revise them. Your proposal, like the second scenario above, is intended to become the basis of an advance contract if it proves acceptable to the Press and outside readers.

What goes into a proposal?

1. Your CV, and the CVs of your contributors, if this is an edited volume. Do not pad the CV; include essential information about occupation, education, publications, and papers.

2. Overview / Summary of the Project. In not more than 5 double-spaced pages, describe in concise, clear language:
· The content of the work. What is it about? Get to the point and don't ramble. Say what needs to be said and move on.
· The organizational plan behind the work. How does the work cohere as a whole? How do the chapters connect to one another? This issue is particularly critical for edited volumes (especially those arising from symposia), where chapters tend to be of inconsistent quality and do not hang together well as a book.
· The scholarly significance and context of the work. Why does it need to be published? Why would anyone care to read it? How does it connect to and depart from current scholarship in this area? It is very important in your proposal that you depict the content and significance of the work as accurately as possible. An editor needs to know exactly what is being offered; if you misrepresent the work at this stage, sooner or later either the Press or reviewers will see the discrepancy and reject the manuscript.

3. Format / Specifications of the Project. Address these topics, if relevant:
· The length or projected length of the work (assuming double-spaced manuscript pages, in 12 pt. Courier)
· The number and type of illustrations, photos, maps, tables
· The possibility of subvention sources to support publication
· The possibility of text, illustrations, maps, or tables being produced camera-ready

4. Timetable. If the work has not been written, when will it be completed if an advance contract is offered? If the work is finished, how soon could it be sent to the Press for review if an editor is interested in looking at it?

5. Audience/Market. Who will read and buy this book? Be realistic about its audience. Don't misrepresent the appeal of the work. If it is a monograph that will be read by other scholars in your profession, state its prospects up front and let an editor decide whether his or her Press is interested in that type of book and in acquiring in that field of scholarship.

6. Fit with the Press's List of Publications. Explain how the proposed work would fit in with the current publishing strategy and efforts of the Press.
· Is the Press a leading publisher in this field of scholarship and/or subject matter covered by the proposed book?
· Does the Press publish the type of book you are proposing (for example, a monograph, memoir, primary source)?
· Does the Press publish the type of scholarship / interpretive theory you are proposing? For example, does it do cutting edge, theoretical work in your field of scholarship and is this the type of book you are proposing? If so, mention this resonance. It shows your knowledge of the Press and sensitivity to its concerns.

7. Detailed Chapter Outline. Summarize each chapter in some detail, giving about 1-2 paragraphs for each chapter. Discuss content and how each chapter fits into the organizational plan of the book as a whole.

8. Sample Bibliography. List complete references for all works cited in your proposal and provide additional bibliography as needed to demonstrate your knowledge of the field.

9. Sample Chapters. If such are available, provide one or two chapter drafts that are representative of the work as a whole.

Send your proposal to address listed at the end.

Copyright and Permission Information

Author   _____
Title   _____
Contributor   _____

We need the following information in order to ensure that previously copyrighted material is properly acknowledged in your book. Thank you for taking the time to supply complete and accurate answers.

Have any portions of your manuscript previously been published? ( )Yes ( )No

If so, where? (Please specify the chapters or portions of your manuscript that have appeared in print, and, for each, the title under which it was published, the title of the journal or book, and full publishing information—volume number, season or month, year, and page numbers for periodicals; place of publication, publisher, year, and page numbers for books.)

Permission is required for the use of two kinds of copyrighted material; your own material that has previously been published and copyrighted by someone other than yourself; and other people's material that is in copyright and does not come under the principle of fair use. Most quotations from copyrighted sources are covered by fair use; most tables, maps, graphs, and other items of illustrative material are not. If in doubt whether permission is required for a particular item, please check with your editor. Unnecessarily requesting permission endangers the principle of fair use. Please send copies of letters granting you permission for the use of copyrighted material so that we can see that any special requirements with regard to form of credit, gratis copies, cropping, and so forth are fulfilled.

Formatting Your Final Manuscript

In preparing electronic files, simpler is better. Your manuscript (MS) will be easier for us to work with if it does not include extra styles and formatting. Please do not use hidden text, the indexing feature, the table-of-contents generator, or other sophisticated features of your word-processing program. We prefer that you prepare your MS follow-

**Books
M-Z**

ing these general guidelines:

File setup

Use the same software from beginning to end. We accept files saved as Word or Word Perfect documents or saved in rich text format (RTF).

Do not put the entire MS in one file:

Save the preliminary pages (table of contents, preface, acknowledgments) together in a single file.

Save each chapter as a separate file. Include the chapter number in the file name (e.g., 00prelim, 01chap1, 02chap2), so they fall in order. If your MS contains part divisions, place each part-title page before the chapter it precedes, in the same electronic file.

Page setup

Set all margins (top, bottom, left, and right) to 1 inch.

Use left justification, not full justification. Begin all paragraphs with a single tab.

Number the pages of the MS straight through from beginning to end; do not number the pages of each chapter independently or use roman numerals for introductory matter. Do not use headers to insert chapter names or numbers, or dates.

Text formatting

Set all parts of the MS in double-spaced 12-point Courier or Courier New.

Avoid boldface, small caps, or other font formatting.

Do not use the styles feature of your word processing program to format headings, extracts, epigraphs, or other sections of the MS; use "normal" style throughout the text.

Do not use automatic hyphenation; the only hyphens in your MS should be those required by the conventions of spelling and grammar.

Do not add extra lines between paragraphs.

Headings and section breaks

Ensure that headings are treated consistently.

Make different subhead levels easy to distinguish from one another (e.g., first level centered, second level flush left).

Use title-style capitalization, not full caps, for subheadings.

If you wish to include a space break to indicate a change of subject, type "" on its own line between paragraphs.

If you have text that needs to start on a new page, insert a page break (Ctrl + Enter) rather than adding extra hard returns to carry the text to a new page.

Extracts

Prose quotations of 100 words or more should be set off from the text with an extra line before and after the extract. Quotations of less than 100 words should be run into the body of the text.

Verse quotations of more than two lines should be set off from the text with an extra line before and after the extract. If the extract requires special spacing, provide a photocopy of the original showing the correct line spacing and alignment.

Notes and bibliography

Begin note numbering with "1" for each chapter.

Set note numbers in the text as superscript. In the notes section, set note numbers on the line (not superscript).

Do not insert extra hard returns before or after each note in the notes section. Use the same formatting as for the text.

Use the hanging indent feature to format the bibliography. Do not insert tabs, hard returns, or spaces to achieve a hanging indent.

Illustrations

Suggest placement for figures, tables, maps, and other illustrations, using call-outs in the text: "<Figure 1 about here>," "<Table 1 about here>."

Create separate files for tables and figures. Do not insert them into the main text.

Include, at the end of the MS, a printout of each table or figure on its own page. Make certain that the printout shows the accurate layout of the tables, such as proper alignment of columns.

Provide table, figure, and map captions, including source and credit lines, in a captions file.

If you are providing instructions for us to prepare a map, include a file that contains a list of all labels that should be used on the map, grouped according to type of element (e.g., list rivers together, state names together, towns and cities together).

Printouts and disks

Submit files on a CD or 3.5" diskette, labeled with your last name, manuscript title, the date, and the word-processing program, with version number.

Submit two hard copies of the MS.

Make sure that the files you submit on disk match exactly the hard copy printouts that you submit. That is, print out the hard copy of the final manuscript only after you have made all corrections to the computer files.

Make sure that all the elements of your manuscript are on the disks you send to us. This includes all chapters, all preliminary matter, notes and bibliography, all captions, and lists of labels for any maps that we are preparing.

If you have questions about these guidelines or are concerned that following them will require a great deal of your time, please contact your acquisitions editor or call the press at (402) 472-3581 and ask to speak with a member of the Manuscript Editorial Department, who will be able to answer questions, offer some assistance with your word-processing software, or explain which of the items discussed here are most critical.

University of Nebraska Press Manuscript Checklist

Before you submit the final version of your manuscript, please complete the following checklist.

Author_____

Title   of   manuscript_____

Manuscript Format

____1. 1-inch margins

____2. Left justification

____3. 12-point Courier

____4. Double-spaced throughout

____5. Pages are numbered consecutively through the manuscript

____6. No extra lines between paragraphs; space breaks indicating subject changes are marked

____7. Subheading levels are easy to distinguish

____8. Prose and verse extracts are set off from text (follow 100-word rule)

____9. Notes begin with 1 in each chapter

____10. Note numbers are superscript in the text and on the baseline in the notes

____11. Chapters are saved as separate electronic files

For specific, detailed instructions see Formatting Your Final Manuscript

Art

____1. Originals and photocopies are included

____2. Captions explain content and contain credit lines

____3. Numbering coincides with captions list and call-outs in the text

____4. List of illustrations includes all elements (photos, maps, tables, etc.)

____5. Call-outs are inserted in the manuscript

For specific, detailed instructions see UNP's art preparation guidelines (blue sheets)

Other

____1. Preliminary pages (table of contents, dedication, acknowledgments) are included

____2. Chapter titles in text match the table of contents exactly

____3. Notemarkers in the text and the notes themselves match exactly and none are missing, repeated, or out of order

____4. Direct quotations have been checked against their sources, and source citations in the notes have been checked against the bibliography

What to Send

1. 2 copies of the final printout
2. Disks, labeled with software used
3. Originals and photocopies of all art
4. Previously Published Work form
5. Photocopies of permissions for text and art
6. Author Information Form (if not submitted electronically)
7. This checklist

Preparing Your Index

The following instructions are based on University of Nebraska Press house style, which follows chapter 18 of the *Chicago Manual of Style*, 15th edition (hereafter CMS); many of them, however, are standard guidelines for an index submitted to any university press. Please note that some instructions may not be relevant for the topic of your book. If you think your index would serve your readers better in an alternate format, please consult your project editor. An index submitted to the press that does not follow these guidelines will be edited to conform to them. It's always a good idea to run a draft of your index by your project editor.

Please use the following formats:

· letter-by-letter alphabetization (see *CMS* 18.57);

· lowercase for words that are lowercase in the text (if a word appears both capitalized and lowercased in the text, index as lowercase so that readers know that they will be looking for a lowercased term on some pages);

· extra space between alphabet breaks;

· underlining for words that should be set in italics;

· run-in style for subheadings (see CMS 18.24);

· hanging indent (that is, the first line of the entry should be on the margin, the rest of the lines should be indented);

· no end punctuation;

· double-spaced, single (page-width) column, in non-proportional font.

There is no prescribed length for an index: some texts warrant a detailed index, others need only a short, simple one. CMS suggests that the length of a typical scholarly index is usually about 2 to 5 percent of the length of the text. Since indexes are usually set in two columns and in a typeface smaller than that in the text, your draft index can be up to about 10 percent of the length of your original manuscript. Another way to gauge length is by number of entries: five or six references per text page will yield a fairly short, basic index; fifteen to twenty references per page will make a long, more comprehensive index. Keep in mind that it's easier to cut entries than to add them, so it;s better to err on the side of inclusion in the beginning.

Choose your main entries and subheadings carefully. Put yourself in the position of your reader and try to determine what terms and concepts would be most useful for someone using your book. Likewise, consider what terms a potential reader would want to search for in your book.

Main entries and subheadings should all lead to a discussion of the subject, not to peripheral references. Readers should be directed only to a page on which they will find significant information on a topic, not just a passing mention. Main entries will almost always be nouns; adjectives alone should not be main entries but should modify nouns, and verbs should use the gerund form (e.g., use running rather than run).

Avoid solidus constructions in main entries and subheadings (e.g., religion/religiosity): the reader will not know whether to interpret such entries as x and y, x or y, or x and/or y. Choose one heading, make the entries separate, or make one a cross-reference of the other.

For titles beginning with articles in any language, we prefer that the articles be left at the head of the title rather than inverted ("The End," not "End, The"; La dolce vita, not dolce vita, La); of course, the articles should be ignored in alphabetization.

If discussion of a topic continues for more than a page, join the first and last page of the discussion with a hyphen: 344-405. If a topic appears on consecutive pages, but other topics intervene between the

mentions, provide the individual page numbers, separated by commas: 127, 128, 129.

Please follow *CMS* number style (see *CMS* 18.13) when eliding consecutive numbers*:

200-204 (first number is an even hundred; do not elide)
206-7 (both numbers x01 through x09, in multiples of a hundred)
198-203
67-92
3-20
178-81

* Exception: if your book used MLA or APA style, use that style for eliding consecutive numbers in the index.

Subheadings

· Alphabetize your subheadings, but disregard introductory articles, prepositions, and conjunctions (see *CMS* 18.66). Example: justice: for eternity, 123, 139; and the past, 45, 59

· It is best to furnish at least one subheading for every five to ten references (a range of pages, such as 53-58, is considered one reference).

· Subheadings should have a logical and grammatical relationship to the main entry (see *CMS* 18.9). Usually a conjunction or a preposition will suffice as a link. The subheading should not repeat the main heading.

· Readers should be able to find topics with a quick scan, so subheadings should be concise-three or four words are usually enough. The key word should be the first word or the first word after the conjunction or preposition that links the subheading to the main heading. More often than not, modifiers are unnecessary. You need only guide readers to the topic; it is not necessary to tell readers what argument they will find on the page. Example: in a book of literary criticism, under the heading "aesthetics," the subheading "imitation vs. invention as fundamental modern problem of" could be shortened to "imitation vs. invention in" or "fundamental modern problem of," depending on which concept is more important, and the reader will find the full argument.

· If subheadings include dates or numbers (such as military regiments), it is acceptable to sort them in chronological or numerical order; in this case, numerical subheadings should precede alphabetical subheadings. Example: allotment, xiv-xv, 18-19; and 1882 legislation, xiv, 16-17; and Dawes Act, 4, Alternatively, dates and numbers may be alphabetized as if spelled out. Example: allotment, xiv-xv, 18-19; and Dawes Act, 4; and 1882 legislation, xiv, 16-17

· If all subheadings for an entry reflect a sequence of time, a chronological rather than an alphabetical arrangement can be used. Example: Minch, Mary: birth of, 12; childhood of, 16-34, 126; at art school, 6, 38-60; and death of parents, 55

· A subheading that introduces an author's works should appear after all other subheadings, on a new line, preceded by an em-dash (two hyphens) and the word "Works": Example:Benjamin, Walter, 9, 10; and assimilation, 108, 111; on memory, 121-31; on modernity, 106-7; on Zionism, 109, 112—Works: Berliner Chronik, 130; Moscow Diary, 144

Cross-references

· Cross-references should exactly match the entry they lead to.

· Guard against blind cross-references, that is, a cross-reference that leads to an entry with no page references. For example, if an entry for "German shepherd" says "See dogs," the entry "dogs" should include page references, not an additional cross-reference such as "See household pets."

· Avoid generic cross-references such as See also individual examples. Such cross-references require the reader to guess at these examples, and a non-expert reader may not know the precise terminology you have used.

· If the cross-reference is to be italicized (for example, a title or foreign word), See or See also can be left roman. Example: See *War and Peace*

· A string of cross-references should be listed in alphabetical order, with entries separated by semicolons. Example: See also Brown, John; grave: moldering in (note that the second cross-reference leads to the subheading "moldering in" under the main headine "grave")

UNP style for indexing titles of works

· If the work was published only in a language other than English and is referred to in the text by its original title, please use only the original title in the index. First references to such works generally offer a translation for convenience, set in roman type with no quotation marks and with sentence, rather than title, capitalization; this translation need not appear in the index.

· If the work has been published in English (English title given in quotation marks or italics, with title capitalization) and is generally referred to in the text by its English title, please use only the English title in the index.

· If any work is presented as having been published in translation (English title in quotes or italics, with title capitalization) but is referred to in the text by its original title, use the original title in the index, followed by the translated title in parentheses. Please call any such cases to our attention.

· For titles beginning with articles in any language, we prefer that the articles be left at the head of the title rather than inverted; of course, they should be ignored in alphabetization.

UNP style for indexing notes

Index the chapter endnotes only when they present information, other than bibliographic information, that is not found in the text (see *CMS* 18.111).

· Indexed word or phrase appears in a single note: Example: 177n1, . . .

· Indexed word or phrase appears in consecutive notes: Example: 177nn1-3, . . .

· Indexed word or phrase appears in nonconsecutive notes: Example: 177n1, 177n3, 177n7, . . .

UNP style for indexing illustrations

Our usual style is to underline page references on which illustrations appear:

· Indexed word or phrase refers only to an illustration: Example: 27, 28

· Indexed word or phrase appears in main text and refers to an illustration on the same page: Example: 27, 27-28

Your book is unique, and as you complete your index you will probably come upon a situation not mentioned here. As always, don't hesitate to get in touch with your project editor if you have any questions.

Categories: Nonfiction—African-American—Agriculture—Arts—Biography—Civil War—Conservation—Culture—Ecology—Environment—Feminism—Film/Video—Government—Hispanic—History—Jewish Interest—Language—Literature—Military—Music—Native American—Politics—Psychology—Regional—Rural America—Sports/Recreation—Western—Women's Issues—Ethnic—Philosophy—Public Policy

CONTACT: Ladette Randolph, Associate Director
Material: All
1111 Lincoln Mall
Lincoln NE 68588-0630
Phone: 402-472-3584
Fax: 402-472-0308
E-mail: lrandolph@unl.edu
Website: www.unp.unl.edu

University of Nevada Press

The University of Nevada Press is a public service division of the Nevada System of Higher Education. Its mission is to make a contribution to the State of Nevada, as well as to the national and international scholarly communities, by publishing books in the humanities, sciences, and social sciences that deal with the history, literature, natural history and resources, environment, economy, politics, anthropology, ethnic groups and cultures of Nevada and the West; the Basque people of Europe and the Americas; Native Americans; gambling and commercial gaming; and contemporary affairs.

In addition to books of general and scholarly interest, the Press publishes seven distinguished series of books: the Basque Series; the Wilbur S. Shepperson Series in Nevada History; the Western Literature Series; the Max C. Fleischmann Series in Great Basin Natural History; and the Gambling Studies Series. The Press also publishes original fiction, and creative nonfiction; and books on regional themes for a general audience.

INITIAL REVIEW

We ask authors interested in submitting their work to the University of Nevada Press to send us first a manuscript proposal, which should consist of a table of contents; a summary or chapter outline of the manuscript; information about its length, number and type of illustrations (if any are planned), and any special components, such as footnotes, bibliography, appendices, tables, glossaries, etc.; information about the book's intended audience and any competing works already in publication; and a representative sample section of the text, consisting of a chapter or two, or in the case of short fiction, a couple of sample stories. A brief vita of the author should accompany this material.

Once we have reviewed the proposal, we shall, if the project seems suited for our publishing program, invite the author to submit the entire manuscript for formal consideration.

FORMAL REVIEW

When we invite an author to submit a full manuscript for our consideration, we ask for two clean paper copies of the entire manuscript, including all notes, bibliography, appendices, and any other components.

If the book is to include illustrations, please send only photocopies at this time.

If the manuscript exists on an electronic disk, we do not need to have access to the disk during the review process. If the manuscript exists only on paper, please provide us with two clear photocopies.

Do not bind the manuscript or enclose it in a binder. Double-space everything (all text, quotations, footnotes, bibliography, figure captions, tables, lists, appendices, etc.). Number the pages consecutively from the beginning to the end of the manuscript. Long quotations (10 lines or more) should be indented an extra five spaces. Use paragraph indents if the quotations were indented in the original. Notes should be placed at the end of the manuscript (not at the bottoms of the pages or ends of the chapters).

Photographs, figures, charts, graphs, tables, etc., should be on separate pages, not on pages with text.

Authors of manuscripts that contain illustrations or large amounts of quoted material and editors of anthologies will be responsible, if the Press makes a publishing commitment, for obtaining all necessary permissions to reprint and for paying any related fees. Fiction authors should include information about any previous publication of this material, including date of first publication and titles of venue.

If the Press makes a publishing offer, the author is required to provide two paper copies of the final draft of the manuscript (which incorporates all revisions recommended by the Press's editors and outside readers) and a disk containing the manuscript formatted to the Press's specifications.

Helpful reference book: *The Chicago Manual of Style*, available at most libraries and books stores.

MANUSCRIPT EVALUATION PROCESS

The review process consists of several stages. Manuscripts are read first by an in-house editor. If they appear suited for our publishing program, they are evaluated by readers from outside the house who are recognized authorities in the subject matter of the manuscript or, in the case of literary work, by distinguished critics or writers in the genre of the manuscript (usually both). After two favorable outside evaluations, the manuscript is presented to the Press's Editorial Board, which consists of eight representatives from the campuses of the Nevada System of Higher Education, which controls the Press's imprint. Only after Board approval is the Press able to make a publishing commitment.

Publication takes place after negotiation and acceptance of a formal contract between the Press and the author or his/her agent. In most cases, the author receives a royalty on book sales, the amount of which is negotiated at the time the contract is offered.

Categories: Fiction—Nonfiction—Biography—Ecology—Environment—General Interest—History—Literature—Native American—Politics—Regional—Science—Ethnic

CONTACT: Joanne O'Hare, Director
Material: All
MS 166
Reno NV 89557-0076
Phone: 775-784-6573
Fax: 775-784-6200
Website: www.nvbooks.nevada.edu

University of North Texas Press

The University of North Texas Press was established in August 1987, and its first books were published in 1989. We publish approximately 15 books a year, with more than 200 books currently in print. Our books are distributed and marketed nationally and internationally through a university press consortium.

The University of North Texas Press is dedicated to producing the highest quality scholarly, academic and general interest books for the Dallas-Fort Worth-Denton metroplex, state, national and international communities. As a part of the largest and most comprehensive research university in North Texas, UNT Press holds to the philosophy that university presses should be on the cutting edge of publishing and thus is not averse to the different and unusual in its publishing agenda.

We are committed to serving all peoples by publishing stories of their cultures and their experiences that have been overlooked. We seek to nurture the development of writers by publishing first books and by publishing poetry. We strive to advance understanding and appreciation of the historical, intellectual, scientific and cultural milieu through our publications. **Publishing Emphasis**

The University of North Texas Press is the publisher of the Texas Folklore Society Publications. We also publish the following series: War and the Southwest, Texas Writers (critical biography), Western Life, Practical Guide, the Katherine Anne Porter Prize in Short Fiction, the Vassar Miller Prize in Poetry, and the North Texas Crime and Criminal Justice Series.

Please consult our website for details about our Vassar Miller and Katherine Ann Porter prizes.

Note that manuscripts for the Katherine Anne Porter Prize in Short Fiction should be sent, along with the entry fee to: KAP contest, Department of English, University of North Texas, P.O. Box 311307, Denton, TX 76203.

Procedures

The decision-making process at UNT Press is like that at other university presses. If we feel your proposal fits with our publishing list

and publishing schedule, we will ask for a complete manuscript, which will then be evaluated by at least two expert readers. These confidential reports are taken to the UNT Press Editorial Board, which has the final say on whether or not we will publish the book. Both the readers and the Editorial Board may have suggestions on revising and improving the manuscript. Sometimes their approval may be contingent on whether or not these changes are made.

The review process can take several months, depending upon the time necessary to receive and compile reports from the readers and the Editorial Board. Once the Editorial Board recommends publication, we will send you a contract for your consideration. Once the contract is signed by both parties, the publication process will usually take from nine months to a year.

Publication Process

UNT Press books are all printed on acid-free paper, according to the American National Standard for Permanence of paper for printed library materials.

Editing is done by both in-house and freelance editors, with the author being given an opportunity to check the edited manuscript, answer questions asked by the editor and offer input on changes made. The author also sees the book in page proofs, for the final chance to correct typographical errors and other problems that may arise. If the book is to be indexed, it will be done at this time.

Once the book goes to the printer, it usually takes around 40 working days for a hardback book and around 35 working days for a paperback book to be printed, bound, wrapped and shipped to the warehouse for distribution to bookstores.

Marketing

You will be sent an author biography form to fill out which will help in marketing your book. You are encouraged to become actively involved in marketing. It is our experience that the most successful books are the ones in which the author has been particularly aggressive in seeking out markets arranging speaking engagements with appropriate groups, and arranging book signings and other venues offering opportunities for book sales. Contacting your sources for book reviews is another effective marketing tool.

We will have your book at most of the major conferences and will consider taking it to other meetings you notify us about.

Since we consider our backlist books the backbone of our publishing house, we actively promote the backlist titles and seek course adoptions. Your book will be kept in print as long as demand justifies.

We have sales representatives throughout the United States, including Hawaii and Alaska. We have representation in Canada, Europe, Latin America, Asia, Australia, New Zealand, and the Pacific Islands.

We are part of a university press consortium that actively markets our books to major bookstore and library accounts and to national and regional distributors, as well as to individuals, through both extensive mailing lists and professional sales representation.

The Final Manuscript

Manuscripts submitted should be prepared according to the guidelines given here.

Hard Copy:
• Once a contract is signed, we need two hard copies of the ms.
• Word-processed manuscripts printed with letter-quality or near letter-quality printer. No dot matrix.
• No right-justification or proportional interspacing on word-processed manuscripts.
• Number pages consecutively through the manuscript; DO NOT begin renumbering with each chapter.
• Include photocopies, with captions, of any photographs or illustrations. (If you have already signed a contract with us, at this point we need original photos or duplicate prints.)

Computer Disks:
• These are not necessary until after a decision to publish the book has been made. (At that time, we will also need actual photographs and art work submitted with disks and hard copy.)

Books
M-Z

• Use the same hardware and software systems from start to finish.

• Keep formatting and fonts to a minimum. Most of it must be removed before typesetting.

• Once you have printed out the hard copy, do not make further changes on the computer disks.

• Name files sequentially ("A. Front matter," "B. Ch 1," "C. Ch 2," etc.) Submit a list of file names with disks. Do not put an entire manuscript in a single document.

• Front matter (title page, dedication, book epigraph, table of contents, lists of illustrations or tables, preface, acknowledgments, introduction, and foreword) and back matter (notes, bibliography, appendixes, index, and/or glossary) should be in separate files.

• Use endnotes at the end of chapters rather than footnotes at the bottom of the page.

• Double-space endnotes and bibliography.

• Do not put two spaces after periods as you do in a type-written document. This causes formatting problems. Do not put two spaces after colons, or anywhere else in the manuscript.

• Do not double-space between paragraphs.

• Use tabs, not spaces, to indent paragraphs.

Style Manual:

In general, the University of North Texas Press follows *The Chicago Manual of Style.* However, we like to remain flexible to the needs of each manuscript, so alternate styles are open for discussion.

Categories: Fiction—Nonfiction—African-American—Cooking—Crime—Environment—Folklore—General Interest—History—Literature—Military—Multicultural—Music—Poetry—Regional—Short Stories—True Crime—Women Studies

CONTACT: Acquisitions Editor
Material: All
PO Box 311336
Denton TX 76203-1336
Phone: 940-565-2142
Fax: 940-565-4590
Website: www.unt.edu/untpress

University of Oklahoma Press

During its more than seventy years of continuous operation, the University of Oklahoma Press has gained international recognition as an outstanding source of scholarly literature. It was the first university press established in the Southwest, and the fourth in the western half of the country.

The Press began as an idea of a man of vision, William Bennett Bizzell, the fifth president of the University of Oklahoma and a wide-ranging humanist and book collector. Over the years, the Press has grown from a staff of one—the first director, Joseph A. Brandt—to an active and capable team of more than forty members.

The OU Press continues its dedication to the publication of outstanding scholarly works.

Under the guidance of the present director, John Drayton, the major editorial goal of the Press is to maintain its position as a preeminent publisher of books about the American West and American Indians, while expanding its program in other scholarly disciplines, including archaeology, classical studies, military history, language and literature, natural science, and women's studies.

GUIDELINES FOR AUTHORS
Introduction

The mission of the University of Oklahoma Press is to publish scholarly books of significance to the state, region, nation, and world both to convey the results of current research to other scholars and to offer broader presentations for the general public.

Founded in 1928, the University of Oklahoma Press was the first university press established in the Southwest and the fourth founded in the western half of the nation. Over time the Press has grown from a staff of one to a team of more than forty people who work in acquisitions, editing, design and production, marketing and sales, rights, distribution, accounting, and administration.

The University of Oklahoma Press is dedicated to publishing outstanding scholarly works by national and international scholars. The Press's ongoing editorial goal is to maintain its preeminent position as a publisher of books about the West and the American Indian and to expand its program in other scholarly disciplines, including archaeology, classical studies, energy studies, language and literature (excluding unsolicited fiction and poetry), natural sciences, political science, and women's studies. Books published by the Press, including those in the series listed below, have accumulated an impressive array of honors and awards.

Series currently published by the Press include:
• American Exploration and Travel
• American Indian Literature and Critical Studies
• Animal Natural History
• Campaigns and Commanders
• Centers of Civilization
• Chicana and Chicano Visions of the Americas
• Civilization of the American Indian
• Congressional Studies
• Gilcrease-Oklahoma Series on Western Art and Artists
• Julian J. Rothbaum Distinguished Lecture Series
• Literature of the American West
• Oklahoma Museum of Natural History Publications
• Oklahoma Series in Classical Culture
• Oklahoma Western Biographies
• Series for Science and Culture
• Variorum Chaucer
• Western Frontier Library

Manuscript Submission and the Review Process

Our decision to publish a book is based chiefly on its contribution to knowledge in fields compatible with our list, sound scholarship, clear writing style, and financial feasibility.

The Press often solicits manuscripts and manuscript proposals. For unsolicited inquiries we prefer to receive:

1. A letter of inquiry that briefly describes the manuscript, its approximate length (including number and kinds of illustrations), its purpose, and its relationship to other books in its field;

2. The author's qualifications to write such a book;

3. A table of contents or, in the case of a proposal, a description of projected contents;

4. A sample chapter.

Upon receipt of your proposal, we will evaluate it and respond to you. If we wish to pursue the project, we will ask to see the complete manuscript. Unless we are told otherwise, we will assume that no other publisher has it under consideration while we consider it for publication.

Manuscripts that pass initial in-house scrutiny are sent to experts in the subject area for evaluation and then considered by an in-house Editorial Committee. Authors of manuscripts not recommended for publication are informed immediately. Manuscripts still under consideration are either presented to the

Press's Faculty Advisory Board or returned to the author for revision and re- submission. If the Board approves publication, the Press offers the author a contract for publication. An in- house decision to publish a book is usually made in approximately three to six months.

Manuscript proposals should be directed to the appropriate editor at the University of Oklahoma.

Categories: Nonfiction—Biography—Civil War—History—Literature—Native American—Regional—Western—Archaeology

CONTACT: John Drayton, Director
Material: Classics
CONTACT: Charles Rankin, Editor-in-Chief
Material: History of the American West, military history, Oklahoma history
CONTACT: Jean Hurtado, Acquisitions Editor
Material: History of the American West, natural history, political science, women's studies
CONTACT: Jo Ann Reece, Acquisitions Editor
Material: American Indian anthropology and history, Mesoamerican studies, Latin American studies
CONTACT: Daniel Simon, Acquisitions Editor
Material: Literature and paperback reprints of previously published works in the above fields
1005 Asp Ave.
Norman OK 73019-6051
Phone: 405-325-5114
Fax: 405-325-4000
Website: www.oupress.com

UpstartBooks
Creative Ideas for Library and Classroom Learning

General

UpstartBooks is an imprint of Highsmith Press. UpstartBooks accepts unsolicited proposals and manuscripts from prospective authors, and we welcome your inquiries. We recommend that you review our online catalog to see the types of materials we publish. Essentially, our primary interests are resources that aid media specialists, librarians and teachers to develop and stimulate reading interests, and facilitate library and information-seeking skills among youth (preschool through high school).

UpstartBooks has over 80 titles currently in print, and we publish approximately twelve new titles a year. We seek to reach a decision on each submission or proposal within 60 days, but in order to achieve this goal we need your cooperation by following these submission guidelines.

Specifics

For manuscripts which are less than 100 pages, we would like to receive the entire work for review, including illustrations.

For longer manuscripts, please send selected sections and illustrations that best describe the project, including the introduction.

We also welcome outlines of prospective projects, particularly if the manuscript is very lengthy.

Please include a cover letter summarizing the purpose of the work and its potential market. Identify any other recent books which have been published on a similar topic, and describe how your book differs.

In your letter state which computer software and platform you used (or plan to use) to develop your manuscript. We can accept a wide variety of Windows and Macintosh software programs. We do not need to receive an electronic version of your manuscript for initial evaluation, but we do require that final manuscripts be in an electronic format.

Attach a current resume listing your qualifications.

Include a self-addressed stamped envelope so we may return your material if we do not accept your manuscript for publication.

Do not send your only manuscript copy; send us a photocopy.

We are not troubled by manuscripts which are being simultaneously submitted to other publishers. We do not have any guidelines for artwork, although we will consider artwork submitted with manuscripts.

At present, we are interested in proposals or manuscripts on the following subjects:

• Creative reading activity books that can be used by children's and school librarians, and teachers to stimulate reading among youth.

• Basic guides for teachers and librarians that offer instructional activities, lesson plans and resources that develop library, information-

seeking and computer skills among youth.

• Guides to library-realted resources on the Internet for youth.

• Storytelling resources for children's librarians, teachers and professional storytellers that feature interesting and easy-to-learn stories and storytelling techniques.

• The specific terms we can offer authors and illustrators will vary with the nature of each project. However, we do provide very competitive royalties and advances, and we emphasize quality design and high production standards. Please call Matt Mulder at (920) 563-9571 if you have any questions or concerns.

Categories: Fiction—Nonfiction—Children—Education—Juvenile—Teen

CONTACT: Matt Mulder, Director of Publications
Material: All
Highsmith Press
PO Box 800
Ft. Atkinson WI 53538-0800
Phone: 920-563-9571
Fax: 920-563-4801(8 pages or less only)
E-mail: mmulder@highsmith.com (4 pages or less)
Website: www.hpress.highsmith.com

USA Books, Inc

We publish: children's, non-fiction, and historical fiction (no crime) with a strong accent on current affairs.

Send two-page synopsis of the work + 3 sample chapters + 1-paragraph author's bio in word format by email to:

Reading committee; Att: Sean Besanger (sbesanger@aol.com).

Do not send whole work.

We respond within a week.

Categories: Fiction—Nonfiction—Biography—Children—History—Mystery—Self Help—Western

CONTACT: Submissions Editor

Material: All
244, Fifth Ave.
New York NY 10001-7604
Phone: 212-561 0849
E-mail: sbesanger@aol.com

Vandamere Press

Thank you for your interest in Vandamere Press. These guidelines are provided assist you in the preparation and submission of manuscripts for publication consideration. Vandamere Press publishes in the areas of history, biography, disability studies/healthcare issues, military, fiction and the Nation's Capital for a national audience. These are only intended as a general guide, as the actual material submitted is fully at the discretion of the author, and we accept no responsibility for the material.

We do not require use of a specific style manual, but request that all authors pick a standard manual and use it consistently. For manuscripts that are selected for publication, authors should be prepared to review and enter all editorial corrections, and plan on rewriting problem areas. Vandamere Press authors are fully involved in the publication process until typesetting.

We cannot be responsible for original art or photos submitted with manuscripts and prefer only Xerox copies be sent.

Preferred submission formats should include the following:

A one-page summary

Books
M-Z

An author resume including a list of all published works (Very Important).

Author contacts for possible book endorsements.

The book's Table of Contents, first chapter and two other sample chapters

A self-addressed, stamped return envelope if negative response is needed (Mandatory).

We will not review or consider electronic submissions in any form.

We are no longer able to provide catalogs upon request to all authors due to the numbers involved. Please visit our website at www.vandamere.com for a full list and description of titles.

Please do not submit material "return receipt requested" or "registered," as waiting in Post Office lines is very time consuming. These submissions will not be reviewed.

Please do not call to request the status of your manuscript. We do not track manuscripts internally, and we will be able to provide you any information. We regret that the selection process can be very slow, but review of manuscripts can only be done time permitting.

All authors must be able to provide their final edited manuscript on a PC or Mac platform using a standard word processing program.

Submissions must be double-spaced and printed with a dark ribbon or high contrast laser/inkjet/Xerox. We will not review faded or hard to read copies. Type size should be no smaller than the type used in these guidelines.

We do not publish children's or young adult titles, accept for books of special interest to the Washington, DC or mid-Atlantic area.

We do not publish poetry.

We do not plan to begin publication of a mystery genre line until 2002 at the earliest.

We are not presently accepting any science fiction or fantasy manuscripts.

We are always interested in Washington regional titles.

Please remember that while we review 2,500 unsolicited manuscripts a year, we only will publish one or two at most in our annual line of about ten new titles.

16. Many of the manuscripts that we do not select for publication are excellent works that do not happen to fit our current needs or marketing strategy. As a result, we encourage authors not to become discouraged and to try other publishers. We recognize that from an author's point of view, the process may seem unfair, but promise that we will give all submissions appropriate consideration.

Categories: Fiction—Biography—Disabilities—Health—History—Military

CONTACT: Jerry Frank, Senior Acquisitions Editor
Po Box 17446
Clearwater, FL 33762
Website: www.vandamerepress.com

Vanwell Publishing

Please refer to Howell Press, Inc.

Via Dolorosa Press

Background

Via Dolorosa Press began in February of 1994. It was originally created to showcase dark works for the goth music scene, but eventually took a more philanthropic role by providing quality reading material to suicidal and depressed individuals. VDP continues to fill this niche in the small press with our selection of cathartic works.

Our specialty is work that is dark, painful, and anguished. We take the opposite stance of conventional therapy as we feel that the sharing of catharsis is more helpful than mainstream inspirational work. (Please be aware that, despite the religious connotations of our name, VDP is *not* a Christian publisher.) It has been our mission to present quality literature helping suffering people see that they are not alone in their struggle and that they can conquer their pain through solidarity.

The majority of our readers are between the ages of 18 and 40. They are extremely well-read and veer from traditional styles and subject matter. Most are in college or have completed degrees. Also, many of our readers are writers themselves, so they pay closer attention to the quality and style of writing than does the average person. Our readers demand higher-level writing, and this makes us very particular about the work we accept.

What We Are Looking For

While we strongly encourage *all* people to write as catharsis, we primarily print writing that *results from* catharsis, not necessarily that *is* catharsis. There is a huge difference between the two and we expect writers to be able to distinguish this difference.

It is necessary to note that we are not interested in work which deals with recovery from abuse (be it physical, mental, sexual, etc.) nor mental health issues. VDP is not qualified to handle such subjects.

We will not accept works which involve incest, rape, abuse, mental health, or geriatric issues as primary subjects.

Works which are directed to children or which feature children as main characters are inappropriate. As stated before, we cater to an adult audience. However, works which feature *excessive* sexual scenes are also inappropriate. Erotica is a great genre (and you can send us some if you really want to put us in good moods!), but we don't print it. We have no aversions to obscene language, just make sure it fits the work.

It is also extremely necessary to reiterate that we are not a Christian publisher. This means that we do not and will not print works about Christianity or works with a Christian slant. We repeatedly receive manuscripts that are supposedly directed to an open audience—Christians and non-Christians alike—but have really only been glorified religious propaganda. There are many new and successful magazines and publishers these days which specialize in Christian-themed work (and the demand is high), so if your manuscript has that slant, we encourage you to submit to those places, not VDP. Our stance does not only apply to Christianity; however, we do not support *any* organized religion or political ideology. Any work which slants toward religion or politics is inappropriate for VDP and will be rejected.

Art will be reviewed with the manuscript as a whole. Please note that we do not print in color. Also, pen and ink drawings are preferred to photographs and paintings as they reproduce best with our mode of printing. Permission to use someone else's artwork must be obtained prior to submitting the manuscript; we do not contact the artist(s) on the author's behalf and will request written proof of permission before accepting the artwork for printing.

There are also specific details for each genre we print:

Poetry

As poetry is our specialty, we are very particular about the manuscripts we accept. We publish dark, introspective writing only. It is *highly* recommended that you read a selection of our books to see what we prefer. We do not accept traditional (rhyming) verse or concrete poetry. We will review and consider experimental poetry, but if it's too elusive we may decline it. Our preference is towards confessional, free verse poetry (like the style of Anne Sexton). We receive a high volume of poetry submissions that are quickly rejected because the style is not like something we'd publish. Please be familiar with our work.

Fiction

We only print fiction that is thematically and stylistically like what Nathanael West would write if he were still alive. Any work unlike that will not be reviewed. As with our usual style, we look for darker material. We are interested in existential, humanist, nihilist, phenomenologist, and solipsist slants.

Non-Fiction

We are looking primarily for literary and philosophical essays. Literary criticisms should cover writers, works, or movements from the 20th century that were typically ignored by mainstream America. We are interested in more works covering Scandinavian poets and novelists of 1930-50, especially Swedish writers. Philosophical criticisms should cover existentialism, humanism, nihilism, phenomenology, and/or solipsism. We are not interested in works on any other philosophical ideologies. We prefer thesis-length works that include a healthy bibliography/works cited section.

How to Submit

For poetry, we suggest that you submit the entire manuscript, along with a cover letter and a list of publishing credits.

For fiction, we suggest that you send a query letter with the approximate word count, a short synopsis, the first 3 pages of your story, and a list of publishing credits.

For non-fiction, we suggest that you send a query letter with the approximate word count, a short synopsis, your table of contents, a few sample pages from one of the chapters, and a list of publishing credits.

Please note: At this time we are only accepting works under 12,500 words. (VDP primarily prints chapbooks which we hand-bind or staple saddleback. This word count limit is in place as have volume limitations. Within the next few years we will begin outsourcing our printing and all books will be trade paperbacks, at which time our word/page limit will be lifted.)

We do not accept submissions by email or fax; all manuscripts should be sent via post or courier with sufficient postage. Please do not send submissions by certified mail, registered mail, or any other form that requires signed receipt, as we are often unavailable when the mail is delivered. If you want confirmation of receipt prior to our acceptance/rejection letter, please include an additional SASE with your manuscript (foreign addresses send an IRC and SAE).

Agented submissions are *not* accepted. We work directly with writers and will reject any and all manuscripts submitted by agents.

All manuscripts should be formatted in the proper MLA style and typed; we do not accept handwritten manuscripts. Double-space lines for fiction and non-fiction. Poetry should be single-spaced. Please indicate on poems longer than one page where the stanza breaks should be.

Excessive spelling, punctuation, &/or grammatical errors will warrant rejection.

On a minor note, please refrain from using "he/she" and variations of it. Despite how politically-correct that form may be, we find it awkward and annoying. We prefer to see either "he" or "she" used consistently throughout the work. Pick a sex! If in doubt, use the masculine form. We also frown upon politically-correct forms of words when the original word is more recognized and sounds better. We will edit out all laborious politically-correct terms.

Rejected manuscripts are only returned to authors when a SASE with sufficient postage (or IRCs for foreign submissions) has been sent with the work.

One last word before submitting…

All magazines and publishing companies say this, and it's true: know your market. We can't stress enough how important it is to know the style and theme of the places you submit your work to. No editor wants to review something that has nothing to do with the type of work he prints. You should always read through the last year's worth of issues from a magazine you're planning to query or read recent books a publishing company you are interested in has released. We are reminding writers of this as 95% of the manuscripts we receive are not stylistically or thematically fitting for VDP.

Submission Address:

Submit all manuscripts to the address below. Include a SASE (or IRC) for a response; we do not respond via email and do not acknowledge submissions sent without a SASE.

Terms of Acceptance

Via Dolorosa Press has very straightforward terms which are standard for all works. We do not work on a negotiation basis as do many other publishing companies (which is why we discourage agented submissions). Our terms are listed below so that you may decide prior to submission if VDP is a worthwhile market for your work.

Like any other small press, our budget is very limited. We used to pay in copies only, but we are established enough now to also pay royalties. We cannot pay advances on works and do not purchase manuscripts outright. Please keep in mind, however, that we are not funded by any state or national grants, and we do not require authors to subsidize the printing of their works. We expect, though, that you know the plight of small presses and the difference between them and large publishing companies if you are considering VDP as your publisher.

Our terms are as follows:

We ask for first print rights and limited reprint rights. Authors retain all other rights to their work.

Authors receive initial payment as copies equaling 10% of the first print run. Our first print runs are small, usually between 50 and 250 copies. Many of the remaining 90% of copies are sent out to other journals and magazines for public review. Any remainders are for sale to the public and help fund the second printing.

Beginning with the first book of the second printing (and continuing until the book is no longer published), the author will receive a 25% royalty payment on the sale price of each copy sold.

Additional compensation may be provided based on each contract, and at the editor's discretion.

Royalty payments are made quarterly.

Specific information such as sale price, royalty amount, and royalty payment dates are different for each work accepted. These details are provided on our acceptance letter.

Categories: Fiction—Nonfiction—Experimental Fiction—Language—Literature—Poetry—Religion

CONTACT: Ms. Hyacinthe L. Raven, Editor
Material: All
701 E. Schaaf Rd.
Cleveland, OH 44131-1227

Virginia Foundation for the Humanities Press

Please refer to Howell Press, Inc.

Books M-Z

Volcano Press

No formal guidelines available.

A BRIEF HISTORY OF VOLCANO PRESS

We are often asked how Volcano Press began, inasmuch as the subject of domestic violence thirty years ago was hardly a household word.

Actually, I was on the publications staff of the Glide Foundation in San Francisco, back in the 70s. Glide was a very forward-looking pro-active organization, engaged in many avant-garde programs. It reflected the mood and spirit of San Francisco and the Bay Area of that time, where almost anything new and innovative seemed possible. And, since we had adequate funding, it was like Camelot—"...where it only rained at night".

So we published many books which were the first of their kind. "Battered Wives", "Lesbian Woman, Menopause~Naturally, Senior Power: Growing Old Rebelliously, Jury Woman, Learning to Live Without Violence: A Workbook for Men, to name a few.

But eventually the Glide Foundation encountered other financial pressing needs in the community, including feeding the poor and homeless, and the publications program was acquired by me. What had been Glide Publications became Volcano Press, a woman-owned California corporation. Today, of course, I now have a wonderful partner, my son Adam, whose energy and skills are once again re-vitalizing our publishing activities. He is now the publisher, and I am the Publisher Emerita.

A review of our ever-changing, expanding website is the best way to learn about us. And as ever, we welcome comments, queries-even pats on the back.

Categories: Nonfiction—Disabilities—Family—Feminism—Health—Human Rishts—Law—Men's Issues—Parenting—Senior Citizens—Women's Issues—Domestic Violence

CONTACT: Ruth Gottstein, Publisher Emerita
Material: All
PO Box 270
Volcano, CA 95689
Website: www.volcanopress.com

Voyageur Press

Welcome to Voyageur Press, publisher of quality nonfiction books on nature, travel, and American heritage. Founded in 1972, Voyageur takes pride in publishing titles featuring exceptional four-color photography and informative, entertaining text. With more than two hundred titles in print and foreign editions throughout the world, Voyageur publishes an average of forty new books a year.

Nature

Voyageur's large-format natural history books detail the behavior, habitat, and conservation of the world's wildlife, including wolves, bears, deer, dolphins, sea turtles, reptiles, raptors, hummingbirds, and bluebirds. Our nature authors include wilderness experts Dr. L. David Mech, Doug Perrine, Dr. Leonard Lee Rue III, and the late Erwin Bauer.

Voyageur also publishes a range of titles on the natural world, including Ken Libbrecht's bestselling pop science book, The Snowflake, and Ted Kerasote's modern wilderness adventure, Out There: In the Wild in a Wired Age. In addition, we have a successful series celebrating our nation's wild places and promoting conservation, led by Judith Sellers's Colorado Wild.

Travel

Our travel titles take readers throughout the United States, exploring historic landmarks and natural wonders through stunning photography and narrative text. Destinations range from canoe country to wine country, from the graceful plantation homes of the South to the fascinating ghost towns of the West. Our popular state backroads series explores secluded roads and unique sites, while our regional lighthouses series tours the historic sentries of America's coasts. We also have an established series of city and state photography books. Titles include Joseph Arrigo's Louisiana Plantation Homes, Philip Varney's Ghost Towns of Northern California, Shawn Perich's Backroads of Minnesota, Jon Marcus's Lighthouses of New England, and J. C. Leacock's Our Colorado.

American Heritage

Voyageur celebrates our national heritage with an extensive list of books on country life and popular culture. Paying tribute to the tractors that cultivated America, our booklist features informative field guides, how-to texts on tractor restoration, and in-depth histories such as Ralph Sanders's Ultimate John Deere. We also look at the lighter side of rural living with titles such as Dolly Mu's The Tao of Cow, Pam Percy's The Complete Chicken, and Roger Welsch's Old Tractors Never Die.

Our popular culture line includes a diverse range of books on transportation, crafts, sports, and other Americana titles. Within transportation, we publish titles on railroading and Harley-Davidson, as well as Mustangs, Corvettes, and hot rods. Our craft books, including Helen Kelley's Every Quilt Tells a Story, celebrate the arts of quilting and knitting through narrative, pictures, and history; we hope to develop a how-to line of craft titles in the future. In sports, we publish entertaining titles on the nostalgic appeal of baseball, hunting, and fishing.

Proposing a Book

If you have a manuscript or book idea that fits our publishing categories, we invite you to submit a proposal. Please note that we specialize in nonfiction. We do not publish poetry and rarely publish fiction; we also do not publish children's books or self-help books. We are especially eager at this time to review proposals on wildlife, the natural world, the Southwest, Michigan, Chicago, railroading, quilting, knitting, and baseball. With your proposal, please submit the following:

• Cover letter introducing your book idea in 250 words or less, your writing qualifications, and an analysis of the potential audience. Who would buy your book and why? What's the appeal or hook?

• Outline or table of contents

• Sample chapter, if written (do not submit an entire manuscript at this stage)

• Published clips

• Sample photography, if applicable

• Self-addressed, stamped return envelope

Mail your proposal to Voyageur Press, Attn: Mary LaBarre/Book Proposals, 123 N. Second St., Stillwater, MN 55082. Please keep in mind that every book idea is unique. We attempt to respond to each proposal within thirty days but ask for your patience if the process takes longer. We'll let you know as soon as we've made a decision. Thank you for your interest in Voyageur Press, and we look forward to reviewing your proposal

Categories: Adventure—Agriculture—Animals—Automobiles—Crafts/Hobbies—Fishing—Photography—Science—Sports/Recreation

CONTACT: Mary LaBarre/Book Proposals
Material: All
123 N. 2nd St.
Stillwater, MN 55082
Phone: 651-430-2210
Website: www.voyageurpress.com

Walter Foster Publishing, Inc.

ARTIST SUBMISSIONS

Walter Foster Publishing welcomes art submissions from individual artists. Please send color copies of illustrations, paintings, and other works for us to review and keep on file. Do not send original images and other original materials as they cannot be returned unless you provide a self-addressed, stamped envelope.

Some categories that we're interested in (but we're open to others):
- painting (oil, acrylic, watercolor)
- drawing (ink, pencil, charcoal)
- illustrations (serious or whimsical)
- crafts for children
- crafts for adults

Fees will be discussed only after your art has been accepted for publication.

Categories: Nonfiction—Arts—Crafts/Hobbies

CONTACT: Artist Submissions
Material: All
A Quarto Group Company
23062 La Cadena Dr.
Laguna Hills CA 92653
Phone: 949-380-7510

Waltsan Publishing, LLC

Publishes 10-20 titles/year. Receives 1,500 queries and 1,000 mss/year. 95% of books from first-time authors; 95% from unagented writers. Pays 20% royalty on invoiced price. Publishes book 9 months to 2 years after acceptance of ms. Accepts simultaneous submissions. Responds in 1 month to queries; 1 month to proposals; 2 months to mss or needed.

Book catalog online at: www.waltsan.com

Ms guidelines: Waltsan Publishing does not charge a reading fee or any other type of fee to the author. We offer industry standard royalty contracts. We do not give advances against royalties Genres include non-fiction, fiction, science fiction, how-to's, romance, children's stories, cook books and collections of short stories and poetry. We do not publish porn of any kind.

When querying, please advise availability of illustrations and/or photos. Author must own the copyrights or have obtained permission to use any and all material utilized in the manuscripts. Queries may be accompanied with the first two and last chapters of books or by three of the best works from a collection. 50,000 word minimum. Multiple submissions OK.

Nonfiction: Subjects include general nonfiction. "We look at any nonfiction subject." Query with SASE or via website or submit proposal package, including outline and 3 sample chapters or submit complete ms. Reviews artwork/photos as part of ms package. Send photocopies. Fiction: "We look at all fiction." Full-length or collections equal to full-length only. Query with SASE or submit proposal package including 3 sample chapter(s), synopsis or submit complete ms. Recent Title(s): *Shadows and Stones*, by Bernita Stark (dark fiction of shape changers and vampires); *Kite Paper, Papel de Barrilete*, by Sue Littleton (love poem with Spanish and English texts); *Jules Verne Classics*, edited by Walter Wellborn. Tips: Audience is computer literate, generally higher income and intelligent. "When possible, authors record

their manuscript to include audio on the CD. Check our website for guidelines and sample contract." Only publishes on CDs and other removable media, including audio books.

Categories: Fiction—Nonfiction

5000 Barnett St.
Fort Worth, TX 76103-2006
E-mail: service@waltsan.com
Website: www.waltsan.com

Warner Books

Due to the volume of submissions we receive, our policy is not to accept anything unsolicited, so we generally request that authors seek an agent. For our subject requirements, we are specifically interested in EPIC fantasy and science fiction for adults. Otherwise, the standard book proposal format applies: We prefer to receive a cover letter with the whole manuscript and a synopsis but are happy to review at least 3 chapters and a synopsis. We strongly encourage including a self addressed, stamped return package. When we are reviewing submissions, we are looking at both the plot and subject of the project as well as the author's writing ability and style.

—Jaime Levine, Editorial Director

Categories: Fiction—Fantasy—Science Fiction

CONTACT: Devi Pillai, Associate Editor
Material: All
1271 Avenue of the Americas
New York NY 10020
Phone: 212-522-5113
Fax: 212-522-7990
Website: www.twbookmark.com

Warner Business Books

Please refer to Time Warner Book Group.

Warner Faith

Please refer to Time Warner Book Group.

Washington State University Press

Washington State University Press, a member of the Association of American University Presses, invites manuscripts focusing on the American West, particularly the prehistory, history, environment, politics, and culture of the greater Northwest region. The Press publishes in a wide variety of genres, including scholarly and trade monographs, reminiscences, essays, and biographies. We seek imaginative works that tell the story of the West in innovative ways. We are not at this time accepting novels, poetry, or literary criticism.

The secret to publishing with WSU Press is to write in a lively fashion. The WSU Press adheres to the belief that good scholarship and good writing are compatible. We are unlikely to spend much time with a manuscript exhibiting extensive academic jargon. On the other hand, when you write a work that requires documentation, we expect to see evidence that your research has been thorough and sound.

The Press publishes an average of 8-10 titles a year. First-time authors are encouraged to submit proposals. The majority of our submissions come from unagented authors, but we also accept agent queries. We respond to queries within two months; simultaneous submissions are acceptable, but please tell us if you are making a multiple submission. On average we publish 12 to 18 months after a contract has been finalized for a manuscript. In general, royalties start on the sale of the first book, and graduate up according to sales.

When querying the Press about a possible manuscript, please submit a cover letter, chapter outline, and sample chapter or chapters. Please do not send the entire manuscript or original artwork/photographs at the query stage. Although we will respond to general questions via e-mail, we prefer that manuscript submissions be submitted via regular mail.

Categories: Nonfiction—Biography—Culture—Environment—History—Native American—Politics—Regional

CONTACT: Glen Lindeman , Acquisitions Editor
Material: All
PO Box 645910
Pullman WA 99164-5910
Phone: 509- 335-3518
Fax: 509-335-8568
E-mail: lindeman@wsu.edu
Website: www.wsu.edu

WATERBROOK
PRESS

Waterbrook Press
A Division of Random House, Inc.

Guidelines for Submitting Fiction Proposals
The creativity, craftsmanship and care reflected in your proposal will help us see how those same qualities would be evidenced in your book. Your book must have a Christian message/theme (Psalm 15:2). This does not mean we want to be hit over the head with the Gospel—weave it in where you can naturally do so. We find the best way is to subtly show your readers what your characters are learning, and how that impacts their lives.

We are seeking quality fiction.
If it competes with the best you've read in our market, we want to see it:
• *Big Concept Fiction:* 90-120,000 words; strong theme or issue addressed; plays to either male or female audience.
• *Women's Fiction:* 100-120,000 words; strong romantic element, but love story does not necessarily have to be the central focus.
• *Suspense:* 90-120,000 words, a la Clancy, Grisham, etc.
• *Literary or Allegorical Fiction:* Must be truly incredible for us to consider. Undaunted by that warning? Send it in.
• *No Short Stories, Anthologies*

Your Proposal Must Include:
1) A cover letter detailing: writing experience and sales; educational or professional qualifications to write the book; why your book is unique or compelling; targeted reader profile; your name, address, and phone number; competition or similar novels already on the market.
2) A two page synopsis of the story. Emphasize message/theme within
3) Your first three chapters (not more, not less)
4) A SASE with enough postage to cover the package, should you wish to see your full proposal returned, a SASE (legal-size envelope)

should you simply be seeking a reply. It is our experience that paper is less expensive than postage and would recommend you include a legal envelope only. Include SASE postcard if you want to verify that we received the package. *Response in four months. No query necessary.*

Guidelines for Submitting Children's Book Proposals
The creativity, craftsmanship and care reflected in your proposal will help us see how those same qualities would be evidenced in your book. There are a variety of proposal approaches that can work, so let your proposal demonstrate the uniqueness of both you and your children's book idea. Demonstrate your style, your enthusiasm, your expertise, and your professionalism.

Within this wide range of creative possibilities, here are some of your most important goals to accomplish in your project proposal:
1. Summarize in thirty words or less the unique, compelling appeal of your book. (Why would children enjoy it? What will make your book intriguing? What's fresh and unusual about yoru approach?)
2. Describe the realistic audience for this book. What age if the typical child who most enjoys the book?
3. Survey the competition. Give a content and market analysis of the major children's books now in print which would compete significantly with yours.
4. Outline your writing experience and provide an updated report on the market performance of your previously published works.
5. Outline your educational and career background.
6. Explain your qualifications to write this children's book and tell us about your natural "platform" (such as a speaking ministry) that allows you to promote the book.
7. Tell why you've written this book. What does it truly mean to you personally?
Please remember to include an SASE.
Categories: Fiction—Nonfiction—Adventure—African-American—Christian Interests—Drama—Family—Inspirational—Marriage—Men's Fiction—Mystery—Parenting—Relationships—Religion—Romance—Self Help—Society—Spiritual—Women's Fiction—Writing

CONTACT: Submissions Editor
Material: All
1226 Oracle Blvd., Suite 200
Colorado Springs CO 80921
Phone: 719-590-4999
Fax: 719-590-8977
Website: www.randomhouse.com/waterbrook

Wescott Cove Publishing Co.

We only publish books on:
• Nautical
• Cruising guides
Please query first. No email submissions.
Categories: Nonfiction—Adventure—Boating—Outdoors—Recreation—Sports/Recreation—Travel

CONTACT: Editor
Material: All
PO Box 130
Stamford CT 06904
Phone: 203-353-8142
Fax: 203-353-8143

Westcliffe Publishers

BOOK PROPOSAL GUIDELINES
When you submit a book proposal to Westcliffe Publishers, your proposal should contain the following items in order to convey a solid "snapshot" of your book idea and its anticipated audience.

• A working title
• A brief description of the concept of the book
• A sample table of contents page, with a general idea of the ratio of text to photography, art, or illustrations
• A sample chapter or two, with at least two samples of proposed photographs or artwork • A resume, tear sheets from previously published work (if available), and brief description of your background and credibility as author/photographer/artist
• A list of similar books in print on a related subject or approach (include the year published, size, and price) • How your book idea differs from other similar books on the market
• Target market: Who would buy this book? Do you see this as potentially a mass-market book, or one targeted to a regional audience?
• A proposed date for completion of the manuscript.

ABOUT WESTCLIFFE

As an eco-publisher, Westcliffe's mission is to foster environmental awareness by showing the beauty and diversity of the natural world. Westcliffe specializes in high-quality nature photography books, calendars, recreational guidebooks, and books with a regional focus. To learn more about Westcliffe's current titles, please browse our catalog. Because production of large-format photography books is costly, Westcliffe is interested in co-publishing ventures whenever possible. If you have support for your book proposal from an environmental or nonprofit organization or a corporate entity, please be sure to include that information. You are invited to call or email also: Linda@westcliffepublishers.com /800-523-3692.

PHOTOGRAPHY PROPOSAL GUIDELINES

For the most part, Westcliffe books and calendars are single-photographer works focusing on states or regions within the United States. The majority of our photographers have established national reputations and are published regularly in magazines such as Sierra, Wilderness, and National Geographic. We generally publish large-format photography (4x5 or 2 1/4), though on occasion we publish 35 mm work. Westcliffe does not use stock photography.

If you would like to submit work for review by Westcliffe, it is suggested that you submit a specific book or calendar proposal, a concise overview of the project following the book proposal guidelines described above. Please look through our catalog and familiarize yourself with the types of titles we publish.

Westcliffe's current list of calendar titles focuses on individual states. We are, however, open to new ideas. Calendar proposals should be in line with or similar to the type of work Westcliffe publishes - regional nature photography. Submit calendar proposals with a resume and tear sheets. Westcliffe will contact you if we would like you to submit transparencies. If you have questions or require further information, please contact the production manager at: craig@westcliffepublishers.com or 1-800-523-3692.

Thank you for your interest in Westcliffe Publishers.

Categories: Nonfiction—Ecology—Environment—Photography—Recreation—REgional

CONTACT: Linda Doyle, Associate Publisher
Material: All
PO Box 1261
Englewood, CO 80150-1261
Phone: 800-523-3692
Fax: 303-935-0903
Website: www.westcliffepublishers.com

Westwinds Press

Please refer to Graphic Arts Center Publishing Company

Whispering Coyote

Please refer to Charlesbridge Publishing.

White Cliffs Media, Inc.

White Cliffs Media publishes quality material about African, World and Popular Music that withstands the test of time.

White Cliffs Media works with the best authorities and performers in the world.

The content of our books and CDs is excellent, and now we're improving the graphics.

White Cliffs Media has been around for over fifteen years.

Categories: Nonfiction—Arts—Biography—Culture—Entertainment—Music

CONTACT: Editorial Dept.
Material: All
PO Box 6083
Incline Village NV 89450
E-mail: wcm@wc-media.com
Website: www.wc-media.com

White Mane Publishing Co., Inc.

What We Are Looking for:

White Mane Publishing Co., Inc. consists of four imprints. White Mane Books publishes quality military history non-fiction titles for the avid collector. Burd Street Press publishes general non-fiction military history books for the enjoyment of reading history. White Mane Kids publishes historical children's fiction for middle grade and young adult readers. Each book contains accurate historical information while captivating the readers with fascinating stories. White Mane Kids does not, however, publish picture books at this time. Finally, Ragged Edge Press aims to make a difference in people's lives with topics that focus on relationships and religion.

How to Submit Your Proposal:

Do not send a computer disk. Please submit printed proposals/manuscripts. Please note only materials accompanied by a self-addressed, postage paid shipping envelope will be returned to you. While every care will be taken of the manuscript, we cannot be responsible for loss or damages, whether it be in our possession or in transit. If concerned about receipt of manuscript please send it by a carrier that provides tracking services.

Submissions should include the following:

• Title/subtitle of Manuscript
• Number of pages and/or words, photos, maps
• Does the manuscript include a bibliography or index?
• Statement of Purpose: A brief paragraph describing why you feel this topic is important. What new information, insights, or approach does your work add to existing works on this topic?
• Marketing Ideas: A brief paragraph outlining the marketing potential of your work. What types of contacts have you made in this field? Indicate any organizations or associations that may help in promoting the book.

Sample Dust Jacket Paragraph: A brief paragraph that describes your book to a potential buyer.

• Contact information including address, day/evening telephone numbers, fax, and email.

When to Expect an Answer:

Review of proposals generally takes one month. Review of full manuscripts generally takes 3 months.

Categories: Fiction—Civil War—Historical—Military—Religion—Self-Help—Young Adult

CONTACT: Acquisitions Department
Material: All
73 West Burd St.
PO Box 708
Shippensburg, PA 17257
Phone: 717-532-2237
Fax: 717-532-6110
E-mail: marketing@whitemane.com
E-mail: editorial@whitemane.com
Website: www.whitemane.com

Wild Flower Press

Please refer to Granite Publishing Group, LLC

Wilder Publishing Center

What We're Looking for

Wilder Publishing Center is looking for book proposals from experts in community development, nonprofit management and organizational development, and human services.

We want manuscripts that identify "best practice" and make it easy to understand. We feel our publications are successful if the reader can pick one up and put it to work immediately. Thus our publications emphasize practical experience and step-by-step directions. *To date, we've used three formats, although we are open to others:*

• Workbooks that explain a process and provide worksheets to guide the reader through that process.

• Research reports and literature reviews that sift through many studies to distill basic trends useful for community organizers and policy makers.

• Curricula that human services professionals can easily follow and adapt for their programs.

Our publications are used by nonprofit managers, community organizers, grassroots groups, policy makers, consultants, trainers, funders, and human service professionals. We seek proposals that appeal to one or more of these audiences.

How to Submit Your Proposal

Do not send a computer disk. You need not send an entire manuscript.

Your proposal should specify the following:

• Audience—who you see as the users of your information.

• Objective—one paragraph that describes the impact your book will make on its readers.

• Market-types of organizations most likely to purchase the book, and your estimate of the number of such organizations.

• Competing publications—competing or similar titles, if any; be sure to describe how your book will differ from them.

• Contents, including:

• A chapter outline with paragraphs or lists of all topics to be covered in each chapter.

• A sample worksheet, if worksheets are to be part of the book. Appendix headings, partial bibliography, and headings for other back matter.

• A description of any illustrations you feel are necessary.

• Sample chapter(s). This is optional. You may enclose a sample chapter if you've already written one, or save yourself the postage by waiting for us to respond to your detailed outline.

• Process—a brief description of the sources you will use as you write.

• Author qualifications—a brief description of yourself, relevant experience, any previous publications, and why you are qualified to write this book.

We encourage you to look through our publications brochure before sending us a proposal. Better still, get a hold of our books and review them first.

When to Expect an Answer

Within three months of receiving your proposal, we will respond telling you either:

We are not interested in the proposal, or we have an interest in the proposal, but need more time to study it.

If we have an interest in the proposal, the actual decision to publish may take another two to three months. During this time we will evaluate the manuscript for its fit with our mission, niche, existing publications, and marketing capacities; its uniqueness, contribution to the field, and impact on readers; and your qualifications as an author and expert. We may also send the proposal for peer review, ask for writing samples, request sample chapters (or a complete manuscript if available), and speak with you about timelines, funding, and other information as appropriate.

What Happens When We Accept Your Book

If we're interested in publishing the book, we work with you to develop a contract we're both happy with. In some cases, we are able to raise funds to pay for the writing of the book, in which case we prefer to purchase the manuscript outright. In others, we are able to work out a royalty agreement. Once you deliver the manuscript, expect rigorous editing and revision; your manuscript will be reviewed by a minimum of three outside experts and often many more. The amount of time it takes to produce the book varies with the scope and size of the work. Once the book is printed, it will be promoted a minimum of four times each year through direct mail.

About the Wilder Publishing Center

Based in St. Paul, Minnesota, the Wilder Publishing Center is a part of the Amherst H. Wilder Foundation, one of the oldest and largest nonprofit human service agencies in North America. Our first book, *Strategic Planning Workbook for Nonprofit Organizations*, has become a classic. Among our other titles are *Collaboration Handbook: Creating, Sustaining, and Enjoying the Journey* and *Community Economic Development Handbook*.

Categories: Nonfiction—Trade—Nonprofit—Nonprofit Management

CONTACT: Acquisitions Editor
Material: Nonprofit Management, Community Development
Wilder Publishing Center
919 Lafond Ave.
St. Paul MN 55104
Phone: 612-659-6013
Website: www.wilder.org

Will Hall Books

The mission of Will Hall, Inc. is threefold: books for children;, chapbooks for emerging writers (handmade, hand-sewn, 25 pp.) who manifestly deserve a broader readership; and, third, educational assistance to any artists, regardless of discipline, for the opportunity to travel, attend conferences, or complete course work.

Will Hall, Inc., which includes the title, Will Hall Books, is a 501(c)3 tax deductible public foundation whose mission is literary and cultural. Our philosophy holds that encouragement to authors, photographers, artists, and musicians is essential to the well-being of a civilized world. We publish books, donate to libraries, and, in doing so, give a "boost" to children and individual artists.

Our most recent endeavors have been supplying an honorarium for Irish Poet, Matthew Sweeney, to read in Fayetteville, donating money to enable a scholar to complete the editing of a book, and providing a scholarship fund for a music student to study in Italy. We are proud to be able to support the efforts of these and other talented individuals.

Will Hall Books publishes chapbooks in any genre. 20 poems submission all year round. once in a while we publish full length books in runs of 1,000 in any genre.

Categories: Nonfiction—Arts—Children—Education—Poetry

CONTACT: Rebecca Newth
Material: Queries
611 Oliver Ave.
Fayetteville AR 72701
E-mail: rharriso@uark.edu
Website: www.willhallbooks.com

Willow Creek Press

Willow Creek Press is a publisher whose primary commitment is to publish nonfiction books specializing in wildlife, nature, the outdoors, gardening, pets, fishing, and some cookbooks. We also publish nature, wildlife, fishing, and sporting calendars.

Personal memoirs and manuscripts dealing with limited regional subject matter may be considered, but generally stand little chance of acceptance. Children's books and fiction manuscripts are not being considered at the present time.

Please include the following details when submitting book proposals:

• Brief synopsis of the book being proposed
• Detailed outline or table of contents
• One or two sample chapters if available
• Samples of art, photos, or transparencies intended for use in the book (no originals, please)
• Author's background, credentials, other publications relevant to the project

Notation as to whether or not proposal is a simultaneous submission

SASE with sufficient postage for response and/or return of materials

Proposals submitted to Willow Creek Press are reviewed for style, content, appropriateness, conceptual integrity, author expertise, and marketability. Therefore, a rejection does not necessarily reflect any judgment regarding the literary merit of an author's work. Please note that Willow Creek Press is not responsible for the loss or damage of any materials submitted for consideration.

We use a standardized author contract, which may be modified upon mutual agreement by the author and publisher. Advances against royalties are negotiable, and royalties are paid semi-annually.

Please provide SASE with all correspondence if you want your materials returned.

Thank you for your interest in Willow Creek Press!

Categories: Nonfiction—Animals—Cooking—Fishing—Gardening—Outdoors—Recreation—Hunting/Birding

CONTACT: Andrea Donner, Managing Editor
Material: All
PO Box 147, 9931 Highway 70 W.
Minocqua WI 54548
Phone: 715-358-7010

Willowgate Press

Willowgate Press currently has six additional novels in press, which will occupy our time through calendar year 2003. We are therefore closed to new submissions until further notice. All submissions received prior to October 1, 2002 will be considered. All submissions received after that date will be returned without examination or comment.

As indicated, we are seeking book length fiction in all categories. We welcome both agented and unagented submissions. *We will be making judgments as to literary merit and commercial viability on the basis of submissions that should include the following:*

• A cover letter identifying the work, and giving a brief biographical sketch of the author and his or her history of publications;
• A brief (one to two page) double-spaced synopsis covering the entire plot, theme and structure of the book, including the conclusion (the synopsis should also identify the genre of the work, if appropriate, the length of the work in words and pages, and whether it is written in the first or third person);
• A chapter outline of no more than 4-5 pages, single-spaced, that gives us the pace and plot of the novel in detail;
• The first ten pages of the manuscript;
• Ten additional consecutive pages of the manuscript of the author's choosing;
• A self-addressed, stamped envelope sufficient to contain all submitted materials.

We will not editorialize, critique or communicate gratuitous judgments about the quality of the work on the basis of this submission. We will either return the material to you with our thanks or ask to see the entire manuscript.

If we do request the manuscript, we ask that it be forwarded in an envelope marked "requested material," and that it be one-sided, double-spaced and contain a "slug line" at the top stating title and author. It must contain an SASE or email address, to which we shall be happy to respond.

Due to the difficulties of supplying a SASE from countries other than the United States, we suggest that submissions from such nations be sent with an email address, rather than return postage.

We hope to respond to queries within two months, and to requested manuscripts within a six months of receipt.

Categories: Fiction—Adventure—Crime—Fantasy—General Interest—Horror—Literature—Mystery—Science Fiction

CONTACT: Submissions Editor
Material: All
PO Box 6529
Holliston MA 01746
Phone: 508-429-8774
Website: www.willowgatepress.com

Wilshire Book Co.

Publisher: Melvin Powers. **Acquisitions:** Rights Department. Estab. 1947. Publishes trade paperback originals and reprints. Publishes 25 titles/year. Receives 1,000 submissions/year. 80% of books from first-time authors; 75% from unagented writers. Pays standard royalty. Offers advance. Publishes 6 months after acceptance of ms. Accepts simultaneous submissions. Responds in 2 months.

Nonfiction: How-to, self-help, motivational, recovery. Subjects include psychology, personal success, entrepreneurship, humor, Internet marketing, mail order, horsemanship, trick training for horses. Minimum 50,000 words. Query or submit outline (synopsis for fiction) and 3 sample chapters or complete ms. Include SASE and e-mail address. No e-mail submissions. Reviews artwork/photos as part of ms package. Photocopies only. Guidelines online.

Fiction: Adult allegories that teach principles of psychological growth or offer guidance in living. Minimum 30,000 words. No standard fiction or short stories.

Recent Title(s): *The Dragon Slayer with a Heavy Heart* by Marcia Powers, *The Secret of Overcoming Verbal Abuse* by Albert Ellis, Ph.D. and Marcia Grad Powers, *The Princess Who Believed in Fairy Tales* by Marcia Grad, *The Knight in Rusty Armor* by Robert Fisher, *Think and Grow Rich* by Napoleon Hill.

Tips: "We are vitally interested in all new material we receive. Just as you are hopeful when submitting your manuscript for publication, we are hopeful as we read each one submitted, searching for those we believe could be successful in the marketplace. Writing and publishing must be a team effort. We need you to write what we can sell. We suggest you read successful books similar to the one you want to write. Analyze them to discover what elements make them winners. Duplicate those elements in your own style, using a creative new approach and fresh material, and you will have written a book we can catapult onto the bestseller list. You are welcome to telephone or e-mail us for immediate feedback on any book concept you may have. To learn more about us and what we publish, visit our website."

Categories: Fiction—Nonfiction—Animals—Business—Health—Hobbies—Humor—Inspirational—Internet—Psychology—Relationships—Romance—Self Help—Sexuality

CONTACT: Submissions Editor
Material: All
9731 Variel Avenue
Chatsworth, CA 91311-4315
Phone: 818-700-1522
Fax: 818-700-1527
E-mail: mnpowers@mpowers.com
Website: www.mpowers.com

Woodbine House

Woodbine House welcomes submissions from all writers-agented and unagented, previously published and unpublished. We will gladly consider book-length, nonfiction manuscripts on almost any subject related to disabilities, but we do not publish and will not consider fiction, poetry, and personal accounts.

We favor books that are one of a kind, but will also consider books that take fresh slants on old subjects. Regardless of a book's subject, we are always impressed by authors who 1) can write with clarity, authority, and style; and 2) can demonstrate that their book has a clearly defined market that they know how to reach.

To submit a proposal, please send a query letter. *If you would like to submit more than a query letter, you can send the following information:*

1. The table of contents;
2. 2-3 sample chapters;
3. An annotated list of books in print on the subject, explaining how your book differs from the competition;
4. A list of potential markets, including specific organizations, book clubs, and groups of individuals that would buy your book;
5. A short biographical note describing your qualifications to write this book;
6. Estimated length and completion date.

Manuscripts should be typed. Send illustrations or copies if applicable. Photocopies and computer printouts are acceptable, as are simultaneous submissions, if so marked. Allow 8-12 weeks for a response.

Categories: Children—Disabilities—Education—Parenting—Self Help—Special Needs

CONTACT: Nancy Gray Paul, Acquisitions Editor
Material: All
6510 Bells Mill Rd.
Bethesda MD 20817
Phone: 301-897-3570
Fax: 301-897-5838

WoodenBoat Books

If you have a manuscript to submit, please take a look at these basic guidelines.

We publish books on boat building, design, nautical history, woodworking, as well as books with great photography.
If your book fits in that area, then you should send:
• A detailed outline / extended table of contents
• Sample chapters / photos / drawings
• Who you feel the target audience is
• What competition is already out there for this topic
• Format: length of the project, types and amount of illustrations
• What specialty marketing would you suggest
• Your information, contact, including email, as well as background
• Postage paid envelope, if you would like the materials returned
Categories: Nonfiction—Boating—History—Photography

CONTACT: Scot Bell
Material: All
Naskeag Rd.
PO Box 78
Brooklin ME 04616
Phone: 207-359-4651
Fax: 207-359-2058
E-mail: books@woodenboat.com
Website: www.woodenboat.com

Woodland Publishing

Does Woodland accept unsolicited manuscripts?

Yes, but we prefer that potential authors query first. Queries should be between 250 and 300 words and should convince us that your topic is timely and of interest to our readers, offer a description on how you would treat the subject and what research or other data you would use. Your query should also tell us if any other books have been written recently on your topic. Background information and credentials are also helpful. Also, because of the high volume of queries we receive, it may take us a while to get back to you.

We endeavor to respond to every query, but the high volume of queries and submissions can delay response time. Furthermore, queries for newsletter articles are not guaranteed a response. Do know that if you send a SASE with your manuscript submission, we will return your manuscript if it is not accepted. Please do not send us the only copy of your manuscript!

Categories: Diet/Nutrition—Health

CONTACT: Cord Udall, Managing Editor
Material: All
PO Box 160
Pleasant Grove, UT 84062
Phone: 801-785-8100
Fax: 801-785-8511
Website: www.woodlandpublishing.com

Word Dancer Press

Please refer to Quill Driver Books/Word Dancer Press, Inc.

World Leisure Corporation

Here are the submission guidelines you requested. We are publishing sports travel, family travel, gift/self-help books and some children's books.

Before any submissions will be considered please prepare:
• an introduction explaining why someone should read the materials you are presenting
• an annotated table of contents outlining each chapter of your proposed book
• at least one sample chapter so I can see your writing style

If I feel your book will fit into our coming book lists I will contact you. Do not send queries.

Send a SASE if you wish to have your manuscript returned or just your cover letter with my notes to you.

Sincerely, Charles Leocha, Publisher

Categories: Nonfiction—Children—Relationships—Sports/Recreation—Travel

CONTACT: Charles Leocha, Publisher
Material: All
177 Paris St.
Boston MA 02128
Phone: 617-569-1966
Fax: 617-561-7654
E-mail: WLEISURE@aol.com

The Writer Gazette

Please refer to The Writer Gazette, in the Periodical Section of this directory.

YMAA Publication Center

The proposed work should address some aspect of Chinese culture—martial arts, Qigong (Chi Kung), medicine, etc. No children's stories, please.

For fastest response, please use the following guidelines:

• Send a brief summary of each chapter and one complete sample chapter. Include sample photos or drawings, if available (photocopies or facsimiles acceptable).

• Include a one page (maximum) author biography. Relate salient experience and qualifications.

• Include a one page (maximum) cover letter. State your intention for writing the book, the proposed audience, and describe the unique, compelling features of the book.

• Letter quality computer printouts acceptable.

Categories: Nonfiction—Health—History—Military—New Age—Sports/Recreation—Martial Arts

CONTACT: David Ripianzi, Acquisitions Editor
Material: Chinese Martial Arts, Chinese Healing Arts
4354 Washington St.
Roslindale MA 02131
Phone: 617-323-7215
Fax: 617-323-7417
E-mail: ymaa@aol.com
Website: www.YMAA.com

YogaVidya.com

What We're Looking For

Authoritative books on Yoga written for the intelligent general public.

The Procedure

First, send us an email briefly describing your proposal. We'll then let you know if we're interested.

Second, if we've answered affirmatively, snail mail us the following materials. (Let's assume here it is a translation of a Sanskrit text, although we are looking for other types of books as well.)

1) A complete and up-to-date curriculum vitae (aka résumé or biodata). Even if we know who you are, we'll need this information to promote your book.

2) A description of the text.

3) Why you think it is worthy of publication.

4) At least ten verses of both the source text and your translation.

5) If it has been translated before, include previous translations for the same sample you translated. Explain how both your source text and translation are better than previously published versions.

6) A brief note on where the project stands and when it might be completed.

Third, if we accept your work for publication, we'll then begin communicating about permissions, schedules, fonts, file formats, contracts, etc.

All communication with us should be in English. Don't send us your only copy of anything. Include an SASE if you want your materials returned, otherwise they will be recycled.

Categories: Health—Physical Fitness—Religion—Spiritual—Yoga

CONTACT: Submissions
YogaVidya.com
PO Box 569
Woodstock NY 12498-0569
USA
Fax: 1-586-283-4680
Email: info@yogavidya.com
Website: www.yogavidya.com

Zondervan Publishing House
A Division of HarperCollins*Publishers*

Zondervan and Zonderkidz

Zondervan and Zonderkidz No Longer Accepting Unsolicited Manuscripts and Book Proposals Sent by Air or Surface Mail

Since the events of 9-11-2001, Zondervan and Zonderkidz have established a new policy concerning unsolicited manuscripts and book proposals. We will no longer open and review any envelope or package that is not addressed to a particular individual or that does not come from an identified source that we recognize. Any such packages that we receive will be returned to the sender unopened; if there is no return address, such packages will be discarded.

We encourage you to submit your book proposal electronically to First Edition, The ECPA Manuscript Service on the ECPA website (www.ECPA.org). Book proposals posted on this website are available for review by all the member publishers of the Evangelical Christian Publishers Association, and Zondervan and Zonderkidz have assigned an editor to regularly review all new proposals posted on First Edition.

If you feel you must submit your book proposal directly to Zondervan or Zonderkidz, you may do so by faxing it to us. Your proposal should include the book title; a table of contents, including a 2 or 3 sentence description of each chapter; a brief description of the proposed book, including the unique contribution of the book and why you feel it must be published; your intended reader; and your Vita, including your qualifications to write the book. The proposal should be no more than 5 pages. If we are interested in reviewing more material from you, we will respond within 6 weeks. You may fax your proposal to the Book Proposal Review Editor, 616-698-3454.

Please note that we've never accepted email proposals.

Categories: Fiction—Nonfiction—Adventure—African-American—Biography—Children—Christian Interests—Family—Marriage—Parenting—Relationships—Spiritual—Women's Fiction

CONTACT: Acquisitions Editor
Material: All
Fax: 616-698-3454
Website: www.zondervan.com

Remember: Editors change jobs and publishers change addresses. It is wise to invest in a phone call for the current information before submitting.

Books M-Z

Topic Index

This index provides the names of publishers interested in seeing
material on or relating to the topics listed.

-A-

Adventure

Periodicals:

*America West Magazine, American Fitness, Arizona Highways, Artemis
Magazine, Asimov's Science Fiction, Aspen Magazine, Backroads,
Bibliophilos, Bike Magazine, Blue Ridge Country Magazine, Boating Life,
Boys' Life, BOYS' QUEST, Cadet Quest, Canoe & Kayak
Magazine, Cascades East Magazine, Chesapeake Bay Magazine,
COBBLESTONE Magazine, Country Magazine, Creative With Words!,
Happy Times Monthly, Heartland USA, Home Times Family Newspaper,
House, Home and Garden, Iconoclast, Insider Magazine, Lake Michigan
Travel Guide, Lake Superior Magazine, Lifeglow, Long Story Short, A
Magazine for Writers, Marlin, Men's Journal, My Legacy, National
Enquirer, Outdoor Life, Paddler, Passport, Persimmon Hill, Rack, Rocky
Mountain Sports Magazine, Sandlapper, Short Stuff Magazine, SKATING
Magazine, SKI, Sport Fishing
Magazine, Springfield! Magazine, Surfer, Texas Parks & Wildlife, Times
News Service, Today's Christian, Transitions Abroad, Western RV News &
Recreation, Whole Life Times, Willow Springs, World & I, Young & Alive*

Book Publishers:

American Literary Press, Inc. Noble House, Black Forest Press,
Bridge Works, Charlesbridge Publishing, Clover Park Press, Conservatory
of American Letters, Council for Indian Education, Denlinger's
Publishers, Ltd., Dial Books for Young Readers, Dutton Children's Books,
Graphic Arts Center Publishing Company, ImaJinn Books, Lobster Press,
Lyons Press, Mayhaven Publishing, Menasha Ridge Press, Mountain N'
AirBooks, Mountaineers Books, Paladin Press: Sycamore Island
Books, Flying Machines Press, PREP Publishing, Printing Industries of
America / Graphic Arts Center Publishing Company, PSI Research/Hellgate
Press, Puget Sound Books/Angel Fire Press, Ragged Mountain Press,
Voyageur Press, Waterbrook Press, A Division of Random House, Inc.,
Wescott Cove Publishing Co., Willowgate Press, Zondervan and Zonderkid

African-American

Periodicals:

*Affaire De Coeur, , African American Pulpit!, African American Re-
view, Arkansas Review, Blackfire, Calyx Journal, Carolina Quarterly,
Clubhouse, Equal Opportunity Publications, Inc., Essence, Feminist
Studies: University of Maryland, Footsteps, Futures Mysterious Anthology Magazine, Home Times Family Newspaper, Jewish Currents,
Message Magazine, Metro Parent, Mother Jones, New Centennial Review, Obsidian III, Other Side, Passport, Reunions Magazine, South
American Explorer, Southern Humanities Review, Springfield! Magazine, Teaching Tolerance, Tequesta, Vibe, Willow Springs*

Book Publishers:

Barricade Books, Branden Publishing Company, Calyx Books, Clarity
Press, Dial Books for Young Readers, Face to Face Press, Fairleigh
Dickinson University Press, Great Quotations Publishing, Holloway House
Publishing Group, Hunter House Publishers, Intercultural Press, Judson
Press, Just Us Books, Lerner Publishing, McFarland & Company, Inc.,
Midmarch Arts Press, Mississippi, University Press of Mississippi, Pelican
Publishing Company, Rutledge Hill Press, Safari Press, Scarecrow
Press, Soho Press Inc, Temple University Press, Texas A&M University
Press, Third World Press, Transactions Publishers: Rutgers The State
University of New Jersey, University of Nebraska Press, University of
North Texas Press, Waterbrook Press, A Division of Random House,
Zondervan and Zonderkid

Agriculture

Periodicals:

*Artemis Magazine, Capper's, Country Magazine, Digger Magazine,
Environment, Farm & Ranch Living, Feed-Lot, Futurific Magazine, Grit
Magazine, Growing Edge, Maine Organic Farmer & Gardener, Mon-
tana, Mother Earth News, New Centennial Review, Old Farmer's Alma-
nac, Onion World, Slipstream, Stone Soup, Toy Farmer, Whole Life
Times, Wines & Vines*

Book Publishers:

Fairleigh Dickinson University Press, Green Nature Books, Island Press,
Stenhouse Publishers, Ten Speed Press, Texas A&M University Press,
University of Maine Press, University of Nebraska Press, Voyageur
Press

Alternate Lifestyle

Periodicals:

*American Fitness, Body & Soul, Frontiers, Futures Mysterious Anthol-
ogy Magazine, Genre, Gray Areas, In the Family, Maine Organic Farmer
& Gardener, National Enquirer, Penthouse Variations, Rainbow Review, Symploke, Willow Springs*

Book Publishers:

Alyson Publications, Face to Face Press, HiddenSpring, New Horizons Press, Small Horizons Imprint

Animals

Periodicals:

*America West Magazine, American Hunter, Animal People, Animals'
Agenda, Animals Magazine, ASPCA Animal Watch, Back Home,
Bibliophilos, Birds & Blooms, Boys' Life, Boys' Quest, Bugle, Califor-
nia Wild, Cat Fancy, Country Magazine, Creative With Words!, De-
fenders of Wildlife, Dog Gone, Environment, Equine Journal, Florida
Wildlife Magazine Newsletter, Fun for Kidz, Fur-Fish-Game, Gaited
Horse, Grit Magazine, Guideposts for Kids, Happy Times Monthly,
Heartland USA, Hopscotch for Girls, Horse Illustrated, House, Home
and Garden, I Love Cats, Lutheran Digest, Maine Organic Farmer &
Gardener, Mushing, My Legacy, National Enquirer, Outdoor Life, Per-
simmon Hill, Polo Players' Edition, Saturday Evening Post,
Songwriter&Aelig;s Monthly, Spider The Magazine for Children, Spring-
field! Magazine, Stone Soup, Timeline, Transitions, Whole Life Times,
Wildlife Art, Young & Alive*

Book Publishers:

Alpine Publications, Angel Bea Publishing, Barrons Educational Se-
ries, Brookline Books, Chronicle Books LLC, Creative Publishing In-
ternational, Cruden Bay Books, DIMI Press, Dutton Children's Books,
Eclipse Press, Great Quotations Publishing, Green Nature Books,
Hancock House, J.N. Townsend Publishing, Lerner Publishing, Lyons
Press, Magni Group, Mayhaven Publishing, Richard C. Owen Publish-
ers, Safari Press, Sphinx Publishing, Temple University Press, Ten Speed
Press, University of North Texas Press, Voyageur Press, Willow Creek
Press, Wilshire Book Co.

Antiques

Periodicals:

*Antique Trader Weekly, Antiques & Collecting Magazine, Appraisers
Standard, Art & Antiques, Atlanta Homes and Lifestyles, Back Home,
Budget Living, Classic Toy Trains, Collectors News, Country Living,
Early American Life, House, Home and Garden, Long Island Woman,
Mountain Living, New Yorker, Persimmon Hill, River Town Gazette, Rug
Hooking, South Florida History, Town & Country*

Architecture

Periodicals:

Adirondack Life, American Bungalow, Architectural Digest, Artemis

Magazine, Atlanta Homes and Lifestyles, Back Home, Charleston Magazine, Colorado Homes & Lifestyles, Early American Life, Futurific Magazine, Home Improver Magazine, House Beautiful, House, Home and Garden, Joiners' Quarterly, LA Architect, Log Home Living, Metropolis, Metropolitan Home, Montana, Mountain Living, New Centennial Review, Persimmon Hill, River Town Gazette, Seattle Homes and Lifestyles, South Florida History, Springfield! Magazine, Stone Soup, Timeline, Town & Country, Whole Life Times

Book Publishers:

Allworth Press, Balcony Press, Chronicle Books LLC, David R. Godine, Fairleigh Dickinson University Press, Mage Publisihers, Mississippi, University Press of Mississippi, Pelican Publishing Company, Stenhouse Publishers, Texas A&M University Press

Arts

Periodicals:

5678 Country, 5678 Swing, 96 Inc., Alberta Views, Alive Now, American Artist, American Indian Art Magazine, American Scholar, The, American Theater, American Style, Antiques & Collecting Magazine, Appraisers Standard, The, Arkansas Review, Art & Antiques, Art Papers, Art Times, Artemis Magazine,, Artist's Magazine, The, Asian Pacific American Journal, The, Aspen Magazine, Atlanta Homes and Lifestyles, BabyTalk, Back Home, Beadwork, Beauty Spot, The: News You Can Use, Black Warrior Review, Body & Soul, Bridge, Buffalo Spree Magazine, Central PA Magazine, Ceramics Monthly, Charleston Magazine, Chattahoochee Review:, Chiron Review, Chronogram, Chrysalis Reader, Cincinnati Woman Magazine, Circle, The, Click Magazine, Crab Creek Review, Cream City Review, The, Cross & Quill,, Dance Spirit, Dance Teacher, Decorative Artist's Workbook, Devo'Zine, Doll World, Dream Network:, Drum Business, Early American Life, East End Lights, Fiberarts Magazine, Futures Mysterious Anthology Magazine, Game Developer, Georgia Review, The, Gist Review, Grit Magazine, Handwoven, Harper's Magazine, Home Times Family Newspaper, Hope Magazine, House, Home and Garden, Hudson Review, The, Iconoclast, The, Insider Magazine, Interior Design Magazine, Jam Rag, Journal of Asian Martial Arts, The, Kalliope: A Journal of Women's Art, Kentucky Monthly, Kenyon Review, The, LA Architect, Ladies' Home Journal, Ladybug Parent's Companion, Left Curve, Letter Arts Review, Light of Consciousness, Liquid Ohio, Literal Latte, Long Island Woman, Lynx eye, Metropolis, Mountain Living, National Enquirer, The, Native Peoples Magazine, New Centennial Review, New Letters, New Millennium Writings, New Yorker, The, Nimrod:, Northwest Review: University of Oregon, Other Side, The, Over the Back Fence, Passages North, Persimmon Hill, Phi Delta Kappan, Popular Photography, Potomac Review, Quilting Arts Magazine, Rearview, Redbook, River Town Gazette, RiverSedge, Roanoker, The, Rosebud, Rug Hooking, Salon, Sandlapper, SchoolArts, Short Stuff Magazine, Small Farm Today, Smoke Magazine, Life's Burning Desires, South American Explorer, South Florida History, Southern California Anthology, Southwest Fly Fishing, Springfield! Magazine, Stock Car Racing, Stone Soup, Swimming World, symploke, Teaching Tolerance, Tequesta, The World & I, Thema, Threepenny Review, The, Town & Country, Tradition, Vanity Fair, Vibe, Watercolor Magic, Weavings, Wildlife Art, William and Mary Review: College of William and Mary, The, Willow Springs, Women Artists News Book Review, Zoetrope: All-Story

Book Publishers:

Allworth Press, Anchorage Press Plays, International Agency of Plays for Young People, Art Direction Book Company, Balcony Press, Branden Publishing Company, Chronicle Books LLC, Collectors Press, David R. Godine, Down East Books, Fairleigh Dickinson University Press, Lerner Publishing, Limelight Editions, Maisonneuve Press, Meriwether Publishing Ltd, Contemporary Drama Service, Michael Wiese Productions, Midmarch Arts Press, Mississippi, University Press of Mississippi, Pelican Publishing Company, QED Press, Santa Monica Press LLC, Scarecrow Press, Shambhala Publications, Stone Bridge Press, University of Maine Press, University of Nebraska Press, Walter Foster Publishing, White Cliffs Media, Will Hall Books

Asian-American

Periodicals:

Asian Pacific American Journal, Calyx Journal, Clubhouse, Equal Opportunity Publications, Inc., Filipinas, Futures Mysterious Anthology Magazine, Japanophile, Evoking the old and the new Japan, Journal of Asian Martial Arts, Kuumba, Manoa, A Pacific Journal of International Writing, Mother Jones, Passport, South American Explorer, Springfield! Magazine, T'ai Chi, Teaching Tolerance, Tequesta, Turtle, Willow Springs

Book Publishers:

Bridge Works, Calyx Books, Clarity Press, Cross Cultural Publications, Fairleigh Dickinson University Press, Intercultural Press, Lehigh University Press, Lerner Publishing, Mayhaven Publishing, McFarland & Company, Pacific View Press, Pelican Publishing Company, Richard C. Owen Publishers, Shambhala Publications, Soho Press Inc, Stone Bridge Press, Temple University Press, Turtle Press

Associations

Periodicals:

Christian Camp & Conference Journal, Commercial Investment Real Estate Magazine, Cross & Quill, Elks Magazine, The Equal Opportunity Publications, Hawaii, Highways, Hope Magazine, Lion Magazine, The Midwest Traveler, Muzzle Blasts, New Mexico Journey, Old Farmer's Almanac, The Paddler Short, Stuff Magazine, Southern Review, Springfield! Magazine, Teaching Tolerance, Toastmaster, The VFW Magazine, Westways, Southern California Lifestyle, Win-Informer, Women In Business

Book Publishers:

Abbott, Langer & Associates, GATF Press, International Foundation of Employee Benefit Plans, Pineapple Press, Sourcebooks

Automobiles

Periodicals:

4-Wheel Drive & Sport Utility, Aspen Magazine, Auto Sound & Security, Automobile Quarterly, Beauty Spot, News You Can Use, Better Homes and Gardens, Boys' Life, Business Fleet, Car and Driver, CC Motorcycle News Magazine, Circle Track, Corvette Fever, Custom Rodder, Futurific Magazine, Go Magazine, Good Old Days, Hawaii, Westways, Heartland USA, Insider Magazine, Midwest Traveler, Mopar Muscle, Motor Trend, Motorcycling, Muscle Mustang & Fast Fords, Mustang & Fords, Mustang Monthly, New Mexico Journey, Poptronics, Popular Mechanics, Popular Science, River Town Gazette, Southern Review, Specialty Travel Index, Toy Cars & Models, Via, Western RV News & Recreation, Southern California Lifestyle

Book Publishers:

Howell Press, Iconografix, Smithsonian Oceanic Collection, Smithsonian Backyard, Smithsonian Lets Go to the Zoo!, Voyageur Press

Aviation

Periodicals:

Artemis Magazine,, Aviation Maintenance, Balloon Life, Boys' Life, Elks Magazine, Futurific Magazine, General Aviation News, Heartland USA, Kitplanes, Popular Mechanics, Popular Science, Primedia History Group, Southern Aviator, Southern Humanities Review, Timeline

Book Publishers:

Aeronitcal Publishers, Branden Publishing Company, Hancock House, Howell Press, Naval Institute Press, Potomac Books, Texas A&M University Press

-B-

Beauty

Periodicals:

Christian Women Today, Elle, First for Women, Harper's Bazaar, Lucky Magazine, Redbook, Seek, Town & Country, Woman's Day, Woman's World, Women Today Magazine

Book Publishers:

Harvard Common Press

Biography

Periodicals:

Acoustic Guitar Magazine, Back Home, Black Forest Press, Cobblestone Magazine, Crone Chronicles, Doll World, Early American Life, East End Lights, Elks Magazine, Freeman, Ideas on Liberty, Grit Magazine, Heartland USA, Iconoclast, Jewish Currents, Kalliope A Journal of Women's Art, Kentucky Monthly, Kung Fu Tai Chi, Ladies' Home Journal, Lifeglow, Lilith, Minnesota Memories, National Enquirer, New Centennial Review, Nine, Nineteenth-Century French Studies, Old Farmer's Almanac, Persimmon Hill, Plus Magazine, Redbook, Rosebud, Sandlapper, South American Explorer, Springfield! Magazine, Tequesta, Timeline, Tiny Lights A Journal of Personal Essay, Transitions, Vanity Fair, Woman's Day, Women Today Magazine, Young & Alive

Book Publishers:

In Print Publishing, Safari Press, Serendipity Systems Books-on-disks, Southern Illinois University Press, Tricycle Press, Trinity Foundation

Boating

Periodicals:

Canoe & Kayak Magazine, Chesapeake Bay Magazine, Cruising World, Florida Wildlife Magazine Newsletter, Heartland USA, Houseboat, Marlin, Offshore, Paddler, Popular Mechanics, Power & Motoryacht, River Town Gazette, Sailing Magazine, Sailing World, Sea Kayaker, Sea The Magazine of Western Boating, Sport Fishing Magazine, Texas Parks & Wildlife, Trailer Boats, Yachting

Book Publishers:

Bristol Fashion Publications, Cornell Maritime Press, David R. Godine, Howell Press, International Marine, Lyons Press, Naval Institute Press, Paradise Cay, Pelican Publishing Company, Ragged Mountain Press, Wescott Cove Publishing Co., WoodenBoat Books

Book Reviews

Periodicals:

Absolute Write, African American Pulpit!, African American Review, American Profile, American Turf Monthly, Anvil Magazine, Atlanta Homes and Lifestyles, Audubon, BabyTalk, Balanced Living Magazine, Beauty Spot, News You Can Use, Bibliophilos, Black Warrior Review, Bloomsbury Review, Body & Soul, Book/Mark Quarterly Review, Boston Magazine, Carolina Quarterly, Chattahoochee Review, Chesapeake Bay Magazine, Cicada, Cincinnati Woman Magazine, Clamor, CompulsiveReader.com, Confrontation, A Literary Journal, Fellowship, First Things, French Forum, Genre, Georgia Review, Gist Review, Glamour, Gray Areas, Green Hills Literary Lantern, Green Mountains Review, Home Times Family Newspaper, Hudson Review, Indiana Review, Iris A Journal about Women, Japanophile, Evoking the old and the new Japan, Jewish Currents, Kentucky Monthly, Legacy Journal, Light, Long Island Woman, Maelstrom, Maine Organic Farmer & Gardener, Mental Floss, Mid-American Review, Minnesota Review, Missouri Review, Montana, Native Peoples Magazine, New Yorker, Nine, Northwest Family News, Obsidian III, Outdoor Life, Parenting, Persimmon Hill, Pleiades A Journal of New Writing, Poetry Magazine, Quarterly West, Redbook, River Town Gazette, Ruminator Review, Salon, Sew News, Shape Magazine, Shenandoah, South Florida History, Springfield! Magazine, Stock Car Racing, Student Leader, Sycamore Review, symploke, Teaching Tolerance, The World & I, Threepenny Review, Transitions, West Coast Magazine, Willow Springs, Win-Informer

Book Publishers:

In Print Publishing, Safari Press, Serendipity Systems Books-on-disks, Southern Illinois University Press, Tricycle Press, Trinity Foundation

Business

Periodicals:

Alaska Business Monthly, American Business Review, American Salesman, Area Development, Artemis Magazine, Artist's Magazine, Aspen Magazine, Automated Builder, Beauty Spot, News You Can Use, Benefits & Compensation Digest, Black Forest Press, Boston Magazine, Business 2.0, ColoradoBiz Magazine, Commercial Investment Real

Estate Magazine, Contract Management, Cooperator, DECA Dimensions, Drum Business, Entrepreneur Magazine, Entrepreneur.com, Equities Magazine, Financial Planning, Florida Hotel & Motel Journal, Forester Communications, Fresh Cut, Futurific Magazine, Government Executive, Happy Times Monthly, Harper's Magazine, Home Business Magazine, Home Business Journal, Home Times Family Newspaper, Labor Paper, Long Island Woman, Model Retailer, Mortgage Banking, New Mexico Woman Magazine, Onion World, Oregon Business, Perdido, Personal Branding Magazine, Playboy, Podiatry Management, Popular Mechanics, Presentations Magazine, Radio World, Redbook, River Town Gazette, Salon, Sandlapper, Script Magazine, Skin Inc. Magazine, Space and Time, Sunset Magazine, Supervision, Supply Chain Systems Magazine, Wines & Vines, Woman's Day, Woman's World

Book Publishers:

Abbott, Langer & Associates, Addicus Books, Aegis Publishing Group, Algora Publishing, Imprint Agathon Press, Allworth Press, Americas Group ATL Press Science Technology, B. Klein Publications, Barrons Educational Series, Bay Tree Publishing, Berrett-Koehler Publishers, Black Forest Press, Bonus Books, Inc., Bookhaven Press LLC, Branden Publishing Company, Business Group, Capital Books, Contemporary Books, A Division of McGraw-Hill Companies, Craftsman Book Company, Emerald Ink Publishing, Forum Publishing Company, Frederick Fell Publishers, Globe Pequot Press, Graduate Group, Harvard Common Press, Intercultural Press, International Foundation of Employee Benefit Plans, JIST Works, Jodere Group Inc., Lehigh University Press, Metamorphous Press, Millennium Publishing Company, New Society Publishers, New World Library, Origin Media, Books for the Integral Age, Pelican Publishing Company, Personal Branding Press, Prep Publishing, Prima Publishing, Quill Driver Books, Stenhouse Publishers, Stone Bridge Press, Success Publishing, Ten Speed Press, Texas A&M University Press, The Oasis Press, Hellgate Press, Tower Publishing, Wilshire Book Co.

-C-

Campus Life

Periodicals:

Campus Life, Circle K, College Bound Teen, Kentucky Monthly, River Town Gazette, Studies in American Jewish Literature, symploke, Young & Alive

Careers

Periodicals:

America West Magazine, American Careers, American Salesman, Artemis Magazine, Beauty Spot, News You Can Use, Black Forest Press, Boys' Life, Christian Women Today, Cross & Quill,, DECA Dimensions, Dialouge, Equal Opportunity Publications, Futurific Magazine, Glamour, Happy Times Monthly, Insider Magazine, Instructor, LA Architect, Labor Paper, Lifeglow, Long Island Woman, Men's Health, Modern Maturity, The Magazine AARP, Natural Beauty and Health, New Centennial Review, Persimmon Hill, Personal Branding Magazine, Springfield! Magazine, Strategic Health Care Marketing, Sunset Magazine, Times News Service, Today's Christian, Transitions, Unique Opportunities, Wines & Vines, Woman's Day, Women In Business, Women Today Magazine, Working Mother Magazine, Young & Alive

Book Publishers:

Barrons Educational Series, Berrett-Koehler Publishers, Black Forest Press, Bookhaven Press LLC, Capital Books, Contemporary Books, A Division of McGraw-Hill Companies, Garth Gardner Company, Globe Pequot Press, Graduate Group, Harvard Common Press, Impact Publishers, JIST Works, Millennium Publishing Company, Mustang Publishing Company, Pathfinder Publishing of California, PREP Publishing, Prima Publishing, Quill Driver Books, Ronin Publishing,

Soundprints, Ten Speed Press

Cartoons

Periodicals:

Artemis Magazine, BabyTalk, Beauty Spot, News You Can Use, Black Warrior Review, Boys' Life, Boys' Quest, Chronogram, Funny Times, Futures Mysterious Anthology Magazine, Happy Times Monthly, Heartland USA, Home Times Family Newspaper, Hopscotch for Girls, Iconoclast, Jewish Currents, Light, Liquid Ohio, Maelstrom, Model Retailer, New Yorker, Passport, Phi Delta Kappan, Protooner, River Town Gazette, Saturday Evening Post, Sport Fishing Magazine, Sunset Magazine, Teaching Tolerance, Thema, With The Magazine for Radical Christian Youth, Young & Alive

Book Publishers:

Elderberry Press, Garth Gardner Company, Pelican Publishing Company, Success Publishing

Children

Periodicals:

All About Kids, American Fitness, Appleseeds, Artemis Magazine, Atlanta Parent, Babybug, Black Forest Press, Boys' Life, Boys' Quest, Calliope Magazine, Cat Fancy, Chess Life, Child Magazine, Christian Parenting Today, Click Magazine, Club Connection, Clubhouse, Creative With Words!, Cricket, Dream Network, Faces The Magazine About People, Family Circle, Family Digest, Footsteps, Fun for Kidz, Girls' Life, Grit Magazine, Guide, Guideposts for Kids, Happy Times Monthly, Highlights for Children, Home Education Magazine, Home Times Family Newspaper, Hopscotch for Girls, House, Home and Garden, Instructor, Kung Fu Tai Chi, Ladies' Home Journal, Ladybug Parent's Companion, Ladybug The Magazine for Young Children, Metro Parent, Muse Magazine, My Legacy, Natural Beauty and Health, New Moon, Northwest Family News, Odyssey Magazine, Old Farmer's Almanac, Pack-o-Fun, Parenting, Parents Magazine, Parents' Press, Passport, Pediatrics For Parents, Pockets, Potluck Children's Literary Magazine, Potomac Review, Redbook, Reunions Magazine, River Town Gazette, Sandlapper, SchoolArts, Scouting, Songwriters Monthly, Spider The Magazine for Children, Springfield! Magazine, Stock Car Racing, Swimming Technique, Teaching Tolerance, United Parenting Publications, West Coast Magazine, Woman's Day, Woman's World, Wonderful Ideas for Teaching, Learning, and Enjoying Mathematics!, Working Mother Magazine

Book Publishers:

American Literary Press, Noble House, Anchorage Press Plays, International Agency of Plays for Young People, Angel Bea Publishing, Atheneum Books, Barbed Wire Publishing, Barrons Educational Series, Bethany House Publishers, Beyond Words Publishing, Black Forest Press, Branden Publishing Company, Carolrhoda Books, Charlesbridge Publishing , Talewinds, Whispering Coyote, Christian Ed. Publishers, Council for Indian Education, David R. Godine, Dawn Publications, Down East Books, Dutton Children's Books, Edupress, Farrar, Straus and Giroux, Publishers, Books for Young Readers, Free Spirit Publishing, Front Street, G.P. Putnam's Sons, Books for Young Readers, Hachai Publishing, Hearts 'N Tummies Cookbook Company, Holiday House, Incentive Publications, Jodere Group Inc., Judson Press, Kar-Ben Publishing, Kids Books By Kids, Legacy Press, Lerner Publishing, Little Simon, Mayhaven Publishing, Milkweed Editions, Munchweiler Press, Quality Books for Young Readers, New Horizons Press, Small Horizons Imprint, Pacific View Press, Pauline Books & Media, Pelican Publishing Company, Perspectives Press, The Infertility and Adoption Publisher, Piano Press, Printing Industries of America Graphic Arts Center Publishing Company, Rainbow Publishers, Richard C. Owen Publishers, Roberts Rinehart, Running Press Kids, Sasquatch Books, Sphinx Publishing, Ten Speed Press, The Millbrook Press, Tilbury House Publishers, UpstartBooks, Waterbrook Press, Will Hall Books, Woodbine House, WoodenBoat Books, World Leisure Corporation, Zondervan and Zonderkid

Christian Interests

Periodicals:

African American Pulpit!, Alive! A Magazine for Christian Senior Adults, Bible Advocate, Black Forest Press, Books & Culture, Cadet Quest, Christian Camp & Conference Journal, Christian Century, Christian New Age Quarterly, Christian Parenting Today, Christian Single, Christian Social Action, Christianity Today, Chronicles A magazine of American Culture, Club Connection, Clubhouse, CNEWA World, Cornerstone, Cross & Quill, Devo'Zine, Discipleship Journal, Door Magazine, Evangel, First Things, Guide, Guideposts, Guideposts for Kids, Home Times Family Newspaper, Insight, Journal of Adventist Education, Kung Fu Tai Chi, Leadership Journal, LifeWayonline.com, Ligourian, Living Church, Living With Teenagers, Lookout For Today's Growing Christian, Lutheran Digest, Marriage Partnership, Mature Living, Mature Years, Men of Integrity, Message Magazine, Moody Magazine, My Legacy, Oblates, On Mission, Other Side, Passport, Plain Truth, Pockets, Presbyterians Today, Secret Place, Stamats Meetings Media, Teaching Tolerance, Today's Christian Woman, Today's Pentecostal Evangel, Upper Room, Weavings, Win-Informer, With The Magazine for Radical Christian Youth, Woman's Touch, Women Alive!, Christian Interestsù, Young & Alive

Book Publishers:

Angel Bea Publishing, Baker Books, Beyond Words Publishing, Black Forest Press, Broadman & Holman Publishers, Christian Publications, Horizon Books, Cross Cultural Publications, Crossway Books, Daily Guideposts, ETC Publications, Genesis Communications, Evergreen Press & Gazelle Press, God Allows U Turns Book Series, IHS Press, Judson Press, Just Us Books, Legacy Press, Loyola Press, Nelson Reference & Electronic Publishing, Prep Publishing, Rainbow Publishers, Shambhala Publications, Square One Publishers, Tricycle Press, Trinity Foundation, Waterbrook Press, Zondervan and Zonderkid

Civil War

Periodicals:

Back Home, Bibliophilos, Black Forest Press, Grit Magazine, Heartland USA, Kentucky Monthly, My Legacy, Primedia History Group, Sandlapper, Southern Humanities Review, Springfield! Magazine, Tequesta, Timeline, Times News Service, Today's Christian, Willow Springs, Young & Alive

Book Publishers:

Black Forest Press, Branden Publishing Company, Bridge Works, Conservatory of American Letters, Fairleigh Dickinson University Press, Fordham University Press, Heritage Books, Mayhaven Publishing, McFarland & Company, University Press of Mississippi, Pelican Publishing Company, Potomac Books, Rutledge Hill Press, Texas Western Press, Tom Doherty Associate, Tor Books, Forge Books, Orb, Starscape, University of Maine Press, University of Nebraska Press, University of Oklahoma Press, White Mane Publishing Company

Collectibles

Periodicals:

American Bungalow, AmericanStyle, Antique Trader Weekly, Appraisers Standard, Back Home, Classic Toy Trains, Collector Editions, Collectors News, Country Living, Doll World, Early American Life, Grit Magazine, House, Home and Garden, Kentucky Monthly, Model Retailer, Persimmon Hill, Plus Magazine, River Town Gazette, Toy Shop, Wildlife Art

Book Publishers:

Collectors Press, Hobby House Press, Kregel Kidzone

College

Periodicals:

Black Forest Press, Change, Circle K, College Bound Teen, Equal Opportunity Publications, Insider Magazine, Iris A Journal about Women, Kentucky Monthly, Liquid Ohio, New Centennial Review, New Millennium Writings, Oregon Quarterly, Oxendine Publishing, Sandlapper, Springfield! Magazine, Teaching Tolerance, Young & Alive

Book Publishers:

Topics

Barrons Educational Series, Black Forest Press, Cross Cultural Publications, Denali Press, Frederick Fell Publishers, Garth Gardner Company, Graduate Group, Intercultural Press, Mustang Publishing Company, Nova Press, Soundprints, Ten Speed Press

Comedy

Periodicals:

America West Magazine, Artemis Magazine, Cadet Quest, The Creative With Words!, Happy Times Monthly, Home Times Family Newspaper, Lutheran Digest, The New Millennium Writings, Playgirl, Plus Magazine, Protooner River Town Gazette, Springfield! Magazine, Transitions, Whole Life Times, Young & Alive

Book Publishers:

Bridge Works, CCC Publications, Diogenes Publishing, Great Quotations Publishing, Piccadilly Books, Success Publishing

Computers

Periodicals:

American Hunter, Artemis Magazine,, Aspen Magazine, Beauty Spot, News You Can Use, Better Homes and Gardens, Boys' Life, ComputorEdge, Desktop Engineering, Dialogue , Game Developer, Genealogical Computing, House, Home and Garden, Insider Magazine, Memory Makers, Model Retailer, Mom Guess What Newspaper, PC World, Popular Mechanics, Popular Science, Presentations Magazine, River Town Gazette, Supervision, Wired, Women In Business, Writer Gazette, Young & Alive

Book Publishers:

29th Press, Abbott, Langer & Associates, ATL Press Science Technology, Franklin, Beedle & Associates, Garth Gardner Company, Graduate Group, Millennium Publishing Company, Osborne/McGraw-Hill, Pathfinder Publishing of California, Prima Publishing, Scarecrow Press

Confession

Periodicals:

Complete Woman, Lutheran Digest, Springfield! Magazine

Conservation

Periodicals:

Adirondack Life, America West Magazine, American Forests, Artemis Magazine,Aspen Magazine, Audubon, BabyTalk, Bear Deluxe Magazine, Boys' Life, Bugle, California Wild, Country Living, Defenders of Wildlife, E Magazine, Field & Stream, Florida Wildlife Magazine Newsletter, Flyfisher, Grit Magazine, Heartland USA, HerbalGram, Insider Magazine, Kentucky Monthly, Lutheran Digest, Maine Organic Farmer & Gardener, Marlin, Montana, Mother Earth News, Mountain Living, Natural Beauty and Health, Northwest Fly Fishing, Outdoor America, Outdoor Life, Paddler, Persimmon Hill, Safari, Sandlapper, Scouting, Small Farm Today, South American Explorer, Southern Traveler, Sport Fishing Magazine, Texas Parks & Wildlife, Transitions Abroad, Whole Life Times, Wildlife Art

Book Publishers:

Beyond Words Publishing, Conservatory of American Letters, Cross Cultural Publications, Green Nature Books, Hancock House, Island Press, McDonald & Woodward Publishing Company, Milkweed Editions, Mountaineers Books, New Society Publishers, Ragged Mountain Press, Sierra Club Books, Sourcebooks, University of Nebraska Press, University of North Texas Press

Consumer

Periodicals:

American Fitness, Artemis Magazine, Arthritis Today, Automobile Quarterly, Beauty Spot, News You Can Use, Budget Living, Canoe & Kayak Magazine, Child Magazine, Cincinnati Woman Magazine, Country Home, Country Woman Magazine, Dialouge, Dollar Stretcher, Go Magazine, Guns & Ammo, Hawaii, Westways, Home Improver Magazine, Insider Magazine, Kentucky Monthly, Labor Paper, Ladies' Home Journal, Lake Superior Magazine, Leather Crafters & Saddlers Jour-

nal, Lutheran Digest, Maine Organic Farmer & Gardener, Marlin, Marriage Partnership, Men's Fitness, Message Magazine, Metropolis, Midwest Traveler, Modern Bride, National Geographic Traveler, Native Peoples Magazine, Natural Beauty and Health, New Mexico Journey, North Dakota Horizons, Oklahoma Today Magazine, Old Farmer's Almanac, Outdoor Life, Parenting, Playgirl, Popular Mechanics, River Town Gazette, Roanoker, Rosebud, Seventeen, SKI, Southern Review, Sport Fishing Magazine, Toy Shop, Travel & Leisure, Veggie Life, Via, Southern California Lifestyle, Woman's Day, Woman's World, Women In Business

Book Publishers:

Berrett-Koehler Publishers, Branden Publishing Company, Kregel Kidzone, Mustang Publishing Company, Santa Monica Press LLC, Success Publishing

Cooking

Periodicals:

Alaska Business Monthly, America West Magazine, American Girl, Artemis Magazine, Atlanta Homes and Lifestyles, Back Home, Beauty Spot, News You Can Use, Better Homes and Gardens, Black Forest Press, Central PA Magazine, Cincinnati Woman Magazine, Clubhouse, Colorado Homes & Lifestyles, Cooking Light, Country Home, Country Living, Country Magazine, Country Woman Magazine, First for Women, Food & Wine, Glamour, Good Old Days, Gourmet, GRIT Magazine, Happy Times Monthly, Health, Home Cooking, House, Home and Garden, Italian Cooking and Living, Kentucky Monthly, Ladies' Home Journal, Long Island Woman, Lutheran Digest, Magazine of La Cucina Italiana, Maine Organic Farmer & Gardener, Modern Maturity, AARP, The Magazine, Mother Earth News, Mountain Living, Natural Beauty and Health, Northwest Palate, Old Farmer's Almanac, Outdoor Life, Persimmon Hill, Prevention Magazine, Redbook, Sandlapper, Saveur, Stone Soup, Veggie Life, West Coast Magazine, Whole Life Times, Wild Foods Forum, Woman's Day, Woman's World, Women Today Magazine, Working Mother Magazine, Yankee, Young & Alive

Book Publishers:

American Literary Press, Noble House, Barrons Educational Series, Berkshire House Publishers, Black Forest Press, Bonus Books, Bristol Publishing Enterprises nitty gritty Cookbooks, Champion Press, Chronicle Books LLC, Collectors Press, Cornell Maritime Press, Crossing Press, David R. Godine, Down East Books, Falcon Publishing, Frederick Fell Publishers, Globe Pequot Press, Golden West Publishers, Hancock House, Harvard Common Press, Hay House, Hearts 'N Tummies Cookbook Company, Howell Press, Jewish Lights Publishing, Llewellyn Publications, LYONS PRESS, Mage Publisihers, Magni Group, Mayhaven Publishing, Mountain N' Air Books, Paradise Cay, Pelican Publishing Company, Pineapple Press, Prima Publishing, Printing Industries of America /Graphic Arts Center Publishing Company, Rutledge Hill Press, Serendipity Systems; Books-on-disks, Southern Illinois University Press, Taylor Trade, Imprints, Cooper Square Press, Derrydale Press, Madison Books, Ten Speed Press, University of North Texas Press, Willow Creek Press

Counseling

Periodicals:

Family Therapy

Book Publishers:

Baywood Publishing Company, Hazelden Publishing

Crafts/Hobbies

Periodicals:

American Girl, AmericanStyle, Antiques & Collecting Magazine, Art Times, Artemis Magazine, Back Home, Backwoodsman Magazine, Bead&Button Magazine, Beadwork, Boys' Life, Budget Living, Cat Fancy, Ceramics Monthly, Cincinnati Woman Magazine, Classic Toy Trains, Cloth Paper Scissors, Clubhouse, Country Living, Country Woman Magazine, Creative Crafter, Crochet World, Decorative Artist's Workbook, Doll World, Fast & Fun Crochet, Fiberarts Magazine, Fine

Woodworking, Girls' Life, Grit Magazine, Guideposts for Kids, Handwoven, House, Home and Garden, Interweave Knits, Kentucky Monthly, Knives Illustrated, Ladies' Home Journal, Ladybug The Magazine for Young Children, Leather Crafters & Saddlers Journal, Long Island Woman, Maine Organic Farmer & Gardener, Memory Makers, Model Railroader, Modeler's Resource, Modern Bride, Mother Earth News, Old Farmer's Almanac, Outdoor Life, Pack-o-Fun, Passport, PieceWork, Plastic Canvas Today, Popular Mechanics, Popular Woodworking, Quilting Arts Magazine, River Town Gazette, Rug Hooking, Scouting, Seventeen, Short Stuff Magazine, Spider The Magazine for Children, Spinning Jenny, Spin-Off, Stone Soup, Threads Magazine, Toy Farmer, Transitions, Woman's Day, Woman's World, Young & Alive

Book Publishers:

Allworth Press, Barrons Educational Series, Chronicle Books LLC, Down East Books, Gem Guides Book Company, Green Nature Books, Hobby House Press, Howell Press, Interweave Press, Jewish Lights Publishing, Legacy Press, Magni Group, Naturegraph Publishers, Rainbow Publishers, Sphinx Publishing, Success Publishing, Ten Speed Press, Voyageur Press, Walter Foster Publishing, WoodenBoat Books

Crime

Periodicals:

Alfred Hitchcock Mystery Magazine, Corrections Compendium, FBI Law Enforcement Bulletin, Futures Mysterious Anthology Magazine, Good Housekeeping, Gray Areas, Gryphon Books, Harper's Magazine, Heartland USA, Kentucky Monthly, My Legacy, Redbook, Society of American Baseball Research, Springfield! Magazine, Teaching Tolerance

Book Publishers:

American Correctional Association, Bridge Works, David R. Godine, Graduate Group, Holloway House Publishing Group, Howells House, Mayhaven Publishing, New Horizons Press, Small Horizons Imprint, PREP Publishing, Smithsonian Oceanic Collection, Smithsonian Backyard, Smithsonian Lets Go to the Zoo!, Soho Press Inc, Tom Doherty Associate, Tor Books, Forge Books, Orb, Starscape, University of North Texas Press, Willowgate Press

Culture

Periodicals:

Adirondack Life, Alaska Business Monthly, Alberta Views, America West Magazine, American Indian Quarterly, Arizona Highways, Arkansas Review, Art Times, Aspen Magazine, Beauty Spot, News You Can Use, Bible Advocate, Black Forest Press, Blue Ridge Country Magazine, Books & Culture, Boston Magazine, Boston Review, Bridge, Capper's, Caribbean Travel & Life, Central PA Magazine, Chronicles A magazine of American Culture, Chronogram, Cimarron Review, Cincinnati Woman Magazine, Circle, CNEWA World, Commonweal, Creative With Words!, Crone Chronicles, Dream Network, Faces The Magazine About People, Family Digest, Feminist Studies University of Maryland, First Things, German Life, Girlfriends Magazine, Gray Areas, Grit Magazine, Harper's Magazine, Home Times Family Newspaper, Iconoclast, Insider Magazine, Italian Cooking and Living, Journal of Asian Martial Arts, Kentucky Monthly, Kuumba, LA Architect, Lake Michigan Travel Guide, Left Curve, Magical Blend, Metro Parent, Metropolis, Minnesota Review, Montana, MORE, Mother Jones, Mountain Living, My Legacy, Native Peoples Magazine, Natural Beauty and Health, New Centennial Review, New Letters, new renaissance, New Yorker, Nimrod, Nine, Nineteenth-Century French Studies, North Dakota Horizons, Obsidian III, Old Farmer's Almanac, Oregon Quarterly, Playboy, Playgirl, Points North, Potomac Review, River Town Gazette, Russian Life, San Francisco, Sandlapper, Shenandoah, Short Stuff Magazine, Small Farm Today, Smoke Magazine, Life's Burning Desires, South American Explorer, Southern Review, Southwest Fly Fishing, Southwest Review, Specialty Retail Report, Springfield! Magazine, Student Leader, Sycamore Review, symploke, Teaching Tolerance, Tequesta, Texas Highways, The Black Table, The World & I, Tikkun, Transitions, Vanity Fair, Vibe, Vogue, Washington Monthly, Whole Life Times, Wil-

low Springs, Women and Music,

Book Publishers:

Algora Publishing, Imprint Agathon Press, BenBella Books, Beyond Words Publishing, Black Forest Press, Branden Publishing Company, Chronicle Books LLC, Cross Cultural Publications, Denali Press, Diogenes Publishing, Fairleigh Dickinson University Press, HiddenSpring, Intercultural Press, Jewish Lights Publishing, Just Us Books, Lerner Publishing, Mage Publisihers, Maisonneuve Press, Mississippi, University Press of Mississippi, Mustang Publishing Company, Paulist Press HiddenSpring, Printing Industries of America Graphic Arts Center Publishing Company, Ronin Publishing, Santa Monica Press LLC, Scarecrow Press, Sphinx Publishing, Stone Bridge Press, Temple University Press, Texas A&M University Press, Texas Western Press, Tricycle Press, Trinity Foundation, University of Nebraska Press, Washington State University Press, White Cliffs Media

Current Affairs

Periodicals:

Newsweek, Ruminator Review, Salon, The Black Table, The World & I

Book Publishers:

Bay Tree Publishing, North Ridge Books

-D-

Dance

Periodicals:

5678 Country, 5678 Swing, Art Times, Cincinnati Woman Magazine, Dance Spirit, Dance Teacher, Dramatics, Hudson Review, Kentucky Monthly, Teaching Tolerance, Threepenny Review, Tradition, Willow Springs

Book Publishers:

Allworth Press, Meriwether Publishing Ltd, Contemporary Drama Service, Players Press, Temple University Press

Diet/Nutrition

Periodicals:

Beauty Spot, News You Can Use, Body & Soul, Cincinnati Woman Magazine, Complete Woman, Diabetes Self-Management, Elle, Good Housekeeping, Health, House, Home and Garden, Ladies' Home Journal, Long Island Woman, Lutheran Digest, Maine Organic Farmer & Gardener, Men's Fitness, Men's Health, Muscle & Fitness, National Enquirer, Natural Beauty and Health, New Times, New York Runner, ParentLife, PLUS Magazine, Prevention Magazine, River Town Gazette, Roanoker, Rocky Mountain Sports Magazine, Skin Inc. Magazine, Syracuse New Times, Veggie Life, Weight Watchers Magazine, West Coast Magazine, Whole Life Times, Wild Foods Forum, Wines & Vines, Woman's Day, Woman's World, Women In Business, Working Mother Magazine, Young & Alive

Book Publishers:

Barrons Educational Series, Contemporary Books, Crossing Press, Empire Publishing Service, Fairview Press, Frederick Fell Publishers, Great Quotations Publishing, Hay House, Hohm Press, Hunter House Publishers, Llewellyn Publications, Piccadilly Books, Quill Driver Books, Renders Wellness/Publishing, Shambhala Publications, Silver Dagger Mysteries, Soundprints, Southern Illinois University Press, Success Publishing, Swedenborg Foundation, Chrysalis Books, Ten Speed Press Woodland Publishing

Directories

Periodicals:

Beauty Spot, News You Can Use, Springfield! Magazine, Teaching Tolerance

Book Publishers:

Black Forest Press, Branden Publishing Company, Brookline Books, Fairview Press, Free Spirit Publishing, Future Horizons, High Tide Press, Hunter House Publishers, In Print Publishing, Mayhaven Pub-

Topics

lishing, Pathfinder Publishing of California, Quill Driver Books, Temple University Press, Woodbine House

Disabilities

Periodicals:

Abilities, Atlanta Parent, Black Forest Press, Dialouge, Equal Opportunity Publications, Heartland USA, Lifeglow, Ragged Edge, River Town Gazette, Teaching Tolerance, Transitions

Book Publishers:

Black Forest Press, Branden Publishing Company, Brookline Books, Fairview Press, Free Spirit Publishing, Future Horizons, High Tide Press, Hunter House Publishers, In Print Publishing, Mayhaven Publishing, Pathfinder Publishing of California, Temple University Press, Woodbine House

Drama

Periodicals:

American Theater, Art Times, Asian Pacific American Journal, Beauty Spot, News You Can Use, Black Forest Press, Cincinnati Woman Magazine, Dance Teacher, Dramatics, Fourteen Hills, Futures Mysterious Anthology Magazine, Hudson Review, Iconoclast, Kentucky Monthly, Kenyon Review, Lilith, New Centennial Review, Obsidian III, Pleiades A Journal of New Writing, Rockford Review, Rosebud, Southern Humanities Review, Springfield! Magazine, Swimming World, Sycamore Review, Teaching Tolerance, Threepenny Review, Willow Springs

Book Publishers:

Allworth Press, Anchorage Press Plays, International Agency of Plays for Young People, Black Forest Press, Branden Publishing Company, Bridge Works, Conservatory of American Letters, Fairleigh Dickinson University Press, Limelight Editions, Mayhaven Publishing, Meriwether Publishing Ltd, Contemporary Drama Service, Players Press, Santa Monica Press LLC, Temple University Press, Waterbrook Press

-E-

Ecology

Periodicals:

Adirondack Life, American Forests, American Gardener, Artemis Magazine, Audubon, BabyTalk, Back Home In Kentucky, Bear Deluxe Magazine, Boys' Life, Bugle, California Wild, Chronogram, Defenders of Wildlife, E Magazine, Environment, Florida Wildlife Magazine Newsletter, Flyfisher, Fur-Fish-Game, Girls' Life, GritMagazine, Heartland USA, Jewish Currents, Kentucky Monthly, Magical Blend, Montana, Mountain Living, National Geographic Traveler, New Centennial Review, New Times, Old Farmer's Almanac, Outdoor Life, Potomac Review, River Town Gazette, Scouting, Small Farm Today, Sport Fishing Magazine, Springfield! Magazine, Timeline, Whole Life Times

Book Publishers:

Beyond Words Publishing, Charlesbridge Publishing , Talewinds, Whispering Coyote, Chelsea Green Publishing Company, Cross Cultural Publications, DIMI Press, Down East Books, Granite Publishing Group, Green Nature Books, Hancock House, HiddenSpring, In Print Publishing, Island Press, Jewish Lights Publishing, McDonald & Woodward Publishing Company, Mountain Press Publishing Company, Naturegraph Publishers, New Society Publishers, Sourcebooks, Stenhouse Publishers, Temple University Press, University of Nebraska Press, University of Nevada Press, Westcliffe Publishers

Economics

Periodicals:

Alberta Views, American Salesman, Artemis Magazine, Boston Magazine, Boston Review, Dollar Stretcher, Equities Magazine, Freeman, Ideas on Liberty, Futurific Magazine, Home Times Family Newspaper, Insider Magazine, Jewish Currents, Labor Paper, Long Island Woman, Mortgage Banking, Mother Jones, National Geographic Traveler, New Centennial Review, The World & I, Tikkun, Woman's World

Book Publishers:

Algora Publishing, Imprint Agathon Press, Berrett-Koehler Publishers, Clarity Press, Cross Cultural Publications, Fordham University Press, IHS Press, Paragon House, Texas A&M University Press, Tricycle Press, Trinity Foundation

Education

Periodicals:

American Careers, American Libraries, American Profile, Artemis Magazine, Atlanta Parent, Bibliophilos, Black Forest Press, Boston Magazine, Boston Review, Boys' Life, Calliope Magazine, Campus Life, Central PA Magazine, Change, Christian Home & School, Chronicles A magazine of American Culture, Circle K, Click Magazine, College Bound Teen, Corrections Compendium, Creative With Words!, Cross & Quill, DECA Dimensions, Education in Focus, Education Week, Educational Leadership, Electron, Equal Opportunity Publications, Et cetera, First Things, Florida Leader, Flyfisher, Footsteps, Futurific Magazine, Growing Edge, Guideposts for Kids, Home Education Magazine, Home Times Family Newspaper, Hope Magazine, Ideas on Liberty, Instructor, Jewish Currents, Journal of Adventist Education, Kentucky Monthly, Kung Fu Tai Chi, Ladies' Home Journal, Ladybug Parent's Companion, Mental Floss, Mercury, Muse Magazine, Muzzle Blasts, National Enquirer, National Geographic Traveler, New Centennial Review, New Millennium Writings, Onion World, Oregon Quarterly, Parenting, Parent Life, Pastoral Life, Phi Delta Kappan, Presentations Magazine, Radio World, Reader's Digest, Sandlapper, SchoolArts, Scouting, Short Stuff Magazine, Skin Inc. Magazine, Songwriters Monthly, Springfield! Magazine, Stock Car Racing, Strategic Health Care Marketing, Studies in American Jewish Literature, Teacher Magazine, Teachers of Vision, Teaching Tolerance, The World & I, Tikkun, Timeline, Today's Catholic Teacher, Today's School, Transitions, Transitions Abroad, West Coast Magazine, Whole Life Times, Woman's Day, Wonderful Ideas for Teaching, Learning, and Enjoying Mathematics!

Book Publishers:

Barrons Educational Series, Black Forest Press, Branden Publishing Company, Brookline Books, Bye Publishing, Carson-Dellosa Publishing Co., Champion Press, Contemporary Books, Cottonwood Press, Council for Indian Education, Cross Cultural Publications, Edupress, ETC Publications, Fordham University Press, Free Spirit Publishing, Graduate Group, Great Quotations Publishing, Gryphon House, Human Kinetics, In Print Publishing, Incentive Publications, Intercultural Press, International Foundation of Employee Benefit Plans, Lerner Publishing, Maupin House, Metamorphous Press, Michael Wiese Productions, Morgan Reynolds Publishing, Nova Press, Orange Frazer Press, Perron Press, Phi Delta Kappa Educational Foundation, Pineapple Press, Players Press, Rainbow Publishers, Redleaf Press, Rodnik Publishing Co., Running Press Kids, Scarecrow Press, Steeple Hill Love Inspired, Stylus Publishing, LLC, Temple University Press, The Millbrook Press, Tricycle Press, Trinity Foundation, UpstartBooks, Will Hall Books, Woodbine House

Electronics

Periodicals:

Artemis Magazine, Boys' Life, Electron, Electronic Servicing & Technology, Futurific Magazine, House, Home and Garden, New Centennial Review, Poptronics, Popular Mechanics, Popular Science, Wired

Engineering

Periodicals:

Artemis Magazine, Cutting Tool Engineering, Desktop Engineering, Engineering Economist, Equal Opportunity Publications, Futurific Magazine, Game Developer, Joiners' Quarterly, Montana, New Centennial Review, Poptronics, Popular Mechanics, Progressive Engineer, Radio World, Timeline

Book Publishers:

Craftsman Book Company, Stenhouse Publishers

Entertainment

Periodicals:

5678 Country, 5678 Swing, America West Magazine, American Girl, American Profile, Art Times, Artemis Magazine, Aspen Magazine, Bear Deluxe Magazine, Beauty Spot, News You Can Use, Boston Magazine, Boys' Life, Buffalo Spree Magazine, Caribbean Travel & Life, Central PA Magazine, Cincinnati Woman Magazine, Coastal Living, Complete Woman, Country Living, Dance Spirit, Doll World, Dramatics, East End Lights, Elle, Food & Wine, Futures Mysterious Anthology Magazine, Girlfriends Magazine, Girls' Life, Glamour, Gourmet, Happy Times Monthly, Home Cooking, Home Times Family Newspaper, Horror Tales, House, Home and Garden, Insider Magazine, Jam Rag, Kentucky Monthly, Lacunae, Ladies' Home Journal, More, National Enquirer, New Yorker, Northwest Palate, Penthouse, Persimmon Hill, Playboy, Playgirl, Plus Magazine, Redbook, River Town Gazette, Salon, Sandlapper, Surfer, Symploke, Teaching Tolerance, Timeline, Times News Service, Today's Christian, Tradition, Transitions, Vampire Tales, Vibe, West Coast Magazine, Willow Springs, Woman's World

Book Publishers:

Charlesbridge Publishing , Talewinds, Whispering Coyote, Chelsea Green Publishing Company, Cross Cultural Publications, Denali Press, DIMI Press, Falcon Publishing, Graduate Group, Granite Publishing Group, Green Nature Books, Hay House, In Print Publishing, Island Press, McDonald & Woodward Publishing Company, McFarland & Company, Milkweed Editions, Naturegraph Publishers, Pruett Publishing Company, Ragged Mountain Press, Richard C. Owen Publishers, Sierra Club Books, Sphinx Publishing, Sulgrave Press, Texas A&M University Press, Transnational Publishers, University of Nebraska Press, University of Nevada Press, University of North Texas Press, Washington State University Press, Westcliffe Publishers

Environment

Periodicals:

Adirondack Life, American Forests, American Gardener, Archaeology, Arizona Highways, Artemis Magazine, Audubon, BabyTalk, Back Home In Kentucky, Balanced Living Magazine, Better Homes and Gardens, Blue Ridge Country Magazine, Body & Soul, Boys' Life, Bugle, California Wild, Central PA Magazine, Chesapeake Bay Magazine, Chronicles A magazine of American Culture, Defenders of Wildlife, E Magazine, Environment, Field & Stream, Florida Wildlife Magazine Newsletter, Flyfisher, Forester Communications, Fur-Fish-Game, Happy Times Monthly, Heartland USA, Insider Magazine, Jewish Currents, Joiners' Quarterly, Kentucky Monthly, LA Architect, Maine Organic Farmer & Gardener, Metropolis, Montana, Mother Jones, Mountain Living, Natural History, Natural Home, New Millennium Writings, New Times, Offshore, Other Side, Outdoor America, Paddler, Persimmon Hill, Popular Mechanics, Popular Science, Potomac Review, Power & Motoryacht, Sandlapper, Scouting, Shuttle Spindle & Dyepot, Sport Fishing Magazine, Springfield! Magazine, Texas Parks & Wildlife, Tikkun, Transitions, Weatherwise Magazine, Whole Life Times, Wildlife Art, Willow Springs, Wisconsin Trails

Book Publishers:

Charlesbridge Publishing , Talewinds, Whispering Coyote, Chelsea Green Publishing Company, Cross Cultural Publications, Denali Press, DIMI Press, Falcon Publishing, Graduate Group, Granite Publishing Group, Green Nature Books, Hay House, In Print Publishing, Island Press, McDonald & Woodward Publishing Company, McFarland & Company, Milkweed Editions, Naturegraph Publishers, Pruett Publishing Company, Ragged Mountain Press, Richard C. Owen Publishers, Sierra Club Books, Sphinx Publishing, Sulgrave Press, Texas A&M University Press, Transnational Publishers, University of Nebraska Press, University of Nevada Press, University of North Texas Press, Washington State University Press, Westcliffe Publishers

Erotica

Periodicals:

Blackfire, Horrorfind, In Touch/Indulge, Penthouse, Penthouse Variations, Rosebud, Springfield! Magazine, Surfer

Book Publishers:

Bella Books, Conservatory of American Letters, March Street Press, Parting Gifts

Experimental Fiction

Periodicals:

AGNI, Black Warrior Review, Confrontation, A Literary Journal, New Millennium Writings, Willow Springs

Book Publishers:

Dalkey Archive Press, Via Dolorosa Press

-F-

Family

Periodicals:

America West Magazine, American Profile, Ancestry Magazine, Atlanta Parent, Better Homes and Gardens, Birds & Blooms, Black Forest Press, Blue Ridge Country Magazine, Bride's Magazine, Cadet Quest, Canoe & Kayak Magazine, Capper's, Catholic Digest, Central PA Magazine, Christian Home & School, Christian Parenting Today, Christian Women Today, Cincinnati Woman Magazine, Clubhouse, Country Living, Country Woman Magazine, Creative With Words!, Dialouge, Doll World, Dovetail, Family Circle, Family Digest, Family Fun, Family Safety and Health, Family Therapy, Genealogical Computing, Good Housekeeping, Grit Magazine, Guideposts for Kids, Happy Times Monthly, Health, Home Education Magazine, Home Times Family Newspaper, Hope Magazine, House, Home and Garden, In the Family, Kung Fu Tai Chi, Ladies' Home Journal, Ligourian, Long Island Woman, Lookout For Today's Growing Christian, Lutheran Digest, Marriage Partnership, Mature Years, Men of Integrity, Metro Parent, Military Officer, Modern Bride, My Legacy, Northwest Family News, Over the Back Fence, Parenting, ParentLife, Parents Magazine, Passport, Pockets, Rememberance, Reunions Magazine, River Town Gazette, Rosebud, Sandlapper, Saturday Evening Post, Scouting, Spider The Magazine for Children, Springfield! Magazine, Teaching Tolerance, Today's Christian Woman, Today's Pentecostal Evangel, Transitions, United Parenting Publications, West Coast Magazine, Woman's Day, Woman's World, Women Today Magazine, Working Mother Magazine, Young & Alive

Book Publishers:

Alba House, Bethany House Publishers, Beyond Words Publishing, Black Forest Press, Blue Mountain Arts , Branden Publishing Company, Broadman & Holman Publishers, Capital Books, Charlesbridge Publishing , Talewinds, Whispering Coyote, Cross Cultural Publications, Dial Books for Young Readers, Diogenes Publishing, Excelsior Cee Publishing, Fairview Press, Free Spirit Publishing, Globe Pequot Press, God Allows U-Turns Book Series, Hazelden Publishing, Health Communications, Hunter House Publishers, Impact Publishers, Jewish Lights Publishing, Judson Press, Just Us Books, Mayhaven Publishing, McBooks Press, Mustang Publishing Company, New Horizons Press, Small Horizons Imprint, Pathfinder Publishing of California, Pelican Publishing Company, Perspectives Press, The Infertility and Adoption Publisher, Prep Publishing, Square One Publishers, Success Publishing, Temple University Press, Waterbrook Press, Zondervan and Zonderkid

Fantasy

Periodicals:

Asimov's Science Fiction, Black Forest Press, Blackfire, Complete Woman, Fantasy & Science Fiction, Horrorfind, Ladybug The Magazine for Young Children, Magazine of Fantasy & Science Fiction, Magazine of Speculative Poetry, My Legacy, Rosebud, Spilogale Inc, The magazine of Fantasy & Science Fiction, Tales of the Talisman, Weird Tales, With The Magazine for Radical Christian Youth

Book Publishers:

Topics

Baen Books, BenBella Books, Black Forest Press, Carolrhoda Books, Charlesbridge Publishing , Talewinds, Whispering Coyote, Conservatory of American Letters, DAW Books, Highlands Keep Publishing, ImaJinn Books, Sphinx Publishing, Tom Doherty Associate, Tor Books, Forge Books, Orb, Starscape, Warner Books, Willowgate Press

Fashion

Periodicals:

Artemis Magazine, Beauty Spot, News You Can Use, Boston Magazine, Budget Living, Cincinnati Woman Magazine, Complete Woman, Diamond Registry Bulletin, Doll World, Elle, First for Women, Genre, Glamour, Harper's Bazaar, House, Home and Garden, Kentucky Monthly, Ladies' Home Journal, Long Island Woman, Lucky Magazine, Men's Health, Modern Bride, More, National Enquirer, Parents Magazine, Penthouse, Persimmon Hill, Playboy, Redbook, River Town Gazette, Seventeen, Short Stuff Magazine, Springfield! Magazine, Town & Country, Travel & Leisure, Vibe, Vogue, Wall Fashions, Weight Watchers Magazine, West Coast Magazine, Whole Life Times, Woman's Day, Woman's World, Working Mother Magazine

Book Publishers:

Players Press

Feminism

Periodicals:

Affilia Journal of Women in Social Work, Beauty Spot, News You Can Use, Calyx Journal, Crone Chronicles, Feminist Studies, University of Maryland, Frontiers, Girlfriends Magazine, House, Home and Garden, Insider Magazine, Iris A Journal about Women, Jewish Currents, Liquid Ohio, Magical Blend, Minnesota Review, Mom Guess What Newspaper, New Centennial Review, New Moon, New Times, Other Side, Playgirl, Rosebud, Shenandoah, Springfield! Magazine, Student Leader, Teaching Tolerance, Tikkun, Whole Life Times

Book Publishers:

American Literary Press, Noble House, Beyond Words Publishing, Bridge Works, Calyx Books, Cross Cultural Publications, David R. Godine, Hay House, Maisonneuve Press, Mississippi, University Press of Mississippi, New Society Publishers, New Victoria Publishers, Scarecrow Press, Spinsters Ink, Temple University Press, University of Nebraska Press

Fiction

Periodicals:

5678 Country, 5678 Swing, 96, ACM Another Chicago Magazine, Affaire De Coeur, AGNI, Alfred Hitchcock Mystery Magazine, Alive! A Magazine for Christian Senior Adults, America West Magazine, American Girl, American Letters & Commentary, Analog Science Fiction and Fact, Antioch Review, AQR Alaska Quarterly Review, Arkansas Review, Artemis Magazine, Artful Dodge, Asimov's Science Fiction, Atlantic Monthly, Babybug, BabyTalk, Bellevue Literary Review, Bellingham Review, Bellowing Ark, Bibliophilos, Birds & Blooms, Black Forest Press, Black Warrior Review, Blackfire, Bloomsbury Review, Boston Review, Boys' Life, Boys' Quest, Bridal Guide, Bridge, Buffalo Spree Magazine, Bugle, ByLine, Cadet Quest, Calyx Journal, Carolina Quarterly, Cat Fancy, CC Motorcycle News Magazine, Chattahoochee Review, Chesapeake Bay Magazine, Chicago Magazine, Chicago Review, Chrysalis Reader, Cicada, Cimarron Review, Circle, Clubhouse, Coal People Magazine, Cobblestone Magazine, Conversely, Cooperator, Cream City Review, Creative With Words!, Cricket, CutBank, Downstate Story, Dream Network, East End Lights, Elle, Ellery Queen's Mystery Magazine, Erased, Sigh, Sigh., Essence, Field & Stream, Flesh & Blood, Fourteen Hills, French Forum, Fun for Kidz, Futures Mysterious Anthology Magazine, Georgia Review, Gettysburg Review, Gist Review, Golf Journal Magazine, Good Housekeeping, Green Hills Literary Lantern, Green Mountains Review, Greensboro Review, GRIT Magazine, Gryphon Books, Hanging Loose, Harper's Bazaar, Harper's Magazine, Hawaii Review, Hayden's Ferry Review, Highlights for Children, Home Business Magazine, Home Times Family Newspaper, Hopscotch for Girls, Horror Tales, Horrorfind, Hudson Review, I Love Cats,

Iconoclast, In the Family, In Touch/Indulge, Indiana Review, Iris A Journal about Women, Japanophile, Evoking the old and the new Japan, Jewish Currents, Kalliope A Journal of Women's Art, Kenyon Review, Lacunae, Ladies' Home Journal, Ladybug The Magazine for Young Children, Legacy Journal, Light of Consciousness, Lilith, Liquid Ohio, Literary Review, Fairleigh Dickinson University, MacGuffin, Maelstrom, Magazine of Fantasy & Science Fiction, Massachusetts Review, Mature Years, Melic Review, Message Magazine, Mid-American Review, Minnesota Review, Mississippi Review, Missouri Review, My Legacy, Nebo A Literary Journal, Nebraska Review, New England Review, Middlebury College, New Letters, New Millennium Writings, New Moon, new renaissance, New Yorker, Nimrod, NINE, Northwest Review, University of Oregon, Obsidian III, Ohio Writer, Other Side, Other Voices, Over the Back Fence, Passages North, Passport, Pearl, Pedestal Magazine, Penthouse, Penthouse Variations, Peregrine, Phantasmagoria, Phoebe, Playgirl, Pleiades A Journal of New Writing, Ploughshares, Emerson College, Potomac Review, Prairie Schooner, Primavera, Quarterly West, Red Rock Review, Redbook, Rockford Review, Rosebud, Running Times, Saturday Evening Post, Secret Place, Senior Living, Sew News, Sewanee Review, Smoke Magazine, Life's Burning Desires, Society of American Baseball Research, Southern Accents, Southern California Anthology, Southern Lumberman, Southwest Fly Fishing, Southwest Review, Spider The Magazine for Children, Spilogale Inc, The magazine of Fantasy & Science Fiction, Sport Fishing Magazine, Sun Valley Magazine, Surfer, Swimming World, Sycamore Review, Tales of the Talisman, Tampa Review, Thema, Threepenny Review, Tikkun, Troika Magazine, True Romance, Urbanite, Vampire Tales, Verses Magazine, Virginia Quarterly Review, Weavings, Western Humanities Review, William and Mary Review College of William and Mary, Willow Springs, Wired, With The Magazine for Radical Christian Youth, Woman's Day, Worcester Review, Yalobusha Review, Zoetrope All-Story, ZYZZYVA

Book Publishers:

Agony in Black, Alyson Publications, American Book Publishing, American Literary Press, Noble House, Anchorage Press Plays, International Agency of Plays for Young People, Apage4You Book Publishing, Arte Público Press, The University of Houston, Atheneum Books, Avalon Books, Baen Books, Bella Books, Bethany House Publishers, Bkmk Press, Black Forest Press, Book Peddlers, Branden Publishing Company, Bridge Works, Brookline Books, Calyx Books, Carolrhoda Books, CCC Publications, Charlesbridge Publishing , Talewinds, Whispering Coyote, Christian Ed. Publishers, Chronicle Books LLC, Conservatory of American Letters, Council for Indian Education, Crossway Books, Dalkey Archive Press, David R. Godine, Daw Books, Denlinger's Publishers, Dial Books for Young Readers, Dorchester Publishing Co., Down East Books, Dutton Children's Books, Edupress, Elderberry Press, Emquad International, Farrar, Straus and Giroux, Publishers, Books for Young Readers, Fiesta City Publishers, Front Street, G.P. Putnam's Sons, Books for Young Readers, Genesis Communications, Evergreen Press & Gazelle Press, Hampton Roads Publishing Co, Hannover House, Harlequin, Hillbrook Publishing, Hilliard & Harris, Holiday House, Holloway House Publishing Group, ImaJinn Books, Intercontinental Publishing New Amsterdam Publishing, J.N. Townsend Publishing, John Daniel & Company, JoNa Books, Just Us Books, Latin American Literary Review Press, LionHearted Publishing, Llewellyn Publications, Lumen Editions, MacAdam/Cage, Mage Publisihers, Maisonneuve Press, Mayhaven Publishing, McBooks Press, Meriwether Publishing Ltd, Contemporary Drama Service, Metropolis Ink, Milkweed Editions, Mississippi, University Press of Mississippi, Moondance Publishing, Naval Institute Press, New Victoria Publishers, Origin Media, Books for the Integral Age, Padlock Mystery Press, Peachtree Publishers, Pelican Publishing Company, Permanent Press, Second Chance Press, Pineapple Press, Possibility Press, Post-Apollo Press, Prep Publishing, Puget Sound Books/Angel Fire Press, QED Press, Quality Words In Print, Red Dress InkTM, Richard C. Owen Publishers, Roberts Rinehart, Running Press Kids, Sarabande Books, Silhouette Desire, Silhouette Intimate Moments, Silhouette Romance, Silhouette Special Edition, Skinner House Books, Soundprints,

A Division of Trudy Corporation, Sphinx Publishing, Spinsters Ink, Square One Publishers, Thriller Press, Tilbury House Publishers, Time Warner Book Group, Tom Doherty Associate, Tor Books, Forge Books, Orb, Starscape, Truman State University Press, Unity House, University of Nevada Press, University of North Texas Press, Upstart Books, USA Books, Via Dolorosa Press, Waltsan Publishing, Warner Books, Waterbrook Press, Willowgate Press, Wilshire Book Co., Zondervan and Zonderkid

Film/Video

Periodicals:

Art Times, Bibliophilos, Cincinnati Woman Magazine, Cineaste, Clamor, Culture, Media and Life., Dramatics, Film Quarterly, Girls' Life, Good Old Days Good Old Days Specials, Gray Areas, Home Times Family Newspaper, The Hudson Review, Insider Magazine, Lilith: The Independent Jewish Women's Magazine, The Minnesota Review: University of Missouri, Columbia, Mom Guess What Newspaper, Mother Jones, The New Renaissance, New Yorker, River Town Gazette, Springfield! Magazine, Teaching Tolerance, The Threepenny Review, Times News Service, Vanity Fair, Zoetrope: All-Story

Book Publishers:

Allworth Press, Arden Press, Inc., Chronicle Books LLC, Companion Press, Fordham University Press, Garth Gardner Company, Hannover House, In Print Publishing, Intercultural Press, Lehigh University Press, Maisonneuve Press, McFarland & Company, Inc., Michael Wiese Productions, Mississippi University Press of Mississippi, Players Press, Inc., Rutledge Hill Press, Santa Monica Press LLC, Scarecrow Press, Inc., Southern Illinois University Press, Stone Bridge Press, Temple University Press, University of Nebraska Press

Fishing

Periodicals:

Adirondack Life, American Hunter, Bass West, Boating Life, Boys' Life, Cascades East Magazine, Chesapeake Bay Magazine, Dakota Outdoors, Field & Stream, Fishing Facts, Fly Fisherman, Fly Fishing in Salt Waters, Flyfisher, Flyfishing & Tying Journal, Fur-Fish-Game, Grit Magazine, Happy Times Monthly, Heartland USA, Houseboat, Marlin, MidWest Outdoors, Montana, Mountain Living, Northwest Fly Fishing, Offshore, Outdoor America, Outdoor Life, Outdoor World, Pacific Fishing, Paddler, Power & Motoryacht, River Town Gazette, Salmon-Trout-Steelheader, Sandlapper, Scouting, Southern Traveler, Sport Fishing Magazine, Springfield! Magazine, Texas Parks & Wildlife

Book Publishers:

Conservatory of American Letters, Cornell Maritime Press, Down East Books, Falcon Publishing, Frank Amato Publications, Hancock House, Hearts 'N Tummies Cookbook Company, Kregel Kidzone, Lyons Press, Mayhaven Publishing, Paradise Cay, Ragged Mountain Press, Smithsonian Oceanic Collection, Smithsonian Backyard, Smithsonian Lets Go to the Zoo!, Stackpole Books, Voyageur Press, Willow Creek Press

Folklore

Periodicals:

Blue Ridge Country Magazine, Fate magazine, Grit Magazine, Old Farmer's Almanac, Parabola, Parenting, Persimmon Hill, River Town Gazette, Sandlapper, Spider The Magazine for Children, Springfield! Magazine, Teaching Tolerance, Tradition, Willow Springs

Book Publishers:

Dial Books for Young Readers, Granite Publishing Group, Mayhaven Publishing, Santa Monica Press LLC, University of Idaho Press, University of North Texas Press

Food/Drink

Periodicals:

All for You, America West Magazine, American Fitness, Artemis Magazine, Atlanta Homes and Lifestyles, Beauty Spot, News You Can Use, Blue Ridge Country Magazine, Boston Magazine, Budget Living, Cen-

tral PA Magazine, Chef Magazine, Cooking Light, Country Home, Country Living, Country Magazine, First for Women, Food & Wine, Fresh Cut, Futurific Magazine, Glamour, Good Old Days, Health, Home Cooking, House, Home and Garden, Insider Magazine, Italian Cooking and Living, Ladies' Home Journal, Lake Michigan Travel Guide, Long Island Woman, Magazine of La Cucina Italiana, Maine Organic Farmer & Gardener, Modern Maturity, Magazine AARP, Mom Guess What Newspaper, Mother Earth News, National Geographic Traveler, Native Peoples Magazine, New Yorker, Northwest Palate, Penthouse, Points North, Prevention Magazine, Redbook, River Town Gazette, Roanoker, Sandlapper, Saveur, Seek, Springfield! Magazine, Symploke, Transitions, Travel & Leisure, Whole Life Times, Wines & Vines, Wisconsin Trails, Woman's Day, Woman's World, Women Today Magazine, Working Mother Magazine, Yankee

Book Publishers:

Bristol Publishing Enterprises nitty gritty Cookbooks, Charlesbridge Publishing , Talewinds, Whispering Coyote, Chronicle Books LLC, Collectors Press, David R. Godine, Frederick Fell Publishers, Gûrze Books, Hearts 'N Tummies Cookbook Company, Lerner Publishing, Lyons Press, Mayhaven Publishing, Mustang Publishing Company, Rutledge Hill Press, Sasquatch Books, Serendipity Systems; Books-on-disks, Smithsonian Oceanic Collection, Smithsonian Backyard, Smithsonian Lets Go to the Zoo!, Southern Illinois University Press, Ten Speed Press

Games

Periodicals:

American Girl, American Turf Monthly, Artemis Magazine, Boys' Life, Boys' Quest, Card Player, Cat Fancy, Chess Life, Clubhouse, Cobblestone Magazine, Game Developer, Guideposts for Kids, Happy Times Monthly, Ladybug The Magazine for Young Children, Passport, Reunions Magazine, River Town Gazette, Spider The Magazine for Children, Young & Alive

Book Publishers:

Bonus Books, Chess Enterprises, Legacy Press, Mustang Publishing Company, Rainbow Publishers, Sphinx Publishing

Gardening

Periodicals:

Adirondack Life, Alaska Business Monthly, American Gardener, American Profile, Atlanta Homes and Lifestyles, Back Home in Kentucky, Better Homes and Gardens, Birds & Blooms, Blue Ridge Country Magazine, Bride's Magazine, Capper's, Central PA Magazine, Coastal Living, Colorado Homes & Lifestyles, Country Living, Creative With Words!, Fine Gardening, Gardening How-To, GRIT Magazine, Growing Edge, Happy Times Monthly, Heartland USA, Home Improver Magazine, Horticulture, House, Home and Garden, Ladies' Home Journal, Long Island Woman, Lutheran Digest, Maine Organic Farmer & Gardener, Mother Earth News, Mountain Living, Old Farmer's Almanac, PLUS Magazine, Points North, River Town Gazette, Sandlapper, Saturday Evening Post, Seattle Homes and Lifestyles, Springfield! Magazine, Stone Soup, Texas Gardener, Transitions, Veggie Life, Wild Foods Forum, Woman's World, Yankee

Book Publishers:

Barrons Educational Series, Bristol Publishing Enterprises nitty gritty Cookbooks, Chelsea Green Publishing Company, Cornell Maritime Press, David R. Godine, Down East Books, Globe Pequot Press, Hearts 'N Tummies Cookbook Company, HiddenSpring, Llewellyn Publications, Mage Publisihers, Mississippi, University Press of Mississippi, Naturegraph Publishers, Sasquatch Books, Southern Illinois University Press, Stenhouse Publishers, Taylor Trade, Imprints, Cooper Square Press, Derrydale Press, Madison Books, Ten Speed Press, Willow Creek Press

Gay/Lesbian

Periodicals:

And Baby Magazine, Blackfire, Calyx Journal, Carolina Quarterly, Chiron Review, East End Lights, Feminist Studies, University of Maryland, Fourteen Hills, Frontiers, Genre, Girlfriends Magazine, In the

Topics

Family, In Touch Indulge, Iris A Journal about Women, Minnesota Review, Mom Guess What Newspaper, New Times, Other Side, Penthouse Variations, Rainbow Review, Teaching Tolerance

Book Publishers:

Alyson Publications, Barricade Books, Bella Books, Calyx Books, Chronicle Books David R. Godine, New Victoria Publishers, Scarecrow Press, Spinsters Ink, Temple University Press

General Interest

Periodicals:

America West Magazine, American Forests, American Hunter, American Legion Magazine, American Profile, American Scholar, Arizona Foothills Magazine, Artemis Magazine,, Atlantic Monthly, Attaché, Austin Monthly Magazine, Baltimore Magazine, Beauty Spot, News You Can Use, Black Forest Press, Blue Ridge Country Magazine, Boys' Life, Braveheart, Calyx Journal, Capper's, Charleston Magazine, Cincinnati Woman Magazine, Colorado Homes & Lifestyles, Complete Woman, Creative Knitting, Dollar Stretcher, Dovetail, Dream Network, Elks Magazine, Essence, Et cetera, Family Circle, First Things, Futures Mysterious Anthology Magazine, Good Housekeeping, Grit Magazine, Guideposts for Kids, Happy Times Monthly, Heartland USA, HerbalGram, Home Education Magazine, Home Times Family Newspaper, Hope Magazine, Hudson Review, Iconoclast, Insider Magazine, Kentucky Monthly, Kenyon Review, Ligourian, Liquid Ohio, Literary Magazine Review, Lutheran Digest, Men's Journal, Metropolis, Military Officer, Modern Bride, More, Mother Jones, New Renaissance, Ohio Magazine, Old Farmer's Almanac, Over the Back Fence, Parade, Passages North, Playboy, Popular Science, Reader's Digest, Reunions Magazine, River Town Gazette, Rosebud, San Francisco, Sandlapper, Seneca Review, Short Stuff Magazine, Sycamore Review, Teaching Tolerance, Threepenny Review, Timeline, Toastmaster, Today's Christian Woman, Town & Country, Transitions, West Coast Magazine, Whole Life Times, Willow Springs, Yankee, Young & Alive

Book Publishers:

Addicus Books, Arden Press, Beyond Words Publishing, Black Forest Press, Branden Publishing Company, Bridge Works, Bright Mountain Books, Calyx Books, Chronicle Books LLC, Cross Cultural Publications, Down East Books, Excelsior Cee Publishing, God Allows U-Turns Book Series, Graduate Group, Hay House, HiddenSpring, Howells House, Human Kinetics, In Print Publishing, Johnston Associates International, Kregel Kidzone, Mayhaven Publishing, Millennium Publishing Company, Mississippi, University Press of Mississippi, Mustang Publishing Company, Paulist Press, HiddenSpring, Roberts Rinehart, Santa Monica Press LLC, Soundprints, Temple University Press, Ten Speed Press, Trinity Press International, University of Nevada Press, University of North Texas Press, Willowgate Press

Government

Periodicals:

American City & County, Artemis Magazine, Bear Deluxe Magazine, Bibliophilos, Black Forest Press, California Journal, California Lawyer, Chronicles A magazine of American Culture, Contract Management, FBI Law Enforcement Bulletin, First Things, Futures Mysterious Anthology Magazine, Government Executive, Home Times Family Newspaper, Ideas on Liberty, Insider Magazine, Jewish Currents, Kentucky Monthly, Long Term View, Massachusetts School of Law, Mother Jones, National Enquirer, New Centennial Review, Penthouse, Presentations Magazine, Springfield! Magazine, Teaching Tolerance, Tikkun, Timeline, Washington Monthly, Wines & Vines, Women In Business

Book Publishers:

Algora Publishing, Imprint, Agathon Press, Americas Group Berrett-Koehler Publishers, Black Forest Press, Branden Publishing Company, Clarity Press, Cross Cultural Publications, Fairleigh Dickinson University Press, Fordham University Press, Graduate Group, IHS Press, Lehigh University Press, Lerner Publishing, Potomac Books, Quill Driver Books, Texas A&M University Press, Tricycle Press, Trinity Foundation, University of Nebraska Press

Graphics

Periodicals:

Futures Mysterious Anthology Magazine, Game Developer, Letter Arts Review, Light, Sycamore Review

Book Publishers:

Garth Gardner Company, GATF Press

-H-

Health

Periodicals:

Alive! A Magazine for Christian Senior Adults, All for You, American Fitness, American Indian Quarterly, American Medical News, American Profile, Artemis Magazine, Arthritis Today, Aspen Magazine, Balanced Living Magazine, Beauty Spot, News You Can Use, Benefits & Compensation Digest, Better Homes and Gardens, Black Forest Press, Body & Soul, Boston Magazine, Boys' Life, Bridal Guide, Buffalo Spree Magazine, Cat Fancy, Catholic Digest, Central PA Magazine, Children's Better Health Institute, Christian Women Today, Cooking Light, Crone Chronicles, Dermascope, Diabetes Self-Management, Discover, Dream Network, Elle, Equal Opportunity Publications, Essence, Family Circle, Family Safety and Health, Firehouse Magazine, Fitness Management, Futurific Magazine, Glamour, Golfer, Good Housekeeping, Good Old Days, Grit Magazine, Health, HerbalGram, Home Times Family Newspaper, HomeLife, House, Home and Garden, International Sports Journal, Journal of Asian Martial Arts, Kentucky Monthly, Kuumba, Ladies' Home Journal, Llewellyn Journal, Long Island Woman, Lutheran Digest, Magical Blend, Maine Organic Farmer & Gardener, Massage & Bodywork, Massage Magazine, Mature Years, Men's Fitness, Men's Health, Midwifery Today, Military Officer, Modern Bride, Modern Maturity, Magazine AARP, More, Mother Earth News, Muscle & Fitness, National Enquirer, National Geographic Traveler, Natural Beauty and Health, Natural Home, New Times, Onion World, Outdoor Life, Parenting, Parents Magazine, Pediatrics For Parents, Playgirl, Plus Magazine, Podiatry Management, Prevention Magazine, Psychology Today, Reader's Digest, Redbook, River Town Gazette, Rock and Ice, Rocky Mountain Sports Magazine, Runner's World, Running Times, Saturday Evening Post, Scouting, Seek, Seneca Review, Skiing Magazine, Skin Inc. Magazine, Springfield! Magazine, Swim Magazine, Swimming Technique, Syracuse New Times, T'ai Chi, Town & Country, Trail Runner, Transitions, Turtle, Veggie Life, Volleyball Magazine, Weight Watchers Magazine, West Coast Magazine, Whole Life Times, Wines & Vines, Woman's Day, Woman's World, Women In Business, Women Today Magazine, Yoga Journal, Young & Alive

Book Publishers:

Addicus Books, American Literary Press, Noble House, Barrons Educational Series, Baywood Publishing Company, Black Forest Press, Blue Poppy Press, Branden Publishing Company, Champion Press, Contemporary Books, Crossing Press, Emerald Ink Publishing, Fairview Press, Frederick Fell Publishers, Free Spirit Publishing, Graduate Group, Gûrze Books, Hampton Roads Publishing Co, Harbor Press, Harvard Common Press, Hatherleigh Press, Hay House, Health Communications, Hohm Press, Human Kinetics, Hunter House Publishers, Jodere Group, Llewellyn Publications, Lyons Press, Magni Group, Mayhaven Publishing, Metamorphous Press, Millennium Publishing Company, Mississippi, University Press of Mississippi, New Harbinger Publications, New Horizons Press, Small Horizons Imprint, New World Library, North Street Publishers, Pathfinder Publishing of California, Perspectives Press, The Infertility and Adoption Publisher, Piccadilly Books, Players Press, Prima Publishing, Quill Driver Books, Ronin Publishing, Safer Society Press, Soundprints, A Division of Trudy Corporation, Swedenborg Foundation, Chrysalis Books, Temple University Press, Wilshire Book Co., Woodland Publishing, YMAA Publication Center, Yogavidya.com

Hispanic

Topics

Periodicals:

Annals of Improbable Research, Bugle, Catholic Digest, CC Motorcycle News Magazine, Coastal Living, Iconoclast, Minnesota Memories, Penthouse, Rosebud, Sandlapper, Saturday Evening Post, Small Farm Today, Sport Fishing Magazine, Tameme, The Black Table, Thoughts for All Seasons, Wittenburg Door

Book Publishers:

CCC Publications, JoNa Books, Moondance Publishing, North Ridge Books, Rutledge Hill Press, Sphinx Publishing, Ten Speed Press, Wilshire Book Co.

-I-

Inspirational

Periodicals:

African American Pulpit!, Alive Now, America West Magazine, American Fitness, American Profile, Angels on Earth, Benefits & Compensation Digest, Black Forest Press, Body & Soul, Braveheart, Capper's, Christian Parenting Today, Club Connection, Crone Chronicles, Devo'Zine, Discipleship Journal, Dream Network, Evangel, Grit Magazine, Guide, Guideposts, Guideposts for Kids, Happy Times Monthly, Heartland USA, Home Times Family Newspaper, Kentucky Monthly, Kung Fu Tai Chi, Lifeglow, Light of Consciousness, Lutheran Digest, Magical Blend, Mature Years, Memory Makers, Men's Fitness, Message Magazine, Minnesota Memories, My Legacy, New Times, Oblates, Other Side, Pastoral Life, Plain Truth, Reader's Digest, Science of Mind, Secret Place, Seneca Review, Springfield! Magazine, Today's Christian Woman, Transitions, Upper Room, Weight Watchers Magazine, West Coast Magazine, Whole Life Times, Win-Informer, With The Magazine for Radical Christian Youth, Woman's Touch, Young & Alive

Book Publishers:

Berrett-Koehler Publishers, Beyond Words Publishing, Black Forest Press, Broadman & Holman Publishers, Bye Publishing, Christian Publications, Horizon Books, Cross Cultural Publications, Daily Guideposts, Emerald Ink Publishing, Excelsior Cee Publishing, Frederick Fell Publishers, Genesis Communications, Evergreen Press & Gazelle Press, God Allows U Turns Book Series, Great Quotations Publishing, Green Nature Books, Hampton Roads Publishing Co, Harbor Press, Hay House, Health Communications, HiddenSpring, In Print Publishing, Jewish Lights Publishing, Jodere Group Judson Press, Legacy Press, Llewellyn Publications, Mayhaven Publishing, New Horizons Press, Small Horizons Imprint, Paulist Press, HiddenSpring, Pelican Publishing Company, PREP Publishing, Rainbow Publishers, Red Wheel/Weiser, Rutledge Hill Press, Square One Publishers, Waterbrook Press, Wilshire Book Co.

Internet

Periodicals:

American Hunter, Annals of Improbable Research, Beauty Spot, News You Can Use, Cross & Quill, Gray Areas, Insider Magazine, Memory Makers, Poptronics, Presentations Magazine, Radio World, River Town Gazette, Senior Living, Sycamore Review, Teaching Tolerance, Women In Business

Book Publishers:

Branden Publishing Company, Franklin, Beedle & Associates, Graduate Group, Osborne/McGraw-Hill, Scarecrow Press, Wilshire Book Co

Interview

Periodicals:

Absolute Write, American Fitness, AmericanStyle, Annals of Improbable Research, Artemis Magazine,, Audubon, Beauty Spot, News You Can Use, Black Warrior Review, Bloomsbury Review, Carolina Quarterly, Central PA Magazine, Chronogram, Circle, Complete Woman, Crone Chronicles, Doll World, Dream Network, Green Hills Literary Lantern, Green Mountains Review, Home Times Family Newspaper, Iconoclast, Insider Magazine, LA Architect, Labor Paper, Lacunae, Ladybug Parent's Companion, Magical Blend, Maine Organic Farmer

& Gardener, Memory Makers, Minnesota Review, Missouri Review, Mother Jones, Natural Beauty and Health, new renaissance, New Times, New York Stories, Obsidian III, Outdoor Life, Passages North, Penthouse, Playboy, Quarterly West, Reader's Digest, Redbook, Ruminator Review, Sandlapper, Southern Lumberman, Southwest Fly Fishing, Southwest Review, Springfield! Magazine, Sun Valley Magazine, Sun, Supply Chain Systems Magazine, SWIM Magazine, Swimming World, The Black Table, Today's Christian Woman, Transitions, Whole Life Times, Willow Springs, Wines & Vines, Wired, Writer Gazette, Yankee, Young & Alive

Book Publishers:

Graduate Group, Jist Works, Square One Publishers, Ten Speed Press

-J-

Jewish Interest

Periodicals:

Calyx Journal

Book Publishers:

Branden Publishing Company, Brookline Books, Calyx Books, Cross Cultural Publications, David R. Godine, Denali Press, Fairleigh Dickinson University Press, Frederick Fell Publishers, Hachai Publishing, Jewish Lights Publishing, Latin American Literary Review Press, Lehigh University Press, Lumen Editions, Pelican Publishing Company, Temple University Press, University of Nebraska Press

Juvenile

Periodicals:

American Girl, Appleseeds, Atlanta Parent, Boys' Life, Cadet Quest Campus Life, Cicada, Classic Toy Trains, Click Magazine, Clubhouse, Creative With Words!, Faces The Magazine About People, Guide, Guideposts for Kids, Instructor, Kung Fu Tai Chi, Muse Magazine, Northwest Family News, Odyssey Magazine, Parents' Press, Passport, Potluck Children's Literary Magazine, River Town Gazette, SchoolArts, Springfield! Magazine, Stock Car Racing, Teaching Tolerance, United Parenting Publications, Wonderful Ideas for Teaching, Learning, and Enjoying Mathematics!

Book Publishers:

American Correctional Association, American Literary Press, Noble House, Anchorage Press Plays, International Agency of Plays for Young People, Arte Público Press The University of Houston, Atheneum Books, ATL Press Science Technology, Barrons Educational Series, Bethany House Publishers, Carolrhoda Books, Charlesbridge Publishing , Talewinds, Whispering Coyote, Council for Indian Education, David R. Godine, Farrar, Straus and Giroux, Publishers, Inc, Books for Young Readers, Free Spirit Publishing, Front Street, ImaJinn Books, Just Us Books, Kids Books By Kids, Legacy Press, Mayhaven Publishing, Morgan Reynolds Publishing, Richard C. Owen Publishers, Ten Speed Press, UpstartBooks

-L-

Language

Periodicals:

America West Magazine, Cross & Quill, Erased, Sigh, Sigh., Et cetera, French Forum, Futures Mysterious Anthology Magazine, Kenyon Review, New Centennial Review, Obsidian III, Rosebud, Southern Humanities Review, Springfield! Magazine, Teaching Tolerance, Thoughts for All Seasons, Transitions Abroad

Book Publishers:

Barbed Wire Publishing, Barrons Educational Series, Branden Publishing Company, Contemporary Books, Council for Indian Education, Great Quotations Publishing, Lerner Publishing, Rodnik Publishing Co., Stone Bridge Press, University of Nebraska Press, Via Dolorosa Press

Law

Periodicals:

Aba Journal, American Hunter, Artemis Magazine,, California Lawyer, Cincinnati Woman Magazine, Corrections Compendium, FBI Law Enforcement Bulletin, FirehouseMagazine, First Things, Gray Areas, Insider Magazine, Long Island Woman, Long Term View, Massachusetts School of Law, Police and Security News, Referee, Springfield! Magazine, Strategic Health Care Marketing, Teaching Tolerance

Book Publishers:

BNA Books, Branden Publishing Company, Clarity Press, Do-It-Yourself Legal Publishers, Fordham University Press, Graduate Group, In Print Publishing, Maisonneuve Press, Soundprints, A Division of Trudy Corporation, Temple University Press, Tower Publishing, Transnational Publishers, Trinity Foundation

Lifestyle

Periodicals:

Abilities, Adirondack Life, Arizona Foothills Magazine, Artemis Magazine, Aspen Magazine, Atlanta Homes and Lifestyles, Austin Monthly Magazine, Balanced Living Magazine, Beauty Spot, News You Can Use, Bible Advocate, Birds & Blooms, Boating Life, Body & Soul, Boston Magazine, Braveheart, Campus Life, Capper's, CC Motorcycle News Magazine, Central PA Magazine, Charleston Magazine, Christian Single, Christian Women Today, Cincinnati Woman Magazine, Coastal Living, Colorado Homes & Lifestyles, Complete Woman, Country Home, Country Magazine, Country Woman Magazine, Crone Chronicles, Cruising World, Elle, Farm & Ranch Living, FirehouseMagazine, Freeskier, Futures Mysterious Anthology Magazine, Genre, Glamour, Good Housekeeping, Grit Magazine, Happy Times Monthly, Highways, Home Improver Magazine, Home Times Family Newspaper, HomeLife, House Beautiful, Houseboat, Italian Cooking and Living, Kentucky Monthly, Lilith, Log Home Living, Magazine of La Cucina Italiana, Magical Blend, Maine Organic Farmer & Gardener, Marriage Partnership, Men of Integrity, Military Officer, Mom Guess What Newspaper, Motorcycling, Mountain Living, Natural Beauty and Health, New Times, New York Runner, Northwest Palate, Paddler, Penthouse, Persimmon Hill, Playgirl, Points North, Rainbow Review, Remembrance, Reunions Magazine, River Town Gazette, SageWoman, Salon, San Francisco, Sandlapper, Seattle Homes and Lifestyles, Skating Magazine, Skin Inc. Magazine, South American Explorer, Springfield! Magazine, Supply Chain Systems Magazine, Swank, Syracuse New Times, Teaching Tolerance, The World & I, Transitions, Travel & Leisure, Vibe, Westchester Magazine, Western RV News & Recreation, Whole Life Times, Wired, Woman's Day

Book Publishers:

Apage4You Book Publishing, Book Peddlers, Capital Books, Champion Press, Chronicle Books LLC, Eclipse Press, Face to Face Press, Genesis Communications, Evergreen Press & Gazelle Press, God Allows U-Turns Book Series, HiddenSpring, Hunter House Publishers, Mustang Publishing Company, New Horizons Press, Small Horizons Imprint, New Society Publishers, Paulist Press HiddenSpring, Prima Publishing, Ronin Publishing, Success Publishing, Swedenborg Foundation, Chrysalis Books, Trinity Press International

Literature

Periodicals:

AGNI, America West Magazine, American Dissident, American Poetry Review, American Scholar, Anhinga Press, Antioch Review, Arkansas Review, Art Times, Artemis Magazine, Asimov's Science Fiction, Babybug, Bear Deluxe Magazine, Beauty Spot, News You Can Use, Bellowing Ark, Black Forest Press, Black Warrior Review, Bloomsbury Review, Book/Mark Quarterly Review, Books & Culture, Boston Review, Bridge, ByLine, Calyx Journal, Carolina Quarterly, Chattahoochee Review, Chicago Magazine, Chiron Review, Chronicles A magazine of American Culture, Chrysalis Reader, Cimarron Review, Cincinnati Woman Magazine, Circle, Commonweal, Confrontation, A Literary Journal, Cream City Review, Creative Knitting, Cricket, Cross

& Quill, Ellery Queen's Mystery Magazine, Et cetera, Fantasy & Science Fiction, Feminist Studies University of Maryland, Fourteen Hills, French Forum, Futures Mysterious Anthology Magazine, Gist Review, Glimmer Train Stories, Grain, Harper's Magazine, Hollins Critic, Home Times Family Newspaper, Hudson Review, Iconoclast, Indiana Review, Jewish Currents, Journal of Asian Martial Arts, Journal of Modern Literature Temple University, jubilat, Kaleidoscope, Kalliope A Journal of Women's Art, Kentucky Monthly, Kenyon Review, LADYBUG Parent's Companion, Left Curve, Legacy Journal, Light, Literary Magazine Review, Literary Review, Fairleigh Dickinson University, Lucky Magazine, MacGuffin, Magazine of Speculative Poetry, Manoa, A Pacific Journal of International Writing, Minnesota Review, Native Peoples Magazine, Nebraska Review, New Centennial Review, New England Review Middlebury College, New Letters, New Millennium Writings, new renaissance, New York Stories, Nineteenth-Century French Studies, Northwest Review University of Oregon, Obsidian III, Ohio Writer, Parnassus Poetry in Review, Passages North, Persimmon Hill, Phantasmagoria, Phoebe, Pleiades A Journal of New Writing, Potluck Children's Literary Magazine, Potomac Review, Primavera, Quarterly West, Rosebud, Senior Living, Sew News, Sewanee Review, Shenandoah, Society of American Baseball Research, Southern California Anthology, Southern Humanities Review, Southern Lumberman, Southwest Fly Fishing, Southwest Review, Spider The Magazine for Children, Springfield! Magazine, Stock Car Racing, Student Leader, Sun Valley Magazine, Sun, Swimming World, Sycamore Review, Tales of the Talisman, Tampa Review, The World & I, Thema, Threepenny Review, Tikkun, Town & Country, Vanity Fair, Virginia Quarterly Review, Western Humanities Review, William and Mary Review College of William and Mary, Willow Springs, Women Artists News Book Review, Worcester Review, Yalobusha Review

Book Publishers:

Arte Público Press The University of Houston, Atheneum Books, Bkmk Press, Black Forest Press, Branden Publishing Company, Brookline Books, Calyx Books, Chatoyant, Chronicle Books LLC, Conservatory of American Letters, Cross Cultural Publications, David R. Godine, Dutton Children's Books, Front Street, In Print Publishing, Ivan R. Dee, Publisher, John Daniel & Company, Latin American Literary Review Press, Lumen Editions, Lyons Press, Mage Publisihers, Maisonneuve Press, March Street Press, Parting Gifts, Mayhaven Publishing, Milkweed Editions, Mississippi, University Press of Mississippi, Prep Publishing, QED Press, Skinner House Books, Soho Press Inc, Temple University Press, Trinity Press International, University of Idaho Press, University of Nebraska Press, University of Nevada Press, University of Oklahoma Press, Willowgate Press

-M-

Marriage

Periodicals:

Bridal Guide, Bride's Magazine, Christian Home & School, Christian Women Today, Cincinnati Woman Magazine, Complete Woman, Country Living, Diamond Registry Bulletin, Family Therapy, Futurific Magazine, Good Housekeeping, Happy Times Monthly, Health, Home Times Family Newspaper, Kung Fu Tai Chi, Ladies' Home Journal, Lifeglow, Long Island Woman, Lutheran Digest, Marriage Partnership, Modern Bride, Natural Beauty and Health, Parenting, Parents Magazine, Redbook, River Town Gazette, Springfield! Magazine, Today's Christian Woman, Transitions, Woman's World, Women Today Magazine, Working Mother Magazine

Book Publishers:

Alba House, Christian Publications, Horizon Books, Genesis Communications, Evergreen Press & Gazelle Press, God Allows U-Turns Book Series, Great Quotations Publishing, Hay House, Impact Publishers, Soundprints, Square One Publishers, Waterbrook Press, Zondervan and Zonderkid

Mass Communications

Periodicals:

Clamor, Journal of Asian Martial Arts, Radio World, Redbook, Springfield! Magazine

Book Publishers:

Barricade Books, Players Press, Santa Monica Press LLC

Men's Fiction

Periodicals:

African American Pulpit!, Beauty Spot, News You Can Use, Blackfire, Carolina Quarterly, Esquire, Genre, Happy Times Monthly, Heartland USA, Insider Magazine, Magical Blend, Men of Integrity, Men's Journal, Mom Guess What Newspaper, Muscle & Fitness, Natural Beauty and Health, New Times, River Town Gazette, Rosebud, Springfield! Magazine, Surfer, Teaching Tolerance, Transitions, Whole Life Times

Book Publishers:

Conservatory of American Letters, David R. Godine, March Street Press, Parting Gifts, Waterbrook Press

Men's Issues

Periodicals:

African American Pulpit!, Beauty Spot, News You Can Use, Blackfire, Carolina Quarterly, Esquire, Genre, Happy Times Monthly, Heartland USA, Insider Magazine, Magical Blend, Men of Integrity, Men's Journal, Mom Guess What Newspaper, Muscle & Fitness, Natural Beauty and Health, New Times, River Town Gazette, Rosebud, Springfield! Magazine, Surfer, Teaching Tolerance, Transitions, Whole Life Times

Book Publishers:

God Allows U-Turns Book Series, Hay House, Health Communications, Hunter House Publishers, Kregel Kidzone, Pathfinder Publishing of California, Smithsonian Oceanic Collection, Smithsonian Backyard, Smithsonian Lets Go to the Zoo!

Military

Periodicals:

Army Magazine, Artemis Magazine, Black Forest Press, Heartland USA, Journal of Asian Martial Arts, Marine Corps Gazett, MHQ, Military Officer, Parameters, Popular Mechanics, Primedia History Group, Springfield! Magazine, Timeline, Times News Service, Today's Christian, VFW Magazine

Book Publishers:

B. Klein Publications, Black Forest Press, Branden Publishing Company, Elderberry Press, Graduate Group, Highlands Keep Publishing, Howells House, JoNa Books, Lyons Press, Mayhaven Publishing, McBooks Press, Naval Institute Press, Paladin Press, Sycamore Island Books, Flying Machines Press, Players Press, Potomac Books, Prep Publishing, PSI Research/Hellgate Press, Scarecrow Press, Stackpole Books, Texas A&M University Press, Texas Western Press, The Oasis Press, Hellgate Press, University of Nebraska Press, University of North Texas Press, White Mane Publishing Company, YMAA Publication Center

Multicultural

Periodicals:

African American Pulpit!, America West Magazine, Arkansas Review, Art Times, Black Forest Press, Boston Review, Calyx Journal, Central PA Magazine, Clubhouse, Country Magazine, Equal Opportunity Publications, Faces The Magazine About People, Filipinas, Frontiers, In the Family, IRIS A Journal about Women, Journal of Asian Martial Arts, Kenyon Review, Left Curve, Legacy Journal, Magical Blend, Manoa, A Pacific Journal of International Writing, Minnesota Review, Mother Jones, Native Peoples Magazine, New Centennial Review, New Renaissance, Obsidian III, Passport, South American Explorer, Southwest Fly Fishing, Southwest Review, Springfield! Magazine, Teaching Tolerance, Tequesta, Transitions Abroad, Turtle, Vibe, Whole Life Times, Willow Springs

Book Publishers:

Arte Público Press The University of Houston, Black Forest Press,

Branden Publishing Company, Calyx Books, Clarity Press, Clover Park Press, Council for Indian Education, Cross Cultural Publications, Denali Press, Face to Face Press, HiddenSpring, Hunter House Publishers, Intercultural Press, Judson Press, Just Us Books, Lerner Publishing, Mage Publisihers, McFarland & Company, Naturegraph Publishers, New Horizons Press, Small Horizons Imprint, New World Library, Pacific View Press, Paulist Press HiddenSpring, Pelican Publishing Company, Scarecrow Press, Temple University Press, Texas A&M University Press, Tilbury House Publishers, University of North Texas Press

Music

Periodicals:

5678 Country, 5678 Swing, Acoustic Guitar Magazine, African American Pulpit!, American Profile, Arkansas Review, Art Times, Body & Soul, Bridge, Campus Life, Chronogram, Circle, Clamor, Drum Business, East End Lights, Girls' Life, Gray Areas, Grit Magazine, Heartland USA, Home Times Family Newspaper, Insider Magazine, Jam Rag, Kentucky Monthly, Lacunae, Ladybug The Magazine for Young Children, Lilith, Lutheran Digest, Modern Drummer, new renaissance, New Yorker, Playboy, River Town Gazette, Rosebud, Shenandoah, Southern California Anthology, Springfield! Magazine, Student Leader, Teaching Tolerance, Threepenny Review, Timeline, Tradition, Vibe, Whole Life Times, Willow Springs, Women and Music

Book Publishers:

Allworth Press, Centerstream Publishing, Charlesbridge Publishing, Talewinds, Whispering Coyote, Chronicle Books LLC, Fiesta City Publishers, Lehigh University Press, Limelight Editions, Mage Publisihers, Mel Bay Publications, Meriwether Publishing Ltd, Contemporary Drama Service, Mississippi, University Press of Mississippi, Pelican Publishing Company, Piano Press, Players Press, Santa Monica Press LLC, Scarecrow Press, Schirmer Trade Book, Soundprints, Stenhouse Publishers, Temple University Press, University of Nebraska Press, University of North Texas Press, White Cliffs Media

Mystery

Periodicals:

Alfred Hitchcock Mystery Magazine, Black Forest Press, Capper's, Ellery Queen's Mystery Magazine, Futures Mysterious Anthology Magazine, Grit Magazine, Lacunae, My Legacy, Passport, River Town Gazette, Rosebud, Society of American Baseball Research

Book Publishers:

Avalon Books, Bella Books, Black Forest Press, Conservatory of American Letters, David R. Godine, Denlinger's Publishers, Ltd., Empire Publishing Service, Hilliard & Harris, Holloway House Publishing Group, Intercontinental Publishing New Amsterdam Publishing, Mayhaven Publishing, New Victoria Publishers, Padlock Mystery Press, Prep Publishing, Puget Sound Books/Angel Fire Press, Quality Words In Print, Silhouette Desire, Silhouette Intimate Moments, Silhouette Romance, Silhouette Special Edition, Soho Press Inc, Spinsters Ink, Tom Doherty Associate, LLC, Tor Books, Forge Books, Orb, Starscape, USA Books, Waterbrook Press, Willowgate Press

-N-

Native American

Book Publishers:

Hancock House

Nature

Periodicals:

Audubon, Birds & Blooms, Boys' Quest, Click Magazine, Country Magazine, Defenders of Wildlife, Florida Wildlife Magazine Newsletter, Flyfisher, HerbalGram, Lake Michigan Travel Guide, Lifeglow, Manoa, A Pacific Journal of International Writing, Northwest Fly Fishing, Small Farm Today, Songwriters Monthly, Southern Traveler, Woman's World

Book Publishers:

Creative Publishing International, Dawn Publications, Dimi Press, Harvard Common Press, Menasha Ridge Press, Primer Publishers, Pruett Publishing Company, Roberts Rinehart, Sasquatch Books, Sourcebooks, Sphinx Publishing, Sulgrave Press, Taylor Trade, Imprints, Cooper Square Press, Derrydale Press, Madison Books

New Age

Periodicals:

Body & Soul, Christian New Age Quarterly, Dream Network, Fate Magazine, Futurific Magazine, Light of Consciousness, Llewellyn Journal, Magical Blend, My Legacy, National Enquirer, New Millennium Writings, New Times, River Town Gazette, Rosebud, SageWoman, Science of Mind, Turtle, Whole Life Times, Yoga Journal

Book Publishers:

American Literary Press, Inc. Noble House, Beyond Words Publishing, Chronicle Books LLC, Cross Cultural Publications, Crossing Press, Frederick Fell Publishers, Granite Publishing Group, Great Quotations Publishing, Gryphon House, Hampton Roads Publishing Co, Harbor Press, Hay House, In Print Publishing, Llewellyn Publications, New Horizons Press, Small Horizons Imprint, New World Library, Paragon House, Soundprints, Turtle Press, Unity House, YMAA Publication Center

Nonfiction

Periodicals:

4-Wheel Drive & Sport Utility, 5678 Country, 5678 Swing, Aba Journal, Abilities, Absolute Write, Acoustic Guitar Magazine, Adirondack Life, Affilia Journal of Women in Social Work, African American Pulpit!, AGNI, Alaska Business Monthly, Alberta Views, Alive! A Magazine for Christian Senior Adults, All About Kids, America West Magazine, American Artist, American Bungalow, American Business Review, American Careers, American City & County, American Dissident, American Fitness, American Forests, American Girl, American Hunter, American Indian Art Magazine, American Indian Quarterly, American Legion Magazine, American Letters & Commentary, American Profile, American Rifleman, American Scholar, American Snowmobiler, American Theater, American Turf Monthly, AmericanStyle, Ancestry Magazine, Angels on Earth, Anhinga Press, Antioch Review, Antique Trader Weekly, Antiques & Collecting Magazine, Appleseeds, Appraisers Standard, AQR Alaska Quarterly Review, Archaeology, Architectural Digest, Arkansas Review, Art & Antiques, Artemis Magazine,, Arthritis Today, Artist's Magazine, Asian Pacific American Journal, Aslan Publishing, Aspen Magazine, Atlanta Homes and Lifestyles, Audio Video Interiors, Audubon, Austin Monthly Magazine, Authorship, Auto Sound & Security, Automated Builder, Automobile Quarterly, Aviation Maintenance, Babybug, BabyTalk, Back Home, Balanced Living Magazine, Balloon Life, Baltimore Magazine, Beadwork, Beauty Spot, News You Can Use, Bellevue Literary Review, Bellingham Review, Bend of the River Magazine, Benefits & Compensation Digest Better Homes and Gardens, Bibliophilos, Bike Magazine, Black Forest Press, Black Warrior Review, Bloomsbury Review, Blue Ridge Country Magazine, Boating Life, Body & Soul, Book/Mark Quarterly Review, Boston Review, Boys' Life, Boys' Quest, Braveheart, Bridal Guide, Bride's Magazine, Budget Living, Buffalo Spree Magazine, Bugle, Business Fleet, Cadet Quest, California Lawyer, Calliope Magazine, Calyx Journal, Canoe & Kayak Magazine, Car and Driver, Card Player, Caribbean Travel & Life, Carolina Quarterly, Cat Fancy, Catholic Digest, CC Motorcycle News Magazine, Central PA Magazine, Ceramics Monthly, Change, Charleston Magazine, Chattahoochee Review, Chesapeake Bay Magazine, Chicago Magazine, Chicago Review, Child Magazine, Children's Better Health Institute, Christian Century, Christian New Age Quarterly, Christian Parenting Today, Christian Single, Christian Social Action, Christian Women Today, Christianity Today, Chronicle of the Old West, Chronicles A magazine of American Culture, Chronogram, Chrysalis Reader, Cicada, Cimarron Review, Cincinnati Woman Magazine, Circle Track, Circle, Click Magazine, Club Connection, Clubhouse, Clubmex, CNEWA World, Coastal Living, Collectors News, College Bound Teen, Colorado Homes & Lifestyles, ColoradoBiz

Magazine, Colored Stone, Commercial Investment Real Estate Magazine, Commonweal, CompulsiveReader.com, ComputorEdge, Conscience, Contract Management, Conversely, Corrections Compendium, Corvette Fever, Country Home, Country Living, Country Magazine, Crab Creek Review, Cream City Review, Creative Crafter, Creative Knitting, Creative Nonfiction, Cricket, CrochetWorld, Crone Chronicles, Cross & Quill, Cruising World, Custom Rodder, CutBank, Cutting Tool Engineering, Dance Spirit, Defenders of Wildlife, Dermascope, Desktop Engineering, Dialouge, Diamond Registry Bulletin, Digger Magazine, Discipleship Journal, Discover, Diver, Dog Gone, Doll World, Dollar Stretcher, Door Magazine, Dream Network, Drum Business, East Bay Monthly, East End Lights, East Texas Historical Journal, Education Week, Educational Leadership, Elks Magazine, Endless Vacation RCI, Engineering Economist, Enrichment, Entrepreneur.com, Environment, Equal Opportunity Publications, Equine Journal, Equities Magazine, Essence, Fabricator National Ornamental & Miscellaneous Metal Association, Family Circle, Family Digest, Family Safety and Health, Family Therapy, Farm & Ranch Living, Fast & Fun Crochet, Fate magazine, Fellowship, Fiberarts Magazine, Field & Stream, Filipinas, Financial Planning, Fine Gardening, Fine Homebuilding, Fine Woodworking, FineScale Modeler, FirehouseMagazine, First for Women, First Things, Fishing Facts, Florida Hotel & Motel Journal, Fly Fisherman, Flyfisher, Food & Wine, Footsteps, Forester Communications, Fourteen Hills, Freelance Philosophy, Freeman, Ideas on Liberty, Freeskier, French Forum, Fresh Cut, Frontiers, Fun for Kidz, FurFish-Game, Futurific Magazine, Gaited Horse, Game Developer, Genre, Georgia Review, German Life, Gettysburg Review, Girlfriends Magazine, Glamour, Go Magazine, Golf Digest, Golf Journal Magazine, Gourmet, Government Executive, Green Mountains Review, GRIT Magazine, Growing Edge, Guide, Guideposts, Guns & Ammo, Handwoven, Happy Times Monthly, Hard Hat News, Harper's Bazaar, Harper's Magazine, Hawaii Review, Hawaii Westways, Health, Heartland USA, HerbalGram, Highlights for Children, Hollins Critic, Home Business Journal, Home Cooking, Home Improver Magazine, Home Times Family Newspaper, HomeLife, Hopscotch for Girls, Horticulture, Houseboat, Hudson Review, I Love Cats, Iconoclast, In the Family, Indiana Review, Insider Magazine, Insight, Instructor, Interior Design Magazine, International Railway Traveler, International Sports Journal, Interweave Knits, IRIS A Journal about Women, Islands, Japanophile, Evoking the old and the new Japan, Jewish Currents, Joiners' Quarterly, Journal of Adventist Education, Journal of Asian Martial Arts, Kentucky Monthly, Kenyon Review, Kitplanes, Knives Illustrated, Kung Fu Tai Chi, Kuumba, LA Architect, Labor Paper, Ladies' Home Journal, Lake Michigan Travel Guide, Lake Superior Magazine, Leadership Journal, Leather Crafters & Saddlers Journal, Legacy Journal, Letter Arts Review, Lifeglow, LifeWayonline.com, Light of Consciousness, Lilith Linn's Stamp News, Literal Latte, Literary Review, Fairleigh Dickinson University, Living Church, Llewellyn Journal, Log Home Living, Long Island Woman, Long Term View Massachusetts School of Law, Lucky Magazine, Lutheran Digest, MacGuffin,Magazine of La Cucina Italiana, Magical Blend, Maine Organic Farmer & Gardener, Manoa, A Pacific Journal of International Writing, Marlin, Marriage Partnership, Massage & Bodywork, Mature Years, Memory Makers, Men of Integrity, Men's Fitness, Men's Health, Mental Floss, Metropolis, Mid-American Review, MidWest Outdoors, Midwifery Today, Minnesota Memories, Minnesota Review, Missouri Review, Modeler's Resource, Modern Bride, Modern Drummer, Modern Maturity, Magazine AARP, Moment, Montana, Montana Catholic, Montana Magazine, Moody Magazine, Mopar Muscle, More, Mortgage Banking, Mother Earth News, Mother Jones, Motor Trend, Motorcycling, Muscle Mustang & Fast Fords, Muse Magazine, Mushing, Mustang & Fords, Mustang Monthly, National Enquirer, National Geographic Traveler, Native Peoples Magazine, Natural Beauty and Health, Natural History, Natural Home, Nebraska Review, Nevada Magazine, New Centennial Review, New England Review Middlebury College, New Letters, New Mexico Journey, New Millennium Writings, New Moon, new renaissance, New Times, New York Runner, Newsweek, Nimrod,

NINE, *Nineteenth-Century French Studies, Nomma Fabricator, North Dakota Horizons, Northwest Fly Fishing, Northwest Palate, Northwest Regional Magazines, Obsidian III, Odyssey Magazine, Offshore, Ohio Writer, Oklahoma Today Magazine, Old Farmer's Almanac, On Mission, Onion World, Orange Coast Magazine, Oregon Quarterly, Other Side, Outdoor America, Outdoor Life, Outdoor World, Over the Back Fence, Overland Journal, Pacific Fishing, Paddler, Parabola, Parade, Parameters, Parenting, ParentLife, Parents Magazine, Parents' Press, Passages North, Passport, PC World, Pedestal Magazine, Pediatrics For Parents, PEN America, Penthouse, Perdido, Persimmon Hill, Phi Delta Kappan, PieceWork, Plain Truth, Plastic Canvas Today, Playboy, Playgirl, Pleiades A Journal of New Writing, Plus Magazine, Podiatry Management, Poetry Magazine, Points North, Police and Security News, Poptronics, Popular Mechanics, Popular Photography, Popular Science, Popular Woodworking, Potomac Review, Prairie Schooner, Presentations Magazine, Prevention Magazine, PRIMEDIA History Group, Progressive Engineer, Psychology Today, Quarterly West, Rack, RADIO WORLD, Reader's Digest, Redbook, Referee, Reminisce Magazine, Reunions Magazine, River Town Gazette, Roanoker, Rock and Ice, Rocky Mountain Sports Magazine, Rosebud, Rug Hooking, Ruminator Review, Runner's World, Running Times, Rural Heritage, Russian Life, Sailing Magazine, Salon, Sandlapper, Saturday Evening Post, Saveur, SchoolArts, Science of Mind, Scouting, Sea Kayaker, Sea The Magazine of Western Boating, Seattle Homes and Lifestyles, Secret Place, Seneca Review, Senior Living, Seventeen, Sew News, Sewanee Review, Shape Magazine, Shenandoah, Shuttle Spindle & Dyepot, Sierra The Magazine of the Sierra Club, Skating Magazine, Ski, Skiing Magazine, Slipstream, Small Farm Today, Society of American Baseball Research, South American Explorer, Southern California Anthology, Southern Humanities Review, Southern Lumberman, Southern Review, Southern Traveler, Southwest Fly Fishing, Southwest Review, Specialty Retail Report, Specialty Travel Index, Spider The Magazine for Children, Spinning Jenny, Spin-Off, Sport Fishing Magazine, Springfield! Magazine, Stamats Meetings Media, Stone Soup, Strategic Health Care Marketing, Student Leader, Studies in American Jewish Literature, Sun Valley Magazine, Supervision, Supply Chain Systems Magazine, Supply Chain Systems Magazine, Surfer, Swank, Swim Magazine, Swimming Technique, Swimming World, Sycamore Review, symploke, Syracuse New Times, T'ai Chi, Tameme, Tampa Review, Teacher Magazine, Teachers of Vision, Technical Analysis of Stocks & Commodities, Tennis Magazine, Tequesta, Texas Gardener, Texas Highways,, Texas Parks & Wildlife, The Black Table, The World & I, Threads Magazine, Threepenny Review, Tikkun, Timeline, Times News Service, Tiny Lights A Journal of Personal Essay, Toastmaster, Today's Catholic Teacher, Today's Christian, Today's Pentecostal Evangel, Today's School, Town & Country, Toy Farmer, Tradition, Trail Runner, Transitions, Transitions Abroad, Travel & Leisure, True West, Turtle, Unique Opportunities, Upper Room, USA Cycling, UU World, Veggie Life, VFW Magazine, Via, Virginia Quarterly Review, Volleyball Magazine, Voyageur, Washington Monthly, Weavings, Weight Watchers Magazine, West Coast Magazine, Western Humanities Review, Western RV News & Recreation, Westways, Southern California Lifestyle, Whole Life Times, William and Mary Review College of William and Mary, Willow Springs, Wines & Vines, Wired, Wisconsin Trails, With The Magazine for Radical Christian Youth, Wittenburg Door, Woman's Day, Woman's Touch, Woman's World, Women Alive!, Women and Music, Women In Business, Women Today Magazine, Wonderful Ideas for Teaching, Learning, and Enjoying Mathematics!, Working Mother Magazine, Writer Gazette, Yalobusha Review, Yankee, Young & Alive, ZYZZYVA*

Book Publishers:

29th Press, Abbott, Langer & Associates, Addicus Books, Aegis Publishing Group, Ltd., Aeronitcal Publishers, Alba House, Algora Publishing, Imprint Agathon Press, Allworth Press, Alpine Publications, Alyson Publications, American Book Publishing, AMG Publishers, Anchorage Press Plays, International Agency of Plays for Young People, Angel Bea Publishing, Apage4You Book Publishing, Arden Press, Arte Público Press The University of Houston, Aslan Publishing, Atheneum

Books, B. Klein Publications, Balcony Press, Barbed Wire Publishing, Barricade Books, Barrons Educational Series, Bay Tree Publishing, Baywood Publishing Company, BenBella Books, Berkshire House Publishers, Berrett-Koehler Publishers, Bethany House Publishers, Beyond Words Publishing, BkMk Press, Black Forest Press, Blue Poppy Press, BNA Books, Bonus Books, Book Peddlers, Branden Publishing Company, Bridge Works, Bright Mountain Books, Bristol Fashion Publications, Broadman & Holman Publishers, Brookline Books, Business Group, Bye Publishing, Calyx Books, Carolrhoda Books, Carson-Dellosa Publishing Co., Caxton Press, CCC Publications, Champion Press, Charles River Media, Charlesbridge Publishing , Talewinds, Whispering Coyote, Chelsea Green Publishing Company, Chess Enterprises, Christian Ed. Publishers, Chronicle Books LLC, Clarity Press, Clover Park Press, Collectors Press, Commonwealth Editions, Conservatory of American Letters, Contemporary Books, A Division of McGraw-Hill Companies, Council for Indian Education, Creative Publishing International, Crossing Press, Crossway Books, Cruden Bay Books, Daily Guideposts, David R. Godine, Dawn Publications, Denali Press, Denlinger's Publishers, Ltd., Dial Books for Young Readers, DIMI Press, Diogenes Publishing, Do-It-Yourself Legal Publishers, Down East Books, Dutton Children's Books, Eclipse Press, Edupress, Elderberry Press, LLC, Emerald Ink Publishing, Emquad International, Ltd., ETC Publications, Excelsior Cee Publishing, Fairview Press, Falcon Publishing, Fiesta City Publishers, Fordham University Press, Forum Publishing Company, Franklin, Beedle & Associates, Frederick Fell Publishers, Free Spirit Publishing, Front Street, Future Horizons, G.P. Putnam's Sons, Books for Young Readers, Garth Gardner Company, GAFT Press, Gem Guides Book Company, Genesis Communications, Evergreen Press & Gazelle Press, Globe Pequot Press, God Allows U-Turns Book Series, Graduate Group, Granite Publishing Group, Green Nature Books, Gryphon House, Gûrze Books, Hachai Publishing, Hampton Roads Publishing Co, Hancock House, Hannover House, Harbor Press, Harvard Common Press, Hatherleigh Press, Hay House, Hazelden Publishing, Health Communications, Heritage Books, HiddenSpring, Hillbrook Publishing, Hilliard & Harris, Historical Resources Press, Hobby House Press, Hohm Press, Holiday House, Holloway House Publishing Group, Howell Press, Human Kinetics, Hunter House Publishers, Iconografix, IHS Press, Impact Publishers, Incentive Publications, Intercultural Press, International Foundation of Employee Benefit Plans, International Marine, Interweave Press, Iron Horse Free Press, Island Press, Ivan R. Dee, Publisher, J.N. Townsend Publishing, Jewish Lights Publishing, Jist Works, Jodere Group John Daniel & Company, Johnston Associates International, Jona Books, Judson Press, Just Us Books, Kids Books By Kids, Kregel Kidzone, Lake Claremont Press, Legacy Press, Lehigh University Press, Lerner Publishing, Llewellyn Publications, Loyola Press, Lumen Editions, Lyons Press, MacAdam Cage, Mage Publisihers, Magni Group, Maisonneuve Press, Markowski International Publishers, Possibility Press, Mayhaven Publishing, McDonald & Woodward Publishing Company, McKenna Publishing Group, Mel Bay Publications, Metamorphous Press, Metropolis Ink, Michael Wiese Productions, Milkweed Editions, Millennium Publishing Company, Mississippi, University Press of Mississippi, Mountain N' Air Books, Mountain Press Publishing Company, Mountaineers Books, Mustang Publishing Company, Naturegraph Publishers, Naval Institute Press, New Harbinger Publications, New Horizons Press, Small Horizons Imprint, New Society Publishers, New World Library, North Ridge Books, Northern Publishing, Nova Press, Orange Frazer Press, Orchises Press, Overmountain Press, Pacific View Press, Paladin Press Sycamore Island Books, Flying Machines Press, Paradise Cay, Parenting Press, Parkway Publishers, Pathfinder Publishing of California, Paulist Press HiddenSpring, Peachtree Publishers, Pelican Publishing Company, Perron Press, Perspectives Press,-The Infertility and Adoption Publisher, Phi Delta Kappa Educational Foundation, Piccadilly Books, Ltd., Pineapple Press, Players Press, Possibility Press, Potomac Books, Potomac Books, Inc. , PREP Publishing, Prima Publishing, Printing Industries of America / Graphic Arts Center Publishing Company, Pructt Publishing Company, PSI Research/Hellgate Press, QED Press, Quality

Words In Print, Quill Driver Books, Ragged Mountain Press, Rainbow Publishers, Really Great Books, Red Wheel/Weiser, Redleaf Press, Renders Wellness Publishing, Republic of Texas Press, Resurrection Press, Richard C. Owen Publishers, RLN & Company, Roadman Press, Roberts Rinehart, Rodnik Publishing Co., Running Press Kids, Rutledge Hill Press, Safari Press, Safer Society Press, Santa Monica Press LLC, Sarabande Books, Sasquatch Books, Scarecrow Press, Schirmer Trade Book, Serendipity Systems; Books-on-disks, Shambhala Publications, Sierra Club Books, Smithsonian Oceanic Collection, Smithsonian Backyard, Smithsonian Lets Go to the Zoo!, Solas Press, Soundprints, A Division of Trudy Corporation, Sourcebooks, Southern Illinois University Press, Sphinx Publishing, Spinsters Ink, Square One Publishers, Stackpole Books, Stenhouse Publishers, Success Publishing, Sulgrave Press, Swedenborg Foundation, Chrysalis Books, Taylor Trade, Imprints, Cooper Square Press, Derrydale Press, Madison Books, Temple University Press, Ten Speed Press, Texas A&M University Press, Texas Western Press, The Americas Group, The Millbrook Press, The Oasis Press, Hellgate Press, Tilbury House Publishers, Tower Publishing, Towlehouse Publishing Co., Transaction Publishers Rutgers, The State University of New Jersey, Tricycle Press, Trinity Foundation, Trinity Press International, Truman State University Press, Turtle Press, Unity House, University of Idaho Press, University of Maine Press, University of Nebraska Press, University of Nevada Press, University of North Texas Press, University of Oklahoma Press, UpstartBooks, USA Books, Via Dolorosa Press, Voyageur Press, Walter Foster Publishing, Waltsan Publishing, Washington State University Press, Waterbrook Press, Wescott Cove Publishing Co., Westcliffe Publishers, White Cliffs Media, Wilder Publishing Center, Will Hall Books, Willow Creek Press, Wilshire Book Co., World Leisure Corporation, YMAA Publication Center, Zondervan and Zonderkid

-O-

Occult

Periodicals:

Fate magazine, SageWoman

Book Publishers:

Hampton Roads Publishing Co, In Print Publishing, Tom Doherty Associate, Tor Books, Forge Books, Orb, Starscape

Outdoors

Periodicals:

Adirondack Life, Alaska Business Monthly, American Forests, American Hunter, American Snowmobiler, Artemis Magazine,, Aspen Magazine, Audubon, Backpacker Magazine, Balloon Life, Birds & Blooms, Blue Ridge Country Magazine, Boating Life, Boys' Life, Boys' Quest, Bugle, California Wild, Canoe & Kayak Magazine, Capper's, Cascades East Magazine, Central PA Magazine, Country Magazine, Creative With Words!, Cruising World, Dog Gone, Field & Stream, Florida Wildlife Magazine Newsletter, Flyfishing & Tying Journal, Fur-Fish-Game, Gaited Horse, Girls' Life, Grit Magazine, Guns & Ammo, Happy Times Monthly, Heartland USA, Highways, House, Home and Garden, Inside Texas Running, Insider Magazine, Kentucky Monthly, Lifeglow, Lutheran Digest, Marlin, MidWest Outdoors, Montana, Montana Catholic, Mushing, Muzzle Blasts, Nevada Magazine, Northwest Regional Magazines, Old Farmer's Almanac, Outdoor America, Outdoor Life, Outdoor World, Over the Back Fence, Paddler, Persimmon Hill, Popular Mechanics, Power & Motoryacht, Rack, River Town Gazette, Rocky Mountain Sports Magazine, Safari, Sailing Magazine, Sailing World, Salmon-Trout-Steelheader, Sandlapper, Scouting, SKI, SongwriterÆs Monthly, Sport Fishing Magazine, Springfield! Magazine, Texas Parks & Wildlife, Transitions, USA Cycling, Western RV News & Recreation, Whole Life Times, Wild Foods Forum, Wilelife Art, Willow Springs, Young & Alive

Book Publishers:

Bright Mountain Books, Charlesbridge Publishing , Talewinds, Whis-

pering Coyote, Conservatory of American Letters, Cornell Maritime Press, Council for Indian Education, Creative Publishing International, David R. Godine, Down East Books, Falcon Publishing, Frank Amato Publications, Gem Guides Book Company, Globe Pequot Press, Hancock House, Hatherleigh Press, Hearts 'N Tummies Cookbook Company, International Marine, Johnston Associates International, Kregel Kidzone, Lyons Press, Menasha Ridge Press, Mountain N' Air Books, Mountain Press Publishing Company, Mountaineers Books, Naturegraph Publishers, Northern Publishing, Paladin Press Sycamore Island Books, Flying Machines Press, Pelican Publishing Company, Primer Publishers, Printing Industries of America Graphic Arts Center Publishing Company, Pruett Publishing Company, Ragged Mountain Press, Rutledge Hill Press, Sierra Club Books, Stackpole Books, Sulgrave Press, Ten Speed Press, Tilbury House Publishers, Wescott Cove Publishing Co., Willow Creek Press

-P-

Paranormal

Periodicals:

Circle, Crone Chronicles, Dream Network, Futures Mysterious Anthology Magazine, Horrorfind, New Times, Surfer

Book Publishers:

Beyond Words Publishing, Conservatory of American Letters, Granite Publishing Group, Gryphon House, Hampton Roads Publishing Co, Hillbrook Publishing, ImaJinn Books, Llewellyn Publications, Mayhaven Publishing, Tom Doherty Associate, Tor Books, Forge Books, Orb, Starscape

Parenting

Periodicals:

All About Kids, And Baby Magazine, Atlanta Parent, Better Homes and Gardens, Bride's Magazine, Child Magazine, Christian Parenting Today, Christian Women Today, Cincinnati Woman Magazine, Dovetail, Dream Network, Family Digest, Family Fun, Grit Magazine, Happy Times Monthly, Home Education Magazine, Home Times Family Newspaper, HomeLife, Kung Fu Tai Chi, Ladies' Home Journal, Ladybug Parent's Companion, Ligourian, Lutheran Digest, Men of Integrity, Metro Parent, Natural Beauty and Health, Northwest Family News, Parenting, ParentLife, Parents' Press, Redbook, River Town Gazette, Scouting, Springfield! Magazine, Teaching Tolerance, Transitions, United Parenting Publications, West Coast Magazine, Whole Life Times, Women Today Magazine, Working Mother Magazine

Book Publishers:

Barrons Educational Series, Bethany House Publishers, Beyond Words Publishing, Brookline Books, Capital Books, Charlesbridge Publishing , Talewinds, Whispering Coyote, Chronicle Books LLC, Contemporary Books, Free Spirit Publishing, Genesis Communications, Evergreen Press & Gazelle Press, God Allows U-Turns Book Series, Gryphon House, Harbor Press, Harvard Common Press, Impact Publishers, Jewish Lights Publishing, McBooks Press, Meadowbrook Press, Mustang Publishing Company, New Society Publishers, New World Library, Parenting Press, Perspectives Press, The Infertility and Adoption Publisher, Soundprints, Square One Publishers, Waterbrook Press, Woodbine House, Zondervan and Zonderkid

Philosophy

Periodicals:

Journal of Asian Martial Arts, Mental Floss, Swank, The World & I, Yoga Journal

Book Publishers:

Alba House, Algora Publishing, Imprint Agathon Press, Hazelden Publishing

Photography

Periodicals:

Adirondack Life, Alive Now, America West Magazine, Artemis Magazine, Blue Ridge Country Magazine, Bugle, Circle, Devo 'Zine, Doll World, Gist Review, Happy Times Monthly, Letter Arts Review, Liquid Ohio, Memory Makers, National Geographic Traveler, Northwest Fly Fishing, Outdoor Life, Popular Mechanics, Popular Photography, Popular Science, Rearview, Reminisce Magazine, River Town Gazette, Rock and Ice, Sandlapper, Southern Traveler, Springfield! Magazine, Sun Valley Magazine, Sun, Supply Chain Systems Magazine, Swimming World, Sycamore Review, Texas Highways, Timeline

Book Publishers:

Allworth Press, Amherst Media, Beyond Words Publishing, Chronicle Books LLC, David R. Godine, Down East Books, Green Nature Books, Mississippi, University Press of Mississippi, Printing Industries of America Graphic Arts Center Publishing Company, Santa Monica Press LLC, Voyageur Press, Westcliffe Publishers, WoodenBoat Books

Physical Fitness

Periodicals:

American Fitness, Artemis Magazine, Balanced Living Magazine, Better Homes and Gardens, Body & Soul, Cascades East Magazine, Children's Better Health Institute, Cincinnati Woman Magazine, Complete Woman, Glamour, Golf Digest, Golfer, Happy Times Monthly, Health, Home Times Family Newspaper, Inside Texas Running, International Sports Journal, Journal of Asian Martial Arts, Kuumba, Long Island Woman, Massage Magazine, Men's Fitness, Men's Health, Men's Journal, Military Officer Modern Bride, Muscle & Fitness, National Enquirer, Natural Beauty and Health, Outdoor Life, Paddler, Parenting, Parents Magazine, Prevention Magazine, Reader's Digest, Rock and Ice, Rocky Mountain Sports Magazine, Runner's World, Saturday Evening Post, Scouting, Seek, Seneca Review, Skin Inc. Magazine, Swimming Technique, Syracuse New Times, T'ai Chi, Tennis Magazine, Trail Runner, Transitions, Turtle, Veggie Life, Volleyball Magazine, Weight Watchers Magazine, West Coast Magazine, Whole Life Times, Woman's Day, Woman's World, Women Today Magazine, Yoga Journal, Young & Alive

Book Publishers:

Contemporary Books, Fairview Press, Front Row Experience, Human Kinetics, International Marine, Lyons Press, Ragged Mountain Press, Silver Dagger Mysteries, Swedenborg Foundation, Chrysalis Books, Turtle Press, Yogavidya.com

Poetry

Periodicals:

12th Planet Literary Journal, 96 ACM Another Chicago Magazine, African American Pulpit!, AGNI, Alive Now, American Dissident, American Letters & Commentary, American Poetry Review, Anhinga Press, Antioch Review, AQR Alaska Quarterly Review, Arkansas Review, Art Times, Artful Dodge, Asian Pacific American Journal, Atlantic Monthly, Babybug, Baltimore Review, Bear Deluxe Magazine, Beauty Spot, News You Can Use, Bellevue Literary Review, Bellingham Review, Bellowing Ark, Beloit Poetry Journal,Bibliophilos, Birmingham Poetry Review, Black Forest Press, Black Warrior Review, Blackfire, Boston Review, Bridal Guide, Bridge, Buffalo Spree Magazine, ByLine, Calyx Journal, Capper's, Carolina Quarterly, Cat Fancy, Chattahoochee Review, Chicago Magazine, Chicago Review, Chiron Review, Chronicles A magazine of American Culture, Chronogram, Chrysalis Reader, Cicada, Cimarron Review, Circle, Cobblestone Magazine, Cornerstone, Crab Creek Review, Cream City Review, Creative With Words!, Cricket, Crone Chronicles, Cross & Quill,, CutBank, Devo 'Zine, Erased, Sigh, Sigh., Field, Flesh & Blood, Fourteen Hills, Futures Mysterious Anthology Magazine, Georgia Review, Gist Review, Grain, Green Hills Literary Lantern, Green Mountains Review, Greensboro Review, Grit Magazine, Guideposts for Kids, Hanging Loose, Harper's Magazine, Hawaii Review, Hayden's Ferry Review, Hollins Critic, Home Times Family Newspaper, House, Home and Garden, Hudson Review, Iconoclast, Indiana Review, IRIS A Journal about Women, Japanophile, Evoking the old and the new Japan, Jewish Currents, jubilat, Kalliope A

Journal of Women's Art, Kentucky Monthly, Kenyon Review, Ladybug The Magazine for Young Children, Ledge Magazine, Left Curve, Light, Light of Consciousness, Lilith, Liquid Ohio, Literal Latte, Literary Magazine Review, Lutheran Digest, Lynx Eye, MacGuffin,Maelstrom, Magazine of Speculative Poetry,Manoa, A Pacific Journal of International Writing, Massachusetts Review, Mature Years, Melic Review, Mid-American Review, Minnesota Review, Mississippi Review, Missouri Review, Modern Haiku, Nebo A Literary Journal, Nebraska Review, New England Review Middlebury College, New Letters, New Millennium Writings, new renaissance, New Yorker, Nimrod, Nineteenth-Century French Studies, Northwest Review University of Oregon, Oblates, Obsidian III, Ohio Writer, Omnific, Other Side, Parnassus Literary Journal, Parnassus Poetry in Review, Passages North, Pearl, Pedestal Magazine, Peregrine, Phantasmagoria, Phoebe, Pleiades A Journal of New Writing, Ploughshares Emerson College, Poem, Poetic Realm, Poetry Magazine, Potluck Children's Literary Magazine, Potomac Review, Prairie Schooner, Primavera, Quarterly West, Rearview, Red Rock Review, Rhino, RiverSedge, Rockford Review, Rosebud, Secondwind, Self, Seneca Review, Sewanee Review, Shape Magazine, Smoke Magazine, Life's Burning Desires, Southern Accents, Southern California Anthology, Southern Humanities Review, Southern Lumberman, Southwest Fly Fishing, Southwest Review, Spider The Magazine for Children, Spoon River Poetry Review, Stamats Meetings Media, Standard, Stock Car Racing, Student Leader, Sun Valley Magazine, Sun, Swimming World, Sycamore Review, Tales of the Talisman, Tameme, Tampa Review, Teaching Tolerance, Thema, Thoughts for All Seasons, Threepenny Review, Tikkun, True West, Urbanite, Verses Magazine, Virginia Quarterly Review, Weavings, Weird Tales, Western Humanities Review, William and Mary Review College of William and Mary, Willow Springs, Women Artists News Book Review, Worcester Review, Yalobusha Review, ZYZZYVA

Book Publishers:

American Literary Press, Inc. Noble House, Backwaters Press, Bkmk Press, Black Forest Press, Blue Mountain Arts, Branden Publishing Company, Brookline Books, Bye Publishing, Calyx Books, Chatoyant, Council for Indian Education, David R. Godine, Front Street, John Daniel & Company, Latin American Literary Review Press, March Street Press, Parting Gifts, Mayhaven Publishing, Midmarch Arts Press, Milkweed Editions, Moondance Publishing, Orchises Press, Perugia Press, Piano Press, Post-Apollo Press, QED Press, Sarabande Books, Skinner House Books, Sphinx Publishing, Square One Publishers, Third World Press, Two Dot, University of North Texas Press, Via Dolorosa Press, Will Hall Books

Politics

Periodicals:

Alberta Views, American Forests, American Hunter, Archaeology, Artemis Magazine, Bear Deluxe Magazine, Black Forest Press, Boston Magazine, Boston Review, California Journal, California Lawyer, Chronicles A magazine of American Culture, Commonweal, Corrections Compendium, Defenders of Wildlife, E Magazine, Fellowship, First Things, Freeman, Ideas on Liberty, Futures Mysterious Anthology Magazine, Girlfriends Magazine, Government Executive, Harper's Magazine, Home Times Family Newspaper, Insider Magazine, Jam Rag, Jewish Currents, Kentucky Monthly, Left Curve, Long Term View Massachusetts School of Law, Minnesota Review, Mom Guess What Newspaper, Mother Jones, Natural Beauty and Health, New Centennial Review, new renaissance, New Yorker, Newsweek, Other Side, Parameters, Pen America, Playboy, River Town Gazette, Salon, The World & I, Threepenny Review, Tikkun, Timeline, Transitions, Vanity Fair, Vibe, Virginia Quarterly Review, Washington Monthly

Book Publishers:

Algora Publishing, Imprint Agathon Press, Americas Group Barbed Wire Publishing, Black Forest Press, Branden Publishing Company, Chelsea Green Publishing Company, Clarity Press, Cross Cultural Publications, Denali Press, Elderberry Press, Howells House, IHS Press, In Print Publishing, Ivan R. Dee, Publisher, Maisonneuve Press, Mayhaven Publishing, Origin Media, Inc. , Books for the Integral Age,

Topics

Press, Texas A&M University Press, Truman State University Press, University of Idaho Press, University of Maine Press, University of Nebraska Press, University of Nevada Press, University of North Texas Press, University of Oklahoma Press, Washington State University Press, Westcliffe Publishers

Relationships

Periodicals:

Alive! A Magazine for Christian Senior Adults, All About Kids, Beauty Spot, The News You Can Use, Bridal Guide, Bride's Magazine, Campus Life, Catholic Digest, Christian Women Today, Cincinnati Woman Magazine, Complete Woman, Conversely, Creative With Words!, Crone Chronicles, Dovetail, Essence, Family Circle, Family Digest, Family Therapy, Girls' Life, Glamour, Happy Times Monthly, Health, Home Times Family Newspaper, HomeLife, In the Family, Insider Magazine, Kung Fu Tai Chi, Ladies' Home Journal, Lifeglow, Ligourian, Long Island Woman, Lutheran Digest, The, Magical Blend, Marriage Partnership, Mature Years, Men's Health, Modern Bride, Modern Maturity, Magazine AARP, Mom Guess What Newspaper, National Enquirer, The, Natural Beauty and Health, Parenting, Parents Magazine, Reunions Magazine, River Town Gazette, Springfield! Magazine, Sunset Magazine, Teaching Tolerance, Today's Christian Woman, Transitions, True Romance, West Coast Magazine, Whole Life Times, Woman's Day, Women Today Magazine, Working Mother Magazine, Young & Alive

Book Publishers:

Algora Publishing, Imprint Agathon Press, Barricade Books, Bethany House Publishers, Beyond Words Publishing, Blue Mountain Arts, Bye Publishing, Contemporary Books, Face to Face Press, Harbor Press, Hatherleigh Press, Hay House, Hazelden Publishing, Health Communications, Hunter House Publishers, Impact Publishers, Jodere Group, Loyola Press, Mayhaven Publishing, New Horizons Press, Small Horizons Imprint, Perron Press, Prep Publishing, Soundprints, Success Publishing, Waterbrook Press, Wilshire Book Co., World Leisure Corporation, Zondervan and Zonderkid

Religion

Periodicals:

African American Pulpit!, Alive Now, Angels on Earth, Bible Advocate, Black Forest Press, Books & Culture, Braveheart, Cadet Quest, Catholic Digest, Christian Century, Christian New Age Quarterly, Christian Parenting Today, Christian Single, Christian Social Action, Christian Women Today, Christianity Today, Clubhouse, Cnewa World, Conscience, Crone Chronicles, Cross & Quill, Devo'Zine, Discipleship Journal, Door Magazine, Dovetail, Enrichment, Fate magazine, Fellowship, First Things, Grit Magazine, Guide, Guideposts, Home Times Family Newspaper, Insight, Jewish Action, Kung Fu Tai Chi, Leadership Journal, LifeWayonline.com, Light of Consciousness, Ligourian, Living Church, Lutheran Digest, Magical Blend, Mature Years, Men of Integrity, Message Magazine, Moment, Montana, New Times, Oblates, On Mission, Oregon Business, Other Side, Parabola, Passport, Pastoral Life, Plain Truth, Pockets, Presbyterians Today, SageWoman, Science of Mind, Secret Place, Shenandoah, Sierra The Magazine of the Sierra Club, Springfield! Magazine, St. Anthony Messenger, Stamats Meetings Media, Student Leader, Swank, Teachers of Vision, Teaching Tolerance, Tikkun, Timeline, Today's Catholic Teacher, Today's Pentecostal Evangel, Transitions, True West, Upper Room, UU World, Weavings, Whole Life Times, Win-Informer, With The Magazine for Radical Christian Youth, Wittenburg Door

Book Publishers:

ACTA Publications Assisting, Alba House, American Literary Press, Inc. Noble House, AMG Publishers, Apage4You Book Publishing, Baker Books, Barbed Wire Publishing, Bethany House Publishers, Beyond Words Publishing, Black Forest Press, Branden Publishing Company, Bye Publishing, Christian Publications, Horizon Books, Cross Cultural Publications, Daily Guideposts, David R. Godine, Fordham University Press, Genesis Communications, Evergreen Press & Gazelle Press, God Allows U-Turns Book Series, Hachai Publish-

ing, HiddenSpring, Hohm Press, IHS Press, Jewish Lights Publishing, Judson Press, Legacy Press, Llewellyn Publications, Loyola Press, Meriwether Publishing Ltd, Contemporary Drama Service, Nelson Reference & Electronic Publishing, New World Library, Paragon House, Pauline Books & Media, Paulist Press HiddenSpring, Pelican Publishing Company, Prep Publishing, Resurrection Press, Shambhala Publications, Solas Press, Square One Publishers, St. Bede's Publications, Temple University Press, Tricycle Press, Trinity Foundation, Unity House, Waterbrook Press, White Mane Publishing Company

Romance

Periodicals:

Affaire De Coeur, Black Forest Press, Braveheart, Capper's, Grit Magazine, Happy Times Monthly, Springfield! Magazine, True Romance

Book Publishers:

American Literary Press, Inc. Noble House, Avalon Books, Bella Books, Black Forest Press, Conservatory of American Letters, Dorchester Publishing Co., Great Quotations Publishing, Harlequin, ImaJinn Books, LionHearted Publishing, Prep Publishing, Red Dress InkTM, Waterbrook Press, Wilshire Book Co.

Rural America

Periodicals:

America West Magazine, American Profile, Aspen Magazine, Back Home, Back Home in Kentucky, Blue Ridge Country Magazine, Capper's, Country Home, Country Magazine, Country Woman Magazine, Elks Magazine, Farm & Ranch Living, Grit Magazine, Heartland USA, Home Times Family Newspaper, Lutheran Digest, Maine Organic Farmer & Gardener, Montana, My Legacy, North Dakota Horizons, Old Farmer's Almanac, Over the Back Fence, Persimmon Hill, Rosebud, Rural Heritage, Sandlapper, Teaching Tolerance, Timeline, Tradition, True Romance, Young & Alive

Book Publishers:

Conservatory of American Letters, David R. Godine, Falcon Publishing, Globe Pequot Press, Mayhaven Publishing, University of Nebraska Press

-S-

Satire

Periodicals:

Artemis Magazine, Funny Times, Futures Mysterious Anthology Magazine, Home Times Family Newspaper, Iconoclast, Rockford Review, Spilogale Inc, The magazine of Fantasy & Science Fiction, Springfield! Magazine, The Black Table, Thoughts for All Seasons, Willow Springs, Wittenburg Door

Book Publishers:

Diogenes Publishing, Elderberry Press, Mayhaven Publishing

Periodicals:

America West Magazine, Analog Science Fiction and Fact, Annals of Improbable Research, Appleseeds, Archaeology, Artemis Magazine, Boys' Life, Bugle, California Wild, Catholic Digest, Circle, Click Magazine, Discover, Elks Magazine, Environment, Fate magazine, Growing Edge, Harper's Magazine, HerbalGram, Home Times Family Newspaper, Journal of Asian Martial Arts, Magazine of Speculative Poetry, Magical Blend, Maine Organic Farmer & Gardener, Men's Fitness, Mental Floss, Mercury, National Enquirer, Natural History, Odyssey Magazine, Playboy, Poptronics, Popular Mechanics, Popular Science, Psychology Today, Small Farm Today, Spider The Magazine for Children, Springfield! Magazine, The World & I, Transitions, Weatherwise Magazine, Whole Life Times, Young & Alive

Book Publishers:

ATL Press Science Technology, Bay Tree Publishing, Charlesbridge Publishing , Talewinds, Whispering Coyote, Dawn Publications, Green Nature Books, HiddenSpring, Island Press, Lerner Publishing, Lyons

Press, Mountain Press Publishing Company, Sphinx Publishing, The Millbrook Press, Tilbury House Publishers, Tricycle Press, Trinity Foundation, University of Idaho Press, University of Nevada Press, Voyageur Press

Science Fiction

Periodicals:

Analog Science Fiction and Fact, Artemis Magazine, Asimov's Science Fiction, Black Forest Press, Boys' Life, Circle, Fantasy & Science Fiction, Futures Mysterious Anthology Magazine, Horrorfind, Magazine of Fantasy & Science Fiction, Magazine of Speculative Poetry, My Legacy, Rosebud, Smoke Magazine, Life's Burning Desires, Spider The Magazine for Children, Spilogale Inc, The magazine of Fantasy & Science Fiction, Tales of the Talisman

Book Publishers:

American Literary Press, Inc. Noble House, Baen Books, Bella Books, BenBella Books, Black Forest Press, Carolrhoda Books, Collectors Press, Conservatory of American Letters, Daw Books, ImaJinn Books, Jona Books, Mayhaven Publishing, Tom Doherty Associate, Tor Books, Forge Books, Orb, Starscape, Warner Books, Willowgate Press

Self Help

Periodicals:

Angels on Earth, Body & Soul, Complete Woman, Dream Network, Health, Home Times Family Newspaper, House, Home and Garden, Ladies' Home Journal, Men's Fitness, Modern Bride, National Enquirer, Natural Beauty and Health, River Town Gazette, Self-Help & Psychology Magazine, Springfield! Magazine, Today's Christian Woman, Transitions, Weight Watchers Magazine, West Coast Magazine, Woman's Day, Women In Business, Young & Alive

Book Publishers:

Allworth Press, American Correctional Association, Berrett-Koehler Publishers, Beyond Words Publishing, Blue Mountain Arts, Bye Publishing, Capital Books, CCC Publications, Champion Press, Contemporary Books, Do-It-Yourself Legal Publishers, Free Spirit Publishing, Genesis Communications, Evergreen Press & Gazelle Press, God Allows U-Turns Book Series, Gûrze Books, Hampton Roads Publishing Co, Harbor Press, Hatherleigh Press, Hay House, Hazelden Publishing, HiddenSpring, Hunter House Publishers, Impact Publishers, Jodere Group Markowski International Publishers, Possibility Press, Metamorphous Press, New Horizons Press, Small Horizons Imprint, Origin Media, Inc. , Books for the Integral Age, Pathfinder Publishing of California, Possibility Press, Prima Publishing, Quill Driver Books, Red Wheel Weiser, Ronin Publishing, Safer Society Press, Shambhala Publications, Soundprints, Success Publishing, USA Books, Waterbrook Press, Wilshire Book Co., Woodbine House

Senior Citizen

Periodicals:

Jewish Currents, Reunions Magazine, Transitions

Book Publishers
Quill Driver Books

Sexuality

Periodicals:

Blackfire, Bridal Guide, Campus Life, Complete Woman, Crone Chronicles, Genre, Girlfriends Magazine, Harper's Bazaar, In the Family, Insider Magazine, Ladies' Home Journal, Long Island Woman, Men's Fitness, Mom Guess What Newspaper, National Enquirer, Natural Beauty and Health, New Millennium Writings, Penthouse, Penthouse Variations, Playboy, Playgirl, Redbook, Salon, Smoke Magazine, Life's Burning Desires, Springfield! Magazine, Tikkun, Transitions

Book Publishers:

Barricade Books, Bethany House Publishers, Frederick Fell Publishers, Hunter House Publishers, March Street Press, Parting Gifts, Metamorphous Press, Safer Society Press, Temple University Press, Wilshire Book Co.

Short Stories

Periodicals:

12th Planet Literary Journal, 96 ACM Another Chicago Magazine, AGNI, Alfred Hitchcock Mystery Magazine, Alive! A Magazine for Christian Senior Adults, America West Magazine, American Letters & Commentary, Arkansas Review, Art Times, Artemis Magazine, Asian Pacific American Journal, Asimov's Science Fiction, Babybug, BabyTalk, Baltimore Review, Bear Deluxe Magazine, Bibliophilos, Black Forest Press, Black Warrior Review, Boston Review, Boys' Life, Buffalo Spree Magazine, Bugle, ByLine, Calyx Journal, Carolina Quarterly, Cat Fancy, CC Motorcycle News Magazine, Chattahoochee Review, Chicago Magazine, Cimarron Review, Circle, Confrontation, A Literary Journal, Conversely, Crab Creek Review, Cream City Review, Creative With Words!, Cricket, CutBank, Downstate Story, Ellery Queen's Mystery Magazine, Erased, Sigh, Sigh., Fantasy & Science Fiction, Flesh & Blood, Fourteen Hills, Futures Mysterious Anthology Magazine, Genre, Glimmer Train Stories, Golf Journal Magazine, Good Housekeeping, Grit Magazine, Guideposts for Kids, Happy Times Monthly, Home Times Family Newspaper, Horror Tales, Horrorfind, House, Home and Garden, Hudson Review, Iconoclast, Indiana Review, IRIS A Journal about Women, Japanophile, Evoking the old and the new Japan, Kentucky Monthly, Kenyon Review, Ladybug The Magazine for Young Children, Literary Magazine Review, Literary Review, The , Fairleigh Dickinson University, Lynx Eye, MacGuffin, Manoa, A Pacific Journal of International Writing, Mature Years, Melic Review, Minnesota Memories, Minnesota Review, My Legacy, Nebraska Review, New Letters, New Millennium Writings, new renaissance, New York Stories, Nine, Obsidian III, Ohio Writer, Over the Back Fence, Paddler, Passages North, Passport, Pearl, Peregrine, Phantasmagoria, Pleiades A Journal of New Writing, Potluck Children's Literary Magazine, Potomac Review, Quarterly West, Red Rock Review, Reminisce Magazine, Rhino, RiverSedge, Rosebud, Secret Place, Sew News, Shape Magazine, Southern California Anthology, Southern Lumberman, Southwest Review, Spider The Magazine for Children, Spilogale Inc, The magazine of Fantasy & Science Fiction, St. Anthony Messenger, Stamats Meetings Media, Stock Car Racing, Student Leader, Sun Valley Magazine, Sun, Swimming World, Sycamore Review, Tales of the Talisman, Tameme, Teaching Tolerance, Thema, Threepenny Review, True Romance, Vampire Tales, Verses Magazine, Weird Tales, West Coast Magazine, William and Mary Review College of William and Mary, Willow Springs, Zoetrope All-Story, ZYZZYVA

Book Publishers:

American Literary Press, Inc. Noble House, Angel Bea Publishing, BkMk Press, Black Forest Press, Brookline Books, Calyx Books, Conservatory of American Letters, David R. Godine, God Allows U-Turns Book Series, John Daniel & Company, Latin American Literary Review Press, Mage Publisihers, March Street Press, Parting Gifts, Mayhaven Publishing, Milkweed Editions, Piano Press, Safari Press, Skinner House Books, Square One Publishers, University of North Texas Press, Via Dolorosa Press

Singles

Periodicals:

Christian Single, Complete Woman, Home Times Family Newspaper, Kung Fu Tai Chi, Long Island Woman, Playgirl, River Town Gazette, Springfield! Magazine

Book Publishers:

God Allows U-Turns Book Series, Soundprints, Success Publishing

Society

Periodicals:

America West Magazine, Angels on Earth, Appleseeds, Artemis Magazine, Atlanta Homes and Lifestyles, Beauty Spot, News You Can Use, Black Forest Press, Boston Review, California Lawyer, Christian Social Action, Freeman, Ideas on Liberty, Futurific Magazine, Glamour, Gray Areas, Grit Magazine, Harper's Magazine, Home Times Family Newspaper, In the Family, Insider Magazine, Jam Rag, Jewish Cur-

rents, *Ladies' Home Journal, Left Curve, Legacy Journal, Modern Maturity, Magazine AARP, Natural Beauty and Health, New Centennial Review, Nine, North Dakota Horizons, Penthouse, Reader's Digest, Redbook, River Town Gazette, Small Farm Today, Student Leader, Teaching Tolerance, Thoughts for All Seasons, Tikkun, Timeline, Town & Country, Transitions, Vanity Fair, Vibe, Whole Life Times, Willow Springs*

Book Publishers:

Algora Publishing, Imprint Agathon Press, Black Forest Press, Branden Publishing Company, Clarity Press, Cross Cultural Publications, Diogenes Publishing, Face to Face Press, Pathfinder Publishing of California, Square One Publishers, Transaction Publishers Rutgers, The State University of New Jersey, Waterbrook Press

Software

Periodicals:

Artemis Magazine, Better Homes and Gardens, Memory Makers, Poptronics, Wired

Book Publishers:

Franklin, Beedle & Associates

Spiritual

Periodicals:

African American Pulpit!, Alive Now, Alive! A Magazine for Christian Senior Adults, All for You, Balanced Living Magazine, Black Forest Press, Body & Soul, Books & Culture, Braveheart, Campus Life, Catholic Digest, Christian New Age Quarterly, Christian Parenting Today, Christian Single, Christian Social Action, Christian Women Today, Christianity Today, Chrysalis Reader, Cincinnati Woman Magazine, Clubhouse, Cnewa World, Crone Chronicles, Devo'Zine, Discipleship Journal, Door Magazine, Dream Network, Enrichment, Fate magazine, Fellowship, First Things, Guide, Guideposts, Home Times Family Newspaper, Kung Fu Tai Chi, Leadership Journal, LifeWayonline.com, Light of Consciousness, Ligourian, Llewellyn Journal, Lutheran Digest, Magical Blend, Mature Years, Men of Integrity, Message Magazine, Moment, My Legacy, Natural Beauty and Health, New Millennium Writings, New Times, Other Side, Parabola, ParentLife, Pastoral Life, Plain Truth, Pockets, SageWoman, Science of Mind, Shenandoah, Stamats Meetings Media, Student Leader, Swank, Teaching Tolerance, Tikkun, Today's Christian Woman, Today's Pentecostal Evangel, Transitions, Upper Room, UU World, Weavings, Whole Life Times, Wittenburg Door, Women Today Magazine, Yoga Journal, Young & Alive

Sports/Recreation

Periodicals:

4-Wheel Drive & Sport Utility, Adirondack Life, American Fitness, American Hunter, American Snowmobiler, American Turf Monthly, Artemis Magazine,, Aspen Magazine, Backpacker Magazine, Balloon Life, Bike Magazine, Black Forest Press, Boating Life, Boys' Life, Boys' Quest, Bugle, Cadet Quest, Canoe & Kayak Magazine, Car and Driver, Cascades East Magazine, Chess Life, Circle Track, Cruising World, Dakota Outdoors, Dialogue, Diver, Dog Gone, Elks Magazine, Field & Stream, Fishing Facts, Fly Fisherman, Fly Fishing in Salt Waters, Flyfisher, Freeskier, Fur-Fish-Game, Girls' Life, Golf Digest, Golf Journal Magazine, Golfer, Guideposts for Kids, Guns & Ammo, Heartland USA, Home Times Family Newspaper, Inside Texas Running, Insider Magazine, International Sports Journal, Journal of Asian Martial Arts, Kentucky Monthly, Kuumba, Long Island Woman, Marlin, Men's Health, Men's Journal, MidWest Outdoors, Mom Guess What Newspaper, Mushing, Muzzle Blasts, National Geographic Traveler, Natural Beauty and Health, New York Runner, Nine, Northwest Fly Fishing, Outdoor America, Outdoor Life, Pacific Fishing, Paddler, Penthouse, Playboy, Points North, Polo Players' Edition, Power & Motoryacht, Referee, River Town Gazette, Rock and Ice, Rocky Mountain Sports Magazine, Runner's World, Running Times, Sailing Magazine, Sailing World, Salmon-Trout-Steelheader, Sandlapper, Scouting, Sea Kayaker, Sea The Magazine of Western Boating, Seneca Review, Skating Magazine, Ski, Southern Humanities Review, Southern Traveler, Specialty Travel In-

dex, *Sport Fishing Magazine, Sports Illustrated for Kids, Sports Spectrum, Springfield! Magazine, Supply Chain Systems Magazine, Swim Magazine, Swimming Technique, Syracuse New Times, T'ai Chi, Tennis Magazine, Timeline, Trail Runner, Transitions, Turtle, USA Cycling, Volleyball Magazine, Young & Alive*

Book Publishers:

American Literary Press, Inc. Noble House, Black Forest Press, Bonus Books, Branden Publishing Company, Bristol Fashion Publications, Conservatory of American Letters, Contemporary Books, Down East Books, Eclipse Press, Falcon Publishing, Globe Pequot Press, Hatherleigh Press, Human Kinetics, International Marine, Lyons Press, McBooks Press, McFarland & Company, Menasha Ridge Press, Mountain N' Air Books, Mustang Publishing Company, Northern Publishing, Orange Frazer Press, Paradise Cay, Pelican Publishing Company, Potomac Books, Potomac Books, Inc. Sports, Prima Publishing, Pruett Publishing Company, Ragged Mountain Press, Rutledge Hill Press, Silver Dagger Mysteries, Smithsonian Oceanic Collection, Smithsonian Backyard, Smithsonian Lets Go to the Zoo!, Soundprints, A Division of Trudy Corporation, Stackpole Books, Stenhouse Publishers, Sulgrave Press, Swedenborg Foundation, Chrysalis Books, Taylor Trade, Imprints, Cooper Square Press, Derrydale Press, Madison Books, Temple University Press, Towlehouse Publishing Co., Truman State University Press, Turtle Press, University of Nebraska Press, Voyageur Press, Wescott Cove Publishing Co., World Leisure Corporation, YMAA Publication Center

-T-

Technical

Periodicals:

4-Wheel Drive & Sport Utility, Artemis Magazine, Audio Video Interiors, ComputorEdge, Corvette Fever, Cutting Tool Engineering, Firehouse Magazine, Futurific Magazine, Game Developer, LA Architect, Labor Paper, Memory Makers, Muscle Mustang & Fast Fords, Mustang & Fords, Mustang Monthly, Poptronics, Popular Woodworking, Progressive Engineer

Book Publishers:

Baywood Publishing Company, Charles River Media, GATF Press, Medical Physics Publishing, Millennium Publishing Company, Stenhouse Publishers

Technology

Periodicals:

Audio Video Interiors, Business 2.0, Chesapeake Bay Magazine, Circle Track, Click Magazine, ComputorEdge, Doll World, Electronic Servicing & Technology, Fresh Cut, Industrial Management, IR World, PC World, Popular Science, Radio Worlk, Salon, Small Farm Today, Supervision, Supply Chain Systems Magazine

Book Publishers:

Aegis Publishing Group, ATL Press Science Technology, Franklin, Beedle & Associates, Sphinx Publishing

Teen

Periodicals:

All About Kids, Cicada, College Bound Teen, Complete Woman, Creative With Words!, DECA Dimensions, Florida Leader, Girls' Life, Happy Times Monthly, Home Times Family Newspaper, Insight, Instructor, Kung Fu Tai Chi, Living With Teenagers, Lutheran Digest, Metro Parent, Muse Magazine, New Moon, Northwest Family News, Odyssey Magazine, Oxendine Publishing, Parents' Press, Passport, Potluck Children's Literary Magazine, River Town Gazette, SchoolArts, Scouting, Springfield! Magazine, Swimming Technique, Teaching Tolerance, United Parenting Publications, With The Magazine for Radical Christian Youth

Book Publishers:

Atheneum Books, Beyond Words Publishing, Blue Mountain Arts,

Branden Publishing Company, Council for Indian Education, Dial Books for Young Readers, Free Spirit Publishing, Front Street, God Allows U-Turns Book Series, Harbor Press, Hunter House Publishers, ImaJinn Books, Just Us Books, Kids Books By Kids, Mayhaven Publishing, Millennium Publishing Company, Scarecrow Press, Success Publishing, UpstartBooks

Television/Radio

Periodicals:

Film Quarterly, Futurific Magazine, Home Times Family Newspaper, Kentucky Monthly, new renaissance, Plus Magazine, Poptronics, Radio World, River Town Gazette, Springfield! Magazine, Teaching Tolerance, Times News Service, Today's Christian

Book Publishers:

BenBella Books, Fordham University Press, McFarland & Company, Players Press, Santa Monica Press LLC, Temple University Press

Textbooks

Periodicals:

Black Forest Press, Northwoods Journal, Springfield! Magazine, Teaching Tolerance

Book Publishers:

American Correctional Association, Barrons Educational Series, Baywood Publishing Company, Black Forest Press, Bonus Books, Bookhaven Press LLC, Branden Publishing Company, Conservatory of American Letters, Cornell Maritime Press, Cottonwood Press, Council for Indian Education, ETC Publications, Garth Gardner Company, GATF Press, Intercultural Press, Orchises Press, Paragon House, Pelican Publishing Company, Players Press, Potomac Books, Scarecrow Press, Stenhouse Publishers, Trinity Foundation

Theatre

Periodicals:

Art Times, Beauty Spot, News You Can Use, Cincinnati Woman Magazine, Confrontation, A Literary Journal, Dramatics, Futures Mysterious Anthology Magazine, Home Times Family Newspaper, Insider Magazine, Kentucky Monthly, New Centennial Review, new renaissance, New Yorker, Nineteenth-Century French Studies, Obsidian III, Rosebud, Southern Humanities Review, Springfield! Magazine, Teaching Tolerance, Vanity Fair, Willow Springs

Book Publishers:

Allworth Press, Anchorage Press Plays, International Agency of Plays for Young People, Branden Publishing Company, Fairleigh Dickinson University Press, Ivan R. Dee, Publisher, Limelight Editions, McFarland & Company, Meriwether Publishing Ltd, Contemporary Drama Service, Mississippi, University Press of Mississippi, Piccadilly Books, Players Press, Santa Monica Press LLC, Temple University Press

Trade

Periodicals:

American Libraries, Artemis Magazine,, Automated Builder, Aviation Maintenance, Backroads, Business Fleet, Chesapeake Bay Magazine, Colored Stone, Cutting Tool Engineering, Desktop Engineering, Diamond Registry Bulletin, Digger Magazine, Doll World, Equine Journal, Fabricator National Ornamental & Miscellaneous Metal Association, Fiberarts Magazine, Firehouse Magazine, Florida Hotel & Motel Journal, Forester Communications, Handwoven, Hard Hat News, Instructor, LA Architect, Labor Paper, Leather Crafters & Saddlers Journal, Log Home Living, Montana, Nomma Fabricator, Oildom Publishing, Party & Paper Retailer, Police and Security News, Short Stuff Magazine, Space and Time, Toastmaster, Unique Opportunities, Wall Fashions

Book Publishers:

Bristol Publishing Enterprises nitty gritty Cookbooks, Christian Publications, Horizon Books, Forum Publishing Company, GATF Press, Human Kinetics, Paradise Cay, Serendipity Systems, Books-on-disks, Wilder Publishing Center

Travel

Periodicals:

Adirondack Life, Alaska Business Monthly, Alive! A Magazine for Christian Senior Adults, America West Magazine, American Fitness, American Profile, Arizona Highways, Artemis Magazine,, Aspen Magazine, ASU Travel Guide, Atlanta Homes and Lifestyles, Back Home, Backpacker Magazine, Backroads, Beauty Spot, News You Can Use, Better Homes and Gardens, Blue Ridge Country Magazine, Boating Life, Bridal Guide, Budget Living, Canoe & Kayak Magazine, Capper's, Caribbean Travel & Life, CC Motorcycle News Magazine, Clubmex, Coast to Coast, Country Living, Country Magazine, Creative With Words!, Dog Gone, Early American Life, Endless Vacation RCI, Florida Wildlife Magazine Newsletter, Fly Fishing in Salt Waters, Freeskier, German Life, Glamour, Go Magazine, Going Places, Golfer, GRIT Magazine, Hawaii Westways, Highways, House, Home and Garden, Inside Texas Running, Insider Magazine, International Railway Traveler, Islands, Italian Cooking and Living, Kentucky Monthly, Ladies' Home Journal, Lake Michigan Travel Guide, Lifeglow, Log Home Living, Magazine of La Cucina Italiana, Mature Years, Men's Health, Men's Journal, MidWest Outdoors, Midwest Traveler, Modern Bride, Modern Maturity, Magazine AARP, Montana, Montana Catholic, MORE, Motorcycling, Mountain Living, National Geographic Traveler, Natural Beauty and Health, Nevada Magazine, New Mexico Journey, New Yorker, North Dakota Horizons, Northwest Family News, Northwest Fly Fishing, Northwest Palate, Northwest Regional Magazines, Offshore, Oklahoma Today Magazine, Outdoor Life, Over the Back Fence, Paddler, Persimmon Hill, Playgirl, Plus Magazine, Points North, Power & Motoryacht, Premier Tourism Marketing, Reunions Magazine, River Town Gazette, Russian Life, Sandlapper, Saturday Evening Post, Scouting, Sea The Magazine of Western Boating, Ski, Small Farm Today, Southern Review, Southern Traveler, Specialty Retail Report, Springfield! Magazine, Supply Chain Systems Magazine, Tameme, Tennis Magazine, Texas Highways, Texas Parks & Wildlife, Times News Service, Today's Christian, Town & Country, Transitions, Transitions Abroad, Via, Western RV News & Recreation, Westways, Southern California Lifestyle, Whole Life Times, Wisconsin Trails, Woodall Publications, Corp., Working Mother Magazine, Yankee, Young & Alive

Book Publishers:

Berkshire House Publishers, Brookline Books, Capital Books, Chronicle Books LLC, Clover Park Press, Dimi Press, Down East Books, Falcon Publishing, Gem Guides Book Company, Globe Pequot Press, Green Nature Books, HiddenSpring, Jewish Lights Publishing, Johnston Associates International, Lake Claremont Press, Lumen Editions, Lyons PReAmerican Literary Press, Inc. Noble House, Arte Público Press The University of Houston, Atheneum Books, Barrons Educational Series, Beyond Words Publishing, Branden Publishing Company, Carolrhoda Books, Chronicle Books LLC, Council for Indian Education, David R. Godine, Farrar, Straus and Giroux, Publishers, Books for Young Readers, Free Spirit Publishing, Front Street, G.P. Putnam's Sons, Books for Young Readers, God Allows U-Turns Book Series, Harbor Press, Hilliard & Harris, Just Us Books, Lerner Publishing, Little, Brown Children's Books, Mayhaven Publishing, Morgan Reynolds Publishing, Prep Publishing, Scarecrow Press, Success Publishing, White Mane Publishing Company, McDonald & Woodward Publishing Company, Menasha Ridge Press, Millennium Publishing Company, Mountain N' Air Books, Mustang Publishing Company, North Ridge Books, Paradise Cay, Pelican Publishing Company, Pruett Publishing Company, PSI Research/Hellgate Press, Roadman Press, Rutledge Hill Press, Santa Monica Press LLC, Sasquatch Books, Sourcebooks, Southern Illinois University Press, Stone Bridge Press, Ten Speed Press, Wescott Cove Publishing Co., World Leisure Corporation

True Crime

Periodicals:

Futures Mysterious Anthology Magazine

Topics

Book Publishers:

Addicus Books, Branden Publishing Company, Jona Books, Mayhaven Publishing, New Horizons Press, Small Horizons Imprint, University of North Texas Press

-W-

Western

Periodicals:

America West Magazine, Arizona Highways, Backwoodsman Magazine, Black Forest Press, California Wild, Capper's, Chronicle of the Old West, GRIT Magazine, Horrorfind, Montana, Montana Magazine, My Legacy, Overland Journal, Persimmon Hill, Primedia History Group

Book Publishers:

American Literary Press, Inc. Noble House, Avalon Books, Black Forest Press, Branden Publishing Company, Caxton Press, Conservatory of American Letters, Council for Indian Education, Denlinger's Publishers, Dorchester Publishing Co., Eclipse Press, JoNa Books, Mayhaven Publishing, Mountain N' Air Books, Pelican Publishing Company, Tom Doherty Associate, Tor Books, Forge Books, Orb, Starscape, University of Nebraska Press, University of Oklahoma Press, USA Books

Women's Fiction

Periodicals:

Affaire De Coeur, Calyx Journal, Carolina Quarterly, Cincinnati Woman Magazine, Feminist Studies University of Maryland, Fourteen Hills, Frontiers, Good Housekeeping, Home Times Family Newspaper, Kalliope A Journal of Women's Art, Kentucky Monthly, Legacy Journal, New Millennium Writings, Obsidian III, Playgirl, Primavera, Rosebud, Society of American Baseball Research, Swimming World, True Romance, Willow Springs

Book Publishers:

American Literary Press, Inc. Noble House, Calyx Books, David R. Godine, Latin American Literary Review Press, March Street Press, Parting Gifts, University of Nebraska Press, Waterbrook Press

Women's Issues

Periodicals:

African American Pulpit!, All About Kids, Beauty Spot, News You Can Use, Calyx Journal, Carolina Quarterly, Cincinnati Woman Magazine, Complete Woman, Cosmopolitan, Crone Chronicles, Elle, Equal Opportunity Publications, Feminist Studies University of Maryland, Frontiers, Futures Mysterious Anthology Magazine, Glamour, Good Housekeeping, Home Times Family Newspaper, Insider Magazine, Iris A Journal about Women, Kalliope A Journal of Women's Art, Kentucky Monthly, Ladies' Home Journal, Legacy Journal, Lilith, Long Island Woman, Magical Blend, More, National Enquirer, Natural Beauty and Health, New Mexico Woman Magazine, New Moon, New Times, Parents Magazine, Playgirl, Redbook, Rosebud, Skin Inc. Magazine, Springfield! Magazine, Teaching Tolerance, Town & Country, Transitions, Whole Life Times, Woman's Day, Woman's Touch, Woman's World, Women and Music, Women Artists News Book Review, Women In Business, Working Mother Magazine

Book Publishers:

American Correctional Association, Arden Press, Arte Público Press The University of Houston, Beyond Words Publishing, Branden Publishing Company, Calyx Books, Champion Press, Clover Park Press, Cross Cultural Publications, Fairleigh Dickinson University Press, God Allows U-Turns Book Series, Hay House, Health Communications, Hunter House Publishers, Impact Publishers, Jewish Lights Publishing, Jodere Group Judson Press, New Horizons Press, Small Horizons Imprint, New World Library, Prep Publishing, Red Dress InkTM, Rutledge Hill Press, Soundprints, A Division of Trudy Corporation, Spinsters Ink, Temple University Press, Transnational Publishers, University of Nebraska Press, Volcano Press, Waterbrook Press, Zondervan and Zonderkid

Writing

Periodicals:

Ability Magazfine, Absolute Write, AGNI, America West Magazine, American Poetry Review, Authorship, BabyTalk, Bibliophilos, Black Forest Press, Black Warrior Review, Bloomsbury Review, Boston Review, ByLine, Carolina Quarterly, Chicago Magazine, Cimarron Review, Circle, CompulsiveReader.com, Cream City Review, Creative Knitting, Creative With Words!, Cross & Quill,, Et cetera, Flesh & Blood, Freelance Writer's Report, Green Mountains Review, Happy Times Monthly, Home Times Family Newspaper, Indiana Review, Iris A Journal about Women, Kalliope A Journal of Women's Art, Kenyon Review, Lacunae, Literary Magazine Review, MacGuffin,My Legacy, Nebraska Review, New Millennium Writings, Nimrod, Obsidian III, Ohio Writer, Passages North, PEN America, Peregrine, Phoebe, Potluck Children's Literary Magazine, Potomac Review, Quarterly West, Rearview, Rosebud, Script Magazine, Senior Living, Smoke Magazine, Life's Burning Desires, Springfield! Magazine, Stock Car Racing, Swimming World, Sycamore Review, Tameme, Teaching Tolerance, Thoughts for All Seasons, Tikkun, Verses Magazine, Willow Springs, Win-Informer, Writer Gazette, Writer's Digest, Writers' Journal, Yalobusha Review

Book Publishers:

Black Forest Press, Brookline Books, Conservatory of American Letters, David R. Godine, Excelsior Cee Publishing, Front Street, Lumen Editions, Marion Street Press, Maupin House, Mountain N' Air Books, Players Press, Prep Publishing, Quill Driver Books, Via Dolorosa Press

-Y-

Young Adult

Periodicals:

American Girl, Cadet Quest, Calliope Magazine, Campus Life, Chess Life, Cicada, Circle K, College Bound Teen, Creative With Words!, DECA Dimensions, Faces The Magazine About People, Fantasy & Science Fiction, Girls' Life, Home Times Family Newspaper, Ligourian, Living With Teenagers, New Moon, Potluck Children's Literary Magazine, School Mates, Scouting, Spilogale Inc, The magazine of Fantasy & Science Fiction, Springfield! Magazine, Stock Car Racing, Swimming Technique, Teaching Tolerance

Book Publishers:

American Literary Press, Inc. Noble House, Arte Público Press, The University of Houston, Atheneum Books, Barrons Educational Series, Beyond Words Publishing, Branden Publishing Company, Carolrhoda Books, Chronicle Books LLC, Council for Indian Education, David R. Godine, Farrar, Straus and Giroux, Publishers, Books for Young Readers, Free Spirit Publishing, Front Street, G.P. Putnam's Sons, Books for Young Readers, God Allows U-Turns Book Series, Harbor Press, Hilliard & Harris, Just Us Books, Lerner Publishing, Little, Brown Children's Books, Mayhaven Publishing, Morgan Reynolds Publishing, Prep Publishing, Scarecrow Press, Success Publishing, White Mane Publishing Company

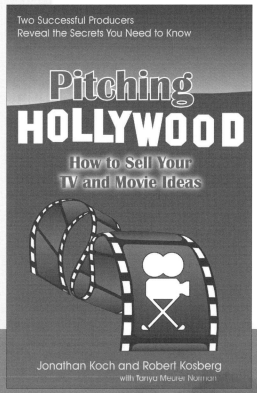

Writers' and Artists' Hideouts
Great Getaways for Seducing the Muse
—by Andrea Brown

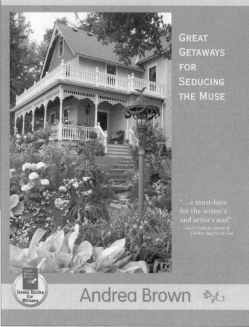

The desire to be creative is often at odds with the routines of daily life. Literary agent Andrea Brown combines her love of travel and adventure with her search for perfect places to seduce the muse and delivers a charming, practical guide that enlightens the curious traveler and provides astute advice from editors, literary agents, authors, illustrators, art directors and other creative people on harnessing one's creativity.

Listed are locations all over the country, from $19 per night hostels to $1,000 per night luxury hotels. There are ranches, lighthouses, boats, bed and breakfasts, and even a museum to sleep in, all listed by region.

> ❝This book is a double treat—both a valuable and unique travel guide but also a useful writer's and artist's manual for accomplishing one's goals to publish or produce lasting creative works. A must have for the writer's and artist's soul—and bookshelf.❞
>
> —Jack Canfield, author of *Chicken Soup for the Soul* series

$14.95 ($23.50 Canada) · ISBN 1-884956-34-3

Quit Your Day Job!
How to Sleep Late, Do What You Enjoy, and Make a Ton of Money *as a Writer!*
—by Jim Denney

A Writer's Digest Book Club Selection

Resolution and perseverance are required to build a writing career and if you're going to succeed, you don't need the hype or hyperbole so often dished out in other writer's guides. You need a candid, no-nonsense appraisal of the daily grind of the writer's life, with the potholes and pitfalls clearly marked.

This book is your road map, written by someone who's lived the writing life for years, with more than sixty published novels and nonfiction books to his credit.

> ❝While there are always a few charmed souls, most career-bent writers are destined to struggle. Jim Denney has been there, done that. Read his book and save yourself much of the anguish.❞
>
> —James N. Frey, author of *How to Write a Damn Good Novel*

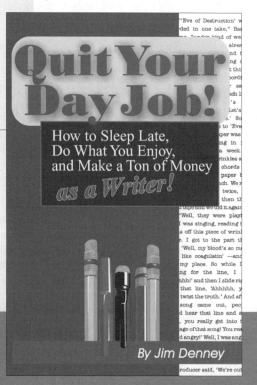

$14.95 (29.95 Canada) · ISBN 1-884956-04-1

Available at better brick and mortar bookstores, online bookstores, at QuillDriverBooks.com or by calling 1-800-497-4909

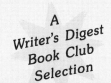

Use This Book To:

- ### Find a publisher

  Search *The American Directory of Writer's Guidelines'* "Topic Index" to find a publisher interested in the subject you wish to write about, then turn to that publisher's guidelines for more information, including the name and address of the editor to whom you should send query letters, manuscripts, book proposals or other submissions. Periodical publisher guidelines are listed alphabetically beginning on page 1. Guidelines for book publishers begin on page 559.

- ### Polish your submission

  When you already know which periodical you would like to target or which book publisher you wish to approach, look up the appropriate guidelines and use the information provided to fine-tune your submission.

- ### Brainstorm ideas

  A primary value of *The American Directory of Writer's Guidelines* is its ability to be browsed. Use the guidelines and the "Topic Index" to brainstorm ideas for everything from nonfiction articles to short stories, from brief fillers to full-length books.

- ### Exploit your expertise

  Many regularly published writers use the same material for more than one article or project. If you are an expert in a certain area or have collected an abundance of material on a subject about which you would like to write, use the "Topic Index" to locate a number of publishers interested in your subject and then contact each individually slanting your approach to fit the individual publisher's wants and needs.

- ### Look like a pro

  Anything less than a businesslike manuscript format will brand you as a beginner. See page xxi for an example of proper manuscript format.

- ### Track your submissions

  A "Submission Tracking Sheet" appears on page xxiii. Photocopy this form to record the progress of each of your submissions.